American Casebook Series
Hornbook Series and Basic Legal Texts
Nutshell Series

of

WEST PUBLISHING COMPANY
P.O. Box 64526
St. Paul, Minnesota 55164–0526

ACCOUNTING

Faris' Accounting and Law in a Nutshell, 377 pages, 1984 (Text)

Fiflis, Kripke and Foster's Teaching Materials on Accounting for Business Lawyers, 3rd Ed., 838 pages, 1984 (Casebook)

Siegel and Siegel's Accounting and Financial Disclosure: A Guide to Basic Concepts, 259 pages, 1983 (Text)

ADMINISTRATIVE LAW

Davis' Cases, Text and Problems on Administrative Law, 6th Ed., 683 pages, 1977 (Casebook)

Gellhorn and Boyer's Administrative Law and Process in a Nutshell, 2nd Ed., 445 pages, 1981 (Text)

Mashaw and Merrill's Cases and Materials on Administrative Law–The American Public Law System, 2nd Ed., 976 pages, 1985 (Casebook)

Robinson, Gellhorn and Bruff's The Administrative Process, 3rd Ed., 978 pages, 1986 (Casebook)

ADMIRALTY

Healy and Sharpe's Cases and Materials on Admiralty, 2nd Ed., 876 pages, 1986 (Casebook)

Maraist's Admiralty in a Nutshell, about 362 pages, 1988 (Text)

Schoenbaum's Hornbook on Admiralty and Maritime Law, Student Ed., 692 pages, 1987 (Text)

Sohn and Gustafson's Law of the Sea in a Nutshell, 264 pages, 1984 (Text)

AGENCY—PARTNERSHIP

Fessler's Alternatives to Incorporation for Persons in Quest of Profit, 2nd Ed., 326 pages, 1986 (Casebook)

AGENCY—PARTNERSHIP—Cont'd

Henn's Cases and Materials on Agency, Partnership and Other Unincorporated Business Enterprises, 2nd Ed., 733 pages, 1985 (Casebook)

Reuschlein and Gregory's Hornbook on the Law of Agency and Partnership, 625 pages, 1979, with 1981 pocket part (Text)

Selected Corporation and Partnership Statutes and Forms, 621 pages, 1987

Steffen and Kerr's Cases and Materials on Agency-Partnership, 4th Ed., 859 pages, 1980 (Casebook)

Steffen's Agency-Partnership in a Nutshell, 364 pages, 1977 (Text)

AGRICULTURAL LAW

Meyer, Pedersen, Thorson and Davidson's Agricultural Law: Cases and Materials, 931 pages, 1985 (Casebook)

ALTERNATIVE DISPUTE RESOLUTION

Kanowitz' Cases and Materials on Alternative Dispute Resolution, 1024 pages, 1986 (Casebook)

Riskin and Westbrook's Dispute Resolution and Lawyers, 223 pages, 1987 (Coursebook)

Riskin and Westbrook's Dispute Resolution and Lawyers, Abridged Ed., 223 pages, 1988 (Coursebook)

Teple and Moberly's Arbitration and Conflict Resolution, (The Labor Law Group), 614 pages, 1979 (Casebook)

AMERICAN INDIAN LAW

Canby's American Indian Law in a Nutshell, 288 pages, 1981 (Text)

Getches and Wilkinson's Cases on Federal Indian Law, 2nd Ed., 880 pages, 1986 (Casebook)

List current as of January, 1988

T7202—1g

I

LAW SCHOOL PUBLICATIONS—Continued

ANTITRUST LAW

Gellhorn's Antitrust Law and Economics in a Nutshell, 3rd Ed., 472 pages, 1986 (Text)

Gifford and Raskind's Cases and Materials on Antitrust, 694 pages, 1983 with 1985 Supplement (Casebook)

Hovenkamp's Hornbook on Economics and Federal Antitrust Law, Student Ed., 414 pages, 1985 (Text)

Oppenheim, Weston and McCarthy's Cases and Comments on Federal Antitrust Laws, 4th Ed., 1168 pages, 1981 with 1985 Supplement (Casebook)

Posner and Easterbrook's Cases and Economic Notes on Antitrust, 2nd Ed., 1077 pages, 1981, with 1984–85 Supplement (Casebook)

Sullivan's Hornbook of the Law of Antitrust, 886 pages, 1977 (Text)

See also Regulated Industries, Trade Regulation

ART LAW

DuBoff's Art Law in a Nutshell, 335 pages, 1984 (Text)

BANKING LAW

Lovett's Banking and Financial Institutions in a Nutshell, 409 pages, 1984 (Text)

Symons and White's Teaching Materials on Banking Law, 2nd Ed., 993 pages, 1984, with 1987 Supplement (Casebook)

BUSINESS PLANNING

Painter's Problems and Materials in Business Planning, 2nd Ed., 1008 pages, 1984 with 1987 Supplement (Casebook)

Selected Securities and Business Planning Statutes, Rules and Forms, about 475 pages, 1987

CIVIL PROCEDURE

American Bar Association Section of Litigation—Reading on Adversarial Justice: The American Approach to Adjudication, edited by Landsman, about 204 pages, 1988 (Coursebook)

Casad's Res Judicata in a Nutshell, 310 pages, 1976 (text)

Cound, Friedenthal, Miller and Sexton's Cases and Materials on Civil Procedure, 4th Ed., 1202 pages, 1985 with 1987 Supplement (Casebook)

Ehrenzweig, Louisell and Hazard's Jurisdiction in a Nutshell, 4th Ed., 232 pages, 1980 (Text)

Federal Rules of Civil-Appellate Procedure—West Law School Edition, 596 pages, 1987

Friedenthal, Kane and Miller's Hornbook on Civil Procedure, 876 pages, 1985 (Text)

Kane's Civil Procedure in a Nutshell, 2nd Ed., 306 pages, 1986 (Text)

CIVIL PROCEDURE—Cont'd

Koffler and Reppy's Hornbook on Common Law Pleading, 663 pages, 1969 (Text)

Marcus and Sherman's Complex Litigation—Cases and Materials on Advanced Civil Procedure, 846 pages, 1985 (Casebook)

Park's Computer-Aided Exercises on Civil Procedure, 2nd Ed., 167 pages, 1983 (Coursebook)

Siegel's Hornbook on New York Practice, 1011 pages, 1978 with 1987 Pocket Part (Text)

See also Federal Jurisdiction and Procedure

CIVIL RIGHTS

Abernathy's Cases and Materials on Civil Rights, 660 pages, 1980 (Casebook)

Cohen's Cases on the Law of Deprivation of Liberty: A Study in Social Control, 755 pages, 1980 (Casebook)

Lockhart, Kamisar, Choper and Shiffrin's Cases on Constitutional Rights and Liberties, 6th Ed., 1266 pages, 1986 with 1987 Supplement (Casebook)—reprint from Lockhart, et al. Cases on Constitutional Law, 6th Ed., 1986

Vieira's Civil Rights in a Nutshell, 279 pages, 1978 (Text)

COMMERCIAL LAW

Bailey's Secured Transactions in a Nutshell, 2nd Ed., 391 pages, 1981 (Text)

Epstein, Henning and Nickles' Basic Uniform Commercial Code Teaching Materials, 3rd Ed., about 720 pages, 1988 (Casebook)

Henson's Hornbook on Secured Transactions Under the U.C.C., 2nd Ed., 504 pages, 1979 with 1979 P.P. (Text)

Murray's Commercial Law, Problems and Materials, 366 pages, 1975 (Coursebook)

Nickles, Matheson and Dolan's Materials for Understanding Credit and Payment Systems, 923 pages, 1987 (Casebook)

Nordstrom, Murray and Clovis' Problems and Materials on Sales, 515 pages, 1982 (Casebook)

Nordstrom, Murray and Clovis' Problems and Materials on Secured Transactions, 594 pages, 1987 (Casebook)

Selected Commercial Statutes, 1527 pages, 1987

Speidel, Summers and White's Teaching Materials on Commercial Law, 4th Ed., 1448 pages, 1987 (Casebook)

Speidel, Summers and White's Commercial Paper: Teaching Materials, 4th Ed., about 578 pages, 1987 (Casebook)—reprint from Speidel, et al. Commercial Law, 4th Ed.

Speidel, Summers and White's Sales: Teaching Materials, 4th Ed., 804 pages, 1987 (Casebook)—reprint from Speidel, et al. Commercial Law, 4th Ed.

LAW SCHOOL PUBLICATIONS—Continued

COMMERCIAL LAW—Cont'd

Speidel, Summers and White's Secured Transactions—Teaching Materials, 4th Ed., 485 pages, 1987 (Casebook)—reprint from Speidel, et al. Commercial Law, 4th Ed.

Stockton's Sales in a Nutshell, 2nd Ed., 370 pages, 1981 (Text)

Stone's Uniform Commercial Code in a Nutshell, 2nd Ed., 516 pages, 1984 (Text)

Uniform Commercial Code, Official Text with Comments, 994 pages, 1978

UCC Article 9, Reprint from 1962 Code, 128 pages, 1976

UCC Article 9, 1972 Amendments, 304 pages, 1978

Weber and Speidel's Commercial Paper in a Nutshell, 3rd Ed., 404 pages, 1982 (Text)

White and Summers' Hornbook on the Uniform Commercial Code, 3rd Ed., 1988 (Text)

COMMUNITY PROPERTY

Mennell and Boykoff's Community Property in a Nutshell, about 475 pages, 1988 (Text)

Verrall and Bird's Cases and Materials on California Community Property, 4th Ed., 549 pages, 1983 (Casebook)

COMPARATIVE LAW

Barton, Gibbs, Li and Merryman's Law in Radically Different Cultures, 960 pages, 1983 (Casebook)

Glendon, Gordon and Osakive's Comparative Legal Traditions: Text, Materials and Cases on the Civil Law, Common Law, and Socialist Law Traditions, 1091 pages, 1985 (Casebook)

Glendon, Gordon, and Osakwe's Comparative Legal Traditions in a Nutshell, 402 pages, 1982 (Text)

Langbein's Comparative Criminal Procedure: Germany, 172 pages, 1977 (Casebook)

COMPUTERS AND LAW

Maggs and Sprowl's Computer Applications in the Law, 316 pages, 1987 (Coursebook)

Mason's An Introduction to the Use of Computers in Law, about 275 pages, 1988 (Text)

CONFLICT OF LAWS

Cramton, Currie and Kay's Cases-Comments-Questions on Conflict of Laws, 4th Ed., 876 pages, 1987 (Casebook)

Scoles and Hay's Hornbook on Conflict of Laws, Student Ed., 1085 pages, 1982 with 1986 P.P. (Text)

Scoles and Weintraub's Cases and Materials on Conflict of Laws, 2nd Ed., 966 pages, 1972, with 1978 Supplement (Casebook)

CONFLICT OF LAWS—Cont'd

Siegel's Conflicts in a Nutshell, 469 pages, 1982 (Text)

CONSTITUTIONAL LAW

Barron and Dienes' Constitutional Law in a Nutshell, 389 pages, 1986 (Text)

Engdahl's Constitutional Federalism in a Nutshell, 2nd Ed., 411 pages, 1987 (Text)

Lockhart, Kamisar, Choper and Shiffrin's Cases-Comments-Questions on Constitutional Law, 6th Ed., 1601 pages, 1986 with 1987 Supplement (Casebook)

Lockhart, Kamisar, Choper and Shiffrin's Cases-Comments-Questions on the American Constitution, 6th Ed., 1260 pages, 1986 with 1987 Supplement (Casebook)—abridgment of Lockhart, et al. Cases on Constitutional Law, 6th Ed., 1986

Manning's The Law of Church-State Relations in a Nutshell, 305 pages, 1981 (Text)

Miller's Presidential Power in a Nutshell, 328 pages, 1977 (Text)

Nowak, Rotunda and Young's Hornbook on Constitutional Law, 3rd Ed., Student Ed., 1191 pages, 1986 (Text)

Rotunda's Modern Constitutional Law: Cases and Notes, 2nd Ed., 1004 pages, 1985, with 1987 Supplement (Casebook)

Williams' Constitutional Analysis in a Nutshell, 388 pages, 1979 (Text)

See also Civil Rights, Foreign Relations and National Security Law

CONSUMER LAW

Epstein and Nickles' Consumer Law in a Nutshell, 2nd Ed., 418 pages, 1981 (Text)

Selected Commercial Statutes, 1527 pages, 1987

Spanogle and Rohner's Cases and Materials on Consumer Law, 693 pages, 1979, with 1982 Supplement (Casebook)

See also Commercial Law

CONTRACTS

Calamari & Perillo's Cases and Problems on Contracts, 1061 pages, 1978 (Casebook)

Calamari and Perillo's Hornbook on Contracts, 3rd Ed., 904 pages, 1987 (Text)

Corbin's Text on Contracts, One Volume Student Edition, 1224 pages, 1952 (Text)

Fessler and Loiseaux's Cases and Materials on Contracts, 837 pages, 1982 (Casebook)

Friedman's Contract Remedies in a Nutshell, 323 pages, 1981 (Text)

Fuller and Eisenberg's Cases on Basic Contract Law, 4th Ed., 1203 pages, 1981 (Casebook)

Hamilton, Rau and Weintraub's Cases and Materials on Contracts, 830 pages, 1984 (Casebook)

LAW SCHOOL PUBLICATIONS—Continued

CONTRACTS—Cont'd

Jackson and Bollinger's Cases on Contract Law in Modern Society, 2nd Ed., 1329 pages, 1980 (Casebook)

Keyes' Government Contracts in a Nutshell, 423 pages, 1979 (Text)

Schaber and Rohwer's Contracts in a Nutshell, 2nd Ed., 425 pages, 1984 (Text)

Summers and Hillman's Contract and Related Obligation: Theory, Doctrine and Practice, 1074 pages, 1987 (Casebook)

COPYRIGHT

See Patent and Copyright Law

CORPORATE FINANCE

Hamilton's Cases and Materials on Corporate Finance, 895 pages, 1984 with 1986 Supplement (Casebook)

CORPORATIONS

Hamilton's Cases on Corporations—Including Partnerships and Limited Partnerships, 3rd Ed., 1213 pages, 1986 with 1986 Statutory Supplement (Casebook)

Hamilton's Law of Corporations in a Nutshell, 2nd Ed., 515 pages, 1987 (Text)

Henn's Teaching Materials on Corporations, 2nd Ed., 1204 pages, 1986 (Casebook)

Henn and Alexander's Hornbook on Corporations, 3rd Ed., Student Ed., 1371 pages, 1983 with 1986 P.P. (Text)

Jennings and Buxbaum's Cases and Materials on Corporations, 5th Ed., 1180 pages, 1979 (Casebook)

Selected Corporation and Partnership Statutes, Regulations and Forms, 621 pages, 1987

Solomon, Schwartz' and Bauman's Materials and Problems on Corporations: Law and Policy, 2nd Ed., about 900 pages, 1988 (Casebook)

CORRECTIONS

Krantz's Cases and Materials on the Law of Corrections and Prisoners' Rights, 3rd Ed., 855 pages, 1986 with 1988 Supplement (Casebook)

Krantz's Law of Corrections and Prisoners' Rights in a Nutshell, 2nd Ed., 386 pages, 1983 (Text)

Popper's Post-Conviction Remedies in a Nutshell, 360 pages, 1978 (Text)

Robbins' Cases and Materials on Post Conviction Remedies, 506 pages, 1982 (Casebook)

CREDITOR'S RIGHTS

Bankruptcy Code, Rules and Forms, Law School Ed., 792 pages, 1988

Epstein's Debtor-Creditor Law in a Nutshell, 3rd Ed., 383 pages, 1986 (Text)

CREDITOR'S RIGHTS—Cont'd

Epstein, Landers and Nickles' Debtors and Creditors: Cases and Materials, 3rd Ed., 1059 pages, 1987 (Casebook)

LoPucki's Player's Manual for the Debtor-Creditor Game, 123 pages, 1985 (Coursebook)

Riesenfeld's Cases and Materials on Creditors' Remedies and Debtors' Protection, 4th Ed., 914 pages, 1987 (Casebook)

White's Bankruptcy and Creditor's Rights: Cases and Materials, 812 pages, 1985, with 1987 Supplement (Casebook)

CRIMINAL LAW AND CRIMINAL PROCEDURE

Abrams', Federal Criminal Law and its Enforcement, 882 pages, 1986 (Casebook)

Carlson's Adjudication of Criminal Justice, Problems and References, 130 pages, 1986 (Casebook)

Dix and Sharlot's Cases and Materials on Criminal Law, 3rd Ed., 846 pages, 1987 (Casebook)

Federal Rules of Criminal Procedure—West Law School Edition, 567 pages, 1987

Grano's Problems in Criminal Procedure, 2nd Ed., 176 pages, 1981 (Problem book)

Israel and LaFave's Criminal Procedure in a Nutshell, 4th Ed., about 500 pages, 1988 (Text)

Johnson's Cases, Materials and Text on Criminal Law, 3rd Ed., 783 pages, 1985 (Casebook)

Johnson's Cases on Criminal Procedure, 859 pages, 1987 (Casebook)

Kamisar, LaFave and Israel's Cases, Comments and Questions on Modern Criminal Procedure, 6th Ed., 1558 pages, 1986 with 1987 Supplement (Casebook)

Kamisar, LaFave and Israel's Cases, Comments and Questions on Basic Criminal Procedure, 6th Ed., 860 pages, 1986 with 1987 Supplement (Casebook)—reprint from Kamisar, et al. Modern Criminal Procedure, 6th ed., 1986

LaFave's Modern Criminal Law: Cases, Comments and Questions, 2nd Ed., about 1000 pages, 1988 (Casebook)

LaFave and Israel's Hornbook on Criminal Procedure, Student Ed., 1142 pages, 1985 with 1987 P.P. (Text)

LaFave and Scott's Hornbook on Criminal Law, 2nd Ed., Student Ed., 918 pages, 1986 (Text)

Langbein's Comparative Criminal Procedure: Germany, 172 pages, 1977 (Casebook)

Loewy's Criminal Law in a Nutshell, 2nd Ed., 321 pages, 1987 (Text)

Saltzburg's American Criminal Procedure, Cases and Commentary, 3rd Ed., about 1200 pages, 1988 (Casebook)

LAW SCHOOL PUBLICATIONS—Continued

CRIMINAL LAW AND CRIMINAL PROCEDURE—Cont'd

Uviller's The Processes of Criminal Justice: Investigation and Adjudication, 2nd Ed., 1384 pages, 1979 with 1979 Statutory Supplement and 1986 Update (Casebook)

Uviller's The Processes of Criminal Justice: Adjudication, 2nd Ed., 730 pages, 1979. Soft-cover reprint from Uviller's The Processes of Criminal Justice: Investigation and Adjudication, 2nd Ed. (Casebook)

Uviller's The Processes of Criminal Justice: Investigation, 2nd Ed., 655 pages, 1979. Soft-cover reprint from Uviller's The Processes of Criminal Justice: Investigation and Adjudication, 2nd Ed. (Casebook)

Vorenberg's Cases on Criminal Law and Procedure, 2nd Ed., 1088 pages, 1981 with 1987 Supplement (Casebook)

See also Corrections, Juvenile Justice

DECEDENTS ESTATES

See Trusts and Estates

DOMESTIC RELATIONS

Clark's Cases and Problems on Domestic Relations, 3rd Ed., 1153 pages, 1980 (Casebook)

Clark's Hornbook on Domestic Relations, 2nd Ed., Student Ed., about 1100 pages, 1988 (Text)

Krause's Cases and Materials on Family Law, 2nd Ed., 1221 pages, 1983 with 1986 Supplement (Casebook)

Krause's Family Law in a Nutshell, 2nd Ed., 444 pages, 1986 (Text)

Krauskopf's Cases on Property Division at Marriage Dissolution, 250 pages, 1984 (Casebook)

ECONOMICS, LAW AND

Goetz' Cases and Materials on Law and Economics, 547 pages, 1984 (Casebook)

See also Antitrust, Regulated Industries

EDUCATION LAW

Alexander and Alexander's The Law of Schools, Students and Teachers in a Nutshell, 409 pages, 1984 (Text)

Morris' The Constitution and American Education, 2nd Ed., 992 pages, 1980 (Casebook)

EMPLOYMENT DISCRIMINATION

Jones, Murphy and Belton's Cases on Discrimination in Employment, 1116 pages, 1987 (Casebook)

Player's Cases and Materials on Employment Discrimination Law, 2nd Ed., 782 pages, 1984 (Casebook)

EMPLOYMENT DISCRIMINATION—Cont'd

Player's Federal Law of Employment Discrimination in a Nutshell, 2nd Ed., 402 pages, 1981 (Text)

Player's Hornbook on the Law of Employment Discrimination, Student Ed., about 650 pages, 1988 (Text)

See also Women and the Law

ENERGY AND NATURAL RESOURCES LAW

Laitos' Cases and Materials on Natural Resources Law, 938 pages, 1985 (Casebook)

Rodgers' Cases and Materials on Energy and Natural Resources Law, 2nd Ed., 877 pages, 1983 (Casebook)

Selected Environmental Law Statutes, about 654 pages, 1987

Tomain's Energy Law in a Nutshell, 338 pages, 1981 (Text)

See also Environmental Law, Oil and Gas, Water Law

ENVIRONMENTAL LAW

Bonine and McGarity's Cases and Materials on the Law of Environment and Pollution, 1076 pages, 1984 (Casebook)

Findley and Farber's Cases and Materials on Environmental Law, 2nd Ed., 813 pages, 1985 (Casebook)

Findley and Farber's Environmental Law in a Nutshell, 343 pages, 1983 (Text)

Rodgers' Hornbook on Environmental Law, 956 pages, 1977 with 1984 pocket part (Text)

Selected Environmental Law Statutes, 654 pages, 1987

See also Energy Law, Natural Resources Law, Water Law

EQUITY

See Remedies

ESTATES

See Trusts and Estates

ESTATE PLANNING

Kurtz' Cases, Materials and Problems on Family Estate Planning, 853 pages, 1983 (Casebook)

Lynn's Introduction to Estate Planning, in a Nutshell, 3rd Ed., 370 pages, 1983 (Text)

See also Taxation

EVIDENCE

Broun and Meisenholder's Problems in Evidence, 2nd Ed., 304 pages, 1981 (Problem book)

Cleary and Strong's Cases, Materials and Problems on Evidence, 3rd Ed., 1143 pages, 1981 (Casebook)

LAW SCHOOL PUBLICATIONS—Continued

EVIDENCE—Cont'd

Federal Rules of Evidence for United States Courts and Magistrates, 370 pages, 1987

Graham's Federal Rules of Evidence in a Nutshell, 2nd Ed., 473 pages, 1987 (Text)

Kimball's Programmed Materials on Problems in Evidence, 380 pages, 1978 (Problem book)

Lempert and Saltzburg's A Modern Approach to Evidence: Text, Problems, Transcripts and Cases, 2nd Ed., 1232 pages, 1983 (Casebook)

Lilly's Introduction to the Law of Evidence, 2nd Ed., about 600 pages, 1987 (Text)

McCormick, Sutton and Wellborn's Cases and Materials on Evidence, 6th Ed., 1067 pages, 1987 (Casebook)

McCormick's Hornbook on Evidence, 3rd Ed., Student Ed., 1156 pages, 1984 with 1987 P.P. (Text)

Rothstein's Evidence, State and Federal Rules in a Nutshell, 2nd Ed., 514 pages, 1981 (Text)

Saltzburg's Evidence Supplement: Rules, Statutes, Commentary, 245 pages, 1980 (Casebook Supplement)

FEDERAL JURISDICTION AND PROCEDURE

Currie's Cases and Materials on Federal Courts, 3rd Ed., 1042 pages, 1982 with 1985 Supplement (Casebook)

Currie's Federal Jurisdiction in a Nutshell, 2nd Ed., 258 pages, 1981 (Text)

Federal Rules of Civil-Appellate Procedure—West Law School Edition, 596 pages, 1987

Forrester and Moye's Cases and Materials on Federal Jurisdiction and Procedure, 3rd Ed., 917 pages, 1977 with 1985 Supplement (Casebook)

Redish's Cases, Comments and Questions on Federal Courts, 878 pages, 1983 with 1986 Supplement (Casebook)

Vetri and Merrill's Federal Courts, Problems and Materials, 2nd Ed., 232 pages, 1984 (Problem Book)

Wright's Hornbook on Federal Courts, 4th Ed., Student Ed., 870 pages, 1983 (Text)

FOREIGN RELATIONS AND NATIONAL SECURITY LAW

Franck and Glennon's United States Foreign Relations Law: Cases, Materials and Simulations, 941 pages, 1987 (Casebook)

FUTURE INTERESTS

See Trusts and Estates

HEALTH LAW

See Medicine, Law and

IMMIGRATION LAW

Aleinikoff and Martin's Immigration Process and Policy, 1042 pages, 1985, with 1987 Supplement (Casebook)

Weissbrodt's Immigration Law and Procedure in a Nutshell, 345 pages, 1984 (Text)

INDIAN LAW

See American Indian Law

INSURANCE

Dobbyn's Insurance Law in a Nutshell, 281 pages, 1981 (Text)

Keeton's Cases on Basic Insurance Law, 2nd Ed., 1086 pages, 1977

Keeton and Wydiss' Insurance Law, Student Ed., about 1024 pages, 1988 (Text)

Wydiss and Keeton's Case Supplement to Keeton and Wydiss Insurance Law, 425 pages, 1988 (Casebook)

York and Whelan's Cases, Materials and Problems on Insurance Law, 715 pages, 1982, with 1985 Supplement (Casebook)

INTERNATIONAL LAW

Buergenthal and Maier's Public International Law in a Nutshell, 262 pages, 1985 (Text)

Folsom, Gordon and Spanogle's International Business Transactions – a Problem-Oriented Coursebook, 1160 pages, 1986, with Documents Supplement (Casebook)

Henkin, Pugh, Schachter and Smit's Cases and Materials on International Law, 2nd Ed., 1517 pages, 1987 with Documents Supplement (Casebook)

Jackson and Davey's Legal Problems of International Economic Relations, 2nd Ed., 1269 pages, 1986, with Documents Supplement (Casebook)

Kirgis' International Organizations in Their Legal Setting, 1016 pages, 1977, with 1981 Supplement (Casebook)

Weston, Falk and D'Amato's International Law and World Order—A Problem Oriented Coursebook, 1195 pages, 1980, with Documents Supplement (Casebook)

Wilson's International Business Transactions in a Nutshell, 2nd Ed., 476 pages, 1984 (Text)

INTERVIEWING AND COUNSELING

Binder and Price's Interviewing and Counseling, 232 pages, 1977 (Text)

Shaffer and Elkins' Interviewing and Counseling in a Nutshell, 2nd Ed., 487 pages, 1987 (Text)

INTRODUCTION TO LAW STUDY

Dobbyn's So You Want to go to Law School, Revised First Edition, 206 pages, 1976 (Text)

LAW SCHOOL PUBLICATIONS—Continued

INTRODUCTION TO LAW STUDY—Cont'd

Hegland's Introduction to the Study and Practice of Law in a Nutshell, 418 pages, 1983 (Text)

Kinyon's Introduction to Law Study and Law Examinations in a Nutshell, 389 pages, 1971 (Text)

See also Legal Method and Legal System

JUDICIAL ADMINISTRATION

Nelson's Cases and Materials on Judicial Administration and the Administration of Justice, 1032 pages, 1974 (Casebook)

JURISPRUDENCE

Christie's Text and Readings on Jurisprudence—The Philosophy of Law, 1056 pages, 1973 (Casebook)

JUVENILE JUSTICE

Fox's Cases and Materials on Modern Juvenile Justice, 2nd Ed., 960 pages, 1981 (Casebook)

Fox's Juvenile Courts in a Nutshell, 3rd Ed., 291 pages, 1984 (Text)

LABOR LAW

Atleson, Rabin, Schatzki, Sherman and Silverstein's Collective Bargaining in Private Employment, 2nd Ed., (The Labor Law Group), 856 pages, 1984 (Casebook)

Gorman's Basic Text on Labor Law—Unionization and Collective Bargaining, 914 pages, 1976 (Text)

Grodin, Wollett and Alleyne's Collective Bargaining in Public Employment, 3rd Ed., (the Labor Law Group), 430 pages, 1979 (Casebook)

Leslie's Labor Law in a Nutshell, 2nd Ed., 397 pages, 1986 (Text)

Nolan's Labor Arbitration Law and Practice in a Nutshell, 358 pages, 1979 (Text)

Oberer, Hanslowe, Andersen and Heinsz' Cases and Materials on Labor Law—Collective Bargaining in a Free Society, 3rd Ed., 1163 pages, 1986 with Statutory Supplement (Casebook)

See also Employment Discrimination, Social Legislation

LAND FINANCE

See Real Estate Transactions

LAND USE

Callies and Freilich's Cases and Materials on Land Use, 1233 pages, 1986 (Casebook)

Hagman's Cases on Public Planning and Control of Urban and Land Development, 2nd Ed., 1301 pages, 1980 (Casebook)

LAND USE—Cont'd

Hagman and Juergensmeyer's Hornbook on Urban Planning and Land Development Control Law, 2nd Ed., Student Ed., 680 pages, 1986 (Text)

Wright and Gitelman's Cases and Materials on Land Use, 3rd Ed., 1300 pages, 1982, with 1987 Supplement (Casebook)

Wright and Wright's Land Use in a Nutshell, 2nd Ed., 356 pages, 1985 (Text)

LEGAL HISTORY

Presser and Zainaldin's Cases on Law and American History, 855 pages, 1980 (Casebook)

See also Legal Method and Legal System

LEGAL METHOD AND LEGAL SYSTEM

Aldisert's Readings, Materials and Cases in the Judicial Process, 948 pages, 1976 (Casebook)

Berch and Berch's Introduction to Legal Method and Process, 550 pages, 1985 (Casebook)

Bodenheimer, Oakley and Love's Readings and Cases on an Introduction to the Anglo-American Legal System, 2nd Ed., about 165 pages, 1988 (Casebook)

Davies and Lawry's Institutions and Methods of the Law—Introductory Teaching Materials, 547 pages, 1982 (Casebook)

Dvorkin, Himmelstein and Lesnick's Becoming a Lawyer: A Humanistic Perspective on Legal Education and Professionalism, 211 pages, 1981 (Text)

Greenberg's Judicial Process and Social Change, 666 pages, 1977 (Casebook)

Kelso and Kelso's Studying Law: An Introduction, 587 pages, 1984 (Coursebook)

Kempin's Historical Introduction to Anglo-American Law in a Nutshell, 2nd Ed., 280 pages, 1973 (Text)

Kimball's Historical Introduction to the Legal System, 610 pages, 1966 (Casebook)

Murphy's Cases and Materials on Introduction to Law—Legal Process and Procedure, 772 pages, 1977 (Casebook)

Reynolds' Judicial Process in a Nutshell, 292 pages, 1980 (Text)

See also Legal Research and Writing

LEGAL PROFESSION

Aronson, Devine and Fisch's Problems, Cases and Materials on Professional Responsibility, 745 pages, 1985 (Casebook)

Aronson and Weckstein's Professional Responsibility in a Nutshell, 399 pages, 1980 (Text)

Mellinkoff's The Conscience of a Lawyer, 304 pages, 1973 (Text)

Mellinkoff's Lawyers and the System of Justice, 983 pages, 1976 (Casebook)

LAW SCHOOL PUBLICATIONS—Continued

LEGAL PROFESSION—Cont'd

Pirsig and Kirwin's Cases and Materials on Professional Responsibility, 4th Ed., 603 pages, 1984 (Casebook)

Schwartz and Wydick's Problems in Legal Ethics, 2nd Ed., about 330 pages, 1988 (Casebook)

Selected Statutes, Rules and Standards on the Legal Profession, 449 pages, 1987

Smith's Preventing Legal Malpractice, 142 pages, 1981 (Text)

Wolfram's Hornbook on Modern Legal Ethics, Student Edition, 1120 pages, 1986 (Text)

LEGAL RESEARCH AND WRITING

Child's Materials and Problems on Drafting Legal Documents, about 276 pages, 1988 (Text)

Cohen's Legal Research in a Nutshell, 4th Ed., 450 pages, 1985 (Text)

Cohen and Berring's How to Find the Law, 8th Ed., 790 pages, 1983. Problem book by Foster, Johnson and Kelly available (Casebook)

Cohen and Berring's Finding the Law, 8th Ed., Abridged Ed., 556 pages, 1984 (Casebook)

Dickerson's Materials on Legal Drafting, 425 pages, 1981 (Casebook)

Felsenfeld and Siegel's Writing Contracts in Plain English, 290 pages, 1981 (Text)

Gopen's Writing From a Legal Perspective, 225 pages, 1981 (Text)

Mellinkoff's Legal Writing—Sense and Nonsense, 242 pages, 1982 (Text)

Ray and Ramsfield's Legal Writing: Getting It Right and Getting It Written, 250 pages, 1987 (Text)

Rombauer's Legal Problem Solving—Analysis, Research and Writing, 4th Ed., 424 pages, 1983 (Coursebook)

Squires and Rombauer's Legal Writing in a Nutshell, 294 pages, 1982 (Text)

Statsky's Legal Research and Writing, 3rd Ed., 257 pages, 1986 (Coursebook)

Statsky and Wernet's Case Analysis and Fundamentals of Legal Writing, 2nd Ed., 441 pages, 1984 (Text)

Teply's Programmed Materials on Legal Research and Citation, 2nd Ed., 358 pages, 1986. Student Library Exercises available (Coursebook)

Weihofen's Legal Writing Style, 2nd Ed., 332 pages, 1980 (Text)

LEGISLATION

Davies' Legislative Law and Process in a Nutshell, 2nd Ed., 346 pages, 1986 (Text)

Eskridge and Frickey's Cases on Legislation, 937 pages, 1987 (Casebook)

Nutting and Dickerson's Cases and Materials on Legislation, 5th Ed., 744 pages, 1978 (Casebook)

LEGISLATION—Cont'd

Statsky's Legislative Analysis and Drafting, 2nd Ed., 217 pages, 1984 (Text)

LOCAL GOVERNMENT

McCarthy's Local Government Law in a Nutshell, 2nd Ed., 404 pages, 1983 (Text)

Reynolds' Hornbook on Local Government Law, 860 pages, 1982, with 1987 pocket part (Text)

Valente's Cases and Materials on Local Government Law, 3rd Ed., 1010 pages, 1987 (Casebook)

MASS COMMUNICATION LAW

Gillmor and Barron's Cases and Comment on Mass Communication Law, 4th Ed., 1076 pages, 1984 (Casebook)

Ginsburg's Regulation of Broadcasting: Law and Policy Towards Radio, Television and Cable Communications, 741 pages, 1979, with 1983 Supplement (Casebook)

Zuckman, Gaynes, Carter and Dee Mass Communications Law in a Nutshell, 3rd Ed., 538 pages, 1988 (Text)

MEDICINE, LAW AND

Furrow, Johnson, Jost and Schwartz' Health Law: Cases, Materials and Problems, 1005 pages, 1987 (Casebook)

King's The Law of Medical Malpractice in a Nutshell, 2nd Ed., 342 pages, 1986 (Text)

Shapiro and Spece's Problems, Cases and Materials on Bioethics and Law, 892 pages, 1981 (Casebook)

Sharpe, Fiscina and Head's Cases on Law and Medicine, 882 pages, 1978 (Casebook)

MILITARY LAW

Shanor and Terrell's Military Law in a Nutshell, 378 pages, 1980 (Text)

MORTGAGES

See Real Estate Transactions

NATURAL RESOURCES LAW

See Energy and Natural Resources Law

NEGOTIATION

Edwards and White's Problems, Readings and Materials on the Lawyer as a Negotiator, 484 pages, 1977 (Casebook)

Peck's Cases and Materials on Negotiation, 2nd Ed., (The Labor Law Group), 280 pages, 1980 (Casebook)

Williams' Legal Negotiation and Settlement, 207 pages, 1983 (Coursebook)

OFFICE PRACTICE

Hegland's Trial and Practice Skills in a Nutshell, 346 pages, 1978 (Text)

Strong and Clark's Law Office Management, 424 pages, 1974 (Casebook)

LAW SCHOOL PUBLICATIONS—Continued

OFFICE PRACTICE—Cont'd

See also Computers and Law, Interviewing and Counseling, Negotiation

OIL AND GAS

Hemingway's Hornbook on Oil and Gas, 2nd Ed., Student Ed., 543 pages, 1983 with 1986 P.P. (Text)

Kuntz, Lowe, Anderson and Smith's Cases and Materials on Oil and Gas Law, 857 pages, 1986, with Forms Manual (Casebook)

Lowe's Oil and Gas Law in a Nutshell, 443 pages, 1983 (Text)

See also Energy and Natural Resources Law

PARTNERSHIP

See Agency—Partnership

PATENT AND COPYRIGHT LAW

Choate, Francis and Collins' Cases and Materials on Patent Law, 3rd Ed., 1009 pages, 1987 (Casebook)

Miller and Davis' Intellectual Property—Patents, Trademarks and Copyright in a Nutshell, 428 pages, 1983 (Text)

Nimmer's Cases on Copyright and Other Aspects of Entertainment Litigation, 3rd Ed., 1025 pages, 1985 (Casebook)

PRODUCTS LIABILITY

Fischer and Powers' Cases and Materials on Products Liability, about 700 pages, 1988 (Casebook)

Noel and Phillips' Cases on Products Liability, 2nd Ed., 821 pages, 1982 (Casebook)

Phillips' Products Liability in a Nutshell, 3rd Ed., about 350 pages, 1988 (Text)

PROPERTY

Bernhardt's Real Property in a Nutshell, 2nd Ed., 448 pages, 1981 (Text)

Boyer's Survey of the Law of Property, 766 pages, 1981 (Text)

Browder, Cunningham and Smith's Cases on Basic Property Law, 4th Ed., 1431 pages, 1984 (Casebook)

Bruce, Ely and Bostick's Cases and Materials on Modern Property Law, 1004 pages, 1984 (Casebook)

Burke's Personal Property in a Nutshell, 322 pages, 1983 (Text)

Cunningham, Stoebuck and Whitman's Hornbook on the Law of Property, Student Ed., 916 pages, 1984, with 1987 P.P. (Text)

Donahue, Kauper and Martin's Cases on Property, 2nd Ed., 1362 pages, 1983 (Casebook)

Hill's Landlord and Tenant Law in a Nutshell, 2nd Ed., 311 pages, 1986 (Text)

Kurtz and Hovenkamp's Cases and Materials on American Property Law, 1296 pages, 1987 (Casebook)

PROPERTY—Cont'd

Moynihan's Introduction to Real Property, 2nd Ed., 239 pages, 1988 (Text)

Uniform Land Transactions Act, Uniform Simplification of Land Transfers Act, Uniform Condominium Act, 1977 Official Text with Comments, 462 pages, 1978

See also Real Estate Transactions, Land Use

PSYCHIATRY, LAW AND

Reisner's Law and the Mental Health System, Civil and Criminal Aspects, 696 pages, 1985, with 1987 Supplement (Casebooks)

REAL ESTATE TRANSACTIONS

Bruce's Real Estate Finance in a Nutshell, 2nd Ed., 262 pages, 1985 (Text)

Maxwell, Riesenfeld, Hetland and Warren's Cases on California Security Transactions in Land, 3rd Ed., 728 pages, 1984 (Casebook)

Nelson and Whitman's Cases on Real Estate Transfer, Finance and Development, 3rd Ed., 1184 pages, 1987 (Casebook)

Nelson and Whitman's Hornbook on Real Estate Finance Law, 2nd Ed., Student Ed., 941 pages, 1985 (Text)

Osborne's Cases and Materials on Secured Transactions, 559 pages, 1967 (Casebook)

REGULATED INDUSTRIES

Gellhorn and Pierce's Regulated Industries in a Nutshell, 2nd Ed., 389 pages, 1987 (Text)

Morgan, Harrison and Verkuil's Cases and Materials on Economic Regulation of Business, 2nd Ed., 666 pages, 1985 (Casebook)

See also Mass Communication Law, Banking Law

REMEDIES

Dobbs' Hornbook on Remedies, 1067 pages, 1973 (Text)

Dobbs' Problems in Remedies, 137 pages, 1974 (Problem book)

Dobbyn's Injunctions in a Nutshell, 264 pages, 1974 (Text)

Friedman's Contract Remedies in a Nutshell, 323 pages, 1981 (Text)

Leavell, Love and Nelson's Cases and Materials on Equitable Remedies and Restitution, 4th Ed., 1111 pages, 1986 (Casebook)

McCormick's Hornbook on Damages, 811 pages, 1935 (Text)

O'Connell's Remedies in a Nutshell, 2nd Ed., 320 pages, 1985 (Text)

York, Bauman and Rendleman's Cases and Materials on Remedies, 4th Ed., 1029 pages, 1985 (Casebook)

LAW SCHOOL PUBLICATIONS—Continued

REVIEW MATERIALS

Ballantine's Problems

Black Letter Series

SECURITIES REGULATION

Hazen's Hornbook on The Law of Securities Regulation, Student Ed., 739 pages, 1985, with 1988 P.P. (Text)

Ratner's Securities Regulation: Materials for a Basic Course, 3rd Ed., 1000 pages, 1986 (Casebook)

Ratner's Securities Regulation in a Nutshell, 3rd Ed., about 335 pages, 1988 (Text)

Selected Securities and Business Planning Statutes, Rules and Forms, 493 pages, 1987

SOCIAL LEGISLATION

Hood and Hardy's Workers' Compensation and Employee Protection Laws in a Nutshell, 274 pages, 1984 (Text)

LaFrance's Welfare Law: Structure and Entitlement in a Nutshell, 455 pages, 1979 (Text)

Malone, Plant and Little's Cases on Workers' Compensation and Employment Rights, 2nd Ed., 951 pages, 1980 (Casebook)

SPORTS LAW

Schubert, Smith and Trentadue's Sports Law, 395 pages, 1986 (Text)

TAXATION

Dodge's Cases and Materials on Federal Income Taxation, 820 pages, 1985 (Casebook)

Dodge's Wills, Trusts and Estate Planning, 700 pages, 1988 (Casebook)

Garbis, Struntz and Rubin's Cases and Materials on Tax Procedure and Tax Fraud, 2nd Ed., 687 pages, 1987 (Casebook)

Gelfand and Salsich's State and Local Taxation and Finance in a Nutshell, 309 pages, 1986 (Text)

Gunn's Cases and Materials on Federal Income Taxation of Individuals, 785 pages, 1981 with 1985 Supplement (Casebook)

Hellerstein and Hellerstein's Cases on State and Local Taxation, 4th Ed., 1041 pages, 1978 with 1982 Supplement (Casebook)

Kahn and Gann's Corporate Taxation and Taxation of Partnerships and Partners, 2nd Ed., 1204 pages, 1985 (Casebook)

Kaplan's Federal Taxation of International Transactions: Principles, Planning and Policy, about 600 pages, 1988 (Casebook)

Kragen and McNulty's Cases and Materials on Federal Income Taxation: Individuals, Corporations, Partnerships, 4th Ed., 1287 pages, 1985 (Casebook)

TAXATION—Cont'd

McNulty's Federal Estate and Gift Taxation in a Nutshell, 3rd Ed., 509 pages, 1983 (Text)

McNulty's Federal Income Taxation of Individuals in a Nutshell, 3rd Ed., 487 pages, 1983 (Text)

Pennell's Cases and Materials on Income Taxation of Trusts, Estates, Grantors and Beneficiaries, 460 pages, 1987 (Casebook)

Posin's Hornbook on Federal Income Taxation of Individuals, Student Ed., 491 pages, 1983 with 1987 pocket part (Text)

Rose and Chommie's Hornbook on Federal Income Taxation, 3rd Ed., about 875 pages, 1988 (Text)

Selected Federal Taxation Statutes and Regulations, 1399 pages, 1988

Solomon and Hesch's Cases on Federal Income Taxation of Individuals, 1068 pages, 1987 (Casebook)

TORTS

Christie's Cases and Materials on the Law of Torts, 1264 pages, 1983 (Casebook)

Dobbs' Torts and Compensation—Personal Accountability and Social Responsibility for Injury, 955 pages, 1985 (Casebook)

Green, Pedrick, Rahl, Thode, Hawkins, Smith, and Treece's Advanced Torts: Injuries to Business, Political and Family Interests, 2nd Ed., 544 pages, 1977 (Casebook)

Keeton, Keeton, Sargentich and Steiner's Cases and Materials on Tort and Accident Law, 1360 pages, 1983 (Casebook)

Kionka's Torts in a Nutshell: Injuries to Persons and Property, 434 pages, 1977 (Text)

Malone's Torts in a Nutshell: Injuries to Family, Social and Trade Relations, 358 pages, 1979 (Text)

Prosser and Keeton's Hornbook on Torts, 5th Ed., Student Ed., 1286 pages, 1984, with 1988 pocket part (Text)

See also Products Liability

TRADE REGULATION

McManis' Unfair Trade Practices in a Nutshell, 444 pages, 1982 (Text)

Oppenheim, Weston, Maggs and Schechter's Cases and Materials on Unfair Trade Practices and Consumer Protection, 4th Ed., 1038 pages, 1983 with 1986 Supplement (Casebook)

See also Antitrust, Regulated Industries

TRIAL AND APPELLATE ADVOCACY

Appellate Advocacy, Handbook of, 2nd Ed., 182 pages, 1986 (Text)

Bergman's Trial Advocacy in a Nutshell, 402 pages, 1979 (Text)

LAW SCHOOL PUBLICATIONS—Continued

TRIAL AND APPELLATE ADVOCACY— Cont'd

Binder and Bergman's Fact Investigation: From Hypothesis to Proof, 354 pages, 1984 (Coursebook)

Goldberg's The First Trial (Where Do I Sit?, What Do I Say?) in a Nutshell, 396 pages, 1982 (Text)

Haydock, Herr and Stempel's, Fundamentals of Pre-Trial Litigation, 768 pages, 1985 (Casebook)

Hegland's Trial and Practice Skills in a Nutshell, 346 pages, 1978 (Text)

Hornstein's Appellate Advocacy in a Nutshell, 325 pages, 1984 (Text)

Jeans' Handbook on Trial Advocacy, Student Ed., 473 pages, 1975 (Text)

Martineau's Cases and Materials on Appellate Practice and Procedure, 565 pages, 1987 (Casebook)

McElhaney's Effective Litigation, 457 pages, 1974 (Casebook)

Nolan's Cases and Materials on Trial Practice, 518 pages, 1981 (Casebook)

Parnell and Shellhaas' Cases, Exercises and Problems for Trial Advocacy, 171 pages, 1982 (Coursebook)

Sonsteng, Haydock and Boyd's The Trialbook: A Total System for Preparation and Presentation of a Case, Student Ed., 404 pages, 1984 (Coursebook)

See also Civil Procedure

TRUSTS AND ESTATES

Atkinson's Hornbook on Wills, 2nd Ed., 975 pages, 1953 (Text)

Averill's Uniform Probate Code in a Nutshell, 2nd Ed., 454 pages, 1987 (Text)

Bogert's Hornbook on Trusts, 6th Ed., Student Ed., about 794 pages, 1987 (Text)

Clark, Lusky and Murphy's Cases and Materials on Gratuitous Transfers, 3rd Ed., 970 pages, 1985 (Casebook)

McGovern, Rein and Kurtz' Hornbook on Wills, Trusts and Estates, 1988 (Text)

TRUSTS AND ESTATES—Cont'd

McGovern's Cases and Materials on Wills, Trusts and Future Interests: An Introduction to Estate Planning, 750 pages, 1983 (Casebook)

Mennell's Wills and Trusts in a Nutshell, 392 pages, 1979 (Text)

Simes' Hornbook on Future Interests, 2nd Ed., 355 pages, 1966 (Text)

Turano and Radigan's Hornbook on New York Estate Administration, 676 pages, 1986 (Text)

Uniform Probate Code, Official Text With Comments, 615 pages, 1982

Waggoner's Future Interests in a Nutshell, 361 pages, 1981 (Text)

Waterbury's Materials on Trusts and Estates, 1039 pages, 1986 (Casebook)

WATER LAW

Getches' Water Law in a Nutshell, 439 pages, 1984 (Text)

Sax and Abram's Cases and Materials on Legal Control of Water Resources, 941 pages, 1986 (Casebook)

Trelease and Gould's Cases and Materials on Water Law, 4th Ed., 816 pages, 1986 (Casebook)

See also Energy and Natural Resources Law, Environmental Law

WILLS

See Trusts and Estates

WOMEN AND THE LAW

Kay's Text, Cases and Materials on Sex-Based Discrimination, 2nd Ed., 1045 pages, 1981, with 1986 Supplement (Casebook)

Thomas' Sex Discrimination in a Nutshell, 399 pages, 1982 (Text)

See also Employment Discrimination

WORKERS' COMPENSATION

See Social Legislation

THE LAW OF
DOMESTIC RELATIONS
IN THE UNITED STATES
Second Edition

By

Homer H. Clark, Jr.

Moses Lasky Professor of Law Emeritus
University of Colorado

This book is an abridgement of Clark's, "The Law of Domestic Relations in the United States, Second Edition, Volumes 1 & 2, Practitioner's Edition".

HORNBOOK SERIES
STUDENT EDITION

WEST PUBLISHING CO.
ST. PAUL, MINN., 1988

This is an abridgement of Clark's, "*The Law of Domestic Relations in the United States, Second Edition, Volumes 1 & 2, Practitioner's Edition*", West Publishing Co. 1987.

COPYRIGHT © 1968 By WEST PUBLISHING CO.
COPYRIGHT © 1988 By WEST PUBLISHING CO.
        50 West Kellogg Boulevard
        P.O. Box 64526
        St. Paul, Minnesota 55164-0526

Library of Congress Cataloging-in-Publication Data

Clark, Homer Harrison, 1918–
  The law of domestic relations in the United States / by Homer H.
  Clark, Jr. — Student ed., 2nd ed.
    p.   cm.
  ISBN 0-314-61281-5
  1. Domestic relations—United States. I. Title.
  KF504.C55 1988
  346.7301'5—dc19   87-22389
  [347.30615]   CIP

ISBN 0-314-61281-5

  Clark, Domestic Rel., 2nd Ed. HBSE

For Ann, Richard and Sarah

*

Preface

During the twenty years since the publication of the first edition of this work the law of domestic relations has changed enormously. Many forms of discrimination against women have been mitigated or removed. The power of the individual to control many of his personal relationships by contract has been increased. The discrimination against the illegitimate child has been removed, while the relationships between parents and illegitimate children have been altered in many respects. The old fault based grounds for divorce have largely been replaced by such non-fault grounds as marriage breakdown in many states. The financial aspects of divorce have changed in the direction of placing more emphasis on divisions of property and less on alimony. The enforcement of child support and to some extent the computation of awards have received attention from legislatures both state and federal. An entirely new jurisprudence of child custody jurisdiction has developed out of the Uniform Child Custody Jurisdiction Act. A region of the law which was formerly left exclusively to the states is now subject to federal regulation in many ways. Many other changes could be listed, but the foregoing are enough to indicate why this edition has had to be almost entirely rewritten. The present text contains little that remains unchanged from the first edition other than the general arrangement of the work.

The most obvious consequence of all this rapid change in a subject once surprisingly resistant to change is the uncomfortable awareness that change will continue. What forms the new developments will take and what forces will bring them about can hardly be predicted with any assurance. The present volume has had the limited purpose of attempting to indicate what the law of domestic relations looks like at the end of 1986 and so far as possible to suggest how it came to look that way. A strenuous effort has been made to bring the citations of statutes and cases up to that date, leaving to the reader the opportunity to make what assumptions he may wish about the future of the subject.

Although the citations in this edition are numerous, it has been impossible to include all of the possibly relevant authorities. Examples of both cases and statutes were chosen with the purpose of suggesting the general state of the law. I have not tried to avoid expressing my views of the wisdom or desirability of the legal principles revealed by either statutes or cases where I thought those views might be relevant. A law book containing no reflections of the author's opinions would certainly be a dull book to write and probably a dull one to read.

I am glad to acknowledge the help of a large number of colleagues in research and the preparation of the manuscript. Four deans of the

University of Colorado Law School, Don W. Sears, Courtland H. Peterson, Thomas G. Brown and Betsy Levin have been most understanding in scheduling classes and in providing student assistance for research over a period so long that I am sure they often thought that the project would never end. The University of Colorado Law Library staff, Professors Oscar Miller, Lois Calvert and Barbara Bintliff, have acquired many much needed materials and provided the expert research guidance that I have often depended upon. Several generations of law students have done excellent work on this edition. They are Rhonda Smith, Kenton Kuhlman, Corin Wood, Robin Taylor, Peter Blood, Lois Remcho, Marjorie Sloan, Chris Santistevan, Marcia Wade and Cynthia Cappel. The book could not have been written at all without the unfailing cooperation, kindness and expertise of the faculty secretaries, Anne Guthrie, Marge Brunner, Marcia Murphy and Kay Wilkie.

I should also like to acknowledge once again the encouragement and the indispensable help on the manuscript of my wife, Jean Clark. Her support greatly lightened the inevitable burdens attendant on any long legal research.

HOMER H. CLARK, Jr.

September 18, 1987

WESTLAW Introduction

Clark's, *The Law of Domestic Relations in the United States, Second Edition,* offers a detailed and comprehensive treatment of basic rules, principles, and issues in domestic relations law. However, readers occasionally need to find additional authority. In an effort to assist with comprehensive research of the law of domestic relations, preformulated WESTLAW references are included after most sections of the text in this edition. The WESTLAW references are designed for use with the WESTLAW computer-assisted legal research service. By joining this publication with the extensive WESTLAW databases in this way, the reader is able to move straight from the hornbook into WESTLAW with great speed and convenience.

Some readers may desire to use only the information supplied within the printed pages of this hornbook. Others, however, will encounter issues in domestic relations law that require further information. Accordingly, those who opt for additional material can rapidly and easily gain access to WESTLAW, an electronic law library that possesses extraordinary currency and magnitude.

The preformulated WESTLAW references in this text provide illustrative searches for readers who wish to do additional research on WESTLAW. The WESTLAW references are approximately as general as the material in the text to which they correspond. Readers should be cautioned against placing undue emphasis upon these references as final solutions to all possible issues treated in the text. In most instances, it is necessary to make refinements to the search references, such as the addition of other search terms or the substitution of different proximity connectors, to adequately fit the particular needs of an individual reader's research problem. The freedom, and also the responsibility, remains with the reader to "fine tune" the WESTLAW references in accordance with his or her own research requirements. The primary usefulness of the preformulated references is in providing a basic framework upon which further query construction can be built. The Appendix gives concise, step-by-step instruction on how to coordinate WESTLAW research with this book.

THE PUBLISHER

*

Summary of Contents

*

Table of Contents

CHAPTER 11. PROTECTION FOR RIGHTS OF CONSORTIUM

CHAPTER 12. JURISDICTION FOR DIVORCE, ALIMONY AND CUSTODY

CHAPTER 13. DIVORCE—GROUNDS AND DEFENSES

CHAPTER 14. DIVORCE PROCEDURE

CHAPTER 15. THE DIVISION OF PROPERTY ON DIVORCE

CHAPTER 16. ALIMONY, TEMPORARY AND PERMANENT

CHAPTER 17. CHILD SUPPORT ORDERS IN DIVORCE DECREES

CHAPTER 18. SEPARATION AGREEMENTS

CHAPTER 19. CUSTODY OF CHILDREN

CHAPTER 20. TERMINATION OF PARENTAL RIGHTS AND ADOPTION

*

THE LAW OF
DOMESTIC
RELATIONS
IN THE UNITED STATES
Second Edition

*

Chapter 1

ANTENUPTIAL AGREEMENTS

Table of Sections

---

§ 1.1 Antenuptial Agreements

The typical antenuptial agreement is made by an older man and woman who are about to be married, who have previously been married and who have property the disposition of which they wish to control.[1] The agreement which they make as they approach marriage generally limits the rights each is to have in the property of the other, during the marriage and upon the death of either. People in circumstances other than these might find it useful to execute an agreement regulating their property rights, but most such agreements are made against this background. Since divorce is on the increase and a large proportion of divorced persons remarry, the circumstances calling for an antenuptial agreement are arising more frequently. This kind of agreement is therefore of greater importance for the attorney today than in the past. For the same reasons a new use for antenuptial agreements has recently developed. The attorney today will often be asked to draw provisions regulating the rights of the parties not only with respect to inheritance of property on death but also with respect to both property and maintenance in the event they should later be divorced. This section will discuss the validity and construction of both the agreement regulating property rights on death and the agreement governing the consequences of divorce, leaving to the law of contracts those general principles which are common to all contracts.

In addition to the traditional antenuptial contract just described, there have recently been proposals for the use and legal enforcement of another kind of pre-marital contract, in which the spouses-to-be would attempt to regulate in detail most or all aspects of their marital relationship. Although the purposes and provisions of these contracts differ dramatically from the conventional antenuptial contract, they are antenuptial contracts of a sort and they will be discussed at the end of this section.

§ 1.1

1. Gamble, The Antenuptial Contract, 26 U.Miami L.Rev. 692, 730 (1972). An extreme example of the sort of person who finds the antenuptial contract useful occurs in Eule v. Eule, 24 Ill.App.3d 83, 320 N.E.2d 506 (1974), where the wife had been married six times, the husband nine times and where they had been married to each other three times.

Agreements having similar purposes and provisions are sometimes made after marriage. These are referred to as post-nuptial agreements. They are governed by principles similar to those governing antenuptial agreements and in general receive favorable treatment by the courts. See, e.g., Rockwell v. Estate of Rockwell, 24 Mich.App. 593, 180 N.W.2d 498 (1970).

Bartke, Marital Sharing—Why Not Do It By Contract? 67 Geo.L.J. 1131 (1979) suggests another function for antenuptial agreements, i.e. that they should be used to create a system of community property between spouses which would govern the ownership, management and disposition of property acquired by either during the marriage.

Broadly speaking antenuptial contracts of the kind described as typical are valid and enforceable and in fact are favored by the law as tending to promote marital harmony, if they meet certain requirements of form and substance.[2] They provide a useful method by which the spouses may be assured that their property will be disposed of in accordance with their wishes.

Statute of Frauds

The initial restriction to be observed in the execution of antenuptial agreements is the Statute of Frauds.[3] The third clause of that Statute has been enacted in most of the American states.[4] It requires promises made in consideration of marriage, other than mutual promises to marry, to be in writing signed by the party to be charged.[5] The reason for including antenuptial contracts among those for which a writing is required seems to be the greater risk that where marriage is part of the bargain the parties will give it less thought or consideration than would be the case with ordinary contracts.[6] If this is the

reason for including these agreements in the Statute, then the Statute should apply in all cases in which there is a substantial risk that the contract will be hasty or ill considered. This means that the contract should be held to be within the Statute whenever the proposed marriage is a substantial factor inducing the formation of the contract. The cases bear out this analysis by construing the statute to mean that if the consideration for the contract is either in whole or in part the marriage of the parties, it is unenforceable unless in writing.[7] A further consequence of this requirement of a writing is that if a conveyance is made by the husband pursuant to an oral agreement, unenforceable because not in writing, it may be fraudulent if it leaves the transferor insolvent.[8]

As is true under other clauses of the Statute of Frauds, a writing properly signed may make the oral antenuptial agreement enforceable even though it is executed subsequent to the oral agreement and subsequent to the parties' marriage.[9] But a will has been held

---

2. Boxberger v. Cotten, 206 Kan. 456, 479 P.2d 869 (1971); Fincham v. Fincham, 160 Kan. 683, 165 P.2d 209 (1946); Hartz v. Hartz, 248 Md. 47, 234 A.2d 865 (1967); Buettner v. Buettner, 89 Nev. 39, 505 P.2d 600 (1973); In re Hillegass' Estate, 431 Pa. 144, 244 A.2d 672 (1968); Lightman v. Magid, 54 Tenn.App. 701, 394 S.W.2d 151 (1965).

For an extensive treatment of antenuptial agreements, see A. Lindey, Separation Agreements and Antenuptial Contracts, section 90 (Revised ed. 1982).

For a good discussion of the antenuptial agreement provision of the Uniform Marital Property Act, see Oldham, Premarital Contracts Are Now Enforceable, Unless * * *, 21 Hous.L.Rev. 757 (1984).

Where the female party to an antenuptial agreement was an unemancipated minor, and was not assisted by her parents, the court in Wilkinson v. Wilkinson, 323 So. 2d 120 (La.1975) held that the agreement was a nullity.

An antenuptial agreement in which a spouse promised to appear before a religious tribunal was enforced in Avitzur v. Avitzur, 58 N.Y.2d 108, 459 N.Y.S.2d 572, 446 N.E.2d 136 (1983), cert. denied 464 U.S. 817, 104 S.Ct. 76, 78 L.Ed.2d 88 (1983), the court holding that this did not violate the First Amendment.

3. 29 Car. II, c. 3 (1677).

4. E.g., West's Ann. Cal.Civ.Code § 1624 (West 1973); N.Y.–McKinney's Gen.Oblig.L. § 5–701 (1978 & Supp. 1983). The Uniform Marital Property Act § 10, 9A Unif. L.Ann. 37 (Supp.1985) requires a "document." Some states have other statutes regulating the form or execu-

tion of antenuptial agreements, or marriage settlements as they are sometimes called. See, e.g., West's Ann. Cal. Civ.Code § 5134 (West 1983); V.T.C.A., Fam.Code § 5.41 (1975) (Supp.1984). Cases construing these requirements are collected in Annot., 16 A.L.R.3d 370 (1967). See also In re Loftin's Estate, 285 N.C. 717, 208 S.E.2d 670 (1974). Section 2–204 of the Uniform Probate Code, 8 Unif.L. Ann. 82 (1983) permits waiver by a surviving spouse of various rights in the estate of a deceased spouse by a written, signed agreement after fair disclosure. The parol evidence rule may exclude oral testimony inconsistent with the written agreement. Annot., 81 A.L.R.3d 453 (1977).

5. 2 A. Corbin, Contracts §§ 460, 461, 462 (1950); 3 S. Williston, Contracts §§ 485, 486 (3d ed. Jaeger 1960); Restatement 2nd Contracts §§ 110(1)(c), 124 (1981).

6. Miller v. Greene, 104 So.2d 457 (Fla.1958). This case permitted a recovery in quantum meruit, however.

7. Miller v. Greene, 104 So.2d 457 (Fla.1958); Herr v. Herr, 13 N.J. 79, 98 A.2d 55 (1953); Matter of Goldberg's Estate, 275 N.Y. 186, 9 N.E.2d 829 (1937). Other cases are cited in Annot., 75 A.L.R.2d 633 (1961).

As with other agreements falling within the Statute of Frauds, if the writing was lost, its contents may be proved by parol evidence. Whitenton v. Whitenton, 659 S.W.2d 542 (Mo.App.1983).

8. Jones v. Williams, 94 Vt. 175, 109 A. 803 (1920).

9. Ayoob v. Ayoob, 74 Cal.App.2d 236, 168 P.2d 462 (1946); Lee v. Central Bank & Trust Co. of Rockford, 56

not to suffice for a writing when it failed to refer to the oral agreement.[10]

The consensus of the cases seems to be that the celebration of the marriage does not constitute such part performance as to justify the enforcement of the oral antenuptial agreement,[11] even when a party has undergone a change of position other than the change of marital status.[12] If there has been full performance on both sides, the agreement may not be rescinded, however, merely on the ground that the agreement was originally oral and therefore unenforceable.[13]

The Requirement of Disclosure

As is the case with any other contract, the antenuptial agreement is not binding upon a party who was induced by fraudulent misrepresentations to sign it, as where the prospective husband falsely understates the amount of his property.[14] In addition it is clear that there is an affirmative duty imposed upon each spouse to disclose his or her financial status and that this duty goes beyond what is normally required for commercial contracts. Many courts take the view that the prospective spouses are in a confidential relationship,[15] and this seems clearly correct. The other relationships which the law finds confidential and in which it imposes affirmative duties of disclosure, such as trustee and beneficiary, agent and principal or the director and his corporation involve a special trust or reliance placed by one of the parties in the other. The same is true of the circumstances surrounding the antenuptial agreement. There the spouses-to-be are normally influenced by mutual affection on the eve of marriage to place a great deal of trust in each

Ill.2d 394, 308 N.E.2d 605 (1974); In re Weber's Estate, 170 Ohio St. 567, 167 N.E.2d 98 (1960).

10. Busque v. Marcou, 147 Me. 289, 86 A.2d 873 (1952).

11. Busque v. Marcou, 147 Me. 289, 86 A.2d 873 (1952); Herr v. Herr, 13 N.J. 79, 98 A.2d 55 (1953); Fuson, Marriage as Part Performance in Relation to the Statute of Frauds, 18 Ky.L.J. 281 (1930). Other cases are cited in Annot., 30 A.L.R.2d 1419 (1953). For criticism of these cases, see 2 A. Corbin, Contracts, § 463 (1950). See also Estate of Sheldon, 75 Cal.App.3d 364, 142 Cal.Rptr. 119 (1977) finding an estoppel to assert the statute of frauds.

12. Hutnak v. Hutnak, 78 R.I. 231, 81 A.2d 278 (1951). Here the wife was induced to come to America from Europe and marry the husband by an oral antenuptial contract, but the court nevertheless refused enforcement. But full performance by the husband and part performance by the wife were held to warrant enforcement of an oral antenuptial agreement in Sun Life Assurance Co. of Canada v. Hoy, 174 F.Supp. 859 (E.D.Ill.1959). And McGrath v. Hilding, 41 N.Y.2d 625, 394 N.Y.S.2d 603, 363 N.E.2d 328 (1977) held that a constructive trust on behalf of the wife may be imposed where the oral antenuptial induced a transfer of property to the husband resulting in unjust enrichment.

Campbell v. Campbell, 371 So.2d 55 (Ala.Civ.App.1979) enforced an oral antenuptial agreement where the defense of the statute of frauds was first raised on appeal and where both parties conceded that the oral agreement had been made.

13. Busque v. Marcou, 147 Me. 289, 86 A.2d 873 (1952). Herr v. Herr, 13 N.J. 79, 98 A.2d 55 (1953) is an extreme example of this and seems wrongly decided. The husband made an oral antenuptial contract, induced by the wife's misrepresentations that she was beneficiary of a trust whose benefits to her would cease on her remarriage. After marriage the husband made a settlement of property on her still in ignorance of her fraud. The court refused to set it aside, holding that since the oral agreement was unenforceable, the post-nuptial settlement was voluntary and not open to attack even though fraudulently induced. The case may be explainable on the ground of failure to prove the fraud, but if it was proved, the gift should be recoverable by the donor. See Restatement, Restitution § 26 (1937).

14. Mathis v. Crane, 360 Mo. 631, 230 S.W.2d 707 (1950); In re McClellan's Estate, 365 Pa. 401, 75 A.2d 595 (1950); In re Harris' Estate, 431 Pa. 293, 245 A.2d 647 (1968), cert. denied 393 U.S. 1065, 89 S.Ct. 718, 21 L.Ed.2d 707 (1969); In re Gelb's Estate, 425 Pa. 117, 228 A.2d 367 (1967).

15. In re Estate of Lopata, 641 P.2d 952 (Colo.1982); Watson v. Watson, 5 Ill.2d 526, 126 N.E.2d 220 (1955); In re Broadie's Estate, 208 Kan. 621, 493 P.2d 289 (1972); Hartz v. Hartz, 248 Md. 47, 234 A.2d 865 (1967); Rosenberg v. Lipnick, 377 Mass. 666, 389 N.E.2d 385 (1979); In re Estate of Strickland, 181 Neb. 478, 149 N.W.2d 344 (1967); Kosik v. George, 253 Or. 15, 452 P.2d 560 (1969); In re Hillegass' Estate, 431 Pa. 144, 244 A.2d 672 (1968). Lightman v. Magid, 54 Tenn.App. 701, 394 S.W.2d 151 (1965) takes the view that the relationship of prospective spouses is not a confidential one in some circumstances, as where the marriage is one of "convenience" between persons who are well along in years. Other courts have rejected the characterization of the relationship as confidential but have nevertheless imposed an affirmative duty of disclosure. Del Vecchio v. Del Vecchio, 143 So.2d 17 (Fla.1962); Lutgert v. Lutgert, 338 So.2d 1111 (Fla. App.1976), appeal after remand 362 So.2d 58 (Fla.App. 1978), cert. denied 367 So.2d 1125 (Fla.1979); In re Estate of Borton, 393 P.2d 808 (Wyo.1964). See also In re Marriage of Dawley, 17 Cal.3d 342, 131 Cal.Rptr. 3, 551 P.2d 323 (1976). Florida has in part abolished any affirmative duty of disclosure by a recent statute. See Weintraub v. Weintraub, 395 So.2d 302 (Fla.App.1981).

other, and in many cases they are unequal in their knowledge and understanding of one another's property and financial affairs. The courts therefore have ample reason to label the relationship confidential and to require a full disclosure of the financial circumstances of the parties and of the consequences of the antenuptial agreement, as a condition upon enforcing it.

When this generalization is applied to individual cases with their endless variety of facts, it is not surprising that the results are varied and at times inconsistent. In some instances, for example, the husband is relatively more experienced or more competent in business affairs than the wife.[16] In other instances the wife may be more competent and therefore correspondingly less in need of protection from the courts,[17] and if the disparity is great, he may be the one who needs protection.

16. E.g., Linker v. Linker, 28 Colo.App. 131, 470 P.2d 921 (1970); Watson v. Watson, 5 Ill.2d 526, 126 N.E.2d 220 (1955); Kosik v. George, 253 Or. 15, 452 P.2d 560 (1969); Hamlin v. Merlino, 44 Wash.2d 851, 272 P.2d 125 (1954); In re Marriage of Hadley, 88 Wash.2d 649, 565 P.2d 790 (1977).

17. E.g., In re Cantrell's Estate, 154 Kan. 546, 119 P.2d 483 (1941); In re Estate of Borton, 393 P.2d 808 (Wyo.1964).

18. Herman v. Goetz, 204 Kan. 91, 460 P.2d 554 (1969); Matter of Marriage of Knoll, 65 Or.App. 484, 671 P.2d 718 (1983); In re Marriage of Hadley, 88 Wash.2d 649, 565 P.2d 790 (1977), 53 Wash.L.Rev. 763 (1978) (post-nuptial agreement).

19. Del Vecchio v. Del Vecchio, 143 So.2d 17 (Fla. 1962); In re Broadie's Estate, 208 Kan. 621, 493 P.2d 289 (1972); In re Spieth's Estate, 181 Neb. 11, 146 N.W.2d 746 (1966); Schutterle v. Schutterle, 260 N.W.2d 341 (S.D.1977); In re McClellan's Estate, 365 Pa. 401, 75 A.2d 595 (1950); In re Hillegass' Estate, 431 Pa. 144, 244 A.2d 672 (1968); Hamlin v. Merlino, 44 Wash.2d 851, 272 P.2d 125 (1954). Other cases are collected in Annot., 27 A.L.R.2d 883 (1953), and Note, 33 Ky.L.J. 197 (1945). Illinois cases have raised a presumption of concealment from the fact that the wife received a disproportionately small share of the property. Fleming v. Fleming, 85 Ill. App.3d 532, 40 Ill.Dec. 676, 406 N.E.2d 879 (1980). But see West's Fla.Stat.Ann. § 732.702(2) (1976) and Weintraub v. Weintraub, 417 So.2d 629 (Fla.1982).

20. Wylie v. Wylie, 249 Ark. 316, 459 S.W.2d 127 (1970); Linker v. Linker, 28 Colo.App. 131, 470 P.2d 921 (1970); Potter v. Collin, 321 So.2d 128 (Fla.App.1975), cert. denied 336 So.2d 1180 (Fla.1976); Lutgert v. Lutgert, 338 So.2d 1111 (Fla.App.1976), appeal after remand 362 So.2d 58 (Fla.App.1978), cert. denied 367 So.2d 1125 (Fla. 1979); Matter of Marriage of Norris, 51 Or.App. 43, 624

The position which many courts have taken is to require essential fairness under all the relevant circumstances.[18] Thus if the agreement makes a fair and reasonable provision for the wife, taking into account her needs and the husband's means, it will be upheld.[19] But if the agreement does not appear to provide adequately for the wife, then the husband must make a full, accurate and specific disclosure of the extent of his property.[20] In the latter case the court may also be influenced in disapproving the antenuptial agreement by the fact that it was drawn by the husband's lawyer and not thoroughly explained to the wife, or by the fact that she was not advised by counsel of her own.[21] On the other hand, where the wife is fully advised of her rights and of the effect upon them of the antenuptial agreement, or where she is experienced in business and used to handling her own affairs, the agreement

P.2d 636 (1981); Bauer v. Bauer, 1 Or.App. 504, 464 P.2d 710 (1970). In In re Perelman's Estate, 438 Pa. 112, 263 A.2d 375 (1970) the court held that the husband was not at fault for failing to disclose property in which he had only a life estate, since this was not an interest over which he had a power of testamentary disposition. For other similar cases see note 19 supra. The Uniform Marital Property Act § 10(g), 9A Unif.L.Ann. 38 (Supp. 1985) requires that the agreement not be unconscionable, that there was a fair disclosure, and no waiver, and no notice of the spouse's property. The Uniform Premarital Agreement & Act, § 556, 9A Unif.L.Ann. 336 (Supp.1985) is similar.

Matter of Lebsock's Estate, 44 Colo.App. 220, 618 P.2d 683 (1980) disapproved a jury charge that a wife would be presumed to have knowledge of the husband's property if she had information which would lead a reasonably prudent person to make inquiry and failed to make such an inquiry.

In re Estate of Lopata, 641 P.2d 952 (Colo.1982) takes the position that it is sufficient if each spouse provides the other with general and approximate information about his net worth.

21. Kosik v. George, 253 Or. 15, 452 P.2d 560 (1969); Matter of Estate of Crawford, 107 Wash.2d 493, 730 P.2d 675 (1986); Friedlander v. Friedlander, 80 Wash.2d 293, 494 P.2d 208 (1972). But if the agreement is fair and reasonable, it will be upheld even where the wife did not have the advice of her own counsel. Whitney v. Seattle-First National Bank, 90 Wash.2d 105, 579 P.2d 937 (1978); Note, 54 Wash.L.Rev. 135 (1978); Gant v. Gant, ___ W.Va. ___, 329 S.E.2d 106 (1985).

Matter of Marriage of Adams, 240 Kan. 315, 729 P.2d 1151 (1986) upheld an agreement which was presented to the wife one hour before the wedding.

should be upheld even though the details of the husband's finances are not disclosed to her.[22] In such a case it is sufficient that she knows her husband is rich, even though she does not know the exact extent of his wealth.[23]

Since, as has been indicated in this section, antenuptial agreements are generally viewed with favor by the courts, it is likewise generally held that the party who is asserting the invalidity of the agreement for lack of disclosure or other unfairness has the burden of proof on this issue,[24] and in fact may be required to establish his claim by clear and convincing evidence.[25] But the party attacking the agreement may be handicapped in sustaining the burden of proof by the Dead Man's Statute which excludes the testimony of a person making a claim against the estate of a deceased person as to transactions with the deceased.[26]

When the antenuptial agreement is looked at from the point of view of the draftsman, the foregoing authorities clearly point to the necessity of ensuring both a full disclosure by each party and an opportunity for each to obtain independent legal advice if he or she wishes it.[27] The full disclosure may best be

made by attaching a complete and accurate account of each party's property to the agreement itself. This is especially important in those cases where the parties wish to make an agreement which might later be considered to provide inadequately for one of them. The practice of having the agreement drawn by the husband's lawyer, without giving the wife an adequate opportunity to obtain independent advice and counsel should certainly be avoided, even though the husband's lawyer views himself as merely performing the function of "scrivener". It seems very doubtful whether one lawyer can purport to represent both parties in such a situation without risking a violation of the Canons of Ethics.[28]

Conflict of Laws

Since the laws of the various states differ to some extent respecting either the formal requirements or the duty of disclosure in the execution of antenuptial agreements, and more importantly respecting the validity of provisions relating to divorce or separation, difficult questions of the conflict of laws may arise. The case law is scanty. One case seems to adopt the view that the law of the state having the most "contacts" with the

22. Matter of Lewin's Estate, 42 Colo.App. 129, 595 P.2d 1055 (1979); In re West's Estate, 194 Kan. 736, 402 P.2d 117 (1965); Hartz v. Hartz, 248 Md. 47, 234 A.2d 865 (1967); McFerron v. Trask, 3 Or.App. 111, 472 P.2d 847 (1970); Schutterle v. Schutterle, 260 N.W.2d 341 (S.D. 1977); Laird v. Laird, 597 P.2d 463 (Wyo.1979). A long delay in attacking the agreement will also leave the court reluctant to upset it. In re Estate of Strickland, 181 Neb. 478, 149 N.W.2d 344 (1967).

At least one case has held that if a full disclosure is made when the antenuptial agreement is executed, the agreement may not be upset later on the ground that circumstances have so changed as to leave a spouse with inadequate resources. Youngblood's Estate v. Youngblood, 457 S.W.2d 750 (Mo.1970).

23. In re Estate of Borton, 393 P.2d 808 (Wyo.1964); Annot., 27 A.L.R.2d 883, 896 (1953).

24. Linker v. Linker, 28 Colo.App. 131, 470 P.2d 921 (1970); In re Estate of Strickland, 181 Neb. 478, 149 N.W.2d 344 (1967).

25. In re Hillegass' Estate, 431 Pa. 144, 244 A.2d 672 (1968). But Kosik v. George, 253 Or. 15, 452 P.2d 560 (1969) takes the position that if the evidence shows that the provision for the wife is clearly inadequate in view of the husband's wealth, this raises a presumption of concealment and places the burden on the husband of prov-

ing full knowledge of all the material facts on the wife's part when she signed the agreement. In Matter of Benker's Estate, 416 Mich. 681, 331 N.W.2d 193 (1982) the court held that the burden of proof is on the party attacking the argument, but also held that evidence of seven specified factors creates a rebuttable presumption of non-disclosure. The factors include a waiver of all rights by the spouse; a disparity between the estates of the spouses; a secretive spouse; no provision in the agreement as to disclosure; no legal representation for the spouse and similar factors. The presumption so created is clearly unnecessary and confusing, since it seems to result in a sort of travelling burden of proof. The rule is better stated in the text at note 18.

26. In re Estate of Lopata, 641 P.2d 952 (Colo.1982); In re Estate of Strickland, 181 Neb. 478, 149 N.W.2d 344 (1967) (semble). In re Gelb's Estate, 425 Pa. 117, 228 A.2d 367 (1967) indicates that the Dead Man's Statute would normally apply to exclude testimony of the widow, but in the particular case her testimony was admissible under an exception to the Statute.

27. See Cathey, Antenuptial Agreements in Arkansas—A Drafter's Problem, 24 Ark.L.Rev. 275 (1970).

28. ABA Model Code of Professional Responsibility, DR 5-105, EC 5-15, 5-16 (1981).

agreement should control its validity.[29] Another applies the law of the state in which the contract was made.[30] If the parties express a wish concerning the applicable law in the contract, their wish might control. The Restatement (Second) of Conflict of Laws would apply the law of the state chosen by the parties in most cases, unless that state has no substantial relation to the contract or unless the law of that state offends a fundamental policy of a state having a greater interest in the particular issue, and in the absence of an expressed intention as to the law to be applied, it would apply the law of the state having the most significant relationship to the transaction and the parties.[31] Where the issue is the formal requisites for an antenuptial agreement, or the validity of the disclosure made by a party, it would seem that the law of the place of execution of the agreement ought to be the governing law. The reason for this is that the parties presumably acted with reference to that law. But where the issue is whether the antenuptial agreement may validly control alimony or the division of property on divorce, the state having the most significant relationship to the controversy would seem to be that of the parties' domicile at the time of divorce, and therefore the law of that state should apply. It is that state which will have the greatest interest in the welfare of the parties and the support of the spouses.

Antenuptial Agreements and Divorce

The typical antenuptial agreement has been described as one which controls the devolution of the parties' property on death.[32] So long as it has only that function, the agreement is unobjectionable if other requirements already discussed have been met.[33] Additional problems are created when the agreement purports to govern the obligations of the parties to pay alimony or child support after divorce, their obligations respecting the disposition of their property on divorce, or even their obligations to support each other during marriage.

Antenuptial agreements attempting to establish the amount of alimony or maintenance payable in the event that the marriage should end in separation or divorce were, until quite recently, almost universally held to be invalid.[34] In some of the cases the agreements provided that the wife waived all claims for support or alimony, and these cases might therefore be explained as making inadequate provision for her, a ground of invalidity which would exist whether or not divorce were involved.[35] But the opinions in these cases generally rest upon a broader principle than this. The assertion is that such an agreement, as one case put it, "invites dispute, encourages separation and incites divorce." [36] What this seems to amount to is the argument that an agreement made before marriage is conducive to divorce when it includes alimony or maintenance provisions intended to become effective upon separation or

29. Osborn v. Osborn, 10 Ohio Misc. 171, 226 N.E.2d 814 (1966), affirmed 18 Ohio St.2d 144, 248 N.E.2d 191 (1969).

30. Hill v. Hill, 262 A.2d 661 (Del.Ch.1970), affirmed 269 A.2d 212 (Sup.1970).

31. Restatement (Second) of Conflict of Laws §§ 187, 188 (1971). See also DeLorean v. DeLorean, 211 N.J. Super. 432, 511 A.2d 1257 (1986).

32. See the text at note 1, supra.

33. Lefevers v. Lefevers, 240 Ark. 992, 403 S.W.2d 65 (1966); In re Estate of Borton, 393 P.2d 808 (Wyo.1964).

34. Norris v. Norris, 174 N.W.2d 368 (Iowa 1970); Fincham v. Fincham, 160 Kan. 683, 165 P.2d 209 (1946); Holliday v. Holliday, 358 So.2d 618 (La.1978); Hilbert v. Hilbert, 168 Md. 364, 177 A. 914 (1935); French v. McAnarney, 290 Mass. 544, 195 N.E. 714 (1935); Crouch v.

Crouch, 53 Tenn.App. 594, 385 S.W.2d 288 (1964); Caldwell v. Caldwell, 5 Wis.2d 146, 92 N.W.2d 356 (1958); Fricke v. Fricke, 257 Wis. 124, 42 N.W.2d 500 (1950). Other cases are collected in Annots., 98 A.L.R. 533 (1935) and 70 A.L.R. 826 (1931). The only case in which such a contract was upheld was Hudson v. Hudson, 350 P.2d 596 (Okl.1960). A few cases held that such contracts could be admitted in evidence as a guide to the court in the divorce suit, but without having binding force on the parties. See, e.g. Moats v. Moats, 168 Colo. 120, 450 P.2d 64 (1969); Krejci v. Krejci, 191 Neb. 698, 217 N.W.2d 470 (1974) (dictum).

35. See, e.g., Fincham v. Fincham, 160 Kan. 683, 165 P.2d 209 (1946), in which the court seems to place emphasis on the inadequacy of the provision for the spouse.

36. Fricke v. Fricke, 257 Wis. 124, 127, 128, 42 N.W.2d 500, 502 (1950).

divorce.[37] Some cases would hold the entire antenuptial agreement invalid on this ground,[38] while others would find the invalid provisions separable and enforce the remainder of the agreement.[39] The latter approach would seem to be preferable unless it could not be taken without altering the impact of the valid provisions to the prejudice of one party or the other.

It is certainly not demonstrable as a general proposition that an agreement respecting alimony made before marriage promotes divorce. On the contrary it may promote marital stability, providing it is arrived at fairly and makes adequate provision for both spouses.[40] In any event it will reduce the hostility and destructiveness of a divorce if one should occur. Furthermore, in the many states which now have adopted marriage breakdown or a similar ground for divorce there is no longer as much reason as formerly to be hostile to agreements which facilitate divorce. By adopting this ground for divorce these states have recognized that nothing is to be gained by trying to hold spouses together when in fact their marriage has broken down. The antenuptial agreement in such states can hardly be more conducive to divorce than the divorce grounds themselves.

For some such reasons as these, since 1970 a line of cases has developed in which the courts have held that antenuptial agreements fixing maintenance on divorce or separation are valid. The first case was Posner v. Posner[41] in which the antenuptial agreement, made by an impecunious wife and a wealthy husband, provided for support to the wife of six hundred dollars per month on divorce. The court found that the state's opposition to divorce and insistence on the preservation of marriage had become attenuated over the years. It then held that this change in public policy should have the effect of validating antenuptial agreements settling alimony and property rights upon divorce. The court emphasized two points, however. In the first place the agreement must meet the tests of fairness and adequacy already discussed.[42] In the second place the agreement was held valid only as to conditions existing at the time

---

37. In addition to the cases cited supra note 34, see In re Murdock's Estate, 213 Kan. 837, 519 P.2d 108 (1974), and Ranney v. Ranney, 219 Kan. 428, 548 P.2d 734 (1976). But see Matlock v. Matlock, 223 Kan. 679, 576 P.2d 629 (1978). The situation in California in this respect has become confused by virtue of In re Marriage of Dawley, 17 Cal.3d 342, 131 Cal.Rptr. 3, 551 P.2d 323 (1976), which purported to disapprove a statement in In re Higgason's Marriage, 10 Cal.3d 476, 110 Cal.Rptr. 897, 516 P.2d 289 (1973) to the effect that antenuptial agreements must be made in contemplation of lifelong marriage in order to be valid. The Dawley case upheld an agreement respecting property which clearly contemplated divorce. The court said that it was not the parties' subjective intent not to remain married which invalidated such agreements, but rather that the terms of the agreement itself encouraged or promoted divorce. It is not clear from the case whether an antenuptial agreement attempting to set alimony in the event of divorce would be held to have promoted divorce.

38. E.g., Fincham v. Fincham, 160 Kan. 683, 165 P.2d 209 (1946); Cord v. Neuhoff, 94 Nev. 21, 573 P.2d 1170 (1978).

39. E.g., In re Higgason's Marriage, 10 Cal.3d 476, 110 Cal.Rptr. 897, 516 P.2d 289 (1973); In re Muxlow's Estate, 367 Mich. 133, 116 N.W.2d 43 (1962).

40. See the dissent in Fricke v. Fricke, 257 Wis. 124, 128, 42 N.W.2d 500, 502 (1950). It is possible in some circumstances that specific provisions in an antenuptial agreement might provide a financial incentive to one of the spouses to obtain a divorce. For example, an agree-

ment by which the wife agrees to accept alimony for three years at fifteen hundred dollars per month, and a property settlement of fifteen thousand dollars in full settlement of all claims, the agreement to expire after eight years of marriage, might be thought to invite the husband to seek a divorce, if he had a large amount of property, before the expiration of the agreement. In such circumstances it might be argued that he would profit by ending the marriage on the contract terms if a court, after the end of eight years, would be likely to give the wife far more alimony or property than the amounts specified in the agreement. But of course this argument would apply in any case in which the contract provides for payments less than a divorce court might award. Invalidating such a contract really amounts to a decision that the sums provided for the wife were unfair.

41. 233 So.2d 381 (Fla.1970). This case was decided at a time when Florida still had the conventional grounds for divorce. Later Florida adopted irretrievable breakdown and mental incompetence as the sole grounds for divorce. West's Fla.Stat.Ann. § 61.052 (1973), (West Supp.1984).

42. A later appeal in the Posner case held that where an inadequate provision (in proportion to the husband's means) is made for the wife in the agreement, the husband has the burden of proving that the wife had full knowledge of his property at the time she executed the agreement. Finding that the burden of proof was not sustained, and in fact that there may have been concealment of assets, the court invalidated the antenuptial agreement. Posner v. Posner, 257 So.2d 530 (Fla.1972).

the agreement was made. A Florida statute in force when the case was decided authorized the courts of that state to enter orders increasing or decreasing support payments provided by agreement between the spouses when it appeared that the circumstances of the parties or the financial ability of the husband had changed since the execution of the agreement.[43]

Since the Posner case was decided many cases have followed it advancing much the same arguments as did the Florida court and being equally careful to insist that the antenuptial agreement must be fair and based upon full knowledge on the part of each party concerning the property of the other.[44] In one case decided since Posner but not citing it the California Supreme Court has adhered to the pre-Posner rule that an antenuptial contract which relieves one spouse of the duty of supporting the other on separation or divorce is invalid.[45] The case relies to some extent on certain California statutes,[46] however, and may not stand for the proposition that an agreement setting a fair and adequate figure

for alimony would be invalid. The court does repeat the old argument that contracts which facilitate divorce or separation are void.

In short, the law now seems to be developing in the direction of permitting spouses, by means of an antenuptial agreement, to control their obligations for alimony or maintenance on divorce or separation, provided the agreement meets the requirements of fairness made for all such agreements, and with the additional qualification that the agreement makes adequate provision for each spouse in view of the needs and resources of each. In other words the rules for antenuptial agreements are being assimilated to those applicable to separation agreements.[47]

One further question is raised by Posner and the cases which follow it. These cases insist that the antenuptial agreement must be fair and must make adequate provision for the spouses. The question thus is, are the fairness and adequacy of the agreement to be determined as of the date on which the agreement was executed, or as of the date on which enforcement is sought, or perhaps as of both

43. West's Fla.Stat.Ann. § 61.14 (1973).

44. In re Marriage of Ingels, 42 Colo.App. 245, 596 P.2d 1211 (1979) (property division only); McHugh v. McHugh, 181 Conn. 482, 436 A.2d 8 (1980) (property only); Parniawski v. Parniawski, 33 Conn.Supp. 44, 359 A.2d 719 (1976); Burtoff v. Burtoff, 418 A.2d 1085 (D.C. App.1980); Belcher v. Belcher, 307 So.2d 918 (Fla.App. 1975); Cert. denied 317 So.2d 762 (Fla.1975); Scherer v. Scherer, 249 Ga. 635, 292 S.E.2d 662 (1982); Volid v. Volid, 6 Ill.App.3d 386, 286 N.E.2d 42 (1972); In re Marriage of Boren, 475 N.E.2d 690 (Ind.1985); Frey v. Frey, 298 Md. 552, 471 A.2d 705 (1984); Osborne v. Osborne, 384 Mass. 591, 428 N.E.2d 810 (1981); Ferry v. Ferry, 586 S.W.2d 782 (Mo.App.1979); Buettner v. Buettner, 89 Nev. 39, 505 P.2d 600 (1973); Marschall v. Marschall, 195 N.J.Super. 16, 477 A.2d 833 (1984); Gross v. Gross, 11 Ohio St.3d 99, 464 N.E.2d 500 (1984), appeal after remand 23 Ohio App.3d 172 (1985); Unander v. Unander, 265 Or. 102, 506 P.2d 719 (1973) (overruling Reiling v. Reiling, 256 Or. 448, 474 P.2d 327 (1970), with the qualification that the antenuptial agreement will not be enforced if it deprives the spouse of her only source of support); Gant v. Gant, ___ W.Va. ___, 329 S.E.2d 106 (1985). Eule v. Eule, 24 Ill.App.3d 83, 320 N.E.2d 506 (1974), stated that the "trend in the law" is to uphold these antenuptial agreements if they are fair and reasonable, but then went on to hold that the agreement in suit was not fair and reasonable when it provided that the wife waived all claims for alimony or support if the marriage should be dissolved within seven years. The court drew an analogy to separation agreements, which it held would not be valid in Illinois if they contained

similar provisions. Cf. Flora v. Flora, 166 Ind.App. 620, 337 N.E.2d 846 (1975). And see the discussion in Note, 11 Ga.L.Rev. 406 (1977).

Some cases contra Posner include In re Gudenkauf's Marriage, 204 N.W.2d 586 (Iowa 1973); Sousley v. Sousley, 614 S.W.2d 942 (Ky.1981); Mulford v. Mulford, 211 Neb. 747, 320 N.W.2d 470 (1982); Connolly v. Connolly, 270 N.W.2d 44 (S.D.1978).

The Uniform Marital Property Act § 10(c)(3) and (4), 9A Unif.L.Ann. 37 (Supp.1985) seems to follow the Posner case. The Uniform Premarital Agreement Act § 3, 9A Unif.L.Ann. 335 (Supp.1985) is similar.

45. In re Higgason's Marriage, 10 Cal.3d 476, 110 Cal. Rptr. 897, 516 P.2d 289 (1973). In re Marriage of Dawley, 17 Cal.3d 342, 131 Cal.Rptr. 3, 551 P.2d 323 (1976) disapproved a statement in the Higgason case to the effect that antenuptial agreements are invalid unless the parties contemplated a marriage lasting until the death of one of them, but it did not cite Posner, and did not retreat from the general doctrine that antenuptial agreements whose terms encourage or promote divorce are invalid. See also Cord v. Neuhoff, 94 Nev. 21, 573 P.2d 1170 (1978) holding invalid a post-nuptial agreement limiting the husband's duty of support, and Connolly v. Connolly, 270 N.W.2d 44 (S.D.1978), 24 S.D.L.Rev. 495 (1979), rejecting the Posner result.

46. West's Ann.Cal.Civ.Code §§ 4801, 5132 (1983 and Supp.1984).

47. See sections 15.1 and 15.2, infra.

dates? There may be a long period between the signing of the antenuptial agreement and the parties' divorce action.[48] Of course the question does not normally arise until the divorce action is brought and the argument is made that alimony or maintenance must be awarded in an amount equal to that called for by the agreement. If, as many courts have said,[49] the state has an interest in the support of its citizens, then the antenuptial agreement should be held valid only when it is found to have been fair both at the time of execution and at the time of the divorce. In most states a separation agreement, when presented to the court in divorce proceedings, will only be incorporated in the divorce decree if it is found to make adequate provision for the spouses, although there are some cases holding that such an agreement must be enforced unless fraud, duress or breach of the confidential relation have entered into its execution.[50] Due to the greater period of time which will usually intervene between execution and enforcement of antenuptial agreements, there is all the more reason for the courts to scrutinize their adequacy at the time of the divorce than in the case of separation agreements. It therefore seems logical to adopt a rule that

the antenuptial agreement will only be enforced if it makes adequate provision for the spouses in view of the circumstances existing both at the date of execution and the date of enforcement. Some courts have taken this position, in whole or in part.[51]

The antenuptial agreement may approach the question of what effect a divorce or separation is to have upon the devolution of the spouses' property (as distinguished from alimony or maintenance) in either of two ways. The distinction between the two types of agreement is significant, since the first raises no questions concerning validity, while the second is analogous to the agreement considered in the Posner case and those cases following it. The first of these agreements merely provides that the property of the parties is to be divided in a prescribed way upon their death, and that the division is only to occur if the parties remain married to each other and living together as husband and wife at the time of death. Such an agreement is clearly valid and the courts so hold.[52] In fact the antenuptial contract should usually contain such a provision, since without it there is some risk that a court would give a surviving ex-spouse his or her agreed share of the de-

48. In In re Murdock's Estate, 213 Kan. 837, 519 P.2d 108 (1974) it was twenty-four years between execution of the antenuptial agreement and the parties' separation.

49. E.g., Unander v. Unander, 265 Or. 102, 506 P.2d 719 (1973).

50. See the discussion in section 18.2, infra. The Uniform Marriage and Divorce Act § 306, 9A Unif.L. Ann. 135 (1979), provides that a separation agreement is binding on the divorce court unless "unconscionable". Perhaps the rule should be the same for antenuptial agreements, although the Uniform Act does not purport to apply to such agreements.

51. Scherer v. Scherer, 249 Ga. 635, 292 S.E.2d 662 (1982). Newman v. Newman, 653 P.2d 728 (Colo.1982); Hill v. Hill, 356 N.W.2d 49 (Minn.App.1984); and Gross v. Gross, 11 Ohio St.3d 99, 464 N.E.2d 500 (1984), appeal after remand 23 Ohio App.3d 172, 492 N.E.2d 476 (1985) hold that the antenuptial agreement is binding on the parties with respect to the division of property if fair and equitable when executed and may not be reviewed for unconscionability at the time of the divorce. But these cases also hold that the maintenance provisions in the agreement *may* be reviewed for unconscionability at the time of the divorce in response to the sort of argument made in the text. Unconscionability seems to be defined as occurring when enforcement of the agreement would leave the spouse without sufficient property, mainte-

nance, or appropriate employment to support himself. The necessity for making this distinction between a division of property and maintenance which these cases impose leaves the courts with the same essentially impossible task which arises in other contexts. The impossibility results from the fact that in most states the purposes of the property division and those of maintenance are the same, providing for the future support of the obligee spouse. This problem is explored in section 15.1, infra.

Contra the text statement: Youngblood's Estate v. Youngblood, 457 S.W.2d 750 (Mo.1970), holding that the validity and applicability of the antenuptial agreement are to be judged at the time it is made, and that later changes in circumstances do not affect the application of the agreement.

Gant v. Gant, ___ W.Va. ___, 329 S.E.2d 106 (1985) reaches a result not unlike that outlined in the text by holding that the antenuptial agreement governs the financial incidents of the divorce so long as the circumstances at the time of divorce are roughly what the parties foresaw when they made the agreement.

52. E.g., Rosenstiel v. Rosenstiel, 368 F.Supp. 51 (S.D. N.Y.1973), affirmed 503 F.2d 1397 (2d Cir.1974) (citing New York cases); Hughes v. Hughes, 251 Ark. 63, 471 S.W.2d 355 (1971); Boxberger v. Cotten, 206 Kan. 456, 479 P.2d 869 (1971); In re Murdock's Estate, 213 Kan. 837, 519 P.2d 108 (1974).

ceased's estate even though that would usually not be the wish of the parties.[53]

The second form of agreement is like that in Posner, except that it provides for a specified distribution of property in the event of divorce rather than for a specified level of alimony or maintenance. Before Posner the courts generally held that such agreements were invalid, for the same reasons as were advanced in support of the alimony cases.[54] It is argued in a later section of this work that very often the property division decreed by the divorce court performs essentially the same function as alimony.[55] If so, the antenuptial agreement concerning the disposition of the parties' property on divorce should share the same fate as the agreement concerning alimony. Under the pre-Posner rule it was sensible to hold such an agreement invalid. If, as seems to be the case, Posner is to be widely followed and alimony agreements are valid, then agreements governing the property division should likewise be held valid.[56]

Effect of Divorce or Separation

Today, as the result of the Posner case and others like it, antenuptial agreements are being drafted to include provisions on the effect of divorce or separation. In the absence of such provisions, however, a question arises as to the effect on the parties' rights when the marriage ends in divorce or separation. As might be predicted, courts disagree on this. Some hold that since the antenuptial agreement is made in contemplation of marriage, and since divorce terminates the marriage, the divorce also terminates the agreement.[57] Another way of dealing with the problem is to say that the antenuptial agreement assumes that the parties will live up to their marriage contract. The losing defendant in the divorce action is barred from relief under the antenuptial contract because he has been found guilty of a breach of the marriage contract.[58] Still other cases hold that the later separation or divorce does not affect obligations under the antenuptial contract where that contract contains no express provisions on the point.[59]

---

53. Sims v. Sims, 186 Neb. 780, 186 N.W.2d 491 (1971), overruled 224 Neb. 510, 398 N.W.2d 722 (1987). The cases are not in agreement on whether an annulment of the marriage makes an otherwise valid antenuptial agreement unenforceable, in the absence of a provision in the agreement expressly dealing with the problem. The correct result would seem to be that the agreement should not be enforced after an annulment, just as it should not be after divorce, but the draftsman cannot rely on the courts to reach this result. See, e.g., In re Estate of Simms, 26 N.Y.2d 163, 309 N.Y.S.2d 170, 257 N.E.2d 627 (1970), 9 Duq.L.Rev. 135 (1970); Annot., 46 A.L.R.3d 1403 (1972).

54. Fricke v. Fricke, 257 Wis. 124, 42 N.W.2d 500 (1950) seems so to hold. In re Muxlow's Estate, 367 Mich. 133, 116 N.W.2d 43 (1962) in effect reads out of the agreement a provision respecting the division of property on divorce, presumably because the inclusion of such a provision would cast doubt on the validity of the agreement. Annot., 57 A.L.R.2d 942 (1958) collects cases which hold invalid agreements that the innocent spouse forfeits property rights on suing for divorce. See also Oliphant v. Oliphant, 177 Ark. 613, 7 S.W.2d 783 (1928).

55. See section 13.7, infra.

56. Spector v. Spector, 23 Ariz.App. 131, 531 P.2d 176 (1975). In re Marriage of Dawley, 17 Cal.3d 342, 131 Cal. Rptr. 3, 551 P.2d 323 (1976) enforced on divorce an agreement that all property acquired by either party during the marriage would remain separate property, the court distinguishing between agreements made in subjective contemplation of divorce, which it said are valid, and those having the objective effect of promoting or facilitating divorce, which it said are invalid. Tomlinson v.

Tomlinson, 170 Ind.App. 331, 352 N.E.2d 785 (1976) upheld an antenuptial agreement providing that upon divorce the husband would retain the property he owned at the time of the marriage. This agreement did not purport to limit alimony. Newman v. Newman, 653 P.2d 728 (Colo.1982) held that an antenuptial agreement providing for a specified division of property on divorce did not violate any public policy and could be enforced on divorce so long as no fraud, overreaching or sharp dealing was proved. See also In re Marriage of Ingels, 42 Colo. App. 245, 596 P.2d 1211 (1979).

57. Seuss v. Schukat, 358 Ill. 27, 192 N.E. 668 (1934); New Jersey Title Guarantee & Trust Co. v. Parker, 85 N.J.Eq. 557, 96 A. 574 (1916). Other cases are cited in Annot., 29 A.L.R. 198 (1924).

58. Southern Ohio Sav. Bank & Trust Co. v. Burkhart, 148 Ohio St. 149, 74 N.E.2d 67 (1947). See also Annot., 29 A.L.R. 198 (1924).

59. Crise v. Smith, 150 Md. 322, 133 A. 110 (1926); In re Cavazza's Estate, 169 Pa.Super. 246, 82 A.2d 331 (1951). In Turner v. Turner, 242 N.C. 533, 89 S.E.2d 245 (1955) the parties separated and made a separation agreement, and then resumed cohabitation. The case held that the separation and the separation agreement did not abrogate their antenuptial contract or affect property rights created by it. In Application of Liberman, 4 A.D.2d 512, 167 N.Y.S.2d 158 (1st Dep't 1957), affirmed 5 N.Y.2d 719, 177 N.Y.S.2d 707, 152 N.E.2d 665 (1958) the court held an antenuptial agreement unaffected by the parties' divorce and remarriage to each other.

In re Estate of Simms, 26 N.Y.2d 163, 309 N.Y.S.2d 170, 257 N.E.2d 627 (1970) held that rights under an antenup-

As has been indicated,[60] the best solution to this problem is to include a provision in the antenuptial agreement to the effect that rights under the agreement do not survive divorce or separation, if that is the desire of the parties. None of the usual objections apply to such a provision and it should be held valid by the courts.[61]

Construction and Application of Antenuptial Agreements

Perhaps the most common question arising under antenuptial agreements is just what claims are being relinquished by the agreement. A surprising number of agreements are drafted so as merely to read that each spouse waives all rights which he may have in the property of the other by virtue of the marriage, without specifying just what claims are being given up. The Uniform Probate Code deals with this problem by providing that unless the contrary is stated in the agreement, such a waiver waives rights to the elective share, exempt property and family allowance and renounces all benefits which would otherwise pass to the surviving spouse by intestate succession or by the provisions of any will executed before the antenuptial agreement was made.[62] In the absence of statute, the cases reached different conclusions. Some held that the widow's allowance, for example, would not be effectively waived by general language in the agreement, but that the waiver must be clearly and specifically expressed.[63] Others have found a waiver in more or less general terms.[64] The obvious lesson to be learned by the draftsman of antenuptial agreements is that the agreement should spell out in detail the claims which each party is relinquishing.

A breach of the antenuptial agreement entitles the other party to a judgment for damages,[65] or, more commonly, since the legal remedy is often inadequate, to an equity decree for specific performance.[66] If the breach of the agreement is material and so substantial as to defeat the purposes of the agreement, the other party may have the alternative remedy of treating the agreement as at an end and claiming his intestate share from the spouse's estate.[67] The parties may, by mutual consent, rescind the agreement, ex-

---

tial agreement were not affected by the annulment of the parties' marriage.

60. See the text at note 53, supra.

61. See the text at note 53, supra. Other cases are collected in Annot., 57 A.L.R.2d 942 (1958).

62. Uniform Probate Code § 2–204, 8 Unif.Laws Ann. 82 (1983).

63. Maher v. Knauss, 150 Colo. 108, 370 P.2d 1017 (1962); In re Griffee's Estate, 108 Colo. 366, 117 P.2d 823 (1941). In re Estate of Taylor, 205 Kan. 347, 469 P.2d 437 (1970) appears to take the position that no right of inheritance may be cut off by an antenuptial agreement unless the language relied upon is clear and unmistakable. Other cases are collected in Annots., 30 A.L.R.3d 858 (1970) and 65 A.L.R.2d 727 (1959).

Williams v. Williams, 569 S.W.2d 867 (Tex.1978) held that the parties may not validly provide in their agreement that property acquired during marriage shall remain the separate property of each of them. The case is criticized in Note, 56 Tex.L.Rev. 861 (1978).

64. Taylor v. United States National Bank, 248 Or. 538, 436 P.2d 256 (1968) (wife's statutory right to remain in the homestead waived); In re Moore's Estate, 210 Or. 23, 307 P.2d 483 (1957) (probate homestead waived); Williams v. Williams, 569 S.W.2d 867 (Tex.1978) (probate homestead waiver held valid.) See also annotations cited, supra, note 63. An agreement which provided that each spouse waived the right to inherit from the other was held sufficient to bar the widow's statutory forced share

in Remington v. Remington, 69 Colo. 206, 193 P. 550 (1920).

An antenuptial agreement relinquishing any interest in the husband's estate other than whatever provision might be made for the wife by will was enforced against the wife even though the husband clearly intended to leave all his property to her but failed to execute a will in time, in Friedman's Estate, 483 Pa. 614, 398 A.2d 615 (1978).

65. Farris v. Farris, 269 Ky. 466, 107 S.W.2d 299 (1937).

66. Kurys v. Kurys, 25 Conn.Supp. 495, 209 A.2d 526 (1965); Price v. Price, 341 Mass. 390, 170 N.E.2d 346 (1960); Sanders v. Sanders, 40 Tenn.App. 20, 288 S.W.2d 473 (1956). Morris v. Masters, 349 Ill. 455, 182 N.E. 406 (1932) held that an antenuptial agreement could be enforced by collateral relatives of the wife.

67. In re Johnson's Estate, 202 Kan. 684, 203 Kan. 262, 452 P.2d 286 (1969). See also Matter of Eisner's Will, 15 Misc.2d 361, 181 N.Y.S.2d 327 (Surr.Ct.1959).

The existence of an antenuptial agreement may limit the freedom of the spouse to dispose of his property under certain circumstances. In Dubin v. Wise, 41 Ill.App.3d 132, 354 N.E.2d 403 (1976) the husband executed an antenuptial agreement providing that he would leave his wife by will one-quarter of his property. During his life the husband gave substantial amounts of his property to his sons. In holding that wife could recover from the sons one-quarter of the property given them, the court

cept where the rescission would deprive third parties of property interests given them by the agreement.[68] The rescission may be by parol or in writing and either express or inferred from the parties' conduct.[69]

Since the consideration for an antenuptial agreement is usually said to be the marriage of the parties,[70] it would seem to follow that if the marriage does not take place there is a failure of consideration and the agreement would consequently be unenforceable. There is authority in support of this view.[71] But there may be limits to this rule. If the party seeking to enforce the agreement is willing and able to go through with the marriage, it has been held that he may enforce the agreement even though the other party is unwilling.[72] Where the agreement is not wholly executory, as in the case where a transfer of property is made at the time the agreement is executed, before the marriage occurs, at least some courts would permit the property to be retained if the party seeking to recover it is the one refusing to go through with the marriage.[73] There is an obvious analogy here to the recovery of antenuptial gifts.[74] The case is similar when the marriage is contracted but for one reason or another it turns out to be invalid, as, for example, where one of the

parties has a prior subsisting marriage. In those circumstances some courts have held that the consideration has failed and the contract is unenforceable.[75] Others have upheld the contract at the instance of a party who had no reason to know of the invalidity, or where both parties acted on the assumption that the marriage was valid.[76] In short, the technical rule of contracts yields to the court's desire to vindicate the reliance or the expectations of the parties to the marriage. Although the problem is not a common one, the best solution to it would lie in a provision in the antenuptial agreement expressing the parties' wishes in the event the marriage is found to be invalid.

Tax Consequences of Antenuptial Agreements

The relevant section of the Internal Revenue Code provides that "Where property is transferred for less than an adequate and full consideration in money or money's worth, then the amount by which the value of the property exceeded the value of the consideration shall be deemed a gift * * * " [77]

Although a transfer of property made pursuant to an antenuptial agreement is supported by consideration in the contract law

said that the promisee under an antenuptial agreement may attack inter vivos gifts by the promisor where the promisor actually intended to subvert the agreement by the gifts, or where the transfers were disproportionately and unreasonably large in relation to the balance of the promisor's property. See also Dickinson v. Lane, 193 N.Y. 18, 85 N.E. 818 (1908); In re Estate of Chayka, 47 Wis.2d 102, 176 N.W.2d 561 (1970).

68. Turner v. Black, 19 Ill.2d 296, 166 N.E.2d 588 (1960); Dean v. Jeisma, 316 P.2d 599 (Okl.1957), overruled on other grounds, Davis v. Davis, 536 P.2d 915 (Okl. 1975). In Bartle v. Bartle, 121 Colo. 388, 216 P.2d 649 (1950) the court refused to find a trust in favor of the children of the marriage and for that reason held that the children could not complain when the husband gave most of his property to his wife during his life. The children's contention was that her interest in the husband's property should be limited to that given to her in the antenuptial agreement.

In In re Marriage of Young, 682 P.2d 1233 (Colo.App. 1984) the parties were held to have rescinded or abandoned an antenuptial agreement providing for no community of property between the spouses when they pooled all their property and funds during the marriage, taking title in joint tenancy, maintaining joint checking accounts and using all funds for family expenses.

69. In re Reed's Estate, 414 S.W.2d 283 (Mo.1967).

70. E.g., Sanders v. Sanders, 40 Tenn.App. 20, 288 S.W.2d 473 (1956).

71. Evans v. Neumann, 278 Fed. 1013 (App.D.C.1922) (semble).

72. Conner v. Stanley, 65 Cal. 183, 3 P. 668 (1884).

73. Id.

74. See section 1.6, Practitioner's Edition.

75. Hosmer v. Tiffany, 115 App.Div. 303, 100 N.Y.S. 797 (1st Dep't 1906); Brunel v. Brunel, 64 N.Y.S.2d 295 (1946). Other cases are collected in Annots., 46 A.L.R.3d 1403 (1972) and 14 A.L.R.2d 918 (1950).

Brunel v. Brunel, 64 N.Y.S.2d 295 (1946); Lang v. Reetz-Lang, 22 Ohio App.3d 77, 488 N.E.2d 929 (1985); Annots., 46 A.L.R.3d 1403 (1972), 14 A.L.R.2d 918 (1950).

76. Ogden v. McHugh, 167 Mass. 276, 45 N.E. 731 (1897); In Re Estate of Simms, 26 N.Y.2d 163, 309 N.Y.S.2d 170, 257 N.E.2d 627 (1970). See also American Surety Co. of N.Y. v. Conner, 251 N.Y. 1, 166 N.E. 783 (1929).

77. I.R.C. § 2512(b).

sense if it is made in consideration of marriage or in consideration of the transferee's release of claims to the property of the transferor by way of inheritance or otherwise, it is now settled that this is not "consideration in money or money's worth" *for gift tax purposes.*[78] Therefore a gift is made for gift tax purposes by such a transfer.[79] A provision of the estate tax chapter specifically states that a relinquishment of dower or curtesy or statutory rights in lieu of dower or curtesy or other marital rights in a decedent's property or estate does not constitute consideration in money or money's worth.[80] The courts have held that the same rule should be applied to the gift tax on the ground that the gift tax supplements the estate tax, was enacted to prevent evasion of the estate tax by inter vivos transfers, and therefore should be construed in the same fashion as the estate tax.

Both the cases and the regulations impose the gift tax where the only consideration is relinquishment of claims to the property of the other spouse. They do not, however, purport to deal with the transfer of property made as consideration for the release of support claims. An agreement under which property is transferred in return for the release of support claims, if made in a state which does not follow *Posner* and which therefore holds such agreements invalid, would clearly rest upon insufficient consideration

and the transfer would be treated as a gift for gift tax purposes.[81] The question then arises whether an antenuptial transfer of property would be a gift for gift tax purposes if made in a state following the *Posner* case[82] where the consideration was the wife's promise that in the event of divorce she would make no claim for maintenance or support. There is some authority that the release of a claim for support is deemed to be consideration in money or money's worth for gift tax purposes.[83] Some of these precedents deal with the release of support claims in separation agreements and therefore are not directly apposite here. The difficulty with accepting these decisions on their faces is that under the laws of many states there is little practical difference between agreements respecting property and agreements respecting support. But if the release of support claims is held to be good consideration for tax purposes, then the *Posner*-type agreement would not involve a gift for gift tax purposes to the extent of the value of these claims.

Although the gift tax treatment of transfers pursuant to an antenuptial agreement may depend on the classification of the rights released as consideration, the distinction between support and property rights is abandoned where the income tax consequences of such transfers are concerned. It has been held in an old case that upon such a transfer

---

78. Merrill v. Fahs, 324 U.S. 308, 65 S.Ct. 655, 89 L.Ed. 963 (1945), rehearing denied 324 U.S. 888, 65 S.Ct. 863, 89 L.Ed. 1436 (1945); Commissioner v. Wemyss, 324 U.S. 303, 65 S.Ct. 652, 89 L.Ed. 958 (1945); Commissioner v. Bristol, 121 F.2d 129 (1st Cir.1941); Krause v. Yoke, 89 F.Supp. 91 (N.D.W.Va.1950). See also Treas.Reg. § 25.2512–8.

79. 1 H. Harris, Federal Estate and Gift Taxes, § 444 (2d ed. Rasch 1972); Note, Federal Tax Consequences of Antenuptial Contracts, 53 Wash.L.Rev. 105 (1977).

80. I.R.C. § 2043(b).

It has similarly been held that sums payable to a surviving spouse out of the estate of a deceased pursuant to an antenuptial agreement are not "claims against the estate" for federal estate tax purposes, and are therefore not deductible from the gross estate of the deceased in determining the taxable estate. I.R.C. § 2053(a)(3); Empire Trust Co. v. Commissioner, 94 F.2d 307 (4th Cir. 1938); Conner v. Bender, Exrs., 125 F.2d 796 (6th Cir. 1942); Estate of Morse v. Commissioner, 625 F.2d 133 (6th Cir.1980). But the sums so payable apparently would be held to be "claims against the estate" to the

extent that they were payment to the survivor in return for a release of the survivor's claims against the deceased for support as distinguished from property claims. Rev. Rul. 75–395, 1975–2 C.B. 370. See also C. Lowndes, R. Kramer, J. McCord, Federal Estate and Gift Taxes, § 15.14 (1974).

An antenuptial agreement which was framed for the purpose of making it appear that the wife would have a power of appointment over half of the husband's residuary estate, although in fact she had no such power, was held illegal and unenforceable as an attempt to evade the estate tax in Frederick v. Frederick, 44 Ill.App.3d 578, 3 Ill.Dec. 231, 358 N.E.2d 398 (1976).

81. Ellis, Jr. v. Commissioner of Internal Revenue, 51 T.C. 182 (1968), affirmed 437 F.2d 442 (9th Cir.1971).

82. See the discussion note 41 supra.

83. McWilliams v. Harrison, 44–1 U.S.Tax.Cas. Par. 10,119 (N.D.Ill.1944); Paul Rosenthal v. Commissioner of Internal Revenue, 17 T.C. 1047 (1951), reversed on other grounds 205 F.2d 505 (2d Cir.1953) (dictum); Rev.Rul. 75–395, 1975–2 C.B. 370.

the transferee takes as his basis the fair market value of the property at the time of the transfer because the transfer is for an adequate consideration, the release of marital property claims.[84] It would seem to follow from this that the transferor in this situation is liable for a tax on the capital gain if he transfers appreciated property under the antenuptial agreement. Some support for this position may be drawn from the *Davis* case, dealing with transfers of appreciated property pursuant to separation agreements.[85] We are thus apparently left with the result that when property is transferred pursuant to an antenuptial agreement, the transfer may be a gift for gift and estate tax purposes and a sale for income tax purposes. The humble domestic relations lawyer may perhaps be pardoned for his bewilderment.

Antenuptial Agreements Regulating Some or All Aspects of Marriage

The discussion to this point has dealt with attempts by the parties to control by their agreement the property or financial consequences of the termination of their marriage by death or divorce. As has been shown, the antenuptial agreement has traditionally been useful in establishing the devolution of property when the marriage ends on the death of a spouse. And recently the courts have become receptive to the use of the agreement as a means of providing for the financial impact of divorce.

Logically the next question is, why should not the antenuptial agreement also be viewed as an appropriate device for governing the parties' relationships, financial or otherwise, during the marriage? Several law review articles have advocated this extension of the use of antenuptial agreements on a variety of grounds, most commonly as a way of eliminating what the authors perceive to be some remaining forms of discrimination against married women.[86] One suspects that such agreements may also appeal to the desire for some structure in marriage at a time when the law has eliminated nearly all structure from the relationship. Although it is too early to predict how the courts might respond to such agreements, lawyers will undoubtedly be asked to draft them and litigation will then follow. It is therefore necessary at least to suggest some of the difficulties which may arise out of the use of antenuptial agreements for these purposes. The assumption here is that the parties intend to contract a valid marriage. The replacement of conventional marriage with various other types of relationships based on contract is discussed in a later section.[87]

Antenuptial agreements which purport to regulate the amount of support to be paid by one spouse to the other during marriage have in the past generally been held invalid.[88] The same is true of agreements made after marriage but before separation, the courts holding that the spouses may not contract with re-

---

84. Farid-Es-Sultaneh v. Commissioner, 160 F.2d 812 (2d Cir.1947). The Commissioner's argument in this case that the wife had received a gift and therefore took the donor's basis was rejected by the court.

85. United States v. Davis, 370 U.S. 65, 82 S.Ct. 1190, 8 L.Ed.2d 335 (1962), rehearing denied 371 U.S. 854, 83 S.Ct. 14, 9 L.Ed.2d 92 (1967), holding that a husband who transferred appreciated property to his wife pursuant to a property settlement agreement executed as an incident to divorce realized a taxable gain to the extent that the property's value at transfer exceeded the husband's basis. The Court cited *Farid-Es-Sultaneh* with approval, stating that the Court was "unfettered" by considerations incident to gift and estate tax.

86. The most thorough and well considered of the articles is Weitzman, Legal Regulation of Marriage, 62 Cal.L.Rev. 1169 (1974). See also L. Weitzman, The Marriage Contract (1981) and Krauskopf and Thomas, Partnership Marriage: The Solution to an Ineffective and

Inequitable Law of Support, 35 Ohio St.L.J. 558 (1974); Note, Marriage Contracts for Support and Services: Constitutionality Begins at Home, 49 N.Y.U.L.Rev. 1161 (1975).

87. See section 2.2, infra.

88. Fincham v. Fincham, 160 Kan. 683, 165 P.2d 209 (1946); Hilbert v. Hilbert, 168 Md. 364, 177 A. 914 (1935) (antenuptial agreement invalid in providing that neither party would claim alimony or attorney fees in the event of a separation); French v. McAnarney, 290 Mass. 544, 195 N.E. 714 (1935); Garlock v. Garlock, 279 N.Y. 337, 18 N.E.2d 521 (1939) (relying on the New York statute) Motley v. Motley, 255 N.C. 190, 120 S.E.2d 422 (1961); Crouch v. Crouch, 53 Tenn.App. 594, 385 S.W.2d 288 (1964); Caldwell v. Caldwell, 5 Wis.2d 146, 92 N.W.2d 356 (1958); Fricke v. Fricke, 257 Wis. 124, 42 N.W.2d 500 (1950). Other cases are cited in Annots., 98 A.L.R. 530 (1935) and 164 A.L.R. 1236 (1946).

spect to support or alimony unless they have actually separated or until separation is imminent.[89] Many of the agreements in these cases provide that the wife waives all support claims during marriage, and so the decision that an agreement is invalid may turn on the inadequacy of the provision for the wife.[90] But other decisions rest on the broad assertion that agreements respecting support obligations during marriage are conducive to divorce,[91] or on the principle that since the husband has a legal duty to support the wife in any event, there is no consideration when he promises to do what he is already bound to do.[92] The Posner case [93] seems to have satisfactorily answered the argument that such contracts are conducive to divorce, although in Florida antenuptial agreements by which the wife waives her claims for support are still held to be invalid.[94]

Furthermore, the husband is no longer solely responsible for the support of the wife and their children. The Supreme Court has recently invalidated statutes making distinctions based upon sex. The effect of these cases is to impose duties of support on both spouses rather than on the husband alone.[95] Many states have enacted equal rights amendments to their state constitutions. Some states have already responded to the demand for equality by amending their alimo-

ny statutes so as to provide that both husband and wife have duties of support.[96] The effect of all these changes seems to be to impose the duty of support on both spouses, to the extent of their respective needs and means. In these circumstances an antenuptial agreement transforming duties so uncertain and so difficult of evaluation in dollars into specific contractual obligations can hardly be described as lacking in consideration.

Although these reasons for not enforcing antenuptial agreements dealing with support during marriage are not persuasive, other considerations may be more troublesome. One is the traditional reluctance of the courts to adjudicate disputes arising in an unbroken family.[97] Judicial economy is an important value in these days of over-burdened courts. The state should not have to bear the expense of providing a forum in which to hear essentially minor disputes between husband and wife over which spouse is to support the family and what the level of support should be. These disputes should occupy the time of courts and lawyers only when compelled by the impending dissolution of the relationship either by separation or divorce. It has been suggested that an arbitration clause in the antenuptial agreement would solve this problem.[98] If the parties are able and wish to pay the arbitrator's expenses, this may be a satis-

89. See section 15.1, infra.

90. E.g., French v. McAnarney, 290 Mass. 544, 195 N.E. 714 (1935). This case ostensibly took the broad position taken by other courts that none of the obligations of marriage established by the law may be varied by agreement. This is of course not a reason but a restatement of the result.

91. E.g., Crouch v. Crouch, 53 Tenn.App. 594, 385 S.W.2d 288 (1964).

92. In re Ryan's Estate, 134 Wis. 431, 114 N.W. 820 (1908). The analysis relied on by this case seems wrong purely as a matter of contract law. A promise to pay a liquidated sum in discharge of a claim for an unliquidated amount is generally held to be valid consideration for the counter-promise. Balfour v. Balfour, [1919] 2 K.B. 571. Decisions like In re Ryan's Estate may have been using, or misusing, doctrines of consideration to invalidate contracts thought to be undesirable for other than purely contract reasons.

93. Discussed supra at note 41.

94. Belcher v. Belcher, 271 So.2d 7 (Fla.1972), the court there stating that the wife's right of support during

marriage "cannot be conclusively supplanted by * * * advance summary disposition by agreement." For a later appeal in the same case see Belcher v. Belcher, 307 So.2d 918 (Fla.App.1975), cert. denied 317 So.2d 762 (Fla.1975).

95. Orr v. Orr, 440 U.S. 268, 99 S.Ct. 1102, 59 L.Ed.2d 306 (1979); Reed v. Reed, 404 U.S. 71, 92 S.Ct. 251, 30 L.Ed.2d 255 (1971); Frontiero v. Richardson, 411 U.S. 677 (1973). But see Kahn v. Shevin, 416 U.S. 351, 94 S.Ct. 1734, 40 L.Ed.2d 189 (1974).

96. E.g., Uniform Marriage and Divorce Act, § 308, 9A Uniform L.Ann. 160 (Supp.1979).

97. See section 5.1, infra.

98. Weitzman, Legal Regulation of Marriage: Tradition and Change, 62 Cal.L.Rev. 1169, 1271 (1974). The same author suggests that the contract would, in most cases, not be sued on until after the parties have separated, which of course would avoid burdening the courts, since presumably the contract claim could be adjudicated in the same proceeding as the divorce. See also L. Weitzman, The Marriage Contract (1981). Arbitration was upheld in DeLorean v. DeLorean, 211 N.J.Super. 432, 511 A.2d 1257 (1986).

factory solution, although in some instances court time would be required to compel arbitration, or to enforce the arbitration award. But judicial enforcement of the arbitration award might still be denied in those jurisdictions in which the invalidity of these support contracts is predicated upon policies other than judicial economy.[99]

There are reasons apart from economy of court time which may well deter courts from enforcing these agreements. There is the possibility, perhaps even the probability, that any level or conditions of support agreed upon before marriage will turn out to be so unfair to one spouse or the other as the years run on and fortunes change that enforcement would impose hardship on either or both spouses. Of course the contract can always be revised, but in many instances it will not be, either through inadvertence or because the spouses are unable to agree upon a new set of terms. This is in effect the same problem which was discussed in connection with the enforcement of antenuptial agreements relating to alimony.[1] The consequences of the unfairness and hardship do not fall upon the spouses alone, but may affect the children of the marriage or the community generally if one of the parties is left destitute thereby.

More fundamentally, there is serious question whether a relationship so intimate, so many-sided and so fluid as marriage can or should be confined within the limits of contractual rules, even in its purely financial aspect. Of course the contract could be general in its terms, providing, for example, that the spouses will have an equal share of all property acquired by either, and will contribute equally to the expenses of the family. Such a contract is largely hortatory in its effect and would be difficult for a court to apply to particular marital disagreements. Other contracts which have been proposed are more specific. One provides, for example, that each spouse will contribute half of his income for living expenses each month, with responsibility for the payment of these expenses being rotated, other expenses being denominated as separate and payable by the spouse incurring them.[2] The objections to enforcement of this kind of contract are equally grave. The major objection is that enforcement would produce extensive and detailed legal regulation of the marriage, a greater interference with the freedom of husband and wife in their daily life together than would have occurred under the most rigid Nineteenth Century marriage and divorce laws. It is indeed a paradox that the effort to give the spouses greater control over their marriage should result in a broader state regulation of the relationship than ever before in

---

99. Arbitration clauses in separation agreements have been generally upheld where they pertain to the support of spouse or child. E.g., Schneider v. Schneider, 17 N.Y.2d 123, 269 N.Y.S.2d 107, 216 N.E.2d 318 (1966); Hirsch v. Hirsch, 45 A.D.2d 167, 356 N.Y.S.2d 884 (1st Dep't 1974), affirmed 37 N.Y.2d 312, 372 N.Y.S.2d 71, 333 N.E.2d 371 (1975). Other cases are collected in Annot., 18 A.L.R.3d 1264 (1968) and in M. Domke, Commercial Arbitration, § 13.09 (1968). In the arbitration of commercial and labor disputes some cases have held that an award which violates a statute or a recognized public policy will not be enforced. See, e.g., Black v. Cutter Laboratories, 43 Cal.2d 788, 278 P.2d 905 (1955), cert. denied 351 U.S. 292, 76 S.Ct. 824, 100 L.Ed. 1188 (1956). But there are cases which do enforce such awards. See Note, Judicial Review of Arbitration: The Role of Public Policy, 58 Nw.U.L.Rev. 545 (1963). See also the Uniform Arbitration Act, §§ 1 and 2, 7 Uniform L.Ann. 4, 23 (1978), which authorizes the enforcement of "a provision in a written contract to submit to arbitration any controversy thereafter arising between the parties". This statute has now been adopted in about twenty states.

1. See the text at note 48, supra. The proponents of such contracts may be assuming rather short-lived mar-

riages, in which the probability of substantial change in conditions might be slight. The courts might take the same approach here as with agreements controlling alimony and enforce the agreement only where circumstances have not so changed as to make the agreement unconscionable or unfair. But this frustrates the major purpose of the agreement in the eyes of its proponents, which is to take from the courts and place in the hands of the spouses the incidents of their marriage.

2. Such a provision is found in the reconciliation agreement used at one time by the Conciliation Court of Los Angeles. See R. Pfaff, The Conciliation Court of Los Angeles County, 16 (1960), and J. White, The Legal Imagination, 558 (1973). Other sample agreements are set out in Weitzman, Legal Regulation of Marriage: Tradition and Change, 62 Cal.L.Rev. 1169, 1278 (1974). Contracts of this sort have been widely publicized as an important discovery, but of course, like so many other contemporary discoveries they are not new. An example of such a contract may be found in Act IV, Scene 1 of William Congreve's play, "The Way of the World", written in 1700.

our history. A major value of marriage as an institution has been the opportunity which it presents for spouses to develop their understanding of personal relationships and to grow in maturity. Shifting to the courts the responsibility for the daily adjustments which marriage entails destroys that value and encourages the sort of immaturity which is already such a prominent factor in marital failure in the United States.

Where the antenuptial contract purports to regulate aspects of the marriage other than support or finances, the foregoing objections to judicial enforcement apply with equal force. The few cases which have arisen in the past have refused to enforce agreements to obtain a divorce,[3] agreements not to defend divorce actions,[4] agreements respecting sexual relations between the spouses,[5] and in one unusual case the agreement that the children of the wife's prior marriage would not live with the parties.[6] Most such cases rest on the traditional view that the incidents of marriage are established by law and may not be altered by the parties. This of course is not a reason but merely another way of stating the result, and it is somewhat inconsistent with the courts' contemporary willingness to permit control of alimony and maintenance by antenuptial agreement. Nevertheless, the results of these cases may be justified as saving the time and energies of courts and as taking the realistic position that the intimate day to day conduct of married persons cannot be controlled by judicial decision, whether or not the decision is based upon the parties' own contract.[7]

Whether these agreements are useful even if not enforceable by the courts depends upon the spouses' attitude and their lawyers' counselling skill. One may be skeptical of the value of contracts as a guide to daily marital conduct without denying that in the hands of a skillful lawyer they may be a helpful means of revealing the expectations, desires and possible conflicts of people contemplating marriage, of acquiring some understanding of the demands that marriage makes upon the marital partners and of expressing, perhaps in general terms, a willingness to make the marriage succeed.

 WESTLAW REFERENCES

di antenuptial

Statute of Frauds

statute +2 fraud /s ante-nuptial pre-nuptial
sy,di(ante-nuptial pre-nuptial /s agreement contract /s oral)

The Requirement of Disclosure

sy,di(ante-nuptial pre-nuptial /s requir! /s disclos!)

Antenuptial Agreements and Divorce

sy(ante-nuptial pre-nuptial /s alimony support maintenance /s divorce dissolution separated separation)

3. In Re Duncan's Estate, 87 Colo. 149, 285 P. 757 (1930); Annot., 70 A.L.R. 826 (1931). But in Davis v. Davis, 191 A.2d 138 (D.C.App.1963) the court granted a divorce on the ground of living separate and apart for five years, holding that the parties' agreement to get a divorce was not collusive.

In Avitzur v. Avitzur, 58 N.Y.2d 108, 459 N.Y.S.2d 572, 446 N.E.2d 136 (1983), cert. denied 464 U.S. 817, 104 S.Ct. 76, 78 L.Ed.2d 88 (1983), the court specifically enforced a religious antenuptial agreement, drawing an analogy between the agreement in suit and an ordinary arbitration provision in an antenuptial agreement. The effect of the court's judgment was to require the plaintiff husband, after obtaining a civil divorce, to appear before a Jewish tribunal, the "Beth Din". Doing so freed the defendant wife to remarry under Jewish law. The complexities of Jewish divorce law and the constitutional implications of this case are explored in Lieberman, Avitzur v. Avitzur, The Constitutional Implications of Judicially Enforcing Religious Agreements, 33 Cath.U.L.Rev. 219 (1983); Note,

Jewish Divorce and Secular Courts: The Promise of Avitzur, 73 Geo.L.J. 193 (1984). New York has passed a statute requiring the filing of a verified statement in divorce actions to the effect that the plaintiff has taken all steps in his power to remove barriers to the defendant's remarriage as a condition on obtaining a civil divorce. N.Y.–McKinney's Dom.Rel.L. § 253 (Supp.1984–1985).

4. 6A A. Corbin, Contracts § 474 (1962).

5. Favrot v. Barnes, 332 So.2d 873 (La.App.1976), reversed on other grounds 339 So.2d 843 (La.1976), cert. denied 431 U.S. 966, 97 S.Ct. 2922, 53 L.Ed.2d 1061 (1976); Restatement (Second) of Contracts § 190 (1981).

6. Mengal v. Mengal, 201 Misc. 104, 103 N.Y.S.2d 992 (Dom.Rel.Ct.1951).

7. For a somewhat similar view, based on different reasons, see Rheinstein, The Transformation of Marriage and the Law, 68 Nw.U.L.Rev. 463, 466–467 (1973).

Construction and Application of Antenuptial Agreements
di(waiv! /s right /s property /s ante-nuptial pre-nuptial)

---

§ 1.2 Agreements Contemplating Meretricious Relations

Traditionally contracts between unmarried men and women made in consideration of their living together and engaging in sexual relations were held to be contrary to public policy and unenforceable.[1] The reason was doubtless the courts' desire to discourage immorality. Perhaps there was also a wish to make a clear distinction between marriage and what used to be called meretricious relationships, as a way of recognizing the crucial importance of marriage in our society.

In the last decade the traditional rule has been eroded to the point where it no longer

has much practical significance, as a judicial reflection of the abandonment by many segments of society of the older rules about sexual morality, and of the tendency in the statutes to remove existing prohibitions on the sexual conduct of consenting adults.[2] This change in the case law also has been influenced by the courts' view that the women in such relationships should receive some compensation for their services even though sexual relations may have constituted one aspect of those "services".[3] The result is that the rule is now stated to be that the contract is enforceable if there is consideration for it other than sexual relations.[4] Or, to put it another way, the agreement is invalid only where the sexual relations are the only or the primary consideration.[5]

The case which goes the farthest in the enforcement of such contracts is Marvin v. Marvin.[6] The plaintiff in that case, a woman

§ 1.2

1. 15 S. Williston, Contracts § 1745 (3d ed. Jaeger 1972); Restatement, Contracts § 589 (1932).

2. Latham v. Latham, 274 Or. 421, 547 P.2d 144 (1976), appeal after remand 281 Or. 303, 574 P.2d 644 (1978). For a discussion of the recognition of these changes in the law, see Bruch, Nonmarital Cohabitation in the Common Law Countries: A Study in Judicial-Legislative Interaction, 29 Am.J.Comp.L. 217 (1981); J. Eekelaar and S. Katz, Marriage and Cohabitation in Contemporary Societies (1980); Karst, The Freedom of Intimate Association, 89 Yale L.J. 624 (1980).

Matter of Linda Ann A., 126 Misc.2d 43, 480 N.Y.S.2d 996 (1984) held that an unmarried woman would not be allowed to change her name to that of her "lover" whom she was not free to marry, on the assumption that the lover was married to someone else and the relationship was presumably adulterous.

3. Tyranski v. Piggins, 44 Mich.App. 570, 205 N.W.2d 595 (1973); Latham v. Latham, 274 Or. 421, 547 P.2d 144 (1976).

4. Cook v. Cook, 142 Ariz. 573, 691 P.2d 664 (1984); Glasgo v. Glasgo, 410 N.E.2d 1325 (Ind.App.1980); Tyranski v. Piggins, 44 Mich.App. 570, 205 N.W.2d 595 (1973); Kinkenon v. Hue, 207 Neb. 698, 301 N.W.2d 77 (1981); Joan S. v. John S., 121 N.H. 96, 427 A.2d 498 (1981) (dictum); Kozlowski v. Kozlowski, 80 N.J. 378, 403 A.2d 902 (1979); Dominguez v. Cruz, 95 N.M. 1, 617 P.2d 1322 (1980) (oral contract); Beal v. Beal, 282 Or. 115, 577 P.2d 507 (1978), 58 Ore.L.Rev. 245 (1979); Rogelis v. Pettis, 49 Or.App. 537, 619 P.2d 1339 (1980); Knauer v. Knauer, 323 Pa.Super. 206, 470 A.2d 553 (1983); Matter of Steffes' Estate, 95 Wis.2d 490, 290 N.W.2d 697 (1980); Kinnison v. Kinnison, 627 P.2d 594 (Wyo.1981) (oral contract). Contra: Rehak v. Mathis, 239 Ga. 541, 238 S.E.2d 81 (1977), 12 Ga.L.Rev. 361 (1978); Hewitt v. Hewitt, 77 Ill.

2d 49, 31 Ill.Dec. 827, 394 N.E.2d 1204 (1979); Schwegmann v. Schwegmann, 441 So.2d 316 (La.App.1983). See also Cougler v. Fackler, 510 S.W.2d 16 (Ky.1974), and Spafford v. Coats, 118 Ill.App.3d 566, 74 Ill.Dec. 211, 455 N.E.2d 241 (1983).

New York has taken the intermediate position that express contracts of persons living together are enforceable so long as illicit sexual relations are not part of the consideration, but that contracts merely implied from the rendition of services are not. The New York Court of Appeals has said that claims of the latter kind must rest on evidence too "evanescent" to be judicially evaluated. Morone v. Morone, 50 N.Y.2d 481, 429 N.Y.S.2d 592, 413 N.E.2d 1154 (1980). A similar result was reached in Carnes v. Sheldon, 109 Mich.App. 204, 311 N.W.2d 747 (1981), and Tapley v. Tapley, 122 N.H. 727, 449 A.2d 1218 (1982), and Merrill v. Davis, 100 N.M. 552, 673 P.2d 1285 (1983). This seems a sensible approach to a difficult issue. Minnesota requires an express written agreement before it will be enforced. Minn.Stat.Ann. §§ 513.075, 513.076 (Supp.1984); Hollom v. Carey, 343 N.W.2d 701 (Minn.App.1984).

A case holding that property would be divided between cohabitants of the same sex on the basis of an oral contract is Ireland v. Flanagan, 51 Or.App. 837, 627 P.2d 496 (1981).

5. Latham v. Latham, 274 Or. 421, 547 P.2d 144 (1976), appeal after remand 281 Or. 303, 574 P.2d 644 (1978); 6A A. Corbin, Contracts § 1476 (1962).

6. 18 Cal.3d 660, 134 Cal.Rptr. 815, 557 P.2d 106 (1976). See also Carlson v. Olson, 256 N.W.2d 249 (Minn. 1977); Kozlowski v. Kozlowski, 80 N.J. 378, 403 A.2d 902 (1979) and Latham v. Hennessey, 87 Wash.2d 550, 554 P.2d 1057 (1976). On the remand of the Marvin case the trial court found no contract had been proved, but did award the plaintiff $104,000 for rehabilitation purposes,

who had been an entertainer and singer, alleged that she gave up her career in order to devote full time to being a "companion, homemaker, housekeeper and cook" for the defendant, who in turn agreed to provide for her financial support and needs for the remainder of her life. In reversing a dismissal of the plaintiff's complaint the California Supreme Court took the position that such an agreement is enforceable except to the extent that it explicitly provides that the consideration for the defendant's financial agreements is meretricious sexual services. The court's decision was based in part upon its finding that many more men and women now live together without marrying than used to be the case, and in part upon the view that any other principle would be too uncertain to be workable. The community property rights of the defendant's wife were held not to bar the enforcement of the contract because they had been fixed in a divorce decree and as so fixed would not be impaired by the agreement. The court in fact gave greater force to this contract than would be given to an ordinary antenuptial agreement, since it held this contract could be enforced even though oral, while an antenuptial contract would be within the statute of frauds.

The assumption underlying cases like Marvin v. Marvin seems to be that contracts between cohabiting men and women are not different from other contracts by which adults control their financial or property affairs and should therefore be enforced unless the sexual aspect of their relationship is clearly expressed. Since sexual relations between persons who live together can usually be taken for granted, as the court in Marvin seems to concede, it is hardly likely that their contract will refer to the subject. It does seem curious, in view of the court's recognition that such relationships are common and of its acceptance of them, that it was not able to muster up the candor to hold all such contracts valid whether or not sexual relations formed an explicit part of the consideration. In any event the practical effect of the Marvin case is to enforce such contracts as readily (or more readily in some instances) as it would enforce a true antenuptial agreement.

In view of the second branch of the Marvin case, which held that even in the absence of a contract persons living together without being married [7] might assert equitable claims in each other's property, such persons must be advised to give serious consideration to a contract settling their financial and property relationships. Numerous articles have been published which offer suggestions as to what should be included in this sort of contract.[8] At the least there should be provisions covering the consequences of a break-up of the relationship, of the death of a party, and, where the amount of property is large, of the

---

to enable her to retrain herself for the resumption of her career. Marvin v. Marvin, 5 Fam.L.Rep. 3077 (1979). See also Foster and Freed, Marvin v. Marvin: New Wine in Old Bottles, 5 Fam.L.Rep. 4001 (1979). The $104,000 award to the plaintiff was appealed and reversed by a Court of Appeal on the ground that it was not within the issues framed by the pleadings in the case. Marvin v. Marvin, 122 Cal.App.3d 871, 176 Cal.Rptr. 555 (1981).

A few cases have even awarded temporary support to a plaintiff pending a Marvin type of suit. Annot., 35 A.L.R.4th 409 (1985). Crowe v. De Gioia, 203 N.J.Super. 22, 495 A.2d 889 (1985), certification granted 102 N.J. 320, 508 A.2d 201 (1985) awarded what looks like alimony on the basis of a Marvin agreement, but denied counsel fees.

The closely related question whether, in the absence of contract, persons who live together without being married thereby acquire rights in property accumulated by either of them during the period of cohabitation, is discussed infra, in section 15.7. The Marvin case of course deals with that question as well as the contracts question.

7. The terminology for describing these relationships is still not available to lawyers. Some possibilities include cohabitation, de facto marriage, domestic partnerships, LTA's or living together arrangements, Marvinizing, but there is no general agreement on what they should be called.

Although the Marvin case seems to open broad possibilities for the recovery of property by unmarried cohabitants, at least one case has held that for purposes of workers' compensation benefits such a cohabitant is not to be considered either a lawful or a putative spouse. Powell v. Rogers, 496 F.2d 1248 (9th Cir.1974), cert. denied 419 U.S. 1032, 95 S.Ct. 514, 42 L.Ed.2d 307 (1974) (relying upon California law).

8. Bruch, Property Rights of De Facto Spouses Including Thoughts on the Value of Homemakers' Services, 10 Fam.L.Q. 101 (1976); Kay and Amyx, Marvin v. Marvin: Preserving the Options, 65 Cal.L.Rev. 937 (1977); Weitzman, Legal Regulation of Marriage: Tradition and Change, 62 Cal.L.Rev. 1169 (1974); L. Weitzman, The Marriage Contract Chs. 10, 11, 12 (1981).

federal and state estate taxes.[9] Presumably, if Marvin is to be followed, the contract should not contain any mention of sexual relations, since any express provision on this score would make a finding of invalidity likely. Some couples who are on the point of forming such a relationship may also wish to include provisions governing their financial affairs while the relationship continues. Such provisions, if placed in the ordinary antenuptial agreement, would not be enforceable in the courts.[10] Whether the courts would enforce them if the parties were not married is impossible to predict at this stage. Even if not, they may have some value to the parties in providing an informal structure for their relationship.

 WESTLAW REFERENCES

contract /s unmarried /s man /s woman
ti(marvin +s marvin)

---

9. Not only would such relationships involve estate tax complications, but they would also raise difficult income tax questions. For example, John J. Whalen, Jr. v. Commissioner, T.C.M. 1976–137 held that a man could not use head of household rates when he lived with a woman not related to him, but that he could claim the woman as a dependent under I.R.C. § 152(a)(9). On the other hand Cassius L. Peacock v. Commissioner, T.C.M. 1978–30 held that the woman with whom the taxpayer lived was not a "spouse", and that she was not a dependent either where the living together was a violation of the state criminal law. And Lyna Kathryn Jones v. Commissioner, T.C.M. 1977–329 held that a woman received income when she was given cash and property in return for sexual relations by the man with whom she was living.

10. See section 1.1, supra.

Chapter 2

MARRIAGE

Table of Sections

---

§ 2.1 Marriage—History and Background

Some knowledge of the history of our marriage law is essential to an understanding of its contemporary form, although the historical record is beset with gaps, obscurities and contradictions.[1] The beginnings themselves are obscure, but it seems probable that the Anglo-Saxon form of marriage was the prototype of our own. It included first a betrothal, by which the bride's father or relatives agreed to transfer to the bridegroom the *mund,* or custody for protection, of the bride to the bridegroom. In return the bridegroom agreed to make a transfer of property to them, according to some versions, or, according to others, to make a settlement of property upon the bride, and, in addition, to care for and protect her. Following the betrothal, the bride's family made the delivery of the bride to the groom, who made the promised settlement in return. This settlement was the forerunner of dower. As Christianity's influence grew in Britain, and especially after the Norman Conquest when the power to regulate marriage was put in the hands of the Church,

§ 2.1

1. This section does not aim at more than a brief account of some historical influences. It relies heavily upon II Pollock and Maitland, History of English Law 364–399 (1898); I Howard, A History of Matrimonial Institutions ch. IV, chs. VI–X (1904); II Holdsworth, History of English Law 87–90 (1922); Koegel, Common Law Marriage (1922); R. Helmholz, Marriage Litigation in Medieval England (1974); and 1 Bishop, Marriage, Divorce and Separation 108–114 (1891). For most interesting statistical studies of American marriage trends, see Jacobson, American Marriage and Divorce, ch. 1 (1959), and H. Carter and P. Glick, Marriage and Divorce (1970).

this ceremony took place in the presence of a priest. The wedding ring came to be given as a pledge that the bridegroom would perform his covenants. This Anglo-Saxon form of marriage is reproduced surprisingly closely in the form of wedding ceremony still used in the Anglican (and many other) churches.[2] The additional ecclesiastical requirement of thrice publishing the banns for all church marriages was imposed at the end of the twelfth century, together with the requirement that marriages had to be conducted in church and by a priest.[3] When the English Reformation transformed the Roman Church and ecclesiastical establishment into an English church, the form of the marriage ceremony and the church's requirements remained unchanged.

One of the most striking, and most disputed, historical developments in the law of marriage was the growth from custom into law of informal marriages. Although the Church insisted upon observance of its rules for the performance of Church marriages, it was at the same time willing to recognize as equally valid and binding the two kinds of informal marriage known as *sponsalia per verba de praesenti* and *sponsalia per verba de futuro*. The first of these took place when the parties exchanged promises that they would be man and wife from that moment on. The second form required an exchange of promises to be man and wife in the future, followed by sexual union. When the parties presently took each other as man and wife, a valid marriage was thereby formed. Consummation of the union was not required for validity of this kind of informal marriage, the views of Peter Lombard prevailing on this point over the earlier insistence of Gratian that sexual union was an essential element for a valid

marriage. In the case of the promise to marry in the future, a valid marriage only resulted when at some later time the parties consummated their promise by intercourse.

We have it on the best historical authority [4] that until the middle of the eighteenth century these informal marriages were held valid by the ecclesiastics whose jurisdiction it was to determine the validity of marriages. In fact an earlier informal marriage would prevail over a later marriage performed in church with full observance of the Church's formalities. Why the Church should sanction these wholly informal non-religious unions, with all the difficulties of proof and opportunities for fraud which they presented, can only be the subject of speculation. It may have been done merely out of a recognition that it was better to regularize than to condemn unions which would be formed regardless of what the law might say. If so, this is another example of the law's willingness to conform once rigorous rules to the unruly demands of human nature, a process many times repeated in the history of marriage and divorce.

Although the recognition of informal marriages is clearly shown by historical sources, it was asserted by three English judges, in the case of Regina v. Millis,[5] that informal marriage was never recognized by English law, and their argument has had some impact in America.[6] A partial explanation for this misconception may be found in the fact that the temporal courts did not recognize such marriages as entitling the wife to dower, hence the expression that the wife must be endowed at the church door. But the temporal courts did not have jurisdiction over marriages other than indirectly through the enforcement of dower rights, so that ecclesiastical rules were

---

2. Book of Common Prayer Authorized for Use in the Protestant Episcopal Church 300 ff. (1928). Cf. St. Joseph Daily Missal 1300 (1953), bearing the imprimatur of Cardinal Spellman, for the Catholic marriage ceremony.

3. II Pollock and Maitland, History of English Law 370 (1898).

4. Id. at 368. Canon law on the Continent was changed by the Council of Trent (1543–1563) to require that marriage occur in the presence of a priest, but this had no effect in England. For an exhaustive study of

early English marriage law, see Engdahl, English Marriage Conflicts Law Before the Time of Bracton, 15 Am.J. of Comp.Law 109 (1967).

5. Regina v. Millis, 10 Cl. & F. 534, 8 Eng.Rep. 844 (1843). See also Beamish v. Beamish, 9 H.L.C. 274, 11 Eng.Rep. 735 (1861).

6. Estate of Baldwin, 162 Cal. 471, 123 P. 267 (1912); In re Roberts Estate, 58 Wyo. 438, 133 P.2d 492 (1943) presents the historical arguments against informal marriage in very persuasive terms.

controlling. In any event informal marriage came to the United States as a continuation of the English experience.

In 1753 Lord Hardwicke's Act [7] did require a church ceremony, publication of banns, and a license as a condition of the validity of marriages. The purpose of the Act was to prevent clandestine marriages, "Fleet" marriages and other fraudulent or irregular unions. It governed only marriages contracted in England, however, leaving Scottish and Irish marriages subject to the earlier rules allowing informal marriage.[8]

In the American colonies marriage was regulated by the civil authorities, and informal marriages were recognized as valid,[9] at least in the absence of statute requiring a ceremony.[10] In fact the informal marriage was a more useful device on the American frontier than in England, since it enabled parties to contract valid marriages when no clergyman or civil officer was at hand to perform a ceremony.

The history of English marriage law also produced some rules for the validity of marriages which have largely affected American law. The English law recognized several impediments to the formation of valid marriages. Relationship between the parties, either by blood or marriage, was the one most

commonly asserted as a cause for declaring the marriage invalid.[11] At first the range of relationship which disqualified the parties to marry was extremely broad. It was narrowed somewhat in 1215, and then in the early sixteenth century, after the Reformation, it was limited to the Levitical degrees.[12]

Infancy was likewise a disqualification for marriage, children below the age of seven being incapable of marrying. After that age they might marry, but the marriage was voidable until they became able to consummate it, which the law presumed to be at age fourteen for boys and twelve for girls. Beyond those ages the marriages were valid, even though the parties were under twenty-one and though they did not have their parents' consent. Later statutes imposed the requirement of parents' consent.[13]

A distinction was made by some authorities between canonical disabilities which were said to make marriages only voidable, and civil disabilities making marriages void.[14] The former, resulting from the ecclesiastical rules, included consanguinity, affinity, and impotence. The latter included prior marriage, infancy, fraud, duress, and insanity. Though this distinction is not universally accepted even as a statement of historical fact,[15] it has retained enough vitality in American

---

7. Lord Hardwicke's Act, 1753, 26 Geo. II, c. 33. Fleet Marriages, performed without formalities by disreputable parsons imprisoned in the Fleet Prison, had become a public scandal and the desire to eliminate them influenced the passage of Lord Hardwicke's Act.

8. See Dalrymple v. Dalrymple, 2 Hagg.Con. 54, 161 Eng.Rep. 665 (1811).

9. 1 Bishop, Marriage, Divorce and Separation 177 (1891); II Howard, History of Matrimonial Institutions, ch. XII (1904), and III Id., ch. XVIII. Maryland was an exception. See Denison v. Denison, 35 Md. 361 (1872). But see Koegel, Common Law Marriage, ch. V. (1922), and Lorenzen, Marriage by Proxy and the Conflict of Laws, 32 Harv.L.Rev. 473, 482 (1919).

10. See the discussion in Hoage v. Murch Bros. Const. Co., 60 App.D.C. 218, 50 F.2d 983 (1931), and in Goebel, Development of Legal Institutions, 519, 525 (1946). Massachusetts had such a statute, Laws and Liberties of Massachusetts, Reprinted from 1648 Edition in the Henry E. Huntington Library (Cambridge 1929) pp. 37, 38, requiring banns and a ceremony.

11. II Pollock & Maitland, History of English Law 386 (1898).

12. 32 Hen. VIII, c. 38 (1541). See 1 Blackstone, Commentaries 434; 5 Bacon's Abridgement 291 (7th ed. 1832).

13. 5 Bacon's Abridgement 289 (7th ed. 1832).

14. 1 Blackstone, Commentaries 433; 1 Bishop, Marriage, Divorce and Separation 112 (1891); Elliot v. Gurr, 2 Phill.Ecc. 16, 161 Eng.Rep. 1064 (1812); Bowers v. Bowers, 10 Rich.Eq. 551 (S.C.1858). The basis for the distinction apparently was that the common law courts would consider the civil disabilities in connection with collateral attacks upon the marriage, while they would not consider the canonical disabilities. The canonical disabilities, being only available in annulment suits in the ecclesiastical courts, thus were only raised in direct attacks upon marriages. The fact is, however, that only confusion results today from referring to nonage marriages, or marriages induced by fraud, as void rather than voidable. For a useful recent discussion of the distinction, see Tolstoy, Void and Voidable Marriages, 27 Mod.L.Rev. 385 (1964).

15. See II Burns, Ecclesiastical Law 408, 445 (4th ed. 1781) stating that marriages are void for lunacy, consanguinity, affinity, impotence, nonage, and prior subsisting marriage.

law to produce unnecessary confusion in the law of annulment.[16] The ancient void-voidable distinction still plagues us.

American law largely adopted, either as part of the common-law heritage or expressly by statute, the principles by which English law determined the validity of marriage. The chief difficulty in this country was in finding a tribunal authorized to apply the rules so inherited. The rules had all been enforced in the ecclesiastical courts in England, but we had no such courts here. One solution, in the absence of statute, was to make this body of law part of equity jurisdiction.[17] At least such defects in marriage as fraud and duress resembled matters of acknowledged equitable cognizance,[18] and equity courts were accustomed to a broader range of remedies than the courts of law. But if these matters cannot be considered equity, then any jurisdiction over the annulment of marriages has to await specific statutory authorization.[19]

Thus it was that the three major elements of our marriage law were sharply influenced by our English inheritance: a) the method of entering the relationship; [20] b) the factors making marriages invalid; and c) the jurisdiction of courts to rule on the validity of marriages. Until very recently American courts and legislatures tenaciously held on to this inheritance in the face of enormous changes in our material, social and cultural world.

According to the English law, and to its American counterpart, the legal definition of

marriage was clear and quite specific, although its outlines had to some extent to be inferred from the judicial resolution of marital conflicts rather than being directly stated in statutory provisions. As so defined, marriage was a permanent, monogamous relationship between a man and woman, divorce being virtually impossible in England until the latter half of the Nineteenth Century.[21] A major purpose of marriage was the procreation of children,[22] and perhaps for that reason sexual relations were permitted only between spouses. The exclusive nature of sexual relations between spouses is shown by the fact that adultery was a ground for legal separation in England and for divorce in this country,[23] and was frequently made a crime.[24] Adultery was also the basis for the curious old tort of criminal conversation, available only to the husband in England and to both spouses in the United States.[25] The spouses were expected to inhabit a joint domicile, the unjustified refusal to do so constituting desertion, also grounds for separation or divorce.[26] The husband was responsible for the support of wife and children,[27] his obligation usually being embodied in a decree for alimony or child support when the marriage ended in divorce or separation. Marriage could be contracted in England only by a ceremony after 1753.[28] In this country they could also be contracted by agreement followed by the open assumption of the marital relationship in many states.[29] Underlying all aspects of the definition of marriage was the principle, fre-

---

16. See section 2.9, infra, with respect to nonage.

17. This was the approach of Wightman v. Wightman, 4 Johns.Ch. 343 (1820). See also Pretlow v. Pretlow, 177 Va. 524, 14 S.E.2d 381 (1941).

18. Cf. Ridgely v. Ridgely, 79 Md. 298, 29 A. 597 (1894).

19. Burtis v. Burtis, Hopk.Ch. 557 (1825), expressing some doubt about Wightman v. Wightman, supra, note 17.

20. Even in those parts of the United States acquired from Mexico or having a Spanish history, the formal requirements for contracting marriage were affected only slightly by the Spanish law prevailing before these territories became part of the United States. The Spanish or Mexican law did have some influence upon the acceptance of common law marriage in Texas, Florida, and New Mexico. For an extensive and detailed account of the historical background of this subject see Baade, The Form

of Marriage in Spanish North America, 61 Corn.L.Rev. 1 (1975).

21. Mueller, Inquiry Into the State of a Divorceless Society, 18 U.Pitt.L.Rev. 545 (1957).

22. Skinner v. Oklahoma, 316 U.S. 535, 62 S.Ct. 1110, 86 L.Ed. 1655 (1942).

23. See section 12.2, Practitioner's Edition.

24. R. Perkins, Criminal Law, 454–456 (3d ed. 1982).

25. W. Prosser and W.P. Keeton, Law of Torts, § 15 (5th ed. 1984).

26. See section 12.3, Practitioner's Edition.

27. See section 5.1, infra.

28. Lord Hardwicke's Act, 1753, 26 Geo. II, C. 33.

29. Weyrauch, Informal and Formal Marriage—An Appraisal of Trends in Family Organization, 28 U.Chi.L. Rev. 88 (1960).

quently announced by the courts, that the method of contracting marriage and the incidents of the relationship were the province of the law and were not within the control of the parties.[30]

Today, however, attitudes toward marriage on the part of some segments of the population are changing so drastically and publicized so widely and so rapidly that the law can hardly remain oblivious to them. Attacks upon the institution of marriage are being made with more or less vehemence by leaders of the women's rights movement on the ground that it is an instrument by which women are prevented from achieving a personal identity,[31] or by which they are made the property of men and are enslaved.[32] More subtle and equally devastating analysis by widely read psychiatrists has it that marriage and family life produce an "unlivable situation", the natural response to which is schizophrenia.[33] The nation's newspapers and popular magazines have given these opinions even more extensive currency than would be accounted for by the limited number of persons reading the original works.

Parallel to these attacks upon marriage, and not uninfluenced by them, have come several significant social changes. One is a sharp reduction in the rate of marriage for the years since 1960,[34] accompanied by an increasing tendency to marry at later ages,[35]

and a continuing increase in the divorce rate.[36] A second is the emergence of various relationships proposed by their adherents as alternatives to conventional monogamous marriage. These include cohabitation without marriage, often but not always as a prelude to marriage between young people not yet ready for a more permanent commitment; various forms of communal living with or without marriage; group "marriage" involving three or more persons who consider themselves married to each other; and "open-ended marriage", a marriage in which it is understood that each spouse is free to engage in sexual relations with persons outside the marriage.[37] Still another significant change is the trend toward elimination of sex stereotypes, as a result of which the roles which custom has assigned to men and women in marriage (as well as in other aspects of life) are becoming identical,[38] which is to say that each spouse will feel free to decide for himself what his marital role will be, unencumbered by social custom. And finally there is the change in the functions of marriage itself which has been going on for a long time, from the days when it was an economic producing unit of society with responsibilities for child rearing and training to the present, when its chief functions seem to be furnishing opportunities for affection, companionship and sexual satisfaction.[39] Most marriages today do serve

30. Maynard v. Hill, 125 U.S. 190, 8 S.Ct. 723, 31 L.Ed. 654 (1888).

31. B. Friedan, The Feminine Mystique, Chapters 7, 10 (1963).

32. K. Millett, Sexual Politics, Chapter 3 (1969); S. Firestone, The Dialectic of Sex, Chapter 2 (1970).

33. R.D. Laing, The Politics of Experience, Chapter 5 (1967); D. Cooper, The Death of the Family (67 Vintage Books ed. 1971).

34. Statistical Abstract of the United States, 1986, at page 79 indicates that the marriage rate for 1960 was 148 per 1,000 unmarried women, and that the rate for 1982 was 101.9 per 1,000 unmarried women.

35. Statistical Abstract of the United States, 1986, p. 79.

36. Statistical Abstract of the United States, 1986, p. 79, gives the divorce rate for 1960 as 2.2 per 1,000 population, for 1977 as 5.0 per 1,000 population and for 1982 as 5.0 per 1,000 population. This exceeded the highest divorce rate ever before recorded in this country, which was 4.3 per 1,000 population in 1946.

37. R. Mazur, The New Intimacy, Open-Ended Marriage and Alternative Life-Styles (1973); L. and J. Constantine, Group Marriage: A Study of Contemporary Multilateral Marriage (1973); J. and L. Smith, Beyond Monogamy (1974); The Family in Search of a Future: Alternative Models for Moderns (A. Otto ed. 1970). For an account of the fate of the children of various kinds of alternative relationships, see J. Rothchild and S. Wolf, The Children of the Counter-culture (1976). That such relationships are not without their emotional difficulties is suggested by Gross, Marriage Counseling for Unwed Couples, New York Times Magazine, April 24, 1977, p. 52.

38. Weitzman, Legal Regulation of Marriage: Tradition and Change, 62 Cal.L.Rev. 1169, 1216 (1974); Rheinstein, The Transformation of Marriage and the Law, 68 Nw.U.L.Rev. 463 (1973); Glendon, Power and Authority in the Family: New Legal Patterns as Reflections of Changing Ideologies, 23 Am.J.Comp.L. 1 (1975).

39. R. Blood and D. Wolfe, Husbands and Wives, Ch. 6 (1960).

to care for children but chiefly from birth to their entrance into school, after which the parents' role diminishes. Their role may diminish further if the current demand for day care centers succeeds in providing an alternative method of caring for small children. Recently marriage has come to resume some importance as a producing economic unit, since nearly half of all wives work at some time, thereby providing the benefits of two sources of income for the maintenance of a single home. But the fact is that the most significant function of marriage today seems to be that it furnishes emotional satisfactions to be found in no other relationships. For many people it is a refuge from the coldness and impersonality of contemporary existence.

Notwithstanding these developments, a majority of Americans still marry in the traditional way and continue to regard marriage as the most important relationship in their lives.[40] It therefore seems that contemporary attitudes toward marriage differ fundamentally between a minority taking an essentially hostile view of it and a majority upholding it with equal fervor, with perhaps a third group of indeterminate size who see some merit in the arguments on both sides but who do not take a fixed position.[41] If we could analyze the individuals in all three groups we might discover much greater ambivalence in their feelings about marriage than would be suspected from their public utterances. Ambivalence has always characterized people's reactions to this complex relationship, and there is no reason to suppose that our contemporaries are subject to any less conflicting emotions than our ancestors.

From the earliest times in America the concept that marriage was a permanent relationship was limited by the existence of divorce laws in nearly all the states. Even so, for a long time divorce was not within the spouses' control, since it could only be granted upon proof of such serious matrimonial misconduct as adultery, desertion or cruelty.[42] During the late Nineteenth Century and the first half of the Twentieth Century the advent of migratory divorce and the more relaxed treatment of cruelty as a ground for divorce gave many spouses an increased opportunity to end their marriages with considerable freedom.[43] In the last five years divorce has been further liberalized in over half of the states by the enactment of statutes authorizing the termination of marriage whenever the relationship has broken down.[44] In practice this came to mean that either spouse could obtain a divorce at will. It is therefore accurate to say that today the concept of permanence has been eliminated from the legal definition of marriage. Marriages may last for life or for a few years or a few months.

The idea that sexual relations may occur only within marriage has also been eliminated from the legal definition of marriage. In those states having "no-fault" divorce, adultery is no longer a reason for ending a marriage. Under the influence of the Model Penal Code [45] adultery is no longer a crime in many states and even in those states where it still is a crime it is seldom prosecuted. The tort of criminal conversation is likewise in nearly complete disuse. Looking at the present situation realistically, it seems clear that there is no legal prohibition upon the sexual

---

40. A. Skolnick, The Intimate Environment, Chapter 6 (1973); R. Blood, Jr. and D. Wolfe, Husbands and Wives (1960); Wall Street Journal, p. 1, col. 1, March 18, 1976.

41. An expression of the views of the middle group may be found in the best-selling book, N. and G. O'Neill, Open Marriage 43 (1972) which advocates the best of both worlds, an "expanded monogamy, retaining the fulfilling and rewarding aspects of an intimate in-depth relationship with another, yet eliminating the restrictions we were formerly led to believe were an integral part of monogamy."

42. 1 J. Bishop, Marriage, Divorce, and Separation, Chs. 48, 49, 50 (1891).

43. M. Rheinstein, Marriage Stability, Divorce and the Law, Ch. 10 (1972); N. Blake, The Road to Reno (1962).

44. See, Uniform Marriage and Divorce Act §§ 302, 305, 9A Unif.L.Ann. 121, 132 (1979).

45. Model Penal Code §§ 213.6, Note on Adultery and Fornication, Model Penal Code and Commentaries, Part II, 430 (1980) describes the current status of criminal statutes in adultery. Colorado neatly compromises the conflict of old and new views of adultery by prohibiting it but providing no penalty for its commission. Colo.Rev. Stat. 18–6–501 (1973).

conduct of married persons outside their marriage.

Since the courts read the newspapers and have always been sensitive to political movements, their decisions reflect the same conflicts and ambivalence concerning marriage which are prevalent in our society. This is particularly true of the United States Supreme Court.[46] Several of its recent opinions contain statements of a traditional kind in praise of marriage, such as the peroration from Griswold v. Connecticut:[47]

"Marriage is a coming together for better or for worse, hopefully enduring, and intimate to the degree of being sacred. It is an association that promotes a way of life, not causes; a harmony in living, not political faiths; a bilateral loyalty, not commercial or social projects. Yet it is an association for as noble a purpose as any involved in our prior decisions."

Similarly, the miscegenation case characterized marriage as "one of the 'basic civil rights of man,' fundamental to our very existence and survival",[48] and the Boddie case referred to "the basic position of the marriage relationship in this society's hierarchy of values."[49]

In contrast to these lofty sentiments, the Supreme Court, followed by other courts, has taken decisions which can be read either as significantly reducing the legal importance of marriage, or as drastically altering its definition.[50] The Griswold case[51] itself began the

alteration of the traditional incidents to marriage when, by an extraordinary piece of judicial legerdemain, it created a "zone of privacy" within which marriage is constitutionally immune to regulation, at least in the absence of some unspecified degree of social need. This extremely vague doctrine opened to potential constitutional scrutiny many of the rules concerning marriage which had long been taken for granted, particularly those governing sexual relationships in marriage. Griswold's right of privacy, ostensibly based upon the nobility of marriage as a social institution, was converted by Eisenstadt v. Baird[52] into the right of the individual, married or unmarried, to be free of unwarranted governmental intrusion into his sexual conduct. The Court in that case held that no distinction between married and unmarried persons was constitutionally permissible for purposes of regulating the distribution of contraceptives. Although no one can say how broadly Supreme Court opinions are to be applied, Griswold and Eisenstadt could be read to impose constitutional limits upon the extent to which the law may base its regulation of consensual sexual conduct on the presence or absence of marriage.[53] The two cases together seemed to mean that sexual acts of both married and unmarried persons are within a zone of privacy largely immune to state control. But this reading of the cases is not justified in view of the Court's decision upholding the constitutionality of a state prohibition of homosexual conduct between con-

46. See Noonan, The Family and the Supreme Court, 23 Cath.U.L.Rev. 255 (1973); Note, Reaching Equal Protection Under Law; Alternative Forms of Family and the Changing Time of Monogamous Marriage, 1975 Det.Coll. of L.Rev. 95; Glendon, Marriage and the State: The Withering Away of Marriage, 62 Va.L.Rev. 663 (1976).

47. 381 U.S. 479, 486, 85 S.Ct. 1678, 1682, 14 L.Ed.2d 510 (1965).

48. Loving v. Commonwealth of Virginia, 388 U.S. 1, 12, 87 S.Ct. 1817, 1824, 18 L.Ed.2d 1010 (1967).

49. Boddie v. Connecticut, 401 U.S. 371, 374, 91 S.Ct. 780, 784, 28 L.Ed.2d 113 (1971), mandate conformed to 329 F.Supp. 844 (D.Conn.1971).

50. Noonan, The Family and the Supreme Court, 23 Cath.U.L.Rev. 255 (1973) documents this point in greater detail.

51. Griswold v. Connecticut, 381 U.S. 479, 85 S.Ct. 1678, 14 L.Ed.2d 510 (1965); Zablocki v. Redhail, 434 U.S.

374, 98 S.Ct. 673, 54 L.Ed.2d 618 (1978). See also Mentek v. State, 71 Wis.2d 799, 807, 238 N.W.2d 752, 757 (1976) and Jones v. State, 55 Wis.2d 742, 200 N.W.2d 587 (1972), stating that the Wisconsin sodomy statute has no application to acts of consenting married persons in private.

52. 405 U.S. 438, 453, 92 S.Ct. 1029, 1038, 31 L.Ed.2d 349 (1972).

53. The length to which these doctrines could be carried is suggested by a dissenting opinion of Mr. Justice Marshall in California v. LaRue, 409 U.S. 109, 132, 93 S.Ct. 390, 404, 34 L.Ed.2d 342 (1972), rehearing denied 410 U.S. 948, 93 S.Ct. 1351, 35 L.Ed.2d 615 (1973); "However, I have serious doubts whether the State may constitutionally assert an interest in regulating any sexual act between consenting adults." See also Lovisi v. Slayton, 539 F.2d 349 (4th Cir.1976), cert. denied 429 U.S. 977, 97 S.Ct. 485, 50 L.Ed.2d 585 (1976), 44 Tenn.L.Rev. 179 (1977); and State v. Pilcher, 242 N.W.2d 348 (Iowa 1976), 1977 Wash.U.L.Q. 337.

senting adults in private.[54] The Court's opinion emphasized that the right of privacy created in Griswold does not bear "any resemblance to the claimed right of homosexuals to engage in acts of sodomy."

Another aspect of marriage has been altered by those cases which invalidate on constitutional grounds most of the traditional forms of discrimination against illegitimate children.[55] Most of the cases are explainable as removing the inequities of illegitimate status, though in its inscrutable wisdom the Court did not remove the most important inequity by which the illegitimate is prevented from inheriting from his father.[56] One of them, Stanley v. Illinois,[57] does not have that effect, but equalizes the rights of unmarried parents with those of married parents respecting the care and custody of their children. The Court there is saying in effect that marriage has no legal significance for the claims of parents to their children's custody. The Court says this under circumstances in which not only does the child's welfare not call for this result, but in which the child's interests will usually be prejudiced by this doctrine.

The Supreme Court has been somewhat inconsistent on the effect of marriage where public benefits or public regulation has been involved. In United States Department of Agriculture v. Moreno [58] the Court held that the Federal Food Stamp Act could not constitutionally limit the benefits of the food stamp program to households of related individuals. The Court took the position that the classification made by the statute between persons just living together and persons married to each other has no rational basis. And in New Jersey Welfare Rights Organization v. Cahill [59] the Court held that a state statute limiting welfare benefits to traditional families, composed of husband and wife and their children by birth or adoption, denied equal protection of the laws by discriminating against illegitimate children. Another way of describing this result is that it holds that marriage has no legal effect on the entitlement to state benefits.

Village of Belle Terre v. Boraas [60] makes a curious contrast with Moreno and Cahill. In this case the Supreme Court held constitutional a village ordinance limiting land use to

54. Bowers v. Hardwick, ___ U.S. ___, 106 S.Ct. 2841, 92 L.Ed.2d 140 (1986), rehearing denied ___ U.S. ___, 107 S.Ct. 29, 92 L.Ed.2d 779 (1986). The New Jersey Supreme Court held, in State v. Saunders, 75 N.J. 200, 381 A.2d 333 (1977), that the New Jersey fornication statute was unconstitutional. That statute was held to invade the individual right of privacy which under the United States Constitution applies to sexual activities between consenting adults in private. The state interests in preventing venereal disease, preventing the birth of illegitimate children, protecting the marital relationship and preserving public morality were all held to be insufficient to justify the statutory prohibition. The Saunders case is notable for its limitation of the state's right to enforce a moral standard by means of the criminal law. Likewise People v. Onofre, 51 N.Y.2d 476, 434 N.Y.S.2d 947, 415 N.E.2d 936 (1980), reargument denied 52 N.Y.2d 1072, 438 N.Y.S.2d 1028, 420 N.E.2d 412 (1981) held that the New York statute forbidding consensual sodomy constituted an unwarranted invasion of privacy under the federal Constitution. See Baker v. Wade, 553 F.Supp. 1121 (N.D.Tex.1982), appeal dismissed 743 F.2d 236 (5th Cir.1984), district court reversed on rehearing 769 F.2d 289 (5th Cir.1985). Contra, State v. Poe, 40 N.C.App. 385, 252 S.E.2d 843 (1979), appeal dismissed 298 N.C. 303, 259 S.E.2d 304 (1979). See also Morales v. Superior Court of Kern County, 99 Cal.App.3d 283, 160 Cal.Rptr. 194 (1979) limiting the scope of interrogatories in a wrongful death action so as to protect sexual privacy. On the other hand Commonwealth v. Stowell, 389 Mass. 171, 449 N.E.2d 357 (1983) has held that a statute imposing criminal sanctions

for adultery is not unconstitutional even as applied to the conduct of adults in private.

55. E.g., Levy v. Louisiana, 391 U.S. 68, 88 S.Ct. 1509, 20 L.Ed.2d 436 (1968), rehearing denied 393 U.S. 898, 89 S.Ct. 65, 21 L.Ed.2d 185 (1968); Glona v. American Guarantee & Liability Ins. Co., 391 U.S. 73, 88 S.Ct. 1515, 20 L.Ed.2d 441 (1968), rehearing denied 393 U.S. 898, 89 S.Ct. 66, 21 L.Ed.2d 185 (1968); Weber v. Aetna Casualty & Surety Co., 406 U.S. 164, 92 S.Ct. 1400, 31 L.Ed.2d 768 (1972); Gomez v. Perez, 409 U.S. 535, 93 S.Ct. 872, 35 L.Ed.2d 56 (1973). Cf. Labine v. Vincent, 401 U.S. 532, 91 S.Ct. 1017, 28 L.Ed.2d 288 (1971), rehearing denied 402 U.S. 990, 91 S.Ct. 1672, 29 L.Ed.2d 156 (1971).

56. Labine v. Vincent, 401 U.S. 532, 91 S.Ct. 1017, 28 L.Ed.2d 288 (1971), rehearing denied 402 U.S. 990, 91 S.Ct. 1672, 29 L.Ed.2d 156 (1971) had this effect but it may be overruled by Trimble v. Gordon, 430 U.S. 762, 97 S.Ct. 1459, 52 L.Ed.2d 31 (1977). But see Lalli v. Lalli, 439 U.S. 259, 99 S.Ct. 518, 58 L.Ed.2d 503 (1978), and the discussion in section 4.2, infra.

57. 405 U.S. 645, 92 S.Ct. 1208, 31 L.Ed.2d 551 (1972). A tendency to retreat from Stanley appears in Quilloin v. Walcott, 434 U.S. 246, 98 S.Ct. 549, 54 L.Ed.2d 511 (1978), rehearing denied 435 U.S. 918, 98 S.Ct. 1477, 55 L.Ed.2d 511 (1978).

58. 413 U.S. 528, 93 S.Ct. 2821, 37 L.Ed.2d 782 (1973).

59. 411 U.S. 619, 93 S.Ct. 1700, 36 L.Ed.2d 543 (1973).

60. 416 U.S. 1, 94 S.Ct. 1536, 39 L.Ed.2d 797 (1974). For other cases dealing with the definition of "family" for

one-family dwellings. The ordinance defined "family" to mean one or more persons related by blood, adoption or marriage, but it did also include in the definition of "family" not more than two unmarried and unrelated persons. The effect of the ordinance was to permit only traditional families to live in the village, with the single exception that two unrelated and unmarried persons could also live there. The latter provision, in the Court's view, absolved the ordinance from the charge that it reeked "with an animosity to unmarried couples who live together." The attack upon this ordinance, which was upheld by the Second Circuit,[61] was based upon the contention that the interest of the local community in the maintenance of traditional family patterns had no relevance to public health, safety and welfare. The Second Circuit took the position that the village of Belle Terre was attempting to compel its inhabitants to conform to the prevailing notions of proper "lifestyle". The Supreme Court's rejection of this line of reasoning seems to have been based in part upon an affirmation of the social values inherent in marriage and the traditional family.[62] The opinion denied that the ordinance affected any right of privacy, or that Griswold or Eisenstadt required invalidation of the ordinance. Of course Moreno and Cahill may be distinguished from Boraas, but they are quite inconsistent in the extent to which they permit or refuse to permit the legislative bodies to encourage the maintenance of marriage and families.

An important incident of traditional marriage relates to the claims which one spouse has to maintenance from the other, or to a share in the property of the other.[63] The courts generally do not honor such claims where the parties were not married in the usual sense, unless the claimant can bring himself within the putative spouse doctrine.[64] Recently, however, some cases have given persons living together but never married the same rights to a division of property which would be given to a legally married spouse.[65]

This brief account of recent judicial treatment of marriage reveals a profound ambivalence paralleling the ambivalence toward marriage exhibited by our society itself. While some cases express a recognition of the importance of marriage sounding almost Victorian in tone, many others hold, in effect if not expressly, that marriage is no longer a legal category on which rules concerning sexual relations, rules concerning the relationship of parent and child, or rules concerning the distribution of financial assistance by state or federal governments may be based. The Marvin case seemed to establish property rights for persons living together very similar to those enjoyed by persons validly married to each other, thereby making marriage an irrelevant circumstance for purposes of property claims. In a sense therefore all these cases may be regarded as diminishing the significance of marriage as a social institution.

zoning purposes, see Annot., 71 A.L.R.3d 693 (1976); Moore v. East Cleveland, Ohio, 431 U.S. 494, 97 S.Ct. 1932, 52 L.Ed.2d 531 (1977); City of Santa Barbara v. Adamson, 27 Cal.3d 123, 164 Cal.Rptr. 539, 610 P.2d 436 (1980); White Egret Condominium, Inc. v. Franklin, 379 So.2d 346 (Fla.1979).

61. Boraas v. Village of Belle Terre, 476 F.2d 806 (2d Cir.1973).

62. 416 U.S. at 9, 94 S.Ct. at 1541. See also Town of Durham v. White Enterprises, Inc., 115 N.H. 645, 348 A.2d 706 (1975), in which the court said, 115 N.H. at 649, 348 A.2d at 709: "The State has a clear interest, however, in preserving the integrity of the biological or legal family." Cf. Atkisson v. Kern County Housing Authority, 59 Cal.App.3d 89, 130 Cal.Rptr. 375 (1976).

63. See sections 13.5, 14.8, Practitioner's Edition.

64. For cases denying alimony to the claimant who did not have a valid marriage, see section 3.4, infra.

Keene v. Keene, 57 Cal.2d 657, 21 Cal.Rptr. 593, 371 P.2d 329 (1962) and Vallera v. Vallera, 21 Cal.2d 681, 134 P.2d 761 (1943) refused to uphold a claim of community property where the parties had lived together for some time but had never married. See Note, Illicit Cohabitation: The Impact of the Vallera and Keene Cases on the Rights of the Meretricious Spouse, 6 U.C.D.L.Rev. 354 (1973); Note, Property Rights Between Unmarried Cohabitants, 50 Ind.L.J. 389 (1975). The doctrine of putative spouse is discussed, infra, in section 2.4. Many courts still adhere to the rule that contracts to devise property are illegal and unenforceable if sexual intercourse is part of the consideration. Cf. Green v. Richmond, 369 Mass. 47, 337 N.E.2d 691 (1975).

65. Marvin v. Marvin, 18 Cal.3d 660, 134 Cal.Rptr. 815, 557 P.2d 106 (1976). The case and its aftermath are discussed in detail in section 1.2, supra, and in section 15.7, infra.

Looked at from another point of view, the law appears to be in the process of redefining marriage. If relationships differing substantially from conventional marriage carry the same legal incidents as marriage, it is fair to say that such relationships may be called marriage. The new definition seems to have abandoned most of the traditional characteristics of marriage. Sexual exclusivity is no longer insisted upon by the law. A joint domicile of husband and wife is no longer required, since under the influence of state Equal Rights Amendments[66] and of recent decisions under the Equal Protection Clause[67] married women are presumably able as a matter of constitutional right to choose a domicile separate from their husbands. The duties of support are no longer imposed upon the husband, but are shared by both husband and wife to the extent of their abilities, which means that in practice it is impossible to determine the extent of those duties until litigation defines them. More importantly, if the California cases granting community property rights to cohabiting persons are followed, presumably support rights between cohabiting persons will be imposed upon those who choose to live together. Underlying these developments in the case law is the premise that entry into marriage is no longer required to be signalized by a ceremony, although the state statutes all contain provisions regulating the entry into marriage. And finally, if, as seems at least possible, the effect of existing state Equal Rights Amend-

ments[68] or the federal amendment[69] (should it be adopted) is to make marriage between homosexuals constitutionally permissible,[70] the most fundamental of all characteristics of marriage, that it is a relationship between a man and a woman, will have been altered. The result seems to be that contemporary marriage cannot be legally defined any more precisely than as some sort of relationship between two individuals, of indeterminate duration, involving some kind of sexual conduct, entailing vague mutual property and support obligations, a relationship which may be formed by consent of both parties and dissolved at the will of either.[71]

The law is committed to this definition to some degree by constitutional limitations and by statutes already in force in many states. The uncertainty which it generates, both for the courts and for individuals and their children is obvious. It is impossible to say, for example, how long such a relationship must continue before it will be given the attributes of marriage, or what effect the courts might be persuaded to give to contracts made by persons living together in which they attempt to control the nature of their relationship.[72] If men and women are encouraged by these legal doctrines to live together informally on the assumption that some or all of the incidents of marriage will result, children born of such relationships will face serious practical difficulties in proving paternity in many instances, difficulties which either do not exist

---

66. See, e.g., Alaska Const. Art. I, § 3; Colo. Const. Art. II, § 29; Hawaii Const. Art. I, § 4; Ill.—S.H.A.Const. Art. I, § 18; N.M. Const. Art. II, § 18; Vernon's Ann. Tex. Const. Art. I, § 3a; Utah Const. Art. IV, § 1 (semble); Va. Const. Art. I, § 11; West's Rev.Code Wash.Ann. Const. Art. XXXI, § 1; Wyo. Const. Art. I, § 3 (semble).

67. E.g., Reed v. Reed, 404 U.S. 71, 92 S.Ct. 251, 30 L.Ed.2d 225 (1971), mandate conformed to 94 Idaho 542, 493 P.2d 701 (1972); Frontiero v. Richardson, 411 U.S. 677, 93 S.Ct. 1764, 36 L.Ed.2d 583 (1973). Cf. Cleveland Board of Education v. LaFleur, 414 U.S. 632, 94 S.Ct. 791, 39 L.Ed.2d 52 (1974); Turner v. Department of Employment Security and Board of Review of Indus. Comm'n of Utah, 423 U.S. 44, 96 S.Ct. 249, 46 L.Ed.2d 181 (1975).

68. See note 69, infra. West's Ann.Cal.Civ.Code § 4452 (1983).

69. U.S.Code Ann., Constitution, Amendments 14 to End (1984 p. 1239).

70. The argument that the Twenty-Seventh Amendment would have this effect is persuasively made and extensively documented in a Note, The Legality of Homosexual Marriage, 82 Yale L.J. 573, 583 (1973).

71. This definition resembles that given in the Uniform Marriage and Divorce Act, section 201, 9A Uniform L.Ann. 101 (1979): "Marriage is a personal relationship between a man and a woman arising out of a civil contract to which the consent of the parties is essential." This section adheres in part to the law's traditional insistence on controlling the formation and termination of the relationship, in the following language: "A marriage may be contracted, maintained, invalidated, or dissolved only as provided by law."

72. For a discussion of contracts in lieu of marriage, and the suggestion that the Uniform Partnership Act might serve as a model for such contracts, see Weitzman, Legal Regulation of Marriage: Tradition and Change, 62 Calif.L.Rev. 1169, 1255 (1974).

or exist to a much slighter degree where traditional marriage or even common law marriage have occurred.

The consequence of these developments seems to be that notwithstanding occasional judicial expressions like those in the Griswold,[73] Loving [74] and Boddie [75] cases, marriage as a legal institution is being transformed from a clearly defined and legally regulated relationship into an imprecisely defined relationship whose incidents are either uncertain or left largely to the control of the parties to the relationship. The transformation is occurring as a result of individual statute and judicial decision, without, so far as appears, any general consideration by either courts or legislatures of the total effect which the judicial decisions and statutes will have on the institution of marriage.[76]

 WESTLAW REFERENCES

find 62 sct 1110
find 85 sct 1678

§ 2.2 Marriage—The State's Power to Control the Relationship

Although historically in English law marriage was the exclusive concern of ecclesiastical courts and the canon law, and although we received a substantial amount of our marriage law from this source, in America marriage has always been regulated by the civil authorities. In many states statutes making this plain have been enacted, providing that marriage is a civil contract.[1] Therefore, the various religious denominations, in spite of their continuing interest in the marital status and its obligations, are clearly subordinate to the law with respect to marriage. Their precepts may be enforced by appeals to conscience, or by other religious sanctions, but the ultimate power to regulate marriage rests with the state.[2]

The assertion by the various state legislatures of a broad, plenary power to regulate marriage was often held constitutional [3] until 1965. In that year, in Griswold v. Connecticut [4] the Supreme Court held that the Connecticut statute forbidding the use of contraceptives was unconstitutional as applied to married persons. Mr. Justice Douglas' opinion, with which four other justices more or less agreed, held that the specific guarantees in the Bill of Rights have "penumbras" which create a zone of marital privacy. The Connecticut statute was said to invade marital privacy in a particularly destructive way and therefore to be invalid. Mr. Justice Goldberg's concurring opinion [5] agreed that the statute intruded upon marital privacy in an impermissible way, but also relied upon the

73. See note 47, supra.

74. See note 48, supra.

75. See note 49, supra.

76. For an argument that some structure should be restored to marriage by private contracts, enforceable by the state, see Shultz, Contractual Ordering of Marriage: A New Model for State Policy, 70 Cal.L.Rev. 204 (1982).

§ 2.2

1. E.g., West's Ann.Cal.Civ.Code § 4100 (1983); [West's Ann.Ind.Code § 31–1–1–1 (1980)]; Iowa Code Ann. § 595.1 (West 1981); Kan.Stat.Ann. § 23–101 (1981); La.Stat.Ann.–Civ.Code Arts. 86, 87 (1952); Mich.Comp. Laws Ann. § 25.2 (1984); Minn.Stat.Ann. § 517.01 (Supp. 1984); N.Y.—McKinney's Domestic Relations Law § 10 (1977); West's Rev.Code Wash.Ann. § 26.04.010 (Supp. 1984); Wis.Stat.Ann. § 765.01 (1981).

For an interesting case asserting the supremacy of state law over the ecclesiastical law respecting the contracting of marriage, see Hames v. Hames, 163 Conn. 588, 316 A.2d 379 (1972).

2. The law of a particular state may leave some authority to the churches, as in Colorado where the statute provides marriages may be solemnized in accordance with the practices of any religious denomination or Indian tribe. Colo.Rev.Stat. § 14–2–109 (Supp.1986).

3. E.g., Maynard v. Hill, 125 U.S. 190, 8 S.Ct. 723, 31 L.Ed. 654 (1888); Estin v. Estin, 334 U.S. 541, 68 S.Ct. 1213, 92 L.Ed. 1561 (1948); Crouch v. Crouch, 28 Cal.2d 243, 169 P.2d 897 (1946); Stokes v. County Clerk of Los Angeles County, 122 Cal.App.2d 229, 264 P.2d 959 (1953); In re Duncan, 83 Idaho 254, 360 P.2d 987 (1961); Siegall v. Solomon, 19 Ill.2d 145, 166 N.E.2d 5 (1960); Pry v. Pry, 225 Ind. 458, 75 N.E.2d 909 (1947); Ladd v. Commonwealth, 313 Ky. 754, 233 S.W.2d 517 (1950); First Nat. Bank in Grand Forks v. North Dakota Workmen's Compensation Bureau, 68 N.W.2d 661 (N.D.1955).

4. 381 U.S. 479, 85 S.Ct. 1678, 14 L.Ed.2d 510 (1965). See Note, Developments in the Law—The Constitution and the Family, 93 Harv.L.Rev. 1157 (1980).

5. Griswold v. Connecticut, 381 U.S. 479, 486, 85 S.Ct. 1678, 1682, 14 L.Ed.2d 510 (1965).

Ninth Amendment [6] as supporting the view that the rights protected by the Fifth [7] and Fourteenth [8] Amendments are not limited to those spelled out in the first eight amendments, but may include such a "fundamental personal right" as the right of marital privacy. Shorn of metaphors and fancy language, these opinions seemed to mean that the states may not make laws regulating at least the sexual relations in marriage without showing a "subordinating state interest which is compelling." [9] No such interest was shown to underlie the Connecticut ban on contraceptives.

Since Griswold was an abrupt departure from prior cases, and since its rationale was not precise, it could, if rigorously applied, be read to invalidate a considerable number of state statutes regulating marriage. It has been suggested, for example that statutes forbidding marriages between first cousins or between persons related by affinity may be invalid under the Griswold reasoning. [10] The same point has been made with respect to public health regulations forbidding the marriage of epileptics or those having tuberculosis, since such statutes have no valid medical or genetic basis. [11] On the other hand, it is equally possible to read Griswold as applying only to regulation of sexual relations within marriage. Sex in marriage is and has been a matter of the utmost privacy in our culture and in that respect is to be distinguished from qualifications for entry into marriage or from requirements of ceremony and licensing, which have always been considered subjects of state and public interest. This distinction between relationships within marriage and the entry into marriage has not been relied upon by the courts, and marriage regulation has not been widely invalidated since Griswold. [12] Some cases have either held or indicated [13] that prohibition of sodomy between consenting married persons is unconstitutional, and this seems within the most limited reading of the Griswold case. But requirements of ceremony, of license, of various kinds of pre-marital medical examination, and the prescription of various qualifications

---

6. U.S.C.A. Const. Amend. IX: "The enumeration in the Constitution, of certain rights, shall not be construed to deny or disparage others retained by the people."

7. U.S.C.A. Const. Amend. V: "No person shall be * * * deprived of life, liberty, or property, without due process of law; * * *"

8. U.S.C.A. Const. Amend. XIV: "* * * nor shall any State deprive any person of life, liberty, or property, without due process of law; * * *"

9. Griswold v. Connecticut, 381 U.S. 479, 497, 85 S.Ct. 1678, 1689, 14 L.Ed.2d 510 (1965) (concurring opinion).

10. Foster, Marriage: A "Basic Civil Right of Man", 37 Ford L.Rev. 51, 61 (1968).

11. Id. at 63.

12. Zablocki v. Redhail, 434 U.S. 374, 98 S.Ct. 673, 54 L.Ed.2d 618 (1978) invalidated a Wisconsin statute which prevented the marriage of persons who failed to comply with child support decrees. But Moe v. Dinkins, 533 F.Supp. 623 (S.D.N.Y.1981), judgment affirmed 669 F.2d 67 (2d Cir.1982), cert. denied 459 U.S. 827, 103 S.Ct. 61, 74 L.Ed.2d 64 (1982) has upheld New York's requirement of parental consent for marriages of persons between fourteen and eighteen.

13. Cotner v. Henry, 394 F.2d 873 (7th Cir.1968), cert. denied 393 U.S. 847, 89 S.Ct. 132, 21 L.Ed.2d 118 (1968); Buchanan v. Batchelor, 308 F.Supp. 729 (N.D.Tex.1970), vacated and remanded 401 U.S. 989, 91 S.Ct. 1221, 28 L.Ed.2d 526 (1971); State v. Lair, 62 N.J. 388, 301 A.2d 748 (1973); State v. Elliott, 88 N.M. 187, 539 P.2d 207 (App.1975), reversed 89 N.M. 305, 551 P.2d 1352 (1976),

appeal after remand 89 N.M. 756, 557 P.2d 1105 (1977); Mentek v. State, 71 Wis.2d 799, 238 N.W.2d 752 (1976).

A few courts have relied upon Griswold, and upon Eisenstadt v. Baird, 405 U.S. 438, 92 S.Ct. 1029, 31 L.Ed.2d 349 (1972) to hold unconstitutional statutes prohibiting homosexual conduct between consenting adults in private. Commonwealth v. Balthazar, 366 Mass. 298, 318 N.E.2d 478 (1974); People v. Onofre, 51 N.Y.2d 476, 434 N.Y.S.2d 947, 415 N.E.2d 936 (1980), cert. denied 451 U.S. 987, 101 S.Ct. 2323, 68 L.Ed.2d 845 (1981); Commonwealth v. Bonadio, 490 Pa. 91, 415 A.2d 47 (1980). See also California v. LaRue, 409 U.S. 109, 132, 93 S.Ct. 390, 404, 34 L.Ed.2d 342 (1972), rehearing denied 410 U.S. 948, 93 S.Ct. 1351, 35 L.Ed.2d 615 (1973) (dissenting opinion); Commonwealth v. MacKenzie, 386 Mass. 613, 334 N.E.2d 613, 617 (1975) (dissenting opinion); and Note, The Constitutionality of Laws Forbidding Private Homosexual Conduct, 72 Mich.L.Rev. 1613 (1975). Other cases have held such statutes constitutional, notwithstanding Griswold. State v. Bateman, 113 Ariz. 107, 547 P.2d 6 (1976), cert. denied 429 U.S. 1302, 97 S.Ct. 1, 50 L.Ed.2d 32 (1976); Dixon v. State, 256 Ind. 266, 268 N.E.2d 84 (1971); State v. Lair, 62 N.J. 388, 301 A.2d 748 (1973). The Supreme Court has settled the question in favor of constitutionality in Doe v. Commonwealth's Attorney for City of Richmond, 403 F.Supp. 1199 (E.D.Va.1975), affirmed per curiam, 425 U.S. 901, 96 S.Ct. 1489, 47 L.Ed.2d 751 (1976), rehearing denied 425 U.S. 985, 96 S.Ct. 2192, 48 L.Ed.2d 810 (1976), and in Bowers v. Hardwick, ____ U.S. ____, 106 S.Ct. 2841, 92 L.Ed.2d 140 (1986), rehearing denied ____ U.S. ____, 107 S.Ct. 29, 92 L.Ed.2d 779 (1986).

for marriage [14] have thus far survived the Griswold doctrine. These, and such other regulations of marriage as statutes dealing with marital property, with support, with the care of children all attempt to achieve a perceptible state interest of one kind or another, usually the interest in supporting and strengthening the family.[15] So far as such an interest appears, the regulation ought to be upheld, whether or not the interest may be characterized as a "compelling" one.

This construction of Griswold is supported by Carey v. Population Services, International,[16] which states that " * * * the teaching of Griswold is that the Constitution protects individual decisions in matters of childbearing from unjustified intrusion by the State." [17] In its subsequent term, however, the Court invalidated a Wisconsin statute which provided that a person subject to a court order for support of his children could not marry without court permission. The Court held that the right to marry is of "fundamental importance" so that state statutes significantly interfering with that right must be subjected to "critical examination." [18] Having imposed what appears to be a rigorous constitutional limitation upon the right to marry, the Court at once retreated from its position with the following language:

"By reaffirming the fundamental character of the right to marry, we do not mean to suggest that every state regulation which

relates in any way to the incidents of or prerequisites for marriage must be subjected to rigorous scrutiny. To the contrary, reasonable regulations that do not significantly interfere with decisions to enter into the marital relationship may legitimately be imposed." [19]

In this case the Court went on to find that since the means chosen by the statute to effectuate the state's purpose of providing child support impinged unnecessarily upon the right to marry, the statute was unconstitutional. The Court held that the statute was both "overinclusive" and "underinclusive" in its choice of technique.

The Supreme Court has thus left us in even greater confusion about the extent of the state's power to regulate marriage than was created by Griswold. Its opinions provide ample proof, if any were needed, that the simplistic application of constitutional shibboleths to complex family relationships handicaps state regulation of those relationships, and is harmful to the relationships themselves.[20]

WESTLAW REFERENCES

state /s church ecclesiastic! canon /s law /s marri! marital marry!

ti(hames +s hames)

griswold /s connecticut /s privacy /7 marri! marry! martial

---

14. The California requirement of pre-marital counseling for persons under eighteen who are about to marry may be questioned as an invasion of privacy, but presumably it too would be upheld on the ground of the obvious state interest which the requirement serves. See West's Ann.Cal.Civ.Code § 4101(c) (1983).

15. Some courts have continued to assert a plenary state power to regulate marriage even after the Griswold decision. See, e.g., In re Marriage of Franks, 189 Colo. 499, 542 P.2d 845 (1975), stay denied 423 U.S. 1043, 96 S.Ct. 766, 46 L.Ed.2d 632 (1976). But see United States v. Orito, 413 U.S. 139, 142, 93 S.Ct. 2674, 2677, 37 L.Ed.2d 513 (1973): "The Constitution extends special safeguards to the privacy of the home, just as it protects other special privacy rights such as those of marriage, procreation, motherhood, child rearing and education."

Prison regulations restricting inmates' right to marry have been held unconstitutional under Zablocki in Salisbury v. List, 501 F.Supp. 105 (D.Nev.1980). Similar regulations have been held valid in Department of Corrections v. Roseman, 390 So.2d 394 (Fla.App.1980).

Clark, Domestic Rel., 2nd Ed. HBSE—3

16. 431 U.S. 678, 97 S.Ct. 2010, 52 L.Ed.2d 675 (1977).

17. 431 U.S. at 687, 97 S.Ct. at 2017.

18. Zablocki v. Redhail, 434 U.S. 374, 98 S.Ct. 673, 54 L.Ed.2d 618 (1978).

19. 434 U.S. at 386, 98 S.Ct. at 681. In Salisbury v. List, 501 F.Supp. 105 (D.Nev.1980) a prison regulation restricting the right of inmates to marry was held invalid in reliance upon the Zablocki case.

20. For an interesting and thorough analysis of the Supreme Court's treatment of marriage and the family, reaching conclusions different from those in the text, see Hafen, The Constitutional Status of Marriage, Kinship, and Sexual Privacy—Balancing the Individual and Social Interests, 81 Mich.L.Rev. 463 (1983).

sodomy (oral +2 sex) fellatio cunnilingus /s marry!
  marri! martial /s unconstitutional! constitution!

find 98 sct 673

constitution! unconstitutional! /p homosexual! consent!
  consensual

find 97 sct 2010

---

§ 2.3 Marriage—Licensing and Solemnization [1]

In order to effectuate a variety of social policies, a great deal of statutory regulation has grown up in all states around entrance into matrimony. Part of this regulation is solely for the collection of vital statistics. A larger part has more important purposes. It has become a commonplace of discussion that one way of reducing the divorce rate and of increasing the stability of marriages is to prevent hasty or ill-advised marriages. Some of the statutes impose waiting periods for this reason. The requirement of a certain amount of formality, delay, and public notice incident to the ceremony and the obtaining of a license serves the same purpose. Licensing statutes are also intended to assist in the enforcement of other marriage laws by requiring persons who are not qualified to marry, because, for example, of age, or a prior subsisting marriage, to reveal such fact before the marriage is contracted. Both license and ceremony serve the additional purpose of providing objective proof that the marriage has occurred,

avoiding the problems of evidence and accusations of fraud which often arise out of informal marriages. Finally, some statutes are public health measures aimed at preventing the marriages of parties who, by reason of venereal or other contagious disease, would be likely to infect the spouse or the children of the marriage.

Although these policies are appealing to the person interested in improvement of marriage, the statutes seem to have accomplished little toward effectuating some of them. This is primarily due to the availability of methods of evasion. The parties can generally evade blood test and waiting period statutes by going to another state. There have been many "Gretna Greens" in the United States, in the business of providing fast and easy marriages.[2] In any event the waiting period is never long enough to do any good. In addition the sanctions behind the regulatory statutes are either rarely invoked or too slight to deter violations.[3]

A complete list of the laws of all states on licensing and the solemnization of marriage would be unduly long, since there is a large variety of such statutes. The present section will attempt to describe the main features of such statutes, in order to illustrate the types of regulation currently in legislative favor.

The laws of all states require the parties to procure a license before marriage.[4] In a few

---

§ 2.3

1. For a comprehensive treatment of the subject of this section, see Richmond and Hall, Marriage and the State (1929), based upon field studies as well as investigation of the law.

2. P. Jacobson, American Marriage and Divorce, 50–53 (1959). For a graphic description of Elkton, Maryland, a notorious "Gretna Green", see State v. Clay, 182 Md. 639, 35 A.2d 821 (1944). For accounts of other purveyors of quick marriages see M. Richmond and F. Hall, Marriage and the State, 84–105 (1929); Wall St. Journal, Feb. 27, 1967, page 1 (Las Vegas) and March 24, 1972 (Clintwood, Virginia). Nevada has taken the profit out of marriage mills by recent statutory changes, however. Nev.Rev.Stat. §§ 122.171, 122.173, 122.175, 122.181 (1979).

3. The licensing statutes make it a crime to falsify the application for license, but prosecutions are understandably rare. One such case, upholding a perjury conviction for falsely reporting the age of the bride in a marriage license application, is State v. Randall, 166 Minn. 381,

208 N.W. 14 (1926). Criminal penalties are also imposed by most statutes for solemnizing marriages where no license has been issued, or with knowledge that either party is legally incompetent to contract the marriage, but prosecutions under these statutes are even more rare. State v. Clay, 182 Md. 639, 35 A.2d 821 (1944) affirmed a conviction for maintaining signs and billboards soliciting a marriage business in violation of the statute. An additional sanction exists in some states in the form of a statutory penalty recoverable by the parents of a minor from one who performs a marriage of the minor without the parents' consent. See Mitchell v. McGuire, 244 Ala. 73, 12 So.2d 180 (1943); Maryland Cas. Co. v. Teele, 70 Ga.App. 259, 28 S.E.2d 193 (1943). For trenchant criticism of the blood test requirement, see Monahan, State Control and Legislation on Marriage, A.B.A. Family Law Section Proceedings 57, 60 (1961).

4. E.g., Colo.Rev.Stat. §§ 14–2–104, 14–2–105, 14–2–106, 14–2–107 (1973 & Supp.1984); Md.Code 1957, Art. 62, §§ 4 to 19; Mich.Comp.Laws Ann. §§ 25.31 to 25.42 (Callaghan 1984); N.Y.—McKinney's Dom.Rel.L. § 13 (1977);

jurisdictions exceptions are made, as in California where no license is required if the parties have previously been living together as husband and wife without having been married.[5] Licenses are issued by a county officer, such as the county clerk, in most states.[6] In other states a clerk of court,[7] a minor court judge,[8] a justice of the peace[9] or a city clerk[10] may be the licensing authority. There is equal diversity as to the place where the license must be obtained. Under some statutes it may be obtained anywhere in the state.[11] Under others it may be issued only in the county where the marriage is to take place,[12] or in the county where the woman resides,[13] or in the county where either party resides.[14] Relatively small fees are charged for licenses in all states.[15]

The usual practice is for both parties to apply in person for the marriage license, but this is not always required by the statute.[16] Statutes are frequently not explicit on the point, but in some states only one applicant need apply in person,[17] while in others neither party need appear before the issuing authority.[18]

The licensing statutes prescribe the information to be furnished by the applicant, and require that it be given under oath.[19] This information includes not only facts which go into the compilation of vital statistics, but also facts which reveal whether the parties are eligible to marry each other, such as age, relationship between them if any, prior marriages and whether such marriages have ended by death or divorce. When this information is received by the issuing officer, it is his duty to deny the license if it appears that the parties are not legally eligible to marry.[20] According to the case law of some states, the

Wis.Stat.Ann. § 765.05 (West Supp.1984); Uniform Marriage and Divorce Act §§ 201–204, 9A Unif.L.Ann. 100–105 (1979). The Uniform Act has been enacted in Arizona, Kentucky and Montana in addition to Colorado.

5. West's Ann.Cal.Civ.Code § 4213 (Supp.1984) and Burt v. Burt, 187 Cal.App.2d 36, 9 Cal.Rptr. 440 (1960). The exception applies to persons over eighteen. Encinas v. Lowthian Freight Lines, 69 Cal.App.2d 156, 158 P.2d 575 (1945). See also Official Code Ga.Ann. § 19–3–39 (Supp.1984) (publication of banns may be substituted for the license); Iowa Code Ann. § 595.17 (Supp.1984) (exemption for certain religious denominations); Md.Code 1957, Art. 27, § 395 (Quakers exempt from penal sanctions for marrying without a license).

6. E.g., Colo.Rev.Stat. § 14–2–106 (Supp.1984); Wis. Stat.Ann. § 765.05 (West Supp.1984).

7. E.g., Ariz.Rev.Stat. §§ 25–121, 25–126 (Supp.1984); Minn.Stat.Ann. § 517.07 (West Supp.1984).

8. West's Fla.Stat.Ann. § 741.01 (Supp.1984); Kan. Stat.Ann. § 23–106 (1981); N.D.Cent.Code § 14–03–10 (1981).

9. Del.Code art. 13, §§ 108, 109 (1981 and Supp.1982).

10. N.Y.–McKinney's Dom.Rel.L. § 13 (1977).

11. Idaho Code § 32–401 (1983); Ill.–S.H.A. ch. 40, § 203 (Supp.1984).

12. Conn.Gen.Stat.Ann. § 46b–24 (1986).

13. Miss.Code 1983, § 93–1–5 (Supp.) (where the woman is under twenty-one and a resident of Mississippi).

14. West's Ann.Ind.Code § 31–1–1–3 (Supp.1984); Mich.C.L.A. § 25.31 (Callaghan 1984).

15. Colo.Rev.Stat. § 14–2–106 (Supp.1984); West's Fla. Stat.Ann. §§ 741.01, 741.02 (1984); N.J.Stat.Ann. § 37:1–12, 37:1–12.1 (1968 and Supp.1984). The use of marriage license fees to fund shelters for battered wives was held unconstitutional as a special tax having no rational relation to the persons on whom it was imposed in Boynton v. Kusper, 112 Ill.2d 356, 98 Ill.Dec. 208, 494 N.E.2d 135 (1986).

16. Ill.–McKinney's Ann.Stat. ch. 40, § 203 (1980 & Supp.1984) requires both parties to apply.

17. E.g., Idaho Code § 32–403 (Supp.1983); Nev.Rev. Stat. § 122.040 (1981).

18. Mass.Gen.Laws Ann. ch. 207, § 19 (1981). Vernon's Ann.Mo.Stat. § 451.040 (1977). N.H.Rev.Stat.Ann. § 457:22 (1968).

19. E.g., Wis.Stat.Ann. § 245.09 (1981 and Supp.1984). The state may not constitutionally require information as to race on the marriage license. Pedersen v. Burton, 400 F.Supp. 960 (D.D.C.1975). Contra: Stokes v. County Clerk of Los Angeles County, 122 Cal.App.2d 229, 264 P.2d 959 (1953).

20. E.g., N.Y.–McKinney's Dom.Rel.L. § 15 (1977); Pa.Stat. tit. 48, § 1–5 (1965 and Supp.1984).

In a few states the licensing procedure has been used to deal with problems of non-payment of child support and alimony. In Wisconsin, for example, no resident of the state may marry without a court order if he is subject to a child support order in a prior divorce proceeding, although a hearing may be waived if it appears that the child is being properly supported. The Wisconsin statute was held unconstitutional in Zablocki v. Redhail, 434 U.S. 374, 98 S.Ct. 673, 54 L.Ed.2d 618 (1978). See also Miller v. Morris, 270 Ind. 505, 386 N.E.2d 1203 (1979).

Disqualification as an applicant for a marriage license may occasionally be based upon other supposed social grounds. E.g., N.D.Cent.Code § 14–03–17 (Supp.1983) requires a showing that the applicant is not an habitual criminal, and Pa.Stat. tit. 48, § 1–5 (Supp.1984) disqualifies indigents.

An attempt to further population control is incorporated in some licensing statutes, as in New Hampshire

officer has more than a ministerial function in issuing licenses, his duty being characterized as judicial or quasi-judicial. In practice this means that he may be obliged to satisfy himself that the applicant is entitled to a marriage license before he issues one.[21] If he doubts the validity of a divorce, for example, he may refuse to issue the license.[22] The question then may ultimately be determined in an action for mandamus brought by the applicant, or by other appropriate legal remedy.[23]

The great majority of states impose a waiting period between the application for the license and its issuance. The length of the period ranges from twenty-four hours[24] to five days.[25] The time usually chosen is three days,[26] hardly long enough to constitute a deterrence to hasty marriage. The suggestion is often made that pre-marital counselling should be required as a device for reducing hasty or ill-considered marriages, but this has not generally been done except in California, where it is required for persons under eighteen years old.[27] In a few states the waiting period is made longer for non-residents than for residents, as a means of discouraging mi-

gratory marriages.[28] In about five states the waiting period intervenes after the license has been issued and before the ceremony may be performed.[29] It is usual to provide for waiver of the waiting period under certain circumstances, usually with the approval of a public official or a court.[30] It should also be noted that many statutes provide for the expiration of the marriage license if the marriage is not performed within a relatively short period.[31]

Nearly all states require some sort of physical examination as a condition upon the issuance of a marriage license.[32] Most of the statutes require an examination for venereal disease alone.[33] A few also require tests for tuberculosis,[34] for mental incompetence,[35] for rubella immunity[36] and for sickle cell anemia.[37] In all instances except the examination for rubella immunity and for sickle cell immunity the physician's statement certifying freedom from the specified disease is required to be presented before the license may issue. There is usually provision in the statutes for waiver of the examination by a court upon proof of circumstances warranting such

where the clerk is required to give couples a list of the family planning agencies in the state. N.H.Rev.Stat. Ann. § 457:28–a (Supp.1973). See also Md.Code 1983, art. 62, § 7B.

21. Antunes v. Antunes, 23 N.J.Super. 150, 92 A.2d 653 (1952). The clerk has the burden of proving that the parties are not eligible to marry. Adelman v. Hubbard, 60 N.Y.S.2d 387 (Sup.Ct.1945). See Uniform Marriage and Divorce Act §§ 203, 9A Unif.L.Ann. 102 (1979).

22. Alzmann v. Maher, 231 App.Div. 139, 246 N.Y.S. 60 (2d Dep't 1930).

23. The leading case granting mandamus is Perez v. Lippold, 32 Cal.2d 711, 198 P.2d 17 (1948). Under the Wisconsin statute the clerk must submit the application for a license to a court for an opinion when he is not satisfied with the sufficiency of the supporting data. Wis.Stat.Ann. § 765.09 (Supp.1984).

24. S.C.Code 1977, § 20–1–220 (Supp.).

25. E.g., N.H.Rev.Stat.Ann. § 457–26 (1968); Wis.Stat. Ann. § 765.08 (Supp.1984). The effective delay in New York seems to be ten days. N.Y.–McKinney's Dom.Rel.L. § 13–b (Supp.1983).

26. E.g., Alaska Stat. § 25.05.091 (1983); West's Fla. Stat.Ann. § 741.04 (Supp.1984); Mass.G.Law Ann. ch. 207, § 19 (Supp.1981); Mont.Code Ann. 40–1–212 (1983); N.J.Stat.Ann. § 37:1–4 (1968). See also Uniform Marriage and Divorce Act § 204, 9A Unif.L.Ann. 104 (1979).

27. West's Ann.Cal.Civ.Code § 4101(c) (1983).

28. E.g., Del.Code tit. 13, § 107 (1981) (one day for residents, four days for non-residents).

29. E.g., LSA–Rev.Stat. § 9:203 (1965); Vt.Stat.Ann. tit. 18, § 5145 (Supp.1984); Uniform Marriage and Divorce Act § 204, 9A Unif.L.Ann. 104 (1979).

30. E.g., N.Y.–McKinney's Dom.Rel.L. § 13–b (Supp. 1983); Ohio Rev.Code § 3101.05 (Supp.1984); Wis.Stat. Ann. § 765.08 (Supp.1984).

31. E.g., West's Ann.Cal.Civ.Code § 4204 (1983) (ninety days); West's A.I.C. § 31–1–1–3 (1984) (sixty days); Ky. Rev.Stat. § 402.105 (1984) (thirty days); N.Y.–McKinney's Dom.Rel.L. § 13–b (Supp.1983) (sixty days); Wis. Stat.Ann. § 765.12 (Supp.1984) (thirty days).

32. Nevada is one of the few states which require no medical examination. Nev.Rev.Stat. § 122.040 (1983).

33. E.g., Ill.–S.H.A. ch. 40, §§ 204, 205 (Supp.1984); Tenn.Code Ann. § 36–3–202 (1984).

34. E.g., N.C.Gen.Stat. § 51–9 (Supp.1983).

35. E.g., N.C.Gen.Stat. § 51–9 (Supp.1983); Pa.Stat. tit. 48, § 1–5 (Supp.1984).

36. E.g., Colo.Rev.Stat. § 14–2–106 (Supp.1984); Mass. Gen.Laws Ann. ch. 207, § 28A (1981).

37. E.g., Ill.–S.H.A. ch. 40, § 204 (Supp.1984); West's Ann.Ind.Code § 31–1–1–7 (1984).

action.[38] As part of the scheme of regulation all states requiring a physical examination also fix a maximum period within which the license must issue. If he permits the period to expire without obtaining a license, the applicant must undergo another examination. The period ranges from ten days to forty days, the most commonly chosen limit being thirty days.[39]

The solemnization of marriages is also governed by statute in all states. The question whether these statutes exclude the possibility of valid informal or common law marriages is considered in another section.[40] At this point we are solely concerned with the form of the statutory regulation. All states authorize named persons, both religious leaders and specified civil officers, to solemnize marriages. Such civil officers include judges,[41] justices of the peace,[42] court clerks,[43] and others.[44] Some statutes attempt to define what is meant by a religious leader or minister of the gospel, usually giving quite broad authority to such persons for the celebration of marriages.[45] The few cases which have arisen have been concerned with those denominations which take the position that every member is a minister. One case held that a member of the Jehovah's Witnesses could perform marriages since all members of the sect were designated as ministers.[46] More recently members of the Universal Life Church, who, under the rules of that sect, may become ministers for life merely by asking to be ordained and without any qualifications, were held not to be eligible to perform marriages under a statute requiring proof of ordination and of the person's being in regular communion with his religious society.[47] The difference in the cases may largely be explained by differences in statutory language. Some states also have statutes authorizing the solemnization of marriages before religious denominations which do not have ministers or priests, such as the Quakers or the Ethical Culture Society.[48]

There is a popular impression that ship captains have authority to perform marriages on the high seas. No American statute authorizing this has been found. One case, Fisher v. Fisher,[49] has held such marriages

38. E.g., Alaska Stat. § 25.05.181 (1983) (licensing officer may waive); West's Ann.Cal.Civ.Code § 4306 (1983).

39. Conn.Gen.Stat.Ann. § 46b–26 (Supp.1986) (thirty-five days); LSA–Rev.Stat. § 9:241 (1965) (ten days); Mich. C.L.A. § 14.15 (5241) (1980) (thirty days); Okl.Stat.1979, tit. 43, § 31 (thirty days); R.I.Gen.L.1986, § 15–2–3 (Supp.) (forty days).

40. See section 2.4, infra. Iowa Code Ann. § 595.11 (1983) provides that marriages are valid though solemnized other than as the statute requires, but imposes a fine for a violation of the statute. See Nelson v. Minner, 604 F.Supp. 590 (S.D.Iowa 1985).

41. E.g., West's Ann.Cal.Civ.Code § 4205 (Supp.1983); Colo.Rev.Stat. § 14–2–109 (Supp.1984); Ill.–S.H.A. ch. 40, § 209 (Supp.1984); V.T.C.A., Fam.Code § 1.83 (Supp. 1984); Wis.Stat.Ann. § 765.16 (Supp.1984).

42. E.g., Mass.Gen.L.Ann. ch. 207, § 38 (Supp.1984).

43. Md.Code 1983, art. 62, § 3A.

44. E.g., West's Ann.Cal.Civ.Code § 4205.1 (1983) (commissioners of civil marriages); West's Ann.Cal.Civ. Code § 4205.5 (1983) (officials of a nonprofit religious institution who have a Ph.D. degree and perform religious services on a regular basis); N.Y.–McKinney's Dom. Rel.L. § 11 (1977) and (Supp.1983) (mayor or city clerk of specified cities).

45. E.g., N.Y.–McKinney's Dom.Rel.L. § 11 (1977) and (Supp.1983) and N.Y.–McKinney's Rel.Corps.L. § 2 (1952) and (Supp.1983): "The term 'clergyman' and the term 'minister' include a duly authorized pastor, rector, priest, rabbi, and a person having authority from, or in accordance with, the rules and regulations of the governing ecclesiastical body of the denomination or order, if any, to which the church belongs, or otherwise from the church or synagogue to preside over and direct the spiritual affairs of the church or synagogue." Ohio Rev.Code § 3101.08 (1980): "An ordained or licensed minister * * * licensed to perform marriages * * *" Code § 3101.10 (1980) (ministers licensed by the probate judge). Wis.Stat.Ann. § 765.002 (Supp.1984): "Unless the context clearly indicates otherwise 'clergyman' in this chapter means spiritual adviser of any religion, whether he is termed priest, rabbi, minister of the gospel, pastor, reverend or any other official designation."

46. State ex rel. Hayes v. O'Brien, 160 Ohio St. 170, 114 N.E.2d 729 (1953).

47. State v. Lynch, 301 N.C. 479, 272 S.E.2d 349 (1980); Cramer v. Commonwealth, 214 Va. 561, 202 S.E.2d 911 (1974), cert. denied 419 U.S. 875, 95 S.Ct. 137, 42 L.Ed.2d 114 (1974). The opinion in the case indicated that this denomination has over one million ordained ministers for only nine thousand churches. Accord, Ravenal v. Ravenal, 72 Misc.2d 100, 338 N.Y.S.2d 324 (1972). See also Paramore v. Brown, 84 Nev. 725, 448 P.2d 699 (1968).

48. E.g., Colo.Rev.Stat. § 14–2–109 (1984); Ill.–S.H.A. ch. 40, § 209 (Supp.1984); Mass.Gen.L.Ann. ch. 207, § 38 (Supp.1984); Wis.Stat.Ann. § 765.16 (1981 and Supp. 1984).

49. 250 N.Y. 313, 165 N.E. 460 (1929). A New York statute does require a report to be filed with the clerk of the county of the bride's residence when a New York

are valid in the absence of any proper law condemning such marriages. This seems to create a common law of marriage solemnization controlling those cases where no contrary law can be found. A leading California case rejects the analysis, however, finding that marriage by a ship captain of California domiciliaries was invalid because the California statute does not include ship captains in the list of persons authorized to perform marriages.[50]

With the exception of West Virginia, where there is an explicit statutory ceremony for civil officials to follow,[51] the states do not require any special form for the marriage ceremony. Several states have statutes expressly providing that no particular form of ceremony is necessary, except that the parties, in the presence of the solemnizing official, must declare that they take each other as husband and wife.[52] Other states allow the marriage to be performed according to the customs of any religious society.[53]

No particular place for the marriage ceremony is generally required, although this may be indirectly affected by those licensing statutes which require that the license be obtained in the county where the marriage is

to occur.[54] In some states the civil officials authorized to perform marriages may do so only in their respective jurisdictions.[55] The statutes do not expressly require the presence of both parties in the same place for the ceremony to be valid. It would thus seem that a valid marriage could be contracted by means of a conference telephone call, although no such cases have been found.

Many states require witnesses for the marriage ceremony, the usual number being two.[56] This requirement is made only indirectly in some states by virtue of a blank on the marriage certificate for the signatures of witnesses.

Finally, all states have statutes relating to the recording of marriage licenses or marriage certificates. A common procedure is for the person solemnizing the marriage to fill in the blanks on the marriage certificate, which is sometimes printed on the back of the license and then send it to the place of recording.[57] The record of the marriage so made, or a certified copy thereof, then may be used as evidence of the marriage in the courts, according to most statutes.[58] Other methods of proving the fact of a ceremonial marriage are by the testimony of witnesses to the ceremo-

---

resident is married at sea. N.Y.–Domestic Relations Law 19–a. 1977.

50. Norman v. Norman, 121 Cal. 620, 54 P. 143 (1898). Richmond and Hall, Marriage and the State 233 (1929) also suggest that there is a common law of marriage on the high seas, not referable to the law of any particular place. Of course, if the marriage can be upheld as a valid common law marriage, i.e. an informal, consensual marriage, the problem is solved. But there remains to be determined what law will govern such a marriage. Fisher v. Fisher, 250 N.Y. 313, 165 N.E. 460 (1929) seems to have applied the law of the owner's domicile, as did Bolmer v. Edsall, 90 N.J.Eq. 299, 106 A. 646 (1919). The Norman case applied the law of the parties' domicile. It takes the position that there is no general law of marriage on the high seas. See also Restatement, Second, Conflict of Laws § 283, com. e–i (1971); 1 Rabel, Conflict of Laws 260 (2d ed. 1958); Menefee, "Getting Spliced": A Re-Evaluation of Marriage at Sea, 10 Okla.City U.L.Rev. 267 (1985).

51. W.Va.Code, § 48–1–12b (1980).

52. E.g., Alaska Stat. § 25.05.301 (1983); West's Ann. Cal.Civ.Code § 4206, 4206.5 (1983); Mich.C.L.A. § 25.9 (1984); N.Y.–McKinney's Dom.Rel.L. § 12 (1977); West's Rev.Code Wash.Ann. § 26.04.070 (1961).

53. E.g., Neb.Rev.Stat. § 42–115 (1978); N.J.Stat.Ann. § 37:1–13 (Supp.1984); Pa.Stat. tit. 48, § 1–13 (Supp.

1984). See Uniform Marriage and Divorce Act § 206, 9A Unif.L.Ann. 107 (1979).

54. Supra, note 12.

55. E.g., West's Ann.Cal.Civ.Code § 4205.1 (Supp. 1983); Nev.Rev.Stat. § 122.080 (1983); N.Y.–McKinney's Dom.Rel.L. § 11 (1977 and Supp.1983); Or.Rev.Stat. § 106.120 (1983). See Helfond v. Helfond, 53 Misc.2d 974, 280 N.Y.S.2d 990 (1967).

56. E.g., Alaska Stat. § 25.05.321 (1983); Del.Code tit. 13, § 106 (Supp.1982); Kan.Stat.Ann. § 23–104a (1981); Mich.C.L.A. § 25.9 (1984); N.Y.–McKinney's Dom.Rel.L. § 12 (1977) (one witness in addition to the person officiating); West's Rev.Code Wash.Ann. § 26.04.070 (1961); Wis.Stat.Ann. (§ 765.16) (1981 and Supp.1984).

57. E.g., Alaska Stat. § 25.05.321 (1983); West's Ann. Cal.Civ.Code § 4208 (1983); Colo.Rev.Stat. § 14–2–109 (Supp.1984); Ill.–S.H.A. ch. 40, § 210 (1980); Minn.Stat. Ann. § 517.10 (1984); N.Y.–McKinney's Dom.Rel.L. § 14a (1977 and Supp.1983); V.T.C.A., Fam.Code § 1.84 (1975). See also Uniform Marriage and Divorce Act § 206, 9A Unif.L.Ann. 107 (1979).

58. E.g., Alaska Stat. § 18.50.320 (1981); Conn.Gen. Stat.Ann. § 461–35 (Supp.1984); Hawaii Rev.Stat. § 572–13 (Supp.1983); Kan.Stat.Ann. § 23–117 (1981); Mass. Gen.L.Ann. ch. 207, § 45 (1981); N.H.Rev.Stat.Ann. § 457:38 (1981); N.Y.–McKinney's Dom.Rel.L. § 14–0

ny,[59] or by the testimony of witnesses that the parties were known in the community and to their friends to be married. The latter evidence is known as evidence of habit and repute in the community.[60]

Although not mentioned in marriage statutes, the question occasionally arises whether consummation is an essential to a valid marriage. The question is clouded by the ignorance of some courts and legislatures, who evidently think that "consummation" refers to the ceremony.[61] Expressions based on this misconception are the source of some unconscious levity,[62] but the fact is that "consummation" means the physical act of coition.[63] The conventional view is that a ceremonial marriage is valid notwithstanding that it is not consummated.[64] The rule is otherwise for common law marriages, whose validity depends upon evidence of marital cohabitation.[65] The necessities of proof do not warrant making this requirement for ceremonial marriages, the fact of whose existence can be

proved clearly enough in most cases. Yet there are expressions in isolated cases, particularly in New Jersey, which suggest that an unconsummated ceremonial marriage is "little more than an engagement to marry."[66] In the writer's view such statements have no basis in reason or law. A distinction between a marriage in which there are children, and one in which there are none might be understandable in terms of the public interest in the relationship, which might be stronger when children are born. But the fact of consummation, not resulting in pregnancy, has no such effect. Of course in some jurisdictions the lack of consummation may be taken as evidence of a pre-existing intent not to consummate which would justify an annulment for fraud, but that does not mean that the lack of consummation of itself invalidates the ceremonial marriage, or makes it any less a marriage.

In the past it has of course been the custom for the wife to take the surname of her hus-

(1977 and Supp.1983); Pa.Stat. tit. 48, § 1–20 (1965); Va. Code 1983, § 20–20; Wis.Stat.Ann. § 891.09 (1966 and Supp.1984). Compare West's Ann.Cal.Civ.Code § 4103 (1983). It is regrettable that the Uniform Marriage and Divorce Act does not contain a similar section. Without a statute expressly authorizing the proof of marriage by official record, at least some cases would permit this method of proof. For a full discussion of the issue see V J. Wigmore, Evidence §§ 1642–1645 (Chadbourn rev. 1974).

59. VII J. Wigmore, Evidence § 2082 (Chadbourn rev. 1978); McMorrow v. Schweiker, 561 F.Supp. 584 (D.N.J.1982).

60. II J. Wigmore, Evidence § 268 (Chadbourn rev. 1979); VII id. § 2083 (Chadbourn rev.1978). See also In re Nowak's Estate, 130 Ill.App.2d 573, 264 N.E.2d 307 (1970); In re Tomlinson's Estate, 493 S.W.2d 402 (Mo. App.1973); Shankle v. Shankle, 26 N.C.App. 565, 216 S.E.2d 915 (1975), cert. denied 288 N.C. 394; 218 S.E.2d 467 (1975).

61. E.g., Lefkoff v. Sicro, 189 Ga. 554, 6 S.E.2d 687 (1939); Mills v. Mills, 186 Misc. 885, 62 N.Y.S.2d 344 (Dom.Rel.Ct.1946) ("Consummation of the marriage is not always the ceremonial.").

62. As in the report of a wedding from a British newspaper: "With appropriate music and in the presence of a well-filled church the marriage was consumated (sic)," and in Cosulich Societa Triestina Di Navigazione v. Elting, 66 F.2d 534 (2d Cir.1933) where one of the parties spoke of consummation by proxy.

63. Webster's Third New International Dictionary (1961), at page 490, defines to consummate as "to complete (marital union) by the first act of sexual intercourse

after marriage." "Cohabitation" is sometimes used as a synonym for consummation, but it is also used to mean merely sharing a marital domicile without any indication of physical union. See, e.g., Hunt v. Hunt, 172 Miss. 732, 161 So. 119 (1935). Apparently cohabitation may properly be used either to mean living together as husband and wife, or to mean coition. See Webster's Third New International Dictionary 440 (1961).

64. Payne v. Payne, 54 App.D.C. 149, 295 Fed. 970 (1924); Robertson v. Robertson, 262 Ala. 114, 77 So.2d 373 (1955); Berdikas v. Berdikas, 54 Del. (4 Storey) 297, 178 A.2d 468 (Super.1962); Mitchell v. Mitchell, 136 Me. 406, 11 A.2d 898 (1940); Martin v. Otis, 233 Mass. 491, 124 N.E. 294 (1919); Ferraro v. Ferraro, 192 Misc. 484, 77 N.Y.S.2d 246 (Dom.Rel.Ct.1948) (semble); In re Zanfino's Estate, 375 Pa. 501, 100 A.2d 60 (1953). English ecclesiastical law seems to have followed Peter Lombard rather than Gratian in the view that consummation is not essential to the validity of marriage. See 1 Howard, History of Matrimonial Institutions 336 (1904).

65. See section 2.4, infra.

66. Akrep v. Akrep, 1 N.J. 268, 63 A.2d 253 (1949), cited with approval in Houlahan v. Horzepa, 46 N.J. Super. 583, 135 A.2d 232 (1957), in which a stricter standard of fraud was imposed for the annulment of a consummated marriage than for the annulment of an unconsummated marriage. Both Akrep and Houlahan find that the community acquires a grave and weighty interest in the consummated marriage, but what that interest can be or why it should arise at any point short of pregnancy or the birth of children remains an impenetrable mystery.

band on marriage. Today, under the influence of the women's rights movement, some women prefer to retain their own names after marriage. There seems to be no legal reason why they should not be able to do this, although the older cases refused to permit it.[67] Today state courts have begun to recognize the right of married women to continue using their birth names after marriage.[68] They should be authorized to do this by statute containing appropriate provisions for making both the woman's status and her name clear for record keeping purposes.[69]

The existence of comprehensive marriage regulations in all American jurisdictions makes it necessary to ask what the consequences will be when the statutory scheme is not fully complied with. The question whether the various statutes abolish common law marriage is discussed in a later section.[70] At this point the question is confined to whether a valid marriage results when there is a ceremony without a license, or without a valid license, or when the ceremony is celebrated by a person who is not in fact authorized to perform marriages.

The validity of a ceremonial marriage contracted without a license depends in the first instance on the language of the license statute. Some licensing statutes make it plain that no marriage in the jurisdiction is valid without a license,[71] and if so, the courts hold the unlicensed marriage invalid.[72] Where the licensing statute does not explicitly say this, however, the cases find the policy favoring valid marriages sufficiently strong to justify upholding the unlicensed ceremony.[73] This seems the correct result. Most such cases arise long after the parties have acted upon the assumption that they are married, and no useful purpose is served by avoiding the longstanding relationship. Compliance with the licensing laws can better be attained by safeguards operating before the license is issued, as by a more careful investigation by the issuing authority or the person marrying the parties. The same policy of upholding marriages underlies the presumption of validity of second marriages and the doctrine of estoppel against jurisdictional attack on divorces, a policy which pervades the entire law of marriage and divorce. That policy also explains the universal rule that a defective or invalid license, or one obtained by perjury does not affect the validity of the marriage.[74] This is true even in those jurisdictions where the

---

67. L. Kanowitz, Women and the Law 41–43 (1969), citing cases.

68. Stuart v. Board of Supervisors of Elections for Howard County, 266 Md. 440, 295 A.2d 223 (1972); Traugott v. Petit, 122 R.I. 60, 404 A.2d 77 (1979). The married woman's claim of a constitutional right to retain her birth name was rejected in Forbush v. Wallace, 341 F.Supp. 217 (M.D.Ala.1971), affirmed per curiam 405 U.S. 970, 92 S.Ct. 1197, 31 L.Ed.2d 246 (1972), in which the court upheld the right of the Alabama Department of Public Safety to issue drivers' licenses to married women only in their husbands' names. But the court did suggest that the married woman might have a remedy in the state law's change of name procedure.

69. Secretary of the Commonwealth v. City Clerk of Lowell, 373 Mass. 178, 366 N.E.2d 717 (1977).

70. See section 2.4, infra.

71. E.g., West's Ann.Cal.Civ.Code § 4100 (1983); Minn.Stat.Ann. § 517.01 (Supp.1984); Miss.Code 1973, § 93–1–15; Vernon's Ann.Mo.Stat. § 451.040 (Supp.1984); Neb.Rev.Stat. § 42–104 (1978); N.J.Stat.Ann. § 37:1–2 (1968). But see West's Ann.Cal.Civ.Code § 4213 (Supp. 1984). Williams v. Williams, 460 N.E.2d 1226 (Ind.App. 1984) held void a marriage contracted without a license.

72. In re Abate's Estate, 166 Cal.App.2d 282, 333 P.2d 200 (1958); Irwin v. Vick, 203 Miss. 44, 34 So.2d 725

(1948) (semble); State v. Eden, 350 Mo. 932, 169 S.W.2d 342 (1943); Scott v. Scott, 153 Neb. 906, 46 N.W.2d 627 (1951) (dictum); Dacunzo v. Edgye, 19 N.J. 443, 117 A.2d 508 (1955).

73. De Potty v. De Potty, 226 Ark. 881, 295 S.W.2d 330 (1956); Carabetta v. Carabetta, 182 Conn. 344, 438 A.2d 109 (1980); In re Parsons' Estate, 44 Del. (5 Terry) 406, 59 A.2d 709 (1948); Haderaski v. Haderaski, 415 Ill. 118, 112 N.E.2d 714 (1953); Browning v. Browning, 224 Md. 399, 168 A.2d 506 (1961); State v. Brem, 51 N.M. 63, 178 P.2d 582 (1947); Maxwell v. Maxwell, 51 Misc.2d 687, 273 N.Y.S.2d 728 (1966). Many other cases are collected in Annot., 61 A.L.R.2d 847 (1958). In some states, e.g. New York, the statute provides expressly that lack of a license will not invalidate a ceremonial marriage. N.Y.–McKinney's Domestic Relations Law 25.

A case contra the statement in the text is Kisla v. Kisla, 124 W.Va. 220, 19 S.E.2d 609 (1942), holding a marriage invalid for lack of a license, the statute not expressly calling for this result. See W.Va.Code, 4683.

74. Payne v. Payne, 54 App.D.C. 149, 295 Fed. 970 (1924); McDonald v. Employers Mutual Cas. Co., 73 F.Supp. 198 (W.D.La.1947) (license not signed by the parties or returned to the issuing authority); Saunders v. Saunders, 49 Del. (10 Terry) 515, 120 A.2d 160 (Sup.1956) (misstatements on license application); Long v. Long, 15

marriage without a license is invalid.[75] The failure to obtain a physical examination likewise should not invalidate the ceremonial marriage.[76] The authorities are then thrown back upon prosecutions for perjury as a means of enforcing the license regulations.[77] Criminal sanctions may also be applied against the person who officiates at an unlicensed marriage.[78]

The fact that a marriage is solemnized by one not legally qualified to perform marriages normally does not impair its validity provided that the spouses are not aware of the disqualification.[79] The leading case for this principle [80] rests upon the analogy to de facto public officers. The acts of one appearing to occupy a public office may be relied upon by the public even though the particular person has no legal right to the office.[81] This doctrine of the law of public officers is produced by the social policy which deems it desirable to make good the expectations of those who deal with such officers and who have no opportunity to determine the legality of their claim to the office. The same policy applies with equal force to the validation of marriages solemnized by unauthorized persons. Where the person officiating is authorized to perform marriages, but such formalities as the waiting period after issuance of the license are not strictly observed, the marriage should not be held invalid.[82] This assumes, however, that something which may be described as a ceremony has occurred. In default of a ceremony, defining that term as the present manifestation of consent by the parties before the officiating person or religious group, no marriage can be said to have occurred.[83]

The variety of state regulation and modern facility of movement from state to state make it necessary to determine what law governs the licensing and solemnization of marriages.[84] The rule has been stated in the past to be that the law of the place of celebration

Ill.App.2d 276, 145 N.E.2d 509 (1957) (false statements as to age); In re Silverman's Estate, 94 N.J.Super. 189, 227 A.2d 519 (1967); Johnson v. Johnson, 104 N.W.2d 8 (N.D.1960) (false statements in license application as to applicant's mental health); In re Estate of Campbell, 260 Wis. 625, 51 N.W.2d 709 (1952) (false statements as to age). Many other cases are cited in Annot., 61 A.L.R.2d 847 (1958). See also Estate of Crittenden, 29 Or.App. 189, 562 P.2d 609 (1977) containing dictum that marriage before expiration of the statutory waiting period is voidable.

75. In re Estate of Kinkead, 239 Minn. 27, 57 N.W.2d 628 (1953); Thompson v. Monteiro, 58 N.J.Super. 302, 156 A.2d 173 (1959).

76. Christensen v. Christensen, 144 Neb. 763, 14 N.W.2d 613 (1944).

77. Cases involving such perjury prosecutions are collected in Annot., 1C1 A.L.R. 1263 (1936).

78. E.g., Alaska Stat. § 25.05.371 (1965); Conn.Gen. Stat.Ann. § 46–4 (1960); N.J.Stat.Ann. § 37:1–15 (1968); N.Y.–McKinney's Dom.Rel.L. § 17 (1964); Pa.Stat. tit. 48, § 1–21 (1965); Wis.Stat.Ann. § 245.30 (Supp.1975–1976).

79. Arthurs v. Johnson, 280 S.W.2d 504 (Ky.1955); Knapp v. Knapp, 149 Md. 263, 131 A. 329 (1925); In re Silverstein's Estate, 190 Misc. 745, 75 N.Y.S.2d 144 (Surr. Ct.1947). This rule is embodied in statutes in some states. See e.g. V.A.M.S. § 451.040; W.S.A. 245.22. Even if only one party believes the minister qualified, the marriage is valid. State v. Eden, 350 Mo. 932, 169 S.W. 2d 342 (1943). Cases contra the statement in the text are State ex rel. Felson v. Allen, 129 Conn. 427, 29 A.2d 306 (1942), and Ladd v. Commonwealth, 313 Ky. 754, 233 S.W.2d 517 (1950), both resting on statutory construction.

80. Knapp v. Knapp, 149 Md. 263, 131 A. 329 (1925).

81. 3 E. McQuillin, Municipal Corporations §§ 12.102, 12.106 (3d ed. rev. volume 1973).

82. In Parker v. Saileau, 213 So.2d 190 (La.App.1968) the court found the marriage valid though the statutory three witnesses were not present and the prescribed seventy-two hours did not elapse between issuance of the license and performance of the ceremony. The court also found that the bride had been able to understand the ceremony in spite of being somewhat under the influence of alcohol. To the same effect is Coulter v. Melady, 489 S.W.2d 156 (Tex.Civ.App.1972), cert. denied 414 U.S. 823, 94 S.Ct. 123, 38 L.Ed.2d 56 (1973), where the court held that the bride had consented to the ceremony although her responses to the minister were not audible. See also Portwood v. Portwood, 109 S.W.2d 515 (Tex.Civ.App. 1937).

83. Hames v. Hames, 163 Conn. 588, 316 A.2d 379 (1972).

84. General discussions of this question may be found in Ehrenzweig, Conflict of Laws 379–380 (1962); 1 Rabel, The Conflict of Laws: A Comparative Study 222–262 (2d ed. 1958); Taintor, Marriage in the Conflict of Laws, 9 Vand.L.Rev. 607, 608–610 (1956); Da Costa, The Formalities of Marriage in the Conflict of Laws, 7 Int. & Comp. L.Q. 217 (1958).

The question of what law governs when there is a complete failure to observe ceremonial or other requirements, i.e. common law marriage in the conflict of laws, is discussed infra, section 2.4. Proxy marriages in the conflict of laws are discussed infra, section 2.5.

governs the formalities of marriage.[85] It is certainly true that a marriage which complies with the formalities imposed in the state of celebration will be held valid elsewhere,[86] even though the parties were never domiciled in the state of celebration and in fact went there solely to get married without complying with the formalities imposed by the law of the domicile.[87] The reason for this rule may be to give effect to the parties' presumed intention,[88] or to take account of the obvious fact that officials of the state of celebration will solemnize marriages in accordance with the rules there prevailing because they know and can be expected to conform their procedure to no other law.[89] For either reason the rule is sensible. It is embodied in the statutes of several states.[90]

Statutes in four states provide that a marriage of domiciliaries contracted in another state which is void by the law of the domicile will not be recognized in the domicile.[91] Of course if the domicile's formal requirements are merely directory and not mandatory, such marriages are valid.[92] But if the domicile's formal requirements are of such importance that marriages which do not meet them are invalid, there may be doubt whether a valid foreign marriage will be upheld in the domicile, where the parties contracted the marriage to avoid the domicile's formalities.[93] Such a marriage would seem to be void rather than voidable by the law of the domicile, but as will be pointed out elsewhere in this work[94] the whole void-voidable distinction in the law of marriage is a source of confusion and ought to be discarded. In the writer's view the Marriage Evasion Statute should not apply to a marriage contracted in a state other than the domicile where the parties fail to comply with mandatory licensing or solemnization requirements of the domicile.[95] It is everywhere accepted that marriages should be invalidated only for the most compelling reasons. Failure to comply with the domicile's formal rules is not such a compelling reason.

The converse question, whether a marriage which does not fulfill the mandatory licensing or solemnization requirements of the place of

---

85. Restatement (Second) of Conflict of laws § 283, comment f (1971). For other authorities supporting the text statement, see the sources cited supra in note 84, and Sturm v. Sturm, 111 N.J.Eq. 579, 163 A. 5 (1932); Ferret v. Ferret, 55 N.M. 565, 237 P.2d 594 (1951); and the cases cited in Annots., 61 A.L.R.2d 847, 856 (1958) and 57 L.R.A. 155 (1903). The rule originated in the following line of English cases: Scrimshire v. Scrimshire, 2 Hagg. Cons. 395, 161 Eng.Rep. 782 (1752); Butler v. Freeman, 1 Ambl. 301, 27 Eng.Rep. 204 (1756) (dictum); Middleton v. Janverin, 2 Hagg.Cons. 437, 161 Eng.Rep. 797 (1802).

86. Henderson v. Henderson, 199 Md. 449, 87 A.2d 403 (1952); Hartman v. Valier & Spies Milling Co., 356 Mo. 424, 202 S.W.2d 1 (1947); Johnson v. Johnson, 104 N.W.2d 8 (N.D.1960). See also Restatement (Second) of Conflict of Laws § 283, comment f (1971). The marriage of tribal Indians in a reservation is governed by Indian custom. Yakima Joe v. To-Is-Lap, 191 Fed. 516 (C.C.Or. 1910); Marris v. Sockey, 170 F.2d 599 (10th Cir.1948), cert. denied 336 U.S. 914, 69 S.Ct. 605, 93 L.Ed. 1078 (1949). See also Ponina v. Leland, 85 Nev. 263, 454 P.2d 16 (1969), and Foster, Indian and Common Law Marriages, 3 Am. Indian L.Rev. 83 (1975).

87. Noble v. Noble, 299 Mich. 565, 300 N.W. 885 (1941); Keith v. Pack, 182 Tenn. 420, 187 S.W.2d 618 (1945) (dictum). To the same effect is In re Perez' Estate, 98 Cal.App.2d 121, 219 P.2d 35 (1950), but it was based at least in part on the California statute. If the lex loci says that the marriage of a foreign domiciliary is to be governed by the law of his domicile, then the marriage will be so judged by the domicile. In re Lando's Estate, 112 Minn. 257, 127 N.W. 1125 (1910).

88. Kochanski v. Kochanska, [1958] P. 147.

89. Taintor, Marriage in the Conflict of Laws, 9 Vand. L.Rev. 607, 609 (1956).

90. These statutes provide that marriages contracted outside the state which are valid by the law of the state in which they were contracted are valid in the state enacting the statute. Ark.Stat. § 55–110 (1971) (semble); West's Ann.Cal.Civ.Code § 4104 (1983); Colo.Rev.Stat. § 14–2–112 (1973) (semble); N.M.Stat.Ann. 1983, § 40–1–4.

91. Ill.–S.H.A. ch. 40, §§ 216–218 (1980); Mass.Gen.L. Ann. ch. 207, §§ 10 to 13 (1981); Vt.Stat.Ann. tit. 15, §§ 5, 6 (1974); Wis.Stat.Ann. § 765.04 (1981). This is the Uniform Marriage Evasion Act, 9 Uniform L.Ann. 480 (1942).

92. Boysen v. Boysen, 301 Ill.App. 573, 23 N.E.2d 231 (1939).

93. Boysen v. Boysen, 301 Ill.App. 573, 23 N.E.2d 231 (1939) applied Illinois law to a marriage contracted in Indiana for the purpose of avoiding the Illinois medical examination, but the question is not thoroughly discussed and in fact the marriage was not invalid by Illinois law. The case of Lyannes v. Lyannes, 171 Wis. 381, 177 N.W. 683 (1920) squarely held that the Marriage Evasion Act did not invalidate the Michigan marriage of Wisconsin domiciliaries though the marriage would not have complied with the formalities required by Wisconsin law.

94. See section 3.1, infra.

95. Lyannes v. Lyannes, 171 Wis. 381, 177 N.W. 683 (1920).

celebration may nevertheless be upheld under the law of some other state, may only be answered tentatively and with caution because of the lack of agreement among the relatively few authorities where the question has been discussed. Some expressions to the effect that the lex loci contractus always governs with respect to marriage formalities stand as authority for the proposition that if the marriage does not meet those formalities, it will not be recognized as valid elsewhere.[96] But even in relatively early times there were cases which did not accept this view.[97] The reason for the apparent illogicality of saying that a marriage good where contracted is good everywhere but that a marriage bad where contracted is not necessarily bad everywhere is again the very strong public policy in favor of upholding marriages, especially where the parties have behaved in all respects as if married.

Perhaps the strongest case for upholding a marriage which does not meet the formal requirements of the lex loci occurs when the parties remain at all times domiciled in one state but marry in another. A few cases suggest that such marriages are valid,[98] but they are anything but persuasive authorities.

Nevertheless, the interest of the domicile should prevail in this case, and probably in any case where its law validates the marriage.[99] The courts sometimes get substantially this result by "presuming" that the law of the place of celebration is the same as that of the domicile.[1] If the spouses have different domiciles at the time of the marriage, the law of that domicile which favors the validity of the marriage might govern,[2] though admittedly this choice cannot be justified on the basis of stronger "contacts" with the marriage, but only on the ground that it produces a valid rather than an invalid marriage. In fact there are many cases today in which it is artificial to argue that the parties have any closer relation to one state than to another. If so, a frank selection of that legal rule which upholds the marriage, from among several possible governing rules, is more sensible than a frustrating search for the state having the most "contacts."

This assertion is borne out by two recent British cases which relied on the English common law to validate the marriages of Polish nationals celebrated in Europe. In the first of these, Taczanowska v. Taczanowski,[3] the parties were members of the Polish armed forces,

96. Bronislawa K. v. Tadeusz K., 90 Misc.2d 183, 393 N.Y.S.2d 534 (Fam.Ct.1977) (Polish law, as lex loci contractus, applied to invalidate a marriage without a civil ceremony); Singh v. Singh, 67 Misc.2d 878, 325 N.Y.S.2d 590 (1971) (lex loci applied to invalidate a Hindu marriage without citation of authority); Scrimshire v. Scrimshire, 2 Hagg.Cons. 395, 161 Eng.Rep. 782 (1752); Butler v. Freeman, 1 Ambl. 301, 27 Eng.Rep. 204 (1756); Middleton v. Janverin, 2 Hagg.Cons. 437, 161 Eng.Rep. 797 (1802). See also Sturm v. Sturm, 111 N.J.Eq. 579, 163 A. 5 (1932); Restatement (Second) of Conflict of Laws § 283, comment i (1971); Maddaugh, Validity of Marriage and the Conflict of Laws, 23 U.Tor.L.Rev. 117 (1973).

Randall v. Randall, 216 Neb. 541, 345 N.W.2d 319 (1984) applied the rule of lex loci in a particularly harmful way, without adequate consideration of the policies or precedents involved in such a determination.

97. Phillips v. Gregg, 10 Watts 158 (Pa.1840). See also Lautour v. Teesdale, 8 Taunt. 830, 129 Eng.Rep. 606 (1816).

98. Ferret v. Ferret, 55 N.M. 565, 237 P.2d 594 (1951) (semble); Sullivan v. American Bridge Co., 115 Pa.Super. 536, 176 A. 24 (1935); Portwood v. Portwood, 109 S.W.2d 515 (Tex.Civ.App.1937) (dictum).

99. A. Ehrenzweig, Conflict of Laws § 139 (1962) states that the marriage is valid if it is (a) valid by the lex loci; or (b) valid by the law of the domicile of either party

at the time of the marriage; or (c) valid by the law of the place where both parties are domiciled at the time of suit. The statutes of the domicile may authorize marriages in other places, and if followed, such marriages will be recognized as valid in the domicile. See, e.g., The Foreign Marriages Act 1947, 10 & 11 Geo. 6, ch. 33, and Collett v. Collett, [1967] 2 All Eng.Rep. 426, [1968] P. 482 upholding under the Foreign Marriages Act a marriage performed in the British Embassy in Prague, even though some requirements of the Act were not complied with. For an interesting account of a misconception on the issue of the validity of foreign marriages, see Parry, A Conflicts Myth: The American "Consular" Marriage, 67 Harv.L.Rev. 1187 (1954), dealing with a statute thought by some officials to authorize American consuls to perform marriages abroad, 12 Stat. 79, 22 U.S.C.A. § 4192. Massachusetts does recognize such marriages, however, Mass.Gen.Laws Ann. ch. 207, § 43 (1981).

1. Cosulich Societa Triestina Di Navigazione v. Elting, 66 F.2d 534 (2d Cir.1933); In Re Lando's Estate, 112 Minn. 257, 127 N.W. 1125 (1910); Sturm v. Sturm, 111 N.J.Eq. 579, 163 A. 5 (1932).

2. A. Ehrenzweig, Conflict of Laws § 139 (1962).

3. [1957] P. 301 (C.A.). A case following Taczanowska is Preston v. Preston, [1963] P. 411 (C.A.), in which a man in the Polish armed forces and a woman civilian were married in a military camp in Germany in 1945, the

and were married in Italy by a Catholic priest in a Catholic ceremony. The ceremony did not comply with Italian law, nor did it comply with Polish law. The court found the rule of the lex loci not absolute but based on the presumed intent of the parties. Since the parties were in the army in this case, they did not choose Italy as the place of marriage, and the presumption that they intended Italian law to govern was rebutted. As the court said, the parties did not subject themselves to the law of Italy. The law of Poland, the parties' domicile, was not relied upon, though the reason for this is not very clear. The court did say that this might lead to difficulties if the parties should have different domiciles, but that problem was not present in this case. In any event the court wound up by holding that the common law of England was the applicable law. With endearing parochialism the court gave as its reason that "such is the law prima facie to be administered in the courts of this country." The Kochanski [4] case was decided only a year later with identical result, the only difference on the facts being that the marriage was performed in Germany and the parties were displaced persons rather than members of the armed forces. Here again the marriage was held valid as complying with the English common law. One can hardly avoid concluding that

the controlling reason for the results in these two cases was the policy favoring the validity of marriages. It remains to be seen whether the same result will be reached where the parties are voluntarily in the lex loci but do not follow its form of marriage.[5] Certainly these two cases in terms are limited to the uncommon situation where the parties are not voluntarily present in the lex loci. Yet by converting the principle that the law of the place of celebration governs the form of marriages from a rule of law to a rebuttable presumption they make it possible for courts in the future to base a finding that the presumption is rebutted upon evidence other than that the parties were members of the armed forces or inmates of a displaced persons camp. In this way the impact of the lex loci has been reduced and the influence of both the law of the domicile and of the forum has been augmented by the Taczanowska and Kochanski cases.

   **WESTLAW**
          REFERENCES

sy(marriage /s solemni! /p invalid! valid!)

di(marriage /s invalid! valid! /s consummat!)

woman wife /s retain! keep! /s birth own +2 name

di(foreign abroad /3 martial marry! marri! /s valid! invalid!)

---

ceremony not complying with German law. The court held this to be a valid English common law marriage. But Merker v. Merker, [1963] P. 283 held that the marriage of Polish nationals in Germany in 1946 was invalid on the ground that before the English proceeding was brought a German court had held the marriage a nullity. The court said that in the absence of the prior German decree Taczanowska would have been followed, but that in the circumstances it was bound by the German judgment.

4. Kochanski v. Kochanska [1958] P. 147. For a critical discussion of both cases see Da Costa, The Formalities of Marriage in the Conflict of Laws, 7 Int. & Comp.L.Q. 217 (1958). A case which, on very similar facts, refuses to apply any law other than that of the place of celebration, thus holding the marriage void, is Fokas v. Fokas, (1952) S.A.S.R. 152.

5. Lazarewicz v. Lazarewicz, 1962 P. 171 suggests an answer to this question, although the reasoning of the case is not persuasive. The parties were married in a

Polish civilian refugee camp in Italy in 1945 by a Catholic priest. The husband was Polish and the wife Italian. The marriage was not valid by either Polish or Italian law. The parties lived together in England until 1956 and had one child. The wife sued to annul the marriage, the case going uncontested. The court, in granting the annulment and holding the marriage null and void, said that the lex loci is the general rule, but that under Taczanowska there may be an exception if the parties did not purport to submit themselves to the lex loci and if the marriage satisfies the requirements of the English common law. But the court found that in this case the parties clearly did choose to submit to the Italian law and intended to contract a marriage in accordance with that law. Since they failed to comply with Italian law, the marriage was invalid. This takes much too narrow a view of Taczanowska and completely ignores the strong reasons for upholding the validity of marriages of this kin.

§ 2.4 Common Law Marriage, Putative Marriage, and Other Informal Unions [1]

Common law marriage, a term with vaguely disreputable connotations for many laymen, was adopted by American law from England. Its name does not accurately reflect its history, since it developed not in the courts of common law but in the English ecclesiastical courts. The name does indicate, however, that this method of contracting marriage was originally the product of judicial decision rather than statutory enactment. The English history of common law marriage is outlined in another section.[2] It is sufficient to say at this point that such marriages were recognized as valid by the ecclesiastical courts before the enactment of Lord Hardwicke's Act in 1753.[3] After that date they were valid if contracted in Scotland or Ireland, where the statute did not govern.[4] In 1843 in Regina v. Millis [5] an evenly divided House of Lords affirmed the decision of a lower court holding that common law marriages had never been valid in England. Despite the clear historical evidence to the contrary,[6] this view prevailed in the subsequent English cases.[7] In America common law marriage was recognized in some of the colonies and in a number of the states after independence from England.[8]

At present in this country common law marriage is on the decline. Of the fifty states, thirty-seven have decided, either by statute or case law, that common law marriages will not be recognized,[9] although in some of these states the non-recognition is

§ 2.4

1. For treatment of the earlier authorities, see Koegel, Common Law Marriage (1922). An article discussing common law marriage is Weyrauch, Informal and Formal Marriage—An Appraisal of Trends in Family Organization, 28 Univ.Chi.L.Rev. 88 (1960).

2. See section 2.1, supra.

3. Lord Hardwicke's Act, 1753, 26 Geo. II, c. 33.

4. Dalrymple v. Dalrymple, 2 Hagg.Cons. 54, 161 Eng. Rep. 665 (1811).

5. 9 H. of L.Cas. 319, 8 Eng.Rep. 844 (1843).

6. See, e.g., II Pollock & Maitland, History of English Law 364–399 (1898).

7. Beamish v. Beamish, 9 H. of L.Cas. 274, 11 Eng. Rep. 735 (1861). For a discussion of this case's peculiar treatment of stare decisis, see Wasserstrom, The Judicial Decision, 58–61 (1961).

8. Koegel, Common Law Marriage 54–90 (1922). Leading early cases discussing common law marriage include Meister v. Moore, 96 U.S. (6 Otto) 76, 24 L.Ed. 826 (1877); Dumaresly v. Fishly, 10 Ky. (3 A.K. Marsh) 368 (1821); Denison v. Denison, 35 Md. 361 (1872); Inhabitants of Milford v. Inhabitants of Worcester, 7 Mass. 48 (1810); Londonderry v. Chester, 2 N.H. 268 (1820); Dunbarton v. Franklin, 19 N.H. 257 (1848); Fenton v. Reed, 4 Johns. 52 (N.Y.1809).

9. As follows:

Alaska:	Alaska Stat. § 25.05.011 (1983); Edwards v. Franke, 364 P.2d 60 (Alaska 1961).
Arizona:	Ariz.Rev.Stat.Ann. § 25–111 (1976).
Arkansas:	Ark.Stat. § 55–201 (1971); Furth v. Furth, 97 Ark. 272, 133 S.W. 1037 (1911).
California:	West's Ann.Cal.Civ.Code § 4100 (1983).
Connecticut:	Conn.Gen.Stat. § 46b–22 (Supp.1984); State ex rel. Felson v. Allen, 129 Conn. 427, 29 A.2d 306 (1942).
Delaware:	Owens v. Bentley, 40 Del. (1 Terry) 512, 14 A.2d 391 (Sup.1940).
Florida:	West's Fla.Stat.Ann. § 741.211 (1984).
Hawaii:	Hawaii Rev.Stat. § 572–1 (1983); Halsey v. Ho Ah Keau, 295 Fed. 636 (9th Cir.1924).
Illinois:	Ill.–S.H.A. ch. 40, § 214 (Supp.1980).
Indiana:	West's Ann.Ind.Code § 31–1–6–1 (1973).
Kentucky:	Ky.Rev.Stat. § 402.020 (1984).
Louisiana:	La.Stat.Ann.–Civ.Code art. 88 (Supp. 1984).
Maine:	Pierce v. Secretary of U.S. Department of Health, Education and Welfare, 254 A.2d 46 (Me.1969).
Maryland:	Henderson v. Henderson, 199 Md. 449, 87 A.2d 403 (1952); Md.Code 1983, art. 62, § 4.
Massachusetts:	Milford v. Worcester, 7 Mass. 48 (1910).
Michigan:	Mich.G.L.A. § 25.2 (1984).
Minnesota:	Minn.Stat.Ann. § 517.01 (1984).
Mississippi:	Miss.Code 1973, § 93–1–15.
Missouri:	Vernon's Ann. Mo.Stat. § 451.040 (Supp.1984). But see Thomson v. Thomson, 236 Mo.App. 1223, 163 S.W.2d 792 (1942), and In re Tomlinson's Estate, 493 S.W.2d 402 (Mo.App. 1973), where, by stating the result in terms of a rule of evidence, the courts come very close to allowing proof of a common law marriage.

qualified in various ways.[10] Thirteen states and the District of Columbia continue to rec-

Nebraska:	Neb.Rev.Stat. § 42–104 (Supp.1978).
Nevada:	Nev.Rev.Stat. § 122.010 (1981).
New Hampshire:	Dumbarton v. Franklin, 19 N.H. 257 (1848).
New Jersey:	N.J.Stat.Ann. § 37:1–10 (1968).
New Mexico:	N.J.Stat.Ann. § 40–1–1 (1986); Gallegos v. Wilkerson, 79 N.M. 549, 445 P.2d 970 (1968); In re Gabaldon's Estate, 38 N.M. 392, 34 P.2d 672 (1934).
New York:	N.Y.–McKinney's Dom.Rel.L. § 11 (Supp.1977 and 1984).
North Carolina:	N.C.Gen.Stat. § 51–1 (Supp.1983).
North Dakota:	N.D.Cent.Code § 14–03–01 (Supp.1981); Schumacher v. Great Northern Ry. Co., 23 N.D. 231, 136 N.W. 85 (1912); N.D. Laws 1975, ch. 126, § 1.
Oregon:	Ore.Rev.Stat. § 106.041 (1975); Wadsworth v. Brigham, 125 Or. 428, 259 P. 299 (1927).
South Dakota:	S.D.Comp.L. § 25–1–1 (1984). But cf. Matter of Miller's Estate, 90 S.D. 554, 243 N.W.2d 788 (1976).
Tennessee:	Tenn.Code Ann. § 36–3–101 (Supp. 1986); Troxel v. Jones, 45 Tenn.App. 264, 322 S.W.2d 251 (1959). But see King v. Clinchfield R.R. Co., 131 F.Supp. 218 (E.D.Tenn.1955).
Utah:	Utah Code Ann.1983, § 30–1–2.
Vermont:	Morrill v. Palmer, 68 Vt. 1, 33 A. 829 (1895).
Virginia:	Va.Code 1983, § 20–13.
Washington:	West's Rev.Wash.Code §§ 26.04.070, 26.04.140 (1961); In re Gallagher's Estate, 35 Wash.2d 512, 213 P.2d 621 (1950).
West Virginia:	W.Va.Code, § 48–1–5 (1980); Kisla v. Kisla, 124 W.Va. 220, 19 S.E.2d 609 (1942).
Wisconsin:	Wis.Stat.Ann. § 765.16 (West 1981 and Supp.1986).
Wyoming:	In re Roberts' Estate, 58 Wyo. 438, 133 P.2d 492 (1943).

Many other cases are cited in Annots., 39 A.L.R. 538 (1925); 60 A.L.R. 541 (1929); 94 A.L.R. 1000 (1935); and 133 A.L.R. 758 (1941).

The Uniform Marriage and Divorce Act takes no position on whether common law marriage should be abolished or retained. The drafters included alternative provisions, leaving the choice to the individual states. 9A Uniform L. Ann. 117, 118 (1979).

10. E.g., Del.Code tit. 13, § 126 (1981) (nothing in the law to be construed to render any common law marriage, otherwise lawful, invalid for failure to take out a license); Owens v. Bentley, 40 Del. (1 Terry) 512, 14 A.2d 391 (1940) (marriage may be proved by cohabitation and repute); West's Ann.Ind.Code § 22–3–3–19 (1984) (a com-

ognize common law marriage.[11]

mon law marriage may be recognized for workmen's compensation purposes if it existed before 1958 and openly and notoriously for five years before the death of a party); Reger v. Reger, 242 Ind. 302, 177 N.E.2d 901 (1961), rehearing denied 242 Ind. 302, 178 N.E.2d 749 (1961) (though common law marriage is not recognized, an invalid ceremonial marriage may ripen into a valid marriage when the impediment is removed); N.H.Rev. Stat.Ann. § 457:39 (1968) (persons cohabiting and acknowledging each other as husband and wife and generally reputed to be such for three years and until the decease of one of them are deemed to have been married); Andrews v. New London, 117 N.H. 747, 379 A.2d 441 (1977); Wis.Stat.Ann. § 765.24 (Supp.1984) (a marriage contracted in good faith when a prior marriage is in force becomes valid when the impediment is removed); Davidson v. Davidson, 35 Wis.2d 401, 151 N.W.2d 53 (1967).

Several states have statutes providing that marriages are valid if entered in good faith notwithstanding the lack of authority of the person performing the ceremony. E.g., Va.Code 1983, § 20–31. Louisiana seems to recognize a relationship which it calls "concubinage" and which resembles common law marriage, at least for workmen's compensation purposes. Henderson v. Travelers Insurance Co., 354 So.2d 1031 (La.1978).

11. As follows:

Alabama:	Ala.Code 1983, § 30–1–9, tit. 34; Krug v. Krug, 292 Ala. 498, 296 So.2d 715 (1974).
Colorado:	Moffat Coal Co. v. Industrial Commission, 108 Colo. 388, 118 P.2d 769 (1941); Deter v. Deter, 484 P.2d 805 (Colo.App. 1971).
District of Columbia:	Matthews v. Britton, 303 F.2d 408 (D.C. Cir.1962).
Georgia:	Official Ga.Code Ann. § 53–101 (1982); Askew v. Dupree, 30 Ga. 173 (1860).
Idaho:	Idaho Code § 32–201 (1983); Hamby v. J.R. Simplot Co., 94 Idaho 794, 498 P.2d 1267 (1972).
Iowa:	Iowa Code Ann. § 595.11 (West Supp. 1984); In re Long's Estate, 251 Iowa 1042, 102 N.W.2d 76 (1960).
Kansas.	Kan.Stat.Ann. § 23–101 (1981); State v. Johnson, 216 Kan. 445, 532 P.2d 1325 (1975).
Montana:	Mont.Code Ann. § 40–1–403 (1983).
Ohio:	Ohio Rev.Code § 3101.08 (1980); Umbenhower v. Labus, 85 Ohio St. 238, 97 N.E. 832 (1912).
Oklahoma:	Okl.Stat. tit. 43, §§ 1, 4 (1979); Quinton v. Webb, 207 Okl. 133, 248 P.2d 586 (1952).
Pennsylvania:	Pa.Stat. tit. 48, § 1–23 (1965); In re McGrath's Estate, 319 Pa. 309, 179 A. 599 (1935).
Rhode Island:	Souza v. O'Hara, 121 R.I. 88, 395 A.2d 1060 (1978).

A sharp division of opinion has arisen among the states on the question whether common law marriage is abolished by the type of statute which sets up a scheme of licensing, solemnization and perhaps other regulation, but which does not in so many words state that common law marriages are invalid. The early leading case of Meister v. Moore [12] construed a Michigan statute of this kind as "merely directory". It held that the public policy which encourages marriage and favors the legitimacy of children upholds common law marriage as against the argument that such a general statute had abolished it. Perhaps the case is explainable as the product of frontier ways of thinking. It has been widely described as stating the prevailing view on the question,[13] and some recent cases have taken the same position.[14] A large number of authorities are contra, however.[15] Today the majority view seems to be that such regulatory statutes are mandatory, and do abolish common law marriage, thereby reflecting the contemporary disapproval of common law marriage.

The thirteen recognizing states are scattered throughout the country. With a highly mobile population, those states which do authorize common law marriage can, under the prevailing conflict of law rules,[16] validate the marriages of a disproportionately large number of persons. For these reasons the doctrines of common law marriage continue to have greater practical consequences than might be expected solely from a count of the states which cling to such doctrines.

Under English law there were two methods of contracting a common law, or non-ceremonial marriage. By the first of these "the consent of two parties expressed in words of present mutual acceptance constituted an actual and legal marriage technically known by the name of sponsalia per verba de praesenti." [17] It was this method which, with some additions, has been relied upon in the United States.[18] The second type of English common law marriage, called sponsalia per verba de futuro, required an engagement for a future marriage, followed by consummation. The fact of consummation converted what had been merely an engagement into a binding marriage.[19] This form of marriage has not been explicitly recognized in the United States,[20] although the facts of some of the cases upholding informal marriages resemble this form more closely than the accepted form of common law marriage.[21] The distinction between a present acceptance and an engage-

South Carolina: Ex parte Romans, 78 S.C. 210, 58 S.E. 614 (1907). But cf. S.C.Code 1977, § 20–21 providing that it is unlawful to contract matrimony without a license.

Texas: V.T.C.A., Fam.Code § 1.91 (1975); Ex Parte Threet, 160 Tex. 482, 333 S.W.2d 361 (1960).

12. 96 U.S. (6 Otto) 76, 24 L.Ed. 826 (1877), construing the Michigan statute.

13. In re Gabaldon's Estate, 38 N.M. 392, 34 P.2d 672 (1934).

14. E.g. In re Estate of Stopps, 244 Iowa 931, 57 N.W.2d 221 (1953); Buradus v. General Cement Products Co., 356 Pa. 349, 52 A.2d 205 (1947).

15. E.g. Edwards v. Franke, 364 P.2d 60 (Alaska 1961); Schumacher v. Great Northern Ry. Co., 23 N.D. 231, 136 N.W. 85 (1912); Huard v. McTeigh, 113 Or. 279, 232 P. 658 (1925); Kisla v. Kisla, 124 W.Va. 220, 19 S.E.2d 609 (1942). Many other cases are cited in Annots., 39 A.L.R. 538 (1925), 60 A.L.R. 541 (1929), 94 A.L.R. 1000 (1935), and 133 A.L.R. 758 (1941).

16. See the text at notes 77–80, infra.

17. Dalrymple v. Dalrymple, 2 Hagg.Cons. 54, 64, 161 Eng.Rep. 665, 669 (1811). This case is the leading English authority on the law of informal marriage.

18. The agreement must express a present intent to marry in the usual sense of that term. It is not sufficient if the parties merely agree to live together so long as they find it mutually agreeable. Peck v. Peck, 155 Mass. 479, 30 N.E. 74 (1892), and Arnold v. Arnold, 219 Mo.App. 8, 267 S.W. 950 (1925). On the other hand, if the parties exchange mutual agreements of marriage, a secret intent not to contract a valid marriage would not prevent the formation of a common law marriage. Ex parte Ver Pault, 86 F.2d 113 (2d Cir.1936); In re Trigg's Estate, 102 Ariz. 140, 426 P.2d 637 (1967).

19. Dalrymple v. Dalrymple, 2 Hagg.Cons. 54, 65, 161 Eng.Rep. 665, 669 (1911).

20. In re Danikas' Estate, 76 Colo. 191, 230 P. 608 (1924); Duey v. Duey, 343 So.2d 896 (Fla.App.1977), Cert. denied 353 So.2d 674 (Fla.1977); In re Estate of Fisher, 176 N.W.2d 801 (Iowa 1970); Cavanaugh v. Cavanaugh, 135 Okl. 204, 275 P. 315 (1929); Peck v. Peck, 12 R.I. 485 (1880). But see Jambrone v. David, 16 Ill.2d 32, 156 N.E.2d 569 (1959) (dictum).

21. E.g. Moffat Coal Co. v. Industrial Com., 108 Colo. 388, 118 P.2d 769 (1941), in which the woman testified that "I thought if he would come and live with me he would marry me and he kept putting it off and he never did." This looks like a promise to marry in the future, followed by consummation, but the court held it a valid

ment for the future is not always obvious, and may be considerably blurred by a court which is anxious, for other reasons, to find that a marriage existed.

In theory there is general agreement among American cases as to the requirements for a valid common law marriage. These include, in addition to the bare present consent of the Dalrymple case, a mutual assumption of the marital relationship.[22] Or, as some cases put it, not only must there be a present agreement to be man and wife, but the parties must "hold themselves out" to the world as married,[23] or they must publicly and professedly live as husband and wife.[24] A few scattered cases confine themselves to the single requirement of agreement, but they are explainable for the most part as being merely dictum.[25] The reason for the additional requirement of a mutual and open assumption of the marital relationship is clear and sound. It is to prevent, or at least to minimize the fraudulent claims of common law marriage which could be made if an agreement alone

were sufficient to prove such a marriage. The problem did not arise in the Dalrymple case where the agreement, though secret, was amply attested to by letters and documents. But if a secret, verbal agreement alone would support a finding of common law marriage, false or fraudulent claims could seldom be detected.[26] Adding the requirement of open marital cohabitation gives assurance that some objective evidence of the relationship will have to be introduced in every case to establish that the parties did consider themselves husband and wife.

There is in many jurisdictions the safeguard of the Dead Man's Statute, which provides that a party to a suit against the executor of a deceased person is disqualified from testifying as to transactions or communications with the deceased.[27] A number of cases have held that this type of statute excludes the testimony of an alleged common law wife as to an agreement of marriage with the deceased when she is making a claim to a share of the estate of her deceased husband.[28]

common law marriage. For similar facts, see Campbell v. Christain, 235 S.C. 102, 110 S.E.2d 1 (1959).

22. United States Fidelity & Guaranty Co. v. Britton, 269 F.2d 249 (D.C.Cir.1959); National Union Fire Ins. Co. v. Britton, 187 F.Supp. 359 (D.D.C.1960), judgment affirmed 289 F.2d 454 (D.C.Cir.1961); Beck v. Beck, 286 Ala. 692, 246 So.2d 420 (1971); Toye v. Toye, 170 A.2d 778 (D.C.Mun.Ct.App.1961); In re Dallman's Estate, 228 N.W.2d 187 (Iowa 1975); State v. Johnson, 216 Kan. 445, 532 P.2d 1325 (1975); In re Walls' Estate, 358 Mich. 148, 99 N.W.2d 599 (1959); Ridley v. Compton, 215 Miss. 532, 61 So.2d 341 (1952); Miller v. Sutherland, 131 Mont. 175, 309 P.2d 322 (1957); Nestor v. Nestor, 15 Ohio St.3d 143, 472 N.E.2d 1091 (1984); Quinton v. Webb, 207 Okl. 133, 248 P.2d 586 (1952). Many other cases are collected in Annot., 133 A.L.R. 758 (1941); Black, Common Law Marriage, 2 Cin.L.Rev. 113 (1928); Weyrauch, Informal Marriage and Common Law Marriage, in R. Slovenko, ed., Sexual Behavior and the Law 297 (1965); Kendrick, Informal Marriages in Tennessee, 3 Vand.L.Rev. 610 (1950); Howery, Marriage by Proxy and Other Informal Marriages, 13 U.Kan.City L.Rev. 48 (1944); Note, 23 Iowa L.Rev. 75 (1937).

23. Anderson v. Anderson, 235 Ind. 113, 131 N.E.2d 301 (1956); In re Dallman's Estate, 228 N.W.2d 187 (Iowa 1975); Tarter v. Medley, 356 S.W.2d 255 (Ky.1962); Borton v. Burns, 11 Ohio Misc. 200, 230 N.E.2d 156 (Ohio 1967); Collora v. Navarro, 574 S.W.2d 65 (Tex.1978).

24. People v. Lucero, 707 P.2d 1040 (Colo.App.1985); In re Foster, 77 Idaho 26, 287 P.2d 282 (1955); In re Long's Estate, 251 Iowa 1042, 102 N.W.2d 76 (1960); O'Malley v. O'Malley, 46 Mont. 549, 129 P. 501 (1913); Cavanaugh v. Cavanaugh, 135 Okl. 204, 275 P. 315 (1929);

Ex parte Threet, 160 Tex. 482, 333 S.W.2d 361 (1960); Grigsby v. Reib, 105 Tex. 597, 153 S.W. 1124 (1913). Lefkoff v. Sicro, 189 Ga. 554, 6 S.E.2d 687 (1939) holds that cohabitation is an essential for common law marriage but "public" cohabitation is not.

25. Great Northern Ry. v. Johnson, 166 C.C.A. 181, 254 Fed. 683 (1918) was a square holding that a secret marriage, based on a written contract of marriage, was valid, without any marital cohabitation. See also In re Gower's Estate, 445 Pa. 554, 284 A.2d 742 (1971). Dictum to this effect can be found in Hayes v. Hay, 92 Ga.App. 88, 88 S.E.2d 306 (1955); Shattuck v. Shattuck's Estate, 118 Minn. 60, 136 N.W. 409 (1912); Gatterdam v. Gatterdam, 86 Ohio App. 29, 85 N.E.2d 526 (1949). A discussion of the question may also be found in Jambrone v. David, 16 Ill.2d 32, 156 N.E.2d 569 (1959), dealing with Iowa law.

26. Grigsby v. Reib, 105 Tex. 597, 153 S.W. 1124 (1913). It is worth noting that in Great Northern Ry. v. Johnson, 166 C.C.A. 181, 254 Fed. 683 (1918), which upheld a common law marriage without evidence of cohabitation, there was no chance of fraud because the agreement was in writing.

27. For a discussion of such statutes in general, see C. McCormick, Handbook of the Law of Evidence § 65 (Cleary 3d ed. 1984).

28. Azimow v. Azimow, 146 Ind.App. 341, 255 N.E.2d 667 (1970); In re Long's Estate, 251 Iowa 1042, 102 N.W.2d 76 (1960); In re Wagner's Estate, 398 Pa. 531, 159 A.2d 495 (1960); Berger v. Kirby, 105 Tex. 611, 153 S.W. 1130 (1913). Contra: In re McKanna's Estate, 106 Cal. App.2d 126, 234 P.2d 673 (1951). See also In re Estate of

The dangers of fraudulent claims are also reduced by the rule of some cases that common law marriage must be proved by "clear and convincing" evidence.[29] This is obviously an imprecise standard of proof, but one which apparently demands evidence of a more reliable and persuasive quality than that of the ordinary civil lawsuit. Pennsylvania and Colorado have added to this vague standard the even more vague qualification that if the alleged common law marriage is a remarriage of parties previously divorced from each other, it is to be encouraged, and therefore evidence of a less clear and convincing character is sufficient to prove it.[30] There seems to be no substantial reason why remarriages should be any more strongly favored by the law than marriages, but these cases probably are of little practical consequence.

Stauffer, 315 Pa. 591, 462 A.2d 750 (1983), affirmed 504 Pa. 626, 476 A.2d 354 (1984).

29. In re Wakefield's Estate, 19 Ill.App.3d 98, 311 N.E.2d 242 (1974) (Michigan law); In re Dallman's Estate, 228 N.W.2d 187 (Iowa 1975); In re Estate of Fisher, 176 N.W.2d 801 (Iowa 1970); In re Hammond's Estate, 39 Ohio Misc. 96, 315 N.E.2d 843 (Com.Pl.1973); Richard v. Richard, 172 Okl. 397, 45 P.2d 101 (1935), 21 Corn.L.Q. 122 (1935); In re Estate Erickson, 75 S.D. 345, 64 N.W.2d 316 (1954). In re Watts' Estate, 31 N.Y.2d 491, 294 N.E.2d 195 (1973), applying Florida law seems to require only that the proponent of the marriage establish a prima facie case for the marriage in the usual situation, with the burden then shifting to the opposing party to rebut the prima facie case.

The same suspicion of claims of common law marriage is reflected in cases which place a heavy burden on the party alleging it and which subject the claim of marriage to "great scrutiny". Estate of Gavula, 490 Pa. 535, 417 A.2d 168 (1980). But see McKenzie v. Harris, 679 F.2d 8 (3d Cir.1982) (Pennsylvania law).

30. In re Peterson's Estate, 148 Colo. 52, 365 P.2d 254 (1961); In re Wagner's Estate, 398 Pa. 531, 159 A.2d 495 (1960); Commonwealth ex rel. McDermott v. McDermott, 236 Pa.Super. 541, 345 A.2d 914 (1975). Matter of Miller's Estate, 90 S.D. 554, 243 N.W.2d 788 (1976) and Carter v. Carter, 309 So.2d 625 (Fla.App.1975) seem to follow the Pennsylvania rule. A case rejecting the rule is In re Keimig's Estate, 215 Kan. 869, 528 P.2d 1228 (1974). Cases involving remarriage without discussion of the quantum of proof include Williams v. Dade County, 237 So.2d 776 (Fla.App.1970); In re Hornback's Estate, 475 P.2d 184 (Okl.1970).

Humphrey v. Humphrey, 293 Ala. 118, 300 So.2d 376 (1974), rather than favoring common law remarriage, seems to make it more difficult to prove than an ordinary common law marriage. The court there seemed to hold that a couple who continued to cohabit after divorce could not establish the necessary understanding to be

It is simple enough to state in abstract terms the elements of a common law marriage as they have been established in American law. But this is only the beginning of analysis. The next step is to discover what sort of evidence is sufficient to prove that the elements of common law marriage exist in a particular case. At this point a subtle change of emphasis can be discerned in the cases. In many cases the parties have made no express agreement to be husband and wife, either in writing or orally. The alternative then is either to say there is no marriage for lack of evidence of agreement, or to infer an agreement from the fact that they have lived together for all intents and purposes as husband and wife, perhaps for a very long time. The courts have generally taken the second alternative.[31] This produces the curious re-

husband and wife. The case is otherwise explainable as being based upon conflicting evidence as to just what the parties' understanding was.

31. Kelly v. Metropolitan Life Insurance Co., 352 F.Supp. 270 (S.D.N.Y.1972); Chatman v. Ribicoff, 196 F.Supp. 931 (N.D.Cal.1961) (Texas law); National Union Fire Ins. Co. v. Britton, 187 F.Supp. 359 (D.D.C.1960); Moffat Coal Co. v. Industrial Com., 108 Colo. 388, 118 P.2d 769 (1941); Chaachou v. Chaachou, 73 So.2d 830 (Fla.1954); Gammelgaard v. Gammelgaard, 247 Iowa 979, 77 N.W.2d 479 (1956) (wife admitted she had not known there was such a thing as common law marriage, but the court found a common law marriage on the basis of cohabitation); Mission Insurance Co. v. Industrial Commission, 114 Ariz. 170, 559 P.2d 1085 (App.1976); In re Benjamin's Estate, 34 N.Y.2d 27, 355 N.Y.S.2d 356, 311 N.E.2d 495 (1974), reargument denied 34 N.Y.2d 916, 359 N.Y.S.2d 1028, 316 N.E.2d 723 (1974); Fischer v. Endres Delivery Co., Inc., 45 A.D.2d 892, 357 N.Y.S.2d 222 (3rd Dep't.1974) (living together creates a presumption of marriage); Mortensen v. Mortensen, 225 N.Y.S.2d 323 (1962) (Georgia law); In re McGrath's Estate, 319 Pa. 309, 179 A. 599 (1935); Commonwealth ex rel. McDermott v. McDermott, 236 Pa.Super. 541, 345 A.2d 914 (1975); Sardonis v. Sardonis, 106 R.I. 469, 261 A.2d 22 (1970); Claveria's Estate v. Claveria, 615 S.W.2d 164 (Tex.1981); Reilly v. Jacobs, 536 S.W.2d 406 (Tex.Civ.App.1976).

Contra, insisting on direct proof of agreement: Marcus v. Director, Office of Workers' Compensation Programs, U.S. Dept. of Labor, 548 F.2d 1044 (D.C.Cir.1976); Williamson v. Williamson, 48 Del. (9 Terry) 379, 104 A.2d 463 (Sup.1954); McCoy v. District of Columbia, 256 A.2d 908 (D.C.App.1969); Anderson v. Anderson, 235 Ind. 113, 131 N.E.2d 301 (1956); Schrader v. Schrader, 207 Kan. 349, 484 P.2d 1007 (1971); Doyle v. Doyle, 497 S.W.2d 846 (Mo. App.1973); Miller v. Townsend Lumber Co., 152 Mont. 210, 448 P.2d 148 (1968); Peart v. T.D. Bross Line Construction Co., 45 A.D.2d 801, 357 N.Y.S.2d 53 (3rd Dep't. 1974) (Pennsylvania law); Abramson v. Abramson,

sult that evidence of marital cohabitation, not an element in common law marriage under the traditional English view, has replaced the agreement which was the sole test for such marriages according to the English law. To put the change in another way, the rules of evidence have largely supplanted the rules of substantive law as a means of determining the existence of common law marriage.

There is another reason for this tendency to obscure the distinction between the substantive and the evidentiary rules for establishing common law marriage. Any marriage, whether ceremonial or common law, may be proved by "habit and repute", that is by the testimony of relatives, friends or acquaintances of the married couple that they conducted themselves as husband and wife, and that they were reputed in the community to be married.[32] Once this sort of evidence is introduced, the court may make a finding of marriage without being very particular about whether any agreement to be husband and wife was made. In fact two cases have held that evidence of habit and repute will support a finding of marriage without any claim that a ceremony occurred even in a state where common law marriage has been abolished.[33] This helpful rule of evidence thus obviates

any close investigation into just how the particular marriage came about.

It is frequently said that although evidence of cohabitation alone will not prove a common law marriage, and that an agreement must also be proved, the agreement may be inferred from the cohabitation, or from other circumstantial evidence.[34] If there is direct evidence that there was no agreement of marriage, some courts hold that this negatives any inference which might otherwise be drawn from the cohabitation.[35] But there are cases which go a long way toward basing a holding of common law marriage upon well established and long continued cohabitation in the face of evidence that no express agreement was ever made.[36]

In short, the existence of common law marriage has come to depend to a very great extent upon the duration and character of the relationship between the parties. This parallels a change in the underlying public policy. Originally perhaps common law marriage was upheld because the agreement was an acceptable substitute for a ceremony which might often be beyond the parties' reach, due to distances, difficulties of travel or the opposition of parents (as in the Dalrymple case).[37] Today, if common law marriage can be justi-

---

161 Neb. 782, 74 N.W.2d 919 (1956); Jolley v. Jolley, 46 Ohio Misc. 40, 347 N.E.2d 557 (1975); McKee v. State, 452 P.2d 169 (Okl.Crim.App.1969); David v. Bellevue Locust Garage, 12 Pa.Cmwlth. 602, 317 A.2d 341 (1974); State v. Miller, 248 N.W.2d 61 (S.D.1976); Gary v. Gary, 490 S.W.2d 929 (Tex.Civ.App.1973). Many of the cases insisting upon proof of an express agreement to be husband and wife are obviously doing so out of a general hostility to the institution of common law marriage. A strict requirement of express agreement in all cases would make it virtually impossible to find a common law marriage.

The cases involving the removal of impediments to common law marriage are also authority that an express agreement need not be insisted upon. See the text at notes 48–62.

32. II J. Wigmore, Evidence § 268 (3d ed. 1940); VII id. § 2083; In re Tomlinson's Estate, 493 S.W.2d 402 (Mo. App.1973); Fischer v. Endres Delivery Co., Inc., 45 A.D.2d 892, 357 N.Y.S.2d 222 (3rd Dep't.1974); Shankle v. Shankle, 26 N.C.App. 565, 216 S.E.2d 915 (1975), cert. denied 288 N.C. 394, 218 S.E.2d 467 (1975). But see Matter of Wilmarth's Estate, 27 Or.App. 303, 556 P.2d 990 (1976).

33. Thomson v. Thomson, 236 Mo.App. 1223, 163 S.W.2d 792 (1942); Suddeth v. Hawkins, 202 S.W.2d 572 (Mo.App.1947).

34. See cases cited supra, note 31, especially National Union Fire Ins. Co. v. Britton, 187 F.Supp. 359 (D.D.C.1960). The classic statement of this principle is Fenton v. Reed, 4 Johns. 52 (N.Y.1809). Texas seems to follow the rule that while no specific evidence of agreement is required for residents, it is required for nonresidents. See Tatum v. Tatum, 241 F.2d 401 (9th Cir. 1957). The logic of this distinction is obscure.

35. In re Danikas' Estate, 76 Colo. 191, 230 P. 608 (1924); Toye v. Toye, 170 A.2d 778 (D.C.Mun.Ct. of App. 1961); Panneton v. Panneton, 323 Mass. 477, 82 N.E.2d 595 (1948); Rush v. Travelers Ins. Co., 347 S.W.2d 758 (Tex.Civ.App.1961). In United States Fidelity & Guaranty Co. v. Britton, 269 F.2d 249 (D.C.Cir.1959) the court refused to uphold a finding of common law marriage where one of the parties was available to testify as to their agreement but did not do so, even though they lived together as husband and wife for eleven years.

36. Radovich v. Radovich, 84 Colo. 250, 269 P. 22 (1928); Moffat Coal Co. v. Industrial Comm., 108 Colo. 388, 118 P.2d 769 (1941); In re Foster, 77 Idaho 26, 287 P.2d 282 (1955); Chivers v. Couch Motor Lines, Inc., 159 So.2d 544 (La.App.1964); Campbell v. Christain, 235 S.C. 102, 110 S.E.2d 1 (1959).

37. Dalrymple v. Dalrymple, 2 Hagg.Cons. 54, 161 Eng.Rep. 665 (1811).

fied at all, it is as a means of making good the bona fide expectations of the parties. The argument which supports this form of marriage is familiar and is made in support of several other rules in the law of domestic relations, such as putative marriage,[38] the presumption of validity of the latest marriage,[39] and the estoppel to attack divorces.[40] This argument asserts that if the parties have in good faith and for an appreciable period behaved like husband and wife, if they have assumed the burdens of marriage in the expectation of receiving the benefits (such as they may be), the law should treat them as married.

It has been argued that this policy weighs more heavily in some cases than in others, so that for example, a common law marriage will be more likely to be found where a wife is claiming workmen's compensation than where she is claiming a share in the alleged husband's estate by intestacy, or than where she is suing for divorce, alimony or separate maintenance.[41] A careful reading of the more recent cases fails to uncover much support for this assertion, nor is there any apparent reason why the policy favoring marriage should have greater influence in one case than another. It does seem true that the law is stretched to protect children born of irregular unions. If the legitimacy of children is at stake, a finding of common law marriage may be rested upon evidence less substantial than would otherwise be required.[42] But in the majority of cases the courts seem to place greater reliance upon such factors as the duration and quality of the relationship,[43] whether the parties maintained it up until the death of one of them or the time of the litigation,[44] and whether they were consistent in their own characterization of it.[45] There are some cases where these generalizations do

38. See the text at notes 63–66, infra.

39. See section 2.7, infra.

40. See section 11.3, Practitioner's Edition.

41. Jacobs and Goebel, Cases and Other Materials on Domestic Relations, 96–97 (4th ed. 1961).

42. Tarter v. Medley, 356 S.W.2d 255 (Ky.1962); Gatterdam v. Gatterdam, 86 Ohio App. 29, 85 N.E.2d 526 (1949).

43. In the following cases a long continued and consistent marital cohabitation persuaded the courts that a common law marriage had been contracted: Kelly v. Metropolitan Life Insurance Co., 352 F.Supp. 270 (S.D. N.Y.1972) (lived together thirty-nine years, had one child); Chatman v. Ribicoff, 196 F.Supp. 931 (N.D.Cal. 1961) (lived together nine years, had one child, then separated); Radovich v. Radovich, 84 Colo. 250, 269 P. 22 (1928) (lived together five years); Moffat Coal Co. v. Industrial Commission, 108 Colo. 388, 118 P.2d 769 (1941) (lived together five years); Gammelgaard v. Gammelgaard, 247 Iowa 979, 77 N.W.2d 479 (1956) (lived together twelve years); In re Estate of Fisher, 176 N.W.2d 801 (Iowa 1970) (lived together less than one year); Shattuck v. Shattuck's Estate, 118 Minn. 60, 136 N.W. 409 (1912) (lived together about three years); In re Swanson's Estate, 160 Mont. 271, 502 P.2d 33 (1972) (lived together eight years, though some inconsistency in the wife's use of her married name); Mortensen v. Mortensen, 225 N.Y.S.2d 323 (1962) (lived together four years); In re McGrath's Estate, 319 Pa. 309, 179 A. 599 (1935) (lived together ten years); Sardonis v. Sardonis, 106 R.I. 469, 261 A.2d 22 (1970) (lived together three years, had two children); Campbell v. Christain, 235 S.C. 102, 110 S.E.2d 1 (1959) (lived together twenty-four years). In Smith v. Smith, 247 Ala. 213, 23 So.2d 605 (1945) the court found a valid common law marriage based upon an extremely brief cohabitation and for this reason the case seems doubtful, as, for the same reason, does Graham v. Graham, 130 Colo. 225, 274 P.2d 605 (1954). Another doubtful case is In re Madia's Estate, 6 Ohio Misc. 109, 215 N.E.2d 72 (Prob.Ct.1966), where the parties' treatment of their relationship was not consistent.

In the following cases claims of common law marriages were rejected largely for lack of evidence of marital cohabitation: Goodman v. McMillan, 258 Ala. 125, 61 So. 2d 55 (1952); Bishop v. Bishop, 57 Ala.App. 619, 330 So.2d 443 (1976); Whetstone v. Whetstone, 178 Kan. 595, 290 P.2d 1022 (1955); Edgewater Coal Co. v. Yates, 261 Ky. 335, 87 S.W.2d 596 (1935); Whitman v. Whitman, 206 Miss. 838, 41 So.2d 22 (1949); Ridley v. Compton, 215 Miss. 532, 61 So.2d 341 (1952); O'Malley v. O'Malley, 46 Mont. 549, 129 P. 501 (1913); Grigsby v. Reib, 105 Tex. 597, 153 S.W. 1124 (1913); Ex parte Threet, 160 Tex. 482, 333 S.W.2d 361 (1960); Claveria v. Estate of Claveria, 597 S.W.2d 434 (Tex.Civ.App.1980), reversed 615 S.W.2d 164 (Tex.1981).

44. Whitman v. Whitman, 206 Miss. 838, 41 So.2d 22 (1949); Miller v. Sutherland, 131 Mont. 175, 309 P.2d 322 (1957); Dondero v. Queensboro News Agency, 270 App. Div. 279, 60 N.Y.S.2d 140 (3d Dep't 1946).

45. Marcus v. Director, Office of Workers' Compensation Programs, U.S. Dept. of Labor, 548 F.2d 1044 (D.C. Cir.1976); In re Marriage of Grother, 242 N.W.2d 1 (Iowa 1976); In re Dallman's Estate, 228 N.W.2d 187 (Iowa 1975); In re Long's Estate, 251 Iowa 1042, 102 N.W.2d 76 (1960); State v. Johnson, 216 Kan. 445, 532 P.2d 1325 (1975); In re Keimig's Estate, 215 Kan. 869, 528 P.2d 1228 (1974); Sullivan v. Sullivan, 196 Kan. 705, 413 P.2d 988 (1966); Damron v. Damron, 301 Ky. 636, 192 S.W.2d 741 (1945); Pittman v. Scullin Steel Co., 289 S.W.2d 57 (Mo.1956); In re McClelland's Estate, 168 Mont. 160, 541 P.2d 780 (1975); Miller v. Townsend Lumber Co., 152 Mont. 210, 448 P.2d 148 (1968); In re Kearns' Estate, 16

not hold, and where there is a continued insistence upon direct proof of agreement to be man and wife.[46] A considerable number of these cases evince such hostility to the entire institution of common law marriage as to justify the conclusion that this, rather than the lack of evidence of agreement, is the real reason for the holding of no marriage.[47] In nearly all of these cases there were additional factors beyond the mere absence of present agreement which support the finding of no marriage, such as a denial by one of the parties that they intended to be married, or conduct during the course of the relationship which was inconsistent with the claim of marriage. And many of the decisions were content to accept the characterization of the relationship by the trial court, on the theory that a question of fact was involved.

The most revealing test of common law marriage occurs in the "impediment" cases, cases in which the parties attempt to marry but are prevented from accomplishing their purpose by some legal impediment. The question then is, if they continue living together with no further ceremony or agreement, do they succeed in contracting a common law marriage? The problem arises most frequently when the impediment consists of a prior subsisting marriage on the part of one or both of the spouses. If both parties believe in good faith that they are married, being ignorant that a prior marriage still exists, it is held that a valid common law marriage comes into existence when the prior marriage ends.[48] The reason for this result is obviously the policy already mentioned,[49] to make good the bona fide expectations of the parties. The same policy has led most courts to find a common law marriage upon the termination of the prior marriage when only one party has acted in good faith and in ignorance of the impediment, notwithstanding the other party's awareness of the impediment.[50] Of

N.Y.S.2d 560 (Surr.Ct.1939); Brastein v. Sedivy, 153 N.E.2d 541 (Ohio Prob.1957); In re Hornback's Estate, 475 P.2d 184 (Okla.1970); Gary v. Gary, 490 S.W.2d 929 (Tex.Civ.App.1973). Cases which go to considerable lengths to uphold common law marriages are In re Marriage of Winegard, 278 N.W.2d 505 (Iowa 1979), cert. denied 444 U.S. 951, 100 S.Ct. 425, 62 L.Ed.2d 321 (1979), and Metropolitan Life Ins. Co. v. Johnson, 103 Idaho 122, 645 P.2d 356 (1982).

46. Tatum v. Tatum, 241 F.2d 401 (9th Cir.1957) (Texas law); Duey v. Duey, 343 So.2d 896 (Fla.App.1977), cert. denied 353 So.2d 674 (Fla.1977); Jambrone v. David, 16 Ill.2d 32, 156 N.E.2d 569 (Iowa 1959); Anderson v. Anderson, 235 Ind. 113, 131 N.E.2d 301 (1956); Schrader v. Schrader, 207 Kan. 349, 484 P.2d 1007 (1971); Hutchins v. Kimmell, 31 Mich. 126, 18 Am.Rep. 164 (1875); Doyle v. Doyle, 497 S.W.2d 846 (Mo.App.1973); Abramson v. Abramson, 161 Neb. 782, 74 N.W.2d 919 (1956) (Iowa law); Peart v. T.D. Bross Line Construction Co., 45 A.D.2d 801, 357 N.Y.S.2d 53 (3rd Dep't.1974); Jolley v. Jolley, 46 Ohio Misc. 40, 347 N.E.2d 557 (Com.Pl.1975); McKee v. State, 452 P.2d 169 (Okl.Crim.App.1969); David v. Bellevue Locust Garage, 12 Pa.Cmwlth. 602, 317 A.2d 341 (1974); In re Estate of Erickson, 75 S.D. 345, 64 N.W.2d 316 (1954).

47. McCoy v. District of Columbia, 256 A.2d 908 (D.C. App.1969); Anderson v. Anderson, 235 Ind. 113, 131 N.E.2d 301 (1956); Jolley v. Jolley, 46 Ohio Misc. 40, 347 N.E.2d 557 (Com.Pl.1975); In re Estate of Erickson, 75 S.D. 345, 64 N.W.2d 316 (1954) (parties lived together in all respects as husband and wife for twenty-five years).

48. Parrella v. Parrella, 74 App.D.C. 161, 120 F.2d 728 (1941); Reger v. Reger, 242 Ind. 302, 177 N.E.2d 901 (1961); In re Haffner's Estate, 254 N.Y. 238, 172 N.E. 483 (1930) (applying the law of New York before the abolition of common law marriage in that state). Other cases are

cited in Note, 18 Minn.L.Rev. 86 (1933). It is worth noting that the Reger case was decided in a jurisdiction which had abolished common law marriage. But in New Jersey it has been held that the abolition of common law marriage prevents any marriage from arising after the removal of the impediment, unless a new ceremony is performed. Dacunzo v. Edgye, 19 N.J. 443, 117 A.2d 508 (1955). The rule of the text is enacted by statute in Iowa and Massachusetts. See Iowa Code Ann. § 595.19(4) (West 1981) and Mass.Gen.Laws Ann. ch. 207, § 6 (1981), construed in Hanford v. Hanford, 214 Iowa 839, 240 N.W. 732 (1932), and Van Bibber's Case, 343 Mass. 443, 179 N.E.2d 253 (1962). See also Tex.Fam.Code § 2.22 (1975). In In re Crandall's Estate 214 App.Div. 363, 212 N.Y.S. 210 (4th Dep't 1925), Weisel v. National Transportation Co., 14 A.D.2d 621, 218 N.Y.S.2d 725 (3rd Dep't 1961), appeal denied 10 N.Y.2d 708, 221 N.Y.S.2d 1028, 178 N.E.2d 192 (1961) and Krug v. Krug, 292 Ala. 498, 296 So.2d 715 (1974) the common law marriage was upheld when the parties were initially prevented from marrying by a divorce decree prohibiting remarriage, but continued to live together after the prohibition expired.

Perhaps the earliest application of the rule stated in the text was in Fenton v. Reed, 4 Johns. 52 (N.Y.1809), where the parties married in the belief that the wife's first husband was dead. When the first husband returned, the parties continued living together, and the court held that a common law marriage was contracted when the first husband finally did die. Cf. the cases on putative marriage, infra at note 63.

49. See the discussion supra at note 40.

50. Hill & Range Songs, Inc. v. Fred Rose Music, Inc., 403 F.Supp. 420 (M.D.Tenn.1975); Metropolitan Life Insurance Co. v. Holding, 293 F.Supp. 854 (E.D.Va.1968); Hackmeyer v. Hackmeyer, 268 Ala. 329, 106 So.2d 245 (1958); Jones v. Jones, 119 Fla. 824, 161 So. 836 (1935);

course in all such cases there must be that evidence of an open and well-known assumption of the relationship which is required by the general rules of common law marriage. But it is striking that in this context the courts seldom insist upon direct evidence that a new agreement of marriage was made *after* the removal of the impediment. In fact in some cases one or both parties may not even know that the impediment has been removed.[51] In other words, there is even less insistence upon agreement and more reliance upon cohabitation than in the ordinary common law marriage case. The agreement is inferable from the cohabitation, particularly if the parties' good faith was attested by their contracting a ceremonial marriage at the outset.[52] This certainly is sound. It would place a wholly unjustifiable emphasis on form to require the parties to say, "we hereby agree to be husband and wife," when they are already giving ample evidence by their conduct that this is their understanding.

If the marriages of those who act in good faith and in ignorance of any impediment are upheld, what is to be done with people who begin living together with full knowledge that one or both of them are bound by a previous marriage? At this point righteous indignation enters the picture. A substantial number of courts strongly express their disapproval of such conduct by holding that if the relationship began meretriciously, it cannot ripen into a valid common law marriage, except upon proof of an explicit agreement of marriage made after the prior marriage ended.[53] In nearly all cases proof of such an agreement is impossible.[54] The parties are thus punished for their sins by withholding legal recognition of their marriage. It must be conceded that this is a very uneven sort of punishment. It generally falls on the woman, excluding her from an inheritance or from workmen's compensation or social security benefits.[55] On occasion the punishment of the woman may be coupled with a reward to the

In re Walls' Estate, 358 Mich. 148, 99 N.W.2d 599 (1959); Stevenson v. Detroit, 42 Mich.App. 294, 201 N.W.2d 688 (1972); Earley v. State Industrial Commission, 269 P.2d 977 (Okla.1954) (semble); LeRoy Roofing Co. v. Workmen's Compensation Appeal Board, 15 Pa.Cmwlth. 396, 327 A.2d 876 (1974). In Parkinson v. J. & S. Tool Co., 64 N.J. 159, 313 A.2d 609 (1974) the parties had been divorced but became reconciled and wished to remarry each other. Their priest told them he would not marry them, however, because they were already married in the eyes of God. Although New Jersey did not recognize common law marriage, the court held they had a "de facto" marriage for workmen's compensation purposes. In Davidson v. Davidson, 35 Wis.2d 401, 151 N.W.2d 53 (1967) the court held that a marriage contracted by the wife in good faith and in ignorance of the husband's prior subsisting marriage was not voidable when the husband's marriage was terminated by divorce and the parties continued living together, under Wis.Stat.Ann. § 765.24 (West Supp.1984). See also Smith v. Smith, 52 Wis.2d 262, 190 N.W.2d 174 (1971).

51. Hess v. Pettigrew, 261 Mich. 618, 247 N.W. 90 (1933).

52. In re Haffner's Estate, 254 N.Y. 238, 172 N.E. 483 (1930).

53. Mellon v. Richardson, 466 F.2d 524 (3d Cir.1972) (Pennsylvania law); Cairns v. Richardson, 457 F.2d 1145 (10th Cir.1972) (Kansas law); Friedenwald v. Friedenwald, 16 F.2d 509 (D.C.Cir.1926), 12 Corn.L.Q. 513 (1926), 13 Va.L.Rev. 579 (1927); Kersey v. Gardner, 264 F.Supp. 887 (M.D.Ga.1967) (no marriage under Georgia law where the parties erroneously thought the man's prior marriage still subsisted); Green v. Ribicoff, 201 F.Supp. 721 (S.D. Miss.1961); Williamson v. Williamson, 48 Del. (9 Terry) 379, 104 A.2d 463 (1954); Dandy v. Dandy, 234 So.2d 728

(Fla.App.1970); Anderson v. Anderson, 235 Ind. 113, 131 N.E.2d 301 (1956) (semble); Kennedy v. Damron, 268 S.W.2d 22 (Ky.1954); Brinson v. Brinson, 233 La. 417, 96 So.2d 653 (1957); In re Widenmeyer's Estate, 134 N.J. Super. 307, 340 A.2d 676 (1975); In re Watts' Estate, 31 N.Y.2d 491, 341 N.Y.S.2d 609, 294 N.E.2d 195 (1973) (Florida law); Hill v. Vrooman, 215 App.Div. 847, 213 N.Y.S. 256 (3rd Dep't 1926), affirmed 242 N.Y. 549, 152 N.E. 421 (1926); Maiorana v. Salerno, 133 N.Y.S.2d 521 (1954); Castellani v. Castellani, 176 Misc. 763, 28 N.Y.S.2d 879 (Dom.Rel.Ct.1941), affirmed sub nom. Capaldo v. Capaldo, 263 App.Div. 984, 34 N.Y.S.2d 400 (1st Dep't 1942); In re Garges' Estate, 474 Pa. 237, 378 A.2d 307 (1977); Donaldson v. P.J. Oesterling & Sons, Inc., 199 Pa.Super. 637, 186 A.2d 653 (1962); Early v. Commonwealth, Department of Public Welfare, 13 Pa. Cmwlth. 17, 317 A.2d 677 (1974); Byers v. Mount Vernon Mills, Inc., 268 S.C. 68, 231 S.E.2d 699 (1977); Williams v. Williams, 46 Wis. 464, 1 N.W. 98 (1879). Two cases which have taken this position are of doubtful authority in view of later decisions, although they have not been expressly overruled. They are United States Fidelity & Guaranty Co. v. Britton, 269 F.2d 249 (D.C.Cir.1959) and Collins v. Voorhees, 47 N.J.Eq. 555, 22 A. 1054 (1890).

54. Some courts have found such a new agreement on extremely flimsy evidence, presumably as a means of avoiding an otherwise highly undesirable result. See, e.g. Schaffer v. Krestovnikow, 88 N.J.Eq. 192, 102 A. 246 (1917); In re Stauffer's Estate, 372 Pa. 537, 94 A.2d 726 (1953); In re Garges' Estate, 474 Pa. 237, 378 A.2d 307 (1977); Kirby v. Kirby, 270 S.C. 137, 241 S.E.2d 415 (1978).

55. As in United States Fidelity & Guaranty Co. v. Britton, 269 F.2d 249 (D.C.Cir.1959), where the woman was refused workmen's compensation death benefits al-

man, as where she seeks a divorce and alimony and he counterclaims for an annulment which would free him from financial responsibility to her.[56] Or the punishment may also fall on children of the parties, making them illegitimate, the law in such case very neatly bearing out the Biblical injunction about the iniquity of the fathers.[57] In addition to their desire to punish immorality, cases have relied upon the argument that if the parties begin living together meretriciously, their illicit intent is presumed to continue even after any impediment to their marriage has been removed.[58] As a matter of psychology this is a non sequitur. In many instances they may have begun living together meretriciously only because the divorce laws of some states, such as New York, prevented them from ending a prior marriage, because they were prevented from forming a legitimate relationship by the abominable type of statute which forbids remarriage after divorce, or because they had no money for a divorce. Their intent

may have been to live as much like husbands and wives as the law would allow. When the obstacle is finally removed, it is not inconsistent with this intent to declare them validly married.

The courts in some jurisdictions have done just that.[59] The leading case is Matthews v. Britton.[60] In this case the man and woman lived together for twenty-two years, from 1935 until his death in 1957, in all respects as if they were husband and wife. She had a prior marriage, as he knew, which ended in divorce in 1951. The court awarded her death benefits under the workmen's compensation law of the District, holding that the removal of an impediment to their marriage resulted in a valid common law marriage, whether or not they had known of the impediment at the time they began living together. No new agreement of marriage was held necessary, the court saying, "It is not to be expected that parties once having agreed to be married will deem it necessary to agree to do so again

---

though she had lived with the deceased in all respects as his wife for eleven years.

56. As in Castellani v. Castellani, 176 Misc. 763, 28 N.Y.S.2d 879 (Dom.Rel.Ct.1941), affirmed sub nom. Capaldo v. Capaldo, 263 App.Div. 984, 34 N.Y.S.2d 400 (1st Dep't 1942).

57. As in Anderson v. Anderson, 235 Ind. 113, 131 N.E.2d 301 (1956), where the court found that the relationship had begun meretriciously, although it is not clear whether this was due to a preexisting marriage of one of the parties, or merely to the fact that they began living together without an intention of being married. A similar case, denying social security benefits, is Lester v. Celebrezze, 221 F.Supp. 607 (E.D.Ark.1963).

58. E.g. Williamson v. Williamson, 48 Del. (9 Terry) 379, 104 A.2d 463 (1954).

59. Thomas v. Murphy, 107 F.2d 268 (D.C.Cir.1939); Walls v. Celebrezze, 215 F.Supp. 414 (S.D.Tex.1963); Krug v. Krug, 292 Ala. 498, 296 So.2d 715 (1974); Brown v. Brown, 234 Ga. 300, 215 S.E.2d 671 (1975); In re Estate of Fisher, 176 N.W.2d 801 (Iowa 1970); Jennings v. Jennings, 20 Md.App. 369, 315 A.2d 816 (1974); Schaffer v. Krestovnikow, 88 N.J.Eq. 192, 102 A. 246 (1917), 28 Yale L.J. 515 (1919) (the law review note arguing that this case overrules Collins v. Voorhees, supra, note 53); Tegenborg v. Tegenborg, 26 N.J. 467, 98 A.2d 105 (1953) (semble); Olinghouse v. Olinghouse, 265 P.2d 711 (Okl.1954); Dowell v. Welch, 574 P.2d 1089 (Okl.App.1978); In re Stauffer's Estate, 372 Pa. 537, 94 A.2d 726 (1953); Sardonis v. Sardonis, 106 R.I. 469, 261 A.2d 22 (1970); Rodriguez v. Avalos, 567 S.W.2d 85 (Tex.Civ.App.1978); Howard v. Howard, 459 S.W.2d 901 (Tex.Civ.App.1970); In re Gallagher's Estate, 35 Wash.2d 512, 213 P.2d 621

(1950). The Gallagher case illustrates the disregard for fine distinctions of intention indulged by some courts, since the wife in this case did not know her prior marriage had ended in divorce until after the death of her second husband. The court based its holding on the fact that she had lived with her second husband for fifteen years. But see Lester v. Celebrezze, 221 F.Supp. 607 (E.D.Ark.1963), and Kersey v. Gardner, 264 F.Supp. 887 (M.D.Ga.1967), where it was held that no marriage was contracted when the parties erroneously believed that a prior marriage continued, not knowing of the prior divorce.

It is worth noting that the leading historical precedent on this question, Campbell v. Campbell (The Breadalbane Case), L.R. I H.L.Scot.App. 182, V Scots Rev.Rep. 107 (1867) held that a common law marriage resulted upon the removal of the impediment with only the slightest evidence of a renewed exchange of consents, so that properly it belongs with those cases which say that a continued cohabitation after removal of the impediment automatically gives rise to a common law marriage. The parties in The Breadalbane Case began their relationship in the utmost bad faith, i.e. by eloping when the woman was married to another. It is also interesting to note the facts in the celebrated early case of Fenton v. Reed, 4 Johns. 52 (N.Y.1809), the opinion in which is generally attributed to Chancellor Kent. There the parties began living together in good faith, the woman thinking her husband was dead. The husband turned up, however, but the woman continued living with her second "husband". At that point she can hardly be described as acting in good faith. Yet the court held that a valid common law marriage arose when the first husband died.

60. 112 U.S.App.D.C. 397, 303 F.2d 408 (1962).

when an earlier marriage is terminated or some other bar to union is eliminated." [61] This seems to settle for the District of Columbia what had looked like a conflict in the decisions,[62] and to put the District among the more enlightened jurisdictions on this question.

In the civil law jurisdictions of California, Louisiana and Texas, the device of putative marriage is used to reach results much like those reached in the common law marriage cases.[63] It is significant that both legal systems found it necessary to devise a doctrine of de facto marriage to take care of persons who fail to observe the technical legal requirements for contracting valid marriages. Putative marriage is a more restricted doctrine than common law marriage. It is usually defined as a marriage which has been solemnized when one or both parties were ignorant of an impediment which made the marriage either void or voidable.[64] The good faith of the party who asserts a claim based on the marriage is required.[65] If the impediment is later removed, the putative marriage becomes a true de jure marriage.[66]

A putative marriage may also occur when, after a divorce, the parties are reconciled and the wife believes in good faith that a remarriage is not necessary and that she is still married. In re Marriage of Monti, 135 Cal. App.3d 50, 185 Cal.Rptr. 72 (1982). Galbraith v. Galbraith, 396 So.2d 1364 (La.App.1981) (good faith requires an honest and reasonable belief that the marriage was valid and that no legal impediment existed).

61. 303 F.2d at page 409.

62. Thomas v. Murphy, 71 U.S.App.D.C. 69, 107 F.2d 268 (1939) had seemed to hold that a meretricious relationship could become a valid common law marriage upon the removal of the legal obstacle. United States Fidelity & Guaranty Co. v. Britton, 269 F.2d 249 (D.C.Cir. 1959), in circumstances of particular hardship, held that proof of a new agreement of marriage must be adduced, casting considerable doubt on the Thomas case. Matthews v. Britton, 112 U.S.App.D.C. 397, 303 F.2d 408 (1962) purports to distinguish the U.S. Fidelity & Guaranty case, but its language and result seem so inconsistent with that case as to indicate that the prior case is in fact overruled.

63. For the relationship between putative and common law marriage, see Curtin v. State, 155 Tex.Cr.R. 625, 238 S.W.2d 187 (1950). On putative marriage generally, see Blakesley, The Putative Marriage Doctrine, 60 Tul.L. Rev. 1 (1985); Note, The Rights of the Putative and Meretricious Spouse in California, 50 Cal.L.Rev. 866 (1962); Note, The Putative Marriage Doctrine in Louisiana, 12 Loyola L.Rev. 89 (1967); Annot., Rights in Decedent's Estate Between Lawful and Putative Spouses, 81 A.L.R.3d 6 (1977).

64. Sanguinetti v. Sanguinetti, 9 Cal.2d 95, 69 P.2d 845 (1937) (putative wife may get the value of her services); In re Vargas' Estate, 36 Cal.App.3d 714, 111 Cal. Rptr. 779 (1974); In re Foy's Estate, 109 Cal.App.2d 329, 240 P.2d 685 (1952); In re Krone's Estate, 83 Cal.App.2d 766, 189 P.2d 741 (1948); Funderburk v. Funderburk, 214 La. 717, 38 So.2d 502 (1949); Smith v. Smith, 1 Tex. 621 (1846); Laughran and Laughran, Property and Inheritance Rights of Putative Spouses in California: Selected Problems and Suggested Solutions, 11 Loyola of L.A.L. Rev. 45 (1977).

The doctrine of putative marriage may be based upon a common law marriage in those states which recognize common law marriage. Sancha v. Arnold, 114 Cal.App. 2d 772, 251 P.2d 67 (1952), rehearing denied 114 Cal.App. 2d 772, 252 P.2d 55 (1953); Curtin v. State, 155 Tex.Cr.R. 625, 238 S.W.2d 187 (1950); Succession of Marinoni, 183 La. 776, 164 So. 797 (1935), 10 Tulane L.Rev. 435 (1935).

The putative spouse doctrine is enacted in the Uniform Marriage and Divorce Act, 9A Unif.L.Ann. 115 (1979). In re Marriage of Flores, 96 Ill.App.3d 279, 51 Ill.Dec. 885, 421 N.E.2d 393 (1981). See also West's Ann.Cal.Civ.Code § 4452 (Supp.1983).

65. Spearman v. Spearman, 482 F.2d 1203 (5th Cir. 1973) (wife was not in good faith when she was aware of the possibility, if not the likelihood, that an earlier marriage existed); Adduddell v. Board of Administration, Public Emp. Retirement System, 8 Cal.App.3d 243, 87 Cal.Rptr. 268 (1970); Gathright v. Smith, 368 So.2d 679 (La.1978) (husband in good faith in accepting wife's statement that her prior marriage had ended in divorce); Succession of Pigg, 228 La. 799, 84 So.2d 196 (1955) (wife acting in good faith when she was ignorant of husband's fraud in obtaining a divorce from his first wife); Super v. Burke, 367 So.2d 93 (La.App.1979) (wife in good faith in relying upon a Dominican divorce); Succession of Hopkins, 114 So.2d 742 (La.App.1959) (wife not in good faith when she had reason to know of husband's prior subsisting marriage); Texas Co. v. Stewart, 101 So.2d 222 (La.App.1958) (good faith means only the absence of knowledge of the impediment); Humphreys v. Marquette Cas. Co., 95 So.2d 872 (La.App.1957); Dean v. Goldwire, 480 S.W.2d 494 (Tex.Civ.App.1972) (wife in good faith when she believed her Mexican divorce was valid).

66. Smith v. Smith, 1 Tex. 621 (1846); Lee v. Smith, 18 Tex. 141 (1956).

The converse question, the point at which the putative spouse ceases to be entitled to benefits, is answered variously. Some cases hold that this occurs when the putative spouse learns of the defect in the marriage. Gallaher v. State Teachers' Retirement System, 237 Cal. App.2d 510, 47 Cal.Rptr. 139 (1965) (semble); Succession of Hopkins, 114 So.2d 742 (La.App.1959); Davis v. Davis, 507 S.W.2d 841 (Tex.Civ.App.1974), reversed on other grounds 521 S.W.2d 603 (Tex.1975). Jackson v. Swift & Co., 151 So. 816 (La.App.1934) holds that benefits may accrue until the defective marriage is annulled. The Uniform Marriage and Divorce Act § 209, 9A Unif.L. Ann. 115 (1979) adopts the rule of the former cases.

Originally the consequence of a finding of putative marriage was that the putative spouse had a valid claim to his share of the community property.[67] More recently putative spouses have been given other benefits of a sort which are normally incident to marriage, such as the right to inherit,[68] the right to sue for the wrongful death of the spouse,[69] and benefits under the Social Security Act.[70] Children of the putative marriage are legitimate.[71] In some states whose common law traditions do not permit them to adopt putative marriage, similar results are reached by drawing analogies to putative marriage or to the law of partnership.[72]

The effect of the removal of an impediment comes up in another context, where again evidence of marital cohabitation is controlling and the requirement of an agreement of marriage is virtually ignored. In its simplest form the problem arises when a man and woman begin living together in a state which does not recognize common law marriage. Later they move to a state which does recognize such a marriage. When they acquire a domicile in the second state, do they also, without making any further agreement of marriage, acquire a valid common law marriage? Travers v. Reinhardt [73] held that they do. The parties in that case had contracted a

ceremonial marriage in Virginia which was invalid for failure to observe the prescribed formalities. They then moved to Maryland, where common law marriage is not recognized, and later moved to New Jersey, where common law marriage was recognized at that time. At all times until the man's death they lived as man and wife and were reputed to be married. The Supreme Court held that they contracted a valid common law marriage during their residence in New Jersey. They had lived together as husband and wife for a total of eighteen years, less than a year of which was in New Jersey. The Supreme Court conceded that there was no evidence of an express agreement to live as husband and wife made after moving to New Jersey. But it found that the entire conduct of the parties during their life together amounted to an implicit agreement to be man and wife, and that this was sufficient to support a finding of common law marriage. This is certainly the proper outcome. When every aspect of the parties' life together attests to their intention of living as man and wife it is superfluous and unnecessary to require proof of an express agreement to this effect. Other cases agree with Travers that the change in domicile and a continued marital cohabitation results in a common law marriage.[74]

67. Schneider v. Schneider, 183 Cal. 335, 191 P. 533 (1920); Texas Co. v. Stewart, 101 So.2d 222 (La.App.1958). Where a spouse dies leaving both a de jure spouse and a putative spouse, the decedent's property has been divided equally between them by the California court. In re Ricci's Estate, 201 Cal.App.2d 146, 19 Cal.Rptr. 739 (1962). See also Sousa v. Freitas, 10 Cal.App.3d 660, 89 Cal.Rptr. 485 (1970), and Price v. Price, 326 So.2d 545 (La. App.1976). The Uniform Marriage and Divorce Act § 209 provides that in such cases the property, maintenance and support rights are to be apportioned as the circumstances make appropriate. 9A Uniform L.Ann. 115 (1979). Unlike ordinary support rights, however, those of the putative spouse may be discharged in bankruptcy. Note, Putative Spousal Support Rights and the Federal Bankruptcy Law, 25 U.C.L.A.L.Rev. 96 (1977).

68. Estate of Leslie, 37 Cal.3d 186, 207 Cal.Rptr. 561, 689 P.2d 133 (1984); Succession of Fields, 222 La. 310, 62 So.2d 495 (1952); Annot., 81 A.L.R.3d 6 (1977). Recently Louisiana has held that the putative wife may also be awarded alimony. Cortes v. Fleming, 307 So.2d 611 (La. 1973), 36 La.L.Rev. 704 (1976); Super v. Super, 397 So.2d 1084 (La.App.1981).

69. Kunakoff v. Woods, 166 Cal.App.2d 59, 332 P.2d 773 (1958); King v. Cancienne, 316 So.2d 366 (La.1975), 36 La.L.Rev. 704 (1976).

70. Aubrey v. Folsom, 151 F.Supp. 836 (N.D.Cal.1957); Speedling v. Hobby, 132 F.Supp. 833 (N.D.Cal.1955).

71. Texas Co. v. Stewart, 101 So.2d 222 (La.App.1958).

72. Some states have enacted putative marriage statutes. E.g., West's Fla.Stat.Ann. § 741.211 (Supp.1984); Mont.Rev.Codes § 40–1–404 (1983); Uniform Marriage and Divorce Act § 209, 9A Uniform L.Ann. 115 (1979). In other states putative marriage has been recognized to varying degrees by judicial decision. E.g., Werner v. Werner, 59 Kan. 399, 53 P. 127 (1898); Walker v. Walker, 330 Mich. 332, 47 N.W.2d 633 (1951); Chrismond v. Chrismond, 211 Miss. 746, 52 So.2d 624 (1951), cert. denied 342 U.S. 878, 72 S.Ct. 167, 96 L.Ed. 659 (1951); King v. Jackson, 196 Okl. 327, 164 P.2d 974 (1945); Buck v. Buck, 19 Utah 2d 161, 427 P.2d 954 (1967); Knoll v. Knoll, 104 Wash. 110, 176 P. 22 (1918); and cases cited in Annot., 31 A.L.R.2d 1255 (1953).

73. 205 U.S. 423, 27 S.Ct. 563, 51 L.Ed. 865 (1907).

74. E.g., Hill & Range Songs, Inc. v. Fred Rose Music, Inc., 403 F.Supp. 420 (M.D.Tenn.1975), motion denied 413 F.Supp. 967 (M.D.Tenn.1976); National Union Fire Ins. Co. v. Britton, 187 F.Supp. 359 (D.D.C.1960), affirmed 289 F.2d 454 (D.C.Cir.1961); Grammas v. Kettle, 306 Mich. 308, 10 N.W.2d 895 (1943); Walker v. Matthews, 191 Miss. 489, 3 So.2d 820 (1941); Matter of Estate of Mur-

The question next in logical order is one concerning the conflict of laws. If the parties either begin living together in a state which recognizes common law marriage, or if they live in such a state under circumstances justifying the application of the Travers rule, and the validity of the marriage is later called in question in a jurisdiction which does not recognize common law marriage, what will be the outcome? It appears to be settled that if they acquired a domicile in a state which held common law marriages valid, and if their conduct was such as to meet the requirements of this state's law governing such marriages, other states will recognize their marriage as valid.[75] This is so even though the state in which the validity of the marriage is litigated would not uphold common law marriages contracted within its own boundaries. Most of the opinions which deal with this question rely on the rule that the law of the place of marriage controls rather than that of the domicile, but in all of them the parties were domiciled at some stage of their lives in a state whose law validated common law marriage, and in at least one case [76] this factor was determinative.

A more difficult problem arises when parties who are domiciled in a state which has abolished common law marriage go into another state where such marriages are valid, remain there for a time and then return to their domicile.[77] Have they, by conducting themselves as husband and wife in the second state, succeeded in contracting a common law marriage which their domicile will recognize? A superficial reliance on the rule that the law of the place of contract governs the formalities of marriage would produce an affirmative answer. But this is not just a question of a choice between different requirements of form. It involves recognizing a marriage contracted without any formalities at all on the basis of evidence which may be hard to evaluate. The court of the domicile may find that such an important public policy underlies the prohibition on common law marriage that it will not honor such marriages by its citizens when contracted in other states. As we have seen, the proof of a common law marriage under modern cases requires evidence of a course of conduct, of marital cohabitation. At the least, this would entail a stay of some duration in the nondomiciliary state before evidence of the requisite kind and amount could become available. For all these reasons an automatic application of the law of the place of contract fails to take account of the relevant factors.

The cases on this point fall into three groups. In the first group, exemplified by the New York authorities, there is a brief reference to the law of the place of contract followed by a decision that the common law

nion, ___ Mont. ___, 686 P.2d 893 (1984); Sullivan v. American Bridge Co., 115 Pa.Super. 536, 176 A. 24 (1935), 83 U.Pa.L.Rev. 801 (1935).

75. Franzen v. E.I. du Pont De Nemours Co., 146 F.2d 837 (3d Cir.1944); Chatman v. Ribicoff, 196 F.Supp. 931 (N.D.Cal.1961); Atkinson v. Valley National Bank of Arizona, 22 Ariz.App. 297, 526 P.2d 1252 (1974); Colbert v. Colbert, 28 Cal.2d 276, 169 P.2d 633 (1946); Henderson v. Henderson, 199 Md. 449, 87 A.2d 403 (1952); Boltz v. Boltz, 325 Mass. 726, 92 N.E.2d 365 (1950); Pope v. Pope, 520 S.W.2d 634 (Mo.App.1975); La Plant v. La Plant, 99 N.H. 357, 111 A.2d 325 (1955); Weisel v. National Transp. Co., 14 A.D.2d 621, 218 N.Y.S.2d 725 (3rd Dep't 1961), appeal denied 10 N.Y.2d 708, 221 N.Y.S.2d 1028, 178 N.E.2d 192 (1961); Mortensen v. Mortensen, 225 N.Y.S.2d 323 (1962); Troxel v. Jones, 45 Tenn.App. 264, 322 S.W.2d 251 (1959).

In re Reed's Marriage, 226 N.W.2d 795 (Iowa 1975) may be contra the statement in the text, although the discussion of law and facts in the opinion is inadequate. In that case the parties apparently began living together in California and then came to Iowa, where they lived together for an unspecified period. California does not recognize common law marriage but Iowa does. The court held that no marriage had been contracted, relying upon a lex loci contractus rule but without discussion of whether a domicile in Iowa would result in a marriage and without citation of the authorities. Restatement (Second) Conflict of Laws § 283 (1971), cited in this case announces the rule that the validity of a marriage is governed by the law of the state having the most significant relationship to the parties and to the marriage, not a helpful rule in the present context. Comments f and g to that section seem to adopt a lex loci rule for common law marriages, but this too is not helpful, since it omits consideration of the crucial question, namely, where was the marriage contracted? The Restatement's inadequacies on this issue are unfortunately not uncommon in its general treatment of marriage in the conflict of laws.

76. Boltz v. Boltz, 325 Mass. 726, 92 N.E.2d 365 (1950).

77. For some general discussion of the conflicts problems raised by common law marriage, see Ehrenzweig, Conflict of Laws, 380 (1962); 1 Rabel, The Conflict of Laws, 241 (2d ed. 1958); Taintor, Marriage in the Conflict of Laws, 9 Vand.L.Rev. 607, 609 (1956).

marriage contracted elsewhere, while the parties were domiciled in New York, is valid.[78] In some of these cases the marriage is upheld on the basis of remarkably vague evidence of short visits to the other state. The explanation seems to be that the prohibition against common law marriage represents no very strong policy in these states, and in the courts' view nothing more important is at stake than the form which a marriage contract takes.

The second group of cases places greater emphasis on the evils of common law marriage. They hold that where the parties retain their domicile but visit another state and attempt to contract a common law marriage there, the marriage will not be recognized.[79] Although these cases have been criticized, they are merely giving appropriate effect to their own state's public policy. One may disagree with their hostility to common law marriage, but if they are right in their assessment of the policy abolishing it, they are equally right to apply that policy to their domiciliaries regardless of where the marriage was contracted.

The third group of cases is exemplified by Kennedy v. Damron.[80] The parties in that case began living together in Kentucky, where they were domiciled. They had no ceremonial marriage although Kentucky is a state which has abolished common law marriage. Over the course of several years they made visits to Ohio, staying as long as a month at a time. At all times, both in Kentucky and Ohio, they conducted themselves openly as husband and wife. Common law marriages are recognized in Ohio, but the Kentucky court held that these parties had not contracted a common law marriage dur-

---

78. Shea v. Shea, 294 N.Y. 909, 63 N.E.2d 113 (1945) is the leading case. See also Ventura v. Ventura, 53 Misc. 2d 881, 280 N.Y.S.2d 5 (1967); Skinner v. Skinner, 4 Misc. 2d 1013, 150 N.Y.S.2d 739 (1956); In re Schneiders' Will, 206 Misc. 18, 131 N.Y.S.2d 215 (Surr.Ct.1954); Matter of Van Valkenburg's Estate, 184 Misc. 949, 54 N.Y.S.2d 897 (Surr.Ct.1945); Matter of Sokoloff's Estate, 166 Misc. 403, 2 N.Y.S.2d 602 (Surr.Ct.1938). But the New York cases are not unanimous, as is evidenced by the contrary opinions in Seagriff v. Seagriff, 21 Misc.2d 604, 195 N.Y.S.2d 718 (Dom.Rel.Ct.1960); and Ray v. Ray, 193 Misc. 131, 83 N.Y.S.2d 126 (1948).

Other cases holding that a common law marriage may be contracted by visits to states recognizing such marriages, without acquiring a domicile there, and that such marriages will be upheld in states which do not have common law marriage include Albina Engine and Machine Works v. J.J. O'Leary, 328 F.2d 877 (9th Cir.1964), cert. denied 379 U.S. 817, 85 S.Ct. 35, 13 L.Ed.2d 29 (1964); Old Republic Insurance Co. v. Christian, 389 F.Supp. 335 (E.D.Tenn.1975); Metropolitan Life Insurance Co. v. Holding, 293 F.Supp. 854 (E.D.Va.1968); In re Trigg's Estate, 102 Ariz. 140, 426 P.2d 637 (1967); Brown's Administrator v. Brown, 308 Ky. 796, 215 S.W.2d 971 (1948); Matter of Willard's Estate, 93 N.M. 352, 600 P.2d 298 (1979); Estate of Smart v. Smart, 676 P.2d 1379 (Okl.App.1983). Damron v. Damron, 301 Ky. 636, 192 S.W.2d 741 (1945) held that Texas law, as the place of marriage, governed, but that no marriage had been contracted under that law. A similar case is Tatum v. Tatum, 241 F.2d 401 (9th Cir.1957).

79. Metropolitan Life Ins. Co. v. Chase, 294 F.2d 500 (3d Cir.1961) is the leading case, applying New Jersey law. See also Walker v. Yarbrough, 257 Ark. 300, 516 S.W.2d 390 (1974); Peirce v. Peirce, 379 Ill. 185, 39 N.E.2d 990 (1942) (dictum); Laikola v. Engineered Concrete, 277 N.W.2d 653 (Minn.1979); Winn v. Wiggins, 47 N.J.Super. 215, 135 A.2d 673 (1957) (dictum); Walker v.

Hildenbrand, 243 Or. 117, 410 P.2d 244 (1966); Matter of Marriage of Wharton, 55 Or.App. 564, 639 P.2d 652 (1982), review denied 293 Or. 146, 651 P.2d 143 (1982); Bridgman v. Stout, 5 Or.App. 558, 485 P.2d 1101 (1971); In re Vetas' Estate, 110 Utah 187, 170 P.2d 183 (1946). In the latter case the court relied upon the Utah statute. Goldin v. Goldin, 48 Md.App. 154, 426 A.2d 410 (1981) emphasizes the parties' intent in finding no marriage resulted from weekend visits to a common law marriage state.

The Uniform Marriage Evasion Act was construed to invalidate a common law marriage allegedly contracted in Texas by Wisconsin domiciliaries in In re Van Schaick's Estate, 256 Wis. 214, 40 N.W.2d 588 (1949).

80. 268 S.W.2d 22 (Ky.1954). A case following Kennedy is Vaughn v. Hufnagel, 473 S.W.2d 124 (Ky.1971), cert. denied 405 U.S. 1041, 92 S.Ct. 1313, 31 L.Ed.2d 582 (1972). The Kennedy case omits to cite the earlier case of Brown's Administrator v. Brown, 308 Ky. 796, 215 S.W.2d 971 (1948) which seems inconsistent with Kennedy. A case in agreement with Kennedy is In re Estate of Binger, 158 Neb. 444, 63 N.W.2d 784 (1954). In re Bivian's Estate, 98 N.M.App. 722, 652 P.2d 744 (1982), cert. quashed 98 N.M. 762, 652 P.2d 1213 (1982) held that a common law marriage had not resulted from business and pleasure trips to Texas and Colorado, where the parties had conducted themselves as husband and wife, although it also held that residence in state which recognizes common law marriage is not necessary for the contracting of such a marriage.

Vandever v. Industrial Commission of Arizona, 148 Ariz. 373, 714 P.2d 866 (App.1985) held that the law of the state in which the common law marriage was alleged to have occurred must determine whether it did in fact exist, and on that basis rejected a claim that the marriage occurred during a three-week visit to Colorado.

ing their Ohio visits. The court expressly disclaimed exclusive reliance on the law of the parties' domicile. But it held that the parties must prove they had an established place of abode outside the domicile, and that mere visits to the recognizing state were not enough. Only then, in the court's view, would evidence of habit and repute be available sufficient to meet objective standards of proof of common law marriage. In this instance the conflicts rule is based upon the relevant policy considerations. The objection usually advanced against common law marriage is that it leads to fraud and uncertainty in the most important of human relationships. Presumably this is the reason why Kentucky and other states have abolished it. But Kentucky says in this case, we will recognize such a marriage when contracted in another state, provided the parties establish a connection with the other state of a kind and duration which will minimize the evils of common law marriage. It is not enough that they made occasional visits to Ohio, since such visits would not furnish convincing evidence of marital cohabitation in Ohio. They must spend sufficient time there to give rise to the testimony of friends, neighbors, acquaintances that they had publicly assumed *in Ohio* the relationship of husband and wife. The evidence must relate to conduct and reputation originating in Ohio, not to conduct and reputation originating in Kentucky and carried on momentarily in Ohio. The result

of Kennedy v. Damron [81] has the defect of being uncertain, since no one can predict in advance how much of a stay in the recognizing state will be enough to produce a common law marriage. It has advantages which more than outweigh this defect, however, in placing the conflicts rule on a sensible policy footing. It avoids the unreality of an exclusive reliance on domicile, since many persons today spend long periods away from their domicile. At the same time it avoids the questions raised by the New York rule, such as, does a common law marriage arise when the parties pass through the recognizing state and spend one night there? [82] Or when they ride through on a train? Or when they fly over it in an airplane?

In closing this section, a word needs to be said about the merits and demerits of common law marriage. As has been shown, it seems to be an unpopular institution today. It is easy to find criticisms of it, not only in judicial opinions,[83] but in the writings of social scientists.[84] They say that common law marriage encourages fraud and vice, that it debases conventional marriage.[85] This depends upon the context in which the issue arises. In most instances in the past people drifted into common law marriage either because one of the parties persuaded the other that they could really be married in this fashion, or because the customs of their social class sanctioned this kind of union.[86] In such cases they had no contact with the law until

81. 268 S.W.2d 22 (Ky.1954).

82. Madewell v. United States, 84 F.Supp. 329 (E.D. Tenn.1949) upheld a common law marriage on the basis of a few days and nights spent together in Alabama, where the husband was stationed as a serviceman. On the other hand In re Keig's Estate, 59 Cal.App.2d 812, 140 P.2d 163 (1943) held that since the parties had just registered in a Nevada hotel when the man died, they had not lived together long enough to contract a common law marriage in Nevada.

83. See cases cited in note 47, supra, and McCoy v. District of Columbia, 256 A.2d 908 (D.C.App.1969); Jolley v. Jolley, 46 Ohio Misc. 40, 347 N.E.2d 557 (1975).

84. E.g., Baber, Marriage and the Family, 69–71 (2d ed. 1953); Folsom, The Family and Democratic Society, 468 (1943); Kephart, The Family, Society and the Individual, 415 (1961); Sait, New Horizons for the Family, 538 (1938); R. Williamson, Marriage and Family Relations, 289–290 (2d ed. 1972). Nimkoff, Marriage and the Fami-

ly, 592 (1947) lists common law marriage as an example of cultural lag.

Stein, Common-Law Marriage: Its History and Certain Contemporary Problems, 9 J.Fam.L. 271 (1969), attacks the institution of common law marriage on the ground that it creates uncertainty and gives the courts too much discretion in characterizing a given relationship as constituting marriage.

85. Groves, The Contemporary American Family, 540 (1947).

86. Nimkoff, Marriage and the Family, 219 (1947) and Sirjamaki, The American Family in the Twentieth Century, 69 (1953), both pointing to the prevalence of common law marriage among blacks and whites of lower economic classes. See also Flores Gonzalez v. Viuda De Gonzalez, 466 S.W.2d 839 (Tex.Civ.App.1971); Valeri, Informal Marriages and Other Curative Devices, 17 Howard L.Rev. 558 (1972); Foster, Indian and Common Law Marriages, 3 Am.Indian L.Rev. 83 (1975); Weyrauch, Informal Mar-

one of them died or a divorce action was brought, at which point the real issues were financial or property issues. If the courts continue to insist upon objective evidence that the parties have lived openly as man and wife for a substantial period, there will be no greater risk of fraud or imposition on the court here than in the trial of any other question of fact. The argument that common law marriage encourages fraud rests upon the false premise that the courts; using the established legal rules, will be unable to separate fraudulent from legitimate claims of marriage.

The assertion that common law marriage encourages vice is hardly worthy of serious regard in an age when sexual morality no longer occupies a prominent place in our scheme of values. But a more telling objection to common law marriage arises from this very fact. Today many people, both old and young, live together under circumstances which in some respects resemble marriage, but without a ceremony. Often, although they have no intention of marrying, they represent themselves to their friends as husband and wife and assume some of the benefits of marriage, such as filing a joint income tax return. The frequent result is that when the relationship breaks up and legal advice is sought by one of the parties, the attorney faces such an ambiguous state of facts that he is unable to respond with any assurance that the parties either were or were not married. The remedy for this difficulty is not abolition of common law marriage but a rigorous insistence by the courts upon proof of all of its elements. Ambiguity in the parties' conduct or doubt about their real intentions should be reason to reject a claim of common law marriage. Many cases already take this position, in particular requiring specific evidence of present agreement to be man and wife.[87]

As for debasing conventional marriage, there seems little risk that common law marriage will have this effect, so long as the traditional evidence of the relationship is required. When that is done, there is no ostensible difference between common law marriage and ceremonial marriage in the lives of the spouses. In fact we debase the institution of marriage when we place conclusive significance on the occurrence of a ceremony. When a woman has performed the obligations of a wife for thirty-five years and then is brutally deprived of all the financial benefits of marriage on the sole ground that the relationship was not signalized by some sort of a ceremony,[88] this debases marriage. It is far better in such cases to hold that the parties were married.

In short, most of the objections to common law marriage mistake its purpose. As a doctrine it has little or no effect at the outset of the parties' relationship. It comes into play after that relationship has existed for some time, for the purpose of vindicating the parties' marital expectations. There are other legal devices having the same purpose, but common law marriage plays an important part. Without it there would be more injustice and suffering in the world than there is with it. This is particularly true among those social and economic classes who have not accepted middle class standards of marriage. Certainly American marriage law should tolerate this much cultural diversity.

It is somewhat paradoxical that some courts, in the face of much prior history of hostility to common law marriage expressed in both statutes and judicial decisions, have now moved in the opposite direction, conferring the benefits of marriage upon persons who clearly were not married, and who had no intention of being married.[89] The impetus for this movement has come from some law review articles [90] and from the celebrated case

riage and Common Law Marriage, in Slovenko, Sexual Behavior and the Law, 297 (1965); O. Lewis, Five Families: Mexican Case Study in the Culture of Poverty (1959), and The Children of Sanchez (1961); M. Harrington, The Other America (1963); Borah and Cook, Marriage and Legitimacy in Mexican Culture: Mexico and California, 54 Cal.L.Rev. 946 (1966).

87. See note 31, supra.

88. As in Seagriff v. Seagriff, 21 Misc.2d 604, 195 N.Y.S.2d 718 (Dom.Rel.Ct.1960).

89. See the discussion in § 2.1, supra, at note 37.

90. E.g., Bruch, Property Rights of De Facto Spouses, Including Thoughts on the Value of Homemakers' Ser-

of Marvin v. Marvin.[91] At the end of the opinion in that case the court suggested that the plaintiff might recover a part of the property standing in the defendant's name even in the absence of proof of an agreement. The court's language is far from lucid, referring to "an implied contract or implied agreement of partnership or joint venture", or "some other tacit understanding between the parties" at one point, and to constructive trust, or resulting trust, or a quantum meruit claim for the value of household services less the value of support received, at another point. In a footnote the court also left open the possibility that additional equitable remedies might evolve for the benefit of the parties to such non-marital relationships. It is hard to know whether the court was still talking of actual agreement in this part of the opinion, or was saying that some of the financial benefits of marriage might be legally enforceable without agreement by persons living together in some undefined relationship.

It is a well documented fact that men and women are now living together outside wedlock in greater numbers than ever before.[92] This has clearly had an effect upon the courts, leading some of them to say that such relationships can no longer be labeled "meretricious" as would have been the case twenty or thirty years ago.[93] Notwithstanding the greater prevalence of such relationships,

however, cases since Marvin v. Marvin (and some before that case) have taken differing positions on whether they should be legally recognized. Some of the uncertainty is due to the vagueness or ambiguity of the reasoning in the Marvin opinion. It follows from this that if non-marital relationships are to be recognized by the law, no one can predict in advance which relationships will be recognized or to what extent they will be recognized. There is a multitude of legal questions which depend upon the existence of marriage for their answer. Rights to support, alimony, division of property, inheritance, to sue for wrongful death, to claim workmen's compensation, social security, to immigrate into the United States, to file joint tax returns and many others have traditionally been dependent upon the proof of marriage. Are any of these or all of them to be dependent also upon the fact that a man and a woman have lived together without marrying for a greater or lesser period, under a wide variety of circumstances? If Marvin is followed, no one can answer these questions until an enormous amount of litigation has occurred. For some such reasons it is not surprising that although some courts have been willing to confer some of the benefits of marriage upon unmarried couples,[94] no court has held that all such benefits will be conferred, and some have

vices, 10 Fam.L.Q. 101 (1976); Note, Common Law Marriage and Unmarried Cohabitation: An Old Solution to a New Problem, 39 U.Pitt.L.Rev. 579 (1978); Casad, Unmarried Couples and Unjust Enrichment: From Status to Contract and Back Again? 77 Mich.L.Rev. 47 (1978).

91. 18 Cal.3d 660, 134 Cal.Rptr. 815, 557 P.2d 106 (1976).

92. Bureau of Census, U.S. Dep't of Commerce, Current Population Reports, Marital Status and Living Arrangements, Series P–20, No. 306, at pp. 4, 5, Table F (1977).

93. Cord v. Gibb, 219 Va. 1019, 254 S.E.2d 71 (1979) (living with a person of the opposite sex out of wedlock is not ground to deny admission to the bar).

94. Markham v. Colonial Mortge. Serv. Co., Associates Inc., 605 F.2d 566 (D.C.Cir.1979) (parties living together are entitled to have their incomes aggregated for purposes of obtaining a mortgage loan, as if they were married, under the Equal Credit Opportunity Act); McCullon v. McCullon, 96 Misc.2d 962, 410 N.Y.S.2d 226 (1978); McCullon v. McCullon, 96 Misc.2d 962, 410 N.Y.S.2d 226 (1978) (court found a common law marriage,

but said that even if there were none, a woman who lived with a man out of wedlock for twenty-eight years could recover temporary alimony when the relationship ended); Beal v. Beal, 282 Or. 115, 577 P.2d 507 (1978), 58 Ore.L. Rev. 245 (1979) (property acquired while the parties lived together divided on the basis of implicit intent, without express contract); Omer v. Omer, 11 Wash.App. 386, 523 P.2d 957 (1974) (court divides property between unmarried couple on a constructive trust theory on the ground that their intent was to share property). Kozlowski v. Kozlowski, 80 N.J. 378, 403 A.2d 902 (1979) enforced a contract for support between unmarried persons living together, but a dissenting judge would have gone further and held that other equitable remedies should be available to the parties even in the absence of contract. For cases dealing with compensation for services between unmarried persons living together, see Annots. 94 A.L.R.3d 552 (1979) and 92 A.L.R.3d 726 (1979).

The remand in the Marvin case resulted in an award to the plaintiff of $104,000 for her rehabilitation, resembling the sort of alimony which a wife might receive. Marvin v. Marvin, 5 Fam.L.Rep. 3077 (1979).

refused to recognize the relationship for any purpose.[95]

This is one legal problem that does not seem amenable to statutory solution. It is hard to imagine a statute which could satisfactorily define the sort of non-marital relationships which ought to be recognized and which could distinguish from them the short term or ephemeral relationships which ought not to have the same legal consequences as marriage. Whatever one thinks of marriage in the conventional sense, it does have the great virtue for administration of the law that it provides a reasonably workable basis for allocating rights and duties.

 WESTLAW REFERENCES

di common law marriage
sy("common law marriage" /s recogni!)
sy,di(common-law /s marriage /s impediment)
di(putative /2 marriage)

---

§ 2.5 Proxy Marriages [1]

Marriage by proxy is a legal institution of variable importance. During times of war it has proved useful to enable men who are away in the services to marry, and often to legitimate children, when they could not contract a valid marriage in any other way.[2] In more normal times, it is seldom used.

For the purposes of this discussion proxy marriage is defined as a marriage contracted or celebrated through agents acting on behalf of one or both parties.[3] In most of the proxy marriages which have reached the courts there has been a civil or religious ceremony with a duly authorized agent participating in the place of one of the spouses,[4] but non-ceremonial or common law marriage might be attempted in the same fashion, with the agreement of marriage being executed by an agent for one of the spouses. Marriages contracted in this way, at least where a ceremony was performed, were recognized as valid in England until the eighteenth century.[5] They are still recognized by some churches,[6] and by many civil law countries.[7] Whether proxy marriages became a part of American common law by virtue of the English experience is an interesting question, but one which has become academic by the enactment of exten-

---

95. Hager v. Hager, 553 P.2d 919 (Alaska 1976) (property acquired before marriage, while the parties lived together may not on that ground be divided on divorce, but spouse may be awarded a share of it if the award is "not clearly unjust"); McCall v. Frampton, 99 Misc.2d 159, 415 N.Y.S.2d 752 (1979) (refuses to impose a constructive trust on land acquired while the parties lived together, rejecting the McCullon case, cited supra, note 94); Grishman v. Grishman, 407 A.2d 9 (Me.1979) (property acquired before marriage, while the parties were living together, may not be considered marital property on divorce); Hewitt v. Hewitt, 77 Ill.2d 49, 31 Ill.Dec. 827, 394 N.E.2d 1204 (1979) (rejects a claim that property accumulated while parties lived together out of wedlock should be divided between them on the basis of some sort of implied contract theory).

§ 2.5

1. For an excellent discussion of proxy marriage, see Note, 55 Yale L.J. 735 (1946). Other general discussions may be found in Howery, Marriage By Proxy and Other Informal Marriages, 13 U.Kan.City L.Rev. 48 (1944); Carter, Proxy Marriages, 35 Can.Bar Rev. 1195 (1957); Lorenzen, Marriage By Proxy and the Conflict of Laws, 32 Harv.L.Rev. 473 (1919).

2. Note, 55 Yale L.J. 735, 736 (1946). During World War II Minnesota had a statute expressly authorizing proxy marriages during the war, upon proof that the woman was pregnant. See M.S.A. § 517.09. West Supp. 1984.

3. Howery, Marriage by Proxy and Other Informal Marriages, 13 U.Kan.City L.Rev. 48 (1944). The term "absentee marriage" is sometimes used to include proxy marriages. It seems to mean a marriage contracted by parties who are in different places but without the aid of an agent or proxy, as for example by mail or over the long distance telephone. Such marriages raise the same issues of validity, either as ceremonial or common law marriages as do proxy marriages. An absentee marriage was upheld as a valid common law marriage in Great Northern Ry. v. Johnson, 166 C.C.A. 181, 254 Fed. 683 (1918).

4. For this reason it is erroneous to refer to proxy marriages as informal marriages. Usually they are contracted with all the formalities of the regular ceremonial marriage.

5. Swinburne, Treatise on Spousals, 162–163 (1686); Lorenzen, Marriage by Proxy and the Conflict of Laws, 32 Harv.L.Rev. 473, 481 (1919).

6. Lorenzen, op. cit. supra note 4 at 474–481.

7. The most important of these for American purposes is Mexico. See Stern, Marriages by Proxy in Mexico, 19 So.Cal.L.Rev. 109 (1945), and The Morris Plan Company of California v. Converse, 15 Cal.App.2d 399, 93 Cal.Rptr. 103 (1971), which found that proxy marriages are not valid under the law of two Mexican states, Baja California and Tlaxcala.

sive statutory regulations governing the entry into marriage.[8]

There is remarkably little case authority on the validity of proxy marriages contracted in American states. Such marriages may be upheld either as valid ceremonial marriages, if they comply with the statutes, or as valid common law marriages if such marriages are recognized in the jurisdiction and if the requirements for common law marriage are met. The obstacle which usually prevents proxy marriages from qualifying as valid ceremonial marriages is the construction placed upon the statutes requiring both parties to be present in person, either at the time of obtaining the license or at the ceremony.[9] But many statutes are not explicit as to this requirement, merely stating that the parties must obtain a license and then must have the marriage solemnized by a named religious or civil official. The form of the ceremony is not usually prescribed. Such a statute might very well be construed to allow proxy marriages, and in one case it has been.[10] This result does not seem to violate any of the policies underlying such statutes. The information required by the licensing statute is provided, there is a ceremony with the accompanying notoriety and public record, and there is no opportunity for fraudulent claims. The only substantial objection seems to lie in the fact that the power of attorney authorizing the proxy to act is revocable under the

usual agency principles, without notice either to the other party or to the proxy himself, thus creating some risk of uncertainty whether the marriage is valid.[11] It is doubtful, however, whether this is a risk of any appreciable magnitude, since no reported case has been found in which it was even contended that revocation had occurred. None the less the prevailing opinion among attorneys general in the various states is that proxy marriages fail to meet the statutory requirements for valid ceremonial marriages.[12]

In states which recognize common law marriage there is some possibility that proxy marriages can be held valid as common law marriages. At least one case, U.S. v. Layton,[13] has so held. The difficulty with this result is that by the law of most, though perhaps not all, states, one of the essentials for a valid common law marriage is open and well known marital cohabitation between the parties.[14] If the parties to the proxy marriage later do live together as husband and wife, then this requirement is met, and they have a valid common law marriage. In most instances, however, they do not live together. In fact they choose to be married by proxy because they are physically separated and are thus unable to celebrate the marriage in the normal way. If this is the case, they cannot meet the cohabitation requirement, and by the great weight of authority they do not have a valid common law marriage.[15] It could be argued that the

8. For a discussion of the various forms of statute see section 2.3, supra.

9. Respole v. Respole, 70 N.E.2d 465 (Ohio Com.Pl. 1946) (applying West Virginia law). The views of many attorneys general as to the laws of their states on this point are cited in Howery, Marriage by Proxy and Other Informal Marriages, 13 U.Kan.City L.Rev. 48 (1944). The author indicates that the states of Idaho, New Hampshire, New Mexico, North Dakota, Pennsylvania and Texas would uphold proxy marriages contracted within their boundaries. See also Annot., 170 A.L.R. 947 (1947).

The Uniform Marriage and Divorce Act § 206 authorizes proxy marriages and at least one state has enacted the uniform provision. Mont.Rev.Code Ann. § 40–1–301(2) (1983).

10. Barrons v. United States, 191 F.2d 92 (9th Cir. 1951) (applying Nevada law). State v. Anderson, 239 Or. 200, 396 P.2d 558 (1964) held a proxy marriage sufficiently valid to allow the husband to invoke the husband-wife privilege against testifying. Torres v. Torres, 144 N.J.

Super. 540, 366 A.2d 713 (1976) held a proxy marriage valid where it was performed in Cuba in accordance with Cuban law. See also Matter of Marriage of Holemar, 27 Or.App. 613, 557 P.2d 38 (1976).

11. This possibility is referred to in Lorenzen, Marriage by Proxy and the Conflict of Laws, 32 Harv.L.Rev. 473, 482–3 (1919), and in Apt v. Apt [1948] P. 83, 35 Can. B.Rev. 1195 (1957). In the Apt case this possibility did not prevent the English court from recognizing a proxy marriage contracted in Argentina.

12. Howery, Marriage by Proxy and Other Informal Marriages, 13 U.Kan.City L.Rev. 48 (1944). One may be skeptical whether the courts of these states would all reach the result indicated by the attorneys general.

13. 68 F.Supp. 247 (S.D.Fla.1946), 33 Corn.L.Q. 129 (1947) (applying Florida law).

14. See section 2.4, supra, at notes 23, 24, 25.

15. See section 2.4, supra at notes 23, 24.

requirement of marital cohabitation, being insisted upon for the purpose of preventing fraudulent marriage claims, could be dispensed with when the proxy marriage is contracted with full ceremony. In such a case there is no danger of fraud and thus no need of further proof that the parties intend a bona fide marriage. No case seems to have made this point, although the Layton case did hold that a proxy marriage was valid without any discussion of the need for subsequent cohabitation.

As a matter of policy, persuasive arguments support the recognition of proxy marriages. They provide a useful means of vindicating the claims of women and children in the circumstances so often existing during wars or national emergencies when a love affair results in pregnancy and the man's army duties in distant parts make the ordinary ceremonial marriage impossible. The proxy marriage then can give the woman and child both status and financial protection. The objections raised to informal marriages do not apply to proxy marriages contracted ceremonially, as most of them seem to be.

Some support for the position that proxy marriages do not conflict with sound public policy may be drawn from the conflict of laws cases. These, virtually without exception, hold that if a proxy marriage is celebrated in a country whose law validates such marriages, other states, such as the state of the domicile of one of the parties, will recognize

the marriage.[16] This result is not affected by the fact that one of the parties was at all times domiciled in the state of the forum and never lived in the state where the marriage was performed. In the well known case of Hardin v. Davis [17] a proxy marriage contracted in Mexico was held valid in Ohio notwithstanding the fact that neither party had ever been domiciled in Mexico. The court found that such a marriage was valid by the law of Mexico, although on this point it may have been mistaken, Mexican law apparently validating such marriages only where one spouse has a Mexican domicile.[18] But if the marriage is valid where contracted, it will be valid elsewhere, on the theory that the issue is merely one of form, as to which the lex loci is the governing law. The English case of Apt v. Apt [19] is the leading authority for this position, saying that there is no English public policy which would forbid the recognition of a proxy marriage performed in Argentina and that such marriages are widely accepted in Christian countries.

 **WESTLAW REFERENCES**

marri! marry! marital /2 proxy

§ 2.6 Successive Marriages

The starting point for a discussion of successive marriages is the Christian precept of monogamy. It is laid down as an elementary principle, both by statute [1] and case law,[2] that

---

16. See the cases collected in Annot., 170 A.L.R. 947, 949 (1947). The leading cases on this point are Ex parte Suzanna, 295 Fed. 713 (D.Mass.1924); In re Valente's Will, 18 Misc.2d 701, 188 N.Y.S.2d 732 (Surr.Ct.1959); Ferraro v. Ferraro, 192 Misc. 484, 77 N.Y.S.2d 246 (Dom. Rel.Ct.1948); Hardin v. Davis, 16 Ohio Supp. 19 (Ohio Com.Pl.1945); Ponticelli v. Ponticelli, L.R. [1958] P. 204; Apt v. Apt [1948] P. 83, 35 Can.B.Rev. 1195 (1957).

The Morris Plan Company of California v. Converse, 15 Cal.App.3d 399, 93 Cal.Rptr. 103 (1971) approved the doctrine of lex loci for the validity of proxy marriages, and, finding that the marriage contracted in Mexico was invalid there, held it invalid in California also. The case contains some suggestion that even if the lex loci principle were not applied, the proxy marriage would not be recognized in California, since it did not comply with licensing and solemnization requirements of the California statutes.

17. 16 Ohio Supp. 19 (Ohio Com.Pl.1945).

18. Stern, Marriages By Proxy in Mexico, 19 So.Cal.L. Rev. 109 (1945).

19. [1948] P. 83, 35 Can.B.Rev. 1195 (1957).

§ 2.6

1. E.g., Alaska Stat. § 25.05.021 (1983); West's Ann Cal.Civ.Code § 4401 (1983); Colo.Rev.Stat. § 14–2–110 (1973); D.C.Code 1981, § 30–101; Official Ga.Code Ann. § 53–104 (1982); Iowa Code Ann. § 595.19 (1981); Mass. Gen.Laws Ann. ch. 207, § 4 (1981); Mich.C.L.A. § 25.5 (1984); Minn.Stat.Ann. § 517.03 (1984); N.J.Stat.Ann. § 2A:34–1 (Supp.1984); N.Y.–McKinney's Dom.Rel.L. § 6 (1977); Ohio Rev. § 3101.01 (1980); V.T.C.A., Fam.Code § 2.22 (1975); W.Va.Code, § 48–2–1 (1984); Wis.Stat.Ann. § 765.03 (West 1981). See also Uniform Marriage and Divorce Act § 207, 9A Uniform L.Ann. 108 (1979). Mississippi has an interesting statute making it a crime to teach polygamy. Miss.Code Ann.1973, § 97–29–43.

2. E.g., Castor v. United States 174 F.2d 481 (8th Cir. 1949), cert. denied 338 U.S. 836, 70 S.Ct. 45, 94 L.Ed. 511 (1949); Sparling v. Industrial Commission, 48 Ill.2d 332, 270 N.E.2d 411 (1971); Beaudin v. Suarez, 365 Mich. 534, 113 N.W.2d 818 (1962) (the text rule applies even though the first marriage was a common law marriage and the

a person may at any time have but a single spouse. A marriage is wholly null and void if contracted when either party already has a spouse living and undivorced.[3] Such a purported marriage needs no decree to establish its invalidity.[4] It is without legal force even though it may have been contracted in the bona fide and reasonable belief that both parties were eligible to marry.[5] All this is summed up in the label "void marriage" which is applied to such attempts at contracting bigamous or polygamous marriages.[6]

Having said this, however, it should be emphasized that we do not apply these rules with their full severity in all cases. The legal qualifications on the principle of monogamy are described in various other sections of this work. They include the doctrine of estoppel against attack upon an admittedly invalid decree of divorce;[7] the presumption that the latest marriage is valid;[8] the Sherrer rule by which an invalid divorce is immune to attack by the parties;[9] the Estin and Vanderbilt rules by which a man may be required to

support a woman no longer his wife;[10] the rule which prevails in some jurisdictions that the doctrines of unclean hands or in pari delicto will bar a suit for annulment;[11] and the Enoch Arden statutes described below.[12] All of them have the purpose of mitigating the hardships caused by a rigid insistence upon monogamy.

Violations of the monogamous principle are not only said under certain circumstances to be ineffectual to create legal rights and duties, but they are also criminal. The felony of bigamy is committed when an attempt is made to contract a second marriage while a valid first marriage is still in existence.[13] The offense is punishable even though committed under the influence of religious belief.[14] In fact in some jurisdictions the crime of bigamy is considered so offensive to morality that the defendant may be found guilty notwithstanding a perfectly innocent intent, as for example where he contracts the second marriage in the bona fide belief that the first marriage had ended by death or divorce.[15] Some of the

second a ceremonial marriage); Heffner v. Heffner, 23 Pa. 104 (1854); Commonwealth ex rel. Knode v. Knode, 149 Pa.Super. 563, 27 A.2d 536 (1942). See also Riddlesden v. Wogan, Trin. 43 Eliz.Roll 145, 78 Eng.Rep. 1084 (1601).

3. Davis v. Green, 91 N.J.Eq. 17, 108 A. 772 (1919); Day v. Day, 216 S.C. 334, 58 S.E.2d 83 (1950). Cases denying workmen's compensation to the bigamous wife are collected in Annot., 80 A.L.R. 1425 (1932). New York allows the first spouse to sue for annulment of a subsequent bigamous marriage. N.Y.–McKinney's Dom.Rel.L. § 140(a) (1977), and Sacks v. Sacks, 47 Misc.2d 1050, 263 N.Y.S.2d 891 (1965).

4. Townsend v. Morgan, 192 Md. 168, 63 A.2d 743 (1949).

5. Johnson v. Johnson, 245 Ala. 145, 16 So.2d 401 (1944) (collecting many other cases); Townsend v. Morgan, 192 Md. 168, 63 A.2d 743 (1949); Price v. Price, 124 N.Y. 589, 27 N.E. 383 (1891); Simpson v. Simpson, 404 Pa. 247, 172 A.2d 168 (1961).

6. Some of the difficulties created by referring to void marriages will be discussed in the section dealing with the consequences of annulment, infra, section 3.6. It is sufficient at this point to say that even a void marriage may under some circumstances have legal consequences.

7. Section 12.3, Practitioner's Edition.

8. Section 2.7, infra.

9. Section 12.2, infra.

10. Section 12.4, infra.

11. Section 3.3, Practitioner's Edition.

12. Infra, this section, at notes 34–40.

13. E.g., West's Ann.Cal.Penal Code § 281 (1970) defines the offense: "Every person having a husband or wife living, who marries any other person * * * is guilty of bigamy". It is not necessary under some statutes that the parties live together in the bigamous relationship, but it is sufficient that they attempted to contract the forbidden marriage. See Beggs v. State, 55 Ala. 108 (1876) and State v. Najjar, 2 N.J.Super. 208, 63 A.2d 807 (1949), affirmed 2 N.J. 208, 66 A.2d 37 (1949). Under other statutes bigamous cohabitation may also constitute a crime. E.g., Tenn.Code Ann. § 39–4–301 (1982). For general discussions of bigamy see R. Perkins, Criminal Law 456–459 (3d ed. 1982); Clark and Marshall, Crimes 786–790 (7th ed. 1967); Model Penal Code 220–230 (Tent. Draft No. 4, 1955).

14. Reynolds v. United States, 98 U.S. (8 Otto) 145, 25 L.Ed. 244 (1878); Davis v. Beason, 133 U.S. 333, 10 S.Ct. 299, 33 L.Ed. 637 (1890); Long v. State, 192 Ind. 524, 137 N.E. 49 (1922). Other cases are cited in Annot., 24 A.L.R. 1237 (1932). See also Davis, Plural Marriage and Religious Freedom: The Impact of Reynolds v. United States, 15 Ariz.L.Rev. 287 (1973).

15. Many cases are collected in Annot., 56 A.L.R.2d 915 (1957). Perhaps the most celebrated such cases are Williams v. North Carolina, I, 317 U.S. 287, 63 S.Ct. 207, 87 L.Ed. 279 (1942) and Williams v. North Carolina, II, 325 U.S. 226, 65 S.Ct. 1092, 89 L.Ed. 1577 (1945), in the second of which the parties' bigamy conviction was affirmed in spite of the fact that no experienced divorce lawyer would have been able to advise them with certainty whether their marriage was bigamous or not, since the applicable constitutional principles were in great confusion.

more enlightened courts today require a guilty intent to be proved as an element of the crime, however.[16]

Most of the persons committing this crime do not attempt to maintain more than one family at one time. They contract successive marriages either out of emotional dependence, neurotically searching for the ideal mate, or as a means of swindling money from gullible wives.[17] The less frequent form of bigamy, or as it is more commonly called, polygamy, occurs when a man marries and lives with several wives, and their children) at one time.[18] Instances of this in the United States have chiefly been connected with the various forms of the Mormon religion.[19] Mormonism as originally practiced encouraged men to take more than one wife. This was of course repugnant to Christian morality [20] and statutes were passed imposing criminal penalties. In Reynolds v. U.S.[21] the Supreme Court of the United States upheld the constitutionality of such statutes against the contention that they interfered with the free exercise of religion. The case makes an unsatisfactory distinction between religious beliefs, which are protected by the Constitution, and religious practices which are not. The true rationale for the decision is that some marriage

customs are so at variance with widely accepted moral precepts that they will not be tolerated whether or not they are enjoined by religious teachings. Polygamy is such a custom, one which is odious to English and American people.

The enforcement of criminal statutes in the early days of Mormon settlement did cause the abandonment of polygamy by the main body of the church, but some fundamentalist Mormon sects still persist in maintaining polygamous families. The most recent well known episode occurred in Short Creek, Arizona, a small community on the Utah-Arizona border.[22] In 1953 the Arizona authorities investigated accounts of polygamy at Short Creek. More than one hundred police were sent to the small town to deal with what the governor of Arizona called an "insurrection," and "this foulest of conspiracies." [23] Twenty or thirty of the men were convicted on pleas of guilty of conspiracy to violate the state's sex offense laws. Children from the polygamous families were removed from their parents and cared for by the state, on the ground that they had been subjected to inadequate care and immoral teaching, but they had to be returned to their parents when the expense of their care became burdensome. In

---

16. People v. Vogel, 46 Cal.2d 798, 299 P.2d 850 (1956), per Traynor, J. But it is not a defense that the defendant acted on rumor, without making a bona fide effort to discover whether his first wife had obtained a divorce, White v. State, 157 Tenn. 446, 9 S.W.2d 702 (1928), or that he relied on a Mexican mail order divorce, State v. De Meo, 20 N.J. 1, 118 A.2d 1 (1955).

17. Karpman, The Sexual Offender and His Offenses, 131 (1954).

18. Webster's Third New International Dictionary, 1758 (1961). The more specific term to describe the family composed of one husband and two or more wives is polygyny. See Webster's Third New International Dictionary, 1758 (1961). Some statutes treat bigamy and polygamy as synonymous. E.g. Mich.C.L.A. §§ 28.694 to 28.696 (1982).

19. A brief account of this may be found in Late Corporation of the Church of Jesus Christ of Latter-Day Saints v. United States, 136 U.S. 1, 10 S.Ct. 792, 34 L.Ed. 478 (1890). Mormon doctrine is discussed in Hilton v. Roylance, 25 Utah 129, 69 P. 660 (1902). The story is more fully told in Linford, The Mormons and the Law: The Polygamy Cases, 9 Utah L.Rev. 308, 543 (1964). See also West, The Kingdom of the Saints (1957).

Discussion of recent developments in plural marriage law in other countries of the world, particularly in Africa

and Islamic countries, may be found in Hartley, Polygamy and Social Policy, 32 Mod.L.Rev. 155 (1969), and in Zabel, Hyde v. Hyde in Africa: A Comparative Study of the Law of Marriage in the Sudan and Nigeria, 1969 Utah L.Rev. 22, 1970 Utah L.Rev. 526.

20. The repugnance and hostility to polygamy which are felt in Anglo-American countries are forcefully expressed by the Supreme Court in Reynolds v. United States, 98 U.S. (8 Otto) 145, 25 L.Ed. 244 (1878), and Davis v. Beason, 133 U.S. 333, 10 S.Ct. 299, 33 L.Ed. 637 (1890).

21. 98 U.S. (8 Otto) 145, 25 L.Ed. 244 (1878). See also Potter v. Murray City, 585 F.Supp. 1126 (D.Utah 1984).

22. This account of the Short Creek events in summarized from the Hearings Before the Subcommittee to Investigate Juvenile Delinquency of the Committee on the Judiciary of the U.S. Senate, 84th Cong., 1st Sess., pursuant to S.Res. 62 (1955).

Even more recently reports have indicated that polygamy continues to spread in Short Creek, now called Colorado City, and in other parts of Utah, Arizona and Idaho, without much opposition from law enforcement authorities. New York Times, October 9, 1977, page 1, col. 1.

23. Id. at pages 13–16.

spite of the governor's inflammatory effort to arouse public opinion, and of the successful prosecutions, the net effect of the Short Creek proceedings seems to have been slight. The number of persons continuing to practice polygamy under the influence of religious doctrine remains substantial by some accounts, although accurate figures are obviously not available. These people continue to be firmly convinced of the rightness of their beliefs. Prosecutions are difficult, because evidence is not easy to collect [24] and because polygamous families may be scattered through more than one state. It therefore appears that a certain (though relatively insignificant) amount of polygamy is to remain a permanent part of the American scene regardless of the moral indignation with which it is viewed by the powers that be. The most harmful consequence of this is the exploitation, both sexual and economic, of women and children which seems to be an inseparable feature of polygamy.

Another interesting problem created by our strict insistence upon monogamy is that of Enoch Arden.[25] Now that the world is shrinking and governments keep more closely in touch with every citizen, this problem may trouble the law less, but it still seems occasionally to arise. The classic case is Glass v. Glass.[26] The parties were married, lived together two months and the husband then went off on a whaling voyage. The wife did not hear from him or of him for ten years. At the end of that time, believing with some reason that he was dead, she remarried. Her first husband was not dead, however, and in

fact when he lost touch with his first wife he also remarried. The wife's second husband apparently tired of the marriage and sued to annul it when he found the first husband was still alive. The court held, as it had to under the Massachusetts statute and the existing case law, that the wife's second marriage was void notwithstanding her good faith and the fact that this marriage had produced children. Since the marriage was void, a decree of nullity had to be granted. This result, harsh as it seems, is unavoidable in the absence of curative statute because of the rule already referred to [27] that under our law a person may have only one spouse at a time.

From an early date the law did provide a defense to bigamy prosecutions when second marriages were contracted in circumstances like those in Glass v. Glass.[28] This was a statute of James I which provided that a person who remarried seven years after the disappearance of his first spouse and with no knowledge that the first spouse was alive would not be guilty of bigamy.[29] Many American states have adopted similar statutes, some of them reducing the period to five years or less.[30]

It is settled, however, that these statutes are limited in their effect to the criminal charge of bigamy. They do not validate the second marriage if it turns out that the first husband or wife is alive after all.[31] They are therefore of only partial help to the spouse who is deserted and wishes to remarry.

---

24. See Miles v. United States, 103 U.S. (93 Otto) 304, 26 L.Ed. 481 (1880), and Wright v. State, 198 Md. 163, 81 A.2d 602 (1951), the latter case setting up "trigamy" as a defense to bigamy.

25. See Tennyson's famous poem telling the story of the sailor who returned from ten years' shipwreck to find his wife married to another, and who nobly refrained from breaking in on their contentment. Poems of Tennyson, 318 (Riverside ed., Jerome H. Buckley ed. 1958). For a contemporary version of the Enoch Arden story, See L. Compton-Burnet, A Father and His Fate (1957). The law has naturally come to refer to cases of second marriage following a long unexplained absence of the first husband as Enoch Arden cases. See Feit, The Enoch Arden: A Problem of Family Law, 6 Bklyn.L.Rev. 423 (1937).

26. 114 Mass. 563 (1874). Similar cases with similar results include Townsend v. Morgan, 192 Md. 168, 63

A.2d 743 (1949) (husband waited nine years after separating from first wife, yet husband granted an annulment of the second marriage); Price v. Price, 124 N.Y. 589, 27 N.E. 383 (1891); Anonymous v. Anonymous, 186 Misc. 772, 62 N.Y.S.2d 130 (1946).

27. Supra, notes 1–4.

28. 114 Mass. 563 (1874).

29. 1 James I, ch. 11, § 2 (1603).

30. E.g., West's Ann.Cal.Penal Code § 282 (1970) (five years); Del.Code tit. 11, § 1002 (1979) (seven years); West's Fla.Stat.Ann. § 826.02 (1976) (three years); Ill.–S.H.A. ch. 38, § 11–12 (Supp.1984) (five years); Mass.Gen. L.Ann. ch. 272, § 15 (1980) (seven years).

31. Townsend v. Morgan, 192 Md. 168, 63 A.2d 743 (1949); Price v. Price, 124 N.Y. 589, 27 N.E. 383 (1891).

One remedy for some of the Enoch Arden cases is an action for divorce on the ground of desertion. But the plaintiff in many cases may be unable to prove that the other spouse deserted him.[32] In Glass v. Glass,[33] for example, the husband did not voluntarily and unjustifiably absent himself from home. And of course in New York, where many of these cases arose desertion was not a ground for divorce.

Several states, including New York, have enacted statutes to solve the Enoch Arden problem. The New York statute provides that a court may dissolve a marriage when it is proved that the spouse has absented himself for five successive years without being known to be alive, that the petitioner believes the spouse to be dead, and that a diligent search has been made and no evidence found that the absent spouse is alive.[34] This statute really authorizes divorce on the ground of a five-year unexplained absence with certain

additional safeguards. After obtaining such a dissolution the deserted spouse is free to remarry.[35] But a second marriage contracted without obtaining dissolution of the first in accordance with the statute will be held invalid if the first spouse proves still to be alive.[36] On the whole the New York statute is useful, although it does not cover all cases of unexplained absence.[37] Other states have tried to solve the problem in various ways.[38] The Pennsylvania statute is the latest and best considered. It provides that when the spouse of an applicant for a marriage license has disappeared or has been absent without being heard of after diligent inquiry, the appropriate court may make a finding that the absentee is dead, after notice by publication.[39] A presumption of death from seven years' absence is created, but a finding of death may be based upon absence of lesser duration. If, after such a finding is made and license issued, the first spouse returns, the second mar-

---

32. See section 12.3, Practitioner's Edition, for a discussion of what must be proved for a divorce based on desertion.

33. 114 Mass. 563 (1874).

34. N.Y.–McKinney's Dom.Rel.L. §§ 220, 221 (1964 and Supp. 1975–1976). Cases under the statute are discussed in Felt, The Enoch Arden: A Problem of Family Law, 6 Bklyn.L.Rev. 423 (1937).

35. Anonymous v. Anonymous, 186 Misc. 772, 62 N.Y.S.2d 130 (1946) (dictum). But if the first wife returns, she may be able to assert claims for support, property or the custody of children notwithstanding the § 220 proceeding, where the service in that proceeding was by publication, since such service does not cut off her in personam rights. See Stanton v. Stanton, 193 Misc. 140, 82 N.Y.S.2d 839 (1948). This is another example of the courts' refusal to adhere strictly to monogamy, the husband in such a case being required to support two "wives".

36. Anonymous v. Anonymous, 186 Misc. 772, 62 N.Y.S.2d 130 (1946). See also Hatfield v. United States, 127 F.2d 575 (2d Cir.1942); Brown v. Brown, 51 Misc.2d 839, 274 N.Y.S.2d 484 (1966).

37. Thus the plaintiff must make a bona fide search for the absent spouse before bringing a § 220 proceeding, mere casual inquiries not being sufficient. Application of Delaney, 7 Misc.2d 316, 164 N.Y.S.2d 170 (1957). The cases are in conflict as to whether the proceeding may be used when the absence may be explained on the ground that the absent spouse just deserted the other spouse rather than on the ground of death. Compare Matter of Entenman, 122 Misc. 441, 204 N.Y.S. 100 (1924), with Rahill v. Rahill, 249 App.Div. 753, 291 N.Y.S. 967 (2d Dep't 1936); Lane v. Lane, 232 App.Div. 690, 247 N.Y.S.

577 (2d Dep't 1931); and In re Heilweil, 232 App.Div. 610, 250 N.Y.S. 670 (1st Dep't 1931), 9 N.Y.U.L.Q.Rev. 101 (1931). The plaintiff must be a resident of New York to bring the suit, though the statute does not require this. Dodge v. Campbell, 223 App.Div. 471, 228 N.Y.S. 618 (3d Dep't 1928).

38. The most common statutory provision authorizes remarriage without a legal proceeding when the spouse has been absent and not known to be living for a specified time, usually five years. E.g., Ark.Stat. § 55–109 (1971); West's Ann.Cal.Civ.Code § 4401 (1970); N.D.Cent.Code § 14–03–06 (1981); S.C.Code 1977, § 20–1–80; Tenn.Code Ann. § 36–3–102 (1984). The Uniform Marriage and Divorce Act contains no provision dealing with the Enoch Arden problem. Many of these statutes contain provisions which may prevent them from applying to cases in which a spouse may rely on them. For example the Arkansas statute has been construed not to permit the second marriage when the parties to the first marriage separated by mutual consent, since one did not then "abandon" the other as the statute requires. Watson v. Palmer, 219 Ark. 178, 240 S.W.2d 875 (1951); Cole v. Cole, 249 Ark. 824, 462 S.W.2d 213 (1971). And under most, if not all of this type of statute, if the first spouse turns up after the second marriage, the second marriage may be invalid. See, e.g., West's Ann.Cal.Civ.Code § 4425 (1970); and Day v. Day, 216 S.C. 334, 58 S.E.2d 83 (1950) (dictum). In In re Lemont's Estate, 7 Cal.App.3d 437, 86 Cal.Rptr. 810 (1970) the court held that the annulment of the second marriage did not operate retroactively. If it occurs before the death of the first husband, the first marriage is left in force, but if it occurs after his death, the first marriage is not revived.

39. Pa.Stat. tit. 48, § 1–8 (1965), applied in Pest & Kolesnik Marriage License, 4 D. & C.2d 12 (Pa.1955).

riage is still valid.[40] The virtue of this statute is that it attempts to prevent the issuance of a license for a marriage which cannot be valid, thus forestalling the Enoch Arden problem before it arises.

Successive marriage may be affected by civil death statutes. These statutes, found in a few states, provide that a person sentenced to a life term in the penitentiary shall be deemed civilly dead.[41] The question then is, does this free the husband or wife of such a person to contract a second marriage? The leading New York case, Matter of Lindewall's Will,[42] holds that it does. A better solution is adopted by Villalon v. Bowen,[43] a Nevada case applying Oregon law, which holds that since conviction of a felony is a ground for divorce in Oregon, this gives the spouse of the convicted person a method of ending the marriage, and makes it unnecessary for the civil death statute to have any effect upon marital relations.

Bigamous and polygamous marriages raise troublesome questions of the conflict of laws,[44] primarily because the courts' abhorrence of such marriages conflicts with principles normally applicable to the recognition of foreign marriages. If marriage is contracted by polygamous rites in a jurisdiction which does not recognize such marriages as valid, it will not be likely to be recognized in other jurisdictions which forbid polygamy.[45] And perhaps it will not be recognized in jurisdictions which do allow polygamous marriages, on the theory that a marriage invalid where contracted is invalid everywhere,[46] although a contrary argument could be made, based on the policies involved. That is, if the state of the parties' domicile or of their intended matrimonial domicile does not disapprove a polygamous marriage, such a state's policy should be controlling rather than that of the place of marriage.[47]

The difficult case arises when persons domiciled in a country which recognizes polygamy are married there and later come to England or the United States where the validity of their marriage is called in question. The early leading case of Hyde v. Hyde and Woodmansee [48] involved essentially this situation. The parties, both Mormons and living in Utah, were married in accordance with Mormon customs, which at that time permitted polygamy. The husband later renounced the Mormon faith, and came to England. The wife obtained a Mormon divorce from him and remarried. He then sued for divorce in England. The divorce was denied on the ground that this was not a marriage as understood in English law, Christian marriage being defined as "the voluntary union for life of one man and one woman, to the exclusion of all other." [49] The case can be construed to mean that English courts will not recognize, for any purpose, a polygamous marriage, even though contracted in a place which sanctions such marriages,[50] but later cases have made it

40. Pa.Stat. tit. 48, § 1–8 (1965).

41. For the consequences of such statutes, see Annot., Civil Effects of Sentence to Life Imprisonment, 139 A.L.R. 1308 (1942).

42. 287 N.Y. 347, 39 N.E.2d 907 (1942).

43. 70 Nev. 456, 273 P.2d 409 (1954).

44. The leading treatment of the subject is Morris, The Recognition of Polygamous Marriages in English Law, 66 Harv.L.Rev. 961 (1953). See also Ehrenzweig, Conflict of Laws, 386–387 (1962); Pearl, Muslim Marriages in English Law, 30 Cambridge L.J. 120 (1972). Cases are collected in Annot., 74 A.L.R. 1533 (1931). Whether a marriage is to be characterized as bigamous is determined by the law of the place where the marriage was contracted, according to Zwerling v. Zwerling, 270 S.C. 685, 244 S.E.2d 311 (1978).

45. Morris, The Recognition of Polygamous Marriages in English Law, 66 Harv.L.Rev. 961, 978–983 (1953).

46. Ibid.

47. Radwan v. Radwan (No. 2) [1973] Fam. 35 recognized a polygamous marriage and granted a divorce to the wife where the wife had been a domiciliary of England at the time of the marriage but immediately thereafter the parties became domiciled in Egypt, where such marriages were valid. The marriage was contracted in the Egyptian consulate in Paris. The marriage was actually and not merely potentially polygamous. For a discussion of the case see Jaffey, The Essential Validity of Marriage in the English Conflict of Laws, 41 Mod.L.Rev. 38 (1978).

48. L.Rep. 1 P. & D. 130 (1866).

49. Id. at 133. But see Nachimson v. Nachimson, [1930] P. 217.

50. This was the view of the Restatement of Conflict of Laws. Restatement, Conflict of Laws §§ 132, 134 (1934). But this view has apparently changed. The

clear that the Hyde case will not be given this broad construction.

The later English cases and the American cases hold that the recognition of marriages like that in the Hyde case depends upon the purpose of the litigation. If anything is left of the Hyde case, it means only that matrimonial remedies, such as divorce, will not be available where the marriage is polygamous.[51] But such marriages are now recognized as valid for the purpose of barring a later English marriage,[52] or of legitimating children of the marriage,[53] or of inheriting property.[54] The reason for the change is most clearly put in In re Dalip Singh Bir's Estate.[55] The California court, in the course of holding that the deceased Hindu's two wives could share his estate equally, said that this result did no violence to California's public policy and therefore the polygamous marriage should be recognized for this purpose. The court went on to say that California's policy would be violated if a polygamist should bring several wives into the state and attempt to cohabit with them, in which case the marriage would not be recognized as valid. This is a sensible solution which effectuates the local policy without indulging in the gratuitous provincialism of the Hyde case. The rationale of the case also suggests a way out of the difficulty which has resulted from the rule that marriages are characterized as polygamous or not by reference to the law of the country in

which they are contracted. By this view a marriage contracted in a Mohammedan country under a law allowing plural wives would be considered polygamous although the husband never attempted to take a second wife.[56] It would seem, adopting the reasoning of Dalip Singh Bir's Estate, that such a marriage, though potentially polygamous, could be recognized for all purposes by an American jurisdiction without prejudice to its own local policies. One Iowa case contains language supporting this argument.[57] If this reasoning prevails, most of the difficulties would disappear, since few cases seem to involve husbands who have actually taken more than one wife.

 **WESTLAW REFERENCES**

di(polygam! bigam! /s marriage /s void)
felony /s bigamy polygamy
find 98 us 145
"enoch arden"

§ 2.7 Presumptions in Support of Marriage

Proof that a marriage has been contracted or that the parties have cohabited as husband and wife raises a number of presumptions. In effect they amount to but a single presumption, which is that purported marriages are presumed valid.[1] In specific situations this broad presumption is reduced to more specific

---

difficulty is that one cannot be sure just what the Restatement's view on the various aspects of bigamous or polygamous marriage may now be. Restatement (Second) Conflict of Laws § 283, comment k (1971).

Where the marriage is contracted in a jurisdiction recognizing polygamy, but one or both of the parties are domiciled elsewhere, such a marriage would probably not be valid. See Morris, op. cit. supra note 44, at 983–988.

51. There is support for this construction in the Hyde case itself. See Hyde v. Hyde and Woodmansee, L.Rep. 1 P. & D. 130, at page 138 (1866), and Morris, The Recognition of Polygamous Marriages in English Law, 66 Harv.L. Rev. 961, 967, 1002 (1953), and Radwan v. Radwan (No. 2) [1973] Fam. 35 recognizes a polygamous marriage for purposes of granting the wife a divorce.

52. Srini Vasan v. Srini Vasan, [1947] P. 62; Baindail v. Baindail, [1946] P. 122. See also Application of Sood, 142 N.Y.S.2d 591 (1955), affirmed 1 App.Div.2d 939, 150 N.Y.S.2d 578 (4th Dep't 1956).

53. Sinha Peerage Claim [1946] 1 All Eng.Rep. 348.

54. In re Dalip Singh Bir's Estate, 83 Cal.App.2d 256, 188 P.2d 499 (1948).

55. Ibid.

56. Morris, The Recognition of Polygamous Marriages in English Law, 66 Harv.L.Rev. 961, 973–977 (1953).

57. Royal v. Cudahy Packing Co., 195 Iowa 759, 190 N.W. 427 (1922) (workmen's compensation awarded to the wife).

§ 2.7

1. Panzer v. Panzer, 87 N.M. 29, 528 P.2d 888 (1974); Schacht v. Schacht, 435 S.W.2d 197 (Tex.Civ.App.1968). Other cases are collected in Annots., 34 A.L.R. 464 (1925) and 77 A.L.R. 729 (1932). For a general discussion of the presumptions see Note, 82 U.Pa.L.Rev. 508 (1934); Note, Presumption of Validity of a Second Marriage, 20 Baylor L.Rev. 206 (1968). This presumption applies to common law marriages. Roy v. Industrial Commission, 97 Ariz. 98, 397 P.2d 211 (1964); Cross v. Rudder, 380 So.2d 766 (Ala.1980), appeal after remand 404 So.2d 8 (1981).

terms. There is a presumption that the legal formalities of marriage were complied with,[2] and that the ceremony was a proper one.[3] There is another presumption that the parties had capacity to marry.[4] There is still another presumption that the person who celebrated the marriage had authority to do so.[5]

All of these presumptions having the effect of validating marriages are based upon the same public policy. This is described in a famous early case: "The law presumes morality, and not immorality; marriage, and not concubinage; legitimacy, and not bastardy." [6] There is the additional basis of probability for these presumptions. Generally speaking it is more likely than not that a purported marriage is a valid one. If the presumption were otherwise, it might be very difficult or impossible to prove that the many requirements for a valid marriage had been complied with. Finally there is the need to vindicate expectations on which the parties have arranged their lives, as in so many other marital cases.[7] For these reasons the law says that a person who is attacking the existence of a marriage has the burden of rebutting the presumption that the marriage was validly contracted. Although these presumptions are rebuttable, a substantial amount of evidence is necessary to overthrow them. The mere absence of any record of a marriage, for example, is not sufficient to establish that the marriage is invalid.[8]

The presumption that the latest of successive marriages is valid [9] is more important than the other presumptions validating mar-riage, is more frequently relied upon, and has a somewhat different policy for its basis. This presumption conflicts with the presumption that a marriage once contracted continues until proved to have ended by death or divorce. The usual way of resolving the conflict is to say that the presumption of validity of the latest marriage is the stronger one and will prevail.[10] Another way of describing this situation is to say that once an earlier marriage is proved we normally draw the inference that it continues in force, but that the normal inference must yield to the presumption [11] if a later marriage is proved. The precise formulation of the rules does not matter, as long as we remember that the latest marriage is presumed valid.

The policies underlying this presumption include those leading to the validation of marriages generally, but here the need to make good the parties' expectations is particularly acute. The typical case illustrates this.[12] A man marries early in life, lives with his wife briefly and then leaves her. He marries again, lives with his second wife for many years, they have children, and the man dies. Without the presumption the first wife would be very likely to prevail over the second in her claim to the man's estate, in spite of the fact that all three parties have behaved for years as if the first marriage had ended and the second was valid. With the presumption, the first wife has far less chance to make good her claim, and the parties' expectations have a correspondingly greater likelihood of being vindicated. A careful reading of the numer-

---

2. Annots., 34 A.L.R. 464, 472 (1925), and 77 A.L.R. 729, 735 (1932).

3. Annot., 34 A.L.R. 464, 474 (1925).

4. Annots., 34 A.L.R. 464, 474 (1925), and 77 A.L.R. 729, 735 (1932).

5. State v. Martinez, 43 Idaho 180, 250 P. 239 (1926); Annot., 34 A.L.R. 464, 473 (1925).

6. Hynes v. McDermott, 91 N.Y. 451, 459 (1883).

7. E.g. estoppel to attack divorce decrees. See section 11.3, Practitioner's Edition.

8. Vest's Adm'r v. Vest, 234 Ky. 587, 28 S.W.2d 782 (1930).

9. Cases on this presumption are collected in Annot., 14 A.L.R.2d 7 (1950). See also Tex.Fam.Code § 2.01 (1975).

10. Holland America Insurance Co. v. Rogers, 313 F.Supp. 314 (N.D.Cal.1970); In re Marriage of Sumners, 645 S.W.2d 205 (Mo.App.1983); Schacht v. Schacht, 435 S.W.2d 197 (Tex.Civ.App.1968); C. McCormick, Evidence 976–978 (3d ed. Cleary 1984). Pennsylvania seems to reach about the same result by using a somewhat different verbal formula. See Commonwealth ex rel. Alexander v. Alexander, 445 Pa. 406, 289 A.2d 83 (1971); In re Watt's Estate, 409 Pa. 44, 185 A.2d 781 (1962); Cupler v. Secretary of Health, Education and Welfare, 252 F.Supp. 178 (W.D.Pa.1966).

11. Note, 82 U.Pa.L.Rev. 508, 512 (1934); Panzer v. Panzer, 87 N.M. 29, 528 P.2d 888 (1974).

12. Spears v. Spears, 178 Ark. 720, 12 S.W.2d 875 (1928).

ous cases applying this presumption leaves a very strong impression that in all probability the prior marriage had not ended, but that the courts were holding that it must be presumed to have ended for the purpose of protecting the legitimacy of children or honoring the financial or property claims of women who had assumed for many years that they were married and had performed the obligations of marriage.[13] This is another instance of the law's treating the de facto assumption of the marital status as paramount to compliance with legal forms. Yet there are cases which purport to reject the presumption. Some of these might not have reached a different result even if the presumption had been applied,[14] while others seem clearly wrong both in theory and result.[15] Aside from these very few cases, the presumption is accepted by the overwhelming majority of au-

thorities. The majority of authorities also hold that the presumption may be based on a common law marriage as well as a ceremonial one, if the common law marriage occurred in a state recognizing such marriages.[16]

The presumption of validity of the latest marriage has been applied in all sorts of cases, including the administration of estates,[17] workmen's compensation,[18] insurance claims,[19] annulments,[20] divorces,[21] and proceedings involving the legitimacy of children.[22] It does not apply in criminal prosecutions for bigamy.[23] The reason for the distinction is not clear, unless it is to make the prosecution's task easier. The same policy factors are present in both civil and criminal cases.

In order to invoke this presumption, the party must put in some evidence that the second marriage occurred, either evidence

13. The policy is discussed in Dolan v. Celebrezze, 381 F.2d 231 (2d Cir.1967), which applied New York law. In this case a woman married H–1, later married H–2, and then resumed living with H–1 after the death of H–2. It was argued that the presumption of the validity of the second marriage was strong and was not rebutted, and that therefore the woman was not entitled to social security benefits as a widow upon the death of H–1. But in this situation, practically speaking, the marriage to H–1 was the later marriage, since that was the marriage in de facto existence when H–1 died and the claim for social security was made. Though the court found the presumption rebutted, it need not have, since the policy underlying the presumption would cause it to be applied in support of the marriage to H–1.

14. E.g., Gainey v. Flemming, 279 F.2d 56 (10th Cir. 1960).

15. Rice v. Randlett, 141 Mass. 385, 6 N.E. 238 (1886); Williams v. Williams, 254 N.C. 729, 120 S.E.2d 68 (1961); 40 N.C.L.Rev. 118 (1961); Domany v. Otis Elevator Co., 369 F.2d 604 (6th Cir.1966), cert. denied 387 U.S. 942, 87 S.Ct. 2073, 18 L.Ed.2d 1327 (1967) (Ohio law); Hilton v. Roylance, 25 Utah 129, 69 P. 660 (1902); Williams v. Williams, 63 Wis. 58, 23 N.W. 110 (1885). A few other cases are collected in Annot., 14 A.L.R.2d 7, 29 (1950). Pennsylvania does not seem either to accept or reject the presumption very clearly, the cases leaving a confused impression. Compare In re Watt's Estate, 409 Pa. 44, 185 A.2d 781 (1962) and Commonwealth ex rel. Alexander v. Alexander, 445 Pa. 406, 289 A.2d 83 (1971), with In re D'Ippolito's Estate, 420 Pa. 541, 218 A.2d 224 (1966) and Estate of Henry, 466 Pa. 518, 353 A.2d 812 (1976).

16. Warner v. Warner, 76 Idaho 399, 283 P.2d 931 (1955); Anderson-Tully Co. v. Wilson, 221 Miss. 656, 74 So.2d 735 (1954); Phillips v. Wilson, 298 Mo. 186, 250 S.W. 408 (1923); Hill v. Shreve, 448 P.2d 848 (Okl.1968); Texas Employers' Ins. Ass'n v. Elder, 155 Tex. 27, 282 S.W.2d 371 (1955). Contra: Lumbermen's Mutual Casu-

alty Co. v. Reed, 84 Ga.App. 541, 66 S.E.2d 360 (1951); In re Leonard's Estate, 45 Mich.App. 679, 207 N.W.2d 166 (1973) (semble). Rosetta v. Rosetta, 525 S.W.2d 255 (Tex. Civ.App.1975) seems to say that the presumption is stronger when it arises out of a ceremonial marriage than when it is based upon a common law marriage.

17. Sims v. Powell's Estate, 245 Ark. 493, 432 S.W.2d 838 (1968); Spears v. Spears, 178 Ark. 720, 12 S.W.2d 875 (1928); Hill v. Shreve, 448 P.2d 848 (Okl.1968); Wood v. Paulus, 524 S.W.2d 749 (Tex.Civ.App.1975).

18. Wilson v. Wilson, 1 Ariz.App. 77, 399 P.2d 698 (1965); Dawson v. Hatfield Wire & Cable Co., 59 N.J. 190, 280 A.2d 173 (1971); Parker v. American Lumber Corp., 190 Va. 181, 56 S.E.2d 214 (1949). The presumption was held to have been rebutted in Sparling v. Industrial Commission, 48 Ill.2d 332, 270 N.E.2d 411 (1971).

19. Metropolitan Life Ins. Co. v. Manning, 568 F.2d 922 (2d Cir.1977); Yarbrough v. United States, 341 F.2d 621 (Ct.Cl.1965); Tatum v. Tatum, 241 F.2d 401 (9th Cir. 1957); Pittinger v. Pittinger, 28 Colo. 308, 64 P. 195 (1901); Stuerze v. State Division of Pensions, 120 N.J. Super. 31, 293 A.2d 227 (1972).

20. Ellis v. Ellis, 50 Ala.App. 67, 277 So.2d 102 (1973); Smiley v. Smiley, 247 Ark. 933, 448 S.W.2d 642 (1970); Leslie v. Leslie, 244 Cal.App.2d 516, 53 Cal.Rptr. 402 (1966); Williamson v. Williamson, 48 Del. (9 Terry) 277, 101 A.2d 871 (1954); Rutledge v. Rutledge, 41 Tenn.App. 158, 293 S.W.2d 21 (1953).

21. Jackson v. Jackson, 49 Ala.App. 702, 275 So.2d 683 (1973); Smith v. Smith, 256 A.2d 833 (D.C.App.1969) (separate maintenance); Warner v. Warner, 76 Idaho 399, 283 P.2d 931 (1955); Frelingstad v. Frelingstad, 134 N.Y.S.2d 63 (Dom.Rel.Ct.1954) (separate maintenance).

22. Ladner v. Pigford, 138 Miss. 461, 103 So. 218 (1925), 23 Ill.L.Rev. 188 (1928), 24 Mich.L.Rev. 194 (1925).

23. Annot., 14 A.L.R.2d 7, 19, 34 (1950).

that there was a ceremony,[24] or evidence of habit and repute in the community indicating that the parties lived as husband and wife.[25] A few states impose the additional requirement that there must be some affirmative evidence that the later marriage was valid or that the earlier marriage had ended, before the presumption may come into play.[26]

The crucial question about the presumption is, what is required to rebut it?[27] On this point there seems to be no single generalization which will explain all the cases. Most of them contain language to the effect that this is one of the strongest presumptions known to the law[28] or that it can only be rebutted by "strong, distinct, satisfactory and conclusive" evidence that the prior marriage still subsists,[29] or by cogent and conclusive evidence.[30] One unusual feature of this presumption is that, according to some cases, its strength increases with the lapse of time and the birth of children of the later marriage.[31] Under a New Jersey case[32] the presumption may also be especially strong, perhaps even conclusive, when the attack on the later marriage is made by an employer, a stranger to the mar-

riage, in a workmen's compensation case. These special rules testify to the policy basis for the presumption, since particular hardship results when a marriage of long standing is upset, when the husband's employer asserts after the husband's death that there was no marriage, or when children of such a marriage are held to be illegitimate.

The cases can be roughly divided into two groups with respect to their position on the kind and amount of evidence needed to rebut the presumption. The first and larger group require the production of evidence which proves beyond a reasonable doubt that neither death nor divorce terminated the prior marriage[33] or which at least makes it appear highly probable that the earlier marriage was still in existence when the later marriage was contracted.[34]

If the first spouse remains absent and unheard from at the time of the litigation, the presumption is that he is no longer alive and its rebuttal is virtually impossible.[35] More commonly, however, it is proved that he is still alive, and the presumption is that he

---

24. Bowman v. Little, 101 Md. 273, 61 A. 223 (1905).

25. Warner v. Warner, 76 Idaho 399, 283 P.2d 931 (1955); Hill v. Shreve, 448 P.2d 848 (Okl.1968); Hill v. Jones, 180 Okl. 330, 69 P.2d 324 (1937). But doubt whether there was a ceremony may help rebut the presumption. Bruno v. Bruno, 221 Ark. 759, 256 S.W.2d 341 (1953).

26. Headen v. Pope & Talbot, Inc., 252 F.2d 739 (3d Cir.1958); Eygabrood v. Gruis, 247 Iowa 1346, 79 N.W.2d 215 (1956); In re Watt's Estate, 409 Pa. 44, 185 A.2d 781 (1962).

27. Steele v. Richardson, 472 F.2d 49 (2d Cir.1972).

28. Jackson v. Jackson, 49 Ala.App. 702, 275 So.2d 683 (1973); Smith v. Smith, 169 Or. 650, 131 P.2d 447 (1942); Texas Employers' Ins. Assn. v. Elder, 155 Tex. 27, 282 S.W.2d 371 (1955); Wood v. Paulus, 524 S.W.2d 749 (Tex.Civ.App.1975).

29. Harsley v. United States, 187 F.2d 213 (D.C.Cir. 1951); Sims v. Powell's Estate, 245 Ark. 493, 432 S.W.2d 838 (1968) (may be overcome only by "positive proof"); Johnson v. Young, 372 A.2d 992 (D.C.App.1977); In re Marriage of Sumners, 645 S.W.2d 205 (Mo.App.1983).

30. Williamson v. Williamson, 48 Del. (9 Terry) 277, 101 A.2d 871 (1954); Panzer v. Panzer, 87 N.M. 29, 528 P.2d 888 (1974) (requires "Clear and convincing" evidence). New Jersey has used the "clear and convincing" language, and has also said that the person attacking the later marriage must disprove every reasonable possibility

that could vitiate the prior marriage. Newburgh v. Arrigo, 88 N.J. 529, 443 A.2d 1031 (1982).

31. Ladner v. Pigford, 138 Miss. 461, 103 So. 218 (1925); 23 Ill.L.Rev. 188 (1928); 24 Mich.L.Rev. 194 (1925); Dawson v. Hatfield Wire & Cable Co., 59 N.J. 190, 280 A.2d 173 (1971) (concurring and dissenting opinion); In re Meehan's Estate, 150 App.Div. 681, 135 N.Y.S. 723 (1st Dep't 1912); Texas Employers' Ins. Assn. v. Elder, 155 Tex. 27, 282 S.W.2d 371 (1955); Wood v. Paulus, 524 S.W.2d 749 (Tex.Civ.App.1975); In re Pilcher's Estate, 114 Utah 72, 197 P.2d 143 (1948).

32. Dawson v. Hatfield Wire & Cable Co., 59 N.J. 190, 280 A.2d 173 (1971).

33. O'Rourke v. Merry Queen Transfer Co., 370 F.2d 781 (2d Cir.1967) (New York Law); Thompson v. Monteiro, 58 N.J.Super. 302, 156 A.2d 173 (1959). See also Yarbrough v. Celebrezze, 217 F.Supp. 943 (M.D.N.C. 1963) (Mississippi Law), and Esmond v. Thomas Lyons Bar & Grill, 26 A.D.2d 884, 274 N.Y.S.2d 225 (3d Dep't 1966).

34. E.g., Wilson v. Wilson, 1 Ariz.App. 77, 399 P.2d 698 (1965); Leslie v. Leslie, 244 Cal.App.2d 516, 53 Cal. Rptr. 402 (1966); Wood v. Paulus, 524 S.W.2d 749 (Tex. Civ.App.1975). New York's position on this is unclear. See Milano v. Secretary of Health and Human Services, 586 F.Supp. 1431 (E.D.N.Y.1984).

35. E.g., Eygabrood v. Gruis, 247 Iowa 1346, 79 N.W.2d 215 (1956).

obtained a divorce.[36] Most of the cases are concerned with the issue of what sort of evidence is required to satisfy the court that no divorce was obtained. There is agreement that testimony by one spouse that he never got a divorce himself, that he never received service or notice of divorce proceedings by the other spouse, and that he never was guilty of conduct which would be grounds for divorce is not sufficient to rebut the presumption.[37] But evidence that court records in all of the places

where the other spouse lived failed to disclose any divorce obtained by him is normally held sufficient to rebut the presumption.[38] Other cases in the group which give maximum force to the presumption hold that various kinds of evidence (often by virtue of its cumulative force) may serve to rebut it.[39] On the other hand, rebuttal is not usually found on the basis of testimony of friends as to their opinion that a divorce had not been granted [40] or of statements by the parties to the same ef-

36. E.g., Ellis v. Ellis, 50 Ala.App. 67, 277 So.2d 102 (1973). In Oregon rebuttal of the presumption apparently requires that the party attacking the later marriage prove that the parties to the earlier marriage were eligible to contract it. In re Estate of Davis, 55 Or.App. 982, 640 P.2d 692 (1982).

37. Yarbrough v. United States, 341 F.2d 621 (Ct.Cl. 1965); Jackson v. Jackson, 49 Ala.App. 702, 275 So.2d 683 (1973); Jordan v. Copeland, 272 Ala. 336, 131 So.2d 696 (1961); Freed v. Sallade, 245 Ala. 505, 17 So.2d 868 (1944); Sims v. Powell, 245 Ark. 493, 432 S.W.2d 838 (1968); Spears v. Spears, 178 Ark. 720, 12 S.W.2d 875 (1928); Pittinger v. Pittinger, 28 Colo. 308, 64 P. 195 (1901); Warner v. Warner, 76 Idaho 399, 283 P.2d 931 (1955); Rainier v. Snider, 174 Ind.App. 615, 369 N.E.2d 666 (1977); Pigford Bros. Constr. Co. v. Evans, 225 Miss. 411, 83 So.2d 622 (1955); Matter of Booker's Estate, 27 Or. App. 779, 557 P.2d 248 (1976); In re Pilcher's Estate, 114 Utah 72, 197 P.2d 143 (1948). But see Blythe v. Blythe, 241 Ark. 768, 410 S.W.2d 379 (1967); Application of Carr, 134 N.Y.S.2d 513 (Sur.Ct.1953), affirmed 284 App.Div. 930, 134 N.Y.S.2d 280 (4th Dep't. 1954).

38. Spearman v. Spearman, 482 F.2d 1203 (5th Cir. 1973); Hewitt v. Firestone Tire & Rubber Co., 490 F.Supp. 1358 (E.D.Va.1981) (semble); Gaddy v. Louisville & Nashville R.R. Co., 249 F.Supp. 305 (E.D.Ky.1965), affirmed in part, reversed in part 386 F.2d 772 (6th Cir. 1967) (presumption rebutted by central divorce records from 23 states); Batts v. United States, 120 F.Supp. 26 (E.D.N.C.1954); Lott v. Toomey, 477 So.2d 316 (Ala.1985); Sloss-Sheffield Steel & Iron Co. v. Watford, 245 Ala. 425, 17 So.2d 166 (1944); Ellis v. Ellis, 50 Ala.App. 67, 277 So. 2d 102 (1973); Cole v. Cole, 249 Ark. 824, 462 S.W.2d 213 (1971); Quinn v. Miles, 124 So.2d 883 (Fla.1960); Roberts v. Roberts, 124 Fla. 116, 167 So. 808 (1936); In re Colton's Estate, 129 Iowa 542, 105 N.W. 1008 (1906); Pigford Bros. Constr. Co. v. Evans, 225 Miss. 411, 83 So.2d 622 (1955); Stuerze v. State, Division of Pensions, 120 N.J.Super. 31, 293 A.2d 227 (1972); Brokeshoulder v. Brokeshoulder, 84 Okl. 249, 204 P. 284 (1921); Payne v. Payne, 142 Tenn. 320, 219 S.W. 4 (1920); Davis v. Davis, 521 S.W.2d 603 (Tex.1975); Caruso v. Lucius, 448 S.W.2d 711 (Tex.Civ. App.1969); In re Grauel's Estate, 70 Wash.2d 870, 425 P.2d 644 (1967). But see Spears v. Spears, 178 Ark. 720, 12 S.W.2d 875 (1928), holding the presumption was not rebutted by evidence that the deceased husband had not obtained a divorce in any of the counties in which he resided. This case places an impossible burden of proof upon the proponent of the earlier marriage, making the

presumption virtually conclusive. See also Rutledge v. Rutledge, 41 Tenn.App. 158, 293 S.W.2d 21 (1954).

39. E.g., Dolan v. Celebrezze, 381 F.2d 231 (2d Cir.1967) (relying on the fact that the wife had resumed living with her first husband after the death of her second, so that in effect the first marriage was the later marriage); Howard v. Pike, 290 Ala. 213, 275 So.2d 645 (1973) (testimony of both husband and first wife that neither obtained a divorce rebuts the presumption); Bruno v. Bruno, 221 Ark. 759, 256 S.W.2d 341 (1953) (relying chiefly on the shortness of duration of the second marriage and the fact that the absent spouse was in New York where it would have been difficult to get a divorce); In re Atherley's Estate, 44 Cal. App.3d 758, 119 Cal.Rptr. 41 (1975) (testimony of both wives and affidavit of husband that no divorce was obtained rebuts the presumption); Vargas v. Superior Court of Los Angeles County, 9 Cal.App.3d 470, 88 Cal.Rptr. 281 (1970) (fact that husband simultaneously purported to be married to, and to some extent lived with, both wives rebuts the presumption, where neither knew of the relationship to the other); Appeal of O'Rourke, 310 Minn. 373, 246 N.W.2d 461 (1976) (presumption not applied where second marriage of very short duration); Fowler v. Fowler, 96 N.H. 494, 79 A.2d 24 (1951) (presumption overcome by evidence that a divorce ending the first marriage was only granted *after* the second marriage was contracted); Lopez v. Bonner, 439 P.2d 687 (Okl.1967) (similar to the Fowler case); Watt v. Watt, 409 Pa. 44, 185 A.2d 781 (1962) (presumption rebutted by proof that a divorce ending the first marriage was set aside for fraud, the inference being that the absent husband would not have obtained another divorce, and by evidence of a resumption of marital relations); Schacht v. Schacht, 435 S.W.2d 197 (Tex.Civ.App. 1968) (evidence the husband obtained an invalid Mexican divorce rebuts the presumption). But see Williamson v. Williamson, 48 Del. (9 Terry) 277, 101 A.2d 871 (1954), holding that a divorce terminating the first marriage, granted after the second marriage, did not rebut the presumption. This conflict with the Fowler and Lopez cases shows how little uniformity there is in the case by case application of this presumption. A great many more cases on rebuttal are cited in Annot., 14 A.L.R.2d 7, 45–60 (1950).

40. Hill v. Jones, 180 Okl. 330, 69 P.2d 324 (1937). Matter of Yee's Estate, 98 Idaho 147, 559 P.2d 763 (1977) (testimony of the son that no divorce had occurred failed to rebut the presumption where the second marriage had lasted 36 years). But see Henderson v. Finch, 300 F.Supp. 753 (W.D.La.1969).

fect,[41] particularly if there is evidence tending to support the validity of the second marriage, as where a first wife fails to make any claim,[42] or where she herself remarries.[43]

The second group of cases, much smaller in number, gives the presumption much less force. They hold that once rebutting evidence is introduced, the question whether the prior marriage prevails is to be answered on the basis of the preponderance of evidence just as any other question of fact would be.[44] This position gives too little effect to the important policy factors underlying the presumption, since it makes the presumption indecisive except where little or no evidence is presented in rebuttal.

The courts dealing with rebuttal of this presumption, whatever theory they may ostensibly adopt, have an extremely wide area of discretion within which they may hold the presumption rebutted or not. In other words the real significance of the presumption is that it gives the courts the opportunity to weigh all the elements of the second spouse's claim in order to reach an equitable result without being hindered either by rule or precedent.[45]

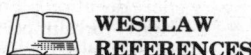 **WESTLAW REFERENCES**

successive /s marriage /s presum! /s valid

find 241 f2d 401

§ 2.8   Same-Sex Marriage

As recently as ten years ago it would have been inconceivable to deal seriously with the question of the validity of marriages between persons of the same sex. The fact that a discussion of this subject must now be included in a legal text testifies to the rapid and drastic social changes which have occurred in that period. That the changes have occurred does not mean, however, that everyone accepts them as desirable, or that there are not highly emotional reactions to them on the part of many people.

Some background information may provide a useful introduction to the subject. For general purposes homosexuality may be defined as a sexual attraction between persons of the same sex.[1] It includes the love of women for women as well as the love of men for men, although the former is often referred to as lesbianism.[2] It is difficult to determine just how large a proportion of the general population may accurately be characterized as homosexual, for two reasons. The first is that since there is still a social stigma, accompanied by material or financial or legal penalties, attached to being a homosexual, many homosexuals naturally choose to conceal, or not to reveal, their identities. The second reason is that a precise definition of homosexuals has never been formulated and perhaps cannot be, since many people feel attracted to members of the same sex at one time or another in their lives and at

---

41. In re Jubala's Estate, 40 N.M. 312, 59 P.2d 356 (1936). Where the testimony of the parties is combined with other facts, some courts have held the presumption rebutted. See, e.g., Dixon v. Gardner, 302 F.Supp. 395 (E.D.Pa.1969); Leslie v. Leslie, 244 Cal.App.2d 516, 53 Cal.Rptr. 402 (1966); Sparling v. Industrial Commission, 41 Ill.2d 332, 270 N.E.2d 411 (1971). But Steele v. Richardson, 472 F.2d 49 (2d Cir.1972) held such evidence did not rebut the presumption when it appeared that the earlier marriage itself was bigamous, the court suggesting that part of the burden of rebutting the presumption was the duty to prove that the earlier marriage was valid.

42. In re Jubala's Estate, 40 N.M. 312, 59 P.2d 356 (1936).

43. Baer v. De Berry, 31 Ill.App.2d 86, 175 N.E.2d 673 (1961).

44. The following cases seem to adopt this view of the presumption; Tatum v. Tatum, 241 F.2d 401 (9th Cir.

1957); Hewitt v. Firestone Tire & Rubber Co., 490 F.Supp. 1358 (E.D.Va.1980); Woolery v. Metropolitan Life Insurance Company, 406 F.Supp. 641 (E.D.Va.1976); Dorsey v. Dorsey, 259 Ala. 220, 66 So.2d 135 (1953); Mccord v. Mccord, 13 Ariz. 377, 114 P. 968 (1911); Patrick v. Simon, 237 Ga. 742, 229 S.E.2d 746 (1976) (semble); Estate of Claveria v. Claveria, 615 S.W.2d 164 (Tex.1981); Parker v. American Lumber Corp., 190 Va. 181, 56 S.E.2d 214 (1949); Deryder v. Metropolitan Life Ins. Co., 206 Va. 602, 145 S.E.2d 177 (1965), 7 W. & M.L.Rev. 403 (1966).

45. Appeal of O'Rourke, 310 Minn. 373, 246 N.W.2d 461 (1976).

§ 2.8

1. D. West, Homosexuality 10–13 (1967); E. Chesser, Live and Let Live 30 (1958). A comprehensive historical account of homosexuality may be found in A. Karlen, Sexuality and Homosexuality (1971).

2. D. West, Homosexuality 12, 13 (1967).

other times are attracted with greater or lesser intensity to members of the other sex.[3] The population seems to be distributed along a continuum at one end of which is the exclusively heterosexual person and at the other end the exclusively homosexual person, with many falling somewhere in between. Not withstanding these difficulties the Kinsey report set up a classification according to which about four percent of white males in the United States were found to be homosexual.[4] A smaller proportion of white females were so characterized.[5] Others have estimated the proportions to be somewhat larger.[6] It thus appears that a substantial number of men and women in this country can be described as homosexual even though they form only a relatively small part of the total population.

In the past the attitude of society, religion and the law toward homosexuals has been one of emotionally charged hostility. Discrimination against homosexuals in employment has been widespread.[7] Religious authorities regarded homosexuality as a sin.[8] And statutes in many states imposed serious penalties upon homosexual conduct.[9] Some changes in these attitudes are beginning to be visible in some parts of the United States. The publication of the Wolfenden Report [10] in England has been influential in advancing the view that homosexual acts between consenting adults ought not to be a criminal offense.[11] Although studies of homosexuality by sociologists, psychiatrists, psychologists and others have been numerous in recent years, they have not produced agreement either concerning the origins of homosexuality or the possibilities for treatment.[12] These studies have, however, led to a greater understanding of

3. E. Chesser, Live and Let Live 32–35 (1958); Report of the Committee on Homosexual Offenses and Prostitution, Cmnd. No. 247, at 11–13 (1957), hereinafter cited as The Wolfenden Report. The same Report was published as The Wolfenden Report in an authorized American edition in 1963, with introduction by Karl Menninger, M.D.

4. Kinsey, Pomeroy, Martin, Sexual Behavior in the Human Male ch. 21 (1948).

5. Kinsey, Pomeroy, Martin, Gebhard, Sexual Behavior in the Human Female ch. 11 (1953).

6. Hooker, Male Homosexuals and Their "Worlds", ch. 5 in Sexual Inversion, J. Marmor ed. (1965); A. Karlen, Sexuality and Homosexuality 511 (1971).

7. E.g., Singer v. United States Civil Service Commission, 530 F.2d 247 (9th Cir.1976), judgment vacated 429 U.S. 1034, 97 S.Ct. 725, 50 L.Ed.2d 744 (1977); Note, Government Employment and the Homosexual, 45 St. John's L.Rev. 303 (1970); Note, Government-Created Disabilities of the Homosexual, 82 Harv.L.Rev. 1738 (1969). But see Morrison v. State Board of Education, 1 Cal.3d 214, 82 Cal.Rptr. 175, 461 P.2d 375 (1969); McConnell v. Anderson, 451 F.2d 193 (8th Cir.1971), cert. denied 405 U.S. 1046, 92 S.Ct. 1312, 31 L.Ed.2d 588 (1972).

8. A. Karlen, Sexuality and Homosexuality ch. 4 (1971); Ford, Homosexuals and the Law: Why the Status Quo, 5 Cal.Western L.Rev. 232 (1969); W. Barnett, Sexual Freedom and the Constitution ch. 4 (1973); D. Bailey, Homosexuality and the Western Christian Tradition (1975).

9. Note, Homosexuality and the Law—An Overview, 17 N.Y.L.F. 273 (1971); Rivera, Our Straight-Laced Judges: The Legal Position of Homosexual Persons in the United States, 30 Hastings L.J. 799 (1979) contains an extensive discussion and citation of cases.

10. See note 3, supra.

11. See, e.g., Model Penal Code, comment on § 207.5, at 276 (Tent. Draft No. 4 1955), and Model Penal Code § 213.2, 1 Unif.L.Ann. 543 (1974) making deviate sexual intercourse a crime only where force or imposition are involved; Harris, Private Consensual Adult Behavior: The Requirement of Harm to Others in the Enforcement of Morality, 14 U.C.L.A.L.Rev. 581 (1967); Note, California "Consenting Adults" Law: The Sex Act in Perspective, 13 San Diego L.Rev. 439 (1976); Chappell and Wilson, Public Attitudes to the Reform Relating to Abortion and Homosexuality, 42 Austr.L.J. 120, 175 (1968), 46 Austr.L.J. 22 (1972). But see the Supreme Court has recently refused to hold unconstitutional statutes which punish sexual conduct between consenting adults in private. Doe v. Commonwealth's Attorney for City of Richmond, 403 F.Supp. 1199 (E.D.Va.1975), affirmed per curiam 425 U.S. 901 96 S.Ct. 1489, 47 L.Ed.2d 751 (1976).

12. E.g., D. Altman, Homosexual: Oppression and Liberation (1971); M. Baisden, The Dynamics of Homosexuality (1975); W. Barnett, Sexual Freedom and the Constitution Chs. 6, 7 (1973); I. Bieber, ed., Homosexuality: A Psychoanalytic Study (1962) (this work takes the older conventional view of homosexuality as "abnormal"); P. Gebhard, Sex Offenders (1965); E. Goode ed., Sexual Deviance and Sexual Deviants Chs. IV, V (1974); L. Humphreys, Tearoom Trade (1970); A. Karlen, Sexuality and Homosexuality, ch. 28 (1971) (this work contains an extensive bibliography on homosexuality); D. Klaich, Woman + Woman (1974); J. Marmor, ed., Sexual Inversion; The Multiple Roots of Homosexuality (1965); M. Weinberg and C. Williams, Male Homosexuals: Their Problems and Adaptations (1974); D. West, Homosexuality (1967). Other journalistic or personal accounts of homosexuality include J. Gerassi, The Boys of Boise (1966); M. Schofield, A Minority: A Report on the Life of the Male Homosexual in Great Britain (1960); J. Stearn, The Sixth Man (1961).

the difficulties which homosexuals face in society and to somewhat more tolerance of homosexuality.[13]

As a result of these changes in law and society, some of the bolder homosexuals have openly identified themselves,[14] and in a few instances have sought to contract marriage with persons of the same sex as themselves.[15] Whether such marriages are valid depends upon two considerations. The first is the marriage statute in the particular state. A few such statutes limit marriages to unions of a man and a woman.[16] In such states it is easy for the courts to hold same-sex marriages invalid, although no cases involving these statutes have been found. But even where the state's marriage statute does not expressly provide that marriage may only be contracted between a man and a woman, the relatively few cases on the question have held that same-sex marriages are not authorized.[17] The reasoning is that the ordinary definition

of marriage, sustained by dictionaries and long custom, whether or not spelled out in the statutes, is that it is a union of a man and a woman.[18] Therefore the union of man and man or of woman and woman cannot be a marriage.

More difficult questions arise when the contention is made that this restriction upon the capacity to marry violates various constitutional provisions. The proponents of same-sex marriage have relied upon several such provisions in support of their position. The argument has been made that the prohibition of same-sex marriages amounts to the establishment of religion, in violation of the Establishment Clause of the First Amendment, as applied to the states by the Fourteenth Amendment.[19] This argument rests upon the assertion that the prohibition of homosexual marriage arises out of and reflects the historical Christian view of marriage and the Judaeo-Christian abhorrence of homosexual

---

13. A nice example of the change in attitude toward homosexuality, which certainly has not gone very far and which still reflects much ambivalence in feeling is the action taken in 1973 by the American Psychiatric Association removing homosexuality from the category of "mental illness" and defining it as a "sexual orientation disturbance." Gould, What We Don't Know About Homosexuality, The New York Times Magazine, February 24, 1974, 13. For changes in the attitude of religious denominations toward homosexuality, see New York Times, December 3, 1967, page E 7, column 4, reporting the views of various religious authorities.

14. Parker, Homosexual in American Society Today: The Homophile—Gay Liberation Movement, 8 Crim.L. Bull. 692 (1972); Wall Street Journal, July 17, 1968, page 1, column 1.

15. Views differ on whether homosexuals, male or female, wish to form long-lasting unions or to contract "marriages". See A. Karlen, Sexuality and Homosexuality 526–528 (1971). An interview with one lesbian woman who expressed scorn for marriage is reproduced in D. Klaich, Woman + Woman 32 (1974). For an account of one church in Los Angeles which performs same-sex marriages, see New York Times, February 15, 1970, page 58, column 1. For a short time in 1975 the County Clerk of Boulder County, Colorado issued marriage licenses to homosexual couples. Boulder Daily Camera, March 27, 1975, page 1, column 1.

16. E.g., La.Stat.Ann.—Civ.Code art. 88 (Supp.1976); Md.Code, Family Law, art. 62, § 2–201 (Supp.1984). The Uniform Marriage and Divorce Act § 201, 9A Unif.L. Ann. 106 (Supp.1979) also expressly provides that marriage must be between a man and a woman. See also, e.g., Colo.Rev.Stat. § 14–2–104 (1973). Note, Homosexuals' Right To Marry: A Constitutional Test and a Legisla-

tive Solution, 128 U.Pa.L.Rev. 193 (1979) proposes a statute creating a quasi-marital statute for homosexuals.

17. Jones v. Hallahan, 501 S.W.2d 588 (Ky.1973); Baker v. Nelson, 291 Minn. 310, 191 N.W.2d 185 (1971), appeal dismissed for want of a substantial federal question, 409 U.S. 810, 93 S.Ct. 37, 34 L.Ed.2d 65 (1972); M.T. v. J.T., 140 N.J.Super. 77, 355 A.2d 204 (1976), certification denied 71 N.J. 345, 364 A.2d 1076 (1976); Frances B. v. Mark B., 78 Misc.2d 112, 355 N.Y.S.2d 712 (1974); Singer v. Hara, 11 Wash.App. 247, 522 P.2d 1187 (1974). The Baker, Jones and Singer cases denied marriage licenses to homosexual couples. The Frances B. case was a suit for an annulment by a woman married to a transsexual where the defendant did not have male genital organs, and where apparently, from the complaint, the defendant had fraudulently misrepresented his condition. Although the issues in the case are only preliminary procedural ones, the court in its opinion states that a marriage of two males would not be valid in New York. Adams v. Howerton, 486 F.Supp. 1119 (C.D.Cal.1980) judgment affirmed 673 F.2d 1036 (9th Cir.1982), cert. denied 458 U.S. 1111, 102 S.Ct. 3494, 73 L.Ed.2d 1373 (1982) held the marriage of homosexuals void for immigration purposes. See also Annot., 63 A.L.R.3d 1199 (1975); Note, The Legality of Homosexual Marriage, 82 Yale L.J. 573 (1973); Harper, Clifton, Heterosexuality: A Prerequisite for Marriage in Texas? 14 So.Tex.L.J. 220 (1973).

18. Jones v. Hallahan; Baker v. Nelson, supra, note 17.

19. U.S. Const. amends. I, XIV, § 1. The First Amendment is applied to the states by the Fourteenth under Cantwell v. Connecticut, 310 U.S. 296, 60 S.Ct. 900, 84 L.Ed. 1213 (1940).

conduct. As a matter of history this assumption seems to be correct.[20] Nonetheless the cases have summarily rejected this constitutional argument.[21] Presumably the courts deciding these cases think that some legitimate secular purpose is served by forbidding same-sex marriage, but they do not tell us what that purpose might be.[22] Various purposes are conceivable. One is to ensure that only those marriages are contracted which can produce offspring. But of course it must be conceded that the marriages of sterile couples are valid.[23] And today it can hardly be argued that procreation is the only function of marriage and the family. Therefore this purpose is hardly sufficient to sustain the cases. Another purpose is to discourage people, especially young people, from becoming homosexual, thereby placing themselves outside the mainstream of society and incurring the many difficulties and hardships which the homosexual faces. Whether this purpose is sufficient to justify the prohibition depends at least in part upon our knowledge of the origins of homosexuality. At the moment that knowledge is not comprehensive. If in fact the prohibition of same-sex marriage would have this effect, then perhaps it is constitutionally justified.

More realistically, forbidding homosexual marriage seems to constitute an attempt to enforce traditional morality, a morality based on strongly felt emotions with religious overtones.[24] Most states still have statutes imposing criminal penalties for sexual activities between men or (more rarely) between women, although these laws are enforced only sporadically and infrequently. Their continued presence in the statute books does suggest, however, that society still views such conduct as immoral. Permitting marriage between homosexuals would amount to affirmatively approving such conduct, and we are apparently not ready to take this step.

The Equal Protection Clause of the Fourteenth Amendment[25] may also be advanced as the basis for a contention that forbidding same-sex marriages is unconstitutional. The argument is that forbidding these marriages constitutes a denial by reason of sex of the right to marry, this right having been characterized by the Supreme Court on several occasions as a fundamental right.[26] A variety of verbal formulae then become available for discussing the issue, all of them resembling the now officially discredited doctrine of substantive due process. Under some cases, which may now have been repudiated by the Supreme Court, a classification resulting in the denial of a fundamental right may only be upheld where it is necessary to accomplish a compelling state interest.[27] And in evaluat-

---

20. See the authorities cited in note 8, supra.

21. Baker v. Nelson, 291 Minn. 310, 191 N.W.2d 185 (1971), appeal dismissed 409 U.S. 810, 93 S.Ct. 37, 34 L.Ed.2d 65 (1972), in a footnote, dismisses the First Amendment argument without discussion. Jones v. Hallahan, 501 S.W.2d 588 (Ky.1973) states that no constitutional issue is involved.

22. A variety of possible purposes are suggested in W. Barnett, Sexual Freedom and the Constitution ch. 5 (1973), in a discussion dealing with the criminal law respecting sodomy. See also Note, The Legality of Homosexual Marriage, 82 Yale L.J. 573, 580 (1973); and Note, Same Sex Marriage and The Constitution, 6 V.C.D.L.Rev. 275 (1973).

23. See section 2.12, Practitioner's Edition. Of course impotence, the inability to engage in sexual relations is a basis for invalidating marriages. The objection to homosexuality is not that homosexuals cannot engage in sexual relations but that they engage in sexual conduct different from that of heterosexual persons.

24. Cf. H.L.A. Hart, Law Liberty and Morality (1963); P. Devlin, The Enforcement of Morals (1959); Dworkin, Lord Devlin and the Enforcement of Morals, 75 Yale L.J.

986 (1966). See also Reynolds v. United States, 98 U.S. (8 Otto) 145, 25 L.Ed. 244 (1878).

25. U.S. Const. amend. XIV, § 1.

26. E.g., Skinner v. Oklahoma, 316 U.S. 535, 62 S.Ct. 1110, 86 L.Ed. 1655 (1942); Griswold v. Connecticut, 381 U.S. 479, 85 S.Ct. 1678, 14 L.Ed.2d 510 (1965); Loving v. Virginia, 388 U.S. 1, 87 S.Ct. 1817, 18 L.Ed.2d 1010 (1967); Boddie v. Connecticut, 401 U.S. 371, 91 S.Ct. 780, 28 L.Ed.2d 113 (1971).

27. E.g. Griswold v. Connecticut, 381 U.S. 479, 486, 85 S.Ct. 1678, 1682, 14 L.Ed.2d 510 (1965) (Goldberg, J., concurring). Another factor which might lead the Court to indulge in a strict scrutiny of the classification is that gender is its basis. A majority of the Court has not thus far, however, held that gender is a "suspect classification" like race. See, e.g. Frontiero v. Richardson, 411 U.S. 677, 93 S.Ct. 1764, 36 L.Ed.2d 583 (1973) (in this case a plurality but not a majority of the Court thought that sex is a "suspect classification"); Reed v. Reed, 404 U.S. 71, 92 S.Ct. 251, 30 L.Ed.2d 225 (1971); Cleveland Board of Education v. LaFleur, 414 U.S. 632, 94 S.Ct. 791, 39 L.Ed.2d 52 (1974); Stanton v. Stanton, 421 U.S. 7, 95 S.Ct. 1373, 43 L.Ed.2d 688 (1975), appeal after remand 555 P.2d

ing that interest, the state law is subjected to "strict scrutiny." Whether the prohibition on same-sex marriage is necessary to accomplish some compelling state interest depends upon the existence and seriousness of the purposes outlined in the preceding paragraphs. The issue here is not unlike that posed by the Establishment Clause. More recent Supreme Court opinions suggest that in determining the validity of such classifications the interests of society should be compared with the harm inflicted on those individuals subjected to the rule, and if societal interests outweigh those harms, the prohibition should be upheld.[28] In view of the continuing hostility toward homosexuality still evident in the United States, it seems likely that society's interest will be considered paramount to those of the homosexual and that therefore the ban on same-sex marriage will be held constitutional. The few cases which have considered this issue have in fact reached this conclusion, although without any thorough consideration of the various arguments. Baker v. Nelson,[29] perhaps the leading case, contents itself with the statement that the Fourteenth Amendment does not require "abstract symmetry" in legislative classifications, and that there is a clear difference between distinctions based upon race which are of course unconstitutional and those based upon sex. It contains no discussion of the possible purposes underlying the prohibition of same-sex

marriage or of whether those purposes reflect some substantial social interest.

Finally, the proposed Equal Rights Amendment to the United States Constitution and similar amendments to the various state constitutions may be relied upon to validate same-sex marriages. These amendments usually state that "Equality of rights under the law shall not be denied or abridged * * * on account of sex."[30] Unlike the Equal Protection Clause, the Equal Rights Amendments purport to be absolute. In fact there would be little reason to propose them if they were not absolute, since the Supreme Court has already shown that it will eliminate most sex-based classifications in reliance upon the Equal Protection Clause.[31] A leading proponent of the Amendment has stated that it bars sex-based classifications even though they might be based on compelling state interests.[32] Therefore on its face the Amendment would seem clearly to invalidate any state's attempt to limit the right to marry on the basis of sex. The only cases which have dealt with the question have held that the Equal Rights Amendment does not prevent the state from forbidding same-sex marriage.[33] In reasoning more ingenious than persuasive the Washington Court of Appeals took the view that no right was being denied to the two male plaintiffs on the basis of sex when they were refused a marriage license. Instead, the court said, they were being denied entry into marriage because the definition of marriage

112 (Utah 1976), judgment vacated 429 U.S. 501, 97 S.Ct. 717, 50 L.Ed.2d 723 (1977), on remand 564 P.2d 303 (Utah 1977), rehearing denied 567 P.2d 625 (Utah 1977); Orr v. Orr, 440 U.S. 268, 99 S.Ct. 1102, 59 L.Ed.2d 306 (1979), on remand 374 So.2d 895 (Ala.Civ.App.1979), writ denied 374 So.2d 898 (1979).

28. San Antonio Ind. School District v. Rodriguez, 411 U.S. 1, 70, 93 S.Ct. 1278, 1315, 36 L.Ed.2d 16 (1973) (Marshal, J., dissenting), rehearing denied 411 U.S. 959, 93 S.Ct. 1919, 36 L.Ed.2d 418 (1973); Weber v. Aetna Casualty & Surety Co., 406 U.S. 164, 92 S.Ct. 1400, 31 L.Ed.2d 768 (1972).

29. 291 Minn. 310, 191 N.W.2d 185 (1971), appeal dismissed 410 U.S. 810, 93 S.Ct. 37, 34 L.Ed.2d 65 (1972); Jones v. Hallahan, 501 S.W.2d 588 (Ky.1973); Adams v. Howerton, 673 F.2d 1036 (9th Cir.1982), cert. denied 458 U.S. 1111, 102 S.Ct. 3494, 73 L.Ed.2d 1373 (1982) refused to recognize a homosexual marriage for immigration purposes and held that such refusal was not unconstitutional.

30. H.R.J.Res. 208, S.R.J. 8, 92d Cong., 1st Sess. (1971). The state constitutional provisions are, in most states which have adopted such provisions, almost identical to the federal amendment. See, e.g., Colo. Const. art. II, § 29; Vernon's Ann.Tex. Const. Art I, §§ 3a; West's Ann.R.C.Wash.A. Const. Art. 31, § 1.

31. See the cases cited in note 27, supra. The validity of such marriages under the state ERA's is comprehensively and ably discussed in Kurtz, The State Equal Rights Amendments and Their Impact on Domestic Relations Law, 11 Fam.L.Q. 101 (1977).

32. Emerson, In Support of the Equal Rights Amendment, 6 Harv.Civ.Rights—Civ.Lib.L.Rev. 225, 231 (1971).

33. De Santo v. Barnsley, 328 Pa.Super. 181, 476 A.2d 952 (1984); Singer v. Hara, 11 Wash.App. 247, 522 P.2d 1187 (1974).

did not include the relationship which they proposed to form. One may sympathize with the court's discomfort without approving of the way in which it begged the question. The fact is that the two plaintiffs were denied the opportunity to form the desired relationship because one of them was not a woman. An important right was denied on account of sex.[34] A more candid way of dealing with the issue would be to say that such unions are so clearly contrary to contemporary notions of morality that they may not be recognized, notwithstanding the Equal Rights Amendment. Perhaps other courts may take that course. In any event, at the present it seems unlikely that the courts will be bold enough to give effect to the plain language of the Equal Rights Amendment in this context.

A related problem concerns the marriage of transsexuals. A transsexual is a person who is convinced he is of one sex but who is anatomically of the other sex.[35] By complex and expensive surgical and medical procedures it has become possible to transform the anatomy of the transsexual so that he can assume his psychological gender. The few cases dealing with the marriages of transsexuals seem to have judged the validity of the marriage by reference to the transsexual's anatomical sex. If a person has had a successful sex change operation from male to female and is able to function sexually as a female, marriage with a male has in one case been held valid.[36] Presumably the same result would be reached if a woman had a sex

change operation and married a woman. But if no such operation has occurred, the marriage of a person anatomically male with another male has been held invalid even though one of the parties considers himself psychologically a woman and wishes to be a woman.[37] In the latter case the courts have treated the transsexual as they have the homosexual, focussing upon the anatomical rather than the psychological sex and treating the marriage as between two persons of the same sex.

 WESTLAW REFERENCES

constitution! unconstitutional! /s same-sex lesbian homosexual! /s marri! martial marry!

find 191 nw2d 185

topic(253) /p transsexual! homosexual! lesbian same-sex /s marri! marital marry!

§ 2.9 Incest [1]

A universal feature of the societies which have been studied by anthropologists is the existence of incest regulations. In every society there are rules, both of great complexity and great diversity, governing sexual relations between persons who are related by blood or marriage.[2] In fact, in the opinion of some scholars, certain specific incest regulations are universally found, for example, those prohibiting sexual relations between siblings and between parent and child, prohibitions which for convenience are referred to as operating within the nuclear family.[3] All societies, including our own, go be-

34. For a thorough and persuasive argument that the Equal Rights Amendment does validate same-sex marriage, see Note, The Legality of Homosexual Marriage, 82 Yale L.J. 573 (1973).

35. A. Karlen, Sexuality and Homosexuality ch. 22 (1971); Holloway, Transsexuals—Their Legal Sex, 40 U.Colo.L.Rev. 282 (1968); W. Barnett, Sexual Freedom and the Constitution 147–148 (1973); Green and Money, Transsexualism and Sex Reassignment (1969).

36. M.T. v. J.T., 140 N.J.Super. 77, 355 A.2d 204 (1976), certification denied 71 N.J. 345, 364 A.2d 1076 (1976). But in the famous English case of Corbett v. Corbett [1970] 2 All Eng.Rep. 33, a man was granted an annulment of his marriage to a transsexual who had had a sex change operation and was apparently able to function to some extent as a female.

37. Frances B. v. Mark B., 78 Misc.2d 112, 355 N.Y.S.2d 712 (1974), 8 Akron L.Rev. 369 (1975); Anony-

mous v. Anonymous, 67 Misc.2d 982, 325 N.Y.S.2d 499 (1971). See also Note, Heterosexuality: A Prerequisite to Marriage in Texas? 14 So.Tex.L.J. 220 (1973).

§ 2.9

1. See Storke, The Incestuous Marriage—Relic of the Past, 36 Univ. of Colo.L.Rev. 473 (1964).

2. M. Mead, Male and Female 35, 153 (Mentor ed. 1955); M. Mead, Incest, 7 International Encyclopedia of the Social Sciences 115 (1968), including a useful bibliography.

3. G. Murdock, Social Structure Ch. 10 (1949). The nuclear family, according to Murdock and other social scientists, is composed of a husband, his wife and their offspring. H. Maisch, Incest 33 (1972) discusses the exceptions to the incest taboo within the nuclear family, which he finds to have been quite extensive in many of

yond this and forbid sexual intercourse between persons related in other ways, such as between grandparent and grandchild, between cousins, between uncle and niece or aunt and nephew. Here there is diversity. Once we move beyond the nuclear family we can find little general agreement among the societies studied as to the relationships which should disqualify persons for marriage.

The prohibition of intercourse within the nuclear family evokes feelings of great emotional intensity which have been expressed in literature and myth [4] and sometimes by judges in opinions which are certainly not literature.[5] The emotion diminishes in intensity where relationships outside the nuclear family are concerned. Since the word "incest" is used to describe sexual relations between any persons related in the forbidden degrees, however, there is sometimes a failure to distinguish between the kind of incest which is abhorrent to all persons and all societies and the kind as to which there may be a legitimate difference of opinion. In order to emphasize this distinction it is sometimes useful to refer to intercourse within the nuclear family as true incest and to label as technical incest sexual relations between persons related in more distant degrees.[6]

Many students of human behavior have asked why incest taboos are found in all societies. What functions do they serve? Why are violations viewed with such horror? Why have they taken such diverse forms? The responses to such questions and the explana-

tions for the origins of incest taboos are more numerous than the questions. Some explanations treat the incest taboo as giving institutional form to pre-existing incest avoidance arising from "instinct" [7] or from the dulling of sexual desire due to closeness of the family association.[8] Such theories either fail to explain or are self-contradictory. Others have speculated that for early man inbreeding was originally impossible, due to short life spans relative to the length of time needed for maturation, to the small proportion of individuals reaching maturity and to the spacing and random sex ratios of offspring, and that incest avoidance was later institutionalized as the incest taboo because of its social advantages in forming ties outside the family, in preventing sexual rivalries within the family and perhaps also because of its genetic benefits.[9] Freudian explanations of the incest taboo account for its emotional intensity as being the result of the parents' rejection and frustration of the young child's sexual attraction to the parent or sibling of the opposite sex, causing the child to repress the forbidden attraction by defense mechanisms. This process sets up such intense conflicts of fear and longing in the child that thereafter any thoughts of incest are accompanied by the deep-seated emotions which even now surround all discussions of the subject.[10] Other more teleological theories emphasize the survival value of incest taboos in strengthening the nuclear family, and in producing adaptive and self-sufficient

the societies studied by historians and anthropologists. But see R. Masters, Patterns of Incest 39, 224 (1963).

4. E.g., Sophocles, Oedipus Rex; D. Defoe, Moll Flanders. Mullahy, Oedipus Myth and Complex (1948) discusses incest from the standpoint of psychoanalytic theory. See also H. Maisch, Incest 12–21 (1972).

5. E.g., Weiss v. Weiss, 8 D. & C. 534 (Pa.1924); Johnson v. Johnson, 57 Wash. 89, 106 P. 500 (1910).

6. This distinction is made by Chancellor Kent in Wightman v. Wightman, 4 Johns. Ch. 343 (N.Y.1820).

7. R. Lowie, Primitive Society 15, 105 (1920).

8. II E. Westermarck, The History of Human Marriage 192 (5th ed. 1921); Wolf, Childhood Association and Sexual Attraction: A Further Test of the Westermarck Hypothesis, 72 American Anthropologist 503 (1969). See also L. White, The Definition and Prohibition of Incest,

50 American Anthropologist, New Series 416 (1948); R. Masters, Patterns of Incest 39 (1963); Talmon, Mate Selection in Collective Settlements, 29 American Sociological Review 491 (1964); Stephen, Mate Selection Among Second Generation Kibbutz Adolescents and Adults: Incest Avoidance and Negative Imprinting, 1 Archives of Sexual Behavior 293 (1971).

9. Aberle, Bronfenbrenner, Hess, Miller, Schneider and Spuhler, The Incest Taboo and the Mating Patterns of Animals, 65 American Anthropologist 253 (1963); Parker, The Precultural Basis of the Incest Taboo: Toward a Biosocial Theory, 78 American Anthropologist 285, 286, 288–289, 299 (1976).

10. G. Murdock, Social Structure 292–313 (1949). See also Model Penal Code 232 (Tent.Draft No. 4, 1955); T. Parsons and R. Bales, Family, Socialization and Interaction Process 397–398 (1955).

children.[11] None of these explanations is capable of verification at this point, but they do throw some light on the possible social functions of incest rules which may be helpful when contemporary prohibitions on first cousin marriages and marriages between persons related by affinity are being questioned.[12]

A genetic explanation for the origin of incest taboos has occasionally been advanced.[13] Since nothing was known about genetics in the remote historical periods when incest rules originated, it seems clear that those rules could not have purposely been based on their genetic benefits. Furthermore the rules of many advanced societies forbid marriages which involve no inbreeding or bear no relation to possible genetic consequences, as for example the prohibitions upon marriage between persons related by affinity. Genetics therefore will hardly explain the origin or development of incest regulations. On the other hand, if inbreeding within human populations has harmful genetic consequences, incest taboos may in the past have had significant survival value, particularly among small or isolated societies. In that sense the evolutionary effect of genetics may have brought about the avoidance of incest.

Although one may still find statements to the effect that inbreeding is not genetically harmful,[14] most geneticists today seem to agree that it sharply increases the probability of appearance of detrimental or even lethal characteristics in offspring.[15] The reason for this is that many, if not all, persons carry recessive genes, some of which arise as muta-

tions, which are either detrimental or lethal, but which are masked so long as they occur in heterozygous form. Inbreeding dramatically increases the chance that the offspring will be homozygous for the harmful gene, the degrees of probability that this will occur being mathematically computable for intermarriage between persons related in varying degrees.[16] The closer the inbreeding, the greater will be the probability of genetic harm, but as a practical matter we need only be concerned with such relationships as first cousins or uncle-niece and aunt-nephew, since no one advocates permitting closer relatives to marry.[17] It therefore appears that present statutes prohibiting such marriages are amply supported by genetic theory.

The prevailing influence upon incest prohibitions in Anglo-American law has been religion. Until the time of the English Reformation the Roman Catholic canon law, which was the source of all rules on the subject, disqualified for marriage those within the fourth degree of consanguinity, by the Church's method of computing degrees as acts of generation from the common ancestor.[18] Relationship by affinity also was a disqualification, within broad limits. The rules were enforced in the ecclesiastical courts, as they continued to be even after the Reformation. The impediments to marriage based on relationship were (until 1835) said to be canonical, making the marriage merely voidable rather than void.[19] The extreme breadth of the forbidden relationships meant that divorces, or as we would say, annulments, for

---

11. T. Parsons, The Incest Taboo, 5 British J. of Sociology 101 (1954); Schwartzman, The Individual, Incest, and Exogamy, 37 Psychiatry 171 (1974); Aberle, Bronfenbrenner, Hess, Miller, Schneider and Spuhler, The Incest Taboo and the Mating Patterns of Animals, 65 American Anthropologist 253, 262 (1963); H. Maisch, Incest 58–64 (1972).

12. E.g., H. Maisch, Incest 81–85 (1972).

13. C. Stern, Principles of Human Genetics 492 (3d ed. 1973).

14. H. Maisch, Incest 80 (1972).

15. W. Bodmer and L. Cavalli-Sforza, Genetics, Evolution and Man Ch. 11 (1976); C. Stern, Principles of Human Genetics 607, 625 (3d ed. 1973); W. Boyd, Genetics and the Races of Man 123 (1950); A. Montagu, Human Heredity Ch. 17 (1963).

16. C. Stern, Principles of Human Genetics 493 (3d ed. 1973); W. Bodmer and L. Cavalli-Sforza, Genetics, Evolution and Man 372 (1976).

17. The frequency of deaths, diseases and physical and mental defects are markedly greater for the offspring of first cousin mating than for the population as a whole, according to Stern. C. Stern, Principles of Human Genetics 494 (3d ed. 1973).

18. II Pollock and Maitland, History of English Law, 387–389 (2d ed. 1898).

19. 2 Burns, Ecclesiastical Law 408 (4th ed. 1781); Wightman v. Wightman, 4 Johns. Ch. 343 (1820); Bowers v. Bowers, 10 Rich.Eq. 551, 73 Am.Dec. 99 (S.C.1858). In 1835 Lord Lyndhurst's Act, 5 & 6 Wm. IV, ch. 54, made consanguineous and affinal marriages void rather than merely voidable. By requiring the retrospective invalida-

consanguinity or affinity were so readily available as to provide a relatively easy way of escaping from a burdensome marriage. The legislation of Henry VIII reduced the prohibited relationships to those found in the Bible,[20] still an extensive list. It included those related both by blood and by marriage in the ascending and descending line, brothers and sisters, uncles and nieces and aunts and nephews.[21] In 1907 the statute permitting marriage with the deceased wife's sister was passed,[22] ending a long and vehement controversy.[23] The present English law has restricted the list of prohibited relationships by allowing marriage between most of those related by affinity whose marriages were formerly proscribed.[24]

American incest statutes are based upon the English experience and the Levitical degrees. The religious and moral background of the law of incestuous marriage has led some courts to discuss difficult questions of statutory construction or the conflict of laws in

terms of divine or natural law when the opinions expressed may have little more basis than the court's personal predilection.[25] This is particularly true of those cases dealing with technical incest in terms more appropriate for true incest. In fact technical incest is the only kind of incest which is seen in the law of marriage. All states prohibit marriage between parent and child, brother and sister and between grandparent and grandchild,[26] but no cases involving such marriages have arisen or are likely to arise. Incest in the sense of sexual intercourse does occur between persons so related, usually between father and daughter, and is dealt with by the criminal law.[27] The relationships which have produced litigation in the law of marriage include first cousins, uncle and niece or aunt and nephew, and certain relationships by affinity. It would be desirable, in view of the difficult conflicts questions raised by existing law, if the states could enact uniform legislation on incestuous marriages, but this has not

---

tion of marriage and bastardizing of issue, this statute succeeded in doing a good deal of social harm.

20. The governing statute was 32 Hen. VIII, ch. 38 (1540), which was repealed in 1554, 1 & 2 Phillip and Mary, ch. 8, but reenacted in 1558, 1 Eliz., ch. 1. It then remained substantially in force until 1907. The Levitical degrees, to which the statute refers are found in 18th Leviticus, verses 6–18. See 4 Holdsworth, History of English Law, 490–492 (1924), and 5 Bacon's Abridgement, 289–294 (7th ed. 1832).

21. A detailed list of the forbidden relationships can be found in 2 Burns, Ecclesiastical Law 400 (4th ed. 1781).

22. Deceased Wife's Sister's Marriage Act, 7 Edw. VII, ch. 47 (1907).

23. Gilbert and Sullivan, Iolanthe, Act 1: "He shall prick that annual blister/Marriage with deceased wife's sister."

24. The basic statute was 12 & 13 Geo. 6, ch. 76 (1949), since amended by The Marriage (Enabling) Act, 1960, 8 & 9 Eliz. 2, ch. 29, which enacted the recommendations of The Report of the Royal Commission on Marriage and Divorce, 298–302 (1956). The list of forbidden relationships is now that found in Jackson, The Formation and Annulment of Marriage, 127–129 (1951), as modified by the 1960 Act.

25. As in Brook v. Brook, 9 H.L.C. 193, 11 Eng.Rep. 703 (1861), in which the House of Lords found that a marriage of a man to his deceased wife's sister had been declared to be contrary to God's law. Presumably the English Parliament was able to change God's law in 1907 when it permitted such marriages to be contracted. Another example is United States ex rel. Devine v. Rodgers, 109 Fed. 886 (E.D.Pa.1901), in which the judge seemed to

think the community's moral sense would be shocked by the marriage of uncle and niece.

26. The general rule is that this includes persons related by the half as well as the whole blood, whether or not that is made explicit in the statute. See, e.g., People v. Womack, 167 Cal.App.2d 130, 334 P.2d 309 (1959); Commonwealth v. Riegel, 22 Pa.Dist.Rep. 903 (1911), and other cases in Annot., 72 A.L.R.2d 706 (1960). Likewise the prohibitions apply to illegitimate as well as legitimate children. See Robertson v. Channing, 1928 Scots Law Times 376, 40 Jurid.Rev. 283 (1928), and 1 Bishop, Marriage, Divorce and Separation sec. 745 (1891). Statutes in some states explicitly provide that the prohibited relationships include persons related by the half blood. See, e.g., West's Ann.Cal.Civ.Code § 4400 (1983); Ill.—Smith Hurd Ann. ch. 40, § 212 (1984); Mont.Code Ann. § 40–1–401 (1983); N.Y.—McKinney's Dom.Rel.Law § 5 (1977); V. Tex.C.A., Fam.Code § 2.21 (Supp.1985).

27. For a discussion of the criminal law on this point see Model Penal Code 231–240 (Tent.Draft No. 4, 1955); R. Perkins, Criminal Law 459 (3d ed. 1982). People v. Baker, 69 Cal.2d 44, 69 Cal.Rptr. 595, 442 P.2d 675 (1968) held that the criminal incest statute did not prohibit sexual relations between uncle and niece where they were related by the half blood only. And State v. Moore, 158 Conn. 461, 262 A.2d 166 (1969) held that relations by affinity were not covered by the criminal statute.

Where a child is involved, incest may be more effectively dealt with by the family court, as has been recognized in some states. See, e.g., N.Y.—McKinney's Fam.Ct. Act §§ 117, 812, 1012, 1013 (1983) (1983 & Supp. 1987); (Supp. 1984); S. v. S., 63 Misc.2d 1, 311 N.Y.S.2d 169 (Fam.Ct. 1970); People v. Lewis, 29 N.Y.2d 923, 329 N.Y.S.2d 100, 279 N.E.2d 856 (1972).

yet occurred.[28] Many states presently forbid uncle-niece and aunt-nephew marriages.[29] Relatively few states forbid first cousin marriage,[30] although genetic considerations seem to dictate the prohibition of such marriages.[31] Stepchildren and adopted children should be treated like natural children and their attempted marriages (fortunately very rare) to adoptive parents or stepparents should be prohibited, since they are in practical effect members of the nuclear family even though not related by blood. Marriages of this sort are socially as objectionable as any marriage of parent and child. Although it has been held that a statute forbidding the marriage of parent and child does not apply to adopted children,[32] a few statutes have been drafted so as specifically to cover the problem.[33] And some statutes also specifically forbid marriages between stepparents and stepchildren.[34]

---

28. The Uniform Marriage and Divorce Act sec. 207, 9A Unif.L.Ann. 108 (1979) prohibits marriages between ancestor, brother and sister whether by whole or half blood or by adoption, and between uncle and niece and aunt and nephew, with an exception for marriages permitted by the customs of aboriginal cultures. This statute has been adopted in only a few states, however.

29. E.g., West's Ann.Cal.Civ.Code § 4400 (1983); Colo. Rev.Stat. § 14–2–110 (1973); Ill.—Smith Hurd Ann. ch. 40, § 212 (1984); Mont.Code Ann. § 40–1–401 (1983); N.H.Rev.Stat.Ann. §§ 457:1, 457:2 (1968); N.Y.—McKinney's Dom.Rel.Law § 5 (1977); Pa.Stat. tit. 48, § 1–5 (1965); V.Tex.C.A., Fam.Code § 2.21 (1985). These prohibitions apply to relatives of the half blood and to illegitimates also. See note 26, supra.

30. E.g., Ill.—Smith Hurd Ann. ch. 40, § 212 (1983); Minn.Stat.Ann. § 517.03 (Supp.1984); Mont.Rev.Codes § 40–1–401 (1983); Okl.Stat. tit. 43, § 2 (1979); Pa.Stat. tit. 48, § 1–5 (1965); West Rev.Code Wash.Ann. § 26.04.020 (1961); Wis.Stat.Ann. § 765.03 (West 1981). In Thomas v. Brown, 239 F.Supp. 350 (E.D.Okl.1965) the court held that persons whose mothers were step-sisters were not related by blood and therefore were not prohibited from marrying under the statute which forbade the marriage of first cousins. In re Kathrein's Estate, 16 Ill. 2d 621, 158 N.E.2d 599 (1959) upheld the marriage where the wife's mother was the husband's cousin, making the parties either second cousins or first cousins once removed. A similar case is In re Jacobsen Marriage License, 8 D. & C.2d 144 (Pa.Orphan's Court 1957).

31. See the authorities cited in notes 16, 17, supra. Wisconsin deals with the genetic objection by permitting first cousins to marry when the woman has reached the age of fifty-five. Wis.Stat.Ann. § 765.03 (West 1981).

32. State v. Lee, 196 Miss. 311, 17 So.2d 277 (1944). The case seems to be in error. In view of the obvious intent of the adoption statute, usually expressed in very broad terms, that the adopted child shall be for all purposes the child of the adoptive parents, the incest prohibition should apply to such children without specific statutory language. See also State v. Rogers, 260 N.C. 406, 133 S.E.2d 1 (1963) and Wadlington, The Adopted Child and Intra-Family Marriage Prohibitions, 49 Va.L. Rev. 478 (1963).

33. E.g., Miss.Code 1973, § 93–1–1; V.Tex.C.A.Fam. Code § 2.21 (1985). The Uniform Marriage and Divorce Act § 207, 9A Unif.L.Ann. 108 (1979) prohibits marriage between ancestor and descendant and between brother and sister where the relationship is by adoption as well as by blood. Israel v. Allen, 195 Colo. 263, 577 P.2d 762 (1978) held that the prohibition in the Uniform Act, so far as it applied to marriage between adopted brother and sister, did not meet the "test of minimum rationality" and so was a violation of the Equal Protection Clause of the Fourteenth Amendment to the United States Constitution. The court cited no authority for this position except for an affidavit from the Roman Catholic Bishop of Denver stating that his Church did not object to such a marriage. The court also seems to have thought it relevant that the parents of the persons seeking to marry favored the marriage. It drew an analogy to prohibitions upon marriage between persons related by affinity, although such prohibitions a) have not generally been held unconstitutional and b) they are not at all analogous to those involved in Israel. The purpose of the Uniform Act's prohibition is to preserve the integrity of the adoption process and to exclude from adoptive families sexual relations, rivalries and conflicts. 9A Unif.L.Ann. 109 (1979). This purpose is consistent with the general treatment of adoptive relationships and with the purposes underlying incest prohibitions as revealed by the extensive research and writing on the subject. R. Masters, Patterns of Incest 60 (1963); M. Mead, Anomalies in American Post Divorce Relationships, in Divorce and After, 104–108 (1970); S. Weinberg, Incest Behavior (1955). The Israel case therefore stands as an extreme example of the substitution of a court's view of the wisdom of the statute for that of the legislature. The case also casts doubt on the constitutionality of the Uniform Act's prohibition of marriage between adopting parent and adopted child.

34. E.g., Conn.Gen.Stat.Ann. § 46b–21 (1984); Iowa Code Ann. § 595.19 (1981); Mass.Gen.Laws Ann. ch. 207, §§ 1, 2 (1984); Mich.Comp.Law Ann. §§ 25.3, 25.4 (1984); N.H.Rev.Stat.Ann. §§ 457:1, 457:2 (1968); Pa.Stat. tit. 48, § 1–5 (1965); Tenn.Code Ann. § 36–3–101 (1984). See Rhodes v. McAfee, 224 Tenn. 495, 457 S.W.2d 522 (1970) invalidating a marriage of stepfather and stepdaughter after the stepfather's divorce from the mother. Henderson v. State, 26 Ala.App. 263, 157 So. 884 (1934) held that where there were no issue of the marriage, the stepmother's relation by affinity to her stepson ended on the death of the stepson's father, so that the marriage of the stepmother with the stepson did not violate the incest statute. But see Tyler v. Andrews, 40 App.D.C. 100 (1834).

A few states prohibit some other marriages between persons related by affinity. See, e.g., Iowa Code Ann. § 595.19 (1981); Mass.Gen.Law Ann. ch. 207, §§ 1, 2 (1984); Miss.Code 1973, § 93–1–1.

The great majority of states, either by statute or case law, pronounce those marriages void which violate the incest statute.[35] The meaning of "void" in this context seems to be that the purported marriage is an absolute nullity, which cannot be ratified by the parties, and which may be attacked at any time, either collaterally or directly, either before or after the death of a party.[36] The reason for taking this strong position is partly the assumption that incest means the marriage of brother and sister, or parent and child, and a failure to see that the practical problems all arise out of marriages between persons less closely related. There is also the argument found in some cases that incest is a crime, and that a criminal relationship should not be given any legal sanction, even the limited one of calling it voidable.[37] The consequences of this position are extremely harsh in specific cases. For example, a marriage of first cousins is contracted and the parties live together in all respects for some years, when the husband is killed in an accident arising out of his employment. If the marriage is void, the wife receives no workmen's compensation.[38] The cases of this sort are by no means rare.[39] A better solution would be to set up two classes

of incest, making marriages within the nuclear family void, but all others merely voidable.

The most difficult problem raised by the incest statutes is that of the conflict of laws. The cases are in hopeless disagreement, both in outcome and in rationale. Here again much of the difficulty arises out of the courts' failure to discriminate between true and technical incest, against the background of Story's famous principle. Story stated the applicable rule to be that the law of the place of celebration governs the validity of marriages unless they are incestuous according to the general consent of all Christendom, or are positively prohibited by the public law of a country from motives of policy.[40] The first Restatement of Conflicts substantially adopted this rule.[41] The second Restatement adopts a dual rule. It first provides that the validity of marriage is to be determined by the law of the state which has the most significant relationship to the spouses and the marriage, and then provides that a marriage valid by the law of the place in which it was contracted will be valid elsewhere unless it violates the strong public policy of another state which had the most significant relationship to the spouses and the marriage.[42] Professor Ehrenzweig has proposed that the marriage should be upheld if it

35. Osoinach v. Watkins, 235 Ala. 564, 180 So. 577 (1938); In re Mortenson's Estate, 83 Ariz. 87, 316 P.2d 1106 (1957); Ragan v. Cox, 208 Ark. 809, 187 S.W.2d 874 (1945); Catalano v. Catalano, 148 Conn. 288, 170 A.2d 726 (1961); Arado v. Arado, 281 Ill. 123, 117 N.E. 816 (1917); Sclamberg v. Sclamberg, 220 Ind. 209, 41 N.E.2d 801 (1942); McIlvain v. Scheibley, 109 Ky. 455, 59 S.W. 498 (1900); Blaisdell v. Bickum, 139 Mass. 250, 1 N.E. 281 (1885); Meisenhelder v. Chicago & N.W. Ry. Co., 170 Minn. 317, 213 N.W. 32 (1927); In re Marriage of Adams, 185 Mont. 63, 604 P.2d 332 (1979); Bucca v. State, 43 N.J. Super. 315, 128 A.2d 506 (1957); In re Estate of Stiles, 59 Ohio St.2d 73, 391 N.E.2d 1026 (1979); Rhodes v. McAfee, 224 Tenn. 495, 457 S.W.2d 522 (1970); Johnson v. Johnson, 57 Wash. 89, 106 P. 500 (1910).

Holding the marriage voidable: Tyler v. Andrews, 40 App.D.C. 100 (1834); Harrison v. State, 22 Md. 468 (1864); Mazzolini v. Mazzolini, 168 Ohio St. 357, 155 N.E.2d 206 (1958); Bowers v. Bowers, 10 Rich.Eq. 551 (S.C.1858); Martin v. Martin, 54 W.Va. 301, 46 S.E. 120 (1903).

36. Mazzolini v. Mazzolini, 168 Ohio St. 357, 155 N.E.2d 206 (1958). For a discussion of the void-voidable problem, see Note, 17 Iowa L.Rev. 254 (1932).

37. Catalano v. Catalano, 148 Conn. 288, 170 A.2d 726 (1961); McIlvaine v. Scheibley, 109 Ky. 455, 59 S.W. 498 (1900).

38. Meisenhelder v. Chicago & N.W. Ry. Co., 170 Minn. 317, 213 N.W. 32 (1927), 26 Mich.L.Rev. 327 (1928).

39. Osoinach v. Watkins, 235 Ala. 564, 180 So. 577 (1938) (question of inheritance); In re Mortenson's Estate, 83 Ariz. 87, 316 P.2d 1106 (1957) (inheritance); Catalano v. Catalano, 148 Conn. 288, 170 A.2d 726 (1961) (widow's allowance); Arado v. Arado, 281 Ill. 123, 117 N.E. 816 (1917) (divorce); Jeffery v. Jeffery, 55 Ill.App.2d 387, 204 N.E.2d 582 (1965) (separate maintenance denied to the "wife"); McIlvaine v. Scheibley, 109 Ky. 455, 59 S.W. 498 (1900) (dower); Rhodes v. McAfee, 224 Tenn. 495, 457 S.W.2d 522 (1970) (dower and homestead rights denied).

40. 1 J. Story, Conflict of Laws, 205–218 (5th ed. 1857).

41. Restatement, Conflict of Laws § 132 (1934).

42. Restatement (Second) of Conflict of Laws sec. 283 (1971). The state having the most significant relationship to the spouses and marriage is to be located in accordance with section 6 of the Restatement, which lists a variety of factors such as the relevant policies of the forum and of other interested states, the protection of justified expectations, predictability and uniformity of result and the like. Section 6 does little to assist the courts in solving this problem other than to direct their attention to factors which they probably would have

is valid either according to the law of the place of celebration, or of the domicile of one of the parties at the time of the marriage, or of the domicile of the parties at the time of commencement of the suit, providing it does not run counter to a strong policy of the forum.[43] This proposal has virtues, but it gives us no clue as to how strong the forum's policy must be in order to override the principle of validation.

Many of the cases do, in result at least, support Ehrenzweig's principle of validation. Thus if the parties' marriage is valid by the law of the place of celebration, and if that is also their domicile at the time of the marriage, other states often uphold it.[44] In this situation the forum is apparently disposed to be tolerant of marriages which, if contracted

within their borders, would be incestuous.[45] The result should be the same where the marriage is valid by the domicile's law though not by the lex loci, but at least one case has denied validity in such circumstances.[46]

When the domicile of the parties is in the forum, and they go outside in order to evade the forum's incest regulations, the courts are not so tolerant. Some cases in this situation hold the marriage invalid, insisting that the forum's domiciliaries must observe its laws.[47] Even if only one party was domiciled in the forum these courts would invalidate the marriage, at least where the forum is also the marital domicile.[48] There are many other cases, however, the leading one being In re May's Estate [49] which accept such marriages as valid notwithstanding the parties' intent to

considered without the help of the Restatement. The effect is to leave the issue at large.

43. A. Ehrenzweig, Conflict of Laws, 378 (1962).

44. Dannelli v. Dannelli, 4 Bush 51 (Ky.1868) (semble); Sutton v. Warren, 10 Metc. 451 (Mass.1845) (marriage in England of English domiciliaries, voidable by English law, cannot be collaterally attacked in Massachusetts though would be void by Massachusetts law); Garcia v. Garcia, 25 S.D. 645, 127 N.W. 586 (1910) (marriage of first cousins in California, between California domiciliaries valid in South Dakota, on the lex loci theory, this not being incestuous by the general consent of Christendom); Brook v. Brook, 9 H.L.C. 193, 11 Eng.Rep. 703 (1861) (dictum); In re Bozzelli's Settlement, [1902] 1 Ch. 751 (Italian marriage between Italian citizens valid in England, though invalid by English law, on the theory of lex loci, the marriage not being incestuous by the general consent of Christendom); In re Green, 25 Times L.Rep. 222 (Ch.Div.1909) (marriage in England of man and deceased wife's sister, both English domiciliaries, followed by change of domicile to New York where they contracted a common law marriage valid by New York law, held would be recognized as valid in England.) But cf. State v. Nakashima, 62 Wash. 686, 114 P. 894 (1911) containing dictum that a marriage of first cousins in another state would not be recognized if they later moved to Washington. In United States ex rel. Devine v. Rodgers, 109 Fed. 886 (E.D.Pa.1901) the court refused to recognize the marriage of uncle and niece in Russia, where such marriages were valid, without discussion of the parties' domicile, on the broad principle that incestuous marriages are exceptions to the rule of the lex loci, since the moral sense of the community would be shocked at the sight of an uncle and niece living together as husband and wife.

45. Mazzolini v. Mazzolini, 168 Ohio St. 357, 155 N.E.2d 206 (1958), in which one spouse was a resident of Ohio and one of Massachusetts and the marriage was celebrated in Massachusetts, where the marriage of first cousins was permitted. The parties intended to live in Ohio and did live there, Ohio forbidding the marriage of first cousins. The court held that the marriage was valid

even though the parties were first cousins. See also In Re Green, 25 Times L.Rep. 222 (Ch.Div.1909).

46. In re Levie's Estate, 50 Cal.App.3d 572, 123 Cal. Rptr. 445 (1975). The decision applies the lex loci principle without any discussion of the policy arguments the other way or of Professor Ehrenzweig's analysis.

47. The leading case is Brook v. Brook, 9 H.L.C. 193, 11 Eng.Rep. 703 (1861). See also Osoinach v. Watkins, 235 Ala. 564, 180 So. 577 (1938); Commonwealth v. Riegel, 22 Pa.Dist.Rep. 903 (1911); Weiss v. Weiss, 8 D. & C. 534 (Pa.1924); Johnson v. Johnson, 57 Wash. 89, 106 P. 500 (1910); Martin v. Martin, 54 W.Va. 301, 46 S.E. 120 (1903); In re Loveland [1906] 1 Ch. 542; De Wilton v. Montefiore [1900] 2 Ch. 481; Chapman v. Bradley, 4 De G. & S. 71, 46 Eng.Rep. 842 (1863).

48. Catalano v. Catalano, 148 Conn. 288, 170 A.2d 726 (1961) (uncle-niece marriage in Italy, where the niece was domiciled and where she remained domiciled for five years after the marriage, invalid in Connecticut, the domicile of the husband); Sclamberg v. Sclamberg, 220 Ind. 209, 41 N.E.2d 801 (1942) (uncle-niece marriage in Russia, niece's domicile, invalid in Indiana); Bucca v. State, 43 N.J.Super. 315, 128 A.2d 506 (1957) (uncle-niece marriage in Italy, niece's domicile, invalid on the ground that they intended to establish the marital domicile in New Jersey); Sottomayor v. De Barros, 5 Prob.Div. 94 (1879); In re Paine [1940] Ch.Div. 46; Mette v. Mette, 1 Sw. & Tr. 416, 164 Eng.Rep. 792 (1859). Cf. Campione v. Campione, 201 Misc. 590, 107 N.Y.S.2d 170 (1951), holding an uncle-niece marriage in Italy valid; with Incuria v. Incuria, 155 Misc. 755, 280 N.Y.S. 716 (Dom.Rel.Ct. 1935), holding an aunt-nephew marriage in Italy invalid. Presumably the Campione case now represents the New York position as a result of In re May's Estate, 305 N.Y. 486, 114 N.E.2d 4 (1953).

49. 305 N.Y. 486, 114 N.E.2d 4 (1953) (marriage of uncle and niece, domiciled in New York, celebrated in Rhode Island and valid under the Rhode Island statute). See also Tyler v. Andrews, 40 App.D.C. 100 (1834) (holds marriage of man and stepdaughter only voidable when

evade the local prohibition. In the conflict of policies, that in favor of validating a long-standing marriage is by these courts felt to be paramount over that which discourages technical incest. The May's case is particularly appealing on this score since the parties lived together as husband and wife thirty-two years and had six children. No useful purpose is served on such facts by holding that the husband has no rights in his wife's estate because they were never married. Another way of avoiding such an undesirable result is to declare such marriages voidable only, making a collateral attack of this sort impossible.[50]

The Uniform Marriage Evasion Act,[51] or statutes resembling it prevent a court from validating the sort of marriage involved in the May's case. These statutes provide, in general, that if domiciliaries of one state go into another state and contract a marriage which is void by the law of the domicile, with intent to evade the law of the domicile, the marriage will not be recognized even if valid

by the law of the place of celebration. They exist in a significant number of states.[52] A leading case denied Federal Employers' Liability Act compensation by virtue of the Illinois Marriage Evasion Act, holding that it covered a first cousin marriage contracted in Kentucky when the parties were domiciled in Illinois.[53]

Conversely, a number of states have statutes which provide that a marriage valid where contracted is valid at the domicile, thus upholding those marriages in which the parties go outside the domicile for the purpose of contracting a marriage condemned by the domicile's law.[54] A further scattering of states have enacted statutes dealing with the problem in a variety of ways.[55]

In the rare case where the law of the place of celebration makes the marriage invalid, but the law of the parties' domicile (either at the time of the marriage or at the time of the suit) does not forbid such marriages, Professor Ehrenzweig's principle of validation should be

---

contracted in Ohio by Maryland domiciliaries, though it would be void by Maryland law); Stevenson v. Gray, 17 B.Mon. 193 (Ky.1856) (seems to apply the lex loci, finding no intent to evade Kentucky law although the parties were domiciled in Kentucky and married in Tennessee); Fensterwald v. Burk, 129 Md. 131, 98 A. 358 (1916) (marriage of uncle and niece in Rhode Island valid though parties domiciled at all times in Maryland); In re Miller's Estate, 239 Mich. 455, 214 N.W. 428 (1927), 12 Minn.L.Rev. 70 (1927) (lex loci governs the marriage of first cousins, which is not within Story's exceptions); Leefeld v. Leefeld, 85 Or. 287, 166 P. 953 (1917) (lex loci governs, first cousin marriage not within Story's exceptions); Schofield v. Schofield, 51 Pa.Super. 564 (1912) (lex loci governs, first cousin marriage not within Story's exceptions); Commonwealth v. Isaacman, 16 Pa.Dist.Rep. 18 (1906), affirmed 33 Pa.Super. 384 (1907) (no intent to evade Pennsylvania law).

Where the marriage is invalid by both the lex loci and the domicile's law, the domicile will not recognize it. McIlvain v. Scheibley, 109 Ky. 455, 59 S.W. 498 (1900); Rhodes v. McAfee, 224 Tenn. 495, 457 S.W.2d 522 (1970).

50. E.g. Tyler v. Andrews, 40 App.D.C. 100 (1834); Harrison v. State, 22 Md. 468 (1864).

51. 9 Uniform L.Ann. 480 (1942), withdrawn id. at page XXI (1943).

52. Ariz.Rev.Stat. § 25–112 (1976); Conn.Gen.Stat. Ann. § 46b–28 (1984); D.C.Code 1981, § 30–105; Ga.Code § 53–214 (1984); Ill.—Smith Hurd Ann.Stat. ch. 40, §§ 216–218 (1980); Me.Rev.Stat.Ann. tit. 19, § 91 (1981); Mass.Gen.L.Ann. ch. 207, §§ 10–13 (1981); Miss.Code 1973, § 93–1–3 (1973); N.D.Cent.Code § 14–03–08 (1981); Vt.Stat.Ann. tit. 15, §§ 5, 6 (1974); Va.Code 1983, § 20–

40 (Supp.); W.Va.Code, § 48–1–17 (1980); Wis.Stat.Ann. § 765.04 (1981); Wyo.Stat. § 1977, 20–1–111. The Uniform Marriage Evasion Act as originally drafted only applied to those marriages which by the law of the domicile were void. Thus it would have no application to marriages where incest renders them only voidable. The Wisconsin version of the Act is broader, applying to marriages either prohibited or declared void.

53. Meisenhelder v. Chicago & N.W. Ry. Co., 170 Minn. 317, 213 N.W. 32 (1927), 26 Mich.L.Rev. 327 (1928). See also In re Mortenson's Estate, 83 Ariz. 87, 316 P.2d 1106 (1957); and Weinberg v. Weinberg, 242 Ill.App. 414 (1926). But see People ex rel. Schutt v. Siems, 198 Ill. App. 342 (1916), recognizing as valid a first cousin marriage contracted in Wisconsin when the husband was domiciled in Minnesota, the wife was domiciled in Illinois, and the intended matrimonial domicile was Minnesota. It should be noted that the Uniform Act refers to "any person", meaning that if one spouse were domiciled in Illinois, and they both returned to Illinois to live, the statute would invalidate the marriage.

54. West's Ann.Cal.Civ.Code § 4104 (1983); Idaho Code § 32–209 (1983); Kan.Stat.Ann. § 23–115 (1981); Ky.Rev.Stat. § 402.040 (1984); Neb.Rev.St. § 42–117 (1984); N.M.Stat.Ann. 1983, § 40–1–4; S.D.Comp.L. § 25–1–38 (1984); Utah Code Ann. 1984, § 30–1–4; Wyo.Stat. Ann. § 20–1–111 (1977).

55. E.g., N.D.Cent.Code § 14–03–08 (1981), which provides that marriages valid where contracted are valid in North Dakota, but that this does not apply where residents of North Dakota contract a marriage in another state which is prohibited by North Dakota law.

applied and the marriage upheld. Some courts, relying on Story and a rigid application of the lex loci, might reach the opposite result.[56]

In the writer's view no simple verbal formula will solve the conflicts problem. The principle of validation helps but does not tell us how the courts would or should evaluate the policies involved in incest prohibitions. Further help would be afforded by making technically incestuous marriages merely voidable rather than void, so that collateral attacks long after the marriage was contracted would be impossible. In the last analysis, however, courts which look with horror upon any marriage in violation of the incest statute will invalidate such marriages in the evasion case, and perhaps in others, thereby proving that matters of policy lie at the root of the problem. This being true, greater weight should be given to the desirability of upholding long-standing marriages. That should outweigh the evils of permitting marriage between uncle and niece or first cousins.

WESTLAW REFERENCES

di incest

sy,di(marri! marry! marital /s void! /s incest!)

di(marry! marri! marital /s affinity consanguinity (blood /2 relati! related) /s prohibit! invalid! void!)

"uniform marriage evasion"

§ 2.10   Nonage [1]

Historical Background

By the English law prevailing before the colonization of America children under the age of seven were deemed entirely incapable of consenting to marriage. An attempted marriage of a child under that age was therefore said to be void.[2] At the age of seven the child became capable of consenting, but the marriage remained "inchoate and imperfect" until he reached fourteen if a boy or twelve if a girl.[3] Above the ages of fourteen and twelve children could contract valid marriages. Nonage was classified as a civil rather than a canonical disability.[4] In general civil disabilities were said to make marriages void, while canonical disabilities merely made them voidable.[5] In the case of the marriage of a boy between seven and fourteen, or a girl between seven and twelve, this seems to have meant that the parties themselves could declare the marriage void without obtaining a decree of nullity, at any time before reaching the age of consent.[6] On the other hand, if the parties wished to continue the marriage, they might agree to do so after both were of full age, i.e., fourteen and twelve respectively, and the marriage then became valid without further ceremony. This possibility of affirmance or disaffirmance upon reaching the age of consent was doubtless what led some authorities to characterize the nonage marriage as voidable rather than void notwithstanding that the disability was civil and not canonical. The resulting confusion over whether nonage rendered marriages void or voidable remains to plague us to this day, as will appear.

The common law rules currently have little influence in American law, although they still might apply to the extent that they have not been altered by statute. For example, if the applicable statute establishes the age of consent for marriage but neglects to state that the marriage of a person under that age is

---

56. In re Levie's Estate, 50 Cal.App.3d 572, 123 Cal. Rptr. 445 (1975), relying in part, paradoxically, on West's Ann.Cal.Civ.Code § 4104 (1983); Blaisdell v. Bickum, 139 Mass. 250, 1 N.E. 281 (1885).

§ 2.10

1. For a thorough discussion of this subject see Kingsley, The Law of Infant Marriages, 9 Vand.L.Rev. 593 (1956).

2. Swinburne, Treatise of Spousals, 20 (1686); 2 Burns, Ecclesiastical Law, 394 (4th ed. 1781).

3. 1 Blackstone, Commentaries on the Laws of England 436 (Cooley's ed. 1884). To the same effect, see 2

Burns, Ecclesiastical Law 394 (4th ed. 1781), and Swinburne, Treatise of Spousals 29–31 (1686).

4. See Elliot v. Gurr, 2 Phill.Ecc. 16, 161 Eng.Rep. 1064 (1812).

5. Ibid.

6. According to Blackstone either party could disaffirm the marriage on the ground that one spouse was under age. 1 Blackstone, Commentaries on the Laws of England 436 (Cooley's ed. 1884). Pollock and Maitland assert, however, that only the party under age could avoid the marriage. 2 Pollock and Maitland, History of English Law, 389–390 (2d ed. 1898).

void or voidable, the cases commonly treat the statute as directory only rather than mandatory, leaving the validity of the marriage to be determined by the common law rules.[7] Since nearly all states have now enacted statutes not only establishing the minimum ages for marriage but also providing for invalidating marriages in which one or both parties have not reached the prescribed age, the common law rules will only rarely have any effect.[8]

The Statutory Pattern

For a time after World War II there was a perceptible trend toward earlier marriages for both men and women which was the subject of comments by students of social movements.[9] As with so many other social trends in the United States, this one was no sooner noticed than it was reversed, so that since

about 1965 the ages at which men and women contract first marriages have been rising.[10] Much legislative activity has accompanied these trends, although it is doubtful that the statutory changes either reflect or have caused changes in the ages at which people marry. One suspects that the new statutes have been more influenced by the Uniform Marriage and Divorce Act [11], the studies which preceded it,[12] the change in voting age brought about by the Twenty-Sixth Amendment,[13] and the reduction in the age of majority from twenty-one to eighteen which has occurred in many states in the past few years.[14] Whatever the cause, the result has been a substantial consensus among the states that the marriageable age should be eighteen and that it should be the same for women as for men.[15]

7. Green v. Green, 77 Fla. 101, 80 So. 739 (1919); Browning v. Browning, 89 Kan. 98, 130 P. 852 (1913); Parton v. Hervey, 67 Mass. (1 Gray) 119 (1854); State v. Ward, 204 S.C. 210, 28 S.E.2d 785 (1944); Ex parte Hollopeter, 52 Wash. 41, 100 P. 159 (1909); Tisdale v. Tisdale, 121 Wash. 138, 209 P. 8 (1893).

8. In Massachusetts and South Carolina the common law ages apparently still have relevance for determining the validity of nonage marriages. See Parton v. Hervey, 67 Mass. (1 Gray) 119 (1854); State v. Ward, 204 S.C. 210, 28 S.E.2d 785 (1944). See also State v. Johnson, 216 Kan. 445, 532 P.2d 1325 (1975) which seems to hold that the ages for consent to common law marriage are fourteen for males and twelve for females.

9. See, e.g., Moss and Gingles, The Relationship of Personality to the Incidence of Early Marriage, 21 Marriage and Family Living 373 (1959); Moss and Gingles, Teen-Age Marriage—The Teacher's Challenge, 23 Marriage and Family Living 187 (1961); Furlong, Youthful Marriage and Parenthood: A Threat to Family Stability, 19 Hast.L.J. 105 (1967).

10. Statistical Abstract of the United States (1975) 67 indicates that the median age for first marriage declined from 1940 to 1965, and since 1965 has been rising but without returning to the 1940 level. Monthly Vital Statistics Report, Vol. 25, No. 2, May 5, 1976, 1, giving the marriage statistics for 1974, shows a median age for first marriage for women of 20.6 and for men of 22.5. See also H. Carter and P. Glick, Marriage and Divorce: A Social and Economic Study 78–82 (1970). This same trend is described as encouraging for the reduction of the birth rate in J. Bernard, The Future of Marriage 183–190 (1972). The same author finds encouraging also the tendency of men to marry women nearer to their own age than in the past. See also Glick, A Demographer Looks at American Families, 37 J. of Marriage and the Family 15, 17 (1975). For statistical evidence that youthful marriages are less stable than others, see Schoen, California

Divorce Rates By Age at First Marriage and Duration of First Marriage, 37 J. of Marriage and the Family 548 (1975).

11. Uniform Marriage and Divorce Act §§ 203, 208, 9A Unif.L.Ann. 102, 110 (1979); setting eighteen as the marriageable age.

12. R. Levy, Uniform Marriage and Divorce Legislation: A Preliminary Analysis, Appendix C: Youth Marriage: Summary and Critique of the Data and Literature, Gallaher and Levy.

13. U.S.Const. amend. XXVI.

14. See section 8.1, infra.

15. E.g., Alaska Stat. § 25.05.011 (1983); Ariz.Rev. Stat.Ann. §§ 25–102 (1976); West's Ann.Cal.Civ.Code § 4101 (1983); Colo.Rev.Stat. § 14–2–106 (1973); Conn. Gen.Stat.Ann. § 46b–30 (Supp.1984) D.C.Code 1981, §§ 30–103 (Supp.); Official Code Ga.Ann. §§ 19–3–2, 19–3–37, 19–3–36, 39–1–1 (Supp.1984); Hawaii Rev.Stat. § 572–2 (1976); Idaho Code § 32–202 (1983); Ill.—Smith Hurd Ann. ch. 40 § 203 (Supp.1984); West's Ann.Ind. Code § 31–1–1–4 (1980); Iowa Code Ann. § 595.2 (1981); Kan.Stat.Ann. § 23–106 (1981); Ky.Rev.Stat. § 402.210 (1984); La.S.A.—Civ.Code art. 37 (Supp.1984); Me.Rev. Stat.Ann. tit. 19, § 62 (Supp.1984); Code, Fam.Law, § 2–301 (1984); Mass.Gen.Laws Ann. ch. 207, § 7 (Supp.1984); Mich.Comp.Laws Ann. § 25.33 (1984); Minn.Stat.Ann. § 517.02 (Supp.1986); Vernon's Ann.Mo.Stat. § 451.090 (Supp.1976); Mont.Code Ann. 40–1–202 (1983); Nev.Rev. Stat. § 122.020 (1981); N.H.Rev.Stat.Ann. § 457:5 (Supp. 1973); N.M.Stat.Ann.1983, § 40–1–6; N.Y.—McKinney's Dom.Rel.Laws §§ 7, 15 (1977 and Supp.1984); N.C.Gen. Stat. § 51–2 (1984); N.D.Cent.Code § 14–03–02 (1981); Ohio Rev.Code §§ 3101.01, 3109.01 (1980); Or.Rev.Stat. § 106.060 (1983); Pa.Stat.tit. 48, § 1–5 (Supp.1984); R.I. Gen.Laws 1981, §§ 15–2–11, 15–12–1; S.C.Code 1977, § 20–1–250; S.D.Comp.L. § 25–1–9 (1977); Tenn.Code Ann. § 36–3–106 (1984); V.Tex.C.A., Fam.Code § 1.51

Presumably the purposes of setting a minimum age for marriage are to prevent unwise marriages of immature persons, to reduce the divorce rate and promote marital stability, it being generally acknowledged that youthful marriages are more likely to end in divorce than other marriages,[16] and to provide children with the care of mature and responsible parents. It is impossible to be certain that the widespread imposition of eighteen as the marriageable age will be effective in accomplishing these purposes, but at least it constitutes an advance from earlier statutes permitting marriage at younger ages. It undoubtedly has some value as an expression of society's judgment that some maturity is important for marriage. And the very fact that there is wide agreement about it and therefore general acceptance among the states sharply reduces the chance that the requirement can be evaded by going to another state where the marriageable age is lower.

The few states which formerly set the marriageable age at twenty-one now have reduced it to eighteen.[17] A very few states still impose different age requirements for males than for females.[18] This group of statutes raise the question whether making this distinction between men and women violates the Equal Protection Clause of the United States Constitution.[19] The Supreme Court adheres to the view that discriminations based upon sex are not, unlike those based upon race, "inherently suspect" and that they may be upheld if reasonable, that is, if they "rest upon some ground of difference having a fair and substantial relation to the object of the legislation, so that all persons similarly circumstanced shall be treated alike." The case from which this quotation comes, Stanton v. Stanton,[20] held unconstitutional the Utah statute establishing the age of majority at twenty-one for men and eighteen for women, where the effect of the statute was to provide parental support for women only until the earlier age. The Court found the statute not to be reasonable because the age difference it imposed was unrelated to the purpose of requiring support, namely the education and training of the child. In the course of the opinion the Court doubted that women mature earlier than men.

Similar arguments can be advanced against age differentials for marriage. It is sometimes asserted that women mature earlier than men,[21] whatever that may mean, but evidence on the point is not easy to come by. The fact that women's ages at marriage do generally continue to be somewhat younger than those of the men they marry is of little consequence. The time has long passed when mere social custom carried weight with the Supreme Court.[22] The argument will be that permitting women to marry at ages younger

(Supp.1985); Utah Code Ann.1984, § 30–1–9; Vt.Stat. Ann.tit. 18, § 5142, tit. 1, § 173 (Supp.1984) Va.Code 1983, §§ 20–48, 20–49; West's Rev.Code Wash.Ann. § 26.04.010 (1985); W.Va.Code, § 48–1–1 (Supp.1984); Wis.Stat.Ann. § 765.02 (Supp.1981).

16. Schoen, California Divorce Rates By Age at First Marriage and Duration of First Marriage, 37 J. of Marriage and the Family 548 (1975); Note, The Uniform Marriage and Divorce Act-Marital Age Provisions, 57 Minn.L.Rev. 179, 181–186 (1972).

On the basis of the state interests listed in the text the New York statute requiring parental consent for the marriages of persons under eighteen was held constitutional in Moe v. Dinkins, 669 F.2d 67 (2d Cir.1982).

17. E.g., West's Fla.Stat.Ann. § 741.04 (Supp.1984); Ala.Code § 30–1–5 (1983).

18. E.g., Ark.Stats. § 55–102 (Supp.1985); Del.Code tit. 13, § 123 (1981).

19. U.S.Const. amend. XIV, § 1.

20. 421 U.S. 7, 95 S.Ct. 1373, 43 L.Ed.2d 688 (1975). The opinion of the Utah Supreme Court upon remand is

Stanton v. Stanton, 552 P.2d 112 (Utah 1976). The decision of that court on the remand is vacated by Stanton v. Stanton, 429 U.S. 501, 97 S.Ct. 717, 50 L.Ed.2d 723 (1977) and upon the second remand the Utah Supreme Court held that both males and females would be treated as adults at age eighteen but that its decision would not be retroactive. Stanton v. Stanton, 564 P.2d 303 (Utah 1977). See also Craig v. Boren, 429 U.S. 190, 97 S.Ct. 451, 50 L.Ed.2d 397 (1976), rehearing denied 429 U.S. 1124, 97 S.Ct. 1161, 51 L.Ed.2d 574 (1977). The former Oklahoma statute establishing different ages of majority for men and women was held unconstitutional in Bassett v. Bassett, 521 P.2d 434 (Okl.App.1974).

21. L. Kanowitz, Women and the Law 10–13 (1969). In this passage Professor Kanowitz expresses no opinion upon the constitutionality of age differentials for marriage.

22. In Stanton v. Stanton, 421 U.S. 7, 14, 95 S.Ct. 1373, 1378, 43 L.Ed.2d 688 (1975), appeal after remand 552 P.2d 112 (Utah 1976), vacated 429 U.S. 501, 97 S.Ct. 717, 50 L.Ed.2d 723 (1977) the Court sneers at the "old

than men reflects the law's willingness to frustrate women's preparation for careers and to relegate them to the despised role of homemaker, despised, that is, by some segments of the women's movement. This argument is supported by evidence that early marriage goes together with dropping out of school and with the consequent reduction in education and training.[23] It therefore seems likely that statutes creating age differentials for marriage will be held unconstitutional.[24] So long as the trend toward setting equal ages for both men and women persists, the issue is not one of great importance.

In addition to prescribing minimum ages below which marriages are in some respects invalid, the statutes of nearly all states require, as a condition upon obtaining a marriage license, the consent of parents or guardians if the applicant is under the prescribed age.[25] The typical statute provides that a person under eighteen may only be issued a marriage license with the written consent of a parent or guardian, but it does not provide for the legal consequences of failure to get such consent. The parents' decision on the matter is final, at least where not entirely unreasonable, and a guardian will not be appointed as a

means of overruling that decision.[26] The Uniform Marriage and Divorce Act provides a means of overruling the parents' refusal to consent to the marriage by stating that if the person is between sixteen and eighteen, he may marry if he obtains the consent of either his parents or the approval of a court.[27] Court approval may be given only where the court finds that the person is capable of assuming the responsibilities of marriage and that the marriage will serve his best interests.[28] As a further safeguard against improvident marriage the California statute provides that the person under eighteen must obtain the permission of the superior court in addition to the consent of a parent or guardian before he may marry. The court in its order granting the permission must require the parties to have counselling concerning the social, economic and personal responsibilities of marriage if it deems such counselling to be necessary.[29] This type of statute reflects the opinion of some persons that the requirement of parental consent alone does not constitute a sufficient deterrent to youthful marriages, since parental consent often is given too readily.[30]

---

notions" which the Utah Supreme Court relied upon to uphold the statute.

23. Gallaher and Levy, Youth Marriage: Summary and Critique of the Data and Literature C–35 to C–41, in R. Levy, Uniform Marriage and Divorce Legislation: A Preliminary Analysis, Appendix C.

24. Phelps v. Bing, 58 Ill.2d 32, 316 N.E.2d 775 (1974). Two lower court cases in New York have reached differing conclusions on the issue. Friedrich v. Katz, 73 Mis.2d 663, 341 N.Y.S.2d 932 (1973), reversed as moot 34 N.Y.2d 987, 360 N.Y.S.2d 415, 318 N.E.2d 606 (1974) held that the statute requiring a male under twenty-one and a female under eighteen to obtain written parental consent to marry was constitutional. The same statute was held unconstitutional in Berger v. Adornato, 76 Misc.2d 122, 350 N.Y.S.2d 520 (1973) on the ground that the statute afforded no assurance that the parents would exercise their responsibility so as to effectuate the state's policy.

25. See the statutes cited, supra, note 15, for Arizona, Colorado, Connecticut, Georgia, Hawaii, Idaho, Illinois, Indiana, Iowa, Kansas, Kentucky, Louisiana, Maine, Maryland, Massachusetts, Michigan, Missouri, Nevada, New Mexico, New York, North Carolina, North Dakota, Ohio, Oregon, Pennsylvania, Rhode Island, South Carolina, South Dakota, Tennessee, Texas, Vermont, Virginia, West Virginia, Wisconsin. The New York statute has been held constitutional in Moe v. Dinkins, 533 F.Supp.

623 (S.D.N.Y.1981), judgment affirmed 669 F.2d 67 (2d Cir.1982).

26. Application of Gilbert, 5 Lycoming 130 (Pa.County Ct.1955). A parent who acts wholly without regard to the welfare of his child in arranging the child's marriage at an age below the statutory minimum may be criminally liable, however. People v. Benu, 87 Misc.2d 139, 385 N.Y.S.2d 222 (Crim.Ct.1976); State v. Gans, 168 Ohio St. 174, 151 N.E.2d 709 (1958), certiorari denied 359 U.S. 945, 79 S.Ct. 722, 3 L.Ed.2d 678 (1959). But State v. Austin, 160 W.Va. 337, 234 S.E.2d 657 (1977) holds that an adult who marries an underage girl without obtaining her parents' consent is not guilty of contributing to delinquency.

27. Uniform Marriage and Divorce Act § 203, 9A Unif.L.Ann. 100–103 (1979). Note, The Uniform Marriage and Divorce Act—Marital Age Provisions, 57 Minn. L.Rev. 179 (1972).

28. Uniform Marriage and Divorce Act § 205, 9A Unif.L.Ann. 105 (1979).

29. West's Ann.Cal.Civ.Code § 4101 (1983).

30. Grover and Jones, Requirement of Parental Consent: A Deterrent to Marriage? 26 J. of Marr. and the Fam. 205 (1964). A premarital counselling program in Iowa was found not to be very successful. Adams, Mar-

The cases hold that the statutes requiring parental consent do not invalidate a marriage contracted without consent, if the parties are above the minimum marriageable age.[31] Although the courts label such statutes directory rather than mandatory, the real reason for this result seems to be the desire to validate marriages whenever possible. Of course if the statute specifically provides, as California's does,[32] that a marriage without the parent's consent is invalid, then such a marriage may be annulled.[33]

In a number of states marriages may be validly contracted by children under the minimum ages if the girl is pregnant and if consent to the marriage is given by a named official, usually the judge of a court of record.[34] The parents' consent is also often required for such a marriage. The obvious purpose of this type of statute is to protect the unborn child by "giving him a name". This policy is generally conceded to be mistaken since such marriages are very often even less stable or successful than other youthful marriages and it has been expressly repudiated in

the Uniform Marriage and Divorce Act.[35] Failure to obtained the judge's approval where the parties are under the age prescribed for valid marriage is a ground for annulment.[36]

Direct Attack: Annulment

Once the statutory pattern has been described, the question is, what are the consequences of attempting to marry before reaching the ages mentioned in the statute? The answer to this question has been obscured by the tendency of many courts to describe the marriage as void or voidable. In some instances the applicable statute may characterize the marriage as void or voidable.[37] We have our historical background to thank for this language.[38] In order to avoid confusion the cases should be discussed in terms of the specific issues which they raise, even though the outcome of particular cases may be more or less influenced by the void-voidable distinction, whether embodied in statute or common law rule.

riage of Minors: Unsuccessful Attempt to Help Them, 3 Fam.L.Q. 13 (1969).

31. Castor v. United States, 174 F.2d 481 (8th Cir. 1949), cert. denied 338 U.S. 836, 70 S.Ct. 45, 94 L.Ed. 511 (1949); Witherington v. Witherington, 200 Ark. 802, 141 S.W.2d 30 (1940); In re Ambrose, 170 Cal. 160, 149 P. 43 (1914) (construing an earlier California statute); Browning v. Browning, 89 Kan. 98, 130 P. 852 (1913); Parton v. Hervey, 67 Mass. (1 Gray) 119 (1854); Noble v. Noble, 299 Mich. 565, 300 N.W. 885 (1941); Teague v. Allred, 119 Mont. 193, 173 P.2d 117 (1946); Melcher v. Melcher, 102 Neb. 790, 169 N.W. 720 (1918); Berry v. Winistorfer, 55 N.D. 310, 213 N.W. 26 (1927); Needam v. Needam, 183 Va. 681, 33 S.E.2d 288 (1945), 31 Va.L.Rev. 210 (1944). A fortiori, consent which does not meet the statute's formal requirements is sufficient basis for a valid marriage. Cross v. Cross, 110 Mont. 300, 102 P.2d 829 (1940) (applying Idaho law).

32. West's Ann.Cal.Civ.Code § 4425 (1983). See also Idaho Code § 32–501 (1983); Mont.Code Ann. 40–1–402 (1983); Uniform Marriage and Divorce Act § 208, 9A Unif.L.Ann. 110 (1979); Mays v. Folsom, 143 F.Supp. 784 (D.Idaho 1956).

33. West v. West, 62 Cal.App. 541, 217 P. 567 (1923) so held, even though the parents who did not consent in advance did encourage the young people to continue living together after the marriage. Blunt v. Blunt, 198 Okl. 138, 176 P.2d 471 (1947) seems contra. In Turner v. Turner, 167 Cal.App.2d 636, 334 P.2d 1011 (1959) the marriage was annulled when the consent of the parent was obtained by fraud. Ruiz v. Ruiz, 6 Cal.App.3d 58, 85

Cal.Rptr. 674 (1970) held that the minor could have the marriage annulled even though he had misrepresented his age. Greene v. Williams, 9 Cal.App.3d 559, 88 Cal. Rptr. 261 (1970) denied an annulment of the minor's marriage after the minor's death.

34. E.g., statutes cited, supra, note 15, for Georgia, Illinois, Indiana, Maryland, New Mexico, North Carolina, South Carolina, South Dakota. Careless statutory drafting is exemplified by State ex rel. Leffingwell v. Superior Court, No. 2 of Grant County, 262 Ind. 574, 321 N.E.2d 568 (1974), which held that a court could not order the issuance of a marriage license to an underage woman who had already borne a child under a statute authorizing such an order if the woman is "pregnant". The statute has since been amended. Ind.Stat.West's Ann. Ind.Code 31–1–1–1 (Supp.1984).

35. Uniform Marriage and Divorce Act § 205, 9A Unif.L.Ann. § 105 (1979), after authorizing the court to issue a marriage license under certain circumstances in which marriage will serve the best interest of the underage party, states: "Pregnancy alone does not establish that the best interest of the party will be served."

36. Carlton v. Carlton, 76 Ohio App. 338, 64 N.E.2d 428 (1945); Morgan v. Lere, 20 D. & C.2d 441 (Pa.County Ct.1959) (semble).

37. E.g., Alaska Stat. § 25.05.011 (1983) (voidable); Ark.Stats. § 55–102 (Supp.1981) (voidable); Mich.Comp. Laws Ann. § 25.82 (1984) (void); West's Rev.Code Wash. Ann. § 26.04.010 (Supp.1985) (void).

38. See notes 3–6, supra.

The first and most obvious consequence of the fact that a marriage was contracted when one of the parties was under the age of consent prescribed by statute is that the party under age may have it annulled.[39] He need not wait to sue until he reaches the age of consent, but he may sue at once.[40] According to one case he may have the marriage annulled even though he lied about his age in order to obtain the marriage license.[41] But if the statute relates only to the age for obtaining a license and does not provide that marriages under such age are invalid, the courts may hold such a statute directory only and deny an annulment even though the statute has not been complied with.[42] The reason for this is apparently the courts' reluctance to upset marriages without a clear statutory mandate.

Collateral Attack

Assuming that the marriage of a person under a specified age is invalid in the sense that it may be annulled, may it also be attacked collaterally, in actions other than annulment? The answer to this question depends upon the language of the applicable statute, as construed by the courts.

Here the void-voidable distinction becomes significant. If the statute is construed to mean that such marriages are void, then the party under age [43] may assert the invalidity of the marriage at any time and in any proceeding where its invalidity may be relevant.[44] If, in a criminal proceeding, the guilt of a party turns on the existence of a marriage, he may be entitled to show that the marriage is void because he was under age.[45] Or where the defendant contracts a first marriage when he is under age, and later contracts a second marriage without obtaining an annulment of the first, it has been held that he cannot be convicted of bigamy if the first marriage was void.[46] In other words, for this purpose, "void" is given its literal meaning.

On the other hand, where, either by statute or common law, the marriage of a person under age is characterized as voidable, it remains a marriage until annulled. Therefore it cannot be collaterally attacked.[47] If a first marriage is contracted when a party is under age, and he later contracts a second marriage without getting the first annulled, character-

---

39. Taylor v. Taylor, 249 Ala. 419, 31 So.2d 579 (1947); Von Felden v. Von Felden, 212 Minn. 54, 2 N.W.2d 426 (1942); Willits v. Willits, 76 Neb. 228, 107 N.W. 379 (1906); Quinzi v. Quinzi, 261 App.Div. 929, 25 N.Y.S.2d 435 (2d Dep't 1941); Carlton v. Carlton, 76 Ohio App. 338, 64 N.E.2d 428 (1945); Hunt v. Hunt, 23 Okl. 490, 100 P. 541 (1909). See also Note, 26 Yale L.J. 622 (1917).

40. Owen v. Coffey, 201 Ala. 531, 78 So. 885 (1918); In re Anonymous, 32 N.J.Super. 599, 108 A.2d 882 (1954).

41. Ruiz v. Ruiz, 6 Cal.App.3d 58, 85 Cal.Rptr. 674 (1970).

42. E.g., In re State in Interest of Goodwin, 214 La. 1062, 39 So.2d 731 (1949) (statute prohibiting a minister from marrying a female under sixteen does not invalidate the marriage); People v. Heine, 12 App.Div.2d 36, 208 N.Y.S.2d 188 (2d Dep't 1960), affirmed 9 N.Y.2d 925, 217 N.Y.S.2d 93, 176 N.E.2d 102 (1961) (statute forbidding justice of the peace to perform marriages of persons under twenty-one does not invalidate the marriage); State v. Ward, 204 S.C. 210, 28 S.E.2d 785 (1944) (statute prescribing certain age limits for marriage license does not invalidate the marriage); Tisdale v. Tisdale, 121 Wash. 138, 209 P. 8 (1893) (statute providing males of twenty-one and females of eighteen may marry does not invalidate marriages below that age).

43. On the question whether the party over age may assert the invalidity of the marriage, see the discussion at notes 56, 57, infra.

44. Ragan v. Cox, 210 Ark. 152, 194 S.W.2d 681 (1946); Crapps v. Smith, 9 Ga.App. 400, 71 S.E. 501 (1911); Griffin v. Griffin, 225 Mich. 253, 196 N.W. 384 (1923).

45. People v. Schoonmaker, 119 Mich. 242, 77 N.W. 934 (1899); Ex parte Tucker, 91 Okl.Cr.App. 391, 219 P.2d 245 (1950); Hardy v. State, 37 Tex.Cr. 55, 38 S.W. 615 (1897).

46. Shafher v. State, 20 Ohio 1 (1851). This case does not treat the problem in the same terms as the text, but the result supports the text statement. The case says that the marriage of one under age is invalid unless he engages in conduct indicating assent to the marriage after he reaches the age of consent. In other, more common terms, the marriage is void unless ratified.

47. Raske v. Raske, 92 F.Supp. 348 (D.Minn.1950) (dictum); People v. Souleotes, 26 Cal.App. 309, 146 P. 903 (1915); State v. Volpe, 113 Conn. 288, 155 A. 223 (1931); Mangrum v. Mangrum, 310 Ky. 226, 220 S.W.2d 406 (1949) (dictum); State ex rel. Scott v. Lowell, 78 Minn. 166, 80 N.W. 877 (1899); Territory v. Harwood, 15 N.M. 424, 110 P. 556 (1910) (dictum); Anonymous v. Anonymous, 176 Misc. 850, 29 N.Y.S.2d 331 (Dom.Rel.Ct.1941); Sawyer v. Slack, 196 N.C. 697, 146 S.E. 864 (1929) (dictum); Peefer v. State, 42 Ohio App. 276, 182 N.E. 117 (1931); Abbott v. Industrial Commission, 80 Ohio App. 7, 74 N.E.2d 625 (1946).

izing the first marriage as voidable has the consequence that the party is a bigamist, and so criminally responsible.[48] For this purpose, "voidable" is also given its usual meaning. A few authorities qualify this view of nonage marriages, holding that they are voidable, but that they may be avoided by acts of disaffirmance other than suits for annulment, though it is by no means clear what conduct constitutes disaffirmance.[49] But until the marriage is disaffirmed, it remains in force.

Though the effect of the void-voidable distinction is clear enough, the distinction itself is not clear. Statutes may specifically provide that nonage marriages are void, but courts, to avoid hardship, construe them as voidable.[50] Or the statutes themselves may be silent as to whether such marriages are void or voidable.[51] Or they may contain inconsistent provisions which say at one point the marriage is void, but at another that it is voidable.[52] Faced with this sort of confusion, one can only urge constructions which best effectuate the statutory policy. The remedy

lies not with the courts but in a comprehensive revision of the nonage statutes. In the writer's view the statutes should provide that nonage marriages be given effect until annulled, and that no sort of disaffirmance other than annulment be recognized.[53] Theoretically there could be marriages of children so young that they should have no effect for any purpose (that is, be void in the strictest sense), but in fact such marriages are so rare as not to be a factor in legislative regulation. Sanctions preventing such marriages are in any event provided by the delinquency and contributory delinquency statutes.[54]

Who May Attack

The question of who can assert the invalidity of a marriage on the ground of nonage is seriously confused by labelling such marriages void. Logically, if the marriage really is void, then either party to it, and perhaps third parties, should be entitled to attack it.[55] But the purpose of the nonage statute is the protection of the party who is under age. It

---

48. State v. Sellers, 140 S.C. 66, 134 S.E. 873 (1926), 40 Harv.L.Rev. 654 (1927), 36 Yale L.J. 426 (1927); State v. Cone, 86 Wis. 498, 57 N.W. 50 (1893).

49. Beggs v. State, 55 Ala. 108 (1876).

50. Sawyer v. Slack, 196 N.C. 697, 146 S.E. 864 (1929); Note, Child Marriages in Kentucky, 37 Ky.L.J. 282 (1949).

51. E.g., Del.Code tit. 13, § 123 (1981) which establishes eighteen as the age for marriage but which fails to state whether a marriage under that age is void or voidable or even annullable.

52. E.g., Ark.Stats. § 55–102 (Supp.1981) and § 55–106 (1971).

53. Cf. Vernon, Annulment of Marriage: A Proposed Model Act, 12 J. of Pub.L. 143, 167–169, 180–182 (1963). The Uniform Marriage and Divorce Act § 208, 9A Unif.L. Ann. 110 (1979) avoids this confusion by providing that certain marriages, including those of persons under age, may be declared invalid, thereby presumably foreclosing any contention that such marriages might be collaterally attacked.

54. There is a conflict in the cases as to whether contracting a voidable marriage can be the basis for a delinquency proceeding. Holding it may: In re Kemp, 192 Misc. 267, 78 N.Y.S.2d 588 (Dom.Rel.Ct.1948), and Williams v. State, 219 S.W.2d 509 (Tex.1949). State v. Huntsman, 115 Utah 283, 204 P.2d 448 (1949) held that a man who married a girl under eighteen could be prosecuted for carnal knowledge, rejecting his argument that the marriage emancipated her and thus took her out of the scope of the statute. But Peefer v. State, 42 Ohio App. 276, 182 N.E. 117 (1931) and State v. Austin, 160 W.Va. 337, 234 S.E.2d 657 (1977) held that a girl who

contracted a voidable marriage was not a delinquent and therefore her husband did not contribute to her delinquency. State v. Graves, 228 Ark. 378, 307 S.W.2d 545 (1957) reached the same result with respect to the parents of a girl who contracted, with their consent, a marriage voidable in Arkansas but valid in Mississippi where contracted. Contra on this point is State v. Gans, 168 Ohio St. 174, 151 N.E.2d 709 (1958), cert. denied 359 U.S. 945, 79 S.Ct. 722, 3 L.Ed.2d 678 (1959), the court saying that parents who actively participate in enabling one under sixteen to marry are guilty of contributing to delinquency. See also Annots., 84 A.L.R.2d 1254 (1962), and 68 A.L.R.2d 745 (1959).

People v. Benu, 87 Misc.2d 139, 385 N.Y.S.2d 222 (Crim. Ct.1976) held that a father could be guilty of the crime of endangering the welfare of a child by arranging a marriage for his thirteen-year-old daughter.

55. Evans v. Ross, 309 Mich. 149, 14 N.W.2d 815 (1944) seems to take this position, allowing the husband, 27, to annul his marriage to a girl of 15 on the ground of her nonage. The case is contrary to other Michigan authorities, and as is shown in the text, inconsistent with the purpose of the nonage statute. Tigner v. Tigner, 90 Mich.App. 787, 282 N.W.2d 481 (1979) avoids this result by finding that a common law marriage was contracted after the woman reached sixteen. Samluk v. Gorecki, 265 A.2d 46 (Del.Super.1970) held that the husband, who was 21, could not get an annulment of his marriage to his underage wife, but the court emphasized that he had known she was under age and had helped her get a license by forgery. Apparently no Delaware statute authorized annulment of a marriage for nonage.

was not enacted to allow a person of full age to escape from an unwanted marriage. For this reason only the party under age has standing to sue to annul the marriage,[56] or to attack it collaterally.[57] This is so even where the statute makes the marriage "void."[58] Under the local practice he may be required to be represented by a guardian or next friend, but the suit is his, not the guardian's.[59]

The only exception to this is for parents, who are given the right by some statutes to bring suits to annul the marriages of their children on the ground of nonage.[60] If the statute expressly authorizes the parent to sue, he may.[61] Without express authorization, however, the parent has no standing to sue.[62] If he does sue, the parent must make both parties to the marriage parties to the annulment suit.[63] The right of the parent to sue under such express statutory authority creates the possibility of conflict between the parent who thinks the marriage should be annulled and the child who wishes the marriage to continue. No case has been found dealing directly with such a conflict, but it would seem to be the duty of the court under these circumstances to determine, upon a full presentation of the facts, what the child's best interests require and grant or deny the annulment accordingly. Under the voidable type of nonage statute the court would clearly have that authority,[64] though there might be some doubt of it if the statute made the marriage void.[65]

Confirmation and Other Defenses

It is universally held that a marriage defective because one of the parties was under age at the time it was contracted becomes wholly valid if there is marital cohabitation beyond the age of consent.[66] Some nonage statutes expressly enact this rule,[67] but it is followed whether expressed in the statute or not, and whether the statute makes such marriages

56. Crummies Creek Coal Co. v. Napier, 246 Ky. 569, 55 S.W.2d 339 (1932), 37 Ky.L.J. 282 (1949); Fodor v. Kunie, 92 N.J.Eq. 301, 112 A. 598 (1920). See Utah Code Ann. § 30–1–17 (1984); Vt.Stat Ann tit. 15 § 513 (1974); Va.Code § 20.89.1 (1983) Wyo.Stat. § 20–2–21 (1977).

57. People v. Pizzura, 211 Mich. 71, 178 N.W. 235 (1920).

58. Ragan v. Cox, 210 Ark. 152, 194 S.W.2d 681 (1946) stated that although the statute made nonage marriages "absolutely void," only the party under age might sue to annul.

59. Kirby v. Gilliam, 182 Va. 111, 28 S.E.2d 40 (1943). See also Owen v. Coffey, 201 Ala. 531, 78 So. 885 (1918), and Annot., 150 A.L.R. 609, 610 (1944).

60. E.g., West's Ann.Cal.Civ.Code § 4426 (1983); Colo. Rev.Stat. § 14–10–111(2)(c) (1973); N.Y.—McKinney's Dom.Rel.Laws § 140 (1977). The Uniform Marriage and Divorce Act § 208(b)(3), 9A Unif.L.Ann. 110 (1979) also permits the parent or guardian to sue.

61. Turner v. Turner, 167 Cal.App.2d 636, 334 P.2d 1011 (1959); Feldman v. Intrator, 175 Misc. 632, 24 N.Y.S.2d 665 (1941). Greene v. Williams, 9 Cal.App.3d 559, 88 Cal.Rptr. 261 (1970) held that the parent could not sue after the death of the underage child, however.

62. Niland v. Niland, 96 N.J.Eq. 438, 126 A. 530 (1924); Fink v. Fink, 70 S.D. 366, 17 N.W.2d 717 (1945); Williams v. White, 263 S.W.2d 666 (Tex.Civ.App.1954); Kirby v. Gilliam, 182 Va. 111, 28 S.E.2d 40 (1943); Ex parte Hollopeter, 52 Wash. 41, 100 P. 159 (1909) (dictum). See also Annot., 150 A.L.R. 609, 612 (1944).

63. Feldman v. Intrator, 175 Misc. 632, 24 N.Y.S.2d 665 (Sup.Ct.1941).

64. Cf. State ex rel. Scott v. Lowell, 78 Minn. 166, 80 N.W. 877 (1899), holding that the father of the under age wife could not legally detain her against the husband's claims, where the marriage was voidable only at the suit of the party under age.

65. See Crapps v. Smith, 9 Ga.App. 400, 71 S.E. 501 (1911).

66. Kibler v. Kibler, 180 Ark. 1152, 24 S.W.2d 867 (1930); Jones v. Jones, 200 Ga. 571, 37 S.E.2d 711 (1946); Andrews v. Andrews, 91 Ga.App. 659, 86 S.E.2d 669 (1955); May v. Meade, 236 Mich. 109, 210 N.W. 305 (1926); Taylor v. Taylor, 355 S.W.2d 383 (Mo.App.1962); Powell v. Powell, 97 N.H. 301, 86 A.2d 331 (1952); Jimenez v. Jimenez, 93 N.J.Eq. 257, 116 A. 788 (1922) (cohabitation for three months is sufficient for ratification); Matturro v. Matturro, 111 N.Y.S.2d 533 (1952); Koonce v. Wallace, 52 N.C. (7 Jones Law) 194 (1859). See also Annot., 159 A.L.R. 104 (1945). One extraordinary case, Ehrlich v. Ehrlich, 112 N.Y.S.2d 244 (1952) held that the parties did not "freely cohabit" when they used contraceptives, and therefore no ratification occurred under N.Y.Dom.Rel.Law § 140b (1977). In Hardware Mutual Casualty Co. v. Mims, 82 Ga.App. 210, 60 S.E.2d 501 (1950) it was held that the person asserting ratification has the burden of proof.

67. E.g., West's Ann.Cal.Civ.Code § 4426 (1983); Idaho Code § 32–501 (1983); Mont.Code Ann. 40–1–402 (1983); Nev.Rev.Stat. § 125.320 (1983); N.H.Rev.Stat. § 457:5 (Supp.1973); N.J.Stat.Ann. § 2A:34–1 (Supp. 1984); N.Y.—McKinney's Dom.Rel.Laws § 140 (1977); N.D.Cent.Code § 14–04–01 (1981); Okl.Stat.1961, tit. 12, § 1283; Or.Rev.Stat. § 107.015 (1983). See also the Uniform Marriage and Divorce Act § 208(b)(3), 9A Unif.L. Ann. 110 (1979).

voidable [68] or wholly void,[69] although the result is inconsistent with the characterization of nonage marriages as void. There is some authority that conduct other than marital cohabitation may amount to confirmation of the marriage if it occurs after the party reaches full age. Powell v. Powell states the general principle to be that confirmation requires "some unequivocal and voluntary act, statement or course of conduct after reaching the age of consent." [70] It held that bringing suit for divorce did not indicate an intention to continue the marriage and therefore did not constitute confirmation, nor did acceptance of temporary support in the divorce action. But presumably bringing an action to enforce continuing duties of the marriage would confirm it.[71] Other than this, and the usual method of confirmation by cohabitation, it is difficult to imagine conduct which would confirm the marriage.

It is more uncertain whether other defenses may be raised against annulment for nonage. Where the statute makes such marriages void or in some other way indicates that the court is to have no discretion to deny annulment, no equitable defenses are available.[72] Where the statute is construed to confer some discretion, it is some times held that annulment is

equitable in nature [73] and that the defenses of estoppel,[74] unclean hands,[75] or laches [76] are available. The better considered opinions are reluctant to apply such defenses, since they often have no relevance to the total marital situation of the parties.[77] In particular it is clear that a misrepresentation of age on a marriage license does not justify refusing annulment to the party under age.[78] One case does make a distinction between this and misrepresentations made directly to the other spouse, holding that the latter would be a defense to the annulment.[79] It has also been held that the death of one of the parties bars a suit to annul the marriage, although strictly speaking this may not be considered a defense.[80]

Choice of Law [81]

Due to the shopping around which young couples engage in to avoid the age restrictions on marriage, most of the conflicts problems arise in a context of evasion of the local law. The parties, domiciled in state A and under the age of consent for marriage by A's law, go to state B to be married in order to take advantage of state B's lower age limit. They return immediately to A. The question then is whether state A, the state of their domicile

68. Kibler v. Kibler, 180 Ark. 1152, 24 S.W.2d 867 (1930).

69. Powers v. Powers, 138 Ga. 65, 74 S.E. 759 (1912).

70. 97 N.H. 301, 303, 86 A.2d 331, 332 (1952).

71. Terrky v. Terrky, 96 Misc. 594, 160 N.Y.S. 1016 (1916) refused annulment when the plaintiff-wife had previously sued for and obtained a decree of separation, holding that this confirmed the marriage.

72. Duley v. Duley, 151 A.2d 255 (D.C.Mun.App.1959); Swenson v. Swenson, 179 Wis. 536, 192 N.W. 70 (1923). But see Mitchell v. Mitchell, 219 Ark. 69, 239 S.W.2d 748 (1951).

73. Gibbs v. Gibbs, 92 N.J.Eq. 542, 113 A. 704 (1921).

74. Duley v. Duley, 151 A.2d 255 (D.C.Mun.App.1959).

75. Gibbs v. Gibbs, 92 N.J.Eq. 542, 113 A. 704 (1921).

76. Carroll v. De Martini, 19 N.J.Super. 136, 88 A.2d 26 (1952), holding a five and one-half year delay in bringing suit constituted laches.

77. Quinzi v. Quinzi, 261 App.Div. 929, 25 N.Y.S.2d 435 (2d Dep't 1941); Swenson v. Swenson, 179 Wis. 536, 192 N.W. 70 (1923).

78. Ruiz v. Ruiz, 6 Cal.App.3d 58, 85 Cal.Rptr. 674 (1970); Vaughan v. Gideon, 56 Cal.App.2d 158, 132 P.2d

529 (1942); Gibbs v. Gibbs, 92 N.J.Eq. 542, 113 A. 704 (1921); Swenson v. Swenson, 179 Wis. 536, 192 N.W. 70 (1923). But cf. Samluk v. Gorecki, 265 A.2d 46 (Del. Super.1970).

79. Gibbs v. Gibbs, 92 N.J.Eq. 542, 113 A. 704 (1921). In Duley v. Duley, 151 A.2d 255 (D.C.Mun.App.1959) the annulment was denied apparently on the ground that the parties lived together before the plaintiff-husband reached full age, and that he was emancipated and mature for his age. But Eliot v. Eliot, 77 Wis. 634, 46 N.W. 806 (1890) holds that cohabitation before reaching the age of consent does not raise a defense to annulment.

80. Greene v. Williams, 9 Cal.App.3d 559, 88 Cal.Rptr. 261 (1970). A parent was suing in this case.

81. The cases on this subject are collected in Annot., 71 A.L.R.2d 687 (1960). The question here is, what law governs the validity of marriages attacked for nonage. The question of what court has jurisdiction to hear the annulment suit is quite different and is discussed infra, section 3.2, though some courts confuse it with choice of law. See Levy v. Downing, 213 Mass. 334, 100 N.E. 638 (1913) and Roop v. Roop, 91 N.H. 47, 13 A.2d 474 (1940), 14 So.Cal.L.Rev. 70 (1940) in which the question was choice of law, but in which the courts wrote as if the problem was one of jurisdiction.

both before and after marriage, will recognize the marriage as valid. If state A has a marriage validating statute, the marriage is recognized.[82] If state A has the Uniform Marriage Evasion Act, or a similar statute,[83] recognition of the marriage turns on (a) whether the marriage is void or only voidable by the law of state A;[84] and (b) whether the parties returned to state A and cohabited there as husband and wife.[85] It is too bad that a statute aimed at solving this difficult problem has adopted the confusing void-voidable distinction. But the statute clearly provides that the marriage is invalidated only if it is "void" by the law of the parties' domicile, and must be given effect according to its terms.

Without the help of statute, the courts have treated the evasion problem in different ways. A substantial number of them have relied on the dogmatic assertion (popularized by the first Restatement of Conflicts)[86] that the law of the place of celebration governs in all cases. This is applied to mean that if the marriage is valid by that law, the domicile will recognize it as valid in spite of the parties' evasion of the domicile's requirements.[87] The case of Wilkins v. Zelichowski[88] takes a different view. In holding the marriage invalid the court reasoned that New Jersey's nonage statute is based on the well considered social policy that child marriages ought to be discouraged. This policy applies to marriages contracted outside New Jersey just as strongly as to those contracted in New Jersey, so long as the parties continue to live in New Jersey. As the court said, the state of Indiana, where the marriage occurred, had no interest in its continuance. If in fact the policy of discouraging child marriages is to be taken seriously, this case is eminently sensible. The cases refusing to annul marriages which are valid by the lex loci, though contrary to the domicile's law, and which are contracted for the purpose of evading the domicile's policy seem to take the underlying policy much too lightly. One further point supports the Wilkins decision. The cases in which nonage marriages are attacked usually involve an action for annulment brought soon after the marriage ceremony. In such circumstances there is less force to the argument, persuasive in other contexts,[89] that marriages should be upheld wherever possible. It is this argument which underlies Professor Ehrenzweig's Rule of Validation.[90] In

82. E.g., West's Ann.Cal.Civ.Code § 4104 (1983); Colo.Rev.Stat. § 14–2–112 (1973); Uniform Marriage and Divorce Act § 210, 9A Unif.L.Ann. 116–117 (1979). Cases applying this type of statute to validate a marriage invalid by the law of the domicile are McDonald v. McDonald, 6 Cal.2d 457, 58 P.2d 163 (1936); Payne v. Payne, 121 Colo. 212, 214 P.2d 495 (1950); and Mangrum v. Mangrum, 310 Ky. 226, 220 S.W.2d 406 (1949). The same principles apply where the alleged defect in the marriage is the failure to obtain a parent's consent. Vaughn v. Vaughn, 62 Cal.App.2d 260, 144 P.2d 658 (1944) (semble). Other similar statutes are cited in section 2.9, supra, at note 54.

83. The basic statute is found in 9 Unif.L.Ann. 480 (1942). It was withdrawn as a uniform act in 1943. 9 Unif.L.Ann. XXI (1942). States which have adopted it are referred to in section 2.9, supra, at note 51.

84. E.g., Mass.Gen.Laws Ann. ch. 207, § 10 (1981).

85. Bell v. Bell, 122 W.Va. 223, 8 S.E.2d 183 (1940).

86. Restatement, Conflict of Laws §§ 121, 129 (1934). For extensive criticism of this view see Ehrenzweig, Conflict of Laws 376–378 (1962). See also Restatement (Second) Conflict of Laws § 283 (1971), which takes a much less definite position. It first states that the validity of marriage is determined by the local law of the state which with respect to the particular issue has the most significant relationship to the spouses and the marriage.

Clark, Domestic Rel., 2nd Ed. HBSE—5

It then provides that if the marriage satisfies the requirements of the state in which it was contracted, it will be recognized in other states unless it violates the strong public policy of some other state which had the most significant relationship to it. Factors relating to the significance of the relationship are listed in section 6 of this Restatement. The Reporter's Notes to comments j–k of section 283 cite the authority upon which this section relies.

87. State v. Graves, 228 Ark. 378, 307 S.W.2d 545 (1957); McDonald v. McDonald, 6 Cal.2d 457, 58 P.2d 163 (1936) (alternative ground of decision); Noble v. Noble, 299 Mich. 565, 300 N.W. 885 (1941); Needam v. Needam, 183 Va. 681, 33 S.E.2d 288 (1945), 31 Va.L.Rev. 210 (1944). Other cases are cited in Annot., 71 A.L.R.2d 687, 708 (1960). The question of who has standing to sue is decided by reference to the law of the forum. Vaughan v. Gideon, 56 Cal.App.2d 158, 132 P.2d 529 (1942).

88. 26 N.J. 370, 140 A.2d 65 (1958). See also State in Interest of I, 68 N.J.Super. 598, 173 A.2d 457 (Juv. & Dom.Rel.Ct.1961); Cunningham v. Cunningham, 206 N.Y. 341, 99 N.E. 845 (1912), 26 Harv.L.Rev. 253 (1913); Ross v. Bryant, 90 Okl. 300, 217 P. 364 (1923), 23 Colum.L.Rev. 782 (1923). Sirois v. Sirois, 94 N.H. 215, 50 A.2d 88 (1946) contains language supporting this point of view.

89. See, e.g., section 2.7 supra.

90. Ehrenzweig, Conflict of Laws, 378–384 (1962).

the nonage cases, however, there usually has been no reliance on the marriage, and little or no de facto assumption of the relationship. Therefore the conflict of laws cases relating to incestuous marriages, or bigamous marriages are not relevant to marriages contracted under the age of consent. Effectuation of policy is more important in solving the conflicts problems created by marriage legislation than the formulation of symmetrical, logical rules.

The cases which do not involve evasion of the local law ought to be decided by the application of similar criteria, but they often are not. Mechanical application of the lex loci principle is common, at least where the result is to validate the marriage.[91] It is also sometimes applied where it makes the marriage invalid,[92] though this is particularly undesirable if the parties have no other relation to the state than that they were married there. In the writer's view the lex loci should be applied if it makes the marriage valid, because in most cases where there is no intent to evade a domiciliary law the parties will have had no law other than that of the place of celebration in view. To apply the law of a domicile chosen later, or of a marital domicile, would therefore upset legitimate expectations. But if the lex loci makes the marriage invalid, it is preferable to apply the law of the domicile as of the date of the action for annulment. If at that time the parties are domi-

ciled in different states, the domicile of the party alleged to be under age should control. The reason for the seemingly inconsistent choice of law rules is to carry out the domicile's policy with respect to child marriages so far as that can be done without unfairly upsetting expectations of the parties developed in reliance upon some other law.

 WESTLAW REFERENCES

common-law /s age /s consent! /s marry! marri! marital

di(nonage /s marri! marry! marital)

The Statutory Pattern

differen! /s age /s marry! marri! marital /s man male /s women female

find 421 us 7

di(consent! approv! /5 parent guardian /s marri! marry! marital)

Direct Attack: Annulment

he(marri! marry! marital /s minor juvenile /s annul!)

---

§ 2.11 Venereal Disease [1]

Many states have statutes which require the applicant for a marriage license to furnish a physician's certificate stating that he is free from venereal disease, as a condition upon the issuance of the license.[2] If he has the disease but it is not communicable, the marriage license may issue.[3] The requirement of a physical examination may be waived under some statutes if the female applicant is pregnant.[4]

---

91. Castor v. United States, 174 F.2d 481 (8th Cir. 1949), cert. denied 338 U.S. 836, 70 S.Ct. 45, 94 L.Ed. 511 (1949); Canale v. People, 177 Ill. 219, 52 N.E. 310 (1898); Abbott v. Industrial Commission, 80 Ohio App. 7, 74 N.E.2d 625 (1946); Ex parte Chace, 26 R.I. 351, 58 A. 978 (1904); Ogden v. Ogden [1908] P. 46, 20 Harv.L.Rev. 412 (1907). In Keith v. Pack, 182 Tenn. 420, 187 S.W.2d 618 (1945) the lex loci was applied to validate a marriage on the ground of ratification, although the acts of ratification occurred in the domicile, not in the state of celebration. Other cases are cited in Annot., 71 A.L.R.2d 687, 692 (1960). A case contra is Pugh v. Pugh [1951] P. 482, invalidating the Austrian marriage of a Hungarian girl of 15 and a British citizen. The girl was under age by English law and the court held the marriage void, though this result certainly seems to have no relation to any rational policy.

92. Cruickshank v. Cruickshank, 193 Misc. 366, 82 N.Y.S.2d 522 (1948), 49 Colum.L.Rev. 693 (1949). The case turned on an owlish application of the lex loci. The husband was 19 and domiciled in New York. The marriage occurred in California. By California law the marriage was invalid for lack of any consent by the husband's

parents. By New York law the marriage was valid. It would seem clear that New York's policy should control with respect to its domiciliary in this situation. Cf. Bays v. Bays, 105 Misc. 492, 174 N.Y.S. 212 (1918), 4 Corn.L.Q. 200 (1919).

§ 2.11

1. See Note, Pre-Marital Tests for Venereal Disease, 53 Harv.L.Rev. 309 (1939).

2. E.g., Ala.Code 1984, § 22–16–5; Conn.Gen.Stat. Ann. § 46b–26 (1984); West's Fla.Stat.Ann. § 741.051 (Supp.1984); Ill.—Smith Hurd Ann.Stat. ch. 40 §§ 204, 205 (Supp.1984); Mass.Gen.Laws Ann. ch. 207, § 28A (1981); Mich.Comp.Laws Ann. § 14.15(5241) (1980); N.J. Rev.Stat.Ann. § 37:1–9 (Supp.1984); N.Y.—McKinney's Dom.Rel.Law § 13–a (Supp.1984).

3. Ibid.

4. E.g., Ill.—Smith Hurd Ann. ch. 40, §§ 204, 205 (Supp.1984). A few states also authorize waiver if the test is in conflict with the person's religious beliefs. See Mich.Comp.Laws Ann. §§ 14.15(5241), 14.15(5245) (1980).

The only reported case dealing with the constitutionality of these statutes has held them valid, undoubtedly a sound result.[5]

The sanctions imposed by these statutes are usually criminal. Ordinarily they do not purport to invalidate marriages contracted without compliance with the physical examination requirement. Presumably the courts would hold that, since the requirement appears only as a prerequisite to obtaining a license, non-compliance does not affect the validity of the marriage.[6] In states continuing to allow common law marriages, the physical examination may be easily avoided. In any event it may be avoided by contracting the marriage in another state. If the other state makes no such requirement, it seems probable that the lex loci would be applied to hold the marriage valid even where the parties intentionally evaded the domicile's law.[7]

In a few states there are statutes which provide that a person having a communicable venereal disease does not have capacity to marry.[8] Where the statute clearly does provide that the disease affects the capacity to marry, it may be a ground for annulment.[9] There is also authority that a venereal disease produces physical incapacity to enter the marriage state and for that reason warrants a decree of annulment.[10] The relative paucity of cases on venereal disease as a ground for annulment is partly due to the fact that the disease is often concealed from the spouse. It is asserted, if at all, in annulment suits based on fraud, rather than as a ground for annulment itself. Whether the concealment of venereal disease is the sort of fraud which justifies the annulment of marriage is discussed in another section.[11]

 WESTLAW REFERENCES

annul! /s marri! marital marry! /s venereal "sexually transmitted" s.t.d.

§ 2.12 Impotence

Impotence of either party made a marriage voidable according to the English ecclesiastical law.[1] It was a canonical disability,[2] entitling either party to a decree of nullity.[3]

Since, in the view of most courts, the English ecclesiastical law never became a part of American common law, impotence is not a ground for annulment in this country in the absence of statute.[4] The contrary position could be persuasively based on the argument that we took most of our marriage law from

---

5. Peterson v. Widule, 157 Wis. 641, 147 N.W. 966 (1914), 28 Harv.L.Rev. 112 (1914).

6. Berenson v. Berenson, 198 Misc. 398, 98 N.Y.S.2d 912 (Dom.Rel.Ct.1950).

7. Presumably this would be considered a question of marriage formality, as to which the lex loci generally governs. See section 2.3, supra, at note 85.

8. Del.Code tit. 13, § 101(b) (1981) (marriage prohibited and void from the time its nullity is declared where either party is venereally diseased, or suffering from some other disease, the nature of which is unknown to the other party); Mich.Comp.Laws Ann. § 25.6 (1984) (no person afflicted with syphilis or gonorrhea shall be capable of marrying); Neb.Rev.St. § 42–102 (1984) (no person afflicted with venereal disease shall marry in this state).

9. Stratos v. Stratos, 317 Mich. 113, 26 N.W.2d 729 (1947) (dictum); Brown v. Greer, 293 Mich. 219, 291 N.W. 640 (1940) (semble); Christensen v. Christensen, 144 Neb. 763, 14 N.W.2d 613 (1944). See also Doe v. Doe, 35 Del. (5 W.W.Harr.) 301, 165 A. 156 (Del.Super.1933). The Stratos case held that if the parties continued to cohabit until after the disease was cured, a valid common law marriage resulted and no annulment would be granted. The Christensen case held that the marriage was voidable, not void, and the person afflicted could not have it annulled.

10. Ryder v. Ryder, 66 Vt. 158, 28 A. 1029 (1892). See Annot., 5 A.L.R. 1016, 1021 (1920).

11. See section 2.15, infra.

§ 2.12

1. Greenstreet v. Cumyns, 2 Phill.Ecc. 10, 161 Eng. Rep. 1062 (1812). See other cases collected in Harthan v. Harthan [1948] 2 All Eng.Rep. 639 (C.A.).

2. 1 Blackstone, Commentaries on the Laws of England, 433, 439 (Sharswood ed. 1876); 2 Burns, Ecclesiastical Law, 445, 446 (4th ed. 1781).

3. Harthan v. Harthan [1948] 2 All Eng.Rep. 639 (C.A.) (impotent party may annul provided he was ignorant of his condition at the time of the marriage.) See for critical comment on this case Bevan, Limitations on the Right of an Impotent Spouse to Petition for Nullity, 76 L.Q.Rev. 267 (1960).

4. D. v. D., 41 Del. (2 Terry) 263, 20 A.2d 139 (1941); Linneman v. Linneman, 1 Ill.App.2d 48, 116 N.E.2d 182 (1953); Steerman v. Snow, 94 N.J.Eq. 9, 118 A. 696 (1922), 9 Va.L.Rev. 464 (1923); Burtis v. Burtis, 1 Hopk.Ch. 557 (N.Y.1825). Smith v. Morehead, 59 N.C. 360 (1863) may be contra.

In Dolan v. Dolan, 259 A.2d 32 (Me.1969) the court held that statutory authority for annulment is required, but that jurisdiction to hear a claim for annulment on the

the English ecclesiastical system even though we never had ecclesiastical courts, and that as soon as jurisdiction over the validity of marriages is lodged in a particular court, that court may annul marriages on the established ecclesiastical grounds.[5] It is plain in other contexts that ecclesiastical rules have been imported into our marriage law without express statutory sanction.[6] There is no compelling reason why impotence as a ground for annulment should not be similarly imported, but it seems not to have been.

In any event, many states have statutes making impotence a ground for annulment.[7] Most such statutes require that the impotence be incurable,[8] and add that it must be "physical," or arise from physical causes.[9] These statutes make an interesting contrast with the statutes found in a substantial number of states listing impotence as a ground for di-

vorce.[10] The divorce statutes generally speak solely of impotence, without qualifying adjectives. They should, however, be construed to read the same as the annulment statutes.[11] It would be anomalous to grant divorces on less evidence of impotence than would be required in annulment suits.

Various questions of construction arise out of statutes authorizing annulment for impotence. The first is, what is meant by impotence. It is clear that in general it means inability to copulate.[12] Sterility, or the inability to have children, is not impotence and does not constitute a ground for annulment.[13] But if ability to copulate is so impaired that sexual relations are imperfect or painful or unnatural, this amounts to impotence.[14] Capacity for intercourse means, in this context, the ability to have normal sexual relations with the spouse. If the lack of ability to have

---

ground of impotence could be based on a general statute which merely authorized annulment "whenever the validity of a marriages is denied or doubted". See Me.Rev. Stat.Ann. tit. 19, § 632 (1981).

5. See Le Barron v. Le Barron, 35 Vt. 365 (1862).

6. The doctrine of recrimination is the most egregious example. See section 13.11, infra.

7. Alaska Stat. § 25.24.030 (1983); Ark.Stats. sec. 55–106 (1971); West's Cal.Civ.Code § 4425(f) (1983); Del.Code tit. 13, § 1506(a)(2) (1981); Hawaii Rev.Stat. § 580–21, 580–28 (1976); Idaho Code § 32–204 (1983); Iowa Code Ann. § 598.29 (1981); Mass.Gen.Laws ch. 208, § 1 (1981) (divorce); Miss.Code 1973, § 93–7–3; Mont.Code Ann. 40–1–402 (1983); N.J.Stat.Ann. § 2A:34–1(c) (1984); N.Y.—McKinney's Dom.Rel.Laws § 7(3) (1977); N.C.Gen.Stat. § 51–3 (1984); N.D.Cent.Code § 14–04–01 (1981); S.D. Codified L. 25–1–39 (1984); V.Tex.C.A., Fam.Code § 2.43 (1975); Vt.Stat.Ann. tit. 15, § 512 (1974); W.Va.Code, § 48–2–1 (1984); Wis.Stat.Ann. § 767.03 (1981).

The Uniform Marriage and Divorce Act, section 208, 9A Unif.L.Ann. 110 (1979) authorizes a declaration of invalidity of marriage where a party lacks physical capacity to consummate the marriage by sexual intercourse and at the time of the marriage the other party did not know of the incapacity.

The ground for annulment found in English law and known as wilful refusal to consummate the marriage is not known in this country. Sasserno v. Sasserno, 240 Mass. 583, 134 N.E. 239 (1922). For the English law see, e.g., Napier v. Napier, [1915] P. 184, holding that this ground does not exist in the absence of statute. But it is found in Matrimonial Causes Act 1973 sec. 12(b).

8. E.g., California, Delaware, Mississippi, New Jersey, North Dakota, Texas, West Virginia, Wisconsin, supra, note 7.

9. E.g., Arkansas, California, Delaware, Hawaii, Idaho, Montana, New Jersey, New York, North Carolina,

North Dakota, South Dakota, Vermont, Wisconsin, supra, note 7.

10. See section 14.8, infra, at note 36, Practitioner's Edition, and statutes cited supra, note 7.

11. Cases are collected in Annot., 65 A.L.R.2d 776, 780 (1959).

12. Helen v. Thomas, 52 Del. (2 Storey) 1, 150 A.2d 833 (1959); Dolan v. Dolan, 259 A.2d 32 (Me.1969); Donati v. Church, 13 N.J.Super. 454, 80 A.2d 633 (1951); Schroter v. Schroter, 56 Mis. 69, 106 N.Y.S. 22 (1907); G. v. G., 1924 A.C. 349. See also Annot. 52 A.L.R.3d 589, 599 (1973) and Annot., 65 A.L.R.2d 776 (1959).

13. Kirschbaum v. Kirschbaum, 92 N.J.Eq. 7, 111 A. 697 (1920); Donati v. Church, 13 N.J.Super. 454, 80 A.2d 633 (1951); Korn v. Korn, 229 App.Div. 460, 242 N.Y.S. 589 (1st Dep't 1930); G. v. G. [1924] A.C. 349; D-e v. A-g, 1 Rob.Ecc. 279, 163 Eng.Rep. 1039 (1845). The English case of L. v. L., [1949] 1 All Eng.Rep. 141, 2 Vand.L.Rev. 489 (1949) held that annulment would be granted to the wife for the husband's psychogenic impotence after the wife had become pregnant through artificial insemination, using the husband's semen.

Further authority that one may be legally impotent, though not sterile, is provided by T v. M, 100 N.J.Super. 530, 242 A.2d 670 (1968), where the annulment was granted notwithstanding that the wife, suffering from vaginismus, had become pregnant as a result of ejaculation against the opening of her vagina.

14. Stepanek v. Stepanek, 193 Cal.App.2d 760, 14 Cal. Rptr. 793 (1961) (dictum); S. v. S., 192 Mass. 194, 77 N.E. 1025 (1906) (annulment granted where intercourse caused the wife such distress that it endangered her health); Schroter v. Schroter, 56 Misc. 69, 106 N.Y.S. 22 (Sup.Ct. 1907) (annulment denied where intercourse was painful but still normal); D. v. D., [1954] 2 All Eng.Rep. 598 (annulment granted where only partial and incomplete intercourse possible); Snowman v. Snowman, [1934] P.

sexual relations is attributable to psychogenic causes, it is none the less impotence, just as where the causes are organic.[15] Even where the applicable statute refers to "physical" impotence, or impotence from physical causes, the courts grant annulments upon proof that the impotence arose from psychogenic causes, so long as these causes produce a physical inability to copulate.[16] In Tompkins v. Tompkins,[17] the leading case on this point, the court granted the annulment when it appeared that the defendant's impotence not only arose from psychogenic causes, but related solely to the spouse. He was apparently capable with respect to women other than his wife.

The requirement is made by the cases as well as the statutes that impotence must be shown to be incurable to justify annulment.[18] Since most physicians are too cautious to testify in absolute terms that any condition is incurable, this requirement might present difficulties of proof if literally applied. The plaintiff, having the burden of proof,[19] would lose in such a case. However, in practice this

requirement is met by evidence that no cure of the condition is presently likely.[20] In addition the old presumption of incurable impotence based on evidence the parties lived together for three years without consummating the marriage, the so-called doctrine of triennial cohabitation, may be relied upon.[21] Persistent refusal of intercourse may also be evidence of incurable impotence.[22] On the other hand, it is clear that if the parties have lived together only a very short time, and there is no evidence as to what treatment might accomplish, the annulment may be denied.[23] It may also be denied where a surgical operation can correct an organic impotence of the wife, even though the operation might be painful and result merely in physical ability to copulate without sexual pleasure.[24] Since proof of impotence is very largely dependent upon medical testimony, many courts hold that they have authority to order defendants to submit to medical examination, even though such an examination may be somewhat distasteful to the person undergoing it.[25] A refusal to submit to such an examination when

186. The English cases say that the only requirement is the ability to engage in *copula vera*, a term never very clearly defined. Apparently it means, so far as the wife is concerned, that she must be physically capable of intercourse without pain or serious distress, though she may not enjoy it. See S.Y. v. S.Y., [1962] 3 Weekly L.Rep. 526 (C.A.), 16 Vand.L.Rev. 955 (1963). For a similar case, in which the question was raised but not decided, see S. v. S., 211 Ga. 365, 86 S.E.2d 103 (1955). Here the wife was capable of intercourse and bearing children, but had no sexual pleasure in intercourse because paralyzed.

15. Kaufman v. Kaufman, 82 U.S.App.D.C. 397, 164 F.2d 519 (1947); Helen v. Thomas, 52 Del. (2 Storey) 1, 150 A.2d 833 (1959); Tompkins v. Tompkins, 92 N.J.Eq. 113, 111 A. 599 (1920), 6 Corn.L.Q. 333 (1921), 69 U.Pa.L. Rev. 388 (1921); G. v. G., [1924] A.C. 349. See also Annot., 65 A.L.R.2d 776, 783 (1959).

16. Rickards v. Rickards, 53 Del. (3 Storey) 134, 166 A.2d 425 (1960) (husband unable to copulate as a "pure form sexual deviate"); T. v. M., 100 N.J.Super. 530, 242 A.2d 670 (1968); Manbeck v. Manbeck, 339 Pa.Super. 493, 489 A.2d 748 (1985); Annot., 52 A.L.R.3d 589, 611 (1973).

17. 92 N.J.Eq. 113, 111 A. 599 (1920). See also D. v. C., 91 N.J.Super. 562, 221 A.2d 763 (1966).

18. Stepanek v. Stepanek, 193 Cal.App.2d 760, 14 Cal. Rptr. 793 (1961); Lorenz v. Lorenz, 93 Ill. 376 (1879); In re Marriage of Naguit, 104 Ill.App.3d 709, 433 N.E.2d 296 (1982); Dolan v. Dolan, 259 A.2d 32 (Me.1969); Annot., 52 A.L.R.3d 589, 602 (1973); D-e v. A-g, 1 Rob.Ecc. 279, 163 Eng.Rep. 1039 (1845).

19. Helen v. Thomas, 52 Del. (2 Storey) 1, 150 A.2d 833 (1959).

20. Rickards v. Rickards, 53 Del. (3 Storey) 134, 166 A.2d 425 (1960); Helen v. Thomas, 52 Del. (2 Storey) 1, 150 A.2d 833 (1959).

21. Tompkins v. Tompkins, 92 N.J.Eq. 113, 111 A. 599 (1920); 6 Corn.L.Q. 333 (1921), 69 U.Pa.L.Rev. 388 (1921); Kay v. Kay, 152 L.T.Rep. 264 (1934). Other cases are cited in Annot., 28 A.L.R.2d 499, 514 (1953), and in Annot., 52 A.L.R.3d 589, 604 (1973).

22. Manbeck v. Manbeck, 339 Pa.Super. 493, 489 A.2d 748 (1985). Cases are collected in Annot., 28 A.L.R.2d 499, 511 (1953).

23. Stepanek v. Stepanek, 193 Cal.App.2d 760, 14 Cal. Rptr. 793 (1961); S. v. E., 3 Sw. & Tr. 240, 164 Eng.Rep. 1266 (1863).

24. Godfrey v. Shatwell, 38 N.J.Super. 501, 119 A.2d 479 (1955); S.Y. v. S.Y., [1962], 3 Weekly L.Rep. 526 (C.A.), 16 Vand.L.Rev. 955 (1963).

25. Devanbagh v. Devanbagh, 5 Paige 554 (N.Y.1836) (examination will not be ordered if the party has already been examined by a doctor whose testimony is readily available); Anonymous v. Anonymous, 69 Misc. 489, 126 N.Y.S. 149 (1910); Le Barron v. Le Barron, 35 Vt. 365 (1862). Under modern rules of procedure this power is general. See Fed.Rules Civ.Proc. rule 35(a), 28 U.S.C.A. Corroboration of the parties' testimony may be required here as in other annulment suits. See Annot., 71 A.L.R. 2d 620 (1960).

ordered by the court may be taken as evidence of impotence.[26]

Impotence, being a canonical disability, is generally said to make the marriage only voidable.[27] This seems to mean that such a marriage may only be attacked directly, in a suit to annul,[28] and that various defenses may be raised. Thus, if the plaintiff knew or should have known of the impotence, annulment will be denied.[29] Likewise if the plaintiff continues to live with the defendant for a long time after learning of the impotence, some courts will refuse annulment on the theory that this constitutes ratification or laches.[30] It hardly seems good social policy, however, to impose on parties who make an attempt to surmount the problem of impotence the risk that their efforts will be the basis for denying the annulment if they fail.[31] Ratification or laches would seem to have no legitimate place in this context.

There is a leading English case holding that the impotent party himself may sue to annul the marriage, providing he did not know of the defect when the marriage was contracted.[32] This logically follows from the cases granting annulment when the impotence relates only to a particular spouse.[33] This seems a sound result, and a few American cases agree, at least in the absence of statutory language to the contrary.[34]

 WESTLAW REFERENCES

topic(253) /p impoten! /s annul!

§ 2.13   Mental Incompetence

Mental incompetence, which in many jurisdictions is a ground for divorce,[1] has long been a ground for annulment both in England and the United States.[2] Annulment for this reason is now governed by statute in all jurisdictions but the common law cases still have great influence. It is an interesting paradox that the statutes authorizing annulment on this ground do not contain nearly as strong

26. S. v. S., 42 Del. (3 Terry) 192, 29 A.2d 325 (1942).

27. Anonymous v. Anonymous, 24 N.J.Eq. 19 (1873); Harthan v. Harthan, [1948] 2 All Eng.Rep. 639 (C.A.).

28. Martin v. Otis, 233 Mass. 491, 124 N.E. 294 (1919).

29. D. v. D., 41 Del. (2 Terry) 263, 20 A.2d 139 (1941); Rickards v. Rickards, 53 Del. (3 Storey) 134, 166 A.2d 425 (1960) (evidence failed to show that the wife knew of the impotence before marriage); Anonymous v. Anonymous, 74 N.Y.S.2d 899 (1947) (wife should have been able to tell that the husband was feeble and had physically deteriorated through age). Other cases are cited in Annot., 15 A.L.R.2d 706, 709 (1951). In Hatch v. Hatch, 58 Misc. 54, 110 N.Y.S. 18 (1908) the court refused annulment to a fifty-six-year-old wife, where the husband was sixty-nine, on the ground that the marriage of persons of this age should be based on motives of support and companionship rather than sex, so that the wife had no just cause for complaint when the husband proved to be impotent. The impotent wife obtained an annulment in D. v. C., 91 N.J. Super. 562, 221 A.2d 763 (1966), 52 Iowa L.Rev. 767 (1967).

30. Jwaideh v. Jwaideh, 140 A.2d 303 (D.C.Mun.App. 1958) (delay of nine years amounted to laches, where the wife's difficulty came from a "phobic fear" of sexual intercourse, the husband being motivated by the desire to help her); Godfrey v. Shatwell, 38 N.J.Super. 501, 119 A.2d 479 (1955) (husband's delay in suing amounted to ratification, though there was some chance the wife's condition might yield to treatment); Donati v. Church, 13 N.J.Super. 454, 80 A.2d 633 (1951) (ratification by continuing to have imperfect intercourse); Kirschbaum v. Kirschbaum, 92 N.J.Eq. 7, 111 A. 697 (1920) (ratification by eleven years' cohabitation); Cofer v. Cofer, 287 S.W.2d

212 (Tex.Civ.App.1956). Contra: Manbeck v. Manbeck, 339 Pa.Super. 493, 489 A.2d 748 (1985). There is a statute of limitations on annulment suits in a few jurisdictions. See, e.g., Deitch v. Deitch, 161 App.Div. 492, 146 N.Y.S. 782 (2d Dep't 1914), and Annot., 52 A.L.R.2d 1163, 1166 (1957).

31. Cf. Singer v. Singer, 9 N.J.Super. 397, 74 A.2d 622 (1950), in which the court held there was no ratification when the husband continued to live with the wife for some time while she was under treatment in the hope of improvement in her condition. And the wife's bearing a child by AID did not bar her from getting an annulment for her husband's impotence in Gursky v. Gursky, 39 Misc.2d 1083, 242 N.Y.S.2d 406 (1963).

32. Harthan v. Harthan, [1948] 2 All Eng.Rep. 639 (C.A.), 76 L.Q.Rev. 267 (1960).

33. E.g., Tompkins v. Tompkins, supra note 17. In such cases, it is impossible to say that one or the other party is impotent, the only accurate characterization being that a normal sexual relationship between them is impossible.

34. Anonymous v. Anonymous, 69 Misc. 489, 126 N.Y.S. 149 (1910); D v. C, 91 N.J.Super. 562, 221 A.2d 763 (1966), 52 Iowa L.Rev. 767 (1967); Annot., 52 A.L.R.3d 589, 621 (1973).

§ 2.13

1. See section 14.8, Practitioner's Edition.

2. For a discussion of the common law developments and the older cases see, McCurdy, Insanity as a Ground for Annulment in English and American Law, 29 Va.L. Rev. 771 (1943).

safeguards for the mentally incompetent party as do the statutes authorizing divorce for mental incompetence.[3] This is particularly notable because, by virtue of the general lack of authority to grant alimony in annulment suits, wives receive much less financial protection from annulment decrees than they do from divorce decrees. It seems clear that a carefully drawn annulment statute should provide the same protection for the mentally incompetent as the existing divorce statute does, although some of the divorce statutes on this subject contain qualifications and restrictions that appear highly technical and unnecessary.

 **WESTLAW REFERENCES**

sy,di(annul! /7 marriage /s mental! /s incompeten! incapacit!)

§ 2.14　Duress

Like other consensual relationships, a marriage contract may be set aside in an action for annulment where it is shown that either party entered the marriage as a result of duress. Duress is a statutory ground for annulment in many states,[1] but even in the absence of statute it can be the basis for annulment under the general equity jurisdiction of the courts.[2]

3. See section 14.8, Practitioner's Edition.

§ 2.14

1. E.g., Alaska Stat. § 25.24.030 (1983); Ark.Stats. § 55–106 (1971); West's Ann.Cal.Civ.Code § 4425 (1983); Colo.Rev.Stat. § 14–10–111 (1973); Del.Code tit. 13, § 1506 (1981); Ky.Rev.Stat. § 402.030 (1984); La.Stat. Ann.—Civ.Code art. 110 (1952); Mich.Comp.Laws Ann. § 25.82 (1984); Minn.Stat.Ann. § 518.02 (Supp.1985); Miss.Code 1973, § 93–7–3; N.J.Stat.Ann. § 2A:34–1 (Supp.1984); N.Y.—McKinney's Dom.Rel.Law § 7(4) (1977); Ohio Rev.Code § 3105.31 (1980); Or.Rev.Stat. § 106.030 (1983); Pa.Stat. tit. 23, § 205 (1984) (divorce); S.D.Codified Laws § 25–1–39 (1984); V.Tex.C.A., Fam. Code § 2.44 (1975); Vt.Stat.Ann. tit. 15, § 512, 516, 517 (1974); Va.Code (1983), § 20–89.1; West's Rev.Code Wash.Ann. § 26.04.130 (1961); Wis.Stat.Ann. § 767.03 (1981).

2. Worthington v. Worthington, 234 Ark. 216, 352 S.W.2d 80 (1961); Jewett v. Jewett, 196 Pa.Super. 305, 175 A.2d 141 (1961). See also Kingsley, Duress As A Ground For Annulment of Marriage, 33 So.Cal.L.Rev. 1 (1959).

The clearest example of duress is the use of physical force or the threat of such force sufficient to overcome the will of one of the parties to the marriage. This entitles the party against whom the force was used to an annulment.[3] In fact the use of such force or its threat against third parties may be grounds for annulment where there is such a close relationship between the plaintiff and the third party that the duress exercised against the third party overcomes the will of the plaintiff.[4] Conversely, it is also true that if the force or threat of force comes from a third party, without either the participation or knowledge of the defendant, it may constitute sufficient duress to be a ground for annulment.[5] Other forms of duress than actual force or threat of force may be sufficient to annul a marriage if they have the necessary effect upon the plaintiff's will, causing the marriage to be undertaken involuntarily.[6]

The claim of duress is most commonly made by husbands who have been induced to marry by various forms of "persuasion" following their seduction of the wife. If the "persuasion" takes the form of violence or threats of violence, this still may constitute duress.[7] The true shotgun marriage may be annulled. But if the marriage is brought about by threats of criminal prosecution for seduction or bastardy, the courts generally hold that this is not duress.[8] A few cases go to great

3. E.g., Fratello v. Fratello, 118 Misc. 584, 193 N.Y.S. 865 (1922).

4. Warren v. Warren, 199 N.Y.S. 856 (1923) (husband threatened to tell wife's father, who had heart condition, that he had taken liberties with her. Wife feared father would die; held: annulment granted.)

5. Parojeic v. Parojeic [1959] All Eng.Rep. 1; H. vs. H [1954] P. 258. See also Note, 30 Colum.L.Rev. 714 (1930).

6. Avakian v. Avakian, 69 N.J.Eq. 89, 60 A. 521 (1905), affirmed 69 N.J.Eq. 834, 66 A. 1133 (1905); H. v. H. [1954] P. 258.

7. Quealy v. Waldron, 126 La. 479, 52 So. 479 (1910). In a similar case the duress was held not to have been proved. Stakelum v. Terral, 126 So.2d 689 (La.App.1961). See also Wadlington, Shotgun Marriage By Operation of Law, 1 Ga.L.Rev. 183 (1967), and Brown, The Shotgun Marriage, 42 Tulane L.Rev. 837 (1968).

8. E.g., Smith v. Saum, 324 Ill.App. 299, 58 N.E.2d 248 (1944); Figueroa v. Figueroa, 110 N.Y.S.2d 550 (Sup.Ct. 1952); Jones v. Jones, 314 S.W.2d 448 (Tex.Civ.App.1958); Harrison v. Harrison, 110 Vt. 254, 4 A.2d 348 (1939).

lengths to uphold marriages brought about in this way,[9] although such marriages offer little prospect of success or happiness. If the threat of arrest or criminal prosecution is made maliciously, or without good cause, however, it is held that this is duress and the marriage may be annulled.[10] The reasoning usually advanced to uphold marriages entered into as a result of threats of criminal prosecution is that there is no interference with the husband's will when he is confronted with a choice between marriage or a legal proceeding.[11] This is of course not a reason but merely another way of stating the result. The real reason underlying these cases is that the courts are convinced that the proper course of action, both from the point of view of social policy and of morality, when there has been pre-marital intercourse and perhaps also a pregnancy, is for the parties to marry.[12] The child must be given a name. This same policy is expressed by those statutes which authorize courts to waive nonage requirements in the event of a pre-marital pregnancy,[13] and by other statutes which bar prosecution for seduction when the parties marry.[14] Certainly today, when pre-marital sexual relations have become almost a matter of course, this policy and this attempt to impose outdated notions of morality should be abandoned.[15] Marriages contracted solely out of

fear of legal proceedings should therefore be annulled under the same circumstances as would any marriage induced by force or threats.

In general where acts of duress are alleged, the courts have made the rule that the effect of duress must be perceptible at the time of the marriage ceremony and must be of such an extent that the complaining party was unable to act as a free agent in entering the marriage.[16] There has been some conflict, particularly in the English cases, as to whether the test is to be a subjective or an objective one, that is whether it is enough that the particular plaintiff was acting only out of a fear of the harmful consequences or whether it must also be shown that the circumstances were such as to produce such fear in the mind of an ordinary reasonable person.[17] Most of the cases seem to take the view that only the particular plaintiff's state of mind is in question, and that his fear is sufficient to justify the annulment even though it may not be a reasonable fear.[18] If it is true that marriage is a relationship of such importance that it should only be undertaken voluntarily, then this majority view would seem to be correct.

The modern view of the effect of duress upon the marriage is that the marriage is

Other cases are cited in Kingsley, Duress as a Ground for Annulment, 33 So.Cal.L.Rev. 1, 3 (1959).

9. E.g., In Figueroa v. Figueroa, 110 N.Y.S.2d 550 (Sup.Ct.1952) the court stated that such persuasion merely induces the right conduct and prevents illegitimate births and ruined womanhood.

10. Smith v. Saum, 324 Ill.App. 299, 58 N.E.2d 248 (1948). As the facts in this case indicate, however, the courts are often reluctant to find that such threats are made without good cause. Another case granting annulment when the threat of legal proceedings was made without cause is apparently Buckland v. Buckland, [1968] P.D. 296, discussed in Manchester, The Case of the Reluctant Bridegroom, 29 Mod.L.Rev. 622 (1966).

11. Mottley v. Vittitow, 251 Ky. 197, 64 S.W.2d 448 (1933); Marckley v. Marckley, 189 S.W.2d 8 (Tex.Civ.App. 1945).

12. Wadlington, Shotgun Marriage By Operation of Law, 1 Ga.L.Rev. 183, 196 (1967).

13. See section 2.10, supra, at note 34.

14. Note, Coercive Power of the Criminal Seduction Statute, 16 S.D.L.Rev. 166 (1971), collecting the statutes.

See also Wadlington, Shotgun Marriage By Operation of Law, 1 Ga.L.Rev. 183, 187 (1967).

15. See Wadlington, Shotgun Marriage By Operation of Law, 1 Ga.L.Rev. 183, 201 (1967).

16. E.g., Phipps v. Phipps, 216 S.C. 248, 57 S.E.2d 417 (1950). For the types of conduct amounting to duress, see Annot., 16 A.L.R.2d 1430 (1951).

17. Cf. Scott v. Sebright, 12 P.D. 21 (1886) with Buckland v. Buckland [1968] P.D. 296. See also Davies, Duress and Nullity of Marriage, 88 L.Q.Rev. 549 (1972), and Brown, The Shotgun Marriage, 42 Tulane L.Rev. 837 (1968).

18. Avakian v. Avakian, 69 N.J.Eq. 89, 60 A. 521 (1905), affirmed 69 N.J.Eq. 834, 66 A. 1133 (1905); Fratello v. Fratello, 118 Misc. 584, 193 N.Y.S. 865 (1922); H. v. H., 1954 P. 258; Scott v. Sebright, 12 P.D. 21 (1886). Thus if the plaintiff has been subjected to pressure but has resisted it and married voluntarily, the court would hold that duress had not induced the marriage and would therefore deny the annulment. Phipps v. Phipps, 216 S.C. 248, 57 S.E.2d 417 (1950). For other cases see Annot., 16 A.L.R.2d 1430 (1951).

voidable rather than void ab initio.[19] In some states the statutory language makes this clear.[20] As a consequence the rights and obligations created by the ceremony are preserved until the time of the annulment decree. Although there are no cases directly in point, it follows that such a marriage may be attacked only by the aggrieved party, and only while both parties are living.[21]

 WESTLAW REFERENCES

sy,di(duress /s marriage /s annul!)

§ 2.15   Fraud [1]

Statutes

Annulments on the ground of fraud are authorized by statute in thirty states and the District of Columbia.[2] Where no specific statutory authority exists, the authority of the courts to annul marriages for fraud is sometimes rested upon doctrines of inherent equity power borrowed from the law of contracts. Since equity exercised authority to set aside contracts for fraud, the argument runs, it may also set aside marriages for fraud.[3] The trouble is that historically equity did *not* set aside marriages for fraud. The ecclesiastical courts alone had this power in England, and we have never had ecclesiastical courts in this country. Therefore the equity analogy is not really apposite. The fact is, however, that some court should be endowed with annulment jurisdiction, and in default of a statutory grant of power the equity courts are the most convenient repository of that jurisdiction. They thus have the jurisdiction from necessity, and if an air of legitimacy is given to the situation by specious historical arguments, perhaps no harm is done.

In a few states the divorce statutes include fraudulent contract as a ground for divorce.[4] In some others it is a ground for divorce that the wife was pregnant by a man other than

19. In re Ruff's Estate, 159 Fla. 777, 32 So.2d 840 (1947); Norvell v. State, 149 Tex.Cr.App. 213, 193 S.W.2d 200 (1946).

20. E.g., West's Ann.Cal.Civ.Code § 4425 (1983); Minn.Stat.Ann. § 518.02 (Supp.1985); N.Y.—McKinney's Dom.Rel.Law § 7(4) (1977).

21. See In re Ruff's Estate, 159 Fla. 777, 32 So.2d 840 (1947).

§ 2.15

1. The leading article on annulments for fraud is Kingsley, Fraud as a Ground for Annulment of Marriage, 18 So.Cal.L.Rev. 213 (1945). See also Vanneman, Annulment of Marriage for Fraud, 9 Minn.L.Rev. 497 (1925); Sayre, A Rationale of Antenuptial Representations and Promises, 91 U.Pa.L.Rev. 735 (1943); and Tolstoy, Void and Voidable Marriages, 27 Mod.L.Rev. 385 (1964). The New York experience has been the subject of much writing. See Gershenson, Fraud in the New York Law of Annulment, 9 Bklyn.L.Rev. 51 (1939); Crouch, Annulment of Marriage for Fraud in New York, 6 Corn.L.Q. 401 (1921); Note, Annulment of Marriage in New York for Fraud Based Upon Religious Factors, 30 Ford.L.Rev. 776 (1962) and Note, Annulments for Fraud—New York's Answer to Reno? 48 Colum.L.Rev. 900 (1948).

2. Alaska Stat. § 25.05.031 (1983); Ark.Stats. § 55-106 (1971); West's Ann.Cal.Civ.Code § 4425 (1983); Colo. Rev.Stat. § 14–10–111(1)(d) (1973); Del.Code tit. 13, § 1506 (1981); D.C.Code 1981, § 30–103; Official Ga.Code Ann. §§ 19–3–4, 19–3–5 (1982); Hawaii Rev.Stat. § 580–21 (1976); Idaho Code § 32–501 (1983); West's Ann.Ind. Code § 31–1–7–6 (1980); Kan.Stat.Ann. § 60–1602 (1983); Ky.Rev.Stat. § 402.030 (1984); Mich.Comp.Laws Ann. § 25.82 (1984); Minn.Stat.Ann. § 518.02 (Supp.1985);

Miss.Code 1973, § 93–7–3; Mont.Code Ann. § 40–1–402 (1983); Neb.Rev.Stat. § 42–118 (1984); Nev.Rev.St. § 125.340 (1983); N.J.Stat.Ann. § 2A:34–1 (Supp.1984); N.Y.—McKinney's Dom.Rel.Law § 7(4) (1977); N.D.Cent. Code § 14–04–01 (1981); Ohio Rev.Code § 3105.31 (1980); Or.Rev.Stat. § 106.030 (1983); S.D.Codified Laws § 25–1–39 (1984); V.Tex.C.A., Fam.Code § 2.44 (1975); Vt.Stat. Ann. tit. 15, §§ 512, 516, 517 (1974); Va.Code 1983, § 20–89.1; West's Rev.Code Wash.Ann. § 26.04.130 (1961); W.Va.Code, §§ 48–2–2, 48–2–3 (1980 and Supp.1984) (semble); Wis.Stat.Ann. § 767.03 (1981); Wyo.Stat.1977, § 20–2–101. The Uniform Marriage and Divorce Act § 208, 9A Unif.L.Ann. 110 (1979) also authorizes annulment for fraud going to the essentials of the marriage.

3. Raia v. Raia, 214 Ala. 391, 108 So. 11 (1926); Means v. Industrial Commission, 110 Ariz. 72, 515 P.2d 29 (1973) (overruling earlier cases); Corder v. Corder, 141 Md. 114, 117 A. 119 (1922); Romatz v. Romatz, 355 Mich. 81, 94 N.W.2d 432 (1959) (dictum); Gatto v. Gatto, 79 N.H. 177, 106 A. 493 (1919); Costello v. Porzelt, 116 N.J.Super. 380, 282 A.2d 432 (1971); Pretlow v. Pretlow, 177 Va. 524, 14 S.E.2d 381 (1941). Contra, where the statute provided for annulment under certain circumstances, the court saying that this left no residuum of inherent equity jurisdiction: Lyannes v. Lyannes, 171 Wis. 381, 177 N.W. 683 (1920). See also Nice v. Nice, 71 D. & C. 167 (Pa.County Ct.1948). For a discussion of annulment for fraud under an early Connecticut colonial statute, see II Howard, History of Matrimonial Institutions 355 (1904).

4. Conn.Gen.Stat.Ann. § 466–40 (1986). The kinds of fraud sufficient to justify divorce under these statutes seem similar to those discussed in the annulment cases. Browning v. Browning, 89 Kan. 98, 130 P. 852 (1913).

her husband at the time of the marriage,[5] a fact which would normally entitle him to annulment for fraud.[6] Although there may be some logical objection to a ground for divorce which avoids the marriage ab initio, the obvious purpose of these statutes is to enable the courts to give the wife the financial protection of temporary and permanent alimony in appropriate cases. In order to effectuate this purpose, divorce should be held to be the exclusive remedy.[7]

It is clear that if fraud sufficient to invalidate the marriage has occurred, the marriage is voidable rather than void.[8] This means that it must be attacked directly in a suit to annul by the injured spouse[9] and that the suit must be brought during the lives of both spouses.[10]

General Principles in Fraud Cases

The statutes authorizing annulment for fraud do not, with a few exceptions, limit the

types of fraud which may make a marriage invalid.[11] Reading them one might therefore expect that any material fraud would qualify as a ground for annulment, defining materiality as in the law of contracts or the law of securities.[12] In fact, however, the courts have not applied the statutes in this way. Whether operating under statute, or applying common law principles, the courts have, at least in the past, held that annulment may not be granted for every material sort of fraud. They have more or less severely limited the frauds which may qualify as a ground for annulment, using a variety of terms to describe the extent of the limitation. Since there is a great deal of diversity and confusion on the point, and since the principles, such as they are, seem to be in the process of changing, it is important to examine the reasons for the earlier limitations on annulment for fraud.

5. Ala.Code 1983, § 30–2–1(a)(10); Tenn.Code Ann. § 36–4–101(9) (Supp.1986). See Burdine v. Burdine, 236 Miss. 886, 112 So.2d 522 (1959). There is a scattering of other statutes dealing with aspects of fraudulent marriage. E.g., La.Stat.Ann. Civ.Code art. 110 (1952) (consent to marriage is not free if there is a mistake as to the person); McKee v. McKee, 262 So.2d 111 (La.App.1972); Note, Nullity of Marriage Because of Simulated Consent, 29 La.L.Rev. 576 (1969); N.J.Stat.Ann. § 2A:34–1 (Supp. 1984) (authorizing annulment when allowable under the general equity jurisdiction of the superior court); N.C. Gen.Stat. § 51–3 (1984) (marriage is voidable if entered under a representation that the wife is pregnant when she is not); R.I.Gen.Laws 1981, § 15–5–1 (divorce may be decree for marriages which are void or voidable).

6. See the cases infra at notes 70, 71.

7. Clayton v. Clayton, 231 Md. 74, 188 A.2d 550 (1963); Abelt v. Zeman, 16 O.O.2d 87, 86 O.L.A. 109, 173 N.E.2d 907 (Com.Pl.1961), 13 West.Res.L.Rev. 404 (1962). Contra: Schwartz v. Schwartz, 113 Ohio App. 275, 17 O.O.2d 267, 173 N.E.2d 393 (1960). Where the annulment statute allows alimony to be awarded to the wife, there seems to be no reason to prefer divorce as a remedy. See Bernstein v. Bernstein, 25 Conn.Supp. 239, 201 A.2d 660 (1964), and Conn.Gen.Stat.Ann. § 46b–82 (1986).

8. Kingsley, Fraud as a Ground for Annulment of a Marriage, 18 So.Cal.L.Rev. 213, 236 (1945).

9. Many of the statutes state this requirement expressly. See Alaska, Delaware, Minnesota statutes cited, supra, note 2. The Michigan statute, Mich.Comp.Laws Ann. § 25.82 (1984) seems to say that a marriage induced by fraud is void without a decree of divorce or other legal process. The Uniform Marriage and Divorce Act § 208, 9A Unif.L.Ann. 110–111 (1979) is clumsily drafted but may be intended to reach this result. See also McLarty v. McLarty, 433 S.W.2d 722 (Tex.Civ.App.1968), 21 Baylor

L.Rev. 391 (1969), holding that a parent has no standing to annul his child's marriage on the ground of fraud. The party deceived must sue under V.Tex.C.A., Fam.Code § 2.44 (1975).

10. Patey v. Peaslee, 99 N.H. 335, 111 A.2d 194 (1955); Kingsley, Fraud as a Ground for Annulment of a Marriage, 18 So.Cal.L.Rev. 213, 236 (1945).

11. See the statutes cited supra, note 2. The exceptions are Colorado, Montana, New Jersey and the Uniform Marriage and Divorce Act § 208, 9A Unif.L.Ann. 110 (1979).

12. The contracts rule seems to be that if a misrepresentation is fraudulent or if it is material, it makes the contract voidable. A fraudulent misrepresentation is defined as one intended to induce the assent of the other party and either known to be false or known to be without basis. Misrepresentations are material when they are likely to induce a reasonable person to contract, or when the speaker knows that they would be likely to induce the other party to contract. See, e.g., Restatement of Contracts §§ 304, 306 (Tent.Draft No. 11, 1976); 12 S. Williston, Contracts § 1490 (3d ed. Jaeger 1970). Cf. Restatement of Contracts §§ 471, 476 (1932). The securities cases define material misrepresentations as those of such a character as would probably have been considered important by a reasonable shareholder in deciding how to vote, or by a reasonable investor in deciding whether to invest. Mills v. Electric Auto-Lite Co., 396 U.S. 375, 90 S.Ct. 616, 24 L.Ed.2d 593 (1970), appeal after remand 552 F.2d 1239 (7th Cir.1977), cert. denied 434 U.S. 922, 98 S.Ct. 398, 54 L.Ed.2d 279 (1977), rehearing denied 434 U.S. 1002, 98 S.Ct. 649, 54 L.Ed.2d (1977); TSC Industries, Inc. v. Northway, Inc., 426 U.S. 438, 96 S.Ct. 2126, 48 L.Ed.2d 757 (1976), motion denied 429 U.S. 810, 97 S.Ct. 48, 50 L.Ed.2d 70 (1976).

The first and most obvious reason is the English background. The only fraud which the English cases, even as late as 1897, would recognize as justifying annulment of marriage was misrepresentation as to the identity of the spouse.[13] Only in the highly unlikely event that W, in marrying X, was deceived into thinking she was marrying Y would the English courts annul.[14] Misrepresentations inducing the marriage, of no matter what variety, did not suffice as grounds. This had also been the canon law rule.[15] It has been changed by statute in England which now authorizes annulment for the wife's pregnancy by someone other than the husband, or for the defendant's affliction with a venereal disease where either condition was not known to the plaintiff.[16]

The social policy underlying the English doctrine was undoubtedly to prevent the dissolution of marriage, to make the status of marriage permanent and unassailable.[17] The same policy is observable in English divorce law before 1857.[18] If fraud had been recognized as a ground for annulment, a way out of marriage would have been provided in a form capable of considerable expansion. This would have seriously weakened the English concept of the indissolubility of marriage. It is something of a paradox that although marriage was often looked upon by the English upper and middle classes as primarily a financial and property transaction,[19] fraud was condoned in the negotiations leading to marriage which would not have been tolerated in commercial contracts. The English man of business was held to a higher ethical standard when selling a bale of cloth than when arranging the marriage of his daughter.[20] If, as seems plain enough, the rule concerning marriage was of ecclesiastical origin, we have a striking example of the immorality produced by certain kinds of officially sanctioned moral rules.

In the United States the early cases were not as restrictive as the English cases had been, but they were influenced by the English precedents and did limit annulments to those forms of fraud which went to the "essentials" of the marriage. The reasons for our more liberal rule were perhaps that we never had a canon law tradition and that in most American states we never took the view that marriage should be entirely indissoluble. Yet the American courts were also fearful of opening too wide an avenue of escape from marriage via the annulment for fraud. In addition some courts have purported to rest their decisions on the words of the marriage service, by which the parties promise to take each other "from this day forward, for better for worse, for richer for poorer, in sickness and in health, to love and to cherish, till death do us part. * * * "[21] The argument seems to be that by this language the parties are saying they have relied upon no pre-marital representations or statements. It seems at least equally likely, however, that the marital vow refers to future vicissitudes rather than to past representations.

The most influential American case has been Reynolds v. Reynolds.[22] An examination of the opinion reveals some of the reasoning already discussed, and some additional assumptions about the nature of marriage

---

13. Moss v. Moss [1897] P. 263; Sullivan v. Sullivan, 2 Hagg.Cons. 238, 161 Eng.Rep. 728 (1818); Ewing v. Wheatley, 2 Hagg.Cons. 175, 161 Eng.Rep. 706 (1814). The Moss case questioned Scott v. Sebright, [1886] 12 P.D. 21.

14. Wakefield v. Mackay, 1 Phillim. 134, 161 Eng.Rep. 937 (1807).

15. Moss v. Moss [1897] P. 263, 271.

16. Matrimonial Causes Act 1973 § 12. This Act also makes the marriage voidable where there has been no valid consent due to mistake.

17. This seems to be the meaning of the opinion in the Moss case which emphasizes that marriage is a status, not merely a contract. Moss v. Moss [1897] P. 263, 267.

18. Mueller, Inquiry Into the State of a Divorceless Society, 18 U.Pitt.L.Rev. 545 (1957).

19. L. Stone, The Family, Marriage and Sex England 1500–1800 Ch. 7 (1977).

20. That English marriage was often a battle in which the chief weapons on both sides were misrepresentation and concealment is evident from Daniel Defoe's Moll Flanders, first published in 1722.

21. The quotation is from the Episcopalian marriage service. Book of Common Prayer, 301 (1929). See Ozark v. Ozark, 191 Misc. 172, 75 N.Y.S.2d 430 (1947).

22. 85 Mass. (3 Allen) 605 (1862), 13 Harv.L.Rev. 110 (1899).

which are both less obvious and more startling. The case arose on a demurrer to the complaint in which the husband, seventeen years old, alleged that the wife, who was thirty, had represented before marriage that she was chaste when in fact she was pregnant by another man. By these representations she had induced the plaintiff to marry her. The court overruled the demurrer, holding that the complaint had alleged fraud of a sort which would justify granting the annulment. After announcing the general rule to be that there must be a fraudulent misrepresentation of a material fact, the court went on to list many facts not "deemed" material, and arrived at the conclusion that nothing may avoid the marriage except a fraud in the *essentialia* of the marriage relation. No definition of *essentialia* is attempted, but certain language in the opinion suggests that the term includes only those qualities essential to sexual relations and the bearing of children. The court then held that such fraud was committed in this case because the wife, being unable to bear a child, had incapacitated herself from executing a valid marriage contract. It emphasized the dilemma of the husband, who if the annulment were refused, would be forced either to accept another's child as his own, or, by rejecting the child, publish to the world the unchastity of his wife. It has been argued that this reasoning, turning on the impossible position of the husband should the annulment be refused, is the true basis for the result in Reynolds.[23] Certainly it is not persuasive that the wife misrepresented her ability to engage in sexual relations, since her condition was only temporary. Temporary or curable impotence is not a ground for annulment,[24] so that misrepresentation or concealment of such a disability would not seem to be. Likewise the inability to have children by the husband was only a temporary condition whose concealment should not constitute

fraud as to the essentials of marriage.[25] Therefore the basis for the holding in Reynolds is in considerable doubt.

Whatever may be the rationale for the Reynolds holding, the case's dictum to the effect that misrepresentations about character, health, fortune or temper are deemed immaterial and furnish no ground for annulment presents even more interesting and important issues. The court's reasoning on this score seems to be that (a) this result is necessary to insure the permanence of marriage; (b) " * * * it would lead to disastrous consequences if a woman who had once fallen from virtue could not be permitted to represent herself as continent, and thus restore herself to the rights and privileges of her sex, and enter into matrimony without incurring the risk of being put away by her husband on discovery of her previous immorality;"[26] (c) one who relies upon representations of this kind acts out of "blind credulity" and deserves no relief from the courts; and (d) one should inquire into the character of a prospective spouse.

The first of these reasons is unanswerable if one accepts the premise that the permanence of marriage must be secured at all costs. But today more than half of the states have enacted "marriage breakdown" divorce statutes of one kind or another. What this means in practical effect is that in those states a divorce may be had for the asking. In such circumstances insistence upon the permanence of marriage as a goal for annulment law seems unreal to say the least.

The second reason is an extraordinary plea for redemption through fraud rather than through penitence. The end justifies the means: It is so important for persons with unsavory pasts to marry that they are entitled to accomplish it by fraud if necessary. This is not far from saying that the foundation of American marriage is deceit, that we

---

23. Fessenden, Nullity of Marriage, 13 Harv.L.Rev. 110, 119 (1899).

24. E.g. Stepanek v. Stepanek, 193 Cal.App.2d 760, 14 Cal.Rptr. 793 (1961); Lorenz v. Lorenz, 93 Ill. 376 (1879).

25. Concealment of sterility seems to be grounds for annulment, but all the cases found involve permanent

and incurable inability to have children. See Kingsley, Fraud as a Ground For Annulment of a Marriage, 18 So. Cal.L.Rev. 213, 219 (1945).

26. 85 Mass. at page 609.

must deceive ourselves into entering the most serious, lasting and socially significant of all contracts. Surely the law cannot provide a more striking paradox than this.[27]

The last two reasons advanced in Reynolds are different ways of asserting one fundamental proposition, that persons who are about to marry should take the trouble to become well acquainted and that the law gives them advance warning that if they do not, it will not release them from ties to a person who turns out to be quite different from their expectations.[28] One can hardly disagree with the insistence upon a sober and realistic approach to marriage. In fact the period of engagement is often justified as providing an opportunity for just this sort of preparation for marriage.[29] It will undoubtedly be objected, however, that the romantic view of marriage [30] makes the court's position hopelessly unreal. Young people in particular marry out of passion, or physical attraction or as a result of love at first sight.[31] Is it not futile for the law to say to them, "You must make your choice of a mate in a rational way?" How can young people manage this in the face of the overwhelming pressures from society, from mass communications and from their peers in the direction of less rationality, rather than more, in the decision to marry? [32] Is not the proposition also unreal by virtue of the difficulty, in an urban, mobile society, of getting sufficient information about the background and past life of a fiancé to make a rational decision to marry? Finally, there is the objection that the law's warning will not be heard, since laymen, particularly of marriageable age, do not know or care what esoteric rules the law may contain as to annulment of marriages for fraud.

In spite of all the counter-arguments, this aspect of the Reynolds rationale seems to be the explanation for the case's dictum, and to underlie most of the later decisions on annulment for fraud. And in fact most of the objections turn out, on close examination, not to be as forceful as they appear at first. Young people today often do have the chance (and take advantage of it) to know each other very well before marriage. In many circles there is an informality and freedom of association between the sexes which makes this possible. Although there is still a large element of romanticism in our official attitudes toward marriage, it is also true that many people take a realistic view of the decision to marry.[33] The legal rules about annulment for fraud may not have a very wide influence on people's attitudes, but they may have some educational value, and certainly do have a healthier influence than would a rule that annulment could be granted whenever one's rosy expectations about the character of one's spouse turned out to be illusory.

The trend of the law since the Reynolds case has been to add to the kinds of fraud which entitle one to annulment. In part this undoubtedly reflects the change of American opinion concerning the indissolubility of marriage, and the recognition that it may be futile to deny the annulment where the marriage has obviously no prospect of success or

---

27. Cf. Oscar Wilde, The Picture of Dorian Gray, Ch. 1: "The one charm of marriage is that it makes a life of deception absolutely necessary for both parties."

28. See Benjamin Franklin, Poor Richard, 1738: "Keep thy eyes wide open before marriage, and half shut afterwards." In Massachusetts apparently annulment is refused no matter how the plaintiff tries to find out the facts, if the misrepresentation is not as to essentials. Arno v. Arno, 265 Mass. 282, 163 N.E. 861 (1928).

29. See section 1.1, Practitioner's Edition.

30. Denis De Rougemont, Love in the Western World, 287–288 (Anchor Book ed. 1957); Beigel, Romantic Love, reprinted in Sussman, Sourcebook in Marriage and the Family, 86 (2d ed. 1962).

31. Groves and Groves, The Contemporary American Family, 321–324 (1947). Some cases recognize limits to the kinds of premarital investigations which people can properly be expected to make. See e.g. Winner v. Winner, 171 Wis. 413, 177 N.W. 680 (1920), and Jackson v. Ruby, 120 Me. 391, 115 A. 90 (1921), 6 Minn.L.Rev. 416 (1922).

32. Van Den Haag, Love or Marriage, reprinted in Coser, The Family, 192 (1964).

33. Statistically it appears that marriages tend to occur between people who resemble each other in age, social class, religious affiliation, national and racial background, and who live near each other. See Kephart, The Family, Society, and the Individual, 267–292 (1961).

even of continued de facto existence.[34] In part the trend also reflects the influence of the New York cases. In that state, due to the former difficulty of obtaining a divorce, annulment was relied upon to end unsuccessful marriages far more than in other states having more liberal divorce laws. Fraud being the only ground for annulment capable of much expansion, in New York the annulment for fraud has come to be a partial substitute for divorce.[35] New York cases are often relied upon as precedents in other states for the very reason that they are so numerous, and thus the New York influence has had its effect in other parts of the country. Massachusetts, on the other hand, has, with some wavering,[36] held to a much stricter rule on annulments for fraud.[37] Its decisions have sometimes been persuasive in other states, at least to the extent that the doctrine of essentials continues to be insisted upon.

Although nearly all courts still purport to adhere to the doctrine of essentials, the doctrine itself seems to be undergoing a change of content. Cases defining the doctrine in general terms have always been rare, but it was originally limited to those misrepresentations related to the sexual obligations of marriage, that is, the ability or willingness to have sexual relations and the ability to bear children.[38] It is perhaps odd that Victorian society should have adopted a rule of law which suggests that sex is the only really essential feature of marriage. More recently some states have expanded the doctrine of essentials to include misrepresentations relating to matters which might prevent the fulfillment of an essential purpose of marriage or result in the practical destruction of the relationship.[39] This goes beyond the sexual aspect of marriage and evinces the courts' concern for the effect of the fraud on the continuing viability of the marriage rather than for the circumstances in which the marriage was originally contracted. This version of the doctrine of essentials makes it possible to use annulment for fraud to accomplish the same purpose as does the marriage break-

34. E.g., Craun v. Craun, 112 U.S.App.D.C. 145, 300 F.2d 737 (1962) and Douglass v. Douglass, 148 Cal.App.2d 867, 307 P.2d 674 (1957). Two cases rejecting this view and adhering to a strict limitation on annulment for fraud are Husband v. Wife, 257 A.2d 765 (Del.Super.1969) and Fortin v. Fortin, 106 N.H. 208, 208 A.2d 447 (1965).

35. The process is described and statistics given in Note, Annulments for Fraud—New York's Answer to Reno?, 48 Colum.L.Rev. 900 (1948). The leading cases expanding the grounds for annulment are Di Lorenzo v. Di Lorenzo, 174 N.Y. 467, 67 N.E. 63 (1903), Shonfeld v. Shonfeld, 260 N.Y. 477, 184 N.E. 60 (1933), 1 U.Chi.L.Rev. 128 (1933), 46 Harv.L.Rev. 1034 (1933), and Kober v. Kober, 16 N.Y.2d 191, 264 N.Y.S.2d 364, 211 N.E.2d 817 (1965). See also Gershenson, Fraud in the New York Law of Annulment, 9 Bklyn.L.Rev. 51 (1939).

36. Smith v. Smith, 171 Mass. 404, 50 N.E. 933 (1898) (annulment for concealment of syphilis); Anders v. Anders, 224 Mass. 438, 113 N.E. 203 (1916) (granted annulment where the wife misrepresented her purpose in marrying).

37. Crehore v. Crehore, 97 Mass. 330 (1867) (no annulment for misrepresentation of paternity); Vondal v. Vondal, 175 Mass. 383, 56 N.E. 586 (1900) (no annulment for concealment of venereal disease); Safford v. Safford, 224 Mass. 392, 113 N.E. 181 (1916) (no annulment for misrepresentation of paternity); Chipman v. Johnston, 237 Mass. 502, 130 N.E. 65 (1921), 19 Mich.L.Rev. 881 (1921) (no annulment for misrepresentation of identity); Richardson v. Richardson, 246 Mass. 353, 140 N.E. 73 (1923) (no annulment for concealment of epilepsy); Arno v. Arno, 265 Mass. 282, 163 N.E. 861 (1928), 42 Harv.L. Rev. 1081 (1929) (no annulment for misrepresentation of

paternity). Damaskinos v. Damaskinos, 325 Mass. 217, 89 N.E.2d 766 (1950) relied upon New York law, since New York was the place of marriage, to annul a marriage where the husband married solely to avoid deportation. See also Levy v. Levy, 309 Mass. 230, 34 N.E.2d 650 (1941), in which the court purports to apply New York law.

38. Kingsley, Fraud as a Ground for Annulment of a Marriage, 18 So.Cal.L.Rev. 213, 214 (1945). Some language in Reynolds v. Reynolds, 85 Mass. (3 Allen) 605 (1862) supports the text statement, though it cannot be considered an adequate general definition of "essentials". See also Aufort v. Aufort, 9 Cal.App.2d 310, 49 P.2d 620 (1935); Fattibene v. Fattibene, 183 Conn. 433, 441 A.2d 3 (1981); Lyon v. Lyon, 230 Ill. 366, 82 N.E. 850 (1907); Costello v. Porzelt, 116 N.J.Super. 380, 282 A.2d 432 (1971); Lindquist v. Lindquist, 130 N.J.Eq. 11, 20 A.2d 325 (Err & App.1941); Wells v. Talham, 180 Wis. 654, 194 N.W. 36 (1923), 33 Yale L.J. 209 (1923).

39. The text paraphrases language from Zutavern v. Zutavern, 155 Neb. 395, 52 N.W.2d 254 (1952). See also In re Rabie's Marriage, 40 Cal.App.3d 917, 115 Cal.Rptr. 594 (1974); Handley v. Handley, 179 Cal.App.2d 742, 3 Cal.Rptr. 910 (1960); Schaub v. Schaub, 71 Cal.App.2d 467, 162 P.2d 966 (1945); Lyman v. Lyman, 90 Conn. 399, 97 A. 312 (1916), 16 Colum.L.Rev. 604 (1916); Wolfe v. Wolfe, 62 Ill.App.3d 498, 19 Ill.Dec. 306, 378 N.E.2d 1181 (1978), judgment affirmed 76 Ill.2d 92, 27 Ill.Dec. 735, 389 N.E.2d 1143 (1979); Reynolds v. Reynolds, 171 Minn. 340, 214 N.W. 650 (1927); Jordan v. Jordan, 115 N.H. 545, 345 A.2d 168 (1975); Fortin v. Fortin, 106 N.H. 208, 208 A.2d 447 (1965).

down statute, that is, to end the marriage which is no longer viable, with the important difference that a clearer, more objective showing must be made for annulment. A useful aspect of this doctrine is that since no very comprehensive or precise definition is attempted by the cases, it can be expanded or contracted as individual courts may find equitable.

Finally, there are cases which approach or even adopt a standard of materiality resembling that which is applied to ordinary contracts.[40] Under these cases the only question to be asked is whether the court is convinced that the plaintiff would not have married had it not been for the fraud. The courts adopting this test do not usually discuss the question whether the test of materiality is an objective or a subjective one. But in view of the emphasis in many of the decisions upon the youthful age or inexperience of the plaintiff,[41] one may legitimately draw the inference that the test is subjective, with the qualification that if the misrepresentation is one which no reasonable person would give credence, the courts will likewise be skeptical of assertions that it induced the marriage.[42]

New York is in a special category. In the Shonfeld case [43] the Court of Appeals appeared to make materiality the test. In the later Woronzoff case [44] the court beat an ill concealed retreat and took up a position somewhere between essentials and materiality, saying that only misrepresentations "vital" to the marriage would justify annulment. Later still Kober v. Kober [45] seems to have returned to the materiality test. Naturally this has produced confusion among the lower New York courts.[46] Fortunately the volume of annulments in New York has decreased since the state enacted a modern divorce law in 1967. Due to its large volume of earlier cases, however, New York has had a somewhat greater influence on the law of other states than is warranted by the quality of its courts' reasoning.

In the opinions of many courts a distinction is made, for purposes of establishing a standard of fraud in annulment cases, between the consummated and the unconsummated marriage. If the marriage has not been consummated, it is held that misrepresentations of much less seriousness (so long as they are material) will constitute grounds to annul.[47]

40. State Compensation Fund v. Foughty, 13 Ariz. App. 381, 476 P.2d 902 (1970), 1971 Wash.U.L.Q. 469; Masters v. Masters, 13 Wis.2d 332, 108 N.W.2d 674 (1961), 45 Mar.L.Rev. 447 (1962). This is apparently now the New York position. Kober v. Kober, 16 N.Y.2d 191, 211 N.E.2d 817 (1965).

41. See the text discussion at note 8, infra. Bilowit v. Dolitsky, 124 N.J.Super. 101, 304 A.2d 774 (1973) discusses the point and expressly adopts a subjective test when applying the doctrine of essentials.

42. This may be the explanation for Avnery v. Avnery, 50 A.D.2d 806, 375 N.Y.S.2d 888 (2d Dep't 1975), appeal dismissed 38 N.Y.2d 997, 384 N.Y.S.2d 439, 384 N.E.2d 915 (1976), which denied annulment where the plaintiff-wife's claim was that the husband had married her for money and not for love, the court stating broadly, however, that fraud must be such as to deceive the ordinary prudent person to be a ground for annulment.

43. Shonfeld v. Shonfeld, 260 N.Y. 477, 184 N.E. 60 (1933), 1 U.Chi.L.Rev. 128 (1933), 46 Harv.L.Rev. 1034 (1933).

44. Woronzoff-Daschkoff v. Woronzoff-Daschkoff, 303 N.Y. 506, 104 N.E.2d 877 (1952).

45. 16 N.Y.2d 191, 264 N.Y.S.2d 364, 211 N.E.2d 817 (1965), 32 Bklyn.L.Rev. 419 (1966), 11 Vill.L.Rev. 632 (1966), 12 Wayne L.Rev. 661 (1966).

46. Many examples could be given, but the following are representative: Johnson v. Johnson, 10 Misc.2d 561,

169 N.Y.S.2d 97 (1957) (annulment denied where the representations related to the home and level of support which the husband would furnish); Di Pillo v. Di Pillo, 17 Misc.2d 673, 184 N.Y.S.2d 892 (1959) (similar misrepresentations, annulment denied); Tuchsher v. Tuchsher, 16 Misc.2d 1, 184 N.Y.S.2d 131 (1959) (annulment granted where the husband misrepresented his earnings and the existence of a paid-up life insurance policy); Madden v. Madden, 204 Misc. 170, 125 N.Y.S.2d 384 (1953) (annulment granted where the husband secretly put a chattel mortgage on the wedding presents). A case which epitomizes the text statement, though decided just before Woronzoff, is Croce v. Croce, 199 Misc. 635, 100 N.Y.S.2d 97 (1950).

47. Husband v. Wife, 257 A.2d 765 (Del.Super.1969); Christlieb v. Christlieb, 71 Ind.App. 682, 125 N.E. 486 (1919); Smith v. Smith, 171 Mass. 404, 50 N.E. 933 (1898); Houlahan v. Horzepa, 46 N.J.Super. 583, 135 A.2d 232 (1957) (where the marriage is unconsummated, the only test is one of materiality); Dooley v. Dooley, 93 N.J.Eq. 22, 115 A. 268 (1921) (where marriage is unconsummated, the standard is the same as for ordinary contracts); Bilowit v. Dolitsky, 124 N.J.Super. 101, 304 A.2d 774 (1973); Lopez v. Lopez, 102 N.J.Super. 253, 245 A.2d 771 (1968); Rutstein v. Rutstein, 221 App.Div. 70, 222 N.Y.S. 688 (1st Dep't 1927), 27 Colum.L.Rev. 1001 (1927); Moore v. Moore, 94 Misc. 370, 157 N.Y.S. 819 (1916), 2 Corn.L.Q. 39 (1916).

New Jersey, which has emphasized this distinction more than most other states, has gone so far as to say in one case that an unconsummated marriage is little more than an engagement.[48]

On the other hand, where the marriage has been consummated, that fact is relied upon by many courts, including those of New Jersey, to justify application of a strict version of the doctrine of essentials.[49] The cases are not very enlightening on the reasons for this distinction. In some instances, of course, consummation may be evidence that the alleged fraud was not really material. So, for example, if the ground for annulment is the defendant's promise to have a religious ceremony, made with intent not to perform it, and it appears that the plaintiff consummated the marriage, an inference may fairly be drawn that the plaintiff did not really consider the religious ceremony important.[50] Or, consummation with knowledge of the facts may amount to a ratification or confirmation of the marriage.[51] In other situations it is difficult to see why consummation should matter so much. Bishop, and other authorities after him, say that although an unconsummated marriage is valid, it is only after consummation that unborn children and the community

acquire "specially grave and weighty interests" in the marriage.[52] A distinction based upon the existence of children, born or unborn, is understandable, since the courts wish to protect them, and might be more reluctant to annul a marriage where there were children than a childless marriage. But today it can be established with very high reliability whether there are unborn children,[53] and the occurrence of consummation is of no evidentiary importance on this point, though it may once have been. It therefore appears that this emphasis on consummation is either a relic of ancient notions about the importance of virginity, or, more likely, a survival of canon law doctrines to the effect that marriage became indissoluble only after consummation.[54] In either event it has no relevance to modern conditions, and the more recent cases tend to recognize this by placing little or no significance on the question whether consummation has occurred.[55]

Since there undoubtedly are differences among the various states as to what constitutes fraud for annulment, or as to the effect of consummation or perhaps other factors, it may be of some significance to know what law applies if more than one state is involved. Most cases hold that the law of the place of

48. Akrep v. Akrep, 1 N.J. 268, 63 A.2d 253 (1949). As a general proposition this dictum is much too broad. See also Lopez v. Lopez, 102 N.J.Super. 253, 245 A.2d 771 (1968).

49. Husband v. Wife, 257 A.2d 765 (Del.Super.1969); Chipman v. Johnston, 237 Mass. 502, 130 N.E. 65 (1921), 19 Mich.L.Rev. 881 (1921); Reynolds v. Reynolds, 3 Allen (85 Mass.) 605 (1862), 13 Harv.L.Rev. 110 (1899); Robertson v. Roth, 163 Minn. 501, 204 N.W. 329 (1925); Brown v. Brown, 34 N.J.Super. 261, 112 A.2d 1 (1954); Rhoades v. Rhoades, 10 N.J.Super. 432, 77 A.2d 273 (1950); Lindquist v. Lindquist, 130 N.J.Eq. 11, 20 A.2d 325 (Err. & App.1941); Caruso v. Caruso, 104 N.J.Eq. 588, 146 A. 649 (1929), 28 Mich.L.Rev. 85 (1929). The Caruso case adopts the interesting notion that a marriage may be consummated before it is contracted.

50. Watkins v. Watkins, 197 App.Div. 489, 189 N.Y.S. 860 (1st Dep't 1921) (dictum); Cart v. Cart, 176 Misc. 457, 28 N.Y.S.2d 58 (1941); Rozsa v. Rozsa, 117 Misc. 728, 191 N.Y.S. 868 (1922); Akrep v. Akrep, 1 N.J. 268, 63 A.2d 253 (1949) was a case of this kind, which would explain the court's heavy reliance upon consummation, but the language of the opinion is very broad and has been applied by other New Jersey cases to quite different facts.

51. The defense of ratification is set up by many of the statutes cited supra, note 2. See also Curtis v. Curtis,

82 Cal.App.2d 965, 187 P.2d 921 (1947); Saunders v. Saunders, 49 Del. 515, 120 A.2d 160 (1956). Many other cases are cited in Kingsley, Fraud as a Ground for Annulment of a Marriage, 18 So.Cal.L.Rev. 213, 235, 236 (1945).

52. 1 Bishop, Marriage, Divorce and Separation, 194 (1891), and, e.g. Chipman v. Johnston, 237 Mass. 502, 130 N.E. 65 (1921), 19 Mich.L.Rev. 881 (1921).

53. 2 Gray, Attorneys' Textbook of Medicine, § 58.09 (3d ed. 1964), describing the Ascheim-Zondek method of testing for pregnancy.

54. See, e.g. Bouscaren and Ellis, Canon Law, 449–450 (3rd rev. ed. 1957); Jackson, Formation and Annulment of Marriage, 208 (1951); James, Marriage and Society, 114 (1952); 3 Westermarck, The History of Human Marriage, 328 (5th ed. 1922).

55. E.g., Handley v. Handley, 179 Cal.App.2d 742, 3 Cal.Rptr. 910 (1962); Douglass v. Douglass, 148 Cal.App. 2d 867, 307 P.2d 674 (1957); Masters v. Masters, 13 Wis. 2d 332, 108 N.W.2d 674 (1961), 45 Mar.L.Rev. 447 (1962). But consummation, or the lack of it, had some influence in Craun v. Craun, 112 U.S.App.D.C. 145, 300 F.2d 737 (1962), applying Maryland law.

contracting the marriage governs annulments for fraud.[56] Presumably the analysis is that the law of the place where consent was given logically should control the validity of that consent. Some courts have held that the law of the forum governs, however.[57] It would seem that if the policy underlying the doctrine of essentials is, as suggested above,[58] to influence the parties' pre-marital behavior, then the law of their domicile before marriage is relevant. If, on the other hand, the purpose is to preserve the indissolubility of marriage, then the law of the domicile after marriage (which would usually be the forum) is relevant. It is difficult to see any overwhelming reasons for the choice of one law rather than another in this situation, however.

One other question of general significance has to do with the form which the alleged fraud assumes. It is clear that if there is an affirmative misrepresentation, this is fraud in its conventional form, and if it relates to a matter which the jurisdiction considers essential, the annulment should be granted.[59] But many of the alleged frauds amount to no more than non-disclosure. The question then is, is there a legal obligation on the part of engaged persons to reveal information which, if it were misrepresented, would justify granting an annulment? To what extent does the law require pre-marital baring of the soul? The discussions of this question in the cases are remarkably rare and uninformative. One approach is to hold that the more fundamental kinds of information must be disclosed, on the theory that the contracting of marriage of itself implies that a person has certain capabilities and intentions. This would require the affirmative disclosure of pregnancy, venereal disease, sterility and possibly a few other kinds of information.[60] Probably the majority of cases give the matter no consideration at all, either granting or denying the annulment on the basis of the particular conditions involved, whether there was affirmative misrepresentation, concealment or mere nondisclosure.[61] It does seem that if the defendant's circumstances are such that a misrepresenta-

---

56. Riedl v. Riedl, 153 A.2d 639 (D.C.Mun.App.1959); Osborne v. Osborne, 134 A.2d 438 (D.C.Mun.App.1957); Levy v. Levy, 309 Mass. 230, 34 N.E.2d 650 (1941); Jewett v. Jewett, 196 Pa.Super. 305, 175 A.2d 141 (1961); Wells v. Talham, 180 Wis. 654, 194 N.W. 36 (1923), 33 Yale L.J. 209 (1923).

57. Du Pont v. Du Pont, 47 Del. (8 Terry) 231, 90 A.2d 468 (1952), cert. denied 344 U.S. 836, 73 S.Ct. 46, 97 L.Ed. 651 (1952); Lyon v. Lyon, 230 Ill. 366, 82 N.E. 850 (1907) (semble). In Chipman v. Johnston, 237 Mass. 502, 130 N.E. 65 (1921) the court seems to have relied upon Massachusetts law although the marriage occurred in Washington.

58. See the text at note 28, supra.

59. See, e.g. Reynolds v. Reynolds, 85 Mass. (3 Allen) 605 (1862), in which the complaint alleged affirmative misrepresentation and the allegation was admitted by demurrer.

60. See Kingsley, Fraud as a Ground for Annulment of a Marriage, 18 So.Cal.L.Rev. 213, 244 (1945), and Aufort v. Aufort, 9 Cal.App.2d 310, 49 P.2d 620 (1935), 9 So.Cal.L.Rev. 412 (1936) (non-disclosure of sterility is grounds for annulment); Houlahan v. Horzepa, 46 N.J. Super. 583, 135 A.2d 232 (1957) (non-disclosure of prior mental illness is not deceit); Lembo v. Lembo, 193 Misc. 1055, 86 N.Y.S.2d 206 (1949) (secret intent not to have children is sufficient); Schulman v. Schulman, 180 Misc. 904, 46 N.Y.S.2d 158 (1943) (wife's silence before marriage justified the inference she intended to have children).

61. Craun v. Craun, 112 U.S.App.D.C. 145, 300 F.2d 737 (1962); Millar v. Millar, 175 Cal. 797, 167 P. 394 (1917) (secret intent not to consummate); Handley v. Handley, 179 Cal.App.2d 742, 3 Cal.Rptr. 910 (1960) (secret intent not to live with the husband); Douglass v. Douglass, 148 Cal.App.2d 867, 307 P.2d 674, (1957) (treats fraudulent representation and concealment on equal terms); Bernstein v. Bernstein, 25 Conn.Supp. 239, 201 A.2d 660 (1964) (secret intent not to consummate); Jones v. Jones, 119 Fla. 824, 161 So. 836 (1935) (concealment of prior marriage); Damaskinos v. Damaskinos, 326 Mass. 217, 89 N.E.2d 766 (1950) (marriage to avoid deportation); Smith v. Smith, 171 Mass. 404, 50 N.E. 933 (1898) (nondisclosure of syphillis); Sampson v. Sampson, 332 Mich. 214, 50 N.W.2d 764 (1952) (husband married wife for her money; some evidence of non-disclosure of homosexuality by the husband); Stegienko v. Stegienko, 295 Mich. 530, 295 N.W. 252 (1940) (secret intent not to have children); Brillis v. Brillis, 4 N.Y.2d 125, 173 N.Y.S.2d 3, 149 N.E.2d 510 (1958) (husband married solely to obtain entry into the United States); Svenson v. Svenson, 178 N.Y. 54, 70 N.E. 120 (1904) (non-disclosure of venereal disease); Schaeffer v. Schaeffer, 20 Misc.2d 662, 192 N.Y.S.2d 275 (1959) (non-disclosure of prior mental illness); Courreges v. Courreges, 229 N.Y.S.2d 73 (1961) (non-disclosure of prior mental illness); Santos v. Santos, 80 R.I. 5, 90 A.2d 771 (1952) (secret intent not to consummate, some evidence of undisclosed homosexuality); C. v. C., 158 Wis. 301, 148 N.W. 865 (1914) (non-disclosure of venereal disease).

The following cases denying annulment seem to place some vague emphasis on the fact that only non-disclosure, rather than misrepresentation, was proved: Wesley v. Wesley, 181 Ky. 135, 204 S.W. 165 (1918) (divorce for fraud denied); Robertson v. Roth, 163 Minn. 501, 204

tion of them would relate to essentials, or if the state so holds, to material matters, then nondisclosure should be on the same footing as a misrepresentation. If marriage is to rest upon a reasonably firm basis of understanding and mutual trust, there should be a duty to disclose this sort of facts.[62] It must be conceded that articulate case authority for any such duty is lacking, however.

Defenses

It is clearly a defense in fraud cases that the plaintiff continued marital cohabitation with knowledge of the true circumstances. If this is proved, the annulment will not be granted.[63] Even if the plaintiff does not know all the facts, a continued cohabitation for a substantial time ought to have the same effect. When the spouses live together for a long period, it is a fair assumption that they come to take each other as they are. The significance of any misrepresentations diminishes with the passage of time to the point

where eventually it can no longer be said to be material.[64] Perhaps the same result should be reached even if the parties are not living together, where the plaintiff waits a long time to sue.[65]

Various other defenses may also occasionally be recognized, such as collusion,[66] or proof that the misrepresentation was made in good faith, as a result of a mistake about the facts.[67] One defense which is often raised in those cases involving misrepresentations about pregnancy is that of prior knowledge,[68] or that the plaintiff, by engaging in pre-marital sexual relations with the defendant is in pari delicto.[69] The argument seems to be that the plaintiff, knowing the defendant was unchaste, should also have known that she was capable of deceiving him,[70] and that by engaging in pre-marital sex the plaintiff disqualified himself for help from the courts.[71] Most courts reject such arguments and hold that the plaintiff who is deceived as to the paternity of a child conceived before marriage may

N.W. 329 (1925); Lindquist v. Lindquist, 130 N.J.Eq. 11, 20 A.2d 325 (Err. & App.1941); Brown v. Brown, 34 N.J. Super. 261, 112 A.2d 1 (1954); Yucabezky v. Yucabezky, 111 N.Y.S.2d 441 (1952).

62. Vernon, Annulment of Marriages in New Mexico: Part II–Proposed Statute, 2 Nat.Res.J. 270, 299 (1962).

A brief and unsatisfactory opinion in Potter v. Potter, 27 A.D.2d 634, 275 N.Y.S.2d 499 (4th Dep't 1966) asserts that there is an affirmative duty to disclose.

63. Many of the statutes cited supra, note 2, require that annulment be denied where there is cohabitation by the plaintiff after learning the facts. See also the cases cited supra, note 51, and Koehler v. Koehler, 137 Ark. 302, 209 S.W. 283 (1919); Goree v. Goree, 187 Neb. 774, 194 N.W.2d 212 (1972); Jones v. Jones, 189 Misc. 145, 69 N.Y.S.2d 223 (1947); McLarty v. McLarty, 433 S.W.2d 722 (Tex.Civ.App.1968), 21 Baylor L.Rev. 391 (1969). But a mere suspicion or belief founded upon inconclusive circumstances is not sufficient to constitute ratification. In re Rabie's Marriage, 40 Cal.App.3d 917, 115 Cal.Rptr. 594 (1974). Some cases characterize this defense as "condonation", but the factual basis seems to be the same in any event. See Avnery v. Avnery, 50 A.D.2d 806, 375 N.Y.S. 2d 888 (2d Dep't 1975), appeal dismissed 38 N.Y.2d 997, 384 N.Y.S.2d 439, 348 N.E.2d 915 (1976).

64. Maslow v. Maslow, 117 Cal.App.2d 237, 255 P.2d 65 (1953); Freitag v. Freitag, 40 Misc.2d 163, 242 N.Y.S.2d 643 (1963); Primmer v. Primmer, 37 Misc.2d 589, 234 N.Y.S.2d 795 (1962); Roger v. Roger, 24 Misc.2d 566, 203 N.Y.S.2d 576 (1960); Jennings v. Jennings, 186 Misc. 1021, 63 N.Y.S.2d 294 (1946). See also the curious case of Travis v. Travis, 183 Pa.Super. 273, 130 A.2d 724 (1957), in which the husband waited nineteen years to sue, alleging that his wife had failed to disclose the birth

of an illegitimate child before their marriage. Contra: Vendetto v. Vendetto, 115 Conn. 303, 161 A. 392 (1932).

65. Cf. Mace v. Mace, 67 R.I. 301, 23 A.2d 185 (1941) (husband waived his right by waiting six and one-half years).

66. Hannibal v. Hannibal, 23 Conn.Supp. 201, 179 A.2d 838 (1962); Schumer v. Schumer, 205 Misc. 235, 128 N.Y.S.2d 119 (1954).

67. Cole v. Cole, 268 App.Div. 564, 52 N.Y.S.2d 100 (3d Dep't 1944). But see Hardesty v. Hardesty, 193 Cal. 330, 223 P. 951 (1924), in which an annulment was granted for a premarital pregnancy by someone other than the husband even though the wife had not known she was pregnant. The court seemed to find that the wife had concealed the pregnancy even though she had been ignorant of it, an odd use of the term "conceal."

68. Cases are collected in Annot., 15 A.L.R.2d 706, 715 (1951). See also Clickner v. Clickner, 95 N.J.Eq. 479, 123 A. 373 (1924); Anderson v. Anderson, 37 Ohio Op.2d 108, 8 Ohio Misc. 97, 219 N.E.2d 317 (1966).

69. Westfall v. Westfall, 100 Or. 224, 197 P. 271 (1921).

70. Safford v. Safford, 224 Mass. 392, 113 N.E. 181 (1916); Crehore v. Crehore, 97 Mass. 330 (1867); Nice v. Nice, 71 D. & C. 167 (Pa.County Ct.1948).

71. The full flavor of judicial self-righteousness comes through in Westfall v. Westfall, 100 Or. 224, 230, 197 P. 271, 275 (1921): "A licentious man cannot call upon a court of equity as a guarantor of the paternity of a child conceived in the lewdness of antenuptial intercourse. * * * Marriage shall not be made a mockery, to shield the licentious from acts penalized by law, and then annulled when it has served his purpose." See also Arno v.

have his annulment.[72] An interesting analogous question might arise where misrepresentations as to character or past life are considered sufficient to justify annulment. Would a plaintiff suing on this ground be barred if it appeared that his past life also had been discreditable, particularly if the plaintiff is the husband? Is there still a double standard? One New York case says there is,[73] but such an attitude seems a relic of Victorian times. Any application of the defense of unclean hands or in pari delicto in these circumstances would resemble the now generally discredited doctrine of recrimination. Therefore such a defense ought not to be recognized in annulment cases either.

The Kinds of Fraud Which Warrant Annulment

The foregoing discussion of general principles is not very meaningful unless it is considered with reference to specific states of fact. Conversely, an investigation limited to the kinds of facts on which annulments for fraud have been granted may be misleading without a constant awareness of policy factors, the history of this branch of annulment, and the general arguments which may be made pro and con a particular result. A particular

decision may be the resultant of several different influences, so that it would be an oversimplification to attribute it merely to the type of fraud proved. In addition, there are infinite variations and gradations of fraud, so that any attempt at classification is at best an approximation.

This being understood, there follows a brief description of the various kinds of fraud with which the annulment cases have been concerned.

1. Misrepresentations as to Pregnancy

The Reynolds case [74] and others make it clear that a misrepresentation or concealment or non-disclosure of the wife's pregnancy by someone other than the husband is the sort of fraud which warrants annulling the marriage.[75] There is less agreement where the misrepresentation relates to paternity, the wife inducing the marriage by telling the husband she is pregnant by him when in fact she is pregnant by another man. But most cases of this kind grant the annulment.[76]

When the wife tells the husband she is pregnant by him, thereby causing him to marry her, when in fact she is not pregnant at all, the majority of the cases deny the annulment.[77]

Arno, 265 Mass. 282, 163 N.E. 861 (1928), 42 Harv.L.Rev. 1081 (1929), and Rhoades v. Rhoades, 10 N.J.Super. 432, 77 A.2d 273 (1950). An assumption of risk argument was relied on to get the same result in Mason v. Mason, 164 Ark. 59, 261 S.W. 40 (1924).

72. E.g., Lyman v. Lyman, 90 Conn. 399, 97 A. 312 (1916); Symonds v. Symonds, 385 Mass. 540, 432 N.E.2d 700 (1982); Gard v. Gard, 204 Mich. 255, 169 N.W. 908 (1918); Zutavern v. Zutavern, 155 Neb. 395, 52 N.W.2d 254 (1952); Masters v. Masters, 13 Wis.2d 332, 108 N.W.2d 674 (1961), 45 Marq.L.Rev. 447 (1962); Winner v. Winner, 171 Wis. 413, 177 N.W. 680 (1920).

73. Burdes v. Burdes, 195 Misc. 265, 90 N.Y.S.2d 97 (Dom.Rel.Ct.1949).

74. Reynolds v. Reynolds, 85 Mass. (3 Allen) 605 (1862), 13 Harv.L.Rev. 110, 118 (1899). The case is discussed in detail, supra at note 22.

75. A.C. v. B.C., 12 Misc.2d 1, 176 N.Y.S.2d 794 (1958), and other cases cited in Kingsley, Fraud as a Ground for Annulment of a Marriage, 18 So.Cal.L.Rev. 213, 215 (1945). A case which may be contra is Clickner v. Clickner, 95 N.J.Eq. 479, 123 A. 373 (1924). Annulment was granted in Hardesty v. Hardesty, 193 Cal. 330, 223 P. 951 (1924) even though the wife apparently did not know she was pregnant.

76. Granting the annulment: Lyman v. Lyman, 90 Conn. 399, 97 A. 312 (1916), 16 Colum.L.Rev. 604 (1916); Arndt v. Arndt, 336 Ill.App. 65, 82 N.E.2d 908 (1948); Jackson v. Ruby, 120 Me. 391, 115 A. 90 (1921), 20 Mich. L.Rev. 454 (1922), 6 Minn.L.Rev. 416 (1922); Gard v. Gard, 204 Mich. 255, 169 N.W. 908 (1918); Zutavern v. Zutavern, 155 Neb. 395, 52 N.W.2d 254 (1952); Goree v. Goree, 187 Neb. 774, 194 N.W.2d 212 (1972) (dictum); B. v. S., 99 N.J.Super. 429, 240 A.2d 189 (1968); Winner v. Winner, 171 Wis. 413, 177 N.W. 680 (1920).

Denying the annulment: Shatford v. Shatford, 214 Ark. 612, 217 S.W.2d 917 (1949); Arno v. Arno, 265 Mass. 282, 163 N.E. 861 (1928), 42 Harv.L.Rev. 1081 (1929); Safford v. Safford, 224 Mass. 392, 113 N.E. 181 (1916).

77. Denying the annulment: Mason v. Mason, 164 Ark. 59, 261 S.W. 40 (1924); Husband v. Wife, 262 A.2d 656 (Del.Super.1970); Hill v. Hill, 79 Ill.App.3d 809, 35 Ill.Dec. 98, 398 N.E.2d 1048 (1979); Levy v. Levy, 309 Mass. 230, 34 N.E.2d 650 (1941); Diamond v. Diamond, 101 N.H. 338, 143 A.2d 109 (1958); Rhoades v. Rhoades, 10 N.J.Super. 432, 77 A.2d 273 (1950); Cole v. Cole, 268 App.Div. 564, 52 N.Y.S.2d 100 (3d Dep't 1944); Donovan v. Donovan, 147 Misc. 134, 263 N.Y.S. 336 (1933), appeal dismissed 241 App.Div. 906, 272 N.Y.S. 157 (4th Dep't

2. *Misrepresentations Concerning Physical or Mental Health*

Where one of the spouses misrepresents or conceals the fact that he is afflicted with a venereal disease, the annulment is usually granted.[78] The concealment of impotence or sterility is also a ground for annulment.[79] Concealment of a prior history of epilepsy [80] or of tuberculosis [81] has been held not to justify annulment.

The concealment of prior mental illness has generally been held not to be grounds for annulment.[82] Whether a marriage would be annulled for concealment of homosexuality by one of the spouses is not clear from the cases,[83] but this would seem to relate to an essential matter and therefore to justify annulment. Non-disclosure of drug addiction has been held to be a basis for annulment,[84] but misrepresentations as to a history of heavy drinking has been held not to be action-

able fraud.[85] If the drinking is sufficiently heavy to amount to alcoholism, the result might be different, however.

Since some of the cases involving non-disclosure of matters of health and non-disclosure of pregnancy place considerable emphasis on the obligation of the petitioner for annulment to make an investigation before the marriage, the question arises whether a physician treating the prospective spouse could reveal that person's medical or psychological history to his fiancee without violating medical ethics or risking liability in tort. The very few cases which have been found on this point suggest that there would be a privilege available to the physician in such circumstances, according to which he could furnish relevant information to a spouse-to-be acquired as a result of the physician-patient relationship.[86] At present the qualifications and limits of any privilege to disclose such

---

1934); Tyminski v. Tyminski, 8 Ohio Misc. 202, 221 N.E. 2d 486 (1966).

Granting the annulment: Parks v. Parks, 418 S.W.2d 726 (Ky.1967), 9 Ariz.L.Rev. 481 (1968), 57 Ky.L.J. 272 (1968), 21 Vand.L.Rev. 567 (1968); Di Lorenzo v. Di Lorenzo, 174 N.Y. 467, 67 N.E. 63 (1903); Masters v. Masters, 13 Wis.2d 332, 108 N.W.2d 674 (1961), 45 Marq.L. Rev. 447 (1962).

The cases are collected and discussed in Note, Fraudulent Representation of Pregnancy—Marriage and Annulment, 13 S.D.L.Rev. 146 (1968).

78. Granting the annulment: Stone v. Stone, 78 U.S. App.D.C. 5, 136 F.2d 761 (1943); Smith v. Smith, 171 Mass. 404, 50 N.E. 933 (1898); Watson v. Watson, 143 S.W.2d 349 (Mo.App.1940), 26 Wash.U.L.Q. 274 (1941); Svenson v. Svenson, 178 N.Y. 54, 70 N.E. 120 (1904); C. v. C., 158 Wis. 301, 148 N.W. 865 (1914).

Denying the annulment: Vondal v. Vondal, 175 Mass. 383, 56 N.E. 586 (1900); Mace v. Mace, 67 R.I. 301, 23 A.2d 185 (1941) (may have turned on waiver).

79. Mutter v. Mutter, 123 Ky. 754, 97 S.W. 393 (1906) (divorce for concealment of impotence). Aufort v. Aufort, 9 Cal.App.2d 310, 49 P.2d 620 (1935), 9 So.Cal.L.Rev. 412 (1936) (annulment for concealment of sterility); Chavias v. Chavias, 194 App.Div. 904, 184 N.Y.S. 761 (2d Dep't 1920), 21 Colum.L.Rev. 99 (1921) refused annulment where the defendant was not aware he was sterile.

80. Lyon v. Lyon, 230 Ill. 366, 82 N.E. 850 (1907); Richardson v. Richardson, 246 Mass. 353, 140 N.E. 73 (1923). Vendetto v. Vendetto, 115 Conn. 303, 161 A. 392 (1932) granted a divorce for concealment of epilepsy, but the case probably turned on the statute making it a crime for an epileptic to marry.

81. Ozark v. Ozark, 191 Misc. 172, 75 N.Y.S.2d 430 (1947).

82. Denying annulment: Lyon v. Lyon, 230 Ill. 366, 82 N.E. 850 (1907) (dictum); Robertson v. Roth, 163 Minn. 501, 204 N.W. 329 (1925); Houlahan v. Horzepa, 46 N.J. Super. 583, 135 A.2d 232 (1957). Concealment of mental illness in the wife's family was held not to warrant annulment in Natoli v. Natoli, 72 N.Y.S.2d 708 (1947).

Granting the annulment: Courreges v. Courreges, 229 N.Y.S.2d 73 (1961); Schaeffer v. Schaeffer, 20 Misc.2d 662, 192 N.Y.S.2d 275 (1959); Potter v. Potter, 27 A.D.2d 634, 275 N.Y.S.2d 499 (4th Dep't. 1966) (concealment of voyeurism).

83. See Freitag v. Freitag, 40 Misc.2d 163, 242 N.Y.S.2d 643 (1963) (turning on a failure of proof), and Santos v. Santos, 80 R.I. 5, 90 A.2d 771 (1952), denying annulment where the wife was a lesbian. Sampson v. Sampson, 332 Mich. 214, 50 N.W.2d 764 (1952) raises but does not decide the question of the effect of homosexuality.

84. Costello v. Porzelt, 116 N.J.Super. 380, 282 A.2d 432 (1971), 30 Mo.L.Rev. 287 (1973); Courreges v. Courreges, 229 N.Y.S.2d 73 (1961). Contra, Husband v. Wife, 257 A.2d 765 (Del.Super.1969), where the wife had concealed a misdemeanor conviction and "periodic disabling use of drugs", the court saying this did not involve essentials of the marriage.

85. Jones v. Jones, 189 Misc. 145, 69 N.Y.S.2d 223 (1947).

86. See Curry v. Corn, 52 Misc.2d 1035, 277 N.Y.S.2d 470 (1966); Berry v. Moench, 8 Utah 2d 191, 331 P.2d 814 (1958); Annot., Physician's Tort Liability, Apart From Defamation, For Unauthorized Disclosure of Confidential Information About Patient, 20 A.L.R.3d 1109, 1120 (1968).

information either to a spouse or a prospective spouse are unclear. For example, it is not clear whether the privilege exists only because the patient expressed no desire to keep the information confidential, or whether the information could be revealed even where the patient explicitly instructed the physician not to reveal it. One would hope that the importance of the relationship between husband and wife would convince the courts that such information should be revealed in any case where it is relevant to that relationship or to its formation, but one cannot be confident that this result will be reached.

3. Misrepresentations Concerning the Intent With Which the Marriage Is Contracted

It is generally accepted that misrepresentation of an existing state of mind or intention constitutes fraud.[87] In the field of marriage the cases have applied this doctrine to several kinds of misrepresentation, the most common being the misrepresentation of intention to consummate the marriage. The analysis is that since sexual intercourse and the procreation of children are fundamental to marriage, misrepresentation of intent with respect to these matters is essential fraud for which

annulment may be granted.[88] Even without affirmative misrepresentation, the concealment or non-disclosure of an intent not to consummate justifies annulment, since the contracting of a marriage, of itself, implies the intent to consummate and if that intent does not exist, there is actionable fraud.[89] In some cases of this type the courts have found that the intent not to consummate was not satisfactorily proved, the difficulties of proof being unusually great here.[90]

Annulments are also granted where the spouse has a secret intent not to have children, although the problems of proof involved in such cases are equally great or greater than where non-consummation is the issue.[91] It does seem, however, that a suit for annulment is not an appropriate way to settle a marital disagreement over the employment of birth control, which is what many of the cases really amount to.[92]

There are a surprising number of cases in which it is alleged in general that the spouse never intended to fulfill any of the duties of marriage. Even if consummation occurs, evidence of this sort of motive is often sufficient to support a decree of annulment.[93] This situation may arise when the marriage is

87. W. Prosser and W. Keeton, Torts 762–765 (5th ed. 1984).

88. Anders v. Anders, 224 Mass. 438, 113 N.E. 203 (1916); Zerk v. Zerk, 257 Wis. 555, 44 N.W.2d 568 (1950). But the annulment will be denied when the defendant makes his intentions clear. Hanson v. Hanson, 287 Mass. 154, 191 N.E. 673 (1934).

89. Millar v. Millar, 175 Cal. 797, 167 P. 394 (1917), 6 Cal.L.Rev. 224 (1918); Rathburn v. Rathburn, 138 Cal. App.2d 568, 292 P.2d 274 (1956); Bernstein v. Bernstein, 25 Conn.Supp. 239, 201 A.2d 660 (1964); Lopez v. Lopez, 102 N.J.Super. 253, 245 A.2d 771 (1968); Santos v. Santos, 80 R.I. 5, 90 A.2d 771 (1952).

90. Mayer v. Mayer, 207 Cal. 685, 279 P. 783 (1929); Sasserno v. Sasserno, 240 Mass. 583, 134 N.E. 239 (1922); Harding v. Harding, 11 Wash.2d 138, 118 P.2d 789 (1941). For a case which discusses in detail the problems of proof and the New York requirement of corroboration in annulment suits, see De Baillet-Latour v. De Baillet-Latour, 301 N.Y. 428, 94 N.E.2d 715 (1950).

91. Zoglio v. Zoglio, 157 A.2d 627 (D.C.Mun.App.1960); Stegienko v. Stegienko, 295 Mich. 530, 295 N.W. 252 (1940); Richardson v. Richardson, 200 Misc. 778, 103 N.Y.S.2d 219 (1951); Lembo v. Lembo, 193 Misc. 1055, 86 N.Y.S.2d 206 (1949); Schulman v. Schulman, 180 Misc. 904, 46 N.Y.S.2d 158 (1943); Coppo v. Coppo, 163 Misc. 249, 297 N.Y.S. 744 (1937). Intercourse with contracep-

tives for a substantial period will bar the annulment on grounds of condonation or acquiescence. Maslow v. Maslow, 117 Cal.App.2d 237, 255 P.2d 65 (1953); Roger v. Roger, 24 Misc.2d 566, 203 N.Y.S.2d 576 (1960).

Some courts require that proof of this sort of fraud must be made by "clear and convincing" evidence. This strict standard of proof is not met by evidence that the defendant insisted upon the use of birth control pills after marriage. Williams v. Witt, 98 N.J.Super. 1, 235 A.2d 902 (1967); Heup v. Heup, 45 Wis.2d 71, 172 N.W.2d 334 (1969).

92. Riedl v. Riedl, 153 A.2d 639 (D.C.Mun.App.1959); Pisciotta v. Buccino, 22 N.J.Super. 114, 91 A.2d 629 (1952); Frost v. Frost, 15 Misc.2d 104, 181 N.Y.S.2d 562 (1958); Bohok v. Bohok, 186 Misc. 991, 63 N.Y.S.2d 560 (1946); Longtin v. Longtin, 22 N.Y.S.2d 827 (1940). This ground for annulment also seems to furnish a temptation to indulge in collusive suits. E.g., Hannibal v. Hannibal, 23 Conn.Supp. 201, 179 A.2d 838 (1962); Primmer v. Primmer, 37 Misc.2d 589, 234 N.Y.S.2d 795 (1962); Lopez v. Lopez, 10 Misc.2d 367, 169 N.Y.S.2d 74 (1957); Schumer v. Schumer, 205 Misc. 235, 128 N.Y.S.2d 119 (1954); Hafner v. Hafner, 66 N.Y.S.2d 442 (1946).

93. Handley v. Handley, 179 Cal.App.2d 742, 3 Cal. Rptr. 910 (1960); Security-First Nat. Bank of Los Angeles v. Schaub, 71 Cal.App.2d 467, 162 P.2d 966 (1945); Osborne v. Osborne, 134 A.2d 438 (D.C.Mun.App.1957);

contracted by one spouse wholly for ulterior purposes, as for example to gain entry into the United States or to avoid being deported, with no intent whatever to enter into married life.[94] If the secret intent relates only to part of the marital duties, to the manner of performing those duties, or to the conduct of a party after marriage, there is more diversity in the cases, but some nevertheless grant the annulment. One of the leading cases is Shonfeld,[95] in which the New York court granted an annulment by reason of the wife's promise that she would loan her husband a sum of money to enable him to buy a business of his own, when it was clear she never had the money and never intended to make the loan. There is some doubt whether this case would be followed even in New York, however.[96] Where more general misrepresentations are made concerning the way in which the husband intends to support the wife, or the kind of home he intends to provide for her, the cases, chiefly from New York, are more reluctant to annul the marriage.[97] In one recent case [98] the husband told the wife before marriage that they would live in an apartment he had rented, but immediately after the ceremony he took her to a three-room apartment where they were to live with three

other couples, all unmarried. The court, relying partly on the fact that the marriage was not consummated, entered a decree of annulment.

In the very rare instance where the plaintiff's claim is that the defendant said before marriage that he loved her when in fact he did not, the few New York cases in existence hold no annulment will be granted,[99] though analytically these cases are similar to those in which the defendant marries for an ulterior purpose.[1] The difference in outcome may turn on the absence of credible evidence where the claim is that affection was misrepresented. Most of these cases produce laughter rather than serious legal treatment.

Still another form of misrepresentation of intent is both more frequent and more likely to be recognized as a ground for annulment. This is the promise by a defendant to participate in a subsequent religious marriage ceremony after a civil one. At least where it is shown that the plaintiff is a person whose belief emphasizes the importance of the religious ceremony, such a promise made without intent to perform it is held to be material and to justify annulling the marriage.[2] There is some tendency in New York to annul when

---

Sampson v. Sampson, 332 Mich. 214, 50 N.W.2d 764 (1952); Fundaro v. Fundaro, 272 App.Div. 825, 70 N.Y.S.2d 510 (2d Dep't 1947); Thurber v. Thurber, 186 Misc. 1022, 63 N.Y.S.2d 401 (1946); Moore v. Moore, 94 Misc. 370, 157 N.Y.S. 819 (1916), 2 Corn.L.Q. 39 (1916). Cf. Hallock v. Hallock, 62 N.Y.S.2d 558 (1946), where the annulment was denied for lack of proof as to intent.

94. In re Rabies Marriage, 40 Cal.App.3d 917, 115 Cal. Rptr. 594 (1974); Babis v. Babis, 45 Del. (6 Terry) 496, 75 A.2d 580 (Del.Super.1950); Damaskinos v. Damaskinos, 326 Mass. 217, 89 N.E.2d 766 (1950); Brillis v. Brillis, 4 N.Y.2d 125, 173 N.Y.S.2d 3, 149 N.E.2d 510 (1958).

95. Shonfeld v. Shonfeld, 260 N.Y. 477, 184 N.E. 60 (1933), 1 U.Chi.L.Rev. 128 (1933), 46 Harv.L.Rev. 1034 (1933).

96. See Woronzoff-Daschkoff v. Woronzoff-Daschkoff, 303 N.Y. 506, 104 N.E.2d 877 (1952). Mitchell v. Mitchell, 310 A.2d 837 (D.C.App.1973), applying New York law, refused to annul the marriage on the ground of false representation that defendant would perform an antenuptial agreement, where that agreement was invalid by New York law. See also Annot., 66 A.L.R.3d 1282 (1975).

A casual and wholly unsupported Colorado case seems to say that marrying for money and not for love constitutes fraud going to the essentials, but this seems most doubtful. In re Blietz's Marriage, 538 P.2d 114 (Colo. App.1975).

97. Denying annulment: Di Pillo v. Di Pillo, 17 Misc. 2d 673, 184 N.Y.S.2d 892 (1959); Johnson v. Johnson, 10 Misc.2d 561, 169 N.Y.S.2d 97 (1957); King v. King, 198 Misc. 674, 98 N.Y.S.2d 686 (1950); Berardino v. Berardino, 156 Misc. 203, 280 N.Y.S. 13 (1935); Smelzer v. Smelzer, 147 Misc. 413, 265 N.Y.S. 220 (1933).

Granting the annulment: Tuchsher v. Tuchsher, 16 Misc.2d 1, 184 N.Y.S.2d 131 (1959); Siek v. Siek, 196 Misc. 165, 93 N.Y.S.2d 470 (1949), affirmed 276 App.Div. 1035, 95 N.Y.S.2d 234 (3 Dep't 1950); Madden v. Madden, 204 Misc. 170, 125 N.Y.S.2d 384 (1953); Waff v. Waff, 189 Misc. 372, 71 N.Y.S.2d 775 (1947).

98. Craun v. Craun, 112 U.S.App.D.C. 145, 300 F.2d 737 (1962).

99. Cantor v. Cantor, 234 N.Y.S.2d 600 (1962); Jennings v. Jennings, 186 Misc. 1021, 63 N.Y.S.2d 294 (1946) (dictum). But see Schinker v. Schinker, 271 App.Div. 688, 68 N.Y.S.2d 470 (4th Dep't 1947), and In re Blietz's Marriage, 538 P.2d 114 (Colo.App.1975).

1. See notes 93 and 94, supra.

2. Akrep v. Akrep, 1 N.J. 268, 63 A.2d 253 (1949); Aufiero v. Aufiero, 222 App.Div. 479, 226 N.Y.S. 611 (1st Dep't 1928), 76 U.Pa.L.Rev. 1002 (1928); Rutstein v. Rutstein, 221 App.Div. 70, 222 N.Y.S. 688 (1st Dep't 1927), 27 Colum.L.Rev. 1001 (1927); Watkins v. Watkins, 197 App. Div. 489, 189 N.Y.S. 860 (1st Dep't 1921); Rozsa v. Rozsa,

one spouse promises to be converted to the other's faith, or to bring up the children in a particular faith, if there is evidence that the defendant did not intend to fulfill his promise when he made it.[3] It must be borne in mind that virtually all these cases dealing with intent are from New York and may (and perhaps should) have very little force as precedents in other jurisdictions.

4. Misrepresentations of Character, Marital History, or Past Life in General

The starting point for discussion of these factors is the dictum in the Reynolds case [4] to the effect that character, fortune, health or temper are "accidental qualities", whatever that means, and that misrepresentations as to them do not constitute fraud sufficient for annulment. Other cases have announced the same principle.[5] Yet there have been a substantial number of cases granting annulments for this sort of falsehood. For example, concealment or misrepresentation of one's religion may, under circumstances in which this is very important to the plaintiff, be a ground for annulment.[6] And although the weight of authority is the other way, a few cases may grant annulments where there has been misrepresentation of prior marital status.[7] Many such cases turn on the youth or inexperience of the plaintiff.[8] A few may be read as repu-

117 Misc. 728, 191 N.Y.S. 868 (1922); Rubinson v. Rubinson, 110 Misc. 114, 181 N.Y.S. 28 (1920), 20 Colum.L.Rev. 708 (1920). All of these cases emphasize the nonconsummation of the marriage, except for the Aufiero case where the parties cohabited only one day.

But see Mirizio v. Mirizio, 242 N.Y. 74, 150 N.E. 605 (1926), 26 Colum.L.Rev. 483 (1926), 39 Harv.L.Rev. 778 (1926), 35 Yale L.J. 758 (1926), holding that the wife's refusal of cohabitation until they should have a religious ceremony was misconduct on her part justifying the husband in refusing to support her. Apparently it was not proved that the husband never had intended to have a religious ceremony.

3. Villani v. Villani, 207 Misc. 629, 139 N.Y.S.2d 724 (1955) (dictum).

4. Reynolds v. Reynolds, 85 Mass. (3 Allen) 605, 607 (1862).

5. Barnes v. Barnes, 110 Cal. 418, 42 P. 904 (1895) (pre-marital unchastity is not grounds to annul); Du Pont v. Du Pont, 47 Del. (8 Terry) 231, 90 A.2d 468 (Del.1952), cert. denied 73 S.Ct. 46, 97 L.Ed. 651, 344 U.S. 836 (1952) (pre-marital unchastity not sufficient); Wesley v. Wesley, 181 Ky. 135, 204 S.W. 165 (1918) (divorce refused where pre-marital unchastity alleged); McKee v. McKee, 262 So. 2d 111 (La.App.1972) (mistake as to spouse's name not sufficient for annulment, cited and discussed in Annot., 50 A.L.R.3d 1295 (1973); Levy v. Levy, 309 Mass. 230, 34 N.E.2d 650 (1941) (pre-marital unchastity insufficient); Robertson v. Roth, 163 Minn. 501, 204 N.W. 329 (1925) (quotes the Reynolds dictum with approval); Diamond v. Diamond, 101 N.H. 338, 143 A.2d 109 (1958) (concealment of prior marriage not sufficient); Patey v. Peaslee, 99 N.H. 335, 111 A.2d 194 (1955) (dictum that fraud as to character, morality, habits, wealth or social position is not sufficient); Heath v. Heath, 85 N.H. 419, 159 A. 418 (1932) (misrepresentations as to character and finances are not sufficient, limiting Gatto v. Gatto, 79 N.H. 177, 106 A. 493 (1919)); Lindquist v. Lindquist, 130 N.J.Eq. 11, 20 A.2d 325 (1941) (misrepresentations as to chastity and character not sufficient); Brown v. Brown, 34 N.J.Super. 261, 112 A.2d 1 (1954) (non-disclosure of criminal record not sufficient); Woronzoff-Daschkoff v. Woronzoff-Daschkoff, 303 N.Y. 506, 104 N.E.2d 877 (1952) (misrepresentations of character and social position not sufficient); Travis v. Travis, 183 Pa.Super. 273, 130 A.2d 724 (1957)

(non-disclosure of illegitimate child not sufficient); Jakar v. Jakar, 113 S.C. 295, 102 S.E. 337 (1920) (misrepresentations as to wealth, social position and character not sufficient); Rascop v. Rascop, 274 Wis. 254, 79 N.W.2d 828 (1956) (misrepresentations as to paternity of a child born before marriage not sufficient). Other cases are collected in Annot., Concealed Pre-marital Unchastity or Parenthood as a Ground for Divorce or Annulment, 64 A.L.R.2d 742 (1959).

6. State Compensation Fund v. Foughty, 13 Ariz.App. 381, 476 P.2d 902 (1970), 1971 Wash.U.L.Q. 469; Bilowit v. Dolitsky, 124 N.J.Super. 101, 304 A.2d 774 (1973); Annot., 44 A.L.R.3d 972 (1972).

7. The cases granting annulment on this ground usually do so at the suit of the wife. Such cases include Jones v. Jones, 119 Fla. 824, 161 So. 836 (1935); Wolfe v. Wolfe, 76 Ill.2d 92, 27 Ill.Dec. 735, 389 N.E.2d 1143 (1979) (husband granted annulment); Wemple v. Wemple, 170 Minn. 305, 212 N.W. 808 (1927); Jordan v. Jordan, 115 N.H. 545, 345 A.2d 168 (1975); Baiter v. Baiter, 21 Misc. 2d 207, 194 N.Y.S.2d 189 (1959); Gambacorta v. Gambacorta, 136 N.Y.S.2d 258 (1954). The claim in these cases usually is that the spouse was in fact divorced when he represented that his first marriage had ended through the death of his first wife, and that the plaintiff's religious convictions forbid marriage to a divorced person.

Cases denying annulments for this reason include Oswald v. Oswald, 146 Md. 313, 126 A. 81 (1924), 73 U.Pa.L. Rev. 195 (1925), 34 Yale L.J. 207 (1924); Cassin v. Cassin, 264 Mass. 28, 161 N.E. 603 (1928); Hess v. Pettigrew, 261 Mich. 618, 247 N.W. 90 (1933); Diamond v. Diamond, 101 N.H. 338, 143 A.2d 109 (1958); Fortin v. Fortin, 106 N.H. 208, 208 A.2d 447 (1965); Villasenor v. Villasenor, 201 Misc. 286, 107 N.Y.S.2d 951 (1951); Sanderson v. Sanderson, 212 Va. 537, 186 S.E.2d 84 (1972) (annulment at suit of the husband denied where the wife had represented she had been married and divorced once when in fact she had been married and divorced five times); Wells v. Talham, 180 Wis. 654, 194 N.W. 36 (1923), 33 Yale L.J. 209 (1923) (applying Massachusetts law). Other cases are collected in Annot., 15 A.L.R.3d 759 (1967).

8. Raia v. Raia, 214 Ala. 391, 108 So. 11 (1926); Christlieb v. Christlieb, 71 Ind.App. 682, 125 N.E. 486 (1919); Brown v. Scott, 140 Md. 258, 117 A. 114 (1922). A

diating the *Reynolds* dictum and standing for the proposition that misrepresentations of character and past life, if flagrant enough to be clearly material, are grounds for annulment.[9] It is notable, however, that in the cases which reach this result the wife is usually the plaintiff. Few cases annul marriages at the suit of the husband for misrepresentations of this kind made by the wife.[10] Apparently a double standard respecting this sort of case persists in the law. We tolerate tricks practised by women in their pursuit of husbands which we condemn when used by men.

 **WESTLAW REFERENCES**

General Principles in Fraud Cases
reynolds +s reynolds /p fraud! /s marriage marry! marital
di(material! /s fraud! /s marry! marital marriage)

Defenses
sy,di(fraud! /s marriage marry! marital /s cohabit!)

The Kinds of Fraud Which Warrant Annulment

1. Misrepresentations as to Pregnancy
sy,di(misrepresent! misled mislead! conceal! non-disclosure disclos! /s pregnan! /s annul!)

4. Misrepresentations of Character, Marital History, or Past Life in General
conceal! misrepresent! fraud! disclos! misled mislead! non-disclosure /s past former previous /2 marriage life /s annul!

husband whose judgment was weakened by age was granted an annulment for misrepresentations by the wife about her character and background, in Entsminger v. Entsminger, 99 Kan. 362, 161 P. 607 (1916).

9. Douglass v. Douglass, 148 Cal.App.2d 867, 307 P.2d 674 (1957) (concealment of a criminal past); People v. Godines, 17 Cal.App.2d 721, 62 P.2d 787 (1936) (dictum concerning racial origin); Corder v. Corder, 141 Md. 114, 117 A. 119 (1922) (misrepresentations as to character); Dooley v. Dooley, 93 N.J.Eq. 22, 115 A. 268 (1921) (misrepresentations as to character and past life; marriage not consummated); Kober v. Kober, 16 N.Y.2d 191, 264 N.Y.S.2d 364, 211 N.E.2d 817 (1965) (concealment of antisemitic Nazi past); Lockwood v. Lockwood, 29 Misc. 2d 114, 220 N.Y.S.2d 718 (1961) (concealment of criminal record); Yucabezky v. Yucabezky, 111 N.Y.S.2d 441 (1952) (concealment of prior illegitimate child); Laage v. Laage, 176 Misc. 190, 26 N.Y.S.2d 874 (1941) (misrepresentations of husband's national origin).

§ 2.16 Marriage for a Limited Purpose[1]

All authorities agree that in general terms a valid marriage may only result from the consent of the parties. On accasion this requirement is elaborated by adding that the consent must be free, voluntary and understanding.[2] As a general proposition this does well enough, but at some points the requirement of consent has to be further refined. For example, the fraud cases demonstrate that some marriages may be valid though consent is not strictly voluntary when they are induced by misrepresentations not relating to "essentials."[3] The cases on marriage in jest hold that a consent which is apparent, but in the particular context not real because it is known to both parties to be no more than a joke, does not produce a valid marriage.[4] Now in the present section our ideas of consent must be defined with even greater preciseness, since we are concerned with marriages contracted on the express understanding that no cohabitation is to occur, that none of the usual marital obligations will be performed and that the marriage is for appearance's sake only.

The problem can best be described by putting a common case.[5] A man and woman have an affair as a result of which the woman becomes pregnant. To legitimize the child they agree to go through a marriage ceremony, agreeing also that they will not live together as husband and wife or undertake any other obligations of marriage and that they

10. See, e.g., cases cited supra, note 7.

§ 2.16
1. The marriages discussed in this section are sometimes referred to as sham marriages. See Note, 20 U.Chi.L.Rev. 710 (1953). It seems better to call them limited purpose marriages in order to avoid begging the questions involved.

2. Johnson v. Johnson, 104 N.W.2d 8 (N.D.1960).

3. See section 2.15, supra.

4. See section 2.15, Practitioner's Edition, and Crouch v. Wartenberg, 91 W.Va. 91, 112 S.E. 234 (1922).

5. These are substantially the facts of Franklin v. Franklin, 154 Mass. 515, 28 N.E. 681 (1891) and Bishop v. Bishop, 62 Misc.2d 436, 308 N.Y.S.2d 998 (1970) and many other cases in between.

will take steps to end the marriage at the earliest opportunity. The marriage is performed, the child is born and then one of the parties sues for an annulment, or otherwise attacks the validity of the marriage. His claim is that the marriage is invalid for lack of consent, since the parties never intended to assume any of the usual incidents of marriage, and they went through the ceremony only for the limited purpose of "giving the child a name."

The legal problem which this case presents can be viewed as merely a semantic one: What do we mean by "consent" in this context? Do we mean merely consent to participate in the ceremony? Or do we mean a consent to assume all or most of the obligations of the marital status? Looked at in this way the problem is one of resolving ambiguities in the term "consent."

An exclusively semantic approach to this problem is not possible, however. The reason is that the meaning attributed to the requirement of "consent" is significantly affected by such policy considerations as the nature and purposes of marriage, and in some cases by policy considerations having little to do with marriage. In the example given, one such consideration might be the court's desire to protect the child by ensuring his legitimacy. This would depend upon what effect an annulment decree would have on his status under local law. If the local statute preserves the legitimacy of children of annulled marriages,[6]

the annulment can be granted and the child's interests protected at the same time. A court in such a state would be more likely to hold the marriage invalid therefore than a court in a state in which the legitimacy of children of annulled marriages is not preserved.[7] To what extent these or other policy considerations should be decisive in establishing consent requirements in marriage law will be discussed further along in this section.

One way of looking at marriages contracted for a limited purpose, what might be labeled the traditional way, was to say that if the parties were competent and participated in a proper marriage ceremony, they were validly married, regardless of their motives or of an agreement not to perform the marital obligations. The English cases seem to have taken this position,[8] as have many of the American cases.[9] Their reasoning is not altogether clear. The courts may have been persuaded by the fact that the parties did consent to and intend a marriage of sorts, since that was necessary to accomplish even the limited purpose.[10] That being so, collateral agreements to the effect that they would not conduct themselves as husband and wife normally do were said to be invalid, the assertion being that the incidents of marriage are imposed by law and cannot be left to the agreement of the parties.[11] And, as has been suggested,[12] the effect of an annulment decree upon the child's legitimacy may have had great influence. It is interesting, however, that the canon law's

---

6. For a discussion of such statutes see section 3.3, infra.

7. Bove v. Pinciotti, 46 D. & C. 159 (Pa.1942) denies annulment where that would bastardize the child, as does Schibi v. Schibi, 136 Conn. 196, 69 A.2d 831 (1949). In Stone v. Stone, 159 Fla. 624, 32 So.2d 278 (1947), 1 Vand. L.Rev. 643 (1948) the annulment was granted without discussion of the issue, but apparently the local law would protect the child's legitimacy. Davis v. Davis, 191 A.2d 138 (D.C.App.1963) granted a divorce where the marriage was contracted solely to legitimate the child.

8. Bell v. Graham, 13 Moore P.C. 242, 15 Eng.Rep. 91 (1859) (dictum); H. v. H. [1954] P. 258 (dictum); Silver v. Silver [1955] 2 All Eng.Rep. 614, [1955] 1 Weekly L.Rep. 728, 69 Harv.L.Rev. 768 (1956). See also Jackson, The Formation and Annulment of Marriage, 196 (1951), and Bromley, Family Law, 71 (2d ed. 1962).

9. Schibi v. Schibi, 136 Conn. 196, 69 A.2d 831 (1949); de Vries v. de Vries, 195 Ill.App. 4 (1915); Hanson v.

Hanson, 287 Mass. 154, 191 N.E. 673 (1934); Franklin v. Franklin, 154 Mass. 515, 28 N.E. 681 (1891); Bishop v. Bishop, 62 Misc.2d 436, 308 N.Y.S.2d 998 (1970); Anonymous v. Anonymous, 49 N.Y.S.2d 314 (1944); Erickson v. Erickson, 48 N.Y.S.2d 588 (1944); Delfino v. Delfino, 35 N.Y.S.2d 693 (1942); Gregg v. Gregg, 133 Misc. 109, 231 N.Y.S. 221 (1928); Barker v. Barker, 88 Misc. 300, 151 N.Y.S. 811 (1914); Interest of Miller, 301 Pa.Super. 511, 448 A.2d 25 (1982) (common law marriage); Bove v. Pinciotti, 46 D. & C. 159 (Pa.1942); Campbell v. Moore, 189 S.C. 497, 1 S.E.2d 784 (1939); McKinney v. Clark, 2 Swan (32 Tenn.) 321 (1852); Rascop v. Rascop, 274 Wis. 254, 79 N.W.2d 828 (1956) (semble). See also Annot., 14 A.L.R.2d 624 (1950).

10. As in Bove v. Pinciotti, 46 D. & C. 159 (Pa.1942).

11. de Vries v. de Vries, 195 Ill.App. 4 (1915); Franklin v. Franklin, 154 Mass. 515, 28 N.E. 681 (1891).

12. See note 7, supra.

position seems to be otherwise, holding that a consent so qualified does not result in true marriage.[13]

In contrast with the traditional approach, a substantial number of cases have held marriages contracted for a limited purpose to be invalid,[14] for a variety of reasons. Some emphasis is placed on the lack of intent to assume the *status* of marriage, as contrasted with intent to participate in the ceremony.[15] The absence of consummation is persuasive to some courts.[16] So also is the obvious fact that marriages contracted in this manner have no social utility, providing no real home for the child if there is a child, and having no prospect of a normal marital relationship for the man and woman.[17] Finally, in one major class of cases, those involving attempts to circumvent the immigration laws, there is a natural desire to punish the parties for marriages which are essentially subterfuges.[18]

The conflicting pressures are best illustrated by the immigration cases. In the earliest of these, United States v. Rubinstein,[19] the parties went through a ceremony solely for the purpose of preventing the deportation of the wife, she paying the husband $200 for his cooperation. The ceremony was held in New Jersey and fully complied with New Jersey law. Since the parties expressly agreed they would never live together as husband and wife, there was no consummation. A lawyer who arranged the marriage was charged with the crime of conspiring to bring an alien into the country by misrepresentation and concealment. One of his defenses was that since the marriage was valid he had made no misrepresentations. Judge Learned Hand held, among other things, that the parties here had never consented to enter the marital relationship as it is generally understood. Relying on contract analogies requiring mutual consent, and on cases invalidating marriages in jest, he went on to say that the limited consent which they expressed did not amount to consent to be married and thus no marriage occurred. The defendant's conviction was therefore affirmed.

The second of the immigration cases, United States v. Lutwak,[20] involved marriages of a similar kind, that is, contracted for money with the purpose of bringing aliens into the country. The Seventh Circuit followed Rubinstein in holding the marriages invalid. When the case went to the Supreme Court, the majority found it unnecessary to pass on the validity of the marriages, holding that "marriage" as used by Congress in the applicable statute means a union of two parties who agree to establish a life together, assum-

---

13. See, e.g. Encyclical Letter on Christian Marriage of Pope Pius XI, reprinted in Association of American Law Schools, Selected Essays on Family Law, 132, 134 (1950); Bouscaren and Ellis, Canon Law, 556 (3d ed. 1957).

14. United States v. Apodaca, 522 F.2d 568 (10th Cir. 1975); United States v. Rubenstein, 151 F.2d 915 (2d Cir. 1945), cert. denied 326 U.S. 766, 66 S.Ct. 168, 90 L.Ed. 462 (1945); Archina v. People, 135 Colo. 8, 307 P.2d 1083 (1957); Stone v. Stone, 159 Fla. 624, 32 So.2d 278 (1947), 1 Vand.L.Rev. 643 (1948); Faustin v. Lewis, 85 N.J. 507, 427 A.2d 1105 (1981) (granting annulment and rejecting a defense of unclean hands); Amsden v. Amsden, 202 Misc. 391, 110 N.Y.S.2d 307 (1952); Dorgeloh v. Murtha, 92 Misc. 279, 156 N.Y.S. 181 (Sup.Ct.1915); Conley v. Conley, 14 Ohio Supp. 22, 28 Ohio Ops. 289 (Ohio Com.Pl.1943); Osgood v. Moore, 38 D. & C. 263 (Pa.1940); Crouch v. Wartenberg, 91 W.Va. 91, 112 S.E. 234 (1922). See also Annot., 14 A.L.R.2d 624 (1950).

15. Archina v. People, 135 Colo. 8, 307 P.2d 1083 (1957). A similar view seems to underlie United States v. Rubenstein, 151 F.2d 915 (2d Cir.1945), cert. denied 326 U.S. 766, 66 S.Ct. 168, 90 L.Ed. 462 (1945), and Faustin v. Lewis, 85 N.J. 507, 427 A.2d 1105 (1981), relying on the New Jersey statute.

16. Amsden v. Amsden, 202 Misc. 391, 110 N.Y.S.2d 307 (1952).

17. Conley v. Conley, 14 Ohio Supp. 22, 28 Ohio Ops. 289 (Ohio Com.Pl.1943).

18. The best illustration of this point of view is Lutwak v. United States, 344 U.S. 604, 73 S.Ct. 481, 97 L.Ed. 593 (1952), rehearing denied 345 U.S. 919, 73 S.Ct. 726, 97 L.Ed. 1352 (1953), 2 U.Chi.L.Rev. 710 (1953), although it did not pass on the validity of the marriages. The opinion is full of emotional question-begging, referring to fraudulent schemes, fake marriages and the like.

19. 151 F.2d 915 (2d Cir.1945), cert. denied 326 U.S. 766, 66 S.Ct. 168, 90 L.Ed. 462 (1945).

Congress has attempted to deal with this problem directly in the Immigration and Marriage Fraud Amendments of 1986, Pub.L.99–639, 100 Stat. 3537 (1986). The chief feature of the Act imposes a conditional period of two years before an alien may be fully accepted on the basis of marriage to a United States citizen.

20. 195 F.2d 748 (7th Cir.1952), affirmed 344 U.S. 604, 73 S.Ct. 481, 97 L.Ed. 593 (1953), 2 U.Chi.L.Rev. 710 (1953).

ing the usual duties and obligations, and that marriage in this sense had not occurred. The cases upholding limited purpose marriages in other contexts were rejected as inapposite. Mr. Justice Jackson, speaking for himself and Mr. Justices Black and Frankfurter, dissented on the ground that the marriages were valid so far as appeared and, that being so, no crime had been committed.

The next case is United States v. Diogo.[21] The Second Circuit, after making a tenuous distinction between the case at bar and Rubinstein and Lutwak,[22] held that a marriage contracted in consideration for a cash payment and for the purpose of gaining entry into the United States was valid under the law of New York where the marriage occurred. On that basis the convictions for misrepresentation of marital status were reversed. A vigorous dissent by Judge Clark asserted that the case should have been governed by Lutwak and Rubinstein. Whether or not the cases are distinguishable, it is by no means clear that the law of New York validates limited purpose marriages. No decisions of the New York Court of Appeals on the point have been found, and decisions of the New York Supreme Court are in disagreement.[23] The best that can be said therefore is that New York's position is doubtful.

Subsequent federal decisions seem for the most part to be following the Lutwak case, and holding either that the validity of the marriage is irrelevant where evasion of the immigration laws is the motive, and that "marriage" in those laws is to be defined as meaning a continuing relationship in which the parties have established a life together, with the usual rights and obligations of such a relationship.[24] The Diogo case seems to have had little influence upon later immigration decisions.

The foregoing short summary shows that the courts, confronted with limited purpose marriages in the immigration context, have at one time or another fallen back on all three of the possible theories. They have held such marriages invalid, they have held them valid, and they have held that validity is irrelevant. The reason for the confusion is the conflict between the desire to implement immigration policy and considerations relevant to the law of marriage. It seems quite plain that Congress, if its attention had been directed to the problem, would have applied criminal penalties to persons entering the country by virtue of marriages of this sort. The trouble is that Congress did not say so, and the courts, succumbing to the temptation to punish unsavoury conduct, chose to manip-

21. 320 F.2d 898 (2d Cir.1963).

22. The distinction was that in the two prior cases the charge had included concealment of intent not to live together as husband and wife, whereas in Diogo the charge was limited to misrepresentation of marital status, so that in the earlier cases the defendants could be convicted without determining the validity of the marriages. This distinction may explain Lutwak, but it does not seem to apply to Rubinstein, where the opinion explicitly said that the marriage was invalid for lack of an effective consent.

23. Holding marriages invalid: Amsden v. Amsden, 202 Misc. 391, 110 N.Y.S.2d 307 (1952); Dorgeloh v. Murtha, 92 Misc. 279, 156 N.Y.S. 181 (1915). Holding marriages valid: Bishop v. Bishop, 62 Misc.2d 436, 308 N.Y.S.2d 998 (1970) (annulment refused where the parties married to legitimate their children, treating the case as one of fraud or non-consummation); Anonymous v. Anonymous, 49 N.Y.S.2d 314 (1944) (marriage apparently consummated); Erickson v. Erickson, 48 N.Y.S.2d 588 (1944) (no discussion of consent, finds no fraud or duress); Delfino v. Delfino, 35 N.Y.S.2d 693 (1942); Gregg v. Gregg, 133 Misc. 109, 231 N.Y.S. 221 (1928); Barker v. Barker, 88 Misc. 300, 151 N.Y.S. 811 (1914). See also Faustin v. Lewis, 85 N.J. 507, 427 A.2d 1105 (1981), which granted an annulment of a marriage contracted for immigration purposes, relying on a statute authorizing annulment for lack of mutual assent.

24. E.g., Garcia-Jaramillo v. INS, 604 F.2d 1236 (9th Cir.1979), cert. denied 449 U.S. 828, 101 S.Ct. 94, 66 L.Ed. 2d 32 (1980); Bark v. Immigration and Naturalization Service, 511 F.2d 1200 (9th Cir.1975); De Figueroa v. Immigration and Naturalization Service, 501 F.2d 191 (7th Cir.1974); United States v. Sacco, 428 F.2d 264 (9th Cir.1970), cert. denied 400 U.S. 903, 91 S.Ct. 141, 27 L.Ed. 2d 140 (1970), rehearing denied 401 U.S. 926, 91 S.Ct. 864, 27 L.Ed.2d 831 (1971); Johl v. United States, 370 F.2d 174 (9th Cir.1966); United States v. Abdel-Khaleq, 354 F.2d 642 (7th Cir.1965); United States v. Pantelopoulos, 336 F.2d 421 (2d Cir.1964); Manarolakis v. Coomey, 416 F.Supp. 532 (D.Mass.1976); McLat v. Longo, 412 F.Supp. 1021 (D.Virgin Islands 1976), 15 J.Family L. 602 (1977).

Whetstone v. Immigration and Naturalization Service, 561 F.2d 1303 (9th Cir.1977) upheld a marriage where the parties separated shortly after being married.

United States v. Mathis, 559 F.2d 294 (5th Cir.1977) held, relying on Lutwak among other cases, that where a marriage is a sham, there is no husband-wife testimonial privilege.

ulate the law of marriage in order to reach the desired result. But is it justifiable to make the validity of marriages turn upon policies underlying the immigration laws? If those laws required a determination of marital status, should not that determination be made solely on the basis of the proper meaning of consent to marry as that meaning may be influenced by our views of the nature and function of marriage. Otherwise the confusion becomes overwhelming, with persons being held unmarried for immigration purposes, and married for other purposes.[25] There is enough uncertainty about marital status as an unavoidable result of our federal system without injecting it into such fundamental issues as the definition of consent.

If this is so, the question is, what sort of consent does marriage require? As should now be clear, the cases are in such disagreement that they cannot furnish a single definite answer to the question. But on principle the correct answer is that a valid marriage ought to be based upon consent to be husband and wife as that phrase is usually construed in our society. That is, the parties must agree that they will assume the usual obligations of marriage. In the absence of such agreement, the ceremony should result in no marriage. This not only does not frustrate legitimate policies, but it helps to effectuate them. No useful purpose is served by insisting that limited purpose marriages are valid. In fact very often this insistence arises from a wish to punish the parties by withholding the desired annulment. Certainly punishment or

vindictiveness has no place here. Such marriages are clearly not viable, as the parties have no intention of living together whether or not an annulment is granted. They furnish no real protection to children for the same reason, since the child of such a marriage will have to be reared by a single parent, usually his mother. They do have the single benefit of assuring the child of legitimacy, but this can and should be accomplished in other ways, as by a statute legitimizing children of annulled marriages.

Where the limited purpose marriage is contracted for reasons other than to legitimize a child, the foregoing arguments have even greater force. Added to a very limited consent is the fact that the parties have at no time behaved as spouses. Just as, in the converse situation, the law is willing to consider persons married who behave as if they were, though there may be serious technical defects in the method by which they contracted marriage,[26] so here, when the parties have agreed to be married only for very limited purposes, and have never acted as if they were married, the law should consider them not married. One hopes this point of view may gradually come to prevail, thereby eliminating the admittedly extensive authority holding limited purpose marriages valid and ending the uncertainty and confusion.

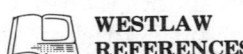 **WESTLAW REFERENCES**

marri! marital marry! /s prevent! /s deport!

find 73 sct 481

---

25. For example, in Lutwak, as the dissent points out, it was apparently conceded that the parties could only terminate the "marriages" by some legal proceeding, presumably divorce. Lutwak v. United States, 344 U.S. 604, 620, 73 S.Ct. 481, 490, 97 L.Ed. 593 (1953), rehearing denied 345 U.S. 919, 73 S.Ct. 726, 97 L.Ed. 1352 (1953). This is borne out by Mpiliris v. Hellenic Lines, Ltd., 323 F.Supp. 865 (S.D.Tex.1969), affirmed per curiam 440 F.2d 1163 (5th Cir.1971), in which a marriage was contracted solely to enable the "husband" to gain entry into the United States, with the understanding that neither party would undertake any of the normal responsibilities of marriage. Nevertheless the court held that these facts did not make the marriage void, for purposes of enabling the wife to bring an action under the maritime law for the wrongful death of the husband. See also Silver v. Silver, 1955 2 All Eng.Rep. 614, 1955 1 Weekly L.Rep. 728, 69 Harv.L.Rev. 768 (1956), where the court held that

the parties to a similar marriage were married for the purpose of obtaining a divorce. But Ramshardt v. Ballardini, 129 N.J.Super. 445, 324 A.2d 69 (1974) held a similar marriage to be void and granted an annulment, without, however, either citing or discussing any of the prior cases on sham marriage.

The statement in the text is quite explicitly supported by Archina v. People, 135 Colo. 8, 307 P.2d 1083 (1957), involving the question whether the wife could be required to testify against her husband. In finding the parties were not married the court expressly stated that its decision was limited to the application of the evidence statute, implying that for other purposes the parties' marriage might have been recognized.

26. As for example where parties are estopped to attack clearly invalid divorces, thereby validating subsequent marriages. See section 11.3, Practitioner's Edition.

Chapter 3

THE SUIT TO ANNUL

Table of Sections

---

§ 3.1 The Suit to Annul—Nature and History

From the middle of the Twelfth Century until 1857 jurisdiction to annul marriages in England lay exclusively with the ecclesiastical courts,[1] although on occasion the courts of law or equity might be faced with a collateral attack on marriage as an incident to an issue within their cognizance, such as dower.[2] The action to annul was not called annulment, but was known as divorce *a vinculo matrimonii*.[3] Divorces *a vinculo* were given for reasons which today would entitle persons to annulments, that is, for conditions at the time of the marriage which made the marriage invalid. Since absolute divorce as we know it was not available in England before 1857 (except for the relatively insignificant parliamentary divorce), annulment or divorce *a vinculo* provided the only escape from unhappy marriages. This was particularly true before the English Reformation, due to the prevailing broad incest prohibitions making it comparatively easy to annul marriages for consanguinity or affinity.[4] In those times therefore annulments performed what we would think of as the function of divorces.

Annulment, still generally referred to as divorce, was not unknown in the American colonies. It was authorized by statute in New England and was granted by both courts and legislatures.[5] In the southern colonies and New York the law was more conservative.[6] Since annulment jurisdiction in England was ecclesiastical, and since we had no ecclesiastical courts in this country, it was held in those states that there were no courts competent to hear such cases in the absence of statute.[7] The result was that no annulments could be granted other than by individual legislative act.

§ 3.1

1. I Holdsworth, History of English Law, 621 (1922); II Pollock and Maitland, History of English Law, 367 (1898).

2. Id., 622.

3. II Burns, Ecclesiastical Law, 445 (4th ed. 1781); Coke on Littleton 235a; II Pollock and Maitland, History of English Law, 393 (1898); Blackstone, Commentaries on the Law, Book I, Ch. XV., Note 7 Stanf.L.Rev. 529 (1955).

4. II Howard, History of Matrimonial Institutions, 56 (1904).

5. II Howard, History of Matrimonial Institutions, 330 ff (1904).

6. Id., 366, 376.

7. Fornshill v. Murray, 1 Blands Ch. 479 (Md.1828); 2 Kent, Commentaries on American Law, 97 (3d ed. 1836).

After independence several views of annulment jurisdiction were announced by courts in the various states.[8] The diversity was produced by the conflict between the obvious need for decrees nullifying invalid marriages, and the strong desire for legitimacy and continuity in our legal institutions. Unless a court's jurisdiction could be traced back to English origins, its legitimacy was suspect. As we have said, the annulment jurisdiction could not be so traced because we did not create ecclesiastical courts in this country, and it was impossible to say that either the common law courts or the equity courts had exercised jurisdiction in matrimonial cases in the mother country. This led some courts to hold that until a statute expressly conferred authority to hear annulments, no court could do so.[9] One answer to this assertion was that annulment of invalid marriages is a necessity in order to terminate relationships clearly violating public policy. Therefore some court must be competent to act. The state cannot tolerate, for example, the maintenance of incestuous marriages, and must have some means for declaring them invalid. This answer was suggested in a dictum by Chancellor Kent in the well-known case of Wightman v. Wightman.[10] An intermediate position taken by some courts was that equity, by analogy to its powers over contracts in general, and by a moderate extension of those powers, could exercise jurisdiction to invalidate marriage contracts on the established equitable grounds of fraud, duress or insanity.[11]

After statutes expressly conferred jurisdiction to annul upon courts of the various states, the closely related question sometimes arose whether the substantive and procedural rules of the ecclesiastical law prevailed in this country. It would seem clear from the more fully developed law of divorce that they did, but some courts refused so to find.[12] On the whole, however, most courts were willing to follow ecclesiastical doctrines even if they did not recognize their origin.[13]

During the Nineteenth Century, perhaps with the spread of statutes governing annulment, the action came to be distinguished from divorce.[14] The distinction turns on the nature and effect of the two decrees. The divorce decree terminates for the future a valid existing marriage. Annulment, however, constitutes a declaration that no marriage ever occurred, due to an impediment existing at the time of the ceremony. On these terms the two types of decree are mutually exclusive. Until recently the distinction was fundamental to the law of domestic relations, and was thought to be both logical and plain.[15] Today the distinction has become blurred and its logic is seen to be very largely an illusion. Many so-called void or voidable marriages have important legal consequences for the parties.[16] We seem to be on the way back to the medieval position, according to which annulment was merely a way of ending a marriage, and was called divorce. The Uniform Marriage and Divorce Act has changed the terminology somewhat by referring to annulment as the declaration of invalidity of a

---

8. For a full discussion see Speca, Jurisdiction in Annulment of Marriage, 22 U.Kan.City L.Rev. 109 (1954).

9. E.g., Brown v. Westbrook, 27 Ga. 102 (1859); Pitcairn v. Pitcairn, 201 Pa. 368, 50 A. 963 (1902).

10. 4 Johns. Ch. 343 (N.Y.1819). See also, e.g. Westerman v. Westerman, 121 Kan. 501, 247 P. 863 (1926) and Estes v. Estes, 194 Tenn. 96, 250 S.W.2d 32 (1952) holding that equity courts have inherent jurisdiction to annul marriages.

11. Burtis v. Burtis, 1 Hopk. Ch. 557 (N.Y.1825); Romatz v. Romatz, 355 Mich. 81, 94 N.W.2d 432 (1959) (dictum).

12. E.g., Burtis v. Burtis, 1 Hopk. Ch. 557 (N.Y.1825).

13. E.g., Harper v. Dupree, 185 Kan. 483, 345 P.2d 644 (1959).

14. See II Pollock and Maitland, History of English Law, 393 (1898).

15. Although in many states the divorce statutes authorize divorces for reasons relevant only to annulment, such as prior subsisting marriage, or fraudulent contract. For a discussion of these statutes, see section 14.8, Practitioner's Edition, infra.

16. See, e.g., sections 3.3, 3.4, 3.5, infra, and Perlstein v. Perlstein, 152 Conn. 152, 204 A.2d 909 (1964). Hall v. Hall, 32 Md.App. 363, 362 A.2d 648 (1976) refused to annul a clearly bigamous marriage but granted a divorce instead, as more "appropriate", apparently on the theory that the parties had had a "normal marital relationship". The case thus somewhat inarticulately recognizes that the distinction between annulment and divorce is no longer so plain.

marriage,[17] but its provisions have moved the states adopting it closer to the position that annulment and divorce have important similarities.

One other distinction has to be made. This is the distinction between the annulment of a void marriage and the annulment of a merely voidable marriage. Professor Ehrenzweig refers to these as "declaratory" and "constitutive" annulments, as have other authorities.[18] Theoretically declaratory annulment declares that no marriage ever existed for any purpose. It establishes in an official manner what the situation has been all along, i.e., that there never was any relationship. Constitutive annulment changes the parties' relationship, however. It declares that because of an impediment or incapacity antedating the purported marriage, that marriage is invalid. But if an action for constitutive annulment is not brought, the voidable marriage continues and is valid for all purposes.[19] When the decree of constitutive annulment is granted, the traditional analysis was that it "related back," and established that there never was a marriage. In this respect, the consequences of the two kinds of annulment decree were the same.

Today this distinction also is beginning to be seen as contrary to the facts, unworkable and productive of endless confusion.[20] Perhaps it can be completely done away with by the enactment of thorough and well-considered annulment statutes, although at the

present statutes which might be described in that style are rare indeed.[21]

As a method of terminating marriages, annulment is not statistically significant in most states, account for approximately only three percent of marriage dissolutions during the nineteen fifties.[22] New York was one exception to this. Before the 1967 amendments of its divorce statutes, annulments were nearly as numerous as divorces.[23]

§ 3.2   The Suit to Annul—Jurisdiction

Jurisdiction Over the Subject Matter

"Jurisdiction" is a word of many meanings in the law.[1] Very broadly, for present purposes, it may be defined as referring to the court's authority to hear a case. That authority may vary in its source, and in the conditions precedent to its coming into existence. "Jurisdiction over the subject matter" in the present context is intended to raise two questions: a) Does *any* court within a particular state have authority, by statute or otherwise to hear annulments? and b) What events must occur within a particular state in order to give that state's courts authority to hear annulments?

The first of these questions can be easily answered in those states where statutes expressly confer on specific courts the authority to decide annulment cases. Such statutes are found in the large majority of states.[2] Without an express statutory grant of authority,

---

17. Uniform Marriage and Divorce Act § 208, 9A Unif.L.Ann. 110 (1979).

18. Ehrenzweig, Conflict of Laws, 300, 301 (1962). See also Storke, Annulment in the Conflict of Laws, 43 Minn. L.Rev. 849 (1959). Professor Ehrenzweig refers to a third type of annulment having only prospective consequences, but this type is really a development from, or transformation of the other two.

19. The void-voidable distinction took its origin in English ecclesiastical law, the canonical impediments being said to make the marriage only voidable. See Elliot v. Gurr, 2 Phill.Ecc. 16, 161 Eng.Rep. 1064 (1812). Part of the existing confusion on the subject arises from the fact that modern statutes sometimes characterize as void marriages to which the impediment was originally canonical, so that it is impossible to define the void-voidable categories in any general way.

20. As for example is the case with nonage marriages. See section 2.10, supra.

21. The Uniform Marriage and Divorce Act section 208, 9A Unif.L.Ann. 110 (1979) is a beginning, but it does not deal with jurisdiction and with many other troublesome aspects of annulment. See Vernon, Annulment of Marriages in New Mexico: Part II Proposed Statute, 2 Nat.Res.J. 270 (1962). A review of the Ohio statute, exploring its virtues and defects is in Note, The Ohio Annulment Law: A Beginning But Not an End, 16 West. Res.L.Rev. 915 (1965).

22. Jacobson, American Marriage and Divorce, 90 (1959).

23. Id. at 113.

§ 3.2

1. Ehrenzweig, Louisell and Hazard, Jurisdiction in a Nutshell, 6–7, 9–16 (4th ed. 1980).

2. E.g., Ariz.Rev.Stat. § 25.311 (Supp.1977); Colo.Rev. Stat. § 14–10–111 (1973); Conn.Gen.Stat.Ann. § 46b–42 (1986); Del.Code tit. 13, § 1504 (1981); D.C.Code 1981,

the problem discussed in the preceding section arises. That is, does our common law include principles which were developed in the English ecclesiastical practice? Most of the few states which do not have statutes have held there is jurisdiction to annul marriages in the equity courts, at least where the defect alleged is a civil impediment.[3]

The second of these questions has been discussed by scholars of the conflict of laws for many years. An early influential article by Judge Goodrich argued that the state of celebration and the state of the domicile at the time of the marriage (if different from the state of celebration) should have jurisdiction over the subject matter of annulment.[4] The state of subsequent domicile of the parties in his view is not a proper place in which to annul the marriage.

As the law has developed, however, Judge Goodrich's views have not prevailed. The basis for annulment jurisdiction has very generally come to be domicile at the time of the suit (that is, domicile of at least one of the parties), with a substantial number of cases holding that the state in which the marriage was celebrated also has jurisdiction to annul.[5] The statutes in a number of states adopt the rule that the domicile of one of the parties is sufficient for jurisdiction.[6] In addition some statutes authorize annulment if the marriage was contracted within the state.[7] The cases in those states having no statutes reach the same result, basing jurisdiction either upon the domicile of one of the spouses[8] or upon

---

§ 16–901; Hawaii Rev.Stat. § 580–1 (Supp.1983); Iowa Code Ann. § 598.2 (1981); Kan.Stat.Ann. § 60–1602 (1983); Me.Rev.Stat.Ann. tit. 19, § 635 (1981); Mich.C.L. A. § 25.83 (1984); Miss.Code 1973, § 93–7–11; Mont.Code Ann. § 40–1–402 (1983); N.J.Stat.Ann. § 2A:34–8 (Supp. 1984); N.C.Gen.Stat. § 50–4 (1984); N.D.Cent.Code § 14–04–01 (1981); Ohio Rev.Code § 3105.011 (1980); Pa.Stat. tit. 23, § 301 (Supp.1984); Utah Code Ann. 1984, § 30–3–16.1; Vt.Stat.Ann. tit. 15, § 591 (1974); Va.Code 1983, § 20–96; West's Rev.Code Wash.Ann. § 26.09.010 (Supp. 1985); Wis.Stat.Ann. § 767.01 (1981).

3. E.g., Harper v. Dupree, 185 Kan. 483, 345 P.2d 644 (1959); Romatz v. Romatz, 355 Mich. 81, 94 N.W.2d 432 (1959). Cf. D. v. D., 41 Del. (2 Terry) 263, 20 A.2d 139 (1941), and Lyannes v. Lyannes, 171 Wis. 381, 177 N.W. 683 (1929).

4. Goodrich, Jurisdiction to Annul a Marriage, 32 Harv.L.Rev. 806 (1919). For other early cases see 3 Freeman, Judgments, SS 1512 (5th ed. 1925).

5. The most thorough review of the authorities is Vernon, Labyrinthine Ways: Jurisdiction to Annul, 10 J.Pub.L. 47 (1961). See also A. Ehrenzweig, Conflict of Laws 301 (1962); H. Goodrich and E. Scoles, Conflict of Laws 268–271 (4th ed. 1964). The Restatement (Second) of Conflict of Laws § 76 (1971) states the rule to be that a state has jurisdiction to annul in those circumstances in which it could grant a divorce or, if the defendant is personally subject to the jurisdiction, where it is the state where the marriage was contracted or the state whose law governs the validity of the marriage. The second of the two major bases for jurisdiction stated in the Restatement is not supported by the case law, at least in the form in which the Restatement states the rule.

6. E.g., Alaska Stat. § 25.24.080 (1983); Colo.Rev.Stat. § 14–10–111 (1983); Del.Code tit. 13, § 1504 (1981); D.C. Code 1981, § 16–902; Iowa Code Ann. §§ 598.2, 598.28 (1981); Nev.Rev.Stat. § 125.370 (1983); N.J.Stat.Ann. § 2A:34–9 (1952); N.Y.–McKinney's Dom.Rel.Law § 230 (1977) (complex rules, including residence of either party); Or.Rev.Stat. § 107.075 (1983); V.T.C.A., Fam.Code § 2.24

(1975); Va.Code 1983, § 20–97; W.Va.Code, § 48–2–6 (1980); Wis.Stat.Ann. § 767.05 (1981). In some states, such as Iowa and Wisconsin, the cited statutes refer to residence in the county, which seems to sound more like a requirement of venue than jurisdiction. And in some states, such as Colorado, Nevada, Oregon and New York, the statutes prescribe periods of residence for annulment jurisdiction.

7. E.g., Colo.Rev.Stat. § 14–10–111 (1973); D.C.Code, § 16–902 (1981); Nev.Rev.Stat. § 125–360 (1983); N.H. Rev.Stat.Ann. § 458:3 (1968); V.T.C.A., Fam.Code § 2.24 (1975); W.Va.Code, § 48–2–6 (1980); Wis.Stat.Ann. § 767.05 (1981).

8. Constantine v. Constantine, 261 Ala. 40, 72 So.2d 831 (1954) (plaintiff domiciled in Alabama, marriage in the Bahamas); Gwin v. Gwin, 219 Ala. 552, 122 So. 648 (1929) (parties domiciled in Alabama, married in Louisiana); Bing Gee v. Chan Lai Yung Gee, 89 Cal.App.2d 877, 202 P.2d 360 (1949), 22 So.Cal.L.Rev. 457 (1949) (plaintiff domiciled in California, marriage in Hong Kong); Owen v. Owen, 127 Colo. 359, 257 P.2d 581 (1953) (plaintiff domiciled in Colorado, marriage in Texas); Perlstein v. Perlstein, 152 Conn. 152, 204 A.2d 909 (1964), on remand 26 Conn.Supp. 257, 217 A.2d 481 (1966); Roth v. Roth, 104 Ill. 35 (1882); Christlieb v. Christlieb, 71 Ind.App. 682, 125 N.E. 486 (1919); Westerman v. Westerman, 121 Kan. 501, 247 P. 863 (1926); Cross v. Cross, 110 Mont. 300, 102 P.2d 829 (1940) (parties domiciled in Montana, married in Idaho); Sirois v. Sirois, 94 N.H. 215, 50 A.2d 88 (1946) (parties domiciled in New Hampshire, married in Massachusetts); Rinaldi v. Rinaldi, 94 N.J.Eq. 14, 118 A. 685 (1922); Avakian v. Avakian, 69 N.J.Eq. 89, 60 A. 521 (1905) (plaintiff domiciled in New Jersey, marriage in England); Cunningham v. Cunningham, 206 N.Y. 341, 99 N.E. 845 (1912) (parties domiciled in New York, married in New Jersey); Everly v. Baumil, 209 S.C. 287, 39 S.E.2d 905 (1946) (court of domicile may annul a marriage celebrated elsewhere, in this case South Carolina being the defendant's domicile); Estes v. Estes, 194 Tenn. 96, 250 S.W.2d 32 (1952) (plaintiff domiciled in Tennessee, mar-

the fact that the marriage was celebrated within the state.[9]

One important case, Whealton v. Whealton,[10] has qualified the foregoing rules by holding that an annulment may be granted by a state which is the domicile of neither party and in which the marriage did not occur, if there is personal jurisdiction over both parties. In other words, where both are personally before the court, the case is treated as an ordinary transitory action. The same case adds that any unfairness of such a rule may be avoided by applying the doctrine of *forum non conveniens,* either at the request of the defendant or on the court's own motion. Thus as a result of Whealton an annulment suit might be heard in the state of the plaintiff's or defendant's domicile, in the state in which the marriage occurred, or in the state in which both parties are personally before the court.

There seem to be at least two reasons for the jurisdictional rules. The first is the growing realization that annulment is similar to divorce in that the decree in either proceeding ends a marital relationship which, in the case of annulment, had an ostensible existence. Some evidence of this realization occurs in the statutes which provide that the jurisdictional requirements for annulment will be the same as for divorce.[11] Without an express provision to this effect, however, it is generally held that the divorce statutes do not control and that domicile within the jurisdiction need not have continued for any particular period in order to justify a suit for annulment.[12] Some of the cases, most notably Whealton,[13] take the position that divorce and annulment are different and should be governed by different jurisdictional rules. The Whealton case rests this assertion on the different choice of law rules which are applicable to divorce and annulment. Divorce is generally governed by the law of the forum. Whealton asserts that annulment is governed by the law of the place where the marriage occurred. This is not true in all cases.[14] But in any event the choice of law rules differ as between the two kinds of proceeding sufficiently that there is much less opportunity for forum-shopping in annulment than in divorce.

---

riage in Mississippi); Heflinger v. Heflinger, 136 Va. 289, 118 S.E. 316 (1923) (parties domiciled in Virginia, married in Maryland); Johnson v. Johnson, 57 Wash. 89, 106 P. 500 (1910); Salvesen v. Administrator, [1927] A.C. 641, 16 Cal.L.Rev. 38 (1927). See also Ehrenzweig, Conflict of Laws, 301 (1962); McMurray and Cunningham, Jurisdiction to Pronounce Null a Marriage Celebrated in Another State or Foreign Country, 18 Cal.L.Rev. 105 (1930); Note, 16 Minn.L.Rev. 398 (1932); and Annot., 128 A.L.R. 61, 64 (1940). A case which seems contra is Bell v. Bell, 122 W.Va. 223, 8 S.E.2d 183 (1940), relying on Judge Goodrich's article. An early Massachusetts case, Levy v. Downing, 213 Mass. 334, 100 N.E. 638 (1913) refused jurisdiction to annul a New Hampshire marriage where the parties were domiciled in Massachusetts, but the case is clearly wrong and probably can be accounted for as confusing jurisdiction with choice of law. Later Massachusetts cases go the other way: Davis v. Seller, 329 Mass. 385, 108 N.E.2d 656 (1952); Damaskinos v. Damaskinos, 325 Mass. 217, 89 N.E.2d 766 (1950); Cohn v. Carlisle, 310 Mass. 126, 37 N.E.2d 260 (1941); Hanson v. Hanson, 287 Mass. 154, 191 N.E. 673 (1934). The question now is controlled by statute, Mass.G.L.A. ch. 207, § 14 (1981) providing that annulment is governed by the same rules as divorce. But see Whealton v. Whealton, 67 Cal.2d 656, 63 Cal.Rptr. 291, 432 P.2d 979 (1967).

9. Jordan v. Courtney, 248 Ala. 390, 27 So.2d 783 (1946); Feigenbaum v. Feigenbaum, 210 Ark. 186, 194 S.W.2d 1012 (1946); Mayer v. Mayer, 207 Cal. 685, 279 P. 783 (1929) (dictum); Mazzei v. Cantales, 142 Conn. 173, 112 A.2d 205 (1955); Corder v. Corder, 141 Md. 114, 117

A. 119 (1922); State ex rel. Pavlo v. Scoggin, 60 N.M. 111, 287 P.2d 998 (1955); Sawyer v. Slack, 196 N.C. 697, 146 S.E. 864 (1929), 7 N.C.L.Rev. 458 (1929); McDade v. McDade, 16 S.W.2d 304 (Tex.Civ.App.1929), 8 Tex.L.Rev. 136 (1929). In the cases cited the parties were domiciled outside the annulling state, and the marriages celebrated within it. Cases holding that jurisdiction does not exist at the place of celebration include Antoine v. Antoine, 132 Miss. 442, 96 So. 305 (1923); Foster v. Nordman, 244 S.C. 485, 137 S.E.2d 600 (1964), and Turner v. Turner, 85 N.H. 249, 157 A. 532 (1931), the latter case being overruled by statute.

10. 67 Cal.2d 656, 63 Cal.Rptr. 291, 432 P.2d 979 (1967), 22 Ark.L.Rev. 509 (1968), 4 San Diego L.Rev. 401 (1968).

11. E.g., Official Code Ga.Ann. § 19–4–4 (Supp.1984); Mass.Gen.Laws Ann. ch. 207, § 14 (1981); Minn.Stat. Ann. § 518.03 (Supp.1985); Pa.Stat. tit. 23, § 301 (Supp. 1984).

12. Whealton v. Whealton, 67 Cal.2d 656, 63 Cal.Rptr. 291, 432 P.2d 979 (1967). Other cases are collected in Annot., 32 A.L.R.2d 734 (1953).

13. Whealton v. Whealton, 67 Cal.2d 656, 63 Cal.Rptr. 291, 432 P.2d 979 (1967). See also Gordon v. Gordon, 35 Ariz. 357, 278 P. 375 (1929), motion to modify denied 35 Ariz. 532, 281 P. 215 (1929).

14. See, e.g. the nonage cases, supra, section 2.10 following note 81.

Since the reliance upon domicile as the basis for subject matter jurisdiction in divorce has as its purpose the prevention of forum-shopping, there is less reason to insist on domicile as a basis for jurisdiction in annulment. Nevertheless the similarity between divorce and annulment in their practical aspects continues to provide strong reason for applying the same rules for subject matter jurisdiction in both types of proceeding.

The chief reason for the adoption of domicile as the jurisdictional basis for annulment is no doubt the recognition that the domicile has the primary governmental interest in the marital status of its citizens, the same reason which has prevailed in the law of divorce.[15] A conceptual way of putting the same reason is adopted by those courts who say that annulment is an in rem action, the marital status is the res, and it is located at the domicile.[16] As will be argued below, this sort of talk is not only fictional, but leads to the worst sort of confusion. Nevertheless, the underlying governmental interest is real enough, at least in theory. The state where the spouses live, or where one of them lives, does have an interest in their status. In practice the drawback is that the spouses often do not live at their domicile, domicile being an increasingly irrelevant concept in a highly mobile society. Basing jurisdiction upon residence as distinguished from domicile might be preferable, if no constitutional limitations forbid, as some states have done with divorce.

If the state's interest in the marital status of its citizens is the basis for jurisdictional rules, it follows that the cases allowing annulment by the state of celebration, when the spouses are both domiciled elsewhere, are wrong. The state of celebration has no interest in the status of persons married within its boundaries, solely by virtue of that fact.[17] As indicated in other sections of this work,[18] there is a tendency (though by no means a universal one) to apply the lex loci as the appropriate choice of law rule in determining the validity of marriages. The persistence of the rule that the place of celebration has jurisdiction to annul is perhaps due to confusion between choice of law and jurisdiction.[19] Such confusion is certainly to be avoided, although it is understandable in some circumstances. Both jurisdictional and choice of law rules may be affected by the presence of very strong public policies. For example, where individuals leave the domicile and go to another state to marry in order to avoid the domicile's law, the domicile may not only assert jurisdiction to annul the marriage, but also apply its own law.[20] Nonetheless, the two questions are different and should be separately considered. The ultimate source of power over the marriage is not in the place of celebration, as Judge Goodrich argued,[21] but in the domicile, or, more realistically, in the place of residence where that differs from the domicile. But perhaps no harm is done when the place of celebration asserts jurisdiction, since that merely gives the annulment plaintiff another opportunity to have the invalidity, or the validity, of his marriage established.

The courts are certainly on sound ground in refusing to apply the divorce statutes so as to impose a specific time period on domicile as a requisite for annulment jurisdiction. Such requirements are sensible in divorce as a means of preventing the forum-shopping which is invited by the rule that the law of the forum governs the grounds for the divorce. In annulment, however, the law of the

15. H. Goodrich, E. Scoles, Conflict of Laws 268 (4th ed. 1964).

16. E.g., Salvesen v. Administrator [1927] A.C. 641.

17. Sirois v. Sirois, 94 N.H. 215, 50 A.2d 88 (1946); Note, 6 Stanf.L.Rev. 153 (1953).

It is interesting that New York's former statute authorized a divorce on the basis that the place of marriage was New York. David-Zieseniss v. Zieseniss, 205 Misc. 836, 129 N.Y.S.2d 649 (1954).

18. See sections 2.3, 2.9, 2.10, supra.

19. As in Levy v. Downing, 213 Mass. 334, 100 N.E. 638 (1913), Roop v. Roop, 91 N.H. 47, 13 A.2d 474 (1940), and Dodds v. Pittsburg, M. & B. Rys. Co., 107 Pa.Super. 20, 162 A. 486 (1932), 33 Colum.L.Rev. 149 (1933).

20. As in Wilkins v. Zelichowski, 26 N.J. 370, 140 A.2d 65 (1958).

21. Goodrich, Jurisdiction to Annul a Marriage, 32 Harv.L.Rev. 806, 814 (1919): "Only the law by which the marriage came into being has power to annul it."

forum normally does not apply, so that there is little reason for the parties to indulge in forum-shopping.[22] Furthermore, it is generally desirable to adjudicate the validity of questioned marriages with as little delay as possible so that the parties will know what their status is. But many of the statutes on annulment do require a specified residence period as for divorce.[23]

The question might be raised whether the same requirements for subject matter jurisdiction exist for suits to affirm marriages as for suits to annul. The two actions are really alike in all essential respects. In both the validity of the marriage is at issue, and in both the decree either establishes its validity or invalidity. The only difference between them is that in annulment the plaintiff asserts the marriage is invalid, while in the suit to affirm, he asserts it is valid. But the merely formal position of the plaintiff does not affect the nature of the suit. The suit to affirm the marriage should therefore be gov-

erned by the same jurisdictional principles as the suit to annul.[24]

Although the cases are not numerous, it seems clear that annulment decrees rendered with jurisdiction are within the Full Faith and Credit Clause[25] and entitled to respect in other states.[26] By analogy to the law of divorce, it would seem that an annulment decree rendered without jurisdiction over the subject matter would not be entitled to full faith and credit.[27] But if both parties were before the court and had a chance to litigate the jurisdictional issue, the Sherrer rule[28] would deny to them the right to attack the decree for lack of subject matter jurisdiction.

Service of Process

In several states the annulment statutes contain provisions regulating the method of service of process. They usually authorize substituted service under certain circumstances, as where the defendant cannot be personally served in the state.[29] At the risk

22. Whealton v. Whealton, 67 Cal.2d 656, 63 Cal.Rptr. 291, 432 P.2d 979 (1967); Estes v. Estes, 194 Tenn. 96, 250 S.W.2d 32 (1952).

23. Vernon, Labryinthine Ways: Jurisdiction to Annul, 10 J.Pub.L. 47, 59 (1961).

24. Some statutes so provide: Mass.Gen.Laws Ann. ch. 207, § 14 (1981); Va.Code 1983, § 20–97; Wis.Stat. Ann. § 767.05 (1981).

Carr v. Carr, 46 N.Y.2d 270, 413 N.Y.S.2d 305, 385 N.E. 2d 1234 (1978) does not support the text statement. In that case W-1 sued W-2, after H had died, to establish the validity of the first marriage, which entailed also establishing the invalidity of H's Honduran divorce from W-1 and of his subsequent marriage to W-2. The sole purpose of the suit was to assert the claim of W-1 to survivor benefits in H's retirement plan. W-1 was domiciled in New York and W-2 in California. The court held there was not sufficient contacts between W-2 and New York to support in personam jurisdiction and that the marital res was not sufficient to support jurisdiction for an in rem adjudication, since H was deceased. Perhaps the real basis for this case is that it was essentially an in personam claim to property rights rather than a case involving the status of marriage. Whatever marriages might have formerly existed had ended with the death of H.

25. U.S.Const. Art. IV, section 1.

26. Sutton v. Leib, 342 U.S. 402, 72 S.Ct. 398, 96 L.Ed. 448 (1952), holding that the annulment decree of the domicile of the parties was entitled to full faith and credit though it annulled a marriage contracted elsewhere. See also McCormack v. McCormack, 175 Cal. 292, 165 P. 930 (1917). Presumably the text statement would

be true whether jurisdiction was based on domicile or place of celebration. H. Goodrich, E. Scoles, Conflict of Laws 271 (4th ed. 1964).

27. Cummington v. Belchertown, 149 Mass. 223, 21 N.E. 435 (1899) (semble).

28. Sherrer v. Sherrer, 334 U.S. 343, 68 S.Ct. 1087, 92 L.Ed. 1429 (1948). See also Johnson v. Muelberger, 340 U.S. 581, 71 S.Ct. 474, 95 L.Ed. 552 (1951).

29. For purposes of the present discussion "personal service" means that form of service which is generally required in order to give the court power to enter a judgment binding the person of the defendant. This includes delivering the summons and complaint in person to the defendant within the state or the entry by the defendant of a general appearance in the action. See Ehrenzweig, Louisell and Hazard, Jurisdiction in a Nutshell, 17 (4th ed. 1980). "Constructive service" is the term used in this discussion to describe those forms of service sufficient to confer jurisdiction in what are traditionally referred to as in rem actions. A. Ehrenzweig, D. Louisell and G. Hazard op. cit. 53. Statutes authorizing constructive service in annulment: Del.Code tit. 13, §§ 1504, 1508 (1981); Official Code Ga.Ann. § 19–4–4 (Supp.1984); Iowa Rules Civ.Proc., 60 (1951); Kan.Stat. Ann. § 60–307 (1983); Mich.C.L.A. §§ 25.83, 25.89(1) (1984); Minn.Stat.Ann. § 518.03 (Supp.1985), Minn.Rules Civ.Proc., 4.04(3) (1979), Wilson v. Wilson, 95 Minn. 464, 104 N.W. 300 (1904); Neb.Rev.Stat. § 42–119 (1984); Nev. Rev.Stat. § 125.400 (1983); N.J.Rules of Court, 4:78–2 (1969); N.Y.–McKinney's Dom.Rel.Law § 232 (1977 and Supp.1984); Okl.Stat. 1981, tit. 12, § 2004 (Supp.); Pa. Rules Civ.Proc., Rule 1124 (1975); Vt. Rules Civ.Proc., 4(e), 4(f), 4(g) (1971 and Supp.1984); Va.Code 1983, § 20–

of creating some confusion, one might say that these statutes allow the sort of service generally available for in rem actions.

In the absence of statute, the cases disagree on what service is required for annulment. The larger number of courts hold that personal service within the state is necessary.[30] The reasoning of this majority is unreal in the extreme.[31] They start with the assertion that annulment differs from divorce because in divorce there is a res, the marital status, on which the court may act, while in annulment the existence of a res is the very point in issue, with the plaintiff, who invokes the jurisdiction, alleging that there is no res. Since there is no res, the action cannot be in rem. It follows that the suit is in personam, and personal service within the jurisdiction is necessary. Curiously enough, most of the cases do not discuss the question in constitutional terms, but only in terms of the local rule of court. But if their reasoning is correct, it is unconstitutional to grant annulments on constructive service, under Pennoyer v. Neff.[32] Any holding to this effect would have disastrous consequences, since it would invalidate on jurisdictional grounds many annulments in the states whose statutes authorize constructive service. If these annulments are invalid, then of course subsequent marriages of the parties are invalid under some condi-

tions. The announcement of any legal doctrine which casts doubt on such a wide range of marital relationships is certainly to be avoided if possible.

There are other serious grounds for objecting to legal reasoning which labels actions as in rem or in personam, and which determines the service required by reference to the label. The entire notion of in rem actions is a fiction, though a fiction of some historical respectability.[33] Where real estate is concerned, a superficially plausible argument may be made that a decree can be in rem, that is, that it can affect the land or the title to the land. This is the traditional way of referring to decrees quieting title to land.[34] When the same sort of reasoning is applied to matrimonial actions, such as divorce, its fictional nature becomes too obvious for modern courts to accept. The "res" then is not a tangible, visible piece of real estate, but a status, the marriage. And, it is plain, the status is nothing more than a set of relationships between two parties. A complex of legal relationships is hypostatized by a verbal trick. Giving it a Latin name helps to conceal what is really going on. If we use English, and refer to marriage as a "thing," the fiction is too transparent to be tolerated. In fact, the same is true of the land cases, since the decree quieting title does not operate

104; Wis.Stat.Ann. §§ 767.05, 767.085 (1981 and Supp. 1984); Wis.Stat.Ann. § 801–13 (1977), Wyo.Stat. § 20–2–101 (1977), Wyo.Rules Civ.Proc., Rule 4(e)(9) (1984).

30.   Gwin v. Gwin, 219 Ala. 552, 122 So. 648 (1929); Owen v. Owen, 127 Colo. 359, 257 P.2d 581 (1953), 6 Stanf.L.Rev. 153 (1953); Mazzei v. Cantales, 142 Conn. 173, 112 A.2d 205 (1955) (personal service required where suit is brought in the state of celebration); Shafe v. Shafe, 101 Ind.App. 200, 198 N.E. 826 (1935); Bisby v. Mould, 138 Iowa 15, 115 N.W. 489 (1908); Prothro v. Prothro, 265 S.W.2d 39 (Ky.1953); Gayle v. Gayle, 301 Ky. 613, 192 S.W.2d 821 (1946); Cummington v. Belchertown, 149 Mass. 223, 21 N.E. 435 (1899); Antoine v. Antoine, 132 Miss. 442, 96 So. 305 (1923); State ex rel. Pavlo v. Scoggin, 60 N.M. 111, 287 P.2d 998 (1955); Pepper v. Shearer, 48 S.C. 492, 26 S.E. 797 (1897). An earlier secondary authority has had some influence by stating, much more broadly than was warranted by the existing case law, that the cases were practically unanimous in requiring personal service. Annot., 128 A.L.R. 61, 71 (1940). The same authority characterized the state of the law differently in Annot., 43 A.L.R.2d 1086 (1955). Restatement (Second) of Conflict of Laws § 76 (1971) seems to take no official position on this question, but the

reporter's note advocates the view that constructive service is sufficient when the basis for subject matter jurisdiction is domicile, but not where the forum is the state of celebration, in which case personal service is required.

For cases upholding constructive service, see note 43 infra.

Compare Detzel v. Detzel, 22 Misc.2d 76, 190 N.Y.S.2d 244 (1959), holding that after an annulment is granted the decree is a "res" which can later be vacated on constructive service, after the death of a party.

31.   E.g. Owen v. Owen, 127 Colo. 359, 257 P.2d 581 (1953), Gayle v. Gayle, 301 Ky. 613, 192 S.W.2d 821 (1946), and Sacks v. Sacks, 47 Misc.2d 1050, 263 N.Y.S.2d 891 (1965).

32.   95 U.S. (5 Otto) 714, 24 L.Ed. 565 (1877).

33.   The classic statement of the fictional nature of the in rem-in personam distinction is by Mr. Justice Holmes in Tyler v. Judges of the Court of Registration, 175 Mass. 71, 55 N.E. 812, 814 (1900).

34.   H. Goodrich, E. Scoles, Conflict of Laws 103 (4th ed. 1964).

against the land. It adjudicates people's legal relations centering around the land. In this case also the in rem label is a fiction.

The more sophisticated courts have expressly recognized that calling divorce in rem solves no problems.[35] At best it is merely a short way of summing up the legal conditions and consequences of such decrees, a description rather than an explanation.

One further development is relevant at this point. This is the contemporary tendency to dispense with personal service in certain types of cases. Personal service within the jurisdiction was originally required in actions labelled in personam on the theory that by this means the state symbolically asserted its power over the defendant's person.[36] The symbolic assertion of power was regarded as a constitutional prerequisite to a valid personal judgment, a judgment without it being a violation of the Due Process Clause.[37] Today, however, we have become accustomed to an extensive erosion of the personal service requirement. Thus if statutes permit, and if notice is given, a domiciliary may be sued without personal service,[38] notwithstanding the fact that domicile is not a realistic concept in many instances. Again, a person who has an auto accident in a state may be sued there

without personal service for claims arising out of the accident, if adequate notice is provided for.[39] Under some broad "long-arm statutes" a person may be sued without personal service for torts occurring within the state when the defendant himself has not at any time been present in the state.[40] And finally, the concept of doing business within the state, according to which corporations may be suable there, has been very considerably extended.[41] In these situations the older strict requirements of personal service in the state would make the action impossible. Since in the cases mentioned there is a strongly felt social demand that the action be brought within the state, the personal service requirement has had to yield, sometimes with the aid of some pretty transparent fictions.[42]

To return to the question of service in annulment suits, it being unacceptable to rely on the in rem—in personam labels as a reason for requiring personal service, what should the courts do? A minority of courts has held that annulment is so similar to divorce that the service requirements should be the same for both.[43] This is the result dictated by many statutes.[44] There is force in this argument. After both annulment and divorce decrees, the parties are single. The fact that

---

35. Williams v. North Carolina, 317 U.S. 287, 63 S.Ct. 207, 87 L.Ed. 279 (1942); Perlstein v. Perlstein, 152 Conn. 152, 204 A.2d 909 (1964). The idea of divorce as in rem, so far as it affects status, gained wide currency from Bishop's work. See II Bishop, Marriage, Divorce and Separation, 2–14 (1891). It is interesting that in this discussion Bishop characterized annulment as being in rem like divorce.

36. McDonald v. Mabee, 243 U.S. 90, 37 S.Ct. 343, 61 L.Ed. 608 (1917).

37. Pennoyer v. Neff, 95 U.S. (5 Otto) 714, 24 L.Ed. 565 (1877).

38. Milliken v. Meyer, 311 U.S. 457, 61 S.Ct. 339, 85 L.Ed. 278 (1940).

39. Hess v. Pawloski, 274 U.S. 352, 47 S.Ct. 632, 71 L.Ed. 1091 (1927).

40. Under the Illinois statute it was held that a foreign corporation could be served by constructive service in a suit arising out of the explosion of a water heater manufactured outside Illinois, the explosion occurring in Illinois and the plaintiff an Illinois resident. The defendant in this case did not even sell the water heater in Illinois and did not do business in Illinois. Gray v. American Radiator & Standard Sanitary Corp., 22 Ill.2d 432, 176 N.E.2d 761 (1961).

41. McGee v. International Life Ins. Co., 355 U.S. 220, 78 S.Ct. 199, 2 L.Ed.2d 223 (1957).

42. Perhaps the most transparent is the non-resident motorist statute, which provides that as one drives his car across the state line he appoints the secretary of state his agent for the service of process.

43. Buzzi v. Buzzi, 91 Cal.App.2d 823, 205 P.2d 1125 (1949); Bing Gee v. Chan Lai Yung Gee, 89 Cal.App.2d 877, 202 P.2d 360 (1949), 22 So.Cal.L.Rev. 457 (1949); Perlstein v. Perlstein, 152 Conn. 152, 204 A.2d 909 (1964) (where plaintiff domiciled in the state); Winter v. Winter, 256 N.Y. 113, 175 N.E. 533 (1931); Piper v. Piper, 46 Wash. 671, 91 P. 189 (1907). See also Annot., 43 A.L.R.2d 1086, 1090 (1955); Restatement (Second) of Conflict of Laws § 76 (1971) (reporter's notes). Whealton v. Whealton, 67 Cal.2d 656, 63 Cal.Rptr. 291, 432 P.2d 979 (1967) recognizes that where the annulment suit is brought at the domicile of the plaintiff, constructive service is and should be sufficient, although it also takes the position that where there is in personam jurisdiction over both parties the annulment may be granted without domicile.

44. See note 29, supra.

in some cases the annulment decree declares there never was a marriage is very often of no practical consequence to the parties, who are only interested in their future status. In fact, the retroactive nature of annulment, which is the element chiefly distinguishing it from divorce, has lately been seriously questioned.[45] Therefore, the supposed distinctions between divorce and annulment are not so great as they used to seem.

The position which favors constructive service in annulment is reinforced by a look at the social policies involved.[46] All rules as to jurisdiction and service are ultimately the result of policy pressures working against a background of authority. The only rational policy supporting the requirement of personal service is that personal service best insures that the defendant has notice of the suit. The argument against personal service is that insistence upon it in annulment cases effectively prevents the plaintiff from getting an annulment in a variety of situations: 1) If the defendant has left the plaintiff or the parties are living separately and the defendant's whereabouts is not known, he cannot be personally served at all. 2) If the defendant is living neither at his domicile nor at the plaintiff's domicile nor in the state of the celebration of the marriage, he cannot be personally served in any state where subject matter jurisdiction exists. 3) If the defendant is living at a distance from the plaintiff, the expense and inconvenience of a suit at the place of defendant's residence, where alone he may be served, will often be prohibitive.

The question then becomes, does the desirability of insuring notice to the defendant more than outweigh the drawbacks to the plaintiff of requiring personal service? This is the issue to which the courts should address themselves instead of asking the meaningless question whether there is a res. In the writer's view it is essential that annulment be freely available so that one who is in doubt as to his marital status has every chance to have it finally adjudicated. Social policy certainly favors the clarification of marital status. This being so, it is more important that the obstacles to the annulment suit created by requirements of personal service be removed than that there be complete certainty of notice. Substantial probability of notice can be achieved in any event by registered mail if the courts take care to see that constructive service statutes are complied with. It must be conceded that where service by publication is relied upon, there is a good chance that notice will not reach the defendant, and that this undesirable situation can never be completely avoided except by requiring personal service. But the risk is no greater in annulment than in divorce.

The view that annulment need not be preceded by personal service best accords with the relevant policies.[47] It does not run counter to established constitutional doctrines, since, as has been shown,[48] those doctrines have proved capable of change where change is demanded by policy, and where reasonably effective notice-giving techniques have been provided. Since Pennoyer v. Neff [49] has already been deeply undermined, there is ample precedent for adding annulment actions to the list of those in which personal service is not necessary. In the writer's view the same principles should govern the action, authorized by some statutes, for the declaration of marital status. For all

---

45. See, e.g., Gaines v. Jacobsen, 308 N.Y. 218, 124 N.E.2d 290 (1954) and other cases discussed infra, section 3.5.

46. For a somewhat different, but well-reasoned and well-documented argument as to policy, see Vernon Labyrinthine Ways: Jurisdiction to Annul, 10 J.Pub.L. 47 (1961).

47. One further argument based upon res judicata might be made. If annulment is characterized as in personam, the decree would presumably bind only the parties to the suit, since that is the normal consequence of an in personam judgment. Ehrenzweig, Conflict of

Laws, 76 (1962). But it is essential, for the protection of the parties and others, that an annulment decree be conclusive upon third persons as well as the parties, in any later action in which the validity of the marriage may be called in question. This is the usual effect of in rem decrees. For this reason annulment ought to be classified as in rem rather than in personam. A case which does this is Headen v. Pope & Talbot, 252 F.2d 739 (3d Cir.1958).

48. See the discussion at notes 36–42, supra.

49. 95 U.S. (5 Otto) 714, 24 L.Ed. 565 (1877).

essential purposes this is only annulment called by another name.

§ 3.3 The Suit to Annul—Custody, Support and Legitimacy of Children of Annulled Marriages

Custody and Support

The usual analysis of annulment as a decree which establishes that no marriage ever existed between the parties breaks down when children enter the picture. If there are children of the "marriage," some provision for their custody and maintenance has to be made. These problems will not vanish merely because a court says there never was a marriage. Therefore by statute in many states the courts have been given authority to include orders, both temporary and permanent, for custody and support of children in the annulment decree.[1] Even without express statutory authority, the courts have inherent power, by virtue of their authority to protect children, to enter custody and child

support orders in annulment cases.[2] Once made, such orders are modifiable as they would be if made as part of a divorce decree.[3] In short, with respect to the custody and care of children, the annulment decree is like the divorce decree.

Legitimacy

The obvious logical consequence of the conventional characterization of annulment is that children of a void marriage are illegitimate. As Bishop said, whatever depends on the void marriage is also void.[4] Even if the marriage is only voidable, the retroactive nature of the annulment decree would, in the absence of statute, bastardize any children born of the marriage. This in fact was the common law position.[5]

A line of cases decided by the Supreme Court has established the unconstitutionality of many of the disabilities suffered by the illegitimate child.[6] Therefore the plight of the child of an annulled marriage is not now

---

§ 3.3

1. E.g., Alaska Stat. § 25.24.160 (1983); West's Ann. Cal.Civ.Code §§ 7004, 7010 (1983) (Uniform Parentage Act); Colo.Rev.Stat. § 14–10–111 (1973); Conn.Gen.Stat. Ann. § 46b–60 (Supp.1984); Idaho Code §§ 32–503, 32–504 (1983); Me.Rev.Stat.Ann. tit. 19, § 752 (Supp.1984); Mass.G.L.A. ch. 207, § 18 (1981); Mich.C.L.A. § 25.96 (1984); Minn.Stat.Ann. § 518.17 (Supp.1985); Miss.Code 1973, § 93–7–7; Neb.Rev.Stat. § 42–351 (1984); N.H.Rev. Stat.Ann. § 458:17 (Supp.1981); N.Y.–McKinney's Dom. Rel.Law § 240 (Supp.1984); Or.Rev.Stat. § 107.105 (1983); Tenn.Code Ann. §§ 36–6–101, 36–6–102 (1984); Va.Code 1983, § 20–107.2; Wis.Stat.Ann. §§ 767.23, 767.24 (1981 and Supp.1984). The Uniform Marriage and Divorce Act § 208, 9A Unif.L.Ann. 111 (1979) has a curiously limited provision on custody and support of children in annulment decrees. It provides that the court decreeing a marriage invalid may declare the marriage invalid nonretroactively, in which case orders for the care and maintenance of children may be included. In the absence of findings that it would be just to make the decree not retroactive, it is retroactive, in which no provisions for the children may be included. This seems a cumbersome and unnecessary provision. The Uniform Parentage Act, 9A Unif.L.Ann. 597 (1979) makes the parent-child relationship independent of marriage and provides that the courts may enter support and custody orders when the existence of the parent-child relationship is found.

2. Cardenas v. Cardenas, 12 Ill.App.2d 497, 140 N.E.2d 377 (1956); Abelt v. Zeman, 179 N.E.2d 176 (Ohio Com.Pl. 1962); Greenwood v. Greenwood, 387 P.2d 615 (Okl.1963); Sanders v. Sanders, 232 S.C. 625, 103 S.E.2d 281 (1958). Many other cases on custody are cited in Annot., 63 A.L.R.2d 1008 (1959), and on child support in Annot., 63

A.L.R.2d 1029 (1959). See also Note, The Aftereffects of Annulment: Alimony, Property Division, Provisions for Children, 1968 Wash.U.L.Q. 148, 159. Contra: Eskew v. Eskew, 199 Ga. 513, 34 S.E.2d 697 (1945) (semble).

3. Grubaugh v. Grubaugh, 200 Cal.App.2d 151, 19 Cal. Rptr. 141 (1962); Harder v. Harder, 162 Neb. 433, 76 N.W.2d 260 (1956).

4. 1 Bishop, Marriage, Divorce and Separation, 313 (1891).

5. Warrenberger v. Folsom, 140 F.Supp. 610 (M.D.Pa. 1956), affirmed 239 F.2d 846 (3d Cir.1956) (Pennsylvania law); Watts v. Owens, 62 Wis. 512, 22 N.W. 720 (1885). One of the best known cases on this point is Matter of Moncrief's Will, 235 N.Y. 390, 139 N.E. 550 (1923), holding that a marriage contracted after the birth of a child did not legitimate the child when the marriage was subsequently annulled for duress, in spite of the statute which provided that the marriage of parents of an illegitimate child legitimated the child. The court took the position that since the annulment of a marriage, whether void or voidable, declares that there never was a marriage, the purported marriage had no effect. A case apparently contra the text statement is Sirois v. Sirois, 94 N.H. 215, 50 A.2d 88 (1946), in which the court, without relying upon statute, held that the annulment of a voidable marriage is not retroactive and therefore does not bastardize issue. See also In re Ruff's Estate, 159 Fla. 777, 32 So.2d 840 (1947), and Taylor v. Taylor, 249 Ala. 419, 31 So.2d 579 (1947). For general discussion see Note, Status of Issue of Void Marriages, 56 Harv.L.Rev. 624 (1943).

6. See the discussion of these cases in section 4.2, infra.

as severe as it was formerly. But the Supreme Court has not yet excluded all forms of discrimination against the illegitimate child [7] and so it is still important to examine the attempts at protecting the children of annulled marriages.

Fortunately for the fate of many children, the common law has been extensively altered by statute in nearly all states.[8] It is less fortunate, however, that the statutes even today do not give children of defective marriages anything like complete protection. Many such children are still considered to be illegitimate, and the status of others is placed in doubt by the drafting of some statutes, which is so inept as to create difficult questions of construction.

A detailed discussion of each state's statute is beyond the scope of this work. Since the legislative solutions to this problem fall pretty clearly into several classes, however, a review of each class of statute furnishes an adequate basis for understanding the entire problem. All such statutes should be given a liberal construction in order to accomplish their humanitarian purpose.[9]

The first type of statute provides that the issue of annulled marriages are legitimate.[10] This language takes care of the problem created by the traditional nature of annulment decrees, but it immediately raises the question of what is to be the status of children of defective marriages where no suit to annul is brought, and where the parties continue living together until, for example, the death of one of them. It would seem obvious that if the children are legitimate when the marriage has been annulled, they should be equally so where the parents have not attempted to invalidate the marriage, and some cases have so held.[11] There is authority the other way, however, based upon a literal reading of the statute, and upon what appears to be some courts' compulsion to punish children for their parents' immoralities.[12]

A larger number of states have enacted broader statutes of a second type, which simply provide that the children of void or voidable marriages or of marriages deemed null in law are legitimate.[13] At first glance this sort of statute appears reasonably satisfactory, but it too raises questions of construction which any well-drawn statute ought to avoid. The term "voidable marriages" is clear enough and causes no trouble.[14] But what is meant by "void marriage"? It is plain that the term covers ceremonial marriages which are void because of the parties' incapacity [15] or lack of

7. E.g., Labine v. Vincent, 401 U.S. 532, 91 S.Ct. 1017, 28 L.Ed.2d 288 (1971), rehearing denied 402 U.S. 990, 91 S.Ct. 1672, 29 L.Ed.2d 156 (1971); Trimble v. Gordon, 430 U.S. 762, 97 S.Ct. 1459, 52 L.Ed.2d 31 (1977); Fiallo v. Bell, 430 U.S. 787, 97 S.Ct. 1473, 52 L.Ed.2d 50 (1977).

8. Rhode Island may be the exception. Far from protecting the legitimacy of children, its statute expressly states that children of bigamous marriages, and of marriages of lunatics (sic) or insane persons shall be illegitimate. R.I.Gen.Laws § 15–1–5 (1981); Scalzi v. Folsom, 156 F.Supp. 838 (D.C.R.I.1957).

9. Brown v. Commonwealth ex rel. Custis, 218 Va. 40, 235 S.E.2d 325 (1977).

10. E.g., Colo.Rev.Stat. § 14–10–111 (1973); Tenn.Code Ann. § 36–4–125 (1984); Uniform Marriage and Divorce Act § 208(d), 9A Unif.L.Ann. 111 (1979).

11. Bernheimer v. First Nat. Bank of Kansas City, 359 Mo. 1119, 225 S.W.2d 745 (1949) (under prior form of statute); Taliaferro v. Rogers, 35 Tenn.App. 521, 248 S.W.2d 835 (1951).

12. Valdez v. Shaw, 100 Colo. 101, 66 P.2d 325 (1937), holding an earlier version of the Colorado statute did not legitimate the child unless the marriage was annulled. See also Crenshaw v. Gardner, 277 F.Supp. 427 (D.N.J.1967), construing the earlier New Jersey statute.

13. E.g., West's Ann.Ind.Code §§ 31–1–7–2, 31–1–7–6 (1980); Vernon's Ann.Mo.Stat. § 474.080 (1956); N.J. Stat.Ann. § 2A:34–20 (Supp.1984); N.Y.–McKinney's Dom.Rel.Law § 24 (1977); Okl.Stat.1984, tit. 84, § 215 (Supp.); Pa.Stat. tit. 48, § 169.1 (1965); V.A.T.S.Prob. Code, § 42 (1980); Va.Code 1983, § 20–31.1; Wis.Stat. Ann. § 767.60 (Supp.1984).

14. Assuming that the courts in the particular jurisdiction are able to distinguish between void and voidable marriages. They are not always able to do so, as in Ragan v. Cox, 208 Ark. 809, 187 S.W.2d 874 (1945) and other Arkansas cases where the court was unable to decide whether "void" in the statute meant void or voidable. But if the court does know which marriages are void and which are voidable, then it is clear that the issue of voidable marriages are legitimate before annulment since by definition such marriages are valid till annulled, and after annulment by virtue of the legitimation statute. See Turner v. Turner, 167 Cal.App.2d 636, 334 P.2d 1011 (1959).

15. Daniels v. Johnson, 216 Ark. 374, 226 S.W.2d 571 (1950); Connor v. Rainwater, 200 Ga. 866, 38 S.E.2d 805 (1946); Abelt v. Zeman, 173 N.E.2d 907 (Ohio Com.Pl. 1961); Green v. Green, 309 P.2d 276 (Okl.1957); Bernier v. Bernier, 101 R.I. 697, 227 A.2d 112 (1967); Brown v.

valid consent.[16] It is probably also clear that it covers common law marriages (where they are recognized) which are void for lack of capacity.[17] But what about the other kinds of relationships which purport to be marriages but are not? For example, does the statute legitimize children when a common law marriage is claimed but is not proved because there is insufficient evidence of present intention to be married?[18] Or does it legitimize the children of a purported common law marriage which is invalid because the state does not recognize common law marriage?[19] Or does it legitimize the children of a liaison which was concededly not a marriage, but which was thought by some friends of the parties to be a marriage, and which lasted for an appreciable time? In fact the language of this second type of statute offers little assistance in answering these questions since, being self-contradictory, it is essentially meaningless. If words are given their usual meaning, a void marriage is a non-existent marriage. This being so, the literal meaning of the statutes is that all children of nonexistent marriages are legitimate. Presumably no court would so construe the statutes. The most sensible construction is that such statutes legitimize the children of all de facto marriages, that is of all relationships which look like marriages and in which the parties behave as husband and wife.

A few cases have chosen to construe this type of statute restrictively, either by requiring some evidence of good faith on the part of the parents,[20] a requirement quite irrelevant to the purpose of the statute, or by requiring that the de facto marriage be contracted before the child's birth, also an irrelevant and unnecessary requirement.[21] The more enlightened contemporary courts have refused to do this, and have insisted that the statute be construed liberally to legitimize the children wherever possible.[22]

A third type of legitimation statute found in a few states[23] provides that children of a void marriage are legitimate if the parents acted in the good faith belief that their marriage was valid, or, if only one acted in good faith, the children are legitimate as to that parent. If neither parent had an honest and reasonable belief in the validity of the marriage, then the child is illegitimate as to both.[24] This form of statute has the doubtful virtue of making it plain that the law's pur-

Commonwealth ex rel. Custis, 218 Va. 40, 235 S.E.2d 325 (1977).

16. Henderson v. Henderson, 187 Va. 121, 46 S.E.2d 10 (1948).

17. Wolf v. Gardner, 386 F.2d 295 (6th Cir.1967); Allen v. Campbell, 208 Ga. 274, 66 S.E.2d 226 (1951); Copenhaver v. Hemphill, 314 Ky. 356, 235 S.W.2d 778 (1951); Santill v. Rossetti, 178 N.E.2d 633 (Ohio Com.Pl. 1961); Whaley v. Peat, 377 S.W.2d 855 (Tex.Civ.App. 1964). The Santill and Wolf cases inject an irrelevant requirement of "good faith" on the part of one of the "spouses" into the statute. This is both unnecessary under the statutory language and undesirable, since the purpose of the statute is to protect children. See Kasey v. Richardson, 462 F.2d 757 (4th Cir.1972).

18. Lester v. Celebrezze, 221 F.Supp. 607 (E.D.Ark. 1963) seems to hold that the legitimation statute does not cover this situation, as does Pace v. Celebrezze, 243 F.Supp. 317 (S.D.W.Va.1965). See also Stutts v. Stutts' Estate, 194 So.2d 229 (Miss.1967).

19. Lester v. Celebrezze, 221 F.Supp. 607 (E.D.Ark. 1963) seems to hold the children of such marriages illegitimate notwithstanding the legitimizing statute, as does Pendleton v. Pendleton, 531 S.W.2d 507 (Ky.1975), judgment vacated 431 U.S. 911, 97 S.Ct. 2164, 53 L.Ed.2d 220 (1977). But Kasey v. Richardson, 462 F.2d 757 (4th Cir. 1972) held a child of a bigamous common law marriage

legitimate where the state (Virginia) did not recognize common law marriage. To the same effect is State v. Bragg, 152 W.Va. 372, 163 S.E.2d 685 (1968), upholding the legitimacy of the child of an invalid common law marriage contracted in West Virginia, which did not recognize such relationships as marriages. This result is clearly correct, since it accomplishes the purpose of the statute.

20. Kasey v. Richardson, 462 F.2d 757 (4th Cir.1972) supports the position of the text, stating that this type of statute applies when the parents of the child have agreed to live together as husband and wife and have represented themselves to the community as married.

21. Bernheimer v. First Nat. Bank of Kansas City, 359 Mo. 1119, 225 S.W.2d 745 (1949); Santill v. Rossetti, 178 N.E.2d 633 (Ohio Com.Pl.1961); Esparza v. Esparza, 382 S.W.2d 162 (Tex.Civ.App.1964).

22. In re Weeast's Estate, 72 N.J.Super. 325, 178 A.2d 113 (1962), overruled by statute, N.J.Stat.Ann. § 2A:34–20 (Supp.1984). Other cases are cited in Annot., 84 A.L.R. 499 (1933).

23. Kasey v. Richardson, 462 F.2d 757 (4th Cir.1972); Home of the Holy Infancy v. Kaska, 397 S.W.2d 208 (Tex. 1965), 44 Tex.L.Rev. 1028 (1966); Brown v. Commonwealth ex rel. Custis, 218 Va. 40, 235 S.E.2d 325 (1977).

24. E.g., La.Civ.Code Ann. arts. 117, 118 (1952).

pose is not to protect the children but to punish them for their parents' wrongs.

A few other legitimation statutes do not fit in any of the foregoing classes. The most important of these is Arizona's, which deals broadly with the problem of legitimacy by providing that every child is the legitimate child of its natural parents and as such is entitled to support and education as if born in lawful wedlock.[25] The most comprehensive and well drawn modern statute on legitimacy also deals with the subject broadly, as it should be dealt with, rather than attacking the narrow issue of the child of an annulled marriage. This is the Uniform Parentage Act,[26] now in force in at least six states.[27] The crux of this Act is section 2, which provides that the parent-child relationship extends to every child and every parent, regardless of the parents' marital relationship. The Act is discussed in detail in a later section of this work.[28] It is only by this form of statute that the troublesome issues of construction raised by more limited statutes can be eliminated and that ordinary justice can be achieved for all children regardless of the accident of their birth.

§ 3.4 The Suit to Annul—Alimony, Temporary and Permanent, and Division of Property

If annulment is viewed as a declaration that no marriage ever existed, it follows that alimony may not be granted, since alimony is

usually described as the substitute for the support which a man owes his wife. If she never was his wife, he owes her no support and no alimony. This section explores the extent to which this is still true in American law.

In the Absence of Statute

Even without statutory authority, most courts are willing to grant temporary alimony and attorney fees to defendant-wives sued by their husbands for annulment, at least when there is a substantial dispute as to the validity of the marriage.[1] The argument is that so long as the wife can make a prima facie showing of a marriage,[2] as by denying under oath the husband's allegations of invalidity,[3] she is entitled to support, including the expenses of litigation, until the invalidity of the marriage is finally established.[4] For this purpose it does not matter whether the marriage is alleged to be void or only voidable.[5] This rule conflicts with the retroactive nature of annulment since if the husband ultimately succeeds in proving there was no valid marriage, he will have been forced to support a woman not his wife and in most instances will be unable to recover back the amounts so paid. Nonetheless the courts evidently feel that the need for supporting wives during litigation is so great as to justify a certain amount of illogic. Conversely, if the defendant-wife concedes that no valid marriage existed, or is unable to deny the husband's alle-

25. Ariz.Rev.Stat. § 8–601 (Supp.1986). See also Alaska Stat. § 25.20.050 (Supp.1984).

26. 9A Unif.L.Ann. 588 (1979). The Act was approved by the National Conference of Commissioners on Uniform State Laws in 1973).

27. California, Colorado, Hawaii, Montana, North Dakota, Washington.

28. See section 4.4, infra.

§ 3.4

1. Peacock v. Peacock, 264 Ala. 332, 87 So.2d 626 (1956); Dietrich v. Dietrich, 41 Cal.2d 497, 261 P.2d 269 (1953), cert. denied 346 U.S. 938, 74 S.Ct. 378, 98 L.Ed. 426 (1954); Middlecoff v. Middlecoff, 171 Cal.App.2d 286, 340 P.2d 331 (1959); Reger v. Reger, 242 Ind. 302, 177 N.E.2d 901 (1961), rehearing denied 242 Ind. 302, 178 N.E.2d 749 (1961); Pickard v. Pickard, 241 Iowa 1307, 45 N.W.2d 269 (1950); Ricard v. Ricard, 143 Iowa 182, 121 N.W. 525 (1909); Zutavern v. Zutavern, 155 Neb. 395, 52

N.W.2d 254 (1952); Callaghan v. Leonard, 152 N.J.Super. 95, 377 A.2d 789 (1977); Barnes v. Barnes, 138 N.J.Eq. 504, 48 A.2d 890 (1946); Bell v. Bell, 122 W.Va. 223, 8 S.E.2d 183 (1940). Other cases are cited in Annot., 110 A.L.R. 1283 (1937), and 4 A.L.R. 926 (1919). Contra: Arndt v. Arndt, 399 Ill. 490, 78 N.E.2d 272 (1948); Smith v. Smith, 99 N.H. 362, 111 A.2d 531 (1955). But see Fowler v. Fowler, 97 N.H. 216, 84 A.2d 836 (1951).

2. Dietrich v. Dietrich, 41 Cal.2d 497, 261 P.2d 269 (1953) cert. denied 346 U.S. 938, 74 S.Ct. 378, 98 L.Ed. 426 (1954).

3. Barnes v. Barnes, 138 N.J.Eq. 504, 48 A.2d 890 (1946).

4. Reger v. Reger, 242 Ind. 302, 177 N.E.2d 901 (1961), rehearing denied 242 Ind. 302, 178 N.E.2d 749 (1961).

5. State ex rel. Reger v. Superior Court of Madison County No. 2, 242 Ind. 241, 177 N.E.2d 908 (1961).

gations, she is given no temporary alimony or attorney fees.[6]

If the wife sues for annulment, the fact that she herself is contending that the marriage is invalid is generally held to defeat her claim for temporary alimony or attorney fees.[7] The courts will not allow her to maintain two inconsistent positions, on the one hand alleging that she is not married to the defendant and never has been, and on the other hand asking that she receive the support due only to a wife.

Where permanent alimony is sought as an incident to a decree annulling a marriage, the great majority of cases have held that it cannot be granted without statutory authority.[8] The reason usually given is the nature of annulment and its dissimilarity to divorce. It would be inconsistent, the courts say, to hold that no marriage ever existed, due to some antecedent incapacity or lack of consent, and then impose on the husband a duty which can only rest upon a valid marriage.[9]

The results of this logic have been so harsh, however, that several courts have chosen to evade them by manufacturing various devices for compensating the "wife". One of the most transparent of these is to order the "husband" to pay the "wife" a fair compensation for the services she performed while they lived together, relying upon a quasi-contractual theory.[10] Another such device is the implied part-

nership. An important Washington case, In re Estate of Thornton,[11] held that a woman who had lived with the deceased for sixteen years and in that time worked successfully to acquire and improve ranch property could be awarded a share of that property on his death as an "implied partner". Since the parties undoubtedly never contemplated the formation of a partnership, this is essentially fictional. Still another technique, this one found in states having a civil law tradition, is the doctrine of putative marriage, which says that a woman who enters into a bigamous or other invalid marriage in good faith, without knowing of the impediment to the marriage, is entitled to community property rights.[12] The doctrine may not be relied upon by a woman who knew the facts which invalidated her marriage, no matter how deserving she might otherwise be.[13] There has been some tendency to rely on this civil law doctrine in common law states as well.[14] Many of these cases do not arise in the context of an annulment proceeding, but since the courts in such a proceeding are faced with the same strong pressure to provide financial protection for the deserving "spouse" as in other marital litigation, there is no reason why these theories should not be as available in annulment as in other proceedings.

An increasing number of courts have taken the broader and less fictional position of divid-

---

6. Kienitz v. Sager, 38 Hawaii 647 (1950); Brown v. Brown, 223 Ind. 463, 61 N.E.2d 645 (1945); Prince v. Freeman, 45 N.M. 143, 112 P.2d 821 (1941).

7. Parmann v. Parmann, 56 Cal.App.2d 67, 132 P.2d 851 (1942); Jones v. Brinsmade, 183 N.Y. 258, 76 N.E. 22 (1905). Other cases are collected in Annots., 110 A.L.R. 1283, 1290 (1937) and 4 A.L.R. 926, 932 (1919).

But if the judicial tendency to treat meretricious relationships as equivalent to marriage persists and is developed further to permit property divisions and permanent alimony without proof of marriage, then it would seem to follow that temporary alimony should also be granted in appropriate circumstances, whether the claimant is plaintiff or defendant in the annulment suit. See the discussion of permanent alimony below, and also section 1.2, supra.

8. Cases are collected in Annots., 54 A.L.R.2d 1410 (1957), and 81 A.L.R.3d 281 (1977), and in Note, The Aftereffects of Annulment: Alimony, Property Division, Provision for Children, 1968 Wash.U.L.Q. 148.

9. Whitebird v. Luckey, 180 Okl. 1, 67 P.2d 775 (1937).

10. Sanguinetti v. Sanguinetti, 9 Cal.2d 95, 69 P.2d 845 (1937). See also Annot., 111 A.L.R. 348 (1937), and Note, 33 Minn.L.Rev. 321 (1949).

11. 81 Wash.2d 72, 499 P.2d 864 (1972), 48 Wash.L. Rev. 635 (1973). See also Brandt v. Brandt, 215 Or. 423, 333 P.2d 887 (1958); and Marvin v. Marvin, 18 Cal.3d 660, 134 Cal.Rptr. 815, 557 P.2d 106 (1976) discussed in § 1.2, supra.

12. Annot., 34 A.L.R.2d 1255, 1291 (1953). A further discussion of putative marriage may be found in section 2.4, supra, at note 63. See also Wilkinson v. Wilkinson, 12 Cal.App.3d 1164, 91 Cal.Rptr. 372 (1970).

13. Shore v. Shore, 43 Cal.2d 677, 277 P.2d 4 (1954).

14. Sclamberg v. Sclamberg, 220 Ind. 209, 41 N.E.2d 801 (1942). The Uniform Marriage and Divorce Act § 209, 9A Unif.L.Ann. 115 (1979) adopts the doctrine of the putative spouse. And Buck v. Buck, 19 Utah 2d 161, 427 P.2d 954 (1967) seems to apply a putative spouse theory without calling it that in order to give the woman an equitable share of the man's property in an annulment suit.

ing the property of the parties, as they would in divorce. If this is done solely on the basis of equitable ownership, giving to each that property to which he has equitable or legal title, it can hardly be said to be a substitute for alimony.[15] But there are cases which use criteria for the division of property more appropriate to alimony than to the ascertainment of ownership.[16] Such factors as the needs of the "spouse", the length of time during which the parties have lived together, the services in or out of the home performed by the "spouse" are all considered in arriving at a share of the property, as would be true in a divorce suit.[17] The much discussed case of Marvin v. Marvin[18] divided property between persons having what the court calls a nonmarital relationship on theories of implied contract, constructive trust or other even less precisely defined equitable doctrines. The reasons for doing so, as expressed in the court's opinion, were the pervasiveness of nonmarital relationships in modern society, the desire to vindicate the expectations of the parties, and a recognition that both parties by their efforts contributed (perhaps in quite indirect ways) to the accumulation of the property. If Marvin is correct in holding that property may be divided when the relationship involved makes no pretense of being a marriage, then it would seem to follow a fortiori that this may be done where the par-

ties have had their marriage annulled. In fact the reasons given for the result in Marvin would support an award of alimony just as well as a division of property. If this final step is taken, however, the courts will have placed themselves in the uncomfortable position of destroying the significance of marriage so far as it concerns money or property. Even the Marvin court was unwilling to go this far, although it never explained why it would not other than by including a disingenuous sentence or two on the social importance of marriage.

Statutory Authority for Alimony in Annulment

One method by which the legislatures of some states have tried to solve this problem is to include some of the grounds for annulment in the divorce statute, as for example by authorizing divorce on the ground of bigamous marriage. Aside from the violence done to the logical distinction between the two actions, this is a sensible method, and allows the court to grant alimony unless it is so bound up in its logic as to refuse, as some courts have.[19]

Other states have attacked the problem more directly by providing for the granting of alimony in annulment suits in the trial court's discretion.[20] This is certainly the best way to provide the necessary financial protec-

15. Short v. Short, 102 N.E.2d 719 (Ohio App.1951). See also Rickards v. Rickards, 53 Del. (3 Storey) 134, 166 A.2d 425 (1960); Kantor v. Kantor, 133 N.J.Eq. 491, 33 A.2d 110 (1943) (wedding gifts). Other cases are cited in Annot., 31 A.L.R.2d 1255 (1953), and Note, 76 U.Pa.L.Rev. 439 (1928).

16. E.g., Coats v. Coats, 160 Cal. 671, 118 P. 441 (1911); Fung Dai Kim Ah Leong v. Lau Ah Leong, 27 F.2d 582 (9th Cir.1928); Walker v. Walker, 330 Mich. 332, 47 N.W.2d 633 (1951); Chrismond v. Chrismond, 211 Miss. 746, 52 So.2d 624 (1951), cert. denied 342 U.S. 878, 72 S.Ct. 167, 96 L.Ed. 659 (1951); White v. White, 283 S.C. 348, 323 S.E.2d 521 (1984); Jenkins v. Jenkins, 107 Utah 239, 153 P.2d 262 (1944). Other cases are cited in Annot., 31 A.L.R.2d 1255 (1953). For sweeping dictum that the wife may have no part of the husband's property as a result of annulment, see Burnett v. Burnett, 192 Kan. 247, 387 P.2d 195 (1963).

17. See section 13.7, infra.

18. 18 Cal.3d 660, 134 Cal.Rptr. 815, 557 P.2d 106 (1976). See also Latham v. Hennessey, 87 Wash.2d 550, 554 P.2d 1057 (1976) (Dictum that if a "long-term, stable,

nonmarital family relationship" exists the court could assume that both parties contributed to the acquisition of property and could therefore divide the property on a "just and equitable" basis.) For a discussion of these cases and an argument for judicial recognition of nonmarital relationships, see Bruch, Property Rights of De Facto Spouses Including Thoughts on the Value of Homemakers' Services, 10 Fam.L.Q. 101 (1976). A case which limits the division of property to instances of express contract is Tyranski v. Piggins, 44 Mich.App. 570, 205 N.W.2d 595 (1973).

19. See section 14.8, Practitioner's Edition, infra, and Burger v. Burger, 166 So.2d 433 (Fla.1964); Clayton v. Clayton, 231 Md. 74, 188 A.2d 550 (1963); Roth v. Roth, 49 Md.App. 433, 433 A.2d 1162 (1981). For a discussion of the unusual Georgia statute, see Wallace v. Wallace, 221 Ga. 510, 145 S.E.2d 546 (1965).

20. E.g., Alaska Stat. § 25.24.160 (1983) (permanent alimony); West's Ann.Cal.Civ.Code § 4455 (1983) (temporary alimony may be awarded to a putative spouse); Colo. Rev.Stat. § 14–10–111 (1973) (maintenance); Conn.Gen. Stat.Ann. § 46b–60 (1986) (alimony may be awarded as in

tion to deserving "wives." It is difficult to understand why more states have not enacted these statutes.

Some of the alimony statutes impose slightly different standards for the granting of alimony in annulment than in divorce, as by authorizing alimony only to the innocent spouse.[21] In most cases, however, the criteria leading to the determination of the amount of alimony are the same.[22] And the installment alimony awarded in annulment is modifiable as it would be in divorce.[23]

By virtue of these statutes, therefore, one more of the supposed distinctions between divorce and annulment has been eliminated, and one more step taken in the direction of the assimilation of the two actions.

§ 3.5   The Suit to Annul—Effect of the Decree

Res Judicata

The question here is whether or to what extent the annulment decree is to be treated as being a conclusive adjudication of the validity or invalidity of the marriage, binding not only on the parties to the suit but on all other persons whose rights or obligations may turn on the asserted marriage.[1] Here again the in rem-in personam distinction creates unnecessary difficulty. Some courts have labelled annulment in personam when faced

with questions of the method of service,[2] without considering that the label might control the effect to be given to the decree by courts for whom labels are controlling. In fact the two issues are distinct and are affected by somewhat different considerations, although the opportunity to be heard is, broadly speaking, at the heart of both.

A choice between values has to be made when rules of res judicata are under examination. One such value is the opportunity to be heard, to present one's case. On the other side, in addition to the need for finality, which is the countervailing element in ordinary cases, there is in matrimonial cases the factor that the parties to the marriage are the persons most concerned with its existence. This is true even though the rights of third persons often do depend on whether a marriage exists or not. The rights of such third persons are in a real sense derivative, or secondary. No matter how clearly these rights may depend on the existence of a marriage, they are not of the same degree of importance, seriousness or consequence as the interests of the spouses themselves in the marriage. It is perhaps this factor that has led to the well-established rule that a decree of divorce is conclusive on third parties with respect to the termination of the marriage.[3] It is the writer's view that a decree of annulment should have the same effect. The di-

---

divorce); Iowa Code Ann. § 598.32 (1981); N.H.Rev.Stat. Ann. § 458.19 (Supp.1981); N.Y.–McKinney's Dom.Rel. Law § 236 (Supp.1984) (temporary and permanent alimony); Or.Rev.Stat. §§ 107.095, 107.105 (1983) (temporary and permanent alimony); West's Rev.Code Wash.Ann. § 26.09.090 (Supp.1985); Wis.Stat.Ann. § 767.26 (1981). See also Callaghan v. Leonard, 152 N.J.Super. 95, 377 A.2d 789 (1977).

The Uniform Marriage and Divorce Act § 208, 9A Unif.L.Ann. 111 (1979) provides that the court may declare the marriage invalid non-retroactively if it finds the interests of justice require this. If the court enters a non-retroactive decree, it may then also grant maintenance and a division of property to the spouse. The injection of the retroactivity issue into this question may be logical but it is quite senseless. A well drawn statute should authorize alimony in all annulment cases, in the discretion of the trial court.

21. See the Iowa and Wisconsin statutes cited supra, note 20, which permit alimony only to the spouse who did not know of the condition making the marriage invalid. See also Wald v. Wald, 239 Or. 351, 397 P.2d 541 (1964),

requiring a finding of unusual circumstances under the Oregon statute.

22. For example, fault may be relevant, Jacobson v. Jacobson, 36 Misc.2d 59, 232 N.Y.S.2d 467 (Sup.Ct.1962), but it is not necessarily conclusive. Thus in Johnson v. Johnson, 295 N.Y. 477, 68 N.E.2d 499 (1946) alimony was awarded to a woman who had contracted a bigamous marriage.

23. Rhinehart v. Rhinehart, 274 App.Div. 898, 82 N.Y.S.2d 796 (2d Dep't 1948). See also Roe v. Doe, 68 Misc.2d 833, 328 N.Y.S.2d 506 (1972).

§ 3.5

1. Throughout the discussion in this section it is assumed that the annulment decree was based upon proper jurisdiction, both of person and subject matter.

2. See section 3.2, supra.

3. Restatement, Judgments § 74 (1942). See also Blumenthal v. Blumenthal, 97 Cal.App. 558, 275 P. 987 (1929), and 2 Freeman, Judgments, § 910 (5th ed. 1925).

vorce cases have reached this result in spite of the fact, now often conceded,[4] that the parties in divorce cases are usually not really adversaries and do not actively litigate the question of grounds. This means that what amounts to a consent decree is given a broader effect by way of res judicata than the ordinary personal judgment arrived at after a vigorous contest. The likelihood that issues will not be actively litigated is less in annulment, but it does exist. Since it is less, there is all the more reason to give annulment decrees the same binding effect upon non-parties in subsequent litigation which is given to divorce decrees.

An illustration may make the position clearer.[5] H–1 and W are married. In a suit based upon jurisdiction the court annuls the marriage for W's nonage. She later marries H–2 and subsequently sues him for non-support. It would be intolerable if, in the non-support action, H–2 were allowed to present evidence that W had not been under age when she married H–1, that she was still married to him, and that she was not married to H–2. Certainty and finality concerning the marital relationship are to be desired in such cases far beyond H–2's claim to have a day in court on the validity of the first marriage.

Most of the cases hold that annulment decrees are binding upon non-parties as well as parties respecting the validity of the marriages involved.[6] A small minority of state statutes provide, however, that annulment decrees bind only the parties or those claiming under them.[7] Such statutes express an unsound policy. They would, for example, allow H–2 in the illustrative case to prove that the first marriage was valid and that the second marriage was therefore invalid, since H–2 would not seem to be "claiming under" either party to the annulment suit.[8]

Although the annulment decree should be, and usually is, binding on third persons as to the marital status, it is not, and should not be, binding on such persons with respect to the facts underlying the decree.[9] Thus, for example, a decree annulling a marriage for fraud, based upon a false representation of paternity, does not bind the child with respect to the finding of non-paternity, though it does bind him with respect to the termination of the marriage.[10] One significant case reached the opposite conclusion in applying an earlier decree validating a marriage, but it appears to be based upon an erroneous reading of precedent.[11] The needs for certainty and finality which require a broad application of res judicata to the decision on the marital status do not apply with respect to the find-

4. A leading judicial discussion is by Judge Goodrich in Alton v. Alton, 207 F.2d 667 (3d Cir.1953).

5. This is substantially Post v. Post, 71 Misc. 44, 129 N.Y.S. 754 (1911), affirmed 149 App.Div. 452, 133 N.Y.S. 1057 (1st Dep't 1912), affirmed 210 N.Y. 607, 104 N.E. 1139 (1914).

6. Luke v. Hill, 137 Ga. 159, 73 S.E. 345 (1911) (dictum); Commonwealth v. Shaman, 223 Mass. 62, 111 N.E. 720 (1916); Burlen v. Shannon, 69 Mass. (3 Gray) 387 (1855) (dictum); Presbrey v. Presbrey, 6 A.D.2d 477, 179 N.Y.S.2d 788 (1st Dep't 1958) (dictum); Post v. Post, 71 Misc. 44, 129 N.Y.S. 754 (Sup.Ct.1911), affirmed 149 App. Div. 452, 133 N.Y.S. 1057 (1st Dep't 1912), affirmed 210 N.Y. 607, 104 N.E. 1139 (1914); Commonwealth ex rel. Di Donato v. Di Donato, 156 Pa.Super. 385, 40 A.2d 892 (1945); Cecil v. Cecil, 11 Utah 2d 155, 356 P.2d 279 (1960); 2 Freeman, Judgments, 1919 (5th ed. 1925); The Restatement of Judgments § 74 (1942) may be construed to support the text statement though it applies the rule, unfortunately, only to actions in rem, without stating whether annulment is in rem. As has been urged throughout this work, the in rem-in personam language should never be used as a reason for reaching one result or another in matrimonial actions.

One case, Hallford v. Industrial Commission, 63 Ariz. 40, 159 P.2d 305 (1945), permitted the industrial commission to attack on non-jurisdictional grounds a wife's annulment decree, but the court failed to give any real consideration to the issue of third-party attack on such decrees. The case has been overruled in part by Jackson v. Industrial Commission, 121 Ariz. 602, 592 P.2d 1258 (1979).

7. E.g., West's Ann.Cal.Civ.Code § 4451 (1983); Idaho Code § 32–505 (1983); N.D.Cent.Code § 14–04–05 (1981).

8. Cf. Briggs v. United States, 116 Ct.Cl. 638, 90 F.Supp. 135 (1950).

9. Blumenthal v. Blumenthal, 97 Cal.App. 558, 275 P. 987 (1929); In re Holmes' Estate, 291 N.Y. 261, 52 N.E.2d 424 (1943); Post v. Post, 71 Misc. 44, 129 N.Y.S. 754 (Sup. Ct.1911), affirmed 149 App.Div. 452, 133 N.Y.S. 1057 (1st Dep't 1912), affirmed 210 N.Y. 607, 104 N.E. 1139 (1914); Restatement, Judgments § 74, comment c (1942).

10. Shatford v. Shatford, 214 Ark. 612, 217 S.W.2d 917 (1949).

11. Headen v. Pope & Talbot, Inc., 252 F.2d 739 (3d Cir.1958), relying upon In re Holben's Estate, 300 Pa. 169, 150 A. 604 (1930).

ings of fact underlying that decision. Therefore the person who was not a party to the annulment suit should be given his day in court with respect to such facts. Hence the distinction in the cases.

Retroactivity [12]

The problem here is, assuming that annulment decrees are binding upon persons not parties to the suit, to what extent may such decrees affect rights and obligations which have accrued before the decree was rendered? This problem arises in a bewildering variety of situations, but a single illustration is sufficient at this point.[13] W and H–1 are married and divorced, the decree ordering H–1 to pay alimony until W remarries. W later does remarry, and H–1 stops paying alimony. Still later W's second marriage is annulled and she brings the appropriate proceeding for requiring H–1 (a) to resume alimony payments; and (b) pay her the installments which accrued during the time she lived with her second "husband." W's argument is plain and logical: The conventional analysis of annulment is that it "relates back," it establishes that there never was a marriage, and that the purported marriage was null and void ab initio. If this is so, the legal position is as if no second marriage had ever occurred. H–1 therefore owes alimony for the entire period during which the purported second marriage existed and from that time on into the future. Given the premise as to the legal nature of annulment, the conclusion seems to be inescapable.

The rub comes from the fact that the conduct of the persons involved has not been consistent with the legal nature of annulment. For a time at least, W and H–2 have acted as if they were married, and H–1, believing they were married, also acted on that assumption. If later on a court decides they never were married, H–1's expectations about his own legal obligations will be upset. The stage is then set for an application of what may be called the de facto principle, familiar in many different legal contexts.[14] This principle determines the parties' rights and duties on the basis of their own characterization of their situation, rather than on the basis of the existing legal characterization. In the present context it means that persons not "really" married are treated as if they were.

When people behave in a manner inconsistent with their legal relations, the courts face the difficult issue of choosing between the law's demands and the parties' expectations. In such cases the reconciliation of law and conduct is not possible. One interest must be sacrificed to the other. It is not surprising that all courts do not choose between the conflicting principles on the same grounds or with the same results. In fact, it is this sort of conflict which produces more diversity and confusion in the decisions than any other with which the law must deal.[15]

We may therefore expect the cases on annulment to be far from agreement on the matter of "relation back". This is not a recent development. Some of the older cases refused to apply the traditional analysis of annulment as declaring that no marriage ever existed,[16] while others did apply that analysis.[17] Today there is still some disagreement, but one line of cases suggests a rationale for dealing with the conflict which is being accepted in many jurisdictions. Many of the

---

12. See Note, The Void and Voidable Marriage: A Study in Judicial Method, 7 Stanf.L.Rev. 529 (1955). For a brief discussion of this issue as related to separation agreements, see section 16.6, infra.

13. This illustration is substantially Sleicher v. Sleicher, 251 N.Y. 366, 167 N.E. 501 (1929), and other cases cited infra, notes 18–26.

14. Perhaps best known is the de facto corporation. See Frey, Legal Analysis and the "De Facto" Doctrine, 100 U.Pa.L.Rev. 1153 (1952).

15. Again de facto corporations are a notorious example. See Frey, op. cit. note 14.

16. E.g. State v. Richards, 175 Minn. 498, 221 N.W. 867 (1928); Jordan v. Missouri & Kansas Tel. Co., 136 Mo. App. 192, 116 S.W. 432 (1909); Wolf v. Wolf, 111 Misc. 391, 181 N.Y.S. 368 (1920), reversed on other grounds, 194 App.Div. 33, 185 N.Y.S. 37 (2d Dep't 1920); Burney v. State, 111 Tex.Cr.R. 599, 13 S.W.2d 375 (1929), 8 Tex.L. Rev. 142 (1929).

17. Henneger v. Lomas, 145 Ind. 287, 44 N.E. 462 (1896); Eichhoff v. Eichhoff, 101 Cal. 600, 36 P. 11 (1894); Taylor v. White, 160 N.C. 38, 75 S.E. 941 (1912).

hard cases could be solved by carefully drawn statutes.

The line of cases referred to begins with Sleicher v. Sleicher.[18] The facts of the case were like those in the illustration.[19] The New York Court of Appeals, although faced with precedent which adopted the relation back analysis in sweeping (and very harsh) terms,[20] took a compromise position. It held that the alimony payments revived as of the date of the annulment decree, but that alimony was not payable for the period during which the woman lived with her second husband. The logic of relation back was thus in part abandoned. The reason given was that the woman had in fact received support from her second husband while she lived with him, and it would have been unfair to duplicate that support by a fully retroactive alimony order. In other words, the second "marriage" was treated as a marriage so long as it existed. The second case, Gaines v. Jacobsen,[21] was decided after New York enacted a statute authorizing alimony in annulment suits.[22] The Gaines case held that this in effect altered the Sleicher rule, and justified a termination of the first husband's alimony obligation when the ex-wife contracted an invalid second marriage. Since she could obtain alimony from her second "husband," the argument went, he became her source of support, so that there would be no more reason to revive the alimony decree than if the second marriage had ended in divorce. The court expressly disclaimed any distinction for this purpose between void and voidable marriages, although there are a few cases which make the result turn on that distinction.[23] Finally, the California court in Sefton v. Sefton [24] followed Gaines v. Jacobsen even though California has no statute authorizing alimony in annulment suits. The reasoning was that the first husband, when his ex-wife remarries, has no way of knowing that the marriage is invalid, is entitled to assume that his alimony obligation is at an end, and to recommit his assets to other uses if he so desires. In other words, the court fully adopted the de facto principle and vindicated the expectations of the parties. The great majority of authorities reach the same result, whether or not the particular state has a statute authorizing alimony in annulment proceedings.[25] The Uniform Marriage and Divorce Act contains a provision

---

18. 251 N.Y. 366, 167 N.E. 501 (1929).

19. See note 13, supra.

20. In re Moncrief's Will, 235 N.Y. 390, 139 N.E. 550 (1923).

21. 308 N.Y. 218, 124 N.E.2d 290 (1954), 41 Corn.L.Q. 141 (1955), 68 Harv.L.Rev. 1076 (1955).

22. N.Y.–McKinney's Dom.Rel.Law § 236 (Supp.1984).

23. E.g., Broadus v. Broadus, 361 So.2d 582 (Ala.Civ. App.1978); Reese v. Reese, 192 So.2d 1 (Fla.1966); Kelley v. Kelley, 350 So.2d 11 (Fla.App.1977), cert. denied 358 So.2d 131 (Fla.1978); Wertheim v. Wertheim, 262 So.2d 723 (Fla.App.1972); State v. Richards, 175 Minn. 498, 221 N.W. 867 (1928); Darling v. Darling, 44 Ohio App.2d 5, 335 N.E.2d 708 (1975); McConkey v. McConkey, 216 Va. 106, 215 S.E.2d 640 (1975), though the court disclaims making any decision as to the effect of a void marriage. Callow v. Thomas, 322 Mass. 550, 78 N.E.2d 637 (1948) relied on the void-voidable distinction, but seems to have been overruled on this point by Glazer v. Silverman, 354 Mass. 177, 236 N.E.2d 199 (1968). Likewise Minder v. Minder, 83 N.J.Super. 159, 199 A.2d 69 (1964) relied on the distinction but that analysis seems to have been disapproved by Flaxman v. Flaxman, 57 N.J. 458, 273 A.2d 567 (1971). Boren v. Windham, 425 So.2d 1353 (Miss.1983) also disclaimed any reliance in the distinction and terminated the alimony. Needless to say, in the writer's view the void-voidable distinction should not be relevant on the issue of relation back. Even though it is only voidable, if the marriage is in fact annulled, the decree logically establishes that no marriage ever existed because of the pre-marital condition or incapacity. Analytically the problem is the same as for void marriages, so long as an annulment decree has been entered. And the expectations of the parties may well be the same where the marriage is void as where it is voidable, in both instances the first husband being likely to assume that his obligation ends when his ex-wife goes through a ceremony. In any event he should be given specific advance assurance that he can make that assumption, without being concerned about possible future events.

A very few cases solve the relation back problem by the specious device of referring to the intent of the parties, where a separation agreement is the source of the alimony obligation. Of course if the parties expressed their intentions about the effect of an invalid subsequent marriage, this would indeed solve the problem. But when the agreement or decree merely refers to "remarriage", there is no expression of intention and the courts must then decide, on the reasoning suggested in the text, whether the alimony terminates upon the occurrence of an invalid remarriage. A case purporting to rely upon this sort of specious reasoning is Dodd v. Dodd, 210 Kan. 50, 499 P.2d 518 (1972).

24. 45 Cal.2d 872, 291 P.2d 439 (1955).

25. Hodges v. Hodges, 118 Ariz. 572, 578 P.2d 1001 (App.1978); Fry v. Fry, 5 Cal.App.3d 169, 85 Cal.Rptr. 126

which enables the court to get this result.[26] To this extent therefore annulment has the same effect on a prior alimony order as divorce would have.

It is important to notice that Sefton did not turn on a finding that the first husband had in fact relied on the validity of the second marriage. The facts were that this marriage lasted only one week, so that he could hardly have changed his position in reliance upon it. The meaning of the case is that it gives ex-husbands notice that they may assume the validity of the second marriage and act accordingly. If it had not gone that far, as a recent Utah case refused to do,[27] it would

have set up a trap for the unwary, since ex-husbands in this position would then never be able to decide with certainty at what point they could safely assume that their alimony obligations had come to an end. This is the kind of common law principle therefore which does not and should not rest on the conduct of the particular parties, but rather which gives all parties assurance that they may rely on appearances. In other words, the court announces a rule for the future rather than one based on events in the past.

There are cases contrary to those just described.[28] They turn partly upon a desire to provide the ex-wife with support at any cost,

(1970); Berkely v. Berkely, 269 Cal.App.2d 872, 75 Cal. Rptr. 294 (1969); In re Marriage of Kolb, 99 Ill.App.3d 895, 55 Ill.Dec. 128, 425 N.E.2d 1301 (1981); Beebe v. Beebe, 227 Ga. 248, 179 S.E.2d 758 (1971); Surabian v. Surabian, 362 Mass. 342, 285 N.E.2d 909 (1972); Glazer v. Silverman, 354 Mass. 177, 236 N.E.2d 199 (1968); Gerrig v. Sneirson, 344 Mass. 518, 183 N.E.2d 131 (1962); Bridges v. Bridges, 217 So.2d 281 (Miss.1968); Glass v. Glass, 546 S.W.2d 738 (Mo.App.1977); Ballew v. Ballew, 187 Neb. 397, 191 N.W.2d 462 (1971); Flaxman v. Flaxman, 57 N.J. 458, 273 A.2d 567 (1971) (semble); Sharpe v. Sharpe, 57 N.J. 468, 273 A.2d 572 (1971); Richards v. Richards, 139 N.J.Super. 207, 353 A.2d 141 (1976); Chavez v. Chavez, 82 N.M. 624, 485 P.2d 735 (1971); Denberg v. Frischman, 17 N.Y.2d 778, 270 N.Y.S.2d 627, 217 N.E.2d 675 (1966), cert. denied 385 U.S. 884, 87 S.Ct. 176, 17 L.Ed.2d 111 (1966). See also Annots., 48 A.L.R.2d 270, 296, 318, 329 (1956), and 45 A.L.R.3d 1033 (1972). Contra, holding the alimony revived, Peters v. Peters, 214 N.W.2d 151 (Iowa 1974). The Utah court seems uncertain on the problem, but may be taking the position that revival of the alimony turns on how much the wife is in need of it. Cf. Kent v. Kent, 28 Utah 2d 34, 497 P.2d 652 (1972) with Ferguson v. Ferguson, 564 P.2d 1380 (Utah 1977). And McCord v. McCord, 558 S.W.2d 624 (Ky.1977) held that the alimony did not revive, but the court relied in part upon the void-voidable distinction, and in part upon a "balancing of the equities", whatever that may mean.

In In re Marriage of Weintraub, 167 Cal.App.3d 420, 213 Cal.Rptr. 159 (1985) a woman alleged that she contracted a second marriage against her will and as a result of an abduction, physical beatings and coercion. This second marriage was annulled on the ground of duress, and she then sought to reinstate spousal support pursuant to a prior divorce decree. The court held that the basis for Sefton was to accomplish substantial justice between the parties. Therefore if the woman could prove that her second marriage was not due to any voluntary act on her part, the spousal support should be reinstated.

26. Uniform Marriage and Divorce Act § 208, 9A Unif.L.Ann. (1979), providing that unless the court finds after a consideration of all relevant circumstances that the interests of justice would be served by making the decree not retroactive, it shall declare the marriage inval-

id as of the date of the marriage. This is a clumsy way of partially dealing with the problem. In many cases the court granting the annulment may have difficulty determining the relevant circumstances, since the first husband may not be before him. The Colorado statute is even less satisfactory, since it provides that in all cases the marriage is to be declared invalid retroactively, thereby presumably requiring a result contrary to most courts' ideas of equity. Colo.Rev.Stat. § 14–10–111 (1973).

27. Cecil v. Cecil, 11 Utah 2d 155, 356 P.2d 279 (1960), in which the woman lived with her second "husband" for only a few weeks, then obtaining an annulment for mental incompetence. The court was persuaded that in this particular instance the first husband had not changed his position in reliance upon her second marriage. But this leaves in uncertainty the question of how much time must elapse, or what action must be taken, before the court will find that there has been reliance and hence that it is inequitable to revive the alimony. It is far better under the circumstances to use the Sefton approach, although obviously this does deprive the woman of support. The woman's mental incompetence made this particularly unfortunate in Cecil, but the proper remedy is a statute authorizing alimony in annulment suits, as in New York. After all, the first husband is not the state welfare department. A case like Cecil is Robbins v. Robbins, 343 Mass. 247, 178 N.E.2d 281 (1961).

Cecil was distinguished and alimony held not to revive after annulment in Ferguson v. Ferguson, 564 P.2d 1380 (Utah 1977). See also Russell v. Russell, 587 P.2d 133 (Utah 1978).

28. The most egregious is Sutton v. Leib, 199 F.2d 163 (7th Cir.1952), on remand from 342 U.S. 402, 72 S.Ct. 398, 96 L.Ed. 448 (1952), 26 So.Cal.L.Rev. 448 (1953), applying Illinois law. Here the woman lived with her second husband about three years and then got an annulment on the ground of a prior subsisting marriage. The court not only revived the alimony as against the first husband, but made him pay the arrears which had accrued during the time she lived with her second husband and during which she was presumably supported by the second husband. See also Peters v. Peters, 214 N.W.2d 151 (Iowa 1974); Kent v. Kent, 28 Utah 2d 34, 497 P.2d 652 (1972);

overlooking the facts that she had some support from her second husband and that such a holding may upset long-standing expectations. For the most part, however, such cases merely sacrifice the de facto principle to the logic of relation back.

It is possible that under certain conditions relation back and the de facto principle may both point to the same result rather than being in opposition to each other. For example, H and W–1 are married. H then goes through a ceremony with W–2. If W–1 later gets an annulment of her marriage to H, and the decree is retroactive, this would validate the marriage to W–2 and at the same time vindicate the expectations of H and W–2.[29] Therefore, the proper result in such a case is to make the decree retroactive.

The conflicts problem created by the diversity of approach among the states seems not to have come before the courts.[30] The case would arise where the alimony decree is entered in state A and the wife's second marriage annulled in state B, the question then being which state's law should govern as to the effect of the annulment on the alimony judgment. The conventional full faith and credit analysis is that the annulment decree should be given that effect in other states which it would be given in the state of rendition.[31] This result would be the more likely if state B permitted alimony to be awarded in

annulment suits. But if the wife remained domiciled in state A at the time the question arose, that state's interest in her status, coupled with the fact that the effect of its own judgment is at stake, might very well lead state A to apply its own law to the case.[32] This is a situation, however, in which the usual uncertainty of conflicts issues is highly undesirable because of the need for both parties to know, without extensive litigation, what their rights and obligations are as a result of the annulment. For that reason it is submitted that the rule should be that state A should give that effect to the annulment decree which state B would give, under the Full Faith and Credit Clause.[33] In this case certainty should prevail over local chauvinism, "minimum contacts" or other conflicts arguments.

In contrast with the alimony cases, in which the conduct and expectations of the parties have largely led the courts to rely on the de facto principle, are the pension, workmen's compensation and social security cases, in which the absence of these factors has resulted in adherence to the principle of retroactivity. The leading case is Folsom v. Pearsall.[34] There W received social security benefits as the widow of H–1. She married H–2 and the payments stopped, since the statute provides that they shall continue only until the widow's remarriage.[35] This second

---

Broadus v. Broadus, 361 So.2d 582 (Ala.Civ.App.1978); Thomas v. Thomas, 111 Ill.App.3d 1032, 67 Ill.Dec. 590, 444 N.E.2d 826 (1983) (based on a construction of the divorce decree by the parties).

29. Eichhoff v. Eichhoff, 101 Cal. 600, 36 P. 11 (1894); Taylor v. White, 160 N.C. 38, 75 S.E. 941 (1912). See also Jordan v. Missouri & Kansas Tel. Co., 136 Mo.App. 192, 116 S.W. 432 (1909). Contra: Tetterton v. Arctic Tankers, Inc., 116 F.Supp. 429 (E.D.Pa.1953).

30. One case, MacPherson v. MacPherson, 496 F.2d 258 (6th Cir.1974), deals with the choice of law issue when the alimony is based upon a separation agreement rather than a decree, finding that the law of the place where the agreement was executed governs. The divorce decree was not involved in that case, however.

31. Aldrich v. Aldrich, 378 U.S. 540, 84 S.Ct. 1687, 12 L.Ed.2d 1020 (1964).

32. Cf. Colby v. Colby, 78 Nev. 150, 369 P.2d 1019 (1962), cert. denied 371 U.S. 888, 83 S.Ct. 186, 9 L.Ed.2d 122 (1962), 63 Colum.L.Rev. 560 (1963). This seems to be the result in Johnston v. Johnston, 3 Kan.App.2d 208, 592 P.2d 132 (1979).

33. U.S. Const. art. IV, § 1. Denberg v. Frischman, 17 N.Y.2d 778, 270 N.Y.S.2d 627, 217 N.E.2d 675 (1966), cert. denied 385 U.S. 884, 87 S.Ct. 176, 17 L.Ed.2d 111 (1966), in a dissenting opinion by Keating, J., suggests that the law of the state of the annulment might apply, but the question is not thoroughly discussed, nor is the constitutional point considered at all.

34. 245 F.2d 562 (9th Cir.1957). On the determination of marital status for federal law purposes, see Seidelson and Bowler, Determination of Family Status in the Administration of Federal Acts: A Choice of Law Problem for Federal Agencies and Courts, 33 G.W.L.Rev. 863 (1965).

For an extensive discussion of the definition of marriage and of remarriage for purposes of veterans' benefits, social security benefits and railroad retirement pensions, see Rombauer, Marital Status and Eligibility for Federal Statutory Income Benefits: A Historical Survey, 52 Wash.L.Rev. 227 (1977).

35. 42 U.S.C.A. § 402(e).

marriage was then annulled for fraud. The court held, applying California law, that no factor of reliance by the parties was involved, that the basis of the Sefton case did not exist here, and therefore the annulment decree should have retroactive effect. In consequence, the social security benefits revived. The outcome of the case was influenced by the broad policy underlying the social security laws, of protecting and providing support from public funds for aged and dependent persons. It is a very different thing to support the widow by this means than to support her out of the usually limited resources of a first husband. Most of the other cases involving social security and state workmen's compensation claims have reached the same result, making the annulment retroactive in order to protect the woman.[36] In New York, however, Nott v. Flemming [37] has held that the annulment is not retroactive, so that social security benefits do not revive when the second marriage is annulled. The court in that case reasoned that the purpose of the social security system is to give the widow a minimum level of support, until she acquires another source of support by remarriage. Re-

marriage in New York gives her this support even though the marriage later turns out to be invalid, since there is statutory authority to give her alimony in the annulment suit.[38] There is thus no more need for social security benefits when she contracts a second invalid marriage than when she contracts a second marriage which is valid.

In situations intermediate between alimony and public support programs, the few cases seem to find the annulment retroactive, on the ground that no expectations or reliance are thereby upset. In some instances, however, it would seem that there might be reliance upon the appearance of the second marriage, and if so, the de facto principle would oppose retroactivity. For example, where a trust is set up for W until her remarriage, she remarries and then gets an annulment,[39] there might very well be such reliance by the trustee as to justify a refusal to revive the payments when the annulment occurred.

A scattering of other cases involve the question of relation back in circumstances where it is difficult to see the need for application of the de facto principle, but where other policy

---

36. Stamer v. United States, 148 Ct.Cl. 482 (1960) (soldier's death gratuity); Starace v. Celebrezze, 233 F.Supp. 452 (W.D.Pa.1964) (social security); Holland v. Ribicoff, 219 F.Supp. 274 (D.Or.1962) (social security); Sparks v. United States, 153 F.Supp. 909 (D.Vt.1957) (social security); Mays v. Folsom, 143 F.Supp. 784 (D.Idaho 1956) (social security); Means v. Industrial Commission, 110 Ariz. 72, 515 P.2d 29 (1973) (workmen's compensation); United States Fidelity & Guaranty Co. v. Industrial Commission, 25 Ariz.App. 244, 542 P.2d 825 (1975) (workmen's compensation); State Compensation Fund v. Foughty, 13 Ariz.App. 381, 476 P.2d 902 (1970) (workmen's compensation); Cottam v. Los Angeles, 184 Cal.App.2d 523, 7 Cal.Rptr. 734 (1960) (policeman's pension); Eureka Block Coal Co. v. Wells, 83 Ind.App. 181, 147 N.E. 811 (1925) (workmen's compensation); Renzo v. Reid Ice Cream Corp., 254 App.Div. 794, 4 N.Y.S.2d 274 (3d Dep't 1938) (workmen's compensation); Foster v. American Radiator Co., 249 App.Div. 460, 292 N.Y.S. 894 (3d Dep't 1937) (workmen's compensation); First Nat. Bank in Grand Forks v. North Dakota Workmen's Compensation Bureau, 68 N.W.2d 661 (N.D.1955) (workmen's compensation). Contra: Northrup v. St. Paul Fire Department Relief Ass'n, 193 Minn. 623, 259 N.W. 185 (1935) (fireman's pension).

There are some limits on relation back in these cases. Where the annulment is not obtained until after the death of the person who is insured or in whose name the death payments are claimed, two cases have held the decree not retroactive, Castor v. United States, 174 F.2d

481 (8th Cir.1949), cert. denied 338 U.S. 836, 70 S.Ct. 45, 94 L.Ed. 511 (1949), and Cummings v. U.S., 34 F.2d 284 (D.Minn.1929), both denying claims for government life insurance. As the Castor case said, a man cannot have a posthumous wife. See also Scarboro v. Morgan, 233 N.C. 449, 64 S.E.2d 422 (1951).

Where the wife's second marriage was annulled on the ground of her own fraud, it has been held that she is barred by estoppel from reviving her former workmen's compensation benefits. State Compensation Fund v. Reed, 12 Ariz.App. 317, 470 P.2d 465 (1970).

37. 272 F.2d 380 (2d Cir.1959). Accord: Schroeder v. Celebrezze, 244 F.Supp. 375 (E.D.N.Y.1965).

38. Yeager v. Flemming, 282 F.2d 779 (5th Cir.1960) refused to follow Nott, where an annulment had been granted in Connecticut, a state like New York which authorizes alimony in annulment suits. The court held the annulment retroactive so as to revive social security benefits.

39. Johnson County Nat. Bank & Trust Co. v. Bach, 189 Kan. 291, 369 P.2d 231 (1962) and In re Newlin's Estate, 231 Pa. 312, 80 A. 255 (1911) held the annulment related back to revive the payments. The Johnson County case indicated it might not be if the trustee had relied on the marriage and wound up the trust. Stoner v. Nethercutt, 8 Cal.App.3d 667, 87 Cal.Rptr. 659 (1970) followed Sefton and held that the trust payments did not revive. See also Scarboro v. Morgan, 233 N.C. 449, 64 S.E.2d 422 (1951).

factors affect the outcome. Two of these are tort actions between the parties, brought after the marriage was annulled and thus raising the question whether the inter-spousal immunity should apply.[40] Their refusal to allow the suits, based on a rejection of the retroactive analysis of annulment was partly due to a finding that the marriages were only voidable. Since after annulment none of the alleged evils of interspousal suits in tort could exist, these cases seem erroneous. Another case applied the privilege against revealing marital communications to a communication made while the parties were living together though the question arose after annulment.[41] This seems clearly correct, since the communication was confidential when made and its character was not changed by the annulment. Likewise it has been held that the annulment does not relate back so as to exonerate the husband from paying for necessaries furnished to the wife while they appeared to be married.[42] And the annulment has been held not to affect the prior adoption of children by the spouses.[43]

In the field of criminal law annulments have been treated variously. One case, Burney v. State,[44] held that a defendant prosecuted for seduction could rely upon the defense that he married the girl even though the marriage was later annulled at his suit, the court emphasizing that the marriage was not void. There seems little room for the de facto

principle here but the case may merely evince dislike for such prosecutions. In another case relation back was rejected though it would have provided a defense to a prosecution for bigamous cohabitation.[45]

The discussion thus far demonstrates that annulment decrees are still given retroactive effect except where that conflicts with the de facto principle. When it does, when retroactivity would upset expectations of the parties, then annulment operates prospectively. As a guide for the determination of future cases this seems to be adequate, but the decision of such cases would be made easier if all states would enact statutes authorizing alimony in annulment suits. Then the expectations of the parties could be as completely vindicated in annulment as in divorce.

The foregoing discussion also demonstrates the extent of the fallacy involved in the conventional distinction between divorce and annulment. Courts still say, not infrequently, that divorce terminates a valid marriage, while annulment establishes that no marriage ever existed.[46] The numerous cases dealing with the effect of annulment decrees make it clear that such a neat, logical distinction is a false and misleading over-simplification. In a great many respects today divorce and annulment are similar. In the writer's view the cause of fairness and equity would be advanced if by statute annulment and divorce were made similar in all respects.

---

40. Callow v. Thomas, 322 Mass. 550, 78 N.E.2d 637 (1948); Gordon v. Pollard, 207 Tenn. 45, 336 S.W.2d 25 (1960). See also Henneger v. Lomas, 145 Ind. 287, 44 N.E. 462 (1896) holding that a wife could sue her husband for her own seduction after their marriage had been annulled, under a statute authorizing an unmarried female to sue for her own seduction.

American Surety Co. of New York v. Conner, 251 N.Y. 1, 166 N.E. 783 (1929) held that the granting of an annulment did not mean that gifts from husband to wife made in consideration of the marriage could be recovered back on the theory of a failure of consideration.

41. People v. Godines, 17 Cal.App.2d 721, 62 P.2d 787 (1936).

42. Kurtis v. Desiervo, 46 Misc.2d 1014, 261 N.Y.S.2d 679 (County Ct.1965).

43. Cowhey v. Tator, 36 Ill.App.3d 962, 344 N.E.2d 501 (1976).

44. 111 Tex.Cr.App. 599, 13 S.W.2d 375 (1929), 8 Tex. L.Rev. 142 (1929).

45. State v. Richards, 175 Minn. 498, 221 N.W. 867 (1928). H married W–1 in South Dakota, and later married W–2 in New York without bothering to obtain a divorce. Some time later he got the first marriage annulled for nonage. The court held that this was not a defense to bigamous cohabitation, since the cohabitation had occurred before the annulment, but suggested the result would be different if the first marriage were void. The result might also be different if the charge were bigamy rather than bigamous cohabitation.

Interesting questions of relation back can be imagined in the tax field. For example, after annulment, should the parties who had filed joint income tax returns be required to go back, file separate returns and pay additional tax? Compare Turnipseed v. Commissioner, 27 T.C. 758 (1957), and Borax', Estate v. C.I.R., 349 F.2d 666 (2d Cir.1965), cert. denied 383 U.S. 935, 86 S.Ct. 1064, 15 L.Ed.2d 852 (1966).

46. E.g., De Rosay v. De Rosay, 162 Pa.Super. 333, 57 A.2d 685 (1948).

Chapter 4

THE ILLEGITIMATE CHILD

Table of Sections

---

§ 4.1 Illegitimacy—Background and Definition

As an original proposition one might expect that a child's legal rights and obligations respecting his parents would depend upon and be a function of the biological fact of parentage. As we all know, however, this has not been true in Anglo-American law, although there is some reason for saying it was more nearly true in pre-Christian times than later.[1] Either because the all-important fact of blood relationship could be proved with greater certainty, or even assumed, where the offspring was born to married parents, or because of the influence of the Church's doctrine of the sanctity of marriage, or for both these and other reasons,[2] the distinction arose early in English law between the legitimate child and the bastard. The bastard was not as badly treated by that law as in other legal systems, a fact which Pollock and Maitland suggest was due to William the Conqueror's being a bastard,[3] but he had no rights of inheritance from his father[4] or from his mother.[5] For long it has been supposed that he had no claim upon his father for support,[6] but a recent article argues persuasively that there were remedies in the English ecclesiastical courts by which fathers could be and were ordered to support their illegitimate chil-

§ 4.1

1. Hooper, The Law of Illegitimacy 2, 3 (1911); Fritz, Judging the Status of the Illegitimate Child in Various Western Legal Systems, 23 Loyola L.Rev. 1 (1977).

2. 2 Pollock and Maitland, The History of English Law, 394–396 (1895); Hooper, The Law of Illegitimacy, 2–4 (1911). Ayer, Legitimacy and Marriage, 16 Harv.L.Rev. 22, 37 (1902) suggests that the disability of the child was designed to punish the immorality of the parent. For a contemporary expression of the view that the disability of the illegitimate child serves to promote marriage and family life, see New York State Legislative Document (1960) No. 27, p. 47, Report of the Joint Legislative Committee on Matrimonial and Family Laws.

3. 2 Pollock and Maitland, The History of English Law, 395 (1895).

4. James, The Illegitimate and Deprived Child: Legitimation and Adoption, in Graveson and Crane eds., A Century of Family Law, 39, 42 (1957); 1 Blackstone, Commentaries on the Law of England, 446 (Cooley 4th ed. 1899); Birtwhistle v. Vardill, 7 C. & F. 895, 7 Eng.Rep. 1308 (1840).

5. 1 Blackstone, Commentaries on the Law of England, 459 (Cooley 4th ed. 1899); 2 Kent, Commentaries on American Law, 212 (6th ed. 1858).

6. Moncrief v. Ely, 19 Wend. 405 (N.Y.1838). His mother had a duty at common law to support him, however. Wright v. Wright, 2 Mass. 109 (1806); State ex rel. Mattes v. Juvenile Court, 147 Minn. 222, 179 N.W. 1006 (1920).

dren.[7] In 1576 the Elizabethan Poor Law gave the illegitimate child a civil law claim for support from his father.[8] Upon the death of the bastard without wife or legitimate heirs, his property escheated to the crown.[9] Aside from the disabilities of inheritance, he had full legal capacity.[10]

The origin of the distinction between legitimate and illegitimate children is perhaps not so remarkable, in view of Christian doctrines of marriage, as is the tenacity with which the distinction has persisted in our law and custom. Until recently it has seemed that the stigma which accompanies illegitimacy is greater than in the Middle Ages. Commencing in 1968, however, a line of cases in the United States Supreme Court has held many of the legal disabilities of the illegitimate child to be in violation of the Fourteenth Amendment.[11] Perhaps influenced by these cases many states have by statute begun to treat the illegitimate child as the equal of the legitimate child.[12] The Uniform Parentage Act, since its approval in 1973, has been enacted in several states.[13] Its key provision extends the parent-child relationship to every parent and every child, regardless of the par-

ents' marital status.[14] It is therefore accurate to say that the law in the United States has during the past few years made substantial progress in improving the status of the illegitimate child.[15] Equal progress has been made in other countries, some of their efforts antedating the developments in the United States.[16]

Any discussion of the law of illegitimacy must be related to contemporary conditions. The most striking thing about our present situation is the sharp increase which has occurred in the rate of illegitimacy over the past three decades. The rate of illegitimate births in the United States per thousand unmarried women within the ages of fifteen to forty-four has more than trebled between 1940 and 1974.[17] In absolute numbers the latest available figures show 418,100 illegitimate births in 1974.[18] The social and psychological factors influencing these developments are undoubtedly complex, as revealed, for example, by the facts that the rates of illegitimacy are higher for non-white than for white women, and that a large proportion of illegitimate children are born to teenage girls.[19] One factor underlying the increase in illegiti-

---

7. Helmholz, Support Orders, Church Courts, and the Rule of Filius Nullius: A Reassessment of the Common Law, 63 Va.L.Rev. 431 (1977).

8. 18 Eliz.I, c. 3 (1576). One enlightened American case, Doughty v. Engler, 112 Kan. 583, 211 P. 619 (1923), has held that the father has a common law duty to support his illegitimate child, enforceable by a civil suit brought by the child.

9. James, The Illegitimate and Deprived Child: Legitimation and Adoption, in Graveson and Crane, A Century of Family Law 39, 43 (1957).

10. 2 Pollock and Maitland, The History of English Law, 394 (1895). At one time he was apparently disqualified from holding office in the church. 1 Blackstone, Commentaries on the Law of England, 459 (Cooley 4th ed. 1899).

11. The first case was Levy v. Louisiana, 391 U.S. 68, 88 S.Ct. 1509, 20 L.Ed.2d 436 (1968), rehearing denied 393 U.S. 898, 89 S.Ct. 65, 21 L.Ed.2d 185 (1968). The cases are discussed in section 4.4, infra.

12. E.g., Or.Rev.Stat. § 109.060 (1984). The Uniform Probate Code § 2–109, 8 Unif.L.Ann. 328 (1972) provides that the illegitimate child may inherit from his mother, and from his father when paternity is established before the father's death, or after his death by clear and convincing proof. The Code has been widely adopted.

13. 9A Unif.L.Ann. 587 (Supp.1979). This statute has been adopted in California, Colorado, Hawaii, Montana,

North Dakota and Washington. The Reporter for the Act was Professor Harry D. Krause of the University of Illinois whose writings and advocacy have done more than anyone else's to bring about the reforms in the treatment of the illegitimate child which are discussed in the text.

14. Uniform Parentage Act § 2, 9A Unif.L.Ann. 588 (1979).

15. For an extensive discussion of the whole subject, see H. Krause, Illegitimacy: Law and Social Policy (1971).

16. H. Krause, Illegitimacy: Law and Social Policy ch. 6 (1971).

17. Schachter and McCarthy, Illegitimate Births: United States 1938–1957, 47 Vital Statistics (Special Reports) 225 (1960) gives the rates as 7.1 illegitimate births per 1,000 unmarried females aged fifteen to forty-four in 1940 and 20.9 in 1957. The Statistical Abstract of the United States 1976, 58 gives the rates as 21.6 for 1960 and 24.1 for 1974. The Statistical Abstract for 1976 indicates that in 1950 illegitimate births amounted to 3.9% of all births, while in 1974 they were 13.2% of all births. Even though some authorities are critical of statistics on illegitimacy, these figures show that significant changes in social custom have occurred. See A. Skolnick, The Intimate Environment 23 (1973).

18. Statistical Abstract of the United States 1976, 58.

19. Statistics on illegitimacy, broken down by race and by age of the mother are found in U.S. Department

mate births may be the growing tendency for young people to live together without marrying, although the extent of this tendency cannot be measured and may be over-emphasized by the popular press.[20] And illegitimate births might be even higher if abortions had not been as readily available after 1973 as they have been.[21] Although both the methods and delivery of contraceptive devices and information have improved markedly in the past thirty years,[22] there is evidence of surprising ignorance or carelessness concerning contraception among many of the young men and women who have had illegitimate children.[23] Not only are the magnitude and influence of all such factors upon the incidence of illegitimacy obscure and impossible to measure with any precision, but we do not know what effect they have had and are having upon the changes in legal doctrine already mentioned. It may be that as the numbers of illegitimate children in the population increase, judges, legislators and lawyers become more sensitive to the hardships inflicted on the illegitimate by the law as it has stood in the past and that as a result they have all moved to change the law. But we cannot be sure of this. The most likely hypothesis is

that the law's development has been both an effect and a cause of the social conditions leading to a rise in illegitimacy. At the least the law is now doing much to remove the social stigma with which the illegitimate child used to be regarded in society.

The legal definition of illegitimacy is of long standing. Traditionally the legitimate child was one "born in lawful wedlock or within a competent time afterwards".[24] More precisely, the law required that the child's parents be married before his birth as the essential condition for legitimacy.[25] The child was not illegitimate if conception occurred before marriage, so long as marriage occurred before birth. The posthumous child of a married man was of course legitimate. But conversely, the child conceived and born before his parents married remained illegitimate even though his parents married after his birth.[26] These same definitions still hold in our law except so far as they have been altered by statutes providing various methods of legitimating the illegitimate child or limiting the concept of illegitimacy.[27]

Along with this definition of legitimacy went the strong presumption that the child born to a married woman was legitimate.

of Health, Education & Welfare, Public Health Service, National Center for Health Statistics, Vital Statistics of the United States 1973, Vol. 1–Natality, Tables 1–30, 1–31. These tables show, for example, that in 1973 there were 22.9 illegitimate births per 1,000 unmarried women aged 15–19, the corresponding figure for 1940 being 7.4. The best known discussion of rates of illegitimacy among blacks is in United States Department of Labor, Office of Policy Planning and Research, The Negro Family, The Case for National Action 8–19 (1965) (The Moynihan Report), stating that nearly one-quarter of all negro births are illegitimate. For a discussion of some of the issues raised by the Moynihan Report, see H. Krause, Illegitimacy: Law and Social Policy 257–267 (1971).

For discussion of some of the factors leading to illegitimacy see L. Young, Out of Wedlock (1954), which contains a short bibliography, and Josselyn, The Unmarried Mother, in R. Slovenko, Sexual Behavior and the Law 356 (1965). See also Child Welfare League of America, Research Perspectives on the Unmarried Mother (1961).

20. See, e.g., Clayton and Voss, Shacking Up: Cohabitation in the 1970's, 39 J. of Marriage and the Family 273 (1977).

21. Roe v. Wade, 410 U.S. 113, 93 S.Ct. 705, 35 L.Ed.2d 147 (1973), rehearing denied 410 U.S. 959, 93 S.Ct. 1409, 35 L.Ed.2d 694 (1973) gave women the constitutional right to abortion during the first trimester of pregnancy.

22. C.T. Dienes, Law, Politics and Birth Control, passim (1972).

23. See, e.g., Evans, Selstad and Welcher, Teenagers: Fertility Control Behavior and Attitudes Before and After Abortion, Childbearing or Negative Pregnancy Test, 8 Family Planning Perspectives 192 (1976); Selnik, Kantner, Sexual and Contraceptive Experience of Young Unmarried Women in the United States, 1976 and 1971, 9 Family Planning Perspective 55 (1977).

24. 1 Blackstone, Commentaries on the Law of England, 446, 454 (Cooley 4th ed. 1899).

A child born to a married woman as a result of her adultery is illegitimate. Fitzsimmons v. Decicco, 44 Misc. 2d 307, 253 N.Y.S.2d 603 (Fam.Ct.1964); State v. Coliton, 73 N.D. 582, 17 N.W.2d 546 (1945). See also Nicolas, Adulterine Bastardy (1836).

25. James, The Illegitimate and Deprived Child: Legitimation and Adoption, in Graveson and Crane, A Century of Family Law, 39, 42 (1957). See Home of the Holy Infancy v. Kaska, 397 S.W.2d 208 (Tex.1965).

26. 1 Blackstone, Commentaries on the Law of England, 454, 455 (Cooley 4th ed. 1899).

27. H. Krause, Illegitimacy: Law and Social Policy 9–21 (1971). See also section 5.2, infra, and F. v. H., 24 Or. App. 517, 546 P.2d 765 (1976), reversed 275 Or. 91, 549 P.2d 1117 (1976).

Although the presumption was rebuttable, at one point in English legal history it could be rebutted only by proof that the mother's husband was impotent or out of England.[28] In the colorful legal phrase he had to be proved to be "beyond the four seas". The presumption survives in our law in various forms, none of them imposing such strict standards for rebuttal as in earlier days.[29]

Illegitimacy occurs in a different context when the child is born to parents who are married but whose marriage is later annulled. According to the traditional view of annulment such marriages are avoided ab initio, any children of the marriage being thereby rendered illegitimate. As is indicated elsewhere,[30] however, statutes generally in force prevent this result and preserve the legitimate status of such children.

The legal definition of illegitimacy is put to its severest test by the development and use of medical techniques for artificial insemination where the donor of semen is a man other than the mother's husband, the process known as heterologous insemination or AID.[31] According to the traditional definition the child conceived in this way, even with the husband's consent, is illegitimate, inimical as this may be to the child's interests and frustrating to the parties' expectations.[32] Case authority on the point is scanty. Several of the earlier cases held the child illegitimate, but at the same time found ways to vindicate the claim which the child raised.[33] Although the legitimation statutes do not help matters because they only furnish the means for recognition of the illegitimate child by his own father and in these cases the child is asserting claims with respect to a man who is clearly not his father,[34] the courts have come up with a variety of legal expedients of more or less persuasiveness. Gursky v. Gursky[35] found the child to be illegitimate but upheld her right to be supported by her mother's husband on theories of implied contract and equitable estoppel. The most frequently cited of the cases, People v. Sorensen,[36] held that a

---

28. Hooper, The Law of Illegitimacy, 13 (1911). Pollock and Maitland indicate the force of this presumption in English law by the remark that " * * * we may almost say that every child born to a married woman is in law the legitimate child of her husband." 2 Pollock and Maitland, The History of English Law, 395 (1895).

29. See the discussion in section 5.4, infra, and Curry v. Felix, 276 Minn. 125, 149 N.W.2d 92 (1967).

30. See section 3.3, supra.

31. Artificial insemination with semen of the husband is referred to as AIH and may be used where conception is prevented by the husband's impotence or physical defect. It is relatively rarely used. Artificial insemination with semen of a third person donor is called AID and is used where the husband is sterile, or where there is danger of transmitting an inheritable defect or where there is an RH incompatibility between husband and wife. The literature on artificial insemination is vast and still growing. A useful bibliography has been issued by the Los Angeles County Law Library on August 11, 1961. Other works include Wadlington, Artificial Conception: The Challenge for Family Law, 69 Va.L.Rev. 465 (1983); W. Finegold, Artificial Insemination (1964); R. Snowden and G. Mitchell, The Artificial Family (1981); Wadlington, Artificial Insemination: The Dangers of a Poorly Kept Secret, 64 Nw.U.L.Rev. 777 (1970); Smith, Through a Test Tube Darkly: Artificial Insemination and the Law, 67 Mich.L.Rev. 127 (1968); Note, The Legal Status of Artificial Insemination: A Need for Policy Formulation, 19 Drake L.Rev. 409 (1970); Note, A Legislative Approach to Artificial Insemination, 53 Corn.L.Q. 497 (1968); Note, Artificial Insemination and the Law, 1968 U.Ill.L.F. 203; Note, Legal Consequences of Artificial Insemination: The California Answer, 3 U.S.F.L.Rev. 178 (1968); Note, Legal Consequences of Artificial Insemination in New York, 19 Syracuse L.Rev. 1009 (1968); Note, Social and Legal Aspects of Human Artificial Insemination, 1965 Wis.L.Rev. 859; Note, Eugenic Artificial Insemination: A Cure for Mediocrity? 94 Harv.L.Rev. 1850 (1981).

32. For discussion of the related question whether artificial insemination constitutes adultery, see section 13.2, infra.

33. Doornbos v. Doornbos, unreported, decided in the Superior Court of Cook County, Ill. on Dec. 13, 1954, noted in 43 Geo.L.J. 517 (1955); Anonymous v. Anonymous, 41 Misc.2d 886, 246 N.Y.S.2d 835 (1964); Gursky v. Gursky, 39 Misc.2d 1083, 242 N.Y.S.2d 406 (1963). The earlier New York case of Strnad v. Strnad, 190 Misc. 786, 78 N.Y.S.2d 390 (1948) is not clear, characterizing the child first as semi-adopted, and then later as not illegitimate. A fortiori the child would be illegitimate in the rare case of artificial insemination without the husband's consent. See also Biskind, Legitimacy of Children Born By Artificial Insemination, 5 J.Fam.Law 39 (1965).

34. Strnad v. Strnad, 190 Misc. 786, 78 N.Y.S.2d 390 (1948) seems to have overlooked this distinction, saying that the child born of AID is like the illegitimate child whose parents later marry.

35. Gursky v. Gursky, 39 Misc.2d 1083, 242 N.Y.S.2d 406 (1963), 30 Bklyn.L.Rev. 126 (1963), 52 Geo.L.J. 633 (1964).

36. 68 Cal.2d 280, 66 Cal.Rptr. 7, 437 P.2d 495 (1968). The result of the Sorensen has now been approved by

husband was responsible, under the criminal non-support statute, for the support of a child born to his wife as the result of AID to which the husband had given his written consent. The court's opinion is far from lucid. At one point it asserts that "father" in the statute does not mean the biological father but the "lawful father", and that the husband in this case was the "lawful father". The court also emphasizes that the husband had given his consent, but it does not seem to rely on estoppel. Although there is some discussion of whether the child is legitimate and of the impact of legitimation statutes, the court seems not to decide whether he was legitimate. It is not surprising that such judicial opinions are unsatisfactory, since there is no very clearly applicable legal principle which would uphold the child's claim in this situation. Perhaps the most useful is the doctrine of equitable adoption, provided that an agreement to adopt could be implied from the circumstances.[37] If, as is sometimes done, the artificial insemination is accomplished by mingling the semen of the donor with that of the husband, at the same time taking care to match the donor's blood group with that of the husband, then the presumption that the child of a married woman living with her husband is legitimate would protect the child

and could be rebutted only with difficulty.[38] It has also been suggested that the husband could become the father of the child by filing an adoption petition and going through statutory adoption proceedings.[39] There are two difficulties with this solution, one being that the parents generally are anxious to avoid even the limited notoriety entailed by adoption, and the other that the usual adoption statute requires either the consent of the natural parent or the involuntary termination of that parent's rights. Since the identity of the donor of semen is usually kept confidential by the physician performing the operation, his consent cannot be obtained. A proceeding for the termination of his parental rights takes on the aspect of a farce in addition to requiring publication of some sort of notice under Stanley v. Illinois.[40]

The obvious response to the law's inadequacy in the face of this particular scientific development is to enact a statute. A good many states [41] and the Uniform Parentage Act [42] do attempt to solve the problem by statute. The statutes all follow the same general pattern. They authorize the performance of heterologous artificial insemination by physicians upon the written consent of husband and wife and provide that a child so conceived is to be treated as the natural child

statute in California. West's Ann.Cal.Civ.Code § 7005 (1983); West's Ann.Cal.Penal Code § 270 (Supp.1985).

L.M.S. v. S.L.S., 105 Wis.App.2d 118, 312 N.W.2d 853 (1981) cited Sorensen and held that a husband who consents to artificial insemination with the understanding that the child will be treated as their own has the legal responsibilities of fatherhood, including the duty of support.

37. For a discussion of equitable adoption see section § 20.9 infra.

38. This presumption is discussed infra, section 4.4.

39. Note, 1965 Wis.L.Rev. 858, 879.

40. Stanley v. Illinois, 405 U.S. 645, 92 S.Ct. 1208, 31 L.Ed.2d 551 (1972) held that the father of the illegitimate child could not be deprived of his parental rights without notice and an opportunity to be heard, under the Fourteenth Amendment to the United States Constitution. It is discussed in section 20.2, infra. Its status as authority has now been called in question by Quilloin v. Walcott, 434 U.S. 246, 98 S.Ct. 549, 54 L.Ed.2d 511 (1978), rehearing denied 435 U.S. 918, 98 S.Ct. 1477, 55 L.Ed.2d 511 (1978).

41. Alaska Stat. § 25.20.045 (1983); Ark.Stat. §§ 61–141(c) (1971); West's Ann.Cal.Civ.Code § 7005 (1983);

Colo.Rev.Stat. § 19–6–106 (1978); Conn.Gen.Stat.Ann. §§ 45–69f to 45–69n (1981); West's Fla.Stat.Ann. § 742.11 (Supp.1985); Official Code Ga.Ann. §§ 19–7–21, 43–34–42 (1984); Kan.Stat.Ann. § 23–130 (1981); LSA–Civ.Code art. 188 (Supp.1985); Md.Code, Est. & Trusts, § 1–206(b) (1975); Mich.C.L.A. § 14.15 (2824) (Supp.1980); Mont. Code Ann. § 40–6–106 (1983); N.Y.–McKinney's Dom.Rel. L. § 73 (1977); N.C.Gen.Stat. § 49A–1 (1984); Okl.Stat. 1984, tit. 10, §§ 551, 552, 553 (Supp); Or.Rev.Stat. §§ 109.239, 109.243, 109.247, 677.355, 677.360, 677.365, 677.370, 677.990 (1983 and 1984); Tenn.Code Ann. § 53–446 (1983); V.T.C.A., Fam.Code § 12.03 (1975); Va.Code 1980, § 64.1–7.1; West's Rev.Code Wash.Ann. § 26.26.050 (Supp.1985); Wyo.Stat.1978, § 14–2–103.

Consent once given is presumed to continue until pregnancy occurs, unless the husband sustains the burden of proving it was revoked. K.S. v. G.S., 182 N.J.Super. 102, 440 A.2d 64 (1981).

42. Uniform Parentage Act § 5, 9A Unif.L.Ann. 592 (1979). This Act is in force in about six states. See, e.g., West's Ann.Cal.Civ.Code § 7005 (1983); Colo.Rev.Stat. § 19–6–106 (1978). A model act dealing with some of the issues is in Note, 24 Cleveland St.L.Rev. 341 (1975).

of the husband. There is sometimes the further provision that the donor of semen is to be treated as not the natural father of the child. In some states there are also provisions for acknowledgment and filing of the parties' consents and for the confidentiality of the records so made. Presumably these statutes convey the negative inference that if the artificial insemination is performed without the husband's consent, the child is illegitimate and gets no rights against the mother's husband. The argument could also be made that the same inference should be drawn where the husband consents to the procedure but where his consent is not in writing and therefore not in accordance with the statute. The better solution to that sort of case would seem to be to rely on the common law authorities, such as Sorensen,[43] unsatisfactory though they are, and to hold that the child is to be treated as the child of his mother's husband. This approach has the virtue of construing a remedial statute in such a liberal spirit as to achieve its basic objective rather than to frustrate that objective.

There are many other "complex and serious legal problems raised by the practice of artificial insemination" [44] which these statutes do not attempt to answer, and which have not yet appeared in litigation. Although it seems highly desirable to permit the procedure to be performed only by licensed physicians, few statutes so provide.[45] Granting the desirability of this restriction, the more difficult questions concern the breadth to be given the physician's discretion. Should he alone choose the donors of semen? Should he be required to maintain the confidentiality of

donor records? What tests, if any, should he be required to make in order to assure himself that genetic harm will not occur? Should the law impose any limitations upon the use of artificial insemination or of frozen semen for the purpose of genetic improvement as distinguished from its use in cases of infertility?

One of the most troublesome situations is that of the unmarried woman who wishes a child through artificial insemination. The first question is whether there are any moral or legal reasons why the physician should refuse to perform the procedure for her. Some physicians, drawing an analogy from adoption,[46] might refuse on the ground that bringing a child into a one-parent family would be likely to prejudice his normal development. Many women would respond that this is a decision for the woman alone to make, and that it is no part of the physician's function to impose his moral or social views on his patients. There seem to be no legal principles which would provide any guidance for the solution to this question, but if we are really concerned for the welfare of children, it seems safe to say that as a general proposition the child is better off in a family with both a mother and a father than with a mother alone. If the unmarried mother does conceive a child by artificial insemination, there is the further question whether the donor of semen, if he should be identified, would have any parental rights or duties with respect to the child. The logical answer is that he is no less a father biologically, and therefore he should be so considered by the law and should have both the rights and the obligations of any

43. See notes 32, 34, 35, supra.

44. The quotation is from the comment to section 5 of the Uniform Parentage Act, 9A Unif.L.Ann. 593 (1979). In addition to the questions which are raised by artificial insemination itself, there is the host of related legal and ethical questions posed by the process of in vitro fertilization, that is, the test-tube baby procedure. This consists in removing ova from a woman (who has in some cases been treated with hormones to increase ova production), placing the ova in a medium and introducing sperm, allowing the fertilized ova to develop for a short period, and then implanting the fertilized ovum in the woman's uterus to grow and be born in the usual manner. The process first resulted in the birth of a live, normal baby

in England in 1978. N.Y. Times, July 26, 1978, p. 1, col. 5. Some of the constitutional, statutory, and common law issues which this method of procreation raises are discussed in Flannery, Weisman, Lipsett, Braverman, Test Tube Babies: Legal Issues Raised by *In Vitro* Fertilization, 67 Geo.L.J. 1295 (1979).

45. See Official Code Ga.Ann. § 19–7–21(b) (Supp. 1984); Okl.Stat.1984, tit. 10, § 553 (Supp.); Or.Rev.Stat. § 677.360 (1983); Wyo.Stat.1978, § 14–2–103.

46. Some adoption agencies would be reluctant to place a child with a single parent or at least would give a single parent applicant for placement a relatively low priority. See section 20.7, infra.

father of an illegitimate child. One lower court has reached this conclusion, relying on Sorensen and other cases,[47] and on the argument that a child should have a father as well as a mother if that is possible. In this situation, however, if the father and the mother refuse to marry and continue to quarrel over the father's relation to the child, the child's acquisition of a father by operation of law does not seem greatly conducive to his future happiness. In all such cases one can only conclude that medical techniques have presented us with dilemmas which the law is not only not equipped to resolve at the moment but which it does not have any rational or satisfactory principles for resolving in the immediate future.

WESTLAW REFERENCES

find 88 sct 1509

defin! /3 illegitima! bastard

sy,di(presum! /s child /s married /2 woman /s legitimate)

find 92 sct 1208

---

§ 4.2 Illegitimacy—Constitutional Protection for the Illegitimate Child

Introduction

Since 1968 the United States Supreme Court has repeatedly had before it the constitutionality of various disabilities imposed upon the illegitimate child by legislative or judicial action both state and federal.[1] In that year the Court held, in Levy v. Louisiana,[2] that a state court's construction of the Louisiana wrongful death statute denying an illegitimate child the right to recover for the death of his mother violated the Equal Protection Clause of the Fourteenth Amendment. The Court's opinion characterized as invidious discrimination having no rational basis Louisiana's refusal to permit the illegitimate child to recover for his mother's death, saying that the child was dependent upon her and was her child "in the biological and in the spiritual sense." The long history of different treatment of the illegitimate was brushed aside as irrelevant. The majority opinion made no attempt to respond to the arguments in Mr. Justice Harlan's dissent,[3] and in fact contained very little reasoning to support its conclusion. It is perhaps not surprising, in view of the summary nature of the Levy opinion, that many lawyers, including some experienced observers of the Supreme Court, construed the case to mean that no distinctions between legitimate and illegitimate children could pass muster under the Equal Protection Clause.[4] Subsequent Supreme Court decisions have exhibited such confusion and vacillation that it is very difficult to predict what statutory distinctions might survive, but it is at least clear that Levy has not been so applied as to outlaw all differences in legal treatment between legitimate and illegitimate children.

47. C.M. v. C.C., 152 N.J.Super. 160, 377 A.2d 821 (Juv. and Dom.Rel.Ct.1977). The facts in this case were unusual in that the child's father and mother accomplished the artificial insemination without the intervention of a physician. Where the procedure is performed by a physician the identity of the donor of semen and of the recipient should not, and presumably would not, be known to the other, so that the donor would not be able to make a claim for custody or visitation.

§ 4.2

1. The constitutional implications of the illegitimate's disabilities are discussed in Krause, Equal Protection for the Illegitimate, 65 Mich.L.Rev. 477 (1967). The Supreme Court cases to 1975 are collected in Annot., 41 L.Ed.2d 1228 (1975). See also Note, Illegitimates and Equal Protection, 10 U.Mich.J.Law Reform 543 (1977).

2. 391 U.S. 68, 88 S.Ct. 1509, 20 L.Ed.2d 436 (1968), rehearing denied 393 U.S. 898, 89 S.Ct. 65, 21 L.Ed.2d 185 (1968), 35 Bklyn.L.Rev. 135 (1968), 47 Tex.L.Rev. 326 (1968), 43 Tulane L.Rev. 383 (1969).

3. The dissent, 391 U.S. at 76, 88 S.Ct. at 1512, pointed out that the Louisiana statute made many distinctions respecting those who could recover for the wrongful death of another. These distinctions were based upon legal rather than biological relationships and had nothing whatever to do with ties of affection or dependency. The dissent went on to say that the obvious justification for the distinction between legitimate and illegitimate children was the state's purpose of affording recognition to formal marriage as the basis for family relationships. The court's recent treatment of marriage ignores this state interest in several different contexts. Clark, The New Marriage, 12 Willamette L.J. 441 (1976).

4. E.g., Henkin, Foreword, The Supreme Court, 1967 Term, 82 Harv.L.Rev. 63, 91, n. 92 (1968); Semmel, Social Security Benefits for Illegitimate Children After Levy v. Louisiana, 19 Buff.L.Rev. 289, 290 (1970): In re Jensen's Estate, 162 N.W.2d 861 (N.D.1968).

One consequence of Levy does seem predictable. The case held that the illegitimate child could not be deprived of the right to sue for the wrongful death of his mother where that right was given to the legitimate child. It should be equally true that he should be entitled to sue for the wrongful death of his father, if legitimate children are given that right by the applicable statute, and several cases have so held.[5]

Inheritance Rights

In 1971 the most important form of discrimination against the illegitimate child, discrimination respecting his rights of inheritance,[6] was held not to violate the Equal Protection Clause in Labine v. Vincent.[7] In this case the illegitimate child had been acknowledged by her parents, the effect of which under Louisiana law was to give her the right to support from her parents. But under the applicable Louisiana statutes the acknowledged illegitimate child could inherit from her father only if he died leaving no legitimate descendants, no parents or grandparents, and no collateral relatives. The Louisiana court had held in this case that the illegitimate daughter could inherit nothing from her father, since he had died leaving collateral relatives. The Supreme Court, in an opinion which reads very much like Mr. Justice Harlan's dissent in Levy v. Louisiana, said that the Constitution

does not require that there be a biological difference between individuals as a condition on treating them differently in the intestacy statute. The Court characterized one set of relationships, those of legitimate children, as socially sanctioned, legally recognized and producing legal rights and obligations. The other relationships, those of the illegitimate child, were characterized as "illicit and beyond the recognition of the law."[8] The opinion also seemed to place some weight upon a distinction from the statute in Levy, saying that the wrongful death statute in that case barred the illegitimate from recovery, whereas in this case the illegitimate was not barred from inheriting because the father could have left her one-third of his property by will, or he could have legitimated her. Finally, the opinion said specifically that Levy cannot be read to say that a state may never treat an illegitimate child differently from a legitimate child. Four justices dissented in this case and Mr. Justice Harlan concurred specially.

As the dissent in Labine amply demonstrated, there was no possible way of distinguishing the Levy and Labine results. If Levy was right, Labine was wrong and vice versa. Lower courts reached differing conclusions as to which case should be followed and as to whether Labine had been overruled by subsequent cases.[9] The confusing consequences of the case are made most obvious by those state

---

5. Cannon v. Transamerican Freight Lines, 37 Mich. App. 313, 194 N.W.2d 736 (1971); Jordan v. Delta Drilling Co., 541 P.2d 39 (Wyo.1975). Other cases are collected in Annot., 78 A.L.R.3d 1230 (1977).

Influenced by Levy and other cases discussed below, Missouri has held that its wrongful death statute is to be construed so as to permit the father and mother of an illegitimate child to recover for the child's death. Cobb v. State Security Insurance Co., 576 S.W.2d 726 (Mo.1979). But the wrongful death statutes in some states provide that the action may be brought by those who would inherit from the deceased. Where that is the case, and where the intestacy statute is constitutional, then it seems to follow that the wrongful death statute may be valid in not permitting some illegitimate children to recover for the wrongful death of their fathers. This is the case in Wisconsin. Robinson v. Kolstad, 84 Wis.2d 579, 267 N.W.2d 886 (1978), appeal dismissed 441 U.S. 939, 99 S.Ct. 2154, 60 L.Ed.2d 1041 (1979); Estate of Blumreich, 84 Wis.2d 545, 267 N.W.2d 870 (1978), appeal dismissed 439 U.S. 1061, 99 S.Ct. 822, 59 L.Ed.2d 26 (1979). Contra: S.M.V. v. Littlepage, 443 N.E.2d 103 (Ind.App.1982).

6. The chief common law disability of the illegitimate child was his inability to inherit from either his mother or his father. See section 4.1, supra.

7. 401 U.S. 532, 91 S.Ct. 1017, 28 L.Ed.2d 288 (1971), rehearing denied 402 U.S. 990, 91 S.Ct. 1672, 290 L.Ed.2d 156 (1971), 38 Bklyn.L.Rev. 428 (1971), N.Dame Law. 392 (1971).

8. 401 U.S. at 538, 91 S.Ct. at 1020.

9. Eskra v. Morton, 524 F.2d 9 (7th Cir.1975), per Stevens, J., took the position that cases subsequent to Labine had severely limited its holding, and that it applied only to inheritance from the father. The court then held that a federal statute governing intestate succession to Indian Trust Land which had the effect of barring the inheritance by an illegitimate through her mother was in violation of the Due Process Clause of the Fifth Amendment. On the other hand, In re Karas' Estate, 61 Ill.2d 40, 329 N.E.2d 234 (1975) held that Labine did not require holding an Illinois statute unconstitutional where it permitted the illegitimate child to inherit from his mother but not from his father. Karas was overruled by Trimble

statutes which provide that the wrongful death action is for the benefit of those persons entitled to take the intestate personal property of the decedent.[10] In that situation it is impossible to say which case, Levy or Labine, governs the constitutionality of the statute, since Levy purports to invalidate the wrongful death statute, but Labine upholds the intestate provision.

The Supreme Court decided other cases dealing with the rights of the illegitimate child between its Labine decision in 1971 and 1977,[11] but it did not again pass on a state inheritance statute until the latter year. The case was Trimble v. Gordon [12] which, by a five to four majority, held unconstitutional the Illinois statute providing that the illegitimate child could inherit from his mother but not from his father.[13] Under Illinois law the legitimate child could inherit from both parents. Suit had been brought by the child's mother on the child's behalf to establish the

child's right to inherit a $2500 Plymouth automobile from her father. Although the child's mother and father had never married, the father before his death had been found to be the child's father in an Illinois paternity proceeding, had complied with the court's order for the support of the child and had acknowledged the child as his own.

The proponents of the statute of course relied upon the Labine case. They also argued that the statute served several state interests. They urged that the purpose of the statute was to ameliorate the status of the illegitimate child by changing the common law rule that he could inherit from neither parent, so far as this could be done consistently with the state's interest in encouraging and preserving family relationships and its interest in establishing an accurate and efficient method of intestate disposition of property. The Supreme Court found that the statute had little connection with the preservation of

v. Gordon, 430 U.S. 762, 97 S.Ct. 1459, 52 L.Ed.2d 31 (1977). See the discussion at note 13, infra.

10. Schmoll v. Creecy, 54 N.J. 194, 254 A.2d 525 (1969), decided before Labine, involved such a statute. It held the statute was unconstitutional under Levy. What the result might be or should be if the case had come up after Labine is impossible to say. Presumably if it came up today, after Trimble v. Gordon, 430 U.S. 762, 97 S.Ct. 1459, 52 L.Ed.2d 31 (1977), the statute would be held invalid.

11. These cases are discussed infra at notes 26, ff.

12. 430 U.S. 762, 97 S.Ct. 1459, 51 L.Ed.2d 31 (1977).

13. In re Karas' Estate, 61 Ill.2d 40, 329 N.E.2d 234 (1975), was overruled by Trimble v. Gordon, 430 U.S. 762, 97 S.Ct. 1459, 52 L.Ed.2d 31 (1977). See note 9 supra. The Illinois statute was recodified after *Trimble* arose but the treatment of the illegitimate child was not changed. Ill.–S.H.A.Ann.Stat. Ch. 110½, § 2–2 (Smith-Hurd Cum. Supp.1984). Many other cases which had relied upon Labine v. Vincent, 401 U.S. 532, 91 S.Ct. 1017, 28 L.Ed.2d 288 (1971), rehearing denied 402 U.S. 990, 91 S.Ct. 1672, 29 L.Ed.2d 156 (1971) are doubtless also overruled. See, e.g., In re Ginochio's Estate, 43 Cal.App.3d 412, 117 Cal. Rptr. 565 (1974); Murray v. Murray, 549 S.W.2d 839 (Ky. App.1977), reversed 564 S.W.2d 5 (Ky.1978); Hanson v. Markham, 371 Mass. 262, 356 N.E.2d 702 (1976); Matter of Thompson's Estate, 136 N.J.Super. 412, 346 A.2d 442 (1975); Moore v. Dague, 46 Ohio App.2d 75, 345 N.E.2d 449 (1975).

Two other cases from the state courts were vacated and remanded for consideration in the light of *Trimble*. Pendleton v. Pendleton, 531 S.W.2d 507 (Ky.1975), vacated and remanded 431 U.S. 911, 97 S.Ct. 2164, 53 L.Ed.2d 270 (1977); Matter of Lalli's Estate, 38 N.Y.2d 77, 340 N.E.2d

721 (1975), vacated and remanded 431 U.S. 911, 97 S.Ct. 2164, 53 L.Ed.2d 220 (1977). The subsequent decision in Lalli is discussed infra at notes 18–22.

Following the remand in Pendleton v. Pendleton, the Kentucky Supreme Court, in a sardonic opinion with which one cannot but sympathize, held that Trimble had made the Kentucky statute unconstitutional. That statute provided that illegitimate children could inherit from their mothers, but could only inherit from their fathers if they had been legitimated by the marriage of their natural parents with each other. The Kentucky court found this to be unconstitutional discrimination between men and women. Pendleton v. Pendleton, 560 S.W.2d 538 (Ky.1977).

The peculiar Louisiana statute forbidding gifts or legacies to adulterine children has been held unconstitutional in Succession of Robins, 349 So.2d 276 (La.1977) in reliance upon the Supreme Court decisions discussed in the text.

The Florida intestacy statute was held unconstitutional on the authority of Trimble v. Gordon in In re Burris Estate, 361 So.2d 152 (Fla.1978).

The Massachusetts statute provided that an illegitimate child could inherit from his mother on the same basis as a legitimate child, but that he could inherit from his father only if his parents married each other and his father either acknowledged paternity or paternity was adjudged. This statute was held to violate the state Equal Rights Amendment in a case in which paternity was conceded as a discrimination based upon sex. But the court reserved the question whether a distinction of this kind might be valid under other, more restrictive limitations. Lowell v. Kowalski, 380 Mass. 663, 405 N.E.2d 135 (1980).

the family since penalizing the children does not influence the parents and since the distinction made by the statute between inheritance from the mother and from the father is not logically connected to the preservation of the family. Presumably the Court was of the view that preservation of the family would require that the child inherit from neither parent. That, with some qualifications, was the effect of the Louisiana statute in Labine. The Court mentioned this difference between the Louisiana and Illinois statutes in a footnote, but did not seem to attach much significance to it. The Illinois Supreme Court's analysis of this state interest was characterized as "most perfunctory".[14]

The state interest in controlling the intestate disposition of property was also held insufficient to justify Illinois in barring the illegitimate's inheritance from his father. The Court conceded that the uncertainty of establishing paternity in some cases might warrant a "more demanding standard"[15] for inheritance by illegitimates from their fathers, but it held that this uncertainty did not apply to all illegitimates. The difficulty of proving paternity in some cases did not justify the Illinois legislature in enacting a statute which forbade inheritance in all cases. Finally, the Court disavowed the argument found in Labine that these statutes are saved by the possibility that other methods of transmitting the property to the illegitimate could have

been used, such as by will or legitimation. This argument never did make any constitutional sense and it was as well that the Court gave it a decent burial.

The Trimble opinion did not in so many words overrule Labine. In a footnote the Court affirmed the view which it found in Labine that deference should be given to the state interest in the stability of land titles and the devolution of property on death.[16] Notwithstanding that saving language, Labine must be taken as substantially limited if not overruled. The most plausible view of the two cases is that state inheritance statutes *may* still pass muster if they only bar the illegitimate child's inheritance from or through his father, and then only in those precise kinds of cases in which paternity is actually in doubt. As in so many other recent cases, the Supreme Court was in effect drafting a statute for the state legislatures. In Trimble paternity was not in doubt because it had been both adjudicated and acknowledged. Of course this was also true in Labine, where the child's father had publicly acknowledged paternity.[17] Thus the facts in the two cases were identical, a point which the Trimble opinion failed to mention.

The uncertainty created by Trimble's treatment of Labine has not been reduced by the Supreme Court's approval of the New York inheritance statute in Lalli v. Lalli.[18] That

---

14. 430 U.S. at 768, 97 S.Ct. at 1464.

15. 430 U.S. at 770, 97 S.Ct. at 1465.

16. The Court was relying upon the view of Labine taken in Weber v. Aetna Casualty & Surety Co., 406 U.S. 164, 92 S.Ct. 1400, 31 L.Ed.2d 768 (1972), which had attempted to justify the Labine decision on the basis of the state's interest in land titles and the determination of ownership, although neither case explains why this state interest is of greater importance than other state interests such as the interest in controlling wrongful death claims or workmen's compensation claims. Nor is it explained why, if the illegitimate child can establish paternity in the wrongful death action, he is not permitted to do the same in the probate proceeding.

17. Labine v. Vincent, 401 U.S. 532, 533, 91 S.Ct. 1017, 1018, 28 L.Ed.2d 288 (1971), rehearing denied 402 U.S. 990, 91 S.Ct. 1672, 29 L.Ed.2d 156 (1971). The analysis suggested in the text is supported by Estate of Blumreich, 84 Wis.2d 545, 267 N.W.2d 870 (1978), appeal dismissed 439 U.S. 1061, 99 S.Ct. 822, 59 L.Ed.2d 26 (1979), which held constitutional the Wisconsin intestacy

statute which provided that the illegitimate child could inherit from his father if paternity had been a) adjudicated; b) admitted in open court; or c) acknowledged by the father in writing. The court held that this was a "carefully tuned" statute in accordance with the Supreme Court's requirements.

18. Lalli v. Lalli, 439 U.S. 259, 99 S.Ct. 518, 58 L.Ed.2d 503 (1978). The confusion generated in the state courts by these cases is graphically demonstrated by Lucas v. Handcock, 583 S.W.2d 491 (Ark.1979), Nagle v. Wood, 178 Conn. 180, 423 A.2d 875 (1979), which followed Trimble, and Everage v. Gibson, 372 So.2d 829 (Ala.1979), cert. denied 445 U.S. 931, 100 S.Ct. 1322, 63 L.Ed.2d 765 (1980); Hayes v. Smith, 194 Conn. 52, 480 A.2d 425 (1984); Poulos v. McMahan, 250 Ga. 354, 297 S.E.2d 451 (1982); Tekulve v. Turner, 181 Ind.App. 295, 391 N.E.2d 673 (1979); and Davis v. Jones, 626 S.W.2d 303 (Tex.1982), 391 N.E.2d 673 (1979), which followed Lalli. Handley, By and Through Herron v. Schweiker, 697 F.2d 999 (11th Cir.1983) rejects Everage and seems to say the issue is governed by Mills v. Habluetzel, 456 U.S. 91, 102 S.Ct.

statute provided that an illegitimate child could inherit from his father only if a court of competent jurisdiction had, during the father's lifetime, made a finding of paternity in a filiation suit brought during the mother's pregnancy or within two years after the child's birth. The child in Lalli had been acknowledged by his father and paternity was conceded by all parties. But since paternity had not been established by a court in a filiation proceeding, the statute did not permit him to inherit from his father. The Supreme Court's position was that the state has an important interest in ensuring the orderly disposition of property on death, and in the finality of intestate distribution.[19] The Court found that the New York statute was calculated to accomplish these objectives whereas the Illinois statute held invalid in Trimble went beyond the accomplishment of similar objectives.

Mr. Justice Blackmun concurred in the Lalli judgment on the ground that it in effect overruled Trimble and resurrected Labine.[20] Mr. Justice Rehnquist concurred in the Lalli judgment for the reason stated in his dissent in Trimble, which was in general that the Court was using the Equal Protection Clause

to second-guess legislatures with respect to issues on which the Court has no greater expertise than the legislators who enacted the statutes.[21] And finally four justices dissented on the ground that the statute in Lalli did not differ from that in Trimble, and that both statutes inflicted injustice upon illegitimate children unnecessarily.[22] The result is that the plurality opinion in Lalli speaks for only three justices. Two justices had the view that Labine was correct, while four justices would hold all such statutes unconstitutional unless very carefully tailored to deal with the problem of proving paternity.

One further justification for the Illinois statute was advanced by its supporters in Trimble but was expressly not passed upon by the Court.[23] The argument was made that the intestacy statute distinguished between legitimate and illegitimate children because of a presumed desire on the part of decedents to have their property go to legitimate children or other relatives in preference to illegitimate children. The Court refused to respond to this argument on the ground that the Illinois statute had not been enacted for this purpose. It is not clear what basis there was for this view of the statutory purpose.[24] No

---

1549, 71 L.Ed.2d 770 (1982). The height of confusion or perhaps incomprehensibility, is exemplified by White v. Randolph, 59 Ohio St.2d 6, 391 N.E.2d 333 (1979), appeal dismissed for want of a substantial federal question, 444 U.S. 1061, 100 S.Ct. 1000, 62 L.Ed.2d 743 (1980). The Ohio statute in this case is indistinguishable from the Illinois statute held unconstitutional in Trimble and yet the Ohio Supreme Court held it valid and the United States Supreme Court apparently thought its validity obvious. Lowell v. Kowalski, 380 Mass. 663, 405 N.E.2d 135 (1980) held the Massachusetts statute unconstitutional under the state Equal Rights Amendment, but intimated that a statute requiring the marriage of the parents before a child could inherit from his father would be unconstitutional under Trimble, but that a statute requiring an acknowledgment of paternity as a condition on inheritance would be valid under Lalli.

A Louisiana case has now held that the statute which Labine found constitutional is in fact unconstitutional under Trimble, although Labine has never been overruled. Succession of Brown, 388 So.2d 1151 (La.1980), cert. denied 450 U.S. 998, 101 S.Ct. 1703, 68 L.Ed.2d 199 (1981).

19. This justification for discriminating against the illegitimate child does not seem adequate. The Uniform Probate Code, for example, has no difficulty in ensuring an orderly distribution of property and the finality of probate decrees even though it permits the illegitimate

child to inherit from his father. This is done by provisions for notice and for statutes of limitation restricting attack upon intestate distribution. See Uniform Probate Code §§ 2–109, 8 Unif.L.Ann. 66 (1983); 1–401, 8 Unif.L. Ann. 47 (1983); 3–1001, 8 Unif.L.Ann. 398 (1983); 3–1003, 8 Unif.L.Ann. 402 (1983); 3–1005, 8 Unif.L.Ann. 405 (1983). Any scheme of probate administration must obviously provide for unknown heirs or devisees who might turn up during or after probate. The illegitimate child creates no greater difficulty in the administration of estates than does the unexpected claimant.

20. 439 U.S. at 276, 99 S.Ct. at 528.

21. Id. at 276, 99 S.Ct. at 528.

22. Id. at 277, 99 S.Ct. at 529. (Brennan, White, Marshall, Stevens, JJ., dissenting.)

23. 430 U.S. at 774, 97 S.Ct. at 1467.

24. It is curious that the discredited notion that a statute is to be construed by reference to "the intent of the legislature" should put in a new appearance in Equal Protection cases. Obviously no one can know what the intent of a legislature was in passing a particular statute. In most instances there will have been no single intent. If by "intent of the legislature" is meant the purpose of the statute, to be gathered from its provisions taken in their context, that is of course a legitimate and sensible aid in statutory construction. But the Court in Trimble was not approaching the statute in this way, but rather

evidence on this point seems to have been offered in the trial court, probably because no such evidence was available. It does seem reasonably plain that the underlying aim of any legislature enacting an intestacy statute must be to reflect "the normal desire of the owner of wealth regarding the disposition of his property at death." [25] In fact the draftsmen of the Uniform Probate Code relied upon the "prevailing patterns of wills" in order to determine what these normal desires might be.[26] If we can assume that this is so, what effect does this have on the validity of intestacy provisions concerning the illegitimate child? If the deceased makes a will excluding his illegitimate child from any share in the property, presumably there is no state action and therefore no violation of the Equal Protection Clause.[27] But when this occurs by operation of the intestacy statute, there clearly is state action. The question then is, as the Court has several times said,[28] whether a legitimate governmental interest is served by regulating the intestate devolution of property in a way of which presumably most decedents would have approved if they had considered the matter. The state, it may be said, is only doing what the decedent would have wanted to do if he had not omitted to make a will. On the other hand it was exactly this sort of classification, made without reference to biological relationships, which the Court held unconstitutional in Levy v. Louisiana [29] and in Weber v. Aetna Casualty & Surety Co.[30] Mr. Justice Harlan's dissent in the for-

mer case urged that what the legislature was doing in enacting the wrongful death statute was trying to define the interest which one person has in the death of another. This involved drawing somewhat arbitrary lines based on family relationships, without reference to affection or loss in particular cases. His argument was rejected, though not answered, by the majority. Intestacy statutes could be described in the same way. They too are attempting to define the interest which one person has in the death of another. The wrongful death statutes may also have been drafted with some thought to the probable affections of decedents, but that did not save them from invalidity. Therefore if wrongful death statutes may not define this interest in the death of another person to exclude the illegitimate, it would seem that intestacy statutes may not either. A similar argument could be based on the Weber case which involved workmen's compensation claims for the death of an insured worker. It held invalid a statutory scheme of payments on the death of a worker which excluded illegitimates under certain circumstances and which may well have been based on some notion of the decedent's probable desires. This statute also can be described as defining the interest which certain relatives have in the death of another. If neither the wrongful death statutes nor the workmen's compensation statutes may define this interest so as to exclude the illegitimate child, it would seem logical to hold that the intestacy statute may not ei-

was concerned with the subjective desire of the Illinois legislature, with its motivation.

25. The quotation is from R. Wellman, 1 Uniform Probate Code Practice Manual 59 (1977). See also Wellman and Gordon, Uniformity in State Inheritance Laws: How UPC Article II Has Fared in Nine Enactments, 1976 B.Y.U.L.Rev. 357; J. Woerner, American Law of Administration 183 (3d ed. 1923).

26. R. Wellman, 1 Uniform Probate Code Practice Manual 59 (1977).

27. Cf. Commonwealth of Pennsylvania v. Brown, 392 F.2d 120 (3d Cir.1968), cert. denied 391 U.S. 921, 88 S.Ct. 1811, 20 L.Ed.2d 657 (1968), and cases cited.

28. E.g. in Trimble v. Gordon, 430 U.S. 762, 97 S.Ct. 1459, 52 L.Ed.2d 31 (1977); Mathews v. Lucas, 427 U.S. 495, 504, 96 S.Ct. 2755, 2761, 49 L.Ed.2d 651 (1976); Weber v. Aetna Casualty & Surety Co., 406 U.S. 164, 172, 173, 92 S.Ct. 1400, 1405, 31 L.Ed.2d 768 (1972).

29. 391 U.S. 68 (1968), rehearing denied 393 U.S. 898, 89 S.Ct. 65, 21 L.Ed.2d 185 (1968).

30. 406 U.S. 164, 92 S.Ct. 1400, 31 L.Ed.2d 768 (1972). The suggestion was made in this case also that the Workmen's Compensation statute was merely distinguishing between dependents enjoying greater familial care and affection and those enjoying less, placing illegitimates in the latter category. The Court held this not sufficient to uphold the statute because the illegitimate child "may be nourished and loved." 406 U.S. at 174, 92 S.Ct. at 1406. The argument outlined in the text was adopted by the court in King v. Commonwealth, 221 Va. 251, 269 S.E.2d 793 (1980) in support of its decision that a statute was constitutional in permitting maternal relatives but not paternal relatives to inherit from illegitimate children.

ther. But since factors other than logic influence these cases, the law's future course of development remains uncertain.

Social Security Act

The Supreme Court has had about as much difficulty in determining the constitutionality of various provisions of the Social Security Act as it has had with state inheritance laws. Of course in these cases the Fifth Amendment rather than the Fourteenth Amendment is the applicable constitutional provision, but under Bolling v. Sharpe [31] the constitutional principles are the same. The first cases to come before the Court concerned the validity of the complex provisions of the Act which regulate the benefits payable to a child of a deceased insured wage earner. The statute defined a "child" of the wage earner by reference to three tests: A "child" is one (a) who by state law would take the personal property of the deceased wage earner by intestacy; [32] or (b) one whose parents went through a marriage ceremony which would result in a valid marriage but for a prior subsisting marriage or some procedural defect; [33] or, (c) who is a child of the deceased wage earner and who has been acknowledged as such by the wage earner, or has been adjudicated as such, or who has been ordered to be supported by the wage earner by a court, or who is shown to the satisfaction of the Secretary of Health, Education and Welfare to be the child of the wage earner and who was living with or being supported by the wage earner. [34] The statute also provided, however, that if the claims of persons entitled under the Act exceed the

maximum amount payable on the death of the wage earner, then those entitled under (c) in the foregoing list must have their payments reduced (or even eliminated) to the extent necessary to bring the total claims of survivors within the amount payable. [35] The practical effect of this was that if the wage earner left a spouse and legitimate children whose allowable claims exceeded the payments due on the wage earner's death, any illegitimate child of the wage earner would receive less than his entitlement, or in some cases nothing at all. In this fashion the Act clearly discriminated against illegitimate children, vis à vis the spouse and legitimate children.

In 1972 two three-judge federal district courts held that the discrimination so imposed by the Social Security Act was arbitrary and violated the Fifth Amendment. Both cases were affirmed per curiam by the Supreme Court [36] on the authority of Weber v. Aetna Casualty & Surety Co. [37]

Two years later the Supreme Court, in Jimenez v. Weinberger [38] similarly decided that the disability provision of the Social Security Act violated the Fifth Amendment in excluding from insurance benefits on the disability of a wage earner illegitimate children born after the onset of the father's disability. Since they were born after the disability occurred, they could not come within the provision of the statute requiring that their paternity be acknowledged or that they were living with and being supported by their father before his disability occurred. [39] The effect of

---

31. 347 U.S. 497, 74 S.Ct. 693, 98 L.Ed. 884 (1954), holding that although the Fifth Amendment does not contain an Equal Protection Clause as does the Fourteenth Amendment, the standards of the Equal Protection Clause have been judicially imported into the Due Process Clause of the Fifth Amendment.

32. 42 U.S.C.A. § 416(h)(2)(a).

33. 42 U.S.C.A. § 416(h)(2)(b).

34. 42 U.S.C.A. § 416(h)(3).

35. 42 U.S.C.A. § 403(a)(3).

36. Davis v. Richardson, 342 F.Supp. 588 (D.Conn. 1972), affirmed 409 U.S. 1069, 93 S.Ct. 678, 34 L.Ed.2d 659 (1972); Griffin v. Richardson, 346 F.Supp. 1226 (D.Md.1972), affirmed 409 U.S. 1069, 93 S.Ct. 689, 34 L.Ed.2d 660 (1972).

Clark, Domestic Rel., 2nd Ed. HBSE—7

37. 406 U.S. 164, 92 S.Ct. 1400, 31 L.Ed.2d 768 (1972), discussed infra at note 54.

38. 417 U.S. 628, 94 S.Ct. 2496, 41 L.Ed.2d 363 (1974), appeal after remand 523 F.2d 689 (7th Cir.1975). A similar case reaching the same result as Jimenez is Beaty v. Weinberger, 478 F.2d 300 (5th Cir.1973), affirmed p.c. 418 U.S. 901, 94 S.Ct. 3190, 41 L.Ed.2d 1150 (1974). The Fifth Circuit opinion in this case took a broader view of the issue, holding that once dependency is established, the Constitution requires that all dependents must be treated alike. 478 F.2d at 308.

39. The applicable portions of the statute are 42 U.S.C.A. § 402(d)(3) and 402 U.S.C.A. § 416(h)(3)(B)(ii).

this provision was therefore to discriminate between two classes of illegitimate children, those born before and those born after the occurrence of the father's disability, as well as between legitimate and illegitimate children. The argument made in support of the Act's validity was that its purpose was to prevent spurious claims by illegitimate children not really dependent upon the disabled wage earner. The Supreme Court found this argument unpersuasive because the exclusion of the after-born illegitimates was not reasonably related to this purpose. The opinion asserted that for all that appeared in the case some illegitimate children entitled under the statute to benefits might not be dependent upon the wage earner, while some excluded because born after the disability might be dependent. It appeared that in this particular case the excluded children had been acknowledged as his by the wage earner and had lived with and been supported by him after the onset of his disability.

Jimenez exemplifies, perhaps to a greater degree even than Trimble v. Gordon,[40] the Supreme Court's intermittent tendency to second guess legislative bodies and rewrite statutes. As Mr. Justice Rehnquist points out in dissent the decision seems to be based not only upon equal protection but also upon the very dubious notion that irrebuttable presumptions violate the Due Process Clause, and finally upon an argument that the government had failed to present sufficient evidence to demonstrate that the classification of illegitimates did in fact serve a valid purpose. As a guide to the further legislative treatment of the illegitimate child the case is therefore of limited significance.

By 1976 then the Court had upset two kinds of discrimination imposed by the Social Security Act, one which gave a priority in social security benefits to the spouse, the legitimate children and some classes of illegitimate children over other classes of illegitimate children,[41] and the other which excluded from disability benefits illegitimate children born after the occurrence of the disability.[42] In 1976 the Supreme Court, in Mathews v. Lucas[43] held constitutional a section of the Social Security Act[44] which had been indirectly involved in the earlier cases. Mathews v. Lucas arose out of the claims by two illegitimate children for children's insurance benefits on the wage earner's death. The trial court found that the claimants were the children of the deceased wage earner. It also found that the deceased had lived with the children's mother from 1948 to 1966, and apparently with the children from their birth to 1966. It found that in 1966 the deceased left his "family" and lived apart from them until his death in 1968, and at his death he was not contributing to their support. The deceased never acknowledged the children in writing as his own, nor were his paternity or support obligations ever the subject of a court decree. Under those circumstances the Act excluded the children from insurance at the death of the deceased. Reversing a trial court holding of unconstitutionality,[45] the Supreme Court found that the statute has as its purpose the financial protection of children actually dependent upon the wage earner at his death, and that the classification in the statute is valid because reasonably related to the likelihood of dependency at death. The obvious difficulty with this result is that the statute

40. 430 U.S. 762, 97 S.Ct. 1459, 52 L.Ed.2d 31 (1977). See discussion at note 12, supra.

41. See cases cited in note 31, supra.

42. Jimenez v. Weinberger, 417 U.S. 628, 94 S.Ct. 2496, 41 L.Ed.2d 363 (1974), appeal after remand 523 F.2d 689 (7th Cir.1975), cert. denied 427 U.S. 912, 96 S.Ct. 3200, 49 L.Ed.2d 1204 (1976), cited supra, note 33.

43. 427 U.S. 495, 96 S.Ct. 2755, 49 L.Ed.2d 651 (1976). The decision was by a six to three vote, Justices Stevens, Brennan and Marshall dissenting. A case dealing with the same provision of the Social Security Act likewise upheld the statute in the same term of court. Norton v. Mathews, 427 U.S. 524, 96 S.Ct. 2771, 49 L.Ed.2d 672

(1976). See also Kimbrell v. Mathews, 429 F.Supp. 440 (D.La.1977).

44. 42 U.S.C.A. § 416(h)(3)(c)(ii). See the text discussion at note 33, supra.

United States v. Clark, 445 U.S. 23, 100 S.Ct. 895, 63 L.Ed.2d 171 (1980) construed a similar provision in the Civil Service Retirement Act so as to cover illegitimate children who had lived with the deceased employee at any time, thereby avoiding a decision on its constitutionality. The relevant provision is 5 U.S.C.A. § 8341(a)(4)(A).

45. Lucas v. Secretary, Department of Health, Education & Welfare, 390 F.Supp. 1310 (D.R.I.1975).

permits children's insurance benefits to be paid to legitimate children without any showing that they lived with or were receiving support from the wage earner when he died.[46] The Court's solution of this difficulty was to say that what amounts to a presumption of dependency in the statute is justifiable on the ground of administrative convenience.[47] These categories of children, including legitimate ones, said the Court, who need not prove actual dependency in order to receive benefits, are children as to whom there is a likelihood of actual dependency. The presumption that legitimate children are ipso facto dependent is characterized as "rational".

Involved in all of the cases on the rights of illegitimate children but especially emphasized in the Mathews case is the question (to put it in the currently fashionable cant phrase) of the strictness of the "scrutiny" with which the Court is to regard the legislation before it. In Trimble v. Gordon,[48] Jimenez v. Weinberger,[49] and Mathews v. Lucas,[50] the Court was urged to characterize illegitimacy as a "suspect classification", which, according to the prevailing reasoning, would require that statutes discriminating between the legitimate and the illegitimate child be given the "strictest scrutiny".[51] The argument was that illegitimacy as a basis for classification is like race in that it turns on personal characteristics for which the individual is not responsible, which he cannot change, and which have no relation to his abilities, or his worth as a citizen. While conceding the aptness of the analogy, the Court has nevertheless refused to accept the

argument. The reason seems to be that although the illegitimate has in the past endured legal disabilities, they have never been as severe or pervasive as those imposed upon women and blacks.[52] This might be a reason for a legislature not to remove some of the disabilities, but it certainly is irrelevant on the issue of the validity of those disabilities which continue to exist. The only apparent reason for invalidating statutes which discriminate against the illegitimate child is that they are irrelevant to his worth and that he is not responsible for the circumstances of his birth. Therefore if any classification is to be given "strictest scrutiny", that turning on legitimacy should be.

Perhaps in partial recognition that the rejection of the "strictest scrutiny" test makes little sense, the Court has taken what might be viewed (if one can discern what it is) a middle position somewhere between "strictest scrutiny" and the minimum requirement that the statute bear some rational relation to a legitimate state purpose.[53] The scrutiny which is to be directed at a classification based upon legitimacy is characterized in both Mathews[54] and Trimble v. Gordon[55] as "not a toothless one." There is no indication in either opinion that the Court was being facetious, but some amusement is irresistible at the image of the justices engaging in either the "toothless scrutiny" of a statute, or one that is not "toothless". In any event, what this seems to mean as a practical matter is that where the illegitimate child claims that the statute creates an unconstitutional distinction between legitimate and illegitimate

46. 42 U.S.C.A. §§ 402(d)(1), 416(h)(2)(A), the latter section providing that benefits go to a child who would be entitled, under the applicable state law, to take the wage earner's property by intestacy. This of course would include legitimate children in all states, plus some illegitimate children in some states.

47. Cf. Stanley v. Illinois, 405 U.S. 645, 656, 92 S.Ct. 1208, 1215, 31 L.Ed.2d 551 (1972), in which administrative convenience was found to be insufficient justification for a statute which deprived fathers of illegitimate children of parental rights. The argument from administrative convenience was stronger in Stanley than in Mathews, leading one to conclude that the Court applied the wrong scale of priorities in both cases.

48. 430 U.S. 762, 97 S.Ct. 1459, 52 L.Ed.2d 31 (1977).

49. 417 U.S. 628, 94 S.Ct. 2496, 41 L.Ed.2d 363 (1974), appeal after remand 523 F.2d 689 (7th Cir.1975), cert. denied 427 U.S. 912, 96 S.Ct. 3200, 49 L.Ed.2d 1204 (1976).

50. 427 U.S. 495, 96 S.Ct. 2755, 49 L.Ed.2d 651 (1976).

51. E.g., Loving v. Virginia, 388 U.S. 1, 11, 87 S.Ct. 1817, 1823, 18 L.Ed.2d 1010 (1967), holding that classifications based upon race must be subjected to the "most rigid scrutiny".

52. Mathews v. Lucas, 427 U.S. 495, 506, 96 S.Ct. 2755, 2762, 49 L.Ed.2d 651 (1976).

53. Id. at 510, 96 S.Ct. at 2764.

54. Ibid.

55. 430 U.S. 762, 97 S.Ct. 1459, 52 L.Ed.2d 31 (1977).

children, he has the burden of establishing that the distinction bears no substantial relation to a proper state interest.[56] Although Supreme Court opinions do seem to emphasize the level of scrutiny to be addressed to a particular statute, perhaps this is not a controlling factor in the illegitimacy cases after all. To the skeptical reader it looks very much like a rhetorical device for putting a good face on a decision already taken for other reasons.

The question remains whether Jimenez and Mathews can be reconciled. In both cases the statute excluded a class of illegitimate children from benefits which were available to legitimate children. Both cases turned in part upon the same provision of the statute. The purpose of the discrimination in Jimenez was to exclude from disability benefits children born after the occurrence of the disability because their claims might be spurious. The argument was that claims are more likely to be trumped up after the benefits have accrued by children who are either not the children of the wage earner, or who are not dependent upon him, the overriding aim of the statute being to provide support for dependent children. The Court in Jimenez rejected this argument, saying that some of the included illegitimates may not be dependent, and some of the excluded ones may be. In other words the statutory distinction does not precisely correspond with the statutory purpose. In Mathews, however, the same condition existed. Some of the children, either legitimate or illegitimate, included by the statute in the list of those entitled to death benefits might not in fact be dependent on the wage earner. Yet they received benefits. Those excluded were children not living with nor being supported by the wage earner, but they may well have been dependent upon him

in the sense of having no other source of support. Thus in both cases a distinction was made between legitimate and illegitimate children which was not related to the statutory purpose. If ever the facts and legal issues in two cases were alike, they are in these cases. The two cases therefore cannot be reconciled. Mathews is also inconsistent with Trimble v. Gordon, with the result in Levy v. Louisiana,[57] and with the result and much of the language in Weber v. Aetna Casualty & Surety Co.[58] Mathews withholds a statutory benefit, in other words, on the basis of illegitimacy of birth, a condition for which the child is not responsible, and one which has no relation to the withholding of the benefit. Such a result belies all that one thought the prior cases (other than Labine) had established.

Other Discrimination Against the Illegitimate

On three other occasions the Supreme Court has upset state legislation which discriminated against the illegitimate child by denying benefits granted to the legitimate child. The first of the cases, Weber v. Aetna Casualty & Surety Co.[59] has already been mentioned. This decision held unconstitutional the Louisiana workmen's compensation statute which provided that illegitimate children not acknowledged by their father could only receive benefits on the death of their father if there were not enough surviving dependents of other classes, including legitimate children and acknowledged illegitimate children, to exhaust the maximum allowable benefits. The Court, relying heavily on Levy v. Louisiana,[60] and distinguishing Labine v. Vincent,[61] suggested that fundamental personal rights were involved calling for a "stricter scrutiny" of the statute, a position which has

56. Mathews v. Lucas, 427 U.S. 495, 510, 96 S.Ct. 2755, 2764, 49 L.Ed.2d 651 (1976).

57. 391 U.S. 68, 88 S.Ct. 1509, 20 L.Ed.2d 436 (1968), rehearing denied 393 U.S. 898, 89 S.Ct. 65, 21 L.Ed.2d 185 (1968).

58. 406 U.S. 164, 92 S.Ct. 1400, 31 L.Ed.2d 768 (1972).

59. 406 U.S. 164, 92 S.Ct. 1400, 31 L.Ed.2d 768 (1972).

60. 391 U.S. 68, 88 S.Ct. 1509, 20 L.Ed.2d 436 (1968), rehearing denied 393 U.S. 898, 89 S.Ct. 65, 21 L.Ed.2d 185 (1968).

61. 401 U.S. 532, 91 S.Ct. 1017, 28 L.Ed.2d 288 (1971), rehearing denied 402 U.S. 990, 91 S.Ct. 1672, 29 L.Ed.2d 156 (1971).

now apparently been repudiated.[62] Louisiana had stated the purpose of the statute to be the protection of legitimate family relationships. Construing this expression of purpose, the Court attributed to Louisiana the obviously absurd notion that persons contemplating illicit sexual relations would abstain because they knew that any children resulting from the union would be denied workmen's compensation death benefits. Finding it inconceivable that the statute would have this effect upon people, the Court was led to say that the statute bore no rational relation to its purpose and therefore violated the Equal Protection Clause. Later in the opinion the Court took a more sensible view of this and similar statutes, saying that they express "society's condemnation of irresponsible liaisons beyond the bonds of marriage."[63] It then disclosed what must be the real meaning of the case, which is that it is illogical and unjust to enforce this condemnation by imposing disabilities upon the innocent illegitimate child. This violates the fundamental legal principle that burdens should be related to responsibility or wrongdoing. No analysis is apparent by which this decision can be reconciled with the decision and the Court's discussion in Mathews v. Lucas.[64] In both cases the broad statutory purpose was the financial relief of dependents of the wage earner. In Mathews the Court indulged in a presumption that illegitimates were less likely than legitimates to be dependent. But in Weber, where a similar presumption would have been just as appropriate, the statutory classification was condemned.

The impression one gets from Weber that it was broadly condemning all statutory disabilities of the illegitimate is reinforced by Gomez v. Perez,[65] decided less than a year later,

holding that the state of Texas violated the Equal Protection Clause by not permitting the illegitimate child to recover support from his father when the legitimate child had such a right to support.

Weber was likewise relied upon to hold, in the same Term of Court, that a New Jersey welfare statute was unconstitutional when it limited benefits to those families composed of married persons and their children.[66] Although the legislation was obviously aimed at the preservation of families in the traditional sense of the term, the Court held that its effect was to exclude illegitimate children from benefits, that the benefits were as indispensable to them as to legitimate children, and therefore the statute violated the Equal Protection Clause. The brevity of the opinion in this case leaves unanswered the question why the traditional definition of "family" has suddenly turned out to be unfairly discriminatory. The statutory benefit here, involving financial assistance, might well be an inducement for the parties to marry, and therefore the relation between the statute and its goal was certainly rational. One can only conclude that the goal, the encouragement of traditional family relationships, in which the parents were validly married, was not a legitimate one in the Court's view.

Immigration

The immigration laws give a preferred status to aliens who are either "children" or "parents" of United States citizens or permanent residents.[67] One section of those laws defines "child" in such a way, however, as to exclude the illegitimate child seeking preferred status by virtue of his relation to his father.[68] Likewise the father of an illegitimate child who is seeking such status by

---

62. Trimble v. Gordon, 430 U.S. 762, 97 S.Ct. 1459, 52 L.Ed.2d 31 (1977); Mathews v. Lucas, 427 U.S. 495, 96 S.Ct. 2755, 49 L.Ed.2d 651 (1976).

63. 406 U.S. at 175, 92 S.Ct. at 1406.

64. 427 U.S. 495, 96 S.Ct. 2755, 49 L.Ed.2d 651 (1976).

65. 409 U.S. 535, 93 S.Ct. 872, 35 L.Ed.2d 56 (1973). Texas law has been brought into conformity with the rule of this case by In Interest of R___ V_____ M_____, 530 S.W.2d 921 (Tex.Civ.App.1975). Idaho, the only other state in which the illegitimate formerly had no claim on

his father for support, now has a statute which gives him such a claim. Idaho Code §§ 7–1101 to 7–1123 (1979 and Supp.1984).

66. New Jersey Welfare Rights Organization v. Cahill, 411 U.S. 619, 93 S.Ct. 1700, 36 L.Ed.2d 543 (1973).

67. 8 U.S.C.A. §§ 1151(a), (b), 1182(a), (b).

68. 8 U.S.C.A. § 1101(b)(1). This section does grant preferred status to the illegitimate child seeking to enter the United States by virtue of his relation to his mother.

virtue of a child who is a United States citizen may not receive the preferred treatment if the child is illegitimate.[69] The effect of obtaining preferred status is that the alien may enter the United States independently of either a numerical quota, or a labor certification requirement, if his relative is a United States citizen, or independently of the labor certification requirement if his relative is a resident alien.[70] In Fiallo v. Bell [71] several fathers of illegitimate children and several illegitimate children sued to invalidate these provisions of the immigration laws on the ground that they violated the Equal Protection Clause, in that they discriminated on the basis of illegitimacy (among other factors) without either compelling or rational justification. The Court's response relied upon "the limited scope of judicial inquiry into immigration legislation," and the established doctrine that Congress' "power over aliens is of a political character and therefore subject only to narrow judicial review." [72] The Court, in that context, then held that it could not consider the claim of unconstitutional discrimination against illegitimate children, statutory distinctions of this kind being within the exclusive authority of the political branches of the government. This was so notwithstanding the obvious fact, urged by the plaintiffs, that the statute discriminated against United States citizens and permanent residents as well as against aliens, since it prevented such citizens and residents from being united with their relatives. This aspect of the case is peculiar in its refusal to give the slightest consideration to biological relationships after those relationships had been so heavily emphasized in the Levy [73] and Weber [74] cases.

Discrimination Against Parents of Illegitimate Children

A companion case to Levy, Glona v. American Guarantee & Liability Insurance Co.,[75] held unconstitutional a Louisiana statute under which the mother of an illegitimate child was not permitted to recover for the wrongful death of her child. Recognizing that this statute raised different issues from that in Levy, the Court nevertheless found no rational basis for it, so long as the mother of a legitimate child was permitted to recover for his death. The only possible basis which the Court could see for the distinction was that it was aimed at discouraging illegitimacy, a basis which the Court found far-fetched. The Court gave no consideration to the obvious basis for all such statutes, which is that they recognize family relationships in the traditional sense and do not recognize them when no marriage has occurred between the parents. One of the major purposes of our law of marriage and legitimacy is to give legal significance to the commitment undertaken when a man and woman marry, a commitment which is absent when they do not marry but merely have sexual relations which may or may not produce offspring. To say that the states may not, under the Constitution, require such a legal commitment, one having traditional moral and social aspects as well, is bizarre in the extreme.

In contrast to Glona, which invalidated a statutory distinction between married and unmarried mothers, the Supreme Court has upheld against constitutional attack a Georgia statute denying fathers of illegitimate children the right to sue for the wrongful death of their children, when the mothers of such children were permitted to sue.[76] Under the statute fathers could sue if they had previously

Thus it discriminates on the basis of sex as well as of legitimacy.

69. 8 U.S.C.A. § 1101(b)(2).

70. See the sections cited supra, note 62. As of January 1, 1977 the parent-child relationship does not confer preferred status with respect to the labor certification requirement. 8 U.S.C.A. § 1182(a)(14).

71. 430 U.S. 787, 97 S.Ct. 1473, 52 L.Ed.2d 50 (1977).

72. 430 U.S. at 792, 97 S.Ct. at 1477.

73. Levy v. Louisiana, 391 U.S. 68, 88 S.Ct. 1509, 20 L.Ed.2d 436 (1968), rehearing denied 393 U.S. 898, 89 S.Ct. 65, 21 L.Ed.2d 185 (1968).

74. Weber v. Aetna Casualty & Surety Co., 406 U.S. 164, 92 S.Ct. 1400, 31 L.Ed.2d 768 (1972).

75. 391 U.S. 73, 88 S.Ct. 1515, 20 L.Ed.2d 441 (1968), rehearing denied 393 U.S. 898, 89 S.Ct. 66, 21 L.Ed.2d 185 (1968).

76. Parham v. Hughes, 441 U.S. 347, 99 S.Ct. 1742, 60 L.Ed.2d 269 (1979).

availed themselves of the statutory legitimation procedure. Four of the justices dissented. The statute was attacked both as creating an impermissible discrimination between men and women, and between fathers of legitimate children and fathers of illegitimate children. Under the Georgia statute the father of a legitimate child could sue for the child's death if the mother were no longer alive. The state's interests which the Court held were sufficient to justify the statutory classification were the prevention of fraudulent claims of paternity and the avoidance of multiple suits by plaintiffs all claiming to be fathers of the deceased. Glona was distinguished because the discrimination there, between married and unmarried mothers, involved no risk of fraudulent claims, and because the statute there foreclosed all mothers of illegitimate children, while the Georgia statute in Parham barred only the father who had failed to legitimate his child. Although the factual distinction between the two cases does exist, the reasoning in Glona would lead to a different result in Parham, as the Parham dissent points out. And the risk of fraudulent claims exists in all cases where paternity is in issue, such as, for example, Gomez, Weber, Levy and Jimenez. Yet the prevention of fraudulent claims was not thought a sufficient state interest to warrant the statutory classification in those cases. In short Parham constitutes still another example of the Court's confusion and inability to deal with illegitimacy in a sensible way.

The rights of fathers with respect to their illegitimate children have also arisen in a line of cases dealing with the termination of parental rights and consent to adoption. These cases, Stanley v. Illinois,[77] Quilloin v. Walcott,[78] and Caban v. Mohammed,[79] are as difficult to understand as the cases discussed in this section. Since they are basic to the

operation of the adoption process, an analysis of these cases will be attempted in a later section.[80]

We are in a period when moral values are rapidly changing and when there is a wide tendency to question and to criticize marriage as an institution. At the same time marriage is the way of life chosen by the overwhelming majority of the people in the United States. A legislature might well decide that it is wiser in such circumstances to give the father of the illegitimate child some rights with respect to custody. Other legislatures might decide that the father of such a child who is not willing to make the commitment which marriage represents should not have such rights. To hold that the second legislature may not make that choice without violating the Constitution of the United States unwisely and unnecessarily restricts the diversity of response to social problems which is one of the chief benefits of a federal form of government.

Further Application of Equal Protection to Illegitimates

The Supreme Court's treatment of the illegitimate child raises many questions, both practical and constitutional, having significance both for illegitimate children and for family relations in general. The Court has already confronted one such question and has been unable to resolve it. An illegitimate child sought to recover the proceeds of a serviceman's life insurance policy authorized by federal statute which provided that such policies should be paid first to the serviceman's widow, or if none to any child of the deceased, or if none to the deceased's parents.[81] The Georgia Court of Appeals held that the illegitimate child was entitled to the proceeds of the

77.   405 U.S. 645, 92 S.Ct. 1208, 31 L.Ed.2d 551 (1972), 34 U.Pitt.L.Rev. 303 (1973); 1973 Wis.L.Rev. 908; 59 Va. L.Rev. 517 (1973). See Schwartz, Rights of a Father With Regard to His Illegitimate Child, 36 Ohio St.L.J. 1 (1975).

78.   434 U.S. 246, 98 S.Ct. 549, 54 L.Ed.2d 511 (1978), rehearing denied 435 U.S. 918, 98 S.Ct. 1477, 55 L.Ed.2d 511 (1978).

79.   441 U.S. 380, 99 S.Ct. 1760, 60 L.Ed.2d 297 (1979), on remand 47 N.Y.2d 880, 419 N.Y.S.2d 74, 392 N.E.2d 1257 (1979).

80.   See § 20.2, infra.

81.   38 U.S.C.A. § 770.

policy [82] but the Georgia Supreme Court reversed in a brief per curiam opinion which seemed to take the position that Georgia law controlled on the meaning of the policy and that under that law "child" did not include illegitimate children.[83] The Supreme Court affirmed this decision by an equally divided court.[84] It is hard to see why the Weber case [85] does not imply that, regardless of whether state or federal law governs the construction of the insurance policy, the Equal Protection Clause requires that the illegitimate child be included in the class of beneficiaries described as "children" in the statute. The purpose of the workmen's compensation act in Weber and of the servicemen's insurance statute here are surely the same, to provide some security or support for the dependents of deceased workmen in the one instance and of deceased servicemen in the other.[86] The Court's treatment of the case produces further uncertainty about what the relevant factors in evaluating these statutes can be.

One is equally puzzled by the Supreme Court's decisions on the constitutionality of statutes of limitation in paternity suits. Many states have such statutes, which provide that the paternity suit may not be brought after a relatively short period following the birth of the child.[87] In 1972 the Colorado Supreme Court held that the state's five-year statute of limitations was constitutional, and the United States Supreme Court dismissed the appeal for want of a substantial federal question.[88] But in Pickett v. Brown [89] the Supreme Court held that a two-year statute of limitations on Tennessee paternity suits was a violation of the Equal Protection Clause. The Court did not wholly rule out the possibility that periods of limitation long enough to be justified as preventing the assertion of stale claims might be valid, but it seems unlikely that any statute can now be upheld, particularly since the Court presently emphasizes the technical advances in blood test evidence as making stale claims less of a risk. It is thus doubtful that the affirmance of the earlier Colorado case is still authoritative.[90]

Although the Court has been unable to develop a coherent law on the application of

---

82. Prudential Insurance Co. of America v. Willis, 123 Ga.App. 150, 179 S.E.2d 688 (1970), reversed 227 Ga. 619, 182 S.E.2d 420 (1971).

83. Prudential Insurance Co. of America v. Willis, 227 Ga. 619, 182 S.E.2d 420 (1971), cert. granted 404 U.S. 937, 92 S.Ct. 290, 30 L.Ed.2d 249 (1971).

84. Willis v. Prudential Insurance Co. of America, 405 U.S. 318, 92 S.Ct. 1257, 31 L.Ed.2d 273 (1972), on remand 126 Ga.App. 378, 190 S.E.2d 625 (1972). See also Annot., Insurance: Term "Children" as Used in Beneficiary Clause of Life Insurance Policy as Including Illegitimate Child, 62 A.L.R.3d 1329 (1975).

85. Weber v. Aetna Casualty & Surety Co., 406 U.S. 164, 92 S.Ct. 1400, 31 L.Ed.2d 768 (1972), decided slightly more than a month after the Willis case.

86. Cf. Gentry v. United States, 546 F.2d 343 (Ct.Cl. 1976), rehearing denied 551 F.2d 852 (Ct.Cl.1977), and Tenny v. United States, 441 F.Supp. 224 (E.D.Mo.1977), holding unconstitutional a provision of the Civil Service Retirement Act which excluded from death benefits an illegitimate child of a civil service employee who did not live with his father.

87. Annot., Statute of Limitations in Illegitimacy or Bastardy Proceedings, 59 A.L.R.3d 685 (1974); Note, 15 J.Fam.L. 611 (1977). See section 5.4 infra.

88. In re People in Interest of L.B., 179 Colo. 11, 498 P.2d 1157 (1972), dismissed for want of a substantial federal question, 410 U.S. 976, 93 S.Ct. 1497, 36 L.Ed.2d 173 (1973). Colorado has since enacted the Uniform Parentage Act, which allows the child to sue for support until he reaches 21. Colo.Rev.Stat. §§ 19–6–101 et seq. (1978 and Supp.1984).

In contrast with these cases are those which hold that the support to which the illegitimate child is entitled from his father cannot constitutionally be limited more strictly than the support to which the legitimate child is entitled. Some states have statutes providing that the illegitimate child need only be supported to age sixteen, while the legitimate child must be supported to age eighteen or twenty-one. Such statutes were held unconstitutional in Rias v. Henderson, 342 So.2d 737 (Miss. 1977), and State v. Booth, 15 Wash.App. 804, 551 P.2d 1403 (1976).

See also In re Estate of Parkarinen, 287 Minn. 330, 178 N.W.2d 714 (1970), dismissed for want of a substantial federal question, 402 U.S. 903, 91 S.Ct. 1384, 28 L.Ed.2d 644 (1971), holding constitutional the Minnesota statute requiring an attested, written acknowledgment for legitimation of illegitimate children.

89. Pickett v. Brown, 462 U.S. 1, 103 S.Ct. 2199, 76 L.Ed.2d 372 (1983). In Mills v. Habluetzel, 456 U.S. 91, 102 S.Ct. 1549, 71 L.Ed.2d 770 (1982) the Court held unconstitutional the one-year statute of limitations on paternity suits in Texas.

90. The Colorado case was not cited in either Mills or Pickett, supra, note 89, suggesting that the Supreme Court has silently overruled it. Presumably the Court has also overruled Thompson v. Thompson, 285 Md. 488,

statutes of limitation to paternity suits, Congress has stepped in to require the states to permit the establishment of paternity until the child's eighteenth birthday, superseding any inconsistent state statutes of limitation. This has been accomplished by amending the Social Security Act so as to authorize AFDC grants to states only on condition that they enact the appropriate legislation.[91]

Orders for the support of legitimate children are almost universally modifiable upon proof of changed circumstances occurring after entry of the original order.[92] But many states have enacted legislation providing that paternity suits may be compromised by agreement between the child's mother and the putative father, and that such agreements when approved by a court are final and not modifiable.[93] The effect is to give the man alleged to be the father of the illegitimate child a chance to "buy his peace". The justification for such statutes is the same as for statutes of limitation, that is, that paternity is often uncertain and charges of paternity are not always made on the basis of convincing evidence.[94] Where the illegitimate child's paternity was not uncertain, the father having acknowledged him, the statute providing for non-modifiable compromise of the support claim has been held invalid under the Equal Protection Clause, as lacking in any justification, by the New York City Family Court in

Shan F. v. Francis F.[95] The court in this case expressly refused to decide whether such a statute would be constitutional as applied to situations in which paternity was uncertain.[96] Another case has applied the same doctrine conversely, by holding that the putative father's constitutional rights are violated when the nature of his support obligation to the illegitimate child differs from that owed to the legitimate child.[97] His argument was that a judgment for support of a legitimate child is modifiable, and therefore the award to the illegitimate child must also be modifiable. He was presumably contemplating the possibility that he might succeed in having the award reduced later on if his ability to make the payments should be impaired.

It is difficult, if not impossible, to predict what the final verdict on the modifiability question will be. The problem is really the same here as in many other cases, that there is a practical difference between the legitimate and the illegitimate child. One knows or can in most instances easily prove who his father is. The other, in many instances, either does not know or has greater difficulty in proving paternity. State law in these circumstances may take one of three forms: a) State statutes might provide that all illegitimate children must be treated like legitimate children in all respects relating to support by their fathers.[98] b) They might provide that

404 A.2d 269 (1979), dismissed for want of a substantial federal question, 444 U.S. 1062, 100 S.Ct. 1002, 62 L.Ed.2d 745 (1980), upholding a two-year statute of limitations. Cessna v. Montgomery, 63 Ill.2d 71, 344 N.E.2d 447 (1976), upholding the two-year Illinois statute is also overruled. Dornfeld v. Julian, 104 Ill.2d 261, 84 Ill.Dec. 471, 472 N.E.2d 431 (1984).

91. 42 U.S.C.A. § 666(a)(5). This section is part of title IV–D of the Social Security Act, passed in 1974 and amended in 1984. It is described in detail in section 17.3, infra. Before the enactment of this provision a large number of state courts had reached inconsistent conclusions concerning state statutes of limitation containing a variety of limitation periods.

92. See section 17.2, infra.

93. E.g., Ill.–S.H.A. ch. 40, §§ 1359, 1360 (1980); Iowa Code Ann. § 675.30 (1950); N.Y.–McKinney's Fam.Ct.Act § 516 (1983); Utah Code Ann.1977, § 78–45a–13. Under the Uniform Parentage Act § 18(2), 9A Unif.L.Ann. 611 (1979), a judgment for a lump sum may specify that it is not modifiable. See also S. Schatkin, 1 Disputed Paternity Proceedings § 12.05 (4th ed. 1977). Cases construing

these and similar statutes are collected in Annot., 20 A.L.R.3d 500 (1968).

94. H. Krause, Illegitimacy: Law and Social Policy 106, 107 (1971); S. Schatkin, 1 Disputed Paternity Proceedings § 4.01 (4th ed. 1977).

95. 88 Misc.2d 165, 387 N.Y.S.2d 593 (Fam.Ct.1976). But the New York statute was held constitutional in Bacon v. Bacon, 46 N.Y.2d 477, 414 N.Y.S.2d 307, 386 N.E.2d 1327 (1979).

96. A case holding that a contract between mother and father could not constitutionally foreclose the child's claim in any circumstances is Walker v. Walker, 266 So. 2d 385 (Fla.App.1972).

97. Munn v. Munn, 168 Colo. 76, 450 P.2d 68 (1969). A similar case is Boyles v. Brown, 69 Mich.App. 480, 245 N.W.2d 100 (1976).

98. This is the effect of the Uniform Parentage Act §§ 15, 18, 9A Unif.L.Ann. 607–8, 611 (1979), except that a lump sum award or the award of an annuity may specify that it is not modifiable.

only illegitimate children who have been acknowledged by their fathers or legitimated by a prior judicial proceeding, as to whom there is no uncertainty as to paternity, must be treated like legitimate children for support purposes. c) They might provide (as some now do) that judicially approved compromises respecting the support of all illegitimate children are final and non-modifiable, relying upon the Supreme Court's apparent view that statutes of limitations restricting support of illegitimate children are valid, presumably on the ground that proof of paternity in some cases is difficult and becomes more so with the lapse of time. One may surmise that with much inconsistency and vacillation the Supreme Court is working toward the principle that the illegitimate child must, under the Equal Protection Clause, have the same rights as the legitimate child except in those categories of case where the difficulties of proving paternity justify some limitation of those rights. If that is true, then the second alternative is constitutionally permissible but the third is not. This result is also consonant with the Supreme Court's frequently exhibited tendency to demand greater precision and less generality of effect in legislation.[99] But one can do no more than speculate at this stage of the law's development.

No less uncertainty exists respecting the constitutional rights of the parents of illegitimate children. The problems created by the Gomez case and its relation to other constitutional decisions are illustrated in Doe v. Norton.[1] Several mothers of illegitimate children brought that case in order to establish the unconstitutionality of a Connecticut statute requiring such mothers to disclose the name of the child's father to state officials where the mother was receiving welfare assistance. Failure to disclose was punishable by contempt but did not involve the forfeiture of the welfare payments. After finding that the state statute did not conflict with the AFDC program created by the Social Security Act,[2] the court held that it did not infringe the mother's right to privacy created by Griswold v. Connecticut,[3] nor did it violate the Equal Protection Clause. The right to privacy was not invaded, the court said, because the government has broad power to compel testimony and because any invasion of privacy caused by the statute was relatively minor. The equal protection claim was rejected on the ground that this statute operated to assist illegitimate children to receive the support to which Gomez v. Perez[4] entitled them. The difficulty here is that the constitutionalization of the relationships between mother, father and illegitimate child has introduced rigidity into the legal regulation of those relationships, making impossible a flexible statutory or administrative handling of them. For example in the Doe v. Norton situation it might well be that under some circumstances it would be detrimental not only to the mother but to the child to reveal the father's identity.[5] All parties might be better off if, in

---

99. As, for example, in Trimble v. Gordon, 430 U.S. 762, 97 S.Ct. 1459, 52 L.Ed.2d 31 (1977), and Jimenez v. Weinberger, 417 U.S. 628, 94 S.Ct. 2496, 41 L.Ed.2d 363 (1974), appeal after remand 523 F.2d 689 (7th Cir.1975), cert. denied 427 U.S. 912, 96 S.Ct. 3200, 49 L.Ed.2d 1204 (1976).

1. 365 F.Supp. 65 (D.Conn.1973), vacated and remanded for consideration in the light of an amendment to the Social Security Act sub nom. Roe v. Norton, 422 U.S. 391, 95 S.Ct. 2221, 45 L.Ed.2d 268 (1975). A case involving the similar Wisconsin statute is Burdick v. Miech, 385 F.Supp. 927 (E.D.Wis.1974), dismissed on the authority of Huffman v. Pursue, Ltd., 420 U.S. 592, 95 S.Ct. 1200, 43 L.Ed.2d 482 (1975), rehearing denied 421 U.S. 971, 95 S.Ct. 1969, 44 L.Ed.2d 463 (1975), in Burdick v. Miech, 409 F.Supp. 982 (E.D.Wis.1975).

2. This is the Aid to Families With Dependent Children Program described in King v. Smith, 392 U.S. 309, 88 S.Ct. 2128, 20 L.Ed.2d 1118 (1968), in which federal funds are contributed to the states whose programs for the support of such families comply with federal statutory and administrative standards. The Social Security Act has been amended since Roe v. Norton was decided so as to require the states to provide, as a condition of eligibility for aid, that the applicant for aid cooperate in establishing the paternity of the child and in obtaining support payments. 42 U.S.C.A. § 602(9)(26). Thus the Social Security Act now requires substantially the same cooperation by the mother as did the Connecticut statute in Roe v. Norton. Of course this raises the question whether that Act is constitutional.

3. 381 U.S. 479, 85 S.Ct. 1678, 14 L.Ed.2d 510 (1965).

4. 409 U.S. 535, 93 S.Ct. 872, 35 L.Ed.2d 56 (1973).

5. Poulin, Illegitimacy and Family Privacy: A Note on Maternal Cooperation in Paternity Suits, 70 Nw.U.L. Rev. 910 (1976) suggests many reasons why the mother would not wish to identify the illegitimate child's father.

such a case, his name were not revealed. But it would be unwise to reason from those cases that the statute is unconstitutional, since in many other circumstances the child would be benefited by having his father's identity known and orders for support entered. It is unworkable to deal with such cases in constitutional terms, and yet the Supreme Court's decisions seem to have left the courts no alternative. At the same time they have provided little guidance where the interests of mother, father and child are at variance.

A further illustration of these conflicting interests occurs in Slawek v. Stroh.[6] Here the Wisconsin Supreme Court held that the father of an illegitimate child had a constitutional right, under Stanley v. Illinois,[7] to establish his paternity and to assert his parental rights against the child's mother who had custody of the child and who resisted the father's claim. Here again the assertion of the father's claim may well be harmful to both mother and child in some cases, and one suspects from the facts given in Slawek that it was such a case, since the mother filed a counterclaim in the same suit for seduction and damages. If Stanley is to be given the expansive reading which the majority of the Wisconsin Supreme Court adopted, this is unavoidable. It is the dubious distinction of the Stanley case that there is little agreement among lawyers on just how it is to be read.

Conclusion

Ten years of Supreme Court litigation have undeniably eliminated many of the legal disabilities formerly afflicting the illegitimate child. The cases seem to rest on the rationale, often articulated more precisely by lower courts than by the Supreme Court, that the illegitimate child, by virtue of a status for which he is not responsible and which has no relation to his worth as an individual, has been the object of discriminatory legal doctrines having no substantial social purpose.

A Note, The Social Services Amendments of 1974: Constitutionality of Conditioning AFDC Grant Eligibility on Disclosure of Paternity of Illegitimate Child, 64 Geo.L.J. 947 (1976) argues the new provision is constitutional.

6. 62 Wis.2d 295, 215 N.W.2d 9 (1974).

The implication, seldom spelled out, is that the recognition by the law of the special position of the traditional family, composed of a married man and woman and their offspring, is not a social purpose which could warrant the discrimination. This being so, the question is, why was not this rationale sufficient to justify the elimination of all forms of discrimination against the illegitimate child? Why were not the early students of Levy v. Louisiana correct in assuming that that case did end differential treatment of the illegitimate?[8] The Supreme Court has certainly provided no satisfactory answer to these questions. The only reason which comes to mind is the obvious practical consideration that paternity of the illegitimate child is often uncertain while that of the legitimate child is usually (though by no means always) clear. But this does not explain why some statutes have been held valid while most have been found wanting. If this is to be the final result, it would have been preferable for the Supreme Court to abstain entirely. The position of the illegitimate child could have been more effectively, and more efficiently, protected by state statutes which were coming to be passed before the Levy case was decided, and are now exemplified by the Uniform Parentage Act.[9] As matters now stand, it is unclear to what extent some states' statutes are valid. It will remain unclear until we have another round of Supreme Court pronouncements, and perhaps even beyond that point.

There is another consequence of the Supreme Court's activity in this field which should not be overlooked. Turning so many aspects of parent-child relationships into constitutional issues, particularly as in the Stanley and Glona cases, is likely to have unforeseen effects in the future, especially in view of the current fashion for giving constitutional decisions broad readings. The result is that techniques for dealing with social problems

7. 405 U.S. 645, 92 S.Ct. 1208, 31 L.Ed.2d 551 (1972).

8. See note 4, supra.

9. 9A Unif.L.Ann. 587 (1979).

in the future may be limited to what the Supreme Court or some other court decides is wise. In the light of later experience the approved techniques may turn out to be unworkable or unsuited to social conditions, and more effective techniques may be disapproved. This is especially true of the law as it affects family relationships, where the implications are subtle and far-reaching and where the Supreme Court and other federal courts have had little experience. For example, it may not be long until the uncertainty of paternity is either sharply reduced or eliminated by new developments in blood testing. In these days of rapid social change it is therefore hardly a sensible policy to limit future legal responses to social problems by constitutional principles having the dual disadvantages of rigidity and uncertainty.

WESTLAW REFERENCES

Introduction

levy /s louisiana & sy,di(illegitima! /p constitution! unconstitutional! ''equal protection'' ''fourteenth amendment'')

Inheritance Rights

discriminat! distinction /s illegitima! /s right /3 inherit!

labine /s vincent & sy,di(illegitima!)

sy,di(statute /s illegitima! /s inherit! /s unconstitutional! constitution!)

find 97 sct 1459

lalli +s lalli & sy,di(acknowledg! recogni! admit! admission /s illegitima!)

Social Security Act

find 96 sct 2755

Further Application of Equal Protection to Illegitimates

statute action period /2 limit! /s paternity /s unconstitutional! constitution!

---

§ 4.3

1. Ester, Illegitimate Children and Conflict of Laws, 36 Ind.L.J. 163, 164–169 (1961); Note 26 Bklyn.L.Rev. 45 (1959). An extensive citation of statutes is in H. Krause, Illegitimacy: Law and Social Policy 19–20 (1971).

2. Uniform Parentage Act, 9A Unif.L.Ann. 587 (1979). The Act is in force in California, Colorado, Hawaii, Montana, North Dakota and Washington.

3. Uniform Parentage Act § 2, 9A Unif.L.Ann. 588 (1979). Oregon has a similar provision. Or.Rev.Stat. § 109.060 (1984).

§ 4.3 Illegitimacy—Legitimation Statutes and Their Application

Statutes

Every one of the fifty states has a statute of one kind or another enabling parents to legitimate their illegitimate children.[1] Since there is great diversity in legitimation statutes, lack of space prevents a detailed consideration of each one and of the numerous cases construing it. The attempt here is to classify the statutes in several broad groups and indicate how the courts have disposed of the problems common to each group.

The best considered and most effective statute is the Uniform Parentage Act[2] which has already been adopted by several states. The Act deals with the problem of legitimation in two steps. In the first step the statute provides that the parent-child relationship extends to every child and every parent, regardless of the parents' marital status.[3] This leaves only the ascertainment of paternity to be dealt with. Paternity, under the Act, may be established either by a civil suit[4] or by the existence of facts giving rise to a rebuttable presumption of paternity.[5] In general the presumption may be based upon the marriage of the child's parents plus the father's acknowledgment of paternity,[6] or by the father's reception of the child into his home,[7] or by the father's acknowledgment of paternity with certain formalities.[8]

Several states also have enacted the Uniform Probate Code in its first version,[9] which, for purposes of intestate succession provides that a child born out of wedlock is a child of his mother, and also a child of his father if the parents were married after his birth, or paternity was established before the death of

---

4. Id. §§ 6, 14, 15, 9A Unif.L.Ann. 593–4, 606, 607–8 (1979).

5. Id. § 4, 9A Unif.L.Ann. 590–1 (1979).

6. Id. § 4(3), 9A Unif.L.Ann. 590–1 (1979).

7. Id. § 4(4), 9A Unif.L.Ann. 591 (1979).

8. Id. § 4(5), 9A Unif.L.Ann. 591 (1979).

9. Uniform Probate Code § 2–109, 8 Unif.L.Ann. 328 (1972) and 8 Unif.L.Ann. 80 (Supp.1977). The later version of this provision has been amended to agree with the Uniform Parentage Act. The Uniform Probate Code in

the father, or was established thereafter by clear and convincing proof.

In other states legitimation may result either from the marriage of the child's parents after his birth,[10] or from their marriage plus some form of acknowledgment of paternity by the father.[11] In still another group of states legitimation may result from acknowledgment alone,[12] or in conjunction with other acts, such as receiving the child into the family.[13] Where acknowledgment is required, either in conjunction with marriage or without marriage, there is great variety in the methods prescribed for making the acknowledgment. In some states it must be in writing and witnessed;[14] in others it must be executed before a notary or other officer;[15] in others it must be merely in writing;[16] and in still others it must be "general and notorious".[17] Finally, there are some states in which legitimation may be accomplished by a special statutory proceeding.[18]

Under most of the legitimation statutes cited compliance with the statutory procedure legitimates the child for all purposes.[19] A few statutes so limit the effect of legitimation as to make the child only partially legitimate, as, for example, by providing that he inherits from his parents but not from their kindred.[20] And at least one case holds that a statute providing for legitimation by acknowledgment or court proceedings for the purpose of determining inheritance by the illegitimate child does not legitimate the child for other purposes.[21] There is no good reason for such limitations. Legitimation statutes should be

some version has been adopted by Alaska, Arizona, Colorado, Florida, Idaho, Minnesota, Montana, Nebraska, New Mexico, North Dakota, and Utah. Some states have legitimation statutes other than the provision found in the Uniform Probate Code.

10. E.g., Alaska Stat. § 25.20.050 (Supp.1984); Conn. Gen.Stat.Ann. § 45–274 (1981); West's Fla.Stat.Ann. § 742.091 (Supp.1985); Mich.C.L.A. § 27.3178(153) (Supp. 1977); Minn.Stat.Ann. § 257.55(1)(c) (1985); N.Y.–McKinney's Dom.Rel.L. § 24 (1977); Wis.Stat.Ann. § 767.60 (Supp.1984).

11. E.g., Ala. Code 1977, § 26–11–1; Ill.–S.H.A. ch. 110½, § 2–2 (Supp.1984); West's Ann.Ind.Code § 29–1–2–7 (1972); Md. Code, Estates and Trusts, § 1–208 (1974); Mass.Gen.Laws Ann. ch. 190, § 7 (1981); Vernon's Ann. Mo.Stat. § 474.070 (1956); N.J.Stat.Ann. § 9:17–43 (1984); Va. Code 1983, § 20–31.1.

12. E.g., Ala. Code 1984, § 26–11–2; Alaska Stat. § 25.20.050 (Supp.1984); Iowa Code Ann. § 633.222 (1964).

13. Idaho Code § 16–1510 (Supp.1979); Okl.Stat.1966, tit. 10, § 55; S.D.Codified Laws § 25–6–1 (1984). These statutes state that the child who is acknowledged and received into the father's family is "adopted", but properly speaking they are legitimation statutes rather than adoption statutes.

14. E.g., Ala. Code 1984, § 26–11–2 (Supp.); Minn. Stat.Ann. § 525.172 (1985).

15. E.g., Me.Rev.Stat.Ann. tit. 18A, § 2–109 (1981).

16. E.g., Alaska Stat. § 25.20.050 (Supp.1984).

17. E.g., Iowa Code Ann. § 633.222 (1964).

18. E.g., Alaska Stat. § 25.20.050 (Supp.1984); West's Ann.Ind.Stat. § 29–1–2–7 (1972); Ohio Rev.Code § 2105.18 (Supp.1984); V.T.C.A., Fam.Code § 13.21 (Supp.1985).

A proceeding which is compromised with a judicial determination of paternity does not legitimate, however. Burnett v. Camden, 253 Ind. 354, 254 N.E.2d 199 (1970),

cert. denied 399 U.S. 901, 90 S.Ct. 2202, 26 L.Ed.2d 556 (1970); In re Case's Estate, 180 Kan. 53, 299 P.2d 589 (1956). Residence in the state on the plaintiff's part was held necessary in Queen v. Jolley, 219 Tenn. 427, 410 S.W.2d 416 (1966).

Under the Texas statute cited above, a court may deny legitimation where it finds that would not be in the child's best interests, as, for example, it finds that adoption would better serve the child's welfare. In re Baby Girl S., 628 S.W.2d 261 (Tex.App.1982). This case appears to assume that legitimation and custody of the child are synonymous. Such a decision has been held not to violate the constitution. In Interest of T.E.T., 603 S.W.2d 793 (1980), cert. denied 450 U.S. 1025, 101 S.Ct. 1732, 68 L.Ed.2d 220 (1981).

19. E.g., Ala. Code 1977 and 1984, §§ 26–11–1, 26–11–2 (and Supp.); Alaska Stat. § 25.20.050 (Supp.1984); Conn.Gen.Stat.Ann. § 45–274 (1981); West's Fla.Stat. Ann. § 742.091 (Supp.1985); Idaho Code § 16–1510 (Supp. 1979); Ill.–S.H.A. ch. 110½, § 2–2 (Supp.1984); Md.Code, Estates and Trusts, § 1–208 (1974); Mass.Gen.Laws Ann. ch. 190, § 7 (1981); N.J.Stat.Ann. § 9:17–43 (1984); N.Y.– McKinney's Dom.Rel.L. § 24 (1977); Okl.Stat. tit. 10, § 55 (1966). See also Knauer v. Barnett, 360 So.2d 399 (Fla.1978); In re Adoption of a Minor, 338 Mass. 635, 156 N.E.2d 801 (1959); Harmon v. D'Adamo, 195 Va. 125, 77 S.E.2d 318 (1953).

20. E.g., Minn.Stat.Ann. § 525.172 (1985). See also Ballentine v. De Sylva, 226 F.2d 623 (9th Cir.1955), decided under the former California statute, and Annot., Right of Child Legitimated by Marriage of Parents to Take By Inheritance From Kindred of Parents, 64 A.L.R. 1124 (1930).

21. A_____. B_____. v. C_____. D_____., 150 Ind.App. 535, 277 N.E.2d 599 (1971), 48 Ind.L.J. 478 (1973). This case takes an unnecessarily narrow view of the inheritance law. The same undesirable result could be reached by a court which was disposed to take the same narrow view of the earlier version of the Uniform Probate Code § 2–109, 8 Unif.L.Ann. 328 (1972).

drafted so as to provide a means by which the child can attain to all the rights of a legitimate child.

Where the statute expressly so provides, the court's decree in a paternity or filiation proceeding may give the child legitimate status.[22] Without statutory authority it has been held that the judicial establishment of paternity in the usual paternity suit does not legitimate the child.[23] Here again the statute should be phrased to include the paternity suit as a source of legitimation for all purposes.[24] Even without statutory authority there should be a procedure by which either the child or his father can judicially establish paternity and some courts have responded to this need by permitting the establishment of paternity in a suit for a declaratory judgment.[25]

 WESTLAW REFERENCES

Statutes

sy,di("uniform parentage" /s paternity)

§ 4.4 Illegitimacy—Proceedings to Establish Paternity-Support of the Illegitimate Child

Nature of the Action and Procedure in General

It has often been asserted that at common law a father had no duty to support his illegitimate child.[1] Recent research has shown that although technically there was no common law action for the support of the illegitimate, the father did have an obligation to support his illegitimate child under the canon law which was enforceable in the ecclesiastical courts.[2] In 1576 the Elizabethan Poor Law, by creating the strange hybrid called a bastardy proceeding, provided a method by which fathers could be forced to support their illegitimate children in the civil courts.[3] The procedure looked criminal, commencing with the arrest of the defendant and including a preliminary hearing before a justice of the peace.[4] Its chief purpose was not so much the protection of the child as the relief of the parish from the expense of supporting the child. Yet it did supply a remedy of sorts. Unfortunately legal conservatism preserved the ancient form when the remedy was brought to this country, thereby creating some wholly unnecessary problems and producing many harsh and unworkable consequences.

Today in all states some method is provided either by statute or case law for compelling fathers to support their illegitimate children.[5] The statutes exhibit considerable variety. Although some retain aspects of the old bastardy proceeding,[6] most statutes authorize an ordinary civil suit, to be brought either by the

---

22. See statutes and cases cited supra, note 18. See also Uniform Parentage Act § 15, 9A Unif.L.Ann. 607–8 (1979), and Griffith v. Gibson, 73 Cal.App.3d 465, 142 Cal. Rptr. 176 (1977).

23. In re Estate of Karger, 253 Minn. 542, 93 N.W.2d 137 (1958). But a plea of guilty to a bastardy proceeding has been held to amount to an acknowledgment of paternity sufficient to legitimate the child in In re Lasarge's Estate, 526 P.2d 930 (Okl.1974). And In re Minor of Martin, 51 Ohio App.2d 21, 365 N.E.2d 892 (1977) takes a broader view of the statute on legitimation and holds that in order to meet constitutional requirements it must be construed to establish paternity for all purposes when a suit for support results in a judgment of paternity.

24. As is done in the Uniform Parentage Act, supra, note 22.

25. Slawek v. Stroh, 62 Wis.2d 295, 215 N.W.2d 9 (1974). See also A._____ B._____ v. C._____ D._____, 150 Ind.App. 535, 277 N.E.2d 599 (1971).

§ 4.4

1. Moncrief v. Ely, 19 Wend. 405 (N.Y.1838); Allen v. Hunnicutt, 230 N.C. 49, 52 S.E.2d 18 (1949). Contra: Doughty v. Engler, 112 Kan. 583, 211 P. 619 (1923).

2. Helmholz, Support Orders, Church Courts, and the Rule of Filius Nullius: A Reassessment of the Common Law, 63 Va.L.Rev. 431 (1977); Helmholz, Bastardy Litigation in Medieval England, 13 Am.J.Legal Hist. 360 (1969).

3. 18 Eliz.I, c. 3 (1576).

4. 1 W. Blackstone, Commentaries on the Laws of England 459 (Cooley 4th ed.1899).

5. For a collection of statutes, see Note, 30 Mo.L.Rev. 154, 155 (1965). Support for the illegitimate is constitutionally required by Gomez v. Perez, 409 U.S. 535, 93 S.Ct. 872, 35 L.Ed.2d 56 (1973), holding that Texas could not deny the illegitimate a claim for support when it permitted the legitimate child to assert such a claim. Texas has conformed to the rule of this case in In Interest of R____ V____ M____, 530 S.W.2d 921 (Tex.Civ.App.1975). But see S. v. D., 410 U.S. 614, 93 S.Ct. 1146, 35 L.Ed.2d 536 (1973). A case holding such a statute constitutional is State ex rel. Wingard v. Sill, 223 Kan. 661, 576 P.2d 620 (1978).

6. E.g., Ark.Stat. §§ 34–701.1 to 34–719 (1962 and Supp.1981). For the odd Pennsylvania procedure see Commonwealth ex rel. Yentzer v. Carpenter, 240 Pa. Super. 202, 362 A.2d 1101 (1976).

child's mother or, at least where public assistance is or will be supplied to mother and child, by a public agency or office.[7] Some states provide for more than one remedy and according to some of the cases the remedies may be cumulative.[8] Other statutes create a criminal remedy for the wilful non-support of an illegitimate child, a remedy which resembles but is not identical with the bastardy proceeding.[9] In a few states the child's mother is allowed to sue in equity to obtain support for the child.[10] According to the law of most states, if the father agrees to make support payments and if there is consideration for his promise, such as by refraining from bringing a paternity suit, he may be held liable on the contract so made.[11]

It is usually held that the general criminal or civil non-support statutes, imposing sanctions or liability for the failure to support wife and children, do not apply to illegitimate children, the term "children" being construed to mean legitimate children only.[12] The states disagree as to whether the Uniform

7. The Uniform Parentage Act § 6 et seq., 9A Unif.L. Ann. 593 (1979) is the most modern statute and is now in force in California, Colorado, Hawaii, Montana, North Dakota, Washington, and Wyoming. The cases disagree on whether this Act may be applied to children born before its passage. Cf. State v. Douty, 92 Wash.2d 930, 603 P.2d 373 (1979) with Vigil v. Tafoya, 600 P.2d 721 (Wyo.1979).

The Uniform Act on Paternity § 2 likewise provides for the enforcement of paternity claims by a civil suit on complaint of the mother, the child or a public agency. 9A Unif.L.Ann. 628 (1979). This Act is in force in Kentucky, Maine, Mississippi, New Hampshire and Utah. See Thut v. Grant, 281 A.2d 1 (Me.1971). Other states authorizing a civil suit to establish paternity include Ariz.Rev.Stat. §§ 12–841 to 12–849 (1982 and Supp.1984); D.C.Code 1981, § 16–909; West's Fla.Stat.Ann. §§ 742.011 et seq. (Supp.1985); Ill.–S.H.A. ch. 40, §§ 2507 et seq. (Supp.1985); Minn.Stat.Ann. §§ 257.57 et seq. (1982 and Supp.1985); N.Y.–McKinney's Fam.Ct.Act §§ 511 to 571 (1983 and Supp.1984). See also Robertson v. Apuzzo, 170 Conn. 367, 365 A.2d 824 (1976), cert. denied 429 U.S. 852, 97 S.Ct. 142, 50 L.Ed.2d 126 (1976).

The leading text on paternity suits is S. Schatkin, Disputed Paternity Proceedings (4th ed. revised 1977), with frequent supplementation, emphasizing New York law.

8. Kopak v. Polzer, 4 N.J. 327, 72 A.2d 869 (1950); M. v. F., 60 N.J.Super. 156, 158 A.2d 334 (1960). See also Rozgall v. Dorrance, 147 Neb. 260, 23 N.W.2d 85 (1946). Raysor v. Gabbey, 57 A.D.2d 437, 395 N.Y.S.2d 290 (4th Dep't 1977) held that paternity may be determined in a habeas corpus proceeding.

9. E.g., Mass.Gen.Laws Ann. ch. 273, § 15 (1980); Vernon's Ann.Mo.Stat. § 568.040 (1979). The section of the Massachusetts statute making it a crime for a man to beget an illegitimate child was held to deny the father equal protection of the laws because the distinction between men and women in this context had no relation to a permissible legislative purpose. But the statute was held constitutional to the extent that it provided a means to determine paternity and to force fathers to support their illegitimate children in Commonwealth v. MacKenzie, 368 Mass. 613, 334 N.E.2d 613 (1975).

State v. Grace, 286 A.2d 754 (Del.1971) and State v. Clay, 160 W.Va. 651, 236 S.E.2d 230 (1977) held that an offense under this type of statute must be proved beyond a reasonable doubt.

One court has held that support for an illegitimate child may be ordered as part of a juvenile delinquency proceeding. In re State in Interest of O.W., 110 N.J. Super. 465, 266 A.2d 142 (1970).

Where both the criminal statute and the bastardy statute exist in the same state, it has been held that the remedies may be cumulative. Commonwealth v. Pewatts, 200 Pa.Super. 22, 186 A.2d 408 (1962). Conviction under such statutes requires proof that the nonsupport be willful, which often involves a demand by the person seeking support, or at least evidence that the father knew of the child's existence and need. In State v. Summerlin, 224 N.C. 178, 29 S.E.2d 462 (1944) the father was held not guilty when the criminal charge was brought on the day following the child's birth since in that short time he could not willfully have failed to support the child. See also State v. Ellis, 262 N.C. 446, 137 S.E.2d 840 (1964), State v. Robinson, 245 N.C. 10, 95 S.E.2d 126 (1956), and State v. McDay, 232 N.C. 388, 61 S.E.2d 86 (1950).

10. Doughty v. Engler, 112 Kan. 583, 211 P. 619 (1923); Craig v. Shea, 102 Neb. 575, 168 N.W. 135 (1918). Such an action is not maintainable against the father's estate, under Carlson v. Bartels, 143 Neb. 680, 10 N.W.2d 671 (1943). Contra, holding there is no equitable remedy at all against the father, Baugh v. Maddox, 266 Ala. 175, 95 So.2d 268 (1957); James v. Hutton, 373 S.W.2d 167 (Mo.App.1963), 30 Mo.L.Rev. 154 (1965). Other cases are cited in Annot., 30 A.L.R. 1069 (1924).

11. Schumn by Whyner v. Berg, 37 Cal.2d 174, 231 P.2d 39 (1951); Fiege v. Boehm, 210 Md. 352, 123 A.2d 316 (1956); Allen v. Hunnicutt, 230 N.C. 49, 52 S.E.2d 18 (1949) (dictum); Peterson v. Eritsland, 69 Wash.2d 588, 419 P.2d 332 (1966). Other cases are cited in Annot., 20 A.L.R.3d 500 (1968), and in Note, The Illegitimate Child Support Contract: A Prophylactic, 1970 Law and the Social Order 641.

The Uniform Parentage Act § 22, 9A Unif.L.Ann. 613 (1979) authorizes such contracts and provides that they are enforceable.

Where the consideration for the contract is found to have been illicit intercourse, however, the contract will not be enforced. Naimo v. La Fianza, 146 N.J.Super. 362, 369 A.2d 987 (1976).

12. Allen v. Hunnicutt, 230 N.C. 49, 52 S.E.2d 18 (1949). Cases are collected in Annots., 99 A.L.R.2d 746 (1965) (criminal statutes) and 30 A.L.R. 1075 (1924) (civil

Reciprocal Enforcement of Support Act [13] remedies are available to enforce the illegitimate child's claim for support from his alleged father, before paternity has been adjudicated in some other proceeding.[14] Since that Act states that its remedies are in addition to others which may be available,[15] and, in section seven,[16] that the duties of support are those imposed by any state in which the obligor was present during the period for which support was sought, a correct construction of the Act should permit paternity to be adjudicated in the URESA proceeding. Imposition of unnecessary limitations on the effectuation of the illegitimate child's support claims seems particularly unwise in view of the fact that if the child is not supported by his father he will probably have to be supported by the state.

Although the support of the illegitimate child has in the past been primarily the responsibility of the father where he could be identified, there were cases imposing a similar common law obligation upon the mother.[17] Some of these cases made the father's obligation the primary one, with the mother having only a secondary duty.[18] The mother's obligation may now be assuming greater importance due to women's increased opportunities for employment. A few states are beginning to enact statutes which impose a support duty upon the mother of the illegitimate child as well as the father, perhaps in response to the change in economic circumstances and more likely in response to constitutional pressures.[19] It is clear that the Equal Protection Clause of the Fourteenth Amendment [20] as construed by the Supreme Court requires that the burden of supporting the illegitimate child rest equally upon mother and father.[21]

statutes). In Colorado the former statute on contributing to dependency was construed to apply to illegitimate children. Dikeou v. People, 95 Colo. 537, 38 P.2d 772 (1934). See also Imperial v. State, 65 Ariz. 150, 176 P.2d 688 (1947). Contra, holding the criminal statute does apply: State v. Russell, 68 Wash.2d 748, 415 P.2d 503 (1966).

Whether this discrimination with respect to remedies would be unconstitutional under Gomez v. Perez, 409 U.S. 535, 93 S.Ct. 872, 35 L.Ed.2d 56 (1973) seems not to have been decided. See the discussion in section 4.2, supra, at note 54.

13. 9A Unif.L.Ann. 643 (1979).

14. Nye v. District Court for Adams County in Seventeenth Judicial Dist., 168 Colo. 272, 450 P.2d 669 (1969), and Aguilar v. Holcomb, 155 Colo. 530, 395 P.2d 998 (1964) held that paternity may not be established in such a proceeding, but they have been overruled by Colo.Rev. Stat. § 14–5–128 (Supp.1984). The better view that paternity may be litigated in a URESA suit is taken by Hodge v. Maith, 435 So.2d 387 (Fla.App.1983); M. v. W., 352 Mass. 704, 227 N.E.2d 469 (1967); Borchers v. McCarter, 181 Mont. 169, 592 P.2d 941 (1979); Clarkston v. Bridge, 273 Or. 68, 539 P.2d 1094 (1975). See also Annot., 81 A.L.R.3d 1175 (1977).

15. Uniform Reciprocal Enforcement of Support Act § 3, 9A Unif.L.Ann. 659 (1979).

16. Id. § 7, 9A Unif.L.Ann. 672 (1979).

17. E.g., State ex rel. Mattes v. Juvenile Court of Ramsey County, 147 Minn. 222, 179 N.W. 1006 (1920); S. v. K., 70 Misc.2d 803, 335 N.Y.S.2d 124 (Fam.Ct.1972); Commonwealth v. Staub, 461 Pa. 486, 337 A.2d 258 (1975); State v. Wood, 89 Wash.2d 97, 569 P.2d 1148 (1977).

18. See section 5.2, infra, dealing with child support in general.

19. E.g., West's Ann.Cal.Civ.Code § 4700 (1983), which authorizes the courts in child support proceedings to order either or both parents to pay any amount needed for support of the child. This section applies to all children, not merely to the illegitimate child. See also Stargell v. Stargell, 263 Cal.App.2d 504, 69 Cal.Rptr. 715 (1968). Oddly, the Uniform Parentage Act contains no express provision making the mother liable for support, although the provision on judgments speaks of the "parent" at one point. Uniform Parentage Act § 15(a), 9A Unif.L.Ann. 607 (1979).

20. U.S.Const. amend XIV, § 1.

21. Orr v. Orr, 440 U.S. 268, 99 S.Ct. 1102, 59 L.Ed.2d 306 (1979), on remand 374 So.2d 898 (Ala.Civ.App.1979); State on Behalf of Forslund v. Bronson, 305 N.W.2d 748 (Minn.1981). The effect of the Equal Protection Clause upon child support obligations is more fully discussed in section 6.2, infra. Although it seemed to concede that the Equal Protection Clause requires that both mother and father be responsible for support of an illegitimate child, Crookham v. Smith, 63 Cal.App.3d 773, 137 Cal. Rptr. 428 (1977) held that this did not require the district attorney to join the mother when he brings suit against the father for support. Nor does this make the procedure in the usual paternity suit unconstitutional, according to Commonwealth v. MacKenzie, 368 Mass. 613, 334 N.E.2d 613 (1975).

The obligation of the father to support an illegitimate child may not be avoided by offering to pay the costs of an abortion during the first trimester of the pregnancy. Imposing this duty upon the father does not violate the Equal Protection Clause of the Fourteenth Amendment. People in Interest of S.P.B., 651 P.2d 1213 (Colo.1982).

Discrimination on the basis of sex has usually been held to violate that Clause, although the Supreme Court has not had before it the support question. What this means in practice is that each of the parents should be required to contribute to support to the extent he or she is able. Where the mother has the care and custody of the child, she is obviously providing support in kind, and this should be taken into account in determining the extent to which she should contribute financial support also. The obligation upon the mother is even clearer in those states having a state Equal Rights Amendment in their constitutions.[22]

Jurisdiction and Service

Unless a statute dictates otherwise as some formerly did [23] neither mother nor child need be domiciled in the state in order to institute either a bastardy proceeding or a civil paternity suit,[24] nor need the child have been born or conceived in the state.[25] Although there is authority that one state will not enforce the bastardy laws of another state,[26] the forum may and should apply its own bastardy law even though the child was born elsewhere.[27]

Since the usual purpose of a paternity proceeding is to obtain an order against the father for the payment of support for the child, the cases hold that there must be personal jurisdiction over the defendant, the putative father, based upon personal service within the jurisdiction or its equivalent.[28] Several cases have held that personal jurisdiction over a nonresident father in a paternity suit may be had under the state's general "long-arm" statute where that statute provides that a nonresident submits to the jurisdiction of the state's courts by committing a "tortious act" in the

22. State v. Wood, 89 Wash.2d 97, 569 P.2d 1148 (1977) held that the paternity statute did not violate the state Equal Rights Amendment because the responsibility for the illegitimate child's support rested upon both parents. For a thorough discussion of the effect of the state Equal Rights Amendments upon child support, see Kurtz, The State Equal Rights Amendments and Their Impact on Domestic Relations Law, 11 Fam.L.Q. 101, 143 (1977). See also Coleman v. State, 37 Md.App. 322, 377 A.2d 553 (1977), holding the state's criminal non-support statute unconstitutional on the ground that it applied only to husbands and not to wives, and Commonwealth v. Baggs, 258 Pa.Super. 133, 392 A.2d 720 (1978), holding that the criminal non-support statute applied to both mothers and fathers of illegitimate children.

23. Vt.Stat.Ann. tit. 15, § 331 (1974); W.Va.Code, § 48–7–1 (1976).

24. Pelak v. Karpa, 146 Conn. 370, 151 A.2d 333 (1959); Davis v. District of Columbia, 102 A.2d 842 (D.C. Mun.Ct.App.1954); Wall v. Johnson, 78 So.2d 371 (Fla. 1955); Commonwealth v. Gross, 324 Mass. 123, 85 N.E.2d 249 (1949); State v. Tetreault, 97 N.H. 260, 85 A.2d 386 (1952); Urbancig v. Pipitone, 23 App.Div.2d 193, 259 N.Y.S.2d 625 (1st Dep't 1965), 17 Syra.L.Rev. 92 (1965); Yuin v. Hilton, 165 Ohio St. 164, 134 N.E.2d 719 (1956); State ex rel. Patterson v. Pickering, 29 S.D. 207, 136 N.W. 105 (1912). See also Buckeridge v. Hall [1963] 2 W.L.R. 354, 26 Mod.L.Rev. 304 (1963), and Ehrenzweig, Conflict of Laws, 391–401 (1962). But cf. Feyler v. Mortimer, 299 N.Y. 309, 87 N.E.2d 273 (1949).

25. Commonwealth v. Gross, 324 Mass. 123, 85 N.E.2d 249 (1949); B. v. O., 50 N.J. 93, 232 A.2d 401 (1967).

26. Kowalski v. Wojtkowski, 19 N.J. 247, 116 A.2d 6 (1955) (dictum).

27. Yuin v. Hilton, 165 Ohio St. 164, 134 N.E.2d 719 (1956). Kowalski v. Wojtkowski, 19 N.J. 247, 116 A.2d 6 (1955) held that the law of the mother's domicile controlled on the question whether she had standing to assert her child, born while she was married to a man other than the father, was illegitimate. This holding was disapproved in B. v. O., 50 N.J. 93, 232 A.2d 401 (1967). See also G. Stumberg, Principles of Conflict of Laws 333 (3d ed.1963); A. Ehrenzweig, Conflict of Laws 391–401 (1962).

28. In re Hindi, 71 Ariz. 17, 222 P.2d 991 (1950); Schilz v. Superior Court, 144 Ariz. 65, 695 P.2d 1103 (1985); Seuring v. Cook, 16 Utah 2d 219, 398 P.2d 690 (1965). See also Note, Developments in the Law-Jurisdiction, 73 Harv.L.Rev. 909, 979–980 (1960), and Ehrenzweig, Conflict of Laws, 80 (1962). In Hartford v. Superior Court In and For Los Angeles County, 47 Cal.2d 447, 304 P.2d 1 (1956), 30 So.Cal.L.Rev. 336 (1957), 4 U.C.L.A.L. Rev. 647 (1957) the court held that a suit by a child to obtain a declaratory judgment that a certain person was his father could not be based upon substituted service because it asserts an in personam claim.

State ex rel. Karr v. Shorey, 281 Ore. 453, 575 P.2d 981 (1978) held that personal jurisdiction could be based upon an agreement acknowledging paternity and providing for the payment of specified child support, together with a stipulation for the entry of a court order in the terms of the agreement.

On the use of long-arm statutes to acquire jurisdiction in paternity suits, see Bartlett v. Superior Court of Santa Barbara County, 86 Cal.App.3d 72, 150 Cal.Rptr. 25 (1978). Long-arm jurisdiction in child support suits generally is discussed in Kulko v. Superior Court of California In and For City and County of San Francisco, 436 U.S. 84, 98 S.Ct. 1690, 56 L.Ed.2d 132 (1978), rehearing denied 438 U.S. 908, 98 S.Ct. 3127, 57 N.E.2d 1150 (1978), more fully stated infra, § 12.4.

state.[29] Such cases define a tortious act as any act committed in the state involving a breach of duty to another person such that the person committing the act would be responsible in damages. The tort, in other words, is the failure of the father to support the child. Other cases have taken the position that this form of "long-arm" statute is not to be construed to reach the nonresident defendant in a paternity suit.[30] The Uniform Parentage Act deals with this problem by providing that a person who has sexual intercourse within the state thereby submits to the jurisdiction of the state's courts with respect to a child who may have been conceived by that act of intercourse.[31]

The application of "long-arm" statutes to paternity suits involves two related questions. One is whether the particular statute may be construed to cover this kind of suit. The other is whether, if the statute does cover it, an act, or acts of intercourse followed by the birth of a child living in the state and not supported by the alleged father constitute sufficient contacts with the state to confer personal jurisdiction over him pursuant to current constitutional doctrines.[32] The first question is one of local law on which the courts have taken different views. The second question seems likely to be answered in the affirmative since the contacts with the state are little if any less substantial than

---

29. Poindexter v. Willis, 87 Ill.App.2d 213, 231 N.E.2d 1 (1967) is the leading case. The Illinois judgment in Poindexter was held to be a valid one and was enforced in Poindexter v. Willis, 51 Ohio Op.2d 157, 23 Misc. 199, 256 N.E.2d 254 (1970), although the Ohio court could have decided the case on the narrower ground that the jurisdictional issue had been fully litigated in Illinois and therefore was not open to relitigation in Ohio. See Baldwin v. Iowa State Traveling Men's Ass'n., 283 U.S. 522, 51 S.Ct. 517, 75 L.Ed. 1244 (1931). Cases refusing to follow Poindexter are People v. Flieger, 125 Ill.App.3d 604, 80 Ill.Dec. 739, 465 N.E.2d 1376 (1984), affirmed 106 Ill.2d 546, 88 Ill.Dec. 640, 478 N.E.2d 1366 (1985) and State ex rel. Stone v. Court of Common Pleas, 14 Ohio St.3d 32, 470 N.E.2d 899 (1984). An Illinois case seems to question whether a bastardy proceeding, as distinguished from a civil paternity suit, could be brought under the long-arm statute. Alsen v. Stoner, 114 Ill.App.2d 216, 252 N.E.2d 488 (1969). But see State v. Judd, 27 Utah 2d 79, 493 P.2d 604 (1972).

For a discussion of the cases see Levy, Asserting Jurisdiction Over Nonresident Putative Fathers in Paternity Actions, 45 U.Cin.L.Rev. 207 (1976).

Other cases upholding the application of the long-arm statute to paternity suits include Backora v. Balkin, 14 Ariz.App. 569, 485 P.2d 292 (1971) (held within a statute providing for personal jurisdiction over one who caused an event to occur in this state out of which the claim arose); Neill v. Ridner, 153 Ind.App. 149, 286 N.E.2d 427 (1972) (held within a statute providing for personal jurisdiction over one who caused personal injury or property damage by an act or omission done within the state); Bouchard v. Klepacki, 116 N.H. 257, 357 A.2d 463 (1976) (held within the statute basing jurisdiction upon a tortious act within the state; defendant was a resident of the state when the child was conceived).

30. A.R.B. v. G.L.P., 180 Colo. 439, 507 P.2d 468 (1973); Whisenant v. Whisenant, 219 Kan. 387, 548 P.2d 470 (1976); State ex rel. Carrington v. Schutts, 217 Kan. 175, 535 P.2d 982 (1975); State ex rel. Larimore v. Snyder, 206 Neb. 64, 291 N.W.2d 241 (1980); State ex rel.

McKenna v. Bennett, 28 Or.App. 155, 558 P.2d 1281 (1977); Taylor v. Texas Dept. of Public Welfare, 549 S.W.2d 422 (Tex.Civ.App.1977).

31. Uniform Parentage Act § 8, 9A Unif.L.Ann. 598 (1979). Holding that acts of intercourse within the state are sufficient for personal jurisdiction: Neill v. Ridner, 153 Ind.App. 149, 286 N.E.2d 427 (1972); Lake v. Butcher, 37 Wash.App. 228, 679 P.2d 409 (1984). Contra: State ex rel. Carrington v. Schutts, 217 Kan. 175, 535 P.2d 982 (1975). Larsen v. Scholl, 296 N.W.2d 785 (Iowa 1980) held that acts of intercourse within the state, plus the birth of the child and the mother's residence there were sufficient contacts to confer personal jurisdiction. Nilsa B.B. v. Clyde Blackwell H., 84 A.D.2d 295, 445 N.Y.S.2d 579 (2d Dep't 1981) held there was no personal jurisdiction where the acts of intercourse and birth of the child occurred in New York, but the defendant was a nonresident. See also Levy, Asserting Jurisdiction Over Non-resident Putative Fathers in Paternity Actions, 45 U.Cin.L.Rev. 207, 217 (1976).

This question is of course affected by Kulko v. Superior Court of California In and For City and County of San Francisco, 436 U.S. 84, 98 S.Ct. 1690, 56 L.Ed.2d 132 (1978), rehearing denied 438 U.S. 908, 98 S.Ct. 3127, 57 L.Ed.2d 1150 (1978), which seems to have adopted a narrower standard of what contacts with a state are sufficient to support personal jurisdiction by that state's courts. For a discussion of that case see section 12.4, infra, at note 17. It is hard to know what effect the case will have on the case law decided before 1978. See, for example, State ex rel. McKenna v. Bennett, 28 Or.App. 155, 558 P.2d 1281 (1977), containing dictum that a statute making sexual intercourse in the state a basis for personal jurisdiction in paternity suits would be constitutional.

32. See, e.g., McGee v. International Life Insurance Co., 355 U.S. 220, 78 S.Ct. 199, 2 L.Ed.2d 223 (1957), and International Shoe Co. v. Washington, Office of Unemployment Compensation & Placement, 326 U.S. 310, 66 S.Ct. 154, 90 L.Ed. 95 (1945).

those in other types of tort or contract actions.[33]

Parties

The usual plaintiff in paternity suits is the child's mother.[34] The fact that the child's mother is married may disqualify her to bring a paternity suit under some statutes which are so poorly drafted as to authorize only the "unmarried woman" to bring a paternity suit.[35] In the absence of such a statute she may bring the suit, however.[36] If the woman obtains an abortion, she may not recover the expenses of her pregnancy or hospital costs, according to one New York case.[37] On the other hand the cases are not in agreement as to whether the fact that the child is stillborn bars the mother's claim for her expenses.[38] The mother's marriage to the father of the child after the suit has been brought abates her claim.[39] A bastardy proceeding may be brought against a married man as well as a single man.[40] But in the absence of a statute providing for the liability of the father's estate, the suit may not be brought or maintained after the father's death.[41]

Under the statutes prevailing in some states the paternity proceeding may be brought by the mother before the child is born.[42] Both the Uniform Parentage Act and the Uniform Act on Paternity allow the suit to be brought before the child's birth, but require a stay of the proceedings until after the birth so that blood test evidence may be available.[43]

In several states the child himself may bring a paternity suit, acting through a

---

33. Bouchard v. Klepacki, 116 N.H. 257, 357 A.2d 463 (1976) held that the requirements of federal due process were complied with, although there was more contact with the state than a single act of intercourse in this case. State ex rel. McKenna v. Bennett, 28 Or.App. 155, 558 P.2d 1281 (1977) contains dictum that the legislature could constitutionally make sexual intercourse within the state the basis for personal jurisdiction over a nonresident.

34. Baby X. v. Misiano, 373 Mass. 265, 366 N.E.2d 755 (1977), holding that the child had no common law right to bring the action, and that therefore any such right is wholly statutory. Historically the court was not entirely correct about this, there being an ecclesiastical right to support in the illegitimate child.

35. State v. Hunt, 13 Utah 2d 32, 368 P.2d 261 (1962); State v. Tucker, 79 Wash.2d 451, 486 P.2d 1072 (1971). But Franklin v. Julian, 30 Ohio St.2d 228, 283 N.E.2d 813 (1972), 34 Ohio St.L.J. 428 (1973), held that the married woman could sue to obtain support for her illegitimate child, notwithstanding the statute authorizing the *unmarried woman* to sue, overruling the earlier case of State ex rel. Hoerres v. Wilkoff, 157 Ohio St. 286, 105 N.E.2d 39 (1952).

In Gammon v. Cobb, 335 So.2d 261 (Fla.1976) the court held that the statute which authorized the unmarried woman to bring a paternity suit, without giving the same authority to the married woman who bears an illegitimate child, was unconstitutional since it denied the children of the married woman the equal protection of the laws.

36. Gomez v. State ex rel. Larez, 157 Neb. 738, 61 N.W.2d 345 (1953). Other cases are cited in Annot., 98 A.L.R.2d 256 (1964). Under section 6 of the Uniform Parentage Act the child's mother may bring an action to establish paternity, without qualification as to her marital status. 9A Unif.L.Ann. 593 (1979).

37. B. v. S., 70 Misc.2d 728, 335 N.Y.S.2d 131 (Fam.Ct. 1972).

38. Cases are collected in Annot., 7 A.L.R.2d 1397 (1949).

39. Overseer of the Poor, Borough of Kenilworth v. Koznowicz, 50 N.J.Super. 218, 141 A.2d 567 (1958), holding that it was immaterial that the father married the mother solely to avoid prosecution in the bastardy proceeding.

40. Beattie v. Traynor, 114 Vt. 238, 42 A.2d 435 (1945).

The Uniform Parentage Act § 19, 9A Unif.L.Ann. 611 (1979) provides for the appointment of counsel for any party unable to afford counsel.

41. Schumm v. Berry, 100 Cal.App.2d 407, 224 P.2d 54 (1950); Hayes v. Smith, 194 Conn. 52, 480 A.2d 425 (1984); Toms v. Lohrentz, 37 Ill.App.2d 414, 185 N.E.2d 708 (1962); Estate of Kidd v. Kidd, 435 So.2d 632 (Miss. 1983); Gross v. Vanlerberg, 231 Kan. 401, 646 P.2d 471 (1982); K.K. v. Estate of M.F., 145 N.J.Super. 250, 367 A.2d 466 (1976). Other cases are cited in Annot., 58 A.L.R.3d 188 (1974). Contra: Sondra S. v. Jay O., 126 Misc.2d 322, 482 N.Y.S.2d 660 (Fam.Ct.1984); Joseph A. v. Gina L., 126 Misc.2d 63, 481 N.Y.S.2d 203 (Fam.Ct. 1984). But apparently a contract settling a paternity suit may be enforced against the estate of the father. Beattie v. Traynor, 114 Vt. 238, 42 A.2d 435 (1945). The Uniform Act on Paternity § 4, 9A Unif.L.Ann. 632 (1979) allows recovery against the father's estate only of amounts accrued up to his death.

42. Richter v. Superior Court for Los Angeles County, 214 Cal.App.2d 821, 29 Cal.Rptr. 826 (1963); People v. Estergard, 169 Colo. 445, 457 P.2d 698 (1969); McCoy v. People in Interest of Child, 165 Colo. 407, 439 P.2d 347 (1968).

43. Uniform Parentage Act § 6, 9A Unif.L.Ann. 593 (1979); Uniform Act on Paternity § 6, 9A Unif.L.Ann. 633 (1979).

guardian or next friend.[44] Both the Uniform Parentage Act and the Uniform Act on Paternity permit the child to bring the suit and this would seem to be sound practice.[45] The Uniform Parentage Act also requires that the child be made a party to the action, presumably a party plaintiff.[46] This requirement also represents the better practice, since the outcome of the suit directly affects the status and financial claims of the child.[47] If the child is made a party, then obviously he should be represented by counsel, although case law on

this point is scanty.[48] Whether there is a constitutional requirement that the child be made a party and be provided with counsel at state expense when he or his mother cannot afford counsel has not been decided by the Supreme Court, but it is at least arguable that the cases dealing with the rights of illegitimate children decided by the Court since 1968 might support such a requirement.[49]

Paternity proceedings may also be initiated by state agencies under some statutes, usually where the child has received support from the

44. E.g., Lawrence v. Boyd, 207 Kan. 776, 486 P.2d 1394 (1971); McGregor v. Turner, 205 Kan. 386, 469 P.2d 324 (1970); Franklin v. Julian, 30 Ohio St.2d 228, 283 N.E.2d 813 (1972); Wiczynski v. Maher, 48 Ohio App.2d 224, 356 N.E.2d 770 (1976); Annot., 19 A.L.R. 4th 1082 (1983). But C.L.W. v. M.J., 254 N.W.2d 446 (N.D.1977) held that the child could not sue. In Lucey v. Torrence, 62 Misc.2d 714, 309 N.Y.S.2d 755 (Fam.Ct.1970) the court held that when the mother, who originally brought the suit, failed to prosecute it, the proceeding would be continued on behalf of the child.

45. Uniform Parentage Act § 6, 9A Unif.L.Ann. 593 (1979); Uniform Act on Paternity § 2, 9A Unif.L.Ann. 628 (1979).

46. Uniform Parentage Act § 9, 9A Unif.L.Ann. 599 (1979); Smith v. Casey, 198 Colo. 433, 601 P.2d 632 (1979). The statute provides that the court may align the parties. But Hayward v. Hansen, 29 Wash.App. 400, 628 P.2d 1326 (1981) held that the child need not be personally served under the Act and that the mother, as plaintiff, could function as the child's representative long enough to bring the child before the court as a party.

47. J.M.L. v. C.L., 536 S.W.2d 944 (Mo.App.1976) held that the child must be made a party when a suit is brought by his putative father against his mother to establish paternity. But People v. Kilbride, 16 Ill.App.3d 820, 306 N.E.2d 879 (1974) held that the child had no right to be represented in a paternity proceeding, thereby implying that he had no right to be made a party.

For persuasive statements that the child's interest is the interest which is most important in paternity suits, see H. Krause, Illegitimacy: Law and Social Policy 112–114 (1971), and Lucey v. Torrence, 62 Misc.2d 714, 309 N.Y.S.2d 755 (Fam.Ct.1970).

48. Ford v. Ford, 191 Neb. 548, 216 N.W.2d 176 (1974) held that in a divorce action in which the legitimacy of a child was at stake the child was entitled to counsel, under a statute generally providing for counsel for children in divorce suits. The Uniform Parentage Act § 19, 9A Unif. L.Ann. 611 (1979) provides that any party is entitled to be represented by counsel and that the court shall appoint counsel for anyone unable to afford counsel. The same statute in section 9, 9A Unif.L.Ann. 599 (1979) provides that neither the mother nor the father of the child may represent the child, as guardian or otherwise.

The courts are not in agreement on whether an indigent defendant in a paternity suit is entitled to have counsel appointed for him at state expense. Holding that

counsel must be appointed: Reynolds v. Kimmons, 569 P.2d 799 (Alaska 1977); Salas v. Cortez, 24 Cal.3d 22, 154 Cal.Rptr. 529, 593 P.2d 226 (1979), cert. denied 444 U.S. 900, 100 S.Ct. 209, 62 L.Ed.2d 136 (1979) (defendant has a constitutional right to counsel in cases where the state appears as a party or appears on behalf of mother or child); Lavertue v. Niman, 196 Conn. 403, 493 A.2d 213 (1985); Artibee v. Cheboygan Circuit Judge, 397 Mich. 54, 243 N.W.2d 248 (1976); Hepfel v. Bashaw, 279 N.W.2d 342 (Minn.1979) (defendant must be given counsel where the mother is represented by the county attorney); Madeline G. v. David R., 95 Misc.2d 273, 407 N.Y.S.2d 414 (Fam.Ct.1978) (defendant must be given counsel where the state controls the suit). Holding that counsel need not be appointed: State ex rel. Hamilton v. Snodgrass, 325 N.W.2d 740 (Iowa 1982); Miller v. Gordon, 58 A.D.2d 1027, 397 N.Y.S.2d 500 (4th Dep't 1977); Sheppard v. Mack, 68 Ohio App.2d 95, 427 N.E.2d 522 (1980); State v. Walker, 87 Wash.2d 443, 553 P.2d 1093 (1976). Most of the cases requiring the appointment of counsel are strongly influenced by the current trend toward having the state enforce the child's right to support.

The Supreme Court has held, in a curiously limited opinion, that the defendant in a paternity suit has a due process right to have blood tests made at state expense if he is indigent, and if a) the state is involved in the case on behalf of the mother or child, and b) the defendant's testimony alone is insufficient to overcome the plaintiff's prima facie case, as was true in some states under the ancient bastardy procedure. The Court relied for this result upon the difficulties of getting proof other than blood tests, the risks of erroneous judgments and the importance of the defendant's interests in such cases. Little v. Streater, 452 U.S. 1, 101 S.Ct. 2202, 68 L.Ed.2d 627 (1981). The Uniform Parentage Act § 16, 9A Unif.L. Ann. 609 (1979), gives the indigent defendant the right to have blood tests made at state expense. See also Cheryl B. v. Alfred W.D., 99 Misc.2d 1085, 418 N.Y.S.2d 271 (Fam.Ct.1979); Commissioner of Social Services of Onondaga County v. Lardeo, 100 Misc.2d 220, 417 N.Y.S.2d 665 (Fam.Ct.1979).

49. See cases cited in section 4.3, supra. The Commissioners' Comment to section 9 of the Uniform Parentage Act, 9A Unif.L.Ann. 599 (1979) states that its requirement that the child be made a party is considered to be the necessary consequence of the Supreme Court's decisions. State v. Santos, 104 Wash.2d 142, 702 P.2d 1179 (1985) holds that the child has a constitutional right to be made a party.

state.[50] And a few statutes authorize the proceeding to be brought by any interested person.[51] Whether the child's mother, in the event the suit is brought by someone else, has a duty to reveal the name of the child's father depends in the first instance upon local statutes,[52] and whether, if her cooperation is required, the requirement is constitutional may depend upon the sanction underlying the requirement.[53] Depriving the child of benefits because his mother refused to assist in the prosecution of a paternity suit raises serious constitutional questions, to say the least.[54]

Although not a paternity suit in the usual sense of the term and so not, strictly speaking, within the scope of this section, the suit by the putative father of the illegitimate child to establish paternity should be discussed at this point for the sake of completeness. A growing body of authority, statutory and judicial, permits the father to bring such a suit.[55] As has been indicated in an earlier section, the father's assertion of a claim of paternity may in some cases be detrimental to the child's interests, opposed to the mother's desires and infringe the mother's privacy.[56] The Supreme Court has created a welter of amorphous constitutional rights surrounding family relationships, such as the child's right to establish his family relationships,[57] the fa-

50. Commonwealth v. Lobo, 385 Mass. 436, 432 N.E.2d 496 (1982); Taylor v. Morris, 88 Wash.2d 586, 564 P.2d 795 (1977). Other statutes are collected in H. Krause, Illegitimacy: Law and Social Policy 112 (1971).

51. Uniform Parentage Act § 6, 9A Unif.L.Ann. 594 (1979). See also statutes cited in H. Krause, Illegitimacy: Law and Social Policy 113 (1971).

52. H. Krause, Illegitimacy: Law and Social Policy 118–121 (1971); In re Putnam, 62 Misc.2d 426, 308 N.Y.S.2d 896 (Fam.Ct.1970).

53. See the discussion of this issue in section 4.2, supra, and Doe v. Norton, 365 F.Supp. 65 (D.Conn.1973), vacated and remanded sub nom. Roe v. Norton, 422 U.S. 391, 95 S.Ct. 2221, 45 L.Ed.2d 268 (1975).

54. Doe v. Swank, 332 F.Supp. 61 (N.D.Ill.1971), affirmed p.c. 404 U.S. 987, 92 S.Ct. 537, 30 L.Ed.2d 539 (1971) held that a state's denial of AFDC benefits to the mother who refused to cooperate in prosecuting the paternity suit was a violation of the Social Security Act and therefore void. See also Doe v. Shapiro, 302 F.Supp. 761 (D.Conn.1969), dismissed for failure to docket in time, 396 U.S. 488, 90 S.Ct. 641, 24 L.Ed.2d 677 (1970), rehearing denied 397 U.S. 970, 90 S.Ct. 991, 25 L.Ed.2d 264 (1970). See also Grow v. Smith, 511 F.2d 1146 (9th Cir.1975) and Saiz v. Goodwin, 325 F.Supp. 23 (D.N.M.1971), vacated 450 F.2d 788 (10th Cir.1971).

Where fornication is still a crime, the child's mother would of course be entitled to refuse to reveal the details of the child's paternity on the ground of the Fifth Amendment privilege against self-incrimination. See State v. Clark, 58 N.J. 72, 275 A.2d 137 (1971); Matter of Grant, 83 Wis.2d 77, 264 N.W.2d 587 (1978).

The Social Security Act now contains a requirement of cooperation by the child's mother unless she has good cause for not cooperating. 42 U.S.C.A. § 602(a)(26) (Supp.).

55. E.g., Mich.C.L.A. § 25.494 (1984); V.T.C.A.Fam. Code Ann. § 13.21 (Supp.1985); Donald J. v. Evna M.W., 81 Cal.App.3d 929, 147 Cal.Rptr. 15 (1978); Pritz v. Chesnul, 106 Ill.App.3d 969, 62 Ill.Dec. 605, 436 N.E.2d 631 (1982); A.B. v. C.D., 150 Ind.App. 535, 277 N.E.2d 599 (1971); Johannesen v. Pfeiffer, 387 A.2d 1113 (Me.1978); Thomas v. Solis, 263 Md. 536, 283 A.2d 777 (1971); J.M.L. v. C.L., 536 S.W.2d 944 (Mo.App.1976); In Interest of K,

535 S.W.2d 168 (Tex.1976), cert. denied 429 U.S. 907, 97 S.Ct. 273, 50 L.Ed.2d 189 (1976), rehearing denied 429 U.S. 1010, 97 S.Ct. 542, 50 L.Ed.2d 620 (1976). Roe v. Roe, 65 Misc.2d 335, 316 N.Y.S.2d 94 (Fam.Ct.1970) held that the child's father did not have standing to bring a proceeding to establish paternity.

The Uniform Parentage Act § 6, 9A Unif.L.Ann. 593 (1979), provides that a man presumed to be the child's father under § 4(a)(1), (2) or (3) may bring suit to establish paternity. The paragraphs of § 4(a) referred to establish a presumption that a man is the natural father of a child if he and the child's mother have been married to each other (with certain other qualifications not relevant here). In R.McG. v. J.W., 200 Colo. 345, 615 P.2d 666 (1980) a man sued to establish paternity of a child born to a woman who was married to someone else. The trial court, in reliance upon § 6 of the Act, granted summary judgment for the defendant, holding that the plaintiff had no standing to bring the suit since he was not the presumed father of the child. The Colorado Supreme Court reversed, holding that the statute, in making a distinction respecting the establishment of parentage between men and women, created a form of gender discrimination which was in violation of the Equal Protection Clauses of the state and federal constitutions and the Equal Rights Amendment of the state constitution. The court rejected the mother's argument that permitting the plaintiff to sue infringed upon her right of privacy as established in Griswold v. Connecticut, infra, note 59. The case illustrates graphically the impossibility of drafting sensible statutes in the face of constitutional decisions which ignore the complex interests involved in family relationships. A case contra is A v. X, Y and Z, 641 P.2d 1222 (Wyo.1982), cert. denied 459 U.S. 1021, 103 S.Ct. 388, 74 L.Ed. 2d 518 (1982).

56. See section 4.2, supra, and Poulin, Illegitimacy and Family Privacy: A Note on Maternal Cooperation in Paternity Suits, 70 Nw.U.L.Rev. 910 (1976). In Interest of K, 535 S.W.2d 168 (Tex.1976), cert. denied 429 U.S. 907, 97 S.Ct. 273, 50 L.Ed.2d 189 (1976), rehearing den. 429 U.S. 1010, 97 S.Ct. 542, 50 L.Ed.2d 620 (1976), the court's account of the facts makes it quite plain that permitting the father to assert parental rights by legitimating the child would not have been in the child's best interests.

57. E.g., Weber v. Aetna Casualty & Surety Co., 406 U.S. 164, 92 S.Ct. 1400, 31 L.Ed.2d 768 (1972).

ther's right to be recognized as such,[58] and the mother's and child's right of family privacy.[59] These constitutional rights operate at cross purposes when the father sues to establish paternity. The Supreme Court's position now seems to be, however, that it is the child's best interests which prevail when the father seeks to assert his paternity, qualifying, or perhaps even rejecting, earlier contrary expressions.[60] Under this decision therefore the father's claim may be denied if the court, after a hearing, finds that such a denial would serve the child's interests, even though the state's law would not similarly cut off the rights of the father of a legitimate child.

Defenses

One obvious consequence of holding that bastardy is a civil rather than a criminal proceeding is that the prohibition on double jeopardy is not applicable to the suit.[61]

Since the old bastardy action and the modern paternity suit are *sui generis,* the courts have had some difficulty in determining what statute of limitations should apply to them. Of course if the state has a statute expressly defining the period within which the action must be brought, it will control.[62] There may be a question whether these statutes bar actions other than paternity suits, having as their purpose the establishment of paternity.[63] In the absence of an express statute most

---

58. E.g., Stanley v. Illinois, 405 U.S. 645, 92 S.Ct. 1208, 31 L.Ed.2d 551 (1972).

59. E.g., Griswold v. Connecticut, 381 U.S. 479, 85 S.Ct. 1678, 14 L.Ed.2d 510 (1965); Eisenstadt v. Baird, 405 U.S. 438, 92 S.Ct. 1029, 31 L.Ed.2d 349 (1972).

In P.B.C. v. D.H., 396 Mass. 68, 483 N.E.2d 1094 (1985), cert. denied ___ U.S. ___, 106 S.Ct. 1286, 89 L.Ed.2d 593 (1986) the court held that a putative father did not have a constitutional right to assert paternity of a child who was conceived while the child's mother was married to another man. The court relied upon the state's interest in preserving and strengthening family ties rather than on the mother's interest in privacy in reaching this result.

60. Quilloin v. Walcott, 434 U.S. 246, 98 S.Ct. 549, 54 L.Ed.2d 511 (1978), affirming the decision of the Georgia Supreme Court in 238 Ga. 230, 232 S.E.2d 246 (1977). The Quilloin opinion appears to limit Stanley v. Illinois, 405 U.S. 645 (1972) by, implicitly at least, rejecting the notion that fathers of illegitimate children have the same rights with respect to their children as the fathers of legitimate children under the Equal Protection Clause.

Perez v. Department of Health, 71 Cal.App.3d 923, 138 Cal.Rptr. 32 (1977) held that the child is an indispensable party to a suit by the putative father to assert his paternity, and that persons in loco parentis are proper parties. It would seem that the child's mother should also be an indispensable party, if it is correct that she has important interests which will be affected by the proceeding.

61. State v. Bowman, 231 N.C. 51, 55 S.E.2d 789 (1949) (semble); Rufus, State ex rel., v. Easley, 129 W.Va. 410, 40 S.E.2d 827 (1946), overruled by State ex rel. Toryak v. Spagnuolo, ___ W.Va. ___, 292 S.E.2d 654 (1982).

62. Jensen v. Voshell, 193 N.W.2d 86 (Iowa 1971); Johns v. Johns, 236 Md. 278, 203 A.2d 704 (1964); Deckert v. Burns, 75 S.D. 229, 62 N.W.2d 879 (1954); Hurst v. Wagner, 181 Wash. 498, 43 P.2d 964 (1935).

One case, Huss v. Demott, 215 Kan. 450, 524 P.2d 743 (1974), held that the statute of limitations on paternity suits related only to suits by mothers and did not bar a nonstatutory suit by the child against his alleged father for support.

The Uniform Act on Paternity § 3, 9A Unif.L.Ann. 631 (1979) contains no limitation on the bringing of the action, but provides that the father's liabilities are limited to a period of four years next preceding the bringing of the action.

The Uniform Parentage Act § 7, 9A Unif.L.Ann. 596 (1979) has a confusing statute of limitations, but the effect of it is that actions by the child or by anyone suing on his behalf may be brought until three years after he reaches majority. In other suits in which there is no presumed father, the period is three years from the birth of the child. And suits by the father to declare the nonexistence of paternity may not be brought beyond a reasonable time after obtaining knowledge of the relevant facts, and in no event later than five years after the child's birth. Uniform Parentage Act § 6(a)(2), 9A Unif. L.Ann. 593 (1979); Miller v. Sybouts, 29 Wash.App. 663, 630 P.2d 477 (1981), remand by 97 Wash.2d 445, 645 P.2d 1082 (1982). The Act was given retroactive effect in Roe v. Doe, 59 Hawaii 259, 581 P.2d 310 (1978), and in In Interest of W.M.V., 268 N.W.2d 781 (N.D.1978).

Cases are collected in Annot., Statutes of Limitations in Illegitimacy or Bastardy Proceedings, 59 A.L.R.3d 685 (1974).

Cases dealing with the constitutionality of statutes of limitations are cited and discussed in section 4.2, note 82, supra.

63. Martinez v. Lopez, 153 Colo. 425, 386 P.2d 595 (1963) barred a suit for support of an illegitimate child brought under the statute dealing with contributing to dependency although that statute contained no period of limitations. The court rested its decision on the statute of limitations in the paternity statute. But Huss v. Demott, 215 Kan. 450, 524 P.2d 743 (1974) held that the limitations provision in the paternity statute applied only to suits by the mother and did not bar a suit by the child himself. To the same effect is Sandifer v. Womack, 230 So.2d 212 (Miss.1970). And in C.L.W. v. M.J., 254 N.W.2d 446 (N.D.1977) it was held that the statute of limitations governing paternity suits did not apply to an illegitimate child's suit against the estate of her father to establish her claim as an heir. The child was also allowed to sue

courts applied a general civil statute of limitations,[64] which could be tolled by an acknowledgment of paternity.[65] Many of these questions and the cases have been rendered obsolete by the enactment of title IV–D of the Social Security Act, which imposes as a condition upon a state's receiving federal money for Aid to Families With Dependent Children that the state enact a statute permitting the establishment of paternity until the child's eighteenth birthday.[66] Since all states wish to participate in this program, the federal law becomes the applicable period of limitation for paternity suits.

A defense peculiar to paternity proceedings has the euphonious title of exceptio plurium concubentium.[67] In general this defense means that if the mother of the illegitimate child had sexual relations with a man or men other than the defendant at about the time the child was conceived, the defendant cannot be found to be the father. The argument is that the child's mother has the burden of proof in bastardy, and she has not sustained it where the evidence shows that any one of several men could have been the child's father. In fact the defense is less often successful than is popularly supposed.[68] If the child's mother admits that she had intercourse with others during the period when conception must have occurred, the suit will be dismissed as a matter of law.[69] If, however, there is evidence to that effect which she denies, the case still goes to the jury who may find the defendant guilty if they believe the mother's testimony.[70] The evidence of inter-

after the death of his father in Weber v. Anderson, 269 N.W.2d 892 (Minn.1978).

64. Wall v. Johnson, 78 So.2d 371 (Fla.1955); State ex rel. Patterson v. Pickering, 29 S.D. 207, 136 N.W. 105 (1912). Where the paternity suit was brought under the criminal nonsupport statute, the court held that the criminal statute of limitations applies, but that the duty of support is a continuing one and the action is therefore not barred so long as the father willfully fails to support the child. State v. Cordrey, 49 Del. (10 Terry) 281, 114 A.2d 805 (1955). See also cases collected in Annot., 59 A.L.R.3d 685, 709 (1974).

65. N.Y.–McKinney's Fam.Ct.Act § 517 (1983); D. v. D., 69 Misc.2d 689, 330 N.Y.S.2d 907 (Fam.Ct.1972). The alleged father's communication was held not a sufficient acknowledgment in Jensen v. Voshell, 193 N.W.2d 86 (Iowa 1971).

Other cases are cited in Annot., 59 A.L.R.3d 685, 739 (1974). Many statutes also provide that the period of limitations may be tolled while the alleged father is absent from the jurisdiction. Frazier v. Castellani, 130 Mich.App. 9, 342 N.W.2d 623 (1983); Annot., 59 A.L.R.3d 685, 753 (1974).

66. 42 U.S.C.A. § 666(a)(5). A father may be estopped to raise the issue of limitations if his conduct leads the child's mother to delay the bringing of proceedings in the belief that he intended to support the child voluntarily. People ex rel. Adams v. Mitchell, 89 Ill.App.3d 1023, 45 Ill.Dec. 327, 412 N.E.2d 678 (1980); Johnson v. State, 186 Okl. 89, 96 P.2d 313 (1939); Commonwealth ex rel. Gonzalez v. Andreas, 245 Pa.Super. 307, 369 A.2d 416 (1976); Annot., 59 A.L.R.3d 685, 707 (1974).

67. Commonwealth v. Rankin, 226 Pa.Super. 37, 311 A.2d 660 (1973); 2 S. Schatkin, Disputed Paternity Proceedings § 24.18 (4th ed. 1977); Note, The Exceptio Plurium Concubentium in English Affiliation Proceedings, 111 Law Journal 736 (1961); Sass, The Defense of Multiple Access (Exceptio Plurium Concubentium) in Paternity Suits: A Comparative Analysis 51 Tulane L.Rev. 468 (1977).

The Uniform Parentage Act § 14(c), 9A Unif.L.Ann. 606 (1979) makes some changes in the defense. That section provides that evidence of intercourse by the mother with a man not subject to the court's jurisdiction is admissible only if blood tests are available showing he is not excluded as the child's father. A man who is identified and subject to the jurisdiction must be made a defendant in the suit. Section 14(b) of the same Act provides that testimony as to sexual access to the mother by an unidentified man at any time, or by an identified man at a time other than the probable time of conception is inadmissible unless offered by the mother.

New York Family Court Act § 531 (1983) requires corroboration of any testimony concerning sexual access by men other than the defendant in the paternity suit.

68. Earlier cases are collected in Annot., 104 A.L.R. 84 (1936).

69. Yarmark v. Strickland, 193 So.2d 212 (Fla.App. 1966), cert. denied 201 So.2d 559 (Fla.1967); Commonwealth v. Sloan, 177 Pa.Super. 178, 110 A.2d 827 (1955) (dictum); Commonwealth v. Young, 163 Pa.Super. 279, 60 A.2d 831 (1948). The question of probable period of gestation may arise in such cases. See Steed v. State, 80 Ga.App. 360, 56 S.E.2d 171 (1949) where the mother admitted intercourse with another man three hundred and twenty days before the child's birth.

70. Nott v. Bender, 246 Ind. 186, 202 N.E.2d 745 (1964), rehearing denied 246 Ind. 186, 204 N.E.2d 219 (1965); Loggins v. Bundy, 248 Iowa 153, 79 N.W.2d 545 (1956); Commonwealth v. Harbaugh, 201 Pa.Super. 360, 191 A.2d 844 (1963); Commonwealth v. Sloan, 177 Pa. Super. 178, 110 A.2d 827 (1955). In Rebmann v. Muldoon, 23 A.D.2d 163, 259 N.Y.S.2d 257 (1st Dep't 1965) the court dismissed the action where the mother was shown to have been intimate with several men at about the time of conception. See also cases in Annot., 104 A.L.R. 84 (1936).

course with others must normally be limited to the period of conception, since evidence which only tends to prove the mother's unchastity at other times is irrelevant and inadmissible.[71] And since the state's prosecutor represents the mother in many states, the lot of those men who testify to intercourse with her may be unexpectedly hard.[72] In other countries the exceptio defense is not used, but all men who are proved to be possible fathers of the child are held liable to contribute to its support, further indicating that the major purpose of the action is the child's welfare rather than the establishing of fault.[73]

Trial and Evidence

Bastardy cases or paternity suits are triable by jury in some states [74] and by the court in

others.[75] Under the Uniform Parentage Act an informal private pre-trial hearing is held which may result in a recommendation for settlement of the case.[76] Some cases hold that since the paternity suit is a civil proceeding, paternity need only be proved by a preponderance of the evidence.[77] Other cases require proof beyond a reasonable doubt on the theory that the action is criminal.[78] The latter rule is undoubtedly influenced by the courts' recognition that the charge of paternity is only disproved with difficulty and is at times made without much basis.[79] The same recognition has led some courts to hold that the testimony of the mother in a paternity suit must be corroborated.[80] Other courts hold that while corroboration is not required, the standard of proof is higher where the sole

71. Thomas v. United States, 74 App.D.C. 167, 121 F.2d 905 (1941); Peterson v. Peterson, 121 Cal.App.2d 1, 262 P.2d 613 (1953); Kyne v. Kyne, 38 Cal.App.2d 122, 100 P.2d 806 (1940); Ellison v. United States, 85 A.2d 917 (D.C.Mun.App.1952); State v. Patton, 102 Mont. 51, 55 P.2d 1290 (1936); I. v. D., 60 N.J.Super. 211, 158 A.2d 716 (1960); State v. Rook, 10 Wash.App. 484, 519 P.2d 252 (1974); I Wigmore, Evidence § 133 (3d ed.1940). In order to prove his defense, the defendant may offer evidence of both the desire and opportunity of intercourse with other men. Huntingdon v. Crowley, 64 Cal.2d 647, 51 Cal.Rptr. 254, 414 P.2d 382 (1966). A few cases allow evidence of intercourse with others at times before conception if there is further evidence to indicate that the relationships had continued until the period of conception. Annot., 104 A.L.R. 84, 94 (1936); Leach v. State ex rel. Cooper, 398 P.2d 848 (Okla.1965). See also Annot., Admissibility, In Disputed Paternity Proceedings, of Evidence to Rebut Mother's Claim of Prior Chastity, 59 A.L.R.3d 659 (1974).

72. As in Commonwealth v. Harbaugh, 201 Pa.Super. 360, 191 A.2d 844 (1963), where the prosecutor had the witnesses prosecuted and convicted for fornication after they testified to acts of intercourse with the plaintiff in the bastardy case.

73. See Note, Liability of Possible Fathers: A Support Remedy for Illegitimate Children, 18 Stan.L.Rev. 859 (1966). But see 1 S. Schatkin, Disputed Paternity Proceedings § 3.01 (4th ed.1977).

An unusual New York case also emphasized the child's welfare in holding that the defendant could not prevail on a defense that the child's mother had falsely told him that she was using the "pill" in order to accomplish her purpose of having a baby. L. Pamela P. v. Frank S., 59 N.Y.2d 1, 462 N.Y.S.2d 819, 449 N.E.2d 713 (1983). See also Hughes v. Hutt, 500 Pa. 209, 455 A.2d 623 (1983), and Linda D. v. Fritz C., 38 Wash.App. 288, 687 P.2d 223 (1984).

74. E.g., Robertson v. Apuzzo, 170 Conn. 367, 365 A.2d 824 (1976), cert. denied 429 U.S. 852, 97 S.Ct. 142, 50

L.Ed.2d 126 (1976) (no denial of equal protection to require an indigent defendant to pay a jury fee); Commonwealth v. Dillworth, 431 Pa. 479, 246 A.2d 859 (1968); Commonwealth ex rel. Yentzer v. Carpenter, 240 Pa. Super. 202, 362 A.2d 1101 (1976).

75. E.g., Uniform Parentage Act § 14(d), 9A Unif.L. Ann. 606 (1979).

76. Uniform Parentage Act §§ 10 to 13, 9A Unif.L. Ann. 600, 605 (1979).

77. People ex rel. Elkin v. Rimicci, 97 Ill.App.2d 470, 240 N.E.2d 195 (1968); Beaman v. Hedrick, 146 Ind.App. 404, 255 N.E.2d 828 (1970); People v. Finks, 343 Mich. 304, 72 N.W.2d 250 (1955); State v. E.A.H., 246 Minn. 299, 75 N.W.2d 195 (1956); State v. Overby, 227 Minn. 111, 34 N.W.2d 355 (1948); State ex rel. Klostermeier v. Klostermeier, 161 Neb. 247, 72 N.W.2d 848 (1955); X v. Y, 482 P.2d 688 (Wyo.1971). The preponderance of the evidence standard was held to meet the requirements of due process in Rivera v. Minnich, 107 S.Ct. 3001 (1987).

78. State v. Dixon, 257 N.C. 653, 127 S.E.2d 246 (1962); State ex rel. Toryak v. Spagnuolo, __ W.Va. __, 292 S.E.2d 654 (1982); Timm v. State, 262 Wis. 162, 54 N.W.2d 46 (1952). But this rule may still allow a verdict of guilty on the mother's uncorroborated testimony. State ex rel. Sarnowski v. Fox, 19 Wis.2d 68, 119 N.W.2d 451 (1963). A few cases may adopt an intermediate rule, that paternity must be proved by clear and convincing evidence. See, e.g., Thom v. Bailey, 257 Or. 572, 481 P.2d 355 (1971).

79. See 1 S. Schatkin, Disputed Paternity Proceedings § 18.01 (4th ed. 1977), referring to the prevalence of false claims of paternity.

80. Lockman v. Fulton, 162 Neb. 439, 76 N.W.2d 452 (1956) (holding the requirements similar to those in criminal cases such as statutory rape); State ex rel. Klostermeier v. Klostermeier, 161 Neb. 247, 72 N.W.2d 848 (1955). For the New York rule see 1 S. Schatkin, Disputed Paternity Proceedings § 3.01 (4th ed.1977).

evidence of paternity is the mother's testimony.[81] But still other courts allow convictions to rest upon the uncorroborated testimony of the mother without further safeguards.[82]

Some courts have held that bastardy proceedings are civil to the extent that the defendant may be required to testify.[83] In those states which have retained the crimes of fornication or adultery, he may refuse to testify on the ground that his testimony would tend to incriminate, if he makes the claim at the proper time.[84] If he does make such a claim, the cases are divided as to whether his refusal may be the subject of comment to the jury.[85] The Uniform Parentage Act deals with the privilege against self-incrimination by providing that the court may order the party claiming the privilege to testify and grant him immunity from prosecution for criminal acts revealed by his testimony.[86]

Various issues relating to the admissibility of evidence are peculiar to paternity suits. One is the question whether the child should be exhibited to the jury in order to demonstrate a resemblance to the defendant. The cases are not in agreement on the issue, some holding that this may not be done,[87] some that it may be done,[88] and a third group adopting the rule that the child may be exhibited or the similarity proved if the child is old enough to have well defined features and thus to make a comparison of his appearance with that of the defendant meaningful.[89] A preferable approach would be to require expert anthropological testimony concerning any alleged resemblance between the child and the defendant.[90] Other kinds of evidence held admissible as tending to prove or disprove paternity include declarations by deceased members of the family as to paternity,[91] ad-

81. State v. E.A.H., 246 Minn. 299, 75 N.W.2d 195 (1956), and State v. Engstrom, 226 Minn. 301, 32 N.W.2d 553 (1948) holding that if the mother's evidence is uncorroborated it must be "clear and convincing". State v. Overby, 227 Minn. 111, 34 N.W.2d 355 (1948) reversed a conviction where the mother's testimony was not corroborated and there was much evidence the other way. See also Roth v. Melzer, 34 A.D.2d 751, 310 N.Y.S.2d 275 (1st Dep't 1970), and 1 S. Schatkin, Disputed Paternity Proceedings § 4.01 (4th ed. 1977).

82. McGuire v. State, 84 Ariz. 242, 326 P.2d 362 (1958); Medina v. Gonzales, 141 Colo. 118, 347 P.2d 138 (1959); State ex rel. Sarnowski v. Fox, 19 Wis.2d 68, 119 N.W.2d 451 (1963).

83. State ex rel. Johnson v. Mooney, 171 N.E.2d 918 (Ohio App.1961). In the celebrated miscarriage of justice, Berry v. Chaplin, 74 Cal.App.2d 652, 169 P.2d 442 (1946), it was held not error to require the defendant to stand in front of the jury with mother and child so the jury could judge the resemblance.

84. People ex rel. Elkin v. Rimicci, 97 Ill.App.2d 470, 240 N.E.2d 195 (1968); Taylor v. Mosley, 178 N.E.2d 55 (Ohio Juv.Ct.1961).

85. People v. Stoeckl, 347 Mich. 1, 78 N.W.2d 640 (1956) held comment on the refusal to testify was improper. Smith v. Lautenslager, 15 Ohio App.2d 212, 240 N.E.2d 109 (1968) permitted such comment. Where the paternity suit is clearly civil, as distinguished from the old bastardy proceeding which had criminal elements, such comment would seem to be proper. See Baxter v. Palmigiano, 425 U.S. 308, 96 S.Ct. 1551, 47 L.Ed.2d 810 (1976), on remand 536 F.2d 305 (9th Cir.1976), on remand 471 F.Supp. 1113 (N.D.Cal.1979).

86. Uniform Parentage Act § 10(b), 9A Unif.L.Ann. 600–601 (1979).

87. In re People in Interest of R.D.S., 183 Colo. 89, 514 P.2d 772 (1973); Almeida v. Correa, 51 Hawaii 594, 465

P.2d 564 (1970); State ex rel. Schlehlein v. Duris, 54 Wis. 2d 34, 194 N.W.2d 613 (1972). Other cases are cited in Annot., 55 A.L.R.3d 1087 (1974). Some older cases admitted evidence of the race or color of the child to show paternity, without very clearly dealing with the issue of just how such evidence should be presented. Annot., 32 A.L.R.3d 1303 (1970). In Hess v. Whitsitt, 257 Cal.App.2d 552, 65 Cal.Rptr. 45 (1967) the California conclusive presumption of legitimacy was held not rebuttable by evidence of racial difference.

88. Comish v. Smith, 97 Idaho 89, 540 P.2d 274 (1975); Dorsey v. English, 283 Md. 522, 390 A.2d 1133 (1978) (leaves it to the trial court's discretion); Glascock v. Anderson, 83 N.M. 725, 497 P.2d 727 (1972) (comparison to be limited to specific traits or features); State ex rel. Fitch v. Powers, 75 S.D. 209, 62 N.W.2d 764 (1954). In Hall v. Centolznaz, 28 N.J.Super. 391, 101 A.2d 44 (1953) it was held proper for the mother to testify that the child resembled the defendant in certain specific ways, but that she could not give general statements of opinion as to the resemblance. Other cases are cited in Annot., 55 A.L.R.3d 1087 (1974).

89. Thomas v. United States, 121 F.2d 905 (D.C.Cir. 1941) (may not exhibit the child unless he has physical characteristics peculiar to him and the resemblance to the defendant is so striking as to leave no reasonable doubt as to its existence); Green v. Commonwealth ex rel. Helms, 297 Ky. 675, 180 S.W.2d 865 (1944). An exhaustive citation of cases and discussion of the issue may be found in I Wigmore, Evidence, § 166 (3d ed.1940).

90. In re People in Interest of R.D.S., 183 Colo. 89, 514 P.2d 772 (1973); Almeida v. Correa, 51 Hawaii 594, 465 P.2d 564 (1970); Commonwealth v. Kennedy, 389 Mass. 308, 450 N.E.2d 167 (1983); The Uniform Parentage Act § 12(4), 9A Unif.L.Ann. 602 (1979) seems to permit this sort of evidence.

91. Annot., 31 A.L.R.2d 989 (1953).

missions or acknowledgments of paternity by the father,[92] medical testimony respecting the sterility of the defendant,[93] and medical testimony concerning the probability of paternity in view of the elapsed time between intercourse and birth.[94] One lower court in New York has admitted polygraph tests,[95] but such evidence is generally not considered sufficiently scientific to be admissible.[96] It may be useful in the preparation of a paternity suit, however.[97] The cases relying upon admissions or acknowledgments by the defendant make it extremely risky for a man accused of being the father of an illegitimate child to attempt to settle the claim.

The content and present status of Lord Mansfield's Rule is discussed in another part of this work.[98] This rule forbids testimony by a married person to the effect that he had no sexual relations with his spouse, where that testimony would tend to bastardize a child.[99]

Where this rule is still in force, it applies in bastardy proceedings to exclude the mother's testimony if she is a married woman.[1] It does not, however, disqualify her to bring the suit.[2]

The use of blood-grouping tests as evidence in paternity suits has produced much discussion in the cases, statutes and texts. The general problem can be analyzed into three specific issues: (a) Is evidence of the results of blood-grouping tests admissible in paternity suits? (b) May the parties be required to submit to the test against their wills? (c) If the evidence is admitted, under what circumstances (if at all) is it conclusive of the paternity question, and if not conclusive, how much weight must it be given?

The scientific theory underlying blood-grouping tests is complex and has been described in detail elsewhere.[3] The principles can be simply summarized. Human blood can today be classified with reference to cer-

92. Briano v. Rubio, 141 Colo. 264, 347 P.2d 497 (1959) (evidence of declarations by defendant that he was the father); Pitts v. United States, 95 A.2d 588 (D.C.Mun. App.1953) (although offers of compromise may not be proved, can put in evidence a contract of compromise actually made and later violated); Fowler v. State, 111 Ga.App. 856, 143 S.E.2d 553 (1965) (admits evidence that defendant offered the mother money to pay her hospital bill); Rousseau v. Bartell, 224 La. 601, 70 So.2d 394 (1954) (admits evidence defendant made payments for the child's support); People v. Finks, 343 Mich. 304, 72 N.W.2d 250 (1955) (no error to admit evidence that defendant promised to marry the child's mother); Rossmiller v. Becker, 157 Neb. 756, 61 N.W.2d 393 (1953) (admits evidence of defendant's offers of help, and of his silence when he might have been expected to deny paternity); Commissioner of Social Services v. Philip De G., 59 N.Y.2d 137, 463 N.Y.S.2d 761, 450 N.E.2d 681 (1983) on remand 97 A.D.2d 760, 468 N.Y.S.2d 390 (1983) (adverse inference may be based on defendant's failure to testify); State v. Bowman, 231 N.C. 51, 55 S.E.2d 789 (1949) (admits defendant's declarations that he was the father). A defendant's offer to pay for an abortion was held admissible in Commonwealth v. Kennedy, 389 Mass. 308, 450 N.E.2d 167 (1983).

93. Parker v. State, 189 Md. 244, 55 A.2d 784 (1947) (defendant testified he was sterile); Thom v. Bailey, 257 Or. 572, 481 P.2d 355 (1971).

94. Beaman v. Hedrick, 146 Ind.App. 404, 255 N.E.2d 828 (1970). Under the Uniform Parentage Act § 10(c), 9A Unif.L.Ann. 601 (1979), such medical testimony is not privileged.

95. A. v. B., 71 Misc.2d 719, 336 N.Y.S.2d 839 (Fam.Ct. 1972). Contra: Anonymous v. Anonymous, 75 Misc.2d 823, 348 N.Y.S.2d 938 (Fam.Ct.1973); Tree v. Ralston, 62 Misc.2d 582, 309 N.Y.S.2d 229 (Fam.Ct.1970).

96. 3A J. Wigmore, Evidence § 999 (rev. ed. Chadbourn, 1970); State v. Molina, 117 Ariz. 454, 573 P.2d 528 (App.1977).

97. 1 S. Schatkin, Disputed Paternity Proceedings §§ 18.01 to 18.17 (4th ed. 1977).

98. See section 14.4, infra.

99. 7 J. Wigmore, Evidence §§ 2063, 2064 (3d ed. 1940 and Supp.1977). Where the effect of the testimony, in the peculiar circumstances of the case, would not bastardize the child, it may be admitted. Commonwealth ex rel. Leider v. Leider, 434 Pa. 293, 254 A.2d 306 (1969), 43 Temp.L.Q. 97 (1969). The Rule is being abolished in some states. See, e.g., Serafin v. Serafin, 401 Mich. 629, 258 N.W.2d 461 (1977); Davis v. Davis, 521 S.W.2d 603 (Tex. 1975). Cases are collected in Annots., 60 A.L.R. 380 (1929), 68 A.L.R. 421 (1930), 89 A.L.R. 911 (1934), and 49 A.L.R.3d 212 (1973).

1. State ex rel. Worley v. Lavender, 147 W.Va. 803, 131 S.E.2d 752 (1963), 112 U.Pa.L.Rev. 613 (1964), overruled on other grounds, State ex rel. Toryak v. Spagnuolo, ___ W.Va. ___, 292 S.E.2d 654 (1982).

2. Ventresco v. Bushey, 159 Me. 241, 191 A.2d 104 (1963) (dictum); Annot., 53 A.L.R.2d 572 (1957). A case contra is Sanders v. Yancey, 122 So.2d 202 (Fla.App. 1960), but it appears to be clearly wrong and contrary to an express statute.

See State ex rel. J.L.K. v. R.A.I., ___ W.Va. ___, 294 S.E.2d 142 (W.Va.1982), holding constitutional the statute which provides that a married woman may only accuse a man other than her husband of being the father of her child if the child is born after the expiration of one year from the time she ceased cohabiting with her husband.

3. 1 J. Wigmore, Evidence §§ 165a, 165b (3d ed. 1940, Supp.1977); L. Sussman, Paternity Testing by Blood

tain qualities which have been isolated by various tests. The blood of all persons has been found to exhibit one or another of these qualities. It has also been established that the qualities so classified are genetically determined. Therefore if the blood types of a mother and father are known, it is possible to predict that their children will have one of several possible blood types and will not have certain other blood types. It is not possible, however, to predict that their children will have a single specific blood type. There are three systems of classifications presently in common use, the ABO system, the MN system, and the Rh system, each resulting from somewhat different testing methods. There are several additional less well known classification systems, so that today one can classify blood groups in about thirteen different systems. Still other scientific tests based upon genetic principles have become available in some laboratories and could provide further evidence excluding the paternity of particular individuals, but they have not yet been accepted for use in litigation.[4]

The application of blood typing to the proof of paternity is thus extremely useful. By determining the blood groupings of the mother, the child, and the defendant in the paternity suit, and applying to them the genetic principles governing inheritance of blood groups, it may be possible to establish that the defendant could not be the child's father.

If the child's blood group is such that it could not have been inherited from the alleged father, the alleged father cannot be the biological father. The probability that the blood-grouping test will establish non-paternity in a given case depends upon the blood types of the individuals involved and increases if all three of the common tests are used, to the point where it is slightly above fifty percent.[5] If further tests are also made, this probability increases still further.[6] If the test does not establish non-paternity, it will merely show that the defendant could be the father, but will not prove that he is the father. If several tests are used, however, they may have some utility in proving that a particular person is the child's father, depending upon the rarity of the genotypes of parent and child, and upon the existence of other evidence of paternity, but great care must be taken to avoid over-stating the probabilities.[7] In any event of course the tests must be conducted by qualified technicians using generally accepted methods.[8]

If the blood tests do show non-paternity, their reliability is very high, on the order of 99.99%.[9] That is, in only one case out of ten thousand will there be a father-child relationship where the blood tests show there could not be. The tests can be performed without risk, suffering or inconvenience to the parties. All that is needed is a few drops of the blood of each.

Grouping (2d ed. 1976); H. Krause, Illegitimacy: Law and Social Policy 123–137 (1971); Ratimorszky, Blood Tests in Paternity Cases, 19 Cleveland St.L.Rev. 491 (1970); 1 S. Schatkin, Disputed Paternity Proceedings chs. 5, 6 (4th ed. 1977).

A thorough technical discussion of present testing methods, their use and procedures for introducing them in evidence may be found in Krause, Abbott, Miale, Sell, Jennings, Rettberg, Joint AMA–ABA Guidelines: Present Status of Serologic Testing in Problems of Disputed Parentage, 10 Fam.L.Q. 247 (1976); and Peterson, A Few Things You Should Know About Paternity Tests (But Were Afraid to Ask), 22 Santa Clara L.Rev. 667 (1982). See also Polesky and Krause, Blood Typing in Disputed Paternity Cases—Capabilities of American Laboratories, 10 Fam.L.Q. 287 (1976), and Note, Blood Test Evidence in Disputed Paternity Cases: Unjustified Adherence to the Exclusionary Rule, 59 Wash.U.L.Q. 977 (1981).

4. 1 S. Schatkin, Disputed Paternity Proceedings ch. 8 (4th ed. 1977).

5. H. Krause, Illegitimacy: Law and Social Policy 126 (1971); L. Sussman, Paternity Testing by Blood Grouping 139 (2d ed. 1976).

6. H. Krause, Illegitimacy: Law and Social Policy 126–127 (1971).

7. See note 15, infra.

8. L. Sussman, Paternity Testing by Blood Grouping 147–151 (2d ed.1976); H. Krause, Illegitimacy: Law and Social Policy 133–136 (1971); 1 S. Schatkin, Disputed Paternity Proceedings § 9.03 (4th ed.1977).

9. H. Krause, Illegitimacy: Law and Social Policy 124 (1971); Ross, The Value of Blood Tests as Evidence in Paternity Cases, 71 Harv.L.Rev. 466 (1958); L. Sussman, Paternity Testing by Blood Grouping 14, 15 (2d ed.1976); 1 S. Schatkin, Disputed Paternity Proceedings § 9.04 (4th ed.1977).

Two thirds of the states and the District of Columbia now have statutes authorizing the admission of blood-grouping tests in evidence in paternity suits, at least where the test excludes paternity on the defendant's part.[10] Several of these states have the Uniform Act on Blood Tests to Determine Paternity[11] and others have the Uniform Parentage Act,[12] both of which Acts authorize the admission of blood-grouping evidence in the court's discretion not only where it proves that the defendant could not be the child's father, but also when it indicates the statistical probability that he could be the father.

Without express statutory authorization, there is still every reason to admit blood test evidence if it excludes paternity and if the tests are made in accordance with accepted medical procedure.[13] It is more reliable than any other evidence on the paternity issue. Courts therefore generally do hold it admissible.[14]

Where the tests do not exclude paternity but are of a nature which indicates the probability that a particular man is the child's father, the older cases excluded the evidence, on the ground that the jury might be misled, but there is a growing body of cases which now admits evidence based upon HLA testing as an indication of the probability of paternity.[15]   Care should be taken in such

10. Ala.Code 1984, § 26–17–12 (Supp.); Ariz.Rev.Stat. § 12–847 (Supp.1984) (semble); Ark.Stat. § 34–705.1 (Supp.1981); West's Ann.Cal.Evid.Code §§ 890 to 897 (1966 and Supp.1985); Colo.Rev.Stat. §§ 13–25–126, 19–6–112, 19–6–113 (1978 and Supp.1984); Conn.Gen.Stat.Ann. § 46b–168 (1986); D.C.Code 1985; § 16–2343 (Supp.); Hawaii Rev.Stat. § 584–11 (1976); Idaho Code §§ 7–1115, 7–1116 (Supp.1985); Ill.–S.H.A. ch. 40 § 2511 (Supp.1985); West's Ann.Ind.Code § 31–6–6.1–8 (Supp.1984); Kan.Stat. Ann. § 23–131 (1981); Ky.Rev.Stat. §§ 406.081, 406.091 (1984); La.Stat.Ann.–Rev.Stat.Ann. §§ 9.396 to 9.398 (Supp.1985); Me.Rev.Stat.Ann. tit. 19, §§ 277 to 280 (1981); Md.Code, Fam.Law, § 1021 (1984); Mass.Gen. Laws Ann. ch. 273, § 12A (1980); Mich.C.L.A. § 25.496 (1984); Miss.Code 1973, §§ 93–9–21 to 93–9–27; Mo.Rules of Court Rule 60.01 (1977); Mont.Code Ann. §§ 40–6–112 to 40–6–115 (1983); Nev.Rev.Stat. § 126.121 (1983); N.H. Rev.Stat.Ann. §§ 522:1 to 522:10 (1974); N.J.Stat.Ann. § 9:17–51 (Supp.1985); N.Y.–McKinney's Fam.Ct.Act § 532 (1983) N.C.Gen.Stat. § 49–7 (1984); N.D.Cent.Code § 14–17–10 (1981); Ohio Rev.Code § 3111.09 (Supp.1984); Or.Rev.Stat. §§ 109.250 to 109.262 (1984); Pa.Stat. tit. 42, §§ 6133 to 6137 (1982); R.I.Gen.Laws § 15–8–11 (Supp. 1984); Tenn.Code Ann. §§ 24–7–112, 36–2–107 (1984 and Supp.1984); V.T.C.A., Fam.Code §§ 13.02, 13.06 (Supp. 1985); Utah Code Ann. 1977 and 1983, §§ 78–45a–7 to 78–45a–10 (Supp.); Va.Code 1983, § 20–61.2; West's Rev. Code Wash.Ann. § 26.26.100 (Supp.1985); W.Va.Code, § 48–7–4 (Supp.1984); Wis.Stat.Ann. § 885.23 (Supp. 1984); Wyo.Stat.1978, § 14–2–109. The New York statute authorizing the courts to require HLA testing has been held constitutional in Linda K.L. v. Robert S., 109 Misc.2d 628, 440 N.Y.S.2d 825 (Fam.Ct.1981).

11. Illinois, New Hampshire, Oregon, Pennsylvania. There is also a Uniform Act on Paternity, 9A Unif.L.Ann. 626 (1979), which resembles the Act on Blood Tests and is in force in Maine, Mississippi and Utah.

12. 9A Unif.L.Ann. 579 (1979), in force in California, Colorado, Hawaii, Montana, North Dakota, Washington and Wyoming. California does not have the blood-grouping provisions of this statute because it has those of the Uniform Act on Blood Tests to Determine Paternity. See Note, The Use of Blood Tests to Prove Paternity in California, 3 U.S.F.L.Rev. 297 (1969).

13. Alf Ross, The Value of Blood Tests as Evidence in Paternity Cases, 71 Harv.L.Rev. 466 (1958).

14. Hanson v. Hanson, 311 Minn. 388, 249 N.W.2d 452 (1977); State v. Summers, 489 S.W.2d 225 (Mo.App.1972) (evidence admissible under court rule); Houghton v. Houghton, 179 Neb. 275, 137 N.W.2d 861 (1965); Groulx v. Groulx, 98 N.H. 481, 103 A.2d 188 (1954); 1 J. Wigmore, Evidence § 165a (3d ed. 1940); Annot., 46 A.L.R.2d 1000 (1956).

In Price v. Simpson, 205 So.2d 642 (Miss.1968) it was held error to comment to the jury on the defendant's failure to request a blood test, since no adverse inference may be drawn from his failure to request the test.

15. Admitting human leukocyte antigen (HLA) testing to show a probability of paternity: State ex rel. Munoz v. Bravo, 139 Ariz. 393, 678 P.2d 974 (App.1984); Cramer v. Morrison, 88 Cal.App.3d 873, 153 Cal.Rptr. 865 (1979); Carlyon v. Weeks, 387 So.2d 465 (Fla.App.1980); State ex rel. Buechler v. Vinsand, 318 N.W.2d 208 (Iowa 1982); Crain v. Crain, 104 Idaho 666, 662 P.2d 538 (1983); State ex rel. Hausner v. Blackman, 233 Kan. 223, 662 P.2d 1183 (1983); Perry v. Commonwealth ex rel. Kessinger, 652 S.W.2d 655 (Ky.1983); Commonwealth v. Beausoleil, 397 Mass. 206, 490 N.E.2d 788 (1986); Hennepin County Welfare Board v. Ayers, 304 N.W.2d 879 (Minn.1981); Smith v. Jones, 120 Misc.2d 834, 466 N.Y.S.2d 643 (Fam. Ct.1983); Owens v. Bell, 6 Ohio St.2d 46, 451 N.E.2d 241 (1983); Callison v. Callison, 687 P.2d 106 (Okl.1984). Excluding such evidence: Hurd v. State, 125 Ga.App. 353, 187 S.E.2d 545 (1972); Phillips v. Jackson, 615 P.2d 1228 (Utah 1980); Jones v. Robinson, 229 Va. 276, 329 S.E.2d 794 (1985); State ex rel. Isham v. Mullally, 15 Wis.2d 249, 112 N.W.2d 701 (1961); The Uniform Parentage Act § 12(3), 9A Unif.L.Ann. 602 (1979) provides for the admission of the blood test in this situation as does the Uniform Act on Blood Tests to Determine Paternity § 10.

The method of testing is described in Terasaki, Resolution by HLA Testing, 16 J.Fam.L. 543 (1978); Note, Use of Human Leukocyte Antigen Results to Establish Paternity, 14 Ind.L.Rev. 831 (1981); Reisner and Bolk, A Layman's Guide to Blood Group Analysis, 20 J.Fam.L. 657 (1981–1982); Imms v. Clarke, 654 S.W.2d 281 (Mo.App. 1983).

cases to ensure that correct methods of computing probability are used, however.

According to many cases evidence of blood grouping tests is also admissible in actions other than paternity proceedings, where it excludes paternity.[16] Cases holding the contrary rest on the view that there is some sort of estoppel which prevents a husband from proving that his wife's child is illegitimate. The Pennsylvania cases in particular have refused to let the husband demand blood tests in certain circumstances,[17] even after the passage of the Uniform Act which authorizes blood tests in all civil actions in which paternity is a relevant fact.[18] Such an approach seems mistaken.

The next question is whether the parties to the paternity suit may be required to submit to blood testing against their will. If bastardy proceedings are characterized as civil, as is generally the case today, there would seem to be no reason why the test may not be required.[19] In the Uniform Act on Blood

Tests to Determine Paternity the requirement of blood tests may be enforced either by the court's enforcing its order, presumably by contempt, or by the court's resolving the question of paternity against the party refusing to submit to the blood test.[20] The Uniform Parentage Act contains no specific provision on this point, but it does provide for enforcement of the court's orders by contempt proceedings.[21] Some other statutes contain weaker provisions, to the effect that a refusal to take the test may be disclosed at the trial and commented on.[22] Where bastardy is considered a criminal action in all its aspects, or where blood grouping tests are sought in some other criminal action, the contention that the involuntary use of blood test evidence violates the defendant's privilege against self-incrimination has been denied, as has (in non-criminal cases) the contention that it constitutes an unreasonable search and seizure, so long as probable cause to make the test exists, and

The ambiguities lying behind discussions of "probability" in this context are explained in Ellman and Kaye, Probabilities and Proof: Can HLA and Blood Group Testing Prove Paternity? 54 N.Y.U.L.Rev. 1131 (1980); Peterson, A Few Things You Should Know About Paternity Tests (But Were Afraid to Ask), 22 Santa Clara L.Rev. 667 (1982); Note, Blood Test Evidence in Disputed Paternity Cases, 59 Wash.U.L.Q. 977 (1981); Davis v. State, 476 N.E.2d 127 (Ind.App.1985); Cole v. Cole, 74 N.C.App. 247, 328 S.E.2d 446 (1985), affirmed 314 N.C. 660, 335 S.E.2d 897 (1985); Plemel v. Walter, 303 Or. 262, 735 P.2d 1209 (1987).

For more general discussion of the use of probability theory in proving the occurrence of events in various kinds of litigation, see Finkelstein and Fairley, A Bayesian Approach to Identification Evidence, 83 Harv.L.Rev. 489 (1970); Tribe, Trial by Mathematics: Precision and Ritual in the Legal Process, 84 Harv.L.Rev. 1329 (1971); Finkelstein and Fairley, A Comment on "Trial by Mathematics", 84 Harv.L.Rev. 1801 (1971).

Everett v. Everett, 150 Cal.App.3d 1053, 201 Cal.Rptr. 351 (1984), cert. denied 469 U.S. 849, 83 L.Ed.2d 102 (1984) approved a detailed charge to the jury on the method of determining probability based upon HLA testing.

16. Richardson v. Richardson, 252 Ark. 244, 478 S.W.2d 423 (1972); Annot., 46 A.L.R.2d 1000, 1025 (1956).

17. Commonwealth ex rel. O'Brien v. O'Brien, 390 Pa. 551, 136 A.2d 451 (1957), holding that where the husband was sued for child support he could not insist on blood tests under the statute then in force.

18. Commonwealth ex rel. Hall v. Hall, 215 Pa.Super. 24, 257 A.2d 269 (1969); Commonwealth ex rel. Weston v.

Weston, 201 Pa.Super. 554, 193 A.2d 782 (1963), 68 Dick. L.Rev. 90 (1963). See also Watts v. Watts, 115 N.H. 186, 337 A.2d 350 (1975); Hill v. Hill, 20 A.D.2d 923, 249 N.Y.S.2d 751 (2d Dep't 1964). Contra: Hansom v. Hansom, 75 Misc.2d 3, 346 N.Y.S.2d 996 (Fam.Ct.1973). See Harris, Some Observations on the Un-Uniform Act on Blood Tests to Determine Paternity, 9 Vill.L.Rev. 59, 62 (1965).

19. Cortese v. Cortese, 10 N.J.Super. 152, 76 A.2d 717 (1950) held that the child's mother could be ordered to submit to the blood test. State ex rel. Lyons v. De Valk, 47 Wis.2d 200, 177 N.W.2d 106 (1970) held that the mother's refusal to submit to the test violated the defendant's constitutional right to a fair trial and warranted the dismissal of the paternity suit. Even at this late date the courts seem unable to rid themselves of the long outdated notion that the paternity suit is criminal and not civil. See, e.g., Franklin v. District Court of Tenth Judicial Dist. In and For Pueblo County, 194 Colo. 189, 571 P.2d 1072 (1977), characterizing the paternity suit as "quasi-criminal". The Uniform Parentage Act § 14, 9A Unif.L.Ann. 606 (1979) expressly provides that the suit is a civil action.

20. Uniform Act on Paternity § 7, 9A Unif.L.Ann. 633 (1979). Sections 7, 8, 9 and 10 of this Act are substantially the same as the Uniform Act on Blood Tests to Determine Paternity.

21. Uniform Parentage Act § 17, 9A Unif.L.Ann. 610 (1979), providing that wilful failure to obey the court's order is a civil contempt.

22. See statutes cited supra at note 21. Whether such statutes violate the privilege against self-incrimination is discussed below at note 24.

that it invades the defendant's privacy.[23] But the state courts are not in agreement as to whether, if a blood test is refused, the refusal may be admitted in evidence, most of the cases being concerned with the admissibility of such evidence in prosecutions for driving under the influence of liquor.[24] The argument against admitting the evidence does not seem convincing since it is conceded that the test itself may constitutionally be required of the defendant. There is beginning to be some authority for the position that where the parties are unable to afford blood tests in paternity suits, the tests may be made at state expense.[25]

The final and most disputed question on blood test evidence is its effect once admitted. More precisely, if the blood test excludes paternity, is that conclusive of the issue, or is it merely one item of evidence which the trier of fact may consider along with other evidence? Some earlier authorities particularly in California, held that the blood test was not conclusive and that the jury could disregard it if they wished to.[26] This was such an idiotic result that some of the statutes subsequently enacted,[27] including the Uniform Act,[28] expressly provide that if the blood test excludes paternity, this requires a finding of no paternity by the trier of fact. The better reasoned case authority also holds that a properly performed blood grouping test which negatives paternity is conclusive.[29] Where the presumption of legitimacy is a rebuttable one, the effect of a blood test excluding paternity by the husband should likewise be sufficient to rebut the presumption.[30] California has a "conclusive" presumption of legitimacy where the child was born while husband and wife were living together, and the husband was

23. Rose v. District Court of Eighth Judicial Dist. of Montana, ___ Mont. ___, 628 P.2d 662 (1981); State v. Alexander, 7 N.J. 585, 83 A.2d 441 (1951), cert. denied 343 U.S. 908, 72 S.Ct. 638, 96 L.Ed. 1326 (1952); Jane L. v. Rodney B., 108 Misc.2d 709, 438 N.Y.S.2d 726 (Fam.Ct. 1981); State v. Meacham, 93 Wash.2d 735, 612 P.2d 795 (1980); 8 J. Wigmore, Evidence §§ 2216, 2220, 2265 (McNaughton rev. ed. 1961); Annot., 46 A.L.R.2d 1000, 1014 (1956). See also Schmerber v. California, 384 U.S. 757, 86 S.Ct. 1826, 16 L.Ed.2d 908 (1966) and Malloy v. Hogan, 378 U.S. 1, 84 S.Ct. 1489, 12 L.Ed.2d 653 (1964).

24. State v. Andrews, 297 Minn. 260, 212 N.W.2d 863 (1973), cert. denied 419 U.S. 881, 95 S.Ct. 146, 42 L.Ed.2d 121 (1974) and Dudley v. State, 548 S.W.2d 706 (Tex.Crim. App.1977) held that in a prosecution for drunken driving the defendant's refusal to take a breathalyzer or blood test could not constitutionally be the subject of testimony. In Commonwealth v. Krutsick, 151 Pa.Super. 164, 30 A.2d 325 (1943) the court held that a mother's refusal to have a blood test in a paternity suit could not be commented on. Cases permitted evidence of refusal to take such tests are cited by the dissent in State v. Andrews, supra.

25. Franklin v. District Court of Tenth Judicial Dist. In and For Pueblo County, 194 Colo. 189, 571 P.2d 1072 (1977); Walker v. Stokes, 45 Ohio App.2d 275, 344 N.E.2d 159 (1975), appeal after remand 54 Ohio App.2d 119, 375 N.E.2d 1258 (1977). Oddly enough, the Uniform Parentage Act contains no provision authorizing state payment for the expense of blood testing.

26. Arais v. Kalensnikoff, 10 Cal.2d 428, 74 P.2d 1043 (1937); Berry v. Chaplin, 74 Cal.App.2d 652, 169 P.2d 442 (1946); Annot., 163 A.L.R. 939, 960 (1946).

27. E.g., in Kentucky, Mississippi, Montana, Wisconsin, the statutes of which are cited supra in note 10.

28. The Uniform Act on Blood Tests to Determine Paternity resembles sections 7 to 10 of the Uniform Act on Paternity, section 10 of which provides that if the blood tests exclude paternity, the question of paternity must be resolved accordingly. This Act is found in Illinois, New Hampshire, Oregon, Pennsylvania and Utah, the statutes being cited supra in note 10. It is odd that the Uniform Parentage Act contains no provision concerning the effect to be given the blood test.

29. Jordan v. Mace, 144 Me. 351, 69 A.2d 670 (1949); Commonwealth v. D'Avella, 339 Mass. 642, 162 N.E.2d 19 (1959); Houghton v. Houghton, 179 Neb. 275, 137 N.W.2d 861 (1965), 23 W. & L.L.Rev. 411 (1966); Annot., 46 A.L.R.2d 1000, 1028 (1956). Contra, holding that the blood test evidence is not conclusive, but is to be considered along with other evidence, State v. Camp, 286 N.C. 148, 209 S.E.2d 754 (1974); State v. Fowler, 277 N.C. 305, 177 S.E.2d 385 (1970). See also 1 J. Wigmore, Evidence §§ 165a, 165b (3d ed. 1940); H. Krause, Illegitimacy: Law and Social Policy 136 (1971); 1 S. Schatkin, Disputed Paternity Proceedings §§ 9.04 to 9.21 (4th ed. 1977).

30. Richardson v. Richardson, 252 Ark. 244, 478 S.W.2d 423 (1972); Kusior v. Silver, 54 Cal.2d 603, 7 Cal. Rptr. 129, 354 P.2d 657 (1960); Beck v. Beck, 153 Colo. 90, 384 P.2d 731 (1963); Beck v. Beck, 159 Ind.App. 20, 304 N.E.2d 541 (1973) (blood test accompanied by other evidence rebutted the presumption); Shepherd v. Shepherd, 81 Mich.App. 465, 265 N.W.2d 374 (1978); Hanson v. Hanson, 311 Minn. 388, 249 N.W.2d 452 (1977); Houghton v. Houghton, 179 Neb. 275, 137 N.W.2d 861 (1965), 23 W. & L.L.Rev. 411 (1966); B. v. Ben, 70 Misc.2d 572, 334 N.Y.S.2d 229 (Fam.Ct.1972); Moore v. Murray, 63 Misc.2d 401, 311 N.Y.S.2d 794 (Fam.Ct.1969); Wright v. Wright, 281 N.C. 159, 188 S.E.2d 317 (1972) (semble); Garrett v. Garrett, 54 Ohio App.2d 25, 374 N.E.2d 654 (1977). Contra: Prochnow v. Prochnow, 274 Wis. 491, 80 N.W.2d 278 (1957); Rasco v. Rasco, 447 S.W.2d 10 (Mo.App.1969), although the latter case seems to be doubted in State v. Summers, 489 S.W.2d 225 (Mo.App.1972).

neither impotent nor sterile, but even this "conclusive" presumption may be rebutted by a blood test which excludes paternity on the part of the husband.[31]

The Presumption of Legitimacy

Apparently out of a desire to make amends for its shabby treatment of illegitimate children generally, the law has created the presumption that a child born to a married woman is legitimate, and has made it one of the strongest of presumptions. At one point in English legal history the presumption was conclusive if the husband was not impotent and was within the four seas, that is, was in England.[32] Today in most of the United States it is a rebuttable presumption, the effect of which is to place the burden of persuasion on the party arguing for illegitimacy.[33] It applies to a child conceived before marriage as well as to a child conceived after marriage,[34] but in the view of some courts it is weaker under the former circumstances.[35] There is also authority that the marriage of the mother after the child's birth creates some presumption that her husband is the

31. West's Ann.Cal.Evid.Code § 621 (Supp.1985); Keaton v. Keaton, 7 Cal.App.3d 214, 86 Cal.Rptr. 562 (1970); Wareham v. Wareham, 195 Cal.App.2d 64, 15 Cal.Rptr. 465 (1961), 11 Kan.L.Rev. 267 (1962). In Jackson v. Jackson, 67 Cal.2d 245, 60 Cal.Rptr. 649, 430 P.2d 289 (1967), 19 Hast.L.J. 963 (1968), it was held that the conclusive presumption of paternity did not control where husband and wife had cohabited only 3½ to 4 days and where the blood test showed the husband could not be the child's father. The reasoning was that the short period of cohabitation and the blood test together tended to show that conception could not have occurred during cohabitation. The statute and the Jackson case are discussed in Note, California's Tangled Web: Blood Tests and the Conclusive Presumption of Legitimacy, 20 Stan. L.Rev. 754 (1968). The California conclusive presumption was held constitutional in Estate of Cornelious, 35 Cal.3d 461, 198 Cal.Rptr. 543, 674 P.2d 245 (1984), appeal dismissed 466 U.S. 967, 104 S.Ct. 2337, 80 L.Ed.2d 812 (1984), where the person attacking the presumption wished to inherit from a deceased person not her presumed father, and in Michelle W. v. Ronald W., 39 Cal.3d 354, 216 Cal.Rptr. 748, 703 P.2d 88 (1985), appeal dismissed for want of a substantial federal question __ U.S. __, 106 Sup.Ct. 774, 88 L.Ed.2d 754 (1986).

32. In re Findlay, 253 N.Y. 1, 170 N.E. 471 (1930). See also section 4.1, supra, at note 16.

33. Happel v. Mecklenburger, 101 Ill.App.3d 107, 56 Ill.Dec. 569, 427 N.E.2d 974 (1981). The rebuttable version of the presumption was held constitutional in Brown v. Danley, 263 Ark. 480, 566 S.W.2d 385 (1978), cert. denied 439 U.S. 983, 99 S.Ct. 572, 58 L.Ed.2d 654 (1978); State v. White, 300 N.C. 494, 268 S.E.2d 481 (1980), rehearing denied 301 N.C. 107, 273 S.E.2d 443 (1980); Etchison v. Greathouse, 596 S.W.2d 233 (Tex.Civ.App. 1980).

The standard of proof required to rebut the presumption varies from state to state. A preponderance of the evidence is sufficient according to Mock v. Mock, 411 So. 2d 1063 (La.1982). Clear and convincing evidence is required by West's Ann.Cal.Civ.Code § 7004 (Supp.1986); Holland v. Holland, 188 Conn. 354, 449 A.2d 1010 (1982); Happel v. Mecklenburger, 101 Ill.App.3d 107, 56 Ill.Dec. 569, 427 N.E.2d 974 (1981). Proof by "overwhelming evidence" is required by McKenzie v. Harris, 679 F.2d 8 (3d Cir.1982) (Pennsylvania law). Proof beyond a reasonable doubt is required by P.B.C. v. D.H., 396 Mass. 68, 483 N.E.2d 1094 (1985), cert. denied __ U.S. __, 106 S.Ct. 1286, 89 L.Ed.2d 593 (1986).

Some states limit the persons who have standing to dispute the legitimacy of a child born to a married woman. P.B.C. v. D.H., 396 Mass. 68, 483 N.E.2d 1094 (1985), cert. denied __ U.S. __, 106 Sup.Ct. 1286, 89 L.Ed.2d 593 (1986) held that a natural father has no constitutional right to a judicial determination of paternity of a child conceived while the mother was married to another man. But see Finnerty v. Boyett, 469 So.2d 287 (La.App.1985), holding that the natural father had a right to prove paternity even though the child was presumed to be the child of the mother's husband. Matter of Legitimation of Locklear by Jones, 314 N.C. 412, 334 S.E.2d 46 (1985) held that the presumption did not apply at all where the natural father asserted his paternity and brought suit to establish it. Other cases on standing to rebut the presumption of legitimacy are cited in Annots., 53 A.L.R.2d 572 (1957) and 90 A.L.R.3d 1032 (1979).

The presumption was held to be conclusive when the mother was living with her husband in Wake County Child Support Enforcement ex rel. Bailey v. Matthews, 36 N.C.App. 316, 244 S.E.2d 191 (1978); Wedgman v. Wedgman, 541 S.W.2d 522 (Tex.Civ.App.1976).

In some states the presumption resembles a statute of limitations. See Murphy v. Houma Well Service, 409 F.2d 804 (5th Cir.1969), rehearing denied 413 F.2d 509 (5th Cir.1969); Tannehill v. Tannehill, 261 La. 933, 261 So.2d 619 (1972); Speight v. Wheeler, 310 So.2d 716 (Miss. 1974).

Under the Uniform Parentage Act § 4(a), 9A Unif.L. Ann. 590 (1979) there is a rebuttable presumption of paternity if the child is born during the marriage of his parents or within 300 days after its termination.

34. State v. E.A.H., 246 Minn. 299, 75 N.W.2d 195 (1956); Curry v. Felix, 276 Minn. 125, 149 N.W.2d 92 (1967); Johnson v. Adams, 18 Ohio St.3d 48, 479 N.E.2d 866 (1985); L.A.M. v. M.L.M., 162 W.Va. 273, 250 S.E.2d 40 (1978); Annots., 57 A.L.R.2d 729 (1958), 8 A.L.R. 427 (1920); Note, Presumptions of Legitimacy in Texas, 27 Baylor L.Rev. 340 (1975).

35. Clark v. State, 208 Md. 316, 118 A.2d 366 (1955), and Annots. cited supra, note 35.

child's father, but in this instance the presumption is much weaker.[36]

There is a line of cases in a few states which holds that if a man marries a woman knowing she is pregnant by another man, or knowing that she has an illegitimate child by another man, he becomes responsible for the child's support.[37] The reasoning of these cases seems to be that the husband is estopped, or has agreed to recognize the child as his.[38] In such cases the child is not presumed legitimate but the support obligation is imposed irrespective of biological paternity. The Uniform Parentage Act deals with this situation in a more satisfactory manner by creating a rebuttable presumption of paternity where the child's father has married the mother and has acknowledged the child in prescribed ways.[39]

Where a child is conceived during marriage but not born until after the marriage has been terminated by divorce or annulment, there is also a rebuttable presumption of legitimacy.[40]

The major problem in connection with this presumption is the determination of the sort of evidence which will be held to rebut it. The courts have used various general terms to describe the strength of the presumption, perhaps the most famous being Judge Cardozo's "that the presumption will not fail unless common sense and reason are outraged by a holding that it abides."[41] Other authorities have held that it may only be rebutted by evidence which shows beyond a reasonable doubt that the husband could not have been the child's father,[42] and still others that the evidence relied on to disprove paternity must be clear and convincing.[43] The specific kinds of evidence which have been held sufficient to rebut the presumption include evidence of impotence or non-access on the part of the husband,[44] evidence that the husband had had a vasectomy before the child was conceived,[45] evidence that another man was living with the child's mother and acknowledged the child,[46] and evidence that the time intervening between intercourse with the husband and the birth of the child made it unlikely that the husband was the child's father.[47] As

---

36. Cases are collected in Annots., 57 A.L.R.2d 729, 761 (1958) and 8 A.L.R. 427 (1920). This presumption is related to, but not identical with, the process of legitimation under those statutes which provide that a child is legitimated by the marriage of his parents. See section 4.3, supra.

37. In re Marriage of Johnson, 88 Cal.App.3d 848, 152 Cal.Rptr. 121 (1979); In re Marriage of Valle, 53 Cal.App. 3d 837, 126 Cal.Rptr. 38 (1975); Brugman v. Prejean, 288 So.2d 702 (La.App.1974); L. v. L., 497 S.W.2d 840 (Mo. App.1973), 43 U.Mo.K.C.L.Rev. 104 (1974); T v. T, 216 Va. 867, 224 S.E.2d 148 (1976). Contra: R.D.S. v. S.L.S., 402 N.E.2d 30 (Ind.App.1980).

38. E.g., T. v. T., 216 Va. 867, 224 S.E.2d 148 (1976). See M.H.B. v. H.T.B., 100 N.J. 567, 498 A.2d 775 (1985).

39. Uniform Parentage Act § 4, 9A Unif.L.Ann. 590 (1979).

40. Alber v. Alber, 93 Idaho 755, 472 P.2d 321 (1970), 1971 Wash.U.L.Q. 492; Annot., 46 A.L.R.3d 158 (1972). See also Uniform Parentage Act § 4(a), 9A Unif.L.Ann. 590 (1979), and Note, Presumptions of Legitimacy in Texas, 27 Baylor L.Rev. 340 (1975).

41. In re Findlay, 253 N.Y. 1, 8, 170 N.E. 471, 473 (1930). See also Stone v. Stone, 76 Wash.2d 586, 458 P.2d 183 (1969).

42. Ventresco v. Bushey, 159 Me. 241, 191 A.2d 104 (1963); Buzzell v. Buzzell, 235 A.2d 828 (Me.1967); Commonwealth v. Leary, 345 Mass. 59, 185 N.E.2d 641 (1962); Madden v. Madden, 338 So.2d 1000 (Miss.1976); Gibson v.

Gibson, 207 Va. 821, 153 S.E.2d 189 (1967); Annot., 128 A.L.R. 713, 717 (1940).

43. Taylor v. Richardson, 354 F.Supp. 13 (M.D.La. 1973) (California law); State v. Mejia, 97 Ariz. 215, 399 P.2d 116 (1965); Miller v. Robertson, 147 Ind.App. 68, 258 N.E.2d 420 (1970); Torres v. Gonzales, 80 N.M. 35, 450 P.2d 921 (1969); Cochran v. Cochran, 2 Wash.App. 514, 468 P.2d 729 (1970). See also Uniform Parentage Act § 4(b), 9A Unif.L.Ann. 591 (1979).

44. Ingalls Shipbuilding Corp. v. Neuman, 322 F.Supp. 1229 (S.D.Miss.1970), affirmed 448 F.2d 773 (5th Cir.1971) (Mississippi law); Coffman v. Coffman, 121 Ariz.App. 522, 591 P.2d 1010 (1979); People in Interest of A.M.D. v. R.C.D., 29 Colo.App. 202, 481 P.2d 123 (1971); Commonwealth v. Kitchen, 299 Mass. 7, 11 N.E.2d 482 (1937); Annot., 57 A.L.R.2d 729, 743 (1958).

45. E.S. _____ v. G.M.S. _____, 520 S.W.2d 652 (Mo.App.1975). Contra: Whitman v. Whitman, 140 Ind. App. 289, 215 N.E.2d 689 (1966).

46. Sacks v. Sacks, 267 So.2d 73 (Fla.1972); People ex rel. Smith v. Cobb, 33 Ill.App.3d 68, 337 N.E.2d 313 (1975).

47. Anderson v. Anderson, 214 Cal. 414, 5 P.2d 881 (1931); Commonwealth v. Leary, 345 Mass. 59, 185 N.E.2d 641 (1962); Commonwealth v. Kitchen, 299 Mass. 7, 11 N.E.2d 482 (1937); Hinterman v. Stine, 55 Mich. App. 282, 222 N.W.2d 213 (1974); Commissioner of Public Welfare of New York on Complaint of Vincent v. Koehler, 284 N.Y. 260, 30 N.E.2d 587 (1940). See also State ex

has been indicated,[48] the presumption may be rebutted by evidence of a properly conducted blood test.

Conversely some courts have held that where the child's mother was living with her husband at the date of conception, the presumption will not be rebutted by evidence of dates or even intercourse with other men.[49] And strong evidence of sterility on the husband's part has likewise been held not to rebut the presumption,[50] although many of these cases seem doubtful by reason of their apparent rejection of quite clear medical testimony.

Compromise or Settlement

Where the paternity statutes are silent on the question of settlement of the suit, the courts are in disagreement as to whether the mother can make a compromise agreement with the alleged father which will

bind all parties including the child.[51] The father of the legitimate child is not able to compromise his support obligation in this way.[52] There is a difference between the two cases, however. Where the child is illegitimate, there is always potentially a question of paternity. In a particular case the question may be doubtful or it may be clear. For this reason, and in order to give the defendants in paternity claims a way of avoiding scandal and notoriety, the statutes in some states authorize a settlement which is binding if made with court approval.[53] When the statute is complied with, subsequent claims are generally foreclosed, sometimes with the exception that the alleged father may be responsible for payments in excess of the settlement figure if the child should later become a public charge.[54] But, as has been shown in an

rel. Worley v. Lavender, 147 W.Va. 803, 131 S.E.2d 752 (1963), 112 U.Pa.L.Rev. 613 (1964), overruled on other grounds, State ex rel. Toryak v. Spagnuolo, ___ W.Va. ___, 292 S.E.2d 654 (1982); and Annots., 57 A.L.R.2d 729, 743 (1958) and 7 A.L.R. 329, 330 (1920).

48. See the cases cited in note 30, supra.

49. Dugas v. Henson, 307 So.2d 650 (La.App.1975), affirmed p.c. 310 So.2d 851 (La.1975); Melvin v. Kazhe, 83 N.M. 356, 492 P.2d 138 (1971); Mannain v. Lay, 33 A.D.2d 1024, 308 N.Y.S.2d 248 (2d Dep't 1970), affirmed p.c. 27 N.Y.2d 690, 262 N.E.2d 216, 314 N.Y.S.2d 9 (1970).

50. Pyeatte v. Pyeatte, 21 Ariz.App. 448, 520 P.2d 542 (1974), citing other cases.

51. People v. Makar, 25 Ill.App.2d 246, 166 N.E.2d 467 (1960) (settlement not binding without statutory authority); State v. Bowen, 80 Wash.2d 808, 498 P.2d 877 (1972) (settlement not binding). Warner v. Burke, 137 Ga.App. 185, 223 S.E.2d 234 (1976) held a settlement binding, but the result has been changed by statute, Official Code Ga.Ann. § 74–9902 (Supp.1984) and by Worthington v. Worthington, 250 Ga. 730, 301 S.E.2d 44 (1983), on remand 166 Ga.App. 424, 305 S.E.2d 187 (1983). Cf. Montgomery v. Ledesma, 12 Or.App. 535, 507 P.2d 405 (1973), apparently holding that a compromise could not be modified, with Fox v. Hohenshelt, 19 Or.App. 617, 528 P.2d 1376 (1974), holding that a compromise is not binding without court approval. Other cases pro and con are cited in Annot., 84 A.L.R.2d 524 (1962), and Note, The Illegitimate Child Support Contract: A Prophylactic, 1970 Law & Social Order 641.

In Shinall v. Pergeorelis, 325 So.2d 431 (Fla.App.1975) the argument was made (but rejected by the court) that since, under Roe v. Wade, 410 U.S. 113, 93 S.Ct. 705, 35 L.Ed.2d 147 (1973), rehearing denied 410 U.S. 959, 93 S.Ct. 1409, 35 L.Ed.2d 694 (1973), the woman was held to have the sole right, during the first trimester of pregnancy, to decide whether or not to bear the child, she should

have the sole right to control other rights of the fetus, including the claim for support. The court relied upon an earlier case to hold that the mother's release of the father did not bind the child.

52. See section 17.3, infra.

53. E.g., Official Code Ga.Ann. § 74–9902 (Supp.1984); Ill.–S.H.A., ch. 40, § 2512.1 (Supp.1985); Iowa Code Ann. § 675.30 (1950); Or.Rev.Stat. § 109.230 (1984); Note, Support of the Illegitimate Child—Judicial Approval of Settlement Agreements, 50 Iowa L.Rev. 924 (1965).

A statute authorizing settlement, to be followed by the entry of a judgment for support was held unconstitutional because it failed to provide for notice and a hearing or for waiver of those rights, but the statute was later amended. See County of Los Angeles v. Soto, 35 Cal.3d 483, 198 Cal.Rptr. 779, 674 P.2d 750 (1984).

54. Annot., 84 A.L.R.2d 524, 534, 542 (1962). Haag v. Barnes, 9 N.Y.2d 554, 216 N.Y.S.2d 65, 175 N.E.2d 441 (1961) held that a settlement binding under Illinois law would be given the same effect in New York, even though a similar settlement made in New York would not have been binding. See Ehrenzweig, The "Bastard" in the Conflict of Laws, 29 U.Chi.L.Rev. 498 (1962). Where the converse question is involved, that is, whether the contract may be enforced against the father, the courts generally enforce it, holding the consideration is adequate. See Peterson v. Eritsland, 69 Wash.2d 588, 419 P.2d 332 (1966) and cases cited supra, note 99. Of course if the applicable statute is not complied with, the settlement will not be enforced. Lennon v. Walrod, 250 N.W.2d 33 (Iowa 1977); Petit v. Ratner, 92 Nev. 421, 551 P.2d 426 (1976).

Bancroft v. Court of Special Sessions of New York, 278 App.Div. 141, 103 N.Y.S.2d 779 (1st Dep't 1951), affirmed 303 N.Y. 728, 103 N.E.2d 344 (1951) held the settlement not binding where the child was in danger of becoming dependent upon the state.

earlier section,[55] there is some question whether, or under what circumstances, such statutes are constitutional. The Uniform Parentage Act deals with this problem by providing that the child must be made a party to the action, and that if the action is compromised by agreement, judgment is entered in accordance therewith.[56] This avoids the objection that the mother should not be permitted to settle a claim which is essentially for the child's benefit without the child's participation. It does not, however, avoid the objection that support decrees for the benefit of legitimate children are modifiable where the child's needs increase and the father is able to afford increased support, and that discrimination between legitimate and illegitimate children may offend the Equal Protection Clause.

Where the settlement is binding under the applicable law, it may be set aside for fraud, duress or mistake on familiar contract principles, but it may not be set aside on the ground that the alleged father later turned out not to be the father in fact.[57] Contracts principles may produce such a result, but it does seem harsh.

Under the law of some states a compromise by the mother may not bind the child. Tuer v. Niedoliwka, 92 Mich.App. 694, 285 N.W.2d 424 (1979). And a settlement agreement between mother and alleged father may not protect the father against a claim by the state if the state has to furnish support to the child later on. State Dep't of Human Services v. Webster, 398 A.2d 792 (Me.1979).

55. See the discussion in section 4.2, supra, at notes 85 to 92.

56. Uniform Parentage Act §§ 9, 13, 9A Unif.L.Ann. 599, 604 (1979). Section 9 also provides that the child, if a minor, shall be represented by a guardian, and section 19 authorizes the appointment of counsel for any party unable to afford counsel.

57. Jordan v. Johnson, 138 Ind.App. 53, 211 N.E.2d 623 (1965); Fiege v. Boehm, 210 Md. 352, 123 A.2d 316 (1956); State ex rel. M.L.B. v. D.G.H., 122 Wis.2d 536, 363 N.W.2d 419 (1985); Annot., 84 A.L.R.2d 593 (1962).

58. People v. Sweet, 346 Mich. 684, 78 N.W.2d 598 (1956).

59. Annot., 40 A.L.R.2d 961 (1955); Uniform Parentage Act §§ 15, 16, 9A Unif.L.Ann. 607–608, 609 (1979). Where necessary for the care of the child, the support of

Judgment or Decree

The judgment in the old-fashioned bastardy proceeding reflects the same confusing hybrid background as do other aspects of the suit. In such a proceeding the jury enters a verdict of guilty or not guilty on the issue of paternity. If the verdict is guilty, the court then determines how much the defendant must pay to the mother for her medical expenses and for the support of the child.[58] Under more modern statutes the paternity suit is a civil action and the court, after a finding of paternity, makes an order for the support of the child, the medical expenses of the mother incurred as the result of the birth and, in some states, for her attorney fees.[59]

The level of support which the older cases ordered for the illegitimate child was often affected by the history of bastardy. The old notion was that the only purpose of the bastardy proceeding was the relief of the community from the burden of supporting the illegitimate child, and this led some courts to limit support to a mere subsistence level.[60] The modern view is that no such limit should be imposed. The support of the illegitimate child should be fixed in the same manner as the support of the legitimate child, that is, with reference to the child's needs and the father's and mother's resources.[61] Indeed it

the mother may also be ordered. Faraday v. Dube, 175 Conn. 438, 399 A.2d 1262 (1978).

60. E.g., Baugh v. Maddox, 266 Ala. 175, 95 So.2d 268 (1957). Alabama now has a civil paternity proceeding. Ala.Code 1984, § 26–17–6 (Supp.).

61. Kilcrease v. Kilcrease, 132 Cal.App.2d 869, 283 P.2d 300 (1955) (father cannot escape liability on the ground mother could earn enough to support the child); Kyne v. Kyne, 70 Cal.App.2d 80, 160 P.2d 910 (1945) (court should admit all relevant evidence on the child's needs and the parents' finances); Isaacson v. Obendorf, 99 Idaho 304, 581 P.2d 350 (1978); Whybra v. Gustafson, 365 Mich. 396, 112 N.W.2d 503 (1961) (error to limit support to 35% of what would be given for a legitimate child); People v. Sweet, 346 Mich. 684, 78 N.W.2d 598 (1956) (error to charge that father and mother must each pay half of support); Race v. Mrsny, 155 Neb. 679, 53 N.W.2d 88 (1952) (child entitled to same benefits and training as other children); Schaschlo v. Taishoff, 2 N.Y.2d 408, 161 N.Y.S.2d 48, 141 N.E.2d 562 (1957), 57 Colum.L.Rev. 1191 (1957) (statutory purpose is the promotion of the child's welfare, so that awards may reflect the father's financial condition). But the child's father is not responsible for the mother's support beyond the expenses

seems likely that any tendency to limit the support of the illegitimate child to levels below those prevailing for legitimate children would violate the Equal Protection Clause of the United States Constitution's Fourteenth Amendment.[62] Where statutory authority exists, the decree for support may be modified to reflect changes in circumstances as may be done with other child support orders.[63]

The usual method of enforcing orders for support in paternity suits is by imprisonment in the case of the old bastardy proceeding, or contempt in the case of the more modern civil paternity proceeding.[64] Most cases have held that these sanctions do not constitute imprisonment for debt under state constitutional provisions.[65] Enforcement by the execution of a bond may also be authorized.[66]

The paternity orders of one state should be enforceable by the courts of other states in the same manner as other child support orders.[67] The remedies for this purpose should include those made available by the Uniform Reciprocal Enforcement of Support Act.[68] Similarly the courts of American states should enforce paternity judgments of foreign countries, if the foreign judgment is based upon reasonable notice and opportunity to be heard and complies with the essentials of due process.[69]

Res Judicata

Put in its broadest aspect, the question here is, what are the consequences for later litigation of a judicial determination that a particular person is or is not the father of an illegitimate child? This question can arise and has arisen in many different contexts, resulting in decisions which are anything but consistent.[70] In its simplest form it arises when the child's mother brings a paternity suit against the putative father, and a judgment of paternity is entered. If there is personal jurisdiction over the defendant,[71] the matter is litigated,[72]

of birth. Mitchell v. Maurer, 328 Mich. 233, 43 N.W.2d 921 (1950). Child support may be made payable to the mother. Wong v. Wong Hing Young, 80 Cal.App.2d 391, 181 P.2d 741 (1947). A rule of law like that in Miner v. Miner, 192 A.2d 811 (D.C.App.1963), to the effect that a man's legitimate children are entitled to preference over his illegitimate children would doubtless be unconstitutional today. See section 4.2, supra.

Harris v. State, 356 So.2d 623 (Ala.1978) held that the defendant may not limit his liability to the cost of an abortion by requiring the plaintiff to have an abortion as a method of mitigating damages.

62. See section 4.2, supra, especially the discussion of Gomez v. Perez, 409 U.S. 535, 93 S.Ct. 872, 35 L.Ed.2d 56 (1973). But Ellen N. v. Stuart K., 88 Misc.2d 280, 387 N.Y.S.2d 367 (Fam.Ct.1976) held that there was no violation of constitutional principles in having a somewhat more limited standard of support for illegitimate children than for legitimate children, under N.Y.–McKinney's Fam.Ct. Act §§ 413, 513 (Supp.1984, 1983). This result seems dubious, however. Equally dubious is Mitchell v. Mitchell, 445 F.2d 722 (D.C.Cir.1971) giving legitimate children priority for support over illegitimate children.

63. Uniform Parentage Act § 18, 9A Unif.L.Ann. 611 (1979); Kyne v. Kyne, 70 Cal.App.2d 80, 160 P.2d 910 (1945); State ex rel. Wall. v. Sovinski, 234 Wis. 336, 291 N.W. 344 (1940). Whether it is constitutional to make support orders for illegitimates non-modifiable when support orders for legitimate children are modifiable is discussed in section 4.2, supra, at note 85.

64. Uniform Parentage Act § 17, 9A Unif.L.Ann. 610 (1979).

65. State v. Brewer, 38 S.C. 263, 16 S.E. 1001 (1893); Acker v. Adamson, 67 S.D. 341, 293 N.W. 83 (1940);

Annot., 118 A.L.R. 1109 (1939). Contra: State ex rel. Bissell v. Devore, 225 Iowa 815, 281 N.W. 740 (1938).

66. State v. Calder, 117 Utah 358, 215 P.2d 912 (1950).

67. Mocher v. Rasmussen-Taxdal, 180 So.2d 488 (Fla. App.1965); Peterson v. Paoli, 44 So.2d 639 (Fla.1950); Bjorgo v. Bjorgo, 402 S.W.2d 143 (Tex.1966); Annot., 16 A.L.R.2d 1098 (1951).

68. Uniform Reciprocal Enforcement of Support Act §§ 2(n), 3, 9, 9A Unif.L.Ann. 657, 659, 677 (1979).

69. Nicol v. Tanner, 310 Minn. 68, 256 N.W.2d 796 (1976).

70. For thorough and well reasoned discussions of this problem, see Note, Res Judicata and Paternity, 37 Univ. Colo.L.Rev. 479 (1965), and Note, Privity, Preclusion and the Parent-Child Relationship, 1977 B.Y.U.L.Rev. 612.

71. As has been shown, personal jurisdiction is generally required for a valid judgment in a paternity suit. See the discussion at note 28, supra.

72. Whether it is sufficient that the matter might have been litigated is not clear under the cases. Note, Res Judicata and Paternity, 37 Univ.Colo.L.Rev. 479, 483 (1965). The preference stated in the text for a requirement of actual litigation is based upon the need to protect the interests of all parties and a desire to make the rule as definite as possible. But the broader rule would not seem to be seriously objectionable. Cases holding that the alleged father may not later assert non-paternity after stipulating in earlier litigation that he was the child's father include De Weese v. Unick, 102 Cal.App.3d 100, 162 Cal.Rptr. 259 (1980); Brown v. Superior Court In and For San Francisco, 98 Cal.App.3d 633, 159 Cal.Rptr. 604 (1979); In re Marriage of Guardino, 95 Cal.App.3d 77, 156 Cal.Rptr. 883 (1979).

and a finding made, this ought to be conclusive in a later action involving other parties, as for example one in which the child seeks to inherit from the father's estate.[73] In other words, the adjudication of paternity in such a case should be given the effect of a judgment in rem, binding in all subsequent actions where the issue of paternity may arise, regardless of the identity of the parties.[74] This is so even though for purposes of acquiring jurisdiction the paternity suit is characterized as one in personam. This may appear inconsistent in terms of the old in personam-in rem categories, but adjudications of paternity have to be treated as sui generis in this respect, like other kinds of family litigation.[75] As in other proceedings, once mother, father and child have litigated the paternity issues, they being the persons most concerned with the child's status, the matter should be concluded.

Where the paternity suit ends in the determination that the defendant is not the child's father, the judgment should likewise be binding upon mother and child, with one important proviso: provided that the child was

made a party to the paternity suit and was independently represented in it.[76] In all cases in which a child's paternity is brought in issue a guardian ad litem should be appointed for him and he should be independently represented by counsel.[77] It is not clear why this is not done as a matter of course in all courts, but if it is done, there seems to be no reason why the rejection of the child's claim of relationship to the defendant should not be final.

Similar principles apply where the initial determination of status is made in a suit other than a paternity proceeding, such as divorce. Such cases are discussed in the later section of this work dealing with child support in general.[78]

Federal Remedies

Congress passed in 1974 and the president signed in early 1975 amendments to the Social Security Act constituting part D of title IV and Title XX of that act.[79] The purpose of this legislation was to provide more effective techniques for the enforcement of child support obligations owed both to legitimate and

---

73. Holding the judgment on paternity binding, with the help of a statute: In re Estate Devine, 255 Iowa 726, 123 N.W.2d 898 (1963). Holding that the paternity proceeding is not res judicata: In re Estate of Karger, 253 Minn. 542, 93 N.W.2d 137 (1958), on the theory that the paternity suit is intended only to relieve the local community from the expense of supporting the child. In Tidwell v. Booker, 290 N.C. 98, 225 S.E.2d 816 (1976) a criminal non-support proceeding was brought against the father of an illegitimate child, he was convicted and was ordered to make certain support payments. He failed to do this and the mother later brought a civil suit for support of the child. The court held that the finding of paternity in the earlier criminal proceeding was not binding on the court in the later civil suit. The case seems clearly wrong, as a cogent dissent pointed out. The defendant here had his day in court on the paternity issue and should not be entitled to another attempt to disprove paternity. But see Wilkins v. Kelly, 108 Misc.2d 598, 438 N.Y.S.2d 72 (Fam.Ct.1981) where a paternity decree based on the defendant's acknowledgement was vacated after nine years. See Note, Effect of a Criminal Conviction in Subsequent Civil Suits, 50 Yale L.J. 499 (1941).

74. The Uniform Parentage Act § 15(a), 9A Unif.L. Ann. 607 (1979) seems to have that effect. Thus, if the mother obtained a paternity judgment, the state should be entitled to rely upon it in a later suit against the father for reimbursement of payments made for the support of the child.

75. Cf. Restatement, Judgments § 74 (1942).

76. State ex rel. Acorman v. Pitner, 42 N.J. 251, 200 A.2d 104 (1964); Brown v. Marrelli, 527 P.2d 230 (Utah 1974). Expressions of doubt that the state would be bound by a prior finding that the defendant was not the child's father, made in the concurring opinion in this case, seem wrong, since the state's claim is derivative in the sense that it is made for the benefit of the child.

Where the child was not made a party to the mother's suit, Johnson v. Norman, 66 Ohio St.2d 186, 421 N.E.2d 124 (1981) properly held that the child's suit was not barred.

In Everett v. Everett, 57 Cal.App.3d 65, 129 Cal.Rptr. 8 (1976) the court held that an earlier judgment that the defendant was not the child's father was not binding in a later suit by the child where the earlier judgment was based upon a compromise not approved by the court. The opinion is quite unclear, but apparently the child was not made a party in the earlier proceeding. See also Arsenault v. Carrier, 390 A.2d 1048 (Me.1978); Ruddock v. Ohls, 91 Cal.App.3d 271, 154 Cal.Rptr. 87 (1979).

77. Annot., 65 A.L.R.2d 1381, 1392 (1959); Uniform Parentage Act § 9, 9A Unif.L.Ann. 599 (1979).

78. See section 14.1, infra. Cases are collected in Annot., 78 A.L.R.3d 846 (1977). See Withrow v. Webb, 53 N.C.App. 67, 280 S.E.2d 22 (1981); Williams v. Holland, 39 N.C.App. 141, 249 S.E.2d 821 (1978); Thompson v. Thompson, 572 S.W.2d 761 (Tex.Civ.App.1978).

79. Act of Jan. 4, 1975, Pub.L. No. 93–647, 88 Stat. 2337.

illegitimate children. Financial inducements to the states to set up enforcement agencies were authorized,[80] a Parent Locator Service was established, debts owed to states for child support were made not dischargeable in bankruptcy,[81] and the United States District Courts were given jurisdiction to hear civil actions for the enforcement of court orders for support where such actions are certified by the Secretary of Health, Education and Welfare.[82] This legislation is discussed in somewhat greater detail in a later section.[83] One section of these statutes which applies specifically to protection of the illegitimate child requires the mother to cooperate with the state in establishing the paternity of the child and in obtaining support for him,[84] unless it is found that the mother had good cause for refusing to cooperate. The sanction against non-cooperation is that the mother will be denied the benefits to which she would otherwise be entitled. But in that case protective payments for which the child is eligible will be continued, so that the child will not suffer for the fault of his parent. The constitutional validity of statutes attempting to coerce parents to cooperate with the state is discussed in an earlier section.[85]

 **WESTLAW
REFERENCES**

Nature of the Action and Procedure in General
sy(illegitima! /s duty right obligat! entitl! /5 support /s father dad)

80. 42 U.S.C.A. §§ 652, 654, 655.

81. 42 U.S.C.A. §§ 653, 656.

82. 42 U.S.C.A. § 660.

83. See section 6.2, infra. The federal legislation is discussed in some detail in Note, Child Support Enforcement and Establishment of Paternity as Tools of Welfare Reform—Social Services Amendments of 1974, pt. B, 42 U.S.C.A. §§ 651–60 (Supp.V), 52 Wash.L.Rev. 169 (1976), and Note, Enforcement of Child Support Obligations of Absent Parents-Social Services Amendments of 1974, 30 S.W.L.J. 625 (1976). Regulations implementing these statutory provisions have been promulgated in 45 C.F.R. Parts 205, 232 to 235, 301 to 304 (1985). A study of state procedure for the determination of paternity was commissioned by the Department of Health, Education and Welfare, Office of Child Support Enforcement, was conducted by the University of Southern California Center for Health Services Research, and published under the title Paternity Determination: Techniques and Procedures to Establish the Paternity of Children Born Out of Wedlock (1976).

"uniform reciprocal enforcement of support" /s illegitima!

Jurisdiction and Service
sy(jurisdiction /s bastard* paternity /3 suit action proceeding lawsuit)
personal /2 service /s bastard* paternity /3 action proceeding suit lawsuit

Parties
child /3 bring /s paternity bastard* /3 suit action proceeding lawsuit

Trial and Evidence
sy(paternity /s jury /2 trial)
child /s exhibit! /s paternity bastard*
sy(admissi! admit! /s blood +2 test /s paternity)

The Presumption of Legitimacy
sy(rebut! /s presum! /10 legitima!)

Res Judicata
sy(res +1 adjudicata judicata /s paternity)

Federal Remedies
42 +5 654 /p paternity

---

§ 4.5 The Consequences of Illegitimacy

Custody and Support

The traditional rule was that the mother of an illegitimate child had the primary, or in some jurisdictions even the exclusive, right to his custody.[1] That rule is now of questionable constitutional validity under Stanley v. Illinois.[2] Even though Stanley has been qualified to some indeterminate extent by Quilloin v. Walcott[3], a flat rule excluding the father

84. 42 U.S.C.A. § 602(a)(26)(B) (Supp.).

85. See section 4.2, supra, at note 97.

§ 4.5

1. Cases are collected in Annots., 45 A.L.R.3d 216 (1972) and 98 A.L.R.2d 417 (1964).

2. 405 U.S. 645, 92 S.Ct. 1208, 31 L.Ed.2d 551 (1972), discussed in § 4.2, supra, at note 72.

3. 434 U.S. 246, 98 S.Ct. 549, 54 L.Ed.2d 511 (1978), rehearing denied 435 U.S. 918, 98 S.Ct. 1477, 55 L.Ed.2d 511 (1978). This case held that a Georgia statute was not unconstitutional when it authorized the adoption of an illegitimate child without the consent of the father notwithstanding that the father was not shown to be an unfit parent and notwithstanding that the father of a legitimate child in the same position could block an adoption by withholding his consent. But see Caban v. Mohammed, 441 U.S. 380, 99 S.Ct. 1760, 60 L.Ed.2d 297 (1979), on remand 47 N.Y.2d 880, 419 N.Y.S.2d 74, 392 N.E.2d 1257 (1979).

without regard to his conduct or interest in the child would still seem to be in violation of the Equal Protection Clause as the Supreme Court has applied it to illegitimates.[4] At the minimum, the father of the illegitimate child would, under Stanley, be entitled to notice and a hearing as to his fitness before being deprived of custody or before being denied custody. It would also seem correct to say that in those states which have adopted a state Equal Rights Amendment [5] there could not constitutionally be a preference given to the mother over the father of the illegitimate child with respect to custody.[6]

Whatever the constitutional position may be, changing social conditions have caused many courts, either explicitly or implicitly, to abandon maternal preference as a guide to the award of custody of illegitimate children. Illegitimacy has become much more prevalent than ever before in the United States.[7] And more fathers of illegitimate children are taking an interest in their children and seeking custody or rights of visitation, although one suspects that these fathers are still a small proportion of all fathers of illegitimate children. The result has been that in a growing body of cases the courts are awarding custody of illegitimate children on the basis of the same sort of reasoning they would use in awarding custody of legitimate children.[8] In many instances, perhaps the majority, the

4. In view of the confusion, lack of understanding of the relationships involved and the excessive breadth exhibited by the Stanley opinion, it is not surprising that the lower courts have been unable to agree on the effect of the Stanley case on the father's claim to custody. A few of them have held, under the influence of Stanley, that the father has a constitutional claim to custody which must be recognized by the courts as equivalent to the mother's claim, at least where there is no question of paternity. See, e.g., Orezza v. Ramirez, 19 Ariz.App. 405, 507 P.2d 1017 (1973); Pi v. Delta, 175 Conn. 527, 400 A.2d 709 (1978); In Matter of Mark T., 8 Mich.App. 122, 154 N.W.2d 27 (1967) (a pre-Stanley case); Raysor v. Gabbey, 57 A.D.2d 437, 395 N.Y.S.2d 290 (1977); Pierce v. Yerkovich, 80 Misc.2d 613, 363 N.Y.S.2d 403 (Fam.Ct. 1974); J.M.S. v. H.A., 161 W.Va. 433, 242 S.E.2d 696 (1978); Hammack v. Wise, 158 W.Va. 343, 211 S.E.2d 118 (1975). But Petitioner F. v. Respondent R., 430 A.2d 1075 (Del.1981) refused to apply Stanley to custody and held that a putative father has no constitutionally protected interest in the determination of his parental status where the child was born to a married woman living with her husband.

A case giving relief under 42 U.S.C.A. § 1983, on the ground that in the circumstances a father's interest in his illegitimate child was constitutionally protected is Dennison v. Vietch, 560 F.Supp. 435 (D.Minn.1983). Likewise Cheryl Lynn H. v. Superior Court for Los Angeles County, 41 Cal.App.3d 273, 115 Cal.Rptr. 849 (1974), while it noted that Stanley would have an effect on state law concerning the custody of illegitimate children, suggested that the case's effect would be upon the change of custody rather than upon the initial award of custody. No reason for this limitation of Stanley was offered. In this case, however, the child's interests seem to have indicated that the father should not be given custody. The effect of Stanley was noted but not decided in In re Richard M., 14 Cal.3d 783, 122 Cal.Rptr. 531, 537 P.2d 363 (1975) since the court held that the child had been legitimated. The Cheryl Lynn H. case was disapproved to the extent that it was inconsistent with the court's opinion, an extent which is not clear.

State v. Hill, 91 Wis.2d 446, 283 N.W.2d 451 (1979) upheld the constitutionality of a criminal statute forbid-

ding the removal of an illegitimate child from the custody of his mother, as applied to the child's father.

5. These states include Alaska, Colorado, Connecticut, Hawaii, Illinois, Louisiana, Maryland, Massachusetts, Montana, New Hampshire, New Mexico, Pennsylvania, Texas, Utah, Virginia, Washington, Wyoming. Kurtz, The State Equal Rights Amendments and Their Impact on Domestic Relations Law, 11 Fam.L.Q. 101 (1977). Although there is some variation in their language, these constitutional provisions generally provide that equality of rights under the law shall not be abridged or denied because of sex. A similar provision has been proposed for the United States Constitution, to be the Twenty-Seventh Amendment, Proposed Amendment to the United States Constitution, S.J.Res. 8, S.J.Res. 9, and H.R.J.Res. 208, 92d Cong., 1st Sess. (1971). The amendment failed of ratification, but has been reintroduced in both Houses of Congress and referred to the two Committees on the Judiciary. S.J.R.1, 1 CCH Cong.Index 16,151 (Status of Senate Resolutions Section) (February 27, 1987); H.J.R.1, 2 CCH Cong.Index 30,501 (Status of House Joint Resolutions) (February 27, 1987).

6. People ex rel. Irby v. Dubois, 41 Ill.App.3d 609, 354 N.E.2d 562 (1976); Kurtz, State Equal Rights Amendments and Their Impact on Domestic Relations Law, 11 Fam.L.Q. 101, 140 (1977).

7. See section 4.1, supra, at note 16.

8. The Uniform Parentage Act § 25(c), 9A Unif.L. Ann. 325 (Supp.1985) provides that when the child's father is identified and claims custody, the court shall then determine custodial rights to the child. See also Or.Rev. Stat. § 109.094 (1984). Custody may even be awarded to the father in order to give him the status of "presumed father" under the Act, the result of which is to require his consent to the child's adoption. Matter of Tricia Marie M., 74 Cal.App.3d 125, 141 Cal.Rptr. 554 (1977), cert. denied 435 U.S. 996, 98 S.Ct. 1649, 56 L.Ed.2d 86 (1978).

But see People v. Carrillo, 162 Cal.App.3d 585, 208 Cal. Rptr. 684 (1984) holding that the natural mother may constitutionally be preferred for custody over an alleged natural father who is not the "presumed" father.

mother's claim is found to be most conducive to the child's welfare and custody is awarded to the mother.[9] In other instances the father is given custody when that is found to be in the child's best interests.[10] And in a few cases custody may be awarded to neither parent but to some other person or an agency if neither parent appears to be a suitable custodian,[11] although some courts at least insist that the parents of the illegitimate child have a paramount claim to custody which can only be defeated on proof of his "unfitness", a term seldom defined.[12] This latter view receives support from a literal reading of Stanley v. Illinois.[13]

Where the mother is awarded custody of her illegitimate child, an increasing number

of fathers are seeking visitation rights. Permitting such visitation may have an adverse impact on the child's welfare, since it emphasizes the child's illegitimacy by placing him in the company of a father who obviously is not married to his mother. It may make the adjustment of mother and child more difficult [14] and may place an obstacle in the way of her marriage to a man who would adopt the child. Notwithstanding these difficulties a substantial number of courts are willing to grant visitation to the father where he has a sincere interest in the child and where, in the court's view, the visits are beneficial or at least not detrimental to the child's welfare.[15] Here also some cases have held that the father has a constitutional right to visitation

Cases which seem to award custody of the illegitimate child in much the same manner as they would the custody of the legitimate child include Orezza v. Ramirez, 19 Ariz.App. 405, 507 P.2d 1017 (1973); People ex rel. Irby v. Dubois, 41 Ill.App.3d 609, 354 N.E.2d 562 (1976); Creppel v. Thornton, 230 So.2d 644 (La.App.1970); Marshall v. Stefanides, 17 Md.App. 364, 302 A.2d 682 (1973) (semble); In re Adoption of B., 152 N.J.Super. 546, 378 A.2d 90 (1977); Sparks v. Phelps, 22 Or.App. 570, 540 P.2d 397 (1975); Hammack v. Wise, 158 W.Va. 343, 211 S.E.2d 118 (1975); Slawek v. Stroh, 62 Wis.2d 295, 319, 215 N.W.2d 9, 22 (1974) (dissenting opinion).

For a full discussion of the factors relevant to custody awards see sections 19.1 to 19.6, infra, which deal with the custody of legitimate children, but which are important also where illegitimate children are concerned.

A case holding that habeas corpus will lie to determine the custody of an illegitimate child is People ex rel. Elmore v. Elmore, 46 Ill.App.3d 504, 5 Ill.Dec. 292, 361 N.E.2d 615 (1977), 16 J.Fam.L. 627 (1978).

9. E.g., Marshall v. Stefanides, 17 Md.App. 364, 302 A.2d 682 (1973); In the Matter of Brenda H., 37 Ohio Misc. 123, 305 N.E.2d 815 (1973); In re Guardianship of Harp, 6 Wash.App. 701, 495 P.2d 1059 (1972). Many cases continue to grant custody to the mother after referring to her paramount claim, but most such cases rest on facts which strongly suggest that the child's welfare is best served by honoring the mother's claim. See, e.g., Commonwealth ex rel. Gifford v. Miller, 213 Pa. Super. 269, 248 A.2d 63 (1968) (this case is in any event overruled by Pennsylvania's adoption of an Equal Rights Amendment); Turner v. Saka, 90 Nev. 54, 518 P.2d 608 (1974); Anonymous v. Anonymous, 26 N.Y.2d 740, 309 N.Y.S.2d 40, 257 N.E.2d 288 (1970); Z. v. A, 36 A.D.2d 995, 320 N.Y.S.2d 997 (3d Dep't 1971); Roe v. Doe, 58 Misc.2d 757, 296 N.Y.S.2d 865 (Fam.Ct.1968); In re Gutman, 22 Ohio App.2d 125, 259 N.E.2d 128 (1969).

10. Orezza v. Ramirez, 19 Ariz.App. 405, 507 P.2d 1017 (1973); People ex rel. Irby v. Dubois, 41 Ill.App.3d 609, 354 N.E.2d 562 (1976); Creppel v. Thornton, 230 So. 2d 644 (La.App.1970); In the Matter of Robert P., 36 Mich.App. 497, 194 N.W.2d 18 (1971); In the Matter of

Mark T., 8 Mich.App. 122, 154 N.W.2d 27 (1967); In re State in Interest of M., 25 Utah 2d 101, 476 P.2d 1013 (1970) (mother deprived of parental rights, father gets custody); Hammack v. Wise, 158 W.Va. 343, 211 S.E.2d 118 (1975).

11. State ex rel. Paul v. Department of Public Welfare, 170 So.2d 549 (La.App.1965); In re Zink, 269 Minn. 535, 132 N.W.2d 795 (1964); S. v. H.M., 111 N.J.Super. 553, 270 A.2d 48 (1970); In re Guardianship of Morgan, 70 Misc.2d 1063, 335 N.Y.S.2d 226 (Surr.Ct.1972). In Cheryl Lynn H. v. Superior Court for Los Angeles County, 41 Cal.App.3d 273, 115 Cal.Rptr. 849 (1974) the court found that an award of custody to the father would be detrimental to the child and therefore held that the mother could place the child for adoption.

12. In some cases at least unfitness seems to be equated with the child's best interests. Hyatte v. Lopez, 366 N.E.2d 676 (Ind.App.1977); In re P., 36 Mich.App. 497, 194 N.W.2d 18 (1971); In re Guardianships of Morgan, 70 Misc.2d 1063, 335 N.Y.S.2d 226 (Surr.Ct.1972). See also Raysor v. Gabbey, 57 A.D.2d 437, 395 N.Y.S.2d 290 (4th Dep't 1977). Johnson v. Lloyd, 211 A.2d 764 (D.C.App. 1965) held that the mother was not unfit by virtue of having had five illegitimate children by four different men.

13. 405 U.S. 645, 92 S.Ct. 1208, 31 L.Ed.2d 551 (1972).

14. E.g., Pierce v. Yerkovich, 80 Misc.2d 613, 363 N.Y.S.2d 403 (Fam.Ct.1974), in which rights of visitation were given to the father of an illegitimate child although the mother had married and there was testimony by Dr. Albert J. Solnit, co-author of J. Goldstein, A. Freud, A. Solnit, Beyond the Best Interests of the Child, to the effect that the visitation would have an adverse effect on the child's development. Sullivan v. Bonafonte, 172 Conn. 612, 376 A.2d 69 (1977) upheld the denial of visitation rights to the father on the ground that visitation would not be in the child's best interests.

15. Griffith v. Gibson, 73 Cal.App.3d 465, 142 Cal. Rptr. 176 (1977); Forestiere v. Doyle, 30 Conn.Supp. 284, 310 A.2d 607 (1973) (father is entitled to be heard on visitation); In re One Minor Child, 295 A.2d 727 (Del.

upon the same terms as would the father of a legitimate child, under Stanley v. Illinois.[16] This is all very well so long as the courts keep in mind that the illegitimate child is not in the same position as a legitimate child, and that visitation by his father may be detrimental to him more often than would be true of the legitimate child, for the reasons outlined.

The mother of the illegitimate child had the duty of supporting him at common law,[17] and still has such a duty under the statutes of many states.[18] As is shown in another section the father also has the obligation of supporting the child, an obligation enforceable by a bastardy or paternity suit.[19] Irrespective of statute it now seems clear that as the Supreme Court has construed the Equal Protec-

tion Clause, both mothers and fathers have equivalent obligations to support their illegitimate children just as they must support their legitimate children.[20] Each parent should contribute to support to the extent of his or her ability.

Although no duty of support is generally imposed upon a man who marries an illegitimate child's mother if he is not the child's father,[21] a few cases have held that he must support the child.[22] These decisions are based either upon an application of estoppel, the theory being that the husband knew about the child and agreed to recognize it as his,[23] or upon vague notions of implied consent to be considered the child's father.[24] There may also be a true estoppel to deny the obligation

1972) (father entitled to visitation if in the child's best interests); Mixon v. Mize, 198 So.2d 373 (Fla.App.1967), cert. denied 204 So.2d 211 (Fla.1967) (father who acknowledges paternity and exhibits an interest in the child's welfare may have visitation rights); People ex rel. Vallera v. Rivera, 39 Ill.App.3d 775, 351 N.E.2d 391 (1976) (father entitled to visitation if in the child's best interests); Carty v. Martin, 233 Kan. 7, 660 P.2d 540 (1983); State ex rel. Wingard v. Sill, 223 Kan. 661, 576 P.2d 620 (1978); Maxwell v. LeBlanc, 434 So.2d 375 (La.1983); Gardner v. Rothman, 370 Mass. 79, 345 N.E.2d 370 (1976) (court may grant visitation to the father, citing many cases); R. v. F., 113 N.J.Super. 396, 273 A.2d 808 (1971); M. v. M., 112 N.J.Super. 540, 271 A.2d 919 (1970); In re Gerald G.G., 61 A.D.2d 521, 403 N.Y.S.2d 57 (2d Dep't 1978) (reversing the trial court, this court refused to permit adoption of the child by mother and stepfather in order to preserve the natural father's relationship with the child); Commonwealth ex rel. Peterson v. Hayes, 252 Pa.Super. 487, 381 A.2d 1311 (1977); Commonwealth v. Rozanski, 206 Pa.Super. 397, 213 A.2d 155 (1965).

The Uniform Parentage Act § 24, 9A Unif.L.Ann. 322 (Supp.1985), seems to contemplate that the father may be given visitation in an appropriate case, when paternity has either been presumed or established. Griffith v. Gibson, 73 Cal.App.3d 465, 142 Cal.Rptr. 176 (1977).

See also Note, 35 Bklyn.L.Rev. 307 (1969); Annot., 15 A.L.R.3d 887 (1967). The strange case of C.M. v. C.C., 152 N.J.Super. 160, 377 A.2d 821 (1977) held that the father of a child produced by artificial insemination was entitled to visitation.

16. La Grone by Bridger v. La Grone, 238 Kan. 630, 713 P.2d 474 (1986) (custody of one child to the mother, of the other to the father); Phillips v. Horlander, 535 S.W.2d 72 (Ky.1975); R v. F, 113 N.J.Super. 396, 273 A.2d 808 (1971); Pierce v. Herkovich, 80 Misc.2d 613, 363 N.Y.S.2d 403 (Fam.Ct.1974); J.M.S. v. H.A., 161 W.Va. 433, 242 S.E.2d 696 (1978).

17. In re Guardianship of Smith, 42 Cal.2d 91, 265 P.2d 888 (1954); Wright v. Wright, 2 Mass. 109 (1806); In re Vieweger, 93 N.J.Eq. 527, 117 A. 291 (1922).

18. E.g., Ill.–S.H.A. ch. 40, §§ 2501.1, 2502, 2503 (Supp.1985); N.Y.–McKinney's Dom. Rel. Law § 33 (1977). It is odd that the Uniform Parentage Act, 9A Unif.L.Ann. 587 (1979) contains no explicit provision imposing a duty of support on the mother. Section 21 of that Act, 9A Unif.L.Ann. 612 (1979), does provide a method for determining the existence of the mother-child relationship but says nothing about the mother's duty to support.

19. See section 4.4, supra.

20. See the cases discussed in section 5.2, supra, and sections 6.2 and 14.1, infra.

21. Clevenger v. Clevenger, 189 Cal.App.2d 658, 11 Cal.Rptr. 707 (1961); Byers v. Byers, 618 P.2d 930 (Okl. 1980); Mace v. Webb, 614 P.2d 647 (Utah 1980); Taylor v. Taylor, 58 Wash.2d 510, 364 P.2d 444 (1961). Other cases are collected in Annot., 90 A.L.R.2d 583 (1963).

22. In re Marriage of Valle, 53 Cal.App.3d 837, 126 Cal.Rptr. 38 (1975); L v. L, 497 S.W.2d 840 (Mo.App. 1973), 43 U.Mo.K.C.L.Rev. 104 (1974); Burse v. Burse, 48 Ohio App.2d 244, 356 N.E.2d 755 (1976); Gustin v. Gustin, 108 Ohio App. 171, 161 N.E.2d 68 (1958); T. v. T., 216 Va. 867, 224 S.E.2d 148 (1976); Hartford v. Hartford, 53 Ohio App.2d 79, 371 N.E.2d 591 (1977).

23. Perkins v. Perkins, 34 Conn.Supp. 187, 383 A.2d 634 (1977); L. v. L., 497 S.W.2d 840 (Mo.App.1973), collecting other cases.

24. Hall v. Rosen, 50 Ohio St.2d 135, 363 N.E.2d 725 (1977). This case also took the view that if the husband is liable for the child's support, the biological father would not be. It seems doubtful that a rule of law cutting off the child's claim against his true father without a hearing in which he is represented could pass muster constitutionally. In any event the case is overruled by Johnson v. Adams, 18 Ohio St.3d 48, 479 N.E.2d 866 (1985), which preserved a rebuttable presumption that the husband is the child's father.

where the husband represents to the child that he is the child's father and the child relies upon the representation.[25]

Inheritance

The most significant disability under which the illegitimate child suffered in earlier times was that he could not inherit property from either his father or his mother.[26] Today in nearly all, if not all, states the illegitimate child may inherit both from and through his mother.[27] Those states whose statutes continue to bar illegitimates from inheriting from their fathers are unconstitutional under Trimble v. Gordon.[28] But there may be some statutes which do not go so far as to bar the inheritance absolutely. For example, the New York statute provides that the illegiti-

mate child may inherit from his father only if a court of competent jurisdiction has entered a decree of filiation in a paternity suit during the life of the father.[29] The New York Court of Appeals has held this statute constitutional, distinguishing it from the Illinois statute held unconstitutional in Trimble on the ground that it goes only to proof of paternity and does not exhibit such a strong hostility to the illegitimate child.[30] Statutes in other states may likewise be unconstitutional in limiting the illegitimate child's right to inherit from or through his father, but reliable predictions are impossible on the current state of the law.[31]

The determination of status for inheritance purposes is governed by the law of the child's domicile.[32]

---

25. In re Marriage of Valle, 53 Cal.App.3d 837, 126 Cal.Rptr. 38 (1975); Clevenger v. Clevenger, 189 Cal.App. 2d 658, 11 Cal.Rptr. 707 (1961) (dictum). A similar doctrine was relied upon to prevent a mother from asserting the illegitimacy of her children in Gossett v. Ullendorff, 114 Fla. 159, 154 So. 177 (1934).

26. See section 4.1, supra, at notes 4, 5.

27. T. Atkinson, Handbook of the Law of Wills § 22 (2d ed. 1953). Cases are collected in Annots., 24 A.L.R. 570 (1923), 83 A.L.R. 1330 (1933). Vallin v. Bondesson, 346 Mass. 748, 196 N.E.2d 191 (1964) held that the illegitimate child could inherit from other illegitimate children of his mother. See also Annot., 7 A.L.R.3d 677 (1966). For cases allowing the illegitimate child to inherit from his mother's legitimate children, see Annot., 60 A.L.R.2d 1182 (1958). Inheritance by the illegitimate from or through his mother's ancestors or collateral kindred is permitted by many statutes. See Annot., 97 A.L.R.2d 1101 (1964).

The Uniform Probate Code § 2–109, 8 Unif.L.Ann. 66 (1983) now defines "child" for purposes of intestate succession to include illegitimate children, so that they clearly would take from or through their mothers.

28. 430 U.S. 762, 97 S.Ct. 1459, 52 L.Ed.2d 31 (1977). This case and others dealing with the constitutionality of various disabilities of the illegitimate child are discussed in section 4.2, supra.

29. N.Y. Est., Powers & Trusts Law § 4–1.2 (1981).

30. Matter of Lalli's Estate, 38 N.Y.2d 77, 378 N.Y.S.2d 351, 340 N.E.2d 721 (1975), vacated and remanded 431 U.S. 911, 97 S.Ct. 2164, 53 L.Ed.2d 220 (1977), decision adhered to 43 N.Y.2d 65, 400 N.Y.S.2d 761, 371 N.E.2d 481 (1977), affirmed 439 U.S. 259, 99 S.Ct. 518, 58 L.Ed.2d 503 (1978).

31. The Uniform Probate Code § 2–109, 8 Unif.L.Ann. 67 (1983), as presently drafted, permits the illegitimate child to inherit from or through his father if paternity is established before the father's death, or afterwards by clear and convincing proof.

See also Foster v. Anderson, 287 Ala. 111, 248 So.2d 707 (1971) (illegitimate child not entitled to share as pretermitted heir); Burnett v. Camden, 253 Ind. 354, 255 N.E.2d 650 (1970), cert. denied 399 U.S. 901, 90 S.Ct. 2202, 26 L.Ed.2d 556 (1970) (statute valid in regulating proof of paternity for inheritance purposes); McKay's Estate v. Davis, 208 Kan. 282, 491 P.2d 932 (1971) (illegitimate whose paternity is established may inherit through his father); In re Estate of Breole, 298 Minn. 116, 212 N.W.2d 894 (1973) (statute allowing inheritance by illegitimate not retroactive); Thom v. Bailey, 257 Or. 572, 481 P.2d 355 (1971) (paternity may be established in a variety of ways for inheritance purposes); Williford v. Downs, 270 S.C. 110, 240 S.E.2d 654 (1978) (statute limits devises to illegitimate children when there is a wife or legitimate child); Annot., Eligibility of Illegitimate Child to Receive Family Allowance Out of Estate of His Deceased Father, 12 A.L.R.3d 1140 (1967).

Whether the illegitimate child is within a class gift to "children" depends upon the intent of the testator as revealed by the will and the surrounding circumstances. Walton v. Lindsey, 349 So.2d 41 (Ala.1977); Vincent v. Sutherland, 691 P.2d 85 (Okl.App.1984); In re Parsons' Trust, 56 Wis.2d 613, 203 N.W.2d 40 (1973). Naimo v. La Fianza, 146 N.J.Super. 362, 369 A.2d 987 (1976) held that an agreement by a father to make a testamentary gift to his illegitimate child was vitiated by the fact that consideration for the agreement was illicit acts of intercourse, the father being married.

A statute precluding inheritance *from* the illegitimate child by his paternal kindred in the absence of a filiation decree was held constitutional in Estate of Fay, 44 N.Y.2d 137, 404 N.Y.S.2d 554, 375 N.E.2d 735 (1978), appeal dismissed 439 U.S. 1059, 99 S.Ct. 820, 59 L.Ed.2d 25 (1979), rehearing denied 440 U.S. 968, 99 S.Ct. 1521, 59 L.Ed.2d 784 (1979).

32. In re Duquesne's Estate, 29 Utah 2d 94, 505 P.2d 779 (1973).

Other Financial Benefits

Spurred on by the Supreme Court's decisions on the constitutional rights of illegitimate children, the state courts have proceeded to eliminate many of the disabilities under which such children have suffered in the past. For example, illegitimate children have been held entitled to sue for the wrongful death of a parent,[33] to make claims for workmen's compensation on the death of a parent,[34] to be included as beneficiaries in life insurance policies,[35] and to have other dependency claims.[36]

Names and Birth Records

Social changes which have occurred in the past few years, such as the increase in the rate of illegitimacy, the accompanying reduction in the stigma attached to illegitimacy, and the move toward greater personal freedom, particularly on the part of women, have led to some uncertainty concerning the names to be given illegitimate children. The usual practice is for the mother to give the child her surname.[37] Where the father consents, some statutes and a little judicial authority approve the child's taking the father's surname.[38] The same may be true if a paternity suit establishes the father's paternity.[39] Unfortu-

nately the Uniform Parentage Act does not provide for these questions, other than to permit an amended birth certificate upon order of court, presumably as the result of a decree establishing paternity.[40]

Many states have statutes dealing in a variety of ways with the manner in which an illegitimate birth is to be recorded. Their purpose is often to prevent a public record of the child's status from being available.[41] When the child is legitimated, or paternity established, statutes often permit the birth record to be changed to indicate the father's name, the fact of change being kept confidential again to avoid any reflection upon the child.[42]

The Tort of "Wrongful Life"

Recently it has been suggested that the law might improve the condition of the illegitimate child by giving him an action in tort against his father which would result in damages compensating him for the material harm and mental suffering caused by being born a bastard. The first case, Zepeda v. Zepeda,[43] held that although the child's complaint alleged the elements of a willful tort, characterized by the court as wrongful life, the recogni-

33. Weaks v. Mounter, 88 Nev. 118, 493 P.2d 1307 (1972); Carroll v. Sneed, 211 Va. 640, 179 S.E.2d 620 (1971).

34. S.L.W. v. Alaska Workmen's Compensation Board, 490 P.2d 42 (Alaska 1971).

35. Metropolitan Life Insurance Co. v. Thompson, 368 F.2d 791 (3d Cir.1966), cert. denied 388 U.S. 914, 87 S.Ct. 2127, 18 L.Ed.2d 1355 (1967), rehearing denied 389 U.S. 891, 88 S.Ct. 22, 19 L.Ed.2d 206 (1967); Butcher v. Pollard, 32 Ohio App.2d 1, 288 N.E.2d 204 (1972); Annot., 62 A.L.R.3d 1329 (1975).

36. Miller v. Laird, 349 F.Supp. 1034 (D.D.C.1972) (Illegitimate child may participate in armed services dependents' medical benefits).

37. Secretary of the Commonwealth v. City Clerk of Lowell, 373 Mass. 178, 366 N.E.2d 717 (1977) (In the absence of objection from the father, mother has the same right to control the child's initial surname as the parents of a legitimate child); Doe v. Dunning, 87 Wash. 2d 50, 549 P.2d 1 (1976). A statute providing the father's name may not be entered on the birth certificate unless the father consented or paternity was adjudicated was held constitutional in Oglesby v. Williams, 484 F.Supp. 865 (M.D.Fla.1980).

38. E.g., Official Code Ga.Ann. § 74–103 (Supp.1984); Application of M., 91 N.J.Super. 296, 219 A.2d 906 (1966).

39. Matter of G.L.A., 430 N.E.2d 433 (Ind.App.1982) and Application of Biegaj, 25 N.Y.S.2d 85 (City Ct.1941) (mother may give the child the father's surname, but court refuses to grant an application for change of name to that of the father as not being in the child's best interests); Eversole v. Strait, 591 S.W.2d 752 (Mo.App. 1979) (court refuses to order unwilling mother to give the child the father's name). Jones v. McDowell, 53 N.C.App. 434, 281 S.E.2d 192 (1981) held unconstitutional a statute requiring the child to be given the father's name on establishing paternity. Contra, ordering the child's name to be changed to that of the father who acknowledged paternity and made some support payments, on the ground that this was for the child's best interests, D.R.S. v. R.S.H., 412 N.E.2d 1257 (Ind.App.1980).

40. Uniform Parentage Act § 23, 9A Unif.L.Ann. 614 (1979). Other statutes on names are cited in H. Krause, Illegitimacy: Law and Social Policy 32–33 (1971).

41. H. Krause, Illegitimacy: Law and Social Policy 33–34 (1971); Doe v. Dunning, 87 Wash.2d 50, 549 P.2d 1 (1976).

42. Ibid.

43. 41 Ill.App.2d 240, 190 N.E.2d 849 (1963), cert. denied 379 U.S. 945, 85 S.Ct. 444, 13 L.Ed.2d 545 (1964), 2 Duquesne L.Rev. 125 (1963) 49 Iowa L.Rev. 1005 (1964), 112 U.Pa.L.Rev. 780 (1964). Notes on the issues raised by

tion of such a tort would be lawmaking of too sweeping a kind to be judicially created. It is not clear from the case what the elements of the tort or the nature of the wrong were thought to be. Conceivably it could be the father's failure to marry the child's mother, except that in Zepeda he was already married and thus could hardly be charged with failure to do what the law would not permit. Presumably it consisted in the adultery which resulted in the child's conception, since the court characterized it as a willful tort, passing over the argument that the use of contraception could have prevented conception and that therefore the father might have been guilty merely of negligence so far as the plaintiff was concerned. The court's reasoning that no substantial objection to recognition of the tort can be found in the fact that conception and tort were simultaneous seems correct, but there are other reasons for denying relief. The damages are difficult if not impossible to compute, the child as a plaintiff is in the logically untenable position of asserting that the very act which gave him life was a wrong to him, and the consequences of a rule that a child can sue his parents when their activities impair his home life or cause social or emotional damage are extremely far-reaching. Should a child, for example, be entitled to sue his parents when their divorce handicaps his care and upbringing? Should a black child be

entitled to sue his parents for bringing him into a world full of racial prejudice? To some extent we must take the world as we find it. Therefore the court in Zepeda reached the right result. A later case, Williams v. State,[44] likewise refused the illegitimate child relief where he was conceived as a result of a sexual assault on his mother in a state operated mental institution. The child's claim here was that the state was liable for its negligence in caring for his mother, but the New York Court of Appeals decided that there had been no tort to him even though his mother might have had a claim. It is far better for the law to go about improving the lot of the illegitimate child, as it has been doing recently, by removing his disabilities than by compensating him on the theory that he was tortiously injured by being born.

 WESTLAW REFERENCES

Custody and Support

sy,di(father dad /s right /3 custody /s illegitima!)
sy,di(visit! /s right /s father dad /s illegitima!)

Other Financial Benefits

sy(illegitima! /s wrongful! /2 death /5 parent father mother)

Tort of "Wrongful Life"

"wrongful life" /s illegitima!

the child's claim may be found in 66 Colum.L.Rev. 127 (1966), 18 Stan.L.Rev. 530 (1966), 22 U.Miami L.Rev. 884 (1968), and 43 N.D.L.Rev. 99 (1966). Relief was denied to a similar claim in Pinkney v. Pinkney, 198 So.2d 52 (Fla. App.1967), overruled on other grounds, Brown v. Bray, 300 So.2d 668 (Fla.1974).

The term "wrongful life" has also been applied to claims of tortious injury caused by various kinds of medical negligence. The suit which most closely resembles Zepeda occurs when a child sues a physician alleging that the physician's negligence in failing to diagnose hereditary defects or in failing to perform genetic tests resulted in

the child's being born with serious defects. In such cases the child is claiming that if it had not been for the doctor's negligence he would not have been born. In most cases the courts have denied recovery. Different legal issues arise when the suit is brought by the affected child's parents. Both kinds of suit are discussed infra, in section 5.4.

44. 46 Misc.2d 824, 260 N.Y.S.2d 953 (Ct.Cl.1965), 18 Stan.L.Rev. 530 (1966), reversed and dismissed Williams v. State, 25 A.D.2d 907, 269 N.Y.S.2d 786 (3d Dep't 1966), affirmed 18 N.Y.2d 481, 276 N.Y.S.2d 885, 223 N.E.2d 343 (1966).

Chapter 5

CONTRACEPTION,
STERILIZATION AND ABORTION

Table of Sections

§ 5.1 Contraception

Historical Background

In 1798 Thomas Robert Malthus published An Essay on the Principle of Population.[1] Although he was by no means the first person to be concerned about the possibility of an over-populated world, his book was so widely read, attacked and defended that he may fairly be said to have been the first to bring that possibility to public attention.[2] He was writing during a period of sharp population growth in Britain, a growth which accelerated during the Nineteenth Century in Britain and in many other parts of the world as well.[3] With the advances in medicine which have occurred in the Twentieth Century, the death rate in the industrialized countries and in some developing countries has fallen rapidly.[4] As a consequence of this, and of continued high birth rates in many nations, the world population has continued to climb in this Century to the point where it not only may outrun the means of subsistence, as Malthus foretold, but may also threaten the exhaustion of water and energy resources.[5]

§ 5.1

1. This was first published as a pamphlet, with later editions in book form. 9 International Encyclopedia of the Social Sciences 549 (1968); 11 Encyclopedia Britannica 394 (1974).

2. W. Petersen, The Politics of Population 26–89 (1964); Morris, Professor Malthus and His Essay, in K. Kammeyer, Population Studies: Selected Essays and Research 54 (1969); For a Marxist attack upon Malthus, see Sokolov, Prospects of Agricultural Development in Connexion With Population Growth, in III United Nations, World Population Conference 414 (1967).

3. Id. at 60; D. Bogue, Principles of Demography 47–51 (1969).

4. D. Bogue, Principles of Demography 74–77 (1969).

5. III United Nations, World Population Conference, 1965, 309–435 (1967); P. Ehrlich, The Population Bomb (1968); L. and A. Day, Too Many Americans (1964); Burton, A Philosopher Looks at the Population Bomb, in W. Blackstone, ed., Philosophy and Environmental Crisis 105 (1974); D. Price, ed., The 99th Hour (1967); D. Wrong, Population and Society (2d ed. 1961); Hardin, The Tragedy of the Commons, 162 Science 1243 (1968); G. Hardin, ed., Population, Evolution and Birth Control (2d ed. 1969). For a theologian's view, see H. Montefiore, The Question Mark (1969). A writer who emphasizes the impact of technology in the context of the economic and social system rather than over-population is B. Commoner, The Closing Circle (1971). A work which argues that over-population is not a social problem and that man's salvation lies in technology is H. Bahr, D. Chadwick, D. Thomas, eds., Population, Resources and The Future (1972).

For historical data on population growth, see D. Bogue, Principles of Demography Ch. 3 (1969). The rate of population growth now appears to be declining. New York Times May 26, 1978, page 18 E, Col. 1.

Population growth in the United States has been equally great, due to the combination of immigration during the Nineteenth Century with the reduction of the death rate and the maintenance, until recently, of high birth rates.[6] The post-World War II "baby boom" was the latest spurt in American population growth, leading to a figure for the United States population, according to the 1970 census, of more than two hundred and three million, as compared with the 1940 figure of one hundred and thirty-one million.[7] Although the United States birth rate has recently declined, the population will still increase for a period through this century, due to the fact that those persons born during the "baby boom" are still relatively young and presumably will continue having children.[8] One must also remember that population projections for periods of any length have been notably unreliable in the past, so that current projections must be viewed with scepticism.

Malthus thought that the chief method of preventing population growth was what he called "moral restraint", by which he meant late marriage. We are now seeing an increase in the age of first marriage in the United States [9] but it is accompanied by an increase in the rate of illegitimate births [10] and is therefore less of a check upon population growth than might be expected. Malthus disapproved of the obvious method of controlling population, contraception, which offers the best prospects for avoiding the harmful consequences of over-population.

Some methods of contraception have been known and used since Roman times,[11] but they were not widely practiced by married couples until the late Nineteenth Century.[12]

In the early Nineteenth Century, as a result of Malthus' book among other influences, advocates of contraception for social and economic betterment began to appear.[13] In England the earliest of these was Jeremy Bentham, and somewhat later Francis Place, who distributed handbills urging the sponge method of contraception as a way of controlling population growth and relieving the poor of the burden of large families.[14] As the movement gained adherents and began to make itself heard, it became the target of state criminal action. The Crown's prosecution of Charles Bradlaugh and Annie Besant for the sale of a book called Fruits of Philosophy whose author was an American, Charles Knowlton, resulted in a conviction by a jury for the publication of an obscene libel. The conviction was reversed in the Court of Appeal on the ground that the indictment was insufficient, the court being extremely careful to state that it was expressing no opinion upon the merits of the case.[15] As with so many obscenity prosecutions, the major effect of the case was to attract wide public interest in the campaign for voluntary birth control.

The law's reaction in the United States to the emerging issue of birth control was even more foolish and hysterical than in Britain. Dr. Knowlton, a leader of the movement early in the century, was convicted several times in Massachusetts for violation of the obscenity

6. D. Bogue, Principles of Demography Ch. 6 (1969).

7. Statistical Abstract of the United States 6 (1985) gives the 1970 census population of this country as 203,302,031, and the 1940 figure as 131,669,275.

8. Statistical Abstract of the United States 8, 9 (1985).

9. See section 2.10, supra, at note 10.

10. See section 4.1, supra, at note 16. But the increase in non-marital births may not outweigh the decline in marital fertility. See Gibson, The U.S. Fertility Decline, 1961–1975: The Contribution of Changes in Marital Status and Marital Fertility, 8 Family Planning Perspectives 249 (1976).

11. J. Noonan, Contraception 18–20, 200–230 (1965). Many of the methods described by Professor Noonan could not have been effective.

12. G. Williams, The Sanctity of Life and the Criminal Law 37 (1957).

13. N. Himes, Medical History of Contraception 211 (1936).

14. G. Williams, The Sanctity of Life and the Criminal Law 37–41 (1957).

15. The Queen v. Bradlaugh, L.R. 2 Q.B.D. 569 (1877), reversed, L.R. 3 Q.B.D. 607 (1878). The jury in this case found that the book was calculated to deprave public morals.

laws and sentenced to jail terms in addition to being fined.[16] In 1873, influenced by the skillful lobbying of Anthony J. Comstock who was supported by many religious groups such as the New York Society for the Suppression of Vice, Congress passed what came to be known as the Comstock law, whose major provisions prohibited the importation into the United States and the transmittal through the mails of articles designed for the prevention of conception and writings describing such articles.[17] The prohibition was enforceable by fine or imprisonment of up to five years, and all such material was declared to be nonmailable matter. This monument to legislative fatuity remained in the United States Code until 1971.[18] As a result of it the authorities seized many books on contraception and contraceptive materials, and brought many criminal prosecutions.[19] Undoubtedly many persons, including physicians, were discouraged by this statute and prosecutions pursuant to it from disseminating information about both the safe and the unsafe or ineffective methods of birth control.[20]

The same combination of forces which brought about the enactment of the federal Comstock law produced legislation in the states which restricted the dissemination of birth control information and materials in a variety of ways.[21] Many of these statutes prohibited sales of contraceptives, in some instances with exceptions in favor of sales by physicians or pharmacists.[22] Connecticut's notorious statute was apparently unique in forbidding the use of contraceptives.[23] Many such statutes remained in force until the 1960's and 1970's, although long before then they had ceased to be consistently enforced. They, like the Comstock law, survived vigorous efforts at repeal, their chief support in states like New York, Massachusetts and Connecticut whose statutes were the most rigorous, being the Roman Catholic Church.[24]

Although federal and state legislatures clung to the notion that birth control could and should be prevented long after that notion had been recognized as ridiculous, and long after most people who could get access to contraceptives used them, some mitigation of the statutes' effects was provided by the federal courts. The cases decided after 1900 generally construed the statutes to forbid only the transmittal or importation of writings or materials which were obscene under the then prevailing criteria.[25] The leading case, dealing with importation, held that the statute was not applicable where the contraceptives

---

16. C. Dienes, Law, Politics and Birth Control 22, 25 (1972).

17. 18 U.S.C.A. §§ 1461, 1462. See also 18 U.S.C.A. § 334; 19 U.S.C.A. § 1305. The events leading to the passage of the Act are concisely described in C. Dienes, Law, Politics and Birth Control 20–48 (1972). An amusing biography of Comstock is H. Brown, M. Leech, Anthony Comstock (1927).

18. Act of Jan. 8, 1971, Pub.L. No. 91–662, §§ 3, 4, 84 Stat. 1973 repealed the prohibition on the transmittal of contraceptives. This same repealing act contained a prohibition upon the mailing of unsolicited birth control information or material, unless sent to a physician or nurse or to certain other listed persons. There were earlier attempts to persuade Congress to repeal the prohibition, but they were not successful.

19. C. Dienes, Law, Politics and Birth Control Ch. 2 (1972).

20. Ibid.

21. Id. at 42–47.

22. A list of the states having such statutes in 1960 is found in C. Dienes, Law, Politics and Birth Control, Appendix B (1972).

23. Conn.Gen.Stat.Ann. § 53–32 (1960); Note, 70 Yale L.J. 322 (1960).

24. C. Dienes, Law, Politics and Birth Control 116–147, 193–209 (1972); Sulloway, The Legal and Political Aspects of Population Control in the United States, 25 L. and Contemp. Prob. 593, 607–613 (1960); St. John-Stevas, A Roman Catholic View of Population Control, 25 L. and Contemp. Prob. 445 (1960); J. Noonan, Contraception, A History of Its Treatment by the Catholic Theologians and Canonists (1965).

25. E.g., United States v. Dennett, 39 F.2d 564 (2d Cir. 1930); United States v. One Obscene Book Entitled "Married Love", 48 F.2d 821 (D.N.Y.1931); United States v. One Book Entitled "Contraception", 51 F.2d 525 (S.D.N.Y. 1931). See also Youngs Rubber Corp. v. C.I. Lee & Co., 45 F.2d 103 (2d Cir.1930); Davis v. United States, 62 F.2d 473 (6th Cir.1933); and Consumers Union of United States v. Walker, 145 F.2d 33 (D.C.Cir.1944). The New York Court of Appeals took the tack of broadly defining "disease" so that physicians could furnish contraceptive advice to their patients. But this did not prevent the court from affirming the conviction of Margaret Sanger for violation of the New York statute. People v. Sanger, 222 N.Y. 192, 118 N.E. 637 (1918). See Stone and Pilpel, The Social and Legal Status of Contraception, 22 N.C.L. Rev. 212 (1944).

were not intended for an immoral purpose, finding that in this instance they were not because they were being shipped to a physician for use in her professional practice.[26] These decisions therefore made it possible for birth control information to be disseminated to a limited extent, and for medical science to carry on research in contraceptive methods. They did not, however, permit the widest and most needed public education concerning birth control, since free or low cost clinics were still reluctant to brave the statutory penalties, both state and federal. The result was that the rich and well educated had access to contraceptives while the poor and uneducated did not. This is precisely the same form of class legislation which we are seeing today, forty years later, with respect to the availability of abortion.[27]

Notwithstanding the law's hostility to contraception, its use increased during the Twentieth Century and at the same time research in the physiology of reproduction was carried on in a limited way. It was not until 1959, however, that the great expansion in research occurred, influenced by the availability, in amounts larger than ever before, of financing from government and private foundations, and by the recognition on all sides that overpopulation was a world-wide social problem.[28] The contraceptive pill was tested in the late 1950's and was put on the market in 1960.[29] In 1963 distribution of the intrauterine device (IUD) began, and since that time there have

been constant efforts to improve these methods of contraception and to discover new ones. The pill and the IUD have reduced unwanted births in the United States by thirty-six percent, and they are major factors in family planning programs in other countries.[30] Both have been criticized on the score of safety and have been very extensively tested. Both have been found to have troublesome side effects, but for most women the qualified medical judgment seems to be that the pill is generally safe and that mortality from its use is lower than that from pregnancy; while at the present writing sales of all except one type of IUD have halted in the United States due to the high expenses and great financial risks caused by product liability suits against the manufacturers.[31] Sterilization has become the most widely used method of contraception, having the advantages of safety and reliability.[32] There remains a great need for research and development of other methods of contraception, especially for males, at the very time when governmental funding for such research is being sharply reduced.

The Catholic Church has continued its opposition to all forms of contraception except continence and the "rhythm" method, Pope Paul VI reaffirming this position in the encyclical Humanae Vitae in 1968.[33] Its opposition often affects the decisions of legislative bodies when they consider appropriations for contraceptive research, or for family planning ser-

26. United States v. One Package, 86 F.2d 737 (2d Cir. 1936), opinion by Augustus Hand, J. Judge Learned Hand doubted the result but did not dissent.

27. See section 5.3, infra.

28. R. Greep, M. Koblinsky, F. Jaffe, Reproduction and Human Welfare: A Challenge to Research 1, 4, 16, 47 (1976) (hereinafter cited as Reproduction and Human Welfare). For legal attempts around the world at controlling population growth, see L. Lee, A. Larson, Population and Law (1971).

29. Reproduction and Human Welfare 4.

30. Reproduction and Human Welfare Ch. 2; C. Westoff, N. Ryder, The Contraceptive Revolution Ch. IX, X (1977).

31. Tietze, The Pill and Mortality From Cardiovascular Disease: Another Look, 11 (2) Family Planning Perspectives 80 (1979); Reproduction and Human Welfare 60; C. Westoff, N. Ryder, The Contraceptive Revolution 44 (1977); Mishell, Assessing the Intrauterine Device, 7

(3) Family Planning Perspectives 103 (1975); Note, The Intrauterine Device: A Criticism of Governmental Compliance and an Analysis of Manufacturer and Physician Liability, 24 Clev.St.L.Rev. 247 (1975). The A.H. Robins Company, maker of the Dalkon Shield IUD was forced into bankruptcy by damage awards and out of court settlements of litigation against it. Other manufacturers then faced numerous lawsuits. At the same time liability insurance became enormously expensive or unobtainable. The result was that all firms making popular types of IUD stopped manufacturing and sales. This has had a serious effect on the more than two million women using the IUD. See Forrest, The End of IUD Marketing in the United States: What Does it Mean for American Women? 18 (2) Family Planning Perspectives 52 (1986).

32. C. Westoff and N. Ryder, The Contraceptive Revolution 18 (1977). See section 5.2 infra.

33. The New York Times, July 30, 1968, page 20, col. 1. See also J. Noonan, Contraception Ch. XIV (1965).

vices in the United States or abroad.[34] On the other hand the Church does not seem able to prevent its own members from using various methods of contraception, the available evidence indicating that nearly as large a proportion of Catholics use artificial methods of birth control as do non-Catholics.[35] Other religions, Protestant, Moslem, Hindu, Buddhist, do not generally oppose methods of contraception, family planning and population control short of abortion.[36]

The Impact of the Constitution

By 1965 some of the state regulations limiting or excluding the sale or use of contraceptives had been modified or repealed, but many remained in force.[37] Before that time two unsuccessful attempts were made to bring the constitutional validity of such statutes before the United States Supreme Court. In 1943 an attack on the Connecticut statute failed when the Court held that the plaintiff, a physician, had no standing to raise the issue.[38] And in 1961 an attack by various individuals on the same statute failed when the Court held that no justiciable controversy existed because

there was no immediate indication that the statute was being or would be enforced.[39] In 1965 the Court finally consented to decide the validity of the Connecticut statute on the merits. The result was the famous opinion in Griswold v. Connecticut [40] in which the statute forbidding the *use* of contraceptives was held to be an unwarranted invasion of a "penumbral" right of privacy deduced from the First, Third, Fourth, Fifth and Ninth Amendments of the United States Constitution, entitling married persons to use contraceptives. Justice Douglas' opinion was a tour de force, since no such limits upon legislative regulation of marriage had ever before been imagined. The Justice created the right of privacy in marriage out of sections of the Bill of Rights which on their face had nothing to do with either privacy or marriage, citing cases which likewise had nothing to do with privacy in marriage. But whatever one may think of the opinion's reasoning, it did have the virtue of disposing of Connecticut's "uncommonly silly" [41] statute, at least so far as it applied to married persons. Unfortunately it was written in terms which (as later events

34. E.g., Hearings on S. 1676 Before the Subcommittee on Foreign Aid Expenditures of the Senate Committee on Government Operations, 89th Congress, 1st Sess., Part I, 280–358 (1965); C. Dienes, Law, Politics and Birth Control 268–284 (1972).

35. C. Westoff, N. Ryder, The Contraceptive Revolution 22–30 (1977) indicates that practices of contraception among Catholic women are converging with those of non-Catholic women, and that by 1970 two-thirds of all Catholic women were using methods not approved by the Church. To the same effect is a news story in the New York Times, April 16, 1978, page 27, col. 1.

36. Regulations in the various countries where these religions are in the majority are described in L. Lee and A. Larson, eds., Population and Law (1971). See also Population Crisis Committee, Population, No. 6, January, 1977.

37. A comprehensive review of the statutes, state and federal, in force as of September, 1971 is found in United States Department of Health, Education and Welfare, The National Center for Family Planning Services, Family Planning, Contraception and Voluntary Sterilization: An Analysis of Laws and Policies in the United States, Each State and Jurisdiction (1974).

38. Tileston v. Ullman, 318 U.S. 44, 63 S.Ct. 493, 87 L.Ed. 603 (1943).

39. Poe v. Ullman, 367 U.S. 497, 81 S.Ct. 1752, 6 L.Ed. 2d 989 (1961), rehearing denied 368 U.S. 869, 82 S.Ct. 21, 7 L.Ed.2d 69 (1961). In the eighty years in which the

Connecticut statute had been in force the Court found only one instance of enforcement, in State v. Nelson, 126 Conn. 412, 11 A.2d 856 (1940).

40. 381 U.S. 479, 85 S.Ct. 1678, 14 L.Ed.2d 510 (1965). The case has been noted in 1966 Duke L.J. 562; 79 Harv. L.Rev. 162 (1965); 64 Mich.L.Rev. 197 (1965); 6 J.Fam.L. 371 (1966) and 30 U.Colo.L.Rev. 267 (1966). See also Pilpel, Birth Control and a New Birth of Freedom, 27 Ohio St.L.J. 679 (1966). Mr. Justice Douglas' opinion is generally regarded as that of the Court, obtaining the broad assent of Justices Clark, Goldberg, Brennan and Chief Justice Warren although the last three justices also concurred in Justice Goldberg's separate opinion. Justices White and Harlan concurred on different grounds and Justices Black and Stewart dissented.

The difficulties of the earlier Tileston and Poe cases with standing and justiciable question were obviated in Griswold because in the later case a state criminal prosecution had been brought against the appellants and they had been convicted as accessories to violation of the statute, and because the strict view of standing adhered to in the earlier case was relaxed. The defendants in Griswold were a physician prescribing contraceptives for married persons and the director of Connecticut's Planned Parenthood League. They were held qualified to raise the Constitutional rights of their patients.

41. The phrase is from Justice Stewart's dissent in Griswold. 381 U.S. at 527, 85 S.Ct. at 1705.

proved) could be expanded and contracted at the will of the courts to include or exclude a great variety of legislative attempts to regulate sexual relations in and out of marriage.[42]

Seven years after Griswold the Supreme Court held unconstitutional the Massachusetts statute regulating the distribution of contraceptives on grounds different from those in Griswold, in Eisenstadt v. Baird.[43] The case began with a state court conviction of Baird after he had given a lecture on contraception to a group of university students at the end of which he gave a package of vaginal foam to a young woman from the audience. After losing state appeals,[44] Baird filed a petition for habeas corpus in the federal courts. The writ was denied in the United States District Court,[45] the denial was reversed in the Court of Appeals,[46] and on appeal the Supreme Court affirmed the Court of Appeals' grant of the writ. The Massachusetts statute under which Baird was convicted in general terms first prohibited the sale or giving away of any article for the prevention of conception, but then provided that a physician might prescribe such articles for married persons and a registered pharmacist might furnish such articles to married persons upon a physician's prescription.[47] The statutes apparently carried the negative implication that either married or single persons could be supplied with contraceptives by anyone so long as this was done to prevent the spread of disease rather than to prevent conception or pregnancy.

After deciding, in reliance upon Griswold, that Baird had standing to raise the constitutionality of the statutes, the Court held that there was no ground upon which the different statutory treatment of married and unmarried persons could rationally be explained and therefore the statutes violated the Equal Protection Clause of the Fourteenth Amendment.[48] The Court gave three reasons for finding no rational basis for these statutes: a) One suggested basis for the statute, that it was aimed at discouraging premarital sexual relations, could not be the real basis because it would be unreasonable to punish fornication by pregnancy and the birth of a child, because contraceptives were available for the prevention of disease and thus the statute had so many exceptions it could not accomplish its supposed purpose. Finally, this conclusion is reinforced by the fact that fornication itself was punishable only as a misdemeanor, the sanctions being a thirty dollar fine or three months in jail, while the contraceptive statute carried a penalty of five years in prison. The Court found it impossible to believe that the Massachusetts legislature would wish to punish an accessory to the misdemeanor twenty times more harshly than the fornicator, and therefore it could not believe that the contraception statute had as its purpose preventing illicit intercourse. b) The Court rejected the argument that the purpose of the statute was the protection of health by preventing the distribution of harmful articles. If that were the purpose, the statute was both discriminatory and overbroad, since it did not permit physicians to prescribe for unmarried persons, and since it applied to all contraceptives, not merely those which might involve risks to health. In addition other state and federal statutes were found to provide effective protection against potentially harmful articles. c) Finally, the statute could not be sustained as a simple prohibition upon contraception because to discriminate between married and unmarried persons on this score would violate the Equal Protection Clause. If Griswold forbids a prohibition on the distribution of contraceptives to married persons, the Court

---

42. The effect of Griswold upon marriage regulations is discussed in sections 2.1 and 2.2, supra.

43. 405 U.S. 438, 92 S.Ct. 1029, 31 L.Ed.2d 349 (1972). The Court's opinion, written by Justice Brennan, was joined in by Justices Douglas, Stewart and Marshall. Justices White and Blackmun filed a concurring opinion and Chief Justice Burger dissented. Justices Powell and Rehnquist took no part in the consideration or decision of the case.

44. Commonwealth v. Baird, 355 Mass. 746, 247 N.E.2d 574 (1969), cert. denied 396 U.S. 1029, 90 S.Ct. 580, 24 L.Ed.2d 524 (1970).

45. Baird v. Eisenstadt, 310 F.Supp. 951 (D.Mass. 1970).

46. Baird v. Eisenstadt, 429 F.2d 1398 (1st Cir.1970).

47. Mass.Ann.L. Ch. 272, §§ 21, 21A (1968).

48. U.S. Const.amend. XIV, § 1.

says, then it equally forbids such a prohibition as applied to unmarried persons. At this point the Court uses language which is more easily quoted than explained:

"It is true that in *Griswold* the right of privacy in question inhered in the marital relationship. Yet the marital couple is not an independent entity with a mind and heart of its own, but an association of two individuals each with a separate intellectual and emotional makeup. If the right of privacy means anything, it is the right of the *individual,* married or single, to be free from unwarranted governmental intrusion into matters so fundamentally affecting a person as the decision whether to bear or beget a child." [49]

The Court did not in this passage reveal why a distinction between married and unmarried persons with respect to the use of contraceptives had no rational basis. The laws prohibiting fornication have made this distinction, which of course is deeply rooted in the traditional notion that sexual relations should occur only in marriage. Obviously this notion has always had its detractors and today it seems to be on its way to being discarded entirely. But there still is a substantial segment of our society which adheres to it and it therefore does not seem to be totally irrational. The quoted passage is equally unclear on how the doctrine of marital privacy announced in Griswold became transformed into a doctrine of general sexual privacy applicable to unmarried as well as married people. No reason for this expansion is given us. The only conclusion one may draw from all this is that a general restriction

on the distribution of contraceptives to unmarried persons is invalid. The effect of this ruling as a precedent is not readily predictable, except that it would probably invalidate also any prohibition on the use of contraceptives by unmarried persons. It seems to be an example of the elimination of an obsolete piece of legislation by a Court which, perhaps because of its earlier experience with the evils of substantive due process as a basis for constitutional decisions, was reluctant to admit that the real ground for its decision was that our society's changing mores have made the obsolescence of the statute too plain to ignore.[50]

The Supreme Court sharply limited the states' power to regulate the distribution, in contrast to the use, of contraceptives in Carey v. Population Services International in 1977.[51] The statute involved [52] had been enacted in New York and provided that a) contraceptives could only be sold by licensed pharmacists; b) contraceptives could not be sold to persons under sixteen years old; and c) any advertisement or display of contraceptives was prohibited. After finding that the plaintiff in the case, a retail mail-order seller of contraceptives located in North Carolina, had standing to raise the constitutional issues,[53] the Court held that all three of the New York regulations were invalid. Justice Brennan's opinion for the Court received the agreement of a majority in both reasoning and result with respect to these parts of the statute limiting sale to pharmacists and forbidding advertising.[54] The provision of the statute forbidding sale to those under sixteen was held unconstitutional by six of the justices, but only three

49. 405 U.S. at 453, 92 S.Ct. at 1038.

50. For critical analysis of the reasoning in Baird see Note, Legislative Purpose, Rationality and Equal Protection, 82 Yale L.J. 123 (1972). See also Note, The Supreme Court, 1971 Term, 86 Harv.L.Rev. 1, 116 (1972).

51. 431 U.S. 678, 97 S.Ct. 2010, 52 L.Ed.2d 675 (1977), 6 Ford.Urb.L.J. 371 (1978). A case which follows Carey is Postscript Enterprises, Inc. v. Whaley, 658 F.2d 1249 (8th Cir.1981). A federal statute forbidding the mailing of unsolicited advertisements for contraceptives was held to violate the First Amendment in Bolger v. Youngs Drug Products Corp., 463 U.S. 60, 103 S.Ct. 2875, 77 L.Ed.2d 469 (1983).

52. N.Y.—McKinney's Educ.L. § 6811(8) (1972).

53. Population Planning Associates Inc. was a mail order house selling contraceptives in New York in violation of the statute. The New York authorities had threatened it with legal action if it did not cease selling in the state. The Court held that this constituted sufficient injury to raise a case or controversy and to enable this plaintiff to challenge the statute on behalf of its potential customers. That being so, the Court did not pass on the standing of other plaintiffs in the suit.

54. Part I of the opinion, finding that there was standing, received the assent of seven justices. Part II, in which Justice Brennan found that the right of privacy protected the decision whether to bear or beget children and that this decision could only be regulated in order to

agreed with Justice Brennan's analysis of this issue.[55] The Chief Justice and Justice Rehnquist dissented on all issues.

The Carey case thus cleared away broad restrictions upon the advertising and sale of contraceptives, but it failed to provide a definitive resolution of the difficult and important question of their availability to minors. Minors are today engaging in sexual intercourse at younger ages, in greater numbers and more frequently than ever before.[56] The harmful social consequences are well known and often described, and include high rates of illegitimate births, of venereal disease, of early and unstable marriages and of babies who do not receive proper care.[57] The response of the New York statute was to forbid the sale of contraceptives to young people on the theory, as described in the Carey opinion, that this would discourage sexual activity either by increasing the risks of pregnancy or by providing a "symbolic" expression of the state's

disapproval of early sexual activity.[58] Evidence on this issue is either not available or tends to show that the availability of contraceptives has little to do with the frequency of sexual activity among teen-agers.[59] Nevertheless it does not seem entirely irrational to suppose that a teen-ager's willingness to engage in sexual intercourse on a given occasion might be affected by the knowledge that he or she had a contraceptive readily available.[60] In any event Justice Brennan's opinion in the Carey case relied chiefly upon the failure of the state to furnish evidence that there was a relation between the statute's prohibition and its purpose, finding that the state's burden of proving a "compelling state interest" for the prohibition was not sustained.

The difficult question left open by the Carey case is the extent to which a state might require parental consent for the sale of contraceptives to minors.[61] The same question is

vindicate a "compelling state interest", was assented to by five justices. Part III, holding that sales could not be limited to pharmacists, was assented to by six justices on Justice Brennan's reasoning and by Justice Powell on more limited grounds. And Part V, invalidating the prohibition upon advertising, was assented to by six justices plus Justice Powell who agreed with the result.

55. Part IV of the plurality opinion, invalidating the prohibition of sales to those under sixteen, received the assent of Justices Brennan, who wrote it, Marshall, Stewart and Blackmun. Justice White concurred in the result on this issue on the ground that the state had failed to show a relation between the prohibition and the state's asserted justification. Justice Powell also concurred in this result, but thought that there was considerable room for state regulation of such sales, more room than Justice Brennan's opinion would allow.

56. Zelnick and Kantner, Sexual and Contraceptive Experience of Young Unmarried Women in the United States, 1976 and 1971, 9 (2) Family Planning Perspectives 55 (1977) found that sexual activity among never-married teenage women increased by 30% between 1971 and 1976. Zero Population Growth, Teenage Pregnancy: A Major Problem for Minors (1978) states that more than one million teenagers become pregnant each year. Other studies are cited in Note, A Minor's Right to Contraceptives, 7 U.C.D.L.Rev. 270 (1974), and Note, Parental Consent Requirements and Privacy Rights of Minors: The Contraceptive Controversy, 88 Harv.L.Rev. 1001 (1975). See also Carey v. Population Services International Inc., 431 U.S. 678, 696, 97 S.Ct. 2010, 2022, 52 L.Ed.2d 675 (1977).

57. See section 4.1, supra; Furstenberg, The Social Consequences of Teenage Parenthood, 8 (4) Family Planning Perspectives 148 (1976); Trussell, Economic Conse-

quences of Teenage Childbearing, 8 (4) Family Planning Perspectives 184 (1976).

58. 431 U.S. at 694, 715, 97 S.Ct. at 2021.

59. Justice Brennan's opinion in Carey cited some studies supporting the view that teenage sexual activities do not increase with the increased access to contraceptives. But a leading study on this subject draws no such conclusion, and in fact draws no conclusion at all on the subject. Zelnick and Kantner, Sexual and Contraceptive Experience of Young Unmarried Women in the United States, 1976 and 1971, 9 (2) Family Planning Perspectives 55 (1977).

60. Some respectable commentators have certainly thought that there was some relationship between the "sexual revolution" and the "contraceptive revolution". See, e.g., W. Lippmann, A Preface to Morals 228 (1939); A. Skolnick, The Intimate Environment 189 (1973); R. Klemer, Marriage and Family Relationships 140 (1970). The Zelnick and Kantner study, supra, note 59, indicated that the increase in sexual activity by teenage women from 1971 to 1976 was accompanied by a dramatic increase in the use of contraception, but the authors properly draw no conclusions about cause and effect from these facts. There really seems to be no convincing proof that the availability of contraceptives either does or does not lead to increased sexual intercourse among teenagers.

61. State courts and lower federal courts have reached different results in the different contexts in which this issue has arisen. Doe v. Planned Parenthood Association of Utah, 29 Utah 2d 356, 510 P.2d 75 (1973), appeal dismissed for want of jurisdiction and cert. denied 414 U.S. 805, 94 S.Ct. 138, 38 L.Ed.2d 42 (1973), held, in a cryptic opinion, that Planned Parenthood's refusal to provide family planning services to minors except with

raised by some state abortion statutes.[62] One source of difficulty in resolving the question is that there may be a wide range of maturity between a girl of thirteen and a young woman of eighteen, both of whom are technically "minors". In order to arrive at an answer the courts must confront two conflicting policies. The first of these is the policy favoring the integrity of the family which the Supreme Court has often described in glowing terms and recently has nearly as often ignored.[63] If the courts should hold that the states may not constitutionally require at least some participation by parents in their children's purchase and use of contraceptives, thereby permitting children to ignore their parents' guidance in a matter of importance to the children's welfare, the family structure would be further weakened. The second policy, of equal significance, is that favoring the widest availability of contraceptives, as a means of reducing the harmful social consequences of teenage pregnancy already mentioned.[64] This policy requires for its implementation the removal of

restrictions upon the distribution of contraceptives, whether imposed by the state or by parents. These competing policies necessarily underlie any determination of the constitutional issue even though that determination may be phrased in some such terms as "compelling state interest" or "minimum rationality", terms which unfortunately obscure the real difficulties, as in the Carey case. It would seem sensible to leave a matter having such complex social, psychological and moral implications to be worked out in the legislative process unimpeded by constitutional limitations which often turn out to be either too rigid or too vaguely expressed to be workable.[65]

The wisdom of leaving matters to the legislatures is at least partially vindicated by the current trend in state legislation in the direction of removing restrictions upon the sale, distribution and advertising of contraceptives.[66] Several states expressly permit minors to obtain contraceptives without parental consent.[67] In addition a substantial

---

parental consent did not violate the Equal Protection Clause. The same rule of Planned Parenthood was held to violate the Social Security Act's family planning provision (42 U.S.C.A. § 1396d(a)(4)(C) (1970 Supp. IV)) and also to violate the minor's right to privacy in T_____ H_____ v. Jones, 425 F.Supp. 873 (D.Utah 1975), 1976 B.Y.U.L.Rev. 296. This case was affirmed, on the statutory ground only, in Jones v. T.H., 425 U.S. 986, 96 S.Ct. 2195, 48 L.Ed.2d 811 (1976). In Doe v. Irwin, 615 F.2d 1162 (6th Cir.1980), cert. denied 449 U.S. 829, 101 S.Ct. 95, 66 L.Ed.2d 33 (1980), the court held that the practice of a public family planning agency in distributing contraceptives to minors without notification to or consultation with their parents did not violate the rights of the parents to the custody and care of their children, rights protected by the First, Fifth, Ninth and Fourteenth Amendments to the United States Constitution. Among other claims, the parent-plaintiffs in this case asserted that their religious beliefs had been violated. See also Doe v. Pickett, 480 F.Supp. 1218 (S.D.W.Va.1979); Planned Parenthood Fed. of America v. Heckler, 712 F.2d 650 (D.C.Cir.1983).

For a discussion of these and other cases, concluding that the minor's right of privacy precludes any requirement of notice to or consent by his parents, see Note, Parental Consent Requirements and Privacy Rights of Minors: The Contraceptive Controversy, 88 Harv.L.Rev. 1001 (1975), and Note, The Minor's Right of Privacy: Limitations on State Action After Danforth and Carey, 77 Colum.L.Rev. 1216 (1977).

M.S. v. Wermers, 557 F.2d 170 (8th Cir.1977), 1978 Wash.U.L.Q. 431, held that in a suit by a minor seeking to receive contraceptives from a public agency without

her parents' consent it was proper to appoint a guardian ad litem, but the parents should not be appointed guardians and the minor should not be required to notify her parents of the suit, since that would violate the right of privacy she was trying to establish.

State laws dealing with the availability of contraceptive services to minors are collected in Department of Health, Education and Welfare, Family Planning, Contraception, and Voluntary Sterilization: An Analysis of Laws and Policies in the United States, Each State and Jurisdiction 70–81 (1974). A substantial number of states expressly authorize women of eighteen or over to obtain contraceptives without their parents' consent.

62. See Bellotti v. Baird, 428 U.S. 132, 96 S.Ct. 2857, 49 L.Ed.2d 844 (1976); Baird v. Attorney General, Mass., 371 Mass. 741, 360 N.E.2d 288 (1977), 16 J.Fam.L. 116 (1977).

63. See the discussion in section 2.1, supra.

64. See the discussion at note 57, supra.

65. The Supreme Court's vacillations over the position of the illegitimate child are a good example. See section 4.2, supra, and Stanley v. Illinois, 405 U.S. 645, 92 S.Ct. 1208, 31 L.Ed.2d 551 (1972) and Quilloin v. Walcott, 434 U.S. 246, 98 S.Ct. 549, 54 L.Ed.2d 511 (1978), rehearing denied 435 U.S. 918, 98 S.Ct. 1477, 55 L.Ed.2d 511 (1978).

66. U.S. Dep't of Health, Education and Welfare, Family Planning, Contraception, and Voluntary Sterilization: An Analysis of Laws and Policies in the United States, Each State and Jurisdiction 58–61 (1974).

67. Note, A Minor's Right to Contraceptives, 7 U.C. D.L.Rev. 270, 279 (1974).

number of states have statutes affirmatively encouraging the distribution of contraceptives by providing state supported family planning services either for the indigent or for all citizens of the state.[68] The federal Social Security Act also provides such services for those who are eligible.[69] Such statutes are evidence of the growing awareness in the United States of the necessity not merely to reduce teenage childbearing but more importantly to control population growth generally.[70]

Court-Ordered Contraception

It has been suggested that where a young woman has had two illegitimate children and is unable to care for them properly, the courts should order that she use contraceptives.[71] As a practical matter this would mean the compulsory insertion of an intrauterine contraceptive device (IUCD or IUD). The juvenile court acts generally do not specifically authorize court-ordered contraception and without specific authorization there would seem to be no jurisdiction to enter such an order.[72] Furthermore, in view of the position taken in Carey and other cases [73] surrounding the process of procreation with a zone of privacy, to be invaded only where there is a compelling state interest, it seems likely that any court-ordered contraception would be held to be an unconstitutional infringement on that right of privacy.[74] Finally, the IUD

could be removed by a physician ignorant of the court order, making the whole process futile. The only effective contraception, in other words, would be sterilization, and this raises even more difficult legal and constitutional issues.[75]

 **WESTLAW REFERENCES**

The Impact of the Constitution

poe /s ullman
find 85 sct 1678
find 97 sct 2010

Court-Ordered Contraception

"guardianship of kemp"

§ 5.2 Sterilization

Voluntary Sterilization

In the relatively recent past there have been widespread doubts concerning the legality of voluntary sterilization undertaken purely for contraceptive rather than medical reasons.[1] This may have been in part a reflection of the position of the Catholic Church, which still forbids this type of sterilization.[2] For these and perhaps other reasons, such as ignorance of the nature and effect of the operation, sterilization was not a significant method of birth control. Today, however, sterilization has taken its place among the most used methods of contraception, particu-

---

68. U.S. Dep't of Health, Education and Welfare, Family Planning, Contraception and Voluntary Sterilization: An Analysis of Laws and Policies in the United States, Each State and Jurisdiction 58 (1974); Note, Toward Greater Reproductive Freedom: Wisconsin's New Family Planning Act, 1979 Wis.L.Rev. 509. But see Planned Parenthood of Minn. v. State, 612 F.2d 359 (8th Cir.1980), judgment affirmed 448 U.S. 901, 100 S.Ct. 3039, 65 L.Ed.2d 1131 (1980).

69. 42 U.S.C.A. § 602(a)(15).

70. For a discussion of other methods of population control, see Rabin, Population Control Through Financial Incentives, 23 Hast.L.J. 1353 (1972). The constitutionality of such methods is advocated in Miller and Davidson, Observations on Population Policy-Making and the Constitution, 40 G.W.L.Rev. 618 (1972).

71. Young, Alverson and Young, Court-Ordered Contraception, 55 A.B.A.J. 223 (1969).

72. See Guardianship of Kemp, 43 Cal.App.3d 758, 118 Cal.Rptr. 64 (1974), dealing with sterilization. But see In re Simpson, 180 N.E.2d 206 (Ohio Prob.Ct.1962) which based a sterilization order on general statutory language.

73. Carey v. Population Services International, 431 U.S. 678, 97 S.Ct. 2010, 52 L.Ed.2d 675 (1977) and cases cited supra, note 61.

74. Note, Court-Ordered Contraception in California, 23 Hast.L.J. 1505 (1972) and cases there cited; Note, 1970 Wisconsin L.Rev. 899.

75. See section 5.2, infra.

§ 5.2

1. G. Williams, The Sanctity of Life and the Criminal Law 102–110 (1957); Bravenec, Voluntary Sterilization as a Crime: Applicability of Assault and Battery and of Mayhem, 6 J. of Fam.L. 94 (1966); Christensen v. Thornby, 192 Minn. 123, 255 N.W. 620 (1934).

Sterilization for medical reasons, for example because a woman's life or health would be endangered by pregnancy, is often referred to as therapeutic sterilization and has generally been accepted as a lawful operation where consented to by the patient.

2. J. Noonan, Contraception 430–431, 451–459 (1965); C. Westoff and N. Ryder, The Contraceptive Revolution 99 (1977). See Padin v. Fordham Hospital, 392 F.Supp.

larly among older couples who have had as many children as they wish. In 1973, for example, sterilization and the "pill" were equally popular among couples practicing contraception where the wife was twenty-five or older.[3] Where the wife was between thirty and forty-four, sterilization was the most popular method.[4]

Sterilization for males (vasectomy) is a relatively simple procedure which can be done in the physician's office. It consists of cutting and tying the vas deferens, the tube carrying the sperm from the testes to the urinary canal, thereby preventing sperm from being included in the semen when ejaculation occurs.[5] For females the procedure is more complicated and normally requires hospitalization for a short time. The abdominal cavity is opened and the fallopian tubes are either tied (tubal ligation), or cut (salpingectomy) so as to prevent the passage of ova from the ovaries thus making union with the male

sperm impossible.[6] Male sterilization is quite safe and female sterilization relatively so, although medical opinion differs somewhat on the degree of risk, since for the female at the present stage of medical technique the operation is considered major surgery.[7] The effectiveness of sterilization as a contraceptive method is also the subject of some disagreement, but there is persuasive authority that it is more effective than any other form of contraception, since the only risk is that the severed or tied tubes will grow back together, a slight risk for males and even slighter for females.[8] The major objection to sterilization as a contraceptive measure is that it must as a practical matter be considered permanent. In the majority of cases the operation cannot be reversed.[9] Another objection which is sometimes raised but which is of much less importance is that in a small proportion of instances sterilization may be accompanied by emotional or psychiatric disturbances of vary-

447 (S.D.N.Y.1975), in which an anesthesiologist refused to participate in the sterilization of a female patient because he was a Catholic. But there may be some disagreement on the Church's position. See Murdock, Sterilization of the Retarded—A Problem or a Solution? 62 Cal.L.Rev. 917 (1974).

3. C. Westoff, Trends in Contraceptive Practice: 1965–1973, 8(2) Family Planning Perspectives 54 (1976).

4. Ibid. See also Pratt, The Practice of Sterilization in the United States: Preliminary Findings From the 1973 National Survey of Family Growth, digested in 7(3) Family Planning Perspectives 113 (1975), stating that in 1973 more than seven million women were no longer at risk of conception due to their own or their husbands' sterilization.

5. R. Morris, A. Moritz, Doctor and Patient and the Law 105–109 (5th ed. 1971); C. Westoff, N. Ryder, The Contraceptive Revolution Ch. V (1977); R. Greep, M. Koblinsky, F. Jaffe, Reproduction and Human Welfare: A Challenge to Research Ch. 4, 5 (1976).

6. Ibid.; Overstreet, Female Sterilization, in Manual of Family Planning and Contraceptive Practice 404 (M. Calderone ed. 1970). Still another method is the "silastic band" procedure, described in Clay v. Brodsky, 148 Ill. App.3d 63, 101 Ill.Dec. 701, 499 N.E.2d 68 (1986).

7. Tietze, Bongaarts, Schearer, Mortality Associated With the Control of Fertility, 8(1) Family Planning Perspectives 6 (1976) indicates the mortality from tubal ligation for women as ranging from 10 to 20 per 100,000 operations at ages 25 to 29 up to 15 to 30 per 100,000 at ages 40 to 44, running well below the mortality for childbirth at the higher ages, and about the same for ages 25 to 29. The same article indicates the mortality rate for male vasectomy to be zero. Sherlock and Sherlock,

Voluntary Contraceptive Sterilization: The Case for Regulation, 1976 Utah L.Rev. 115, 117 suggests that there may be long term harmful effects without producing much evidence. New methods of female sterilization not requiring hospitalization are being investigated and involve less risk. Digest 9(2) Family Planning Perspectives 85 (1977); R. Greep, M. Koblinsky, F. Jaffe, Reproduction and Human Welfare: A Challenge to Research Ch. 6 (1976).

8. Tietze, Bongaarts, Schearer, Mortality Associated With the Control of Fertility, 8(1) Family Planning Perspectives 6, 7 (1976) states that failures after sterilization both male and female are sufficiently rare to assume a one hundred percent effectiveness. The failure rate for vasectomies is found to be under one percent by a number of investigators. P. Gillette, The Vasectomy Information Manual 52 (1972); Lee, Technique and Results of Vasectomy in Control of Male Fertility 74 (J. Scram, C. Markland, J. Speidel eds. 1975). The failure rate for female sterilizations varies slightly with the method used but remains well under two percent. Najar, Culdoscopy as an Aid to Family Planning, in Female Sterilization 45 (1972); Laufe and Summerson, Internal Vaginal Tubal Ligation, in Female Sterilization 75 (1972); McCann, Laparoscopy Versus Minilaparotomy, in Risks Benefits and Controversies in Fertility Control 74 (1978). See also C. Westoff, N. Ryder, The Contraceptive Revolution 71 (1977); Note, Elective Sterilization, 113 U.Pa.L.Rev. 415, 417 (1965). Sherlock and Sherlock, Voluntary Contraceptive Sterilization: The Case for Regulation, 1976 Utah L.Rev. 115, 116 asserts that sterilization is not superior in effectiveness to oral contraceptives, but this seems doubtful.

9. G. Williams, The Sanctity of Life and The Criminal Law 75 (1957).

ing severity.[10] It is not clear whether these difficulties are caused by the sterilization or by other contemporaneous factors. So far as can be determined, sterilization in the great majority of cases should have no adverse effect upon sexual drives or sexual satisfaction.[11] For many people it seems to increase sexual satisfaction by removing anxiety about pregnancy.[12]

Although it now seems clear that sterilization for contraceptive purposes is legal in nearly all, if not all, states in the sense that it is neither a crime nor a tort,[13] this does not mean it is easily available in all parts of the United States. For one thing the statutes in

some states impose such limitations as that the person be over 21,[14] that the operation be requested in writing,[15] that the spouse of the patient consent,[16] that the physician consult with another physician,[17] and that the physician provide the patient with a full and reasonable medical explanation of the operation.[18]

The matter of sterilization of minors is greatly complicated by the question whether they are capable of consenting to the operation, no matter how carefully the procedure has been explained to them and no matter how mature they may be. This question was raised in connection with attacks upon regu-

---

10. C. Westoff, N. Ryder, The Contraceptive Revolution 102 (1977); Roberto, Marital and Family Planning Expectancies of Men Regarding Vasectomy, 36 J. of Marriage and the Family 698 (1974); Rodgers, Ziegler, Changes in Sexual Behavior Consequent to Use of Noncoital Procedures of Contraception, 30 Psychosomatic Medicine 495 (1968); Ferber, Tietze, Lewit, Men With Vasectomies: A Study of Medical, Sexual and Psychosocial Changes, 29 Psychosomatic Medicine 354 (1967); Rodgers, Ziegler, Altrocchi, Levy, A Longitudinal Study of the Psycho-Social Effects of Vasectomy, 27 J. of Marriage and the Family 59 (1965); Landis, Poffenberger, The Marital and Sexual Adjustment of 330 Couples Who Chose Vasectomy as a Form of Birth Control, 27 J. of Marriage and the Family 57 (1965); Johnson, Social and Psychological Effects of Vasectomy, 121 Am.J. of Psychiatry 482 (1964); Wolf, Legal and Psychiatric Aspects of Voluntary Sterilization, 3 J. of Fam.L. 103 (1963).

11. See Landis, Poffenberger, The Marital and Sexual Adjustment of 330 Couples Who Chose Vasectomy as a Form of Birth Control, 27 J. of Marriage and the Family 57 (1965).

12. See Note, A Woman's Right To Voluntary Sterilization 22 Buff.L.Rev. 291 (1972).

13. A collection and discussion of statutes and cases may be found in United States Department of Health, Education and Welfare, Family Planning, Contraception and Voluntary Sterilization: An Analysis of Laws and Policies in the United States, Each State and Jurisdiction 63 (1974). Utah, which has a statute which might be construed to forbid voluntary sterilization, has determined that it does not, and that such sterilization is not restricted. See Utah Code Ann. § 64–10–16 (Supp.1985), and Parker v. Rampton, 28 Utah 2d 36, 497 P.2d 848 (1972). Jessin v. Shasta County, 274 Cal.App.2d 737, 79 Cal.Rptr. 359 (1969) held that voluntary, non-therapeutic sterilization is lawful in California, and suggests that a contrary rule might be unconstitutional under Griswold v. Connecticut, 381 U.S. 479, 85 S.Ct. 1678, 14 L.Ed.2d 510 (1965). Today this latter conclusion seems clear in view of Roe v. Wade, 410 U.S. 113, 93 S.Ct. 705, 35 L.Ed.2d 147 (1973), rehearing denied 410 U.S. 959, 93 S.Ct. 1409, 35 L.Ed.2d 694 (1973). For other opinions that contraceptive sterilization is not unlawful, see Greenawalt, Criminal

Law and Population Control, 24 Vand.L.Rev. 465, 476 (1971); Note, Elective Sterilization 113 U.Pa.L.Rev. 415, 427 (1965), although the three states listed in this Note as forbidding the operation have all changed their laws.

Several states have statutes expressly authorizing voluntary sterilization, sometimes with certain conditions. See, e.g., Ark.Stats. § 59–501(M) (1971); West's Ann.Cal. Health and Safety Code §§ 1232, 1258, 32128.10 (1979); Colo.Rev.Stat. § 25–6–102 (1982); Conn.Gen.Stat.Ann. §§ 19a–112 (Supp.1985); Ga.Code § 84–932 (1985); N.C. Gen.Stat. § 90–271 (1985); Or.Rev.Stat. § 435.305 (1985); Va.Code 1982, § 54–325.9 (Supp.1985). Either implicitly or explicitly these statutes make it plain that sterilization is to be performed only by a licensed physician. In most states there are no statutes either permitting or forbidding voluntary sterilization. See also Stepan and Kellogg, The World's Laws Concerning Voluntary Sterilization for Family Planning Purposes, 5 Cal.West.Internat.L.J. 72 (1974).

14. E.g., Va.Code 1982, § 54–325.9 (Supp.1985). Other statutes may put the age of consent at eighteen, which is the age of consent in most states. E.g., N.C.Gen.Stat. § 90–271 (1985), permitting sterilization of a person over eighteen, or under eighteen and married. Such statutes do not state whether the sterilization of one under eighteen could be performed on consent of a parent or guardian, but it would seem that it could not be in absence of express statutory authority. The Colorado statute requires the consent of a parent or guardian for the sterilization of an unmarried person under eighteen. Colo.Rev. Stat. § 25–6–102(6) (1973).

15. E.g., Ga.Code § 84–931 (1985).

16. E.g., Ga.Code § 84–931 (1985) (spousal consent required if spouse can be found after a reasonable effort); N.M.Stat.Ann. § 24–9–1 (1981) (spousal consent not required if spouse has abandoned the person), noted in 7 N.M.L.Rev. 121 (1976–1977). Oregon has a statute specifically obviating spousal consent. Or.Rev.Stat. § 435.305(2) (1985).

17. E.g., Ga.Code § 84–932 (1985).

18. E.g., Ga.Code § 84–932 (1985); Va.Code 1982, § 54–325.9.

lations of the Department of Health, Education and Welfare which authorized funding for the sterilization of minors under certain rules designed to ensure informed consent.[19] In Relf v. Weinberger [20] the court held that these regulations were invalid and that the Department has no authority under the applicable statutes to fund the sterilization of any person who is incompetent under state law to consent to the operation, whether because of minority or of mental deficiency. The basis for this holding was that the statutes authorizing federal financial support for family planning services required that such services be voluntarily requested,[21] and that minors are lacking in the knowledge, maturity and judgment required to make a voluntary decision concerning sterilization. It seems implicit in this case that state law and not federal law is to govern on whether a minor is competent in this respect, and therefore whether sterilizations of minors may be funded by the HEW programs.[22] In any event the case is of great importance because of the tendency of decisions made for Medicaid and similar federal purposes to become general guides to medical procedures and to exercise great influence on state law.

The Relf opinion seems to assume that under state law minors may not give a binding consent to medical or surgical procedures. Although the law generally on minors' consent to surgery is not well developed, this assumption is not warranted by what case

and statutory law there is. The relatively few cases which have considered the question conclude that a mature minor may give binding consent to operations, at least less serious operations.[23] Minors who are not mature must have the consent of their parents.[24] The Relf case seems to take it for granted that these principles would not cover sterilization procedures. The opinion in fact does not discuss cases involving other kinds of surgery. If they do apply to sterilization, then the controlling issues are two: a) Whether the minor is mature or not; and b) Whether the operation is considered a serious one. The answer to the second question would seem to be that it is serious, since it must be considered irreversible. That being so, if state law on surgical treatment of minors is to be followed, the minor could be sterilized with the consent of his parents. If sterilization is considered sui generis because of its irreversible nature and its effect upon the future life of the minor, so that the general principles relating to surgery on minors do not apply to it, there may be no lawful method for arranging the sterilization of a minor, no matter how strongly the interests of the minor, his parents and of society may indicate the need for the operation. The same impasse may be created if it should be held that the Danforth case applies to sterilization, so that a parent may not constitutionally give a binding consent to his child's sterilization.[25] The best solution to this difficulty would seem to be to

19. The proposed regulations, which never came into operation, are printed in 39 Fed.Reg. 4730 (1974). Present regulations are published in 43 Fed.Reg. 52,146 ff. (1978), to be codified in 42 C.F.R. §§ 50.203, 50.205.

20. 372 F.Supp. 1196 (D.D.C.1974), proposed modifications denied, Relf v. Mathews, 403 F.Supp. 1235 (D.D.C. 1975), vacated and remanded with directions to dismiss the complaints, Relf v. Weinberger, 565 F.2d 722 (D.C.Cir. 1977). In none of this litigation was the possible constitutional impact considered, although at the time of the Court of Appeals decision Planned Parenthood v. Danforth, 428 U.S. 52, 96 S.Ct. 2831, 49 L.Ed.2d 788 (1976) had been decided. See also Voe v. Califano, 434 F.Supp. 1058 (D.Conn.1977).

21. 42 U.S.C.A. §§ 300a–5, 602(a)(15), 1396d(a)(4).

22. See Relf v. Weinberger, 565 F.2d 722 (D.C.Cir. 1977).

23. Smith v. Seibly, 72 Wash.2d 16, 431 P.2d 719 (1967); Baird v. Attorney General, 371 Mass. 741, 360

N.E.2d 288 (1977); W. Prosser and W. Keeton Handbook on the Law of Torts, 114–115 (5th Ed.1984). See also section 8.1, infra.

24. id. Cf. Baird v. Bellotti, 450 F.Supp. 997 (D.Mass. 1978).

25. Planned Parenthood v. Danforth, 428 U.S. 52, 96 S.Ct. 2831, 49 L.Ed.2d 788 (1976), holding that a statute requiring parental consent to abortion for a minor was unconstitutional. Ruby v. Massey, 452 F.Supp. 361 (D.Conn.1978) held that a parent could not constitutionally consent to the sterilization of a minor under the abortion cases, even though the parent normally may consent to surgical operations on his child. In this case the minors involved were not mentally competent, which meant that they could not effectively consent to the procedure. The court seems to have assumed that the minors, if competent, might have been able to give a binding consent by themselves, since it referred to the fact that "the Constitution protects the freedom of even

permit a mature minor to make the decision about sterilization himself, but to require some counseling or consultation with parents wherever possible. If the minor is not mature, or is incompetent by reason of medical or psychiatric defects, statutory procedures involving both parental and court approval of sterilization should be adequate to provide sufficient protection for the minor as well as the parents and society. But such statutes would have to meet stringent constitutional standards which are only just beginning to evolve in the cases dealing with involuntary sterilization.

It should be noted that by the law of most states today the age of majority is eighteen.[26] The lowering of the age from twenty-one substantially enlarges the group of young persons who may consent to sterilization. The question is also affected by the existence in some states of specific statutes authorizing minors to consent to medical care.[27]

The requirement of spousal consent would seem to be unconstitutional under the principles announced in Planned Parenthood v. Danforth,[28] in which the Supreme Court reasoned that since the state could not proscribe abortion during the first trimester, it could not delegate to the spouse the authority to prevent abortion. The sterilization case, which involves less sensitive issues, there being no fetus involved, follows a fortiori from Danforth, and in fact the Danforth opinion

refers to the sterilization issue.[29] The requirement of consultation with another physician likewise appears to be unconstitutional under Doe v. Bolton.[30] That case held that the state's requirement of approval for abortions from a hospital committee, and from two licensed physicians in addition to the patient's doctor was an unconstitutional interference with the woman's right to a first trimester abortion established by Roe v. Wade.[31] The requirements that the patient request sterilization in writing and that the physician give a reasonable medical explanation of the operation would not seem to be unconstitutional. Neither imposes an undue burden on obtaining sterilization and both are reasonably calculated to ensure that there is an informed consent to a procedure which has long-lasting consequences for the individual. The Danforth case upheld a state requirement of written and informed consent to abortion.[32] The same result should obtain with respect to sterilization, where an informed and deliberate consent is particularly desirable, because of the irreversible nature of the procedure.

The prohibition upon the voluntary sterilization of minors raises difficult constitutional questions which have not yet been faced by the courts.[33] The Danforth case held that the Missouri parental consent requirement for abortions of unmarried women under eighteen could not be justified by any significant state interest and was therefore unconstitu-

---

an immature teenager to decide for herself whether to bear or beget a child * * *" 452 F.Supp. at 366. The court went on to hold, however, that the parents could apply to a state court for approval of the operation, under a statutory procedure applicable to inmates of state institutions which, the court said, must be extended to similar individuals not in institutions in order to be constitutional.

26. See section 8.1, infra.

27. See, e.g., West's Ann.Cal.Civ.Code § 34.5 (1982), requiring parental consent to sterilization; Colo.Rev.Stat. § 13–22–103 (Supp.1984), authorizing some classes of minor to consent to operations.

28. 428 U.S. 52, 96 S.Ct. 2831, 49 L.Ed.2d 788 (1976). Ponter v. Ponter, 135 N.J.Super. 50, 342 A.2d 574 (1975), 7 Capital U.L.Rev. 117 (1977) held that a woman has a constitutional right to be sterilized without her husband's consent, although no state statute was involved in the case and husband and wife had been living apart. See

also Murray v. Vandervander, 522 P.2d 302 (Okl.App. 1974); Note, Sterilization: Who Says No? 29 Mercer L.Rev. 821 (1978); and Note, A Woman's Right to Voluntary Sterilization, 22 Buff.L.Rev. 291 (1972).

29. 428 U.S. at 68, 96 S.Ct. at 2840.

30. 410 U.S. 179, 93 S.Ct. 739, 35 L.Ed.2d 201 (1973), rehearing denied 410 U.S. 959, 93 S.Ct. 1410, 35 L.Ed.2d 694 (1973).

31. 410 U.S. 113, 93 S.Ct. 705, 35 L.Ed.2d 147 (1973), rehearing denied 410 U.S. 959, 93 S.Ct. 1409, 35 L.Ed.2d 694 (1973).

32. Planned Parenthood v. Danforth, 428 U.S. 52, 96 S.Ct. 2831, 49 L.Ed.2d 788 (1976).

33. Voe v. Califano, 434 F.Supp. 1058 (D.Conn.1977) held that the Medicaid ban on funds for sterilization of minors is constitutional, but did not pass on the constitutionality of a complete prohibition of sterilization for minors.

tional.[34] There are obvious differences between abortion and sterilization, however. It may be argued that sterilization has longer term consequences than abortion, since it terminates the power to procreate, while abortion does not. Therefore a more sweeping limitation upon sterilization is an appropriate method for achieving the state interest in protecting the welfare of minors than would be tolerated for abortions. Further it may be argued that forbidding sterilization does not necessarily prevent the minor from practicing contraception, other methods of more or less efficacy and more or less safety being available. On the other hand the decision to abort a fetus also involves serious ethical and medical consequences, and if a parental veto of that decision is unconstitutional, one can easily imagine that a state prohibition of the decision to be sterilized might also be held unconstitutional, especially since less sweeping limitations, such as a parental consent or parental consultation requirement could be used.[35]

In addition to the statutory restrictions upon voluntary sterilization imposed by some states, there are other obstacles facing a person wishing to be sterilized for contraceptive reasons. Some physicians apparently still think they may be risking tort liability and refuse to perform the operation for that reason.[36] Some hospitals may have local rules imposing various conditions upon the per-

formance of tubal ligations, conditions having nothing to do with the medical aspects of the operation.[37] And of course some hospitals supported by the Catholic Church may refuse to perform sterilizations out of religious conviction and in some cities these may be the only hospitals.[38]

The constitutionality of special hospital rules respecting sterilization has in the past been in some doubt. Hathaway v. Worcester City Hospital[39] held that a municipal hospital's rule forbidding consensual sterilizations was warranted by no compelling state interest and therefore violated the Equal Protection Clause of the Fourteenth Amendment. But Chrisman v. Sisters of St. Joseph of Peace[40] held that it was not unconstitutional for a Catholic hospital to refuse to do sterilizations since no state action was involved in the refusal. The Ninth Circuit also relied for its decision upon an amendment to the federal statutes making grants to private, non-profit hospitals which provides that the receipt of any such grant does not authorize a court to require the individual or the hospital to perform sterilizations if the performance of the operation would be contrary to the religious beliefs or moral convictions of the individual or the organization owning the hospital.[41] Since the decision in Poelker v. Doe,[42] it appears that even where the hospital's relation to the state is such that the denial of sterilization may be held to constitute state action,

34. 428 U.S. at 72, 96 S.Ct. at 2842.

35. See Bellotti v. Baird, 428 U.S. 132, 96 S.Ct. 2857, 49 L.Ed.2d 844 (1976). Colo.Rev.Stat.Ann. § 25–6–102 (1982) requires parental consent for sterilization of an unmarried person under eighteen.

36. The physicians in Ponter v. Ponter, 135 N.J.Super. 50, 342 A.2d 574 (1975), 7 Capital U.L.Rev. 117 (1977), 7 Rut.-Cam.L.Rev. 771 (1976) refused to perform the operation without spousal consent for fear they would be open to civil liability. See also McKenzie, Contraceptive Sterilization: The Doctor, the Patient and the United States Constitution, 25 U.Fla.L.Rev. 327 (1973).

37. See Note, A Woman's Right to Voluntary Sterilization, 22 Buff.L.Rev. 291, 295 (1972) describing the criteria of the American College of Obstetricians and Gynecologists for sterilization, which among other conditions require the woman to have had five children. This rule was apparently applied by the hospital in McCabe v. Nassau County Medical Center, 453 F.2d 698 (2d Cir. 1971). West's Ann.Cal.Health and Safety Code § 1258 (1979) forbids hospitals to set up special non-medical

qualifications for sterilizations not required for other operations. Colo.Rev.Stat. § 25–6–102(3) (1973) is similar.

38. This was apparently the situation in Taylor v. St. Vincent's Hospital, 523 F.2d 75 (9th Cir.1975), cert. denied 424 U.S. 948, 96 S.Ct. 1420, 47 L.Ed.2d 355 (1976), the Catholic hospital in Billings being, by agreement, the only hospital with a maternity department. N.J.Stat. Ann. § 30:11–9 (1981) provides that a hospital is not required to perform sterilizations where that is contrary to religious beliefs.

39. 475 F.2d 701 (1st Cir.1973).

40. 506 F.2d 308 (9th Cir.1974). The Chrisman case collects earlier authorities and was followed in Taylor v. St. Vincent's Hospital, 523 F.2d 75 (9th Cir.1975), cert. denied 424 U.S. 948, 96 S.Ct. 1420, 47 L.Ed.2d 355 (1976).

41. 42 U.S.C.A. § 300a–7.

42. 432 U.S. 519, 97 S.Ct. 2391, 53 L.Ed.2d 528 (1977), on remand 558 F.2d 1346 (8th Cir.1977).

this would not amount to an invasion of the person's right of privacy. The reason for this is the Supreme Court's view that a distinction must be made between state action which "unduly burdens" the right to abortion (or in this instance sterilization) and state action which merely encourages an alternative activity as outlined in Maher v. Roe.[43] The latter form of state action need meet only the test of rationality applicable to regulations infringing no fundamental right, and in the abortion case it was held that the state's interest in protecting potential life meets this test. Whether the state's interest in protecting potential life is sufficient to justify state hospitals' denial of sterilization is not wholly clear, but the factual similarity between Poelker and the sterilization case is close. In the last analysis, as Justice Marshall has eloquently said,[44] Poelker and Maher were largely the product of political pressure. Predictions based on such decisions cannot be reached by the conventional processes of legal analysis.

In short, although sterilization is now a crucial method of contraception in the United States, and although its importance as such will doubtless increase in the future, there are still substantial practical and legal limitations upon its availability, especially for those men and women whose poverty relegates them to a reliance upon public hospitals and clinics. For these men and women access to sterilization is also affected by the cases, statutes and regulations governing federal aid to state family planning services. Due to the complexities of state-federal relationships, to the delays of litigation and bureaucratic action and to constitutional uncertainties, many

of these men and women have been and will be deprived of any opportunity to have a vasectomy or tubal ligation because it cannot be funded by Medicaid.[45] It does seem curious that the courts and the HEW regulations should insist that people under twenty-one lack the judgment to decide on sterilization when the age of consent for other purposes is eighteen and when the Supreme Court has decided that a minor woman may not be prevented from having an abortion.

Involuntary Sterilization

Obviously no hard and fast line can be drawn in practice between voluntary and involuntary sterilization. The sterilization of minors illustrates this since there is doubt whether a minor can give effective consent to the operation.[46] And even with respect to an adult there may be a question whether the consent was voluntary or coerced in some way, as in the Relf case,[47] where there was evidence that sterilization was induced by threats of withholding welfare payments. The Relf case itself defines "voluntary" to require that "the individual have at his disposal the information necessary to make his decision and the mental competence to appreciate the significance of that information."[48] The meaning of that decision is that the operation should not be performed when it is not "voluntary" by that definition, the determination of which may involve the resolution of difficult questions of fact. If the operation is not "voluntary", then the physician performing it and any hospital participating may be liable in tort to the person upon whom it is performed.[49] This risk of liability naturally

---

43. 432 U.S. 464, 97 S.Ct. 2376, 53 L.Ed.2d 484 (1977).

44. Marshall, J., dissenting in Beal v. Doe, 432 U.S. 438, 454, 462, 97 S.Ct. 2366, 2376, 53 L.Ed.2d 464 (1977).

45. The Department of Health, Education and Welfare's "moratorium" on funding for sterilization of all persons under twenty-one, in response to the Relf case, but going beyond it, is found in 38 Fed.Reg. 20930 (1973). For a case illustrating the hardships involved, see Voe v. Califano, 434 F.Supp. 1058 (D.Conn.1977).

The HEW regulations governing medicaid payments for sterilizations as presently adopted require a thirty-day waiting period between the giving of consent and the performance of sterilization, with certain exceptions. They continue the prohibition upon payment for steriliza-

tions of persons under the age of twenty-one and contain provisions limiting the circumstances in which sterilization of mental incompetents may be paid for. 43 Fed. Reg. 52,146 ff. (1978) (to be codified in 42 C.F.R. §§ 50.203, 50.205.

46. See the discussion at footnote 19, supra.

47. Relf v. Weinberger, 372 F.Supp. 1196 (D.D.C.1974), motion denied 403 F.Supp. 1235 (1975).

48. 372 F.Supp. at 1202.

49. W. Prosser and W. Keeton, Handbook on the Law of Torts 112–115 (5th ed. 1984); Bonner v. Moran, 126 F.2d 121 (D.C.Cir.1941); Annot., 139 A.L.R. 1370, 1371 (1942). See Smith v. Seibly, 72 Wash.2d 16, 431 P.2d 719

generates reluctance among physicians to perform sterilizations whenever there is any doubt of the patient's capacity to consent.

The further question arises whether the operation for sterilization may ever be lawfully performed upon an individual who does not or cannot consent. In other words, is involuntary sterilization ever lawful? It is obvious that it is not lawful for a physician to perform the operation upon a non-consenting patient without some state sanction.[50] The issue therefore is whether a state may authorize involuntary sterilization, and if so, under what circumstances.

The cases are divided on whether the courts may order an involuntary sterilization, of a mentally retarded person, for example, without express statutory authority.[51] Most such cases have involved the sterilization of individuals whose mental incompetence prevented them from giving a binding consent, and in some of them even the consent of a parent or guardian was held not sufficient to warrant the operation.[52] The basis for the decisions denying sterilization has been either that the particular court whose aid was invoked had only limited statutory jurisdiction and therefore had no power to enter the order,[53] or the broader ground that an operation of such great and permanent importance to the individual should not be assumed under the general common law power given to courts of general jurisdiction.[54] In any event the refus-

(1967), in which the court held that it was a question for the jury whether a married minor of eighteen, emancipated, was able to consent to sterilization. In that case the jury gave a verdict in favor of the defendant physician whom the minor sued for assault, claiming a lack of consent. In the unusual case of Downs v. Sawtelle, 574 F.2d 1 (1st Cir.1978), cert. denied 439 U.S. 910, 99 S.Ct. 278, 58 L.Ed.2d 255 (1978) the court held that a community hospital and its chief of medical staff could be held liable under the Civil Rights Act, 42 U.S.C.A. § 1983, for sterilizing a young woman without her consent, thereby depriving her of a constitutional right. The case was remanded for jury trial on various issues, including that of immunity of the state officials involved. See also Ruby v. Massey, 452 F.Supp. 361 (D.Conn.1978), and Beck v. Lovell, 361 So.2d 245 (La.App.1978), writ of review denied 362 So.2d 802 (La.1978), holding that in the absence of an emergency a husband may not give binding consent to his wife's sterilization.

50. See cases cited supra note 49.

51. Holding the courts do not have such authority: Wade v. Bethesda Hospital, 337 F.Supp. 671 (S.D.Ohio 1971), motion denied 356 F.Supp. 380 (S.D.Ohio 1973); Guardianship of Kemp, 43 Cal.App.3d 758, 118 Cal.Rptr. 64 (1974); A.L. v. G.R.H., 163 Ind.App. 606, 325 N.E.2d 501 (1975), cert. denied 425 U.S. 936, 96 S.Ct. 1669, 48 L.Ed.2d 178 (1976); Holmes v. Powers, 439 S.W.2d 579 (Ky.1968); In Interest of M.K.R., 515 S.W.2d 467 (Mo. 1974); Application of A.D., 90 Misc.2d 236, 394 N.Y.S.2d 139 (Sur.1977); Frazier v. Levi, 440 S.W.2d 393 (Tex.Civ. App.1969). See also Annot., Jurisdiction of Court to Permit Sterilization of Mentally Defective Person in Absence of Specific Statutory Authority, 74 A.L.R.3d 1210 (1976). Nine cases have held the courts do have authority to order involuntary sterilization without specific statutory provisions. Matter of A.W., 637 P.2d 366 (Colo. 1981); Wentzel v. Montgomery Gen. Hospital, Inc., 293 Md. 685, 447 A.2d 1244 (1982), cert. denied 459 U.S. 1147, 103 S.Ct. 790, 74 L.Ed.2d 995 (1983); Matter of Moe, 385 Mass. 555, 432 N.E.2d 712 (1982); In re Penny N., 120 N.H. 269, 414 A.2d 541 (1980); Matter of Grady, 85 N.J. 235, 426 A.2d 467 (1981); Matter of Sallmaier, 85 Misc.2d 295, 378 N.Y.S.2d 989 (1976); In re Simpson, 180 N.E.2d 206 (Ohio Prob.1962); Matter of Guardianship of Hayes, 93 Wash.2d 228, 608 P.2d 635 (1980); Matter of Guardianship of Eberhardy, 102 Wis.2d 539, 307 N.W.2d 881 (1981). In re D [1976] Fam.Div. 185, [1976] 2 W.L.R. 279 seems to assume the English courts have this power, although it refused to enter the order on the ground it would not be for the minor's best interests. People v. Blankenship, 16 Cal.App.2d 606, 61 P.2d 352 (1936) ordered the sterilization of a convicted rapist as a condition of probation, but this decision is characterized as dubious in People v. Dominguez, 256 Cal.App.2d 623, 64 Cal.Rptr. 290 (1967). An involuntary hysterectomy of a mentally disabled adult as a means of preventing cancer of the cervix was authorized by Butte County Public Guardian v. Superior Court, 135 Cal.App.3d 626, 185 Cal.Rptr. 516 (1982), in the face of a statute prohibiting the sterilization of a person under conservatorship. Involuntary sterilization of a mentally retarded child was ordered without specific statutory approval, where sterilization was in the child's best interests, in P.S. by Harbin v. W.S., 452 N.E. 2d 969 (Ind.1983).

Matter of Guardianship of Eberhardy, 102 Wis.2d 539, 307 N.W.2d 881 (1981) takes the metaphysical position that although the state trial court had jurisdiction, even in the absence of statutory authority, to order the sterilization of an adult, mentally retarded daughter at the request of her parents, that jurisdiction should not be exercised. In part the court was moved by the absence of any "guidelines" for such a decision and in part by the fear that a decision ordering sterilization would have a broad precedential effect in the state.

52. E.g., Guardianship of Kemp, 43 Cal.App.3d 758, 118 Cal.Rptr. 64 (1974); A.L. v. G.R.H., 163 Ind.App. 636, 325 N.E.2d 501 (1975), cert. denied 425 U.S. 936, 96 S.Ct. 1669, 48 L.Ed.2d 178 (1976).

53. E.g., In Interest of M.K.R., 515 S.W.2d 467 (Mo. 1974) (juvenile court); Frazier v. Levi, 440 S.W.2d 393 (Tex.Civ.App.1969).

54. E.g., Guardianship of Kemp, 43 Cal.App.3d 758, 118 Cal.Rptr. 64 (1974); In Interest of M.K.R., 515 S.W.2d 467 (Mo.1974); Application of A.D., 90 Misc.2d 236, 394 N.Y.S.2d 139 (Sur.1977) (suggests such an order would be

al to act without specific statutory authority seems justified, particularly since any such action must, if it is to be constitutional, be taken only with strict adherence to due process requirements which are best spelled out in statutory terms.

The strength of the doctrine that involuntary sterilization cannot be ordered without express statutory authority is evidenced by the court's decision in Wade v. Bethesda Hospital [55] that a judge entering such an order could be held liable to the individual sterilized. But the Supreme Court has held a judge to be immune from liability to a minor whose sterilization he ordered without statutory authority and without notice or a hearing, in Stump v. Sparkman.[56] The Court there held that the judge had jurisdiction over the subject matter and that his order was a "judicial act" because it was a function normally performed by a judge. It therefore fell within the normal limits of judicial immunity.

In the early part of the Twentieth Century, primarily as a result of the eugenics movement, a substantial number of states enacted statutes authorizing involuntary sterilization of various classes of persons, usually the mentally retarded, the mentally incompetent, and in some instances certain classes of criminal.[57] Eugenics may be defined as the application of

genetic principles to the improvement of human populations.[58] The involuntary sterilization statutes were aimed at implementing the negative aspects of eugenics by preventing the reproduction of individuals possessing inheritable mental or physical defects.[59] As this Century progressed, two developments diminished, in fact nearly eliminated, the earlier optimism about the possibilities of eugenics. The first of these was the recognition that eugenics could be used as a pretext for the sterilization of unpopular political or racial groups, as was done in Nazi Germany. The second was the discovery, as the science of genetics became more sophisticated, that human qualities may be the product of many genetic factors and also of some environmental ones, making the prediction of inheritance of such qualities more difficult than they had been thought to be. As a result the statutes providing for involuntary sterilization fell into some disrepute and many were repealed. Some remained, however. Recently the eugenics movement has regained strength as genetic research had advanced.[60] A new rationale for such statutes has also come to be recognized. In the view of some persons involuntary sterilization may be justified where the individual suffers from such severe mental retardation or incompetence as to be

---

unconstitutional under Griswold v. Connecticut, 381 U.S. 479, 85 S.Ct. 1678, 14 L.Ed.2d 510 (1965), unless it would be required by a compelling state interest).

Cases which find the authority to order involuntary sterilization to lie within the general equitable powers of the courts may rely upon the idea that the incompetent person has some sort of constitutional right to be sterilized and that the courts can decide for him whether this right should be exercised. Matter of Moe, 385 Mass. 555, 432 N.E.2d 712 (1982).

55. Wade v. Bethesda Hospital, 356 F.Supp. 380 (S.D. Ohio 1973).

56. 435 U.S. 349, 98 S.Ct. 1099, 55 L.Ed.2d 331 (1978), rehearing denied 436 U.S. 951, 98 S.Ct. 2862, 56 L.Ed.2d 795 (1978). Presumably this overrules Wade v. Bethesda Hospital, supra note 55, although the Supreme Court did not cite the earlier case. See Nagel, Judicial Immunity and Sovereignty, 6 Hast.Const.L.Q. 237 (1978).

But it has been held that a physician in a community hospital may be liable for performing a sterilization without the patient's consent if he acted with knowledge that he was violating the patient's constitutional rights. Downs v. Sawtelle, 574 F.2d 1 (1st Cir.1978), cert. denied 439 U.S. 910, 99 S.Ct. 278, 58 L.Ed.2d 255 (1978). But see

Walker v. Pierce, 560 F.2d 609 (4th Cir.1977), cert. denied 434 U.S. 1075, 98 S.Ct. 1266, 55 L.Ed.2d 782 (1978).

57. For a description of the early statutes see H. Laughlin, Eugenical Sterilization in the United States (1922). Some of the statutes had an obviously punitive purpose, such as the Oklahoma statute held unconstitutional in Skinner v. Oklahoma, 316 U.S. 535, 62 S.Ct. 1110, 86 L.Ed. 1655 (1942).

58. Eugenics, 5 International Encyc. of the Social Sciences 193 (1968); Vukowich, The Dawning of the Brave New World—Legal, Ethical, and Social Issues of Eugenics, 1971 U. of Ill.L.F. 189.

59. Ferster, Eliminating the Unfit—Is Sterilization the Answer? 27 Ohio St.L.J. 591 (1966). A positive form of eugenics is now talked of, and, to some extent practiced by the use of artificial insemination with the sperm of "superior" donors. Note, Eugenic Artificial Insemination: A Cure for Mediocrity? 94 Harv.L.Rev. 1850 (1981).

60. See, e.g., G. Wolstenholme, ed., Man and His Future (1963), especially pages 247–298; J. Bresler, ed. Genetics and Society (1973); J. Robitscher, ed., Eugenic Sterilization (1973); Vukowich, The Dawning of the Brave New World—Legal, Ethical, and Social Issues of Eugenics, 1971 U. of Ill.L.F. 189.

incapable of caring for any children he or she might have.[61] As in the case of the eugenic basis for the statute, this may call for difficult and subtle medical and psychological judgments.[62]

At present there are statutes authorizing, in a great variety of terms, the sterilization of limited classes of persons in at least fourteen states.[63] Some of these statutes apply only to inmates of state institutions,[64] although there may well be constitutional objections to providing for sterilization of institutionalized persons without making the same provision for similar persons outside of institutions.[65] The statutes set up standards of varying preciseness, ranging from those which authorize sterilization when procreation by the individual would be "inadvisable" [66] to those requiring proof of inheritable mental disease or of such mental incompetence as to disable the person from caring for children.[67] One or two of the statutes have as their purpose the punishment for crimes,[68] but their constitutionality is questionable under Skinner v. Oklahoma.[69] Others authorize the sterilization of epileptics, not an inheritable or even disabling condition in many instances, and these also are of doubtful validity.[70]

All such statutes raise complex questions of constitutional validity. The Supreme Court has dealt with these questions on two occasions, but neither of the cases provides a complete answer applicable to all statutes. The Supreme Court's approach to the validity of statutes has in recent years become so strict that these earlier cases may in fact be of little value as precedents. The first case, Buck v. Bell,[71] held that the Virginia statute was constitutional when it authorized the sterilization of mental defectives who were inmates of state institutions. The patient in this case was a "feeble-minded" woman, daughter of a "feeble-minded" mother and mother of a "feeble-minded" child, leading to Justice Holmes' often quoted statement that "Three generations of imbeciles are enough." [72] The assumption of the opinion seems to have been that the patient's condition was inheritable and would be further passed on without sterilization.

The second case, Skinner v. Oklahoma,[73] held unconstitutional the Oklahoma statute authorizing the sterilization of certain classes

---

61. An example of this statutory purpose is found in the Georgia statute, cited infra, note 63. West's Ann.Cal. Probate Code § 2356(d) (Supp.1984) provides that a ward or conservatee may *not* be sterilized. This statute was held to deprive a mentally retarded adult of her right to privacy and liberty under the state and federal constitutions in Conservatorship of Valerie N., 40 Cal.3d 143, 219 Cal.Rptr. 387, 707 P.2d 760 (1985).

62. See In re D, [1976] Fam.Div. 185, [1976] 2 W.L.R. 279, for a judge's conscientious attempt to deal with such a problem.

63. Ark.Stats. §§ 59–501, 59–502 (1971); Del.Code tit. 16, §§ 5701 to 5705 (1983 and Supp.1984); Ga.Code §§ 84–932 to 84–935.2 (1985); Minn.Stat.Ann. §§ 252A.11, 252A.13 (1982); Miss.Code 1981, §§ 41–45–1 to 41–45–19 (Supp.1984); N.C.Gen.Stat. §§ 35–36 to 35–50 (1984); Or.Rev.Stat. §§ 436.205 to 436.335 (1983); S.C. Code 1985, §§ 44–47–10 to 44–47–100; Utah Code Ann. 1985, §§ 64–10–1 to 64–10–16; Vt.Stat.Ann. tit. 18, §§ 8705 to 8716 (Supp.1985); Va.Code 1982, §§ 54–325.9 to 54–325.15; West's Rev.Code Wash.Ann. § 9.92.100 (1977); W.Va.Code, §§ 27–16–1 to 27–16–5 (1980).

64. E.g., the Mississippi statute cited supra, note 63.

65. Ruby v. Massey, 452 F.Supp. 361 (D.Conn.1978) held this distinction, found in the Connecticut statute, to violate the right of privacy of those not in institutions. Conservatorship of Valerie N., 40 Cal.3d 143, 219 Cal. Rptr. 387, 707 P.2d 760 (1985) held that a young woman

afflicted with Down's Syndrome and mentally retarded, and therefore unable to use birth control devices, was unconstitutionally deprived of her right to be sterilized by the statutory scheme in California which provided for no such procedure on persons unable to consent. The right of privacy and liberty interests of such persons pursuant to the Fourteenth Amendment of the United States Constitution and the corresponding sections of the California constitution were thus held to have been violated. The court also held, however, that the evidence in the record did not show a need for sterilization.

66. E.g., the Delaware statute cited supra, note 63.

67. E.g., the West Virginia statute cited supra, note 63.

68. The Washington statute cited supra, note 63.

69. 316 U.S. 535, 62 S.Ct. 1110, 86 L.Ed. 1655 (1942).

70. E.g., the Delaware, Mississippi, and South Carolina statutes cited supra in note 63. See 3B R. Gray, Attorneys' Textbook of Medicine ch. 92 (1978) and R. Barrow, Epilepsy and the Law ch. V, (2d ed. 1966).

71. 274 U.S. 200, 47 S.Ct. 584, 71 L.Ed. 1000 (1927).

72. 274 U.S. at 207, 47 S.Ct. at 584.

73. 316 U.S. 535, 62 S.Ct. 1110, 86 L.Ed. 1655 (1942).

of habitual criminals. The basis for the decision was that the exclusion of certain offenders from the class of habitual criminal and the inclusion of others guilty of very similar offenses constituted an "invidious" discrimination [74] and therefore violated the Equal Protection Clause of the Fourteenth Amendment. The Skinner case retains importance as a precedent because in his opinion Justice Douglas first announced that this statute dealt with "one of the basic civil rights of man", marriage and procreation, and therefore that it must be subjected to strict scrutiny.[75] This doctrine has since been expanded and refined in Griswold v. Connecticut,[76] Eisenstadt v. Baird,[77] Roe v. Wade,[78] and Carey v. Population Services [79] so as to characterize procreation as a "fundamental right", which may only be restricted by the state where necessary to the accomplishment of a compelling state interest.

A logically prior constitutional issue may be raised by some sterilization statutes which fail to provide an acceptable measure of procedural due process to the individual whose sterilization is sought. Buck v. Bell [80] held that the Virginia statute did provide due process in that case, when it provided for notice and an administrative hearing to be participated in by the patient and his guardian, followed by judicial review de novo of the administrative decision. The condition of the patient, who is usually either a minor or mentally incompetent or both, and the gravi-

ty of the operation certainly justify a requirement of the utmost procedural protection for anyone subjected to involuntary sterilization.[81] This should include those steps outlined in Buck v. Bell, with clear authority for an attorney to represent the patient at all stages, his services to be provided at state expense where the patient is unable to pay an attorney himself. In addition, wherever necessary, transcripts of proceedings and expert medical testimony should be provided at state expense. Many of the present statutes do include most of these safeguards.[82] This should then constitute compliance with the requirements of the Due Process Clause.

Assuming that the statute does provide due process for the patient, the more difficult question arises whether the statute is necessary to effectuate a compelling state interest.[83] The interests involved are two, as has been indicated: a) To prevent the transmission of inheritable mental defects; and b) To prevent the birth of children to parents who are incapable of caring for them. These would seem to be compelling interests, although one cannot predict with any confidence how the Supreme Court might view them. If they are, then one would have to scrutinize the particular statute to determine whether it stated these purposes with sufficient clarity to guide the courts in deciding specific cases. Some of the statutes do not state these purposes with sufficient preciseness.[84] Others may.[85]

---

74. 316 U.S. at 541, 62 S.Ct. at 1113.

75. Id.

76. 381 U.S. 479, 85 S.Ct. 1678, 14 L.Ed.2d 510 (1965).

77. 405 U.S. 438, 92 S.Ct. 1029, 31 L.Ed.2d 349 (1972).

78. 410 U.S. 113, 93 S.Ct. 705, 35 L.Ed.2d 147 (1973), rehearing denied 410 U.S. 959, 93 S.Ct. 1409, 35 L.Ed.2d 694 (1973).

79. 431 U.S. 678, 97 S.Ct. 2010, 52 L.Ed.2d 675 (1977).

80. 274 U.S. 200, 47 S.Ct. 584, 71 L.Ed. 1000 (1927).

81. Cf. Application of Gault, 387 U.S. 1, 87 S.Ct. 1428, 18 L.Ed.2d 527 (1967); Heryford v. Parker, 396 F.2d 393 (10th Cir.1968).

A leading case establishing procedural requirements for sterilization of mentally retarded minors, in the absence of a statute on the subject is Matter of A.W., ___ Colo. ___, 637 P.2d 366 (1981). The court there required the appointment of a guardian ad litem for the minor, and the appointment of expert witnesses in the field of

mental retardation to examine the minor and testify on relevant points. The court also held that the minor's wishes should be taken into account, and that the court must determine whether the minor's ability to decide about sterilization is likely to improve. Finally, the court must find by clear and convincing evidence that the sterilization is medically necessary.

82. E.g., North Carolina, Utah statutes, cited supra, note 63.

83. See the discussion at notes 74 to 79, supra.

84. E.g., the Delaware statute cited supra, note 63, seems vague in its statement of purposes.

85. E.g., the Georgia statute cited supra, note 63. The Utah statute authorizes the court to compel sterilization where it finds a "compelling state interest". The North Carolina statute, which has been held constitutional, merely authorizes sterilization where it is for the best interests of the patient or for the public good.

In order to establish that sterilization is "necessary" to the effectuation of these purposes, there would have to be evidence (a) that the particular mental condition of the patient was inheritable, or (b) that the patient would be unable to give proper care to any child he or she might have, (c) that the patient's condition was not curable, (d) that the patient was likely to have sexual relations, and (e) that contraception was not an effective alternative to sterilization. Presumably the statute, in order to pass muster, would have to spell out these requirements as well, or at least be written in such terms that the requirements could be construed to be present. Much of the evidence on these points would necessarily be expert medical, psychiatric or psychological testimony, the burden of proof being upon the authority seeking sterilization. A further procedural safeguard of a higher than normal burden of proof might be imposed, such as proof "by clear and convincing evidence". If all these qualifications can be met, it has been held that such statutes are constitutional.[86] Perhaps the Supreme Court will reaffirm the position taken in Buck v. Bell that these are important state interests. Some commentators take the other view, however, urging the constitutional invalidity of involuntary sterilization.[87] It is possible that the requirements of proof outlined here will make any substantial program of involuntary sterilization impractical. At the moment the statutes are not being extensively used.

86. North Carolina Assn. for Retarded Children v. State, 420 F.Supp. 451 (M.D.N.C.1976); In re Moore's Sterilization, 289 N.C. 95, 221 S.E.2d 307 (1976); Matter of Truesdell, 63 N.C.App. 258, 304 S.E.2d 793 (1983). The court in the federal case construed the statute to require proof of the factors listed as (a) through (e) in the text. See also Matter of Grady, 85 N.J. 235, 426 A.2d 467 (1981) and Cook v. State, 9 Or.App. 224, 495 P.2d 768 (1972). But see In re Cavitt, 182 Neb. 712, 157 N.W.2d 171 (1968), rehearing denied 183 Neb. 243, 159 N.W.2d 566 (1968); and Annot. 53 A.L.R.3d 960 (1973). Matter of A.W., 637 P.2d 366 (Colo.1981) authorized the sterilization of a mentally retarded minor where it could be proved, by clear and convincing evidence, that the sterilization was medically necessary.

87. E.g., Murdock, Sterilization of the Retarded: A Problem or a Solution? 62 Cal.L.Rev. 917 (1974); Vukowich, The Dawning of the Brave New World—Legal, Ethical, and Social Issues of Eugenics, 1971 U. of Ill.L.F. 189; Ferster, Eliminating the Unfit—Is Sterilization the

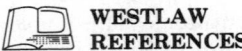

WESTLAW REFERENCES

Voluntary Sterilization

steriliz! /7 voluntar! /10 consent! capab! right competen!

ruby /s massey

find 475 f2d 701

Involuntary Sterilization

statut! law legislat! /s steriliz! /s constitution! unconstitutional

steriliz! /s incompeten! (mental! develop! +3 handicap! retarded disabled delayed)

find 337 fsupp 671

eugenic /s steriliz!

§ 5.3 Abortion

Historical Background

For the lawyer's purposes abortion may be defined as the deliberate, premature interruption of a pregnancy with the intention of destroying the fetus.[1] Medically the term is often used to cover the premature termination of a pregnancy from any cause.[2] In this section the word will be used in the legal sense.

Abortion in this sense has been practised to some extent in most societies we know anything about.[3] Although the authorities agree that abortion was an ecclesiastical offense in

Answer? 27 Ohio St.L.J. 591 (1966). A note, Sexual Sterilization—Constitutional Validity of Involuntary Sterilization and Consent Determinative of Voluntariness, 40 Mo.L.Rev. 509 (1975) seems to take the position that involuntary sterilization is constitutional where it effectuates a compelling state interest and where procedural due process is provided for as does Note, Sterilization, Retardation, and Parental Authority, 1978 B.Y.U.L. Rev. 380.

§ 5.3

1. Black's Law Dictionary 20 (4th rev. ed. 1968); I Oxford English Dictionary 27 (1961); G. Williams, The Sanctity of Life and the Criminal Law 146 (1957).

2. 4B R. Gray, Attorneys' Textbook of Medicine ch. 311 (3d ed. 1978); R. Sloane, ed., Abortion Changing Views and Practice 65 (1970).

3. See G. Devereux, A Study of Abortion in Primitive Societies (rev. ed. 1976).

English law,[4] there is some uncertainty as to whether it was a common law crime. There is a statement in Bracton to the effect that it was a crime when accomplished after the fetus had quickened.[5] Lord Coke relied upon Bracton to characterize abortion after quickening as a "great misprision", that is, a misdemeanor.[6] On the other hand it has been persuasively argued that abortion was not a crime at all at the common law.[7] It seems to be agreed by all authorities that abortion of a fetus before quickening was not a common law crime. In 1803 abortion was made a felony by statute in England, with a lighter punishment when the operation occurred before the fetus had quickened.[8] This statute was amended in 1861 to prescribe the maximum punishment of life imprisonment for abortions, whether or not the child had quickened.[9] That remained the English law until 1967, when years of effort for reform culminated in the Abortion Act, which permitted abortions by medical practitioners where the pregnancy involved risk to the life or the physical or mental health of the mother or of existing children, or where there was substantial risk that the child would be seriously handicapped.[10]

In the United States there was similar disagreement on whether abortion was a common law crime when the child had not quickened. The leading case of Commonwealth v. Parker [11] held that it was not. Courts in other states took the same position.[12] In Pennsylvania and North Carolina, however, it was held that abortion was a common law crime whether or not the child had quickened at the time the abortion occurred.[13]

New York in 1830 enacted the first general statute making abortion a crime.[14] Over the next decades other states followed until by 1880 all states had such statutes, the chief influence in their passage being physicians' organizations. All such statutes forbade the operation whether performed by a physician using medically approved methods or by an

---

4. Davies, The Law of Abortion and Necessity, 2 Mod. L.Rev. 126 (1938); Means, The Phoenix of Abortional Freedom, 17 N.Y.L.F. 335 (1971).

5. Davies, The Law of Abortion and Necessity, 2 Mod. L.Rev. 126, 133 (1938). Quickening is the first movement of the fetus in the womb as felt by the mother. It usually occurs toward the end of the fourth month or at the beginning of the fifth month, although its timing varies somewhat. Since early medicine had no tests by which pregnancy could be conclusively determined, quickening provided a convenient time for making that determination. And quickening also was a point at which philosophers could say that the fetus possessed a "soul," or had become "alive." J. Mohr, Abortion in America 3–4 (1978).

6. Part III, E. Coke, Institutes 50 (ed. 1797); G. Williams, The Sanctity of Life and the Criminal Law 152 (1957). See also 1 W. Blackstone, Commentaries on the Law of England 129 (3d ed. Cooley 1884), and H. Storer and F. Heard, Criminal Abortion 151–153 (1868). An extensive discussion of the history may be found in Roe v. Wade, 410 U.S. 113, 130–138, 93 S.Ct. 705, 715–719, 35 L.Ed.2d 147 (1973), rehearing denied 410 U.S. 959, 93 S.Ct. 1409, 35 L.Ed.2d 694 (1973).

7. Means, The Phoenix of Abortional Freedom, 17 N.Y.L.F. 335, 337–352 (1971).

8. 43 Geo. III, ch. 58 (1803). Needless to say, the lighter punishment was not very light, consisting of whipping, the pillory or transportation for up to fourteen years. If the child had quickened, the punishment was execution.

9. Offenses Against the Person Act, 1861, 24 & 25 Vict. c. 100, §§ 58, 59. See B. Dickens, Abortion and the

Law (1966); G. Williams, The Sanctity of Life and the Criminal Law 152–156 (1957). See the famous case of Rex v. Bourne, (1939) 1 K.B. 687 in which Macnaghten, J. created a defense for therapeutic abortions.

10. Abortion Act 1967, § 1. This Act contains other qualifications, but the text statement describes the major authority for the performance of abortions. For a description of the reform campaign, see K. Hindell and M. Simms, Abortion Law Reformed (1971). Experience with this Act is described in A. Hordern, Legal Abortion: The English Experience (1971).

11. 50 Mass. (9 Metc.) 263 (1845). See also Commonwealth v. Bangs, 9 Mass. 387 (1812).

12. Smith v. Gaffard, 31 Ala. 45, 51 (1857) (dictum); Abrams v. Foshee, 3 Iowa (3 Clarke) 274 (1856); Mitchell v. Commonwealth, 78 Ky. 204 (1879); In re Vince, 2 N.J. 443, 67 A.2d 141 (1949).

13. State v. Slagle, 83 N.C. 630 (1880); Mills v. Commonwealth, 13 Pa. 631 (1850).

14. Means, The Law of New York Concerning Abortion and the Statutes of the Foetus, 1664–1968: A Case of Cessation of Constitutionality, 14 N.Y.L.F. 411 (1968). For an account of the American experience with abortion, see J. Mohr, Abortion in America (1978). Actually the first anti-abortion legislation was passed in Connecticut in 1821, but it forbade only the abortion of a quickened fetus, Roe v. Wade, 410 U.S. 113, 138, 93 S.Ct. 705, 719, 35 L.Ed.2d 147 (1973), rehearing denied 410 U.S. 959, 93 S.Ct. 1409, 35 L.Ed.2d 694 (1973), and it applied only to abortion accomplished by the use of drugs.

untrained, unskilled "back-room" abortionist, and most statutes provided that the performance of an illegal abortion was a ground for revoking a physician's license to practice medicine.[15] Statutes in a few states prohibited all abortions, but most statutes permitted abortions to save the life of the mother, and some included even broader exemptions, such as abortions to save the life of the child, or to protect the health of the mother.[16] The distinction between the case in which the fetus had quickened and that in which it had not was retained only for purposes of fixing the penalty.[17] In many states the woman herself was made criminally responsible for procuring her own abortion.[18] As a means of enforcing the prohibition on abortions indirectly, many states also enacted legislation forbidding the sale, distribution or advertising of abortifacients.[19]

Forbidding abortions of course did not prevent them from occurring. Women who became pregnant but were unwilling to bear the child still resorted to abortion in large numbers.[20] Since the operation was illegal, however, no precise figures for the numbers of abortions can be arrived at, and all such statements can be no more than estimates. For well-to-do women it was sometimes possible to obtain an abortion from a physician in a hospital, the operation being disguised as a routine dilatation and curettage, which is an accepted gynecological procedure as well as an abortion technique.[21] Women who were not well-to-do or who had no connections in the medical community were forced to employ untrained abortionists whose lack of skill combined with the unsanitary conditions in which they operated resulted in the sterility, serious illness, or death of many women.[22]

The hardship, the suffering, and the egregious class bias which were caused by the existing criminal abortion laws led to strong movements for reform, both in the United States and England, in the 1950's and 1960's. In 1955 the Planned Parenthood Federation held a conference on abortion at which forty-three participants discussed the social, medical and legal aspects of the problem. The report of this conference became a useful source of information for later changes in the law.[23] Many other books and articles were written on the social, legal, philosophical, theological and humanitarian aspects of the abortion problem.[24]

A focus for reform efforts was provided by the Model Penal Code project, which included a section on "justifiable abortion", permitting an abortion by a physician where there is substantial risk that the pregnancy would

15. George, Current Abortion Laws: Proposals and Movements for Reform, in D. Smith, ed., Abortion and the Law 1, 5, 14 (1967).

16. Id. at 5–8; G. Williams, The Sanctity of Life and the Criminal Law 160 (1957).

17. George, Current Abortion Laws: Proposals and Movements for Reform, in D. Smith, ed., Abortion and the Law 1, 10 (1967).

18. J. Mohr, Abortion in America 124–129, 207–211, 218 (1978).

19. George, Current Abortion Laws: Proposals and Movements for Reform, in D. Smith, ed., Abortion and the Law 1, 14–16 (1967).

20. Estimates of the total number of abortions per year in the United States in the 1950's ranged from 200,000 to 1,500,000. L. Lader, Abortion 2 (1966). Other estimates are that 800,000 to 1,000,000 illegal abortions were occurring each year in the United States before the statutes were liberalized. D. Callahan, Abortion: Law, Choice, and Morality 132–133 (1970). Callahan also estimates thirty to thirty-five million abortions, legal and illegal each year throughout the world. Id. at 285. J. Mohr, Abortion in America ch. 3 (1978) describes the "great upsurge in abortion" which occurred in the United States between 1840 and 1880. On the evidence of contemporary estimates the author concludes that in the later decades of this period abortions were terminating from one-fifth to one-third of all pregnancies. Abortion had become a method of contraception. The same work, in chapters 6, 7, and 8, documents the campaign against abortion led by doctors and the newly formed American Medical Association from 1857 to 1880.

21. D. Callahan, Abortion: Law, Choice, and Morality 136–139 (1970). Dilatation and curettage is described in A. Hordern, Legal Abortion: The English Experience 91–92 (1971).

22. D. Callahan, Abortion: Law, Choice, and Morality 136–139 (1970).

23. Planned Parenthood Federation, M. Calderone, ed., Abortion in the United States (1958).

24. See C. Dollen, Abortion in Context: A Select Bibliography (1970). An extensive bibliography may also be found in L. Lader, Abortion 196–202 (1966), which also had an important influence for reform, as did G. Williams, The Sanctity of Life and the Criminal Law (1957), A. Guttmacher, ed., The Case for Legalized Abortion Now (1967), and Packer and Gampel, Therapeutic Abortion, 11 Stan.L.Rev. 417 (1959).

gravely impair the physical or mental health of the mother, or that the child would be born with grave physical or mental defect, or where the pregnancy resulted from rape, incest or other felonious intercourse.[25] This provision was the model for the first liberalized abortion statute in the United States, that of Colorado.[26] In the very same year, 1967, similar statutes were passed in California[27] and North Carolina.[28] Although there was opposition to these statutes and to any abortion reform, chiefly led by the Catholic Church, it was not sufficiently organized or financed to prevent their passage. In fact the wide support for the Colorado statute from diverse political groups suggested that the population generally favored reform more strongly than the legislation's proponents had realized. In the immediately ensuing years other states broadened their therapeutic abortion laws.[29] In 1970 New York, Hawaii, Alaska and Washington enacted statutes permitting abortions to be performed by a physician at the request of the woman at variously defined early stages of pregnancy.[30] Nearly as broad authority existed in states like California and Colorado by virtue of the provision, widely relied upon, permitting abortions to preserve the mother's mental health. The

effects of these statutes were to increase the number of legal abortions, and, more important, to drastically reduce the risk of injury or illness which had formerly been created by illegal abortions.[31] Early abortion by a physician in medically approved conditions is conceded to be safer than carrying the pregnancy to term.[32]

Abortion as a Constitutional Question

While the statutory reforms just outlined were being accomplished, the proponents of abortion reform were also active in the courts. The right of privacy announced in Griswold v. Connecticut[33] seemed to offer a slender foothold for constitutional attack on restrictive statutes, although only a rash lawyer in 1965 would have dared to predict how far the doctrines of that case would be carried. The first case to deal with the issue held that the earlier California statute imposing criminal penalties for performing abortions except where necessary to preserve the mother's life was unconstitutionally vague. In response to the argument that the statute should be construed to permit the abortion only when death from the pregnancy was certain, the court in People v. Belous[34] said that such a

25. Model Penal Code § 230.3(2) Proposed Official Draft (1962).

26. Colo.Rev.Stat.1963, § 40–2–50 (Supp.1967). The Colorado statute did not follow the terminology of the Model Penal Code exactly, but provided for abortion where the pregnancy was likely to result in the death of the woman, or in the serious permanent impairment of her physical or mental health, or in the birth of a child with grave and permanent physical deformity or mental retardation, or where it resulted from rape or incest. The statute also required approval of a hospital committee of three physicians, and, where impairment of mental health was the ground, the written approval of a psychiatrist.

27. Therapeutic Abortion Act, 1967 Cal.Ses.L. c. 327. A provision authorizing abortion where there was probability that the child would be deformed was omitted in order to get the bill passed. Thus the statute allowed abortion where there was substantial risk that the pregnancy would gravely impair the physical or mental health of the mother or where it resulted from rape or incest. Detailed accounts of the statute and its passage are Leavy and Charles, California's New Therapeutic Abortion Act: An Analysis and Guide to Medical and Legal Procedure, 15 U.C.L.A.L.Rev. 1 (1967); and Note, The California Therapeutic Abortion Act, 19 Hast.L.J. 242 (1967).

28. N.C.Gen.Stat. § 14–45.1 (1967).

29. See the statutes cited in Roe v. Wade, 410 U.S. 113, 140 n. 37, 93 S.Ct. 705, 720 n. 37, 35 L.Ed.2d 147 (1973), rehearing denied 410 U.S. 959, 93 S.Ct. 1409, 35 L.Ed.2d 694 (1973).

30. Alaska Stat. § 18.16.010 (1981); Hawaii Rev.Stat. § 453–16 (1976); N.Y.—McKinney's Penal Law § 125.05 (1975); West's Rev.Code Wash.Ann. §§ 9.02.060 to 9.02.080 (1977). Some period of residence in the state was generally required by these statutes. The New York statute was held constitutional in Byrn v. New York City Health and Hospitals Corp., 31 N.Y.2d 194, 335 N.Y.S.2d 390, 286 N.E.2d 887 (1972), motion denied 409 U.S. 821, 93 S.Ct. 86, 34 L.Ed.2d 78 (1972).

31. See D. Callahan, Abortion: Law, Choice and Morality 287–289 (1970).

32. Id.; Roe v. Wade, 410 U.S. 113, 149, 93 S.Ct. 705, 724, 35 L.Ed.2d 147 (1973), rehearing denied 410 U.S. 959, 93 S.Ct. 1409, 35 L.Ed.2d 694 (1973).

33. 381 U.S. 479, 85 S.Ct. 1678, 14 L.Ed.2d 510 (1965), discussed supra in section 5.1.

34. 71 Cal.2d 954, 80 Cal.Rptr. 354, 458 P.2d 194 (1969), cert. denied 397 U.S. 915, 90 S.Ct. 920, 25 L.Ed.2d 96 (1970), 48 Tex.L.Rev. 937 (1970), 118 U.Pa.L.Rev. 643 (1970). This was a four to three decision, with dissent by

construction would amount to an unconstitutional invasion of the woman's right to privacy as established in the Griswold case. The protection of the mother's health was rejected as a possible state interest since the abortion, under modern conditions, is safer than continuing the pregnancy. And the state's interest in protecting the fetus or the unborn child was held insufficient to support the statute on the ground that the state may not require the woman to take the risk of bearing the child where the risk of death from childbirth would be substantially certain or more likely than not. The court seemed to indicate that the amended California Therapeutic Abortion Act [35] would be constitutional, but a later California case held that the standards for establishing permissible abortions in this statute were also unconstitutionally vague.[36] The Belous case is important because it rehearsed legal arguments later found decisive in the United States Supreme Court.

After an earlier case in which it held the District of Columbia abortion statute not to be unconstitutionally vague in permitting abortions where necessary for the preservation of the mother's life or health,[37] the Supreme Court of the United States directly faced the issue of the states' power to prohibit abortions in Roe v. Wade.[38] This was a class action, brought by a pregnant woman who wished an abortion in Texas, seeking a declaratory judgment that the Texas abortion statute was unconstitutional, and an injunction restraining its enforcement. A physician intervened in the action, seeking the same relief, alleging that prosecutions against him for violation of the statute were pending. A consolidated action was brought by a married couple

alleging that the wife had been advised by her physician to avoid pregnancy, that she had discontinued birth control pills for medical reasons, and that if she should become pregnant she would want an abortion performed by a physician under safe circumstances. The Court held that Jane Roe, the pregnant woman, had standing to raise the constitutional issue, but that the physician and the married couple did not.

The Texas statute at issue in Roe v. Wade provided that the only circumstance in which abortion could be performed was upon medical advice for the purpose of saving the mother's life. In a decision concurred in by seven of the justices, the Supreme Court held the statute unconstitutional.[39] The majority opinion, which reads more like the report of a legislative committee than a judicial opinion, reviewed the history of abortion in this country and then held that the Constitution gives women a right of privacy which protects their decision to terminate a pregnancy. The source of this right of privacy was located either in the "Fourteenth Amendment's concept of personal liberty" in the Court's view, or perhaps in the "Ninth Amendment's reservation of rights to the people."[40] This right, the Court suggested, is a "fundamental right", which means that it may be regulated by the state only to achieve a "compelling state interest."[41] The Court identified the state's interests in this context as the interest in protecting the pregnant woman's health, and the interest in protecting the "potentiality of human life",[42] that is, the fetus. The Court held that the first of these interests becomes "compelling" at the end of the first trimester

---

Justice Burke. The case arose out of the prosecution of Dr. Belous for referring a couple desiring an abortion to a doctor who was not licensed to practice in California.

35. See note 27, supra.

36. People v. Barksdale, 8 Cal.3d 320, 105 Cal.Rptr. 1, 503 P.2d 257 (1972).

37. United States v. Vuitch, 402 U.S. 62, 91 S.Ct. 1294, 28 L.Ed.2d 601 (1971).

38. 410 U.S. 113, 93 S.Ct. 705, 35 L.Ed.2d 147 (1973), rehearing denied 410 U.S. 959, 93 S.Ct. 1409, 35 L.Ed.2d 694 (1973), 63 Cal.L.Rev. 1250 (1975), 74 Colum.L.Rev. 237 (1974), 87 Harv.L.Rev. 75 (1973), 26 Stan.L.Rev. 1161

(1974), 60 Va.L.Rev. 305 (1974). See Perry, Abortion, The Public Morals and the Police Power: The Ethical Function of Substantive Due Process, 23 U.C.L.A.L.Rev. 689 (1976).

39. Justice Blackmun wrote for the majority. Justices Burger and Douglas wrote brief concurring opinions not inconsistent with the majority opinion. Justices White and Rehnquist dissented.

40. 410 U.S. at 153, 93 S.Ct. at 726.

41. 410 U.S. at 155, 93 S.Ct. at 727.

42. 410 U.S. at 162, 93 S.Ct. at 731.

of pregnancy.[43] The second becomes "compelling" at the time of viability, that is, at the point at which the fetus is capable of existing outside the womb.[44]

The principles or rather rules to which this reasoning led the Court [45] were that a) until the end of the first trimester the decision whether to abort must be left to the woman and her physician; b) after the end of the first trimester the state may regulate abortion in ways reasonably related to maternal health; and c) during the state of pregnancy after viability the state may regulate or even forbid abortion except where necessary to preserve the life or health of the mother. The Court also held that at all stages of pregnancy the state may forbid the performance of abortions by anyone other than a physician.[46] Since the Texas statute went beyond these rules in its proscription of abortion, it was unconstitutional.

A companion case to Roe v. Wade, Doe v. Bolton,[47] was concerned with the validity of the Georgia abortion statute which was modeled on the Model Penal Code [48] and which permitted abortions to preserve the health of the mother, or where the fetus would suffer a grave mental or physical de-

---

43. The first trimester is the first three months of pregnancy, ending at about the end of the first twelve weeks. 4B R. Gray, Attorneys' Textbook of Medicine §§ 311.20, 311.41 (3d ed. 1978).

44. The Court defined viability as the point at which the fetus becomes "potentially able to live outside the mother's womb, albeit with artificial aid" and placed this point at about twenty-eight weeks, but said it might occur as early as twenty-four weeks. 410 U.S. at 160. The difficulty with attempts to locate viability is that at all stages of pregnancy it is a matter of probability rather than certainty. At twenty-eight weeks the probability that the fetus will live outside the womb may be greater than at twenty-four weeks, but in neither case is it certain that it will live. The difficulty is illustrated in Floyd v. Anders, 440 F.Supp. 535 (D.S.C.1977), judgment vacated 440 U.S. 445, 99 S.Ct. 1200, 59 L.Ed.2d 442 (1979), rehearing denied 441 U.S. 928, 99 S.Ct. 2043, 60 L.Ed.2d 403 (1979), in which an abortion was performed at about twenty-five weeks and the child lived twenty days after being removed from the womb and then died. The physician was indicted for murder under a statute which forbade abortions after the twenty-fourth week except in certain circumstances. In holding that the physician could not be prosecuted, the district court said the statute was unconstitutional so far as it applied to a non-viable fetus, and that viability could not be placed at a specific point in the period of gestation. A somewhat similar case is Commonwealth v. Edelin, 371 Mass. 497, 359 N.E.2d 4 (1976), in which the fetus may or may not have lived a short period after removal from the womb. See Annot., Proof of Live Birth in Prosecution for Killing Newborn Child, 65 A.L.R.3d 413 (1975).

At the moment, it appears that medical opinion regards twenty-six to twenty-eight weeks as the point at which the fetus has at least a fifty percent chance of survival outside the womb, provided that there has been normal fetal development and growth up to that point, and provided that facilities for care of the fetus are available in the hospital. With the best modern neonatal care techniques available, twenty-five and twenty-six week fetuses also stand a good chance of survival, especially if their weight is slightly ahead of normal growth at that point. The earliest point at which a fetus has survived without severe or harmful malformation or retardation, again with intensive neonatal care, has been indicated by one author to be at twenty-one weeks. See Hoffman, Analysis of Birth Weight, Gestational Age, and Fetal Viability, U.S. Births 1968, 29 Obstetrical and Gynecological Survey 651 (1974). Other medical writing on this issue includes Elwood and Thompson, Fetal Viability, Lancet, April 12, 1975, at page 862; Glantz, The Legal Aspects of Fetal Viability, in A. Milunsky, G. Annas, Genetics and the Law 29 (1975); Rush, Keirse, Howat, Baum, Anderson, Turnbull, Contribution of Preterm Delivery to Perinatal Mortality, British Medical Journal, October 23, 1976 at page 965; Gordon, Premature Baby Statistics, British Medical Journal, May 21, 1977 at page 1313.

45. 410 U.S. at 164, 165, 93 S.Ct. at 732.

A relatively new procedure called menstrual extraction makes it possible for women, using simple equipment, to bring about menstruation at the time when it is due. No professional help is needed. This may have the obvious advantage of avoiding protracted and painful menstruation. In addition it may amount to a kind of self-induced abortion in those women who may have become pregnant during the preceding period. The extent to which this technique is being used and the hazards of its use are the subject of controversy among both women and members of the medical profession. See E. Frankfort, Vaginal Politics 215–242 (1972).

46. 410 U.S. at 165, 93 S.Ct. at 732. See also People v. Franklin, 683 P.2d 775 (Colo.1984).

47. 410 U.S. 179, 93 S.Ct. 739, 35 L.Ed.2d 201 (1973), rehearing denied 410 U.S. 959, 93 S.Ct. 1410, 35 L.Ed.2d 694 (1973). The district court in this case had held that the substantive limitations on the circumstances in which abortions might be performed unconstitutionally restricted women's rights of privacy under Griswold v. Connecticut, 381 U.S. 479, 85 S.Ct. 1678, 14 L.Ed.2d 510 (1965), but it upheld the procedural requirements of the statute. The state's appeal from this ruling was dismissed for want of jurisdiction, so that the only issues before the Supreme Court were the procedural aspects of the statute, that is, the requirements that the abortion must be performed in an accredited hospital, that various physicians other than the woman's own must approve, and that the procedure could only be made available to Georgia residents.

48. See note 25, supra.

fect, or where the pregnancy resulted from rape. The Court held unconstitutional this statute's requirement that abortions might only be performed in *accredited* hospitals, its requirement that abortions might be performed only in hospitals during the first trimester, its requirement that abortions had to be approved by a committee of the staff of the hospital in which the abortion was to be performed, and its requirement that abortions had to be approved by two physicians in addition to the woman's own physician and the hospital committee. The Court also held unconstitutional the provision that only legal residents of Georgia could have an abortion pursuant to this statute.

One question which has been much discussed, in the argument of Roe v. Wade and subsequently, is whether the fetus is a "person", or, in somewhat different terms, when "life" begins. The Catholic Church's position, and that of many "right to life" advocates, is that the fetus is a "person" from the moment of conception.[49] This implies also that this "person" has "life" from that moment. If this position is accepted, as Roe v. Wade acknowledged,[50] no abortion could constitutionally be permitted for any reason, (assuming that some state action is involved in the decision) since abortion would deprive a person of life without due process of law in violation of the Fourteenth Amendment. Roe v. Wade dealt with this problem in an equivocal way. The opinion states at one point that "We need not resolve the difficult question of when life begins."[51] It holds, at another point, howev-

er, that the fetus is not a "person" under the Fourteenth Amendment.[52] Neither the Court nor many of the numerous authorities who have taken positions on abortion seem to have realized that the question whether a fetus is a "person" is essentially circular. The answer depends upon the definition given to "person", or to "life," which brings the discussion back to the starting point. The meanings of these terms are far from self-evident, either at law or in popular usage.[53] That being so, it would be preferable to cease arguing the question of whether the fetus is a "person" and to concentrate on the crucial issues. They involve one's moral and philosophical values and whether one group's set of values are so fundamental that they should be the basis for legislation in the face of determined opposition by a group of equal or greater numbers in the community. For a person holding utilitarian principles the issue might be characterized as whether, or at what point, the interests of the unborn child outweigh those of the mother, perhaps with some consideration also for the evils of over-population and the dangers of returning abortions to unskilled practitioners. In other words the issue should be placed in its individual and social context rather than be discussed in abstract terms.[54]

Roe v. Wade did not decide what effect, if any, a woman's family relationships would have upon her decision whether to have an abortion. The Supreme Court dealt with these and other questions in Planned Parenthood of Central Missouri v. Danforth.[55]

---

49. E.g., J. Noonan, An Almost Absolute Value in History, in J. Noonan, ed., The Morality of Abortion 1–59 (1970); Roe v. Wade, 410 U.S. 113, 161, 93 S.Ct. 705, 730, 35 L.Ed.2d 147 (1973), rehearing denied 410 U.S. 959, 93 S.Ct. 1409, 35 L.Ed.2d 694 (1973). Although the official position of the Catholic Church continues to oppose abortion, a Gallup poll indicates that 44% of American Catholics want the ban eased, while 47% want it kept as it is. New York Times, March 3, 1978, p. 8, col. 5.

50. 410 U.S. at 156, 157, 93 S.Ct. at 728.

51. Id. at 159, 93 S.Ct. at 729. See Eubanks v. Brown, 604 F.Supp. 141 (W.D.Ky.1984).

52. Id. at 158, 93 S.Ct. at 729.

53. As already indicated, the common law only protected the fetus after quickening, if then. See the discussion at notes 5–7, supra. The Court in Roe cites authori-

ties for the position that a fetus is not a "person" under the Fourteenth Amendment. 410 U.S. at 158, 93 S.Ct. at 729. In various other legal contexts the fetus is also not held to be a "person." See, e.g., Justus v. Atchison, 19 Cal.3d 564, 139 Cal.Rptr. 97, 565 P.2d 122 (1977) (fetus is not a "person" under the wrongful death statute, citing many cases both ways on this question); State v. Dickinson, 28 Ohio St.2d 65, 275 N.E.2d 599 (1971) (viable fetus not a "person" under the vehicular homicide statute). For an attempt to struggle with this definition see D. Callahan, Abortion: Law, Choice and Morality ch. X (1970).

54. D. Callahan, Abortion: Law, Choice and Morality chs. XII, XIII, XIV (1970).

55. 428 U.S. 52, 96 S.Ct. 2831, 49 L.Ed.2d 788 (1976).

The suit was brought by Planned Parenthood and two Missouri physicians seeking a declaration that the Missouri statute was invalid and an injunction against its enforcement. After finding that the physicians had standing to bring the suit, the Court answered a question expressly left open in Roe v. Wade by holding that the statute's requirement that the woman's spouse consent to the abortion was inconsistent with the standards set up in Roe v. Wade and therefore invalid. The Court's reasoning was that since the state could not veto the woman's decision to have an abortion, it could not give that power to her spouse, and further that she should have the exclusive right to make the decision because it is she who is "the more immediately and directly affected by the pregnancy." [56] Since there may well be reasons for permitting a husband to have something to say about the abortion of the fetus which do not apply to the state, state and husband being in entirely different relationships to the woman, the Court's first line of reasoning is not impressive. This is particularly true in view of the language in Stanley v. Illinois,[57] a case which was still an authority at the time Planned Parenthood v. Danforth was decided, although it now seems to have been partially repudiated.[58] The other line of reasoning which the Court adopts does seem persuasive, however.

The Missouri statute also required, for women under eighteen and unmarried, that no abortion could be performed without the consent of the woman's parents. This provision Planned Parenthood v. Danforth also held to be unconstitutional. Here again the Court found that the state had no constitutional power to authorize a third person, the parent, to veto a woman's decision to have an abortion. This reasoning is faulty for the same reason the reasoning related to spousal consent is faulty. The Court's decision on

this point is somewhat qualified by its remark that it "does not suggest that every minor, regardless of age or maturity, may give effective consent for termination of her pregnancy." [59]

In the companion case of Bellotti v. Baird [60] the Court held that the United States District Court should have abstained from passing on the constitutionality of a comprehensive Massachusetts statute requiring parental consent for abortions of unmarried women under eighteen, since that statute might be construed not to give the parent a veto power, but merely to require consultation. The proper course, the Court held, was to certify appropriate questions of construction of the statute to the Massachusetts Supreme Judicial Court before attempting to deal with any constitutional issues which the statute might raise. This was done and the Massachusetts Supreme Judicial Court responded in the following vein: [61] a) If the woman's parents refuse consent, a court order of consent may be obtained where that would serve the woman's best interests. b) Parental consultation is required in all cases other than emergencies, or where no parent is available. c) Notification of the parents is required unless that requirement should be found unconstitutional. d) Various procedural requirements of the statute were spelled out, including a provision authorizing appointment of counsel for the woman. The Massachusetts court added the general observation that if its construction had unconstitutionally burdened the minor's freedom of choice respecting the abortion, the statute should be so construed as to be valid.

The Massachusetts statute as so construed returned to the United States Supreme Court in the case which has come to be known as Bellotti II.[62] After a general discussion of the rights of minors, and the permissible limits on those rights, and of the rights of parents to control the conduct of their children, the

56. 428 U.S. at 71, 96 S.Ct. at 2842.

57. 405 U.S. 645, 92 S.Ct. 1208, 31 L.Ed.2d 551 (1972).

58. By Quilloin v. Walcott, 434 U.S. 246, 98 S.Ct. 549, 54 L.Ed.2d 511 (1978), rehearing denied 435 U.S. 918, 98 S.Ct. 1477, 55 L.Ed.2d 511 (1978).

59. 428 U.S. at 75, 96 S.Ct. at 2843.

60. 428 U.S. 132, 96 S.Ct. 2857, 49 L.Ed.2d 844 (1976). See also Wynn v. Carey, 582 F.2d 1375 (7th Cir.1978).

61. Baird v. Attorney General, 371 Mass. 741, 360 N.E.2d 288 (1977).

62. Bellotti v. Baird, 443 U.S. 622, 99 S.Ct. 3035, 61 L.Ed.2d 797 (1979), rehearing denied 444 U.S. 887, 100

Court held the statute constitutional in some respects and unconstitutional in others, the underlying question being whether the statute "unduly" burdened the minor's right to seek an abortion. In view of the potentially serious consequences of inability to obtain an abortion, the Court said that the statute may not require the minor to obtain her parents' consent in all cases, but must provide an alternative procedure, here obtaining a court's approval, obviating parental consent. The minor must therefore be permitted to go directly to court for permission to have the abortion without first consulting or notifying her parents. If the court finds that she is mature and well informed enough to make the abortion decision intelligently, it must authorize her to undertake it. If she is not mature enough, she must be permitted to convince the court that the abortion is in her interest, and if she succeeds in this, the abortion must be permitted. If she does not succeed, the court may refuse its permission.[63] To the extent that the Massachusetts statute did not provide the minor with these opportunities, it was held unconstitutional as imposing an undue burden upon the minor's right to an abortion.

The Supreme Court faced the question of abortions for minors and the role of parents again in 1981.[64] In that year a Utah statute required the attending physician to notify the

minor's parents, if possible, before performing the abortion. A fifteen-year-old girl dependent upon her parents and living at home sued for a declaratory judgment that this statute was unconstitutional on its face. After holding that the plaintiff did not have standing to attack the statute as applied to mature or emancipated women because she failed to offer any evidence that she was either mature or emancipated, the Court held that the requirement of parental notification was constitutional as applied to the immature, dependent minor. The decision was rested upon both the constitutional protection afforded parental rights respecting their children, and upon the benefits to the child of obtaining the mature advice and counsel of her parents. The state interest in protecting both parental rights and minors' welfare was sufficient to uphold the statute even though the Court had to concede that the notice requirement would prevent some minors from obtaining abortions.

Due to the decision on standing in the Matheson case, the decision appears to apply only to immature, unemancipated minors. It therefore does not have application to a woman who could allege that she was emancipated, mature, or that it is in her best interests to have an abortion without notifying her parents, since in those circumstances it is at least an open question whether she could be

S.Ct. 185, 62 L.Ed.2d 121 (1979). Justice Powell wrote for the Court, and was joined by the Chief Justice and Justices Stewart and Rehnquist. Justices Stevens, Marshall, Brennan and Blackmun concurred in the judgment. Justice White dissented.

63. A Missouri statute was construed to come within the limits imposed by Bellotti II in Planned Parenthood Association of Kansas City, Missouri, Inc. v. Ashcroft, 462 U.S. 476, 490, 103 S.Ct. 2517, 2524, 76 L.Ed.2d 733 (1983). The Supreme Court in Bellotti II also indicated that if the minor seeks parental consent and it is refused, she may then try to obtain judicial consent. The manner in which the courts have dealt with the petitions of minors who are unwilling or unable to obtain parental consent is illustrated by Matter of T.H., 484 N.E.2d 568 (Ind.1985); In re T.P., 475 N.E.2d 312 (Ind.1985); Matter of Moe, 18 Mass.App.Ct. 727, 469 N.E.2d 1312 (1984); Matter of Mary Moe, 15 Mass.App.Ct. 966, 446 N.E.2d 740 (1983); Matter of Mary Moe, 12 Mass.App.Ct. 298, 423 N.E.2d 1038 (1981). An Ohio statute was held unconstitutional under Belotti II by permitting too long a delay in obtaining judicial relief in Akron Center for Reproductive Health v. Rosen, 633 F.Supp. 1123 (N.D.Ohio 1986).

A city ordinance prohibiting a physician from performing an abortion on a woman under the age of fifteen unless he obtained the informed written consent of her parents or guardian, or unless she obtained a court order that the abortion be performed was held unconstitutional in City of Akron v. Akron Center for Reproductive Health, 462 U.S. 416, 103 S.Ct. 2481, 76 L.Ed.2d 687 (1983), on remand 604 F.Supp. 1268 (N.D.Ohio 1984).

64. H.L. v. Matheson, 450 U.S. 398, 101 S.Ct. 1164, 67 L.Ed.2d 388 (1981), 50 U.Cin.L.Rev. 867 (1982). The Chief Justice wrote the Court's opinion which was concurred in by Justices White and Rehnquist. Justices Powell, Stewart and Stevens concurred specially and Justices Marshall, Brennan and Blackmun dissented. Subsequent application of the Utah statute is illustrated in H___ B___ v. Wilkinson, 639 F.Supp. 952 (D.Utah 1986). See also Glick v. McKay, 616 F.Supp. 322 (D.Nev.1985); Indiana Planned Parenthood v. Pearson, 716 F.2d 1127 (7th Cir.1983).

required to notify her parents of her proposed abortion.[65]

The vigorous campaign against abortion has produced many statutes whose purpose is to regulate the physician performing abortion in ways which make it more difficult or more expensive to carry out the procedure. The Missouri statute of this kind was held unconstitutional in part by Planned Parenthood v. Danforth.[66] The section of the statute prohibiting the use of the saline amniocentesis technique for abortion after the first twelve weeks of pregnancy was held arbitrary on the ground that this method was safer than childbirth, other safe methods were not readily available and because other less safe methods were not forbidden. For these reasons this provision was held unconstitutional. In another perplexing provision the statute required the physician performing an abortion to exercise that care and skill to preserve the life of the fetus which he would be required to exercise in assisting at a live birth. This section carried manslaughter penalties and civil damages as sanctions. The Court found this to be excessively broad since it was not limited to a viable fetus, and therefore held it unconstitutional. A later Pennsylvania statute having the same purpose attempted to cure the defect by limiting the statute's impact to viable fetuses, but the Court held that unconstitutional also on the ground that it was ambiguous and vague, and that the standard of care provision was unconstitutionally vague.[67] Various reporting and record-keeping requirements and the requirement of a

prior written and "informed" consent in the Missouri statute were held constitutional in the Danforth case.[68]

The consent required in the Danforth case was no more than the normal consent required for many medical or surgical procedures. A later Akron, Ohio ordinance required consent to the abortion, but also required the physician to inform the woman in great detail concerning many of the aspects of her pregnancy and of the abortion, such as the development of the fetus, the date of viability, the complications resulting from abortions, the risks of her pregnancy, and the abortion technique to be employed. The Supreme Court held this ordinance unconstitutional.[69] The Court found that much of the information described had the purpose of persuading the woman not to have the abortion rather than to inform her consent, and interfered with the physician's discretion by requiring him to give information which might often be irrelevant to the particular woman's condition. Other information directly related to the patient's own pregnancy and to care following the abortion was held related to maternal health and the state's legitimate purposes, but the Court decided that it was unconstitutional to require that it be provided by the attending physician. It found that this form of counseling could be delegated to other qualified persons.[70]

The Akron case also held unconstitutional a requirement of the ordinance that abortions after the first trimester of pregnancy be performed in hospital, on the ground that this

---

65. This is the position taken by the dissent. See H.L. v. Matheson, 450 U.S. 398, 425, 426 n. 1, 101 S.Ct. 1164, 1179 n. 1, 67 L.Ed.2d 388 (1981). Nevertheless the Matheson and Bellotti II decisions make it somewhat more difficult for minors to obtain abortions especially since the state courts to whom the minor may have to apply have been given wide discretion in determining whether the abortion is in the minor's best interests. See In re T.P., 475 N.E.2d 312 (Ind.1985). Conversely, it has been held that the minor may not be ordered to have an abortion at the suit of her parents. In re Smith, 16 Md. App. 209, 295 A.2d 238 (1972); Matter of Mary P., 111 Misc.2d 532, 444 N.Y.S.2d 545 (Fam.Ct.1981).

66. 428 U.S. 52, 96 S.Ct. 2831, 49 L.Ed.2d 788 (1976). See also Wood and Durham, Counseling, Consulting, and Consent: Abortion and the Doctor-Patient Relationship, 1978 B.Y.U.L.Rev. 783.

67. Colautti v. Franklin, 439 U.S. 379, 99 S.Ct. 675, 58 L.Ed.2d 596 (1979).

68. See also Planned Parenthood Association v. Fitzpatrick, 401 F.Supp. 554 (E.D.Pa.1975), affirmed sub nom. Franklin v. Fitzpatrick, 428 U.S. 901, 96 S.Ct. 3202, 49 L.Ed.2d 1205 (1973).

69. City of Akron v. Akron Center for Reproductive Health, Inc., 462 U.S. 416, 103 S.Ct. 2481, 76 L.Ed.2d 687 (1983), on remand 604 F.Supp. 1268 (N.D.Ohio 1984). Plaintiffs making contentions like those in the Akron case and in other abortion cases may of course face difficult questions of standing, discussion of which is beyond the scope of this work. See, e.g., Diamond v. Charles, ___ U.S. ___, 106 S.Ct. 1697, 90 L.Ed.2d 48 (1986).

70. 462 U.S. at 448, 103 S.Ct. at 2502.

placed a significant obstacle of expense on the woman and was not necessary for protection of her health under available approved procedures.[71] Other provisions of the Akron ordinance imposing a twenty-four hour waiting period and dealing with the disposal of the remains of the fetus were also held unconstitutional as not being supported by a legitimate state interest and as being impermissibly vague.[72] The requirement of a Missouri statute that abortions performed after twelve weeks be done in a hospital was held unconstitutional in a companion case to City of Akron.[73] But the requirement in the same statute that a second physician be present at all abortions of viable fetuses was held constitutional as effectuating the state's interest in preserving the life of the viable fetus where that is possible.[74]

In 1986 the Supreme Court was faced with claims of unconstitutionality of the Pennsylvania abortion statute.[75] The "informed consent" provision of this statute was held unconstitutional on the authority of City of Akron, on the ground that it was designed to influence the woman not to have the abortion. Another section requiring that the attending physician make various reports concerning the viability of the fetus, and extensive information concerning the patient was also held unconstitutional as going beyond any legiti-

mate state interest in maternal health. The reports were to be available for copying in a form which would not make possible the identification of a person filing the report.[76] The Court distinguished between the Pennsylvania requirements and those approved in the Danforth case on the ground that in Danforth the statute was directly related to the preservation of material health.[77] Two other provisions requiring imposing a degree of care for postviability abortions and requiring a second physician to be present when the fetus is viable were also held unconstitutional, on the ground that they failed to accord paramount importance to maternal health, and that they failed to provide for a medical emergency in which the second physician might not be present, thereby risking the health of the woman.[78]

Another common form of attack on the performance of abortion has been addressed to abortion clinics. Zoning ordinances either prohibiting them outright or excluding them from business or other seemingly appropriate zones have usually been held unconstitutional as unduly burdening the woman's right to an abortion.[79] Although the Supreme Court has held that there is no violation of the constitution when a city chooses to provide publicly financed hospital services for childbirth without providing corresponding services for non-

71. 462 U.S. at 434, 103 S.Ct. at 2494.

72. 462 U.S. at 449, 451, 103 S.Ct. at 2502–2503. See also Margaret S. v. Edwards, 794 F.2d 994 (5th Cir.1986).

73. Planned Parenthood Association of Kansas City, Missouri, Inc. v. Ashcroft, 462 U.S. 476, 481, 103 S.Ct. 2517, 2520, 76 L.Ed.2d 733 (1983).

74. 462 U.S. at 482, 103 S.Ct. at 2520.

75. Thornburgh v. American College of Obstetricians and Gynecologists, ___ U.S. ___, 106 S.Ct. 2169, 90 L.Ed. 2d 779 (1986).

76. The Court, ___ U.S. at ___, 106 S.Ct. at 2182 found that the reports were sufficiently detailed that the woman's identity could in fact be discovered and that this might make her and her physician more reluctant to choose abortion.

77. ___ U.S. at ___, 106 S.Ct. at 2179.

78. ___ U.S. at ___, to ___, 106 S.Ct. at 2182 to 2184.

79. Deerfield Medical Center v. Deerfield Beach, 661 F.2d 328 (5th Cir.1981) (zoning ordinance invalid when it barred the abortion clinic from a business zone); Mahoning Women's Center v. Hunter, 610 F.2d 456 (6th Cir. 1979), judgment vacated 447 U.S. 918, 100 S.Ct. 3006, 65

L.Ed.2d 1110 (1980) (ordinance imposing expensive code regulations on abortion clinics unconstitutional); Planned Parenthood Association of Cincinnati, Inc. v. Cincinnati, 635 F.Supp. 469 (S.D.Ohio 1986) (fetal disposal ordinance unconstitutional); National Education Association of Rhode Island v. Garrahy, 598 F.Supp. 1374 (D.R.I. 1984), opinion affirmed 779 F.2d 790 (1st Cir.1986) (unconstitutional to exclude from comprehensive health insurance most induced abortions); Family Planning Clinic v. Cleveland, 594 F.Supp. 1410 (N.D.Ohio 1984) (ordinance forbidding abortion clinics in residence-office districts is invalid); West Side Women's Services, Inc. v. Cleveland, 573 F.Supp. 504 (N.D.Ohio 1983) (ordinance prohibiting abortion clinics in retail business districts unconstitutional); Village of Oak Lawn v. Marcowitz, 86 Ill.2d 406, 55 Ill.Dec. 916, 427 N.E.2d 36 (1981) (ordinance requiring a license of abortion clinics unconstitutional); Framingham Clinic v. Board of Selectmen of Southborough, 373 Mass. 279, 367 N.E.2d 606 (1977) (zoning law prohibiting abortion clinics unconstitutional). See also Birth Control Centers, Inc. v. Reizen, 743 F.2d 352 (6th Cir.1984), upholding some regulations and invalidating others.

therapeutic abortions,[80] the Eighth Circuit has held that a city could not prohibit staff physicians from performing abortions for paying patients at the only hospital in the community.[81] The court in the latter case distinguished the Supreme Court's decision on the ground that that case merely held that the city need not spend public funds for abortions, and that it did not hold that a city or state hospital could refuse to allow physicians to perform paid abortions on its premises. State prohibition of abortion referrals [82] or of advertisements for abortion services [83] have also been held unconstitutional. And in one case the organized campaign of obstruction and harassment aimed at an abortion clinic by physicians, hospitals and insurers was held to be actionable under the California constitution's guarantee of privacy.[84]

State and federal restrictions on the funding of abortions have led to discussions in the law reviews [85] and litigation in the courts, including the United States Supreme Court. The first of the Supreme Court cases, Beal v. Doe,[86] held that a Pennsylvania regulation limiting medicaid payments to those physicians performing abortions which were "medically necessary" [87] did not violate those provisions of the Social Security Act which set up the medicaid program and which authorized federal reimbursement to the states for medical care furnished to needy persons. The controlling federal statute said nothing specif-

ically about abortions but merely required that a state plan for medical assistance "include reasonable standards * * * for determining eligibility for and the extent of medical assistance under the plan which * * * are consistent with the objectives of" the Act.[88] Although the Court agreed that abortion was both cheaper and safer than childbirth, it held the exclusion of nontherapeutic abortions from medicaid was "reasonable" because of the state's interest in encouraging childbirth. At the same time the Court conceded that this state interest did not, until the third trimester, justify "unduly burdensome" state restrictions upon the woman's right of privacy. What this amounts to is that the Social Security Act permits "burdensome" but not "unduly burdensome" state limitations upon abortion. It is not clear from the opinion, which is indeed short and unenlightening, whether more extensive state limits on abortion, such as, for example, the complete exclusion of abortion from medicaid coverage, would violate the Social Security Act.[89] It is fair to say, however, that Beal v. Doe set the tone for the Supreme Court's treatment of the validity, statutory and constitutional, of abortion funding.

The companion case to Beal v. Doe was Maher v. Roe,[90] in which the Supreme Court held constitutional the Connecticut Welfare Department regulation which provided that abortions could be paid for out of state medi-

---

80. Poelker v. Doe, 432 U.S. 519, 97 S.Ct. 2391, 53 L.Ed.2d 528 (1977), on remand 558 F.2d 1346 (8th Cir. 1977).

81. Nyberg v. Virginia, 667 F.2d 754 (8th Cir.1982), appeal dismissed for want of jurisdiction and cert. denied 462 U.S. 1125, 103 S.Ct. 3102, 77 L.Ed.2d 1358 (1983).

82. Valley Family Planning v. North Dakota, 661 F.2d 99 (8th Cir.1981).

83. Meadowbrook Women's Clinic v. Minnesota, 557 F.Supp. 1172 (D.Minn.1983).

84. Chico Feminist Women's Health Center v. Butte Glenn Medical Society, 557 F.Supp. 1190 (E.D.Cal.1983).

85. Tribe, The Abortion Funding Conundrum: Inalienable Rights, Affirmative Duties, and the Dilemma of Dependence, 99 Harv.L.Rev. 330 (1985); Perry, Why the Supreme Court Was Plainly Wrong in the Hyde Amendment Case: A Brief Comment on Harris v. McRae, 32 Stan.L.Rev. 1113 (1980); Fahy, The Abortion Funding Cases: A Response to Professor Perry, 67 Geo.L.J. 1205 (1979); Yarborough, The Abortion-Funding Issue: A

Study in Mixed Constitutional Cues, 59 N.C.L.Rev. 611 (1981).

86. 432 U.S. 438, 97 S.Ct. 2366, 53 L.Ed.2d 464 (1977).

87. "Medically necessary" was defined by the regulation to mean abortions where the mother's health was threatened, or where the child would be deformed or mentally deficient, or where the pregnancy resulted from rape or incest.

88. 42 U.S.C.A. § 1396a(a)(17).

89. See Zbaraz v. Quern, 596 F.2d 196 (7th Cir.1979), cert. denied 448 U.S. 907, 100 S.Ct. 3048, 65 L.Ed.2d 1136 (1980), holding that Illinois could not restrict funding of abortions to an extent greater than the restrictions found in the applicable federal statute.

90. 432 U.S. 464, 97 S.Ct. 2376, 53 L.Ed.2d 484 (1977). Another companion case was Poelker v. Doe, 432 U.S. 519, 97 S.Ct. 2391, 53 L.Ed.2d 528 (1977), on remand 558 F.2d 1346 (8th Cir.1977), which held, on the authority of Maher v. Roe, that the refusal of the St. Louis authorities to permit abortions in the city hospital was not unconsti-

caid funds only if, in the physician's opinion, they were "medically necessary". The regulation defined "medically necessary" to include "psychiatric necessity".[91] The Court defined the issue in the case to be whether the regulation impinged upon a fundamental constitutional right. Recognizing that women do have such a fundamental right to abortion under Roe v. Wade,[92] the Court held that that case did not declare an "unqualified right" to an abortion, but rather protected the woman only from "unduly burdensome" state interference with her decision whether to abort or to bear a child. The Connecticut regulation, said the Court, placed no obstacle in the woman's path to an abortion and therefore did not restrict her fundamental right. Since for that reason the fundamental right-strict scrutiny formula did not apply, the regulation then had to be evaluated against the "less demanding" test of rationality. The Court held that the regulation passed this test because it vindicated the state's "legitimate interest in encouraging normal childbirth." [93] Justices Brennan, Marshall and Blackmun dissented from this decision on the ground that the regulation infringed the right of privacy of indigent women, forcing them to bear children they would not otherwise have without the justification of a compelling state interest.[94]

The Supreme Court's position on the funding of abortions taken in these earlier cases was reaffirmed in Harris v. McRae.[95] In 1980 Congress enacted what has come to be called the Hyde Amendment as an amendment to the appropriations bill for the Department of Health, Education and Welfare.[96] The Hyde

Amendment provided that none of the funds appropriated should be used to fund abortions except where the mother's life would otherwise be endangered, or for the victims of rape or incest where the rape or incest was promptly reported to a law enforcement agency. There had been earlier similar amendments which restricted abortion funding in somewhat less severe respects.[97] The Hyde Amendment for fiscal 1980 came before the Supreme Court in the Harris case. The Court first held that the medicaid provisions of the Social Security Act[98] did not require the states to fund all abortions for which funding reimbursement was not permitted by the Hyde Amendment. Its reasoning was that the Act was not intended by Congress to require in its plan any services for which a later Congress might withhold federal reimbursement. Although this "reasoning" merely restates the result, the Court did find support for it in the legislative history.

The more important decision in the Harris case was that the Hyde Amendment did not violate any constitutional provision, a decision which was based largely on Maher v. Roe.[99] The contention that this Amendment violated the Due Process Clause was rejected on the ground that although Roe v. Wade[1] forbids the state from interfering with a woman's freedom to end her pregnancy, it does not require the state to provide her with the means of doing so when the constraints which restrict her freedom "are the product not of governmental restrictions on access to abortions, but rather of her indigency." [2] As the Court put it, the Hyde Amendment left the indigent woman the same range of choice in

---

tutional. See the discussion of this case at note 80, supra.

91. 432 U.S. at 466, 97 S.Ct. at 2378.

92. See the discussion at note 38, supra.

93. 432 U.S. at 478, 97 S.Ct. at ___.

94. 432 U.S. at 482, 97 S.Ct. at ___.

95. 448 U.S. 297, 100 S.Ct. 2671, 65 L.Ed.2d 784 (1980), rehearing denied 448 U.S. 917, 101 S.Ct. 39, 65 L.Ed.2d 1180 (1980).

96. Pub.L. No. 96–123, § 109, 93 Stat. 926 (1979).

97. See Zbaraz v. Quern, 596 F.2d 196 (7th Cir.1979), cert. denied 448 U.S. 907, 100 S.Ct. 3048, 65 L.Ed.2d 1136

(1980), dealing with an earlier version of the Hyde Amendment.

98. Medicaid is provided for in Title XIX of the Social Security Act, more specifically 42 U.S.C.A. § 1396a(a)(17).

99. 432 U.S. 464, 97 S.Ct. 2376, 53 L.Ed.2d 484 (1977).

1. 410 U.S. 113, 93 S.Ct. 705, 35 L.Ed.2d 147 (1973), rehearing denied 410 U.S. 959, 93 S.Ct. 1409, 35 L.Ed.2d 694 (1973).

2. 448 U.S. at 316, 100 S.Ct. at 2687.

deciding whether to abort as she would have had if Congress had subsidized no health care costs at all. The Court also found that the Hyde Amendment did not violate the Establishment Clause of the First Amendment [3] because it had a secular purpose, even though its effect may have coincided with the tenets of the Catholic Church.[4] Finally, the Court held there was no violation of the Equal Protection Clause [5] because a) the indigent woman is not within a constitutionally suspect classification; and b) the Amendment bears a rational relation to a legitimate government objective, the protection of the life of the fetus.[6]

The Supreme Court's treatment of the abortion question reveals many surprises, ironies and political influences. Roe v. Wade [7] was surprising, at least to many lawyers, in its expansive application of the Griswold case,[8] and in its lack of any clearly articulated principle.[9] The opinion itself takes the form of a statute, laying down specific rules governing abortions. The rule with the greatest practical significance, that permitting abortion without qualification during the first trimester, bears a striking resemblance to the ancient common law treatment of abortion, according to which it was freely permitted until (at least) quickening.[10] But though Roe v. Wade may be open to criticism as a piece of judicial craftsmanship, it certainly expanded

the freedom of choice available to women in the United States at a time when that expansion was of the utmost importance to their self-realization. The decision seems also to have been the product of a recognition by the Court, whether conscious or unconscious it is hard to say, that public opinion was ready for an end to the earlier strict prohibitions upon abortion.[11]

It is ironical that the broad impact of Roe v. Wade, Danforth,[12] Akron,[13] and Thornburgh [14] should be in such sharp contrast with the Beal, Maher and Harris cases.[15] The reasoning in the three latter cases, so far as it attempts to distinguish the other cases, is forced, illogical and was contrary to the expectations of most of the lower courts who had faced the issues of state and federal funding limitations.[16] These cases have encouraged some of the states to impose their own limits on the funding of abortions, thereby augmenting the anti-abortion influence of the Supreme Court's opinions.[17] The emphasis in those opinions upon the state's interest in promoting childbirth over abortion is irreconcilable with the decision in Roe v. Wade, since that case held that for the first trimester the state was not constitutionally permitted to assert that interest. The distinction proposed by the Beal, Maher and Harris cases between those restrictions which burden the decision to abort and those which "unduly"

3. 448 U.S. at 317, 100 S.Ct. at 2688.

4. 448 U.S. at 319, 100 S.Ct. at 2689.

5. 448 U.S. at 321, 100 S.Ct. at 2690.

6. 448 U.S. at 324, 100 S.Ct. at 2692.

7. 410 U.S. 113, 93 S.Ct. 705, 35 L.Ed.2d 147 (1973), rehearing denied 410 U.S. 959, 93 S.Ct. 1409, 35 L.Ed.2d 694 (1973).

8. Griswold v. Connecticut, 381 U.S. 479, 85 S.Ct. 1678, 14 L.Ed.2d 510 (1965).

9. See Cox, The Supreme Court and Abortion, 2 Human Life Rev. 15, 18 (1976).

10. See the discussion at note 5, supra.

11. By 1973 several states, including New York, had passed liberal abortion laws, as indicated, supra, notes 26–30. And public opinion polls had demonstrated that nearly half of the public favored liberalized abortion laws. See, e.g., New York Times, January 28, 1973, page 45, column 3, for an account of such a poll.

12. Planned Parenthood of Central Missouri v. Danforth, 428 U.S. 52, 96 S.Ct. 2831, 49 L.Ed.2d 788 (1976).

13. City of Akron v. Akron Center for Reproductive Health, Inc., 462 U.S. 416, 103 S.Ct. 2481, 76 L.Ed.2d 687 (1983), on remand 604 F.Supp. 1268 (N.D.Ohio 1984).

14. Thornburgh v. American College of Obstetricians and Gynecologists, ___ U.S. ___, 106 S.Ct. 2169, 90 L.Ed. 2d 779 (1986).

15. See notes 86, 90, 95, supra.

16. See, e.g., Doe v. Wohlgemuth, 376 F.Supp. 173 (W.D.Pa.1974), cause remanded, judgment modified 523 F.2d 611 (3d Cir.1975), reversed 432 U.S. 438, 97 S.Ct. 2366, 53 L.Ed.2d 464 (1977); McRae v. Califano, 491 F.Supp. 630 (E.D.N.Y.1980).

17. E.g., Colo. Const. Art. V, § 50, prohibiting public funding for abortion, with the exception that the legislature may authorize funds for medical services to prevent the death of the pregnant woman or her unborn child. A similar proposed constitutional amendment was held invalid on the ground that the ballot name was improper in Arkansas Women's Political Caucus v. Riviere, 283 Ark. 463, 677 S.W.2d 846 (1984). See also Planned Parenthood of Central and Northern Arizona v. Arizona, 718 F.2d 938 (9th Cir.1983), appeal after remand 789 F.2d 1348 (1986).

burden it is hard to regard as seriously as its consequences demand. In the usual constitutional context the question is, what is the effect of the statute or regulation on the individual? Here the effect of the statute or regulation is to say to the indigent woman, we will pay your childbirth expenses but we will not pay for your abortion. One or the other of these medical procedures is obviously inevitable for the pregnant woman. So situated, the indigent pregnant woman has no choice. She must bear the child. If that does not "unduly" burden her decision to have an abortion, it must be because the term "unduly" is being used in some Pickwickian sense understood only by Supreme Court justices.

In short the practical result of the Supreme Court's abortion decisions has been to create a freedom of choice for women in America concerning whether to bear or not to bear a child, and almost at once to permit restrictions upon the exercise of that choice in practice which render it virtually non-existent for large numbers of indigent women in all states.[18] Although the legalization of abortion has had a significant influence in reducing our rate of population growth,[19] that influence is obviously not as great as it would have

been had abortion been available for women of all classes. To a shocking extent the result of the Supreme Court's efforts in this field has been to perpetuate the class distinctions which prevailed when abortion could not legally be obtained by any but wealthy and well connected women. Since denial of abortion and the birth of an unwanted child will often have serious psychological consequences for the child,[20] the harms inflicted by the Court's funding decisions are significant and long lasting.

At the present writing the future of abortion in the United States is an open issue. Several resolutions have been introduced in Congress proposing amendments to the Constitution which would either forbid all abortions or would severely limit them by providing that the fetus is a "person" from the moment of fertilization and entitled to the right to life.[21] Other methods of amending the Constitution initiated by the states may also be resorted to.[22] And of course the composition of the Supreme Court may well change in such a way as to lead to judicial restrictions upon, or even abolition, of abortion, by decisions overruling some or all of the earlier cases.

18. Over one million legal abortions were performed in the United States in 1975, but another half to three-quarters of a million women who wished abortions were unable to obtain them. It is still impossible for many poor, rural and teenage women to obtain abortions. Less than 20% of the public hospitals will perform abortions. Weinstock, Tietze, Jaffe, Dryfoos, Abortion Need and Services in the United States, 1974–1975, 8(2) Family Planning Perspectives 58 (1976); Pakter, Nelson, Svigir, Legal Abortion: A Half-Decade of Experience, 7(6) Family Planning Perspectives 248 (1975). In 1977 1.3 million abortions were performed in the United States, but 30% of women who wished abortions were unable to obtain them. Forrest, Tietze, Sullivan, Abortion in the United States, 1976–1977, 10(5) Family Planning Perspectives 27 (1978). The hardships of indigent women caused by the prohibition in medicaid funding for abortions are described in the New York Times, December 25, 1977, p. 20, col. 1.

19. Tietze, The Effect of Legalization of Abortion on Population Growth and Public Health, 7(3) Family Planning Perspectives 123 (1975).

20. Dytrych, Matejcek, Schuller, David, Friedman, Children Born to Woman Denied Abortion, 7(4) Family Planning Perspectives 165 (1975).

21. S.J. Res. 6, 94th Cong., 1st Sess. (1975), 121 Cong. Rec. 726 (1975), is the best known of the proposals and is

often referred to as the Helms Amendment, after Senator Helms, its sponsor. It is important to note that this proposal and those like it might well make it unlawful to use an intra-uterine device for contraception or any other device which operates to prevent the implantation of a fertilized ovum. This proposal would not permit an abortion even to save the mother's life. S.J. Res. 10, 94th Cong., 1st Sess. (1975), 121 Cong.Rec. 965 (1975), is the Buckley Amendment, and would permit an abortion to prevent the death of the mother. Still another proposed amendment would allow the states to restrict or prohibit abortion. For discussion of these proposals, see Goodman and Price, Abortion and the Constitution: An Examination of the Proposed Anti-Abortion Amendments, 7 Rutgers-Camden L.Rev. 671 (1976).

22. This involves requests from legislatures of two-thirds of the states to Congress asking that a convention be called for proposing amendments. Congress must then call the convention which may propose amendments, which may then be ratified by three-fourths of the state legislatures or by conventions in three-fourths of the states. See C. Antieau, Modern Constitutional Law §§ 12:173 to 12:179 (1969). Some state legislatures have passed resolutions of this kind. See the Kentucky Resolution in 120 Cong.Rec. 4594 (1974); West's La.Sess.L. Serv. 215 (1978); R.I. Acts and Resolves 123 (1977).

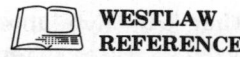

WESTLAW REFERENCES

Historical Background

di abortion

abortion /s unborn foetus fetus child /s quick! /s crime criminal!

Abortion as a Constitutional Question

people +s belous

griswold /s connecticut & di (constitution! unconstitutional! /p abortion)

find 93 sct 705

parent! /s consent! /s abortion /s juvenile child minor

bellotti /s baird

di(constitution! unconstitutional! /p abortion /s rape incest!)

abortion /s medicaid /s medical! /3 necess!

poelker /s doe

§ 5.4　Tort Claims Arising Out of Contraception, Sterilization and Abortion

Introduction

The phrase "wrongful life" has been coined to cover several kinds of tort claims which have some resemblance to each other, but which also have important differences. The first of these is a suit by an illegitimate child asking for damages from his parents or others to compensate him for the stigma or deprivation which the status of illegitimacy generally carries with it. These cases have been discussed in an earlier section.[1] Another kind of suit to which the same label is sometimes attached is that which arises when a man or woman engages a physician to perform an operation for sterilization or to supply contraceptive devices and a child is later born as a result of the physician's alleged negligence in performing the operation or in providing the contraception. This claim is made by the parents, not the child, and therefore involves quite different issues from those in the suit by the illegitimate child. It is sometimes also referred to as a suit for "wrongful birth" or "wrongful conception". A third type of claim arises when a woman gives birth to a defective or deformed or mentally retarded child as a result of the alleged negligence of her physician either in not preventing the birth or in not informing her of the risk that the child will not be normal. In that situation a suit may be brought by the parents or by the child. The parents' claim is similar to that asserted in the cases involving negligent failure to sterilize, although the elements of damage are different. The child's claim is similar to that asserted by the illegitimate child, in which he says he was wrongfully born, or born with a serious handicap. This section is concerned with the second and third of these types of suits, and with the claims brought by either the parents or the child.[2]

Possible Bases of Liability

Since the suits which are the subject of this section are brought against physicians, hospitals, occasionally pharmacists, or other medical personnel, they involve specific applications of the general principles which govern the tort liability of that sort of professional person or entity. The four legal theories upon which this sort of tort liability may be based are negligence, which is also often referred to under the general heading of malpractice; breach of express contract or warranty; absence of informed consent; and misrepresentation or fraud. Although a full treatment of these theories is beyond the scope of this work, a brief discussion of them, as they are relied on in assertions of liability for unwanted pregnancy, is essential to an understanding of the cases, and it therefore follows:

a. Negligence.

Negligence of a medical professional may be defined as conduct which lacks that degree of care, skill and knowledge which it is customary for ordinary physicians to exercise in sim-

---

§ 5.4

1. See section 4.5, supra. These cases and the cases which are the subject of this section are sometimes lumped together in discussion. Kashi, The Case of The Unwanted Blessing: Wrongful Life, 31 U.Miami.L.Rev. 1409 (1977).

2. A collection of cases dealing with these claims may be found in Annot., 83 A.L.R.3d 15 (1978).

ilar cases.[3] Endless variations of this standard are possible as well as considerable quibbling over its nuances. In recent years it has been seriously weakened by some courts.[4] One thoughtful article indicates its elements to be five:

"(1) a reasonable or ordinary degree of skill or learning;

"(2) commonly possessed and exercised by members of the profession

"(3) who are of the same school or system as the defendant

"(4) and who practice in the same or similar localities;

"(5) and exercise of the defendant's good judgment." [5]

The limitation as to the locality in which the defendant practices is inserted apparently on the theory that the country doctor is less skilled or has fewer facilities than the big city practitioner, but in the view of one authority the contemporary tendency is to minimize or abandon it and to impose a broad, general standard of competence.[6] When the physician represents himself as a specialist, in the cases here involved, for example, as a specialist in obstetrics and gynecology, he is held to the standard of skill and knowledge normally exercised by other OB–GYN specialists, presumably a somewhat higher standard than that of a general practitioner.[7]

This negligence theory of liability is sometimes confused by the courts with a theory based upon contract, usually an "implied contract". This confusion could and should be avoided, since an "implied undertaking" to use due care in the treatment of the patient is indistinguishable from ordinary negligence liability.[8] On the other hand, if a specific contract or warranty is asserted, it must be proved in express terms and vague claims of implied undertakings will not suffice.[9]

Negligence is the theory most often relied upon in the sterilization cases.[10] Some examples of conduct which could be found to be negligent when it resulted in an unwanted pregnancy include the removal of a section of an artery rather than a Fallopian tube, followed by an assumption that the tube had been blocked in any event;[11] the failure of a physician to warn the plaintiff that after their first child had died of a fatal hereditary kidney disease a later child might have the same disease;[12] the obvious case of the pharmacist who supplied a tranquillizer on a prescription for birth control pills;[13] and a physician's failure to diagnose a mother's illness as

3. W. Prosser and W. Keeton Handbook of the Law of Torts 185–193 (5th ed. 1984): Howard v. Lecher, 42 N.Y.2d 109, 397 N.Y.S.2d 363, 366 N.E.2d 64 (1977) (dissenting opinion); Shaheen v. Knight, 11 D. & C.2d 41 (Pa. County Court 1957); Note, Liability for Failure of Birth Control Methods, 76 Colum.L.Rev. 1187 (1976). The standard for the particular case is established, unless obvious even to a layman, by the expert testimony of other physicians. Cobbs v. Grant, 8 Cal.3d 229, 104 Cal.Rptr. 505, 502 P.2d 1 (1972); 2 F. Harper and F. James, The Law of Torts 968–969 (1956). See also Restatement (Second) of Torts § 299A, comments b, e (1965). But recent cases may be more liberal in admitting testimony as to the applicable standard. Brown v. Colm, 11 Cal.3d 639, 522 P.2d 688, 114 Cal.Rptr. 128 (1974).

4. See, e.g., Helling v. Carey, 83 Wash.2d 514, 519 P.2d 981 (1974), which appears to have been overruled by West's Rev.Code Wash.Ann. §§ 7.70.010 to 7.70.080 (Supp.1985).

5. McCoid, The Care Required of Medical Practitioners, 12 Vand.L.Rev. 549, 559 (1959). See also D. Louisell and H. Williams, Medical Malpractice §§ 8.04, 8.05 (1977).

6. W. Prosser and W. Keeton Handbook of the Law of Torts 187–188 (5th ed. 1984). A case which does include in the standard a reference to the locality in which the physician practices is Custodio v. Bauer, 251 Cal.App.2d 303, 59 Cal.Rptr. 463 (1967). See also Pearson, The Role of Custom in Medical Malpractice Cases, 51 Ind.L.J. 528 (1976); McCoid, The Care Required of Medical Practitioners, 12 Vand.L.Rev. 549, 569–575 (1959); D. Louisell and H. Williams, Medical Malpractice § 8.06 (1977); Annot., 99 A.L.R.3d 1133 (1980).

7. Restatement (Second) of Torts § 299A, comment d (1965); McCoid, The Care Required of Medical Practitioners, 12 Vand.L.Rev. 549, 566–569 (1959).

8. D. Louisell and H. Williams, Medical Malpractice § 8.03 (1977).

9. See the discussion infra, at note 24, and D. Louisell and H. Williams, Medical Malpractice § 8.10 (1977).

10. Annot., Malpractice in Relation to Contraception and Sterilization, 27 A.L.R.3d 906 (1969).

11. Martineau v. Nelson, 311 Minn. 92, 247 N.W.2d 409 (1976).

12. Park v. Chessin, 88 Misc.2d 222, 387 N.Y.S.2d 204 (1976), modified and affirmed 60 A.D.2d 80, 400 N.Y.S.2d 110 (2d Dep't 1977).

13. Troppi v. Scarf, 31 Mich.App. 240, 187 N.W.2d 511 (1971), 8 Wake Forest L.Rev. 159 (1971).

rubella which led to the birth of a deformed child.[14] The courts thus far seem to have been reluctant to charge physicians with negligence in failing to perform tests or to evaluate patients' medical histories sufficiently to engage in genetic counseling which would prevent the birth of defective children. Johnson v. Yeshiva University[15] held that it was not negligent for the physician not to perform an amniocentesis which would have revealed a fetus' chromosomal defect. Howard v. Lecher[16] assumed, when the case arose upon a motion to dismiss the complaint, that negligence was alleged in that the defendant failed to advise parents of the risk that a child would be born with Tay-Sachs disease, a genetic disease of the nervous system to which people of the plaintiffs' genetic background were particularly susceptible, but the court nevertheless refused to permit the child's parents to recover. As genetic counseling develops, however, this reluctance to recognize failure to engage in it as negligence may diminish, at least in those cases in which specialist may be expected to be familiar with the current learning on the subject.[17]

As with any claim based upon negligence, it must be proved that the negligence was the proximate cause of the injury. An application of this principle occurs in Renslow v. Mennonite Hospital,[18] in which a girl of thirteen was given a blood transfusion with Rh-positive blood when she had Rh-negative blood. Due to this alleged negligence, when the girl became pregnant eight years later, the baby was born with defects of the brain and nervous system. The court, in reversing a dismissal of the complaint, held that the effect upon the baby was reasonably foreseeable even though the child had not even been conceived at the time of transfusion, and that therefore a cause of action was stated. It should be obvious also that an argument that the plaintiff's sexual relations with her husband are an intervening cause cannot succeed, since this was the same act whose effect the sterilization was to prevent.[19] Presumably contributory negligence would be a defense to a malpractice claim wherever contributory negligence is still recognized. In Martineau v. Nelson[20] the court held that the plaintiffs were not contributorily negligent when they refused the offer of a vasectomy for the husband after it appeared that there was a possibility that the wife's own sterilization had not been effective.

b. Breach of Contract or Warranty.

Although it is unusual, it is possible for doctor and patient to contract for a specific result or for the doctor to guarantee a result.[21] Since there is considerable risk that the doctor's general statements aimed at reassuring

---

14. Dumer v. St. Michael's Hospital, 69 Wis.2d 766, 233 N.W.2d 372 (1975). The court held that this case was properly dismissed as against the hospital, since its employees are not responsible for making diagnoses, that being the physician's responsibility.

15. 53 A.D.2d 523, 384 N.Y.S.2d 455 (1st Dep't 1976), affirmed 42 N.Y.2d 818, 396 N.Y.S.2d 647, 364 N.E.2d 1340 (1977), rehearing denied 42 N.Y.2d, 398 N.Y.S.2d 1033, 368 N.E.2d 289 (1977). But see Park v. Chessin, supra, note 12.

16. 42 N.Y.2d 109, 397 N.Y.S.2d 363, 366 N.E.2d 64 (1977). Gleitman v. Cosgrove, 49 N.J. 22, 227 A.2d 689 (1967) held that a woman could not recover from the physician who failed to advise her of the risk that she might have a defective child as a result of having had rubella while pregnant, but the court was influenced by the fact that the plaintiff could not legally have obtained an abortion even if she had known of the risk.

17. Gildiner v. Thomas Jefferson University Hospital, 451 F.Supp. 692 (E.D.Pa.1978) denied a motion to dismiss the complaint, holding that a claim was stated for negligence in genetic counseling. For an argument in support of tort liability for negligent genetic counseling, see Note,

Father and Mother Know Best: Defining the Liability of Physicians for Inadequate Genetic Counseling, 87 Yale L.J. 1488 (1978). For a general discussion of genetic counseling, see P. Reilly, Genetics, Law, and Social Policy ch. 6 (1977).

18. 67 Ill.2d 348, 10 Ill.2d 348, 367 N.E.2d 1250 (1977).

19. Bishop v. Byrne, 265 F.Supp. 460 (S.D.W.Va.1967); Custodio v. Bauer, 251 Cal.App.2d 303, 59 Cal.Rptr. 463 (1967).

20. 311 Minn. 92, 247 N.W.2d 409 (1976).

There is a conflict in the cases concerning when the statute of limitations begins to run on such malpractice claims, some cases holding the period begins at the time of the negligence, others that it begins when the plaintiff discovers the operation was not effective. See Annot., 93 A.L.R.3d 218 (1979).

21. Robins v. Finestone, 308 N.Y. 543, 127 N.E.2d 330 (1955); Annot., Recovery Against Physician on Basis of Breach of Contract to Achieve Particular Result or Cure, 43 A.L.R.3d 1221 (1972); D. Louisell and H. Williams, Medical Malpractice § 8.10 (1977).

the patient may later be characterized as promises if the patient feels the result is unsatisfactory, the courts are skeptical of claims that an express contract has been made, and often require the claim to be supported by clear and convincing evidence.[22] This risk is particularly acute in the sterilization cases, since it is so easy to allege that the physician, in discussing the operation, warranted that there would be no chance of pregnancy as a result. Sterilization cases are sometimes brought as breach of contract actions, either to obtain a favorable statute of limitations or to avoid having to prove negligence.[23] Such claims are very carefully scrutinized by the courts.[24]

The law of warranty may also be asserted against the manufacturer of birth control pills or devices in the same manner as in other products liability cases.[25] The harm caused may either be the failure of the device to prevent conception, or the occurrence of harmful side effects. Where the plaintiff's suit is based upon the pill's failure to prevent conception, the claim is peculiarly susceptible to fabrication, since no evidence other than the plaintiff's own testimony will normally be available on the issue of whether the pill was

taken regularly in accordance with the manufacturer's directions. Perhaps this is partly the reason why, notwithstanding the great recent expansion in the liability of manufacturers for their products,[26] the courts have been unwilling to hold that drug companies warranted the effectiveness of birth control pills.[27] Some courts have also been reluctant to hold drug companies responsible for the harmful side effects which sometimes are produced by birth control pills or devices. Liability in such cases is asserted on several theories, including failure of the duty to warn, breach of implied warranty, breach of express warranty, negligence, fraud, and strict liability for a dangerous product. Two cases have granted summary judgments for the drug companies, on the ground that warnings addressed to physicians were adequate, that warnings covering the use of prescription drugs are properly addressed to the physician rather than the user, on the ground that no express warranties were made, on the ground that no negligence was proved in manufacture, and that no evidence proved that the pill was inherently dangerous.[28] Other cases have imposed liability on one or another of these theories.[29] Although the facts that the

22. Sullivan v. O'Connor, 363 Mass. 579, 296 N.E.2d 183 (1973).

23. Cf. Hackworth v. Hart, 474 S.W.2d 377 (Ky.1971), in which the court found that the statute of limitations was the same for all suits against physicians, whether based upon contract or tort.

In either the negligence or the contract case the statute of limitations only begins to run when the plaintiff learns of the negligence or the breach, or in the exercise of due diligence should have learned of it. Bishop v. Byrne, 265 F.Supp. 460 (S.D.W.Va.1967); Hackworth v. Hart, 474 S.W.2d 377 (Ky.1971); Hays v. Hall, 488 S.W.2d 412 (Tex. 1972).

24. Garcia v. Von Micsky, 602 F.2d 51 (2d Cir.1979); Bishop v. Byrne, 265 F.Supp. 460 (S.D.W.Va.1967) (summary judgment for defendant on the breach of contract or warranty claim); Herrera v. Roessing, 533 P.2d 60 (Colo. App.1975) (statements after surgery just reassurances, not warranties, and without consideration); Rogala v. Silva, 16 Ill.App.3d 63, 305 N.E.2d 571 (1973) (contract must be set forth explicitly in the complaint and proved by clear and convincing evidence); Clevenger v. Haling, 379 Mass. 154, 394 N.E.2d 1119 (1979) (doctor's statements held not to constitute a contract); Clegg v. Chase, 89 Misc.2d 510, 391 N.Y.S.2d 966 (1977) (warranty claim dismissed); Shaheen v. Knight, 11 Pa.D. & C.2d 41 (Pa. County Ct.1957) (no warranty of cure will be implied);

Annot., Recovery Against Physician on Basis of Breach of Contract to Achieve Particular Result or Cure, 43 A.L.R.3d 1221, 1251 (1972).

25. Annot., Liability of Manufacturer or Seller For Injury or Death Allegedly Caused by Use of Contraceptive, 70 A.L.R.3d 315 (1976); Note, Unwanted Pregnancy and the Pill—The Question of Liability of the Manufacturer, 41 U.Cin.L.Rev. 335 (1972).

26. E.g., Henderson, Expanding the Negligence Concept: Retreat from the Rule of Law, 51 Ind.L.J. 467 (1976).

27. Whittington v. Eli Lilly & Co., 333 F.Supp. 98 (S.D.W.Va.1971) held that the defendant's statement in a pamphlet that the pill was "virtually" 100% effective did not constitute a warranty of effectiveness. The court said that the manufacturer cannot be held to insure the pill's effectiveness.

28. Dunkin v. Syntex Laboratories, Inc., 443 F.Supp. 121 (W.D.Tenn.1977); Chambers v. G.D. Searle & Co., 441 F.Supp. 377 (D.Md.1975), affirmed on the district court's opinion 567 F.2d 269 (4th Cir.1977). A case which held that a claim was alleged on the basis of failure to warn of the risks is Jorgenson v. Meade Johnson Laboratories, Inc., 483 F.2d 237 (10th Cir.1973).

29. Cases are collected in Annot., Liability of Manufacturer or Seller For Injury or Death Allegedly Caused

drugs must be approved by the United States Food and Drug Administration and that the warnings are likewise subject to federal scrutiny do not necessarily protect the manufacturer from civil liability, it does seem that they should lead the courts to be cautious in their acceptance of damage claims in such cases.[30]

c. Lack of Informed Consent.

One aspect of the physician's duty of care is his obligation to disclose to the patient the extent of the risks and consequences of the treatment which is proposed.[31] Formerly the failure to obtain an informed consent from the patient meant that the physician would be liable for an operation without consent, or in other words, a battery,[32] but today this is treated as a form of medical malpractice so that the physician is liable for all of the harmful consequences of the operation as in other malpractice cases.[33] Several cases have found liability where the physician failed to warn a woman of the risks of continuing a pregnancy,[34] or where he failed to advise her fully of the statistical probability that sterilization might not be effective.[35] Since the danger of trumped up claims is as great here as in the case of an alleged warranty, and since there may be good reason for not dwelling upon the risks of the operation to a degree which frightens the patient, the courts should require the same clear and convincing evidence that informed consent was not obtained as is required for proof of an express warranty.[36]

d. Fraud or Deceit.

False representations by the physician to the patient may also be the basis for a suit against the physician.[37] Only two of the sterilization cases have been based upon allegations of deceit. In one of these, Custodio v. Bauer,[38] the court found that the elements of a case for deceit had been properly alleged. These included allegations that (a) the physician made representations of material facts; (b) the representations were false; (c) the physician knew they were false or at least did not believe them to be true; (d) the representations were intended to induce action by the plaintiff; and (e) the plaintiff acted in reliance on the representations to his or her damage. The other case, Christensen v. Thornby,[39] held that none of the elements of an action for deceit had been alleged and therefore sustained a demurrer to the complaint. It seems very unlikely that the necessary fraud allegations could be proved in most sterilization cases. If fraud is alleged, the claim should be subjected to the same strict requirements of proof which have been made for claims of express warranty.[40]

"Public Policy" and Damages

The crucial issue which has to be faced when claims of negligence in sterilization are made is whether, even if one or more of the

by Use of Contraceptive, 70 A.L.R.3d 315 (1976). A physician may also be liable for prescribing birth control pills where they cause injury to the woman. Annot., 9 A.L.R.4th 372 (1981).

30. Note, Unwanted Pregnancy and the Pill—The Question of Liability of the Manufacturer, 41 U.Cin.L. Rev. 335 (1972) presents other arguments against the manufacturer's liability in these cases.

31. W. Prosser and W. Keeton, Handbook of the Law of Torts 189–190 (5th ed. 1984); Annot., Malpractice: Physician's Duty to Inform Patient of Nature and Hazards of Treatment in Pregnancy and Childbirth Cases Under the Doctrine of Informed Consent, 69 A.L.R.3d 1250 (1976).

32. D. Louisell, H. Williams, Medical Malpractice § 8.09 (1977); Karlsons v. Guerinot, 57 A.D.2d 73, 394 N.Y.S.2d 933 (4th Dep't 1977).

33. W. Prosser and W. Keeton, Handbook of the Law of Torts 189–190 (5th ed. 1984).

34. Park v. Chessin, 88 Misc.2d 222, 387 N.Y.S.2d 204 (1976), modified and affirmed 60 A.D.2d 80, 400 N.Y.S.2d 110 (2d Dep't 1977); Jacobs v. Theimer, 519 S.W.2d 846 (Tex.1975); Dumer v. St. Michael's Hospital, 69 Wis.2d 766, 233 N.W.2d 372 (1975).

35. Custodio v. Bauer, 251 Cal.App.2d 303, 59 Cal. Rptr. 463 (1967); Sard v. Hardy, 281 Md. 432, 379 A.2d 1014 (1977) (physician failed to mention vasectomy as a method of birth control, and also failed to tell the plaintiff the failure rates of various methods of female sterilization, directed verdict for the defendant reversed).

36. See notes 23, 24, supra.

37. D. Louisell, H. Williams, Medical Malpractice § 8.11 (1977).

38. 251 Cal.App.2d 303, 59 Cal.Rptr. 463 (1967).

39. 192 Minn. 123, 255 N.W. 620 (1934).

40. See note 24, supra.

recognized theories of physicians' liability have been alleged and proved, the case is one in which the courts should give relief. This question may be phrased as one of standing to bring the suit, or as one of damages, or as one controlled by that vaguest of all legal principles, "public policy". Put in specific terms, the question is whether, and how much, a particular plaintiff should recover when medical procedures for the prevention of pregnancy have failed or been made unavailable due to the legal fault of a physician or other health professional.

Where the physician's negligence has resulted in the birth of a defective or retarded or otherwise less than normal child, an important New York case has taken the position that the child's parents may not recover for their emotional distress from the allegedly negligent physician, on the ground that such a recovery would extend traditional tort concepts beyond manageable limits, and also on the ground that a parent may not recover for the emotional suffering to which he is subjected when physical harm is negligently inflicted upon his child.[41] In this case the alleged negligence was that the physician had failed to take a complete genealogical history, which would have revealed that there was a risk that the child would have Tay-Sachs disease. If the history had been taken, the contention was, the likelihood of the disease would have been known to the parents and the mother would have had an abortion. As it turned out, the child was born with this progressive degenerative disease and died within two years of birth. In other similar cases relief has been denied on the ground that at the time the physician's negligence occurred abortion was not legal in the state.[42] But some cases do permit the father and mother of the retarded child to recover for negligent failure to diagnose the mother's illness as rubella, or to perform tests which would reveal that the child would be abnormal, provided that the plaintiffs prove that the mother would have been able to obtain an abortion and that she would in fact have obtained one.[43] The court in one such case held only that the medical and hospital expenses occasioned by the child's birth defects could be recovered.[44] No claim was made for the mental suffering caused by the wife's bearing a retarded child.

41. Howard v. Lecher, 42 N.Y.2d 109, 397 N.Y.S.2d 363, 366 N.E.2d 64 (1977). Contra, allowing recovery for mental anguish: Smith v. Cote, 128 N.H. 231, 513 A.2d 341 (1986) (but the parents were not permitted to recover the expenses of raising the child); Berman v. Allan, 80 N.J. 421, 404 A.2d 8 (1979). See also Capron, Tort Liability in Genetic Counseling, 79 Colum.L.Rev. 618 (1979).

42. Stewart v. Long Island College Hospital, 35 A.D.2d 531, 313 N.Y.S.2d 502 (2d Dep't 1970), affirmed 30 N.Y.2d 695, 332 N.Y.S.2d 640, 283 N.E.2d 616 (1972). But Jacobs v. Theimer, 519 S.W.2d 846 (Tex.1975) held that the parents had a claim against the physician who failed to diagnose rubella, even though at that time abortion was not legally available in Texas in those circumstances.

43. Phillips v. United States, 575 F.Supp. 1309 (D.S.C.1983) (South Carolina law); Gildiner v. Thomas Jefferson University Hospital, 451 F.Supp. 692 (E.D.Pa. 1978) (Pennsylvania law); Blake v. Cruz, 108 Idaho 253, 698 P.2d 315 (1984); Siemieniec v. Lutheran Gen. Hosp., 134 Ill.App.3d 823, 89 Ill.Dec. 484, 480 N.E.2d 1227 (1985); Goldberg v. Ruskin, 128 Ill.App.3d 1029, 84 Ill.Dec. 1, 471 N.E.2d 530 (1984), judgment affirmed on another point, 113 Ill.2d 482, 101 Ill.Dec. 818, 499 N.E.2d 406 (1986); Smith v. Cote, 128 N.H. 231, 513 A.2d 341 (1986); Berman v. Allan, 80 N.J. 421, 404 A.2d 8 (1979) (parents may recover only for their emotional distress); Becker v. Schwartz, 46 N.Y.2d 401, 413 N.Y.S.2d 895, 386 N.E.2d 807 (1978); Speck v. Finegold, 497 Pa. 77, 439 A.2d 110 (1981) (parents may recover for expense of care, and for emotional distress); Stribling v. de Quevedo, 288 Pa. Super. 436, 432 A.2d 239 (1980) (negligent sterilization led to birth of a child with a physical defect); Naccash v. Burger, 223 Va. 406, 290 S.E.2d 825 (1982); Harbeson v. Parke-Davis, Inc., 98 Wash.2d 460, 656 P.2d 483 (1983) (parents may recover for medical expenses of birth and those attributable to the child's defective condition and for their mental distress); James G. v. Caserta, ___ W.Va. ___, 332 S.E.2d 872 (1985); Dumer v. St. Michael's Hospital, 69 Wis.2d 766, 233 N.W.2d 372 (1975).

Schroeder v. Perkel, 87 N.J. 53, 432 A.2d 834 (1981), held that parents could recover the expenses of therapy for the negligence of a physician in failing to diagnose cystic fibrosis in their first child when a second child was born with the disease. Azzolino v. Dingfelder, 315 N.C. 103, 337 S.E.2d 528 (1985), cert. denied ___ U.S. ___, 107 S.Ct. 131, 93 L.Ed.2d 75 (1986) held that the siblings of a Down's Syndrome child could not recover from a physician who allegedly negligently failed to provide adequate prenatal information to their mother, as a result of which she did not have an abortion, citing other cases.

44. Dumer v. St. Michael's Hospital, 69 Wis.2d 766, 233 N.W.2d 372 (1975). In this case the plaintiff-parents asked only for medical, hospital and treatment expenses occasioned by the child's deformity. Since the parents would presumably have desired a normal child, only the additional expense of caring for the abnormal child should be the basis for the damages. To the same effect is Moores v. Lucas, 405 So.2d 1022 (Fla.App.1981).

It is difficult to articulate persuasive reasons for denying recovery to the parents in these cases. They should at least recover their out of pocket expenses for the care of the child to the extent that these exceed the expense of caring for a normal child.[45] The reasoning of *Howard v. Lecher*,[46] that this is an unwarranted extension of tort law will hardly do. The liability is well within the normal tort principles. The one real difficulty with permitting recovery is that the assertion that the mother would have had an abortion may be an afterthought indulged in for litigation purposes. Evidence of this should therefore be required to be clear and convincing. As for the claim that mental anguish cannot be compensated when caused by negligent injury to a third person, the dissent in *Howard v. Lecher* argues that the negligent injury is not inflicted upon a third person, but on the mother at a time when she is pregnant.[47] She is the patient and it is she who is not informed of the risks of continuing the pregnancy. The majority's refusal to permit

damages to compensate her for her mental suffering as well as for her expenses is therefore not justified.

A different issue is raised when the suit against the physician is brought by the defective child. His claim is that, due to the alleged negligence of the physician or hospital, he was born with a deformity or birth defect and that if the negligence had not occurred his parents could have prevented his being born at all. If this claim is recognized, the court is placed in the impossible position of attempting to determine whether the suffering endured by the deformed or defective child is greater than the harm which would have been done him if he had not been born at all, and if so, to assess the difference in dollars. The question to be answered is whether it is better not to be born than to be born with a birth defect of greater or lesser seriousness. Since this is an essentially unanswerable question, it is not surprising that most courts have held that the child has no cause of action in such cases.[48] This is of

45. See note 44, supra.

46. See note 41, supra. New York now permits recovery for the parents' expenses in caring for the child. Becker v. Schwartz, 46 N.Y.2d 401, 413 N.Y.S.2d 895, 386 N.E.2d 807 (1978).

47. Howard v. Lecher, 42 N.Y.2d 109, 113, 397 N.Y.S.2d 363, 366, 366 N.E.2d 64, 66 (1977). Karlsons v. Guerinot, 57 A.D.2d 73, 394 N.Y.S.2d 933 (4th Dep't 1977) makes the same point, but presumably it has been overruled by Howard v. Lecher.

48. Gildiner v. Thomas Jefferson University Hospital, 451 F.Supp. 692 (E.D.Pa.1978) (Pennsylvania law); Elliott v. Brown, 361 So.2d 546 (Ala.1978); Moores v. Lucas, 405 So.2d 1022 (Fla.App.1981); Blake v. Cruz, 108 Idaho 253, 698 P.2d 315 (1984); Goldberg By and Through Goldberg v. Ruskin, 128 Ill.App.3d 1029, 84 Ill.Dec. 1, 471 N.E.2d 530 (1984), judgment affirmed 113 Ill.2d 482, 101 Ill.Dec. 818, 499 N.E.2d 406 (1986); Eisbrenner v. Stanley, 106 Mich.App. 357, 308 N.W.2d 209 (1981); Strohmaier v. Associates in Obstetrics & Gynecology, 122 Mich.App. 116, 332 N.W.2d 432 (1982); Berman v. Allan, 80 N.J. 421, 404 A.2d 8 (1979); Smith v. Cote, 128 N.H. 231, 513 A.2d 341 (1986); Schroeder v. Perkel, 87 N.J. 53, 432 A.2d 834 (1981); Stewart v. Long Island College Hospital, 35 A.D.2d 531, 313 N.Y.S.2d 502 (2d Dep't 1970), affirmed 30 N.Y.2d 695, 332 N.Y.S.2d 640, 283 N.E.2d 616 (1972); Karlsons v. Guerinot, 57 A.D.2d 73, 394 N.Y.S.2d 933 (4th Dep't 1977); Azzolino v. Dingfelder, 315 N.C. 103, 337 S.E.2d 528 (1985), cert. denied ___ U.S. ___, 107 S.Ct. 131, 93 L.Ed.2d 75 (1986); Speck v. Finegold, 497 Pa. 77, 439 A.2d 110 (1981) (by an equally divided court); Nelson v. Krusen, 635 S.W.2d 582 (Tex.App.1982), judgment affirmed in part, reversed in part 678 S.W.2d 918 (1984);

James G. v. Caserta, ___ W.Va. ___, 332 S.E.2d 872 (1985); Dumer v. St. Michael's Hospital, 69 Wis.2d 766, 233 N.W.2d 372 (1975). Allowing recovery: Curlender v. Bio-Science Laboratories, 106 Cal.App.3d 811, 165 Cal.Rptr. 477 (1980). But see Foy v. Greenblott, 141 Cal.App.3d 1, 190 Cal.Rptr. 84 (1983).

In Turpin v. Sortini, 31 Cal.3d 220, 182 Cal.Rptr. 337, 643 P.2d 954 (1982) the court denied general damages on the grounds advanced in the text, but quite inconsistently held that the child could recover special damages, that is, the cost of treating the hereditary defect, thereby apparently overruling Curlender, cited in the preceding paragraph. Siemieniec v. Lutheran Gen. Hosp., 134 Ill.App. 3d 823, 89 Ill.Dec. 484, 480 N.E.2d 1227 (1985); Procanik By Procanik v. Cillo, 97 N.J. 339, 478 A.2d 755 (1984), on remand 206 N.J.Super. 270, 502 A.2d 94 (1985). Azzolino v. Dingfelder, 71 N.C.App. 289, 322 S.E.2d 567 (1984) reach similar results.

A different type of claim was held maintainable by the child in Renslow v. Mennonite Hospital, 67 Ill.2d 348, 10 Ill.Dec. 484, 367 N.E.2d 1250 (1977) where the child's mother, long before the pregnancy, had been given a blood transfusion with Rh-positive blood when her blood was Rh-negative, causing the child to have birth defects. Here the child was not asserting that she should not have been born but that the negligence of the physician, occurring some eight years before the child's conception, had later caused the birth defects. The damages in this sort of case are manageable. Similar cases include Bergstreser v. Mitchell, 577 F.2d 22 (8th Cir.1978); Jorgenson v. Meade Johnson Laboratories, Inc., 483 F.2d 237 (10th Cir.1973); Harbeson v. Parke-Davis, Inc., 98 Wash.2d 460, 656 P.2d 483 (1983). Albala v. New York, 54 N.Y.2d 269,

course the same result reached in other "wrongful birth" cases, in which the illegitimate child asserts that he would be better off not having been born than being born a bastard.[49] The harm of which the child complains is beyond the courts' powers to evaluate.

An entirely different sort of harm is complained of by the parents who have a normal, healthy child as a consequence of a physician's negligence in performing a vasectomy or a tubal ligation. The injury of which they complain is not the grief, anguish and additional expense of caring for a retarded or defective child, but just the cost of feeding, clothing and educating one more child. The assertion that the physician has inflicted an injury upon them in this fashion runs counter to the traditional view that a major purpose of marriage is to have children,[50] and that children are a source of pleasure, comfort and support, moral and material, to their parents.[51] Courts in the various states have recognized the value of children to their parents

by construing wrongful death statutes to permit the award of damages to the parent for the pecuniary loss he suffers when his child is negligently killed,[52] although it is clear that today most children are a financial liability rather than an asset.[53] In a growing number of states wrongful death awards may in addition include sums to compensate the parent for such non-pecuniary harm as the loss of society, companionship or affection of his child.[54] And some courts are now holding that wrongful death claims may be made when the defendant's negligence causes the destruction of a viable unborn child.[55]

In the face of so much authority attesting to the importance of children to their parents, how can a parent be heard to complain that he was harmed by the birth of a child? Some courts have answered the question by holding that a parent cannot, as a matter of law, be damaged when a child is born as the result of a physician's negligence respecting contraception or sterilization.[56] According to these cases no damages can be awarded either be-

---

445 N.Y.S.2d 108, 429 N.E.2d 786 (1981) erroneously denied recovery in a case analytically similar to Renslow.

The child's claim is discussed in Note, 39 Alb.L.Rev. 221, 233 (1975), and an argument for the child's recovery is made in Capron, Tort Liability in Genetic Counseling, 79 Colum.L.Rev. 618 (1979).

49. See section 4.5, supra.

50. E.g., Reynolds v. Reynolds, 85 Mass. (3 Allen) 605, 610 (1862): " * * * one of the leading and most important objects of marriage under our laws is the procreation of children * * *" Kreyling v. Kreyling, 20 N.J.Misc. 52, 56, 23 A.2d 800, 803 (1942): "The controlling purpose of marriage is to enable the sexes to gratify lawfully the natural desire for procreation which has been implanted in them, that the race may be preserved upon the earth."

51. "Lo, children are an heritage of the Lord: and the fruit of the womb is his reward. As arrows are in the hand of a mighty man; so are children of his youth. Happy is the man that hath his quiver full of them * * *" Bible, Psalms, Ch. 127, Verses 3–5. See also Cockrum v. Baumgartner, 95 Ill.2d 193, 69 Ill.Dec. 168, 447 N.E.2d 385 (1983), cert. denied 464 U.S. 846, 104 S.Ct. 149, 78 L.Ed.2d 139 (1983).

52. W. Prosser and W. Keeton, Handbook of the Law of Torts 949–956 (5th ed. 1984).

53. Wycko v. Gnodtke, 361 Mich. 331, 105 N.W.2d 118 (1960) explicitly recognized that in our society a child is a financial burden to his parents, not a benefit. The court nevertheless approved damages of $14,000 for the wrongful death of a child on the ground that this was the value of the child's companionship and society. See also F. Harper, F. James, The Law of Torts 1330–1331 (1956).

Espenshade, The Value and Cost of Children, 32 Population Bulletin 3 (1977) calculates the total direct costs of raising a child in the United States in 1977 as ranging between $44,000 and $64,000, and also estimates the earnings which the wife would have to forego in order to care for a child as between $34,000 and $54,000.

54. E.g., West's Rev.Code Wash.Ann. § 4.24.010 (Supp. 1985); Wilson v. Lund, 80 Wash.2d 91, 491 P.2d 1287 (1971). See also Finkelstein, Pickrel, Glasser, The Death of Children: A Nonparametric Statistical Analysis of Compensation for Anguish, 74 Colum.L.Rev. 884 (1974); Speiser, Malawer, American Tragedy: Damages for Mental Anguish of Bereaved Relatives in Wrongful Death Actions, 51 Tul.L.Rev. 1 (1976).

55. Presley v. Newport Hospital, 117 R.I. 177, 365 A.2d 748 (1976); Moen v. Hanson, 85 Wash.2d 597, 537 P.2d 266 (1975). Contra: Justus v. Atchison, 19 Cal.3d 564, 139 Cal.Rptr. 97, 565 P.2d 122 (1977). Other cases on both sides of this question are collected in Annot., 15 A.L.R.3d 992 (1967).

56. La Point v. Shirley, 409 F.Supp. 118 (W.D.Tex. 1976) (Texas Law); Boone v. Mullendore, 416 So.2d 718 (Ala.1982); Coleman v. Garrison, 349 A.2d 8 (Del.1975); Public Health Trust v. Brown, 388 So.2d 1084 (Fla.App. 1980), review denied 399 So.2d 1140 (Fla.1981); Cockrum v. Baumgartner, 95 Ill.2d 193, 69 Ill.Dec. 168, 447 N.E.2d 385 (1983), cert. denied 464 U.S. 846, 104 S.Ct. 149, 78 L.Ed.2d 139 (1983); Byrd v. Wesley Medical Center, 237 Kan. 215, 699 P.2d 459 (1985); Weintraub v. Brown, 98 A.D.2d 339, 470 N.Y.S.2d 634 (2d Dep't 1983); Clegg v. Chase, 89 Misc.2d 510, 391 N.Y.S.2d 966 (1977); Shaheen v. Knight, 11 D. & C.2d 41 (Pa.County Ct.1957); Terrill v. Garcia, 496 S.W.2d 124 (Tex.Civ.App.1973), cert. denied

cause as a matter of legal doctrine the birth of a child is a blessing, not a burden, or because it is incongruous for the physician to be paying for the support of a child not his own who is being cared for and educated and enjoyed by the child's parents.[57]

The most obvious and far-reaching tendency in contemporary domestic relations law has been the breakdown of general principles and the substitution, in the place of those principles, of highly individualized decisions. This tendency is reflected in the number of cases which do permit the parents of the unwanted child to recover damages, including in some instances the cost of supporting the child to maturity, from the negligent physi-

cian or medical professional.[58] These cases take the position that the only relevant factor is the desire of the individual plaintiffs to avoid further childbearing. Conceding that many parents do consider their children a benefit rather than a burden, these courts accept the fact that many other parents do not wish to have children, or more often do not wish to have more children, and that when an unwanted child is born it is a burden both to the parents and to the other children in the family. As evidence that parents today do not universally desire children in unlimited numbers, the courts point to the widespread use of contraceptives.[59] They cite the Supreme Court's cases on abortion and contraception as holding that there is a constitu-

415 U.S. 927, 94 S.Ct. 1434, 39 L.Ed.2d 484 (1974); McKernan v. Aasheim, 102 Wash.2d 411, 687 P.2d 850 (1984); James G. v. Caserta, ___ W.Va. ___, 332 S.E.2d 872 (1985); Rieck v. Medical Protective Co. of Fort Wayne, Ind., 64 Wis.2d 514, 219 N.W.2d 242 (1974). The early case of Christensen v. Thornby, 192 Minn. 123, 255 N.W. 620 (1934), denied relief in part on the argument that the plaintiff had been blessed with the fatherhood of another child, but the later Minnesota cases do not characterize this as an authority rejecting the parent's claim. See the cases cited in note 58, infra. Wilczynski v. Goodman, 73 Ill.App.3d 51, 29 Ill.Dec. 216, 391 N.E.2d 479 (1979), allowed a mother to recover the expenses of childbirth after a negligent and ineffective abortion, but not the expenses of caring for the unwanted child.

57. See Rieck v. Medical Protective Co., 64 Wis.2d 514, 219 N.W.2d 242 (1974), which also argues that the liability imposed in such cases would be wholly out of proportion to the physician's culpability, as does Berman v. Allan, 80 N.J. 421, 404 A.2d 8 (1979), and P. v. Portadin, 179 N.J.Super. 465, 432 A.2d 556 (1981). The Berman case does permit the parents to recover for their emotional anguish caused when the child was born with Down's Syndrome, however. See also White v. United States, 510 F.Supp. 146 (D.Kan.1981) (Georgia law), citing other cases.

58. University of Arizona v. Superior Court, 136 Ariz. 579, 667 P.2d 1294 (1983); Custodio v. Bauer, 251 Cal. App.2d 303, 59 Cal.Rptr. 463 (1967); Anonymous v. Hospital, 33 Conn.Supp. 125, 366 A.2d 204 (1976); Jones v. Malinowski, 299 Md. 257, 473 A.2d 429 (1984); Sherlock v. Stillwater Clinic, 260 N.W.2d 169 (Minn.1977); Martineau v. Nelson, 311 Minn. 92, 247 N.W.2d 409 (1976); Green v. Sudakin, 81 Mich.App. 545, 265 N.W.2d 411 (1978); Troppi v. Scarf, 31 Mich.App. 240, 187 N.W.2d 511 (1971), 8 Wake Forest L.Rev. 159 (1971); Betancourt v. Gaylor, 136 N.J.Super. 69, 344 A.2d 336 (1975); Rivera v. State, 94 Misc.2d 157, 404 N.Y.S.2d 950 (Ct.Cl.1978); Ziemba v. Sternberg, 45 A.D.2d 230, 357 N.Y.S.2d 265 (4th Dep't 1974). Other cases are cited and discussed in Annot., 27 A.L.R.3d 906 (1969); Note, Liability for Failure of Birth Control Methods, 76 Colum.L.Rev. 1187 (1976); Note, Redressing a Blessing: The Question of

Damages for Negligently Performed Sterilization Operations, 33 U.Pitt.L.Rev. 886 (1972).

Hartke v. McKelway, 707 F.2d 1544 (D.C.Cir.1983), cert. denied 464 U.S. 983, 104 S.Ct. 425, 78 L.Ed.2d 360 (1983), citing many cases, has held that where the wife sought sterilization for therapeutic reasons, because she feared pregnancy, and where the birth of the child turned out to be a "positive experience" for her, the parents could not recover the cost of rearing a healthy child. But there are suggestions in the opinion that if the reason for seeking sterilization is to avoid the expense of rearing the child, particularly where the parents' financial situation changed in reliance on the sterilization, then the child-rearing expenses might be recoverable. On the other hand the court also said that the defendant should be permitted to introduce evidence of the benefits accruing from the child's birth in mitigation of damages. But it expressly refused to rule on whether the availability of abortion or adoption would justify reducing or denying damages.

Boone v. Mullendore, 416 So.2d 718 (Ala.1982) held that although the cost of raising the child could not be recovered, the parents could recover their medical expenses, and damages for physical and mental suffering from the pregnancy and for impairment of the husband's rights of consortium caused by the pregnancy.

It has been held that the statute of limitations on such claims begins to run when the pregnancy of the woman is discovered. Christ v. Lipsitz, 99 Cal.App.3d 894, 160 Cal. Rptr. 498 (1979).

A few states have attempted to deal with these questions by statute, but it is far from clear what effect the statutes would have where the parent is suing for negligent sterilization and a healthy child was born, except that they do seem to foreclose any defense based on the availability of abortion. E.g., Minn.Stat.Ann. § 145.424 (Supp.1984); S.D.Codif.L. §§ 21–55–1, 21–55–2, 21–55–3 (Supp.1983); Utah Code Ann. 1983, §§ 78–11–24, 78–11–25.

59. See Section 5.1, supra. Sherlock v. Stillwater Clinic, 260 N.W.2d 169 (Minn.1977) emphasizes this point.

tional right to limit family size.[60] Such social and legal developments do show that many people's attitudes toward the joys of parenthood have changed, and that it is unrealistic today to insist that in all circumstances parenthood is a benefit rather than a burden to the parent.

Logically, it seems to follow that if the plaintiffs in these cases did not want the child, they were damaged when the child was born, and the negligent physician who caused the damage should pay for it. Logic is not the only thing to be considered, however. For one thing, the damages can be very large if they include the cost of feeding, clothing, housing and educating the child until he is eighteen or twenty-one.[61] And juries are too often excessively generous with other people's money. The result may well be to discourage physicians from undertaking sterilizations, a most undesirable result in view of our need to limit population growth.[62] In order to avoid excessive verdicts, a few cases have limited recovery to the medical costs of childbirth, together with an amount to compensate the mother for any pain or suffering during childbirth, and to compensate the father for any loss of consortium.[63]

If a court takes the position that the plaintiffs should recover all costs, including the support of the child during minority, then

certainly the defendant should be allowed to introduce evidence of any benefits which the parents enjoy as a result of the child's birth.[64] The difficulty of course is that these benefits are nearly impossible to evaluate in dollars and evidence that they exist at all may be unavailable.[65]

In many cases the defendant may argue that if the child really was unwanted, the plaintiffs could have avoided the burden by an abortion or by placing the child for adoption. This argument has a double effect. In the first place it amounts to an assertion that the plaintiffs could have mitigated their damages by either of these methods. Secondly, it tends to prove that the child was not unwanted, and that the plaintiffs have in fact found the birth of the child to be a benefit rather than a burden. The argument is appealingly realistic. It is consistent with the willingness of the courts to look at the plaintiffs as individuals who may not wish to have another child. It carries that tendency a step further by scrutinizing all of the evidence as to their emotions without stopping at bare assertions concerning their feelings. For all these reasons a defendant should be permitted to produce evidence that abortion and adoption were practical alternatives which were available to the plaintiffs. If the plaintiffs are able to convince the trier of fact that strong ethi-

60. E.g., Roe v. Wade, 410 U.S. 113, 93 S.Ct. 705, 35 L.Ed.2d 147 (1973), rehearing denied 410 U.S. 959, 93 S.Ct. 1409, 35 L.Ed.2d 694 (1973); Eisenstadt v. Baird, 405 U.S. 438, 92 S.Ct. 1029, 31 L.Ed.2d 349 (1972); Griswold v. Connecticut, 381 U.S. 479, 85 S.Ct. 1678, 14 L.Ed.2d 510 (1965). Rivera v. State, 94 Misc.2d 157, 404 N.Y.S.2d 950 (Ct.Cl.1978) relies in part on these cases.

61. In Green v. Sudakin, 81 Mich.App. 545, 265 N.W.2d 411 (1978) a jury verdict for $95,000 was affirmed.

62. Sherlock v. Stillwater Clinic, 260 N.W.2d 169 (Minn.1977) takes the odd position that it is socially desirable to hold the physician liable and thereby discourage physicians generally from performing contraceptive sterilizations, although the opinion recognizes that sterilization is becoming the preferred method of birth control for married persons. The court neglects to explain why the law should adopt a rule which tends to limit a popular, safe and effective method of birth control in our over-populated age.

63. Bishop v. Byrne, 265 F.Supp. 460 (S.D.W.Va.1967); Bushman v. Burns Clinic Medical Center, 83 Mich.App. 453, 268 N.W.2d 683 (1978) (plaintiff seeking only dam-

ages for mental distress, anxiety, discomfort and other effects of the pregnancy); Kingsbury v. Smith, 122 N.H. 237, 442 A.2d 1003 (1982); West v. Underwood, 132 N.J.L. 325, 40 A.2d 610 (1945); Mason v. Western Pennsylvania Hospital, 499 Pa. 484, 453 A.2d 974 (1982); Beardsley v. Weirdsma, 650 P.2d 288 (Wyo.1982); McKernan v. Aasheim, 102 Wash.2d 411, 687 P.2d 850 (1984); James G. v. Caserta, ___ W.Va. ___, 332 S.E.2d 872 (1985).

64. Ochs v. Borrelli, 187 Conn. 253, 445 A.2d 883 (1982); Jones v. Malinowski, 299 Md. 257, 473 A.2d 429 (1984); Troppi v. Scarf, 31 Mich.App. 240, 187 N.W.2d 511 (1971); Sherlock v. Stillwater Clinic, 260 N.W.2d 169 (Minn.1977); permit this sort of evidence in mitigation of damages, as does Coleman v. Garrison, 281 A.2d 616 (Del. Super.1971), although the Delaware Supreme Court seems to have disapproved the latter decision in 298 A.2d 320 (Del.1972), mandate conformed 327 A.2d 757 (1974), judgment affirmed 349 A.2d 8 (1975).

65. Bushman v. Burns Clinic Medical Center, 83 Mich. App. 453, 268 N.W.2d 683 (1978). This case excluded evidence of possible benefits where the plaintiffs' claim was limited to those damages resulting from the pregnancy and did not cover the cost of raising the child.

cal or religious principles, held seriously and in good faith, prevented them from considering abortion, then perhaps the defendant should not be allowed to rely upon that alternative as a defense to the damage claim. But he should still be entitled to prove that the infant could readily have been placed for adoption, if that was in fact the case. In many parts of the country adoptable infants are in great demand. Evidence of this sort does no more than take at face value the plaintiffs' claim that the child was unwanted. The welfare of the child is hardly promoted by his parents' public announcement in their lawsuit that they did not want him to be born. In such circumstances the interests of all parties, plaintiffs, defendant and, most important of all the child, are best vindicated by placing the child for adoption. This being so, there is no reason why the defendant should be foreclosed from making this defense, and the defense should ordinarily limit the physician's liability to the expenses of childbirth.

Notwithstanding the cogency of these arguments, several cases have held that neither abortion nor adoption placement is a defense to the plaintiffs' claim.[66] The reasoning of the cases is not very persuasive, suggesting that the courts think that if the defense were recognized this might amount to coercing the

parents to have an abortion or to relinquish the child. But of course there is no element of coercion or anything resembling it. If the defense is recognized, the court is merely saying that the plaintiffs have to accept the responsibility of their choice. Although it might be nice to have the pleasure of raising a child without the financial burden, there seems to be no social utility in providing that option for parents who find themselves in these circumstances.

 WESTLAW REFERENCES

Possible Bases of Liability

    a. Negligence

sy,di(negligen! malpractice /s steriliz!)

renslow /s mennonite

    b. Breach of Contract or Warranty

di,sy(negligen! liab! /s contraceptive "birth control" prophylactic)

    c. Lack of Informed Consent

informed /2 consent /s steriliz!

    d. Fraud or Deceit

find 59 cal rptr 463

    Public Policy and Damages

howard /s lecher

sy,di(damages /p wrongful +2 conception life birth pregnancy)

---

66. Jones v. Malinowski, 299 Md. 257, 473 A.2d 429 (1984); Troppi v. Scarf, 31 Mich.App. 240, 187 N.W.2d 511 (1971) (would be unreasonable to require the plaintiff to mitigate damages by placing the child for adoption); Sherlock v. Stillwater Clinic, 260 N.W.2d 169 (Minn.1977) (no duty to mitigate damages by abortion or placing the child for adoption); Rivera v. State, 94 Misc.2d 157, 404 N.Y.S.2d 950 (Ct.Cl.1978) (requiring mitigation of damages by having an abortion would be a gross invasion of the plaintiff's privacy). But see Ziemba v. Sternberg, 45 A.D.2d 230, 357 N.Y.S.2d 265 (4th Dep't 1974).

See West's Ann.Cal.Civ.Code § 43.6 (1982), which provides that the failure or refusal of a parent to prevent a live birth of his or her child shall not be a defense in an action against a third party, nor shall it be considered in awarding damages in such an action. This seems to apply in cases in which the parent sues the physician for negligence causing the birth of a defective child as well as a normal healthy child.

Chapter 6

SUPPORT OBLIGATIONS IN THE FAMILY

Table of Sections

---

§ 6.1 Duties of Support Between Husband and Wife—In General

Background and History

Anglo-American law has for centuries prescribed rules for the proper behavior of husbands and wives in marriage. These rules were often stated in the abstract. Specifically, the courts have said that the husband has a duty to support his wife, that she has a duty to render services in the home, and that these duties are reciprocal.[1] In a sense such a statement is misleading, because rules take on a different aspect when one examines the remedies available for their enforcement and the circumstances in which they operate. Since the remedies are usually indirect and the rules come into play only when the marriage has broken down, one might describe them as predictions of what courts will do on divorce or separation rather than as models of the well conducted marriage. But these rules have acquired much of their force and vitality from the fact that they have constituted a pattern for correct behavior in marriage. They have been regarded as moral precepts.

Up until the 1960's it was accurate to characterize these rules as extraordinarily conservative. Until then they described the traditional roles of husband and wife. The husband was to provide the family with food, clothing, shelter and as many of the amenities of life as he could manage, either (in earlier days) by management of his estates or (more recently) by working for wages or a salary. The wife was to be mistress of the household, maintaining the home with the resources furnished by the husband, and caring for the children. One could only account for the tenacity of the rules on the theory that since they expressed moral precepts backed up by religious teachings, they were independent of time, place and circumstances. This conservatism was reinforced by the reciprocal nature of the duties imposed, making it easier to

§ 6.1

1. E.g., Manby v. Scott, 1 Lev. 4, 86 Eng.Rep. 781 (1659); Lungworthy v. Hockmore, 1 Ld.Raym. 444, 91 Eng.Rep. 1195 (1698); Bolton v. Prentice, 2 Str. 1214, 93 Eng.Rep. 1136 (1745); Bromley, Family Law, 195–196 (2d ed. 1962); 1 Blackstone, Commentaries on the Laws of England, 442 (Cooley 3d ed. 1884); 2 Pollock and Maitland, History of English Law, 405 (1898).

treat deviations as evidence of moral fault and of breach of faith.[2]

In the English law the husband's duty of support was enforced either at law by allowing the wife to pledge his credit for necessaries,[3] or in the ecclesiastical courts by a suit for divorce a mensa et thoro.[4] The grounds recognized for the divorce a mensa were adultery and cruelty.[5] The wife's remedy for desertion was to bring the ecclesiastical action for restitution of conjugal rights, which ultimately could lead to the requirement that the husband support her.[6] There was apparently no direct right of action in equity for nonsupport,[7] although equity would give specific performance of articles of separation in which support payments were provided for.[8] The level of support was defined as that at which the parties lived,[9] and the husband was not required to furnish support if the wife should elope and live away from home without justification.[10]

2. McCutchen v. McGahay, 11 Johns. 281 (N.Y.1814) (wife's duties are in consideration for those of the husband).

3. Lungworthy v. Hockmore, 1 Ld.Raym. 444, 91 Eng. Rep. 1195 (1698); Read v. Legard, [1851] 6 Exch. 636, 155 Eng.Rep. 698.

4. 2 Burns, Ecclesiastical Law, 447 (4th ed. 1781).

5. Ibid. See also Evans v. Evans, 1 Hagg.Cons. 35, 161 Eng.Rep. 466 (1790); Harris v. Harris, 2 Hagg.Cons. 148, 161 Eng.Rep. 697 (1813); 1 Blackstone, Commentaries on the Laws of England, 440 (Cooley 3rd ed. 1884).

6. Segelbaum v. Segelbaum, 39 Minn. 258, 259, 39 N.W. 492, 493, (1888); Bromley, Family Law, 81 (2d ed. 1962).

7. 1 Bacon's Abridgment, 723 (7th ed. 1832). Cf. 1 Bishop, Marriage, Divorce and Separation, § 1389 (1891). But see Watkyns v. Watkyns, 2 Atk. 96, 26 Eng.Rep. 460 (1740), and Lasbrook v. Tyler, 1 Chan.Rep. 44, 21 Eng. Rep. 502 (1630).

8. Williams v. Callow, 2 Vern. 752, 23 Eng.Rep. 1091 (1717); Angier v. Angier, Gilb.Ch. 152, 25 Eng.Rep. 107 (1718); Head v. Head, 3 Atk. 295, 26 Eng.Rep. 972 (1745).

9. Read v. Legard, [1851] 6 Exch. 636, 155 Eng.Rep. 698.

10. Manby v. Scott, 1 Lev. 4, 86 Eng.Rep. 781 (1659); Lungworthy v. Hockmore, 1 Ld.Raym. 444, 91 Eng.Rep. 1195 (1698); Child v. Hardyman, 2 Str. 875, 93 Eng.Rep. 909 (1731); McCutchen v. McGahay, 11 Johns. 281 (N.Y.1814); 1 Blackstone, Commentaries on the Laws of England, 442 (Cooley 3d ed. 1884).

11. McCutchen v. McGahay, 11 Johns. 281 (N.Y.1814); 1 Bishop, Marriage, Divorce and Separation § 1184 (1891).

The English model of the well conducted marriage and the duties of husband and wife which went with it were adopted in this country.[11] Changes have been made in the methods of enforcement in order to provide the wife with more effective and convenient remedies,[12] but the rules themselves remained substantially the same until the late 1960's.[13]

Contemporary Status of Support Obligations Between Husband and Wife

Since the late 1960's, however, changes in statutory and constitutional law accompanying the influence of the women's rights movement and the changes in the economic position of women have been reflected in new legal rules governing support obligations of husbands and wives. In a substantial number of states statutory amendments provide that the duty of support rests equally upon husband and wife, to be shared in proportion to their individual abilities.[14] The Uniform

12. See sections 6.4, 6.5, 6.6, infra.

13. A thorough account of the traditional rules of support as between husband and wife, with emphasis on the law of Ohio, may be found in Krauskopf and Thomas, Partnership Marriage: The Solution to an Ineffective and Inequitable Law of Support, 35 Ohio St.L.J. 558 (1974).

14. E.g., West's Ann.Cal.Civ.Code § 5100 (1983); Conn.Gen.Stat.Ann. § 46b–37 (1985); V.T.C.A., Fam.Code § 4.02 (1985). In the majority of states today the divorce statutes provide that alimony may be granted to either spouse, thereby implying that the support obligation rests upon both husband and wife. See, e.g., Alaska Stat. § 25.24.160 (1983); Ariz.Rev.Stat. § 25.313 (Supp.1984) (separate maintenance); Colo.Rev.Stat. § 14–10–114 (1973); West's Fla.Stat.Ann. § 61.08 (Supp.1985); Hawaii Rev.Stat. § 580–47 (Supp.1984); Ill–S.H.A. ch. 40, § 504 (Supp.1985); Ky.Rev.Stat. § 403.140 (1984); Mass.Gen. Laws Ann. ch. 208, § 34 (Supp.1985); Mich.C.L.A. § 25.103 (1984 and Supp.1985); Minn.Stat.Ann. § 518.54 (Supp.1985); Neb.Rev.Stat. § 42–365 (1984); N.J.Stat. Ann. § 42–365 (Supp.1985); Ohio Rev.Code § 3105.18 (1980); Va.Code 1983, § 20–107.1 (Supp.); West's Rev. Code Wash.Ann. § 26.09.090 (Supp.1985); Wis.Stat.Ann. § 767.26 (1981). There is a small minority of states in which the husband is still solely responsible for the support of his wife. E.g., N.Y.–McKinney's Fam.Ct.Act § 412 (1983).

The Uniform Civil Liability for Support Act, 9 Unif.L. Ann. 174 (1979) likewise imposes a duty of support on both spouses. It has been adopted in California, Maine, New Hampshire and Utah.

Marriage and Divorce Act enacts the same rule by providing that a court in a divorce proceeding or a suit for legal separation may award maintenance to either spouse, taking into account the spouses' needs and resources.[15] In states having constitutional provisions forbidding the denial or abridgment of rights on account of sex, it has been held that the duty of support cannot be exclusively imposed upon husbands, since this amounts to a form of sexual discrimination.[16] The same result should be reached under the Equal Protection Clause of the Fourteenth Amendment. The Supreme Court has held that a state statute authorizing alimony only for wives violates that Clause in Orr v. Orr,[17] relying upon prior cases[18] invalidating various state statutes on the basis of sex. Although in two cases[19] the Court has upheld statutes which discriminated against men, on the ground that the statutes merely recognized and alleviated the economic disadvantages which women have suffered, it is diffi-

cult to see any legitimate state purpose to be served by continuing to place upon the husband the sole duty of supporting his wife and children. For this reason and on the authority of Orr v. Orr, it seems plain that the duty of support must constitutionally rest equally upon husband and wife. A large proportion of married women work.[20] Continuing to insist that they have no responsibility for support tends to preserve their former subordinate status in the legal definition of the family, while a rule which makes them jointly responsible with the husband to the extent of their ability emphasized the position of equality to which women today legitimately aspire.[21]

Scope and Limitations of the Spousal Duty of Support

Postponing to later sections the discussion of remedies,[22] it is useful here to outline generally the principles governing the spouses' duties.[23] These principles are largely judge-

15. Uniform Marriage and Divorce Act § 308, 9A Unif.L.Ann. 160 (1979).

16. Rand v. Rand, 280 Md. 508, 374 A.2d 900 (1977), on remand 40 Md.App. 550, 392 A.2d 1149 (1978); Coleman v. State, 37 Md.App. 322, 377 A.2d 553 (1977); Henderson v. Henderson, 458 Pa. 97, 327 A.2d 60 (1974) (dictum); Commonwealth v. Stein, 487 Pa. 1, 406 A.2d 1381 (1979); Conway v. Dana, 456 Pa. 536, 318 A.2d 324 (1974); Smith v. Smith, 13 Wash.App. 381, 534 P.2d 1033 (1975) (dictum). See also Wiegand v. Wiegand, 226 Pa. Super. 278, 310 A.2d 426 (1973), reversed on other grounds 461 Pa. 482, 337 A.2d 256 (1975). Louisiana's decisions, on the basis of a more loosely worded equal rights amendment reach the same result. Lovell v. Lovell, 378 So.2d 418 (La.1979). See also Kurtz, The State Equal Rights Amendments and Their Impact on Domestic Relations Law, 11 Fam.L.Q. 101, 128 (1977) and Note, The Support Law and the Equal Rights Amendment in Pennsylvania, 77 Dick.L.Rev. 254 (1973).

17. Orr v. Orr, 440 U.S. 268, 99 S.Ct. 1102, 59 L.Ed.2d 306 (1979), cases holding there is not a violation of equal protection when husbands are required to support their wives include People v. Elliott, 186 Colo. 65, 525 P.2d 457 (1974); Stern v. Stern, 165 Conn. 190, 332 A.2d 78 (1973); Murphy v. Murphy, 232 Ga. 352, 206 S.E.2d 458 (1974), cert. denied 421 U.S. 929, 95 S.Ct. 1656, 44 L.Ed.2d 87 (1975); Eagerton v. Eagerton, 265 S.C. 90, 217 S.E.2d 146 (1975); Hendricks v. Hendricks, 535 S.W.2d 668 (Tex.Civ.App.1976).

State cases holding that imposing a support duty exclusively upon men violates the Equal Protection Clause are Beal v. Beal, 388 A.2d 72 (Me.1978); Thaler v. Thaler, 89 Misc.2d 315, 391 N.Y.S.2d 331 (1977), reversed on other grounds 58 A.D.2d 890, 396 N.Y.S.2d 815 (1977).

18. E.g., Reed v. Reed, 404 U.S. 71, 92 S.Ct. 251, 30 L.Ed.2d 225 (1971); Craig v. Boren, 429 U.S. 190, 97 S.Ct. 451, 50 L.Ed.2d 397 (1976), rehearing denied 429 U.S. 1124, 97 S.Ct. 1161, 51 L.Ed.2d 574 (1977); Stanton v. Stanton, 421 U.S. 7, 95 S.Ct. 1373, 43 L.Ed.2d 680 (1975), appeal after remand 552 P.2d 112 (Utah 1976); Weinberger v. Wiesenfeld, 420 U.S. 636, 95 S.Ct. 1225, 43 L.Ed. 2d 514 (1975); Frontiero v. Richardson, 411 U.S. 677, 93 S.Ct. 1764, 36 L.Ed.2d 583 (1973); Califano v. Webster, 430 U.S. 313, 97 S.Ct. 1192, 51 L.Ed.2d 360 (1977).

19. Schlesinger v. Ballard, 419 U.S. 498, 95 S.Ct. 572, 42 L.Ed.2d 610 (1975), rehearing denied 420 U.S. 966, 95 S.Ct. 1363, 43 L.Ed.2d 446 (1975); Kahn v. Shevin, 416 U.S. 351, 94 S.Ct. 1734, 40 L.Ed.2d 189 (1974).

20. Peterson, Working Women, 93 Daedalus 671 (1964) gives a figure as about 13.5 million working married women at that time. According to J. Kreps and R. Clark, Sex, Age and Work 8–9 (1975) by 1974 married women with husband present comprised 22.5% of the total labor force.

21. This point is forcefully made in Thaler v. Thaler, 89 Misc.2d 315, 391 N.Y.S.2d 331 (1977), reversed on other grounds 58 A.D.2d 890, 396 N.Y.S.2d 815 (1977).

22. See sections 6.4, 6.5, 6.6, infra.

23. The duty of support is discussed in Krauskopf and Thomas, Partnership Marriage: The Solution to an Ineffective and Inequitable Law of Support, 35 Ohio St.L.J. 558 (1974); Paulsen, Support Rights and Duties Between Husband and Wife, 9 Vand.L.Rev. 709 (1956); Brown, The Duty of the Husband to Support the Wife, 18 Va.L.Rev. 823 (1932); Crozier, Marital Support, 15 B.U.L.Rev. 28 (1935); Sayre, A Reconsideration of a Husband's Duty to Support and a Wife's Duty to Render Services, 29 Va.L.

made,[24] although in some states there are Family Expense Acts [25] which impose obligations upon both spouses to furnish support for their family. The principles were developed in earlier times when the duty of support was solely the husband's, but many of them remain applicable notwithstanding that both husband and wife now have a duty of support in most states. Since many wives still do not work, and those who do often do not earn as much as their husbands, as a practical matter most support litigation is brought by the wife against her husband. For convenience in terminology therefore, the discussion which follows will refer to the husband's duty of support, with the unspoken understanding that the principles outlined apply equally to the rarer suit by the husband against the wife for non-support.

In describing the extent of the husband's obligation the courts sometimes use either archaic or unrealistic terms. Thus the husband is required to provide support suitable to the wife's rank and station in life,[26] or commensurate with their circumstances or standard of living.[27] The difficulty is that unless the husband's means are relatively large, both parties cannot continue to live at their accustomed level of expenditure after separation. The same difficulty arises in alimony litigation.[28] All the courts can realistically do is to give the wife a fair proportion of the husband's income, having regard to her needs.[29] It is clear, however, that she is not limited to an amount which barely furnishes her with the necessities of food, clothing and shelter.[30] She is entitled to have the comforts and even the luxuries of life to the extent that the husband is able to supply them.[31] His ability is to be determined not solely by looking at his present earnings, but also by taking account of property which he owns which might provide support.[32] In cases where it appears he is not in good faith earning as much as he is able, his ability to provide support is judged by his capacity to earn rather than by his actual earnings.[33] Gifts from others are not ordinarily considered in determining his ability to pay,[34] but funds exempt from creditors are so considered.[35]

Rev. 857 (1943); Cretney, The Maintenance Quagmire, 33 Mod.L.Rev. 662 (1970); Note, Support of the Wife: Statutory Rights and Remedies, 28 Bklyn.L.Rev. 108 (1961).

On the tax consequences of support obligations, see Note, Federal Tax Aspects of the Obligation to Support, 74 Harv.L.Rev. 1191 (1961).

24. E.g., Branson v. Branson, 190 Okl. 347, 123 P.2d 643 (1942).

25. See the discussion infra, at notes 69 to 79.

26. Gimbel Bros., Inc. v. Pinto, 188 Pa.Super. 72, 145 A.2d 865 (1958).

27. State v. Moran, 99 Conn. 115, 121 A. 277 (1923); Ewell v. State, 207 Md. 288, 114 A.2d 66 (1955); Jordan Marsh Co. v. Cohen, 242 Mass. 245, 136 N.E. 350 (1922); De Brauwere v. De Brauwere, 203 N.Y. 460, 96 N.E. 722 (1911); Grishaver v. Grishaver, 225 N.Y.S.2d 924 (1961). The husband's minority does not relieve him of his obligation. Butler v. Breck, 7 Metc. (48 Mass.) 164 (1843).

28. See section 13.5, infra. There is obviously a close relation between the problems of support and of alimony.

29. du Pont v. du Pont, 34 Del.Ch. 267, 103 A.2d 234 (1954); Bonanno v. Bonanno, 4 N.J. 268, 72 A.2d 318 (1950). For a very comprehensive collection of cases, see Annot., Adequacy or Excessiveness of Amount of Money Awarded as Separate Maintenance, Alimony or Support for Wife Where No Absolute Divorce Is or Has Been Granted, 1 A.L.R.3rd 208 (1965).

30. State v. Waller, 90 Kan. 829, 136 P. 215 (1913); Capodanno v. Capodanno, 58 N.J. 113, 275 A.2d 441 (1971); Grishaver v. Grishaver, 225 N.Y.S.2d 924 (1961).

31. Ewell v. State, 207 Md. 288, 114 A.2d 66 (1955); Gimbel Bros., Inc. v. Pinto, 188 Pa.Super. 72, 145 A.2d 865 (1958) (mink coat). State v. Moran, 99 Conn. 115, 121 A. 277 (1923) holds the wife entitled to suitable clothing, lodging, food and medical attendance. du Pont v. du Pont, 34 Del.Ch. 267, 103 A.2d 234 (1954) states that she is entitled to support as a wife, not as an inferior person.

32. Pezas v. Pezas, 151 Conn. 611, 201 A.2d 192 (1964).

Sample awards may be found in Wife v. Husband, 270 A.2d 180 (Del.Ch.1970); Scott v. Scott, 129 Ill.App.2d 176, 262 N.E.2d 728 (1970); Gould v. Gould, 359 Mass. 29, 267 N.E.2d 652 (1971); Schloss v. Schloss, 273 N.C. 266, 160 S.E.2d 5 (1968).

33. Ewell v. State, 207 Md. 288, 114 A.2d 66 (1955); Commonwealth ex rel. DiSanti v. DiSanti, 221 Pa.Super. 435, 293 A.2d 115 (1972); Zitlow v. State, 213 Wis. 493, 252 N.W. 358 (1934). See also Pencovic v. Pencovic, 45 Cal.2d 97, 287 P.2d 501 (1955), dealing with child support. In Painter v. Commonwealth, 140 Va. 459, 124 S.E. 431 (1924) the husband's mental and physical condition was held to disable him from supporting his wife and so to provide a defense, as to which the husband had the burden of proof. The fact that the husband was supporting his parents did not excuse his failure to support his wife in Commonwealth ex rel. Wieczorkowski v. Wieczorkowski, 155 Pa.Super. 517, 38 A.2d 347 (1944).

34. Turi v. Turi, 34 N.J.Super. 313, 112 A.2d 278 (1955).

35. Commonwealth v. Berfield, 160 Pa.Super. 438, 51 A.2d 523 (1947); E. Griswold, Spendthrift Trusts 388–403

More precisely, the factors relied upon in fixing support are similar to those relevant to fixing alimony. They include such considerations, in addition to the economic circumstances of the spouses, as the duration of the marriage, the extent to which the wife helped the husband during the marriage particularly in accumulating property, and the effect of the decree in encouraging or discouraging a reconciliation.[36] One factor which has given the courts much trouble and which has not been very satisfactorily dealt with is the wife's property and earnings. Many cases say that the married woman is entitled to support notwithstanding that she has property or earnings of her own.[37] This is too broadly stated in view of the increased economic opportunities open to women and of the current legal emphasis upon equality between husband and wife with respect to support rights and duties.[38] Although employment discrimination against women has not been eliminat-

ed,[39] many married women can and do work.[40] There is no reason why, if the married woman is working or is qualified to work and able to get a job, her earnings should not enter into the computation of the amount of support to which she is entitled from her husband.[41] And if she owns property the income from which is substantial, this also should reduce the amount otherwise due from her husband.[42] In fact, the husband should not have to support his wife at all if she has sufficient income from earnings or property to support herself adequately, but in the past the courts have been unwilling to come to this conclusion. The same should be true in the converse situation where the husband seeks support from the wife.

In the past fault has always been a highly relevant issue in non-support cases. It usually arose by way of defense.[43] The cases held that the wife's adultery[44] or her desertion or abandonment of her husband[45] excused him

(2d ed. 1947). See also Annot., 91 A.L.R.2d 262 (1963) on trust assets or income as subject to support claims.

36. For a comprehensive collection of cases on these points, see Annot., 1 A.L.R.3rd 208 (1965). The Uniform Civil Liability For Support Act, §§ 6, 9, Unif.L.Ann. 180 (1979) includes a list of relevant factors.

37. Poole v. People, 24 Colo. 510, 52 P. 1025 (1898); Pezas v. Pezas, 151 Conn. 611, 201 A.2d 192 (1964); Churchward v. Churchward, 132 Conn. 72, 42 A.2d 659 (1945) (wife is entitled to support even though she had property producing large income originally given to her by her husband); Ewell v. State, 207 Md. 288, 114 A.2d 66 (1955); Ott v. Hentall, 70 N.H. 231, 47 A. 80 (1900); Bonanno v. Bonanno, 4 N.J. 268, 72 A.2d 318 (1950); Manufacturers' Trust Co. v. Gray, 278 N.Y. 380, 16 N.E. 2d 373 (1938); Grishaver v. Grishaver, 225 N.Y.S.2d 924 (1961); Commonwealth ex rel. Fedor v. Fedor, 157 Pa. Super. 305, 43 A.2d 363 (1945); Heflin v. Heflin, 177 Va. 385, 14 S.E.2d 317 (1941). The husband is liable for his wife's support even though she is currently being supported by her relatives. He cannot shift the burden to them. Ulrich v. State, 44 Del. (5 Terry) 400, 59 A.2d 460 (1948). See also Annot., 1 A.L.R.3d 208, 224 (1965).

38. See the discussion at notes 14 through 21, supra.

39. Rossi, Equality Between the Sexes: An Immodest Proposal, 93 Daedalus 607 (1964); Krauskopf and Thomas, Partnership Marriage: The Solution to an Ineffective and Inequitable Law of Support, 35 Ohio St.L.J. 558 (1974).

40. See note 20, supra.

41. Grubb v. Grubb, 200 Md. 452, 90 A.2d 175 (1952); Brownstein v. Brownstein, 25 A.D.2d 205, 268 N.Y.S.2d 115 (1st Dep't 1966); Commonwealth ex rel. Volinski v. Volinski, 180 Pa.Super. 348, 119 A.2d 648 (1956).

42. State v. Waller, 90 Kan. 829, 136 P. 215 (1913); Benjamin v. Benjamin, 283 App.Div. 455, 128 N.Y.S.2d 401 (1st Dep't 1954); Hunt v. Hayes, 64 Vt. 89, 23 A. 920 (1891). See also Annot., 10 A.L.R.2d 466, 529 (1950).

43. For a comprehensive collection of cases, see Annot., 10 A.L.R.2d 466 (1950). The Uniform Civil Liability for Support Act makes no mention of fault as a relevant factor.

44. M. Martin Polokow Corp. v. Industrial Commission, 336 Ill. 395, 168 N.E. 271 (1929); Poppe v. Poppe, 3 N.Y.2d 312, 165 N.Y.S.2d 99, 144 N.E.2d 72 (1957). Annot., 10 A.L.R.2d 466, 498 (1950). But vague allegations of the wife's infidelity, without proof of adultery, does not justify the husband in his refusal to support her. Cram v. Cram, 116 N.C. 288, 21 S.E. 197 (1895).

45. Rearden v. Rearden, 210 Ala. 129, 97 So. 138 (1923) (dictum); McCutchen v. McGahay, 11 Johns. 281 (N.Y.1814); Fernandez v. Fernandez, 53 Misc.2d 73, 278 N.Y.S.2d 75 (Fam.Ct.1966), affirmed 27 A.D.2d 905, 280 N.Y.S.2d 898 (1967) (dictum); Kurpiewski v. Kurpiewski, 254 Pa.Super. 489, 386 A.2d 55 (1978); Whitcomb v. Whitcomb, 86 R.I. 62, 133 A.2d 746 (1957). The Rearden case held that if the husband aided or approved or consented to the wife's leaving home, he could be required to support her. Sengstack v. Sengstack, 4 N.Y.2d 502, 176 N.Y.S.2d 337, 151 N.E.2d 887 (1958), 12 Vand.L. Rev. 493 (1959) seems to hold that the wife who left her husband as a result of her mental illness could sue him for non-support. On the other hand, Richardson v. Stuesser, 125 Wis. 66, 103 N.W. 261 (1905) takes the harsh position that the husband's duty is only to support his wife in their home, so that he is not liable for her support in a state mental institution. Glover v. Glover, 64 Misc.2d 374, 314 N.Y.S.2d 873 (Fam.Ct.1970) held that a husband need not support his wife when she had been

from providing her with support. Even if he was the one who left home, he had a defense to her claims if she had by her conduct made cohabitation intolerable or prevented it without justification.[46] On the other hand the wife could prevail if she could show that the separation was not her fault.[47] If the parties separated by mutual consent, or as the result of fault on both sides, the wife was held not to be entitled to support, at least in some states.[48] Though the husband was originally in the wrong by having deserted or abandoned his wife, if he made a bona fide offer of reconciliation which she refused without justification, he had a defense.[49] The same principle operated in the wife's favor if she made an offer of reconciliation.[50]

Under some statutes a state furnishing welfare payments to a spouse may recover the amount of such payments from the other spouse.[51] Unless the statute expressly requires otherwise, the state's claim is generally held to be derivative [52] so that, for example, the state could not recover where the indigent spouse would have been barred from recovery by her own fault.[53]

The cases have distinguished between marital fault which is serious enough to excuse the husband from the performance of his marital obligations and less serious unkindness or bickering or unpleasantness which presumably lie within the normal, foreseeable range of marital relationships and do not excuse the failure to support.[54] This distinction is neither easy to describe in general terms nor to apply in specific cases. In fact the reliance upon fault is to some extent artificial, since there is usually some fault on both sides, and perhaps for this reason the cases have been criticized.[55] The objections to the reliance upon fault in support cases are somewhat mitigated by the position which some courts take, that although fault may not disqualify the wife for support entirely, it may be taken into account in determining the amount of support she is to receive.[56]

One of the striking changes which has occurred since the first edition of this work was published has been the minimization, even the virtual elimination of fault in marital litigation. The Uniform Marriage and Divorce Act, parts or all of which are now in force in many states, expressly provides that

guilty of "grievous and loathsome" misconduct toward him.

46. Martin v. Martin, 134 Conn. 354, 57 A.2d 622 (1948); Haberman v. Haberman, 267 A.2d 818 (D.C.App. 1970); Annot., 10 A.L.R.2d 466, 481 (1950).

47. Mode v. Mode, 8 N.C.App. 209, 174 S.E.2d 30 (1970). For the complicated Pennsylvania rules concerning fault see Larkin v. Larkin, 262 Pa.Super. 294, 396 A.2d 761 (1978).

48. State v. Lucas, 242 N.C. 84, 86 S.E.2d 770 (1955); Commonwealth ex rel. Young v. Young, 213 Pa.Super. 515, 247 A.2d 659 (1968); Annot., 10 A.L.R.2d 466, 478, 479 (1950). A case suggesting that the wife could require the husband to support her where both had been guilty of adultery is Hellman v. Hellman, 246 Pa.Super. 536, 371 A.2d 964 (1977).

In California mutual obligations of support between spouses are terminated if the parties live apart by agreement, unless they have expressly provided for support in their agreement. See Bruch, The Legal Import of Informal Separations: A Survey of California Law and a Call for Change, 65 Cal.L.Rev. 1015 (1977).

49. Annot., 10 A.L.R.2d 466, 506 (1950). Cf. Nicholas v. Bickford, 44 N.M. 210, 100 P.2d 906 (1940).

50. Annot., 10 A.L.R.2d 466, 509 (1950).

51. E.g., Alaska Stat. § 47.25.580 (1984); Conn.Gen. Stat.Ann. § 17–82e (Supp.1985); N.Y.–McKinney's Soc.

Serv.L. §§ 101, 101–a (1983); Utah Code Ann. § 78–45–9 (1977).

52. Mecham v. Mecham, 570 P.2d 123 (Utah 1977).

53. State v. Lugg, 144 Conn. 21, 127 A.2d 52 (1956); State v. Jordan, 142 Conn. 375, 114 A.2d 694 (1955), 36 B.U.L.Rev. 134 (1956); Edge v. Commissioner of Welfare, 34 Conn.Supp. 284, 388 A.2d 1193 (1978). But compare People v. Schenkel, 258 N.Y. 224, 179 N.E. 474 (1932) with Mellen v. Mellen, 46 A.D.2d 790, 361 N.Y.S.2d 28 (2d Dep't 1974).

54. Compare Martin v. Martin, 134 Conn. 354, 57 A.2d 622 (1948); State v. Kelly, 100 Conn. 727, 125 A. 95 (1924); and State v. Newman, 91 Conn. 6, 98 A. 346 (1916), in all of which cases the same court is struggling to make the distinction clear, with very indifferent success. In du Pont v. du Pont, 34 Del.Ch. 267, 103 A.2d 234 (1954) the wife's perjury in the support action was held not relevant nor was her premarital immorality. See also Larkin v. Larkin, 262 Pa.Super. 294, 396 A.2d 761 (1978).

55. For a typical criticism see Paulsen, Support Rights and Duties Between Husband and Wife, 9 Vand.L.Rev. 709, 727 (1953), suggesting that at least in some cases it would be better to consider fault merely in setting the amount or duration of support, rather than to make it an absolute bar.

56. Annot., 10 A.L.R.2d 466, 501 (1950).

marital misconduct is not to be taken into account in determining maintenance in proceedings for dissolution of marriage or for legal separation.[57] The inference from this provision, if not its plain meaning, is that in these states marital fault is no longer relevant to the issue of spousal support.[58] This result has many advantages, such as avoiding the difficult distinctions between degrees of marital fault described in the preceding paragraph, and, more importantly, avoiding essentially unrealistic allocations of fault in marriages where the responsibility for separation or failure to support is attributable to the attitudes or conduct of both parties. On the other hand, there are bound to be some cases in which the exclusion of all fault considerations will strike some lawyers and judges as unfair. The most obvious case is where the wife leaves her husband and, after commencing to live with another man, sues her husband for support. Of course a thorough inquiry might reveal that her departure from the marital domicile was not entirely her fault. If not, this sort of case might be covered by express statutory provision, as has been done in a couple of states.[59] In any event the occurrence of a relatively few cases

of this kind does not invalidate the conclusion that the current trend toward the elimination of fault as a consideration in support cases is wise. On balance its advantages far outweigh its disadvantages. Having said this, however, it must be conceded that some states do adhere to the former rule that fault may be considered in granting support and in determining its amount.[60]

If the parties have executed a valid separation agreement, which the husband is performing, this is also a defense to the wife's claims for support.[61] Although the spouses may not contract concerning support so long as they are living together,[62] they may do so upon separation.[63] The separation agreement is not a defense, however, if the husband has failed to comply with it. Under those circumstances the wife is entitled to disregard the agreement and sue for support as if no agreement had been made.[64]

One further qualification on the wife's right to support arises out of the courts' reluctance to enter a support decree when the parties are living together. Some cases have gone far to refuse relief in such circumstances on the theory that the courts should not make deci-

---

57. Uniform Marriage and Divorce Act § 308, 9A Unif.L.Ann. 160 (Supp.1979). See also, e.g., West's Ann. Cal.Civ.Code § 4801 (Supp.1983 and Supp.1985) which is construed to exclude fault from consideration in awarding maintenance on dissolution of marriage. In re Cosgrove's Marriage, 27 Cal.App.3d 424, 103 Cal.Rptr. 733 (1972).

58. A case contra the statement in the text is Gordon v. Gordon, 139 N.J.Super. 23, 351 A.2d 811 (1976), affirmed in part, remanded in part on other grounds 147 N.J.Super. 585, 371 A.2d 791 (1977), which said that even though fault would not be a bar to alimony in divorce, it remained a bar to support. It is difficult to discern any reason for this distinction, other than, perhaps, that the statutes on divorce and support contained differing terms. But if there is no clear statement as to the effect of fault in the support statute, the alimony statute would seem to imply that alimony and support should be determined upon the same basis.

59. E.g., West's Ann.Cal.Civ.Code § 4801 (1983 and Supp.1985); N.Y.–McKinney's Dom.Rel.L. § 248 (1977).

60. E.g., Official Code Ga.Ann. § 19–6–4 (1980); Ill.– S.H.A. § 40–402 (1985); West's Ann.Ind.Ann. § 31–1–9– 10 (1980); Me.Rev.Stat.Ann. tit. 19, §§ 581, 582 (Supp. 1984); Nev.Rev.Stat. § 123.100 (1979); Noyes v. Noyes, 108 N.H. 462, 237 A.2d 692 (1968); Gordon v. Gordon, 139 N.J.Super. 23, 351 A.2d 811 (1976), affirmed in part, remanded in part on other grounds 147 N.J.Super. 585,

371 A.2d 791 (1977); Madderom v. Madderom, 44 A.D.2d 828, 355 N.Y.S.2d 24 (2d Dep't 1974); Commonwealth D'Andrea v. D'Andrea, 262 Pa.Super. 302, 396 A.2d 765 (1978); Larkin v. Larkin, 262 Pa.Super. 294, 396 A.2d 761 (1978).

Even in states in which fault is not normally considered in determining support obligations, it may be relevant if the proceeding is a criminal one. See, e.g., West's Ann.Cal.Penal Code § 270a (Supp.1978); Jones, The Problem of Family Support: Criminal Sanctions for the Enforcement of Support, 38 N.C.L.Rev. 1 (1959).

61. See section 16.2, infra, dealing with separation agreements, and Note, Contractual Liquidations of the Husband's Duty to Support His Wife, 40 Colum.L.Rev. 677 (1940). Cases are cited in Annot., 10 A.L.R.2d 466, 535 (1950). Cf. Churchward v. Churchward, 132 Conn. 72, 42 A.2d 659 (1945). The separation agreement is not a defense if conditioned on a divorce which has not been obtained, however. Ewell v. State, 207 Md. 288, 114 A.2d 66 (1955).

62. French v. McAnarney, 290 Mass. 544, 195 N.E. 714 (1935); Lacks v. Lacks, 12 N.Y.2d 268, 238 N.Y.S.2d 949, 189 N.E.2d 487 (1963); Ritchie v. White, 225 N.C. 450, 35 S.E.2d 414 (1945).

63. See section 16.3, infra.

64. Cram v. Cram, 116 N.C. 288, 21 S.E. 197 (1895); Annot., 10 A.L.R.2d 466, 536 (1950).

sions for the parties concerning the details of their marital conduct when the marriage is still a going concern,[65] and on the old-fashioned ground that the husband is entitled to determine the level of family expenditure.[66] The courts have taken a similar position with respect to custody disputes.[67] Within limits this reluctance is certainly sensible. The courts can hardly allow themselves to be drawn into deciding whether the family budget will cover the purchase of a car or a television set. On the other hand, there may be good reason for the court to enter an order even though the parties are neither separated nor contemplating a separation if, over a substantial period, the husband has consistently failed and refused to furnish support at a level clearly within his means.[68] Such cases are rare, however.

Family Expense Statutes

Now that both husbands and wives have mutual obligations of support in the majority of states,[69] family expense statutes, in force in about twenty states,[70] have less practical significance then in the past. The wording of these statutes varies, but they generally provide that the expenses of the family and of the education of children are chargeable against the property of both husband and wife and (under some statutes) that both husband and wife may be held jointly or severally liable for such expenses.

Many questions of construction arise under the Family Expense Statutes, the answers of course depending on the wording of the individual statute. For example, under some statutes the liability of husband and wife extends to any article which in fact is used by the family, whether or not it may be considered a necessary,[71] and the husband's liability may not be contingent on proof that he neglected to provide for his family.[72] Some of the statutes impose no personal liability on the wife but merely impose a liability against property which she owned at the time of the contract.[73] Attorney fees in divorce cases have been said not to be family expenses on the ground that they are incurred in an attempt to disrupt family unity, but the same case held that attorney fees for services in a habeas corpus proceeding by which the wife sought to obtain child custody were family expenses.[74] And expenses of the husband's burial have been held not family expenses, so that the wife was not liable, on the ground

---

65. McGuire v. McGuire, 157 Neb. 226, 59 N.W.2d 336 (1953), 33 Neb.L.Rev. 103 (1953); Commonwealth v. George, 358 Pa. 118, 56 A.2d 228 (1948). The McGuire case is criticized in Paulsen, Support Rights and Duties Between Husband and Wife, 9 Vand.L.Rev. 709, 719 (1956), and both cases are criticized in Krauskopf and Thomas, Partnership Marriage: The Solution to an Ineffective and Inequitable Law of Support, 35 Ohio St.L.J. 558, 565 (1974).

66. Pattberg v. Pattberg, 94 N.J.Eq. 715, 120 A. 790 (1923) (dictum).

67. E.g., Kilgrow v. Kilgrow, 268 Ala. 475, 107 So.2d 885 (1958).

68. Relief was granted in Miller v. Miller, 320 Mich. 43, 30 N.W.2d 509 (1948), where the discrepancy between the husband's income and the level of maintenance was great, and in Caras v. Caras [1955] 1 All Eng.Rep. 624, where the parties lived in the same house but slept apart. See also West's Fla.Stat.Ann. § 61.09 (Supp.1979) authorizing suits for support apart from divorce.

69. See the discussion at notes 14–21, supra.

70. See, e.g., West's Ann.Cal.Civ.Code §§ 5120.130, 5120.140 (Supp.1985); Colo.Rev.Stat. § 14–6–110 (1973); Conn.Gen.Stat.Ann. § 46b–37 (Supp.1985); Ill.–S.H.A. ch. 40, § 1015 (Supp.1985); Iowa Code Ann. § 597.14 (1981); Mass.Gen.Laws Ann. ch. 209, § 7 (1981); Minn.Stat.Ann.

§ 519.05 (Supp.1985); Vernon's Ann.Mo.Stat. § 451.250 (1977); Neb.Rev.Stat. § 42–201 (1984); N.D.Cent.Code § 14–07–08 (Supp.1983); Or.Rev.Stat. § 108.040 (Supp. 1983); S.D.Codified L. § 25–2–11 (1984); Utah Code Ann. 1984, § 30–2–9; West's Rev.Code Wash.Ann. § 26–16–205 (Supp.1985); W.Va.Code, § 48–3–22 (1980); Wyo.Stat. 1977, § 20–1–201.

The family expense statute was held constitutional in Carson Pirie Scott & Co. v. Hyde, 39 Ill.2d 433, 235 N.E. 2d 643 (1968).

71. Fitzmaurice v. Buck, 77 Conn. 390, 59 A. 415 (1904); Lyman v. Harbaugh, 117 Ill.App.3d 732, 73 Ill. Dec. 81, 453 N.E.2d 906 (1983). In Neasham v. McNair, 103 Iowa 695, 72 N.W. 773 (1897) the wife was held liable on the statute for a diamond stud purchased and worn by the husband, and in Louis Berman & Co. v. Dahlberg, 336 Ill.App. 233, 83 N.E.2d 380 (1948) the husband was held liable for the wife's purchase of a mink coat.

72. Gorco Const. Co. v. Stein, 256 Minn. 476, 99 N.W.2d 69 (1959).

73. Dreamer v. Oberlander, 122 Neb. 335, 240 N.W. 435 (1932), 18 Va.L.Rev. 680 (1932).

74. Morrison v. Federico, 120 Utah 75, 232 P.2d 374 (1951). Expenses of defending the wife against a criminal charge were held within the family expense statute in State v. Clark, 88 Wash.2d 533, 563 P.2d 1253 (1977).

that the liability was incurred after the family had been dissolved by the husband's death.[75]

The position in most states is that although the Family Expense Statute imposes upon the wife, or upon her property, liability for family expenses, it does not absolve the husband of the ultimate responsibility for support of the wife and children.[76] Thus, an outsider furnishing goods or services to the family may recover the cost from the wife, but she is entitled to be reimbursed by the husband,[77] unless she has paid for them under circumstances showing she intended to make a gift or that she intended to make a nonreimbursable contribution to the household expenses.[78] Iowa takes the contrary view, that unless there is an agreement for repayment, neither husband nor wife may get reimbursement for money expended for family support.[79]

Support Between Unmarried Couples

In the celebrated case of Marvin v. Marvin,[80] the California Supreme Court held that a woman who had lived with a man without being married to him could be awarded a share of the property which he acquired during the time they lived together. The basis for the court's ruling was vague, being expressed in such terms as implied contract, implied agreement of partnership or joint venture, constructive trust, or compensation for the reasonable value of household services rendered. If this result is sound, one might ask why the woman should not, on similar vague principles, be entitled to support from a man with whom she had lived. No answer comes readily to mind, other than the obvious one that rights of support have always rested upon marriage. The objection to the abandonment of that principle, as well as to the Marvin case itself, is that there is no other principle which can guide the courts in deciding what sort of relationship between a man and a woman, or perhaps between men and between women, will justify ordering one of the couple to support the other. Perhaps for this reason the courts have thus far not chosen to create rights of support between unmarried couples.[81]

WESTLAW REFERENCES

Contemporary Status of Support Obligations Between Husband and Wife

equal! /3 responsib! duty /s support! /s husband wife spous!)

Scope and Limitations of Spousal Duty of Support

di(husband /s support! /s wife /s station rank +2 life)

Family Expense Statutes

"family expense" /2 law statute act

Support Between Unmarried Couples

marvin +s marvin & promise right /s support!

---

§ 6.2 Support of Children

Most of the questions which commonly arise concerning the support of children are discussed in later sections in connection with divorce.[1] At this point only a few issues relat-

---

75. Dennis v. Shaw, 137 Conn. 450, 78 A.2d 691 (1951).

76. In some states this is spelled out in the statute. E.g., Conn.Gen.Stat.Ann. § 46b–37 (Supp.1985). See also Cantiello v. Cantiello, 136 Conn. 685, 74 A.2d 199 (1950); Bennett v. Bennett, 27 Ill.App.2d 24, 169 N.E.2d 172 (1960); Kosanke v. Kosanke, 137 Minn. 115, 162 N.W. 1060 (1917). The statute applies to a husband and wife who are estranged but living in the same house. Nichol v. Clema, 188 Neb. 74, 195 N.W.2d 233 (1972).

77. Spalding v. Spalding, 361 Ill. 387, 198 N.E. 136 (1935).

78. Petersen v. Swan, 239 Minn. 98, 57 N.W.2d 842 (1953); Kosanke v. Kosanke, 137 Minn. 115, 162 N.W. 1060 (1917).

79. Truax v. Ellett, 234 Iowa 1217, 15 N.W.2d 361 (1944).

80. 18 Cal.3d 660, 134 Cal.Rptr. 815, 557 P.2d 106 (1976), 62 Minn.L.Rev. 449 (1978), 53 Wash.L.Rev. 145 (1977). The case has been followed in Carlson v. Olson, 256 N.W.2d 249 (Minn.1977). On the remand in Marvin the trial court awarded $104,000.00 a kind of rehabilitative alimony, suggesting that perhaps there is some right of support arising from such relationships. Marvin v. Marvin, 5 Fam.L.Rep. 3077 (1979).

81. Davis v. Misiano, 373 Mass. 261, 366 N.E.2d 752 (1977).

§ 6.2

1. See Chapter 17, infra.

ing to the underlying parental duty to support will be raised.

At common law there seems to have been no legal obligation on the father's part to support his child,[2] but the statutes making provision for the poor imposed such a duty from a relatively early date.[3] Until recently in the United States the father was primarily liable for the support of his children,[4] with the mother liable in the event that the father failed or refused to furnish support.[5] This is no longer the case. Today both mother and father are responsible for the support of their children, to the extent of their respective resources and abilities. Some states have made this change by statute,[6] some by judicial decision.[7] In those states having an Equal Rights Amendment in the state constitution equality of responsibility is thereby imposed.[8] And finally, the Equal Protection Clause of the United States Constitution [9] also requires that this obligation be equally imposed upon husband and wife.[10]

About twenty states have family expense statutes providing that expenses of the family are chargeable against the property of both husband and wife.[11] Now that both spouses are constitutionally responsible for child sup-

port, these statutes are no longer of great significance.

The amount of support which a parent will be ordered to pay is at least theoretically a function of the child's needs and the parent's ability to pay,[12] although several cases have held that a father must furnish child support even though the child has property of his own.[13] In practice, however, awards of child support may vary widely between comparable situations due to the tendency of trial judges to reach disparate judgments about what children need and what parents can afford.[14] And in some cases the court may award child support on the basis of what the parent could earn rather than on what he actually was earning.[15]

The breakdown in parental authority and the conflict between parent and child which are not uncommon nowadays have led to the question whether a parent is required to support a child who disobediently leaves home and insists upon living in a manner of which the parent disapproves. The New York Court of Appeals has held in such a case that a father is not obliged to support his daughter, a college student who refused to live in the college dormitory, who was old enough (twen-

2. Bazeley v. Forder, 3 Q.B. 559, 565 (1968) (dissenting opinion); 1 Blackstone, Commentaries on the Laws of England 447 (Cooley 3d ed. 1884).

3. Shelton v. Springett, 11 C.B. 452, 138 Eng.Rep. 549 (1851); 1 Blackstone, Commentaries on the Laws of England 448 (Cooley 3d ed. 1884).

4. Earlier cases are cited in Rand v. Rand, 280 Md. 508, 374 A.2d 900 (1977), on remand 40 Md.App. 550, 392 A.2d 1149 (1978) and Conway v. Dana, 456 Pa. 536, 318 A.2d 324 (1974). See also Merlino v. Merlino, 33 Misc.2d 462, 227 N.Y.S.2d 262 (1962).

5. Cassas v. Cassas, 73 Wyo. 147, 276 P.2d 456 (1954).

6. E.g., West's Ann. Cal. Civ. Code § 4700 (Supp.1980); Uniform Civil Liability for Support Act §§ 2, 3, 9 U.L.A. 174, 177 (1979). See § 6.1, supra, at note 14.

7. Barnhard v. Barnhard, 252 Ark. 167, 477 S.W.2d 845 (1972), 27 Ark.L.Rev. 157 (1973); Carter v. Carter, 58 A.D.2d 438, 397 N.Y.S.2d 88 (2d Dep't 1977); Murredu v. Murredu, 160 W.Va. 610, 236 S.E.2d 452 (1977).

8. Rand v. Rand, 280 Md. 508, 374 A.2d 900 (1977), on remand 40 Md.App. 550, 392 A.2d 1149 (1978); Conway v. Dana, 456 Pa. 536, 318 A.2d 324 (1974).

9. U.S.Const. amend XIV, § 1.

10. Orr v. Orr, 440 U.S. 268, 99 S.Ct. 1102, 59 L.Ed.2d 306 (1979), on remand 374 So.2d 895 (Ala.Civ.App.1979),

writ denied 374 So.2d 898 (Ala.1979), holding that a statute authorizing alimony exclusively for wives violates the Equal Protection Clause. See also In re Aguilar, 80 Cal.App.3d 58, 145 Cal.Rptr. 197 (1978); Cotton v. Municipal Court of San Diego Judicial Dist., 59 Cal.App.3d 601, 130 Cal.Rptr. 876 (1976), and section 6.1, supra, at note 17.

11. See section 6.1, supra, at note 70.

12. See the discussion in section 17.1, infra; Note, Calculation of Child Support in Pennsylvania, 81 Dick. L. Rev. 793 (1977); Foster, Freed, Midonick, Child Support: The Quick and the Dead, 26 Syracuse L. Rev. 1157, 1163 (1975).

13. Armstrong v. Armstrong, 15 Cal.3d 942, 126 Cal. Rptr. 805, 544 P.2d 941 (1976); Gold v. Gold, 96 Misc.2d 481, 409 N.Y.S.2d 114 (1978); White v. White, 226 Pa. Super. 499, 313 A.2d 776 (1973); Commonwealth ex rel. Byrne v. Byrne, 212 Pa.Super. 566, 243 A.2d 196 (1968).

14. Yee, What Really Happens in Child Support Cases: An Empirical Study of Establishment and Enforcement of Child Support Orders in the Denver District Court, 57 Den.L.J. 21 (1979).

15. See Rapson v. Rapson, 165 Colo. 188, 437 P.2d 780 (1968).

ty) to be employable, and who was determined to live off campus in disregard of her father's wishes.[16] The court held that the New York Family Court was not warranted in setting its standards of behavior for the daughter in substitution for those of the father. A few other cases have similarly held that the father is not liable for support when his child leaves home against his wishes and lives in a fashion of which he disapproves, even when the state has furnished support for the child and sues the parent for reimbursement.[17] On the other hand, there are cases in which the parent is held liable to the child or to the public authorities in such circumstances, the courts taking the position that the child had not been emancipated.[18] In view of the courts' frequent emphasis upon the importance of the family, it does seem that a parent who, in good faith and without any intention of evading his support obligations, conditions support upon what he reasonably considers to be proper behavior by the child, should be entitled to withhold support from a child who refuses to meet his conditions. In cases of this sort the state should uphold rather than undermine parental authority. If the state does not uphold their authority, at least with-

in very broad limits parents can hardly be expected to meet their responsibility for the care and training of their children. This is particularly true in contemporary society, where there are so many competing sources of authority for child behavior outside the family.

One of the most frequently litigated questions in the law of child support concerns the extent of the parent's obligation to support his child beyond the age of majority and, more specifically, to pay the expenses of the child's education in private school or college. The question has been made more acute by the almost universal lowering of the age of majority from twenty-one to eighteen. Since the bulk of the litigation occurs in connection with divorce against a background of the divorce statutes, discussion of this question is postponed to a later section of this work.[19] It suffices to say at this point that although there is disagreement among the courts, a substantial number of cases require the parent to pay the child's college expenses.[20] And some cases impose a duty to support the adult child where he is unable to support himself through illness or incapacity.[21]

---

16. Roe v. Doe, 29 N.Y.2d 188, 324 N.Y.S.2d 71, 272 N.E.2d 567 (1971), 46 St. John's L.Rev. 139 (1971).

17. Parker v. Stage, 43 N.Y.2d 128, 400 N.Y.S.2d 794, 371 N.E.2d 513 (1977); St. Lawrence County Department of Social Services v. Menard, 86 Misc.2d 126, 381 N.Y.S.2d 939 (Fam.Ct.1975); Haight v. Haight, 241 Or. 532, 405 P.2d 622 (1965) (mother left home without cause and took the children); Annot., 98 A.L.R.3d 334 (1979).

One case has held that a father is responsible for the medical expenses of his daughter incurred as a result of the birth of an illegitimate child, without any discussion of whether the father would have been entitled to refuse on the ground of his disapproval of her conduct, and notwithstanding that the baby's father would also be responsible for these expenses. Allison v. Fulton-Dekalb Hospital Authority, 245 Ga. 445, 265 S.E.2d 575 (1980), appeal dismissed 449 U.S. 939, 101 S.Ct. 339, 66 L.Ed.2d 206 (1980).

18. Byrd v. O'Neill, 309 Minn. 415, 244 N.W.2d 657 (1976); Fevig v. Fevig, 90 N.M. 51, 559 P.2d 839 (1977); Thompson v. Thompson, 94 Misc.2d 911, 405 N.Y.S.2d 974 (Fam.Ct.1978) (parent still liable where the child does not leave home voluntarily); Matter of Bylow, 92 Misc.2d 509, 400 N.Y.S.2d 451 (Fam.Ct.1977); Annot., 32 A.L.R.3d 1055 (1970).

It is generally true that emancipation of the child ends the parent's duty to support him. See section 17.1, infra.

But the issue raised in the text relates to the child's conduct irrespective of emancipation.

But if the parents are unable to support a child, the state may have a duty to support him, at least where the state takes custody pursuant to a dependency decree. In re Welfare of Feldman, 94 Wash.2d 244, 615 P.2d 1290 (1980).

19. See section 17.1, infra.

20. See, e.g., Hutchinson v. Hutchinson, 263 Pa.Super. 299, 397 A.2d 1218 (1979); Childers v. Childers, 89 Wash. 2d 592, 575 P.2d 201 (1978); Veron, Parental Support of Post-Majority Children in Colleges: Changes and Challenges, 17 J. Fam. L. 645 (1979).

21. Scott v. Superior Court (Scott by Scott), 156 Cal. App.3d 577, 202 Cal.Rptr. 920 (1984) (relying on West's Ann.Cal.Civ.Code § 206 (1982); Feinberg v. Diamant, 378 Mass. 131, 389 N.E.2d 998 (1979); Kamp v. Kamp, 640 P.2d 48 (Wyo.1982). The Scott case, supra, held that California law would be applied to require the parent to furnish support where the parent was a resident of California and the child seeking support was a resident of New York. Under the N.Y.–McKinney's Social Serv.L. § 101(1) (Supp.1984–1985) the parent's obligation of support ends when the child reaches twenty-one.

A variety of remedies are available for the enforcement of the duty to support one's child. One such remedy, clumsy and ineffective but still occasionally used, is to have the child purchase necessaries, and to hold the father liable in equity for their cost to the tradesman or other person furnishing them.[22] A more effective remedy is provided in most states by allowing the child, or one suing on his behalf, to bring a direct civil suit against the parent.[23] The outcome of such a suit is a decree ordering the parent to make specific periodic payments for the child's support. The failure to make the payments, if wilful and if the parent is able to make the payments, may constitute a civil contempt of court.[24] The amounts due under a support order may also be collectible by garnishment under the statutes of some states.[25] In addition to these remedies, the criminal non-support statutes in force in most states [26] and the Uniform Reciprocal Enforcement of Support Act,[27] some version of which is in force in all states, are available to enforce child support obligations.

An important source of support for children in this country is the cooperative program known as Aid to Families With Dependent Children (AFDC). It is conducted pursuant to the Social Security Act,[28] financed largely by the federal government, and administered by the states. As is made clear by the statutory definition of "dependent child" [29] it is designed to provide support for those children who, by reason of the absence of a parent or of other circumstances, are not being properly supported by their parents. All states participate in the program.

Since AFDC is administered under complex state and federal statutes whose interaction has been the subject of much litigation, a detailed account of how it operates is beyond the scope of this work. An earlier section [30] has dealt briefly with the constitutional implications of its treatment of the illegitimate child. But a program so pervasive must necessarily affect family life in many ways and a few instances of this may be described at this point.[31] Much of the litigation has arisen out of the states' attempts to limit the circumstances in which payments will be made on behalf of needy children. For example, some states enacted a rule that in computing the needs of a child, the income of a man living with the child's mother although not married to her, would be taken into account. The

---

22. Greenspan v. Slate, 12 N.J. 426, 97 A.2d 390 (1953). See section 6.3, infra.

23. McQuade v. McQuade, 145 Colo. 218, 358 P.2d 470 (1960); Johnson v. Norman, 66 Ohio St.2d 186, 421 N.E.2d 124 (1981); Annot., 13 A.L.R.2d 1142 (1950). But see Weinman v. Larsh, 5 Ohio St.3d 85, 448 N.E.2d 1384 (1983) holding that a husband could not recover at common law for necessaries furnished to illegitimate children of his wife, the defendant being the children's natural father.

24. E.g., In the Matter of Proceeding for Support Under Article 4 of Family Court Act, 94 Misc.2d 891, 405 N.Y.S.2d 961 (Fam.Ct.1978). For a study of the actual incidence of contempt penalties in one court, see Yee, What Really Happens in Child Support Cases: An Empirical Study of Establishment and Enforcement of Child Support Orders in the Denver District Court, 57 Den.L.J. 21, 44 (1979).

25. Note, Remedies-Domestic Relations: Garnishment for Child Support, 56 N.C.L. Rev. 169 (1978).

26. See section 6.5, infra. The Model Penal Code § 207.14 (Tent.Draft No. 9, 1959) makes it a misdemeanor persistently to fail to support one's children, where the defendant is capable of furnishing support. See also State v. Ducey, 25 Ohio App.2d 50, 266 N.E.2d 233 (1970) (criminal conviction does not violate constitutional provision prohibiting imprisonment for debt); Day v. State,

481 P.2d 807 (Okl.Crim.App.1971) (non-support of child is a continuing criminal offense).

27. 9A U.L.A. 643, 747 (1979). See section 7.6, infra.

28. 42 U.S.C.A. §§ 601 to 644. AFDC is described in King v. Smith, 392 U.S. 309, 88 S.Ct. 2128, 20 L.Ed.2d 1118 (1968) and A. Kadushin, Child Welfare Services ch. 5 (2d ed. 1974). See also Note, Developments in Welfare Law-Aid to Families With Dependent Children, 61 Cornell L.Rev. 777 (1976).

29. 42 U.S.C.A. § 606, defining "dependent child" as a needy child who has been deprived of parental support or care by reason of the death, continued absence from the home or physical or mental incapacity of a parent and who is living with certain named relatives. See Annot., 23 A.L.R.Fed. 232 (1975). "Child" has been held to mean a child who has been born, so that benefits are not available for unborn children. Burns v. Alcala, 420 U.S. 575, 95 S.Ct. 1180, 43 L.Ed.2d 469 (1975), on remand 514 F.2d 1002 (8th Cir.1975), on remand 410 F.Supp. 1024 (S.D.Iowa 1976), affirmed 545 F.2d 1101, cert. denied 431 U.S. 920, 97 S.Ct. 2187, 53 L.Ed.2d 232 (1977); Green v. Stanton, 451 F.Supp. 567 (N.D.Ind.1978).

30. See the discussion in section 4.2, supra, at note 31.

31. Caplow, The Loco Parent: Federal Policy and Family Life, 1976 B.Y.U. L. Rev. 709 argues that AFDC has had the effect of breaking up families.

Supreme Court on two occasions held this sort of regulation inconsistent with the standards in the Social Security Act.[32] These decisions make an interesting contrast with other cases which are beginning to give to some unmarried couples' relationships some of the legal attributes of marriage and which require as a matter of constitutional right that unmarried couples living together receive benefits earmarked for families.[33] The AFDC program also provides financial support for a foster care program, for children living in foster homes with either relatives or non-relatives.[34]

Another way in which the AFDC program affects families is illustrated by Wyman v. James[35] which held that a woman receiving AFDC benefits could be deprived of those benefits if she refused a home visit of inspection by a state case worker. The Supreme Court said that such a visit did not involve a "search" under the Fourth Amendment, but that even if it did, it was not an unreasonable search and therefore did not violate the Fourth and Fourteenth Amendments, when it was conducted without a warrant. Justice Douglas wrote a strong dissent, taking the position that this was an invasion of the privacy of the home and a violation of the Fourth Amendment when it occurred without a warrant.

The statutes of many states impose upon parents liability to the state for reimbursement of any support which the state has furnished to their children, to the extent of the parents' means.[36] These statutes and the issue of their constitutionality, are discussed in a later section.[37]

The recognition of child support as a national social problem led, in 1974, to the enactment of legislation by Congress, effective on August 1, 1975, which provided federal assistance to the states, both financial and procedural, in the enforcement of claims for child support against parents.[38] This legislation set up, in the Department of Health, Education and Welfare, an organization charged with the responsibility to establish state standards for locating absent parents and obtaining child support, and authorized appropriations of federal funds to carry out the purposes of the statute.[39] In order to receive the benefit of this legislation the states are required to adopt a plan for effective location of parents and collection of child support payments from them and for cooperation with other states in such activities all subject to standards set by the Department of Health, Education and Welfare.[40]

The federal district courts are given jurisdiction to enforce court orders for child support after approval of applications for such action by the Secretary of Health, Education

32. King v. Smith, 392 U.S. 309, 88 S.Ct. 2128, 20 L.Ed.2d 1118 (1968); Lewis v. Martin, 397 U.S. 552, 90 S.Ct. 1282, 25 L.Ed.2d 561 (1970). See also Van Lare v. Hurley, 421 U.S. 338, 95 S.Ct. 1741, 44 L.Ed.2d 208 (1975).

33. New Jersey Welfare Rights Organization v. Cahill, 411 U.S. 619, 93 S.Ct. 1700, 36 L.Ed.2d 543 (1973) held that a state welfare program was unconstitutional when it limited its benefits to families composed of two married adults and their children. See also United States Department of Agriculture v. Moreno, 413 U.S. 528, 93 S.Ct. 2821, 37 L.Ed.2d 782 (1973); Chavez v. Shea, 185 Colo. 400, 525 P.2d 1148 (1974).

34. Miller v. Youakim, 440 U.S. 125, 99 S.Ct. 957, 59 L.Ed.2d 194 (1979).

35. 400 U.S. 309, 91 S.Ct. 381, 27 L.Ed.2d 408 (1971), 85 Harv. L. Rev. 258 (1971); Burt, Forcing Protection on Children and Their Parents: The Impact of Wyman v. James, 69 Mich.L. 1259 (1971). For an excellent account of a welfare family in New York see Sheehan, A Welfare Mother, The New Yorker Magazine, September 29, 1975, page 42.

36. E.g., State Division of Family Services v. Clark, 554 P.2d 1310 (Utah 1976). See also Tucker v. Toia, 43 N.Y.2d 1, 400 N.Y.S.2d 728, 371 N.E.2d 449 (1977) holding that a New York statute requiring a suit and judgment against the responsible parent as a condition upon state aid to a needy child was a violation of the state constitutional provision imposing upon the state a duty to aid the needy. See also 42 U.S.C.A. § 656.

37. See section 7.7, Practitioner's Edition.

38. 42 U.S.C.A. §§ 651 to 662; Note, Child Support Enforcement and Establishment of Paternity as Tools of Welfare Reform-Social Services of 1974, pt. B, 42 U.S.C.A. §§ 651-60, 52 Wash.L.Rev. 169 (1976); Bernet, The Child Support Provisions: Comments on the New Federal Law, 9 Fam.L.Q. 491 (1975).

39. 42 U.S.C.A. § 652.

40. 42 U.S.C.A. § 654.

and Welfare.[41] This may only be done when it has been found that the state of the absent parent's residence has failed to enforce the order and that the federal courts provide the only reasonable method of enforcing the order.[42] The Congressional intent was presumably to provide the additional remedy of district court suit in cases where the support obligor had gone to another state and where existing remedies were inadequate. But the statute is not limited to suits in which the parties are citizens of different states and therefore may, to the extent that diversity does not exist, raise constitutional doubts.[43] Another section of the Social Security Act, enacted contemporaneously, provided that wages or salaries for employment due from the United States may be the subject to garnishment for the payment of child support or alimony.[44] This provision does not authorize garnishment in the federal courts,[45] nor does it permit garnishment of debts due from the United States on obligations other than wages or salaries.[46] The effect of this statute is to waive the United States' sovereign immunity, leaving the question whether garnishment is to be granted in a particular case to the law of the state.[47]

The Social Security Act amendments also require the Secretary of Health, Education and Welfare to set up and operate a Parent Locator Service, using information not only from the records of that Department, but also from those of other government agencies, including the Internal Revenue Service, to aid the states and named authorized persons to find parents for purposes of enforcing support obligations against them.[48] In aid of this provision, the statute requires the applicant for or recipient of aid to assign to the state any rights to support which he may have and to cooperate with the state in obtaining support payments.[49]

The prevalence of divorce and remarriage in today's society greatly increases the number of families in which there are stepchildren. In addition to the well known psychological tensions, this creates an important legal issue, the extent to which the stepparent is to be responsible for the support of his stepchildren. A few states have enacted statutes imposing a duty of support upon the stepparents, generally for the purpose of reducing the state's welfare liabilities rather than from any notion of treating the stepchild like a natural child.[50] Some of these statutes

---

41. 42 U.S.C.A. § 660.

42. 42 U.S.C.A. § 652(a)(8).

43. U.S. Const. art. III, § 2.

44. 42 U.S.C.A. § 659; Note, Remedies-Domestic Relations: Garnishment for Child Support, 56 N.C.L.Rev. 169 (1978). Regulations covering the procedure in such garnishment proceedings are authorized by 42 U.S.C.A. § 661.

45. Overman v. United States, 563 F.2d 1287 (8th Cir. 1977); Golightly v. Golightly, 410 F.Supp. 861 (D.Neb. 1976); Jizmerjian v. Department of the Air Force, 457 F.Supp. 820 (D.S.C.1978), affirmed 607 F.2d 1001 (4th Cir. 1979), cert. denied 444 U.S. 1082, 100 S.Ct. 1036, 62 L.Ed. 2d 766 (1980). For cases dealing with all aspects of this statute, see Annot., 44 A.L.R.Fed. 494 (1979).

46. Brockelman v. Brockelman, 478 F.Supp. 141 (D.Kan.1979) (spouse may not garnish amounts owed to the other spouse as income tax refunds.)

47. Diaz v. Diaz, 568 F.2d 1061 (4th Cir.1977); Cunningham v. Department of Navy, 455 F.Supp. 1370 (D.Conn.1978); Clemons v. Morris, 350 So.2d 519 (Fla. App.1977); Hall v. Air Force Finance Center, Dept. of Air Force of United States, 344 So.2d 1340 (Fla.App.1977).

48. 42 U.S.C.A. § 653.

49. 42 U.S.C.A. § 602(a)(26), the support rights so assigned being made an obligation owed to the state, col-

lectible under all applicable state and local processes, by 42 U.S.C.A. § 656.

50. E.g., N.H.Stat.Ann. §§ 546–A:1, 546–A:2 (1974); N.Y.–McKinney's Soc.Serv.L. § 101 (1983 & Supp.1986); S.D.Comp.L. § 25–7–8 (1984); Utah Code Ann. 1986, § 78–45–4.1 (Supp.); West's Rev.Code Wash.Ann. § 26.16.205 (Supp.1986). The Uniform Civil Liability for Support Act, 9 U.L.A. 171 (1979), in force in a few states, contains no provision for the support liability of stepparents, but as enacted in New Hampshire it does contain such a provision, one which has been construed to place stepchildren on the same footing for support purposes as natural or adopted children. Logan v. Logan, 120 N.H. 839, 424 A.2d 403 (1980).

The welfare purpose of the Indiana statute is clear on its face. That of the New York statute is explained in Sugarman v. Burns, 76 Misc.2d 813, 350 N.Y.S.2d 99 (Fam.Ct.1973), and Slochowsky v. Lavine, 73 Misc.2d 563, 342 N.Y.S.2d 525 (1973).

The state recovered from a stepparent sums paid for the support of a stepchild in Sugarman v. Burns, 76 Misc. 2d 813, 350 N.Y.S.2d 99 (Fam.Ct.1973); Eagen v. Robb, 72 Misc.2d 364, 339 N.Y.S.2d 526 (Fam.Ct.1972); Komm v. Department of Social and Health Services, 23 Wash.App. 593, 597 P.2d 1372 (1979).

limit the stepparent's liability to situations where the stepchild is living in his household,[51] or terminate the stepparent's responsibility when the marriage to the child's natural parent ends.[52] The Washington statute has been held constitutional.[53] These statutes have been construed to mean that the obligation exists only where the natural parents are dead or are unable or unwilling to support the child.[54] Where the stepparent is living in a family with the stepchild and is, under state law, required to support the stepchild upon the same terms as a natural child, the natural parent and child are not entitled to AFDC.[55]

In the absence of statute the common law does not impose a liability for support upon stepparents except where the stepparent voluntarily takes the stepchild into his family and assumes the duty of support, the cases often describing the stepparent in this situation as being in loco parentis.[56] Even under those circumstances, however, the stepparent can end his support obligation at will. If he ceases to maintain the stepchild or is

separated from his spouse, or if the marital relationship with the child's natural parent ends in death or divorce, he is held no longer to be responsible for the stepchild's support.[57] There are a few exceptional cases in which the courts have relied upon equitable estoppel to hold the stepparent liable for the stepchild's support, finding that the child believed that the stepparent was his father and that the stepparent fostered that belief by representing himself to be the father.[58] In such cases there would be more than usual hardship to the child if the support obligation were not imposed.

In the rare cases in which an adult assumes the position of a parent for a child who is neither his natural child nor his stepchild, the courts have applied similar principles. The adult in such cases is referred to as acting in loco parentis. Most of these cases have held that the adult in this position may abandon his support obligation at any time, in effect that he is subject to no legally enforceable obligation.[59] The similarity between this situ-

51. Van Dyke v. Thompson, 95 Wash.2d 726, 630 P.2d 420 (1981) held that although the Washington family expense statute does refer to stepparents, it does not impose child support obligations upon a noncustodial, nonobligated stepparent.

52. E.g., the Utah statute, supra, note 50.

53. Washington Statewide Organization of Stepparents v. Smith, 85 Wash.2d 564, 536 P.2d 1202 (1975). Other cases construing these statutes are cited in Annot., 75 A.L.R.3d 1129 (1977).

54. Department of Welfare of New York v. Siebel, 6 N.Y.2d 536, 190 N.Y.S.2d 683, 161 N.E.2d 1 (1959), dismissed for want of a substantial federal question, 361 U.S. 535, 80 S.Ct. 586, 4 L.Ed.2d 538 (1960).

55. Archibald v. Whaland, 555 F.2d 1061 (1st Cir. 1977). Where the statute is not so broad, AFDC is not barred by the presence of a stepparent in the home. Slochowsky v. Lavine, 73 Misc.2d 563, 342 N.Y.S.2d 525 (Sup.Ct.1973).

56. Chapin v. Superior Court In and For Kern County, 239 Cal.App.2d 851, 49 Cal.Rptr. 199 (1966); Ladd v. Welfare Commissioner, 3 Conn.Cir. 504, 217 A.2d 490 (1965); Fussell v. Douberly, 206 So.2d 231 (Fla.Dist.Ct. App.1968); Kelley v. Iowa Department of Social Services, 197 N.W.2d 192 (Iowa 1972), appeal dismissed for want of a substantial federal question, 409 U.S. 813, 93 S.Ct. 170, 34 L.Ed.2d 69 (1972); Zeller v. Zeller, 195 Kan. 452, 407 P.2d 478 (1965); In re Besondy, 32 Minn. 385, 20 N.W. 366 (1884); Falzo v. Falzo, 84 N.J.Super. 343, 202 A.2d 192 (1964); In re Estate of Turer, 27 Wis.2d 196, 133 N.W.2d 765 (1965); In re Fowler, 130 Vt. 176, 288 A.2d 463 (1972).

57. Franklin v. Franklin, 75 Ariz. 151, 253 P.2d 337 (1953); Clevenger v. Clevenger, 189 Cal.App.2d 658, 11 Cal.Rptr. 707 (1961); Remkiewicz v. Remkiewicz, 180 Conn. 114, 429 A.2d 833 (1980); Kelley v. Iowa Department of Social Services, 197 N.W.2d 192 (Iowa 1972), dismissed for want of a substantial federal question, 409 U.S. 813, 93 S.Ct. 170, 34 L.Ed.2d 69 (1972); Zeller v. Zeller, 195 Kan. 452, 407 P.2d 478 (1965); Chestnut v. Chestnut, 247 S.C. 332, 147 S.E.2d 269 (1966); Annot., 75 A.L.R.3d 1129, 1137 (1977).

Brown v. Brown, 287 Md. 273, 412 A.2d 396 (1980) conceded that a stepparent has no legal duty of support, but found such a duty on the basis of a separation agreement incorporated in a divorce decree in which the stepfather promised to support his stepchild. But the court held that this obligation could not be enforced by contempt since that would violate Maryland's constitutional prohibition upon imprisonment for debt.

58. Miller v. Miller, 97 N.J. 154, 478 A.2d 351 (1984), citing other cases. Wiese v. Wiese, 699 P.2d 700 (Utah 1985) conceded the principle but found no basis for an estoppel on the facts. Arguments for and against the imposition of support duties on stepparents may be found in Lewis and Levy, Family Law and Welfare Policy: The Case for "Dual Systems", 54 Cal.L.Rev. 748, 762 (1966), and Mahoney, Support and Custody Aspects of the Stepparent-Child Relationship, 70 Corn.L.Rev. 38 (1984). See also J. Goldstein, A. Freud, A. Solnit, Beyond the Best Interests of the Child (1973) for emphasis on psychological as distinguished from natural parentage.

59. Franklin v. Franklin, 75 Ariz. 151, 253 P.2d 337 (1953); In re Carney's Marriage, 206 N.W.2d 107 (Iowa

ation and that in equitable adoption is striking and would seem to justify imposing the support duty in at least those cases where a promise to adopt can be proved.[60] In cases of this kind, where the child's natural parents are either unknown or dead, certainly the persons who have voluntarily taken him into their care should be responsible for his support. To a degree at least he has a stronger claim upon them than he would have upon a stepparent.

WESTLAW REFERENCES

di,sy(father /s primar! /s liab! /s support! /s child)

equal /3 duty responsib! /3 support!

sy,di(amount measure /3 support! /s ability /2 pay /s mother father parent!)

sy,di(parent! father mother /s support! /s adult post-majority /s child /s disab! handicap! ill**** incapacit!)

di(child /s suit sue*** action lawsuit /s comp*l! enforc! /s support! /s parent! mother father)

sy,di(statut! /s garnish! attach! /s enforc! comp*l! /s support!)

find 88 sct 2128

step-parent /s duty obligat! responsib! /s support! /s step-child

---

1973); Sargeant v. Sargeant, 88 Nev. 223, 495 P.2d 618 (1972).

60. Two cases imposed a duty of support on the basis of equitable estoppel and a finding that the adult stood in loco parentis to the child. A.S. v. B.S., 139 N.J.Super. 366, 354 A.2d 100 (1976), affirmed p.c. 150 N.J.Super. 122, 374 A.2d 1259 (1977); Wener v. Wener, 35 A.D.2d 50, 312 N.Y.S.2d 815 (2d Dep't 1970), 15 N.Y.L.F. 973 (1970). The New York case refused to rely upon equitable estoppel. For a discussion of equitable adoption, see section 20.9, infra.

Cf. West's Ann.Cal.Welf. & Inst.Code § 11351.5 (1980), which provides that an unrelated adult male residing in a family applying for or receiving state aid must contribute to the family an amount not less than the cost of an independent living arrangement.

§ 6.3

1. Manby v. Scott, 1 Lev. 4, 86 Eng.Rep. 781 (1659); Lungworthy v. Hockmore, 1 Ld.Raym. 444, 91 Eng.Rep. 1195 (1698); Child v. Hardyman, 2 Str. 875, 93 Eng.Rep. 909 (1731); Bolton v. Prentice, 2 Str. 1214, 93 Eng.Rep. 1136 (1745); Read v. Legard, 6 Exch. 636, 155 Eng.Rep. 698 (1851); McCutchen v. McGahay, 11 Johns. 281 (N.Y.

§ 6.3 The Spouse's Duty to Furnish Necessaries for His Spouse and Child

At common law the customary method for enforcing the husband's duty to support his family was for the wife or child to buy what they needed and charge it to the husband.[1] According to what became the doctrine of necessaries, the husband was thereby made responsible directly to the merchant who supplied the goods to the wife or child. In some early cases this procedure was referred to as the wife's agency by necessity,[2] perhaps as a fictional way of lending respectability to the doctrine of necessaries, perhaps out of confusion between that doctrine and agency. The fact is, however, that the doctrine of necessaries is not a doctrine of agency at all. The husband is liable for his wife's necessaries regardless of whether he authorized or apparently authorized her to buy them.[3] His liability is imposed by law, on principles of restitution or quasi-contract, in order to provide wives and children with support, and is not dependent upon his consent. The wife may also be liable for necessaries purchased by her.[4]

Now that the duty of support has, under the federal and state constitutions, been held to rest equally upon husband and wife,[5] the common law doctrine of necessaries also ap-

---

1814). See also 1 Blackstone, Commentaries on the Laws of England, 442 (Cooley 3d ed. 1884); 2 Pollock and Maitland, History of English Law, 405 (1898); Bromley, Family Law, 195–196 (2d ed. 1962). The foregoing apply to the wife's right to pledge the husband's credit. The history of the child's right to buy necessaries is discussed in Greenspan v. Slate, 12 N.J. 426, 97 A.2d 390 (1953), and Porter v. Powell, 79 Iowa 151, 44 N.W. 295 (1890).

2. See, e.g., some of the language in Debenham v. Mellon. L.R., 6 App.Cas. 24 (1880); Paquin, Ltd. v. Beauclerk, [1906] A.C. 148; Mathews Furniture Co. v. La Bella, 44 So.2d 160 (La.App.1950); Jordan Marsh Co. v. Hedtler, 238 Mass. 43, 130 N.E. 78 (1921).

3. Hodgson v. Harris, 8 N.J.Misc. 188, 149 A. 830 (1930); Restatement, Second, Agency § 14I, com. b (1958); Restatement, Restitution § 113 (1937); Seavey, Law of Agency, § 11D (1964). According to Greenspan v. Slate, 12 N.J. 426, 97 A.2d 390 (1953) the husband's liability is quasicontractual.

4. Cooke v. Adams, 183 So.2d 925 (Miss.1966), 38 Miss. L.J. 150 (1966); Annot., 15 A.L.R. 833 (1921).

5. See the authorities discussed supra, § 6.1, at note 14.

plies to both spouses, according to their respective means and ability to perform the duty.[6] This change in the law makes obsolete, or at least open to different interpretation, much of the language in the cases which deal with the doctrine of necessaries. But since nearly all the cases speak of the husband's liability under the doctrine of necessaries, and since many of them involve suits against the husband, the discussion in this section will continue to refer to the husband's liability, albeit with the understanding that the responsibility now rests upon both spouses.

Of course in an appropriate case the husband can be held liable on agency principles for goods purchased by his wife or child, as where he has authorized or apparently authorized the purchase.[7] But the relationship of husband and wife does not *ipso facto* constitute the wife an agent for her husband. The effect of the relationship is to make it more likely that other circumstances will create the inference of agency, where such circumstances would not have that effect if the parties were not married to each other.[8] If the husband is held liable on agency principles, then the court need not find the articles necessaries.

The doctrine of necessaries, stated in somewhat greater detail, is that if the husband fails or refuses to supply his wife or child with necessaries, the wife or child may purchase them, charging them to the husband, and he will be liable to the supplier for their cost. The merchant has the burden of proof respecting the various factors controlling liability, according to most authorities.[9]

§ 6.4 Separate Maintenance and Other Civil Remedies for Non-support

Nature of the Action

There are a number of civil remedies for nonsupport, but without too much obscuring of detail they may be accounted for in three classes. The first is the statutory suit for separate maintenance or alimony without divorce or separate support. The second class is the nonstatutory suit for support. The third is the statutory suit which is variously named divorce from bed and board, or divorce a mensa et thoro, or judicial separation. There is no difference between the first two kinds of action except that one is based upon statute and the second upon inherent equity jurisdiction. Whether and to what extent, there is a real difference between separate maintenance and divorce from bed and board is a more difficult question. The difficulties

---

6. United States v. O'Neill, 478 F.Supp. 852 (E.D.Pa. 1979) (Pennsylvania law); Manatee Convalescent Center, Inc. v. McDonald, 392 So.2d 1356 (Fla.App.1980); Memorial Hospital v. Hahaj, 430 N.E.2d 412 (Ind.App.1982); Annot., 11 A.L.R.4th 1160 (1982). Jersey Shore Medical Center-Fitkin Hospital v. Baum's Estate, 84 N.J. 137, 417 A.2d 1003 (1980), 20 Washburn L.Rev. 638 (1981) held that in the absence of agreement between creditor and spouses, the creditor may have recourse to the property of both spouses only when the property of the spouse who incurred the debt is insufficient to pay the claim. The duty to pay for necessaries may be imposed upon both spouses by statute in some states. Swogger v. Sunrise Hospital, Inc., 88 Nev. 300, 496 P.2d 751 (1972). Maryland and Virginia have taken the odd position that the state Equal Rights Amendment or the Equal Protection Clause abolish the doctrine of necessaries altogether. Condore v. Prince George's County, 289 Md. 516, 425 A.2d 1011 (1981); Schilling v. Bedford County Mem. Hospital, Inc., 225 Va. 539, 303 S.E.2d 905 (1983). Wisconsin and a few other states take the position that the husband is primarily liable for necessaries, and the wife only secondarily liable. Marshfield Clinic v. Discher, 105 Wis.2d 506, 314 N.W.2d 326 (1982). A Note, Inequality in Marital Liabilities: The Need for Equal Protection When Modify-

ing the Necessaries Doctrine, 17 U.Mich.J. of Law Reform 43 (1983).

For cases dealing with the duty of stepparents to support their stepchildren, see § 6.2, supra, at note 50, and § 7.7, Practitioner's Edition, at note 16.

7. Saks & Co. v. Bennett, 12 N.J.Super. 316, 79 A.2d 479 (1951). In this case the court properly held that the husband could be liable either on agency principles or under the doctrine of necessaries. Seavey, Law of Agency § 14C (1964) states that a child may be an agent.

8. Moehlenkamp v. Shatz, 396 N.E.2d 433 (Ind.App. 1979); Gorco Corst. Co. v. Stein, 256 Minn. 476, 99 N.W.2d 69 (1959); Saks & Co. v. Bennett, 12 N.J.Super. 316, 79 A.2d 479 (1951); Restatement, Second, Agency § 22 (1958); W. Seavey, Law of Agency § 14D (1964).

9. Jordan Marsh Co. v. Cohen, 242 Mass. 245, 136 N.E. 350 (1922). Other cases are cited in Annot., 60 A.L.R.2d 7, 68 (1958).

In a few states the tradesman has the burden of proof only where husband and wife are living separate and apart. Cole v. Adams, 56 N.C.App. 714, 289 S.E.2d 918 (1982).

are caused by a lack of precision in statutes and a tendency in the cases to repeat clichés without examining their meaning.

The action for separate maintenance is often said to have as its purpose the support of the wife, while divorce from bed and board is to affect the requirement of marital cohabitation.[1] The fact is, however, that both actions contemplate that the parties will live apart, but that they will remain married to each other in the sense that they will not be free to marry anyone else.[2] And both actions can result in decrees which order the husband to support the wife.[3] The grounds for the two actions are also quite similar,[4] although not completely so, since the grounds for both vary considerably from state to state.[5] The two actions are sometimes distinguished by saying that separate maintenance permits the parties to live apart, while divorce from bed and board compels them to,[6] but this distinction is unrealistic. If the parties wish to live apart they will do so whether a court permits them to or not. If they wish to live together they will do so whether a court has previously forbidden them to. The real issue is not whether they are permitted or commanded to live apart, but rather which of their marital rights and obligations are affected by their living apart.[7] On this score the two kinds of suit bear a close similarity.

In a few states the applicable statutes authorize broader decrees for judicial separation than for separate maintenance, so as to permit orders relating to custody of children and division of property in the former type of suit.[8]

The most important distinction between the two suits turns on the effect of reconciliation, however. Reconciliation terminates obligations under most separate maintenance decrees[9] but not under decrees for divorce from

§ 6.4

1. Williams v. Williams, 33 Ariz. 367, 265 P. 87 (1928); Goodwine v. Superior Court of Los Angeles County, 63 Cal.2d 481, 47 Cal.Rptr. 201, 407 P.2d 1 (1965), 39 So.Cal. L.Rev. 137 (1966), 39 Temp.L.Q. 372 (1966); Wilson v. Wilson, 349 Mass. 29, 206 N.E.2d 155 (1965); Lavino v. Lavino, 23 N.J. 635, 130 A.2d 369 (1957); Wolford v. Wolford, 133 W.Va. 403, 56 S.E.2d 614 (1949); Rosenthal v. Rosenthal, 12 Wis.2d 190, 107 N.W.2d 204 (1961). See also Bromley, Family Law, Ch. X (2d ed.1962).

2. People ex rel. Com'rs of Public Charities and Correction v. Cullen, 153 N.Y. 629, 47 N.E. 894 (1897). See also Courson v. Courson, 213 Md. 183, 129 A.2d 917 (1957), holding that the wife forfeits her payments under a decree of divorce a mensa et thoro when she is guilty of adultery. Brown, The Duty of the Husband to Support the Wife, 18 Va.L.Rev. 823, 846 (1932).

3. Myers v. Williams, 225 Ark. 290, 281 S.W.2d 944 (1955); Clifford v. Clifford, 42 Hawaii 279 (1958); Sanford v. Sanford, 173 Neb. 835, 115 N.W.2d 451 (1962). People ex rel. Com'rs of Public Charities and Correction v. Cullen, 153 N.Y. 629, 47 N.E. 894 (1897) holds that the obligation under the decree supplants the duty of support.

4. Rosenthal v. Rosenthal, 12 Wis.2d 190, 107 N.W.2d 204 (1961).

5. See the statutes cited in notes 13, 14, infra.

6. Radermacher v. Radermacher, 61 Idaho 261, 100 P.2d 955 (1940); Rudin v. Rudin, 104 N.J.Eq. 524, 146 A. 351 (1929).

7. The form of decree used in the two actions is substantially the same. Cf. Murphy, Newkirk, O'Brien, New York Domestic Relations Manual, 677 (1953) with Weinberg, Illinois Divorce, Separate Maintenance and Annulment, 594 (1954). Under some statutes a distinction is made between permanent and temporary separations, one being authorized for some reasons and the other for other reasons. See Chipman v. Chipman, 241 Or. 393, 406 P.2d 150 (1965). This adds further confusion to the other problems of separation.

Sanford v. Sanford, 173 Neb. 835, 115 N.W.2d 451 (1962), indicates there is no real difference between the two remedies and that the purpose is support for the wife. But Rosenthal v. Rosenthal, 12 Wis.2d 190, 107 N.W.2d 204 (1961) states that while separate maintenance is aimed at supporting the wife, divorce from bed and board affects the marital status in some undisclosed way. The point is that they both affect status and in nearly identical ways. It compounds the confusion to persist in referring to some undefined distinction in this inarticulate fashion.

In some states separate maintenance is considered a temporary remedy, while divorce from bed and board is permanent. See, e.g., Chipman v. Chipman, 241 Or. 393, 406 P.2d 150 (1965), and Rudin v. Rudin, 104 N.J.Eq. 524, 146 A. 351 (1929). But Clifford v. Clifford, 42 Hawaii 279 (1958) takes the position that the divorce from bed and board does not contemplate a permanent status, and that either party may have a divorce after thirty days.

8. E.g., Nichols v. Nichols, 538 S.W.2d 727 (Mo.App. 1976); Mercer v. Mercer, 183 Neb. 515, 162 N.W.2d 230 (1968).

9. E.g., Hester v. Hester, 239 N.C. 97, 79 S.E.2d 248 (1953). But sporadic or occasional cohabitation will not amount to a reconciliation. Hawn v. Hawn, 505 S.W.2d 459 (Mo.App.1974).

bed and board.[10] But the parties may have their decree of divorce from bed and board vacated if they have become reconciled.[11] Therefore this distinction is not very significant, except as a trap for the unwary. The effect of an offer of reconciliation constitutes a more important distinction between the two decrees. If the parties are living apart by virtue of a separate maintenance decree, an offer of reconciliation made in good faith by the losing defendant (that is, the wrongdoer) places upon the plaintiff the duty of accepting the offer or being labelled a deserter and losing the benefits of the separate maintenance decree.[12] An offer of reconciliation has no such effect, apparently no effect at all, if the parties are living apart under a divorce from bed and board.[13]

About half of the states have statutes authorizing divorces from bed and board or legal separations.[14] The Uniform Marriage and Divorce Act authorizes a decree of legal separation where one spouse requests it and the other does not object.[15] A similar number of states have enacted separate maintenance statutes.[16] In addition many states recognize a non-statutory right to separate maintenance.[17] As a result of Orr v. Orr [18] there is a constitutional requirement that the right to separate maintenance be made available equally to husbands and wives and many of the recently enacted statutes accomplish this. If equality is attained, the statutes are constitutional.[19]

The remedy of divorce from bed and board has been criticized for decades as creating a situation in which the parties are bound by marital ties but are not living together, in which they have the burdens but not the comforts of marriage, in which they are neither married nor single.[20] The same objections can be raised against separate maintenance and are well taken. The only valid social purpose for such remedies is to provide support and incidental relief for the spouse whose husband or wife fails or refuses to

---

10. E.g., Cecil v. Farmers Nat. Bank, 245 S.W.2d 430 (Ky.1951); Rozycki v. Rozycki, 102 N.Y.S.2d 217 (1951). See note 81, infra.

11. See cases cited in note 10, supra.

12. E.g., Williams v. Williams, 33 Ariz. 367, 265 P. 87 (1928); Wilson v. Wilson, 249 Mass. 29, 206 N.E.2d 155 (1965).

13. Monroe v. Superior Court of Los Angeles County, 28 Cal.2d 427, 170 P.2d 473 (1946), 35 Cal.L.Rev. 153 (1947).

14. Ala.Code 1983, § 30–2–30; Ariz.Rev.Stat. § 25–313 (Supp.1986); West's Ann.Cal.Civ.Code §§ 4506, 4508 (1983); Colo.Rev.Stat. § 14–10–106 (1973 and Supp.1986); Conn.Gen.Stat.Ann. § 46b–40 (Supp.1986); D.C.Code 1981, § 16–904 (1981); Hawaii Rev.Stat. § 580–71 (1976); Ill.–S.H.A. Ch. 40, § 402 (1980); Ky.Rev.Stat. § 403.050 (1984); La.Stat.Ann.-Civ.Code art. 138 (1952 and 1986 Supp.); Md. Code, Fam.Law, § 7–102 (1984); Neb.Rev. Stat. §§ 42–347, 42–350, 42–353 (1984); N.H.Rev.Stat. Ann. § 458:26 (1983 and Supp.1985); N.J.Stat.Ann. § 2A:34–3 (1952); N.Y.–McKinney's Dom.Rel.Law § 200 (1977 and Supp.1986); N.C.Gen.Stat. § 50–7 (1984 and Supp.1985); N.D.Cent.Code § 14–06–01 (1981); Or.Rev. Stat. § 107.025 (1984); R.I.Gen.Laws § 15–5–9 (1981); Tenn.Code Ann. § 36–4–102 (1984); Vt.Stat.Ann. tit. 15, § 555 (1974 and Supp.1985); Va.Code 1983, § 20–95; Wis. Stat.Ann. § 767.07 (1981). Hamel v. Hamel, ___ R.I. ___ 426 A.2d 259 (1981) holds that a decree of divorce from bed and board may be awarded to the husband on the ground of "irreconcilable differences" the decree to be in effect until the parties should be reconciled. The court examined the history and nature of divorce from bed and board, recognized the apparent lack of logic in such a decree, but found that the legislature had authorized the action, explaining it on the theory that what might look like irreconcilable differences at one time may later turn out to be reconcilable after all.

15. Uniform Marriage and Divorce Act § 302, 9A Unif.L.Ann. 121 (1979).

16. D.C.Code (1981, § 16–916; West's Fla.Stat.Ann. § 61.09 (1985); Official Code Ga.Ann. § 19–6–10 (1980); Ind.Code § 31–1–9–10 (1980); Kan.Stat.Ann. § 60–1601 (1983); Me.Rev.Stat.Ann. tit. 19, § 581 (1981 and Supp. 1986); Mass.Gen.Laws Ann. ch. 209, § 32 (1981 and Supp. 1986); Mich.C.L.Ann. § 25–87 (1984); Vernon's Ann.Mo. Stat. § 452.130 (1986); Nev.Rev.Stat. § 125.190 (1986); N.J. Stat.Ann. § 2A:34–24 (1952 and Supp. 1986); N.C. Gen.Stat. § 50–16.2 (1984); Ohio Rev.Code § 3105.17 (1980); Okl.Stat.1961, tit. 12, § 1284; R.I.Gen.Laws 1981 and 1986, § 15–5–19 (Supp.); S.D.Codified Laws § 25–4–40 (1984); Tenn.Code Ann. § 36–5–101 (1984); Utah Code Ann.1984, § 30–4–1; W.Va.Code, § 48–2–28 (1986); Wis. Stat.Ann. § 767.28 (1981); Wyo.Stat.1977, § 20–2–102.

17. Annot., 141 A.L.R. 399 (1942).

18. 440 U.S. 268, 99 S.Ct. 1102, 59 L.Ed.2d 306 (1979), on remand 374 So.2d 895 (Ala.Civ.App.1979), holding that a statute providing for alimony to wives alone is a violation of the Equal Protection Clause. See also George v. George, 487 Pa. 133, 409 A.2d 1 (1979).

19. Reese v. Reese, 2 Ill.App.3d 1054, 278 N.E.2d 122 (1971).

20. E.g., Kunze v. Kunze, 153 Minn. 5, 189 N.W. 447 (1922); 1 Bishop, Marriage, Divorce and Separation § 67 (1891).

support him or her, or who for religious or other reasons does not want a divorce.[21] Some courts also argue that separate maintenance encourages reconciliation,[22] but this seems doubtful. If, after such a decree has been entered, either party wishes a divorce, then it should be available. The Uniform Marriage and Divorce Act accomplishes this by requiring the court to convert legal separation decrees into divorces on motion of either party after the expiration of six months from the date of the separation decree.[23] Other statutes also authorize divorce after a period of legal separation.[24]

§ 6.5 Criminal Remedies for Non-support

Although desertion and non-support of wife and child were apparently not crimes at common law,[1] the statutes in all states contain provisions making such acts or failure to act crimes with respect to children, and in nearly all states with respect to spouses.[2] About half the states have adopted as their statutes, with more or less modification, the Uniform Desertion and Nonsupport Act,[3] a uniform law now nearly sixty years old. The Model Penal Code also contains a criminal non-support provision.[4] Somewhat more than half of the states treat the offense as a misdemeanor. In those states where non-support is a felony, the max-

---

21. Where the separation of the spouses is informal in the sense that no proceeding has been brought by either of them, there may be many pitfalls relating to property, support, custody, and other matters which impose hardship on one or both of them. See Bruch, The Legal Import of Informal Marital Separations: A Survey of California Law and a Call for Change, 65 Cal.L.Rev. 1015 (1977).

22. McWilliams v. McWilliams, 216 Ala. 16, 112 So. 318 (1927); Lavino v. Lavino, 23 N.J. 635, 130 A.2d 369 (1957); Weber v. Weber, 257 Wis. 613, 44 N.W.2d 571 (1950).

23. Uniform Marriage & Divorce Act § 314, 9A Unif. L.Ann. 180 (1979). See Rojas v. Rojas, 595 S.W.2d 729 (Mo.App.1980).

24. E.g., N.Y.–McKinney's Dom.Rel.Law § 170(5) (1977).

§ 6.5

1. Brooke v. State, 99 Fla. 1275, 128 So. 814 (1930) (abandonment of wife not a common law crime); Ewell v. State, 207 Md. 288, 114 A.2d 66 (1955); Regina v. Hogan, 5 Cox Crim.Cas. 255, 169 Eng.Rep. 504 (1851) (desertion of a child no crime). Contra: In re Ryder's Petition, 11 Paige 185 (N.Y.1844) (dictum that parent's neglect to support his child is a common law misdemeanor). But if the desertion or nonsupport caused injury or death to the child, the parent could be convicted of a crime. Regina v. Nicholls, 13 Cox Crim.Cas. 75 (1874) (manslaughter); Regina v. Conde, 10 Cox Crim.Cas. 547 (1867) (manslaughter); Regina v. Hogan, supra.

2. Alaska Stat. § 11.51.120 (1983); Ariz.Rev.Stat. § 13–3610 (1978); Ark.Stat. § 41–2405 (1977 and Supp. 1986); West's Ann.Cal. Penal Code §§ 270, 270a (1970 and Supp.1986); Colo.Rev.Stat. § 14–6–101 (1973); Conn. Gen.Stat.Ann. § 53–304 (1985); Del.Code tit. 13, §§ 521 to 524 (1981); West's Fla.Stat.Ann. § 856.04 (1976); Official Code Ga.Ann. § 19–9–64 (1981 and Supp.1986); Hawaii Rev.Stat. §§ 709–902, 709–903 (1976); Idaho Code §§ 18–401 to 18–405 (1979); Ill.–S.H.A. ch. 40, § 1101 (1980); West's Ann.Ind.Code § 35–46–1–4 (1985); Iowa Code Ann. § 726.5 (1979); Kan.Stat.Ann. § 21–3605 (1981); Ky.Rev. Stat. § 530–050 (1985); La.S.A.—Rev. Stat. tit. 14, § 74

(1986); Me.Rev.Stat.Ann. tit. 19, § 481 (1981); Mass.Gen. Laws Ann. ch. 273, § 1 (1980); Mich.C.L.A. Stat. Ann. § 28.358 (1981 and Supp.1986); Minn.Stat.Ann. § 609.375 (1964 and Supp.1986); Miss.Code 1973, § 97–5–3; Vernon's Ann.Mo.Stat. § 568.040 (1979); Mont.Code Ann. § 45–5–621 (1984); Neb.Rev.Stat. § 28–705 (1985); Nev. Rev.Stat. § 201.020 (1986); N.H.Rev.Stat.Ann. § 639.4 (1986); N.J.Stat.Ann. § 2C:24–5 (1982); N.Y.–McKinney's Penal Law § 260.05 (1980); N.C.Gen.Stat. §§ 14–322, 14–322.1, 14–322.2, 14–322.3, 14–323, 14–324 (1986); N.D. Century Code §§ 14–07–15, 14–07–16 (1981); Ohio Rev. Code § 2919.21 (1975); Okl.Stat.1983, tit. 21, §§ 851 to 853; Or.Rev.Stat. § 163.555 (1985); Pa.Stat. tit. 18, §§ 4321, 4322 (1985); R.I.Gen.Laws § 11–2–1 (1981); S.C. Code 1985, § 20–7–40; S.D.Codified Laws §§ 25–7–4, 25–7–16 (1985); Tenn.Code Ann. §§ 39–4–101, 39–4–102 (1982); V.T.C.A.Penal Code § 25.05 (1974); Utah Code Ann.1978, § 76–7–201; Vt.Stat.Ann. tit. 15, §§ 202 to 207 (1974 and Supp.1986); Va.Code 1983, § 20–61; West's Rev.Code Wash.Ann. § 26.20.030 (1986); Wyo.Stat.1977, § 20–3–101.

A few of these statutes continue to refer to the duty of husbands to support their wives, but of course a statute applied in such terms would violate the Equal Protection Clause of the Fourteenth Amendment to the United States Constitution, Orr v. Orr, 440 U.S. 268, 99 S.Ct. 1102, 59 L.Ed.2d 306 (1979), on remand 374 So.2d 895 (Ala.Civ.App.1979), or the Equal Rights Amendment to the state constitution, Commonwealth v. Baggs, 258 Pa. Super. 133, 392 A.2d 720 (1978).

For a discussion of all aspects of criminal non-support, see Jones, The Problem of Family Support: Criminal Sanctions for the Enforcement of Support, 38 N.C.L.Rev. 1 (1959).

3. This Act is reproduced in volume 10 of the old set of Uniform Laws Annotated at page 1 (1922).

4. Model Penal Code § 230.5 (1974): "A person commits a misdemeanor if he persistently fails to provide support which he can provide and which he knows he is legally obliged to provide to a spouse, child or other dependent."

imum penalties are set most often at about three years, but in a few states they are higher.

Several objections to the use of criminal sanctions in non-support cases can be made and have been made, the most obvious of which is that the defendant will not be providing any support during the time that he is in jail, so that the sanction is to that extent self-defeating. But many of the criminal statutes authorize the court to suspend sentence on condition that the defendant make specified payments to his dependents, thereby giving a conviction an effect somewhat similar to that of a civil contempt citation.[5] Other objections relate to the unfairness or hardship to defendants, who are often unskilled workers, in many instances alcoholics, and who are incarcerated in the worst institutions of the correctional system, county jails, where overcrowding, violence and beastly conditions are prevalent. The effect of a prosecution and jail sentence may be to damage or destroy the relationship of parent and child, but it is impossible to say how often this occurs. A thoughtful study of this social problem has concluded that where two factors exist together, a public agency which can quickly and efficiently initiate prosecutions, and courts

which will impose jail sentences for non-payment of support, the rate of violation of support orders is significantly reduced.[6] In other words the combination of a probability of prosecution with that of a jail sentence seems to be a deterrent, not a startling conclusion. Whether this is enough to justify the preservation of criminal non-support legislation remains an open question but one which all legislatures have answered in the same way. It is important to note that the statutes do have a dual purpose, that is, punishment for past non-support and enforcement of the defendant's support obligations in the future.[7]

These statutes have been subjected to constitutional attack upon a variety of grounds but have generally been upheld. They have been held not to violate the prohibition upon imprisonment for debt,[8] and not to be unconstitutionally vague under the Due Process Clause of the Fourteenth Amendment.[9] As has been indicated,[10] the Equal Protection Clause would today require that the statute apply to men and women alike. An argument that conviction under the statute violated the Freedom of Religion clause of the First Amendment by requiring the defendant to abandon his religious activities and go to work has been rejected.[11] The provision

---

5. For civil contempt enforcement of support orders, see § 6.4, supra. The criminal statutes also often authorize the court to order performance secured by a bond, and to modify support orders in the same fashion as a civil order. The criminal sentence may be enforced in the event the support order is later violated. See the Uniform Desertion and Nonsupport Act § 4, 10 Unif.L. Ann. 57 (1922).

6. Chambers, Men Who Know They Are Watched: Some Benefits and Costs of Jailing for Nonpayment of Support, 75 Mich.L.Rev. 900 (1977).

7. State v. Kempner, 51 Del. (1 Storey) 109, 138 A.2d 504 (Super.1957) (dual nature, criminal aspect predominant); State v. Savastini, 14 N.J. 507, 103 A.2d 249 (1954). In Pennsylvania, apparently the two purposes are served by two different statutes. Commonwealth v. George, 358 Pa. 118, 56 A.2d 228 (1948); Commonwealth v. Widmeyer, 149 Pa.Super. 91, 26 A.2d 125 (1942).

But even though the action may result in a support order, it is not a personal judgment which the wife may enforce against the husband, the only sanction being a criminal sentence. In re Cameron's Estate, 306 Mass. 138, 27 N.E.2d 696 (1940).

See also State v. Berry, 287 Md. 491, 413 A.2d 557 (1980).

8. People v. Elliott, 186 Colo. 65, 525 P.2d 457 (1974); Commonwealth v. Pouliot, 292 Mass. 229, 198 N.E. 256 (1935); State v. Davis, 469 S.W.2d 1 (Mo.1971); State v. Wright, 4 Ohio App.3d 291, 448 N.E.2d 499 (1982); Zitlow v. State, 213 Wis. 493, 252 N.W. 358 (1934).

9. State v. Joyce, 361 So.2d 406 (Fla.1978); State v. Wright, 4 Ohio App.3d 291, 448 N.E.2d 499 (1982); State v. Turner, 3 Ohio App.2d 5, 209 N.E.2d 475 (1965); Commonwealth v. Baggs, 258 Pa.Super. 133, 392 A.2d 720 (1978). Other cases on constitutionality are cited in Annot., 48 A.L.R. 1193 (1927).

Contentions that the statute violates the Equal Protection Clause by discriminating against the poor were rejected in State v. Meyer, 14 Ohio App.3d 69, 470 N.E.2d 156 (1983).

10. See note 2, supra. Cases which held that either the Equal Rights Amendment of state constitutions or the Equal Protection Clause do not require equal treatment of men and women in this respect must be taken to have been implicitly overruled. See, e.g., People v. Elliott, 186 Colo. 65, 525 P.2d 457 (1974); State v. Barton, 315 So.2d 289 (La.1975), overruled in 377 So.2d 335 (La.1979).

11. State v. Sprague, 23 Ore.App. 621, 550 P.2d 769 (1976).

found in some statutes that the failure to furnish support is prima facie evidence that the failure was wilful has been held not to violate the Due Process Clause of the Fourteenth Amendment.[12] But the distinction which some other statutes make between the failure to support by a resident of the state and the same failure by one who remains out of the state for a specified period, the first being only a misdemeanor and the second a felony, has been held to violate the Equal Protection Clause of the state constitution.[13] Attacks upon criminal non-support statutes come both from advocates for husbands and from advocates for wives and sometimes are phrased in constitutional terms.[14] Most of the attacks are really directed at particular unfair or erroneous decisions which can be expected to continue occurring until someone is clever enough to devise a legal system requiring no human intervention.

There is considerable variation in language among criminal non-support statutes, but some generalizations can be made. Most such statutes impose criminal penalties upon husbands or wives who desert or fail to support their spouses, and upon parents who desert or fail to support their children.[15] An adopted child is a "child" within the meaning of the statutes.[16] A few statutes also authorize punishment of the parent who fails to support his incapacitated adult child.[17] Nearly all statutes refer to the offense as either abandonment, desertion or non-support, the only real distinction being that the latter is a continuing offense, while the offenses of desertion and abandonment occur at a single point in time.[18] In the majority of states the crime is defined (so far as children are concerned) as the desertion or non-support of a child under a stated age, usually sixteen or eighteen.[19] If the age of majority is eighteen, as is now generally the case, it is not clear why the criminal liability for non-support should end at sixteen.

Under the great majority of statutes the offense of criminal non-support of a spouse is only committed when the spouse is left in "destitute or necessitous circumstances."[20] A similar phrase is also sometimes found in the statutes relating to the non-support of children.[21] The quoted phrase means that the wife or child has been left without necessary food, clothing or shelter.[22] The fact that a

---

12. State v. Shaw, 96 Idaho 897, 539 P.2d 250 (1975); State v. Bauer, 92 Wash.2d 162, 595 P.2d 544 (1979). The California conclusive presumption of legitimacy has been held constitutional as applied in a criminal proceeding in People v. Thompson, 89 Cal.App.3d 193, 152 Cal.Rptr. 478 (1979). Contra: State v. Jones, 481 So.2d 598 (La.1986).

13. In re King, 3 Cal.3d 226, 90 Cal.Rptr. 15, 474 P.2d 983 (1970), cert. denied 403 U.S. 931, 91 S.Ct. 2249, 29 L.Ed.2d 709 (1971).

14. E.g., Willging & Ellsmore, The "Dual System" in Action: Jail for Nonsupport, 1969 U. Toledo L.Rev. 348, taking the position that these statutes are unfair to husbands and that they violate the Due Process and Equal Protection Clauses of the Fourteenth Amendment, and the Eighth Amendment. An article which finds the law of support unfair to wives is Krauskopf & Thomas, Partnership Marriage: The Solution to an Ineffective and Inequitable Law of Support, 35 Ohio St.L.J. 558 (1974). They recommend equality of obligation as between husband and wife, which has now been achieved by constitutional interpretation, modification of the husband–wife relationship by contract, and enforcement of support obligations while the spouses remain together.

15. E.g., Uniform Desertion and Nonsupport Act § 1, 10 Unif.L.Ann. 1 (1922).

16. Commonwealth v. Kirk, 212 Ky. 646, 279 S.W. 1091 (1926); Annot., 44 A.L.R. 820 (1926).

17. E.g., Va.Code 1983, § 20–61.

18. People v. Winn, 94 Cal.App.2d 169, 210 P.2d 75 (1949); State v. James, 203 Md. 113, 100 A.2d 12 (1953); State v. Echavarria, 101 N.H. 458, 146 A.2d 256 (1958). There is some authority that a father cannot be convicted of deserting a child not in his custody though he could be guilty of non-support. Manners v. State, 210 Ind. 648, 5 N.E.2d 300 (1936). Abandonment is not an element of the crime of non-support, however. People v. Haralson, 26 Mich.App. 353, 182 N.W.2d 636 (1970).

19. The Uniform Desertion and Nonsupport Act, § 1, 10 Uniform Laws Ann. 1 (1922) uses age 16. The Model Penal Code, § 230.5 (Proposed Official Draft 1962) contains no age limit. Where the statutory language is "refuses or neglects to support", conviction of a refusal requires evidence of some sort of a demand for support. State v. Boyd, 4 Conn.Cir. 544, 236 A.2d 476 (1967).

20. See the statutes cited supra, note 2.

21. The Uniform Desertion and Nonsupport Act § 1, 10 Unif.L.Ann. 1 (1922) makes this requirement for both spouses and children. Fitzgerald v. Commonwealth, 403 S.W.2d 21 (Ky.1966) suggests that a statute not so limited would be unconstitutional. But State v. Davis, 469 S.W.2d 1 (Mo.1971) holds that a statute making it a crime to fail to provide "adequate" support is constitutional.

22. Turner v. State, 343 So.2d 591 (Ala.1977), on remand 343 So.2d 594 (Ala.Crim.App.1977); Poke v. State, 369 So.2d 840 (Ala.1979), on remand 369 So.2d 841 (Ala. Crim.App.1979); State v. Weyant, 149 Iowa 457, 128 N.W.

friend or relative steps in with help does not excuse the spouse or parent from criminal liability.[23] But now that both spouses are equally responsible for the support of their children, it does not seem that one of them could be convicted of non-support if the other were adequately supporting the children, even if the non-supporting spouse were able to provide support.[24] Of course the supporting spouse might well have a civil claim against the other for contribution to the support of the children.[25]

Several conclusions seem to follow from that statutory language which imposes criminal liability upon a person only when his spouse or child is destitute. One is that if sentence is suspended and an order for support entered, support is to be placed at a level sufficient to cover the spouse's or child's bare necessities and no more.[26] One might also conclude that the purpose of such a statute, or at least its major purpose, is the protection of state welfare funds rather than the protection of the welfare of dependents.[27] If, as has been

suggested,[28] the criminal sanction can be effective when initiated by state authorities, then it should be available for the full protection of spouses and children, without such severe limits on the size of support orders.

Conversely, in some states the prosecution need not prove that the spouse or child is destitute in order to obtain a criminal conviction.[29] In these states the implication from the statute is that its purpose is the protection of the dependents by providing support for them commensurate both with their needs and the defendant's ability to pay.[30] Consequently orders made in these states take account of both the spouse's or child's needs and the defendant's means, very much as in civil non-support cases.[31]

The requirement that the abandonment or non-support be wilful is either explicit or implicit in all criminal statutes. This means that the defendant must be proved capable of furnishing support before he can be convicted for his failure.[32] But under some statutes proof of failure to furnish support is prima

839 (1910); State v. Breaux, 227 La. 417, 79 So.2d 502 (1955). Failure to provide medical care also violates the statutes. Annot., 12 A.L.R.2d 1047 (1950).

23. People v. Winn, 94 Cal.App.2d 169, 210 P.2d 75 (1949); Kistler v. State, 190 Ind. 149, 129 N.E. 625 (1921); State v. Herring, 200 Iowa 1105, 205 N.W. 861 (1925); State v. Freiberg, 35 Wis.2d 480, 151 N.W.2d 1 (1967). But the court in City of Cincinnati v. Meade, 22 Ohio App.2d 176, 259 N.E.2d 505 (1970) held that a mother could not be charged with abandonment when she left her children in a foster home.

24. State v. Oppenheimer, 46 Ohio App.2d 241, 348 N.E.2d 731 (1975) (semble); Fitzgerald v. Commonwealth, 403 S.W.2d 21 (Ky.1966). But see State v. Ozanne, 75 Wash.2d 546, 452 P.2d 745 (1969). Earlier cases are collected in Annot., 131 A.L.R. 482 (1941). The early cases were in some disagreement as to a parent's criminal liability when his children are cared for by a charitable institution, although the policy and intent of the statutes dictate that this should be no defense. State v. Freiberg, 35 Wis.2d 480, 151 N.W.2d 1 (1967); Annot., 24 A.L.R. 1075 (1923).

25. State v. Oppenheimer, 46 Ohio App.2d 241, 348 N.E.2d 731 (1975) (dictum).

26. Greggo v. Greggo, 41 Del.Ch. 289, 194 A.2d 58 (1963).

27. Turner v. State, 343 So.2d 591 (Ala.1977), on remand 343 So.2d 594 (Ala.Crim.App.1977).

28. See note 6, supra.

29. E.g., Md.Code 1984, Fam.Law, §§ 10–201, 10–203 (1984); S.C.Code 1985, § 20–7–40; West's Rev.Code Wash.

Ann. § 26.20.030 (1986); Shaw v. State, 27 Ariz. 9, 229 P. 395 (1924); Commonwealth v. Whiston, 306 Mass. 65, 27 N.E.2d 703 (1940). Earlier cases holding that a wife's means are not to be taken into account presumably are no longer to be followed, in view of the principle that wives are equally responsible with husbands for support. E.g., Ewell v. State, 207 Md. 288, 114 A.2d 66 (1955).

30. State v. Boyd, 4 Conn.Cir. 544, 236 A.2d 476 (1967); State v. Davis, 469 S.W.2d 1 (Mo.1971); State v. Freiberg, 35 Wis.2d 480, 151 N.W.2d 1 (1967). State v. Berry, 287 Md. 491, 413 A.2d 557 (1980) states the statutory purpose to be "to assist spouses and children in directly procuring support and thereby preventing them from becoming public burdens * * *", although the Maryland statute does not require proof that the dependents were destitute as a condition on conviction. See also S.C.Code 1985, § 20–7–40.

31. State v. Moran, 99 Conn. 115, 121 A. 277 (1923). State v. Davis, 469 S.W.2d 1 (Mo.1971) construed the statute making it a crime to fail to provide "adequate" support as follows: " * * * it has been held that adequate support means personal support, maintenance, food, clothing, et cetera, reasonably suitable to the condition in life and commensurate with the defendant's ability." See also Krauskopf & Thomas, Partnership Marriage: The Solution to an Ineffective and Inequitable Law of Support, 35 Ohio St.L.J. 558, 575 (1974).

32. State v. Greer, 259 Iowa 367, 144 N.W.2d 322 (1966); Ewell v. State, 207 Md. 288, 114 A.2d 66 (1955); People v. Bittner, 32 Misc.2d 750, 224 N.Y.S.2d 222 (County Ct.1961); Zitlow v. State, 213 Wis. 493, 252 N.W. 358 (1934). Burris v. State, 178 Ind.App. 327, 382 N.E.2d

facie evidence that the failure was wilful, the presumption so created being rebuttable by evidence of incapacity or lawful excuse.[33] The defendant may be guilty of non-support of a child even after a divorce decree has placed custody of the child with an ex-spouse, if the divorce decree is silent on child support, or if the defendant fails to comply with a child support order.[34] According to most cases, however, he is not guilty if he does comply with the child support order even though the child does not thereby receive as much for support as he needs.[35]

There is also explicitly or implicitly in the statutes the requirement that the non-support or abandonment must have been without good cause or without lawful excuse. The effect of this, if it requires any more than the proof of the defendant's ability to furnish support,[36] is to retain in the criminal proceeding the whole issue of marital fault which formerly played such a large role in civil non-support cases.[37] It is difficult to define in general terms what is meant by "good cause" or "lawful excuse" if

they do refer to marital fault.[38] Perhaps they mean that the defendant is not guilty if the spouse has refused to live with him.[39] And compliance with a valid separation agreement should constitute a lawful excuse.[40] Although fault has in most states been eliminated from the civil non-support cases,[41] perhaps it is reasonable to retain it in the criminal cases where there is a stronger probability of a prison term. Some courts would go so far as to absolve the father from criminal liability for non-support of a child who is living apart through no fault of the father.[42] The difficulty with all this is that there are no longer any generally accepted norms of behavior for the husband-wife and parent-child relationships in the United States, so that it is impossible to say what some court might decide is a "lawful excuse" for not providing support for a spouse or a child.

The procedural and constitutional principles applicable to criminal non-support actions are those of the criminal law generally, even though the action has a remedial pur-

---

963 (1978) requires proof of wilfulness beyond a reasonable doubt and defines it as being a deliberate or perverse design, malice, or an intentional or deliberate breach of the duty to provide support.

33. E.g., Uniform Desertion and Nonsupport Act § 6, 10 Unif.L.Ann. 71 (1922); Commonwealth v. Marino, 343 Mass. 725, 180 N.E.2d 662 (1962); State v. Wright, 4 Ohio App.3d 291, 448 N.E.2d 499 (1982); State v. Bauer, 92 Wash.2d 162, 595 P.2d 544 (1979); State v. Ozanne, 75 Wash.2d 546, 452 P.2d 745 (1969).

34. Cases are collected in Annot., 73 A.L.R.2d 960 (1960).

35. Id. at 967. But Williamson v. State, 138 Ga.App. 306, 226 S.E.2d 102 (1976) held that a husband could be convicted of non-support even though his divorce decree incorporated a separation agreement by which his ex-wife agreed to assume the full responsibility for supporting their child. If husband and wife now have equal responsibility for child support, this decision can hardly be approved.

36. State v. Conway, 182 Iowa 1236, 166 N.W. 596 (1918); State v. Davis, 469 S.W.2d 1 (Mo.1971); State v. Russell, 73 Wash.2d 903, 442 P.2d 988 (1968) all seem to suggest that "good cause" refers to the defendant's ability to support the spouse or child.

37. For general discussion of fault in this context, see Jones, The Problem of Family Support: Criminal Sanctions for the Enforcement of Support, 38 N.C.L.Rev. 1, 33–35 (1959), and Model Penal Code, § 207.14, comments (Tent.Draft No. 9, 1959).

38. See, e.g., State v. Weymiller, 197 Iowa 1273, 198 N.W. 780 (1924); and State v. Stout, 139 Iowa 557, 117

N.W. 958 (1908), the latter indicating that "cause" refers to the kind of conduct which would justify a legal separation.

39. Commonwealth v. Marino, 343 Mass. 725, 180 N.E.2d 662 (1962); People v. Jansen, 264 N.Y. 364, 191 N.E. 17 (1934) (husband has no duty to support where he had a decree of legal separation). Many other cases are collected in Annots., 3 A.L.R. 107 (1919) and 8 A.L.R. 1314 (1920) (husband not criminally liable where wife refuses to live with him); 17 A.L.R. 999 (1922) (husband not guilty if wife engages in conduct which would be ground for divorce). For cases discussing "cause" as used in the Uniform Desertion and Nonsupport Act, see 10 Uniform Laws Ann. 14 (1922). But cf. People v. Schenkel, 258 N.Y. 224, 179 N.E. 474 (1932).

If the husband by conduct which would defeat the purposes of marriage causes the wife to leave home, he may be criminally liable for abandonment or non-support. State v. Newman, 91 Conn. 6, 98 A. 346 (1916); Bingham v. State, 488 P.2d 603 (Okl.Crim.App.1971). But see Russ v. State, 242 So.2d 148 (Fla.App.1970).

40. State v. Prince, 42 Wash.2d 314, 254 P.2d 731 (1953). Cf. Ewell v. State, 207 Md. 288, 114 A.2d 66 (1955). But see Williamson v. State, 138 Ga.App. 306, 226 S.E.2d 102 (1976), and State v. Karagavoorian, 32 R.I. 477, 79 A. 1111 (1911).

41. See §§ 6.1 and 6.4, supra.

42. Cases, which are now hardly up to date, are collected in Annot., 23 A.L.R. 864 (1923).

pose. Thus the action is begun by indictment or information,[43] the presumption of innocence applies,[44] the elements of the offense must be proved beyond a reasonable doubt,[45] and the criminal statute of limitations applies.[46] Since the offense of non-support, as distinguished from abandonment or desertion, is a continuing one, however, the statute of limitations may not run so long as the defendant fails to give support.[47] Former jeopardy is also a defense, as to acts charged up to the date of the first prosecution.[48] Here also the continuing nature of the offense of non-support is relevant, since the failure to support occurring after the first prosecution is a new and separate offense which may be the basis for a subsequent prosecution without subjecting the defendant to double jeopardy.[49] An acquittal of the charge of criminal non-support does not, however, bar subsequent civil suits for non-support.[50] In some states the defendant may be placed on probation on condition that he provide support to his dependents, and the probation may be revoked when he fails to comply with the condition.[51] An order so entered may be modified when the parties' circumstances change where the

applicable statute so provides.[52] Many criminal non-support statutes also provide that husband and wife are competent to testify against each other in such proceedings.[53]

 WESTLAW REFERENCES

sy,di(non-support support /s misdemeanor)
sy,di(non-support support /s felon*)
sy,di(constitution! unconstitutional! /s non-support /5 statute)

§ 6.6   The Uniform Reciprocal Enforcement of Support Act

Concern for destitute wives and children who were not being supported by their husbands and fathers led to the drafting in the Nineteen Forties of the prototype of this statute, whose outstanding feature is its provision for a two-state lawsuit. The statute was first passed in New York state where it was called the Uniform Support of Dependents Law.[1] The Commissioners on Uniform State Laws then took up the idea and produced the first Uniform Reciprocal Enforcement of Support Act.[2] The latest version of this statute was

---

43. State v. Kempner, 51 Del. (1 Storey) 109, 138 A.2d 504 (1958). See also Annot., 24 A.L.R. 1002, 1014 (1923). The offense may be charged substantially in the language of the statute. People v. Bittner, 32 Misc.2d 750, 224 N.Y.S.2d 222 (County Ct.1961). See Annot., 5 A.L.R.2d 444, 499 (1949) on the right to a bill of particulars.

44. State v. Kempner, 51 Del. (1 Storey) 109, 138 A.2d 504 (1958).

45. State v. Newman, 91 Conn. 6, 98 A. 346 (1916). Keener v. People, 194 Colo. 244, 572 P.2d 463 (1977) held that a report of testimony given by the defendant in a prior civil contempt proceeding for failure to comply with a support order in a divorce case could be admitted in the criminal non-support proceeding without violating the Fifth Amendment, where the defendant had been represented in the prior case.

46. State v. Kempner, 51 Del. (1 Storey) 109, 138 A.2d 504 (1958).

47. Jones, The Problem of Family Support: Criminal Sanctions for the Enforcement of Support, 38 N.C.L.Rev. 1, 33 (1959).

48. State v. Kempner, 51 Del. (1 Storey) 109, 138 A.2d 504 (1958).

49. People v. Winn, 94 Cal.App.2d 169, 210 P.2d 75 (1949); State v. Morgan, 155 Iowa 482, 136 N.W. 521 (1912); State v. James, 203 Md. 113, 100 A.2d 12 (1953). (Prosecution in Delaware is no bar to a prosecution in Maryland).

50. State v. Lugg, 144 Conn. 21, 127 A.2d 52 (1956); Greggo v. Greggo, 41 Del.Ch. 289, 194 A.2d 58 (1963).

51. State v. Berry, 287 Md. 491, 413 A.2d 557 (1980).

52. See the statutes cited, supra, note 2, and State v. Guillot, 256 La. 751, 238 So.2d 191 (1970). State v. Mansy, 6 Conn.Cir. 24, 262 A.2d 817 (1969) held that a spouse could not file a motion for modification in such a criminal case, although the Connecticut statute authorizes modification. Presumably the state alone would be the proper party to take such action.

53. E.g., Uniform Desertion and Nonsupport Act, § 6, 10 Uniform Laws Ann. 71 (1922).

§ 6.6

1. The New York statute is now N.Y.–McKinney's Dom.Rel.L. §§ 30 to 43 (1977 and Supp.1987). For brief accounts of the origins of these statutes, see W. Brockelbank, Interstate Enforcement of Family Support 3–7 (2d ed. Infausto 1971). Briggs, The Reciprocal Enforcement of Support Act in Montana, 15 Mont.L.Rev. 40 (1954); Note, Uniform Reciprocal Legislation to Enforce Familial Duties of Support, 25 Drake L.Rev. 206 (1975); Note Uniform Reciprocal Enforcement of Support Act, 20 Washburn L.Rev. 409 (1981).

2. 9A Unif.L.Ann. 747 (1979). For convenience the Act will hereafter be referred to as RURESA (Revised Uniform Reciprocal Enforcement of Support Act), meaning the 1968 version. If the reference is to an earlier version, it will be described as URESA.

promulgated by the Commissioners in 1968.[3] The New York type of statute was at one time in force in about ten states. At present one form or another either of the New York statute, URESA or RURESA is in force in every state, territory and the District of Columbia.[4] The different versions are all sufficiently similar so that there is reciprocity among all states and territories.[5] An action begun in one state or territory may thus be continued in any other state or territory.

Perhaps because of its novel procedure URESA has been subjected to constitutional attack in several cases. It has been upheld in all instances, successfully meeting the test of due process,[6] equal protection of the laws,[7] and the argument that it is in effect an interstate compact which does not comply with the requirements for such compacts.[8] In fact, there seems to be no serious constitutional question about the procedure which the Act sets up, although provisions concerning choice of law, discussed below, may have constitutional implications.

In applying RURESA or URESA it is important to remember that they are procedural rather than substantive statutes. They do not establish duties of support, but, as the statutes put it, "Duties of support applicable under this Act are those imposed under the laws of any state where the obligor was present for the period during which support is sought."[9] The effect of these Acts is to provide new, cheaper and more efficient techniques for enforcing those duties of support which the various state laws may create.

It is also significant that URESA and RURESA are essentially civil and not criminal statutes. They do contain provisions facilitating interstate rendition (extradition) for criminal non-support violations,[10] but the only direct remedies which they authorize are civil. Although their chief purpose is to reach the spouse or parent who runs out on his support obligations,[11] they may be invoked by the spouse or children who have moved into another state against the spouse or parent who has remained at home.[12] The courts are committed to a liberal construction of the Acts in order to effectuate their purpose of providing for support across state and county lines, the emphasis in the statute on support leads one to wonder whether it would be available to enforce a division of property of

3.   9A Unif.L.Ann. 643 (1979).

4.   Statutory citations may be found in 9A Unif.L.Ann. 643, 747 (1979) and 37, 46 (Supp.1980).

5.   Landes v. Landes, 1 N.Y.2d 358, 153 N.Y.S.2d 14, 135 N.E.2d 562 (1956); Commonwealth ex rel. Shaffer v. Shaffer, 175 Pa.Super. 100, 103 A.2d 430 (1954); W. Brockelbank, Interstate Enforcement of Family Support 5 (2d ed. Infausto, 1971).

6.   Harmon v. Harmon, 160 Cal.App.2d 47, 324 P.2d 901 (1958), cert. denied 358 U.S. 881, 79 S.Ct. 120, 3 L.Ed. 2d 110 (1958); Smith v. Smith, 125 Cal.App.2d 154, 270 P.2d 613 (1954); Proctor v. Sachner, 143 Conn. 9, 118 A.2d 621 (1955); Ivey v. Ayers, 301 S.W.2d 790 (Mo.1957); Martin v. Martin, 213 Tenn. 345, 373 S.W.2d 609 (1963). For general discussion of constitutionality, see Brockelbank, Is the Uniform Reciprocal Enforcement of Support Act Constitutional, 31 Ore.L.Rev. 97 (1952); Note, Uniform Reciprocal Enforcement of Support Act, 17 U.Pitts.L.Rev. 261, 275 (1956). Kulko v. Superior Court of Cal. In and For San Francisco, 436 U.S. 84, 98 S.Ct. 1690, 56 L.Ed.2d 132 (1978), rehearing denied 438 U.S. 908, 98 S.Ct. 3127, 57 N.E.2d 1150 (1978) by suggesting reliance on URESA as a way of dealing with the child support problem, seems to assume URESA is constitutional.

7.   Aberlin v. Domestic Relations Court of New York, 159 F.Supp. 59 (S.D.N.Y.1958); Harmon v. Harmon, 160 Cal.App.2d 47, 324 P.2d 901 (1958), cert. denied 358 U.S.

881 (1958); Proctor v. Sachner, 143 Conn. 9, 118 A.2d 621 (1955); Landes v. Landes, 1 N.Y.2d 358, 153 N.Y.S.2d 14, 135 N.E.2d 562 (1956).

8.   Ivey v. Ayers, 301 S.W.2d 790 (Mo.1957); Landes v. Landes, 1 N.Y.2d 358, 153 N.Y.S.2d 14, 135 N.E.2d 562 (1956); Fraser v. Fraser, ___ R.I. ___, 415 A.2d 1304 (1980).

9.   RURESA § 7, 9A Unif.L.Ann. 672 (1979). See also Chance v. Lapausky, 43 Md.App. 84, 402 A.2d 1329 (1979).

10.   RURESA §§ 5, 6, 9A Unif.L.Ann. 664 (1972). For a discussion of extradition see § 6.5, supra. On the civil nature of the act, see W. Brockelbank, Interstate Enforcement of Family Support ch. 3 (2d ed. Infausto 1971), and Phillips v. Phillips, 336 Mass. 561, 146 N.E.2d 919 (1958).

11.   Although the Act was christened the "Runaway Pappy Act" by its principal draftsman, Professor Brockelbank, it may no longer be so referred to in view of the Supreme Court's holding that duties of support rest equally upon husband and wife. Orr v. Orr, 440 U.S. 268, 99 S.Ct. 1102, 59 L.Ed.2d 306 (1979), on remand 374 So.2d 895 (Ala.Civ.App.1979).

12.   Harmon v. Harmon, 160 Cal.App.2d 47, 324 P.2d 901 (1958), cert. denied 358 U.S. 881, 79 S.Ct. 120, 3 L.Ed. 2d 110 (1958); Commonwealth v. Mexal, 201 Pa.Super. 457, 193 A.2d 680 (1963); Bushway v. Riendeau, 137 Vt. 455, 407 A.2d 178 (1979) citing other cases.

the spouses, even though such a division often serves the same purpose as a support order.[13]

The civil remedies provided by RURESA are two: a) The person or agency claiming support may bring a suit in his or her home state, the initiating state, and obtain a judgment for support in the state in which the obligor is present, the responding state.[14] The same procedure may be used when obligee and obligor are in different counties of the same state.[15] The Act may be used whenever the parties are in different states or different counties, even though they may be just across a state or county line and therefore be living

13. State ex rel. Whatley v. Mueller, 288 S.W.2d 405 (Mo.App.1956); Bushway v. Riendeau, 137 Vt. 455, 407 A.2d 178 (1979); Davidson v. Davidson, 66 Wash.2d 780, 405 P.2d 261 (1965) (also states that URESA may be used to accomplish a division of community property).

14. RURESA §§ 9, 11, 14, 18, 9A Unif.L.Ann. 677 ff. (1979); Fox, The Uniform Reciprocal Enforcement of Support Act, 12 Fam.L.Q. 113 (1978); Note, Uniform Reciprocal Legislation to Enforce Familial Duties of Support, 25 Drake L.Rev. 206 (1975).

15. RURESA § 33, 9A Unif.L.Ann. 737 (1979). This provision was not in the original Act, but first appeared in the 1958 version.

16. Bushway v. Riendeau, 137 Vt. 455, 407 A.2d 178 (1979).

17. RURESA §§ 35 to 40, 9A Unif.L.Ann. 741 ff. (1979); O'Halloran v. O'Halloran, 580 S.W.2d 870 (Tex. Civ.App.1979); Morway v. Morway, 460 S.W.2d 531 (Tex. Civ.App.1970).

But URESA does not provide the only method for enforcing alimony decrees of other states. They may also be enforced by a suit on the decree in the state where the obligor may be served. Barrell v. Barrell, 288 Md. 19, 415 A.2d 579 (1980).

The standards for enforcing, as contrasted with modifying, the decrees of other states have been held to differ, depending upon whether the method of enforcement chosen is registration or the two-state lawsuit procedure. State on Behalf of McDonnell v. McCutcheon, 337 N.W.2d 645 (Minn.1983).

Enforcement by registration may only be had where the judgment being enforced was itself based upon jurisdiction, In re Marriage of McMahan, 660 P.2d 515 (Colo. App.1983), and where the state registering the judgment has personal jurisdiction over the judgment debtor. Stephens v. Stephens, 229 Va. 610, 331 S.E.2d 484 (1985).

18. The discussion of procedure assumes that two states are involved. The procedure is essentially the same where URESA § 33 is being relied upon and the parties are living in different counties in the same state. The procedure in states having the Uniform Support of Dependents Law may vary in some respects. See, e.g., State of Colorado, ex rel. Graham v. Brammer, 301 N.W. 2d 715 (Iowa 1981).

close to each other.[16] b) If there is an outstanding support judgment of another state, the beneficiary of that judgment may register it in the state of the obligor's presence and by a summary procedure have it enforced there as if it were the judgment of a court of that state.[17]

An action under RURESA is begun in the initiating state [18] by the filing of a petition, just as one would begin any other civil suit.[19] The plaintiff may be a spouse or child of the obligor [20] or an ex-spouse seeking to enforce an alimony judgment [21] or a state suing to recover reimbursement for support furnished

19. RURESA § 11, 9A Unif.L.Ann. 681 (1979). Assessment of filing fees and costs against the defendant is discretionary under § 15 of RURESA, but they may not be charged to the obligee.

20. Harmon v. Harmon, 160 Cal.App.2d 47, 324 P.2d 901 (1958), cert. denied 358 U.S. 881, 79 S.Ct. 120, 3 L.Ed. 2d 110 (1958), holding that suit may be brought on behalf of a minor without making him a party. Contra: Mahan v. Read, 240 N.C. 641, 83 S.E.2d 706 (1954). RURESA § 13 provides that a petition may be filed on behalf of a minor by one having custody without appointment of a guardian ad litem. See also Lambrou v. Berna, 154 Me. 352, 148 A.2d 697 (1959). Byrd v. O'Neill, 309 Minn. 415, 244 N.W.2d 657 (1976) held that a child's guardian was entitled to recover support for the child in a RURESA suit. Campbell v. Campbell, 126 Ariz. 558, 617 P.2d 66 (Ariz.1980) held that a child's mother did not have standing to bring a URESA proceeding for support of the child where the divorce decree had given custody to the father and the mother was holding the child in violation of the decree.

21. Scott v. Sylvester, 220 Va. 182, 257 S.E.2d 774 (1979), appeal after remand 225 Va. 304, 302 S.E.2d 30 (1983), cert. denied 464 U.S. 961, 104 S.Ct. 395, 78 L.Ed.2d 338 (1983) enforcing a modifiable decree of another state for the full amount due, not just the amount accrued after the defendant became a resident of Virginia; Mancini v. Mancini, 136 Vt. 231, 388 A.2d 414 (1978), holding that arrears may be collected in a URESA proceeding when specifically prayed for in the petition. But see Schlecht v. Schlecht, 387 A.2d 575 (D.C.App.1978), limiting the recovery of arrears due under the divorce decree to those which accrued after the filing of the petition in the initiating state. This is typical of the tendency of so many courts to impose senseless and unauthorized limits on the scope of RURESA. The case seems clearly wrong on this point.

The divorced spouse may recover alimony or child support by the RURESA procedure even where the divorce decree was entered in the responding state, without being required to seek a modification of the divorce decree from the court which entered it. Paul v. Paul, 439 S.W.2d 746 (Mo.1969); Maskil v. Green, 25 Utah 2d 187, 479 P.2d 343 (1971) (allowing recovery even though the

to dependents of the out-of-state obligor.[22] No service on or notice to the defendant is made by the court of the initiating state, since an adversary hearing is not held at this stage.[23] The petition so filed must state the names, addresses, and circumstances of the plaintiff and defendant, plus any other information concerning the defendant which might be of help in finding him.[24] The plaintiff may, on request by the court, be represented by a designated public official, often the district or county attorney.[25]

Those administering the Reciprocal Support Act have found the greatest source of difficulty to be a proper understanding of the function of the court in the initiating state. The Act provides that this court is only concerned with whether the petition (or complaint) sets forth facts from which it may be determined that the defendant owes a duty of support and that a court of the responding state may obtain jurisdiction over the defendant.[26] If it so

finds, it must so certify and transmit three copies of the complaint, of its certification and of the Act to the appropriate court in the responding state.[27] This does not amount to a finding by the initiating court that support is due, nor does it constitute evidence against the defendant. It has been described by one case as saying only that further proceedings are warranted.[28] Yet some courts in initiating states persist in entering an order that the defendant is liable.[29] When this occurs, and when the defendant enters no denial in the responding court, the responding court may enter an order for support without further evidence or findings, not because the initiating court's action justifies it, but only because of the defendant's default.[30] If the defendant denies liability in the responding court, then no support order may be entered without evidence and a finding in that court which warrants the order.[31] If the initiating court erroneously enters an order for support,

prior Utah divorce decree had been silent on the question of alimony and child support.)

The New York courts have also had difficulty in enforcing their own statute in ways effectuating its obvious purposes. Martin v. Martin, 58 Misc.2d 459, 296 N.Y.S.2d 453 (Fam.Ct.1968) refused to enforce an alimony order of a Mexican court based upon a separation agreement incorporated in the Mexican decree. See also the confusion created by counsel seeking to have a New York court upset the judgment of a California court, the latter being the responding state, in Matter of a Proceeding for Support Under Uniform Support of Dependents Law, 94 Misc.2d 588, 405 N.Y.S.2d 225 (Fam.Ct.1978). The New York statute differs in some respects from RURESA.

22. RURESA § 8, 9A Unif.L.Ann. 675 (1979). Paredes v. Paredes, 118 Ill.App.3d 27, 73 Ill.Dec. 765, 454 N.E.2d 1014 (1983), appeal after remand 150 Ill.App.3d 692, 104 Ill.Dec. 10, 502 N.E.2d 273 (1986); Santa Clara County, Cal. v. Hughes, 43 Misc.2d 559, 251 N.Y.S.2d 579 (Fam.Ct.1964); County of Stanislaus v. Ross, 41 N.C.App. 518, 255 S.E.2d 229 (1979). But see Department of Mental Hygiene, State of Cal. v. Judd, 45 N.J. 46, 211 A.2d 198 (1965), holding that the California Department of Mental Hygiene could not recover from a New Jersey father the cost of supporting his mentally ill son when the California statute authorizing such recovery had been held unconstitutional in Department of Mental Hygiene v. Kirchner, 60 Cal.2d 716, 36 Cal.Rptr. 488, 388 P.2d 720 (1964), and 62 Cal.2d 586, 43 Cal.Rptr. 329, 400 P.2d 321 (1965), even though the law of New Jersey would have allowed the state to recover.

23. Allain v. Allain, 24 Ill.App.2d 400, 164 N.E.2d 611 (1960).

24. RURESA § 11, 9A Unif.L.Ann. 681 (1979).

25. RURESA § 12, 9A Unif.L.Ann. 683 (1979).

26. RURESA § 14, 9A Unif.L.Ann. 688 (1979); Huffman v. Huffman, 93 Misc.2d 790, 403 N.Y.S.2d 850 (Fam.Ct.1978). If the proper court in the responding state is not known, the file may be sent to a designated information agency in that state, which will transmit it to the proper court. Such agencies are authorized by § 17 of the Act.

27. Ibid. See State ex rel. Johnson v. Reeves, 234 Ind. 225, 125 N.E.2d 794 (1955).

28. Pfueller v. Pfueller, 37 N.J.Super. 106, 117 A.2d 30 (1955). See also Prager v. Smith, 195 A.2d 257 (D.C. App.1963); State ex rel. Lyon v. Lyon, 75 Nev. 495, 346 P.2d 709 (1959); State v. Perry, 198 Tenn. 389, 280 S.W.2d 919 (1955).

29. E.g., Cobbe v. Cobbe, 163 A.2d 333 (D.C.Mun.App. 1960), in which the court seems to have thought its function as initiating court was to pass on the plaintiff's standing to sue.

30. Clark v. Clark, 139 So.2d 195 (Fla.App.1962); People ex rel. Hartshorn v. Hartshorn, 21 Ill.App.2d 91, 157 N.E.2d 563 (1959). Some cases have held, however, that the initiating court's certification of the RURESA petition which sets out the needs of the child and the amount of that need is prima facie evidence of the needs and circumstances of the obligee. State of Minnesota, Clay County, on Behalf of Licha v. Doty, 326 N.W.2d 74 (N.D. 1982). But if the defendant files an answer denying the allegations of the complaint, an order for support may not be entered without evidence, on the basis of the verified complaint alone, according to O'Hara v. Floyd, 41 Ala.App. 619, 259 So.2d 673 (1972).

31. Carpenter v. Carpenter, 231 La. 638, 92 So.2d 393 (1956).

the responding court may disregard such an order and go on to handle the case correctly without prejudice to the defendant.[32]

The court in the responding state, upon receipt of the complaint, certification and copies of the act from the initiating court, is required to docket the case and notify the appropriate public officer.[33] This officer must then take the usual steps under the practice of the responding state to acquire jurisdiction over the defendant or his property.[34] In most states this would involve service of a summons and a copy of the complaint on the defendant.[35] In the responding state as well as in the initiating state, the plaintiff is represented by the designated official. Among his other duties under the Act, this official must try to trace the defendant, and arrange to forward the file either to another county, or to another state if he finds that the defendant is or has property in such other county or state.[36] The duties so imposed have been made increasingly explicit by the Act in order to correct the short-sighted tendency of some officials to give up further effort as soon as difficulties arise in locating defendants.[37]

Another example of unnecessary frustration of the statute is Mahan v. Read.[38] The wife started her suit under the Act in Arkansas, with North Carolina as the responding state. The husband was served there. Before a hearing was held the wife and children moved to Virginia. The trial court's support order was reversed, in part on the ground that the court had no authority to make an order for transmittal to Arkansas and from that state to Virginia. There is no reason either in the statute or in the interests of the parties why such an order should not be made. Certainly no interest of the defendant would be affected by the roundabout transmittal. The case exhibits the vice of "hometowning", the refusal to enforce the legitimate claims to support of a person from another state in order to protect the local domiciliary. The same sort of thing is familiar to experienced lawyers in custody litigation. It is surprising how partial some courts are to their own domiciliaries, particularly when they are administering a statute whose chief purpose is to accomplish an even-handed enforcement of support duties in all states.

Once jurisdiction over the defendant has been acquired by the responding state, the case proceeds like other civil actions for non-support.[39] Where the defendant defaults or appears and admits liability, an order of support may be entered in accordance with the information available from the petition.[40] The assumption of the statute, borne out by the experience under it, is that most defendants will default or admit liability.

Obviously the defendant must be permitted to raise any defenses he may have. For example, if the defendant is making payments in accordance with a separation agreement or divorce decree and circumstances have not so changed as to justify a modification, he would have a defense to a RURESA suit.[41] The same result would be appropriate where the agreement or decree placed the obligation of supporting children upon the petitioning

32. State ex rel. Whatley v. Mueller, 288 S.W.2d 405 (Mo.App.1956).

33. RURESA § 18, 9A Unif.L.Ann. 694 (1979).

34. Ibid. Jurisdiction by arrest is authorized by § 16 of the Act, 9A Unif.L.Ann. 691 (1979), if the defendant is about to flee the state. For a discussion of jurisdiction in non-support cases, see § 6.4, supra.

35. Pousson v. Superior Court In and For San Diego County, 165 Cal.App.2d 750, 332 P.2d 766 (1958).

36. RURESA § 19, 9A Unif.L.Ann. 698 (1979).

If the defendant moves to another state after he has been personally served in the responding state, the responding state does not lose jurisdiction to enter a judgment, and in an appropriate case may elect to exercise that jurisdiction. Sedelmeyer v. Sedelmeyer, 167 N.J. Super. 175, 400 A.2d 571 (1979).

37. W. Brockelbank, Interstate Enforcement of Family Support 46–51 (2d ed. Infausto 1971).

38. 240 N.C. 641, 83 S.E.2d 706 (1954).

39. RURESA § 20, 9A Unif.L.Ann. 700 (1979). If the support obligation relied on is that of a spouse, the court of the responding state has the power to determine the validity of the marriage. Bushnell v. Bushnell, 393 Mass. 462, 472 N.E.2d 240 (1984).

40. W. Brockelbank, Interstate Enforcement of Family Support 51 (2d ed. Infausto 1971). A default will not be set aside where the record reveals no dispute as to the liability. Dorsey v. Dorsey, 86 Ill.App.3d 1043, 42 Ill.Dec. 124, 408 N.E.2d 502 (1980).

41. Huffman v. Huffman, 93 Misc.2d 790, 403 N.Y.S. 2d 850 (Fam.Ct.1978).

spouse.[42] The statute of limitations may also provide a defense, although to meet the requirements of equal protection it must not make unreasonable distinctions between residents and non-residents of the state.[43] On rare occasions a court has held that it is a defense to a URESA proceeding that the spouse seeking child support had removed the child from the state in violation of a custody order, or in some other way improperly frustrated the obligor's visitation rights.[44] A provision of RURESA and other cases have held that this is not a defense.[45] It has also been held that the child's misconduct is not a defense.[46]

If the defendant files an answer and defends the suit, a trial must be had in the responding state's court. This creates practical difficulties, since the plaintiff in the case will often (though not always) be unavailable to testify.[47] The defendant of course will be available and may be cross-examined by the public official who represents the plaintiff. In rare cases the plaintiff may prevail on the testimony of the defendant alone.[48] In most contested cases, however, the plaintiff's testimony will be necessary and may be obtained either by taking her deposition or by interrogatories,[49] the Act requiring the court of the responding state to continue the case while this is done.[50] Even so, this form of hearing is not wholly satisfactory.

The RURESA proceeding being equitable in nature, trial is to the court and not by jury and a jury trial is not constitutionally required.[51] The Act provides that the court may grant immunity from criminal prosecution to the obligor, so that he may not decline to answer on the ground that his testimony might incriminate him.[52] The privilege for communications between husband and wife is expressly made inapplicable to RURESA cases.[53]

Defendants in URESA or RURESA cases have sometimes attempted to bring aspects of the family relationship other than support into the proceedings, but courts have generally not been receptive to such attempts.

But where the divorce court has entered an order terminating child support because of the custodian's interference with the obligor's visitation rights, it has been held that this is res judicata on the issue of the right to child support in the RURESA proceeding. Moffat v. Moffat, 27 Cal.3d 645, 165 Cal.Rptr. 877, 612 P.2d 967 (1980); People ex rel. Oetjen v. Oetjen, 92 Ill.App.3d 699, 48 Ill.Dec. 247, 416 N.E.2d 278 (1980).

42. Chance v. Lapausky, 43 Md.App. 84, 402 A.2d 1329 (1979). One case, Martin v. Coffey, 83 Mich.App. 113, 268 N.W.2d 307 (1978) quashed a mother's petition for support of an illegitimate child on the ground that an agreement had discharged the defendant from any support obligation, Michigan being the initiating state, but this seems doubtful since the defenses to a petition should normally be heard and decided in the responding state.

43. Haughton v. Haughton, 76 Ill.2d 439, 31 Ill.Dec. 183, 394 N.E.2d 385 (1979), cert. denied 444 U.S. 1102, 100 S.Ct. 1069, 62 L.Ed.2d 789 (1980).

44. Hethcox v. Hethcox, 146 Ga. 430, 246 S.E.2d 444 (1978); Watkins v. Springsteen, 102 Mich.App. 451, 301 N.W.2d 892 (1980) (plaintiff must be given notice of intention of defendant to raise denial of visitation rights); State on Behalf of McDonnell v. McCutcheon, 337 N.W.2d 645 (Minn.1983). Moffat v. Moffat, 27 Cal.3d 645, 165 Cal.Rptr. 877, 612 P.2d 967 (1980) is contra the text statement.

45. RURESA § 23: "The determination or enforcement of a duty of support owed to one obligee is unaffected by any interference by another obligee with rights of custody or visitation granted by a court." See also Clearwater County, Minn. v. Petrash, 198 Colo. 231, 598 P.2d 138 (1979); Vigil v. Vigil, 30 Colo.App. 452, 494 P.2d 609 (1972); People ex rel. Argo v. Henderson, 97 Ill.App.3d 425, 52 Ill.Dec. 796, 422 N.E.2d 1005 (1981); Dorsey v. Dorsey, 86 Ill.App.3d 27, 42 Ill.Dec. 124, 408 N.E.2d 502 (1980); Brown v. Turnbloom, 89 Mich.App. 162, 280 N.W.2d 473 (1979). For similar cases dealing with enforcement of child support orders in divorce proceedings, see § 17.1, infra.

46. Byrd v. O'Neill, 309 Minn. 415, 244 N.W.2d 657 (1976).

47. Fox, The Uniform Reciprocal Enforcement of Support Act, 12 Fam.L.Q. 112, 128 (1978).

48. Phillips v. Phillips, 336 Mass. 561, 146 N.E.2d 919 (1958); Kinney v. Kinney, 122 N.H. 1165, 453 A.2d 1321 (1982).

49. The method of operation is described in Prager v. Smith, 195 A.2d 257 (D.C.App.1963); Carpenter v. Carpenter, 231 La. 638, 92 So.2d 393 (1956); Lambrou v. Berna, 154 Me. 352, 148 A.2d 697 (1959); Pfueller v. Pfueller, 37 N.J.Super. 106, 117 A.2d 30 (1955); W. Brockelbank, Interstate Enforcement of Family Support 52–61 (2d ed. Infausto 1971); Fox, The Uniform Reciprocal Enforcement of Support Act, 12 Fam.L.Q. 112, 123–129 (1978).

50. RURESA § 20, 9A Unif.L.Ann. 700 (1979).

51. Reynolds v. Reynolds, 86 Cal.App.3d 732, 150 Cal. Rptr. 423 (1978).

52. RURESA § 21, 9A Unif.L.Ann. 710 (1979).

53. RURESA § 22, 9A Unif.L.Ann. 711 (1979).

RURESA itself contains a cryptic provision which may forbid such a move.[54] So a defendant has been denied permission to file a counterclaim for divorce when sued for nonsupport under URESA.[55] Some courts have refused to condition an award of support upon compliance with rights of visitation,[56] or to permit a custody issue to be litigated in the URESA proceeding.[57] A few courts have recognized that a rigid rule on this issue may be both unwise and unnecessary, since it is desirable to dispose of all issues in marital litigation where that is feasible and URESA defendants (usually fathers) have vital interests in custody and visitation rights to their children.[58] If the contacts with the responding state are sufficiently close to justify either a divorce or a custody proceeding, and if all issues are or can be brought before the same court, there seems good reason to permit the court to deal with the other matters in addition to support.

If the court of the responding state finds that the defendant had a duty to support the spouse or child who brought the action, it may enter an appropriate order, which may reimburse the spouse for support provided by her[59] or order support for the future,[60] or both.[61] The order so made must then be transmitted to the initiating court.[62] Payments in compliance with the order must be made to the responding court and sent to the obligee via the initiating court.[63] The usual sanctions are available to the responding court for the enforcement of orders for support, including contempt and the furnishing of a bond,[64] and they are available throughout the responding state.[65] Foreign support orders registered under Part IV of RURESA are enforceable in the same manner as a support order issued by a court of the responding state.[66]

It is clear under the Act as it is now drafted that it may be used to collect arrearages accrued under the divorce or maintenance decrees of other states.[67] This provides an alternative to registration under Part Four where the plaintiff already has obtained a support decree in another jurisdiction. Some conflict has arisen in the cases where the decree being enforced is that of the responding state. In the typical case the wife obtains an alimony decree in County A of State X. She then moves to State Y and brings a Reciprocal Support Act suit to collect arrears due on the State X judgment. The defendant has moved to County B in State X, and the question is, which county of the responding state has ju-

---

54. RURESA § 32: "Participation in any proceeding under this Act does not confer jurisdiction upon any court over any of the parties thereto in any other proceeding." For a discussion of these issues see Note, Counterclaims and Defenses Under the Uniform Reciprocal Enforcement of Support Act, 15 Ga.L.Rev. 143 (1980).

55. Blois v. Blois, 138 So.2d 373 (Fla.App.1962); State ex rel. Schwartz v. Buder, 315 S.W.2d 867 (Mo.App.1958).

56. In re Marriage of Ryall, 154 Cal.App.3d 743, 201 Cal.Rptr. 504 (1984); Patterson v. Patterson, 2 Kan.App. 2d 447, 581 P.2d 824 (1978); Hoover v. Hoover, 271 S.C. 177, 246 S.E.2d 179 (1978).

57. Watson v. Dreadin, 309 A.2d 493 (D.C.App.1973), cert. denied 415 U.S. 959, 94 S.Ct. 1488, 39 L.Ed.2d 574 (1974); State ex rel. Hubbard v. Hubbard, 110 Wis.2d 683, 329 N.W.2d 202 (1983). See also Brown v. Turnbloom, 89 Mich.App. 162, 280 N.W.2d 473 (1979): "The Act does not contemplate that the custodial parent come to the responding state to defend against claims arising from other domestic relations matters."

58. Ray v. Pentlicki, 375 So.2d 875 (Fla.App.1979); Chandler v. Chandler, 109 N.H. 477, 256 A.2d 157 (1969). See also the dissenting opinion in Brown v. Turnbloom, 89 Mich.App. 162, 280 N.W.2d 473 (1979).

59. State ex rel. Whatley v. Mueller, 288 S.W.2d 405 (Mo.App.1956).

60. Phillips v. Phillips, 336 Mass. 561, 146 N.E.2d 919 (1958).

61. For a discussion of the res judicata effects of a RURESA order, see In re Marriage of Hight, 67 Cal.App. 3d 498, 136 Cal.Rptr. 685 (1977); D.L.M. v. V.E.M., 438 N.E.2d 1023 (Ind.App.1982).

62. RURESA § 25, 9A Unif.L.Ann. 727 (1979).

63. RURESA §§ 28, 29, 9A Unif.L.Ann. 732, 733 (1979).

64. RURESA § 26, 9A Unif.L.Ann. 727 (1979); Scott v. Scott, 220 A.2d 95 (D.C.App.1966), affirmed 382 F.2d 461 (D.C.Cir.1967).

65. RURESA § 24, 9A Unif.L.Ann. 713 (1979).

66. See note 17, supra, and RURESA § 40, 9A Unif.L. Ann. 744 (1979). See also Kelso, Reciprocal Enforcement of Support: 1958 Dimension, 43 Minn.L.Rev. 875, 880 (1959).

67. RURESA § 9, 9A Unif.L.Ann. 635 (1979). See note 21, supra.

risdiction? A Florida decision,[68] holding that the court in the county of the defendant's residence is the appropriate court, seems to be correct, since the action is brought under the Act and is not an attempt to have the original court enforce its own judgment. But this is a matter of local procedure.

Much confusion arises when an obligee has an outstanding support order (for example in a prior divorce decree) and she seeks to enforce it under RURESA, either by registration or by bringing an independent RURESA proceeding, disregarding the divorce decree.[69] If the outstanding support order has been complied with by the obligor, and if, as is usually the case, its installments become final judgments when they accrue, the defendant would certainly have a defense as to all past and paid installments. Any attempt in the RURESA proceeding to order him to pay additional amounts in excess of the arrears under the divorce decree would violate the full faith and credit obligations due to that decree.[70] Even if the accrued installments have not been paid, this would be true, since the Full Faith and Credit Clause [71] forbids modification of final judgments and has been construed to mean that such judgments must be given that effect by other courts which the rendering courts would give.[72] Conversely, if,

under the law of the state where the divorce was granted, accrued installments of maintenance are not final and are modifiable, there would be no Full Faith and Credit Clause obstacle to a retroactive award of a different amount under RURESA. This is because of the curious position taken by the United States Supreme Court that full faith and credit is not applicable to non-final decrees and judgments.[73]

There are cases in which a decree for support is final for the future as well as for the accrued installments. One example might be the divorce decree which provides that the spouse is not entitled to alimony, in which event many courts would say that it cannot later be modified so as to revive support rights.[74] Another example is the Georgia child support decree which may apparently be made final notwithstanding later changes in circumstances and continued need on the child's part.[75] The question then is, may a subsequent RURESA proceeding award support to a spouse or child when the earlier decree has terminated any right to support? The question has been answered in the affirmative by Elkind v. Byck.[76] In that case there was a Georgia divorce, the decree incorporating the parties' agreement under which the husband set up trusts for the support and

---

68. Thompson v. Thompson, 93 So.2d 90 (Fla.1957). Contra, holding that the court originally granting the alimony is the correct responding court, Freeland v. Freeland, 313 S.W.2d 943 (Tex.Civ.App.1958).

69. RURESA § 3 seems to permit an obligee to bring a new and independent suit for support even when there is already a support order outstanding, by providing, "The remedies herein provided are in addition to and not in substitution for any other remedies."

The confusion is exemplified by State on Behalf of McDonnell v. McCutcheon, 337 N.W.2d 645 (Minn.1983), which seems to hold that if the form of the suit is the two-state variety, as contrasted with registration, even if the plaintiff seeks enforcement of an existing divorce decree, the responding state must apply its own law in determining the level of support. It is not to enter an order just enforcing the divorce decree, even with respect to arrears which are due under that decree. The result is to make the support recoverable entirely dependent upon the form the suit takes.

70. See note 41, supra.

71. United States Constitution Art. IV, § 1.

72. Aldrich v. Aldrich, 378 U.S. 540, 84 S.Ct. 1687, 12 L.Ed.2d 1020 (1964); Yarborough v. Yarborough, 290 U.S.

202, 54 S.Ct. 181, 78 L.Ed. 269 (1933); Sullivan v. Sullivan, 98 Ill.App.3d 928, 54 Ill.Dec. 207, 424 N.E.2d 957 (1981).

73. See Sistare v. Sistare, 218 U.S. 1, 30 S.Ct. 682, 54 L.Ed. 905 (1910).

74. See section 16.5, infra.

75. Official Code Ga.Ann. §§ 19–6–18, 19–6–21 (1980 and Supp.1986), providing that alimony and child support orders are not modifiable where the award is made from the corpus of the defendant's estate in lieu of periodic payments. This provision seems to be unique, at least so far as child support is concerned, other states making child support orders modifiable on proof of changed circumstances.

76. 68 Cal.2d 453, 67 Cal.Rptr. 404, 439 P.2d 316 (1968).

A case following Elkind on very dubious grounds is Commonwealth of Virginia ex rel. Halsey v. Autry, 293 Md.App. 53, 441 A.2d 1056 (1982). A prior New Jersey decree had held that no child support was due from the defendant, but the Maryland court, in a URESA proceeding, held that the New Jersey decree, which seems to have been final, could be disregarded and further child support ordered.

education of their child. The agreement and the decree provided explicitly that there should be no modification of the agreement or the decree even if the circumstances should change. There was also a Georgia statute seeming to make such decrees final and not modifiable. The wife moved to New York, where she brought a URESA proceeding to increase the amounts payable for child support. The husband was then a resident of California, the responding state, and argued that any modification of the final Georgia decree would violate the Full Faith and Credit Clause. The California Supreme Court rejected his defense on the ground that the conflict of laws provision of URESA [77] which authorizes the courts to apply the law of any state in which the obligor was present during the relevant period. This, the court held, prevents any state from freezing the child support obligation, and Georgia assented to this principle by enacting URESA. The court also held that the father's move to California entitled the California courts to impose further child support obligations upon him in disregard of the Georgia decree and of the fact that he had fully complied with that decree. The court said that its disregard of the Georgia decree did not violate the Full Faith and Credit Clause because California was justified in applying its law of support to the father after he had established a "sub-stantial relationship" with the state, relying upon the Supreme Court's reservation of a similar question in Yarborough v. Yarborough.[78] In view of the Supreme Court's repeated strict construction of the Full Faith and Credit Clause as requiring out-of-state judgments to be given the same effect as they would have in the state of rendition,[79] the California court's decision on this issue seems mistaken. But the Elkind result is warranted by Georgia's enactment of the URESA conflicts provision. The rationale of the Elkind case would apply equally to final alimony decrees, but most courts would presumably agree that a final denial of alimony could not be modified.[80] The law of the responding state would therefore not produce a different result from that of the state in which the divorce was granted. For that reason Elkind may well be limited in its effect to child support orders.

Where the support order in the divorce or other prior decree is not final, it follows *a fortiori* from Elkind v. Byck that a subsequent URESA or RURESA proceeding may result in an order for a different amount. Several cases have held that prior awards may be increased by URESA actions.[81] Other URESA cases have reduced support awards made earlier in divorce actions or prior

---

77. This provision is now in RURESA § 7, 9A Unif.L. Ann. 672 (1979): "Duties of support applicable under this Act are those imposed under the laws of any state where the obligor was present for the period during which support is sought. The obligor is presumed to have been present in the responding state during the period for which support is sought until otherwise shown."

78. 290 U.S. 202, 54 S.Ct. 181, 78 L.Ed. 269 (1933). See also Gilbert v. Gilbert, 245 Ga. 674, 266 S.E.2d 490 (1980) holding that Georgia support orders which would be final and non-modifiable under the Georgia statute may be modified by other states when the obligor has become domiciled in a state other than Georgia.

79. E.g., Aldrich v. Aldrich, 378 U.S. 540, 84 S.Ct. 1687, 12 L.Ed.2d 1020 (1964) which held that an alimony decree must be given the effect in other states which it had in the rendering state even though the second state would not give its own decrees that effect. But the position of Elkind v. Byck is supported by Restatement (Second) of Conflict of Laws § 103 (1971) stating the rule to be that "A judgment * * * need not be recognized or enforced in a sister State if such recognition or enforcement is not required by the national policy of full faith

and credit because it would involve an improper interference with important interests of the sister State." The cases cited in support of this rule are generally dissenting or concurring opinions, and of course the rule itself, like many other Restatement "rules", contains clauses ("*improper* interference with *important* interests") opening escape routes from the rule for any court wishing to take them. A case which recognizes that a final decree of another state could not, consistently with the Full Faith and Credit Clause, be modified in a URESA proceeding is Gruber v. Wallner, 198 Colo. 235, 598 P.2d 135 (1979). See also People ex rel. Kerl v. Kerl, 75 Ill.App.3d 347, 30 Ill.Dec. 958, 393 N.E.2d 1305 (1979).

80. See § 16.5, infra.

81. Gruber v. Wallner, 198 Colo. 235, 598 P.2d 135 (1979); Proctor v. Sachner, 143 Conn. 9, 118 A.2d 621 (1955); State of Georgia v. McKenna, 253 Ga. 6, 315 S.E.2d 885 (1984), on remand 171 Ga.App. 918, 322 S.E.2d 369 (1984); Moore v. Moore, 252 Iowa 404, 107 N.W.2d 97 (1961), 47 Iowa L.Rev. 177 (1961); Koehler v. Koehler, 559 S.W.2d 944 (Tenn.App.1977); Jaramillo v. Jaramillo, 27 Wash.App. 391, 618 P.2d 528 (1980).

URESA suits.[82] Although RURESA is far from lucid on the issue, some of the courts which have modified earlier judgments of other states have relied upon § 31 of the Act, which provides that a support order under the Act does not nullify and is not nullified by a support order made by a court of any other state.[83] Whatever the basis, the results of these cases are correct, since the very purpose of making support orders modifiable is to provide for future changes in circumstance which cannot be foreseen at the time the original order is entered. If the court which entered the order retains the power to modify, courts applying RURESA or URESA should have no less power, in order to carry out the purposes of the Act.

The more difficult question is, what are the consequences with respect to enforcement of the original order when it is modified in a URESA proceeding? Some examples may make the position clearer. An Illinois divorce decree orders the husband to pay fifty dollars per month in child support. The wife moves to Alabama and the husband to Iowa. The wife begins a URESA suit in Alabama, asking for seventy-five dollars a month in child support. The Iowa court enters a decree in the higher amount.[84] The Act makes it clear that the total payments due would then be seventy-five dollars, payments under the earlier order being credited on the later one.[85] If both parties should move back to Illinois, the amount due should still be seventy-five dollars unless an Illinois court with jurisdiction over the parties should in turn modify the URESA judgment by reducing the amount of future payments.

Neither RURESA nor URESA deals with the converse situation, in which the Iowa court decides that support payments should be only twenty-five dollars.[86] If the Illinois payments continue to accrue at fifty dollars per month, and if, as is true in most states, the accrued installments have the status of final judgments, it might be argued that all other states, including Iowa must enforce the accrued installments ordered by the Illinois court, including those accruing after the Iowa modification, in order to comply with the Full Faith and Credit Clause.[87] A substantial number of cases have reached that result, often in reliance upon the ambiguous lan-

82. Chisholm v. Chisholm, 197 Neb. 828, 251 N.W.2d 171 (1977); State ex rel. Louisiana v. Phillips, 39 Or.App. 325, 591 P.2d 1196 (1979). A case which seems to say that the responding state has no power to modify a prior order is Craft v. Hertz, 182 N.W.2d 293 (N.D.1970). The beneficiary of the support order must be given notice and an opportunity to be heard before it may be reduced. Bjugan v. Bjugan, 710 P.2d 213 (Wyo.1985).

Where the registration procedure set up by RURESA is relied upon the cases do not agree on whether the judgment being registered may be modified. The statute provides that the obligor may petition the court to vacate the registration "or for other relief." RURESA § 40(b), 9A Unif.L.Ann. 744 (1979). Monson v. Monson, 85 Wis.2d 794, 271 N.W.2d 137 (1978) held that the quoted language authorized a reduction in the registered judgment. O'Halloran v. O'Halloran, 580 S.W.2d 870 (Tex.Civ.App. 1979) holds to the contrary, saying that the responding state's only course of action is to register the judgment as is.

83. RURESA § 31, 9A Unif.L.Ann. 734 (1979). W. Brockelbank, Interstate Enforcement of Family Support 67 (2d ed. Infausto 1971) states that the purpose of § 31 is to confer "the power upon the courts to nullify or modify prior orders or support provisions contained in divorce decrees." One can only say that language much more apt for the purpose could easily be devised. For cases dealing with this section of URESA, see Annot., Construction and Effect of Provision of URESA That No Support Order Shall Supersede or Nullify Any Other Order, 31 A.L.R.4th 347 (1984).

84. Moore v. Moore, 252 Iowa 404, 107 N.W.2d 97 (1961), 47 Iowa L.Rev. 177 (1961).

85. RURESA § 31, 9A Unif.L.Ann. 734 (1979: " * * * Amounts paid for a particular period pursuant to any support order made by the court of another state shall be credited against the amounts accruing or accrued for the same period under any support order made by the court of this State."

86. RURESA § 31, 9A Unif.L.Ann. 734 (1979) provides that "A support order made by a court of this State pursuant to this Act does not nullify * * * a support order made by a court of any other state pursuant to a substantially similar act or any other law, * * * unless otherwise specifically provided by the court." This provision may be construed to apply to the reduction of prior orders, although it is difficult to see why "nullify" was used if modification was intended. In any event the courts in RURESA cases do not seem to specifically provide for the modification of prior orders. RURESA § 3, 9A Unif.L.Ann. 659 (1979) provides that "The remedies herein provided are in addition to and not in substitution for any other remedies." It is certainly not clear that this section was aimed at the modification problem.

87. See Sistare v. Sistare, 218 U.S. 1, 30 S.Ct. 682, 54 L.Ed. 905 (1910) holding that full faith and credit must be

guage of RURESA,[88] rather than the Full
Faith and Credit Clause.[89] This result is inconsistent with the purpose of RURESA and
with its provision permitting modification of
prior support orders.[90] A proceeding under
the Act is an exercise in futility if it results in
a decree which says to the defendant, "We
think you should pay twenty-five dollars in
child support, but you really should be paying
fifty dollars in compliance with the Illinois
decree." The only sensible solution to the
problem is to hold that the later decree supersedes the earlier, and that twenty-five dollars
per month is the measure of the obligor's
liability until a subsequent order with jurisdiction revises the amount upward again.[91]
The Full Faith and Credit Clause need present no obstacle to this result if, as in Elkind v.
Byck,[92] the enactment of URESA or RURESA
is construed as giving consent to the modification (either upward or downward) of each
state's support orders. Of course the responding state in a URESA proceeding should give
considerable weight to the prior support decree, should not modify it without good reason, and should not indulge in the sort of
"home-towning" which before the enactment
of the Uniform Child Custody Jurisdiction
Act [93] was such a prominent and distasteful
feature of many custody cases.

URESA has from the start contained provisions governing the choice of law which is to
be applied by the responding state. The original statute provided two alternatives, either
the law of the place in which the obligor was
present during the relevant period, or, at the
election of the obligee, the law of the place
where the obligee was present when the failure to support commenced.[94] As presently
drafted, the statute states that the duties of
support enforced by the statute are those imposed by the law of any state in which the
obligor was present during the relevant period, and that he is presumed to have been
present in the responding state unless otherwise proved.[95] In other words, in most instances the law of the responding state will be
controlling. The cases often state this to be
the rule without any thorough consideration
or discussion.[96] In the vast majority of cases
there is no difference between the laws of the
various states, but where there is, there is no
entirely satisfactory way of resolving the conflict thus created. The usual solution is
merely to apply the responding state's law in
order to effectuate policies which the responding court as the forum prefers to the policies
of the initiating state.[97] A few cases suggest
that any other result would violate the Equal

given to the alimony decrees of other states to the extent
that such decrees are final.

88. See note 86, supra.

89. Ibach v. Ibach, 123 Ariz. 507, 600 P.2d 1370 (1979);
In re Marriage of Enewold, 709 P.2d 1385 (Colo.App.
1985); Despain v. Despain, 78 Idaho 185, 300 P.2d 500
(1956); Banton v. Mathers, 159 Ind.App. 634, 309 N.E.2d
167 (1974); Howard v. Howard, 191 So.2d 528 (Miss.1966);
Foster v. Marshman, 96 Nev. 475, 611 P.2d 197 (1980);
Peot v. Peot, 92 Nev. 388, 551 P.2d 242 (1976); Nichols v.
Bardua, 74 A.D.2d 566, 424 N.Y.S.2d 288 (2d Dep't 1980);
Thompson v. Thompson, 366 N.W.2d 845 (S.D.1985);
Oglesby v. Oglesby, 29 Utah 2d 419, 510 P.2d 1106 (1973).
W. Brockelban, Interstate Enforcement of Family Sup-
port 13 (2d ed. Infausto 1971) seems to agree with these
cases.

San Diego County v. Elavsky, 58 Ohio St. 81, 388 N.E.
2d 1229 (1979) compounds the confusion by holding that a
later modification of the support order in the divorce suit
has no effect on the amount awarded in the URESA
proceeding. See also Wilson v. Wilson, 274 S.C. 516, 266
S.E.2d 65 (1980).

90. See notes 81 and 82, supra.

91. See Southard v. Southard, 305 F.2d 730 (2d Cir.
1962). Cf. Colby v. Colby, 78 Nev. 150, 369 P.2d 1019
(1962), cert. denied 371 U.S. 888, 83 S.Ct. 186, 9 L.Ed.2d
122 (1962), 63 Colum.L.Rev. 560 (1963), and Note, 68
Harv.L.Rev. 719 (1955), and Pace v. Pace, 222 Va. 524,
281 S.E.2d 891 (1981). The possibility of conflict between
support decrees arises outside the Reciprocal Support
Act, as is illustrated by Lopez v. Avery, 66 So.2d 689 (Fla.
1953).

92. See note 76, supra.

93. 9 Unif.L.Ann. 99 (1973).

94. URESA § 7, 9C Unif.L.Ann. 26, 27 (1957). The
section was amended in 1952. See 9A Unif.L.Ann. 767
(1979). For criticism of this position see Ehrenzweig,
Interstate Recognition of Support Duties, 42 Cal.L.Rev.
382, 390 (1954).

95. RURESA § 7, 9A Unif.L.Ann. 672 (1979).

96. E.g., Rosenberg v. Rosenberg, 152 Me. 161, 125
A.2d 863 (1956); Davidson v. Davidson, 66 Wash.2d 780,
405 P.2d 261 (1965).

97. Commonwealth of Pa. ex rel. Dept. of Public Assistance, Mercer County Board of Assistance v. Mong, 160

Protection Clause,[98] but this is clearly wrong.[99] That Clause only requires a reasonable and non-arbitrary classification system. The fact that the dependent is located in another state is a perfectly rational basis on which to treat the obligor differently from other persons living in the responding state. But the tendency of the forum to apply its own law and to favor its own policies is not necessarily objectionable. At least this settles the choice of law issue with some certainty. One qualification on the rule might be added, however. In the rare case in which it appears that the obligor moved to the responding state in order to take advantage of a favorable legal rule respecting support obligations, the law of the dependent's domicile, normally the initiating state, might be applied. This would prevent forum-shopping and evasion by the obligor.

Looked at in the abstract, URESA and RURESA seem to be ingenious devices for dealing with child and spousal support in a federal state having a highly mobile population. In operation the statutes may or may not be so successful. Their efficiency depends in large part upon the willingness of the authorities in responding states to perform the obligations which the statutes impose upon them. Some of the enforcing agencies do their work expeditiously and well. A substantial number of them do not. In such circumstances it is unrealistic to assume, as Kulko does for example,[1] that an obligee always can fall back on the URESA proceeding when long-arm jurisdiction is unavailable. In many instances the child or spouse may find that in practice URESA just does not work well.

 WESTLAW REFERENCES

purpose /3 u.r.e.s.a. "uniform reciprocal enforcement of support" r.u.r.e.s.a.

u.r.e.s.a. "uniform reciprocal enforcement of support" r.u.r.e.s.a. /s visit!

u.r.e.s.a. "uniform reciprocal enforcement of support" r.u.r.e.s.a. /s constitution! unconstitutional!

u.r.e.s.a. "uniform reciprocal enforcement of support" r.u.r.e.s.a. /s "full faith and credit"

Ohio St. 455, 117 N.E.2d 32 (1954). Here Pennsylvania was the initiating state, the state seeking reimbursement for support supplied to the defendant's father. By Ohio law the defendant had the defense that his father had abandoned him in his youth. No such defense was recognized in Pennsylvania. Cf. Vincenza v. Vincenza, 197 Misc. 1027, 98 N.Y.S.2d 470 (Dom.Rel.Ct.1950). But Department of Mental Hygiene, State of Cal. v. Judd, 45 N.J. 46, 211 A.2d 198 (1965) seems to have applied the law of the initiating state.

98. U.S.Const. Amend. XIV, § 1.

99. Commonwealth of Pa. ex rel. Dept. of Public Assistance, Mercer County Board of Assistance v. Mong, 160 Ohio St. 455, 117 N.E.2d 32 (1954). See also State of California v. Copus, 158 Tex. 196, 309 S.W.2d 227 (1958), cert. denied 356 U.S. 967, 78 S.Ct. 1006, 2 L.Ed.2d 1074 (1958). Texas seems to make a distinction for this purpose between support obligations incurred before moving into Texas and those incurred after the defendant moves into the state. The former may be enforced though incurred under the law of the initiating state, while the latter are apparently governed by the law of Texas. See Bjorgo v. Bjorgo, 402 S.W.2d 143 (Tex.1966) in which this distinction is announced (though it is pure dictum, not being at all necessary to the decision of the case). In Bjorgo the plaintiff had a Kentucky judgment ordering the defendant to support his illegitimate child. She brought a Reciprocal Support Act proceeding to enforce the judgment, and the Texas Supreme Court, reversing a lower court decision, granted enforcement. Among other dicta the court made statements inconsistent with its opinion on Equal Protection in the Copus case.

1. Kulko v. Superior Court of California In and For San Francisco, 436 U.S. 84, 98 S.Ct. 1690, 56 L.Ed.2d 132 (1978), rehearing denied 438 U.S. 908, 98 S.Ct. 3127, 57 L.Ed.2d 1150 (1978).

Chapter 7

THE LEGAL POSITION OF
MARRIED WOMEN

Table of Sections

---

§ 7.1 The Legal Position of Married Women Before the Enactment of Modern Legislation

At Common Law

A brief look at the position of married women at common law and in equity is necessary to provide the background for a later account of the effect of modern legislation enlarging her legal capacity. What follows is merely a summary,[1] omitting many details and qualifications, but it should serve this limited purpose.

Unmarried women at common law had considerable legal capacity, being competent to make contracts, hold property and sue or be sued.[2] But this was no great reason for complacency, since their rights of inheritance were limited,[3] they could not serve on juries, could not vote, and could not hold public office.[4] These disabilities were only removed in the first quarter of the Twentieth Century as a result of the long and bitter struggles of the feminist movement.[5] Furthermore, the unmarried woman's economic prospects were chiefly dependent upon marriage, on which event she could look forward to losing all of her legal capacity in exchange for whatever value the guardianship or protection of her husband might have.[6]

The disabilities of the married woman at common law, according to Blackstone, were deducible from the principle that upon marriage husband and wife became one, acquired

§ 7.1

1. See for good general accounts, 3 W. Holdsworth, History of English Law 520–533 (3d ed. 1923); 2 F. Pollock, F. Maitland History of English Law 399–436 (2d ed. 1898); Bromley, Family Law 347–355 (4th ed. 1971).

2. Graveson, Status in the Common Law 21 (1953).

3. 2 Blackstone, Commentaries on the Laws of England 212–213 (Cooley 3d ed. 1884).

4. N. St. John-Stevas, Women in Public Law, printed in Graveson and Crane, A Century of Family Law 256 (1957); 3 Blackstone, Commentaries on the Laws of Eng-

land 362 (Cooley 3d ed. 1884); 23 Encyc. Britannica 704–708 (14th ed. 1930).

5. N. St. John-Stevas, Women in Public Law, op. cit. supra note 4; Pankhurst, Suffragette Movement (1931); 29 Encyc. Americana 89–96 (1963); 15 Encyc. of Social Sciences 439–450 (1934).

6. Pollock and Maitland state the principle underlying the married woman's disabilities as being that the husband was the wife's guardian. 2 F. Pollock, F. Maitland, History of English Law 406 (2d ed. 1898).

a "unity of person".[7] Such a notion may have been both useful and comforting as a summary of the legal situation in a less sophisticated age, but it hardly accounts for the rules which gave the husband extensive rights in his wife's property and which deprived her of power to contract or to engage in litigation.[8] A realist might be pardoned for thinking that the rules were the result of male economic, social and legal power.[9]

Upon her marriage the wife's personal property and possession became the property of her husband, and on his death passed to his personal representatives.[10] The same was true of personal property which she acquired during marriage.[11] Even her paraphernalia, clothing and jewelry, belonged to him, but this sort of property did come back to her on her husband's death.[12] Her choses in action, claims which she might assert in law or in equity, could be enforced by him and also became his absolutely when he acquired possession of them.[13] If he failed to take possession of them, they remained her own, and passed to her personal representative, who would be her husband if he survived her.[14]

The rules were different with respect to the married woman's real property, but no more favorable to her interests. The use of her estates of inheritance in land belonged to her husband during the marriage, and for that time he was entitled to the rents and profits of the land.[15] If the marriage produced a child born alive, the husband became a tenant by the curtesy, as a result of which he was entitled to the rents and profits of the land during his life.[16] The estate of inheritance remained the wife's property, but the husband could convey his interest, and the wife could not convey hers without his consent, nor could any conveyance be made between husband and wife.[17] On his death the property passed to the wife or her heirs. Land in which the wife held a life estate was the husband's in the right of his wife and he became entitled to the use, rents and profits.[18] Land in which the wife had only a leasehold interest or a term for years became the property of the husband, which he could convey, but if he did not do so, it survived to the wife.[19]

In other respects the wife's capacity was equally limited by the common law. She could not make contracts, either with her husband or with others,[20] although she could

7. 1 Blackstone, Commentaries on the Laws of England 445 (Cooley 3d ed. 1884).

8. 2 F. Pollock, F. Maitland, History of English Law 406 (2d ed. 1898).

9. 1 R. Powell, Real Property § 117 (1985 & Supp. 1986). Since Anglo-Saxon law recognized a regime of marital property resembling what is now known as community property, and since similar regimes existed among Germanic peoples on the continent, it is curious that community property did not prevail in Britain. For discussions of this question, with suggested answers, see Donahue, What Causes Fundamental Legal Ideas? Marital Property in England and France in the Thirteenth Century, 78 Mich.L.Rev. 59 (1979); Buckstaff, Married Women's Property in Anglo-Saxon and Anglo-Norman Law and Origin of the Common-Law Dower, 4 Annals of the American Academy of Political and Social Science 233 (1894); Young, The Anglo-Saxon Family Law, in H. Adams, ed., Essays in Anglo-Saxon Law 121 (1876); 2 F. Pollock and F. Maitland, The History of English Law 397–431 (1895). The development of community property systems in the western United States is described in Kirkwood, Historical Background and Objectives of the Law of Community Property in the Pacific Coast States, 11 Wash.L.Rev. 1 (1936).

10. Jordan v. Jordan, 52 Me. 320 (1864); 2 Kent's Commentaries on American Law, 130 (13th ed. 1884).

11. Ibid.; 3 Holdsworth, History of English Law, 526 (3d ed. 1923); 2 Pollock & Maitland, History of English Law, 404 (2d ed. 1898); Commonwealth v. Davis, 63 Mass. (9 Cush) 283 (1852).

12. Tipping v. Tipping, 1 P.Wms. 730, 24 Eng.Rep. 589 (1721).

13. 2 Kent's Commentaries on American Law, 135 (13th ed. 1884).

14. Ibid.; Judge of Probate v. Chamberlain, 3 N.H. 129 (1824).

15. 3 Holdsworth, History of English Law, 525 (3rd ed. 1923); 2 Pollock & Maitland, History of English Law, 403 (2d ed. 1898). See also Sayre, Property Rights of Husband and Wife, 6 Marr. & Family Living 17 (1944); and 1 Powell, Real Property, § 117 (1985 and Supp.1986).

16. I American Law of Property §§ 5.57–5.74 (1952).

17. 1 Powell, Real Property, § 117 (1985 & Supp. 1986). On the married woman's incapacity to convey land, see Concord Bank v. Bellis, 10 Cush. 276 (Mass. 1852).

18. 1 Schouler, Marriage, Divorce and Domestic Relations, § 194 (6th ed. 1921).

19. 3 Holdsworth, History of English Law, 410 (1909).

20. 2 Pollock & Maitland, History of English Law, 405 (2d ed. 1898); Robinson v. Reynolds, 1 Aikens 174 (Vt.

contract as her husband's agent,[21] and she could pledge his credit for necessaries.[22] She was not able to sue or be sued without joining her husband.[23] It followed that she could not sue her husband at all, since he could hardly be joined as a plaintiff in a suit against himself, except that she could bring matrimonial actions in the ecclesiastical courts.[24] She could not make a will,[25] nor could she testify either for or against her husband in civil or criminal suits.[26]

Marriage did give to the wife certain benefits under the common law. She became entitled to dower, a life estate in one-third of the land of which her husband held the fee at any time during marriage.[27] The husband also was responsible for the wife's antenuptial debts,[28] and for any torts she might commit either before or during marriage.[29] And of course he was required to support her.[30]

The wife was fully responsible at common law for her criminal conduct.[31] One curious rule had it that if the wife committed a crime in her husband's presence, it was presumed at his direction, and this provided her with the defense of coercion.[32] The same presumption applied to her torts.[33] The fiction of the unity

of husband and wife had one consequence for criminal law: Husband and wife, being one, could not be guilty of a conspiracy with each other.[34]

The Wife's Separate Estate in Equity

The worst features of the common law's treatment of married women in matters of property were softened by equitable principles originating in the Seventeenth Century [35] and developing during the Eighteenth Century.[36] The purpose of these equitable principles was to preserve to the married woman her personal property and the rents and profits of her real estate. In order to accomplish this, the equitable principles had to take precedence over the common law rules. The married woman's separate estate in equity was the more remarkable since it was entirely judge-made, created and existing without statutory sanction.

The technique used by equity to reach this highly desirable result was that of the trust, although as the doctrine developed the trust was largely fictional.[37] An example makes the point most clearly.[38] A father whose daughter married a spendthrift made a will

1826); 1 Blackstone, Commentaries on the Laws of England, 442 (Cooley 3d ed. 1884).

21. 1 Schouler, Marriage, Divorce, Separation and Domestic Relations, § 137 (6th ed. 1921); 2 Pollock & Maitland, History of English Law, 405 (2d ed. 1898).

22. See section 5.3, supra.

23. 1 Blackstone, Commentaries on the Laws of England, 443 (Cooley 3d ed. 1884); Cole v. Shurtleff, 41 Vt. 311 (1868).

24. Ibid.

25. 1 Page, Wills, § 12.10 (Bowe-Parker Rev.1960); Marston v. Norton, 5 N.H. 205 (1830); Dudley v. Staton, 257 N.C. 572, 126 S.E.2d 590 (1962).

26. 1 Blackstone, Commentaries on the Laws of England, 443 (Cooley 3d ed. 1884); 1 Schouler, Marriage, Divorce, Separation and Domestic Relations, § 62 (6th ed. 1921).

27. 2 Pollock & Maitland, History of English Law, 404 (2d ed. 1898); I American Law of Property, §§ 5.1–5.49 (1952).

28. 1 Schouler, Marriage, Divorce, Separation and Domestic Relations, § 76 (6th ed. 1921).

29. Id., § 122.

30. See section 5.1, supra.

31. 1 Schouler, Marriage, Divorce, Separation and Domestic Relations, § 55 (6th ed. 1921).

32. 1 Schouler, Marriage, Divorce, Separation and Domestic Relations § 56 (6th ed. 1921). See also Farrell v. Turner, 25 Utah 2d 351, 482 P.2d 117 (1971); Wiener, Is a Spinster an Unmarried Woman, 20 Am.J.Legal Hist. 27 (1976).

33. Id. at § 123.

34. United States v. Dege, 364 U.S. 51, 80 S.Ct. 1589, 4 L.Ed.2d 1563 (1960), rehearing denied 364 U.S. 854, 81 S.Ct. 29, 5 L.Ed.2d 77 (1960).

35. See Sanky v. Golding, Cary 86, 21 Eng.Rep. 46 (1579), and L. Bonfield, Marriage Settlements, 1601–1740 (1983).

36. 1 Schouler, Marriage, Divorce, Separation and Domestic Relations, § 247 (6th ed. 1921); III Pomeroy, Equity Jurisprudence, § 1098 (1883).

37. III Pomeroy, Equity Jurisprudence, § 1098 (1883). There may also have been roots in the wife's equity to a settlement. That doctrine held that if the husband sought the aid of equity to make good his claim to his wife's property, he was required to do equity, that is, to settle a part of the property upon his wife and children for their separate use. See 1 Schouler, Marriage, Divorce, Separation and Domestic Relations, § 175 (6th ed. 1921), and Howard v. Moffatt, 2 Johns.Ch. 206 (N.Y.1816).

38. These are the facts of Bennet v. Davis, 2 P.Wms. 316, 24 Eng.Rep. 746 (1725). See also Picquet v. Swan, Fed.Cas. No. 11133 (Cir.Ct.D.Mass.1827).

leaving his land to the daughter, "for her separate and peculiar use exclusive of her husband", spelling out his desire that the husband's usual common law right of curtesy shall not apply. The Master of the Rolls in this case held that there was a trust in the husband in favor of his wife, since the father expressed the clear intention that she should enjoy the land herself and that her husband should be barred from his usual common law rights. In other words, the daughter was held to have a separate estate in equity in this land. Her separate estate was further held not to be subject to the claims of her husband's creditors.

Under English law a separate estate in equity could be set up by the husband or by others, the only requirement being that the intention to provide the separate estate for the wife had to be clearly expressed.[39] But no particular verbal formula had to be used, and the separate estate might comprise either real or personal property, tangible or intangible.[40]

Not only did the married woman have the use of the property in her separate estate, but she could convey it by deed or will,[41] and she could make contracts which, though not enforceable against her personally, were enforceable against the separate estate.[42] She could also sue or be sued with respect to the separate estate.[43]

Thus, in summary, equity gave back to the married woman many of the legal rights which the common law took from her, and as a result she possessed extensive rights to property, to make contracts and to sue or be sued.

 WESTLAW REFERENCES

At Common Law

to(205) /p wife woman /10 capacity /7 sue* contract will /s common-law

The Wife's Separate Estate in Equity

woman wife /s separate /s estate /s equity /s common-law

§ 7.2 The Legal Position of Married Women Under Constitutions and Modern Statutes

The Married Women's Property Acts

Perhaps because the married woman's separate estate in equity was not as widely and consistently used by American courts as by the English to avoid the hardships of the common law disabilities of married women,[1] it became apparent quite early in this country that other reforms were needed. As a result, the state legislatures began enacting statutes even before 1850 which had as their purpose the reduction or elimination of the married woman's disabilities.[2] By the end of the Century all states had such statutes in one form or another. But they by no means succeeded in conferring full legal capacity upon married women. The general and sometimes inappropriate language which they contained was often used by the courts as an excuse for restrictive interpretation.[3] Part of this judicial conservatism reflected a desire to protect the married woman and to preserve family

---

39. 1 Schouler, Marriage, Divorce, Separation and Domestic Relations, §§ 254, 262 (6th ed. 1921).

40. 2 Story, Equity Jurisprudence, 709–712 (13th ed. 1886).

41. Taylor v. Meads, 4 De Gex J. & S. 597, 46 Eng.Rep. 1050 (1865); 1 Schouler, Marriage, Divorce, Separation and Domestic Relations, § 274 (6th ed. 1921).

42. 1 Schouler, Marriage, Divorce, Separation and Domestic Relations, § 274 (6th ed. 1921); 2 Story, Equity Jurisprudence, 725–735 (13th ed. 1886). Her intent to charge her separate estate had to be shown, however, according to some cases. Batchelder v. Sargent, 47 N.H. 262 (1867); Yale v. Dederer, 22 N.Y. 450 (1860).

43. 2 Kent, Commentaries on American Law, 163–170 (13th ed. 1884). See also Burdeno v. Amperse, 14 Mich. 91 (1866).

§ 7.2

1. 1 Schouler, Marriage, Divorce, Separation and Domestic Relations, § 248 (6th ed. 1921).

2. 1 Id., § 287; Younger, Marital Regimes: A Story of Compromise and Demoralization, Together With Criticism and Suggestions for Reform, 67 Corn.L.Q. 45 (1981).

3. See, e.g., Warren, Husband's Right to Wife's Services, 38 Harv.L.Rev. 421, 622 (1925), which gives numerous examples. Some of the early statutes were themselves limited in effect, for example the sole trader statute, which authorized the wife under certain circumstances to carry on business on her separate account, freeing her property from her husband's claims. 1 Schouler, Marriage, Divorce, Separation and Domestic Relations, Ch. XVII (6th ed. 1921).

institutions, but it none the less ran counter to the clear spirit and purpose of the statutes. The legislatures were thereby led, over a long period, to pass specific provisions correcting the courts' mistakes. The outcome of this interaction between case law and statutes was that most of the married women's disabilities were ultimately removed.[4]

Broadly speaking then, the Married Women's Property Acts have given the married woman the right to acquire, own and transfer all kinds of property, to make contracts, to engage in business or be employed and keep her own earnings, and to sue or be sued.[5] She may also make a will,[6] may testify in civil or criminal suits,[7] (although there is still a privilege for either spouse not to testify against the other in a criminal case in some jurisdictions),[8] and she is fully responsible for her own criminal and tortious conduct.[9]

The Effect of State and Federal Constitutions Upon the Legal Rights of Married Women

Well publicized developments in constitutional law over the past fifteen years have had as their purpose conferring upon women full equality with men. Although this work cannot explore all aspects of the discrimination against women as affected by constitu-

4. These statutes, generally referred to as Married Women's Property Acts, include the following, the list being as complete as possible although probably not exhaustive: Ala.Code 1975, §§ 30–4–1 to 30–4–16; Alaska Stat. §§ 25.15.010 to 25.15.060, 25.15.100, 25.15.110 (1983 and Supp.1985); Ariz.Rev.Stat. §§ 25–213 to 25–215, 25–217 (1976); Ark.Stat. §§ 55–401 to 55–415 (Supp.1985); West's Ann.Cal.Civ.Code §§ 4802, 5102, 5103, 5104, 5105, 5107, 5108, 5118, 5120.110, 5120.130, 5120.140 (1983 and Supp.1985) and West's Ann.Cal.Prob.Code § 6412 (Supp. 1987); Colo.Rev.Stat. §§ 14–2–201 to 14–2–210 (1973); Conn.Gen.Stat.Ann. § 46b–36 (Supp.1986); Del.Code tit. 13, §§ 311 to 314 (1981); D.C.Code 1981, §§ 30–201; West's Fla.Stat.Ann. §§ 708.08, 708.09 (Supp.1986); Official Code Ga.Ann. §§ 19–3–8, 19–3–9, 19–3–10, 51–1–10 (Supp.1984); Hawaii Rev.Stat. §§ 572–22—572–24, 573–1, 573–3, 573–8 (1976 and Supp.1984); Idaho Code §§ 32–903 to 32–912 (1983); Ill.–S.H.A.Ann.Stat. ch. 40, §§ 1000, 1007, 1009 (1980 and Supp.1986); West's Ann.Ind.Code §§ 31–7–10–1 to 31–7–10–4 (Supp.1986); Iowa Code Ann. §§ 597.1 to 597.11 (1981); Kan.Stat.Ann. §§ 23–201 to 23–206 (1981); Ky.Rev.Stat. §§ 404.010 to 404.060 (1984); La.S.A.–Rev.Stat. §§ 9:101 to 9:105 (1965); Me.Rev.Stat. Ann. tit. 19, §§ 161 to 166 (1981); Md.Fam.Law, Code, §§ 4–203 to 4–206, 4–301, 4–302 (1984); Mass.Gen.Laws Ann. ch. 209, §§ 1 to 9, 13 (1981); Mich.C.L.A. §§ 26.165(1) to 26.165(8) (1984); Minn.Stat.Ann. §§ 519.101, 519.111 (1969 and Supp.1986); Miss.Code 1973, §§ 93–3–1 to 93–3–13; Vernon's Ann.Mo.Stat. §§ 451.250, 451.260, 451.270, 451.290 (1986); Mont.Code Ann. §§ 40–2–201 to 40–2–210, 40–2–301, 40–2–302 (1985); Neb.Rev.Stat. §§ 42–201 to 42–207 (1984); Nev.Rev.Stat. §§ 123.010 to 123.230 (1986); N.H.Rev.Stat.Ann. §§ 460:1 to 460:21 (1983); N.J.Stat.Ann. §§ 37:2–12 to 37:2–30 (1968); N.M.Stat.Ann.1983 and 1985, §§ 40–2–2, 40–2–3, 40–3–3, 40–3–8 to 40–3–10, 40–3–12, 40–3–13 (Supp.); N.Y.–McKinney's Dom.Rel.L. § 50 (1977) and N.Y.–McKinney's Gen.Obl.L. §§ 3–301 to 3–315 (1978); N.C.Gen. Stat. §§ 52–1, 52–7 to 52–12 (1984); N.D.Cent.Code §§ 14–07–03 to 14–07–17, 14–07–19 to 14–07–22 (1981 and Supp. 1985); Ohio Rev.Code §§ 2307.09, 2307.10 (1981), and §§ 3103.04, 3103.05, 3103.06, 3103.07, 3103.08 (1980); Okl.Stat.1985, tit. 12, § 2017, tit. 16, § 13 (1953), tit. 32, §§ 4 to 15 (1976); Or.Rev.Stat. §§ 108.010 to 108.100 (1983); Pa.Stat. tit. 48, §§ 32.1, 34, 64, 70, 71, 111 (1965);

and Pa.Cons.Stat.Ann. § 5927 (1982); R.I.Gen.L.1981, §§ 15–4–1 to 15–4–16; S.C.Code 1985, §§ 20–5–10 to 20–5–80; S.D.Codif.L. ¶¶ 25–2–3 to 25–2–15 (1984); Tenn. Code Ann. §§ 36–3–501 to 36–3–505 (1984); V.T.C.A., Fam.Code §§ 4.04, 5.01, 5.61 (1975); Utah Code Ann.1984, §§ 30–2–1 to 30–2–10; Vt.Stat.Ann. tit. 15, §§ 61 to 69 (1974); Va.Code 1981 §§ 55–35 to 55–47.1 (1981 and Supp. 1985); West's Rev.Wash.Code Ann. §§ 26.16.010 to 26.16.125, 26.16.140 to 26.16.160, 26.16.180 to 26.16.210 (1986); W.Va.Code, §§ 48–3–1 to 48–3–7, 48–3–8 to 48–3–25 (1980 and Supp.1985); Wis.Stat.Ann. §§ 766.001 to 766.75, 766.95 to 766.97 (Supp.1985) and (Interim Supp. 1986); Wyo.Stat.1977, §§ 20–1–201, 20–1–202.

A few states have constitutional provisions guaranteeing the married woman her rights in her property. E.g., Ark. Const. Art. 9, § 7; West's Ann.Cal. Const. Art. 1, § 21; West's Fla.Stat.Ann. Const. Art. 10, § 5; Kan.Stat. Ann. Const. Art. 15, § 6; N.C. Const. Art. X, § 4; Utah Const. Art. XXII, § 2.

5. The married woman's rights respecting property, contracts, earnings and litigation are discussed in detail below. The broad purpose of the statutes was to place the wife in a position of equality with her husband. In re Estate of Nickolay, 249 Wis. 571, 25 N.W.2d 451 (1946).

6. 1 Page on Wills, § 12.14 (Bowe-Parker Rev.1960). See Dudley v. Staton, 257 N.C. 572, 126 S.E.2d 590 (1962).

7. II J. Wigmore, Evidence §§ 488, 620 (Chadbourn rev. 1979).

8. VIII J. Wigmore, Evidence ch. 79 (McNaughton rev. 1961). The United States Supreme Court has held that this privilege may be asserted only by the witness spouse, overruling an earlier case which held that both spouses had to consent before the testimony could be admitted. Trammel v. United States, 445 U.S. 40, 100 S.Ct. 906, 63 L.Ed.2d 186 (1980), collecting cases and statutes on the privilege from the various states. See also Note, 8 Fla. State Univ.L.Rev. 319 (1980); Note, 59 B.U.L.Rev. 894 (1979); Annot., 46 A.L.R.Fed. 735 (1980). This privilege should be distinguished from the privilege for confidential communications between husband and wife. VIII J. Wigmore, Evidence ch. 83 (McNaughton rev. 1961).

9. See the discussion infra, at notes 29–37.

tional law, an attempt will be made to indicate ways in which married women have benefited by these developments. They occurred against a background of earlier reforms giving women the right to vote, to hold office, and to sit on juries.

A major development, but one which still has not come to fruition, is the submission to the states by Congress of the federal Equal Rights Amendment in 1972.[10] The proposed Twenty-Seventh Amendment would provide that "Equality of rights under the law shall not be denied or abridged by the United States or by any State on account of sex."[11] The proposal required ratification within seven years. At the end of that time only thirty-five of the needed thirty-eight states had ratified the Amendment and Congress then extended the time of ratification to June 30, 1982. The extension period expired without ratification and a resubmission may yet occur.[12]

Seventeen state constitutions now include provisions forbidding discrimination by the state on the basis of sex.[13] The standard of review under these state constitutions has varied considerably, ranging from those cases which uphold state legislation if it has a rational relation to a legitimate state purpose[14] to others which hold state statutes invalid unless they are essential to the effectuation of a "compelling state interest",[15] or even to a few cases which seem to say that all statutes discriminating on the basis of sex are invalid,[16] with the possible exception of those taking account of physical differences between the sexes. The reasoning of the Massachusetts Supreme Judicial Court is persuasive that when the state Equal Rights Amendments were adopted the people must have intended to impose a stricter standard of review than the United States Supreme Court was then imposing under the Equal Protection Clause.[17] Therefore statutes which do not meet the compelling state interest test at least must be considered to violate the Equal Rights Amendments. And even an absolute ban upon any classification relating to sex may be justified by the literal language of

10. H.J.Res. 208, 92d Cong. 1st Sess., 117 Cong.Rec. H 35815, 92d Cong. 2d Sess., 118 Cong.Rec. S 9598, S 9809, S 9907 (1972). For the legislative history of the Amendment, see Report of the House Judiciary Committee, H.R. Rep. 92–359, 92d Cong.2d Sess. (1971); Equal Rights for Men and Women, S.R. No. 92–689, 92d Cong., 2d Sess., Senate Committee on the Judiciary (1972); C. Stimpson, ed., Women and the "Equal Rights" Amendment (1972).

11. U.S.C.A., Constitution, Amendment 14 to End (Supp.1984), containing the text of the Amendment and the list of ratifying states. The leading article urging adoption of the Amendment is Brown, Emerson, Falk, Freedman, The Equal Rights Amendment: A Constitutional Basis for Equal Rights for Women, 80 Yale L.J. 871 (1971), construing the Amendment to mean that sex is a prohibited classification, but that legislation might take into account a physical characteristic unique to one sex.

12. H.J.Res. 638, 95th Cong.2d Sess., 124 Cong.Rec. H 8664–5, S 17318 (1978).

13. Alaska Const. Art. I, § 3; Colo. Const. Art. II, § 29; Conn.Gen.Stat.Ann. Const. Art. I, § 20; Hawaii Const. Art. I, § 3; Ill.–S.H.A. Const Art. I, § 18; La.Stat. Ann.–Const. Art. I, § 3; Md. Const. Declaration of Rights, Art. 46; Mass. Const. Declaration of Rights Pt. 1, Art. I; Mont. Const. Art. II, § 4; N.H. Const. Pt. I, art. 2; N.M. Const. Art. II, § 18; Pa. Const. Art. I, § 28; Vernon's Ann.Tex. Const. Art. I, § 3a; Utah Const. Art. IV, § 1; Va. Const. Art. I, § 11; West's RCWA Const. Art. XXXI, § 1; Wyo. Const. Art. I, § 3. The California Constitution, Art. I, § 8 forbids discrimination in vocations or employment on the ground of sex. Most of the constitutional provisions cited are phrased in ways similar to the proposed federal Amendment. Discussion of the effect of these state constitutional provisions may be found in Kurtz, The State Equal Rights Amendments and Their Impact on Domestic Relations Law, 11 Fam.L.Q. 101 (1977) and Note, Equal Rights Provisions: The Experience Under State Constitutions, 65 Cal.L.Rev. 1086 (1977); Annot., 90 A.L.R.3d 158 (1979), collecting many cases.

The Florida Constitution, Art. X, § 5 prohibits any distinction between married men and married women respecting the holding, control, disposition or encumbrance of property. Hallman v. Hospital & Welfare Bd. of Hillsborough Co., 262 So.2d 669 (Fla.1972).

14. Archer v. Mayes, 213 Va. 633, 194 S.E.2d 707 (1973).

15. Attorney General v. Massachusetts Interscholastic Athletic Ass'n, Inc., 378 Mass. 342, 393 N.E.2d 284 (1979) (Sex is a classification to be scrutinized as strictly as race would be under the Equal Protection Clause of the Fourteenth Amendment); Mercer v. Board of Trustees, North Forest Independent School District, 538 S.W.2d 201 (Tex. Civ.App.1976).

16. Sail'er Inn, Inc. v. Kirby, 5 Cal.3d 1, 95 Cal.Rptr. 329, 485 P.2d 529 (1971) (semble); Hopkins v. Blanco, 457 Pa. 90, 320 A.2d 139 (1974) (semble); Darrin v. Gould, 85 Wash.2d 859, 540 P.2d 882 (1975). But In re Marriage of Bouquet, 16 Cal.3d 583, 128 Cal.Rptr. 427, 546 P.2d 1371 (1976) states that Sail'er Inn stands for the rule that sex is a suspect classification.

17. Attorney General v. Massachusetts Interscholastic Athletic Ass'n, Inc., 378 Mass. 342, 393 N.E.2d 284 (1979).

those Amendments.[18] In any event, either of the two more restrictive standards should be sufficient to invalidate the remaining forms of discrimination against married women.

Some of the sex-based forms of discrimination have been discussed in other sections of this work.[19] In the few instances in which a state rule regulating the property of spouses has been attacked under the Equal Rights Amendment, the result has usually been to invalidate any distinction based upon sex. The presumption that the husband dominates the family, as a reason for looking with disfavor upon gifts from wife to husband was held to violate the Equal Rights Amendment [20] as was the old common law presumption that the husband as purchaser of household goods was their owner.[21] Similarly the presumption that where a husband receives a wife's property without consideration a trust for the wife

is created has been replaced with a presumption that when either spouse contributes to the purchase of entireties property, the amount of the contribution is a gift.[22]

Commencing with Reed v. Reed in 1971,[23] the United States Supreme Court has decided in a succession of cases that legislation basing legal distinctions upon sex violates the Equal Protection Clause of the Fourteenth Amendment, or the similar requirement of the Fifth Amendment.[24] The Court has upheld some sex-based distinctions favoring women, however, on the ground that such statutes were attempting to make amends for society's prior unfavorable treatment of women.[25] Although this sort of reasoning could logically support all kinds of state action discriminating against men, perhaps these cases should not be considered more than aberrations.[26] In any event the Court has resisted characteriz-

18. See note 13, supra, and Brown, Emerson, Falk, Freedman, The Equal Rights Amendment: A Constitutional Basis for Equal Rights for Women, 80 Yale L.J. 871 (1971).

19. E.g., equality in support, sections 6.1, 6.2, supra; equality in alimony, section 16.1 infra; equality in age for marriage, section 2.10, supra; equality in custody proceedings, section infra; domicile of the married woman, section 4.3, Practitioner's Edition; equality in actions for loss of consortium, section 11.3, ch. 11 infra. The discussion of the married woman's choice of a name will be found infra, at notes 38–42. Cases dealing with these and other aspects of state Equal Rights Amendments are cited in Annot., 90 A.L.R.3d 158 (1979).

20. Bell v. Bell, 38 Md.App. 10, 379 A.2d 419 (1977).

21. DiFlorido v. DiFlorido, 459 Pa. 641, 331 A.2d 174 (1975).

22. Butler v. Butler, 464 Pa. 522, 347 A.2d 477 (1975).

23. 404 U.S. 71, 92 S.Ct. 251, 30 L.Ed.2d 225 (1971), mandate conformed to 94 Idaho 542, 493 P.2d 701 (1972), holding unconstitutional an Idaho statute which required that men be preferred to women in appointments to administer the estates of decedents.

24. A representative sample of these cases includes Frontiero v. Richardson, 411 U.S. 677, 93 S.Ct. 1764, 36 L.Ed.2d 583 (1973) (federal statute unconstitutional in providing different standards for the dependency benefits of men and women in the armed forces); Weinberger v. Wiesenfeld, 420 U.S. 636, 95 S.Ct. 1225, 43 L.Ed.2d 514 (1975) (distinction in the Social Security Act between benefits payable to survivors of deceased husband and those payable to survivors of deceased wife violates the Fifth Amendment); Stanton v. Stanton, 421 U.S. 7, 95 S.Ct. 1373, 43 L.Ed.2d 688 (1975), appeal after remand 552 P.2d 112 (Utah 1976), judgment vacated 429 U.S. 501, 97 S.Ct. 717, 50 L.Ed.2d 723 (1977), on remand 564 P.2d 303 (1977), rehearing denied 567 P.2d 625 (1977) (Utah

statute setting the age of majority as twenty-one for males and eighteen for females, for child support purposes violates equal protection); Craig v. Boren, 429 U.S. 190, 97 S.Ct. 451, 50 L.Ed.2d 397 (1976), rehearing denied 429 U.S. 1124, 97 S.Ct. 1161, 51 L.Ed.2d 574 (1977) (Oklahoma statute prohibiting the sale of 3.2 beer to males under twenty-one and females under eighteen violates equal protection); Califano v. Goldfarb, 430 U.S. 199, 97 S.Ct. 1021, 51 L.Ed.2d 270 (1977) (Social Security Act unconstitutional in discriminating between widows and widowers with respect to survivors' benefits); Orr v. Orr, 440 U.S. 268, 99 S.Ct. 1102, 59 L.Ed.2d 306 (1979), on remand 374 So.2d 895 (Ala.Civ.App.1979), writ denied 374 So.2d 898 (1979) (Alabama statute violates equal protection by authorizing alimony for wives but not for husbands).

See also Cleveland Board of Education v. LaFleur, 414 U.S. 632, 94 S.Ct. 791, 39 L.Ed.2d 52 (1974), holding that a school board regulation imposing mandatory five-month pregnancy leaves violated the Due Process Clause. And Taylor v. Louisiana, 419 U.S. 522, 95 S.Ct. 692, 42 L.Ed.2d 690 (1975) held that a state statute discriminating between men and women with respect to jury service violated the Sixth and Fourteenth Amendments.

25. Kahn v. Shevin, 416 U.S. 351, 94 S.Ct. 1734, 40 L.Ed.2d 189 (1974) (Florida statute giving a tax exemption for widows but not for widowers is constitutional); Schlesinger v. Ballard, 419 U.S. 498, 95 S.Ct. 572, 42 L.Ed.2d 610 (1975), rehearing denied 420 U.S. 966, 95 S.Ct. 1363, 43 L.Ed.2d 466 (1975) (stricter promotion requirements for male than for female naval officers held constitutional); Califano v. Webster, 430 U.S. 313, 97 S.Ct. 1192, 51 L.Ed.2d 360 (1977) (Social Security Act provisions giving women of certain ages greater benefits than men of the same ages and earnings records held constitutional).

26. In Orr v. Orr, supra, note 24, the Court invalidated a statute discriminating against men respecting alimo-

ing distinctions based upon sex as "suspect", the code word which triggers the Court's most rigid constitutional scrutiny.[27] Instead it has continued to hold that the issues in such cases are whether the statute serves important governmental objectives and, if so, whether the statute is substantially related to the achievement of those objectives.[28] This less rigid approach to legislation still would appear to invalidate any remaining forms of discrimination against wives in the law of marital property.[29]

The Married Woman's Property

The Married Woman's Property Acts ordinarily provide that the married woman's property remains her own notwithstanding her marriage, that it may be conveyed by her, and that it is not subject to claims against her husband.[30] Her own property is defined as that which she owned before marriage as well as that which she acquires during marriage.[31] The few remaining qualifications on the principle of equality between husband and wife in the holding and conveyance of property seem now to have been eliminated. As has been

well said, this equality still has aspects of unfairness to the married woman who is not employed outside the home and who therefore is never able to accumulate property of her own.[32] The community property regimes of eight states take a different approach to equality, by giving each spouse an equal interest in the property acquired during the marriage.[33]

Obviously questions of ownership and the ability to convey property as between husband and wife do not often arise so long as the marriage is harmonious and not disrupted by death, separation, or divorce. The effect of death is rather arbitrarily placed beyond the scope of this work, since it is customarily characterized as part of the subject called wills and estates. The consequences of separation and divorce for marital property are considered in other sections of the work.[34]

Nevertheless the law does have something to say about the property of husbands and wives even before the marriage ends. Thus it is clear that she may convey property to him and he to her,[35] although conveyances from one spouse to the other are closely scrutinized

ny (and, by inference respecting obligations of support) and this may represent a change in the Court's view of the supposed justification for such forms of discrimination.

27. In Frontiero v. Richardson, 411 U.S. 677, 93 S.Ct. 1764, 36 L.Ed.2d 583 (1973) a plurality of four justices, Brennan, Douglas, White and Marshall, held that sex is a suspect classification, but this view has not been able to attract a majority of the Court.

28. Craig v. Boren, 429 U.S. 190, 97 S.Ct. 451, 50 L.Ed. 2d 397 (1976), rehearing denied 429 U.S. 1124, 97 S.Ct. 1161, 51 L.Ed.2d 574 (1977).

29. Some doubt about the text statement may be based upon Geduldig v. Aiello, 417 U.S. 484, 94 S.Ct. 2485, 41 L.Ed.2d 256 (1974), holding constitutional a California state disability insurance system which excluded pregnancy from coverage. See also D'Ercole v. D'Ercole, 407 F.Supp. 1377 (D.Mass.1976).

30. See statutes cited supra, note 4; Herzog v. Ross, 358 Mo. 177, 213 S.W.2d 921 (1948); Beard v. Myers, 136 Mont. 350, 347 P.2d 719 (1959); Note, 32 Minn.L.Rev. 262 (1948).

31. Shaw v. Shaw, 122 Mont. 593, 208 P.2d 514 (1949). The presumption that household goods were owned by the husband has been abolished by judicial decision or has been held in violation of the constitution. du Pont v. du Pont, 33 Del.Ch. 571, 98 A.2d 493 (1953); Fine v. Fine, 366 Pa. 227, 77 A.2d 436 (1951). See cases cited supra, note 21.

32. M. Glendon, State, Law and Family 149 (1977); Prager, Sharing Principles and the Future of Marital Property Law, 25 U.C.L.A.L.Rev. 1 (1977); Kulzer, Law and the Housewife: Property, Divorce and Death, 28 U.Fla.L.Rev. 1 (1975).

33. M. Glendon, State, Law and Family 147 (1977). For a thorough and critical discussion of the California community property regime as it applies during marriage, see Bruch, Management Powers and Duties Under California's Community Property Laws: Recommendations for Reform, 34 Hast.L.J. 227 (1982).

The Uniform Marital Property Act classifies property of married persons as either marital or individual, and provides that each spouse has a present undivided one half interest in the marital property. Uniform Marriage and Divorce Act § 4, 9A Unif.L.Ann. 29 (Supp.1985). This results in a marital property regime very similar to community property. Reppy, The Uniform Marital Property Act: Some Suggested Revisions for a Basically Sound Act, 21 Hous.L.Rev. 679 (1984).

34. See sections 6.4, supra, on separation, and Chapter 15, infra, dealing with the division of property on divorce.

35. Warner v. Florida Bank & Trust Co. at West Palm Beach, 160 F.2d 766 (5th Cir.1947); Perry v. Stancil, 237 N.C. 442, 75 S.E.2d 512 (1953); Rice v. Shank, 382 Pa. 396, 115 A.2d 210 (1955); Webb v. Webb, 148 Tex. 405, 224 S.W.2d 868 (1949).

by the courts on the theory that the confidential relationship of husband and wife makes such transactions particularly suspect.[36] Likewise property may often be acquired by one spouse or the other without giving much attention to the form in which title is taken. The property may be taken in joint tenancy, in tenancy by the entireties or in the name of either spouse individually. The consideration. for the property may have been furnished by either spouse or by both together. For a variety of purposes it may be necessary later to determine which spouse is the owner of the property.

Since the evidence of ownership is often conflicting, or inconclusive, the courts have adopted the familiar device of the presumption based upon the parties' probable intention to aid in establishing ownership. For-

merly it was held that when the husband buys property and takes title in his wife's name, he is presumed to have made a gift to her and she thereby acquires an interest in the property.[37] Today, in order to meet the requirements of the Equal Protection Clause or of state Equal Rights Amendments, the presumption is applied when either spouse acquires property and takes title wholly or partially in the name of the other.[38] The presumption is relied upon in many states,[39] but has been rejected in some, at least in certain circumstances.[40] The presumption may be rebutted by evidence that the parties had some other intention,[41] such as the desire to avoid probate.[42]

Where one spouse makes improvements on property belonging to the other, there is also a rebuttable presumption that the improve-

36. Sidebotham v. Robison, 216 F.2d 816 (9th Cir. 1954); O'Quin v. O'Quin, 217 Ark. 321, 230 S.W.2d 16 (1950); Erdmann v. Erdmann, 127 Mont. 252, 261 P.2d 367 (1953); Peardon v. Peardon, 65 Nev. 717, 201 P.2d 309 (1948); Link v. Link, 278 N.C. 181, 179 S.E.2d 697 (1971); Shapiro v. Shapiro, 424 Pa. 120, 224 A.2d 164 (1966).

Whether the relationship between husband and wife is a confidential one has been held to be a question of fact, turning on whether one spouse places confidence in the other. Yohe v. Yohe, 466 Pa. 405, 353 A.2d 417 (1976).

A transfer of property before marriage may be set aside as in fraud of the prospective spouse if it is without adequate consideration, is made with fraudulent intent, and if the prospective spouse relied upon the transferor's interest in it as an inducement to the marriage. See Haynie v. Byrd, 429 So.2d 973 (Ala.1983); Strong v. Wood, 306 N.W.2d 737 (Iowa 1981).

The Uniform Marital Property Act § 7, 9A Unif.L.Ann. 34 (Supp.1984) abolishes all restrictions on the transfer of property between spouses.

37. Nickoloff v. Nickoloff, 384 Ill. 377, 51 N.E.2d 565 (1943); Greenberg v. Greenberg, 141 Me. 320, 43 A.2d 841 (1945); Graham v. Onderdonk, 33 N.J. 356, 164 A.2d 749 (1960); O'Brien v. O'Brien, 73 R.I. 1, 53 A.2d 501 (1947); Bates v. Bates, 213 S.C. 26, 48 S.E.2d 612 (1948). See also Note, 53 Nw.L.Rev. 781 (1959); and Note, 32 Minn.L.Rev. 262 (1948). In Smith v. Smith, 255 N.C. 152, 120 S.E.2d 575 (1961) it was held that money deposited in a joint savings account was presumed to be owned half by the wife and half by the husband, except that if the husband furnished the deposit he would be presumed the owner. The presumption of gift to the wife was not applied because the deposit in that form did not constitute a completely executed transfer to her. See also Scanlon v. Scanlon, 6 Ill.2d 224, 127 N.E.2d 435 (1955).

38. Butler v. Butler, 464 Pa. 522, 347 A.2d 477 (1975); Yohe v. Yohe, 466 Pa. 405, 353 A.2d 417 (1976) (state Equal Rights Amendment).

39. E.g., Husband R.T.G. v. Wife G.K.G., 410 A.2d 155 (Del.1979); In re Marriage of Severns, 93 Ill.App.3d 122, 48 Ill.Dec. 713, 416 N.E.2d 1235 (1981); D'Amico v. D'Amico, 1 Mass.App.Ct. 561, 303 N.E.2d 737 (1973) (presumption applied to joint bank accounts); Ross v. Ross, 2 Mass.App.Ct. 502, 314 N.E.2d 888 (1974), cert. denied 420 U.S. 947, 95 S.Ct. 1329, 43 L.Ed.2d 425 (1975), rehearing denied 421 U.S. 1017, 95 S.Ct. 2426, 44 L.Ed.2d 686 (1975); Marco v. Marco, 196 Neb. 313, 242 N.W.2d 867 (1976); Susan W. v. Martin W., 89 Misc.2d 681, 392 N.Y.S.2d 957 (Sup.Ct.1977) (presumption applied to joint bank account, but not to works of art); Palmer v. Protrka, 257 Or. 23, 476 P.2d 185 (1970).

40. Ball v. Ball, 335 So.2d 5 (Fla.1976) (presumption not applicable where the consideration for property held by entireties came from a source unconnected with the marriage, i.e. from an inheritance); Wright v. Wright, 388 So.2d 1319 (Fla.App.1980); In re Marriage of Dietz, 76 Ill.App.3d 1029, 32 Ill.Dec. 532, 395 N.E.2d 762 (1979) (presumption abolished by Dissolution of Marriage Act); Note, 67 Ky.L.J. 173 (1978) (Kentucky law). Cases which seem simply to ignore any presumption are United States v. Cotier, 403 F.Supp. 397 (D.N.J.1975), and Peterson v. Peterson, 571 P.2d 1360 (Utah 1977).

41. Roberson v. Roberson, 261 Ala. 371, 74 So.2d 445 (1954); Ashbaugh v. Ashbaugh, 222 Ga. 811, 152 S.E.2d 888 (1966); Scanlon v. Scanlon, 6 Ill.2d 224, 127 N.E.2d 435 (1955); Miethe v. Miethe, 410 Ill. 226, 101 N.E.2d 571 (1951); Insoda v. Insoda, 400 Ill. 596, 81 N.E.2d 473 (1948); Nelson v. Nelson, 139 N.J.Eq. 329, 51 A.2d 251 (1947); Waddell v. Carson, 245 N.C. 669, 97 S.E.2d 222 (1957).

The burden of proof in rebutting the presumption lies on the spouse who is presumed to have made a gift. Ross v. Ross, 2 Mass.App.Ct. 502, 314 N.E.2d 888 (1974), cert. denied 420 U.S. 947, 95 S.Ct. 1329, 43 L.Ed.2d 425 (1975), rehearing denied 421 U.S. 1017, 95 S.Ct. 2426, 44 L.Ed.2d 686 (1975).

42. See note 42 on page 295.

ments constitute a gift to the other spouse.[43] It follows that if the improvements are made when the spouse is insolvent, his creditors may be able to upset it as a fraudulent conveyance.[44] A spouse's creditors may also be able to assert that the other spouse is estopped to assert his ownership if he has led them to rely on the appearance of title in the debtor spouse, even if the debtor was not insolvent.[45]

Legal recognition of marital interests as contrasted with individual interests in property has taken many forms. Common law dower was one such form. By virtue of her dower right the wife, on her husband's death, took a life estate in one-third of all land in which the husband had held an estate of inheritance at any time during the marriage.[46] Today most states have abolished dower and substituted some other form of protection for the wife on

the death of her husband, such as, for example, the statutory forced share in all his property, real and personal.[47] The courts have safeguarded these rights of the wife by developing the principle that a husband may not convey away his property for the purpose of defrauding his wife.[48] There is disagreement as to whether the test of validity of such transfers is the husband's motive, or whether the court should look only at the reality of the transfer and upset it if it is found to be a sham.[49]

The law also recognized the family as a property-owning unit in the tenancy by the entireties, a tenancy which resulted at common law whenever property was conveyed to husband and wife by name, by the same conveyance, and to take effect at the same time.[50] Neither spouse could convey or encumber entireties property independently of the other,

---

42. Blanchette v. Blanchette, 362 Mass. 518, 287 N.E.2d 459 (1972). See also Doucette v. Doucette, 361 Mass. 156, 279 N.E.2d 901 (1972). A case holding the presumption not rebutted is In re Frapwell's Marriage, 49 Cal.App.3d 597, 122 Cal.Rptr. 718 (1975), appeal after remand 53 Cal.App.3d 479, 125 Cal.Rptr. 878 (1975).

Krasner v. Krasner, 362 Mass. 186, 285 N.E.2d 398 (1972) held that the presumption was rebutted by evidence that the purchasing spouse paid the taxes and expenses of the property, dealt with prospective buyers and put the property in the spouse's name solely to insulate the property from creditors' claims.

43. Hoef v. Hoef, 323 Ill. 170, 153 N.E. 658 (1926).

44. Banister v. Solomon, 126 F.2d 740 (2d Cir.1942); Mullins v. Riopel, 322 Mass. 256, 76 N.E.2d 633 (1948).

45. Wilson v. Grey, 131 Cal.App.2d 58, 280 P.2d 29 (1955). The wife is not estopped if the creditors did not rely on the appearance of title in the husband. Creason v. Wells, 158 Neb. 78, 62 N.W.2d 327 (1954).

But aside from these doctrines a judgment obtained against one spouse may not be enforced against the other spouse's property. Freeman v. Heiman, 426 F.2d 1050 (10th Cir.1970), citing other cases.

46. Beitzell v. Frishman, 427 F.2d 605 (D.C.Cir.1970); 2 R. Powell, Real Property § 209 (Rev. ed. 1985 and Supp. 1986).

47. 2 R. Powell, Real Property § 213(1) (Rev. ed. 1985) (Supp.1986). For a typical and thoroughly worked out statute on distributive shares for spouses see Uniform Probate Code §§ 2–201 to 2–207, 8 Unif.L.Ann. 331–340 (1972). Cf. Annot., 1 A.L.R.3d 446, 486 (1967) on the effect of a spouse's adultery or desertion upon his right to share in the other spouse's estate.

48. Scavello v. Scott, 194 Colo. 64, 570 P.2d 1 (1977) ("colorable" transfer); Montgomery v. Michaels, 54 Ill.2d 532, 301 N.E.2d 465 (1973), 23 DeP.L.Rev. 1247 (1974)

(Totten trust); Estate of Tomaso v. Tomaso, 82 Ill.App.3d 286, 37 Ill.Dec. 700, 402 N.E.2d 702 (1980) (question whether the conveyance was made without the spouse's knowledge or consent); Dzialowy's Estate v. Dzialowy, 53 Ill.App.3d 585, 11 Ill.Dec. 229, 368 N.E.2d 780 (1977); Sanditen v. Sanditen, 496 P.2d 365 (Okl.1972); Smigell v. Brod, 366 Pa. 612, 79 A.2d 411 (1951). Other cases are collected in Annot., 49 A.L.R.2d 521 (1956).

A conveyance by a spouse may also be invalid under the Uniform Fraudulent Conveyance Act ¶¶ 4, 6, 7, 7A Unif.L.Ann. 474, 507, 509 (1985) or similar statutes, if made without fair consideration and if the spouse is or will thereby be rendered insolvent, or if he believes he will incur debts beyond his ability to pay, or if he has an actual intent to defraud his creditors.

49. Most cases seem to determine the validity of the transfer on the basis of whether it is illusory, or a sham, rather than by reference to the transferor's intent. E.g., Scavello v. Scott, 194 Colo. 64, 570 P.2d 1 (1977); Lesnik v. Lesnik's Estate, 82 Ill.App.3d 1102, 38 Ill.Dec. 452, 403 N.E.2d 683 (1980); Irvin v. Thompson, 500 P.2d 283 (Okl. 1972); Robinson v. Leonard, 274 Or. 635, 547 P.2d 629 (1976). See the discussion in In re Estate of Jeruzal, 269 Minn. 183, 130 N.W.2d 473 (1964) and in 1 A. Scott, Trusts § 58.5 (3d ed. 1967). The Uniform Probate Code § 2–202, 8 Unif.L.Ann. 75 (1985) deals with this problem by including in the decedent spouse's "augmented estate" property transferred by him inter vivos in specified ways.

50. Kahn v. Kahn, 43 N.Y.2d 203, 401 N.Y.S.2d 47, 371 N.E.2d 809 (1977); Koster v. Boudreaux, 11 Ohio App.3d 1, 463 N.E.2d 39 (1982). A statute preserving the tenancy by the entireties was held not to discriminate against women on the basis of sex in Klein v. Mayo, 367 F.Supp. 583 (D.Mass.1973), affirmed p.c. 416 U.S. 953, 94 S.Ct. 1964, 40 L.Ed.2d 303 (1974). See Annot., Estate Created by Deed to Persons Described as Husband and Wife But Not Legally Married, 9 A.L.R.4th 1189 (1981).

nor use it to the exclusion of the other spouse.[51] On the death of one spouse title to the property passed to the survivor.[52] The tenancy by the entireties was converted by a divorce or annulment into a tenancy in common.[53] The tenancy by the entireties has been abolished in many states, some courts reaching this result in reliance upon the Married Women's Property Acts.[54]

Still another form of protection for family ownership as contrasted with individual ownership of property is found in the homestead statutes of the various states. These protect a prescribed amount of the value of the family home (usually a relatively small amount) from the claims of some types of creditors.[55] They also restrict the legal title holder's right to convey the property without the consent of his or her spouse.[56] Specific property may be designated as homestead property in accordance with the local statute.[57]

Eight states have adopted community property as a means of providing equitably for the property interests of married persons.[58] The principle underlying community property is that the efforts of both spouses are instrumental in contributing to the welfare of the family, and that therefore property acquired by either spouse during the marriage, with certain exceptions, should belong to both spouses.[59] Community property was originally a Spanish institution and was enacted first in those states whose law was influenced by Spanish law, spreading later to other states.[60] It has also had an influence on common law property states which did not directly adopt it but which for divorce purposes have classified the property of the spouses as either separate or marital property and have authorized the marital property to be divided on divorce.[61]

Although a full account of the law of community property cannot be included in this work, especially since there are many variations among the eight states which have adopted it, a word or two concerning its main outlines is essential. It arises when the spouses are married [62] and includes property acquired by either spouse during the marriage except property acquired by gift, devise or inheritance.[63] Property which does not fall within the definition of community property is characterized as separate property of the spouse who has acquired it.[64] The difficulty of applying this ostensibly simple definition to

---

51. In re Wall's Estate, 440 F.2d 215 (D.C.Cir.1971); Koster v. Boudreaux, 11 Ohio App.3d 1, 463 N.E.2d 39 (1982). Fascione v. Fascione, 272 Pa.Super. 530, 416 A.2d 1023 (1979).

52. Cohen v. Goldberg, 431 Pa. 192, 244 A.2d 763 (1968).

53. Kahn v. Kahn, 43 N.Y.2d 203, 401 N.Y.S.2d 47, 371 N.E.2d 809 (1977). See also Klein v. Mayo, 367 F.Supp. 583 (D.Mass.1973), affirmed p.c. 416 U.S. 953, 94 S.Ct. 1964, 40 L.Ed.2d 303 (1974).

54. 4A R. Powell, Real Property § 621 (Rev. ed. 1982); Note, Tenancy By the Entirety in Illinois: A Reexamination, 1980 So.Ill.L.J. 83.

55. 1 American Law of Property § 5.85 (1952).

56. Id. § 5.101.

57. Id. § 5.80.

58. These are Arizona, California, Idaho, Louisiana, Nevada, New Mexico, Texas and Washington. 4A R. Powell, Real Property § 625[2] (Rev.ed.1982). At one time Wisconsin was considering the adoption of a community property system. Barke and Zurvalec, Wisconsin, Illinois, Ontario-Three Roads to Marital Property Law Reform, 1 Loyola Univ. of Chi.L.Rev. 1 (1980). The Uniform Marital Property Act adopts what is substantially a community property regime, although the statute uses the terms marital and individual rather than community and separate property. Uniform Marital

Property Act § 4, 9A Unif.L.Ann. 29 (Supp.1985). See Reppy, The Uniform Marital Property Act: Some Suggested Revisions for a Basically Sound Act, 21 Hous.L. Rev. 679 (1984).

59. 4A R. Powell, Real Property § 625[1], [2] (Rev.Ed. 1982).

60. W. De Funiak and M. Vaughn, Principles of Community Property ch. IV (2d ed.1971).

61. E.g., Colo.Rev.Stat. § 14–10–113 (1973 and Supp. 1985); Ill. Smith-Hurd Ann. ch. 40, ¶ 503 (Supp.1986). See sections 15.1, 15.2, infra.

62. 4A R. Powell, Real Property § 625.1 (Rev.ed. Rohan 1982). In states such as Texas and Idaho which recognize common law marriage, such a marriage may be a sufficient basis for acquiring community property. For the civil law doctrine of putative marriage, see section 2.4, supra, at note 63.

63. Id. at § 625.2[1]. The Uniform Marital Property Act § 4, 9A Unif.L.Ann. 29 (Supp.1985) defines marital property in substantially the same way. Under that Act the parties may by agreement vary the manner in which property is held. Uniform Marital Property Act § 3, 9A Unif.L.Ann. 28 (Supp.1985) Community property states permit this also. Spector v. Spector, 23 Ariz.App. 131, 531 P.2d 176 (1975).

64. 4A R. Powell, Real Property § 624.3 (Rev.ed. Rohan 1979).

the many forms in which property is acquired has led to the development of a rebuttable presumption that property acquired by either spouse during the marriage, whether title is taken in the name of either spouse or of both, is community property.[65] The presumption may be rebutted if it can be proved that the funds with which the property was acquired were the separate funds of one of the spouses.[66]

In most community property states the parties may by agreement vary the usual rules. They may agree that all property acquired by either of them is separate property, or that it is all community property, or they may agree on the characterization of particular items of property.[67]

Some examples indicate the difficulties of determining whether particular property is community or separate property. Thus veterans' education benefits have been held to be separate property when they were earned before marriage, but paid after marriage, even though the statute provided for increased benefits for dependents, including spouses.[68] There is a conflict in the decisions concerning

damages for personal injury. The Texas authorities classify such damages as separate property, but they hold that the medical expenses and loss of earnings recovered in such a suit are community property.[69] Other courts hold that the entire recovery is community property.[70] Where property is purchased before marriage but paid for in part after marriage out of community funds, its classification as community or separate varies among the community property states. Some would characterize it as separate property, some as separate or community depending upon when title vested, and some would apply complex calculations to establish the proportion of separate to community funds going into the purchase.[71]

The diversity in characterization of property as community or separate, and the differences between the community property states and the common law states, have created difficult questions of the conflict of laws. An early case, Saul v. His Creditors,[72] established the rule that when the marriage occurred in a common law state, where the parties were then domiciled, but they later became domi-

65. In re Marriage of Lucas, 27 Cal.3d 808, 166 Cal. Rptr. 853, 614 P.2d 285 (1980); Wiggins v. Rush, 83 N.M. 133, 489 P.2d 641 (1971); Cockerham v. Cockerham, 527 S.W.2d 162 (Tex.1975); W. de Funiak, M. Vaughn, Principles of Community Property § 60 (2d ed. 1971). There may be other presumptions, such as the statutory presumption in California that where a single family residence is acquired by husband and wife as joint tenants, it is community property. See the Lucas case, supra and In re Marriage of Neal, 153 Cal.App.3d 117, 200 Cal.Rptr. 341 (1984). See also Uniform Marital Property Act § 4(b), 9A Unif.L.Ann. 29 (Supp.1985).

66. In re Marriage of Lucas, 27 Cal.3d 808, 166 Cal. Rptr. 853, 614 P.2d 285 (1980); Cockerham v. Cockerham, 527 S.W.2d 162 (Tex.1975). Of course property acquired by gift during marriage is separate property. Enrich v. Barton, 2 Wash.App. 954, 471 P.2d 700 (1970). Henry S. Miller Co. v. Evans, 452 S.W.2d 426 (Tex.1970) held that property conveyed to a wife by a deed which recited that it was conveyed as her sole and separate estate was separate property.

67. West's Ann.Cal.Civ.Code § 5200 (Supp.1986); Vernon's Ann.Tex. Const. Art. XVI, § 15; Spector v. Spector, 23 Ariz.App. 131, 531 P.2d 176 (1975); In re Marriage of Dawley, 17 Cal.3d 342, 131 Cal.Rptr. 3, 551 P.2d 323 (1976); 4 A R. Powell, Real Property § 625.2[1] (Rev. ed. 1982). Uniform Marital Property Act §§ 3, 10, 9A Unif. L.Ann. 28, 37 (Supp.1985).

68. In re Marriage of Shea, 111 Cal.App.3d 713, 169 Cal.Rptr. 490 (1980).

69. Vernon's Tex.Code Ann., Fam.Code § 5.01 (1975); Lester v. United States, 487 F.Supp. 1033 (N.D.Tex.1980); Graham v. Franco, 488 S.W.2d 390 (Tex.1972). Cases which also take this position include Soto v. Vandeventer, 56 N.M. 483, 245 P.2d 826 (1952) and Jurek v. Jurek, 124 Ariz. 596, 606 P.2d 812 (1980).

70. Doggett v. Boiler Engineering and Supply Co., 93 Idaho 888, 477 P.2d 511 (1970); In re Marriage of Parsons, 28 Wash.App. 276, 622 P.2d 415 (1981). See also West's Ann.Cal.Civ.Code §§ 4800, 5126 (Supp.1981).

71. In re Marriage of Moore, 28 Cal.3d 366, 168 Cal. Rptr. 662, 618 P.2d 208 (1980); Succession of Fay, 161 La. 1022, 109 So. 824 (1926); Gillespie v. Gillespie, 84 N.M. 618, 506 P.2d 775 (1973); McCurdy v. McCurdy, 372 S.W.2d 381 (Tex.Civ.App.1963).

For a detailed discussion of the related question of the classification of property acquired on credit during the marriage, see Young, Community Property Classification of Credit Acquisitions in California: Law Without Logic, 17 Cal.West.L.Rev. 173 (1981).

72. 5 Mart. (N.S.) 569, 16 Am.Dec. 212 (La.1827). For a discussion of conflict of laws as applied to community property, see 4A R. Powell, Real Property § 626 (Rev. ed. 1982); Restatement (Second) of Conflict of Laws §§ 233, 234 (1971); H. Marsh, Marital Property in the Conflict of Laws (1952); R. Leflar, American Conflicts Law ch. 23 (3d ed. 1977); Philip, Hague Draft Convention on Matrimonial Property, 24 Am.J.Comp.L. 307 (1976).

ciled in the community property state, property acquired after the change in domicile had the status of community property. California has carried this a step further by enacting a statute creating the institution of "quasi-community property". This is defined as real or personal property, wherever situated, which was acquired by either spouse while domiciled outside California, and which would have been community property if the spouse who acquired it had been domiciled in California at the time of acquisition.[73] Quasi-community property is divisible on divorce in the same fashion as community property.

The right to manage and control community property is a subject for differing statutory provisions among the various community property states. Traditionally the husband alone had this power. The United States Supreme Court, in Kirchberg v. Feenstra,[74] was presented with an Equal Protection Clause challenge to the former Louisiana statute which made the husband the "head and master" of the community and gave him the power to convey community property without the wife's consent. The Court held that such gender-based classifications cannot stand in the absence of proof that they further some important governmental interest. Finding no such interest in this case, the Court held that

the statute violated the Fourteenth Amendment. Within the constitutional limit so laid down, the states have provided for management and control by each spouse,[75] have required the consent of both spouses for certain transfers of community property,[76] and have authorized joint management of at least some forms of community property.[77] The obvious analogy here is to the law of partnership, since the spouses owe each other fiduciary duties of good faith and fair treatment in dealing with community property, as do partners with respect to partnership property.[78]

The enforcement of spouses' liability in community property states is subject to wide variations as between the various states. It is governed in some respects by statute, and depends upon the nature of the liability and the time at which the liability was incurred. For example, there may be specific statutory provisions covering the enforcement of tort liability arising during the marriage.[79] And in some states a debt of either spouse incurred during the marriage is presumed a community obligation, enforceable out of community property.[80] On this subject generalizations are impossible and the particular state statute and case law must be the basis for any legal opinion.[81]

---

73. West's Ann.Cal.Civ.Code § 4803 (1983).

74. 450 U.S. 455, 101 S.Ct. 1195, 67 L.Ed.2d 428 (1981). The Supreme Court's opinion is unclear whether the decision applies retroactively. The Court of Appeals' decision expressly was made prospective only. Kirchberg v. Feenstra, 609 F.2d 727 (5th Cir.1979).

75. E.g., West's Ann.Cal.Civ.Code § 5125(a) (1983); Vernon's Tex.Code Ann., Fam.Code § 5.22 (1975); West's Rev.Code Wash.Ann. § 26.16.030 (1986). For the New Mexico provisions, see N.M.Stat.Ann.1978, §§ 40–3–13, 40–3–14, 40–3–16. See also Note, Section 5.22 of the Vernon's Texas Code Ann., Family Code, 27 S.W.L.J. 837 (1973), and Uniform Marital Property Act §§ 5, 9A Unif. L.Ann. 32 (Supp.1985).

76. E.g., West's Ann.Cal.Civ.Code § 5125(b), (c) (1983); N.M.Stat.Ann.1978, § 40–3–13(A); West's Rev.Code Wash.Ann. § 26.16.030 (1986).

77. E.g., West's Ann.Cal.Civ.Code § 5127 (1983). For general discussion of management and disposition of community property, see 4A R. Powell, Real Property § 625.3 (Rev.ed.1982).

78. West's Ann.Cal.Civ.Code § 5125(e) (1983); Peters v. Skalman, 27 Wash.App. 247, 617 P.2d 448 (1980).

79. E.g., Ariz.Rev.Stat. § 25.215B (1976); West's Ann. Cal.Civ.Code § 5122 (Supp.1986); West's Rev.Code Wash. Ann. § 26.16.200 (1986). A broader form of regulation for separate and community debts is found in N.M.Stat. Ann.1978, §§ 40–3–9, 40–3–10, 40–3–11 and Vernon's Tex. Code Ann., Fam.Code § 5.61 (1975).

80. Oil Heat Co. of Port Angeles, Inc. v. Sweeney, 26 Wash.App. 351, 613 P.2d 169 (1980).

81. For general treatment see 4A R. Powell, Real Property § 625.4 (Rev.ed.1982) and W. de Funiak and M. Vaughn, ch. IX (2d ed. 1971).

Illustrative cases include Garrett v. Shannon, 13 Ariz. App. 332, 476 P.2d 538 (1970) (community property may be liable for an intentional tort of a spouse where the purpose was to benefit the community); Williams v. Paxton, 98 Idaho 155, 559 P.2d 1123 (1976) (married woman's separate property chargeable for a contract claim based on a contract signed by husband and wife to buy community property); Benson v. Bush, 3 Wash.App. 777, 477 P.2d 929 (1970) (community property is chargeable for a tort of the husband committed in management of the community property). Pacific Gamble Robinson Co. v. Lapp, 95 Wash.2d 341, 622 P.2d 850 (1980) held that

Finally brief mention must be made of the ubiquitous Marvin case,[82] in which the California Supreme Court held that a share of property accumulated while two unmarried persons cohabited could be recovered by the non-acquiring party. The court did not place its decision on community property grounds, but first on contract in fact and, failing proof of contract, on vague notions of equity.[83]

The Married Woman's Contracts and Earnings

It is commonly provided in the Married Women's Property Acts that the wife may make contracts as if she were sole.[84] The statutes have been construed to give her complete power to make contracts with people other than her husband.[85] Vestiges of her former disability which a few courts preserved for a surprisingly long time, such as the rule that her contract must be shown to relate to her separate estate to be valid, which apparently meant that it had to benefit her own property or augment her own earnings,[86] would undoubtedly be held today to violate the Equal Protection Clause of the Fourteenth Amendment on the authority of Orr v. Orr.[87] The assumption made by such rules is that a married woman is either not competent to make business decisions or cannot be trusted to judge her own interests, and the Supreme Court has made it clear that an

assumption of this kind can no longer be tolerated in the age of equality of the sexes. The point would be even clearer in those states having state Equal Rights Amendments in their constitutions.

The wife may also enter into contracts of employment with persons other than her husband and thereby become entitled to wages which are her own and not her husband's.[88] The issue usually arises when the wife is tortiously injured and sues the tortfeasor, including in her damages a claim for lost wages.[89] The bare legal right to make employment contracts was of course of little value to married women, or women generally, so long as they were discriminated against by employers. Sex discrimination in employment was first attacked on a national scale in 1964, when Congress included in the Civil Rights Act of that year a provision making it unlawful for an employer

> "to fail or refuse to hire or to discharge any individual, or otherwise to discriminate against any individual with respect to his compensation, terms, conditions, or privileges of employment, because of such individual's * * * sex".[90]

The Act applies to those employers in industries affecting interstate commerce who have fifteen or more employees.[91]

Colorado law would govern liability on a promissory note executed in Colorado by the husband, at a time when husband and wife were domiciled there, although suit was brought in Washington after husband and wife had moved to that state. By Colorado law, the court held, the note was enforceable against all property of the husband, including property which later became community property in Washington.

82. Marvin v. Marvin, 18 Cal.3d 660, 134 Cal.Rptr. 815, 557 P.2d 106 (1976).

83. Marvin and cases subsequent to it are discussed in § 1.2, supra, and in § 15.7, infra.

84. See the statutes cited in note 4, supra.

85. Residential Industrial Loan Co. v. Brown, 559 F.2d 438 (5th Cir.1977); Hamilton v. Hamilton, 255 Ala. 284, 51 So.2d 13 (1950); Cabot v. First National Bank of Santa Fe, 81 N.M. 793, 474 P.2d 476 (1970); Montsinger v. White, 240 N.C. 441, 82 S.E.2d 362 (1954); Short v. Oklahoma Farmers Union Insurance Co., 619 P.2d 588 (Okl.1980); Kitten v. Vaughn, 397 S.W.2d 530 (Tex.Civ. App.1965); In re Estate of Nickolay, 249 Wis. 571, 25 N.W.2d 451 (1946).

86. Frost v. Mead, 86 Idaho 155, 383 P.2d 834 (1963), finally overruled by Williams v. Paxton, 98 Idaho 155, 559 P.2d 1123 (1976); National Bank of Rochester v. Meadowbrook Heights, Inc., 80 Mich.App. 777, 265 N.W.2d 43 (1978).

87. 440 U.S. 268, 99 S.Ct. 1102, 59 L.Ed.2d 306 (1979), on remand 374 So.2d 895 (Ala.Civ.App.1979), writ denied 374 So.2d 898 (1979). See also Kirchberg v. Feenstra, 450 U.S. 455, 101 S.Ct. 1195, 67 L.Ed.2d 428 (1981), and Greschler v. Greschler, 71 A.D.2d 322, 422 N.Y.S.2d 718 (2d Dep't 1979, modified on other grounds 51 N.Y.2d 368, 434 N.Y.S.2d 194, 414 N.E.2d 694 (1980).

88. McCarthy v. McKechnie, 152 Me. 420, 132 A.2d 437 (1957). See also Ill.—Smith-Hurd Ann. ch. 40, § 1007 (1980).

89. Payne v. Kinder, 147 W.Va. 352, 127 S.E.2d 726 (1962).

90. 42 U.S.C.A. § 2000e–2(a)(1), as amended by the Equal Employment Opportunity Act of 1972.

91. 42 U.S.C.A. § 2000e(b). For data on discrimination against women, see United States Congress, House

The large body of law concerning sex discrimination in employment which has grown up since 1964 is beyond the scope of this work, but there are some points at which the Civil Rights Act has affected the rights of married women specifically. For example, the Supreme Court held, in Phillips v. Martin Marietta Corp., that an employer's refusal to hire women with pre-school-age children when it did hire men having such children could constitute a violation of the statute.[92] But the Court went on to say that the existence of such conflicting family obligations could be the basis for a "bona fide occupational qualification" under the statute,[93] and remanded the case for findings on this issue. And the policy formerly adhered to by most airlines of not hiring or discharging female flight attendants while not applying a similar policy to male flight attendants received a mixed treatment by the courts, some cases holding that this violated the statute,[94] while others held that so long as only female flight attendants were employed, the policy was not unlawful.[95]

Although employers, public and private, have lately relaxed their rules governing the hiring of spouses, one case, Yuhas v. Libbey-Owens-Ford Co.,[96] has held that a rule forbidding the hiring of spouses of hourly workers at plants in which the applicant's spouse is already employed in the same capacity is justifiable as job-related and therefore does not violate the Civil Rights Act. The same case did find that the no-spouse rule had a substantially discriminatory effect as shown by the fact that seventy-one of the last seventy-four people disqualified by it were women.

Married women are also sharply affected in their chances for retaining their jobs by the employers' policies concerning pregnancy. Both the Constitution and the Civil Rights Act may be infringed by such policies. The initial question is whether the policy, as for example where it restricts or mandates maternity leaves, arbitrarily infringes the woman's constitutional freedom of personal choice in deciding whether to have children. Cleveland Board of Education v. LaFleur[97] held that a school board's rule that teachers had to take maternity leave commencing five months before the birth of a child, during which leave they received no pay, bore no reasonable relation to the need for continuity of instruction or to the necessity of keeping physically unfit teachers out of the classroom. Therefore, the Court held, the rule violated the Due Process Clause of the Fourteenth Amendment. The Court reached a similar conclusion respecting limitations on the teacher's eligibility to return to work after having a child. Other cases have held that

Committee on Education and Labor, Special Subcommittee on Education, Discrimination Against Women, Congressional Hearings on Equal Rights in Education and Employment (Stimpson ed. 1973).

92. Phillips v. Martin Marietta Corp., 400 U.S. 542, 91 S.Ct. 496, 27 L.Ed.2d 613 (1971).

93. 42 U.S.C.A. § 200e–2(e) (1982): "Notwithstanding any other provision of this subchapter, (1) it shall not be an unlawful employment practice for an employer to hire and employ employees * * * on the basis of * * * sex * * * in those certain instances where * * * sex * * * is a bona fide occupational qualification reasonably necessary to the normal operation of that particular business or enterprise * * *."

94. Sprogis v. United Air Lines, Inc., 444 F.2d 1194 (7th Cir.1971), cert. denied 404 U.S. 991, 92 S.Ct. 536, 30 L.Ed.2d 543 (1971). For other cases, see Annot., Distinctions Based on Marital Status as Constituting Sex Discrimination Under § 703(a) of Civil Rights Act of 1964 (42 U.S.C.A. § 2000e–2(a)), 34 A.L.R.Fed. 648 (1977).

95. Stroud v. Delta Air Lines, Inc., 544 F.2d 892 (5th Cir.1977), rehearing denied 548 F.2d 356 (5th Cir.1977). For one reason or another most airlines have dropped the no-marriage employment policy for flight attendants. For discussion of some of these issues, see Kanowitz, Sex-Based Discrimination in American Law II: Law and the Married Woman, 12 St.L.L.J. 3 (1967); Binder, Sex Discrimination in the Airline Industry: Title VII Flying High, 59 Cal.L.Rev. 1091 (1971); Note, Marital Restrictions on Stewardesses: Is This Any Way to Run an Airline? 117 U.Pa.L.Rev. 616 (1969).

96. 562 F.2d 496 (7th Cir.1977), cert. denied 435 U.S. 934, 98 S.Ct. 1510, 55 L.Ed.2d 531 (1978). For discussion of a similar problem faced by Congress, see Note, Conflicts of Interest and the Changing Concept of Marriage: The Congressional Compromise, 75 Mich.L.Rev. 1647 (1977). State cases dealing with rules on the employment of spouses include Application of Gaulkin, 69 N.J. 185, 351 A.2d 740 (1976); Thomson v. Sanborn's Motor Express, Inc., 154 N.J.Super. 555, 382 A.2d 53 (1977); Kraft, Inc. v. State, 284 N.W.2d 386 (Minn.1979).

97. 414 U.S. 632, 94 S.Ct. 791, 39 L.Ed.2d 52 (1974). Other forms of maternity leave may bear some relation to reasonable employment purposes, however. deLaurier v. San Diego Unified School District, 588 F.2d 674 (9th Cir.1978).

various discriminatory provisions in employer pregnancy leave policies violate the Civil Rights Act.[98] Oddly enough, however, in view of the number of cases dealing with pregnancy leave policies, the Supreme Court has held that the exclusion of disabilities arising out of pregnancy from a medical disability benefit plan provided by an employer did not violate the Civil Rights Act.[99] The Court's reasoning was that no gender-based discrimination could be found in the benefit plan, which merely included some disabilities and excluded others.[1] How it is that a classification based upon the occurrence of pregnancy could be said not to be related to gender was never adequately explained.

The married woman's capacity to contract has also been aided in an important practical way by the federal Equal Credit Opportunity Act[2] which became effective in 1975, and by similar statutes in some states.[3] Women, married, single or divorced, have in the past had difficulty in applying for credit in all forms.[4] Married women were usually unable to obtain credit cards except in their husbands' names. Divorced women, who had relied on their husband's credit and so had no credit history to be the basis for credit applications, were denied credit entirely. To deal with these and similar problems the federal Act provides that it is unlawful for any creditor to discriminate against any applicant with respect to any aspect of a credit transaction on the ground of sex or marital status.[5] Administrative enforcement of the Act is delegated to the Federal Trade Commission and to other agencies having jurisdiction over banks, credit unions and other enterprises involving credit.[6] The Act imposes civil liabilities for both compensatory and punitive damages for violations, with jurisdiction in the appropriate United States district court or other court of competent jurisdiction.[7] Where the plaintiff is successful, she may also receive costs and attorney fees.[8]

The foregoing discussion indicates that the law has made considerable progress in giving married women capacity to make contracts and to free them from discrimination in employment and in credit transactions. Where she attempts to contract with her husband, she continues to meet with difficulties, however. Although most states give broad powers to the spouses to contract with each other,[9]

98. Nashville Gas Co. v. Satty, 434 U.S. 136, 98 S.Ct. 347, 54 L.Ed.2d 356 (1977) (employer's policy that women on pregnancy leave received no sick pay, unlike other leaves for nonoccupational disabilities, and that the woman lost all accumulated job seniority, violated the Act); Burwell v. Eastern Air Lines, Inc., 633 F.2d 361 (4th Cir. 1980), cert. denied 450 U.S. 965, 101 S.Ct. 1480, 67 L.Ed. 2d 613 (1981); Hanson v. Hoffmann, 628 F.2d 42 (D.C.Cir. 1980); Harper v. Thiokol Chemical Corp., 619 F.2d 489 (5th Cir.1980); In re Consolidated Pretrial Proceedings in Airline Cases, 582 F.2d 1142 (7th Cir.1978). See also Jacobs v. Martin Sweets Co., Inc., 550 F.2d 364 (6th Cir. 1977), cert. denied 431 U.S. 917, 97 S.Ct. 2180, 53 L.Ed.2d 227 (1977); Cerra v. East Stroudsburg Area School District, 450 Pa. 207, 299 A.2d 277 (1973). Other cases are collected in Annot., Pregnancy Leave or Maternity Leave Policy, or Lack Thereof, as Unlawful Employment Practice Violative of Title VII of the Civil Rights Act of 1964, 27 A.L.R.Fed. 537 (1976).

99. General Electric Co. v. Gilbert, 429 U.S. 125, 97 S.Ct. 401, 50 L.Ed.2d 343 (1976), rehearing denied 429 U.S. 1079, 97 S.Ct. 825, 50 L.Ed.2d 799 (1977).

1. The Court also relied upon its own decision in Geduldig v. Aiello, 417 U.S. 484, 94 S.Ct. 2485, 41 L.Ed.2d 256 (1974), which had held that a similar classification in a disability benefits plan did not violate the Equal Protection Clause of the Fourteenth Amendment.

2. 15 U.S.C.A. §§ 1691 to 1691f. Regulations of the Federal Reserve System Board of Governors implement-

ing the Act are found in 12 C.F.R. § 202. For a brief account of the statute, see Koon, Skimming the Equal Credit Opportunity Act, 5 Colo.Law. 1065 (1976). And see Annot., 55 A.L.R.Fed. 458 (1981).

3. The state statutes are cited in Gates, Credit Discrimination Against Women: Causes and Solutions, 27 Vand.L.Rev. 409, 436 (1974).

4. Brown, The Discredited American Woman: Sex Discrimination in Consumer Credit, 6 U.Cal.Davis L.Rev. 61 (1973).

5. 15 U.S.C.A. § 1691(2)(1).

6. 15 U.S.C.A. § 1691c.

7. 15 U.S.C.A. § 1691e.

8. Id.

9. E.g., Conn.Gen.Stat.Ann. § 46b–3 (Supp.1981); Del. Code. tit. 13, § 311 (1981); West's Fla.Stat.Ann. § 708.09 (Supp.1986); Md.Code, Fam.Law, §§ 4–204, 4–205(a) (1984); Mass.Gen.Laws Ann. c. 209, § 2 (Supp.1981); Nev. Rev.Stat. § 123.070 (1986); N.Y.—McKinney's Gen.Oblig. L. § 3–301 (1978); Ohio Rev.Code. § 3103.05 (1980); Okl. Stat.Ann. tit. 32, § 5 (1976).

It is usually held that the contract obligations or indebtedness existing between two persons are not affected by their subsequent marriage to each other. In re Marriage of Reilly, 176 Mont. 239, 577 P.2d 840 (1978), citing other cases.

there are a few in which some kinds of contract between husband and wife are still invalid.[10] Contracts of partnership between husband and wife are generally valid.[11] And a wife may be an agent for her husband, although the mere fact that they are married does not constitute her his agent.[12]

Notwithstanding the existence of a general power of husband and wife to contract with each other, at least some courts seem still to be unwilling to recognize their contracts when they relate to what are regarded as essential aspects of the marital relationship. Contracts with respect to the duty of support have in the past only been recognized when they were made at a time when the spouses were on the point of separation or divorce.[13] It is true that there is a growing acceptance of antenuptial agreements which provide for alimony or a division of property on divorce, but

even the courts which approve of these contracts do not permit them to regulate the level of support in the going marriage.[14]

Conversely, the wife's traditional obligation to perform household services has been held not to be within the parties' contractual powers, either because the wife would be contracting to do only what the law already requires her to do and the contract is therefore without consideration,[15] or because such a contract is against some public policy.[16] The policy is left largely undefined.

This line of cases imposes especial hardship on wives when the wives work for their husbands outside the home. Many courts have been incapable of making the distinction between household work and work in the husband's business, and have held that the wife has no contractual rights against her husband in either event.[17] Although she works in the

---

10. E.g., Hawaii Rev.L. § 572–22 (Supp.1984) (apparently husband and wife may contract with each other only by deed, or by agreement in contemplation of divorce relating to property or alimony); Minn.Stat.Ann. § 519.06 (Supp.1986) (contract between husband and wife is not valid as to land).

11. E.g., West's Fla.Stat.Ann. § 708.09 (Supp.1986); Md.Code, Fam.Law, § 4–204(4) (1984); Vt.Stat.Ann. tit. 15, § 61 (1974). See also In re Jarodsky's Estate, 122 Ill. App.2d 243, 258 N.E.2d 365 (1970); McGehee v. McGehee, 227 Miss. 170, 85 So.2d 799 (1956); Klotz v. Klotz, 202 Va. 393, 117 S.E.2d 650 (1961); Annot. 157 A.L.R. 652 (1945). Contra, under Louisiana law, City National Bank of Baton Rouge v. United States, 383 F.2d 341 (5th Cir.1967).

12. State Farm Mutual Automobile Insurance Co. v. Long, 16 Ariz.App. 222, 492 P.2d 718 (1972); Pierce v. Horvath, 142 Ind.App. 278, 233 N.E.2d 811 (1968); Bergh v. Warner, 47 Minn. 250, 50 N.W. 77 (1891); Barber v. Carolina Auto Sales, 236 S.C. 594, 115 S.E.2d 291 (1960); W. Seavey, Law of Agency § 14D (1964).

For a discussion of the distinction between agency and a spouse's power to buy necessaries at the other spouse's expense see § 6.3, supra.

13. For a discussion of separation agreements and the requirement that they may only be made when the parties are separating, see § 18.1, infra.

For arguments favoring control of support as well as other aspects of marriage by contract, see Weitzman, Legal Regulation of Marriage: Tradition and Change, 62 Cal.L.Rev. 1169 (1974); Krauskopf and Thomas, Partnership Marriage: The Solution to an Ineffective and Inequitable Law of Support, 35 Ohio St.L.J. 558 (1974); Note, Marriage Contracts for Support and Services: Constitutionality Begins at Home, 49 N.Y.U.L.Rev. 1161 (1974).

One case, Greschler v. Greschler, 71 A.D.2d 322, 422 N.Y.S.2d 718 (2d Dep't 1979) modified on other grounds 51 N.Y.2d 368, 434 N.Y.S.2d 194, 414 N.E.2d 694 (1980) held unconstitutional N.Y.—McKinney's Gen.Oblig.L.

§ 5–311, which forbids contracts between spouses relieving the husband of his duty of support. The court said that this was impermissible gender discrimination, since the statute did not forbid contracts relieving the wife of her duty of support.

14. See Posner v. Posner, 233 So.2d 381 (Fla.1970), mandate conformed to 234 So.2d 378 (1970), appeal after remand 237 So.2d 186 (1970) and other cases cited supra, § 1.1.

15. Youngberg v. Holstrom, 252 Iowa 815, 108 N.W.2d 498 (1961); Sprinkle v. Ponder, 233 N.C. 312, 64 S.E.2d 171 (1951) (dictum); Frame v. Frame, 120 Tex. 61, 36 S.W.2d 152 (1931), 16 Minn.L.Rev. 443 (1932); see also Havighurst, Services in the Home—A Study of Contract Concepts in Domestic Relations, 41 Yale L.J. 386, 397 (1932).

16. Bendler v. Bendler, 3 N.J. 161, 69 A.2d 302 (1949), overrule on another point by Romeo v. Romeo, 84 N.J. 289, 418 A.2d 258 (1980); Matter of Lord's Estate, 93 N.M. 543, 602 P.2d 1030 (1979). In Snaith v. Snaith, 282 Pa.Super. 450, 422 A.2d 1379 (1980) the court refused to enforce an alleged agreement by which the husband promised to share the proceeds of the family business (in which the wife had formerly worked) with the wife and she agreed to devote full time to housework and caring for their children. The court seemed to think that the contract was not pleaded with sufficient particularity, or perhaps that the wife should have made her claim in a divorce action.

Dunaj v. Harry Becker Co., 52 Mich.App. 354, 217 N.W. 2d 397 (1974) held that although a wife may not generally recover compensation for household services performed for her husband, she may recover from his employer under the workers' compensation law when she nursed the husband after he was injured in a compensable accident.

17. Ladden v. Ladden, 59 N.J.Super. 502, 158 A.2d 189 (1960); Bendler v. Bendler, 3 N.J. 161, 69 A.2d 302 (1949), overruled on this point by Romeo v. Romeo, 84 N.J. 289, 418 A.2d 258 (1980); Blaechinska v. Howard Mission & Home for Little Wanderers, 130 N.Y. 497, 29 N.E. 755

business just as any other employee would, she may be unable to collect any wages from her husband.[18] Some cases have given her partial relief by holding she may recover if she can prove a contract, but that she may not recover on the basis of any implied obligation to pay her.[19] More enlightened courts have held that she is entitled to the full status of an employee with the rights which that implies.[20]

Today developments in constitutional law have made much of the foregoing reasoning obsolete. Since the Supreme Court in Orr v. Orr [21] has held that the duty of support cannot be imposed exclusively on the husband, there seems to be no substantial reason why the courts should continue to hold that husband and wife may not contract with respect to their support obligations. Certainly such a contract would be based upon consideration in that it would transform an inchoate responsibility resting on both spouses into a definite legal obligation expressed in a specific sum. And there seems to be no public policy which would be infringed by such contracts. On the contrary, they are compatible with the contemporary tendency to abandon rigid rules of marital conduct.[22] It also seems to follow that if the duty of support may not be imposed upon the husband alone, the duty to render marital services may not be imposed upon the wife alone. This is especially true in those states having an Equal Rights Amendment to their constitutions. This being so, the parties ought also to have the

power to agree upon the allocation of household services and payment therefor, and their contracts should be enforceable at least in their financial aspects.[23]

The diversity of rules respecting married women's contracts carries the seeds of some difficult conflict of laws problems. These are most fully and rationally discussed by Professor Currie,[24] who rejected the traditional rule that the law of the place where the contract was made is to be applied. He favored instead, with respect to those cases in which there is no conflict between the interests of the states involved, a choice of law which turns on the residence of the married woman and of her creditor. With respect to cases involving conflicts of state interests, which he regarded as not susceptible of rational solution under existing circumstances, he suggested that the court apply its own law, at the same time urging that such conflicts should be ultimately dealt with by legislative implementation of the Full Faith and Credit Clause.

The Married Woman's Right to Sue and Be Sued

Here again the married woman may, with respect to persons other than her husband, sue and be sued as if she were unmarried. The statutes make this clear.[25] And suits between husband and wife are permitted when they concern breach of contract,[26] or divorce, or controversies relating to the prop-

---

(1892). Other early cases are collected in Warren, Husband's Right to Wife's Services, 38 Harv.L.Rev. 421, 622 (1925).

18. In the extraordinary case of Leatherman v. Leatherman, 297 N.C. 618, 256 S.E.2d 793 (1979) the court held that the wife could receive no compensation for working full time in the family business for about fourteen years, during which period it grew from small beginnings to substantial worth. The wife was unable to prove a specific contract for compensation and the court relied upon a presumption that her services were intended to be gratuitous!

19. Ferris v. Barrett, 250 Iowa 646, 95 N.W.2d 527 (1959); Brodsky v. Brodsky, 132 Neb. 659, 272 N.W. 919 (1937); Leatherman v. Leatherman, 297 N.C. 618, 256 S.E.2d 793 (1979); Dorsett v. Dorsett, 183 N.C. 354, 111 S.E. 541 (1922), 32 Yale L.J. 188 (1922).

20. Reid v. Reid, 216 Iowa 882, 249 N.W. 387 (1933) (semble); McCarthy v. McKechnie, 152 Me. 420, 132 A.2d

437 (1957); Flynn v. State Compensation Com'r, 141 W.Va. 445, 91 S.E.2d 156 (1956).

21. 440 U.S. 268, 99 S.Ct. 1102, 59 L.Ed.2d 306 (1979), on remand 374 So.2d 895 (Ala.Civ.App.1979), writ denied 374 So.2d 898 (1979).

22. See the law review articles cited supra, note 13.

23. For methods of valuation of such services, see Annot., Admissibility and Sufficiency of Proof of Value of Housewife's Services, in Wrongful Death Action, 77 A.L.R.3d 1175 (1977).

24. Currie, Married Women's Contracts: A Study in Conflict-of-Law Method, 25 U.Chi.L.Rev. 227 (1958).

25. See the statutes cited supra, note 4, and Kitten v. Vaughn, 397 S.W.2d 530 (Tex.Civ.App.1965). Cf. Reeves v. Schulmeier, 303 F.2d 802 (5th Cir.1962).

26. Hamilton v. Hamilton, 255 Ala. 284, 51 So.2d 13 (1950).

erty of the wife.[27] But torts to the wife's person, most frequently suits for negligence, even today may not be the subject of litigation between the spouses in some jurisdictions. Discussion of inter-spousal tort immunity is postponed to a later section [28] because it involves policies broader than the married woman's legal capacity.

The Married Woman's Responsibility for Torts and Crimes

Under the Married Women's Property Acts the married woman today is fully responsible for her own torts and crimes.[29] Her husband is no longer liable for her torts, whether committed before or after marriage, unless of course he participated in them or is liable on the basis of some other recognized tort principle.[30] The archaic rule that torts or crimes committed by the wife in her husband's presence are presumed to be the result of his coercion has been almost entirely discarded,[31] as has the rule that husband and wife, being one, may not conspire with each other.[32]

An indirect result of the Married Women's Property Acts is that the husband may now

be guilty of larceny if he appropriates his wife's property.[33]

There was some authority for the proposition that at common law a husband could not be guilty of rape against his wife, the reason being either that the wife gave some sort of universal consent to sex in any form when she married,[34] or that in some sense the intercourse is not "unlawful" when it occurs between spouses.[35] It seems extraordinary that this sort of nonsense is still occasionally repeated.[36] Certainly any criminal code which is not barbaric should find no room for the so-called marital exemption to the offense of rape, and the contemporary trend seems headed in this direction.[37]

The Married Woman's Name

The symbolic importance of names is demonstrated by the amount of litigation and of law review writing concerning married women's names. Traditionally of course married women took their husbands' surnames.[38] Even in fairly recent times cases can be found which seemed to require them to adopt their husbands' names.[39] Today, however, the overwhelming weight of authority is that the mar-

27. Notes v. Snyder, 55 App.D.C. 233, 4 F.2d 426 (1925); Langley v. Schumacker, 46 Cal.2d 601, 297 P.2d 977 (1956); Eddleman v. Eddleman, 183 Ga. 766, 189 S.E. 833 (1937); Baxt v. Baxt, 320 Mass. 762, 70 N.E.2d 799 (1946); Levy v. Levy, 309 Mass. 486, 35 N.E.2d 659 (1941); Brobst v. Brobst, 384 Pa. 530, 121 A.2d 178 (1956). For other cases, see Annot., 109 A.L.R. 882 (1937). But see Bruner v. Hart, 178 Okl. 222, 62 P.2d 513 (1936), and M.G.L.A. c. 209, § 6. See W. Prosser & W. Keeton, The Law of Torts 902 (5th Ed. 1984); McCurdy, Property Torts Between Spouses, 2 Vill.L.Rev. 447 (1957).

28. See section 10.1, infra.

29. See the statutes cited supra, note 4.

30. Ruth v. Rhodes, 66 Ariz. 129, 185 P.2d 304 (1947); Barber v. Hochstrasser, 136 N.J.L. 76, 54 A.2d 458 (1947).

31. United States v. Dege, 364 U.S. 51, 80 S.Ct. 1589, 4 L.Ed.2d 1563 (1960), rehearing denied 364 U.S. 854, 81 S.Ct. 29, 5 L.Ed.2d 77 (1960); People v. Pierce, 61 Cal.2d 879, 40 Cal.Rptr. 845, 395 P.2d 893 (1964); Matter of Gault, 546 P.2d 639 (Okl.Crim.App.1976); 9 J. Wigmore, Evidence § 2514 (Chadbourn Rev.1981).

32. United States v. Anthony, 145 F.Supp. 323 (M.D. Pa.1956); People v. Pierce, 61 Cal.2d 879, 40 Cal.Rptr. 845, 395 P.2d 893 (1964); Annot., Criminal Conspiracy Between Spouses, 74 A.L.R.3d 838 (1976).

33. People v. Morton, 308 N.Y. 96, 123 N.E.2d 790 (1954), 21 Bklyn.L.Rev. 271 (1955), 30 N.Y.U.L.Rev. 198 (1955); Stewart v. Commonwealth, 219 Va. 887, 252 S.E.2d 329 (1979), citing other cases.

34. This is the reason given by Lord Hale, who apparently originated this peculiar legal rule. 1 M. Hale, Pleas of the Crown 628 (J. Dougherty ed. 1800).

35. R. Perkins, Criminal Law 203 (3d ed. 1982) relies on this reason.

36. Hilf, Marital Privacy and Spousal Rape, 16 N.Eng. L.Rev. 31 (1980), suggesting that abolition of the spousal immunity in rape would invade constitutional rights of marital privacy, and that in any event, its abolition would be unwise. No adequate response to these suggestions occurs to the writer at the moment.

37. State v. Smith, 85 N.J. 193, 426 A.2d 38 (1981), reviews the history of the supposed exemption, finding it neither as clear nor as broad as was thought, and in any case holding that it does not apply when husband and wife are living apart. New Jersey has now abolished it, as have other states. N.J.Stat.Ann. § 2C:14–5(b) (Supp. 1982); Clancy, Equal Protection Considerations of the Spousal Sexual Assault Exclusion, 16 N.Eng.L.Rev. 1, 2 (1981).

38. Malone v. Sullivan, 124 Ariz. 469, 605 P.2d 447 (1980).

39. Forbush v. Wallace, 341 F.Supp. 217 (M.D.Ala. 1971), affirmed p.c. 405 U.S. 970, 92 S.Ct. 1197, 31 L.Ed. 2d 246 (1972); Whitlow v. Hodges, 539 F.2d 582 (6th Cir. 1976), cert. denied 429 U.S. 1029, 97 S.Ct. 654, 50 L.Ed.2d 632 (1976), 38 Ohio St.L.J. 157 (1977).

ried woman may retain her maiden name, or take what name she chooses, so long as her choice is neither fraudulent nor unlawful.[40] In fact it would seem clear that she should have a constitutional right to do this, since married men may do so and there is no rational basis for distinguishing between men and women on this score.[41] The state's only conceivable interest is in regularity of records concerning names. It has no interest in what names a person may choose and therefore has no constitutional justification for preventing the married woman from making a non-fraudulent, lawful choice of name.[42]

WESTLAW REFERENCES

The Married Woman's Property Acts

sy,di("married woman property act")

The Effect of State and Federal Constitutions Upon the Legal Rights of Married Women

frontiero /s richardson & sy,di(wife (marri! marry! marital /s woman female) % divorc!)

craig /s boren & sy,di(wife (marri! marry! marital /s woman female) % divorc!)

The Married Woman's Property

tenan! +3 entirety /s abrogat! abolish!

homestead /s property /s convey! /s consent! /s spous! wife husband

find 101 sct 1195

The Married Woman's Contracts and Earnings

phillips /s "martin marietta"

"equal credit opportunity"

The Married Woman's Name

malone /s sullivan

woman female wife /s requir! /s assum! /s name /4 husband man male

§ 7.3   The Battered Wife

The term "battered wife", by analogy to the "battered child syndrome",[1] has become a popular way of referring to wives who have been subjected to physical violence by their husbands.[2] This section deals with the attempts currently being made by legal institutions to prevent and to provide remedies for this kind of violence. Since the same sort of violence occurs between unmarried cohabitants, the term "battered wife" is intended to include women who have been abused by men with whom they have been living. Although we do not usually speak of battered husbands, many of the remedies discussed in this section are available also for husbands who have been the target of violence from their wives.

The incidence of domestic violence between husbands and wives has been variously estimated, but by all estimates it occurs often enough to be a serious social problem. One study produced evidence that nearly four women out of one hundred are physically abused by their husbands every year.[3] Another account estimated that in 1975 of the forty-seven million couples living together in the United States more than one million

40. Ball v. Brown, 450 F.Supp. 4 (N.D.Ohio 1977); Malone v. Sullivan, 124 Ariz. 469, 605 P.2d 447 (1980); Petition of Hauptly, 262 Ind. 150, 312 N.E.2d 857 (1974); Secretary of Commonwealth v. City Clerk of Lowell, 373 Mass. 178, 366 N.E.2d 717 (1977); Application of Lawrence, 133 N.J.Super. 408, 337 A.2d 49 (1975); Application of Halligan, 46 A.D.2d 170, 361 N.Y.S.2d 458 (4th Dep't 1974); Traugott v. Petit, 122 R.I. 60, 404 A.2d 77 (1979); In re Erickson, 547 S.W.2d 357 (Tex.Civ.App. 1977); In re Miller, 218 Va. 939, 243 S.E.2d 464 (1978); Kruzel v. Podell, 67 Wis.2d 138, 226 N.W.2d 458 (1975), 59 Mar.L.Rev. 876 (1976), 50 Tul.L.Rev. 967 (1976). Other cases are collected in Annot., 67 A.L.R.3d 1266 (1975).

41. A case contra the text statement is Forbush v. Wallace, 341 F.Supp. 217 (M.D.Ala.1971), affirmed p.c. 405 U.S. 970, 92 S.Ct. 1197, 31 L.Ed.2d 246 (1972), but the Supreme Court's decision is based on no opinion and is inconsistent with other Supreme Court cases on gender discrimination. For the constitutional arguments, see Note, Married Woman's Right to Her Maiden Name: The Possibilities for Change, 23 Buff.L.Rev. 243 (1973); Note, Married Women and the Name Game, 11 U.Rich.L.Rev. 121 (1976); Note, A Woman's Right to Her Name, 21 U.C.

L.A.L.Rev. 665 (1973); Note, Domestic Relations—The Right of a Married Woman to Retain Her Maiden Name, 79 W.Va.L.Rev. 108 (1976). For other discussions of the question, see Note, Pre-Marriage Name Change, Resumption and Reregistration Statutes, 74 Colum.L.Rev. 1508 (1974); Hughes, And Then There Were Two, 23 Hast.L.J. 233 (1971); Carlsson, Surnames of Married Women and Legitimate Children, 17 N.Y.L.F. 552 (1971); Note, Surname Alternatives in Pennsylvania, 82 Dick.L.Rev. 101 (1977).

42. Cases dealing with the sort of fraud or illegality which would warrant denial of a name change are collected in Annot., 79 A.L.R.3d 562 (1977).

§ 7.3

1. The quoted phrase seems to have originated with a group of physicians who studied child injuries. Kempe, Silverman, Steele, Droegmueller, Silver, The Battered Child Syndrome, 181 A.M.A.J. 17 (1962).

2. D. Martin, Battered Wives (1976); L. Walker, The Battered Woman (1979).

3. R. Gelles, Family Violence 92 (1979).

seven hundred thousand had experienced the violence of a spouse using a knife or gun, and more than two million husbands or wives had been beaten by their spouses.[4] These studies and others also make it clear that much of the violence is extreme, not only involving weapons but resulting in serious bodily injury or death.[5] The incidence of violence by wives against husbands has also been reported as surprisingly high, although perhaps the types of violence are not as severe and the plight of the abused husband is not as hopeless as that of the abused wife.[6]

It has often been said that at common law the husband had a legal privilege to beat his wife, so long as he used a stick of a certain

size, either one no larger than his thumb, or on which would pass through a wedding ring.[7] The conclusion is sometimes drawn from this that the common law encouraged family violence.[8] Reliable primary authority for the husband's privilege is not easy to find,[9] and it is doubtful that the common law gave any encouragement to family violence in this way. In other ways, however, the common law failed to do what it could have to protect wives from injury by their husbands. The inter-spousal immunity from suit for personal torts left wives without recourse in tort for injuries caused by their husbands, but as a later section of this work explains, this immunity is being minimized or eliminated in most states.[10]

---

4. Martin, Overview-Scope of the Problem in U.S. Commission on Civil Rights, Battered Women: Issues of Public Policy 206 (1978), Fain, Conjugal Violence: Legal and Psychosociological Remedies, 32 Syra.L.Rev. 497 (1981); Freeman, Le Vice Anglais?—Wife Battering in English and American Law, in S. Katz, M. Inker, Fathers, Husbands and Lovers 183 (1979).

5. E.g., People v. Gray, 69 Ill.2d 44, 12 Ill.Dec. 886, 370 N.E.2d 797 (1977), cert. denied 435 U.S. 1013, 98 S.Ct. 1887, 56 L.Ed.2d 395 (1978) (husband shot wife); Ortmann v. Ortmann, 547 S.W.2d 226 (Mo.App.1977) (husband tore off wife's ear); Commonwealth v. Ulatoski, 472 Pa. 53, 371 A.2d 186 (1977) (husband intentionally shot and killed wife). See also R. Langley and R. Levy, Wife Beating: The Silent Crisis (1977).

6. R. Gelles, Family Violence ch. 8 (1979), indicating that husbands' abuse of wives was likely to be more severe, that a larger proportion of wives' violence was likely to be in self-defense, and that wives, by virtue of economic necessity, had fewer refuges outside the home than husbands.

For a discussion of self-defense in prosecutions of wives for killing their husbands, see Marcus, The Law of Force and the Force of Law, 69 Cal.L.Rev. 1657 (1981); Note, Battered Wife Syndrome: A Potential Defense to a Homicide Charge, 6 Pepperdine L.Rev. 213 (1978); Note, The Use of Expert Testimony in the Defense of Battered Women, 52 U.Colo.L.Rev. 587 (1981); Note, Limits on the Use of Defensive Force to Prevent Intramarital Assaults, 10 Rutgers Cam.L.J. 643 (1979); Schneider and Jordan, Representation of Women Who Defend Themselves in Response to Physical or Sexual Assault, 4 Women's Rights L.Rptr. 149 (1978); Eisenberg and Seymour, The Self Defense Plea and the Battered Woman, 14 Trial Magazine 34 (1978).

7. E.g., Note, Spouse Abuse: A Novel Remedy for a Historic Problem, 84 Dick.L.Rev. 147, 151 (1979); Note, The Battered Wife Syndrome: A Potential Defense to a Homicide Charge, 6 Pepperdine L.Rev. 213, 214 (1978).

8. E.g., Bruno v. Codd, 90 Misc.2d 1047, 396 N.Y.S.2d 974 (Sup.Ct.1977), judgment reversed 64 A.D.2d 582, 407 N.Y.S.2d 165 (1978), judgment affirmed 47 N.Y.2d 582, 419 N.Y.S.2d 901, 393 N.E.2d 976 (1979), appeal denied 48 N.Y.2d 656, 421 N.Y.S.2d 1032, 396 N.E.2d 488 (1979).

9. State v. Oliver, 70 N.C. 60 (1874) referred to "the old law" that a husband could whip his wife provided he used a stick no larger than his thumb, but said that this was not the law in North Carolina, and went on to uphold a criminal conviction of the husband for assault and battery. No authority for the "old law" is given. Perhaps the court was thinking of a statement in Blackstone to the effect that the husband, by the "old law", might give his wife moderate correction, moderate correction not being defined. Blackstone goes on to say that this rule began to be doubted in the politer reign of Charles II, when a wife could be granted security of the peace against her husband. 1 W. Blackstone, Commentaries on the Laws of England 445 (Cooley 4th ed. 1899). In State v. Rhodes, 61 N.C. 453 (1868) the North Carolina court had held that a husband's acquittal of the charge of assault and battery on his wife would be upheld not because a husband had any right to whip his wife, but because the court would "not interfere with family government in trivial cases", a reason somewhat reminiscent of Justice Douglas' remarks on family privacy in Griswold v. Connecticut, 381 U.S. 479, 85 S.Ct. 1678, 14 L.Ed. 2d 510 (1965), but in any event one not of much comfort to battered wives in North Carolina. The case Blackstone was referring to was perhaps Lord Leigh's Case, 3 Keble 433, 84 Eng.Rep. 807 (1675), which granted to a wife the security of the peace against her husband, stating in dictum that when the law permits the husband to engage in moderate chastisement, that merely means admonition and confinement to the house when the wife has been extravagant. Another early American case, Bradley v. State, 1 Miss. (Walker) 156 (1824) affirmed a conviction of a husband for assault and battery against his wife, but said that husbands could use "moderate chastisement" against wives under the "old law". The Bradley case cited two English authorities which did not support its statement and in any event was overruled in Harris v. State, 71 Miss. 464, 14 So. 266 (1894). An early New York case, People v. Winters, 2 Parker's Crim.Cas. 10 (N.Y.1823) stated that a husband has no right to beat his wife. A similar statement, with a thorough review of the early English authorities, may be found in Regina v. Jackson, (1891) 1 Q.B.D. 671.

10. The inter-spousal immunity for torts is discussed infra, section 10.1.

The most egregious example of the law's callous attitude toward intra-family violence is the common law rule, still in existence in many states, that a husband who forcibly rapes his wife cannot be prosecuted for the offense.[11] The origin of the rule in the Seventeenth Century was an unsupported dictum of Lord Hale, who gave as his reason that by consenting to marry the wife grants her consent to intercourse with her husband.[12] This apparently assumed that she consented for all times and all circumstances, certainly a peculiar notion, whose real basis must have been the dominance of husbands over wives which the law imposed upon the marriages of those times. There seems to be no reason to support this rule today, when a wife is certainly able to revoke her consent to intercourse, just as she can unilaterally seek a divorce under the law of most states.[13] Although some modern criminal statutes inexplicably continue to preserve the husband's immunity,[14] other cases and statutes either abolish the immunity entirely[15] or at least refuse to apply it when husband and wife are living apart.[16] One can only hope that all states will abolish it.

The law's most frequent contact with husband-wife violence occurs when police are called to the scene of a domestic quarrel. These calls present difficult, often dangerous situations for the police, and at the same time situations in which battered wives complain about inadequate police protection.[17] When arrests are made, the police sometimes find that the wife later withdraws her complaint, leading the police to avoid making arrests and to attempt mediation or even to take no action at all.[18] Remedies for inadequate police protection have been attempted by legislation which permits officers to make arrests without warrants in domestic disturbances,[19] and by placing greater emphasis in police training on the handling of domestic violence.[20]

---

11. For discussion of the so-called marital rape exemption, see R. Gelles, Family Violence ch. 7 (1979); Freeman, Le Vice Anglais?—Wife-Battering in English and American Law, in S. Katz and M. Inker, Fathers, Husbands and Lovers 183, 196 (1979); Berger, Man's Trial, Woman's Tribulation: Rape Cases in the Courtroom, 77 Colum.L.Rev. 1, 9 (1977); Note, The Marital Rape Exemption, 52 N.Y.U.L.Rev. 306 (1977); Note, The Marital Rape Exemption in Pennsylvania: "With This Ring * * *", 86 Dick.L.Rev. 79 (1981); Note, The Marital Rape Exemption, 27 Loyola L.Rev. 597 (1981); Note, Abolishing the Marital Exemption for Rape: A Statutory Proposal, 1983 U.Ill.L.Rev. 201. Cases are collected in Annot., 24 A.L.R.4th 105 (1983).

12. I M. Hale, Pleas of the Crown 629 (Stokes and Ingersoll ed. 1847). Lord Hale's dictum and its influence on American law are critically discussed in Commonwealth v. Chretien, 383 Mass. 123, 417 N.E.2d 1203 (1981).

13. State v. Smith, 85 N.J. 193, 426 A.2d 38 (1981). Various other reasons for retaining the immunity, most of them being reducible to the difficulty of proving or disproving the charge, are discussed in Note, The Marital Rape Exemption, 27 Loyola L.Rev. 597 (1981). None of them is worthy of serious consideration.

14. E.g., Model Penal Code § 213.1, A.L.I. Model Penal Code and Commentaries Part II, 274 (1980); Colo.Rev. Stat. § 18–3–409 (1978); Ill.—Smith-Hurd Ann. ch. 38, ¶ 12–18(c) (1986). N.Y.—McKinney's Penal Law §§ 130.05, 130.25, 130.30, 130.35 (1975), preserving a qualified immunity, was held a violation of the Equal Protection Clause in People v. De Stefano, 121 Misc.2d 113, 467 N.Y.S.2d 506 (County Court 1983).

Some states have expanded the immunity to include unmarried cohabitants. See, e.g., Conn.Gen.Stat.Ann. § 53a–67(b) (1985); Hawaii Rev.Stat. § 707–700(10) (Supp. 1984); Iowa Code Ann. § 709.4 (1979) (semble); Mont.

Code Ann. § 45–5–511 (1985); Pa.Stat. tit. 18, § 3103 (Supp.1986).

15. E.g., West's Ann.Cal.Penal Code § 262 (Supp.1986) (requiring the rape to be reported to the authorities within ninety days); Neb.Rev.Stat. § 28–319 (1985); N.J. Stat.Ann. § 2C:14–5(b) (1982); Or.Rev.Stat. § 163.375 (1985). Where the statute does not expressly adopt the marital exemption, State v. Smith, 85 N.J. 193, 426 A.2d 38 (1981) and Commonwealth v. Chretien, 383 Mass. 123, 417 N.E.2d 1203 (1981) seem to hold that it will no longer be recognized, but both cases involved husbands and wives who were living apart from each other, so that the decisions could have been put on narrower grounds.

People v. Liberta, 64 N.Y.2d 152, 485 N.Y.S.2d 207, 474 N.E.2d 567 (1984) held the exemption arbitrary and therefore a violation of the Equal Protection Clause.

16. E.g., Colo.Rev.Stat. § 18–3–409 (1978); N.Y.—McKinney's Penal Law § 130.00(4) (Supp.1986); Pa.Cons. Stat.Ann. tit. 18, § 3103 (Supp.1980).

17. Parnas, The Police Response to the Domestic Disturbance, 1967 Wis.L.Rev. 914; see Bruno v. Codd, 90 Misc.2d 1047, 396 N.Y.S.2d 974 (Sup.Ct.1977), judgment reversed 64 A.D.2d 582, 407 N.Y.S.2d 165 (1978), judgment affirmed 47 N.Y.2d 582, 419 N.Y.S.2d 901, 393 N.E.2d 976 (1979), appeal denied 48 N.Y.2d 656, 421 N.Y.S.2d 1032, 396 N.E.2d 488 (1979).

18. Ibid.

19. E.g., Mich.Comp.Laws Ann. § 28.874(1) (1985); Buzawa and Buzawa, Legislative Responses to the Problem of Domestic Violence in Michigan, 25 Wayne L.Rev. 859 (1979).

20. Bard and Connolly, The Police and Family Violence: Policy and Practice, in United States Commission on Civil Rights, Consultation, Battered Women: Issues of Public Policy 304 (1978).

A few communities have established shelters for the victims of domestic violence, using private or public funds for the purpose.[21] These shelters try to provide temporary lodging, food, medical care and assistance in finding work for women who have been abused by husbands or lovers.[22] Usually the resources available for shelters are inadequate, however.[23]

Several states have enacted legislation aimed at providing a variety of legal remedies for the prevention or redress of domestic violence.[24] This legislation may provide the courts with jurisdiction to enter civil injunctions or protective orders against spouse abuse,[25] in some states it may authorize or appropriate money for shelters,[26] it may set up a program for the collection of statistics on domestic violence,[27] and it sometimes imposes criminal penalties specifically for spouse abuse.[28] A carefully drafted statute of this kind should provide protection for unmarried cohabitants as well as spouses.[29]

Some judicial recognition of the problem of wife battering may also be seen in those cases in which the doctrine of self-defense has been somewhat expanded when relied upon by women who have been subjected to abuse by husbands or lovers.[30]

 WESTLAW REFERENCES

"battered wife syndrome"

marital +1 rape

---

21. Note, Spouse Abuse: A Novel Remedy for a Historic Problem, 84 Dick.L.Rev. 147, 153 (1979); D. Martin, Battered Wives ch. 10 (1976).

22. Shelters, Short Term Needs, Long Term Needs, in United States Commission on Civil Rights, Consultation, Battered Women: Issues of Public Policy 98, 126, 371, 409 (1978).

23. Ibid.

24. State Statutes, in United States Commission on Civil Rights, Consultation, Battered Women: Issues of Public Policy 627 (1978); Galvin, Ohio's New Civil Remedies for Victims of Domestic Violence, 8 Ohio No.L.Rev. 248 (1981); Note, Domestic Violence: Illinois Responds to the Plight of the Battered Wife—The Illinois Domestic Violence Act, 16 J.Marsh.L.Rev. 77 (1982); Colo.Rev.Stat. §§ 14–4–101 to 14–4–105 (Supp.1985); Note, Domestic Abuse Legislation in Illinois and Other States: A Survey and Suggestions for Reform, 1983 U.Ill.L.Rev. 261; Note, Duties and Enforcement Mechanisms for the Rights of Battered Women, 16 Suff.U.L.Rev. 937 (1982); Mele, Evidentiary Issues in the Prosecution of Family Abuse Cases, 11 Ohio N.U.L.Rev. 245 (1984).

The Missouri Adult Abuse Act was held constitutional against attack on a variety of grounds in State ex rel. Williams v. Marsh, 626 S.W.2d 223 (Mo.1982). The Illinois Act's authorization of protective orders in the event of domestic violence, Ill.—Smith-Hurd Ann. ch. 40, ¶ 2301–1 (Supp.1984–1985), has been held constitutional against the contention that "abuse" as defined in the Act was too vague to meet due process requirements in In re Marriage of Hagaman, 123 Ill.App.3d 549, 78 Ill.Dec. 922, 462 N.E.2d 1276 (1984). But another section of the Illinois act which increased the fee for marriage licenses in order to fund shelters for battered wives was held unconstitutional as a special tax in Boynton v. Kusper, 122 Ill. 2d 356, 98 Ill.Dec. 208, 494 N.E.2d 135 (1986).

25. E.g., West's Ann.Cal.Civ.Pro.Code §§ 527(b), 527.6, 540, 547 (1986); West's Ann.Cal.Civ.Code § 4359 (Supp.

1987); N.Y.—McKinney's Fam.Ct. Act §§ 812 to 847 (1983 and Supp.1986); Pa.Stat. tit. 35, §§ 10181 to 10190 (Supp.1981–1982). See also Spouse Abuse: A Novel Remedy for a Historic Problem, 84 Dick.L.Rev. 147 (1979); Mills and McNamar, California's Response to Domestic Violence, 21 Santa Clara L.Rev. 1 (1981).

26. E.g. Colo.Rev.Stat. §§ 26–7.5–101 to 26–7.5–105 (Supp.1986); N.J.Stat.Ann. §§ 30:14–1 to 30:14–14 (1981).

27. E.g., Mich.Comp.Laws Ann. §§ 16.611(1) to 16.611(10) (1982 and Supp.1986–1987); Buzawa and Buzawa, Legislative Responses to the Problem of Domestic Violence in Michigan, 25 Wayne L.Rev. 859 (1979).

28. E.g., West's Ann.Cal.Penal Code § 273.5 (Supp. 1986) (physical injury to spouse or cohabitant is a felony); Hawaii Rev.Stat. § 709–906 (Supp.1984); R.I.Gen.L.1956, § 11–5–9. Mich.Comp.Laws Ann. § 28.1167 (1986) provides for the imposition of a bond to keep the peace, with a penalty of criminal contempt in the event of a violation.

29. See, e.g., West's Ann.Cal.Penal Code § 273.5 (Supp.1987); N.Y.—McKinney's Fam.Ct. Act §§ 812 to 847 (Supp.1986).

30. See The Battered Wife Syndrome: A Potential Defense to a Homicide Charge, 6 Pepperdine L.Rev. 213 (1978) citing the relatively few available cases. See also Note, The Use of Expert Testimony in the Defense of Battered Women, 52 Colo.L.Rev. 587 (1981).

Expert testimony on the battered wife syndrome was held admissible in a homicide prosecution when a) the expert was qualified on the subject; b) scientific knowledge on the subject permitted a reasonable opinion by the expert; and c) the subject matter of the expert opinion was sufficiently complex to be beyond the understanding of the average layman. Hawthorne v. State, 408 So.2d 801 (Fla.App.1982), review denied 415 So.2d 1361 (1982), citing other cases; and Annot., 18 A.L.R.4th 1153 (1982).

Chapter 8

THE LEGAL DISABILITIES OF MINORS

Table of Sections

---

§ 8.1 The Child's Legal Disabilities—In General

From early times the common law imposed disabilities upon persons under age.[1] The age at which the disabilities came to an end originally varied for different classes of people,[2] but gradually the age of twenty-one, the age of majority for the knightly class, came to be the standard.[3] Apparently this was the age at which men were thought strong enough to bear the heavy medieval armour.[4] At any rate it became the common law age of majority both in Britain and the United States, establishing the point in the lives of both men and women when full legal capacity is acquired.[5] Persons of both sexes below that age are referred to by the law as infants, minors, or, more recently, children.

During the 1970's all except five states reduced the age of majority to eighteen. Alabama,[6] Nebraska,[7] and Wyoming[8] lowered the age of majority to nineteen. In Mississippi[9] and Pennsylvania[10] it is still twenty-one. In all states the age of majority is the same for females as for males.[11] In some states the statutes expressly provide that marriage confers full adult status.[12] In several the minimum age for purchasing liquor is still twenty-

§ 8.1

1. 3 Holdsworth, History of English Law, 395–404 (1909).

2. 2 Pollock and Maitland, History of English Law, 436–447 (1898).

3. 1 Blackstone, Commentaries on the Laws of England, 463 (3d rev. ed. Cooley 1884).

4. James, The Age of Majority, 4 Am.J. of Legal Hist. 22 (1960).

5. Jones v. Jones, 63 App.D.C. 373, 72 F.2d 829 (1934). At common law most disabilities continued to age twenty-one, but a few did not. An example was the capacity to marry, which was acquired at age twelve for girls and fourteen for boys. See section 2.9, supra.

6. Ala.Code 1977, § 26–1–1.

7. Neb.Rev.Stat. § 38–101 (1984).

8. Wyo.Stat.1978, § 8–1–102.

9. Miss.Code 1972, § 1–3–21.

10. Pa.Stat. tit. 1 App., § 1991 (1986).

11. It seems clear that any attempt to differentiate for this purpose between males and females would be held to violate the Equal Protection Clause of the Fourteenth Amendment. Stanton v. Stanton, 421 U.S. 7, 95 S.Ct. 1373, 43 L.Ed.2d 688 (1975), appeal after remand 552 P.2d 112 (Utah 1976), judgment vacated 429 U.S. 501, 97 S.Ct. 717, 50 L.Ed.2d 723 (1977), on remand 564 P.2d 303 (Utah 1977) rehearing denied 567 P.2d 625 (Utah 1977).

12. E.g., Alaska Stat. § 25.20.020 (1983); Iowa Code Ann. § 599.1 (1981); Kan.Stat.Ann. § 38–101 (1981); Neb.Rev.Stat. § 38–101 (1984).

one.[13]   And in a few states, although the age of attaining legal capacity is only eighteen, parents may have a duty to support their children until age twenty-one.[14]

The reasons for lowering the age of majority probably include the drafting of eighteen-year-olds, the argument being that if they were old enough to risk their lives in a war, they were old enough to vote, and the adoption of the Twenty-Sixth Amendment which gave eighteen-year-olds the right to vote.[15]

Although it is customary to speak of the disabilities and privileges of those under eighteen, it seems clear that the law creates both disabilities and privileges for the same purposes, either to protect the child against the consequences of his own lack of judgment, or to prevent him from acting where he is not considered to have sufficient maturity to act advisedly. The first purpose underlies most of the rules concerning disabilities and privileges, such as the child's privilege to disaffirm his contracts and conveyances, or his privilege of having a guardian ad litem if he sues or is sued.[16] The second purpose underlies the child's incapacity to vote or to hold public office.

It is generally held that a person becomes eighteen at the beginning of the day before the eighteenth anniversary of his birth.[17]

Thus a person born on January fifteenth, 1963, would become eighteen for legal purposes at 12:01 A.M. on January fourteenth, 1981.

A brief account of most of the disabilities imposed upon minors by contemporary American law follows. The purpose of this outline is to indicate as well as possible without an exhaustive study of the law of individual states the extent of the minor's legal capacity. Obviously some of the minor's disabilities are much more important than others.

a) *Property:* The person under age is capable of acquiring and owning property, both real and personal.[18] He may also convey it, but his conveyance may be disaffirmed upon reaching majority or within a reasonable time thereafter.[19] If he owns property, as a practical matter it will normally be necessary at some point to make contracts respecting it or to convey it. Since such contracts or conveyances do not bind him, it is customary to have a guardian of the estate appointed for the infant who owns property.[20] The guardian can administer the property for the child's benefit under the court's supervision. As a means of avoiding the expense and inconvenience of guardianship, the Uniform Gifts to Minors Act was drafted.[21] It is now in force

13. E.g., Ark.Stats. § 57–103 (Supp.1985); Ky.Rev. Stat. § 2.015 (1985); S.C.Const. Art. XVII, § 14; Tenn. Code Ann. § 1–3–105 (1985).

14. E.g., Colo.Rev.Stat. § 13–22–101 (1973 and Supp. 1985); West's Fla.Stat.Ann. § 743.07 (1986); Utah Code Ann.1985, § 15–2–1. See also In re Marriage of Weaver, 39 Colo.App. 523, 571 P.2d 307 (1977); Price v. Price, 395 Mich. 6, 232 N.W.2d 630 (1975), 1976 Det.Coll. of L.Rev. 147.

15. U.S. Const.Amend. XXVI.

The change in the age of majority was held constitutional in Arnold v. Davis, 503 S.W.2d 100 (Tenn.1973). The effect of the change on outstanding child support decrees is discussed infra in section 17.1. See also Annot., Statutory Change of Age of Majority as Affecting Pre-Existing Status or Rights, 75 A.L.R.3d 228 (1977). The change in the age of majority was held prospective only in Walker v. Walker, 116 N.H. 717, 367 A.2d 211 (1976).

In many states the age of majority for certain specified kinds of contracts or transactions may be less than eighteen. See, e.g., Colo.Rev.Stat. §§ 13–22–102, 13–22–103, 13–22–105 (1974) (consent to various kinds of medical and dental care); Conn.Gen.Stat.Ann. § 38–157 (1969) (minor

aged fifteen may make insurance contracts); Vernon's Ann.Mo.Stat. § 431.061 (Supp.1982) (consent medical and surgical treatment). Other examples are cited infra, in section 8.2.

For a thoughtful discussion of the legal status of today's young people, see F. Zimring, The Changing Legal World of Adolescence (1982).

16. 1 Blackstone, Commentaries on the Laws of England 463 (3d rev.ed. Cooley (1884).

17. N.D.Cent.Code § 14–10–01 (Supp.1985); Nelson v. Sandkamp, 227 Minn. 177, 34 N.W.2d 640 (1948); State in Interest of F.W., 130 N.J.Super. 513, 327 A.2d 697 (1974); T. Atkinson, Wills § 50 (1953). But compare Okl.Stat. Ann. tit. 15, § 13 (1972).

18. 1 R. Powell, Real Property §§ 124, 125 (Rev. ed. Rohan 1985). The child may acquire property by adverse possession. Deatherage v. Lewis, 131 Ill.App.3d 685, 86 Ill.Dec. 797, 475 N.E.2d 1364 (1985).

19. Ibid. See also section 8.2, infra, which discusses the right of disaffirmance in detail.

20. See section 9.4, Practitioner's Edition, concerning guardianship.

21. 8A Unif.L.Ann. 317 (1983).

in most states.[22] It provides a method for making gifts of certain kinds of property to minors, after which the property may be administered in a specified manner by a custodian designated in the instrument of gift.

b) *Contracts:* The minor may make contracts and enforce them,[23] but he may disaffirm his contracts (thereby avoiding liability) at any time before reaching majority, or within a reasonable time thereafter.[24] This disability of infancy has proved unsatisfactory in modern conditions. For this reason it has been qualified and limited in many ways by statute and by the judicial doctrine that the minor's contracts are binding where they are entered into for the purchase of necessaries.[25] Where both parties to a contract are under age, either may disaffirm the transaction.[26]

c) *Consent to operations:* Where the infant is well below the age of majority, he is incapable of consenting to medical treatment or surgical procedures and the consent of his parent is required.[27] As he approaches majority, however, the courts have in some states applied the "mature minor" principle to his medical treatment. This may merely be a specific application of the doctrine of informed consent as it has developed in medical malpractice litigation.[28] In any event there is a body of case law which holds that if the minor is mature enough to understand the proposed medical or surgical procedure, he may give a binding consent to it, perhaps with the additional qualification that the procedure is not one involving serious risk to life or health.[29]

d) *Making a will:* Statutes generally regulate the age at which a person becomes qualified to make a will, either by the general prescription of the age of majority (now eighteen)[30] or by a specific wills statute which usually also provides that testamentary capacity is acquired at age eighteen.[31]

e) *Agency and partnership:* It is clear that a minor may be an agent.[32] He may also be a principal, but he has the privilege of disaffirming transactions executed on his behalf by his agent, to the same extent as if he had entered into them himself.[33] He may disaffirm the contract with his agent,[34] but there is a divergence of opinion as to whether the infant master is liable for the torts of his servant committed before any disaffirmance of the relationship.[35] It would seem that he

22. There is a new version of this Act called the Uniform Transfers to Minors Act, 8A Unif.L.Ann. 107 (Supp.1986), which is in force in sixteen states. The Uniform Gifts to Minors Act, 8A Unif.L.Ann. 45 (Supp. 1986) and the new Act are between them in force in more than forty states.

23. Holt v. Ward Clarencieux, 2 Str. 937, 93 Eng.Rep. 954 (1732).

24. 2 S. Williston, Contracts ch. 9 (3d ed. Jaeger 1959). See also section 9.2. infra.

25. Note, Statutory Problems in the Law of Minors' Contracts, 48 Colum.L.Rev. 272 (1948); 2 S. Williston, Contracts §§ 240, 241, 242 (3d ed. Jaeger 1959).

26. Hurwitz v. Barr, 193 A.2d 360 (D.C.App.1963); Drude v. Curtis, 183 Mass. 317, 67 N.E. 317 (1903).

27. W. Prosser and W. Keeton, The Law of Torts 115 (5th ed. 1984).

28. Cf. Younts v. St. Francis Hospital & School of Nursing, Inc., 205 Kan. 292, 469 P.2d 330 (1970).

29. Baird v. Attorney General, 371 Mass. 741, 360 N.E.2d 288 (1977), citing cases; Bach v. Long Island Jewish Hospital, 49 Misc.2d 207, 267 N.Y.S.2d 289 (Sup. Ct.1966); Lacey v. Laird, 166 Ohio St. 12, 139 N.E.2d 25 (1956); W. Prosser and W. Keeton, Torts 103 (4th ed. 1971); Wadlington, Minors and Health Care: The Age of Consent, 11 Osgoode Hall L.J. 115 (1973). See also Smith v. Seibly, 72 Wash.2d 16, 431 P.2d 719 (1967).

30. See the text at notes 6–10, supra.

31. Uniform Probate Code § 2–501, 8 Unif.L.Ann. 102 (1983), in force in fourteen states, 8 Unif.L.Ann. 106 (Supp.1986). See also, e.g., West's Ann.Cal.Prob.Code § 6100 (Supp.1986); Ill.—Smith-Hurd Ann. ch. 110½, ¶ 4–1 (1978); Mass.Gen.L.Ann. c. 191, § 1 (1981); N.Y.—McKinney's Estates, Powers & Trusts L. § 3–1.1 (1981); Pa.Cons.Stat.Ann. tit. 20, § 2501 (1986); Utah Code Ann. 1953, § 75–2–501; West's Rev.Code Wash.Ann. § 11.12.010 (Supp.1986).

32. W. Seavey, Agency § 14 (1964); Restatement, Second, Agency § 21 (1958). But the minor who commits a breach of his agency relation before reaching full age would not be liable to the extent that his breach of duty rested upon contract. To the extent that it rested upon tort, as where he intentionally damaged or misappropriated the principal's property, he could be liable. Cf. II A. Scott, Trusts § 91 (3d ed. 1967).

33. Casey v. Kastel, 237 N.Y. 305, 142 N.E. 671 (1924); Restatement, Second, Agency § 20 (1958); W. Seavey, Agency § 14 (1964).

34. Cases are collected in Annot., 31 A.L.R. 1001 (1924).

35. Cases are collected in Restatement, Second, Agency § 20, Reporter's Notes (1958), and W. Prosser and W. Keeton, Law of Torts 1072 (5th ed. 1984).

should be liable for these as he would be for his own torts.

Minors may be members of partnerships, but they may disaffirm their contracts of partnership as well as transactions between the partnership and outsiders.[36] There is a conflict in the cases, however, as to whether the infant may, after disaffirmance of his partnership contract, recover back his capital contribution without allowing for losses.[37]

f) *Minor as trustee, director or other fiduciary:* In the rare case where a minor is named as trustee, the trust does not fail, but the minor is removed as trustee because his disability to bind himself by contracts and conveyances makes his administration of the trust impracticable.[38] If he attempts to administer the trust, there may also be difficulties in holding him liable for breaches of trust.[39]

Generally minors do not qualify as executors or administrators, since persons in those capacities often must make contracts and conveyances which will be binding, something the minor cannot do.[40]

Statutes sometimes provide that minors may not qualify as directors of corporations,[41] but many states impose no such age limitations.[42] If the statute is silent, and if there are no such limits in articles or by-laws, it would seem that a minor could serve as the director of a corporation,[43] although he might be subject to less severe standards of fiduciary duty than an adult.

g) *Responsibility for torts:*[44] In general children are liable for their torts, but more lenient standards of intent or negligence may be applied to them than to adults.[45] The courts also hold that theories of tort may not be relied on in suits against children in order to get around the rule that the child may disaffirm his contracts. But if the tort exists independently and separately from the contract, the child may be liable.

h) *Responsibility for crimes:* At common law children below the age of seven were conclusively deemed incapable of committing crimes.[46] Between the ages of seven and fourteen the common law presumed that the child was unable to form a criminal intent, but this presumption could be rebutted by the state's proving that the child had sufficient intelligence to form a criminal intent.[47] Children over fourteen were held to have the same capacity to form a criminal intent as an adult.[48]

Today most states attempt to solve the problem of children's criminality by enacting statutes on juvenile delinquency.[49] Under such statutes the child who violates criminal

---

36. Annot., 58 A.L.R. 1366 (1929).

37. J. Crane and A. Bromberg, Partnership 45–46 (1968).

38. II A. Scott, Trusts § 91 (3d ed. 1967).

39. Ibid.

40. Uniform Probate Code § 3–203(f), 8 Unif.L.Ann. 241 (1983) (personal representative must be twenty-one); T. Atkinson, Wills § 110 (2d ed. 1953); Annot. 14 A.L.R. 619 (1921). Some statutes provide that although the minor cannot administer an estate, letters of administration may issue to his guardian. E.g., West's Ann.Cal. Prob.Code § 426 (Supp.1986).

41. H. Henn and J. Alexander, Laws of Corporations § 204 (3d ed. 1983).

42. E.g. American Bar Association, Model Business Corporation Act Ann. § 8.02 (3d ed. 1985); Del.Code tit. 8, § 141 (1983 and Interim Supp.1985).

43. The Model Business Corporation Act § 8.02, Am. Bar Assn., Model Business Corporation Act 752 (3d ed. 1985), in force in many states makes no age requirement for directors, leaving their qualification to the articles or by-laws. See also 2 W. Fletcher, Cyclopedia of Corporations § 297 (Rev. permanent ed. 1982).

44. For a discussion of the minor's liability in tort see W. Prosser and W. Keeton, The Law of Torts § 134 (5th ed. 1984).

45. Horton v. Reaves, 186 Colo. 149, 526 P.2d 304 (1974) (to be liable the infant must have some awareness of the consequences of his intentional acts); DeLuca v. Brown, 42 Ohio St.2d 392, 329 N.E.2d 109 (1975) (infant under seven incapable as a matter of law of negligence); Gremban v. Burke, 33 Wis.2d 1, 146 N.W.2d 453 (1966).

46. G. Williams, Criminal Law—The General Part § 269 (2d ed. 1961).

47. W. LaFave and A. Scott, Criminal Law 351 (1972).

48. Ibid.

49. For a general discussion see S. Fox, Juvenile Courts in a Nutshell (3d ed. 1984); P. Piersma, Law and Tactics in Juvenile Cases (3d ed. 1977). See also Application of Gault, 387 U.S. 1, 87 S.Ct. 1428, 18 L.Ed.2d 527 (1967) and State v. Monahan, 15 N.J. 34, 104 A.2d 21 (1954), and Fourth Annual Juvenile Law Thematic Journal, 7 Pepperdine L.Rev. 801–1057 (1980). An historical account is Fox, Juvenile Justice Reform: An Historical Perspective, 22 Stan.L.Rev. 1187 (1970).

laws is treated not as a criminal but as the subject of a civil proceeding whose purpose is supervision and rehabilitation.[50] The child usually remains subject to the delinquency laws and procedure until the age of sixteen or eighteen,[51] after which he becomes subject to the same criminal responsibilities as the adult, except that his age may be taken into account in deciding to which penal institution he shall be sentenced. In about half the states the delinquency procedure is exclusive for children within the specified age. In the others the courts or other officials may have discretion as to whether the child shall be treated as a criminal or a delinquent.[52]

One other aspect of the child's relation to the criminal law should be mentioned. Some regulatory statutes having criminal or quasi-criminal sanctions in contemporary America apply only to children or young people. The most common examples are those forbidding the driving of an automobile under a stated age, usually sixteen,[53] and forbidding the drinking of intoxicating liquors, the relevant ages here being from eighteen to twenty-one.[54] In addition, some local governments have passed curfew laws, requiring children of stated ages to be off the streets by a certain time in the evening.[55] And many school administrations over the country seem to have taken it upon themselves to be arbiters of dress for children, prescribing the sort of clothing and hair styles to be worn in school.[56]

i) *Participation in litigation:* At common law a minor could only be sued when his guardian was joined as a defendant. He could sue either by his guardian or "next friend", who could be any adult willing to undertake the case.[57] Today these rules have decreased in importance, although it is still true that the litigation is conducted by a guardian on behalf of the minor.[58] The suit is brought or defended in the minor's own name in some states, and in the name of the guardian in others.[59] The chief consideration here

50. Examples of comprehensive legislation are Ill.—Smith-Hurd Ann. ch. 37, ¶¶ 701–1 to 707–6 (1972 and Supp.1986); N.Y.—McKinney's Fam.Ct.Act §§ 711 to 784 (1983 and Supp.1986). National Advisory Committee on Criminal Justice Standards and Goals, Juvenile Justice and Delinquency Prevention (1976) proposes standards for a juvenile justice system. See also Model Penal Code § 4.10 (Proposed Official Draft 1985).

51. S. Fox, Juvenile Courts in a Nutshell § 10 (3d ed. 1984).

52. Id. at § 11.

53. E.g., West's Ann.Cal. Vehicle Code § 12507 (Supp. 1986); N.Y.—McKinney's Vehicle & Traffic L. § 501 (Supp.1986).

54. E.g., West's Ann.Cal.Bus. & Prof.Code § 25658 (1985); N.Y.—McKinney's Alcoholic Bev. Control L. §§ 65, 65–a, 65–b (1970 and Supp.1986).

55. E.g., Boulder, Colorado, Municipal Code § 5–6–5 (1981) (all children under sixteen must be off the streets or out of public places by eleven P.M. and before five A.M.); Or.Rev.Stat. §§ 419.710 (1985) (state-wide curfew). See also Manella, Curfew Laws, 4 Nat.Prob. & Parol Assn.J. 161 (1958); Note, Curfew Ordinances and the Control of Nocturnal Juvenile Crime, 107 U.Pa.L.Rev. 66 (1958). People v. Chambers, 66 Ill.2d 36, 4 Ill.Dec. 308, 360 N.E.2d 55 (1976), held the state curfew law constitutional. See also Note, Juvenile Curfew Ordinances and the Constitution, 76 Mich.L.Rev. 109 (1977), and Note, Assessing the Scope of Minors' Fundamental Rights: Juvenile Curfews and the Constitution, 97 Harv.L.Rev. 1163 (1984). Johnson v. Opelousas, 658 F.2d 1065 (5th Cir. 1981), held a curfew ordinance unconstitutional for overbreadth.

56. Freeman v. Flake, 448 F.2d 258 (10th Cir.1971), cert. denied 405 U.S. 1032, 92 S.Ct. 1292, 31 L.Ed.2d 489 (1972); Leonard v. School Committee of Attleboro, 349 Mass. 704, 212 N.E.2d 468 (1965); Annot., Validity of Regulation by Public School Authorities as to Clothes or Personal Appearance of Pupils, 14 A.L.R.3d 1201 (1967); Goldstein, Reflections on Developing Trends in the Law of Student Rights, 118 U.Pa.L.Rev. 612 (1970); Goldstein, The Scope and Sources of School Board Authority to Regulate Student Conduct and Status: A Nonconstitutional Analysis, 117 U.Pa.L.Rev. 373 (1969); Note, A Student's Right to Govern His Personal Appearance, 17 J.Pub.L. 151 (1968).

57. 1 W. Blackstone, Commentaries on the Laws of England 464 (Cooley 6th ed. 1884).

58. Collins v. York, 159 Conn. 150, 267 A.2d 668 (1970); McDaniel v. Lovelace, 439 S.W.2d 906 (Mo.1969); F. James & G. Hazard, Civil Procedure § 10.7 (3d ed. 1985). The usual practice is that the child sues by his next friend and defends by a guardian ad litem. 3A J. Moore, Federal Practice § 17.26 (2d ed. 1986). Where a child's parents sue and lose an action for loss of the minor's services, the child's action is not foreclosed by res judicata. Whitehead v. General Telephone Co., 20 Ohio St.2d 108, 254 N.E.2d 10 (1969). And generally a guardian ad litem does not have authority to settle the child's suit without court approval. Dacanay v. Mendoza, 573 F.2d 1075 (9th Cir.1978).

59. For the federal practice see 3A J. Moore, Federal Practice § 17.26 (2d ed. 1986).

is to see to it that the minor's interests in the case are adequately represented.

There are no specific ages below which children may not be witnesses in lawsuits. Their capacity to testify turns on the trial judge's evaluation of their ability, first of all, to take and understand the oath,[60] and, secondly, to observe, recollect and communicate the facts concerning which their testimony is offered.[61]

j) *Voting and holding office:* As a result of the Twenty-Sixth Amendment the voting age is now eighteen,[62] paralleling the general reduction in the age of majority over the country.

The age at which one becomes eligible to hold public office depends upon the applicable constitutional or statutory provision. Ages in excess of the age of majority may often be the rule.[63] Where the statute or constitution were silent, the older authority had it that minors could only hold offices not requiring the exercise of judgment, discretion and experience.[64] The issue is academic today.

k) *The child's work and earnings:* At common law the child's earnings were the property of his parent.[65] This followed from the rule that the parent was entitled to his child's

services [66] and is evidenced most commonly by those cases allowing the parent to recover for the loss of the child's services caused by the tort of a third person.[67]

The employment of children is today regulated, where interstate commerce is involved, by the Fair Labor Standards Act,[68] and by child labor statutes in the various states. These acts set up minimum ages below which employment of certain kinds is prohibited.[69] The usual age is sixteen or eighteen.

l) *Domicile:* The child's legal incapacity to choose his own domicile is discussed in another section of this work.[70]

(m) *The child's name:* Questions concerning a child's surname may arise either at birth or on the occasion of the parents' separation or divorce. Of course the custom has been for the legitimate child to take the father's surname.[71] Where both parents wish the child to have some other name and their wishes are resisted by the state agency keeping birth records, there is authority that the parents' choice of name must be respected.[72] This is apparently the case even though parents may choose a whimsical name for their child or one which may not signify the con-

60. VI J. Wigmore, Evidence § 1821 (Rev. ed. Chadbourn 1976).

61. II J. Wigmore, Evidence §§ 505–509 (Rev. ed. Chadbourn 1979).

62. U.S.Const.Amend. XXVI: "Section 1. The right of citizens of the United States, who are eighteen years of age or older, to vote shall not be denied or abridged by the United States or by any State on account of age."

63. E.g., Colo. Const. Art. V, § 4 (legislators must be twenty-five); N.Y. Const. Art. 4, § 2 (governor must be thirty); Pa. Const. Art. 4, § 5 (governor must be thirty); Vernon's Ann.Tex. Const. Art. 4, § 4 (governor must be thirty). See also 2 B. Gassman, Election Law § 99 (2d ed. 1962).

64. F. Mechem, Public Officers § 71 (1890).

65. 1 W. Blackstone, Commentaries on the Laws of England 453 (Cooley 3d ed. 1884). Minors may be employed by their parents, however. Pioneer Casualty Co. v. Bush, 457 S.W.2d 165 (Tex.Civ.App.1970), error refused n.r.e.

According to some courts the parent retains his right to the child's services and earnings only so long as he has custody of and supports the child. Beaudoin v. Beaudoin, 118 N.H. 325, 386 A.2d 1261 (1978).

66. Weeks v. Holmes, 66 Mass. (12 Cush.) 215 (1853); 2 S. Williston, Contracts § 225 (Jaeger 3d ed. 1959).

67. Lessard v. Great Falls Woolen Co., 83 N.H. 576, 145 A. 782 (1929); W. Prosser and W. Keeton, The Law of Torts § 125 (5th ed. 1984).

68. 29 U.S.C.A. §§ 201–219, especially 29 U.S.C.A. §§ 203(e)(1), 212, and 213(c) and (d). See C. Livengood, The Federal Wage and Hour Law 162–163 (1952).

69. U.S. Bureau of Labor Standards, Bulletin No. 114, State Child-Labor Standards (1949).

70. See section 4.3, Practitioner's Edition.

71. Secretary of Commonwealth v. City Clerk of Lowell, 373 Mass. 178, 366 N.E.2d 717 (1977). See also Note, The Controversy Over Children's Surnames: Familial Autonomy, Equal Protection and the Child's Best Interests, 1979 Utah L.Rev. 303, citing many other articles and cases; Carlsson, Surnames of Married Women and Legitimate Children, 17 N.Y.L.F. 552, 563 (1971). Earlier cases, decided before ideas of gender equality had received general legal acceptance, are cited in Annot., 53 A.L.R.2d 914 (1957).

72. Jech v. Burch, 466 F.Supp. 714 (D.Hawaii 1979) (parents' right to name their child is within the right of familial privacy guaranteed by the Fourteenth Amendment). The dissenting opinion in Rice v. Department of Health and Rehabilitative Services, 386 So.2d 844 (Fla. App.1980) took the same position but the majority did not decide the issue. See also O'Brien v. Tilson, 523 F.Supp.

tinuity of identity between the child and his forbears and therefore not serve the child's interests as well as another name. Whether it would also be the case if the question arose after the child was old enough to have an opinion contrary to that of his parents may be doubtful.[73] If the parents of a legitimate child disagree as to the name which the child will take at birth, the authorities are not helpful. Continuing to require the adoption of the paternal surname may well be held to violate the Fourteenth Amendment and the Supreme Court's gender discrimination cases.[74] Various nondiscriminatory solutions have been suggested, such as a hyphenated surname, or giving the child the name of the parent of the same sex, or of the parent in whose custody he is placed.[75] If the child is in the custody of only one parent, it would seem that that parent should decide on the child's name, just as he or she makes other decisions respecting the child's welfare. The whole question may be affected by statute in many states, provided of course that such statutes do not run afoul of constitutional principles.[76]

Where the child is illegitimate and paternity has not been established, the child's mother normally has the right to decide on his surname.[77] If paternity has been established and both parents agree on a name, the result should be the same as for a legitimate child.[78] If the parents are unable to agree on a name, the parent having custody of the child should

be entitled to choose a name for the child.[79] Here again statutes may control the decision, if they are constitutional.[80]

When the controversy over the child's name occurs as the result of divorce, it usually takes the form of a petition by the ex-wife to change from the ex-husband's surname to some other name, either the ex-wife's surname or perhaps the surname of a second husband. The standard here seems to be the child's best interests, a standard too vague to be of much help in specific cases.[81]

WESTLAW REFERENCES

b. Contracts

sy(minor /s disaffirm! /s contract)

c. Consent to Operations

di(minor /s consent! /s operation surgery (medical
   +2 treatment procedure))

g. Responsibility For Torts

to(211) /p minor /s liab! /s tort

m. The Child's Name

surname /s illegitimate /s child infant minor juvenile

§ 8.2   The Child's Contracts and Conveyances

The child's power to disaffirm his contracts and conveyances has already been briefly mentioned.[1] It is available where the contract or conveyance was made before majori-

---

494 (E.D.N.C.1981); Sydney v. Pingree, 564 F.Supp. 412 (S.D.Fla.1983).

73. Secretary of Commonwealth v. City Clerk of Lowell, 373 Mass. 178, 189, 366 N.E.2d 717, 725 (1977) recognized but did not decide the issue.

74. E.g., Orr v. Orr, 440 U.S. 268, 99 S.Ct. 1102, 59 L.Ed.2d 306 (1979), on remand 374 So.2d 895 (Ala.Civ. App.1979), writ denied 374 So.2d 898 (1979). The constitutional question would be even more acute in those states having state Equal Rights Amendments. See section 6.1, supra.

75. Note, The Controversy Over Children's Surnames: Familial Autonomy, Equal Protection and the Child's Best Interests, 1979 Utah L.Rev. 303, 311–312.

76. Id. at 337, collecting state statutes on the naming of children.

77. See section 4.5, supra, at note 37.

78. Note, The Controversy Over Children's Surnames: Familial Autonomy, Equal Protection and the Child's Best Interests, 1979 Utah L.Rev. 303, 314.

79. This is the position taken with respect to legitimate children by Justice Mosk, concurring, in In re Marriage of Schiffman, 28 Cal.3d 640, 169 Cal.Rptr. 918, 620 P.2d 579 (1980). The majority opinion in that case and in Donald J. v. Evna M.W., 81 Cal.App.3d 929, 147 Cal.Rptr. 15 (1978) take the position that the child's best interests should control the choice of name, but in most instances this standard without more is too vague to be very helpful. See Jones v. McDowell, 53 N.C.App. 434, 281 S.E.2d 192 (1981) holding unconstitutional a statute which required a child's name to be changed to that of his father when paternity had been established.

80. See note 76, supra.

81. The cases are discussed infra, in section 14.5.

§ 8.2

1. See section 8.1, supra. On infants' contracts generally see 2 S. Williston, Contracts ch. 9 (3d ed. Jaeger 1959); Edge, Voidability of Minors' Contracts: A Feudal Doctrine in a Modern Economy, 1 Ga.L.Rev. 205 (1967).

ty.[2] Early authorities held that the child's contracts and conveyances were void.[3] Later on they were said to be voidable.[4] Today it is generally conceded that there is no profit in the void-voidable argument and that the matter is best dealt with by referring to the child's power to disaffirm and by concentrating on the conditions in which the power is created and may be exercised.[5] It is clear in any event that if the child chooses not to disaffirm, he may enforce the contract against the other party (if the other party is an adult).[6] Of course if both contracting parties are below the age of majority, they both have the power to disaffirm.[7] If the child is in fact under age, his power to disaffirm the transaction is not affected by the fact that his parent acquiesced in the contract or approved of it.[8]

Now that children in their teens have more money than they used to, and buy correspondingly more things, their power to disaffirm can have harsher effects upon those who deal with them. The purpose of the power was and still is to protect children against the consequences of their own improvidence. In weighing this purpose against the losses caused to those who deal with children in ignorance of their nonage, there has recently been a growing concern with the interests of the adult.[9] It is true that one who sells to a child may often be able to protect himself by requiring proof of age. Others doing business with children may not be able to do this. Further, there is some recognition that in fact minors do engage in many commercial transactions. It makes little sense to say that they are not competent to do what we see them doing all the time.

The common law recognizes this by allowing minors to make binding contracts for necessaries when they are not living with a parent who is furnishing them with necessaries.[10] Some cases hold that if the minor is living with a parent able and willing to supply necessaries, the minor may disaffirm this sort of contract as well as others,[11] but other cases seem to hold that the minor is bound,[12] at least if the purchase of necessaries is on the minor's credit and not that of another.[13] The child may make a binding contract to borrow money if he intends to use the proceeds of the loan to buy necessaries.[14] Necessaries are defined for this purpose as the ordinary and usual goods or services needed

2. International Text-Book Co. v. Connelly, 206 N.Y. 188, 99 N.E. 722 (1912). It is available even to an infant maker of a negotiable instrument as against a holder in due course. Uniform Commercial Code § 3–305, 2 Unif. L.Ann. 239 (1977). The infant may disaffirm his contract to marry, McConkey v. Barnes, 42 Ill.App. 511 (1891), or his antenuptial contract, Wilkinson v. Wilkinson, 323 So.2d 120 (La.1975), even though he is of marriageable age.

3. Burnand v. Irigoyen, 30 Cal.2d 861, 186 P.2d 417 (1947) (contract of infant under eighteen is void); 2 S. Williston, Contracts § 230 (3d ed. Jaeger 1959).

4. E.g., Casey v. Kastel, 237 N.Y. 305, 142 N.E. 671 (1924), 24 Colum.L.Rev. 676 (1924); Coleman v. Coleman, 51 Ohio App. 221, 200 N.E. 197 (1935).

5. 2 S. Williston, Contracts § 231 (3d ed. Jaeger 1959). "Power" is presumably the correct term for describing the infant's legal position respecting his contracts. See W. Hohfeld, Fundamental Legal Conceptions 38–50 (1964); J. Stone, Province and Function of Law 119–122 (1950); 3A A. Corbin, Contracts § 623, n. 1 (1960).

6. Holt v. Ward Clarencieux, 2 Str. 937, 93 Eng.Rep. 954 (1732); 1 A. Corbin, Contracts § 6 (1963).

7. Hurwitz v. Barr, 193 A.2d 360 (D.C.App.1963); Drude v. Curtis, 183 Mass. 317, 67 N.E. 317 (1903).

8. Gage v. Moore, 200 Okl. 623, 198 P.2d 395 (1948), 12 U.Detroit L.J. 99 (1949).

9. See Note, 16 U.Chi.L.Rev. 183 (1948); Note, 48 Colum.L.Rev. 272 (1948); Note, 30 Kan.City L.Rev. 230 (1962); Edge, Voidability of Minors' Contracts: A Feudal Doctrine in a Modern Economy, 1 Ga.L.Rev. 205 (1967).

10. Gregory v. Lee, 64 Conn. 407, 30 A. 53 (1894); Hyman v. Cain, 48 N.C. (3 Jones) 111 (1855); Greenville Hospital System v. Smith, 269 S.C. 653, 239 S.E.2d 657 (1977); Bainbridge v. Pickering, C.P. 20 Geo. III, 2 W.Bl. 1325 (1780).

11. Valencia v. White, 134 Ariz. 139, 654 P.2d 287 (App.1982); Westrate v. Schipper, 284 Mich. 383, 279 N.W. 870 (1938); Greenville Hospital System v. Smith, 269 S.C. 653, 239 S.E.2d 657 (1977).

12. Scott County School District I v. Asher, 263 Ind. 47, 324 N.E.2d 496 (1975) (both child and parent are liable for necessaries).

13. Kennedy v. Kiss, 89 Ill.App.3d 890, 45 Ill.Dec. 273, 412 N.E.2d 624 (1980); Madison General Hosp. v. Haack, 124 Wis.2d 398, 369 N.W.2d 663 (1985).

14. Norwood National Bank v. Allston, 152 S.C. 199, 149 S.E. 593 (1929), 43 Harv.L.Rev. 498 (1930); Annot., 65 A.L.R. 1337 (1930).

for the child's support.[15] The term includes such things as medical care,[16] some kinds of legal services,[17] services of an employment agency,[18] and in rare cases an automobile,[19] in addition to the requirements of food, clothing and shelter.[20] As in the case of spouses,[21] whether a particular item is a necessary depends to some extent on the economic status of the child.[22] And the child's liability is for the fair value of the necessaries, not for the contract price.[23]

Modern statutes testify to a widespread conviction that other limitations on the child's power to disaffirm are necessary.[24] The statutes have not only lowered the age of majority from twenty-one to eighteen, but authorize children under eighteen to bind themselves by specific kinds of transactions. Thus banks are protected when they receive and pay out deposits at the demand of children.[25] In New York and California children may make binding contracts of employment as actors or professional athletes.[26] Certain kinds of educational loans to minors are often made binding on them.[27] And in New York certain business contracts by minors over eighteen may not be disaffirmed.[28] The ad hoc nature of these statutes, which lack any coherent pattern or philosophy, makes it clear that a thorough reexamination of the child's power to make binding contracts is long overdue.

The mechanics of exercising the child's power of disaffirmance produced some litigation in earlier times. For example, it has been held not only that the child himself may exercise the power, but that certain persons representing him may also, including his heirs, executors or administrators.[29] The power must be exercised either before reaching majority or within a reasonable time thereafter.[30] Obviously no fixed limits can be placed upon what is a reasonable time, but

---

15. Sykes v. Dickerson, 216 Ark. 116, 224 S.W.2d 360 (1949); 2 S. Williston, Contracts § 241 (3d ed. Jaeger 1959).

16. Scott County School District I v. Asher, 263 Ind. 47, 324 N.E.2d 496 (1975); Hagerman v. Mutual Hospital Ins., Inc., 175 Ind.App. 293, 371 N.E.2d 394 (1978) (insurer may recover from the child after the child gets a judgment from a tort feasor for his medical expenses); Annot., 71 A.L.R. 226 (1931).

17. Annot., 13 A.L.R.3d 1251 (1967).

18. Gastonia Personnel Corp. v. Rogers, 276 N.C. 279, 172 S.E.2d 19 (1970).

19. Rose v. Sheehan Buick, Inc., 204 So.2d 903 (Fla. App.1967). Cases collected in Annot., 56 A.L.R.3d 1335 (1974) indicate that automobiles are generally not held to be necessaries, however. See also Star Chevrolet Co. v. Green by Green, 473 So.2d 157 (Miss.1985).

20. J. Calamari and J. Perillo, Contracts § 8–8 (2d ed. 1977). But an apartment was held not a necessary where the minor was free to live at home if he wished. Webster St. Partnership, Ltd. v. Sheridan, 220 Neb. 9, 368 N.W.2d 439 (1985).

21. See section 6.3, supra.

22. International Text-Book Co. v. Connelly, 206 N.Y. 188, 99 N.E. 722 (1912).

23. 2 S. Williston, Contracts § 240 (3d ed. Jaeger 1959).

24. Edge, Voidability of Minors' Contracts: A Feudal Doctrine in a Modern Economy, 1 Ga.L.Rev. 205 (1967); Samuels, Special Legislation Removing Disabilities of Infancy, 15 Tenn.L.Rev. 655 (1949); Note, 48 Colum.L.Rev. 272 (1948).

25. E.g., West's Ann.Cal.Fin.Code § 850 (1968); Colo. Rev.Stat. § 11–6–104 (1973 and Supp.1985); Vernon's

Ann.Mo.Stat. § 362.465 (1968). See also Smalley v. Central Trust & Savings Co., Newcastle, Ind., 72 Ind.App. 296, 125 N.E. 789 (1920); Phillips v. Savings Trust Co. of St. Louis, 231 Mo.App. 1178, 85 S.W.2d 923 (1935); Peterson v. Weimar, 181 Wis. 231, 194 N.W. 346 (1923).

26. West's Ann.Cal.Civ.Code § 36 (Supp.1981); N.Y.— McKinney's Gen.Oblig.L. § 3–105 (1978). If a statute permits a parent to contract on behalf of his child, this may be construed to prevent disaffirmance. Shields v. Gross, 58 N.Y.2d 338, 461 N.Y.S.2d 254, 448 N.E.2d 108 (1983), reargument denied 59 N.Y.2d 762, 463 N.Y.S.2d 1030, 450 N.E.2d 254 (1983).

27. Uniform Minor Student Capacity to Borrow Act § 2, 9A Unif.L.Ann. 226 (1979), in force in a few states allows a minor over sixteen to make binding educational loans. See also N.Y.—McKinney's Gen.Oblig.L. § 3–103 (1978); Wis.Stat.Ann. § 39.32 (Supp.1981–1982).

28. N.Y.—McKinney's Gen.Oblig.L. § 3–101 (1978). This provision is now of significance only for contracts made before the age of majority was reduced to eighteen. See Prinze v. Jonas, 38 N.Y.2d 570, 381 N.Y.S.2d 824, 345 N.E.2d 295 (1976).

29. 2 S. Williston, Contracts § 232 (3d ed. Jaeger 1959).

30. Burnand v. Irigoyen, 30 Cal.2d 861, 186 P.2d 417 (1947); Wuller v. Chuse Grocery Co., 241 Ill. 398, 89 N.E. 796 (1909); Boyden v. Boyden, 50 Mass. (9 Metc.) 519 (1845); Casey v. Kastel, 237 N.Y. 305, 142 N.E. 671 (1924), 24 Colum.L.Rev. 676 (1924); Cassella v. Tiberio, 150 Ohio St. 27, 80 N.E.2d 426 (1948); Spencer v. Lyman Falls Power Co., 109 Vt. 294, 196 A. 276 (1938). The statement is made in 2 Williston, Contracts, § 235 (3d ed. 1959) that the conveyance of land may only be disaffirmed at or after majority, but the cases cited do not sustain this proposition. See, e.g., Dulion v. Folkes, 153 Miss. 91, 120

the courts have been quite liberal in this respect. Disaffirmance within six months after reaching twenty-one is clearly effective, according to one case,[31] and another upholds a disaffirmance of a conveyance occurring seven years after reaching majority.[32]

There is substantial authority that the disaffirmance of a conveyance of property is effective even as against a subsequent purchaser of the property for value without notice of the infancy, so that the property may be reclaimed by the infant even against such a subsequent buyer.[33] But the infant who by negotiation transfers a negotiable instrument may not rescind the transfer as against a holder in due course, under the Uniform Commercial Code.[34] One case has held that the child who has conveyed real estate has until a reasonable time after the grantee records the

deed to disaffirm the conveyance, at least where he is unaware of any adverse claims to the property.[35]

There may often be a question as to how disaffirmance must be evidenced in order to be effective. It seems clear that if the contract is wholly executory on both sides, no affirmative action by the child is necessary. He need only raise the defense of infancy when sued on the contract.[36] If the contract has been partially or wholly executed, however, under many cases some action must be taken which clearly expresses his intent to disaffirm.[37] There is some authority the other way, holding that his mere inaction after reaching majority does not amount to ratification.[38] Of course if he acts in a way indicating his approval of the contract, after reaching majority, this constitutes ratification and

So. 437 (1928). See also 1 Powell, Real Property, § 125 (Rohan rev. ed. 1985) and Smith v. Wade, 169 Neb. 710, 100 N.W.2d 770 (1960).

In some states a statute of limitations may set the boundaries for disaffirmance. Gibson v. Hall, 260 Ala. 539, 71 So.2d 532 (1954). On special statutes of limitation covering children's claims, see Jacobson v. Lenhart, 30 Ill.2d 225, 195 N.E.2d 638 (1964).

31. International Text-Book Co. v. Connelly, 206 N.Y. 188, 99 N.E. 722 (1912). But Eastern Airlines, Inc. v. Stuhl, 65 Misc.2d 901, 318 N.Y.S.2d 996 (N.Y.City Civil Ct.1970), affirmed p.c. 68 Misc.2d 629, 327 N.Y.S.2d 752 (Sup.Ct.1971) held that disaffirmance after only five months from majority was not timely, the court relying in part upon the fact that the infant had been involved in business enterprises from his seventeenth birthday, so that he had had business experience. This case also seems to reflect the current judicial disenchantment with the disabilities of infancy.

32. Walker v. Ellis, 212 Ark. 498, 207 S.W.2d 39 (1947). Compare Dolph v. Hand, 156 Pa. 91, 27 A. 114 (1893) (fifteen years not a reasonable time), with Mott v. Iossa, 119 N.J.Eq. 185, 181 A. 689 (1935) (thirteen years is reasonable); Spencer v. Lyman Falls Power Co., 109 Vt. 294, 196 A. 276 (1938) (nine years is unreasonable).

33. Ware v. Mobley, 190 Ga. 249, 9 S.E.2d 67 (1940); Elkhorn Coal Corp. v. Tackett, 261 Ky. 795, 88 S.W.2d 943 (1935); III American Law of Property § 12.69 (1952). Contra: Jones v. Caldwell, 216 Ark. 260, 225 S.W.2d 323 (1949).

On disaffirmance of conveyances by infants in general, see 1 R. Powell, Real Property § 125 (Rev. ed. Rohan 1985).

Sisneros v. Garcia, 94 N.M. 552, 613 P.2d 422 (1980) held that a disaffirmance fourteen years after the conveyance was timely where the infant never had intended to

sell the land and was unaware until that time of any adverse claim.

Presumably the Uniform Commercial Code § 2–403, 1A Unif.L.Ann. 151 (1976) was not intended to change the rule stated in the text.

The child may recover the market value of what he conveyed if the other party has in turn conveyed the property. Carpenter v. Grow, 247 Mass. 133, 141 N.E. 859 (1923). For cases dealing with the method of determining value see Annot., 52 A.L.R.2d 1114 (1951) and Joseph v. Schatzkin, 259 N.Y. 241, 181 N.E. 464 (1932).

34. Uniform Commercial Code § 3–207, 2 Unif.L.Ann. 156 (1977). "Holder in due course" is defined in section 3–302, 2 Unif.L.Ann. 176 (1977).

35. Sisneros v. Garcia, 94 N.M. 552, 613 P.2d 422 (1980).

36. Edmunds v. Mister, 58 Miss. 765 (1881); Cassella v. Tiberio, 150 Ohio St. 27, 80 N.E.2d 426 (1948); Warwick Municipal Employees Credit Union v. McAllister, 110 R.I. 399, 293 A.2d 516 (1972); 1 A. Corbin, Contracts § 6 (1963).

37. Slaney v. Westwood Auto, Inc., 366 Mass. 688, 322 N.E.2d 768 (1975) (any unequivocal repudiation of the contract is sufficient); Edmunds v. Mister, 58 Miss. 765 (1881); Cassella v. Tiberio, 150 Ohio St. 27, 80 N.E.2d 426 (1948); Spencer v. Lyman Falls Power Co., 109 Vt. 294, 196 A. 276 (1938). St. Paul Fire & Marine Insurance Co. v. Muniz, 19 Ariz.App. 5, 504 P.2d 546 (1972) adds the requirement that the disaffirmance must be communicated to the other contracting party. A later inconsistent conveyance may constitute disaffirmance under Teat v. Jones, 126 Tex. 480, 89 S.W.2d 987 (1936). See also 2 S. Williston, Contracts § 234 (3d ed. Jaeger 1959).

38. Cases are collected in Annot., 5 A.L.R.2d 7 (1949).

binds him.[39] No new consideration is required in order to make the ratification binding on the child.[40]

Two further questions relating to the child's disaffirmance have given the courts much difficulty. The first is, does the child's misrepresentation of his age estop him to disaffirm the contract? The answer given to this question is obviously influenced (though often not explicitly so) by the particular court's approval or disapproval of the policy of protecting the child against the consequences of his bargain and its solicitude for the interests of the other party to the bargain. The answer has also been influenced by whether the question arises in the context of an action at law or suit in equity, although certainly this should be entirely irrelevant today when every possible step has been taken by rules of practice in most states to eliminate the distinction between law and equity. The argument for denying the estoppel is of course that most children's contracts probably result from misrepresentations of age, and that applying an estoppel would leave the infant largely unprotected. There is also the argument that the infant's contract should not be enforced against him under the guise of an imposition of tort liability.[41] The argument the other way is that children are responsible for their torts, and thus either should be estopped when they engage in the tort of fraud inducing a change of position, or at least should be liable for the damages caused by their fraud.

The courts in the various states are sharply divided on this issue.[42] Some take the position that estoppel should not apply in any case.[43] Others make an irrelevant distinction between actions at law where estoppel does not apply, and suits in equity, where it does.[44] Still others hold that although the infant is not estopped to disaffirm by his own misrepresentation, he is liable in damages for the harm caused to the other party by the misrepresentation of age.[45] In the typical case the child, by lying about his age, induces a car dealer to sell him a car. He drives the car enough to incur depreciation or perhaps he is involved in a collision. He then disaffirms the transaction and seeks the return of the

---

39. J.I. Case Threshing Machine Co. v. Dulworth, 216 Ky. 637, 287 S.W. 994 (1925), 1 U.Cin.L.Rev. 229 (1927) (giving of renewal note constituted ratification); Boyden v. Boyden, 50 Mass. (9 Metc.) (1845) (retention of property, or sale of it, or neglect to tender it back, constitute ratification); Watzel v. Beardslee, 289 Mich. 522, 286 N.W. 813 (1939), 24 Marq.L.Rev. 223 (1940) (making of payments in fulfillment of prior promise is ratification). Other cases are cited in Annot., 5 A.L.R.2d 7 (1949), and 2 Williston, Contracts, § 239 (3d ed. 1959). In Sawyer Boot & Shoe Co. v. Braveman, 126 Me. 70, 136 A. 290 (1927), 28 Colum.L.Rev. 98 (1928) it was held that listing a claim in bankruptcy did not amount to ratification, and International Text-Book Co. v. Connelly, 206 N.Y. 188, 99 N.E. 722 (1912) held that making one payment after reaching twenty-one did not ratify the contract.

Some later cases find ratification on the basis of relatively brief periods of acceptance of the benefits of the contract. Jones v. Dressel, 623 P.2d 370 (Colo.1981); Bobby Floars Toyota, Inc. v. Smith, 48 N.C.App. 580, 269 S.E.2d 320 (1980).

40. 1A A. Corbin, Contracts § 227 (1963).

41. Where the imposition of tort liability would indirectly enforce a contract obligation which the infant is entitled to disaffirm, the infant may not be held liable. Brown v. Wood, 293 Mich. 148, 291 N.W. 255 (1940) and cases cited in Annot., 127 A.L.R. 1441 (1940). W. Prosser and W. Keeton, The Law of Torts § 134 (5th ed. 1984) points out the difficulty in distinguishing between an independent tort, for which the infant is liable, and the tort which is merely the failure to perform a contract, for which the infant is not liable. In Bunkie Bank & Trust Co. v. Johnston, 385 So.2d 1264 (La.App.1980) the court held that an infant was liable to a bank for fraudulent misrepresentations made in order to persuade the bank to make a loan to the infant. The misrepresentations concerned the existence of property which would be pledged to secure the loan. This seems to be an example of the enforcement of a contract by the use of a tort action, since the damages for the tort would consist of the amount of the loan.

42. The cases are exhaustively collected and tabulated in Miller, Fraudulent Misrepresentations of Age as Affecting the Infant's Contract—A Comparative Study, 15 U.Pitts.L.Rev. 73 (1953). See also Annots., 6 A.L.R. 416 (1920), 18 A.L.R. 520 (1922), 90 A.L.R. 1441 (1934). In Iowa the statute provides that the child may not disaffirm if he misrepresents his age. Iowa Code Ann. § 599.3 (1981).

43. E.g., Sternlieb v. Normandie Nat. Securities Corp., 263 N.Y. 245, 188 N.E. 726 (1934), and authorities cited, supra, note 42.

44. See authorities cited supra, note 42. The cases there cited also make a senseless distinction between the infant as plaintiff and the infant as defendant.

45. Myers v. Hurley Motor Co., 273 U.S. 18, 47 S.Ct. 277, 71 L.Ed. 515 (1927), 75 U.Pa.L.Rev. 570 (1927); Doenges-Long Motors, Inc. v. Gillen, 138 Colo. 31, 328 P.2d 1077 (1958). For other cases see 2 S. Williston, Contracts § 245 (3d ed. Jaeger 1959), and Annot., 12 A.L.R.3d 1174 (1967).

purchase price. A substantial number of courts would hold that the child may recover back the price but that the car dealer may set off the diminution in the car's value, either on the ground that one who seeks equity must do equity, or on the theory that the dealer should recover damages for the fraudulent misrepresentation of age and that the damages equal the loss of value in the car.[46] One function of law is to educate. That being so, it seems clear that the cases holding the infant responsible for his misrepresentation of age are correct, since they teach the lesson that fraud is unacceptable in this society.

The second question is, must the child, as a condition on his right to disaffirm restore to the other party what he has received from the transaction? Most of the cases hold that if the child still has the consideration, he must return it upon disaffirmance,[47] but if he has lost or dissipated it, he may disaffirm without being required to give it back.[48] A few cases take a less receptive approach to the infant's power of disaffirmance by requiring that if he no longer has the consideration for his promise, but has some other property acquired in exchange for the consideration, he must hand over that property before he may disaffirm.[49] And in a very few cases, he may not be permitted to disaffirm without return of the consideration if the consideration is not of a kind capable of return, as where a covenant not to compete is enforced against him.[50]

An analogous issue is presented when the infant disaffirms his contract and tenders back the consideration which he has received but the consideration has been damaged or has depreciated in value so that the seller will incur a substantial loss on the transaction. The seller then seeks restitution from the infant for the difference between the original value of the consideration and the depreciated value. For example, the infant buys a car, damages it in a collision, and seeks the return of the purchase price upon return of the damaged car to the seller. Some of the cases hold that the infant is entitled to disaffirm and to obtain the return of his payment without being liable for the loss incurred by the seller.[51] The theory behind this view seems to be that requiring the minor to make restitution for the diminution in value of the consideration would be to impose upon him the burden (or part of it) of the very improvidence from which the doctrine of infants' disability is designed to protect him. Other cases allow the seller to obtain restitution for the consideration's diminution in value,[52] at least where the transaction was accompanied by the infant's misrepresentation of his age.[53] Even where no misrepresentations are made, a useful lesson in responsibility would be conveyed

---

46. Doenges-Long Motors, Inc. v. Gillen, 138 Colo. 31, 328 P.2d 1077 (1958).

47. Merritt v. Jowers, 184 Ga. 762, 193 S.E. 238 (1937); Star Chevrolet Co. v. Green, 473 So.2d 157 (Miss.1985); Nelson v. Browning, 391 S.W.2d 873 (Mo.1965); Casey v. Kastel, 237 N.Y. 305, 142 N.E. 671 (1924), 24 Colum.L. Rev. 676 (1924). A case the other way is Steinberg v. Scala Ltd., [1923] 2 Ch. 452 (C.A.), 24 Colum.L.Rev. 206 (1924), holding that the child may not recover unless he can restore the consideration. Many other cases are cited in Annots., 16 A.L.R. 1475 (1922), 36 A.L.R. 782 (1925), and 124 A.L.R. 1368 (1940). See also 2 S. Williston, Contracts § 283 (3d ed. Jaeger 1959).

48. Shutter v. Fudge, 108 Conn. 528, 143 A. 896 (1928), 38 Yale L.J. 994 (1929); Terrace Co. v. Calhoun, 37 Ill. App.3d 757, 347 N.E.2d 315 (1976); Mutual Life Ins. Co. of N.Y. v. Schiavone, 63 App.D.C. 257, 71 F.2d 980 (1934); Lawrence v. Baxter, 275 Mich. 587, 267 N.W. 742 (1936); Halbman v. Lemke, 99 Wis.2d 241, 298 N.W.2d 562 (1980). See also cases cited supra, note 47.

49. See Whitman v. Allen, 123 Me. 1, 121 A. 160 (1923); 2 S. Williston, Contracts § 238 (3d ed. Jaeger 1959).

50. Pankas v. Bell, 413 Pa. 494, 198 A.2d 312 (1964); Annot., 17 A.L.R.3d 863 (1968).

51. Central Bucks Aero, Inc. v. Smith, 226 Pa.Super. 441, 310 A.2d 283 (1973); Halbman v. Lemke, 99 Wis.2d 241, 298 N.W.2d 562 (1980), citing many authorities; Annots., 12 A.L.R.3d 1174, 1178 (1967); 50 A.L.R. 1187 (1927); 11 A.L.R. 491 (1921).

52. Annot., 12 A.L.R.3d 1174, 1182 (1967). In some states the infant must account for benefits received though not for the depreciation. Annot., 12 A.L.R.3d 1174, 1187 (1967). It has been suggested that the infant's liability for depreciation should be imposed when he is the plaintiff in the case, but not when he is the defendant resisting the seller's claim for the price. J. Calamari and J. Perillo, Contracts 240–241 (2d ed. 1977). The objection to this view is that it causes the result to turn on wholly adventitious circumstances.

53. E.g., Keser v. Chagnon, 159 Colo. 209, 410 P.2d 637 (1966).

by a legal rule that the infant who returns damaged or depreciated property is liable for the property's decrease in value.

The child's power to disaffirm, as it arises in one special context, needs separate discussion. When a child is tortiously injured, his claim may be settled upon the giving of a release. If the release were merely that of the child, it would be subject to disaffirmance by him on the same basis as his other contracts.[54] The statutes or practice of most states have, however, created a method by which his release may be made binding, with the purpose of encouraging settlement of tort claims. Usually the requirements are that a guardian be appointed for the child and that when he has executed the release, the settlement must be approved by a court.[55] On the face of it these safeguards seem adequate. The difficulty is that some recent cases have created a strong suspicion that the administration of the safeguards is such that the child's interests are often ignored. The guardian's function may be performed in a perfunctory way and the court may approve the settlement as a matter of course without any real investigation or evidence of its fairness. In fact some attorneys purport to act

for the child in the settlement when they represent the insurance company which is paying the claim, and in other ways indulge in questionable tactics.[56]

A leading Minnesota case has held that when the settlement is the product of an unconscionable advantage on the part of the defendant over the child, it may be set aside.[57] The case involved an accident causing serious injuries to the child. The defendant knew, but the plaintiff and his guardian did not know, that some of the injuries would have a permanent effect. The defendant did not disclose this information either to the plaintiff or to the court which approved the settlement. The court held that the settlement should be set aside, saying that the settlement was unconscionable because of the non-disclosure, and that mistake, even though not mutual, might justify vacating such settlements. Other cases on facts nearly as strong have refused to set aside the settlement of infant claims, even when the sums paid were no larger than necessary to take care of the parent's out-of-pocket expenses in providing medical treatment for the child.[58] These latter cases seem to ignore the fact that the guardian's interest may be limited to the re-

---

54. Cases are collected in Annot., 13 A.L.R. 402 (1921). See also Note, Settling the Personal Injury Claim of a Minor, 38 U.Colo.L.Rev. 377 (1966). The guardian ad litem is not usually held competent to give a binding release of the child's claim. Pacheco v. Delgardo, 46 Ariz. 401, 52 P.2d 479 (1935). Of course children over eighteen may now settle their own tort claims. Garrett v. Gay, 394 So.2d 321 (Miss.1981). And a few states would allow the minor to settle in some circumstances. Frank v. Volkswagenwerk, A.G. of West Germany, 522 F.2d 321 (3d Cir.1975) (holding child's release binding under Pennsylvania law where he received benefits); Hamrick v. Hospital Service Corp. of Rhode Island, 110 R.I. 634, 296 A.2d 15 (1972) (minor bound by the subrogation clause in a medical service insurance contract made by his parent).

55. E.g., West's Ann.Cal.Civ.Pro.Code § 372 (Supp. 1986); Ill.—Smith-Hurd Ann.Stat. ch. 110½, ¶¶ 11–13, 19–8 (1978) and (Supp.1986); N.Y.—McKinney's Civ.Prac. L. & R. §§ 1207, 1208 (1976 and Supp.1986); West's Rev. Code Wash.Ann. § 11.92.060 (Supp.1986). See also Annot., 111 A.L.R. 686 (1937) for cases holding that the next friend has no authority to receive payment on behalf of the child. A parent, unless he has been appointed guardian, has no authority to settle a child's claim. Fitzgerald v. Newark Morning Ledger Co., 111 N.J.Super. 104, 267 A.2d 557 (1970). In re Truitt, 269 N.C. 249, 152 S.E.2d 74 (1967) requires payment to be made to a duly appointed

guardian. The court reviewing the settlement must find it fair. Walker v. Killoren Electric Co., 243 Ark. 752, 421 S.W.2d 893 (1967). The court refused to approve a settlement in Rafferty v. Rainey, 292 F.Supp. 152 (E.D.Tenn. 1968).

56. See, e.g., Handley v. Mortland, 54 Wash.2d 489, 498, 342 P.2d 612, 617 (1959), in which the complaint alleged that the attorney for the defendant purported to represent the child in presenting the settlement for court approval. See also Hudson v. Thies, 35 Ill.App.2d 189, 182 N.E.2d 760 (1962), affirmed 27 Ill.2d 548, 190 N.E.2d 343 (1963), in which counsel for the insurance company drew the settlement papers and no one represented either the child or his guardian.

57. Spaulding v. Zimmerman, 263 Minn. 346, 116 N.W.2d 704 (1962). See also Nelson v. Browning, 391 S.W.2d 873 (Mo.1965), and cases cited in Annot., 8 A.L.R.2d 460 (1949).

58. Hudson v. Thies, 35 Ill.App.2d 189, 182 N.E.2d 760 (1962), affirmed 27 Ill.2d 548, 190 N.E.2d 343 (1963); Denison v. Crowley, Milner & Co., 279 Mich. 211, 271 N.W. 735 (1937); Handley v. Mortland, 54 Wash.2d 489, 342 P.2d 612 (1959). The child in such cases might have a remedy against his guardian for the negligent settlement of the claim. See, e.g., In re Jaeger's Will, 218 Wis. 1, 259 N.W. 842 (1935).

covery of his expenses and that the child's interests are not protected by a perfunctory court approval. The tendency of the opinions in many of the cases, though not always clearly expressed, seems to be to treat the judicially approved settlement of the child's claim just as an adult's settlement would be treated.[59] There are persuasive reasons, however, for looking at the child's settlement much more closely. The most obvious reason is that this will ensure that in making settlements of children's claims the defendant, his counsel, and the approving court will fully protect the child's interests, and that the settlement is fair in all respects. Without such close scrutiny, we can expect to see more cases in which the child's claim is settled unfairly.

Where the applicable statute or rule of practice requires judicial approval of the settlement of children's claims, the courts have refused to allow a binding settlement to be made with the child's parent on the basis of the parent's agreement to indemnify the defendant if the child himself should later sue.[60] The reason for the courts' hostility to this expedient is that the indemnity agreement creates a conflict of interest in the parent which may lessen his zeal to enforce the child's claim.

59. For the standards applicable to releases by adults, see the cases cited in Annots., 71 A.L.R.2d 82 (1960), and 48 A.L.R. 1462 (1927).

60. Valdimer v. Mount Vernon Hebrew Camps, Inc., 9 N.Y.2d 21, 210 N.Y.S.2d 520, 172 N.E.2d 283 (1961), 47 Minn.L.Rev. 123 (1962). See also Note, 38 U.Colo.L.Rev. 377, 380 (1966), and Annot., 103 A.L.R. 500 (1936).

§ 8.3

1. Buckland, A Text-Book of Roman Law, 131 (3d ed. Stein 1963); Leage, Roman Private Law, 127 (3d ed. Prichard 1961); Schulz, Classical Roman Law, 158 (1951); Sohm, Institutes of Roman Law, 486–488 (3d ed. 1907).

2. E.g., Rex v. Offchurch, 3 Term Rep. 114, 100 Eng. Rep. 484 (1789), stating that a child is emancipated either where he obtains a settlement for himself, or becomes head of a family, or arrives at the age when he may set up in the world for himself. See also Jones v. Brown, Peake 306, 170 Eng.Rep. 165 (1795), holding that a father is entitled to his son's services so long as the son is living in the father's family and under his protection, suggesting that the case would be different if the child lived apart from the father; and Ex parte Hopkins, 3 P.Wms. 152, 24 Eng.Rep. 1009 (1732) which leaves an implication

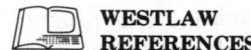

WESTLAW REFERENCES
di(minor child infant juvenile /s contract /s necessary necessity)

§ 8.3 Emancipation

This peculiar and, fortunately, unimportant corner of the law vividly illustrates both the conservatism and the semantic naiveté of much legal reasoning. Emancipation, the legal process by which a child is released from the control and authority of his parent, was a Roman law institution.[1] The Roman law concept seems to have had little influence on the English common law, except in the few cases concerned with the settlement of children for poor law purposes.[2] The influence was a little greater in America, where "emancipation" eventually became a frequently used legal expression. But the earliest cases did not use it. These cases arose out of the father's claim to the services and earnings of his son, a claim which he was normally entitled to assert at common law.[3] In some circumstances, however, it was plainly unfair to enforce the father's claim. If he had let his child work with the express or implied understanding that the child could keep his earnings, no court would be willing to let the father recover from the child's employer,[4] particularly if the employer had already paid the agreed

that the parent's right to custody might be lost if the father let the child live apart for a time. Neither the Jones nor the Hopkins case uses the term "emancipation", however.

3. E.g., Burlingame v. Burlingame, 7 Cowen 92 (N.Y.1827); McCoy v. Huffman, 8 Cowen 84 (N.Y.1827), overruled on another point by Medbury v. Watrous, 7 Hill 110 (N.Y.1845); Canovar v. Cooper, 3 Barb. 115 (N.Y.1848).

For an excellent review of the authorities on emancipation see Katz, Schroeder, Sidman, Emancipating Our Children—Coming of Age in Legal America, 7 Fam.L.Q. 211 (1973). Some of the historical background is discussed in Marks, Detours on the Road to Maturity: A View of the Legal Conception of Growing Up and Letting Go, 39 L. & Contemp. Prob. 78 (Summer 1975).

4. McCoy v. Huffman, 8 Cowen 84 (N.Y.1827); Armstrong v. McDonald, 10 Barb. 300 (N.Y.1851); II Kent, Commentaries on American Law, 194 (13th ed. Holmes 1884). See also Gale v. Parrott, 1 N.H. 28 (1817). The same theory would allow the son to sue for and collect his own wages. Stiles v. Granville, 60 Mass. (6 Cush.) 458 (1850).

wages to the child.[5] Or if the father had failed or refused to support the child, courts were reluctant to let the father recover the child's earnings from an employer, since the father's right to his child's services was usually considered to be a correlative of the father's duty to support the child.[6] Somewhat later the cases began characterizing the circumstances in which the father's claim to the child's earnings was rejected as constituting emancipation.[7] In this narrow context the term and the social policies underlying it are clear, since only a single issue is raised, that is, under what circumstances is the parent's claim to his child's earnings terminated, short of the age of majority.

Difficulties of semantics and policy began to appear, however, when emancipation became a concept sufficiently familiar to have a status of its own. In subsequent cases the emancipated child was often referred to as if he had acquired the legal capacity of an adult, as if achieving emancipation were the equivalent of reaching majority.[8] The pattern of analysis thereafter adopted by many cases was a) to determine whether the facts indicated emancipation, and then b) to hold that the minor's disabilities had been terminated.[9] This

worked well enough when the issues were confined to the child's earnings, or to his domicile, but it early became apparent that there were disabilities which did not and should not end upon emancipation. The solution adopted in some cases was to say that emancipation could be partial as well as total, leaving the child with some of the disabilities of infancy.[10] This is merely a verbal solution, since it suggests no rational basis for deciding which disabilities end on emancipation and which survive. Some cases went somewhat further, to hold that emancipation ended the rights and duties as between parent and child, but did not affect other limits on the child's legal capacity unrelated to relations with his parents.[11] But this distinction is also unworkable, both because it gives emancipation too broad an impact upon some disabilities and too narrow a one on others. For example, it would be intolerable for a court to hold that a parent, by abandoning a child and thereby emancipating him (a method of emancipation for which there is authority),[12] could end his own obligations of support. On the other hand, emancipation by abandonment may very well give the child capacity to choose his own domicile, and cases so hold.[13] So it is

5. Burlingame v. Burlingame, 7 Cowen 92 (N.Y.1827); Huntoon v. Hazelton, 20 N.H. 388 (1850).

6. Canovar v. Cooper, 3 Barb. 115 (N.Y.1848).

7. See McCoy v. Huffman, 8 Cowen 84 (N.Y.1827) and Canovar v. Cooper, 3 Barb. 115 (N.Y.1848) which seem among the earliest cases to label the effect of the father's conduct as emancipation.

8. E.g., Iroquois Iron Co. v. Industrial Commission, 294 Ill. 106, 128 N.E. 289 (1920); Swenson v. Swenson, 241 Mo.App. 21, 227 S.W.2d 103 (1950). For a collection of cases describing the methods of "implied emancipation," as by abandonment, the child's leaving home, the child's marriage, the child's enlistment in the armed forces, see Annot., 165 A.L.R. 723 (1946). Cases taking the conventional view of emancipation generally say that it may be express or implied. See, e.g., Buxton v. Bishop, 185 Va. 1, 37 S.E.2d 755 (1946), involving the father's duty to support an emancipated child. 2 S. Williston, Contracts § 225 (3d ed. Jaeger 1959) contains a discussion of emancipation in conventional terms.

Turner v. McCune, 4 Mass.App.Ct. 864, 357 N.E.2d 942 (1976) states that under both New Jersey and Massachusetts law there is no specific age at which emancipation occurs, that in fact it does not automatically occur even at majority.

Although emancipation may be express or implied, it is not presumed, and the burden of proving it generally

rests on the person asserting that it has occurred. Royall v. Legislation & Policy Division, Bureau of Retirement Ins. and Occupational Health, 610 S.W.2d 377 (Mo.App. 1980); In re Marriage of Heddy, 535 S.W.2d 276 (Mo.App. 1976).

9. See note, 28 Minn.L.Rev. 275 (1944), which describes and criticizes the conventional analysis.

10. E.g., In re Sonnenberg, 256 Minn. 571, 99 N.W.2d 444 (1959); Fevig v. Fevig, 90 N.M. 51, 559 P.2d 839 (1977); Matter of Williams, 106 Misc.2d 280, 431 N.Y.S.2d 334 (Fam.Ct.1980); Wadoz v. United National Indemnity Co., 274 Wis. 383, 80 N.W.2d 262 (1957). For other cases see Katz, Schroeder, Sidman, Emancipating Our Children—Coming of Legal Age in America, 7 Fam.L.Q. 211, 215 (1973). Some cases seem to assume that emancipation is an all or nothing proposition, however. E.g. In re Greer, 184 So.2d 104 (La.App.1966).

11. E.g., Altieri v. Altieri, 21 Conn.Supp. 376, 155 A.2d 758 (1959).

12. Annot., 165 A.L.R. 723, 727 (1946). Some cases hold that in determining whether a child has been emancipated the court should look only to the intention of the parent. E.g., Bates v. Bates, 62 Misc.2d 498, 310 N.Y.S.2d 26 (Fam.Ct.1970).

13. In re Sonnenberg, 256 Minn. 571, 99 N.W.2d 444 (1959).

clear that the traditional method of defining emancipation and its consequences is both confused and productive of undesirable results.[14] Emancipation as a legal term is useful, but only as a means of describing a result already reached, not as an analytical tool.

How then should we define the circumstances in which some or all of the child's disabilities terminate? The answer in general terms is clear: A particular disability should no longer exist whenever the child's circumstances have so changed that the reason for creating the disability no longer exists. This requires separate treatment for each sort of disability, but the existing reliance upon doctrines of emancipation are doing this already, via the theory of partial emancipation. This analysis has the advantage of focussing the courts' attention on relevant circumstances and of avoiding broad generalizations which later have either to be ignored or distinguished away by disingenuous reasoning. Courts are beginning to adopt it in decisions which expressly hold that emancipation has occurred for some purposes but not for others.[15] The best test of this analysis is to apply it to the various fact situations which commonly arise:

a) *The child's right to his own earnings:* This has been partially dealt with in the discussion of the early cases.[16] The basis for giving the parent the right to control the

child's services and earnings is presumably as a corollary of the parent's obligation to support the child. The parent's right to services and earnings was of considerable importance a hundred years ago, when the family was a producing unit and the child worked, either on the farm or in industry. It is of so little importance today that it can be said to be nearly obsolete. If the parent consents to have the child work outside the home and keep his own earnings, he waives his claim.[17] Likewise if the parent fails in his obligations by abandoning the child, he loses any claim to the child's earnings.[18] The cases today more often deal indirectly with the parent's relinquishment of his claim to services, as where suit is brought for a tort to the child and loss of earnings is claimed as part of the damages, but the result is the same as where there is a suit against the employer for the earnings themselves.[19]

b) *The child's choice of a domicile:* The rule that the child's domicile is, as a matter of law, the domicile of his parents has been adopted by the courts because it reflects what is the fact in most instances, assuming the family is unbroken, and also because younger children are incapable of choosing a domicile of their own. It follows that when a child reaches the age at which he can exercise a choice of domicile,[20] and when in fact he does so with the consent of his parents, the law

14. In re Marriage of Robinson, 629 P.2d 1069 (Colo. 1981).

15. In re Marriage of Robinson, 629 P.2d 1069 (Colo. 1981); Florida Board of Regents of Dept. of Educ., Division of Universities v. Harris, 338 So.2d 215 (Fla.App. 1976); Matter of Williams, 106 Misc.2d 280, 431 N.Y.S.2d 334 (Fam.Ct.1980).

16. See cases cited supra, notes 5 and 6, and Note, 28 Minn.L.Rev. 275 (1944).

17. Bonner v. Surman, 215 Ark. 301, 220 S.W.2d 431 (1949); Lottinville v. Dwyer, 68 R.I. 263, 27 A.2d 305 (1942).

18. Annot., 165 A.L.R. 723, 727 (1946).

19. The child was allowed to recover for his own loss of earnings in National City Development Co. v. McFerran, 55 A.2d 342 (D.C.Mun.App.1947), and Romine v. Watseka, 341 Ill.App. 370, 91 N.E.2d 76 (1950). The father was denied recovery where emancipation was found in Roher v. State, 279 App.Div. 1116, 112 N.Y.S.2d 603 (3d Dep't 1952). No emancipation being proved, the parent was allowed to recover in Allen v. Arthur, 139

Ind.App. 460, 220 N.E.2d 658 (1966) (child lived at home, worked on weekends and kept his own earnings); Collis v. Hoskins, 306 Ky. 391, 208 S.W.2d 70 (1948) (suit for seduction of child, she returned home when she became pregnant and her expenses were paid by her father, the plaintiff); McStay v. Przychocki, 10 N.J.Super. 455, 77 A.2d 276 (1950), affirmed 7 N.J. 456, 81 A.2d 761 (1951); Immel v. Richards, 154 Ohio St. 52, 93 N.E.2d 474 (1950). See American Products Co. v. Villwock, 7 Wash.2d 246, 109 P.2d 570 (1941) holding no emancipation could be inferred from the sole fact a father paid his son wages for working in the father's business.

20. This analysis is borne out by several cases which used the term "emancipation" in its conventional sense, but which refused to hold that emancipation of a very young child enabled him to acquire a domicile of choice. Inhabitants of Town of Camden v. Inhabitants of Town of Warren, 160 Me. 158, 200 A.2d 419 (1964) (emancipation at age seven through abandonment by the parent); In re Sonnenberg, 256 Minn. 571, 99 N.W.2d 444 (1959) (child emancipated at birth when abandoned by mother but retained his mother's domicile). In New Jersey Division

respects his domicile of choice. This happens most often when a person under twenty-one marries and sets up his own home,[21] but it may happen when he moves away from his parents' home, gets a job and assumes the activities and responsibilities of an adult.[22] Some cases make unnecessarily strict requirements that the parents must release all control before the child may acquire his own domicile,[23] but the essential issue is only whether the child is old enough to decide on a domicile and whether in fact he does choose a domicile for himself apart from parents or guardian.

c) *Suits by and against the child:* When the question arises whether emancipation allows the child to sue or be sued in his own name, the controlling issue should be, does he have sufficient judgment and discretion to manage the litigation for himself? Emancipation is certainly some evidence that he does, but it is not necessarily conclusive. It is not surprising that the cases take no strong position either way on the question.[24]

In those states where parents and children may not sue each other for personal torts, the question may arise whether the parent may sue or be sued by his emancipated child. Here again the answer turns on the policy underlying the immunity and on whether that policy retains its force when the child is emancipated. Those courts which continue to uphold the immunity seem to think that its purpose is to preserve family unity and solidarity.[25] If so, the emancipated child should be able to sue or be sued when he is no longer part of the family unit.[26] The cases usually reach this result, although most of them find that emancipation has or has not occurred without much awareness of the relevant factors.[27] One case in particular became involved in elaborate consideration of whether emancipation may be revoked and whether in fact it was revoked [28] when the basic question was whether the child was so much a part of the family that a tort action against her by the parents would impair family solidarity.

d) *The child's right to support:* The application of our suggested analysis to the determination of the point at which the child no

of Youth and Family Services v. V., 154 N.J.Super. 531, 381 A.2d 1241 (1977) the court found that a minor's interest and desire to live apart from her mother and the fact that she had lived apart for three years and had a child of her own were sufficient reason to declare her disabilities ended and not to award her custody to her mother. In all of these cases the courts, by looking at the relevant facts, including the minor's desires and needs, avoided harsh results to which an uncritical and rigid definition of "emancipation" would have led them. See also Tencza v. Aetna Casualty & Surety Co., 21 Ariz.App. 552, 521 P.2d 1010 (1974), opinion vacated 111 Ariz. 226, 527 P.2d 97 (1974); Florida Board of Regents v. Harris, 338 So.2d 215 (Fla.App.1976); Matter of Williams, 106 Misc.2d 280, 431 N.Y.S.2d 334 (Fam.Ct.1980). A case which adhered to the erroneous idea that emancipation turns exclusively on the actions or intentions of the parent is Holly v. Maryland Automobile Ins. Fund, 29 Md.App. 498, 349 A.2d 670 (1975).

21. Appelt v. Whitty, 286 F.2d 135 (7th Cir.1961); Town of Milford v. Greenwich, 126 Conn. 340, 11 A.2d 352 (1940); Ex parte Olcott, 141 N.J.Eq. 8, 55 A.2d 820 (1947).

22. Spurgeon v. Mission State Bank, 151 F.2d 702 (8th Cir.1945), cert. denied 327 U.S. 782, 66 S.Ct. 682, 90 L.Ed. 1009 (1946).

23. Hall v. Fall, 235 F.Supp. 631 (W.D.N.C.1964).

24. Holding the child may sue or be sued: Ruiz v. Ruiz, 233 Miss. 192, 101 So.2d 533 (1958) (divorce); Kirby v. Gilliam, 182 Va. 111, 28 S.E.2d 40 (1943) (annulment,

child's mother not entitled to sue). Holding a guardian must be appointed: Altieri v. Altieri, 21 Conn.Supp. 376, 155 A.2d 758 (1959); Nims v. Nims, 305 S.W.2d 875 (Mo. App.1957).

25. See section 10.2, infra.

26. A case making this analysis is Logan v. Reaves, 209 Tenn. 631, 354 S.W.2d 789 (1962), 3 J.Fam.L. 167 (1963). In Detwiler v. Detwiler, 162 Pa.Super. 383, 57 A.2d 426 (1948) the court relied on a rigid and uncomprehending analysis to find that no emancipation had occurred so that the parent could not sue the child in tort. On the proper analysis the result seems correct because the child still lived at home and presumably there remained no family solidarity to preserve against the impact of the tort suit.

It has been properly noted that some cases use the doctrine of emancipation as a disguised device for limiting or eliminating the parent-child immunity entirely. Katz, Schroeder, Sidman, Emancipating Our Children— Coming of Legal Age in America, 7 Fam.L.Q. 211, 219 (1973).

27. Vaupel v. Bellach, 261 Iowa 376, 154 N.W.2d 149 (1967) (child living with his mother not emancipated where the question was whether he would be liable over to a tort feasor for the injury to his mother); Parker v. Parker, 230 S.C. 28, 94 S.E.2d 12 (1956); Annot., 60 A.L.R.2d 1284, 1292 (1958).

28. Wadoz v. United Nat. Indemnity Co., 274 Wis. 383, 80 N.W.2d 262 (1957).

longer has a right to be supported by his parents is both simple and productive. It eliminates confusion and provides clear solutions. The child is given the right to be supported by his parents because he is unable to support himself and because human progress requires that there be a relatively long period of education and training for the young, during which they cannot be productive citizens. If the child's situation is such that he no longer needs to be supported, then his right to that support should no longer exist.[29] We normally, though not always, find that this right ends at majority,[30] but it could end earlier. Since the issue of the right to support arises in many ways, there are situations in which a child who would be considered "emancipated" for other purposes would not be entitled to support and others in which he would be so entitled.

For example, when a young man or woman of seventeen leaves home, gets a job and supports himself or herself, their parents' support is no longer necessary and therefore their parents would no longer be liable to someone furnishing goods or services to them.[31] On the other hand, if the young person worked only part time or during vaca-

tions, remaining essentially dependent upon his parents, he would not be considered emancipated for this purpose and would continue to have a right to be supported by his parents.[32] When a person marries and lives with his spouse, his right to be supported by his parents likewise ends.[33] The reason is that he no longer needs parental support, having a right to support from his spouse. Or when a young man or woman enters the army, he or she ordinarily does not need parental support any longer since support is provided by the army, and the parents' duty of support is said to end.[34] In all such cases the result is attributed to emancipation, a term which does not enlighten us very much about the underlying reasons for the result.

It is clear that a parent who abandons a sixteen-year-old child might be said to have emancipated him for some purposes[35] but such a parent could hardly argue that he had no further duty to support the child. The reason would not be that the child was emancipated, but that, emancipated or not, he needed the support from his parents. So long as that need continues, up to age eighteen (and sometimes beyond), the parents must supply it.

29. In re Marriage of Robinson, 629 P.2d 1069 (Colo. 1981).

30. See section 6.2, supra, and section 17.1, infra, on the obligation of parents to support their children. Colorado recognizes by statute the different interests involved in emancipation by providing that the age of majority for purposes of suing, making contracts and conveyances and handling property is eighteen, but for support purposes it is still twenty-one. Colo.Rev.Stat. § 13–22–101 (1974).

31. Ison v. Florida Sanitarium and Benevolent Assn., 302 So.2d 200 (Fla.App.1974); Iroquois Iron Co. v. Industrial Commission, 294 Ill. 106, 128 N.E. 289 (1920) (workers' compensation); Royall v. Legislation & Policy Division, 610 S.W.2d 377 (Mo.App.1980); Accent Service Co., Inc., v. Ebsen, 209 Neb. 94, 306 N.W.2d 575 (1981); Timmerman v. Brown, 268 S.C. 303, 233 S.E.2d 106 (1977); Buxton v. Bishop, 185 Va. 1, 37 S.E.2d 755 (1946).

32. In re Marriage of Robinson, 629 P.2d 1069 (Colo. 1981); Brundige v. Marcum, 694 S.W.2d 891 (Mo.App. 1985).

33. Lawson v. Brown, 349 F.Supp. 203 (W.D.Va.1972) (social security and AFDC entitlement, citing many cases); Specking v. Specking, 528 S.W.2d 448 (Mo.App. 1975) (right to support under a divorce decree).

The analysis in the text is borne out by In re Marriage of Fetters, 41 Colo.App. 281, 584 P.2d 104 (1978), holding

that a daughter was emancipated by her marriage, but that the emancipation was terminated when the marriage was annulled, thereby reviving her father's duty of support.

34. Corbridge v. Corbridge, 230 Ind. 201, 102 N.E.2d 764 (1952); Green v. Green, 234 S.W.2d 350 (Mo.App. 1950); Dingley v. Dingley, 121 N.H. 670, 433 A.2d 1281 (1981). Where the child lived with his mother during his period of army service, it was held that his father continued to have a duty to support him in Koon v. Koon, 50 Wash.2d 577, 313 P.2d 369 (1957), 15 Wash. & L.L.Rev. 298 (1958), thereby bearing out the argument in the text that that need is the real issue.

35. Byrd v. O'Neill, 309 Minn. 415, 244 N.W.2d 657 (1976); Fevig v. Fevig, 90 N.M. 51, 559 P.2d 839 (1977); Thompson v. Thompson, 94 Misc.2d 911, 405 N.Y.S.2d 974 (Fam.Ct.1978) (daughter left home but not voluntarily and only because there was neither room nor money to permit her to stay); Matter of Bylow, 92 Misc.2d 509, 400 N.Y.S.2d 451 (Fam.Ct.1977); Darene H. v. Patricia S., 90 Misc.2d 558, 394 N.Y.S.2d 807 (Fam.Ct.1977); Bates v. Bates, 62 Misc.2d 498, 310 N.Y.S.2d 26 (Fam.Ct.1970); Annot., 32 A.L.R.3d 1055 (1970).

In these days when we seem to be seeing the breakdown of family unity, there is a further group of cases in which the courts sometimes refer to emancipation as a basis for excusing parents from their support obligations. What makes these cases difficult is the conflict they represent between the child's need for support and the parent's traditional authority over the child's conduct. In the typical case the child leaves home against the parent's wishes, in defiance of parental authority, and then seeks to force the parent to support him. More often than not courts faced with this situation have enforced the obligation of support, no doubt influenced to some extent by the awareness that a contrary result will require the state to support the child. In a few cases, however, involving conduct by the child which is considered a flagrant violation of legitimate parental discipline, the courts have held that the child may not force his parent to support him, even though he may be in need.[36] Here the analysis based upon need which has been suggested in this section breaks down before the recognition that it is unfair to impose the support obligation upon the parent whose child is entirely beyond his control, particularly where the child's choice of a way of life requires higher expenditures for support than the parent's would.[37]

e) *The child's power to disaffirm contracts:* It is sometimes stated that emancipation has no effect on the child's capacity to contract or convey property.[38] On the analysis already suggested, this statement seems too broad, and in fact there are cases in which the child's power to disaffirm is denied on the ground that he has been emancipated.[39] The reason for giving the child this power was to protect him against his own lack of judgment and against adults who might take advantage of his youth. It follows that when his condition is such that this protection is no longer needed, the power should be terminated. Emancipation should at least be some evidence that the child no longer needs this protection. If, for example, he has married, is working and supporting his wife, he would seem to have reached sufficient maturity to enter into binding contracts and conveyances.[40] In other situations, emancipation might not prove capacity, in which case the child would still be entitled to disaffirm.[41] But the ultimate issue ought to be his maturity and judgment rather than a mechanical definition of emancipation. And in weighing his maturity and judgment, some consideration should be given to the contemporary demand for limitation of the infant's power of disaffirmance.[42]

f) *Emancipation by judicial decree pursuant to statute:* Some states have enacted legislation which authorizes a court to enter a decree relieving a minor of his legal disabilities.[43] Most such statutes specify the grounds

36. Parker v. Stage, 43 N.Y.2d 128, 400 N.Y.S.2d 794, 371 N.E.2d 513 (1977) (father not liable to the state for support furnished to a daughter who left home to live with her paramour and have a child when the father urged her to return home and continue her schooling); Roe v. Doe, 29 N.Y.2d 188, 324 N.Y.S.2d 71, 272 N.E.2d 567 (1971), 46 St.J.L.Rev. 139 (1971) (father not required to support college age daughter who refused to live in a dormitory in accordance with the father's wishes); St. Lawrence County Department of Social Services v. Menard, 86 Misc.2d 126, 381 N.Y.S.2d 939 (Fam.Ct.1975).

37. See, e.g., Haight v. Haight, 241 Or. 532, 405 P.2d 622 (1965).

38. Kiefer v. Fred Howe Motors, Inc., 39 Wis.2d 20, 158 N.W.2d 288 (1968); 2 S. Williston, Contracts § 225 (3d ed. Jaeger 1959).

39. E.g., In re Greer, 184 So.2d 104 (La.App.1966) (child of thirteen emancipated by marriage and had legal capacity to sue); Merrick v. Stephens, 337 S.W.2d 713 (Mo.App.1960), 1 J.Fam.L. 140 (1961), 36 Notre Dame

Law. 419 (1961); Schulman v. Villensky, 103 Ohio App. 300, 143 N.E.2d 754 (1957).

40. Merrick v. Stephens, 337 S.W.2d 713 (Mo.App. 1960).

41. Inakay v. Sun Laundry Corp., 180 Misc. 550, 42 N.Y.S.2d 344 (1943).

42. See Edge, Voidability of Minors' Contracts: A Feudal Doctrine in a Modern Economy, 1 Ga.L.Rev. 205 (1967).

43. Ala.Code 1977, §§ 26–13–1 to 26–13–8; Ark.Stats. §§ 34–2001, 34–2002 (Supp.1982); West's Ann.Cal.Civ. Code § 64 (Supp.1981); Conn.Gen.Stat.Ann. §§ 46b–150, 46b–150a, 46b–150b, 46b–150c, 46b–150d, 46b–150e (Supp. 1981); Kan.Stat.Ann. §§ 38–108 to 38–110 (1973); La. Stat.Ann.—Civ.Code art. 385 (Supp.1981) and La.Stat. Ann.—Code Civ.Pro. arts. 3991 to 3994 (1961 and Supp. 1981); Mich.Comp.Laws Ann. § 25.244(4) (1974); Miss. Code 1973, §§ 93–19–1 to 93–19–11; Okla.Stat.1981, tit. 10, §§ 91 to 93; Or.Rev.Stat. §§ 109.555 to 109.565,

on which emancipation may be decreed, often with the additional requirement that it be for the minor's best interests.[44] Some of them require that the minor must be of a certain age in order to bring the suit while others make no such requirement.[45] The consent of a parent or guardian is required for emancipation under some of these statutes [46] while others permit it without such consent.[47]

The effect of a decree of emancipation is generally to remove some or all of the disabilities of minority.[48] The California, Connecticut, and Oregon statutes specifically provide that such a decree also ends the parents' responsibility for the child's support.[49]

Where the decree results in a complete termination of the mutual obligations of parents and child, it may accurately be characterized as a form of parent-child divorce, albeit a one-sided form since the statutes do not ordinarily authorize the parents to divorce their children.

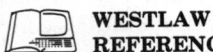 **WESTLAW REFERENCES**

to(285 211) /p emancipat! /s age /2 legal majority

a. The Child's Right to his Own Earnings

to(211 285 /p child juvenile minor infant /s right entitl! /2 earning wage salary

---

419.476, 482.270 (1979); Tenn.Code Ann. §§ 23–1201 to 23.1204 (1955 and Supp.1980). The statutes are discussed in Katz, Schroeder, Sidman, Emancipating Our Children—Coming of Legal Age in America, 7 Fam.L.Q. 211, 232 (1973). The Oregon statute is discussed in detail in Note, Juvenile Law—Emancipation: New Legislation for Oregon's Children, 57 Ore.L.Rev. 573 (1978).

44. E.g. the Alabama, California, Connecticut, Michigan, statutes.

45. The prescribed ages vary from eighteen in Alabama to fourteen in California, with sixteen in Arkansas, Connecticut, Louisiana and Oregon.

46. E.g., in Alabama and California. In Oregon the court must consider whether the parent consents, but the

statute does not say what effect the parent's refusal to consent may have. The Connecticut statute requires a finding that the decree is in the interests of both the minor and his parents.

47. E.g., in Arkansas, Kansas, Louisiana, Mississippi and Oklahoma.

48. See the statutes cited in note 43.

49. West's Ann.Cal.Civ.Code § 63 (Supp.1981) and Connecticut and Oregon statutes cited supra, note 43.

For a discussion of the California statute, see Note, California's Emancipation of Minors Act: The Costs and Benefits of Freedom From Parental Control, 18 Cal.West. L.Rev. 482 (1982).

Chapter 9

THE CARE, EDUCATION AND SUPERVISION OF CHILDREN: THE STATE VS. THE PARENT

Table of Sections

§ 9.1 Introduction

This chapter is devoted to an account of several more or less distinct aspects of the relationship of parent and child. Broadly speaking the question it raises is, to what extent have parents in an unbroken family both the power and the responsibility to care for, educate and discipline their children? Or, since this is a law book, under what circumstances may the legal authorities displace parental authority in the care of children? Obviously there are many other sections of this work which deal with the parent-child relationship in ways closely related to this chapter. The section most closely related is that on the involuntary termination of parental rights [1], since that is the state's ultimate civil sanction for serious parental inadequacy. Termination of parental rights may often lead to the adoption of a child whose relationship with his natural parents has been severed, however, and for that reason

the grounds for and procedure in such termination are discussed in connection with adoption. But the section on termination of parental rights should be considered an intrinsic part of any discussion of child abuse and should be read after the child abuse material. Other sections of this work which also deal with the parent's authority and responsibility to care for his child include those on abortion,[2] contraception,[3] sterilization,[4] custody,[5] intra-family torts,[6] and consortium.[7]

A major reason for the difficulties with parent-child relationships, as the title to this chapter suggests, is that there are three sets of interests in actual or potential conflict, those of the parent, those of the child and those of the state. The cases exhibit such great variety that in one case the interests of the parent seem obviously to predominate, while in another those of the child are clearly dispositive, and in another the state's interests are called into play. One effect of this is

---

§ 9.1

1. See section 20.6, infra.
2. See section 5.3, supra.
3. See section 5.1, supra.
4. See section 5.3, supra.
5. See chapter 19, infra.
6. See section 10, infra.
7. See section 11, infra.

to lead legislatures to enact statutes which are often lacking in precision, the purpose being to permit the courts to exercise wide discretion in mediating between these interests. Another effect is to tempt both courts and commentators to indulge in broad generalizations which may account for a limited group of cases but which may be inappropriate in others.

For example, some statutes define child abuse in ways leaving a great deal to judicial exposition,[8] thereby also authorizing extensive state intervention in the family. There are advocates for this type of broad statute,[9] but more commonly the legal writing emphasizes the rights of the children[10] or the rights of parents [11] with a corresponding minimization of the value of and need for state intervention.[12] Much of the writing by the proponents of one or another view is not very

specific, nor does it define what is meant by "rights" in this context.[13] The policy conflicts do become specific, however, when they arise in litigation involving parent, child, and state, especially where constitutional principles are appealed to.[14] The resolution of such cases is made all the more difficult by the fact that the arguments on behalf of parents' rights or of state intervention are usually justified as ultimately benefiting the child.[15]

In the sections of this chapter which follow these conflicts are explored as they arise in various types of litigation. The discussion of the statutes and cases has been written and should be read with an awareness of social conditions surrounding the American family in the second half of the Twentieth Century, the most striking of which has been the weakening of family relationships, not only be-

8. E.g., Del.Code tit. 16, § 902 (1983); Okl.Stat.1985, tit. 21, § 845 (Supp.). A measure of the criticism of such statutes may be taken by comparing West's Rev.Code Wash.Ann. § 13.04.010 (1962) with § 26.44.020(12) (1986).

9. Paulsen, Child Abuse Reporting Laws: The Shape of the Legislation, 67 Colum.L.Rev. 1 (1967); Paulsen, The Legal Framework for Child Protection, 66 Colum.L. Rev. 679 (1966); McCoid, The Battered Child and Other Assaults Upon the Family, 50 Minn.L.Rev. 1 (1965). See also Delaney, New Concepts of the Family Court in R. Helfer, C. Kempe, Child Abuse and Neglect 335 (1976), and C. Kempe, R. Helfer, Helping the Battered Child and His Family (1972).

10. The most extreme example is Foster and Freed, A Bill of Rights for Children, 6 Fam.L.Q. 343 (1972). The authors, perhaps under the influence of the movement which glorified youth in the early 1970's, suggested that the status of minority is analogous to that of slavery. They argued that among other rights children should have a legal right to parental love, to a suitable home, to be regarded as persons, to be listened to, and to emancipation when the relationship with their parents has broken down. They were apparently not troubled by the likelihood that implementation of any such rights would require frequent and detailed state intrusion into family privacy. The most influential statement of the need for exclusive attention to the child's needs, emphasizing his psychological needs is J. Goldstein, A. Freud, A. Solnit, Beyond the Best Interests of the Child (2d ed. 1979). The authors' views have been somewhat qualified in a later book which took the position that although the child's needs are paramount, those needs are best served by preserving his family. J. Goldstein, A. Freud, A. Solnit, Before the Best Interests of the Child (1979). Other writing which places the child's interests first in importance is Burt, Developing Constitutional Rights of, in, and

for Children, 39 Law & Contemp.Prob. No. 3 118 (1975); Skolnick, The Limits of Childhood: Conceptions of Child Development and Social Context, 39 L. & Contemp.Prob. No. 3 38 (1975); Note, State Intrusion Into Family Affairs: Justifications and Limitations, 26 Stan.L.Rev. 1383 (1974). The Supreme Court decision which first began to limit state intrusion into child care and the family is Application of Gault, 387 U.S. 1, 87 S.Ct. 1428, 18 L.Ed.2d 527 (1967).

11. Hafen, Children's Liberation and the New Egalitarianism: Some Reservations About Abandoning Youth to Their "Rights", 1976 B.Y.U.L.Rev. 605; Levy, The Rights of Parents, 1976 B.Y.U.L.Rev. 693.

12. J. Goldstein, A. Freud, A. Solnit, Before the Best Interests of the Child ch. 5 (1979) urges strict limitations on the state's inquiry into parent-child relationships and upon the state's power to terminate or modify those relationships.

13. For a discussion of the definition of "rights" in this context, see Eekelaar, What Are Parental Rights? 89 L.Q.Rev. 210 (1973).

14. See Tribe, Childhood, Suspect Classifications, and Conclusive Presumptions: Three Linked Riddles, 39 L. & Contemp.Prob. No. 3, 8 (1975), and, e.g., Parham v. J.R., 442 U.S. 584, 99 S.Ct. 2493, 61 L.Ed.2d 101 (1979) and Note, 93 Harv.L.Rev. 60, 89 (1979).

15. Delaney, The Battered Child and the Law in C. Kempe, R. Helfer, Helping the Battered Child and His Family 187, 197 (1972) stresses the courts' function in protecting the child. Wald, State Intervention on Behalf of "Neglected" Children: A Search for Realistic Standards, 27 Stan.L.Rev. 985, 991–993 (1975) argues that parental autonomy in raising children generally is of more benefit to children than state intervention. See generally, S. Katz, When Parents Fail (1971).

tween husband and wife but also between parent and child.[16]

§ 9.2 Parental Authority Over the Child's Education

The conflicting interests of parents, children and state are nowhere more in evidence than in controversies arising out of the compulsory education laws. Every state now has statutes requiring that children be sent to school, usually between the ages of six and sixteen.[1] Sanctions for non-compliance with the statutes include misdemeanor convictions of the parents for wilful failure to send their children to school[2] and civil proceedings in the juvenile courts against the children for their truancy.[3] The statutes often contain

exemptions for mentally or physically handicapped children,[4] and sometimes exemptions for home instruction by qualified teachers.[5]

The parent's interest in directing his child's education has in several cases been referred to as a constitutional right, generally in rather vague terms, presumably as a specific application of the parent's right to liberty guaranteed by the Fourteenth Amendment.[6] It seems paradoxical that if there is such a right, it applies to a subject, the education of children, which is regulated by the state not only by the compulsory school attendance laws but by an extensive and detailed statutory scheme, most aspects of which are beyond the scope of this work.[7] And in one of the three leading cases referring to the parent's

---

16. This development is amply documented in M. Glendon, The New Family and the New Property 36–41 (1981).

§ 9.2

1. E.g., Ala.Code 1985, § 16–28–3 (Supp.); West's Ann. Cal.Educ.Code § 48200 (1978); Colo.Const. Art. IX, § 11; Colo.Rev.Stat. § 22–33–104 (1973 and Supp.1985); Ill.-S.H.A. ch. 122, § 26–1 (Supp.1986); Miss.Code 1985, § 37–13–91 (Supp.); N.Y.—McKinney's Ed.L. § 3205 (1981); S.C.Code 1985, § 59–65–10 (Supp.); Va.Code, § 22.1–254 (1985). For a summary of the school attendance laws, see Steinhilber & Sokolowski, State Law on Compulsory Attendance (U.S. Dept. of Health, Education and Welfare, Office of Education 1966).

2. E.g., N.Y.—McKinney's Educ.L. § 3233 (1981). The parent may also be charged with neglect of the child, a civil remedy leading either to a protective order or in extreme cases to a removal of the child from parental custody. Such a protective order, directing the parent to see that the child was in school, enforceable by contempt, was entered in In Interest of Burr, 119 Ill.App.2d 134, 255 N.E.2d 57 (1970). Charges of neglect were held not to be proved in In re Pima County Juvenile Action No. J-31853, 18 Ariz.App. 219, 501 P.2d 395 (1972); In re Davis, 114 N.H. 242, 318 A.2d 151 (1974); and Matter of Skipwith, 14 Misc.2d 325, 180 N.Y.S.2d 852 (Dom.Rel.Ct.1958).

3. E.g., Colo.Rev.Stat. §§ 22–33–107, 22–33–108 (1973 and Supp.1985); In Matter of George C., 91 Misc.2d 875, 398 N.Y.S.2d 936 (Fam.Ct.1977) (truancy not proved); In re Mario, 65 Misc.2d 708, 317 N.Y.S.2d 659 (Fam.Ct.1971).

4. E.g., Ill.-S.H.A. ch. 122, § 26–1 (Supp.1986). Many states provide for the education of such children in special classes and such a statutory scheme was held constitutional in Cuyahoga County Assn. for Retarded Children and Adults v. Essex, 411 F.Supp. 46 (N.D.Ohio 1976). The classification and placement problems of such children are dealt with in In re White, 103 Ill.App.3d 105, 58 Ill.Dec. 50, 429 N.E.2d 1383 (1982); In the Matter of "A" Family, 184 Mont. 145, 602 P.2d 157 (1979); L. v. State, 70 Misc.2d 660, 335 N.Y.S.2d 3 (Fam.Ct.1972). Newspaper publication of the names of such children in a special

class was held to be an actionable invasion of their privacy in Deaton v. Delta Democrat Pub. Co., 326 So.2d 471 (Miss.1976).

5. E.g., West's Ann.Cal.Educ.L. § 48224 (1978).

6. E.g., Prince v. Massachusetts, 321 U.S. 158, 166, 64 S.Ct. 438, 442, 88 L.Ed. 645 (1944): "It is cardinal with us that the custody, care and nurture of the child reside first in the parents, whose primary function and freedom include preparation for obligations the state can neither supply nor hinder. * * * And it is in recognition of this that these decisions have respected the private realm of family life which the state cannot enter." See also Pierce v. Society of Sisters of the Holy Names of Jesus and Mary, 268 U.S. 510, 535, 45 S.Ct. 571, 573, 69 L.Ed. 1077 (1925): "The child is not the mere creature of the state; those who nurture and direct his destiny have the right, coupled with the high duty, to recognize and prepare him for additional obligations." Meyer v. Nebraska, 262 U.S. 390, 43 S.Ct. 625, 67 L.Ed. 1042 (1923) seems to assume the parent's interest is protected by the right to liberty given in the Fourteenth Amendment. And Wisconsin v. Yoder, 406 U.S. 205, 213–214, 92 S.Ct. 1526, 1532, 32 L.Ed.2d 15 (1972) puts the parent's interest this way: " * * * the values of parental direction of the religious upbringing and education of their children in their early and formative years have a high place in our society."

Halderman, by Halderman v. Pennhurst State School & Hosp., 707 F.2d 702 (3d Cir.1983) makes a manful attempt to give some content to the vague statements of the Supreme Court by saying that a) parents have a substantial constitutional right to control the rearing of their children; b) this right is not constitutionally protected if the parent is guilty of abuse or neglect; and c) without proof of abuse or neglect this right may be subjected to state action only when that action is supported by a significant governmental interest.

7. See generally, G. Johnson, Education Law (1969); M. Sorgen, W. Kaplan, P. Duffy, E. Margolin, State, School and Family Cases and Materials on Law and Education (1979).

right the Court held that that right had to yield to the state's regulation.[8] It therefore is more realistic to say that the parent has an interest in and responsibility for the education of his child, thereby avoiding the connotation of absoluteness carried by the term "right". The parent's interest and responsibility arise out of our traditional assumption that the basic social unit is the nuclear family and that that unit is the best instrument for the transmission of social values to succeeding generations.[9] Notwithstanding that assumption, it is not true that the parents have the sole right and responsibility for their children's education. The state asserts and actively exercises broad powers in all aspects of education.[10]

In one respect the state's intrusion into the child's education is limited by practical considerations. Where the parents disagree over the course the child's education should take and the family remains intact, the courts have been very reluctant to resolve the disagreement, at least so long as the child's health or welfare is not jeopardized.[11] These decisions recognize the obvious fact that courts are neither qualified nor equipped to supervise the details of a child's education. Even after divorce most courts refuse to enter decrees controlling the education of children of the marriage, as for example where one of the parents seeks enforcement of an antenup-

tial agreement concerning the child's religious training,[12] leaving that control to the parent having custody of the child.[13]

The crucial question for the law is the constitutional validity of the various ways in which the state supersedes the parent's power over the child's education. Two much cited Supreme Court cases have held that the state may not require pupil attendance exclusively in public schools [14] and that the state may not forbid the teaching of languages other than English in the public schools until after the eighth grade.[15] Both of these cases found the state statutes to be in violation of the Fourteenth Amendment, and both announced the test of the statutes' validity to be whether they bore a reasonable relation to any purpose within the state's competency. No such purpose was found in either case.

Both the Pierce [16] and Meyer [17] cases assumed that as a general proposition the state may constitutionally require children to attend school. Although it did not directly involve compulsory school attendance, Prince v. Massachusetts [18] contains dictum to the effect that the state may require school attendance. The courts of many states have reached the same conclusion where the parent's refusal to send his child to school was based upon the opinion that he could give the child a better

8. Prince v. Massachusetts, 321 U.S. 158, 64 S.Ct. 438, 88 L.Ed. 645 (1944).

9. E.g., II J. Kent, Commentaries on American Law 195 (12th ed. Holmes 1884). A second assumption is implied, of course, that the parents will generally be competent to direct the child's education. Sugarman and Kirp, Rethinking Collective Responsibility for Education, 39 Law & Contemp.Prob. No. 3,144, 211 (1975).

10. In addition to the compulsory attendance laws, supra, note 1, the states often regulate courses, qualifications of teachers, the medical care of students, provide for special kinds of education and for vocational programs. See, e.g., N.Y.—McKinney's Educ.L., passim.

11. Kilgrow v. Kilgrow, 268 Ala. 475, 107 So.2d 885 (1958); People ex rel. Sisson v. Sisson, 271 N.Y. 285, 2 N.E.2d 660 (1936).

12. E.g., In re Marriage of Wolfert, 42 Colo.App. 433, 598 P.2d 524 (1979).

13. See section 19.4, infra.

14. Pierce v. Society of Sisters of the Holy Names of Jesus and Mary, 268 U.S. 510, 45 S.Ct. 571, 69 L.Ed. 1070

(1925). In this case suit was brought by a society which ran a private school to enjoin the enforcement of the Oregon statute which required all children to be sent to public school. The language of the case concerning the parent's liberty to educate his child is essentially dictum though it is much quoted. The holding of the case was that substantive due process was violated by the statute in that it improperly interfered with the business of operating private schools.

15. Meyer v. Nebraska, 262 U.S. 390, 43 S.Ct. 625, 67 L.Ed. 1042 (1923). The Supreme Court here reversed the conviction of a teacher in a parochial school for violation of the statute making it a crime to teach a language other than English until after the eighth grade. Justice Holmes dissented on the ground that this was a reasonable requirement.

16. See note 14, supra.

17. See note 15, supra.

18. 321 U.S. 158, 166, 64 S.Ct. 438, 442, 88 L.Ed. 645 (1944).

education at home,[19] or upon some reason other than religious scruples.[20] To this extent the state's interest in seeing to it that all children receive an adequate education outweighs the parent's claim under the Fourteenth Amendment to direct his child's training. Many of these decisions are undoubtedly based in part upon the view that attendance at school alone, apart from the subjects taught, has educational value which cannot be achieved at home without contact with other children.[21] This argument focuses the conflict of interests precisely on the parent's objection, since he often thinks that the values he would inculcate at home are preferable to those to which his child would be exposed from peers and teachers at school.[22] To the extent that there is a difference between the cultural, social and psychological atmosphere of home and school, compulsory school attendance weakens the solidarity of the family. The latest expression of the Supreme Court on the question, Wisconsin v. Yoder,[23] gives the state very extensive power to override the parent's decisions about what constitutes a proper education for his child, so long as the state's regulations can be labeled "reasonable" and so long as the parent's decision is not based upon religious conviction.

The Supreme Court has taken an entirely different position where the state's compulsory schooling requirements are resisted on religious rather than secular grounds. Wisconsin v. Yoder [24] arose when Amish parents were convicted of violating the state compulsory attendance law by refusing to permit their child to attend public school beyond the eighth grade. The Court's reasoning, though very discursive, may be accurately summarized as follows: a) The Amish religious beliefs and their way of life, including their way of educating their children, were inseparable and interdependent. b) Compulsory attendance at public school would expose the Amish child to influences which would conflict with his religious training, require him to engage in activity inconsistent with that religion, and would threaten the continued existence of the Amish community. c) Wisconsin failed to show that the child's failure to get the additional schooling would impair his physical or mental health, result in his inability to be self-supporting or to be a responsible citizen, or in any other way materially impair the social welfare. On this last point the Court held that when school attendance conflicts with religious belief the state must show something more than that, as Pierce had

19. Scoma v. Chicago Board of Education, 391 F.Supp. 452 (N.D.Ill.1974) (dictum); People v. Y.D.M., 197 Colo. 403, 593 P.2d 1356 (1979); In re R., 79 Misc.2d 339, 357 N.Y.S.2d 1001 (Fam.Ct.1974); Stephens v. Bongart, 15 N.J.Misc. 80, 189 A. 131 (Juv.Ct.1937); City of Akron v. Lane, 65 Ohio App.2d 90, 416 N.E.2d 642 (1979); State ex rel. Shoreline School District No. 412 v. Superior Court for King County, Juvenile Court, 55 Wash.2d 177, 346 P.2d 999 (1959), cert. denied 363 U.S. 814, 80 S.Ct. 1248, 4 L.Ed.2d 1154 (1960). The inadequacy of public school facilities was held not a defense to a truancy charge in In re Gregory B, 88 Misc.2d 313, 387 N.Y.S.2d 380 (Fam.Ct. 1976). According to most cases instruction at home does not qualify as a "private school" within the school attendance law. Annot., 65 A.L.R.3d 1222 (1975).

For an appealing account of one mother's struggle to educate her child at home, see J. Baker, Children in Chancery (1964).

20. People v. Serna, 71 Cal.App.3d 229, 139 Cal.Rptr. 426 (1977) (parent's claim that public schools were segregated did not justify keeping child from school); Matter of Baum, 86 Misc.2d 409, 382 N.Y.S.2d 672 (Fam.Ct.1976), affirmed 61 A.D.2d 123, 401 N.Y.S.2d 514 (2d Dep't 1978), appeal denied 44 N.Y.2d 647, 407 N.Y.S.2d 1026, 379 N.E.2d 596 (1978) (mother's desire to protest against alleged racial discrimination in school not a sufficient ground for keeping child out of school). But Matter of

Skipwith, 14 Misc.2d 325, 180 N.Y.S.2d 852 (Dom.Rel.Ct. 1958) held that a parent could not be charged with child neglect for refusing to send his child to school where the de facto racial segregation resulted in inferior educational opportunity for the child.

21. Stephens v. Bongart, 15 N.J.Misc. 80, 189 A. 131 (Juv.Ct.1937). Brown v. Board of Education of Topeka, Shawnee County, Kansas, 347 U.S. 483, 493, 74 S.Ct. 686, 691, 98 L.Ed. 873 (1954) describes the functions of public education as providing a foundation for good citizenship, a means of awakening the child to cultural values, preparing him for professional training and helping him to adjust to his environment.

22. This is especially true in the cases involving religion, but is also a factor in other cases. See State v. Massa, 95 N.J.Super. 382, 231 A.2d 252 (1967) and J. Baker, Children in Chancery (1964).

23. 406 U.S. 205, 215, 92 S.Ct. 1526, 1533, 32 L.Ed.2d 15 (1972): "A way of life, however virtuous and admirable, may not be interposed as a barrier to reasonable state regulation of education if it is based on purely secular considerations; * * * "

24. 406 U.S. 205, 92 S.Ct. 1526, 32 L.Ed.2d 15 (1972). The case is carefully analyzed in Kurland, The Supreme Court, Compulsory Education, and the First Amendment's Religion Clauses, 75 W.Va.L.Rev. 213 (1973).

said,[25] the requirement bears a "reasonable relation to some purpose within the competency of the state."

The Court itself characterized the crucial issue in this sort of case as follows:

"* * * in order for Wisconsin to compel school attendance beyond the eighth grade against a claim that such attendance interferes with the practice of a legitimate religious belief, it must appear either that the State does not deny the free exercise of religious belief by its requirement, or that there is a state interest of sufficient magnitude to override the interest claiming protection under the Free Exercise Clause".[26]

The Court emphasized that in these cases only a *religious* objection to school attendance would justify invoking such a strict test of the state's interference. An objection based upon ethical or moral grounds would not be sufficient. The Court was influenced by the long history of Amish communities, their solidarity and care for their members, and their law-abiding habits. It is also not without significance that the Amish were willing to have their children attend public school up to the eighth grade, so that only one or two years of high school were at stake in the case, the

Wisconsin statute requiring attendance only to age sixteen.

What Yoder may mean for future controversies over school attendance remains uncertain, but a few precepts may be deduced from it. It reinforces prior indications that the state's power to require attendance is very broad where religion is not interfered with. Since its special circumstances are not likely to be repeated where religions other than the Amish are involved, it does not seem to limit state power very much even when the parent fails to comply with the statute for religious reasons. The relatively few lower court cases before and since Yoder tend to bear this out.[27] And except for Justice Douglas' dissent, the decision tells us nothing about the difficult problem which would be presented if the child should assert some constitutional claim in opposition to the parent.[28] If, for example, the Amish child should wish to go to the public high school, rather than to remain on the family farm, would the Court find that he had a constitutional right to make that choice? Aside from the abortion cases,[29] which are hardly apposite here, the courts have not recognized constitutional rights in children to make decisions in opposition to

---

25. 268 U.S. at 535, 45 S.Ct. at 573.

26. 406 U.S. at 214, 92 S.Ct. at 1532. Cf. State ex rel. Douglas v. Faith Baptist Church of Louisville, 207 Neb. 802, 301 N.W.2d 571 (1981), dism'd for want of a substantial federal question sub nom. Faith Baptist Church v. Douglas, 454 U.S. 803, 102 S.Ct. 75, 70 L.Ed.2d 72 (1981) (enjoins the non-compliance of private religious schools with reasonable state regulations); Bangor Baptist Church v. State of Maine, Dept. of Educational and Cultural Services, 549 F.Supp. 1208 (D.Me.1982), citing many other cases.

27. E.g., Jernigan v. State, 412 So.2d 1242 (Ala.Crim. App.1982) (affirms parents' conviction for refusing to send children to any public school out of Catholic religious conviction); People v. Levisen, 404 Ill. 574, 90 N.E.2d 213 (1950), 18 U.Chi.L.Rev. 105 (1950) (reversed a conviction of Seventh Day Adventists for not sending their children to school, on the ground that their home teaching was equivalent to a private school); State v. Garber, 197 Kan. 567, 419 P.2d 896 (1966), appeal dismissed and cert. denied 389 U.S. 51, 88 S.Ct. 236, 19 L.Ed. 2d 50 (1967) (compulsory school attendance law as applied to the Amish did not violate the First Amendment); Application of Auster, 198 Misc. 1055, 100 N.Y.S.2d 60 (1950), affirmed 278 App.Div. 784, 104 N.Y.S.2d 65 (2d Dep't 1951), affirmed 302 N.Y. 855, 100 N.E.2d 47 (1951), appeal dismissed 342 U.S. 884, 72 S.Ct. 178, 96 L.Ed. 663

(1951) (held that if a divorced father was to retain custody of the child, he must place the child in public school rather than a Yeshiva, a Jewish school which did not meet state requirements); State v. Shaver, 294 N.W.2d 883 (N.D.1980) (state's interest prevailed over the constitutional claims of members of Bible Baptist Church to educate their children in a Bible Baptist school); State ex rel. Nagle v. Olin, 64 Ohio St.2d 341, 415 N.E.2d 279 (1980) (reverses on constitutional grounds the conviction of a Biblical Christian who refused to send his child to public school); State v. Whisner, 47 Ohio St.2d 181, 351 N.E.2d 750 (1976) (upholds the religious defense to compulsory school attendance laws); State ex rel. Shoreline School District No. 412 v. Superior Court for King County, Juvenile Court, 55 Wash.2d 177, 346 P.2d 999 (1959), cert. denied 363 U.S. 814, 80 S.Ct. 1248, 4 L.Ed.2d 1154 (1960) (rejects the First Amendment claim of members of Seventh Elect Church in Spiritual Israel to keep their children out of public school).

28. 406 U.S. at 241, 92 S.Ct. at 1546. Justice Douglas would have remanded the case for evidence on the child's views about his own education. Presumably in his opinion those views should be decisive in this situation.

29. Bellotti v. Baird, 443 U.S. 622, 99 S.Ct. 3035, 61 L.Ed.2d 797 (1979), rehearing denied 444 U.S. 887, 100 S.Ct. 185, 62 L.Ed.2d 121 (1979). But see H.L. v. Matheson, 450 U.S. 398, 101 S.Ct. 1146, 67 L.Ed.2d 388 (1981).

their parents. It seems preferable, even in times when tradition is being rejected, to continue to permit the parent's judgment about school attendance to prevail over that of the child, at least where serious harm to the child is not threatened.

§ 9.3 Medical, Surgical and Psychiatric Care for the Child

The general principle with which we begin an account of medical and psychiatric care for children is that the parent decides whether care is to be provided and what that care is to be.[1] The most common legal expression of this principle occurs in those cases holding that a physician who treats a child or performs surgery on a child without the parent's consent will be liable to the child in tort.[2] To an increasing degree, however, the principle must be qualified today in response to statutory and case authority giving the child himself, without parental permission, the power to consent to medical treatment in some circumstances. For example, statutes may authorize the child to give permission for certain types of treatment.[3] The mature minor rule, in force in some states, allows children who are mature enough to understand the treatment to consent to it, at least where it does not create a serious risk to life or health.[4]

This general principle is obviously not absolute even where the child is not capable of making a decision about his own treatment. It is limited by the power of the state to intercede for the protection of the child's health, safety or welfare. Although the origins of state power are somewhat obscure,[5] and although the obscurity is not mitigated by the invocation of the magic Latin phrase *parens patriae*, there is no doubt that the power exists.[6] *Parens patriae* is a useful term for describing the state's power, but it provides no explanation for the basis of that power, nor, conversely, does its use warrant a wholesale attack on the state's power.[7] The real issue here is how the legislatures or the courts are to define the circumstances in which the state may override a parent's decision to withhold, or to furnish, medical treatment for the child.

Broad state intervention in children's health occurs pursuant to statutes which require immunization against certain diseases, medical examinations for children entering the public schools, and certain treatments for newborn children.[8] In addition there are often statutes which require treatment of such infectious diseases as venereal disease or tuberculosis.[9] Many of these statutes exempt children whose parents object to the procedures, either on medical or religious grounds.[10] A number of cases have held that such statutes are constitutional where they excuse persons on the ground of religious ob-

§ 9.3

1. Matter of Hofbauer, 47 N.Y.2d 648, 419 N.Y.S.2d 936, 393 N.E.2d 1009 (1979).

2. W. Prosser and W. Keeton, Torts 159 (5th ed. 1984).

3. E.g., Colo.Rev.Stat. § 13–22–103 (Supp.1985) (minor fifteen years or older living apart from his parents may consent); Ill.–S.H.A. ch. 111, § 4503 (Supp.1986) (minor may be given emergency treatment); Or.Rev.Stat. § 109.640 (1985) (minor may be given birth control information; minor fifteen years or older may consent to treatment).

See also Wilkins, Children's Rights; Removing the Parental Consent Barrier to Medical Treatment of Minors, 1975 Ariz.St.L.J. 31; Note, Consent to the Medical Treatment of a Minor Under the Family Code, 27 Baylor L.Rev. 319 (1975); Note, Minors' Rights to Medical Care, 14 J.Fam.L. 581 (1976).

4. E.g., Miss.Code 1985, § 41:41–3(g), (h) (Supp.); cases cited supra, § 8.1 at note 29.

5. 2 J.Story, Equity §§ 1328 to 1337 (13th ed. 1886) states that the chancery authority to protect infants was an outgrowth of the Crown's parens patriae power to protect all persons unable to care for themselves, and indicates that the authority was of long standing in the English practice. But see 1 Coke on Littleton 88b, Harg. note 16 (16th ed. 1853) and Smith v. Smith, 3 Atk. 304, 26 Eng.Rep. 977 (1745).

6. Jehovah's Witnesses in the State of Wash. v. King County Hospital Unit No. 1, 278 F.Supp. 488 (W.D.Wash. 1967), affirmed 390 U.S. 598, 88 S.Ct. 1260, 20 L.Ed.2d 158 (1968).

7. Cf. Goldstein, Medical Care for the Child at Risk: On State Supervention of Parental Autonomy, 86 Yale L.J. 645, 650 (1977).

8. Statutes are collected in Bennett, Allocation of Child Medical Care Decision-Making Authority: A Suggested Interest Analysis, 62 Va.L.Rev. 285, 294–299 (1976).

9. Id. at 301.

10. Id. at 297.

jection to the procedures,[11] and also where they contain no such exemptions.[12] And where they excuse those having religious objections, it is not unconstitutional to require the immunization of those having philosophical objections.[13]

More difficult issues arise when the state seeks to persuade a court to authorize medical or surgical treatment for an individual child whose parents have refused to consent to such treatment, often on religious grounds. The legal procedure employed in such cases usually consists of a petition by state child welfare officials alleging that the child is dependent or neglected by reason of being denied necessary medical care, and asking for the appoint-

ment of a temporary guardian with authority to consent to the treatment.[14]

If the treatment which the state seeks involves little or no risk to the child, and if the failure to provide it would substantially endanger the child's life or health, the courts will order the operation to be performed. The best example is the case in which a blood transfusion was required to save the life of a new-born child, the parent, a Jehovah's Witness, refusing to consent for religious reasons based upon certain Biblical language. The Illinois Supreme Court ordered the operation to be performed, holding such an order to be within the state's power to protect its children from neglect as defined in the dependency statute.[15] This case and others like it are

---

11. Jacobson v. Massachusetts, 197 U.S. 11, 25 S.Ct. 358, 49 L.Ed. 643 (1905). Many cases are cited in Annot., 93 A.L.R. 1413 (1934). Avard v. Dupuis, 376 F.Supp. 479 (D.N.H.1974) takes the very dubious position that a statute which authorized the school board to exempt a child from immunization for "religious reasons" is unconstitutionally vague.

12. Brown v. Stone, 378 So.2d 218 (Miss.1979), cert. denied 449 U.S. 887, 101 S.Ct. 242, 66 L.Ed.2d 112 (1980), citing many other cases; Board of Education of Mountain Lakes v. Maas, 56 N.J.Super. 245, 152 A.2d 394 (1959), affirmed per curiam 31 N.J. 537, 158 A.2d 330 (1960), cert. denied 363 U.S. 843, 80 S.Ct. 1613, 4 L.Ed.2d 1727 (1960).

13. Syska v. Montgomery County Board of Education, 45 Md.App. 626, 415 A.2d 301 (1980), dismissed for want of a substantial federal question, 450 U.S. 961, 101 S.Ct. 1475, 67 L.Ed.2d 610 (1981); In re Elwell, 55 Misc.2d 252, 284 N.Y.S.2d 924 (Fam.Ct.1967).

14. E.g., In re Green, 448 Pa. 338, 292 A.2d 387 (1972), appeal after remand 452 Pa. 373, 307 A.2d 279 (1973).

15. People ex rel. Wallace v. Labrenz, 411 Ill. 618, 104 N.E.2d 769 (1952), cert. denied 344 U.S. 824, 73 S.Ct. 24, 97 L.Ed. 642 (1952), 47 Nw.U.L.Rev. 541 (1952). Accord: In Interest of Ivey, 319 So.2d 53 (Fla.App.1975); Morrison v. State, 252 S.W.2d 97 (Mo.App.1952); Raleigh Fitkin-Paul Morgan Mem. Hosp. and Ann May Memorial Foundation in Town of Neptune v. Anderson, 42 N.J. 421, 201 A.2d 537 (1964), cert. denied 377 U.S. 985, 84 S.Ct. 1894, 12 L.Ed.2d 1032 (1964); State v. Perricone, 37 N.J. 463, 181 A.2d 751 (1962), cert. denied 371 U.S. 890, 83 S.Ct. 189, 9 L.Ed.2d 124 (1962); Matter of Storar, 52 N.Y.2d 363, 438 N.Y.S.2d 266, 420 N.E.2d 64 (1981), cert. denied 454 U.S. 858, 102 S.Ct. 309, 70 L.Ed.2d 153 (1981) (dictum) Hoener v. Bertinato, 67 N.J.Super. 517, 171 A.2d 140 (Juv.Ct.1961); But see Or.Rev.Stat. § 419.500 (1981).

In In re Sampson, 65 Misc.2d 658, 317 N.Y.S.2d 641 (Fam.Ct.1970), affirmed 37 A.D.2d 668, 323 N.Y.S.2d 253 (3d Dep't 1971), affirmed 29 N.Y.2d 900, 328 N.Y.S.2d 686, 278 N.E.2d 918 (1972) the child's mother consented to a risky operation to correct a disfiguring facial condi-

tion of the child, but she refused to consent to possible blood transfusions incident to the surgery. The court held that the transfusions would be ordered, thereby making the surgery medically possible, although not without risk. Presumably if the child's mother had consented to blood transfusions, the physicians would have gone ahead with the operation without seeking judicial approval. Thus although the court treated the case as one for approval of the whole surgical procedure, the effect of the court's decision was only to reduce the risk and make the procedure safe enough to be undertaken.

See also Jehovah's Witnesses in the State of Wash. v. King County Hospital Unit No. 1, 278 F.Supp. 488 (W.D. Wash.1967), affirmed 390 U.S. 598, 88 S.Ct. 1260, 20 L.Ed. 2d 158 (1968), which refused to enjoin the giving of blood transfusions to Jehovah's Witnesses, holding that the state statutes which empowered judges to order such transfusions for children needing them were not unconstitutional since transfusions were both safe and necessary in many kinds of cases.

Custody of a Minor, 375 Mass. 733, 379 N.E.2d 1053 (1978) ordered chemotherapy for a child suffering from leukemia, where that was necessary to save his life and where the parents had refused to have the child treated. See also Application Cicero, 101 Misc.2d 699, 421 N.Y.S.2d 965 (1979), in which a spinal operation on a newborn child was authorized by the court over the religiously based objection of the parents, where the spinal disorder created serious risk of infection, paralysis and death.

In Matter of Appeal in Cochise County, Juvenile Action No. 5666-J, 133 Ariz. 157, 650 P.2d 459 (1982) the court held that the state had failed to prove dependency when the evidence showed that one of eight children had died for want of medical attention, and the children's mother said that she would not seek medical help for any of the other seven children if they should become ill, since her religious belief was that miracles would protect her children. The state was seeking to have custody of the seven children awarded to the state Department of Eco-

certainly correct in refusing to permit a child to die or suffer a serious impairment of health solely to vindicate the parents' religious beliefs, no matter how firmly or sincerely held. In fact if state intervention did not occur and the child was seriously harmed or died, the parents might properly be held criminally responsible.[16] One case has applied the principle of the transfusion cases to an unborn child, ordering the mother to submit to a caesarean delivery where the medical testimony was that a normal delivery would almost certainly result in the death of the child and would also involve a high risk of death for the mother.[17] The mother's objection to the operation was based upon religious beliefs, but it would seem that the result should be the same where her objection was based upon a fear of the surgery.

Courts are, not surprisingly, more reluctant to order medical treatment for children over the objections of their parents when the proposed treatment involves substantial risk or suffering and when the condition being treated does not threaten a comparatively greater probability of harm to life or health. Although it has been argued that the principle of parental autonomy should be so construed as to bar state intervention in cases where denial of the treatment would not result in death,[18] the courts reject such an absolute approach and attempt to deal with the merits of the cases, weighing the risks and the benefits of treatment against the risks and consequences of denying treatment. In doing so, they take into account the feelings of the child himself and the possible consequences of postponing the treatment to a time when the child would be mature enough to decide for himself whether to undertake it.[19] Reported cases of this kind are not numerous, but the opinions exhibit great restraint in authorizing surgery which inflicts substantial risk and suffering on the child.

Some examples include In re Hudson,[20] in which the court refused to order the amputation of a child's deformed arm where the medical testimony was that the operation was dangerous but necessary to improve the child's health and enable her to lead a more normal life; In re Seiferth [21], in which the court left the decision to the fourteen-year-old boy whether to undergo an operation for harelip and cleft palate, an operation which was not dangerous but desirable to enable him to lead a useful life, but which required his cooperation in subsequent speech therapy for full benefits; In re Green,[22] in which the court refused to order an operation for curvature of the spine on a seven-year-old boy when the operation may have been dangerous but would have been beneficial in increasing the boy's range of activity, leaving the decision to the boy himself. The Green case mistakenly relied upon Wisconsin v. Yoder,[23] although that case involves entirely different interests and considerations. Green is also unusual in that the child's mother did not object to the operation, but for religious reasons would not consent to any blood transfusion which might become necessary.[24] The court gave some

---

nomic Security but was not seeking a final termination of parental rights.

16. See Trescher and O'Neil, Medical Care for Dependent Children: Manslaughter Liability of the Christian Scientist, 109 U.Pa.L.Rev. 203 (1960).

17. Jefferson v. Griffin Spalding County Hospital Authority, 247 Ga. 86, 274 S.E.2d 457 (1981).

18. J. Goldstein, A. Freud, A. Solnit, Before the Best Interests of the Child ch. 6 (1979).

19. This factor seems to have been present in In re Seiferth, 309 N.Y. 80, 127 N.E.2d 820 (1955), 16 Ohio St. L.J. 629 (1955).

20. 13 Wash.2d 673, 126 P.2d 765 (1942). See also Annot., 30 A.L.R.2d 1138 (1953).

21. In re Seiferth, supra, note 19. See also In re Karwath, 199 N.W.2d 147 (Iowa 1972), in which a court

ordered the surgical removal of children's tonsils and adenoids over the objection of their father. His objection was based upon unspecified religious reasons, and also upon a preference for chiropractic treatment. Here the children were already in state custody, and the court found the surgery necessary for their welfare, even though no immediate threat to their lives was involved. Matter of Jensen, 54 Or.App. 1, 633 P.2d 1302 (1981), review denied 291 Or. 662, 639 P.2d 1280 (1981) authorized surgery for hydrocephalus over a parent's religious objection.

22. 448 Pa. 338, 292 A.2d 387 (1972), appeal after remand 452 Pa. 373, 307 A.2d 279 (1973).

23. 406 U.S. 205, 92 S.Ct. 1526, 32 L.Ed.2d 15 (1972), discussed supra, section 10.2 at note 23.

24. In this respect the case resembles In re Sampson, supra, note 15.

weight to the fact that her objection was based on religious grounds.

Most of the cases cited rightly hold that the religious basis of the parent's objection to medical treatment does not, of itself, warrant refusing to order the treatment if the court finds that on balance the welfare of the child will be served by ordering it.[25] The parent's objection in such cases has little to do with the child's welfare. Where religion is not the basis for the parent's refusal, that refusal may be closely related to the child's welfare. A good example is In re Phillip B.[26] The child in this case was afflicted both with Down's Syndrome producing mental retardation and with a congenital heart defect. His retardation led his parents to place him in an institution. The heart defect, it was testified, would lead to lung damage, progressive incapacity and death at an early age. The parents refused to consent to heart surgery apparently on the ground that it was better to let him die by age thirty than to perform an operation whose effect, if successful, would be to condemn him to further years of suffering in institutions for the mentally retarded.[27] The trial court refused to order the operation and the appellate court affirmed, without explicitly dealing with the basis for the parental objection, basing its decision on the fact that the operation would involve more than the usual risks for a Down's syndrome child, and upon the legal principle that in such cases the parent's decision may only be overriden by the courts where there is clear and convincing evidence that the child's welfare would there-

by be promoted. The parents' reason for refusing their consent to the surgery raised a question like that in the "wrongful birth" cases, that is, whether life with serious handicaps is to be preferred to no life at all.[28] Since this is a question which the law is not equipped to answer, the court was right to leave it to the parents, at least where their decision was not clearly prejudicial to the child's interests.

It does seem, however, that the courts should be willing to order treatment for illnesses or physical conditions which are not life-threatening where the treatment likewise creates no risk to life or health. A child should not be required to endure such conditions if in the opinion of competent physicians they can be corrected without risk of harm or suffering to the child, solely because the parents have religiously based scruples about medical or surgical care.

Considerable leeway for parental decision has been extended by the courts where the question is not whether any treatment for a child is to be provided but rather what kind of treatment should be given. Matter of Hofbauer,[29] the laetrile case, denied the state's petition to have a child suffering from Hodgkin's disease treated with chemotherapy and radiation after the parents chose to employ nutritional or metabolic therapy, including injections of laetrile. There was medical testimony in favor of the latter kinds of treatment, and the parents had not entirely ruled out the possibility of more conventional ther-

---

25. Where a statute excludes from the definition of dependency or neglect the denial of medical treatment for religious reasons, the religious basis for the parent's refusal to provide treatment may lead the court to refuse to order it. People in the Interest of D.L.E., 200 Colo. 244, 614 P.2d 873 (1980) so held, although the court advanced the risk of adverse side effects from the treatment as an additional ground for refusal. The court intimated that the result might be different if the child's life were in danger. But a subsequent appeal in this same case held that where the failure to provide medical treatment, in this instance failure to administer medication to control epileptic seizures, endangered the child's life, the child could be found dependent and neglected notwithstanding the very ill drawn statute which provided that no child who is under treatment solely by spiritual means shall for that reason alone be considered to have been neglected. People in Interest of D.L.E., 645

P.2d 271 (Colo.1982). See also Matter of Jensen, 54 Or. App. 1, 633 P.2d 1302 (1981), review denied 291 Or. 662, 639 P.2d 1280 (1981), and Matter of Hamilton, 657 S.W.2d 425 (Tenn.App.1983).

26. In re Phillip B., 92 Cal.App.3d 796, 156 Cal.Rptr. 48 (1979), cert. denied 445 U.S. 949, 100 S.Ct. 1597, 63 L.Ed.2d 784 (1980). But see Guardianship of Phillip B., 139 Cal.App.3d 407, 188 Cal.Rptr. 781 (1983), approving heart catheterization of the child at the instigation of his "de facto" parents, and revealing the facts of the earlier hearing in a somewhat different aspect.

27. New York Times, Nov. 26, 1978, page 38, col. 1.

28. The cases are discussed in section 5.4, supra.

29. 47 N.Y.2d 648, 419 N.Y.S.2d 936, 393 N.E.2d 1009 (1979).

apy. The court adopted a standard of the "ordinarily prudent and loving parent, 'solicitous for the welfare of his child and anxious to promote [the child's] recovery'"[30] and found that the parents' choice in this case met that standard.

The child's own wishes may assume greater importance in some types of cases than in the usual one where his parent is failing or refusing to provide treatment.[31] For example, one case has held that a child may not be required against her will to have an abortion at the demand of a parent, even though abortion is generally safer than childbirth and even though the birth of the baby may entail increased support obligations, either morally or legally, upon the parent.[32] The child's wishes may also have a crucial impact on the organ transplant cases. In those cases the surgery does not physically benefit the organ donor, who is often a sibling of the donee. When the donor is a child, he may consent to the operation, and the courts have usually then authorized it on the ground that there is a psychological benefit to the donor in preserving the life of his sibling.[33] It has been suggested that the critical question for the courts is whether the donor would consent if he were competent,[34] but basing the authorization upon a benefit to the donor, if such a benefit really exists, seems preferable.

The most troublesome questions regarding the medical and surgical care of children are raised when the child, usually a newborn child, suffers from such serious birth defects that he is likely not to survive beyond a few

months or a year, or, if he does survive, that his capacity for normal mental and physical activity will be drastically curtailed.[35] As has already been described in this section, a child's parents usually have the obligation to provide medical and surgical care for him when such care is necessary. The law on the books makes no exception for the child with serious birth defects, so that the parent who refuses to authorize the procedures for treating the defects, as well as the physician who participates in the withholding of treatment is, theoretically at least, risking criminal and civil sanctions.[36] Nevertheless, it is now recognized that in some instances parents and physicians do withhold extraordinary medical and surgical procedures where those procedures would not be likely to produce a lasting improvement in the child's condition.[37]

In the past these infants would not have lived long past birth because medical treatment for the preservation of their lives was not available. Today, however, medical and surgical procedures are known which can correct the defects to the extent of prolonging life in some cases but which generally cannot appreciably improve the quality of that life. In this way science has presented us with dauntingly difficult ethical and ultimately legal questions: In these cases should medical care be withheld? If there are cases in which the withholding of medical care is proper, who should make these decisions, and on the basis of what standards? Similar questions have arisen regarding terminally ill adults who are not competent to decide whether

---

30. 47 N.Y.2d at 655, 419 N.Y.S.2d at 940, 393 N.E.2d at 1013. The New York court qualified this statement at the same point in its opinion by saying that great deference must be given the parent's decision as to the kind of treatment and the physician chosen to care for the child.

31. See In re Seiferth, supra, note 21, where the child's cooperation in the operation was an important factor in the court's decision not to order it.

32. In re Smith, 16 Md.App. 209, 295 A.2d 238 (1972), 7 Suff.U.L.Rev. 1157 (1973).

33. Hart v. Brown, 29 Conn.Supp. 368, 289 A.2d 386 (1972); Strunk v. Strunk, 445 S.W.2d 145 (Ky.1969); Little v. Little, 576 S.W.2d 493 (Tex.Civ.App.1979).

34. Robertson, Organ Donations by Incompetents and the Substituted Judgment Doctrine, 76 Colum.L.Rev. 48 (1976).

35. Many such defects of the central nervous system are described in Robertson, Involuntary Euthanasia of Defective Newborns: A Legal Analysis, 27 Stan.L.Rev. 213, footnotes 2 through 8 (1975).

36. The sanctions are discussed in detail in Robertson, Involuntary Euthanasia of Defective Newborns: A Legal Analysis, 27 Stan.L.Rev. 213 (1975).

37. Duff and Campbell, Moral and Ethical Dilemmas in the Special-Care Nursery, 289 New England J. of Medicine 890 (1973); Legislative History of the Child Abuse Amendments of 1984, P.L. 98–457, 98 Stat. 1749, 4 U.S.Cong. and Admin.News 2918, 98th Cong., 2d Sess. (1984).

extraordinary measures for prolonging life without the prospect of a cure should be continued.[38] In a highly publicized case the New Jersey Supreme Court authorized the removal of life support systems from an unconscious adult woman at the request of her parents, on the basis of medical evidence that no treatment could improve her condition and that she could not live very long after the support systems were removed.[39] The court required that the decision be concurred in by the parents, the physicians and an ethics committee of the hospital. In fact she lived for almost ten years after the removal of support systems without recovering consciousness.[40]

Notwithstanding the extensive publicity given to some of the cases in which treatment for newborns has been withheld, the existing legal sanctions are seldom invoked.[41] When the cases do come to court, it is usually in the context of a proceeding to seek court approval for the action or nonaction which the parents and perhaps the physicians wish to adopt. One must conclude from this that the state officials responsible for civil or criminal proceedings recognize that the parents' decision to withhold treatment is morally justified in some circumstances, a recognition which is shared by at least some commentators.[42] If the treatment involves intrusive, painful or very uncomfortable procedures for the child without countervailing benefits, or substantial risk of death or a further impairment of physical or mental capacity, the parental refusal to authorize it seems justified.[43] This is

the same sort of consideration which is relevant to any decision respecting medical care for the child.[44] In the cases of defective newborns it is also sometimes asserted that the psychological, physical and financial burdens imposed on the parents and siblings of the infant by the demands of extraordinary and possibly long-term care outweigh the benefits to the infant of a possibly longer but seriously handicapped existence. Although one can sympathize with the feelings of parents when confronted with the difficulties of caring for a seriously handicapped infant, surely it is the infant's interests which should determine whether treatment is withheld in a particular case.[45] But even where his interests alone are considered, they raise the question whether an existence which is drastically limited in time or quality or both is to be preferred to an early death.

Handicapped children have made the converse argument in "wrongful birth" suits against physicians, claiming that the physician's negligence in failing to foresee or warn against birth defects caused the child suffering which could have been prevented by an abortion. The courts have generally refused relief in such cases,[46] sensibly concluding that there are no standards by which a court can decide whether nonexistence is preferable to a short and painful life. The same restraint should be exercised by legal institutions where treatment is proposed to be withheld from infants. Although circumstances can be imagined in which treatment clearly should

---

38. Childress, Refusal of Lifesaving Treatment by Adults, 23 J.Fam.L. 191 (1984); Capron, Borrowed Lessons: The Role of Ethical Distinctions in Framing Law on Life-Sustaining Treatment, 1984 Ariz.St.L.J. 647. See Superintendent of Belchertown State School v. Saikewicz, 373 Mass. 728, 370 N.E.2d 417 (1977).

39. Matter of Quinlan, 70 N.J. 10, 355 A.2d 647 (1976), cert. denied 429 U.S. 922, 97 S.Ct. 319, 50 L.Ed.2d 289 (1976). See also Matter of Conroy, 98 N.J. 321, 486 A.2d 1209 (1985).

40. Karen Ann Quinlan died on June 11, 1985. New York Times, June 12, 1985, p. 1, col. 2.

41. Mnookin, Two Puzzles, 1984 Ariz.St.L.J. 667, 668–671.

42. Goldstein, Not for the Law to Approve or Disapprove—A Comment on Professor Mnookin's Paper, 1984 Ariz.St.L.J. 685.

43. E.g., Custody of a Minor, 385 Mass. 697, 434 N.E.2d 601 (1982).

44. See the discussion in this section supra, at note 18.

45. Fost, Baby Doe and Solutions, 1984 Ariz.St.L.J. 637; Annas, Refusal of Lifesaving Treatment for Minors, 23 J.Fam.L. 217 (1984).

46. These cases are discussed in section 5.4, supra. Contra the text, Procanik by Procanik v. Cillo, 97 N.J. 339, 478 A.2d 755 (1984), on remand 206 N.J.Super. 270, 502 A.2d 94 (1985).

not be withheld,[47] in most of the cases the parents' decision is only reached after sincerely and painfully weighing the possible courses of action and their consequences.[48] In this situation it is as impossible to make a general rule that any life is better than death as it is to adopt a rule in the wrongful birth cases that death is better than life.

In some cases most people would agree that it is preferable to withhold the treatment. It is not possible to define those cases in general terms. The crucial issue therefore is, who should decide? Since the parents best know all the relevant facts and have the greatest psychological stake in the outcome, they should decide most cases. No court or state official and certainly no legislature is able to experience the moral dilemma the parents face in these cases with the profound concern which informs the parents' decision. These considerations dictate that the parental decision should be respected except in those cases in which the treatment promises a better and longer life for the infant.

For the most part the cases in the state courts, which have arisen when a physician seeks judicial authority for withholding treatment in order to protect himself from later legal sanctions, have taken the kind of restrained approach advocated here.[49] Undoubtedly more cases have been decided by parents and physicians without court intervention which also evidences a proper acceptance of the parents as the primary source of decision respecting the treatment of their child. Although the decision is essentially an ethical rather than a medical one, it should be made in reliance upon the best available medical advice.

The law on this issue has been complicated by the injection of federal administrative regulations into what had formerly been an exclusively state law province. A federal statute prohibits hospitals or health care programs receiving federal financial assistance from discriminating against the handicapped.[50] In response to the widely publicized "Baby Doe" and "Baby Jane Doe" cases,[51] the Secretary of Health and Human Services has promulgated regulations pursuant to this statute purporting to govern hospitals receiving federal aid with respect to the medical treat-

---

47. In re Phillip B., 92 Cal.App.3d 796, 156 Cal.Rptr. 48 (1979), cert. denied 445 U.S. 949, 100 S.Ct. 1597, 63 L.Ed.2d 784 (1980), may have been such a case. See the later case concerning the same child, Guardianship of Phillip B., 139 Cal.App.3d 407, 188 Cal.Rptr. 781 (1983).

48. This was true of the parents of Phillip B., whose decision was litigated in the case cited in note 47, supra. See New York Times, Nov. 26, 1978, p. 38, col. 1.

49. In re Phillip B., 92 Cal.App.3d 796, 156 Cal.Rptr. 48 (1979), cert. denied 445 U.S. 949, 100 S.Ct. 1597, 63 L.Ed.2d 784 (1980); In re Guardianship of Barry, 445 So. 2d 365 (Fla.App.1984); In re L.H.R., 253 Ga. 439, 321 S.E. 2d 716 (1984); In re P.V.W., 424 So.2d 1015 (La.1982); Custody of a Minor, 385 Mass. 697, 434 N.E.2d 601 (1982). Application of Cicero, 101 Misc.2d 699, 421 N.Y.S.2d 965 (1979), ordered the operation but emphasized the importance of the family in decisions of this kind. Some unreported lower court cases are cited in Mnookin, Two Puzzles, 1984 Ariz.St.L.J. 667, 670.

50. Rehabilitation Act of 1973, § 504, 29 U.S.C.A. § 794.

51. The "Baby Doe" case in 1982 involved a Down's Syndrome baby who also had a separation between the esophagus and the stomach, and a blockage of the esophagus, so that surgery was required in order to permit him to be fed by mouth. The parents refused to permit the operation and the baby died. Mathieu, The Baby Doe Controversy, 1984 Ariz.St.L.J. 605. The "Baby Jane Doe" case arose in New York. The baby was born in 1983 with multiple birth defects, including spina bifida, microcephaly, hydrocephalus, a malformed brain stem, upper extremity spasticity, a thumb entirely within her fist, and a "weak face" which prevented her from closing her eyes or making a full suck with her tongue. Her rectal, bladder and sensory functions were impaired. Due to her brain defects there was an extremely high risk that she would be so greatly retarded as to be unable to interact either with other people or with her environment. Her physicians recommended surgical procedures which could increase her life expectancy from six weeks to twenty years, but she would remain severely retarded, epileptic, paralyzed, bedridden and subject to constant urinary tract infections. After consultations the parents refused to consent to the surgery, choosing conservative procedures instead. Annas, The Case of Baby Jane Doe: Child Abuse or Unlawful Federal Intervention? 74 Am.J.Pub. H. 727 (1984); Mathieu, The Baby Doe Controversy, 1984 Ariz.St.L.J. 605, 615. A man from Vermont unrelated to Baby Jane Doe brought suit in New York to require that surgery be done on the infant. Weber v. Stony Brook Hospital, 60 N.Y.2d 208, 469 N.Y.S.2d 63, 456 N.E.2d 1186 (1983), cert. denied 464 U.S. 1026, 104 S.Ct. 560, 78 L.Ed.2d 732 (1983), held that under the applicable state statutes the plaintiff had no standing to bring the suit and that the statutory scheme for the protection of children had not been followed in the case.

ment of infants.[52] These regulations "encourage" hospitals to set up Infant Care Review Committees. The functions of such Committees are a) to develop standards for the treatment of handicapped infants such that treatment will not be withheld solely on the basis of medical or physical impairment, and b) to make decisions "concerning medically beneficial treatment in specific cases." [53] The Committees are required to include a physician, a nurse, a hospital administrator, a lawyer, a representative of a "disability group," a lay community member, and a member of the hospital's organized medical staff as chairman.[54] The regulations specify in detail the action the Committee is authorized to take in the event of disagreement concerning treatment between the child's family, the attending physicians, and the Committee itself, including in certain circumstances the referral of the case to an appropriate court.[55] Substantive provisions in the regulations respecting the withholding of treatment are contained in a notice which the hospital must post, and in a statement of principles adopted by various medical groups.[56] The notice states that it is the hospital's policy, consistent with federal law, that nourishment and medically beneficial treatment (as determined with respect for reasonable medical judgments) should not be withheld from handicapped infants solely on the basis of their present or anticipated mental or physical impairments.

A second federal statute [57] which authorizes grants to the states for the prevention and treatment of child abuse and neglect now includes a provision that in order to qualify for federal assistance the state must have in place procedures for reporting suspected instances of withholding medically indicated treatment from disabled infants with life-threatening conditions and for pursuing legal remedies to prevent the withholding of such treatment. The term "withholding of medically indicated treatment" is defined in unclear language.[58]

Although one may have doubts about the informal and private way in which physicians and parents have decided on the amount and quality of treatment appropriate for defective infants in the past, placing primary responsibility for treatment in the hands of the parents still seems the best of the various alternatives. The parents' traditional right to decide on the proper medical treatment for their child should be respected here just as it is where the parents' judgment concerns other kinds of medical treatment for their child. Where the parental decision is brought before a court, the court should also respect the parents' decision except in the rare case where one can say that the decision is clearly wrong. Unfortunately that degree of respect for the parents' judgment may no longer be possible, due to the intrusion of federal rules and their related publicity into the operation of hospitals. Of all the ways of dealing with these questions, the federal solution of a committee is certainly the worst. It interferes with the parents' traditional authority which should be exercised in decent privacy, and it replaces that authority with the diffused judgment of a group of people who have no emo-

---

52. 45 C.F.R. § 84.55; 49 Fed.Reg. 1622–1654. Earlier regulations on the same subject were held invalid on various grounds by American Academy of Pediatrics v. Heckler, 561 F.Supp. 395 (D.D.C.1983), and United States v. University Hospital of New York at Stony Brook, 729 F.2d 144 (2d Cir.1984). The present regulations have been held invalid as being unsupported by the authority of the statute in American Hospital Association v. Heckler, 585 F.Supp. 541 (S.D.N.Y.1984), affirmed __ U.S. __, 106 S.Ct. 2102, 90 L.Ed.2d 584 (1986). See also Mathieu, The Baby Doe Controversy, 1984 Ariz.St.L.J. 605, 606–619; Annas, Refusal of Lifesaving Treatment for Minors, 23 J.Fam.L. 217, 224–233 (1984).

See also Ariz.Rev.Stat. §§ 13–3620, 36–2281 to 36–2284 (Supp.1986), and Mathieu, The Baby Doe Controversy, 1984 Ariz.St.L.J. 605, 619–624.

53. 45 C.F.R. § 84.55(f).

54. 45 C.F.R. § 84.55(f)(2).

55. 45 C.F.R. § 84.55(f)(3)(ii).

56. 45 C.F.R. § 84.55(b), (f)(1)(ii). This section of the regulations and 45 C.F.R. § 84.55(c), (d) and (e) were held invalid as not being authorized by the anti-discrimination provisions of the Rehabilitation Act of 1973 § 504, 29 U.S.C.A. § 794, in Bowen v. American Hospital Association, __ U.S. __, 106 S.Ct. 2101, 90 L.Ed.2d 584 (1986).

57. 42 U.S.C.A. § 5103(b)(2)(K).

58. 42 U.S.C.A. § 5102(2)(B)(3).

tional stake in the decision, and many of whom will have no competence in deciding such sensitive questions. The use of a committee may bring delay and procedural complication into the situation. Worst of all, the committee, unlike a court, is not responsible to anyone for its decisions, need not state why it acted as it did, and is controlled by no set of standards or principles. A careful reading of the federal regulations makes it apparent that their major purpose is the elimination or minimization of the parents' ability to withhold treatment by this unwise reliance on the institution of a committee.

The parent has both a right and a duty to provide psychiatric care for his child for the same reasons that he has a right and a duty to provide medical or surgical care.[59] He may normally arrange for psychiatric care, including institutional care, without seeking state permission.[60] And if he fails to provide proper care where clear and convincing evidence shows that the child needs it, the state may bring a proceeding as result of which the courts may order the psychiatric treatment to be provided.[61] The state should observe greater caution in overriding parental decisions where psychiatric rather than medical or surgical treatment is proposed, since the former involves greater uncertainties of both diagnosis and prognosis than the latter. In such cases deference to parental judgment and proof by clear and convincing evidence are appropriate.

The extent and even the existence of parental authority over psychiatric treatment for children, although apparently accepted by the courts, is the subject of vehement disagreement among commentators. Dr. Szasz views treatment in psychiatric hospitals as a form of involuntary confinement as to which children should have all the constitutional protections available to adults against involuntary confinement.[62] On the other hand, Professor Goldstein and Drs. Freud and Solnit seemingly would not permit any interference with the parent's decision on such matters except perhaps where the child's life is endangered.[63]

This disagreement is reflected in lawsuits which have been brought on behalf of children to assert claims that their liberty has been infringed in violation of the constitution when they have been hospitalized for mental illness, either by their parents or by the state. It is obvious that commitment to a psychiatric hospital, whether by the state or the parent, may result from erroneous diagnosis, from a mistaken expert opinion about its desirability in the circumstances, or, in the parent's case, from a parent's selfish wish to rid himself of the burden of caring for a difficult child. These risks and the physical and psychological harms which may often result from commitment to mental institutions have been graphically described by Justice Brennan in his dissent to the Parham case.[64] The California Supreme Court has responded to these dangers by holding that before a minor fourteen years of age or older may be committed

---

59. See the foregoing discussion at notes 1 to 24, supra. For a general account of child mental health, see Report of the Joint Commission on Mental Health of Children, Crisis in Child Mental Health: Challenge for the 1970's (1969, 1970).

60. In re Roger S., 19 Cal.3d 921, 141 Cal.Rptr. 298, 569 P.2d 1286 (1977); In re John S., 66 Cal.App.3d 343, 135 Cal.Rptr. 893 (1977); Note, The Mental Hospitalization of Children and the Limits of Parental Authority, 88 Yale L.J. 186 (1978), collecting statutes. In re CFB, 497 S.W.2d 831 (Mo.App.1973) upheld the parent's choice of psychiatric care when the state authorities sought to impose a different kind of care. Guardianship of a Minor, 11 Mass.App.Ct. 1027, 419 N.E.2d 1075 (1981) seems to approve hospitalization of a minor child for psychiatric reasons by action of his mother and a co-guardian. Compare Guardianship of Roe, 383 Mass. 415, 421 N.E.2d 40 (1981), in which the court held that the parents and guardians had no power by virtue of that relationship to

consent to the forcible administration of drugs to their adult psychotic son, saying that this could only be done after authorization by a court.

61. Bjerke v. D.T. and W.T., 248 N.W.2d 808 (N.D. 1976).

62. Szasz, The Child as Involuntary Mental Patient: The Threat of Child Therapy to the Child's Dignity, Privacy and Self-Esteem, 14 San Diego L.Rev. 1005 (1977).

63. J. Goldstein, A. Freud, A. Solnit, Before the Best Interests of the Child (1979), as interpreted by Watson, Children, Families and Courts: Before the Best Interests of the Child and Parham v. J.R., 66 Va.L.Rev. 653 (1980).

64. Parham v. J.R., 442 U.S. 584, 625, 99 S.Ct. 2493, 2515, 61 L.Ed.2d 101 (1979). See also Note, The Mental Hospitalization of Children and the Limits of Parental Authority, 88 Yale L.J. 186 (1978).

by his parent to a state-run mental institution, he is entitled under the Due Process Clauses of the state and federal constitutions to a pre-commitment administrative hearing before a neutral fact-finder.[65] This means, the court said, that the child must have counsel, the right to present evidence and cross-examine witnesses, adequate written notice of the basis for the commitment, and findings based on a preponderance of the evidence. The court expressly refrained from deciding what due process might require for children under fourteen.

The federal constitutional requirements for the commitment of children to state psychiatric hospitals have been established by Parham v. J.R.,[66] thereby superseding Roger S. so far as that case relied upon the United States Constitution but not affecting its authority as to the effect of the California Constitution except perhaps indirectly. The United States Supreme Court's position in Parham v. J.R. was that the Due Process Clause requires only an independent medical decision-making procedure, to be conducted after a thorough psychiatric investigation, for admission of children to state mental hospitals. The Court also held that there should be periodic review by the hospital staff of a child's status to warrant the child's retention in the hospital, where the child was in the legal custody of his parents. Where the child

was a ward of the state, the Court indicated that more formal procedures might be required for his continued hospitalization and remanded for findings on this point. The Court refused to require a formal, trial-type, adversary hearing as a condition on the child's admission to or retention in the hospital.

As in some other cases, the Court analyzed this issue in terms of the costs and the benefits to the parents, the child and the state. It found the costs involved in more formal procedural requirements high, both in money and time, and in diverting hospital personnel from the more important function of providing therapy. It emphasized the parent's role in child care and the fact that neither the courts nor other state agencies are well equipped to review parental decisions concerning the child's mental health. The result of this case has been heavily criticized as being inconsistent with such other decisions as Bellotti v. Baird,[67] Application Gault,[68] and Addington v. Texas,[69] and as failing to protect the child's interests in a situation where those interests would often conflict with those of the parent and therefore would not receive parental protection.[70] The case does lend some support to traditional parental authority respecting child care decisions but in such qualified terms, and in such a narrowly defined context that it may have only a limited effect.

---

65. In re Roger S., 19 Cal.3d 835, 141 Cal.Rptr. 298, 569 P.2d 1286 (1977), 66 Cal.L.Rev. 344 (1978). See also Bartley v. Kremens, 402 F.Supp. 1039 (E.D.Pa.1975), reversed and remanded sub nom. Secretary of Public Welfare v. Institutionalized Juveniles, 442 U.S. 640, 99 S.Ct. 2523, 61 L.Ed.2d 142 (1979).

66. 442 U.S. 584, 99 S.Ct. 2493, 61 L.Ed.2d 101 (1979).

In P.F. v. Walsh, 648 P.2d 1067 (Colo.1982) the Colorado Supreme Court held that the Colorado statutory scheme for the admission of minors to state psychiatric hospitals did not meet the requirements of the Due Process Clause as set out in Parham because, unlike the Georgia statute in Parham, the Colorado statute contained no standard for application by the hospitals in determining whether to accept a minor for treatment.

The extent of deference which must be given to parental decisions about psychiatric care for children is discussed in Halderman, by Halderman v. Pennhurst State School & Hosp., 707 F.2d 702 (3d Cir.1983).

67. 443 U.S. 622, 99 S.Ct. 3035, 61 L.Ed.2d 797 (1979), rehearing denied 444 U.S. 887, 100 S.Ct. 185, 62 L.Ed.2d

121 (1979). This case invalidated a Massachusetts statute requiring parental consultation before a minor could obtain an abortion. See also Planned Parenthood of Central Missouri v. Danforth, 428 U.S. 52, 96 S.Ct. 2831, 49 L.Ed.2d 788 (1976).

68. 387 U.S. 1, 87 S.Ct. 1428, 18 L.Ed.2d 527 (1967). This case imposed extensive due process requirements upon juvenile delinquency proceedings.

69. 441 U.S. 418, 99 S.Ct. 1804, 60 L.Ed.2d 323 (1979), on remand 588 S.W.2d 569 (Tex.1979). This case held that due process required clear and convincing evidence for the involuntary commitment of an adult to a state mental hospital.

70. See Note, 93 Harv.L.Rev. 60, 89 (1979); Note, A Chance to be Heard: An Application of Bellotti v. Baird to the Civil Commitment of Minors, 32 Hast.L.J. 1285 (1981). Parham v. J.R. is approved by Watson, Children, Families and Courts: Before the Best Interests of the Child and Parham v. J.R., 66 Va.L.Rev. 653 (1980).

The law on medical and psychiatric care for children has thus rejected absolute solutions, and has continued to give the parent substantial authority but continues to permit state agencies to scrutinize and, when the child's welfare demands it, to override, parental decisions concerning that care. It is difficult to formulate standards having greater certainty or greater humanity than this.[71]

WESTLAW REFERENCES

di parens patriae

statut! law legislat! act policy /s requir! /s immuniz! innoculat! vaccin! /s child minor student pupil /s school

blood /2 transfus! /s child /s "jehovah witness"

"re hudson"

ti(matter /s quinlan)

"baby jane doe"

find 99 sct 2493

§ 9.4 Child Abuse and Neglect: The Battered Child

Introduction

The maltreatment of children by their parents or by others entrusted with their care has existed in most societies and in most periods of history.[1] It may result from customs having the affirmative sanction of the society, as where rites of initiation are required of the young.[2] It may be the product of economic forces which seem at the time to be inevitable or even desirable, as with child labor in Nineteenth Century England and America.[3] Or it may occur under the influence of complex social and psychological factors only partially identified or understood.[4]

In the United States cruelty to children has always existed,[5] but it has only been impressed upon public consciousness in the years since World War II. During the 1950's several pediatricians began to notice injuries in children whom they treated which could not be explained as due to accidents.[6] Then in 1962 a group of physicians published an article in which they coined the phrases "battered child" and "battered child syndrome" to describe the children, and the injuries inflicted upon them, who are the victims of the violence of their parents or their custodians.[7] The leaders of this group of physicians, Drs. Kempe and Helfer, published other works on the battered child,[8] as have many others in all the professions concerned with such social problems.[9] The subject also receives extensive attention in newspapers, magazines, radio and television.

Much of the writing about child abuse has been done by physicians, psychologists, psy-

71. For an attempt to formulate such standards, see Note, Choosing for Children: Adjudicating Medical Care Disputes Between Parents and the State, 58 N.Y.U.L.Rev. 157 (1983).

§ 9.4

1. Child Abuse and Neglect Part I: Historical Overview, Legal Matrix, and Social Perspectives, 50 N.C.L. Rev. 293 (1972).

2. Radbill, Children in a World of Violence: A History of Child Abuse, in C. Kempe and R. Helfer, The Battered Child 3 (3d ed. 1980).

3. S. Wood, Constitutional Politics in the Progressive Era: Child Labor and the Law ch. 1 (1968); III Encyclopedia of the Social Sciences 412–424 (1930); Radbill, Children in a World of Violence, supra, note 2.

4. L. Stone, The Family, Sex and Marriage in England, 1500–1800 pp. 105–114, 449–478 (1977); Steele, Psychodynamic Factors in Child Abuse, in C. Kempe and R. Helfer, The Battered Child 49 (3d ed. 1980); J. Garbarino and G. Gilliam, Understanding Abusive Families ch. 2 (1980).

5. Williams, Cruelty and Kindness to Children: Documentary of a Century, 1874–1974, in G. Williams and J.

Money, Traumatic Abuse and Neglect of Children at Home 68 (1980).

6. E.g., Caffey, Multiple Fractures in the Long Bones of Infants Suffering from Chronic Subdural Hematoma, 56 Am.J. Roentgenol. 163 (1946).

7. Kempe, Silverman, Steele, Droegemueller, Silver, The Battered-Child Syndrome, 181 J.Am.Med.Assn. 17 (1962), reprinted in G. Williams and J. Money, Traumatic Abuse and Neglect of Children at Home 89 (1980). It should come as no surprise that the use of "the battered-child syndrome" has been criticized as inhumane in Newberger, The Myth of the Battered Child Syndrome, in R. Bourne and E. Newberger, Critical Perspectives on Child Abuse 15 (1979), since pioneers in any discipline are usually targets for academic sniping.

8. C. Kempe and R. Helfer, eds. Helping the Battered Child and His Family (1972); R. Helfer and C. Kempe, Child Abuse and Neglect: The Family and The Community (1976).

9. D. Wells, Child Abuse: An Annotated Bibliography (1980) contains four hundred and fifty pages of citations to books and articles on the subject.

chiatrists, social workers and sociologists in an effort to explore some of its causes and origins. Although it is obviously impossible to give a detailed account of this research here, it is equally obvious that some awareness of its broad outlines is essential for a lawyer's ability to understand and deal with child abuse either as an advocate, a judge or a legislator. Understanding is made especially difficult for most people by the anger, repulsion and outrage which they feel so strongly when they see the marks of brutality left on the bodies of young children.

The conditions surrounding a particular case of child abuse are complex, but certain psychological factors have been identified as being present in nearly all cases.[10] The abusing parent (or other caretaker of the child) is generally found to have been himself mistreated as a child, so that he failed to learn how to form a normal attachment to and empathy for his own child. Very often his expectations for the behavior of his child are impossibly high or entirely inappropriate for a small child, leading him either to punish the child heavily or to neglect the child as worthless when those expectations are not fulfilled. Against this psychological background the mistreatment is often precipitated by some crisis or stress in the life of the parent, coupled with an absence of help for the parent and conduct by the child which is perceived as unsatisfactory.

The lack of attachment or empathy for the child felt by the abusing or neglecting parent may be aggravated if the child was the product of a difficult pregnancy, was the product of an unwanted pregnancy, was illegitimate, or was in some sense abnormal as by having early illnesses, or by being born prematurely, or was hyperactive or difficult to feed or care

for.[11] Such children have come to be characterized as "high-risk" children,[12] apparently meaning that they have a greater than normal likelihood of being abused or neglected. But this does not mean that such children are likely to be abused or neglected unless their parents exhibit the psychological symptoms found in most abusing parents.

A relatively small proportion of adults who maltreat the children in their care are either suffering from mental illness or are accustomed to acting with unchecked brutality toward other people generally.[13] The latter class has been labeled sociopaths and their maltreatment of children is often particularly cruel and severe and without reason. Both classes of person offer little chance of becoming acceptable parents no matter what therapy or assistance may be given them.

The sexual exploitation of children in the family may involve various kinds of acts and relationships. The adults who engage in it generally had poor family relationships as children, may have suffered themselves from sexual abuse, and are frequently isolated and alone.[14] The use of alcohol and drugs is often connected with sexual abuse. The most commonly reported type of this abuse is between father and daughter or stepfather and stepdaughter. It may be difficult to prove, since it results in psychological rather than physical harm in most instances, and since some of the authorities who deal with it go to extraordinary (and quite unwarranted) lengths to assert that the child victim, by her own seductive conduct, brought about the sexual exploitation by the adult.

The foregoing necessarily superficial description of some of the social and psychological conditions surrounding child abuse and neglect would undoubtedly be the subject

---

10. Steele, Psychodynamic Factors in Child Abuse, in C. Kempe and R. Helfer, The Battered Child 49 (3d ed. 1980), [hereinafter cited as Steele].

11. Friedrich and Boriskin, The Role of the Child in Child Abuse: A Review of the Literature, in G. Williams and J. Money, Traumatic Abuse and Neglect of Children at Home 188 (1980); Schwarzbeck, Identification of Infants at Risk for Child Abuse: Observations and Inferences in the Examination of the Mother-Infant Dyad, id. at 240.

12. Steele, supra note 10, at 67.

13. Id. at 71.

14. Steele, supra note 10, at 72; D. Finkelhor, Sexually Victimized Children ch. 2 (1979). For a review of the literature on incest within the nuclear family, see Katz, Incestuous Families, 1983 Det.Coll. of L.L.Rev. 79. An example of the difficulty of proving sexual molestation is found in Matter of Cheryl H., 153 Cal.App.3d 1098, 200 Cal.Rptr. 789 (1984).

of qualification or disagreement on the part of some writers. For example, the incidence of child abuse has been attributed to such environmental factors as poverty, unemployment and adverse living conditions.[15] The difficulties with this explanation are that it does not account either for those parents in adversity who do not abuse their children or for those more affluent parents who do engage in child abuse. On the other hand, environmental factors can produce the stress which may cause a parent having the right psychological traits to mistreat his child.[16] Others have laid a large portion of the responsibility for widespread child abuse upon the competitive, exploitative values prevailing in our society.[17] Although there may be some basis for this view, it does not offer much help in the diagnosis and treatment of child abuse cases.

The Reporting Acts

Since child abuse generally occurs in the privacy of the home out of sight and hearing of witnesses, legal remedies could only become effective after methods of acquiring evidence of the mistreatment were developed. The method adopted was to enact statutes, known as the child abuse reporting acts, which required persons who might be expected to come in contact with instances of child abuse to report them to the legal authorities. Such statutes now exist in all states.[18]

Although the details of such statutes vary, the general pattern of them is more or less uniform. After a declaration of purposes[19] they require of medical and school personnel[20] a report to a central office of injuries to children under eighteen which the reporting person suspects or has reason to believe were caused by child abuse.[21] In addition to *requiring* reports from such persons, the statutes often also *permit* reports of such injuries to be made by any person.[22] The reports must be made immediately upon discovery of the injuries, usually with the requirement of a later written report.[23] The agency to whom the report must be made varies in the several states, but most commonly the agency chosen is the state department of social services.[24] Most of the statutes impose a minor criminal

---

15. J. Garbarino and G. Gilliam, Understanding Abusive Families ch. 2 (1980).

16. Steele, supra note 10, at 51. The Wall Street Journal for August 6, 1982, page 17, col. 3, describes the effect of economic stress resulting from high unemployment in increasing the incidence of child abuse.

17. Gil, Unraveling Child Abuse, in R. Bourne and E. Newberger, Critical Perspectives on Child Abuse 69 (1979).

18. For a review of the earlier versions of these statutes, see Paulsen, The Legal Framework of Child Protection, 66 Colum.L.Rev. 679 (1966); Paulsen, Child Abuse Reporting Laws: The Shape of the Legislation, 67 Colum. L.Rev. 1 (1967). Later forms of the statutes are described in Beshrov, The Legal Aspects of Reporting Known and Suspected Child Abuse and Neglect, 23 Vill.L.Rev. 458 (1978); Fraser, A Glance at the Past, A Gaze at the Present, A Glimpse at the Future: A Critical Analysis of the Development of Child Abuse Reporting Statutes, 54 Chi.-Kent L.Rev. 641 (1978). Citations to all such statutes may be found in D. Besharov, ed., The Abused and Neglected Child Multi-Disciplinary Court Practice 591 (Practising Law Institute 1978).

19. E.g., Colo.Rev.Stat. § 19–10–102 (1978), stating the purposes to be the protection of children's best interests, the provision of protective services, and the dissemination of public information about child abuse.

20. The statutes usually contain an extensive list of such persons. E.g., Ill.–S.H.A. ch. 23, § 2054 (Supp.1986): Physician, hospital, hospital administrator, personnel engaged in the examination, care and treatment of persons, surgeon, dentist, osteopath, chiropractor, podiatrist, Christian Science practitioner, coroner, medical examiner, school personnel, truant officers, social workers, social services administrator, registered nurse, nursery school and day care center personnel, law enforcement officer, and some others.

21. E.g., West's Ann.Cal.Penal Code § 11166 (Supp. 1986).

22. E.g., West's Ann.Cal.Penal Code § 11166 (Supp. 1986); N.Y.–McKinney's Soc.Serv.Law § 414 (1983). The purpose of permitting all persons to make such reports is that it encourages such reports by giving such persons the immunity from civil and criminal liability which other sections of the statutes provide. The Texas statute *requires* that a report be made by any person having cause to believe that child abuse or neglect has occurred. V.T.C.A., Fam.Code § 34.01 (1975).

For an enlightening discussion of the ethical dilemma facing the lawyer who represents a parent charged with child neglect and who learns in the course of that representation that his client has been having sexual relations with his child, see Thurman, Incest and Ethics: Confidentiality's Severest Test, 61 Den.L.J. 619 (1984).

23. E.g., West's Ann.Cal.Penal Code § 11166 (Supp. 1986); Colo.Rev.Stat. § 19–10–108 (Supp.1985); Mass. Gen.Law.Ann. ch. 119, § 51A (Supp.1986).

24. E.g., Ill.–S.H.A. ch. 23, § 2054 (Supp.1986) (Department of Children and Family Services); N.Y.–McKinney's Soc.Serv.Law § 415 (1983) (reports to be made to the statewide central register of child abuse or to the local child protective service).

penalty for non-reporting by making it a misdemeanor [25] but apparently the penalty is rarely invoked.

In order to make the reporting requirements effective, the statutes provide for immunity from civil and criminal liability for those making reports.[26] For the same reason the privileges against revealing communications between doctor and patient [27] and between husband and wife [28] are often abrogated where the communications concern child abuse or neglect.

In most states a central registry of information based on reports of child abuse is maintained.[29] Records in the registry and in the hands of other state agencies concerning child abuse are made confidential, to be released only to limited persons or under limited conditions.[30]

In view of the statutes' reporting requirements, their criminal provisions, their immunity provisions, and their requirements for investigation and action by state agencies,[31] it

is clear that they raise substantial likelihood of civil liability for those whose activities are either authorized or required.[32] First there is the question whether a physician or hospital treating a child who has been abused or neglected may be liable if he or it does not make a child abuse report. A leading California case, Landeros v. Flood [33], has held that a complaint alleging malpractice against a physician and a hospital in failing to report serious injuries to a child being treated stated a cause of action against both parties when the child, on her return to her mother, was again seriously injured, after which her mother and her mother's common law husband were convicted of child abuse and the child plaintiff was removed to a foster home.

Landeros identified several issues of fact which it left to be tried on the remand to the trial court before the child would be entitled to recover. In the first place, the plaintiff would have to prove that the defendants' failure to report the injuries amounted to a failure to meet the standard of care required for

---

25. E.g., Mich.C.L.A. § 25.248(13)(2) (Supp.1986–1987); N.Y.–McKinney's Soc.Serv.Law § 420(1) (1983).

26. E.g., West's Ann.Cal.Penal Code § 11172 (Supp. 1986); Mass.G.L.A. ch. 119, § 51A (Supp.1986); V.T.C.A., Fam.Code § 34.03 (1975).

27. E.g., West's Ann.Cal.Penal Code § 11171 (1982); Matter of the Parental Rights of PP, 648 P.2d 512 (Wyo. 1982). Cf. State v. R.H., 683 P.2d 269 (Alaska App.1984); People v. Stritzinger, 34 Cal.3d 505, 194 Cal.Rptr. 431, 668 P.2d 738 (1983).

28. E.g., Colo.Rev.Stat. § 19–10–112 (Supp.1985). Some states have just abolished all privileges where child abuse is concerned. E.g., Ill.–S.H.A. ch. 23, § 2054 (Supp. 1986); V.T.C.A., Fam.Code § 34.04 (1975) (abolishes all privileges except that of attorney and client).

The abrogation of the privileges was held to apply to criminal prosecutions for child abuse in State v. Suttles, 287 Or. 15, 597 P.2d 786 (1979).

29. E.g., Ill.–S.H.A. ch. 23, § 2057.7 (Supp.1986); Mich.C.L.A. § 25.248(7) (Supp.1986–1987); N.Y.–McKinney's Soc.Serv.Law § 422 (1983); V.T.C.A., Fam.Code § 34.06 (Supp.1986). See also Besharov, Putting Central Registers to Work: Using Modern Management Information Systems to Improve Child Protective Services, 54 Chi.-Kent L.Rev. 687 (1978).

The Texas statute dealing with reports of child abuse in the absence of any judicial determination of abuse was held unconstitutional in Sims v. State Department of Public Welfare of State of Texas, 438 F.Supp. 1179 (S.D. Tex.1977), reversed on the basis of Younger v. Harris, 401 U.S. 37, 91 S.Ct. 746, 27 L.Ed.2d 669 (1971), in Moore v. Sims, 442 U.S. 415, 99 S.Ct. 2371, 60 L.Ed.2d 994 (1979).

30. E.g., Colo.Rev.Stat. § 19–10–115 (1978 and Supp. 1985); Ill.–S.H.A. ch. 23, §§ 2061, 2061.1 (Supp.1986); Pa. Stat. tit. 11, § 2215 (Supp.1985).

31. All states' statutes contain provisions requiring investigation and legal action by state agencies upon receipt of child abuse and neglect reports. See the discussion infra at note 84.

32. For general discussions of these liabilities, see Brown and Truitt, Civil Liability in Child Abuse Cases, 54 Chi.-Kent L.Rev. 753 (1978); Note, Civil Liability for Failing to Report Child Abuse, 1977 Det.C. of L.L.Rev. 135; Note, A Damages Remedy for Abuses by Child Protection Workers, 90 Yale L.J. 681 (1981).

A few states have included a provision for civil liability for failure to make reports in their reporting statutes. Ark.Stat. § 42–816(b) (Supp.1985) (wilful failure to report actionable); Colo.Rev.Stat. § 19–10–104(4)(b) (1978) (wilful violation of the reporting law actionable); Iowa Code Ann. § 232.75(2) (1985) (knowing failure to report actionable); Mich.C.L.A. § 25.248(13)(1) (Supp.1986–1987) (civil liability for failure to report); N.Y.–McKinney's Soc.Serv. Law § 420(2) (1983) (liability for knowing and wilful failure to report).

The child's right to recover from his parents for child abuse or neglect involves questions of the parent-child immunity in tort and is discussed infra, in section 10.2.

33. 17 Cal.3d 399, 131 Cal.Rptr. 69, 551 P.2d 389 (1976). Cf. Tarasoff v. Regents of the University of California, 17 Cal.3d 425, 131 Cal.Rptr. 14, 551 P.2d 334 (1976).

malpractice recovery. That standard is normally described as being the knowledge and skill ordinarily exercised by other members of the profession in similar circumstances.[34] The effect of the reporting statute was held to be the creation of a rebuttable presumption that the defendants failed to exercise due care if it were proved that the violation of the statute proximately caused the injuries and if the plaintiff were one of the class of persons for whose protection the statute was passed.[35] The California reporting statute in force at the time required a report of "physical * * * injuries which appear to have been inflicted * * * by other than accidental means".[36] The court held that this imposed a subjective test which meant that there would only be a duty to report if the physician actually observed the injuries and formed the opinion that they were intentionally inflicted.[37] Finally, the court held that the plaintiff would have to prove proximate cause, that is, would have to convince the trier of fact that the defendants should reasonably have foreseen that the plaintiff's mother would resume her brutality to the plaintiff if the plaintiff should be returned to the mother's custody. The court failed to mention another aspect of

proximate cause. It would seem that the plaintiff should also have to prove that if a report were made, it would be reasonably foreseeable that the authorities would act to prevent further injury to the plaintiff, either by removing the child from the parent's custody or by some other protective order.

When the state agency, usually the department of social services, which is charged with the duty of investigating and enforcing the child abuse reporting act fails to perform its obligations under the statute, thereby exposing a child to injury or death, the child or his estate may sue the agency or its employees. Suits of this kind involve not only the issues of negligence and proximate cause found in suits against nonreporting physicians, but also questions of state employees' immunity to suits.[38] Some courts have held that a state agency which is alleged to have been negligent in placing a child with incompetent or abusive foster parents may be held liable to the child for injuries inflicted by the foster parents, the opinions either ignoring the immunity issue,[39] or finding that the placement does not involve the sort of "discretionary acts" which fall within the immunity extend-

34. W. Prosser and W. Keeton, Torts 185–189 (5th ed. 1984).

35. The effect given to this statute was weaker than the usual "negligence per se" doctrine, according to which the violation of a statute designed to protect persons like the plaintiff is conclusive on the issue of negligence. See W. Prosser, and W. Keeton, Torts 220–234 (5th ed. 1984). But this may not have been a negligence case at all, since the court held that there would only be a duty to report if the physician or hospital actually observed the injuries and decided that they had been intentionally inflicted, thus suggesting that only a wilful failure to report would be actionable under the statute. The opinion in Landeros is far from clear on this issue.

36. West's Ann.Cal.Penal Code § 11166(a) (Supp. 1986).

37. Other reporting acts contain different language, raising the question whether they would justify the courts in imposing a less subjective standard of civil liability. The current version of the California statute requires a report of the specified professional person "who has knowledge of or observes a child * * * whom he or she knows or reasonably suspects has been the victim of child abuse." West's Ann.Cal.Penal Code § 11166(a) (Supp.1986). Other states have adopted provisions requiring reports when the professional person has "reasonable cause to suspect" that the child has been

abused. E.g., N.Y.–McKinney's Soc.Serv.Law § 413 (Supp.1986). Such a statute would be susceptible to the construction that a physician who examined a child and concluded that his injuries did not result from child abuse might be liable to the child for failing to report if that conclusion could be proved not to have been reasonable, or in other words to have been negligent.

38. For a comparative discussion of judicial, legislative and executive immunities from suit in the federal courts, see Nagel, Judicial Immunity and Sovereignty, 6 Hast. Const.L.Q. 237 (1978).

39. Vonner v. State Department of Public Welfare, 273 So.2d 252 (La.1973) held that a child's mother could recover for the child's death resulting from a beating by a foster mother with whom the state department had placed the child. The opinion is far from clear, but the department had apparently been negligent in disregarding warnings that the foster mother was abusing the children in her care. The opinion seems to go beyond negligence and holds the department liable on some theory of respondeat superior, however.

For a discussion of the liability of social agencies and their employees for negligence in the protection of abused or neglected children, see Besharov, Protecting Abused and Neglected Children: Can Law Help Social Work? 9 Fam.L.Rep. 4029 (1983).

ed to employees of the executive branch of state government.[40]

Where the state agency's negligence or failure to supervise the placement of a child leads to acts of abuse which can be characterized as depriving the child of his constitutional rights, the child may have a claim based on the federal Civil Rights Act.[41] The leading case is Doe v. New York City Department of Social Services,[42] which held that a placement agency, the Catholic Home Bureau, could be liable under the Civil Rights Act to a girl whom the Bureau placed in a foster home where she was beaten and sexually abused by her foster father. The court stated that the requirements for recovery under the federal statute are that a government official's non-performance of his custodial duties infringed a constitutionally protected liberty or property interest of the plaintiff, and that the official had a mental state of "deliberate indifference" to the harm being done to the plaintiff.[43] Ordinary negligence on the official's part was held not sufficient to meet the "deliberate indifference" standard, but the court suggested that gross negligence by such a person might be enough. There was little doubt in this case that the child had been denied her constitutional rights by being subjected to violence and sexual exploitation in the foster home, and that the placement agency's supervision of the foster home failed to satisfy the requirements of the child abuse reporting statute. The case was therefore remanded for a new trial in which the major issue would presumably be whether the placement agency employees had exhibited a deliberate unconcern for the plaintiff's plight. The court did not address the question whether the agency and its employees would have a qualified immunity from suit, but other cases have held that such an immunity does exist, where the defendants both acted with good intentions and had reasonable grounds for believing that their conduct was constitutional.[44]

Social workers who are attempting to administer the child abuse reporting acts may risk liability not only when they do not act with sufficient speed and decision to protect a child, but also when they act in a way which may be characterized as excessively zealous.[45] A social worker's lot is not a happy one.[46]

Defining Child Abuse and Neglect: Constitutional Limitations

The definitions of child abuse and neglect vary greatly from state to state. Some statutes are quite general, defining abuse as physical injury, sexual abuse or maltreatment.[47] Others are specific, spelling out in detail the kinds of conduct which may constitute abuse or neglect.[48] Still other statutes fall some-

40. Elton v. Orange County, 3 Cal.App.3d 1053, 84 Cal.Rptr. 27 (1970); Bartels v. Westchester County, 76 A.D.2d 517, 429 N.Y.S.2d 906 (2d Dep't 1980). Koepf v. York County, 198 Neb. 67, 251 N.W.2d 866 (1977) indicates that the county could be liable for the death of a child killed by a foster parent, but held that its employees were not negligent in the placement or supervision of the child and therefore were not liable in this case.

Agency employees have in a few cases been charged with criminal misconduct in connection with child abuse, but have generally been acquitted on one ground or another. See People v. Beruman, 638 P.2d 789 (Colo. 1982); Steinberger v. District Court, In and For Tenth Judicial Dist., 198 Colo. 59, 596 P.2d 755 (1979). Pope v. State, 284 Md. 309, 396 A.2d 1054 (1979) held that a woman who was present while a child was killed by her mother was not guilty of any crime.

41. 42 U.S.C.A. § 1983.

42. 649 F.2d 134 (2d Cir.1981), appeal after remand 709 F.2d 782 (2d Cir.1983). See also Dixey v. Jewish Child Care Association, 522 F.Supp. 913 (S.D.N.Y.1981).

43. 649 F.2d at 141.

44. Duchesne v. Sugarman, 566 F.2d 817 (2d Cir.1977); Langton v. Maloney, 527 F.Supp. 538 (D.Conn.1981).

45. Darryl H. v. Coler, 585 F.Supp. 383 (N.D.Ill.1984); Martin v. Weld County, 43 Colo.App. 59, 598 P.2d 532 (1979) (reverses summary judgment for the defendants in a slander suit brought by a parent against a social worker who investigated a child abuse report). But see Roman v. Appleby, 558 F.Supp. 449 (E.D.Pa.1983), and Fitzgerald v. Williamson, 787 F.2d 403 (8th Cir.1986).

46. W.S. Gilbert and A. Sullivan, The Pirates of Penzance, Act II (1879).

47. E.g., Alaska Stat. § 47.17.070 (Supp.1985). See also Official Ga.Code Ann. § 74–111 (Supp.1985), and Kan.Stat.Ann. § 38–717 (1981).

48. E.g., Colo.Rev.Stat. § 19–10–103 (1978 and Supp. 1985), which lists skin bruising, bleeding, malnutrition, failure to thrive, burns, fractures, subdural hematoma, soft tissue swelling, death, sexual assault, molestation or exploitation, or the failure to provide adequate food, clothing, shelter or supervision which a prudent parent would provide. See also Hawaii Rev.Stat. § 587–2 (Supp. 1984); Ill.–S.H.A. ch. 23, § 2053 (Supp.1986).

where between these extremes.[49] The form which child abuse statutes should take has been the center of controversy, both scholarly and political, partly because of the availability of the drastic civil remedy of involuntary termination of the parent's rights in his child.[50] The charge has been made that child abuse statutes have such a broad reach that they permit state social or law enforcement agencies to impose middle class standards of behavior upon families who, by reason of ethnic or class origins, fail or refuse to observe such standards.[51] The state's intervention in child abuse and neglect cases has also been criticized on the ground that American law has traditionally and correctly taken the position that a child's parents are better able to understand and promote his welfare than agents of the state.[52] One response to these claims has been a proposed statute which would sharply restrict the occasions on which a state agency would be permitted to intervene in families to protect children from abuse or neglect.[53] Although family autonomy is most important, considerable leeway must be left to state agencies responsible for child protection. It is naive for the draftsman to suppose that he can produce a statute which will obviate the exercise of discretion by those charged with enforcing it. Although it is certainly true that in general the family is better able to care for children than state agencies, the cases on child abuse and neglect provide convincing evidence that many families are not only not able to perform this function but are inflicting such serious harm upon children that state intervention is essential to their welfare.

In two respects there is general agreement among the states respecting the definition of child abuse. First, "child" is almost universally defined as a person under eighteen.[54] Second, many of the statutes provide that a child shall not be considered to be neglected if he is under treatment in good faith solely by spiritual means through prayer in accordance with the tenets of a recognized religious denomination.[55] It is difficult to determine what this latter exemption from the neglect statutes can mean, since it seems obvious that the state cannot permit a child to die or suffer serious injury when conventional medical treatment would provide an effective cure, solely because his parent's religious belief rejects medical or surgical treatment.[56]

49. E.g., West's Ann.Cal.Penal Code § 11165(b)–(g) (Supp.1986); Conn.Gen.Stat.Ann. § 17–38a (Supp.1986); D.C.Code 1981, § 22–901; Mich.G.L.A. § 25.248(2) (Supp. 1986–1987); Wis.Stat.Ann. § 48.981(1) (Supp.1985). Many of these statutes include in the definition that the harm was caused by other than accidental means. See, e.g., Or.Rev.Stat. § 418.740 (1985); Pa.Stat. tit. 11, § 2203 (Supp.1985); Va.Code, § 63.1–248.2A (Supp.1985).

50. For a more extensive discussion of the involuntary termination of parental rights, see § 20.6, infra.

51. See Smith v. Organization of Foster Families for Equality and Reform, 431 U.S. 816, 833, 97 S.Ct. 2094, 2103, 53 L.Ed.2d 14 (1977); R. Bourne and E. Newberger, Critical Perspectives on Child Abuse 141 (1979). Cf. Korbin, The Cross-Cultural Context of Child Abuse and Neglect, in C. Kempe and R. Helfer, The Battered Child 21 (3d ed. 1980).

52. Wald, State Intervention on Behalf of "Neglected" Children: A Search for Realistic Standards, 27 Stan.L. Rev. 985 (1975); Wald, State Intervention on Behalf of "Neglected" Children: Standards for Removal of Children from Their Homes, Monitoring the Status of Children in Foster Care and Terminating Parental Rights, 28 Stan.L.Rev. 623 (1976). But see Olsen, The Myth of State Intervention in the Family, 18 U.Mich.J.L.Ref. 835 (1985).

53. Institute of Judicial Administration and American Bar Association, Juvenile Justice Standards Project,

Standards Relating to Abuse and Neglect, 16–17 (Rev.ed. 1981). The purpose of this draft is to limit state intervention to those cases in which there is disfigurement, impairment of bodily functioning, or serious physical or emotional harm. The proposal has been criticized in Bourne and Newberger, "Family Autonomy" or "Coercive Intervention"? Ambiguity and Conflict in the Proposed Standards for Child Abuse and Neglect, 57 B.U.L.Rev. 670 (1977). The proposed standards are defended in McCathren, Accountability in the Child Protection System: A Defense of the Proposed Standards Relating to Abuse and Neglect, 57 B.U.L.Rev. 707 (1977). The proposed standards seem to have had some influence on the New Jersey and New York definitions of abuse and neglect. N.J.Stat.Ann. § 9:6–8.21 (Supp.1985); N.Y.–McKinney's Fam.Ct.Act § 1012(e) (1983 and Supp.1986).

Myers, The Legal Response to Child Abuse: In the Best Interests of Children? 24 J.Fam.L. 149 (1985) argues for a greater emphasis on a therapeutic approach as an alternative to criminal prosecutions on the ground that the latter harm the child and work against treatment in individual cases.

54. See the statutes cited in notes 47 and 49, supra.

55. E.g., Colo.Rev.Stat. § 19–1–114 (1986); N.J.Stat. Ann. § 9:6–821 (Supp.1985).

56. See People in Interest of D.L.E., 645 P.2d 271 (Colo.1982), which held that the exemption did not pre-

The reported cases on abuse and neglect exhibit as much variety as might be anticipated in view of the differences in statutory language, but at the same time there are recurring patterns in their holdings which suggest that much of the criticism of statutory deficiencies is exaggerated. The most obvious form of abuse, a form often seen by physicians, occurs when a child is physically beaten, burned or tortured by his parents or caretakers, sometimes in ways so brutal as to be almost inconceivable, particularly when the injuries are revealed by photographs.[57] The courts in such cases have little difficulty in finding violations of the child abuse statutes,[58] or of the general criminal law.[59] The finding of violation is not affected by the excuse sometimes given that the parent was

merely disciplining the child.[60] Excessive punishment is an all too familiar type of child abuse.[61] Somewhat more difficult issues may be presented by the cases in which a parent is prosecuted for failure to prevent injuries inflicted by another person, often a stepparent. Some statutes may explicitly cover this sort of case,[62] but the courts usually hold, even in the absence of such provisions, that a parent who is able to prevent the injuries and fails to do so is chargeable with child abuse or neglect.[63]

Once we move beyond physical violence to children, the definition of child abuse becomes more difficult. Thus it seems clear that drug or alcohol use by a pregnant woman can have seriously harmful effects on her child, leading in extreme cases to drug addiction on the part

vent a finding of neglect where a child's life was in danger. The validity of such a statute was raised but not decided in People v. Lybarger, 700 P.2d 910 (Colo.1985), when a child died of pneumonia after her parents relied upon prayer rather than medical treatment in caring for her. Commonwealth v. Barnhart, 345 Pa.Super. 10, 497 A.2d 616 (1985) affirmed convictions for involuntary manslaughter and child endangering after a parent refused to obtain medical treatment for his two-year-old son on the ground that such treatment violated his religious beliefs, and the son died. No statute was involved in the case but the court discussed the First Amendment guaranty of religious freedom and held that the convictions did not violate that Amendment.

57. E.g., C. Kempe and R. Helfer, eds., The Battered Child chs. 8, 9, 13, 14 (3d ed. 1980); A. Franklin, ed., Concerning Child Abuse 18 (1975).

58. State v. Campbell, 102 Wis.2d 243, 306 N.W.2d 272 (1981) (throwing baby against a wall constituted cruel treatment even though no injury was alleged).

59. Commonwealth v. Gallison, 383 Mass. 659, 421 N.E.2d 757 (1981) (mother convicted of manslaughter in killing a two-year-old daughter and of assault with a dangerous weapon in attack on a three-year-old son); Commonwealth v. Cadwell, 374 Mass. 308, 372 N.E.2d 246 (1978), 14 N.Eng.L.J. 812 (1979) (man living with child's mother convicted of second degree murder of child); State v. Loss, 295 Minn. 271, 204 N.W.2d 404 (1973) (father convicted of manslaughter in death of his son). But People v. Steger, 16 Cal.3d 539, 128 Cal.Rptr. 161, 546 P.2d 665 (1976) reversed a conviction of first degree murder under the torture murder statute on the ground that the defendant, who beat her three-year-old child to death did not have the required cold blooded intent to inflict extreme and prolonged pain.

60. In re Edward C., 126 Cal.App.3d 193, 178 Cal.Rptr. 694 (1981) (repeated beatings of an eight-year-old girl by her father, using a leather strap, because "God wanted him to", caused the child to be held a dependent child); In Matter of Rodney C., 91 Misc.2d 677, 398 N.Y.S.2d 511 (Fam.Ct.1977) (various forms of punishment held unrea-

sonable and to constitute neglect). Allegations of spanking were held insufficient to support a finding of neglect in Interest of Aaronson, 65 Ill.App.3d 729, 22 Ill.Dec. 463, 382 N.E.2d 853 (1978). But see In Interest of D.M.C., 107 Ill.App.3d 902, 63 Ill.Dec. 516, 438 N.E.2d 254 (1982). Confinement of children for considerable periods as a method of discipline was held to violate criminal statutes in People v. Warner, 98 Ill.App.3d 433, 53 Ill.Dec. 956, 424 N.E.2d 747 (1981). But see Whitt v. Commonwealth, 479 S.W.2d 646 (Ky.1972).

61. Steele, Violence Within the Family, in R. Helfer and C. Kempe, eds., Child Abuse and Neglect, The Family and the Community 3, 16–19 (1976); Gelles, Violence Toward Children in the United States, in J. Cook and R. Bowles, Child Abuse: Commission and Omission 35 (1980); Gil, Unraveling Child Abuse, in R. Bourne and E. Newberger, Critical Perspectives on Child Abuse 69 (1979).

In view of the widespread use of corporal punishment both by parents and by institutions caring for children, there may be cases in which it is difficult to determine what forms and degrees of punishment should be labeled excessive. J. Garbarino and G. Gilliam, Understanding Abusive Families 5–11 (1980). But the majority of cases involve such extreme violence that it is impossible to deny that it is excessive. E.g. In re Edward C., supra, note 60.

62. E.g., Colo.Rev.Stat. § 18–6–401 (Supp.1985); Va. Code 1985, § 63.1–248.2A (Supp.).

63. People v. Figueroa, 167 Cal.App.3d 981, 213 Cal. Rptr. 676 (1985) (suggests proper jury instruction); Smith v. State, 408 N.E.2d 614 (Ind.App.1980) (mother guilty of manslaughter when she failed to prevent her male friend from beating her son to death, the court refusing to accept her excuse that she was "meek, timid and dependent" in personality); Pope v. State, 284 Md. 309, 396 A.2d 1054 (1979) (mother's friend held guilty of child abuse in failing to prevent the mother from killing her child during psychotic episodes). But see State v. McLaughlin, 42 Or.App. 215, 600 P.2d 474 (1979).

of the child or the fetal alcohol syndrome and brain damage to the child.[64] But most of the child abuse statutes do not explicitly apply to these forms of harm to children,[65] and the relatively few decisions on the point are in conflict.[66] This method of injuring a child ought to be within the definition of either abuse or neglect.

Statutory definitions of child neglect are necessarily even less specific than the definitions of abuse.[67] They do cover failure to provide food for the child,[68] "failure to thrive" cases,[69] and failure to provide medical care.[70] But vague claims that the child's environment is unsatisfactory, or that his parents are providing a less than ideal education are not sufficient to support a finding of neglect.[71] Maltreatment of an emotional or psychological nature may constitute abuse or neglect under some statutes,[72] even though it is extremely difficult to define.[73]

Sexual abuse or sexual exploitation of children is generally included in the definition of abuse in reporting and criminal statutes.[74] When it occurs outside the family, it is the concern of the criminal law.[75] When it occurs within the family, it is often not reported, often takes the form of father-daughter or stepfather-stepdaughter incest, and is extremely difficult for the law to deal with in an

---

64. Black and Mayer, Parents With Special Problems: Alcoholism and Opiate Addiction, in C. Kempe and R. Helfer, The Battered Child 103 (3d ed. 1980).

65. N.Y.–McKinney's Fam.Ct.Act § 1012(f)(i)(B) (1983) includes drug and alcohol use in the definition of neglect, but such provisions are rare in the statutes.

See Myers, Abuse and Neglect of the Unborn: Can the State Intervene? 23 Duq.L.Rev. 1 (1984).

66. Reyes v. Superior Court In and For San Bernardino County, 75 Cal.App.3d 214, 141 Cal.Rptr. 912 (1977) ("child" is not an unborn fetus, so mother not guilty of endangering child when her heroin use caused twins to be addicted after birth); In re P., 123 Cal.App.3d 734, 176 Cal.Rptr. 708 (1981) (prenatal heroin addiction caused by mother's addiction is child abuse); Matter of Baby X, 97 Mich.App. 111, 293 N.W.2d 736 (1980) (child held neglected when suffered drug withdrawal due to the mother's drug addiction during pregnancy); Matter of Smith, 128 Misc.2d 976, 492 N.Y.S.2d 331 (Fam.Ct.1985) (unborn child is a "person" and neglected when afflicted with fetal alcohol syndrome).

67. See the statutes cited, supra, notes 47, 48, 49. The IJA–ABA standards contain no specific definition of neglect, but they would authorize state intervention when parental failure to supervise or protect the child causes serious physical injury, or where the child suffers serious emotional damage and the parents are unwilling to provide treatment for him, or where the parents are unwilling to provide medical treatment for serious physical harm. Institute of Judicial Administration-American Bar Assn., Juvenile Justice Standards Project, Standards Relating to Abuse and Neglect 16–17 (Rev.2d 1981). It is not clear whether these definitions would cover instances of infant failure to thrive or of emotional maltreatment.

68. Harrington v. State, 547 S.W.2d 616 (Tex.Crim. App.1977) (mother convicted of murder for the starvation of her two-year-old child). On diagnosis of neglect, see Cantwell, Child Neglect, in C. Kempe and R. Helfer, The Battered Child 183 (3d ed. 1980).

69. In re R.J.M., 164 W.Va. 496, 266 S.E.2d 114 (1980). Kempe, Cutler, Dean, The Infant With Failure-to-Thrive, in C. Kempe and R. Helfer, The Battered Child 163 (3d ed. 1980) defines this condition as one in which a child during the first three years of life suffers a marked retardation or cessation of growth. See also Koel, Failure to Thrive and Fatal Injury as a Continuum, in J. Cook and R. Bowles, Child Abuse: Commission and Omission (1980).

70. State v. Clark, 5 Conn.Cir. 699, 261 A.2d 294 (1969). See also cases cited, supra, in section 9.3.

71. Doe v. G.D., 146 N.J.Super. 419, 370 A.2d 27 (1976), affirmed 74 N.J. 196, 377 A.2d 626 (1977).

State v. Goff, 297 Or. 635, 686 P.2d 1023 (1984) held a mother guilty of child neglect when she left her two children, ages twenty-two months and eight years, unattended for five hours in a house containing flammable materials. The house caught fire and both children were killed.

72. E.g., Conn.Gen.Stat.Ann. § 17–38a (Supp.1986). The IJA–ABA standards take the curious position that serious emotional damage to the child does not constitute child abuse when it is inflicted by the parents, but only when the parents fail to provide treatment for it. Institute of Judicial Administration-American Bar Assn., Juvenile Justice Standards Project, Standards Relating to Abuse and Neglect 16 (Rev.ed. 1981). A mother's threats to kill a child were held neglect in Matter of Jason B., 117 Misc.2d 480, 458 N.Y.S.2d 180 (Fam.Ct.1983).

73. J. Garbarino and G. Gilliam, Understanding Abusive Families 67–78 (1980) attempts a non-legal definition. People v. D.A.K., 198 Colo. 11, 596 P.2d 747 (1979), appeal dismissed for want of a substantial federal question, 444 U.S. 987, 100 S.Ct. 515, 62 L.Ed.2d 416 (1979) held that there could be a conviction for emotional abuse under general statutory language proscribing "mistreatment or abuse". See also Note, Emotional Neglect in Connecticut, 5 Conn.L.Rev. 100 (1972).

74. See the statutes cited supra, in notes 47, 48, 49.

In re Interest of Hollenbeck, 212 Neb. 253, 322 N.W.2d 635 (1982) held that a mother's failure to protect her child from sexual abuse by the child's father constituted child abuse justifying termination of the mother's parental rights. See also Katz, Incestuous Families, 1983 Det. Coll. of L.L.Rev. 79, and In re Sabrina M., 460 A.2d 1009 (Me.1983).

75. D. Finkelhor, Sexually Victimized Children (1979).

effective way.[76] Sexual abuse is seldom defined in the statutes, but a suggested definition is "contacts or interactions between a child and an adult when the child is being used for the sexual stimulation of the perpetrator or another person when the perpetrator is in a position of power or control over the victim." [77] Needless to say sexual abuse may have extremely serious harmful effects on the child, and often accompanies physical abuse.[78]

In view of the difficulties of definition, of the conflicting considerations of child welfare and parental control, and of the contemporary tendency to express all conflicts in terms of constitutional doctrines, it is not surprising that many constitutional attacks have been made on the child abuse and neglect statutes

of the various states. The attack is most often based upon the claim that the statute is void for vagueness under the Due Process Clause of the Fourteenth Amendment of the United States Constitution, or under the corresponding provision of the state constitution. Although of course the question turns primarily on the precise language of the statute, the cases have nearly always held that the statutes are sufficiently definite to give persons of ordinary intelligence fair notice of what the legislature is forbidding.[79] This is so even where the parents' right to discipline or punish a child is held to be a fundamental right justifying strict scrutiny of the statutory language.[80] Other constitutional attacks upon these statutes, usually based upon the argument that they violated equal protection by

76. Kempe, Incest and Other Forms of Sexual Abuse in C. Kempe and R. Helfer, The Battered Child 198 (3d ed. 1980). See also D. Walters, Physical and Sexual Abuse of Children 111–154 (1975). A father was excluded from contact with his child where sexual abuse had occurred in Matter of Cheryl H., 153 Cal.App.3d 1098, 200 Cal.Rptr. 789 (1984).

77. J. Garbarino and G. Gilliam, Understanding Abusive Families 151 (1980). Colo.Rev.Stat. § 18–6–403 (Supp.1985) contains a detailed definition of sexual abuse and exploitation. Clear and convincing evidence of the abuse is required by Matter of Dawn B., 114 Misc.2d 834, 452 N.Y.S.2d 817 (Fam.Ct.1982). In Interest of Cook, 208 Neb. 549, 304 N.W.2d 390 (1981) held that a mother's parental rights could be terminated where for a considerable time she failed to prevent her husband from sexually molesting their daughter. See also Chesebrough v. State, 255 So.2d 675 (Fla.1971), cert. denied 406 U.S. 976, 92 S.Ct. 2427, 32 L.Ed.2d 676 (1972) holding that parents who engaged in sexual intercourse in the presence of their young son were guilty of committing a lewd and lascivious act in violation of the criminal statute.

78. Kempe, Incest and Other Forms of Sexual Abuse, in C. Kempe and R. Helfer, The Battered Child 198 (3d ed. 1980).

79. People v. Smith, 35 Cal.3d 798, 201 Cal.Rptr. 311, 678 P.2d 886 (1984); In re P., 123 Cal.App.3d 734, 176 Cal.Rptr. 708 (1981) ("cruelly treated or neglected" not unconstitutionally vague as applied to mother's use of heroin causing addiction in her daughter); People v. Ewing, 72 Cal.App.3d 714, 140 Cal.Rptr. 299 (1977) (abuse causing great bodily harm or death not unconstitutional); People v. Schwartz, 678 P.2d 1000 (Colo.1984); People v. Mann, 646 P.2d 352 (Colo.1982) (child abuse statute punishing one who "negligently" places child in a situation which "may" endanger his life or health is not too vague); People v. Jennings, 641 P.2d 276 (Colo.1982) (prohibition of "cruel punishment" is not unconstitutional); People v. Taggart, 621 P.2d 1375 (Colo.1981) (use of "negligently" and "may" in statute does not render it unconstitutional), rejected on other grounds James v. People, 727 P.2d 850

(Colo.1986); People v. Hoehl, 193 Colo. 557, 568 P.2d 484 (1977) (use of "may" and "without justifiable excuse" in statute does not render it unconstitutional); State v. Riker, 376 So.2d 862 (Fla.1979) (statute forbidding one to deprive a child of "necessary" food, clothing, shelter, etc., is not unconstitutionally vague); State v. Shamrani, 370 So.2d 1 (Fla.1979) (statute constitutional in prohibiting acts causing a child to be dependent); State v. Joyce, 361 So.2d 406 (Fla.1978) (negligently permitting child's health to be "materially endangered" not unconstitutionally vague); People v. Virgin, 60 Ill.App.3d 964, 18 Ill.Dec. 361, 377 N.E.2d 846 (1978) (statute constitutional as applied to a mother who whipped her child in providing for penalty to one "who * * * shall in any other manner injure in health or limb, any child"); State v. Fisher, 230 Kan. 192, 631 P.2d 239 (1981) ("unreasonably * * * permitting a child * * * to be placed in a situation in which its life, body or health may be injured or endangered" is not unconstitutionally vague); Bowers v. Maryland, 283 Md. 115, 389 A.2d 341 (1978) ("cruel or inhumane treatment" is not unconstitutionally vague); State v. Brown, 660 S.W.2d 694 (Mo.1983); State v. Sinica, 220 Neb. 792, 372 N.W.2d 445 (1985); State v. Coe, 92 N.M. 320, 587 P.2d 973 (1978), cert. denied 92 N.M. 353, 588 P.2d 554 (1978) ("negligently" placing child in a situation that may endanger his life or health is not unconstitutional); State v. Sammons, 58 Ohio St.2d 460, 391 N.E.2d 713 (1979), appeal dismissed for want of a substantial federal question, 444 U.S. 1008, 100 S.Ct. 655, 62 L.Ed.2d 637 (1980) ("substantial risk" to health or safety, and violating a "duty of care" not unconstitutionally vague); State v. Mills, 52 Or.App. 777, 629 P.2d 861 (1981), review denied 291 Or. 662, 639 P.2d 1280 (1981) (leaving a child in a place for such a time as is "likely to endanger" his health or welfare is not too vague); Keser v. State, 706 P.2d 263 (Wyo.1985) ("physical injury" and "mental trauma" not too vague. Contra, holding "unjustifiable physical pain" is unconstitutionally vague, State v. Meinert, 225 Kan. 816, 594 P.2d 232 (1979).

80. Bowers v. Maryland, 283 Md. 115, 389 A.2d 341 (1978).

imposing heavier penalties for child abuse than for other crimes have also usually been unsuccessful.[81]

Procedure and Remedies

Child abuse cases, under the law of most states, begin when suspected abuse or neglect is reported in accordance with the reporting statutes.[82] The reports are usually required to be made to the local law enforcement agency, police department or sheriff's office, or to an office of the state department of social services.[83] The statutes generally require one of these agencies to make an investigation to determine whether there is any basis for the report.[84] In emergencies, when the child is in danger, a state agency may be authorized to take custody of the child without court action,

but it is usually required to bring the matter before a court for preliminary orders without delay.[85] The statutes vary considerably with respect to the persons who are authorized to file petitions in abuse or neglect cases. The more carefully drafted of them limit those who may file,[86] or give the juvenile court the authority to control its own intake.[87]

Service of the petition must be made on the parent or other defendant in the case in accordance with local rules.[88] It would seem logical that substituted service of a kind most likely to give the defendant notice would be sufficient where personal service cannot be made.[89]

Under the statutes in many states a guardian ad litem or other representative must be

---

81. Jones v. Helms, 452 U.S. 412, 101 S.Ct. 2434, 69 L.Ed.2d 118 (1981) (statute is valid in providing that a parent who abandons a child is guilty of only a misdemeanor, while one who does so and leaves the state is guilty of a felony); People v. Mann, 646 P.2d 352 (Colo. 1982) (no violation of equal protection in imposing a heavier penalty for child abuse than for criminally negligent homicide); People v. Noble, 635 P.2d 203 (Colo.1981) (no violation of equal protection in imposing a heavier penalty for child abuse than for reckless manslaughter). State v. Lucero, 98 N.M. 204, 647 P.2d 406 (1982) held that the child abuse statute was constitutional notwithstanding that it did not require proof of a criminal intent. But it did require proof that the conduct was engaged in knowingly, intentionally or negligently and without justifiable cause. And vague claims of unconstitutional "overbreadth" were rejected in State v. Daniels, 61 Ohio St.2d 220, 400 N.E.2d 399 (1980), cert. denied 449 U.S. 851, 101 S.Ct. 142, 66 L.Ed.2d 63 (1980).

The claim that the reporting act unconstitutionally violated a parent's right to treatment for his illness was rejected in People v. Younghanz, 156 Cal.App.3d 811, 202 Cal.Rptr. 907 (1984).

82. See, e.g., notes 19–22, supra. The reference in the text is to civil child abuse cases.

83. E.g., Colo.Rev.Stat. § 19–10–104 (1986); Ill.–S.H.A. ch. 23, § 2054 (Supp.1986); Mich.C.L.A. § 25.248(3) (Supp. 1986–1987). West's Ann.Cal.Penal Code § 11166(2) (Supp.1986) requires reports to be made to a child protection agency.

84. E.g., Alaska Stat. § 47.17.030 (1979); West's Ann. Cal.Welf. & Inst.Code § 309 (1984); Colo.Rev.Stat. § 19–10–109 (1986); Conn.Gen.Stat.Ann. § 17–38a(e) (Supp. 1986); Ill.–S.H.A. ch. 23, § 2057 (Supp.1986); Mass.Gen. Law Ann. ch. 119, § 51B (Supp.1986); Mich.C.L.A. § 25.248(8) (Supp.1986–1987); Or.Rev.Stat. § 418.760 (1985); Pa.Stat. tit. 11, § 2217 (Supp.1985); V.T.C.A., Fam.Code § 34.05 (Supp.1986); Va.Code 1985, § 63.1–248.6 (Supp.); Wis.Stat.Ann. § 48.981(3) (Supp.1985).

85. E.g., Alaska Stat. § 47.17.030(d) (1979); Colo.Rev. Stat. § 19–10–107 (1986); Conn.Gen.Stat.Ann. § 17–38a(e) (Supp.1986); Ill.–S.H.A. ch. 23, § 2055 (Supp.1986); N.J.Stat.Ann. § 9:6–8.16 (1976); N.Y.–McKinney's Fam. Ct.Act § 1024 (1983 and Supp.1986); V.T.C.A., Fam.Code § 17.03 (Supp.1986).

Failure to observe due process standards carefully in taking custody of children without a hearing on a plea of emergency may produce decisions holding the procedure unconstitutional. See Sims v. State Department of Social Welfare of State of Texas, 438 F.Supp. 1179 (S.D.Tex. 1977), reversed on the authority of Younger v. Harris, 401 U.S. 37, 91 S.Ct. 746, 27 L.Ed.2d 669 (1971) in Moore v. Sims, 442 U.S. 415, 99 S.Ct. 2371, 60 L.Ed.2d 994 (1979). See Institute of Judicial Administration-American Bar Assn., Juvenile Justice Standards Project, Standards Relating to Abuse and Neglect 91–102 (Rev. ed. 1981) for proposed statutes dealing with the state's authority to take emergency custody of endangered children.

86. E.g., N.J.Stat.Ann. § 9:6–8.34 (Supp.1985); N.Y.–McKinney's Fam.Ct.Act § 1032 (1983). Or.Rev.Stat. § 419.482 (1985) allows anyone to allege the child is within the court's jurisdiction, but permits only the court to direct that a petition be filed.

87. E.g., Colo.Rev.Stat. §§ 19–3–101, 19–10–113 (1986); Wis.Stat.Ann. § 48.24 (1985).

88. E.g., West's Ann.Cal.Welf. & Inst.Code § 337, (Supp.1986); Colo.Rev.Stat. § 19–3–103 (1986); Ill.–S.H.A. ch. 37, §§ 704–3, 704–4 (Supp.1986); N.J.Stat.Ann. § 9:6–8.38 (Supp.1985); N.Y.–McKinney's Fam.Ct.Act § 1036 (1983).

89. Reliance on substituted service in some cases may be essential if the parent or other defendant is out of the state. But some doubt may be raised concerning the requirements of due process by May v. Anderson, 345 U.S. 528, 73 S.Ct. 840, 97 L.Ed. 1221 (1953), discussed infra, section 12.5.

appointed to represent the child.[90] In view of the Lassiter case,[91] the question whether a guardian ad litem or counsel for the child must be appointed in order to meet constitutional requirements is an open one. The Supreme Court in that case held that the Due Process Clause does not require appointment of counsel for the parent in every case in which parental rights may be terminated, but it went on to say that in some cases, particularly where the parent faces a criminal charge which might lead to imprisonment, there may be a constitutional right to appointed counsel. Cases in the state courts are in disagreement on the question.[92] Due regard for the importance of the interests of both child and parents, and for the complexity of the cases and the relative inability of both parents and child to protect their inter-

ests should lead the courts to require the appointment of counsel for both parents and child in all cases in which the parties are unable to provide counsel for themselves,[93] notwithstanding the cost to the state which this may entail.

Primarily as a result of initiatives from the medical profession, organizations known variously as child abuse protection teams or child protective service teams have been set up in some states.[94] Their functions also vary in detail, but their general purpose is to bring to bear on child abuse and neglect cases the expertise of the several disciplines which might be able to contribute to diagnosis, evaluation, proof and treatment of such cases.[95] Some such teams are based in hospitals and are concerned chiefly with the treatment of

90. E.g., Alaska Stat. § 47.17.030(e) (1979); West's Ann.Cal.Welf. & Inst.Code § 349 (West 1984); Ill.–S.H.A. ch. 37, § 704–5 (Supp.1986); Mich.G.L.A. § 25.248(10) (1984); Wis.Stat.Ann. § 48.23 (1979 and Supp.1985). For a discussion of the guardian ad litem and his functions, see Davidson, The Guardian Ad Litem, An Important Approach to the Protection of Children, in American Bar Association, National Legal Resource Center for Child Advocacy and Protection, National Resource Center on Child Abuse, and National Association of Counsel for Children, Protecting Children Through the Legal System 835 (1981) (hereinafter cited as Protecting Children Through the Legal System.) See also, Isaacs, The Role of the Lawyer in Child Abuse Cases, in C. Kempe and R. Helfer, Helping the Battered Child and His Family 225 (1972).

91. Lassiter v. Department of Social Services of Durham County, N.C., 452 U.S. 18, 101 S.Ct. 2153, 68 L.Ed.2d 640 (1981), rehearing denied 453 U.S. 927, 102 S.Ct. 889, 69 L.Ed.2d 1023 (1981). The Court engaged in a "balancing of the competing private and public interests", which consisted of the parties' interests, the risks of error, and the expense involved.

92. The leading case holding that counsel must be appointed for the parent, at least where there is a possibility of criminal charges is In re B, 30 N.Y.2d 352, 285 N.E.2d 288, 334 N.Y.S.2d 133 (1972). Other cases on the point are collected in the Lassiter opinion.

New Jersey Division of Youth & Family Services v. Wandell, 155 N.J.Super. 302, 382 A.2d 711 (Juv. & Dom. Rel.Ct.1978) held the child entitled to counsel. Matter of D., 24 Or.App. 601, 547 P.2d 175 (1976), cert. denied 429 U.S. 907, 97 S.Ct. 273, 50 L.Ed.2d 189 (1976) held that counsel is not required by due process, and that the trial court should assign counsel on a case by case basis.

The function of the children's representative is not clearly defined. One case states that at the outset of the proceeding he should be neutral and not take a position

as to what the child's interests demand, but that as the proceeding goes on, he may advocate a particular disposition. Matter of Apel, 96 Misc.2d 839, 409 N.Y.S.2d 928 (Fam.Ct.1978). This seems to assume that he will have no knowledge of the facts in the case until he hears the evidence, and relegates him to a somewhat passive role. It would seem preferable for him to prepare the case as any lawyer would, investigating the facts and presenting evidence to the court as a basis for arguing whatever position he concludes would best serve the child's welfare. For other discussions of counsel's role in representing the child, see Isaacs, The Role of the Lawyer in Child Abuse Cases, in C. Kempe and R. Helfer, Helping the Battered Child and His Family 225 (1972); National Legal Resource Center for Child Advocacy and Protection, and American Bar Association, Protecting Children Through the Legal System ch. 7 (1981).

93. That these interests far outweigh the expense to the state is attested to by the fact that so many state statutes require counsel to be appointed. And the Child Abuse Prevention and Treatment Act of 1974, as amended, requires the states to appoint counsel to represent the child in all cases of abuse or neglect, as a condition upon receiving federal grants for various state programs.

This question is discussed in greater detail in connection with involuntary termination of parental rights infra, section 20.6.

94. E.g., Colo.Rev.Stat. § 19–10–109(6) (1986); Ill.–S.H.A. ch. 23, § 2057.2 (Supp.1986); Mass.Gen.Laws Ann. ch. 119, § 51D (Supp.1986); Pa.Stat. tit. 11, §§ 2216, 2217 (Supp.1985).

95. National Center on Child Abuse and Neglect, Multidisciplinary Teams in Child Abuse and Neglect Programs (1978); Schmitt, Grosz, Carroll, The Child Protection Team: A Problem Oriented Approach, in R. Helfer and C. Kempe, Child Abuse and Neglect: The Family and the Community 91 (1976).

the child.[96] Others play a more general role in compiling information and suggesting improvements in the state's whole child protection system.[97] Whatever their precise purpose in a particular state, they offer a useful method for mobilizing community resources for dealing with this pervasive and difficult social problem.

Of course the final legal step in child abuse and neglect cases is the hearing. In some states the hearing occurs in two steps, the first being concerned with adjudication or finding whether or not the abuse or neglect actually took place, the second being concerned with disposition, with what should be done with the child and his parents.[98] Where the charge of child abuse or neglect may result in the total termination of the parent's rights or the removal of the child from the parent's control, the statutes of some states require, at some point in the hearing procedure, that the state show that it has made an effort to encourage and promote the parent-child relationship.[99]

Since most instances of alleged child abuse and neglect occur in a family setting where there are few or no witnesses to the crucial events other than the parents themselves, a major legal problem presented by the cases is what standard of proof the courts should apply. Of course where child abuse is prosecuted as a crime, either under a specific child abuse criminal statute or under the criminal assault or homicide statutes, the standard of proof is that for any criminal case, and the offense must be proved beyond a reasonable doubt.[1] But where the state brings a civil suit seeking the various non-criminal forms of

relief provided for child abuse and neglect, there is conflict among the states as to what standard of proof should be required. The majority of states, either by statute or case law, require that where the remedy is to be termination of parental rights, the state must prove its allegations by clear and convincing evidence, or, in a few instances, beyond a reasonable doubt.[2] Relying in part upon this majority rule, the Supreme Court in Santosky v. Kramer[3] has held that the clear and convincing evidence standard is mandated by the Due Process Clause of the Fourteenth Amendment to the Constitution, in cases in which the state is seeking to terminate parental rights. The Court's reasoning was that the standard of proof required by the Due Process Clause turns on the relative weight of the public and private interests affected and also upon the determination of how the risk of error should be apportioned between the litigants. Here, the Court found, the parental interest outweighs that of the state, the risk of error is great and that risk should be imposed more heavily upon the state than upon the parents. In consequence of these arguments the Court decided that the "clear and convincing evidence" standard properly allocates the risk of error, while a "preponderance of evidence" standard would not.

Obviously many civil child abuse cases do not result in the termination of the parents' rights in their child and are not brought to reach that result. Whether the Santosky ruling would apply to such cases is not clear. In Colorado, where the parents' rights may only be terminated after a second proceeding which requires proof of other facts in addition

96. Delnero, Hopkins, Drews, The Medical Center Child Abuse Team, in C. Kempe and R. Helfer, Helping the Battered Child and His Family 161 (1972).

97. For a broad account of all such teams, see Bross, Multi-Disciplinary Child Protection Teams and Effective Legal Management of Abuse and Neglect, in Protecting Children Through the Legal System 495 (1981), cited supra, note 90. See also Bourne, The Role of Attorneys on Child Abuse Teams, 54 Chicago-Kent L.Rev. 773 (1978).

98. E.g., Colo.Rev.Stat. §§ 19–3–106, 19–3–111 (1986); N.J.Stat.Ann. § 9:6–8.47 (Supp.1985); N.Y.–McKinney's Fam.Ct.Act § 1047 (1983). Under Or.Rev.Stat. §§ 419.498, 419.505 (1985) a single hearing is held.

99. See, e.g., West's Ann.Cal.Welf. & Inst.Code §§ 358.1, 16501 (Supp.1986); Colo.Rev.Stat. § 19–11–105 (1986); N.Y.–McKinney's Fam.Ct.Act § 614.1(c) (1983); West's Rev.Code Wash.Ann. § 13.34.120 (Supp.1986).

1. See, e.g., State v. Loss, 295 Minn. 271, 204 N.W.2d 404 (1973) (manslaughter).

2. The cases and statutes are collected in Santosky v. Kramer, 455 U.S. 745, 749, 102 S.Ct. 1388, 1392, 71 L.Ed. 2d 599, 604 (1982), on remand 89 A.D.2d 738, 453 N.Y.S.2d 942 (1982).

3. Id.

to those constituting abuse or neglect, it has been held that the initial proceeding for child dependency or neglect, which of itself does not support a decree for termination of parental rights, may still be based upon a preponderance of the evidence standard.[4] This is a proper result in view of the child's need, which is often exigent, and of the fact that the dependency or neglect decree does not have the final and irrevocable effect upon the parents' interests which a decree terminating their rights would have.

The typical child abuse case rests upon evidence of an examining physician or other medical expert to the effect that the injuries could not have been the result of accident, countered by the parent's testimony that the injuries were accidental. Evidence in this posture is generally enough to get the case to the trier of fact, particularly if there is some other testimony supporting the state's version of the facts, whether the standard of proof is beyond a reasonable doubt or clear and convincing evidence.[5] Expert medical testimony is of course admissible on such issues.[6] When

the state seeks to introduce evidence that a parent had abused other children or had engaged in child abuse on other occasions, the evidence will not be admitted if the proceeding is a criminal one,[7] but at least some courts will admit it if the proceeding is civil in nature.[8]

Under most child abuse statutes there is no husband-wife testimonial privilege.[9] And the privilege against self-incrimination may be avoided by an immunity provision in the statute.[10] Where sexual abuse is alleged the child may be permitted to testify out of the presence of her parents if the proceeding is civil in nature and the parents' attorney has an opportunity to cross-examine.[11]

Consideration of the remedies for child abuse leads initially to the question whether the particular case should be handled as a criminal prosecution, or a civil proceeding, or both. The use of the criminal law in child abuse cases has been vigorously criticized on the ground that it is ineffective, does not get at the underlying causes of the abuse by the particular parent, does not provide therapy

---

4. People in Interest of A.M.D., 648 P.2d 625 (Colo. 1982); People in Interest of O.E.P., 654 P.2d 312 (Colo. 1982). See also In re Linda C, 86 A.D.2d 356, 451 N.Y.S.2d 268 (3d Dep't 1982) and Matter of Cheryl H., 153 Cal.App.3d 1098, 200 Cal.Rptr. 789 (1984).

5. E.g., People v. Watson, 107 Ill.App.3d 691, 63 Ill. Dec. 522, 438 N.E.2d 453 (1982) (sexual abuse of three-year-old child); State v. Loss, 295 Minn. 271, 204 N.W.2d 404 (1973); In re J.Z., 190 N.W.2d 27 (N.D.1971); Matter of S.J.Z., 252 N.W.2d 224 (S.D.1977); Sanderson v. State, 548 S.W.2d 337 (Tenn.Crim.App.1976) (incest); State v. Pennewell, 23 Wash.App. 777, 598 P.2d 748 (1979).

Contra, holding the evidence not sufficient: Fabritz v. Traurig, 583 F.2d 697 (4th Cir.1978), cert. denied 443 U.S. 915, 99 S.Ct. 3106, 61 L.Ed.2d 879 (1979) (violation of due process for mother to be convicted of child abuse in failing to obtain medical treatment for child injured by another); Pickering v. State, 596 S.W.2d 124 (Tex.Crim. App.1980) (circumstantial evidence failed sufficiently to connect defendant with the injuries, which were dreadful). State v. Loebach, 310 N.W.2d 58 (Minn.1981) held that evidence of the "battering parent" profile should be excluded, but that in this case it was not prejudicial.

Due to the difficulties of proving child abuse, especially sexual abuse, the courts are often faced with hearsay objections. Cases dealing with such objections in various contexts include United States v. Renville, 779 F.2d 430 (8th Cir.1985) (admitted child's statement to a physician); In re Estrella R., 167 Cal.App.3d 704, 213 Cal.Rptr. 198 (1985) (probation report admissible and may be used to sustain a finding of dependency); In re Amanda I., 166

Cal.App.3d 248, 212 Cal.Rptr. 317 (1985) (social worker's report admissible where opportunity to rebut was given, but could not be relied upon to sustain a finding of abuse); State v. Smith, 315 N.C. 76, 337 S.E.2d 833 (1985) (admits child's statement to her grandmother); Goldade v. State, 674 P.2d 721 (Wyo.1983), cert. denied 467 U.S. 1253, 104 S.Ct. 3539, 82 L.Ed.2d 844 (1984) (admits child's statement to nurse and physician). Matter of X, 110 Idaho 44, 714 P.2d 13 (1986) has held admissible the result of a polygraph test of a defendant charged with child abuse where it indicated his denial of abuse was truthful, where most of the evidence against him consisted of statements from counselors and psychologists who had interviewed the child, a four-year-old.

6. Annot., 98 A.L.R.3d 306 (1980). See also Collins v. Superior Court In and For Los Angeles County, 74 Cal. App.3d 47, 141 Cal.Rptr. 273 (1977); Ruppert v. Dinin, 49 Misc.2d 585, 267 N.Y.S.2d 953 (1966).

7. Worthen v. State, 42 Md.App. 20, 399 A.2d 272 (1979). But see Harrington v. State, 547 S.W.2d 616 (Tex. Crim.App.1977).

8. In Interest of Long, 313 N.W.2d 473 (Iowa 1981); Matter of T.Y.K., 183 Mont. 91, 598 P.2d 593 (1979).

9. See note 28, supra; Commonwealth v. Boarman, 610 S.W.2d 922 (Ky.1980); Annot., 93 A.L.R.3d 1018 (1979).

10. Matter of Vance A., 105 Misc.2d 254, 432 N.Y.S.2d 137 (Fam.Ct.1980).

11. Matter of T.E.R., 180 Mont. 340, 590 P.2d 1117 (1979).

for the parent or care for the child, is expensive in time and resources, and is often very difficult to prove.[12] These criticisms are so severe that one might conclude that child abuse should not be made a crime at all, but as one author has pointed out, it would be a most peculiar legal system that permitted a person charged with homicide or criminal assault and battery to defend on the ground that the object of his violence was only his child.[13] This being so, the question then becomes under what circumstances a particular case should be treated as one for the criminal courts. The decision to prosecute should be based upon such factors as whether the child died or suffered permanent injury, whether there were mitigating circumstances in the parents' conduct, whether there would be reasonable prospects for holding the family together with outside help or therapy, and whether the criminal prosecution might be used to force the parents to undertake therapy.[14] Certainly when the child has been killed, it would be difficult to justify a failure to prosecute except for the presence of very clear and very strong mitigating facts.[15]

The disposition stage of a civil child abuse or neglect proceeding presents the court with a broad range of alternative remedies. Most statutes authorize in greater or lesser detail various protective orders, supervision of the parents, an award of temporary custody to foster parents or to the state, orders for the medical treatment or psychiatric therapy of the child or the parents, and as a last resort the permanent termination of parental rights.[16] Under the federal Child Abuse Prevention and Treatment Act of 1974 in order to receive federal grants the states must show that they provide programs and personnel making these remedies effective.[17] In appropriate cases many of these remedies may be available without court action, as a result of negotiation and voluntary agreement between the parents and the state agency,[18] but of course in such negotiations the agency always has the leverage produced by the awareness that a civil proceeding can be brought if the negotiations break down.

In making its decision on disposition the court is faced with the same difficult conflict of interests which arises in child custody cases. The primary concern is the child's welfare, or, as Goldstein, Freud and Solnit would have it, the least detrimental alternative for the child,[19] but at the same time the parents' interest may not be ignored. As some cases rather simplistically put it, the

12. Paulsen, The Legal Framework for Child Protection, 66 Colum.L.Rev. 679, 692 (1966); Delaney, The Battered Child and the Law, in C. Kempe and R. Helfer, Helping the Battered Child and His Family 187, 192 (1972).

13. Rosenthal, Physical Abuse of Children by Parents: The Criminalization Decision, 7 Am.J.Crim.L. 141, 168 (1979). But see Myers, The Legal Response to Child Abuse: In the Best Interests of Children? 24 J.Fam.L. 149 (1985).

14. McKenna, A Case Study of Child Abuse: A Former Prosecutor's View, 12 Am.Crim.L.Rev. 165 (1974); Allott, The District Attorney, in C. Kempe and R. Helfer, Helping the Battered Child and His Family 256 (1972).

15. Examples of the proper use of the criminal sanction are Commonwealth v. Cadwell, 374 Mass. 308, 372 N.E.2d 246 (1978) and Commonwealth v. Labbe, 6 Mass. App.Ct. 73, 373 N.E.2d 227 (1978). A case which perhaps should not have been prosecuted, although the child died, is Fabritz v. Traurig, 583 F.2d 697 (4th Cir.1978), cert. denied 443 U.S. 915, 99 S.Ct. 3106, 61 L.Ed.2d 879 (1979).

16. E.g., Alaska Stat. § 47.10.080 (1979); West's Ann. Cal.Welf. & Inst.Code §§ 361, 362 (Supp.1986); Colo.Rev. Stat. §§ 19–3–111, 19–11–105 (1986); Conn.Gen.Stat.Ann. § 17–43a (Supp.1986); Ill.–S.H.A. ch. 37, §§ 705–1, 705–2,

705–7 (Supp.1986); N.J.Stat.Ann. §§ 9:6–8.50, 9:6–8.51, 9:6–8.54, 9:16–8.58 (1976 and Supp.1985); N.Y.–McKinney's Fam.Ct.Act §§ 1052, 1054, 1055, 1056, 1057 (1983 and Supp.1986); Or.Rev.Stat. §§ 419.507, 419.523 (1985); Pa.Stat. tit. 35, § 10186 (Supp.1986); West's Rev.Code Wash.Ann. § 13.34.130 (Supp.1986); Wis.Stat.Ann. §§ 48.427, 48.428, 48.43 (Supp.1985). The Institute of Judicial Administration-American Bar Assn., Juvenile Justice Standards Project, Standards Relating to Abuse and Neglect 124, 128, 159 (Rev. ed. 1981) provide for similar dispositional alternatives.

17. 42 U.S.C.A. § 5103(b)(2). See Hoffman, Policy and Politics: The Child Abuse Prevention and Treatment Act, in R. Bourne and E. Newberger, Critical Perspectives on Child Abuse 157 (1979).

18. E.g., Colo.Rev.Stat. § 19–3–101(2)(c) (1986); Ill.–S.H.A. ch. 23, § 2058.2 (Supp.1986); Institute of Judicial Administration-American Bar Assn., Juvenile Justice Standards Project, Standards Relating to Abuse and Neglect 183–195 (Rev. ed. 1981). See Carroll, The Function of Protective Services in Child Abuse and Neglect, in C. Kempe and R. Helfer, The Battered Child 275 (3d ed. 1980).

19. J. Goldstein, A. Freud, A. Solnit, Beyond the Best Interests of the Child ch. 4 (1973).

parent may not be deprived of the custody and control of his child solely because the state could find someone else who might do a better job as a parent.[20] Perhaps a more precise formulation of the applicable principle would be to say that if it is reasonably likely that the child's welfare can be served by methods of treatment which do not require permanently or temporarily taking him away from his parents, these methods should be used. If this cannot be accomplished, then removal from his parents must be resorted to, but the extent of the interference with parental control and custody should be no greater than is reasonably necessary to provide for the child's physical, emotional and developmental needs.[21]

The success or failure of the court's effort at helping the abused or neglected child depends upon the range of community resources which

are available to treat the child and his parents, and upon the extent to which the lawyers can cooperate with other professionals in the diagnosis and treatment of the child.[22] The medical and mental health professions have been active in devising and developing interdisciplinary approaches to the prediction, diagnosis and prevention of child abuse, as the extensive literature on the subject demonstrates.[23] It is essential for lawyers and judges to be familiar with these approaches and to use them whenever they are available and offer prospects for success.[24] This is especially true for the cases in which sexual exploitation or abuse of the child are alleged.[25] At the same time the legal profession should continue to do all that it can to provide encouragement and public support for the efforts of the other professions to control child abuse and neglect.

20.   E.g., In re N.H., 135 Vt. 230, 373 A.2d 851 (1977).

21.   For examples of the application of this kind of standard, see, e.g., Martin v. Sand, 444 A.2d 309 (Del. Fam.Ct.1982); Matter of T.J.D., 189 Mont. 147, 615 P.2d 212 (1980); New Jersey Div. of Youth and Family Services v. Huggins, 148 N.J.Super. 86, 371 A.2d 841 (Juv. & Dom.Rel.Ct.1977), affirmed on the reasoning of the court below, 160 N.J.Super. 159, 388 A.2d 1338 (1978). A similar position is taken by McQuiston and Kempe, Treatment of the Child, in C. Kempe and R. Helfer, The Battered Child 379, 381 (3d ed. 1980). Research on the efficacy of service to children in their own homes is reported on in M. Phillips, A. Shyne, E. Sherman, B. Haring, Factors Associated With Placement Decisions in Child Welfare (Child Welfare League of America 1971), and E. Sherman, M. Phillips, B. Haring, A. Shyne, Service to Children in Their Own Homes: Its Nature and Outcome (Child Welfare League of America 1974).

A current tendency to adopt a more rigid standard than that in the text, one which imposes much stricter limits on intervention in the family by state agencies, is reflected in the Institute of Judicial Administration-American Bar Assn., Juvenile Justice Standards Project, Standards Relating to Abuse and Neglect (Rev. ed. 1981). Criticism of this approach as providing inadequate protection for children is expressed in the dissent to that work, at pages 197 and 200, by Commissioners Wilfred W. Nuernberger and Justine Wise Polier. Similar criticism may be found in R. Bourne and E. Newberger, Critical Perspectives on Child Abuse 97 (1979).

22.   Bross, Multi-Disciplinary Child Protection Teams and Effective Legal Management of Abuse and Neglect, in Protecting Children Through the Legal System 495 (1981); Ten Broeck, Casework and Supervision in Child Protective Services, id. at 439.

23.   Some of the approaches are described in the following works: C. Kempe and R. Helfer, Helping the Battered Child and His Family chs. 1, 3, 11, 12 (1972); R. Helfer and C. Kempe, Child Abuse and Neglect, The Family and the Community Parts II and III (1976); G. Williams and J. Money, Traumatic Abuse and Neglect of Children at Home Part VIII (1980); J. Garbarino and G. Gilliam, Understanding Abusive Families ch. 14 (1980); C. Kempe and R. Helfer, The Battered Child Parts III and IV (3d ed. 1980).

24.   Stein, The Role of the Court in Case Planning, in Protecting Children Through the Legal System 409 (1981).

25.   Some of the additional difficulties inherent in incest and sexual abuse cases are explored in D. Walters, Physical and Sexual Abuse of Children chs. 8, 9 (1975); D. Finkelhor, Sexually Victimized Children ch. 6 (1979); G. Williams and J. Money, Traumatic Abuse and Neglect of Children at Home Part VI (1980); J. Garbarino and G. Gilliam, Understanding Abusive Families ch. 11 (1980); C. Kempe and R. Helfer, The Battered Child ch. 12 (3d ed. 1980). See also In re Courtney S., 130 Cal.App.3d 567, 181 Cal.Rptr. 843 (1982).

A serious difficulty in the law's treatment of sexual abuse cases is the harm done to the child by requiring him to testify in open court about the details of the abuse. Some use of videotape or closed circuit television has been suggested as a way of lessening this harm. See Bulkley, Evidentiary and Procedural Trends in State Legislation and Other Emerging Legal Issues in Child Sexual Abuse Cases, 89 Dick.L.Rev. 645 (1985). For new approaches to preventive measures, see Davidson, Protection of Children Through Criminal History Record Screening: Well-Meaning Promises and Legal Pitfalls, 89 Dick.L.Rev. 577 (1985).

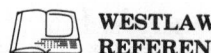

§ 9.5 Parental Discipline and the Child in Need of Supervision

The subjects of juvenile delinquency and juvenile courts are too extensive to be dealt with in this work. One aspect of those subjects is so closely related to the relationships between parents and children and the state, however, that it must briefly be discussed here. All or nearly all states have as part of their juvenile court legislation statutes which give those courts jurisdiction over children whose conduct fails to meet traditional standards of children's behavior even though it does not amount to a violation of the criminal law. Specifically, these statutes authorize juvenile proceedings respecting children (generally defined as persons under eighteen) who are habitually truant from school, who habitually disobey their parents' lawful and reasonable instructions, or who persistently run away from home.[1] A few years ago children in this category were sometimes included in the definition of juvenile delinquents, but this is rarely the case today.[2] Today these children are generally referred to as children in need of supervision,[3] children in need of oversight,[4] persons in need of supervision,[5] dependent children,[6] or are not given any general designation at all.[7] Most such statutes now contain disposition provisions expressly applicable only to such children, distinguishing them from delinquents and not permitting the more drastic court orders authorized for delinquents, such as commitment to institutions.[8]

The conduct forbidden by these statutes has been somewhat inaccurately referred to as "status offenses", although these statutes do turn on conduct rather than status.[9] The statutes themselves and court proceedings taken pursuant to them have been vigorously criticized in the law reviews and elsewhere. A fair sample of the criticism would include assertions that the statutes are so general that they permit all sorts of harmless conduct to be prosecuted;[10] that the courts process as CHINS or PINS children who should be han-

§ 9.5

1. E.g., Ala.Code 1986, § 12–15–1(4); Ariz.Rev.Stat. § 8–201(13) (Supp.1985); West's Ann.Cal.Welf. & Inst. Code § 601 (1984); Colo.Rev.Stat. § 19–1–103(20)(e)(f); Conn.Gen.Stat.Ann. § 46b–120 (Supp.1986); West's Fla. Stat.Ann. § 39.01(9) (Supp.1986); West's Ann.Ind.Code § 31–6–4–1 (Supp.1986); Mass.G.L.A. ch. 119, § 39E (1975 and Supp.1986); Minn.Stat.Ann. §§ 260.015(19), (20) (1982); Miss.Code 1981, § 43–21–105(k); N.H.Rev.Stat. § 169–D:2 IV (Supp.1983); N.Y.–McKinney's Fam.Ct.Act § 712(a) (1983); Pa.Stat. tit. 42, § 6302 (1982); V.T.C.A., Fam.Code § 51.03(b) (Supp.1986); W.Va.Code, § 49–1–4 (1980).

2. West's Ann.Ind.Code § 31–6–4–1 (Supp.1986) and W.Va.Code, § 49–1–4 (1980) continue to classify these children as delinquents.

3. The Alabama statute, supra, note 1, uses this term, which is often abbreviated as CHINS. Illinois, see supra, note 1, refers to such children as minors requiring authoritative intervention.

4. See the New Hampshire statute, supra, note 1.

5. See the New York statute, supra, note 1. Children in this category are known as PINS.

6. See the Florida statute, supra, note 1.

7. As in the California and Minnesota statutes, supra, note 1.

8. The California, Colorado, Massachusetts, Mississippi, Pennsylvania and Texas statutes, listed supra, note 1, contain provisions which foreclose commitment of children to institutions on the basis of the status offenses.

9. Institute of Judicial Administration-American Bar Assn., Juvenile Justice Standards Project, Standards Relating to Noncriminal Misbehavior 2 (1982), hereinafter referred to as IJA–ABA Standards. Cf. In Interest of Gras, 337 So.2d 641 (La.App.1976).

10. Rosenberg and Rosenberg, The Legacy of the Stubborn and Rebellious Son, 74 Mich.L.Rev. 1097, 1110 (1976).

dled as either neglected or delinquent;[11] conversely that these children are treated like delinquents with respect to disposition;[12] that the courts permit the proceedings to be used as a threat or as punishment for the child without making an investigation of the causes and circumstances of the child's conduct, the implication being that the fault often lies with the parents rather than the child;[13] that the remedies available to and applied by the courts are not effective, or harm rather than help the child;[14] and that the ungovernable child should be a responsibility of other community organizations or of the schools rather than the courts.[15] The obvious conclusion from these criticisms is that the jurisdiction over children in need of supervision ought to be abolished.[16] This has not occurred, but the criticism has probably had some influence in causing the statutes to be amended so as to remove some of the archaic or trivial bases for the jurisdiction and so as to limit the range of remedies available to the courts. On the other hand it seems clear that community resources for helping children in need of super-

vision have not increased but have been reduced, as have the financial resources available to the schools. To the extent that these children's difficulties are a product of poverty and despair on the part of their parents and themselves, the problems are not likely to be solved very soon.

Although it may be conceded that there is force to these criticisms of CHINS or PINS jurisdiction, there is also logic to providing state support for parental authority.[17] In other contexts the law places heavy responsibility upon parents, to support their children,[18] to determine what medical or surgical care they should receive,[19] to make important decisions about their education[20] and to retain custody of their children in the face of state attempts to terminate parental rights.[21] It is hardly unreasonable for the state to provide such remedies as it can to help parents meet these responsibilities.

Notwithstanding all the criticism, the courts have generally upheld these statutes when they have been attacked as void for vagueness under the Due Process Clause.[22]

11. Note, Ungovernability: The Unjustifiable Jurisdiction, 83 Yale L.J. 1383, 1391 (1974).

12. IJA–ABA Standards 5.

13. Note, Ungovernability: The Unjustifiable Jurisdiction, 83 Yale L.J. 1383, 1394 (1974).

14. IJA–ABA Standards 3.

15. Bazelon, Beyond Control of the Juvenile Court, 21 Juv.Ct.Judges J. 42 (1970).

16. IJA–ABA Standards 2. The Standards propose that juvenile court jurisdiction over children in need of supervision be abolished, with a system of voluntary referrals to be substituted. The commentary to the standards contains sweeping criticism of the jurisdiction and statutes, collecting articles also critical but without citation of authority on the other side of the question.

For other discussion of these issues, see L. Teitelbaum, A. Guogh, eds., Beyond Control-Status Offenders in the Juvenile Court (1977).

17. Gregory, Juvenile Court Jurisdiction Over Noncriminal Behavior: The Argument Against Abolition, 39 Ohio St.L.J. 242 (1978) makes a strong case for the retention of the PINS jurisdiction in the juvenile courts.

L.A.M. v. State, 547 P.2d 827 (Alaska 1976) has described the purpose of the CHINS statute as vindicating the parent's right to custody of the child and consequently protecting the child against the harms resulting from running away or from rejecting parental supervision.

18. See section 6.2, supra.

19. See section 9.3, supra.

20. See section 9.2, supra.

21. See section 20.6, infra. See also the statutes and cases holding parents responsible for their children's torts cited in section 10.6 Practitioner's Edition.

22. D.T.H. v. State, 345 So.2d 703 (Fla.1977) ("ungovernable child" as defined in the statute not too vague); In Interest of Gras, 337 So.2d 641 (La.App.1976) ("habitually disobeys the reasonable and lawful demands of his parents" is not too vague); S_____ S_____ v. State, 299 A.2d 560 (Me.1973) ("living in circumstances of manifest danger of falling into habits of vice or immorality" not too vague); A. v. New York, 31 N.Y.2d 83, 335 N.Y.S. 2d 33, 286 N.E.2d 432 (1972) ("habitual truant", "incorrigible", "ungovernable" and "habitually disobedient and beyond * * * lawful control" are not too vague); In re Napier, 532 P.2d 423 (Okl.1975) ("habitually truant", "beyond the control of his parents", and "habitually deports himself so as to injure or endanger the health or morals of himself or others" is not too vague); Blondheim v. State, 84 Wash.2d 874, 529 P.2d 1096 (1975) ("incorrigible" not too vague).

Roybal, Void for Vagueness: State Statutes Proscribing Conduct only for a Juvenile, 1 Pepperdine L.Rev. 1 (1973) cites an unreported United States District Court case, Gonzalez v. Mailliard, which held unconstitutional the phrase "who from any cause is in danger of leading an idle, dissolute, lewd, or immoral life." The case was vacated and remanded, Mailliard v. Gonzalez, 416 U.S. 918, 94 S.Ct. 1915, 40 L.Ed.2d 276 (1974). See also Gesicki v. Oswald, 336 F.Supp. 371 (S.D.N.Y.1971), af-

The statutes have also been held valid when attacked for overbreadth,[23] or on the ground that they violate the Eighth Amendment by punishing status alone.[24] Older versions of the statutes are now held to violate the Equal Protection Clause if they prescribed different maximum ages for males and females, however.[25] The Due Process Clause may be violated if the court's decree abridges the child's freedom more extensively than is necessary, the court being required, according to one case, to adopt the least restrictive remedy appropriate for correcting the child's behavior.[26] In doing so the court may restrict the child's associations with others without infringing the child's right of free association given by the First Amendment.[27]

Some of the phrases defining the child in need of supervision require proof of repeated acts or a course of conduct by the child before he can be adjudicated.[28] Other statutory language may be satisfied by a single act of disobedience, for example, or running away.[29] Running away may violate the statute if the child leaves a foster home rather than the home maintained by his parents,[30] but it is not an offense if the child has a good reason for leaving home,[31] or if there is no evidence that he does not intend to return home.[32] Likewise failure to attend school does not amount to truancy in violation of the statute

if the child is made miserable by the conditions to which he is subjected at school.[33]

One much discussed case, In re Snyder's Welfare,[34] raises difficult questions concerning the proper definition and use of the CHINS or PINS jurisdiction. Cynthia Snyder, sixteen years old, was subjected to strict discipline by her parents, discipline which she found difficult to endure. She filed a petition in dependency and after a hearing was returned to her parents' home. Shortly thereafter Cynthia had further trouble with her parents and sought help from an organization for troubled juveniles. As a result a social worker at a youth service center filed a petition in juvenile court alleging that Cynthia was incorrigible. At the hearing she testified that she was refusing to return to her parents, that she could not live with them. After ordering some counseling for Cynthia and her parents, the trial court concluded that she was incorrigible and ordered her placed in a foster home. The Supreme Court of Washington affirmed, holding that the question of why the parent-child relationship broke down is irrelevant to the disposition of the case, and finding that substantial evidence supported the juvenile court's finding of incorrigibility. There was apparently no evidence that the parents' discipline was abusive or unreasona-

firmed mem. 406 U.S. 913, 92 S.Ct. 1773, 32 L.Ed.2d 113 (1972).

23. Blondheim v. State, 84 Wash.2d 874, 529 P.2d 1096 (1975).

24. In Interest of Gras, 337 So.2d 641 (La.App.1976); S_____ S_____ v. State, 299 A.2d 560 (Me.1973); Blondheim v. State, 84 Wash.2d 874, 529 P.2d 1096 (1975).

25. A. v. New York, 31 N.Y.2d 83, 335 N.Y.S.2d 33, 286 N.E.2d 432 (1972). See Stanton v. Stanton, 421 U.S. 7, 95 S.Ct. 1373, 43 L.Ed.2d 688 (1975), appeal after remand 552 P.2d 112 (Utah 1976).

26. Chicago Board of Education v. Terrile, 47 Ill.App. 3d 75, 5 Ill.Dec. 455, 361 N.E.2d 778 (1977).

27. People in Interest of C.S.M., 194 Colo. 76, 570 P.2d 229 (1977).

28. In re S., 12 Cal.App.3d 1124, 91 Cal.Rptr. 261 (1970); Matter of Morrison, 110 Misc.2d 329, 442 N.Y.S.2d 43 (Fam.Ct.1981).

29. In re S., 12 Cal.App.3d 1124, 91 Cal.Rptr. 261 (1970) (single serious act may show child is "beyond control of his parents").

30. Matter of Williams, 55 Or.App. 951, 640 P.2d 675 (1982).

31. Matter of Price, 94 Misc.2d 345, 404 N.Y.S.2d 821 (Fam.Ct.1978) (child was not "habitually disobedient" or "beyond lawful control" of her parent when she left a dirty and unpleasant home to live with her maternal grandparent). See also In re G., 28 Cal.App.3d 276, 104 Cal.Rptr. 585 (1972).

32. In re R., 73 Misc.2d 390, 341 N.Y.S.2d 998 (Fam. Ct.1973).

33. Matter of Ian D., 109 Misc.2d 18, 439 N.Y.S.2d 613 (Fam.Ct.1981).

34. 85 Wash.2d 182, 532 P.2d 278 (1975). The case is discussed critically in Note, Status Offenses and the Status of Children's Rights: Do Children Have the Legal Right to be Incorrigible? 1976 B.Y.U.L.Rev. 659. Cynthia Snyder apparently remained apart from her parents as a result of this case. 1976 B.Y.U.L.Rev. 659, 691, n. 138.

ble or unduly harsh.[35]   Although Cynthia's parents argued that the juvenile court had taken Cynthia's part in disregard of their parental rights, the Supreme Court found this contention unsupported by the evidence.

The difficulty with the Snyder case lies both in its definition of incorrigibility and in the juvenile court's decree.   Incorrigibility is defined by the Washington statute [36] as applying to a child who is beyond the control of his parents.   As has been indicated,[37] some courts would require repeated conduct as evidence that the child was beyond control, while others would say that a single serious act would be sufficient.   There seems not to have been repeated conduct on Cynthia's part here, but it is at least conceivable that her refusal to return home meets the statutory test.   The more serious issue is created by the Washington Supreme Court's apparent assumption that her refusal was just as entitled to vindication as her parents' insistence upon disciplinary rules, insistence which was never shown to be unreasonable.   The effect of this was that a statute whose clear purpose is the

reinforcement of parental custody and control was so applied as to frustrate parental custody and control.   The case therefore must be read as inconsistent with the well settled principle that the state should not remove children from the custody and care of their parents in the absence of clear evidence that the parents have behaved in a way which has harmed or threatens to harm the child.   A later Illinois case, In Interest of Polovchak,[38] in analogous circumstances refused to permit the child to remain away from his parents, holding that the child was not beyond the control of his parents.

The procedure in PINS and CHINS cases is much like that in cases involving charges of dependency or neglect.[39]   The proceeding begins with a petition setting forth the child's acts.[40]   The cases are in conflict as to whether the child in such cases is entitled to have counsel appointed for him.[41]   Although detention of some sort may not always be a possible disposition of the case, still the effect upon the child is in any case sufficiently serious to warrant providing him with counsel at state

35.   This is made clear by the fact that the earlier petition alleging dependency, filed by Cynthia, was held not supported by the juvenile court.

36.   West's Rev.Code Wash.Ann. § 13.04.010(7) (1962).   This statute was repealed in 1977.   The Washington legislature apparently disapproved of Snyder, since in 1979 it enacted a statute entitled Procedure for Families in Conflict, West's Rev.Code Wash.Ann. §§ 13.32A.170 ff. (Supp.1987).   This statute provides for both voluntary reconciliation services and court action where child and parent cannot agree upon where the child is to live.   West's Rev.Code Wash.Ann. § 13.32A.170 (Supp.1987) authorizes a hearing on a petition by child or parent for an alternative residential placement of the child, but it expressly provides that the court may not grant such a petition filed by the child or the department of social and health services where it is based solely on the child's dislike of reasonable rules or reasonable discipline by his parents.

37.   See notes 28, 29, supra.

38.   104 Ill.App.3d 203, 59 Ill.Dec. 929, 432 N.E.2d 873 (1981).   This case arose when a twelve-year-old son of Soviet citizens left his parents' home because he did not wish to return with them to the Soviet Union.   The juvenile court held that the boy was beyond the control of his parents and therefore a minor otherwise in need of supervision as defined in the applicable statute.   The appellate court reversed, holding that the case presented merely an instance of family disagreement concerning whether they should all return to Russia.   The court held the question whether the child should be given political

asylum in the United States to be outside of its competence.   Although the case is obviously distinguishable from Snyder, the court's approach to it is more in accord with our traditional ideas of parent-child relations than that of the Washington court in Snyder.

For a discussion of the related subject of emancipation and the statutes in some states which permit the child to remove himself from the custody and control of his parents, see section 8.3, supra, at note 43.

39.   An outline of the usual procedure is found in Rosenberg and Rosenberg, The Legacy of the Stubborn and Rebellious Son, 74 Mich.L.Rev. 1097, 1102–1109 (1976).   The New York procedure is described in Note, Ungovernability: The Unjustifiable Jurisdiction, 83 Yale L.J. 1383, 1387–1391 (1974).   An example of abuse of the PINS jurisdiction occurs in Matter of Andrew R., 115 Misc.2d 937, 454 N.Y.S.2d 820 (Fam.Ct.1982).

40.   In re R., 73 Misc.2d 390, 341 N.Y.S.2d 998 (Fam. Ct.1973);   Matter of Morrison, 110 Misc.2d 329, 442 N.Y.S.2d 43 (Fam.Ct.1981).

41.   Wagstaff v. Superior Court, Family Court Division, 535 P.2d 1220 (Alaska 1975) requires counsel to be appointed.   In re Walker, 282 N.C. 28, 191 S.E.2d 702 (1972) held that counsel for the child is not constitutionally required.   In Interest of Hutchins, 345 So.2d 703 (Fla. 1977) held that counsel need not be furnished in an initial hearing which could only result in a finding of dependency, but must be furnished in later hearings which might lead to a finding of delinquency.

expense.[42] There is also some conflict concerning the standard of proof which must be observed in these cases, a few courts or statutes requiring proof by a mere preponderance of the evidence,[43] or by clear and convincing evidence,[44] but most insisting on proof beyond a reasonable doubt.[45]

The final step in a proceeding against a child in need of supervision is the decision on the remedy. This normally occurs after a separate hearing concerned only with the disposition of the case.[46] Most statutes provide the court with a range of possible dispositions. These include leaving the child with his parents, with or without some sort of protective order or order for medical or psychiatric treatment or counseling; placing him on probation or under the supervision of a social

worker; placing him in the custody of a relative or other suitable person; placing him in a foster home; or placing him in the control of a state agency.[47] In some states he may be committed to a state institution, such as a training school for juveniles.[48] Some courts have held that in framing a remedy the trial judge should adopt the least restrictive viable alternative.[49] The court's orders are enforceable by contempt proceedings.[50]

Of course this extensive battery of remedies is only of theoretical interest unless the state or the community provides the resources for making the remedies effective, and many of them do not.[51] One response to the lack of appropriate facilities for children in need of supervision has been the practice of some courts of placing such children in the same

---

42. Well drafted statutes provide for the appointment of counsel for children in need of supervision. E.g., Colo. Rev.Stat. § 19–1–106 (1986). See also Application Gault, 387 U.S. 1, 87 S.Ct. 1428, 18 L.Ed.2d 527 (1967). Cf. Lassiter v. Department of Social Services of Durham County, N.C., 452 U.S. 18, 101 S.Ct. 2153, 68 L.Ed.2d 640 (1981).

The function of the lawyer for the child is not really different from his function in relation to adult clients. He should advise the child respecting the child's best interests, but if the child wishes to oppose the petition, the lawyer should do all that he fairly can to defend the suit. See Institute of Judicial Administration-American Bar Association, Juvenile Justice Standards Project, Standards Relating to Counsel for Private Parties 77–81 (1980). Of course if the child is unable to make a judgment about his own interests, the attorney must either maintain a neutral stance, merely investigating and presenting the evidence he finds; or he may follow the instructions of the guardian ad litem if there is one; or if there is not one, he must independently decide what course best serves the child's interests. Id. at 81–83.

43. E.g., Md.Code, Cts. & Jud.Proc. § 3–819 (1984).

44. E.g., In Interest of Potter, 237 N.W.2d 461 (Iowa 1976).

45. E.g., Ala.Code 1986, § 12–15–65; Colo.Rev.Stat. § 19–3–106 (1986); West's Fla.Stat.Ann. § 39.40 (Supp. 1982); Mass.G.L.A. ch. 119, § 39G (Supp.1986); Miss.Code 1972, § 43–21–561; In re R., 73 Misc.2d 390, 341 N.Y.S.2d 998 (Fam.Ct.1973).

For the considerations controlling the proper constitutional standard for the burden of proof in somewhat similar cases, see Santosky v. Kramer, 455 U.S. 745, 71 L.Ed.2d 599, 102 S.Ct. 1388 (1982).

46. Rosenberg and Rosenberg, The Legacy of the Stubborn and Rebellious Son, 74 Mich.L.Rev. 1097, 1106 (1976).

47. E.g., Ala.Code 1986, § 12–15–71; Ariz.Rev.Stat. § 8–241 (Supp.1985); West's Ann.Cal.Welf. & Inst.Code

§§ 725, 726 (1984); Colo.Rev.Stat. § 19–3–111 (1986); Conn.Gen.Stat.Ann. § 46b–149(g) (Supp.1986); West's Fla.Stat.Ann. § 39.41 (Supp.1986); Ill.–S.H.A. ch. 37, § 705–2(b) (Supp.1986); West's Ann.Ind.Code §§ 31–6–4–15.4, 31–6–4–15.5 (Supp.1986); Mass.G.L.A. ch. 119, § 39G (1975 and Supp.1986); Minn.Stat.Ann. § 260.194 (1982); Miss.Code 1981, § 43–21–607; N.H. Rev. Stat. § 169–D:17 (Supp.1983); N.Y.–McKinney's Fam.Ct.Act §§ 754, 756 (1983 and Supp.1986); Pa.Stat. tit. 42, § 6351 (1982); V.T.C.A., Fam.Code §§ 52.03, 54.04, 54.041 (1975 and Supp.1986); W.Va.Code, § 49–5–13 (Supp.1985).

It has been asserted that all of the battery of remedies are ineffective. Note, Ungovernability: The Unjustifiable Jurisdiction, 83 Yale L.J. 1383, 1401 (1974).

48. Official Ga.Code Ann. §§ 24A–2302, 24A–2303 (1986). Although it is sometimes claimed that a large number of children in need of supervision are confined in institutions, Institute of Judicial Administration-American Bar Assn., Juvenile Justice Standards Project, Standards Relating to Noncriminal Misbehavior 6–8 (1982), statutes expressly authorizing such commitments are hard to find.

For cases dealing with the constitutionality of confining children in need of supervision in the same facility with juvenile delinquents, see note 53 infra.

49. Chicago Board of Education v. Terrile, 47 Ill.App. 3d 75, 5 Ill.Dec. 455, 361 N.E.2d 778 (1977); State ex rel. H.K. v. Taylor, 169 W.Va. 639, 289 S.E.2d 673 (1982).

50. State v. Norlund, 31 Wash.App. 725, 644 P.2d 724 (1982). Disobedience of a court order may transform a child in need of supervision into a juvenile delinquent. Vann v. Scott, 467 F.2d 1235 (7th Cir.1972); In Interest of Gras, 337 So.2d 641 (La.App.1976).

51. Rosenberg and Rosenberg, The Legacy of the Stubborn and Rebellious Son, 74 Mich.L.Rev. 1097, 1128, 1129 (1976); Note, Ungovernability: The Unjustifiable Jurisdiction, 83 Yale L.J. 1383, 1398–1400 (1974).

institutions with juvenile delinquents. This practice has been approved in some jurisdictions,[52] but in others has been held either to violate the statutes or constitution.[53]

The closely related judicial creation known as the "right to treatment" first appeared during the Nineteen Sixties and Seventies. It was initially devised to protect persons who were being involuntarily committed to mental institutions.[54] The doctrine was then applied to juvenile delinquents confined in institutions [55] and somewhat later to children in need of supervision.[56] The doctrine has been widely discussed in the law reviews, almost

always favorably.[57] It is the creature of the lower federal courts and some state courts.[58] In O'Connor v. Donaldson [59] the United States Supreme Court was asked to rule on the existence of a constitutional right to treatment as applied to a patient in a mental hospital, but held that the issue was not presented and ordered the patient released on other grounds. Chief Justice Burger wrote a separate concurring opinion indicating his view that there is not such a constitutionally based doctrine.[60]

The impression that the Supreme Court of the United States does not recognize *any* con-

52. Vann v. Scott, 467 F.2d 1235 (7th Cir.1972); Martarella v. Kelley, 349 F.Supp. 575 (S.D.N.Y.1972).

53. C. v. Redlich, 32 N.Y.2d 588, 347 N.Y.S.2d 51, 300 N.E.2d 424 (1973) (confinement is not "supervision" or "treatment" in accordance with the statute on disposition); State ex rel. Harris v. Calendine, 160 W.Va. 172, 233 S.E.2d 318 (1977) (confinement of status offenders violates the Equal Protection Clause because it discriminates invidiously on the basis of social class, sex, and geographic location, since such a child would go to a private, less restrictive institution if he were from an upper class family in a large city; also status offenders must be treated in a manner consistent with the state's parens patriae power to be constitutional; there is also sex discrimination because the statute can be used to punish young women for promiscuity; confinement with juvenile delinquents constitutes cruel and unusual punishment). Accord: State ex rel. H.K. v. Taylor, 169 W.Va. 639, 289 S.E.2d 673 (1982); State ex rel. C.A.H. v. Strickler, 162 W.Va. 535, 251 S.E.2d 222 (1979).

But placement of children in need of supervision in an institution exclusively for such children is permissible. Lavette M. v. Corporation Counsel of New York, 35 N.Y.2d 136, 359 N.Y.S.2d 20, 316 N.E.2d 314 (1974).

54. Rouse v. Cameron, 373 F.2d 451 (D.C.Cir.1966). A subsequent decision in the same case is Rouse v. Cameron, 387 F.2d 241 (D.C.Cir.1967).

55. Creek v. Stone, 379 F.2d 106 (D.C.Cir.1967).

56. Martarella v. Kelley, 349 F.Supp. 575 (S.D.N.Y. 1972). The later decision on the form of an injunction in this case is Martarella v. Kelley, 359 F.Supp. 478 (S.D. N.Y.1973).

57. E.g. Levine, Disaffirmance of the Right to Treatment Doctrine: A New Juncture in Juvenile Justice, 41 U.Pitt.L.Rev. 159 (1980); Note, A Right to Treatment for Juveniles? 1973 Wash.U.L.Q. 157; Note, Persons in Need of Supervision: Is There a Constitutional Right to Treatment? 39 Bklyn.L.Rev. 624 (1973); Gough, The Beyond-Control Child and the Right to Treatment: An Exercise in the Synthesis of Paradox, 16 St.L.U.L.J. 182 (1971); Kittrie, Can the Right to Treatment Remedy the Ills of the Juvenile Process? 57 Geo.L.J. 848 (1969).

58. Nelson v. Heyne, 491 F.2d 352 (7th Cir.1974), cert. denied 417 U.S. 976, 94 S.Ct. 3183, 41 L.Ed.2d 1146 (1974);

D.B. v. Tewksbury, 545 F.Supp. 896 (D.Or.1982) (semble); Johnson v. Solomon, 484 F.Supp. 278 (D.Md.1979) (citing many cases); Gary W. v. Louisiana, 437 F.Supp. 1209 (E.D.La.1976); State in Interest of Doe, 169 N.J.Super. 585, 405 A.2d 448 (Juv. & Dom.Rel.Ct.1979); Matter of L., 24 Or.App. 257, 546 P.2d 153 (1976); Janet D. v. Carros, 240 Pa.Super. 291, 362 A.2d 1060 (1976); State ex rel. Harris v. Calendine, 160 W.Va. 172, 233 S.E.2d 318 (1977).

Closely related cases have on occasion held that particularly harsh or unreasonable punishment inflicted on juveniles violates the Eighth Amendment's prohibition on cruel and unusual punishment. E.g., Nelson v. Heyne, 491 F.2d 352 (7th Cir.1974), cert. denied 417 U.S. 976, 94 S.Ct. 3183, 41 L.Ed.2d 1146 (1974); Morales v. Turman, 364 F.Supp. 166 (E.D.Tex.1973), 383 F.Supp. 53 (E.D.Tex. 1974), vacated and remanded 535 F.2d 864 (5th Cir.1976), reversed and remanded 430 U.S. 322, 97 S.Ct. 1189, 51 L.Ed.2d 368 (1977), remanded for further hearing 562 F.2d 993 (5th Cir.1977), rehearing denied 565 F.2d 1215 (5th Cir.1977); D.B. v. Tewksbury, 545 F.Supp. 896 (D.Or. 1982).

59. 422 U.S. 563, 95 S.Ct. 2486, 45 L.Ed.2d 396 (1975), on remand reversed and remanded per curiam sub. nom. Donaldson v. O'Connor, 519 F.2d 59 (5th Cir.1975).

60. 422 U.S. at 580–589, 95 S.Ct. at 2496–2500. The Chief Justice, at 422 U.S. 580, stated that the district court had held that an involuntarily committed person has a constitutional right to such treatment as will give him a realistic chance to be cured, and that the Fifth Circuit had approved this holding. He then said: "The Court's opinion plainly gives no approval to that holding and makes clear that it binds neither the parties to this case nor the courts of the Fifth Circuit. . . . Moreover, in light of its importance for future litigation in this area, it should be emphasized that the Court of Appeals' analysis has no basis in the decisions of this Court."

Perhaps influenced by the Chief Justice's remarks, some later cases have denied claims for a right to treatment. L.H. v. Jamieson, 643 F.2d 1351 (9th Cir.1981); Maryland State Department of Health and Mental Hygiene v. Prince George's County Department of Social Services, 47 Md.App. 436, 423 A.2d 589 (1980).

stitutional right to treatment has been corrected by Youngberg v. Romeo.[61] In this case a young man was involuntarily committed to an institution for the mentally retarded. The Court held that his "liberty interests require the State to provide minimally adequate or reasonable training to ensure safety and freedom from undue restraint."[62] But the opinion emphasizes that the training referred to was only that which was necessary to protect the young man from his own violence and that of others in the institution and to give him some freedom of movement within the institution. Whether the Court would uphold any broader version of the right to treatment is doubtful.

The bases for a right to treatment are either statutory or constitutional. If based upon statute, any such right obviously depends upon the language of the particular statute. The statute may specifically require treatment of a juvenile.[63] Or the court may be able to infer a duty to provide treatment from less specific language calling for "rehabilitation" of the juvenile.[64] And the purpose clause of the statute may be helpful in indicating a legislative requirement that some treatment be provided.[65] In all such cases the statute furnishes a more definite and less intrusive rationale for the right to treatment than does doubtful constitutional exegesis.

The constitutional right to treatment, if it exists, rests on the Due Process and Equal Protection Clauses of the Fourteenth Amendment, and on the Eighth Amendment. One theory has it that when the state assumes to

act as *parens patriae* in confining those who have committed no crimes, its action can only be justified on the ground that it is providing treatment for such persons. If the treatment is not provided, the confinement is without justification and amounts to a deprivation of liberty without due process.[66] This seems to be a substantive due process argument. A variation of it refers to the treatment as the *quid pro quo* which the person involuntarily confined is entitled to receive in exchange for his loss of liberty.[67] A procedural due process argument is also advanced in support of the right to treatment. The strict procedural requirements prevailing in the criminal law are relaxed in the cases of juveniles or the mentally ill on the ground that they are being treated rather than imprisoned. If the treatment is not forthcoming, they are being imprisoned without procedural due process.[68]

The Equal Protection theory of the right to treatment is even more difficult to define than the Due Process theory. It seems to be that since upper class or wealthy juveniles are treated in private institutions, placing less fortunate or poorer children in public institutions without adequate treatment constitutes an invidious discrimination which violates the Equal Protection Clause.[69] It has also been asserted that if the state confines juveniles longer than adults would be confined for the same offense, this constitutes a violation of the Equal Protection Clause unless the juvenile receives some treatment.[70] Since the child in need of supervision has violated no criminal statute, presumably this

---

61. 457 U.S. 307, 102 S.Ct. 2452, 73 L.Ed.2d 28 (1982), on remand 687 F.2d 33 (3d Cir.1982).

62. 457 U.S. at 319, 102 S.Ct. at 2460, 73 L.Ed.2d at 39. The Court did not discuss the O'Connor case, supra, note 59, or the Chief Justice's concurrence in that case.

63. E.g., Matter of L., 24 Or.App. 257, 546 P.2d 153 (1976).

64. State in Interest of Doe, 169 N.J.Super. 585, 405 A.2d 448 (Juv. & Dom.Rel.Ct.1979).

65. Janet D. v. Carros, 240 Pa.Super. 291, 362 A.2d 1060 (1976). See, e.g., V.T.C.A., Fam.Code § 51.01(3) (Supp.1982).

66. Nelson v. Heyne, 491 F.2d 352 (7th Cir.1974), cert. denied 417 U.S. 976, 94 S.Ct. 3183, 41 L.Ed.2d 1146 (1974); D.B. v. Tewksbury, 545 F.Supp. 896 (D.Or.1982); Johnson

v. Solomon, 484 F.Supp. 278 (D.Md.1979); Gary W. v. Louisiana, 437 F.Supp. 1209 (E.D.La.1976); Kittrie, Can the Right to Treatment Remedy the Ills of the Juvenile Process? 57 Geo.L.J. 848, 864 (1969).

67. Martarella v. Kelley, 349 F.Supp. 575 (S.D.N.Y. 1972).

68. Levine, Disaffirmance of the Right to Treatment Doctrine: A New Juncture in Juvenile Justice, 41 U.Pitt. L.Rev. 159, 166 (1980).

69. State ex rel. Harris v. Calendine, 160 W.Va. 172, 233 S.E.2d 318 (1977).

70. In re Wilson, 438 Pa. 425, 264 A.2d 614 (1970); Levine, Disaffirmance of the Right to Treatment Doctrine: A New Juncture in Juvenile Justice, 41 U.Pitt.L. Rev. 159, 168 (1980).

argument would apply with greater force to him than to the juvenile delinquent.

The Eighth Amendment has been violated in some cases in which institutional facilities have been particularly inadequate or the behavior of staffs particularly brutal.[71] The effect of this is to bring about adequate treatment by enforcing negative sanctions rather than by imposing affirmative standards of what treatment should be provided.

When one asks just what sort of treatment is being insisted upon in these cases, no very specific answer emerges. The following general principles do seem to be adhered to in the cases, however. a) The right to treatment applies only to those children in need of supervision who are involuntarily committed to institutions. It apparently does not apply to those for whom the court orders some other disposition, such as probation, placement in a foster home or placement with the child's own parents. This seems to follow from the constitutional bases for the doctrine. It may be that if the basis for the right is statutory, the child may be entitled to insist on some appropriate treatment even though he is not committed to an institution.

b) The treatment required is not of an individualized kind, tailored to the needs of the specific child. It is merely a requirement that the physical facilities, the staff, and the internal procedures meet a general standard of adequacy for the rehabilitation of the child in need of supervision who is committed to the institution.[72] For example, one case held that one facility was inadequate and should

be closed, that the ratio of staff to children was inadequate, that the staff was not properly trained, that the institution's intake procedure was inadequate, and that some treatment had to be provided for all children committed to the institution for more than thirty days.[73]

c) The fact that the state has failed to provide adequate financing or staff for the institution is not a justification for failure to provide adequate treatment.[74] At this point of course there occurs the most serious conflict between the judicial branch on the one hand and the legislative and executive branches on the other. It is this conflict which generates the greatest scepticism concerning the merits of the right to treatment as a judge-made principle.

The foregoing is sufficient to demonstrate that the child in need of supervision is the focus of profound conflicts in our society. In the first place we cannot agree that he should come within the purview of the courts at all. A substantial body of opinion would abolish the so-called status offenses entirely. This seems to have influenced some legislatures to limit the offenses and reduce the severity of the possible sanction. When the cases do come to court, there is still a tendency to commit the children to institutions in which there may be harsh treatment and little chance for rehabilitation or therapy. We are also uncertain whether the child in need of supervision is in need of protection from unreasonable parents, or whether he should be required to obey parental discipline. And fi-

---

71. Nelson v. Heyne, 491 F.2d 352 (7th Cir.1974), cert. denied 417 U.S. 976, 94 S.Ct. 3183, 41 L.Ed.2d 1146 (1974); Morales v. Turman, 364 F.Supp. 166 (E.D.Tex.1973), 383 F.Supp. 53 (E.D.Tex.1974), vacated and remanded 535 F.2d 864 (5th Cir.1976), reversed and remanded 430 U.S. 322, 97 S.Ct. 1189, 51 L.Ed.2d 368 (1977), remanded for further hearing 562 F.2d 993 (5th Cir.1977), rehearing denied, 565 F.2d 1215 (5th Cir.1977); State ex rel. Harris v. Calendine, 160 W.Va. 172, 233 S.E.2d 318 (1977).

72. Youngberg v. Romeo, 457 U.S. 307, 102 S.Ct. 2452, 73 L.Ed.2d 28 (1982), on remand 687 F.2d 33 (3d Cir.1982); Patton v. Dumpson, 425 F.Supp. 621 (S.D.N.Y.1977) (dictum); Martarella v. Kelley, 349 F.Supp. 575 (S.D.N.Y. 1972); State ex rel. Harris v. Calendine, 160 W.Va. 172, 233 S.E.2d 318 (1977). See also Levine, Disaffirmance of the Right to Treatment Doctrine: A New Juncture in Juvenile Justice, 41 U.Pitt.L.Rev. 159, 172 (1980).

Cases contra the text statement and appearing to require that the treatment be adapted to the special needs of individual children are Nelson v. Heyne, 491 F.2d 352 (7th Cir.1974), cert. denied 417 U.S. 976, 94 S.Ct. 3183, 41 L.Ed.2d 1146 (1974); Johnson v. Solomon, 484 F.Supp. 278 (D.Md.1979); Gary W. v. Louisiana, 437 F.Supp. 1209 (E.D.La.1976). Any such requirement as this would impose intolerable supervisory burdens on the courts, and would exacerbate the conflict between the judicial and executive departments of government.

73. Martarella v. Kelley, 359 F.Supp. 478 (S.D.N.Y. 1973).

74. Wyatt v. Stickney, 325 F.Supp. 781 (M.D.Ala. 1971).

nally, if he is committed to an institution, we cannot seem to decide whether he is entitled to treatment appropriate to his condition.

These conflicts and this confusion are not unique to this branch of domestic relations. They reflect the uncertainties of a troubled society in which some people try to preserve traditional parent-child relationships, others cling to the worship of youth prevalent in the nineteen sixties and seventies, and still others try more or less unsuccessfully to reach workable compromises in specific situations. The legislators, lawyers and judges can do little more than attempt to minimize the physical and psychological harm to children and parents who come before the courts, in the hope that perhaps some agreement may ultimately be achieved.

 WESTLAW REFERENCES

ungovernab! incorrigib! (habitual! /2 truan!) /p vague! "interest of polovchak"

juvenile child minor youth /10 right /2 treatment

Chapter 10

TORT LIABILITY WITHIN THE FAMILY

Table of Sections

§ 10.1 Tort Actions Between Husband and Wife

The legal disabilities of the married woman at common law made it impossible for her to sue her husband in tort, and for him to sue her, for several reasons. One was the concept that husband and wife were one, so much beloved by Blackstone.[1] Another was the rule that the husband was liable for his wife's torts,[2] which, if he were to sue, would place him in the position of suing himself. And there was the rule that she could only sue by joining him as plaintiff,[3] which again would place him on both sides of the litigation if she should sue him in tort.

None of these objections had any force after the adoption of the Married Women's Property Acts, however. A prediction might have been made that those Acts would make it possible for husband and wife to sue each other for torts as well as for breaches of contract. But this would underestimate the ingenuity generated by judicial conservatism. It has already been shown that suits between spouses for breach of contract were only permitted with reluctance and with some qualifications.[4] The courts were even more grudging in their treatment of tort actions.

Tort actions between the spouses have been held by all courts to be authorized by the Married Women's Property Acts where they concern the wife's property.[5] This is undoubtedly because those statutes very plainly confer on the married woman the right to own, control and dispose of property. The right to invoke the aid of courts to get redress for interference with ownership is inseparable from ownership. It is inconceivable that a married woman may own personal property but that she may not sue her husband for conversion or replevin when he appropriates the property. In some cases the definition of torts affecting property has been expanded so far as to include torts to the person.[6]

§ 10.1

1. 1 W. Blackstone, Commentaries on the Laws of England 445 (Cooley 3d ed. 1884).

2. See section 7.1, supra.

3. Ibid.

4. See section 7.2, supra.

5. W. Prosser & W. Keeton, The Law of Torts 902 (5th ed. 1984); McCurdy, Property Torts Between Spouses, 2

Vill.L.Rev. 447 (1957); Note, Litigation Between Husband and Wife, 79 Harv.L.Rev. 1650 (1966); Tobias v. Tobias, 225 Miss. 392, 83 So.2d 638 (1955).

6. See Langley v. Schumacker, 46 Cal.2d 601, 297 P.2d 977 (1956), holding that a suit seeking damages for inducing the plaintiff to contract an invalid marriage, essentially based upon a claim of fraud, was a suit for a property tort.

Where the tort consisted in harm to the person of a spouse, for a long time the majority of American courts persisted in refusing relief.[7] Specifically, this meant that in most states husband and wife could not sue each other for negligence, assault, defamation, false imprisonment or malicious prosecution.[8] The courts which adhered to this position no longer relied upon the historical grounds for disallowing the action,[9] but instead advanced a number of public policy arguments: a) Such suits disturb the harmony of the marital relationship.[10] b) They involve the courts in trivial disputes between the spouses.[11] c) They encourage fraud and collusion between spouses where the conduct constituting the tort is covered by insurance, as in the case of the negligent operation of an automobile.[12] d) The criminal law provides an adequate remedy.[13] e) The divorce law provides an adequate remedy.[14] f) Such suits reward the defendant for his own wrong, since if the parties are living together, they both share in the benefits of any judgment.[15] g) A further consideration not often mentioned in judicial opinions but perhaps in the minds of some judges is that it appears broadly inconsistent with family solidarity, or unseemly, to have husbands and wives suing each other.[16]

The kindest thing to be said about the first five of these policy arguments is that they are frivolous.[17] The argument from marital harmony, the one most often relied upon, is particularly hard to take seriously. Either marital harmony has ended before the suit is brought, as for example where the spouses have separated,[18] or the situation is such that marital harmony will not be affected by the suit. The typical case occurs when the wife sues the husband for injuries caused by his negligent operation of an automobile and the husband is insured. This kind of suit has no effect on the relations between the parties. In fact it is impossible to find a case in which the bringing of a suit has impaired marital harmony. The argument that the immunity prevents fraud and collusion against insurance companies may have a sounder psychological basis, but it assumes that all such suits are decided upon evidence within the parties' control. Certainly courts and juries are capable of distinguishing between meritorious and collusive claims. Insurance companies are normally capable of protecting their own interests.[19] The suggestion that trivial litiga-

---

7. The leading case is Thompson v. Thompson, 218 U.S. 611, 31 S.Ct. 111, 54 L.Ed. 1180 (1910). Other earlier cases are collected in W. Prosser & W. Keeton, Torts § 122 (5th ed. 1984); 2 F. Harper and F. James & O. Gray, The Law of Torts § 8.10 (2d ed. 1986); McCurdy, Personal Injury Torts Between Spouses, 4 Vill.L.Rev. 303 (1959). Later cases are collected in Annot., 92 A.L.R.3d 901 (1979).

8. W. Prosser & W. Keeton, Torts 902 (5th ed. 1984).

9. As late as 1970 Pickens' Estate v. Pickens, 255 Ind. 119, 263 N.E.2d 151 (1970), since overruled, adhered to the immunity on the ground that husband and wife are one.

10. Thompson v. Thompson, 218 U.S. 611, 31 S.Ct. 111, 54 L.Ed. 1180 (1910); Rubalcava v. Gisseman, 14 Utah 2d 344, 384 P.2d 389 (1963).

11. Goode v. Martinis, 58 Wash.2d 229, 361 P.2d 941 (1961).

12. Lyons v. Lyons, 2 Ohio St.2d 243, 208 N.E.2d 533 (1965).

13. Goode v. Martinis, 58 Wash.2d 229, 361 P.2d 941 (1961).

14. Hill v. Hill, 415 So.2d 20 (Fla.1982).

15. Austin v. Austin, 136 Miss. 61, 100 So. 591 (1924).

16. Hill v. Hill, 415 So.2d 20 (Fla.1982).

17. These policy arguments have been demolished over and over again by legal scholars, by dissenting opinions and by the majority opinions in those cases which have rejected the immunity. For trenchant examples see W. Prosser & W. Keeton, Torts 902, 903 (5th ed. 1984); McCurdy, Personal Injury Torts Between Spouses, 4 Vill.L.Rev. 303 (1959); Bonkowsky v. Bonkowsky, 69 Ohio St.2d 152, 155, 431 N.E.2d 998, 1000 (1982), cert. denied 457 U.S. 1135, 102 S.Ct. 2963, 73 L.Ed.2d 1352 (1982) (dissenting opinion); Hack v. Hack, 495 Pa. 300, 433 A.2d 859 (1981).

18. See, e.g., Taibi v. De Gennaro, 65 N.J.Super. 294, 167 A.2d 667 (1961), where the spouses had separated before suit, but the court refused to let the wife sue because a suit might prevent a reconciliation! New Jersey has since abolished the immunity, while Kansas has limited it to actions for negligence.

19. N.Y.—McKinney's Gen.Oblig.Law § 3–313 (1978) abolishes the interspousal immunity, but N.Y.—McKinney's Ins.Law § 3420(g) (Supp.1981–1982) provides that liability of the spouses to each other is not covered unless the policy contains an express provision including such coverage. See also Note, Interspousal Immunity and the Effect of Liability Insurance in Automobile Accidents, 11 S.D.L.Rev. 144 (1966).

tion will result if the immunity is abandoned is fanciful, and one need hardly comment on the argument that the criminal remedy or the divorce remedy are adequate.

The sixth argument makes a little more sense in terms of the traditional view of tort law as turning on the fault of the defendant and the freedom from fault of the plaintiff. Undoubtedly if the wife collects from her husband's insurance carrier for the husband's negligence, the proceeds may often go into the family treasury. To that extent the tort-

feasor will benefit. But this risk is inherent in the wife's legal capacity. She may do what she likes with her property. The fact that she may decide to give the proceeds of the judgment to her husband is not a reason to deny her compensation in all cases. As tort law becomes more consonant with the realities of contemporary life,[20] this argument loses all force.

Recognition of the insubstantiality of the arguments for the immunity has led a majority of the states to abolish it [21] or to limit

20. See, e.g., R. Keeton and J. O'Connell, Basic Protection for the Traffic Victim (1965); Morris, Negligence in Tort Law, 53 Va.L.Rev. 899 (1967); Franklin, Replacing the Negligence Lottery: Compensation and Selective Reimbursement, 53 Va.L.Rev. 774 (1967).

21. U.S. admiralty jurisdiction: Byrd v. Byrd, 657 F.2d 615 (4th Cir.1981).

Alabama:	Johnson v. Johnson, 201 Ala. 41, 77 So. 335 (1917).
Alaska:	Drickersen v. Drickersen, 546 P.2d 162 (Alaska 1976).
Arizona:	Fernandez v. Romo, 132 Ariz. 447, 646 P.2d 878 (1982).
Arkansas:	Leach v. Leach, 227 Ark. 599, 300 S.W.2d 15 (1957).
California:	Klein v. Klein, 58 Cal.2d 692, 26 Cal.Rptr. 102, 376 P.2d 70 (1962).
Colorado:	Rains v. Rains, 97 Colo. 19, 46 P.2d 740 (1935).
Connecticut:	Silverman v. Silverman, 145 Conn. 663, 145 A.2d 826 (1958).
Idaho:	Rogers v. Yellowstone Park Co., 97 Idaho 14, 539 P.2d 566 (1974).
Indiana:	Brooks v. Robinson, 259 Ind. 16, 284 N.E. 2d 794 (1972), 6 Ind.L.Rev. 558 (1973).
Iowa:	Shook v. Crabb, 281 N.W.2d 616 (Iowa 1979).
Kentucky:	Brown v. Gosser, 262 S.W.2d 480 (Ky.1953).
Maine:	MacDonald v. MacDonald, 412 A.2d 71 (Me.1980). Boblitz v. Boblitz, 269 Md. 242, 462 A.2d 506 (1983) (semble), The opinion in this case contains an exhaustive list of citations from other states.
Massachusetts:	Brown v. Brown, 381 Mass. 231, 409 N.E.2d 717 (1980).
Michigan:	Hosko v. Hosko, 385 Mich. 39, 187 N.W.2d 236 (1971).
Minnesota:	Beaudette v. Frana, 285 Minn. 366, 173 N.W.2d 416 (1969).
Missouri:	Townsend v. Townsend, 708 S.W.2d 646 (Mo.1986).
Montana:	Miller v. Fallon County, ___ Mont. ___, 721 P.2d 342 (1986).

Nebraska:	Imig v. March, 203 Neb. 537, 279 N.W.2d 382 (1979).
Nevada:	Rupert v. Stienne, 90 Nev. 397, 528 P.2d 1013 (1974) (semble).
New Hampshire:	Taylor v. Bullock, 111 N.H. 214, 279 A.2d 585 (1971).
New Jersey:	Merenoff v. Merenoff, 76 N.J. 535, 388 A.2d 951 (1978).
New Mexico:	Maestas v. Overton, 87 N.M. 213, 531 P.2d 947 (1975).
New York:	N.Y.—McKinney's Gen.Oblig.Law § 3–313 (1978).
North Carolina:	N.C.Gen.Stat. § 52–5 (1984).
North Dakota:	Fitzmaurice v. Fitzmaurice, 62 N.D. 191, 242 N.W. 526 (1932).
Ohio:	Shearer v. Shearer, 18 Ohio St.3d 94, 480 N.E.2d 388 (1985).
Oklahoma:	Courtney v. Courtney, 184 Okl. 395, 87 P.2d 660 (1938).
Pennsylvania:	Hack v. Hack, 495 Pa. 300, 433 A.2d 859 (1981).
South Carolina:	Algie v. Algie, 261 S.C. 103, 198 S.E.2d 529 (1973).
South Dakota:	Scotvold v. Scotvold, 68 S.D. 53, 298 N.W. 266 (1941).
Tennessee:	Davis v. Davis, 657 S.W.2d 753 (Tenn. 1983).
Utah:	Stoker v. Stoker, 616 P.2d 590 (Utah 1980).
Virginia:	Va.Code 1950, § 8.01–220.1.
Washington:	Freehe v. Freehe, 81 Wash.2d 183, 500 P.2d 771 (1972), overruled on other grounds Brown v. Brown, 100 Wash.2d 729, 675 P.2d 1207 (1984).
West Virginia:	Coffindaffer v. Coffindaffer, 161 W.Va. 557, 244 S.E.2d 338 (1978).
Wisconsin:	Zelinger v. State Sand & Gravel Co., 38 Wis.2d 98, 156 N.W.2d 466 (1968).
Wyoming:	Tader v. Tader, 737 P.2d 1065 (Wyo.1987).

The federal Omnibus Crime Control and Safe Streets Act of 1968, 18 U.S.C.A. § 2511(1)(a) and (d), forbids wiretapping. Although this Act does contain certain

it.[22] Some states do persist in keeping the immunity, largely out of regard for stare decisis.[23] It has been held that the existence of the immunity violates no constitutional provisions, state or federal.[24]

Even in those states which continue to adhere to the interspousal immunity the courts have recognized some exceptions to it. There are cases which allow the suit where the tort occurred before the parties were married,[25] or where the parties were divorced at the time the suit was brought.[26] If one of the spouses

has died before the suit is brought, the suit can hardly impair family harmony. For this reason some courts have held that the suit may be brought in such cases,[27] but others have persisted in applying the immunity in these circumstances.[28]

The abolition of the interspousal immunity in many states has led to the insertion in some liability insurance policies of a "family exclusion clause" according to which the policy coverage does not apply to any member of the family of the insured living in the same

exceptions, it does not make any exception for wiretaps used by one spouse to eavesdrop on the conversations of the other spouse. The Act also provides for civil liability for those whose conversations are tapped in violation of its prohibitions. 18 U.S.C.A. § 2520. One case has held, however, that the Act does not apply to interspousal wiretaps placed on phones in the marital home. Simpson v. Simpson, 490 F.2d 803 (5th Cir.1974), rehearing denied 493 F.2d 664 (5th Cir.1974). In circuits following that case, the spouses are unable to sue each other for violations of the Act. Anonymous v. Anonymous, 558 F.2d 677 (2d Cir.1977). The rationale seems to be that the wiretap was a "purely domestic conflict", which did not rise to the level of a violation of the Act. Other courts have held that no such implied exception can be read into the Act, however. United States v. Jones, 542 F.2d 661 (6th Cir.1976), appeal after remand 580 F.2d 219 (6th Cir. 1978). In circuits where that rule prevails, a spouse may recover from the other spouse even though the state where the offense occurred still adheres to the interspousal tort immunity. Heyman v. Heyman, 548 F.Supp. 1041 (N.D.Ill.1982).

22.

Illinois:　Ill.—Smith-Hurd Ann. ch. 40, § 1001 (Supp. 1982–1983) (interspousal tort actions permitted where physical injury has been intentionally inflicted).

Kansas:　Stevens v. Stevens, 231 Kan. 726, 647 P.2d 1346 (1982); Ebert v. Ebert, 232 Kan. 502, 656 P.2d 766 (1983); (creates exception to the immunity for wilful and intentional torts).

Oregon:　Davis v. Bostick, 282 Or. 667, 580 P.2d 544 (1978) (creates exception to the immunity for intentional torts even where no physical injury is inflicted).

Texas:　Bounds v. Caudle, 560 S.W.2d 925 (Tex.1977) (no immunity for intentional torts).

Vermont:　Richard v. Richard, 131 Vt. 98, 300 A.2d 637 (1973) (creates exception to the immunity for injuries arising out of auto accidents).

The former Illinois statute imposing the interspousal tort immunity for torts to the person was held unconstitutional as having no rational relation to the preservation of marital harmony in a case involving assault and battery to a wife, Moran v. Beyer, 734 F.2d 1245 (7th Cir. 1984), 58 Temp.L.Q. 709 (1985).

23. E.g., Alfree v. Alfree, 410 A.2d 161 (Del.1979), appeal dismissed 446 U.S. 931, 100 S.Ct. 2145, 64 L.Ed.2d 783 (1980); Hill v. Hill, 415 So.2d 20 (Fla.1982); Peters v. Peters, 63 Hawaii 653, 634 P.2d 586 (1981); Bonkowsky v. Bonkowsky, 69 Ohio St.2d 152, 431 N.E.2d 998 (1982), cert. denied 457 U.S. 1135, 102 S.Ct. 2963, 73 L.Ed.2d 1352 (1982).

24. Alfree v. Alfree, 410 A.2d 161 (Del.1979), appeal dismissed for want of a substantial federal question 446 U.S. 931, 100 S.Ct. 2145, 64 L.Ed.2d 783 (1980); Tyrken v. Tyrken, 63 Ill.App.3d 199, 19 Ill.Dec. 932, 379 N.E.2d 804 (1978); Renfrow v. Gojohn, 600 S.W.2d 77 (Mo.App.1980). Contra, where intentional tort is involved, preserving the immunity violates the Equal Protection Clause, Moran v. Beyer, 734 F.2d 1245 (7th Cir.1984).

25. O'Grady v. Potts, 193 Kan. 644, 396 P.2d 285 (1964), 14 Kan.L.Rev. 124 (1965); Moulton v. Moulton, 309 A.2d 224 (Me.1973); Mosier v. Carney, 376 Mich. 532, 138 N.W.2d 343 (1965); Hamilton v. Fulkerson, 285 S.W.2d 642 (Mo.1955); Childress v. Childress, 569 S.W.2d 816 (Tenn.1978); Juaire v. Juaire, 128 Vt. 149, 259 A.2d 786 (1969). Contra: Taibi v. De Gennaro, 65 N.J.Super. 294, 167 A.2d 667 (1961); Thomas v. Herron, 20 Ohio St. 2d 62, 253 N.E.2d 772 (1969). Gaston v. Pittman, 224 So. 2d 326 (Fla.1969) held that the immunity barred the suit even where the tort occurred before marriage and the suit occurred after divorce.

26. Soedler v. Soedler, 89 Ill.App.3d 74, 44 Ill.Dec. 425, 411 N.E.2d 547 (1980); Sanchez v. Olivarez, 94 N.J.Super. 61, 226 A.2d 752 (1967); Kobe v. Kobe, 61 Ohio App.2d 67, 399 N.E.2d 124 (1978); Turner v. Turner, 487 Pa. 403, 409 A.2d 412 (1979); Goode v. Martinis, 58 Wash.2d 229, 361 P.2d 941 (1961). Contra: West v. West, 414 So.2d 189 (Fla.1982); Ensminger v. Campbell, 242 Miss. 519, 134 So. 2d 728 (1961); Counts v. Counts, 221 Va. 151, 266 S.E.2d 895 (1980). Hill v. Hill, 415 So.2d 20 (Fla.1982) held that the immunity applied even though the spouses were separated.

27. Pickens' Estate v. Pickens, 255 Ind. 119, 263 N.E.2d 151 (1970); Mosier v. Carney, 376 Mich. 532, 138 N.W.2d 343 (1965).

28. Saunders v. Hill, 202 A.2d 807 (Del.1964); Horton v. Unigard Ins. Co., 355 So.2d 154 (Fla.App.1978). See also Annot., 92 A.L.R.3d 901, 952 (1979).

household.[29] One court has held such a clause invalid as contrary to public policy, the policy being the interest of society in favor of permitting the victims of negligence to recover from those at fault, including spouses among such victims.[30] On the other hand the New York statute provides that liability policies do not cover injuries to the insured's spouse unless they expressly include such coverage.[31] But where the immunity continues to exist, it has been held that the liability insurer can assert the spouse's immunity.[32]

In those states where the interspousal immunity is adhered to, the courts have often permitted the wife to sue her husband's employer for negligent conduct of the husband occurring in the scope of his employment, on essentially metaphysical grounds.[33] The leading case is Schubert v. August Schubert Wagon Co.,[34] in which Judge Cardozo held that the husband's conduct was tortious even though the law exempted him from liability to his wife, and therefore his employer could be liable. The judge admitted that the husband might be liable over to the employer but said that the husband's liability would rest on a violation of duty owed to the employer rather than to the wife. But the fact remains that if the husband is liable over the courts are doing indirectly what they have disclaimed the authority to do directly. If marital harmony is prejudiced in the one case, it will be prejudiced in the other. One case justifies holding the employer liable on the theory that as a practical matter the employee's liability over to the employer is never enforced or expected to be enforced,[35] but this assumption cannot be made in all cases.[36] Similar problems arise where the wife sues a partnership of which her husband is a member,[37] and where contribution is sought from the husband under the Uniform Contribution Among Tortfeasors Act.[38] The courts' inability to agree on how these cases should be disposed of is further evidence, if any were needed, of the absence of any realistic policy basis for the interspousal immunity in torts.

 WESTLAW REFERENCES

inter-spousal /5 immun! /s harmon! /s marri! marry! marital

to(205) /p inter-spousal /5 immun! /s negligen! tort tortious! /s action sue* suit suing lawsuit

di(inter-spousal /5 immun! /s aboli! abrogat!)

di("family exclusion" /p valid! invalid! null! void! avoid!)

---

29. Ashdown, Intrafamily Immunity, Pure Compensation, and the Family Exclusion Clause, 60 Iowa L.Rev. 239 (1974).

30. Mutual of Enumclaw Ins. Co. v. Wiscomb, 95 Wash.2d 373, 622 P.2d 1234 (1980), adhered to on reconsideration 97 Wash.2d 203, 643 P.2d 441 (1982). See also Transamerica Ins. Co. v. Royle, 202 Mont. 173, 656 P.2d 820 (1983) (parent-child immunity).

31. State Farm Mutual Automobile Ins. Co. v. Westlake, 35 N.Y.2d 587, 364 N.Y.S.2d 482, 324 N.E.2d 137 (1974). But see N.Y.—McKinney's Ins. Law § 3240(g) (1985).

32. Williams v. Williams, 108 Ill.App.3d 936, 64 Ill.Dec. 390, 439 N.E.2d 1055 (1982), affirmed as modified 98 Ill.2d 128, 74 Ill.Dec. 495, 455 N.E.2d 1388 (1983). Where the policy contained both a family exclusion clause and uninsured motorist coverage, however, the wife was held entitled to be paid under the uninsured motorist provision when her injuries were caused by the negligence of her husband. See also Broy v. Inland Mutual Ins. Co., 160 W.Va. 138, 233 S.E.2d 131 (1977). Contra: Patrons Mut. Ins. Ass'n v. Norwood, 231 Kan. 709, 647 P.2d 1335 (1982).

33. Fields v. Synthetic Ropes, Inc., 59 Del. 135, 215 A.2d 427 (1965), on remand 59 Del. 302, 219 A.2d 374 (1966), 17 Syracuse L.Rev. 729 (1966); Kowaleski v. Kowaleski, 227 Or. 45, 361 P.2d 64 (1961). Other cases are cited in Annot., 1 A.L.R.3d 677 (1965). See also Restatement (Second) of Agency § 217 (1958). Contra: Riegger v. Bruton Brewing Co., 178 Md. 518, 16 A.2d 99 (1940).

34. 249 N.Y. 253, 164 N.E. 42 (1928).

35. Eule v. Eule Motor Sales, 34 N.J. 537, 170 A.2d 241 (1961), 10 Kan.L.Rev. 478 (1962).

36. See Steffen, The Employer's "Indemnity" Action, 25 U.Chi.L.Rev. 465 (1958).

37. Holding the partnership liable: Eule v. Eule Motor Sales, 34 N.J. 537, 170 A.2d 241 (1961), 10 Kan.L.Rev. 478 (1962). Holding the partnership not liable: Caplan v. Caplan, 268 N.Y. 445, 198 N.E. 23 (1935). See Note, 47 Va.L.Rev. 1450 (1961).

In May v. Palm Beach Chemical Co., 77 So.2d 468 (Fla. 1955) the wife was allowed to recover from the owner of a car for the negligence of her husband.

38. Holding the tortfeasor may recover over against the spouse of the injured person: Smith v. Southern Farm Bureau Cas. Ins. Co., 247 La. 695, 174 So.2d 122 (1965); Daly v. Buterbaugh, 416 Pa. 523, 207 A.2d 412 (1964); Zarrella v. Miller, 100 R.I. 545, 217 A.2d 673 (1966). Holding the tortfeasor may not recover over: Ennis v. Donovan, 222 Md. 536, 161 A.2d 698 (1960); Martinez v. Lankster, 595 S.W.2d 316 (Mo.App.1980); Kennedy v. Camp, 14 N.J. 390, 102 A.2d 595 (1954). See also Annot., 19 A.L.R.2d 1003 (1951). The Uniform Act is set out in 12 Unif.L.Ann. 57 (1975).

§ 10.2   Tort Actions Between Parent and Child

Child versus Parent

There is no question but that a child, emancipated or not, may sue his parent for breach of contract [1] and for torts affecting his property.[2] There is also no doubt that the emancipated child may sue his parent for torts to his person.[3]

Unlike its treatment of the married woman, the common law placed no legal obstacles in the way of suits by the unemancipated child. The only English case on the point made no difficulty concerning his capacity to sue his parent for a tort to his person.[4] But for the first two-thirds of the Twentieth Century the rule in the United States has been that a child could not sue his parent for such torts.[5] The history of this rule began in 1891 with an ipse dixit in Hewlett v. George,[6] based upon no authority whatever and supported by no reasoning other than a vague reference to the need for family repose and the incredible

statement that the criminal law provides an adequate remedy. The court in that case held that a minor daughter could not recover damages from her mother for her wrongful confinement in an insane asylum. The parent-child tort immunity quickly reached its full development in Roller v. Roller,[7] a landmark of American jurisprudence which, after finding that the policy underlying the immunity was the preservation of family harmony, held that a daughter could not recover from her father for rape.

A substantial number of American states continue to adhere to the immunity in some form, notwithstanding its doubtful origins.[8] Where it is still recognized, it generally also applies to prevent suits by a child against a person who is in loco parentis with respect to him.[9]

The policy arguments relied upon to support the parent-child immunity in some respects resemble those underlying the husband-wife immunity. Permitting such suits is said to impair the harmony of the family and

§ 10.2

1. Hilbish v. Hilbish, 71 Ind. 27 (1880); Hall v. Hall, 44 N.H. 293 (1862); Ayer v. Ayer, 41 Vt. 302 (1868). See Smith v. Smith, 38 Cal.App. 388, 176 P. 382 (1918), and McCurdy, Torts Between Persons in Domestic Relation, 43 Harv.L.Rev. 1030, 1058 (1930).

2. McLain v. McLain, 80 Okl. 113, 194 P. 894 (1921); McCurdy, Torts Between Persons in Domestic Relation, 43 Harv.L.Rev. 1030, 1057–1058 (1930); W. Prosser & W. Keeton, Torts 904 (5th ed. 1984); McCurdy, Torts Between Parent and Child, 5 Vill.L.Rev. 521, 527 (1960).

3. Brumfield v. Brumfield, 194 Va. 577, 74 S.E.2d 170 (1953); Smith v. Kauffman, 212 Va. 181, 183 S.E.2d 190 (1971) (dictum), 49 N.D.L.Rev. 179 (1972); Annot., 19 A.L.R.2d 423, 437 (1951). If emancipation occurs after the tort, but before the suit, the child may not sue. Reingold v. Reingold, 115 N.J.L. 532, 181 A. 153 (1935). Reaching the age of majority may not amount to emancipation, according to Wilkosz v. Wilkosz, 124 Ill.App.3d 904, 80 Ill.Dec. 249, 464 N.E.2d 1232 (1984).

4. Ash v. Ash, Comb. 357, 90 Eng.Rep. 526 (1696); T. Reeve, Domestic Relations 288 (1816); P. Bromley, Family Law 309 (4th ed. 1971); 1 J. Schouler, Marriage, Divorce, Separation and Domestic Relations § 691 (6th ed. 1921).

5. The earlier cases are cited in Annots., 19 A.L.R.2d 423 (1951) and 41 A.L.R.3d 904 (1972); W. Prosser & W. Keeton, Torts 904 (5th ed. 1984); 1 F. Harper, F. James & O. Gray, The Law of Torts § 8.11 (2d ed. 1986); McCurdy, Torts Between Parent and Child, 5 Vill.L.Rev. 521 (1960).

6. 68 Miss. 703, 9 So. 885 (1891). See also 1 J. Schouler, Marriage, Divorce, Separation and Domestic Relations § 691 (6th ed. 1921).

7. 37 Wash. 242, 79 P. 788 (1905). Another influential early case is McKelvey v. McKelvey, 111 Tenn. 388, 77 S.W. 664 (1903).

8. Karam v. Allstate Ins. Co., 70 Ohio St.2d 227, 231, 436 N.E.2d 1014, 1017 (1982), cert. denied 459 U.S. 1070, 103 S.Ct. 490, 74 L.Ed.2d 632 (1982) lists eighteen states which continue to uphold the parent-child immunity. For an extensive collection of the cases see Annot., 6 A.L.R.4th 1066 (1981); Mauk v. Mauk, 12 Ohio St.3d 156, 466 N.E.2d 166 (1984), overruled by Kirchner v. Crystal, 15 Ohio St.3d 326, 474 N.E.2d 275 (1984) and Unah By and Through Unah v. Martin, 676 P.2d 1366 (Okl.1984).

9. E.g., Mathis v. Ammons, 453 F.Supp. 1033 (E.D. Tenn.1978) (Tennessee law, child's uncle in loco parentis); Plesnicar v. Kovach, 102 Ill.App.3d 867, 58 Ill.Dec. 616, 430 N.E.2d 648 (1981) (school district in loco parentis); Hush v. Devilbiss Co., 77 Mich.App. 639, 259 N.W.2d 170 (1977); Wooden v. Hale, 426 P.2d 679 (Okl.1967) (stepfather) overruled on other grounds Unah v. Martin, 676 P.2d 1366 (Okl.1984); Van Wart v. Cook, 557 P.2d 1161 (Okl.App.1976) (stepmother); Lyles v. Jackson, 216 Va. 797, 223 S.E.2d 873 (1976) (stepfather). Busillo v. Hetzel, 58 Ill.App.3d 682, 16 Ill.Dec. 315, 374 N.E.2d 1090 (1978) held that a grandparent was not in loco parentis.

Although a child may not recover from a parent for negligent supervision, Andrews v. Otsego County, 112 Misc.2d 37, 446 N.Y.S.2d 169 (Sup.Ct.1982), has held that the child may recover from a foster parent for negligent supervision.

create discord.[10] Conversely, the argument is made that there will be too much harmony between parent and child, as a result of which they will engage in collusion to defraud the parent's insuror.[11] Still other courts have upheld the immunity on the ground that if the child's suit is successful it will result in an inequitable distribution of family resources.[12] All of these arguments have been refuted by many commentators and by both majority and dissenting judicial opinions.[13]

One consequence of the critical attacks on these policy bases for the immunity has been that in the states which continue to preserve the immunity various exceptions to it have been created. In some states the child has been permitted to sue his parent for intentional torts [14] or for torts involving "wanton and reckless" conduct.[15] In some states he may sue the estate of a deceased parent, on the theory that such a suit could have no adverse

effect on family harmony.[16] For the same reason a few cases have held that the child may sue his parent where there has been a divorce and the tort is committed by the parent who does not have custody of the child.[17] And a substantial number of courts have created an exception for automobile accident cases, on the ground that the parent is probably insured and therefore the suit could not disturb family harmony.[18] The latter group of cases seldom considers the possibility (which may often be quite significant) that the tort claim may exceed the limits of the insurance policy, in which event the suit would have all of the supposed undesirable effects upon the family.[19] Of course those cases which reject the immunity where auto accidents are the source of the injury necessarily also reject any argument that there is a serious risk of collusion or fraud on the insurance company when the child sues his parent.[20]

---

10. E.g., Thomas v. Inmon, 268 Ark. 221, 594 S.W.2d 853 (1980); Gerrity v. Beatty, 71 Ill.2d 47, 15 Ill.Dec. 639, 373 N.E.2d 1323 (1978); Karam v. Allstate Ins. Co., 70 Ohio St.2d 227, 436 N.E.2d 1014 (1982), cert. denied 459 U.S. 1070, 103 S.Ct. 490, 74 L.Ed.2d 632 (1982); Wright v. Wright, 213 Va. 177, 191 S.E.2d 223 (1972).

11. Cases relying on this argument are cited in Annot., 41 A.L.R.3d 904, 934 (1972).

12. Borst v. Borst, 41 Wash.2d 642, 251 P.2d 149 (1952) emphasized this argument, although Washington has now largely repudiated the immunity. Merrick v. Sutterlin, 93 Wash.2d 411, 610 P.2d 891 (1980).

13. W. Prosser & W. Keeton, Torts § 122 (5th ed. 1984); McCurdy, Torts Between Persons in Domestic Relations, 43 Harv.L.Rev. 1030 (1930); Williams v. Williams, 369 A.2d 669 (Del.1976); Turner v. Turner, 304 N.W.2d 786 (Iowa 1981); Hastings v. Hastings, 33 N.J. 247, 163 A.2d 147 (1960) (dissenting opinion). Henderson, Expanding the Negligence Concept: Retreat from the Rule of Law, 51 Ind. L.J. 467, 502 (1976) provides a partial defense of the immunity, but not on the traditional policy bases.

14. Small v. Rockfeld, 66 N.J. 231, 330 A.2d 335 (1974) (child could recover from father for feloniously killing mother). Cases rejecting this exception and adhering to the immunity include Jones v. Swett, 244 Ga. 715, 261 S.E.2d 610 (1979) (child could not recover from stepfather for killing his mother); Maxey v. Sauls, 242 S.C. 247, 130 S.E.2d 570 (1963).

15. Attwood v. Attwood's Estate, 276 Ark. 230, 633 S.W.2d 366 (1982), 35 Ark.L.Rev. 509 (1982) (drunken driving); Gerrity v. Beatty, 71 Ill.2d 47, 15 Ill.Dec. 639, 373 N.E.2d 1323 (1978) (dictum); Horton v. Reaves, 186 Colo. 149, 526 P.2d 304 (1974) (dictum); Oldman v. Bartshe, 480 P.2d 99 (Wyo.1971) (drunken driving). Nolechek v. Gesuale, 46 N.Y.2d 332, 413 N.Y.S.2d 340, 385 N.E.2d 1268 (1978) held that there is no liability for a parent who negligently entrusts his child with a dangerous instrumentality.

16. Barnwell v. Cordle, 438 F.2d 236 (5th Cir.1971) (Georgia law); Brinks v. Chesapeake & Ohio Ry. Co., 295 F.Supp. 1318 (W.D.Mich.1969) (Michigan law); Thurman v. Etherton, 459 S.W.2d 402 (Ky.1970); Annot., 6 A.L.R.4th 1066, 1096 (1981). Contra: Karam v. Allstate Ins. Co., 70 Ohio St.2d 227, 436 N.E.2d 1014 (1982), cert. denied 459 U.S. 1070, 103 S.Ct. 490, 74 L.Ed.2d 632 (1982); Wooley v. Parker, 222 Tenn. 104, 432 S.W.2d 882 (1968). Cf. Bonner v. Williams, 370 F.2d 301 (5th Cir.1966) (Alabama law).

The cases are also divided where the child dies and suit is brought against the parent for wrongful death. Permitting the suit: Harlan Nat. Bank v. Gross, 346 S.W.2d 482 (Ky.1961). Denying the suit: Maxey v. Sauls, 242 S.C. 247, 130 S.E.2d 570 (1963); Annot. 6 A.L.R.4th 1066, 1100 (1981).

17. Buffalo v. Buffalo, 441 N.E.2d 711 (Ind.App.1982); Fugate v. Fugate, 582 S.W.2d 663 (Mo.1979), 45 Mo.L.Rev. 186 (1979). Contra: Coleman v. Coleman, 157 Ga.App. 533, 278 S.E.2d 114 (1981).

18. Hebel v. Hebel, 435 P.2d 8 (Alaska 1967); Ard v. Ard, 414 So.2d 1066 (Fla.1982); Johnson v. Myers, 2 Ill. App.3d 844, 277 N.E.2d 778 (1972); Transamerica Ins. Co. v. Royle, 202 Mont. 173, 656 P.2d 820 (1983); France v. A.P.A. Transport Corp., 56 N.J. 500, 267 A.2d 490 (1970); Unah By and Through Unah v. Martin, 676 P.2d 1366 (Okl.1984), limited Sixkiller v. Summers, 680 P.2d 360 (Okl.1984); Smith v. Kauffman, 212 Va. 181, 183 S.E.2d 190 (1971). See N.C.Gen.Stat. § 1–539.21 (Supp.1985), S.C.Code 1976, § 15–5–210.

19. Cases which do consider this possibility, and which limit the child's right of recovery to the policy limits are Ard v. Ard, 414 So.2d 1066 (Fla.1982) and Sorensen v. Sorensen, 369 Mass. 350, 339 N.E.2d 907 (1975).

20. E.g., Sorensen v. Sorensen, 369 Mass. 350, 339 N.E.2d 907 (1975).

A substantial number of jurisdictions have agreed that the policy arguments advanced in support of the immunity [21] are not persuasive and therefore have purported to abolish it.[22] At the same time many of the courts taking this position have been careful to concede that there may still be certain kinds of cases in which it is undesirable to permit tort actions by children against their parents.[23] For this reason it is difficult if not impossible to classify the various states as retaining or abolishing the parent-child immunity. All that can be said is that a majority of states have expanded in varying degrees the extent to which children may sue their parents.

The rationale for continued insistence upon some limited version of the immunity is not the preservation of family harmony or the prevention of fraud on insurance companies. Instead the courts are concerned with family privacy. They are reluctant to substitute their judgment for that of parents respecting the care, supervision, training or protection of children. As in those cases in which a state agency seeks to require medical or surgical treatment for a child over his parent's objection,[24] the assumption is that generally speaking the parent is a better judge of what a child's welfare requires than a court or some other agency of the state.[25]

The obvious difficulty which the adoption of this policy creates for appellate courts is the articulation of a workable principle which will enable trial courts and litigants to distinguish the personal torts for which children may sue their parents from those for which they may not sue. California's Supreme Court has adopted a familiar solution to the problem. It held in Gibson v. Gibson [26] that the trier of fact must decide what an ordinarily reasonable and prudent *parent* would have done in the same circumstances. This standard is really no standard at all and provides little guidance for either the trial courts or individuals in such cases. It has the additional defect that nearly any parental conduct

---

21. See the discussion at notes 10 to 13, supra.

22. Karam v. Allstate Ins. Co., 70 Ohio St.2d 227, 436 N.E.2d 1014 (1982), cert. denied 459 U.S. 1070, 103 S.Ct. 490, 74 L.Ed.2d 632 (1982) cites cases from twenty-eight states which have abolished the immunity in whole or in part. See also cases cited in 6 A.L.R.4th 1066, 1113 (1981). Four cases seem to abolish the immunity without qualification, but perhaps they should not be taken at face value. They are Briere v. Briere, 107 N.H. 432, 224 A.2d 588 (1966); Gelbman v. Gelbman, 23 N.Y.2d 434, 297 N.Y.S.2d 529, 245 N.E.2d 192 (1969); Kirchner v. Crystal, 15 Ohio St.3d 326, 474 N.E.2d 275 (1984); Falco v. Pados, 444 Pa. 372, 282 A.2d 351 (1971). Lee v. Comer, 159 W.Va. 585, 224 S.E.2d 721 (1976) may also abrogate the immunity entirely. Holodook v. Spencer, 36 N.Y.2d 35, 364 N.Y.S.2d 859, 324 N.E.2d 338 (1974) qualifies Gelbman by holding that the parent is not liable for negligent supervision of the child.

Restatement (Second) of Torts § 895G (1979) takes the position that there is no tort immunity by virtue of the parent-child relationship, but that this does not establish liability for acts otherwise privileged or not tortious. The Restatement, comment k, explaining this somewhat vague rule, suggests that some conduct of the parent which would be tortious or negligent absent the relationship should not be so characterized where it involves parental discretion or occurs in the family home.

Winn v. Gilroy, 296 Or. 718, 681 P.2d 776 (1984) follows The Restatement.

23. Goller v. White, 20 Wis.2d 402, 122 N.W.2d 193 (1963) is an influential case taking this position. It held that children could recover from their parents for negligence except a) where the tort involved the exercise of parental authority over the child, or b) where the tort

involved the exercise of ordinary parental discretion respecting the provision of food, clothing, housing, or medical or dental services. Other similar cases are cited infra, notes 26 and 28.

24. See section 9.3, supra.

25. See, e.g., Chaffin v. Chaffin, 239 Or. 374, 381, 397 P.2d 771, 774 (1964):

"Necessarily then, a parent in performing his duties of providing support, discipline and education to his children must have wide discretion. Wealth or poverty, physical strength or weakness, wisdom or mental incapacity are not in themselves criteria for fixing guide lines by which the law judges the performance of parental duties. Physical, mental or financial weakness may cause parents to provide what many a reasonable man would consider substandard maintenance, guidance, education and recreation for their children, and in many instances to provide a family home which is not reasonably safe as a place of abode. But it would be clearly wrong to permit the minor child to hold the parent liable for these unintended injuries. The wide scope of the family life in day to day living should not be subjected to the scrutiny of the courts for each failure to exercise the care and attention that is required of one individual toward another as a member of the public." But Chaffin has been repudiated by Winn v. Gilroy, 296 Or. 718, 681 P.2d 776 (1984).

See also Black v. Solmitz, 409 A.2d 634 (Me.1979).

26. 3 Cal.3d 914, 92 Cal.Rptr. 288, 479 P.2d 648 (1971). Anderson v. Stream, 295 N.W.2d 595 (Minn.1980) follows Gibson. It was given only prospective application in American Family Mut. Ins. Co. v. Ryan, 330 N.W.2d 113 (Minn.1983).

may be characterized as unreasonable under the particular circumstances. The only parental conduct likely to be within the immunity is that which is not negligent and therefore not tortious.[27] If this is the desired result, it would be more straightforward to abolish the immunity entirely.

Courts in other states distinguish between torts occurring in the exercise of parental discretion and authority, as to which the immunity persists, and other kinds of tortious activity which are not immune to suit by the child.[28] Some courts have described the cases in which the immunity does not apply as those in which in some sense the family relation has been abandoned or has terminated or somehow has become logically irrelevant to the tort,[29] but the fictional nature of this formulation precludes any usefulness as a guide to the decision of cases.[30]

27. This seems to be the implication in both Gibson v. Gibson and Anderson v. Stream, supra, note 26. Both cases involved situations in which the alleged parental negligence consisted in failure to supervise children. The terms of remand in both cases seem to leave it to the trial courts to determine whether the parents' conduct was negligent. Both decisions rejected the distinction based on parental discretion or authority made by the cases cited infra, note 28.

28. E.g., Streenz v. Streenz, 106 Ariz. 86, 471 P.2d 282 (1970); Turner v. Turner, 304 N.W.2d 786 (Iowa 1981) (semble); Nocktonick v. Nocktonick, 227 Kan. 758, 611 P.2d 135 (1980) (semble); Rigdon v. Rigdon, 465 S.W.2d 921 (Ky.1970); Black v. Solmitz, 409 A.2d 634 (Me.1979); Plumley v. Klein, 388 Mich. 1, 199 N.W.2d 169 (1972); Merrick v. Sutterlin, 93 Wash.2d 411, 610 P.2d 891 (1980). Most of these cases arose out of auto accidents in which there was liability insurance.

29. Holodook v. Spencer, 36 N.Y.2d 35, 364 N.Y.S.2d 859, 324 N.E.2d 338 (1974).

30. The New York court in Holodook characterizes the parent inflicting an intentional injury as having abandoned the family relation, and the auto accident cases as being logically irrelevant to the family relation. But in many child abuse cases the parent has clearly not abandoned the parent-child relation and it is a fiction to say he has. In the auto accident cases there is no logical irrelevance, since in nearly all of them the parent is transporting or in some other way caring for the child. See also Illinois National Bank and Trust Co. v. Turner, 83 Ill.App.3d 234, 38 Ill.Dec. 652, 403 N.E.2d 1256 (1980).

31. See the cases cited in note 28, supra.

32. Cummings v. Jackson, 57 Ill.App.3d 68, 14 Ill.Dec. 848, 372 N.E.2d 1127 (1978) (mother liable for negligence in failing to trim trees near her home, obstructing an auto driver's view, and causing him to injure the child);

In application the distinction between torts involving parental discretion or authority and other torts has been of limited value in explaining the cases. Where the child is injured in an auto accident through the negligent driving of his parent, the courts generally seem to hold that this does not involve parental discretion or authority and therefore the parent may be held liable,[31] although the parent in such circumstances is certainly exercising his authority with respect to the child, and in a sense is also engaged in discretionary activity. Even more difficult are the cases in which the child is injured either by negligently maintained conditions in or around the home, or by his parent's negligent failure to instruct or supervise him. In both categories of cases there are decisions holding the parent liable,[32] and decisions holding him not liable on the ground that he was exercising discretion or authority.[33] The in-

Horn v. Horn, 630 S.W.2d 70 (Ky.1982) (father liable when negligent on the highway in trying to protect his son on a motorbike); Romanik v. Toro Co., 277 N.W.2d 515 (Minn.1979) (father liable under the former Minnesota rule when he negligently supervised his son's operation of a snowblower); Carey v. Davison, 181 N.J.Super. 283, 437 A.2d 338 (1981) (father liable when he negligently let his infant daughter cross a street); Convery v. Maczka, 163 N.J.Super. 411, 394 A.2d 1250 (1978) (son could recover from his mother for negligent failure to supervise his play); Gross v. Sears, Roebuck & Co., 158 N.J.Super. 442, 386 A.2d 442 (1978) (child could recover from father for negligent operation of a power lawnmower where the negligence was in part the father's failure to warn the child to stay away); Thomas v. Kells, 53 Wis.2d 141, 191 N.W.2d 872 (1971) (child could recover for his mother's failure to supervise him, leading to a stairway fall); Cole v. Sears Roebuck & Co., 47 Wis.2d 629, 177 N.W.2d 866 (1970) (two-year-old child could recover from his parents for their negligent supervision of his play, leading to an injury on a neighbor's swing).

Under the New York rule, which absolves the parent of any liability for failure to supervise the child, it was held that a mother could be held liable when a two-year-old child was burned when a pan on the stove caught fire, the child having been left in a nearby room. Hurst v. Titus, 99 Misc.2d 205, 415 N.Y.S.2d 770 (Sup.Ct.1979), affirmed 77 A.D.2d 157, 432 N.Y.S.2d 938 (4th Dep't 1980).

33. Bell v. Schwartz, 422 F.Supp. 257 (D.Minn.1976) (under former Minnesota rule parent not liable for negligent supervision); Sandoval v. Sandoval, 128 Ariz. 11, 623 P.2d 800 (1981) (child could not recover when hit by a car after going through a gate negligently left open by his parents); Schneider v. Coe, 405 A.2d 682 (Del.1979) (child could not recover when kicked by a horse as a result of negligent parental supervision); Cosmopolitan National

consistency of results in these cases suggests that the "discretion or authority" formulation is not serving its purpose very well. The reason seems to be that it is possible to say in any case that the tort occurs in the course of the parent's exercise of discretion or authority, and yet some of the cases holding the parent not liable seem to be an unwarranted restriction of the child's rights.[34]

A better way of dealing with this admittedly difficult problem would seem to be to focus on the policy underlying the immunity, asking in every case whether allowing the recovery would constitute such an invasion of family privacy as to interfere with the parent's ability to care for, train and protect his child, and conversely, whether denying recovery would leave the child without a source of funds for the treatment of and rehabilitation from his injuries. The interests of the child seem often to be ignored by the cases as the courts concentrate their attention upon the effects of the lawsuit on the family. The emphasis should be primarily on the child's

interests and only secondarily on possible intrusion into family privacy.

This analysis may be tested by the rare case in which a child sues his parent for abusing him or neglecting or abandoning him. In Burnette v. Wahl [35] the court held that children who were in the custody of a state agency could not recover from their mothers for emotional and psychological harm caused by the defendants' failure to support and care for them. The court found that tort actions are not appropriate vehicles for establishing good emotional relationships between parent and child, and that a tort recovery might well interfere with the state's attempts to reestablish family relationships. It also relied on the argument that many parents could be said to fail in some degree to meet the emotional and psychological needs of their children, so that permitting such suits would create the possibility of great numbers of suits, as for example, by children against parents who inflict emotional trauma on their children by getting divorces. Although this latter argument is

Bank of Chicago v. Heap, 128 Ill.App.2d 165, 262 N.E.2d 826 (1970) (child could not recover for injuries from a negligently maintained stairway rug in the home); McCallister v. Sun Valley Pools, Inc., 100 Mich.App. 131, 298 N.W.2d 687 (1980) (child could not recover when injured in a dangerous swimming pool owned by his parents; case comes within the exercise of parental discretion in providing housing; parents had liability insurance but the claim far exceeded the policy limits); Hush v. Devilbiss Co., 77 Mich.App. 639, 259 N.W.2d 170 (1977) (child could not recover when, due to negligent supervision, he spilled hot water on himself); Paige v. Bing Construction Co., 61 Mich.App. 480, 233 N.W.2d 46 (1975) (child's estate could not recover from parents for child's death due to negligent supervision); Cherry v. Cherry, 295 Minn. 93, 203 N.W.2d 352 (1972) (under the former Minnesota rule the child could not recover from her parents when injured by a negligently maintained extension cord in the home); Foldi v. Jeffries, 182 N.J.Super. 90, 440 A.2d 58 (1981), judgment affirmed 93 N.J. 533, 461 A.2d 1145 (1983) (child of two could not recover from her parents when their negligent supervision allowed her to be bitten by a dog); Sixkiller v. Summers, 680 P.2d 360 (Okl.1984) (child could not recover for parent's negligence in supervising another child); Lemmen v. Servais, 39 Wis.2d 75, 158 N.W.2d 341 (1968) (child could not recover for parent's failure to instruct her how to cross the road after leaving the school bus; parents held not to be negligent).

Some courts make a distinction between injuries in the course of the parent's occupation, as to which there is no immunity, and injuries caused by parental care, as to which there is immunity. E.g., Trevarton v. Trevarton,

151 Colo. 418, 378 P.2d 640 (1963); Signs v. Signs, 156 Ohio St. 566, 103 N.E.2d 743 (1952); Wright v. Wright, 213 Va. 177, 191 S.E.2d 223 (1972).

34. E.g., McCallister v. Sun Valley Pools, Inc., 100 Mich.App. 131, 298 N.W.2d 687 (1980), where one might argue that the parents should be liable at least to the extent of their liability insurance. In many of the cases the parents' liability is asserted by way of a claim for contribution brought by a third party tortfeasor, and it seems very likely that this factor often leads the courts to deny parental liability. The assumption in such cases is that even though the parent is protected by the immunity, the child's claim will be paid by the third party.

35. 284 Or. 705, 588 P.2d 1105 (1978), 48 U.Cin.L.Rev. 940 (1979), affirming summary judgment for the defendant parents. The plaintiffs' theory of tort liability here was that the parents had violated the child dependency and neglect statutes, raising the question whether such a violation would give rise to a private right of action for damages when the statutes themselves failed to specify any such right of action. The court was unwilling to imply such a right of action, but it was influenced by the impact such a suit would have on the parent-child relationship and on the other civil remedies provided by the statutes.

Another sort of claim which should be within the parent-child immunity is that asserted by a defective child on the ground that his parents were negligent in allowing him to be born. See the cases discussed in section 5.4, at note 48, and Note, Child v. Parent: A Viable New Tort of Wrongful Life? 24 Ariz.L.Rev. 391 (1982).

somewhat fanciful, a broad principle that children could recover for their parent's deficiencies as parents would certainly be an objectionable interference with family autonomy. Therefore the Burnette result seems correct so long as there is a possibility that the family involved will continue to exist, with or without the aid of state social agencies. On the other hand the child should be entitled to sue his parent in tort for the sort of physical harm which commonly constitutes child abuse,[36] and also for neglect and abandonment when the parent-child relationship has deteriorated to an extent sufficient to warrant the involuntary termination of parental rights.[37]

As in the case of the husband-wife immunity, the parent-child immunity, where it still exists, does not prevent suits by the child against his parent's employer, even though this may result in the father's indirect liability.[38] The cases are in disagreement on whether a third party tortfeasor may recover contribution from the parent when sued by

the child in those jurisdictions which still preserve the immunity.[39]

Parent vs. Child

The parent may sue his emancipated child for personal torts.[40] Where the child is not emancipated, a suit by the parent for such a tort would not conflict with the policy favored by the more recent cases,[41] that is, respect for the parent's discretion and judgment in the care and protection of his children. Where the parent sues, he has obviously made the decision to seek the intervention of the courts in his family, and there can be no unwarranted invasion of family privacy. The cases are not numerous, but some have for this reason abolished the immunity where the parent is the plaintiff.[42] Others have chosen to treat the case like that in which the child brings suit and have therefore adhered to the immunity,[43] but still others have recognized some of the exceptions discussed in connection with suits by the child.[44]

36. See the injuries described supra, in section 9.4, notes 57 to 63.

37. Cf. Note, The Child's Right to "Life Liberty and the Pursuit of Happiness": Suits By Children Against Parents for Abuse, Neglect, and Abandonment, 34 Rutgers L.Rev. 154 (1981).

38. Cases are collected in Annot., 1 A.L.R.3d 677, 699 (1965).

39. Holding that there can be no contribution where the immunity exists: Schneider v. Coe, 405 A.2d 682 (Del. 1979); Petersen v. City and County of Honolulu, 51 Hawaii 484, 462 P.2d 1007 (1969); Barry v. Schorling, 2 Ohio App.3d 110, 440 N.E.2d 1216 (1981). Holding that the third party may have contribution notwithstanding the immunity: Larson v. Buschkamp, 105 Ill.App.3d 965, 61 Ill.Dec. 732, 435 N.E.2d 221 (1982); Walker v. Milton, 263 La. 555, 268 So.2d 654 (1972).

The New York cases on this point exhibit a tortuous rationale. Gelbman v. Gelbman, 23 N.Y.2d 434, 297 N.Y.S.2d 529, 245 N.E.2d 192 (1969) purported to abolish the immunity. Holodook v. Spencer, 36 N.Y.2d 35, 364 N.Y.S.2d 859, 324 N.E.2d 338 (1974) reinstated the immunity where the parent negligently supervised the child. Nolechek v. Gesuale, 46 N.Y.2d 332, 413 N.Y.S.2d 340, 385 N.E.2d 1268 (1978) held that this immunity extended to cases where the parent entrusted the child with a dangerous instrumentality, in this instance by permitting a child with badly impaired vision to have a motorcycle. But the court in this case then held that the parent was liable to a third party defendant for contribution where the third party stood to be responsible in damages for the child's death. The court reasoned that although the

parent would not be liable to his child, he had a duty to protect third parties from loss resulting from the child's improvident use of the dangerous instrumentality.

Where the immunity is abolished on the ground that the parent has liability insurance, it has been held that the third party may recover contribution from the parent, but only to the extent of the insurance coverage. Joseph v. Quest, 414 So.2d 1063 (Fla.1982), on remand 416 So.2d 27 (1982).

40. Fitzgerald v. Valdez, 77 N.M. 769, 427 P.2d 655 (1967); Gillikin v. Burbage, 263 N.C. 317, 139 S.E.2d 753 (1965).

41. See the text supra, at notes 24, 25.

42. Tamashiro v. De Gama, 51 Hawaii 74, 450 P.2d 998 (1969); Balts v. Balts, 273 Minn. 419, 142 N.W.2d 66 (1966); Gaudreau v. Gaudreau, 106 N.H. 551, 215 A.2d 695 (1965); Silva v. Silva, ___ R.I. ___, 446 A.2d 1013 (1982); Ertl v. Ertl, 30 Wis.2d 372, 141 N.W.2d 208 (1966). In most of these cases the defendant-child was covered by liability insurance. See also Deshotel v. Travelers Indemnity Co., 257 La. 567, 243 So.2d 259 (1971); Jagers v. Royal Indemnity Co., 257 So.2d 806 (La.App.1972); Guterman v. Guterman, 66 N.J. 69, 328 A.2d 233 (1974).

43. E.g., Kirtz v. Kirtz, 52 Md.App. 136, 447 A.2d 492 (1982). See also cases collected in Annot., 60 A.L.R.2d 1284 (1958).

44. See the discussion supra, at notes 14–18, and cases cited in Annot., 60 A.L.R.2d 1284, 1288, 1290 (1958). For cases on suits for wrongful death by the parent against the child, see Annot., 62 A.L.R.3d 1299 (1975).

Choice of Law

The law has seen the same development here as in the case of the husband-wife immunity.[45] The older tendency was to apply the law of the place of the tort, but more recently the law of the parties' domicile has come to be the controlling law in deciding whether or to what extent the parent-child immunity exists.[46]

45. See section 10.1 at note 39, supra.

46. Sweeney v. Sweeney, 402 Mich. 234, 262 N.W.2d 625 (1978); Balts v. Balts, 273 Minn. 419, 142 N.W.2d 66

WESTLAW REFERENCES

Child Versus Parent

hewlett /s george /s child!

(parent /2 child) intra-famil! inter-famil! /5 immun! /p harmon!

"loco parentis" /s immun! /s child step-child!

(1966). See Restatement (Second) of Conflict of Laws § 169 (1971).

Chapter 11

PROTECTION FOR RIGHTS OF CONSORTIUM

Table of Sections

§ 11.1 Consortium—In General

Consortium is a useful though ambiguous term. As between husband and wife it used to denote the husband's right to his wife's services, society, companionship, assistance and sexual relations, and the wife's corresponding right to her husband's society, companionship, affection, sexual relations [1] and, according to some authorities, financial support.[2] It arose in cases which permitted the husband to recover for injuries to his wife on an analogy to the action given to a master for injuries to his servant.[3]

Today, when the obligation of support [4] and presumably all other obligations of marriage have been held to be equal for husbands and wives as a matter of constitutional law, consortium refers to the total of tangible and intangible relationships prevailing between husbands and wives. The parties to contemporary marriages view their roles in many different ways. In about half of all marriages the wife works outside the home, while in other marriages she is still a homemaker in the traditional sense. In still other marriages the parties adopt variations of these models to meet their economic and psychological needs. In most marriages the spouses' functions change over the years. The feature common to all, however, is the belief that marriage partners should be free to work out their own modus vivendi without hindrance from legal rules. For the most part the law has come to accept this diversity as the modern definition of consortium demonstrates. The term includes material and moral support, sexual relations, mutual assistance of all kinds, companionship and affection, all expressed in whatever manner the spouses themselves

§ 11.1

1. For an historical account of consortium, see Lippman, The Breakdown of Consortium, 30 Colum.L.Rev. 651 (1930); Holbrook, The Change in the Meaning of Consortium, 22 Mich.L.Rev. 1 (1923). For traditional accounts of the concept see 1 J. Schouler, Marriage, Divorce, Separation and Domestic Relations ch. 2 (6th ed. 1921); Pound, Individual Interests in the Domestic Relations, 14 Mich.L.Rev. 177 (1916); Riggs v. Smith, 52 Idaho 43, 11 P.2d 358 (1932).

2. E.g., Daily v. Parker, 152 F.2d 174 (7th Cir.1945); Fischer v. Mahlke, 18 Wis.2d 429, 118 N.W.2d 935 (1963).

3. Hyde v. Scyssor, Cro.Jac. 539, 79 Eng.Rep. 462 (K.B.1620); Guy v. Livesay, Cro.Jac. 501, 79 Eng.Rep. 428 (K.B.1619).

4. Orr v. Orr, 440 U.S. 268, 99 S.Ct. 1102, 59 L.Ed.2d 306 (1979), on remand 374 So.2d 895 (Ala.Civ.App.1979), writ denied 374 So.2d 898 (1979).

have chosen to adopt.[5] The result is a genuinely pluralistic law of marital relations.

It is useful to refer also to the parent-child relationship as constituting consortium. Here again the word summarizes the multitude of rights and duties binding parents to their children and vice versa. The law's view of these rights and duties has changed over the last one hundred years but not nearly as much as has family custom. It is still not uncommon to find courts writing as if the parent's right to the child's services were the crux of the relationship.[6] Yet we know that this is of minimal consequence in most families. The important aspects of the parent-child relationship, apart from the parent's duty of support, are the intangibles which follow from living together as a family, the affection, society, companionship, the mutual learning, the moral support given and received. Perhaps the greatest weakness of the law's treatment of this aspect of consortium has been the failure to recognize that the relation between parents and children is constantly changing, sometimes slowly, sometimes very rapidly. The relationship between a parent of twenty-five and his two-year-old child is entirely different from that between a parent of forty and his twenty-year-old "child". It may therefore be wise to refer to this changing relationship, composed of many variables and differing from family to family by an ambiguous term like consortium. By so doing the law may avoid rigidity and may develop more workable principles.

It is a commonplace, largely but not entirely true, that the law does not enforce the claims of consortium directly in actions between members of a family. A person who abandons his spouse or is not affectionate, or who, through negligence injures himself to such an extent that he cannot meet his marital obligations, is not open to a suit for deprivation of consortium.[7] But of course under some circumstances one spouse may sue the other for non-support.[8] A parent who abandons or abuses his children may be required to care for them properly by criminal or civil sanctions,[9] but the courts will not generally attempt to supervise the details of his relationship with his children.[10]

Direct enforcement of the child's obligations to his parents is available in the form of juvenile proceedings for delinquency or for children in need of oversight.[11] The child who runs away or is disobedient may be the subject of such proceedings which will result in the application of appropriate sanctions.[12] Although the parent is not technically the plaintiff in such proceedings, he often instigates them and they are really brought to enforce his discipline and control.

Granting that rights of consortium are not usually enforced directly, at least as between husband and wife, they may be enforced indirectly. In times past they were enforced by divorce, the spouse who did not live up to his obligations in certain ways often finding himself the losing defendant in a divorce action. Now that no-fault divorce is almost universally accepted that is no longer true, but in some

---

5. A case which outlines marital obligations in these terms is Pickens-Bond Constr. Co. v. Case, 266 Ark. 323, 584 S.W.2d 21 (1979). These obligations include the duty of a spouse to obtain medical help for the other spouse when needed, according to Commonwealth v. Konz, 265 Pa.Super. 570, 402 A.2d 692 (1979), order reversed 489 Pa. 639, 450 A.2d 638 (1982). Conversely, the courts have held that the wife's decision not to have a child is her own, to be respected notwithstanding her husband's objection. E.g., Planned Parenthood of Central Missouri v. Danforth, 428 U.S. 52, 96 S.Ct. 2831, 49 L.Ed.2d 788 (1976) (abortion); Murray v. Vandevander, 522 P.2d 302 (Okl.App.1974) (hysterectomy). Severns v. Wilmington Medical Center, 421 A.2d 1334 (Del.1980) held that a husband could be appointed guardian for his seriously injured wife, with authority to assert her right to privacy by having the hospital disconnect life-sustaining systems.

The wife in this case was not capable of making this decision for herself.

6. E.g., Blackman v. Iles, 4 N.J. 82, 71 A.2d 633 (1950). A more modern approach is Magierowski v. Buckley, 39 N.J.Super. 534, 121 A.2d 749 (1956).

7. Plain v. Plain, 307 Minn. 399, 240 N.W.2d 330 (1976).

8. See section 6.4, supra.

9. See chapter 9, supra.

10. Burnette v. Wahl, 284 Or. 705, 588 P.2d 1105 (1978), discussed in section 10.2, supra, at note 35.

11. See section 9.5, supra.

12. Ibid.

states marital fault is still considered by the courts in determining the amount of alimony or of property a spouse will receive.[13] Other methods of indirect enforcement are discussed in the succeeding sections. These methods result in judgments for damages against persons outside the family who interfere with consortium in various ways. The cases share a common feature; they are brought to vindicate the interest of family members in the family consortium. For that reason there has been a tendency to lump them all together and to minimize their differences.[14] But since the cases involve different kinds of interference with consortium, different parties and different defenses, clarity is better served by treating them separately. It is important to remember, however, that a single interest is at stake—that of consortium.

---

13. See sections 15.3, 16.5, infra.

14. W. Prosser, Torts § 124 (4th ed. 1971); Wright v. Lester, 105 Ga.App. 107, 123 S.E.2d 672 (1961), modified 218 Ga. 31, 126 S.E.2d 419 (1962), on remand 106 Ga.App. 452, 127 S.E.2d 193 (1962).

§ 11.2

1. See section 19.3, infra.

2. A typical statute is Model Penal Code § 212.4. Part II (1985), Model Penal Code and Commentaries 248 (Am. L.Inst.1980) making it an offense to take or entice a child under eighteen from the custody of his parent without a privilege to do so. The comment to this statute, id. at 249, cites many state statutes of similar effect. See also Ark.Stats. § 41–2411 (1977); Colo.Rev.Stat. § 18–3–304 (1973). It is not clear whether a parent would be in violation of such a statute if he should remove the child from the custody of the other parent at a time when there was no custody decree outstanding. It is true that both parents are equally entitled to custody, but conceivably a court might hold there is no privilege for one parent to exercise his custody rights in such a way as to frustrate the rights of the other parent. Cf. Rosefield v. Rosefield, 221 Cal.App.2d 431, 34 Cal.Rptr. 479 (1963), a tort case for abduction in which the court indicated the parent would be acting wrongfully in such circumstances, and People v. Harrison, 82 Ill.App.3d 530, 37 Ill.Dec. 820, 402 N.E.2d 822 (1980), in which a father was convicted under the statute for removal of his child notwithstanding that he had custody jointly with the mother. Contra, State v. Edmiston, 43 Or.App. 13, 602 P.2d 282 (1979), holding that a person who took a child from its mother at the direction of the father who was the mother's husband

§ 11.2 Intentional Interference With the Parent-Child Relationship

Action by the Parent

The parent's interest in the custody, society, companionship, affection and services of his child is protected by the law in a variety of ways. A direct and specific remedy for obtaining custody is given the parent by such procedures as habeas corpus or an equity action for custody.[1] A large number of states now have statutes imposing criminal sanctions upon one who takes a child from his parent either without a privilege to do so,[2] or in violation of a court's custody decree.[3] Where the parent's interest is interfered with by strangers, the parent also has at least two actions for damages, the suit for abduction or enticement and the suit for seduction.

The common law provided remedies in damages, remedies which are still enforced in most states, for parents whose children were forcibly abducted from the parents' custody,[4]

was not guilty of kidnapping since the father himself would not be guilty. Statutes making such conduct criminal have been held constitutional. State v. Musumeci, 116 N.H. 136, 355 A.2d 434 (1976).

The federal kidnapping statute, the Lindbergh Act, 18 U.S.C.A. § 1201, expressly excludes parents from its provisions. But Congress in the Parental Kidnapping Prevention Act of 1980, Pub.L. 96–611, 94 Stat. 3573, section 10, provided that 18 U.S.C.A. § 1073 will apply to parental kidnapping. That section makes it a crime to engage in interstate or international flight to avoid prosecution. The practical effect of this is to enlist the Federal Bureau of Investigation in the tracing and apprehension of parents who abduct their own children in violation of state statutes.

3. S Katz, Child Snatching 155–187 (1981) contains a comprehensive citation to and summary of these statutes. See also R. Perkins and R. Boyce, Criminal Law 234–236 (3d ed. 1982); Annot., 20 A.L.R.4th 823 (1983); State v. Kracker, 123 Ariz.App. 294, 599 P.2d 250 (1979); People v. Carrillo, 162 Cal.App.3d 585, 208 Cal.Rptr. 684 (1984).

4. Magee v. Holland, 27 N.J.L. 86 (1858); Pickle v. Page, 252 N.Y. 474, 169 N.E. 650 (1930); Howell v. Howell, 162 N.C. 283, 78 S.E. 222 (1913). See also III W. Blackstone, Commentaries on the Laws of England 140 (Cooley 3d ed. 1884); 1 J. Schouler, Marriage, Divorce, Separation and Domestic Relations § 750 (6th ed. 1921); W. Prosser & W. Keeton, Torts § 924 (5th ed. 1984); 2 F. Harper, F. James & O. Gray, Torts § 8.6 (2d ed. 1986); Pound, Individual Interests in the Domestic Relations, 14 Mich.L.Rev. 177 (1916).

or whose children were enticed away,[5] or whose children were harbored by the defendant after they had left home.[6] In order to recover for the tort of harboring the child the parents need not prove that the defendant enticed the child away, but need only prove that the defendant knew that the child had left home against the will of his parents and had persuaded the child not to return home.[7] The early cases held that the parents had to prove that the defendant had caused them to lose the child's services in order to recover.[8] The modern cases have come to recognize that in today's world the child generally performs no substantial services, so that any claim for loss of services is largely fictional, and that the essence of the suit is the interference with the totality of the relationship between parent and child, with what may be called the parent's right of consortium.[9]

The older cases also held that the child's father alone was a proper plaintiff,[10] but now that gender discrimination has been held unconstitutional in nearly all instances it seems clear that either father or mother may bring the action, since both are equally entitled to the custody of the child until a court decree determines otherwise.[11] Adoptive parents are entitled to these tort remedies as well as natural parents.[12]

The damages recoverable in suits for abduction or enticement include compensation for loss of the child's services,[13] for loss of the child's society,[14] for the parent's mental and emotional distress,[15] for expenses incurred in trying to regain custody of the child,[16] and for treatment of medical conditions resulting from the abduction.[17] Punitive damages may also be recovered where malice is proved.[18]

An action for abduction or enticement is maintainable by a parent having custody of his child pursuant to a court's decree, against the other parent who has removed the child from that custody and against any third per-

---

5. Hare v. Dean, 90 Me. 308, 38 A. 227 (1897); Kipper v. Vokolek, 546 S.W.2d 521 (Mo.App.1977); Restatement (Second) of Torts § 700 (1977).

6. Hinton v. Hinton, 436 F.2d 211 (D.C.Cir.1970); W. Prosser & W. Keeton, Torts 925 (5th ed. 1984).

7. Hinton v. Hinton, 436 F.2d 211 (D.C.Cir.1970); Restatement (Second) of Torts § 700, comment b (1977).

8. Magee v. Holland, 27 N.J.L. 86 (1858); Rogers v. Smith, 17 Ind. 323 (1861); Pickle v. Page, 252 N.Y. 474, 169 N.E. 650 (1930); W. Prosser & W. Keeton, Torts 924 (5th ed. 1984).

9. Steward v. Gold Medal Shows, 244 Ala. 583, 14 So. 2d 549 (1943); Pickle v. Page, 252 N.Y. 474, 169 N.E. 650 (1930); Willeford v. Bailey, 132 N.C. 402, 43 S.E. 928 (1903); Idleman v. Groves, 89 W.Va. 91, 108 S.E. 485 (1921).

10. Soper v. Igo, Walker & Co., 121 Ky. 550, 89 S.W. 538 (1905).

11. See, e.g., Orr v. Orr, 440 U.S. 268, 99 S.Ct. 1102, 59 L.Ed.2d 306 (1979), on remand 374 So.2d 895 (Ala.Civ. App.1979), writ denied 374 So.2d 898 (1979). LaGrenade v. Gordon, 46 N.C.App. 329, 264 S.E.2d 757 (1980), appeal dismissed 300 N.C. 557, 270 S.E.2d 109 (1980) seems clearly wrong in saying that the father's right to custody is superior to the mother's, but the case does allow the mother to recover from the father for abduction where the parents had made a contract giving the mother custody.

12. Pickle v. Page, 252 N.Y. 474, 169 N.E. 650 (1930). It is not clear whether the courts would recognize a claim for abduction on behalf of one not a natural parent and not an adoptive parent, but who has custody of the child. Such a person, if he stands in loco parentis with the child and has ties of affection similar to those of a parent,

would seem to have an interest which should be protected by the tort law. See Ellis v. Hamilton, 669 F.2d 510 (7th Cir.1982), cert. denied 459 U.S. 1069, 103 S.Ct. 488, 74 L.Ed.2d 631 (1982).

13. Brown v. Brown, 338 Mich. 492, 61 N.W.2d 656 (1953), cert. denied 348 U.S. 816, 75 S.Ct. 27, 99 L.Ed. 644 (1954); Tavlinsky v. Ringling Bros. Circus, 113 Neb. 632, 204 N.W. 388 (1925); Little v. Holmes, 181 N.C. 413, 107 S.E. 577 (1921); Magnuson v. O'Dea, 75 Wash. 574, 135 P. 640 (1913).

14. Fenslage v. Dawkins, 629 F.2d 1107 (5th Cir.1980); Brown v. Brown, 338 Mich. 492, 61 N.W.2d 656 (1953), cert. denied 348 U.S. 816, 75 S.Ct. 27, 99 L.Ed. 644 (1954); Tavlinsky v. Ringling Bros. Circus, 113 Neb. 632, 204 N.W. 388 (1925); Little v. Holmes, 181 N.C. 413, 107 S.E. 577 (1921); Magnuson v. O'Dea, 75 Wash. 574, 135 P. 640 (1913).

15. Fenslage v. Dawkins, 629 F.2d 1107 (5th Cir.1980); Lloyd v. Loeffler, 539 F.Supp. 998 (E.D.Wis.1982), judgment affirmed 694 F.2d 489 (7th Cir.1982) (father recovered amount paid to psychologists for treatment of his emotional distress); Howell v. Howell, 162 N.C. 231, 78 S.E. 222 (1913).

16. Lloyd v. Loeffler, 539 F.Supp. 998 (E.D.Wis.1982), judgment affirmed 694 F.2d 489 (7th Cir.1982); Rice v. Nickerson, 91 Mass. 478 (1864); Howell v. Howell, 162 N.C. 231, 78 S.E. 222 (1913).

17. Fenslage v. Dawkins, 629 F.2d 1107 (5th Cir.1980), relying on Restatement (Second) of Torts § 700, comm. g (1977).

18. Fenslage v. Dawkins, 629 F.2d 1107 (5th Cir.1980); Howell v. Howell, 162 N.C. 231, 78 S.E. 222 (1913). The jurisdiction of federal courts in such cases is discussed, infra, section 12.2.

son who assists the removing parent.[19] In the converse situation where the parent removing the child is entitled to custody under a court's decree, the action for abduction may not be brought.[20] Where custody has been jointly conferred on both parents after divorce, and one parent removes the child from custody or contact with the other parent, an action for abduction should lie since the removal frustrates the underlying premise of the decree, that both parents are to have equal access to the child, but the authorities are not in agreement on the point.[21] In the somewhat analogous case where one parent prevents the other from exercising his visitation rights after divorce the courts have not granted recovery in tort.[22] Parents have on occasion recovered for the false arrest or imprisonment of their

child,[23] or for civil conspiracy to abduct their child.[24]

Although obviously neither the criminal sanctions nor damages in tort actions guarantees the return of the child, the prospect of both forms of legal process very likely serves as a deterrent to child snatching.[25] Tort actions serve the additional function of providing the funds with which the parent may pay the expenses incurred in regaining custody of the child.[26]

Where no abduction or enticement or harboring is alleged, but the parent sues for the alienation of the affections of his child, most of the cases have denied relief, whether the child is an adult [27] or a minor.[28] The courts give as reasons for refusing to entertain the

19. Lloyd v. Loeffler, 694 F.2d 489 (7th Cir.1982) (Wisconsin law); Fenslage v. Dawkins, 629 F.2d 1107 (5th Cir. 1980); Abdul-Rahman Omar Adra v. Clift, 195 F.Supp. 857 (D.Md.1961); Gibson v. Gibson, 15 Cal.App.3d 943, 93 Cal.Rptr. 617 (1971); Oversmith v. Lake, 295 Mich. 627, 295 N.W. 339 (1940); Plante v. Engel, 124 N.H. 213, 469 A.2d 1299 (1983). See Note, The Tort of Custodial Interference—Toward A More Complete Remedy for Parental Kidnapping, 1983 U.Ill.L.Rev. 229. Punitive damages may be awarded if the defendant spouse shows a reckless disregard of the plaintiff's rights. Kramer v. Leineweber, 642 S.W.2d 364 (Mo.App.1982). In the Lloyd case, supra, the trial court awarded punitive damages, with the proviso that they would increase by $2000 for each month the child was withheld from the plaintiff's custody.

State v. Al-Turck, 220 Kan. 557, 552 P.2d 1375 (1976) held that a father was not guilty of violating the parental interference statute when he took his daughter to a foreign country without the mother's knowledge or consent during the pendency of a divorce suit but before any custody order had been entered. The court relied on the principle that each parent is equally entitled to the custody of their child. This result obviously encourages the spouses to "seize and run" when divorce is in the offing.

20. Aberlin v. Zisman, 244 F.2d 620 (1st Cir.1957), cert. denied 355 U.S. 857, 78 S.Ct. 84, 2 L.Ed.2d 63 (1957); Kipper v. Vokolek, 546 S.W.2d 521 (Mo.App.1977); McGrady v. Rosenbaum, 62 Misc.2d 182, 308 N.Y.S.2d 181 (1970), affirmed 37 A.D.2d 917, 324 N.Y.S.2d 876 (1st Dep't 1971). But see Rosefield v. Rosefield, 221 Cal.App. 2d 431, 34 Cal.Rptr. 479 (1963).

21. Note, Abduction of Child by Noncustodial Parent: Damages for Custodial Parent's Mental Distress, 46 Mo.L. Rev. 829, 841 (1981). People v. Harrison, 82 Ill.App.3d 530, 37 Ill.Dec. 820, 402 N.E.2d 822 (1980) held that a father could be convicted under the statute prohibiting child-snatching even though he and his former wife had a joint custody decree. But the Restatement (Second) of Torts § 700, com. c (1977) states that when both parents have a joint custody decree neither can recover from the

other for the abduction or enticement of the child. See also Annot., 20 A.L.R.4th 823 (1983).

22. McGrady v. Rosenbaum, 62 Misc.2d 182, 308 N.Y.S.2d 181 (1970), affirmed 37 A.D.2d 917, 324 N.Y.S.2d 876 (1st Dep't 1971); Friedman v. Friedman, 79 Misc.2d 646, 361 N.Y.S.2d 108 (1974). But see Sheltra v. Smith, 136 Vt. 472, 392 A.2d 431 (1978), in which the court held that a mother could recover for her mental distress caused when the defendant prevented her from having any contact or communication with her daughter. Suits by parents against government agencies for violation of the Civil Rights Act allegedly occurring when the parents' relationship with their children has been interfered with have generally been unsuccessful. Wise v. Bravo, 666 F.2d 1328 (10th Cir.1981); Leonhard v. United States, 633 F.2d 599 (2d Cir.1980), cert. denied 451 U.S. 908, 101 S.Ct. 1975, 68 L.Ed.2d 295 (1981).

23. Kajtazi v. Kajtazi, 488 F.Supp. 15 (E.D.N.Y.1978); Conoly v. Imperial Tobacco Co., 63 Ga.App. 880, 12 S.E.2d 398 (1940); Oversmith v. Lake, 295 Mich. 627, 295 N.W. 339 (1940); Drabek v. Sabley, 31 Wis.2d 184, 142 N.W.2d 798 (1966); Annot., 20 A.L.R.3d 1441 (1968).

24. Lloyd v. Loeffler, 694 F.2d 489 (7th Cir.1982); Rosefield v. Rosefield, 221 Cal.App.2d 431, 34 Cal.Rptr. 479 (1963); Brown v. Brown, 338 Mich. 492, 61 N.W.2d 656 (1953), cert. denied 348 U.S. 816, 75 S.Ct. 27, 99 L.Ed. 644 (1954).

25. S. Katz, Child Snatching 89–102 (1981).

26. Kajtazi v. Kajtazi, 488 F.Supp. 15 (E.D.N.Y.1978) ordered the father's relatives to pay $50 per day for the period during which the child was abducted. Lloyd v. Loeffler, 694 F.2d 489 (7th Cir.1982) held the defendant mother, husband and grandparents jointly and severally liable for $70,038.45. The mother and husband were held liable also for $25,000 in punitive damages, to be increased by $2,000 each month until the child should be returned to the father, but the increasing feature of punitive damages was disapproved.

27.–28. See notes 27–28 on page 387.

suit that the parent-child relationship does not constitute consortium,[29] that permitting the suit would produce too much litigation,[30] that the child is not allowed to recover for the alienation of his parent's affections,[31] and that the suit is barred by the Heart Balm Statute.[32] Phrasing the claim as one for the intentional infliction of emotional distress has not been successful.[33]

A few cases have held that a parent may recover for the alienation of the affections of his child, arguing that the action is analogous to the suit for abduction or enticement, that today there is no requirement that the plaintiff in such a case prove a loss of the child's services, and that some courts are beginning to allow the child to recover for the alienation of his parent's affections.[34] Certainly the distinction between an action for enticement and one for alienation of affections is a fine one, not easy to draw in some circumstances. And

the effect of the alienation of affections upon the parent may be an element of damage when the parent sues for abduction or enticement.[35] Whether this kind of a suit is open to the same objections as the spousal action for alienation of affections is a difficult question. In any event the Heart Balm Statutes, where they exist, do apply to it.

Another remedy for intentional interference with the parent-child relationship is the action for seduction. At common law a woman could not sue for her own seduction, being barred by her consent, except where force or duress was used.[36] Today statutes in some states permit her to sue.[37] The common law did recognize a cause of action in a father for the seduction of his minor daughter.[38] Occasionally the mother was allowed to bring the action,[39] and now statutes in some states provide that either parent or a guardian may sue.[40] There is no reason why either parent

---

27. Orlando v. Alamo, 646 F.2d 1288 (8th Cir.1981) (semble); Schuppin v. Unification Church, 435 F.Supp. 603 (D.Vt.1977), affirmed 573 F.2d 1295 (2d Cir.1977); French v. Safeway Stores Inc., 247 Or. 554, 430 P.2d 1021 (1967).

28. Note, Torts—A Parent's Cause of Action for the Alienation of a Child's Affections, 22 U.Kan.L.Rev. 684 (1974), citing cases. See also Restatement (Second) of Torts § 699 (1977); and Annot., Right of Child or Parent to Recover for Alienation of Other's Affections, 60 A.L.R.3d 931 (1974).

29. Pyle v. Waechter, 202 Iowa 695, 210 N.W. 926 (1926); Edwards v. Edwards, 43 N.C.App. 296, 259 S.E.2d 11 (1979).

30. Bock v. Lindquist, 278 N.W.2d 326 (Minn.1979).

31. Edwards v. Edwards, 43 N.C.App. 296, 259 S.E.2d 11 (1979). Ronan v. Briggs, 351 Mass. 700, 220 N.E.2d 909 (1966) just denies that there is any such cause of action, without giving any reasons.

32. Schuppin v. Unification Church, 435 F.Supp. 603 (D.Vt.1977), affirmed 573 F.2d 1295 (2d Cir.1977); McGrady v. Rosenbaum, 62 Misc.2d 182, 308 N.Y.S.2d 181 (1970), affirmed 37 A.D.2d 917, 324 N.Y.S.2d 876 (1st Dep't 1971). Orlando v. Alamo, 646 F.2d 1288 (8th Cir. 1981) held the suit barred by the statute of limitations.

33. Orlando v. Alamo, 646 F.2d 1288 (8th Cir.1981).

34. Strode v. Gleason, 9 Wash.App. 13, 510 P.2d 250 (1973), 22 U.Kan.L.Rev. 684 (1974); Snyder v. State, 19 Wash.App. 631, 577 P.2d 160 (1978). The Strode case denied recovery on the ground that the statute of limitations had run, holding that the statute begins to run when the parent becomes aware of the loss of affections. Hammond v. Peden, 224 Ark. 1053, 278 S.W.2d 96 (1955) seems to have recognized the cause of action when it was

coupled with a claim for loss of a spouse's affections, but the case is far from clear on the point.

35. Little v. Holmes, 181 N.C. 413, 107 S.E. 577 (1921) (semble).

36. Kirkpatrick v. Parker, 136 Fla. 689, 187 So. 620 (1939); Magierowski v. Buckley, 39 N.J.Super. 534, 121 A.2d 749 (1956). But the seduction could be proved in an action for breach of promise of marriage, in order to augment the damages. See section 1.4, Practitioner's Edition. Slawek v. Stroh, 62 Wis.2d 295, 215 N.W.2d 9 (1974) holds that a woman may recover for her seduction if it was accomplished by false or fraudulent representations.

37. E.g., Ala.Code 1975, § 6–5–350 (unmarried woman under age nineteen may sue); Ariz.Rev.Stat. § 12–541 (1982); Idaho Code § 5–308 (1979) (unmarried woman may sue); Miss.Code 1972, § 11–7–9; Mont.Code Ann. § 27–1–514(3) (1985); Tenn.Code Ann. § 20–1–106(a)(1) (1980); Utah Code Ann. 1977, § 78–7–11.

38. 2 F. Harper, F. James & O. Gray, Torts § 8.6 (2d ed. 1986); W. Prosser & W. Keeton, Torts 926–928 (5th ed. 1984). Of course the daughter's consent is no defense to the father's action. Reutkemeier v. Nolte, 179 Iowa 342, 161 N.W. 290 (1917).

39. Bunker v. Mains, 139 Me. 231, 28 A.2d 734 (1942) (mother could sue for seduction of her illegitimate daughter when father was unknown); Malone v. Topfer, 125 Md. 157, 93 A. 397 (1915) (divorced mother could sue for seduction of daughter); Furman v. Van Sise, 56 N.Y. 435, 15 Am.Rep. 441 (1874).

40. E.g., Alaska Stat. 09.15.020 (1983); Idaho Code § 5–309 (1979); Mont.Code Ann. § 27–1–514(2) (1985); Utah Code Ann.1977, § 78–11–5.

should not be allowed to sue [41] and in fact restricting the right to the father is a form of gender discrimination which would undoubtedly be held a violation of the Equal Protection Clause of the Fourteenth Amendment.[42]

As in the early abduction and enticement cases, the early seduction cases denied recovery unless there was proof that the daughter had performed services for her father.[43] If proof of nominal services were made, the father could recover not only the value of the services but compensation for his own distress caused by the seduction.[44] Recovery of medical expenses resulting from the seduction could also be had,[45] as well as punitive damages.[46] Today the requirement of proof of services is seen to be fictional and the action is essentially for the vindication of the father's consortium.[47] The emancipation or later marriage of the daughter has been held to bar the father's suit.[48]

Although there seems to be no reason why a cause of action should not arise when it is a son who has been seduced, there seems to have been no cases of this kind.[49] Some

states have statutes which allow the parent to sue for his child's seduction with no requirement that the child be female.[50] In other states the Heart Balm Statute provides that the action for seduction be abolished.[51] These statutes have been construed to abolish both the father's and the daughter's action for seduction.[52]

Action by the Child For Alienation of the Affections of His Parent

When a stranger to the marriage captures the affections of a spouse, the other spouse, as we have seen,[53] may have a cause of action for alienation of affections. The resulting break-up of the marriage affects not only the spouse, however, but also any children the spouses may have. If it is proper to speak of the parent-child consortium as we have suggested, that consortium is damaged or destroyed when a parent leaves the home or gets a divorce. The question this raises is whether the children of the marriage thereby acquire a right to sue the stranger for alienation of the affections of the parent.

---

41. Since both parents have equal rights to the custody of their child, infra, section 19.4, the consortium interests of both are the same and should be protected by the same kinds of legal proceeding.

42. U.S. Const. amend. XIV, § 1.

43. Tittlebaum v. Boehmcke, 81 N.J.L. 697, 80 A. 323 (1911); Bartley v. Richtmyer, 4 N.Y. (4 Comst.) 38 (1850); Wendt v. Lentz, 197 Wis. 569, 222 N.W. 798 (1929).

44. Haeissig v. Decker, 139 Minn. 422, 166 N.W. 1085 (1918); Dwire v. Stearns, 44 N.D. 199, 172 N.W. 69 (1919); Anderson v. Aupperle, 51 Or. 556, 95 P. 330 (1908); Davidson v. Abbott, 52 Vt. 570 (1880).

45. Boedges v. Dinges, 428 S.W.2d 930 (Mo.App.1968); Anderson v. Aupperle, 51 Or. 556, 95 P. 330 (1908); Robinson v. Moore, 408 S.W.2d 582 (Tex.Civ.App.1966).

46. Haessig v. Decker, 139 Minn. 422, 166 N.W. 1085 (1918); Piggott v. Miller, 557 S.W.2d 692 (Mo.App.1977); Berghammer v. Mayer, 189 Wis. 197, 207 N.W. 289 (1926).

47. Anthony v. Norton, 60 Kan. 341, 56 P. 529 (1899); Haeissig v. Decker, 139 Minn. 422, 166 N.W. 1085 (1918); Dwire v. Stearns, 44 N.D. 199, 172 N.W. 69 (1919); Lawyer v. Fritcher, 130 N.Y. 239, 29 N.E. 267 (1891). But Restatement (Second) of Torts § 701, comment c (1977) continues to insist upon the fictional requirement that a loss of services resulting from the seduction must be proved.

48. Collis v. Hoskins, 306 Ky. 391, 208 S.W.2d 70 (1948); Aldrich v. Bennett, 63 N.H. 415 (1885). Under Ala.Code 1975, § 6–5–351 a suit by the daughter bars suit

by the father or mother. And under Miss.Code 1972, § 11–7–11 and Tenn.Code Ann. § 20–1–106(b) (1980) recovery by either the mother, father or daughter bars any subsequent suit.

49. W. Prosser & W. Keeton, Torts 926 (5th ed. 1984).

50. E.g., Alaska Stat. § 09.15.020 (1983); Mont.Code Ann. 27–1–514(2) (1985); Utah Code Ann. 1977, § 78–11–5.

51. Ala.Code 1977, § 6–5–331 (no suit for seduction of female over nineteen); West's Ann.Cal.Civ.Code § 43.5 (1982) (no suit for seduction of female over the age of consent); Colo.Rev.Stat. § 13–20–202 (1974) (abolishes actions for seduction); Del.Code tit. 10, § 3924 (1975) (abolishes actions for seduction); West's Fla.Stat.Ann. § 771.01 (1986) (abolishes actions for seduction); West's Ann.Ind.Code § 34–4–4–1 (1986) (no suit for seduction of female over eighteen); Mich.Comp.Laws Ann. § 27A.2901(3) (1980) (no suit for seduction of female over eighteen); Minn.Stat.Ann. § 553.01 (Supp.1987) (abolishes actions for seduction); N.J.Stat.Ann. § 2A:23–1 (1952) (abolishes actions for seduction); N.Y.—McKinney's Civ.Rights Law § 80–a (1976) (abolishes actions for seduction); Ohio Rev.Code § 2305.29 (1981) (no suit for seduction of one eighteen or over); Vt.Stat.Ann. tit. 15, § 1001 (Supp.1986) (abolishes actions for seduction); Wyo. Stat.1977, § 1–23–101 (abolishes actions for seduction).

52. Magierowski v. Buckley, 39 N.J.Super. 534, 121 A.2d 749 (1956).

53. See section 12.3, Practitioner's Edition.

The answer to this question given by most authorities has been that the child may not recover for the alienation of the affections of his parent.[54] Some cases take the position that there is no right of consortium based upon the parent-child relationship as distinguished from the marriage relationship.[55] Other courts fear that recognition of the child's claim would produce a "flood of litigation"[56] or a multiplicity of suits against the same defendant by several family members.[57] Still other reasons for denying a remedy include a fear of fraud or extortion in such suits,[58] and an expectation that damages would be difficult to measure.[59] Problems of damages could be avoided by invoking equitable remedies, but the courts have properly refused to grant injunctions as a means of controlling human emotions and family relations.[60]

A small number of cases have been willing to award damages to children whose parents' affections have been alienated notwithstanding the arguments and authorities to the contrary.[61] These cases recognize that consortium is a concept broader than the husband-wife relationship, that it includes all the relationships within the family. Since, they assert, the children have rights based on these relationships, they should be entitled to enforce these rights against one whose conduct leads to the destruction of the family. The elements of the suit have been held to be evidence of a) affection of the alienated spouse for the plaintiff; b) wilful conduct by the defendant which destroyed that affection; and c) a relationship of proximate cause between the defendant's conduct and the plaintiff's damages.[62]

Many states have enacted Heart Balm Statutes which abolish suits for alienation of affections.[63] The case law in these states has generally held that such statutes prevent suits by children for alienation of the affections of a parent as well as suits by spouses for the alienation of the affections of the other spouse.[64] Although the child is a more appealing plaintiff than the spouse, the prob-

54. Cases are collected in Annots., 60 A.L.R.3d 931 (1974), 12 A.L.R.2d 1178 (1950), and 162 A.L.R. 824 (1946). See also Nelson v. Richwagen, 326 Mass. 485, 95 N.E.2d 545 (1950); Zarrella v. Robinson, ___ R.I. ___, 492 A.2d 833 (1985); Scholberg v. Itnyre, 264 Wis. 211, 58 N.W.2d 698 (1953); Restatement (Second) of Torts § 702A (1977). Henson v. Thomas, 231 N.C. 173, 56 S.E.2d 432 (1949) held that the child could not recover for criminal conversation against his mother's paramour.

55. Taylor v. Keefe, 134 Conn. 156, 56 A.2d 768 (1947); Morrow v. Yannantuono, 152 Misc. 134, 273 N.Y.S. 912 (1934); Kane v. Quigley, 1 Ohio St.2d 1, 203 N.E.2d 338 (1964); Garza v. Garza, 209 S.W.2d 1012 (Tex.Civ.App. 1948); Wallace v. Wallace, 155 W.Va. 569, 184 S.E.2d 327 (1971). The Taylor and Garza cases have begged the question by characterizing the wrong to the child as a moral rather than a legal wrong, as has the Kane case in slightly different terms.

56. Mode v. Barnett, 235 Ark. 641, 361 S.W.2d 525 (1962); Taylor v. Keefe, 134 Conn. 156, 56 A.2d 768 (1947); Hunt v. Chang, 60 Hawaii 608, 594 P.2d 118 (1979); Whitcomb v. Huffington, 180 Kan. 340, 304 P.2d 465 (1956); Nelson v. Richwagen, 326 Mass. 485, 95 N.E.2d 545 (1950); Morrow v. Yannantuono, 152 Misc. 134, 273 N.Y.S. 912 (1934); Henson v. Thomas, 231 N.C. 173, 56 S.E.2d 432 (1949); Kane v. Quigley, 1 Ohio St.2d 1, 203 N.E.2d 338 (1964); Scholberg v. Itnyre, 264 Wis. 211, 58 N.W.2d 698 (1953).

57. Taylor v. Keefe, 134 Conn. 156, 56 A.2d 768 (1947).

58. Hunt v. Chang, 60 Hawaii 608, 594 P.2d 118 (1979); Katz v. Katz, 197 Misc. 412, 95 N.Y.S.2d 863 (1950).

59. Taylor v. Keefe, 134 Conn. 156, 56 A.2d 768 (1947); Hunt v. Chang, 60 Hawaii 608, 594 P.2d 118 (1979); Nelson v. Richwagen, 326 Mass. 485, 95 N.E.2d 545 (1950).

60. White v. Thomson, 324 Mass. 140, 85 N.E.2d 246 (1949).

61. Daily v. Parker, 152 F.2d 174 (7th Cir.1945); Russick v. Hicks, 85 F.Supp. 281 (W.D.Mich.1949); Johnson v. Luhman, 330 Ill.App. 598, 71 N.E.2d 810 (1947); Rudnick v. Vokaty, 84 Ill.App.3d 1003, 40 Ill.Dec. 404, 406 N.E.2d 105 (1980); Miller v. Monsen, 228 Minn. 400, 37 N.W.2d 543 (1949). One other case, Hammond v. Peden, 224 Ark. 1053, 278 S.W.2d 96 (1955) seems to have approved the child's claim without discussion when coupled with a spouse's claim for alienation.

62. Rudnick v. Vokaty, 84 Ill.App.3d 1003, 40 Ill.Dec. 404, 406 N.E.2d 105 (1980).

63. See section 12.3, Practitioner's Edition, at note 46.

64. Rudley v. Tobias, 84 Cal.App.2d 454, 190 P.2d 984 (1948); Kleinow v. Ameika, 19 N.J.Super. 165, 88 A.2d 31 (1952); Katz v. Katz, 197 Misc. 412, 95 N.Y.S.2d 863 (1950). Russick v. Hicks, 85 F.Supp. 281 (W.D.Mich.1949) held that the former Michigan Heart Balm Statute did not bar suits by children for alienation of affections, but the Michigan legislature amended the statute so as to make it entirely clear that such suits were barred. See Mich.Comp.Laws Ann. § 27A.2901(1) (1980). And Wallace v. Wallace, 155 W.Va. 569, 184 S.E.2d 327 (1971) held that the Heart Balm Statute did not apply to these suits, but went on to hold that there is no right in a child to sue for the alienation of the affections of his parent.

lems of causation and of proving damages are as acute here as in the husband-wife cases. For this reason the legislatures and courts are probably right not to recognize the suit.

 WESTLAW REFERENCES

Action by the Parent

"common law" /s kidnap! abduct! /s minor child!

custod! /s forc! /s abduct! kidnap! /s child minor

"parental kidnapping prevention" /s inter-state international!

joint! /s custod! /s child minor /s abduct!

damag! /s recover! /s abduct! /s child!

Action by the Child for Alienation of the Affections of His Parent

henson /s thomas

---

§ 11.3 Negligent Interference With the Husband-Wife Relationship— Actions for Impairment of Consortium

Suit by the Husband

From quite early times it was established that a husband might recover from one who, by assault, battery or imprisonment, so seriously injured the plaintiff's wife as to deprive him of her company and assistance.[1] The action lay not merely for depriving the husband of his wife's services, as some later cases seem to have thought,[2] but for impairment of

loss of the consortium, as is shown by the use of the Latin phrase, *per quod consortium amisit.*[3] The early American authorities recognized this right of action in the husband.[4] As the action for negligence developed, the same doctrine was extended to give the husband a claim against one who injured his wife by negligence.[5] In the negligence cases also the damages consisted of the loss or impairment of the husband's right of consortium, both past and future.[6] This included but was by no means limited to the value of the wife's services.[7] As has already been shown,[8] the idea that a husband has a legal right to his wife's services[9] has been replaced by our contemporary principle that the rights and obligations of marriage are mutual and that they include the interests of each spouse in the support, society, companionship, affection and sexual relationships of the other spouse.[10] It is now apparent that the essence of the husband's claim is that these interests have been invaded by the defendant's tortious conduct.

At one time a substantial minority of jurisdictions refused to recognize the husband's claim for negligent impairment of his consortium caused by the act of a third person.[11] Today, however, all but a handful of jurisdictions allow the husband to recover.[12] The rationale of those courts refusing relief seems to be that the injured spouse may himself

---

§ 11.3

1. Guy v. Livesey, Cro.Jac. 501, 79 Eng.Rep. 428 (1619); III Blackstone, Commentaries on the Laws of England, 140 (Cooley 3d ed. 1884).

2. E.g., Marri v. Stamford St. Ry. Co., 84 Conn. 9, 78 A. 582 (1911).

3. See note 1, supra. See also Lippman, The Breakdown of Consortium, 30 Colum.L.Rev. 651 (1930), and Holbrook, The Change in the Meaning of Consortium, 22 Mich.L.Rev. 1 (1923).

4. T. Reeve, The Law of Baron and Femme 63 (1816).

5. 1 W. Schouler, Marriage, Divorce, Separation and Domestic Relations § 677 (6th ed. 1921), citing many early cases. For general accounts of the action for loss of consortium, see W. Prosser & W. Keeton, Torts § 124 (5th ed. 1984); 2 F. Harper, F. James & O. Gray, The Law of Torts § 8.9 (1986); Foster, Relational Interests of the Family, 1962 U.Ill.L.F. 493; Note 61 Colum.L.Rev. 1341 (1961).

6. Hewitt v. Pennsylvania R. Co., 228 Pa. 397, 77 A. 623 (1910). Other earlier cases are collected in Annots., 21 A.L.R. 1517 (1922) and 133 A.L.R. 1156 (1941).

7. Guevin v. Manchester St. Ry., 78 N.H. 289, 99 A. 298 (1916).

8. See section 11.1, supra.

9. Some contemporary cases continue to emphasize the husband's right to his wife's services, however. Hopson v. St. Mary's Hospital, 176 Conn. 485, 408 A.2d 260 (1979).

10. Nicholson v. Hugh Chatham Mem. Hospital, 300 N.C. 295, 266 S.E.2d 818 (1980); Restatement (Second) of Torts § 693, comment f (1977).

11. The states of California, Connecticut, Kansas, Massachusetts, North Carolina, Rhode Island, Utah, Virginia and Washington refused to permit recovery for loss of consortium when the first edition of this work was published.

12. American Export Lines, Inc. v. Alvez, 446 U.S. 274, 284–285 n. 11, 100 S.Ct. 1673, 1679 n. 11, 64 L.Ed.2d 284 (1980) cites authority from forty-two jurisdictions which recognize the cause of action by the wife or by both spouses, which means of course that the same courts would recognize the husband's right to recover as well. In addition to the authorities there cited three other

recover, as an element of his damages, compensation for being deprived of the ability to perform the functions of marriage.[13] This view ignores the effect on the uninjured spouse and on the marriage relationship brought about by the defendant's negligence. In cases of permanent injury, which is generally the only kind of injury justifying an award for impairment of consortium, a happy marriage may be transformed into a source of serious psychological suffering for the uninjured spouse as she attempts to cope with the day to day consequences of the defendant's tort.[14] It does seem that a humane legal system should take account of such suffering in the only way it can, by awarding damages.

Suit by the Wife

At common law the wife had no cause of action for loss of consortium when her husband was either intentionally or negligently injured. The reason for this was not clear, the view of some authorities being that she had no such proprietary interest in her husband as would support the claim,[15] of others that the essence of the husband's claim was his right to services, a right which the wife did not have,[16] of still others that the wife could not sue in her own name and therefore could not recover for loss of consortium.[17] Until 1950, notwithstanding the Married Women's Property Acts, it was universally true in the United States that the wife could not bring the action.[18]

The enactment of the Married Women's Property Acts giving the wife the capacity to sue and be sued eliminated most of the common law rationalizations for denying her the right to sue for loss of consortium. The courts then raised other objections to her claim, such as that her injury was indirect rather than direct; that double recovery would result if she could sue; that the damages would be too remote and would be incapable of evaluation with accuracy; that the claim was really one for services and she was not entitled to services from her husband; and that the Married Women's Property Acts merely removed her disabilities and did not create new causes of action unknown to the common law.[19] The universality of the rule did not protect it from strong criticism on the part of the commentators.[20]

In 1950 the United States Court of Appeals for the District of Columbia recognized what had been obvious to nearly all the commentators by holding, in Hitaffer v. Argonne Co.,[21] that a wife could recover for loss of consorti-

states now permit suits for impairment of consortium: Nicholson v. Hugh Chatham Mem. Hospital, 300 N.C. 295, 266 S.E.2d 818 (1980); Hughey v. Ausborn, 249 S.C. 470, 154 S.E.2d 839 (1967); Lundgren v. Whitney's, Inc., 94 Wash.2d 91, 614 P.2d 1272 (1980).

Suits for loss of consortium are still not permitted by Kan.Stat.Ann. 23–205 (1981) and Albertson v. Travis, 2 Kan.App.2d 153, 576 P.2d 1090 (1978); Mouton v. Armco, Inc., 417 So.2d 889 (La.App.1982), writ denied 425 So.2d 231 (La.App.1982); Tjas v. Proctor, 591 P.2d 438 (Utah 1979); Va.Code 1986, § 55–36. New Mexico may not permit the suit. Roseberry v. Starkovich, 73 N.M. 211, 387 P.2d 321 (1963).

13. E.g., Tjas v. Proctor, 591 P.2d 438 (Utah 1979).

14. This was the case in Rodriguez v. Bethlehem Steel Corp., 12 Cal.3d 382, 115 Cal.Rptr. 765, 525 P.2d 669 (1974).

For an argument that no actions for loss of consortium should be recognized by the law, whether brought by husband or wife or parent or child, see Note, Negligent Injury to Family Relationships: A Reevaluation of the Logic of Liability, 77 Nw.U.L.Rev. 794 (1983).

15. Best v. Samuel Fox & Co., [1952] A.C. 716, 732.

16. Lynch v. Knight, 9 H.L.Cas. 577, 11 Eng.Rep. 854, 863 (1861).

17. Feneff v. New York Central & Hudson River R.R. Co., 203 Mass. 278, 89 N.E. 436 (1909).

18. Cases are collected in Annot., 23 A.L.R.2d 1378 (1952).

19. Cases on all points are cited in Annot., 23 A.L.R.2d 1378, 1391 (1952). See also Kronenbitter v. Washburn Wire Co., 4 N.Y.2d 524, 176 N.Y.S.2d 354, 151 N.E.2d 898 (1958), and Pound, Individual Interests in the Domestic Relations, 14 Mich.L.Rev. 177, 193–195 (1916).

20. W. Prosser & W. Keeton, Torts 931 (5th ed. 1984), citing many articles; Igneri v. Cie. de Transports Oceaniques, 323 F.2d 257 (2d Cir.1963), cert. denied 376 U.S. 949, 84 S.Ct. 965, 11 L.Ed.2d 969 (1964), citing many articles; 2 F. Harper, F. James & O. Gray, Torts § 8.9 (2d ed 1986). In addition to Dean Pound's article, supra, note 19, the only article favorable to the rule denying relief to the wife is Jaffe, Damages For Personal Injury: The Impact of Insurance, 18 Law & Contemp.Prob. 219, 228–231 (1953).

21. 183 F.2d 811 (D.C.Cir.1950), cert. denied 340 U.S. 852, 71 S.Ct. 80, 95 L.Ed. 624 (1950), 19 Geo.Wash.L.Rev. 463 (1951), 35 Minn.L.Rev. 318 (1951), 26 N.Y.U.L.Rev. 205 (1951). The Hitaffer case also held that the wife's claim for impairment of consortium was not barred by the fact that the husband's accident was covered by

um from a defendant who negligently injured her husband. After full consideration, the court found wanting all of the opposing policy arguments. It condemned the inequity of allowing the husband to sue while denying the same right to the wife and rejected any distinction between the loss of consortium caused by intentional conduct and the loss of consortium caused by negligence.[22] In the years since 1950 Hitaffer has been followed by the great majority of American jurisdictions [23] including, by virtue of a decision of the United States Supreme Court,[24] the federal admiralty jurisdiction. In some of the states, where an Equal Rights Amendment is part of the state constitution, it has been held that that Amendment would be violated if a husband but not a wife were permitted to recover

for loss of consortium.[25] Even without such an Amendment a persuasive case may be made for the position that the Equal Protection Clause of the Fourteenth Amendment to the United States Constitution would be violated if the husband's claim were recognized but the wife's were not.[26] Thus the current law has come to be that both husband and wife may recover when his or her spouse has been injured by the negligence of a third person and the injury produces an impairment or loss of the rights of consortium. In order to avoid the risk of double recovery when one spouse sues for the injury to himself and the other sues for loss of consortium, some states have come to require that the two claims be joined in a single action.[27]

workers' compensation, but on this point the case has been overruled. Smither & Co. v. Coles, 242 F.2d 220 (D.C.Cir.1957), cert. denied 354 U.S. 914, 77 S.Ct. 1299, 1 L.Ed.2d 1429 (1957). Cases in other jurisdictions reach differing results on the question whether workers' compensation coverage bars a spouse's claim for loss of consortium, the difference being attributed to differences in the language of the workers' compensation statutes. Holding the consortium claim barred: England v. Dana Corp., 428 F.2d 385 (7th Cir.1970) (Indiana law); Lunow v. Fairchance Lumber Co., 389 F.2d 212 (10th Cir.1968), cert. denied 392 U.S. 908, 88 S.Ct. 2062, 20 L.Ed.2d 1366 (1968) (Oklahoma law); Underwood v. United States, 207 F.2d 862 (10th Cir.1953) (federal employees' compensation act); Newman v. Gibraltar Coal Corp., 350 F.Supp. 71 (W.D.Ky.1972), affirmed p.c. 471 F.2d 653 (6th Cir.1972); Wright v. Action Vending Co., 544 P.2d 82 (Alaska 1975). Holding the consortium claim not barred: Ferriter v. Daniel O'Connell's Sons, Inc., 381 Mass. 507, 413 N.E.2d 690 (1980); Labonte v. National Gypsum Co., 110 N.H. 314, 269 A.2d 634 (1970).

22. Not only has the wife at common law been given a right of action for alienation of affections and criminal conversation, see sections 12.2 and 12.3, Practitioner's Edition, but she is usually held entitled to recover from sellers of liquor or drugs who sell to her husband with knowledge that he is an alcoholic or drug addict, thereby causing a loss or impairment of her rights of consortium. See, e.g., Pratt v. Daly, 55 Ariz. 535, 104 P.2d 147 (1940), 25 Minn.L.Rev. 113 (1940) (sale of liquor); Flandermeyer v. Cooper, 85 Ohio St. 327, 98 N.E. 102 (1912) (sale of drugs); Swanson v. Ball, 67 S.D. 161, 290 N.W. 482 (1940), 39 Mich.L.Rev. 830 (1941). See also Annot., 130 A.L.R. 352 (1941).

23. American Export Lines, Inc. v. Alvez, 446 U.S. 274, 284–285, 100 S.Ct. 1673, 1679, 64 L.Ed.2d 284 (1980) lists forty-two jurisdictions and the District of Columbia allowing recovery by the wife alone or when joined with her husband. Earlier cases are collected in Annot., 36 A.L.R.3d 900 (1970). Some representative, thoroughly reasoned cases on the point include Schreiner v. Fruit,

519 P.2d 462 (Alaska 1974); Rodriguez v. Bethlehem Steel Corp., 12 Cal.3d 382, 115 Cal.Rptr. 765, 525 P.2d 669 (1974); Gates v. Foley, 247 So.2d 40 (Fla.1971); Troue v. Marker, 253 Ind. 284, 252 N.E.2d 800 (1969); Diaz v. Eli Lilly and Co., 364 Mass. 153, 302 N.E.2d 555 (1973); Millington v. Southeastern Elevator Co., Inc., 22 N.Y.2d 498, 293 N.Y.S.2d 305, 239 N.E.2d 897 (1968); Nicholson v. Hugh Chatham Memorial Hospital, Inc., 300 N.C. 295, 266 S.E.2d 818 (1980); Clouston v. Remlinger Oldsmobile Cadillac, Inc., 22 Ohio St.2d 65, 258 N.E.2d 230 (1970); Whittlesey v. Miller, 572 S.W.2d 665 (Tex.1978). See also Restatement (Second) of Torts § 693 (1977).

In those few states in which the husband may not sue for loss of consortium, presumably the wife may not either. See note 12, supra.

24. American Export Lines, Inc. v. Alvez, 446 U.S. 274, 100 S.Ct. 1673, 64 L.Ed.2d 284 (1980).

25. Hopkins v. Blanco, 457 Pa. 90, 320 A.2d 139 (1974); Whittlesey v. Miller, 572 S.W.2d 665 (Tex.1978), approving Miller v. Whittlesey, 562 S.W.2d 904 (Tex.Civ.App. 1978), judgment affirmed 572 S.W.2d 665 (1978); Lundgren v. Whitney's, Inc., 94 Wash.2d 91, 614 P.2d 1272 (1980).

26. Duncan v. General Motors Corp., 499 F.2d 835 (10th Cir.1974); Karczewski v. The Baltimore & Ohio R.R. Co., 274 F.Supp. 169 (N.D.Ill.1967); Hopson v. St. Mary's Hospital, 176 Conn. 485, 408 A.2d 260 (1979) (semble); Hastings v. James River Aerie No. 2337, etc., 246 N.W.2d 747 (N.D.1976); Lundgren v. Whitney's, Inc., 94 Wash.2d 91, 614 P.2d 1272 (1980).

27. E.g., Swartz v. United States Steel Corp., 293 Ala. 439, 304 So.2d 881 (1974); Schreiner v. Fruit, 519 P.2d 462 (Alaska 1974); Rodriguez v. Bethlehem Steel Corp., 12 Cal.3d 382, 115 Cal.Rptr. 765, 525 P.2d 669 (1974); Brown v. Metzger, 104 Ill.2d 30, 83 Ill.Dec. 344, 470 N.E.2d 302 (1984); Deems v. Western Maryland Ry. Co., 247 Md. 95, 231 A.2d 514 (1967); Thill v. Modern Erecting Co., 284 Minn. 508, 170 N.W.2d 865 (1969); Millington v. Southeastern Elevator Co., 22 N.Y.2d 498, 293 N.Y.S.2d 305, 239 N.E.2d 897 (1968); Nicholson v. Hugh

Nature and Limits of the Action

Since the remedy which the law provides for interference with consortium rests upon the relationship which exists when the parties have made the formal commitment to each other called marriage, most courts have held that there can be no recovery where the injury occurred before the parties were married.[28] For the same reason it has been held, with a few exceptions, that there can be no recovery by a man or woman who have been living together without being married [29] in a Marvin-type relationship.[30] These results seem correct unless the law is to abandon its traditional emphasis upon marriage as the basis for family life.[31] In the converse case, where the parties were married at the time of the injury, but were divorced before the suit was brought, the suit may be barred by local statutes which provide that upon dissolution of marriage the parties lose all rights acquired by the marriage except those specifically preserved in the divorce decree.[32]

The usual consortium case involves physical harm caused to a spouse by the negligence of a third person. A few cases have granted relief for impairment of consortium where the spouse's injury was caused by other actionable conduct, such as products liability,[33] or a physician's breach of warranty that proposed surgery would produce no complications.[34] Other cases have gone a step further to hold that actions for loss of consortium may be brought where the injury to the spouse is not physical but consists in the infliction of emotional distress [35] or defamation.[36] On the other hand some courts have been oddly reluctant to give damages for impairment of consortium where the injury to the spouse was caused by conduct violating a statute, such as a wrongful death act,[37] or the Civil

Chatham Memorial Hospital, Inc., 300 N.C. 295, 266 S.E.2d 818 (1980); Moran v. Quality Aluminum Casting Co., 34 Wis.2d 542, 150 N.W.2d 137 (1967). Contra, holding joinder is not required: Kotsiris v. Ling, 451 S.W.2d 411 (Ky.1970).

28. Navarre v. Wisconsin Barge Line, Inc., 502 F.Supp. 360 (S.D.Ill.1980); Chiesa v. Rowe, 486 F.Supp. 236 (W.D.Mich.1980); Wagner v. International Harvester Co., 455 F.Supp. 168 (D.Minn.1978); Sostock v. Reiss, 92 Ill.App.3d 200, 47 Ill.Dec. 781, 415 N.E.2d 1094 (1980); Sawyer v. Bailey, 413 A.2d 165 (Me.1980); Miller v. Davis, 107 Misc.2d 343, 433 N.Y.S.2d 974 (1980). Haas v. Lewis, 8 Ohio App.3d 136, 456 N.E.2d 512 (1982). Contra: Sutherland v. Auch Inter-Borough Transit Co., 366 F.Supp. 127 (E.D.Pa.1973) (Pennsylvania law). See Annot., 5 A.L.R.4th 300 (1981).

29. Curry v. Caterpillar Tractor Co., 577 F.Supp. 991 (E.D.Pa.1984); Weaver v. G.D. Searle & Co., 558 F.Supp. 720 (N.D.Ala.1983) (Alabama law); Ledger v. Tippitt, 164 Cal.App.3d 625, 210 Cal.Rptr. 814 (1985); Tremblay v. Carter, 390 So.2d 816 (Fla.App.1980), 11 Stetson L.Rev. 161 (1981); Laws v. Griep, 332 N.W.2d 339 (Iowa 1983). Bulloch v. United States, 487 F.Supp. 1078 (D.N.J.1980) purported to rely on New Jersey law to hold that persons living together but not married could recover for loss of consortium. This view of New Jersey law was rejected by Leonardis v. Morton Chemical Co., 184 N.J.Super. 10, 445 A.2d 45 (1982). A case squarely holding that an action for loss of consortium is available to unmarried persons living in "stable and significant" relationships is Butcher v. Superior Court of Orange County, 139 Cal.App.3d 58, 188 Cal.Rptr. 503 (1983), which contains an extensive explication of the question.

30. This reference is to Marvin v. Marvin, 18 Cal.3d 660, 134 Cal.Rptr. 815, 557 P.2d 106 (1976), discussed supra, in § 1.2.

31. See Hafen, The Constitutional Status of Marriage, Kinship, and Sexual Privacy-Balancing the Individual and Social Interests, 81 Mich.L.Rev. 463, 538 (1983).

32. Michael v. Harrison County Rural Elec. Co-op., 292 N.W.2d 417 (Iowa 1980).

33. Timms v. Verson Allsteel Press Co., 520 F.Supp. 1147 (N.D.Ga.1981).

34. Scarzella v. Saxon, 436 A.2d 358 (D.C.App.1981). See also Togstad v. Vesely, Otto, Miller & Keefe, 291 N.W.2d 686 (Minn.1980), in which the loss of consortium was caused by alleged legal malpractice occurring when an attorney gave certain advice in connection with a medical malpractice claim.

35. Molien v. Kaiser Foundation Hospitals, 27 Cal.3d 916, 167 Cal.Rptr. 831, 616 P.2d 813 (1980). In this case the defendant hospital employees were alleged to have negligently informed the wife that she had syphilis when she did not, causing the husband emotional distress and leading to the breakup of the marriage. The court held that this stated a cause of action for loss of consortium. See Annot., Necessity of Physical Injury to Support Cause of Action for Loss of Consortium, 16 A.L.R.4th 537 (1982).

36. Agis v. Howard Johnson Co., 371 Mass. 140, 355 N.E.2d 315 (1976). But see FNB Financial Co. v. Superior Court for Los Angeles County, 80 Cal.App.3d 927, 144 Cal.Rptr. 496 (1978).

37. Liff v. Schildkrout, 49 N.Y.2d 622, 427 N.Y.S.2d 746, 404 N.E.2d 1288 (1980), reargument denied 49 N.Y.2d 1048, 429 N.Y.S.2d 1027, 407 N.E.2d 483 (1980). The court held that the spouse could recover for loss of consortium occurring before death, but that all causes of action arising out of the death had to be maintained in accordance with statutory authority. But Sea-Land Services, Inc. v. Gaudet, 414 U.S. 573, 94 S.Ct. 806, 39 L.Ed. 2d 9 (1974), rehearing denied 415 U.S. 986, 94 S.Ct. 1582,

Rights Act [38] or other special statutory liability. [39]

The nature of the consortium claim and its relationship to the claim of the injured spouse for his own injury raise hard questions on which the courts have not agreed. One such question is whether the contributory negligence of the injured spouse provides a defense to the consortium claim. The courts, notwithstanding strong and nearly unanimous criticism by the commentators, [40] have generally taken the position that contributory negligence is a defense to the consortium claim. [41] The reason seems no more substantial than some inarticulate notion of what is fair, [42] or a characterization of the consortium claim as "derivative" which is merely another way of

describing the result. [43] Of course the consent or contributory negligence of the spouse suing for loss of consortium will also bar his claim. [44] And in the unusual case where the injury occurs through the negligent conduct of the injured spouse himself it has been held that the other spouse may not recover from the injured spouse for loss of consortium. [45]

Similar questions arise in those states which do not require the injured spouse's claim to be joined with the consortium claim. For example, if the injured spouse sues and is unable to prove that the defendant was negligent, and the other spouse then sues for loss of consortium, the defendant will wish to assert the defense of res judicata in one of its forms. The majority of cases [46] and the Re-

---

39 L.Ed.2d 883 (1974) held that a spouse could recover for loss of consortium when her spouse was killed in a maritime accident. And Elliott v. Willis, 92 Ill.2d 530, 65 Ill.Dec. 852, 442 N.E.2d 163 (1982), on remand 113 Ill. App.3d 848, 69 Ill.Dec. 627, 447 N.E.2d 1062 (1983) held that damages for loss of consortium could be awarded in a suit for wrongful death.

38. Walters v. Oak Lawn, 548 F.Supp. 417 (N.D.Ill. 1982).

39. Martin v. Kiendl Construction Co., 108 Ill.App.3d 468, 63 Ill.Dec. 824, 438 N.E.2d 1187 (1982). Beltia v. Sidney Torres Marine Transport, Inc., 701 F.2d 491 (5th Cir.1983) (Jones Act).

40. W. Prosser & W. Keeton, Torts 938 (5th ed. 1984), citing other authors; 2 F. Harper, F. James & O. Gray, Torts 555 (2d ed. 1986).

41. Hall v. United States, 266 F.Supp. 671 (D.Mont. 1967); Pioneer Construction Co. v. Bergeron, 170 Colo. 474, 462 P.2d 589 (1969); Dixon v. Wright, 214 So.2d 787 (Fla.App.1968); Deskins v. Woodward, 483 P.2d 1134 (Okl.1971); Ross v. Cuthbert, 239 Or. 429, 397 P.2d 529 (1964). Where comparative negligence exists the consortium claim is reduced in proportion to the negligence of the injured spouse. McGuire v. Sifers, 235 Kan. 368, 681 P.2d 1025 (1984); Maidman v. Stagg, 82 A.D.2d 299, 441 N.Y.S.2d 711 (2d Dep't 1981). See also Annot., 25 A.L.R.4th 118 (1983); Restatement (Second) of Torts § 693, comment e (1977). Contra, refusing to impute the negligence of the injured spouse to the plaintiff, Feltch v. General Rental Co., 383 Mass. 603, 421 N.E.2d 67 (1981).

For a citation of cases dealing with the similar question whether a child's contributory negligence is a defense to an action for services or consortium by his parent, see section 11.4, infra, at note 19.

See also Note, Loss of Consortium, Contributory Negligence and Contribution: An Old Problem and a New Solution, 24 B.C.L.Rev. 403 (1983).

42. Ross v. Cuthbert, 239 Or. 429, 397 P.2d 529 (1964).

43. Maidman v. Stagg, 82 A.D.2d 299, 441 N.Y.S.2d 711 (2d Dep't 1981). Holding the claim not derivative,

Feltch v. General Rental Co., 383 Mass. 603, 421 N.E.2d 67 (1981).

Another basis for applying contributory negligence in this situation is that the consortium plaintiff is really an assignee of part of the injured spouse's claim and as such takes the claim subject to the defense of contributory negligence which the defendant has against the assignor. White v. Lunder, 66 Wis.2d 563, 225 N.W.2d 442 (1975). The fictional and far-fetched nature of this theory is exposed in W. Prosser & W. Keeton, Torts 937–939 (5th ed. 1984).

44. Restatement (Second) of Torts §§ 694, 694A (1977).

45. Plain v. Plain, 307 Minn. 399, 240 N.W.2d 330 (1976).

46. Roy v. Jasper Corp., 666 F.2d 714 (1st Cir.1981) (holding that the judgment in the first suit conclusively established that the defendant did not cause the injury, under doctrines of collateral estoppel or "issue preclusion"); Jones v. Beasley, 476 F.Supp. 116 (M.D.Ga.1979); Stickney v. E.R. Squibb & Sons, Inc., 377 F.Supp. 785 (M.D.Fla.1974); Hopson v. St. Mary's Hospital, 176 Conn. 485, 408 A.2d 260 (1979); Douberly v. Okefenokee Rural Electric Membership Corp., 146 Ga.App. 568, 246 S.E.2d 708 (1978); Board of Com'rs of Cass County v. Nevitt, 448 N.E.2d 333 (Ind.App.1983); Laws v. Fisher, 513 P.2d 876 (Okl.1973), 27 Okla.L.Rev. 267 (1974). Contra, holding no res judicata effect: Russ Transport, Inc. v. Jones, 104 Ga. App. 612, 122 S.E.2d 282 (1961); Reid v. Spadone Machine Co., 119 N.H. 198, 400 A.2d 54 (1979); W. Prosser & W. Keeton, Torts 937, 938 (5th ed. 1984), citing cases. Crouch v. West, 29 Colo.App. 72, 477 P.2d 805 (1970), held that the claim for consortium was not affected by the injured spouse's settlement of his claim with the defendant, but Brown v. Metzger, 118 Ill.App.3d 855, 74 Ill.Dec. 405, 455 N.E.2d 834 (1983), judgment affirmed 104 Ill.2d 30, 83 Ill.Dec. 344, 470 N.E.2d 1984), held that while the consortium claim is derivative, it is not barred by a release given by the injured spouse. See also Annot., 29 A.L.R.4th 1200 (1984).

The federal cases seem to disagree as to whether this issue is procedural or substantive for Erie Railroad pur-

statement (Second) of Judgments [47] take the position that the consortium claim is precluded unless the first suit was decided on grounds not available to the other spouse. This result has also been heavily criticized, since there is no "privity" in the usual meaning of that term between husband and wife and since the two lawsuits are brought to vindicate different interests.[48] The Restatement's treatment of the question is rested on the argument that the two claims are similar in that they compensate for losses to the family, and that the application of res judicata prevents the family from being given two chances to recover for the same losses.[49] Neither of these arguments is valid, since the losses are not the same and the recoveries do not duplicate each other if properly defined. In the converse situation, where the injured spouse sues first and wins, the cases also disagree as to whether the spouse suing for loss of consortium may rely on the earlier judgment as establishing the defendant's liability for the injuries.[50] A holding that the first judgment precludes reexamination of the issues there litigated may result in unfairness to the defendant in the two suits under some circumstances, as where the plaintiff in the consortium suit has intentionally waited to sue in order to take advantage of the outcome of the injured spouse's suit.[51] All of these problems may be reduced by requiring the joinder of the main claim and the consortium claim in the same action.[52]

The unusual nature of the consortium action has also led to uncertainty concerning the applicable statute of limitations. Thus it has been held that the consortium claim was barred by the running of the statute of limitations on the injured spouse's claim on the ground that the consortium claim is precipitated by and dependent upon the injured spouse's claim.[53] On the other hand some cases hold that the consortium claim is not one for malpractice where the injured spouse was harmed by the alleged negligence of a physician, so that the general tort statute of limitations applies rather than the malpractice statute.[54] Still other cases hold that the consortium claim accrues and the statute of limitations begins to run only when the consortium plaintiff rather than the injured spouse discovers the injury.[55] Although some of these differences are attributable to differences in the language of the statutes and to legislative policies either favorable or unfavorable to medical malpractice suits, the courts' characterization of consortium suits as derivative or independent plays an important part in the results. The uncertainty and ex-

---

poses. Holding it substantive and therefore to be governed by the law of the state in which the court was sitting: Roy v. Jasper Corp., 666 F.2d 714 (1st Cir.1981); Stickney v. E.R. Squibb & Sons, Inc., 377 F.Supp. 785 (M.D.Fla.1974). Holding it procedural: Jones v. Beasley, 476 F.Supp. 116 (M.D.Ga.1979). The question would clearly seem to be substantive for this purpose.

47. Restatement (Second) of Judgments § 48(2) (1982).

48. See note 40, supra.

49. Restatement (Second) of Judgments § 48, comment c (1982).

50. Holding that the consortium plaintiff may take advantage of "offensive" res judicata: Snodgrass v. General Telephone Co. of Northwest, Inc., 275 Or. 79, 549 P.2d 1120 (1976). Holding that res judicata does not apply in this situation: W. Prosser & W. Keeton, Torts 937, 938 (5th ed. 1984), citing cases.

Collins v. Seaboard Coastline R.R. Co., 681 F.2d 1333 (11th Cir.1982) held that whether the defendant should be permitted to relitigate liability in the second case is a matter for the trial court's discretion, to be decided on the basis of what is fair under the circumstances including a determination of whether the consortium plaintiff had been following a "wait and see" course of action.

Restatement (Second) of Judgments § 48, Reporter's Notes to comment c (1982) takes the position that the judgment for the plaintiff in the first suit is preclusive of the issues determined for purposes of the consortium suit.

51. Collins v. Seaboard Coastline R.R. Co., 681 F.2d 1333 (11th Cir.1982).

52. Authorities requiring this are cited, supra, in note 27.

A settlement and release by the injured spouse does not bar the other spouse from bringing his consortium claim. Oldani v. Lieberman, 144 Mich.App. 642, 375 N.W.2d 778 (1985); Haspil v. Church of St. Cyril, 128 Misc.2d 968, 491 N.Y.S.2d 914 (1985).

53. Kolar v. Chicago, 12 Ill.App.3d 887, 299 N.E.2d 479 (1973), citing cases both ways on the question.

54. Holzwart v. Wehman, 1 Ohio St.3d 26, 437 N.E.2d 589 (1982); Amer v. Akron City Hospital, 47 Ohio St.2d 85, 351 N.E.2d 479 (1976).

55. Goodman v. Mead Johnson & Co., 534 F.2d 566 (3d Cir.1976), cert. denied 429 U.S. 1038, 97 S.Ct. 732, 50 L.Ed.2d 748 (1977); Baughman v. Bolinger, 485 F.Supp. 1000 (S.D.Ohio 1980).

penditure of lawyers' and judges' time could easily be avoided by the enactment of statutes of limitations specifically applicable to suits for impairment of consortium.

Suits for loss of consortium have generally survived other tort law doctrines restricting recovery. It has been held that they are not abolished by the no-fault statutes limiting recovery for automobile negligence now in force in some states.[56] Where the spouse of an automobile passenger sues for loss of consortium he has been held not subject to the guest statute.[57] Where liability insurance is involved, coverage of consortium claims turns on the language of the policy.[58]

Damages

The assessment of damages in consortium cases has been one of the obstacles to the recognition of the claim, due to the tendency of some courts to find that the consortium claim necessarily duplicates some of the elements of damage properly recoverable by the injured spouse. Today that obstacle has been removed as a result of more careful definition of the nature of the wrong which the suit for loss of consortium seeks to redress,[59] and by the requirement in many states that the action for loss of consortium be joined with the suit by the injured spouse.[60] As has been

indicated earlier,[61] the term "consortium" has come to be defined as comprising all aspects of the marital relationship. It includes the interests of each spouse in the society, companionship, affection, assistance and sexual relations of the other spouse.[62] Of course the plaintiff has the burden of proving the damages for loss of consortium,[63] and the amount of the damages is a matter for the sound discretion of the trier of fact.[64] And the fact that the injured spouse is awarded damages for his injury does not necessarily mean that the spouse seeking redress for consortium must also be awarded damages since the trier of fact may in some circumstances find that one spouse proved damages and the other failed to do so.[65]

The elements of harm for which damages may be recovered in an action for impairment of consortium are the logical consequences of the contemporary definition of consortium. They normally occur when the injuries to the other spouse are permanent, or at least serious.[66] These elements include the mental distress caused when the consortium claimant sees the suffering of the injured spouse;[67] the deprivation of social and family activities which the injury imposes on the consortium claimant;[68] the adverse impact caused to the marriage relationship by the injury, as where

---

56. Cotton v. Minter, 469 F.Supp. 199 (E.D.Mich.1979) (Michigan law); Rusinek v. Schultz, Snyder & Steele Lumber Co., 411 Mich. 502, 309 N.W.2d 163 (1981); Barker v. Scott, 81 Misc.2d 414, 365 N.Y.S.2d 756 (1975).

57. Naber v. Thompson, 274 Or. 309, 546 P.2d 467 (1976).

58. Bean v. Miller, 122 N.H. 681, 448 A.2d 424 (1982) (loss of consortium is not "bodily injury" under the policy); American Asbestos Textile Corp. v. American Mutual Liability Ins. Co., 114 N.H. 806, 330 A.2d 451 (1974) (loss of consortium is within comprehensive coverage of the policy). Thompson v. Grange Insurance Ass'n, 34 Wash.App. 151, 660 P.2d 307 (1983) (loss of consortium is not "bodily injury" for purposes of the policy limits); Bilodeau v. Lumbermens Mutual Cas. Co., 392 Mass. 537, 467 N.E.2d 137 (1984) (consortium claimant is a separate "person" under policy limits).

59. Diaz v. Eli Lilly and Co., 364 Mass. 153, 302 N.E.2d 555 (1973).

60. See the cases cited in note 27.

61. See section 11.1, supra.

62. Ekalo v. Constructive Service Corp. of America, 46 N.J. 82, 215 A.2d 1 (1965); Millington v. Southeastern

Elevator Co., 22 N.Y.2d 498, 293 N.Y.S.2d 305, 239 N.E.2d 897 (1968); Moran v. Quality Aluminum Casting Co., 34 Wis.2d 542, 150 N.W.2d 137 (1967).

63. Streight v. Conroy, 279 Or. 289, 566 P.2d 1198 (1977).

64. Annot., Measure and Elements of Damages In Wife's Action For Loss of Consortium, 74 A.L.R.3d 805, 811 (1976).

65. Waterfield v. Quimby, 277 Ark. 472, 644 S.W.2d 241 (1982).

66. E.g., Rodriguez v. Bethlehem Steel Corp., 12 Cal. 3d 382, 115 Cal.Rptr. 765, 525 P.2d 669 (1974); General Electric Co. v. Bush, 88 Nev. 360, 498 P.2d 366 (1972).

67. Agis v. Howard Johnson Co., 371 Mass. 140, 355 N.E.2d 315 (1976); Millington v. Southeastern Elevator Co., 22 N.Y.2d 498, 293 N.Y.S.2d 305, 239 N.E.2d 897 (1968).

68. Troue v. Marker, 253 Ind. 284, 252 N.E.2d 800 (1969); Lundgren v. Whitney's, Inc., 94 Wash.2d 91, 614 P.2d 1272 (1980).

it leads to separation,[69] or divorce;[70] the impairment of the sexual relations of the spouses, as where the injury causes impotence;[71] the inability to have children, where the injury has that consequence;[72] and in general, as one well known case has put it, where the injury turns a happily married spouse into a life-long nurse and deprives him or her of the opportunity of rearing children.[73]

Certain elements of damage are not recoverable in the suit for loss of consortium on the ground that they are more properly recovered by the injured spouse and that recovery in the consortium action would result in a double recovery. For this reason the cases generally hold that a diminution in the level of support caused by the injury is not recoverable in the consortium action, since this element of damage is compensated in the injured spouse's claim for lost wages.[74] The same is true of the wife's claim for nursing care which she provides for an injured husband, this being recoverable by the husband as a part of his medical expenses.[75] Presumably the defen-

dant may also mitigate consortium damages by showing that there was little affection between the spouses, so that the injury could have had little effect upon their relationship.[76]

The cases are quite evenly divided on the question whether punitive damages may be awarded in a suit for impairment of consortium.[77] In the usual case these damages are awarded on proof that the tort was committed wilfully, wantonly or maliciously, all these vague terms meaning under outrageous circumstances or with an extreme disregard for the interests of other people.[78] The purpose of punitive damages is said to be, as the name indicates, to punish and so to discourage such highly antisocial conduct [79] but there is also at least a suspicion that they are a means of providing a higher level of compensation for tort victims than is achieved by the ordinary rules of compensatory damages.[80] The reasoning of the cases denying punitive damages to the consortium claimant is that the injured spouse may recover them, and so there is

69. Maxworthy v. Horn Electric Service, Inc., 452 F.2d 1141 (4th Cir.1972).

70. Togstad v. Vesely, Otto, Miller & Keefe, 291 N.W.2d 686 (Minn.1980). In Lankford v. Trust Company Bank, 141 Ga.App. 639, 234 S.E.2d 179 (1977) the court rejected, for lack of proof of proximate cause, an ingenious husband's claim that his marriage was destroyed and consortium thereby impaired when a bank and a hotel negligently billed him on a charge card for a room he did not reserve, his wife saw the bill and refused to believe him innocent.

71. Rodriguez v. Bethlehem Steel Corp., 12 Cal.3d 382, 115 Cal.Rptr. 765, 525 P.2d 669 (1974); Deems v. Western Maryland Ry. Co., 247 Md. 95, 231 A.2d 514 (1967); Togstad v. Vesely, Otto, Miller & Keefe, 291 N.W.2d 686 (Minn.1980).

72. General Electric Co. v. Bush, 88 Nev. 360, 498 P.2d 366 (1972).

73. Millington v. Southeastern Elevator Co., 22 N.Y.2d 498, 293 N.Y.S.2d 305, 239 N.E.2d 897 (1968). For other cases on damages, see Annot., Measure and Elements of Damages in Wife's Action for Loss of Consortium, 74 A.L.R.3d 805 (1976).

74. Troue v. Marker, 253 Ind. 284, 252 N.E.2d 800 (1969); Kotsiris v. Ling, 451 S.W.2d 411 (Ky.1970); Thill v. Modern Erecting Co., 284 Minn. 508, 170 N.W.2d 865 (1969); Tribble v. Gregory, 288 So.2d 13 (Miss.1974); Moran v. Quality Aluminum Casting Co., 34 Wis.2d 542, 150 N.W.2d 137 (1967).

75. Rodriguez v. Bethlehem Steel Corp., 12 Cal.3d 382, 115 Cal.Rptr. 765, 525 P.2d 669 (1974); Kotsiris v. Ling,

451 S.W.2d 411 (Ky.1970); Tribble v. Gregory, 288 So.2d 13 (Miss.1974). But Nichols v. Sonneman, 91 Idaho 199, 418 P.2d 562 (1966) allowed the wife to recover for her own lost wages during the time she cared for her husband.

76. A few cases are collected in Note, Mitigation of Damages for Loss of Consortium, 28 U.Pitt.L.Rev. 366 (1966). But a wife may have a claim for loss of consortium even though the husband lives only a few hours after a tortious injury. Minkley v. MacFarland, 371 Mass. 891, 356 N.E.2d 1391 (1976).

77. Allowing punitive damages on proof of the defendant's outrageous conduct: Butcher v. Robertshaw Controls Co., 550 F.Supp. 692 (D.Md.1981) (Maryland law); Sheats v. Bowen, 318 F.Supp. 640 (D.Del.1970) (Delaware law). Holding punitive damages may not be granted: People's Home Telephone Co. v. Cockrum, 182 Ala. 547, 62 So. 86 (1913); Hammond v. North American Asbestos Corp., 105 Ill.App.3d 1033, 61 Ill.Dec. 843, 435 N.E.2d 540 (1982), judgment affirmed 97 Ill.2d 195, 73 Ill.Dec. 350, 454 N.E.2d 210 (1983); Hughey v. Ausborn, 249 S.C. 470, 154 S.E.2d 839 (1967). These cases often purport to make the issue turn on whether the action for loss of consortium is derivative or direct, but of course this is just another way of describing the result rather than a reason for the result. Consortium suits can be characterized as either derivative or direct with equal plausibility.

78. K. Redden, Punitive Damages § 2.1 (1980).

79. Ibid., id. at §§ 2.2(D), 2.2(E).

80. Id. at §§ 2.2(B) and 2.2(C).

double recovery if they are awarded to both spouses.[81] If the true purpose of the award is punishment, this analysis is correct and the injured spouse alone should be allowed punitive damages. But if the purpose is additional compensation of some uncertain kind, then both spouses might be given punitive damages. The risk of double recovery seems substantial enough, however, to justify denying such damages in consortium cases.

Choice of Law

Since nearly all states now recognize the right of either husband or wife to recover for impairment of consortium, the choice of law question has been reduced in practical importance. There may still be some differences in the law of the various states, however, so that the question of whose law governs may still have some limited interest. Authority may be found to support most of the choice of law rules which have been advanced to govern tort cases, including the lex loci,[82] the law of the state having the most significant contacts with the tort [83] as suggested by the second Restatement [84], and the law of the forum in circumstances where neither state has vital policy interests in the application of substantive rules.[85] Since the conflicts in suits for loss of consortium usually concern such procedural matters as res judicata, defenses, double recovery and statutes of limitations, it would seem most sensible to apply the forum's law as being the law of the state most interested in such issues.

81. Hughey v. Ausborn, 249 S.C. 470, 154 S.E.2d 839 (1967).

82. Folk v. York-Shipley, Inc., 239 A.2d 236 (Del.1968). See other cases collected in Annot., 46 A.L.R.3d 880 (1972).

83. Berghammer v. Smith, 185 N.W.2d 226 (Iowa 1971); Casey v. Manson Construction and Engineering Co., 247 Or. 274, 428 P.2d 898 (1967).

84. Restatement (Second) of Conflict of Laws § 145 (1971).

85. Erwin v. Thomas, 264 Or. 454, 506 P.2d 494 (1973).

§ 11.4

1. Shiels v. Audette, 119 Conn. 75, 174 A. 323 (1934); Bioni v. Haselton, 99 Vt. 453, 134 A. 606 (1926); 1 J.

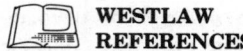 **WESTLAW REFERENCES**

Suit by the Husband

consortium /s husband spous! marry! marital marri! /s
    negligen! + 1 interfer! impair!

Suit by the Wife

hitaffer /s argonne /s wife

wife /s "fourteenth amendment" "equal right" /s
    consortium

Nature and Limits of the Action

consortium /s "product liability"

di(consortium /p unmarried co-habit! (live* living + 1
    together))

consortium /s wife /s wrongful! /2 death

Damages

consortium /s punitive /s wilful! wanton! malic!

---

§ 11.4 Negligent Interference With the Parent-Child Relationship

Suit by the Parent

Traditionally the father of an unemancipated child was entitled to the child's services in the home and to the child's earnings if he worked outside the home.[1] Upon emancipation the child became entitled to the value of his own services and could keep his own earnings.[2] The legal right to the child's services and earnings was most commonly recognized when the child was tortiously injured, in which event the father could recover from the tortfeasor the value of the child's services or earnings.[3] The father could also recover for any medical expenses he was required to pay as a result of the injury to the child, since he was responsible for those expenses as an incident of his duty to support the child.[4] Al-

Schouler, Marriage, Divorce, Separation and Domestic Relations 813–821 (6th ed. 1921).

2. See section 8.3, supra.

3. Smith v. Hewett, 235 N.C. 615, 70 S.E.2d 825 (1952); Norton v. Jason, Style 398, 82 Eng.Rep. 809 (1653); Jones v. Brown, 1 Esp. 217, 170 Eng.Rep. 334 (1794). See also Annots., 32 A.L.R.2d 1055 (1953) and 69 A.L.R.3d 553 (1976). But the parent may not recover if the child is an adult or is emancipated. Schmeck v. Shawnee, 231 Kan. 588, 647 P.2d 1263 (1982); Restatement (Second) of Torts § 703, comment e (1977).

4. Hernandez v. United States, 313 F.Supp. 349 (N.D. Tex.1969); Smith v. Richardson, 277 Ala. 389, 171 So.2d 96 (1965); Lopez v. Waldrum Estate, 249 Ark. 558, 460 S.W.2d 61 (1970); Jackiewicz v. United Illuminating Co.,

though there are few cases, it is clear today that the mother has an equal right to the child's services and earnings and therefore is equally entitled to recover for them when the child is tortiously injured.[5] As social conditions changed so that many children no longer performed substantial services in the home or worked outside the home, the authorities were not of one mind on whether the parent bringing the suit had to prove just what services he had been deprived of [6] or whether he could recover even though the child had not been performing any real services before the injury.[7]

Since the services rendered to the parent by the child are in fact largely insignificant today, the characterization of the parent's suit

as one for the loss of services has become a fiction. If, as some cases hold, an actual loss of services must be proved, there would be no recovery in the great majority of cases. If there is a recovery, the parent is really being permitted to recover for the loss or impairment of the parent-child consortium, that is, the loss of the child's society, companionship, affection, which have already been described.[8] Some courts have been willing to recognize this either implicitly [9] or explicitly.[10] Others have refused, adhering to the old-fashioned position that the action's only purpose is to compensate the parent when he has been deprived of his child's services.[11] Reasons for refusing to award damages for loss of the child's consortium are often not given,[12] but

106 Conn. 310, 138 A. 151 (1927); City Stores Co. v. Langer, 308 So.2d 621 (Fla.App.1975); Gilbert v. Stanton Brewery, 295 N.Y. 270, 67 N.E.2d 155 (1946); McGarr v. National & Providence Worsted Mills, 24 R.I. 447, 53 A. 320 (1902); Boring v. Miller, 215 Tenn. 394, 386 S.W.2d 521 (1965).

The medical expenses may include the cost of nursing the child at home. Smith v. Richardson, 277 Ala. 389, 171 So.2d 96 (1965); Yordon v. Savage, 279 So.2d 844 (Fla. 1973). They may also include travel and lodging expenses and telephone calls necessary to enable the parents to keep in touch with the injured child. Mancino v. Webb, 274 A.2d 711 (Del.Super.1971); Woodman v. Peck, 90 N.H. 292, 7 A.2d 251 (1939). The parents may also recover for the future effects of the child's injury. Kramer v. May Lumber Co., 432 S.W.2d 617 (Mo.1968); Jordan v. Bero, 158 W.Va. 28, 210 S.E.2d 618 (1974).

5. Wright v. Standard Oil Co., Inc., 470 F.2d 1280 (5th Cir.1972), rehearing denied 471 F.2d 650 (5th Cir.1973) (relying on a Mississippi statute). Since under Orr v. Orr, 440 U.S. 268, 99 S.Ct. 1102, 59 L.Ed.2d 306 (1979), on remand 374 So.2d 895 (Ala.Civ.App.1979), writ denied 374 So.2d 898 (1979) both husband and wife have equal responsibilities for support pursuant to the Equal Protection Clause of the Fourteenth Amendment, any discrimination between them respecting the right to recover for the child's services and medical expenses would be unconstitutional to the extent it was based upon gender.

6. Brennan v. Biber, 93 N.J.Super. 351, 225 A.2d 742 (1966), affirmed 99 N.J.Super. 247, 239 A.2d 261 (1968); Meyer v. State, 92 Misc.2d 996, 403 N.Y.S.2d 420 (Ct.Cl. 1978); Lofgren v. Western Washington Corp., 65 Wash.2d 144, 396 P.2d 139 (1964).

7. Restatement (Second) of Torts § 703, comment g (1977) takes this position. It is sometimes asserted that the child today is allowed to keep his earnings if he works outside the home, so that the parent's remedy for loss of earnings is of little importance. Katz, Schroeder, Sidman, Emancipating Our Children—Coming of Legal Age in America, 7 Fam.L.Q. 211 (1973). This is undoubtedly true in many families, but the extent to which it is true depends upon the level of the family fortunes and vitality

of the national economy. See R. Baker, Growing Up (1983).

8. See section 11.1, supra.

9. Wright v. Standard Oil Co., Inc., 470 F.2d 1280 (5th Cir.1972), rehearing denied 471 F.2d 650 (5th Cir.1973) (allowing damages for loss of services of a five-year-old child); Kramer v. May Lumber Co., 432 S.W.2d 617 (Mo. App.1968) (allowing recovery for loss of services of an eight-year-old girl).

10. Drayton v. Jiffee Chemical Corp., 395 F.Supp. 1081 (N.D.Ohio 1975), modified and affirmed 591 F.2d 352 (6th Cir.1978) (Ohio law); Reben v. Ely, 146 Ariz. 309, 705 P.2d 1360 (App.1985); Yordon v. Savage, 279 So.2d 844 (Fla.1973); Stephens v. Weigel, 336 Ill.App. 36, 82 N.E.2d 697 (1948); Shockley v. Prier, 66 Wis.2d 394, 225 N.W.2d 495 (1975). Statutes in some states authorize such damages as may be just under the circumstances. E.g., West's Ann.Cal.Code Civ.Proc. § 376 (1983). This form of statute has been construed to permit damages for loss of consortium in Hayward v. Yost, 72 Idaho 415, 242 P.2d 971 (1952). A few statutes expressly authorize recovery for loss of consortium by the parent when the child is injured. E.g., West's R.C.Wash.A. § 4.24.010 (Supp.1987); Handeland v. Brown, 216 N.W.2d 574 (Iowa 1974).

11. Hernandez v. United States, 313 F.Supp. 349 (N.D. Tex.1969); Smith v. Richardson, 277 Ala. 389, 171 So.2d 96 (1965); Baxter v. Superior Court of Los Angeles County, 19 Cal.3d 461, 138 Cal.Rptr. 315, 563 P.2d 871 (1977); Jackiewicz v. United Illuminating Co., 106 Conn. 310, 138 A. 151 (1927); Butler v. Chrestman, 264 So.2d 812 (Miss. 1972); Siciliano v. Capitol City Shows, Inc., 124 N.H. 719, 475 A.2d 19 (1984); Brennan v. Biber, 93 N.J.Super. 351, 225 A.2d 742 (1966), affirmed 99 N.J.Super. 247, 239 A.2d 261 (1968); Gilbert v. Stanton Brewery, Inc., 295 N.Y. 270, 67 N.E.2d 155 (1946); Kalsow v. Grob, 61 N.D. 119, 237 N.W. 848 (1931); Quinn v. Pittsburgh, 243 Pa. 521, 90 A. 353 (1914); McGarr v. Providence Worsted Mills, 24 R.I. 447, 53 A. 320 (1902).

12. E.g., no reasons were given in Hernandez v. United States, 313 F.Supp. 349 (N.D.Tex.1969) or in Jack-

when they are they include the argument that consortium is not within the definition of "services",[13] that consortium is a relationship applying only to husband and wife,[14] and that the intangible nature of the injury creates the risk that damages will not be adequate, that damages cannot be measured accurately, that there may be double recovery, and that liability may be greatly out of proportion to the real harm suffered.[15]

The arguments for not awarding damages for loss of consortium when the child is tortiously injured are not very persuasive. The parent's interest is obvious even though intangible and is analogous to the interest which is the basis for suits when husband-wife consortium is impaired.[16] The procedural objections to the suit can largely be obviated by requiring that the parent's claim be joined with that of the child, as is done in the husband-wife cases and in some of the parent-child cases.[17] Some courts have shown awareness of the soundness of this position by awarding consortium damages in actions by parents for the wrongful deaths of their children, although in these cases the availability of this remedy depends in part on the language of the wrongful death statutes.[18]

The same difficulties arise out of the relationship between the parent's claim for services or consortium and the child's claim for

his own injuries as arise in the husband-wife consortium cases.[19] These include the effect of the child's contributory negligence, the impact of res judicata on the parent's suit, or the release and settlement of the child's claim before the parent sues. Many courts indulge in a futile attempt to resolve the difficulties by labeling the parent's claim either "derivative" or "independent",[20] apparently failing to see that such labels accomplish no more than to restate the result. A more effective way to deal with such questions is to analyze them individually with a view to their relation to the purposes and consequences of the consortium suit.

Conduct of the child after his injury which disables him from bringing suit on the tort should clearly have no effect on the parent's claim. The reason is that such conduct does not mitigate the harm suffered by the parent, nor does it result in unfairness to the tortfeasor if the parent is allowed to recover. So, for example, where the child married the tortfeasor after the tort occurred and was disabled from suing by the husband-wife immunity, the child's father could still sue for loss of services.[21] Likewise a release by the child or the death of the child would not prevent the parent from suing.[22] Similarly, if the child sues first and loses his case on the merits, most courts hold that the parent's

iewicz v. United Illuminating Co., 106 Conn. 310, 138 A. 151 (1927).

13. E.g., Smith v. Richardson, 277 Ala. 389, 171 So.2d 96 (1965).

14. E.g., Quinn v. Pittsburgh, 243 Pa. 521, 90 A. 353 (1914).

15. Baxter v. Superior Court of Los Angeles County, 19 Cal.3d 461, 138 Cal.Rptr. 315, 563 P.2d 871 (1977); Wilson v. Galt, 100 N.M. 227, 668 P.2d 1104 (N.M.App. 1983), cert. quashed 100 N.M. 192, 668 P.2d 308 (1983).

16. See section 11.3, supra.

17. See section 11.3, supra, at note 27, and Schockley v. Prier, 66 Wis.2d 394, 225 N.W.2d 495 (1975).

18. E.g., Bullard v. Barnes, 102 Ill.2d 505, 82 Ill.Dec. 448, 468 N.E.2d 1228 (1984); Wardlow v. Keokuk, 190 N.W.2d 439 (Iowa 1971), appeal after remand, Pagitt v. Keokuk, 206 N.W.2d 700 (Iowa 1973); Jones v. Flannigan, 270 Or. 121, 526 P.2d 543 (1974), appeal after remand 273 Or. 563, 542 P.2d 907 (1975); Sanchez v. Schindler, 651 S.W.2d 249 (Tex.1983). In the wrongful death cases the damages may be reduced by the amount which the parent would have had to expend for the support of the child.

For a collection of cases dealing with the parent's damages when his child is tortiously injured, see 69 A.L.R.3d 553 (1976). A case using a novel basis for damages in a suit by a parent for the wrongful death of his child is Green v. Bittner, 85 N.J. 1, 424 A.2d 210 (1980).

19. See section 11.3, supra, at note 40.

20. Cases holding the claim derivative: Wineman v. Carter, 212 Minn. 298, 4 N.W.2d 83 (1942); McNally v. Addis, 65 Misc.2d 204, 317 N.Y.S.2d 157 (1970); Norfolk Southern Ry. Co. v. Fincham, 213 Va. 122, 189 S.E.2d 380 (1972). Holding it independent: Welter v. Curry, 260 Ark. 287, 539 S.W.2d 264 (1976); Botelho v. Curtis, 28 Conn.Supp. 493, 267 A.2d 675 (1970); Acevedo v. Acosta, 296 So.2d 526 (Fla.App.1974); Jones v. City Council of Augusta, 100 Ga.App. 268, 110 S.E.2d 691 (1959); Handeland v. Brown, 216 N.W.2d 574 (Iowa 1974); Trevorrow v. Boyer, 56 N.J.Super. 215, 145 A.2d 154 (1958); Meisel v. Little, 407 Pa. 546, 180 A.2d 772 (1962).

21. Orr v. Orr, 36 N.J. 236, 176 A.2d 241 (1961).

22. Restatement (Second) of Torts § 703, comment b (1977).

consortium claim is not barred by res judicata.[23] This decision seems to rest on the assumption that there is no unfairness in subjecting the alleged tortfeasor to two lawsuits. The solution to this is to require that the parent's claim be joined with that of the child and that the verdicts be consistent with respect to both claims.[24]

The cases also generally hold that the child's contributory negligence is a defense to the parent's action for loss of consortium.[25] This result may be based on the definition of the claim for consortium, which is that the claim arises when a third person tortiously injures the child. If the child is contributorily negligent, the injury to the child is not tortious.[26] But the rule has been criticized on the ground that the tort consists in the negligent injury to the child, that contributory negligence is a defense, and that none of the usual bases for imputing negligence exists in this situation.[27]

If the parent himself is contributorily negligent, he is generally held to be unable to recover for his loss of consortium when the child has been tortiously injured.[28] But an important New York case has held that a parent's negligent failure to supervise his child should not be recognized as a tort so that the parent whose child was negligently injured by a defendant would not be liable over to that defendant for contribution or indemnification even though the parent had been negligent in failing to supervise the child.[29] The logic of this decision seems to be that the parent's negligent failure to supervise the child does not prevent the parent from recovering for loss of services or consortium when the child is tortiously injured. Several cases have held that the negligence of one parent does not prevent the other parent from recovering for loss of consortium when the child is negligently injured, except perhaps in community property states where the recovery by one spouse might become community property and thus shared by the negligent spouse.[30]

A special application of the consortium doctrine occurs when an employer places the child in an occupation which is dangerous to

23. Kleibor v. Rogers, 265 N.C. 304, 144 S.E.2d 27 (1965); Boring v. Miller, 215 Tenn. 394, 386 S.W.2d 521 (1965); Annots., 116 A.L.R. 1087 (1938), 133 A.L.R. 181, 185 (1941), 23 A.L.R.2d 710, 737 (1952). See also Restatement (Second) of Judgments § 48(2) (1982) which says the consortium suit is precluded by the earlier judgment. In comment c the Restatement gets into the question-begging issue of whether the consortium claim is derivative or independent.

See also section 11.3, supra, at notes 46 and 47.

24. Jones v. Schmidt, 349 Ill.App. 336, 110 N.E.2d 688 (1953); Dudley v. Phillips, 218 Tenn. 648, 405 S.W.2d 468 (1966). In Welter v. Curry, 260 Ark. 287, 539 S.W.2d 264 (1976) the court said that the verdict in the child's suit would control liability in the consortium suit where joinder had been had. But Kleibor v. Rogers, 264 N.C. 304, 144 S.E.2d 27 (1965) took the position that the two claims may not be joined.

25. Welter v. Curry, 260 Ark. 287, 539 S.W.2d 264 (1976); Schaffner v. Smith, 158 Colo. 387, 407 P.2d 23 (1965); Jones v. Schmidt, 349 Ill.App. 336, 110 N.E.2d 688 (1953); Fontenot v. Pan American Fire & Casualty Co., 209 So.2d 105 (La.App.1968), writ refused 252 La. 460, 211 So.2d 328 (1968); Zarba v. Lane, 322 Mass. 132, 76 N.E.2d 318 (1947) (But see Feltch v. General Rental Co., 383 Mass. 603, 421 N.E.2d 67 (1981)); Wineman v. Carter, 212 Minn. 298, 4 N.W.2d 83 (1942); Kleibor v. Rogers, 265 N.C. 304, 144 S.E.2d 27 (1965); Annot., 21 A.L.R.3d 469 (1968); Gregory, The Contributory Negligence of Plaintiff's Wife or Child in an Action for Loss of Services, 2 U.Chi.L.Rev. 173 (1935).

26. This seems to be the basis for Restatement (Second) of Torts § 703, comment a (1977). Another theory has it that the law assigns part of the child's claim to the parent, certainly a far-fetched notion. See Callies v. Reliance Laundry Co., 188 Wis. 376, 206 N.W. 198 (1925), as discussed in White v. Lunder, 66 Wis.2d 563, 225 N.W.2d 442 (1975). All such theories are rejected by Handeland v. Brown, 216 N.W.2d 574 (Iowa 1974), which holds that contributory negligence of the child is not imputed to the parent.

27. Handeland v. Brown, 216 N.W.2d 574 (Iowa 1974).

28. Wright v. Standard Oil Co., Inc., 470 F.2d 1280 (5th Cir.1972), rehearing denied 471 F.2d 650 (5th Cir. 1973) (Mississippi law); Binette v. Deane, 391 A.2d 811 (Me.1978); Restatement (Second) of Torts § 496 (1965).

29. Holodook v. Spencer, 36 N.Y.2d 35, 364 N.Y.S.2d 859, 324 N.E.2d 338 (1974).

30. Wright v. Standard Oil Co., Inc., 470 F.2d 1280 (5th Cir.1972), rehearing denied 471 F.2d 650 (5th Cir. 1973) (Mississippi law); Acevedo v. Acosta, 296 So.2d 526 (Fla.App.1974); Zach v. Morningstar, 258 Iowa 1365, 142 N.W.2d 440 (1966); Brennan v. Biber, 93 N.J.Super. 351, 225 A.2d 742 (1966), affirmed 99 N.J.Super. 247, 239 A.2d 261 (1968); Restatement (Second) of Torts § 494A (1965); Annot., 66 A.L.R.2d 1325 (1959). Contra: Gillam v. J.C. Penney Co., 341 F.2d 457 (7th Cir.1965). Crane v. Smith, 23 Cal.2d 288, 144 P.2d 356 (1943) represents the view of a community property state.

the child in view of the child's capacity and other circumstances. The employer then is liable to the parent if the child is injured either for loss of services or for loss of consortium in those states recognizing loss of consortium as actionable.[31] The parent's consent to the child's employment in such an occupation is a defense to his claim, however.[32]

Most of the courts which have faced the question have held that the parent may not recover punitive damages as an element of his cause of action for loss of consortium when his child is injured [33] just as the spouse usually may not recover punitive damages in a loss of spousal consortium case.[34] There is authority allowing recovery of punitive damages by a parent, however, on proof of the kind of aggravated or outrageous conduct required for recovery of punitive damages generally.[35]

Suit by the Child

Attempts by children to recover for the loss of parental consortium caused by tortious injury to their parents by third persons have usually failed.[36] The denial of such claims is not open to constitutional objection.[37] The reasons given for denying recovery are that there was no such cause of action at common law; [38] that this is a matter better left to legislative treatment; [39] that the jury will have taken the child's loss into account in the suit by the parent so that there is danger of a double recovery; [40] that the tort would result in many suits and many recoveries where the injured parent has several children; [41] that there would be a consequent sharp increase in insurance premiums; [42] that the injury to the child is indirect, remote or speculative; [43] that damages could not be based upon definite standards and thus would be difficult to assess and often excessive; [44] and that the effect of the litigation and of the award of damages would often be to cause disruption in the family.[45] Some courts have raised the spectre of an ever-widening range of relationships which might become the basis for consortium claims if the child's interest were recognized, imagining suits for loss of consortium by

31. Restatement (Second) of Torts § 707 (1977).

32. Id., comment c; Annot., 94 A.L.R. 1211 (1935).

33. Annot., 25 A.L.R.3d 1416 (1969).

34. See section 11.3, supra, at note 77.

35. Wangen v. Ford Motor Co., 97 Wis.2d 260, 294 N.W.2d 437 (1980).

36. Cases are collected in Annots., 11 A.L.R.4th 549 (1982) and 69 A.L.R.3d 528 (1976). See also Restatement (Second) of Torts § 707A (1977): "One who by reason of his tortious conduct is liable to a parent for illness or other bodily harm is not liable to a minor child for resulting loss of parental support and care." No reasons for this position are given.

37. Borer v. American Airlines, Inc., 19 Cal.3d 441, 138 Cal.Rptr. 302, 563 P.2d 858 (1977); Koskela v. Martin, 19 Ill.App.3d 568, 47 Ill.Dec. 32, 414 N.E.2d 1148 (1980); Norwest v. Presbyterian Intercommunity Hospital, 293 Or. 543, 652 P.2d 318 (1982).

38. Turner v. Atlantic Coast Line R.R. Co., 159 F.Supp. 590 (N.D.Ga.1958) (South Carolina law); Jeune v. Del E. Webb Constr. Co., 77 Ariz. 226, 269 P.2d 723 (1954), overruled on other grounds, Glendale v. Bradshaw By and Through Bradshaw, 108 Ariz. 582, 503 P.2d 803 (1972), appeal after remand 114 Ariz. 236, 560 P.2d 420 (1977); Koskela v. Martin, 91 Ill.App.3d 568, 47 Ill.Dec. 32, 414 N.E.2d 1148 (1980); Duhan v. Milanowski, 75 Misc.2d 1078, 348 N.Y.S.2d 696 (1973).

39. Pleasant v. Washington Sand & Gravel Co., 262 F.Supp. 471 (D.C.Cir.1958); Lewis v. Rowland, 287 Ark. 474, 701 S.W.2d 122 (1985); Clark v. Suncoast Hosp., Inc., 338

So.2d 1117 (Fla.App.1976); Halberg v. Young, 41 Hawaii 634 (1957); General Electric Co. v. Bush, 88 Nev. 360, 498 P.2d 366 (1972); Norwest v. Presbyterian Intercommunity Hospital, 293 Or. 543, 652 P.2d 318 (1982); Roth v. Bell, 24 Wash.App. 92, 600 P.2d 602 (1979).

40. Hoesing v. Sears, Roebuck & Co., 484 F.Supp. 478 (D.Neb.1980); Borer v. American Airlines, Inc., 19 Cal.3d 441, 138 Cal.Rptr. 302, 563 P.2d 858 (1977); Hoffman v. Dautel, 189 Kan. 165, 368 P.2d 57 (1962); Russell v. Salem Transp. Co., 61 N.J. 502, 295 A.2d 862 (1972).

41. Ibid. Mueller v. Hellrung Constr. Co., 107 Ill.App. 3d 337, 63 Ill.Dec. 140, 437 N.E.2d 789 (1982). But see Love, Tortious Interference With the Parent-Child Relationship: Loss of an Injured Parent's Society and Companionship, 51 Ind.L.J. 590 (1976).

42. Koskela v. Martin, 91 Ill.App.3d 568, 47 Ill.Dec. 32, 414 N.E.2d 1148 (1980).

43. Halberg v. Young, 41 Hawaii 634 (1957); Russell v. Salem Transp. Co., 61 N.J. 502, 295 A.2d 862 (1972). See also Note, Torts—Parent-Child-Action by Child for Indirect Interference With Family Relationship, 54 Mich. L.Rev. 1023 (1956).

44. Hoesing v. Sears, Roebuck & Co., 484 F.Supp. 478 (D.Neb.1980); Borer v. American Airlines, Inc., 19 Cal.3d 441, 138 Cal.Rptr. 302, 563 P.2d 858 (1977); Norwest v. Presbyterian Intercommunity Hospital, 293 Or. 543, 652 P.2d 318 (1982).

45. Russell v. Salem Transp. Co., 61 N.J. 502, 295 A.2d 862 (1972), suggesting that the apportionment of any damages among siblings might create discord.

friends or by grandchildren, or by adult children.[46]

It is obvious from this list of policy reasons for denying the child's claim that for the most part the denial is not based upon the view that the child suffers no harm when his parent is injured. At least in instances of serious or permanent injury to the parent, as in the Norwest case for example,[47] one could hardly assert that the child was not harmed, or that his interest in all the tangible and intangible aspects of parental care was not grievously affected. In fact some of the very cases which refuse the child a remedy concede the reality of the harm.[48] It is the reality and seriousness of the harm to the child which has led some commentators to express vigorous criticism of the case law.[49]

The question which then has to be faced is whether such administrative or procedural objections to the remedy as the risk of double recovery, the difficulty of assessing damages, the risk of multiple suits and of family disrup-

tion in the distribution of the damages are sufficiently weighty to justify denying relief for conceded harm to a relationship which in other contexts has been characterized as worthy of constitutional protection.[50] Some courts are now beginning to reach the conclusion that these objections do not support a denial of relief.[51] Such objections as the risk of multiple awards, the remoteness or speculative nature of the damages, as well as the argument that the creation of a cause of action is a matter for the legislature rather than the courts have in many states, as the Ferriter case [52] demonstrates, been found too insubstantial to support a denial of relief where the parent sues for loss of consortium caused by an injury to his child or where a spouse sues for loss of consortium caused by an injury to the other spouse. And the risk of multiple recovery can be minimized by requiring joinder of the child's action with that of the parent.[53] The same procedural requirement may be made to ensure that all children

46. Koskela v. Martin, 91 Ill.App.3d 568, 47 Ill.Dec. 32, 414 N.E.2d 1148 (1980); Russell v. Salem Transp. Co., 61 N.J. 502, 295 A.2d 862 (1972); Norwest v. Presbyterian Intercommunity Hospital, 293 Or. 543, 652 P.2d 318 (1982). See also De Angelis v. Lutheran Medical Center, 58 N.Y.2d 1053, 462 N.Y.S.2d 626, 449 N.E.2d 406 (1983) and Note, Actions for Loss of Consortium in Washington: The Children Are Still Crying, 56 Wash.L.Rev. 487 (1977).

47. Norwest v. Presbyterian Intercommunity Hospital, 293 Or. 543, 652 P.2d 318 (1982), in which the allegation was that the mother and sole surviving parent of the three-year-old plaintiff had been caused brain damage through the defendant's negligence requiring lifelong custodial care.

48. E.g., Hill v. Sibley Memorial Hospital, 108 F.Supp. 739 (D.D.C.1952); Borer v. American Airlines, Inc., 19 Cal.3d 441, 138 Cal.Rptr. 302, 563 P.2d 858 (1977); Hoffman v. Dautel, 189 Kan. 165, 368 P.2d 57 (1962).

Of course the nature of the consortium interest is somewhat different here from the consortium interest as between husbands and wives, where sexual relations are an element of the relationship. A few cases seem to place some emphasis on this difference, but the difference hardly suffices to diminish the importance of the parent-child relationship. Such a case is Borer v. American Airlines, Inc., 19 Cal.3d 441, 138 Cal.Rptr. 302, 563 P.2d 858 (1977).

49. E.g., W. Prosser and W. Keeton, The Law of Torts 935 (5th ed. 1984).

50. See, e.g., Stanley v. Illinois, 405 U.S. 645, 92 S.Ct. 1208, 31 L.Ed.2d 551 (1972); Quilloin v. Walcott, 434 U.S. 246, 98 S.Ct. 549, 54 L.Ed.2d 511 (1978). A curious case, Espinoza v. O'Dell, 633 P.2d 455 (Colo.1981), cert. granted

454 U.S. 1122, 102 S.Ct. 969, 71 L.Ed.2d 109 (1981), has held that a child may recover, under the federal Civil Rights Act, 42 U.S.C.A. §§ 1983, 1985, consortium-like damages when his father is killed by the police in violation of the father's constitutional rights. The court refused to limit recovery to pecuniary damages as would have been required by the state wrongful death statute.

51. Reighley v. International Playtex, Inc., 604 F.Supp. 1078 (D.Colo.1985) (Colorado law); Nelson v. Ludovissy, 368 N.W.2d 141 (Iowa 1985); Audubon-Exira v. Illinois Central Gulf R. Co., 335 N.W.2d 148 (Iowa 1983); Ferriter v. Daniel O'Connell's Sons, 381 Mass. 507, 413 N.E.2d 690 (1980); Berger v. Weber, 411 Mich. 1, 303 N.W.2d 424 (1981), containing a long and vigorous dissent; Hay v. Medical Center Hospital of Vermont, 145 Vt. 533, 496 A.2d 939 (1985); Ueland v. Reynolds Metals Co., 103 Wash.2d 131, 691 P.2d 190 (1984), 21 Williamette L.Rev. 885 (1985); Theama by Bichler v. Kenosha, 117 Wis.2d 508, 344 N.W.2d 513 (1984).

Different issues are raised by the unusual case in which the child sues a physician for negligently performing a vasectomy on the parent, claiming that the birth of a sibling diluted the consortium rights of the first child. Here the child's claim is properly denied, since he has no protectible interest in remaining an only child or a member of a smaller family, this being a matter which must be left to the parents. See Aronoff v. Snider, 292 So.2d 418 (Fla.App.1974); Cox v. Stretton, 77 Misc.2d 155, 352 N.Y.S.2d 834 (1974).

52. Ferriter v. Daniel O'Connell's Sons, 381 Mass. 507, 413 N.E.2d 690 (1980).

53. Ueland v. Reynolds Metals Co., 103 Wash.2d 131, 691 P.2d 190 (1984).

are treated equitably, thereby avoiding family disruption. The risk of further extension of the liability to friends or more remote relatives can be eliminated by limiting the concept of consortium to the nuclear family. Even in these days when the family sometimes appears to be in decline as a legal institution there is a clear and workable distinction between the relationships within the family and those outside it.

The argument is sometimes made that since the child is not permitted to recover from a third party when his parent's affections have been alienated, he should likewise not be permitted to recover when the parent is injured through the negligence of a third person.[54] Although superficially the two claims may seem analogous, the fact is that they are entirely dissimilar and involve different interests and relationships. This has been recognized in the spousal consortium cases.[55] Where a spouse's or parent's affections are alleged to have been alienated, the action of the spouse or parent has been voluntary making it difficult or impossible to characterize the third person as a tortfeasor. In addition, suits for alienation of affections raise much greater risks of scandal, extortion and excessive damages than actions for impairment of consortium.[56] Therefore the courts are not taking inconsistent positions when they disapprove suits for alienation and uphold suits for loss of consortium.

Since the child has important interests which may be prejudiced when the parent is tortiously injured, the law should do what it can to vindicate those interests, just as it does when a spouse sues for impairment of consortium. Now that the courts are becoming more sensitive to the rights of children, their consortium claims may perhaps come to be widely recognized.

 WESTLAW REFERENCES

Suit by the Parent

unemancipat! /s child minor /s parent /s servic!

consortium society companionship /s tort tortious! /s parent! /s child minor (wrongful! /2 death)

Suit by the Child

consortium society companionship /s ''common law'' /s refus! deny! deni** /s parent! child minor

consortium society companionship /s doubl! multiple /2 recover! /s parent! child minor

---

54. Lewis, Three New Causes of Action? A Study of the Family Relationship, 20 Mo.L.Rev. 107 (1955).

55. See sections 12.2, Practitioner's Edition, and 11.3, supra.

56. See section 12.2, Practitioner's Edition.

Chapter 12

JURISDICTION FOR DIVORCE, ALIMONY AND CUSTODY

Table of Sections

§ 12.1 Divorce—Nature and History of the Action

The word "divorce" is used in this chapter in its modern sense, to mean the legal termination of a valid marriage. This is to be distinguished from "annulment", which technically means the declaration by a court that a purported marriage was invalid from its beginning because of defects existing at the time it was contracted. Although "divorce" sometimes used to be applied to actions that were properly annulments,[1] although today some divorce statutes include grounds relevant only to annulment,[2] and although several modern, well-considered decisions assimilate annulment to divorce under certain circumstances,[3] it is still desirable to distinguish between the two for clarity of expression and accuracy of analysis.

Many, if not most, simple societies have established ways of ending marriages that are analogous to divorce.[4] Often, as under our divorce law, there is some provision for a return of property to the parties,[5] or for compensation to the wife.[6] These results are sometimes accomplished by processes that we might call legal, and sometimes only by custom. In any event such societies furnish evidence of a widely felt need for ending unsatisfactory marriages, and of an equally widespread assertion by the community of some control over the process. In few of them do we find the hostility to divorce as such which has permeated English law for hundreds of years.

The view of divorce taken by any society is closely related to that society's ideal of marriage and the family. Any historical account

§ 12.1

1. II G. Howard, A History of Matrimonial Institutions 53 (1904).

2. E.g., Ark.Stats. § 34–1202 (Supp.1985); Ohio Rev. Code § 3105.01 (Supp.1985).

3. E.g., Sefton v. Sefton, 45 Cal.2d 872, 291 P.2d 439 (1955).

4. E.g., Llewellyn and Hoebel, The Cheyenne Way 185 (1941); Gluckman, The Judicial Process Among the Ba-

rotse of Northern Rhodesia 123, 140–147, (1955); Benedict, Patterns of Culture 63, 192 (Pelican ed. 1946); II Howard, A History of Matrimonial Institutions 34 (1904); Murdock, Family Stability in Non-European Cultures 272 Annals 195 (1950).

5. Benedict, Patterns of Culture 68 (Pelican ed. 1946).

6. Gluckman, The Judicial Process Among the Barotse of Northern Rhodesia 123 (1955).

405

of divorce alone therefore involves an artificial division of what is really a single subject. Nevertheless, in order to provide the information necessary to make our present divorce law intelligible, a brief history of Anglo-American divorce is given here,[7] while the history of marriage and the family is discussed elsewhere in this work.[8]

A convenient starting point for this account is the time, probably about the tenth or eleventh century, when Christianity became sufficiently influential in Britain to enable the Church to assert its rules about divorce effectively. Before that time the necessity for compromise had forced the Church to accept, at least in part, the Anglo-Saxon law, which allowed divorce by consent of the spouses or for the wife's adultery or desertion. The Christian doctrine when finally formulated in Britain made divorce as we know it impossible, although it did permit divorce a mensa et thoro, or judicial separation.[9]

The doctrine that a marriage could end only on the death of one of the parties to it was the outcome of centuries of casuistical embellishment upon various passages in the New Testament. Thus at one point Jesus is reported as forbidding the husband to put away his wife except for her unfaithfulness.[10] At another point He seems to say that neither spouse may put away the other and remarry.[11] Paul in one place forbids divorce to either spouse,[12] but in another appears to approve the divorce of an unbeliever by a Christian.[13] The process by which these fragmentary teachings were welded into a coherent body of dogma must have been divinely inspired, since it cannot be accounted for by human reason alone. Two of the most important human instruments in this process were Gratian,[14] who resolved what appear to lesser intellects as irreconcilable contradictions, and Peter Lombard,[15] whose theory of the sacramental nature of marriage accomplished two useful results: It made any reform exceedingly difficult, if not impossible, and it provided a basis for asserting the exclusive jurisdiction of the Church's courts over marriage and divorce.

The doctrines so evolved can be summed up as follows: (a) True divorce in the modern sense of the term could never be granted for any reason. (b) Divorce a mensa et thoro, or limited divorce, without a right of remarriage, could be granted for adultery and cruelty. (c) Annulments sometimes confusingly referred to as divorces *a vinculo*, were granted freely for impediments existing at the time of the marriage. The impediments most commonly relied upon were affinity, consanguinity, and prior informal marriage, and since the Church held very remote degrees of relationship to be objectionable, annulments on these grounds became useful devices for evading the prohibition upon divorce. Even today, in states like New York where divorce has been

---

7. This account is based upon II Howard, A History of Matrimonial Institutions Ch. XI, XV (1904) and III id. Ch. XVII; 2 Pollock and Maitland, History of English Law 392–394 (1898); 1 Holdsworth, History of English Law 622–624 (7th ed. 1956); 2 Id. 90; 4 Id. 34–42; Bryce, Marriage and Divorce Under Roman and English Law, 3 Select Essays on Anglo-American Legal History 728 (1909); Lichtenberger, Divorce 19–140 (1931); Kitchin, A History of Divorce (1912); Barnett, Divorce and the American Divorce Novel 15–69 (1939); Llewellyn, Behind the Law of Divorce: II, 33 Colum.L.Rev. 249 (1933). For valuable statistical data on American marriage and divorce, see P. Jacobson, American Marriage and Divorce (1959); H. Carter and P. Glick, Marriage and Divorce: A Social and Economic Study (1970).

8. See sec. 2.1, supra.

9. II Howard, A History of Matrimonial Institutions 52–54 (1904); Winnett, Divorce and Remarriage in Anglicanism, ch. I–VII (1957); Foliamb's Case, 3 Salk. 138 (1602); 1 Bishop, Marriage, Divorce and Separation, § 1498 (1891).

10. Matthew 5: 31, 32; Matthew 19: 3–12.

11. Mark 10: 2–12; Luke 16: 18.

12. Romans 7: 2, 3; 1 Corinthians 7: 10, 11.

13. 1 Corinthians 7: 12–16.

14. Author of Decretum Gratiani and often referred to as the founder of the canon law. He did his work during the early years of the 12th century.

15. Circa 1100–1160, Bishop of Paris, best known for his book Sententiarum Libri Quatuor which established the doctrine of the seven sacraments.

For an earnest attempt, in the twentieth century, to construct a coherent theory of divorce from Biblical sources, see "Viator," Divorce in Its Ecclesiastical Aspect (1912). Among other opinions the author asserts that there is a law of nature by which one must distinguish the immorality of the male from that of the female spouse.

difficult, annulment was often used as a substitute.[16]

Not only did the Church develop a set of doctrines regulating divorce, but its courts successfully maintained exclusive jurisdiction over the administration of those doctrines. No royal courts had authority to hear cases of divorce or annulment, or to rule on the validity of marriages. Even when the validity of a marriage arose in connection with a claim for dower, the royal courts often referred the question to the ecclesiastical courts for an opinion. The ecclesiastical courts retained this exclusive jurisdiction until the reforms of 1857, except for the years of the Commonwealth, the only effect of Henry VIII's break with Rome being to transfer the ecclesiastical courts from the control of the Catholic Church to that of the Church of England.[17]

The English Reformation and the establishment of the Church of England during the reign of Henry VIII were in part precipitated by the Pope's refusal to grant an annulment of Henry's marriage to Catherine of Aragon. At the same period, both on the Continent and in England Protestants were attacking the Catholic Church's dogmas on marriage and urging that divorces be granted for adultery and desertion.[18] It might be expected that these influences would have produced a liberalization of divorce laws in England, but for the most part this did not occur. In fact the dissolution of marriage became more difficult due to the simplification and reduction of those prohibited degrees of kinship within which a marriage could formerly have been annulled. This change cured one of Protestantism's strongest objections to Catholic mar-riage law. It was not accompanied by any clear authorization of divorce. During the sixteenth century there were apparently some divorces in England, and some cases in which remarriage after a judicial separation was held valid,[19] but at the end of the century the Church reinstated its conservative policy of refusing all divorce.[20] This remained English law until 1857,[21] when divorce jurisdiction was transferred from the ecclesiastical courts to the civil court system and divorces were authorized for adultery. Even here, however, there was sharp discrimination against wives, who could obtain a divorce only if the husband's adultery was aggravated by bigamy, cruelty or incest, while the husband could get his divorce for adultery alone.

One other peculiarly unfair institution originated in the late seventeenth century, the divorce by special act of Parliament.[22] Since it could be obtained only on the ground of adultery after the ecclesiastical court had granted a judicial separation and usually only after the successful prosecution of an action against the paramour for criminal conversation, such a divorce was beyond the reach of any but the very rich. As a practical matter it was seldom obtainable by the wife. Aside from its significance as an illustration of the law's barbarity, it has some historic interest for us, since the English example led to frequent divorces by special legislative act in the United States, both during the colonial period and as late as the middle of the nineteenth century.

English divorce was given a somewhat more modern look by the Matrimonial Causes Act of 1937,[23] which added desertion, cruelty and

---

16. See Note, Annulments for Fraud—New York's Answer to Reno?, 48 Colum.L.Rev. 900 (1948).

17. For a description of this process see 1 Holdsworth, History of English Law 588–614, 621–624 (7th ed. 1956), and 6 Id. 418–419.

18. The most famous of these attacks is in Milton's Doctrine and Discipline of Divorce, in Modern Library ed. of Milton's Complete Poetry and Selected Prose 615 (1950).

19. 1 Holdsworth, History of English Law 623 (7th ed. 1956).

20. II Howard, History of Matrimonial Institutions 83 (1904).

21. The Matrimonial Causes Act of 1857, 20 and 21 Vict. c. 85. See Woodhouse, The Marriage and Divorce Bill of 1857, 3 Am.J. of Legal Hist. 260 (1959). For an account of divorce law and social conditions before 1857, see Mueller, Inquiry into the State of a Divorceless Society, 18 Pitt.L.Rev. 545 (1957). See also A. Horstman, Victorian Divorce (1985).

22. II Howard, History of Matrimonial Institutions 102–109 (1904).

See also Crouch, The Evolution of Parliamentary Divorce in England, 52 Tul.L.Rev. 513 (1978).

23. 1 Edw. 8 and 1 Geo. 6 c. 57.

some other offenses as grounds for divorce and made other changes. Extensive official and unofficial investigations of divorce after World War II [24] led to the curiously ambivalent Divorce Reform Act of 1969, which makes irretrievable breakdown of marriage the sole ground for divorce, but then goes on to provide that the marriage will not be deemed to have broken down unless one of five conditions is proved, namely, adultery, cruelty, desertion, two years' separation and the respondent consents to the decree, or five years' separation.[25]

From its beginnings, American law has allowed divorce more freely than the British, due to a strong Protestant tradition and the absence of any system of ecclesiastical courts. In New England the Protestant doctrine of the civil nature of marriage had as its consequence statutes authorizing divorce for adultery, desertion, sometimes cruelty and some other offenses.[26] Divorces were often granted under these statutes, sometimes by the courts and sometimes by the legislatures, which in colonies like Massachusetts functioned both as legislature and highest court. Judicial separations were not favored, but occasionally were granted. By contrast with New England, divorces were rare in the middle and southern colonies.[27] Although it was conceded that the English common law prevailed in those colonies, no ecclesiastical courts were set up there, and so no judicial body with common law jurisdiction over marital cases existed. The result was that the only divorces or judicial separations were granted by special legislative act.

After the War of Independence and through the nineteenth century the divorce law of the various states was characterized by such diversity and subjected to such frequent change that in this brief account only a few of the more important developments can be mentioned. The grounds for divorce, varying greatly from state to state often included provisions more relevant to annulment than to divorce, such as those authorizing dissolution of the marriage for a prior existing marriage or for fraud.[28] In a few states during the middle of the century the "omnibus clause" appeared, permitting divorce for any cause deemed just and reasonable,[29] thus giving the courts the kind of wide discretion advocated much later by some enthusiasts for "therapeutic" divorce.[30] When, during the second half of the century, the omnibus clauses were

24. Report of Royal Commission on Marriage and Divorce (1956), criticized in Pollard, The Problem of Divorce (1958) and in Kahn-Freund, Divorce Reform? 19 Mod.L.Rev. 573 (1956). Greater impetus toward reform came from The Law Commission, Reform of the Grounds for Divorce, The Field of Choice (Cmd. 3123 1966) and Putting Asunder, A Divorce Law for Contemporary Society, The Report of a Group Appointed by the Archbishop of Canterbury in January 1964 (1966).

25. Divorce Reform Act of 1969, as modified by the Matrimonial Causes Act of 1973 and the Matrimonial Causes Act of 1976. Under these statutes a court may deny the divorce on the basis of "grave hardship" to the respondent even where divorce grounds are proved. But procedures have now been adopted in accordance with which divorces may be granted without a court hearing, on affidavits alone, where the divorce is undefended. See Matrimonial Causes Rules 1973, No. 2016, §§ 16, 33(3), 48; Matrimonial Causes Rules 1976, No. 2166; O.Stone, Family Law 137 (1977).

26. II Howard, History of Matrimonial Institutions 328–366 (1904). For a good account of the history of divorce in the United States see Blake, The Road to Reno (1962).

It is important to note, something often taken for granted by lawyers, that divorce jurisdiction in the United States rests upon statute in the first instance. With-

out statutory authority, no court could grant divorces. Wood v. Wood, 407 A.2d 282 (Me. 1979).

27. II Howard, History of Matrimonial Institutions 366–387 (1904).

28. III Id. 4–18, 50–79, 101–144. Many other curious grounds for divorce are described by Howard, the oddest of which is found in a Mississippi statute of 1862 authorizing divorce for a wife whose husband is in the army or navy of the United States or lives in one of the United States in preference to the Confederacy. This is merely an extreme instance of the common tendency to make the divorce law serve purposes quite foreign to the relations between husband and wife, which has caused so much needless trouble and unhappiness.

29. The wording of these clauses varied, but they all meant substantially the same thing. Connecticut, a leading state in enacting such legislation, provided for divorce for conduct which "permanently destroys the happiness of the petitioner and defeats the purpose of the marriage relation." III Howard, History of Matrimonial Institutions 13 (1904). Maine, Indiana, Illinois, Iowa, and Utah also enacted such clauses. See III Howard, History of Matrimonial Institutions 17, 115, 119, 126, 131 (1904).

30. See, e.g., Alexander, Let's Get the Embattled Spouses Out of the Trenches, 18 Law & Contemp.Prob. 98, 105–106 (1953); Mudd, Contributions to a Therapeutic

repealed, the statutes resumed the historic pattern which they retained until the 1960's and 1970's of requiring that all cases be brought within one or another category of marital offense, the broadest of these being "cruelty" or "indignities" or their equivalent. Many states had adopted this vague and therefore useful ground for divorce by 1900.[31]

The statutory catalog of marital wrongs found in nearly every state in these earlier times suggested that divorce law had been shaped by a carry-over of attitudes from tort law.[32] This was confirmed by the adoption of the defenses of connivance, condonation, collusion and recrimination. These defenses were developed by the English ecclesiastical courts in actions for judicial separation [33] and applied in this country, either by statute or judicial decision, to suits for absolute divorce. They implied consent, forgiveness or fault on the plaintiff's part. The divorce decree thus came to resemble a tort judgment, both being granted for the fault of the defendant causing harm to the plaintiff, and both being denied where the plaintiff either consented or was himself at fault. This development was particularly deplorable since it bore no relation to the causes, consequences and purposes of divorce. It resulted in widespread hypocrisy, perjury or near perjury, and public contempt for the courts.

The nineteenth century also saw divorce firmly established as a judicial and not a legislative function, although the custom of granting divorces by special legislative act survived to a surprisingly late date in spite of

the favoritism, lack of respect for the claims of absent spouses and other abuses which were frequently observed.[34]

Other characteristic features of twentieth century divorce law took shape during the century of legislative tinkering between 1800 and 1900. Alimony, the division of spouses' property, and orders for the support and custody of children were authorized. Residence requirements were imposed, some of them intentionally made short to attract divorce business. Judicial separation and restrictions on the remarriage of divorced persons, both of which created a legal limbo of persons neither married nor unmarried, were widely provided for by statute.[35]

The existence in a few jurisdictions of short residence requirements for divorce produced the phenomenon called migratory divorce, permitting people living in one state to go to one of the divorce mill states, stay the necessary six weeks or ninety days (or, in the case of Alabama, one day) get a divorce and immediately return home. Numerically those divorces were never very significant since migratory divorce was confined to those wealthy enough to pay the expense of a trip to Reno or Miami or the Virgin Islands plus the period of residence. Mexico also offered quickie divorces to those unable to get them at home, and in fact one could even get a mail order divorce there.[36] Mexico has changed its law so that non-residents may no longer be divorced there,[37] but the foreign migratory divorce business now flourishes in Haiti and the Dominican Republic.[38] An extensive body of

---

Solution to the Divorce Problem: Social Work and Marriage Counseling, Univ. of Chicago Conference on Divorce 65 (1952).

31. 2 C. Vernier, American Family Laws 24–29 (1932). The early cases are discussed in Black, Cruelty as a Ground for Divorce, 20 Cent.L.J. 284 (1885).

32. See, e.g., Brown v. Brown, 198 Tenn. 600, 281 S.W.2d 492, 498 (1955), stating that divorce "is conceived as a remedy for the innocent against the guilty."

33. See, e.g., Ferrers v. Ferrers, 1 Hagg.Con. 130, 161 Eng.Rep. 504 (1790); D'Aguilar v. D'Aguilar, 1 Hagg.Ecc. 773, 162 Eng.Rep. 748 (1794); Rogers v. Rogers, 3 Hagg. Ecc. 57, 162 Eng.Rep. 1079 (1830); Crewe v. Crewe, 3 Hagg.Ecc. 123, 162 Eng.Rep. 1102 (1800).

34. III G. Howard, History of Matrimonial Institutions 31–50, 96–101 (1904).

35. Utah required only that the plaintiff show he wished to become a resident. South Dakota was an early divorce mill, with a 90-day residence requirement. II G. Howard, History of Matrimonial Institutions 131, 157 (1904). For separations and restrictions on remarriage see III Id. 20, 78, 79–84, 105, 110, 145–152.

36. An example of a Mexican mail-order divorce was involved in Rosenbaum v. Rosenbaum, 309 N.Y. 371, 130 N.E.2d 902 (1955).

37. Note, Mexican Divorce Law Now More Restricted, 58 A.B.A.J. 86 (1972).

38. A case dealing with the validity of a Dominican divorce is Hyde v. Hyde, 562 S.W.2d 194 (Tenn. 1978). See also Everett v. Everett, 345 So.2d 586 (La. App. 1977), writ denied 349 So.2d 329 (1977), and Note, Caribbean

constitutional and conflicts law grew up to deal with the question of the validity of these divorces.[39] Today, however, they have become of even less significance because the enactment of no-fault divorce laws in so many states has made it unnecessary for the unhappily married to leave home in order to obtain a divorce.[40]

At the time the first edition of this work was published it was accurate to say that American divorce law had exhibited extraordinary conservatism in the face of extensive social changes. In the years since 1968 the social changes have become even more rapid and the law of divorce has responded by attempting to meet the demands which these changes made upon it. No longer may that law be characterized as conservative, whatever other criticisms may be made of it.

The social change of greatest importance has been the sharp growth in the divorce rate, which reached its highest point in 1979 and which has fluctuated somewhat since then.[41] The year 1982 saw a decline in the number of divorces.[42] It is interesting that while divorce rates were increasing, the rate of marriage

was also increasing.[43] A second important development has been the increase in the proportion of married women working outside the home to the point at which more than half of them work, and nearly two-thirds do so at younger ages.[44] Needless to say, an even higher proportion of divorced women work outside the home.[45]

These trends were accompanied by much criticism of our divorce laws, primarily aimed at the emphasis on fault, taking the position that the fault grounds for divorce were usually symptoms rather than causes of the difficulties in marriages, and that the prevalence of uncontested divorces, usually granted on trivial claims of cruelty, made the continued insistence upon fault an essentially dishonest pretence.[46] The earliest legislative response to these criticisms was California's enactment of a statute authorizing divorce on only two grounds, incurable insanity, and "irreconcilable differences which have caused irremediable breakdown of marriage".[47] In 1970, after extensive study and discussion,[48] the Uniform Marriage and Divorce Act [49] was approved by the National Conference of Commissioners on

Divorce for Americans: Useful Device or Obsolescent Institution? 10 Cornell Int.L.J. 116 (1976).

39. The cases are discussed in section 12.2, infra.

40. See Freed and Foster, Family Law in the Fifty States: An Overview as of September 1982, 8 Fam.L.Rep. 4065 (1982), for a list of states having no-fault divorce.

41. In 1945 the rate was 3.5 divorces per 1,000 of the population. The rate declined until 1967 when it began to rise again, reaching 5.4 divorces per 1,000 population in 1979. The rate in 1981 was 5.3 per 1,000 population. Statistical Abstract of the United States 60 (1982–1983).

42. In 1982 the number of divorces declined for the first time since 1962, the rate declining from the 1981 figure of 5.3 to 5.1 per 1,000 of the population. National Center for Health Statistics, Monthly Vital Statistics Report, Vol. 31, No. 12, at 2 (March 14, 1983).

43. The rate of marriage has increased from 8.5 per 1,000 of the population in 1960 to 10.6 in 1981. Statistical Abstract of the United States 60 (1982–1983). The number of marriages has increased over the past seven consecutive years from 1975 to 1982. The rate of marriage in 1982 was 10.8 per 1,000 of the population, except for 1972 and 1973 the highest in the past 32 years. National Center for Health Statistics, Monthly Vital Statistics Report, Vol. 31, No. 12, at 1 (March 14, 1983).

44. Statistical Abstract of the United States 382 (1982–1983).

45. Ibid.

46. Report of the Governor's Commission on the Family, California 1966; Putting Asunder, A Divorce Law For Contemporary Society, The Report of a Group Appointed by the Archbishop of Canterbury in January 1964 (1966), known as the Report of the Mortimer Commission; Tenney, Divorce Without Fault: The Next Step, 46 Neb.L. Rev. 24 (1967); Turner, Retreat from "Fault"?: An English Lawyer's View, 46 Neb.L.Rev. 64 (1967).

47. West's Ann.Cal.Civ.Code § 4506 (1983), enacted in 1969, effective in 1970.

48. One of the Reporters for the Act, Professor Robert J. Levy, wrote Uniform Marriage and Divorce Legislation: A Preliminary Analysis (1969), giving an account of existing statutes and making recommendations for reforms. The Act was debated at length in a Symposium on the Uniform Marriage and Divorce Act, 18 S.D.L.Rev. 531 (1973).

49. 9A Unif.L.Ann. 91 (1979). The Act will hereinafter be cited UMDA § ___, with the understanding that it may be found in volume 9A of the Uniform Laws Annotated. The disputes preceding the American Bar Association's approval of the Act are described in Zuckman, The ABA Family Law Section v. the NCCUSL: Alienation, Separation and Forced Reconciliation Over the Uniform Marriage and Divorce Act, 24 Cath.U.L.Rev. 61 (1974). The provisions of the Act are discussed in Note, The Uniform Marriage and Divorce Act: New Statutory Solutions to Old Problems, 37 Mont.L.Rev. 119 (1976)

Uniform State Laws. It adopted as the sole ground for divorce "that the marriage is irretrievably broken", with the additional requirement of evidence that serious marital discord adversely affects the attitude of the parties toward the marriage.[50] Other states were not long in enacting marriage breakdown as a ground or the only ground for divorce.[51] In still other states divorce was permitted on proof of other non-fault grounds, such as incompatibility [52] or living separate and apart for a specified period.[53] The result is that fault has largely been eliminated from the grounds for divorce, as have those defenses related to fault, such as collusion, connivance, condonation and recrimination.[54]

If fault is no longer an issue in the granting of a divorce, the question arises whether it makes any sense to continue to insist upon the traditional requirement that divorces may not be granted without a judicial hearing, that divorces may not be granted by default, at least in those cases in which there is no controversy over property, maintenance or child custody. Some states have begun to answer that question in the negative by authorizing divorces to be awarded without a hearing where both parties desire a decree, with certain other conditions.[55]

The elimination of fault grounds and the consequent lessening of hostility have not by any means made divorce a painless process for the parties.[56] One reason for this is that sources of dispute other than grounds have remained more intractable to legislative treatment. Nearly all states now have statutes authorizing alimony (or maintenance as it is often called) and the division of property on divorce,[57] and the Supreme Court has outlawed gender discrimination respecting alimony,[58] but there remain many hardships for the spouse who is dependent upon such awards, due to the difficulties of enforcement.[59] Child support has also proved difficult to enforce, to such an extent that Congress has begun to take a hand in the process.[60] The custody aspects of divorce have remained as a source of great difficulty for judges in divorce actions, notwithstanding statutory attempts to deal with interstate conflicts and with child-snatching by the Uniform Child Custody Jurisdiction Act [61] and the federal Parental Kidnaping Prevention Act of 1980.[62] Awarding custody to both parents, that is, joint custody, is often advocated as a panacea but is feasible in only a small proportion of cases.[63]

In the 1960's a critical aspect of the "divorce problem" was seen as the continued high rate of divorce. Several attempts at

50. UMDA § 302.

51. Freed and Foster, Family Law in the Fifty States: An Overview as of September 1982, 8 Fam.L.Rep. 4065, 4074 (1982) lists thirty-five states as having some form of marriage breakdown as a ground for divorce.

52. Id. at 4075 lists seven states as having incompatibility as a ground for divorce.

53. Id. at 4076 lists twenty states as having this ground for divorce in some form.

54. Id. at 4076, 4077 lists seventeen states which have abolished all the fault defenses and several others which have abolished part of these defenses.

55. E.g., West's Ann.Cal.Civ.Code §§ 4550 to 4556 (1983); Colo.Rev.Stat. 14–10–120.3 (Supp.1986); Ohio Rev. Code §§ 3105.61 to 3105.65 (1980). For the English procedure, see note 25, supra.

56. Books written by divorced persons describe in detail the suffering inflicted by the process of divorce. Examples are A. Alvarez, Life After Marriage: Love in an Age of Divorce (1981) and J. Epstein, Divorced in America (1974). The former work contains illuminating accounts of the difficulties undergone by unmarried couples when they broke up.

57. See sections 15.1 and 16.1, infra.

58. Orr v. Orr, 440 U.S. 268, 99 S.Ct. 1102, 59 L.Ed.2d 306 (1979), on remand 374 So.2d 895 (Ala. Civ. App. 1979), writ denied 374 So.2d 898 (1979).

59. Weitzman, The Economics of Divorce: Social and Economic Consequences of Property, Alimony and Child Support Awards, 28 U.C.L.A.L.Rev. 1181 (1981).

60. 42 U.S.C.A. §§ 651 ff. and 1397 ff. (Supp. III 1985). Regulations implementing this legislation are contained in 45 C.F.R. Parts 205, 232–235, 301–304.

61. 9 Unif.L.Ann. 111 (1979). This Act is now in force in all but two states, Massachusetts and Texas. Freed and Foster, Family Law in the Fifty States: An Overview as of September 1982, 8 Fam.L.Rep. 4065, 4087 (1982).

62. 28 U.S.C.A. § 1738A.

63. Various types of statute favoring joint custody decrees have been enacted in about half of the states. Freed and Foster, Family Law in the Fifty States: An Overview as of September 1982, 8 Fam.L.Rep. 4065, 4090 (1982).

dealing with this "problem" were made in various states. In California and some other states it was thought for a time that conciliation courts would induce parties to divorce suits to be reconciled and thereby make substantial reductions in the number of divorces.[64] Unfortunately the conciliation process did not succeed in achieving much in the way of discouraging divorce and we no longer hear much about it. In other states there was a touching but naive faith in marriage counseling or divorce counseling as a way of persuading couples to remain together and not to obtain divorces. Counseling services were set up in conjunction with the divorce courts for this purpose, culminating in the short-lived New York attempt at "compulsory" counseling.[65] These efforts did little to reduce the number of divorces, although they often succeeded in reducing the hostility of the divorcing couples with consequent benefits for the parties and their children. At about the same time there was considerable enthusiasm for family courts, which could deal with the entire family and its problems, using psychiatric and other expert assistance.[66] This movement also seems to have lost impetus.

The latest of the popular divorce reforms seems to be what is elaborately called "alternative dispute resolution". The basic idea is no longer to prevent or reduce divorce but to get it out of the courts. One way of accomplishing this is of course to resort to arbitration.[67] Another is mediation, in which the parties are induced to appear before an impartial mediator or mediators who can then help them to arrive at an agreement resolving their divorce disputes, after which the agreement can be approved by a divorce court more or less as a formality.[68] The virtues of mediation are that it avoids expensive and time-consuming litigation, produces results respecting property and child custody more or less satisfactory to both spouses, and in general avoids the destructive hostility which causes so much suffering and leads to so much post-divorce litigation over property and custody.[69] We have reduced our goals and expectations from the days when we thought we could limit the number of divorces and thereby increase the stability of marriage. We now seem content to make the divorce process less traumatic, hoping thereby to reduce the personal and social damage and expense of family breakup. Whether this more modest program will succeed any better than family courts and counseling programs did remains to be seen.

 **WESTLAW REFERENCES**

"divorce a vinculo" /s annul!

dissol! divorc! /s sex gender /s discriminat! /s alimony maintenance support

---

64. Burke, Conciliation—A New Approach to the Divorce Problem, 30 Cal.S.B.J. 199 (1955); Burke, The Role of Conciliation in Divorce Cases, 1 J.Fam.L. 209 (1961); Elkin, The Conciliation Court: A Pioneering Approach to the Divorce Problem, Student Lawyer Journal 26 (December 1968); Burke, With This Ring (1958); Hartman, Report of the Subcommittee on the Conciliation Court, Matrimonial Actions Committee, Section of Family Law, American Bar Association (1961). The California Conciliation Courts were set up pursuant to West's Ann.Cal. Code Civ.Proc. §§ 1730 to 1772 (1982).

65. See, e.g., Seidelson, Systematic Marriage Investigation and Counselling in Divorce Cases: Some Reflections on Its Constitutionality and General Desirability, 36 G.W.L.Rev. 60 (1967); Foster, Conciliation and Counselling in the Courts in Family Law Cases, 41 N.Y.U.L.Rev. 353 (1966); Bodenheimer, The Utah Marriage Counselling Experiment, 7 Utah L.Rev. 443 (1961); Note, New York Conciliation and Divorce, 37 Alb.L.Rev. 751 (1973).

California has tried a different approach, by authorizing its courts, when asked to approve the marriage of a person under eighteen, to require pre-marital counseling as a condition on the grant of approval. West's Ann.Cal. Civ.Code § 4101 (1983); Hogoboom, Premarital Counselling for Teenagers-One Year's Experience in California, 22 Buff.L.Rev. 145 (1972).

66. W. Gellhorn, Children and Families in the Courts of New York (1954); M. Virtue, Family Cases in Court (1956); Kay, A Family Court: The California Proposal, 56 Cal.L.Rev. 1205 (1968); Chute, Divorce and the Family Court, 18 L. & Contemp.Prob. 49 (1953); Lindsay, A Family Court-Why Not? 51 Minn.L.Rev. 223 (1966). Paulsen, Juvenile Courts, Family Courts and the Poor Man, 54 Cal.L.Rev. 694 (1966) documents disappointment with the operation of these courts.

67. Holman and Noland, Agreement and Arbitration: Relief to Overlitigation in Domestic Relations Disputes in Washington, 12 Willamette L.J. 527 (1976).

68. O. Coogler, Structured Mediation in Divorce Settlement (1978).

69. See, e.g., Riskin, Mediation and Lawyers, 43 Ohio St.L.J. 29 (1982).

§ 12.2　Divorce—Jurisdiction to End the Marital Status

State Statutes Imposing Durational Residence Requirements

Statutes in nearly all states impose, as a condition upon the right to sue for divorce, requirements that either the plaintiff or one of the parties has been a resident of the state for a specified period ranging from six weeks to two years, the most common period being six months.[1] "Residence" as used in these statutes usually means domicile.[2] The cases are not in agreement on whether these statutes must be complied with in order to give the court jurisdiction over the subject matter of the divorce. Most of the cases hold that the requirement of a period of residence is jurisdictional,[3] but a substantial number hold

that it is not, although the fact of residence is necessary for jurisdiction.[4] Since the purpose of the statutes is to provide some objective evidence of the party's domicile in the state,[5] and since domicile *is* essential for subject matter jurisdiction in divorce,[6] it is logical to take the view that statutory compliance is jurisdictional. The point has some importance in view of the settled rule that lack of subject matter jurisdiction may not be waived, that it may be asserted at any stage of the proceeding, and that it may be the basis for collateral attack on the decree.[7]

During the 1970's a number of courts, relying upon some Supreme Court decisions concerned with durational residence requirements,[8] held that statutes imposing such requirements upon suits for divorce were un-

§ 12.2

1. E.g., Ala.Code 1977, § 30–2–5 (six months); West's Ann.Cal.Civ.Code § 4530 (1983) (six months); Conn.Gen. Stat.Ann. § 46b–44 (1986) (twelve months under certain circumstances); Idaho Code § 32–701 (1983) (six weeks); Nevada.Rev.Stat. § 125.020 (1986) (six weeks); N.J. Stat. Ann. § 2A: 34–10 (1952 and Supp. 1986) (one year under some circumstances); N.M.Stat.Ann. 1986, § 40–4–5 (six months); N.Y.—McKinney's Dom.Rel.Law § 230 (1977) (complex provisions, including a two-year residence requirement under some circumstances); Pa.Stat. tit. 23, § 302 (Supp. 1986) (six months); Wis.Stat.Ann. § 767.05 (1981) (six months). Alaska and Washington appear not to have any durational residence requirement. The Uniform Act requires that one of the parties have been domiciled in the state for ninety days preceding the commencement of the suit. UMDA § 302. The Act gives no indication whether this requirement is jurisdictional.

2. Smith v. Smith, 45 Cal.2d 235, 288 P.2d 497 (1955); State v. DeMeo, 20 N.J. 1, 118 A.2d 1 (1955); Raybin v. Raybin, 179 N.J.Super. 121, 430 A.2d 953 (1981); Usher v. Usher, 41 A.D.2d 368, 343 N.Y.S.2d 212 (3d Dept. 1973); Tower v. Tower, 120 Vt. 213, 138 A.2d 602 (1958); Annots., 159 A.L.R. 496 (1945), 106 A.L.R. 6 (1937). In Illinois "residence" is construed not to mean domicile, but the courts define "residence" in a way not easily distinguishable from domicile. Berlingieri v. Berlingieri, 372 Ill. 60, 22 N.E.2d 675 (1939); Garrison v. Garrison, 107 Ill.App.2d 311, 246 N.E.2d 9 (1969). In Arkansas the statute seems to make it clear that "residence" does not mean domicile. Ark. Stats. §§ 34–1208, 34–1208.1 (1962). Residence plus the unavailability of another forum were held to warrant jurisdiction in In re Marriage of Thornton, 135 Cal.App.3d 500, 185 Cal.Rptr. 388 (1982).

Domicile is defined by Reese and Green, That Elusive Word, "Residence", 6 Vand.L.Rev. 561 (1953).

3. Chavis v. Chavis, 394 So.2d 54 (Ala.Civ.App. 1981); Chrastka v. Chrastka, 2 Ill.App.3d 722, 277 N.E.2d 729 (1971); Old Colony Trust Co. v. Porter, 324 Mass. 581, 586, 88 N.E.2d 135 (1949), approved on this point by

Fiorentino v. Probate Court, 365 Mass. 13, 310 N.E.2d 112 (1974); Wyman v. Wyman, 297 Minn. 465, 212 N.W.2d 368 (1973); Crownover v. Crownover, 58 N.M. 597, 274 P.2d 127 (1954); Redrow v. Redrow, 94 Ohio App. 38, 114 N.E.2d 293 (1952); Annot., 2 A.L.R.2d 291, 298 (1948). Particular statutes may state expressly that compliance is essential to subject matter jurisdiction. E.g., Nev.Rev. Stat. § 125.020 (1986).

4. Robinson v. Robinson, 70 Idaho 122, 212 P.2d 1031 (1949); Perry v. Copeland, 323 S.W.2d 339 (Tex.Civ.App. 1959). Lacks v. Lacks, 41 N.Y.2d 71, 390 N.Y.S.2d 875, 359 N.E.2d 384 (1976), reargument denied 41 N.Y.2d 862, 393 N.Y.S.2d 710, 362 N.E.2d 261 (1977) held that noncompliance with the statute on residence deprived the court of power to decide the merits of the case, but did not deprive it of competence to entertain the action, i.e. of subject matter jurisdiction. This is surely a distinction of a technicality worthy of medieval English land law. See also Annot., 2 A.L.R.2d 291 (1948).

5. Sosna v. Iowa, 419 U.S. 393, 95 S.Ct. 553, 42 L.Ed. 2d 532 (1975).

6. Williams v. State of North Carolina, 317 U.S. 287, 63 S.Ct. 207, 87 L.Ed. 279 (1942); Williams v. State of North Carolina, 325 U.S. 226, 65 S.Ct. 1092, 89 L.Ed. 1577 (1945), rehearing denied 325 U.S. 895, 65 S.Ct. 1560, 89 L.Ed. 2006 (1945).

7. Hartman v. Hartman, 89 Ill.App.3d 969, 45 Ill.Dec. 360, 412 N.E.2d 711 (1980). The statement in the text is obviously over-simplified, although the cases often state the rule in this form. There are circumstances in which a court has jurisdiction to decide on its own jurisdiction, and in which a finding of subject matter jurisdiction will be res judicata and not open to subsequent attack. See Restatement (Second) of Judgments §§ 11, 12, 69 (1982); Dobbs, Validation of Void Judgments: Bootstrap Principle, 53 Va.L.Rev. 1003, 1241 (1967).

8. Shapiro v. Thompson, 394 U.S. 618, 89 S.Ct. 1322, 22 L.Ed.2d 600 (1969) (residence requirements for welfare eligibility); Dunn v. Blumstein, 405 U.S. 330, 92 S.Ct.

constitutional on a variety of grounds.[9] In 1975, however, the Supreme Court in Sosna v. Iowa,[10] held that Iowa's one-year residence requirement for divorce jurisdiction was constitutional. The Court found that the statute served valid state purposes by preventing Iowa from becoming a "divorce mill" state which would interfere in the marital relations of spouses living in other states, and by minimizing the chance of collateral attack in other states on Iowa divorce decrees. Therefore the statute did not impermissibily discriminate against persons who had recently exercised their right to travel to Iowa. And since the effect of the statute was merely to delay and not to prevent the divorce action, the Court held there was no deprivation of due process.[11] Sosna seems to establish the validity of residence requirements for divorce which last no longer than one year, but longer or more complex requirements, such as New York's,[12] may still be constitutionally suspect if they go beyond the effectuation of the interests relied on in support of the Iowa statute. The question is largely academic since nearly all state statutes now impose requirements of a year or less.

Federal Jurisdiction in Domestic Relations Matters

The Supreme Court has said on several occasions that the federal courts sitting in the various states do not have jurisdiction to grant divorces, award alimony or determine the custody of children on divorce, even though there may be diversity of citizenship between the parties and the required amount in controversy.[13] The reasons for this judicial restriction upon power which Congress appears to have conferred on the federal courts are not clear although they have been much discussed in the cases. One explanation is historical. It is that a divorce was not a suit "of a civil nature at common law or equity" [14] pursuant to the original Judiciary Act conferring jurisdiction on the federal courts, since at the time that Act as passed divorces *a mensa et thoro* and annulments were the exclusive province of the English ecclesiastical courts, and divorces *a vinculo* were not granted by any English court.[15] Therefore, the argument goes, there being no ecclesiastical courts in the United States, divorces could hardly have been considered part of the business of either the common law or the equity courts.[16] The historical explanation has been

---

995, 31 L.Ed.2d 274 (1972) (voting rights); Memorial Hospital v. Maricopa County, 415 U.S. 250, 94 S.Ct. 1076, 39 L.Ed.2d 306 (1974) (residence requirements for medical care).

9. Cases pro and con on constitutionality are collected in Annot., 57 A.L.R.3d 221 (1974). The grounds for holding unconstitutional a requirement of a specified period of residency generally were that the requirement discriminated against recent arrivals in the state without being necessary to vindicate a compelling state interest and therefore violated the Equal Protection Clause of the Fourteenth Amendment, and that it violated the Due Process Clause by precluding the adjudication of a fundamental human relationship under Boddie v. Connecticut, 401 U.S. 371, 91 S.Ct. 780, 28 L.Ed.2d 113 (1971), mandate conformed 329 F.Supp. 844 (D.Conn.1971).

10. 419 U.S. 393, 95 S.Ct. 553, 42 L.Ed.2d 532 (1975).

11. The Court here distinguished Boddie v. Connecticut, 401 U.S. 371, 91 S.Ct. 780, 28 L.Ed. 113 (1971), mandate conformed 329 F.Supp. 844 (D.Conn.1971). That case had held that when a state required indigent divorce plaintiffs to pay filing fees in order to bring divorce suits this violated the Due Process Clause because it denied them an opportunity to be heard on the claimed dissolution of their marriage without sufficient state justification.

12. N.Y.—McKinney's Dom. Rel. Law § 230 (1977), establishing five different bases for qualification as a divorce plaintiff in New York.

13. Barber v. Barber, 62 U.S.(21 How.) 582, 16 L.Ed. 226 (1858); Ex parte Burrus, 136 U.S. 586, 10 S.Ct. 850, 34 L.Ed. 500 (1890); Simms v. Simms, 175 U.S. 162, 20 S.Ct. 58, 44 L.Ed. 115 (1899); De La Rama v. De La Rama, 201 U.S. 303, 26 S.Ct. 485, 50 L.Ed. 765 (1906); State of Ohio ex rel. Popovici v. Agler, 280 U.S. 379, 50 S.Ct. 154, 74 L.Ed. 489 (1930). See also C. Wright, A. Miller, E. Cooper, Federal Practice and Procedure § 3609 (1975).

14. The quoted language comes from the Judiciary Act of 1789, Ch. 20, § 11, 1 Stat. 78. Later codifications of the diversity jurisdiction do not include this language, but it is clear that they were not intended to change the meaning of the earlier act in this respect. See 28 U.S. C.A. § 1332(a), and Reviser's Note to 28 U.S.C.A. § 1332(a).

15. See the historical account of divorce in section 14.1, supra.

16. This historical explanation was first expressed by the dissenting justices in Barber v. Barber, 62 U.S.(21 How.) 582, 605, 16 L.Ed. 226 (1858). See also Justice Holmes' opinion in State of Ohio ex rel. Popovici v. Agler, 280 U.S. 379, 50 S.Ct. 154, 74 L.Ed. 489 (1930).

characterized as "not convincing" [17] and as "dubious and unhelpful." [18] So far as it rests on the English practice the history is accurate, [19] but there may be a question whether the first Judiciary Act should be construed to confer jurisdiction only to the extent it had existed in England, when in 1789 many American colonies had general divorce laws. [20]

Whether the historical reason for this limitation on federal jurisdiction is sound or not is of relatively little significance, as Judge Friendly has pointed out, since the Supreme Court has not shown any tendency to question its earlier cases and Congress has not amended the statute. [21] Although it remains correct to say that the federal courts do not grant divorces, except where sitting as territorial courts, [22] the courts' analysis of the reasons has changed entirely. The emphasis to-

day is on the federal courts' respect for state competence over divorce and related matters, [23] on the lack of experience with these matters in the federal courts, [24] and on the great additional burdens which would be imposed on the federal courts if divorce jurisdiction were to be assumed by them. [25] This line of reasoning has led some of the lower federal courts to treat the "domestic relations exception" as an instance of abstention or of refusal on the ground of comity to exercise a jurisdiction which they do in fact possess. [26] In any event this exception to federal jurisdiction is sometimes said to be "rather narrowly confined". [27] In many other parts of this work there are examples of the Supreme Court's expansion of its review of state court domestic relations cases on constitutional grounds. [28] This sort of case has never been considered to fall within the "domestic relations exception".

17. Spindel v. Spindel, 283 F.Supp. 797 (E.D.N.Y. 1968). This case contains a scholarly review of federal jurisdiction in domestic relations cases.

18. Lloyd v. Loeffler, 694 F.2d 489, 492 (7th Cir.1982).

19. It is clear that the English ecclesiastical courts had exclusive jurisdiction over marriage, divorce *a mensa*, alimony and annulment until 1857. 1 F. Pollock and F. Maitland, History of English Law 127, 2 Id. 367 (Rev.ed.1968); D. Tolstoy, Divorce 1 (7th ed.1971); A. Winnett, Divorce and Remarriage in Anglicanism passim (1958); F. Emmison, Elizabethan Life 164–168 (1973); 3 W. Blackstone, Commentaries on the Laws of England 87–103 (Lewis ed.1900). Custody jurisdiction as we know it was not often in question due to the rule that the child's father nearly always was entitled to custody, but custody could be litigated in the common law courts in habeas corpus proceedings and in the equity courts by petition. Shelley v. Westbrooke, Jacob 265, 37 Eng.Rep. 850 (ch.1817); Petit, Parental Control and Guardianship, in R. Graveson and F. Crane, A Century of Family Law 56 (1957). But litigation over children was more often concerned with property and with what we would call the guardianship of the estate. Ratcliff's Case, 3 Co.Rep. 37, 76 Eng.Rep. 713 (1592); H. Bell, The Court of Wards and Liveries (1953).

20. II G. Howard, History of Matrimonial Institutions 328–387 (1904).

21. See note 14, supra. Judge Friendly's comment is found in Phillips, Nizer, Benjamin, Krim & Ballon v. Rosenstiel, 490 F.2d 509, 514 (2d Cir.1973).

22. Congress has general legislative power respecting the territories and therefore the federal courts may hear divorces from the territories. Simms v. Simms, 175 U.S. 162, 20 S.Ct. 58, 44 L.Ed. 115 (1899); De La Rama v. De La Rama, 201 U.S. 303, 26 S.Ct. 485, 50 L.Ed. 765 (1906). And of course the federal courts have heard divorce cases coming from the District of Columbia. Bottomley v. Bottomley, 262 F.2d 23 (D.C.Cir.1958).

The federal courts have uniformly denied federal jurisdiction when an attempt has been made to sue for divorce in a federal court sitting in a state or to remove to the federal court a divorce action brought in a state court. Anderson v. State of Nebraska, 530 F.Supp. 19 (D.Neb. 1981), appeal dismissed 668 F.2d 349 (8th Cir.1981); Patterson v. Patterson, 381 F.Supp. 1029 (D.Colo.1974); Blank v. Blank, 320 F.Supp. 1389 (W.D.Pa.1971); In re Wilson, 314 F.Supp. 271 (E.D.Tenn.1970).

23. Crouch v. Crouch, 566 F.2d 486 (5th Cir.1978); Solomon v. Solomon, 516 F.2d 1018 (3d Cir.1975).

24. Phillips, Nizer, Benjamin, Krim & Ballon v. Rosenstiel, 490 F.2d 509 (2d Cir.1973); Firestone v. Cleveland Trust Co., 654 F.2d 1212 (6th Cir. 1981).

25. Armstrong v. Armstrong, 508 F.2d 348 (1st Cir. 1974).

26. Armstrong v. Armstrong, 508 F.2d 348 (1st Cir. 1974); Davis v. Davis, 558 F.Supp. 485 (N.D.Miss.1983); Zimmerman v. Zimmerman, 395 F.Supp. 719 (E.D.Pa. 1975); Lutsky v. Lutsky, 310 F.Supp. 517 (S.D.Fla.1970), judgment affirmed 433 F.2d 346 (5th Cir.1970).

27. Armstrong v. Armstrong, 508 F.2d 348 (1st Cir. 1974); Phillips, Nizer, Benjamin, Krim & Ballon v. Rosenstiel, 490 F.2d 509, 514 (2d Cir.1973).

28. Obviously the Supreme Court may and often does review state court domestic relations cases on constitutional grounds, even where such cases involve divorce, custody, alimony or child support. See, e.g., Williams v. North Carolina, 317 U.S. 287, 63 S.Ct. 207, 87 L.Ed. 279 (1942); Williams v. North Carolina, 325 U.S. 226, 65 S.Ct. 1092, 89 L.Ed. 1577 (1945), rehearing denied 325 U.S. 895, 65 S.Ct. 1560, 89 L.Ed. 2006 (1945) (full faith and credit to divorce decrees); Estin v. Estin, 334 U.S. 541, 68 S.Ct. 1213, 92 L.Ed. 1561 (1948) (full faith and credit to alimony judgments); Kulko v. Superior Court, 436 U.S. 84, 98 S.Ct. 1690, 56 L.Ed.2d 132 (1978), rehearing denied 438 U.S. 908, 98 S.Ct. 3127, 57 L.Ed.2d 1150 (1978) (jurisdic-

And in a few instances the Congress has expressly given the United States district courts jurisdiction in certain domestic relations cases.[29] The question raised by the "domestic relations exception" at this point is how far the district courts may go in taking on the large variety of cases which, although they are not divorces or the property or custody incidents of divorces, can be considered to be domestic relations cases. If the exception is narrowly confined, in other words, how far may it expand?

One might think, in consideration of the cogent reasons advanced in support of the exception, that the federal district courts and courts of appeal would be reluctant to explore the "thicket" [30] of state domestic relations law when for so long the Supreme Court has excused them from doing so. Although the exception has been held to apply to federal question jurisdiction [31] as well as to diversity jurisdiction, the cases do exhibit a tendency to expand into domestic relations in reliance upon both branches of jurisdiction albeit with much uncertainty, confusion and disagree-

ment. The federal district courts seem understandably less willing to take on domestic relations cases than the courts of appeals.

Where the purpose of the federal suit is to enforce a final alimony decree of a state and there is no question of continuing supervision or of modification of the state decree, so that the suit is strictly one for money damages, it is usually held that, diversity and amount in controversy being present, the federal court may hear the case.[32] The same result is reached where the suit is brought to enforce a separation agreement's provisions for alimony, property or child support, so long as no questions of status exist and so long as there is no possibility of conflict with state proceedings in the same case.[33] These are relatively clear cases for the exercise of federal jurisdiction. But if there is still a state proceeding pending,[34] if the federal court's decision may conflict with a state decision in the same case,[35] or if the enforcement of a separation agreement would involve the federal court in the status of wives or children or in continu-

tion to enter child support order); May v. Anderson, 345 U.S. 528, 73 S.Ct. 840, 97 L.Ed. 1221 (1953) (full faith and credit to custody decrees). And see section 4.2, supra, for the Supreme Court's decisions on the status of the illegitimate child.

29. E.g., 42 U.S.C.A. § 660, giving the district courts jurisdiction over child support claims in certain instances, without regard to amount in controversy.

The Parental Kidnapping Prevention Act, 28 U.S.C.A. § 1738A has been held to create federal question jurisdiction in certain custody cases in Flood v. Braaten, 727 F.2d 303 (3d Cir.1984), discussed infra in section 12.5.

30. The word is Judge Friendly's in Phillips, Nizer, Benjamin, Krim & Ballon v. Rosenstiel, 490 F.2d 509, 516 (2d Cir.1973). A good example of the great expenditure of time and effort caused by a federal court's attempt to deal with the intricacies of state divorce law is Fehlhaber v. Fehlhaber, 681 F.2d 1015 (5th Cir.1982), rehearing denied 702 F.2d 81 (5th Cir.1983), cert. denied 464 U.S. 818, 104 S.Ct. 79, 78 L.Ed.2d 90 (1983), in which the Fifth Circuit, sitting en banc reversed a panel decision. But the academic calls for limiting or ending the domestic relations exception continue. Note, The Domestic Relations Exception to Diversity Jurisdiction, 83 Colum.L.Rev. 1824 (1983); Note, Federal Jurisdiction and the Domestic Relations Exception: A Search for Parameters, 31 U.C. L.A.L.Rev. 843 (1984); Wand, A Call for the Repudiation of the Domestic Relations Exception to Federal Jurisdiction, 30 Vill.L.Rev. 307 (1985).

31. Firestone v. Cleveland Trust Co., 654 F.2d 1212 (6th Cir. 1981). Contra: Flood v. Braaten, 727 F.2d 303

(3d Cir. 1984); Ruffalo by Ruffalo v. Civiletti, 702 F.2d 710 (8th Cir. 1983), on remand 565 F.Supp. 34 (W.D.Mo. 1983).

32. Barber v. Barber, 62 U.S.(21 How.) 582, 16 L.Ed. 226 (1858); Harrison v. Harrison, 214 F.2d 571 (4th Cir. 1954), cert. denied 348 U.S. 896, 75 S.Ct. 217, 99 L.Ed. 704 (1954) (the court held a Mexican divorce invalid and then enforced a prior alimony decree); Smith v. Smith, 217 F.2d 917 (6th Cir. 1954).

33. Jagiella v. Jagiella, 647 F.2d 561 (5th Cir.1981), rehearing denied 654 F.2d 723 (5th Cir.1981); Crouch v. Crouch, 566 F.2d 486 (5th Cir.1978); Solomon v. Solomon, 516 F.2d 1018 (3d Cir.1975) (dictum); Korby v. Erickson, 550 F.Supp. 136 (S.D.N.Y.1982); Zimmerman v. Zimmerman, 395 F.Supp. 719 (E.D.Pa.1975); Cain v. King, 313 F.Supp. 10 (E.D.La.1970). In the somewhat unusual case of Cole v. Cole, 633 F.2d 1083 (4th Cir.1980) the court held that the domestic relations exception did not apply to a man's suit against his ex-wife for harassment, malicious prosecution, assault and battery and conspiracy to burn his house, even though her alleged conduct grew out of their former relationship.

34. Bossom v. Bossom, 551 F.2d 474 (2d Cir.1976); Solomon v. Solomon, 516 F.2d 1018 (3d Cir.1975); Robinson v. Robinson, 523 F.Supp. 96 (E.D.Pa.1981).

35. Fusaro v. Fusaro, 550 F.Supp. 1260 (E.D.Pa.1982). The case here involved a husband suing for breach of contract and fraud arising out of a separation agreement. The court said he was trying to play the federal court off against the state court.

ing supervision of its decree,[36] the jurisdiction will normally not be assumed. *A fortiori* the jurisdiction should not be assumed where a divorce decree in state court is silent on the question of alimony or property and the plaintiff spouse seeks such an award from a federal court.[37] The Phillips, Nizer case [38] held that a federal court should abstain from exercise of jurisdiction where a wife's lawyer sued a husband to recover fees for services rendered to the wife in a divorce suit and in other legal matters. Judge Friendly, in so holding, relied not so much on the historical argument as on the impracticality of having federal courts deal with state law concerning the doctrine of necessaries, and on the fact that the domestic relations exception has been a part of judge-made federal jurisprudence for over a century.

The uncertainty in the current status of the domestic relations exception as applied to the financial or property aspects of the husband-wife relationship is illustrated by the Spindel case.[39] The federal district court there held that it had jurisdiction to hear a case in which a wife sought to invalidate her husband's Mexican divorce and to recover damages for his alleged fraud in inducing her to

marry him and in later obtaining the Mexican divorce. The court's opinion is chiefly concerned with establishing that there was both common law and equity jurisdiction over some domestic relations matters in England before 1789 and thus with destroying the historical basis for the exception. The court rejected the argument for state expertise in domestic relations and largely ignored the risk of increasing congestion in federal court dockets if domestic relations cases were to be heard there.

The uncertainty and confusion are compounded where the custody of children, as distinguished from alimony or property, is the subject of the claim in the federal courts. One line of cases holds that the federal district courts may hear a parent's claim for damages against the other parent or against strangers for the enticement or abduction of his child. The leading example is Lloyd v. Loeffler.[40] In that case the father of an illegitimate child who had custody pursuant to a state court decree sued the child's mother and her parents when the mother failed to return the child after a period of visitation, keeping her location and that of the child a secret so effectively that the father was unable to find them. The Seventh Circuit questioned the his-

---

36. Csibi v. Fustos, 670 F.2d 134 (9th Cir.1982) (federal court has no jurisdiction to hear claims to a man's estate which involves determining the status of alleged wives); Firestone v. Cleveland Trust Co., 654 F.2d 1212 (6th Cir. 1981) (should not exercise jurisdiction where the wife and sons were essentially trying to determine the husband's present and future obligations under a property settlement agreement); Armstrong v. Armstrong, 508 F.2d 348 (1st Cir.1974) (abstention appropriate where the claim involved the examination of family needs and the husband's ability to pay support); Davis v. Davis, 558 F.Supp. 485 (N.D.Miss.1983) (federal court should not modify a property settlement agreement); Smith v. Smith, 559 F.Supp. 107 (S.D.Ohio 1982) (no jurisdiction to deal with a husband's defenses to a separation agreement and decree); Lewis v. Lewis, 543 F.Supp. 35 (M.D.Pa.1981) (no jurisdiction to determine husband's past and future obligations under a separation agreement). Contra: Van Gaalen v. Sparks, 555 F.Supp. 325 (E.D.Va.1983) (court has jurisdiction of a suit for breach of a separation agreement though it is conceded that this will involve the wife's needs and the husband's ability to pay).

37. Williamson v. Williamson, 306 F.Supp. 516 (W.D. Okl.1969).

38. Phillips, Nizer, Benjamin, Krim & Ballon v. Rosenstiel, 490 F.2d 509 (2d Cir.1973). The disposition of the case was that since the defendant had failed to make

a timely motion for a stay, it was not an abuse of discretion for the trial court to decide the merits. If a timely motion had been made, it should have been granted.

39. Spindel v. Spindel, 283 F.Supp. 797 (E.D.N.Y. 1968). Vann v. Vann, 294 F.Supp. 193 (E.D.Tenn.1968) also held that a federal court had jurisdiction to determine the validity of a divorce decree attacked for fraud. But Lutsky v. Lutsky, 310 F.Supp. 517 (S.D.Fla.1970), affirmed p.c. 433 F.2d 346 (5th Cir.1970) refused to exercise jurisdiction to declare a state divorce void where the state court had refused to set its decree aside.

40. 694 F.2d 489 (7th Cir.1982). Cases reaching a similar result, where a parent sued under the diversity jurisdiction for abduction or "child-snatching", include Bennett v. Bennett, 682 F.2d 1039 (D.C.Cir.1982), on remand 595 F.Supp. 366 (D.D.C.1984); Raftery v. Scott, 756 F.2d 335 (4th Cir.1985); Wasserman v. Wasserman, 671 F.2d 832 (4th Cir.1982), cert. denied 459 U.S. 1014, 103 S.Ct. 372, 74 L.Ed.2d 507 (1982); Acord v. Parsons, 551 F.Supp. 115 (W.D.Va.1982). The Bennett case illustrates the incongruity of federal court action by holding that the federal court could award damages to a parent when the other parent wrongfully removed the child from the state, but that it could not award an injunction, since that would entail an inquiry into the child's best interests, a matter for the state courts.

torical basis for refusing federal jurisdiction, found that this case did not seek divorce, custody, alimony or child support and therefore lay outside the "core" of the domestic relations exception, and also found that it was not ancillary to any case within that "core". For these reasons the court affirmed an award of compensatory damages against the maternal grandparents on the ground that they had conspired with the child's mother to interfere with the father's custody, in violation of the outstanding custody decree.[41] A number of other cases have held, in a variety of contexts, either that there is no federal jurisdiction respecting custody of children or that such jurisdiction should not be exercised, notwithstanding that diversity of citizenship and amount in controversy exist.[42]

Where the additional factor of an alleged violation of constitutional rights is injected into the domestic relations case, and the plaintiff therefore relies upon the federal Civil Rights Act,[43] the courts have been no less in doubt whether they may provide a remedy. The particular facts of the case may persuade the court that only a typical family law dispute is involved, so that there is no jurisdiction under the Civil Rights Act.[44] On the other hand, if the dispute is of such a nature that complete relief is not available in the state courts, the federal court will be inclined to give relief, especially if the violation of constitutional rights is clear.[45] Still other cases seem to avoid the issue by grounding their decision on other elements of the case.[46]

41. The trial court in Lloyd v. Loeffler, 539 F.Supp. 998 (E.D.Wis.1982) awarded, in addition to compensatory damages, punitive damages against the child's mother and her then husband, adding the ingenious provision that the punitive damages would increase by $2,000 for each month in which the defendants continued to conceal the child from the plaintiff. The Seventh Circuit refused to approve this feature of the punitive damages award, relying upon the Bennett case, cited supra, note 40, and saying that this would involve a ruling as to who should have custody of the child for the future, a matter apparently not within the subject-matter jurisdiction of the federal court. Lloyd v. Loeffler, 694 F.2d 489, 494 (7th Cir.1982).

The situation is vastly complicated by the enactment of the Parental Kidnapping Prevention Act of 1980, 28 U.S. C.A. § 1738A, which attempts to define the circumstances in which state custody decrees are to be given full faith and credit. It has been held that this Act gives the federal courts jurisdiction to decide which of two conflicting state custody decrees is to control a child's custody, thereby putting the federal courts directly into the business of determining custody. Flood v. Braaten, 727 F.2d 303 (3d Cir.1984); DiRuggiero v. Rodgers, 743 F.2d 1009 (3d Cir.1984).

42. Schleiffer v. Meyers, 644 F.2d 656 (7th Cir.1981), cert. denied 454 U.S. 823, 102 S.Ct. 110, 70 L.Ed.2d 96 (1981) (refuses to hear child's claim to enjoin enforcement of a Swedish custody order, the child not wishing to be taken to Sweden); Bergstrom v. Bergstrom, 623 F.2d 517 (8th Cir.1980) (daughter's suit to enjoin her removal to Norway dismissed, on the ground the case was pending in the state courts); Buechold v. Ortiz, 401 F.2d 371 (9th Cir. 1968) (suit to establish paternity dismissed); Kilduff v. Kilduff, 473 F.Supp. 873 (S.D.N.Y.1979) (no federal jurisdiction of wife's suit for false imprisonment of her children, breach of a custody agreement and deprivation of custody); Cherry v. Cherry, 438 F.Supp. 88 (D.Md.1977) (dismisses wife's damage action for breach of visitation provisions of a separation agreement occurring when husband removed child from the state).

43. 42 U.S.C.A. §§ 1983, 1985, 1986.

44. Denman v. Leedy, 479 F.2d 1097 (6th Cir.1973). The case does not deal with the question whether the domestic relations exception applies to federal question cases.

45. Ruffalo by Ruffalo v. Civiletti, 702 F.2d 710 (8th Cir.1983), on remand 565 F.Supp. 34 (W.D.Mo.1983). In this case a mother sued federal officials for keeping her son from her by leaving him with his father who was in hiding under the federal witness protection program and whose whereabouts was being kept from the plaintiff. The court characterized the historical basis for the domestic relations exception as probably incorrect, said it has no application to federal question cases, and that its basic premise is that a state court could give relief. It then found that state relief would not be effective against the federal officials who were defendants here. See also Ruffalo v. United States, 590 F.Supp. 706 (W.D.Mo.1984). Dennison v. Vietch, 560 F.Supp. 435 (D.Minn.1983) granted damages to an unmarried father when police entered his home without a warrant and deprived him of custody of his child. This occurred in the course of a dispute over custody between the father and the child's mother. The case fails to discuss the domestic relations exception to federal jurisdiction. The domestic relations exception was held not applicable to a 1983 suit in Hooks v. Hooks, 771 F.2d 935 (6th Cir.1985).

46. E.g., Ellis v. Hamilton, 669 F.2d 510 (7th Cir.1982), cert. denied 459 U.S. 1069, 103 S.Ct. 488, 74 L.Ed.2d 631 (1982), where the court affirmed a summary judgment for the defendants, partly on the ground that the plaintiffs' custody rights were not clear and therefore the alleged invasion of constitutional right was not clear, and partly on the ground that the state courts provided ample remedies. The court seemed to assume that the domestic relations exception would apply to federal question jurisdiction, but did not discuss the point. Wise v. Bravo, 666 F.2d 1328 (10th Cir.1981) held that the alleged interference with a parent's custody was too insubstantial to amount to a constitutional deprivation. Newton v. Burgin, 363 F.Supp. 782 (W.D.N.C. 1973), affirmed 414 U.S. 1139, 94 S.Ct. 889, 39 L.Ed.2d 96 (1974), a suit for declaratory judgment not brought under the Civil Rights Act,

A federal habeas corpus proceeding pursuant to the statute [47] is another conceivable remedy for a parent wishing to raise constitutional issues arising out of a custody dispute. In the past the lower courts have reached differing conclusion on the availability of this remedy.[48] The Supreme Court has now resolved a conflict in the circuits by holding that federal habeas is not available to a parent whose rights have been terminated by a state court proceeding under an allegedly unconstitutional state statute.[49] The Court in reaching this conclusion reasoned that a child placed in a foster home by the state is not in "custody" in the sense that term is used in the habeas statute; that federal habeas has traditionally not been used to determine custody; and that the use of the federal writ would impair the finality and certainty so much to be desired in custody cases since the doctrine of res judicata does not apply to federal habeas corpus petitions.

It is ironical that the historical argument, so much disputed in the cases dealing with the domestic relations exception to federal diversity jurisdiction, is clear with respect to habeas corpus. The writ was certainly available for the purpose of hearing custody disputes in the English courts before the founding of the United States.[50] The dissent in Lehman makes the point forcefully and the majority opinion acknowledges it, but distinguishes between state habeas corpus, which it characterizes as just another procedure for resolving custody disputes, and federal habeas corpus which, if available, would lead to collateral challenges to state court decisions. The Court in this way seems implicitly to evince respect for state competence in custody matters, but it does not discuss the domestic relations exception to federal jurisdiction in general. And it seems to approve a statement from a First Circuit case [51] that state decisions on custody may be challenged by other procedures, including the civil rights statutes.[52]

The extent to which the federal courts may act in the variety of domestic relations cases which litigants today bring to them remains a baffling question. Although the limitations on their authority are said to be narrowly confined, presumably because not spelled out in the statutory grants of jurisdiction, such considerations as lack of familiarity with the law of domestic relations in general and with local variations on that law, the desirability of avoiding conflicts with state court decisions, the inability of federal courts to provide the continuing supervision which many cases demand and the consequent inability to provide full relief for the parties, and the prospect of a sizable increase in docket congestion in the federal courts resulting from the assumption of jurisdiction in such cases, all suggest that the traditional reluctance of the Supreme Court and of many of the lower courts to act in such cases was and is wise judicial administration. It is the rare case indeed in which the federal remedy is the

resulted in a summary judgment for the defendant on the ground that no constitutional violation was shown, no discussion of the domestic relations exception being mentioned.

47. 28 U.S.C.A. § 2254(a), which authorizes federal judges to entertain applications for habeas corpus on behalf of persons in custody pursuant to a state court judgment on the ground that the custody violates the constitution, laws or treaties of the United States.

48. E.g., Sylvander v. New England Home For Little Wanderers, 584 F.2d 1103 (1st Cir.1978) holding federal habeas not available in custody cases; Davis v. Page, 640 F.2d 599 (5th Cir.1981) holding it was available. The Davis case was vacated and remanded, 458 U.S. 1118, 102 S.Ct. 3504, 73 L.Ed.2d 1380 (1982). The opinion on the remand dealing with the right to counsel in proceedings for the termination of parental rights is Davis v. Page, 714 F.2d 512 (5th Cir.1983), cert. denied 464 U.S. 1052, 104 S.Ct. 735, 79 L.Ed.2d 194 (1984).

49. Lehman v. Lycoming County Children's Services Agency, 458 U.S. 502, 102 S.Ct. 3231, 73 L.Ed.2d 928 (1982). The mother of three children in this case sought federal habeas corpus from a United States District Court after her parental rights had been terminated by a Pennsylvania state court whose decision was affirmed by the Supreme Court of Pennsylvania. Her petition for certiorari seeking review of the Pennsylvania Supreme Court's decision was denied, 439 U.S. 880, 99 S.Ct. 216, 58 L.Ed. 2d 192 (1978). Her claim was that the Pennsylvania statute pursuant to which her rights had been terminated was unconstitutional.

50. See section 19.3, infra.

51. Sylvander v. New England Home For Little Wanderers, 584 F.2d 1103, 1111 (1st Cir.1978).

52. See the cases cited supra, at notes 43 to 46.

only remedy or is superior to the state remedy. Unless it is, the parties should be left to their state remedy. Federal constitutional limitations can be exerted by the Supreme Court through the usual methods of certiorari or appeal.

Indian Divorces

Since early in the history of the United States the Supreme Court has taken the position that the federal government rather than the state governments has primary authority to enact laws regulating the Indian tribes, and that the federal laws and treaties setting aside Indian reservations implicitly reserved to the tribes the power of self-government over tribal territory free of state interference.[53] Subject to that federal power, many tribes have exercised considerable self-government.[54] The consequence is that the question of what courts have jurisdiction over civil proceedings, including divorce, to which Indians are parties and which arise in Indian territory, may be affected by a complex interaction of federal law, Indian tribal law and state law.[55]

A federal statute passed in 1953 gave the consent of the United States to the assumption by the states of jurisdiction over civil actions to which Indians were parties and which arose on reservations.[56] Some states did act to assert jurisdiction pursuant to this statute, and where they did so, the state courts were empowered to grant divorces to Indians, a power which they still retain.[57] On the other hand, in those states which did not pass statutes or constitutional provisions asserting the jurisdiction, the tribal courts retained exclusive jurisdiction over the divorces of Indians on the reservations.[58] In 1968 the 1953 statute was amended to provide that the states could assert jurisdiction respecting civil actions between Indians arising in Indian country only with the consent of the tribe occupying the particular Indian country.[59] Thus if the tribal laws include provisions governing the divorces of Indians, the tribal courts will have exclusive divorce jurisdiction.[60]

Where the spouses seeking a divorce live off the reservation, the state courts would have jurisdiction.[61] The situation is less clear when the spouses live on the reservation but one is an Indian and the other is not. Apparently the rule is that an Indian plaintiff may sue either in the state court or the tribal

---

53. Worcester v. Georgia, 31 U.S. (6 Pet.) 515, 8 L.Ed. 483 (1832); United States v. Kagama, 118 U.S. 375, 6 S.Ct. 1109, 30 L.Ed. 228 (1886); Williams v. Lee, 358 U.S. 217, 79 S.Ct. 269, 3 L.Ed.2d 251 (1959); F. Cohen, Handbook of Federal Indian Law ch. 5 (Rev.ed.1982).

54. Collins, Implied Limitations on the Jurisdiction of Indian Tribes, 54 Wash.L.Rev. 479 (1979).

55. See Begay v. Miller, 70 Ariz. 380, 222 P.2d 624 (1950).

56. Public Law 83–280, Act of Aug. 15, 1953, ch. 505, 67 Stat. 588, part of which is codified as 18 U.S.C.A. § 1162. See F. Cohen, Handbook of Federal Indian Law 362 (Rev.ed.1982); Goldberg, Public Law 280: The Limits of State Jurisdiction Over Reservation Indians, 22 U.C. L.A.L.Rev. 535 (1975).

57. Fisher v. Fisher, 104 Idaho 68, 656 P.2d 129 (1982). Sheppard v. Sheppard, 104 Idaho 1, 655 P.2d 895 (1982) held that in the exercise of this divorce jurisdiction the state court could divide the community property of the spouses. The Idaho statute asserting state jurisdiction over divorce (among other matters) is Idaho Code § 67–5101 (1980).

58. Conroy v. Conroy, 575 F.2d 175 (8th Cir.1978); Whyte v. District Court of Montezuma County, 140 Colo. 334, 346 P.2d 1012 (1959), cert. denied 363 U.S. 829, 80 S.Ct. 1600, 4 L.Ed.2d 1624 (1960).

59. 25 U.S.C.A. § 1322 (1982).

60. Leon v. Numkena, 142 Ariz. 307, 689 P.2d 566 (1984); In re Marriage of Limpy, 195 Mont. 314, 636 P.2d 266 (1981), overruling Bad Horse v. Bad Horse, 163 Mont. 445, 517 P.2d 893 (1974), cert. denied 419 U.S. 847, 95 S.Ct. 83, 42 L.Ed.2d 76 (1974). In Fisher v. District Court of Sixteenth Judicial District, 424 U.S. 382, 96 S.Ct. 943, 47 L.Ed.2d 106 (1976), rehearing denied 425 U.S. 926, 96 S.Ct. 1524, 47 L.Ed.2d 772 (1976) the Supreme Court held that a tribal court had exclusive jurisdiction of an adoption proceeding arising on the reservation, in which all parties were members of the tribe residing on the reservation. The Court stated the controlling issue in such cases to be whether state court jurisdiction would interfere with the powers of self-government conferred upon the tribe by federal law and exercised by the tribal courts. But the state courts will have jurisdiction over the divorces of Indians living on a reservation if the tribal courts relinquish jurisdiction to the state. Desjarlait v. Desjarlait, 379 N.W.2d 139 (Minn.App.1985).

61. Voorhees v. Spencer, 89 Nev. 1, 504 P.2d 1321 (1973). If there are both on- and off-reservation contacts, the courts will balance the contacts to determine whether the state courts may exercise jurisdiction. See Wisconsin Potowatomies of Hannahville Indian Community v. Houston, 393 F.Supp. 719 (W.D.Mich.1973); Wakefield v. Little Light, 276 Md. 333, 347 A.2d 228 (1975).

court where the defendant is the non-Indian, but that the tribal court has exclusive jurisdiction where the Indian is the defendant, and that the state court will recognize the tribal court decree on the basis of comity or of full faith and credit.[62]

The Indian Child Welfare Act [63] might be thought to affect the question of jurisdiction over one aspect of Indian divorces, since it provides that the tribal courts have exclusive jurisdiction over any child custody proceeding involving an Indian child residing or domiciled on the reservation. But the Act's narrow definition of "child custody proceeding"[64] seems to exclude divorce proceedings, so that apparently jurisdiction for divorce is not controlled by this statute.

Notice and Opportunity to be Heard: Due Process

It is elementary that the defendant in divorce, as in other civil actions, must be given notice of the suit and an opportunity to be heard.[65] The Supreme Court has said in the Mullane case that due process demands "notice reasonably calculated, under all the circumstances, to apprise interested parties of the pendency of the action and afford them an opportunity to present their objections".[66] Since divorce is one of those kinds of lawsuit sometimes described as *in rem*, however, the various forms of constructive service are permitted.[67] If the defendant's whereabouts is not known and cannot be discovered by the exercise of diligence, constructive service may take the form of service by publication,[68] a

---

62. See Three Affiliated Tribes of the Fort Berthold Reservation v. Wold Engineering, P.C., 467 U.S. 138, 147–150, 104 S.Ct. 2267, 2274–2275, 81 L.Ed.2d 113 (1984), on remand 364 N.W.2d 98 (N.D.1985) and F. Cohen, Handbook of Federal Indian Law 354–355 (Rev.ed.1982), citing other cases.

On the recognition in state court of tribal court decrees see Mexican v. Circle Bear, 370 N.W.2d 737 (S.D.1985) (comity); Matter of Marriage of Red Fox, 23 Or.App. 393, 542 P.2d 918 (1975) (comity); Sheppard v. Sheppard, 104 Idaho 1, 655 P.2d 895 (1982) (full faith and credit). See generally Lawrence, Service of Process and Execution of Judgments in Indian Reservations, 10 Am.Ind.L.Rev. 257, 274–278 (1982); Ragsdale, Problems in the Application of Full Faith and Credit for Indian Tribes, 7 N.M.L.Rev. 133 (1977).

63. 25 U.S.C.A. § 1911.

64. 25 U.S.C.A. § 1903(1) seems to limit "child custody proceeding" to include only foster care placements, suits terminating parental rights, preadoptive placements and adoptive placements, thereby excluding divorce actions from the operation of the Act.

But a child custody proceeding involving an Indian child living on the reservation with an Indian parent is normally within the jurisdiction of the tribal court, not the state court. Malaterre v. Malaterre, 293 N.W.2d 139 (N.D.1980).

65. Atherton v. Atherton, 181 U.S. 155, 21 S.Ct. 544, 45 L.Ed. 794 (1901); Williams v. State of North Carolina, 317 U.S. 287, 299, 63 S.Ct. 207, 213, 87 L.Ed. 279 (1942); United States v. Smith, 398 F.2d 173 (3d Cir. 1968); Gardner v. Perkins, 41 Md.App. 632, 398 A.2d 480 (1979); Dillon v. Dillon, 46 Wis.2d 659, 176 N.W.2d 362 (1970); Restatement (Second) of Conflict of Laws § 69 (1971).

66. Mullane v. Central Hanover Bank & Trust Co., 339 U.S. 306, 314, 70 S.Ct. 652, 657, 94 L.Ed. 865 (1950).

67. Atherton v. Atherton, 181 U.S. 155, 21 S.Ct. 544, 45 L.Ed. 794 (1901); Rediker v. Rediker, 35 Cal.2d 796, 221 P.2d 1 (1950); Edwards v. Edwards, 481 P.2d 432

(Colo.App. 1970), cert. denied 404 U.S. 850, 92 S.Ct. 79, 30 L.Ed.2d 89; McClellan v. McClellan, 125 Ill.App.2d 477, 261 N.E.2d 216 (1970); Fleek v. Fleek, 270 N.C. 736, 155 S.E.2d 290 (1967). See also N.Y.Civ.Prac.L. & R. 315 (1972).

The *in rem-in personam* distinction is no longer helpful as a reason for making differing service requirements, but it still is useful as a shorthand method of classification of the cass. See Williams v. North Carolina, 317 U.S. 287, 63 S.Ct. 207, 87 L.Ed.2d 279 (1942), and Carr v. Carr, 46 N.Y.2d 270, 413 N.Y.S.2d 305, 385 N.E.2d 1234 (1978). The reason for permitting constructive service in divorce actions is not that some mystical "res" called the status of marriage is involved in such cases, but rather that if it were not permitted one spouse could put the divorce out of the power of the other by leaving the jurisdiction, and, in the extreme case, by ensuring that his whereabouts was not known to the other spouse. Courts have thought that it is sufficiently desirable for a spouse to be able to terminate his marriage when the law of his domicile permits it and when he wishes to do so that the usual rules about personal jurisdiction over the defendant should not apply. Or, to put it another way, the idea is that the state of a spouse's domicile should be able to control that spouse's marital status even though the defendant spouse absents himself or lives in some other state. These forms of public policy are merely summed up by labeling divorce an *in rem* proceeding. See, e.g., Atherton v. Atherton, 181 U.S. 155, 21 S.Ct. 544, 45 L.Ed. 794 (1901).

68. N.Y.Civ.Prac.L. & R. 314, 315 (1972); Fleek v. Fleek, 270 N.C. 736, 155 S.E.2d 290 (1967). Restatement (Second) of Conflict of Laws § 69, com. b (1971) expresses doubt whether service by publication in divorce actions would be constitutional, but the cases cited do not support such doubt, and it seems unlikely that the Supreme Court would take such a position. If the Court did, it would be condemning some spouses to perpetual marriage solely because the other spouse had departed the marriage and could not thereafter be located.

method not likely to come to the notice of the defendant. And some jurisdictions have accepted the suggestion of the Supreme Court in the Boddie case [69] to authorize service by posting a notice, which is equally unlikely to be seen by the divorce defendant.

To this extent therefore the requirement of notice in divorce actions is fictional. The requirement does have important practical consequences in most cases, so that, for example, if a plaintiff knows where the defendant is or could find out where he is but does not serve him by a method calculated to reach him, relying instead upon publication or posting, the decree so obtained will be invalid and may be set aside.[70]

The Due Process Clause may also be violated if the plaintiffs, rather than the defendants, are deprived of the opportunity to have their claims heard in a divorce action. Boddie v. Connecticut [71] involved the application of a state statute to indigent plaintiffs which provided that court fees and costs of service had to be paid into court in order or bring suit for divorce. The plaintiffs, indigent persons who proved that they were unable to pay the fees and therefore unable to obtain a divorce in the state of their domicile, sued to have the

statute declared unconstitutional as applied to them. The Supreme Court held that the statute did violate the Due Process Clause. The Court reasoned that the statute denied this class of plaintiffs an opportunity to be heard without being justified by a significant countervailing state interest. At the same time it appeared to confine its decision to actions for divorce, on the ground that divorce differs from other civil actions in that in Connecticut (and in all other states as well) a divorce proceeding is the only method by which the parties may resolve their dispute and adjust their marital relations. As the Court put it, a divorce is "the exclusive precondition to the adjustment of a fundamental human relationship." [72] Since service by publication often entails considerable expense, the Court suggested that some sort of posted notice might be sufficient in those cases where publication would normally be used, that is, where the defendant's whereabouts was unknown. If publication is required, the Boddie case seems to mean that the state must bear this expense, but the state cases are divided on the point.[73] The state courts have not taken the next logical step of holding that the state must pay the attorney fees of indigents in divorce actions.[74]

---

69. Boddie v. Connecticut, 401 U.S. 371, 91 S.Ct. 780, 28 L.Ed.2d 113 (1971), mandate conformed 329 F.Supp. 844 (D.Conn.1971), leaving the impression that either publication or posting would be sufficient in some circumstances. West's Fla.Stat.Ann. § 49.10(1)(b) (1969 and Supp.1986) permits service by posting and Sheppard v. Sheppard, 329 So.2d 1 (Fla.1976) holds the statute is constitutional. Dungan v. Dungan, 579 S.W.2d 183 (Tenn.1979) permits service by posting where the plaintiff is indigent.

70. M.T.L. v. T.P.L., 414 A.2d 510 (Del.1980); Mayo v. Mayo, 344 So.2d 933 (Fla.App.1977); Murphy v. Murphy, 55 Hawaii 34, 514 P.2d 865 (1973); Baggett v. Baggett, 541 S.W.2d 407 (Tenn.1976); Span v. Span, 52 Wis.2d 786, 191 N.W.2d 209 (1971); West v. West, 82 Wis.2d 158, 262 N.W.2d 87 (1978).

71. 401 U.S. 371, 91 S.Ct. 780, 28 L.Ed.2d 113 (1971), mandate conformed 329 F.Supp. 844 (D.Conn.1971).

72. 401 U.S. at 383, 91 S.Ct. at 788. Cases following Boddie are collected in Annot., Right of Indigent to Proceed in Marital Action Without Payment of Costs, 52 A.L.R.3d 844 (1973).

"Indigent" in this context is construed to require clear evidence that, but for the waiver of the fees, the plaintiff would be unable to bring the suit. Ashley v. Superior Court In and For Pierce County, 82 Wash.2d 188, 509

P.2d 751 (1973), on rehearing 83 Wash.2d 630, 521 P.2d 711 (1974). See also Harris v. Harris, 424 F.2d 806 (D.C. Cir.1970), cert. denied 400 U.S. 826, 91 S.Ct. 50, 27 L.Ed. 2d 55 (1970); Coonce v. Coonce, 356 Mass. 690, 255 N.E.2d 330 (1970); Wilson v. Wilson, 218 Pa.Super. 344, 280 A.2d 665 (1971); Miserak v. Terrill, 130 Vt. 7, 285 A.2d 753 (1971).

73. Holding that the costs of service by publication must be borne by the state, where that method is appropriate: Hart v. Superior Court In and For Pima County, 16 Ariz.App. 184, 492 P.2d 433 (1972); Deason v. Deason, 32 N.Y.2d 93, 343 N.Y.S.2d 321, 296 N.E.2d 229 (1973), on remand 73 Misc.2d 964, 363 N.Y.S.2d 276 (1973); Cook v. Jones, 521 S.W.2d 335 (Tex.Civ.App.1975). The Deason and Cook cases indicated that there might be cheaper alternatives. Refusing to order payment of the costs of publication: Cohen v. Board of Supervisors for Alameda County, 20 Cal.App.3d 236, 97 Cal.Rptr. 550 (1971); Ashley v. Superior Court In and For Pierce County, 82 Wash.2d 188, 509 P.2d 751 (1973), on rehearing 83 Wash. 2d 630, 521 P.2d 711 (1973). But service rules may sometimes be waived to avoid expense to an indigent plaintiff. Bullock v. Roberts, 84 Wash.2d 101, 524 P.2d 385 (1974).

74. In re Smiley, 36 N.Y.2d 433, 369 N.Y.S.2d 87, 330 N.E.2d 53 (1975).

Full Faith and Credit

In addition to the limits imposed by local statute, there are other legal rules which must be taken into account in determining whether there is jurisdiction to grant a divorce. These other rules originated in the common law, but have acquired additional force in the United States by being read into the Constitution.[75] The Full Faith and Credit Clause of the Constitution [76] as interpreted by the Supreme Court of the United States finally determines the conditions under which the decrees of courts in one state are to be recognized in other states. In these days of a mobile population it is highly desirable, if not essential, for a divorce decree to be unchallengable in all states. For this reason the limitation found in the Full Faith and Credit Clause, though it purports only to affect recognition in other states, is in practice nearly as effective in defining the boundaries of divorce court jurisdiction as the state statutes which actually set those boundaries.

After a long and confusing historical development,[77] the United States Supreme Court has arrived at the doctrine that full faith and credit must be given divorce decrees of the various states when one of the parties to the action, usually the plaintiff but conceivably the defendant, was domiciled in the state where the decree was granted.[78] This doctrine was announced in the two opinions in Williams V. North Carolina, known as Williams I [79] and Williams II.[80] It governs only the circumstances under which the marital status may be terminated. Where alimony, property, support and custody of children are involved, additional legal principles become relevant.

The Williams cases arose out of a prosecution in North Carolina for bigamous cohabitation. The two defendants had been domiciled in North Carolina, had gone to Reno and obtained ex parte divorces from their respective spouses, and had then married each other and returned to North Carolina. North Carolina's contention was that the divorces were invalid, so that defendants' subsequent cohabitation was criminal. In the opinion on the first appeal, the Supreme Court held that a divorce obtained in a state where one of the spouses is domiciled is entitled to full faith and credit in other states.[81] Since the record at this stage contained no proof that Nevada was not the domicile of the parties, it followed that these divorces were valid. This over-

---

75. For an interesting examination of the origin of these rules see Rheinstein, The Constitutional Bases of Jurisdiction, 22 U.Chi.L.Rev. 775 (1955), and Note, 76 Harv.L.Rev. 1233 (1963).

76. U.S.Const. art. IV, § 1.

77. For accounts of earlier cases and the changes made by the Williams cases, see Lorenzen, Haddock v. Haddock Overruled, 52 Yale L.J. 341 (1943); Corwin, Out-Haddocking Haddock, 93 U.Pa.L.Rev. 341 (1945).

78. Whether the domicile of one of the parties is the *only* basis for jurisdiction in divorce actions and therefore the only circumstance in which full faith and credit must be given to the divorce decrees of other states is discussed infra, at note 86. Restatement (Second) of Conflict of Laws § 72 (1971) asserts that it is not the only basis, but has little direct authority to support this view.

79. Williams v. North Carolina, 317 U.S. 287, 63 S.Ct. 207, 87 L.Ed. 279 (1942), 43 Colum.L.Rev. 116 (1943), 28 Iowa L.Rev. 362 (1943), 91 U.Pa.L.Rev. 565 (1943). See Sumner, Full Faith and Credit for Divorce Decrees—Present Doctrine and Possible Changes, 9 Vand.L.Rev. 1 (1955).

80. Williams v. North Carolina, 325 U.S. 226, 65 S.Ct. 1092, 89 L.Ed. 1577 (1945), rehearing denied 325 U.S. 895, 65 S.Ct. 1560, 89 L.Ed. 2006 (1945), 45 Colum.L.Rev. 796 (1945). See also Lorenzen, Extraterritorial Divorce—Wil-

liams v. North Carolina, II, 54 Yale L.J. 799 (1945); Powell, And Repeat at Leisure, An Inquiry into the Unhappy Lot of Those Whom Nevada Hath Joined Together and North Carolina Hath Put Asunder, 58 Harv.L. Rev. 930 (1945); Griswold, Divorce Jurisdiction and Recognition of Divorce Decrees—A Comparative Study, 65 Harv.L.Rev. 193, 208 (1951). For collections of cases decided since the Williams Cases, see Annot., 1 A.L.R.2d 1385 (1948) and 28 A.L.R.2d 1301 (1953). Domicile must exist at the outset of the suit. Annot., 7 A.L.R.2d 1414 (1949).

81. Williams v. North Carolina, 317 U.S. 287, 63 S.Ct. 207, 87 L.Ed. 279 (1942). Cases following Williams I and giving full faith and credit to the divorce decrees of other states on the ground of domicile include Smith v. Smith, 174 Conn. 434, 389 A.2d 756 (1978); Spalding v. Spalding, 171 Conn. 220, 368 A.2d 14 (1976); Taylor v. Taylor, 168 Conn. 619, 362 A.2d 795 (1975); Staples v. Staples, 232 So. 2d 904 (La.App.1970); Epstein v. Epstein, 193 Md. 164, 66 A.2d 381 (1949); Nickel v. Nickel, 29 Mich.App. 185 N.W.2d 200 (1970); Kram v. Kram, 52 N.J. 545, 247 A.2d 316 (1968); Maray v. Maray, 35 A.D.2d 603, 313 N.Y.S.2d 488 (2d Dept. 1970); Foss v. Foss, 83 S.D. 574, 163 N.W.2d 354 (1968); Atchley v. Atchley, 585 S.W.2d 614 (Tenn. App.1978); Ford v. Franklin, 129 Vt. 114, 274 A.2d 461 (1971).

ruled the earlier, much criticized case of Haddock v. Haddock.[82]

On a second appeal to the Supreme Court, after a retrial, Williams II [83] held that a state which is requested to recognize a foreign divorce decree may decide for itself whether one of the spouses was domiciled in the foreign state, and, if it finds he was not, may refuse recognition. The North Carolina court therefore was entitled to make its own determination as to the parties' domicile, but since Nevada's finding that it had jurisdiction was entitled "to respect and more",[84] the party attacking the Nevada decree had the burden of proving the absence of a Nevada domicile. The second Williams opinion thus mitigated the extent to which a state having slight or fictional domicile and divorce requirements could impose its views upon other states. Still the difficulty of sustaining the burden of disproving domicile gives the Nevada decree substantial practical effect.[85]

The Supreme Court's current view that "in order to justify an exercise of jurisdiction *in rem*, the basis for jurisdiction must be suffi-cient to justify exercising 'jurisdiction over the interests of persons in a thing' ",[86] might at first glance be thought to alter the principles laid down by the Williams cases. The Supreme Court's position as so expressed is that for *in rem* and *quasi in rem* cases, just as for *in personam* cases, there must be such "minimum contacts" between the parties to the suit and the state to satisfy the dictates of the Due Process Clause.[87] At the same time, however, the Court has disclaimed in its usual cryptic fashion any intention of changing the rules of jurisdiction over status. In a footnote to Shaffer v. Heitner it stated that the rules governing adjudication of status were not being held to be inconsistent with the Court's new position on *in rem* jurisdiction.[88] There is in any event some authority that the domicile of one of the spouses in the state is a sufficient "minimum contact" to meet the requirements of Shaffer v. Heitner.[89] It therefore appears unlikely that Shaffer v. Heitner and its progeny have effected a change in the rules of divorce jurisdiction.

82. 201 U.S. 562, 26 S.Ct. 525, 50 L.Ed. 867 (1906).

83. Williams v. North Carolina, 325 U.S. 226, 65 S.Ct. 1092, 89 L.Ed. 1577 (1945), rehearing denied 325 U.S. 895, 65 S.Ct. 1560, 89 L.Ed. 2006 (1945). See also Rice v. Rice, 336 U.S. 674, 69 S.Ct. 751, 93 L.Ed. 957 (1949), and Esenwein v. Commonwealth, 325 U.S. 279, 65 S.Ct. 1118, 89 L.Ed. 1608 (1945).

84. 325 U.S. at 233, 65 S.Ct. at ___. But the North Carolina court seems not to have lived up to this requirement in the Williams case itself, since the charge to the jury as reported by Justice Frankfurter, placed on the petitioners the burden of satisfying the jury that they had been domiciled in Nevada.

Cases which, following Williams II, find no domicile in the divorcing state and thus deny full faith and credit to the decree, include Keck v. Keck, 56 Ill.2d 508, 309 N.E.2d 217 (1974); Fink v. Fink, 37 Ill.App.3d 604, 346 N.E.2d 415 (1976); In re Marriage of Winegard, 278 N.W.2d 505 (Iowa 1979), cert. denied 444 U.S. 951, 100 S.Ct. 425, 62 L.Ed.2d 321 (1979) (Williams II does not require full faith and credit, but it may be given); Staley v. Staley, 251 Md. 701, 248 A.2d 655 (1968); Ragucci v. Ragucci, 357 Mass. 235, 258 N.E.2d 28 (1970); Henry v. Henry, 362 Mich. 85, 106 N.W.2d 570 (1960).

85. In Zieper v. Zieper, 14 N.J. 551, 103 A.2d 366 (1954), the New Jersey Supreme Court stated that the concept of domicile is to be defined in accordance with federal law for purposes of interstate recognition of divorce decrees, a view which is probably correct, although an argument might be made, based upon Aldrich v. Aldrich, 378 U.S. 540, 84 S.Ct. 1687, 12 L.Ed.2d 1020

(1964) that the divorcing state's definition of domicile should be controlling.

On the problems of attacking Nevada decrees, see Hobbs v. Hobbs, 91 U.S.App.D.C. 68, 197 F.2d 412 (1952), cert. denied 344 U.S. 855, 73 S.Ct. 93, 97 L.Ed. 664 (1952); Elwert v. Elwert, 196 Or. 256, 248 P.2d 847 (1952); Commonwealth ex rel. McVay v. McVay, 383 Pa. 70, 118 A.2d 144 (1955), cert. denied 350 U.S. 995, 76 S.Ct. 544, 100 L.Ed. 860 (1956). In Lanigan v. Lanigan, 78 So.2d 92 (Fla.1955) the lengths to which the court went to prevent an attack on a Reno divorce raises the suspicion that there may be an esprit de corps among the divorce mill states which leads them to protect one another's decrees.

86. Shaffer v. Heitner, 433 U.S. 186, 207, 97 S.Ct. 2569, 2581, 53 L.Ed.2d 683 (1977). The quotation in Shaffer is from Restatement (Second) of Conflict of Laws § 56, Introductory Note (1971). The rule of minimum contacts is more fully discussed in International Shoe Co. v. Washington, Office of Unemployment Comp. & Placement, 326 U.S. 310, 66 S.Ct. 154, 90 L.Ed. 95 (1945). The doubts expressed in the text are also expressed without being pursued in Fehlhaber v. Fehlhaber, 681 F.2d 1015, 1021, note 6 (5th Cir.1982), rehearing denied 702 F.2d 81 (5th Cir.1983), cert. denied 464 U.S. 818, 104 S.Ct. 79, 78 L.Ed.2d 90 (1983).

87. Shaffer v. Heitner, 433 U.S. 186, 212, 97 S.Ct. 2569, 2583, 53 L.Ed.2d 683 (1977).

88. Id. at 208 n. 30, 97 S.Ct. at 2582 n. 30.

89. In re Marriage of Rinderknecht, 174 Ind.App. 382, 367 N.E.2d 1128 (1977).

Subsequent cases [90] raise interesting questions concerning the further application of the principles of Williams II. They involve three marital suits rather than two. First there is an ex parte divorce in State A, the court finding that the plaintiff was domiciled in the state. The defendant then brings another suit in State B attacking the divorce for lack of jurisdiction. As permitted by Williams II, the State B court holds the divorce invalid on the ground that the divorce plaintiff was not domiciled in State A. A third suit is then brought, either in State C, or back in State A, attacking the second judgment on the ground that it failed to give full faith and credit to the State A divorce. The cases have reached different results in such cases. The correct result is that the decision of State B invalidating the divorce is in accord with Williams II and should be given full faith and credit in subsequent litigation either in State A or State C.[91] Some decisions refuse to do this, however, mistakenly adhering to the result reached in State A, either from an erroneous view of Williams II or because they refuse to upset their own divorce decree.[92]

The Williams cases rejected the older mechanical reasoning which first places the *in rem* label on divorce actions and then concludes that the *res* is to be found at the domicile of one of the parties. The Williams opinions did say, however, that a divorce action is different from the ordinary *in personam* lawsuit in that it affects a relationship which is of great concern to the state of the domicile.[93] The American rule allowing husband and wife to acquire separate domiciles [94] creates the difficulty that two states may be interested in their marriage and may have quite different views on how that marriage should be terminated. The Supreme Court permits one of these states to end the marital status notwithstanding the other's view that it should continue. The paradox of the Williams cases is that by their very insistence upon recognition of a state's governmental concern with the marriages of its domiciliaries they enable that concern to be defeated.

One way in which some spouses have attempted to deal with the problem of migratory divorce is to enjoin the other spouse from going to another state or country for the purpose of getting a divorce. If the evidence shows that the defendant does propose to go to Reno, for example, solely for the purpose of getting a divorce and without any intention of acquiring a Nevada domicile, some courts have been willing to enjoin him from doing so.[95] The basis upon which equity intervenes in that case is that under Williams II the stay-at-home spouse would have the burden of rebutting a claim of Nevada domicile if she

90. Southard v. Southard, 305 F.2d 730 (2d Cir. 1962); Levy v. Dickstein, 70 Ill.App.3d 180, 26 Ill.Dec. 473, 388 N.E.2d 97 (1979); Colby v. Colby, 78 Nev. 150, 369 P.2d 1019 (1962), cert. denied 371 U.S. 888, 83 S.Ct. 186, 9 L.Ed.2d 122 (1962); Layton v. Layton, 538 S.W.2d 642 (Tex. Civ. App. 1976), 55 Tex.L.Rev. 127 (1976); Kessler v. Fauquier Nat. Bank, 195 Va. 1095, 81 S.E.2d 440 (1954), cert. denied 348 U.S 834, 75 S.Ct. 57, 99 L.Ed. 658 (1954), rehearing denied 348 U.S. 890, 75 S.Ct. 204, 99 L.Ed. 699 (1954).

91. Sutton v. Leib, 342 U.S. 402, 72 S.Ct. 398, 96 L.Ed. 448 (1952), rehearing denied 343 U.S. 921, 72 S.Ct. 674, 96 L.Ed. 1334 (1952); Southard v. Southard, 305 F.2d 730 (2d Cir. 1962); Di russo v. Di russo, 55 Misc.2d 839, 287 N.Y.S.2d 171 (1968); Layton v. Layton, 538 S.W.2d 642 (Tex. Civ. App. 1976), 55 Tex.L.Rev. 127 (1976). See also Restatement (Second) of Judgments § 15 (1982).

92. Levy v. Dickstein, 70 Ill.App.3d 180, 26 Ill.Dec. 473, 388 N.E.2d 97 (1979); Colby v. Colby, 78 Nev. 150, 369 P.2d 1019 (1962), cert. denied 371 U.S. 888, 83 S.Ct. 186, 9 L.Ed.2d 122 (1962), 63 Colum.L.Rev. 560 (1963), 15 Stan.L.Rev. 331 (1963); Kessler v. Fauquier Nat. Bank, 195 Va. 1095, 81 S.E.2d 440 (1954), cert. denied 348 U.S.

834, 75 S.Ct. 57, 99 L.Ed. 658 (1954), rehearing denied 348 U.S. 890, 75 S.Ct. 204, 99 L.Ed. 699 (1954).

93. Williams v. North Carolina, 317 U.S. 287, 297, 63 S.Ct. 207, 212, 87 L.Ed. 279 (1942). And see Mr. Justice Frankfurter's dissent in Sherrer v. Sherrer, 334 U.S. 343, 356, 68 S.Ct. 1087, 1097, 92 L.Ed. 1429 (1948).

94. See section 4.3, Practitioner's Edition, for authority that today the married woman has a constitutional right to acquire a separate domicile from her husband.

95. Baumann v. Baumann, 250 N.Y. 382, 165 N.E. 819 (1929), 43 Harv.L.Rev. 477 (1930); Garvin v. Garvin, 302 N.Y. 96, 96 N.E.2d 721 (1951); Martin v. Martin, 62 Misc. 2d 703, 309 N.Y.S.2d 477 (1970); Monihan v. Monihan, 438 Pa. 380, 264 A.2d 653 (1970), 32 U.Pitt.L.Rev. 92 (1970). The federal courts will not grant such injunctions against state court divorce suits under 28 U.S.C.A. § 2283. Rosenstiel v. Rosenstiel, 278 F.Supp. 794 (S.D. N.Y.1967). If the defendant intends a bona fide change of domicile, the injunction should not be granted. But see Monihan v. Monihan, 438 Pa. 380, 385, 264 A.2d 653, 655 (1970) (concurring opinion).

wished to attack the divorce, and that therefore her legal remedy is inadequate. If the defendant spouse proposes to get a divorce in a foreign country, however, the injunction is usually denied because Williams II does not apply to foreign divorces and the stay-at-home spouse's remedy of attacking the decree on the other's return is an adequate one.[96] The grant of such an injunction does not unconstitutionally abridge the defendant's freedom to travel since it does not forbid travel but only obtaining a divorce in a state in which the defendant is not domiciled.[97]

In such a suit for injunction the court must have personal jurisdiction over the defendant.[98] An injunction of this sort, for historical reasons, is probably not entitled to full faith and credit in the divorcing state,[99] but that state might recognize it in accordance with notions of comity and therefore refuse to grant the divorce.[1] If the divorcing state should refuse to recognize the injunction and proceed to grant the divorce, the home state's obligation upon the spouse's return would be governed by the Williams cases. The courts of that state, when the divorce is attacked there, must decide whether the spouse acquired a domicile in the other state, giving

the divorce decree the kind of presumptive weight required by Williams II.[2] If it is found that a domicile was acquired, then the divorce must be recognized.[3] In other words, when the out of state divorce is attacked, the attacking spouse gets little or no advantage from having earlier obtained an injunction.

Divorce Without Domicile: A Transitory Action?[4]

A number of states and the Uniform Marriage and Divorce Act have provisions conferring jurisdiction to grant divorces where the plaintiff has a less substantial contact with the state than domicile. For example, the Uniform Act authorizes divorces where the plaintiff is a serviceman who has been stationed in the state for ninety days.[5] Several states have similar provisions allowing divorces to be granted to servicemen on the basis of presence in the state for similar periods.[6] And some states have enacted statutes permitting divorces to be granted where both parties were physically present in the state and personally before the court, without any requirement either of domicile or of any particular period of presence.[7]

96. Rosenbaum v. Rosenbaum, 309 N.Y. 371, 130 N.E.2d 902 (1955), 69 Harv.L.Rev. 1327 (1956); Arpels v. Arpels, 8 N.Y.2d 339, 207 N.Y.S.2d 663, 170 N.E.2d 670 (1960).

97. Monihan v. Monihan, 438 Pa. 380, 385, 264 A.2d 653, 655 (1970) (concurring opinion).

98. Shady v. Shady, 10 Ill.App.3d 801, 295 N.E.2d 130 (1973); Foris v. Foris, 103 N.J.Super. 316, 247 A.2d 156 (1968).

99. Rapoport v. Rapoport, 273 F.Supp. 482 (D.Nev. 1967), reversed for lack of amount in controversy 416 F.2d 41 (9th Cir. 1969), cert. denied 397 U.S. 915, 90 S.Ct. 920, 25 L.Ed.2d 96 (1970); E. Scoles and P. Hay, Conflict of Laws 930 (1982).

1. Friedland v. Friedland, 295 F.Supp. 237 (D. Virgin Islands 1968); Corbin v. Corbin, 26 Conn.Supp. 443, 226 A.2d 799 (1967), various motions denied 155 Conn. 714, 229 A.2d 701 (1967), 155 Conn. 716, 230 A.2d 438 (1968), 156 Conn. 660, 241 A.2d 878 (1968). Contra, refusing to extend comity to such injunction decrees: Cunningham v. Cunningham, 25 Conn.Supp. 221, 200 A.2d 734 (1964); Seabrook v. Seabrook, 264 A.2d 311 (D.C.App.1970); Abney v. Abney, 176 Ind.App. 22, 374 N.E.2d 264 (1978), cert. denied 439 U.S. 1069, 99 S.Ct. 836, 59 L.Ed.2d 34 (1979).

2. See note 84, supra.

3. Lawler v. Lawler, 2 N.J. 527, 66 A.2d 855 (1949); Dominick v. Dominick, 26 Misc.2d 344, 205 N.Y.S.2d 503 (1960); Stambaugh v. Stambaugh, 458 Pa. 147, 329 A.2d 483 (1974); Annot., 74 A.L.R.2d 828 (1960).

4. Garfield, The Transitory Divorce Action: Jurisdiction in the No-Fault Era, 58 Tex.L.Rev. 501 (1980).

5. Uniform Marriage and Divorce Act § 302, 9A Unif. L.Ann. 121 (1979).

6. E.g., Ala.Code 1977, § 6–7–20; Alaska Stat. § 25.24.100 (1983); Ariz.Rev.Stat. § 25–312 (1976 and Supp.1986); West's Fla.Stat.Ann. § 47.081 (Supp.1986); Official Code Ga.Ann. § 30–107 (Supp.1986); Kan.Stat. Ann. § 60–1603 (1983); Ky.Rev.Stat. § 403.140 (1984); Me.Rev.Stat.Ann. tit. 19, § 691 (1981); Miss.Code 1986, § 93–5–5 (Supp.); Neb.Rev.St. § 42–349 (1984); N.M.Stat. Ann.1978, § 40–4–5 (1986 Replacement); N.C.Gen.Stat. § 50–18 (1984); Okl.Stat. tit. 12, § 127 (Supp.1987); Tenn. Code Ann. § 36–4–101 (1984); V.T.C.A.Fam.Code § 3.23 (1975); Utah Code Ann.1984, § 30–3–1; Va.Code 1986 § 20–97 (Supp.).

7. See the statutes cited in Alton v. Alton, 207 F.2d 667 (3d Cir.1953); Jennings v. Jennings, 251 Ala. 73, 36 So.2d 236 (1948); David-Zieseniss v. Zieseniss, 205 Misc. 836, 129 N.Y.S.2d 649 (1954). The Virgin Islands statute in issue in the Alton case was later held unconstitutional

The cases dealing with these statutes have reached disparate conclusions. One leading authority, Judge Goodrich in Alton v. Alton,[8] held that the Virgin Islands statute violated the Due Process Clause of the Fifth Amendment[9] when it authorized divorces for persons not domiciled in the Islands on personal service alone. The opinion conceded that there is a difficult question as to just what the deprivation of due process consisted of, since the defendant was not complaining of any wrong done him, nor was he deprived of liberty or property. Judge Goodrich's answer seemed to be that such statutes as this allow one state to interfere with the proper concerns of another state by altering the marital relations of persons domiciled in the other state. But the Due Process Clause protects persons, not states, and thus has no application to such interstate conflicts. One might suggest that the Full Faith and Credit Clause[10] would be a better basis for holding the Virgin Islands statute unconstitutional. The argument would be that that statute did not give proper respect to the substantive laws of Connecticut, the state of the parties' domicile and therefore violated the Full Faith and Credit Clause.[11] The difficulty with this approach is that the Supreme Court has generally, in other contexts, refused to apply that Clause to substantive choice of law ques-

tions.[12] As a matter of policy, as distinguished from constitutional principle, it does seem undesirable for a state to grant divorces which are not going to be entitled to full faith and credit,[13] and it is no doubt that factor which led Judge Goodrich to hold the statute unconstitutional.

The typical serviceman's statute requires more contact with the divorcing state than the Virgin Islands statute, usually a period ranging from ninety days to six months during which the serviceman was either a resident or stationed in the state.[14] The cases dealing with these statutes are also divided, many of them holding the statute constitutional,[15] while others hold either that the statute is unconstitutional[16] or that it must be construed to require domicile in the state in order to avoid possible constitutional problems.[17] Although these statutes do require a greater state interest than mere presence as a condition on divorce jurisdiction, and although they serve the laudable purpose of enabling the serviceman to obtain a divorce when he is living away from his domicile, they remain open to the objection that they result in divorces which may be valid where granted but not entitled to recognition elsewhere.

The United States Supreme Court has not squarely held that domicile is the only possi-

---

on other grounds in Granville-Smith v. Granville-Smith, 349 U.S. 1, 75 S.Ct. 553, 99 L.Ed. 773 (1955).

8. 207 F.2d 667 (3d Cir.1953), judgment vacated, remanded with directions to dismiss the case as moot, 347 U.S. 610, 74 S.Ct. 736, 98 L.Ed. 987 (1954). Jennings v. Jennings, 251 Ala. 73, 36 So.2d 236 (1948) held a similar Alabama statute to be a violation of due process.

9. U.S.Const.Amend. V.

10. U.S.Const. art. IV, sec. 1.

11. This analysis is discussed in Rheinstein, The Constitutional Bases of Jurisdiction, 22 U.Chi.L.Rev. 775 (1955).

12. Id. at 786–789.

13. Williams v. North Carolina, 325 U.S. 226, 65 S.Ct. 1092, 89 L.Ed. 1577 (1945), rehearing denied 325 U.S. 895, 65 S.Ct. 1560, 89 L.Ed. 2006 (1945) (Williams II) clearly held that North Carolina, if it found the parties had not been domiciled in Nevada, could disregard the Nevada divorce. Under the Virgin Islands statute, although both parties had to be before the court *in personam*, the court did not need to make a finding that they were domiciled in the Virgin Islands. Therefore the doctrine of *res*

judicata as elaborated in Sherrer v. Sherrer, 334 U.S. 343, 68 S.Ct. 1087, 92 L.Ed. 1429 (1948), discussed infra at note 24, cannot be invoked to protect the Virgin Islands type of divorce.

14. See note 6, supra.

15. Lauterbach v. Lauterbach, 392 P.2d 24 (Alaska 1964); Wheat v. Wheat, 229 Ark. 842, 318 S.W.2d 793 (1958), 39 B.U.L.Rev. 462 (1959), 12 Vand.L.Rev. 824 (1959); Craig v. Craig, 143 Kan. 624, 56 P.2d 464 (1936); Schaeffer v. Schaeffer, 175 Kan. 629, 266 P.2d 282 (1954); Crownover v. Crownover, 58 N.M. 597, 274 P.2d 127 (1954); Wallace v. Wallace, 63 N.M. 414, 320 P.2d 1020 (1958); Wood v. Wood, 159 Tex. 350, 320 S.W.2d 807 (1959); Fox v. Fox, 559 S.W.2d 407 (Tex.Civ.App.1977); In re Marriage of Ways, 85 Wash.2d 693, 538 P.2d 1225 (1975), 52 Wash.L.Rev. 369 (1977). See also Annot., 73 A.L.R.3d 431 (1976).

16. Darbie v. Darbie, 195 Ga. 769, 25 S.E.2d 685 (1943).

17. Viernes v. District Court In and For Fourth Judicial Dist., 181 Colo. 284, 509 P.2d 306 (1973); Martin v. Martin, 253 N.C. 704, 118 S.E.2d 29 (1961).

ble basis for divorce jurisdiction, but its opinions have contained dicta to that effect.[18] The Court's view that divorce jurisdiction is based upon domicile has at least two virtues from the point of view of sound divorce policy. In the first place the state of a party's domicile has the closest relation to and the strongest interest in the parties' marriage and is therefore justified in applying its own law to the dissolution of that marriage. Of course if the parties have domiciles in different states, there will be two states having such interests, but this is an unavoidable result of permitting married women to acquire domiciles separate from their husbands'. Secondly, if the domicile requirement is coupled with the availability of substituted service, there will always be some state which can grant a divorce even if one spouse is not amenable to personal service. If divorce were exclusively a transitory action, this would not be true and some marriages could not be terminated, either because the defendant could not be found to be served, or because as a practical matter the plaintiff would often be unable to sue in the only state in which personal jurisdiction over the defendant could be obtained.

Although it is true that the population of the United States is highly mobile, the concept of domicile as presently applied by the courts [19] is sufficiently liberal to be retained as a workable basis for divorce jurisdiction.[20] Its use achieves a workable compromise between the state's interest in regulating mar-

riage and the parties' interest in having an accessible forum for the resolution of their differences. This is especially true now that the national trend toward no-fault divorce has minimized the need of the unhappily married to seek relief in the divorce mill states such as Nevada. Divorce jurisdiction is for that reason rapidly becoming little more than a subject for historical study.

Attack Foreclosed by Res Judicata

In Sherrer v. Sherrer [21] the wife, domiciled with her husband in Massachusetts, went to Florida and sued for divorce. The husband appeared personally in the action, but a divorce was granted. The question of her domicile was not actually litigated before the Florida court, but the decree recited that she was domiciled in the state. The Supreme Court held that the husband could not later attack the validity of the Florida decree in a suit brought in Massachusetts. It stated the rule to be that "the requirements of full faith and credit bar a defendant from collaterally attacking a divorce decree on jurisdictional grounds in the courts of a sister state where there has been participation by the defendant in the divorce proceedings, where the defendant has been accorded full opportunity to contest the jurisdictional issues, and where the decree is not susceptible to such collateral attack in the courts of the State which rendered the decree." [22] This, as Mr. Justice

---

18. E.g., Williams v. North Carolina, 325 U.S. 226, 229, 65 S.Ct. 1092, 1094, 89 L.Ed. 1577 (1945), rehearing denied 325 U.S. 895, 65 S.Ct. 1560, 89 L.Ed. 2006 (1945): "Under our system of law, judicial power to grant a divorce—jurisdiction, strictly speaking—is founded on domicil." Sosna v. Iowa, 419 U.S. 393, 407, 95 S.Ct. 553, 561, 42 L.Ed.2d 532 (1975) quoted this language from Williams II with approval.

19. See section 4.2, Practitioner's Edition.

20. For arguments contra to that in the text, see Garfield, the Transitory Divorce Action: Jurisdiction in the No-Fault Era, 58 Tex.L.Rev. 501 (1980) and E. Scoles and P. Hay, Conflict of Laws §§ 15.6, 15.7 (1982).

21. 334 U.S. 343, 68 S.Ct. 1087, 92 L.Ed. 1429 (1948). The companion case is Coe v. Coe, 334 U.S. 378, 68 S.Ct. 1094, 92 L.Ed. 1451 (1948). An earlier case, Davis v. Davis, 305 U.S. 32, 59 S.Ct. 3, 83 L.Ed. 26 (1938), motion denied ___ U.S. ___, 59 S.Ct. 773, ___ L.Ed. ___ (1939) had held that domicile could not be reexamined when it had

been actively litigated in the divorce suit and the decree had held it to be present, but Sherrer did not involve any litigation on the merits of this question and therefore goes farther than Davis.

Cases following Sherrer include Mackessy v. Mackessy, 15 Alaska 361 (1954); Craig v. Superior Court In and For Sacramento County, 45 Cal.App.3d 675, 119 Cal.Rptr. 692 (1975); Lorant v. Lorant, 366 Mass. 380, 318 N.E.2d 830 (1974); Roskein v. Roskein, 25 N.J.Super. 415, 96 A.2d 437 (1953); Csanyi v. Csanyi, 82 N.M. 411, 483 P.2d 292 (1971) (semble); Thrasher v. Thrasher, 4 N.C.App. 534, 167 S.E.2d 549 (1969); Duncan v. Seay, 553 P.2d 492 (Okl. 1976); Barnes v. Buck, 464 Pa. 357, 346 A.2d 778 (1975). Other cases are collected in Annot., 28 A.L.R.2d 1303, 1318 (1953). See also Restatement (Second) of Conflict of Laws § 73 (1971); E. Scoles and P. Hay, Conflict of Laws 482–484 (1982).

22. 334 U.S. at 351, 68 S.Ct. at 1091. The same reasoning has been applied where the attack is based on

Frankfurter's dissent vigorously urged,[23] goes a long way toward vitiating the domicile requirement since it makes the decree unassailable where the defendant has appeared and had a chance to raise the jurisdictional issue and where the court makes a finding of domicile,[24] even though it is plain on later investigation that neither party was domiciled in the state granting the divorce.

It is important to note that full faith and credit pursuant to the Sherrer rule turns on the doctrines of res judicata prevailing in the divorcing state. If a divorce decree is immune to attack in that state on the ground that both spouses were personally before the court, then under Sherrer it will be immune to attack in other states.[25]

Sherrer v. Sherrer raised hard questions, some of which have been answered. The protection against collateral attacks upon divorce decrees which the Sherrer case provides has been extended by the Supreme Court to attacks made by the children of the parties. In Johnson v. Muelberger[26] a Florida divorce was attacked in New York by the daughter of one of the parties on the ground that the divorce plaintiff had not been domiciled in Florida at the time of the divorce. The divorce defendant had appeared and contested

the divorce action, and the Supreme Court held that since under Florida law the daughter would not be permitted to attack the divorce in that state, the Full Faith and Credit Clause[27] prevented her from attacking it in any other state. Cook v. Cook[28] held that the same principle bars collateral attack by a second husband on his wife's divorce from her first husband.

Other questions remain, however. One is whether the Sherrer doctrine depends on a personal appearance by the defendant in the divorce case or whether it is sufficient that the defendant was personally served in the jurisdiction. Both Cook v. Cook[29] and Johnson v. Muelberger[30] contain language indicating that personal service is enough, although the cases do not directly present the issue. The theory of the Sherrer doctrine is that since the defendant had one opportunity to litigate the jurisdictional question and failed to take advantage of it, he should not have another. Whether he has as much of an opportunity when he is personally served within the jurisdiction as when he appears is an open question. Since in the large majority of cases all his interests demand that he *not* litigate, it is also an extremely artificial question. Although it is stultifying to solemnly

---

a failure to observe due process. Chapman v. Chapman, 5 A.D.2d 257, 168 N.Y.S.2d 872 (3d Dept.1957). For discussion of the general problems of res judicata as applied to jurisdiction over the subject matter, see Bosky & Braucher, Jurisdiction and Collateral Attack: October Term 1939, 40 Colum.L.Rev. 1006 (1940) and Reese & Johnson, The Scope of Full Faith and Credit to Judgments, 49 Colum.L.Rev. 153 (1949). On proof of the foreign law see Note, 8 Buff.L.Rev. 389 (1959).

23. 334 U.S. at 356, 68 S.Ct. at 1097.

24. The requirement of a finding of domicile prevents the application of the Sherrer rule to divorces based solely upon personal service since no such finding is usually required by the statutes in such cases. See note 13, supra.

25. This formerly caused confusion due to uncertainty as to the status of the "Alabama quickie", particularly in New York state. Cf. Weisner v. Weisner, 17 N.Y.2d 799, 271 N.Y.S.2d 252, 218 N.E.2d 300 (1966), reargument denied 18 N.Y.2d 690, 273 N.Y.S.2d 1025, 219 N.E.2d 884 (1966), 16 Buff.L.Rev. 474 (1967), with In re Joseph's Estate, 27 N.Y.2d 299, 317 N.Y.S.2d 338, 265 N.E.2d 756 (1970). See also Richards v. Richards, 2 Misc.2d 596, 153 N.Y.S.2d 979 (1956).

26. 340 U.S. 581, 71 S.Ct. 474, 95 L.Ed. 552 (1951), 46 Ill.L.Rev. 307 (1951), 50 Mich.L.Rev. 465 (1952). Cases following Johnson include In re Marriage of Winegard, 278 N.W.2d 505 (Iowa 1979), cert. denied 444 U.S. 951, 100 S.Ct. 425, 62 L.Ed.2d 321 (1979); Hudman v. Hudman, 259 So.2d 619 (La.App.1972); Magowan v. Magowan, 19 N.Y.2d 296, 279 N.Y.S.2d 513, 226 N.E.2d 304 (1967). Other cases are collected in Annot., 28 A.L.R.2d 1303, 1328 (1953).

27. U.S.Const. art. IV, § 1.

28. 342 U.S. 126, 72 S.Ct. 157, 96 L.Ed. 146 (1951). See Sumner, Full Faith and Credit for Divorce Decrees-Present Doctrine and Possible Changes, 9 Vand.L.Rev. 1 (1955), and Note, Stranger Attack on Sister-State Decrees of Divorce, 24 U.Chi.L.Rev. 376 (1957), suggesting that the Cook case gives broader effect to divorce decrees than would be given to other in rem decrees.

29. 342 U.S. 126, 128, 72 S.Ct. 157, 196 L.Ed. 146 (1951). Zenker v. Zenker, 161 Neb. 200, 72 N.W.2d 809 (1955) also holds that personal service is sufficient. In re Day's Estate, 7 Ill.2d 348, 131 N.E.2d 50 (1955) and Boxer v. Boxer, 7 N.Y.2d 781, 194 N.Y.S.2d 47, 163 N.E.2d 149 (1959) hold that an appearance through an attorney is sufficient to invoke the Sherrer rule.

30. 340 U.S. 581, 71 S.Ct. 474, 95 L.Ed. 552 (1951).

consider whether a party has had an opportunity to litigate a question which he never desired to litigate, there is nevertheless something important to be said for the Sherrer rule when it is taken in the context of divorce policy. At the time it developed, there were many states in which divorce was not readily available except on proof of various kinds of fault. The effect of this was that practically speaking many unhappily married persons either could not get a divorce at all in the state of their domicile or they could not get a divorce without going through a humiliating and demeaning process. The effect of Sherrer was to provide them with the opportunity to get a divorce in a state other than their domicile (Nevada for example) on condition that both cooperated by arranging for the defendant to be personally before the divorcing court. This amounted to recognition of the fact, which seems obvious to us today, that no sensible policy is served by forcing spouses to remain married to each other when one of them has determined that he wants a divorce. This fact has led most states to adopt a nonfault ground for divorce which, as has been indicated, has sharply reduced the practical significance of the Williams cases and likewise of the Sherrer and Johnson cases.

The Sherrer doctrine also leads to the question whether its benefits are available to the spouses who plainly engage in a collusive attempt to take advantage of the liberal divorce laws of a state other than their domicile. Justice Frankfurter's dissent in the Sherrer case suggests that its benefits are available in such circumstances.[31] A scattering of state court cases holds that they are not.[32] The Sherrer opinion itself contains no limitation which would prevent this. And if the Sherrer rule reflects sensible divorce policy, there should be no such limitation. The issue is largely academic, however, since well instructed divorce litigants are generally careful to behave like adversaries even when they are not.

31. Sherrer v. Sherrer, 334 U.S. 343, 68 S.Ct. 1087, 92 L.Ed. 1429 (1948). See Griswold, Divorce Decrees—A Comparative Study, 65 Harv.L.Rev. 193, 217 (1951), where the author says that it is still to be decided whether "active", as distinguished from "passive" fraud would entitle a state court to disregard the Sherrer rule. See Paulsen, Divorce Jurisdiction by Consent of the Parties—Developments Since "Sherrer v. Sherrer", 26 Ind. L.J. 380 (1951).

32. Oberstein v. Oberstein, 217 Ark. 80, 228 S.W.2d 615 (1950) (dictum); Gherardi De Parata v. Gherardi De Parata, 179 A.2d 723 (D.C.Mun.App.1962); Cole v. Cole, 221 Ga. 171, 143 S.E.2d 637 (1965) (semble); Eaton v. Eaton, 227 La. 992, 81 So.2d 371 (1955), cert. denied 350 U.S. 873, 76 S.Ct. 116, 100 L.Ed. 772 (1955) (defendant signed "Waiver of Summons and Entry of Appearance"); Boudreaux v. Welch, 180 So.2d 725 (La.App.1965); Day v. Day, 237 Md. 229, 205 A.2d 798 (1965), 65 Colum.L.Rev. 924 (1965); Winters v. Winters, 236 Miss. 624, 111 So.2d 418 (1959); Zenker v. Zenker, 161 Neb. 200, 72 N.W.2d 809, 69 Harv.L.Rev. (1984 Reissue) 1325 (1956); Guerieri v. Guerieri, 75 N.J.Super. 541, 183 A.2d 499 (1962); Staedler v. Staedler, 6 N.J. 380, 78 A.2d 896 (1951) (now strictly limited to its particular facts by Nappe v. Nappe infra); Chirelstein v. Chirelstein, 8 N.J.Super. 504, 73 A.2d 628 (Ch.1950), modified on other grounds 12 N.J. Super. 468, 79 A.2d 884 (App.Div.1951); Brasier v. Brasier, 200 Okl. 689, 200 P.2d 427 (1948); Davis v. Davis, 259 Wis. 1, 47 N.W.2d 338 (1951) (defendant appeared specially by attorney to contest the jurisdiction). Contra: In re Day's Estate, 7 Ill.2d 348, 131 N.E.2d 50 (1955); Chittick v. Chittick, 332 Mass. 554, 126 N.E.2d 495 (1955) (Virgin Islands decree entitled to full faith and credit although plainly collusive); Nappe v. Nappe, 20 N.J. 337,

120 A.2d 31 (1956); Schlemm v. Schlemm, 31 N.J. 557, 158 A.2d 508 (1960); Commonwealth v. Case, 200 Pa. Super. 200, 189 A.2d 756 (1963); Restatement (Second) of Conflict of Laws § 73, Reporter's Note (1971); E. Scoles, P. Hay, Conflict of Laws § 15.10 (1982). See also Note, 34 Ind.L.J. 592 (1959) and Annot., 28 A.L.R.2d 1303 (1953). An Alabama divorce was held immune to attack in Boxer v. Boxer, 7 N.Y.2d 781, 194 N.Y.S.2d 47, 163 N.E.2d 149 (1959) and Commonwealth v. Case, 200 Pa.Super. 200, 189 A.2d 756 (1963) where the defendant wife had appeared by counsel, but another Alabama divorce was held subject to attack in Donnel v. Howell, 257 N.C. 175, 125 S.E.2d 448 (1962) although the defendant husband filed a "waiver" in the Alabama suit. To the same effect is Pelle v. Pelle, 229 Md. 160, 182 A.2d 37 (1962).

Two earlier cases which refused to uphold a divorce where no domicile existed, in spite of the defendant's personal appearance in the action are Maguier v. Maguier, 37 Ky. (7 Dana) 181 (1838) and Hardy v. Smith, 136 Mass. 328 (1884).

The Sherrer and Coe cases seem to have limited the effect of statutes like the Uniform Divorce Recognition Act and the Massachusetts and New Jersey prototypes, which provide that a foreign divorce is of no force or effect in the forum if both parties remained domiciled in the forum. See, Uniform Divorce Recognition Act, 9 Unif.L.Ann. 644 (1979); West's Ann.Cal.Civ.Code § 5001 (1983); Mass.Gen.L.Ann. c. 208, § 39 (1981); Neb.Rev.St. § 42–341 (1978); Coe v. Coe, 334 U.S. 378, 68 S.Ct. 1094, 92 L.Ed. 1451 (1948), and Note 42 Cal.L.Rev. 503 (1954). Hartenstein v. Hartenstein, 18 Wis.2d 505, 118 N.W.2d 881 (1963) holds that this statute was not intended to be inconsistent with the Sherrer rule.

Another open question, though one of limited practical importance, is whether the state of the domicile, in a prosecution for bigamy, adultery or similar offense, would be entitled to attack the foreign divorce for lack of jurisdiction notwithstanding the divorce defendant's appearance. There is a little inconclusive authority that the state is not prevented from proving that the foreign divorce was without jurisdiction.[33] Persuasive arguments for the opposite view can be found. If the Full Faith and Credit Clause does require, as the Supreme Court has so often said, that the decree be given the effect which it would have had in the rendering state, that should prevent collateral attack in a criminal prosecution, since the rendering state would hardly allow its own prosecuting authorities to contend that a divorce in accordance with its statutes was void.[34] Furthermore, once a decree is held good as against attack by the appearing defendant and all other private individuals, no useful purpose is achieved by preserving the domicile's right to prosecute the parties for crime.

Foreign Country Divorces

Although the recognition in the United States of the divorce decrees of other nations is of course not governed by the Full Faith and Credit Clause,[35] but rather by notions of "comity",[36] the cases decided under the Full Faith and Credit Clause have been influential with courts facing demands for recognition of foreign divorces.[37] Since most such cases concern the effect in the American states of migratory divorces obtained in Mexico,[38] or more recently, in Haiti or the Dominican Republic,[39] it is only natural that the courts consult precedents dealing with the effect of Nevada, Alabama, Florida or other migratory divorces granted by the divorce mill states. It should be borne in mind, however, that such cases involve the factors of evasion of the divorce policy of the parties' home state and of a specious finding of domicile in the divorcing state. For those reasons they are not necessarily to be followed where the divorce is not of the migratory variety.

Foreign migratory divorces fall into three classes. The first class is comprised of Mexi-

33. Sumner, Full Faith and Credit for Divorce Decrees-Present Doctrine and Possible Changes, 9 Vand.L. Rev. 1, 9 (1955). Four cases, decided before Sherrer, held the state could prove the lack of domicile where the divorce defendant had personally appeared. Lipham v. State, 68 Ga.App. 174, 22 S.E.2d 532 (1942); People v. Dawell, 25 Mich. 247 (1872); Van Fossen v. State, 37 Ohio St. 317 (1881) (semble); State v. Westmoreland, 76 S.C. 145, 56 S.E. 673 (1907). One later case contains dictum suggesting that the state would be foreclosed from proving the divorce invalid. Slansky v. State, 192 Md. 94, 63 A.2d 599 (1949).

34. E. Scoles and P. Hay, Conflict of Laws § 15.11 (1982) agrees with the general position in the text but for different reasons. See also Note, Stranger Attack on Sister-State Decrees of Divorce, 24 U.Chi.L.Rev. 376, 387–389 (1957).

35. U.S.Const. art. IV, § 1.

36. Comity may be broadly defined for this purpose as the respect which sovereign nations in a civilized world render to the legal proceedings and judgments of other sovereign nations. II Oxford English Dictionary 666, col. 3. "Comity" is given a more technical definition in discussions of conflict of laws theory. See E. Scoles and P. Hay, Conflict of Laws § 2.4 (1982). Cases dealing with doctrines of comity are collected in Annot., 13 A.L.R.3d 1419 (1967).

37. Juenger, Recognition of Foreign Divorces—British and American Perspectives, 20 Am.J. of Comp.L. 1 (1972) makes this point and also offers a thorough analysis of

the proper bases for recognition of foreign divorces in general. The article also discusses the Hague Convention on Recognition of Divorces and Legal Separations, American Society of International Law, 8 International Legal materials 31 (1968), which has not been signed by the United States.

38. Until March 7, 1971 it was possible to get a divorce in Mexico without being domiciled there. All that was needed was a short visit across the border, just long enough to sign a list of "residents". In some instances Mexican divorces might be obtained by mail order, without even a brief visit to the country. See, e.g., Currie, Suitcase Divorce in the Conflict of Laws, 34 U.Chi.L.Rev. 26 (1966); Leach, Divorce by Plane-Ticket in the Affluent Society, 14 Kan.L.Rev. 549 (1966); New York Times Magazine, Sept. 12, 1965, p. 78. On March 7, 1971 Mexico changed its law so as to require residence for divorce, to be evidenced by a certificate of residence from a government agency which was difficult and expensive to obtain. As a result Mexico is no longer a source of migratory divorces. Juenger, Recognition of Foreign Divorces-British and American Perspectives, 20 Am.J. of Comp.L. 1, 22 (1972).

39. No domicile requirement exists in either of these countries and divorces are granted on either mutual consent or very liberal grounds. See Note, Caribbean Divorce for Americans: Useful Alternative or Obsolescent Institution, 10 Corn.Int.L.J. 117 (1976); Swisher, Foreign Migratory Divorces: A Reappraisal, 21 J.Fam.L. 9 (1982–1983).

can mail-order divorces. These are not recognized in the United States as ending the marital relationship since they exhibit a complete absence of any of the usual bases for divorce jurisdiction.[40] The doctrine of estoppel may in some states be available to prevent attacks upon such divorces, however.[41]

In the second class of cases are those obtained ex parte, solely on the basis of the plaintiff spouse's physical presence in the divorcing nation, without his ever having become domiciled in that nation. By ex parte it is meant that the defendant spouse neither participated in the divorce proceeding, did not make an appearance in the proceeding, nor was personally subject to the jurisdiction of the divorcing court. Divorces of this kind are also generally not recognized by United States courts[42] but may be immune from attack by virtue of the estoppel doctrine.[43] The reason usually given for reaching this result is that jurisdiction for divorce is dependent upon the domicile of at least one of the spouses in the divorcing state, and without jurisdiction over

the subject matter the divorce will not be recognized.[44] The analogy is to Williams II.[45] The law to be applied in such cases is the law of the state of the parties' domicile at the time the foreign divorce was obtained.[46] Of course if by that law the plaintiff did acquire a Mexican domicile, the divorce is valid.[47]

If the plaintiff not only goes to Mexico or other foreign country, and makes a personal appearance in the action, but the defendant does also, a situation analogous to that in the Sherrer case[48] arises. Although the Full Faith and Credit Clause[49] obviously does not protect the divorce decrees of foreign countries, some American courts have relied upon doctrines of comity to reach the same result, drawing on the Sherrer analogy.[50] The same result has been reached when the defendant did not herself go to Mexico but did make an appearance in the divorce action through a Mexican attorney.[51] Other cases have refused to recognize divorces procured in this fashion, however.[52] The estoppel doctrine may also foreclose attack upon these divorces.[53]

40. Cammarota v. Secretary of Health, Education and Welfare, 329 F.Supp. 1087 (N.D.N.Y.1971) (New York law); State v. De Meo, 20 N.J. 1, 118 A.2d 1 (1955); Caldwell v. Caldwell, 298 N.Y. 146, 81 N.E.2d 60 (1948). Other cases are collected in Annot., 13 A.L.R.3d 1419, 1429, 1435 (1967).

41. See section 12.3, infra, in which standing to attack divorce decrees is also discussed.

42. Montemurro v. Immigration and Naturalization Service, 409 F.2d 832 (9th Cir.1969); Farias v. Secretary of Health, Education and Welfare, 390 F.Supp. 480 (D.Puerto Rico 1975); Bethune v. Bethune, 192 Ark. 811, 94 S.W.2d 1043 (1936); Sohnlein v. Winchell, 230 Cal. App. 2d 508, 41 Cal.Rptr. 145 (1964); Litvaitis v. Litvaitis, 162 Conn. 540, 295 A.2d 519 (1972); Butler v. Butler, 239 A.2d 616 (D.C.App.1968); Kittel v. Kittel, 194 So.2d 640 (Fla.App.1967); Shenker v. Shenker, 18 Misc.2d 606, 187 N.Y.S.2d 95 (1959); Yoder v. Yoder, 24 Ohio App.2d 71, 263 N.E.2d 913 (1970). Other cases are collected in Annot., 13 A.L.R.3d 1419, 1431, 1435 (1967).

43. See section 12.3, infra.

44. Litvaitis v. Litvaitis, 162 Conn. 540, 295 A.2d 519 (1972).

45. Williams v. North Carolina, 325 U.S. 226, 65 S.Ct. 1092, 89 L.Ed. 1577 (1945), rehearing denied 325 U.S. 895, 65 S.Ct. 1560, 89 L.Ed. 2006 (1945).

46. Meeker v. Meeker, 52 N.J. 59, 243 A.2d 801 (1968), 1969 Duke L.J. 192.

47. Scott v. Scott, 51 Cal.2d 249, 331 P.2d 641 (1958).

48. Sherrer v. Sherrer, 334 U.S. 343, 68 S.Ct. 1087, 92 L.Ed. 1429 (1948).

49. U.S.Const. art. IV, § 1.

50. Drew v. Hobby, 123 F.Supp. 245 (S.D.N.Y. 1954).

51. Perrin v. Perrin, 408 F.2d 107 (3d Cir.1969); McCarthy v. McCarthy, 361 Mass. 359, 280 N.E.2d 151 (1972) (semble); Greschler v. Greschler, 51 N.Y.2d 368, 434 N.Y.S.2d 194, 414 N.E.2d 694 (1980) (Dominican divorce); Rosenstiel v. Rosenstiel, 16 N.Y.2d 64, 262 N.Y.S.2d 86, 209 N.E.2d 709 (1965), cert. denied 384 U.S. 971, 86 S.Ct. 1861, 16 L.Ed.2d 682 (1966); Ramm v. Ramm, 34 A.D.2d 667, 310 N.Y.S.2d 111 (2d Dept.1970), affirmed p.c. 28 N.Y.2d 892, 322 N.Y.S.2d 726, 271 N.E.2d 558 (1971); Kraham v. Kraham, 73 Misc.2d 977, 342 N.Y.S.2d 943 (1973); Rosen v. Sitner, 274 Pa.Super. 445, 418 A.2d 490 (1980) (New York law); Terrell v. Terrell, 578 S.W.2d 637 (Tenn.1979) (Haitian divorce); Hyde v. Hyde, 562 S.W.2d 194 (Tenn.1978) (Dominican divorce). Other cases are cited in Annot., 13 A.L.R.3d 1419, 1433 (1967).

52. Prudential Insurance Co. of America v. Lewis, 306 F.Supp. 1177 (N.D.Ala.1969); Clagett v. King, 308 A.2d 245 (D.C.App.1973); Everett v. Everett, 345 So.2d 586 (La. App.1977), writ denied 349 So.2d 329 (1977) (Dominican divorce); Weber v. Weber, 200 Neb. 659, 265 N.W.2d 436 (1978) (Dominican divorce); Golden v. Golden, 41 N.M. 356, 68 P.2d 928 (1937); Warrender v. Warrender, 79 N.J. Super. 114, 190 A.2d 684 (1963), affirmed p.c. 42 N.J. 287, 200 A.2d 123 (1964); Bobala v. Bobala, 68 Ohio App. 63, 33 N.E.2d 845 (1940); In re Steffke's Estate, 65 Wis.2d 199, 222 N.W.2d 628 (1974).

53. See section 12.3, infra.

The cases recognizing these bilateral migratory divorces have been heavily criticized by scholars of the conflict of laws.[54] Criticism may be justified from the viewpoint of conflict of laws theory, whatever that may be, but there is a more important consideration which leads to approval of the cases. As a matter of divorce policy there is no substantial state interest to be served by denying recognition to a divorce when both spouses cooperate to obtain it, provided of course that the cooperation is not the product of duress, fraud or overreaching. This is especially true now that fault has largely been banished from the scene and the divorce defenses along with it. Furthermore, as Rosenstiel said,[55] there is no real difference except in the amount of expense involved between a six-week stay in Nevada which the Full Faith and Credit Clause[56] requires the home state to accept, and an even briefer stay in Mexico, Haiti or the Dominican Republic. If Nevada's bilateral decrees must be recognized, the only effect of denying the same recognition to Haiti's is to accentuate the discrimination based upon wealth. Therefore Rosenstiel[57] and its progeny are clearly correct.

Where the foreign nation divorce was not obtained out of a desire to evade the law of the parties' home state, and is valid by the law of the country in which it was obtained, it certainly should be recognized in the United States. Such divorces are generally recognized as valid in the various states, notwithstanding the fact that domicile may not have been the basis for jurisdiction in the foreign nation.[58] The domicile requirement as announced in the cases involving Mexican or similar migratory divorces should not be applied to other cases where no evasion motive exists. In fact the American states have on rare occasions recognized foreign nation religious, non-judicial divorces where those were valid by the law of the foreign nation.[59] A rule favoring recognition has the virtues of vindicating the parties' expectations and achieving certainty in their relationship, and in most instances does not offend the policies of the recognizing state.[60]

 WESTLAW REFERENCES

State Statutes Imposing Durational Residence Requirements

di(divorc! /s resid! /s subject-matter /2 jurisdiction)
sosna /p divorc! dissol!

Federal Jurisdiction in Domestic Relations Matters

sy(domestic family support divorc! /2 matter relation /s (federal /3 court) subject-matter /s jurisdiction!)

Indian Divorces

divorc! domestic! dissol! /s indian trib! /s state /s jurisdiction!

Notice and Opportunity to be Heard: Due Process

"due process" "fourteenth amendment" /s rem /s divorce! dissol! domestic

divorc! /s "fourteenth amendment" "due process" opportunity /s indigen! /s boddie

Full Faith and Credit

divorc! /s "full faith and credit" /s jurisdiction! /s william

54. Currie, Suitcase Divorce in the Conflict of Laws, 34 U.Chi.L.Rev. 26 (1966). Analysis somewhat similar to that in the text is found in E.Scoles, P.Hay, Conflict of Laws § 15.22 (1982).

55. Rosenstiel v. Rosenstiel, 16 N.Y.2d 64, 262 N.Y.S.2d 86, 209 N.E.2d 709 (1965), cert. denied 384 U.S. 971, 86 S.Ct. 1861, 16 L.Ed.2d 682 (1966).

56. U.S.Const. art. IV, § 1.

57. See note 55, supra.

58. Gonzalez v. Beraha, 449 F.Supp. 1011 (D.Canal Zone 1978) (Panama divorce); Schiereck v. Schiereck, 14 Mass.App.Ct. 378, 439 N.E.2d 859 (1982), review denied 387 Mass. 1103, 441 N.E.2d 260 (West German divorce); Chaudry v. Chaudry, 159 N.J.Super. 566, 388 A.2d 1000 (1978), certification denied 78 N.J. 335, 395 A.2d 204 (1978) (Pakistani divorce).

59. Machransky v. Machransky, 31 Ohio App. 482, 166 N.E. 423 (1927). See Note, United States Recognition of Foreign Nonjudicial Divorces, 53 Minn.L.Rev. 612 (1969). The House of Lords recognized, under the Recognition of Divorces and Legal Separations Act of 1971, a Pakistani religious divorce, a *talaq*, obtained by the husband in Pakistan. Quazi v. Quazi, [1979] 3 All.Eng.Rep. 897. See Maidment, The Legal Effect of Religious Divorces, 37 Mod.L.Rev. 611 (1974). Religious divorces obtained in the United States by spouses living here have not been recognized. Shikoh v. Murff, 257 F.2d 306 (2d Cir.1958); Seth v. Seth, 694 S.W.2d 459 (Tex.App.1985).

60. See Peterson, Foreign County Judgments and the Second Restatement of Conflict of Laws, 72 Colum.L.Rev. 220 (1972); Juenger, Recognition of Foreign Divorces-British and American Perspectives, 20 Am.J.Comp.L. 1 (1972).

Attack Foreclosed by Res Judicata

sherrer /s domicil!

domicil! /s res +1 judicata adjudicata /s
jurisdiction! /s divorc! domestic dissol!

Foreign Country Divorces

divorc! /s comity /s foreign! /s country nation
international! /s recogni!

§ 12.3 Divorce—Estoppel Against Jurisdictional Attack on Divorce Decrees

As a general principle a court's judgment given without jurisdiction over the subject matter of the action is void and open to collateral attack,[1] either by the parties to the original suit[2] or by others whose interests may

have been affected thereby.[3] This principle governs divorce decrees as well as other kinds of decrees and judgments,[4] perhaps with even greater force because of the state's often mentioned interest in divorces. Yet there is another conflicting principle, that one who obtains a judgment cannot later collaterally attack it upon jurisdictional grounds.[5] This principle also has long been applied to divorce decrees,[6] (though not without some disagreement), and recently has been rather broadly extended.[7] This second principle is commonly referred to as "estoppel." For convenience it will be so named here, although it sometimes differs from technical equitable estoppel.[8]

One application of estoppel to divorce decrees is discussed in another section.[9] Sher-

---

§ 12.3

1. 1 A. Freeman, Judgments §§ 333, 337 (5th ed.1925); Note, Developments in the Law of Res Judicata, 65 Harv. L.Rev. 818, 851, 853 (1952); Baltimore Mail S.S. Co. v. Fawcett, 269 N.Y. 379, 390, 199 N.E. 628, 633 (1936), cert. denied 298 U.S. 675, 56 S.Ct. 939, 80 L.Ed. 1396 (1936); Restatement (Second) of Conflict of Laws § 105 (1971). The principle is limited today by doctrines of res judicata and rules about timeliness. See Restatement (Second) of Judgments §§ 11, 12, com. b (1982); Bosky and Braucher, Jurisdiction and Collateral Attack, 40 Colum.L.Rev. 1006 (1940). Default judgments are open to collateral attack on broader principles than contested judgments for that reason. Restatement (Second) of Judgments §§ 65, 66 (1982).

2. 1 A. Freeman, Judgments § 317 (5th ed.1925).

3. Id. § 318. Treece v. Treece, 84 Idaho 457, 373 P.2d 750 (1962) (dictum).

4. Jacobs, Attack on Decrees of Divorce, 34 Mich.L. Rev. 749 (1936), reprinted in Association of American Law Schools, Selected Essays on Family Law, 987 (1950); Note, Stranger Attack on Sister-State Decrees of Divorce, 24 U.Chi.L.Rev. 376 (1957). For an example of the rigid treatment of jurisdiction see People v. Dawell, 25 Mich. 247 (1872) (per Cooley, J.).

5. Three States Lumber Co. v. Blanks, 133 Fed. 479 (6th Cir. 1904); Consolidated Home Supply Ditch & Reservoir Co. v. New Loveland & G. Irr. & Land Co., 27 Colo. 521, 62 P. 364 (1900); Ray v. McLain, 106 La. 780, 31 So. 315 (1901); Hewitt v. Northrup, 75 N.Y. 506 (1878); 3 J. Story, Equity Jurisprudence 581 (14th ed. 1918); 1 A. Freeman, Judgments § 320 (5th ed.1925).

6. E.g. Palmer v. Palmer, 1 Sw. & Tr. 551, 164 Eng. Rep. 855 (Ct. for Div. and Matrim. Causes 1859); Ellis v. White, 61 Iowa 644, 17 N.W. 28 (1883). Cases contra often turned on the argument that the application of estoppel would in effect allow spouses to confer jurisdiction and obtain divorces by consent alone. See Smith v. Smith, 79 Mass. (13 Gray) 209 (1859).

Other cases on this point are collected in the following Annotations: 60 L.R.A. 294, 301 (1903); 51 L.R.A.(n.s.)

534 (1914); 109 A.L.R. 1018, 1019 (1937); 122 A.L.R. 1321, 1323 (1939); 140 A.L.R. 914, 915 (1942); 153 A.L.R. 941, 943 (1944); 175 A.L.R. 538, 539 (1948).

7. The extension is nicely illustrated by the successive changes in the Restatement of the Conflict of Laws. The original Restatement, § 112, in 1934 stated that "the validity of a divorce decree cannot be questioned * * * either by a spouse who has obtained such decree of divorce from a court which had no jurisdiction, or by a spouse who takes advantage of such decree by remarrying." A caveat was included, expressing no view on whether a spouse might be precluded from questioning the validity of a divorce for other reasons. In the 1948 supplement to the Restatement, Conflict of Laws, the caveat was removed, and language was added in comment c to section 112: "Any person may be precluded from questioning the validity of a divorce decree if, under all the circumstances, his conduct has led to the obtaining of the divorce decree, or for any other reason has been such as to make it inequitable to permit him to deny the validity of the divorce decree." Restatement (Second) of Conflict of Laws § 74 (1971) finally revises the rule to make it read: "A person may be precluded from attacking the validity of a foreign divorce decree if, under the circumstances, it would be inequitable for him to do so."

8. Equitable estoppel is defined variously. See McClintock, Equity 79 (2d ed. 1948). See also 3 Pomeroy, Equity Jurisprudence 189 (5th ed. 1941): "Equitable estoppel is the effect of the voluntary conduct of a party whereby he is absolutely precluded, both at law and in equity, from asserting rights which might perhaps have otherwise existed, * * * as against another person, who has in good faith relied upon such conduct, and has been led thereby to change his position for the worse * * *." In accord is Bigelow, Estoppel 607 (6th ed. 1913). Short historical sketches of the origins of estoppel can be found in 9 Holdsworth, History of English Law 161 (1926), and 3 Pomeroy, Equity Jurisprudence 179 (5th ed. 1941).

9. See section 12.2, supra.

rer v. Sherrer [10] held that if a state which granted a divorce would deny collateral attack upon it because the defendant had had an opportunity to raise and litigate the question of jurisdiction over the subject matter, then other states must also refuse to entertain collateral attacks upon the same grounds. Sherrer thus announced a principle of full faith and credit whose application depends upon the rule of res judicata or collateral estoppel adopted in the state granting the divorce. The policy underlying this rule is that which demands finality in litigation after a person has had a chance to present his case. The policy underlying the kind of estoppel presently under discussion is different, as will appear. Both doctrines preclude attack on admittedly invalid divorces, but for different reasons.

Logically it would seem that if the Full Faith and Credit Clause [11] requires that a foreign state respect the doctrines of res judicata of the divorcing state, it should likewise require that the foreign state respect the rules of estoppel prevailing in the divorcing state. So, if the divorcing state would exclude collateral attack upon its own decree by the party who obtained it, on a theory of estoppel, the Full Faith and Credit Clause should forbid a similar attack in other states. But in spite of the apparently logical analogy, this is not the law. [12] The reason lies in the difference between res judicata and estoppel. The application of res judicata depends upon the conditions under which the divorce was granted and is really a function of the divorce decree itself. The estoppel under discussion here, however, is an equity principle dependent upon events which may have occurred after the divorce was granted or apart from the divorce action. It is not a function of the decree but a personal disability of the party attacking the decree. It is not a rule of jurisdiction. Therefore its application is not governed by the Full Faith and Credit Clause.

Under what circumstances then will courts invoke or refuse to invoke estoppel? After an examination of these, an attempt can be made to determine the bases and extent of the doctrine.

The circumstance which most obviously calls for application of the estoppel theory is that the divorce was obtained by the very party attempting to attack it. Usually it is held that he is estopped to question the decree. [13] The courts which reach this result are careful not to say that such divorces are valid, but rather say that the attacking party is estopped to assert that they are invalid. In

---

10. 334 U.S. 343, 68 S.Ct. 1087, 92 L.Ed. 1429 (1948).

11. U.S.Const. art. IV, § 1.

12. See Restatement (Second) of Conflict of Laws § 74 (1971): "Unlike the principle of res judicata (see § 73), application of this estoppel doctrine has not to date been held required by any constitutional mandate. Its applicability in a particular case has been held to be determined not by the local law of the state in which the divorce was granted but by the local law of the state in which the divorce is attacked. Each State of the United States has been deemed free, at least within broad limits, to determine the rule's scope and effect. Whether full faith and credit requires that a person who would be estopped from attacking the divorce decree in the State of rendition must likewise be held estopped from attacking the decree in a sister State is a question that appears never to have arisen." The Restatement does not state what it means by the qualification "at least within broad limits." See Gaylord v. Gaylord, 45 So.2d 507 (Fla.1950); Astor v. Astor, 6 Misc.2d 967, 160 N.Y.S.2d 103 (1967).

13. Cohen v. Randall, 137 F.2d 441 (2d Cir.1943), cert. denied 320 U.S. 796, 64 S.Ct. 263, 88 L.Ed. 48 (1943) (New York law); Curry v. Curry, 65 App.D.C. 47, 79 F.2d 172 (1935); Reiss v. Reiss, 46 Ala.App. 422, 243 So.2d 507 (1970), writ denied 286 Ala. 737, 243 So.2d 514 (1971);

Oberstein v. Oberstein, 217 Ark. 80, 228 S.W.2d 615 (1950); Rediker v. Rediker, 35 Cal.2d 796, 221 P.2d 1 (1950); In re Toth's Marriage, 38 Cal.App.2d 205, 113 Cal. Rptr. 131 (1974); Mattos v. Correia, 274 Cal.App.2d 413, 79 Cal.Rptr. 229 (1969); Oakley v. Oakley, 30 Colo.App. 292, 493 P.2d 381 (1972), cert. dismissed 179 Colo. 450, 514 P.2d 633 (1973); Clagett v. King, 308 A.2d 245 (D.C. App. 1973); Bledsoe v. Seaman, 77 Kan. 679, 95 P. 576 (1908); Asbury v. Powers, 23 Ky.L.Rep. 1622, 65 S.W. 605 (1901); Leatherbury v. Leatherbury, 233 Md. 344, 196 A.2d 883 (1964); 24 Md.L.Rev. 215 (1964); Lorant v. Lorant, 366 Mass. 380, 318 N.E.2d 830 (1974); Watson v. Watson, 238 Minn. 403, 57 N.W.2d 691 (1953); In re Ellis' Estate, 55 Minn. 401, 56 N.W. 1056 (1893); Untermann v. Untermann, 19 N.J. 507, 117 A.2d 599 (1955) (unclean hands); Krause v. Krause, 282 N.Y. 355, 26 N.E.2d 290 (1940); Marc v. Marc, 68 Misc.2d 340, 326 N.Y.S.2d 489 (Fam.Ct.1971); Starbuck v. Starbuck, 173 N.Y. 503, 66 N.E. 193 (1903); Brown v. Brown, 242 App.Div. 33, 272 N.Y.S. 877 (4th Dept.1934), affirmed p.c. 266 N.Y. 532, 195 N.E. 186 (1935); Diamond v. Diamond, 501 Pa. 418, 461 A.2d 1227 (1983); In re Romanski's Estate, 354 Pa. 261, 47 A.2d 233 (1946); Smoak v. Smoak, 269 S.C. 313, 237 S.E.2d 372 (1977); Dunn v. Tiernan, 284 S.W.2d 754 (Tex.Civ.App.1955); In re Tamke's Estate, 32 Wash.2d 927, 204 P.2d 526 (1949).

fact one court held that a husband could not assert the invalidity of his divorce from his first wife even after an annulment suit brought by his second wife had established that the divorce was void.[14] What is probably the utmost extension of the estoppel doctrine occurred in an Ohio case which held that a wife who falsely told her husband she had divorced him was estopped to deny that she had, after he had remarried on the faith of her statement.[15] This is divorce by consent with a vengeance, but it does fit the usual requirements for technical equitable estoppel. The defense of connivance may sometimes be used to reach the same result.[16]

Obtaining the decree does not estop the wife from questioning it, however, where she brought the divorce action as the result of the coercion, duress or fraud of her husband,[17] or

where for other reasons she cannot be held responsible for her actions.[18]

Participation in obtaining the divorce, as by persuading a married person to divorce his spouse,[19] or by financing a married woman's divorce with the intention of marrying her,[20] also has been held to estop one from a later collateral attack on the decree. If participation takes the form of an appearance in the case as defendant, then of course the Sherrer rule would immunize the resulting divorce from attack,[21] although the cases occasionally use the language of estoppel here.[22]

Estoppel may also rest upon acts or events occurring after the divorce in question. A long acquiescence in the divorce with knowledge of its jurisdictional defect will often foreclose an attack, whether the rationale of the defense is labeled estoppel or laches.[23]

14. Watson v. Watson, 39 Cal.2d 305, 246 P.2d 19 (1952).

15. Edgar v. Richardson, 33 Ohio St. 581 (1878).

16. Shilman v. Shilman, 105 Misc. 461, 174 N.Y.S. 385 (1918), affirmed without opinion 188 App.Div. 908, 175 N.Y.S. 681 (1919), affirmed without opinion 230 N.Y. 554, 130 N.E. 890 (1920). Here the husband had obtained a Jewish divorce, after which the wife remarried. He then sued her for divorce on the ground of adultery and the court held him barred by his connivance. See also Langewald v. Langewald, 234 Mass. 269, 125 N.E. 566 (1920); Loud v. Loud, 129 Mass. 14 (1880).

17. Meyer v. Meyer, 328 Ill.App. 408, 66 N.E.2d 457 (1946); Burton v. Burton, 176 Okl. 494, 56 P.2d 385 (1936); Graham v. Graham, 54 Wash. 70, 102 P. 891 (1909) (Semble).

18. Meyer v. Meyer, 328 Ill.App. 408, 66 N.E.2d 457 (1946) (wife in a sanatorium for alcoholism).

19. Goodloe v. Hawk, 72 App.D.C. 287, 113 F.2d 753 (1940); Bowen v. Finke, 34 F.Supp. 235 (D.D.C.1940); Kazin v. Kazin, 81 N.J. 85, 405 A.2d 360 (1979) (semble); Margulies v. Margulies, 109 N.J.Eq. 391, 157 A. 676 (1931); Packer v. Packer, 6 A.D.2d 464, 179 N.Y.S.2d 801 (1st Dept.1958). Contra: Jardine v. Jardine, 291 Ill.App. 152, 9 N.E.2d 645 (1937); Golden v. Golden, 41 N.M. 356, 68 P.2d 928 (1937); Ex parte Nimmer, 212 S.C. 311, 47 S.E.2d 716 (1948).

20. In re Coleman's Estate, 132 Cal.App.2d 137, 281 P.2d 567 (1955).

21. See note 10, supra.

22. In re Coleman's Estate, 132 Cal.App.2d 137, 281 P.2d 567 (1955); Scherer v. Scherer, 405 N.E.2d 40 (Ind. App.1980) (participation by obtaining counsel, executing documents consenting to the decree, reliance on the decree); Webb v. Webb, 461 S.W.2d 204 (Tex.Civ.App.1970) (participation by filing jointly with other spouse).

23. Harris v. Harris, 90 U.S.App.D.C. 239, 196 F.2d 46 (1952), cert. denied 344 U.S. 829, 73 S.Ct. 34, 97 L.Ed. 645 (1952), rehearing denied 344 U.S. 888, 73 S.Ct. 182, 97 L.Ed. 687 (1952) (fourteen-year delay); In re Shank's Estate, 154 Cal.App.2d 808, 316 P.2d 710 (1957); Brown v. Brown, 274 Cal.App.2d 178, 79 Cal.Rptr. 257 (1969); Swift v. Swift, 239 Iowa 62, 29 N.W.2d 535 (1947) (defect here consisted of absence of proper service, laches held to operate against the husband, the innocent party); Langewald v. Langewald, 234 Mass. 269, 125 N.E. 566 (1920); Zirkalos v. Zirkalos, 326 Mich. 420, 40 N.W.2d 313 (1949); (husband estopped to question wife's divorce from prior marriage after six-year acquiescence with knowledge of facts); Marvin v. Foster, 61 Minn. 154, 63 N.W. 484 (1895); Van Slyke v. Van Slyke, 186 Mich. 324, 152 N.W. 921 (1915); Krieger v. Krieger, 25 N.Y.2d 364, 306 N.Y.S.2d 441, 254 N.E.2d 750 (1969), motion denied 27 N.Y.2d 741, 314 N.Y.S.2d 990, 263 N.E.2d 389 (1970) (estoppel based upon a twelve-year delay in attacking the divorce, during which time the other spouse remarried); Marcus v. Marcus, 194 Misc. 464, 90 N.Y.S.2d 830 (1949) (semble); Hansen v. Hansen, 185 Misc. 443, 57 N.Y.S.2d 331 (1945); Jannino v. Jannino, 234 S.C. 352, 108 S.E.2d 572 (1959); Caffall v. Caffall, 5 Utah 2d 407, 303 P.2d 286 (1956) (nine-year delay produces estoppel).

Contra: Tarlton v. Tarlton, 262 Ala. 67, 77 So.2d 347 (1955) (no laches or estoppel where the complaining party did not know the facts); Brandt v. Brandt, 76 Ariz. 154, 261 P.2d 978 (1953); In re Atherley's Estate, 44 Cal.App. 3d 758, 119 Cal.Rptr. 41 (1975) (not unconscionable to allow first wife to attack a divorce though she acquiesced in it to some extent); Ludwig v. Ludwig, 413 Ill. 44, 107 N.E.2d 848 (1952); Staley v. Staley, 251 Md. 701, 248 A.2d 655 (1968) (no laches based on non-action for eighteen months); Freda v. Bergman, 77 N.J.Eq. 46, 76 A. 460 (1910); Lorenzo v. Lorenzo, 85 N.M. 305, 512 P.2d 65 (1973); Heckathorn v. Heckathorn, 77 N.M. 369, 423 P.2d 410 (1967); Landsman v. Landsman, 302 N.Y. 45, 96

Acceptance of benefits, usually alimony, under the divorce has the same consequence.[24] Remarriage after the defective decree, either by the person attacking it,[25] or by the other party,[26] will usually raise an estoppel, as will reliance upon the decree by innocent third parties.[27] At this point estoppel to attack a defective divorce begins to resemble estoppel to attack a defective marriage, since both arise from the courts' reluctance to upset relationships formed (by one party at least) in good faith and in ignorance of any defect.[28]

This summary of the kinds of cases in which courts have rejected attacks upon invalid divorce decrees is evidence of a broad

acceptance of the estoppel doctrine. If a mere counting of cases were not irrelevant, or even misleading, one might sum up by saying that the majority of jurisdictions approve of estoppel in this context and let the matter rest there. Nevertheless the cases which do not approve are numerous enough and of sufficient standing as authorities to require further discussion of the basis and extent of the doctrine. The confusion which is found within particular jurisdictions such as New York also demands some clarification.

One rationale, originating in New York[29] and seized upon with relief by troubled judges

N.E.2d 81 (1950); Davis v. Davis, 279 N.Y. 657, 18 N.E.2d 301 (1938), aff'g without opinion 259 App.Div. 719, 4 N.Y.S.2d 996 (1st Dep't 1938); Kiessenbeck v. Kiessenbeck, 145 Or. 82, 26 P.2d 58 (1933); Loiacono v. Loiacono, 179 Pa.Super. 387, 116 A.2d 881 (1955). Cf. also Mercer v. Mercer, 231 Ark. 155, 328 S.W.2d 365 (1959).

24. Anderson v. Anderson, 223 Ark. 571, 267 S.W.2d 316 (1954); In re Marriage of Maxfield, 142 Cal.App.3d 755, 191 Cal.Rptr. 267 (1983); Novak v. Novak, 126 Ind. App. 428, 133 N.E.2d 578 (1956); Langewald v. Langewald, 234 Mass. 269, 125 N.E. 566 (1920); Chapman v. Chapman, 224 Mass. 427, 113 N.E. 359 (1916); Norris v. Norris, 342 Mich. 83, 69 N.W.2d 208 (1955), cert. denied 350 U.S. 903, 76 S.Ct. 182, 100 L.Ed. 793 (1955). Contra: Amplatz v. Amplatz, 289 N.W.2d 164 (Minn.1980).

25. Dietrich v. Dietrich, 41 Cal.2d 497, 261 P.2d 269 (1953), cert. denied 346 U.S. 938, 74 S.Ct. 378, 98 L.Ed. 426 (1954); Bruguiere v. Bruguiere, 172 Cal. 199, 155 P. 988 (1916); Matter of Birch's Estate, 140 Cal.App.3d 776, 189 Cal.Rptr. 796 (1983); Smith v. Smith, 157 Cal.App.2d 46, 320 P.2d 100 (1958); Wendell v. Wendell, 111 Cal.App. 2d 899, 245 P.2d 342 (1952); In re Kyle, 77 Cal.App.2d 634, 176 P.2d 96 (1947); Arthur v. Israel, 15 Colo. 146, 25 P. 81 (1890) (immaterial that attacking party did not know the divorce was void); Reichert v. Appel, 74 So.2d 674 (Fla.1954); Mohler v. Shank's Estate, 93 Iowa 273, 61 N.W. 981 (1895); Chapman v. Chapman, 224 Mass. 427, 113 N.E. 359 (1916); Norris v. Norris, 342 Mich. 83, 69 N.W.2d 208 (1955), cert. denied 350 U.S. 903, 76 S.Ct. 182, 100 L.Ed. 793 (1955); Packer v. Packer, 6 A.D.2d 464, 179 N.Y.S.2d 801 (1st Dep't 1958); Matter of Bingham's Will, 265 App.Div. 463, 39 N.Y.S.2d 756 (2d Dep't 1943), appeal denied 266 A.D. 669, 41 N.Y.S.2d 180 (1943); Kelsey v. Kelsey, 204 App.Div. 116, 197 N.Y.S. 371 (4th Dept. 1922), affirmed without opinion 237 N.Y. 520, 143 N.E. 726 (1923); Dale v. Carson, 141 Okl. 105, 283 P. 1017 (1929); Cummings v. Huddleston, 99 Okl. 195, 226 P. 104 (1924); Rosen v. Sitner, 274 Pa.Super. 445, 418 A.2d 490 (1980); Newberry v. Newberry, 257 S.C. 202, 184 S.E.2d 704 (1971). Other cases are collected in Annots., 12 A.L.R.2d 153 (1950), 81 A.L.R.3d 110 (1977).

Contra: Gardner v. Gardner, 144 W.Va. 630, 110 S.E.2d 495 (1959).

26. In re Shank's Estate, 154 Cal.App.2d 808, 316 P.2d 170 (1957); Neuman v. Neuman, 377 A.2d 393 (D.C.App. 1977); Lanigan v. Lanigan, 78 So.2d 92 (Fla.1955) (remarriage plus delay of sixteen years amounted to laches); Novak v. Novak, 126 Ind.App. 428, 133 N.E.2d 578 (1956); Poor v. Poor, 381 Mass. 392, 409 N.E.2d 758 (1980) (both parties remarried); Langewald v. Langewald, 234 Mass. 269, 125 N.E. 566 (1920); Loud v. Loud, 129 Mass. 14 (1880) (wife connived at or acquiesced in husband's remarriage); Bussey v. Bussey, 95 N.H. 349, 64 A.2d 4 (1949) (semble); Scoufos v. Fuller, 280 P.2d 720 (Okl. 1954). Other cases are cited in Annots., 12 A.L.R.2d 153 (1950) and 81 A.L.R.3d 110 (1977).

Contra: Yost v. Yost, 161 Neb. 164, 72 N.W.2d 689 (1955) (under Uniform Divorce Recognition Act); Sorrentino v. Mierzwa, 25 N.Y.2d 59, 302 N.Y.S.2d 565, 250 N.E.2d 58 (1969).

27. Chapman v. Chapman, 224 Mass. 427, 113 N.E. 359 (1916) (semble).

28. The leading case on the whole question of estoppel, Spellens v. Spellens, 49 Cal.2d 210, 317 P.2d 613 (1957), involved attack on a bigamous marriage contracted before a prior marriage had been finally dissolved. Similar cases relying on estoppel include Higgins v. Higgins, 266 Ark. 953, 588 S.W.2d 454 (1979); Fox v. Fox, 247 Ark. 188, 444 S.W.2d 865 (1969); In re Marriage of Recknor, 138 Cal.App.3d 539, 187 Cal.Rptr. 887 (1982); Szlauzis v. Szlauzis, 255 Ill. 314, 99 N.E. 640 (1912); In re Marriage of Summers, 645 S.W.2d 205 (Mo.App.1983); Rooney v. Rooney, 54 N.J.Eq. 231, 34 A. 682 (1896); White v. Kessler, 101 N.J.Eq. 369, 139 A. 241 (1927); Gress v. Gress, 209 S.W.2d 1003 (Tex.Civ.App.1948). Contra, rejecting estoppel: Anderson v. Anderson, 27 Conn. Supp. 342, 238 A.2d 45 (1967); Rhodes v. Miller, 189 La. 288, 179 So. 430 (1938); Landsman v. Landsman, 302 N.Y. 45, 96 N.E.2d 81 (1950), 51 Colum.L.Rev. 388 (1951); Martin v. Martin, 54 W.Va. 301, 46 S.E. 120 (1903).

See also Z. Chafee, Some Problems of Equity 75–77 (1950).

29. See e.g. Starbuck v. Starbuck, 173 N.Y. 503, 66 N.E. 193 (1903); and Stevens v. Stevens, 273 N.Y. 157, 7 N.E.2d 26 (1937).

in other states,[30] makes the application of estoppel turn upon the nature of the lawsuit, once facts are found to be present which might justify the estoppel. If the action is "matrimonial", estoppel is said to be inappropriate and the state's interest in regulating marriage dictates that the divorce without jurisdiction be held void. On the other hand if the action is merely a "private" dispute over property, even though it may turn upon marital status, estoppel can apply. The New York courts, with an ingenuity which would be praiseworthy if employed in a socially useful cause, have succeeded in constructing upon this ostensibly simple distinction an edifice of inconsistency and confusion unsurpassed elsewhere in the law. Unfortunately for the rest of the nation, their decisions have had some influence in other states.

The distinction between "matrimonial" and "property" or "private" claims seems to have been first suggested in a short opinion by the New York Court of Appeals in Stevens v. Stevens,[31] though not precisely in those terms. In that case the wife sued for a separation and the husband counterclaimed for a divorce on the ground of adultery. It appeared that the husband had already obtained a Nevada divorce, but it was conceded that the Nevada decree was without jurisdiction. The Court held that the husband was not estopped to assert Nevada's lack of jurisdiction even though he had obtained the divorce. The earlier Starbuck case,[32] which held that a wife was estopped to attack a divorce which she herself had obtained and thus could not claim dower in the estate of her ex-husband, was distinguished as being a case "different in character." The two cases were in fact materially different. While in Starbuck the wife

alone attacked the previously obtained divorce as invalid, in Stevens both husband and wife asked the Court to disregard the earlier divorce and to assume the continued existence of the marriage. The wife in Stevens was in no position to invoke estoppel against her husband with respect to his counterclaim for divorce since she could hardly allege that the Nevada divorce was effective in barring any further action by her husband, but wholly inoperative as to her. The New York Court, however, inexplicably chose to ignore this factual distinction, stating rather that in Starbuck the rejection of the wife's attack on the divorce she had obtained was "necessary in the due administration of justice," while in Stevens estoppel would not lie simply because the "court was invoked (sic) to pronounce directly upon the marital status—a relationship which no stipulation or conduct of the parties could alter."

The distinction inarticulately propounded in Stevens to explain what appeared to be an inconsistency in the cases was described in more precise terms by the dissenting opinion in Krause v. Krause.[33] In that case a second wife sued her husband for separation and support, after they had lived together about six years. The husband's defense was that the Reno divorce which he had obtained from his first wife was void for lack of jurisdiction, so that he could not marry the plaintiff. The New York Court of Appeals held, however, that the husband could not thus avoid the responsibility of supporting his second wife, a responsibility which he voluntarily undertook.[34] It specifically disavowed any recognition of the Reno divorce as valid, saying only that although it was invalid, he was estopped (or rather "quasi estopped") to attack it. It

30. E.g. In re Romanski's Estate, 354 Pa. 261, 47 A.2d 233 (1946); Hamm v. Hamm, 30 Tenn.App. 122, 204 S.W.2d 113 (1947), 20 Tenn.L.Rev. 211 (1948), 1 Vand.L. Rev. 161 (1947); In re Englund's Estate, 45 Wash.2d 708, 277 P.2d 717 (1954); In re Tamke's Estate, 32 Wash.2d 927, 204 P.2d 526 (1949); Gardner v. Gardner, 144 W.Va. 630, 110 S.E.2d 495 (1959).

31. 273 N.Y. 157, 7 N.E.2d 26 (1937).

32. Starbuck v. Starbuck, 173 N.Y. 503, 66 N.E. 193 (1903). The facts in this case provide the classic instance of estoppel. The court refuses to let a wife disavow her

divorce in order to profit at the expense of the husband's second wife and the children of the second marriage.

33. 282 N.Y. 355, 26 N.E.2d 290 (1940).

34. In the course of its opinion the court distinguished the Stevens case on the ground that there the husband was not really taking a position inconsistent with the Nevada decree, since in both Nevada and New York suits he was seeking to terminate the marriage. This distinction bears out the analysis suggested below, at notes 92, 93, 94.

also said that the needs of the first wife would be taken into account in determining how much should be awarded to the second wife. The dissent, after a consideration of all the New York precedents, argued that they could be placed in two categories. The first group, including the Stevens case, were "matrimonial actions-cases that primarily involved a marital status asserted as such." [35] Those cases, the dissent said, due to the public policy of the state, must declare the true status of the parties regardless of what hardship may result. The second group, including Starbuck, were "private suits", in which the claim, "though predicated of a marriage—was personal to an individual party." [36] In this second group of cases "equitable inducements conceived as affecting only the several parties to the litigation" could be considered by the courts. The dissenting judge thought, however, that the facts of the Krause case itself brought it into the first group of cases, in which the court was bound to declare the true marital status irrespective of equitable considerations. Although the majority opinion did not discuss the dissent's characterization of the precedents, its holding that estoppel would be applied in an action for separation must certainly be construed as a refusal to embrace the matrimonial-private distinction, for if any action should be labeled "matrimo-

nial" the action for separation should, as the dissenting opinion demonstrates.

Notwithstanding the majority's failure to approve the matrimonial-private distinction in the Krause case, the next case, Querze v. Querze,[37] seemed to assume that this distinction was part of the law of New York, although such an assumption was not necessary to the decision. Querze summed up the prior cases as holding that one who obtains a foreign divorce is estopped to attack it in a private suit, but that he may have a full adjudication of his marital status in a matrimonial action. In this case a wife sued her husband for divorce and alimony. He defended on the ground of a Mexican mail order divorce, which the wife had obtained several years before. The wife argued that this divorce was wholly void. The court held she was not estopped to urge this, even though the husband had since remarried, because this was a matrimonial action. The claim for alimony did not transform it into a "private" suit, that claim being based upon statute not common law. The court failed to explain why an alimony claim in a divorce action is not "private", when support money in a separation suit (under Krause) *is* "private." [38] Querze's characterization of the suit implies that the term "matrimonial" in New York is to be defined as including all those actions conventionally referred to by that name, such

35. 282 N.Y. 355, 361, 26 N.E.2d 290, 294 (1940).

36. Ibid.

37. 290 N.Y. 13, 47 N.E.2d 423 (1943), motion denied 290 N.Y. 765, 50 N.E.2d 102 (1943).

38. Krause v. Krause, 282 N.Y. 355, 26 N.E.2d 290 (1940). Estoppel was rejected in Lefferts v. Lefferts, 263 N.Y. 131, 188 N.E. 279 (1933), and in Fischer v. Fischer, 254 N.Y. 463, 173 N.E. 680 (1930), both actions for separation. And in Stevens v. Stevens, 273 N.Y. 157, 7 N.E.2d 26 (1937), also an action for separation, the court held it a "matrimonial" action, and thus not appropriate for estoppel. Yet a New York case seems to put annulment in the "private" category, so that a wife was estopped to attack a Virginia divorce from her first husband and barred from annulling her second marriage, Packer v. Packer, 6 A.D.2d 464, 179 N.Y.S.2d 801 (1st Dep't 1958). If annulment is not a "matrimonial" action, then the whole scheme of characterization has broken down. This case is in conflict with Landsman v. Landsman, 302 N.Y. 45, 96 N.E.2d 81 (1950), which held a husband could obtain an annulment where he had married before the decree annulling his wife's prior marriage had become final,

even though he knew all the facts and persuaded his second wife to marry him. And Stewart v. Stewart, 188 Misc. 243, 67 N.Y.S.2d 799 (1947) allowed estoppel in an action for divorce, implicitly standing for the proposition that divorce is "private."

Cases in other states have been more consistent in their characterization. E.g. Romanski's Estate, 354 Pa. 261, 47 A.2d 233 (1946) and In re Tamke's Estate, 32 Wash.2d 927, 204 P.2d 526 (1949) held disputes over inheritance to be "private." Hamm v. Hamm, 30 Tenn. App. 122, 204 S.W.2d 113 (1947) held a divorce action with no alimony claim to be "matrimonial." In re Hensgen's Estate, 80 Cal.App.2d 78, 181 P.2d 69 (1947) held a dispute over appointment as administratrix of an estate to be "matrimonial", but a later appeal of the same case held a dispute over the inheritance to be "private." Hensgen v. Silberman, 87 Cal.App.2d 668, 197 P.2d 356 (1948), 21 So.Cal.L.Rev. 201 (1948), 22 So.Cal.L.Rev. 201 (1949). Gardner v. Gardner, 144 W.Va. 630, 110 S.E.2d 495 (1959) held an annulment suit "private" as affecting only status.

as divorce, separation and annulment, and further that the inclusion of money claims in such suits does not alter their "matrimonial" nature. The matrimonial-private distinction is thus made to turn on commonly used labels, rather than on the remedy sought in the particular action. In this respect Querze is completely at variance with the decision in the Krause case.

Perhaps the inconsistency in characterization between Krause and Querze is explicable on the basis of an exception when the divorce under attack is the mail-order variety. At any rate, it now seems to be true in New York that estoppel will not preclude attack on an ex parte Mexican divorce, whether or not the claim involved can be described as "private", and whether or not the divorce was obtained by mail. The case which established this is Caldwell v. Caldwell,[39] an action for separation brought by a second wife against her

husband. He defended by attacking his Mexican mail-order divorce from his first wife as void, on that premise arguing that he never had married his second "wife". The court held that the "quasi-estoppel" of the Krause case could not be relied upon where the divorce was by mail-order, since there was not the slightest semblance of jurisdiction in the Mexican court. Other sections of the opinion suggest that the real basis for this holding was that New York could not tolerate an evasion of its own divorce laws so blatant (and so inexpensive) as that provided by the Mexican mail-order device. The same reasoning does not apply to the Reno divorce, which is relatively expensive, requires a stay of six weeks in Nevada, is beyond the reach of most New Yorkers, and thus offers less of a threat to New York's policies.[40] Doctrines of divorce law which discriminate against the less well-to-do are of course no novelty.

39. 298 N.Y. 146, 81 N.E.2d 60, 61 (1948), 47 Mich.L. Rev. 574 (1949) as amplified by Alfaro v. Alfaro, 5 App. Div.2d 770, 169 N.Y.S.2d 943 (1958), 44 Va.L.Rev. 1167 (1958), affirmed mem. 7 N.Y.2d 949, 198 N.Y.S.2d 318, 165 N.E.2d 880 (1960), 35 N.Y.U.L.Rev. 1404, 1406 (1960); also Vose v. Vose, 280 N.Y. 779, 21 N.E.2d 616 (1939); Marum v. Marum, 8 App.Div.2d 975, 190 N.Y.S.2d 812, (2d Dep't 1959); Whittleton v. Whittleton, 3 Misc.2d 542, 152 N.Y.S.2d 117 (1956). Wood v. Wood, 41 Misc.2d 95, 245 N.Y.S.2d 800 (1963), modified on other grounds 16 N.Y.2d 64, 262 N.Y.S.2d 86, 209 N.E.2d 709 (1965) refused to apply estoppel against a second husband where the Mexican divorce was obtained in person, with an appearance by the defendant through his attorney. To the same effect are two cases applying New York law for the determination of social security claims. Magner v. Hobby, 215 F.2d 190 (2d Cir. 1954), cert. denied 348 U.S. 919, 75 S.Ct. 305, 99 L.Ed. 721 (1955); Dwyer v. Folsom, 139 F.Supp. 571 (E.D.N.Y.1956) wife denied benefits after living with husband twenty-four years). A New York case which does reject attack on a Mexican mail-order divorce is Apelbaum v. Apelbaum, 7 A.D.2d 911, 183 N.Y.S.2d 54 (2d Dep't 1959), but it may be explainable as applying New Jersey law, where the second marriage occurred. It would seem, however, that the law of the forum or the domicile (both New York) should govern the application or non-application of estoppel here. Cross v. Cross, 94 Ariz. 28, 381 P.2d 573 (1963) refused to apply estoppel to prevent attack on a Mexican divorce not obtained by mail. But cf. Unruh v. Industrial Commission, 81 Ariz. 118, 301 P.2d 1029 (1956).

California has also vacillated in dealing with the question of estoppel to attack mail-order divorces. Kegley v. Kegley, 16 Cal.App.2d 216, 60 P.2d 482 (1936) held that they could be attacked. In re Atherley's Estate, 44 Cal. App.3d 758, 119 Cal.Rptr. 41 (1975) held that an ex parte (though not mail-order) Mexican divorce could be attacked, though estoppel was rejected on specific and limited grounds. Harlan v. Harlan, 70 Cal.App.2d 657, 161

P.2d 490 (1945) and In re Shank's Estate, 154 Cal.App.2d 808, 316 P.2d 710 (1957) held estoppel might apply. The question now seems to be settled in favor of estoppel where the circumstances are appropriate. Rediker v. Rediker, 35 Cal.2d 796, 221 P.2d 1 (1950). To the same effect is Trivanovitch v. Hobby, 95 U.S.App.D.C. 80, 219 F.2d 762 (1955), applying Massachusetts law, and Tonti v. Chadwick, 1 N.J. 531, 64 A.2d 436 (1949), 3 Miami L.Q. 629 (1949). Accord: Sears v. Sears, 110 U.S.App.D.C. 407, 293 F.2d 884 (1961), on remand 188 A.2d 298 (D.C.App. 1963), 110 U.Pa.L.Rev. 747 (1962).

40. The analysis in the text is borne out by the fact that Mexican and other divorces have been protected by estoppel if one of the spouses actually goes to the divorcing jurisdiction, no matter how short his visit. Clagett v. King, 308 A.2d 245 (D.C.App.1973) (Mexican divorce); Scherer v. Scherer, 405 N.E.2d 40 (Ind.App.1980) (Dominican divorce, attacking party participated); Poor v. Poor, 381 Mass. 392, 409 N.E.2d 758 (1980) (husband spent one day in Haiti, wife represented); Kazin v. Kazin, 81 N.J. 85, 405 A.2d 360 (1979) (husband accompanied wife on a short visit to Mexico); Bowen v. Bowen, 22 Misc.2d 496, 195 N.Y.S.2d 307 (1959); Diamond v. Diamond, 501 Pa. 418, 461 A.2d 1227 (1983) (husband made a short visit to Alabama); Dunn v. Tiernan, 284 S.W.2d 754 (Tex.Civ. App.1955) (short visit to Mexico).

Drew v. Hobby, 123 F.Supp. 245 (S.D.N.Y.1954) granted social security benefits to a wife on the death of her second "husband", under circumstances almost exactly like those in Dwyer v. Folsom, 139 F.Supp. 571 (E.D.N.Y. 1956), the only difference being that in the Drew case one party to the marriage actually went to Mexico for a very short time, while in the Dwyer case the divorce was obtained by mail.

A wife who visited Mexico briefly was allowed to attack the divorce she obtained in Warrender v. Warrender, 79 N.J.Super. 114, 190 A.2d 684 (1963), certification granted 41 N.J. 119, 195 A.2d 16 (1963).

The estoppel doctrine came into existence against a background of official hostility toward divorce, hostility most clearly and strongly expressed in the statutes of New York, where until 1967 divorce could only be obtained upon proof of adultery. In all states the official view was that only serious marital fault could be the basis for granting a divorce. All states asserted a strong interest in preserving the marital relations of their citizens. It was not surprising that when these citizens attempted to obtain a divorce by consent in one of the migratory divorce jurisdictions or in Mexico, the courts reacted with bursts of righteous indignation [41] and emphatic declarations that such divorces were void. Nevertheless many courts were doubtless aware that the positions which they so stoutly defended were no longer defensible.[42] The estoppel doctrine provided a technique by which the courts could protect spouses against the hardships inflicted by the Victorian divorce laws and at the same time avoid expressing their approval of migratory divorces obtained in evasion of the domiciliary law. Estoppel accomplished this by enabling the courts to say that the divorce was invalid, but that the party attacking it was not permitted to assert its invalidity.[43]

The divorce revolution of the 1960's and 1970's which led to the enactment in nearly all states of non-fault or marriage breakdown grounds for divorce [44] was a product of the views of many commentators, that divorce is a regrettable but necessary legal acceptance of marital failure and that the factors leading to the breakdown of the marriage are generally not all on one side.[45] The doctrine of estoppel reflected these same views, although of course it developed long before these views attained official recognition in the statutes. The doctrine recognized that for certain purposes a marriage had ended de facto and adjusted the legal rights and obligations of the parties accordingly, notwithstanding the fact that the termination of the marriage was not accomplished pursuant to prevailing legal requirements.[46] This had the effect, for most relevant purposes, of allowing the parties to end their marriage by consent,[47] although the courts often attempted to appease tradition by stating that they were not validating a divorce obtained without jurisdiction, but merely refusing to hear an attack upon it.[48] This was bound to create some confusion about the marital status of the parties, confusion which is certainly undesirable. The uncertainty over whether parties are or are not married, or over whether they are married for some purposes, and if so, for what purposes, is a

---

41. E.g. Ainscow v. Alexander, 28 Del.Ch. 545, 39 A.2d 54 (1944); Smith v. Smith, 79 Mass.(13 Gray) 209 (1859); Hollingshead v. Hollingshead, 91 N.J.Eq. 261, 110 A. 19 (1920). See also McKinney's General Obligations Law (N.Y.) 5–311, which prohibits spouses from contracting to alter or dissolve their marriage.

42. See Ainscow v. Alexander, 28 Del.Ch. 545, 39 A.2d 54, 61 (1944), which concedes that the doctrines it enforces may be obsolete, but in familiar fashion places responsibility for changes upon the legislature.

43. As in Spellens v. Spellens, 49 Cal.2d 210, 317 P.2d 613 (1957).

44. See section 12.1, supra.

45. Id. at note 46. See also Lichtenberger, Divorce, A Social Interpretation 16 (1931); M. Nimkoff, Contributions to a Therapeutic Solution to the Divorce Problem, Sociology, Univ. of Chicago Conf. on Divorce 55 (1952); R. Cavan, ed., Marriage and Family in the Modern World ch. 16 (3d ed.1969); M. Mead, Male and Female ch. XVII (1949); Sirjamaki, The American Family in the Twentieth Century ch. 8 (1955); Waller, The Family ch. XX, XXI (1938); R. Williamson, Marriage and Family Relations 527–533 (2d ed. 1972); R. Levy, Uniform Marriage and Divorce Legislation: A Preliminary Analysis 41–111 (1967).

46. See, e.g. Goodloe v. Hawk, 72 App.D.C. 287, 113 F.2d 753, 757 (1940):

"* * * it can no longer be said that public policy requires nonrecognition of all irregular foreign divorces. We have recognized that the interest of the state in many situations may lie with recognition of such divorces and preservation of remarriages rather than a dubious attempt to resurrect the original. From a pragmatic viewpoint, judicial invalidation of irregular foreign divorces and attendant remarriages, years after both events, is a less than ineffective sanction against an institution whose charm lies in its immediate respectability." For somewhat similar views see also Rediker v. Rediker, 35 Cal.2d 796, 221 P.2d 1 (1950), and Cummings v. Huddleston, 99 Okl. 195, 226 P. 104 (1924).

47. See note 41, supra.

48. E.g. Spellens v. Spellens, 49 Cal.2d 210, 317 P.2d 613 (1957); Dietrich v. Dietrich, 41 Cal.2d 497, 261 P.2d 269 (1953), cert. denied 346 U.S. 938, 74 S.Ct. 378, 98 L.Ed. 426 (1954); Rediker v. Rediker, 35 Cal.2d 796, 221 P.2d 1 (1950); Krause v. Krause, 282 N.Y. 355, 26 N.E.2d 290 (1940); Packer v. Packer, 6 A.D.2d 464, 179 N.Y.S.2d 801 (1st Dep't 1958).

legitimate objection to the use of the estoppel theory.[49] Refusal to rely on estoppel may, however, create even greater uncertainty.[50] In any event we are now so committed by the United States Supreme Court to a theory of "divisible divorce"[51] that a large amount of uncertainty about the validity of divorces and ensuing marriages is inevitable.

The estoppel doctrine thus reflected a more realistic analysis of marital relations than the traditional fault-based grounds for divorce, what one might call a sociological analysis of how people behave in marriage. This analysis has become predominant in the United States in the years since 1970, with the general enactment of marriage breakdown grounds for divorce. As might be expected, the estoppel cases decided since that time see the doctrine's purpose more clearly and exhibit less resistance to it.[52] Some of the confusion and uncertainty about its purpose and scope still persists, however.[53]

Notwithstanding the confusion, a principle is emerging from the cases which, with allowances for differences of approach, offers an explanation for the results reached and gives insight into the operative policies. It turns upon the conduct of the parties rather than the type of action. Three factors seem to be involved: 1) The attack on the divorce is inconsistent with prior conduct of the attack-

ing party. 2) The party upholding the divorce has relied upon it, or has formed expectations based upon it. 3) These relations or expectations will be upset if the divorce is held invalid. When either the first and third, or the second and third of these factors exist, one or the other or both of the parties have treated the marriage as at an end, and estoppel to attack the divorce amounts to recognition that such a marriage cannot be resurrected. All three factors will sometimes appear in a single case, making the nature of the situation particularly plain.

To put the principle in concise form, if the person attacking the divorce is, in doing so, taking a position inconsistent with his past conduct, or if the parties to the action have relied upon the divorce, and if, in addition, holding the divorce invalid will upset relationships or expectations formed in reliance upon the divorce, then estoppel will preclude calling the divorce in question. Some cases have imposed an additional qualification on the use of estoppel. They reject estoppel where the party attacking the divorce was ignorant of the facts making the divorce invalid until a short time before bringing the suit to invalidate it.[54] This qualification is based upon the traditional equity view of estoppel, rather than the social policy discussed in this section. It reflects some unwillingness to accept

49. Astor v. Astor, 6 Misc.2d 967, 160 N.Y.S.2d 103 (1957) is perhaps the most striking example of the uncertainty created by estoppel, since here the plaintiff was paying support money to two wives, and brought a declaratory judgment suit to have his relationships cleared up. An unfeeling court denied relief.

50. Dwyer v. Folsom, 139 F.Supp. 571 (E.D.N.Y.1956) is an example. Here a woman was denied social security benefits after living with a man as his wife for twenty-four years. See also Cirone v. Cirone, 82 N.Y.S.2d 780 (1948). In Alfaro v. Alfaro, 5 A.D.2d 770, 169 N.Y.S.2d 943 (2d Dep't 1958), affirmed mem. 7 N.Y.2d 949, 198 N.Y.S.2d 318, 165 N.E.2d 880 (1960), 44 Va.L.Rev. 1167 (1958), a marriage following a Mexican divorce was held void when the parties had lived as husband and wife for twelve years and had three children.

51. E.g. Estin v. Estin, 334 U.S. 541, 68 S.Ct. 1213, 92 L.Ed. 1561 (1948) and Vanderbilt v. Vanderbilt, 354 U.S. 416, 77 S.Ct. 1360, 1 L.Ed.2d 1456 (1957).

52. E.g., Clagett v. King, 308 A.2d 245 (D.C.App.1973); Scherer v. Scherer, 405 N.E.2d 40 (Ind.App.1980); Poor v. Poor, 381 Mass. 392, 409 N.E.2d 758 (1980); Kazin v. Kazin, 81 N.J. 85, 405 A.2d 360 (1979); Diamond v. Diamond, 501 Pa. 418, 461 A.2d 1227 (1983).

53. See Swisher, Foreign Migratory Divorces: A Reappraisal, 21 J. of Fam.L. 9 (1982).

54. This seems to have been the case in Smith v. Foto, 285 Mich. 361, 280 N.W. 790 (1938) and Fischer v. Fischer, 254 N.Y. 463, 173 N.E. 680 (1930), in both of which second husbands were held entitled to upset divorces obtained by their wives from their first husbands. In neither case did the second husband know the circumstances of the divorce when he contracted the marriage. This fact distinguishes Fischer from Krause v. Krause, 282 N.Y. 355, 26 N.E.2d 290 (1940), where the husband was held estopped to attack his own divorce, and therefore liable to his second wife in her action for separation. The Krause opinion emphasized that the husband had voluntarily (i.e. knowingly) undertaken to support his second wife. In the Smith and Fischer cases the second husband had not undertaken this duty voluntarily in that sense of the word. See also Old Colony Trust Co. v. Porter, 324 Mass. 581, 88 N.E.2d 135 (1949) and In re Gibson's Estate, 7 Wis.2d 506, 96 N.W.2d 859 (1959). Jardine v. Jardine, 291 Ill.App. 152, 9 N.E.2d 645 (1937) is similar except that a second wife was suing for annulment, attacking her husband's Reno divorce.

the implications of that policy and to that extent reveals a point of view opposed to the analysis advanced herein.

This additional qualification based on lack of knowledge of the divorce's defects aside, the differences between estoppel in divorce cases and the usual definition of equitable estoppel become clear.[55] The social policy underlying equitable estoppel is the achievement of fairness and the prevention of fraud,[56] whereas here the estoppel accomplishes the purposes of a contemporary theory of marriage and divorce. This illustrates both the use of old doctrine to serve new purposes, and the value of equity as a reforming force in the law.[57]

 WESTLAW REFERENCES

jurisdiction! /5 challeng! attack! /s divorc! dissol! /s estop!

challeng! attack! /s laches /s estop! /s dissol! divorc!

"divisible divorce" /s valid! invalid! void! avoid!

Some cases do not insist on the limitation stated in the text. In Anderson v. Anderson, 121 Utah 237, 240 P.2d 966 (1952) a husband was held subject to an alimony decree arising out of a marriage clearly invalid because contracted before a prior divorce decree had become final. The ground for decision was the presumption that the later marriage was valid. Yet here the second husband was ignorant that the wife was not free to marry him. The effect was the same as if the husband had been held estopped. See also Bussey v. Bussey, 95 N.H. 349, 64 A.2d 4 (1949) where a wife was not allowed to make a direct attack upon the divorce after the husband's remarriage, notwithstanding the lack of jurisdiction and that she moved immediately after she learned the facts.

55. See note 8, supra.

56. 3 Pomeroy, Equity Jurisprudence 176–178 (5th ed. 1941); 3 Story, Equity Jurisprudence 569–570 (14th ed. 1918).

57. Maine, Ancient Law 28 (13th ed. 1890); Stone, Province and Function of Law 459–463 (1950).

§ 12.4

1. Auman v. Auman, 134 Ariz. 40, 653 P.2d 688 (1982); Robertson v. Robertson, 164 Conn. 140, 318 A.2d 106 (1972); In re Marriage of Hudson, 434 N.E.2d 107 (Ind. App. 1982), cert. denied 459 U.S. 1202, 103 S.Ct. 1187, 75 L.Ed.2d 433 (1983); Altman v. Altman, 282 Md. 483, 386 A.2d 766 (1978); Blitzer v. Blitzer, 361 Mass. 780, 282 N.E.2d 918 (1972); Gaffney v. Gaffney, 528 S.W.2d 738 (Mo. 1975); Carnie v. Carnie, 252 S.C. 471, 167 S.E.2d 297 (1969); Restatement (Second) of Conflict of Laws § 77 (1971). Other personal orders incident to divorce decrees may also require personal jurisdiction over the defendant. E.g., Conlon by Conlon v. Heckler, 719 F.2d 788 (5th Cir. 1983); Stanley v. Stanley, 271 A.2d 636 (Me. 1970); Carr v. Carr, 46 N.Y.2d 270, 413 N.Y.S.2d 305, 385

§ 12.4   Divorce—Jurisdiction for Alimony, Property Division and Child Support

A divorce decree in many cases does more than dissolve the marriage. It may provide for temporary or permanent alimony, for a division of the parties' property, for child support, and for the payment of the attorney fees of one spouse by the other. If these additional remedies involving the financial or property incidents of the divorce are to be included in the decree, the court must have personal jurisdiction over the defendant.[1] Traditionally personal jurisdiction could be asserted by personal service of process in the state,[2] or by the defendant's entering a general appearance.[3] The type of service required may be affected by complex local rules[4] as may also the distinction between a general appearance which confers personal jurisdiction and a spe-

N.E.2d 1234 (1978). Personal jurisdiction in divorce is thoroughly discussed in R. Casad, Jurisdiction in Civil Actions Ch. 9 (1983).

2. Meredith v. Meredith, 226 F.2d 257 (D.C. Cir. 1955); Baldwin v. Baldwin, 28 Cal.2d 406, 170 P.2d 670 (1946); LaBow v. LaBow, 171 Conn. 433, 370 A.2d 990 (1976). In any event the provisions of the Soldiers' and Sailors' Civil Relief Act of 1940, 54 Stat. 1178 ff., 50 U.S.C.A.App. §§ 501 ff., especially section 521, must be complied with. See Annot., Soldiers' and Sailors' Civil Relief Act of 1940, as amended, as affecting matrimonial actions, 54 A.L.R. 2d 390 (1957).

Whether a defendant is subject to the jurisdiction when served while in the state to attend a hearing or when induced to come into the state by the plaintiff is not clear on the cases. R. Casad, Jurisdiction in Civil Actions § 9.02(4)(a) (1983). It remains unclear whether in the Supreme Court's view after Shaffer v. Heitner, 433 U.S. 186, 97 S.Ct. 2569, 53 L.Ed.2d 683 (1977) service upon a person present in the state solely as a transient, without other contacts with the state, is sufficient to confer personal jurisdiction. R. Casad, Jurisdiction in Civil Actions § 2.04(2)(c) (1983).

3. Keen v. Keen, 191 Md. 31, 60 A.2d 200 (1948); Crouch v. Crouch, 641 S.W.2d 86 (Mo.1982); Restatement (Second) of Conflict of Laws § 33 (1971). A definition of "general appearance" is given by Creed v. Schultz, 148 Cal.App.3d 733, 196 Cal.Rptr. 252 (1983).

4. Robertson v. Robertson, 164 Conn. 140, 318 A.2d 106 (1972); Liebeskind v. Liebeskind, 86 A.D.2d 207, 449 N.Y.S.2d 226 (1st Dep't 1982), affirmed 58 N.Y.2d 858, 460 N.Y.S.2d 526, 447 N.E.2d 74 (1983); O'Heaney v. O'Heaney, 80 A.D.2d 46, 437 N.Y.S.2d 811 (4th Dep't 1981), appeal dismissed 53 N.Y.2d 1055, 442 N.Y.S.2d 500,

cial appearance which does not.[5] Whatever the local rules may be, the method of service must be such as to be reasonably calculated to give notice to the defendant in order to meet the requirements of the Due Process Clause.[6] Once personal jurisdiction is acquired, it continues throughout the litigation, so that it is sufficient for later proceedings to modify the original decree.[7]

Acquisition of personal jurisdiction in our federal system has a dual importance. In the first place it is essential if the court in the divorce action is to have the authority to enter a decree deciding the financial and property aspects of the case.[8] Secondly, personal jurisdiction must exist before the financial and property aspects of the decree will be entitled to full faith and credit in other states under Article IV, section 1 of the United States Constitution.[9] In our mobile society being assured of full faith and credit is nearly as important as being able to obtain the original decree.

In recent decades the traditional methods of acquiring personal jurisdiction have been greatly expanded as a response to the increased mobility of the American population. The expansion has had an effect upon the jurisdiction for the financial aspects of divorce as well as upon the more widely publicized fields of torts and commercial litigation.[10] The fundamental principle governing the assertion of personal jurisdiction has now come to be that it must be done in accordance with state statute and that it must meet constitutional requirements. The state must have a statute authorizing the exercise of jurisdiction under the circumstances of the particular case and the application of the statute to those circumstances must be in accord with the Due Process Clause as the cases, especially the Supreme Court cases, construe it.[11] Although some states have enacted "long-arm" statutes providing that the courts have personal jurisdiction in all cases where the exercise of such jurisdiction would be in accord with the Due Process Clause,[12] thereby in effect rendering

425 N.E.2d 888 (1981); Carnie v. Carnie, 252 S.C. 471, 167 S.E.2d 297 (1969).

5. A defendant wishing to question the jurisdiction over his person must be careful to observe the local procedural requirements for doing so and not to seek affirmative relief. Vaughan v. Vaughan, 267 Ala. 117, 100 So.2d 1 (1957); Leslie v. Leslie, 174 Conn. 399, 389 A.2d 747 (1978); In re Marriage of Mierlak, 100 Ill.App. 3d 228, 426 N.E.2d 1010 (1981); Bryant v. Bryant, 149 Me. 276, 100 A.2d 663 (1953); Crouch v. Crouch, 641 S.W.2d 86 (Mo.1982); Deich v. Deich, 136 Mont. 566, 323 P.2d 35 (1958); Nocher v. Nocher, 268 S.C. 503, 234 S.E. 2d 884 (1977). In Schroff v. Schroff, 85 Wis.2d 505, 271 N.W.2d 379 (1978) it was held that signing a stipulation for alimony, division of property and child support did not subject the defendant to the jurisdiction.

General appearance is defined by Webber v. Webber, 32 N.C.App. 572, 232 S.E.2d 865 (1977) as an appearance without limit as to its purpose, or as a request for relief which may only be given if the court has personal jurisdiction over the applicant.

A written waiver of service and entry of appearance is often held sufficient to confer personal jurisdiction. Beardsley v. Beardsley, 144 Conn. 725, 137 A.2d 752 (1957); Walsh v. Walsh, 388 So.2d 240 (Fla.App.1980) (current in a separation agreement); Jennings v. Jennings, 337 Ill.App. 647, 86 N.E.2d 287 (1949); Patterson v. Patterson, 164 Kan. 501, 190 P.2d 887 (1948); Sundlun v. Sundlun, 103 R.I. 25, 234 A.2d 358 (1967); Restatement (Second) of Conflict of Laws § 32 (1971).

6. Mullane v. Central Hanover Bank & Trust Co., 339 U.S. 306, 70 S.Ct. 652, 94 L.Ed. 865 (1950); Restatement

(Second) of Conflict of Laws § 25 (1971); Pinebrook v. Pinebrook, 329 So.2d 343 (Fla.App.1976). Service by publication may in some cases convey adequate notice. Gross v. Gross, 56 Misc.2d 286, 288 N.Y.S.2d 674 (1968).

7. Smollar v. Smollar, 267 S.C. 528, 280 S.E.2d 543 (1981); R. Casad, Jurisdiction in Civil Actions § 1.08 (1983).

8. See cases cited in note 1, supra.

9. Vanderbilt v. Vanderbilt, 354 U.S. 416, 77 S.Ct. 1360, 1 L.Ed.2d 1456 (1957); Estin v. Estin, 334 U.S. 541, 68 S.Ct. 1213, 92 L.Ed. 1561 (1948); Conlon v. Heckler, 719 F.2d 788 (5th Cir.1983); State ex rel. State of Oklahoma v. Griggs, 51 Or.App. 275, 625 P.2d 660 (1981), modified on other grounds 52 Or.App. 655, 628 P.2d 791 (1981).

10. See, e.g., Weintraub, Texas Long-Arm Jurisdiction in Family Law Cases, 32 S.W.L.J. 965 (1978); Anderson, Using Long-Arm Jurisdiction to Enforce Marital Obligations, 42 Miss.L.J. 183 (1971); Note, Long-Arm Jurisdiction in Alimony and Custody Cases, 73 Colum.L.Rev. 289 (1973).

11. Conlon v. Heckler, 719 F.2d 788 (5th Cir.1983); Morrill v. Tong, 390 Mass. 120, 453 N.E.2d 1221 (1983); State ex rel. State of Oklahoma v. Griggs, 51 Or.App. 275, 625 P.2d 660 (1981), modified on other grounds 52 Or. App. 655, 628 P.2d 791 (1981); R. Casad, Jurisdiction in Civil Actions § 4.01(1)(b) (1983).

12. E.g., West's Ann.Cal.Code Civ.Proc. § 410.10 (1973): "A court of this state may exercise jurisdiction on any basis not inconsistent with the Constitution of this state or of the United States."

the statute otiose, the requirement that juris-diction comply with the long-arm statute retains force in some cases and may often aid in precision of analysis.

In its contemporary definitions of what the Due Process Clause requires for personal jurisdiction, the Supreme Court has largely abandoned the criterion of physical power over the defendant or his property which it relied upon in its earlier cases.[13] Instead the Court now considers "the relationship among the defendant, the forum, and the litigation"[14] when it has to determine whether personal jurisdiction was acquired by a state court. This extremely vague approach to the problem has been amplified but hardly clarified by further pronouncements which have acquired the character of shibboleths from frequent repetition. In International Shoe Co. v. State of Washington the Court said that "due process requires only that in order to subject a defendant to a judgment *in personam*, if he be not present within the territory of the forum, he have certain minimum contacts with it such that the maintenance of the suit does not offend 'traditional notions of fair play and substantial justice' ".[15] A subsequent opinion stated the position to be that "it is essential in each case that there be some act by which the defendant purposefully avails itself of the privilege of conducting activities within the forum State, thus invoking the benefits and protections of its laws".[16] The consequence of these statements has been significantly to expand the personal jurisdiction

of state courts over defendants who neither consented, appeared nor were served with process within the state. How far this expansion goes or should go remains very uncertain.

Many of the earlier expansive decisions involved suits against large corporations, leading one to suspect that the Supreme Court was making the unspoken assumption that it is not unfair to subject such defendants to suit on the basis of relatively slight relationships with the forum. Whether the same expansive approach would be taken in domestic relations cases where the defendant is an individual, usually less capable of financing a defense in a distant state, was a matter left in some doubt. To some extent that doubt has been resolved against the expansive version of jurisdiction in Kulko v. Superior Court of California.[17]

The husband and wife in Kulko had been married in California, in 1959, some seventeen years before the suit was brought. At that time they stayed in California only three days. While married they were domiciled in New York. In 1972 they separated and the plaintiff wife moved to California, executing a separation agreement providing that their two children would live with the husband during the school year and with the wife during vacations. The wife later obtained a Haitian divorce. The separation agreement also provided that the husband would pay $3000 per year for support of the children,

---

13. E.g., Pennoyer v. Neff, 95 U.S. (5 Otto) 714, 24 L.Ed. 565 (1877); McDonald v. Mabee, 243 U.S. 90, 37 S.Ct. 343, 61 L.Ed. 608 (1917); R. Casad, Jurisdiction in Civil Actions ch. 2 (1983).

14. Shaffer v. Heitner, 433 U.S. 186, 204, 97 S.Ct. 2569, 2579, 53 L.Ed.2d 683 (1977). This case also abolished "quasi in rem" jurisdiction, establishing the rule that personal jurisdiction may no longer be based solely upon the presence of property within the state, but must rest upon the relationship between the defendant, the lawsuit and the state as in other cases. Harris v. Balk, 198 U.S. 215, 25 S.Ct. 625, 49 L.Ed. 1023 (1905) was overruled.

15. 326 U.S. 310, 316, 66 S.Ct. 154, 158, 90 L.Ed. 95 (1945), quoting in part from Milliken v. Meyer, 311 U.S. 457, 463, 61 S.Ct. 339, 342, 85 L.Ed. 278 (1940), rehearing denied 312 U.S. 712, 61 S.Ct. 548, 85 L.Ed. 1143 (1941). The International Shoe language was quoted with approval in McGee v. International Life Insurance Co., 355 U.S. 220, 222, 78 S.Ct. 199, 200, 2 L.Ed.2d 223 (1957).

16. Hanson v. Denckla, 357 U.S. 235, 253, 78 S.Ct. 1228, 1239, 2 L.Ed.2d 1283 (1958), rehearing denied 358 U.S. 858, 79 S.Ct. 10, 3 L.Ed.2d 92 (1958).

17. 436 U.S. 84, 98 S.Ct. 1690, 56 L.Ed.2d 132 (1978), rehearing denied 438 U.S. 908, 98 S.Ct. 3127, 57 L.Ed.2d 1150 (1978). The case is discussed in R. Casad, Jurisdiction in Civil Actions 2–52 (1983). Cases subsequent to Kulko which also run counter to the expansive view of jurisdiction include World-Wide Volkswagen Corp. v. Woodson, 444 U.S. 286, 100 S.Ct. 559, 62 L.Ed.2d 490 (1980) and Rush v. Savchuk, 444 U.S. 320, 100 S.Ct. 571, 62 L.Ed.2d 516 (1980), on remand 290 N.W.2d 633 (Minn. 1980).

But see Ross v. Ross, 371 Mass. 439, 358 N.E.2d 437 (1976), which held, before Kulko, that the term "transaction of business" in the state was not limited to commercial activity.

covering the periods they were in the wife's custody. In 1973, at his daughter's request, the father consented to her going to California to live permanently with her mother, buying her a plane ticket for this purpose. In 1976 the other child asked for and received a plane ticket from his mother, went to California apparently without obtaining the consent of his father, and remained in his mother's custody. The mother then brought suit in California to establish the Haitian divorce decree as a judgment of California, to obtain custody of the children, and to increase the amount of child support from the defendant father. Defendant was served by mail in New York. He appeared specially in the suit and moved to quash service on the ground that the court had no personal jurisdiction over him. The only real issue was whether the California court had jurisdiction to enter a support order,[18] the California Supreme Court holding that it did on the ground that by permitting his daughter to live in California with her mother he had purposely availed himself of the benefit and protection of California law. The court found that this was sufficient to support jurisdiction over a claim for support of both children.

In a six to three decision the United States Supreme Court reversed the California judgment, holding that California's attempt to assert personal jurisdiction over the defendant did not meet the requirements of the Due Process Clause. The major emphasis of the opinion seems to be that although California has interests in the welfare of children residing in California, those interests are not sufficient to make it fair or reasonable to subject a New York father having no other contacts with California to the personal jurisdiction of the California courts. The Court rejected the argument that the defendant had purposely benefited from the protection of California law by sending his daughter to live with her mother, saying that any benefits were con-

ferred on the child rather than the defendant, and that any financial benefit he received arose out of the daughter's absence from her New York home rather than from her presence in California, and also from the mother's failure earlier to seek an increase in support payments. The Court also denied that the defendant's actions had the kind of "effect" in California which should subject him to the jurisdiction of its courts since he had not sought a commercial benefit in the state.

The Supreme Court in Kulko placed some reliance on the argument that the state's interest in the support of its children, and presumably this plaintiff's claim for support, could be vindicated by a proceeding pursuant to the Uniform Reciprocal Enforcement of Support Act.[19] This argument reveals both the Court's ignorance of that Act and naivete concerning its practical operation. The Act as it has been applied may be used only to enforce claims for support. Proceedings under it may not be combined with claims for divorce or for custody or for other types of marital remedy.[20] It would therefore not have been available to the plaintiff in Kulko. Further, the processing of claims under the Act varies greatly from one locality to another. In some places it may offer a fairly efficient way to recover support, while in others it does not receive adequate attention from local officials. It is therefore not an adequate substitute for the kind of suit the plaintiff sought to bring in Kulko.

The effect of Kulko on divorce and non-support claims is that great uncertainty is injected into the litigation at its outset, with respect to a question which ought to be easily and clearly answered, that is, where should the suit be brought? The standard of fairness in this context is not only vague but is unworkable. What is fair for the defendant may be unfair for the plaintiff and unfavorable to the interests of one of the states in-

---

18. The California long-arm statute pursuant to which the plaintiff brought the suit in effect passes the buck to the courts by providing that "A court of this state may exercise jurisdiction on any basis not inconsistent with the Constitution of this state or of the United States." West's Ann.Cal.Code Civ.Proc. § 410.10 (1973).

19. 9A Unif.L.Ann. 643 (1979).

20. See § 6.6, supra, at note 54.

volved. Fairness will generally depend upon the distance between the homes of plaintiff and defendant rather than upon the fact that their homes are in different states. For example, it might be more difficult and expensive for a defendant living in New York to be required to litigate in California than for a defendant living in New York to litigate in New Jersey or Connecticut. In fact there seems no unfairness in requiring the New York domiciliary to litigate in New Jersey. Looked at in this light, the talk of fairness assumes the aspect of an inappropriate surrogate for state sovereignty, the doctrine underlying Pennoyer v. Neff.[21]

The other standard is equally unsatisfactory.[22] In the ordinary sense of the phrase it seems clear that the defendant in Kulko purposely availed himself of the protection and benefits of California law when he sent his daughter there to live. If the defendant here had been an insurance company which sent one of its policies into California, it would have apparently been liable to suit in California.[23] The Kulko opinion suggests that this standard is only met when the defendant has sought a commercial benefit in the forum state. Since no such commercial benefit is at stake in the usual suit for alimony or child support, this meaning of the standard makes it inapplicable to many domestic relations cases. A rule of law which gives greater

weight to the enforcement of commercial contracts than to the enforcement of duties of support in the family can only be characterized as enacting a topsy-turvy system of values.

If the unfairness to the defendant in Kulko consists in forcing him to undergo the expense of litigating at a distance from his home, the Court's solicitude for his interests may be misplaced. If the plaintiff in Kulko were required to go to New York to get an increase in child support, the court might, in some circumstances, require the defendant to pay her expenses, including attorney fees.[24] If so, the burden on the defendant in this sort of domestic relations case might turn out to be about the same regardless of where the litigation occurred.

The lower court cases on the constitutional question decided since Kulko exhibit the sort of uncertainty that one might expect after reading the Kulko opinion. Several of them have held that maintaining a marital domicile in the forum state is a sufficient contact to support personal jurisdiction notwithstanding that at the time of suit the defendant has moved to another state.[25] But the cases are not in agreement where the parties had a marital domicile in the forum, moved to another state, separated, after which the plaintiff spouse returned to the forum state.[26] Nor are they in agreement where the sole basis for

21. 95 U.S.(5 Otto) 714, 24 L.Ed. 565 (1877).

22. Professor Casad analyzes the relationship of the two standards as being that there is a threshold requirement of "purposeful availing" oneself of the benefit of the forum's law, after which the factors of relative inconvenience and state interest may be considered. Some of the language of Worldwide Volkswagen Corp. v. Woodson, 444 U.S. 286, 100 S.Ct. 559, 62 L.Ed.2d 490 (1980) may be susceptible to this interpretation, but Kulko does not follow this analysis. See R. Casad, Jurisdiction in Civil Actions § 2.05 (1983).

23. As in McGee v. International Life Insurance Co., 355 U.S. 220, 78 S.Ct. 199, 2 L.Ed.2d 223 (1957).

24. See section 16.2, infra.

25. In re Marriage of Lontos, 89 Cal.App.3d 61, 152 Cal.Rptr. 271 (1979); Stuckey v. Stuckey, 434 So.2d 513 (La.App.1983), writ denied 440 So.2d 145 (1983) (dictum); Plucker v. Plucker, 338 N.W.2d 842 (S.D.1983).

26. McGlothen v. Superior Court of City and County of San Francisco, 121 Cal.App.3d 106, 175 Cal.Rptr. 129 (1981) and Barker v. Barker, 94 N.M. 162, 608 P.2d 138

(1980) held there was jurisdiction in these circumstances. Hoerler v. Superior Court In and For Santa Clara County, 85 Cal.App.3d 533, 149 Cal.Rptr. 569 (1978) held that California could not assert personal jurisdiction where the parties had lived as husband and wife in California for fourteen years, had moved to Washington, where the defendant remained domiciled at the time of the suit, while the plaintiff returned to California. Visits of the spouses to a state on several occasions was held not sufficient in Crouch v. Crouch, 641 S.W.2d 86 (Mo.1982). See also Hines v. Clendenning, 465 P.2d 460 (Okl.1970), a pre-Kulko case holding that in the circumstances outlined in the text there is personal jurisdiction for constitutional purposes.

The confusion generated by Kulko is aptly illustrated by Ex parte Brislawn, 443 So.2d 32 (Ala.1983). Husband and wife were married in Georgia, where the husband was stationed as an army officer. The wife was then domiciled in Alabama. After the wedding they stayed ten days in Alabama with the wife's parents and then left for his new station in Germany. Less than a year later the wife returned to her parents' home in Alabama,

jurisdiction is that a child of the defendant lives in the forum state and is not being supported there by the defendant,[27] although this state of facts appears very close to that in Kulko. The Kulko rule may also have a restrictive effect upon the degree of participation in litigation which is sufficient to justify subjecting a non-resident to personal jurisdiction.[28]

There are undoubtedly many other common circumstances in which there will be serious question whether there is sufficient personal jurisdiction to warrant a decree for alimony, property division or child support. For example, drawing on the provision in the Uniform Parentage Act,[29] would a statute be constitutional if it should provide that a person having sexual intercourse in the state submits to the jurisdiction for a support action respecting a child conceived as the result of such intercourse?[30] Or is there sufficient contact with the state in the sole fact that a separation agreement was executed there providing for the payment of alimony or child support?[31]

As has been indicated, Shaffer v. Heitner has abolished quasi-in-rem jurisdiction, so that no longer may a plaintiff obtain a judgment enforceable against property located in the state on the sole basis that the property is found and attached there.[32] The same case seems to say, however, that there would be sufficient constitutional jurisdiction to adjudicate interests in that very property notwithstanding that the defendant had no other contacts with the state.[33] That being so, a

---

where their child was born, the husband returning to Georgia. His domicile was at all times in the state of Washington. The Alabama court held that the husband was subject to personal jurisdiction in Alabama, reversing a decision by the Alabama Court of Appeals, finding that he had the necessary "minimum contacts" with Alabama. See also Bergan v. Bergan, 114 Cal.App.3d 567, 170 Cal.Rptr. 751 (1981); Matter of Marriage of Hazen, 74 Or.App. 322, 702 P.2d 1143 (1985).

27. Plucker v. Plucker, 338 N.W.2d 842 (S.D.1983) and Johansen v. Johansen, 305 N.W.2d 383 (S.D.1981) seem to say that the failure to support a minor child residing in the state is sufficient to find personal jurisdiction. In re Marriage of Lontos, 89 Cal.App.3d 61, 152 Cal.Rptr. 271 (1979) says that if a defendant's failure to support his child causes the burden of support to fall on the state, this constitutes purposely deriving a benefit from activities in the state under the Kulko rule. Contra, holding that the mere residence of a spouse or a dependent child is not sufficient for personal jurisdiction, Morton v. United States, 708 F.2d 680 (Fed.Cir.1983); Cotton v. Cotton, 3 Ark.App. 158, 623 S.W.2d 540 (1981); Boyer v. Boyer, 73 Ill.2d 331, 22 Ill.Dec. 747, 383 N.E.2d 223 (1978); In re Marriage of Hudson, 434 N.E.2d 107 (Ind.App.1982), cert. denied 459 U.S. 1202, 103 S.Ct. 1187, 75 L.Ed.2d 433 (1983).

See also Morrill v. Tong, 390 Mass. 120, 453 N.E.2d 1221 (1983), holding that jurisdiction could not constitutionally rest upon the facts that monthly payments were sent to the forum state by the defendant; that the defendant maintained his navy I.D. card for the children's benefit; that gifts, letters, cards and phone calls came to the children in the state from the defendant; and that the forum state was the first marital home.

28. Kumar v. Santa Clara County Superior Court, 124 Cal.App.3d 1003, 177 Cal.Rptr. 763 (1981), vacated on other grounds 32 Cal.3d 689, 186 Cal.Rptr. 772, 659 P.2d 1003 (1982), holding that a father who sought habeas corpus in California to enforce his visitation rights under a New York decree did not subject himself to personal jurisdiction in California for purposes of modification of a

support order. See also Knox v. Knox, 137 Ariz. 494, 671 P.2d 935 (App.1983).

29. Uniform Parentage Act § 8(b), 9A Unif.L.Ann. 598 (1979), providing that one who has sexual intercourse within the state submits to the jurisdiction of the state's courts respecting the paternity of any child conceived by that act of intercourse.

30. See section 4.4, supra, at note 31. Holding that such a contact is sufficient to support in personam jurisdiction under the Constitution is Lake v. Butcher, 37 Wash.App. 228, 679 P.2d 409 (1984).

31. Holding that execution of a separation agreement in the forum state constitutes transaction of business under the long-arm statute and meets the constitutional requirement of purposely availing oneself of the benefit of the forum's laws, Ross v. Ross, 371 Mass. 439, 358 N.E.2d 437 (1976) (decided before Kulko); Hurlbut v. Hurlbut, 101 Misc.2d 571, 421 N.Y.S.2d 509 (1979) (some other contacts with the forum state occurred; cites other cases).

32. 433 U.S. 186, 97 S.Ct. 2569, 53 L.Ed.2d 683 (1977).

33. 433 U.S. at 207–208, 97 S.Ct. at 2581: "This argument, of course, does not ignore the fact that the presence of property in a State may bear on the existence of jurisdiction by providing contacts among the forum State, the defendant, and the litigation. For example, when claims to the property itself are the source of the underlying controversy between the plaintiff and the defendant, it would be unusual for the State where the property is located not to have jurisdiction. In such cases, the defendant's claim to property located in the State would normally indicate that he expected to benefit from the State's protection of his interest. The State's strong interests in assuring the marketability of property within its borders and in providing a procedure for peaceful resolution of disputes about the possession of that property would also support jurisdiction, as would the likelihood that important records and witnesses will be found in the State." (Footnotes omitted).

divorce action could constitutionally distribute property found in the divorcing state even though the defendant had no other contacts with the forum state than a claim to the property located there.[34] There is also a suggestion in Shaffer v. Heitner[35] that there may still be quasi-in-rem jurisdiction based upon the location of property in the state in the unusual case in which the plaintiff has no other forum available to him.[36] One final exception to its abolition to quasi-in-rem jurisdiction consists in the Supreme Court's statement that if a judgment has already been obtained, for example in some other state, such a judgment could be enforced in the forum state against property found there, even though that state would not have had jurisdiction in the constitutional sense sufficient to grant the judgment in the first place.[37] Even with these exceptions, the Shaffer case does enact a substantial limitation on the extent to which a plaintiff may obtain a judgment on property located within the forum state.

The confusion and uncertainty engendered by the Kulko decision can be reduced by the enactment of reasonably specific state long-arm statutes. Of course the type of statute which merely says that personal jurisdiction may be exercised whenever permitted by the United States Constitution, in force in California[38] and some other states,[39] is of no help in this respect. Any long-arm statute addressed to the collection of alimony, maintenance or child support must meet the constitutional requirements of Kulko, but it need not go to the full extent of constitutional limits.

A number of states have in fact adopted statutes expressly governing personal jurisdiction in matrimonial and support actions. Most commonly they provide that personal jurisdiction exists as to obligations for alimony, child support and property settlements, where the parties lived in the state in a marital relationship,[40] although the statutory language varies from state to state,[41] notwithstanding the fact that the defendant is a non-

---

34. Hodge v. Hodge, 178 Conn. 308, 422 A.2d 280 (1979) (semble). In this case and Shaffer a suit claiming an interest in or right to property located in the state is characterized as in rem rather than quasi-in-rem, but no consequences turn on the characterization. Hodge also held that in this situation attachment of the property at the outset of the suit was not essential to the assertion of jurisdiction to deal with the property. In any such case, however, the local procedure must be observed. Navonis v. Navonis, 116 N.H. 505, 363 A.2d 420 (1976). And of course the property must have a situs in the forum state. Morrill v. Tong, 390 Mass. 120, 453 N.E.2d 1221 (1983). For cases exhibiting some confusion about jurisdiction in this situation, see In re Ramsey's Marriage, 34 Colo.App. 338, 526 P.2d 319 (1974); Harrod v. Harrod, 34 Colo.App. 172, 526 P.2d 666 (1974); Gelkop v. Gelkop, 384 So.2d 195 (Fla.App.1980).

On the location of intangible personal property, see Waite v. Waite, 6 Cal.2d 461, 99 Cal.Rptr. 325, 492 P.2d 13 (1972), overruled on other grounds 15 Cal.3d 838, 126 Cal.Rptr. 633, 544 P.2d 561 (1976).

35. Shaffer v. Heitner, 433 U.S. 186, 211 n. 37, 97 S.Ct. 2569, 2583 n. 37, 53 L.Ed.2d 683 (1977): "This case does not raise, and we therefore do not consider, the question whether the presence of a defendant's property in a State is a sufficient basis for jurisdiction when no other forum is available to the plaintiff."

36. Rich v. Rich, 93 Misc.2d 409, 402 N.Y.S.2d 767 (1978) where the New York court asserted jurisdiction against the defendant's New York property partly on the ground the defendant remained in Europe apparently out of reach of any American court, so that the plaintiff had

no other forum in which to enforce her judgment for child support.

37. Shaffer v. Heitner, 433 U.S. 186, 210 n. 36, 97 S.Ct. 2569, n. 36, 53 L.Ed.2d 683 (1977): "Once it has been determined by a court of competent jurisdiction that the defendant is a debtor of the plaintiff, there would seem to be no unfairness in allowing an action to realize on that debt in a State where the defendant has property, whether or not that State would have jurisdiction to determine the existence of the debt as an original matter." The Rich case, supra, note 36 also relied on this language to enforce a child support claim.

38. West's Ann.Cal.Code Civ.Proc. § 410.10 (1973), quoted supra, note 12.

39. E.g., Ala.R.Civ.Proc., Rule 4.2(a)(2)(I) (1984); Ark. Stats. § 27–2502 F (1979); D.C.Code Ann.1986, § 13–423(a)(7)(E) (Supp.); Okl.Stat. tit. 12, § 2004(F) (Supp. 1987); Pa.Stat. tit. 42, § 5322(b) (1981).

40. Ala.R.Civ.Proc., Rule 4.2(a)(2)(I) (1984); Alaska Stat. § 9.05.015(12) (1983); Kan.Stat.Ann. § 60–308(b)(8) (1983); Me.Rev.Stat.Ann. tit. 14, § 704–A(2)(G) (1980); Nev.Rev.Stat. 14.065(2)(e) (1986); N.C.Gen.Stat. § 1–75.4(12) (1983); Wis.Stat.Ann. § 801.05(11) (1977 and Supp.1986).

41. Colo.Rev.Stat. § 13–1–124 (1973 and Supp.1986) (matrimonial domicile in the state); D.C.Code 1981, § 13–423(a)(7)(C), (D) (Supp.1986) (matrimonial domicile, or child conceived in the state, or defendant has resided with child in the state); West's Fla.Stat.Ann. § 48.193(1) (e) (Supp.1986) (maintenance of a matrimonial domicile at time of suit, or defendant resided in state preceding

resident at the time of suit.[42] Ordinarily this requires something like domicile in the state, so that it is not sufficient that the parties stayed briefly in the state at some time in the past.[43] A few statutes have gone farther than others, to provide that the conception of a child in the state is sufficient to assert personal jurisdiction against a parent for child support.[44] As has been indicated,[45] such statutes may raise serious questions of "minimum contacts" and therefore of constitutionality.

Where no statute expressly applies to matrimonial suits, or where the particular facts do not fit the matrimonial long-arm statute, plaintiffs may be able to rely on other provisions of the state's long-arm statute. For example, the defendant's continued domicile

in the state may justify the exercise of jurisdiction notwithstanding his temporary absence.[46] A few cases have held that the execution of a separation agreement constitutes "doing business" in the state for purposes of the general long-arm statute.[47]

Many states have enacted long-arm statutes providing with more or less breadth that doing an act outside the state which causes a tort or inflicts harm within the state is sufficient to warrant personal jurisdiction in the state where the tort or harm takes effect.[48] This raises the question whether a defendant living outside the state who fails or refuses to support a spouse or child within the state is suable in the state of the spouse's or child's residence. The cases have taken diverse posi-

commencement of suit); Ill.R.Civ.Proc., Rule 2–209 (1985) (maintenance of matrimonial domicile in state); La.Stat. Ann.—Courts and Jud.Proc. § 13.3201 (1987) (former residence in state with spouse or child); Mass.Gen.L.Ann. c. 223A, § 3(g) (1986) (Domicile as party to marriage in state for one year in the last two years preceding suit); Mich.C.L.A. § 27A.705 (1986) (maintaining domicile in state while subject to marital family relationship); N.Y.—McKinney's CPLR § 302(b) (1972 and Supp.1987) (matrimonial domicile in state before separation); S.D. Codif.L. § 15–7–2(9) (Supp.1986) (maintenance of matrimonial domicile in state); V.Tex.C.A.Fam.Code § 3.26 (1986 Supp.) (plaintiff is resident and Texas was last state of marital cohabitation); Utah Code Ann.1983, § 78–27–24(6) (Supp.) (maintenance of matrimonial domicile in state).

42. Scott v. Hall, 203 Kan. 331, 454 P.2d 449 (1969); Scott v. Scott, 554 S.W.2d 274 (Tex.Civ.App.1977); Lefkovitz v. Lefkovitz, 341 So.2d 253 (Fla.App.1976), cert. denied 348 So.2d 949 (1977) (Illinois law).

43. Corcoran v. Corcoran, 353 So.2d 805 (Ala.Civ.App. 1978); Thompson v. Thompson, 657 S.W.2d 629 (Mo. 1983).

44. E.g., V.Tex.C.A.Fam.Code § 11.051 (1978); Wis. Stat.Ann. 767.01(2) (1981); Zeisler v. Zeisler, 553 S.W.2d 927 (Tex.Civ.App.1977). See Weintraub, Texas Long-Arm Jurisdiction in Family Law Cases, 32 S.W.L.J. 965 (1978); Dorsaneo, Due Process, Full Faith and Credit, and Family Law Litigation, 36 S.W.L.J. 1085, 1105 (1983).

45. See note 30, supra.

46. Hampson v. Hampson, 271 So.2d 898 (La.App. 1972); Cannon v. Cannon, 242 So.2d 291 (La.App.1970); Kennedy v. Kennedy, 10 Mass.App.Ct. 113, 406 N.E.2d 409 (1980), appeal after remand 17 Mass.App.Ct. 308, 457 N.E.2d 1133 (1983); Stucky v. Stucky, 186 Neb. 636, 185 N.W.2d 656 (1971); Duford v. Duford, 119 N.H. 515, 403 A.2d 431 (1979).

In rare instances the domicile of the plaintiff in the state may satisfy the state's long-arm statute, although it

seems doubtful that it would, by itself, be enough to meet constitutional standards. See, e.g., N.H.Rev.Stat. 458:5 (1968) and Williams v. Williams, 121 N.H. 728, 433 A.2d 1316 (1981), appeal dismissed 455 U.S. 930, 102 S.Ct. 1415, 71 L.Ed.2d 639 (1982). In the Williams case there were other contacts with the state sufficient to meet constitutional standards.

Hines v. Clendenning, 465 P.2d 460 (Okl.1970) upheld personal jurisdiction where the plaintiff was domiciled in the state, but where there were other contacts, including the facts that the marriage was contracted in Oklahoma, the parties had lived together in Oklahoma and the plaintiff wife was abandoned in that state. The long-arm statute was of the California type.

47. Ross v. Ross, 371 Mass. 439, 358 N.E.2d 437 (1976); Hurlbut v. Hurlbut, 101 Misc.2d 571, 421 N.Y.S.2d 509 (1979); Underwood v. Underwood, 92 Misc.2d 359, 399 N.Y.S.2d 967 (1977); Lawrenz v. Lawrenz, 65 Misc.2d 627, 318 N.Y.S.2d 610 (Fam.Ct.1971). Contra: Guccione v. Guccione, 100 Misc.2d 212, 417 N.Y.S.2d 633 (1979). Prybolsky v. Prybolsky, 430 A.2d 804 (Del.Fam.Ct.1981) seems to hold that the "doing business" requirement of the long-arm statute is satisfied by the facts that the state was the last matrimonial domicile and that the plaintiffs, wife and child, remained domiciled in the state.

Washington v. Washington, 486 S.W.2d 668 (Mo.App. 1972) held that the contracting of a marriage in the state is not a sufficient basis for long-arm jurisdiction under a statute which authorized that jurisdiction where a contract was made in the state.

48. E.g., Ala.R.Civ.Proc., Rule 4.2(a)(4) (1984); Ariz.R. Civ.Proc., Rule 4(e)(2) (1973); Colo.Rev.Stat. § 13–1–124(b) (1973); Conn.Gen.Stat.Ann. § 52–59b (Supp.1986); Ill.R. Civ.Proc., Rule 2–209 (1983); V.Mo.Stat.Ann. § 506.500 (Supp.1987); Ohio Rev.Code § 2307.382(A)(6) (1981); Pa. Stat. tit. 42, § 5322(a)(4) (1981).

tions on this question, in part due to the presence or absence of contacts with the state other than the infliction of harm there.[49] It would seem that the more general form of statute is sufficient to support a finding of jurisdiction, and at the same time to meet constitutional requirements.[50] The courts have taken long-arm statutes to considerable lengths to enforce tort claims against non-residents not served within the forum state.[51] They should be willing to do the same with respect to claims for maintenance and support of spouses and children, in view of the important interests involved, and of the widespread evasion of support obligations which causes so much hardship to spouses and children.

The doctrine of forum non conveniens may lead a court to refuse to exercise jurisdiction which it clearly has, where such an exercise of jurisdiction would be inconvenient or cause hardship, and where a more convenient forum is available.[52]

The Estin-Vanderbilt Doctrine

Just as the cases have held that alimony may not be awarded without personal jurisdiction over the defendant, so the Supreme Court has held that alimony may not be foreclosed by a court which does not have personal jurisdiction over the party having a possible claim to alimony. The effect of this doctrine is sometimes characterized as making divorce "divisible", meaning that a court may, under the Williams cases,[53] have jurisdiction to terminate the marital relationship, but may not have jurisdiction to terminate the financial incidents of that relationship.

In Estin v. Estin[54] where this doctrine first appeared, the husband obtained a divorce in Nevada without obtaining personal jurisdiction over her. The Supreme Court held that this decree, notwithstanding the husband's real domicile in Nevada, did not terminate his duty to make payments to the wife under a New York separation order which had been in force from a date before the divorce, the wife being at all times domiciled in New York. Full faith and credit required recognition of the Nevada decree as ending the marriage but not as ending the wife's right under the separation order. The Court based this holding upon the proposition that the wife's rights under the separation decree were in the nature of intangible property rights which could not be cut off by any court which did not have personal jurisdiction over her. Estin has been followed by many lower court decisions,[55] but there are cases which hold that

---

49. Holding personal jurisdiction conferred by the statute: Poindexter v. Willis, 87 Ill.App.2d 213, 231 N.E.2d 1 (1967); Poindexter v. Willis, 23 Ohio Misc. 199, 256 N.E.2d 254 (1970). Contra: Boyer v. Boyer, 73 Ill.2d 331, 22 Ill.Dec. 747, 383 N.E.2d 223 (1978). See also Janni v. Janni, 271 Ark. 953, 611 S.W.2d 785 (1981). Nickerson v. Nickerson, 25 Ariz.App. 251, 542 P.2d 1131 (1975), review denied 113 Ariz. 326, 553 P.2d 1200 (1976) held that this provision of the long-arm statute only applied when the forum state was the last location of the matrimonial domicile.

Where the suit arose out of the defendant's wrongful taking of property, the divorce court had jurisdiction over him pursuant to this provision of the long-arm statute. Wood v. Wood, 369 Mass. 665, 342 N.E.2d 712 (1976).

50. E.g., Conn.Gen.Stat.Ann. § 52–59b(c) (Supp.1986) (commission of a tortious act outside the state which causes injury in the state); Ohio Rev.Code § 2307.382 (1981) (tortious injury in state by an act committed outside the state with the purpose of injury to a person within the state when defendant might reasonably expect some person to be injured in the state); Pa.Stat. tit. 42, § 5322(a)(4) (1981) (causing harm or tortious injury in the state by an act or omission outside the state).

51. R. Casad, Jurisdiction in Civil Actions ch. 4 (1983), discussing, inter alia, the notion of implied consent, the convenient fiction on which many of the tort statutes are based.

52. MacLeod v. MacLeod, 383 A.2d 39 (Me. 1978); Restatement (Second) of Conflict of Laws § 84 (1971).

53. Williams v. State of North Carolina, 317 U.S. 287, 63 S.Ct. 207, 87 L.Ed. 279 (1942) and Williams v. State of North Carolina, 325 U.S. 226, 65 S.Ct. 1092, 89 L.Ed. 1577 (1945), rehearing denied 325 U.S. 895, 65 S.Ct. 1560, 89 L.Ed. 2006 (1945), discussed supra, section 12.2, at notes 79, 80.

54. 334 U.S. 541, 68 S.Ct. 1213, 92 L.Ed. 1561 (1948).

55. Mackessy v. Mackessy, 15 Alaska 361 (1954), 24 Ohio St.L.J. 346 (1963); White v. White, 83 Ariz. 305, 320 P.2d 702 (1958); Herczog v. Herczog, 186 Cal.App.2d 318, 9 Cal.Rptr. 5 (1960) (applying English law); Altman v. Altman, 282 Md. 483, 386 A.2d 766 (1978) (dictum); Phelan v. Phelan, ___ R.I. ___, 443 A.2d 1259 (1982); Annot., 49 A.L.R.3d 1266, 1299 (1973). See also Krauskopf, Divisible Divorce and Rights to Support, Property and Custody, 24 Ohio St.L.J. 346 (1963). A case which erroneously

the foreign ex parte divorce does terminate a spouse's rights under a prior separate maintenance decree.[56]

It follows logically from the argument in Estin that if the wife had been personally served in the Nevada suit, or had appeared generally there, or had been subject to the personal jurisdiction of the Nevada court as by the operation of a valid long-arm statute, the Nevada court could have terminated her right to payments under the New York decree.[57] And conversely, in all states the ex parte divorce would not terminate the obligation under the prior separate maintenance decree if the divorce plaintiff were not domiciled in the divorcing state and that state therefore did not have subject matter jurisdiction to grant the divorce.[58]

"Divisible divorce" was carried a step further by Vanderbilt v. Vanderbilt,[59] which held that a valid ex parte Nevada divorce did not terminate the right to support to which the New York wife was entitled by New York law. Here, as in Estin, the wife did not

appear in the Nevada suit nor was she personally served in Nevada. But unlike Mrs. Estin, Mrs. Vanderbilt had not obtained a New York separate maintenance decree at the time when her husband got his divorce. Nevertheless the Supreme Court held that she could get such an award of support in New York, her domicile, after the Nevada divorce had been granted. The Full Faith and Credit Clause,[60] the Court said, did not require New York to deny her this "personal" claim.

The effect of the Estin and Vanderbilt cases, when taken with the Williams decisions, is that although a divorce granted ex parte at the domicile of one of the spouses must be recognized in all states as ending the marital status, it need not cut off the defendant spouse's right to support, at least where the state of his domicile follows the rule that he may sue for alimony after an ex parte foreign divorce.[61] The majority of states today do permit the spouse to bring such a suit,[62] although there are still some states in which it is held that once the marriage is

refused to follow Estin is Perry v. Perry, 51 Wash.2d 358, 318 P.2d 968 (1958), 10 Stan.L.Rev. 758 (1958).

56. Lewis v. Lewis, 404 So.2d 1230 (La.1981) (ex parte foreign divorce terminates prior support order if filed with the Louisiana court and made a judgment of that court); Ross v. Ross, 385 Mass. 30, 430 N.E.2d 815 (1982) (dictum that a valid ex parte foreign divorce relieves a defendant from liability for separate support payments); Watson v. Watson, 243 Pa.Super. 23, 364 A.2d 431 (1976) (probably overruled by Pa.Stat. tit. 23, § 505 (Supp.1986); Brady v. Brady, 151 W.Va. 900, 158 S.E.2d 359 (1967); Annot., 49 A.L.R.3d 1266, 1295 (1973). Some courts go to extraordinary lengths to frustrate support claims by their own domiciliaries. E.g., Brown v. Brown, 249 Or. 274, 437 P.2d 845 (1968).

57. Barrows v. Barrows, 489 F.2d 661 (3d Cir.1974); Bouchard v. Bouchard, 119 R.I. 656, 382 A.2d 810 (1978). Doctrines of estoppel or waiver may, however, lead the court of the obligee's domicile to retain the separate maintenance obligations. Lappert v. Lappert, 20 N.Y.2d 364, 283 N.Y.S.2d 26, 229 N.E.2d 599 (1967); Belt v. Belt, 67 Misc.2d 679, 324 N.Y.S.2d 623 (Fam.Ct.1971).

58. Madden v. Madden, 359 Mass. 356, 269 N.E.2d 89 (1971), cert. denied 404 U.S. 854, 92 S.Ct. 95, 30 L.Ed.2d 94 (1971).

59. 354 U.S. 416, 77 S.Ct. 1360, 1 L.Ed.2d 1456 (1957). This result was foreshadowed in Armstrong v. Armstrong, 350 U.S. 568, 76 S.Ct. 629, 100 L.Ed. 705 (1956), rehearing denied 351 U.S. 943, 76 S.Ct. 832, 100 L.Ed. 1469 (1956). See also Lewis v. Lewis, 49 Cal.2d 389, 317

P.2d 987 (1957), and Restatement (Second) of Conflict of Laws § 77(2) (1971).

60. U.S.Const. art. IV, § 1.

61. See Justice Douglas' concurring opinion in Esenwein v. Commonwealth, 325 U.S. 279, 65 S.Ct. 1118, 89 L.Ed. 1608 (1945).

62. Fehlhaber v. Fehlhaber, 681 F.2d 1015 (5th Cir. 1982), rehearing denied 702 F.2d 81 (5th Cir.1983), cert. denied 464 U.S. 818, 104 S.Ct. 79, 78 L.Ed.2d 90 (1983) (California law); Kendall v. Kendall, 224 Kan. 624, 585 P.2d 978 (1978); Altman v. Altman, 282 Md. 483, 386 A.2d 766 (1978) (citing other cases); Kram v. Kram, 98 N.J.Super. 274, 237 A.2d 271 (1967), certification granted 51 N.J. 273, 239 A.2d 662 (1968); Rymanowski v. Rymanowski, 105 R.I. 89, 249 A.2d 407 (1969); Newport v. Newport, 219 Va. 48, 245 S.E.2d 134 (1978).

The statutes in some states expressly provide for the award of alimony after a foreign ex parte divorce. E.g., Official Code Ga.Ann. § 30–226 (Supp.1986); Kan.Stat. Ann. § 60–1611 (1983); N.J.Stat.Ann. § 2A:34–24.1 (Supp.1986–1987); Pa.Stat. tit. 23, § 505 (Supp.1986), apparently overruling Stambaugh v. Stambaugh, 458 Pa. 147, 329 A.2d 483 (1974). See Sohmer v. Sohmer, 318 Pa. Super. 500, 465 A.2d 665 (1983).

If the defendant in the divorce action *was* subject to the personal jurisdiction of the divorcing court and that court refused to award alimony, the courts of the defendant's domicile generally respect that refusal and likewise deny alimony pursuant to the Full Faith and Credit Clause.

validly ended, alimony or support may not be awarded.[63]

The Estin-Vanderbilt doctrine of divisible divorce has troubled those who find it illogical to say that two people are at the same time married and not married, depending upon what court is deciding the question and for what purpose. Yet there is nothing unusual about this. In the Middle Ages in England a woman married by the standards of the ecclesiastical courts could be denied dower if her marriage had been contracted without observing certain formalities.[64] She too was in a sense both married and not married. Logical inconsistency need not bother us if a valid social policy is served.

Another criticism can be based upon the Supreme Court's adherence to the *in rem-in personam* distinction. The Court has disclaimed the older tendency to label divorce an action *in rem*.[65] But the effect of its decisions is that the status of marriage can be ended by one party in the absence of the other, while the financial incidents of that status cannot. The termination of the status is thus treated as if it were *in rem*, while termination of the incidents is treated as if *in personam*. Yet a spouse's claims to the society and companionship of the other spouse are, on any realistic view of the matter, as much a "personal" right as the claim for support,[66] although of course the claim to his society is not enforceable in a direct action against the spouse, while the claim for support is so enforceable. The critics of Estin-Vanderbilt then ask, if the spouse must be subject to the court's personal jurisdiction before one right may be cut off, why should not the same requirement be made when the other right is in issue? The answer lies in the contemporary attitude to-ward divorce. The nearly universal adoption of some form of "no-fault" divorce recognizes that even though a spouse's claim to the companionship and affection of the other spouse is a "personal" one of great importance, it has value only when honored voluntarily by the other spouse. If the other spouse is determined to have a divorce, evidencing a choice not to honor the claim for society and affection, the divorce may not be prevented in those states (the great majority of American jurisdictions) in which fault grounds for divorce have been abolished. Happy relations cannot then be restored. Therefore permitting the divorce to be obtained without personal jurisdiction over the defendant spouse causes her little real prejudice so long as her financial claims are preserved, as they are by Estin and Vanderbilt. In short the Supreme Court's gloss on the Full Faith and Credit Clause preserves the spouse's opportunity to contest the divorce at the point where in the modern divorce action the contest has importance, that is, respecting money or property. It does not preserve the opportunity to contest the issue where a contest is in vain, respecting the grant of the divorce itself. That contest the spouse may lose without being present although, as has been shown, some reasonable notice to her is required by the Constitution.[67] This demonstrates that what the Court is really concerned with is the protection of the parties' interests rather than the vindication of some state interest, even assuming that the latter could be defined.

If the Supreme Court is correct in saying that personal jurisdiction over a spouse is essential before her claim for support may be cut off, does it follow that a state which did

---

E.g., Whitaker v. Whitaker, 237 Ga. 895, 230 S.E.2d 486 (1976); Osborne v. Osborne, 215 Va. 205, 207 S.E.2d 875 (1974). Cf. Healey v. Healey, 152 N.J.Super. 44, 377 A.2d 762 (1977).

63. E.g., Loeb v. Loeb, 118 Vt. 472, 114 A.2d 518 (1955).

64. 2 F. Pollock and F. Maitland, History of English Law 372–375 (1898).

65. Williams v. North Carolina, 317 U.S. 287, 297, 63 S.Ct. 207, 212, 87 L.Ed. 279 (1942).

66. Justice Frankfurter's dissent in Vanderbilt v. Vanderbilt, 354 U.S. 416, 424, 77 S.Ct. 1360, 1365, 1 L.Ed. 2d 1456 (1957) makes this point.

67. See section 12.2, supra, at note 65.

rely on an ex parte decree to end her rights of support would be violating the Due Process Clause?[68] The Estin and Vanderbilt cases on their facts only hold that a state which allows alimony to survive a foreign ex parte divorce is not prevented by the Full Faith and Credit Clause from continuing to do so. A minority of states have considered the right to support an inseparable incident to marriage with the consequence that once the marriage has been terminated, even without personal jurisdiction over the defendant spouse, no right to alimony survives.[69] But the reasoning of the Supreme Court seems to be that the right to support is the kind of personal right which may not be cut off without personal jurisdiction over the defendant. In other words, the reason full faith and credit need not be given is that the Due Process Clause would be violated if the ex parte divorce were treated as terminating the right to alimony. This view of the Supreme Court's decisions is supported by a reading of the dissenting opinions in Estin v. Estin[70] which argued against such an extreme position.

68. U.S. Const. amend. XIV, section 1.

69. See the cases cited supra, note 63 and other cases collected in Note, 53 Harv.L.Rev. 1180, 1184 (1940); Annot., 28 A.L.R.2d 1378, 1402 (1953). See also Rodda v. Rodda, 185 Or. 140, 200 P.2d 616 (1949), cert. denied 337 U.S. 946, 69 S.Ct. 1504, 93 L.Ed. 1749 (1949); Meredith v. Meredith, 204 F.2d 64 (D.C.Cir.1953), modified by Hopson v. Hopson, 221 F.2d 839 (D.C.Cir.1955).

Where the claimant for alimony has moved from one state to another between the granting of the ex parte divorce and the assertion of the alimony claim, the effect of the ex parte divorce is apparently to be determined in accordance with the law of the claimant's domicile at the time the divorce was obtained. Loeb v. Loeb, 4 N.Y.2d 542, 176 N.Y.S.2d 590, 152 N.E.2d 36 (1958), reargument denied 5 N.Y.2d 793, 180 N.Y.S.2d 1025, 154 N.E.2d 581 (1958); Morphet v. Morphet, 263 Or. 311, 502 P.2d 255 (1972).

70. 334 U.S. 541, 551–552, 68 S.Ct. 1213, 1219–1220, 92 L.Ed. 1561 (1948). But see Morris, Divisible Divorce, 64 Harv.L.Rev. 1287, 1295 (1951). Cf. Hudson v. Hudson, 52 Cal.2d 735, 344 P.2d 295 (1959), which seems to say that the wife's right to support may not be cut off by the husband's valid foreign ex parte divorce, but that she may not assert this right in a separate maintenance action. She may, however, sue for temporary or permanent alimony. This is a distinction without a difference. See also Fehlhaber v. Fehlhaber, 681 F.2d 1015 (5th Cir.1982), rehearing denied 702 F.2d 81 (5th Cir. 1983), cert. denied 464 U.S. 818, 104 S.Ct. 79, 78 L.Ed.2d 90 (1983).

In nearly all states today the divorce court may divide the property of the spouses as an incident to divorce.[71] Since the provisions of the divorce decree dividing the property must be based upon personal jurisdiction over both spouses,[72] it follows as a logical consequence of Estin and Vanderbilt that after a foreign ex parte divorce the defendant spouse who was not subject to the divorce court's personal jurisdiction may bring a suit for a division of the marital property. The Full Faith and Credit Clause requires that a divorce based upon the domicile of one spouse be recognized in all states as ending the marriage.[73] But just as it does not require other states to give it the effect of ending alimony or support obligations, it likewise does not require them to give it the effect of ending the spouse's obligation to divide the spouses' property. Although the Estin and Vanderbilt cases do not involve this question directly, their reasoning supports this result. A substantial number of decisions in the lower courts take this position.[74]

71. See section 15.1, infra.

72. See note 1, supra.

73. See section 12.2, supra, at note 78.

74. Moucka v. Windham, 483 F.2d 914 (10th Cir.1973); Sidebotham v. Robison, 216 F.2d 816 (9th Cir.1954); Curles v. Curles, 136 F.Supp. 916 (D.D.C.1955), judgment affirmed 241 F.2d 448 (D.C.Cir.1957); Worthley v. Worthley, 44 Cal.2d 465, 283 P.2d 19 (1955) (dictum); In re Williams' Estate, 36 Cal.2d 289, 223 P.2d 248 (1950); Willoughby v. Willoughby, 178 Kan. 62, 283 P.2d 428 (1955) (local statute expressly provided for this); Slodowski v. Slodowski, 156 N.J.Super. 376, 383 A.2d 1188 (1978); Woliner v. Woliner, 132 N.J.Super. 216, 333 A.2d 283 (1975), affirmed p.c. 68 N.J. 324, 344 A.2d 781 (1975); Zimler v. Zimler, 91 Misc.2d 452, 398 N.Y.S.2d 108 (1977), reversed on other grounds 61 A.D.2d 981, 402 N.Y.S.2d 446 (2d Dep't 1978); Kolb v. Kolb, 52 Misc.2d 313, 276 N.Y.S.2d 317 (1966), 17 Buff.L.Rev. 541 (1968); Slapp v. Slapp, 73 Ohio App. 444, 57 N.E.2d 81 (1943), affirmed 143 Ohio St. 105, 54 N.E.2d 153 (1944).

If the divorcing court has personal jurisdiction of the defendant spouse, the decree's provision concerning a division of property may be recognized. Manfrini v. Manfrini, 136 N.J.Super. 390, 346 A.2d 430 (1975), certification denied 70 N.J. 526, 361 A.2d 540 (1976). But see Pierrakos v. Pierrakos, 148 N.J.Super. 574, 372 A.2d 1331 (1977).

The Supreme Court in Simons v. Miami Beach First National Bank [75] has taken a position which on the face of the opinion seems to constitute a retreat from the logic of the Estin-Vanderbilt doctrine.[76] The case held that an ex parte Florida divorce obtained by the husband terminated the wife's claim to dower in Florida real estate owned by the husband at his death. The wife's argument that Florida had no power to cut off her right to dower without personal jurisdiction over her was rejected in the following terms:

"* * * the answer is that under Florida law no dower right survived the decree. The Supreme Court of Florida has said that dower rights in Florida property, being inchoate, are extinguished by a divorce decree predicated on substituted or constructive service * * * It follows that the Florida courts transgressed no constitutional bounds in denying petitioner dower in her ex-husband's Florida estate." [77]

The Simons case may of course be distinguished from Estin and Vanderbilt on the ground that it did not involve the Full Faith and Credit Clause, since in Simons the only issue was the effect in Florida of a Florida divorce decree. But the case does amount to a silent repudiation of the proposition that it is a violation of the Due Process Clause to give an ex parte divorce the effect of cutting off at least this sort of "inchoate" property right. Simons is also concerned with a property right only enforceable on death, rather than the kind of property right enforceable in connection with divorce and having similarities with alimony. The Vanderbilt rationale applies with greater force to the latter kind of property right, although it does seem that both forms of property right are "inchoate" in any proper sense of the word since both require the termination of a marriage to become enforceable, in the one case termination by death, in the other termination by divorce. Perhaps on practical grounds it makes sense to say to a spouse, "You may not evade the obligations of alimony and its equivalent, such as a division of property, by obtaining an ex parte divorce," and at the same time holding that such a divorce does terminate dower rights which would become effective only at some time in the future.

The Supreme Court's zeal for the implementation of the Full Faith and Credit Clause seems at times to be inconsistent with the Estin-Vanderbilt doctrine. The issue is raised by putting an example. Suppose that the law of Nevada clearly is that an ex parte divorce cuts off the wife's rights either to alimony or to payments under an existing separate maintenance decree. But suppose that by New York law, the law of the wife's domicile, the wife's rights are not cut off by the foreign ex parte divorce. The husband obtains a Nevada divorce upon an unassailable finding of domicile. He returns to New York, where his wife sues him for alimony or seeks to enforce a prior separate maintenance decree against him. Which law determines the effect of the Nevada decree on her rights, that of Nevada or that of New York? Estin and Vanderbilt appear to hold that New York law does. But in Aldrich v. Aldrich [78] the Supreme Court held that West Virginia was required, by the Full Faith and Credit Clause, to give a Florida alimony decree as broad a scope as it would have had in Florida. This is in accord with the general rule that full faith and credit means that a sister state judgment must be given the effect it would have in the state where it was rendered.[79] If so, why does not New York have to give a Nevada decree as broad a scope as it would have in Nevada?

---

75. 381 U.S. 81, 85 S.Ct. 1315, 14 L.Ed.2d 232 (1965), rehearing denied 381 U.S. 956, 85 S.Ct. 1797, 14 L.Ed.2d 728 (1965), 33 U.Chi.L.Rev. 837 (1966).

76. Justice Harlan, in his concurring opinion in Simons characterized the majority opinion as constituting "a withdrawal from the due process phase of Vanderbilt". 381 U.S. at 88, 85 S.Ct. at 1319.

77. 381 U.S. at 85, 86, 85 S.Ct. at 1318–1319.

78. 378 U.S. 540, 84 S.Ct. 1687, 12 L.Ed.2d 1020 (1964).

79. See 28 U.S.C.A. § 1738, which provides in relevant part: "Such Acts, records and judicial proceedings or copies thereof, so authenticated, shall have the same full faith and credit in every court within the United States and its Territories and Possessions as they have by law or usage in the courts of such State, Territory or Possession from which they are taken." See also Restatement (Second) of Conflict of Laws § 93 (1971); E. Scoles and P. Hay, Conflict of Laws 934–935 (1982).

The only reason that comes to mind is that in the Nevada-New York conflict the decree was not based upon personal service, while in the Aldrich case the Florida court did have personal jurisdiction over the defendant. But it is not clear why that difference should matter, unless the Estin-Vanderbilt doctrine is based upon a due process analysis. If it is, it is possible to say that in our hypothetical the wife has not had her day in court, while in the Aldrich case the husband had participated in the Florida proceeding and therefore was not unfairly prejudiced by having the decree given the effect called for by Florida law. Other more complex states of fact could be imagined. For example, the wife might move in good faith from the marital domicile to State X, where an ex parte divorce does not cut off alimony rights. The husband then obtains a divorce at the marital domicile, where an ex parte decree is given the effect of cutting off alimony rights. What should be the consequence in State X, under Estin, Vanderbilt and Aldrich? On the basis of the existing law the outcome is hard to predict. One suspects that leaving aside elaborate constitutional and conflicts analysis, the practical solution is for the forum to apply its own law, but this may not be permitted by the present state of authority.

Finally, a foreign ex parte divorce generally has no effect upon claims for child support, for two reasons: a) Neither the child nor his mother or father is, by definition, personally subject to the divorce court's jurisdiction.[80] b) Child support decrees are nearly always modifiable, so that Full Faith and Credit ordinarily does not prevent a second state from later reexamining any decree purporting to deal with child support.[81]

---

80. See, e.g., Conlon by Conlon v. Heckler, 719 F.2d 788 (5th Cir.1983).

81. See Silverstein v. Silverstein, 246 Pa.Super. 503, 371 A.2d 948 (1977) and section 17.2, infra.

§ 12.5

1. A definition of "custody" is attempted in section 19.2, infra. Contemporary statutes contain provisions defining "custody determinations".

2. See, e.g., Rejda v. Rejda, 198 Neb. 465, 253 N.W.2d 295 (1977); Sosso v. Sosso, 196 Neb. 242, 242 N.W.2d 621 (1976); Holderle v. Holderle, 11 Ohio App.2d 148, 229

WESTLAW REFERENCES

divorc! dissol! /s person** /3 jurisdiction /s
    property /s "full faith and credit"
di(person** /3 jurisdiction! /p child spous! wife /s
    support /p inadequa! adequa! insufficien! sufficien!)

The Estin-Vanderbilt Doctrine

person** /3 jurisdiction! /s "marital relationship"
"divisible divorce" /s jurisdiction!
vanderbilt /s "ex parte" /s support

§ 12.5 Divorce—Jurisdiction to Award Custody

Introduction and Scope

Jurisdiction to award custody is an issue in contexts other than divorce. It is discussed here in the divorce chapter for lack of any more obviously convenient place and because it probably arises most often in the divorce or post-divorce context.

The word "jurisdiction" generally refers to the authority of a particular court to decide a custody dispute.[1] This authority may depend upon the extent of the court's power over the parties to the suit (personal jurisdiction) or on the relation between the parties including the child, and the state in which the court is sitting (subject-matter jurisdiction), or on both of these factors. In addition local statutes governing which of the state's courts, district courts, superior courts, juvenile courts, family courts, are authorized to hear custody cases are the source of further rules of jurisdiction.[2]

The decision on whether a court has jurisdiction to determine custody in any of these senses controls not only whether it may give a decree of custody in the first instance, but also the extent to which some other state's court will recognize a decree so given as valid

---

N.E.2d 79 (1967); Richtmyer v. Richtmyer, ___ R.I. ___, 461 A.2d 409 (1983); Paolino v. Paolino, ___ R.I. ___, 420 A.2d 830 (1980). Jurisdiction in this sense varies so much from state to state that it will not be discussed further. It is closely related to the prevailing rule that all divorce jurisdiction is in the first instance based upon statute in the United States. The conflicts and confusion created by multiple local custody remedies is described in Bodenheimer, The Multiplicity of Child Custody Proceedings—The Problems of California Law, 23 Stan.L.Rev. 703 (1971).

and binding upon the parties. These two consequences of the presence or absence of jurisdiction are closely related by the doctrine that the decree of a court which has no jurisdiction will not be respected by other courts [3] and by the natural tendency of many courts not to give decrees which will not be respected elsewhere. The United States Constitution's Full Faith and Credit Clause [4] plays an important part in determining whether a custody decree will be recognized by other states.

Although custody disputes arise most often in suits for divorce, the jurisdictional rules for custody differ sharply from those for the divorce itself. Thus a court may have jurisdiction to grant a husband and wife a divorce but may not have jurisdiction to decide a dispute regarding the custody of their child.[5] Conversely, a court may not have jurisdiction to grant a divorce but may have jurisdiction to determine custody.[6]

History and Background

The traditional and conventional view, advocated by Professor Beale [7] and adopted by the first edition of the Restatement of the Conflict of Laws,[8] was that the court of a state had jurisdiction to grant a custody decree only where the child who was the subject of the decree was domiciled in that state. These authorities did concede, however, that a court could give a temporary protective order where the child had no domicile in the state but was physically present there. The domicile rule had the advantage of certainty since theoretically at least only one court in the world would be the domicile of the child and only that court could determine the child's custody.[9] Its conceptual basis was that custody is a status [10] and only in the state of the domicile was there the permanent relationship between the state and the child sufficient to give the state an interest in regulating that status.

Several penetrating studies criticized the domicile rule.[11] They argued that custody is not properly characterized as a status,[12] that more than one state should and often did assume the authority to deal with custody,[13] and that the courts generally based jurisdiction on factors other than domicile, even those courts which paid lip service to the domicile rule.[14] The most cogent reasons for rejecting the domicile rule were that the child's welfare often required court action in a state other than the domicile, and that courts in states other than the domicile were often in a better position to determine custody and to enforce their decrees than courts of the domicile would be.[15]

The result of these criticisms of the domicile rule was that many courts came to the conclusion that any state having a substantial interest in the child's welfare, the ability to

---

3. The text statement is obviously over-simplified but in general is supported by Restatement (Second) of Conflict of Laws §§ 93, 98 (1971). One important qualification based upon principles of res judicata is discussed infra at note 83.

4. U.S. Const. art. IV, § 1.

5. Jurisdiction for divorce is discussed supra, section 12.2.

6. E.g., Vanneck v. Vanneck, 49 N.Y.2d 602, 427 N.Y.S.2d 735, 404 N.E.2d 1278 (1980); Lynch v. Lynch, 302 N.C. 189, 274 S.E.2d 212 (1981), modified on other grounds 303 N.C. 367, 279 S.E.2d 840 (1981).

7. 2 J. Beale, Conflict of Laws § 144.3 (1935).

8. Restatement, Conflict of Laws § 117 (1934). See also G. Stumberg, Conflict of Laws 319 (3d ed.1963).

9. The domicile of children is discussed in section 4.3, Practitioner's Edition.

10. Restatement, Conflict of Laws §§ 119, 144 (1934).

11. Stumberg, The Status of Children in the Conflict of Laws, 8 U.Chi.L.Rev. 42 (1940); Stansbury, Custody and Maintenance Across State Lines, 10 L. & Contemp. Prob. 818 (1944); Ehrenzweig, Interstate Recognition of Custody Decrees, 51 Mich.L.Rev. 345 (1953); Ratner, Child Custody in a Federal System, 62 Mich.L.Rev. 795 (1964).

12. Stansbury, supra, note 11 at 820.

13. Sampsell v. Superior Court, In and For Los Angeles County, 32 Cal.2d 763, 197 P.2d 739 (1948) (Traynor, J.); Annot., 4 A.L.R.2d 7 (1949); Ehrenzweig, supra, note 11 at 351–352.

14. Professor Ehrenzweig, supra, note 11, at 357, argued that the predominant factor leading courts to refuse recognition to custody decrees of other states was the petitioner's "unclean hands", that is, that the petitioner was violating the existing custody order of the other state.

15. Finlay v. Finlay, 240 N.Y. 429, 148 N.E. 624 (1925) (Cardozo, J.); Sampsell v. Superior Court In and For Los Angeles County, 32 Cal.2d 763, 197 P.2d 739 (1948); Stansbury, Custody and Maintenance Across State Lines, 10 L. & Contemp. Prob. 818, 828 (1944).

determine that welfare through access to the relevant evidence, and the means of effectuating the custody decree so determined would have jurisdiction to decide upon the child's custody. The basis for such an interest and ability might be the domicile of the child within the state,[16] his residence there,[17] occasionally his temporary presence there,[18] the domicile of one or both parents in the state,[19] or the fact that one or both parents were before the court and subject to its power.[20] Many cases combined several of these factors. What this meant was, as the Sampsell case [21] made clear, that the courts of more than one state could concurrently have jurisdiction respecting a particular custody case.

By about 1970 the law of custody jurisdiction had been transformed from the certainty, rigidity and unreality of the Beale-Restatement principle to the child-oriented approach of the Sampsell case,[22] with its attendant uncertainty and diversity. Since the Sampsell analysis provided in many instances several possible courts in which a custody case could be heard, the temptation to shop around for a congenial forum was irresistible for a parent and his lawyer facing a doubtful custody case. The most congenial forum generally proved to be in the home town of the petitioning parent, the phrase "home-towning" being the slang term describing the local favoritism indulged in by too many judges in custody cases.[23] Not

only was it possible to indulge in forum-shopping at the time of the initial proceeding, but if that proceeding produced an unsatisfactory result, the disappointed parent could usually go to another state and attempt to persuade the court in that state to modify the first decree, the law in all states being that custody decrees were modifiable upon a showing of changed circumstances.[24] Too many judges were too ready to grant such petitions for modification.[25] The hope of succeeding with such petitions for modification led many noncustodial parents to seize the child or employ an agent to seize the child and bring him to the second state in order to strengthen jurisdictional claims in that state. Child-snatching, really a form of kidnapping, became a national scandal.[26]

Two non-legal developments aggravated and focused public attention on the evils of custody litigation. The first was the extraordinary mobility of American society which sometimes seemed so great as to convert every divorce suit involving children into an interstate custody case. The second was the publication of an influential book by experts in law and child psychology which vigorously asserted the importance of stability in the lives of children of divorce and the undesirable consequences of shifting them from one parent to the other.[27]

16. Boardman v. Boardman, 135 Conn. 124, 62 A.2d 521 (1948).

17. Sampsell v. Superior Court In and For Los Angeles County, 32 Cal.2d 763, 197 P.2d 739 (1948).

18. Bassett v. Bassett, 56 N.M. 739, 250 P.2d 487 (1952).

19. Van Gundy v. Van Gundy, 244 Iowa 488, 56 N.W.2d 43 (1952).

20. Green v. Green, 351 Mass. 466, 221 N.E.2d 857 (1966).

21. Sampsell v. Superior Court In and For Los Angeles County, 32 Cal.2d 763, 197 P.2d 739 (1948).

22. Ibid. The Sampsell approach was codified in the Restatement (Second) of Conflict of Laws § 79 (1971), which provided that a state had jurisdiction to determine the custody of a child who was domiciled in the state, or who was present in the state, or where the controversy was between two or more persons who were personally subject to the jurisdiction of the state.

23. See, e.g., State v. Stacy, 182 So.2d 119 (La.App. 1966), 12 Loy.L.Rev. 147 (1967), in which the courts of

Louisiana first gave custody of the children to their Louisiana mother, the Iowa court then gave custody to their Iowa father, and finally the Louisiana courts insisted that custody be with the Louisiana mother.

24. E.g., People of State of New York ex rel. Halvey v. Halvey, 330 U.S. 610, 67 S.Ct. 903, 91 L.Ed. 1133 (1947); Kovacs v. Brewer, 356 U.S. 604, 78 S.Ct. 963, 2 L.Ed.2d 1008 (1958); Ford v. Ford, 371 U.S. 187, 83 S.Ct. 273, 9 L.Ed.2d 240, on remand 242 S.C. 344, 130 S.E.2d 916 (1963). See also section 19.9, infra.

25. Bodenheimer, The Rights of Children and the Crisis In Custody Litigation: Modification of Custody In and Out of State, 46 Univ. of Colo.L.Rev. 495 (1975).

26. The situation is described in Hudak, Seize, Run, and Sue: The Ignominy of Interstate Child Custody Litigation in American Courts, 39 Mo.L.Rev. 521 (1974); Foster and Freed, Child Snatching and Custodial Fights: The Case for the Uniform Child Custody Jurisdiction Act, 28 Hast.L.J. 1011 (1977).

27. J. Goldstein, A. Freud, A. Solnit, Beyond the Best Interests of the Child (1973). See also J. Goldstein, A.

Although this undesirable state of the law of custody was made possible by the jurisdictional rules, it was not made inevitable thereby. Judge Traynor's opinion in Sampsell was careful to emphasize the need for restraint in modifying decrees, the necessity for respect and comity for the decrees of other states, and the obvious fact that the existence of concurrent jurisdiction did not mean that the jurisdiction should always be exercised. Many trial courts did not heed his words, however, and their local chauvinism was the primary cause of the child-snatching and relitigation of custody disputes which has just been described.

Since the common law principles of comity and respect for the judgments of other states were ineffectual to reduce the abuses of custody litigation, the obvious next step was legislation. Two statutes entered the field. The Uniform Child Custody Jurisdiction Act [28] was approved by the American Bar Association in 1968. In 1980 Congress passed the Parental Kidnapping Prevention Act of that year.[29] These statutes have transformed the law of custody jurisdiction. Their provisions and their effects will be discussed in detail later in this section.[30]

Constitutional Limitations on Custody Jurisdiction

Another aspect of the history of this subject, but one having more than purely historical importance, is the extent to which jurisdictional principles have been affected by two provisions of the United States Constitution, the Full Faith and Credit Clause,[31] and the Due Process Clause of the Fourteenth Amendment.[32] In the custody context the two clauses are closely related and have generated reams of complicated exegesis.

As a general proposition the Supreme Court of the United States [33] and the state courts [34] have all agreed that due process requires adequate notice and the opportunity to be heard for custody proceedings. The Mullane case amplifies the requirement by prescribing that the notice must be "reasonably calculated, under all the circumstances, to apprise interested parties of the pendency of the action and afford them an opportunity to present their objections." [35] The method of service is spelled out in some detail by the UCCJA,[36] which also specifically describes the persons to whom notice must be given,[37] as does the PKPA.[38] There seems to be some question whether service by publication is permissible,[39] although if it is not, the consequence is

---

Freud, A. Solnit, Before the Best Interests of the Child (1979).

28. 9 Unif.L.Ann. 111 (1979). This act will be referred to in the following form: UCCJA § ___.

29. Pub.L.No. 96–611, 94 Stat. 3568, codified at 28 U.S.C.A. § 1738A. This statute will be referred to as the PKPA and will be cited 28 U.S.C.A. § 1738A followed by the subsection.

30. See the text at notes 66, 90, infra.

31. U.S. Const. art. IV, § 1.

32. U.S. Const. amend. XIV, § 1.

33. Stanley v. Illinois, 405 U.S. 645, 92 S.Ct. 1208, 31 L.Ed.2d 551 (1972); Armstrong v. Manzo, 380 U.S. 545, 85 S.Ct. 1187, 14 L.Ed.2d 62 (1965).

34. Wyatt v. Falhsing, 396 So.2d 1069 (Ala.Cir.App. 1981); Agnello v. Becker, 184 Conn. 421, 440 A.2d 172 (1981); Brown v. Brown, 463 N.E.2d 310 (Ind.App.1984); Application of Felix C, 116 Misc.2d 300, 455 N.Y.S.2d 234 (Fam.Ct.1982).

35. Mullane v. Central Hanover Bank & Trust Co., 339 U.S. 306, 314, 70 S.Ct. 652, 657, 94 L.Ed. 865 (1950).

36. UCCJA § 5, 9 Unif.L.Ann. 131 (1979), authorizes notice to persons outside the state by personal delivery, by a method meeting the requirements of the state in which service is to be made, by mail with a provision for a return receipt, or as directed by the court. Since this statute is specifically addressed to custody cases, it presumably is controlling where in conflict with general service statutes or rules of the states.

37. UCCJA § 4, 9 Unif.L.Ann. 129 (1979) requires notice to any contestants, any parent whose parental rights have not been terminated, and any person having physical custody of the child.

38. 28 U.S.C.A. § 1738A(e), containing a provision like that in UCCJA § 4, supra, note 37.

39. The Commissioners' comments to UCCJA § 5 state that service by publication is not provided for in that section because of doubts about constitutionality, citing Mullane v. Central Hanover Bank & Trust Co., 339 U.S. 306, 70 S.Ct. 652, 94 L.Ed. 865 (1950). The Supreme Court has recently become a little more realistic about notice and hearing where illegitimate children are concerned, so perhaps the Commissioners' doubts are somewhat exaggerated. See Lehr v. Robertson, 463 U.S. 248, 103 S.Ct. 2985, 77 L.Ed.2d 614 (1983). Appointment of a guardian without notice was upheld in Patten v. Patrick, 276 N.W.2d 390 (Iowa 1979), where a hearing after the appointment of a guardian was available. And Stanley v. Illinois, 405 U.S. 645, 657 n. 9, 92 S.Ct. 1208, 1215 n.9, 31 L.Ed.2d 551 (1972) seems to approve of service by publica-

that a court can never enter a custody decree so long as the whereabouts of the respondent is unknown, a highly undesirable state of affairs.

The Supreme Court of the United States has considered the effect of the Full Faith and Credit Clause on custody decrees on several occasions. Although the effect of that Clause is now the subject of detailed treatment in the PKPA,[40] a consideration of the Supreme Court's position at this point is essential to a full understanding of that Act. Many years ago the Court in a line of cases held that since custody decrees are modifiable under the law of all states, the modification of such decrees by the courts of other states is not foreclosed by the Full Faith and Credit Clause.[41] This was an application of the familiar principle that the Full Faith and Credit Clause does not require that a judgment need be given more final or conclusive effect in the state of the forum than in the state where rendered.[42] The Court therefore did not have to decide directly whether full faith and credit must be given to custody decrees in some circumstances. Since those cases were decided the local law of some states has sharply restricted the extent to which custody decrees may be modified.[43] The Full Faith and Credit Clause may now assume a greater importance respecting the decrees of those states than it had when the power to modify decrees was more extensive.[44] Before these more recent

changes in the law of modification of custody decrees some state courts[45] and one Supreme Court Justice[46] went so far as to assert that because of the overriding interest of each state in protecting the children within its territory the Full Faith and Credit Clause has no application whatever to custody decrees.

In one other case, May v. Anderson,[47] the Supreme Court also denied full faith and credit to a custody decree, but on the ground that the decree was entered without personal jurisdiction over the respondent rather than because it was modifiable. In May the husband obtained a divorce in Wisconsin, the decree giving him custody of the children of the marriage. He was domiciled in Wisconsin, which was also the marital domicile until marital discord developed, at which time the wife went to Ohio, taking the children and shortly thereafter informed the husband that she would not return. The Supreme Court assumed that she thereby acquired a domicile in Ohio. She was served with process in the divorce action by personal delivery in Ohio. After the divorce the husband took the decree to Ohio and demanded and obtained custody of the children. He took them back to Wisconsin, where they remained with him for about four years. At the end of that time he took them to Ohio and left them for a visit with their mother, after which she refused to return them to him. He then filed a petition in Ohio for habeas corpus, seeking enforce-

tion in a proceeding to terminate parental rights. Nussbaumer v. Nussbaumer, 442 So.2d 1094 (Fla.App.1983) held that a Pennsylvania decree should be enforced even though based upon service by publication and entered without personal jurisdiction over the respondent.

Notice to a party's attorney of record was held adequate even though the party had a short time earlier left the state and the attorney did not know his whereabouts, in Spaulding v. Spaulding, 460 A.2d 1360 (Me.1983), applying Colorado's version of the UCCJA.

40. 28 U.S.C.A. § 1738A. The Act is discussed infra, at note 90.

41. People of State of New York ex rel. Halvey v. Halvey, 330 U.S. 640, 675 S.Ct. 903, 91 L.Ed. 1133 (1947); Kovacs v. Brewer, 356 U.S. 604, 78 S.Ct. 963, 2 L.Ed.2d 1008 (1958); Ford v. Ford, 371 U.S. 187, 83 S.Ct. 273, 9 L.Ed.2d 240 (1962), on remand 242 S.C. 344, 130 S.E.2d 916 (1963).

42. Restatement (Second) of Conflict of Laws § 109 (1971).

43. See, e.g., Uniform Marriage and Divorce Act § 409, 9A Unif.L.Ann. 211 (1979). Modification of custody decrees is discussed infra, in section 19.9.

44. Some states did give a limited full faith and credit to custody decrees, even though such a position may seem a contradiction in terms. See Miller v. Miller, 158 Conn. 217, 258 A.2d 89 (1969), cert. denied 396 U.S. 940, 90 S.Ct. 374, 24 L.Ed.2d 241 (1969); Rethorst v. Rethorst, 214 Md. 1, 133 A.2d 101 (1957); Application of Lorenz, 194 Or. 355, 241 P.2d 142 (1952), rehearing denied 194 Or. 355, 242 P.2d 200 (1952).

45. E.g., People ex rel. Strand v. Harnetiaux, 46 Ill.2d 424, 263 N.E.2d 30 (1970) (semble); Bachman v. Mejias, 1 N.Y.2d 575, 154 N.Y.S.2d 903, 136 N.E.2d 866 (1956).

46. Justice Frankfurter, dissenting, in Kovacs v. Brewer, 356 U.S. 604, 609, 78 S.Ct. 963, 966, 2 L.Ed.2d 1008 (1958), and concurring in May v. Anderson, 345 U.S. 528, 535, 73 S.Ct. 840, 844, 97 L.Ed. 1221 (1953).

47. 345 U.S. 528, 73 S.Ct. 840, 97 L.Ed. 1221 (1953).

ment of the Wisconsin custody decree. Under the Ohio practice habeas corpus was available only to determine the immediate right to possession of the children, and did not provide a remedy for determining the best interest of the children or for modifying the custody decree of another state. The husband was therefore in the position of asserting the immediate legal right to custody, on the basis of the prior Wisconsin decree. The Supreme Court held that Ohio need not respect the Wisconsin decree because Wisconsin had not had personal jurisdiction over the wife, relying largely on an analogy to the alimony cases which required personal jurisdiction, such as Estin v. Estin.[48] It took this position even though the parties had stipulated that at the time of the divorce the children were domiciled in Wisconsin.

It is not surprising that May v. Anderson has been sharply criticized[49] since it focused on one aspect of the custody problem and entirely overlooked all others. By drawing the analogy to rights of property the Court emphasized its assumption that the only function of a custody decree is to adjudicate parental rights in a child, just as the divorce court must often adjudicate the rights of spouses in a house or an automobile. No attention was given to the protection of the child,[50] to the fact that the courts act in these cases as parens patriae,[51] or to the availability of evidence in the state where personal jurisdiction was obtainable, all of which factors would

seem to be relevant to the formulation of a jurisdictional principle. The Court made no reference to the extensive literature on custody jurisdiction or to the various suggested bases for it.

The most serious consequence of May v. Anderson for custody litigation is that if its reasoning prevails, there will be a substantial number of cases in which no custody decree may be entered by any state. Although the case purports to hold only that full faith and credit may not be accorded a decree in which there is no personal jurisdiction over the respondent, the only possible reason for so holding is that a decree rendered without such jurisdiction is invalid and the only possible ground for invalidity is that such a decree is held to violate the Due Process Clause, just as would be true of any in personam judgment rendered without personal jurisdiction over the defendant.[52] Therefore the only logical meaning of May v. Anderson is that a custody decree, a judgment having the greatest significance to the welfare of the child concerned, may not be given without personal jurisdiction over the respondent. In those cases in which the respondent is not amenable to personal service or its equivalent, under any available long-arm statute, the child's situation must remain unresolved and physical possession becomes not merely nine points of the law but the entire law of the case. Even the law of property does not go to such absurd lengths as this.[53]

48. 334 U.S. 541, 68 S.Ct. 1213, 92 L.Ed. 1561 (1948). The Court's much quoted language drawing the analogy stated: "Rights far more precious to appellant than property rights will be cut off if she is to be bound by the Wisconsin award of custody." 345 U.S. at 533, 73 S.Ct. at 843. See also Vanderbilt v. Vanderbilt, 354 U.S. 416, 77 S.Ct. 1360, 1 L.Ed.2d 1456 (1957) and the discussion of jurisdiction for alimony and property in section 12.4, supra.

49. Hazard, May v. Anderson: Preamble to Family Law Chaos, 45 Va.L.Rev. 379 (1959); Bodenheimer and Neeley-Kvarme, Jurisdiction Over Child Custody and Adoption After Shaffer and Kulko, 12 U.C. Davis L.Rev. 229, 248 (1979). See also Justice Jackson's dissent to May, 345 U.S. at 536, 73 S.Ct. at 844.

50. In fact the Court said that the issue in the case is separated from that of the future interests of the children. 345 U.S. at 533, 73 S.Ct. at 843. It is difficult to see how any decision propounding a rule of jurisdiction

for custody cases can be separated from the interests of the children.

51. See Finlay v. Finlay, 240 N.Y. 429, 148 N.E. 624 (1925).

52. Justice Frankfurter's concurrence in May took the position that the only thing the case decided was that the Full Faith and Credit Clause did not require Ohio to accept the Wisconsin custody decree. 345 U.S. at 535, 73 S.Ct. at 844. Justice Jackson's dissent seems to have taken the correct view of the matter, that is, that the decision held that Wisconsin could not constitutionally adjudicate custody for lack of personal jurisdiction over the defendant wife.

53. Under Shaffer v. Heitner, 433 U.S. 186, 207–208, 97 S.Ct. 2569, 2581, 53 L.Ed.2d 683 (1977), the presence in a state of property over which there is a dispute is sufficient to establish jurisdiction to adjudicate claims to the property. Thus if property rather than a child had

The subsequent treatment of May v. Anderson has been odd, to say the least. Stanley v. Illinois [54] cited it with approval in 1972, although in a footnote in that case the Court seemed to suggest that service by publication in the form "To whom it may concern" would be sufficient for jurisdiction to terminate a parent's right to his child, a suggestion surely inconsistent with the rationale of May v. Anderson.[55] The Kulko case also cited May v. Anderson with approval as holding that a custody decree without personal jurisdiction is void.[56] It therefore appears that the Supreme Court is not disposed to question the holding in May v. Anderson, although there may be considerable question about just what that holding was.[57]

State court responses to May v. Anderson have been even more diverse. Some cases rely on it as their reason for refusing to enforce the custody decrees of other states where there has been no personal jurisdiction over the defendant.[58] Some courts have given the case its full logical effect by holding that without personal jurisdiction over the defendant, they may not enter a custody decree,[59] although the force of this holding may be mitigated by reliance upon the state's long-arm statute to find that personal jurisdiction was in fact acquired.[60] Decisions in other states have taken positions contrary to the apparent holding in May v. Anderson, either by ignoring that case,[61] by giving it a limited construction,[62] or by rejecting its teaching outright.[63] Some of these cases have been decid-

been the subject of litigation in May, the Wisconsin court would have had jurisdiction.

It is worth noting that in the famous footnote 30 to Shaffer v. Heitner, 433 U.S. 186, 208, 97 S.Ct. 2569, 2581, 53 L.Ed.2d 683 (1977), in which the Court appears to recognize an exception to the rules of personal jurisdiction for "status" questions, there is no citation of May v. Anderson. Does this mean that the Court does not consider a custody case to involve status?

54. 405 U.S. 645, 651, 92 S.Ct. 1208, 1212, 31 L.Ed.2d 551 (1972).

55. 405 U.S. at 657 n. 9, 92 S.Ct. at 1215 n. 9.

56. Kulko v. Superior Court of California, 436 U.S. 84, 97, 98 S.Ct. 1690, 1699, 56 L.Ed.2d 132 (1978), rehearing denied 438 U.S. 908, 98 S.Ct. 3127, 57 L.Ed.2d 1150 (1978).

57. Garfield, Due Process Rights of Absent Parents in Interstate Custody Conflicts: A Commentary on In re Marriage of Hudson, 16 Ind.L.Rev. 445 (1983) argues that May v. Anderson be read to require that custody decrees be based upon "minimum contacts" with the state, and that where that is impossible an ex parte decree could be granted but could be reexamined when and where jurisdiction over the defendant could be achieved.

58. E.g., Ex parte Dean, 447 So.2d 733 (Ala.1984), on remand 447 So.2d 737 (1984); Boggus v. Boggus, 236 Ga. 126, 223 S.E.2d 103 (1976); Batchelor v. Fulcher, 415 S.W.2d 828 (Ky.1967); Salmon v. Salmon, 88 N.J.Super. 291, 212 A.2d 171 (1965); McLam v. McLam, 81 N.M. 37, 462 P.2d 622 (1969), appeal after remand 85 N.M. 196, 510 P.2d 914 (1973); McAninch v. McAninch, 39 N.C.App. 665, 251 S.E.2d 633 (1979), review denied 297 N.C. 300, 254 S.E.2d 920 (1979); Pasqualone v. Pasqualone, 63 Ohio St.2d 96, 406 N.E.2d 1121 (1980); Gunther v. Gunther, 478 S.W.2d 821 (Tex.Civ.App.1972).

59. In re Hall's Marriage, 25 Wash.App. 530, 607 P.2d 898 (1980); Cogar v. Cogar, 165 W.Va. 797, 272 S.E.2d 58 (1980).

60. Varney v. Varney, 222 Kan. 700, 567 P.2d 876 (1977) (long-arm statute based jurisdiction on living in a

marital relation in the state); Smith v. Smith, 254 Md. 31, 253 A.2d 719 (1969); Lynch v. Lynch, 303 N.C. 367, 279 S.E.2d 840 (1981) (right to challenge personal jurisdiction waived by a general appearance); Kelly v. Novak, 606 S.W.2d 25 (Tex.Civ.App.1980) (jurisdiction under the omnibus long-arm statute); In re Marriage of Myers, 92 Wash.2d 113, 594 P.2d 902 (1979); In re Custody of Miller, 86 Wash.2d 712, 548 P.2d 542 (1976).

Of course if the defendant did not have "minimum contacts" with the state, the court will not have jurisdiction, under this view of May v. Anderson. State ex rel. Muirhead v. District Court of First Judicial Dist., 169 Mont. 535, 550 P.2d 1304 (1976).

In some states the general long-arm statute may be held to be inapplicable to custody cases. Worland v. Worland, 89 N.M. 291, 551 P.2d 981 (1976).

See also Note, Long-Arm Jurisdiction in Alimony and Custody Cases, 73 Colum.L.Rev. 289 (1973).

61. E.g., Mueller v. Mueller, 259 Ind. 366, 287 N.E.2d 886 (1972); Franciscus v. Franciscus, 31 Md.App. 78, 354 A.2d 454 (1976).

62. In re Marriage of Hudson, 434 N.E.2d 107 (Ind. App.1982), cert. denied 459 U.S. 1202, 103 S.Ct. 1187, 75 L.Ed.2d 433 (1983) (May v. Anderson permits the recognition of custody decrees rendered without personal jurisdiction, but does not require recognition); Morrell v. Giesick, 188 Mont. 89, 610 P.2d 1189 (1980) (holding of May v. Anderson is limited to cases in which neither the child nor the defendant is in the rendering state at the time of the custody proceeding).

63. In re Marriage of Leonard, 122 Cal.App.3d 443, 175 Cal.Rptr. 903 (1981); Goldfarb v. Goldfarb, 246 Ga. 24, 268 S.E.2d 648 (1980); In re Marriage of Schuham, 120 Ill.App.3d 339, 76 Ill.Dec. 159, 458 N.E.2d 559 (1983) (custody is a matter of status, as to which personal jurisdiction is not required); In re Marriage of Hudson, 434 N.E.2d 107 (Ind.App.1982), cert. denied 459 U.S. 1202, 103 S.Ct. 1187, 75 L.Ed.2d 433 (1983), criticized in Garfield, Due Process Rights of Absent Parents in Interstate

ed since the enactment of the UCCJA or the PKPA and have undoubtedly been influenced by a desire to avoid constitutional doubts about those statutes.[64]

In the late 1970's and early 1980's the requirement of personal jurisdiction in custody cases was thus left in a highly confused and confusing condition. The question remained important because in this period a concerted attempt was made by the enactment of the two statutes, the UCCJA and the PKPA, to reduce the amount of forum-shopping and relitigation in custody cases by broadening the application of full faith and credit to custody decrees. The effect of May v. Anderson upon these statutes will be discussed later in this section.[65]

Uniform Child Custody Jurisdiction Act [66]

The UCCJA was drafted principally by the late Professor Brigitte M. Bodenheimer under the supervision of a committee of the National Conference of Commissioners on Uniform State Laws.[67] It was approved by the American Bar Association in 1968, but for some years thereafter it was not widely adopted by

the states. By 1983, however, it had been adopted by all states and the District of Columbia in one form or another,[68] the last two states to do so being Massachusetts[69] and Texas.[70]

The Act must be construed in accordance with its purposes which are nine in number.[71] They may fairly be summed up as emphasizing the avoidance of conflicts between states over custody by assuring that custody litigation will occur in the state where the child and his family have the closest connection and where the best evidence respecting the child's welfare is available, by discouraging relitigation of custody disputes and abductions for the purpose of forum-shopping, and by promoting interstate cooperation and the interstate enforcement of custody decrees.[72] It is of some interest that the listed purposes contain no direct reference to the best interests of the child other than as related to the ill effects of repeated litigation over his custody.

Although the UCCJA is most often invoked in disputes between spouses or former spouses concerning custody of their children, its jurisdictional and other provisions apply to all

---

Custody Conflicts: A Commentary on In re Marriage of Hudson, 16 Ind.L.Rev. 445 (1983); Pratt v. Pratt, ___ R.I. ___, 431 A.2d 405 (1981); Salisbury v. Salisbury, 657 S.W.2d 761 (Tenn.App.1983) (semble); Perry v. Ponder, 604 S.W.2d 306 (Tex.Civ.App.1980); Thornlow v. Thornlow, 576 S.W.2d 697 (Tex.Civ.App.1979), cert. denied 445 U.S. 949, 100 S.Ct. 1596, 63 L.Ed.2d 784 (1980); McAtee v. McAtee, ___ W.Va. ___, 323 S.E.2d 611 (1984). The Indiana decree in In re Marriage of Hudson, supra, was held valid and enforceable by the Washington Court of Appeals in Hudson v. Hudson, 35 Wash.App. 822, 670 P.2d 287 (1983).

64. See the cases cited, supra, note 63.

65. See the text, infra, at note 17.

66. As has been indicated, supra, in note 28, this Act will be referred to as UCCJA § ___. See 9 Unif.L.Ann. 111 (1979).

67. The work on the Act is described in Bodenheimer, The Uniform Child Custody Jurisdiction Act: A Legislative Remedy for Children Caught in the Conflict of Laws, 22 Vand.L.Rev. 1207, 1216 (1969).

Many of the provisions in the UCCJA find an echo in the Parental Kidnaping Prevention Act of 1980, 28 U.S. C.A. § 1738A, but the two Acts are not identical. In an attempt to provide a coherent account of the whole subject of custody jurisdiction as it now appears, the two Acts will be discussed separately, taking the UCCJA first

because it was enacted earlier and because a large number of cases construing it have been decided. The PKPA will then be described. See the text at note 90, infra. It will be argued that where the two Acts are identical, the cases construing the UCCJA will have considerable force as precedents for construing the PKPA. Finally, the relationship between the two Acts will be outlined, so far as that is possible, giving particular attention to that relationship so far as it affects the interstate recognition, enforcement and modification of custody decrees. See the text at note 74, infra.

An excellent discussion of the UCCJA and PKPA may be found in Blakesley, Child Custody—Jurisdiction and Procedure, 35 Emory L.J. 291 (1986).

For a citation of cases on the UCCJA, see Annot., Validity, Construction, and Application of Uniform Child Custody Jurisdiction Act, 96 A.L.R.3d 968 (1980).

68. Citations to the various state versions may be found in 9 Unif.L.Ann. 19 (Supp.1984).

69. Mass.Gen.L.Ann. c. 209B (Supp.1984).

70. V.Tex.C.A.Fam.Code §§ 11.51 to 11.75 (Supp. 1984).

71. UCCJA § 1.

72. See In re Custody of Helwig, 442 N.E.2d 1035 (Ind. 1982); Spaulding v. Spaulding, 460 A.2d 1360 (Me.1983).

custody determinations.[73] The Act defines custody determinations to include any court decision or court order for the custody of a child including visitation orders, but excluding child support and other monetary obligations.[74] Custody proceedings are broadly defined to include not merely divorce and separation but child neglect and dependency proceedings as well.[75] Presumably the Act would apply to proceedings for the appointment of a guardian of the person of a child, but not to the appointment of a guardian of a child's estate.[76] Where the child or the parent are Indians living on a reservation, however, the tribal court, rather than the state court pursuant to UCCJA, has jurisdiction respecting the child's custody.[77] The policy of the Act is expressly made applicable to the decrees of foreign nations, and its provisions apply to such decrees where they rest on reasonable notice and an opportunity to be heard.[78]

The UCCJA (and the PKPA also) have at least three functional sorts of provision. First, they contain provisions governing jurisdiction over the subject matter of custody and prescribing the kind of notice needed for a valid custody decree.[79] Second, they contain provisions dealing with circumstances in which existing jurisdiction over the subject matter should or should not be exercised and with communication between courts both of which appear to have jurisdiction.[80] Third, they contain specific provisions governing the circumstances in which the custody decrees of other states must be enforced or may be modified.[81] In any specific case more than one category of provision may be relevant to whether a decree may be entered. For this reason the decided cases may have limited value as precedents because they contain a mixture of factors which will not often be repeated in the same form. For the same reason a logical analysis of the statutes and case law is extremely difficult and in addition is likely to require the lawyer or court to move, step by step, from one of the Acts to the other, and from one of the provisions in one of the Acts to other provisions in that Act. Nevertheless there can be no understanding of the present law without analysis of the meaning of individual provisions, and it will therefore be undertaken (with considerable uneasiness and many qualifications) in the following pages.

As a general proposition, cases often hold that jurisdiction over the subject matter of a dispute may not be conferred by consent of the parties,[82] the reason being that the state's interest in controlling the business of its

---

73. UCCJA §§ 3, 2(2). The Act has been applied to controversies over the custody of illegitimate children. Brauch v. Shaw, 121 N.H. 562, 432 A.2d 1 (1981). In re Marriage of Trouth, 631 P.2d 1183 (Colo.App.1981) contains dictum that the Act does not apply to actions which are purely intrastate, but the statement seems clearly erroneous, since there is no authority for it in the Act and § 3 applies to all child custody determinations as defined. The Act may apply to contempt proceedings if they are "inextricably interwoven" with issues of custody or visitation. Funk v. Macaulay, 457 N.E.2d 223 (Ind. App.1983).

74. UCCJA § 2(2). See also Lee v. Deshaney, 457 N.E.2d 604 (Ind.App.1983).

75. UCCJA § 2(3). Matter of Welfare of Mullins, 298 N.W.2d 56 (Minn.1980) applied the Act to a dependency proceeding but suggested that the concept of "home state" would have less than its usual importance in such a case. See also Squires v. Squires, 12 Ohio App.3d 138, 468 N.E.2d 73 (1983); E.P. v. District Court of Garfield County, 696 P.2d 254 (Colo.1985).

76. The appointment of a guardian of the person is essentially an order for the custody of the child, while the appointment of a guardian of the estate affects only the child's property. See section 9.4, Practitioner's Edition.

77. Malaterre v. Malaterre, 293 N.W.2d 139 (N.D. 1980). But the Indian Child Welfare Act, 25 U.S.C.A. §§ 1901, 1911 does not apply to custody proceedings arising in divorce.

78. UCCJA § 23. Decisions enforcing the decrees of foreign nations include Woodhouse v. District Court In and For Seventeenth Judicial Dist., 196 Colo. 558, 587 P.2d 1199 (1978); Custody of a Minor (No. 3), 392 Mass. 728, 468 N.E.2d 251 (1984); Commonwealth ex rel. Zaubi v. Zaubi, 492 Pa. 183, 423 A.2d 333 (1980); Middleton v. Middleton, 227 Va. 82, 314 S.E.2d 362 (1984); Oehl v. Oehl, 221 Va. 618, 272 S.E.2d 441 (1980).

Miller v. Superior Court of Los Angeles County, 22 Cal. 3d 923, 151 Cal.Rptr. 6, 587 P.2d 723 (1978) enforced an Australian custody decree where the only service of notice was on the respondent's former attorney and the decree was issued ex parte.

79. E.g., UCCJA §§ 3, 4; 28 U.S.C.A. § 1738A(c) and (e).

80. E.g., UCCJA §§ 6, 7, 8, 9; 28 U.S.C.A. § 1738A(g).

81. E.g., UCCJA §§ 13, 14; 28 U.S.C.A. § 1738A(a) and (f).

82. Campbell v. Campbell, 180 Ind.App. 351, 388 N.E.2d 607 (1979), appeal after remand 182 Ind.App. 661,

courts overrides any desire the parties may have to get the case heard. This broad rule has to be qualified, however, by an important principle of res judicata. If the issue of jurisdiction over the subject matter was litigated in an earlier action, or could have been litigated because both parties were personally before the court, the usual applications of res judicata do not permit jurisdiction to be questioned in a later suit. This has long been established with respect to jurisdiction for divorce.[83] In the divorce cases it has also been held that the Full Faith and Credit Clause requires that if the law of the state granting the decree forbids later attack on it on jurisdictional grounds, the decree is likewise immune to attack in other states.[84] The same principle of res judicata should and does apply to custody decrees.[85]

The UCCJA authorizes subject matter jurisdiction over custody determinations in four categories of cases. The first of these, somewhat reminiscent of Professor Beale's domicile rule,[86] provides for jurisdiction in the

child's "home state" or in the state which had been the "home state" within six months before commencement of the suit and the child was absent from the state because of his removal or retention by a person claiming his custody, with the additional requirement that a parent or person acting as parent continues to live in the state.[87] "Home state" is defined as the state in which the child lived with his parents or a parent for six consecutive months, or, in the case of a child less than six months old, in which he lived from birth.[88] This section of the statute is sufficiently precise to be applied with little controversy. The cases arising under it are relatively few and are largely concerned with computation of the six-month period.[89] It has been held that once the suit is brought in compliance with the statute, the removal of the child from the state pending the suit does not affect the jurisdiction.[90]

As the Commissioners' Comments to the UCCJA indicate [91], the purpose of the drafters was to choose a precise period which bears

396 N.E.2d 142 (1979); St. Clair v. Faulkner, 305 N.W.2d 441 (Iowa 1981). See generally, Restatement (Second) of Judgments § 11 (1982). But see Hattoum v. Hattoum, 295 Pa.Super. 169, 441 A.2d 403 (1982), in which the court gave some weight to an agreement of both spouses to submit to the state's jurisdiction.

83. Sherrer v. Sherrer, 334 U.S. 343, 68 S.Ct. 1087, 92 L.Ed. 1429 (1948); Johnson v. Muelberger, 340 U.S. 581, 71 S.Ct. 474, 95 L.Ed. 552 (1951); Restatement (Second) of Judgments § 12 (1982).

84. Ibid.

85. Lofts v. Superior Court In and For Maricopa County, 140 Ariz. 407, 682 P.2d 412 (1984); In re Custody of Zumbrun, 42 Colo.App. 37, 592 P.2d 16 (1978); Geesbreght v. Geesbreght, 63 Ill.App.3d 37, 19 Ill.Dec. 866, 379 N.E.2d 738 (1978); O'Malley v. O'Malley, 338 A.2d 149 (Me. 1975); McDonald v. McDonald, 74 Mich.App. 119, 253 N.W.2d 678 (1977). But see Salisbury v. Salisbury, 657 S.W.2d 761 (Tenn. App. 1983). The UCCJA does not deal with this question. Cf. UCCJA § 12.

86. See the text at note 7, supra.

87. UCCJA § 3(a)(1). The home state requirement is discussed briefly in Bodenheimer, The Uniform Child Custody Jurisdiction Act: A Legislative Remedy for Children Caught in the Conflict of Laws, 22 Vand.L.Rev. 1207, 1225 (1969).

At least one state has retained the domicile rule as a basis for jurisdiction in addition to the home state rule. Ariz. Rev. Stat. § 8–403 (Supp. 1983–1984). A decree based on domicile has been held not substantially in accord with the UCCJA in O'Neal v. O'Neal, 329 N.W.2d 666 (Iowa 1983).

The language of this section speaks of the home state of the child "at the time of the commencement of the proceeding." This has been held to mean at the time of the pending motion affecting custody or visitation, not the time at which the original dissolution action was brought.

88. UCCJA § 2(5). This subsection also provides that periods of temporary absence of parents or children from the state are to be included as part of the six-month period. See Elder v. Park, 104 N.M. 163, 717 P.2d 1132 (App.1986).

89. Kimmons v. Heldt, 667 P.2d 1245 (Alaska 1983) (petition filed just two days before the end of the child's six-month absence from the state); Allen v. Allen, 64 Hawaii 553, 645 P.2d 300 (1982); Lewis v. Canty, 115 Ill. App.3d 306, 71 Ill.Dec. 176, 450 N.E.2d 864 (1983); Revere v. Revere, 389 So.2d 1277 (La.1980) (close question as to whether the suit was filed within the second six-month period); Bell v. Bell, 682 S.W.2d 892 (Mo.App.1984) (Kansas not the home state where child but not parent there); Mattleman v. Bandler, 123 N.H. 368, 461 A.2d 561 (1983), appeal after remand 125 N.H. 204, 480 A.2d 85 (1984).

As in other situations, the plaintiff must plead and prove the existence of jurisdiction. State ex rel. State of Pennsylvania v. Stork, 56 Or.App. 335, 641 P.2d 660 (1982), review denied 293 Or. 190, 648 P.2d 851 (1982).

Other cases applying the "home state" rule are cited in Annot., 96 A.L.R.3d 968, 979 (1980).

90. Mayer v. Mayer, 91 Wis.2d 342, 283 N.W.2d 591 (App.1979).

91. UCCJA § 3, Commissioners' Comments, 9 Unif.L. Ann. 123 (1979).

some relation to the fact of a child's residence. Necessarily, however, the emphasis upon the two six-month periods will result in many cases in a race to the courthouse, making it inadvisable for a parent to spend time in attempts to work out a compromise of the custody dispute. For example, if the parents and child live in State A for longer than six months and, when the marriage breaks down, one of them takes the child and moves to State B, the stay-at-home spouse has only six months in which to bring the custody proceeding if he wishes to rely on the home state provision, and to have the advantage of litigating at home.[92]

The various categories of jurisdictional basis in the UCCJA were intended, in the opinion of the drafters, to be alternatives, so that even if there is a state which can qualify as the home state of the child, there may be other states having jurisdiction under other subsections of section 3 of the Act.[93] The first of these alternatives, sharply contrasting with the precision of the home state test, has come to be called the "significant connection" test. It reads as follows:

[A court has jurisdiction to make a child custody determination if]

"(2) it is in the best interest of the child that a court of this State assume jurisdiction because (i) the child and his parents, or the child and at least one contestant, have a significant connection with this State, and (ii) there is available in this State substantial evidence concerning the child's present or future care, protection, training and personal relationships;" [94]

On its face the significant connection subsection of the Act seems to require proof of three elements to establish jurisdiction, the best interests of the child, the significant connection between the child, at least one parent, and the state, and existence in the state of substantial evidence concerning the child's welfare, present and future.[95] Some cases have taken the position that there are only two elements, however, significant connection with the state and access to substantial evidence.[96] Others have reduced the issue to a single basic question, does the state have maximum access to substantial evidence respecting the child's welfare? [97] Regardless of the reading of this subsection, it is at least clear that it should be so applied as to effectuate the purposes of the Act as a whole, the dominant purpose being the reduction of interstate conflicts over custody.[98]

Another subsection of the Act limits the significant connection test by providing that the physical presence of the child in the state or of the child and one parent is not alone sufficient to constitute the basis for custody jurisdiction.[99] Conversely, the Act also provides that the presence of the child, while

---

92. See, e.g., Kimmons v. Heldt, 667 P.2d 1245 (Alaska 1983).

93. UCCJA § 3(a)(2), Commissioners' Comments, 9 Unif.L.Ann. 123 (1979), stating that this subsection comes into play either where the home state test cannot be met, or as an alternative to that test.

The Commissioners' Comments are entitled to substantial weight in construing the statute. Smith v. Superior Court of San Mateo County, 68 Cal.App.3d 457, 137 Cal. Rptr. 348 (1977).

The cases agree that jurisdiction may be based either on one or the other or both of these provisions. Brokus v. Brokus, 420 N.E.2d 1242 (Ind.App.1981); William L. v. Michele P., 99 Misc.2d 346, 416 N.Y.S.2d 477 (Fam. Ct. 1979); Holt v. District Court etc., 626 P.2d 1336 (Okl. 1981).

94. UCCJA § 3(a)(2). This subsection may not have been enacted in all states. See, e.g., Alaska Stat. § 25.30.020 (1983).

95. See Griffith v. Griffith, 60 Hawaii 567, 592 P.2d 826 (1979).

96. Allison v. Superior Court of Los Angeles County, 99 Cal.App.3d 993, 160 Cal.Rptr. 309 (1979); Matter of Custody of Ross, 291 Or. 263, 630 P.2d 353 (1981).

97. Schlumpf v. Superior Court of Trinity County, 79 Cal.App.3d 892, 145 Cal.Rptr. 190 (1978); Revere v. Revere, 389 So.2d 1277 (La.1980). The draftsman of the Act seems to have taken this view of the significant connection test since she emphasized the strength of the ties between the parties and the state. Bodenheimer, The Uniform Child Custody Jurisdiction Act: A Legislative Remedy for Children Caught in the Conflict of Laws, 22 Vand.L.Rev. 1207, 1226 (1969).

98. Mattleman v. Bandler, 123 N.H. 368, 461 A.2d 561 (1983), appeal after remand 125 N.H. 204, 480 A.2d 85 (1984); Aldridge v. Aldridge, 326 Pa.Super. 49, 473 A.2d 602 (1984). The Act's purposes are discussed supra, at note 71.

99. UCCJA § 3(b); Bodenheimer, The Uniform Child Custody Jurisdiction Act: A Remedy for Children Caught in the Conflict of Laws, 22 Vand.L.Rev. 1207, 1227 (1969).

desirable, is not essential for jurisdiction to determine his custody.[1]

It is not surprising, in view of the imprecision and vagueness of the significant connection provision in the Act that the cases construing that provision have reached widely diverse results. The point is perhaps best illustrated by a pair of Oregon cases which are as close to being on all fours as two custody cases can ever be. Both cases involved the modification of another state's decree and for that reason may be somewhat atypical of decisions on the bare question of jurisdiction, but they do purport to determine the jurisdictional question. In Settle[2] the spouse lived in Indiana and the divorce action was brought there. Before a final decree the mother brought the children to Oregon, without notifying their father, and kept them there eighteen months before the father located them. In a proceeding in Oregon for enforcement or modification of the Indiana custody award to the father, the Oregon Supreme Court held that Oregon had become the home state and that Indiana no longer had significant connection jurisdiction, not having optimum access to relevant evidence. In the Ross case[3] the parties were married and lived together in Montana. Shortly after they separated the father took their child and went to Oregon, without telling the mother where he was going. The mother got a default divorce and an award of custody ex parte in Montana. Approximately eighteen months later the mother discovered where the father and chil-

dren were and brought suit in Oregon to enforce the Montana custody decree. The Oregon Supreme Court overruled Settle, holding that Montana continued to have significant connection jurisdiction. The court found that there was still substantial evidence in Montana concerning the care and training given the child while the parents had lived in the state. In addition the court found that the child continued to have a significant connection with Montana in that the mother still lived there, and the child's older sister still lived there.[4] One can hardly avoid the suspicion that the court in the Ross case was more concerned with punishing the father for removing the child than with the child's welfare. By the time the case was finally decided the child had been in the custody of her father from the time she was about a year and a half old until she was more than five years old. If Drs. Goldstein, Freud and Solnit are correct in their emphasis on the need for stability in the life of a young child,[5] the Ross child's need was indeed frustrated in this case.

Other courts have exhibited equal diversity in applying the significant connection provision for jurisdiction. The residence of one parent in the state plus the presence of the child for only a short time or for brief visits has generally led the courts to hold that there is not substantial evidence or a significant connection in the state sufficient to warrant a finding of jurisdiction.[6] But where the child and one parent have been in the state a

---

1. UCCJA § 3(c).

2. Matter of Marriage of Settle, 276 Or. 759, 556 P.2d 962 (1976).

3. Matter of Custody of Ross, 291 Or. 263, 630 P.2d 353 (1981).

4. See Bodenheimer, Progress Under the Uniform Child Custody Jurisdiction Act and Remaining Problems: Punitive Decrees, Joint Custody, and Excessive Modifications, 65 Cal.L.Rev. 978, 998 (1977) states that once jurisdiction is acquired, it continues until all parties have moved from the state, citing the Commissioners' Comments to UCCJA § 14, but those comments do not support such a broad statement. 9 Unif.L.Ann. 154 (1979).

5. J. Goldstein, A. Freud, A. Solnit, Beyond the Best Interests of the Child (1973).

6. Rexford v. Rexford, 631 P.2d 475 (Alaska 1980) (California did not have jurisdiction where mother and

child had been in the state only eight days when the petition was filed; but Alaska's trial court did not abuse its discretion in deferring to California, even though Alaska was the home state); Biggers v. Biggers, 11 Ark. App. 62, 666 S.W.2d 714 (1984) (no jurisdiction where children in the state for short visits); In re Marriage of Ben-Yehoshua, 91 Cal.App.3d 259, 154 Cal.Rptr. 80 (1979) (presence of the mother and children in California for a month before suit not sufficient for jurisdiction); Plas v. Superior Court, 155 Cal.App.3d 1008, 202 Cal.Rptr. 490 (1984); Allen v. Allen, 64 Hawaii 553, 645 P.2d 300 (1982) (presence of mother and child in state for six days not sufficient); Bills v. Murdock, 232 Kan. 237, 654 P.2d 406 (1982) (father's residence in the state, together with visits by the child not sufficient for jurisdiction); Mattleman v. Bandler, 123 N.H. 368, 461 A.2d 561 (1983), appeal after remand 125 N.H. 204, 480 A.2d 85 (1984) (residence of father in the state and presence of the children on

somewhat longer time or under slightly different circumstances, other cases have found jurisdiction to exist.[7] Undoubtedly the diversity of result is attributable in many cases to the presence or absence of other factors, factors which invoke other provisions of the Act, and to the courts' view of what the child's interests require. Whatever the forces controlling the outcomes of the cases, it seems impossible to advance any reliable generalization concerning the meaning and application of the significant connection test of jurisdiction, other than to say that this test permits a court to accept or reject a finding of jurisdiction on almost any state of the facts which is likely to arise.

The third category of jurisdiction created by the Act is referred to as emergency jurisdiction. According to this subsection, if the child is physically present in the state and either has been abandoned or is in an emergency because subjected to or threatened with mistreatment, abuse or neglect, the courts of the state have jurisdiction to determine his custody.[8] The Commissioners' Comments[9] and the cases[10] emphasize that where there is neglect without emergency or abandonment, this provision does not apply, and that the provision creates an extraordinary jurisdiction which is reserved for extraordinary circumstances. Where an allegation of abandonment or emergency is made, the court is required to take evidence on the issue.[11] It is usually held, however, that the emergency may not be proved solely by the unsubstantiated testimony of one of the parties.[12] There is substantial authority that if an abandonment or emergency is established, this does not normally warrant a permanent change of custody, but that the proper action is to award custody temporarily to the petitioner with directions or on condition that a proceeding be brought in the home state or in the state of significant connection within a prescribed relatively short, time.[13] Although the

---

summer visits not sufficient for jurisdiction). Conversely, the presence of the child in the state for more than six months did not constitute a significant connection when the applicant for custody was in the state less than six months in In re B.R.F., 669 S.W.2d 240 (Mo.App.1984).

7. Kimmons v. Heldt, 667 P.2d 1245 (Alaska 1983) (father's residence in California and the child's presence there for one month held sufficient for California jurisdiction); Allison v. Superior Court of Los Angeles County, 99 Cal.App.3d 993, 160 Cal.Rptr. 309 (1979) (California had jurisdiction where mother lived there, children born there and lived there until moved to Texas with father, although the children had lived in Texas for eighteen months); Schlumpf v. Superior Court of County of Trinity, 79 Cal.App.3d 892, 145 Cal.Rptr. 190 (1978) (California had jurisdiction even though the children had lived with their father in Wyoming for nine years, where the spouses had lived in California during their marriage, the divorce and original custody order were granted there, and the mother remained a California resident); Brokus v. Brokus, 420 N.E.2d 1242 (Ind.App.1981) (court finds a significant connection in Indiana, based on the residence of the mother and a five-month residence of the children, interrupted by a one-month removal of the children from the state by their father); Revere v. Revere, 389 So.2d 1277 (La.1980) (family domicile in Louisiana is sufficient for jurisdiction even though the child and his mother had lived in Texas for six months); William L. v. Michele P., 99 Misc.2d 346, 416 N.Y.S.2d 477 (1979) (New York has jurisdiction where the father lives there, the child is there on a visit, the divorce decree had been entered in New York four years earlier, even though the home state is Mississippi; but New York held to be an inconvenient forum).

8. UCCJA § 3(a)(3).

9. Id., Commissioners' Comments, 9 Unif.L.Ann. 124 (1979).

10. In re Schwander's Marriage, 79 Cal.App.3d 1013, 145 Cal.Rptr. 325 (1978); Brock v. District Court of Boulder County, 620 P.2d 11 (Colo.1980); Matter of Lemond, 413 N.E.2d 228 (Ind.1980); Dillon v. Medellin, 409 So.2d 570 (La.1982); Hricko v. Stewart, 99 Misc.2d 266, 415 N.Y.S.2d 747 (Fam.Ct.1979).

Cases in which an emergency was held to be proved are rather rare, but include the following: Webb v. Webb, 245 Ga. 650, 266 S.E.2d 463 (1980), cert. dismissed 451 U.S. 493, 101 S.Ct. 1889, 68 L.Ed.2d 392 (1981); Breneman v. Breneman, 92 Mich.App. 336, 284 N.W.2d 804 (1979); Wenz v. Schwartze, 183 Mont. 166, 598 P.2d 1086 (1979), cert. denied 444 U.S. 1071, 100 S.Ct. 1015, 62 L.Ed. 2d 753 (1980); Severio P. v. Donald Y., 128 Misc.2d 539, 490 N.Y.S.2d 439 (Fam.Ct.1985). The court relied in part on the emergency jurisdiction in Carpenter v. Carpenter, 326 Pa.Super. 570, 474 A.2d 1124 (1984).

11. Johnson v. District Court for Jefferson County, 654 P.2d 827 (Colo.1982); Marcrum v. Marcrum, 181 N.J. Super. 361, 437 A.2d 725 (1981), certification granted 89 N.J. 402, 446 A.2d 136 (1982) (emergency jurisdiction may be found even though petitioner wrongfully brings the child into the state); Holt v. District Court for Twentieth Judicial Dist., 626 P.2d 1336 (Okl.1981).

12. Johnson v. District Court for Jefferson County, 654 P.2d 827 (Colo.1982).

13. Iacouzze v. Iacouzze, 137 Ariz. 605, 672 P.2d 949 (1983), affirmed 137 Ariz. 584, 672 P.2d 928 (1983); Nussbaumer v. Nussbaumer, 442 So.2d 1094 (Fla.App.1983); Nelson v. Nelson, 433 So.2d 1015 (Fla.App.1983); Hache v. Riley, 186 N.J.Super. 119, 451 A.2d 971 (1982); Vorpahl v. Lee, 99 Wis.2d 7, 298 N.W.2d 222 (1980).

statute does not limit emergency jurisdiction in this way, many courts seem to think this is a wise compromise between the need to protect children and the desire not to upset existing custody dispositions, especially since the evidence of mistreatment of the child is likely to be conflicting or uncertain.

The fourth category of jurisdiction established by the Act is characterized as "subsidiary in nature" by the Commissioners' Comments.[14] It is clearly intended to provide for situations in which none of the other three bases for jurisdiction applies. It operates when no other state has jurisdiction pursuant to the other sections of the UCCJA or when another state has refused to exercise jurisdiction on the ground that this state is the more convenient forum and when it is in the best interests of the child that this court takes jurisdiction.[15] Judging from the rarity of reported cases, the provision is not often relied upon.

The foregoing discussion demonstrates that the UCCJA imposes requirements of subject matter jurisdiction alone. Although the Act does expressly provide for notice,[16] it does not require that personal jurisdiction over the defendant be obtained in custody proceedings.

This omission raises the question whether a custody decree granted pursuant to the Act but without personal jurisdiction over the defendant would either be invalid as lacking in due process, or would not be entitled to full faith and credit in other states. The case of May v. Anderson,[17] discussed in detail earlier in this section,[18] would, if given its logical meaning, have those highly unfortunate consequences.[19] One way of avoidng those consequences would be to characterize custody adjudications as determinations of status.[20] Determinations of status, according to the Supreme Court, need not meet the requirements of in personam jurisdiction.[21] Some courts have taken this tack.[22] It has also been suggested that custody determinations, like other kinds of lawsuit, be subject to the usual rules of in personam jurisdiction, that is, that there be sufficient connection between the defendant and the forum state to make it fair to require him to defend the action in the forum.[23] If this were the rule, jurisdiction to enter custody decrees would be impossible to obtain in many cases, particularly if the Supreme Court should adhere to its restrictive test of personal jurisdiction adopted in

14. UCCJA § 3(a)(4), Commissioners' Comments, 9 Unif.L.Ann. 124 (1979).

15. UCCJA § 3(a)(4). A case which relies on this basis for jurisdiction is In re B.R.F., 669 S.W.2d 240 (Mo. App.1984).

16. UCCJA §§ 4, 5.

17. 345 U.S. 528, 73 S.Ct. 840, 97 L.Ed. 1221 (1953).

18. See the text at note 47, supra.

19. E.g., no recognition could be given to a custody decree like that in Nussbaumer v. Nussbaumer, 442 So.2d 1094 (Fla.App.1983).

20. This result is persuasively urged in Bodenheimer and Neeley-Kvarme, Jurisdiction Over Child Custody and Adoption After Shaffer and Kulko, 12 U.Cal. Davis L.Rev. 229 (1979).

21. Shaffer v. Heitner, 433 U.S. 186, 208 n. 30, 97 S.Ct. 2569, 2582 n. 30, 53 L.Ed.2d 683 (1977) states as follows: "We do not suggest that jurisdictional doctrines other than those discussed in text, such as the particularized rules governing adjudications of status, are inconsistent with the standard of fairness." The Court cited at the end of this footnote an article of Justice Traynor urging that in personam jurisdiction should not be required for custody proceedings. Traynor, Is This Conflict Really Necessary? 37 Tex.L.Rev. 657, 660–661 (1959).

Shaffer v. Heitner, the Kulko case, and the rules for in personam jurisdiction in other kinds of domestic relations suits are discussed supra, section 13.4. See also Genoe v. Genoe, 205 N.G.Super. 6, 500 A.2d 3 (1985).

22. E.g., In re Marriage of Schuham, 120 Ill.App.3d 339, 76 Ill.Dec. 159, 458 N.E.2d 559 (1983); In re Marriage of Hudson, 434 N.E.2d 107 (Ind.App.1983), cert. denied 459 U.S. 1202, 103 S.Ct. 1187, 75 L.Ed.2d 433 (1983), the decree in this case being enforced in Hudson v. Hudson, 35 Wash.App. 822, 670 P.2d 287 (1983). The Hudson case and the suggestion that custody determinations affect status are criticized in Garfield, Due Process Rights of Absent Parents in Interstate Custody Conflicts: A Commentary on In re Marriage of Hudson, 16 Ind.L. Rev. 445 (1983), and in Coombs, Interstate Child Custody: Jurisdiction, Recognition, and Enforcement, 66 Minn.L. Rev. 711, 742 (1982).

23. Coombs, Interstate Child Custody: Jurisdiction, Recognition, and Enforcement, 66 Minn.L.Rev. 711, 752 (1982), arguing, however, for "broader due process standards than those that the Supreme Court has imposed * * * in child support cases or in commercial litigation." Kulko v. Superior Court of California, 436 U.S. 84, 91, 98 S.Ct. 1690, 1696, 56 L.Ed.2d 132 (1978), rehearing denied 438 U.S. 908, 98 S.Ct. 3127, 57 L.Ed.2d 1150 (1978) states the general principle as indicated in the text.

Kulko.[24] There is the further difficulty that the UCCJA is not a long-arm statute and there has been some judicial unwillingness to apply general long-arm statutes to custody proceedings.[25]

Since the PKPA[26] is open to the same difficulty as the UCCJA in that it does not require in personam jurisdiction for custody decrees as a condition of their receiving full faith and credit, the courts must adopt some rationale for avoiding the application of May v. Anderson[27] and Kulko[28] to custody proceedings. If this is not done, there will be many cases in which the courts cannot give decrees or in which decrees once given will not be recognized in other states, thereby frustrating the purposes of both the PKPA and the UCCJA.

The discussion of UCCJA thus far has been devoted to its jurisdictional rules. Of equal importance are the sections of the Act which either require or permit courts which concededly have jurisdiction not to exercise it.[29] The first such section forbids the exercise of jurisdiction if at the time of filing the petition a custody proceeding was pending in the court of another state exercising jurisdiction substantially in accord with the UCCJA, unless the proceeding in the other state is stayed.[30] In order to comply with this provision, a court must engage in a complex series of steps, involving many provisions of the UCCJA:[31]

a) The court must first determine whether it has jurisdiction under any of the subsections of section 3 of the Act. If it does not, then it should deny the petition without further consideration of the pending proceeding in the other state.[32]

b) If the court does find that it has jurisdiction under either the home state test or the significant connection test, it must then consider whether there is another proceeding in some other state already pending. Of course if the court knows of no such pending case, section 6 of the Act has no application.[33] The Act provides that if a court enters a custody order before learning of a pending suit in another state, it must notify the court of the other state, but it neglects to indicate what the court of either state should do thereafter.[34]

c) The Act requires the courts in all cases to take affirmative steps to determine whether there are custody proceedings pending in other states.[35] If a court finds that there are proceedings pending, it must stay its own suit and communicate with the court in the other state, for the purpose of having the issue litigated in the more appropriate forum.[36] This aspect of the Act exemplifies the contemporary tendency to abandon formal rules of jurisdiction in exchange for pragmatic tests of convenience, state interest and hardship of the parties.[37]

d) Once the court finds that there is a custody proceeding already pending in another state, and communicates with the other court, it must decide whether the court in the other state is exercising jurisdiction "substantially" in accordance with the UCCJA.[38] If the court in the other state is not exercising jurisdiction

---

24. Bodenheimer and Neeley-Kvarme, Jurisdiction Over Child Custody and Adoption After Shaffer and Kulko, 12 U.Cal. Davis L.Rev. 229, 244 (1979).

25. See note 60, supra.

26. 28 U.S.C.A. § 1738A.

27. 345 U.S. 528, 73 S.Ct. 840, 97 L.Ed. 1221 (1953).

28. Kulko v. Superior Court, 436 U.S. 84, 98 S.Ct. 1690, 56 L.Ed.2d 132 (1978), rehearing denied 438 U.S. 908, 98 S.Ct. 3127, 57 L.Ed.2d 1150 (1978).

29. See note 80, supra.

30. UCCJA § 6.

31. Etter v. Etter, 43 Md.App. 395, 405 A.2d 760 (1979).

32. In re Marriage of Ben-Yehoshua, 91 Cal.App.3d 259, 154 Cal.Rptr. 80 (1979); Allen v. Allen, 64 Hawaii 553, 645 P.2d 300 (1982). The Ben-Yehoshua case must

apparently be read as holding that the abduction of the child from the state does not confer jurisdiction on the state if the provisions of section 3 do not apply.

33. Etter v. Etter, 43 Md.App. 395, 405 A.2d 760 (1979). "Pending" in this section means that the first court to enter a decree prevails, and not the first court in which a complaint is filed, according to Peterson v. Peterson, 464 A.2d 202 (Me. 1983).

34. UCCJA § 6(c).

35. UCCJA § 6(b).

36. UCCJA § 6(c).

37. Murphy v. Murphy, 380 Mass. 454, 404 N.E.2d 69 (1980).

38. UCCJA § 6(a). Failure to comply with the requirement of communication does not deprive a court of jurisdiction, according to Lofts v. Superior Court In and

in accordance with the Act, the court in the later of the two proceedings may proceed to hear the case,[39] although on occasion the court in the later of the cases has deferred to the earlier proceeding even though it found that the court in the earlier case had no jurisdiction.[40] It is not clear what "substantially" means in this context, but presumably it is intended to cover situations in which there are minor differences in the various state versions of the UCCJA, or in which the prior proceeding's jurisdictional basis is open to some doubt.

e) Some courts, upon finding that there are pending proceedings in another state in which the court has jurisdiction, take the Act's apparently absolute prohibition literally and dismiss the later suit.[41] Action of this kind aggravates the tendency of the UCCJA to cause a race to the courthouse in custody

For Maricopa County, 140 Ariz. 407, 682 P.2d 412 (1984), but may make exercise of jurisdiction reversible error. Matter of Appeal in Pima County, 147 Ariz. 584, 712 P.2d 431 (1986). But Pasqualone v. Pasqualone, 63 Ohio St.2d 96, 406 N.E.2d 1121 (1980) held that failure of a parent to inform the court of other pending proceedings, under UCCJA § 9, would deprive the court of jurisdiction. But see In re Palmer, 12 Ohio St.3d 194, 465 N.E.2d 1312 (1984).

39. Allison v. Superior Court of Los Angeles County, 99 Cal.App.3d 993, 160 Cal.Rptr. 309 (1979); Brokus v. Brokus, 420 N.E.2d 1242 (Ind.App.1981).

Middleton v. Middleton, 227 Va. 82, 314 S.E.2d 362 (1984) held Virginia properly exercised jurisdiction notwithstanding the existence of a pending English proceeding conducted substantially in accordance with the UCCJA, apparently on the ground that the mother had "spirited" the child away to England. A strong flavor of local chauvinism permeates the opinion.

40. Kimmons v. Heldt, 667 P.2d 1245 (Alaska 1983); Carpenter v. Carpenter, 326 Pa.Super. 570, 474 A.2d 1124 (1984) (Semble). Rexford v. Rexford, 631 P.2d 475 (Alaska 1980) held that Alaska would defer to earlier proceedings in California although the Alaska court found that California did not have jurisdiction in accordance with the UCCJA.

41. Lopez v. District Court, 199 Colo. 207, 606 P.2d 853 (1980); In re Custody of Rector, 39 Colo.App. 111, 565 P.2d 950 (1977); Steele v. Steele, 250 Ga. 101, 296 S.E.2d 570 (1982).

42. UCCJA § 6(a), (c); Peterson v. Peterson, 464 A.2d 202 (Me.1983); Vanneck v. Vanneck, 49 N.Y.2d 602, 427 N.Y.S.2d 735, 404 N.E.2d 1278 (1980). St. Andrie v. St. Andrie, 473 So.2d 140 (La.App.1985), after finding that both Georgia and Louisiana had "significant connection" jurisdiction, held, without more ado, that Louisiana, being prior in time, should exercise jurisdiction.

cases. The Act actually requires, however, that the later court go further and determine whether jurisdiction in the prior proceeding is being properly exercised.[42] This means that the court in the later case must decide not only whether there is jurisdiction in pending proceeding, but also whether that proceeding violates the UCCJA's "unclean hands" provision,[43] and whether that proceeding is being conducted in a convenient forum as defined in the Act.[44] When the question of a convenient forum arises, the seemingly absolute prohibition on the later of two proceedings imposed in the first sentence of section 6 of the Act turns out not to be absolute at all. The UCCJA requires the two courts to communicate with each other and, in some fashion not spelled out, to decide which of them is the more convenient forum.[45]

43. The "unclean hands" provision is UCCJA § 8, which states that jurisdiction should not be exercised in some circumstances because of the moving party's wrongful conduct. This section is further discussed infra, at note 61.

44. The inconvenient forum provision is UCCJA § 7. Loper v. Superior Court In and For the County of Cochise, 126 Ariz. 14, 612 P.2d 65 (1980); In re Marriage of Weinstein, 87 Ill.App.3d 101, 42 Ill.Dec. 243, 408 N.E.2d 952 (1980); Vanneck v. Vanneck, 49 N.Y.2d 602, 427 N.Y.S.2d 735, 404 N.E.2d 1278 (1980) (the court must determine which forum has optimum access to the relevant evidence dealing with the child's welfare). The inconvenient forum provision is discussed further infra, at note 53.

45. UCCJA § 6(c). Communication between courts is also authorized by UCCJA § 7(d). The Commissioners' Comments to this section emphasize the section's provision for interstate communication and cooperation, saying that when there is doubt as to the appropriate forum, the doubt should be resolved by consultation and cooperation between the courts involved.

While the consultation and cooperation provided for by the Act are not often discussed in reported cases, there are statements that such activities are a duty of the courts, as in Loper v. Superior Court In and For the County of Cochise, 126 Ariz. 14, 612 P.2d 65 (1980); Paltrow v. Paltrow, 37 Md.App. 191, 376 A.2d 1134 (1977), affirmed 282 Md. 291, 388 A.2d 547 (1978) (court has an affirmative duty to consider the pendency of proceedings elsewhere, and must do so on its own motion even though the parties do not raise the issue); Vanneck v. Vanneck, 49 N.Y.2d 602, 427 N.Y.S.2d 735, 404 N.E.2d 1278 (1980). Petition of Edilson, 637 P.2d 362 (Colo.1981), however, excuses any duty of communication when the court in the later case is not uncertain as to the appropriate forum.

f) Finally, if the pending proceeding seeks a modification of a still earlier custody order, the court in the later case would have to address the question whether it and the court in the earlier proceeding have jurisdiction to modify the original custody decree. This involves the application of still other intricate provisions of the UCCJA.[46]

Section 7 of the UCCJA, the inconvenient forum section, substantially reduces whatever precision there may be in the basic jurisdictional sections of the Act by authorizing a court having jurisdiction to decline to exercise it if it finds that it is an inconvenient forum and that another state's court is a more appropriate forum.[47] This may be done on the court's own motion as well as on the motion of the parties.[48] The uncertainty created by this possibility is the greater since the application of the inconvenient forum doctrine lies in the discretion of the trial court, although the failure by the trial court to consider the factors relevant to the doctrine is an abuse of discretion.[49] Where the custody issue arises in a divorce action, the UCCJA permits the court to retain jurisdiction over the divorce although it refuses to exercise its jurisdiction respecting custody.[50] And if the court finds that the suit has been brought in a clearly inappropriate forum, it may assess the costs, including attorney fees and travel and other expenses, against the moving party.[51]

Forum non conveniens, as it developed in the general law of procedure, had as its purpose the protection of the state from the expense of litigation not connected with the state and the parties from the hardship and inconvenience caused by the same lack of relation between the suit and the state.[52] Under the UCCJA, however, the court must focus on the question whether it is in the interests of the child that the forum state or another state exercise jurisdiction.[53] The Act lists five factors bearing on this question, the most significant of which are the location of the best evidence concerning the child's present and future care and the effectuation of the statutory purposes.[54] Two of the listed factors just reproduce the home state and significant connection tests for jurisdiction, underlining the similarity between the jurisdictional bases, particularly the significant connection basis, and the question of inconvenient forum.[55] The dominant purpose of the inconvenient forum provision is to encourage restraint in the exercise of jurisdiction.[56]

Many of the cases involving the inconvenient forum provision of the Act come up when one parent lives in state A with the child and the other lives in state B. It is impossible to generalize from the outcome of these cases. Perhaps most of them hold that the state in which the child is living is the appropriate forum,[57] but there are cases hold-

---

The requirement of consultation has not eliminated the "home town" effect in custody cases. See, e.g., In re Marriage of Weinstein, 87 Ill.App.3d 101, 42 Ill.Dec. 243, 408 N.E.2d 952 (1980); Pasqualone v. Pasqualone, 63 Ohio St.2d 96, 406 N.E.2d 1121 (1980).

No case has been found considering the question whether this sort of consultation between judges infringes on the due process right of a hearing. It would seem that at a minimum a record of any communications between courts should be kept and made available to the parties to be the subject of challenge or argument by the parties. See Allen v. Allen, 64 Hawaii 553, 645 P.2d 300 (1982), stating in dictum that the substance of such conversations should be made part of the record, but finding the omission in this case was not prejudicial.

46. UCCJA § 14, discussed infra, at note 74.

47. UCCJA § 7(a).

48. UCCJA § 7(b).

49. Colby v. Colby, 102 Wis.2d 198, 306 N.W.2d 57 (1981); Mayer v. Mayer, 91 Wis.2d 342, 283 N.W.2d 591 (App.1979).

50. UCCJA § 7(f).

51. UCCJA § 7(g).

52. F. James, G. Hazard, Civil Procedure § 12.29 (2d ed.1977).

53. UCCJA § 7(c); William L. v. Michele P., 99 Misc. 2d 346, 416 N.Y.S.2d 477 (Fam.Ct.1979). But Allison v. Superior Court of Los Angeles County, 99 Cal.App.3d 993, 160 Cal.Rptr. 309 (1979) does give some weight to the financial burden on the litigating parties.

54. UCCJA § 7(c)(1) to (5).

55. William L. v. Michele P., 99 Misc.2d 346, 416 N.Y.S.2d 477 (Fam.Ct.1979).

56. UCCJA § 7, Commissioners' Comments, 9 Unif.L. Ann. 139 (1979).

57. Bosse v. Superior Court for Santa Clara County, 89 Cal.App.3d 440, 152 Cal.Rptr. 665 (1979) (Montana was the more appropriate forum since the child and mother had lived there for two and one-half years, even though the original custody decree had been given in California and the court found that California still had jurisdiction);

ing the other way.[58] It may make some difference whether the child has been in the state for a substantial period.[59] It is also of some significance that a parent is claiming that there is continuing jurisdiction in one or the other of the states as a result of the earlier award of custody in that state.[60]

The "unclean hands" provision gives a court another reason for refusing to exercise jurisdiction. It is even more vague than the inconvenient forum provision. The Act says that if a petitioner for an *initial* decree has wrongfully taken the child from another state, or has engaged in similar reprehensible conduct, the court *may* decline to exercise jurisdiction if that would be just and proper under the circumstances.[61] But the court *shall not* exercise its jurisdiction to modify the decree of another state if the petitioner has improperly removed or retained the child, unless the exercise of jurisdiction is required in the interest of the child.[62] If the petitioner has violated any other provision of the decree of another state, the court *may* decline to

exercise its jurisdiction (presumably to modify), if this is just and proper under the circumstances.[63] It would surely be difficult to draft a statute which would give the courts less guidance than this. As the Commissioners' Comments indicate,[64] the general notion that a parent who violates a custody decree should not be assisted by the courts in obtaining custody was first given prominence by Professor Ehrenzweig.[65] Aside from the difficult, if not impossible, problem of weighing the child's interests against the parent's culpability which the doctrine poses, it reintroduces into the lawsuit many of the charges and counter-charges that used to be such a distasteful feature of the fault grounds for divorce.[66]

The initial question of construction raised by section 8(a) is, what is meant by the phrase "has wrongfully taken the child from another state or has engaged in similar reprehensible conduct." The Commissioners' comments on this are not very helpful, being even more

---

In re Marriage of Kern, 87 Cal.App.3d 402, 150 Cal.Rptr. 860 (1978) (Rhode Island the appropriate forum since the child lived there); Schlumpf v. Superior Court of the County of Trinity, 79 Cal.App.3d 892, 145 Cal.Rptr. 190 (1978) (child resided in Wyoming, evidence of his interests was more readily available there, making Wyoming the appropriate forum); Clark v. Superior Court In and For Mendocino County, 73 Cal.App.3d 298, 140 Cal.Rptr. 709 (1977) (though California had continuing jurisdiction, Oregon, where the child lived, was the more appropriate forum); Snider v. Snider, 474 So.2d 1374 (La.App.1985), writ denied 478 So.2d 903 (1985); In re Marriage of Pavelcik, 138 Ill.App.3d 1060, 93 Ill.Dec. 589, 487 N.E.2d 33 (1985). In all of these cases the courts tended to emphasize the importance of the availability of relevant evidence concerning the child's present and future care. See also Annot., 96 A.L.R.3d 968, 995 (1980).

58. Allison v. Superior Court of Los Angeles County, 99 Cal.App.3d 993, 160 Cal.Rptr. 309 (1979) (California was the appropriate forum even though the child had lived in Texas with his father for eighteen months); In re Marriage of Weinstein, 87 Ill.App.3d 101, 42 Ill.Dec. 243, 408 N.E.2d 952 (1980) (Illinois had greater access to evidence although the child had resided in Montana for two and one-half years). See also Annot., 96 A.L.R.3d 968, 999 (1980).

In Brown v. Brown, 195 Conn. 98, 486 A.2d 1116 (1985) the court of the home state, Connecticut, held that it was an inconvenient forum after the state of the mother's residence, Florida, had held that *it* was an inconvenient forum. This seems to be pressing the Alphonse and Gaston tendencies of the UCCJA to their ultimate absurdity.

59. William L. v. Michele P., 99 Misc.2d 346, 416 N.Y.S.2d 477 (Fam.Ct.1979) (Mississippi had the better access to evidence where the children were only in New York on short visits).

60. Palm v. Superior Court of San Diego County, 97 Cal.App.3d 456, 158 Cal.Rptr. 786 (1979) (North Dakota was the more appropriate forum even though mother and child lived in California; strong dissent); Larsen v. Larsen, 5 Kan.App.2d 284, 615 P.2d 806 (1980) (Kansas the more appropriate forum where the children were there on a visit, though they lived in Minnesota; original custody decree was in Kansas).

61. UCCJA § 8(a).

62. UCCJA § 8(b).

63. UCCJA § 8(b). Under UCCJA § 8(c) a court which dismisses a petition in accordance with this section may, in appropriate cases, charge the petitioner with travel and other expenses, including attorney fees, incurred by other parties or their witnesses.

64. UCCJA § 8, Commissioners' Comments, 9 Unif.L. Ann. 142 (1979).

65. Ehrenzweig, Interstate Recognition of Custody Decrees, 51 Mich.L.Rev. 345 (1953).

66. Hafer v. Superior Court, San Diego County, 126 Cal.App.3d 856, 179 Cal.Rptr. 132 (1981) is a good example of this. After a long opinion and a long dissent, the reader is unable to ascertain what the facts of the case were. Another example is Martin v. Martin, 45 N.Y.2d 739, 408 N.Y.S.2d 479, 380 N.E.2d 305 (1978), reargument denied 45 N.Y.2d 839, 409 N.Y.S.2d 1031, 381 N.E.2d 630 (1978).

vague than the statutory language.[67] The Comments do provide an illustration, however, of a kind of taking which is characterized as wrongful.[68] The cases are not in agreement on whether a spouse is guilty of a wrongful taking if he removes the children to another state at a time when there is no custody decree outstanding. The differences in result are at least in part attributable to differences in circumstances, the number of which in custody cases seems infinite.[69] It is even less clear what is meant by "similar reprehensible conduct". Perhaps this would

include the removal of a child in violation of an agreement between the spouses, or the deliberate frustration of a parent's attempts to see or communicate with the child, but there is simply no way to predict how courts might construe language as vague as this.[70]

Section 8 provides no clues to proper court action in the not uncommon case where both parents have been guilty of removing the child from the state and from the custody of the other parent. Some courts sensibly ignore the problem, since it is usually impossible to decide which parent is the more seri-

---

67. UCCJA § 8(a), Commissioners' Comments, 9 Unif. L.Ann. 143 (1979): " 'Wrongfully' taking under this subsection does not mean that a 'right' has been violated- both husband and wife as a rule have a right to custody until a court determination is made- but that one party's conduct is so objectionable that a court in the exercise of its inherent equity powers cannot in good conscience permit that party access to its jurisdiction." The reference to inherent equity powers leads one to recall what a distinguished equity lawyer had to say about the clean hands doctrine: "* * * the concentration of judges on the clean hands maxim does harm by distracting their attention from the basic policies which are applicable to the situation before them. The matrimonial suits are a notable example of this bad tendency." Z. Chafee, Some Problems of Equity 95 (1950).

68. UCCJA § 8, Commissioners' Comments, 9 Unif.L. Ann. 142 (1979): "For example, if upon a de facto separation the wife returned to her own home with the children without objection by her husband and lived there for two years without hearing from him, and the husband without warning forcibly removes the children one night and brings them to another state, a court in that state although it has jurisdiction after 6 months may decline to hear the husband's custody petition." The trouble with this example is that it raises many more questions than it answers. What should be the result if the wife leaves, taking the child, without warning and without saying where she is going? Is this a wrongful taking? What does it mean to say the husband "forcibly" retakes the children? What if both spouses have indulged in self-help? What if the wife, after she removes the children, refuses to permit visitation? Is this "wrongful"?

69. The following cases relied upon section 8(a) to decline the exercise of jurisdiction: Barcus v. Barcus, 278 N.W.2d 646 (Iowa 1979) (father retained child in violation of a temporary custody order); Stevens v. Stevens, 177 N.J.Super. 167, 425 A.2d 1081 (1981) (mother guilty of wrongful taking when she forced her way into the premises, assaulted a baby sitter and removed the child from the state); Marks v. Marks, 281 S.C. 316, 315 S.E.2d 158 (App.1984). Freeman v. Freeman, 547 S.W.2d 437 (Ky. 1977) contains a statement that the period during which a child is hidden in the state may not be counted for computing the home state requirement.

The following cases refused to apply the unclean hands doctrine of section 8(a): Morgan v. Morgan, 666 P.2d 1026

(Alaska 1983) (marriage became strained when parties lived in Virginia; mother removed the children with the intention of going to Alaska; father caught up with them in Washington and took the children back to Virginia; the father's taking was not "wrongful" because no custody proceeding had been brought and both parents were equally entitled to custody); In re Marriage of Severn, 44 Colo.App. 109, 608 P.2d 381 (1980) (father brought children from Florida to Colorado with mother's consent; retained them in Colorado without her consent; trial court erred in refusing to exercise jurisdiction, the paramount consideration being the interests of the children, not the wrongdoing of the parent); In re Marriage of Thompson, 96 Ill.2d 67, 70 Ill.Dec. 214, 449 N.E.2d 88 (1983), cert. denied 464 U.S. 895, 104 S.Ct. 242, 78 L.Ed.2d 232 (1983) (mother removed the child from Illinois to Michigan and tried to hide him from father; father got an order for temporary custody in Illinois and taking it to Michigan forcibly took the child from the mother; the court seems to say this is the kind of conduct section 8(a) is intended to prevent, but that the mother failed to raise the issue in timely fashion); O'Neal v. O'Neal, 329 N.W.2d 666 (Iowa 1983) (clean hands doctrine not to be applied where it would jeopardize the child's welfare); Dean v. Dean, 133 Mich.App. 220, 348 N.W.2d 725 (1984); Brauch v. Shaw, 121 N.H. 562, 432 A.2d 1 (1981) (paramount issue is the welfare of the child, not the tactics of the parents; same principle applies to illegitimate children); Houtchens v. Houtchens, __ R.I. __, 488 A.2d 726 (1985) (father's action may have been wrongful, was not reprehensible), In re Marriage of Verbin, 92 Wash.2d 171, 595 P.2d 905 (1979) (mother took children from Maryland to Washington without notice to father; father removed children from Washington to Maryland without notice to mother; mother removed one child from Maryland to Washington without notice to father; dictum that section 8(a) would not require the court to decline jurisdiction). Other cases are cited in Annot., 96 A.L.R.3d 968, 1000 (1980).

70. Bodenheimer, The Uniform Child Custody Jurisdiction Act: A Legislative Remedy for Children Caught in the Conflict of Laws, 22 Vand.L.Rev. 1207, 1242 (1969) gives a removal in violation of an agreement as an example of wrongful conduct. Williams v. Zacher, 35 Or. App. 129, 581 P.2d 91 (1978) defines section 8(a) as applying to "unconscionable conduct" even though no legal right or duty has been violated.

ously at fault.[71] Others decline to exercise jurisdiction if the parent invoking the jurisdiction has violated a custody order, regardless of the misconduct of the other parent.[72]

While section 8(a) of the UCCJA provides that a court in a proceeding seeking an initial decree *may* decline to exercise jurisdiction on the ground of unclean hands, thereby indicating that the court has some discretion in the matter, section 8(b) states that a court *shall not* exercise jurisdiction to modify a decree entered in another state if the petitioner has improperly removed or retained the child away from the physical custody of the person to whom the decree gave custody.[73] The intention was apparently to make the application of the unclean hands doctrine mandatory in modification proceedings.[74] But section 8(b) is qualified by the opening phrase, "un-

less required in the interest of the child", thereby sharply mitigating the intended mandatory effect of the subsection.[75] The second sentence of section 8(b) does set up a discretionary unclean hands defense when the petitioner has violated a decree's provision other than by removal or retention of the child.[76] The term "petitioner" in section 8(b) has been defined to include a parent who is seeking to have a prior decree modified even though he is technically the respondent in the particular proceeding.[77] Although there are other considerations under the UCCJA and the PKPA where modification of another state's decree is sought,[78] some courts do give much weight in such cases to the petitioner's improper conduct[79] sometimes even in circumstances where the child's welfare might well be prejudiced by the refusal of modifica-

71. E.g., Morgan v. Morgan, 666 P.2d 1026 (Alaska 1983); In re Marriage of Thompson, 96 Ill.2d 67, 70 Ill. Dec. 214, 449 N.E.2d 88 (1983), cert. denied 464 U.S. 895, 104 S.Ct. 242, 78 L.Ed.2d 232 (1983); Appelblom v. Appelblom, 66 A.D.2d 188, 412 N.Y.S.2d 517 (4th Dep't 1979); Williams v. Zacher, 35 Or.App. 129, 581 P.2d 91 (1978); In re Marriage of Verbin, 92 Wash.2d 171, 595 P.2d 905 (1979).

72. Mondy v. Mondy, 428 So.2d 235 (Fla.1983). Van Haren v. Van Haren, 171 N.J.Super. 12, 407 A.2d 1242 (1979) refused to enforce a South Carolina decree obtained by a father who had taken the children there and hidden them, even though the mother had brought them to New Jersey in violation of the South Carolina decree. Hays v. Hays, 117 Misc.2d 541, 458 N.Y.S.2d 440 (1982) seems to say that section 8(b) has no application where both parents have engaged in illegal self-help.

73. UCCJA § 8(b). This section would not apply if the children ran away from their legal custodian to live with the other parent, at least where that parent did not encourage them to do so. In re Marriage of Dunkley, 89 Wash.2d 777, 575 P.2d 1071 (1978) so held, although it was decided before the enactment of the UCCJA. There is also authority that a removal is not improper if the custody decree does not forbid it, even though it makes visitation impracticable, but this view of section 8(b) seems very doubtful. Baird v. Baird, 374 So.2d 60 (Fla. App.1979).

There is authority that a court will not modify its own decree at the petition of a parent who has abducted the child, Hafer v. Superior Court, San Diego County, 126 Cal.App.3d 856, 179 Cal.Rptr. 132 (1981), although section 8(b) does not purport to deal with this kind of case.

74. UCCJA § 8, Commissioners' Comments, 9 Unif.L. Ann. 143 (1979).

75. Mattleman v. Bandler, 123 N.H. 368, 461 A.2d 561 (1983), appeal after remand 125 N.H. 204, 480 A.2d 85 (1984) states that a parent retaining a child after a

visitation period should be permitted to seek modification of custody only on proof of clearly compelling circumstances. See also Murphy v. Murphy, 380 Mass. 454, 404 N.E.2d 69 (1980), a pre-UCCJA case but one influenced by the statute.

76. It is not clear what sort of violation the statute is referring to. Perhaps a refusal to comply with the provisions of a joint custody decree might disqualify a parent from seeking a change in custody in another state, although difficult questions of the child's interests would be raised in such a case.

77. Commonwealth ex rel. Zaubi v. Zaubi, 492 Pa. 183, 423 A.2d 333 (1980).

78. UCCJA § 14; 28 U.S.C.A. § 1738A(f). See the discussion of modification infra at note 74. For example Matter of Marriage of Settle, 276 Or. 759, 556 P.2d 962 (1976) and the overruling case, Matter of Custody of Ross, 291 Or. 263, 630 P.2d 353 (1981) both involved abductions or retentions of the children, but the courts in both cases chose to base their decisions on other aspects of the UCCJA.

79. Denying modification on this ground: Both v. Superior Court In & For Mohave County, 121 Ariz. 381, 590 P.2d 920 (1979); Young v. District Court of Boulder County, 194 Colo. 140, 570 P.2d 249 (1977); Mondy v. Mondy, 428 So.2d 235 (Fla.1983); Bishop v. Bishop, 247 Ga. 56, 273 S.E.2d 394 (1981); Owens, By and Through, Mosley v. Huffaman, 481 So.2d 231 (Miss.1985) (abduction by a grandparent); Clark v. Clark, 67 A.D.2d 388, 416 N.Y.S.2d 330 (3d Dep't 1979), appeal denied 47 N.Y.2d 706, 417 N.Y.S.2d 1027, 391 N.E.2d 305 (1979); Matter of Potter, 56 Ohio Misc. 17, 377 N.E.2d 536 (1978); Terrill v. Terrill, ___ R.I. ___, 431 A.2d 1194 (1981); Tuttle v. Henderson, 628 P.2d 1275 (Utah 1981); In re Custody of Nelsen, 37 Wash.App. 640, 681 P.2d 1302 (1984); Shermer v. Cornelius, ___ W.Va. ___, 278 S.E.2d 349 (1981); Vorpahl v. Lee, 99 Wis.2d 7, 298 N.W.2d 222 (App.1980).

tion.[80] Other cases have found that the interests of the child demanded an exercise of jurisdiction notwithstanding the petitioner's violation of a prior custody decree.[81] It is difficult to draw any general conclusions from the cases pro and con, since many factors in addition to unclean hands were taken into account by the courts in reaching the diverse results.

A few courts have gone beyond the language of section 8(b) to take the position that home state jurisdiction may not be acquired if the child is brought into the state in violation of an outstanding custody order.[82] A consequence of this view is that a decree entered by a state's court on the basis of home state jurisdiction acquired in this manner is without jurisdiction and therefore need not be respected in other states.[83] Such a result is inconsistent with section 8 of the UCCJA, which treats unclean hands as going only to the exercise of jurisdiction, not to its existence. It is also undesirable because it forecloses any consideration of the child's welfare.

The UCCJA contains many other sections designed to promote cooperation between the courts of the various states in the decision of custody cases. These sections provide for the collection and sharing of information concerning custody proceedings,[84] the filing and enforcement of custody decrees,[85] taking testimony and holding hearings in other states,[86] and for compelling the presence of parties who are outside the state.[87] The recognition, enforcement and modification of the decrees of other states are governed by specific sections of the Act [88] which are discussed later in this section in connection with the PKPA.[89]

Parental Kidnapping Prevention Act of 1980

In 1980 Congress passed the PKPA primarily to implement the Full Faith and Credit Clause of the Constitution as it applies to custody decrees.[90] Although some hearings

---

80. E.g., Walker v. Luckey, 474 So.2d 608 (Miss.1985); Martin v. Martin, 45 N.Y.2d 739, 408 N.Y.S.2d 479, 380 N.E.2d 305 (1978), reargument denied 45 N.Y.2d 839, 409 N.Y.S.2d 1031, 381 N.E.2d 630 (1978) (decided before enactment of UCCJA, but follows the statute; majority and dissent disagree as to the child's welfare); Nehra v. Uhlar, 43 N.Y.2d 242, 401 N.Y.S.2d 168, 372 N.E.2d 4 (1977) (child returned to father after abduction by mother, and after child had lived with mother for four years, pursuant to the policy of the UCCJA but before its enactment); Commonwealth ex rel. Zaubi v. Zaubi, 492 Pa. 183, 423 A.2d 333 (1980) (modification denied although three judges thought the child's welfare would be harmed).

81. Berry v. Berry, 466 So.2d 138 (Ala.Civ.App.1985); Bosse v. Superior Court for Santa Clara County, 89 Cal. App.3d 440, 152 Cal.Rptr. 665 (1979); Nelson v. District Court In and For Second Judicial District, 186 Colo. 381, 527 P.2d 811 (1974); Hadley v. Hadley, 394 So.2d 769 (La. App.1981), writ denied 399 So.2d 622 (1981); Bull v. Bull, 109 Mich.App. 328, 311 N.W.2d 768 (1981); Green v. Green, 87 Mich.App. 706, 276 N.W.2d 472 (1978); Tettis v. Boyum, 317 Pa.Super. 8, 463 A.2d 1056 (1983).

82. Winkelman v. Moses, 279 N.W.2d 897 (S.D.1979). A pre-UCCJA case, Murphy v. Murphy, 380 Mass. 454, 404 N.E.2d 69 (1980) held that a child could not acquire a domicile in the state when brought into the state in violation of a custody decree.

83. In re Marriage of Hopson, 110 Cal.App.3d 884, 168 Cal.Rptr. 345 (1980). Where the abducting parent is seeking modification of an earlier decree, other, more complex provisions of the UCCJA come into play. See UCCJA § 14, discussed, infra, at note 74, and Bodenheimer, Progress Under the Uniform Child Custody

Jurisdiction Act and Remaining Problems: Punitive Decrees, Joint Custody, and Excessive Modifications, 65 Cal. L.Rev. 978, 988 (1977).

84. UCCJA § 9 (parties are required to give certain information under oath in pleadings or affidavits); UCCJA § 16 (requires the maintenance of a registry of out-of-state custody decrees); UCCJA § 17 (requires copies of custody decrees to be furnished to courts or persons); UCCJA § 21 (requires the preservation of relevant pleadings, orders, decrees and records in custody cases); UCCJA § 22 (a court taking jurisdiction of a custody case shall request court records from other states involving the same child).

85. UCCJA § 15. A decree of another state filed in accordance with section may be enforced as a decree of the state where filed. This provision is similar to the Uniform Enforcement of Foreign Judgments Act § 2, 13 Unif.L.Ann. 177 (1980). A case discussing but not deciding issues under this section is Kilgore v. Kilgore, 666 S.W.2d 923 (Mo. App. 1984).

86. UCCJA §§ 18, 19.

87. UCCJA § 20.

88. UCCJA §§ 13, 14.

89. See the discussion at note 74, infra.

90. The Act is cited as 28 U.S.C.A. § 1738A, and is found in 94 Stat. 3568. The Full Faith and Credit Clause is U.S.Const. art. IV, § 1. The Act is also known as the Wallop Act, for Senator Wallop of Wyoming, one of its principal sponsors. The PKPA is extensively discussed in Coombs, Interstate Child Custody: Jurisdiction, Recognition, and Enforcement, 66 Minn.L.Rev. 711 (1982), Profes-

were held on the Act,[91] it was passed rather "precipitately" as a rider to a bill dealing with medicare reimbursement.[92] The fact that it does implement the Full Faith and Credit Clause makes the PKPA controlling in any circumstances in which it conflicts with the UCCJA or with other aspects of state law, under the Supremacy Clause of the United States Constitution.[93] It seems fairly clear that in passing the PKPA Congress did not purport to occupy the field of custody jurisdiction, and in fact that it expressly left some

scope for the operation of the UCCJA.[94] And where the PKPA and the UCCJA do not conflict, the state law survives. For example, the PKPA does not appear to forbid a state from enforcing another state's decree even though that enforcement is not required by the PKPA.[95] On the other hand there may be cases in which it is exceedingly unclear whether or to what extent there is the sort of conflict between the two Acts that would warrant invoking the Supremacy Clause.[96]

sor Coombs having been concerned with its drafting and passage in the United States Senate.

The findings made by Congress in the PKPA refer to the Commerce Clause and the Due Process Clause as well as the Full Faith and Credit Clause of the Constitution but the latter clause seems most clearly and closely related to the subject matter and the purpose of the PKPA.

Other sections of the PKPA authorize the Secretary of Health and Human Services to make agreements with the states for the use of the federal parent locator services in connection with locating an absent parent or child for the purpose of enforcing custody decrees or laws dealing with abduction. 42 U.S.C.A. § 663. The Act also contains a provision to the effect that 18 U.S.C.A. § 1073 applies to parental kidnaping and to interstate or international flight to avoid prosecution under state felony statutes. The statute referred to makes it a federal crime to travel interstate or internationally to avoid prosecution for state felonies. The purpose of this provision in the PKPA seems to have been to enlist the aid of the federal law enforcement agencies in cases of interstate parental abduction of children. The Department of Justice opposed the criminal portion of the PKPA. Addendum to Joint Hearing Before the Subcommittee on Criminal Justice of the Committee on the Judiciary and the Subcommittee on Child and Human Development of the Committee on Labor and Human Resources, United States Senate, 9th Cong., 2d Sess., on S. 105 (1980) (Letter of Patricia M. Wald).

91. Joint Hearing Before the Subcommittee on Criminal Justice of the Committee on the Judiciary and the Subcommittee on Child and Human Development of the Committee on Labor and Human Resources, U.S.Senate, 96th Cong., 2d Sess. on S. 105 (1980), and Addendum to Joint Hearing Before the Subcommittee on Criminal Justice of the Committee on the Judiciary and the Subcommittee on Child and Human Development of the Committee on Labor and Human Resources, U.S.Senat, 96th Cong., 2d Sess., on S. 105 (1980).

92. Leslie L. F. v. Constance F., 110 Misc.2d 86, 441 N.Y.S.2d 911 (Fam.Ct.1981), footnote 1 to the opinion.

The effective date of the PKPA is unclear. Although the Act was passed on December 28, 1980, it contains a statement, 94 Stat. at 3567, that, "The amendments made by this Act shall take effect on, and apply to services furnished on or after, July 1, 1981." Holding that the effective date was July 1, 1981: Mitchell v. Mitchell, 437

So.2d 122 (Ala.Cir.App.1982); Kumar v. Superior Court of Santa Clara County, 32 Cal.3d 689, 186 Cal.Rptr. 772, 652 P.2d 1003 (1982). Holding that December 28, 1980, was the effective date: State ex rel. Valles v. Brown, 97 N.M. 327, 639 P.2d 1181 (1981); Bahr v. Bahr, 108 Misc.2d 920, 442 N.Y.S.2d 687 (Fam.Ct.1981), affirmed 91 A.D.2d 1010, 458 N.Y.S.2d 247 (1983); Matter of Custody of Ross, 291 Or. 263, 630 P.2d 353 (1981); Salisbury v. Salisbury, 657 S.W.2d 761 (Tenn.App.1983). See also E.E.B. v. D.A., 89 N.J. 595, 446 A.2d 871 (1982).

93. U.S.Const. art. VI. Cases recognizing the supremacy of the federal Act include Mitchell v. Mitchell, 437 So.2d 122 (Ala.Civ.App.1982); Neger v. Neger, 93 N.J. 15, 459 A.2d 628 (1983); Tufares v. Wright, 98 N.M. 8, 644 P.2d 522 (1982); S. Frederick P. v. Barbara P., 115 Misc. 2d 332, 454 N.Y.S.2d 202 (Fam.Ct.1982); Mebert v. Mebert, 111 Misc.2d 500, 444 N.Y.S.2d 834 (Fam.Ct.1981); Virginia E. E. v. Alberto S.P., 110 Misc.2d 448, 440 N.Y.S.2d 979 (Fam.Ct.1981); Leslie L. F. v. Constance F., 110 Misc.2d 86, 441 N.Y.S.2d 911 (Fam.Ct.1981); Salisbury v. Salisbury, 657 S.W.2d 761 (Tenn.App.1983); Arbogast v. Arbogast, ___ W.Va. ___, 327 S.E.2d 675 (1984); Quenzer v. Quenzer, 653 P.2d 295 (Wyo.1982), cert. denied 460 U.S. 1041, 103 S.Ct. 1436, 75 L.Ed.2d 794 (1983).

For a further but somewhat confusing discussion of preemption by the PKPA, see Coombs, Interstate Child Custody: Jurisdiction, Recognition, and Enforcement, 66 Minn.L.Rev. 711, 822 (1982), which may reach the same ultimate conclusion as the text. For a general discussion of conflicts between state and federal law see L. Tribe, American Constitutional Law § 6–24 (1978).

94. For example, 28 U.S.C.A. § 1738A(c)(1) provides that a custody determination made by a state court is consistent with the PKPA if (among other requirements) the state court has jurisdiction under its own law. Federal occupation of the field is discussed in L. Tribe, American Constitutional Law § 6–25 (1978). See also Coombs, Interstate Child Custody: Jurisdiction, Recognition, and Enforcement, 66 Minn.L.Rev. 711, 827 (1982).

95. Rexford v. Rexford, 631 P.2d 475 (Alaska 1980), for example, deferred to California's earlier proceedings even though California did not have jurisdiction, and this would not seem to violate the PKPA. See Coombs, Interstate Child Custody: Jurisdiction, Recognition, and Enforcement, 66 Minn.L.Rev. 711, 828 (1982). See also Neger v. Neger, 93 N.J. 15, 459 A.2d 628 (1983).

96. See, e.g., Wachter v. Wachter, 439 So.2d 1260 (La. App. 1983).

If the possible conflicts between the PKPA and the UCCJA are not enough to warm the heart of the most technical of lawyers, there is always the question whether the federal courts have jurisdiction in custody matters by virtue of the PKPA. The "domestic relations exception" to federal jurisdiction is discussed in another section,[97] in which are cited numerous cases in which the federal courts have expressed reluctance to decide custody disputes. The enactment of the PKPA provides another occasion for the debate over the "domestic relations exception". In addition it raises the question whether the PKPA itself creates federal question jurisdiction over custody disputes as a way of resolving interstate conflicts. Although there is persuasive material in the legislative history of the PKPA to the effect that that Act was not intended to establish federal jurisdiction over jurisdictional conflicts between state courts in custody cases,[98] some courts have held that where a state court has violated the PKPA by refusing to enforce the custody decree of another state court, a federal court has federal question jurisdiction to enjoin that violation and enforce the Act.[99] Due to the obvious impact which the PKPA and UCCJA have upon the merits of custody decisions, the federal courts

in these cases may well have embarked upon a course which will involve them more deeply in the decision of custody conflicts than many judges will find desirable, and than the usual application of the "domestic relations exception" would permit. The extent of federal involvement in these cases could be reduced to some extent by the imposition of a requirement of the exhaustion of state judicial remedies before recourse to the federal courts.[1]

Congress, in enacting the PKPA, made findings that the laws relating to custody jurisdiction are inconsistent and conflicting, that this inconsistency causes abduction and concealment of children interstate and the excessive relitigation of cases. As a consequence, Congress found that courts fail to give full faith and credit to custody decrees and deprive persons of rights to liberty and property without due process.[2] The Act also contains a list of six purposes, all of which are nearly identical to the purposes of the UCCJA, omitting three of the UCCJA's purposes.[3] Oddly enough these purposes do not include the implementation of the Full Faith and Credit Clause, but in general they amount to the avoidance of interstate conflicts in custody cases, the facilitation of the enforcement of

97. Section 12.2, supra, at note 13.

98. Joint Hearing Before the Subcommittee on Criminal Justice of the Committee on the Judiciary and the Subcommittee on Child and Human Development of the Committee on Labor and Human Resources, U.S. Senate, 96th Cong., 2d Sess. on S. 105 (1980), statement of Congressman Duncan, co-sponsor of the bill, at 19, 20, indicating a desire to keep federal interference in custody to a minimum. See also Coombs, Interstate Child Custody: Jurisdiction, Recognition, and Enforcement, 66 Minn.L. Rev. 711, 825 (1982).

99. Flood v. Braaten, 727 F.2d 303 (3d Cir.1984). This case presented in an extreme form the typical interstate conflict over custody, with North Dakota awarding custody to the father and New Jersey to the mother, neither court apparently paying any attention to either the UCCJA or the PKPA. Contempt decrees were outstanding against both parents, both of whom had engaged in abduction of the children. The court held that (a) the PKPA creates federal question jurisdiction in this sort of a case and (b) that the "domestic relations exception" does not apply to federal question jurisdiction. The court conceded that the legislative history of the PKPA showed that Congress intended custody cases to remain in the state courts. It held nevertheless that the federal courts could enforce compliance with the PKPA, presumably by injunction, although the opinion is notably silent as to

the appropriate remedy. The reason for this result seems to be that "* * * denying parents a district court forum for lawsuits claiming violation of rights under § 1738A would come close to a judicial repeal of those statutory rights." 727 F.2d at 312. The case is discussed in Note, 57 Univ. of Colo.L.Rev. 117 (1985). Similar results were reached in McDougald v. Jenson, 786 F.2d 1465 (11th Cir.1986); cert. denied ___ U.S. ___, 107 S.Ct. 207, 93 L.Ed.2d 137 (1986); Heartfield v. Heartfield, 749 F.2d 1138 (5th Cir.1985); DiRuggiero v. Rodgers, 743 F.2d 1009 (3d Cir.1984). See also Krauskopf, Remedies for Parental Kidnapping in Federal Court, 45 Ohio St.L.J. 429 (1984). A case decided before the PKPA and holding the federal court could not enforce a Swedish decree against a State Court is Schleiffer v. Meyers, 644 F.2d 656 (7th Cir.1981), cert. denied 454 U.S. 823, 102 S.Ct. 110, 70 L.Ed.2d 96 (1981).

1. The court in Flood v. Braaten, 727 F.2d 303, 312 n. 28 (3d Cir. 1984), raised this point but did not decide it.

2. 28 U.S.C.A. § 1738A, note.

3. Ibid. The UCCJA purposes which the PKPA omits are those referring to assuring that litigation occurs in the state where the child and his family have the closest connection; to the avoidance of relitigation of the decisions of other states; and to the accomplishment of uniformity in state laws.

custody decrees, and the deterrence of abduction.

The PKPA also requires that before a child custody determination is made, reasonable notice must be given to the contestants, to any parent whose parental rights have not been terminated, and any person who has physical custody of a child.[4] Unlike the UCCJA, the PKPA does not attempt to define what is meant by reasonable notice. Presumably the UCCJA definition of reasonable notice and the cases dealing with notice in custody determinations will be persuasive authority on the notice requirement of the PKPA.[5]

The PKPA contains no requirement of personal jurisdiction over defendants in custody cases.[6] This omission leaves the law of this Act in the same uncertainty which surrounds the UCCJA. The question is whether May v. Anderson[7] requires personal jurisdiction for interstate custody recognition and whether that case is to be followed in controversies arising under the PKPA.[8] Since the PKPA purports to define each state's duty to enforce the decrees of other states, it would seem that

the Act would be subject to May v. Anderson. This would mean that a state's custody decree would only be enforceable in other states if the defendant had sufficient "contacts" with the first state to meet constitutional requirements for personal jurisdiction, and if the first state had a long-arm statute applicable to custody cases.[9] But it is impossible to say at this point whether this is the law.

Since it is only concerned with interstate enforcement, the PKPA does not purport to establish rules for initial jurisdiction in custody cases.[10] It seems obvious, however, that all states will wish their decrees to have the protection of the rather strict enforcement requirements of the PKPA.[11] It follows that they will be guided by the conditions which that Act imposes for enforcement where those conditions differ from the UCCJA. But in order to be enforceable under the PKPA, a state's decree must also be based upon jurisdiction under its own law, which means, now that the UCCJA is in force in all states, under the UCCJA.[12] Thus for all practical purposes

---

4. 28 U.S.C.A. § 1738A(e).

5. Notice requirements of the common law and the UCCJA are discussed supra, at note 33.

6. There is the cryptic reference in Congress' findings to the result of interstate conflicts as including the deprivation of rights of liberty without due process of law. Perhaps this is an attack on ex parte custody decrees, but the fact remains that Congress did not include a requirement of personal jurisdiction as a condition on the enforcement of decrees. In view of the difficulty the states have had with this problem this seems a serious flaw in the Act.

7. 345 U.S. 528, 73 S.Ct. 840, 97 L.Ed. 1221 (1953).

8. These questions are discussed supra, at note 47. It is indicated in that discussion that the various state courts are sharply divided on the question whether May v. Anderson is still to be followed and on whether the rule of that case must be read into the UCCJA. See also the discussion at note 26, supra.

9. This seems to be the position taken in Coombs, Interstate Child Custody: Jurisdiction, Recognition, and Enforcement, 66 Minn.L.Rev. 711, 836–837 (1982). Ex parte Dean, 447 So.2d 733 (Ala. 1984), on remand 447 So. 2d 737 (1984) held that neither the UCCJA nor the PKPA has a long-arm provision, nor did a general long-arm statute apply, so a Florida decree was not entitled to enforcement.

10. The text statement must be qualified in one respect. The exercise of initial jurisdiction is limited by the PKPA when a proceeding is pending in the court of

another state. 28 U.S.C.A. § 1738A(g). This is similar to, but not identical with, the UCCJA § 6, discussed supra, at note 30. The PKPA provision is discussed infra, at note 27.

11. 28 U.S.C.A. § 1738A(a), the basic provision of PKPA, states: "The appropriate authorities of every State shall enforce according to its terms, and shall not modify except as provided in subsection (f) of this section, any child custody determination made consistently with the provisions of this section by a court of another State." "Child" is defined as a person under the age of eighteen. 28 U.S.C.A. § 1738A(b)(1). Apparently in those few states in which the age of majority is still twenty-one the PKPA would have no application to custody decrees respecting children between eighteen and twenty-one. "Custody determination" is defined as a judgment, decree or court order for the custody or visitation of a child, including temporary or permanent orders, and initial or modification orders. 28 U.S.C.A. § 1738A(b)(3). Presumably this includes judgments in dependency or neglect proceedings where they affect the custody of the children. See the discussion of the corresponding provision of UCCJA at note 73, supra, and E.E.B. v. D.A., 89 N.J. 595, 446 A.2d 871 (1982), holding that habeas corpus is included.

12. 28 U.S.C.A. § 1738A(c)(1) reads: "A child custody determination made by a court of a State is consistent with the provisions of this section only if—

(1) such court has jurisdiction under the law of such State; and * * *"

initial jurisdiction in custody cases must comply with both the PKPA and the UCCJA.

The conditions imposed by the PKPA for enforcement of custody decrees are, in addition to jurisdiction under state law, very similar to the jurisdictional requirements imposed by the UCCJA.[13] These include the "home state" requirement;[14] the "significant connection" requirement;[15] the abandonment-emergency requirement;[16] and the omnibus provision which confers jurisdiction when no other state would have it under the preceding subsections or when another state has declined to exercise jurisdiction.[17] In addition the PKPA confers jurisdiction on a ground not found in the UCCJA, namely, where the court has continuing jurisdiction pursuant to another subsection of PKPA.[18]

A major difference between the PKPA and the UCCJA lies in the relationship between the "home state" jurisdiction and the "significant connection" jurisdiction. Under the UCCJA these are alternatives, so that at one time two states could have jurisdiction, one pursuant to one subsection of the Act, the other pursuant to the other subsection.[19] Under the PKPA, however, there can only be "significant connection" jurisdiction if it appears that there would not be "home state"

jurisdiction in any other state.[20] One potential source of interstate conflict created by the UCCJA is thus removed. And in this difference between the two statutes, the PKPA must control.[21]

As has already been indicated,[22] the UCCJA contains three provisions authorizing courts to decline to exercise jurisdiction which they concededly have, on the grounds of simultaneous proceedings in other states,[23] inconvenient forum,[24] and unclean hands on the petitioner's part.[25] The PKPA includes only one of these provisions. In somewhat different form[26] it forbids a state to exercise jurisdiction in a case already pending in another state where the court of the other state is exercising jurisdiction consistently with the provisions of the PKPA.[27] The PKPA thus preserves the race to the courthouse in custody controversies. One case has held that another suit is not "pending" under the Act until a temporary or permanent decree is entered, and that the filing of a complaint in the case does not cause it to be "pending".[28] This is contrary to the usual meaning of "pending".[29] This construction also makes the result turn on such an adventitious circumstance as the relative congestion in the courts of the two states, and seems clearly

---

13. UCCJA § 3, discussed supra, at note 86.

14. 28 U.S.C.A. § 1738A(c)(2)(A). "Home state" is defined as in the UCCJA. 28 U.S.C.A. § 1738A(b)(4). Where the parents have joint custody, the child's home state is the state in which he spends the greater portion of his time. Patricia R. v. Andrew W., 121 Misc.2d 103, 467 N.Y.S.2d 322 (Fam.Ct.1983).

15. 28 U.S.C.A. § 1738A(c)(2)(B). Differences between this and the UCCJA "significant connection" provision are discussed infra, at note 19.

16. 28 U.S.C.A. § 1738A(c)(2)(C). This subsection is identical to the corresponding provision in UCCJA § 3(a)(3). Presumably the cases construing that section of the UCCJA, discussed supra, at note 8, would be persuasive in construing this section of the PKPA.

17. 28 U.S.C.A. § 1738A(c)(2)(D). This is identical to the corresponding section of the UCCJA. For an unusual application of this provision, see E.E.B. v. D.A., 89 N.J. 595, 446 A.2d 871 (1982), construing it to mean that a home state may defer jurisdiction to another state as the more appropriate forum.

18. 28 U.S.C.A. § 1738A(c)(2)(E). The subsection of the PKPA dealing with continuing jurisdiction is 28 U.S.C.A. § 1738A(d), which will be discussed infra, at note 42.

19. See the discussion of this point supra, at note 93.

20. Mitchell v. Mitchell, 437 So.2d 122 (Ala.Civ.App. 1982); Neger v. Neger, 93 N.J. 15, 459 A.2d 628 (1983) (child may have had no home state so California had significant connection jurisdiction where the child was shifted back and forth from California to New Jersey under a joint custody agreement); Mebert v. Mebert, 111 Misc.2d 500, 444 N.Y.S.2d 834 (Fam.Ct.1981); Voninski v. Voninski, 661 S.W.2d 872 (Tenn.App.1982).

21. Wachter v. Wachter, 439 So.2d 1260 (La.App. 1983).

22. See notes 80 and 29 (this page), supra.

23. UCCJA § 6, discussed at note 30, supra.

24. UCCJA § 7, discussed at note 47, supra.

25. UCCJA § 8, discussed at note 61, supra.

26. UCCJA § 6 contains detailed instructions for the exchange of information concerning the proceedings between the two states, all of which is omitted from the PKPA.

27. 28 U.S.C.A. § 1738A(g).

28. Peterson v. Peterson, 464 A.2d 202 (Me.1983).

29. Black's Law Dictionary 1291 (Rev.4th ed.1968). The UCCJA requirement of exchange of information suggests that that Act was intended to make the filing of the suit the point at which it became pending, since that

wrong. Notwithstanding the difference in language, the simultaneous proceedings provisions in the two statutes should be applied in the same way and with the same results.[30]

Neither the inconvenient forum provision nor the unclean hands provision[31] of the UCCJA is found in the PKPA. But since the two Acts contain largely the same list of statutory purposes, including the encouragement of cooperation between states to the end that custody decisions should be made in the state best able to make them, and the deterrence of interstate abductions, and since both the inconvenient forum provision and the unclean hands provision are conducive to the achievement of those purposes, it seems clear that both provisions would continue to be applicable pursuant to the UCCJA even though they are omitted from the PKPA.[32]

Other sections of the UCCJA are also omitted from the PKPA. Most of these deal with procedural matters creating no conflict with the PKPA and therefore presumably will continue to be operative notwithstanding their omission. The sections include provisions respecting information to be given to the court,[33] parties,[34] appearances by parties and others,[35] the res judicata effect of custody decrees,[36] procedure for the enforcement of out-of-state decrees,[37] maintenance of a registry of custody decrees,[38] and other provisions implementing interstate cooperation.[39]

The PKPA, due to its relationship to the Full Faith and Credit Clause,[40] contains no provision concerning the enforcement of the custody decrees of foreign countries. The UCCJA provision on this subject thus remains controlling for the state courts.[41]

Two important issues, the most important issues in custody litigation today, remain. They are a) the problem of continuing jurisdiction, and b) the question whether, under these two Acts, another state's decree must be enforced or whether it may be modified. Discussion of these two issues follows.

Continuing Jurisdiction

Traditionally all custody decrees were modifiable upon proof that a change in circumstances had occurred after the entry of the initial decree.[42] This is still true except that there has been a tendency for custody statutes to restrict the availability of modification. For example, the Uniform Marriage and Divorce Act forbids any modification for two years after the initial decree except where affidavits indicate that existing custody arrangements endanger the child's physical, mental, moral or emotional health.[43] Modifiability after the expiration of two years is also limited by the Act.[44] These restrictions on modification reflect the views of influential writers on custody who have emphasized continuity in the life of the child and finality in his custody.[45]

enables the two courts to determine whether either or both are proceeding in conformity with the two Acts.

30. This means that under both Acts the same complex series of steps must be undertaken by the later of the two courts to become involved. See the discussion at note 30, supra.

31. UCCJA §§ 7, 8.

32. Patricia R. v. Andrew W., 121 Misc.2d 103, 467 N.Y.S.2d 322 (Fam.Ct.1983) relied on UCCJA § 7 in a case under the PKPA. Any potential conflict between these provisions and the PKPA can easily be avoided by reliance on the qualifying language of the two sections, which is broad enough to cover most of the cases which are likely to arise.

33. UCCJA § 9.

34. UCCJA § 10.

35. UCCJA § 11.

36. UCCJA § 12. This is an important section for the achievement of finality in custody disputes.

Clark, Domestic Rel., 2nd Ed. HBSE—17

37. UCCJA § 15.

38. UCCJA § 16.

39. UCCJA §§ 17 to 22.

40. U.S.Const. art. IV, § 1.

41. UCCJA § 23.

42. People of State of New York ex rel. Halvey v. Halvey, 330 U.S. 610, 67 S.Ct. 903, 91 L.Ed. 1133 (1947); Kovacs v. Brewer, 356 U.S. 604, 78 S.Ct. 963, 2 L.Ed.2d 1008 (1958). See section 19.9, infra.

43. Uniform Marriage and Divorce Act § 409(a), 9A Unif.L.Ann. 211 (1979).

44. Uniform Marriage and Divorce Act § 409(b), 9A Unif.L.Ann. 211 (1979).

45. E.g., J. Goldstein, A. Freud, A. Solnit, Beyond the Best Interests of the Child 37 (1973): "As in adoption, a custody decree should be final, that is, not subject to modification". See also Watson, The Children of Arma-

Before the enactment of the UCCJA there was considerable confusion in the case law when the courts were faced with the problem whether their broad jurisdiction to modify custody decrees continued after one or more of the parties to the custody case moved out of the state. The traditional view was that jurisdiction over the person of the defendant, or over the subject-matter, once properly acquired in an action, is never lost until a final judgment is entered disposing of the litigation. Justice Holmes' famous dictum in Michigan Trust Co. v. Ferry [46] is the leading authority. But the custody cases did not conform to this pattern. Although it was held that once the court took jurisdiction over a custody case, the departure of the parties or the child from the state before the trial or before any decree did not oust the court from jurisdiction to decide the case,[47] some cases held that such a departure *after* the decree was entered deprived the court of jurisdiction to modify the decree.[48] About an equal number of cases held that the jurisdiction to modify persisted notwithstanding the removal of a parent and the child from the state.[49]

With advent of the UCCJA and the PKPA the analysis of the continuing jurisdiction problem has changed but the uncertainty and unpredictability of result in the case law has not been reduced. Although the problem was

recognized by all who dealt with interstate custody, for some unexplained reason it was not explicitly covered by the UCCJA. The crucial section of that Act is section 14 [50] which provides that the custody decree of another state shall not be modified unless 1) the court of the other state does not presently have jurisdiction substantially in accord with the Act or has declined to exercise jurisdiction to modify, and 2) the court of this state does have jurisdiction. The language of this section must of course be construed with the statutory purposes in mind, particularly those purposes related to the avoidance of the relitigation of custody disputes and to the elimination of continuing controversies over custody.[51] The Commissioners' Comments to section 14 assert that in order to achieve those purposes petitions for modification must be submitted to the state rendering the initial decree so long as that state meets the requirements for jurisdiction imposed by section 3 of the Act.[52] Unfortunately those requirements are often so difficult to apply to specific situations that the Commissioners' precepts are not helpful in most instances.

One type of case does seem clear under the UCCJA. When all parties, parents and child, have left the state in which the initial decree was entered, and have been away for an appreciable period, jurisdiction to modify the

---

geddon: Problems of Custody Following Divorce, 21 Syra. L.Rev. 55 (1969).

46. 228 U.S. 346, 353, 33 S.Ct. 550, 552, 57 L.Ed. 867 (1913).

47. Ex parte Butts, 129 Mont. 440, 289 P.2d 949 (1955); Onderdonk v. Onderdonk, 3 Wis.2d 279, 88 N.W.2d 323 (1958).

48. E.g., In re Hughes, 73 Ariz. 97, 237 P.2d 1009 (1951); Hodgen v. Byrne, 105 Colo. 410, 98 P.2d 1000 (1940); Dahlke v. Dahlke, 97 So.2d 16 (Fla.1957); Word v. Word, 236 Ga. 100, 222 S.E.2d 382 (1976); Niccum v. Lawrence, 186 Kan. 223, 350 P.2d 133 (1960); Marlar v. Howard, 312 Ky. 209, 226 S.W.2d 755 (1949); Odom v. Odom, 345 So.2d 1154 (La.1977); Application of Enke, 129 Mont. 353, 287 P.2d 19 (1955), cert. denied 350 U.S. 923, 76 S.Ct. 212, 100 L.Ed. 808 (1955); Heiney v. Heiney, 40 Ohio App.2d 571, 321 N.E.2d 611 (1973); Adams v. Miller, 253 S.C. 118, 169 S.E.2d 391 (1969).

49. E.g., Cox v. Cox, 457 F.2d 1190 (3d Cir.1972); Bergen v. Bergen, 439 F.2d 1008 (3d Cir.1971); Ferguson v. State, 251 Ala. 645, 38 So.2d 853 (1949); Forslund v. Forslund, 225 Cal.App.2d 476, 37 Cal.Rptr. 489 (1964); People ex rel. Koelsch v. Rone, 3 Ill.2d 483, 121 N.E.2d

738 (1954); Haney v. Knight, 197 Md. 212, 78 A.2d 643 (1951); Anonymous v. Anonymous, 62 Misc.2d 758, 309 N.Y.S.2d 966 (1970); Application of Lorenz, 194 Or. 355, 241 P.2d 142 (1952), rehearing denied 194 Or. 355, 242 P.2d 200 (1952); Plumb v. Plumb, 555 P.2d 1205 (Utah 1976).

50. UCCJA § 14 reads: "(a) If a court of another state has made a custody decree, a court of this State shall not modify that decree unless (1) it appears to the court of this State that the court which rendered the decree does not now have jurisdiction under jurisdictional prerequisites substantially in accordance with this Act or has declined to assume jurisdiction to modify the decree and (2) the court of this State has jurisdiction.

"(b) If a court of this State is authorized under subsection (a) and section 8 to modify a custody decree of another state it shall give due consideration to the transcript of the record and other documents of all previous proceedings submitted to it in accordance with section 22."

51. UCCJA § 1(a)(4) and (6).

52. UCCJA § 14, Commissioners' Comments, 9 Unif.L. Ann. 154 (1979).

decree no longer continues in the court of that state.[53] The PKPA does have a provision explicitly defining the extent of continuing jurisdiction, but it just refers to the local law of the state which entered the decree, which of course now means the UCCJA.[54] Thus under the PKPA definition of continuing jurisdiction that jurisdiction would also be lost when all parties leave the state. Conversely, where the custodial parent and the child remain in the state of the initial decree and the other parent leaves that state, it seems clear that the initial state, since it remains the child's home state, would continue to have jurisdiction to modify its own decree.[55]

The more troublesome cases occur when an initial decree awards custody to one parent after which she and the child go to another state and the question arises (which it may do in a variety of circumstances) whether the first state retains its jurisdiction to modify the decree. From the outset confusion respecting this type of case was generated by the proponents of the UCCJA. Professor Bodenheimer, principal draftsman of the UCCJA, quite early stated that the jurisdiction would continue in such a case, as long as the non-custodial parent lived in the first state, unless that parent failed to exercise his visitation rights.[56] The Commissioners' Comments to section 14 state that if the non-custodial parent removes the child from the state and keeps him away for more than six months, the first state's jurisdiction continues even though the second state has become the home state of the child.[57] But this does not tell us why this is so and whether the result would be different if the removal were by the custodial parent. PKPA creates further confusion. Section (d) of the Act [58] provides that jurisdiction continues so long as the UCCJA requirements are met and the state remains the residence of the child or of any contestant. But the PKPA's basic jurisdiction provision makes the home state, where one exists, the

---

53. Bakke v. District Court 4th Jud. Dist., 719 P.2d 313 (Colo.1986); McCarron v. District Court In and For Jefferson County, 671 P.2d 953 (Colo.1983); Bills v. Murdock, 232 Kan. 237, 654 P.2d 406 (1982); McGee v. McGee, 651 S.W.2d 891 (Tex.App.1983). See also UCCJA § 14, Commissioners' Comments, 9 Unif.L.Ann. 154 (1979): "If, however, all persons involved have moved away or the contact with the state has otherwise become slight, modification jurisdiction would shift elsewhere."

54. 28 U.S.C.A. § 1738A(d) reads as follows: "(d) The jurisdiction of a court of a State which has made a child custody determination consistently with the provisions of this section continues as long as the requirement of subsection (c)(1) of this section continues to be met and such State remains the residence of the child or of any contestant." Subsection (c)(1) of the section provides: "(c) A child custody determination made by a court of a State is consistent with the provisions of this section only if— (1) such court has jurisdiction under the law of such State;".

The modification provision of PKPA is similar to that of the UCCJA. 28 U.S.C.A. § 1738A(f) reads as follows: "(f) A court of a State may modify a determination of the custody of the same child made by a court of another State, if—

(1) it has jurisdiction to make such a child custody determination; and

(2) the court of the other State no longer has jurisdiction, or it has declined to exercise such jurisdiction to modify such determination."

55. In re LeMond, 182 Ind.App. 626, 395 N.E.2d 1287 (1979).

56. Bodenheimer, The Uniform Child Custody Jurisdiction Act: A Legislative Remedy for Children Caught in the Conflict of Laws, 22 Vand.L.Rev. 1207, 1237 (1969). The case put is one in which there is a divorce in state A with custody to the wife, visitation to the husband. The wife and children move to state B, with or without the A court's permission. The author states that state A has continuing and exclusive jurisdiction and that state B may not hear the wife's petition for modification. It is not clear why this result is affected by the husband's failure to exercise his rights of visitation. The same view is stated in Bodenheimer, Interstate Custody: Initial Jurisdiction and Continuing Jurisdiction Under UCCJA, 14 Fam.L.Q. 203, 214 (1984). Professor Bodenheimer's view is rejected in Leslie L.F. v. Constance F., 110 Misc.2d 86, 441 N.Y.S.2d 911 (Fam.Ct.1981).

57. UCCJA § 14, Commissioners' Comments, 9 Unif.L. Ann. 154 (1979). The Comments do not state that the first state has exclusive jurisdiction, as Professor Bodenheimer does, but only that it has "preferred" jurisdiction, whatever that may mean. The Comments also state that if the father allowed the mother to keep the children in the second state for several years in violation of the decree, without asserting his rights or visiting the children, the first state would lose its jurisdiction. Reasons for this view are not given.

58. This section is quoted in full in note 54, supra. "Residence" as used in this subsection has been given the doubtful construction of "domicile" by McDougald v. Jenson, 786 F.2d 1465 (11th Cir. 1986), cert. denied ___ U.S. ___, 107 S.Ct. 207, 93 L.Ed.2d 137 (1986), rehearing denied ___ U.S. ___, 107 S.Ct. 614, 93 L.Ed.2d 611 (1986).

exclusive basis for jurisdiction,[59] leading one to think that if the child's home state changes, the first state would lose jurisdiction.[60]

When one looks at the case law, one finds, not surprisingly in view of the complexity and vagueness of the two Acts, that the courts are not in agreement. Cases relying solely on the UCCJA have held that when the custodial parent and child move out of the state, jurisdiction to determine custody persists in that state, as Professor Bodenheimer asserted.[61]

The basis for this often is that it best effectuates the Act's purpose of preventing re-litigation of custody cases.[62] Courts taking this view may also rest the decision on the view that the initial state, even though no longer the child's home state, is still a state with which the child and one contestant have a significant connection.[63] In some circumstances the effect of such a decision may be the exact opposite of stability for the child and may be detrimental to his welfare.[64] On the other hand there is a substantial number

59. 28 U.S.C.A. § 1738A(c)(2)(A) and (B). The home state jurisdiction is exclusive of the significant connection jurisdiction, but not of the abandonment-emergency jurisdiction, or of the omnibus jurisdiction based on the absence of jurisdiction elsewhere, or, apparently, of the continuing jurisdiction under 28 U.S.C.A. § 1738A(d).

60. Since the PKPA seems to make continuing jurisdiction an exception to the exclusive nature of home state jurisdiction, this apparent inconsistency is resolved. What this means is that if there is continuing jurisdiction under UCCJA, even though not based upon the state's being the child's home state, then there is continuing jurisdiction under PKPA. See 28 U.S.C.A. § 1738A(c)(2) (E) and (d).

Boyd v. Boyd, 653 S.W.2d 732 (Tenn.App.1983) takes this view of the PKPA, at least in part, although the opinion also expresses a preference for home state jurisdiction.

61. Palm v. Superior Court of San Diego County, 97 Cal.App.3d 456, 158 Cal.Rptr. 786 (1979) (jurisdiction in North Dakota continued although mother and child had been in California for several years); Smith v. Superior Court of San Mateo County, 68 Cal.App.3d 457, 137 Cal. Rptr. 348 (1977) (California court had continuing jurisdiction although the mother and child had lived in Oregon five years); Kraft v. District Court In and For City and County of Denver, 197 Colo. 10, 593 P.2d 321 (1979); Reeve v. Reeve, 391 So.2d 789 (Fla.App.1980) (Florida retains jurisdiction notwithstanding that the husband and child had lived in New Jersey for five years); Hofer v. Agner, 373 So.2d 48 (Fla.App.1979); Biggers v. Biggers, 103 Idaho 550, 650 P.2d 692 (1982); In re Marriage of Mintle, 294 N.W.2d 564 (Iowa 1980) (Colorado retained jurisdiction even though husband and child had lived in Iowa more than two years); Lustig v. Lustig, 99 Mich. App. 716, 299 N.W.2d 375 (1980); Hricko v. Stewart, 99 Misc.2d 266, 415 N.Y.S.2d 747 (Fam.Ct.1979).

Many cases do not follow the pattern posed in the text, of a custodian and child who move to a second state. For example in Connolly v. Connolly, —— Mont. ——, 680 P.2d 568 (1984) a Montana decree gave custody of two children to the husband and the other two children to the wife, who lived in Wyoming. The court held that Montana had continuing jurisdiction with respect to the custody of all four children. An even more confusing case is Matter of Marriage of Fenn, 63 Or.App. 506, 664 P.2d 1143 (1983). The initial decree in Oregon gave the parents joint custody, pursuant to which the child spent alternate

months in Oregon and California until the mother took her to Texas without the father's knowledge or consent. The mother sought modification in Texas and ultimately got custody. During the pendency of the Texas proceeding the father sought custody in Oregon. During the pendency of both proceedings the father took the child from school in Texas and brought her to Oregon and the mother twice snatched the child from Oregon, the second time disappearing entirely. The Oregon court held that since Oregon had continuing jurisdiction the Texas decree had not been entered substantially in conformity with UCCJA, and therefore did not affect Oregon's continuing jurisdiction.

62. E.g., Kraft v. District Court In and For City and County of Denver, 197 Colo. 10, 593 P.2d 321 (1979); Biggers v. Biggers, 103 Idaho 550, 650 P.2d 692 (1982). Some courts also rest their decision on the policy of choosing the forum having the best access to the evidence. Smith v. Superior Court of San Mateo County, 68 Cal.App.3d 457, 137 Cal.Rptr. 348 (1977).

63. E.g., Larsen v. Larsen, 5 Kan.App.2d 284, 615 P.2d 806 (1980); Lustig v. Lustig, 99 Mich.App. 716, 299 N.W.2d 375 (1980); Matter of Custody of Ross, 291 Or. 263, 630 P.2d 353 (1981). The facts of the Ross case are stated supra, at note 3.

64. Consideration of this possibility led the court to find that the state of initial decree no longer had jurisdiction in the case of Matter of Marriage of Settle, 276 Or. 759, 556 P.2d 962 (1976), the opinion containing the often quoted sentence: "A close reading of the Act discloses a schizophrenic attempt to bring about an orderly system of decision and at the same time to protect the best interests of the children who may be immediately before the court." The case was overruled by Matter of Custody of Ross, 291 Or. 263, 630 P.2d 353 (1981), in which the court seems to have considered the deterrence of abduction a more important policy than protecting the child's interests. See also Clarke v. Clarke, 126 N.H. 753, 496 A.2d 361 (1985). Cf. In re Custody of Dunn, 701 P.2d 158 (Colo.App.1985).

Where these policies conflict, some courts have tried to achieve a compromise, either by holding that jurisdiction continues but will not be exercised, or by staying the exercise of jurisdiction until the court of another state exercises its jurisdiction. In re Marriage of Kern, 87 Cal. App.3d 402, 150 Cal.Rptr. 860 (1978); Fry v. Ball, 190 Colo. 128, 544 P.2d 402 (1975); Moore v. Moore, 24 Or. App. 673, 546 P.2d 1104 (1976).

of cases which hold that the state of the initial decree loses jurisdiction when the child and one parent move to another state.[65] Concern for the child's welfare,[66] insistence on hearing the case in the most convenient forum,[67] and the unclean hands doctrine [68] are all factors which may play a part in such decisions.

The cases decided since the enactment of PKPA exhibit the same ambivalence on the question whether jurisdiction continues after the custodian and the child leave the state. If anything, the injection of the PKPA into the continuing jurisdiction issue has amplified the confusion already evident under the UCCJA.[69] The cases holding that the jurisdiction continues generally are based upon a technical reading of the PKPA.[70] The cases holding that the initial jurisdiction did not continue follow the same pattern,[71] although there is sometimes a tendency to make continuing jurisdiction turn on the continuance of the state as the child's home state,[72] a position which, as has already been stated,[73] is not supported by the language of the PKPA.

This discussion has demonstrated that continuing jurisdiction, which is often a crucial issue when a party seeks modification of a custody decree, involves a complex interaction between the PKPA and the UCCJA. The confusion in the case law as to whether, in a specific instance, jurisdiction does or does not continue is caused by a) failure to read the PKPA closely, and b) by the alternative bases for jurisdiction authorized by the UCCJA. As long as both of these conditions exist the confusion and uncertainty are likely to persist.

Enforcement or Modification: Which Alternative?

In the preceding pages an attempt is made to explore in detail the individual requirements for custody jurisdiction as they have been imposed by the Supreme Court, the state legislatures and the Congress. The ultimate purpose of all such requirements is to guide the courts in determining when they must enforce and when they may modify the custody decrees of other states. In a specific case enforcement and modification are normally mutually exclusive alternatives. In the discussion which follows the provisions of the PKPA and the UCCJA are applied to the facts of particular cases in order to determine

65. Templeton v. Witham, 595 F.Supp. 770 (S.D.Cal. 1984), order vacated 805 F.2d 1039 (9th Cir. 1986) (jurisdiction did not continue because the California court did not comply with the Interstate Compact, so that jurisdiction was lost under California's own law); Kioukis v. Kioukis, 185 Conn. 249, 440 A.2d 894 (1981); Hegler v. Hegler, 383 So.2d 1134 (Fla.App.1980); Matteson v. Matteson, 379 So.2d 677 (Fla.App.1980); Siegel v. Siegel, 84 Ill.2d 212, 49 Ill.Dec. 298, 417 N.E.2d 1312 (1981); Slidell v. Valentine, 298 N.W.2d 599 (Iowa 1980); Moore v. Moore, 379 So.2d 1153 (La.App.1980); Mace v. Mace, 215 Neb. 640, 341 N.W.2d 307 (1983); In re Reynolds, 2 Ohio App.2d 309, 441 N.E.2d 1141 (1982); Boyd v. Boyd, 653 S.W.2d 732 (Tenn.App.1983).

66. Slidell v. Valentine, 298 N.W.2d 599 (Iowa 1980).

67. Siegel v. Siegel, 84 Ill.2d 212, 49 Ill.Dec. 298, 417 N.E.2d 1312 (1981).

68. Matter of Custody of Ross, 291 Or. 263, 630 P.2d 353 (1981). But the unclean hands doctrine may not be followed if it runs counter to the child's best interests. Slidell v. Valentine, 298 N.W.2d 599 (Iowa 1980).

69. E.g., Patricia R. v. Andrew W., 121 Misc.2d 103, 467 N.Y.S.2d 322 (Fam.Ct.1983); Quenzer v. Quenzer, 653 P.2d 295 (Wyo.1982), cert. denied 460 U.S. 1041, 103 S.Ct. 1436, 75 L.Ed.2d 794 (1983).

70. Flannery v. Stephenson, 416 So.2d 1034 (Ala.Civ. App.1982); Kumar v. Superior Court of Santa Clara

County, 32 Cal.3d 689, 186 Cal.Rptr. 772, 652 P.2d 1003 (1982); Belosky v. Belosky, 97 N.M. 365, 640 P.2d 471 (1982); State ex rel. Valles v. Brown, 97 N.M. 327, 639 P.2d 1181 (1981); S. Frederick P. v. Barbara P., 115 Misc. 2d 332, 454 N.Y.S.2d 202 (Fam.Ct.1982); Bahr v. Bahr, 108 Misc.2d 920, 442 N.Y.S.2d 687 (Fam.Ct.1981), affirmed p.c. 91 A.D.2d 1010, 458 N.Y.S.2d 247 (2d Dep't 1983); State ex rel. Cooper v. Hamilton, 688 S.W.2d 821 (Tenn. 1985).

71. Patricia R. v. Andrew W., 121 Misc.2d 103, 467 N.Y.S.2d 322 (Fam.Ct.1983); Leslie L.F. v. Constance F., 110 Misc.2d 86, 441 N.Y.S.2d 911 (Fam.Ct.1981); Voninski v. Voninski, 661 S.W.2d 872 (Tenn.App.1982).

72. Quenzer v. Quenzer, 653 P.2d 295 (Wyo.1982), cert. denied 460 U.S. 1041, 103 S.Ct. 1436, 75 L.Ed.2d 794 (1983) held that a Texas decree modifying an earlier Texas decree was not based upon continuing jurisdiction because Texas was no longer the home state at the time of the modification. Pierce v. Pierce, 197 Mont. 16, 640 P.2d 899 (1982) remanded the case for a finding on whether at the bringing of the Montana proceeding Kentucky was still the residence of the child, apparently on the theory that this is the basis for continuing jurisdiction under the PKPA.

73. See the discussion at note 54, supra.

whether a state must enforce or may modify the custody decree of another state. In this process we must remember that the purpose sections of both statutes [74] indicate a bias in favor of enforcement and against modification.

A court which is asked by one parent to enforce and by the other to modify another state's decree must, under the PKPA and the UCCJA, go through the following analytical steps:

(a) The court must enforce the other state's decree if it was made consistently with the PKPA, except that it may modify that decree as provided in subsection (f) of PKPA.[75] This means that if the first state's decree did not rest on jurisdictional bases outlined in the PKPA [76] or was entered without reasonable notice and an opportunity to be heard,[77] or was entered during the pendency of another proceeding in a court acting pursuant to the PKPA,[78] then the second state need not enforce it. Whether, if the first decree was not based upon in personam jurisdiction as required by May v. Anderson,[79] it may not be enforced, the PKPA does not tell us and the cases reach contradictory conclusions.[80] It is also somewhat unclear whether, if the first court's decree were objectionable under the unclean hands or inconvenient forum provisions of the UCCJA, the second court would be permitted to deny enforcement.[81] Presumably if any of these issues were actually litigated in the earlier proceeding, or if both parties had been before the court so that they could have been litigated, the principles of res

judicata would not permit them to be raised in the second state's court.[82]

(b) If the jurisdictional obstacles just outlined are found to have been surmounted by the court of the first state, its decree is then entitled to enforcement *unless* the PKPA permits it to be modified. The court of the second state must then turn its attention to the modification provision of the Act.

(c) The PKPA permits another state's decree to be modified if i. the court in which modification is sought has jurisdiction to make a child custody determination; and ii. the court of the first state no longer has jurisdiction or has declined to exercise jurisdiction to modify its decree.[83] The court in which modification is sought must therefore determine whether it has jurisdiction under both the PKPA and the UCCJA; whether any other court has a proceeding pending for modification; whether it is an inconvenient forum; whether the party seeking modification has unclean hands; and perhaps, whether it has in personam jurisdiction over the defendant.[84]

(d) If the court of the second state decides that it has jurisdiction, having passed all of the tests just mentioned, it must then determine whether the court of the first state still has jurisdiction in the case. This of course entails a consideration of the continuing jurisdiction issue which has already been dicussed at length.[85] If there is not continuing jurisdiction in the first state, this court may then decide whether or not the decree should be

---

74. 28 U.S.C.A. § 1738A, note; UCCJA § 1, discussed, supra, at notes 71 and 3.

75. 28 U.S.C.A. § 1738A(a) reads: "(a) The appropriate authorities of every State shall enforce according to its terms, and shall not modify except as provided in subsection (f) of this section, any child custody determination made consistently with the provisions of this section by a court of another State."

76. 28 U.S.C.A. § 1738A(c), discussed, supra, at note 13. It is important to notice that in order to comply with the jurisdictional requirements of the PKPA the first state's decree must also comply with the UCCJA. 28 U.S.C.A. § 1738A(c)(1).

77. 28 U.S.C.A. § 1738A(e).

78. 28 U.S.C.A. § 1738A(g).

79. 345 U.S. 528, 73 S.Ct. 840, 97 L.Ed. 1221 (1953).

80. Ex parte Dean, 447 So.2d 733 (Ala.1984), on remand 447 So.2d 737 (1984), a case purporting to follow the PKPA, held that a Florida decree was not entitled to full faith and credit in Alabama where the Florida court had not obtained in personam jurisdiction over the defendant. But see Salisbury v. Salisbury, 657 S.W.2d 761 (Tenn.App.1983). These and other cases are discussed supra, at notes 47 and 6.

81. See the discussion at note 31, supra.

82. See the discussion at note 82, supra.

83. 28 U.S.C.A. § 1738A(f). This subsection is quoted in note 54, supra.

84. These are generally the same questions respecting its own jurisdiction which it must consider in relation to the first court's jurisdiction. See notes 75 to 81, supra.

85. See the discussion at note 42, supra.

modified. Even if there is continuing jurisdiction in the first court, that court may decline to exercise jurisdiction, in which event the second court may proceed to consider the merits of modification. Where the first court's jurisdiction continues, the UCCJA contemplates some communication between the two courts [86] which may result in the first court's declining to act so as to permit the second court to exercise its jurisdiction. Presumably the PKPA does not foreclose this sort of interstate cooperation, although it contains no provision authorizing it.

The analysis of modification procedure is based upon the PKPA since that Act, under the Supremacy Clause,[87] controls the effect to be given to the custody decrees of other states. The UCCJA also contains enforcement and modification provisions. Now that all states have the UCCJA, the enforcement provision is not very different from that in the PKPA.[88] The modification provision is nearly identical to that of the PKPA.[89] Therefore the analytical approach to modification and enforcement under the UCCJA would be substantially like that just outlined.

Professor Bodenheimer has argued that there is an exception to the enforcement requirement of the UCCJA where the decree for which enforcement is sought was entered to punish one of the parents, usually for the offense of leaving the state with the child in violation of the original decree.[90] In her view such "punitive" decrees should not be enforced, even though no such exception to the enforcement provisions exists in either the UCCJA or the PKPA. The Commissioners' Comments to the UCCJA appear to recognize such an exception in a cryptic fashion.[91] There is little authority in support of such an exception.[92] In view of the difficulty of determining whether a particular decree is punitive and of the complete absence of any such exception from the PKPA it seems very doubtful that such an exception will be recognized.[93] There is the additional factor that the unclean hands provision of the UCCJA sanctions the denial of modification as a way of punishing a parent who has removed the child from the state in violation of a court order. Permitting this to be done amounts to approval of the use of a kind of punitive decree. It is therefore inconsistent with the creation of an extra-statutory exception to enforcement of punitive decrees.

It may be helpful to apply the suggested analytical steps to some actual and some hypothetical cases. This is done in the following pages with the caveat, however, that others may reach conclusions different from those

---

86. UCCJA §§ 6, 7.

87. U.S.Const. art. VI. The controlling effect of the PKPA is discussed supra, at note 93.

88. Enforcement is required by UCCJA § 13, as follows: "The courts of this State shall recognize and enforce an initial or modification decree of a court of another state which had assumed jurisdiction under statutory provisions substantially in accordance with this Act * * *"

89. UCCJA § 14(a) "If a court of another state has made a custody decree, a court of this State shall not modify that decree unless (1) it appears to the court of this State that the court which rendered the decree does not now have jurisdiction under jurisdictional prerequisites substantially in accordance with this Act or has declined to assume jurisdiction to modify the decree and (2) the court of this State has jurisdiction. Cf. 28 U.S. C.A. § 1738A(f).

90. Bodenheimer, Progress Under the Uniform Child Custody Jurisdiction Act and Remaining Problems: Punitive Decrees, Joint Custody, and Excessive Modifications, 65 Cal.L.Rev. 978, 1006 (1977).

91. UCCJA § 13, Commissioners' Comments, 9 Unif.L. Ann. 152 (1979): "The mandate of this section could

cause problems if the prior decree is a punitive or disciplinary measure. See Ehrenzweig, Inter-state Recognition of Custody Decrees, 51 Mich.L.Rev. 345, 370 (1953)."

92. Brooks v. Brooks, 20 Or.App. 43, 530 P.2d 547 (1975). Matter of Marriage of Settle, 276 Or. 759, 556 P.2d 962 (1976) seems to approve of the result in Brooks, but the case has been overruled by Matter of Custody of Ross, 291 Or. 263, 630 P.2d 353 (1981). See also In re B. R. F., 669 S.W.2d 240 (Mo.App.1984). Arbogast v. Arbogast, ___ W.Va. ___, 327 S.E.2d 675 (1984) denies that there is such an exception.

93. For example, the Oregon Court of Appeals found the Indiana decree punitive, but the Oregon Supreme Court found no evidence of this in Matter of Marriage of Settle, 276 Or. 759, 556 P.2d 962 (1976). It is a truism of the custody cases that custody should not be awarded as a way of punishing a parent. See section 19.4, infra. It will rarely be the case therefore that a judgment will reveal either expressly or impliedly that the basis for the award was punitive. Spaulding v. Spaulding, 460 A.2d 1360 (Me.1983) contains dictum that a punitive decree should not be enforced, but finds the decree not punitive, in the face of language in the decree to the effect that the "acts of Jon M. Spaulding are reprehensible and in willful disobedience to the Orders of this Court * * *"

suggested here, particularly since there is little agreement in the case law dealing with problems of this kind.

Case 1: We begin with an easy example. Husband and wife lived in Ohio with their two-year-old daughter. In 1973 they were divorced there, the husband being awarded custody of the child. The wife moved to Iowa. In 1974 the wife removed the child to Iowa without authority, but an Iowa court ordered the child returned to the husband. The husband remarried and in 1974 moved to Indiana, where he, his second wife, and the daughter lived until 1979. In 1979 discord arose in his second marriage and the husband took the child to Iowa and left her with her mother. The evidence was in conflict as to what was said and what was intended to be the arrangement when the child was left in Iowa. Three weeks later the child's mother filed a petition in Iowa seeking custody and the modification of the Ohio decree. The father challenged Iowa's jurisdiction. Pending the suit the father and his second wife were reconciled. The Iowa trial court held that it had jurisdiction and gave custody to the child's mother. The Supreme Court of Iowa reversed, holding Iowa did not have jurisdiction under the UCCJA.[94] It found that Ohio had lost jurisdiction because none of the parties had lived there for five years. It also found that Iowa was not the home state, it was not a state having a significant connection with the child and a parent, the child had not been abandoned but only temporarily placed in Iowa, and therefore that Iowa had no jurisdiction under any provision of the UCCJA. The home state of the child was held to be Indiana. This result seems clearly correct and undoubtedly would also be reached under the PKPA, which was not in force when this case was decided. Unfortu-

nately, however, very few reported cases can be found which are as easily decided as this one.

Case 2: The analytical steps involved in determining the availability of modification as outlined above do not include any reference to the ubiquitous May v. Anderson[95] issue, but that issue must always be kept in mind, as the present case illustrates. The case is Eicke v. Eicke,[96] which many lawyers hoped (in vain as it turned out) would produce some clarification from the United States Supreme Court. The parties in this case were married in Alaska and then moved to Texas where two children were born. In 1978 and 1979 they lived in Louisiana for about four months, in April, 1979 moving back to Texas. On August 9, 1979 the mother left the father and moved back to Louisiana with the children. She continued to live there during the remainder of the custody controversy. On October 26, 1979, she sued in Louisiana for a separation and for custody of the children. It is not clear from the opinion whether or how the father was served, but an attorney was appointed to represent him. He apparently did not appear or participate in this proceeding. On December 14, 1979 the Louisiana court entered a decree giving custody to the mother. On June 18, 1980 the father obtained a decree in Texas giving him custody of the children.[97] The mother was served with notice of the Texas proceeding but did not appear or participate in it. The father then brought in Louisiana the suit which became the Eicke case, on July 17, 1980, seeking recognition and enforcement of the Texas decree. The Louisiana trial court refused to enforce the Texas decree and the Court of Appeal affirmed, on the ground that the father's action in obtaining that decree resulted in the sort of conflict which the UCCJA was

94. St.Clair v. Faulkner, 305 N.W.2d 441 (Iowa 1981). A case which likewise holds that the jurisdiction of the state granting the earlier custody decree ended when both spouses moved away from that state is Ex parte Blanton, 463 So.2d 162 (Ala.1985).

95. 345 U.S. 528, 73 S.Ct. 840, 97 L.Ed. 1221 (1953), discussed at length supra, at note 47.

96. 399 So.2d 1231 (La.App.1981), cert. denied with the statement, "The result is correct.", 406 So.2d 607 (La.

1981), cert. granted 456 U.S. 970, 102 S.Ct. 2232, 72 L.Ed. 2d 843 (1982), cert. dismissed as improvidently granted 459 U.S. 1139, 103 S.Ct. 776, 74 L.Ed.2d 987 (1983).

97. The opinion states this date to be June 18, 1960, but this is an obvious typographical error. The father apparently brought this suit in April of 1980. See Coombs, Custody Conflicts in the Courts: Judicial Resolution of the Old and New Questions Raised by Interstate Child Custody Cases, 16 Fam.L.Q. 251, 253 (1982).

designed to prevent. The PKPA was not in force and therefore not discussed in the opinion.

The Louisiana court did not cite May v. Anderson either, and of course the application of that case turns on whether it is still to be regarded as requiring in personam jurisdiction for the recognition of custody decrees. If it is not,[98] then nothing further need be said about it. If it is, that raises the question whether either the first Louisiana case or the Texas case was based on personal jurisdiction over the defendant. There were some "contacts" with Louisiana which could be the basis for such jurisdiction, since the parties had recently lived for four months in the state. Whether that would be enough under the Kulko rationale[99] is an open question. It is, however, clear that Texas had sufficient "contacts" to meet constitutional requirements for personal jurisdiction, since the parties had lived there for some time and the children were born there. And the Texas long-arm statute[1] would seem to cover this situation. This being so, the traditional analysis is that the Texas decree must be given full faith and credit in Louisiana, except that if that decree is not final, Louisiana could modify it to the same extent as Texas could have.[2] It could also be argued that if the mother were personally subject to the Texas court's jurisdiction, as she seems to have been, she had an opportunity to litigate the Texas court's jurisdiction, and not having done so, she is barred from further questioning that jurisdiction under the usual rules of res judicata as applied by the United States Supreme Court.[3]

If the Eicke case is analyzed in accordance with the PKPA, the first question is whether there was jurisdiction in the first Louisiana proceeding. Since the mother and children had been in the state less than three months when she filed her petition, Louisiana was not the home state under that Act. Texas could have been the home state when the Louisiana petition was filed, but only if the stay in Louisiana in early 1979 could be considered temporary.[4] If Texas were the home state at that time, Louisiana had no jurisdiction under PKPA and Texas would not have been required by PKPA to recognize the Louisiana decree. And Louisiana would be required to enforce the Texas decree.[5]

---

98. See the discussion at note 47, supra. Texas seems to have declined to follow May v. Anderson. See Perry v. Ponder, 604 S.W.2d 306 (Tex.Civ.App.1980).

99. Kulko v. Superior Court of California In and For the City and County of San Francisco, 436 U.S. 84, 98 S.Ct. 1690, 56 L.Ed.2d 132 (1978), rehearing denied 438 U.S. 908, 98 S.Ct. 3127, 57 L.Ed.2d 1150 (1978), discussed supra, section 12.4.

1. V.Tex.C.A., Fam.Code § 3.26 (Supp.1984), authorizing jurisdiction over nonresidents in all cases permitted by the United States Constitution.

2. Some Supreme Court cases have held that modifiable custody decrees may be modified by the courts in other states without violating the Full Faith and Credit Clause. E.g., Kovacs v. Brewer, 356 U.S. 604, 78 S.Ct. 963, 2 L.Ed.2d 1008 (1958); People of State of New York ex rel. Halvey v. Halvey, 330 U.S. 610, 67 S.Ct. 903, 91 L.Ed. 1133 (1947).

Whether the Texas decree was modifiable is of course a question now of continuing jurisdiction under the PKPA, which makes the question turn on the local law of Texas, which is now the Texas version of the UCCJA. See V.Tex.C.A., Fam.Code § 11.53 (Supp.1984).

3. Sherrer v. Sherrer, 334 U.S. 343, 68 S.Ct. 1087, 92 L.Ed. 1429 (1948); Johnson v. Muelberger, 340 U.S. 581, 71 S.Ct. 474, 95 L.Ed. 552 (1951); Cook v. Cook, 342 U.S. 126, 72 S.Ct. 157, 96 L.Ed. 146 (1951); Restatement (Second) of Conflict of Laws § 73 (1971). See also Sutton v. Leib, 342 U.S. 402, 72 S.Ct. 398, 96 L.Ed. 448 (1952), rehearing denied 343 U.S. 921, 72 S.Ct. 674, 96 L.Ed. 1334 (1952) and Southard v. Southard, 305 F.2d 730 (2d Cir. 1962). Contra: Colby v. Colby, 78 Nev. 150, 369 P.2d 1019 (1962), cert. denied 371 U.S. 888, 83 S.Ct. 186, 9 L.Ed.2d 122 (1962).

4. If the earlier Louisiana stay had been temporary, it could have been included as part of the six-month home state period, under 28 U.S.C.A. § 1738A(b)(4). If not temporary, then the children lived in Texas only from April, 1979 to August 9, 1979, when the mother took them to Louisiana, a period of less than six months.

5. Under the PKPA if there is a home state, there cannot be jurisdiction based on a significant connection. 28 U.S.C.A. § 1738A(c)(2)(A) and (B), discussed supra, at note 19. Thus if Texas were the home state, Louisiana could not rest its decree on significant connection jurisdiction and no other subsection of the PKPA would be available as a basis for jurisdiction.

Under the UCCJA the father would have been required to inform the Texas court of the Louisiana proceeding, if he had known about it. UCCJA § 9. But even if the Texas court had been informed of the Louisiana proceeding, it would not have been required to decline to exercise jurisdiction if the Louisiana proceeding was not based on jurisdiction consistent with the provisions of the PKPA. 28 U.S.C.A. § 1738A(g).

On the other hand, if Texas were not the home state, then Louisiana could have had jurisdiction by virtue of its significant connection with the children and their mother.[6] That being so, Texas would be required to enforce the Louisiana decree and not to modify it so long as Louisiana's jurisdiction continued and so long as Louisiana had not declined jurisdiction.[7] Texas' attempt at modification, assuming the foregoing analysis is correct, would in turn be without jurisdiction.[8] Therefore the Texas decree would not be entitled to enforcement in the Eicke case and the result of that case would be correct.[9]

The foregoing analysis omits any mention of the unclean hands provision of the UCCJA [10] although conceivably that might have been invoked against the mother in the first Louisiana proceeding since she may have removed the children from Texas "wrongfully". But the UCCJA is so uncertain in this respect that any reference to this section here would be speculative.

One cannot help but be struck by two aspects of this account of Eicke. The first is the intricacy of the analysis.[11] The second is that after four years of litigation in several courts there had not been a single proceeding participated in by both parents authoritatively determining what would best serve the children's interests. The obvious question this raises is, did the intricacy of the analysis contribute to the futility of the litigation?

Case 3: This example presents the familiar issue of continuing jurisdiction in a setting of numerous interstate moves and attempts at relitigation. The case is Quenzer v. Quenzer.[12] In 1975 the parties were divorced in Texas where they lived, the decree giving custody to the mother with rights of visitation to the father. Shortly thereafter the mother left Texas with the daughter, as a result of which the father's visitation rights were often frustrated, particularly since in some periods he was unable to locate mother and daughter. After one visit to Texas he refused to return the child and the mother succeeded in persuading a Texas court to order the return of the child to her. At some point before 1977 mother and child moved to Oregon. The father remained a resident of Texas at all relevant times. In August of 1977 the father sought enforcement of his visitation rights from an Oregon court, the mother asked other relief and the case was expanded by the father's additional motion for a modification giving him custody. The Oregon court entered a decree containing provisions respecting support, the details of visitation and held both parents in contempt, but retained custo-

Enforcement by Louisiana of the Texas decree, assuming the Texas decree was based upon jurisdiction, seems to be required by 28 U.S.C.A. § 1738A(a); (f)(2); (d).

6. If Texas were not the home state, Louisiana was also not the home state. In the absence of a home state, the PKPA permits jurisdiction to be based upon a significant connection between the child and the state. 28 U.S.C.A § 1738A(c)(2)(B). Presumably Louisiana could be said to have such a significant connection, although under the PKPA if there is no home state, more than one state might have a significant connection with the child or, as in this case, there might be a question whether one or the other has such a connection. See Matter of Custody of Ross, 291 Or. 263, 630 P.2d 353 (1981), decided under the UCCJA. In such circumstances the two courts might exchange information in order to determine which of them is the more convenient forum. See UCCJA § 7. The Texas version of this section is V.Tex.C.A., Fam.Code § 11.56 (Supp.1984).

7. 28 U.S.C.A. § 1738A(a), (f). Presumably if Louisiana had jurisdiction initially, it would continue, since mother and children continued to live there.

8. 28 U.S.C.A. § 1738A(f) provides that modification may only occur under the conditions stated, which pre-

sumably means that if it is attempted in the absence of such conditions, it would be without jurisdiction.

9. 28 U.S.C.A. § 1738A(a) only requires enforcement of decrees made consistently with the provisions of the section.

10. UCCJA § 8(a), which provides that a court may decline to exercise jurisdiction if the petitioner has wrongfully taken the child from another state or has engaged in similar reprehensible conduct, but only if that is just and proper under the circumstances.

11. It is interesting that two experts in custody jurisdiction reached contradictory conclusions about the Eicke case. Coombs, Custody Conflicts in the Courts: Judicial Resolution of the Old and New Questions Raised by Interstate Child Custody Cases, 16 Fam.L.Q. 251 (1982); Bruch, Interstate Child Custody Law and *Eicke*: A Reply to Professor Coombs, 16 Fam.L.Q. 277 (1982). The analysis in the text is indebted to but does not follow either of these articles.

12. 653 P.2d 295 (Wyo.1982), cert. denied 460 U.S. 1041, 103 S.Ct. 1436, 75 L.Ed.2d 794 (1983).

dy in the mother.[13] In August of 1979 the mother remarried and moved to Alaska, where she remained until the summer of 1980, when she moved to Wyoming. In June of 1980 while the daughter was visiting her father in Texas, he filed a petition in Texas for modification, seeking custody of the child. The mother then filed a petition for habeas corpus in Texas and it was granted, after which she took the daughter to Wyoming. The same judge who had granted the Texas habeas petition then proceeded to hear the father's motion for modification on the merits. On January 12, 1981 the Texas court awarded custody to the father, with visitation to the mother. On February 23, 1981 the mother brought the Quenzer case in Wyoming, asking that the Texas modification be in turn modified so as to give her custody. The trial court held that it had jurisdiction and awarded custody to the mother. The Wyoming Supreme Court affirmed, relying upon the PKPA and the UCCJA to find that the Texas court had not had jurisdiction to modify its own order.

At the outset it seems clear that under both the PKPA and the UCCJA the Oregon court had lost jurisdiction by the time of the Wyoming proceeding since mother and daughter had left the state permanently and the father never did live there.[14] The question then was whether Wyoming had to enforce the Texas award of custody to the father or whether it could modify that award. The Wyoming court correctly reasoned that the PKPA controlled that issue and required Wyoming to find that it had jurisdiction and that Texas no

longer had jurisdiction before Wyoming would be able to modify the Texas decree.[15] At the time the Wyoming proceeding was begun, mother and daughter had lived in the state for six months, so that Wyoming was the home state and therefore had jurisdiction. The Wyoming court then went on to hold that Texas had not had jurisdiction when it gave custody to the father because at that time Texas was not the home state and therefore did not qualify for jurisdiction under the PKPA.[16] The Wyoming court ignored the continuing jurisdiction provision of the PKPA,[17] however, which makes the issue turn on the local law of the initial state. The Texas local law contained a provision basing jurisdiction on a significant connection between the child, one contestant and the state, as in the UCCJA, and in fact the Wyoming court found that this basis for jurisdiction had existed in Texas when the modification was entered in that state.[18] Since the child had not lived in Texas for about four years at the time of the Wyoming proceeding, it would be possible to argue that there was no longer a significant connection with Texas. On the other hand, the father had had the child with him for visitation on several occasions, and would have done so more often if the mother had not taken steps to prevent it. Thus there was continuing contact between the child and Texas. Other courts have held that jurisdiction continues in circumstances not unlike those in Quenzer.[19]

The Wyoming court also found that Wyoming was the state having the greatest access to the facts and thus the best opportunity to

---

13. The Oregon case is reported in Matter of Marriage of Quenzer, 42 Or.App. 3, 599 P.2d 1217 (1979).

14. See note 53, supra.

15. 28 U.S.C.A. § 1738A(f).

16. Quenzer v. Quenzer, 653 P.2d 295, 301 (Wyo.1982), cert. denied 460 U.S. 1041, 103 S.Ct. 1436, 75 L.Ed.2d 794 (1983).

17. 28 U.S.C.A. § 1738A(d).

18. Quenzer v. Quenzer, 653 P.2d 295, 300 (Wyo.1982), cert. denied 460 U.S. 1041, 103 S.Ct. 1436, 75 L.Ed.2d 794 (1983). Cf. V.Tex.C.A., Fam.Code §§ 11.05(g) and 11.53(d) (Supp.1985), and Heartfield v. Heartfield, 749 F.2d 1138 (5th Cir.1985), distinguishing between continuing jurisdiction for custody and continuing jurisdiction for visitation and child support.

19. E.g., McDougald v. Jenson, 786 F.2d 1465 (11th Cir.1986), cert. denied ___ U.S. ___, 107 S.Ct. 207, 93 L.Ed. 2d 137 (1986), rehearing denied ___ U.S. ___, 107 S.Ct. 614, 93 L.Ed.2d 611 (1986); Kumar v. Superior Court of Santa Clara County, 32 Cal.3d 689, 186 Cal.Rptr. 772, 652 P.2d 1003 (1982); Belosky v. Belosky, 97 N.M. 365, 640 P.2d 471 (1982); Matter of Custody of Ross, 291 Or. 263, 630 P.2d 353 (1981); Arbogast v. Arbogast, ___ W.Va. ___, 327 S.E.2d 675 (1984); Cases holding that jurisdiction did not continue include, e.g., Kudler v. Smith, 643 P.2d 783 (Colo.App.1981), cert. denied 459 U.S. 837, 103 S.Ct. 83, 74 L.Ed.2d 78 (1982); Mace v. Mace, 215 Neb. 640, 341 N.W.2d 307 (1983); Voninski v. Voninski, 661 S.W.2d 872 (Tenn.App.1982). E.E.B. v. D.A., 89 N.J. 595, 446 A.2d 871 (1982) held New Jersey could exercise jurisdiction where Ohio had declined to do so.

judge what the child's interests required.[20] Most importantly, however, there was a trial of the merits in the Wyoming trial court, in which there was apparently evidence that the child was doing well in the custody of her mother. In such circumstances it would have been clearly contrary to the spirit and purpose of both Acts if the child had been removed from the custody of the parent with whom she had lived for four or five years solely on the ground of a technical construction of the PKPA. Perhaps one should be thankful that the Acts are both so full of loopholes that the right result can be reached even if a careful construction of individual provisions might easily produce the wrong result.

Case 4: There is considerable interest in joint custody today. Although courts seem to define the term in different ways, one version of it consists in dividing the physical custody of the child between the two parents for specified periods of time. This may cause unusual jurisdictional problems,[21] as the following hypothetical case illustrates.[22]

The spouses lived in Oregon and were divorced there in November of 1979. The court ordered joint custody of their daughter, aged five, pursuant to the parents' agreement. The agreement and order provided that the child would live with her father in Oregon for one month, then with her mother in California for a month, alternating between her parents at monthly intervals. At the end of the sixth month the mother remarried and moved to Texas with her new husband. Instead of returning the child to the father in Oregon as the decree provided, she took her to Texas in

July of 1980. In October of 1980 the mother filed a petition in Texas seeking modification of the Oregon decree so as to give her custody. The father came to Texas and before a hearing was held in the Texas case took the child from school without the mother's knowledge and returned her to Oregon. The mother and her second husband immediately went to Oregon, seized the child at school, assaulting a school administrator in the process, and departed with the child for Texas. A month later the father filed a motion in Oregon to modify the original Oregon decree so as to give him custody. The mother had notice of the Oregon proceeding and the father had notice of the Texas proceeding, but neither appeared in the out of state case. Before the Oregon motion could be heard the Texas court entered an order awarding custody to the mother. The question then is whether Oregon had jurisdiction to hear the motion, and if so, whether it should exercise jurisdiction.

The initial Oregon decree was based upon both personal and subject matter jurisdiction, since both parents were before the court and Oregon was obviously the home state under the UCCJA.[23] By the time the petition was filed in the Texas proceeding, however, the child had no home state. She had not been living in Oregon for six consecutive months and it does not seem that her absences from the state could be described as "temporary" since they were pursuant to the joint custody decree and would recur every month so long as that decree was in force.[24] When the Texas proceeding was filed, Texas may have had significant connection jurisdiction under the UCCJA[25] and under the PKPA as well since

---

20. Quenzer v. Quenzer, 653 P.2d 295, 304 (Wyo.1982), cert. denied 460 U.S. 1041, 103 S.Ct. 1436, 75 L.Ed.2d 794 (1983).

The Wyoming court also referred to the unclean hands provision of the Wyoming statute, suggesting that the father's retention of the child beyond the period of visitation while he sought the modification was "wrongful" under that statute. But it found that Texas had no such provision in its statute. 653 P.2d at 303. Texas now has such a provision. V.Tex.C.A., Fam.Code § 11.58 (Supp. 1984).

21. Bodenheimer, Progress Under the Uniform Child Custody Jurisdiction Act and Remaining Problems: Punitive Decrees, Joint Custody and Excessive Modifications,

65 Cal.L.Rev. 978, 1009 (1977) points out some of the difficulties but does not offer many solutions.

22. Although the case put is hypothetical, it is suggested by and somewhat similar to Matter of Marriage of Fenn, 63 Or.App. 506, 664 P.2d 1143 (1983).

23. UCCJA § 2(5).

24. UCCJA §§ 2(5), 3(a)(1). It also seems clear that she was not then absent from the state because of her removal by a person claiming her custody under § 3(a)(1)(ii). She was absent from Oregon because of her removal by a person who *had* custody for the month. But cases construing this phrase in the Act have not been found.

25. UCCJA § 3(a)(2).

there was no home state.[26] At the same time Oregon also had significant connection jurisdiction it seems, at least in the view that Oregon courts have taken respecting that phrase.[27] Under the PKPA Texas would only be permitted to modify the initial Oregon decree if it had jurisdiction (as it probably did have) and if Oregon no longer had jurisdiction.[28] Since Oregon's jurisdiction seems to have continued under the PKPA,[29] Texas did not have jurisdiction to modify the Oregon decree. Since Texas did not have jurisdiction to modify, Oregon was not required to observe the pending proceeding provision of the PKPA [30] and could proceed to decide the case on the merits. Under the unclean hands provision of the UCCJA [31] Texas should not have exercised its jurisdiction since the child was only in Texas by virtue of her mother's improper retention of her in violation of the initial Oregon decree. But this factor seems only to affect the *exercise* of jurisdiction, not its existence.[32] Therefore it did not prevent Texas from having jurisdiction. Which of these two states would be the more appropriate forum is an open question since both had about the same degree of contact with the child after the divorce. But the PKPA contains no *forum non conveniens* provision corresponding to the provision in the UCCJA.[33] It is not clear whether in such circumstances the UCCJA controls and the two judges

should communicate with each other on the question, or whether the more rigid rules of the PKPA should be applied without the exercise of discretion.

The foregoing analysis demonstrates the adventitious impact of the two Acts on a situation where two states have approximately equivalent contacts with the child and the parents. In this case stability in the child's life was not a factor because the poor child had never experienced any stability once the divorce was granted.

Summary and Conclusion

The first edition of this work, published in 1968, found great confusion among judicial opinions dealing with custody jurisdiction. Part of the reason for this was that the courts concentrated primarily on the welfare of the children before them and only secondarily on the jurisdictional issue. This state of affairs was accompanied by forum-shopping among litigants, conflicts between states over custody awards and frequent removal of children in violation of custody decrees by parents who hoped for a more favorable result in some other court. The law's first response to what was viewed as a highly unsatisfactory and harmful state of affairs was to produce the UCCJA, which, after about fifteen years was adopted in all states. At a time when many states had accepted the UCCJA, the Congress

26. 28 U.S.C.A. § 1738A(c)(2)(B).

27. UCCJA § 3(a)(2); Matter of Custody of Ross, 291 Or. 263, 630 P.2d 353 (1981), overruling Matter of Marriage of Settle, 276 Or. 759, 556 P.2d 962 (1976).

28. 28 U.S.C.A. § 1738A(f).

29. 28 U.S.C.A. § 1738A(d), stating that jurisdiction continues so long as the state (Oregon) continues to meet the requirements of 28 U.S.C.A. § 1738A(c)(1) and the state continues to be the residence of one contestant. 28 U.S.C.A. § 1738A(c)(1) refers to jurisdictional requirements of the state law, which in this case would be UCCJA 3(a)(2).

30. 28 U.S.C.A. § 1738A(g). This subsection seems to impose a strict rule to the effect that the court of one state shall not exercise jurisdiction while the court of another state is exercising its jurisdiction in accordance with the PKPA. Here Texas was not acting in accordance with the PKPA and on that ground Oregon could disregard the pendency of the Texas proceeding.

31. UCCJA § 8(b), which forbids the exercise of jurisdiction to modify if the petitioner has improperly re-

tained the child after a visit or other temporary relinquishment. The father's conduct in this case was also reprehensible, but he would not be covered by section 8(b) because he was not seeking modification of the decree of "another state" but rather the modification of a decree of the same state, Oregon. This is another example of the whimsical effects achieved by these statutes.

32. UCCJA § 8(b): "∗ ∗ ∗ the court shall not exercise its jurisdiction to modify ∗ ∗ ∗" This provision is also qualified by the introductory clause, "Unless required in the interest of the child ∗ ∗ ∗", which makes the entire provision essentially unworkable.

33. UCCJA § 7 in a long and complex set of provisions authorizes a court to decline to exercise its jurisdiction if it finds that it is an inconvenient forum and that the court of another state is a more appropriate forum. It is unclear whether, pursuant to this provision, Oregon could decline to exercise jurisdiction in favor of Texas' exercise where the PKPA seems to have forbidden Texas to modify the initial Oregon decree.

adopted the PKPA, a statute which differed from the UCCJA sufficiently to create some confusion, particularly since at the time of its passage a large body of case law had arisen construing the UCCJA.

The length of this section testifies to the combination of technical complexity and enormous uncertainty which these developments in the law have produced. The complexity results from the complicated provisions of the two statutes and the necessity for determining what should be the relationship between the two statutes. The uncertainty is due to the facts that there is a constitutional provision in the background, the Full Faith and Credit Clause,[34] and that our only clues to the impact of that Clause on custody jurisdiction come from Supreme Court cases now more than thirty years old. Ordinarily a lawyer operating in a technical field has the consolation that if he can master the technicalities he can rely on at least some assurance of certainty. The lawyer facing questions of custody jurisdiction may learn the details of the two Acts but he will still be unable to predict how the courts will deal with his jurisdictional problem. And it should be emphasized that it is a rare custody case which raises no jurisdictional problems.

It is impossible to tell whether the enactment of the UCCJA and the PKPA have brought about a diminution of the courts' local chauvinism which has been such a troublesome aspect of custody litigation. The reported cases contain so many examples of ex parte trial court decisions awarding custody to the home town parent that one suspects there has been little improvement on this score.[35] There is also a question whether the two Acts have caused any lessening in parental tendencies to seize their children and flee to other states. Here again the reported cases provide some evidence that these activities persist.[36] It is popular to condemn the parent who engages in "child-snatching", but we often forget that most such parents act this way because they love their children, even if, at the same time, they may hate their former spouses.

One result of the enactment of the UCCJA and the PKPA is clear. They have enabled the courts to avoid the extremely difficult and distasteful task of evaluating the parents as candidates for custody and of trying to discover what disposition will best serve or least harm the child. Instead the case can be analyzed in terms technical enough to delight a medieval property lawyer. And if the judge is sufficiently determined, he can often find that the case should be heard in some other state.

---

34. U.S.Const. art. IV, § 1. We also face the confusing issue of whether this Clause is limited by the PKPA, or whether it continues to have a broader application in custody proceedings than that Act indicates.

35. E.g., State ex rel. Marcrum v. Marion County Superior Court, 273 Ind. 222, 403 N.E.2d 806 (1980), the same case relitigated in Marcrum v. Marcrum, 181 N.J. Super. 361, 437 A.2d 725 (1981), certification granted 89 N.J. 402, 446 A.2d 136 (1982); Matter of Marriage of Fenn, 63 Or.App. 506, 664 P.2d 1143 (1983); McDougald v. Jenson, 596 F.Supp. 680 (N.D.Fla.1984), decision affirmed 786 F.2d 1465 (11th Cir. 1986) cert. denied ___ U.S. ___, 107 S.Ct. 207, 93 L.Ed.2d 137 (1986), rehearing denied ___ U.S. ___, 107 S.Ct. 614, 93 L.Ed.2d 611 (1986). Many other cases cited throughout this section would never have arisen but for the fact that one or more courts entered ex parte custody orders favoring the home town parent. Courts rarely reveal their local chauvinism, so that the following quotation is artlessly candid: "We conclude that the Tennessee decree, as modified by this Court, is entitled to enforcement by the state of Texas,

which we would point out would still be a Mexican province had Tennesseans not fought at the Alamo." Salisbury v. Salisbury, 657 S.W.2d 761, 768 (Tenn.App. 1983).

36. E.g., Fenn and Matter of Marriage of Fenn, 63 Or. App. 506, 664 P.2d 1143 (1983), in which the child was improperly removed from a state on three different occasions by one or the other parent. See also Flannery v. Stephenson, 416 So.2d 1034 (Ala.Cir.App.1982); In re Marriage of Ben-Yehoshua, 91 Cal.App.3d 259, 154 Cal. Rptr. 80 (1979); Fry v. Ball, 190 Colo. 128, 544 P.2d 402 (1975); Wenz v. Schwartze, 183 Mont. 166, 598 P.2d 1086 (1979), cert. denied 444 U.S. 1071, 100 S.Ct. 1015, 62 L.Ed. 2d 753 (1980); Neger v. Neger, 93 N.J. 15, 459 A.2d 628 (1983); Tufares v. Wright, 98 N.M. 8, 644 P.2d 522 (1982); State ex rel. Valles v. Brown, 97 N.M. 327, 639 P.2d 1181 (1981); Matter of Custody of Ross, 291 Or. 263, 630 P.2d 353 (1981), in all of which there was at least one improper removal from or retention outside a state. The number of such cases could be multiplied many times.

WESTLAW REFERENCES

History and Background

Constitutional Limitations on Custody Jurisdiction

di(noti! /s hear*** /s "due process" "fourteenth amendment" /s custod!)

stanley /s illinois /s publication noti! publish!

Uniform Child Custody Jurisdiction Act

di("uniform child custody" u.c.c.j.a. /p intra-state inter-state)

"uniform child custody" u.c.c.j.a. /s "full faith and credit" /s jurisdiction!

Parental Kidnapping Prevention Act of 1980

sy("parental kidnapping prevention" p.k.p.a.)

Continuing Jurisdiction

28 +5 1738a(f)

Enforcement or Modification: Which Alternative?

di(modif! /p enforc! /p "uniform child custody" u.c.c.j.a.)

bodenheimer /s punitive punish!

Chapter 13

DIVORCE—GROUNDS AND DEFENSES

Table of Sections

§ 13.1 Divorce Grounds—In General

At the time when the first edition of this work was published there was a wide diversity in the grounds for divorce prevailing in the fifty states. Today the non-fault grounds of marriage breakdown, incompatibility and living separate and apart have been enacted in almost all the states.[1] It is thus fair to say that there is now wide agreement that fault no longer should be relevant in determining whether or not a marriage should be dissolved, even though the fault grounds continue to exist in some states.[2] Since most of the traditional defenses to divorce are logically related to fault in some way, it is also true that they have been largely abolished or ignored today in those states in which the non-fault grounds for divorce prevail.[3]

Although divorce procedure and the divorce defenses developed in large part through the adoption of rules from equity and from the English ecclesiastical law,[4] the grounds for divorce are exclusively statutory. If the conduct which is relied upon to justify the di-

---

§ 13.1

1. See section 12.1, supra, at notes 51 to 53. Illinois, long a resolute adherent to fault grounds, has adopted a non-fault ground which combines living apart, irreconcilable differences and irretrievable breakdown. Ill.—S.H.A. ch. 40, § 401(2) (Supp.1986). South Dakota apparently is determined to retain the fault grounds. S.D. Codif.L. § 25–4–2 (Supp.1986). South Carolina is unique in having the grounds for divorce in its constitution. S.E. Const. art. 17, § 3.

2. Freed and Foster, Family Law in the Fifty States: An Overview as of September, 1982, 8 Fam.L.Rptr. 4065, 4075 (1982) indicates that twenty states have retained fault grounds, either alone as in South Dakota, or in combination with one or another of the non-fault grounds. Independent investigation seems to indicate that between twenty-seven and thirty states have retained one or all of the chief fault grounds of adultery, desertion and cruelty. That investigation also reveals that nearly as many states have retained a great diversity of divorce grounds, many of which are seldom relied upon. One looks in vain for some social policy or policies which might account for all this diversity and for the essential triviality of many of the statutory grounds.

3. Ibid. at 4077, lists seventeen states which have abolished all the divorce defenses.

4. See sections 12.1, infra.

vorce does not fit into one of the statutory causes for divorce, a decree may not be granted.[5] At the same time it has been true that the ecclesiastical law has had a great deal to do with giving specific content to the statutory grounds, especially those of cruelty and desertion.[6] Where the statutes covering the grounds for divorce are amended, it is generally held that a divorce may be granted pursuant to the amended statute even though the conduct on which the divorce is based occurred before the enactment of the amended statute.[7] But of course the conduct or condition relied on as the ground for divorce must have occurred or existed after the marriage,[8] and before the suit for divorce was brought.[9]

The rule is well established that it is the divorce statute of the forum which governs the granting of a divorce.[10] This is true even though all the operative facts occurred in some other state. If those facts constitute grounds for divorce according to the law of the forum, the divorce may be granted. If they do not, it may not be. This choice of law rule provided a strong temptation to indulge in forum-shopping and produced many migratory divorces in the days when there was a large disparity in the strictness with which the various states granted divorces. Now that no-fault divorce is so widely accepted

forum-shopping and migratory divorce are much less prevalent.

The contention has occasionally been made by persons whose religious beliefs do not permit the recognition of divorce that the grant of a divorce pursuant to a state statute in some way violates the Free Expression Clause of the First Amendment.[11] In the relatively rare cases in which this argument has been made it has been rejected.[12] The reasoning is that the effect of a divorce is only to dissolve the civil contract of marriage. It has no effect upon the marriage relationship as defined or regulated by the party's ecclesiastical advisers. Conversely the ecclesiastical authorities have no power to affect the legal relationships of spouses as defined by the state's statutes.

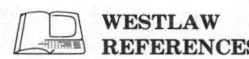

WESTLAW REFERENCES

divorc! /s "civil contract"

§ 13.2   Divorce Grounds—Adultery

Adultery is a subject of interest to novelists[1] and playwrights,[2] and social scientists have found it to be not uncommon in our society,[3] but in the contemporary law of di-

---

5. Moore v. Moore, 101 Ariz. 40, 415 P.2d 568 (1966); Firestone v. Firestone, 263 So.2d 223 (Fla.1972); Graham v. Graham, 44 Ill.App.3d 519, 3 Ill.Dec. 141, 358 N.E.2d 308 (1976); Welling v. Welling, 144 Ind.App. 182, 245 N.E.2d 173 (1969), cert. denied 396 U.S. 929, 90 S.Ct. 266, 24 L.Ed.2d 227 (1969); Liebling v. Liebling, 76 Misc.2d 465, 352 N.Y.S.2d 758 (1973); Williams v. Williams, 543 P.2d 1401 (Okl.1975), appeal dismissed, cert. denied 426 U.S. 901, 96 S.Ct. 2220, 48 L.Ed.2d 826 (1976).

6. See, e.g., the impact of Evans v. Evans, 1 Hagg. Cons. 35, 161 Eng.Rep. 466 (1790) on the American definition of cruelty, discussed in section 13.4, infra.

7. Cases are cited in Annot., 23 A.L.R.3d 626 (1969). Of course the legislature has plenary power to amend the statute. Chalmers v. Chalmers, 65 N.J. 186, 320 A.2d 478 (1974).

8. McKee v. McKee, 262 So.2d 111 (La.App.1972).

9. Johnson v. Johnson, 213 Va. 204, 191 S.E.2d 206 (1972).

10. Torlonia v. Torlonia, 108 Conn. 292, 142 A. 843 (1928), 38 Yale L.J. 381 (1929); D.S. v. J.S., 247 A.2d 125 (Del.1968); E.Scoles, P.Hay, Conflict of Laws 475 (1982); Restatement (Second) of Conflict of Laws § 285 (1971). Contra the statement in the text: Hoffman v. Hoffman, 94 N.J.Super. 292, 228 A.2d 87 (1967). The rule stated in

the text may be qualified by statute. See, e.g., Woodruff v. Woodruff, 114 N.H. 365, 320 A.2d 661 (1974).

11. U.S.Const.amend. I.

12. Sharma v. Sharma, 8 Kan.App.2d 726, 667 P.2d 395 (1983); Williams v. Williams, 543 P.2d 1401 (Okl. 1975), appeal dismissed for want of a substantial federal question, 426 U.S. 901, 96 S.Ct. 2220, 48 L.Ed.2d 826 (1976).

§ 13.2

1. L. Tolstoy, Anna Karenina (1875–1877).

2. E. Albee, Who's Afraid of Virginia Woolf (1961–1962); J. Anouilh, The Waltz of the Toreadors (1956).

3. A. Kinsey, W. Pomeroy, C. Martin, Sexual Behavior in the Human Male 583–594 (1948) estimates that about half of all married males have intercourse with women other than their wives at some time while married. The proportion for married females is about half that for males. See A. Kinsey, C. Martin, P. Gebhard, Sexual Behavior in the Human Female 416 (1953). Tolerance of adultery is suggested by N. and G. O'Neill, Open Marriage ch. 16 (1972). See also W. Masters, V. Johnson, Human Sexual Response (1966); W. Masters, V. Johnson, Human Sexual Inadequacy (1970).

vorce it is statistically unimportant.[4] Although it is a ground for divorce in about twenty-eight states today,[5] for a variety of obvious reasons it is relied upon in only a very small proportion of cases.

The usual definition of adultery is "the commission of an act of sexual * * * intercourse, voluntarily performed by the defendant, with a person other than the plaintiff after the marriage of plaintiff and defendant."[6] In the past there was some tendency of the criminal statutes on adultery to define the offense as intercourse between a man and a married woman, but it now seems clear that either spouse may commit adultery, and the imposition of different standards of conduct for men and women has been abandoned.[7] Many states have in fact abolished the criminal offense of adultery entirely.[8]

The cases are in some disagreement as to whether sexual contacts between a married person and another person of the same sex constitutes adultery for divorce purposes, with the few recent cases holding that this is adultery.[9] Since the reason for making adultery a ground for divorce is the traditional assumption that sexual relations should only occur between spouses as an implication from the prescription of marital loyalty, the cases which include homosexual contacts within the definition of adultery seem correct.

The voluntary character of adultery comes into question in three situations. First, when the wife is the victim of rape, she is clearly not guilty of adultery,[10] but the husband who rapes a woman not his wife is of course an adulterer.[11] The second type of case has caused more difficulty. When one of the parties is insane at the time of intercourse with someone other than his spouse, most cases have held that he is not responsible and therefore that this does not constitute adultery.[12] The test for insanity for this purpose is usually the criminal law test of not knowing right from wrong [13] although there are cases holding that it is sufficient that the alleged adulterer was not able to exercise a rational judgment.[14] The third type of case

---

4. P. Jacobson, American Marriage and Divorce 124 (1959) indicates that adultery accounted for only three percent of all divorces even before the advent of non-fault divorce. Now that nearly all states have one or more non-fault grounds, it is likely that adultery is even less relied upon.

5. A representative sample of states includes Ala. Code, § 30–2–1(a) (1983); Alaska Stat. § 25.24.050 (1983); Conn.Gen.Stat.Ann. § 46b–40 (1986); Official Ga.Code Ann. § 19–5–3 (Supp.1986); Ill.—S.H.A. ch. 40, § 401(2) (Supp.1986); Mass.G.L.A. ch. 208, § 1 (1981); N.H.Rev. Stat.Ann. § 458:7 (1983 Replacement); N.J.Stat.Ann. § 2A:34–2 (Supp.1986); N.Y.—McKinney's Dom.Rel.L. § 170 (1977); Ohio Rev.Code § 3105.01 (Supp.1985); Pa. Stat. tit. 23, § 201 (Supp.1986); S.C.Code 1985, § 20–3–10; S.D.Codif.L. § 25–4–2 (Supp.1986); Tenn.Code Ann. § 36–4–101 (1984); V.T.C.A., Fam.Code § 3.03 (1975); Utah Code Ann. 1984, § 30–3–1 (Replacement); Va.Code 1986, § 20–91 (Supp.).

6. The quotation is from N.Y.—McKinney's Dom.Rel. L. § 170 (1977). See also Milne v. Milne, 266 Ark. 900, 587 S.W.2d 229 (Ark.App.1979); Johnson v. Johnson, 78 N.J.Eq. 507, 80 A. 119 (1911); Ermis v. Ermis, 255 Wis. 339, 38 N.W.2d 485 (1949).

A few English cases have taken the view that an adultery divorce might be based upon "some lesser act of sexual gratification" than intercourse, but American courts have not gone this far. Compare Thompson v. Thompson [1938] P. 162 and Rutherford v. Richardson [1923] A.C. 1, with W v. W, 94 N.J.Super. 121, 226 A.2d 860 (1967).

7. See the statutes cited supra, note 5, making adultery a ground for divorce without qualification as to

parties. Any distinction based on gender in this context would undoubtedly violate the Equal Protection Clause of the United States Constitution. Orr v. Orr, 440 U.S. 268, 99 S.Ct. 1102, 59 L.Ed.2d 306 (1979), on remand 374 So.2d 895 (Ala.Civ.App.1979), writ denied 374 So.2d 898 (Ala. 1979).

8. Model Penal Code § 213.6, Note on Adultery and Fornication, Model Penal Code and Commentaries, Part II, 430 (1980). For a discussion of the constitutional limitations on the states' power to regulate marriage, see section 2.2, supra.

9. Owens v. Owens, 247 Ga. 139, 274 S.E.2d 484 (1981); Adams v. Adams, 357 So.2d 881 (La.App.1978), writ denied 359 So.2d 1309 (La.1978). N.J.Stat.Ann. § 2A:34–2 (Supp.1986) and N.Y.—McKinney's Dom.Rel.L. § 170 (1977) include deviant sexual intercourse in adultery. Earlier cases are cited in Baker v. Baker, 166 Neb. 306, 89 N.W.2d 35 (1958) (dissenting opinion).

10. Johnson v. Johnson, 78 N.J.Eq. 507, 80 A. 119 (1911).

11. Ibid.

12. Kretz v. Kretz, 73 N.J.Eq. 246, 67 A. 378 (1907); Manley v. Manley, 193 Pa.Super. 252, 164 A.2d 113 (1960). Other cases are collected in Annot., 19 A.L.R.2d 174 (1951). But see Matchin v. Matchin, 6 Pa. (6 Barr.) 332 (1847).

13. Hanbury v. Hanbury [1892] P. 222.

14. Kretz v. Kretz, 73 N.J.Eq. 246, 67 A. 378 (1907).

holds that adultery is not excused when the defendant was intoxicated at the time of intercourse, the reason being that the defendant's lack of responsibility was caused by his own fault.[15]

The defendant's state of mind is also relevant in those cases in which the defendant contracts a second marriage on the assumption that his first marriage has ended in divorce. If he remarries on the faith of a divorce which is later set aside, the cohabitation with the second spouse will only be considered adulterous if the defendant knew that the divorce was invalid when he contracted the second marriage [16] or when he obtained the divorce by collusion, fraud or in bad faith.[17]

It also follows from the definition of adultery that if the plaintiff and defendant are married, even though separated or living apart when the defendant engages in intercourse with another person, the defendant is guilty of adultery.[18]

The concept of adultery is put to a sharp test by modern medicine's development and wide use of artificial insemination.[19] The technique known as AID, by which a man other than the husband is the donor of semen, if accomplished without the husband's consent, squarely presents the question whether the operation constitutes adultery. Some rather scanty authority holds that it does, the leading decision being the Canadian case of Orford v. Orford.[20] The argument runs that the essential wrong of adultery consists in the voluntary submission of the wife's reproductory powers to a man other than the husband, with the consequence of bringing a spurious offspring into the family.[21] It is interesting that this is the same argument which was relied on to find the insane wife guilty of adultery in Matchin v. Matchin,[22] and which has since been generally rejected.[23] It is an argument which is quite inconsistent with the usual definition of adultery, and is really theological rather than legal. There is no doubt that intercourse may be adulterous even if there is no possibility that pregnancy will result. Intercourse, not pregnancy, is the essential factor in adultery. If it were not so, then the donor in AID and perhaps the doctor performing the operation, would be adulterers, and criminals in many jurisdictions. The possibility would be humorous if it did not have such serious consequences in frustrating the desire of sterile couples for children, a desire which may not be realizable by adoption and which in any event may be more satisfactorily realized by AID than by adoption.

The attempt to fit AID into the legal concept of adultery is a failure on both logical and policy grounds. In fact AID is a technique which cannot be effectively dealt with

---

15. Miller v. Miller, 140 Md. 60, 116 A. 840 (1922).

16. Meyer v. Meyer, 343 Ill.App. 554, 99 N.E.2d 706 (1951); Harmon v. Harmon, 245 N.C. 83, 95 S.E.2d 355 (1956).

17. Fox v. Fox, 23 Misc.2d 504, 206 N.Y.S.2d 317 (1960). Other cases are collected in Annot., 63 A.L.R.2d 816 (1959). In Wells v. Wells, 41 N.J. 594, 198 A.2d 442 (1964) it was held that the husband did not commit adultery when he remarried in the bona fide belief his first wife was dead.

18. Clark v. Clark, 644 S.W.2d 681 (Tenn.App.1982); Bell v. Bell, 540 S.W.2d 432 (Tex.Civ.App.1976).

19. For a discussion of the process and the problems it creates, see G. Williams, The Sanctity of Life and the Criminal Law 112–145 (1957) and Finegold, Artificial Insemination (1964). Public attitudes toward artificial insemination are described in Vernon & Boadway, Attitudes Toward Artificial Insemination and Some Variables Associated Therewith, 21 Marri. & Fam. Living 43 (1959). Other materials dealing with artificial insemination are cited in section 4.1, supra, at note 30.

20. 58 Dom.L.Rep. 251 (Ont.Sup.Ct.1951). The case suggests considerable suspicion of the wife's claim that she conceived by artificial insemination, so that as authority it is not as strong as it would be had the issue been squarely presented. A dictum in Doornbos v. Doornbos, 12 Ill.App.2d 473, 139 N.E.2d 844 (1956) states that AID with the husband's consent is adultery. Contra: Maclennan v. Maclennan, 1958 Scots.L.T.R. 12 holding AID is not adultery. For further discussion see Rudlow, Legal Aspects of Artificial Insemination 28 Australian L.J. 490 (1955); Note 58 Yale L.J. 457 (1949); Bartholomew, Legal Implications of Artificial Insemination, 21 Mod.L.Rev. 236 (1958); Pollard, Report on the Departmental Committee on Human Artificial Insemination, 24 Mod.L.Rev. 158 (1961).

21. The argument is amplified in Tallin, Artificial Insemination, 34 Can.B.Rev. 1 (1956), and Kelly, Artificial Insemination, 33 U.Det.L.J. 135 (1956). See also Hubbard, Artificial Insemination, 34 Can.B.Rev. 425 (1956).

22. 6 Pa.(6 Barr.) 332 (1847).

23. See note 12, supra.

by any existing legal concepts.[24] If it is to be a basis for divorce, this should be done by statutory amendment, which can take account of the only real objection to the process, the absence of the husband's consent.[25] If his consent is obtained, even those who condemn AID as sinful must concede that he is not entitled to a divorce.[26] The lack of litigation suggests that in most instances the husband's consent is obtained and the operation is performed in a careful manner by reputable physicians.

WESTLAW REFERENCES

adulter*** /2 defin! mean***

adulter! /s ''equal protection''

adulter! /s ''same sex'' homosexual! lesbian /p divorc!

adulter! /s ''artificial inseminat!''

§ 13.3 Divorce Grounds—Desertion

Desertion or its equivalent is a ground for divorce in twenty-nine states.[1] It formerly accounted for a substantial proportion of divorces in many states,[2] but judging from the

paucity of reported cases it is relatively seldom relied upon today.

There is considerable variation in the statutory language describing the offense of desertion. Not only are such adjectives as "wilful",[3] "utter",[4] "continued",[5] and "obstinate"[6] used to qualify the offense, but in some states the offense is called abandonment.[7] In still other states the requirements of absence[8] or total neglect of duty[9] are added. The question then arises whether the difference in language should produce different results in the cases or whether all of these statutes are really describing a single offense, which can broadly be labeled desertion. For the most part the various statutes refer to the same offense, defined in the same way by the cases. There seems to be little or no difference between desertion and abandonment,[10] for example, although it has been argued that they differ in origin.[11] There is no substantial reason why they should mean different things.

Occasionally a difference in the statutory language may lead to a difference in result. Thus where the statute speaks of the defen-

---

24. See, e.g., Strnad v. Strnad, 190 Misc. 786, 78 N.Y.S.2d 390 (1948), which invents the term "semi-adopted" to protect the child who is born of AID.

25. Statutes dealing with AID are cited in section 4.1, supra, at notes 40 and 41.

26. The husband's consent would give rise to the defense of connivance if AID were held to be adultery. See section 14.8, Practioner's Edition.

§ 13.3

1. A representative list of states includes Ala.Code § 30–2–1(a) (1983); Alaska Stat. § 25.24.050 (1983); Conn. Gen.Stat.Ann. § 46b–40 (1986); Official Ga.Code Ann. § 19–5–3 (Supp.1986); Ill.—S.H.A. ch. 40, § 401(2) (Supp. 1986); Md.Code, art. 16, § 7–103 (Supp.1984); Mass.G.L. A. ch. 208, § 1 (1981); N.J.Stat.Ann. § 2A:34–2 (Supp. 1986); N.Y.—McKinney's Dom.Rel.L. § 170 (1977); Ohio Rev.Code § 3105.01 (Supp.1986); Pa.Stat. tit. 23, § 201(a) (1) (Supp.1986); Tenn.Code Ann. § 36–4–101 (1984); V.T. C.A., Fam.Code § 3.05 (1975); Va.Code 1986, § 20–91 (Supp.).

2. P. Jacobson, American Marriage and Divorce 124 (1959) found that desertion accounted for less than eighteen percent of all divorces but that it was the leading ground for divorce in seven states and the District of Columbia.

3. Alaska Stat. § 25.24.050 (1983); Idaho Code § 32–603 (1983); Miss.Code 1973, § 93–5–1; Pa.Stat. tit. 23, § 201 (Supp.1986).

4. Me.Rev.Stat.Ann. tit. 19, § 691(1) (1981); Mass.G.L. A. ch. 208, § 1 (1981).

5. Official Ga.Code Ann. § 19–5–3 (Supp.1986); Miss. Code 1973, § 93–5–1; N.J.Stat.Ann. § 2A:34–2 (Supp. 1986).

6. Miss.Code 1973, § 93–5–1.

7. Ala.Code, § 30–2–1(a) (1983); Md.Code art. 16, § 7–103 (1984); Okl.Stat. tit. 12, § 1271 (1961).

8. Ohio Rev.Code § 3105.01 (Supp.1985); Pa.Stat. tit. 23, § 201 (Supp.1985); Tenn.Code Ann. § 36–4–101 (1984).

9. Conn.Gen.Stat.Ann. § 46b–40 (Supp.1986).

10. In Gannon v. Gannon, 130 Conn. 449, 35 A.2d 204 (1943) and Lewis v. Lewis, 206 Minn. 501, 289 N.W. 60 (1939) the general definition of desertion is identical with the definition of abandonment found in Webb v. Webb, 260 Ala. 426, 70 So.2d 639 (1954), and Schwartz v. Schwartz, 158 Md. 80, 82, 148 A. 259, 260 (1930). In McCurry v. McCurry, 126 Conn. 175, 10 A.2d 365 (1939), Crumlick v. Crumlick, 164 Md. 381, 165 A. 189 (1933) and Bohmert v. Bohmert, 241 N.Y. 446, 150 N.E. 511 (1926), 11 Corn.L.Q. 544 (1926) desertion and abandonment are treated as if synonymous. And in Va.Code, § 20–91 (Supp.1986) § 20–91 the statute authorizes a divorce where either party wilfully deserts or abandons the other for one year.

11. Jacobs and Goebel, Cases and Other Materials on Domestic Relations 464–465 (3d ed. 1952).

dant's absenting himself,[12] or leaving the spouse with the intention of abandonment,[13] the courts would have some difficulty in holding that a mere refusal of marital intercourse is a ground for divorce. The same is true where the statute requires proof of a total neglect of duty.[14] Aside from these special situations it is accurate to say that the definition of desertion is the same under all of these forms of statute.

In order to furnish some assurance that a divorce will not be granted unless the desertion is permanent, most statutes require that the desertion continue for a specified period before it can be the subject of a suit. The length of the required period varies between one and five years, one year being the most common.[15] This means that if a husband deserts his wife, she is not entitled to sue for divorce on the ground of desertion until the statutory period, whatever it may be, has expired. The period begins to run when the desertion first occurs,[16] but if it is interrupted by a period of reconciliation, followed by a second desertion, the two periods cannot be added together to produce the statutory minimum.[17] It may also be interrupted by the misconduct of the deserted spouse.[18] There must be a continuous and uninterrupted separation lasting for the statutory time.

It is often said that time spent in previous marital litigation must be deducted from the time during which the parties have been living apart in order to determine whether the statutory desertion period has run.[19] This is too broad a statement of the rule, which can only be accurately stated after an examination of specific cases. It is true that if the parties separate without fault on the plaintiff's part and one of them sues for divorce in good faith on grounds other than desertion and loses, the time spent in this litigation cannot be counted in arriving at the statutory period which must elapse before the other spouse may sue on the ground of desertion.[20] But if the first suit is not brought in good faith, then the time may be counted.[21] And if one spouse brings about the separation through his own fault, sues, and loses, then the period of the litigation may be included for purposes of establishing a desertion.[22]

There are two reasons for deducting litigation time. One is that the parties to divorce suits were traditionally both expected and required to live apart. Thus there is in such a separation no impropriety which can be the basis for a claim of desertion.[23] The other is that it would unfairly prejudice the plaintiff in the first suit if he should be faced with an action based on desertion solely because he

12. Ohio Rev.Code § 3105.01 (Supp.1985).

13. V.T.C.A., Fam.Code § 3.05 (1975).

14. Conn.Gen.Stat.Ann. § 46b–40 (1986).

15. See the statutes cited in notes 1, 3 to 9, supra, and Me.Rev.Stat.Ann. tit. 19, § 691(1) (1981) (three years); R.I.Gen.L.1981, § 15–5–2 (five years).

16. But see Carroll v. De Martini, 19 N.J.Super. 136, 88 A.2d 26 (1952).

17. Cases are collected in Annot., 155 A.L.R. 132 (1945). Acts of intercourse without any real reconciliation do not interrupt the period of desertion. Campbell v. Campbell, 246 Ala. 107, 19 So.2d 354 (1944); Docotovich v. Docotovich, 125 Mont. 56, 229 P.2d 971 (1951); Sabia v. Sabia, 16 N.J.Super. 273, 84 A.2d 559 (1951). Under Mass.G.L.A. ch. 208, § 22 (1981) the return of the deserter does not interrupt the period if not in good faith.

18. Paulsen v. Paulsen, 243 Iowa 51, 50 N.W.2d 567 (1951).

19. E.g., Roberts v. Roberts, 223 Va. 736, 292 S.E.2d 370 (1982); Vickers v. Vickers, 95 W.Va. 323, 122 S.E. 279 (1924). Other cases are collected in Annot., 80 A.L.R.2d

855 (1961). Ill.—S.H.A. ch. 40, § 401 (Supp.1986) includes periods of litigation.

20. Ewing v. Ewing, 16 Cal.2d 208, 105 P.2d 586 (1940); Ellis v. Ellis, 115 Neb. 685, 214 N.W. 300 (1927); Vickers v. Vickers, 95 W.Va. 323, 122 S.E. 279 (1924). Contra: Quamo v. Quamo, 102 N.H. 410, 157 A.2d 644 (1960), where the desertion occurred before the action for divorce based on cruelty and had continued for the statutory period.

There is a related line of cases holding that a withdrawal from the marital domicile which occurs after a suit for divorce or separation has begun cannot, as a matter of law, constitute desertion. Plattner v. Plattner, 202 Va. 263, 117 S.E.2d 128 (1960), 18 Wash. & L.L.Rev. 245 (1961).

21. Betts v. Betts, 63 So.2d 302 (Fla.1953); Heinemann v. Heinemann, 202 Wis. 639, 233 N.W. 552 (1930) (citing many cases).

22. Daves v. Daves, 576 S.W.2d 4 (Tenn.App.1978).

23. Ellis v. Ellis, 115 Neb. 685, 214 N.W. 300 (1927); Vickers v. Vickers, 95 W.Va. 323, 122 S.E. 279 (1924).

chose in good faith to assert a claim which turned out to be a losing one.[24]

Where the claim of desertion is made by amended complaint, after the action was brought on another ground, only the first of these reasons applies, but that should be enough. The suit should not be maintainable unless the period had run at the time of the original complaint. The cases are in disagreement on the issue, however.[25]

Similar results should be reached when a suit for separation is followed by the divorce action for desertion since similar reasons apply.[26] On the other hand, if the first action is a dispute over custody or property, which does not reaquire the parties to live apart, then the period of that action should be included in determining whether the statutory time has elapsed.

Even though the period of pendency of litigation may not be counted in determining whether the statutory time has run, the time before and after the litigation may be cumulated and if the total exceeds the statutory period, the action will lie.[27]

One further question concerning the time period arises. What is the result if the husband deserts, the wife sues for separate main-tenance or limited divorce, (which she may do under many statutes without having to wait for the expiration of any particular period of time) she gets a decree, and at some later date decides she wants an absolute divorce? May she include in the period of desertion the time during which they lived apart under the separate maintenance decree? There are few cases on this but those which do consider the problem generally favor the position that she cannot get the divorce because the separation decree authorizes the parties to live apart.[28] The separation is therefore not without justification. A fortiori, the wife herself is not a deserter as a result of living apart under the decree.[29] And there is even some doubt whether, if the husband should offer a reconciliation, she would become a deserter by refusing it.[30] The differing results here may be explained by differences between decrees of separate maintenance and decrees of divorce a mensa et thoro[31] although such differences are more form than substance. It would seem that in the usual case, if the husband makes no bona fide offer of reconciliation, the wife should be permitted to include the time under the separation decree for purposes of obtaining a divorce on the ground of desertion.

24. Upah v. Upah, 175 Neb. 606, 122 N.W.2d 507 (1963); White v. White, 185 Pa.Super. 141, 138 A.2d 162 (1958).

25. E.g. Ewing v. Ewing, 16 Cal.2d 208, 105 P.2d 586 (1940); Bennett v. Bennett, 259 Iowa 227, 144 N.W.2d 328 (1966) and Latour v. Latour, 162 Pa.Super. 75, 56 A.2d 332 (1948) held that time in litigation should not be counted. White v. White, 185 Pa.Super. 141, 138 A.2d 162 (1958), disapproving the Latour case, held that it might be counted, on reasons which do not take account of the fact that the separation is justified while the parties are in suit. Hannan v. Hannan, 256 S.W.2d 485 (Ky.1953) seems to take the same position. Analytically Quamo v. Quamo, 102 N.H. 410, 157 A.2d 644 (1960) is a case of this sort, though the second claim was a new action rather than an amended complaint. It was held that the time consumed in the first suit could be included in computing the period of desertion.

26. Van Dolman v. Van Dolman, 378 Ill. 98, 37 N.E.2d 850 (1941). Contra: Hartzog v. Hartzog, 65 So.2d 756 (Fla.1953), though this may be a case in which the first suit was not brought in good faith. See also Cannistraro v. Cannistraro, 352 Mass. 65, 223 N.E.2d 692 (1967).

27. Betts v. Betts, 63 So.2d 302 (Fla.1953).

28. Betts v. Betts, 63 So.2d 302 (Fla.1953) (semble); Weld v. Weld, 27 Minn. 330, 7 N.W.2d 267 (1880); Kyle v. Kyle, 52 N.J.Eq. 710, 29 A. 316 (1894). Contra: Van Dolman v. Van Dolman, 378 Ill. 98, 37 N.E.2d 850 (1941) (dictum); Popovics v. Popovics, 98 N.J.Eq. 350, 129 A. 126 (1925) (semble). Other cases are collected in Annot., 25 A.L.R. 1047 (1923) and 61 A.L.R. 1268 (1929).

In Kunze v. Kunze, 153 Minn. 5, 189 N.W. 447 (1922) the husband's failure to comply with the separate maintenance decree was held desertion. In Courson v. Courson, 208 Md. 171, 117 A.2d 850 (1955) the court found a recriminatory defense in the husband's living apart under a separate maintenance decree obtained by the wife, saying this amounts to desertion by the husband.

29. Bliss v. Bliss, 208 Minn. 84, 293 N.W. 94 (1940); Hanover v. Hanover, 34 Ohio App. 483, 171 N.E. 350 (1929); Koolish v Koolish, 214 Pa.Super. 304, 257 A.2d 680 (1969); Scott v. Scott, 141 W.Va. 533, 91 S.E.2d 621 (1956) (dictum).

30. Martin v. Martin, 66 So.2d 268 (Fla.1953) states that if the prevailing party in the separate maintenance suit refuses a good faith offer of reconciliation, he is a deserter. Contra: Williams v. Williams, 33 Ariz. 367, 265 P. 87 (1928); Perrin v. Perrin, 201 Tenn. 354, 299 S.W.2d 19 (1957).

31. This seems to be the reasoning of Williams v. Williams, 33 Ariz. 367, 265 P. 87 (1928).

Desertion is usually defined by the cases[32] (and some statutes)[33] as requiring four elements: a) a voluntary separation by one spouse from the other; b) with intent not to resume marital cohabitation; c) without the consent of the other spouse; and d) without justification. All of these elements raise questions of interpretation and application.

Cessation of Cohabitation

One of the most vexing questions relates to what we mean by a voluntary separation. In general this means an intentional departure.[34] When one spouse leaves home and has nothing further to do with the other spouse, his action may be easily characterized as a voluntary separation.[35] But where he leaves because he is required to enter the army, this alone does not amount to desertion.[36] Or where he leaves because he has committed a crime and is imprisoned, this should not constitute desertion,[37] although some courts think it does,[38] reasoning that the husband's fault was responsible for his inability to perform his marital responsibilities. And insanity may prevent the departure from being considered voluntary.[39]

Apart from these special cases, whether or not the separation occurred with the necessary intent to withdraw permanently from cohabitation depends upon the facts surrounding the withdrawal.[40] If the defendant showed by his conduct or statements that he did not intend to remain away permanently, he is not a deserter.[41] The length of time during which he did remain away is often evidence of intent to desert.[42] A few cases confuse the intent to desert with justification, holding that if withdrawal is justified by the other's misconduct, it does not amount to desertion.[43]

It is not necessary that the withdrawal from cohabitation and the intent to desert coincide in time. If a separation occurs, followed later by conduct evidencing intent to desert, this constitutes desertion dating from the time when the intent was formed.[44]

Granting that the separation must be voluntary, what then is a separation? Does it entail a complete withdrawal from the marital domicile, or may a refusal to perform some marital obligations while remaining in the home constitute desertion? These questions

---

32. E.g., Gannon v. Gannon, 130 Conn. 449, 35 A.2d 204 (1943); In re Marriage of Jones, 90 Ill.App.3d 95, 45 Ill.Dec. 540, 412 N.E.2d 1122 (1980); Bunger v. Bunger, 249 Iowa 938, 90 N.W.2d 1 (1958); Bergeron v. Bergeron, 372 So.2d 731 (La.App.1979); Crumlick v. Crumlick, 164 Md. 381, 165 A. 189 (1933); Lewis v. Lewis, 206 Minn. 501, 289 N.W. 60 (1939); Peterson v. Peterson, 112 Utah 542, 189 P.2d 961 (1948); Smith v. Smith, 202 Va. 104, 116 S.E.2d 110 (1960). See also Note, 83 U.Pa.L.Rev. 905 (1935). The adjective "wilful" in many statutes is construed to mean "voluntary".

33. E.g., La.Civ.Code art. 143 (Supp.1987).

34. Casale v. Casale, 138 Conn. 490, 86 A.2d 568 (1952); Styka v. Styka, 257 Md. 464, 263 A.2d 555 (1970); Partleton v. Partleton, 169 Pa.Super. 485, 82 A.2d 684 (1951).

35. E.g., Lutticke v. Lutticke, 406 Ill. 181, 92 N.E.2d 754 (1950); Ewing v. Ewing, 154 Md. 84, 140 A. 37 (1928). A departure motivated by religious zeal may be desertion. Wood v. Wood, 227 Md. 211, 176 A.2d 229 (1961). But some courts have insisted on an abnegation of *all* marital duties before a divorce for desertion may be granted, perhaps out of sympathy for an unfortunate defendant. Edmond v. Edmond, 20 Ill.App.3d 40, 312 N.E.2d 766 (1974).

36. Reimer v. Reimer, 160 Pa.Super. 509, 52 A.2d 357 (1947); Moltz v. Moltz, 182 Va. 737, 30 S.E.2d 561 (1944) (dictum); Beeken v. Beeken [1948] P. 302 (C.A.) (internment by enemy). See also Watkins v. Kidds, 261 Ala. 463, 75 So.2d 87 (1954).

37. Truman v. Truman, 36 Del. (6 W.W.Harr.) 104, 171 A. 453 (1934), distinguishing the case where the desertion begins voluntarily and then continues because of the subsequent imprisonment.

38. Liberato v. Liberato, 93 N.H. 219, 38 A.2d 880 (1944); Brady v. Brady, 98 N.J.Super. 600, 238 A.2d 201 (1968), 23 Rut.L.Rev. 389 (1969).

39. Kendall v. Kendall, 268 Ala. 383, 106 So.2d 653 (1958); Preston v. Reed, 142 Me. 275, 50 A.2d 95 (1946); Youmans v. Youmans, 3 N.J.Misc. 576, 129 A. 122 (1925) (dictum); Cahill v. Cahill, 26 Wis.2d 173, 131 N.W.2d 842 (1965), 50 Iowa L.Rev. 1288 (1965) (semble); Annot., 4 A.L.R. 1331 (1919). Cf. Silverness v. Silverness, 270 Minn. 564, 134 N.W.2d 901 (1965).

40. Brown v. Brown, 92 Cal.App. 276, 268 P. 401 (Dist. Ct. of App. 1928); Casale v. Casale, 138 Conn. 490, 86 A.2d 568 (1952); Lutticke v. Lutticke, 406 Ill. 181, 92 N.E.2d 754 (1950).

41. Flohr v. Flohr, 195 Md. 482, 73 A.2d 874 (1950); Machado v. Machado, 220 S.C. 90, 66 S.E.2d 629 (1951).

42. Hagen v. Hagen, 159 Pa.Super. 539, 49 A.2d 193 (1946).

43. Zirpoli v. Zirpoli, 185 Pa.Super. 378, 138 A.2d 295 (1958).

44. Thurlow v. Thurlow, 212 Md. 222, 129 A.2d 170 (1957); Rebar v. Rebar, 165 Pa.Super. 341, 67 A.2d 598 (1949).

have produced the majority of the litigated cases on desertion, without at the same time producing agreement. An early Massachusetts case,[45] following English authority on restitution of conjugal rights, a kind of action not known in America, held that the mere refusal of sexual relations without departure from the marital domicile is not desertion. Desertion, the court held, involves an abandonment of *all* marital duties, a cessation of living together, and anything less is not desertion. This rule has been followed in other jurisdictions.[46] A smaller number of jurisdictions have held that the refusal of sexual relations is desertion.[47] In some of these cases this result is made easier by the parties' breaking off all intercourse with each other, sexual and social, while continuing to live in one house.[48] In others desertion has been held to occur upon the cessation of sexual relations notwithstanding that the spouses continue to take meals together, converse, and in other ways behave as husband and wife.[49] The courts which hold this to be desertion urge that the sexual side of marriage and the propagation of children are so important that their cessation justifies dissolving the relationship entirely.[50] Certainly there

seems to be little social value in preserving a marriage in which one of the parties has persisted in a denial of physical intimacy for the statutory period. As has been indicated, however, the language of some statutes may sometimes make it impossible to hold that this constitutes desertion.[51]

So long as cohabitation continues, the non-performance of other marital duties does not amount to desertion.[52] Mere failure to support the wife is not, without more, desertion by the husband, though it certainly may be a revealing factor in determining his intent.[53] On the other hand, if desertion as defined above has taken place, it is not made any the less desertion by the husband's continuing to support his wife.[54]

Consent and Justification

Desertion, being defined as a marital wrong committed by one spouse against the other, does not occur if the parties live apart by mutual agreement.[55] In this respect it must be distinguished from that other ground for divorce found in several states, according to which the parties may be divorced after hav-

---

45. Southwick v. Southwick, 97 Mass. 327 (1867).

46. E.g., McCurry v. McCurry, 126 Conn. 175, 10 A.2d 365 (1939); Lemon v. Lemon, 14 Ill.2d 15, 150 N.E.2d 608 (1958); Edmond v. Edmond, 20 Ill.App.3d 40, 312 N.E.2d 766 (1974); Howison v. Howison, 128 Ill.App.2d 377, 262 N.E.2d 1 (1970); Watson v. Watson, 291 S.W.2d 198 (Mo. App.1956); Dudley v. Dudley, 225 N.C. 83, 33 S.E.2d 489 (1945); Bennefield v. Bennefield, 263 S.C. 233, 209 S.E.2d 563 (1974); Gallaher v. Gallaher, 147 W.Va. 463, 128 S.E.2d 464 (1962).

Many other cases both ways are cited in Annot., 82 A.L.R.3d 660 (1978); Note 83 U.Pa.L.Rev. 905 (1935); Note, 15 Iowa L.Rev. 477 (1930); Note, 28 Conn.B.J. 112 (1954).

47. Maryland, New Jersey and New York are the leading jurisdictions for this view. See, e.g., Mower v. Mower, 209 Md. 413, 121 A.2d 185 (1956); Scheinin v. Scheinin, 200 Md. 282, 89 A.2d 609 (1952); Benton v. Benton, 197 Md. 373, 79 A.2d 146 (1951); Faulkner v. Faulkner, 176 Md. 692, 4 A.2d 117 (1939); Semely v. Semely, 113 N.J.Super. 411, 274 A.2d 57 (1971); Crowell v. Crowell, 33 N.J.Super. 272, 110 A.2d 57 (1954); Ullrich v. Ullrich, 26 N.J.Misc. 333, 64 A.2d 917 (1947); Rains v. Rains, 127 N.J.Eq. 328, 12 A.2d 857 (1940); Haviland v. Haviland, 114 N.J.Eq. 96, 168 A. 260 (1933); Diemer v. Diemer, 8 N.Y.2d 206, 203 N.Y.S.2d 829, 168 N.E.2d 654 (1960) (separation). See also Whitfield v. Whitfield, 89 Ga. 471, 15 S.E. 543 (1892); Evans v. Evans, 247 Ky. 1, 56 S.W.2d 547 (1933); Graves v. Graves, 88 Miss. 677, 41 So.

384 (1906); Baker v. Baker, 99 Or. 213, 195 P. 347 (1921). No desertion occurs where the refusal is justified by reasons of health. Ullrich v. Ullrich, 26 N.J.Misc. 333, 64 A.2d 917 (1947).

Other cases are cited in Annot., 82 A.L.R.3d 660 (1978).

48. E.g. Reppert v. Reppert, 40 Del. (1 Terry) 492, 13 A.2d 705 (1940); Whitfield v. Whitfield, 89 Ga. 471, 15 S.E. 543 (1892); Graves v. Graves, 88 Miss. 677, 41 So. 384 (1906); Croll v. Croll, 106 W.Va. 691, 146 S.E. 880 (1929).

49. E.g. Mower v. Mower, 209 Md. 413, 121 A.2d 185 (1956); Rains v. Rains, 127 N.J.Eq. 328, 12 A.2d 857 (1940).

50. Diemer v. Diemer, 8 N.Y.2d 206, 203 N.Y.S.2d 829, 168 N.E.2d 654 (1960).

51. See notes 15, 16, supra.

52. Davis v. Davis, 187 Va. 63, 45 S.E.2d 918 (1948); Littlewood v. Littlewood [1943] P. 11. See the discussion of New York cases in Note, 29 Bklyn.L.Rev. 157 (1962).

53. Sause v. Sause, 192 Md. 88, 63 A.2d 632 (1949); Mattox v. Mattox, 43 N.J.Super. 111, 127 A.2d 893 (1956).

54. Webb v. Webb, 260 Ala. 426, 70 So.2d 639 (1954); Magrath v. Magrath, 103 Mass. 577 (1870).

55. See note 32, supra. Nesmith v. Nesmith, 112 Ariz. 248, 540 P.2d 1229 (1975); Pempek v. Pempek, 141 Conn. 602, 109 A.2d 238 (1954); Heikes v. Heikes, 90 Pa. Super. 312 (1926).

ing lived separate and apart for a period of years.[56]

Whether the plaintiff has consented to the separation so as to prevent its constituting desertion depends upon the surrounding circumstances.[57] The cases holding that separation pursuant to a written separation agreement may be held consented to so that a suit for desertion will not lie are cited in another section of this work.[58] The distinction which these cases attempt to make is one between a consent to the separation preventing suit for desertion on the one hand, and a consent to a settlement of financial disputes after a desertion has already occurred or is at least imminent on the other, which does not prevent suit for desertion.[59] The bulk of the cases fall into the first category.

Other evidence of consent to the separation may include declarations or conduct at the time,[60] failure to object to the defendant's departure,[61] offers of reconciliation or lack of

them,[62] and similar circumstances. Consent to a temporary separation is not consent to a permanent one.[63] If the consent is manifested after the separation occurs, but before the statutory period for desertion runs, it has the effect of ending the desertion, and thus prevents any cause of action from arising.[64]

Just as consent makes a cessation of cohabitation unobjectionable, so does justification. In fact conduct which is found to justify the departure of a spouse from the home has a double effect. In the first place it causes the departure not to constitute desertion and therefore not to be a ground for divorce.[65]

Secondly, in those states which accept the doctrine of constructive desertion, the conduct causing a spouse to leave the home, if it is found to justify the departure, is held itself to amount to desertion and therefore to furnish a ground for divorce to the departing spouse.[66] This ground for divorce is usually described as constructive desertion and, since it is a wholly

---

56. Living separate and apart as a ground for divorce is discussed in section 13.7, supra.

57. Fallon v. Fallon, 83 Cal.App.2d 298, 189 P.2d 766 (1948); Flohr v. Flohr, 195 Md. 482, 73 A.2d 874 (1950). Thus where the defendant has determined to end the marriage regardless of the plaintiff's desire, the plaintiff's acquiescence in that decision does not amount to consent such as to foreclose her divorce for desertion. Good v. Good, 135 N.J.Super. 56, 342 A.2d 578 (1975).

58. See section 19.9, Practitioner's Edition and cases cited in Annot., 34 A.L.R.2d 954 (1954).

59. Lort v. Lort, 91 U.S.App.D.C. 118, 198 F.2d 598 (D.C.Cir.1952); Pempek v. Pempek, 141 Conn. 602, 109 A.2d 238 (1954); Wilner v. Wilner, 251 Md. 13, 246 A.2d 273 (1968). If the agreement to separate is induced by misconduct, the offended party may still sue for desertion. Gee v. Gee, 249 Ala. 642, 32 So.2d 657 (1947).

60. Portis v. Portis, 122 Cal.App.2d 36, 264 P.2d 102 (1953); Wilner v. Wilner, 251 Md. 13, 246 A.2d 273 (1968); Espinola v. Espinola, 273 Mass. 450, 173 N.E. 926 (1930); Heikes v. Heikes, 90 Pa.Super. 312 (1926).

61. Fallon v. Fallon, 83 Cal.App.2d 798, 189 P.2d 766 (1948); Munger v. Munger, 130 N.J.Eq. 279, 21 A.2d 784 (1941); Hay v. Hay, 67 Misc.2d 50, 323 N.Y.S.2d 481 (Fam.Ct.1971) (husband acquiesced in wife's refusal of sexual relations).

62. See the text at note 91, infra for a discussion of the requirement of offers of reconciliation. Gee v. Gee, 249 Ala. 642, 32 So.2d 657 (1947) and Chasman v. Chasman, 161 Pa.Super. 77, 53 A.2d 876 (1947) held that no offer of reconciliation need be made by the wronged party.

63. Lutticke v. Lutticke, 406 Ill. 181, 92 N.E.2d 754 (1950); Grace v. Grace, 165 Pa.Super. 336, 68 A.2d 197 (1949).

64. Duncan v. Duncan, 171 Pa.Super. 69, 90 A.2d 357 (1952), affirmed 323 Pa. 308, 96 A.2d 115 (1953).

65. E.g. Hoover v. Hoover, 267 Ala. 76, 100 So.2d 5 (1958); Marshak v. Marshak, 115 Ark. 51, 170 S.W. 567 (1914); Watkins v. Watkins, 202 Ky. 141, 259 S.W. 20 (1923); Hoffhines, v. Hoffhines, 146 Md. 350, 126 A. 112 (1924); Van Houten v. Van Houten, 320 Mich. 604, 31 N.W.2d 734 (1948); Eftimiou v. Eftimiou, 204 N.Y.S.2d 785 (1960); Andrew v. Andrew, 143 Pa.Super. 68, 17 A.2d 673 (1941).

Conduct of the plaintiff was held to justify the defendant's departure from the home in Palese v. Palese, 25 A.D.2d 540, 267 N.Y.S.2d 542 (2d Dep't 1966); Breschel v. Breschel, 221 Va. 208, 269 S.E.2d 363 (1980); Graham v. Graham, 210 Va. 608, 172 S.E.2d 724 (1970). Once the desertion is proved, the duty of going forward with evidence of justification is on the defendant, according to the Breschel case.

The departure from the home was held not to be justified in Cannistraro v. Cannistraro, 352 Mass. 65, 223 N.E.2d 692 (1967); Kuester v. Kuester, 633 S.W.2d 281 (Mo.App.1982).

66. Livani v. Livani, 51 Del. (1 Storey) 515, 148 A.2d 776 (Super.1958) (applying Pennsylvania law); Rice v. Rice, 46 Del. (7 Terry) 175, 81 A.2d 298 (Super.1951); Sharp v. Sharp, 58 Md.App. 386, 473 A.2d 499 (1984), cert. denied 300 Md. 795, 481 A.2d 240 (1984); Hoback v. Hoback, 208 Va. 432, 158 S.E.2d 113 (1967); Annot., 19 A.L.R.2d 1428 (1951); Note, Constructive Desertion—A Broader Basis for Breaking the Bond, 51 Iowa L.Rev. 108 (1965); Note, Constructive Desertion in Virginia, 47 Va.L. Rev. 362 (1961).

judge-made doctrine, is an exception to the commonly expressed view that grounds for divorce are exclusively statutory.[67] In rare circumstances a constructive desertion may even occur notwithstanding that the innocent spouse does not leave the marital home.[68] Typical examples of the sort of conduct which supports a finding of constructive desertion occur when the husband by his cruelty forces his wife to leave their home,[69] or when the wife without justification locks her husband out of the marital home.[70]

WESTLAW REFERENCES

di(divorc! /p desert! /p obstina! /p ground! /p statut!)

divorc! /s desert! /s neglect! /s duty

divorc! /s abandon! /s refus! /s intercourse "sexual relation!"

abandon! desert! /p element /s consen! /s justif!

Cessation of Cohabitation

abandon! desert! /s element /s co-habit! (liv*** /3 together) to(134) /p sane sanity insan! incompeten! incapacit! (mental! /s ill illness competen! capacit!)

Consent and Justification

di(abandon! desert! /p mutual! /3 agree*** agreement consen! assent! /p divorc!)

---

67. See section 13.1, supra, at note 5. Of course where the conduct justifying the departure from the home is in itself an independent ground for divorce, the courts are not constructing a wholly new ground for divorce.

68. Edwards v. Edwards, 356 A.2d 633 (D.C.App.1976). Here the husband assaulted the wife, she brought a criminal proceeding against him, as a result of which he was excluded from the home. She was then granted a divorce on the ground of constructive desertion.

69. Rice v. Rice, 46 Del.(7 Terry) 175, 81 A.2d 298 (Super.1951).

70. Pohren v. Pohren, 13 Ill.App.3d 380, 300 N.E.2d 288 (1973), appeal after, remand 40 Ill.App.3d 1063, 353 N.E.2d 6 (1976); Schirrmann v. Schirrmann, 436 So.2d 1340 (La.App.1983), writ denied 440 So.2d 761 (La.1983); Schine v. Schine, 31 N.Y.2d 113, 335 N.Y.S.2d 58, 286 N.E.2d 449 (1972), reargument denied 31 N.Y.2d 805, 339 N.Y.S.2d 1027, 291 N.E.2d 591 (1972); Fort v. Fort, 270 S.C. 255, 241 S.E.2d 891 (1978).

§ 13.4

1. 2 Burns, Ecclesiastical Law, marriage xi (1791); 2 Howard, History of Matrimonial Institutions 54 (1904).

§ 13.4 Divorce Grounds—Cruelty

Background and General Definitions

Cruelty was a ground for divorce a mensa et thoro in English ecclesiastical law,[1] and from that source was brought into American law as a ground for absolute divorce. It has been a cliché of the profession that at common law a husband was entitled to use some force to discipline his wife, although it is not easy to find persuasive authority that this was the law.[2] Whether it was or was not, it is clear that the use of excessive force amounted to cruelty and gave the wife cause for divorce a mensa. Today the husband is not entitled to use force, moderate or otherwise.[3]

Before the enactment of the various non-fault grounds for divorce commencing about 1970, cruelty was in most states the basis for most divorces.[4] The major reason for this was that hard pressed trial courts were willing to grant divorces on evidence of cruelty falling far short of the requirements of the statutes or of the reported cases so long as the suit was uncontested. In many states, especially in the West, an uncontested divorce for cruelty could be had for the asking, in the face of pronouncements by the appellate courts which would lead one to think that the definition of cruelty had not changed for one hundred and fifty years.[5] In the states which do have one of the non-fault grounds for di-

---

2. 2 Schouler, Marriage, Divorce, Separation and Domestic Relations, § 1574 (6th ed. 1921) makes this statement, but the cases relied upon do not support it. E.g., Barber v. Barber, 168 App.Div. 212, 153 N.Y.S. 256 (2d Dep't 1915). 1 Blackstone, Commentaries on the Laws of England, 445 (Cooley 3d ed. 1884) states that a husband may, by force, keep his wife within the bounds of duty.

3. Scalf v. Scalf, 312 S.W.2d 467 (Ky.1958); Leahy v. Leahy, 208 Or. 659, 669, 303 P.2d 952, 961 (1956); Schmidt v. Schmidt, 51 Wash.2d 753, 321 P.2d 895 (1958).

For other authorities, see section 7.3, supra, at note 7.

4. Jacobson, American Marriage and Divorce 122 (1959) states that in 1950 between 50% and 60% of all American divorces were granted for cruelty. See Note, A Survey of Mental Cruelty as a Ground for Divorce, 15 DePaul L.Rev. 159 (1965).

5. See, e.g. Reed v. Reed, 138 Colo. 74, 329 P.2d 633 (1958), quoting with approval from Evans v. Evans, 1 Hagg.Con. 35, 161 Eng.Rep. 466 (1790). See also Silva v. Silva, 28 Conn.Supp. 336, 260 A.2d 408 (1969).

vorce, cruelty need no longer be so heavily relied upon, but to a limited degree people do still bring suits based upon it and the courts in the reported cases still adhere to relatively strict definitions of the ground. To this extent we can echo the remark in the first edition of this work, that this section is devoted to a fiction, the pretended definition of cruelty as a ground for divorce.

Cruelty is a statutory cause for absolute divorce in about twenty-seven states today.[6] The statutory language is diverse, usually including adjectives connoting severity or aimed at giving greater precision to the offense.[7] A few states use the term indignities rather than cruelty.[8] In spite of the diversity, which cannot but cause differences of result in close cases, there is a tendency to minimize the differences of the statutory language in order to develop a general common law of cruelty over the country.

The starting point for any attempt at defining cruelty must be Evans v. Evans,[9] a case which is still followed although it dealt only with ecclesiastical law, is now more than one hundred and fifty years old, and contains chiefly dictum. Lord Stowell's opinion in Evans v. Evans did two things of importance to

the later development of the law. It first stated what sort of conduct does not amount to cruelty, and then, after disclaiming any intention of defining cruelty affirmatively, went on to define cruelty affirmatively. The essence of the definition is that cruelty occurs only when there is bodily harm or a reasonable apprehension of bodily harm. Injuries to the feelings are not sufficient, nor are "mere austerity of temper, petulance of manners, rudeness of language, a want of civil attention and accommodation, even occasional sallies of passion, if they do not threaten bodily harm. * * *"[10] This limited concept of cruelty arose from the assumption that marital happiness is best secured by making marriage indissoluble except for a very few causes. When the parties know that they are bound together for life, the argument runs, they will resolve their differences and disagreements and make an effort to get along with each other. If they are able to separate legally upon less serious grounds, they will make no such effort, and immorality will result. This reasoning must be understood in the legal context of 1790 when absolute divorce was impossible, so that allowing a separation would not enable the parties to form other, happier relationships, but would condemn

---

6. E.g., Ala.Code 1983, § 30–2–1(a) (when the other party has committed actual violence on the complaining party's person or there is reasonable apprehension of such violence); Alaska Stat. § 25.24.050 (1983) (cruel and inhuman treatment calculated to impair health, or personal indignities rendering life burdensome); Ark.Rev.Stat. § 34–1202 (Supp.1985) (such cruel and barbarous treatment as to endanger life, or offering such indignities to the person of the other as shall render his or her condition intolerable); Conn.Gen.Stat.Ann. § 46b–40 (Supp.1986) (intolerable cruelty); Official Ga.Code Ann. § 19–5–3 (Supp. 1986) (cruel treatment such as to reasonably justify apprehension of danger to life, limb or health); Idaho Code § 32–603 (1983) (extreme cruelty); Ill.—S.H.A. ch. 40, § 401(2) (Supp.1986) (extreme and repeated physical or mental cruelty); Me.Rev.Stat.Ann. tit. 19, § 691(1) (1981) (extreme cruelty); Mass.G.L.A. ch. 208, § 1 (1981) (cruel and abusive treatment); Miss.Code 1973, § 93–5–1 (habitual cruel and inhuman treatment); N.H.Rev.Stat.Ann. § 458.7 (1983 Replacement) (extreme cruelty); N.J.Stat. Ann. § 2A:34–2 (Supp.1986) (extreme cruelty); N.M.Stat. Ann. 1986, § 40–4–1 (Replacement) (cruel and inhuman treatment); N.Y.—McKinney's Dom.Rel.L. § 170 (1977) (cruel and inhuman treatment endangering the physical or mental well being of the plaintiff); N.D.Cent.Code § 14–05–03 (1981 Replacement) (extreme cruelty); Ohio Rev. Code § 3105.01 (Supp.1985) (extreme cruelty); Okl.Stat. 1961, tit. 12, § 1271 (extreme cruelty); Pa.Stat. tit. 23, § 201 (Supp.1986) (cruel and barbarous treatment endan-

gering life or health); R.I.Gen.L. 1981, § 15–5–2 (extreme cruelty); S.C.Code 1985, § 20–3–10 (physical cruelty); S.D. Codif.L. § 25–4–2 (Supp.1986) (extreme cruelty); V.T.C.A., Fam.Code § 3.02 (1975) (cruel treatment that renders further living together insupportable); Utah Code Ann. 1984, § 30–3–1 (Replacement) (cruel treatment to the extent of causing bodily injury or great mental distress); Vt.Stat. Ann. tit. 15, § 551 (1974 and Supp.1986) (intolerable severity); Va.Code 1986, § 20–91 (Supp.) (cruelty); W.Va.Code, § 48–2–4 (1986) (cruel or inhuman treatment).

7. Ibid.

8. E.g., Alaska, Arkansas, Pennsylvania, supra, note 6. "Indignities" has been defined as requiring "a showing of habitual, continuous, permanent and plain manifestation of settled hate, alienation and estrangement on the part of one spouse, sufficient to render the condition of the other intolerable." McNew v. McNew, 262 Ark. 567, 559 S.W.2d 155 (1977). "Indignities" has also been defined as "vulgarities, unmerited reproach, habitual contumely, studied neglect, intentional incivility, manifest disdain, abusive language, or malignant ridicule." Beaver v. Beaver, 313 Pa.Super. 512, 460 A.2d 305 (1983).

9. 1 Hagg.Con. 35, 161 Eng.Rep. 466 (1790). See also Goodhart, Cruelty, Desertion and Insanity in Matrimonial Law, 79 L.Q.Rev. 98 (1963).

10. Id. at 38, 161 Eng.Rep. at 467. See also Holden v. Holden, 1 Hagg.Con. 453, 161 Eng.Rep. 614 (1810).

them either to a single life or to illegal and immoral attachments. In spite of the great differences between English society in 1790 and American society in the mid-Twentieth Century, the ecclesiastical definition of cruelty as announced in Evans v. Evans has had a strong influence on the definition of cruelty found in American statutes and judicial decisions,[11] although today the ground for divorce is rarely limited to physical cruelty.[12]

Cruelty, as it was defined by Evans v. Evans and by the American cases influenced by the English doctrine, was recognized as a ground for divorce in order to protect the spouse from bodily injury,[13] not to enable the parties to escape from an unhappy marriage nor to punish the defendant. This definition immediately suggests the question why the plaintiff spouse is protected only from bodily harm when today we know that equal or greater

suffering may result from psychological causes. Many courts have responded to this question by expanding the definition of cruelty to include conduct having no physical impact on the plaintiff provided either that it produces or is likely to produce an impairment of health or other bodily symptoms.[14]

The question then is, why should the law stop at this point? Suffering may be acute without necessarily producing physical symptoms. If the object of granting divorces for cruelty is the protection of the plaintiff from harm, first physical and now psychological, why should it matter what the symptoms are? Logically and psychologically it should not matter, and for that reason some jurisdictions have been willing to find cruelty without proof of injury to health, at least where the marriage has become unendurable.[15] Other courts, perhaps the majority, have refused to

11. Cases whose language sounds very much like that in Evans v. Evans include Neff v. Neff, 13 Md.App. 128, 281 A.2d 556 (1971); Williams v. Williams, 351 Mich. 210, 88 N.W.2d 483 (1958). The Evans case has also influenced the majority of courts which hold that whatever form the cruelty may take, there must be evidence of its effect on the plaintiff's health before a divorce may be granted. See note 14, infra.

12. South Carolina seems to require that the cruelty be physical in its nature, and not merely in its effect. S.C.Code, § 20–3–10 (1985); Bankhead v. Bankhead, 254 S.C. 78, 173 S.E.2d 372 (1970).

13. Steinbrugge v. Steinbrugge, 2 N.J. 77, 65 A.2d 606 (1949). Language in some of the New York cases also indicates that in that state the adoption of cruelty as a ground for divorce was for the purpose of protecting the complaining spouse. E.g., Warguleski v. Warguleski, 79 A.D.2d 1107, 435 N.Y.S.2d 857 (4th Dep't 1981); Sgroi v. Sgroi, 70 A.D.2d 702, 416 N.Y.S.2d 384 (3d Dep't 1979).

14. E.g., Reed v. Reed, 138 Colo. 74, 329 P.2d 633 (1958); Connor v. Connor, 212 Ga. 92, 90 S.E.2d 581 (1955); In re Marriage of Semmler, 90 Ill.App.3d 649, 46 Ill.Dec. 62, 413 N.E.2d 502 (1980); Christian v. Christian, 69 Ill.App.3d 450, 26 Ill.Dec. 326, 387 N.E.2d 1254 (1979); Young v. Young, 260 Iowa 1018, 151 N.W.2d 340 (1967); Flavell v. Flavell, 324 Mass. 362, 86 N.E.2d 647 (1949); Tschida v. Tschida, 170 Minn. 235, 212 N.W. 193 (1927); Ormachea v. Ormachea, 67 Nev. 273, 217 P.2d 355 (1950); Friedman v. Friedman, 37 N.J.Super. 52, 116 A.2d 793 (1955), certification denied 20 N.J. 135, 118 A.2d 559 (1955); Wolf v. Wolf, 114 R.I. 375, 333 A.2d 138 (1975); Lafko v. Lafko, 127 Vt. 609, 256 A.2d 166 (1969); Upchurch v. Upchurch, 194 Va. 990, 76 S.E.2d 170 (1953); Jacobs v. Jacobs, 42 Wis.2d 507, 167 N.W.2d 238 (1969).

Judicial notice of the effect of defendant's conduct on plaintiff's health may only be taken where the connection is plain. Annot., 72 A.L.R.2d 554, 586 (1960).

If the conduct complained of would have amounted to cruelty had the parties been living together, it is no less

cruelty by having occurred after they had separated. See cases collected in Annot., 129 A.L.R. 160 (1940).

It is not uncommon for courts in cruelty cases to emphasize that evidence of incompatibility is not a sufficient basis for granting the divorce. E.g., Klakk v. Klakk, 41 Ill.App.3d 462, 354 N.E.2d 64 (1976); Churchill v. Churchill, 467 So.2d 948 (Miss.1985); Hessen v. Hessen, 33 N.Y.2d 406, 353 N.Y.S.2d 421, 308 N.E.2d 891 (1974); Brady v. Brady, 64 N.Y.2d 339, 486 N.Y.S.2d 891, 476 N.E.2d 290 (1985).

15. E.g. Obennoskey v. Obennoskey, 215 Ark. 358, 220 S.W.2d 610 (1949) (mental suffering sufficient to make plaintiff's condition intolerable); Carroll v. Carroll, 135 Colo. 379, 311 P.2d 709 (1957) (semble); Hoppe v. Hoppe, 181 Kan. 428, 312 P.2d 215 (1957) (course of conduct which utterly destroys the legitimate ends of marriage); Carter v. Carter, 191 Kan. 80, 379 P.2d 311 (1963) (same); Thompson v. Thompson, 227 Minn. 256, 35 N.W.2d 289 (1948); Russell v. Russell, 157 Miss. 425, 128 So. 270 (1930) (conduct which defeats the purpose of the relationship); Sims v. Sims, 185 Neb. 479, 176 N.W.2d 683 (1970), appeal after remand 186 Neb. 780, 186 N.W.2d 491 (1971) (conduct which nullifies or destroys the legitimate objects and ends of matrimony); Buess v. Buess, 89 Ohio App. 37, 100 N.E.2d 646 (1950); McCullough v. McCullough, 120 Tex. 209, 36 S.W.2d 459 (1931) (conduct such as to render further living together insupportable).

Gazzillo v. Gazzillo, 153 N.J.Super. 159, 379 A.2d 288 (1977), after the 1971 amendment of the New Jersey statute broadening the definition of cruelty, held that a divorce would be granted where the husband was insensitive and unresponsive to the wife's needs, even though he was not guilty of objective fault. The case exemplifies the attempts of some courts, with some legislative help, to reflect changing standards of marital conduct and of divorce grounds. See also Small v. Small, 413 A.2d 1318 (Me. 1980).

In New York it seems that a showing of more serious misconduct is required to constitute cruelty where the

go this far.[16] One explanation of their refusal may be a fear that where the impact on the plaintiff is exclusively psychological, the fabrication or exaggeration of claims for divorce becomes easier. If some bodily harm is required, presumably the court will be better able to judge the effect of the misconduct upon the plaintiff. In fact when the cases are examined the requirement of proof of some physical harm turns out to be largely illusory. This requirement is often met by vague testimony as to impairment of health, loss of sleep, nervousness, loss of weight and similar general symptoms. If this is all that is necessary, and it appears to satisfy most courts, then the requirement becomes a formality, since anyone who is having serious marital conflicts or unhappiness can doubtless testify that they produce these symptoms.

One further influence in the direction of expanding cruelty comes from a change in the underlying policy. A few courts today explicitly recognize that the purpose to be served by making cruelty a ground for divorce is not to protect the plaintiff, but to enable the courts to dissolve marriages which have so far deteriorated that they no longer serve the interests of the parties or of society.[17] On this theory cruelty becomes a synonym for serious, irreconcilable marital differences, and divorces may be granted without further search for bodily symptoms or concern for precisely who is responsible for the differences. Only a few appellate courts have gone this far, but this view of cruelty is undoubtedly widely accepted by trial courts in the adjudication of uncontested cases.

In addition to the broad trends in the cases already discussed, some more specific principles applicable to cruelty should be mentioned. One of these is the often stated notion that in determining the effect of the defendant's conduct on the plaintiff, subjective tests are to be applied. Conduct which might not seriously distress one person, or perhaps many people, might be devastating to the particular plaintiff. The court may take this into consideration.[18] The age, education, and degree of sensitivity of the plaintiff may be considered in assessing the impact of the defendant's conduct.[19] If the plaintiff has such a disposition as not to be hurt by the defendant's conduct, he may not have a divorce even though other plaintiffs might.[20]

If the plaintiff's own conduct has been such as to provoke the defendant's harsh treatment of the plaintiff, the plaintiff is denied the divorce, the defendant's conduct being considered excused, if not wholly excusable, so long as it was not disproportionate to the provocation.[21]

---

marriage has been of long duration than where the marriage has been of short duration. Brady v. Brady, 64 N.Y.2d 339, 486 N.Y.S.2d 891, 476 N.E.2d 290 (1985).

16. See the cases cited in note 14, supra. Clear cut distinctions between the general definitions of cruelty are not made by many cases, nor is there a precise definition of what sort of evidence will suffice to prove cruelty. In some jurisdictions authorities both ways may be found.

The hardships imposed by courts which continue to deny divorces for failure to prove the old-fashioned version of cruelty are well described by the dissent in Gallaspy v. Gallaspy, 459 So.2d 283 (Miss.1984).

17. E.g., Gazzillo v. Gazzillo, 153 N.J.Super. 159, 379 A.2d 288 (1977); Leahy v. Leahy, 208 Or. 659, 303 P.2d 952 (1956); Graziano v. Graziano, 7 Utah 2d 187, 321 P.2d 931 (1958); Freeburn v. Freeburn, 107 Wash. 646, 182 P. 620 (1919). Contra: Miller v. Miller, 58 Wash.2d 193, 361 P.2d 583 (1961).

18. May v. May, 275 Cal.App.2d 264, 79 Cal.Rptr. 622 (1969); Surratt v. Surratt, 12 Ill.2d 21, 145 N.E.2d 594 (1957); Graff v. Graff, 71 Ill.App.3d 496, 27 Ill.Dec. 798, 389 N.E.2d 1206 (1979); Gregory v. Gregory, 24 Ill.App.3d 436, 321 N.E.2d 122 (1974).

Hessen v. Hessen, 33 N.Y.2d 406, 353 N.Y.S.2d 421, 308 N.E.2d 891 (1974) held that such individual factors as the ages of the spouses, the duration of the marriage, the effects of these factors on the physical and mental disposition of the spouses, and the fact that the grant of a divorce would deprive a middle aged spouse of alimony are all to be considered in determining whether cruelty occurred.

19. Diem v. Diem, 141 Fla. 260, 193 So. 65 (1940); Grant v. Grant, 44 R.I. 169, 116 A. 481 (1922); McCullough v. McCullough, 120 Tex. 209, 36 S.W.2d 459 (1931); Daughtry v. Daughtry, 312 S.W.2d 957 (Tex.Civ.App.1958).

Carroll v. Carroll, 135 Colo. 379, 311 P.2d 709 (1957) seems to emphasize the sensitive nature of the plaintiff husband in finding the wife guilty of cruelty.

20. Wilson v. Wilson, 246 Iowa 792, 68 N.W.2d 904 (1955).

21. Iverson v. Iverson, 38 Ill.App.3d 308, 347 N.E.2d 6 (1976) (no provocation found); Collis v. Collis, 355 Mass. 25, 242 N.E.2d 423 (1968); Evans v. Evans, 176 Or. 403, 157 P.2d 495 (1945), 25 Or.L.Rev. 63 (1946); Beaver v. Beaver, 313 Pa.Super. 512, 460 A.2d 305 (1983). Provocation is distinguished from recrimination in Rosenbaum v. Rosenbaum, 38 Ill.App.3d 1, 349 N.E.2d 73 (1976); Lovett v. Lovett, 164 N.W.2d 793 (Iowa 1969).

If the object of granting divorces for cruelty is, as some cases say, the preservation of the plaintiff's physical health, it follows that the defendant's state of mind is irrelevant. Many cases hold that it is relevant, however, and that the defendant's conduct is only cruelty where he acts wilfully or maliciously, by which is apparently meant with intent to hurt the plaintiff.[22] These cases are evidence that divorce is still viewed in some quarters as punishing the defendant for his guilty intent. Although a harsh course of conduct may sometimes inflict greater suffering if it is accompanied by an intent to hurt than if it is merely insensitive to the plaintiff's feelings, in either event the purposes of marriage will usually be frustrated. For this reason a growing number of cases have held that the defendant's state of mind is irrelevant if cruelty has occurred.[23]

It is often said that cruelty involves a course of conduct over a period of time.[24] This means that a single act of violence or threat of violence does not amount to cruelty,[25] but this is of little practical importance since it is rare that such acts do occur but once. Even if there is only a single act, it may still constitute cruelty if the circumstances indicate that it is likely to be repeated,[26] or if it is particularly brutal or severe.[27]

If the complaining spouse knows in advance of marriage of the defendant's propensity to engage in cruelty or abuse, it has occasionally been held that this is a defense to the action for divorce.[28] Such cases are not common, and this rule certainly should not be applied unless there is clear evidence of the knowledge before marriage.

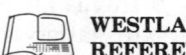

WESTLAW REFERENCES

Background and General Definitions
di cruelty
di(divorc! /p cruel /s actual! /2 violen!)
di indignity

§ 13.5 Divorce Grounds—Incompatibility

Incompatibility as a ground for divorce came into American law first in the Virgin Islands, which adopted it from the Danish law

22. Obennoskey v. Obennoskey, 215 Ark. 358, 220 S.W.2d 610 (1949); Sarafin v. Sarafin, 28 Conn.Supp. 24, 247 A.2d 500 (1968); Connor v. Connor, 212 Ga. 92, 90 S.E.2d 581 (1955); Williams v. Williams, 351 Mich. 210, 88 N.W.2d 483 (1958); Friedman v. Friedman, 37 N.J. Super. 52, 116 A.2d 793 (1955); Buess v. Buess, 89 Ohio App. 37, 100 N.E.2d 646 (1950); Walper v. Walper, 198 Pa.Super. 409, 182 A.2d 209 (1962); Shankles v. Shankles, 445 S.W.2d 803 (Tex.Civ.App.1969).

The courts are divided on whether the defendant's insanity or mental illness is a defense to a charge of cruelty, on the ground that in such circumstances the cruelty could not be intentional. Holding that it is a defense: Vaughan v. Vaughan, 223 Ga. 298, 154 S.E.2d 592 (1967); Loveless v. Loveless, 128 Ill.App.2d 297, 261 N.E.2d 732 (1970) (wife found legally responsible for her actions); Dankers v. Dankers, 285 Minn. 120, 172 N.W.2d 318 (1969) (insanity is a defense, but here it was not proved that the defendant was under such a defect of reason as not to know the nature of her acts or that they were wrong); Hano v. Hano, 5 Mass.App.Ct. 639, 367 N.E. 2d 1190 (1977); Britton v. Britton, 280 Pa.Super. 87, 421 A.2d 417 (1980); Jumper v. Jumper, 240 Pa.Super. 99, 362 A.2d 411 (1976). Holding insanity not a defense: Nunes v. Nunes, 62 Cal.2d 33, 41 Cal.Rptr. 5, 396 P.2d 37 (1964); Pajak v. Pajak, 56 N.Y.2d 394, 452 N.Y.S.2d 381, 437 N.E.2d 1138 (1982). See also Annot., 19 A.L.R.2d 144, 148 (1951); Goodhart, Cruelty, Desertion and Insanity in Matrimonial Law, 79 L.Q.Rev. 98 (1963); Hall, Matrimonial Cruelty and Mens Rea, 1963 Camb.L.J. 104. Other aspects of insanity as a defense to divorce are discussed in section 14.2, infra. Insanity as a ground for divorce is discussed in section 14.8, Practitioner's Edition.

23. Nunes v. Nunes, 62 Cal.2d 33, 41 Cal.Rptr. 5, 396 P.2d 37 (1964), 38 So.Cal.L.Rev. 713 (1965); Grossman v. Grossman, 90 So.2d 115 (Fla.1956); Flavell v. Flavell, 324 Mass. 362, 86 N.E.2d 647 (1949) (is sufficient that harm is the natural consequence of defendant's acts); Nelson v. Nelson, 221 Or. 117, 350 P.2d 702 (1960) (callous want of consideration is equivalent to intentional injury); Note 112 U.Pa.L.Rev. 606 (1964).

24. This is sometimes embodied in the statute. E.g., Ill.—S.H.A. ch. 40, § 401(2) (Supp.1986) providing for extreme and repeated physical or mental cruelty. See also Welling v. Welling, 144 Ind.App. 182, 245 N.E.2d 173 (1969), cert. denied 396 U.S. 929, 90 S.Ct. 266, 24 L.Ed.2d 227 (1969); Brown v. Brown, 248 Iowa 802, 82 N.W.2d 661 (1957); Saunders v. Saunders, 82 N.J.Eq. 491, 89 A. 518 (1914); Richardson v. Richardson, 258 S.C. 135, 187 S.E.2d 528 (1972).

25. Collins v. Collins, 184 Md. 655, 42 A.2d 680 (1945); Brown v. Brown, 215 S.C. 502, 56 S.E.2d 330 (1949). Other cases are cited in Annot., 24 A.L.R. 918 (1923).

26. Johnson v. Johnson, 76 Nev. 318, 353 P.2d 449 (1960); Stephenson v. Stephenson, 111 N.H. 189, 278 A.2d 351 (1971).

27. Ellzey v. Ellzey, 253 So.2d 249 (Miss.1971); Gray v. Gray, 220 Pa.Super. 143, 286 A.2d 684 (1971); Annot., 7 A.L.R.3d 761 (1966).

28. Williamson v. Williamson, 212 Ark. 12, 204 S.W.2d 785 (1947).

which prevailed in the Islands until they were acquired by the United States in 1917.[1] This ground for divorce now exists in six states[2] and, in a qualified form, in a seventh state, Delaware.[3] In those states where it exists, it is often relied upon.[4]

The most quoted definition of incompatibility owes much to Danish law from which the Virgin Islands statute was derived:

"We conclude that while incompatibility of temperament in the Virgin Islands Divorce Law does not refer to those petty quarrels and minor bickerings which are but the evidence of that frailty which all humanity is heir to, it unquestionably does refer to conflicts in personalities and dispositions so deep as to be irreconcilable and to render it impossible for the parties to continue a normal marital relationship with each other. To use the ancient Danish phrase, the disharmony of the spouses in their common life must be so deep and intense as to be irremediable. It is the legal recognition of the proposition long established in the earlier Danish law of the Islands that if the parties are so mismated that their marriage has in fact ended as the result of their hopeless disagreement and discord the courts should be empowered to terminate it as a matter of Law."[5]

Although it seems clear that incompatibility has been adopted as a ground for divorce in order to broaden the circumstances in which

spouses may terminate an unhappy marriage,[6] the courts continue to emphasize that this ground is not to be relied on to provide divorces for minor quarrels and bickering, but rather that it "may be broadly defined as such a deep and irreconcilable conflict in personalities or temperaments of the parties as makes it impossible for them to continue a normal marital relationship. The conflict of personalities and dispositions must be so deep as to be irreconcilable and irremediable."[7] Other courts have expressed the same idea in terms of the elements of the ground, which are said to be (a) that there be a rift or discord in the marriage; (b) that the discord is sufficient to destroy a normal marital relationship; and (c) that reconciliation is improbable.[8] These definitions are reminiscent of the expanded version of cruelty which prevails in some states, the chief difference being that with incompatibility there is no need to prove an adverse effect upon health.

When the courts come to apply these general definitions to specific cases, they look for objective conduct which evidences the serious discord and conflict described in the definitions. As a result divorces for incompatibility have been granted on evidence of repeated and bitter arguments and quarrels accompanied by serious differences in the goals of married life and by refusal to communicate;[9] of threats of violence accompanied by heavy drinking;[10] of harassment, accusations and

§ 13.5

1. Orfield, Divorce for Temperamental Incompatibility, 52 Mich.L.Rev. 659 (1954). The Virgin Islands have now replaced incompatibility with the similar ground of marriage breakdown. Virgin Is.Code tit. 16, § 104 (Supp. 1984–1985).

2. Ala.Code, 1983, § 30–2–1(a); Alaska Stat. § 25.24.050 (1983); Kan.Stat.Ann. § 60–1601(a) (1983); Nev.Rev.Stat. § 125.010 (1986); N.M.Stat.Ann.1986, § 40–4–1 Replacement; Okl.Stat.1961, tit. 12, § 1271.

3. Del.Code tit. 13, § 1505 (1981) provides that divorce shall be granted when the marriage is irretrievably broken and that a marriage is irretrievably broken when it is characterized by a separation caused by incompatibility.

4. P. Jacobson, American Marriage and Divorce 126 (1959) states that incompatibility accounts for seven-eighths of all divorces in New Mexico.

5. Burch v. Burch, 195 F.2d 799, 806–807 (3d Cir. 1952). Accord: Hughes v. Hughes, 363 P.2d 155 (Okl. 1961) and the dissent in Shearer v. Shearer, 356 F.2d 391,

395 (3d Cir.1965), cert. denied 384 U.S. 940, 86 S.Ct. 1463, 16 L.Ed.2d 540 (1966).

6. North v. North, 217 Kan. 213, 535 P.2d 914 (1975), appeal dismissed 423 U.S. 918, 96 S.Ct. 257, 46 L.Ed.2d 245 (1975).

7. LaRue v. LaRue, 216 Kan. 242, 244, 531 P.2d 84, 87 (1975). See also Williams v. Williams, 543 P.2d 1401 (Okl.1975), appeal dismissed for want of a substantial federal question, 426 U.S. 901, 96 S.Ct. 2220, 48 L.Ed.2d 826 (1976).

8. Pruitt v. Pruitt, 445 A.2d 955 (Del.Fam.Ct.1982).

9. Clark v. Clark, 384 So.2d 1120 (Ala.App.1980); Husband, R. S. S. v. Wife, B. J. S., 280 A.2d 705 (Del.1971); H. v. H., 253 A.2d 500 (Del.1969); Pruitt v. Pruitt, 445 A.2d 955 (Del.Fam.Ct.1982); North v. North, 217 Kan. 213, 535 P.2d 914 (1975), appeal dismissed 423 U.S. 918, 96 S.Ct. 257, 46 L.Ed.2d 245 (1975), cert. denied 423 U.S. 940, 96 S.Ct. 299, 46 L.Ed.2d 271 (1975).

10. Rothchild v. Rothchild, 434 So.2d 794 (Ala.Civ. App.1983), cert. denied 434 So.2d 794 (1983).

the refusal of sexual relations;[11] and of the wife's settled dislike, leading her to testify that she had just had enough of her husband.[12] There is some question whether the testimony of one spouse alone as to the marital difficulties is sufficient basis for the divorce.[13] Other cases have granted the divorce on evidence of general marital unkindness, living apart and other conduct indicating a settled lack of affection and harmony.[14] There are cases, however, which refuse to grant divorces for incompatibility where the evidence reveals marital conflicts so severe that any resumption of the marital relationships seems most unlikely.[15]

It should be obvious that incompatibility is a ground for divorce which does not oblige the court to make any finding concerning marital fault. Most of the authorities do take this view.[16] Unfortunately there are a few cases in which divorces for incompatibility have been denied because the plaintiff was found at fault,[17] or because the defendant was found not to be at fault,[18] or even because both were at fault, so that a defense resembling recrimi-

nation was invoked.[19] The Delaware cases, although prevented from considering fault by the state's statute,[20] seem to require that the incompatibility be "mutual", whatever that may mean.[21] Any such continued insistence on the relevance of fault or proof of mutuality is inconsistent with the definition of incompatibility. When one of the spouses seriously and definitively feels that he cannot continue the marriage, there is incompatibility regardless of fault and irrespective of what the other spouse feels about the relationship. This may impose hardship on the spouse who wants to continue the marriage, but that is the price that has to be paid for ending the evils of a fault-based divorce law. And in any case where one spouse is so seriously disaffected as to sustain a claim of incompatibility, the denial of a divorce will not restore the marriage to viability.

 **WESTLAW REFERENCES**

divorc! /s incompatib! /s quarrel! fight! fought
divorc! /s incompatib! /s irreconcilab!

---

11. Dyal v. Dyal, 54 Ala.App. 206, 307 So.2d 17 (1975); Doran v. Doran, 245 A.2d 434 (Del.Super.1968).

12. LaRue v. LaRue, 216 Kan. 242, 531 P.2d 84 (1975).

13. Testimony of the plaintiff alone was held sufficient in Clark v. Clark, 384 So.2d 1120 (Ala.Civ.App. 1980). The court in Owens v. Owens, 435 So.2d 1316 (Ala.Civ.App.1983) said that it would not be, however.

14. Del Peschio v. Del Peschio, 356 F.2d 402 (3d Cir. 1966), cert. denied 385 U.S. 886, 87 S.Ct. 181, 17 L.Ed.2d 113 (1966); Paddock v. Paddock, 16 Alaska 427, 240 F.2d 926 (9th Cir. 1956); Hines v. Hines, 64 N.M. 377, 328 P.2d 944 (1958); Woollett v. Woollett, 57 N.M. 550, 260 P.2d 913 (1953) (physical violence); Poteet v. Poteet, 45 N.M. 214, 114 P.2d 91 (1941); Rakestraw v. Rakestraw, 345 P.2d 888 (Okl.1959); Chappell v. Chappell, 298 P.2d 768 (Okl.1956); Bradley v. Bradley, 284 P.2d 434 (Okl.1955). Other cases are collected in Annots., 58 A.L.R.2d 1218 (1958) and 97 A.L.R.3d 989 (1980).

Incompatibility is perhaps clearest where the evidence shows that there is no probability of reconciliation. See, e.g., Gordon v. Gordon, 218 Kan. 686, 545 P.2d 328 (1976).

15. E.g., Schlesinger v. Schlesinger, 399 F.2d 7 (3d Cir. 1968); Shearer v. Shearer, 356 F.2d 391 (3d Cir.1965), cert. denied 384 U.S. 940, 86 S.Ct. 1463, 16 L.Ed.2d 540 (1966); Della Loggia v. Della Loggia, 264 A.2d 521 (Del. Super.1970).

16. Del Peschio v. Del Peschio, 356 F.2d 402 (3d Cir. 1966), cert. denied 385 U.S. 886, 87 S.Ct. 181, 17 L.Ed.2d 113 (1966); Burch v. Burch, 195 F.2d 799 (3d Cir.1952);

Helton v. Helton, 362 So.2d 257 (Ala.Civ.App.1978); Cooper v. Cooper, 57 Ala.App. 674, 331 So.2d 689 (1976), cert. denied 331 So.2d 695 (Ala.1976); Berry v. Berry, 215 Kan. 47, 523 P.2d 342 (1974); State ex rel. Dubois v. Ryan, 85 N.M. 575, 514 P.2d 851 (1973); Chavez v. Chavez, 39 N.M. 480, 50 P.2d 264 (1935).

17. Schlesinger v. Schlesinger, 399 F.2d 7 (3d Cir. 1968); Colby v. Colby, 283 F.Supp. 150 (D.V.I.1968); Sachs v. Sachs, 155 F.Supp. 860 (D.V.I.1957); T. v. T., 314 A.2d 176 (Del.1973) (decided under the earlier statute). Dowdell v. Dowdell, 463 P.2d 948 (Okl.1969) seems to say that a divorce based on incompatibility established the fault of the defendant. A case which seems to reject any reliance upon fault is Husband, M. v. Wife, M., 295 A.2d 723 (Del.1972).

18. Shearer v. Shearer, 356 F.2d 391 (3d Cir.1965), cert. denied 384 U.S. 940, 86 S.Ct. 1463, 16 L.Ed.2d 540 (1966).

19. Clark v. Clark, 54 N.M. 364, 225 P.2d 147 (1950). Fortunately this case seems to have been overruled by Garner v. Garner, 85 N.M. 324, 512 P.2d 84 (1973).

20. Del.Code tit. 13, § 1503(3) (1981) defines incompatibility as a "marital rift or discord that has destroyed the marital relation, without regard to the fault of either party."

21. Wife S v. Husband S, 413 A.2d 886 (Del.1980); J.A.D. v. P.L.D., 259 A.2d 381 (Del.1969). Contra: Kegley v. Kegley, 355 So.2d 1121 (Ala.Civ.App.1977), cert. denied 355 So.2d 1123 (Ala.1978).

§ 13.6 Divorce Grounds—Marriage Breakdown

This section is concerned with those non-fault grounds for divorce which were enacted in the 1970's as a product of divorce reform movements of the 1960's. They are phrased in such terms as "irretrievable breakdown of marriage" or "irremediable breakdown of marriage" or "irreconcilable differences". Although at first glance this language appears not to differ substantially from incompatibility, these grounds are discussed separately because they have a different history, and because they represent a legislative and judicial acceptance of a broad version of divorce without fault which largely avoids the restrictive kinds construction which incompatibility has sometimes received in the courts.[1]

Criticism of the grounds for divorce and demands for their reform have had a long history,[2] but the appearance of marriage breakdown statutes in many states was precipitated for the most part by three important studies, all completed during the 1960's. Putting Asunder,[3] the report of a group appointed by the Archbishop of Canterbury, took an unfavorable view of the existing English divorce law and recommended that divorces be granted on the ground of breakdown of marriage. In California a commission appointed by the governor to study the state's divorce law was similarly critical of the grounds for divorce and also recommended enactment of a form of marriage breakdown to replace the traditional fault grounds.[4] Such a statute was passed in 1969.[5] And after an extensive monograph had outlined the current and past objections to fault based divorce,[6] the Commissioners on Uniform State Laws recommended a uniform divorce statute which contained irretrievable breakdown of marriage as its sole ground for divorce.[7]

The consequence of these reform proposals was that thirty-three states now have some version of marriage breakdown as a ground or the ground for divorce.[8] The language of

§ 13.6

1. See section 13.5, supra, at note 17.

2. The most extensive critical study of American law and of the law of other countries as well is M. Rheinstein, Marriage Stability, Divorce, and the Law (1972), which cites many other proposals for reform. See also Bodenheimer, Reflections on the Future of Grounds for Divorce, 8 J. of Fam.L. 179 (1968).

3. Putting Asunder, The Report of a Group Appointed by the Archbishop of Canterbury in January 1964 (1966), also known as the Mortimer Report after the Group's chairman, the Right Reverend R. C. Mortimer, D.D., the Lord Bishop of Exeter.

4. California Governor's Commission on the Family, Report of the Governor's Commission on the Family (1966).

5. This statute is now West's Ann.Cal.Civ.Code §§ 4506, 4507, 4508 (1983).

6. R. Levy, Uniform Marriage and Divorce Legislation: A Preliminary Analysis 41 (1969).

7. Uniform Marriage and Divorce Act §§ 302, 305, 9A Unif.L.Ann. 121, 132 (1979).

8. Alaska Stat. § 25.24.050 (1983) (incompatibility of temperament causing the irremediable breakdown of the marriage on joint petition); Ariz.Rev.Stat. §§ 25–312 (Supp.1986) and 25–316 (1976) (marriage is irretrievably broken); West's Ann.Cal.Civ.Code §§ 4506, 4507 (1983) (irreconcilable differences which have caused irremediable breakdown of the marriage); Colo.Rev.Stat. §§ 14–10–106, 14–10–110 (1973 and Supp.1986) (marriage is irretrievably broken); Conn.Gen.Stat.Ann. § 46b–40 (1986) (marriage has broken down irretrievably); Del.Code tit.

13, § 1505 (1981) (marriage is irretrievably broken, which means it is characterized by separation caused in several ways, including by respondent's misconduct and by incompatibility); West's Fla.Stat.Ann. § 61.052 (1985) (marriage is irretrievably broken); Official Ga.Code Ann. § 19–5–3 (Supp.1986) (marriage is irretrievably broken); Hawaii Rev.Stat. § 580–41 (1976 Replacement) (marriage is irretrievably broken); Idaho Code § 32–603 (1983) (irreconcilable differences); Ill.—S.H.A. ch. 40, § 401(2) (Supp.1986) (irreconcilable differences causing irretrievable breakdown of marriage and lived apart two years); West's Ann.Ind.Code § 31–1–11.5–3(a) (Supp.1986) (irretrievable breakdown of marriage); Iowa Code Ann. § 598.5 (1981 and Supp.1986) (breakdown of the marriage to the extent that legitimate objects of matrimony have been destroyed and there remains no reasonable likelihood that the marriage can be preserved); Ky.Rev.Stat. § 403.170 (1984) (marriage is irretrievably broken); Me. Rev.Stat.Ann. tit. 19, § 691(1) (1981) (irreconcilable marital differences); Mass.G.L.A. ch. 208, § 1 (1981) (irretrievable breakdown of the marriage on affidavit of both parties and execution of a separation agreement); Mich. C.L.A. § 25.86 (1984) (similar to the Iowa statute); Minn. Stat.Ann. § 518.06 (Supp.1987) (irretrievable breakdown of the marriage); Miss.Code 1986, § 93–5–2 (Supp.) (irreconcilable differences if the parties file a joint bill and separation agreement); Vernon's Ann.Mo.Stat. §§ 452.305 (1986) and 452.320 (1986) (marriage is irretrievably broken if no spouse objects; if the respondent denies the breakdown, the petitioner must prove adultery, abandonment for six months, behavior such that the petitioner cannot reasonably be expected to live with the respondent, or separation for twelve or twenty-four months); Mont.Code Ann. § 40–4–107 (1985) (marriage is

these statutes varies considerably in ways which will sometimes lead to differing results. Most of them make it clear that fault is no longer relevant to the grant of a divorce.[9] A few expressly exclude from consideration any evidence of marital misconduct respecting the grant or denial of the divorce.[10] And some include provisions encouraging counseling or conciliation before entry of a decree.[11] Although the divorce rate has risen sharply in the years after enactment of marriage breakdown statutes,[12] notwithstanding these attempts at persuading spouses to attempt reconciliation, the causes for the increase in the divorce rate are more likely to lie in the social, ethical, and psychological attitudes toward marriage and divorce which currently

prevail in this country than in the more liberal grounds on which divorce may now be obtained.[13]

Not surprisingly, the marriage breakdown ground for divorce has been subjected to a barrage of constitutional attacks. It has withstood them all. It has been held not to be void for vagueness, being as definite and capable of definition as other grounds for divorce.[14] It has been held not to violate the Contracts Clause of the Constitution [15] since marriage, although often referred to as a contract, is not such a contract as that Clause protects and the legislature has plenary power over the institution of marriage.[16] It does not violate the Equal Protection Clause of the Fourteenth Amendment.[17] And it does not

irretrievably broken); Neb.Rev.Stat. § 42–361 (1984) (marriage is irretrievably broken); N.H.Rev.Stat.Ann. § 458.7–a (1983 Replacement) (irreconcilable differences causing irremediable breakdown of the marriage); N.D. Cent.Code §§ 14–05–03, 14–05–09.1 (1981 Replacement) (irreconcilable differences); Or.Rev.Stat. § 107.025 (1983) (irreconcilable differences causing irremediable breakdown of marriage); Pa.Stat. tit. 23, § 201 (Supp.1986) (marriage is irretrievably broken); R.I.Gen.L.1981, § 15–5–3.1 (irreconcilable differences have caused irremediable breakdown of the marriage); Tenn.Code Ann. § 36–4–101(11) (1984) (irreconcilable differences between the parties); V.T.C.A., Fam.Code § 3.01 (1975) (marriage has become insupportable because of discord or conflict of personalities that destroys the legitimate ends of the marriage relationship); West's Rev.Code Wash.Ann. § 26.09.030 (1986) (marriage is irretrievably broken); W.Va.Code, § 48–2–4 (1986) (agreement of parties that irreconcilable differences have arisen); Wis.Stat.Ann. § 767.12(2) (1981) (marriage is irretrievably broken); Wyo.Stat.1977, § 20–2–104 (1977) (irreconcilable differences in the marital relationship).

The English statute is like that in Missouri, retaining substantial aspects of the fault grounds. Matrimonial Causes Act of 1973, §§ 1 and 2 provides that there may be a petition for divorce if the marriage has broken down irretrievably, but that the petitioner must prove that the respondent has committed adultery and the petitioner finds it intolerable to live with the respondent; or that the respondent has behaved in such a manner that the petitioner cannot reasonably be expected to live with the respondent; or that the respondent has deserted the petitioner for two years; or that the parties have lived apart for two years and the respondent consents to a decree; or that the parties have lived apart for five years.

9. Anderson v. Anderson, 237 Ga. 886, 230 S.E.2d 272 (1976). But the Delaware and Missouri statutes, cited supra, note 8, still cause the finding of marriage breakdown and the grant of a divorce to turn on fault in some circumstances. See In re Marriage of Mitchell, 545 S.W.2d 313 (Mo.App.1976) and C.B.H. v. R.N.H., 571 S.W.2d 449 (Mo.App.1978).

10. E.g., West's Ann.Cal.Civ.Code § 4509 (1983), excluding evidence of specific acts of misconduct.

11. Ariz.Rev.Stat. § 25–381.09 (1976), providing for transfer of cases to a conciliation court; West's Ann.Cal. Civ.Code § 4508 (1983), providing for a continuance if there is a chance of conciliation; Colo.Rev.Stat. § 14–10–110(2)(b) (1974); Idaho Code § 32–716 (1983), providing for conferences of the parties with a view to conciliation; Iowa Code Ann. § 598.16 (Supp.1986), permitting the court to order conciliation in some circumstances; Vernon's Ann.Mo.Stat. § 452.320(3) (1986), suggesting counseling; Neb.Rev.Stat. § 42–360 (1984), forbidding the entry of a decree unless all reasonable efforts at reconciliation have been made; Wis.Stat.Ann. §§ 767.083, 767.12(b)(2) (1981).

12. See section 12.1, supra, at note 41.

13. For a careful and thorough empirical study supporting the text statement, see Frank, Berman, Mazur-Hart, No Fault Divorce and the Divorce Rate: The Nebraska Experience—An Interrupted Time Series Analysis and Commentary, 58 Neb.L.Rev. 1 (1979). See also M. Rheinstein, Marriage Stability, Divorce, and the Law ch. 12 (1972).

14. In re Cosgrove's Marriage, 27 Cal.App.3d 424, 103 Cal.Rptr. 733 (1972); In re Marriage of Franks, 189 Colo. 499, 542 P.2d 845 (1975), stay denied 423 U.S. 1043, 96 S.Ct. 766, 46 L.Ed.2d 632 (1976); Joy v. Joy, 178 Conn. 254, 423 A.2d 895 (1979); Gluck v. Gluck, 181 Conn. 225, 435 A.2d 35 (1980); Donkin v. Donkin, 35 Conn.Supp. 123, 399 A.2d 844 (1978); Cowsert v. Cowsert, 78 Mich.App. 129, 259 N.W.2d 393 (1977).

15. U.S.Const. art. I, § 10.

16. In re Walton's Marriage, 28 Cal.App.3d 108, 104 Cal.Rptr. 472 (1972); In re Marriage of Franks, 189 Colo. 499, 542 P.2d 845 (1975); Joy v. Joy, 178 Conn. 254, 423 A.2d 895 (1979); In re Marriage of Semmler, 107 Ill.2d 130, 89 Ill.Dec. 873, 481 N.E.2d 716 (1985); Cowsert v. Cowsert, 78 Mich.App. 129, 259 N.W.2d 393 (1977).

17. Dickson v. Dickson, 238 Ga. 672, 235 S.E.2d 479 (1977); Roberts v. Roberts, 200 Neb. 256, 263 N.W.2d 449

violate some usually unspecified constitutional provision by abolishing those defenses which are relevant only to the fault grounds for divorce.[18]

The marriage breakdown ground for divorce had to confront the difficulties facing any significant reform in such an emotional field as marital relations from an essentially conservative legal profession. The Uniform Act, which has served as a model for many of the state statutes, was itself the product of heated discussion and compromise.[19] It seems strange after years of experience with the Act and its counterparts in the states, but there was a fear that the wide discretion which marriage breakdown left to trial judges would cause them to deny many divorces which should be granted.[20] Conversely, some lawyers were concerned that the Act would lead to divorce by consent of the parties, eliminating any judicial role in the process.[21]

As the appellate courts have come to deal with marriage breakdown, few disagreements about the impact of the statutes have arisen. It is generally held that divorce remains a matter for the courts, so that except in those few states expressly authorizing divorce without a hearing, the parties must have a hearing and the court must decide whether the marriage is broken.[22] The appellate courts also say that the hearing must not be perfunctory[23] although it is difficult to see how they can be other than perfunctory in view of the pressure on trial courts' time, particularly in those cases where both parties desire the divorce.[24] Even the appellate courts acknowledge that if both parties wish the divorce, the trial court should normally grant it without speculating about the remote chance that a reconciliation might be possible.[25] In the unusual case where one party sues for divorce on the ground of marriage breakdown and the other sues on one of the fault grounds, such as cruelty, the breakdown statute's purpose of avoiding hostility should dictate granting the divorce on the non-fault ground, but the courts seem to leave this to the trial court's discretion.[26]

Attempts at general definitions of marriage breakdown are often made in judicial opinions but usually result in tautology. The reason is that, contrary to the opinions of many commentators, such phrases as "irretrievable marriage breakdown" or "irreconcilable differences" are not in this context either vague or uncertain or ambiguous.[27] They are clear-

---

(1978), appeal dismissed for want of a substantial federal question, 439 U.S. 804, 99 S.Ct. 60, 58 L.Ed.2d 97 (1978); Buchholz v. Buchholz, 197 Neb. 180, 248 N.W.2d 21 (1976).

18. In re Marriage of Franks, 189 Colo. 499, 542 P.2d 845 (1975); Gluck v. Gluck, 181 Conn. 225, 435 A.2d 35 (1980); Buchholz v. Buchholz, 197 Neb. 180, 248 N.W.2d 21 (1976); Hopkins v. Hopkins, 540 S.W.2d 783 (Tex.Civ. App.1976).

19. The debates and compromises which went into the adoption of the Uniform Act are described by the Act's Reporter, Professor Robert J. Levy, in his Introduction to A Symposium on the Uniform Marriage and Divorce Act, 18 S.D.L.Rev. 531 (1973). See also Merrill, Section 305: Genesis and Effect, 18 S.D.L.Rev. 538 (1973).

20. Ibid.

21. Ibid.

22. Laffosse v. Laffosse, 564 S.W.2d 220 (Ky.App. 1978); In re Jackson's Marriage, 506 S.W.2d 261 (Tex.Civ. App.1974).

23. McKim v. McKim, 6 Cal.3d 673, 100 Cal.Rptr. 140, 493 P.2d 868 (1972).

24. See Dickson v. Dickson, 238 Ga. 672, 235 S.E.2d 479 (1977), which held that if the petitioner files an affidavit that the marriage was irretrievably broken and no counter-affidavits were filed by the respondent, a summary judgment granting the divorce might be entered.

25. Whitmire v. Whitmire, 236 Ga. 153, 223 S.E.2d 135 (1976); Craft v. Craft, 226 N.W.2d 6 (Iowa 1975); Kretzschmar v. Kretzschmar, 48 Mich.App. 279, 210 N.W.2d 352 (1973); Baxla v. Baxla, 522 S.W.2d 736 (Tex. Civ.App.1975).

Under the version of marriage breakdown prevailing in some states, if the parties both seek divorce, the trial court is required to enter a decree. Sweet v. Sweet, 190 Conn. 657, 462 A.2d 1031 (1983), the court observing that this has the salutary purpose of preserving the spouses' marital privacy.

26. Loftis v. Loftis, 236 Ga. 637, 225 S.E.2d 685 (1976); Ebbert v. Ebbert, 123 N.H. 252, 459 A.2d 282 (1983). It is difficult to discern any useful social policy in preserving fault grounds when a marriage breakdown statute has been passed, but many states have done this. See note 8, supra. Where one spouse sues for divorce and the other asks for a legal separation, this would seem to prove that the marriage had broken down and the divorce should be granted. See Colabianchi v. Colabianchi, 646 S.W.2d 61 (Mo.1983).

27. Mattson v. Mattson, 376 A.2d 473 (Me.1977), although it states that "irreconcilable differences" lacks precision, holds that a definition is not necessary, strict

er and more definite than "cruelty", for example.[28] Nevertheless it is in the nature of appellate courts to propound definitions whether they are needed or not. So it is here. Some of the decisions take the position that the only important question is whether a reconciliation is likely. If, as it usually turns out, reconciliation is not likely, the marriage has broken down.[29] The same idea is put a bit differently by saying that the question is whether the parties can no longer live together because of difficulties so substantial that no reasonable efforts could succeed in reconciling them.[30] Most courts agree that the test is not an objective but a subjective one, that is, whether these particular spouses are willing to continue living together as husband and wife.[31] The persistent unwillingness to continue the marriage which is the essence of marriage breakdown has been found to exist even though the parties engage in sexual relations occasionally during the pendency of the divorce action,[32] or in spite of the fact that they continue to live in the same house.[33]

Although the definitions of marriage breakdown refer to the spouses' state of mind, evidence of their behavior obviously has probative value with respect to their attitudes toward their marriage. For that reason some

appellate courts rely upon such evidence as a long separation,[34] failure to support the family,[35] the usual manifestations of marital unkindness,[36] refusal of sexual relations,[37] and the failure or refusal of counseling [38] to support findings of marriage breakdown.

The crucial question raised by the marriage breakdown statutes is whether the divorce may be granted on the complaint of one of the spouses when the other spouse strongly asserts that he or she wants the marriage to continue and that it really has not broken down. The same question is even more acute when it appears that the spouse seeking the divorce has been at fault in creating the marital difficulties, as fault was defined in the traditional divorce law. To put the issue concretely, should the divorce be granted to a husband who has left his wife and lives in adultery with another woman, over the wife's objection that she still loves him and thinks that the marriage could be preserved? The answer given by most courts is that if one of the spouses seriously and persistently asserts that the marriage is broken, it is broken, notwithstanding the disagreement of the other spouse and notwithstanding the other spouse's insistence that the marriage could be saved.[39] Since marriage is a relationship re-

definitions often becoming unworkable. This amounts to a concession that the statutory term is precise enough.

28. In re Marriage of Franks, 189 Colo. 499, 542 P.2d 845 (1975).

29. Harwell v. Harwell, 233 Ga. 89, 209 S.E.2d 625 (1974).

30. Flora v. Flora, 166 Ind.App. 620, 337 N.E.2d 846 (1975); Witcig v. Witcig, 206 Neb. 307, 292 N.W.2d 788 (1980). See also In re Walton's Marriage, 28 Cal.App.3d 108, 104 Cal.Rptr. 472 (1972).

31. Riley v. Riley, 271 So.2d 181 (Fla.App.1972); Dunn v. Dunn, 13 Or.App. 497, 511 P.2d 427 (1973).

32. Nooe v. Nooe, 277 So.2d 835 (Fla.App.1973); Smith v. Smith, 322 So.2d 580 (Fla.App.1975); Cowsert v. Cowsert, 78 Mich.App. 129, 259 N.W.2d 393 (1977); Peltola v. Peltola, 79 Mich.App. 709, 263 N.W.2d 25 (1977).

33. Flynn v. Flynn, 120 R.I. 575, 388 A.2d 1170 (1978), where the wife had not enough money to move.

34. Witcig v. Witcig, 206 Neb. 307, 292 N.W.2d 788 (1980); Mathias v. Mathias, 194 Neb. 598, 234 N.W.2d 212 (1975); Condreay v. Condreay, 190 Neb. 513, 209 N.W.2d 357 (1973).

35. In re Collins' Marriage, 200 N.W.2d 886 (Iowa 1972).

36. Harrison v. Harrison, 314 So.2d 812 (Fla.App. 1975), cert. denied 334 So.2d 605 (Fla.1976); Cowie v. Cowie, 628 S.W.2d 727 (Mo.App.1982); Nichols v. Nichols, 538 S.W.2d 727 (Mo.App.1976); Bakken v. Bakken, 503 S.W.2d 315 (Tex.Civ.App.1973). Other cases are cited in Annot., 55 A.L.R.3d 581 (1974).

37. In re Baier's Marriage, 39 Colo.App. 34, 561 P.2d 20 (1977).

38. In re Boyd's Marriage, 200 N.W.2d 845 (Iowa 1972).

39. In re Baier's Marriage, 39 Colo.App. 34, 561 P.2d 20 (1977) (wife testified that they quarreled, that she no longer liked or trusted her husband; husband testified that their relationship was satisfactory and that wife's difficulties could be resolved by counseling); Byers v. Byers, 324 So.2d 164 (Fla.App.1975) (husband seeks divorce, wife suffering from emotional and psychiatric difficulties); McCoy v. McCoy, 236 Ga. 633, 225 S.E.2d 682 (1976) (husband living with another woman, wishes to marry her, wife opposes the divorce); In re Morgan's Marriage, 218 N.W.2d 552 (Iowa 1974) (twenty year marriage; husband living with another woman; eight children of the marriage); In re Tucker's Marriage, 213 N.W.2d 498 (Iowa 1973) (husband testified there was no longer love in the marriage; wife suffering from a deep

quiring the consent and cooperation of both spouses, this result is the obvious and logical outcome of the adoption of marriage breakdown as the basis for divorce. It undeniably imposes a hardship on the objecting spouse, but this is the inevitable consequence of abandoning the fault grounds for divorce and adopting marriage breakdown as the ground.[40] This result also recognizes that in American society today there is little or no likelihood that the law can force married persons to live together when one of them is determined to end the marriage. In this situation the law should concentrate on providing some financial security for the respondent spouse rather than trying to shore up a broken marriage. Even this limited goal may be hard to reach of course.

When they initially faced the marriage breakdown statutes, the appellate courts emphasized that the grant of a divorce on this ground continued to be wholly a judicial function, as it had been when suits were brought on the old fault grounds, with the courts responsible for more than a perfunctory approval of the plaintiff's claim. Trial courts were told that they were not to rubber stamp suits for divorce. As the new ground for divorce became more familiar to the courts and its purposes more clearly understood by them,[41] the appellate courts have generally come to acknowledge that the parties' views about their marriage have to be taken at their face. If they both think the marriage is

broken and cannot be restored, certainly the divorce must be granted. Even if only one spouse takes this position, the court really must grant the divorce and the appellate courts largely accept this as a fact. The result is that in those states where marriage breakdown is a ground for divorce, the question of grounds and whether or not the divorce should be granted has been eliminated from the suit. Trial courts understand this and waste little or no time on testimony concerning the breakdown of the marriage. A logical consequence of all this is that it is virtually impossible to imagine a case in which, if one spouse wishes a divorce, the divorce would be denied. The question then arises whether there is any need for a judicial hearing if the only claim is for a divorce and neither finances nor custody are at stake in the case. The answer given in a few states is that indeed a hearing need not be held in such a case.[42]

WESTLAW REFERENCES

divorc! /p break-down irretrievab! irreconcilab! /s vague! "due process" constitution! unconstitutional! "equal! protect***"

"uniform marriage and divorce" /s fault!

---

§ 13.7   Divorce Grounds—Living Separate and Apart

This ground for divorce exists in about half of the states.[1] It used to account for more

---

depression); Grotelueschen v. Grotelueschen, 113 Mich. App. 395, 318 N.W.2d 227 (1982) (husband living with another woman; thirty-two year marriage); Hagerty v. Hagerty, 281 N.W.2d 386 (Minn.1979) (husband, an alcoholic, seeks divorce after a twenty year marriage, wife claims the marriage could be saved if husband were treated for his alcoholism); Weeks v. Weeks, 124 N.H. 252, 469 A.2d 1313 (1983) (plaintiff husband refused to continue with the marriage); Desrochers v. Desrochers, 115 N.H. 591, 347 A.2d 150 (1975) (plaintiff wife wanted the divorce, husband opposed it); In re Halford's Marriage, 19 Or.App. 508, 528 P.2d 119 (1974) (plaintiff husband living with another woman, wife opposed divorce but sought a legal separation).

The Missouri statute cited supra, note 8, does not permit a divorce to be granted to a plaintiff who has committed adultery or has deserted his spouse except where the parties have lived apart for twenty-four months, and in some instances not even then. Buscher v. Buscher, 659 S.W.2d 587 (Mo.App.1983); In re Marriage

of Mitchell, 545 S.W.2d 313 (Mo.App.1976). Other statutes permit a divorce for marriage breakdown only where the suit is uncontested. E.g., Tenn.Code Ann. § 36–4–103(e) (1984).

40. Clark, Divorce Policy and Divorce Reform, 42 U.Colo.L.Rev. 403, 408 (1971).

41. See Marriage of Franks, 189 Colo. 499, 542 P.2d 845 (1975), stay denied 433 U.S. 1043, 96 S.Ct. 766, 46 L.Ed.2d 632 (1976).

42. See section 14.4, infra.

§ 13.7

1. Ala.Code 1983, § 30–2–1; Ark.Stat. § 34–1202 (Supp.1985); Conn.Gen.Stat.Ann. § 46b–40 (1986); D.C. Code, 1981, § 16–904; Hawaii Rev.Stat. § 580–41 (1986 Replacement); Idaho Code § 32–610 (1983); Ill.—S.H.A. ch. 40, § 401(2) (1986); L.S.A.—Rev.Stat. §§ 9:301, 9:302 (Supp.1987); Md.Code, § 7–103 (1984); Vernon's Ann.Mo. Stat. §§ 452.305, 452.320 (1986); Nev.Rev.Stat. § 125.010

than half of all divorces in a few states which had enacted it,[2] but that no longer seems to be true since the enactment of marriage breakdown statutes in many states. There is some diversity in the language of the statutes, but in general they fall into three classes. The first and most restrictive type of statute authorizes divorce only when the parties have lived apart for a prescribed time under a decree of separation from a court of the same or another state,[3] or under a written separation agreement.[4] The second type of statute, less restrictive, authorizes divorce when the parties have "voluntarily" or "willingly" lived apart for the prescribed time.[5] The third and broadest type of statute allows divorce solely upon proof that the parties have lived apart for the prescribed time.[6] The period during which the separation must continue varies considerably from state to state, ranging from six months in Vermont to five years in Idaho. The most common periods are one or three years. The statutes have usually been construed to be retroactive, so that the period of separation occurring before the statute was

passed may be included in computing the statutory period.[7]

This ground for divorce is often advocated as avoiding the defects of the fault grounds and also being objective.[8] Unfortunately in the hands of the courts neither of these virtues has been achieved. Living separate and apart for the considerable periods required by the statutes also has the disadvantage of imposing serious hardships on non-earning spouses.[9] The statutes have been held constitutional, however.[10]

Courts have been unable to agree upon just what "separation" requires in order to grant a divorce on this ground. Some have held that there can be no separation if the parties continued to live in the same house even though they had no sexual relations.[11] Other courts hold that this can amount to a separation.[12] There is similar conflict over the question whether the occurrence of some sexual relations between the parties during the statutory period prevents the court from granting a divorce.[13]

(1986); N.J.Stat.Ann. § 2A:34–2 (Supp.1986); N.Y.—McKinney's Dom.Rel.L. § 170 (1977); N.C.Gen.Stat. § 50–6 (Supp.1983); Ohio Rev.Code § 3105.01 (Supp.1985); Pa. Stat. tit. 23, § 201 (Supp.1986); R.I.Gen.L. 1981, § 15–5–3; S.C.Code 1985, § 20–3–10; V.T.C.A., Fam.Code § 3.06 (1975); Utah Code Ann. 1984, § 30–3–1 (Replacement); Vt.Stat.Ann. tit. 15, § 551 (1974 and Supp.1986); Va.Code 1986, § 20–91 (Supp.1986); W.Va.Code, § 48–2–4 (1986).

2. P. Jacobson, American Marriage and Divorce 125 (1959).

3. Hawaii, Louisiana, New York and Utah.

4. New York and Virginia. Ohio has a unique provision which authorizes a divorce to be granted when the spouses have executed a separation agreement agreeing to terminate their marriage and resolving all questions of property, maintenance and custody and support of children. Ohio Rev.Code § 3105.65 (1980); Ashley v. Ashley, 1 Ohio App.3d 80, 439 N.E.2d 911 (1981).

5. Arkansas, Maryland, Missouri and the District of Columbia have this type of statute. Some states have statutes of more than one type, setting different time periods for the different types of separation. For example the District of Columbia has a voluntary statute providing for a six month separation and a straight separation statute providing for a period of one year.

6. This type of statute is found in the states listed in note 1, supra, except for those states mentioned in notes 3, 4, or 5.

7. Buckheit v. Buckheit, 10 Md.App. 526, 272 A.2d 54 (1970); Gleason v. Gleason, 26 N.Y.2d 28, 308 N.Y.S.2d

347, 256 N.E.2d 513 (1970) (as so construed the statute is constitutional); Cassaro v. Cassaro, 50 Ohio App.2d 368, 363 N.E.2d 753 (1976); Singley v. Singley, 256 S.C. 117, 181 S.E.2d 17 (1971).

8. Wadlington, Divorce Without Fault Without Perjury, 52 Va.L.Rev. 32 (1966).

9. Bruch, The Legal Import of Informal Marital Separations: A Survey of California Law and a Call for a Change, 65 Cal.L.Rev. 1015 (1977).

10. Harwood v. Harwood, 120 R.I. 145, 385 A.2d 1055 (1978).

11. Jackson v. Jackson, 13 Md.App. 725, 284 A.2d 654 (1971). Ellam v. Ellam, 132 N.J.Super. 358, 333 A.2d 577 (1975) held that the parties were not separated when the husband moved out of the house but continued to spend time with his wife, to take some meals with her, and to attend social engagements with her, although they had no sexual relations. Other cases both ways are collected in Annot., 35 A.L.R.3d 1238 (1970).

12. Heckman v. Heckman, 245 A.2d 550 (Del.1968) (under a statute since repealed); In re Marriage of Uhls, 549 S.W.2d 107 (Mo.App.1977).

13. Holding there is no separation if the parties have sexual relations: Smith v. Smith, 257 Md. 263, 262 A.2d 762 (1970); Pitts v. Pitts, 54 N.C.App. 163, 282 S.E.2d 488 (1981). Holding that a separation may occur notwithstanding sexual relations: Wilkins v. Wilkins, 85 Misc.2d 985, 382 N.Y.S.2d 240 (1976); Thomas v. Thomas, 335 Pa. Super. 41, 483 A.2d 945 (1984).

Since the statutes on living separate and apart provide that the separation must continue for a consecutive period of years, a reconciliation or resumption of cohabitation will interrupt the period and prevent the divorce even though the parties have been separated altogether for a longer time than the statute requires.[14] But bringing a suit for separation does not interrupt the statutory period.[15]

The intention with which the parties separate may be relevant under some of these statutes. If they part because of necessity, as where one is imprisoned or required to perform compulsory military service or is hospitalized for a long illness, there is no ground for divorce.[16] If they part with the understanding that the separation is to be only temporary, this is not the sort of separation on which a divorce may be granted. To qualify, the separation must be final and intentional, and it must have that character for the entire time prescribed by the statute.[17] Where the separation begins as a temporary or provisional one but the parties later decide it is to be permanent, the statutory period does not begin to run until their intentions change.[18] The need for determining whether the separation is permanent leads some

courts to inquire into the prospects for reconciliation,[19] but of course in any separation there may be some remote possibility of reconciliation and absolute finality should not be required.[20] It should be sufficient to show that no reconciliation was at any time likely.[21]

The question of intention also arises when the respondent spouse in the divorce action is mentally incompetent. In those states having a "voluntary" type of statute, the separation can not be voluntary if one spouse is incapable of understanding the nature and consequences of the separation. A few cases in states which do not require the separation to be voluntary have reached the same result, the analysis being that there can be no separation in the statutory sense unless the respondent is conscious that a separation has occurred, at least where the respondent has been committed for mental illness.[22] If the separation is brought about by the commitment of the mentally ill spouse, some courts could find that it occurred out of necessity and could deny the divorce on that ground.[23]

The minority of states which have chosen to require either that the separation be pursuant to a decree or that it be voluntary have had to face a variety of questions not present-

---

14. Varnell v. Varnell, 207 Ark. 711, 182 S.W.2d 466 (1944). And they must live apart. A mere refusal of conjugal rights is not enough to justify a divorce on this ground. McNary v. McNary, 8 Wash.2d 250, 111 P.2d 760 (1941); Oxford v. Oxford, 237 Ark. 384, 373 S.W.2d 707 (1963); Lillis v. Lillis, 235 Md. 490, 201 A.2d 794 (1964).

15. Jones v. Jones, 199 Ark. 1000, 137 S.W.2d 238 (1940); North v. North, 164 La. 293, 113 So. 852 (1927).

16. Gardner v. Gardner, 125 So.2d 463 (La.App.1961) (dictum); Sitterson v. Sitterson, 191 N.C. 319, 131 S.E. 641 (1926); Dailey v. Dailey, 11 Ohio App.3d 121, 463 N.E.2d 427 (1983).

17. France v. Safe Deposit & Trust Co., 176 Md. 306, 4 A.2d 717 (1939); Pearson v. Pearson, 34 A.D.2d 797, 311 N.Y.S.2d 749 (2d Dep't 1970), appeal denied 27 N.Y.2d 485, 315 N.Y.S.2d 1027, 263 N.E.2d 564 (1970); Hooker v. Hooker, 215 Va. 415, 211 S.E.2d 34 (1975).

18. Sutherland v. Sutherland, 75 Nev. 304, 340 P.2d 581 (1959); Hahn v. Hahn, 192 Md. 561, 64 A.2d 739 (1949).

19. Tabakin v. Tabakin, 131 Vt. 234, 303 A.2d 816 (1973).

20. In Maur v. Ciavarro, 154 A.2d 366 (D.C.Mun.App. 1959) the court refused a divorce apparently on this

ground, imposing nearly impossible requirements as to proof of the impossibility of reconciliation. Issarescu v. Issarescu, 82 Nev. 239, 415 P.2d 67 (1966) held that a voluntary separation could be inferred from the fact of separation without cohabitation for the statutory period.

21. Benson v. Benson, 204 Md. 601, 105 A.2d 733 (1954); Baker v. Baker, 76 Nev. 127, 350 P.2d 140 (1960). The question of fault should not be confused with the likelihood of reconciliation. One relates to the cause of the separation, the other to its finality. Some statutes specifically require a finding that there is no likelihood of reconciliation. E.g., Hawaii Rev.Stat. § 580–41 (1976).

22. Shaw v. Shaw, 256 S.C. 453, 182 S.E.2d 865 (1971); Crittenden v. Crittenden, 210 Va. 76, 168 S.E.2d 115 (1969). See Wadlington, A Case of Insanity and Divorce, 56 Va.L.Rev. 12 (1970). Altbrandt v. Altbrandt, 129 N.J. Super. 235, 322 A.2d 839 (1974) took the contrary position, that the mental incompetence of the defendant does not prevent the separation from being a ground for divorce, so long as the respondent was not committed to an institution.

23. See the cases cited in note 16, supra.

ed to the other states. Thus it has been held that if a decree of alimony without divorce is granted to a spouse, this qualifies as a legal separation and an absolute divorce may be obtained when the statutory period has run.[24] Once the separation has been granted, the grounds may not be reexamined to reevaluate possible claims of fault.[25] And the fact that one of the parties to the separation decree attempted to obtain a migratory divorce was held not to foreclose the award of a divorce for separation when the period had run.[26] Under the unique New York statute which authorizes divorce where the parties have separated pursuant to a separation agreement, the divorce may be granted even though the separation agreement has been found to be invalid.[27]

Much of the litigation over divorce on the ground of separation occurs in determining what is the significance of fault. Where the statute requires that the separation be pursuant to a decree or a separation agreement, once the decree or agreement has been obtained and the statutory period has run, either party may get the divorce.[28] The defendant in the separation suit is entitled to sue as well as the plaintiff and fault or responsibility for the separation are immaterial.[29]

Those statutes which authorize a divorce only after a "voluntary" or "willing" separation have been construed to mean that the separation must have occurred at the mutual consent of both parties before it can be a cause for divorce.[30] Under such a statute if one party deserts the other, the deserter may not get a divorce on this ground after the prescribed time has gone by, recrimination being a defense,[31] or perhaps more accurately there has not been a mutual consent to the separation.[32] Later acquiescence may supply the mutual agreement which did not exist at the time of the original separation, but the statutory period only begins to run from the date when consent was given.[33] But the kind of acquiescence which merely consists in recognizing that a spouse is determined to depart and that there is nothing the deserted spouse can do to prevent it is not the sort of consent which meets the statutory requirement.[34] Similarly if one spouse leaves the other because of the other's cruelty or other misconduct, the resulting separation does not give a cause for divorce under this form of statute since it did not occur by consent.[35]

In those states whose statutes do not contain the requirement that the separation must be voluntary, it is generally held that

---

24. Cook v. Cook, 41 N.C.App. 156, 254 S.E.2d 261 (1979).

25. Hautot v. Hautot, 236 So.2d 635 (La.App.1970).

26. Plancher v. Plancher, 35 A.D.2d 417, 317 N.Y.S.2d 140 (2d Dep't 1970), affirmed 29 N.Y.2d 880, 328 N.Y.S.2d 444, 278 N.E.2d 650 (1972). Under the Missouri statute a decree of separation may be converted to one for absolute divorce when the statutory period has run, on the motion of either spouse. Vernon's Ann.Mo.Stat. § 452.360 (1986); Howard v. Howard, 583 S.W.2d 553 (Mo.App. 1979).

27. Christian v. Christian, 42 N.Y.2d 63, 396 N.Y.S.2d 817, 365 N.E.2d 849 (1977). But the agreement must be performed in accordance with its terms. Van Vort v. Van Vort, 62 Misc.2d 981, 310 N.Y.S.2d 641 (1970).

Under the unique Ohio statute by which a divorce may be granted on the basis of a separation agreement signed by both spouses, the agreement must cover all the property of the spouses. If it does not, the decree based upon it has been held to be voidable. In re Murphy, 10 Ohio App.3d 134, 461 N.E.2d 910 (1983).

28. Gleason v. Gleason, 26 N.Y.2d 28, 308 N.Y.S.2d 347, 256 N.E.2d 513 (1970).

29. Gerdts v. Gerdts, 196 Minn. 599, 265 N.W. 811 (1936); Gleason v. Gleason, 26 N.Y.2d 28, 308 N.Y.S.2d 347, 256 N.E.2d 513 (1970).

30. Butler v. Butler, 154 F.2d 203 (D.C.Cir.1946); Wife S. v. Husband S., 375 A.2d 451 (Dec.1977); Seabrook v. Seabrook, 264 A.2d 311 (D.C.App.1970) (requires the defendant to manifest a real desire to continue the marriage); Garner v. Garner, 257 Md. 723, 264 A.2d 858 (1970). Other cases are cited in Annot., 14 A.L.R.3d 502 (1967).

31. Pharr v. Pharr, 223 N.C. 115, 25 S.E.2d 471 (1943); Annot., 152 A.L.R. 336 (1944).

32. Wife S. v. Husband S., 375 A.2d 451 (Del.1977).

33. Parks v. Parks, 116 F.2d 556 (D.C.Cir.1940); Wallace v. Wallace, 290 Md. 265, 429 A.2d 232 (1981); Lukat v. Lukat, 21 Md.App. 354, 319 A.2d 818 (1974).

34. Franklin v. Franklin, 257 Md. 678, 264 A.2d 829 (1970); Sauls v. Sauls, 288 S.C. 387, 218 S.E.2d 338 (1975).

35. Campbell v. Campbell, 174 Md. 229, 198 A. 414 (1938). Consent to the separation is vitiated if obtained by fraud or duress. Pearce v. Pearce, 225 N.C. 571, 35 S.E.2d 636 (1945).

fault is irrelevant.[36] It does not matter whether the suit for divorce is brought by the deserting spouse, or whether one of the spouses is anxious for a reconciliation,[37] so long as the separation is final. The rationale of these cases is that the statutory objective is the recognition of marriage failure, evidence of that failure being the fact that the parties have lived apart for the prescribed time.[38] Here, as with incompatibility and marriage breakdown, there has occurred a fundamental change in the theory of divorce. Marriage breakdown and not fault has become the crucial fact and the doctrine of recrimination is relegated to well-deserved oblivion.[39]

WESTLAW REFERENCES

di(divorc! /p separate! apart /5 liv*** /s period time /s sex conjugal sexual! intercourse relations)

mutual! /3 agree*** agreement! consen! assent /s separat! divorc! /s acquiesc!

---

§ 13.8 Divorce Defenses—Connivance

Like the other traditional divorce defenses, connivance is only of historical significance today. It was adopted by our common law from the English ecclesiastical practice [1] but it was and still is included in some statutes.[2] As a practical matter it was almost entirely limited to suits brought on the ground of adultery.[3] Since the ground of adultery is seldom relied on today and since connivance has no relevance at all to the non-fault grounds for divorce and therefore has been abolished as a defense in many of the states having such grounds,[4] this defense virtually never appears in divorce litigation.

The policy basis underlying connivance was usually described in terms of the Latin maxim, *volenti non fit injuria*.[5] The analogy to torts in the application of this maxim was obvious. If a divorce was claimed by one spouse because of a wrong resembling a tort done to him by the other spouse, it was said

---

36. Gardner v. Gardner, 250 Ala. 251, 34 So.2d 157 (1948); McCormick v. McCormick, 246 Ark. 348, 438 S.W.2d 23 (1969); White v. White, 94 Idaho 26, 480 P.2d 872 (1971); Cotton v. Cotton, 306 Ky. 826, 209 S.W.2d 474 (1948); Pearson v. Pearson, 77 Nev. 76, 359 P.2d 386 (1961). Other cases are cited in Annots., 14 A.L.R.3d 502 (1967) and 152 A.L.R. 336 (1944).

Contra the text statement: Mandigo v. Mandigo, 128 Vt. 446, 266 A.2d 434 (1970); Winslow v. Winslow, 127 Vt. 428, 251 A.2d 419 (1969).

North Carolina seems to have taken a mixed view of this question. See Earles v. Earles, 29 N.C.App. 348, 224 S.E.2d 284 (1976); Oliver v. Oliver, 219 N.C. 299, 13 S.E.2d 549 (1941); Parker v. Parker, 210 N.C. 264, 186 S.E. 346 (1936); Taylor v. Taylor, 257 N.C. 130, 125 S.E.2d 373 (1962). But see Byers v. Byers, 222 N.C. 298, 22 S.E.2d 902 (1942) which seems inconsistent. See also Mallard v. Mallard, 234 N.C. 654, 68 S.E.2d 247 (1951). Fault of the plaintiff is an affirmative defense. Pickens v. Pickens, 258 N.C. 84, 127 S.E.2d 889 (1962). And even though the husband was at fault in causing the separation, he may have a divorce if they live apart for the entire two-year period by virtue of a separation decree obtained by the wife. Sears v. Sears, 253 N.C. 415, 117 S.E.2d 7 (1960), 40 N.C.L.Rev. 340 (1962); Richardson v. Richardson, 257 N.C. 705, 127 S.E.2d 525 (1962).

37. Baker v. Baker, 76 Nev. 127, 350 P.2d 140 (1960).

38. Herrick v. Herrick, 55 Nev. 59, 25 P.2d 378 (1933).

39. Young v. Young, 207 Ark. 36, 178 S.W.2d 994 (1944); Helfer v. Helfer, 342 S.W.2d 8 (Tex.Civ.App.1960).

§ 13.8

1. Morrison v. Morrison, 142 Mass. 361, 8 N.E. 59 (1886); Robbins v. Robbins, 140 Mass. 528, 5 N.E. 837 (1886); II Bishop, Marriage, Divorce and Separation 110–

128 (1891). Cases on connivance are collected in Annot., 17 A.L.R.2d 342 (1951).

2. Ala.Code, § 30–2–3 (1983); Alaska Stat. § 25.24.120 (1983) (applicable to adultery only); Ark.Stat. § 34–1209 (1962); Del.Code tit. 13, § 1505(c) 1981); Official Code Ga. Ann. § 19–5–4 (Supp.1986); Ill.—S.H.A. ch. 40, § 408 (1980); N.Y.—McKinney's Dom.Rel.L. § 171 (1977); N.D. Cent.Code § 14–05–10 (1981); Pa.Stat. tit. 23, § 207 (Supp.1986); R.I.Gen.L. § 15–5–4 (1981); S.C.Code, § 20–3–20 (1985); S.D.Codif.L. § 25–4–19 (1984); Tenn.Code Ann. § 36–4–112 (1984) (applicable to adultery only); Va. Code, § 20–94 (1983) (applicable to adultery, sodomy or buggery only); W.Va.Code, § 48–2–14 (1986).

3. See the statutes cited supra, note 2.

4. E.g., Ariz.Rev.Stat. § 24–314(C) (Supp.1986); Colo. Rev.Stat. § 14–10–107(5) (1973); Conn.Gen.Stat.Ann. § 46b–52 (1986) (abolishes recrimination and condonation, no mention of connivance); West's Fla.Stat.Ann. § 61.044 (Supp.1984); Ky.Rev.Stat. § 403.150(5) (1984); Vernon's Ann.Mo.Stat. § 452.310(5) (1986); Mont.Code Ann. § 105(f)(4) (1985); N.J.Stat.Ann. § 2A:34–7 (Supp. 1986) (semble); Or.Rev.Stat. § 107.055 (1983); Pa.Stat. tit. 23, § 207(a) (Supp.1986) (defenses abolished as to marriage breakdown and living apart grounds); W.Va. Code, § 48–2–14 (1986) (defenses abolished as to non-fault grounds); Wis.Stat.Ann. § 767.085(4) (1981 and Supp. 1986). The Uniform Marriage and Divorce Act § 303(e), 9A Unif.L.Ann. 126 (1979) abolishes all defenses.

5. Dennis v. Dennis, 68 Conn. 186, 36 A. 34 (1896); Robbins v. Robbins, 140 Mass. 528, 5 N.E. 837 (1886); Douglas v. Douglas [1951] P. 85; Rogers v. Rogers, 3 Hagg.Ecc. 57, 162 Eng.Rep. 1079 (1830); Timmings v. Timmings, 3 Hagg.Ecc. 76, 162 Eng.Rep. 1086 (1792); Forster v. Forster, 1 Hagg.Con. 144, 161 Eng.Rep. 504 (1790).

that the plaintiff's willingness that the wrong be done removed the sting and barred the suit. More precisely, this meant that if the plaintiff originally consented to the adultery, he would not later be permitted to change his mind and say that he no longer consented or revoked his consent.

Connivance may also be based on the fact that in certain cases the plaintiff is an actual participant in the defendant's wrong, and thus does not come into court with clean hands.[6] The clean hands rule is always one of dubious soundness,[7] and is particularly suspect in matrimonial litigation.[8]

§ 13.9 Divorce Defenses—Collusion

Collusion as a defense to divorce originated in the English ecclesiastical law[1] and became part of the American law of divorce when our courts adopted ecclesiastical principles to guide them.[2] It was formerly in effect in all states, either by statute or common law, but with the enactment of the various non-fault grounds for divorce it has come to have little practical importance.[3] Some states still refer to it in their statutes,[4] while other states have abolished it.[5]

The defense of collusion was closely related to the traditional view that divorce was a remedy to be granted only to a wronged spouse and only when the wrong was estab-

lished by evidence in a trial. The reason for this was that divorce suits were an aspect of the state's regulation of marriage and divorce, this being expressed by the statement often found in judicial opinions that the state was a party to all divorce actions.[6] Since in most divorce suits both parties wish the marriage to end, the proceeding is not adversary with respect to that issue. The consequence was that the prevention of collusive divorces was essential to the effective administration of the fault oriented divorce laws.

For this reason the policy against collusion pervaded the entire divorce law before the advent of non-fault grounds accounting for many of the rules of trial, evidence[7] and pleading[8] as well as the defense itself. In fact making the presence of collusion a bar to divorce, or a defense as it is usually described, was in practice the least effective of all the methods of preventing collusive divorces for the non-adversary nature of the divorce trial ensured that collusion would rarely be raised by the parties. The remarkable paucity of reported cases made this plain.

The first problem which arises with respect to the defense of collusion is one of definition. Lord Stowell defined collusion as "an agreement between the parties for one to commit, or appear to commit, a fact of adultery, in order that the other may obtain a remedy at law as for a real injury".[9] Other definitions

---

6. E.g., Nacrelli v. Nacrelli, 288 Pa. 1, 136 A. 228 (1927).

7. Z. Chafee, Some Problems of Equity 1–102 (1950).

8. See section 13.11, infra, on recrimination.

§ 13.9

1. Crewe v. Crewe, 3 Hagg.Ecc. 123, 162 Eng.Rep. 1102 (1800).

2. Robbins v. Robbins, 140 Mass. 528, 5 N.E. 837 (1885). For discussions of collusion see Note, Consensual Divorce and the New York Anomaly, 36 Colum.L.Rev. 1121 (1936); Bradway, Collusion and the Public Interest in the Law of Divorce, 47 Corn.L.Q. 374 (1962); Moore, An Analysis of Collusion and Connivance, Bars to Divorce, 36 U.Mo. at Kan.City L.Rev. 193 (1968).

3. For an amusing example of a case in which the court still seemed to think collusion was relevant when the suit was brought on the ground of marriage breakdown, see In re Ried's Marriage, 212 N.W.2d 391 (Iowa 1973). The court emphasized that the plaintiff's claim that the marriage was broken was corroborated by the testimony of others including that of the defendant. As

has been indicated in section 13.6, however, the only sensible meaning of marriage breakdown is that if one of the spouses believes the marriage has broken down, the divorce should be granted.

4. Ala.Code, 1983, § 30–2–3; Ark.Stat. § 34–1209 (1962); Del.Code tit. 13, § 1505(c) (1981); Official Code Ga.Ann. § 19–5–4 (Supp.1986); Hawaii Rev.Stat. § 580–8 (1976) (semble); Idaho Code § 32–611 (1983); Ill.—S.H.A. ch. 40, § 408 (1980); Me.Rev.Stat.Ann. tit. 19, § 691(1) (1981); N.D.Cent.Code § 14–05–10 (1981); Pa.Stat. tit. 23, § 207 (Supp.1986) (defenses retained for the traditional fault grounds); R.I.Gen.L. 1981, § 15–5–4; S.D.Codif.L. Ann. § 25–4–19 (Supp.1986).

5. See the statutes cited in note 4 of section 13.8, supra.

6. E.g., Reed v. Reed, 138 Colo. 74, 329 P.2d 633 (1958).

7. See section 14.4, infra.

8. See section Practitioner's Edition, infra.

9. Crewe v. Crewe, 3 Hagg.Ecc. 123, 130, 162 Eng.Rep. 1102, 1105 (1800).

in similar terms may be found in the cases.[10] The agreement that one party will actually commit a marital wrong in order to give grounds for divorce constitutes connivance.[11] To that extent connivance and collusion are similar, although the policies underlying the two defenses are completely different. In practice, however, collusion seldom takes this form. A valid working distinction between connivance and collusion is that connivance depends on consent that a marital offense actually be committed, while collusion involves an agreement that the marital offense appear to have been committed.

When the general definitions are applied to specific facts, some classes of cases fall pretty clearly on one side or the other. It is clear that an agreement by the parties to fabricate grounds for divorce as by staging a fake adultery scene,[12] or by testifying falsely[13] is collusion. It is equally clear that the parties are not guilty of collusion merely because they both desire a divorce, no matter how ardent-

ly.[14] Nor is it collusion where the defendant, acting unilaterally, decides not to defend the case and withdraws an answer or cross-complaint.[15] As the opinions put it, no man is required to make a defense. And a mere attempt at collusion, which does not result in an improper agreement, is not a bar to the divorce.[16]

Once the easy cases are disposed of, however, collusion becomes a concept which is extremely difficult to apply. What is to be said of the defendant who cooperates with the plaintiff so as to facilitate the divorce, as by furnishing evidence of his own wrong, by entering his appearance and consenting to an immediate decree or by waiving further notice? So long as these things are not done pursuant to agreement between the parties the courts seem to feel they do not amount to collusion.[17] When the parties make an agreement that one will sue and the other will not defend, however, this is held to be collusion.[18] Such agreements are often made as part of

---

10. E.g., Bacon v. Bacon, 233 Ala. 482, 172 So. 632 (1937); Sheehan v. Sheehan, 77 N.J.Eq. 411, 77 A. 1063 (1910). Other cases are cited in Annot., 109 A.L.R. 832 (1939) and 2 A.L.R. 699 (1919). See also 2 Bishop, Marriage, Divorce and Separation §§ 252–266 (1891) for a collection of the older authorities.

11. See section 13.8, supra. Some statutory definitions of collusion look more like connivance than collusion. See Ill.—S.H.A. ch. 40, § 408 (1980).

12. Furst v. Furst, 191 Misc. 699, 78 N.Y.S.2d 608 (1948), affirmed 275 App.Div. 991, 91 N.Y.S.2d 202 (2d Dep't 1949).

13. Oberstein v. Oberstein, 217 Ark. 80, 228 S.W.2d 615 (1950); Maimone v. Maimone, 90 N.E.2d 383 (Ohio App. 1949).

14. McCauley v. McCauley, 88 N.J.Eq. 392, 103 A. 20 (1918); Scott v. Scott [1947] 1 D.L.R. 374.

15. Brainard v. Brainard, 82 Cal.App.2d 478, 186 P.2d 990 (1947); O'Connell v. O'Connell, 27 Ill.App.3d 204, 326 N.E.2d 200 (1975); Wiemer v. Wiemer, 21 N.D. 371, 130 N.W. 1015 (1911); Maimone v. Maimone, 90 N.E.2d 383 (Ohio App.1949). See also Bacon v. Bacon, 233 Ala. 482, 172 So. 632 (1937), in which the court refused to infer collusion from the speed with which the divorce action was conducted.

16. Underwood v. Underwood, 271 Fed. 553 (D.D.Cir. 1921); Rosenfeld v. Rosenfeld, 67 Mo.App. 29 (1896).

17. Vayette v. Myers, 303 Ill. 562, 136 N.E. 467 (1922) (consent to decree not collusive); Rosenzweig v. Rosenzweig, 231 App.Div. 13, 246 N.Y.S. 231 (2d Dep't 1930) (husband's promise to furnish wife with evidence of his past acts of adultery held not collusive); State ex rel. Watson v. Rodgers, 129 W.Va. 174, 39 S.E.2d 268 (1946)

(waiver of maturity and consent to immediate docketing of case held not collusive). The Kentucky cases illustrate the difficulty of distinguishing between proper and improper activity. Denehie v. Denehie, 306 Ky. 787, 209 S.W.2d 309 (1948) found collusion where the husband showed willingness to have the divorce granted, agreed that evidence might be taken without notice to him, and admitted the charge of abandonment. The court had later to repudiate this position in two cases, although it attempted to explain the Denehie case on other grounds. In these later cases it was held not collusion for the divorce defendant to enter his appearance and consent to a decree for the plaintiff. Mitchell v. Mitchell, 312 Ky. 810, 229 S.W.2d 967 (1950); Conyers v. Conyers, 311 Ky. 468, 224 S.W.2d 688 (1949). The Vermont statute contains a unique provision on collusion: "The term 'collusion', as used in divorce actions, shall not be construed to include conversations or negotiations of the parties carried on in good faith in an effort to resolve their marital difficulties, where the purpose or result of the conference is not to hinder or obstruct justice or to suppress evidence as to the merits of the case." For an expression of the conventional, strict view, see Pressney v. Pressney, 339 Ill.App. 371, 90 N.E.2d 119 (1950), disapproving of "divorce by negotiation", that is to say, of about ninety percent of all divorces.

18. Vayette v. Myers, 303 Ill. 562, 136 N.E. 467 (1922) (dictum that agreement not to defend "universally" held collusive); Edleson v. Edleson, 179 Ky. 300, 200 S.W. 625 (1918); Sheehan v. Sheehan, 77 N.J.Eq. 411, 77 A. 1063 (1910) (any agreement as a result of which no defense will be made is collusive, here agreement by husband to furnish wife money with which to get the divorce); Riggle v. Riggle, 148 N.E.2d 72 (Ohio App. 1957); Campbell v. Campbell, 36 Ohio App. 232, 75 N.E.2d 698 (1947), 17 Univ.Cin.L.Rev. 202 (1948); Johnson v. Johnson, 185

the negotiations leading to a settlement of the parties' property claims, or in the settlement itself.[19] This rule results in an essentially meaningless distinction between cases where the defendant merely signifies his intention not to defend, characterized as not collusive, and cases in which he agrees not to defend, characterized as collusive. If the parties receive competent legal advice, they will have no trouble in staying on the right side of this line. A legal rule which is so easily avoided would seem to be of dubious value. Where the parties agree that one of them will sue for divorce, the cases disagree on whether they are guilty of collusion.[20]

A separation agreement which conditions a financial reward upon obtaining a divorce may also be considered collusive,[21] although there is apparently no objection to making a separation agreement conditional upon the divorce being granted.[22] This distinction is equally hard to justify, especially since the compromise of property claims arising out of divorce ought to be encouraged rather than made contingent upon the observation of hairline distinctions.

Once a court has decided how collusion is to be defined, and that it has occurred in a particular case, it faces the second difficult

issue, which is, what disposition is to be made of the case. In the rather rare case where the collusion is discovered during the pendency of the divorce action, the answer is easy: The divorce is just denied.[23] But collusion is more often brought to light after the divorce is granted. Typically, the parties obtain their divorce by collusion, and after the decree has become final, perhaps after one of them has remarried, the other becomes dissatisfied with the alimony provisions of the decree and moves to set them aside on the ground of collusion.[24] The court then faces a dilemma. If it grants the motion and sets the decree aside, it rewards one of the wrongdoers. But if it refuses relief, it gives up any chance to enforce the policy underlying the prohibitions on collusion. Most courts seem to choose the second alternative,[25] thus perhaps revealing a lack of conviction that collusive divorces can be prevented by this means, although they ostensibly based their decisions on the principles of estoppel, unclean hands or in pari delicto. Cases reaching the opposite result argue that there has been a fraud upon the court, and that only by vacating the decree based on that fraud can the state's interest in orderly proceedings be vindicated.[26] As the divorce law now stands there seems to be no

Wash. 677, 56 P.2d 679 (1936); Squier v. Squier, 99 Vt. 452, 134 A. 529 (1926); McNinch v. McNinch, 117 W.Va. 774, 188 S.E. 231 (1936). A pair of Montana cases illustrates the delicate distinctions involved here. Grush v. Grush, 90 Mont. 381, 3 P.2d 402 (1931) held an agreement collusive where the wife promised not to defend in consideration of the husband's promise to insert a provision for alimony in the decree. Schulz v. Fox, 136 Mont. 152, 345 P.2d 1045 (1959) held no collusion had occurred when the wife executed a property settlement only because the husband said that if she did not, he would contest the divorce. Apparently a promise not to contest differs substantially from a threat to contest.

19. Collusion and its relation to separation agreements is discussed infra in section 18.3.

20. Holding collusion: Henderson v. Henderson, 32 N.D. 520, 156 N.W. 245 (1916), 16 Colum.L.Rev. 424 (1916). Holding no collusion: Moore v. Moore, 197 Tenn. 360, 273 S.W.2d 148 (1954).

21. Wolkovisky v. Rapaport, 216 Mass. 48, 102 N.E. 910 (1913); Kull v. Losch, 328 Mich. 519, 44 N.W.2d 169 (1950) (dictum); Niman v. Niman, 15 Misc.2d 1095, 181 N.Y.S.2d 260 (1958), affirmed 8 App.Div.2d 793, 188 N.Y.S.2d 948 (1st Dep't 1959); T. v. B. [1951] 2 All Eng.Rep. 183; Lowndes v. Lowndes [1950] 1 All Eng.Rep. 999. Contra: Nelson v. Nelson, 71 S.D. 342, 24 N.W.2d 327 (1946); Jarrard v. Jarrard, 116 Wash. 70, 198 P. 741 (1921).

22. See the cases cited in section 18.3, infra.

23. Crosby v. Hatten, 213 Miss. 240, 56 So.2d 705 (1952); Maimone v. Maimone, 90 N.E.2d 383 (Ohio App. 1949) (defendant not barred by unclean hands since he did not fully understand the procedure). Other cases are cited in Annot., 109 A.L.R. 832, 848 (1939).

24. E.g., Newcomer v. Newcomer, 199 Iowa 290, 201 N.W. 579 (1925); Grush v. Grush, 90 Mont. 381, 3 P.2d 402 (1931).

25. Oberstein v. Oberstein, 217 Ark. 80, 228 S.W.2d 615 (1950) (refuses to vacate decree, but suggests counsel should be disciplined); Fender v. Crosby, 209 Ga. 896, 76 S.E.2d 769 (1953); Reppert v. Reppert, 214 Iowa 17, 241 N.W. 487 (1932); Todd v. Rhodes, 108 Kan. 64, 193 P. 894 (1920), 5 Minn.L.Rev. 317 (1921); In re Ellis' Estate, 55 Minn. 401, 56 N.W. 1056 (1893); Grush v. Grush, 90 Mont. 381, 3 P.2d 402 (1931); Paffen v. Paffen, 94 N.J.Eq. 356, 120 A. 197 (1923); Riggle v. Riggle, 148 N.E.2d 72 (Ohio App. 1957); Johnson v. Johnson, 185 Wash. 677, 56 P.2d 679 (1936). Other cases are cited in Annot., 109 A.L.R. 832, 849 (1939).

26. Furst v. Furst, 191 Misc. 699, 78 N.Y.S.2d 608 (1948), affirmed 275 App.Div. 991, 91 N.Y.S.2d 202 (2d Dep't 1949); Fuchs v. Fuchs, 64 N.Y.S.2d 487 (1946); Fowler v. Fowler, 190 N.C. 536, 130 S.E. 315 (1925), 74

wholly satisfactory way out of the dilemma illustrated by these opposing lines of cases.[27]

The enactment of the various non-fault grounds for divorce should have been sufficient to relegate the doctrine of collusion to the legal dust bin, and perhaps it has had that effect.[28] Unfortunately, however, the doctrine remains in the statutes of some states and perhaps in the common law of still more states. The careful lawyer must therefore be aware of it and must counsel his client in such a way as to avoid the charge of collusion. This is not difficult to accomplish if he is familiar with the history of collusion and with its peculiar distinctions, especially with respect to separation agreements.

§ 13.10 Divorce Defenses—Condonation

Like connivance and collusion, the defense of condonation came into American law from the English ecclesiastical practice.[1] Today it is expressly provided for by statute in some states,[2] and has been abolished by statute in other states.[3] Where the suit for divorce is brought on non-fault grounds, particularly for breakdown of the marriage, the defense is irrelevant.[4] If the claim of either or both of the spouses is that the marriage is no longer viable, the validity of that claim is not affected by the existence of earlier marital offenses and of their forgiveness by one of the parties. Where the doctrine of condonation still exists it is held to be a good defense to actions for divorce[5] or of separate maintenance.[6] It will also cut off a recriminatory defense where that pernicious doctrine still exists.[7]

Univ.Pa.L.Rev. 627 (1925); Miller v. Miller, 76 N.D. 558, 38 N.W.2d 35 (1949), 2 Ala.L.Rev. 117 (1949) (semble).

27. For further discussion of attack on divorce decrees on non-jurisdictional grounds, see section 14.6, infra.

28. In re Marriage of Collins, 200 N.W.2d 886 (Iowa 1972). But in an extraordinarily unreal opinion the California Supreme Court, in McKim v. McKim, 6 Cal.3d 673, 100 Cal.Rptr. 140, 493 P.2d 868 (1972) said that collusion may still prevent the granting of a marriage breakdown divorce, on the supposition that husband and wife would come into court and give false testimony that their marriage had broken down. Why the spouses might do this wholly irrational act, or why the court felt obliged to resurrect collusion after the legislature had repealed the collusion section of the statute, is not clear.

§ 13.10

1. Delliber v. Delliber, 9 Conn. 233 (1832); Williamson v. Williamson, 1 Johns.Ch. 488 (1815); See also Anonymous v. Anonymous, 6 Mass. 147 (1815). For a discussion of the English rules, see Collins v. Collins, L.R. 9 App.Cas. 205 (1884); II Burns Ecclesiastical Law, tit. Marriage, sec. 11 (4th ed. 1781). As applied in England it was a defense to judicial separation, absolute divorce being unknown, but there seems nothing inappropriate in translating a defense to separation into a defense to divorce.

2. Ala.Code 1983, § 30–2–3 (provides a defense if there has been a condonation of adultery by the admission of the offending party to the conjugal embraces after knowledge of the commission of the crime); Alaska Stat. § 25–24.120 (1983) (the act has been expressly forgiven or impliedly forgiven by the voluntary cohabitation of the parties after knowledge of the act); Del.Code tit. 13, § 1505(c) (1981) (condonation preserved as to misconduct grounds); Official Code Ga. Ann. § 19–5–4 (Supp.1986) (voluntary condonation and cohabitation subsequent to the acts complained of, with notice thereof); Idaho Code § 32–611 (1983); Me.Rev.Stat.Ann. tit. 19, § 69(1) (1981) (condonation is a discretionary defense); Md.Code, § 7–103 (1984) (condonation not an absolute bar, but a factor to be considered); N.Y.—McKinney's Dom.Rel.L. § 171

(1977) (defense where the offense has been forgiven by the plaintiff, forgiveness to be proved either affirmatively or by voluntary cohabitation with knowledge of the fact); N.D.Cent.Code § 14–05–10 (1981); Pa.Stat. tit. 23, § 207 (Supp.1986) (condonation retained as to the fault grounds for divorce); S.D.Codif.L. § 25–4–19 (1984); Tenn.Code Ann. § 36–4–112 (1984) (defense that the complainant admitted the defendant into conjugal society and embraces after having knowledge of the criminal act); V.T.C.A., Fam.Code § 3.08 (1975) (condonation is a defense only if the court finds there is a reasonable expectation of reconciliation); Va.Code, 1983, § 20–94 (defense to adultery, sodomy or buggery if the parties voluntarily cohabit after having knowledge of the offense); W.Va.Code, § 48–2–4 (1986) (no divorce if the parties voluntarily cohabit after knowledge of the adultery).

3. See the statutes cited in note 4 of section 13.8, supra, and Del.Code tit. 13, § 1505(c) (1981) (defenses abolished as to the non-fault grounds); West's Fla.Stat. Ann. § 61–044 (1985); Ill.—S.H.A. ch. 40, § 403(c) (1980) (no condonation after suit is filed); Ohio Rev.Code § 3105.10(c) (1980); Pa.Stat. tit. 23, § 207 (Supp.1986); Vt.Stat.Ann. tit. 15, § 563 (1974).

4. Nardone v. Nardone, 134 N.J.Super. 478, 341 A.2d 698 (1975); Peltola v. Peltola, 79 Mich.App. 709, 263 N.W.2d 25 (1977). See also Tigert v. Tigert, 595 P.2d 815 (Okl.App.1979). Contra: Woods v. Woods, 241 Ga. 393, 245 S.E.2d 651 (1978).

5. Many cases are collected in Annot., 32 A.L.R.2d 107 (1953). Condonation is an affirmative defense which should be pleaded by the defendant, but it will often be considered even though not pleaded. Ollman v. Ollman, 396 Ill. 176, 71 N.E.2d 50 (1947); Eicher v. Eicher, 148 Neb. 173, 26 N.W.2d 808 (1947). Contra: Ayers v. Ayers, 226 Ark. 394, 290 S.W.2d 24 (1956).

6. Commonwealth v. Sanders, 187 Pa.Super. 494, 144 A.2d 749 (1958). Other cases are collected in Annot., 10 A.L.R.2d 466, 526 (1950).

7. Kinek v. Kinek, 331 Mich. 54, 49 N.W.2d 58 (1951).

Condonation is ordinarily a question of fact.[8] It has been variously defined in English and American law. The early English rule was that when a resumption of marital intercourse occurred with knowledge of the defendant's offense, the offense was presumed remitted and the plaintiff could not have a divorce.[9] This definition includes the two elements of marital intercourse and forgiveness of the offense, but it fails to say whether both are essential for condonation. Some of the statutes indicate that either element is sufficient for condonation,[10] some limit condonation to cases in which there has been a resumption of cohabitation,[11] some require both elements to be present,[12] and some are ambiguous.[13] The case law is in similar confusion.[14]

There are two threads of policy running through discussions of condonation. The first is the ethical idea that forgiveness of sins is intrinsically good and that the law should recognize this.[15] The second is that marriages should not be lightly dissolved and that reconciliation should be encouraged.[16] The second of these policies, it is often asserted, is frustrated rather than promoted by the doctrine of condonation.[17] Divorce clients are often correctly advised by their lawyers that if they undertake a reconciliation which fails, any claim for divorce which they may have had will be barred. A prospective plaintiff is much less likely to try a reconciliation after receiving this advice. The first of these policies emphasizes the ethical position of the plaintiff while the second emphasizes the preservation of the marriage.

If this analysis is correct, both policies should be served and both forgiveness and a resumption of marital relations should be required for condonation.[18] A total resumption of marital life together amounts to condonation because it implies that there is both forgiveness and a full reconciliation.[19] But isolated acts of intercourse occurring without evidence of willingness to resume married life should not be sufficient.[20] On the same rea-

---

8. Dion v. Dion, 128 Conn. 416, 23 A.2d 314 (1941); Christensen v. Christensen, 125 Me. 397, 134 A. 373 (1926); Quigley v. Quigley, 310 Mass. 415, 38 N.E.2d 624 (1941); Murray v. Murray, 38 Wash.2d 269, 229 P.2d 309 (1951).

9. II Burns Ecclesiastical Law, tit. Marriage, sec. 11 (pp. 449–450) (4th ed. 1781). See also Beeby v. Beeby, 1 Hagg.Ecc. 789, 162 Eng.Rep. 755 (1799). For an excellent discussion of the principles involved, see Reader, The Meaning of Condonation in the Law of Divorce, 40 Dick. L.Rev. 92 (1936).

10. E.g., the Alaska statute cited supra, note 2.

11. E.g., Tennessee, Virginia and West Virginia statutes cited supra, note 2.

12. E.g., the New York statute cited supra, note 2.

13. E.g., the Delaware, Idaho, Maine, Maryland, North Dakota, Pennsylvania and Texas statutes cited supra, note 2.

14. Holding that condonation occurs on the resumption of sexual relations: Graves v. Graves, 123 Ind.App. 618, 112 N.E.2d 869 (1953). Holding that a single act of intercourse is sufficient for condonation: Collins v. Collins, 194 La. 446, 193 So. 702 (1940); Rushmore v. Rushmore, 114 N.J.Eq. 151, 168 A. 614 (1933); Crittenden v. Crittenden, 214 S.W.2d 670 (Tex.Civ.App.1948); Tarr v. Tarr, 184 Va. 443, 35 S.E.2d 401 (1945) (statute involved); De Berry v. De Berry, 115 W.Va. 604, 177 S.E. 440 (1934) (statute involved). Contra: Ojena v. Ojena, 154 Cal.App.2d 440, 316 P.2d 414 (1957) (statute involved); Mickler v. Mickler, 101 So.2d 157 (Fla.1958); Ramsay v. Ramsay, 69 Nev. 176, 244 P.2d 381 (1952); Kinley v. Kinley, 115 N.Y.S.2d 341 (1952). Holding that if the plaintiff forgives the defendant, it amounts to condonation whether there is a resumption of sexual relations or not: E.g., Bush v. Bush, 135 Ark. 512,

205 S.W. 895 (1918); Seiferth v. Seiferth, 132 So.2d 471 (Fla.App.1961), 19 W. & L.L.Rev. 243 (1962). Contra: Fearn v. Fearn [1948] 1 All Eng.Rep. 459 (C.A.).

15. A leading case on this aspect of policy is Stringfellow v. Stringfellow, 56 Wash.2d 957, 350 P.2d 1003 (1960), rehearing denied 56 Wash.2d 957, 353 P.2d 671 (1960).

16. Christensen v. Christensen, 125 Me. 397, 134 A. 373 (1926), and Fearn v. Fearn [1948] 1 All Eng.Rep. 459 (C.A.) stress this view of condonation.

17. Moore, An Examination of the Condonation Doctrine, 2 Akron L.Rev. 75 (1969); Note, Domestic Relations—Condonation—A Bar to Reconciliation, 20 Mercer L.Rev. 481 (1969).

18. Pope v. Pope, 12 Ill.App.3d 800, 299 N.E.2d 161 (1973). McNamara v. McNamara, 181 N.W.2d 206 (Iowa 1970); Brown v. Brown, 260 So.2d 66 (La.App.1972); Wright v. Wright, 153 Neb. 18, 43 N.W.2d 424 (1950); Tigert v. Tigert, 595 P.2d 815 (Okl.App.1979); McLaughlin v. McLaughlin, 244 S.C. 265, 136 S.E.2d 537 (1964).

19. Hickman v. Hickman, 227 So.2d 14 (La.App.1969); Trevett v. Trevett, 151 Neb. 517, 38 N.W.2d 332 (1949); Huffine v. Huffine, 74 N.E.2d 764 (Ohio Com.Pl.1947); Williams v. Williams, 188 Va. 543, 50 S.E.2d 277 (1948); Murray v. Murray, 38 Wash.2d 269, 229 P.2d 309 (1951).

20. Russell v. Russell, 270 Ala. 662, 120 So.2d 733 (1960); Seiferth v. Seiferth, 132 So.2d 471 (Fla.App.1961), 38 N.D.L.Rev. 354 (1962). See cases cited, note 9, supra. Much of the conflict in these cases may be explained by the analysis suggested in the text. See also cases cited in Annot., 32 A.L.R.2d 107, 133 (1953). Contra the text statement: Littlefield v. Littlefield, 292 A.2d 204 (Me. 1972); Zildjian v. Zildjian, 8 Mass.App.Ct. 1, 391 N.E.2d 697 (1979); Maughan v. Maughan, 184 N.E.2d 628 (Ohio Com.Pl.1961).

soning, an expression of forgiveness made in such clear and believable terms as to indicate a willingness to resume life as husband and wife ought to be sufficient to constitute condonation even before marital relations are in fact resumed.[21] The same is true where express conditions are imposed and not complied with.[22] Where the court has doubts about the sincerity and depth of meaning of the expressions, it should hold that there is no condonation without the more objective evidence provided by a resumption of marital relations.[23]

§ 13.11 Divorce Defenses—Recrimination, Comparative Rectitude and Provocation

Recrimination

Recrimination is the outrageous legal principle which ordains that when both spouses have grounds for divorce, neither may have a decree.[1] Like other rules which have no perceptible basis in social policy, the explanations for it are historical, but the history of recrimination is unusual.[2] It began as a rule of property in the Roman law, governing the circumstances in which a wife could recover her dowry on the dissolution of her marriage. It was never applied to prevent a divorce. In the Eighteenth Century Lord Stowell convert-

ed this doctrine of Roman property law into a defense to divorce a mensa et thoro, with the help of some favorable expressions in the canon law authorities.[3] This use of the doctrine was not as much an extension of the Roman version as might appear, since the effect of it generally, when asserted by the wife, was to require her husband to continue supporting her. Its consequences were still financial. There being no absolute divorce in English law at this period, recrimination was never relied on to prevent the dissolution of marriage. Upon the passage of divorce statutes in America, recrimination was imported along with the body of ecclesiastical law which most courts found to be part of the common law of divorce.[4] At this point, however, recrimination was transformed from a defense to separation into a bar to absolute divorce. No longer is it substantially a rule of property and support. It now prevents the dissolution of those very marriages most appropriate for dissolution, insuring that warring spouses may never form happier attachments. In this way an abstract principle of ancient lineage was transposed from one legal system to another, and from one legal context to another, without justification in reason or logic.

Several legal theories have been advanced in support of recrimination. These include

---

21. Miles v. Miles, 138 W.Va. 513, 48 S.E.2d 669 (1948). See also Annot., 32 A.L.R.2d 107, 145 (1953). See Henning v. Henning, 89 Ariz. 330, 362 P.2d 124 (1961), holding a "probationary reconciliation" not sufficient for condonation.

22. Stringfellow v. Stringfellow, 56 Wash.2d 957, 350 P.2d 1003 (1960), rehearing denied 56 Wash.2d 957, 353 P.2d 671 (1960).

23. See cases in Annot., 32 A.L.R.2d 107, 145 (1953). Other acts short of resumption of cohabitation are not usually sufficient to prove condonation. E.g., Pilgrim v. Pilgrim, 118 Ind.App. 6, 75 N.E.2d 159 (1947); Doyle v. Doyle, 328 Mass. 174, 102 N.E.2d 435 (1951); Reimer v. Reimer, 7 Wis.2d 146, 96 N.W.2d 375 (1959).

§ 13.11

1. Comment critical of recrimination fills the books. See, for example, the following: Chafee, Some Problems of Equity 80–84 (1950): Sherman, The Doctrine of Recrimination in Massachusetts, 35 B.U.L.Rev. 454 (1953); Raskin & Katz, The Dying Doctrine of Recrimination in the United States of America, 35 Can.B.Rev. 1046 (1957); Note, 26 Colum.L.Rev. 83 (1926); Note, 28 Iowa L.Rev. 341 (1943); Beamer, Recrimination in Divorce Proceedings, 10 Kan. City L.Rev. 213 (1942) (the leading treatment of the subject); Note, 29 Mich.L.Rev. 232 (1931);

Feinsinger & Young, Recrimination and Related Doctrines in the Wisconsin Law of Divorce, 6 Wis.L.Rev. 195 (1931); Note, Recrimination and Alimony—Are They Compatible, 13 Syra.L.Rev. 562 (1962).

The case of Wells v. Wells, 73 N.J.Super. 545, 180 A.2d 356 (1962) is an outstanding example of the horrors of recrimination in the hands of an undiscriminating judiciary. In this case the plaintiff's first wife deserted him. After eleven years he married again in the good faith belief his first wife was dead. Many years after the second marriage the first wife turned up and he sued her for divorce, continuing to live with his second wife. The divorce was not contested but on its own motion the court held the husband guilty of adultery and refused the divorce on the ground of recrimination. The case is criticized in a Note, 17 Rutgers L.Rev. 456 (1963). Luckily the case was reversed in 41 N.J. 594, 198 A.2d 442 (1964).

2. Beamer, Recrimination in Divorce Proceedings, 10 Kan. City L.Rev. 213 (1942) contains the most complete account of the doctrine's history.

3. Forster v. Forster, 1 Hagg.Con. 144, 161 Eng.Rep. 504 (1790).

4. E.g., Robbins v. Robbins, 140 Mass. 528, 5 N.E. 837 (1885).

the "clean hands" rule as the most common;[5] the assertion that the parties are in pari delicto;[6] compensatio criminum;[7] breach of mutual dependent covenants;[8] and the assertion that divorce is a remedy for the innocent spouse alone.[9] All of these share the defect of being merely slogans which restate the result without explaining or justifying it. Yet recrimination had a strong emotional appeal for the courts,[10] partly because of its long history, and partly because of the formerly pervasive view that divorce, like a tort action, was a means of compensating the innocent spouse for the wrong caused by the guilty spouse. This view was often clearly revealed in discussions of alimony and property divisions on divorce and even now has not entirely disappeared.[11] The effect of recrimination was to leave the spouses to "stew in their own juice", in other words, to remain married to each other. In such cases marriage became a form of punishment. Recrimination was also sometimes justified as a means of preserving marriages and families, usually with little attention to the question of how viable marriages so preserved would be.[12]

Fortunately the doctrine of recrimination is now almost entirely a thing of the past. In many states it has been expressly abolished by statute.[13] In those states in which the nonfault grounds for divorce exist, it is clearly irrelevant.[14] In a few states it is still technically applicable to the fault grounds for divorce,[15] but the courts often use various expedients for avoiding its impact.[16] Thus although an occasional rare case involving recrimination may still be seen,[17] it is accurate to say that the doctrine has received a well deserved extinction.

5. E.g., Vardon v. Vardon, 266 Mich. 341, 253 N.W. 320 (1934); Smith v. Smith, 146 Or. 600, 31 P.2d 168 (1934). See Chafee, Some Problems of Equity, 80–84 (1950).

6. Beeby v. Beeby, 1 Hagg.Ecc. 789, 162 Eng.Rep. 755 (1799).

7. Chambers v. Chambers, 1 Hagg.Con. 439, 161 Eng. Rep. 610 (1810).

8. Conant v. Conant, 10 Cal. 249 (1858).

9. McMillan v. McMillan, 113 Wash. 250, 193 P. 673 (1920).

10. Reddington v. Reddington, 317 Mass. 760, 59 N.E.2d 775 (1945).

11. See sections 15.3 and 16.4, infra.

12. Kuhfal v. Kuhfal, 318 Mich. 105, 27 N.W.2d 512 (1947); Phillips v. Phillips, 48 Ohio App. 322, 193 N.E. 657 (1933).

13. See the statutes cited in note 4, section 13.8, supra, and Ill.—S.H.A. ch. 40, § 403 (1980); Iowa Code Ann. § 598.18 (1981); Me.Rev.Stat.Ann. tit. 19, § 691 (1981) (recrimination a comparative rather than an absolute defense); Md.Code, § 7–103 (1984) (recrimination not a bar but a factor to be considered in a suit on the ground of adultery, and not a bar where the ground is living separate and apart); Mass.G.L.A. ch. 208, § 1 (1981); Miss.Code, § 93–5–3 (1973) (not mandatory to deny a divorce on the ground of recrimination); Ohio Rev.Code § 3105.10(c) (1980); V.T.C.A., Fam.Code § 3.08 (1975); Vt.Stat.Ann. tit. 15, § 562 (1974). Louisiana seems to have abolished recrimination by judicial decision. Thomason v. Thomason, 355 So.2d 908 (La.1978), 24 Loy.L.Rev. 776 (1978).

14. Vanderhuff v. Vanderhuff, 79 U.S.App.D.C. 153, 144 F.2d 509 (D.C.Cir.1944), 23 Tex.L.Rev. 194 (1945); Young v. Young, 207 Ark. 36, 178 S.W.2d 994 (1944) (living apart); Matysek v. Matysek, 212 Md. 44, 128 A.2d 627 (1957), 17 Md.L.Rev. 268 (1957) (living apart); Fausone v. Fausone, 75 Nev. 222, 338 P.2d 68 (1959) (living apart); Garner v. Garner, 85 N.M. 324, 512 P.2d 84 (1973); Rakestraw v. Rakestraw, 345 P.2d 888 (Okl.1959).

15. Alaska Stat. § 25.24.120 (1983); Ark.Stat. § 34–1209 (1962); Del.Code tit. 13, § 1505(c) (1981); Official Code Ga.Ann. § 19–5–4 (Supp.1986); Idaho Code § 32–611 (1983); N.Y.—McKinney's Dom.Rel.L. § 171 (1977) (plaintiff's adultery is a defense to divorce on the ground of adultery); Pa.Stat. tit. 23, § 207 (Supp.1986); Tenn.Code Ann. § 36–4–112 (1984) (retained for adultery); W.Va. Code, § 48–2–14 (1986).

16. The leading case is De Burgh v. De Burgh, 39 Cal. 2d 858, 250 P.2d 598 (1952) which gave the former California recrimination statute such a limited construction that the defense was virtually eliminated. See, e.g., Mueller v. Mueller, 44 Cal.2d 527, 282 P.2d 869 (1955); Nunes v. Nunes, 62 Cal.2d 33, 41 Cal.Rptr. 5, 396 P.2d 37 (1964). A similar case is Chastain v. Chastain, 559 S.W.2d 933 (Tenn.1977). O'Connor v. O'Connor, 253 Ind. 295, 253 N.E.2d 250 (1969), after an extensive review of the doctrine of recrimination, held that it would no longer be an absolute defense, but that its effect would be in the discretion of the trial court, that discretion to be guided by the same factors outlined by Justice Traynor in De Burgh. And a Georgia case has held that cruelty and desertion are not "like conduct" under that state's recrimination statute, so that the husband could have a divorce for cruelty even though he was guilty of desertion. Blois v. Blois, 234 Ga. 475, 216 S.E.2d 281 (1975).

17. E.g., Champion v. Champion, 47 Ala.App. 565, 258 So.2d 907 (1972); Pereira v. Pereira, 105 R.I. 746, 254 A.2d 436 (1969); Recht v. Recht, 36 A.D.2d 939, 321 N.Y.S.2d 395 (1st Dep't 1971).

Chapter 14

DIVORCE PROCEDURE

Table of Sections

§ 14.1 Divorce Procedure—In General and Constitutional Limitations

Since marital actions were exclusively the province of the ecclesiastical courts in England before the settlement of America,[1] and ecclesiastical courts were never established here, English divorce law and procedure could not be imported into this country as fully as were the doctrines of law and equity.[2] Nevertheless the courts in many cases have followed ecclesiastical procedure to the extent they felt it was appropriate to our different conditions.[3] In this way the ecclesiastical law has had an impact on our own divorce law. Other decisions, especially when statutes placed divorce jurisdiction in the equity courts, have relied on the equity precedents for their procedural rules in divorce cases.[4] Still other cases have said that divorce is primarily statutory.[5] With this background American divorce practice has become a blend of equity, ecclesiastical law and indigenous statutory law.

Today, most jurisdictions having abolished the distinctions between law and equity in favor of a single "civil action", the procedure

---

§ 14.1

1. 1 Holdsworth, History of English Law 622–623 (1922).

2. See Burtis v. Burtis, 1 Hopk.Ch. 557 (N.Y.1825), and Kitchin, A History of Divorce, Ch. X (1912).

3. See, e.g. Bauman v. Bauman, 18 Ark. 320 (1857); Jeans v. Jeans, 2 Harr. 38 (Del.1836); J.G. v. H.G., 33 Md. 401, 406 (1870); Chapman v. Chapman, 269 Mo. 663, 192 S.W. 448 (1917); Le Barron v. Le Barron, 35 Vt. 365, 367 (1862); Latham v. Latham, 71 Va.(30 Grat.) 307 (1878). This is one reason for the critical attitude expressed by many sociologists toward the divorce law. See Sirjamaki, The American Family in the Twentieth Century, 179 (1955).

4. Bremer v. Bremer, 4 Ill.2d 190, 122 N.E.2d 794 (1954); Winston v. Winston, 290 Md. 641, 431 A.2d 1330 (1981); White v. White, 322 Mass. 461, 78 N.E.2d 100 (1948); Fulton v. Fulton, 36 Miss. 517 (1858); Black v. Black, 5 Mont. 15, 2 P. 317 (1883); Thompson v. Thompson, 49 Nev. 375, 247 P. 545 (1926); Pollino v. Pollino, 39 N.J.Super. 294, 121 A.2d 62 (Ch.Div.1956); McCurdy v. McCurdy, 123 Okl. 295, 253 P. 295 (1926); Steiwer v. Steiwer, 112 Or. 485, 230 P. 359 (1924); Scolardi v. Scolardi, 42 R.I. 456, 108 A. 651 (1920); Brown v. Brown, 167 Tenn. 567, 72 S.W.2d 557 (1934); Cast v. Cast, 1 Utah 112 (1873).

5. Krasnow v. Krasnow, 140 Conn. 254, 99 A.2d 104 (1953); People ex rel. Levine v. Shea, 201 N.Y. 471, 94 N.E. 1060 (1911); Ackerman v. Ackerman, 200 N.Y. 72, 93 N.E. 192 (1910); Walker v. Walker, 330 Mich. 332, 47 N.W.2d 633 (1951).

in divorce cases is largely the same as in other civil actions, except so far as statute, court rule or case law specifically dictate otherwise.[6]

To the extent that divorce practice follows the general rules of civil procedure, it is outside the scope of this work.[7] An understanding of those rules which are peculiar to divorce practice is essential for any student of domestic relations, however, and they will be briefly discussed in the following sections. Necessarily these sections can only be a guide and starting point for further investigation. There is great local variation in the rules which govern divorce procedure, and the law of the particular jurisdiction must be examined in detail before any final conclusions can be reached.

One rule of practice found in all states requires the plaintiff in divorce actions to pay a fee for the filing of his complaint with the appropriate court and to pay the costs of serving process on the defendant.[8] Some states have been accustomed to mitigating the hardship of this requirement for indigent plaintiffs by permitting a filing in forma pauperis upon a proper showing of inability to pay the fees.[9] Now, as a result of the decision in Boddie v. Connecticut,[10] all states must permit indigent plaintiffs to sue for divorce without paying the filing fee or the costs of service. Boddie was a class suit brought by

welfare recipients in Connecticut attacking the constitutionality of the state's requirement of fees in divorce actions. It was conceded in this case that the plaintiffs were unable to pay the fees. The Supreme Court held that the requirement, as applied to these indigent plaintiffs, was a violation of the Due Process Clause of the Fourteenth Amendment. The rationale of the case seems to be that since marriage occupies a special position in our society such that it may only be dissolved by a court proceeding, the effect of the rules concerning fees was to deprive the plaintiffs of their right to a hearing on the dissolution of their marriages. The state's interests in preventing frivolous lawsuits and in having litigants pay the expenses generated by litigation were held not sufficient to override the plaintiffs' interest in access to the courts. There is some language in the opinion which might be construed as creating a broad constitutional right of access to the courts, but the opinion is careful to limit its holding to the situation at hand, in which the access to the courts "is the exclusive precondition to the adjustment of a fundamental human relationship",[11] that is, marriage.

In responding to the state's argument in Boddie that the fees were a reasonable method of allocating the costs of litigation, the Supreme Court made a cryptic reference to cheaper methods of serving process than by sheriffs or than by publication. The methods

6. Cohen v. Cohen, 209 Ga. 459, 74 S.E.2d 95 (1953); Harmon v. Harmon, 131 Me. 171, 159 A. 856 (1932); Steiwer v. Steiwer, 112 Or. 485, 230 P. 359 (1924); Hurvitz v. Hurvitz, 44 R.I. 243, 116 A. 661 (1922).

7. Rules of practice or divorce statutes frequently provide that divorce procedure will be the same as in other civil actions except as otherwise specifically provided. See, e.g., Ill.—S.H.A. c. 40, ¶105 (Supp.1986); Mass. Gen.L.Ann. c. 208, § 8 (1981); N.Y.—McKinney's Civ. Prac.L. & R. 101 (1972); West's Rev.Code Wash.Ann. 26.09.010 (1986); Wis.Stat.Ann. § 767.01 (1981); Uniform Marriage and Divorce Act § 301, 9A Unif.L.Ann. 119 (1979).

8. E.g., Colo.Rev.Stat. § 13–32–101(1)(a) (Supp.1986); Conn.Gen.Stat.Ann. §§ 52–257, 52–261 (Supp.1986); Ill.— S.H.A. ch. 25, ¶27.2(1)(d) (Supp.1986); Mass.Gen.L.Ann. c. 262, § 2 (Supp.1984); N.Y.—Civ.Prac.L. & R. § 8020 (1981).

9. E.g., Harris v. Harris, 424 F.2d 806 (D.C.Cir.1970), cert. denied 400 U.S. 826, 91 S.Ct. 50, 27 L.Ed.2d 55 (1970).

10. 401 U.S. 371, 91 S.Ct. 780, 28 L.Ed.2d 113 (1971), 10 Duq.L.Rev. 123 (1971).

The application of the Boddie case to Indian tribal courts is discussed in Cohen, Divorce Filing Fees in Indian Tribal Courts, 1970 Law & Soc. Order 541.

11. 401 U.S. at 383, 91 S.Ct. at 788. The Supreme Court later emphasized the point made in the text in United States v. Kras, 409 U.S. 434, 97 S.Ct. 631, 34 L.Ed. 2d 626 (1973). In that case an indigent petitioner in bankruptcy claimed that he had a constitutional right to be exempt from the usual fees in bankruptcy proceedings, relying on the Boddie case. The lower court, and other lower federal courts, had held that since he was unable to pay the fees he had been deprived of access to the bankruptcy courts in violation of the Due Process Clause of the Fifth Amendment. The Supreme Court rejected this argument, distinguishing Boddie on the ground that it involved marriage which could only be dissolved by court action and which is a fundamental interest of greater constitutional importance than the interest in being discharged from debt.

suggested were service by mail at the defendant's last known address and "posted notice".[12] Although service by publication can be quite expensive, some courts following Boddie have held that an indigent plaintiff has a constitutional right to have those costs paid by the state as well as the sheriff's fees for service, which were the only fees actually involved in the Boddie case.[13] It is not clear what the Court meant by its reference to posted notice, nor is it clear that posting a notice somewhere would meet the notice requirements of the Due Process Clause as elaborated by the Mullane case.[14]

As might be expected, the definition of indigency for purposes of applying the Boddie rule has produced considerable litigation.[15] Few courts have attempted a general definition, other than to hold that the plaintiff, in order to have his fees waived, must show that he would be unable to bring the suit if the fees were assessed.[16] The issue is generally to be decided on affidavits unless a question about the facts arises, in which event a hearing may be required.[17]

The Boddie case also suggests the question whether an indigent plaintiff has a constitutional right to have counsel furnished him in a divorce action. The Supreme Court in that case was careful to express no opinion on the point. Its reasoning might well support a Due Process claim, however, in those cases at least where complex issues control the grant or denial of a divorce.[18] Conversely, in those states which have adopted marriage breakdown as a ground for divorce, access to the courts for the termination of a marriage might not require the assistance of a lawyer.[19] Somewhat different questions are involved where the divorce action includes a dispute over the custody of a child of the marriage. In such a case an indigent party might argue, not that his inability to hire a lawyer deprived him of access to the courts, but that it threatened to deprive him of the care and custody of his child, an interest which some courts might well characterize as fundamental. There is some authority which favors such a due process claim.[20] But the majority of courts, understandably reluctant to impose upon the states the predictably large expenses of providing counsel for indigent divorce liti-

12. Boddie v. Connecticut, 401 U.S. 371, 382, 91 S.Ct. 780, 788, 28 L.Ed.2d 113 (1971).

13. Hart v. Superior Court, 16 Ariz.App. 184, 492 P.2d 433 (1971); King v. King, 21 Ill.App.3d 1062, 316 N.E.2d 555 (1974); State ex rel. Taylor v. Clymer, 503 S.W.2d 53 (Mo.App.1973); Deason v. Deason, 32 N.Y.2d 93, 343 N.Y.S.2d 321, 296 N.E.2d 229 (1973), on remand 73 Misc. 2d 964, 343 N.Y.S.2d 276 (1973). Dungan v. Dungan, 579 S.W.2d 183 (Tenn. 1979) followed the suggestion in Boddie and ordered, in lieu of publication, service by registered mail to the defendant's last address and posting in three public places in the county. Cohen v. Board of Supervisors, 20 Cal.App.3d 236, 97 Cal.Rptr. 550 (1971) refused to order the county to pay the cost of publication but seemed to authorize the trial court to order an alternative method of service. And Johnson v. Johnson, 329 A.2d 451 (D.C.App. 1974) authorized publication in only one newspaper and that the less expensive one.

14. Mullane v. Central Hanover Bank & Trust Co., 339 U.S. 306, 70 S.Ct. 652, 94 L.Ed. 865 (1950).

15. Cases are collected in Annot., 52 A.L.R.3d 844 (1973).

16. Ashley v. Superior Court In & For the County of Pierce, 82 Wash.2d 188, 509 P.2d 751 (1973), on rehearing 83 Wash.2d 630, 521 P.2d 711 (1974). Hightower v. Peterson, 235 N.W.2d 313 (Iowa 1975) took the position that the plaintiff must show that he is unable to pay the fees without losing the capacity to support himself with life's basic necessities. The plaintiff need not be desti-

tute, but something more than financial inconvenience must be shown. The court applied this standard to uphold the trial court's decision that a young woman with seven children living on AFDC and a small monthly wage was able to pay the fees of $27. Other cases holding welfare recipients not indigent are Tomashefski v. Tomashefski, 246 Pa.Super. 118, 369 A.2d 839 (1976) and Nicholson v. Nicholson, 247 Pa.Super. 172, 371 A.2d 1383 (1977). Indigency was found in Coonce v. Coonce, 356 Mass. 690, 255 N.E.2d 330 (1970); Schoepple v. Schoepple, 239 Pa.Super. 557, 361 A.2d 665 (1976); Wilson v. Wilson, 218 Pa.Super. 344, 280 A.2d 665 (1971).

Since indigency was conceded in the Boddie case, the Court was not required to formulate a definition.

17. Earls v. Superior Court of San Luis Obispo County, 6 Cal.3d 109, 98 Cal.Rptr. 302, 490 P.2d 814 (1971).

18. The traditional grounds for divorce and the affirmative defenses, to say nothing of jurisdictional issues, could produce complex legal questions. It would seem futile to give an indigent litigant the right to have his fees paid under the Boddie case so that he had technical access to the divorce court and then refuse to provide the legal counsel necessary to make that access meaningful.

19. See Note, The Unauthorized Practice of Law and Pro Se Divorce: An Empirical Analysis, 86 Yale L.J. 104 (1976).

20. Flores v. Flores, 598 P.2d 893 (Alaska 1979).

gants, have held that there is no constitutional right to counsel in this situation.[21] On the other hand, there is some tendency to permit the divorce court to appoint counsel for indigents as a matter of discretion in appropriate cases.[22]

Legislatures have occasionally imposed greater filing fees in divorce cases than in other kinds of litigation, thereby prompting constitutional challenges on equal protection or due process grounds. A statute which imposed such higher fees was held not to violate the Equal Protection Clause of the Fourteenth Amendment.[23] The rationale of the case was that whether or not the right to a divorce is characterized as "fundamental", that right was not substantially infringed by requiring divorce plaintiffs to pay the higher fee, and that judged under the "rational basis" test the fee was justified as a method of paying for the increased costs to the judicial system caused by divorce litigation. On the other hand an Illinois statute imposing an additional fee in divorce actions was held unconstitutional as an arbitrary use of the police power and a violation of due process when the proceeds from the fee were earmarked by statute to fund shelters for victims of domestic violence.[24] The court concluded that court filing fees could only be imposed for purposes related to the operation and maintenance of the courts.

 **WESTLAW REFERENCES**

divorc! dissol! /s "due process" /s boddie

indigen! /3 defin! mean*** /p divorc! dissol!

di(divorc! dissol! /s counsel lawyer attorney /s right furnish! provid! appoint! assign! /s indigen!)

divorc! dissol! /p fee cost*** expense /7 file* filing /s "equal protection" "rational basis" fundamental! "economic discrimination"

§ 14.2 Divorce Procedure—Parties

Although as a general rule only the two spouses are proper parties to a divorce action,[1] there are circumstances in which other persons may become parties either originally or by intervention. Thus if the divorce action involves property in which third persons claim an interest, such persons may become parties to the suit in order to determine all questions in one litigation.[2] In such a case they have no right to be heard on the granting or denial of the divorce, but only on the disposition of the property. Ordinarily they would not be entitled to be parties to the divorce solely to assert claims against the spouses unrelated to the divorce.[3] If such persons are not made parties, their claims may be decided in a later suit.[4] Likewise third persons may become parties to divorce actions when it is claimed that they have received transfers of property in fraud of the rights of one of the spouses.[5] But persons

21. Meyer v. Meyer, 414 A.2d 236 (Me. 1980); In re Smiley, 36 N.Y.2d 433, 369 N.Y.S.2d 87, 330 N.E.2d 53 (1975); Kiddie v. Kiddie, 563 P.2d 139 (Okl. 1977); Annot., 85 A.L.R.3d 983 (1978).

22. N.Y.—McKinney's Fam.Ct.Act §§ 261, 262 (1983); Kiddie v. Kiddie, 563 P.2d 139 (Okl. 1977).

23. Murillo v. Bambrick, 681 F.2d 898 (3d Cir.1982), cert. denied 459 U.S. 1017, 103 S.Ct. 378, 74 L.Ed.2d 511 (1982), 56 Temp.L.Q. 1013 (1983).

24. Crocker v. Finley, 99 Ill.2d 444, 77 Ill.Dec. 97, 459 N.E.2d 1346 (1984).

§ 14.2

1. Yedinak v. Yedinak, 383 Mich. 409, 175 N.W.2d 706 (1970); Donahue v. Donahue, 134 Mich.App. 696, 352 N.W.2d 705 (1984).

2. Cook v. Cook, 248 Ala. 206, 27 So.2d 255 (1946); Baker v. Baker, 6 Ill.App.2d 557, 128 N.E.2d 616 (1955); Edwards v. Edwards, 182 Kan. 737, 324 P.2d 150 (1958); Cadwell v. Cadwell, 162 Kan. 552, 178 P.2d 266 (1947); Arnold v. Arnold, 214 Neb. 39, 332 N.W.2d 672 (1983); Greathouse v. Greathouse, 64 N.M. 21, 322 P.2d 1075

(1958); Wright v. Wright, 199 Okl. 291, 185 P.2d 915 (1947); Brust v. Brust, 181 Or. 307, 181 P.2d 632 (1947); Lancaster v. Lancaster, 155 Tex. 528, 291 S.W.2d 303 (1956). Other cases are collected in Annots., 63 A.L.R.3d 373 (1975) and 102 A.L.R. 814 (1936), and in Note, The Right of Third Parties to Intervene in Divorce Proceedings, 39 Harv.L.Rev. 1090 (1926). Although third persons may have a right to be parties to the divorce action, that may not make them indispensable parties. See, e.g., Coman v. Coman, 492 F.2d 273 (3d Cir. 1974); Reilly v. Reilly, 671 P.2d 330 (Wyo.1983).

West's Ann.Cal.Civ.Code §§ 4363 and 4363.1 (1983) authorize the joinder of interested persons and of employee pension plans where a pension is involved in a property distribution.

3. Dick v. Dick, 238 So.2d 469 (Fla.App. 1970), cert. denied 240 So.2d 641 (1970).

4. Long v. Long, 88 Cal.App.2d 544, 199 P.2d 47 (1948).

5. Breidenthal v. Breidenthal, 182 Kan. 23, 318 P.2d 981 (1957); Brown v. Brown, 335 Mich. 511, 56 N.W.2d

having only contingent interests or expectancies in property have no right to be parties.[6]

It is clear that any divorce affects the children of the marriage in a variety of ways and that therefore there is good reason to make the children parties to the divorce action. Nevertheless this is not usually done, although there is a growing tendency to appoint guardians ad litem for children in divorce actions.[7]

Influenced by the former English practice,[8] a few states still authorize the co-respondent in an adultery divorce to become a party to the suit,[9] but this is rarely done.[10] Without such a statute the co-respondent may not be a party.[11]

In special circumstances, where their interests may be affected by the decision in a divorce action, prior or subsequent spouses of the parties to the divorce may be made parties to the suit.[12]

In view of the common judicial statement that the state is a party to all divorce actions, one might expect that a representative of the state ought to be served or notified in all cases to protect the state's interests, as may be done in England.[13] In the past when only fault grounds for divorce existed, many American states authorized or required the participation of a state representative in divorce suits as a means of preventing collusion, of ensuring that the grounds relied on were properly proved, and of protecting the interests of the children of the marriage. Today only a few states have statutes of this kind,[14] and representatives of the state's interest play little part in divorce litigation. This is especially true in those states which have enacted marriage breakdown as a ground for divorce.

Questions as to the capacity of parties to divorce actions frequently arise where the party is either a minor or insane. It is settled that minors may bring and defend divorce actions.[15] In many jurisdictions the courts require appointment of a guardian ad litem to protect the minor's interests.[16] In others no guardian need be appointed, on the theory that the minor has been emancipated by his marriage and he thus has full legal capacity.[17]

The fact that the defendant is insane at the time of the divorce action does not of itself prevent hearing the case and granting the

367 (1953); Donahue v. Donahue, 134 Mich.App. 696, 352 N.W.2d 705 (1984); Annot., 63 A.L.R.3d 373 (1975).

6. Bernheimer v. Bernheimer, 87 Cal.App.2d 242, 196 P.2d 813 (1948).

7. This question is discussed infra, in section 19.3. The guardian ad litem of an illegitimate child was not permitted to intervene in the divorce action in which the child's father was a defendant in Maher v. Maher, 64 Ohio App.2d 22, 410 N.E.2d 1260 (1978).

8. Matrimonial Causes Act 1965 § 41, no longer in force.

9. N.J.Stat.Ann. § 2A:34–15 (1952); N.Y.—McKinney's Dom.Rel.L. § 172 (1977); W.Va.Code § 48–2–12 (1986).

10. See, e.g., Branch v. Branch, 188 Pa.Super. 587, 149 A.2d 573 (1959).

11. San Chez v. Superior Court, 153 Cal.App.2d 162, 314 P.2d 135 (1957); Leland v. Leland, 319 Ill. 426, 150 N.E. 270 (1925); Lickle v. Boone, 187 Md. 579, 51 A.2d 162 (1947); Blankenship v. Blankenship, 239 Md. 498, 212 A.2d 294 (1965). Other cases are collected in an Annot., 170 A.L.R. 161 (1948), and 1 A.L.R. 1414 (1919).

12. Harmon v. Harmon, 256 S.C. 328, 182 S.E.2d 300 (1971). But see Vanderson v. Vanderson, 668 S.W.2d 167 (Mo.App.1984).

13. Matrimonial Causes Act 1973 § 8. The official is called the Queen's proctor.

14. Del.Code tit. 13, § 1516 (1981); D.C.Code 1981, § 16–918; Official Code Ga.Ann. § 19–5–10 (1986); Hawaii Rev.Stat. § 580–8 (1976); Ky.Rev.Stat. § 403.090 (1984); Mass.Gen.L.Ann. c. 208, § 16 (1981); Mich.Com.L. Ann. § 25.121 (1984); Wis.Stat.Ann. §§ 767.13, 767.14 (1981 and Supp.1986); Wyo.Stat.1977, § 20–2–105.

The functions of divorce proctors are described in Connolly, Divorce Proctors, 34 B.U.L.Rev. 1 (1954) and Cox, The Divorce Proctor, 33 Tenn.L.Rev. 439 (1966).

15. Bentley v. Bentley, 149 Ga. 707, 102 S.E. 21 (1920); Stephenson v. Stephenson, 196 Okl. 623, 167 P.2d 63 (1945); Bernardi v. Bernardi, 42 Tenn.App. 282, 302 S.W.2d 63 (1956); Holman v. Holman, 35 Tenn.App. 273, 244 S.W.2d 618 (1957). Other cases are collected in Annot., 17 A.L.R. 900 (1922).

16. Whaley v. Whaley, 224 Ark. 632, 275 S.W.2d 634 (1955); Altieri v. Altieri, 21 Conn.Supp. 376, 155 A.2d 758 (1959); Nims v. Nims, 305 S.W.2d 875 (Mo.App.1957); Evans v. Evans, 161 N.E.2d 401 (Ohio App.1959). See also Annot., 17 A.L.R. 900 (1922). This was the procedure under the English ecclesiastical law. Brown v. Brown, 2 Rob.Eccl.Rep. 302, 163 Eng.Rep. 1325 (1850). Service must be made on the minor. Zurowsky v. Zurowsky, 60 D. & C. 160 (Pa.1946).

17. Bentley v. Bentley, 149 Ga. 707, 102 S.E. 21 (1920); Holman v. Holman, 35 Tenn.App. 273, 244 S.W.2d 618 (1951).

divorce upon a showing of proper grounds, provided the court is satisfied that the defendant's interests are properly represented.[18] This generally means that a conservator, guardian or committee must be appointed for the incompetent defendant,[19] and if such a representative is not appointed, the divorce may be set aside.[20] If defendant has not been adjudicated an incompetent, but nevertheless claims to have been insane at the time of trial, the appointment of a guardian ad litem is proper [21] even though refusal to appoint one may not be reversible error.[22]

Insanity may be grounds for denial of the divorce, however, if it is proved that the defendant was insane at the time of the alleged marital misconduct. The reasons for this are variously stated, but they all amount to a logical application of the traditional view that a divorce is granted not to relieve the parties of an intolerable relationship, but because the defendant has been guilty of a specified offense against the marriage. It follows, as the cases usually hold, that if defendant's commission of this wrong was caused by his insanity, he cannot be held responsible.[23]

Where the ground for divorce is cruelty or indignities, the insane defendant is said to be incapable of forming the specific intent to injure the plaintiff or the malevolent motive which is an essential element of the offense of cruelty.[24] Some courts have even adopted the definition of insanity originating in M'Naghten's Case [25] and applied it to divorce.[26] Other courts, however, have held that mental illness of the defendant is not a defense to divorce, on the ground that the purpose of granting divorces for cruelty is the protection of the plaintiff or the recognition that the defendant's conduct has frustrated the purposes of marriage.[27] Insanity itself is a ground for divorce in a number of states, but it is hedged about with so many limitations that it may not be available in a given case.[28] The hardships that all these doctrines may impose are of course mitigated by the existence of the common non-fault grounds for divorce.

In the converse case which arises when the plaintiff in the divorce action has been adjudged insane, the action cannot be brought either by the insane party himself or by a

---

18. Johnson v. First Nat. Bank, 223 F.2d 31 (10th Cir. 1955); Smith v. Smith, 226 N.C. 544, 39 S.E.2d 458 (1946); Harrison v. Harrison, 76 N.W.2d 906 (N.D.1956); Gaines v. Gaines, 234 S.W.2d 250 (Tex.Civ.App.1950). Other cases are cited in Annot., 19 A.L.R.2d 144, 181 (1951).

19. Breen v. Breen, 199 Misc. 366, 103 N.Y.S.2d 554 (1951); Olsen v. Olsen, 197 Misc. 451, 95 N.Y.S.2d 265 (1950).

20. Box v. Box, 253 Ala. 297, 45 So.2d 157 (1950); Stephens v. Stephens, 253 Ala. 315, 45 So.2d 153 (1950); Metcalf v. Metcalf, 301 Ky. 817, 193 S.W.2d 446 (1946); Berg v. Berg, 336 Mich. 284, 57 N.W.2d 889 (1953); Schwarzkopf v. Schwarzkopf, 176 Pa.Super. 441, 107 A.2d 610 (1954).

21. Fischhof v. Fischhof, 135 N.Y.S.2d 599 (1954); In re Miller's Guardianship, 26 Wash.2d 202, 173 P.2d 538 (1946).

22. MacDonald v. MacDonald, 120 Utah 573, 236 P.2d 1066 (1951). Contra: Puterman v. Puterman, 66 Wyo. 89, 205 P.2d 815 (1949).

23. Kendall v. Kendall, 268 Ala. 383, 106 So.2d 653 (1958); Crosby v. Crosby, 186 Kan. 420, 350 P.2d 796 (1960); Rice v. Rice, 332 Mass. 489, 125 N.E.2d 787 (1955); Fansler v. Fansler, 344 Mich. 569, 75 N.W.2d 1 (1956); Niedergerke v. Niedergerke, 271 S.W.2d 204 (Mo.App. 1954). Other cases are collected in Annots., 19 A.L.R.2d 144 (1951) and 4 A.L.R. 1331 (1919). Manley v. Manley, 193 Pa.Super. 252, 164 A.2d 113 (1960) held that insanity

was a defense to the charge of adultery, refusing to follow Matchin v. Matchin, 6 Pa. 332 (1847).

24. Vaughan v. Vaughan, 223 Ga. 298, 154 S.E.2d 592 (1967); Hano v. Hano, 5 Mass.App.Ct. 639, 367 N.E.2d 1190 (1977); Jumper v. Jumper, 240 Pa.Super. 99, 362 A.2d 411 (1976); Barr v. Barr, 232 Pa.Super. 9, 331 A.2d 774 (1974). In Loveless v. Loveless, 128 Ill.App.2d 297, 261 N.E.2d 732 (1970), affirmed 3 Ill.App.3d 967, 279 N.E.2d 531 (1972), the court upheld a finding that the wife was legally responsible for her conduct notwithstanding a history of mental and emotional difficulties on her part.

25. 10 Cl. & Fin. 200, 8 Eng.Rep. 718 (1843).

26. Dochelli v. Dochelli, 125 Conn. 468, 6 A.2d 324 (1939); Fansler v. Fansler, 344 Mich. 569, 75 N.W.2d 1 (1956); Dankers v. Dankers, 285 Minn. 120, 172 N.W.2d 318 (1969); Niedergerke v. Niedergerke, 271 S.W.2d 204 (Mo.App.1954); Annot., 19 A.L.R.2d 144, 151 (1951). Crosby v. Crosby, 186 Kan. 420, 350 P.2d 796 (1960), 10 Kan.L.Rev. 95 (1961) seems to have adopted the Durham rule for divorce cases.

27. Nunes v. Nunes, 62 Cal.2d 33, 41 Cal.Rptr. 5, 396 P.2d 37 (1964); Pajak v. Pajak, 56 N.Y.2d 394, 452 N.Y.S.2d 381, 437 N.E.2d 1138 (1982). See also Williams v. Williams [1964] A.C. 698, [1963] 2 All Eng.Rep. 994.

28. This ground for divorce is discussed in section 14.8, at note 25 Practitioner's Edition.

guardian or representative on his behalf.[29] The reason usually given is that just as entrance into marriage requires a voluntary exercise of will, so also does the decision to end the marriage by divorce. A personal choice of the greatest importance to the individual must be made. The insane person is incapable of making this choice by virtue of his mental condition, and it is too personal and too important to be made for him by a guardian or conservator.[30] There is thus no plaintiff qualified to initiate the suit.

The doctrine that the insane plaintiff may not sue for divorce must be limited in two respects. If a statute specifically authorizes his guardian to sue on his behalf, then the action may be brought notwithstanding an adjudication of incompetency.[31] Specific authorization for divorce actions is required, however, and it is not enough that there is a general statute in the jurisdiction allowing incompetents to sue through a guardian.[32] Secondly, if the plaintiff has not been adjudicated, although admittedly insane, he himself may bring the action,[33] and he may also bring it if he is capable of consenting to the dissolution of the marriage whether or not he has been adjudicated.[34]

It is often held that the death of a party to a divorce action occurring before the decree causes the action to abate automatically.[35] In fact in their zeal some courts have held that the court loses jurisdiction to proceed further when the death occurs,[36] or when the death follows the interlocutory decree of divorce but precedes the final decree.[37] There is considerable over-simplification in such decisions although as a broad statement of the doctrine they are generally correct. Thus if the case was fully adjudicated and decided before the death but for some reason a decree was not entered, a decree nunc pro tunc may be entered.[38] Several cases have held that where a divorce decree was entered but the court reserved jurisdiction to decide the property issues later, the litigation did not abate on the death of a party and the court could proceed to determine the property issues.[39] The same

---

29. In re Higgason's Marriage, 10 Cal.3d 476, 110 Cal. Rptr. 897, 516 P.2d 289 (1973); Scott v. Scott, 45 So.2d 878 (Fla.1950); Sternberg v. Sternberg, 203 Ga. 298, 46 S.E.2d 349 (1948); State ex rel. Quear v. Madison Circuit Court, 229 Ind. 503, 99 N.E.2d 254 (1951); Mohrmann v. Kob, 291 N.Y. 181, 51 N.E.2d 921 (1943); Freeman v. Freeman, 34 N.C.App. 301, 237 S.E.2d 857 (1977); Shenk v. Shenk, 100 Ohio App. 32, 135 N.E.2d 436 (1954). Other cases are cited in Annot., 6 A.L.R.3d 681 (1966). But see In re Marriage of Gannon, 104 Wash.2d 121, 702 P.2d 465 (1985). A decree entered in violation of this rule may be set aside. Jackson v. Bowman, 226 Ark. 753, 294 S.W.2d 344 (1956); Heine v. Witt, 251 Wis. 157, 28 N.W.2d 248 (1947). Contra the general rule: Turner v. Bell, 198 Tenn. 202, 279 S.W.2d 71 (1955), cert. denied 350 U.S. 842, 76 S.Ct. 83, 100 L.Ed. 751 (1955), 28 Rocky Mt.L.Rev. 274 (1956).

Where the relief sought is annulment rather than divorce, the courts have held that the guardian for an incompetent person may bring the suit. And where a divorce is sought for reasons ordinarily entitling a person to annulment, it has been held that a guardian may sue. Jones v. Minc, 77 Wash.2d 381, 462 P.2d 927 (1969), overruled on other grounds In re Marriage of Gannon, 104 Wash.2d 121, 702 P.2d 465 (1985).

30. Scott v. Scott, 45 So.2d 878 (Fla.1950); Mohrmann v. Kob, 291 N.Y. 181, 51 N.E.2d 921 (1943).

31. Cohn v. Carlisle, 310 Mass. 126, 37 N.E.2d 260 (1941).

32. Mohrmann v. Kob, 291 N.Y. 181, 51 N.E.2d 921 (1943). Contra: Campbell v. Campbell, 242 Ala. 141, 5 So.2d 401 (1941).

33. Sengstack v. Sengstack, 4 N.Y.2d 502, 176 N.Y.S.2d 337, 151 N.E.2d 887 (1958), 12 Vand.L.Rev. 493 (1959) (Separation).

34. In re Higgason's Marriage, 10 Cal.3d 476, 110 Cal. Rptr. 897, 516 P.2d 289 (1973); Boyd v. Edwards, 4 Ohio App.3d 142, 446 N.E.2d 1151 (1982).

35. Tillman v. Tillman, 172 F.2d 270 (D.C.Cir.1948), cert. denied 336 U.S. 954, 69 S.Ct. 883, 93 L.Ed. 1108 (1949); Chatsworth Lumber Co. v. White, 214 Ga. 798, 107 S.E.2d 827 (1959); Howard v. Howard, 49 Ill.App.3d 441, 7 Ill.Dec. 303, 364 N.E.2d 464 (1977); Jordan v. Silva, 330 Mass. 165, 112 N.E.2d 258 (1953); Heil v. Rogers, 329 S.W.2d 960 (Mo.App.1959); Jones v. Minc, 77 Wash.2d 381, 462 P.2d 927 (1969), overruled on other grounds In re Marriage of Gannon, 104 Wash.2d 121, 702 P.2d 465 (1985); Annots., 158 A.L.R. 1205 (1945), 104 A.L.R. 654 (1936).

36. Childress v. McManus, 282 Ark. 255, 668 S.W.2d 9 (1984); In re Marriage of Lawrence, ___ Mont. ___, 687 P.2d 1026 (1984).

37. In re Seiler's Estate, 164 Cal. 181, 128 P. 334 (1912).

38. In re Shayman's Marriage, 35 Cal.App.3d 648, 111 Cal.Rptr. 11 (1973); Koester v. Administrator of Estate of Koester, 101 Nev. 68, 693 P.2d 569 (1985); Novotny v. Novotny, 665 S.W.2d 171 (Tex.App. 1984). Refusing to enter such a decree: Pratt v. Pratt, 99 Wash.2d 905, 665 P.2d 400 (1983).

39. Kinsler v. Superior Court, County of Los Angeles, 121 Cal.App.3d 808, 175 Cal.Rptr. 564 (1981); In re Marriage of Davies, 95 Ill.2d 474, 70 Ill.Dec. 4, 448 N.E.2d 882

result has been reached as to the disposition of custody issues after the death of a spouse, there being little purpose to be served in requiring the contestants for custody to bring a new, independent proceeding.[40]

WESTLAW REFERENCES

to(134 211) /p divorc! dissol! /s party /s child /s "guardian ad litem"

divorc! dissol! /s (set setting +1 aside) vacat! /s husband wife spous! /5 insan! sane sanity incompeten! incapacit! (mental +1 ill illness capacity)

di(divorc! dissol! /s abat! /s property /s death dead deceas! dying die*)

§ 14.3 Divorce Procedure—Preliminary Orders

The title to this section is intended to refer to those injunctions pendente lite which may be granted in divorce actions to preserve the status quo or protect the parties or their children from harm. Orders for temporary alimony or counsel fees, though they have a similar purpose, will be discussed in another section.[1]

Authority to enjoin transfers or encumbrances of property, interference with or molestation of the person of a spouse or child, removal of a child from the jurisdiction of the court, or exclusion of a party from the family home is given by statute in many states.[2] Where statutes do not exist, this authority can be rested upon the inherent power of equity courts to give whatever incidental relief may be necessary to make their decrees effective.[3]

Although there may be local variations in practice, it is usually held that restraining orders and preliminary injunctions may only be obtained upon affidavits or verified pleadings [4] stating facts which show the necessity for the injunction.[5] General statements of opinion, conclusion, inference or suspicion, or allegations made upon information and belief are not sufficient, since such injunctions often seriously curtail the freedom of one of the parties and should not be granted except upon clear factual grounds.[6] They also must be specifically prayed for, a general prayer for equitable relief not being sufficient, at least in an uncontested case.[7] They must be based upon personal service within the jurisdiction

---

(1983); Goldman v. Walker, 260 Md. 222, 271 A.2d 639 (1970); Jacobson v. Jacobson, 146 N.J.Super. 491, 370 A.2d 65 (1976). Taylor v. Wells, 265 So.2d 402 (Fla.App. 1972), cert. denied 273 So.2d 767 (1973) held that the divorce action could continue after the death of a husband when the wife had been defaulted through a mistake of her attorney, in order to settle property rights. See also Howsden v. Rolenc, 219 Neb. 16, 360 N.W.2d 680 (1985).

40. Milenkovic v. Milenkovic, 93 Ill.App.3d 204, 48 Ill. Dec. 618, 416 N.E.2d 1140 (1981).

§ 14.3

1. See section 16.2, infra.

2. Some or all such injunctions are authorized by, e.g., West's Ann.Cal.Civ.Code § 4359 (Supp.1986); Colo.Rev. Stat. § 14–10–108 (1974 and Supp.1986); Del.Code tit. 13, § 1509 (1981); Ill.—S.H.A. ch. 40, ¶501 (1980); West's Ann.Ind.Code § 31–1–11.5–7 (Supp.1986); Kan.Stat.Ann. § 60–1607 (1983); Mass.Gen.L.Ann. c. 208, § 18 (1981); Mich.Con.Laws Ann. § 25.94 (Supp.1986–87); Minn.Stat. Ann. § 518.131 (Supp.1987); N.Y.—McKinney's Dom.Rel. L. § 233 (1986); Ohio Civ.R. 75(H)(2) (1982); V.Tex.C.A., Fam.Code § 3.58 (Supp.1987); West's Rev.Code Wash. Ann. § 26.09.060 (1986). See also Uniform Marriage and Divorce Act § 304, 9A Unif.L.Ann. 128 (1979).

3. National Automobile and Casualty Ins. Co. v. Queck, 1 Ariz.App. 595, 405 P.2d 905 (1965); McRae v. McRae, 52 So.2d 908 (Fla.1951); Klajbor v. Klajbor, 398

Ill. 152, 75 N.E.2d 353 (1947); Grayson v. Grayson, 222 Or. 507, 352 P.2d 738 (1960) (inherent power to appoint a receiver); Annot., 164 A.L.R. 321, 341 (1946); Annot., 8 A.L.R. 327 (1920).

See also 2 Story, Commentaries on Equity Jurisprudence 634 (14th ed. 1918), and 3 Id. 510–511, for discussion of preliminary injunctions in divorce actions. For ne exeat see Shaftoe v. Shaftoe, 7 Ves.Jr. 172, 32 Eng.Rep. 70 (1802), and Coglar v. Coglar, 1 Ves.Jr. 94, 30 Eng.Rep. 246 (1790), and Gredone v. Gredone, 361 A.2d 176 (D.C. App. 1976).

See also Winston v. Winston, 290 Md. 641, 431 A.2d 1330 (1981), disapproving Kapneck v. Kapneck, 31 Md. App. 410, 356 A.2d 572 (1976).

4. Harlan v. Superior Court, 94 Cal.App.2d 902, 211 P.2d 942 (1949); Hoda v. Hoda, 122 Ill.App.2d 283, 258 N.E.2d 386 (1970); Annot., 164 A.L.R. 321, 352 (1946).

5. In re Marriage of Schmidt, 118 Ill.App.3d 467, 74 Ill.Dec. 93, 455 N.E.2d 123 (1983); Emery v. Emery, 122 Mont. 201, 200 P.2d 251 (1948).

6. Low v. Low, 143 Cal.App.2d 650, 299 P.2d 1022 (1956); Daniel v. Daniel, 243 So.2d 247 (Fla.App. 1970); State ex rel. George v. Mitchell, 230 S.W.2d 116 (Mo.App. 1950).

7. Viera v. Viera, 107 Cal.App.2d 179, 236 P.2d 630 (1951); Levine v. Levine, 204 Ga. 313, 49 S.E.2d 814 (1948) (semble).

except that where specific property located within the jurisdiction is affected, service may be had upon the person in possession of the property, thus giving jurisdiction to deal with the claims to that property.[8] A bond may or may not be required of the applicant, depending upon local rules.[9]

Since the preliminary order is in aid of the court's divorce jurisdiction, at least a prima facie showing that that jurisdiction exists must be made in order to get the preliminary order.[10] Likewise at least a prima facie showing of grounds for divorce must be made.[11] If the complaint is open to dismissal on either of these grounds, the preliminary injunction cannot be granted.

The grant or denial of a preliminary injunction is within the discretion of the trial courts,[12] but the discretion is held to be abused unless the facts upon which the trial court relies show that the injunction was necessary to protect the applicant from an imminent threat of injury.[13] If an injunction is sought against the transfer of property by the husband, it must be proved that he intended such a transfer,[14] and that the transfer would prejudice the wife's claim to the property either because she had an interest in the

property as such,[15] or because it would disable the husband from making payments for alimony or support.[16] Some courts have appointed a receiver to take possession of the property where the husband has left the state, and a receivership is necessary to the wife's protection.[17] If no property remains within the state, receivership may not be effective against the departing husband, and the court may then be willing to enjoin his departure from the state altogether. This is a drastic remedy and will only be invoked where the husband is threatening to leave in order to evade his marital obligations.[18] It generally results in the husband's posting a bond, but it has been held that such a bond secures only his remaining within the state, and not his payment of the obligation.[19] Thus if he remains in the jurisdiction, but fails to pay his alimony, the bond is not forfeited. It would seem desirable in such cases that the bond be conditioned both upon his appearance and upon his payment of alimony.

Injunctions of this sort have also been granted to prevent the husband from obtaining a foreign divorce upon fraudulent evidence of domicile, where this would cause the wife irreparable injury.[20]

---

8. Shaffer v. Heitner, 433 U.S. 186, 97 S.Ct. 2569, 53 L.Ed.2d 683 (1978); Pennington v. Fourth National Bank, 243 U.S. 269, 37 S.Ct. 282, 61 L.Ed. 713 (1917); Annots., 164 A.L.R. 321, 354 (1946), 65 A.L.R. 886 (1930).

9. Statutes sometimes excuse a bond. V.Tex.C.A., Fam.Code § 3.58(e) (Supp.1987). A bond was held mandatory in Ex parte Cattell, 146 Ohio St. 112, 64 N.E.2d 416 (1945).

10. Annot., 164 A.L.R. 321, 345 (1946). Contra: Hayes v. Towles, 95 Idaho 208, 506 P.2d 105 (1973).

11. Walls v. Walls, 227 Ark. 191, 297 S.W.2d 648 (1957); Annot., 164 A.L.R. 321, 345 (1946).

12. Shively v. Shively, 88 Ohio App. 7, 95 N.E.2d 276 (1950). The court may in its discretion require the deposit of security in lieu of an injunction. Gardiner v. Gardiner, 230 Miss. 778, 93 So.2d 638 (1957).

13. Emery v. Emery, 122 Mont. 201, 200 P.2d 251 (1948). Cf. Janelli v. Janelli, 220 S.W.2d 255 (Tex.Civ. App.1949), affirmed 227 S.W.2d 889 (1950).

14. McRae v. McRae, 52 So.2d 908 (Fla. 1951); Stone v. Stone, 210 Ga. 127, 78 S.E.2d 22 (1953); Brannen v. Brannen, 208 Ga. 88, 65 S.E.2d 161 (1951); Hempel v. Hempel, 225 Minn. 287, 30 N.W.2d 594 (1948); State ex rel. George v. Mitchell, 230 S.W.2d 116 (Mo.App. 1950); Emery v. Emery, 122 Mont. 201, 200 P.2d 251 (1948); Glick v. Glick, 5 A.D.2d 942, 171 N.Y.S.2d 891 (3d Dep't

1958); Bisca v. Bisca, 108 Misc.2d 227, 437 N.Y.S.2d 258 (1981); Johnson v. Johnson, 111 R.I. 46, 298 A.2d 795 (1973); Annot., 164 A.L.R. 321, 322 (1946).

15. McRae v. McRae, 52 So.2d 908 (Fla.1951) (homestead); Messersmith v. Messersmith, 229 La. 495, 86 So. 2d 169 (1956) (community property); Hartnett v. Hartnett, 93 N.H. 406, 43 A.2d 153 (1945) (family car); Witt v. Witt, 205 S.W.2d 612 (Tex.Civ.App.1947).

16. Hempel v. Hempel, 225 Minn. 287, 30 N.W.2d 594 (1948).

17. Nichols v. Superior Court, 1 Cal.2d 589, 36 P.2d 380 (1934); Oles Envelope Co. v. Oles, 193 Md. 79, 65 A.2d 899 (1949); Grayson v. Grayson, 222 Or. 507, 352 P.2d 738 (1960). See also N.Y.—McKinney's Dom.Rel.L. § 243 (1986) and Annot., 95 A.L.R. 902 (1935).

18. National Automobile & Cas. Ins. Co. v. Queck, 1 Ariz.App. 595, 405 P.2d 905 (1965); Gredone v. Gredone, 361 A.2d 176 (D.C.App. 1976); Landy v. Landy, 62 So.2d 707 (Fla. 1953).

19. Gredone v. Gredone, 361 A.2d 176 (D.C.App. 1976); Pan American Surety Co. v. Walterson, 44 So.2d 94 (Fla. 1950), 3 Fla.L.Rev. 374 (1950).

20. Kahn v. Kahn, 325 Ill.App. 137, 59 N.E.2d 874 (1945); Garvin v. Garvin, 302 N.Y. 96, 96 N.E.2d 721 (1951). Contra: Rosenbaum v. Rosenbaum, 309 N.Y. 371, 130 N.E.2d 902 (1955), 69 Harv.L.Rev. 1327 (1956).

Where either spouse has been guilty of violence, threats of violence, or other methods of harassment, the other spouse may obtain an injunction against molestation.[21] In addition the court may exclude the wrongdoer from the family home pending the suit, if that is necessary for the protection of spouse and children.[22] The court may also forbid interference with the custody of the children.[23] The difficulty here is that courts are often so reluctant to grant these orders that wives must suffer a beating or two before qualifying for legal protection. It would seem that no great harm would result from more liberality.[24]

Preliminary injunctions and restraining orders may, upon proof of facts showing need to protect the applicant, be issued against a person other than the spouse.[25] For example, a third person having possession of property of the husband might thus be required to hold it subject to the wife's claims.[26] Service upon such third person would have to be made before he could be bound by the order. One Ohio case goes so far as to issue a restraining order against the husband and his paramour, enjoining them from seeing or talking with each other and enjoining the paramour from interfering with the marriage, pending the suit.[27] The court sustained this order as a means of making effective the six-week "cooling-off" period imposed by statute in Ohio whose purpose the court found to be the promotion of reconciliation. The court's argument was that there could not be opportunity for reconciliation unless husband and paramour were kept apart. One may look with scepticism on attempts to control human affection by restraining order, however.[28]

Where property is transferred in violation of a restraining order, the transferee is protected if he is a bona fide purchaser for

21. Application of Laham, 145 Cal.App.2d 110, 302 P.2d 21 (1956) (husband violated order by trying to seize the children by force); Harlan v. Superior Court, 94 Cal. App.2d 902, 211 P.2d 942 (1949) (molestation order void where not based on violence or threats of violence); Blanton v. Blanton, 163 Ga. 361, 136 S.E. 141 (1926) (wife's harassment of husband justified restraining order); Ex parte Cattell, 146 Ohio St. 112, 64 N.E.2d 416 (1945) (physical attacks, accusations, interference with the children justified injunction).

22. Smith v. Smith, 49 Cal.App.2d 716, 122 P.2d 346 (1942) (trial court could exclude husband from home where he had committed violence, threatened lives of wife and children and destroyed property); Luitwieler v. Luitwieler, 57 Cal.App. 751, 207 P. 931 (1922) (abuse of discretion to exclude husband from home where no violence or threats of violence); Burnett v. Burnett, 158 Fla. 464, 28 So.2d 878 (1947) (husband may be excluded from home if public decency, safety of parties or welfare of children require); Ginsberg v. Ginsberg, 113 So.2d 565 (Fla.App.1959); Huggins v. Huggins, 202 Ga. 738, 44 S.E.2d 778 (1947) (wife given use of home in lieu of alimony pendente lite); Lee v. Lee, 200 Ga. 690, 38 S.E.2d 174 (1946) (husband excluded from home where he had caused noise, disturbance and had interfered with wife's sleep, made her nervous etc., without showing of violence or threats of violence); Singleton v. Singleton, 302 S.W.2d 121 (Ky.1957) (no injunction where husband gave wife no trouble); Carlson v. Carlson, 234 Minn. 258, 48 N.W.2d 58 (1951) and McCauley v. McCauley, 267 Minn. 514, 124 N.W.2d 411 (1963) (husband removed from home where his presence might seriously endanger health or safety of wife or react unfavorably on children); Degenaars v. Degenaars, 186 N.J.Super. 233, 452 A.2d 222 (1982) (hus-

band excluded from the home where his presence was inimical to the children's welfare, even though there was no threat of violence); Babushik v. Babushik, 157 N.J. Super. 128, 384 A.2d 574 (1978) (wife could have husband ordered out of the house in order to establish the eighteen months' separation as a ground for divorce); S. v. A., 118 N.J.Super. 69, 285 A.2d 588 (1972) (mentally disabled and alcoholic mother excluded from the home to protect the children). See also Annot., 164 A.L.R. 321, 338 (1946).

23. Annot., 164 A.L.R. 321, 340 (1946).

24. See Daniel v. Daniel, 236 So.2d 197 (Fla.App. 1970); Di Donna v. Di Donna, 72 Misc.2d 231, 339 N.Y.S.2d 592 (Fam.Ct. 1972), where absence of violence led to a denial of an order. But Sandy v. Sandy, 106 Wis. 2d 230, 316 N.W.2d 164 (1982), affirmed 109 Wis.2d 564, 326 N.W.2d 761 (1982) held that physical violence need not be shown where there is notice and an opportunity to be heard, but that it is only required for ex parte orders. See also Geisinger v. Voss, 352 F.Supp. 104 (E.D.Wis. 1972).

The subject of domestic violence and its treatment by the law is discussed supra, in section 7.3.

25. Kiplinger v. Kiplinger, 172 Mich. 552, 138 N.W. 230 (1912).

26. Annot., 164 A.L.R. 321, 357 (1946). Compare Johnson v. Johnson, 111 R.I. 46, 298 A.2d 795 (1973).

27. Pashko v. Pashko, 35 O.O. 498, 101 N.E.2d 804 (1951), 9 Wash. & Lee L.Rev. 242 (1952); 4 W.Res.L.Rev. 84 (1952).

28. Moreland, Injunctive Control of Family Relations, 18 Ky.L.J. 207 (1930).

value,[29] but not if he either had notice of the order,[30] or was a donee of the property.[31]

It is generally held that preliminary restraining orders and injunctions automatically terminate upon the conclusion of the main suit, whether that ends by the award of a divorce decree [32] or by the death of one of the parties.[33] This may sometimes cause considerable hardship to spouses relying upon such injunctions for their protection.[34]

Enforcement of the orders described in this section is by means of contempt proceedings.[35] The courts have some difficulty in deciding whether the contempt involved is civil or criminal, however.[36]

**WESTLAW
REFERENCES**

di(divorc! dissol! /p preliminar! temporar! /2 enjoin! injuncti! order! /s affidavit)

sy(divorc! dissol! /s preliminar! temporar! /2 enjoin! injuncti! order! /s contempt)

---

29. Gallaway v. Smith, 70 Ariz. 364, 220 P.2d 857 (1950).

30. Western Slavonic Ass'n. v. Videtich, 90 Colo. 230, 8 P.2d 263 (1932).

31. Candler v. Donaldson, 272 F.2d 374 (6th Cir. 1959) (held change in beneficiary of life insurance forbidden by an injunction against assignment). See also Gillespie v. District Court, 119 Colo. 242, 202 P.2d 151 (1949) holding that funds deposited with the clerk of the court after sale of a business subject to a restraining order could not be reached by execution against the husband.

32. Warburton v. Kieferle, 135 Cal.App.2d 278, 287 P.2d 1 (1955); Krmpotich v. Krmpotich, 227 Minn. 567, 35 N.W.2d 810 (1949); Gardner v. Gardner, 87 N.Y. 14 (1882).

33. Milewski v. Milewski, 351 Ill.App. 158, 114 N.E.2d 419 (1953).

34. Ibid., where the wife was held unable to reach proceeds of a life insurance policy transferred in violation of an injunction, where the husband had died after making the illegal transfer.

35. Roberts v. Roberts, 226 Ga. 203, 173 S.E.2d 675 (1970); Ex parte Jackman, 663 S.W.2d 520 (Tex.App. 1983).

36. Marcisz v. Marcisz, 65 Ill.2d 206, 2 Ill.Dec. 310, 357 N.E.2d 477 (1976), holding the particular contempt to have been criminal.

§ 14.4

1. E.g., Official Code Ga.Ann. § 19–5–8 (1986); Ill.—S.H.A. ch. 40, ¶410 (1980); Uniform Marriage and Divorce Act §§ 301, 303, 9A Unif.L.Ann. 119, 125 (1979).

2. Cortese v. Cortese, 163 Pa.Super. 553, 63 A.2d 420 (1949).

§ 14.4 Divorce Procedure—Trial and Evidence

Trial

For the most part the trial of a divorce action follows the procedure established for other civil suits.[1] A few differences do exist, either because divorce is still viewed as a special type of civil suit in which the state has an interest,[2] or because of the heavy burden which divorce litigation imposes on the judicial systems of the states.[3] The state's interest, though generally ill defined, formerly lay in the direction of preserving marriages and ensuring that divorces were only granted after satisfactory proof that conduct constituting one of the fault grounds for divorce had occurred.[4] One of the obvious consequences of this view was the rule that a divorce could not be granted by default.[5] Even though the defendant failed to appear or defend, evidence had to be presented before the trier of fact

---

3. Attempts at dealing with this burden have in some states, especially Pennsylvania, taken the form of extensive use of masters to try divorce cases. Pa.Stat. tit. 23, § 304 (Supp.1986); Decker v. Decker, 102 Pa.Super. 234, 160 A.2d 242 (1960); Note, The Administration of Divorce: A Philadelphia Study, 101 U.Pa.L.Rev. 1204 (1953). Statute or court rule in other states authorize the use of masters under some conditions. Gelfond v. District Court In and For Second Judicial District, 180 Colo. 95, 504 P.2d 673 (1972); Russell v. Thompson, 96 Nev. 830, 619 P.2d 537 (1980); Nagy v. Oakley, ___ W.Va. ___, 309 S.E.2d 68 (1983). In the absence of a statute or court rule the cases are in conflict as to whether the divorce court may refer part or all of the case to a master. Annot., Propriety of Reference in Connection With Fixing Amount of Alimony, 85 A.L.R.2d 801 (1962). On references to masters in general, see La Buy v. Howes Leather Co., 352 U.S. 249, 77 S.Ct. 309, 1 L.Ed.2d 290 (1957), rehearing denied 352 U.S. 1019, 77 S.Ct. 553, 1 L.Ed.2d 560 (1957) (court congestion alone is not a sufficient reason); 5A J. W. Moore, Federal Practice § 53.05(1) (1984); Kaufman, Masters in the Federal Courts: Rule 53, 58 Colum.L.Rev. 452 (1958).

Mediation and arbitration as methods for mitigating the burdens and expense of divorce litigation are discussed in section 14.7, infra.

4. Chisholm v. Chisholm, 98 Fla. 1196, 125 So. 694 (1929); Caye v. Caye, 66 Nev. 78, 211 P.2d 252 (1949) (dictum).

5. Rea v. Rea, 124 F.Supp. 922 (D.D.C.1954) (motion for summary judgment not available in divorce); Kinsley v. Kinsley, 388 Ill. 194, 57 N.E.2d 449 (1944); Ladner v. Ladner, 233 Miss. 222, 102 So.2d 195 (1958); Schillerstrom v. Schillerstrom, 75 N.D. 667, 32 N.W.2d 106 (1948).

proving that the plaintiff was entitled to the decree.[6] And the trial court itself had to take an active part by summoning and examining witnesses and in other ways seeing to it that the material facts were fully brought out.[7]

Now that the fault grounds for divorce have either been abandoned or relegated to a minor role,[8] insistence upon a trial of the issue of termination of the marriage, as distinguished from the issues of custody, property or maintenance, seems no longer to serve any useful purpose, at least where both spouses desire the divorce. In those states where marriage breakdown is a ground or the sole ground for divorce, the assertion of one spouse that the marriage is broken is generally sufficient to warrant granting the decree.[9] If that is so, it is difficult to see why the courts continue to insist upon a hearing on that issue, but the fact is that most of them do,[10] although the hearing requirement has begun to break down in some states. Legislation in these states authorizes a summary divorce procedure dispensing with a trial in certain

limited circumstances.[11] In a few other states summary judgments for divorce are permitted where there is no genuine issue of material fact.[12]

In England the state's interest in the prevention of collusive divorces or divorces not authorized by the statute led to the institution of the Queen's Proctor, whose duty it was to ferret out and prevent such divorces.[13] Divorce proctors were never very numerous or active in the United States[14] and are now entirely obsolete since the enactment of nonfault grounds for divorce has made it clear that the states' policy is to terminate marriages which are no longer viable.

Divorce cases are usually tried to the court without a jury, since historically they resembled suits in equity rather than actions at law.[15] In some states, however, the parties may demand a jury trial.[16] In order to meet the requirements of a fair trial, the parties must not be excluded from the hearing,[17] must be given the opportunity for an orderly

---

6. Zwarensteyn v. Zwarensteyn, 347 Mich. 353, 79 N.W.2d 913 (1956); Schillerstrom v. Schillerstrom, 75 N.D. 667, 32 N.W.2d 106 (1948). See also Dionne v. Dionne, 155 Me. 377, 156 A.2d 393 (1959) holding a divorce could not be granted on the record of a prior trial for alienation of affections.

7. Gosnell v. Gosnell, 329 S.W.2d 230 (Mo.App.1959); Cortese v. Cortese, 163 Pa.Super. 553, 63 A.2d 420 (1949).

8. See sections 13.1, 13.5, 13.6, 13.7, supra.

9. See section 13.6, supra.

10. E.g., Manion v. Manion, 143 N.J.Super. 499, 363 A.2d 921 (1976) (summary judgment denied). Many state statutes expressly continue to require hearings in divorce. See, e.g., Alaska Stat. § 25.24.220 (1983); Ark. Stats. § 34–1207 (1962); Official Code Ga.Ann. § 30–113 (1986); Hawaii Rev.Stat. § 580–45 (1976); Ill.—S.H.A. ch. 40, ¶403(f) (1980); Iowa Code Ann. § 598.7 (1981); R.I. Gen.Laws § 15–5–22 (1981); Tenn.Code Ann. § 36–4–114 (1984); Wis.Stat.Ann. § 767.12 (1981 and Supp.1986). See also Uniform Marriage and Divorce Act § 305, and Commissioners' Note, 9A Unif.L.Ann. 132, 133 (1979).

11. West's Ann.Cal.Civ.Code §§ 4550, 4553 (Supp. 1984); Colo.Rev.Stat. § 14–10–120.3 (Supp.1984); Nev. Rev.Stat. 125.181 to 125.184 (1983); Or.Rev.Stat. §§ 107.485, 107.490, 107.500 (1983). There is a similar "special procedure" available for undefended cases in England. Matrimonial Causes Rules 1977, Rules 33, 48, discussed in Day v. Day [1980] Fam. 29.

12. Miss.Code, § 93–5–7 (Supp.1983); N.Y.—McKinney's Dom.Rel.L. § 211 (Supp.1984–1985); Dickson v.

Dickson, 238 Ga. 672, 235 S.E.2d 479 (1977); Zimmie v. Zimmie, 11 Ohio St.3d 94, 464 N.E.2d 142 (1984).

13. Matrimonial Causes Act 1973 § 8. The earlier activities of this officer are described in A. P. Herbert, Holy Deadlock (1934) and in the Report of the Royal Commission on Marriage and Divorce 249–251 (1956).

14. The history of divorce proctors in the United States is described in Connolly, Divorce Proctors, 34 B.U.L.Rev. 1 (1954).

15. Colo.Rev.Stat. § 14–10–107(6) (1974 & Supp.1986); Del.Code tit. 13, § 1516 (1981); Mich.Com.Laws Ann. § 25.92 (1984); West's Rev.Code Wash.Ann. § 26.09.010 (1986); Wis.Stat.Ann. § 767.12 (1981 and Supp.1986). In Illinois the divorce may be given a bifurcated trial in "appropriate circumstances", in which the court hears and decides on the dissolution of the marriage, and then, after a forty-eight-hour delay, deals with the other issues in the case. Ill.—S.H.A. ch. 40, ¶¶401, 403 (1980 & Supp. 1986). "Appropriate circumstances" are defined in In re Marriage of Cohn, 93 Ill.2d 190, 66 Ill.Dec. 615, 443 N.E.2d 541 (1982). See also Uniform Marriage and Divorce Act § 302(a)(4), 9A Unif.L.Ann. 121 (1979), and Little v. Little, 96 Wash.2d 183, 634 P.2d 498 (1981).

16. N.Y.—McKinney's Dom.Rel.L. § 173 (1977); Pa. Stat. tit. 23, § 305 (Supp.1984–1985); V.Tex.C.A.Fam. Code § 3.61 (Supp.1984).

17. Burts v. Burts, 227 Va. 618, 316 S.E.2d 745 (1984); Bernfeld v. Bernfeld, 41 Wis.2d 358, 164 N.W.2d 259 (1969).

presentation of their case [18] and in general decisions should be made in open court.[19] Since courts have relatively broad discretion to control the course of trials and to dispose of their business in an orderly way, they may exclude part or all of the public from divorce trials where that is necessary to prevent scandal or to protect children, so long as the parties' right to be heard is not infringed.[20]

The requirement of a fair trial has applications which may be peculiar to suits for divorce in some circumstances. The first of these occurs when the judge interviews in his chambers, out of the presence of the parties or their counsel, children whose custody is in issue in the case.[21] This practice obviously excludes the parties from what may be an important right to hear evidence, examine witnesses and make arguments on the basis of evidence. On the other hand the practice is often justified as providing insight into the children's needs and desires, and perhaps more importantly, as protecting them from the trauma of having to stand up in open court and express a wish to live with one parent or the other and then to be cross-examined on the preference so expressed.[22] It is not surprising, in view of the conflicting policies in such cases, that the courts have reached a variety of different results. Where the parties stipulate that the trial judge may interview the child in chambers out of the presence of counsel or parties, the procedure is generally approved.[23] Even without the consent of the parties, some cases have approved such interviews if a record of the interview is made and the record is made available to the parties or their counsel.[24] Other courts have held that the procedure is proper so long as counsel are present at the interview, even though the parties themselves are excluded.[25] Still other courts, emphasizing the interests of the child in opposition to those of the parents, have held that there is no violation of due process to interview the child out of the presence of the parties and their counsel, and futher to promise the child that the results of the interview would not be

18. Lisiten v. Lisiten, 30 Colo.App. 375, 492 P.2d 895 (1972); Hall v. Hall, 708 P.2d 416 (Wyo. 1985).

19. Stout v. Stout, 155 N.J.Super. 196, 382 A.2d 659 (1977), overruled on other grounds by Petersen v. Petersen, 85 N.J. 638, 428 A.2d 1301 (1981); In re Marriage of Ebbighausen, 42 Wash.App. 99, 708 P.2d 1220 (1985).

20. S.N.E. v. R.L.B., 699 P.2d 875 (Alaska 1985); Whitney v. Whitney, 164 Cal.App.2d 577, 330 P.2d 947 (1958); English v. McCrary, 348 So.2d 293 (Fla.1977); Bloomer v. Bloomer, 197 Wis. 140, 221 N.W. 734 (1928); Annot., 79 A.L.R.3d 401, 405 (1977).

21. The practice is discussed in Note, Use of Extra-Record Information in Custody Cases, 24 U.Chi.L.Rev. 349 (1957), and in Lombard, Judicial Interviewing of Children in Custody Cases: An Empirical and Analytical Study, 17 U.Cal. Davis L.Rev. 807 (1984). Interviews with trial judges in the Lombard article revealed that a substantial proportion of them saw the children in chambers, without permitting either parents or counsel to be present and without making a record of the child's statements. In some instances additional significant evidence came out of the conference in chambers and this also was sometimes not revealed to the parties. The author suggests, among other possibilities, that children in custody cases should be interviewed by experts with training in child development rather than by trial judges. The expert could then be called as a witness by the spouses.

22. Burghdoff v. Burghdoff, 66 Mich.App. 608, 239 N.W.2d 679 (1976).

23. High v. High, 288 Minn. 524, 179 N.W.2d 274 (1970). In Ex parte Wilson, 450 So.2d 104 (Ala. 1984), on remand 450 So.2d 107 (1984) the court held there was reversible error when the child's father consented to an in camera interview by the trial court on condition that a court reporter be present, but the trial court did not have the reporter at the interview. Other cases are cited in Annot., 99 A.L.R.2d 954 (1965).

24. DeYoung v. DeYoung, 62 Ill.App.3d 837, 19 Ill. Dec. 732, 379 N.E.2d 396 (1978), holding that the requirement of the presence of a court reporter may not be waived by the parties. Contra, holding that this requirement may be waived, Lehman v. Billman, 178 Mont. 367, 584 P.2d 662 (1978). Other cases approving an in camera interview without the presence of the parties or their counsel, providing a record is kept, include Shapiro v. Shapiro, 54 Md.App. 477, 458 A.2d 1257 (1983); Schiele v. Sager, 174 Mont. 533, 571 P.2d 1142 (1977).

The Uniform Marriage and Divorce Act § 404, 9A Unif.L.Ann. 203 (1979) provides that the court may interview the chambers concerning his preferences, *may* permit counsel to be present, and *shall* cause a record of the interview to be made and to be made part of the record in the case. This seems to permit parties and counsel to be excluded from the interview if a record is made.

25. In re Stanley F., 86 Cal.App.3d 568, 152 Cal.Rptr. 5 (1978), approving the interview so long as counsel were present and the testimony was taken by a reporter. This position seems to have been approved also in Matter of Maricopa County Juvenile Action No. JD–561, 131 Ariz. 25, 638 P.2d 692 (1981), a dependency proceeding involving allegations of a father's sexual contacts with his ten-year-old daughter.

revealed to the parents.[26] Lastly, there are a few cases holding that the Due Process Clause's guarantee of a fair trial is violated when the judge interviews the child in his chambers out of the presence of the parties or their counsel.[27] These last cases seem to take the better reasoned position. Taking secret testimony in a case as important to the parties and as dependent for its result upon the trial judge's discretion as a custody determination is unwise. The protection of the child can largely be achieved by taking the testimony in chambers in the presence of counsel and with a record made.[28]

Social Workers' Reports

Questions of fair trial in divorce actions also arise where the custody aspects of cases are the subject of investigation by social workers or other kinds of professionals. One of the most conspicuous developments in divorce law has been the willingness of legislatures and courts to use techniques and information from disciplines other than law. Specifically, the use of reports of social workers, probation officers, welfare workers, psychiatrists or psychologists to provide information about the children and the claimants for custody in divorce actions has become commonplace in many states.[29] Two questions have arisen out of this practice. The first is whether the

courts may call upon such experts to make an independent investigation. The second is what use may be made of the reports which summarize the investigation.

It is well settled that the court in a suit involving custody may properly request an investigation from an impartial expert agency, such as the welfare department, or a probation officer, or even a private social work agency, to determine the condition of the child involved and the fitness of the contending parents.[30] Where one of the parties lives outside the jurisdiction, the local welfare department may be able to obtain information from another state's welfare department for presentation to the court in a custody case.[31]

Custody cases are of great public interest, they raise difficult psychological issues concerning the capacities of the parents, their relationships with their child and the child's future welfare. The temptation for the courts to use whatever "expert" aid may be available is therefore understandable. The use of custody investigations and of investigators' reports create serious risks, however. The invasion of privacy, the reliance upon gossip, scandal and hearsay are among the risks of which some courts are aware.[32] Other risks are less clearly recognized. There is also the possibility that trial courts, looking for some assistance and influenced by the tendency to

---

26. Parker v. Parker, 467 S.W.2d 595 (Ky. 1971) (semble); Burghdoff v. Burghdoff, 66 Mich.App. 608, 239 N.W.2d 679 (1976); Lincoln v. Lincoln, 24 N.Y.2d 270, 299 N.Y.S.2d 842, 247 N.E.2d 659 (1969). A related case has stated that it is within the trial court's discretion to refuse to permit a minor child of the marriage to testify. Spencer v. Spencer, 242 So.2d 786 (Fla.App. 1970), cert. denied 248 So.2d 169 (1971).

27. Ex parte Wilson, 450 So.2d 104 (Ala. 1984), on remand 450 So.2d 107 (1984) (dictum); Ex parte Berryhill, 410 So.2d 416 (Ala. 1982), on remand 410 So.2d 419 (1982); Gennarini v. Gennarini, 2 Conn.App. 132, 477 A.2d 674 (1984).

28. Gennarini v. Gennarini, 2 Conn.App. 132, 477 A.2d 674 (1984).

29. Gozansky, Court-Ordered Investigations in Child Custody Cases, 12 Willamette L.J. 511 (1976). The most thorough study of the subject is Levy, Custody Investigations in Divorce Cases, 1985 Am. Bar Foundation Res.J. 713. See also Okpaku, Psychology: Impediment or Aid in Child Custody Cases, 29 Rut.L.Rev. 1117 (1976), expressing some skepticism on the value of experts in custody cases.

30. Statutes in many states authorize the court to obtain such assistance. E.g., West's Ann.Cal.Civ.Code § 4602 (Supp.1987); Ill.—S.H.A. ch. 40, ¶605 (Supp.1986); Me.Rev.Stat.Ann. tit. 19, § 751 (Supp.1986); Uniform Marriage and Divorce Act § 405, 9A Unif.L.Ann. 204 (1979). Cases reaching this result include Aylor v. Aylor, 173 Colo. 294, 478 P.2d 302 (1970); Eaton v. Karr, 251 A.2d 640 (D.C.App. 1969) (costs assessed against the parent if he is able to pay); Sabol v. Sabol, 2 Hawaii App. 24, 624 P.2d 1378 (1981); Ziehm v. Ziehm, 433 A.2d 725 (Me. 1981); In re Marriage of Kramer, 177 Mont. 61, 580 P.2d 439 (1978); Kesseler v. Kesseler, 10 N.Y.2d 445, 225 N.Y.S.2d 1, 180 N.E.2d 402 (1962). Other cases are cited in Annot., 35 A.L.R.2d 629, 632 (1954). The use of a private social work agency was approved in In re Marriage of Schulke, 40 Colo.App. 473, 579 P.2d 90 (1978), cert. denied 439 U.S. 861, 99 S.Ct. 181, 58 L.Ed.2d 170 (1978).

31. Onderdonk v. Onderdonk, 3 Wis.2d 279, 88 N.W.2d 323 (1958).

32. E.g., Matter of Lockmondy's Adoption, 168 Ind. App. 563, 343 N.E.2d 793 (1976).

disparage the "adversary system" of which we hear so much,[33] will give undue weight to the investigation or will even abdicate to the investigator the responsibility of deciding the case, particularly if the investigator is a court appointee. A leading study has also produced evidence that many custody investigations are unreliable or inaccurate, compounding the harm they may do when the court uncritically relies upon them to decide the case.[34]

The question of how reports of custody investigations may be used in the courtroom has produced much litigation. It is not easy to draw general conclusions on this from the cases, since many of them do not lay down any ground rules for the use of reports, but content themselves with disapproval of what was done by the trial court.[35] Nevertheless there appear to be two lines of authority on the issue. The stricter cases require compliance with the rules of evidence, including the hearsay rule. This means that the social worker's report must be given to both parties, the author must be available for cross-examination, and anyone whose work or information went into the report must also be available for cross-examination.[36] This certainly is the preferable rule, given the hearsay nature and the inaccuracy of much that is found in such reports, although for a variety of obvious reasons counsel will often not attack reports as vigorously as he might cross-examine other witnesses so that the right of cross-examination is less of a protection here than in other situations.

The other line of cases gives much less protection to the parties. These cases hold that social workers' reports may be relied upon by the courts so long as the parties receive copies of the reports and the persons who wrote them are available for cross-examination.[37] Under this rule persons who furnished information or who examined the child or were interviewed by the social worker do not have to be made available for cross-examination. Where this rule prevails, the only effective recourse for a party who is on the receiving end of an unfavorable report is to employ his own expert to make another investigation and write another report, thereby transforming the litigation into the familiar battle of the experts. Of course if the parties are willing to stipulate on the admission of the report, there is no error in the court's considering it pursuant to the stipulation, even if that waives any right to cross-examination.[38]

33. Watson, The Children of Armageddon: Problems of Custody Following Divorce, 21 Syra.L.Rev. 55 (1969).

34. Levy, Custody Investigations in Divorce Cases, 1985 Am. Bar Foundation Research J. 713. Cases in which trial courts have indulged in this sort of uncritical acceptance of reports are not hard to find. E.g., Draper v. Draper, 39 Md.App. 73, 382 A.2d 1095 (1978); Duro v. Duro, 392 Mass. 574, 467 N.E.2d 165 (1984); State ex rel. Fisher v. Devins, 294 Minn. 496, 200 N.W.2d 28 (1972); Jorgensen v. Jorgensen, 194 Neb. 271, 231 N.W.2d 360 (1975). Professor Levy recommends that custody investigations be used only in cases where both spouses agree, and that the investigating case worker be required to keep a complete record of the investigation. He also takes the position that the chief importance of such investigations lies in the influence they exert in the direction of mediating custody disputes. 1985 Am. Bar Foundation Research J. 735, 792.

35. E.g., Williams v. Williams, 8 Ill.App.2d 1, 130 N.E.2d 291 (1955); Cupp v. Cupp, 302 S.W.2d 371 (Ky. 1957). The question of how social workers' reports are to be used by the courts also arises in adoption cases. See section 21.4, Practitioner's Edition.

36. This is the rule of Uniform Marriage and Divorce Act § 405, 9A Unif.L.Ann. 204 (1979), and Ill.—S.H.A. ch. 40, § 605 (Supp.1986). See also Matter of George G., 68

Cal.App.3d 146, 137 Cal.Rptr. 201 (1977); State ex rel. Fisher v. Devins, 294 Minn. 496, 200 N.W.2d 28 (1972); Stanford v. Stanford, 266 Minn. 250, 123 N.W.2d 187 (1963); Jorgensen v. Jorgensen, 194 Neb. 271, 231 N.W.2d 360 (1975); In Interest of Jones, 286 Pa.Super. 574, 429 A.2d 671 (1981); Lawrence v. Hosfield, 51 Wash.2d 157, 316 P.2d 1102 (1957) (dictum).

37. This seems to be the purport of Me.Rev.Stat.Ann. tit. 19, § 751 (Supp.1986). See also Nance v. Nance, 226 Ark. 682, 292 S.W.2d 74 (1956) (dictum); Fewel v. Fewel, 23 Cal.2d 431, 144 P.2d 592 (1943); Sabol v. Sabol, 2 Hawaii App. 24, 624 P.2d 1378 (1981); Ziehm v. Ziehm, 433 A.2d 725 (Me. 1981); Draper v. Draper, 39 Md.App. 73, 382 A.2d 1095 (1978); Duro v. Duro, 392 Mass. 574, 467 N.E.2d 165 (1984) (semble); Kritzik v. Kritzik, 21 Wis. 2d 442, 124 N.W.2d 581 (1963); Annot., 59 A.L.R.3d 1337 (1974).

Kern v. Kern, 333 So.2d 17 (Fla. 1976) is quite unclear, but may hold that reports are admissible if made available to the parties, even without a right of cross-examination.

38. Tapscott v. Tapscott, 149 Cal.2d 379, 308 P.2d 399 (1957); Kesseler v. Kesseler, 10 N.Y.2d 445, 225 N.Y.S.2d 1, 180 N.E.2d 402 (1962); Commonwealth ex rel. Kuntz v. Stackhouse, 176 Pa.Super. 361, 108 A.2d 73 (1954), cert. denied 348 U.S. 981, 75 S.Ct. 571, 99 L.Ed. 763 (1955)

Competence of Spouses to Testify

The common law gave to each spouse a privilege not to have the other testify against him.[39] This privilege was never supported by any but specious reasons,[40] and has now been sharply limited by statute where divorce actions are concerned.[41] In some cases it still may have to be reckoned with, however.[42]

The marital privilege mentioned in the preceding paragraph should not be confused with the privilege for confidential communications between husband and wife. Communications between husband and wife which are confidential are privileged against courtroom disclosure in order to protect the marital relationship.[43] This privilege not only preserves confidences between husband and wife, but protects the most intimate aspects of their relationship from intrusion by outsiders.[44] The privilege belongs to and may be asserted by the spouse by whom the communication was made, although there is some confusion on this point.[45]

The privilege for confidential communications has also been limited by statute so that it frequently does not apply in actions between the spouses or in divorce actions.[46] There may often be a question whether the statute limits only this privilege, or whether it also applies to the privilege against one spouse's testifying against the other. Some statutes may be broadly construed to apply to both privileges.[47]

A third principle which may prevent spouses from testifying in divorce actions is not a privilege but a rule of competence. This rule, named after Lord Mansfield, who conjured it up from thin air,[48] states that neither spouse may testify in such a manner as to bastardize a child born during the marriage.[49] It is sometimes stated in a more limited form, that neither spouse may testify to non-access where such evidence would make the child illegitimate.[50] In spite of a devastating analysis of the rule by Dean Wigmore,[51] it was followed by many courts in the United States for years.[52] In recent years, however, many courts, influenced by statute

---

(habeas corpus); Austad v. Austad, 2 Utah 2d 49, 269 P.2d 284 (1954). See Note, 24 U.Chi.L.Rev. 349 (1957). The stipulation may, however, limit the scope of review on appeal. Rea v. Rea, 195 Or. 252, 245 P.2d 884 (1952).

39. Stein v. Bowman, 38 U.S.(13 Pet.) 209, 10 L.Ed. 129 (1839). VIII Wigmore, Evidence §§ 2227–2245 (McNaughton rev.1961). See also Trammel v. United States, 445 U.S. 40, 100 S.Ct. 906, 63 L.Ed.2d 186 (1980).

40. VIII J. Wigmore, Evidence § 2228 (McNaughton rev.1961).

41. VIII J. Wigmore, Evidence § 2239 (McNaughton rev.1961); II J. Wigmore, Evidence § 488 (Chadbourn rev. 1979); C. McCormick, Evidence § 66 (Cleary 3d ed.1984); Hickey v. Hickey, 138 Pa.Super. 271, 11 A.2d 187 (1940). Cases in which spouses are allowed to testify in divorce actions based on cruelty are collected in Annot., 70 A.L.R. 499 (1931).

42. E.g., N.Y.—McKinney's Civ.P.L. & R. 4502 (1963); N.C.Gen.S. § 8–56 (1986), in which husbands and wives are not competent to give evidence for or against each other in suits based on adultery, with in the case of New York, certain exceptions. See also Tallent v. Tallent, 22 A.D.2d 988, 254 N.Y.S.2d 722 (3d Dep't 1964) and VIII J. Wigmore, Evidence 250 (McNaughton rev.1961). Children of the parties are competent to testify if sufficiently mature and intelligent to understand and respond to the questions. Annot., 2 A.L.R.2d 1329 (1948).

43. C. McCormick, Evidence ch. 9 (Cleary 3d ed.1984); D. Louisell, C. Mueller, Federal Evidence § 219 (1978). The effect on this and the marital privilege of a separation of the spouses is discussed in United States v. Byrd,

750 F.2d 585 (7th Cir. 1984) and Annot., 98 A.L.R.3d 1285 (1980).

44. C. McCormick, Evidence § 86 (Cleary 3d ed.1984); D. Louisell, C. Mueller, Federal Evidence § 219 (1978).

45. VIII J. Wigmore, Evidence § 2340 (McNaughton rev.1961).

46. United States v. Allery, 526 F.2d 1362 (8th Cir. 1975), citing many cases; T. C. H. v. K. M. H., 693 S.W.2d 802 (Mo.1985) (no privilege in custody cases); Poppe v. Poppe, 3 N.Y.2d 312, 165 N.Y.S.2d 99, 144 N.E.2d 72 (1957); C. McCormick, Evidence § 84 (Cleary 3d ed.1984); II J. Wigmore, Evidence § 488 (Chadbourn rev.1979).

47. E.g., West's Ann.Cal.Evid.Code §§ 972, 984 (1966 and Supp.1987); Colo.Rev.Stat. § 13–90–107(1)(a) (Supp. 1986); Minn.Stat.Ann. § 595.02(1)(a) (Supp.1987).

48. In Goodright v. Moss, 2 Cowp. 291, 98 Eng.Rep. 1257 (1777).

49. C. McCormick, Evidence § 67 (Cleary 3d ed.1984).

50. Ibid., and State ex rel. Worley v. Lavender, 147 W.Va. 803, 131 S.E.2d 752 (1963), overruled on other grounds State ex rel. Toryak v. Spagnuolo, ___ W.Va. ___, 292 S.E.2d 654 (1982). The application of this rule to paternity suits is discussed supra, in section 4.4.

51. VII J. Wigmore, Evidence § 2064 (Chadbourn rev. 1978).

52. Many cases are collected in Annots., 60 A.L.R. 380 (1929), 68 A.L.R. 421 (1930); 89 A.L.R. 911 (1934); 49 A.L.R.3d 212 (1973). See also Note, 112 U.Pa.L.Rev. 613 (1964).

or by their recognition of the unwise nature of the rule, have abolished it.[53] It is fair to say that today the rule's impact is greatly reduced.

WESTLAW REFERENCES

Social Workers' Reports

child minor /s custod! /s impartial! unbiased fair** fairness neutral! /s report! evaluat! profession! investigat! expert!

Competence of Spouses to Testify

divorc! dissol! /s marital spous! (husband /2 wife) /3 privileg!

§ 14.5 Divorce Procedure—Interlocutory and Final Decrees

Interlocutory Decrees [1]

A small minority of states continue to have statutes which provide that divorce decrees are interlocutory when granted and do not become final until the expiration of a stated period.[2] Under some statutes the interlocutory decree (or decree nisi as some states call it)

becomes final automatically while others require the entry of a final decree by the court. Where a final decree must be entered, the local practice may allow entry of a nunc pro tunc order relating back to the date of expiration of the interlocutory period, thereby validating an intervening marriage.[3] But unless the statute allows the party at fault in the divorce to have the nunc pro tunc order entered, this is a right belonging solely to the prevailing party.[4]

During the interlocutory period the parties are considered still to be married.[5] They are authorized but not required to live apart,[6] and orders for temporary alimony for spousal support may be entered. This means that if one of them tries to marry a new spouse during this time, such a marriage is invalid as bigamous, whether contracted in the divorcing state or some other state.[7] It also means that if one of the parties dies during the interlocutory period, they are still married and the

---

53. Coffman v. Coffman, 121 Ariz. 522, 591 P.2d 1010 (1979); In re Marriage of Schneckloth, 320 N.W.2d 535 (Iowa 1982), citing many other cases; Serafin v. Serafin, 401 Mich. 629, 258 N.W.2d 461 (1977); Davis v. Davis, 521 S.W.2d 603 (Tex. 1975); Annot., 49 A.L.R.3d 212, 258, 268 (1973). Cases which limit the rule include Staley v. Staley, 25 Md.App. 99, 335 A.2d 114 (1975); Commonwealth ex rel. Leider v. Leider, 434 Pa. 293, 254 A.2d 306 (1969).

§ 14.5

1. This subject is extensively discussed in Note, Interlocutory Decrees of Divorce, 56 Colum.L.Rev. 228 (1956).

2. E.g., West's Ann.Cal.Civ.Code §§ 4512, 4514 (Supp. 1987) (decree becomes final after six months from the date of service or appearance, whichever occurred first); Mass.Gen.L.Ann. c. 208, § 21 (Supp.1986) (decree nisi becomes absolute after ninety days from entry; Neb.Rev. Stat. 42–363 (1984) (decree becomes final after six months from entry); R.I.Gen.L., § 15–5–23 (1981) (decree not final until three months from trial and decision); Utah Code Ann., 30–3–7 (Supp.1986) (court may impose delay up to six months after entry). Wis.Stat.Ann. 767.37(2) (1981) provides that so far as a divorce affects the marital status, the court may vacate or modify the decree for sufficient cause at any time within six months of entry. Roddis v. Roddis, 18 Wis.2d 118, 118 N.W.2d 109 (1962) holds that the attempt of a party to contract a second marriage within the six months is a sufficient cause to vacate the divorce. The effect of this provision is therefore similar to the usual interlocutory decree statute.

3. In re Estate of Shippy, 37 Wash.App. 164, 678 P.2d 848 (1984), applying the law of the parties' domicile rather than the law of the place where the intervening marriage was contracted. See also Annot., 19 A.L.R.3d 648, 678 (1968). Where a spouse dies after the expiration of the interlocutory period, and a nunc pro tunc order is

entered, the result is that the marriage is treated as having been terminated before the spouse's death. Kern v. Kern, 261 Cal.App.2d 325, 67 Cal.Rptr. 802 (1968).

4. Annot., 151 A.L.R. 849 (1944). But some cases permit even a person not a party to the divorce to apply for an order. Annot., 19 A.L.R.3d 648, 674 (1968).

5. C.I.R. v. Evans, 211 F.2d 378 (10th Cir. 1954); Hendrich v. Anderson, 191 F.2d 242 (10th Cir. 1951); In re Abila's Estate, 32 Cal.2d 559, 197 P.2d 10 (1948); Paulus v. Bauder, 106 Cal.App.2d 589, 235 P.2d 422 (1951) (wife cannot sue husband for tort occurring during interlocutory period); Shinn v. Shinn, 148 Neb. 832, 29 N.W.2d 629 (1947).

6. C.I.R. v. Evans, 211 F.2d 378 (10th Cir. 1954).

7. Hendrich v. Anderson, 191 F.2d 242 (10th Cir.1951); Sullivan v. Sullivan, 219 Cal. 734, 28 P.2d 914 (1934); Roddis v. Roddis, 18 Wis.2d 118, 118 N.W.2d 109 (1962). Parker v. Parker, 29 Conn.Supp. 41, 270 A.2d 94 (1970) held invalid a marriage contracted in Connecticut within the interlocutory period of a Massachusetts divorce which had been obtained by the husband. The court applied the lex loci contractus to reach this result notwithstanding the existing Massachusetts putative marriage statute which might have validated the marriage. But Garrett v. Chapman, 252 Or. 361, 449 P.2d 856 (1969) held valid a marriage contracted in Idaho during the interlocutory period following a Montana divorce. The court relied upon a Montana statute calling for the application of the lex loci, and on the principle that marriages should be validated where entered into in good faith. Courts may on occasion have difficulty in determining whether a decree is interlocutory, or absolute with a prohibition on remarriage. See, e.g., Citrynell v. Citrynell, 86 Misc.2d 60, 382 N.Y.S.2d 256 (1976).

survivor will inherit.[8] If the parties engage in a good faith, unconditional reconciliation during the period, the divorce decree may be set aside.[9] This is true even though the reconciliation later turns out to be unsuccessful and the parties separate for a second time.[10] Although the purpose of the interlocutory period is to encourage reconciliation, these cases, which resemble the defense of condonation,[11] really discourage attempts at reconciliation since the parties know that if the reconciliation is tried and fails, the divorce action will have to be brought all over again. This is why divorce lawyers advise their clients to have nothing to do with the other spouse during the interlocutory period.[12] Partly for this reason the interlocutory decree of divorce has not been a spectacular success in achieving reconciliations and has largely been abandoned.[13]

If the prevailing party engages in sexual relations with someone other than the former spouse during the interlocutory period, this amounts to adultery and may lead the court to set the decree aside on the ground of recrimination, where that doctrine still exists.[14] The divorce decree may be set aside on this ground even though the adultery is not discovered until after the interlocutory decree has become final.[15] There is also authority that a final decree may not be entered at the request of one who is in violation of the interlocutory decree.[16]

The cases conflict as to whether the prevailing party may have the interlocutory decree set aside and the suit dismissed during the interlocutory period, some allowing this to be done with or without cause,[17] and others permitting the trial court to deny the dismissal or to require a showing of cause.[18] Since the right to have the suit dismissed can be used as leverage to force a more advantageous property settlement,[19] the better rule is that dismissal should not be a matter of right. If the

---

8. In re Estate of Watson, 217 Neb. 305, 348 N.W.2d 856 (1984); Keidel v. Keidel, 119 R.I. 726, 383 A.2d 264 (1978); Daly v. Daly, 533 P.2d 884 (Utah 1975); Annots., 158 A.L.R. 1205, 1207 (1945), 104 A.L.R. 654, 658 (1936).

9. Modnick v. Modnick, 33 Cal.3d 897, 191 Cal.Rptr. 629, 663 P.2d 187 (1983) (burden of proof is on the spouse asserting the reconciliation); Cochran v. Cochran, 13 Cal. App.3d 339, 91 Cal.Rptr. 630 (1970); Lawson v. Lawson, 185 Neb. 164, 174 N.W.2d 202 (1970).

10. Nacht v. Nacht, 167 Cal.App.2d 254, 334 P.2d 275 (1959) (reconciliation shown by cohabitation on week ends for about twenty successive weeks); Slusher v. Slusher, 85 Cal.App.2d 626, 193 P.2d 778 (1948) (reconciliation began and ended before decree became final); Angell v. Angell, 84 Cal.App.2d 339, 191 P.2d 54 (1948) (no reconciliation where forgiveness was conditional and the condition violated); Kalmus v. Kalmus, 330 Mass. 41, 110 N.E. 2d 760 (1953) (decree vacated thirty years later); Shinn v. Shinn, 148 Neb. 832, 29 N.W.2d 629 (1947). Contra: Johnson v. Johnson, 116 Utah 27, 207 P.2d 1036 (1949) (resumption of marital relations within the interlocutory period does not justify vacating decree after it became final). Many other cases are collected in Annots., 174 A.L.R. 519 (1948), and 109 A.L.R. 1005, 1007 (1937).

11. Note, 56 Colum.L.Rev. 227, 230 (1956). The court may also base its decision on the fraud of one of the parties in misrepresenting to the other that he will have the decree set aside. See, e.g. Meyer v. Meyer, 326 Mass. 491, 95 N.E.2d 645 (1950), Shinn v. Shinn, 148 Neb. 832, 29 N.W.2d 629 (1947).

12. Johnson, Suppressed, Delayed, Damaging and Avoided Divorces, 18 Law & Contemp.Prob. 72, 82 (1953).

13. See Note, 56 Colum.L.Rev. 228, 249 (1956).

14. Street v. Street, 48 Del. 272, 101 A.2d 803 (Super. 1953); Hellebuyck v. Hellebuyck, 349 Mich. 358, 84 N.W.2d 876 (1957) (trial court's discretion to set aside the

interlocutory decree for the wife's "misconduct" did not mean the case would be dismissed); Roddis v. Roddis, 18 Wis.2d 118, 118 N.W.2d 109 (1962). Other cases are collected in Annots., 174 A.L.R. 519, 523 (1948), 109 A.L.R. 1005, 1009 (1937).

15. Linn v. Linn, 341 Mich. 668, 69 N.W.2d 147 (1955). But see Hull v. Superior Court, 54 Cal.2d 139, 5 Cal.Rptr. 1, 352 P.2d 161 (1960), holding the contracting of a Mexican marriage during the interlocutory period did not justify denial of a final decree.

16. Hull v. Superior Court, 54 Cal.2d 139, 5 Cal.Rptr. 1, 352 P.2d 161 (1960) (dictum). Other cases are collected in Annots., 109 A.L.R. 1005, 1013 (1937), and 174 A.L.R. 519, 523 (1937).

17. Faith v. Faith, 128 Colo. 483, 261 P.2d 225 (1953) (Colorado no longer has the interlocutory decree); Iovino v. Iovino, 58 N.J.Super. 138, 155 A.2d 578 (1959) (New Jersey no longer has the interlocutory decree); Annots., 174 A.L.R. 519 (1948), 109 A.L.R. 1005, 1006 (1937).

18. Labadie v. Labadie, 347 Mich. 592, 81 N.W.2d 367 (1957) (no dismissal after cross-bill except by consent); Colick v. Colick, 148 Neb. 201, 26 N.W.2d 820 (1947). Vinyard v. Vinyard, 43 Del. 422, 48 A.2d 497 (1946) indicated that consent to dismissal would generally be granted, but Husband M. v. Wife M., 293 A.2d 589 (Del. Super. 1972) held that the state's policy toward divorce had changed with the adoption of incompatibility and the continuation of marriage was no longer primary, so that the plaintiff would not be permitted to discontinue the suit.

19. Sheffer v. Sheffer, 316 Mass. 575, 56 N.E.2d 13 (1944). Contra: Mailer v. Mailer, 387 Mass. 401, 439 N.E.2d 811 (1982), appeal after remand 390 Mass. 371, 455 N.E.2d 1211 (1983).

decree is set aside after a property division has been made, difficult and perhaps insoluble problems arise.[20] The only satisfactory solution to such problems is to restore the parties to status quo, but this may not be possible, in which case serious hardship or unfairness may result, usually to the husband.

Final Decree

The final decree should dispose of the issues in controversy in the case. It should grant the dissolution of the marriage to one spouse or the other or, in those states permitting such a decree, to both spouses.[21] The decree should also award alimony[22], divide the property,[23] and make an award of custody[24] where these matters are in issue in the case. Where grounds for dissolution of the marriage exist, the divorce should be granted and should not be denied or deferred because of the wishes of one of the spouses.[25]

The divorce decree should also authorize the wife to resume her maiden name if she wishes to do so. She is normally entitled to make the change in name even though the children's names will then be different from

her own.[26] If she wishes to retain her married name, she is entitled to do that.[27]

The question of what surname children will have when the marriage of their parents ends in divorce often arises in the divorce proceedings and, if the parents are unable to agree, must be resolved in the divorce decree.[28] This question has been difficult for the courts to deal with. If, as is often the case, custody is given to the mother and she remarries, the children may form close ties of affection to their stepfather. Even if the natural father supports them and continues contacts with them, the children, their mother and their stepfather all may wish to have the children take their stepfather's name. As a matter of procedure, most courts have held that where this is attempted, the natural father is entitled to notice that a change of name is being requested.[29]

Although the cases have generally held that the choice of a child's surname after divorce is to be governed by the child's best interests, the traditional view was that there was a sort of presumption or vaguely qualified right in the child's father that the child

---

20. Cases are collected in Note, 56 Colum.L.Rev. 228, 236–242 (1956).

21. See, e.g., Uniform Marriage and Divorce Act § 301(e), 9A Unif.L.Ann. 119 (1979). Where the law provides that the decree state who won the suit, the court's failure to do so does not invalidate the decree. Grimditch v. Grimditch, 71 Ariz. 198, 225 P.2d 489 (1950), opinion modified on rehearing 71 Ariz. 237, 226 P.2d 142 (1951).

22. The award of alimony is discussed infra, in section 16.4.

23. The division of property is discussed infra, in chapter 15.

24. Custody orders are discussed infra, in chapter 19.

25. Marazita v. Marazita, 27 Conn.Supp. 190, 233 A.2d 145 (1967); Kerbis v. Kerbis, 38 Ill.App.3d 866, 350 N.E.2d 1 (1976) (dictum); Psomas v. Psomas, 99 N.M. 606, 661 P.2d 884 (1982), overruled on other grounds, Walentowski v. Walentowski, 100 N.M. 484, 672 P.2d 657 (1983); Husting v. Husting, 54 Wis.2d 87, 194 N.W.2d 801 (1972).

26. In re Marriage of Banks, 42 Cal.App.3d 631, 117 Cal.Rptr. 37 (1974); Brown v. Brown, 384 A.2d 632 (D.C. App. 1977); Pilch v. Pilch, 447 So.2d 989 (Fla.App.1984); Thomas v. Thomas, 100 Ill.App.3d 1080, 56 Ill.Dec. 604, 427 N.E.2d 1009 (1981); Klein v. Klein, 36 Md.App. 177, 373 A.2d 86 (1977); Moskowitz v. Moskowitz, 118 N.H. 199, 385 A.2d 120 (1978); Sneed v. Sneed, 585 P.2d 1363 (Okl.1978); Elwell v. Elwell, 132 Vt. 73, 313 A.2d 394

(1973); Petition for Change of Name of Harris, 160 W.Va. 422, 236 S.E.2d 426 (1977).

27. Welcker v. Welcker, 342 So.2d 251 (La.App.1977), writ denied 343 So.2d 1077 (1977); Richette v. Ajello, 2 Fam.L.Rptr. 2716 (Pa.Com.Pl.1976).

28. Children's names, where no divorce is involved, are discussed in section 8.1, supra.

The divorce court has jurisdiction to decide disputes concerning the names of children of the parties and, where necessary, to enjoin a name change. In re Marriage of Nguyen, 684 P.2d 258 (Colo.App.1983), cert. denied 469 U.S. 1108, 105 S.Ct. 785, 83 L.Ed.2d 779 (1985). In re Marriage of Presson, 102 Ill.2d 303, 80 Ill.Dec. 294, 465 N.E.2d 85 (1984). The question of the child's name may also be decided in a statutory change of name proceeding, Lazow v. Lazow, 147 So.2d 12 (Fla.App. 1962), or in an independent suit for injunction against the change, Degerberg v. McCormick, 41 Del.Ch. 46, 187 A.2d 436 (1963). A comprehensive list of change of name statutes is found in Note, Family Law-Parental Rights in Changing Child's Surname, 9 Wm. Mitchell L.Rev. 484, 485 (1984).

29. Carroll v. Johnson, 263 Ark. 280, 565 S.W.2d 10 (1978); Petition for Change of Name of Harris, 160 W.Va. 422, 236 S.E.2d 426 (1977). Contra: Fulghum v. Paul, 229 Ga. 463, 192 S.E.2d 376 (1972). Newman v. King, 433 S.W.2d 420 (Tex.1968) held that the child need not be represented by a guardian ad litem in such a proceeding.

should continue to have the father's surname.[30] This of course was based on the custom then prevailing that on marriage the wife took the husband's surname and that the children also took his name.[31] The presumption could be rebutted by showing that retaining the father's surname would in some fashion be contrary to the child's welfare.[32] Now that gender discrimination has largely been held to violate the Equal Protection Clause of the Fourteenth Amendment [33] and is certainly invalid under equal rights provisions in state constitutions, it seems reasonably clear that the presumption in favor of the father's surname can no longer control. Without facing the constitutional issue, several cases have refused to be guided by traditional custom, but rather have just held that the child's surname should be chosen in accordance with his best interests.[34] As a means of giving some content to such a vague standard, these courts have suggested a list of factors to be considered in determining what the child's

interests require. These include a) the preservation of the father-child relationship; b) the strength of the mother-child relationship; c) the identification of the child as part of a family unit; d) the wishes of the child; e) the child's age and maturity; f) the nature of the family situation; g) misconduct of or neglect toward the child by the parent opposing the change; h) the name by which the child has customarily been called; i) the opposing party's conduct toward the spouse and the child during the marriage.[35] As in any case in which numerous factors are laid down to guide the courts, there is no way to determine how much or how little weight any of the factors should carry and therefore no way to predict how specific controversies will or should be decided. Both trial courts and the spouses are left at sea in these cases.

One way to avoid this uncertainty, at least to a degree, is to adopt the suggestion of Justice Mosk, concurring in the Schiffman case,[36] that there should be a rebuttable pre-

---

30. Carroll v. Johnson, 263 Ark. 280, 565 S.W.2d 10 (1978) (father has a basic and fundamental interest in his child's name); Degerberg v. McCormick, 41 Del.Ch. 46, 187 A.2d 436 (1963); Lazow v. Lazow, 147 So.2d 12 (Fla. App.1962); Burke v. Hammonds, 586 S.W.2d 307 (Ky. App. 1979); Overton v. Overton, ___ Mont. ___, 674 P.2d 1089 (1983); Firman v. Firman, 187 Mont. 465, 610 P.2d 178 (1980); Petition for Change of Name of Harris, 160 W.Va. 422, 236 S.E.2d 426 (1977). Many other cases are cited in Annot., 92 A.L.R.3d 1091 (1979).

31. Laks v. Laks, 25 Ariz.App. 58, 540 P.2d 1277 (1975); Degerberg v. McCormick, 41 Del.Ch. 46, 187 A.2d 436 (1963). For a discussion of this custom and its origins, see Note, The Controversy Over Children's Surnames: Familial Autonomy, Equal Protection and the Child's Best Interests, 1979 Utah L.Rev. 303.

32. W. v. H., 103 N.J.Super. 24, 246 A.2d 501 (1968) (children's names changed to maiden name of mother where father had sexually abused the children); Petition for Change of Name of Harris, 160 W.Va. 422, 236 S.E.2d 426 (1977) (court suggests that the child's name might be changed from that of the father if the father were a notorious criminal).

33. E.g., Orr v. Orr, 440 U.S. 268, 99 S.Ct. 1102, 59 L.Ed.2d 306 (1979), on remand 374 So.2d 895 (Ala.Civ. App.1979), writ denied 374 So.2d 898 (1979).

34. In re Marriage of Schiffman, 28 Cal.3d 640, 169 Cal.Rptr. 918, 620 P.2d 579 (1980) takes this position in its broadest form, stating that "the rule giving the father, as against the mother, a primary right to have his child bear his surname should be abolished." Other cases which emphasize the child's best interests include In re Marriage of Nguyen, 684 P.2d 258 (Colo.App.1983), cert. denied 469 U.S. 1108, 105 S.Ct. 785, 83 L.Ed.2d 779 (1985);

In re Marriage of Presson, 102 Ill.2d 303, 80 Ill.Dec. 294, 465 N.E.2d 85 (1984); In re Saxton, 309 N.W.2d 298 (Minn.1981), cert. denied 455 U.S. 1034, 102 S.Ct. 1737, 72 L.Ed.2d 152 (1982), 9 Wm. Mitchell L.Rev. 484 (1984); Robinson v. Hansel, 302 Minn. 34, 223 N.W.2d 138 (1974); Cohee v. Cohee, 210 Neb. 855, 317 N.W.2d 381 (1982); Application of Rossell by Yacono, 196 N.J.Super. 109, 481 A.2d 602 (1984). But the Presson case seems to give a sort of presumptive status to the existing name of the child, stating that the name may only be *changed* when the change is shown to be in the child's interests. If, as is often the case, the child has had the father's surname during the marriage, this approach to the question places the father in the same preferred position as under the traditional rule. The Robinson case also seems to take this view, as do Flowers v. Cain, 218 Va. 234, 237 S.E.2d 111 (1977), and Petition of Meyer, 471 N.E.2d 718 (Ind. App.1984).

35. See the cases cited in note 34, especially the Schiffman, Presson and Cohee cases.

36. In re Marriage of Schiffman, 28 Cal.3d 640, 648, 169 Cal.Rptr. 918, 923, 620 P.2d 579, 584 (1980). See also Petition of Schidlmeier by Koslof, 344 Pa.Super. 562, 496 A.2d 1249 (1985).

See also Note, Like Father, Like Child: The Rights of Parents in Their Children's Names, 70 Va.L.Rev. 1303 (1984), which argues for a rebuttable presumption that the child under fourteen should be given a compound surname made up of the names of both parents. The presumption might be rebutted by evidence of abandonment or neglect by one of the parents, and the older child should be permitted to choose what name he wishes.

Clearly the best way of resolving the name question is by the parties' separation agreement. Even there diffi-

sumption that the parent with custody of the child has acted in the child's best interests in choosing the child's name. The burden of rebutting the presumption would lie with the non-custodial parent, by showing that the name chosen was prejudicial to the child's interests. This rule would not be helpful in cases where custody was joint in the strict sense of the word, but in such cases if the parents had sufficient respect for each other to make joint custody work, they presumably would be able to agree on the question of a name for the child.

Although in some jurisdictions the courts are authorized to grant the divorce to both parties,[37] in others it is customary to indicate in the decree that one spouse or the other is the prevailing party, but the failure to do so does not make the decree invalid.[38] Who gets the divorce only matters in those jurisdictions where fault is relevant to the alimony or property award, or so far as guilt or innocence may be relevant to the custody decision.[39] Where the divorce is awarded on a non fault ground it makes no difference who gets it. But whatever relief is granted, it may not, when the defendant defaults, exceed the relief asked in the complaint.[40]

The consequence of an absolute divorce is of course to terminate the marriage of the parties.[41] It also may affect any wills in existence which name the parties as beneficiaries,[42] any insurance policies in which the parties are beneficiaries,[43] and it may alter rights to social security payments.[44] A divorce before judgment may also cut off consortium claims unless they are preserved by agreement of the parties.[45]

An absolute divorce decree, as distinguished from an interlocutory decree,[46] not only terminates the marriage but frees the parties to contract subsequent marriages.[47] In a very few states, however, there are statutes which forbid one or both of the parties to remarry.[48] The purposes of these statutes vary. They may be intended to discourage divorce,[49] or to punish one of the parties to the divorce,[50] or in the case of the strange Wisconsin statute, to enforce outstanding child support orders.[51] The kindest thing to be said about all such statutes is that they are misguided, and of course the Wisconsin version has been held to be an unconstitutional interference with the fundamental right to marry.[52] The other forms of prohibition on remarriage have not

culties may later arise, however. See, e.g., Gershowitz v. Gershowitz, 112 A.D.2d 67, 491 N.Y.S.2d 356 (1st Dep't 1985), appeal dismissed 66 N.Y.2d 915, 498 N.Y.S.2d 1027, 489 N.E.2d 773 (1985), holding that the child's mother violated the separation agreement by changing the child's name from Gershowitz to Hahn-Gershowitz, Hahn being her maiden name.

37. See note 21, supra.

38. Grimditch v. Grimditch, 71 Ariz. 198, 225 P.2d 489 (1950); Fried v. Fried, 208 Ga. 861, 69 S.E.2d 862 (1952); Annot., 133 A.L.R. 556 (1941).

39. See chapters 15, 16, and 19, dealing with alimony division of property and custody.

40. McHan v. McHan, 59 Idaho 496, 84 P.2d 984 (1938).

41. See, e.g., Conn.Gen.Stat.Ann. § 46b–67 (1986); Ohio Rev.Code § 3105.10 (1980).

42. Uniform Probate Code § 2–508, 8 Unif.L.Ann. 122 (1983) (divorce revokes a will of a spouse); Annot., Divorce or Annulment as Affecting Will Previously Executed By Husband or Wife, 71 A.L.R.3d 1297 (1976).

43. Government Personnel Mut. Life Ins. Co. v. Kaye, 584 F.2d 738 (5th Cir.1978).

44. Mathews v. de Castro, 429 U.S. 181, 97 S.Ct. 431, 50 L.Ed.2d 389 (1976).

45. Beeck v. Aquaslide 'N' Dive Corp., 350 N.W.2d 149 (Iowa 1984).

46. Remarriage during the interlocutory period is discussed supra, at note 7.

47. N.Y.—McKinney's Dom.Rel.L. § 8 (1977).

48. Okl.St.Ann. tit. 12, § 1280 (Supp.1987); Pa.Stat. tit. 48, § 169 (Supp.1986); V.Tex.C.A.Fam.Code § 3.66 (Supp.1987); Wis.Stat.Ann. § 765.03 (1981).

49. The Oklahoma, Texas and Wisconsin statutes seem to have this purpose.

50. The Pennsylvania statute, which forbids a spouse guilty of adultery to marry the co-respondent during the life of the former spouse, seems to be penal in nature. See in re Estate of Lenherr, 455 Pa. 225, 314 A.2d 255 (1974).

51. This was Wis.Stat.Ann. § 245.10 (1973), since repealed, which provided that Wisconsin residents who were the obligors under a support order could not marry in Wisconsin or elsewhere until they obtained a court's permission. Permission was not to be granted unless they were in compliance with the support order. Utah Code Ann. § 30–3–8 (1984) is a similar statute.

52. Zablocki v. Redhail, 434 U.S. 374, 98 S.Ct. 673, 54 L.Ed.2d 618 (1978), discussed at length in section 2.2, supra. An expansive approach to constitutional doctrine

been held unconstitutional, perhaps because they have not been challenged.

If the second marriage is contracted within the divorcing state in violation of the statutory prohibition, it is usually held void.[53] Some cases have held such marriages bigamous and therefore a sufficient basis for a criminal prosecution.[54] Where the second marriage is contracted in a state other than the divorcing state, one which does not prohibit remarriage after divorce, it is usually held valid if the parties have acquired a domicile in the second state.[55] On the other hand, if the parties go to the second state solely for the purpose of evading the prohibition and contracting the marriage there, many cases hold such a marriage invalid.[56] Fortunately cases under these statutes rarely arise today.

The divorce courts may have authority to make and enforce other post-decree orders,

depending upon the local law of the particular state.[57] New York's courts have enforced agreements between spouses providing that the parties would appear before a Jewish religious tribunal for counseling, as a preliminary step to enable one of them to obtain a Jewish divorce or "Get".[58] Enforcement of this agreement was held to constitute no violation of the First Amendment to the United States Constitution.

Earlier in this section we have written of the rules permitting dismissal of a divorce action pending the interlocutory period.[59] The same question arises in those jurisdictions which do not give interlocutory decrees when the plaintiff seeks to dismiss the case. Whether he will be allowed to do so depends upon court rule or statute in the particular state.[60] Where the statute does permit dismissal, the courts are in disagreement as to

might lead one to suppose that on the authority of this case, all of the statutes forbidding remarriage after divorce are invalid as not employing closely tailored means for the accomplishment of a compelling state interest. But the uses of constitutional doctrine, especially in the hands of the United States Supreme Court, are far from predictable.

53. Matter of D'Alessio's Estate, 196 Misc. 759, 92 N.Y.S.2d 540 (Sur.Ct.1949); Matter of Miccio's Estate, 193 Misc. 754, 86 N.Y.S.2d 30 (Sur.Ct.1949). But see Chlystek v. Califano, 599 F.2d 1270 (3d Cir.1979).

54. Brand v. State, 242 Ala. 15, 6 So.2d 446 (1941). Contra: Loughran v. Loughran, 292 U.S. 216, 54 S.Ct. 684, 78 L.Ed. 1219 (1934) (dictum).

55. Loughran v. Loughran, 292 U.S. 216, 54 S.Ct. 684, 78 L.Ed. 1219 (1933); Fisher v. Fisher, 250 N.Y. 313, 165 N.E. 460 (1929). Contra: Marek v. Flemming, 192 F.Supp. 528 (S.D.Tex.1961), judgment, vacated and remanded on other grounds 295 F.2d 691 (5th Cir.1961) (applying Virginia law). Early cases are collected in Annots., 51 A.L.R. 325 (1927), and 32 A.L.R. 1116 (1924). See also Citrynell v. Citrynell, 86 Misc.2d 60, 382 N.Y.S.2d 256 (1976), refusing to give effect to a Kansas prohibition on remarriage where the second marriage occurred in New York. The Kansas decree was treated as a prohibition on remarriage even though it read remarkably like an interlocutory decree.

56. Brand v. State, 242 Ala. 15, 6 So.2d 446 (1941); Harvey v. State, 31 Okl.Cr. 229, 238 P. 862 (1925); Maurer v. Maurer, 163 Pa.Super. 264, 60 A.2d 440 (1948); In re Kienstra, 151 Wash. 424, 276 P. 294 (1929) (specific statutory provision). The divorcing state's enactment of the Uniform Marriage Evasion Act makes this result easier to reach. See, e.g., Mass.Gen.Laws Ann. ch. 207, § 10 (1981).

New York and some other states have had so little regard for the policy underlying the prohibition on re-

marriage that they have been willing to hold out-of-state remarriages valid notwithstanding the intent to evade the local law. Estate of Ragone, 116 Misc.2d 993, 459 N.Y.S.2d 649 (Sur.Ct.1981), modified on other grounds 87 A.D.2d 457, 452 N.Y.S.2d 410 (1st Dep't 1982), appeal dismissed 57 N.Y.2d 1046, 457 N.Y.S.2d 788, 444 N.E.2d 38 (1982); In re Palmer's Estate, 192 Misc. 385, 79 N.Y.S.2d 404 (Sur.Ct.1948); Olsen v. Olsen, 27 Misc.2d 555, 209 N.Y.S.2d 503 (1960); Bogen v. Bogen, 261 N.W.2d 606 (Minn.1977); In re Lenherr's Estate, 455 Pa. 225, 314 A.2d 255 (1974). A violation of the Oklahoma prohibition on remarriage was held not be enforcible by contempt in Wasson v. Carden, 594 P.2d 1223 (Okl.1979).

57. E.g., Mathews v. Mathews, 101 Cal.App.3d 811, 161 Cal.Rptr. 879 (1980) (trial court had no authority to require the ex-wife to undergo psychiatric therapy for an indefinite time as an aspect of a custody award); In re Marriage of Peper, 38 Colo.App. 177, 554 P.2d 727 (1976) (trial court had authority to enjoin the ex-wife from proceeding in another jurisdiction).

58. Avitzur v. Avitzur, 58 N.Y.2d 108, 459 N.Y.S.2d 572, 446 N.E.2d 136 (1983), cert. denied 464 U.S. 817, 104 S.Ct. 76, 78 L.Ed.2d 88 (1983). New York has now enacted an "Avitzur" statute, which requires the parties, as a condition on obtaining a divorce, to show that they have taken all necessary steps to remove any barriers to remarriage, including any religious or conscientious barriers. N.Y.—McKinney's Dom.Rel.Law § 253 (Supp. 1984–1985).

59. See the discussion at note 17, supra.

60. Hartley v. Hartley, 435 A.2d 1052 (Del.Fam.Ct. 1981); Werner v. Werner, 186 Neb. 558, 184 N.W.2d 646 (1971); Moore v. Moore, 218 Va. 790, 240 S.E.2d 535 (1978); Annot., 16 A.L.R.3d 283 (1967). In Skitzki v. Skitzki, 114 R.I. 429, 334 A.2d 413 (1975) a voluntary dismissal by the plaintiff husband was denied where it would have cut off temporary alimony. Wiggins v. Wig-

whether the dismissal will be permitted for the purpose of enabling the plaintiff to take advantage of a change in the substantive law which has occurred after his suit was brought.[61]

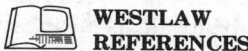 **WESTLAW REFERENCES**

di nisi

divorc! dissol! /s "nunc pro tunc" /s interlocutory

interlocutory /s divorc! dissol! /s reconcil! /s (set setting +1 aside) vacat! overturn!

Final Decree

divorc! dissol! /p maiden surname name /s chang! retain! retention keep! kept /s notice notif!

di(dissol! divorc! /p consortium)

di(divorc! dissol! /3 order decree /s prohibit! forb*d! preclu! restrain! restrict! bar barred barring /7 remarry! remarri***)

§ 14.6 Divorce Procedure—Attack on Divorce Decrees on Non-jurisdictional Grounds [1]

Jurisdictional attack on divorce decrees is treated in other parts of this work,[2] and is therefore excluded here. Similarities do exist between procedural rules applicable to jurisdictional and non-jurisdictional attack, although cases may be found which allow attack for fraud where an attack for lack of jurisdiction would be barred by estoppel.[3] The difference in result may be explained by

the more appealing innocence of the attacking party in the fraud cases.

As has been explained, divorce decrees are not given by default.[4] They may be given ex parte, however, without an appearance by the defendant. In this section such decrees will be referred to as default decrees for lack of a better term, but with the understanding that they are not granted by default in the sense that a hearing is dispensed with.

Most, if not all, jurisdictions have statutes or rules of court which provide that a party may be relieved from a judgment or decree on the ground of mistake, excusable neglect, newly discovered evidence, or fraud.[5] Many of these rules are based on the Federal Rules of Civil Procedure.[6] Their purpose is to provide for relief from final judgments when other methods, such as motions for new trial or appeals, are no longer available. The rules do not limit relief to default judgments but they are most often relied upon where the judgment has been entered by default. In a few states there are statutes specifically authorizing relief from divorce decrees.[7] In any event the general rules on relief from judgments do apply to divorce decrees,[8] although some courts have said that divorce decrees should have a higher degree of stability than other judgments because they affect many collateral rights and interests.[9] Court rules permitting relief from judgments generally

gins, 417 So.2d 691 (Fla.App.1982) held that when the husband took a voluntary dismissal the trial court could order him to pay the wife's attorney fees.

61. Permitting the wife to dismiss her petition voluntarily pursuant to the statute although she wished to do so in order to benefit from the new equitable distribution law, Battaglia v. Battaglia, 90 A.D.2d 930, 457 N.Y.S.2d 915 (3d Dep't 1982), reversed on the opinion of the dissenting judge 59 N.Y.2d 778, 464 N.Y.S.2d 725, 451 N.E.2d 472 (1983). See also Motler v. Motler, 60 N.Y.2d 244, 469 N.Y.S.2d 586, 457 N.E.2d 691 (1983), granting discontinuance of the wife's counterclaim. Holding that a husband-plaintiff could not dismiss his petition in order to benefit from a more favorable new alimony statute, H.C.M. v. E.W.M., 413 A.2d 1271 (Del.Fam.Ct.1980), order affirmed 428 A.2d 1148 (1981), appeal after remanded 455 A.2d 866 (1983).

§ 14.6

1. This subject has been exhaustively dealt with in Jacobs, Attack on Decrees of Divorce, 34 Mich.L.Rev. 749, 959 (1936), reprinted in Selected Essays on Family Law 987 (1950). See also Restatement (Second) of Judgments

ch. 5 (1982), dealing with relief from judgments in general.

2. See sections 12.2 and 12.3, supra.

3. Cases are collected in Annot., Vacating or Setting Aside Divorce Decree After Remarriage of Party, 17 A.L.R.4th 1153 (1982).

4. See section 14.4, supra.

5. F. James, G. Hazard, Civil Procedure §§ 13.13, 13.14 (2d ed.1977). Cases are collected in Annots., 157 A.L.R. 6 (1945) and 22 A.L.R.2d 1312 (1952).

6. Fed.R.Civ.P. 60(b). This rule is extensively discussed in 11 C. Wright, A. Miller, Federal Practice and Procedure §§ 2857 to 2868 (1973).

7. E.g., Wis.Stat.Ann. § 767.37 (1981) (so far as the decree affects the marital status, it may be modified for sufficient cause within six months).

8. Egan v. Egan, 560 P.2d 704 (Utah 1977); Annots., 157 A.L.R. 6 (1945), and 22 A.L.R.2d 1312 (1952).

9. Bachtle v. Bachtle, 468 A.2d 302 (Del.Super.1983), decision affirmed 494 A.2d 1253 (1985); Reville v. Reville,

impose a relatively short time period during which the attack on the judgment may be made.[10] The procedure established is usually a motion in the original suit,[11] which must state the grounds for relief with particularity.[12]

The grant or denial of a motion to set aside a divorce decree is within the sound discretion of the trial court.[13] Where the decree was entered by default, it may be set aside on relatively slight grounds on a motion made pursuant to a rule like that of Federal Rule 60(b). Not only are fraud and duress sufficient to warrant setting the decree aside, but other less serious defects may also suffice.[14] In addition it must appear that the defendant has a meritorious defense to the suit.[15] Even where the default is attacked after the period prescribed in the counterpart of Rule 60(b), the courts make an effort, sometimes in dubious terms, to give the defendant a day in court.[16]

Where the divorce decree under attack was not entered ex parte, the courts are more reluctant to find that the attacking party has fulfilled the requirements of the statute or court rule. For example, where the rule permits a decree to be set aside for newly discovered evidence, this does not apply to facts not in existence at the time of the original decree, and the rule may not be used as a method of obtaining modification of otherwise non-modifiable decrees.[17] Nor is a proceeding under Rule 60(b) to be used as a substitute for appeal.[18] On the other hand, the language of the rule is sufficiently vague to permit a decree to be set aside where a party fails to understand the meaning of a separation agreement.[19] It is really impossible to draw general conclusions about the meaning and application of these rules in divorce litigation. The context in which a particular case arises is often a crucial factor in the court's decision. That is obviously a factor capable of infinite variation.

As has been indicated, the state counterparts of Rule 60(b) usually impose a time limit for motions to set aside judgments for mistake, excusable neglect or fraud.[20] The question then is, may a judgment be attacked on any grounds after the expiration of the time limit? Whether and how this may be done depends on the local law of the various states. Federal Rule 60(b) and some of the state rules

---

370 A.2d 249 (Me.1977). Presumably in these cases the courts were referring to that aspect of divorce decrees which terminates the parties' marriages. This part of a divorce decree does indeed affect the interests of other persons than the spouses. But the financial aspects of divorce decrees may be set aside without normally affecting other persons. Other cases take the position that decrees of divorce may be set aside more readily than other judgments. Lesko v. Lesko, 79 A.D.2d 1100, 435 N.Y.S.2d 847 (4th Dep't 1981), appeal after remand 9 A.D.2d 1176, 459 N.Y.2d 146 (1983).

10. E.g., Ariz.R.Civ.P. 60(c) (six months); Colo.R.Civ. P., Rule 60(b) (six months); Ill.—Smith Hurd Ann. ch. 110, § 2–1401 (1983) (two years); Mass.R.Civ.P., Rule 60(b) (one year); Mich.R.Civ.P. 528.3 (one year). Fed.R. Civ.P., Rule 60(b) imposes a one-year period for such motions.

11. Fed.R.Civ.P., Rule 60(b).

12. Merrill v. Merrill, 449 A.2d 1120 (Me.1982).

13. Galper v. Galper, 162 Cal.App.2d 391, 328 P.2d 487 (1958); Reville v. Reville, 370 A.2d 249 (Me.1977); Rogers v. Rogers, 351 N.W.2d 129 (S.D.1984).

14. Garcia v. Garcia, 105 Cal.App.2d 289, 233 P.2d 23 (1951); Handy v. Handy, 250 Iowa 879, 96 N.W.2d 922 (1959) (defendant's attorney failed to appear at the hearing); Cole v. Cole, 462 S.W.2d 172 (Mo.App.1970) (negligence of defendant's attorney); Baton v. Baton, 109 R.I. 115, 281 A.2d 295 (1971); Moore v. Moore, 224 Tenn. 611,

460 S.W.2d 844 (1970) (negligence of attorney); Lake v. Lake, 63 Wyo. 375 182 P.2d 824 (1947) (answer not filed in time). Courts refused to set decrees aside in Lindsey v. Lindsey, 48 Ala.App. 495, 266 So.2d 298 (1972) (defendant negligent in failing to appear); Damiano v. Damiano, 83 Ariz. 366, 321 P.2d 1027 (1958) (defendant failed to hire a lawyer). The court in Jones v. Jones, 276 Or. 1125, 557 P.2d 239 (1976) indicated that duress would be grounds for setting aside a default decree, but found no duress in this case.

15. Cantwell v. Cantwell, 237 Ind. 168, 143 N.E.2d 275 (1957), appeal dismissed 356 U.S. 225, 78 S.Ct. 700, 2 L.Ed.2d 712 (1958), rehearing denied 356 U.S. 954, 78 S.Ct. 913, 2 L.Ed.2d 847 (1958); Handy v. Handy, 250 Iowa 879, 96 N.W.2d 922 (1959); Lesko v. Lesko, 79 A.D.2d 1100, 435 N.Y.S.2d 847 (4th Dep't 1981), appeal after remand 91 A.D.2d 1176, 459 N.Y.S.2d 146 (1983); Hooker v. Hooker, 8 Wis.2d 331, 99 N.W.2d 113 (1959).

16. F. James, G. Hazard, Civil Procedure § 13.14 (2d ed.1977).

17. Bachtle v. Bachtle, 468 A.2d 302 (Del.Super.1983), decision affirmed 494 F.2d 1253 (1985); Merrill v. Merrill, 449 A.2d 1120 (Me.1982).

18. Reville v. Reville, 370 A.2d 249 (Me.1977).

19. Rogers v. Rogers, 351 N.W.2d 129 (S.D.1984).

20. See note 10, supra.

based upon it provide that the time limit does not apply to motions made for "any other reason justifying relief from the operation of a judgment."[21] Although this provision is even more vague than the other language of Rule 60(b), some cases have attempted to give it content in the divorce context by relying on it to set aside divorce decrees on the ground of various allegations of fraud or misconduct by the prevailing party.[22] Here again, however, it is difficult to predict how the courts will view a particular set of facts, especially in view of the broad discretion conceded to trial courts in such cases.

Rule 60(b) and its counterparts in the various states provide that this rule does not limit the power of the courts to entertain an independent suit to obtain relief from a judgment or to set aside a judgment for fraud upon the court.[23] The cases reach the same result.[24] Traditional methods for obtaining relief from judgments after the appeal time had expired or after term time included the writ of error coram nobis or coram vobis,[25] or the bill in equity for review of the judgment,[26]

but coram nobis and bills of review have been generally abolished by Rule 60(b) in favor of an independent suit in equity.[27] Although some courts have assumed that such an equitable action may only be brought in the same jurisdiction which granted the divorce, there are cases holding that it may be addressed to divorce decrees of other jurisdictions where similar relief would be available under the law of those other jurisdictions.[28] If an independent equity suit is brought, this is of course a new action requiring new service of process,[29] whereas no new service is required of a proceeding brought by motion under Rule 60(b).[30]

Since proceedings of this sort for relief from divorce decrees are equitable in nature, they will be barred by doctrines of laches or estoppel where there has been such prejudicial delay or change in circumstances as would make it unconscionable or unfair to set aside the judgment.[31] There used to be a rather rigid doctrine that a person who received the benefits of a decree was estopped to attack

21. Fed.R.Civ.Proc., Rule 60(b) and rules cited, supra, note 10. See also Utah R.Civ.Proc., Rule 60(b).

22. Coulson v. Coulson, 5 Ohio St.3d 12, 448 N.E.2d 809 (1983) ("fraud on the court", consisting of conduct of the husband's counsel in purporting to represent the wife also); In re Marriage of Watson, 13 Ohio App.3d 344, 469 N.E.2d 876 (1983) (court set aside the decree to the extent of making orders for child custody and support after the wife had concealed her pregnancy or failed to reveal it pending the suit); Egan v. Egan, 560 P.2d 704 (Utah 1977) (mistake of fact may be sufficient to grant relief from the decree).

The federal courts' approach to this section of Rule 60(b) is discussed in 11 C. Wright and A. Miller, Federal Practice and Procedure § 2864 (1973).

23. Fed.R.Civ.Proc., Rule 60(b). See also the rules cited in note 10, supra.

24. Titus v. Nieheiser, 269 Ala. 493, 114 So.2d 242 (1959); Cure v. Southwick, 137 Mont. 1, 349 P.2d 575 (1960); Jelm v. Jelm, 155 Ohio St. 226, 98 N.E.2d 401 (1951); Davis v. Davis, 236 S.C. 277, 113 S.E.2d 819 (1960); Annot., 157 A.L.R. 6, 18 (1945).

25. Orfield, The Writ of Error Coram Nobis in Civil Practice, 20 Va.L.Rev. 423 (1934).

26. Annot., 20 Am.Dec. 160 (1910), 1917B L.R.A. 409, 421; 3 A. Freeman, Judgments 2473–2474 (5th ed.1925). It is important to note that this procedure is a direct attack on the judgment, not a collateral attack.

27. See the rules cited in note 10, supra, and N.C. v. W.R.C., ____ W.Va. ____, 317 S.E.2d 793 (1984).

Where the divorce is vacated, the court is free to provide any appropriate equitable remedy. Brink v. Brink, 155 Cal.App.3d 218, 202 Cal.Rptr. 57 (1984). But it has been held that the party alleging that the divorce was obtained by fraud may not recover damages for the fraud. Hall v. Hall, 455 So.2d 813 (Ala.1984).

28. Jacobs, Attack on Decrees of Divorce, 34 Mich.L. Rev. 749, 794 (1936). But see Azar v. Thomas, 206 Ga. 588, 57 S.E.2d 821 (1950); du Pont v. du Pont, 47 Del. (8 Terry) 231, 90 A.2d 468 (1952), cert. denied 344 U.S. 836, 73 S.Ct. 46, 97 L.Ed. 651 (1952); Golson v. Golson, 351 So. 2d 100 (La.1977). Where the divorce was granted by the court of a foreign country, the Full Faith and Credit Clause does not protect it but ordinary considerations of comity apply to it. In those circumstances a divorce procured by fraud may be set aside by an American court. Greschler v. Greschler, 51 N.Y.2d 368, 434 N.Y.S.2d 194, 414 N.E.2d 694 (1980); Feinberg v. Feinberg, 40 N.Y.2d 124, 386 N.Y.S.2d 77, 351 N.E.2d 725 (1976), on remand 96 Misc.2d 443, 409 N.Y.S.2d 365 (1978), judgment affirmed 70 A.D.2d 612, 415 N.Y.S.2d 1018 (1979). See also Restatement (Second) of Judgments § 82 (1982) and Restatement (Second) of Conflict of Laws § 115 (1971).

29. Edwards v. Edwards, 67 So.2d 661 (Fla.1953).

30. Bussey v. Bussey, 94 N.H. 328, 52 A.2d 856 (1957). But of course notice of the motion must be given to the other party.

31. Lewis v. Lewis, 214 Ark. 454, 217 S.W.2d 346 (1949) (six month delay held not unreasonable); Norris v. Norris, 342 Mich. 83, 69 N.W.2d 208 (1955), cert. denied

it.[32] More modern cases have refused to apply this doctrine to the case which arises when one of the parties to a divorce wishes to have the financial or property aspects of the decree set aside after he has accepted some benefits from the decree. These cases treat the various provisions in the decree as separable and sensibly hold that there is no estoppel in such circumstances.[33]

The death or remarriage of a party are the two kinds of changed circumstances most often urged as a reason for not setting aside a fraudulent decree.[34] It is clear that neither circumstance deprives the court of the power to vacate a fraudulent decree, but the question is whether the court should take either of them into account in attempting to reach an equitable result. The results of the cases, though superficially conflicting, can largely be reconciled. Where the innocent party has waited a long time before attacking the decree, during which time the other spouse has remarried or died, or both, the decree will usually not be set aside.[35] Here, as in other contexts,[36] the courts are inarticulately recognizing that a marriage which has ended and

which both parties have treated as ended, cannot be revived by setting aside the divorce. On the other hand, where the attack on the decree comes soon after it is granted and soon after the innocent party learns of the fraud, the intervening remarriage or death of the fraudulent spouse will ordinarily not prevent the decree from being vacated.[37]

In some instances the divorce defendant may attack the decree in a collateral proceeding. Pronouncements have been made both by courts [38] and text writers [39] that a collateral attack on the decree may not be made by a party to it on the ground of fraud, duress or collusion. The cases relied upon to support such statements are not entirely convincing.[40] It is not clear why, if a party may attack a divorce directly by a suit in equity or a petition to vacate, he should not be allowed to attack it collaterally. Presumably the reason has to do with the ancient law-equity distinction, according to which a judgment obtained by fraud was none the less a judgment (where jurisdiction existed) although equity would prevent the prevailing party from accepting its benefits.[41] Today when most courts are

350 U.S. 903, 76 S.Ct. 182, 100 L.Ed. 793 (1955) (twenty-year delay raises laches); Bredemann v. Bredemann, 253 Minn. 21, 91 N.W.2d 84 (1958) (ten-year delay raises laches); Attebery v. Attebery, 172 Neb. 671, 111 N.W.2d 553 (1961) (twenty years); Bussey v. Bussey, 94 N.H. 328, 52 A.2d 856 (1947) (is within trial court's discretion to refuse to set aside decree after remarriage and death of one of the parties); Patrick v. Patrick, 245 N.C. 195, 95 S.E.2d 585 (1956) (twenty-seven years and the death of a party not laches, where they had lived together all this time, and the husband only learned of existence of the divorce twenty-five days before he filed his petition to set it aside).

32. Cases are cited in Annot., 55 A.L.R.3d 1299 (1974) and 29 A.L.R.3d 1167 (1970), dealing with appeals after receiving the benefit of divorce decrees.

33. Alderson v. Alderson, 258 Ind. 328, 281 N.E.2d 82 (1972) (appeal); Rogers v. Rogers, 351 N.W.2d 129 (S.D.1984); Rose v. Rose, 598 S.W.2d 889 (Tex.Civ.App. 1980).

34. Cases on the effect of death on the suit for relief are cited in Annots., 30 A.L.R. 1466 (1924) and 40 A.L.R. 1118 (1926). Cases on the effect of remarriage and cited in Annot., 17 A.L.R.4th 1153 (1982).

35. Sajich v. Sajich, 128 Ill.App.2d 432, 262 N.E.2d 11 (1970) (sixteen-year delay plus marriage of the other spouse); Wooddy v. Wooddy, 256 Md. 440, 261 A.2d 486 (1970) (twenty-six month delay after the wife learned of the decree plus remarriage of the husband); Johnston v. Johnston, 280 Minn. 81, 158 N.W.2d 249 (1968) (trial

court did not abuse discretion in refusing to vacate the divorce so far as it ended the marriage, but did vacate the financial provisions); Hemphill v. Quigg, 355 S.W.2d 57 (Mo.1962) (fourteen year delay plus remarriage); Bussey v. Bussey, 94 N.H. 328, 52 A.2d 856 (1947) (nearly twenty year delay plus remarriage and death of the other spouse). Other cases are cited in Annot., 17 A.L.R.4th 1153 (1982).

36. See the analysis of estoppel against jurisdictional attack on divorces in section 12.3, supra.

37. Gillen v. Gillen, 117 Mont. 496, 159 P.2d 511 (1945) (wife attacked the decree within one year, not knowing of the divorce until after the husband's death); Jelm v. Jelm, 155 Ohio St. 226, 98 N.E.2d 401 (1951) (second spouse had knowledge of the fraud). But see Anderson v. Dyer, 456 S.W.2d 808 (Mo.App.1970). Other cases are cited in Annot., 17 A.L.R.4th 1153 (1982).

38. E.g., Kalmus v. Kalmus, 330 Mass. 41, 110 N.E.2d 760 (1953); Old Colony Trust Co. v. Porter, 324 Mass. 581, 88 N.E.2d 135 (1949); Ellis v. Ellis, 55 Minn. 401, 56 N.W. 1056 (1893); Rutledge v. Rutledge, 198 Tenn. 665, 281 S.W.2d 666 (1955).

39. Jacobs, Attack on Decrees of Divorce, 34 Mich.L. Rev. 749, 787 (1936).

40. E.g., Rutledge v. Rutledge, 198 Tenn. 665, 281 S.W.2d 666 (1955), which seems to involve direct attack although the court refers to it as a case of collateral attack.

41. Restatement, Judgments § 112, comment c (1942).

courts of both law and equity, this distinction is obsolete and in fact results in a multiplicity of suits, a condition which equity traditionally condemned. There is no reason why the divorce defendant should be required first to bring an equity suit to set aside the decree, and then bring a second suit to assert his property rights,[42] provided that all interested persons can be joined as parties and so bound by the outcome. Both remedies should be available in one action, whether it be labelled a collateral or a direct attack.

It is clear that the parties to a divorce action have standing to have it set aside for fraud, but there is a close and difficult question whether others have such standing. The authorities have confused matters to a considerable degree by using inexact terminology. Thus the general rule is stated by the Restatement (Second) of Judgments to be that a person may seek relief from a judgment if he has an interest affected by the judgment[43] but this does not tell us what sort of interests are meant or how they must be affected. Obvi-ously any person who seeks to set aside a divorce decree will have some sort of an interest which will be affected in some way by the divorce.

According to some cases, direct attack on a divorce by suit in equity or by a petition in the divorce action itself may not be made by persons not parties to the divorce action.[44] There are a substantial number of contrary cases holding that such persons may have the divorce decree set aside for fraud.[45] Freeman,[46] supported by some cases,[47] takes the intermediate position that non-parties may collaterally attack the divorce but only if the decree affects legally enforceable rights in existence before it was entered. This rule would seem to deprive the stranger of standing to attack the decree in the majority of situations, since, for example, a second spouse would not qualify under it, nor would the heirs or personal representatives of a deceased spouse. None of these persons has pre-existing rights.[48]

---

42. Restatement (Second) of Judgments § 80, comment a and Reporter's Note (1982) seems to support the text position.

43. Restatement (Second) of Judgments § 64 (1982). This section refers us to § 76, which states that a person who is not bound by a judgment under the rules of res judicata may have relief from the judgment when the judgment jeopardizes a protectible interest. Protectible interests are not defined but examples are given. One such example is in § 80, illustration 3, according to which the sister of a spouse would be permitted to attack the validity of the spouse's divorce in a dispute over inheritance from the spouse. See also 3 A. Freeman, Judgments 2499 (5th ed.1925) and Jacobs, Attack on Decrees of Divorce, 34 Mich.L.Rev. 959 (1936).

44. Weill v. Weill, 226 Ark. 206, 288 S.W.2d 946 (1956); Shammas v. Shammas, 9 N.J. 321, 88 A.2d 204 (1952); Shaver v. Shaver, 248 N.C. 113, 102 S.E.2d 791 (1958); Crockett v. Crockett, 27 Wash.2d 877, 181 P.2d 180 (1947). Many other cases are collected in Annots., 12 A.L.R.2d 717, 727 (1950), 120 A.L.R. 814, 822 (1939), 99 A.L.R. 1309, 1310 (1935), and in Jacobs, Attack on Decrees of Divorce, 34 Mich.L.Rev. 959 (1936).

In reading the cases great care must be used to determine the precise reason for refusing to allow attack on the decree. The present discussion concerns only refusal on the ground that the attacker was not a party. Refusal may also be based on estoppel, or laches, or on the fact that the fraud alleged does not justify vacating the decree. Attacks for fraud must also be distinguished from attacks for jurisdictional reasons, which are sometimes characterized as fraud on the court. See Old Colony Trust Co. v. Porter, 324 Mass. 581, 88 N.E.2d 135 (1949).

45. State ex rel. Willys v. Chillingsworth, 124 Fla. 274, 168 So. 249 (1936); Azar v. Thomas, 206 Ga. 588, 57 S.E.2d 821 (1950); Allen v. Allen, 341 Mich. 543, 67 N.W.2d 805 (1954) (seems inconsistent with Baugh v. Baugh, 37 Mich. 59, (1877)); Jones v. Goolsby, 218 Miss. 847, 68 So.2d 89 (1953).

See also Smith v. Smith, 68 Nev. 10, 226 P.2d 279 (1951) holding a second wife had standing to set aside an order vacating the husband's divorce from his first wife.

Additional cases are collected in Annots., 12 A.L.R.2d 717, 727 (1950), 120 A.L.R. 815, 822 (1939), 99 A.L.R. 1309, 1310 (1935).

In Berg v. Berg, 336 Mich. 284, 57 N.W.2d 889 (1953) the sister of a party was allowed to make a direct attack on the divorce, but apparently she was acting as a representative of the party.

46. 1 A. Freeman, Judgments 636 (5th ed.1925).

47. Fattibene v. Fattibene, 183 Conn. 433, 441 A.2d 3 (1981); Murphy v. Murphy, 34 Conn.Super. 251, 386 A.2d 274 (1978); du Pont v. du Pont, 47 Del. (8 Terry) 231, 90 A.2d 468 (1952), cert. denied 344 U.S. 836, 73 S.Ct. 46, 97 L.Ed. 651 (1952) (applying Texas law, involving collateral attack); Johnson v. Hartford Insurance Group, 99 Idaho 134, 578 P.2d 676 (1978); Gullo v. Brown, 82 N.M. 412, 483 P.2d 293 (1971). The Johnson case makes a distinction between a "void" decree, which may be attacked by a stranger even though he had no pre-existing rights which were affected by it, and other decrees as to which the text statement is applied.

48. But see In re Kant's Estate, 272 So.2d 153 (Fla. 1972), holding that the children of a husband's first marriage could attack a divorce decree which his second

There being precedent for all possible rules, the sensible course of action is to examine and evaluate the consequences resulting from the choice of one rule over another. Does any of the possible rules serve a desirable social policy? Unfortunately few judicial opinions consider the problem from this angle so that we may look for little help there.

The reason for allowing direct attack on any judgment for fraud is that the defendant has by deception been deprived of his day in court and has thereby suffered harm. The essential factor is the deprivation of a fair trial.[49]

We might then ask whether the same may be said of the stranger to the divorce action when he seeks relief from the decree. A clearer view of the question may result from consideration of a particular set of facts. The following are not unusual.[50] W, married to H–1, sues for divorce, falsely stating to the court that she does not know where he is and thus obtains service by publication which H–1 never sees. H–1 does not appear and the divorce is granted ex parte. H–1 does not hear of it until much later. W marries H–2, who dies not long thereafter. H–2's brother, A, then sues to set aside the divorce of W from H–1 on the ground of fraud. If he succeeds, it will follow that W was not married to H–2 and A will inherit H–2's property. If the divorce is held to be unassailable by A, then the marriage of W and H–2 stands and W inherits as the widow.

On these facts A's suit to set aside the decree meets three objections. In the first place A was not deceived. In the second place the divorce itself did not deprive him of any enforceable right, since at the time it was granted he had at best a mere expectancy in H–2's estate. The loss of this expectancy did not result solely from the fraudulent divorce, but also from the marriage of H–2. If H–2 had chosen to marry a legally more eligible woman, A would certainly have lost his expectancy. Finally, it should not be overlooked that H–2 and W were satisfied to consider themselves married. H–1, the only person plainly wronged by the fraud, is not disposed to attack the divorce. Certainly A would not have been permitted to intervene in the divorce proceeding in order to assert W's fraud, and that being so, it is not easy to see why he should be permitted to get the same effect after an appreciable interval of time during which the persons most intimately concerned thought they were married and behaved as if they were married.

On the other side, it must be conceded that if the divorce is not assailable by A, W has profited by her own fraud. More important perhaps, A has never had a day in court on the validity of the divorce.

The question is thus reduced to this: When a fraud committed by W against H–1 starts a chain of circumstances which later affects the interests of A, should A be entitled to assert this fraud in an action against W? In the writer's view the answer to this question should be no. On balance it seems that greater stability in marital relationships will result from this view, and this is much to be desired. So long as the parties to the divorce have not raised the issue, it ought to be fait accompli. An additional reason for this view is the law's reluctance in other contexts to compensate for the more remote consequences of fraud.[51]

When the stranger to the divorce action attacks it in a collateral, rather than a direct, proceeding,[52] the foregoing considerations of policy ought also to apply. The result should

---

wife had obtained before she married him. The court took the position that the children of the first marriage had existing rights as their father's sole heirs at the time the second wife obtained her divorce from her first husband. This seems an exceedingly dubious proposition, since it was the father's second marriage which infringed on their chance to inherit, not the divorce.

49. E.g., In re Marriage of Park, 27 Cal.3d 337, 165 Cal.Rptr. 792, 612 P.2d 882 (1980). See the discussion of "extrinsic fraud", infra, at note 58.

50. These are the facts of Jones v. Goolsby, 218 Miss. 847, 68 So.2d 89 (1953), simplified in some particulars.

51. 1 F. Harper, F. James, The Law of Torts § 7.2 (1956); W. Prosser, W. Keeton, The Law of Torts 743–745 (5th ed.1984).

52. Restatement (Second) of Judgments §§ 76, 80 (1982) seems not to use the direct-collateral terminology but does distinguish between a suit to set aside the

not differ from the result reached where the attack is direct.[53] But the cases do not so hold. Some of them hold that a stranger may attack the divorce directly but not collaterally,[54] but there is also authority for saying that collateral attack may be possible where direct is not.[55] This distinction may turn on a supposed distinction between "void" and "voidable" decrees which is a relic of older equity theories.[56] If the stranger is considered to have sufficient interest to be allowed to assert the fraud, it seems more sensible to let him assert it either directly or collaterally, whichever is more economical of time and expense.

The final and perhaps anticlimactic question in this section relates to the merits. What sort of fraud will entitle the appropriate party to have a divorce set aside? The traditional doctrine was that in order to set aside a judgment, the fraud must be "extrinsic" as distinguished from "intrinsic."[57] "Extrinsic" fraud was often defined as the sort of fraud which prevented the plaintiff from presenting his case to the court.[58] This defini-

tion may still be found in the cases.[59] The extrinsic-intrinsic distinction has been discarded by the Restatement, and the federal rules permit judgments to be attacked by motion on grounds of fraud whether extrinsic or intrinsic.[60]

It is clear that the courts will vacate divorce decrees where the obvious forms of "extrinsic" fraud were present, as where the plaintiff falsely tells the court that he is ignorant of the defendant's whereabouts, thereby obtaining the divorce without giving her notice,[61] or where he deliberately fails to give notice of the hearing, telling the defendant he will not prosecute the action further.[62] It is likewise clear that duress will justify vacating a decree, where the defendant is forced to withhold a defense or consent to a decree.[63] Divorce decrees may also be set aside if the defendant was deprived of a fair opportunity to present his case, as where an insane party was not represented by a guardian ad litem,[64] or where the defendant received representation so inadequate that he could not be said to

judgment, and attack on the judgment in subsequent litigation.

53. See the discussion at note 26, supra.

54. Couyoumjian v. Anspach, 360 Mich. 371, 103 N.W.2d 587 (1960) (collateral attack refused); Allen v. Allen, 341 Mich. 543, 67 N.W.2d 805 (1954) (direct attack allowed); Jones v. Goolsby, 218 Miss. 847, 68 So.2d 89 (1953) (direct attack allowed); Kirby v. Kent, 172 Miss. 457, 160 So. 569 (1935) (collateral attack refused). Collateral attack was also denied in Fattibene v. Fattibene, 183 Conn. 433, 441 A.2d 3 (1981); Murphy v. Murphy, 34 Conn.Supp. 251, 386 A.2d 274 (1978); Gullo v. Brown, 82 N.M. 412, 483 P.2d 293 (1971), without discussion of whether direct attack would be permitted. The tenor of these cases suggests that it would not be.

55. du Pont v. du Pont, 47 Del. (8 Terry) 231, 90 A.2d 468 (1952), cert. denied 344 U.S. 836, 73 S.Ct. 46, 97 L.Ed. 651 (1952); Carpenter v. Carpenter, 244 N.C. 286, 93 S.E.2d 617 (1956); Matter of Akers' Estate, 541 P.2d 284 (Okl.App.1975); Jacobs, Attack on Decrees of Divorce, 34 Mich.L.Rev. 959, 971–973 (1936). The Restatement seems to approve of collateral attack. Restatement (Second) of Judgments §§ 76, 80, illustration 3 (1982).

56. Johnson v. Hartford Insurance Group, 99 Idaho 134, 578 P.2d 676 (1978).

57. Restatement, Judgments §§ 118 to 121 (1942), and Galper v. Galper, 162 Cal.App.2d 391, 328 P.2d 487 (1958).

58. Restatement, Judgments § 118, comment b (1942).

59. In re Marriage of Park, 27 Cal.3d 337, 165 Cal. Rptr. 792, 612 P.2d 882 (1980), indicating that the term

"extrinsic fraud" is to be given a broad meaning. Considerable confusion can be generated by the use of these terms. See Matter of Bonfils' Estate, 190 Colo. 70, 543 P.2d 701 (1975), taking the view that extrinsic fraud makes a decree void, while intrinsic fraud makes a decree voidable, opening it to direct but not collateral attack. A case finding the alleged fraud to be intrinsic is Haws v. Haws, 96 Nev. 727, 615 P.2d 978 (1980).

60. Restatement (Second) of Judgments § 70, comment c (1982); Fed.R.Civ.P., Rule 60(b); DeClaire v. Yohanan, 453 So.2d 375 (Fla.1984).

61. Titus v. Nieheiser, 269 Ala. 493, 114 So.2d 242 (1959); Peschier v. Peschier, 419 So.2d 923 (La.1982); Patrick v. Patrick, 245 N.C. 195, 95 S.E.2d 585 (1956); Cortese v. Cortese, 163 Pa.Super. 553, 63 A.2d 420 (1949). Other cases are collected in Annots., 22 A.L.R.2d 1312, 1328 (1952), and 157 A.L.R. 6, 63 (1945).

62. Seay v. Seay, 239 Ark. 1115, 396 S.W.2d 838 (1965); Horra v. Horra, 118 So.2d 670 (Fla.App. 1960); Meyer v. Meyer, 326 Mass. 491, 95 N.E.2d 645 (1950); Cure v. Southwick, 137 Mont. 1, 349 P.2d 575 (1960); Jelm v. Jelm, 155 Ohio St. 226, 98 N.E.2d 401 (1951); Davis v. Davis, 236 S.C. 277, 113 S.E.2d 819 (1960).

63. Cary v. Cary, 257 Ala. 431, 59 So.2d 659 (1952); James v. James, 14 Ill.2d 295, 152 N.E.2d 582 (1958), on remand 24 Ill.App.2d 445, 164 N.E.2d 505 (1960); Dunn v. Dunn, 258 Wis. 188, 45 N.W.2d 727 (1951). See also Annot., 22 A.L.R.2d 1312, 1334 (1952).

64. Dei Tos v. Dei Tos, 105 Cal.App.2d 81, 232 P.2d 873 (1951) (excellent review of the cases).

have had a fair trial.[65] Similar results have been reached where an inexperienced or unsophisticated defendant acts on the faith of representations that the lawyer for the other spouse will represent him,[66] or where such a defendant was induced to sign documents by misrepresentations as to the effect of the divorce, leading him not to appear in the proceedings.[67]

Where a party seeks to set aside the property or financial provisions of a divorce decree, some courts have found that misrepresentations concerning the existence or the value of property constitute extrinsic fraud sufficient to support relief.[68] There are other cases characterizing this sort of misrepresentation as intrinsic fraud, but often the outcome seems to have been affected by the credibility of the party seeking relief or the precise nature of the misrepresentation.[69] The extrinsic-intrinsic distinction seems to have caused even more confusion in this than in other contexts.

A scattering of other grounds relevant only to divorce have induced some courts to set aside decrees. These include misrepresentations to the court that the parties had lived apart for the prescribed period when they had not,[70] concealment from the court of the fact that they had been reconciled,[71] or concealment from the court of some form of marital misconduct.[72] When collusion was an important factor in divorce the courts were unable to agree on whether a decree obtained by collusion should be set aside when the collusion later came to light.[73] Some of them were persuaded that the state's interest in seeing that divorces were only granted in strict compliance with statute required collusive decrees to be set aside. Others were reluctant to do this because by definition collusion required that both spouses impose on the divorce court, and setting aside the decree would often reward a wrongdoer.

Several conclusions from the foregoing discussion are reasonably plain. First, the courts are far from agreement about what is extrinsic fraud which will justify setting aside a divorce decree. Part of the reason for this is that some courts are strongly of the opinion that divorce decrees are entitled to as much or perhaps more stability and finality than other judgments.[74] Others, looking at the hardship which occurs in individual cases,

65. Stephens v. Stephens, 251 Ala. 431, 37 So.2d 918 (1948); In re Marriage of Park, 27 Cal.3d 337, 165 Cal. Rptr. 792, 612 P.2d 882 (1980) (defendant had been deported, either no attorney had been properly appointed to represent her or the attorney who was appointed did virtually nothing on her behalf); Edison v. Edison, 178 Cal.App.2d 632, 3 Cal.Rptr. 201 (1960); Hemphill By and Through Burns v. Hemphill, 316 S.W.2d 582 (Mo.1958); Heine v. Witt, 251 Wis. 157, 28 N.W.2d 248 (1947).

66. Daffin v. Daffin, 567 S.W.2d 672 (Mo.App. 1978).

67. In re Marriage of Adkins, 137 Cal.App.3d 68, 186 Cal.Rptr. 818 (1982); Fraunhofer v. Price, 182 Mont. 7, 594 P.2d 324 (1979).

68. Modnick v. Modnick, 33 Cal.3d 897, 191 Cal.Rptr. 629, 663 P.2d 187 (1983); In re Marriage of Madden, ___ Mont. ___, 683 P.2d 493 (1984).

69. Wescott v. Wescott, 444 So.2d 495 (Fla.App. 1984); Masters v. Smythe, 124 Ill.App.2d 474, 259 N.E.2d 399 (1970), appeal dismissed, cert. denied 401 U.S. 969, 91 S.Ct. 1195, 28 L.Ed.2d 318 (1971); Forney v. Forney, 672 S.W.2d 490 (Tex.App. 1983).

70. E.g. Henderson v. Henderson, 232 N.C. 1, 59 S.E.2d 227 (1950) (decree set aside when it appeared parties had gotten their divorce on the ground of living apart for two years, when in fact they had been living together); Weber v. Weber, 260 Wis. 420, 51 N.W.2d 18 (1952) (dictum that relief against divorce decrees is not limited to extrinsic fraud).

71. Kalmus v. Kalmus, 330 Mass. 41, 110 N.E.2d 760 (1953) (resumption of marital relations and concealment from the court held fraud); Meyer v. Meyer, 326 Mass. 491, 95 N.E.2d 645 (1950) (resumption of marital relations pending decree nisi held fraud); Lantinga v. Lantinga, 318 Mich. 78, 27 N.W.2d 504 (1947) (fraud includes perjury as to cohabitation during suit); Contra: Jones v. Jones, 254 S.W.2d 260 (Mo.App.1953) (resumption of cohabitation not sufficient fraud).

72. De Haan v. De Haan, 348 Mich. 199, 82 N.W.2d 432 (1957) (plaintiff's adultery a fraud on the court); Allen v. Allen, 341 Mich. 543, 67 N.W.2d 805 (1954) (plaintiff pregnant by another man at time of divorce, held fraud); Shammas v. Shammas, 9 N.J. 321, 88 A.2d 204 (1952) (fraud in plaintiff's false denial of adultery at the trial: dictum).

73. Melvin v. Melvin, 73 N.H. 602, 58 A. 835 (1904) (refuses to set divorce aside for collusion). Other cases are collected in Annots., 22 A.L.R.2d 1312, 1333 (1952), and 157 A.L.R. 6, 76 (1945). See also Jacobs, Attack on Decrees of Divorce, 34 Mich.L.Rev. 749, 785 (1936).

74. Schneider v. Schneider, 35 Md.App. 230, 370 A.2d 151 (1977). This case and others insist that divorce decrees should only be set aside where extrinsic fraud in the traditional, limited sense, is proved. See Heathman v. Vant, 172 Cal.App.2d 639, 343 P.2d 104 (1959); Chermak v. Chermak, 227 Ind. 625, 88 N.E.2d 250 (1949);

have been willing to expand the category of extrinsic fraud to include kinds of misrepresentation which would not have been included in the past. Second, the result has been some confusion about definitions and about wise policy. This is particularly evident where the attack on the divorce decree is launched by someone who was not a party to it. Only when some consensus on policy can be reached will this confusion and the consequent conflict in the case law be cleared up.

WESTLAW REFERENCES

sy(vacat! (set setting +1 aside) /s discretion! /s divorc! dissol! /3 order decree)

appeal! /s 60(b) /s divorc! dissol! /3 order decree

coram +1 nobis vobis /s divorc! dissol! /3 order decree

sy(dead death die* dying deceas! remarry! re-marri! /s (set setting +1 aside) vacat! /s fraudulen! fraud /s divorc! dissol!)

to(134) /p valu! /s property /s fraud! /s dissol! divorc!

---

§ 14.7   Responsibilities of Counsel in Divorce Litigation

Introduction [1]

The purpose of this section is to explore some of the aspects of the lawyer's professional functions and responsibilities which are peculiar to marital litigation. No attempt is made to review all of the duties of the lawyer as laid down in the rules and opinions of courts and bar association committees, but these authorities will be referred to where they seem to offer assistance in dealing with the divorce lawyer's ethical problems.

F. v. F., 333 S.W.2d 320 (Mo.App.1960); Wisecup v. Wisecup, 190 Pa.Super. 384, 154 A.2d 332 (1959).

§ 14.7

1. For useful treatment of this subject, see H. O'Gorman, Lawyers and Matrimonial Cases (1963); B. Mortlock, The Inside of Divorce (1972) (dealing with an English solicitor's experience but containing many insights of value to American lawyers); Zacher, The Professional Responsibility of the Lawyer in Divorce, 27 Mo.L. Rev. 466 (1962); Crystal, Ethical Problems in Marital Practice, 30 S.C.L.Rev. 321 (1979).

2. H. O'Gorman, Lawyers and Matrimonial Cases Ch. 5 (1963). For a trenchant account of contemporary attacks on divorce lawyers see Note, Trend Analysis: The

It is a cliche of the profession that a divorce practice confronts the lawyer with more and greater challenges than most other kinds of law practice.[2] There are several reasons for this. The interests at stake in divorce affect the parties' lives more deeply than is the case in other kinds of litigation, except perhaps for criminal cases. The parties themselves recognize that the possibility of divorce threatens their material and psychological security and they arrive at the lawyer's office in a highly nervous and emotional state of mind which often grows more acute as the litigation goes on. The client's uncertainty and consequently his fears are increased because he may have had little or no previous contact with the law and lawyers. His ignorance of the law may, however, be combined with misinformation about divorce received from the Sunday supplements and from well meaning but equally ignorant friends. The result of these circumstances for the divorce lawyer is that the client makes heavy demands upon his time, his professional abilities and upon his own emotional resources. The client expects his lawyer to fill the roles of understanding friend, wise counselor and tireless and effective champion. And if these factors are not enough to discourage the divorce practitioner, there is the well known tendency for contemporary divorce litigants to bring malpractice suits or to file grievances when the result of litigation is not wholly to their satisfaction. The fact that most such suits and grievances are unfounded is cold comfort to the lawyer.[3]

In responding to these challenges the lawyer in divorce must, in addition to exercising

"Changed Landscape" of Divorce Practice as Ethical Minefield, 3 Fam.L.Rptr. 4031 (1977).

3. In Colorado in 1983 the largest percentage of grievances filed concerned domestic relations matters. Of those filed almost seventy-two percent were dismissed. 1983 Annual Report of the Colorado Supreme Court Grievance Committee, 13 Colo. Lawyer 772, 774 (1984). Gates, The Newest Data on Lawyers' Malpractice Claims, April, 1984 Am. Bar Assn.J. 78, shows family law claims to be fourth in rank out of thirteen areas of law. On the family law claims $1,000 or less was paid to 78.5% of the claimants. See also In re Conduct of Taub, 298 Or. 46, 688 P.2d 1332 (1984).

professional competence,[4] bring to the client's problems a considerable amount of psychological insight, as a means of ensuring that the divorce process will be as constructive, even therapeutic, for the client as possible.[5] Relatively early in the case he must attempt to determine what his client really wants and what will best serve the client's interests. What the client says he wants may often be far from what those interests dictate. Making this determination involves counseling, but this does not mean that every divorce lawyer must be ready to function as a marriage counselor. The individual lawyer himself is entitled to decide how much counseling he is willing and able to do and to communicate that decision to his client. To whatever degree he engages in client counseling the lawyer must necessarily be aware of his own emotions and limitations, so that any advice he gives will be responsive to the client's needs rather than a product of his own biases. The lawyer should be ready to refer his client to other professionals in the community when the circumstances suggest that such a referral is necessary.[6] For that purpose he should be familiar with the identities and abilities of physicians, counselors, mental health professionals or others to whom clients might helpfully be referred.

Since divorce is such an emotional experience for the client, the lawyer, if he is to represent his client adequately, must approach the client's case with sympathy and understanding. At the same time all lawyers recognize that clients seldom reveal the entire truth about their affairs to their lawyer. Some skepticism about the client's story is

therefore essential to avoid later surprises and embarrassment. The lawyer must maintain a position which might be described as one of sympathetic objectivity. This is easy to say and extremely difficult to apply to particular situations. The client's statements and claims must be checked and tested without destroying lawyer-client rapport. Maintaining such a delicately balanced approach to the client's problems is especially difficult for the lawyer who undertakes to represent a friend in divorce litigation. For this reason some experienced divorce counsel do not take their friends' divorce cases.[7]

With this brief and necessarily superficial account of some of the predominantly psychological pitfalls of divorce practice, we may turn to more specific applications of the doctrines of professional responsibility to divorce litigation.

Conflicts of Interest [8]

The rules governing the conduct of lawyers contain a variety of prohibitions designed to prevent them from acting in cases in which their own interests or the interests of other clients are likely to prevent them from exercising an independent, unbiased judgment.[9] A lawyer may also be forbidden to act in a case or for a client where his action would involve a breach of confidences acquired in the course of representing other clients.[10] Some applications of these principles to divorce litigation are plain. It is a violation of the rules for an attorney to represent one spouse in a divorce when he is contemporaneously representing the other spouse in another proceeding,[11] especially when the two pro-

---

4. The requirement of professional competence is discussed in detail, infra, at note 47.

5. Elkins, A Counseling Model for Lawyer in Divorce Cases, 53 N. Dame L. 229 (1977), citing many useful non-legal materials; Steinberg, The Therapeutic Potential of the Divorce Process, 62 Am. Bar Assn.J. 617 (1976); Harper and Harper, Lawyers and Marriage Counseling, 1 J.Fam.L. 73 (1961).

6. Sachs, What a Family Lawyer Needs to Know About Psychiatry, 3 Fam.L.Rptr. 4013 (1976) discusses techniques of referral. See also Orten and Wilson, Divorce Applicants: Which Ones Should Go to Marriage Counselors? 35 Okla.L.Rev. 403 (1982).

7. B. Mortlock, The Inside of Divorce 93–100 (1972).

8. The conflicts of interest which may arise in connection with lawyers' engaging in mediation are discussed in section 14.8, infra.

9. A.B.A. Code of Professional Responsibility, Canons 4, 5, 9. The Code will henceforth be cited as ABA Code, followed by the number of the Disciplinary Rule or Ethical Consideration. See also A.B.A. Model Rules of Professional conduct 1.6, 1.7, 1.9. These Rules will henceforth be cited ABA Model Rules, followed by the number of the rule.

10. Ibid.

11. People v. Awenius, 653 P.2d 740 (Colo.1982) (attorney acted improperly by representing a husband in bank-

ceedings bear some relation to each other.[12] These rules create an especial obstacle to the lawyer who wishes to engage in counseling as part of his divorce practice. If he holds conferences with both spouses with a view to reconciliation and they do not become reconciled, he will not be able to represent either of them in a subsequent divorce suit.[13] The reason for this is that in the counseling sessions there is a possibility, often a likelihood, that he will be given confidential information from either or both spouses which should not be used adversely in the divorce proceeding.[14]

The lawyer who has represented one of the spouses in the past is usually also disqualified from representing the other when they later decide to end their marriage. The rule is designed to protect confidential information. The inquiry is not whether the cases or issues are identical or similar, but whether in the prior representation confidential information might reasonably have been disclosed which could be useful against the former client in the present proceeding. The crucial factor in such cases is whether there is either a substantial possibility that knowledge acquired in the former representation could be used

against the former client, or a substantial relationship between the former representation and the divorce.[15] Once the former client has established the subject matter of the former representation by the lawyer, the trial court must determine whether confidential information was likely to have been disclosed to the lawyer in the course of that representation, and if it was, whether that information could be used against the former client in the divorce suit. It is not a defense that there is proof that no confidential information was actually acquired in the course of the earlier representation. It is sufficient that there was a substantial possibility that such information was acquired.[16] Thus where a lawyer drew wills for a husband and wife during the marriage, he could not later represent the husband in the divorce, or where he had represented a family corporation in which the wife held an interest, he likewise could not represent the husband in the subsequent divorce.[17]

What constitutes "representation" for this purpose has been given a broad construction in some cases.[18] These principles apply to the partners and associates of the attorney representing the spouses as well as to the attorney

---

ruptcy at the same time he represented the wife in a divorce having disputed property and custody issues).

12. People ex rel. Cortez v. Calvert, 200 Colo. 157, 617 P.2d 797 (1980) (attorney represented one alleged spouse in a divorce and the other alleged spouse in an annulment at approximately the same time); Matter of Thrush, 448 N.E.2d 1088 (Ind.1983) (prosecuting attorney represented husband in a divorce at a time when the husband was being prosecuted for wife-battering). In Ishmael v. Millington, 241 Cal.App.2d 520, 50 Cal.Rptr. 592 (1966) the husband persuaded his lawyer to represent the wife in their divorce proceeding, the lawyer drafting a separation agreement and purporting to represent the wife in the divorce hearing. When the wife later found the provision for her in the agreement to be inadequate, she sued the husband's lawyer for malpractice. The court held that she had made out a sufficient case to go to a jury, relying to some extent on the conflict of interest.

13. In re Braun, 49 N.J. 16, 227 A.2d 506 (1967). This principle has been criticized on the ground that it prevents a lawyer from conferring with both spouses for the purpose of determining whether reconciliation is possible. Harper and Harper, Lawyers and Marriage Counseling, 1 J.Fam.L. 73 (1961). Of course if permission can be obtained from the lawyer representing the other spouse, such a conference may be held. Without permission the risks of overreaching and misunderstanding are so great that the prohibition seems amply justified even if a chance of reconciliation may be lost.

14. ABA Code, EC 4–5; ABA Model Rules 1.9.

15. Gause v. Gause, 613 P.2d 1257 (Alaska 1980); Woods v. Superior Court of Tulare County, 149 Cal.App. 3d 931, 197 Cal.Rptr. 185 (1983); Cleland v. Cleland, 35 Conn.Supp. 215, 404 A.2d 905 (1979).

16. Cleland v. Cleland, 35 Conn.Supp. 215, 404 A.2d 905 (1979); Buntrock v. Buntrock, 419 So.2d 402 (Fla. App.1982). In re Conduct of Jayne, 295 Or. 16, 663 P.2d 405 (1983) it was held improper for the attorney to represent a husband in divorce after she had represented both husband and wife in a variety of matters in the past. But Gause v. Gause, 613 P.2d 1257 (Alaska 1980) held that a law firm was not disqualified from representing a husband in divorce where it had, a year before, represented the wife in a suit to collect a debt.

17. Woods v. Superior Court of Tulare County, 149 Cal.App.3d 931, 197 Cal.Rptr. 185 (1983); Kurbitz v. Kurbitz, 77 Wash.2d 943, 468 P.2d 673 (1970).

18. King v. King, 52 Ill.App.3d 749, 10 Ill.Dec. 592, 367 N.E.2d 1358 (1977) (attorney-client relationship found, based on one half-hour consultation between spouse and attorney concerning marital problems); Ava H. v. Richard H., 7 Fam.L.Rptr. 2663 (N.Y.Fam.Ct.1981) (where partner in a law firm talked to the wife about her case at a social gathering, the firm could not later represent the husband in a support action).

himself.[19] A related rule requires the lawyer to withdraw from the case when it appears that he will become a witness,[20] although it has been held that this rule does not apply when the lawyer is a litigant representing himself.[21]

In general a representation which involves some conflict of interest on the attorney's part may be undertaken if the client, after being fully informed about all the relevant circumstances, consents to the attorney's conduct.[22] The foregoing discussion has assumed that the client did not consent, and this is the usual situation in conflict of interest cases involving divorce. But there is one difficult kind of case in which there is consent by both spouses, the so-called dual representation case. This arises when both spouses ask an attorney to represent them both as a means of obtaining a divorce with the minimum of expense. When divorce was available only on proof of fault grounds, and collusion was not only a defense but was considered to prejudice the state's interest in enforcing its divorce laws, dual representation was forbidden by some authorities.[23] Today, in those states having non-fault grounds for divorce collusion is no longer a factor in the cases and the state's interest can no longer be said to be hostile to divorce.[24] In some statutes express

authority is given for both spouses to join in the divorce petition, in recognition of the obvious fact that in a majority of cases both spouses want the divorce.[25] In such a case the layman and many clients have some difficulty in understanding why they should have to employ and pay two lawyers rather than one. They also may fear that the effect of two lawyers in the case will be to magnify the disagreements and aggravate hostilities.

Unfortunately, as with many other issues of professional ethics, the matter is not quite so easy to resolve as the layman might suppose. If the attorney makes a misrepresentation to the court concerning the spouse whom he is representing, this is a fraud on the court and warrants setting aside the divorce decree.[26] If the attorney purporting to represent both spouses negligently permits one of the spouses to sign a separation agreement which makes a clearly inadequate provision for her, he may be guilty of a variety of negligence which will lead to a judgment of malpractice.[27] And if there is an *existing* dispute between the spouses concerning, for example, alimony or property, or the custody or support of children, it is clearly improper for an attorney to attempt to represent both.[28] It does not matter in this situation that non-fault grounds for the divorce exist and that both spouses want

19. Buntrock v. Buntrock, 419 So.2d 402 (Fla.App. 1982); In re McCaffrey, 275 Or. 23, 549 P.2d 666 (1976); Kurbitz v. Kurbitz, 77 Wash.2d 943, 468 P.2d 673 (1970); ABA Code DR 5–105(D); ABA Model Rules 1.10(a), 1.12(c). See also Connecticut Bar Association Committee on Professional Ethics, Informal Opinion 81–10, ABA/BNA Lawyers' Manual on Professional Conduct 801:2053. This manual will henceforth be cited ABA/BNA Manual, followed by the page number. This Manual merely abstracts the opinions cited. Since the abstracts are necessarily incomplete and sometimes cursory, the original opinions should be consulted if they are to be relied upon.

20. ABA Code DR 5–102. The reason often given for this rule is that the lawyer who is a witness is more easily impeachable for interest and therefore is less effective as a witness for the client. ABA Code EC 5–9. If this were true, the client himself could not testify. A more cogent reason is that the trier of fact might confuse the lawyer's testimony with his argument, so there is a public interest underlying the rule.

21. Borman v. Borman, 378 Mass. 775, 393 N.E.2d 847 (1979), discussing the purpose and extent of this rule as applied to divorce actions where the contention is that the litigant's law partners should be disqualified.

22. ABA Code DR 5–101(A); ABA Model Rules 1.9(a).

23. Drinker, Problems of Professional Ethics in Matrimonial Litigation, 66 Harv.L.Rev. 443, 452 (1953); Note, Developments in the Law—Conflicts of Interest in the Legal Profession, 94 Harv.L.Rev. 1244, 1311 (1981); Annot., 16 A.L.R. 427 (1922).

24. See the discussion of grounds and defenses in chapter 13, supra, especially sections 13.6 and 13.9.

25. E.g., Uniform Marriage and Divorce Act § 303(c), 9A Unif.L.Ann. 126 (1979).

26. Coulson v. Coulson, 5 Ohio St.3d 12, 448 N.E.2d 809 (1983).

27. Ishmael v. Millington, 241 Cal.App.2d 520, 50 Cal. Rptr. 592 (1966).

28. ABA Code DR 5–105 and EC 5–15. Disciplinary Rule 5–105(C) permits the lawyer to represent multiple clients only if it is "obvious" that he can adequately represent the interests of each. It seems clear that he cannot do this if their interests are presently in conflict. EC 5–15 states that he should never represent in litigation multiple clients with differing interests. To the same effect is Klemm v. Superior Court of Fresno County, 75 Cal.App.3d 893, 142 Cal.Rptr. 509 (1977) (dictum).

to obtain a divorce. The authorities do not agree on whether a different principle should apply where the spouses are indigent and seek to be represented by a public agency, such as a legal aid office or a legal services corporation.[29]

Where there is no *existing* dispute between the spouses, the question of dual representation becomes more difficult. The situation may be one in which there is no property to be divided, no possibility of an alimony award, and no children who can be the object of a custody dispute. In such a case it is difficult to envision potentially differing interests if both wish the divorce, and any insistence that each spouse should have his own lawyer does not seem justified. Nevertheless there are authorities which would say flatly that the lawyer may not represent both spouses.[30]

More commonly there are assets in the marriage which must be divided, or there are funds which might be sufficient for alimony, or there are children whose custody and support must be provided for, but the spouses together request a lawyer to represent them both, telling him that they have reached agreement on financial and custody issues. They may also present him with a written agreement and ask him to "put it in legal form". In this case it is possible to characterize the parties' interests as only "potentially" differing.[31] No broad principle for lawyers' responsibilities in this kind of a case may be derived from the cases or the statements of bar association committees. This is due in part to the importance of differing circumstances and in part to a difference in perception of the risks. Many authorities take the position that representing both parties under such circumstances is improper.[32] Some permit it in strictly limited circumstances where real conflict seems very unlikely.[33] It must be remembered that these authorities usually have the benefit of hindsight. The attorney faced with this problem cannot know whether either of his clients may in the future be dissatisfied with the financial or custody result of the divorce and seek to hold the attorney responsible. Even if a court or grievance committee should eventually absolve him from wrongdoing, the attorney must appreciate the obvious fact that his practice does not benefit from litigation over his own conduct. Therefore, even though one suspects that practitioners often do undertake to represent both spouses in divorce suits, this seems very unwise. Certainly attempting to draft a separation agreement for both spouses is not insu-

29. Holding that the same legal services office may not represent both spouses in divorce: Borden v. Borden, 277 A.2d 89 (D.C.App.1971). But Flores v. Flores, 598 P.2d 893 (Alaska 1979) took the position that the legal services office is not an ordinary law firm and that it could represent both spouses if it could set up strict regulations assuring separate record keeping, separation of offices and restricting access to files. Since no such regulations existed in that case, the court held that one spouse had to be represented by a member of the private bar. See also Michigan State Bar Committee on Professional and Judicial Ethics, Opinion CI–506 (1980), ABA/BNA Manual 801:4802 permitting two branch legal aid offices to represent the spouses in divorce under controlled circumstances.

30. Mississippi State Bar Ethics Committee Opinion 80 (1983), ABA/BNA Manual 801:5104; Colorado Bar Assn. Ethics Committee Formal Opinion 47 (1972) seems to take position that where the parties have no conflicting interests, the lawyer may represent both of them, but that there will be conflicts in most cases.

31. ABA Code EC 5–15 suggests that the lawyer may represent multiple clients with potentially differing interests after carefully weighing the effect upon his judgment and loyalty, but that doubts should be resolved against the propriety of the representation.

32. E.g., Blum v. Blum, 59 Md.App. 584, 477 A.2d 289 (1984); Matter of Marriage of Eltzroth, 67 Or.App. 520, 679 P.2d 1369 (1984); Mississippi State Bar Ethics Committee Opinion 80 (1983), ABA/BNA Manual 801:5104; State Bar of Wisconsin Committee on Professional Ethics Opinion E–84–3 (1984), ABA/BNA Manual 801:9111. See also Ishmael v. Millington, 241 Cal.App.2d 520, 50 Cal. Rptr. 592 (1966).

33. Klemm v. Superior Court of Fresno County, 75 Cal.App.3d 893, 142 Cal.Rptr. 509 (1977) permitted the attorney to represent both spouses after they consented in writing where no property was involved, child support was waived and an agreement for joint custody had been made, describing any conflict as "only potential". Halvorsen v. Halvorsen, 3 Wash.App. 827, 479 P.2d 161 (1970) also approved a dual representation, where a large amount of property was involved, as did Levine v. Levine, 56 N.Y.2d 42, 451 N.Y.S.2d 26, 436 N.E.2d 476 (1982). See also State Bar of Montana Ethics Committee Opinion 10 (1980), ABA/BNA Manual 801:5401; New York State Bar Association Committee on Professional Ethics Opinion 478 (1978), 4 Fam.L.Rptr. 2333; District of Columbia Bar Association Ethics Committee Opinion 143 (1984), 11 Fam.L.Rptr. 1101.

lated from criticism by characterizing the attorney's position as merely that of a "scribe" or a "scrivener".[34] At the very least the attorney who undertakes a dual representation should first obtain the written consent of both spouses after describing in writing the potential conflicts of interest and the effect on the parties' rights of any action which might be taken.[35]

One other conflict of interest frequently encountered in divorce concerns the relationship between the attorney for one spouse and the other spouse. It is of course clear that an attorney may not communicate with the opposing party in the case if that party is represented by an attorney.[36] But the opposing spouse in some divorce cases, out of a desire to save expenses or for other reasons, may choose not to be represented. The question is whether the lawyer for one spouse may properly negotiate with the opposing spouse when that spouse is not represented. If he does so, he may be accused of taking advantage of superior legal knowledge or of giving legal advice to the opposing spouse. But if the financial or custody aspects of the divorce can be agreed upon, the statutes of many states

encourage the parties to do so.[37] Under those circumstances some communication between the attorney and the opposing spouse must of necessity occur in spite of some risks for the attorney. The authorities seem to permit this provided that the attorney does not give advice to the spouse other than to advise him to obtain counsel.[38] But there is some authority that the attorney cannot engage in negotiations with the other spouse.[39] This restriction seems highly undesirable in view of the policy favoring the amicable settlement of divorce actions.[40]

Where the divorce suit involves the issue of custody of children, a unique potential for conflict of interests arises. It was traditionally assumed that the interests of children in divorce would be safeguarded either by their parents and the parents' attorneys or by the court itself exercising its *parens patriae* function.[41] Many commentators have criticized these assumptions, taking the position that separate legal counsel for the children should be obtained, at the parents' expense where possible and at the state's expense where necessary.[42] Some states have enacted legislation authorizing the appointment of counsel

34. Blum v. Blum, 59 Md.App. 584, 477 A.2d 289 (1984), stating that the attorney should have discussed the possible implications of the separation agreement and should have considered whether the agreement was unfair, even if he was only acting as a "scribe". See also Matter of Marriage of Eltzroth, 67 Or.App. 520, 679 P.2d 1369 (1984) and Kosik v. George, 253 Or. 15, 452 P.2d 560 (1969) (antenuptial agreement).

35. Klemm v. Superior Court of Fresno County, 75 Cal.App.3d 893, 142 Cal.Rptr. 509 (1977). The attorney should also advise the spouses in writing of the desirability of being individually represented by counsel of their own choosing.

36. ABA Code DR 7–104(A)(1). See also People v. Selby, 156 Colo. 17, 396 P.2d 598 (1964); In re Marietta, 223 Kan. 11, 569 P.2d 921 (1977); State v. Thompson, 206 Kan. 326, 478 P.2d 208 (1970); In re McCaffrey, 275 Or. 23, 549 P.2d 666 (1976). See also ABA Model Rules 4.2; Crystal, Ethical Problems in Marital Practice, 30 S.C.L. Rev. 321, 356 (1979).

37. Uniform Marriage and Divorce Act § 306, and Commissioners' Note, 9A Unif.L.Ann. 135 (1979).

38. ABA Code DR 7–104(A)(2), EC 7–18; ABA Model Rules 4.3. New York State Bar Association Committee on Professional Ethics Opinion 478 (1978), 4 Fam.L.Rptr. 2233 states that the lawyer may prepare a separation agreement negotiated by the parties themselves if he acts

only as a scrivener, and can transmit it to an unrepresented opposing spouse for signature. It also states that where the divorce is actually the subject of litigation, the lawyer may negotiate with the unrepresented opposing spouse.

39. American Bar Association Formal Opinion 58 (1931). This opinion may reflect the view taken in earlier times that separation agreements and the settlement of divorce litigation was not favored because of suspicion of collusion.

40. Crystal, Ethical Problems in Marital Practice, 30 S.C.L.Rev. 321, 354 (1979). See also Davidson v. Davidson, 92 Cal.App.2d 809, 204 P.2d 71 (1949).

41. An extreme example of this assumption is Yarborough v. Yarborough, 290 U.S. 202, 54 S.Ct. 181, 78 L.Ed. 269 (1933), in which a child was held bound by a support decree when she had not been represented or made a party to the suit.

42. Foster and Freed, A Bill of Rights for Children, 6 Fam.L.Q. 343 (1972); Berdon, A Child's Right to Counsel in a Contested Custody Proceeding Resulting from a Termination of the Marriage, 50 Conn.B.J. 150 (1976); Note, A Child's Due Process Right to Counsel in Divorce Custody Proceedings, 27 Hast.L.J. 917 (1976); Note, Lawyering for the Child: Principles of Representation in Custody and Visitation Disputes Arising from Divorce, 87 Yale L.J. 1126 (1978).

for children in divorce suits.[43] The additional expense, the complications and delays in trials caused by the introduction of a third lawyer into the proceeding give rise to serious doubt whether the appointment of a lawyer for the children is either necessary or wise in most custody cases.[44] It seems likely that the parents' counsel usually will make all the arguments and present all the evidence which are relevant to the custody issue.[45] In addition there seems to be confusion in the minds of many lawyers appointed to represent children about their roles in such proceedings, whether they are to be mediators, advocates, counselors or fact finders.[46]

Competence

The lawyer who represents a client in a domestic relations case has the same obligation to exercise reasonable skill, diligence and care as lawyers in other types of representation.[47] This is sometimes expressed as a requirement that the lawyer must use that degree of care, skill and diligence which is commonly possessed and exercised by lawyers in practice in the jurisdiction.[48] If his legal knowledge is questioned, he must possess knowledge of the plain and elementary principles known to other well informed lawyers and must undertake reasonable research to discover other less well known principles.[49] None of these general statements is very helpful in defining the extent of his obligation in specific circumstances, however.

The question of competence usually arises in suits against the lawyer for professional malpractice.[50] In such suits four factors must be established in order to hold the lawyer responsible: a) That the lawyer and client relationship existed; b) That the lawyer acted negligently; c) That the client was damaged; d) That the lawyer's negligence was the proximate cause of the client's damage.[51] Although the lawyer-client relationship may arise out of a single interview,[52] it has been held that in divorce litigation the lawyer is responsible only to the litigant whom he represents and not to the children of the marriage.[53]

Somewhat greater precision in defining professional negligence in the divorce context may be arrived at by looking at individual cases. Some of these cases reveal such obvious examples of negligence as failing to notify a client about a hearing and failing to appear,[54] failing to have the divorce decree entered until after the client had entered a second marriage,[55] or completely failing to

43. E.g., Colo.Rev.Stat. § 14–10–116 (1974); Ill. Ann. Stat. ch. 40, § 506 (Supp.1986); Wis. Stat. Ann. § 767.045 (1981).

44. Dembitz, Beyond Any Discipline's Competence, 83 Yale L.J. 1304, 1312 (1974).

45. For a case in which the parents apparently did not adequately protect the children's interests, see Pelham v. Griesheimer, 92 Ill.2d 13, 64 Ill.Dec. 544, 440 N.E.2d 96 (1982).

46. Note, Lawyering for the Child: Principles of Representation in Custody and Visitation Disputes Arising from Divorce, 87 Yale L.J. 1126 (1978).

47. Smith v. Lewis, 13 Cal.3d 349, 118 Cal.Rptr. 621, 530 P.2d 589 (1975). The general principle is stated somewhat inadequately by ABA Code DR 6–101 and EC 6–1. See also ABA Model Rules 1.1.

48. Spalding v. Davis, 674 S.W.2d 710 (Tenn. 1984).

49. Smith v. Lewis, 13 Cal.3d 349, 118 Cal.Rptr. 621, 530 P.2d 589 (1975).

50. Professional negligence may also be the subject of disciplinary proceedings. Cases are collected in Annot., 96 A.L.R.2d 823, 866 (1964).

51. Togstad v. Vesely, Otto, Miller & Keefe, 291 N.W.2d 686 (Minn.1980). Dunn v. McKay, Burton, McMurray & Thurman, 584 P.2d 894 (Utah 1978) held that the plaintiff could not recover where she failed to prove that her injury was not proximately caused by the defendant's negligence. See also Anderson v. Anderson, 399 N.E.2d 391 (Ind.App.1979).

52. Togstad v. Vesely, Otto, Miller & Keefe, 291 N.W.2d 686 (Minn.1980) (wife became a client of a lawyer whom she consulted once about a possible consortium claim).

53. Pelham v. Griesheimer, 92 Ill.2d 13, 64 Ill.Dec. 544, 440 N.E.2d 96 (1982). The court here also rejected the contention that the children were third party beneficiaries of the attorney-client contract, although it seemed to concede that they might become so under some circumstances.

54. Kuehn v. Garcia, 608 F.2d 1143 (8th Cir.1979), cert. denied 445 U.S. 943, 100 S.Ct. 1340, 63 L.Ed.2d 777 (1980), following Matter of Garcia, 243 N.W.2d 383 (N.D.1976).

55. In re Johnson, 93 Ill.2d 441, 67 Ill.Dec. 114, 444 N.E.2d 153 (1982).

perform any services at all.[56] Advice which is plainly erroneous is also negligence.[57] Although an attorney has authority by virtue of his representation of a client to make stipulations or agreements concerning procedure, he may not do so when the effect is to relinquish a substantial substantive right of his client.[58] Since the attorney is a fiduciary for his client, he may not violate that fiduciary relation for financial or other advantage to himself.[59] The attorney may be held negligent in not investigating the extent of the defendant spouse's property so that his client received only an inadequate share of that property on the divorce.[60]

The duty of the lawyer when faced with an emerging or doubtful legal problem is outlined by the influential case of Smith v. Lewis.[61] The lawyer in this case represented a wife seeking a divorce from a husband who was entitled to both state and federal pensions. The state pension was already being paid in monthly installments at the time of divorce but the federal pension, earned by military service, was vested but not matured. The attorney advised his client that neither pension formed part of community property and no claim for a share of them was made in the divorce proceeding.[62] The California Supreme Court held that since at the time of the divorce vested retirement benefits were clearly held to be community property subject to division on divorce, the jury's verdict of negli-

gence against the attorney and the judgment thereon should be affirmed. The court said that although a lawyer does not guarantee the correctness of his opinions and is not responsible for every mistake he might make in practice, and although he is not responsible for failing to anticipate how uncertainties in the law will be resolved, in this case the answer to the issue concerning the status of the state pension was clear. And although the status of the federal military pension was perhaps not so clear, the attorney had a duty to undertake reasonable research in order to arrive at an informed decision on that status. This he did not do. He assumed the duty to become familiar with the legal status of retirement benefits when he agreed to represent the wife and he gave erroneous advice without doing research in readily available sources. The irony of this case is that as things later turned out, federal military pensions were not community property until Congress changed the law in 1982.[63]

Compliance With the Law and Respect for the Courts

In the days when divorces were granted only on proof of the fault grounds and when the defenses of collusion, connivance and recrimination still existed, it was held to be unethical for a lawyer to assist his client to obtain a divorce by fabricating grounds or to obtain a divorce by collusion.[64] This sort of

---

56. Cases are collected in Annot., 96 A.L.R.2d 823, 866 (1964).

57. Pinkerton v. West, 353 So.2d 102 (Fla.App.1977), cert. denied 365 So.2d 715 (Fla.1978). Other cases are cited in Annot., 78 A.L.R.3d 255, 261 (1977). A mistake in effecting service may be considered negligence according to the dissent in Dunn v. McKay, Burton, McMurray & Thurman, 584 P.2d 894, 899 (Utah 1978).

58. Linsk v. Linsk, 70 Cal.2d 272, 74 Cal.Rptr. 544, 449 P.2d 760 (1969).

59. Barbara A. v. John G., 145 Cal.App.3d 369, 193 Cal.Rptr. 422 (1983).

60. Ishmael v. Millington, 241 Cal.App.2d 520, 50 Cal.Rptr. 592 (1966). See also Annot., Legal Malpractice in Settling or Failing to Settle Client's Case, 87 A.L.R.3d 168, 173, 177 (1978).

61. 13 Cal.3d 349, 118 Cal.Rptr. 621, 530 P.2d 589 (1975).

62. At the request of the client the attorney attempted to have the divorce decree amended on the

ground of mistake, inadvertence, and excusable neglect, but the court denied his motion. Following this the wife brought her malpractice action against the attorney.

63. For a discussion of the confusing development of the law on the divisibility in divorce of federal military pensions, see section infra. A rash of lower court cases on malpractice reflect this confusion. Sharpe v. Superior Court, 143 Cal.App.3d 469, 192 Cal.Rptr. 16 (1983) (attorney is not liable when he inadvertently gave correct legal advice); Jones v. Stevenson, 149 Cal.App.3d 560, 197 Cal. Rptr. 25 (1983) (same result as in Sharpe); Ruchti v. Goldfein, 113 Cal.App.3d 928, 170 Cal.Rptr. 375 (1980) (attorney not negligent in not foreseeing a change in the law respecting non-vested pensions); Gorman v. Gorman, 90 Cal.App.3d 454, 153 Cal.Rptr. 479 (1979) (attorney liable for malpractice in not obtaining for a wife a share in the husband's military retirement benefits).

64. Drinker, Problems of Professional Ethics in Matrimonial Litigation, 66 Harv.L. 443, 445–454 (1953). Annot., 13 A.L.R.3d 1010 (1967).

conduct was considered to constitute a fraud on the court and was not infrequently the subject of disciplinary proceedings.[65] Now that the nonfault grounds are so prevalent there is much less likelihood that these forms of unethical conduct will occur, but in those states where the old grounds and defenses are still occasionally relied upon [66] attorneys should be careful not to engage in these violations of ethics.

The attorney who assisted a client to obtain a migratory divorce on the basis of temporary residence in a state like Nevada or a foreign jurisdiction like Mexico [67] or Haiti or the Dominican Republic also was engaging in conduct considered unethical by the authorities.[68] There were two objections to the attorney's participation in migratory divorce. It aided the client to evade the law and policy of his home state and it resulted in the client's misrepresenting his domicile to the other state.[69] Some fine lines had to be drawn in dealing with the issue, however. It seemed reasonably clear that the attorney was entitled to advise his client on the legal consequences which might be expected to follow from a migratory divorce and from remarriage after such a divorce.[70] Usually that advice ought to have included a warning that migratory divorce was inadvisable because open to attack in the home state under some circumstances.[71] The attorney was thus placed in the uncomfortable position of being able to give advice but not being able to counsel or assist the client in obtaining the migratory divorce, not always an easy distinction to make.[72] These risks are now not so frequently encountered since migratory divorce is less often resorted to, but the attorney who advises divorce clients should be aware of them.

As the preceding paragraphs make plain, the attorney in divorce who makes false statements to the court or presents perjured testimony is guilty of unethical conduct.[73] When the client, without the acquiescence or participation of the lawyer, testifies falsely or engages in other forms of misrepresentation or fraud, the attorney is faced with what appears to be a pair of inconsistent, not to say contradictory precepts. One of them tells him that he must preserve the confidences of his client.[74] In most instances the client's falsehoods will be revealed to the attorney in the course of their confidential relationship. The other precept tells the attorney that when a fraud has been perpetrated upon a person or court, he must seek to have the client rectify the fraud. If the client refuses, the lawyer must reveal the fraud to the person or court unless the information is protected as privileged.[75] As is so often the case the rules of the American Bar Association do not answer the crucial question, which is, is the information privileged. It has been persuasively argued that in this sort of case the information normally would be privileged and therefore should not be revealed by the attorney to the person or the court defrauded.[76] The Oregon Supreme Court has ruled that this is the

---

65. In re Backes, 16 N.J. 430, 109 A.2d 273 (1954) (per Wm. J. Brennan, J.).

66. For a discussion of the fault grounds and defenses, see chapter 13, supra. See also Crystal, Ethical Problems in Marital Practice, 30 S.C.L.Rev. 321, 338 (1979).

67. Mexico is no longer available for migratory divorces. See section 12.2, supra.

68. The authorities, many of them dating from the past when the divorce law and policy were very different from their present condition, are collected in Drinker, Problems of Professional Ethics in Matrimonial Litigation, 66 Harv.L.Rev. 443, 454 (1953); Adams and Adams, Ethical Problems in Advising Migratory Divorce, 16 Hast. L.J. 60 (1964); Crystal, Ethical Problems in Marital Practice, 30 S.C.L.Rev. 321, 340 (1979); Annot., 13 A.L.R.3d 1010 (1967); Nappe v. Nappe, 20 N.J. 337, 120 A.2d 31 (1956).

69. See ABA Code DR 7–102(A)(7).

70. Adams and Adams, Ethical Problems in Advising Migratory Divorce, 16 Hast.L.J. 60 (1964). But see In re Feltman, 51 N.J. 27, 237 A.2d 473 (1968).

71. See sections 12.2 and 12.3, supra.

72. Crystal, Ethical Problems in Marital Practice, 30 S.C.L.Rev. 321, 341 (1979).

73. ABA Code DR 7–102(A)(4), (5), (6), (7). See also ABA Model Rules 3.3. An attorney who files contradictory affidavits and engages in other delaying or harassing tactics may be subject to discipline. Eberly v. Eberly, 489 A.2d 433 (Del.1985).

74. ABA Code DR 4–101. See also ABA Model Rules 1.6.

75. ABA Code DR 7–102(B)(1).

76. Crystal, Ethical Problems in Marital Practice, 30 S.C.L.Rev. 321, 348–351 (1979). American Bar Assn. Formal Opinions 287 and 341 (1953 and 1975) agree. But

correct result, but has also held that the attorney in this situation should withdraw from further representation of the client.[77] This leads one to wonder just what the attorney is to say to the court if he is asked why he wishes to withdraw or if the court refuses to permit withdrawal.[78]

The conflict between the preservation of client confidences and the duty to be forthright and candid with the court has been especially acute in divorce actions where a spouse attempts to conceal his or her whereabouts. The attorney, who has learned where the client is in confidence, is then asked to reveal the information to the court. Not surprisingly, the courts have not been able to arrive at a very satisfactory resolution of the conflict. Such cases as there are seem to make the result turn on the client's intentions in remaining in hiding. If the client is a wife who is hiding from her husband because she fears for her safety, her attorney need not reveal her address to the court.[79] On the other hand if the client is hiding in order to frustrate the enforcement of a custody or child support order, the attorney has been

held to have a duty to reveal his whereabouts.[80] There is little real distinction between these cases and the cases in which the client has committed a fraud on another person or on the court.[81] In both cases the privilege for confidential communications between lawyer and client is relied on to prevent the rectification of a continuing injury to someone. Sophisticated arguments about the importance of the privilege often sound lame when measured against the obvious fact that the law is permitting a wrong to go unredressed.

As has been indicated in a prior section,[82] a parent who takes his child from the custody of the other parent in violation of a court order may be engaging in a tort and may also be criminally responsible under the law of most states. It follows that an attorney who counsels or assists his client to remove his child from the custody of the other parent in such circumstances is guilty of a serious breach of professional ethics.[83] Where there is no outstanding custody order, the impropriety of such advice is less clear. But both the Uniform Child Custody Jurisdiction Act and

---

the Kutak Rules seem to take the position that the attorney must reveal the fraud to the court. ABA Model Rules 3.3, Comment.

77. In re A, 276 Or. 225, 554 P.2d 479 (1976). In the divorce case the attorney represented the husband who lied to the court about some property's status and refused to rectify the fraud when the attorney requested him to do so. The court took notice of the conflict between the rules and held that client confidence should be respected in this case but that the attorney should withdraw. The attorney was not subjected to disciplinary action, however, because of the unsettled nature of the rules. In Livingston v. Livingston, 572 P.2d 79 (Alaska 1977) the court held that counsel's failure to disclose to the court that the child whose custody was in issue had been at all times living in Oregon, thereby depriving Alaska of custody jurisdiction, did not constitute a fraud on the court.

78. ABA Model Rules 1.16, Comment, states: "The lawyer's statement that professional considerations require termination of the representation ordinarily should be accepted as sufficient."

79. Taylor v. Taylor, 45 Ill.App.3d 352, 3 Ill.Dec. 961, 359 N.E.2d 820 (1977); Waldmann v. Waldmann, 48 Ohio St.2d 176, 358 N.E.2d 521 (1976) (semble, also indicating that the person asserting the privilege has the burden of proof).

80. Matter of Jacqueline F., 47 N.Y.2d 215, 417 N.Y.S.2d 884, 391 N.E.2d 967 (1979) (attorney for child's aunt not privileged to reveal the aunt's address where she was keeping the child in violation of a custody order);

Lemley v. Kaiser, 6 Ohio St.3d 258, 452 N.E.2d 1304 (1983) (adoptive parents' attorney ordered to return the child or reveal his location); Fellerman v. Bradley, 192 N.J.Super. 556, 471 A.2d 788 (1983), certification granted 96 N.J. 280, 475 A.2d 579 (1984) (husband's attorney not privileged not to reveal the client's address where the client was avoiding the payment of accountant's fees in divorce).

In Brennan v. Brennan, 281 Pa.Super. 362, 422 A.2d 510 (1980) the court refused to hold a lawyer in contempt for refusing to reveal his client's location even though the client was apparently evading a custody order, but seemed to leave the case open for the plaintiff to show that the interests of justice were being frustrated, whatever that might mean. This case also held that the burden of proof is on the party attacking the privilege.

81. See the text at note 76, supra.

82. See section 11.2, supra.

83. ABA Code DR 7–102(A)(7); Attorney Grievance Commission of Maryland v. Kerpelman, 288 Md. 341, 420 A.2d 940 (1980), cert. denied 450 U.S. 970, 101 S.Ct. 1492, 67 L.Ed.2d 621 (1981). But see the extraordinary case of Maryland Attorney Grievance Commission v. Sait, 301 Md. 238, 482 A.2d 898 (1984), in which a lawyer who was present during the abduction of his client's child by private detectives was held guilty of no breach of ethics although fraud and an assault occurred in the course of the operation. The trial court in this case held that no attorney-client relationship had been formed, but that seems erroneous under the circumstances.

the Parental Kidnapping Prevention Act of 1980 emphasize the orderly handling of custody disputes and strongly indicate disapproval of child-snatching in all its forms.[84] In view of these Acts an attorney who counsels or assists in such conduct even before a proceeding has been brought or a decree obtained would seem to be on doubtful ground. If he is not assisting in illegal conduct, he is at least assisting in conduct which is inconsistent with the policy of all states. His conduct therefore gives the appearance of impropriety.[85]

In their zeal to obtain evidence, lawyers in divorce cases sometimes advise their clients to resort to various forms of interception of communications between their spouses and others. A substantial number of cases have held that wiretapping of this kind is unlawful under a federal statute [86] although others have found an implied exception to the statute for the communications of spouses in the home in the course of domestic conflicts.[87] Given the uncertain legality of such wiretaps, it seems improper for lawyers to counsel their clients or agents of the clients to engage in the practice.[88]

Fees

As in other cases, the attorney in divorce should not charge an excessive fee.[89] Where the fee is questioned, its reasonableness is a matter for the sound discretion of the trial court.[90] Factors which enter into the evaluation of the fee include the time spent on the case, the attorney's skill and standing as a lawyer, the nature of the case, the novelty and difficulty of the issues in it, the importance of the subject matter, the degree of responsibility involved, the usual charge for such cases, and the benefits achieved for the client.[91] Where the fee is reasonable, it may be secured by an attorney's lien.[92] In most states the attorney is held to be responsible for the fees of experts employed by him to testify or otherwise assist in the litigation.[93]

The magnitude of the fee in a divorce case is a matter of more importance than might be true in other cases because very often the client has only limited resources but at the same time is likely to make heavy demands on the time and energy of the lawyer. To some extent the difficulty is mitigated by competition among lawyers, some of whom

Where the lawyer himself is a litigant in divorce and violates the decree, he may be subject to discipline. People v. Kane, 655 P.2d 390 (Colo. 1982) (repeated failure to pay child support resulting in a contempt conviction held to violate ABA Code DR 1–102.)

84. These statutes are cited and extensively discussed in section 12.5, supra.

85. ABA Code EC 9–6.

86. Pritchard v. Pritchard, 732 F.2d 372 (4th Cir. 1984); United States v. Rizzo, 583 F.2d 907 (7th Cir.1978), cert. denied 440 U.S. 908, 99 S.Ct. 1216, 59 L.Ed.2d 456 (1979); United States v. Jones, 542 F.2d 661 (6th Cir. 1976), appeal after remand 580 F.2d 219 (1978); Kratz v. Kratz, 477 F.Supp. 463 (E.D.Pa.1979), 53 Temp.L.Q. 451 (1980) (the husband's lawyer was also a defendant in this case). The federal statute is Title III of the Omnibus Crime Control and Safe Streets Act of 1968, principally 18 U.S.C.A. § 2511 (1982). Cases on the question are collected in Annot., 55 A.L.R.Fed. 936 (1981). Stamme v. Stamme, 589 S.W.2d 50 (Mo.App.1979) held that evidence acquired in this way was not admissible in the divorce proceeding.

An attorney was disciplined partly on the ground that he covertly taped conversations with a judge in chambers in People v. Selby, 198 Colo. 386, 606 P.2d 45 (1979), in which the court said: "A lawyer may not secretly record any conversation he has with another lawyer or person. Candor is required between attorneys and judges. Surreptitious recording suggests trickery and deceit."

87. Anonymous v. Anonymous, 558 F.2d 677 (2d Cir. 1977); Simpson v. Simpson, 490 F.2d 803 (5th Cir.1974), cert. denied 419 U.S. 897, 95 S.Ct. 176, 42 L.Ed.2d 141 (1974).

88. ABA Code DR 7–102(A)(7).

89. ABA Code DR 2–106; McInerney v. Massasoit Greyhound Association, 359 Mass. 339, 269 N.E.2d 211 (1971). See also ABA Model Rules 1.5.

90. Ransom v. Ransom, 102 Ill.App.3d 38, 57 Ill.Dec. 696, 429 N.E.2d 594 (1981).

91. Ransom v. Ransom, 102 Ill.App.3d 38, 57 Ill.Dec. 696, 429 N.E.2d 594 (1981); McInerney v. Massasoit Greyhound Association, 359 Mass. 339, 269 N.E.2d 211 (1971).

92. In re Marriage of Mostow, 126 Ill.App.3d 67, 81 Ill. Dec. 490, 466 N.E.2d 1292 (1984); Campanello v. Mason, 571 P.2d 449 (Okl.1977). But it has been held that an attorney may not enforce a charging lien against a child support award, in Brake v. Sanchez-Lopez, 452 So.2d 1071 (Fla.App.1984).

93. Theuerkauf v. Sutton, 102 Wis.2d 176, 306 N.W.2d 651 (1981), citing other cases.

advertise their fees [94] and by the availability of legal services offices,[95] but the price of a divorce is still a source of hardship for many middle class clients.

Another device which is sometimes advocated as a way of making legal services more readily available to divorce clients is the contingent fee. Although the American Bar Association's Code takes an equivocal position on the propriety of contingent fees in divorce,[96] most of the cases and bar committee pronouncements continue to insist that such fee arrangements are improper when used in connection with divorce litigation.[97] The reasons given are that the contingent fee promotes divorce by giving the lawyer an incentive to discourage or block reconciliations; that its effect may be to bargain away part of the alimony in advance, thereby leaving the client without sufficient support; and that it is likely to result in excessive fees because divorce clients are unlikely to understand the arrangement and are particularly vulnerable.[98] Most of these reasons are not convincing, except for the last.[99] It does appear likely that if contingent fees were customary in divorce, on some occasions the fees would be excessive. Unlike the circumstances in personal injury litigation, there is relatively little property or alimony at stake in most divorces and therefore contingent fees would offer little help to plaintiffs in obtaining representation.

Where some or all of the reasons for condemning contingent fees do not apply, as where, by virtue of the defendant spouse's long absence there is no possibility of reconciliation, where the claim is for past due alimony or child support,[1] or where the plaintiff is suing for property on a claim which he could make absent the divorce,[2] the courts have sometimes been willing to enforce contingent fee contracts. And even where the contingent fee is unenforceable, the attorney may be entitled to a fee for his services based upon quantum meruit.[3]

Do-It-Yourself Divorce

In those states where marriage breakdown or its equivalent is the ground for divorce, a

94. Pagel, A Proposal for Reducing the Cost of Legal Representation in Divorce Proceedings, 11 Willamette L.Rev. 344 (1975).

95. Goldberger, Legal Aid Divorces—A Practical Approach, 20 American U.L.Rev. 30 (1970).

96. ABA Code EC 2–20: "Because of the human relationships involved and the unique character of the proceedings, contingent fee arrangements in domestic relations cases are rarely justified." ABA Model Rules 1.5(d) (1) would forbid contingent fees in domestic relations matters.

97. Avant v. Whitten, 253 So.2d 394 (Miss.1971), 43 Miss.L.Rev. 406 (1972); Thompson v. Thompson, 313 N.C. 313, 328 S.E.2d 288 (1985); Hay v. Erwin, 244 Or. 488, 419 P.2d 32 (1966). Other cases are cited in Annot., 93 A.L.R.3d 523, 526 (1979) and in Note, Professional Responsibility—Contingent Fees in Domestic Relations Actions: Equal Freedom to Contract for the Domestic Relations Bar, 62 N.C.L.Rev. 381 (1984). State bar associations generally continue to condemn contingent fee contracts in divorce. See, e.g., Committee on Rules of Professional Conduct, State Bar of Arizona Opinion 82–9 (1982), ABA/BNA Manual 801:1312; Ethics Committee of the State Bar of Montana Opinion 11 (1980), ABA/BNA Manual 801:5401; Committee on Professional Ethics, The New York County Lawyers' Association Opinion 660 (1984), ABA/BNA Manual 801:6501; Virginia State Bar Council Opinion 423 (1983), ABA/BNA Manual 801:8806.

98. Barelli v. Levin, 144 Ind.App. 576, 247 N.E.2d 847 (1969); Thompson v. Thompson, 70 N.C.App. 147, 319 S.E.2d 315 (1984). The cases emphasize the supposed tendency of contingent fees to discourage reconciliation. The same reasons have persuaded some courts to forbid nonrefundable retainers in divorce proceedings. Volkell v. Volkell, 10 Fam.L.Rptr. 1574 (N.Y.Sup.Ct.1984).

99. Arguing that none of these reasons is convincing is Note, Professional Responsibility—Contingent Fees in Domestic Relations Actions: Equal Freedom to Contract for the Domestic Relations Bar, 62 N.C.L.Rev. 381 (1984).

A case which illustrates excessive fees in divorce actions is Matter of Disciplinary Proceedings Against Kinast, 121 Wis.2d 25, 357 N.W.2d 282 (1984).

1. Burns v. Stewart, 290 Minn. 289, 188 N.W.2d 760 (1971), 56 Minn.L.Rev. 979 (1972); Colorado Bar Association Ethics Committee Formal Opinion 67 (1985), citing cases.

2. Smith v. Armstrong & Murphy, 181 Okl. 293, 73 P.2d 140 (1937). See also Committee on Rules of Professional Conduct, State Bar of Arizona Opinion 82–9 (1982), ABA/BNA Manual 801:1312; Professional Ethics Committee of the Kansas Bar Association Opinion 80–33 (1980), ABA/BNA Manual 801:3803; Committee on Professional and Judicial Ethics of the State Bar of Michigan Opinions C–72, CI–620, CI–712, CI–828 (1983), ABA/BNA Manual 801:4862; Committee on Professional Ethics, The New York County Lawyers' Association Opinion 660 (1984), and Kraus v. Naumburg, 13 Bucks 547 (C. P. Bucks County Pa.1964), criticized in Note, 113 U.Pa.L. Rev. 278 (1964).

3. Morfeld v. Andrews, 579 P.2d 426 (Wyo.1978), citing other cases; Annot., 100 A.L.R.2d 1378, 1390 (1965).

substantial number of persons obtain their divorces without the help of a lawyer, sometimes with the help of a "divorce kit", a book containing instructions and copies of the necessary forms. Although it has been argued that this practice does not result in less satisfactory divorce dispositions than do cases where the parties are represented by lawyers,[4] it does involve risks to the individuals involved which are far from negligible.[5] The risks are not substantially reduced when the divorce is uncontested. The uncontested divorce may often occur after an agreement about property or support which is seriously unfair to one or the other of the parties because of his ignorance either of the law, or of the facts concerning the nature and value of the property concerned. There may also be public costs in pro se divorces which could be avoided if the parties were represented.[6] The criticisms which have been directed at the legal profession's performance in divorce cases[7] can better be met by improving the skill, knowledge, efficiency and sensitivity of the divorce bar than by encouraging litigants to represent themselves in divorce actions.

It is generally agreed that the publication and sale of divorce kits by laymen does not constitute the unauthorized practice of law,[8]

but that unauthorized practice does occur when laymen not only publish the divorce kits but offer advice and assistance to particular individuals in particular situations for the purpose of helping them to obtain divorces.[9] The shortage of lawyers or the unavailability of legal advice for middle income clients has led some commentators to urge that laymen should be permitted to assist individuals in this way without being prosecuted for unlawful practice.[10] What has been said about the risks of pro se divorces applies to this argument as well. The further expansion of legal services offices and of the practice in some of those offices of assisting clients to bring their own cases and of negotiating and drafting agreements are more effective ways of providing representation for divorce litigants than opening the field to laymen. One wonders whether the apparent willingness to let laymen handle some divorce cases reflects the misconception, popular among some elements of the bar, that domestic relations matters involve few legal complexities.

 **WESTLAW REFERENCES**

Conflicts of Interest

conflict +2 interest /s divorc! dissol! /s attorney lawyer counsel

---

4. Note, The Unauthorized Practice of Law and Pro Se Divorce: An Empirical Analysis, 88 Yale L.J. 104 (1976) analyzing the responses to questionnaires submitted to lawyers and divorce clients, comparing the effectiveness of representation with the experiences of those who obtained their own divorces, generally to the disadvantage of the lawyers.

5. Kelley v. Kelley, 73 Cal.App.3d 672, 141 Cal.Rptr. 33 (1977), in which a wife failed to claim part of her husband's military pension in her pro se divorce and was held to have no recourse in a later claim. The case was overruled by Henn v. Henn, 26 Cal.3d 323, 161 Cal.Rptr. 502, 605 P.2d 10 (1980) on the issue of res judicata. See also In re Marriage of Eller, 38 Colo.App. 74, 552 P.2d 30 (1976).

6. Board of County Commissioners of Boulder County v. Barday, 197 Colo. 519, 594 P.2d 1057 (1979), enjoining a husband from proceeding pro se on claims arising out of his marital difficulties, after he had filed many complaints wasting the time of courts, public officials and lawyers.

7. See note 4, supra.

8. State ex rel. Schneider v. Hill, 223 Kan. 425, 573 P.2d 1078 (1978) (by an evenly divided court); State Bar of Michigan v. Cramer, 399 Mich. 116, 249 N.W.2d 1

(1976); In re Thompson, 574 S.W.2d 365 (Mo.1978), citing other cases; New Jersey State Bar Assn. v. Divorce Center of Atlantic County, 194 N.J.Super. 532, 477 A.2d 415 (1984); State v. Winder, 42 A.D.2d 1039, 348 N.Y.S.2d 270 (4th Dep't 1973); Oregon State Bar v. Gilchrist, 272 Or. 552, 538 P.2d 913 (1975); Annot., 71 A.L.R.3d 1000 (1976).

9. Delaware State Bar Assn. v. Alexander, 386 A.2d 652 (Del.1978), dismissed for want of jurisdiction and cert. denied 439 U.S. 808, 99 S.Ct. 65, 58 L.Ed.2d 100 (1978) (men's group held engaged in unauthorized practice by assisting fathers in divorce suits); The Florida Bar v. Furman, 376 So.2d 378 (Fla.1979), appeal dismissed 444 U.S. 1061, 100 S.Ct. 1001, 62 L.Ed.2d 744 (1980); The Florida Bar v. Brumbaugh, 355 So.2d 1186 (Fla.1978); New Jersey State Bar Assn. v. Divorce Center of Atlantic County, 194 N.J.Super. 532, 477 A.2d 415 (1984); State v. Winder, 42 A.D.2d 1039, 348 N.Y.S.2d 270 (4th Dep't 1973); Annot., 12 A.L.R.4th 656 (1982).

10. Note, Lay Divorce Firms and the Unauthorized Practice of Law, 6 U.Mich.J. of Law Reform 423 (1973). See also Kavanagh, C.J., dissenting in State Bar of Michigan v. Cramer, 399 Mich. 116, 140, 249 N.W.2d 1, 10 (1976).

sy,di(malpractice /s attorney lawyer counsel /s
    dissol! divorc!)

Competence

smith /s lewis /p divorc! dissol!

Fees

counsel lawyer attorney /s lien! /s fee /s divorc!
    dissol!

Do-it-Yourself Divorce

divorc! dissol! /s illegal! unlawful! unauthorized /s
    practic!

---

§ 14.8 Divorce Procedure—Conciliation, Arbitration, and Mediation

The three topics discussed in this section constitute three possible ways of dealing with divorce other than by the conventional adversary litigation before a court. Although the three are ostensibly different devices, in some instances the activities which they encourage may be very similar. Sometimes conciliation may operate in ways much like mediation. Arbitrators also may, on occasion, behave like mediators, although such behavior may seem to many to be inconsistent with or in violation of the rules governing the arbitration process. With this as a reminder, the three topics will

§ 14.8

1. Ariz. Rev. Stat. §§ 25–381.01 to 25–381.24 (1976 and Supp.1986); West's Ann. Cal. Civ. Proc. Code §§ 1730 to 1772 (1982 and Supp.1987); Colo. Rev. Stat. § 14–10–110(2)(b) (1973); Conn. Gen. Stat. Ann. § 46b–53 (1986); Del. Code tit. 13, § 1517(b)(2) (1981); Ill.—Smith Hurd Ann. ch. 40, § 404 (1980); Ind. Code Ann. § 31–1–11.5–19 (Supp.1986); Iowa Code Ann. § 598.16 (Supp.1986); Kan. Stat. Ann. § 60–1608(c) (1983); Ky. Rev. Stat. § 403.170 (1984); La. Stat. Ann—Rev. Stat. §§ 9:351 to 9:356 (Supp. 1987); Mich. Stat. Ann. §§ 25.123(1) to 25.123(14) (1984); Mont. Code Ann. §§ 40–3–101 to 40–3–127 (1985); Neb. Rev. Stat. §§ 42–801 to 42–823 (1984); N.H. Rev. Stat. Ann. §§ 167–B:1 to 167–B:5 (1978); N.Y.—McKinney's Fam. Ct. Act §§ 911–926 (1983); Ohio Rev. Code §§ 3105.091, 3117.01 to 3117.08 (1980); Or.Rev. Stat. §§ 107.510 to 107.615 (1983); V. Tex. C.A., Fam. Code § 3.54 (Supp.1987); Utah Code Ann. 1984, §§ 30–3–11.1 to 30–3–18; West's Rev. Code Wash. Ann. §§ 26.12.010 to 26.12.220 (1986); Wis. Stat. Ann. §§ 767.081, 767.082, 767.083 (1981).

2. E.g., the Colorado, Delaware, Indiana, Kentucky, Michigan, Oregon statutes cited, supra, note 1.

3. E.g., the Arizona, California, Nebraska, New York, and Oregon statutes cited in note 1, supra.

4. E.g., the Connecticut, Illinois, Iowa, Kansas, Ohio, Texas, Washington and Wisconsin statutes cited in note 1, supra.

be dealt with separately for purposes of clarity.

Conciliation

Nearly half of the states now have statutes creating some form of a court-related conciliation procedure.[1] There is considerable variety in these statutes. Some of them make the access to conciliation wholly voluntary,[2] while others impose more or less pressure on the parties to participate in it, either by staying the divorce action,[3] or even by directing the parties to attend conciliation conferences.[4] The presence of a minor child of the marriage may be the factor which leads to conciliation.[5] In some states success in conciliation produces a written agreement.[6] The costs of the procedure are often shared by the parties as the court may determine.[7] And several statutes provide that information coming out in the course of conciliation conferences shall be confidential and shall not be revealed in later litigation, surely an essential provision if conciliation is ever to succeed.[8]

Those statutes which contain a statement of purpose for conciliation programs make it clear that the legislatures wished to provide a

5. E.g., the Arizona and Montana statutes cited in note 1, supra. In most of the statutes cited the conciliation process is invoked by a request from one of the parties or from the guardian of a minor child of the parties, or by the action of the divorce court. In most states the attempt at conciliation need only be made where there is a reasonable possibility that the spouses may be reconciled. Sawdey v. Superior Court In and For City and County of San Francisco, 195 Cal.App.2d 729, 16 Cal.Rptr. 156 (1961); Mueller v. Mueller, 203 Neb. 653, 279 N.W.2d 631 (1979).

6. E.g., the Montana and Nebraska statutes cited in note 1, supra. The Montana statute authorizes the court to order compliance with the agreement.

7. E.g., the Connecticut, Iowa, Kansas and Utah statutes cited in note 1, supra.

8. E.g., the Connecticut, Delaware, Illinois, Texas and Utah statutes cited in note 1, supra. But In re Boyd's Marriage, 200 N.W.2d 845 (Iowa 1972) takes the very odd position that a conciliator's report should be received in evidence, thereby confusing conciliation with some sort of pre-trial investigation.

method for reconciling the spouses in divorce, or in other words to try to reduce the number of divorces.[9] This purpose was particularly evident in states like New York and Utah, where the conciliation law accompanied changes in the divorce laws which were expected to make divorce more readily available.[10] Conciliation in that context was seen as a way to compromise with those who opposed any liberalization of the divorce laws. Conciliation could also have another and equally useful purpose. It could be used to reduce the hostility of the litigants and to lead them to arrange the details of the divorce in an amicable, non-litigious way.[11]

The statutes do not generally define what is meant by conciliation. Since they contemplate a process during which the spouses have one or more conferences with someone usually referred to as a counselor, the assumption is that the spouses are to discuss their marital differences in the presence of and with the participation of the counselor. The function of the counselor is to use the techniques developed in psychology or psychiatry or similar disciplines in such a fashion as to cause them to resume marital life together or, failing that, perhaps to cause them to agree on such matters as property, support and custody of children.[12] The similarity between this process and the currently popular mediation process is obvious.[13] Some of the statutes authorize the counseling to be done by private individuals or agencies in addition to the court staff[14] occasionally also with the proviso that the parties may not be required to participate in counseling which would conflict with their religious beliefs.[15] Ordering an unwilling spouse to attend conciliation conferences has been held by one court to be a violation of the Due Process Clause[16] but this seems very doubtful since the effect of the requirement is merely to postpone the divorce hearing. Under most statutes the unwilling spouse has merely to make it clear that he is not interested in conciliation in order to end the process.[17] It is therefore unlikely that an invasion of marital privacy could successfully be asserted.[18]

Although the idea of court-related conciliation has been in existence with varying degrees of support for several decades, there is a remarkable scarcity of reliable information about its effects. At the height of its popularity during the 1960's statistics were published indicating that conciliation was effective in a substantial proportion of the cases referred to

9. West's Ann.Cal.Civ.Proc.Code § 1730 (1982); Mont. Code Ann. § 40–3–102 (1985); Rodriguez v. Rodriguez, 8 Ariz.App. 5, 442 P.2d 169 (1968); In re Smith's Marriage, 207 N.W.2d 548 (Iowa 1973).

10. McLaughlin, Court-Connected Marriage Counseling and Divorce—The New York Experience, 11 J.Fam.L. 517 (1971); Bodenheimer, The Utah Marriage Counseling Experiment: An Account of Changes in Divorce Law and Procedure, 7 Utah L.Rev. 443 (1961).

11. The California, Arizona and Montana statutes speak of the "amicable settlement of family controversies", which sounds like an authorization to engage in the less extensive kind of conciliation. See the statutes cited in note 1, supra.

12. Orten and Wilson, Divorce Applicants: Which Ones Should Go to Marriage Counselors? 35 Okla.L.Rev. 403 (1982) describes some of the clients and marital problems which counselors attempt to deal with. The inability of lawyers to deal with counseling is described in Kargman, The Lawyer as Divorce Counselor, 46 Am. Bar Assn.J. 399 (1960). Some psychiatric techniques useful in counseling are outlined in Bodenheimer, New Approaches of Psychiatry: Implications for Divorce Reform, 1970 Utah L.Rev. 191. More general treatments of the subject include V. Eisenstein, Neurotic Interaction in Marriage

(1956); M. Grotjahn, Psychoanalysis and the Family Neurosis (1960); D. Lansley and D. Kaplan, The Treatment of Families in Crisis (1968); A. Watson, Psychiatry for Lawyers (1968).

13. See the discussion of mediation, infra, at note 65.

14. E.g., the Arizona, Connecticut, Illinois, Indiana, Kansas, Michigan, Nebraska, New York, Ohio, Texas statutes cited in note 1, supra.

15. E.g., the Kansas statute cited in note 1, supra. Without such a safeguard People ex rel. Bernat v. Bicek, 405 Ill. 510, 91 N.E.2d 588 (1950) indicated that the First Amendment would be violated.

16. People ex rel. Bernat v. Bicek, 405 Ill. 510, 91 N.E.2d 588 (1950). Rodriguez v. Rodriguez, 8 Ariz.App. 5, 442 P.2d 169 (1968) has held that filing a petition for conciliation does not constitute consent to the divorce court's jurisdiction over the person of the petitioner.

17. Sawdey v. Superior Court In and For City and County of San Francisco, 195 Cal.App.2d 729, 16 Cal.Rptr. 156 (1961); In re Smith's Marriage, 207 N.W.2d 548 (Iowa 1973); Mueller v. Mueller, 203 Neb. 653, 279 N.W.2d 631 (1979).

18. For a discussion of constitutional protection for marital privacy see section 2.2, supra.

the conciliation courts or agencies,[19] but the process was never shown to have an effect upon the divorce rate.[20] A form of "mandatory" conciliation was attempted in New York but was found to result in nothing more than the filing of one more document in the divorce proceeding.[21] In Utah the most ambitious of programs was repealed after only a few years' trial.[22] There are several possible reasons for this relative lack of success. In some cases the bench and the bar have opposed conciliation or have failed to give it enthusiastic support. In many, probably most, states the legislatures have been unwilling to provide the financial support necessary to hire enough trained counselors to handle the large number of spouses who might profit from counseling. The expense is made the greater by the fact that in many instances the counseling may be quite a long process, requiring many conferences over weeks or perhaps months of time.[23] Perhaps the most important factor is the obvious one. When the parties have reached the point of seriously considering divorce, it is usually too late for counseling or conciliation to succeed in saving the marriage. To be really effective, a conciliation program should be made available to spouses long before divorce is contemplated, but of course that would require a very large expenditure of public funds.[24] On consideration of all these factors, one is led to be skeptical of any very ambitious claims for conciliation,[25] although it may help some couples either to save their marriages or to reduce the material and psychological damage of their divorces.

Arbitration

Arbitration, which has had great influence and wide use in labor law and collective bargaining [26] and to some extent in commercial disputes,[27] is currently being looked to in many jurisdictions as a technique for deciding disputes arising out of divorce.[28] It offers the advantages of savings in time and money where court delays are long, of informality in procedure, and of privacy, over litigation in the courts. Arbitration awards are final and may be confirmed and enforced by the entry of judgments, with few grounds on which they may be set aside or modified.[29]

19. Burke, The Role of Conciliation in Divorce Cases, 1 J.Fam.L. 209 (1961); Burke, Conciliation—A New Approach to the Divorce Problem, 30 Cal. State Bar J. 199 (1955); Henderson, Marriage Counseling in a Court of Conciliation, 3 Fam.L.Q. 6 (1969). For an outline of many of the conciliation programs see Foster, Conciliation and Counseling in the Courts in Family Law Cases, 41 N.Y.U.L.Rev. 353 (1966).

20. Professor Bodenheimer found some evidence that the Utah conciliation program caused some decline in the divorce rate. Bodenheimer, The Utah Marriage Counseling Experiment: An Account of Changes in Divorce Law and Procedure, 7 Utah L.Rev. 443, 469, note 159 (1961).

21. McLaughlin, Court-Connected Marriage Counseling and Divorce—The New York Experience, 11 J.Fam.L. 517 (1971). See also Frazier v. Frazier, 228 S.C. 149, 89 S.E.2d 225 (1955).

22. Bodenheimer, The Utah Marriage Counseling Experiment: An Account of Changes in Divorce Law and Procedure, 7 Utah L.Rev. 443 (1961).

23. McIntyre, Conciliation of Disrupted Marriages By or Through the Judiciary, 4 J.Fam.L. 117 (1964); Bodenheimer, New Approaches of Psychiatry: Implications for Divorce Reform, 1970 Utah L.Rev. 191; Note, Marriage Counseling Through the Divorce Court—Another Look, 28 S.C.L.Rev. 687 (1977).

24. New Hampshire and New York seem to authorize counseling before divorce actions have been brought. See the statutes cited in note 1, supra.

25. Seidelson, Systematic Marriage Investigation and Counseling in Divorce Cases: Some Reflections on Its Constitutional Propriety and General Desirability, 36 G.W.L.Rev. 60 (1967).

26. F. Elkouri and E. Elkouri, How Arbitration Works ch. 1 (3d ed.1973).

27. M. Domke, Domke on Commercial Arbitration chs. 1, 2, and 3 (Rev.ed. Wilner 1984).

28. Holman and Noland, Agreement and Arbitration: Relief to Overlitigation in Domestic Relations Disputes in Washington, 12 Willamette L.J. 527 (1976); Coulson, Family Arbitration—An Exercise in Sensitivity, 3 Fam. L.Q. 22 (1969).

29. Uniform Arbitration Act §§ 12, 13, 7 Unif.L.Ann. 140, 201 (1985), authorizing a court to vacate awards on such grounds as corruption or fraud in procurement of the award, partiality of the arbitrator and other limited grounds. Section 12 of that Act states that it is not ground for vacating or refusing to confirm an arbitration award that "the relief was such that it could not or would not be granted by a court of law or equity". The Act has been adopted in about half of the states. 7 Unif.L.Ann. 1 (Supp.1987). A majority of the states have modern arbitration statutes of similar tenor. M. Domke, Domke on Commercial Arbitration Appendix I (Rev.ed. Wilner 1984).

Arbitration occurs when the parties to a controversy agree to submit it to an impartial third person for a decision based upon evidence and argument.[30] The parties' agreement may be expressed in a contract providing that some or all disputes arising under the contract will be referred to arbitration, or it may be made at the time the controversy arises. In either event the authority of the arbitrator and the questions he is to decide are defined and limited by the agreement which the parties have made.[31] There are statutes in some states providing for "compulsory" arbitration,[32] but the concern in this section is exclusively with voluntary agreements to arbitrate marital controversies arising out of divorce.

Arbitration is usually distinguished from conciliation and mediation in the labor law context in that the arbitrator decides disputes, while the conciliator or mediator merely advises or recommends what should be done exercising what influence he may have to induce the parties to come to an agreement.[33] The role of conciliation in domestic relations has already been described.[34] Its purpose is to persuade the spouses to be reconciled or, according to some authorities, to obtain their divorce without destructive or hurtful behavior. Mediation, described later

in this section,[35] resembles the second of the purposes of conciliation. It has come to mean the process by which a third party presides over conferences with the parties in an effort to induce them to settle differences arising out of divorce concerning property, alimony, child support or child custody and its details. Arbitration of domestic relations disputes, while far from thoroughly worked out, seems to involve the decision by the third party of the controversies arising out of the spouses' agreement. The arbitrator is employed to resolve disputes,[36] while the conciliator or mediator is employed to create a situation in which the spouses will reach an agreement themselves concerning actual or potential differences between them. The arbitrator may also have to be distinguished from an appraiser on occasion, although this distinction is often difficult. The major difference between them seems to be that the arbitrator decides the entire controversy as a judge would do, while the appraiser is more like an expert witness, giving his opinion concerning a specific issue in the controversy.[37]

The arbitrator in labor and commercial cases, and presumably in divorce cases, may be chosen by whatever method the parties specify in their agreement to arbitrate.[38] They may name an individual to act as arbi-

---

30. M. Domke, Domke on Commercial Arbitration 1 (Rev.ed. Wilner 1984). But it has been held that once a dispute has been brought into court, the court has no authority to order arbitration even with the parties' consent. Crutchley v. Crutchley, 306 N.C. 518, 293 S.E.2d 793 (1982).

A form of alternative dispute resolution known as fact-finding is related to arbitration. It consists of referring to an impartial person factual disputes between the parties for determination. When the facts have been so found, the parties may proceed to a settlement of their dispute. This device has not been extensively used in divorce but would seem to offer possibilities in that context, particularly where the characterization and valuation of property is in issue. Still another device is called last-best-offer arbitration, in which each party states the best offer he is willing to make and the arbitrator is authorized to choose between them. In this case the arbitrator may only choose one or the other of the offers as the basis for his award, thereby putting heavy pressure on the parties to be reasonable in their demands. This is another technique which might be useful in arriving at the settlement of marital property disputes.

31. M. Domke, Domke on Commercial Arbitration § 1.01 (Rev.ed.Wilner 1984).

32. F. Elkouri and E. Elkouri, How Arbitration Works 17–22 (3d ed.1973); M. Domke, Domke on Commercial Arbitration § 1.03 (Rev.ed.Wilner 1984).

33. F. Elkouri and E. Elkouri, How Arbitration Works 4–5 (3d ed.1973).

34. See the discussion at notes 9 to 12, supra.

35. See the discussion at note 65, infra.

36. Levine v. Wiss & Co., 97 N.J. 242, 478 A.2d 397 (1984); Holman and Noland, Agreement and Arbitration: Relief to Overlitigation in Domestic Relations Disputes in Washington, 12 Willamette L.J. 527 (1976).

37. Levine v. Wiss & Co., 97 N.J. 242, 478 A.2d 397 (1984). This distinction, as the vigorous dissent in this case points out, is far from clear.

38. Uniform Arbitration Act § 3, 7 Unif.L.Ann. 96 (1985) provides also that if there is no agreement on appointment or if the agreed method fails, the appropriate court may make the appointment on application of a party. See also F. Elkouri and E. Elkouri, How Arbitration Works ch. 4 (3d ed.1973); O. Fairweather, Practice and Procedure in Labor Arbitration ch. V (2d ed.1983); M. Domke, Domke on Commercial Arbitration § 2:02 (Rev.ed.Wilner 1984), describing the American Arbitra-

trator, or they may delegate the choice of arbitrator to the American Arbitration Association, which maintains lists of arbitrators having experience in various kinds of cases.[39] If more than one arbitrator is chosen, their powers may be exercised by a majority of them.[40] Unless otherwise provided by the parties' agreement, the arbitrators must hold hearings, on notice to the parties, at which the parties may be present, present evidence, cross-examine witnesses and present arguments.[41] The parties may be represented by attorneys.[42] The arbitrator may issue subpoenas for the attendance of witnesses which are enforceable by the courts and may permit depositions to be taken.[43] The arbitrator's award must be in writing and must be made within the time set by the parties or within such time as the court orders if not set by the parties.[44] The award must be confirmed by the appropriate court on the application of a party,[45] with only a few grounds on which it may be vacated or modified, none of these going to the substance of the award.[46]

The agreement to arbitrate in divorce cases would normally be inserted in the separation agreement executed by the parties. The standard forms which have been suggested for

separation agreements provide that all controversies arising out of the separation agreement or its breach shall be submitted to arbitration, in accordance with the rules of the American Arbitration Association, and that the parties agree to abide by the award of the arbitrator.[47] In view of the position taken by the courts on the arbitrability of custody and child support, an arbitration provision thus unqualified is likely to mislead the spouses and produce needless controversy. A more specific provision describing the precise issues to be arbitrated in the event of disagreement or breach of the contract is preferable.[48]

Although the courts' traditional hostility toward arbitration has now been transformed into approval,[49] the current enthusiasm for arbitration as a substitute for litigation[50] should not blind us to the fact that in the domestic relations context arbitration involves difficulties which the courts have only just begun to face. The difficulties arise out of the relationship between the arbitration process and the substantive law of divorce. In commercial arbitration it is sometimes said that the arbitrator is not bound by rules of law but that he should decide cases on the basis of his experience of the business, cus-

---

tion Association and containing a typical arbitration clause for commercial contracts, calling for arbitration in accordance with the rules of the Association.

39. M. Domke, Domke on Commercial Arbitration chs. 20, 21 (Rev.ed.Wilner 1984), describing in detail the methods for choosing arbitrators and the qualifications of arbitrators. Of course the arbitrator must be disinterested and should disqualify himself if he finds that he cannot act impartially.

40. Uniform Arbitration Act § 4, 7 Unif.L.Ann. 99 (1985).

41. Id., § 5, 7 Unif.L.Ann. 99 (1985). See also Haughton, Running the Hearing, Jones, Selected Problems of Procedure and Evidence, and Fleming, Due Process and Fair Procedure, in A. Zack, ed., Arbitration in Practice 37, 48, 68 (1984); M. Domke, Domke on Commercial Arbitration ch. 24 (Rev.ed.Wilner 1984).

42. Id., § 6, 7 Unif.L.Ann. 113 (1985).

43. Id., § 7, 7 Unif.L.Ann. 114 (1985).

44. Id., § 8, 7 Unif.L.Ann. 116 (1985).

45. Uniform Arbitration Act § 11, 7 Unif.L.Ann. 133 (1985).

46. See note 29, supra.

47. Coulson, American Arbitration Associations's Family Dispute Services, 2 Fam.L.Rptr. 3083, 3084 (1976).

The Rules of the Association for the interpretation of separation agreements are reproduced in 2 Fam.L.Rptr. 3088 (1976). A similar form for arbitration clauses in separation agreements is proposed in 1 A. Lindey, Separation Agreements and Antenuptial Contracts 29–5 (Rev. 1984, Kaufman, Chernin, Post). See also Note, The Enforceability of Arbitration Clause in North Carolina Separation Agreements, 15 Wake Forest L.Rev. 487 (1979).

48. Susquehanna Valley Central School District v. Susquehanna Valley Teachers' Assn., 37 N.Y.2d 614, 617, 376 N.Y.S.2d 427, 429, 339 N.E.2d 132, 133 (1975): ". . . matters affecting marriage, child custody, and the like, are not subject to unbridled arbitrability . . ." See also Bowmer v. Bowmer, 50 N.Y.2d 288, 428 N.Y.S.2d 902, 406 N.E.2d 760 (1980), holding that a broadly phrased arbitration clause did not, under the circumstances authorize the arbitration of the ex-husband's claim to reduce his alimony and child support payments.

49. See Southland Corp. v. Keating, 465 U.S. 1, 12, 104 S.Ct. 852, 859, 79 L.Ed.2d 1, 13 (1984).

50. Spencer and Zammit, Mediation-Arbitration: A Proposal for Private Resolution of Disputes Between Divorced or Separated Parents, 1976 Duke L.J. 911, proposing that the two steps of mediation and arbitration replace the conventional divorce litigation.

toms of the trade and the equities of the case, unless the arbitration agreement expressly refers to the law to be applied.[51] This reflects one of the often assumed advantages of arbitration, that it enables cases to be decided sensibly, without hindrance from supposedly foolish or hyper-technical rules of law.[52] But when domestic relations controversies arise, the most intimate of human relations are at stake and the rules of law express public policies which most states take very seriously. Does it follow from this that some or all of such controversies should not be arbitrable at all? Or, if they are arbitrable, should the arbitrator continue to ignore the substantive law as in commercial arbitration, or should he decide cases as a judge would do? Or is there some other way of defining his function and his relationship to legal rules?

A hypothetical example (one which could easily be imagined with a multitude of variations) may help to demonstrate the point. H and W are married and have a son six years old. They find their marriage no longer tolerable, separate and in contemplation of divorce execute a separation agreement. The agreement provides that W will have custody of the son, S, that H will have the child with him on weekends and during school vacations, and that H will pay a stated monthly sum for support of S. The agreement also contains the usual blanket arbitration provision.[53] The divorce is granted and the court approves the agreement. In the subsequent months H finds that W is repeatedly frustrating his visits with S on a variety of what appear to be pretexts until finally she informs him that he can no longer see the child at all because he has been teaching S to hate his mother. H then informs her that he will not pay any child support until he can see S again in accordance with their agreement. He also tells her he is asking that their dispute be submitted to arbitration. When she refuses, he brings suit to compel arbitration [54] and she responds by asking for a stay of arbitration.[55]

The first question, and the one the courts have been concerned with, is whether this controversy is arbitrable. The cases in New York, where the popularity of arbitration has caused the issue to arise most often, have exhibited much disagreement. One influential case has held that the custody and support of children are arbitrable, but that arbitration would not infringe on the court's power to protect children as *parens patriae* because the arbitrator's decision would be subject to the court's supervisory jurisdiction, exercisable *de novo*, and because the award would not be given *res judicata* effect as against the child.[56] The same case indicated, however, that the award could only be attacked by showing that it adversely affected the child's welfare. A later thoughtful case in New York expressed serious doubt whether custody disputes should be arbitrable, for the reason that only the courts are capable of protecting the interests of the child and of carefully evaluating the subtle factors relevant to the protection of those interests.[57] Cases in other states have taken the position that custody disputes are arbitrable, but that the arbitrator's award is subject to court review on the merits.[58] The review is said to be

---

51. M. Domke, Domke on Commercial Arbitration § 25:01 (Rev.ed.Wilner 1984).

52. O. Fairweather, Practice and Procedure in Labor Arbitration 1 (2d ed.1983).

53. See note 47, supra.

54. Uniform Arbitration Act § 2, 7 Unif.L.Ann. 68 (1985) authorizes the court to compel compliance with an agreement to arbitrate.

55. Ibid.

56. Sheets v. Sheets, 22 A.D.2d 176, 254 N.Y.S.2d 320 (1st Dep't 1964). The result in Sheets seems to have been approved in Hirsch v. Hirsch, 37 N.Y.2d 312, 372 N.Y.S.2d 71, 333 N.E.2d 371 (1975). See also Schneider v. Schneider, 17 N.Y.2d 123, 269 N.Y.S.2d 107, 216 N.E.2d

318 (1966). Other cases are cited in Annot., 18 A.L.R.3d 1264 (1968).

57. Fence v. Fence, 64 Misc.2d 480, 314 N.Y.S.2d 1016 (Fam.Ct.1970), per Polier, J. See also Agur v. Agur, 32 A.D.2d 16, 298 N.Y.S.2d 772 (2d Dep't 1969), appeal dismissed 32 N.Y.2d 703, 343 N.Y.S.2d 607, 296 N.E.2d 458 (1973) and Nestel v. Nestel, 38 A.D.2d 942, 331 N.Y.S.2d 241 (2d Dep't 1972). The Fence case stated that child support is so inextricably connected with custody that it likewise should not be arbitrable. Biel v. Biel, 114 Wis.2d 191, 336 N.W.2d 404 (App.1983) seems to say that a court cannot compel the parties to arbitrate custody and visitation, but gives no reasons for this view.

58. Faherty v. Faherty, 97 N.J. 99, 477 A.2d 1257 (1984); Crutchley v. Crutchley, 306 N.C. 518, 293 S.E.2d

de novo, but no such review may be granted if it is clear on the face of the arbitrator's award that the award could not adversely affect the substantial best interests of the child.[59] This qualification leaves the grant or denial of *de novo* review very largely to the discretion of the court, since no one can say with assurance whether an award could adversely affect the child's interests, but presumably the tendency will be for the courts to review most awards. The obvious consequence of this rule is to impose on the parties the time and expense burdens of two proceedings instead of one when the purpose of arbitration is supposedly to reduce time and expense. At the least this view of arbitrability should lead the spouses and their lawyers to consider specific provisions concerning arbitration of custody and child support in their separation agreement rather than uncritically to rely on the standard form of arbitration provision.

In the hypothetical case therefore, a few courts would deny arbitration entirely. Others would hold that the husband is entitled to have the arbitrator decide the dispute over custody and child support, but that the wife is entitled to have a court reexamine the question of custody and, since it is closely related to custody, the question of child support as well, except perhaps in the unlikely event that the award on its fact showed that the child's interests could not be adversely affected. There is a further question presented to which the cases provide no answer, however. If we assume, as may be the case in many states,[60] that there is a rule of case law that a father is not justified in failing to pay child support by the mother's frustration of

his visitation rights, the question is whether an arbitrator must or should follow that rule in this case, even if the "equities" might suggest a different result. Certainly if the courts are to review the arbitrator's award, he should follow the legal rules. If he does not, he will generally find his awards vacated, making arbitration a wholly futile exercise. Even if the separation agreement should provide that child support is excused if visitation provisions are violated, the arbitrator should follow the case law, since interests other than the parties' wishes are at stake. There are of course many other legal rules or principles or standards which may affect custody and child support decisions, not least the extensive rules which are embodied in and developed from the Uniform Child Custody Jurisdiction Act and the Parental Kidnapping Prevention Act of 1980,[61] which may have important potential consequences for arbitrators' awards respecting child custody and which certainly must be considered by those arbitrators who propose to make such awards.

Where division of property and alimony are in issue, the cases generally assume without much discussion that arbitration is appropriate.[62] There is less reason to question that view than where custody or child support are concerned, but the same questions about the applicability of the substantive law arise here as with custody. For example if the parties' separation agreement provided that the wife waived any claim to alimony, would the arbitrator be bound by the provision in many state statutes that such agreements are not to be approved if they are unconscionable?[63] Or is he bound by the agreement, as is generally

---

793 (1982); Rustad v. Rustad, 68 N.C.App. 58, 314 S.E.2d 275 (1984), petition for discretionary review denied 311 N.C. 763, 321 S.E.2d 145 (1984). Sheets v. Sheets, 22 A.D.2d 176, 254 N.Y.S.2d 320 (1st Dep't 1964) may also take this position. The courts who do take this position do not seem concerned with the fact that they are violating the express prohibition of many state arbitration statutes, which, as does the Uniform Act, provide that ". . . the fact that the relief was such that it could not or would not be granted by a court of law or equity is not ground for vacating or refusing to confirm the award." Uniform Arbitration Act § 12(a), 7 Unif.L.Ann. 140 (1985). The purpose of this provision clearly is to prevent the courts from reexamining the merits of a dispute which has been arbitrated.

59. Faherty v. Faherty, 97 N.J. 99, 477 A.2d 1257 (1984) spells this out most clearly.

60. See section 17.3, infra.

61. See section 12.5, supra.

62. Faherty v. Faherty, 97 N.J. 99, 477 A.2d 1257 (1984), citing cases; Crutchley v. Crutchley, 306 N.C. 518, 293 S.E.2d 793 (1982); Annot., 18 A.L.R.3d 1264, 1266 (1968).

63. See Uniform Marriage and Divorce Act § 306(c), (d), 9A Unif.L.Ann. 135 (1979).

the case in commercial arbitration? [64] If arbitration is to achieve reliability and begin to take the place of litigation in domestic relations matters, certainly the arbitrators should be familiar with and bound by the substantive law.

Mediation

Mediation is usually defined as a process by which the parties to a divorce are assisted in reaching agreement on such matters as division of property, alimony, and the custody and support of children by an impartial, professional third person.[65] Its major purpose is not to achieve a reconciliation of the spouses, as in conciliation,[66] but to aid in the procurement of the divorce desired by the spouses without the hostility and the psychological and material costs often imposed by adversary litigation. It is therefore distinguished from conciliation,[67] but the fact is that conciliation can have the same aims and use much the same techniques as mediation on occasion.[68] Mediation is in theory at least also distinguishable from arbitration, since the arbitrator decides the parties' disputes [69] while the mediator attempts to bring them to agreement. Some mediation programs encourage the spouses to resort to arbitration when they

reach an impasse in mediation, however, so that there is a practical relationship between the two processes.[70]

Mediation has been the subject of extensive commentary during the 1980's, most of it emphasizing mediation's assumed benefits, much of it superficial rather than critical or analytical.[71] The benefits claimed for mediation are both material and psychological.[72] The process is said to result in savings of both time and money when compared with conventional divorce litigation. Mediation's proponents also argue that by giving the spouses responsibility for their own divorce settlement, mediation reduces hostility and destructive behavior. This in turn leads to a greater tendency to comply with agreements so arrived at, to improved post-divorce relations and especially to custody and visitation arrangements more beneficial to the children of the marriage than would result from a court's decree.

One much quoted study of the effects of mediation found that many of these benefits are in fact achieved, but that the expected cost savings were either slight or non-existent.[73] This study has been sharply criticized on the ground that the information it provides is inadequate and that it was conducted

---

64. E.g., Zack, Weighing the Decision, in A. Zack, Arbitration in Practice 163, 174–176 (1984); M. Domke, Domke on Commercial Arbitration § 25:01 (Rev.ed.Wilner 1984). See also O. Fairweather, Practice and Procedure in Labor Arbitration ch. XVI (2d ed.1983). The arbitrator was held not to have authority to arbitrate a husband's claim for reducing alimony in Bowmer v. Bowmer, 50 N.Y.2d 288, 428 N.Y.S.2d 902, 406 N.E.2d 760 (1980). The court said, among other reasons for the result, that this would amount to rewriting the contract. The question this suggests is whether the court would also deny arbitrability if the law of the state was that alimony based on separation agreements is modifiable.

65. J. Blades, Family Mediation 1 (1985); O. Coogler, Structured Mediation in Divorce Settlement 1 (1978); R. Coulson, Fighting Fair 9 (1983); Folberg, Divorce Mediation—A Workable Alternative, in American Bar Association, Special Committee on Alternative Means of Dispute Resolution 11, 13–15 (1982); Riskin, Mediation and Lawyers 43 Ohio St.L.J. 29 (1982); Taylor, Toward a Comprehensive Theory of Mediation, 19 Conciliation Courts Rev. 1 (1981).

66. See the text at note 9, supra.

67. Folberg, Divorce Mediation—A Workable Alternative, in American Bar Association, Special Committee on Alternative Means of Dispute Resolution 11, 15 (1982).

68. Orlando, Where and How—Conciliation Courts, in American Bar Association, Special Committee on Alternative Means of Dispute Resolution 111, 116 (1982) makes it clear that conciliation and mediation are in practice often indistinguishable. See also Comeaux, Procedural Controls in Public Sector Domestic Relations Mediation, in American Bar Association, Special Committee on Alternative Means of Dispute Resolution 79 (1982).

69. See the text at note 30, supra.

70. O. Coogler, Structured Mediation in Divorce Settlement 129 (1978), setting forth section 42 of the Marital Mediation Rules requiring the submission to arbitration of controversies in which an impasse is reached in mediation.

71. See Selected Mediation Bibliography, in 17 Fam. L.Q. 539 (1984); F. Sander, A Select Annotated Bibliography (1984); R. Coulson, Fighting Fair 183 (1983).

72. J. Blades, Family Mediation 34–35 (1985); K. Schneider and M. Schneider, Divorce Mediation 27–28 (1984); J. Folberg and A. Taylor, Mediation, A Comprehensive Guide to Resolving Conflicts Without Litigation ch. 7 (1984).

73. Pearson and Thoennes, Mediating and Litigating Custody Disputes: A Longitudinal Evaluation, 17 Fam. L.Q. 497 (1984). An account of the same study is in

with a bias favoring mediation.[74] Not only this study but other writing on mediation take as their starting point the familiar clichés about the iniquities of the "adversary process" and of lawyers, who are assumed to devote their energies to stirring up hostility in their clients and to provoking litigation when their clients would be better served by compromising their claims.[75] The continued currency of these clichés is puzzling in view of the well established fact that even before the advent of mediation a very large proportion of divorce cases were uncontested, the function of the courts in such cases being merely to approve arrangements already worked out by the parties and their lawyers.[76] The stereotype of the rashly aggressive divorce lawyer who litigates every case in disregard of the broader long term interests of his clients, like most stereotypes of lawyers, bears little resemblance to one's experience with the practicing divorce bar.

The publicity given to mediation has led some states to provide for it as part of the divorce procedure.[77] Some of these statutes are truly mandatory in that they require mediation in all cases of disputed custody.[78] Others merely authorize the court to order mediation in some circumstances.[79] And still others authorize mediation only at the request of the parties.[80] It should be remembered also that in those states having conciliation procedures the conciliation court may be able to engage in mediation of the incidents to the divorce.[81]

The details of the mediation process vary considerably depending upon the views and experience of the mediator. In general the process is expected to require from five to ten hours of conferences between mediator and client, in weekly sessions of from one and one half to two hours each.[82] Some mediators confer only with the two spouses jointly, while others hold individual conferences with each spouse when those promise to be productive.[83] One method of mediation originating with O. J. Coogler has come to be known as structured mediation and provides a more formal agenda for the mediator than other methods.[84] Rules for the conduct of the mediation

Pearson, Thoennes, and Kooi, Mediation of Child Custody Disputes, 11 Colo.Lawyer 336 (1982).

74. Levy, Comment on the Pearson-Thoennes Study and on Mediation, 17 Fam.L.Q. 525 (1984). The authors of the study responded to the criticism in Pearson and Thoennes, Dialogue: A Reply to Professor Levy's Comment, 17 Fam.L.Q. 535 (1984).

75. Pearson and Thoennes, Mediating and Litigation Custody Disputes: A Longitudinal Evaluation, 17 Fam. L.Q. 497, 498 (1984); J. Blades, Family Mediation, Cooperative Divorce Settlement 18–21 (1985).

76. Mnookin and Kornhauser, Bargaining in the Shadow of the Law: The Case of Divorce, 88 Yale L.J. 950, 951 (1979).

77. Alaska Stat. § 25.24.060 (1984); West's Ann. Cal. Civ. Code § 4607 (Supp.1987); La. Stat. Ann.—Rev. Stat. § 9–351 (Supp.1987); Me. Rev. Stat. Ann. tit. 19, § 636 (Supp.1986); Mich. Stat. Ann. § 25.176(13) (1984); Or. Rev. Stat. §§ 107.755 to 107.795 (1983). Colo. Rev. Stat. §§ 13–22–301 to 13–22–310 (Supp.1986) sets up offices of dispute resolution in judicial districts for the purpose of mediating controversies generally, not merely controversies arising out of divorce. See Maxwell, Keeping the Family Out of Court: Court-Ordered Mediation of Custody Disputes Under Kansas Statutes, 25 Washburn L.J. 203 (1986).

78. See the California and Oregon statutes cited in note 77.

79. See the Alaska, Louisiana and Maine statutes cited in note 77.

80. See the Michigan statute cited in note 77.

81. Comeaux, Procedural Controls in Public Sector Domestic Relations Mediation, in A.B.A. Special Committee on Alternative Means of Dispute Resolution, Alternative Means of Family Dispute Resolution 79 (1982); McIsaac, The Family Conciliation Court of Los Angeles County, in A.B.A. Special Committee on Alternative Means of Dispute Resolution, Alternative Means of Family Dispute Resolution 131 (1982). The Comeaux article discusses many of the procedural requirements of the mediation statutes.

82. J. Blades, Family Mediation, Cooperative Divorce Settlement 37–39, 63 (1985).

83. J. Blades, Family Mediation, Cooperative Divorce Settlement 86–88 (1985).

84. O. Coogler, Structured Mediation in Divorce Settlement ch. 4 (1978) describes the procedure, which begins with intake sessions informing the clients about the process, and is followed by setting the agenda, then by agreement on temporary support and custody, then by sessions on property and finances for four or five hours, then by a meeting with an advisory attorney, then by a session on the final agreement concerning property and money, and concluding with sessions on custody and visitation.

are also promulgated.[85] The operation of this type of mediation has been described in detail by ex-spouses who participated in it.[86]

The question has frequently been raised whether the negotiations of the parties in the course of mediation are to be confidential. Although offers to compromise litigation are not generally admissible in evidence, matters of fact revealed in the course of compromise negotiations may be admissible.[87] It seems clear that the possibility that statements made in mediation might later be evidence in the divorce proceeding would seriously prejudice the mediation process by limiting the spouses' willingness to discuss the facts of their situation freely and thoroughly. This problem has been solved by some statutes which provide that matters revealed in mediation shall not be admissible in evidence and that the entire process shall be confidential.[88] Some mediators attempt to reach the same result by having the spouses sign an agreement to this effect in advance of mediation.[89] The California statute adopts the curiously

inconsistent position that the negotiations are confidential, but that the mediator may make a recommendation to the court concerning custody and visitation, thereby placing the mediator in the role of arbitrator.[90]

It seems clear that if mediation is to work, any divorce proceeding which has been brought should be stayed until mediation is concluded.[91] Some statutes so provide.[92] It also seems clear that a full disclosure of material information by both spouses is essential to effective mediation,[93] but the available writing on mediation leaves largely unclear just how much intervention by the mediator is permissible in order to ensure a full disclosure. For example, should a lawyer-mediator examine one of the spouses as to the value of stock in a close corporation which constitutes part of the marital property? Or should the mediator insist that an accountant be employed to give an independent opinion on its value? These questions are related to the broader issue of the extent to which the lawyer-mediator may actively promote "fairness"

---

85. O. Coogler, Structured Mediation in Divorce Settlement 117–129 (1978). Section 1 of the Rules provides that the parties are deemed to have made the Rules a part of their mediation agreement whenever the agreement so provides or whenever they have agreed that the mediation will be conducted by a facility certified by the Family Mediation Association. Section 17 provides that the parties may not communicate with the mediator or the advisory attorney except in the presence of each other during a mediation session. The appointment and duties of an advisory attorney are outlined in section 12 of the Rules.

86. K. Schneider and M. Schneider, Divorce Mediation ch. 4 (1984). Verbatim examples of the ways in which mediators and mediation work are also included in J. Blades, Family Mediation, Cooperative Divorce Settlement passim (1985). A detailed discussion of the mediation process is also included in Taylor, Toward a Comprehensive Theory of Mediation, 19 Conciliation Courts Rev. 1 (1981).

87. C. McCormick, Evidence 811–813 (3d ed.Cleary 1984).

88. See the California, Louisiana, Michigan and Oregon statutes cited in note 77, supra, and Colo. Rev. Stat. § 13–22–307 (Supp.1986).

89. See section 21 of the Marital Mediation Rules, O. Coogler, Structured Mediation in Divorce Settlement 121 (1978); J. Blades, Family Mediation, Cooperative Divorce Settlement 41–42 (1985); Standards of Practice for Family Mediators II A, 17 Fam.L.Q. 456 (1984). But there may be some question whether such an agreement would be enforceable if one of the parties chose to introduce

evidence in violation of it. See Bishop, The Standards of Practice for Family Mediators: An Individual Interpretation and Comments, 17 Fam.L.Q. 461, 465 (1984). If the mediator is an attorney, this places him in the odd position of persuading the parties to sign an unenforceable contract and of obliging him to tell them that it is unenforceable.

90. West's Ann.Cal.Civ.Code § 4607(c), (e) (Supp.1987). In McLaughlin v. Superior Court for San Mateo County, 140 Cal.App.3d 473, 189 Cal.Rptr. 479 (1983) the court held that if the mediator makes a recommendation, the parties have the right as a matter of due process to subject him to cross-examination. The court said that subsection (c) of the statute did insulate the mediator from cross-examination, but that that subsection could not constitutionally be enforced if the mediator made a recommendation in a contested custody case.

Biel v. Biel, 114 Wis.2d 191, 336 N.W.2d 404 (1983) held that a trial court had discretion to order the parties to mediate a custody dispute, but that it must be shown that there was a reasonable basis for the court's exercise of discretion.

91. Comeaux, Procedural Controls in Public Sector Domestic Relations Mediation, in A.B.A. Special Committee on Alternative Means of Dispute Resolution, Alternative Means of Family Dispute Resolution 79, 86 (1982).

92. Alaska Stat. § 25.24.060 (1984).

93. Standards of Practice for Family Mediators TV, 17 Fam.L.Q. 458 (1984); Marital Mediation Rules, section 23, O. Coogler, Structured Mediation in Divorce Settlement 122 (1978).

in the agreement which the parties make without incurring the risk of representing one at the expense of the other or of giving advice to one of the parties.

Mediators may be appointed by the parties, or by a court, or by an agency such as the Family Mediation Association.[94] Most authorities agree that they should have some training to qualify them for mediation, but there is little agreement on what form that training should take.[95] Some mediators are attorneys and some are mental health professionals belonging to one discipline or another.[96] Not surprisingly, the view is sometimes expressed by people with a mental health orientation that mental health professionals make better mediators than attorneys.[97] In some cases the spouses may wish to appoint a team of mediators, made up of persons from several disciplines, and of both men and women in order to avoid the suspicion of gender discrimination.[98] Since mediators must be paid for their work,[99] this sharply

reduces the saving in expense which is alleged to be a major benefit of mediation.

A major cause of the uncertainty and controversy surrounding mediation in divorce is the notion that the lawyer-mediator should be "impartial" or "neutral" or "fair", depending upon which authority one consults.[1] Obviously these terms are not synonymous. Those who demand impartiality seem to be concerned that the lawyer not mediate where one of the spouses has been his client in the past, and that after the mediation he not represent one of the spouses in the divorce proceeding. It is impossible to say what neutrality or fairness mean in this context. The difficulty is created by the suggestion often made, though in veiled terms, that the mediator has an obligation to prevent the execution of an agreement which is not "fair" to one of the spouses.[2] This seems to mean that if one of the spouses has less experience, less knowledge of business or of property values, is less aggressive in negotiations, or has a less acute

---

94. There are many privately managed mediation agencies in the various states. These are listed in A.B.A. Special Committee on Alternative Dispute Resolution, Dispute Resolution Program Directory (1983). See also A.B.A. Special Committee on Dispute Resolution, Mediation in the Justice System (1983).

95. J. Folberg and A. Taylor, Mediation, A Comprehensive Guide to Resolving Conflicts Without Litigation ch. 9 (1984).

96. O. Coogler, Structured Mediation in Divorce Settlement ch. 9 (1978).

97. J. Blades, Family Mediation, Cooperative Divorce Settlement chs. 4, 5 (1985).

98. Ibid. ch. 7. See also Kubie, Provisions for the Care of Children of Divorced Parents: A New Legal Instrument, 73 Yale L.J. 1197 (1964), and Note, Committee Decision of Child Custody Disputes and the Judicial Test of "Best Interests", 73 Yale L.J. 1201 (1964).

The ethical questions for the lawyer which may arise when he takes part in team mediation or is a member of a mediation "center" are discussed below at note 26.

99. Fees in a structured mediation are estimated in K. Schneider and M. Schneider, Divorce Mediation 48 (1984). Compensation is dealt with in sections 13 and 15 of the Marital Mediation Rules set out in O. Coogler, Structured Mediation in Divorce Settlement 120 (1978).

1. Standards of Practice for Family Mediators III, 17 Fam.L.Q. 457 (1984) states that the mediator has a duty to be impartial. Specific Consideration A explaining that Standard forbids the lawyer to represent either spouse after the mediation and to undertake the mediation if he has represented either spouse before the mediation. But

Specific Consideration D under this Standard states that impartiality is not the same as neutrality, and that "The mediator has an obligation to avoid an unreasonable result." The Marital Mediation Rules section 9, O. Coogler, Structured Mediation in Divorce Settlement 118 (1978) requires the mediators to be neutral in their relations with the spouses. See also Committee on Professional Ethics, Connecticut Bar Association Informal Opinion 83–1 (1982), ABA/BNA Lawyers' Manual on Professional Conduct 801:2058, hereinafter cited as ABA/BNA Manual. This Manual contains only abstracts of opinions. The full opinions should be consulted before they are relied upon.

2. J. Blades, Family Mediation, Cooperative Divorce Settlement 44–45 (1985), indicates that the mediator may need to help balance the parties' negotiating abilities, but that he should be careful "to retain the appearance of neutrality". Riskin, Toward New Standards for the Neutral Lawyer in Mediation, 26 Ariz.L.Rev. 329, 354–357 (1984) recommends that the lawyer-mediator do what is reasonable to promote fairness. Standards of Practice for Family Mediators V, 17 Fam.L.Q. 458–459 (1984) imposes on the mediator the duty to suspend or terminate the mediation when the process would harm or prejudice one of the parties. If the euphemisms and circumlocutions of this kind of talk are translated into plain language, this seems to mean that the lawyer-mediator has an obligation to help the disadvantaged party or even to terminate the mediation. This would appear to be at variance with one of the supposed purposes of mediation, which is to let the parties take responsibility for their own decisions without interference from courts and lawyers. See note 72, supra.

awareness of his advantages or disadvantages in the bargaining process than the other spouse, the mediator should step in and redress the balance, or, as some writers put it, "empower" the less effective spouse. In other words, the mediator in this situation is to act very much as would a lawyer representing that spouse. It is difficult to understand how the lawyer-mediator is to do this without being charged with representing the disadvantaged spouse, and with acting in a way which is neither impartial nor neutral. This leads us to a consideration of the professional and ethical pronouncements which the lawyer must take into account when he undertakes to mediate in divorce cases.

When the lawyer undertakes to act as a mediator, he is venturing into waters which are largely uncharted or, what is worse, where the charts may be unreliable. The dangers are that the position of mediator will involve him in serious conflicts of interest and that his membership on mediation teams or in mediation "centers" may be characterized as participating or aiding in the unauthorized practice of law. The extensive promotion of mediation in legal and non-legal publications has assumed that the expense, delay and hostility of much divorce litigation are caused by the lawyers, and that spouses who mediate will be honest with each other, reasonable in their demands, and ultimately willing to reach agreement.[3] Many lawyers and their bar associations hesitate to question these assumptions because they foresee the charges of featherbedding which often follow any insistence on traditional prohibitions against conflicts of interest and unauthorized practice of law. The result is that the bar associations' pronouncements concerning these issues vary from state to state, contain internal inconsistencies and ambiguities, and appear to approve lawyer participation in mediation on conditions which are often not likely to be met.[4] In addition to the psychological barriers to a realistic definition of the lawyer's duties in mediation, there is the objective fact that mediation in the divorce setting is a new process unlike others in which the lawyer functions as advocate or judge. The terminology describing the lawyer's role as advocate or judge does not seem to be useful to describe his role as mediator, suggesting that perhaps the inquiry should avoid using the traditional terminology and instead focus on exploring in detail precisely what the lawyer should do and should not do when he acts as a mediator.

The objections to the lawyer's representation of both parties to a divorce have already been explored and found to be serious.[5] But the Model Code does permit the lawyer to act as an "impartial arbitrator or mediator" in matters involving present or former clients if he discloses the relationships.[6] The question raised by this in conventional terms would be, is he representing both spouses when he mediates a divorce, or is he representing neither of them? Some bar association opinions have said that he represents neither spouse,[7] or that his representation is only a "limited"

3. K. Schneider and M. Schneider, Divorce Mediation ch. 2 (1984).

4. Compare Committee on Professional Ethics, Connecticut Bar Assn. Formal Opinion 35 (1982), ABA/BNA Manual 801:2002; Committee on Ethics of the Maryland State Bar Assn.Inc.Opinion 80–55A (1980), ABA/BNA Manual 801:4303; Committee on Legal Ethics and Professional Conduct, Ohio State Bar Assn. Opinion 82–2 (1982), ABA/BNA Manual 801:6827; Ethics Committee, Board of Professional Responsibility, Supreme Court of Tennessee Opinion 83–F–39 (1983), ABA/BNA Manual 801:8107; Virginia State Bar Council Opinion 511 (1983), ABA/BNA Manual 801:8815.

5. See section 14.7 at note 31, supra.

6. ABA Model Code of Professional Responsibility EC 5–20, hereinafter cited as ABA Model Code. See also ABA Model Rules of Professional Conduct 2.2, hereinafter cited as ABA Model Rules.

The most thorough and critical analysis of the lawyer's role as mediator is Crouch, Divorce Mediation and Legal Ethics 16 Fam.L.Q. 219 (1982). See also Silberman, Professional Responsibility Problems of Divorce Mediation, 16 Fam.L.Q. 107 (1982), a revision of a similar article in 7 Fam.L.Rptr. 4001 (1981); Gaughan, An Essay on the Ethics of Separation and Divorce Mediation, in American Bar Assn., Special Committee on Alternative Means of Dispute Resolution, Alternative Means of Family Dispute Resolution 321 (1982).

7. Association of the Bar of the City of New York, Committee on Professional and Judicial Ethics, Opinion 80–23 (1981), 7 Fam.L.Rptr. 3097, citing other opinions from Oregon and Boston. Some bar association opinions seem more or less implicitly to assume that the mediator represents both spouses. E.g., Committee on Ethics, Maryland State Bar Association, Inc. Opinion 80–55A (1980), ABA/BNA Manual 801:4303; Committee on Legal Ethics

one.[8] "Representation" does not seem to be an apt term in this context, since the lawyer is not acting as an advocate. The risks to be avoided here are the same, however, as in the case where the lawyer attempts to act for both spouses. The risks are that the lawyer-mediator will be unable to avoid so conducting the mediation as to advance the interests of one spouse, and that either or both spouses will mistakenly assume that he is responsible for protecting their individual interests.[9] Protecting the interests of one spouse can normally be accomplished only at the expense of the other spouse's interests, contrary to the contention sometimes made

that both parties win in mediation.[10] In mediations where the property or custody issues are complex and the parties in sharp disagreement, or where the bargaining position of one spouse is weaker than that of the other, it is highly likely if not inevitable that the interests of one spouse will be favored or will appear to have been favored over the interests of the other.[11] This will especially be true if the lawyer attempts to indicate the legal consequences of a proposed agreement, since this places him in the position of giving legal advice to parties whose interests are in direct conflict.[12] The position of "advisory attorney" in the structured mediation system

and Professional Conduct, Ohio State Bar Assn. Opinion 82–2 (1982), ABA/BNA Manual 801:6827, requiring the lawyer who participates in multiple representation to exercise his independent professional judgment on behalf of both clients, unfortunately without revealing just how that is to be accomplished.

Gaughan, An Essay on the Ethics of Separation and Divorce Mediation, in American Bar Association, Special Committee on Alternative Means of Dispute Resolution, Alternative Means of Family Dispute Resolution 321, 329 (1982) takes the position that the lawyer-mediator is not the common lawyer for the parties and is not to recommend a reasonable solution for them, but at 331 states that the mediator has an obligation to seek a full disclosure if one of the parties appears to be concealing relevant information. Obtaining a full disclosure would seem to be a clear example of the kind of activity one's legal representative should engage in. Of course there is also the question of how the mediator reaches the conclusion that concealment of information has occurred.

8. Legal Ethics Committee, Oregon State Bar Assn. Opinion 488 (1983), ABA/BNA Manual 801:7112. It is not clear what "limited" representation entails in specific circumstances.

9. The client's mistake about whether he is being represented by the mediator is understandable in view of the confusion exhibited by the legal authorities on the subject. As indicated in notes 7 and 8 there is authority that the mediator represents neither party, both parties, or that he represents both in a limited way. The ABA Model Rules 2.2 speaks of a "common representation", and requires the mediator to consult with each "client" concerning the decisions to be made and the considerations relevant to making them, strongly implying that somehow the mediator is to represent both and advance the interests of both, when the divorce context makes it likely that those interests will be in direct conflict.

10. J. Blades, Family Mediation, Cooperative Divorce Settlement 40 (1985) (mediation fosters, "win/win solutions which benefit everyone"); K. Schneider and M. Schneider, Divorce Mediation 88 (1984).

11. Crouch, Divorce Mediation and Legal Ethics, 16 Fam.L.Q. 219, 226 (1982); Association of the Bar of the City of New York, Committee on Professional and Judi-

cial Ethics Opinion 80–23 (1980), 7 Fam.L.Rptr. 3097, The conflict of interests is made more obvious when it is recommended that the lawyer-mediator has a responsibility to promote reasonableness in the spouses' negotiations and agreements. He can only do this by in some way restraining the unreasonableness of one spouse in order to benefit the other, or in other words to behave as if he were representing the second spouse. See J. Folberg and A. Taylor, Mediation 247 (1984); and Standards of Practice for Family Mediators III D, 17 Fam.L.Q. 457 (1984); Bishop, The Standards of Practice for Family Mediators: An Individual Interpretation and Comments, 17 Fam.L.Q. 461, 465, 467 (1984).

12. Some authorities attempt to deal with this problem by making a distinction between giving "legal advice", which is forbidden, and giving "legal information", which is permitted. Gaughan, An Essay on the Ethics of Separation and Divorce Mediation, in American Bar Association, Special Committee on Alternative Means of Dispute Resolution, Alternative Means of Family Dispute Resolution, 321, 328 (1982); Virginia State Bar Council Opinion 511 (1983), ABA/BNA Manual 801:8815. Some such distinction as this may be tenable when it marks the difference between a general discussion of a legal issue in a book or article on the one hand, and on the other the delivery of legal advice by a lawyer to his client when both understand that the client will act in reliance upon the advice. But the distinction resides in the context in which the information is given, not in the generality of the information. Any "legal information", no matter how generally phrased, is "legal advice" when it comes from an individual lawyer to a layman in a context where both know that it will be considered by the layman in determining a future course of conduct. To take Gaughan's example, a general discussion by a lawyer-mediator of the rule in Commissioner v. Lester, 366 U.S. 299, 81 S.Ct. 1343, 6 L.Ed.2d 306 (1961) concerning the tax effects of alimony and child support, addressed to the spouses in mediation, who then use the information to decide what sort of separation agreement they will execute, is legal advice, as much so as if a similar discussion occurred between the lawyer and his client in the lawyer's office. This purported distinction is a striking example of the sophistical reasoning too often advanced by the proponents of mediation to obscure the serious ques-

involves the same or even greater objections,[13] as does the assumption by some proponents of mediation that the lawyer-mediator or the "advisory attorney" may safely "put the parties' agreement in legal form."[14] Putting an agreement in legal form necessarily requires the draftsman to consider the legal consequences of possible alternative provisions in the contract, the choice among which is likely to benefit one spouse rather than the other.[15]

Notwithstanding all of the conflict of interests dangers facing the lawyer-mediator in divorce cases, the bar association opinions permit the lawyer to act as mediator, albeit with many qualifications and conditions.[16] He is required by some bar opinions to ensure that the parties understand that he does not represent either of them, that he will not protect their individual interests in the media-

ation, and that if they wish that sort of protection they must consult independent counsel.[17] He probably should advise them to seek independent counsel and should proceed only after he satisfies himself that the parties consent to the mediation with full awareness and understanding of the process and its risks.[18] The rule of structured mediation which would discourage the parties from consulting anyone, friends or attorneys, during the courts of mediation would seem clearly to be improper.[19] Whether the lawyer may give legal advice during the course of mediation seems to be a matter of dispute, but if he does give it, it seems clear that he should give it to both parties in the presence of each other.[20] "Individual caucusing", that is, conferring with a party out of the presence of the other party, seems to be a doubtful practice.[21] Some au-

tions of professional responsibility lurking in the mediation process.

13. In the Coogler system of structured mediation an advisory attorney is brought into the process near its end to explain to the parties and to the mediator their rights and obligations under the law, including the tax implications of any agreement they have made. He is to be impartial and refrain from influencing either party toward making a particular decision. O. Coogler, Structured Mediation in Divorce Settlement 31, 119 (1978). One wonders how this mythical attorney would respond to the question by one of the spouses as to whether a court would be likely to reach the same division of property or custody arrangement which the parties have arrived at. See also K. Schneider and M. Schneider, Divorce Mediation 138 (1984), stating that the mediator and the advisory attorney in structured mediation give their opinions to the parties on whether the agreement is "appropriate" and indicate its advantages and disadvantages, comparing it to other agreements. If this does not constitute giving legal advice to parties in direct conflict with each other, it is hard to imagine what could be so described.

14. See the discussion of dual representation in section 14.7, at notes 31 to 35, supra. Taking a position contra that in the text is Silberman, Professional Responsibility Problems of Divorce Mediation, 16 Fam.L.Q. 107, 118 (1982). Committee on Ethics of the Maryland State Bar Association, Inc. Opinion 80–55A (1980), ABA/BNA Manual 801:4303 seems to take the position that if the advisory attorney does more than fill in the blank forms, the lawyer is in a position of having conflicts of interests.

15. Crouch, Divorce Mediation and Legal Ethics, 16 Fam.L.Q. 219, 229 (1982).

16. Committee on Professional and Judicial Ethics of the Association of the Bar of the City of New York Opinion 80–23 (1980), 7 Fam.L.Rptr. 3097 imposes the strictest standard so far. It provides that a lawyer may not participate in the divorce mediation process where it

appears that the issues are so complex or difficult that the parties cannot prudently reach a resolution without the advice of separate and independent counsel. It is not clear how the lawyer is to make this determination in advance of undertaking the mediation.

17. Committee on Professional Ethics, Connecticut Bar Association Formal Opinion 35 (1982), ABA/BNA Manual 801:2002; Committee on Professional and Judicial Ethics of the Association of the Bar of the City of New York Opinion 80–23 (1981), 7 Fam.L.Rptr. 3097; Ethics Committee of the North Carolina State Bar Association Opinion 286 (1981), ABA/BNA Manual 801:6604. See also Standards of Practice for Family Mediators I, 17 Fam.L.Q. 455 (1984); Crouch, Divorce Mediation and Legal Ethics, 16 Fam.L.Q. 219, 248 (1982).

18. Ibid.; Ethics Committee, Board of Professional Responsibility, Supreme Court of Tennessee Opinion 83–F–39 (1983), ABA/BNA Manual 801:8107.

19. Coogler's Marital Mediation Rule 26 provides that during mediation the parties shall refrain from discussing the matters in mediation with all third parties, including friends or attorneys. O. Coogler, Structured Mediation in Divorce Settlement 123 (1978).

20. Committee on Professional and Judicial Ethics, Association of the Bar of the City of New York Opinion 80–23 (1980), 7 Fam.L.Rptr. 3097; Virginia State Bar Council Opinion 511 (1983), ABA/BNA Manual 801:8815 (mediator may give legal information but not legal advice); Crouch, Divorce Mediation and Legal Ethics, 16 Fam.L.Q. 219, 249 (1982).

21. J. Blades, Family Mediation, Cooperative Divorce Settlement 68 (1985) indicates that this is sometimes done. Coogler's Marital Mediation Rules section 17 forbid it. O. Coogler, Structured Mediation in Divorce Settlement 121 (1978). Commission on Professional and Judicial Ethics of the Association of the Bar of the City of New York Opinion 80–23 (1980), 7 Fam.L.Rptr. 3097

thorities advocate having the parties sign an agreement to the effect that all communications between them and between them and the mediator are to be confidential and are not to be used in any subsequent litigation between them,[22] although since the mediator is not in an attorney-client relationship with the parties, such an agreement may not be enforceable.[23] The lawyer-mediator should not represent either party in any subsequent proceeding between them which is related to the subject of the mediation.[24] All authorities emphasize that the mediator must be fair and impartial,[25] an adjuration which may give comfort to some laymen but which only adds to the uncertainty of the lawyer's position. Certainly no one can say with any assurance what fairness or impartiality require in this context.

The lawyer who mediates in a team with non-lawyers or who is associated with non-lawyers in a family mediation "center" must be concerned with whether he is aiding non-lawyers in the unauthorized practice of law,[26] and whether he is receiving business from an organization in violation of the canons of ethics.[27] Some of the authorities provide precepts offering guidance on these questions, although it is not possible to determine in advance or in general whether non-lawyers are engaged in the unauthorized practice of law.[28] That depends upon the precise nature of their conduct of mediations and upon whether they give legal advice.[29] Of course it may be argued that in mediation no one, lawyer or non-lawyer, is practicing law.[30] But if the activities engaged in include statements to the parties about the consequences of agreements, about the tax implications of agreements, and include assistance in drafting agreements, this is certainly the practice of law in any sense of the phrase.[31] That being so, the lawyer who acts with a mental health professional in mediation must be certain that his co-mediator does not give legal advice in any form to avoid the charge that he is aiding in the unauthorized practice.[32]

The lawyer who participates in a family mediation "center" must avoid other prohibitions of ethical rules or state statutes. The

---

seems also to forbid it, as do the Standards of Practice for Family Mediators III F, 17 Fam.L.Q. 455, 457 (1984).

22. See the text at notes 87 to 90, supra.

23. New Hampshire Bar Association Ethics Committee Opinion 10 (1982), ABA/BNA Manual 801:5703.

24. Committee on Professional Ethics, Connecticut Bar Association Formal Opinion 35 (1982), ABA/BNA Manual 801:2002; Professional Ethics Committee, Kansas Bar Association Opinion 83–3 (1983), ABA/BNA Manual 801:3813; Ethics Committee of the North Carolina State Bar Association Opinion 323 (1982), ABA/BNA Manual 801:6609 (semble); Committee on Professional and Judicial Ethics of the Association of the Bar of the City of New York Opinion 80–23 (1980), 7 Fam.L.Rptr. 3097. See also Standards of Practice for Family Mediators III A, 17 Fam.L.Q. 455, 457 (1984). But Committee on Legal Ethics and Professional Conduct, Ohio State Bar Association Opinion 82–2 (1982), ABA/BNA Manual 801:6827 would permit the mediator to represent one of the parties under some circumstances.

25. But even here there is disagreement. Gaughan, An Essay on the Ethics of Separation and Divorce Mediation in American Bar Association, Special Committee on Alternative Means of Dispute Resolution, Alternative Means of Family Dispute Resolution 321, 329 (1982) states that the mediator should be as neutral and impartial as possible. But the Standards of Practice for Family Mediators III D, 17 Fam.L.Q. 455, 457 (1984) states that the mediator should be impartial but not neutral, and that he should be concerned with fairness and the prevention of unreasonable results.

26. ABA Model Code DR 3–101 states that a lawyer shall not aid a non-lawyer in the unauthorized practice of law. EC 3–5 defines the practice of law in general terms.

27. ABA Model Code DR 2–103(D)(4).

28. Committee on Ethics of the Maryland State Bar Association, Inc. Opinion 80–55A (1980), ABA/BNA Manual 801:4303; Committee on Legal Ethics and Professional Conduct, Ohio State Bar Association Opinion 82–2 (1982), ABA/BNA Manual 801:6827; Committee on Professional and Judicial Ethics of the Association of the Bar of the City of New York Opinion 80–23 (1980), 7 Fam.L. Rptr. 3097.

29. See Silberman, Professional Responsibility Problems of Divorce Mediation, 16 Fam.L.Q. 107, 123 (1982): "It is hard to imagine that a mental health professional can effectively help the couple reach agreement without some understanding of and advice on the legal issues involved."

30. Id. at 130; J. Folberg, and A. Taylor, Mediation 255–258 (1984).

31. ABA Model Code EC 3–5; Ethics Committee, Board of Professional Responsibility, Supreme Court of Tennessee Opinion 83–F–39 (1983), ABA/BNA Manual 801:8107; Committee on Professional Responsibility, Vermont Bar Association Opinion 80–12 (1980), ABA/BNA Manual 801:8601.

32. Committee on Professional Ethics, Connecticut Bar Association Formal Opinion 35 (1982), ABA/BNA Manual 801:2002.

principle is universal, for example, that a corporation or voluntary association may not practice law.[33] Presumably such centers may be able to operate without practicing law if they are managed with this prohibition well in view. Another rule has it that the lawyer may not be in partnership with non-lawyers if any of the activities of the partnership consist of the practice of law.[34] And a lawyer may not share legal fees with a non-lawyer.[35] These rules may also be complied with by a properly organized family mediation association.[36]

The major difficulty confronting the lawyer who participates in these organizations arises when the organization refers mediation business to him. The Supreme Court of the United States has held that a state bar association could not constitutionally prevent a labor union from employing and paying lawyers whose function it was to represent labor union members who had workers' compensation claims.[37] The theory of the case was that any such prohibition by the bar association would violate the union's rights of free speech, assembly and petition under the First Amendment as applied to the state by the

Fourteenth Amendment. The American Bar Association's Disciplinary Rules have been amended to meet the constitutional requirements as they are now perceived.[38] The traditional opposition of the bar to lay organizations' control of lawyers' services has been based on the fear that such control would prejudice the lawyer's independent judgment and his loyalty to his client.[39] The leading bar association authority which has considered whether the lawyer in the family mediation organization will be subject to this sort of interference has held that if he complies with the applicable Disciplinary Rule [40] his participation in the organization is proper,[41] apparently concluding that there is then no risk that his judgment and loyalty will be affected by his membership in the organization. Vigorous arguments to the contrary have been made, however.[42]

Although mediation in divorce cases is relatively new, it offers substantial potential benefits to divorce litigants and to the divorce process as a whole. At the same time mediation must not be so conducted as to violate the traditional principles preventing lawyers from undertaking work which places them in

33. L. Patterson, E. Cheatham, The Profession of Law 315 (1971). See also N.Y.Judiciary L. § 495 (1983). Of course there may be an exception for professional corporations organized under specific authority of state law.

34. ABA Model Code DR 3–103. Ethics Committee of North Carolina State Bar Association Opinion 316 (1982), ABA/BNA Manual 801:6608 forbids the lawyer to provide mediation services under a trade name, the use of a trade name being considered misleading. See also Committee on Legal Ethics and Professional Conduct, Ohio State Bar Association Opinion 82–2 (1982), ABA/BNA Manual 801:6827.

35. ABA Model Code DR 3–102, with limited exceptions not relevant here.

36. See Virginia State Bar Council Opinion 512 (1983), ABA/BNA Manual 801:8816, stating that a mediation center may refer clients to the lawyer if the lawyer pays a referral fee and the fee for mediation is paid to the lawyer.

37. United Mine Workers of America, District 12 v. Illinois State Bar Association, 389 U.S. 217, 88 S.Ct. 353, 19 L.Ed.2d 426 (1967), citing other cases.

38. ABA Model Code DR 2–103(D)(4).

39. See Justice Harlan's dissent in United Mine Workers of America, District 12 v. Illinois State Bar Association, 389 U.S. 217, 230–232, 88 S.Ct. 353, 360–361, 19 L.Ed.2d 426 (1967). See also Committee on Ethics of

the Maryland State Bar Association, Inc. Opinion 80–55A (1980), ABA/BNA Manual 801:4303; Virginia State Bar Council Opinion 516 (1983), ABA/BNA Manual 801:8816, emphasizing that the lawyer participating in a family mediation organization must exercise his independent professional judgment on behalf of his clients.

40. ABA Model Code DR 2–103(D)(4). These requirements are that a) the organization may obtain no profits from the rendition of legal services; b) the lawyer must not promote the mediation for the primary purpose of obtaining financial benefit to himself or to procure financial benefits for lawyers outside of the program of the organization; c) the party seeking mediation and not the organization is recognized as the lawyer's client; d) the lawyer does not know or have reason to know that the divorce mediation program violates any applicable laws, rules of court or other legal requirements.

41. Committee on Professional and Judicial Ethics of the Association of the Bar of the City of New York Opinion 80–23 (1980), 7 Fam.L.Rptr. 3097. But see Ethics Committee, Board of Professional Responsibility, Supreme Court of Tennessee Opinion 83–F–39 (1983), ABA/BNA Manual 801:8107, which seems to take the position that a lawyer may not engage with a non-lawyer in the business of offering mediation services to the public.

42. Crouch, Divorce Mediation and Legal Ethics, 16 Fam.L.Q. 219, 246–247 (1982).

circumstances involving conflicts of interest or interfering with their loyalty to their clients. These principles are based upon public interests just as important as the interest in having divorcing spouses reach amicable and lasting agreements about property and the custody of children. It does not advance mediation's prospects to assume that these principles are not important, or that they do not apply to mediation.

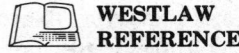 **WESTLAW REFERENCES**

Conciliation

conciliat! /s statut! /s dissol! divorc!

Arbitration

arbitrat! /s divorc! dissol! /s alimony property maintenance

Chapter 15

THE DIVISION OF PROPERTY
ON DIVORCE

Table of Sections

§ 15.1 Division of Property—In General [1]

One consequence of the increased affluence of many Americans in the 1960's and 1970's has been the appearance in many divorce petitions of claims for a division of property between the spouses. Next to custody disputes the property division has become the most litigated aspect of divorce proceedings. It is replacing alimony as a device for adjusting the financial relationships of the spouses, perhaps because of the lessening emphasis on alimony which has resulted from the changed position of women in contemporary society.

The cases have generally held that an order dividing the spouses' property may not be made without statutory authority.[2] If the court in making the order is taking the property of one spouse and transferring it to the other, or is dividing jointly owned property in proportions not representative of the parties' actual title, then express statutory authority is undoubtedly required.[3] But if the court is

§ 15.1

1. For background on this subject see Daggett, Division of Property Upon Dissolution of Marriage, 6 Law & Contemp.Prob. 225 (1939), and Rheinstein, Division of Marital Property, 12 Willamette L.J. 413 (1976).

For an illuminating and thorough study of what courts in California are actually doing when they divide community property on divorce, see L. Weitzman, The Divorce Revolution chs. 3, 4, 5 (1985). Much of what Professor Weitzman says in this important book is relevant to property divisions in other states and in states having a common law property system.

For a critical look at marital property doctrines see Oldham, Is the Concept of Marital Property Outdated? 22 J.Fam.L. 263 (1984).

The enforcement of decrees for property divisions is governed by the same principles (and beset by the same difficulties) as the enforcement of alimony decrees, dis-

cussed infra at sections 15.7 and 16.7 Practitioner's Edition.

2. Dyndul v. Dyndul, 541 F.2d 132 (3d Cir. 1976); McCraney v. McCraney, 208 Miss. 105, 43 So.2d 872 (1950); Britt v. Britt, 119 R.I. 791, 383 A.2d 592 (1978); Smith v. Smith, 264 S.C. 624, 216 S.E.2d 541 (1975); Warne v. Warne, 36 S.D. 573, 156 N.W. 60 (1916); Guy v. Guy, 210 Va. 536, 172 S.E.2d 735 (1970). Other cases are collected in Annot., 133 A.L.R. 860 (1941). Contra: LaRue v. LaRue, ___ W.Va. ___, 304 S.E.2d 312 (1983).

3. Just as statutory authority is required to award alimony in a lump sum, in the view of some courts. Canakaris v. Canakaris, 382 So.2d 1197 (Fla. 1980); Parmly v. Parmly, 125 N.J.Eq. 545, 5 A.2d 789 (1939). It has also been held that a statute giving general authority to divide the property does not allow the court to order the creation of a trust for the parties, but this is contrary to both the letter and spirit of the statute. See Husband

adjudicating the property rights qua property rights, no special statutory authority is needed, the matter lying well within the court's general equity powers.[4] Relief could be given in a separate suit to establish ownership, and there is no reason why a multiplicity of suits should not be avoided by giving the same sort of relief as an incident to the divorce. In this aspect the division of property resembles the winding up of a partnership.[5]

Since today the courts are given the authority to order a division of property by statute in nearly every state,[6] (such statutes often being referred to as equitable distribution statutes) the issue is largely academic. According to some courts, depending of course

upon the particular statutory language, the property of the parties may be divided even if the divorce is denied.[7] Some modern statutes expressly authorize a division of property also in a decree of annulment or of legal separation.[8] And the statutes of several states permit the court in the divorce action to set aside part of the spouses' property for the support of children of the marriage.[9]

There are many variations of detail in the state statutes dealing with property division on divorce, but they can be generally classified at the outset in ways which may be helpful. First there is the broad distinction between the community property states,[10] in which each spouse has an existing interest in

---

C. v. Wife C., 391 A.2d 745 (Del. 1978). Levine v. Levine, 394 Mass. 749, 477 N.E.2d 402 (1985) held that since the court's authority to divide the property is wholly statutory, the trial court could not order an assignment of the husband's property to a child of the marriage.

4. Eakin v. Eakin, 99 So.2d 854 (Fla.1958); Griste v. Griste, 171 Ohio St. 160, 167 N.E.2d 924 (1960); Boehm v. Boehm, 101 Ohio App. 145, 138 N.E.2d 418 (1956). Contra: Flynn v. Flynn, 367 Mich. 625, 116 N.W.2d 907 (1962), holding the court had no authority to decree a life estate to the parties with remainders to the children.

The court may likewise determine in the divorce action the ownership of property held in joint tenancy or tenancy by the entireties. Steinhauer v. Steinhauer, 252 So.2d 825 (Fla.App. 1971); Bowis v. Bowis, 259 Md. 41, 267 A.2d 84 (1970). But see Kahn v. Kahn, 43 N.Y.2d 203, 401 N.Y.S.2d 47, 371 N.E.2d 809 (1977). The not uncommon practice, when divorce is imminent, of a spouse's withdrawal of all the funds from a joint bank account may be remedied by a suit in which the other spouse is able to establish his ownership of the account or part of it. O'Hair v. O'Hair, 109 Ariz. 236, 508 P.2d 66 (1973); Sody v. Sody, 32 Md.App. 644, 363 A.2d 568 (1976).

5. Whitney v. Whitney, 192 Okl. 174, 134 P.2d 357 (1942). See also Sclamberg v. Sclamberg, 220 Ind. 209, 41 N.E.2d 801 (1942).

6. Ala. Code 1983, § 30–2–51; Alaska Stat. § 25.24.160 (1983); Ariz. Rev. Stat. § 25.318 (Supp. 1986); Ark. Stat. § 34–1214 (Supp. 1985); West's Ann. Cal. Civ. Code § 4800 (Supp. 1987); Colo. Rev. Stat. § 14–10–113 (1973, Supp. 1986); Conn. Gen. Stat. Ann. § 46b–81 (1986); Del. Code tit. 13, § 1513 (1981); D.C. Code 1981, § 16–910; Official Code Ga. Ann. § 30–218 (Supp. 1986); Hawaii Rev. Stat. ch. 580, § 47 (Supp. 1984); Idaho Code § 32–713 (1983); Ill.—S.H.A. ch. 40, § 503 (Supp. 1986); West's Ann. Ind. Code § 31–1–11.5–11 (Supp. 1986); Iowa Code Ann. § 598.21 (1981 & Supp. 1986); Kan. Stat. Ann. § 60–1610 (Supp. 1986); Ky. Rev. Stat. § 403.190 (Supp. 1986); L.S.A.—Rev. Stat. § 9:308 (Supp. 1987); Me. Rev. Stat. Ann. tit. 19, § 722–A (1981); Md. Code, Fam. Law § 8–202 (1984 & Supp. 1986); Mass. G.L.A. ch. 208, § 34 (Supp. 1986); Mich. C.L.A. § 25–99 (1984); Minn. Stat. Ann. § 518.58 (Supp. 1987); Vernon's Ann. Mo. Stat.

§ 452.330 (1986); Mont. Code Ann. § 40–4–202 (1985); Neb. Rev. Stat. § 42–365 (1984); Nev. Rev. Stat. § 125.150 (1986); N.H. Rev. Stat. Ann. § 458:19 (Supp. 1986); N.J.Stat. Ann. § 2A:34–23 (Supp. 1986); N.M. Stat. Ann. 1986, § 40–4–7; N.Y.—McKinney's Dom.Rel. Law § 234 (1986); N.C. Gen. Stat. § 50–20 (1984 and Supp. 1985); N.D. Cent. Code § 14–05–24 (1981); Okl. Stat. 1987, tit. 12, § 1278 (Supp.); Or. Rev. Stat. § 107.105 (1983); Pa. Stat. tit. 23, § 401 (Supp. 1986); R.I. Gen. L. 1986, § 15–5–16.1 (Supp.); S.C. Code 1985, § 20–7–420; S.D. Codified Laws § 25–4–44 (1984); Tenn. Code Ann. § 36–4–121 (Supp. 1986); V.T.C.A., Fam. Code § 3.63 (Supp. 1987); Utah Code Ann. 1986, § 30–3–5 (Supp.); Vt. Stat. Ann. tit. 15, § 751 (Supp. 1986); Va. Code 1982, § 20–107.3 (Supp.); West's Rev. Code Wash. Ann. § 26.09.080 (1986); W. Va. Code, § 48–2–21 (1986); Wis. Stat. Ann. § 767.255 (1981 and Supp. 1986); Wyo. Stat. 1986, § 20–2–114 (Supp.). The Uniform Marriage and Divorce Act provision on the division of property is § 307 (Alternative A), 9A Unif.L.Ann. 142 (1979). The New York statute is described in detail in a Note, New York's Equitable Distribution Law; A Sweeping Reform, 47 Bklyn.L.Rev. 67 (1980). The Massachusetts statute is described in Inker and Clower, Towards a New Justice in Marital Dissolution: The Massachusetts Statutory Scheme and Due Process Analysis, 16 Suff.U.L.Rev. 907 (1982).

7. Fincham v. Fincham, 161 Kan. 753, 173 P.2d 244 (1946); Brown v. Brown, 237 Miss. 53, 112 So.2d 556 (1959). Contra: Martin v. Soden, 81 Idaho 274, 340 P.2d 848 (1959); Rothwell v. Rothwell, 219 Or. 221, 347 P.2d 63 (1959).

8. Uniform Marriage & Divorce Act § 307, 9A Unif.L. Ann. 142 (1979).

9. See the statutes of Illinois, Montana, New Mexico, Oklahoma and the Uniform Marriage and Divorce Act, cited supra, note 6.

10. The eight states having community property regimes are Arizona, California, Idaho, Louisiana, Nevada, New Mexico, Texas and Washington. See the statutes cited in note 6, supra. For an excellent review of the Texas law, see McKnight, Division of Texas Marital Property on Divorce, 8 St. Mary's L.J. 413 (1977), and of the

the assets of the community, and the common law property states, in which each spouse owns the property standing in his name. This distinction has come to be blurred at the point of divorce, however, in those common law states having statutes which classify the spouses' property as either marital or separate and which permit the courts to divide the marital property.[11] In such states, for divorce purposes marital property bears a strong resemblance to community property. In other common law states the statutes permit the courts in divorce cases to divide all the property owned by either spouse, regardless of when or how acquired.[12] There are a few states in which the statutes are so brief as to leave matters very largely to the courts.[13]

The property division statutes have generally survived constitutional attack. The argument that they retroactively impair vested property rights has been rejected on the ground that they do not affect the property rights of spouses during the marriage, but merely authorize the disposition of property on divorce.[14] Charges of unconstitutional vagueness have not been upheld.[15] In short, there seems no substantial basis for holding that such statutes have any constitutional infirmities, so long, of course, as they apply even-handedly to both husbands and wives.[16]

It follows from the authority given the courts in these statutes that if one of the spouses makes a fraudulent conveyance to a third party as a means of evading the division

California law see Bruch, The Definition and Division of Marital Property in California; Towards Parity and Simplicity, 33 Hast.L.J. 769 (1982).

11. E.g., Arkansas, Colorado, Delaware, District of Columbia, Illinois, Kentucky, Maine, Maryland, Minnesota, Missouri, New Jersey, New York, North Carolina, Oklahoma, Pennsylvania. Wisconsin's statute authorizes the division of marital property, but then also authorizes the division of separate property in cases of hardship. See the statutes cited in note 6, supra.

Details of the New York statute are discussed in Foster, Commentary on Equitable Distribution, 26 N.Y. School L.Rev. 1 (1981).

In a few of the marital property states there has developed the peculiar institution of a "vested interest" in the marital property on the part of both spouses, occurring when the divorce action is filed. This produces the anomalous situation that after the filing of the divorce complaint each spouse has a vested interest in some proportion of the marital property, the amount of which will not be known until the divorce court enters its final decree. This is a transparent device to evade the consequences of United States v. Davis, 370 U.S. 65, 82 S.Ct. 1190, 8 L.Ed.2d 335 (1962), rehearing denied 371 U.S. 854, 83 S.Ct. 14, 9 L.Ed.2d 92 (1962). See Collins v. Oklahoma Tax Commission, 446 P.2d 290 (Okl. 1968); In re Questions Submitted by United States District Court for District of Colorado Concerning C.R.S. 1963, 41–1–5 and 1971 Perm. Supp., C.R.S. 1963, 46–1–13 in Civil Action No. 26089 Entiled, 184 Colo. 1, 517 P.2d 1331 (1974); Cady v. Cady, 224 Kan. 339, 581 P.2d 358 (1978); Vernon's Ann. Mo.Stat. § 452.330 (Supp. 1983). The tax consequences of this doctrine are discussed infra, in section 16.8.

The distinction between community property and common law property states is further obscured by the Uniform Marital Property Act, which classifies property during marriage as marital or individual, reaching a result much like that in community property states. Uniform Marital Property Act § 4, 9A Unif.L.Ann. 29 (Supp. 1987). That Act also provides that on divorce each

spouse becomes a tenant in common of one half of the marital property, but the act does not provide how the property is to be divided by the divorce court. Uniform Marital Property Act § 17, 9A Unif.L.Ann. 48 (Supp. 1987). See Reppy, The Uniform Marital Property Act: Some Suggested Revisions for a Basically Sound Act, 21 Hous.L.Rev. 679 (1984); Symposium on the Uniform Marital Property Act, 68 Marq.L.Rev. 381–583 (1985).

12. E.g., Alabama, Alaska, Connecticut, Hawaii, Indiana, Kansas, Massachusetts, Montana, Nebraska, New Hampshire, Oregon, Rhode Island, Tennessee, Vermont, Wyoming. The Uniform Act also permits all property to be divided. See the Statutes cited in note 6, supra. Oregon apparently also has adopted the doctrine of vested interests on the filing of the divorce complaint, as in Oklahoma, Colorado, Kansas and Missouri. See the Oregon statute cited supra, note 6.

13. E.g., Georgia, Iowa, Utah, West Virginia.

14. Kujawinski v. Kujawinski, 71 Ill.2d 563, 17 Ill.Dec. 801, 376 N.E.2d 1382 (1978); Fournier v. Fournier, 376 A.2d 100 (Me. 1977).

15. In re Marriage of Thornqvist, 79 Ill.App.3d 791, 35 Ill.Dec. 342, 399 N.E.2d 176 (1979).

16. A case holding the Idaho statute unconstitutional on the ground of gender discrimination is Suter v. Suter, 97 Idaho 461, 546 P.2d 1169 (1976). Contra, M. v. M., 321 A.2d 115 (Del. 1974). Eggemeyer v. Eggemeyer, 554 S.W.2d 137 (Tex. 1977), appeal after remand 623 S.W.2d 462 (Tex.App. 1981), 10 St. Mary's L.J. 37 (1978) and Cameron v. Cameron, 641 S.W.2d 210 (Tex. 1982) intimated that a statute authorizing the court to order separate property of the spouses to be divided on divorce would be unconstitutional as impairing vested property rights, but this seems dubious. And Hatch v. Hatch, 113 Ariz. 130, 547 P.2d 1044 (1976) took the very doubtful position that under certain circumstances the unequal division of community property would be unconstitutional.

For further Texas developments, see McKnight, Family Law: Husband and Wife, 34 S.W.L.J. 115, 147 (1980).

of marital property, the divorce court may reach the property in the hands of the transferee and may divide it in accordance with the statute.[17]

With one exception,[18] the statutes cited do not make any effort to distinguish the division of property between spouses from an award of alimony. It would be nice if this question could be ignored, but unfortunately the law has developed so that important consequences depend upon whether a particular award is labeled alimony or a division of property. These consequences are:

a) Alimony is generally modifiable when it can be proved that there has been a subsequent change in relevant circumstances,[19] while the property division usually may not be modified.[20] Alimony also usually ends on the remarriage of the recipient,[21] while the division of property (for example when payable in installments) does not.[22] b) Alimony is usually enforceable by contempt,[23] while in some states the award of property (at least in the form of a cash payment) is not.[24] c) the obligation to pay alimony is not dischargeable in bankruptcy,[25] while the obligation to comply with a property award is dischargeable.[26]

17. Kaladic v. Kaladic, 41 Colo.App. 419, 589 P.2d 502 (1978); Molitor v. Molitor, 184 Conn. 530, 440 A.2d 215 (1981); Hofmann v. Hofmann, 94 Ill.2d 205, 68 Ill.Dec. 593, 446 N.E.2d 499 (1983), appeal after remand 125 Ill. App.3d 548, 81 Ill.Dec. 12, 466 N.E.2d 598 (1984); In re Marriage of Peshek, 89 Ill.App.3d 959, 45 Ill.Dec. 347, 412 N.E.2d 698 (1980); Wallace v. Wallace, ___ W.Va. ___, 291 S.E.2d 386 (1982). See also Thigpen v. Kennedy, 238 So.2d 744 (Miss. 1970); Krenzelak v. Krenzelak, 503 Pa. 373, 469 A.2d 987 (1983).

A spouse may also be chargeable in the property division if he uses marital property for his own benefit, for a purpose unrelated to the marriage at a time when divorce is imminent. In re Marriage of Smith, 114 Ill.App. 3d 47, 69 Ill.Dec. 287, 448 N.E.2d 545 (1983).

Protection of a spouse from fraudulent conveyances or from the removal of marital property when divorce is imminent may be provided by preliminary court orders restraining the other spouse's access to the property or, in urgent cases, the appointment of a receiver for the property. Annot., 15 A.L.R.4th 224 (1982). If the property is improperly removed by a spouse in order to defeat the other's claims in divorce, the court may include the removed property in its calculations in arriving at a fair division. Kramer v. Kramer, 111 Misc.2d 388, 444 N.Y.S.2d 991 (1981).

18. Neb. Rev. Stat. § 42–365 (1984) provides that the purpose of the property division is to distribute the marital assets equitably between the parties, while the purpose of alimony is to provide maintenance or support where appropriate.

19. E.g., Uniform Marriage & Divorce Act § 316, 9A Unif.L.Ann. 183 (1979). See also § 16.5, infra.

20. Friedman v. Schneider, 52 So.2d 420 (Fla. 1951); Walters v. Walters, 409 Ill. 298, 99 N.E.2d 342 (1951); Wilhelm v. Wilhelm, 397 N.E.2d 1079 (Ind.App. 1979); Drummond v. Drummond, 209 Kan. 86, 495 P.2d 994 (1972); Pierson v. Pierson, 351 Mich. 637, 88 N.W.2d 500 (1958); Mamalis v. Bornovas, 112 N.H. 423, 297 A.2d 660 (1972); Nelson v. Nelson, 181 Or. 494, 182 P.2d 416 (1947); Austad v. Austad, 2 Utah 2d 49, 269 P.2d 284 (1954), 4 Utah L.Rev. 280 (1954) (dictum). But see Lebreton v. Lebreton, 604 P.2d 469 (Utah 1979). Other cases are cited in Annot., 48 A.L.R.2d 270, 302 (1956). The statutes of many states and the Uniform Marriage and Divorce Act expressly provide that property division

decrees are not modifiable. Of course such decrees may be reopened on grounds which warrant the reopening of any other judgment. See, e.g., Ariz. Rev. Stat. § 25–327 (Supp.1986); Colo. Rev. Stat. § 14–10–122 (Supp.1986); Uniform Marriage and Divorce Act § 316, 9A Unif.L. Ann. 183 (1979). On the reopening of judgments for fraud or mistake, see section 14.6, supra.

21. See § 16.5, infra.

22. Hamblett v. Lewis, 114 N.H. 258, 319 A.2d 629 (1974); Nastrom v. Nastrom, 262 N.W.2d 487 (N.D. 1978), appeal after remand 276 N.W.2d 130 (N.D. 1979).

23. See § 16.6, infra.

24. E.g., Proffit v. Proffit, 105 Ariz. 222, 462 P.2d 391 (1969); Bradley v. Superior Court, In and For City and County of San Francisco, 48 Cal.2d 509, 310 P.2d 634 (1957); McAlear v. McAlear, 298 Md. 320, 469 A.2d 1256 (1984); Thomas v. Thomas, 337 Mich. 510, 60 N.W.2d 331 (1953). Contra, permitting contempt enforcement, Harvey v. Harvey, 153 Colo. 15, 384 P.2d 265 (1963); Harris v. Harris, 58 Ohio St.2d 303, 390 N.E.2d 789 (1979); Ex parte Preston, 162 Tex. 379, 347 S.W.2d 938 (1961), 41 Tex.L.Rev. 141 (1962); Decker v. Decker, 52 Wash.2d 456, 326 P.2d 332 (1958), 6 U.C.L.A.L.Rev. 328 (1959), 34 Wash.L.Rev. 192 (1959).

In some states, however, the distinction may be drawn between money decrees, which are not enforceable by contempt, and act decrees, which are so enforceable. See, e.g., Linton v. Linton, 166 Ind.App. 409, 336 N.E.2d 687 (1975), rehearing denied 166 Ind.App. 409, 339 N.E.2d 96 (1975).

25. Bankruptcy Code § 523(a)(5), 11 U.S.C.A. § 523(a) (5). See also section 16.6, infra.

26. Matter of Albin, 591 F.2d 94 (9th Cir.1979); Nitz v. Nitz, 568 F.2d 148 (10th Cir.1977). The property claim passes to the trustee in bankruptcy when it is owed to the bankrupt, in distinction to the alimony claim. Adler v. Nicholas, 381 F.2d 168 (5th Cir.1967).

Community property becomes an asset of the debtor's estate under the Bankruptcy Code § 541(a)(2), 11 U.S. C.A. § 541(a)(2), to be distributed in accordance with § 726(c)(2) of that Code. See Pedlar, Community Property and the Bankruptcy Reform Act of 1978, 11 St. Mary's L.J. 349 (1979) and Matter of Paderewski, 564 F.2d 1353 (9th Cir.1977).

§ 15.1 DIVISION OF PROPERTY ON DIVORCE 593
d) Under the federal income tax until 1984 installments of alimony were deductible by the payer and taxable to the payee, while payments in compliance with an award of property were not taxed to the payee, nor were they deductible by the payer.[27] Fortunately this distinction was eliminated by the Domestic Relations Tax Reform Act of 1984 as to divorce decrees and separation agreements executed after 1984.[28] Pursuant to that Act all payments which comply with the statutory definition of alimony are taxable to the payee and deductible by the payer regardless of whether the purpose of the payments is support or the transfer of property between the spouses.

Given these important differences in consequences between the two aspects of divorce decrees, it is obvious that some attempt should be made to formulate principles which would define the distinction between alimony awards and property distributions. Few of the state court cases discuss the question. Those which do frequently increase rather than reduce one's uncertainty concerning the rationale for characterizing awards. The issue is more often discussed in the federal tax and bankruptcy cases, which presumably are not binding on the state courts. There is the further uncertainty whether the tax cases have any relevance now that the distinction has been eliminated from the tax law.[29] One possible basis for making the distinction between property and alimony might be by reference to the purposes and functions of the two kinds of award. The purposes and functions of alimony are usually said to be the maintenance and support of the spouse and, indirectly, of the children of the marriage.[30] The purpose and function of the division of property was traditionally quite different, to give to each spouse that property which he or she equitably owned, recognizing that in marriage the title to property often does not correspond to the rights of ownership.[31] This purpose of the property division has seemed most obvious in community property states, where each spouse is considered to have a present interest even before divorce in the property of the community.[32] In those states the first step in the division of property is to determine which property is community property and which is the separate property of the spouses, and to set apart to each spouse his separate property. A similar process occurs in those states whose statutes distinguish between marital and separate property, the courts' first step being to award to each spouse his or her separate property.[33]

After each spouse has been awarded his separate property, the community property or the marital property must itself be divided. It is at this point that the difficulty in distinguishing property from alimony awards arises. The purpose of the division of property, under the statutes of many states, is not merely to give to each spouse what he or she equitably owns but is stated in broader terms.[34] In the community property states the court is often enjoined to make an equitable division.[35] In the common law property states the statutes require a division of the marital property (or of all the property where a distinction between marital and separate

---

27. I.R.C. § 71; Wright v. Commissioner, 543 F.2d 593 (7th Cir.1976).

28. I.R.C. § 71, Pub.L. 98–369, 98 Stat. 793, 795 (1984). See the discussion of the changes in section 16.8, infra.

29. See section 16.8, infra.

30. See the discussion in section 16.4, infra.

31. Cases which suggest that this is the basis for the property division include McPhee v. McPhee, 186 Conn. 167, 440 A.2d 274 (1982); Garver v. Garver, 184 Kan. 145, 334 P.2d 408 (1959); Chalmers v. Chalmers, 65 N.J. 186, 320 A.2d 478 (1974); Williams v. Williams, 302 N.W.2d 754 (N.D.1981).

32. Daggett, Division of Property on Dissolution of Marriage, 6 L. & Contemp.Prob. 224, 230 (1939). See also section 7.2, supra. The same would be true under the Uniform Marital Property Act, 9A Unif.L.Ann. 25 (Supp. 1987). See also Koelsch v. Koelsch, 148 Ariz. 176, 713 P.2d 1234 (1986).

33. See note 11, supra.

34. See the statutes cited in note 6, supra, and the text discussion at notes 94 to 14, infra.

35. E.g., V.T.C.A., Fam. Code § 3.63 (Supp. 1987) (property to be divided as the court deems just and right); West's Rev. Code Wash. Ann. § 26.09.080 (1986) (court to make such division as appears just and equitable). West's Ann.Cal.Civ.Code § 4800 (Supp. 1987) differs, requiring an equal division of the community property.

property is not required) which is just, or reasonable, or equitable, after taking into account a list of factors which usually includes the financial and non-financial contributions of both spouses to the marriage, and, in addition, the post-divorce economic circumstances and needs of the spouses.[36]

Statutes enacted in these terms justify the inference that the purpose of the property division is as much to provide for the financial needs of the spouses after the divorce as to award to each what he or she equitably owns. The purpose and function of the property division then looks very much like the purpose and function of alimony or maintenance. The task of making a rational distinction between the two becomes difficult, indeed impossible. The difficulties are compounded by decisions which say that "alimony" has two elements, the division of property and periodic payments for support;[37] or by those which award alimony in gross, that is, in a lump sum, which is often treated like a division of property;[38] or by those insisting that the property award be made first and alimony second, thereby making it plain that if the spouse receives more property, he or she should receive less alimony, or vice versa.[39]

The cases which attempt to characterize property awards made under these statutes

exhibit understandable confusion. Some of them hold that the character of the award depends upon the intent of the parties where the award was based upon a separation agreement, or the intent of the divorce court where only the decree was involved.[40] Other cases say that the label placed on the award by the court or the parties is not controlling, thereby not only frustrating the parties' expectations but also making impossible any rational divorce planning.[41] Still other cases seem to be willing to hold an award to be property only where it appears that both spouses had contributed property to the marriage, apparently being unaware that under modern statutes the contribution of a spouse as homemaker may be the basis for a division of property.[42] The form of the award may be persuasive to some courts.[43] If the award specifically has as its purpose the support of wife or children, it is often held to be alimony, even though that is also one of the purposes of the division of property.[44]

Some of the bankruptcy cases hold that the state law controls the characterization of the award,[45] while others hold that state law governs only the legal relationships created by the divorce decree and that the characterization of those relationships as alimony or property is governed by the federal law.[46] Even in

---

36. See the statutes cited in note 6, supra, and the Uniform Marriage and Divorce Act § 307, 9A Unif.L. Ann. 142 (1979).

37. Cherry v. Cherry, 66 Ohio St.2d 348, 421 N.E.2d 1293 (1981). The ultimate in confusion occurs in Oklahoma, where the courts have created categories of "support alimony" and "property division alimony". Hubbard v. Hubbard, 603 P.2d 747 (Okl.1979). See also Reiss v. Reiss, 200 N.J.Super. 122, 490 A.2d 378 (1984), affirmed 205 N.J.Super. 41, 500 A.2d 24 (1985) which seems to say that reimbursement alimony is neither alimony nor a marital asset.

38. E.g., West's Fla.Stat.Ann. § 61.08 (1985); Rayer v. Rayer, 32 Colo.App. 400, 512 P.2d 637 (1973); Scoville v. Scoville, 179 Conn. 277, 426 A.2d 271 (1979); In re Burks, 100 Ill.App.3d 700, 56 Ill.Dec. 273, 427 N.E.2d 353 (1981). But see Gallagher v. Gallagher, 399 So.2d 75 (Fla.App. 1981).

39. In re Marriage of Jones, 627 P.2d 248 (Colo.1981); In re Marriage of Johnsrud, 181 Mont. 544, 572 P.2d 902 (1977).

40. McAlear v. McAlear, 298 Md. 320, 469 A.2d 1256 (1984) (semble). The tax cases are especially conflicting on this point. Cf. Wright v. Commissioner, 543 F.2d 593

(7th Cir.1976) and Schatten v. United States, 746 F.2d 319 (6th Cir.1984) with Schottenstein v. Commissioner, 75 T.C. 451 (1980). It is not clear what force, if any, these cases will continue to have after the Internal Revenue Code has eliminated the need for the property-alimony distinction.

41. Wright v. Commissioner, 543 F.2d 593 (7th Cir. 1976); In re Smith, 436 F.Supp. 469 (N.D.Ga.1977).

42. Schottenstein v. Commissioner, 75 T.C. 451 (1980).

43. Riley v. Commissioner, 649 F.2d 768 (10th Cir. 1981); Matter of Woods, 561 F.2d 27 (7th Cir.1977); In re Francisco, 1 B.R. 565 (U.S.Bkrtcy.1979); Nitz v. Nitz, 568 F.2d 148 (10th Cir.1977); Hopper v. Hopper, 183 Mont. 543, 601 P.2d 29 (1979).

44. Wright v. Commissioner, 543 F.2d 593 (7th Cir. 1976); Hayutin v. Commissioner, 508 F.2d 462 (10th Cir. 1974); Schatz v. Commissioner, 42 T.C.M. 292 (1981). See also Annot., 19 A.L.R.4th 239 (1983).

45. Nitz v. Nitz, 568 F.2d 148 (10th Cir.1977).

46. Matter of Albin, 591 F.2d 94 (9th Cir. 1979). A tax case, Hayutin v. Commissioner, 508 F.2d 462 (10th Cir. 1974), likewise held that the characterization of the award is for the federal courts, applying federal law, but

the latter cases there are sometimes indications that the court is more influenced by the desire to protect the spouse who is dependent upon the award than by a strictly logical approach to the issue.[47]

Although no one can predict with assurance how awards will be characterized, especially in the bankruptcy context, lawyers can take some steps to vindicate their clients' purposes. The agreement or decree should clearly label the payments, should contain provisions covering both alimony and property, if only nominal ones for either, and should spell out whether either award is modifiable on death or remarriage or other eventuality. If this is done, there is at least a legitimate hope that the courts will treat the awards as the parties intended.[48] It is certainly regrettable that where the parties and the divorce court do clearly characterize the payments, their characterization is not controlling in later litigation, either state or federal. The parties' interest in being able to plan their post-divorce obligations more than outweighs any state or federal interest in giving the payments a characterization different from that of the parties.

**WESTLAW
REFERENCES**

di(statute statutory law legislat! /3 authority authoriz! /s divid! division distribut! /2 property /s divorc! dissol!)

sy,di(property /2 award! division divid! distribut! /s enforc! /3 contempt)

find 591 f2d 94

ti(mcphee +s mcphee)

---

§ 15.2   Division of Property—Marital and Separate Property Defined—In General [1]

As has been indicated,[2] the statutes of many states provide that the division of property on divorce shall proceed in two steps. First, the separate property of each spouse is set over to that spouse. Second, the marital property is divided between the spouses. This form of statute obviously requires that the terms "separate property" and "marital property" be defined. The statutes themselves contain definitions, but the task of applying the ostensibly simple statutory definitions to the variety of property interests which married persons may own is left to the courts.

Marital property is defined by this group of statutes as that property acquired by either spouse during the marriage, with certain named exceptions.[3] Any property which does not fit the definition of marital property is separate property. The exceptions usually consist of property acquired by gift, bequest, devise or inheritance;[4] property acquired in exchange for property acquired by gift, be-

---

this holding may have been disapproved by Imel v. United States, 523 F.2d 853 (10th Cir. 1975).

47. In re Smith, 436 F.Supp. 469 (N.D.Ga. 1977).

48. Riley v. Commissioner, 649 F.2d 768 (10th Cir. 1981) provides some basis for this hope. But see Widmer v. Commissioner, 75 T.C. 405 (1980), in which the Tax Court held that the payments were property after both the parties and the divorce court did everything possible to express the intention that they be alimony.

§ 15.2

1. The discussion which immediately follows deals with the definitions of marital and separate property in general and as applied to some specific circumstances. Some frequently litigated questions, such as the treatment of pensions and retirement income, of professional good will, and of professional education and licenses, will be discussed further along in this Chapter.

2. See the statutes referred to in note 11, and cited in note 6, supra, section 15.1.

3. Most of the marital property statutes contain this definition and these exceptions, although there are some

variations from state to state. The statutes reproduce an early version of the Uniform Marriage & Divorce Act § 307, 9 Unif.L.Ann. 490 (1973), quoted in Zillert v. Zillert, 395 A.2d 1152, 1154 (Me. 1978).

Where the parties live together before marriage, during that time acquire property, later marry and then sue for divorce, the property so acquired is not held to be marital property in those states which permit only marital property to be divided on divorce. E.g., Crouch v. Crouch, 88 Ill.App.3d 426, 43 Ill.Dec. 580, 410 N.E.2d 580 (1980); Grishman v. Grishman, 407 A.2d 9 (Me. 1979).

4. Where the gift or bequest is to *both* spouses, in joint tenancy for example, the property ought to be considered marital rather than separate since both parties share it. The arguments pro and con on this question are given in Grant v. Grant, 424 A.2d 139 (Me. 1981). The same should be true of wedding gifts if they are made to both spouses after the marriage. Cf. Cohan v. Cohan, 172 Colo. 563, 474 P.2d 792 (1970); In re Marriage of Vrban, 359 N.W.2d 420 (Iowa 1984); W. de Funiak and M. Vaughn, Principles of Community Property § 69 (2d ed. 1971).

quest, devise or inheritance; [5] property which is excluded from marital property by a valid agreement of the parties; and in some of the states property acquired by either spouse after a judgment of legal separation.[6] These statutes assist the process of judicial definition by providing that there is a presumption that property acquired during the marriage is marital property, a presumption which may be rebutted by showing that the particular property falls within one of the exceptions.[7]

Due to the relatively recent enactment of marital property statutes, many of the questions which they raise have not been answered by the courts. The rationale of these statutes is similar to that of community property, however. That is, that marriage should be considered analogous to a partnership so that when the marriage ends both spouses should share in whatever property has been produced from their joint efforts.[8] Since there is this similarity in policy, the case law in community property states should be persuasive in deciding questions arising under marital property statutes.[9] Unfortunately this source of authority is not as helpful as it might be, however, because of the diversity of result among the community property states respecting many of the distinctions between community and separate property.

Two related doctrines of community property have made their appearance in the marital property cases. The first of these is commingling, according to which separate property becomes marital property if inextricably mingled with marital property or with the separate property of the other spouse.[10] If the separate property continues to be segregated or can be traced into its product, commingling does not occur. The second doctrine is that of transmutation. This occurs when separate property is treated in such a way as to give evidence of an intention that it become marital property. One method of causing transmutation is to purchase property with separate funds but to take title in joint tenancy.[11] This may also be done by placing separate property in the names of both spouses.[12] The rationale underlying both of these doctrines is that dealing with property in these ways creates a rebuttable presumption of a gift to the marital estate. This presumption is based also upon the provision in many marital property statutes that property acquired during the marriage is presumed marital. The presumption can be rebutted by evidence of cir-

5. Where property of greater value than the separate property is acquired in exchange for the separate property, the acquired property should be separate to the extent of the value of the separate property exchanged for it. Tibbetts v. Tibbetts, 406 A.2d 70 (Me.1979).

6. Statutes containing these exemptions are typified by Colo. Rev. Stat. § 14–10–113(2)(c) (1973); Ill.—S.H.A. ch. 40, § 503(a)(3) (Supp. 1986); Me. Rev. Stat. Ann. tit. 19, § 722–A(2)(c) (1981). See also Schanck v. Schanck, 717 P.2d 1 (Alaska 1986).

7. Without evidence to the contrary, the presumption will cause the property to be treated as marital. Zillert v. Zillert, 395 A.2d 1152 (Me. 1978). The burden of proof is on the spouse asserting that the property is separate. In re Marriage of Emken, 89 Ill.App.3d 667, 44 Ill.Dec. 477, 411 N.E.2d 599 (1980); In re Marriage of Amato, 80 Ill.App.3d 395, 35 Ill.Dec. 729, 399 N.E.2d 1018 (1980). For a case imposing a strict standard of proof for rebuttal of the presumption, see Conrad v. Bowers, 533 S.W.2d 614 (Mo. App. 1975).

8. Krauskopf, Marital Property at Marriage Dissolution, 43 Mo.L.Rev. 157 (1978).

9. See Grant v. Grant, 424 A.2d 139, 144 (Me. 1981).

10. In re Marriage of Marsden, 130 Cal.App.3d 426, 181 Cal.Rptr. 910 (1982); In re Killgore's Marriage, 532 P.2d 386 (Colo.App.1974) (semble); Sturgis v. Sturgis, 663

S.W.2d 375 (Mo.App.1983). See also Ill.—S.H.A. ch. 40, § 503(c) (Supp.1986).

11. Carter v. Carter, 419 A.2d 1018 (Me.1980). The reason for this doctrine is that when property was taken in some form of joint ownership between spouses a gift to the non-acquiring spouse was presumed. But Grant v. Zich, 300 Md. 256, 477 A.2d 1163 (1984) held that this presumption no longer applies to the definition of marital property, and when property is acquired in this form, the source of funds doctrine determines the characterization of the property. See note 15, infra. Ill.—S.H.A. ch. 40, § 503(b) (Supp.1986) provides that all property acquired during marriage is presumed marital, even though title is taken in some form of joint ownership, but that this presumption may be rebutted by proof that the acquisition occurred in one of the ways producing separate property.

See also Krauskopf, Marital Property At Marriage Dissolution, 43 Mo.L.Rev. 157, 190 (1978); Gregory, Marital Property in Illinois, 1982 So.Ill.U.L.J. 159; 4A R. Powell, Real Property § 624.4 (Rev.ed. Rohan 1979); Krauskopf, The Transmutation and Source of Funds Rules in Divisions of Marital Property, 50 Mo.L.Rev. 759 (1985).

12. Goldstein v. Goldstein, 310 So.2d 361 (Fla.App. 1975). But see Smith v. Smith, 472 A.2d 943 (Me.1984).

cumstances or communications clearly indicating an intent that the property remain separate.

It is important to notice that the doctrines of commingling and transmutation may often result in unfairness if, as is usually the case in marriage, the parties do not keep records of what is done with the property they own or acquire. For example, if a wife inherits a large sum and it is commingled with marital property, which is then exchanged for other property and there are no accurate records which could be the basis for tracing the inheritance, she will receive much less on divorce than she normally should in view of her contribution of separate property. The moral for spouses with large amounts of separate property would seem to be that they should not trust each other but should be careful to ensure that separate property does not get commingled or transmuted, a moral very destructive of good marital relations.

Under the marital property statutes the classification of property as separate or marital may turn on whether it was acquired before or after marriage. This creates a large number of problems in many different contexts, on which the cases and statutes reach a variety of different results. The simplest example occurs when a spouse buys or contracts to buy property before marriage but pays for it after marriage in part from marital funds. The community property states do not agree on how such property should be characterized. Some of them hold that the date of the inception of title is the crucial circumstance. If that occurred before the marriage, the proper-

ty is separate and remains so even though paid for after marriage.[13] Other states take the position that the property should be apportioned between separate and community interests in proportion to the sums paid from separate and community funds.[14] The cases in marital property states have generally chosen to follow this "source of funds" rule, allocating the property between separate and marital interests in proportion to the contributions from separate and marital sources.[15] The inception of title rule has the virtue of ease and convenience of application. The source of funds rule requires difficult calculations in many instances, but by recognizing the contributions of both spouses to the property, it is more consonant with the policy underlying both community and marital property regimes.

In the analogous situation, where separate property is improved by the use of community funds or the labor of the non-owning spouse, the community property cases generally hold that this does not affect the property's separate character, but that the community is entitled to reimbursement for the value of the improvements.[16] A few marital property decisions seem to take the same position.[17]

Where separate property is acquired before marriage, but it is mortgaged and the note which the mortgage secures is signed by both spouses, the community property states have been unable to agree on whether the property retains its separate status. Some of them hold that it does, while others attempt to determine the intent of the mortgage lender in relying on the separate property or the

13. See section 7.2, supra, at note 71. McCurdy v. McCurdy, 372 S.W.2d 381 (Tex. Civ. App. 1963); Pritchard v. Snow, 530 S.W.2d 889 (Tex. Civ. App. 1975) (insurance policies).

14. In re Marriage of Moore, 28 Cal.3d 366, 168 Cal. Rptr. 662, 618 P.2d 208 (1980); In re Marriage of Marsden, 130 Cal.App.3d 426, 181 Cal.Rptr. 910 (1982). This is sometimes referred to as the source of funds rule.

See also Note, The Division of Family Residence Acquired with a Mixture of Separate and Community Funds, 70 Cal.L.Rev. 1263 (1982).

15. Brandenburg v. Brandenburg, 617 S.W.2d 871 (Ky. App.1981); Tibbetts v. Tibbetts, 406 A.2d 70 (Me.1979), 45 Mo.L.Rev. 538 (1980); Schweizer v. Schweizer, 301 Md. 626, 484 A.2d 267 (1984); Harper v. Harper, 294 Md. 54,

448 A.2d 916 (1982), appeal after remand 58 Md.App. 193, 472 A.2d 1018 (1984); Hoffman v. Hoffman, 676 S.W.2d 817 (Mo.1984).

Illinois has adopted still a different rule, requiring that the marital estate be reimbursed in the amount of its contribution to the separate property, except where the contribution cannot be traced, or was a gift, or was not significant. Ill.—S.H.A. ch. 40, § 503(c) (Supp.1986).

16. Jensen v. Jensen, 665 S.W.2d 107 (Tex. 1984); W. de Funiak and M. Vaughn, Principles of Community Property 171 (2d ed. 1971); 4A R. Powell, Real Property 741 (Rev. ed. Rohan 1979). But see Wanberg v. Wanberg, 664 P.2d 568 (Alaska 1983).

17. Gaskie v. Gaskie, 188 Colo. 239, 534 P.2d 629 (1975); Higby v. Higby, 538 P.2d 493 (Colo.App. 1975).

credit of the spouses.[18] The marital property cases are also divided on the question, some of them holding that the property remains separate, while others appear to hold that the pledging of the spouse's credit transforms the property into marital property.[19]

Questions about when property was received arise in other contexts in the marital property states. Thus where the husband was the beneficiary of a trust set up before his marriage, but where he did not receive the principal of the trust until after marriage, the principal was held to be acquired during marriage and therefore divisible on divorce.[20] Conversely, property acquired before the divorce action is brought and after marriage is held to be marital property in a variety of situations.[21]

As has been indicated,[22] property acquired before marriage but paid for in whole or in part after marriage from marital funds has been characterized, at least in some cases, as separate property. A related question arises when separate property either appreciates in value or produces income after marriage. Some states have attempted to deal with these questions by statute. The Missouri and Illinois statutes define marital property as property acquired subsequent to the marriage except (inter alia) the increase in value of property acquired before the marriage.[23] On the other hand, the Colorado statute provides that an asset acquired before marriage or by gift, devise, bequest or descent, or acquired in exchange for such property shall be considered marital property to the extent that its present value exceeds its value at the time of

18. Cases are collected and discussed in Young, Community Property Classification of Credit Acquisitions in California: Law Without Logic? 17 Cal.West.L.Rev. 173 (1981).

19. Holding the property separate: Drennan v. Drennan, 93 Ill.App.3d 903, 49 Ill.Dec. 386, 418 N.E.2d 30 (1981); Davis v. Davis, 544 S.W.2d 259 (Mo.App.1976). Appearing to hold the property marital: Wanberg v. Wanberg, 664 P.2d 568 (Alaska 1983).

20. Mey v. Mey, 79 N.J. 121, 398 A.2d 88 (1979). See also Gauger v. Gauger, 73 N.J. 538, 376 A.2d 523 (1977), where the husband became a joint tenant of land before marriage, but acquired the whole parcel by right of survivorship after marriage. The court held that half of the value of the property became marital property on the death of the other joint tenant. The husband's interest by right of survivorship, created before marriage, was held not to be effective or meaningful until the death of the other joint tenant. Other cases holding that various contingent interests are not marital property include In re Marriage of Rosenblum, 43 Colo.App. 144, 602 P.2d 892 (1979); Storm v. Storm, 470 P.2d 367 (Wyo. 1970), appeal after remand 489 P.2d 1167 (Wyo.1971). But In re Marriage of Johnson, 40 Colo.App. 250, 576 P.2d 188 (1977) held that real estate commissions were marital property where the husband had performed the services as a broker before the divorce, but the conveyances of the property had not occurred at that time. And Raney v. Raney, 262 Ark. 747, 561 S.W.2d 287 (1978) held that the trial court properly required the husband to make the wife the beneficiary of a major part of his life insurance. Perhaps the most extraordinary of this kind of case is A.I.D. v. P.M.D., 408 A.2d 940 (Del.1979), in which the court held that the trial court could divide nonexistent marital property, that is, property which the husband had acquired during the marriage but had spent, the order dividing it to be satisfied out of trust income which the husband would receive in the future.

21. In re Marriage of Carruthers, 40 Colo.App. 278, 577 P.2d 773 (1977) (stored corn crop is marital property

though acquired after the parties' separation but before the divorce decree was entered); Rieger v. Christensen, 529 P.2d 1362 (Colo.App. 1974) (bonus earned before the divorce but declared and paid after it is marital property); Wife J. v. Husband J., 367 A.2d 655 (Del.Super. 1976) (property acquired after divorce complaint filed but before decree is marital property); Portner v. Portner, 93 N.J. 215, 460 A.2d 115 (1983) and Brandenburg v. Brandenburg, 83 N.J. 198, 416 A.2d 327 (1980) (property acquired after separation but before divorce complaint is filed is marital property but may be other exceptional situations). Wilkins v. Stout, 588 P.2d 145 (Utah 1978) (wife continues to receive share of royalties on books published before the divorce, but not on editions published after divorce). In California the earnings of a spouse living separate and apart from the other spouse are separate property. In re Marriage of Bouquet, 16 Cal.3d 583, 128 Cal.Rptr. 427, 546 P.2d 1371 (1976).

For the allocation of stock options between marital and separate property, see In re Marriage of Hug, 154 Cal. App.3d 780, 201 Cal.Rptr. 676 (1984).

22. See the text at notes 13 to 15, supra.

23. Ill.—S.H.A. ch. 40, § 503(a)(7) (Supp.1986); In re Marriage of Komnick, 84 Ill.2d 89, 49 Ill.Dec. 291, 417 N.E.2d 1305 (1981); Vernon's Ann.Mo.Stat. § 452.330(2) (5) (1986). Under the Illinois provision either the marital estate or the property of the non-owning spouse may be reimbursed if the separate property's increase is due to contributions from or the efforts of the other spouse. See also Gregory, Marital Property in Illinois, 1982 So.Ill.U.L. J. 159.

Appreciation in separation property which was due at least in part or indirectly to the marital efforts of the non-owning spouse was held to be marital property in Cassiday v. Cassiday, 716 P.2d 1133 (Hawaii 1986); McLeod v. McLeod, 74 N.C.App. 144, 327 S.E.2d 910 (1985), cert. denied 314 N.C. 331, 333 S.E.2d 488 (1985).

the marriage or at the time of acquisition.[24] Stock splits and stock dividends should be considered a form of appreciation in the value of the stock, and therefore treated as separate or marital property as these statutes would require.[25] In the absence of express statute, increases in the value of separate property should probably be held to be separate property, where they result from external economic forces, such as inflation, since this is the position taken in community property states.[26]

Where the increase in the value of separate property is attributable to the use of marital capital or to the labor and industry of the spouses after marriage rather than to general economic conditions or "natural causes", the question of characterization is more difficult. The Illinois statute indicates that the marital estate or the non-owning spouse would be entitled to reimbursement for the increment in value under such circumstances.[27] This is consistent with the policy of marital property by recognizing the contributions of the spouses to the increase in value. Even without specific statutory authority cases in both the community property and marital property states find a way to include the increased value in marital property, using one of several possible formulae for computing the proportion of marital or community property resulting from the application of community capital or labor to the separate property.[28]

The treatment of income, rents or profits from separate property is largely governed by statute in the community property states. Traditional Spanish community property law had it that the income from separate property became community property and some states retain this rule.[29] In other states it remains separate property.[30] The policy of the marital property statutes would seem best vindicated by holding such income to be marital property, particularly in view of the presumption that property acquired during the marriage is marital.[31]

---

24. Colo. Rev. Stat. § 14–10–113(4) (1973).

25. In re Marriage of Smith, 86 Ill.2d 518, 56 Ill.Dec. 693, 427 N.E.2d 1239 (1981); In re Marriage of Scott, 85 Ill.App.3d 773, 41 Ill.Dec. 547, 407 N.E.2d 1045 (1980). But E.C.W. v. M.A.W., 419 A.2d 934 (Del. 1980) makes a distinction for this purpose between stock splits and stock dividends.

26. Elam v. Elam, 97 Wash.2d 811, 650 P.2d 213 (1982); W. de Funiak and M. Vaughn, Principles of Community Property 169–70 (2d ed. 1971). Other cases are cited in Annot., 24 A.L.R.4th 453 (1983). In re Marriage of Komnick, 84 Ill.2d 89, 49 Ill.Dec. 291, 417 N.E.2d 1305 (1981) and Wade v. Wade, 72 N.C.App. 372, 325 S.E.2d 260 (1985), review denied 313 N.C. 612, 330 S.E.2d 616 (1985) take this position in reliance on the statute. But the non-owning spouse is entitled to a share of the increased value where that resulted from marital funds. Honnas v. Honnas, 133 Ariz. 39, 648 P.2d 1045 (1982).

27. See the Illinois statute cited, supra, in note 23. Stark v. Stark, 539 S.W.2d 779 (Mo.App.1976) held that separate property's character remained unchanged even though increases in it were due to efforts occurring after marriage.

28. Beam v. Bank of America, 6 Cal.3d 12, 98 Cal. Rptr. 137, 490 P.2d 257 (1971) (community income is defined as the amount by which the actual income of the separate estate exceeded the return which the separate property would have earned in the absence of the spouse's efforts). Another method would be to determine the reasonable value of the spouse's services, allocating that amount to the marital or community property. See Pereira v. Pereira, 156 Cal. 1, 103 P. 488 (1909); Van Camp v. Van Camp, 53 Cal.App. 17, 199 P. 885 (1921);

Jensen v. Jensen, 665 S.W.2d 107 (Tex.1984). Other cases reaching similar results include Cockrill v. Cockrill, 124 Ariz. 50, 601 P.2d 1334 (1979), appeal after remand 139 Ariz. 72, 676 P.2d 1130 (App.1983); Gravenstine v. Gravenstine, 58 Md.App. 158, 472 A.2d 1001 (1984); Schulman v. Schulman, 92 Nev. 707, 558 P.2d 525 (1976). See also N.Y.—McKinney's Dom.Rel.L. § 236, Part B(d)(3) (1986); Sementilli v. Sementilli, 102 A.D.2d 78, 477 N.Y.S.2d 626 (1st Dep't 1984).

New Mexico takes the position that the community is entitled to the increase in the value of the separate property which is attributable to the community funds or labor of the spouses. Portillo v. Shappie, 97 N.M. 59, 636 P.2d 878 (1981).

For a critical discussion of these rules, see Bodenheimer, The Community Without Community Property: The Need for Legislative Attention to Separate-Property Marriages Under Community Property Laws, 8 Cal.West.L.Rev. 381 (1972).

29. Idaho Code § 32–906 (1983).

30. Ariz.R.S. § 25–213 (1976); West's Ann. Cal. Civ. Code §§ 5107, 5108 (1983); Nev. Rev. Stat. § 123.130 (1979); N.M. Stat. Ann. 1986, § 40–3–8 West's Rev. Code Wash. Ann. §§ 26.16.010, 26.16.020 (1986).

31. See note 7, supra. Cases which support the text are J.D.P. v. F.J.H., 399 A.2d 207 (Dec. 1979) (increase in the retained net earnings of a corporation in which the husband held 65% of the stock as his separate property is marital property); Sousley v. Sousley, 614 S.W.2d 942 (Ky.1981). E.C.W. v. M.A.W., 419 A.2d 934 (Del.1980) held that stock dividends on shares of stock acquired before marriage were marital property, but this seems wrong since the only effect of a stock dividend is to

Damages for personal injury present a special problem of characterization as marital or separate property. The community property states do not agree on whether such damages are to be considered separate or community, or partly separate and partly community property.[32] To the extent that such damages represent recovery for loss of earnings, logic seems to indicate that they should be marital property. The few decisions extant in the marital property states label them marital property on the ground that they do not come within the listed exceptions to marital property, and that they fall within the statutory presumption that property acquired during marriage is marital.[33]

WESTLAW REFERENCES

sy(marital marry! marri! /2 property /3 define* definition defining mean***)

he("separate property" /3 defin! mean***)

di(combin! commingl! /s separate /s marital marry! marri! /5 property)

source /5 fund /s separate /s marital marry! marri! /5 property

increase the number of shares held by each shareholder, without increasing the value of his interest.

32. V.T.C.A., Fam. Code § 5.01 (1975) (personal injury damages are separate property except for loss of earning capacity); Graham v. Franco, 488 S.W.2d 390 (Tex.1972). West's Ann. Cal. Civ. Code § 5126 (Supp. 1987) provide that damages for personal injury received during marriage are community property except where the claim arose while the injured spouse was living separate and apart or after a separation decree. In Washington the damages attributable to physical injury or pain are separate property. Damages for expenses are community property if the community paid the expenses, and damages for lost wages or decreased earning capacity are usually community property because the wages normally would have produced community property if earned. Brown v. Brown, 100 Wash.2d 729, 675 P.2d 1207 (1984).

33. In re Marriage of Fjeldheim, 676 P.2d 1234 (Colo. App. 1983); Gan v. Gan, 83 Ill.App.3d 265, 38 Ill.Dec. 882, 404 N.E.2d 306 (1980); Harmon v. Harmon, 161 N.J. Super. 206, 391 A.2d 552 (1978). In re Marriage of Dettore, 86 Ill.App.3d 540, 42 Ill.Dec. 51, 408 N.E.2d 429 (1980) and Lukas v. Lukas, 83 Ill.App.3d 606, 39 Ill.Dec. 161, 404 N.E.2d 545 (1980) held workers' compensation awards to be marital property, in the former case where the spouse was injured before but not paid until after the divorce. Contra: Cook v. Cook, 102 Idaho 651, 637 P.2d 799 (1981). In re Marriage of Smith, 84 Ill.App.3d 446, 39 Ill.Dec. 905, 405 N.E.2d 884 (1980) held that a disability pension and insurance proceeds covering the loss of a commercial pilot's license were marital property.

---

ti(portillo +s shappie)

---

§ 15.3 Division of Property—Relevant Factors in the Division

Some of the statutes authorizing the division of property on divorce, particularly those based upon the Uniform Marriage and Divorce Act, set forth in detail the factors which the court must consider in arriving at a division.[1] In addition these statutes contain a general requirement that the division be equitable, or just, or reasonable, or a combination of these or similar terms.[2] Other statutes contain only the general terms, leaving to the courts the formulation of specific factors to be deemed relevant.[3]

Although the statutes generally contain no provision concerning the relative functions of trial and appellate courts in making the property division, the case law is settled that the trial court's decision is to be reversed only in the event of an abuse of its discretion or of an erroneous application or definition of the le-

§ 15.3

1. See the statutes cited in section 15.1, notes 6 and 11, supra.

2. The Uniform Marriage and Divorce Act § 307 in the early version authorizes a division of the marital property "in just proportions". 9 Unif.L.Ann. 491 (1973). The later version of the Act authorizes the court to "equitably apportion" the spouses' property between them. The commentary by the commissioners does not indicate what, if any, difference the change in language was intended to make. 9A Unif.L.Ann. 142, 144 (1979).

3. E.g., Alaska Stat. § 25.24.160 (Supp.1986) (court to divide property as may be just); Ariz.Rev.Stat. § 25.318 (Supp.1986) (community property to be divided equitably); Mich.C.L.A. § 25.99 (1984) (just and reasonable division); N.J. Stat. Ann. § 2A:34–23 (Supp.1986) (equitable division); N.Y.—McKinney's Dom. Rel.Law § 236, Part B (1986) (equitable distribution).

California is an exception, since its statute requires an equal division of the community property on divorce. West's Ann.Cal.Civ.Code § 4800 (Supp.1987). The early version of the Uniform Act contains a commissioners' comment to the effect that the division may be equal or unequal. 9 Unif.L.Ann. 492 (1973).

The Oregon statute creates a rebuttable presumption that both spouses have contributed equally to the acquisition of property during the marriage. For a case applying this provision see Matter of Marriage of Jenks, 294 Or. 236, 656 P.2d 286 (1982).

gal principles.[4] In affirming the trial court's discretion, the appellate courts often emphasize that there is no fixed rule as to the proportions in which the property is to be divided,[5] but it is not uncommon for trial courts to develop rules of thumb to aid them in making what are obviously very difficult decisions.[6] As in any case in which the courts must be guided by many factors, however, it is nearly impossible to generalize from the decisions or to predict their outcome. This is particularly true where, as in this instance, the ultimate standard is as vague as "just" or "equitable". There is the additional uncertainty created by the fact that the cases do not agree on the precise date as of which the division shall be made, whether the date of separation,[7] or of the divorce,[8] or the date of the hearing on the property division.[9] The

sensible choice of date would seem to be the date on which the hearing is held since that gives the court the maximum opportunity to evaluate the relevant circumstances.

The Uniform Marriage and Divorce Act, in its earlier version, requires the courts in dividing the marital property to consider the contribution of each spouse to the acquisition of the marital property, including his contribution as a homemaker; the value of their separate property; the duration of the marriage; and the economic circumstances of each spouse when the division is to become effective.[10] The later version of the Act includes a more detailed list of factors, including one or two whose relevance is unclear.[11] Both versions of the statute forbid the courts to take marital misconduct into account. Much of the case law contains factors similar

4. Vanover v. Vanover, 496 P.2d 644 (Alaska 1972); In re Marriage of Graham, 194 Colo. 429, 574 P.2d 75 (1978); Moss v. Moss, 190 Colo. 491, 549 P.2d 404 (1976); Fucci v. Fucci, 179 Conn. 174, 425 A.2d 592 (1979); Almquist v. Almquist, 214 Kan. 788, 522 P.2d 383 (1974); Jaeger v. Jaeger, 547 S.W.2d 207 (Mo.App. 1977) (trial court decision to be sustained unless there was no substantial evidence, or it was against the weight of the evidence or erroneous in law); Erickson v. Erickson, 202 Neb. 345, 275 N.W.2d 287 (1979); Halla v. Halla, 200 N.W.2d 271 (N.D. 1972); Bussewitz v. Bussewitz, 75 Wis.2d 78, 248 N.W.2d 417 (1977); Kane v. Kane, 577 P.2d 172 (Wyo. 1978), affirmed 616 P.2d 780 (Wyo.1980).

5. In re Marriage of Aschwanden, 82 Ill.2d 31, 44 Ill. Dec. 269, 411 N.E.2d 238 (1980); Halla v. Halla, 200 N.W.2d 271 (N.D. 1972); Bussewitz v. Bussewitz, 75 Wis. 2d 78, 248 N.W.2d 417 (1977) (rejecting the earlier one-third rule of thumb).

6. There seems some tendency to make an equal division of property in many cases. E.g., Harrah v. Harrah, 196 Kan. 142, 409 P.2d 1007 (1966); Bollenbach v. Bollenbach, 285 Minn. 418, 175 N.W.2d 148 (1970); Miller v. Miller, 352 N.W.2d 738 (Minn. 1984); In re Marriage of Jacobson, 183 Mont. 517, 600 P.2d 1183 (1979); Cook v. Cook, 159 Mont. 98, 495 P.2d 591 (1972); Kirkland v. Kirkland, 488 P.2d 1222 (Okl. 1971); Winterholler v. Winterholler, 486 P.2d 232 (Wyo. 1971). But In re Marriage of Herron, 186 Mont. 396, 608 P.2d 97 (1980) held that an equal division was error under the circumstances.

In In re Marriage of Kaasa, 181 Mont. 18, 591 P.2d 1110 (1979) the wife was given one-quarter of the property. She was given one-third in Krohn v. Krohn, 284 Minn. 95, 169 N.W.2d 389 (1969), but one-third was held too little in In re Marriage of Johnsrud, 181 Mont. 544, 572 P.2d 902 (1977). A 60%–40% division was approved in In re Marriage of McMahon, 82 Ill.App.3d 1126, 38 Ill. Dec. 499, 403 N.E.2d 730 (1980). And in Allen v. Allen, 554 P.2d 393 (Alaska 1976) the wife was given a life estate in the family home.

Cherry v. Cherry, 66 Ohio St.2d 348, 421 N.E.2d 1293 (1981) suggests that "a potentially equal division should be the starting point of analysis for the trial court." In contrast to this is Herron v. Herron, 573 S.W.2d 342 (Ky. 1978) which holds that the trial court should not indulge in presumptions as to the proportion of the division, but should just apply the statutory standards.

The Uniform Marital Property Act provides that after divorce each spouse owns an undivided half interest in the marital property but it does not purport to state how the divorce court should distribute the property. Uniform Marital Property Act § 17, 9A Unif. L. Ann. 48 (Supp. 1987).

7. Bussell v. Bussell, 623 P.2d 1221 (Alaska 1981); Tucker v. Tucker, 121 N.J.Super. 539, 298 A.2d 91 (1972).

8. Brandenburg v. Brandenburg, 83 N.J. 198, 416 A.2d 327 (1980) (division as of date divorce complaint is filed, in absence of separation agreement). In re Marriage of Frazier, 125 Ill.App.3d 473, 80 Ill.Dec. 838, 466 N.E.2d 290 (1984); Dean v. Dean, 87 Wis.2d 854, 275 N.W.2d 902 (1979).

If there is a separation agreement, executed when the parties have separated, the crucial date is that of the agreement. Smith v. Smith, 72 N.J. 350, 371 A.2d 1 (1977).

9. Colo.Rev.Stat. § 14–10–113(5) (1973) provides that valuation shall be as of the date of the decree, or as of the date of the hearing on disposition of property if such hearing precedes the date of the decree. See notes 17, 18, infra.

10. Uniform Marriage and Divorce Act § 307, 9 Unif. L.Ann. 490 (1973).

11. Uniform Marriage and Divorce Act § 307, 9A Unif.L.Ann. 142 (1979). This statute refers to the prior marriages of either spouse and the "station" of either spouse, both factors hardly appearing to have any bearing on the issue.

to those listed in the Uniform Acts, often in greater detail, and sometimes includes additional factors.[12] A few opinions expressly acknowledge that the relevant factors for the division of property are the same ones which the courts consider in awarding alimony.[13]

The most obvious of the relevant factors in dividing the property of the spouses is the source of the property. Where the spouse claiming a share had a significant role in the acquisition of the property, he is entitled to a share corresponding to his efforts.[14] Conversely, when the spouse acquired the property during a period of financial independence from the other spouse, he is permitted to keep the property so acquired.[15] It should go without saying that the division is not affected by the state of the technical legal title to property as between the parties,[16] except so far as that might indicate a commingling or transmutation of separate into marital property.[17] The fact that part or all of the property was a

gift to one spouse or the other is of course crucial in those states which distinguish between separate and marital property, permitting a division of the marital property alone.[18] But even in those states where all the parties' property may be divided the courts often consider it relevant that the property was given to either spouse or to both.[19] Another important factor, under the Uniform Acts and in many states not having those Acts, is the needs of the spouses, particularly the wife where she is out of the job market or where she has custody of children and is thereby unable to work.[20]

The structure of the property division is important in those cases in which, for example, there is a family business or farm the value of which might be impaired or not realized if a sale were ordered. In such circumstances the courts should award the farm or business to the spouse able to operate it and

12. Of course some states have enacted the Uniform Act in one or other version. See the statutes cited in § 15.1, supra.

For representative cases dealing generally with the relevant factors, see Messer v. Messer, 289 Minn. 449, 184 N.W.2d 801 (1971); Painter v. Painter, 65 N.J. 196, 320 A.2d 484 (1974), 28 Rutgers L.Rev. 447 (1975), 48 Temple L.Q. 397 (1975); Rohde v. Rohde, 154 N.W.2d 385 (N.D. 1967); Lacey v. Lacey, 45 Wis.2d 378, 173 N.W.2d 142 (1970). See also Krauskopf, A Theory for a "Just" Division of Marital Property in Missouri, 41 Mo.L.Rev. 165 (1976); Inker, Walsh, Perrochi, Alimony and Assignment of Property: The New Statutory Scheme in Massachusetts, 10 Suff.L.Rev. 1 (1975); Perlberger, Marital Property Distributions: Legal and Emotional Considerations, 25 Vill.L.Rev. 662 (1980).

A factor not mentioned in the statutes, but one having considerable effect upon what the parties ultimately receive as a result of the division is the federal or state tax liability of each resulting from the form of the division. Where it is speculative whether a party will have a tax liability as a result of the property division, one California case has held that it should not be taken into account in making the division. But where the tax is clearly due as a result of the court's decree or the parties' agreement, the amount of the tax should be considered in determining the share of property each party will receive. In re Marriage of Epstein, 24 Cal.3d 76, 154 Cal.Rptr. 413, 592 P.2d 1165 (1979); In re Marriage of Clark, 80 Cal.App.3d 417, 145 Cal.Rptr. 602 (1978); In re Marriage of Beck, ____ Mont. ____, 631 P.2d 282 (1981). But where the tax liability was not occasioned by the judgment dividing the property, or was incurred in a transaction respecting the property in which the non-owning spouse did not benefit, it has been held that the impact of the tax should not be taken into account in arriving at the division of property.

In re Marriage of Emken, 86 Ill.2d 164, 427 N.E.2d 125 (1981); In re Marriage of Rimmele, 102 Ill.App.3d 88, 57 Ill.Dec. 762, 429 N.E.2d 879 (1981).

13. E.g., Pasquariello v. Pasquariello, 168 Conn. 579, 362 A.2d 835 (1975) (equitable principles apply to both alimony and property division); Libra v. Libra, 157 Mont. 252, 484 P.2d 748 (1971) (alimony provided in lieu of property division); Smith v. Smith, 72 N.J. 350, 371 A.2d 1 (1977) (alimony and property aspects of award "inextricably interrelated").

14. Vanover v. Vanover, 496 P.2d 644 (Alaska 1972); Cooke v. Cooke, 449 S.W.2d 216 (Ky. 1969); Krohn v. Krohn, 284 Minn. 95, 169 N.W.2d 389 (1969); Cozik v. Cozik, 279 Minn. 91, 155 N.W.2d 471 (1968); Brandenburg v. Brandenburg, 83 N.J. 198, 416 A.2d 327 (1980); Beroud v. Beroud, 4 Or.App. 469, 478 P.2d 652 (1971).

15. Marriage of Lemke, 289 Or. 145, 611 P.2d 295 (1980).

16. Cook v. Cook, 159 Mont. 98, 495 P.2d 591 (1972).

17. See the text at notes 10, 11 in sec. 15.2, supra.

18. See the statutes cited in notes 6 and 11, of sec. 15.1, supra.

19. Kirkland v. Kirkland, 488 P.2d 1222 (Okl. 1971); In re Marriage of Herron, 186 Mont. 396, 608 P.2d 97 (1980); In re Marriage of Kaasa, 181 Mont. 18, 591 P.2d 1110 (1979); Winterholler v. Winterholler, 486 P.2d 232 (Wyo. 1971).

20. In re Marriage of Johnsrud, 181 Mont. 544, 572 P.2d 902 (1977); Murff v. Murff, 615 S.W.2d 696 (Tex. 1981). Contra: Durfee v. Durfee, 465 P.2d 161 (Okl.1969). In re Marriage of Hadley, 88 Wash.2d 649, 565 P.2d 790 (1977), a community property case, emphasized the wife's ill health producing total disability in dividing the community property.

compensate the other spouse by an award of other property or of cash.[21]

The partnership theory of marriage which underlies modern marital property statutes necessarily implies that non-economic as well as economic contributions to the marriage be recognized when the marital property comes to be divided on divorce. Both versions of the Uniform Marriage and Divorce Act provide that the "contribution of a spouse as home-maker" is among those factors which the courts must consider in dividing the property.[22] An important Illinois case, while conceding the difficulty of putting a value on the different forms of contribution, has cautioned against placing too much emphasis on monetary as opposed to non-monetary contributions.[23] Other cases place at least as much importance on the contribution of a full time homemaker as on that of a working spouse.[24]

Marital fault or misconduct is one factor as to which there is disagreement among the states. The Uniform Marriage and Divorce Act provides, in both of its versions, that the property division be accomplished "without regard to marital misconduct".[25] In the earlier version the commissioners' commentary states that this means the courts are not to consider marital misconduct "such as adultery or other nonfinancial misdeeds".[26] In

this context fault has also been defined as the sort of conduct which constitutes grounds for divorce.[27] Conversely, where the applicable statute authorizes or requires the court to take account of marital misconduct, that may be done,[28] although it would be unusual to find a court completely denying a share of property to a spouse on such a ground. The proportion of the spouses' shares might, however, be affected under such a statute.

Where the statute is silent on the point, merely authorizing the courts to make a reasonable or an equitable division, some courts have held that marital fault is not to be considered at all in arriving at a property division.[29] The arguments for this position are that divorces are now generally granted without regard to fault; that it is difficult to determine in most cases which spouse is at fault; that fault may merely be evidence of a marriage which is no longer viable; and that the whole concept of fault is one which is not relevant to the basis for the property division, i.e. that it recognizes the contribution which each spouse made to the marriage.[30] Although in some cases it does seem possible, even probable, that marital misconduct is relevant to the spouse's contribution to the marriage,[31] most of these arguments are sufficiently persuasive to justify removing fault from the courts' consideration when they

---

21. In re Marriage of Hellwig, 100 Ill.App.3d 452, 55 Ill.Dec. 762, 426 N.E.2d 1087 (1981); In re Marriage of McMahon, 82 Ill.App.3d 126, 403 N.E.2d 730 (1980); In re Marriage of Jacobson, 183 Mont. 517, 600 P.2d 1183 (1979); In re Marriage of Hadley, 88 Wash.2d 649, 565 P.2d 790 (1977).

Special considerations may also apply to the allocation of the marital home and personal property used by the family. For example, it is common to allow the custodian of children to have the use of or even title to the family home where that is the desirable way to provide housing. See Note, The Marital Home: Equal or Equitable Distribution? 50 U.Chi.L.Rev. 1089 (1983).

22. Uniform Marriage and Divorce Act § 307, 9A Unif.L.Ann. 142 (1979), 9 Unif.L.Ann. 490 (1973).

23. In re Marriage of Aschwanden, 82 Ill.2d 31, 44 Ill. Dec. 269, 411 N.E.2d 238 (1980).

24. Gibbons v. Gibbons, 174 N.J.Super. 107, 415 A.2d 1174 (1980); Wilberscheid v. Wilberscheid, 77 Wis.2d 40, 252 N.W.2d 76 (1977); Bussewitz v. Bussewitz, 75 Wis.2d 78, 248 N.W.2d 417 (1976).

25. 9A Unif.L.Ann. 142 (1979); 9 Unif.L.Ann. 490 (1973).

26. 9 Unif.L.Ann. 492 (1973).

27. Chalmers v. Chalmers, 65 N.J. 186, 320 A.2d 478 (1974).

28. Conrad v. Bowers, 533 S.W.2d 614 (Mo.App. 1975). But see Note, Property Division in Alaska Upon Divorce: An Analysis of the 1968 Statutory Amendments, 6 U.C. L.A.—Alaska L.Rev. 218, 236 (1977), suggesting that fault remains a factor in Alaska cases notwithstanding that the statute provides that the property is to be divided without regard to fault.

29. In re Peterson's Marriage, 227 N.W.2d 139 (Iowa 1975); Boyd v. Boyd, 421 A.2d 1356 (Me. 1980); Chalmers v. Chalmers, 65 N.J. 186, 320 A.2d 478 (1974). M.R.V. v. T.M.R., 115 Misc.2d 674, 454 N.Y.S.2d 779 (1982). Other cases are collected in Annot., 86 A.L.R.3d 1116 (1978).

30. Chalmers v. Chalmers, 65 N.J. 186, 320 A.2d 478 (1974).

31. As, for example, where the misconduct of a spouse has caused a physical or psychological disability in the other spouse. See, e.g., Crume v. Crume, 378 P.2d 183 (Alaska 1963).

come to divide the spouses' property. Notwithstanding the force of these arguments, there are cases which continue to consider marital fault for this purpose, although the weight to be given it is not specified, thereby creating the suspicion that it is not a factor of much weight in comparison with others.[32]

It remains to be seen whether the conduct of the spouses might be considered relevant to the property division where it has an impact on the family's economic fortunes.[33] It does seem that if the underlying issue is the nature of the spouses' contributions to the marriage, this sort of conduct should be taken into account, especially since it is capable of more accurate evaluation than the sort of marital fault which some statutes and cases have excluded from consideration.

WESTLAW REFERENCES

134k252.2 /p husband wife spous! /4 contribut! /s division divid! distribut! /10 property

valu! /3 separate /s property /5 division divid! distribut! /p divorc! dissol!

find 565 p2d 790

sy(farm business /7 division divid! distribut! /s (dissol! /3 marriage) divorc!)

32. Sides v. Sides, 284 Ala. 39, 221 So.2d 677 (1969); Vail v. Vail, 360 So.2d 985 (Ala.Civ.App.1977), judgment reversed on other grounds 360 So.2d 992 (1978); Ferguson v. Ferguson, 202 N.W.2d 760 (N.D. 1972); Swenson v. Swenson, 85 S.D. 320, 181 N.W.2d 864 (1970); Young v. Young, 609 S.W.2d 758 (Tex.1980); Wilberscheid v. Wilberscheid, 77 Wis.2d 40, 252 N.W.2d 76 (1977); Grosskopf v. Grosskopf, 677 P.2d 814 (Wyo.1984). Other cases are collected in Annot., 86 A.L.R.3d 1116 (1978).

The New York courts are permitted to consider fault under a statute which authorizes them to consider "any other factor which the court shall expressly find to be just and proper", but this may only be done in egregious cases which shock the conscience of the court, since only then would it be just and proper to take fault into account. O'Brien v. O'Brien, 66 N.Y.2d 576, 498 N.Y.S.2d 743, 489 N.E.2d 712 (1985).

33. Boyd v. Boyd, 421 A.2d 1356 (Me. 1980) expressly refused to decide whether marital fault would be considered if it had an economic impact. Smith v. Smith, 314 N.C. 80, 331 S.E.2d 682 (1985) suggests that misconduct which dissipates or reduces marital property for nonmarital purposes is relevant to the division of property. See also Annot., 41 A.L.R.4th 416 (1985), Spouse's Dissipation of Marital Assets Prior to Divorce as Factor in Divorce Court's Determination of Property Division.

§ 15.4

1. Olsher v. Olsher, 78 Ill.App.3d 627, 34 Ill.Dec. 32, 397 N.E.2d 488 (1979); In re Marriage of Brown, 179

contribut! /3 home-maker house-wife /s division divid! distribut! /s property

§ 15.4 Division of Property—Valuation

In order to make a just and equitable division of the property between spouses, the trial court must nearly always place a money value upon that property.[1] Failure to do so is generally a ground for reversal.[2]

In these days of fluctuations in property values, it may often be important to determine as of what date the property is to be valued for purposes of making a division. The cases reach a variety of results, adopting the date of the trial of the property questions,[3] the date on which the parties began to live separate and apart when that was the ground for divorce,[4] or the date of the divorce decrees or of the hearing on the property division whichever was earlier.[5] Valuation as of the date of the hearing on the property division would seem to be the most equitable and workable solution to the problem. Where fluctuations in value are so rapid as to be material between the date of hearing and the date on which the actual division is made, the

Mont. 417, 587 P.2d 361 (1978). But see Moss v. Moss, 190 Colo. 491, 549 P.2d 404 (1976). See generally B. Goldberg, Valuation of Divorce Assets (1984).

2. Marriage of Leon, 80 Ill.App.3d 383, 35 Ill.Dec. 717, 399 N.E.2d 1006 (1980).

3. In re Marriage of Priddis, 132 Cal.App.3d 349, 183 Cal.Rptr. 37 (1982); In re Marriage of Walters, 91 Cal. App.3d 535, 154 Cal.Rptr. 180 (1979); Walter W. B. v. Elizabeth P. B., 462 A.2d 414 (Del. 1983); In re Marriage of Hitchcock, 309 N.W.2d 432 (Iowa 1981); Schamber v. Schamber, 41 Mich.App. 589, 200 N.W.2d 454 (1972).

4. In re Marriage of Wagner, —— Mont. ——, 679 P.2d 753 (1984); Tucker v. Tucker, 121 N.J.Super. 539, 298 A.2d 91 (1972); Berish v. Berish, 69 Ohio St.2d 318, 432 N.E.2d 183 (1982).

5. In re Marriage of Femmer, 39 Colo.App. 277, 568 P.2d 81 (1977) (construing the statute); Wilen v. Wilen, 61 Md.App. 337, 486 A.2d 775 (1985) (date of divorce); Berger v. Berger, 713 P.2d 695 (Utah 1985) (date of divorce). In re Marriage of Taylor, 436 N.E.2d 56 (Ind. 1982) takes the odd position that the court is without jurisdiction to designate a specific date for valuation. In re Marriage of Krause, —— Mont. ——, 654 P.2d 963 (1982) holds that the valuation should not be dated as to any specific event; that different dates of valuation might be used for different kinds of property; and that generally speaking valuation should be made as of the time of distribution.

decree should contain a provision permitting modification taking account of the changes.[6]

The valuation of property in the present context is a particular example of a process which courts must go through in many other kinds of litigation.[7] The process is such that few rules of general application can be formulated, and in the present discussion only a few illustrations of the methods the courts have used in marital property cases will be given.[8] The usual method for evaluating real estate is by appraisal,[9] although either rental value or the reasonable value of labor expended on the property may enter into the calculation.[10] Where the value of a partnership interest is involved, the courts first find the value of its assets, subtract the firm liabilities, subtract also the partners' capital accounts, and then apply the spouse-partner's percentage share to the resulting amount. The spouse-partner's capital account is then added to that figure to arrive at the total value of his interest.[11]

Since the purpose of valuation in dividing marital property differs from the purpose of valuation in tort cases, different standards of value may be used in the different kinds of cases. Thus where the value of a wife's jewels and furs was involved, it has been held that neither the retail value, nor the replacement cost less depreciation should be used, on the ground that the wife was not in a position to sell these items at these values.[12] Appraisals of personal property should be made with these differences in mind.[13]

Where the property to be valued consists of a business, the courts rely upon such evidence as financial statements,[14] book value,[15] capitalization of earnings,[16] and the contributions of the spouse to the business.[17] Similar standards of value are used where the property involved is corporate stock. Of course if the stock is regularly traded, market price is the best evidence of value.[18] But in the common case of stock in closely held corporations which has no established market, book value (or asset value) of the underlying corporate assets may be relied upon,[19] as well as capitalization of earnings.[20] If the stock is subject to a first option or buy-sell agreement, the price

6. Bollenbach v. Bollenbach, 285 Minn. 418, 175 N.W.2d 148 (1970).

7. General treatments of valuation include J. Bonbright, The Valuation of Property (1937); L. Orgel, Valuation Under the Law of Eminent Domain ch. II, III, XII, XIV, XV (2d ed. 1953); C. McCormick, Handbook of the Law of Damages ch. 6 (1935).

8. The valuation of pension rights and the goodwill of professional practices will be discussed, infra, in connection with those items of property.

9. Leeder v. Leeder, 46 Wis.2d 464, 175 N.W.2d 262 (1970); Ford, Putting a Value on Farm and Ranch Property, 2 Fam. Advocate 22 (1979); Brown, Putting a Value on Real Estate, 2 Fam. Advocate 28 (1979).

10. Hayner v. Hayner, 91 N.M. 140, 571 P.2d 407 (1977). In valuing real estate exactitude is not required, so long as the value arrived at lies within a reasonable range. Johnson v. Johnson, 277 N.W.2d 208 (Minn. 1979).

11. McDowell v. McDowell, 499 P.2d 1208 (Colo.App. 1972); Johnson v. Johnson, 277 N.W.2d 208 (Minn.1979). See also Johnson v. Johnson, 78 Wis.2d 137, 254 N.W.2d 198 (1977).

12. Carty v. Carty, 87 Wis.2d 759, 275 N.W.2d 888 (1979).

13. On appraisal of personal property, see Jersin, Putting a Value on Personal Property, 2 Fam. Advocate 14 (1979).

14. Courtney v. Courtney, 542 P.2d 164 (Alaska 1975).

15. In re Marriage of Gray, 422 N.E.2d 696 (Ind.App. 1981).

16. Ibid. Where the value of oil and gas interests was involved, one case rejected the capitalization of earnings method of valuation, on the ground that it did not reflect market value and did not take into account the declining asset nature of oil and gas interests. Knigge v. Knigge, 204 Neb. 421, 282 N.W.2d 581 (1979). But see Walker, Putting a Value on Oil and Gas, 2 Fam. Advocate 6 (1979).

17. Fucci v. Fucci, 179 Conn. 174, 425 A.2d 592 (1979).

18. In re Marriage of Moffatt, 279 N.W.2d 15 (Iowa 1979). This case also put some reliance upon financial statements previously prepared for other purposes. In re Marriage of Connolly, 23 Cal.3d 590, 153 Cal.Rptr. 423, 591 P.2d 911 (1979) upheld a valuation based upon prior private sales of $7.50 per share, even though a few months after the trial the corporation "went public," after which the stock sold at prices about $25.00 per share.

19. In re Marriage of Moffatt, 279 N.W.2d 15 (Iowa 1979). In an appropriate case, good will may also be considered. Suther v. Suther, 28 Wash.App. 838, 627 P.2d 110 (1981).

20. For an extensive discussion of this and other valuation methods See Bowen v. Bowen, 96 N.J. 36, 473 A.2d 73 (1984) suggesting reliance in the factors outlined in Rev. Rul. 59–60, 1959–1 C.B. 237. See also Banks, Measuring the Value of Corporate Stock, 11 Cal.W.L.Rev. 1

set in that agreement is admissible in evidence, but it may not be conclusive since the option may not be exercised or the price set may be out of date.[21] But where the agreement binds the corporation to buy and the shareholder to sell, the contract price should normally be controlling evidence of value.

Finally, the spouses' debts are a negative aspect of the value of their property. Logic would suggest that debts should be allocated between separate and marital property in those states which permit only the marital property to be divided between the spouses, and some cases do this, taking into account the receipt of benefits from the indebtedness and the extent of the spouse's participation in the loan.[22] In those states in which all property is subject to division, without distinction as to whether it is separate or marital, responsibility for debts may be imposed upon the spouses in whatever manner is equitable under the circumstances in the light of the amounts of property awarded to each.[23]

 WESTLAW REFERENCES

ti(olsher +s olsher)

134k253(3) /p time date /5 fix fixing establish**** set setting determination determin***

(1974); and Perocchi and Walsh, Putting a Value on Closely Held Corporations, 2 Fam. Advocate 32 (1979).

21. In re Marriage of Moffatt, 279 N.W.2d 15 (Iowa 1979); Rogers v. Rogers, 296 N.W.2d 849 (Minn.1980). Bowen v. Bowen, 96 N.J. 36, 473 A.2d 73 (1984).

22. Cadwell v. Cadwell, 126 Ariz. 460, 616 P.2d 920 (App.1980); Bodie v. Bodie, 590 S.W.2d 895 (Ky.App. 1979); Lacey v. Lacey, 61 Wis.2d 604, 213 N.W.2d 80 (1973). For cases on community debts in community property states, see Annot., 20 A.L.R.4th 211 (1983).

In the case of marital real estate subject to a mortgage, it seems obvious that the value is the amount of the equity. Schweizer v. Schweizer, 301 Md. 626, 484 A.2d 267 (1984).

23. Courtney v. Courtney, 542 P.2d 164 (Alaska 1975); Finley v. Finley, 422 N.E.2d 289 (Ind.App. 1981).

§ 15.5

1. E.g., Wisner v. Wisner, 129 Ariz. 333, 631 P.2d 115 (App.1981); In re Marriage of Slater, 100 Cal.App.3d 241, 160 Cal.Rptr. 686 (1979); Matter of Marriage of Fleege, 91 Wash.2d 324, 588 P.2d 1136 (1979). A case which refuses to recognize the goodwill of a medical practice as community property is Nail v. Nail, 486 S.W.2d 761 (Tex.

to(134) /p valu! /s spouse husband wife /s share interest /10 partnership

to(134) /p valu! /s business corporation company enterprise /s earnings "book value" "financial statement"

§ 15.5 Division of Property—Goodwill and Professional Education as Marital Assets

As an abstract proposition, the goodwill of a spouse's business is generally held to be marital property subject to division on divorce, at least where it was acquired during the marriage. This is true in community property states,[1] and should be equally true in common law property states.[2] It is true where the business consists of the rendition of personal services, as for example the practice of medicine, law or dentistry as well as for ordinary commercial businesses.[3]

The closely related issues of the definition of goodwill and the methods of placing a value upon it are more difficult. The accountant often defines goodwill as the amount by which the earning capacity of a business exceeds the earning capacity of the tangible assets in the business, or sometimes the excess of the total

1972), 10 Hous.L.Rev. 966 (1973), the argument being that goodwill is an attribute of the person, which cannot be transferred.

2. Rostel v. Rostel, 622 P.2d 429 (Alaska 1981); In re Marriage of Nichols, 43 Colo.App. 383, 606 P.2d 1314 (1979); In re Marriage of White, 98 Ill.App.3d 380, 53 Ill. Dec. 786, 424 N.E.2d 421 (1981), appeal after remand 151 Ill.App.3d 778, 104 Ill.Dec. 424, 502 N.E.2d 1084 (1986); Stern v. Stern, 66 N.J. 340, 331 A.2d 257 (1975). Contra: E.E.C. v. E.J.C., 457 A.2d 688 (Dei. 1983); Powell v. Powell, 231 Kan. 456, 648 P.2d 218 (1982); Holbrook v. Holbrook, 103 Wis.2d 327, 309 N.W.2d 343 (1981).

See also Note, Treating Professional Good Will As Marital Property In Equitable Distribution States, 58 N.Y.U.L.Rev. 554 (1983).

3. E.g., Rostel v. Rostel, 622 P.2d 429 (Alaska 1981) (business was selling electrical equipment); In re Foster's Marriage, 42 Cal.App.3d 577, 117 Cal.Rptr. 49 (1974) (medical practice); In re Marriage of Nichols, 43 Colo. App. 383, 606 P.2d 1314 (1979) (dental practice); Stern v. Stern, 66 N.J. 340, 331 A.2d 257 (1975) (law practice); In re Marriage of Hall, 103 Wash.2d 236, 692 P.2d 175 (1984) (medical practice).

value of a business over the value of its tangible assets.[4]

Judicial definitions of goodwill are often confused and confusing. Perhaps the most common definition is that "Goodwill is property of an intangible nature and is commonly defined as the expectation of continued public patronage." [5] One California case which has had considerable influence on other courts so defines goodwill but then goes on to say that the value of goodwill must be established without relying upon the potential or continuing net income of the professional spouse.[6] The effect of this is to ignore one of the two basic elements of goodwill. These are that a) in the past there have been greater than normal earnings from the business; and b) the evidence indicates that such earnings will continue in the future.[7] Another way of putting the same point is to say, as courts have, that goodwill rests on the probability that old customers will continue to patronize the business in the future.[8] Goodwill thus requires both evidence of past history and a forecast of the future. The factors leading to a recognition that goodwill exists include the spouse's reputation for skill and honesty in his profession, the continuity of his name in the business, the continuity of location, and the prospect of his continued exercise of talent and ability.[9]

Placing a value upon the goodwill of the business in which a spouse is engaged obviously requires the exercise of judgment and discretion on the part of the trier of fact. There is no universally accepted calculation which will, by a mathematical process alone, produce a dollar figure representing goodwill. The method of valuation available for and appropriate to a particular business or profession will depend upon such circumstances in the specific case as the nature of the business, its earning history, the existence of comparable businesses and their earnings, evidence concerning the sales of this or similar businesses, and contract provisions relating to withdrawal from the business.

For example, if evidence could be obtained concerning the recent sale of the particular business or practice, or of a similar business or practice, that part of the total consideration for the sale which could not be allocated either to tangible assets or intangible assets other than goodwill would be attributable to the value of goodwill.[10] Where the goodwill of the business or goodwill of comparable businesses has not recently been sold, the accountant's direct method of valuing goodwill may be used.[11] This requires first that he deter-

4. A. Wyatt, A Critical Study of Accounting for Business Combinations 62–64 (Accounting Research Study No. 5, 1963).

5. Matter of Marriage of Fleege, 91 Wash.2d 324, 325, 588 P.2d 1136, 1138 (1979).

6. In re Foster's Marriage, 42 Cal.App.3d 577, 117 Cal. Rptr. 49 (1974). See also In re Marriage of Slater, 100 Cal.App.3d 241, 160 Cal.Rptr. 686 (1979), and In re Marriage of Freedman, 23 Wash.App. 27, 592 P.2d 1124 (1979), appeal after remand 35 Wash.App. 49, 665 P.2d 902 (1983) in which the court said that the expectancy of future earnings is not synonymous with goodwill, but is a factor, whatever that may mean.

7. Matter of Marriage of Fleege, 91 Wash.2d 324, 588 P.2d 1136 (1979).

8. Wisner v. Wisner, 129 Ariz.App. 333, 631 P.2d 115 (1981) held that the definition does not limit the existence of goodwill to those businesses in which old customers would be likely to return, but includes those in which the practitioner's age, health, earning power and reputation in the community were responsible for profits in the practice. In this case the husband was a plastic surgeon who would not normally expect his old patients to return, but who nevertheless could have goodwill in his practice.

In re Marriage of Lukens, 16 Wash.App. 481, 558 P.2d 279 (1976) supports the text statement.

9. Wisner v. Wisner, 129 Ariz.App. 333, 631 P.2d 115 (1981); Levy v. Levy, 164 N.J.Super. 542, 397 A.2d 374 (1978); Matter of Marriage of Fleege, 91 Wash.2d 324, 588 P.2d 1136 (1979); In re Marriage of Freedman, 23 Wash.App. 27, 592 P.2d 1124 (1979), appeal after remand 35 Wash.App. 49, 665 P.2d 902 (1983).

10. In re Marriage of Nichols, 43 Colo.App. 383, 606 P.2d 1314 (1979) (semble); Matter of Marriage of Fleege, 91 Wash.2d 324, 588 P.2d 1136 (1979). Even if the goodwill of a professional practice is not readily salable because it is dependent upon the personality of the practitioner, it still constitutes property whose value should be taken into account on divorce. In re Marriage of Lukens, 16 Wash.App. 481, 558 P.2d 279 (1976).

11. This method is clearly outlined in M. Backer, Modern Accounting Theory 198–201 (Rev. ed. 1966). See also Hurley v. Hurley, 94 N.M. 641, 615 P.2d 256 (1980), overruled on other grounds Ellsworth v. Ellsworth, 97 N.M. 133, 637 P.2d 564 (1981); In re Marriage of Hall, 103 Wash.2d 236, 692 P.2d 175 (1984). In Levy v. Levy, 164 N.J.Super. 542, 397 A.2d 374 (1978) the court adopted this method of valuing goodwill and found that in this

mine the normal rate of return on the tangible assets and the intangible assets other than goodwill in the business, thereby arriving at the normal or typical earnings for such a firm. The estimated future earnings of the firm are then determined, generally by reference to the firm's past earnings history. The difference between the normal earnings and the estimated future earnings is then discounted on the basis of its probable future existence, and the amount so computed is the value of the firm's goodwill. Less precise methods of valuation are also sometimes approved by the courts, relying on opinion evidence,[12] or merely taking a year's profits as the indicium of value,[13] or relying upon contract provisions establishing the amount which the spouse would receive on death or withdrawal from the practice.[14] The fact that it may be difficult to put an exact value on the goodwill should not foreclose the courts from treating it as property divisible on divorce.[15]

If the goodwill of a professional practice is held to be a form of marital or community property, on the ground that it represents the probability that past profits will continue in the future, it should follow that the position of an employee is likewise an element of valuable property since in his case also there may be an equal probability that his lucrative salary will continue in the future. The few cases dealing with this question have held otherwise, however, on the theory that there is no

"vested present interest" in the employee's future earnings.[16] This reasoning hardly supports the result, since of course there is no "vested present interest" in goodwill, either. Although it may seem peculiar to lawyers to characterize as property a spouse's possession of a lucrative position as an employee, it is very difficult to draw any economic distinction between the spouse who practices a profession and thereby acquires goodwill, and the spouse who, for example, practices the same profession as an employee and by his ability achieves the good opinion of his employer and a consequent high salary. In both cases the assumption is that he was assisted in his financial success by the claimant spouse. In both cases, therefore, the claimant spouse should have a share in the financial benefit.

A similar kind of case arises when one spouse works to support the other spouse while the latter studies for and obtains a professional or other degree which leads to a career offering greater financial rewards than the spouse would otherwise expect. In the typical case the wife works as a secretary or airline stewardess while the husband obtains a master's degree in business administration. She supports them both out of her earnings and pays for his books, fees, tuition and other educational expenses. Under the influence of the Graham case,[17] which arose on these facts, other cases have held that the degree is not property and therefore may not be evaluated in the divorce proceeding so as to give the

---

case there were no excess earnings and therefore no goodwill. See B. Goldberg, Valuation of Divorce Assets Ch. 8 (1984).

12. In re Marriage of Freedman, 23 Wash.App. 27, 592 P.2d 1124 (1979), appeal after remand 35 Wash.App. 49, 665 P.2d 902 (1983) (expert testimony of accountants).

13. Rostel v. Rostel, 622 P.2d 429 (Alaska 1981).

14. In re Marriage of Fonstein, 17 Cal.3d 738, 131 Cal. Rptr. 873, 552 P.2d 1169 (1976); Stern v. Stern, 66 N.J. 340, 331 A.2d 257 (1975); Hertz v. Hertz, 99 N.M. 320, 657 P.2d 1169 (1983); Annot., 74 A.L.R.3d 621 (1976).

15. Matter of Marriage of Fleege, 91 Wash.2d 324, 588 P.2d 1136 (1979). For a discussion of valuation of goodwill, see Note, Valuation of Professional Goodwill Upon Marital Dissolution, 7 S.W.U.L.Rev. 186 (1975).

16. Wilcox v. Wilcox, 173 Ind.App. 661, 365 N.E.2d 792 (1977); Nastrom v. Nastrom, 262 N.W.2d 487 (N.D. 1978), appeal after remand 276 N.W.2d 130 (N.D. 1979);

In re Marriage of Hall, 103 Wash.2d 236, 692 P.2d 175 (1984). Although the court in Stern v. Stern, 66 N.J. 340, 331 A.2d 257 (1975) held that a person's earning capacity is not to be considered property, it is a factor to be considered by the trial court in deciding what distribution of property will be equitable. This seems to give earning capacity some qualified recognition as an element of value. The court in the same case observed that the concept of vesting should find no place in the law relating to the equitable distribution of marital property, the important issue being whether the property was acquired during the marriage and not whether it was vested.

For a discussion of this issue see Note, Toward a Property Theory of Future Earning Potential in Dissolution Proceedings, 56 Wash.L.Rev. 277 (1981).

17. In re Marriage of Graham, 194 Colo. 429, 574 P.2d 75 (1978).

wife a sum corresponding to her interest in it.[18] The argument in these cases is that the degree (or the license to practice the profession) is not transferable, or inheritable, and cannot be acquired by the mere expenditure of money, so that it has none of the usual attributes of property.[19] Oddly enough, however, some of the same cases hedge their holdings with statements that the wife may have other remedies,[20] or that the trial court may consider the husband's earning capacity in deciding what distribution of property would be equitable.[21]

These cases are inconsistent with the spirit and purpose of the marital property statutes, to say nothing of being unfair to the wives involved. These courts themselves recognize

this by suggesting other remedies which on examination usually turn out to be inadequate [22] or non-existent.[23] Fortunately there are other cases, more realistic in reasoning, which hold either that the increased earning potential resulting from the professional degree or license to practice is a form of property under the statute,[24] or that the wife is to be compensated for her efforts either on a theory of unjust enrichment, or on some other theory.[25] Whichever legal rationale is used, there is less of a burden on the trial court than in either the goodwill or the pension cases, since the wife's contribution can normally be valued with greater ease and precision than can goodwill or pensions. The value given to that contribution can at the least be valued by

---

18. In re Marriage of Weinstein, 128 Ill.App.3d 234, 83 Ill.Dec. 425, 470 N.E.2d 551 (1984), citing many cases. West's Ann. Cal. Civ. Code § 4800.3 (Supp. 1987) attempts to deal with this problem by providing that the community estate shall be reimbursed for community contributions to the education or training of a spouse which substantially enhanced that spouse's earning capacity. See In re Marriage of Sullivan, 37 Cal.3d 762, 209 Cal. Rptr. 354, 691 P.2d 1020 (1984). California also authorizes the spouse's contribution to education to be considered in awarding alimony. West's Ann. Cal. Civ. Code § 4801 (Supp. 1987). See section 16.4, infra.

19. In re Marriage of Graham, 194 Colo. 429, 574 P.2d 75 (1977).

20. In re Marriage of Graham, 194 Colo. 429, 574 P.2d 75 (1977) suggests that the wife's contribution might be relevant on the issue of maintenance, as does Lovett v. Lovett, 688 S.W.2d 329 (Ky. 1985), and Stevens v. Stevens, 23 Ohio St.2d 115, 492 N.E.2d 131 (1986).

21. In re Marriage of Graham, supra, note 20; In re Marriage of Faulkner, 652 P.2d 572 (Colo. 1982); Stern v. Stern, 66 N.J. 340, 331 A.2d 257 (1975). This suggestion appears to amount to a holding that although the husband's degree or increased earning potential is not property, it will be treated as if it were.

22. See note 21, supra. Taking the wife's contribution into account in dividing other marital property is obviously not a great help to her if there is no other material property to be divided.

23. The wife in Graham, supra, note 20, was clearly not entitled to maintenance under the Colorado statute since she was able to support herself through appropriate employment. See In re Marriage of McVey, 641 P.2d 300 (Colo.App.1981).

24. In re Marriage of Horstmann, 263 N.W.2d 885 (Iowa 1978); O'Brien v. O'Brien, 66 N.Y.2d 576, 498 N.Y.S.2d 743, 489 N.E.2d 712 (1985); Hubbard v. Hubbard, 603 P.2d 747 (Okl.1979). The New York Court of Appeals in the O'Brien case held that the husband's license to practice medicine was marital property subject to distribution where the wife had supported him through

medical school. The court also held that she was entitled to a share of the value of that license, rejecting the argument that she should be limited to the amount of her support. The court relied in part on the New York statute authorizing the court to consider, in dividing the property, services of a spouse to the career or career potential of the other spouse. A distinction between a degree, which is property, and a license to practice a profession, which is not, is maintained by Moss v. Moss, 639 S.W.2d 370 (Ky.App.1982).

In re Marriage of Lundberg, 107 Wis.2d 1, 318 N.W.2d 918 (1982) approves an award of maintenance to the wife who put her husband through medical school on the authority of a specific statutory provision stating that in dividing the spouses' property the court could take into account the contribution by a spouse to the education, training or increased earning power of the other spouse.

25. Pyeatte v. Pyeatte, 135 Ariz. 346, 661 P.2d 196 (App.1982); DeLa Rosa v. DeLa Rosa, 309 N.W.2d 755 (Minn.1981), 66 Minn.L.Rev. 1205 (1982); Scott v. Scott, 645 S.W.2d 193 (Mo.App.1983); Hubbard v. Hubbard, 603 P.2d 747 (Okl.1979). Washburn v. Washburn, 101 Wash. 2d 168, 677 P.2d 152 (1984) held that it would not rest an award on unjust enrichment since the enrichment of the student spouse could not be called unjust. But it also held that compensation could be effected by a division of property or, if there were not sufficient property, by a supplemental award of maintenance. The court also indicated that there might be circumstances in which an award would not be appropriate, for example where the marriage continues for long enough after the degree is obtained so that the supporting spouse benefited from the student spouse's increased earning capacity. Other legal theories supporting an award are suggested by Krauskopf, Recompense for Financing Spouse's Education: Legal Protection for the Marital Investor in Human Capital, 28 Kan.L.Rev. 379 (1980); Erickson, Spousal Support Toward the Realization of Educational Goals: How the Law Can Ensure Reciprocity, 1978 Wis.L.Rev. 943.

An award based on fraud was upheld in Church v. Church, 96 N.M. 388, 630 P.2d 1243 (1981).

reference to the sums which the wife contributed to the husband's expenses. If the goodwill cases are correct, the increase in earning power could also be valued by considering the same sort of evidence as is relied on in those cases.[26]

 WESTLAW REFERENCES

sy,di(good-will /s marital marri! /10 property)
education! profession! /3 degree license /s marital marri! /10 property /s distribut! division divid!

§ 15.6 Division of Property—Pensions and Contingent Benefits as Property

Since many kinds of pension or retirement benefits result either from employment by the federal government or from plans subject to federal regulation, the initial question to be faced in deciding whether the pension is property divisible on divorce is a dual one: a) Does the federal legislation governing the pension preempt the state domestic relations law? b) And if it does, does the federal legislation prevent the state divorce court from assigning an interest in the pension to the non-earner spouse?

The United States Supreme Court first dealt with these questions in Hisquierdo v. Hisquierdo,[1] in which it held that the Railroad Retirement Act preempted California's community property law and that in consequence an employee's pension acquired pursuant to that Act could not be divided between spouses in a California divorce proceeding. Although, the Court conceded, domestic relations law is the province of the states, where the state law conflicts with federal law in such a way that "State family and family-related property law * * * do 'major damage' to 'clear and substantial' federal inter-

ests" then the Supremacy Clause[2] requires that the state law be overridden.[3] The Court found that this conflict existed in this case. It relied in part upon the provision in the Act forbidding any attachment, garnishment, assignment or other legal process addressed to any pension payable under the Act.[4] The purpose of this provision, according to the Court, is to ensure that the pension actually reaches the beneficiary, a purpose which the Court thought would be frustrated by permitting a state divorce court to order part of the pension paid to a spouse. The Court also found the purpose of the Act to be to encourage employees to retire, a purpose which would also be frustrated if part of the employee's retirement benefits were taken from him and ordered paid to his spouse. The Court held that the purposes of the Retirement Act would be impaired whether the divorce court's decree took the form of an order to pay part of the pension to the spouse on the earner's retirement, or whether it directed the payment to the spouse of an offsetting amount of marital property, leaving the earner in complete possession of his pension. The first form of order, the Court said, would violate the non-assignment provision, and the second would constitute an improper anticipation of the benefits, anticipation also being forbidden by the statute.[5] The Court's highly technical analysis ignores the fact that in community property states at least the non-earner spouse acquires an interest in the pension as it is earned, so that there is no assignment on divorce. The divorce court just awards to that spouse what already belongs to her.

In 1981 the Supreme Court in the McCarty case[6] held that federal military retirement laws were in such conflict with state domestic relations law that military pensions could not

---

26. Various methods for valuing the earning spouse's contribution are canvassed in Haugan v. Haugan, 117 Wis.2d 200, 343 N.W.2d 796 (1984).

§ 15.6

1. 439 U.S. 572, 99 S.Ct. 802, 59 L.Ed.2d 1 (1979). Justices Stewart and Rehnquist dissented.

2. U.S.Const. art. VI.

3. 439 U.S. at 581, 99 S.Ct. at 808.

4. 45 U.S.C.A. § 231m. Subsequent amendments to the Railroad Retirement Act have made divorced wives eligible for annuities under the eligibility rules established by the Social Security Act. 45 U.S.C.A. § 231a(c) (4).

5. Ibid.

6. McCarty v. McCarty, 453 U.S. 210, 101 S.Ct. 2728, 69 L.Ed.2d 589 (1981). Although some federal pensions

be divided between spouses on divorce. Congress has partially overruled the McCarty case by enacting the Uniformed Services Former Spouses' Protection Act.[7] This Act provides that if the spouses had been married ten years or more, during which time the serviceman performed at least ten years of service creditable in determining his eligibility for retirement pay, the divorce court may treat the retirement pay as the property of the serviceman and his spouse.[8] This enables the state courts to divide the military retirement benefits as it would divide other retirement pensions, provided the ten-year limitations are met. The statute applied only to retired pay payable to the serviceman for pay periods beginning after June 25, 1981. The McCarty case had been held not to apply to final state divorce decrees entered before McCarty was decided, in which military pensions were ordered to be divided between the spouses.[9]

The Supreme Court has also held that a wife may not be awarded a community property interest in the proceeds of her husband's National Service Life Insurance policy where he had designated his mother as beneficiary, even though the premiums had been paid out of community funds.[10]

The Employee Retirement Income Security Act of 1974 (ERISA) covers employee benefit plans established by employers engaged in commerce or in an industry affecting commerce, or by employee organizations representing employees engaged in commerce in an industry affecting commerce.[11] This Act imposes a comprehensive system of regulation of such employee benefit plans.[12] It has as its general purpose the protection of beneficiaries of such plans by imposing requirements of disclosure, of financial soundness, of funding, of vesting of benefits, of proper conduct by fiduciaries, and standards improving the equitable nature of retirement schemes.[13]

As originally enacted ERISA provided that it "supersedes any and all State laws insofar as they * * * relate to any employee benefit plan" covered by the Act, and that "Each pension plan shall provide that benefits provided under the plan may not be assigned or alienated."[14] These provisions raised the same questions as those arising under the Railroad Retirement Act and under federal military pensions, that is, were ERISA pensions immune to division on divorce in community property or common law property states? The cases were not in agreement on this question, but it seemed that the United States Supreme Court had taken the position, in a case from a community property state, that ERISA's non-alienation provisions did not prevent a divorce court from ordering the distribution to a non-earning spouse of the proceeds of an ERISA pension.[15]

---

may not be divisible under federal law, it has been held that the pension can be taken into account as one of the economic circumstances of the parties when the court divides other community or marital assets. In re Marriage of Dessauer, 97 Wash.2d 831, 650 P.2d 1099 (1982); In re Marriage of Roark, 34 Wash.App. 252, 659 P.2d 1133 (1983).

7. 10 U.S.C.A. § 1408, 96 Stat. 730. Walentowski v. Walentowski, 100 N.M. 484, 672 P.2d 657 (1983) takes the position that this statute operates retroactively, citing other cases.

8. 10 U.S.C.A. § 1408(c)(1), 96 Stat. 731. No more than 50% of the retirement pay may be awarded under this statute. 10 U.S.C.A. § 1408(e)(1). Several courts have held that the ten year limitation merely limits direct payments by the federal service finance centers to the obligee spouse, but does not limit the state courts' authority to divide the military retirement pay. Konzen v. Konzen, 103 Wash.2d 470, 693 P.2d 97 (1985), citing other cases.

9. Erspan v. Badgett, 659 F.2d 26 (5th Cir. 1981).

10. Wissner v. Wissner, 338 U.S. 655, 70 S.Ct. 398, 94 L.Ed. 424 (1950), rehearing denied 339 U.S. 926, 70 S.Ct. 619, 94 L.Ed. 1348 (1950); Ridgway v. Ridgway, 454 U.S. 46, 102 S.Ct. 49, 70 L.Ed.2d 39 (1981).

11. 29 U.S.C.A. § 1003(a).

12. 29 U.S.C.A. § 1001 ff. Discussion of the provisions of this statute and their operation may be found in M. Canan, Qualified Retirement Plans (1977), and S. Thompson, Pension Reform: How to Comply With ERISA (Ill.Inst. for CLE 1976).

13. 29 U.S.C.A. § 1001.

14. 29 U.S.C.A. § 1144(a); 29 U.S.C.A. § 1056(d)(1); Int.Rev.Code § 401(a)(13).

15. In re Marriage of Campa, 89 Cal.App.3d 113, 152 Cal.Rptr. 362 (1979), appeal dismissed for want of a substantial federal question, 444 U.S. 1028, 100 S.Ct. 696, 62 L.Ed.2d 664 (1980). The reason for the guarded statement in the text is that this kind of dismissal by the Supreme Court, although it operates as a decision on the merits, may have less precedential effect that an opinion

In 1984 ERISA was amended by the Retirement Equity Act of 1984 (REA) in several respects. One of REA's provisions authorized the state courts to order the distribution of ERISA benefits in divorce actions pursuant to a "qualified domestic relations order".[16] "Qualified domestic relations order" is defined by REA as the decree of a court relating to alimony, child support, or the division of property made in accordance with state domestic relations law, which meets the highly complicated conditions of that Act.[17] There is therefore now a method by which the many pensions subject to the provisions of ERISA may be reached by non-earning spouses in divorce actions. In order to accomplish this, the lawyers representing these spouses must carefully comply with the detailed rules set out in REA.[18]

The lower courts are not in agreement on whether other pension interests which are regulated by federal statute may be divided on divorce. Social security payments have been held subject to division by some cases [19] and not by others.[20] Disability benefits received by a civil service employee were held

not subject to preemption by the federal law, but not community property in California.[21] Veterans' administration disability benefits have been held to be excluded from division on divorce by the federal statutes authorizing them in several decisions.[22] Federal foreign service retirement benefits were held to be divisible on divorce in another case.[23]

Pensions which are not affected by federal statutes have received a variety of treatment from state divorce courts. To some extent the decisions turn on the nature of the pension and of the rights which the earner spouse has in the pension plan. Pensions are described as "contributory" if the employee spouse has contributed to the plan out of his earnings.[24] "Vested" pensions are those pension rights which survive the discharge or voluntary termination of the employee's employment.[25] "Matured" pension rights are those as to which the employee has an unconditional right to immediate payment.[26] These terms are achieving acceptance in the cases, although some courts may on occasion give them somewhat different meanings.

issued after briefs and arguments. Carpenters Pension Trust for Southern California v. Kronschnabel, 632 F.2d 745 (9th Cir.1980), cert. denied 453 U.S. 922, 101 S.Ct. 3159, 69 L.Ed.2d 1004 (1981). Lower court cases on the effect of ERISA in divorce include Stone v. Stone, 450 F.Supp. 919 (N.D.Cal.1978), affirmed 632 F.2d 740 (9th Cir.1980), 1979 Wis.L.Rev. 277; Francis v. United Technologies Corp., 458 F.Supp. 84 (N.D.Cal.1978); Cody v. Reicker, 594 F.2d 314 (2d Cir.1979); Cartledge v. Miller, 457 F.Supp. 1146 (S.D.N.Y.1978); Biles v. Biles, 163 N.J. Super. 49, 394 A.2d 153 (1978); American Tel. & Tel. Co. v. Merry, 592 F.2d 118 (2d Cir.1979). See also Reppy, Community and Separate Interests in Pensions and Social Security Benefits After Marriage of Brown and ERISA, 25 U.C.L.A.L.Rev. 417 (1978).

16. 29 U.S.C.A. § 1056(d)(3)(A). REA is found in Public L. 98–397, 98 Stat. 1433 (1984). The same provision has been inserted in Int.Rev.Code § 401(a)(13)(B) (Supp. 1985).

17. 29 U.S.C.A. § 1056(d)(3)(B), (C), (D); Int.Rev.Code §§ 401(a)(13), 414(p) (Supp.1985).

18. Some useful examples of the workings of the REA are provided in Troyan, Pension Evaluation in Light of the Retirement Equity Act of 1984, 11 Fam.L.Rptr. 3005 (1985).

19. Evans v. Evans, 96 Mich.App. 328, 296 N.W.2d 248 (1980); Elliott v. Elliott, 274 N.W.2d 75 (Minn.1978).

20. In re Hillerman's Marriage, 109 Cal.App.3d 334, 167 Cal.Rptr. 240 (1980); In re Marriage of Cohen, 105

Cal.App.3d 836, 164 Cal.Rptr. 672 (1980); Umber v. Umber, 591 P.2d 299 (Okl.1979). Udall v. Udall, 613 P.2d 742 (Okl.1980) held that an interest in a state-created pension fund could not be reached to satisfy an alimony judgment.

21. In re Marriage of Samuels, 96 Cal.App.3d 122, 158 Cal.Rptr. 38 (1979). Contra, holding them to be emmunity property, Hughes v. Hughes, 96 N.M. 719, 634 P.2d 1271 (1981).

22. In re Marriage of Orr, 95 Cal.App.3d 561, 157 Cal. Rptr. 301 (1979); Miller v. Miller, 96 N.M. 497, 632 P.2d 732 (1981) (Texas law); Ex parte Burson, 615 S.W.2d 192 (Tex. 1981).

23. Matter and Marriage of Rogers, 45 Or.App. 885, 609 P.2d 877 (1980), modified 47 Or.App. 963, 615 P.2d 412 (1980), modified 50 Or.App. 511, 623 P.2d 1108 (1981).

24. M. Canan, Qualified Retirement Plans § 3.12 (1977).

25. In re Marriage of Brown, 15 Cal.3d 838, 126 Cal. Rptr. 633, 544 P.2d 561 (1976); Copeland v. Copeland, 91 N.M. 409, 575 P.2d 99 (1978). Int. Rev. Code § 411 establishes the vesting requirements for pensions governed by ERISA.

26. In re Marriage of Brown, 15 Cal.3d 838, 126 Cal. Rptr. 633, 544 P.2d 561 (1976); Copeland v. Copeland, 91 N.M. 409, 575 P.2d 99 (1978).

Whether the particular pension is contributory or non-contributory should not affect its disposition on the dissolution of a marriage. Both types of pension realistically represent deferred compensation to the earning spouse and therefore both should be available for division on divorce just as would be the case for savings which the spouses had made from their earnings and placed in the savings bank. The cases generally take this position, with the qualification that the result may be affected by the vested or non-vested character of the pension.[27]

Where a spouse's right to a pension can be said to be vested as that term has just been defined, the great majority of cases, in both community property and common law property states, hold that it is a form of property which may be divided on divorce, whether the pension is matured or non-matured at the time of the divorce.[28] Some of the pensions in the cited cases were military pensions which are no longer divisible under McCarty,[29] but of course that does not alter the effect of these cases as precedents on the state law question. The rationale of these cases is that the vested pension rights are intangible assets of a spouse which have been earned during the marriage, either through the contributions of the spouse which otherwise would have been available as assets during the marriage, or through contributions of the employer which constitute deferred compensation.[30] Intangible rights to receive payments in the future represent an economic resource which is as clearly available for division on divorce as other intangible claims.[31] Of course in those states which make a distinction between marital and separate property the pension would only be divisible if marital, that is, to the extent it was acquired during the marriage. Since ERISA requires full vesting of pensions which it covers within ten years of the employee's service, and a partial vesting after five years' service,[32] the cases dividing only vested pensions still reach a substantial proportion of all pensions.

In spite of the difficulties of valuation which many non-vested pensions present, most of the state courts, under the influence of a leading California case,[33] have held that non-vested pensions constitute a form of property which may be divided between the spouses on divorce.[34] These courts have re-

---

27. Non-contributory pension rights were held divisible on divorce in Foster v. Foster, 589 S.W.2d 223 (Ky. App.1979), and McGrew v. McGrew, 151 N.J.Super. 515, 377 A.2d 697 (1977), the Foster case stating that the vested or non-vested nature of the rights rather than the non-contributory feature was the crucial factor.

28. Day v. Day, 281 Ark. 261, 663 S.W.2d 719 (1984); In re Marriage of Brown, 15 Cal.3d 838, 126 Cal.Rptr. 633, 544 P.2d 561 (1976); In re Marriage of Gillmore, 113 Cal.App.3d 319, 169 Cal.Rptr. 811 (1980); In re Mitchell, 195 Colo. 399, 579 P.2d 613 (1978); In re Marriage of Pope, 37 Colo.App. 237, 544 P.2d 639 (1975); Kuchta v. Kuchta, 636 S.W.2d 663 (Mo.1982), 48 Mo.L.Rev. 245 (1983); Kruger v. Kruger, 73 N.J. 464, 375 A.2d 659 (1977); Kikkert v. Kikkert, 177 N.J.Super. 471, 427 A.2d 76 (1981); Blitt v. Blitt, 139 N.J.Super. 213, 353 A.2d 144 (1976); Pellegrino v. Pellegrino, 134 N.J.Super. 512, 342 A.2d 226 (1975); Copeland v. Copeland, 91 N.M. 409, 575 P.2d 99 (1978); Majauskas v. Majauskas, 61 N.Y.2d 481, 474 N.Y.S.2d 699, 463 N.E.2d 15 (1984); In re Marriage of Haftorson, 49 Or.App. 205, 619 P.2d 655 (1980); Matter of Marriage of Rogers, 45 Or.App. 885, 609 P.2d 877 (1980); Englert v. Englert, 576 P.2d 1274 (Utah 1978).

Other cases are collected in Annot., 94 A.L.R.3d 176 (1979).

Division of a vested state pension was approved notwithstanding a non-assignment provision in Phillipson v. Board of Admin., Pub. Emp. Retire. System, 3 Cal.3d 32, 80 Cal.Rptr. 61, 473 P.2d 765 (1970), limited on other grounds, In re Marriage of Brown, 15 Cal.3d 838, 126 Cal. Rptr. 633, 544 P.2d 561 (1976); Uluhogian v. Uluhogian, 86 Ill.App.3d 654, 41 Ill.Dec. 761, 408 N.E.2d 107 (1980).

29. McCarty v. McCarty, 453 U.S. 210, 101 S.Ct. 2728, 69 L.Ed.2d 589 (1981), discussed supra at note 6.

30. See the Phillipson case, supra, note 28.

31. Kruger v. Kruger, 73 N.J. 464, 375 A.2d 659 (1977).

32. I.R.C. § 411.

33. In re Marriage of Brown, 15 Cal.3d 838, 126 Cal. Rptr. 633, 544 P.2d 561 (1976). For law review discussion of this question, see Bonavich, Allocation of Private Pension Benefits as Property in Illinois Divorce Proceedings, 25 Dep.L.Rev. 1 (1979); Note, Retirement Pay: A Divorce in Time Saved Mine, 24 Hast.L.J. 347 (1972); Bote, 42 Mo.L.Rev. 143 (1977); Pattiz, In a Divorce or Dissolution Who Gets the Pension Rights: Domestic Relations Law and Retirement Plans, 5 Pepp.L.Rev. 191 (1978).

34. Van Loan v. Van Loan, 116 Ariz. 272, 569 P.2d 214 (1977); Guffey v. Lachance, 127 Ariz. 140, 618 P.2d 634 (1980) (Van Loan rule does not warrant reopening a prior judgment to give a spouse a share of the pension); In re Marriage of Stenquist, 21 Cal.3d 779, 148 Cal.Rptr. 9, 582 P.2d 96 (1978) (husband's election of disability benefits does not defeat wife's claim to longevity pension); Robert C. S. v. Barbara J. S., 434 A.2d 383 (Del.1981); Linson v. Linson, 1 Hawaii App. 272, 618 P.2d 748 (1980) (military pension); Shill v. Shill, 100 Idaho 433, 599 P.2d

jected the argument that non-vested pensions are no more than expectancies,[35] or that they have no immediate cash value or sale value.[36] Such pensions are earned by the employee, they are contractual claims, albeit contingent, which will vest or mature if the employee continues to work for the employer until retirement or until the date of vesting. The very existence of the pension offers strong inducement for the employee to remain in the same job, so that even when the pension is not vested, it is not unlikely that the employment will continue until vesting.[37] For these reasons the non-vested pension is an intangible asset of value, in some cases the only valuable asset of the marriage, which properly should be divisible on divorce.

Contingent benefits and contingent interests other than retirement pensions have received differing kinds of treatment by the courts. The crucial factors in determining whether these interests are "property" for divorce purposes seem to be the nature of the spouse's interest, the nature of the benefit, and the purpose for which the benefit was created. Thus an interest in a discretionary trust, of which the spouse was one of two trustees, was held not to be property where the spouse had no enforceable legal claim either to principal or income, although in practice he had used the property as he pleased.[38] Disability benefits have been held not to be divisible property, either because of the federal statute creating them,[39] or because they are held to be compensation for pain or disfigurement rather than for loss of earnings.[40] Death benefits included in a pension plan have been held not to be property because of the spouse's lack of control over the proceeds.[41] On the other hand the spouse's

1004 (1979); Pieper v. Pieper, 79 Ill.App.3d 835, 34 Ill. Dec. 877, 398 N.E.2d 868 (1979); Sims v. Sims, 358 So.2d 919 (La. 1978) (semble); Deering v. Deering, 292 Md. 115, 437 A.2d 883 (1981); Weir v. Weir, 173 N.J.Super. 130, 413 A.2d 638 (1980) (semble); Taggart v. Taggart, 552 S.W.2d 422 (Tex. 1977) (semble, military pension); Wilder v. Wilder, 85 Wash.2d 364, 534 P.2d 1355 (1975) (semble, military pension); Leighton v. Leighton, 81 Wis.2d 620, 261 N.W.2d 457 (1978). Matter of Marriage of Rogers, 45 Or.App. 885, 609 P.2d 877 (1980), modified 47 Or.App. 963, 615 P.2d 412 (1980), modified 50 Or.App. 511, 623 P.2d 1108 (1981), takes the position that retirement benefits are not property to be divided on divorce but that they are marital assets to be considered in reaching the financial aspects of a divorce, whatever that may mean.

Ellis v. Ellis, 191 Colo. 317, 552 P.2d 506 (1976) and Light v. Light, 599 S.W.2d 476 (Ky.App.1980) held that non-vested pensions are not property to be divided on divorce, although the Light case describes such a pension as an "economic circumstance", whatever that is. Presumably those states which hold vested pensions not to be property would take the same position respecting non-vested pensions. See note 91, supra.

Other cases are collected in Annot., 94 A.L.R.3d 176 (1979).

35. In re Marriage of Brown, 15 Cal.3d 838, 126 Cal. Rptr. 633, 544 P.2d 561 (1976).

36. Ellis v. Ellis, 191 Colo. 317, 552 P.2d 506 (1976) held that non-vested pensions are not property because they have no cash surrender value, loan value, redemption value, lump sum value or value realizable after death, without referring to any of the numerous cases which had reached the opposite position. The case graphically illustrates the injustice of this view of pensions since the husband retired on his military pension just after the divorce action was brought, leaving the wife without compensation for the twenty years of marriage during which the pension right was accruing.

37. See M. Glendon, The New Family and the New Property 170–176 (1981) describing the manner in which pension rights tie employees to their jobs, the tie becoming tighter as the employee grows older.

When the divorce court has ordered the earning spouse to pay a portion of his retirement benefits to the other spouse when they come due (normally on the retirement of the earning spouse), it has been held that the earning spouse may not choose among alternative retirement plans in such a way as to impair the non-earning spouse's interest in the benefits. In re Marriage of Gillmore, 29 Cal.3d 418, 174 Cal.Rptr. 493, 629 P.2d 1 (1981) (husband could not postpone his receipt of benefits by postponing his retirement, but would be required to begin making the prescribed payments to his ex-wife when the benefits came due, whether or not he chose to retire at that time).

38. In re Marriage of Rosenblum, 43 Colo.App. 144, 602 P.2d 892 (1979).

39. Luna v. Luna, 125 Ariz. 120, 608 P.2d 57 (1979) (relying on Hisquierdo v. Hisquierdo, 439 U.S. 572, 99 S.Ct. 802, 59 L.Ed.2d 1 (1979)); Ex parte Johnson, 591 S.W.2d 453 (Tex. 1979). See also Perez v. Perez, 587 S.W.2d 671 (Tex. 1979) ("military readjustment" benefits not community property).

40. In re Marriage of Saslow, 40 Cal.3d 848, 221 Cal. Rptr. 546, 710 P.2d 346 (1985) (disability payments are community property to the extent that they were intended to provide retirement income).

Contra: In re Marriage of Smith, 84 Ill.App.3d 446, 39 Ill.Dec. 905, 405 N.E.2d 884 (1980) (disability pension is marital property); Guy v. Guy, 98 Idaho 205, 560 P.2d 876 (1977) (disability payments are partial consideration for past employment and are divided on divorce as community property).

41. Corrigan v. Corrigan, 160 N.J.Super. 400, 390 A.2d 141 (1978). A group term life insurance policy was held

interest in stock option or profit sharing plans has been held to be analogous to pension rights and therefore to constitute divisible property.[42]

The valuation of pension rights, particularly non-vested rights, may often be difficult. One solution to this problem which has been adopted by the Brown case [43] and some others [44] is to award to each spouse the appropriate proportion of each pension payment as it is paid. This avoids having to place a value at the time of the divorce upon such contingencies as whether the earning spouse will continue to work at the same job until vesting or retirement and whether he will survive to or beyond retirement. It has the drawback that it requires the divorce court to reserve jurisdiction to the date when the payments are to be made.

Other courts have found it desirable to make the division of pension rights at the time of the divorce. This requires that two determinations be made: a) The court must place a current value on the pension rights. b) The court must then decide what proportion of that value should go to the non-earn-

ing spouse. In states having community property, or states in which only the marital property may be divided, the courts must also calculate how much of the pension's value is community or marital property and how much separate property of the earner spouse. This last computation is easily made, by multiplying the value of the pension by a fraction whose numerator is the period of time during which the marriage existed and whose denominator is the period of time during which the pension rights have been accruing.[45] Thus if the present value of the pension is ten thousand dollars, it has accumulated over ten years, and the marriage has been in existence during five of those years, the community property or marital property value of the pension would be five thousand dollars.

The cases have used at least two methods for arriving at the current value of pension rights. One such method is merely to rely on the amount to which the earner spouse would be entitled to take from the fund at the time of the divorce.[46] This has the merit of simplicity but of course it fails to take account of the value of the retirement benefits to which

not to be "property" in Metropolitan Life Ins. Co. v. Tallent, 445 N.E.2d 990 (Ind. 1983).

42. Green v. Green, 64 Md.App. 122, 494 A.2d 721 (1985); Callahan v. Callahan, 142 N.J.Super. 325, 361 A.2d 561 (1976); Keig v. Keig, 270 N.W.2d 558 (N.D. 1978). In re Marriage of Skaden, 19 Cal.3d 679, 139 Cal. Rptr. 615, 566 P.2d 249 (1977) held an insurance sales agent's "termination benefits" to be community property divisible on divorce.

43. In re Marriage of Brown, 15 Cal.3d 838, 126 Cal. Rptr. 633, 544 P.2d 561 (1976).

44. Johnson v. Johnson, 131 Ariz. 38, 638 P.2d 705 (1981); Pollick v. Pollick, 52 Hawaii 357, 477 P.2d 620 (1970) (semble); Shill v. Shill, 100 Idaho 433, 599 P.2d 1004 (1979) (recommends this method where the divorce does not occur near the time of retirement); In re Marriage of Hunt, 78 Ill.App.3d 653, 34 Ill.Dec. 55, 397 N.E.2d 511 (1979); In re Marriage of Haftorson, 49 Or.App. 205, 619 P.2d 655 (1980); Rogers and Matter of Marriage of Rogers, 45 Or.App. 885, 609 P.2d 877 (1980), modified 47 Or.App. 963, 615 P.2d 412 (1980), modified 50 Or.App. 511, 623 P.2d 1108 (1981) (this case, while expressly saying the pension is not property, proceeded to divide it, ordering it to be paid when the earner spouse received it.)

The income tax consequences to the parties should also be taken into account in determining how the pension rights are to be divided, according to the Rogers case, supra, and Selchert v. Selchert, 90 Wis.2d 1, 280 N.W.2d 293 (1979).

Where evidence of value is not introduced it has been held that the pension rights may not be divided. In re Marriage of Evans, 85 Ill.2d 523, 55 Ill.Dec. 529, 426 N.E.2d 854 (1981).

The method of dividing pensions is, like other similar questions, within the discretion of the trial court, but some cases have expressed a preference for a division at the time of divorce where that can be done without undue hardship to the spouses. Taylor v. Taylor, 329 N.W.2d 795 (Minn. 1983).

For an attempt to deal with the complexities caused when the employee spouse chooses not to retire when his pension has become vested and mature, see Koelsch v. Koelsch, 148 Ariz. 176, 713 P.2d 1234 (1986).

45. An example of this computation in somewhat complicated form is in In re Marriage of Stenquist, 21 Cal.3d 779, 148 Cal.Rptr. 9, 582 P.2d 96 (1978).

46. Ridgway v. Ridgway, 94 N.M. 345, 610 P.2d 749 (1980) (profit-sharing plan); Bloomer v. Bloomer, 84 Wis. 2d 124, 267 N.W.2d 235 (1978).

Dewan v. Dewan, 17 Mass.App.Ct. 97, 455 N.E.2d 1236 (1983) held that it was reversible error to assign a value to a pension equal to the amount of the earning spouse's contributions to the plan, where the actuarial value greatly exceeded such contributions.

the employee will be entitled if he continues in the same pension plan. Furthermore, if the pension rights are not vested, the employee may not have a right to any present payment. The other solution adopted by the courts is to determine the value of the benefits under the plan when they become payable in the future, and discount that value for both mortality and vesting.[47] This requires an estimate from the appropriate experts of the probability that the employee spouse will live to the date of vesting and that he will remain in the pension plan until that time. This method is obviously uncertain and may result in a range of possible values, depending upon the probabilities arrived at by the experts. But is no more uncertain than other judgments about value which the courts are required to make. And since most of the cases involve marriages of long standing, the probabilities of both survival and continuance in the pension plan are usually high.[48]

WESTLAW REFERENCES

hisquierdo +s hisquierdo & 134k252.3(4) /p marri! community marital /10 property /s divid! division distribut!

sy(vested matured /2 retir! pension /s marital marri! community /10 property)

ti("van loan" +s "van loan")

---

47. Johnson v. Johnson, 131 Ariz. 38, 638 P.2d 705 (1981); Shill v. Shill, 100 Idaho 433, 599 P.2d 1004 (1979) (recommends this method where retirement will occur not long after the divorce); Matter of Marriage of Franzke, 292 Or. 110, 637 P.2d 595 (1981); Derevere v. Derevere, 5 Wash.App. 741, 491 P.2d 249 (1971); Bloomer v. Bloomer, 84 Wis.2d 124, 267 N.W.2d 235 (1978).

48. E.g., In re Marriage of Brown, 15 Cal.3d 838, 126 Cal.Rptr. 633, 544 P.2d 561 (1976), where the employee spouse would be eligible for retirement about three years after the divorce.

§ 15.7

1. See § 1.2, supra.

2. See the discussion in § 1.2, supra, at note 4.

3. Marvin v. Marvin, 18 Cal.3d 660, 134 Cal.Rptr. 815, 557 P.2d 106 (1976). The trial court's decision after the remand is reproduced in 5 Fam.L.Rptr. 3085 (1979), giving the plaintiff $104,000 in rehabilitative alimony. This judgment was reversed in Marvin v. Marvin, 122 Cal. App.3d 871, 176 Cal.Rptr. 555 (1981) on the ground that the award was not within the issues as framed by the pleadings. See Kay and Amyx, Marvin v. Marvin: Preserving the Options, 65 Cal.L.Rev. 937 (1977); Folberg and Buren, Domestic Partnership: A Proposal for Divid-

§ 15.7 Division of Property Between Unmarried Cohabitants

An earlier section of this work[1] has dealt with contracts regulating property rights which have been made by unmarried persons who are living together. The great majority of cases in recent years have enforced such contracts, at least where they do not involve payment for sexual services.[2] The question then is, can the property of unmarried cohabitants be divided upon their separation in the absence of any contract, in reliance upon some other legal rationale?

The celebrated Marvin case[3] is the only case which gives this question any extensive discussion. It concludes that there are several legal theories which justify an equitable division of the property accumulated by unmarried persons while they lived together. These theories include constructive trust, quantum meruit, resulting trust. The court in this case was further at pains to say that it was not basing possible relief upon common law marriage, which had been abolished by statute in California,[4] or upon the California Family Law Act, which authorized the division of community property between spouses upon divorce.[5] A few other cases[6] also authorize the distribution of property acquired by persons living together without having been

---

ing the Property of Unmarried Families, 12 Willamette L.J. 453 (1976); Bruch, Nonmarital Cohabitation in the Common Law Countries: A Study in Judicial-Legislative Interaction, 29 Am.J.Comp.L. 217 (1981).

4. West's Ann.Cal.Civ.Code § 4100 (1983).

5. West's Ann. Cal. Civ. Code § 4800 (Supp. 1987). An earlier case, In re Cary's Marriage, 34 Cal.App.3d 345, 109 Cal.Rptr. 862 (1973) had held that the Family Law Act did provide authority for dividing the property of unmarried persons living together.

6. Eaton v. Johnston, 235 Kan. 323, 681 P.2d 606 (1984); Carlson v. Olson, 256 N.W.2d 249 (Minn.1977); Warden v. Warden, 36 Wash.App. 693, 676 P.2d 1037 (1984). The court in the Carlson case, after extensive quotation from Marvin, talks about an irrevocable gift as the basis for the division of the property.

See Reppy, Property and Support Rights for Unmarried Cohabitants: A Proposal for Creating a New Legal Status, 44 La.L.Rev. 1677 (1984), suggesting several legal theories on which to base property awards to unmarried persons living together.

Taylor v. Taylor, 317 So.2d 422 (Miss.1975) approved an award of alimony to a woman who had lived with a man without being married to him. The court did not devote

married, but it is difficult to discern from the opinions what rationale the courts thought was appropriate to such cases.

The legal basis for the Marvin case must be examined in the light of the allegations in that case. The plaintiff there was a woman who lived for some years with a well known actor and alleged that she had performed various services for the defendant as "companion, homemaker, housekeeper and cook", after having given up a lucrative career as an entertainer and singer. When the court says that she might recover on a theory of quantum meruit in such circumstances, it presumably means that she should receive compensation for the services which she performed. It is not clear whether on this theory she should also receive reimbursement for her opportunity costs, that is, the value of the career which she gave up in order to serve the defendant, but perhaps this is also included in quantum meruit. This basis for the court's decision is also suggested by the court's reference to the expectations of the parties as supporting an award,[7] although it is somewhat difficult to see just how the plaintiff could have had any expectations until she had won her lawsuit, her claim being a novel one. The question this leaves us with is whether, in determining how much compensation for her services the plaintiff should receive, the court is authorized to deduct from the value of those services the value of the support provided by the defendant for the plaintiff during the time they lived together. Conceivably in some cases the defendant may have conferred upon the plaintiff benefits exceeding the value of the plaintiff's services. The Marvin opinion does not answer this question.

If the reliance in cases like Marvin is on such equitable doctrines as resulting trust or constructive trust, the case furnishes even less guidance as to the measure of recovery which is being authorized. A resulting trust has been defined as occurring when a person makes a disposition of property such that he does not intend the transferee to take a beneficial interest.[8] A constructive trust occurs when the person holding property has an equitable duty to convey it, the duty usually arising out of the existence of fraud, duress, undue influence or breach of a fiduciary relation.[9] Since neither of these doctrines seems to fit the Marvin circumstances very well, perhaps all they mean is that some vague equitable duty is being imposed upon the defendant, the details of which are being left to the trial court to work out. After all the early history of equity was distinguished by the equity courts' ingenuity in fashioning new remedies for claims which did not fit into the existing system of actions at law. The trial court in the Marvin case accepted the invitation extended to it by the California Supreme Court by awarding the plaintiff one hundred and four thousand dollars in rehabilitative alimony. As that court put it, the purpose of the award was to enable the plaintiff to acquire training either in her former vocation as an entertainer or in furtherance of some new career.[10]

The meaning of the Marvin case thus seems to be that living together out of wedlock, at least for a substantial period,[11] gives rise to

much discussion to the case but did say the award was based upon a "decent regard for the sensibilities of humanity."

7.   18 Cal.3d at 682, 134 Cal.Rptr. at 830, 557 P.2d at 121. Carlson v. Olson, 256 N.W.2d 249, 255 (Minn.1977) also mentions the reasonable expectations of the parties.

8.   5 A. Scott, The Law of Trusts §§ 404, 404.1 (3d ed. 1967). Professor Scott gives three situations in which resulting trusts arise: (1) where an express trust fails; (2) where an express trust is fully performed without exhausting the trust estate; (3) where property is purchased and the price is paid by one person and at his direction the vendor conveys the property to another person. Restatement of Restitution § 160, com. b (1937) states that "A resulting trust arises where a transfer of

property is made under circumstances which raise an inference that the person making the transfer did not intend the transferee to have the beneficial interest in the property transferred."

9.   5 A. Scott, The Law of Trusts § 462 (3d ed. 1967). The general purpose of the constructive trust is to prevent unjust enrichment. This theory is therefore somewhat more apt when applied to the Marvin situation than is resulting trust.

10.   Marvin v. Marvin, 5 Fam.L.Rptr. 3077, 3085 (1979).

11.   The parties in the Marvin case lived together for seven years. Marvin v. Marvin, 18 Cal.3d 660, 665, 134 Cal.Rptr. 815, 819, 557 P.2d 106, 110 (1976). The court

claims on the part of both parties to share in each other's property on some unspecified equitable basis. The measure of the claim may be the value of services rendered, or it may be just what strikes the trial court as fair under all the circumstances.

A question closely related to the Marvin problem is whether property acquired by either party before marriage, but while they were living together is available for division if they later marry and then seek a divorce. In those states in which only marital property is divisible on divorce and which define marital property as property acquired during marriage (with certain exceptions not relevant here) [12] it seems clear that the acquisition of

property by cohabiting but unmarried spouses cannot be characterized as marital and cannot be divided if the parties later marry and then sue for divorce.[13] But under the form of statute which authorizes the division of all property of either spouse, property acquired before marriage would be divisible.[14] With respect to this property, however, the courts might well be reluctant to consider activities occurring before the marriage as relevant to the share to be allocated to one or the other spouse.[15]

 **WESTLAW REFERENCES**

find 134 cal rptr 815

---

suggests no standards by which one might determine whether the parties had lived together long enough for some equitable duty to arise.

12. See section 15.1, supra, at note 11 for a list of these states.

13. E.g., Grishman v. Grishman, 407 A.2d 9 (Me. 1979). Other cases are cited in Wand, The Relevance of Premarital Cohabitation to Property Division Awards in Divorce Proceedings: An Evaluation of Present Trends and a Proposal for Legislative Reform, 63 B.U.L.Rev. 105 (1983).

But Matter of Marriage of Lindsey, 101 Wash.2d 299, 678 P.2d 328 (1984) held that where property was ac-

quired while the parties lived together and where they later married, the rule is that the courts must "examine the [meretricious] relationship and the property accumulations and make a just and equitable disposition of the property." Washington is of course a community property state.

14. See section 15.1, supra, at note 12 for a list of these states.

15. For example, if a relevant factor in making the division is the services of a spouse as a homemaker, the court may be unwilling to consider services of this sort performed before marriage.

Chapter 16

ALIMONY, TEMPORARY AND PERMANENT

Table of Sections

§ 16.1 Alimony—Historical Background and Constitutional Limitations

American law imported the practice of granting alimony as an incident to divorce from the English ecclesiastical law as it existed before the reform of the English court system in 1857.[1] As with other rules borrowed from England,[2] those relating to alimony were applied in a different context. In England the ecclesiastical courts gave only divorces a mensa et thoro, authorizing husband and wife to live apart, but not freeing them from the marriage bond.[3] The alimony which was awarded by the ecclesiastical courts under those circumstances merely constituted a recognition and enforcement of the husband's duty to support the wife which continued after the judicial separation.[4] The wife's need was the greater in those days because of the control over her property which the law gave to her husband. This was reflected in the courts' willingness to take into account in fixing the amount of alimony the value of the property which the wife brought into the marriage.[5] Alimony was further made necessary by the lack of employment opportunities for married women. In addition to these factors the English courts gave consideration to the degree of the husband's fault in making the award.[6] Where

§ 16.1

1. For a good discussion of the historical background see Vernier and Hurlbut, The Historical Background of Alimony Law and Its Present Statutory Structure, 6 Law & Contemp.Prob. 197 (1939).

2. E.g., recrimination. See section 13.11, supra.

3. 2 Bishop, Marriage, Divorce and Separation §§ 852–857 (1891).

4. Wilson v. Wilson, 3 Hagg.Ecc. 329, 162 Eng.Rep. 1175 (1830) (note); Mytton v. Mytton, 3 Hagg.Ecc. 658, 162 Eng.Rep. 1298 (1831); Fischli v. Fischli, 1 Blackf. 360

(Ind.1825). See also 1 Blackstone Commentaries, Bk. I, ch. 15, p. 189 (Gavit ed. 1941); 2 Burns, Ecclesiastical Law 450–451 (1781); 2 Vernier, American Family Laws 259 (1932).

5. Cooke v. Cooke, 2 Phill.Ecc. 40, 161 Eng.Rep. 1072 (1812); Smith v. Smith, 2 Phill.Ecc. 235, 161 Eng.Rep. 130 (1814).

6. Cooke v. Cooke, 2 Phill.Ecc. 40, 161 Eng.Rep. 1072 (1812); Otway v. Otway, 2 Phill.Ecc. 109, 161 Eng.Rep. 1092 (1813). See Scrimshire v. Scrimshire, 2 Hagg.Con. 395, 161 F.Supp. 782 (1752).

the wife was at fault, she was entitled to no alimony.[7] Thus even in the English law alimony was not solely measured by the wife's need for support.

Alimony was also occasionally given in the only kind of absolute divorce available in England before 1857, the Parliamentary divorce, but it is the ecclesiastical practice rather than the Parliamentary divorce which seems to have influenced the American law. This is shown by the fact that although alimony might be given to the guilty wife as a result of a Parliamentary divorce,[8] the American rule was generally, up until quite recently, that she was entitled to no alimony,[9] following the ecclesiastical precedent.

When the English institution of alimony, which served the plain and intelligible purpose of providing support for wives living apart from their husbands, was utilized in America in suits for absolute divorce, however, its purpose became less clear. As a result of absolute divorce the marriage is entirely dissolved. It is harder to justify imposing on the ex-husband a continuing duty to support his former wife than after a divorce a mensa, which does not dissolve the marriage. This difficulty is not obviated by labelling alimony a "substitute" for the wife's right to support. Why should there be such a substitute? Would it not be more logical to say that when the marriage is dissolved all rights and duties based upon it end? Doubts about the wisdom of alimony or about how long it should continue after the divorce have also arisen as a result of the married woman's full legal capacity to own and control her own property and during the last two decades as a result of her increased participation in work outside the home.[10] For example, this has led some courts to award "rehabilitative alimony", to continue for a relatively short period, with the purpose of enabling the married woman to obtain education or training which will qualify her to obtain a job after the divorce.[11]

Notwithstanding the logical objection to alimony as an incident to absolute divorce, it has been granted in the United States from the earliest colonial times to the present.[12] Today, for some unknown reason, it is sometimes also referred to as "maintenance".[13] Authority to grant it is statutory in origin.[14] A few decisions have said that alimony is within the inherent jurisdiction of equity courts,[15] but these cases are probably limited to alimony in actions for separation rather than absolute divorce. In any event they are based upon a mistaken reading of English legal history. It is clear that alimony was not within the jurisdiction of English courts of equity but was the exclusive province of the ecclesiastical courts.[16]

Although nearly all states have statutes authorizing alimony in appropriate cases,

---

7. 1 Blackstone, Commentaries, Bk. I, ch. 15, p. 189 (Gavit ed. 1941).

8. Fisher v. Fisher, 2 Sw. & Tr. 410, 164 Eng.Rep. 1055 (1861).

9. Cases are collected in Annot., 34 A.L.R.2d 313, 321 (1954).

10. Hopson, The Economics of Divorce: A Pilot Empirical Study at the Trial Court Level, 11 Kan.L.Rev. 107 (1962); Kelso, The Changing Social Setting of Alimony, 6 Law & Contemp.Prob. 186 (1939). The provisions of the Uniform Marriage and Divorce Act § 308, 9A Unif.L. Ann. 160 (1979) and the Commissioners' Comments indicate a purpose to reduce reliance upon alimony.

11. E.g., Roberts v. Roberts, 283 So.2d 396 (Fla.App. 1973); Otis v. Otis, 299 N.W.2d 114 (Minn.1980).

12. II Howard, A History of Matrimonial Institutions 332, 338, 339, 349, 368, 370, 374, 377 (1904); III Id. 28–30, 90–95.

13. Uniform Marriage and Divorce Act § 308, 9A Unif.L.Ann. 160 (1979).

14. Today all states authorize alimony awards except Texas. The statutes often contain a list of factors to be considered in making the award. Freed, Foster, Family Law in the Fifty States: An Overview, 17 Fam.L.Q. 365, 383–388 (1984).

15. Salvato v. Salvato, 195 Cal.App.2d 869, 16 Cal. Rptr. 263 (1961), 50 Cal.L.Rev. 353 (1962); Fornshill v. Murray, 1 Bland 479 (Md.1828); Helms v. Franciscus, 2 Bland 544 (Md.1820); Almond v. Almond, 4 Randolph 662 (Va.1826). See also Machado v. Machado, 220 S.C. 90, 66 S.E.2d 629 (1951).

16. Anonymous, 2 Shower 282, 89 Eng.Rep. 941 (1631); Ball v. Montgomery, 2 Ves.Jun. 195, 30 Eng.Rep. 191 (1793). But equity would enforce separation agreements, Angier v. Angier, Prec. Ch. 497, 24 Eng.Rep. 222 (1718); Head v. Head, 3 Atkyns 547, 26 Eng.Rep. 1115 (1747), and would aid in the enforcement of alimony decrees of the ecclesiastical courts, Dawson v. Dawson, 7 Vesy Jun. 173, 32 Eng.Rep. 71 (1803).

there is a lack of agreement on just what purpose alimony serves. In the opinion of some judges alimony continues the support which the wife was entitled to receive while the marriage existed.[17] Others look on alimony as furnishing damages for the husband's wrongful breach of the marriage contract.[18] Still others speak as if it were a penalty imposed on the guilty husband.[19] Since the purpose of alimony is obviously related to the factors which enter into such questions as whether and when it should be awarded and in what amount, it will be discussed in more detail in a later section.[20]

Assuming that one important purpose of alimony is to provide a substitute for the spousal right of support which exists during marriage, the changed economic position of women cannot help but have an effect upon courts' alimony decrees. Today more than half of all married women are in the labor force.[21] There are statements to be found in judicial opinions suggesting that this is indeed a reason for denying alimony or awarding it only in small amounts or for limited periods.[22] The most thorough recent economic study of the financial aspects of divorce demonstrates that whatever may be the reason, alimony is granted in less than one-fifth of all divorces, and in less than half of those divorces terminating marriages of over fifteen years' duration.[23] Even in those divorces in which there are minor children in the custody of their

mothers, which presumably disables or limits the mothers in their ability to work, alimony awards as distinguished from child support are made in less than one-quarter of the cases.[24] On the other hand there is a greater likelihood of an alimony award where the husband's income exceeds thirty thousand dollars.[25] Where alimony is granted, it is likely to be relatively low even where the marriage is of long duration and the husband's income is above thirty thousand dollars.[26] It is notable that the Uniform Marriage and Divorce Act is framed with the purpose of providing for the spouses by means of a division of property rather than by an award of alimony.[27] Of course it is clear that only a small proportion of divorces involve enough property to be of any benefit to the spouses.[28]

The conclusion which one must draw from these facts is that although divorce may not be financially harmful to spouses in a marriage of short duration where the wife has been working, it can be and often is disastrous for the wife in a marriage of long duration where she has not worked outside the home,[29] or for the wife who has custody of small children. If the husband's income is not large, it is obvious that it cannot be divided between two families in such a way as to provide both with adequate support. Even if it is large, there is the further difficulty for the wife that any award she receives may not

17. E.g., Dayton v. Dayton, 290 Ky. 418, 161 S.W.2d 618 (1942); Wolfe v. Wolfe, 124 N.E.2d 485 (Ohio Com.Pl. 1954); Bray v. Landergren, 161 Va. 699, 172 S.E. 252 (1934).

18. E.g., Driskill v. Driskill, —— Mo.App. ——, 181 S.W.2d 1001 (1944).

19. E.g., Lewis v. Lewis, 202 Ark. 740, 151 S.W.2d 998 (1941); Gusman v. Gusman, 140 Ind. 433, 39 N.E. 918 (1895); Poppe v. Poppe, 114 Ind.App. 348, 52 N.E.2d 506 (1944). Contra: Bonanno v. Bonanno, 4 N.J. 268, 72 A.2d 318 (1950); O'Neill v. O'Neill, 18 N.J.Misc. 82, 11 A.2d 128 (1939); Miles v. Miles, 185 Or. 230, 202 P.2d 485 (1949); Cecil v. Cecil, 179 Va. 274, 19 S.E.2d 64 (1942).

20. See section 15.5, infra.

21. The Statistical Abstract of the United States 399 (1985) indicates that in 1984 52.8% of married women living with their husbands were in the labor force, as contrasted with 40.8% in 1970. The corresponding figures for separated women were 61.1% and 52.1%, and for divorced women were 74.3% and 71.5%.

22. Kover v. Kover, 29 N.Y.2d 408, 328 N.Y.S.2d 641, 278 N.E.2d 886 (1972).

23. L. Weitzman, The Divorce Revolution 169 (1985).

24. Id. at 186.

25. Id. at 179.

26. Id. at 171–173.

27. Uniform Marriage and Divorce Act § 308, Commissioners' Comment, 9A Unif.L.Ann. 161 (1979).

28. L. Weitzman, The Divorce Revolution 61–69 (1985).

29. See, e.g., Orr v. Orr, 458 So.2d 362 (Fla.App.1984), in which the trial court awarded alimony of $800 per month plus payments on a car for a woman fifty-eight years old, after a thirty-six year marriage during which she had not worked outside the home. The husband in this case was a successful lawyer with an income of $60,000 per year. This award was reversed on appeal as an abuse of discretion.

be regularly paid. She must then face the practical legal difficulties and the expense of trying to enforce her decree.[30]

The preceding discussion has assumed the traditional impact of alimony, that the husband pays it and the wife receives it. Even before 1979 this was not the exclusive pattern. In some states by statute either spouse could be awarded alimony if he or she needed it and the other spouse was able to pay it.[31] And in states having an equal rights amendment in the state constitution, it was sometimes held that alimony had to be available to either spouse in order to be constitutional.[32] In 1979 the United States Supreme Court decided Orr v. Orr,[33] which held that the Alabama statute authorizing alimony to be imposed only upon husbands and in favor of wives violated the Equal Protection Clause of the United States Constitution's Fourteenth Amendment. The Court applied the test that gender classifications must serve important governmental objectives and must be substantially related to the achievement of those objectives. It found the state's objective to be the reinforcement of the wife's dependent role in the family, and the recognition of the husband's responsibility for support of the family, and said that these objectives could no longer support the statute. The Court also found that the statutory purposes of compensating the wives for past discrimination and of helping needy spouses, using sex as a proxy for need, could not validate the statute because

individualized hearings on need were also a feature of the procedure, already protecting wives against unfairness and penury. The Court further held that statutory gender classifications tend to reinforce stereotypes about the proper roles of women and are for that reason questionable. The Court remanded the case for further consideration of what effect its ruling would have on the Alabama statute. To no one's surprise, on the remand the Alabama court held that the effect would be to extend alimony rights to needy husbands as well as wives.[34] The effect of Orr has been more symbolic than practical. It has had an extensive educational impact by strengthening the philosophical underpinnings of gender equality in and out of marriage. But it has not led to the award of alimony to husbands in any very large number of cases.[35]

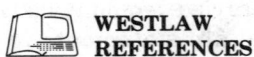

WESTLAW
REFERENCES

alimony /s ecclesiastical canon /2 law

---

§ 16.2 Alimony—Temporary Alimony and Attorney Fees

Jurisdiction

Divorce statutes customarily if not universally authorize the award of alimony pendente lite and attorney fees (or "suit money" as it is often called) to wives who are parties to divorce and separate maintenance suits.[1] Whether the statute is the exclusive

---

30. These are indicated in L. Weitzman, The Divorce Revolution 161–163 (1985). See also sections 16.7 and 16.8, infra.

31. E.g., West's Ann. Cal. Civ. Code § 4801 (1987); Mass. Gen. Laws Ann. c. 208, § 34 (Supp.1986); Uniform Marriage and Divorce Act § 308, 9A Unif.L.Ann. 160 (1979).

32. Henderson v. Henderson, 458 Pa. 97, 327 A.2d 60 (1974).

33. 440 U.S. 268, 99 S.Ct. 1102, 59 L.Ed.2d 306 (1979), on remand 374 So.2d 895 (Ala.Civ.App.1979), writ denied 374 So.2d 898 (1979). Justice Brennan wrote for the Court, with Justices Blackmun and Stevens concurring, and Justices Powell, Rehnquist and Chief Justice Burger dissenting on procedural grounds. Boyles v. Boyles, 268 Ark. 120, 594 S.W.2d 17 (1980) held that Orr did not affect an alimony decree entered before Orr was decided pursuant to a statute which would have been unconstitutional under Orr.

34. Orr v. Orr, 374 So.2d 895 (Ala.Civ.App.1979), cert. denied 444 U.S. 1060, 100 S.Ct. 993, 62 L.Ed.2d 738 (1980).

35. See section 15.5, infra.

§ 16.2

1. Ala. Code 1983, § 30–2–50; Ariz. Rev. Stat. §§ 25–315(B), 25–324 (Supp.1986); West's Ann.Cal.Civ.Code §§ 4357, 4370 (Supp.1987); Conn.Gen.Stat.Ann. §§ 46b–62, 46b–83 (1986); West's Fla.Stat.Ann. § 61.071 (1985); Ill.—Smith Hurd Ann. ch. 40, §§ 501, 508 (1980 and Supp.1986); Mass.Gen.Laws Ann. c. 208, § 17 (Supp. 1986); Minn.Stat.Ann. § 518.14 (Supp.1987); N.J.Stat. Ann. § 2A:34–23 (Supp.1986); N.Y.—McKinney's Dom. Rel. Law §§ 236, Part B 6, 237 (1986); N.C.Gen.Stat. §§ 50–16.3, 50–16.4 (1984); Pa.Stat. tit. 23, § 502 (Supp. 1986); V.Tex.C.A., Fam.Code § 3.59 (Supp.1987); West's Rev.Code Wash.Ann. 1986 Ann. §§ 26.09.060, 26,09.140 (1986); Wis.Stat.Ann. § 767.23 (1981 and Supp.1986).

source of authority to make such awards is a subject of dispute, some courts holding that they have inherent power by virtue of their equity jurisdiction to provide for the support of the wife during suit.[2] Other courts say that the power is exclusively statutory.[3] The question is seldom of importance, since the statutes usually cover the problems most likely to arise, but occasionally the theory of inherent powers must be relied on to make up for statutory deficiencies.[4] Once the legislature has entered upon a general regulation of the subject, it seems preferable to hold that the sole measure of the court's power lies in the statute, leaving it to the legislature to amend if changes appear necessary.

Jurisdiction over the subject matter of the divorce action is sometimes said to be necessary for an award of temporary alimony.[5] This is inaccurate. Certainly the court should be empowered to make awards for maintenance of the wife during the time necessary to determine the jurisdictional question, even though it is later found no jurisdiction over the subject matter existed.[6] After the suit is dismissed for lack of jurisdiction

over the subject matter, however, there is no further power to make temporary alimony or counsel fee orders.[7]

Orders for temporary alimony and attorney fees, being in personam in their effect, must be based upon personal service,[8] on a personal appearance by the defendant,[9] or on a long-arm statute coupled with the minimum contacts required by constitutional doctrine.[10] Such orders should be made only after notice to the defendant and an opportunity to be heard.[11]

Prerequisites

The purpose of temporary alimony used to be described as the maintenance of the wife during the pendency of the divorce action.[12] It arose out of and was a substitute for the husband's common law duty of support. Today, as a result of Orr v. Orr,[13] the duty of support is no longer the sole obligation of the husband but is allocated between the spouses in accordance with their needs and the ability of each to contribute. Therefore temporary alimony (and temporary child support) may

See also the Uniform Marriage and Divorce Act §§ 304(a), 313, 9A Unif.L.Ann. 128, 177 (1979).

2. E.g., Howard v. Howard, 72 App.D.C. 145, 112 F.2d 44 (1940); Brown v. Brown, 42 Del.(3 Terry) 157, 29 A.2d 149 (1942); Williams v. Williams, 537 S.W.2d 107 (Tex. Civ.App.1976); Bray v. Landergren, 161 Va. 699, 172 S.E. 252 (1934). An early English case ordering maintenance pendente lite is Head v. Head, 3 Atk. 295, 26 Eng.Rep. 972 (1745). See Note, 32 Yale L.J. 478 (1923).

3. Loeb v. Loeb, 84 Cal.App.2d 141, 190 P.2d 246 (1948); Lyon v. Lyon, 318 Mass. 646, 63 N.E.2d 459 (1945); Teske v. Teske, 80 N.E.2d 517 (Ohio App.1948), appeal dismissed 150 Ohio St. 126, 80 N.E.2d 677 (1948).

4. E.g. Howard v. Howard, 72 App.D.C. 145, 112 F.2d 44 (1940), in which support pendente lite was awarded for children of the marriage; Branon v. Branon, 247 N.C. 77, 100 S.E.2d 209 (1957), in which a wife as defendant was held to have a common law right to temporary alimony, where the statute authorized such awards only to wives as plaintiffs.

5. People v. District Court, County of Denver, 66 Colo. 438, 182 P. 5 (1919) (dictum).

6. Kirk v. Kirk, 218 Ark. 880, 239 S.W.2d 6 (1951) (dictum); Morgan v. Morgan, 103 Conn. 189, 130 A. 254 (1925).

7. Morgan v. Morgan, 104 Conn. 412, 133 A. 249 (1926).

8. Gaines v. Gaines, 81 U.S.App.D.C. 260, 157 F.2d 521 (1946).

9. Keen v. Keen, 191 Md. 31, 60 A.2d 200 (1948).

10. See the discussion of jurisdiction for alimony, property division and child support in section 12.4, supra, and Pitsenberger v. Pitsenberger, 287 Md. 20, 410 A.2d 1052 (1980), appeal dismissed for want of a substantial federal question 449 U.S. 807, 101 S.Ct. 52, 66 L.Ed.2d 10 (1980), rehearing denied 449 U.S. 1028, 101 S.Ct. 601, 66 L.Ed.2d 491 (1980).

11. Rethorst v. Rethorst, 214 Md. 1, 133 A.2d 101 (1957); Annot., 10 A.L.R.3d 280 (1966). But see Loeb v. Loeb, 84 Cal.App.2d 141, 190 P.2d 246 (1948), Annot., 152 A.L.R. 445, 457 (1944).

12. Howard v. Howard, 72 App.D.C. 145, 112 F.2d 44 (1940); Ex parte Tranum, 255 Ala. 143, 50 So.2d 447 (1951); Whelan v. Whelan, 87 Cal.App.2d 690, 197 P.2d 361 (1948); England v. England, 138 Conn. 410, 85 A.2d 483 (1951); Brown v. Brown, 42 Del.(3 Terry) 157, 29 A.2d 149 (1942); Bannon v. Bannon, 270 N.Y. 484, 1 N.E.2d 975 (1936); Stone v. Stone, 98 Ohio App. 240, 122 N.E.2d 404 (1954), 17 Ohio St.L.J. 150 (1956); Bray v. Landergren, 161 Va. 699, 172 S.E. 252 (1934).

If the spouse complies with the order for temporary alimony, he can no longer be held liable for necessaries furnished to the other spouse. Annot., 60 A.L.R.2d 7, 55 (1958).

13. 440 U.S. 268, 99 S.Ct. 1102, 59 L.Ed.2d 306 (1979), on remand 374 So.2d 895 (Ala.Civ.App.1979), writ denied 374 So.2d 898 (1979), discussed in section 15.1, supra, at note 33.

be imposed upon either spouse and the statutes so provide.[14] As a practical matter, however, it is most often awarded to the wife.

The logical consequence of temporary alimony's purpose would seem to be that the existence of a marriage is the first prerequisite for an award.[15] If there is no marriage, the man has no duty to support the woman, and there is no basis for alimony. On the other hand, if this requirement were strictly adhered to, there might have to be extensive preliminary trials on the marriage issue before temporary alimony could be granted. This would delay and hinder the trial on the merits. Faced with this dilemma, the courts compromise. If the marriage is alleged and not denied, it is assumed to exist and temporary alimony is granted on that basis. If the existence of the marriage is disputed, most courts required the wife to make a "prima facie" case as to its existence,[16] but do not require her to prove it as fully as at a trial on the merits.[17] In practice this means proof that a ceremonial marriage occurred and that the parties lived together as husband and wife.[18] Where the marriage is attacked because an underlying divorce was invalid, the court will not usually deny temporary alimony but will reserve the issue for later trial on

the merits,[19] although a prior divorce might be so clearly invalid in some cases as to justify a denial of temporary alimony.[20] One party or the other may be estopped to assert the validity or invalidity of the marriage and the alimony issue may be determined on that ground.[21]

In dealing with this and other requirements for temporary alimony, appellate courts strongly adhere to the principle that temporary alimony is within the trial court's discretion.[22] A grant or denial of alimony by the trial court will be reversed only for abuse of discretion. What this principle seems to amount to is that the trial courts may consider a broad range of factors in reaching their decision, and their evaluation of those factors will be accepted on appeal unless its error is very clear.

Temporary alimony and attorney fees may be granted to a spouse whether he is plaintiff or defendant in the suit,[23] but an accusation of marital fault may sometimes be made as a defense to the claim. Where either the award of temporary alimony or the grant of a divorce are no longer dependent upon fault, such a defense is of course of no avail.[24] Where fault is still relevant to either claim, the cases hold that if the claimant is suing or

---

14. See the statutes cited in note 1, supra.

15. Ex parte Gurganus, 251 Ala. 361, 37 So.2d 591 (1948); Colbert v. Colbert, 28 Cal.2d 276, 169 P.2d 633 (1946); Fincher v. Fincher, 55 So.2d 800 (Fla.1952); Hill v. Hill, 241 Mo.App. 243, 236 S.W.2d 394 (1951). Other cases are collected in Annot., 11 A.L.R.2d 1040, 1042 (1950).

16. Sweeley v. Sweeley, 28 Cal.2d 389, 170 P.2d 469 (1946); Harris v. Harris, 171 Colo. 233, 466 P.2d 70 (1970); Reger v. Reger, 242 Ind. 302, 177 N.E.2d 901 (1961), rehearing denied 242 Ind. 302, 178 N.E.2d 749 (1961); Alvernes v. Alvernes, 75 R.I. 325, 66 A.2d 373 (1949); Annot., 11 A.L.R.2d 1040 (1950).

17. Ex Parte Gurganus, 251 Ala. 361, 37 So.2d 591 (1948); Colbert v. Colbert, 28 Cal.2d 276, 169 P.2d 633 (1946); Harvey v. Harvey, ___ W.Va. ___, 298 S.E.2d 467 (1982). In McGrath v. McGrath, 387 S.W.2d 239 (Mo. App.1965) failure to prove a valid common law marriage led to the court's refusal of temporary alimony.

18. Dietrich v. Dietrich, 41 Cal.2d 497, 261 P.2d 269 (1953), cert. denied 346 U.S. 938, 74 S.Ct. 378, 98 L.Ed. 426 (1954). A stronger showing may be required if the wife relies on a common law marriage. Fincher v. Fincher, 55 So.2d 800 (Fla.1952). But see Colbert v. Colbert, 28 Cal.2d 276, 169 P.2d 633 (1946).

19. Hill v. Hill, 241 Mo.App. 243, 236 S.W.2d 394 (1951).

20. In Ex parte Gurganus, 251 Ala. 361, 37 So.2d 591 (1948) the court held the parties' prior divorce invalid for fraud, so that the wife was entitled to temporary alimony. An attack on the wife's divorce from her former husband might conversely result in a denial of her claim to alimony.

21. Dietrich v. Dietrich, 41 Cal.2d 497, 261 P.2d 269 (1953), cert. denied 346 U.S. 938, 74 S.Ct. 378, 98 L.Ed. 426 (1954).

22. Ex parte Phillips, 247 Ala. 94, 22 So.2d 611 (1945); Sweeley v. Sweeley, 28 Cal.2d 389, 170 P.2d 469 (1946); Floyd v. Floyd, 91 Fla. 910, 108 So. 896 (1926); Hanson v. Hanson, 177 Pa.Super. 384, 110 A.2d 750 (1955).

23. Rooney v. Rooney, 231 Ind. 443, 109 N.E.2d 93 (1952); Johnson v. Johnson, 237 N.C. 383, 75 S.E.2d 109 (1953).

24. See the statutes cited in note 1, supra. The nonfault grounds for divorce are discussed, supra, in sections 13.5, 13.6, 13.7. See also Wife R. v. Husband R., 310 A.2d 877 (Del.Super.1973), granting temporary alimony on the ground of incompatibility.

making his defense in good faith and with reasonable support in the evidence, he may be granted temporary alimony and attorney fees notwithstanding that a full trial on the merits might find him at fault.[25] If the defense is found to be a sham or not made in good faith, temporary alimony is denied.[26] In this way the claimant is given the financial support necessary to present his case. For the same reason courts may in their discretion grant temporary alimony even after the divorce is denied.[27] It is important to make a distinction here between temporary alimony for the support of a spouse and support pendente lite for the children of the marriage. If the claim is for support of the children, the claimant's marital misconduct is entirely irrelevant.

Most of the cases involving temporary alimony center on the claimant's needs and the obligor's ability to pay. It is clear that the claimant must show that she needs the support before it can be awarded to her,[28] but the definitions of "need" differ widely. Since this is the aspect of temporary alimony most clearly discretionary, it is not surprising that a wide spread of conflicting awards are to be found.[29] In times of substantial inflation the precedential effect of earlier cases is obviously minimal, but this fact may sometimes not be evident to trial courts.

There are some areas of agreement in the cases. If the husband is making payments in accordance with a valid separation agreement, the wife is not entitled to temporary alimony.[30] If she is attacking the separation agreement as invalid, she should be able to get temporary alimony.[31] The purpose of temporary alimony being to maintain the living conditions and standard of living of the parties as close to the status quo as possible during the litigation, the amount awarded has no necessary connection with what might be awarded for permanent alimony and the two kinds of award should be independent of each other.[32]

The more difficult questions arise when it is shown that the claimant has some financial means of his own and the defendant spouse argues that no support is needed. If the claimant has some property, but the income from the property is not sufficient to support her, many cases will grant her temporary alimony.[33] If there are children to be supported, then the obligor spouse should be required to pay enough to care for them to the extent he is able to do so, irrespective of temporary alimony.[34] But of course both spouses must contribute to the support of

25. Ex parte Phillips, 247 Ala. 94, 22 So.2d 611 (1945); Barkley v. Barkley, 42 So.2d 51 (Fla.1949); Floyd v. Floyd, 91 Fla. 910, 108 So. 896 (1926); Edwards v. Edwards, 182 Kan. 737, 324 P.2d 150 (1958); Messer v. Messer, 157 Neb. 312, 59 N.W.2d 395 (1953); Bolin v. Bolin, 242 N.C. 642, 89 S.E.2d 303 (1955); Hanson v. Hanson, 177 Pa.Super. 384, 110 A.2d 750 (1955); Poliakoff v. Poliakoff, 221 S.C. 391, 70 S.E.2d 625 (1952). Other cases are collected in Annot., 2 A.L.R.2d 307 (1948). Some cases seem to adopt a principle of comparative rectitude. Howard v. Howard, 291 S.W.2d 828 (Ky.1956); Eals v. Swan, 221 La. 329, 59 So.2d 409 (1952).

26. Moss v. Moss, 196 Ga. 340, 26 S.E.2d 628 (1943); Lakey v. Lakey, 218 Miss. 697, 67 So.2d 711 (1953); Yost v. Yost, 161 Neb. 164, 72 N.W.2d 689 (1955); Branon v. Branon, 247 N.C. 77, 100 S.E.2d 209 (1957); Poliakoff v. Poliakoff, 221 S.C. 391, 70 S.E.2d 625 (1952). If the wife disobeys other orders of the court, she may be refused temporary alimony. Reibstein v. Reibstein, 220 Ark. 783, 249 S.W.2d 847 (1952).

27. Chlupacek v. Chlupacek, 226 Ga. 520, 175 S.E.2d 834 (1970); Pitsenberger v. Pitsenberger, 287 Md. 20, 410 A.2d 1052 (1980), appeal dismissed for want of a substantial federal question 449 U.S. 807, 101 S.Ct. 52, 66 L.Ed.2d 10 (1980), rehearing denied 449 U.S. 1028, 101 S.Ct. 601,

66 L.Ed.2d 491 (1980). See also Berbiglia v. Berbiglia, 442 S.W.2d 949 (Mo.App.1969), stating that temporary alimony and attorney fees are entirely independent of the merits of the case.

28. Moore v. Moore, 218 Md. 218, 145 A.2d 764 (1958); Annot., 15 A.L.R. 781 (1921).

29. Many cases are collected in Annots., 26 A.L.R.4th 1218 (1983) and 1 A.L.R.3d 280 (1965).

30. Ellis v. Ellis, 67 N.Y.S.2d 845 (1946).

31. Locke Paddon v. Locke Paddon, 194 Cal. 73, 227 P. 715 (1924). But see Patton v. Patton, 32 Cal.2d 520, 196 P.2d 909 (1948), with strong dissent by Justice Traynor.

32. Burlini v. Burlini, 143 Cal.App.3d 65, 191 Cal. Rptr. 541 (1983); MacReynolds v. MacReynolds, 29 Colo. App. 267, 482 P.2d 407 (1971).

33. Whelan v. Whelan, 87 Cal.App.2d 690, 197 P.2d 361 (1948); Loeb v. Loeb, 84 Cal.App.2d 141, 190 P.2d 246 (1948); Jennings v. Jennings, 78 R.I. 139, 79 A.2d 920 (1951); Weiss v. Weiss, 111 Utah 353, 179 P.2d 1005 (1947). Many other cases are collected in Annot., 60 A.L.R.3d 728, 785 (1974).

34. Howard v. Howard, 72 App.D.C. 145, 112 F.2d 44 (1940); Annot., 60 A.L.R.3d 832 (1974).

children to the extent of their means.[35] Where there are no children and the spouse claiming temporary alimony has not sufficient property to produce support for himself without, as the cases say, impairing the capital of his separate estate, no temporary alimony will be awarded.[36]

Although cases can be found which say that the wife is not required to go out and work to support herself,[37] if the husband's income is not large and the wife is relatively young and able to earn her living, the court will grant her less temporary alimony than otherwise, and perhaps will refuse to grant her any.[38] It cannot be over-emphasized that these are matters of degree which turn on such facts as the relative incomes of the parties,[39] their ages and states of health, their future prospects,[40] their debts and obligations, and their accustomed manner of living.[41] In some jurisdictions the courts may develop local guidelines for establishing, at least presumptively, levels of temporary alimony under various conditions.[42] Each case is necessarily somewhat different from every other. Therefore few general rules can be found which will govern particular cases. One useful device is

the concept of "net need", that is, "the wife's actual financial requirements, less her current assets and earnings potential in relation to her husband's capacity to pay",[43] as a measure of temporary alimony. The usefulness of any formula depends upon the court's having complete and accurate evidence of the relative circumstances of the parties and this is sometimes not provided.[44]

Special needs of a spouse caused by the demands of litigation may be included in the award of temporary alimony, such as travel expenses and subsistence away from home during the trial.[45] If feasible, the spouse's needs may be met by giving her the use of property rather than requiring payments in cash.[46] Where the spouse shows a need for support, temporary alimony may be awarded pending appeal in the divorce action.[47]

Enforcement and Termination

Orders for temporary alimony are ordinarily enforceable by contempt proceedings [48] and by execution,[49] and may be enforced against exempt property.[50] To the extent that they are considered final by the law of the state in

35. See section 6.2, supra, and section 17.1, infra.

36. Sweeley v. Sweeley, 28 Cal.2d 389, 170 P.2d 469 (1946); Welsh v. Welsh, 160 Fla. 380, 35 So.2d 6 (1948); Frank v. Frank, 207 Md. 124, 113 A.2d 411 (1955); Annot., 60 A.L.R.3d 728, 766 (1974).

37. Bilello v. Bilello, 240 La. 158, 121 So.2d 728 (1960); Hempel v. Hempel, 225 Minn. 287, 30 N.W.2d 594 (1948); Annot., 60 A.L.R.3d 728, 789 (1974).

38. Howard v. Howard, 72 App.D.C. 145, 112 F.2d 44 (1940); Palmieri v. Palmieri, 8 Misc.2d 396, 168 N.Y.S.2d 48 (1957); Annot., 60 A.L.R.3d 728, 792 (1974). But it may be proper to award a wife temporary alimony to acquire further education. McNulty v. McNulty, 347 Pa. Super. 363, 500 A.2d 876 (1985).

39. Hempel v. Hempel, 225 Minn. 287, 30 S.W.2d 594 (1948).

40. State ex rel. Houtchens v. District Court of Fourth Judicial District in and for Ravalli County, 122 Mont. 76, 199 P.2d 272 (1948); Conrad v. Conrad, 252 N.C. 412, 113 S.E.2d 912 (1960), 39 N.C.L.Rev. 189 (1961).

41. Hempel v. Hempel, 225 Minn. 287, 30 N.W.2d 594 (1948). Cf. England v. England, 138 Conn. 410, 85 A.2d 483 (1951) (need, not manner of living, is the test).

42. Burlini v. Burlini, 143 Cal.App.3d 65, 191 Cal. Rptr. 541 (1983); McNulty v. McNulty, 347 Pa.Super. 363, 500 A.2d 876 (1985).

43. Walton v. Walton, 219 Ga. 729, 135 S.E.2d 886 (1964); Palmieri v. Palmieri, 8 Misc.2d 396, 168 N.Y.S.2d 48, 50 (1957), 33 N.Y.U.L.Rev. 1260 (1958).

44. Ibid.

45. McMillion v. McMillion, 31 Colo.App. 33, 497 P.2d 331 (1972), appeal after remand __ Colo.App. __, 522 P.2d 125 (1974); Greaney v. Greaney, 109 N.H. 305, 250 A.2d 502 (1969); State ex rel. Pearce v. Superior Court for King County, 34 Wash.2d 768, 209 P.2d 906 (1949).

46. Ex parte Gurganus, 251 Ala. 361, 37 So.2d 591 (1948); Huggins v. Huggins, 202 Ga. 738, 44 S.E.2d 778 (1947); Little v. Little, 9 N.C.App. 361, 176 S.E.2d 521 (1970).

47. Bain v. Superior Court for Los Angeles County, 36 Cal.App.3d 804, 111 Cal.Rptr. 848 (1974).

48. In re Robbins, 212 Cal. 534, 299 P. 51 (1931); Moore v. Moore, 207 Ga. 335, 61 S.E.2d 500 (1950).

49. Moore v. Moore, 207 Ga. 335, 61 S.E.2d 500 (1950); Ex parte Asadoorian, 48 R.I. 50, 135 A. 322 (1926). But Edwards v. Edwards, 182 Kan. 737, 324 P.2d 150 (1958) holds that installments of temporary alimony do not become final judgments on which execution may issue.

50. Cases are collected in Annot., 54 A.L.R.2d 1422 (1957).

which they are made, suits to enforce them may be brought in other jurisdictions.[51]

The difficulties which arise in enforcing temporary alimony orders center upon the effect of a final decree in the divorce action. When a final decree is entered, either dismissing the action or granting the divorce, the contention is often made that the trial court loses "jurisdiction" to make further orders for temporary alimony, since the statutes usually authorize such orders only during the pendency of the suit. It is also argued that where the divorce is granted the parties are no longer husband and wife and there is no further duty of support. The answer which the courts give to this contention depends on the precise language of the statute, and also on the court's view of the ultimate source of its power to grant temporary alimony. If the court finds an inherent equity power to grant these orders, it may allow temporary alimony after the final decree, at least where an appeal has been taken.[52] Certainly if the purpose of temporary alimony is what the courts so often say it is, such orders ought to be permitted pending appeals, as the wife is in as much need of support then as during the trial, and her claim for support is not finally terminated until a ruling on the appeal. The trial court is the appropriate forum for granting relief, since it has the best chance to evaluate the needs and circumstances of the parties.

Nevertheless some cases deny the power of the trial court to make such orders,[53] and other authorities leave the wife entirely without remedy by holding that the appellate court has no such power either.[54] This line of cases sacrifices good sense and sound policy to legal technicality. Fortunately there is a large body of authority the other way.[55]

Where no appeal is taken or contemplated, it is usually held that the wife cannot have temporary alimony awarded after the final decree in the action, unless jurisdiction has been previously reserved by the court.[56] This is a pitfall which counsel for the wife should be careful to avoid, either by obtaining temporary alimony before a final decree or, if that is impractical, by drafting the final decree so as to include provision for the wife's support.

In fact some authorities go so far as to hold that temporary alimony due and owing for the period up to the date of final decree cannot be collected after that date, because the temporary alimony order is "merged" in the final decree of divorce and all enforcement proceedings fall with the order.[57] This is an entirely senseless rule since it rewards the recalcitrant husband for non-compliance with the court's order by excusing him from payment of arrears. The majority of cases reach the opposite result.[58]

---

51. Kearney v. Kearney, 224 Ark. 484, 274 S.W.2d 779 (1955); Kelly v. Kelly, 121 N.J.Eq. 361, 189 A. 665 (1937) (dictum).

52. McCaleb v. McCaleb, 177 Cal. 147, 169 P. 1023 (1917) (old order terminates with final decree, but wife could apply for a new allowance pending appeal); Welling v. Welling, 257 Ind. 120, 272 N.E.2d 598 (1971) (old order terminated when the divorce was granted, but the court has inherent power to make a new order independent of statute); Eldridge v. Eldridge, 278 Mass. 309, 180 N.E. 137 (1932) (wife can apply for a new order to carry her through the appeal). Other cases are cited in Annot., 19 A.L.R.2d 703 (1951). The husband may be credited on his permanent alimony obligation with amounts paid as temporary alimony pending the appeal. Annot., 86 A.L.R.2d 696 (1962).

53. Saunders v. Saunders, 140 Conn. 140, 98 A.2d 815 (1953); Hunnicutt v. Hunnicutt, 214 Ga. 834, 108 S.E.2d 279 (1959); Woods v. Woods, 236 Mo.App. 855, 159 S.W.2d 320 (1942). Other cases are collected in Annot., 19 A.L.R.2d 703 (1951).

54. Annot., 136 A.L.R. 502, 511 (1942).

55. Bain v. Superior Court for Los Angeles County, 36 Cal.App.3d 804, 111 Cal.Rptr. 848 (1974); Teske v. Teske, 80 N.E.2d 517 (Ohio App.1948), appeal dismissed 150 Ohio St. 126, 80 N.E.2d 677 (1948) (granting temporary alimony pending a motion to set the divorce aside for fraud). Other cases are cited in Annot., 19 A.L.R.2d 703 (1951).

56. Wilson v. Superior Court, 31 Cal.2d 458, 189 P.2d 266 (1948); Clark v. Clark, 213 Ga. 342, 99 S.E.2d 127 (1957); Hawthorne v. Hawthorne, 214 La. 905, 39 So.2d 338 (1949); Trutnau v. Trutnau, 221 Minn. 462, 22 N.W.2d 321 (1946); Domicolo v. Domicolo, 32 N.J.Super. 330, 108 A.2d 206 (1954); Caldwell v. Caldwell, 189 N.C. 805, 128 S.E. 329 (1925).

57. E.g., Cole v. Cole, 82 U.S.App.D.C. 155, 161 F.2d 883 (1947) (semble); Walter v. Walter, 15 App.D.C. 333 (1834); Richardson v. Richardson, 218 Minn. 42, 15 N.W.2d 127 (1944); Mittman v. Mittman, 263 App.Div. 384, 33 N.Y.S.2d 211 (1942); Colom v. Colom, 58 Ohio St. 2d 245, 389 N.E.2d 856 (1979).

58. Douglas v. Superior Court, In and For Los Angeles County, 143 Cal.App.2d 17, 299 P.2d 285 (1956). Other cases are collected in Annot., 154 A.L.R. 530 (1945).

Where one of the spouses dies pending the divorce, the arrears of temporary alimony may be collected, but the amount due may not be increased on the ground of alleged fraud in the disclosure of the obligor's income.[59]

If the husband and wife reach a reconciliation before the divorce is granted, the temporary alimony order is held waived and terminates.[60] It does not revive upon a later separation, but a new order for maintenance of the wife must be obtained.[61]

Whether or not an order for temporary alimony is appealable depends upon the local procedure. Where the statute or rule allows an appeal from "final" decrees, a substantial group of cases holds that this includes temporary alimony decrees,[62] although such decrees are ordinarily modifiable for changed circumstances.[63] There is considerable authority denying appeal.[64] If such orders are held not to be appealable, they still may be reviewed by appellate courts in some instances through the use of extraordinary writs such as mandamus,[65] prohibition[66] or certiorari.[67]

Attorney Fees

The American legal system requires each party to a suit to pay his own attorney fees except where statutes or contracts provide otherwise.[68] The statutes in most states authorize the courts having jurisdiction in matrimonial litigation to order either spouse to pay the attorney fees of the other spouse for reasons similar to those underlying temporary alimony.[69] Formerly the duty to pay attorney fees was solely that of the husband, as an aspect of his duty to support his wife and children, but since the Orr case the obligation must apply to both spouses in order to meet the demands of the Equal Protection Clause of the Fourteenth Amendment.[70]

The granting of attorney fees is based upon the same policy of providing support for the spouse who needs it at the expense of the spouse who can afford to provide it as is temporary alimony.[71] When the spouse is involved in litigation, legal services are as necessary an element of support as food or lodging.[72] As is the case with temporary alimony, the allowance or disallowance of attor-

59. Howard v. Howard, 49 Ill.App.3d 441, 7 Ill.Dec. 303, 364 N.E.2d 464 (1977).

60. Hill v. District Court of the Seventeenth Judicial District, 189 Colo. 356, 540 P.2d 1079 (1975) (temporary support for minor children payable to Social Services Department terminated when husband and wife became reconciled and dismissed their divorce action); Brown v. Brown, 210 Ga. 233, 78 S.E.2d 516 (1953); Rosen v. Rosen, 2 Misc.2d 905, 149 N.Y.S.2d 512 (Dom.Rel.Ct.1956). See also Uniform Marriage and Divorce Act § 304(f)(3), 9A Unif.L.Ann. 130 (1979).

61. Hester v. Hester, 239 N.C. 97, 79 S.E.2d 248 (1953).

62. Howard v. Howard, 72 App.D.C. 145, 112 F.2d 44 (1940); In re Marriage of Skelley, 18 Cal.3d 365, 134 Cal. Rptr. 197, 556 P.2d 297 (1976); Hizel v. Hizel, 132 Colo. 379, 288 P.2d 354 (1955); England v. England, 138 Conn. 410, 85 A.2d 483 (1951) (semble); Floyd v. Floyd, 91 Fla. 910, 108 So. 896 (1926); State ex rel. Houtchens v. District Court of Fourth Judicial Dist. In and For Ravalli County, 122 Mont. 76, 199 P.2d 272 (1948); Branon v. Branon, 247 N.C. 77, 100 S.E.2d 209 (1957) (semble); Poliakoff v. Poliakoff, 221 S.C. 391, 70 S.E.2d 625 (1952) (semble). Contra: McMahon v. McMahon, 156 Ohio St. 280, 102 N.E.2d 252 (1951) (semble); Hanson v. Hanson, 177 Pa.Super. 384, 110 A.2d 750 (1955). Other cases are collected in Annot., 167 A.L.R. 360 (1947). The wife is not estopped to appeal from the amount of the award by her acceptance of the payments under it. Lewis v. Lewis, 219 Md. 313, 149 A.2d 403 (1959).

63. Warner v. Warner, 34 Cal.2d 838, 215 P.2d 20 (1950); Elmer v. Elmer, 132 Colo. 57, 285 P.2d 601 (1955),

appeal after remand 163 Colo. 430, 431 P.2d 470 (1967); Young v. Young, 65 So.2d 28 (Fla.1953); Edwards v. Edwards, 182 Kan. 737, 324 P.2d 150 (1958) (child support).

64. Cases are collected in Annot., 167 A.L.R. 360, 365 (1947).

65. Ex parte Tranum, 255 Ala. 143, 50 So.2d 447 (1951); Ex parte Gurganus, 251 Ala. 361, 37 So.2d 591 (1948).

66. Douglas v. Superior Court, In and For Los Angeles County, 143 Cal.App.2d 17, 299 P.2d 285 (1956) (husband asks prohibition against execution on allegedly invalid temporary alimony order).

67. Jennings v. Jennings, 78 R.I. 139, 79 A.2d 920 (1951); State ex rel. Pearce v. Superior Court for King County, 34 Wash.2d 768, 209 P.2d 906 (1949).

68. Harrison v. Harrison, 208 Ga. 70, 65 S.E.2d 173 (1951).

69. See the statutes cited in note 1, supra, and House v. House, 368 Mass. 120, 330 N.E.2d 152 (1975). Krasnow v. Krasnow, 140 Conn. 254, 99 A.2d 104 (1953) holds that there is inherent equity power to award attorney fees in divorce. See also Note, Counsel Fees in Matrimonial Actions, 38 Neb.L.Rev. 761 (1959).

70. Orr v. Orr, 440 U.S. 268, 99 S.Ct. 1102, 59 L.Ed.2d 306 (1979), on remand 374 So.2d 895 (Ala.Civ.App.1979), writ denied 374 So.2d 898 (1979), discussed at note 33 in section 15.1, supra. A husband was awarded attorney

—————

71.–72. See notes 71–72 on page 629.

ney fees and the amount of the allowance are within the sound discretion of the trial court, to be reversed on appeal only where the appellate court finds that the discretion was abused.[73]

In order to get attorney fees, as is the case with temporary alimony, a prima facie showing of a valid marriage must be made.[74] The spouse claiming fees may be either plaintiff or defendant in the divorce [75] and in fact may ultimately be the losing party without being disqualified for the award of fees.[76] Since attorneys may often refuse to undertake a representation of a party in divorce without payment of a retainer, many cases have held that attorney fees may be awarded to a spouse in advance of the rendition of attorney's services.[77] If that is not done, the spouse might effectively be deprived of counsel.

Attorney fees may be awarded when one spouse is in need of them and the other spouse has the means to pay them.[78] "Need"

is defined in different ways by different courts. Some cases seem to define it as synonymous with destitution.[79] Others emphasize that the purpose of the award is to enable the spouse to litigate on the same footing with the other spouse, so that fees may be awarded even though the claimant spouse has some resources.[80] Still other cases take the position that attorney fees may be awarded when the failure to do so would substantially reduce the effectiveness of awards of alimony or property made to the claimant spouse,[81] or where the failure to award them would force the claimant spouse to deplete her capital.[82] The apparent diversity of approach is unavoidable where the ultimate considerations are relative means and fairness to both spouses. There is probably no more adequate way of defining the situation in which attorney fees should be awarded than to say that an award is justified when it can be paid with relatively slight hardship by one spouse and

fees in Keister v. Keister, 458 So.2d 32 (Fla.App.1984), petition for review denied 466 So.2d 217 (1985).

71. Denham v. Denham, 285 S.W.2d 176 (Ky.1955); McClanahan v. McClanahan, 197 S.W.2d 581 (Tex.Civ. App.1946). But see the curious remarks in Keister v. Keister, 458 So.2d 32 (Fla.App.1984), petition for review denied 466 So.2d 217 (1985), to the effect that the purpose of awarding attorney fees is not related to maintenance but rather is designed to ensure that both spouses have similar ability to secured competent legal counsel.

72. Phillips, Nizer, Benjamin, Krim & Ballon v. Rosenstiel, 490 F.2d 509 (2d Cir.1973); Read v. Read, 119 Colo. 278, 202 P.2d 953 (1949) (husband must provide the wife with legal services when she is prosecuted for killing their child).

73. In re Marriage of Munguia, 146 Cal.App.3d 853, 195 Cal.Rptr. 199 (1983); Holley v. Holley, 194 Conn. 25, 478 A.2d 1000 (1984); In re Marriage of Smith, 128 Ill. App.3d 1017, 84 Ill.Dec. 242, 471 N.E.2d 1008 (1984); Foster v. Foster, 33 Md.App. 73, 364 A.2d 65 (1976); Lester v. Lester, 452 S.W.2d 269 (Mo.App.1970).

74. Reeves v. Reeves, 34 Cal.2d 355, 209 P.2d 937 (1949); Weitz v. Weitz, 24 N.Y.2d 930, 301 N.Y.S.2d 991, 249 N.E.2d 768 (1969).

75. Walls v. Walls, 232 Ark. 638, 339 S.W.2d 430 (1960); Crute v. Crute, 208 Ga. 724, 69 S.E.2d 255 (1952); Riggers v. Riggers, 81 Idaho 570, 347 P.2d 762 (1959); Denham v. Denham, 285 S.W.2d 176 (Ky.1955); Walker v. Walker, 201 S.W.2d 61 (Tex.Civ.App.1947); McClanahan v. McClanahan, 197 S.W.2d 581 (Tex.Civ.App.1946).

Some cases suggest the wife is more deserving of attorney fees when she is defendant than when she is bringing the suit, Westphal v. Westphal, 122 Cal.App. 388, 10 P.2d 122 (1932); Judd v. Judd, 1 Misc.2d 965, 59 N.Y.S.2d 680

(1946), but there is no substantial basis for such a suggestion.

76. Rosser v. Rosser, 355 So.2d 717 (Ala.Civ.App.1978), cert. denied 355 So.2d 722 (1978); Husband S. v. Wife S., 294 A.2d 89 (Del.1972); Lockard v. Lockard, 193 Neb. 400, 227 N.W.2d 581 (1975) (wife entitled to attorney fees notwithstanding the commission of adultery during the marriage). Annot., 32 A.L.R.3d 1227 (1970).

77. Many cases are collected in Annot., 22 A.L.R.4th 407 (1983).

78. Krasnow v. Krasnow, 140 Conn. 254, 99 A.2d 104 (1953); In re Marriage of Borowczyk, 78 Ill.App.3d 425, 33 Ill.Dec. 738, 397 N.E.2d 71 (1979); Ousley v. Ousley, 264 S.W.2d 62 (Ky.1953); Hempel v. Hempel, 225 Minn. 287, 30 N.W.2d 594 (1948); Lester v. Lester, 452 S.W.2d 269 (Mo.App.1970). Weiss v. Weiss, 111 Utah 353, 179 P.2d 1005 (1947) held that the fact a wife was able to pay her attorney in the first instance did establish that she was not entitled to reimbursement from the husband. Contra on this point: Hopkins v. Hopkins, 47 Del.(8 Terry) 515, 94 A.2d 222 (1953).

79. In re Marriage of Zannis, 114 Ill.App.3d 1034, 70 Ill.Dec. 545, 449 N.E.2d 892 (1983) (wife entitled to attorney fees if she would otherwise be "stripped of her assets").

80. Porter v. Porter, 67 Ariz. 273, 195 P.2d 132 (1948).

81. Holley v. Holley, 194 Conn. 25, 478 A.2d 1000 (1984); Fitzgerald v. Fitzgerald, 190 Conn. 26, 459 A.2d 498 (1983).

82. In re Marriage of Smith, 128 Ill.App.3d 1017, 84 Ill.Dec. 242, 471 N.E.2d 1008 (1984); Donnelley v. Donnelley, 80 Ill.App.3d 597, 35 Ill.Dec. 919, 400 N.E.2d 56 (1980).

its payment will relieve relatively greater hardship for the receiving spouse.

Additional uncertainty is created by the next question, how much should be awarded in attorney fees? The fee awarded may be intended to cover all of the spouse's expenses for counsel [83] or the court may think that in view of the parties' relative means only part of the fees should be paid.[84] The amount of the fees is also within the sound discretion of the trial court,[85] just as is the decision whether to award fees at all. The courts rely on that favorite word of lawyers to define the amount of the fee. It must be reasonable,[86] and the services for which it is given must have been reasonably necessary to the conduct of the spouse's case.[87] The spouse being charged for the fee should have an opportuni-

ty to see the items on the attorney's bill and be heard on the amounts charged.[88] The list of factors which should be considered in setting the fee is similar to that in other cases where fees are awarded and includes such items as the nature of the case, its difficulty, the amount of money or property involved, the degree of skill and experience required and employed on the case, the degree of success attained, and the number of hours employed.[89] Time spent in negotiation may be included in the compensation hours,[90] but there is some authority that the court should carefully scrutinize time spent in conferences with the client.[91] Services rendered to a spouse by a legal services office may be the basis for an award of attorney fees,[92] as may services rendered in representing the children

83. Masters v. Stair, 505 S.W.2d 702 (Tex.Civ.App. 1974), appeal after remand 518 S.W.2d 439 (1975). If this is the case, the attorney may not claim further compensation from the spouse receiving the award.

84. Ibid.; Eizenhoefer v. Eizenhoefer, 292 Minn. 442, 193 N.W.2d 628 (1972).

85. Many cases are collected in an Annot., Amount of Attorneys' Fees in Matters Involving Domestic Relations, 59 A.L.R.3d 152 (1974).

86. In re Marriage of Siegel, 123 Ill.App.3d 710, 79 Ill. Dec. 219, 463 N.E.2d 773 (1984); Mayer v. Mayer, 180 N.J.Super. 164, 434 A.2d 614 (1981), certification denied 88 N.J. 494, 443 A.2d 709 (1981); Hennen v. Hennen, 53 Wis.2d 600, 193 N.W.2d 717 (1972). But it has been said that the trial court is not bound by expert testimony on what is a reasonable fee, judges being experts themselves on this question. In re Marriage of Jayne, 200 N.W.2d 532 (Iowa 1972). It has also been held that an agreement between a wife and her lawyer as to the amount of the fee does not limit the trial court's discretion to grant a reasonable fee, which may be more than the agreed amount. Foster v. Foster, 33 Md.App. 73, 364 A.2d 65 (1976).

87. Mayer v. Mayer, 180 N.J.Super. 164, 434 A.2d 614 (1981), certification denied 88 N.J. 494, 443 A.2d 709 (1981).

88. In re Marriage of Siegel, 123 Ill.App.3d 710, 79 Ill. Dec. 219, 463 N.E.2d 773 (1984); Welsh v. Welsh, 38 Ill. App.3d 35, 347 N.E.2d 512 (1976) (rejects the claimed fee where no written record of the time spent); Mayer v. Mayer, 180 N.J.Super. 164, 434 A.2d 614 (1981), certification denied 88 N.J. 494, 443 A.2d 709 (1981). But Foster v. Foster, 33 Md.App. 73, 364 A.2d 65 (1976) allowed the trial court to rely on its own experience in appraising the value of a lawyer's services, even though no record of the number of hours spent on the case. Chandler v. Chandler, 330 So.2d 190 (Fla.App.1976) held that the appropriate hourly charge was the usual charge prevailing in the place where the case was tried, rather than the place where the attorney usually practiced.

89. Lochridge v. Lochridge, 448 So.2d 378 (Ala.Civ. App.1984); In re Marriage of Munguia, 146 Cal.App.3d 853, 195 Cal.Rptr. 199 (1983); In re Marriage of Siegel, 123 Ill.App.3d 71, 79 Ill.Dec. 219, 463 N.E.2d 773 (1984); In re Marriage of Zannis, 114 Ill.App.3d 1034, 70 Ill.Dec. 545, 449 N.E.2d 892 (1983); In re Marriage of Brophy, 96 Ill.App.3d 1108, 52 Ill.Dec. 236, 421 N.E.2d 1308 (1981); Burkhart v. Burkhart, 169 Ind.App. 588, 349 N.E.2d 707 (1976); Foster v. Foster, 33 Md.App. 73, 364 A.2d 65 (1976). The financial ability of a spouse to pay the other spouse's fee may limit the award, but it does not justify awarding a fee larger than what is reasonable under the circumstances. Green v. Green, 41 Ill.App.3d 154, 354 N.E.2d 661 (1976). A bar association fee schedule was considered in Greiner v. Greiner, 179 Ind.App. 61, 384 N.E.2d 1055 (1979), but this is probably improper after Goldfarb v. Virginia State Bar, 421 U.S. 773, 95 S.Ct. 2004, 44 L.Ed.2d 572 (1975), rehearing denied 423 U.S. 886, 96 S.Ct. 162, 46 L.Ed.2d 118 (1975), which outlawed minimum fee schedules as violations of the antitrust laws.

For a discussion of the determination of the amount of attorney fees in matrimonial litigation, rejecting the use of a "multiplier" to reflect unusually difficult issues and unusually skillful attorneys, see Bellow v. Bellow, 94 Ill. App.3d 361, 50 Ill.Dec. 656, 419 N.E.2d 924 (1981).

90. Cueva v. Cueva, 86 Cal.App.3d 290, 149 Cal.Rptr. 918 (1978). It would seem that expenses of mediation should also be included in attorney fees.

91. Mayer v. Mayer, 180 N.J.Super. 164, 434 A.2d 614 (1981), certification denied 88 N.J. 494, 443 A.2d 709 (1981). The court's reason seems to be that divorce clients place greater than usual demands on their counsel for conferences, but this does not seem ipso facto to justify refusal to include such services in the award.

92. In re Marriage of Brockett, 130 Ill.App.3d 499, 85 Ill.Dec. 794, 474 N.E.2d 754 (1984).

of the marriage in the marital litigation.[93] But the attorney who is a witness for a party to the divorce may not have his fees included as attorney fees.[94] And legal services not related to the divorce action itself, such as fees for services in an earlier suit or in other matters may not be included.[95]

Other expenses incurred in the litigation may be recoverable by a spouse under the general heading of "suit money". These include the expense of depositions, of investigation, travel expenses, living expenses at the place of trial and similar costs.[96]

In some jurisdictions attorney fees may be ordered paid directly to the attorney,[97] while in others they must be paid to the spouse.[98] This is a matter of local practice.

The question sometimes arises whether attorney fees may be awarded to a spouse for services in connection with post-decree litigation such as motions to modify alimony, child support or custody. Most of the statutes in force today give the courts power to award attorney fees in such cases, either by providing that fees may be awarded in any proceed-ing brought under the divorce statute,[99] or by expressly mentioning the various types of modification proceedings.[1] Since the award of attorney fees is discretionary with the trial courts, the award of fees in post-decree proceedings is often influenced by the purpose for which the proceeding is brought, the success or lack of success of the moving party, and the impact of the proceeding on spouses and children of the former marriage, in addition to the considerations which are relevant to an award made as part of the divorce action itself. For example fees are often awarded for litigation to increase alimony or child support, at least where there is a reasonable probability for success.[2] Fees on appeal are often awarded where the appeal is not frivo-lous.[3] Proceedings brought to protect children or to enforce custody orders are also appropriate for requiring a spouse to pay the fees of the other spouse.[4] Where the proceeding is brought to obtain a modification of a custody order, the cases are divided on whether an award of fees should be made, with the claimant's chances somewhat better if he is resisting the modification.[5]

93. Carole K. v. Arnold K., 85 Misc.2d 643, 380 N.Y.S.2d 593 (Fam.Ct.1976); Matter of a Proceeding for Support Under Article 4 of Fam. Court Act, 87 Misc.2d 547, 385 N.Y.S.2d 740 (Fam.Ct.1976); Zande v. Zande, 3 N.C.App. 149, 164 S.E.2d 523 (1968).

94. Hubbard v. Hubbard, 233 So.2d 150 (Fla.App. 1970).

95. In re Zoellner's Marriage, 219 N.W.2d 517 (Iowa 1974); Weseley v. Weseley, 58 A.D.2d 829, 396 N.Y.S.2d 455 (2d Dep't 1977), appeal denied 42 N.Y.2d 809, 398 N.Y.S.2d 1032, 368 N.E.2d 288 (1977).

96. Donigan v. Donigan, 208 Md. 511, 119 A.2d 430 (1956); Green v. Green, 75 Nev. 317, 340 P.2d 586 (1959); Jack v. Jack, 75 N.E.2d 484 (Ohio App.1947); Parker v. Parker, 89 R.I. 300, 152 A.2d 526 (1959); State ex rel. Pearce v. Superior Court, 34 Wash.2d 768, 209 P.2d 906 (1949). Other cases are collected in Annots., 111 A.L.R. 1098 (1937), and 99 A.L.R.2d 264 (1965).

97. E.g., West's Fla.Stat.Ann. § 61.16 (1985); Owens v. Owens, 264 P.2d 341 (Okl.1953).

98. Wong v. Superior Court In and For Los Angeles County, 246 Cal.App.2d 541, 54 Cal.Rptr. 782 (1966); Weil v. Superior Court, 97 Cal.App.2d 373, 217 P.2d 975 (1950) (attorney cannot enforce order for fees); Lloyd v. Lloyd, 60 N.M. 441, 292 P.2d 121 (1956); Application of Waxstein and Gelbman, 130 N.Y.S.2d 285 (1954); McAlister v. McAlister, 253 S.W.2d 483 (Tex.Civ.App.1952).

99. Uniform Marriage and Divorce Act § 313, 9A Unif.L.Ann. 177 (1979).

1. E.g., N.Y.—McKinney's Dom. Rel. Law § 237 (1986).

2. In re Marriage of Davis, 141 Cal.App.3d 71, 190 Cal. Rptr. 104 (1983); Gilmore v. Gilmore, 74 Ill.App.3d 831, 30 Ill.Dec. 378, 393 N.E.2d 33 (1979); Waltrip v. Waltrip, 3 Ill.App.3d 892, 279 N.E.2d 405 (1972); Klipstein v. Klipstein, 47 Wis.2d 314, 177 N.W.2d 57 (1970). Edsall v. Superior Court In & For the County of Pima, 143 Ariz. 240, 693 P.2d 895 (1984) held that a trial court was not required to follow the parties' separation agreement concerning the award of attorney fees in a proceeding to modify a divorce decree. The court's position was that the statute controls the award of fees, giving the courts discretion in this respect and the statute thereby overrides the parties' agreement.

3. Bremer v. Bremer, 4 Ill.2d 190, 122 N.E.2d 794 (1954); Molto v. Molto, 242 Minn. 112, 64 N.W.2d 154 (1954); Annot., 18 A.L.R. 1494 (1922).

4. Payne v. White, 1 Ark.App. 271, 614 S.W.2d 684 (1981); Peterman v. Peterman, 14 Md.App. 310, 286 A.2d 812 (1972). In Fitts v. Fitts, 284 Ala. 109, 222 So.2d 696 (1969) the wife was denied attorney fees for her defense of a contempt charge when she was found guilty of contempt.

5. Granting attorney fees: Lerner v. Superior Court, 38 Cal.2d 676, 242 P.2d 321 (1952) (wife resisting modification); Wenzel v. Wenzel, 76 Idaho 7, 276 P.2d 485 (1954) (wife resisting modification); Wyatt v. Webb, 317 S.W.2d 883 (Ky.1958) (wife counterclaimed for child sup-

Events occurring after the institution of a divorce action may, in the opinion of some courts, prevent the award of attorney fees. These include the death of one of the parties, which technically abates the suit,[6] the reconciliation of the parties and dismissal of the suit,[7] or the claimant's waiver of support and contracting of a second marriage.[8] If the attorney's services were actually performed and if attorney fees would otherwise be appropriate, there seems no substantial reason why any of these events should foreclose the award of a reasonable fee.

The enforcement of orders for attorney fees again raises the question whether they are analogous to decrees for alimony or support of a spouse. The courts reach a variety of results, depending largely on their views of the policies underlying the award of attorney fees. Some cases hold that orders for attorney fees are just money judgments rather than alimony or support judgments, from which it follows that enforcement of them by contempt proceedings would violate the constitutional prohibition against imprisonment for debt.[9] This view seems very doubtful, to say the least.[10] The bankruptcy cases on the other hand generally take the position that attorney fees are analogous to maintenance and are therefore non-dischargeable debts on bankruptcy.[11] There is some confusion in the cases on whether the federal law or state law governs the bankruptcy issue [12] but the correct position would seem to be that the characterization of attorney fees as similar to alimony is a federal question, to be answered on the basis of what state law has to say about the actual functions of attorney fees.[13]

port); Mathews v. Mathews, 337 S.W.2d 529 (Mo.App. 1960) (wife resisting modification); Jones v. Jones, 365 P.2d 1019 (Okl.1961); Loeb v. Loeb, 120 Vt. 489, 144 A.2d 825 (1958) (wife resisting modification). Contra: Turney v. Nooney, 21 N.J.Super. 522, 91 A.2d 418 (1952). Many other cases both ways are collected in Annot., 15 A.L.R.2d 1270 (1951). In re Marriage of Cotton, 103 Ill.2d 346, 83 Ill.Dec. 143, 469 N.E.2d 1077 (1984) stated that the court had authority to award attorney fees to the wife in a proceeding for modification of custody, but refused to do so in this case because the husband had rescued the child from the wife's inadequate care.

6. Holding that the death of the husband deprives the court of jurisdiction to award attorney fees to the wife: Drucker v. Drucker, 7 Or.App. 85, 488 P.2d 1377 (1971); Louthian & Merritt, P. A. v. Davis, 272 S.C. 330, 251 S.E.2d 757 (1979). Holding that the wife's death does not deprive the trial court of responsibility to determine attorney fees to be paid by the husband: State ex rel. Paxton v. Porter Superior Court, 467 N.E.2d 1205 (Ind. 1984); Williams v. Williams, 59 N.J. 229, 281 A.2d 273 (1971); Mayer v. Mayer, 180 N.J.Super. 164, 434 A.2d 614 (1981), certification denied 88 N.J. 494, 443 A.2d 709 (1981).

7. Denying attorney fees after reconciliation: McNutt v. Beaty, 370 So.2d 998 (Ala.1979), on remand 370 So.2d 1001 (1979). Granting attorney fees after reconciliation: In re Marriage of Pallesi, 73 Cal.App.3d 424, 140 Cal. Rptr. 842 (1977); Weiner v. Weiner, 119 N.J.Super. 109, 290 A.2d 307 (1972).

8. Granting attorney fees to the wife after her remarriage: In re Marriage of Newport, 154 Cal.App.3d 915, 201 Cal.Rptr. 647 (1984).

9. Bahre v. Bahre, 248 Ind. 656, 230 N.E.2d 411 (1967), cited with approval in State ex rel. Egger v. Marion County Superior Court Civil Division, Room No. 7, 435 N.E.2d 993 (Ind.1982); Kerr v. Kerr, 287 Md. 363, 412 A.2d 1001 (1980).

10. Decrees ordering the payment of attorney fees serve the same purpose as alimony, that is, the support of the spouse. In fact if the attorney fees are not paid in accordance with the order, the spouse may have to use funds attributable to alimony to pay them. Hartt v. Hartt, 121 R.I. 220, 397 A.2d 518 (1979) approved the contempt enforcement of an order for attorney fees.

11. The applicable section of the Bankruptcy Code is 11 U.S.C.A. § 523(a)(5) (Supp. III 1985), which provides in relevant part: "A discharge . . . does not discharge an individual debtor from any debt . . . to a spouse, former spouse, or child of the debtor, for alimony to, maintenance for, or support of such spouse or child, in connection with a separation agreement, divorce decree, or property settlement agreement . . . .". Cases holding that attorney fees are not dischargeable include In re Williams, 703 F.2d 1055 (8th Cir.1983); Matter of Catlow, 663 F.2d 960 (9th Cir.1981); Steingesser v. Steingesser, 602 F.2d 36 (2d Cir.1979); In re Birdseye, 548 F.2d 321 (10th Cir.1977); Jones v. Tyson, 518 F.2d 678 (9th Cir. 1975); Matter of Coleman, 37 B.R. 120 (Bkrtcy.Wis.1984); In re Mattern, 33 B.R. 566 (Bkrtcy.Ala.1983); In re Whitehurst, 10 B.R. 229 (Bkrtcy.Fla.1981); Goldman v. Roderiques, 370 Mass. 435, 349 N.E.2d 335 (1976).

12. Cf. In re Williams, 703 F.2d 1055 (8th Cir.1983), describing the question as one of federal law, with Matter of Catlow, 663 F.2d 960 (9th Cir.1981) seeming to say that state law controls.

13. This analysis may resolve apparent conflicts in the cases. E.g., In re Williams, 703 F.2d 1055 (8th Cir. 1983) found that the function of the award is to support the wife, even if the payment is to be made to a third person, her attorney. The court reached this conclusion notwithstanding the Missouri position that for garnishment purpose the award is not for support. See Dyche v. Dyche, 570 S.W.2d 293 (Mo.1978).

§ 16.3 Alimony—Divorce as a Bar to Claims for Alimony, Support or Property

The question which this section tries to answer is: May a former wife obtain alimony, support or a division of property after she or her former husband has obtained a divorce decree which makes no mention of financial or property relief?[1] The cases dealing with this question present varying states of fact and the subject is therefore subdivided. A few relatively simple considerations of policy play a controlling part in all the cases.

Divorce Obtained by the Wife

The wife who obtains a divorce from a court having jurisdiction over the subject matter of the suit and over the person of the husband, either by personal service within the jurisdiction or by his making a general appearance, generally will not later be allowed to assert a claim for alimony.[2] Where there is no jurisdiction over the subject matter, the doctrine of estoppel discussed in another section prevents the wife from asserting the defect in a later suit for alimony.[3]

The reasons which lead courts to deny the wife alimony after a divorce based upon personal jurisdiction over the husband are (a) the notion that alimony is an inseparable incident to divorce and (b) the doctrines of res judicata. The first of these reasons is metaphysical, but the second may have merit in a particular case.[4] If the wife has had a chance to assert a claim for alimony, she should not be able to put her husband to the trouble and expense of a second suit on this same claim.[5] The rule barring her alimony claim applies whether the two cases are brought in the same state or in different states,[6] and whether or not she actually did ask for alimony in the divorce

---

§ 16.3

1. Under Orr v. Orr, 440 U.S. 268, 99 S.Ct. 1102, 59 L.Ed.2d 306 (1979), on remand 374 So.2d 895 (Ala.Civ. App.1979), writ denied 374 So.2d 898 (1979), discussed in section 16.1, supra, the traditional rule that only wives were entitled to alimony was held unconstitutional. Today either spouse may be entitled to it if he can prove a need for it and an ability to pay on the part of the other spouse. In practice, however, it is still usually the wife who claims alimony and the husband who pays it. For convenience in avoiding circumlocution the discussion in this section will assume that it is the wife who seeks alimony, with the understanding that the principles discussed apply as well where the husband is seeking it.

A good general discussion of the problems of this section may be found in Note, 24 Iowa L.Rev. 735 (1939). See also Note, 53 Harv.L.Rev. 1180 (1940), and Stumberg, Foreign Ex Parte Divorces and Local Claims for Alimony, 34 Wash.L.Rev. 15 (1959).

This section does not deal with subsequent suits for child support. Since child support is always modifiable and is for the benefit of the child and not the custodian, there is normally no basis for objecting to such a subsequent suit, whether it is brought under the Uniform Reciprocal Enforcement Act or as an ordinary civil suit. See sections 6.6 and 17.4 and Drobney v. Drobney, 146 N.J.Super. 317, 369 A.2d 963 (1977); Powell v. Powell, 63 Misc.2d 748, 313 N.Y.S.2d 523 (Fam.Ct.1970).

2. Whitaker v. Whitaker, 52 Ohio App. 223, 3 N.E.2d 667 (1936). Other cases are collected in Annot., 43 A.L.R.2d 1387 (1955). See also 2 Freeman, Judgments, § 911 (1925). But see Baldridge v. Baldridge, 313 Ky. 604, 233 S.W.2d 95 (1950) granting alimony and stating the wife is not later barred if alimony was not actually litigated. Zuber v. Zuber, 215 Ga. 314, 110 S.E.2d 370 (1959) held the wife could be given alimony where jurisdiction was reserved in the decree.

The rule should be the same for divisions of property as for alimony.

The statement in the text is in agreement with the general principles of res judicata and judgments. See Restatement (Second) of Judgments §§ 17(1), 24, 25 (1982).

3. See section 12.3, supra.

4. For a criticism of this reasoning see Note, 24 Iowa L.Rev. 735 (1939).

5. Stephenson v. Stephenson, 54 Ohio App. 239, 6 N.E.2d 1005 (1936) (dictum).

6. Pollock v. Pollock, 273 Wis. 233, 77 N.W.2d 485 (1956) (dictum). But as suggested below, she should be able to have the original decree modified so as to provide for alimony.

action.[7] The logical consequence of this policy is that if the wife fails to make her claim for alimony in the divorce case because of the fraud of the husband, or even through an honest mistake for which the husband is not responsible, she is allowed to bring a later suit for alimony.[8]

Statutes in a few states provide that a court may make orders for alimony at any time after a divorce decree is granted, but they do not indicate whether this may be done when there had been personal jurisdiction over the defendant in the divorce action, nor do they expressly authorize a new suit.[9] Presumably these statutes are based on the idea that the policy favoring support for wives outweighs principles of res judicata.

A similar question arises when the wife, instead of bringing an independent suit for alimony or property, seeks to modify the original decree so as to insert in it a provision for alimony. Statutes usually provide in general terms that alimony orders in divorce decrees are modifiable upon proof of a change in circumstances.[10] We might expect that under such statutes the wife could have a provision for alimony inserted in a decree which had been silent on the subject. But this may not be done.[11] The usual rationale for this rule is that when there is no alimony in the original decree, there is nothing to modify,[12] or that after the original decree (which ordered no alimony) the parties were no longer husband and wife and there was therefore no further

obligation on one to support the other.[13] A somewhat better reason is that when the divorce decree is silent on the subject of alimony, this assures the husband that he will not have to meet any further money demands and may plan his affairs accordingly. But even this reason does not explain why he should have this assurance when no alimony is awarded but does not have it if one dollar a month in alimony is awarded, in which event the one dollar award could be increased to five hundred dollars if the wife were able to show she needed it.

A preferable approach to these cases would be to decide them by looking at the reason why alimony was omitted from the original decree. It it was omitted because the wife did not ask for it, or because the husband lacked ability to pay it, and if her needs have later become pressing and he is able to pay, there is no reason why the decree should not be modified to give her an appropriate sum.[14] Any change in the husband's financial position subsequent to the divorce in reliance on the original decree should certainly be taken into account in assessing his ability to pay. On the other hand if alimony was omitted for a reason justifying a final and conclusive denial of alimony, then the decree should not later be modifiable.

The spouse is not totally without protection, however. The local statute may authorize a modification inserting a provision for alimony.[15] If the divorce decree expressly reserves

7. Weidman v. Weidman, 57 Ohio St. 101, 48 N.E. 506 (1897) (by failing to claim alimony the wife waived it).

8. Reynierson v. Reynierson, 303 S.W.2d 252 (Ky.1957) (Husband sued here, but the principle applies also to suits by the wife).

9. Mass.Gen.Laws Ann. c. 208, § 34 (Supp.1986); N.J. Stat.Ann. § 2A:34–23 (Supp.1986). The New Jersey statute apparently is construed to authorize modification of the divorce decree so as to include an award of alimony. See Kase v. Kase, 18 N.J.Super. 12, 86 A.2d 587 (1952), where an award of alimony was made twenty years after the divorce.

10. See section 15.6, infra.

11. Simpson v. Simpson, 134 Cal.App.2d 219, 285 P.2d 313 (1955); Comcowich v. Comcowich, 237 So.2d 66 (Fla. App.1970); Bickford v. Bickford, 229 Ga. 229, 190 S.E.2d 70 (1972); In re Marriage of Carlson, 338 N.W.2d 136 (Iowa 1983); Reed v. Reed, 484 S.W.2d 844 (Ky.1972), cert. denied 410 U.S. 931, 93 S.Ct. 1375, 35 L.Ed.2d 594 (1973);

Baird v. Baird, 311 Mass. 329, 41 N.E.2d 5 (1942) (statute permits a separate suit but not modification); Ballentine v. Ballentine, 357 Mich. 7, 97 N.W.2d 620 (1959) (dictum); Berger v. Berger, 308 Minn. 426, 242 N.W.2d 836 (1976); Haug v. Haug, 195 Neb. 377, 238 N.W.2d 455 (1976); Becker v. Becker, 262 N.W.2d 478 (N.D.1978). Many other cases are collected in Annots., 83 A.L.R. 1248 (1933), and 43 A.L.R.2d 1387, 1396 (1955). Contra: Joubert v. Sylvester, 241 So.2d 30 (La.App.1970); Athorne v. Athorne, 100 N.H. 413, 128 A.2d 910 (1957).

12. Howell v. Howell, 104 Cal. 45, 37 P. 770 (1894); Perry v. Perry, 202 Va. 849, 120 S.E.2d 385 (1961).

13. In re Marriage of Carlson, 338 N.W.2d 136 (Iowa 1983).

14. Cody v. Cody, 47 Utah 456, 154 P. 952 (1916).

15. E.g., N.J.Stat.Ann. § 2A:34–23 (Supp.1986). The Uniform Marriage and Divorce Act § 316(a), 9A Unif.L. Ann. 183 (1979) authorizes modification of alimony in general terms, but it does not deal with the question

jurisdiction to modify, alimony may later be awarded.[16] It would be wise to insist upon such a provision in the divorce decree whenever it seems likely that the spouse's needs will increase later on. Finally, alimony may later be inserted in the decree if it was originally omitted through fraud or mistake.[17]

In contrast to the foregoing rules, when the wife's divorce action rests only upon constructive service and the husband fails to appear, most (but not all) courts have enforced the wife's subsequent claim for alimony or property.[18] The result is the same whether the divorce was obtained in the state of the forum or in another state.[19] The cases which allow her to recover hold that since she could not have obtained alimony in the divorce action for lack of personal jurisdiction over the husband, arguments based upon res judicata do not apply.[20] The resulting piecemeal litigation is justified on the ground that to hold otherwise would require the wife to follow her husband into another jurisdiction to sue him for divorce, and this might be impossible because she could not meet the other jurisdiction's domicile requirements.[21] This would often mean that she would have to choose between getting a divorce without alimony or getting support without a divorce. And finally, alimony is said not to be an inseparable part of the divorce action.[22]

Notwithstanding the harsh alternatives which the contrary rule poses for the wife, a surprising number of states hold that she loses her right to alimony by obtaining a divorce on constructive service.[23] The reasoning usually is either that she waivers her right by getting the divorce, or that the right to alimony is such an inseparable feature of divorce that it cannot exist apart from divorce or after the marriage and its support obligations have been terminated. Both of these so-called reasons are tautologies, merely restating the result in different terms. Regardless of the view taken on a new action for alimony, an attempt to modify the decree by inserting a provision for alimony must fail where the original decree was based upon

---

whether a decree which provides for no alimony may be modified to include alimony. The Massachusetts statute cited, supra, note 9, also permits the divorce decree to be modified so as to include a provision for property distribution if one was omitted from the original decree. Hay v. Cloutier, 389 Mass. 248, 449 N.E.2d 361 (1983).

16. Zoercher v. Zoercher, 114 So.2d 728 (Fla.App. 1959); Bickford v. Bickford, 229 Ga. 229, 190 S.E.2d 70 (1972); Reed v. Reed, 11 Md.App. 396, 274 A.2d 652 (1971); Eckert v. Eckert, 299 Minn. 120, 216 N.W.2d 837 (1974); Becker v. Becker, 262 N.W.2d 478 (N.D.1978). Other cases are cited in Annot., 43 A.L.R.2d 1387, 1409 (1955). In re Marriage of Carlson, 338 N.W.2d 136 (Iowa 1983) took the odd position that if the decree is silent, no alimony may later be awarded, but if alimony is initially awarded but then "terminated", it may later be reinstated. Anderson v. Anderson, 289 Minn. 339, 184 N.W.2d 415 (1971) upheld the trial court's refusal to reserve jurisdiction over alimony. But Neal v. Neal, 116 Ariz. 590, 570 P.2d 758 (1977) held it to be error to award nominal alimony for the purpose of retaining jurisdiction later to modify the award, where the wife was able to support herself through employment.

17. Annot., 83 A.L.R. 1248, 1249 (1933).

18. Woods v. Woods, 285 Ark. 175, 686 S.W.2d 387 (1985); Darnell v. Darnell, 212 Ill.App. 601 (1918); Brown v. Brown, 269 N.W.2d 819 (Iowa 1978); Baird v. Baird, 311 Mass. 329, 41 N.E.2d 5 (1942) (under a statute); Mandelberg v. Mandelberg, 187 Neb. 844, 195 N.W.2d 148 (1972); Woods v. Waddle, 44 Ohio St. 449, 8 N.E. 297

(1886); Stephenson v. Stephenson, 54 Ohio App. 239, 6 N.E.2d 1005 (1936); Spradling v. Spradling, 74 Okl. 276, 181 P. 148 (1919); Hutton v. Dodge, 58 Utah 228, 198 P. 165 (1921); Adams v. Abbott, 21 Wash. 29, 56 P. 931 (1889); Pollock v. Pollock, 273 Wis. 233, 77 N.W.2d 485 (1956). Other cases are collected in Annot., 28 A.L.R.2d 1378, 1415 (1953); Note, 24 Iowa L.Rev. 735 (1939). King v. King, 185 Kan. 742, 347 P.2d 381 (1959) held that the wife could obtain separate maintenance in Kansas after getting an ex parte California divorce.

The Uniform Marriage and Divorce Act § 308(a), 9A Unif.L.Ann. 160 (1979) expressly authorizes alimony in a new proceeding following an ex parte divorce.

19. Stephenson v. Stephenson, 54 Ohio App. 239, 6 N.E.2d 1005 (1936); Hutton v. Dodge, 58 Utah 228, 198 P. 165 (1921); Pollock v. Pollock, 273 Wis. 233, 77 N.W.2d 485 (1956).

20. Nelson v. Nelson, 71 S.D. 342, 24 N.W.2d 327 (1946).

21. Hutton v. Dodge, 58 Utah 228, 198 P. 165 (1921).

22. Adams v. Abbott, 21 Wash. 29, 56 P. 931 (1899).

23. Howell v. Howell, 104 Cal. 45, 37 P. 770 (1894); Dimon v. Dimon, 40 Cal.2d 516, 254 P.2d 528 (1953); Staub v. Staub, 170 Md. 202, 183 A. 605 (1936), 50 Harv.L. Rev. 526 (1937); McFarlane v. McFarlane, 43 Or. 477, 73 P. 203 (1903); Darby v. Darby, 152 Tenn. (25 Thom.) 287, 277 S.W. 894 (1925). Other cases are collected in Annot., 28 A.L.R.2d 1378, 1417 (1955).

constructive service.[24] This is because alimony decrees cannot be awarded without jurisdiction over the person of the defendant.

Divorce Obtained by the Husband

Where the husband sues for divorce, and the wife makes a general appearance, but no alimony is awarded, it is generally held she may not bring a later independent suit for alimony, her claim being barred by res judicata.[25] Likewise she may not later have the decree modified so as to give her alimony.[26] The same objections to this result might be raised here as have been raised in criticizing the cases where the wife is the divorce plaintiff.[27]

If the wife is personally served within the jurisdiction, but does not appear, the cases reach the same result, arguing that she could have obtained alimony in the divorce action and her failure to do so should prevent her from bringing a subsequent independent suit.[28] Here her opportunity to litigate the alimony question is not as clear as where she appears in the divorce suit, the fact that she was personally served not necessarily being evidence that she could assert her claim for alimony without hardship or undue expense. This might be the case if she had been served in a state other than that of her domicile for example. This difference would often justify allowing her to bring a later suit for alimony at least if she could show that her initial failure to ask for alimony was due to the hardship of having to litigate at a distance

from her domicile, but few cases follow such reasoning.[29]

If the law says that the husband's prior divorce bars alimony when there is personal jurisdiction over the wife, what is to be the result if the divorce is based upon constructive service? In the typical case the husband leaves home, gets an ex parte Nevada divorce, returns, and is sued for alimony. First of all, if the wife can prove that he never had a Nevada domicile, the divorce itself is not entitled to full faith and credit and her alimony claim is clearly valid.[30] Second, the Vanderbilt case[31] established that even if the husband did have a Nevada domicile the Full Faith and Credit Clause does not require that other states respect the divorce decree to the extent of affecting the wife's right to alimony or property, though they must respect it as terminating the marital status. The divorce is said to be divisible. The theory of the cases seems to be that just as the wife may not get a decree for alimony without personal jurisdiction over her husband, so she may not be deprived of alimony in the absence of personal jurisdiction over herself. In a prior section we have suggested that this argument, logically applied, would mean that no state could deprive the wife of her claim for support by virtue of a foreign ex parte divorce without a violation of due process,[32] but the cases do not go this far. Each state is therefore free, as far as the United States Constitution is concerned, to decide for itself what effect the

24. Kelley v. Kelley, 317 Ill. 104, 147 N.E. 659 (1925), 10 Minn.L.Rev. 254 (1926); Doeksen v. Doeksen, 202 Iowa 489, 210 N.W. 545 (1926).

25. Bates v. Bodie, 245 U.S. 520, 38 S.Ct. 182, 62 L.Ed. 444 (1918); Barber v. Barber, 51 Cal.2d 244, 331 P.2d 628 (1958); Gilbert v. Gilbert, 83 Ohio St. 265, 94 N.E. 421 (1911); Sohmer v. Sohmer, 318 Pa.Super. 500, 465 A.2d 665 (1983). Other cases are cited in Note, 39 Yale L.J. 587 (1930), and Annot., 43 A.L.R.2d 1387 (1955). The rule does not apply if the wife appeared specially in the divorce action for the purpose of contesting the court's jurisdiction. Mackessy v. Mackessy, 15 Alaska 361 (1954).

Contra: Cooper v. Cooper, 314 Ky. 413, 234 S.W.2d 658 (1950), 47 Ky.L.J. 516 (1959).

26. Weiss v. Weiss, 118 So.2d 833 (Fla.App.1960).

27. See the discussion at note 10, supra.

28. Sprague v. Sprague, 73 Minn. 474, 76 N.W. 268 (1898). Other cases are cited in Note, 39 Yale L.J. 587 (1930), Annot., 28 A.L.R.2d 1387 (1955).

29. Crawford v. Crawford, 158 Miss. 382, 130 So. 688 (1930) allowed the wife to sue later for alimony where she had been in a hospital for the insane at the time of the divorce, although apparently service had been made in accordance with the local statute. And in Reynierson v. Reynierson, 303 S.W.2d 252 (Ky.1957), the court allowed the wife to bring a subsequent alimony suit on the ground she had failed through mistake to ask for alimony in the divorce action.

30. Esenwein v. Commonwealth, 325 U.S. 279, 65 S.Ct. 1118, 89 L.Ed. 1608 (1945).

31. Vanderbilt v. Vanderbilt, 354 U.S. 416, 77 S.Ct. 1360, 1 L.Ed.2d 1456 (1957).

32. See section 12.4, supra.

husband's ex parte divorce has upon the wife's claim for alimony.

Of the jurisdictions which have passed on this question, a strong majority have held that the wife's alimony claim survives the husband's ex parte divorce.[33] The leading case is Hudson v. Hudson.[34] There the California Supreme Court held that an Idaho divorce, although valid, did not foreclose the California courts from awarding a wife alimony pendente lite. The court said that alimony could be awarded in an action independent of divorce, that alimony need not be granted simultaneously with the termination of the marriage, and that California's dominant interest in the welfare of its domiciliaries entitles it to adjudicate their support rights after an ex parte divorce. Maryland has taken a similar position, overruling prior decisions.[35] The Hudson case[36] at one point suggests that its result is not merely permitted but required by Vanderbilt v. Vanderbilt,[37] but on this the opinion is not entirely clear.

The decision in the Hudson case broadly means that the wife's support claims survive the husband's valid ex parte divorce. This is true even though the alimony suit is not brought until after the divorce is obtained,[38] and though the wife receives actual notice of the divorce action.[39] This result is contrary to that in a few jurisdictions which adhere to the rule that alimony is an inseparable incident to a divorce action, and that once the marriage ends, all rights to alimony end.[40] Under these cases the wife must follow her husband to his new domicile and present her alimony claims there on pain of losing them, assuming she gets notice of the proceeding. The effect of this is that the state of her domicile, the state having paramount interest in her welfare, abdicates its own interest and sacrifices hers to a metaphysical concept of the nature of alimony.[41] When the wife who is so deprived of support becomes a public charge, she and the taxpayers of the state will no doubt be comforted by the conviction that they are vindicating the logic of alimony decrees.

The Hudson case[42] makes a distinction between alimony, which survives ex parte di-

---

33. Hopson v. Hopson, 95 U.S.App.D.C. 285, 221 F.2d 839 (1955); Hudson v. Hudson, 52 Cal.2d 735, 344 P.2d 295 (1959); Davis v. Davis, 70 Colo. 37, 197 P. 241 (1921); Pollard v. Pollard, 330 S.W.2d 407 (Ky.1959); Altman v. Altman, 282 Md. 483, 386 A.2d 766 (1978) (citing many cases); Searles v. Searles, 140 Minn. 385, 168 N.W. 133 (1918); Squitieri v. Squitieri, 196 N.J.Super. 76, 481 A.2d 585 (1984) (division of property); Armstrong v. Armstrong, 162 Ohio St. 406, 123 N.E.2d 267 (1954), affirmed 350 U.S. 568, 76 S.Ct. 629, 100 L.Ed. 705 (1956); Seely v. Seely, 348 P.2d 1064 (Okl.1959); Rheaume v. Rheaume, 107 R.I. 500, 268 A.2d 437 (1970); Toncray v. Toncray, 123 Tenn. 476, 131 S.W. 977 (1910); Pollock v. Pollock, 273 Wis. 233, 77 N.W.2d 485 (1956). Other cases are cited in Annot., 28 A.L.R.2d 1378 (1953). If the wife waits too long to sue, she may be barred by laches. Corah v. Corah, 246 Minn. 350, 75 N.W.2d 465 (1956).

34. 52 Cal.2d 735, 344 P.2d 295 (1959). See also Restatement (Second) of Judgments § 31 (1982).

35. Altman v. Altman, 282 Md. 483, 386 A.2d 766 (1978).

36. "The Idaho decree, even if valid, did not *and could not* under the Vanderbilt decision, terminate plaintiff's right to alimony under the law of this state." (Emphasis supplied.) Hudson v. Hudson, 52 Cal.2d 735, 743, 344 P.2d 295, 299 (1959).

37. 354 U.S. 416, 77 S.Ct. 1360, 1 L.Ed.2d 1456 (1957), discussed supra, in section 12.4.

38. Weber v. Superior Court of Los Angeles County, 53 Cal.2d 403, 2 Cal.Rptr. 9, 348 P.2d 572 (1960); Davis v.

Davis, 303 S.W.2d 256 (Ky.1957); Pollard v. Pollard, 330 S.W.2d 407 (Ky.1959). Other cases are collected in Annot., 28 A.L.R.2d 1378 (1953).

39. The wife had notice in the Hudson case. In the view of some courts, notice is a critical factor. McCormick v. McCormick, 82 Kan. 31, 107 P. 546 (1910); Shaw v. Shaw, 92 Iowa 722, 61 N.W. 368 (1894). The rule should apply whether the divorce action was brought in a state other than the forum or in the forum, although most of the cases involve the first situation. Cochran v. Cochran, 42 Neb. 612, 60 N.W. 942 (1894). But some of the statutes limit the wife's relief to cases in which the husband obtained an out-of-state ex parte divorce. Pa. Stat. tit. 23, § 505 (Supp.1986). The fact that the wife is found guilty of marital fault in the divorce suit apparently does not have the effect of issue preclusion in the later suit for alimony. Restatement (Second) of Judgments § 31, comment c (1982).

40. Loeb v. Loeb, 118 Vt. 472, 114 A.2d 518 (1955). Other cases are cited in Altman v. Altman, 282 Md. 483, 386 A.2d 766 (1978) and in Annot., 28 A.L.R.2d 1378, 1402 (1953). Pennsylvania was formerly one of the states in which a foreign ex parte divorce cut off rights to alimony, but its rule has been changed by statute. Pa.Stat.Ann. tit. 23, § 505 (Supp.1986), overruling Stambaugh v. Stambaugh, 458 Pa. 147, 329 A.2d 483 (1974).

41. The opinion in Loeb v. Loeb, 118 Vt. 472, 114 A.2d 518 (1955) is particularly open to this reproach.

42. Hudson v. Hudson, 52 Cal.2d 735, 344 P.2d 295 (1959).

vorce, and separate maintenance, which does not. Since both forms of relief have precisely the same purpose, support of the wife, this distinction is entirely without substance, but it is made in other states [43] and seems to have been required by the state of the precedents in California.[44] If the courts feel bound to adhere to it on the ground that separate maintenance is a remedy for wives and not ex-wives, they ought to allow the ex-wives to amend their complaints so as to demand alimony rather than a decree of separate maintenance. Alimony might then be granted.

The wife's claim for alimony or support may be preserved, after the husband gets a divorce, by the statutes already cited in connection with prior divorce actions by the wife.[45] Whether it is or not depends upon the construction placed on the statute and upon the closeness of the wife's contact with the state. New York, whose statute is explicit in authorizing relief to the wife when the husband gets a prior ex parte divorce,[46] has held that this does not furnish a remedy to a woman who was not a resident of New York at any time during her marriage, even though she had become a resident of New York when she sued for maintenance.[47] The court arrived at this result by relying on some ambiguous language from the legislative history of the statute to bolster its abhorrence of "forum-shopping", although in this case it was perfectly clear that the wife was not forum-shopping. The curious consequence of the case is that the husband is allowed to escape his marital obligation by doing some forum-shopping of his own. On the narrowest ground of state interest New York should have given relief here since the plaintiff, if without other means of support, would become the responsibility of New York to support if the husband were not liable.[48] If residence or domicile is relevant to the statute, the important thing is residence at the time of the wife's suit, not residence at the time of the Nevada divorce.

The conflict among jurisdictions over the effect of an ex parte divorce on the wife's support claim makes it necessary to determine which law applies to a given case. The courts which have faced this problem have held that the law of the wife's domicile is the applicable law. The leading case is Worthley v. Worthley,[49] in which the wife sued in California to enforce a New Jersey separate maintenance decree, after the husband had obtained a Nevada divorce on constructive service. The California Supreme Court decided that, the plaintiff being domiciled in New Jersey, New Jersey law should govern the effect of the Nevada divorce on the New Jersey decree. If the wife should change her domicile after the Nevada divorce was granted, it would seem that the law of her new domicile should be controlling on this question, however.[50]

---

43. E.g. Pawley v. Pawley, 46 So.2d 464 (Fla.1950). In Kansas the attempt to make this essentially meaningless distinction seems to have baffled the courts completely. Cf. Lowry v. Lowry, 174 Kan. 526, 256 P.2d 869 (1953), Willoughby v. Willoughby, 178 Kan. 62, 283 P.2d 428 (1955), and King v. King, 185 Kan. 742, 347 P.2d 381 (1959). White v. White, 83 Ariz. 305, 320 P.2d 702 (1958) allows a separate maintenance decree, at least where the suit was brought while the divorce action was still pending.

44. E.g. De Young v. De Young, 27 Cal.2d 521, 165 P.2d 457 (1946).

45. See the statutes cited in note 9, supra, and Kan. Stat.Ann. § 60–1611 (1983); N.Y.—McKinney's Dom. Rel. Law § 236, Part B(2) (1986); N.C.Gen.Stat. § 50–11 (1984); Pa.Stat. tit. 23, § 505 (Supp.1986); Uniform Marriage and Divorce Act § 308(a), 9A Unif.L.Ann. 160 (1979).

46. N.Y.—McKinney's Dom. Rel. Law § 236, Part B(2) (1986).

47. Loeb v. Loeb, 4 N.Y.2d 542, 176 N.Y.S.2d 590, 152 N.E.2d 36 (1958). The plaintiff in this case had the dubious distinction of seeing the courts of two different states reject her claim. Loeb v. Loeb, 118 Vt. 472, 114 A.2d 518 (1955).

48. Cf. the same court's discussion of the statute in Vanderbilt v. Vanderbilt, 1 N.Y.2d 342, 153 N.Y.S.2d 1, 135 N.E.2d 553 (1956), cert. granted 352 U.S. 820, 77 S.Ct. 67, 1 L.Ed.2d 45 (1956).

49. Worthley v. Worthley, 44 Cal.2d 465, 283 P.2d 19 (1955). See also Lewis v. Lewis, 49 Cal.2d 389, 317 P.2d 987 (1957), and Hudson v. Hudson, 52 Cal.2d 735, 344 P.2d 295 (1959). Cf. Note, 26 Univ.Chi.L.Rev. 136, 143 (1958).

50. Cf. Yarborough v. Yarborough, 290 U.S. 202, 213, 54 S.Ct. 181, 185, 78 L.Ed. 269 (1933) (dissenting opinion).

Effect of Divorce on Separate Maintenance Orders

The question here is what effect a divorce decree has on a prior decree of separate maintenance, a question which, upon analysis, depends on the same factors as the cases previously under discussion in this section. Thus if the divorce decree is obtained without jurisdiction over the subject matter, it does not affect outstanding maintenance orders.[51] If it is based upon jurisdiction over the subject matter, but the wife is not personally subject to the divorce court's jurisdiction, the decree is entitled to full faith and credit, but this does not require the state of the separate maintenance decree to terminate the husband's duties under the decree.[52] The doctrine of "divisible divorce" says that the divorce ends the marital status, but does not necessarily end the obligations imposed by the decree of separate maintenance. Whether it does affect those obligations depends on the law of the state issuing the separate maintenance decree.[53]

For the most part a domestic divorce granted upon the wife's petition, or with personal jurisdiction over the wife, is held to terminate the wife's rights under an existing decree of separate maintenance.[54] The reason seems to be that the wife has an opportunity to make a claim for alimony in the divorce action, and when she does not, or when her claim is decided against her, that terminates all rights which depend on the marriage. The rights under the separate maintenance decree are of that nature, although they are embodied in the decree. This reasoning does not apply

with such force, however, where the wife gets an ex parte divorce after her husband has left the state. In such a case her rights under the separate maintenance decree ought to remain unimpaired.

The same result is reached where the divorce is granted in a foreign jurisdiction, provided again that the wife is personally subject to the court's power.[55] The theory here is the same as for the domestic divorce decree, there being no reason to treat the two differently.

Where the divorce decree is given with jurisdiction over the subject matter, but not over the wife's person, many states hold that it does not affect the prior separate maintenance order.[56] Although normally the maintenance obligation ends with divorce, the doctrine of divisible divorce has made it easier to say that this is a personal claim of the wife which should not be cut off without personal jurisdiction over her. More realistically, the courts are recognizing that the wife should not be faced with the hardship and expense of following her husband to a different state to litigate the financial side of their marital dispute. Just as she is today generally allowed to sue him for alimony after he gets an ex parte foreign divorce, she should be entitled to continue receiving the payments ordered by the separate maintenance decree. In fact where the obligation is embodied in a decree there is all the greater reason why it should continue, as some cases have held.[57] Notwithstanding the force of these arguments, there are cases which hold that the separate maintenance decree is only authorized (under the applicable statute) when and so

---

51. Esenwein v. Commonwealth, 325 U.S. 279, 65 S.Ct. 1118, 89 L.Ed. 1608 (1945).

52. Estin v. Estin, 334 U.S. 541, 68 S.Ct. 1213, 92 L.Ed. 1561 (1948). See section 12.4, supra.

53. Worthley v. Worthley, 44 Cal.2d 465, 283 P.2d 19 (1955); Rodda v. Rodda, 185 Or. 140, 200 P.2d 616 (1948), cert. denied 337 U.S. 946, 69 S.Ct. 1504, 93 L.Ed. 1749 (1949). But cf. the suggestion made supra at note 37.

54. Cases are collected in Annot., 166 A.L.R. 1004 (1947). Contra the text statement, where the wife got an ex parte divorce; Allred v. Allred, 12 Utah 2d 325, 366 P.2d 478 (1961).

55. Lynn v. Lynn, 302 N.Y. 193, 97 N.E.2d 748 (1951), cert. denied 342 U.S. 849, 72 S.Ct. 72, 96 L.Ed. 641 (195).

Other cases are collected in Annot., 1 A.L.R.2d 1423 (1948), and 28 A.L.R.2d 1346 (1953).

56. Hudson v. Hudson, 52 Cal.2d 735, 344 P.2d 295 (1959) (dictum, overruling Cardinale v. Cardinale, 8 Cal. 2d 762, 68 P.2d 351 (1937); Estin v. Estin, 296 N.Y. 308, 73 N.E.2d 113 (1947), affirmed 334 U.S. 541, 68 S.Ct. 1213, 92 L.Ed. 1561 (1948); Morris v. Morris, 118 Vt. 270, 108 A.2d 258 (1954). Other cases are collected in Annot., 1 A.L.R.2d 1423 (1948), and 28 A.L.R.2d 1346 (1953).

57. Hudson v. Hudson, 52 Cal.2d 735, 344 P.2d 295 (1959); Morris v. Morris, 118 Vt. 270, 108 A.2d 258 (1954), as distinguished in Loeb v. Loeb, 118 Vt. 472, 114 A.2d 518 (1955).

long as the parties are husband and wife.[58] When the status ends, the maintenance order must end also.

The Divorce Decree as an Adjudication of Property Rights

Property rights based on the marital relationship are conclusively determined if actually litigated in the divorce action or if the decree makes a specific finding on property, and both parties are personally subject to the court's jurisdiction.[59] This is an application of ordinary rules of res judicata. Some cases extend this rule to include any divorce in which the parties are personally subject to the court's jurisdiction, whether or not the decree disposes of the property.[60] This is a mistake, especially where the divorce complaint contains no prayer for relief with respect to the property and the defendant allows the decree to be taken by default, since in that situation the defendant is entitled to assume there will be no adjudication of property rights.[61] But if the wife obtains

divorce on a complaint alleging there is no marital property, she will be estopped to claim such property in a later case.[62]

One qualification on the res judicata rule must be made where the divorce decree orders conveyance of land located in another state. If the conveyance is actually made, the courts of the land's situs will recognize the transferee's title.[63] But if the conveyance is not made, Fall v. Eastin [64] has held that the decree ordering the conveyance is not entitled to full faith and credit at the situs of the land. And some state courts have refused to recognize such decrees as a matter of comity.[65] There is no reason why the decree, being based on personal jurisdiction, should not be given effect at the situs as a final adjudication of the parties' title, however, and some recent cases have been willing to do this.[66]

Where the divorce decree does not show that property rights were adjudicated,[67] or where the parties in the divorce action were not personally subject to the court's jurisdic-

---

58. Johnson v. Johnson, 202 Md. 547, 97 A.2d 330 (1953); Rodda v. Rodda, 185 Or. 140, 200 P.2d 616 (1949), cert. denied 337 U.S. 946, 69 S.Ct. 1504, 93 L.Ed. 1749 (1949). Other cases are cited in Annot., 1 A.L.R.2d 1423 (1948), and 28 A.L.R.2d 1346 (1953).

59. Maxwell v. Maxwell, 66 Cal.App.2d 549, 152 P.2d 530 (1944); Moore v. Zelic, 338 Ill. 583, 170 N.E. 664 (1930); Steele v. Steele, 189 N.W.2d 660 (N.D.1971).

Henn v. Henn, 26 Cal.3d 323, 161 Cal.Rptr. 502, 605 P.2d 10 (1980) may be contra the statement in the text. In that case the husband got a divorce in 1971, the decree incorporating a property settlement which divided the community property. The decree made no mention of a military pension which the husband was receiving and which had been partially earned during the marriage. In 1973 the wife moved in the suit for a division of the pension. This was denied in 1974. In 1976 the wife brought this independent suit seeking a share of the pension and the court held that she was entitled to make this claim. The opinion is far from clear in its reasons. It may turn on the legal uncertainty surrounding military pensions in 1971 and therefore be based on the rationale of Restatement (Second) of Judgments § 28(2)(b) (1982). It also seemed to say that a spouse's interest in community property arises during marriage and if not mentioned in the pleadings, is left unadjudicated by the divorce, the spouses then becoming tenants in common in the property until further litigation. But it is not clear why the denial of the wife's motion in 1974 was not res judicata of her claim to an interest in the pension. There is the additional factor that she had sued her former attorneys for malpractice for failing to obtain an interest in the pension and had received a settlement in that case.

60. Cummings v. Cummings, 138 Kan. 359, 26 P.2d 440 (1933) (dictum). See Annot., 22 A.L.R.2d 724 (1952) for cases on the effect of a default divorce decree.

61. Lang v. Lang, 190 P. 181 (Cal.1920); Tarien v. Katz, 216 Cal. 554, 15 P.2d 493 (1932); Green v. Green, 66 Cal.App.2d 50, 151 P.2d 679 (1944).

62. Spurr v. Daniels, 152 Cal.App.2d 867, 313 P.2d 621 (1957).

63. Fall v. Fall, 75 Neb. 104, 106 N.W. 412 (1915), affirmed 215 U.S. 1, 30 S.Ct. 3, 54 L.Ed. 65 (1909) (dictum).

64. 215 U.S. 1, 30 S.Ct. 3, 54 L.Ed. 65 (1909). Cf. Buswell v. Buswell, 377 Pa. 487, 105 A.2d 608 (1954).

65. Porter v. Porter, 101 Ariz. 131, 416 P.2d 564 (1966), cert. denied 386 U.S. 957, 87 S.Ct. 1028, 18 L.Ed.2d 107 (1967), rehearing denied 386 U.S. 1027, 87 S.Ct. 1371, 18 L.Ed.2d 472 (1967); Wayne v. Reynolds, 125 So.2d 223 (La.App.1960). Cf. Cooper v. Cooper, 314 Ky. 413, 234 S.W.2d 658 (1950).

66. Allis v. Allis, 378 F.2d 721 (5th Cir.1967), cert. denied 389 U.S. 953, 88 S.Ct. 337, 19 L.Ed.2d 363 (1967); Ivey v. Ivey, 183 Conn. 490, 439 A.2d 425 (1981); Weesner v. Weesner, 168 Neb. 346, 95 N.W.2d 682 (1959); Owen v. Stewart, 111 N.H. 350, 283 A.2d 492 (1971); McElreath v. McElreath, 162 Tex. 190, 345 S.W.2d 722 (1961), 50 Geo. L.J. 157 (1961), 47 Iowa L.Rev. 712 (1962); Kane v. Kane, 577 P.2d 172 (Wyo.1978), affirmed 616 P.2d 780 (Wyo. 1980). See also Annots., 32 A.L.R.3d 1340 (1970) and 34 A.L.R.3d 967 (1970).

67. In re Estate of Williams, 36 Cal.2d 289, 223 P.2d 248 (1950).

tion, the divorce decree is not a binding adjudication of the property rights.[68]

WESTLAW REFERENCES

Divorce Obtained by the Wife

weidman +s weidman

sy(suit action cause claim /5 res +1 adjudicata judicata /s alimony)

di(statute /s modif! /s alimony /s change /3 circumstance)

Divorce Obtained by the Husband

find 77 sct 1360

alimony /s surviv! /s "ex parte" /s divorce

ti(worthley +s worthley)

Effect of Divorce on Separate Maintenance Orders

theory principle doctrine rule /3 "divisible divorce" /p "ex parte"

sy(divorce /s "separate maintenance" /2 order decree)

The Divorce Decree as an Adjudication of the Property Rights

fall /s eastin

§ 16.4   Relevant Factors in Awarding Alimony

The Functions of Alimony

An earlier section has described how difficult it is to assign a single social policy to alimony when it is awarded as an incident to absolute divorce.[1] The practical consequences of this difficulty are revealed in this section.

If we do not know what we are trying to accomplish by giving a spouse alimony, we will not easily be able to decide whether it should be granted in a particular case, or, if granted, in what amount. The situation is not clarified by statutes which vary widely in listing the relevant facts to be considered,[2] and by appellate decisions which likewise state or assume that alimony has many different functions.[3] The idea that alimony is a substitute for the traditional duty of a husband to support his wife still has great currency in the cases [4] but today alimony can be only partially explained on this ground.

A start at clarifying the subject may be made by recognizing that alimony serves several functions. In any given case one or more of these functions may be relevant, thereby requiring that a broad range of factors be taken into account.

The first and most important of the functions of alimony relates to the care of children. Even in these days of gender equality the mother will most often be given custody of small children.[5] If she has custody, she will also normally be awarded a sum for child support, but if she is to care for the child adequately she may be unable to work outside the home, at least on a full time schedule. What is perhaps more likely, she will be forced to work outside the home but what she earns will not be sufficient to support herself

---

68. Sidebotham v. Robison, 216 F.2d 816 (9th Cir. 1954). Contra: Holdorf v. Holdorf, 198 Iowa 158, 197 N.W. 910 (1924).

§ 16.4

1. See section 15.1, supra.

2. A sampling of the alimony statutes follows: Ala. Code 1983, § 32–2–51; Alaska Stat. § 25.24.160 (Supp. 1986); West's Ann.Cal.Civ.Code § 4801 (Supp.1987); Conn.Gen.Stat.Ann. § 46b–82 (1986); West's Fla.Stat. Ann. § 61.08 (1985 and Supp.1987); Official Code Georgia Ann. §§ 30–201, 30–209 (Supp.1986); Ill.—S.H.A. ch. 40, § 504 (Supp.1986); West's A.I.C. §§ 31–1–11.5–11(*l*), 31–1–11.5–9(c) (Supp.1986); Iowa Code Ann. § 598.21 (1981 & Supp.1986); Mass.Gen.Laws Ann. c. 208, § 34 (Supp. 1986); Mich.C.L.A. § 25.103 (Supp.1986–1987); V.A.Mo. Stat. § 452.335 (1986); N.J.Stat.Ann. § 2A:34–23 (Supp. 1986); N.Y.—McKinney's Dom.Rel.Law § 236, Part B(6) (1986); N.C.Gen.Stat. § 50–16.1 (1984); Or.Rev.Stat. § 107.105(1)(d) (1983); Pa.Stat. tit. 23, § 501 (Supp.1986); Wis.Stat.Ann. § 767.26 (1981); Uniform Marriage and Divorce Act § 308, 9A Unif.L.Ann. 160 (1979).

3. E.g., Roberts v. Roberts, 283 So.2d 396 (Fla.App. 1973) (purpose is rehabilitation); Bellow v. Bellow, 94 Ill. App.3d 361, 50 Ill.Dec. 656, 419 N.E.2d 924 (1981) (purpose is support); Fisher v. Fisher, 320 So.2d 326 (La.App. 1975) (alimony is a gratuity or pension!); Pyke v. Pyke, 212 Neb. 114, 321 N.W.2d 906 (1982) (purpose is to avoid disruption); English v. English, 565 P.2d 409 (Utah 1977) (purpose is support); Mose v. Mose, 4 Wash.App. 204, 480 P.2d 517 (1971) (permanent alimony is disfavored, perhaps because viewed as having no function).

4. Bellow v. Bellow, 94 Ill.App.3d 361, 50 Ill.Dec. 656, 419 N.E.2d 924 (1981); Donigan v. Donigan, 208 Md. 511, 119 A.2d 430 (1956); Prosser v. Prosser, 156 Neb. 629, 57 N.W.2d 173 (1953); English v. English, 565 P.2d 409 (Utah 1977); Hawkins v. Hawkins, 187 Va. 595, 47 S.E.2d 436 (1948).

5. J. Wallerstein and J. Kelly, Surviving the Breakup 25 (1980): "But by and large, child-care responsibilities belonged entirely to the mother." The authors were speaking of the approximately sixty families whom they studied.

as well as the children.[6] In this situation she should be entitled to alimony as a way of providing for the care of the children in a family setting. Some statutes make this function of alimony explicit.[7] The Uniform Marriage and Divorce Act seems to contemplate that an award of child support might include a sum for the support of the child's custodian.[8]

Where no children are involved or where they are otherwise taken care of, it is customary for the courts and the statutes to speak of alimony as a way of providing support for the wife.[9] In fact in California alimony is referred to as "spousal support".[10] Where alimony is necessary in order to keep a spouse, generally the wife, from becoming dependent upon the state for support, its function is clear enough. What is not clear is why this single obligation of marriage should continue beyond divorce when all other marital obligations are terminated by divorce. Furthermore the support provided as alimony is not limited to a subsistence level if the husband's means permit a larger award.[11] It is not easy to state in general terms, not only why the husband's duty to support his wife should continue, but also why it should continue at a level above subsistence, but specific cases can be imagined in which most people would agree that it should. For example, there might be little dissent from the award of

substantial alimony to a woman of fifty who has been married for twenty-five years to an affluent husband, during which time she worked as a homemaker and cared for their children, when she has no property of her own or qualifications for employment.[12] The function of alimony in such a case, and very likely in most cases, is to accomplish the divorce with the least possible social and financial hardship and disruption. This is made clear by the statements in cases [13] and statutes [14] that alimony should, within the limits of the husband's resources, be such as to maintain the wife's standard of living as nearly as possible at the same level she enjoyed during the marriage. The husband, having entered one of the strongest and most fundamental relationships known to the law, must continue to bear its financial burden where he can reasonably do so and where that is necessary in order to prevent a relatively greater hardship to the wife. Divorce inevitably produces painful alterations in the lives of the spouses. A major function of alimony is to reduce its financial impact.[15]

Although this is less often recognized, alimony can also serve as compensation to the wife for faithful service during marriage. In the traditional marriage this meant that she kept house, cared for the children and did what she could to assist her husband in his work. Modern statutes not only authorize

6. Weitzman, The Economics of Divorce: Social and Economic Consequences of Property, Alimony and Child Support Awards, 28 U.C.L.A.L.Rev. 1181 (1981).

7. E.g., the California, Connecticut, Indiana, Iowa, New York, Oregon, Pennsylvania, Wisconsin statutes and the Uniform Marriage and Divorce Act, cited in note 2, supra.

8. Uniform Marriage and Divorce Act § 308(b)(1), 9A Unif.L.Ann. 160 (1979) includes as a factor to be considered in awarding alimony any provision for support of a child which includes a sum for the custodian. It is not entirely clear whether this does authorize an inclusion in child support of an amount for alimony and the Commissioners' Comment does not discuss the point.

9. E.g., California, Georgia, Indiana, Iowa, North Carolina, Oregon, Pennsylvania statutes, supra note 2. See also Matter of Marriage of Grove, 280 Or. 341, 571 P.2d 477 (1977), modified 280 Or. 769, 572 P.2d 1320 (1977), 57 Or.L.Rev. 566 (1978).

10. Rosan v. Rosan, 24 Cal.App.3d 885, 101 Cal.Rptr. 295 (1972); Weitzman, The Economics of Divorce: Social and Economic Consequences of Property, Alimony and

Child Support Awards, 28 U.C.L.A.L.Rev. 1181, 1221 (1981).

11. E.g., Bellow v. Bellow, 94 Ill.App.3d 361, 50 Ill. Dec. 656, 419 N.E.2d 924 (1981); Williams v. Williams, 299 N.C. 174, 261 S.E.2d 849 (1980); English v. English, 565 P.2d 409 (Utah 1977); Bahr v. Bahr, 107 Wis.2d 72, 318 N.W.2d 391 (1982). It is not unusual for alimony statutes to authorize the courts to take into account the standard of living maintained during the marriage as a factor in setting the level of alimony. E.g. the California and Oregon statutes cited in note 2, supra.

12. In re Marriage of Brantner, 67 Cal.App.3d 416, 136 Cal.Rptr. 635 (1977); Note, The Displaced Homemaker and the Divorce Process in Wisconsin, 1982 Wis.L.Rev. 941.

13. E.g., English v. English, 565 P.2d 409 (Utah 1977); Bahr v. Bahr, 107 Wis.2d 72, 318 N.W.2d 391 (1982).

14. E.g., the California and Oregon statutes cited in note 2, supra.

15. Pyke v. Pyke, 212 Neb. 114, 321 N.W.2d 906 (1982).

the courts to consider this aspect of alimony,[16] but some of them and some cases permit the alimony to compensate the wife for contributing to the husband's education or training.[17] The latter statutes are attempting to redress what some people think is a deficiency in the case law of property divisions, many of those cases having held that the husband's professional degree or license to practice is not a form of property of which the wife can be given a share on divorce.[18]

The notion of alimony as compensation for service in marriage can readily be, and sometimes is, transformed into a negative precept. When divorce was based upon marital fault, it was not surprising to find that marital fault was an important factor in the award or denial of alimony.[19] The wife's fault either disqualified her entirely for alimony or justified only a reduced amount. The husband's fault might permit an increased award.[20] It is surprising to find that even when fault has largely been eliminated from the grounds for divorce, it still may be considered a relevant factor in the alimony decision.[21] The tendency of some courts to refuse alimony to a wife who has been guilty of adultery is perhaps

understandable although this (and the corresponding tendency to increase the award if the husband is guilty of adultery) makes alimony appear to be a form of punishment at a time when many states are removing adultery from their criminal statutes.[22] Since facile judgments about who is responsible for the breakup of a marriage are notoriously unreliable, basing alimony awards upon marital fault risks being guided by nothing more substantial than prejudice or sentimentality. The statutes which, influenced by the Uniform Marriage and Divorce Act, exclude fault as a consideration in the alimony decision therefore reflect the more sensible policy.[23]

An outline of the functions of alimony would be incomplete without a reference to the contemporary body of opinion which holds that alimony has few or no useful functions and therefore ought either to be abolished or very strictly limited. This seems to be the position of the Uniform Marriage and Divorce Act.[24] The same view underlies other statutes permitting alimony to be awarded for limited periods only,[25] and judicial opinions which either deny alimony or grant it in small amounts.[26] Various reasons are given

---

16. E.g., Florida, Georgia, Indiana, Massachusetts, New York, Pennsylvania statutes cited in note 2, supra. Contra the text statement: Skelton v. Skelton, 490 A.2d 1204 (Me. 1985).

17. E.g., Georgia, Iowa, New York, Oregon, Pennsylvania, Wisconsin statutes cited in note 2, supra. See also Reiss v. Reiss, 195 N.J.Super. 150, 478 A.2d 441 (1984), modification on the wife's remarriage denied 200 N.J.Super. 122, 490 A.2d 378 (1984), affirmed 205 N.J. Super. 41, 500 A.2d 24 (1985).

18. See section 15.5, supra.

19. Cases are collected in Annot., 34 A.L.R.2d 313 (1954).

20. E.g., Poppe v. Poppe, 114 Ind.App. 348, 52 N.E.2d 506 (1944).

21. E.g., Connecticut, North Carolina, Pennsylvania statutes cited in note 2, supra. Cases are collected in Annots., 86 A.L.R.3d 1116 (1978) and 83 A.L.R.3d 97 (1978).

22. Compare Mahne v. Mahne, 147 N.J.Super. 326, 371 A.2d 314 (1977), certification denied 75 N.J. 22, 379 A.2d 253 (1977) with Lynn v. Lynn, 165 N.J.Super. 328, 398 A.2d 141 (1979), cert. denied 81 N.J. 52, 404 A.2d 1152 (1979).

23. E.g., Alaska, California, Illinois, Uniform Marriage and Divorce Act, as cited in note 2, supra. But Chapman v. Chapman, 498 S.W.2d 134 (Ky.1973) takes

the very odd position that the Uniform Act forbids consideration of marital fault in determining whether alimony should or should not be granted, but permits its consideration in determining the amount of alimony.

24. Uniform Marriage and Divorce Act § 308(a), 9A Unif.L.Ann. 160 (1979) permits alimony only where the person claiming it meets two conditions. She must show she does not have sufficient property to provide for her reasonable needs, and that she is unable to support herself through appropriate employment, or has custody of a child whose circumstances make it appropriate that she not seek a job outside the home. The views of the Reporter for the Act are given in R. Levy, Uniform Marriage and Divorce Legislation: A Preliminary Analysis 144–150 (1969). This statute, like other alimony statutes, gives to trial courts who are hostile to alimony sufficient leeway to deny it in a broad range of circumstances.

25. E.g., the Indiana statute cited in note 2, supra, limiting alimony to two years in some circumstances. See also Del.Code tit. 13, § 1512(a)(3) (1981); Md.Code, Fam.Law, § 11–106(a) (1984); N.H.Rev.Stat.Ann. § 458:19 (Supp.1986).

26. Olsen v. Olsen, 98 Idaho 10, 12, 557 P.2d 604, 606 (1976) (dissenting opinion); Kover v. Kover, 29 N.Y.2d 408, 328 N.Y.S.2d 641, 278 N.E.2d 886 (1972); Mose v. Mose, 4 Wash.App. 204, 480 P.2d 517 (1971). The statement in the text is often reflected in trial court decisions

for the current hostility to alimony. The most common is that women today have greater opportunities for employment and for becoming self-supporting than in the past.[27] The facts that alimony has in the past been awarded in only a relatively small proportion of the cases and that it is often not paid even when it is awarded are also sometimes offered as justification for restricting the use of alimony.[28] It is perhaps a reflection of the difficulties of enforcement that while alimony awards are declining, the courts are more willing to award to wives substantial proportions of their husband's property on divorce.[29] The substitution of property awards for alimony is of course not helpful to the large majority of wives whose husbands have little or no property at the time of divorce.[30] Courts are also more sensitive to the needs of children for support after divorce than to the needs of wives for alimony, although as has been indicated, child support awards may sometimes include a component intended to support the child's custodian.[31] One must recognize that to some extent similar functions are served by awards of alimony, property and child support, but the three forms of award have sufficiently different purposes and different proce-

dural implications so that clarity of analysis requires that they be separately considered.

None of the arguments advanced in opposition to alimony confutes its functions and purposes or shows them in any way unworthy of the law's attention. The statutes of most states continue to recognize this by authorizing the courts to take account of a broad range of circumstances in deciding alimony claims.[32] It is therefore still clear that alimony should be and will be granted in a proper case. That being so, we are left with the question familiar to lawyers: What is a proper case? In order to arrive at an answer we must look at the ways in which alimony's functions are performed in particular circumstances.

Factors to be Considered in Awarding Alimony

1. The Trial Court's Discretion

It is axiomatic that the trial courts have a wide discretion in determining the propriety and the amount of alimony.[33] The relevant factors are so numerous and their influence so incapable of precise evaluation that the trial court's decision in a particular case will be affirmed unless it amounts to an abuse of

---

on alimony. See, e.g., Cromwell v. Cromwell, 180 Mont. 40, 588 P.2d 1010 (1979); Johnson, Divorce, Alimony, Support and Custody: A Survey of Judges' Attitudes in One State, 3 Fam.L.Rptr. 4001 (1976).

27. See the Kover case, supra, note 26.

28. See R. Levy, Uniform Marriage and Divorce Legislation: A Preliminary Analysis 144–145 (1969).

29. See section 15.3, supra.

30. Weitzman, The Economics of Divorce: Social and Economic Consequences of Property, Alimony and Child Support Awards, 28 U.C.L.A.L.Rev. 1181, 1188–1196 (1981) indicates that even in marriages of eighteen years' duration and longer the median value of the marital property was only about $50,000, which is hardly enough to provide much support for a wife when divided in half.

31. See note 7, supra.

32. See, e.g., the Oregon and Pennsylvania statutes cited in note 2, supra. See also Matter of Marriage of Grove, 280 Or. 341, 571 P.2d 477 (1977), modified on another point 280 Or. 769, 572 P.2d 1320 (1977), taking the position that some women marry with the understanding that they will sacrifice their own career plans in favor of homemaking and child care on the assumption that their husbands will support them, in which instance alimony is appropriate.

33. The following are samples of a large number of cases which support this statement: In re Marriage of Epstein, 24 Cal.3d 76, 154 Cal.Rptr. 413, 592 P.2d 1165 (1979); Stoner v. Stoner, 163 Conn. 345, 307 A.2d 146 (1972); Olsen v. Olsen, 98 Idaho 10, 557 P.2d 604 (1976); Clark v. Clark, 236 Kan. 703, 696 P.2d 1386 (1985); Eberly v. Eberly, 12 Md.App. 117, 278 A.2d 107 (1971); Rice v. Rice, 372 Mass. 398, 361 N.E.2d 1305 (1977); Kover v. Kover, 29 N.Y.2d 408, 328 N.Y.S.2d 641, 278 N.E.2d 886 (1972); Quick v. Quick, 305 N.C. 446, 290 S.E.2d 653 (1982); Graham v. Graham, 253 S.C. 486, 171 S.E.2d 704 (1970); Bahr v. Bahr, 107 Wis.2d 72, 318 N.W.2d 391 (1982). Appellate courts usually require trial courts to make findings indicating the basis for their alimony awards. See the Rice and Quick cases supra. In a few states the old equity practice still obtains and alimony is triable de novo on appeal, but even in those cases considerable weight is given to the trial court's determination. Behrle v. Behrle, 228 N.W.2d 25 (Iowa 1975); Pound, Appellate Procedure in Civil Cases 298 (1941). See also Covey, The Exercise of Judicial Discretion in the Award of Alimony, 6 Law & Contemp.Prob. 213 (1939).

discretion [34] or is based upon an erroneous application of legal principles.[35] For the same reason precedents are of relatively slight value in arriving at alimony judgments, each case turning on its own circumstances.[36] Rules of thumb to guide trial courts in awarding alimony have occasionally been advanced, but they are only of limited usefulness in specific cases.[37] As a result claims for alimony are won or lost in the trial courts, which have a correspondingly heavy responsibility to deal fairly with spouses in such cases.[38]

Many of the alimony statutes list the variety of factors which courts are to consider in passing on alimony claims.[39] Where the statute of the state omits to enumerate the relevant factors, the courts' opinions provide a similar catalogue for the guidance of trial judges.[40] The factors are so numerous and it is so unlikely that a single factor in isolation from the others will control the outcome of a case that a discussion of each factor separately may incur the reproach that we are indulg-

ing in abstractions unrelated to the world of litigation. Notwithstanding the risk, an attempt to analyze each factor in as precise terms as possible will be made, in the hope of clarifying the statute and case law.

2. The Defendant's Ability to Pay

The defendant's (usually the husband's) ability to pay alimony places an upper limit upon what can be awarded.[41] The statutes often do not speak of ability to pay but more specifically refer to the resources and property of the parties as relevant considerations.[42] However it may be expressed, the term "ability to pay" is one of those legal phrases whose meaning seems obvious at first glance but which raises many questions when one applies it to specific situations.

The first step in reaching a judgment about the defendant's ability to pay alimony is a determination of how much property and income he possesses. If there has been a division of property in the divorce, the share of

---

34. Lindsay v. Lindsay, 115 Ariz. 322, 565 P.2d 199 (App.1977); Carlson v. Carlson, 178 Colo. 283, 497 P.2d 1006 (1972); In re Marriage of Smith, 77 Ill.App.3d 858, 33 Ill.Dec. 332, 396 N.E.2d 859 (1979); Hillery v. Hillery, 342 Mass. 371, 173 N.E.2d 269 (1961); Martin v. Martin, 271 So.2d 391 (Miss.1972); Swanson v. Swanson, 464 S.W.2d 225 (Mo.1971).

35. Benner v. Benner, 37 Md.App. 367, 377 A.2d 582 (1977); Rosenbaum v. Rosenbaum, 86 Nev. 550, 471 P.2d 254 (1970); Commonwealth ex rel. Burns v. Burns, 232 Pa.Super. 295, 331 A.2d 768 (1974) (non-support case); State ex rel. Cecil v. Knapp, 143 W.Va. 896, 105 S.E.2d 569 (1958).

36. Turi v. Turi, 34 N.J.Super. 313, 112 A.2d 278 (1955).

37. Mueller v. Mueller, 44 Cal.2d 527, 282 P.2d 869 (1955); Carlson v. Carlson, 178 Colo. 283, 497 P.2d 1006 (1972); O'Neill v. O'Neill, 18 N.J.Misc. 82, 11 A.2d 128 (1939); Brasier v. Brasier, 200 Okl. 689, 200 P.2d 427 (1948). See 3 Fam.L.Rptr. 3185 (1977) for a schedule of spousal and child support suggested by the Family Law Department of the Los Angeles County Superior Court. The amounts for spousal support alone range from one-fourth of the lowest income to one-third of the highest.

38. An extensive collection of cases on the excessiveness or adequacy of alimony awards may be found in Annot., 28 A.L.R.4th 786 (1984).

39. E.g., the California, Connecticut, Florida, Georgia, Illinois, Iowa, Massachusetts, Missouri, New York, Oregon, Pennsylvania, and Wisconsin statutes cited supra in note 2. The Uniform Marriage and Divorce Act § 308, 9A Unif.L.Ann. 160 (1979) first restricts the award of alimony to a spouse who has neither property nor income

sufficient for his support, and then lists six factors to be considered in arriving at an equitable award.

40. E.g., Eberly v. Eberly, 12 Md.App. 117, 278 A.2d 107 (1971); Martin v. Martin, 271 So.2d 391 (Miss.1972); Graham v. Graham, 253 S.C. 486, 171 S.E.2d 704 (1970).

Although the purpose of temporary alimony is the support of the spouse, and there is a similar component of support in "permanent" alimony, it does not follow that permanent alimony should be awarded in the same amount as temporary alimony. MacReynolds v. MacReynolds, 29 Colo.App. 267, 482 P.2d 407 (1971).

41. E.g., Byerly v. Byerly, 363 Ill. 517, 2 N.E.2d 898 (1936); Flanders v. Flanders, 241 Iowa 159, 40 N.W.2d 468 (1950); Donigan v. Donigan, 208 Md. 511, 119 A.2d 430 (1956); Wood v. Wood, 288 Mich. 14, 284 N.W. 627 (1939); Holmes v. Holmes, 255 Minn. 270, 96 N.W.2d 547 (1959); Nickerson v. Nickerson, 152 Neb. 799, 42 N.W.2d 861 (1950); Van Horn v. Van Horn, 189 Okl. 624, 119 P.2d 825 (1941); Miles v. Miles, 185 Or. 230, 202 P.2d 485 (1949); MacDonald v. MacDonald, 120 Utah 573, 236 P.2d 1066 (1951).

42. See, e.g., West's Ann.Cal.Civ.Code § 4801 (Supp. 1987) (earning capacity, obligations and assets of the defendant); Conn.Gen.Stat.Ann. § 46b–82 (1986) (amount and sources of income, estate and needs of the defendant); Pa.Stat. tit. 23, § 501 (Supp.1986) (containing a long list of quite specific factors relating to property and income). The Uniform Marriage and Divorce Act § 308(b)(6), 9A Unif.L.Ann. 161 (1979) defines this element as "the ability of the spouse from whom maintenance is sought to meet his needs while meeting those of the spouse seeking maintenance."

property awarded to him is of course to be considered.[43] Income from this and other property is to be taken into account,[44] including income from sources exempt from the claims of creditors, such as pensions,[45] or spendthrift trusts.[46] But the fact that the defendant may have an expectancy of inheritance is normally not to be considered, since this class of property is outside his control.[47] The defendant's earnings from employment are of course taken account of[48] although if they fluctuate from year to year, the court might be more inclined to look at the earning history or take an average figure.[49] Obligations should normally be deducted in determining the income available for alimony[50], including income taxes[51] although the claimed debts should be scrutinized to determine whether they have been incurred in good faith and whether they really affect the defendant's ability to pay alimony.[52] If the defendant's property is not productive of income, it may still be considered in assessing

alimony,[53] although the courts are sometimes reluctant to order it sold to pay alimony.[54] It does not matter that part or all of his property is located outside the state in which the divorce is granted.[55]

Some courts are willing to consider large resources or a high income on the defendant's part not as a factor limiting alimony, but as a factor justifying a larger award than might otherwise be proper.[56] The same result may occur if the court emphasizes the standard of living which the parties enjoyed during marriage rather than the defendant's earnings,[57] although of course the earnings were the source of the high standard of living. This result seems justified if it produces a comfortable standard of living for the wife of a marriage of long duration who has an uncertain future in the job market, but even in these circumstances the wife's property, including property awarded in the divorce, and her earning prospects should not be ignored.

---

43. Matter of Marriage of Grove, 280 Or. 341, 571 P.2d 477 (1977), opinion modified, rehearing denied 280 Or. 769, 572 P.2d 1320 (1977). Under the law of most states the court should distribute the property of the spouses before it passes on the alimony issue. See the discussion in section 15.1, supra.

44. Donigan v. Donigan, 208 Md. 511, 119 A.2d 430 (1956).

45. Pyke v. Pyke, 212 Neb. 114, 321 N.W.2d 906 (1982); DeRevere v. DeRevere, 5 Wash.App. 446, 488 P.2d 763 (1971); Mose v. Mose, 4 Wash.App. 204, 480 P.2d 517 (1971); Annot., 22 A.L.R.2d 1421 (1952). Contra, where the pension was contingent at the time of trial with respect to any amounts other than his own contributions. Robbins v. Robbins, 463 S.W.2d 876 (Mo.1971). Whether such pensions are subject to attachment or garnishment by the plaintiff is another question. See section 16.6, infra.

46. Bacardi v. White, 463 So.2d 218 (Fla.1985); Athorne v. Athorne, 100 N.H. 413, 128 A.2d 910 (1957).

47. Hillery v. Hillery, 342 Mass. 371, 173 N.E.2d 269 (1961); Turi v. Turi, 34 N.J.Super. 313, 112 A.2d 278 (1955); Robertson v. Robertson, 215 Va. 425, 211 S.E.2d 41 (1975).

48. Rosan v. Rosan, 24 Cal.App.3d 885, 101 Cal.Rptr. 295 (1972) (court considered the husband's earnings, but not his gambling winnings); Hillery v. Hillery, 342 Mass. 371, 173 N.E.2d 269 (1961). Quinn v. Quinn, 11 Md.App. 638, 276 A.2d 425 (1971) refused to take into account the earnings of a corporation all of whose stock was owned by the husband, where the corporation was not used to perpetrate a fraud, but the result seems doubtful. Where the spouses' standard of living during marriage was

higher than the husband's apparent earnings would justify, the court in Bucci v. Bucci, 350 So.2d 786 (Fla.App. 1977) based an award of alimony on the standard of living, on the ground that the husband had had earnings which were not "visible" in his tax return. Fringe benefits should be included in earnings, according to Hirth v. Hirth, 48 Wis.2d 491, 180 N.W.2d 601 (1970).

49. English v. English, 565 P.2d 409 (Utah 1977).

50. Clark v. Clark, 236 Kan. 703, 696 P.2d 1386 (1985); Graham v. Graham, 253 S.C. 486, 171 S.E.2d 704 (1970).

51. Aaron v. Aaron, 281 N.W.2d 150 (Minn.1979) stated that taxes in general may be considered, but that they may not be if the tax liability is speculative. See Annot., Divorce and Separation: Consideration of Tax Liability or Consequences in Determining Alimony or Property Settlement Provisions, 51 A.L.R.3d 461 (1973).

52. Thus a depreciation deduction on the husband's income tax return may be disregarded as reducing disposable income, since it does not affect the dollars available for alimony. Stoner v. Stoner, 163 Conn. 345, 307 A.2d 146 (1972); Eberly v. Eberly, 12 Md.App. 117, 278 A.2d 107 (1971).

53. Mack v. Mack, 112 So.2d 861 (Fla.App.1959).

54. Miles v. Miles, 185 Or. 230, 202 P.2d 485 (1949).

55. Fuller v. Fuller, 175 Or. 136, 151 P.2d 979 (1944).

56. Ingram v. Ingram, 217 Va. 27, 225 S.E.2d 362 (1976); Bahr v. Bahr, 107 Wis.2d 72, 318 N.W.2d 391 (1982) (award of $18,000 unreasonably low where the husband earned $300,000 per year).

57. See Bahr v. Bahr, 107 Wis.2d 72, 318 N.W.2d 391 (1982) and cases cited infra in note 76.

Troublesome questions arise when it appears that the defendant's earnings have been sharply reduced at the time of the divorce, leading the claimant for alimony to argue that he is capable of earning much more, and therefore paying much more alimony than his current earnings would permit. The outcome of the cases turns on what the evidence shows as to the reason for the reduction in earnings. If it has been produced by a bona fide career change, for example when a physician moves from private practice into an academic position, the lower income will be the proper measure of alimony.[58] The same is true where he is at the normal retirement age and retires,[59] or where circumstances beyond his control confine him to the lower income.[60] But if there is evidence that the defendant has intentionally chosen the lower income to frustrate alimony claims or without an independent career justification, or is making his income appear to be lower for that purpose, the courts are properly unsympathetic, ordering alimony on the basis of what he could earn rather than what he actually earns or appears to earn.[61] Needless to say, the evidence is often unclear in such cases, thereby making the trial judge's task all the more

difficult.[62] Caution should be used in estimating the defendant's future income in any case, and speculative income prospects should not be the basis for alimony awards.[63]

The foregoing is sufficient to demonstrate that the term "husband's ability to pay" is ambiguous. The ambiguity arises from the fact that his ability cannot be evaluated in isolation from the wife's needs. Obviously he must retain a large enough portion of his income to support himself so that he can continue to work and provide for his ex-wife and their children. Reading between the lines of the opinions, one gets the impression that the courts are being careful not to kill the goose that lays the golden eggs, even if the eggs may not be very nourishing. Perhaps for this reason it often appears that the alimony being awarded leaves the wife in a financial position substantially inferior to that of the husband, even though some authorities assert that equality should be the norm.[64]

3. *The Plaintiff's Needs*

Given the purposes of alimony outlined earlier in this section, the plaintiff's (usually the wife's) need is the most influential of the

58. This was the situation in Butler v. Butler, 217 Va. 195, 227 S.E.2d 688 (1976), in which the trial court's award was affirmed notwithstanding the husband's claim that it exceeded his ability and his concession that he could double his compensation by going into private practice. But the Virginia Supreme Court's decision was based primarily on its finding that the amount awarded was essential to the support of the wife and children, and on the view that some of the husband's claimed expenses were not legitimate. If the spouses had remained married to each other, the wife would have had to live on the reduced salary. It does not seem that she should be entitled to insist that he work in a more highly paid job unless his decision is based on a desire to deprive her of support rather than upon a good faith decision about his career.

59. Commonwealth ex rel. Burns v. Burns, 232 Pa. Super. 295, 331 A.2d 768 (1974). This question often arises when the defendant seeks to have a court reduce an award entered in the past. E.g., Smith v. Smith, 419 A.2d 1035 (Me. 1980), and cases discussed infra in section 16.5.

60. Rosenbaum v. Rosenbaum, 86 Nev. 550, 471 P.2d 254 (1970).

61. In re McCarthy's Marriage, ___ Colo.App. ___, 533 P.2d 928 (1975); In re Marriage of Smith, 77 Ill.App.3d 858, 33 Ill.Dec. 332, 396 N.E.2d 859 (1979) (husband's

motives were suspect and the higher award was necessary to meet the wife's needs); Donigan v. Donigan, 208 Md. 511, 119 A.2d 430 (1956); Hess v. Hess, 134 N.J.Eq. 360, 35 A.2d 677 (1944); Kay v. Kay, 37 N.Y.2d 632, 376 N.Y.S.2d 443, 339 N.E.2d 143 (1975) (court based alimony on the income the husband was capable of earning, indicating some skepticism concerning his calculation of his income); Hawkins v. Hawkins, 187 Va. 595, 47 S.E.2d 436 (1948).

62. Bowes v. Bowes, 287 N.C. 163, 214 S.E.2d 40 (1975).

63. Bratnober v. Bratnober, 48 Cal.2d 259, 309 P.2d 441 (1957); Richards v. Richards, 44 Hawaii 491, 355 P.2d 188 (1960); Schwartz v. Schwartz, 38 Ill.App.3d 959, 349 N.E.2d 567 (1976).

64. See Weitzman, The Economics of Divorce: Social and Economic Consequences of Property, Alimony and Child Support Awards, 28 U.C.L.A.L.Rev. 1181, 1246–1253 (1981) describes statistics showing how divorce in California results in a higher standard of living for husbands and a much lower one for wives in most cases. Epstein v. Epstein, 24 Cal.3d 76, 154 Cal.Rptr. 413, 592 P.2d 1165 (1979) contains dictum to the effect that it is an abuse of discretion for a trial court to give one spouse a standard of living significantly higher than it gives to the other.

factors to be considered in framing a decree for alimony.[65] It was formerly accurate to say that within the limits of the husband's ability to pay the wife was entitled to an amount of alimony which would support her as nearly as possible at the standard of living which she enjoyed during the marriage.[66] Now that a larger proportion of women, including married women, work, that statement must be qualified. Although the standard of living during the marriage is still a factor to be considered,[67] many courts place much more emphasis upon the wife's ability or potential ability to find work and support herself than would have been true twenty years ago.[68] The result is that alimony awards are generally either not made at all or are smaller in amount or shorter in duration than in the past. This judicial approach may impose hardships on the older wife who has been out of the labor force for a long time.[69]

Any evaluation of the plaintiff's needs must start by considering her property, including any property distributed to her by the divorce decree itself.[70] If her property is ample for her support, she should receive no alimony,[71] although there is some authority that if the income from her property is not sufficient for her maintenance, she need not use up the principal for that purpose but may be awarded alimony.[72]

Where the evidence shows that the plaintiff is able to support herself adequately and to a degree comparable with the standard of living enjoyed during the marriage, alimony may be denied.[73] In any event earnings which the

---

65. See, e.g., West's Ann.Cal.Civ.Code § 4801 (Supp. 1987); Conn.Gen.Stat.Ann. § 46b–82 (1986); West's Fla. Stat.Ann. § 61.08 (1985 and Supp.1987); Official Code Georgia Ann. § 30–201 (Supp.1986); Iowa Code Ann. § 598.21 (1981 and Supp.1986); Mass.Gen.Laws Ann. 208, § 34 (Supp.1986); N.Y.—McKinney's Dom.Rel.L. § 236 Part B(6) (1986). The wife's need is made an essential condition for the award of alimony by the Uniform Marriage and Divorce Act § 308(a), 9A Unif.L.Ann. 160 (1979), which provides that a spouse may not be awarded alimony unless she lacks property sufficient for her reasonable needs, *and* is either unable to support herself through appropriate employment, or is the custodian of a child making it inappropriate that she work outside the home.

66. Hall v. Hall, 42 Cal.2d 435, 267 P.2d 249 (1954); Byerly v. Byerly, 363 Ill. 517, 2 N.E.2d 898 (1936); Flanders v. Flanders, 241 Iowa 159, 40 N.W.2d 468 (1950); Wood v. Wood, 288 Mich. 14, 284 N.W. 627 (1939); Schwent v. Schwent, 209 S.W.2d 546 (Mo.App. 1948); Nickerson v. Nickerson, 152 Neb. 799, 42 N.W.2d 861 (1950); Polyckronos v. Polyckronos, 17 N.J.Misc. 250, 8 A.2d 265 (1939); MacDonald v. MacDonald, 120 Utah 573, 236 P.2d 1066 (1951).

67. See, e.g., West's Ann.Cal.Civ.Code § 4801 (Supp. 1987), and other statutes cited in note 2, supra.

68. E.g., Kover v. Kover, 29 N.Y.2d 408, 328 N.Y.S.2d 641, 278 N.E.2d 886 (1972), in which the court quoted with apparent approval the remark in another opinion that women have "practically unlimited opportunities . . . in the business world of today". The Uniform Marriage and Divorce Act cited supra in note 65 bars alimony entirely to the wife who is able to find appropriate employment, whatever that may be.

69. A good example is Abuzzahab v. Abuzzahab, 359 N.W.2d 12, 14 (Minn.1984), as spelled out in the dissenting opinion. But very substantial alimony awards to wives who also have large amounts of property can still be seen. E.g., Rice v. Rice, 372 Mass. 398, 361 N.E.2d 1305 (1977).

70. See Chapter 15, supra, on the division of property on divorce. See also Barnett v. Barnett, 292 Ky. 840, 168 S.W.2d 17 (1942); Donigan v. Donigan, 208 Md. 511, 119 A.2d 430 (1956); Swanson v. Swanson, 464 S.W.2d 225 (Mo.App.1971); Phillips v. Phillips, 1 A.D.2d 393, 150 N.Y.S.2d 646 (1st Dept. 1956), affirmed 2 N.Y.2d 742, 157 N.Y.S.2d 378, 138 N.E.2d 738 (1956), 23 Bklyn.L.Rev. 131 (1956), 8 Syra.L.Rev. 128 (1956).

The confusion between a property division and alimony is graphically demonstrated by Hunt v. Hunt, 698 P.2d 1168 (Alaska 1985), which held that a property division could be relied upon in lieu of rehabilitative alimony.

Taylor v. Taylor, 329 N.W.2d 795 (Minn.1983) held that the wife's social security entitlement should be taken into account in assessing her alimony.

71. See note 70, supra. But Benner v. Benner, 37 Md. App. 367, 377 A.2d 582 (1977) held that a court should not take into account in awarding alimony to a wife the fact that she expected to inherit some property from her mother's estate, at least where there was no evidence as to when the estate would be settled or what the property would be worth.

72. Williams v. Williams, 299 N.C. 174, 261 S.E.2d 849 (1980).

73. Neal v. Neal, 116 Ariz. 590, 570 P.2d 758 (1977); Brueggemann v. Brueggemann, 551 S.W.2d 853 (Mo.App. 1977). The courts sometimes use the device of rehabilitative alimony where the wife seems capable of returning to work outside the home but needs a period of education or training. See the discussion infra at note 84. Permanent alimony was rejected in favor of rehabilitative alimony in Campbell v. Campbell, 432 So.2d 666 (Fla.App. 1983), petition for review dismissed 453 So.2d 1364 (1984); Matter of Marriage of Watrous, 23 Or.App. 241, 541 P.2d 1082 (1975). But see Walter v. Walter, 464 So.2d 538 (Fla. 1985).

Where the divorce ends a brief marriage of a few months only, the cases generally grant little or no alimony presumably on the theory that the wife's capacity to

plaintiff is receiving or is capable of receiving will in a proper case serve to reduce the amount of alimony.[74] But vague speculation about the general availability of work for women or the changing status of women in the work force should not be the basis for denying or reducing alimony.[75] Where the plaintiff has been married a long time and has worked as a homemaker, so that any employment skills she may once have had could no longer enable her to find a job, she should receive sufficient alimony, within the husband's means, to provide her with support on a scale comparable with the married standard of living.[76] If she is in such poor health that she is unable to work, this also may entitle her to alimony.[77] Even if she is able to find a job, she may be awarded alimony if she chooses to care for the children of the marriage rather than to work outside the home, provided again that the husband is able to pay alimony.[78]

Perhaps the most difficult case concerns the wife who is able to work and earn but whose earnings are far below the standard of living provided by the husband during marriage. Statutes like the Uniform Marriage and Divorce Act [79] seem to forbid alimony in such a case if the wife's work is "appropriate". One might argue that it is not appropriate if it produces earnings much lower than the level of marital support.[80] The cases are not in agreement when faced with this question, some of them granting alimony,[81] while others deny or sharply limit it.[82] Assuming that the wife's security cannot be provided for by a property division, it ought to be within the trial court's discretion to grant substantial alimony in such cases even if we agree with the judges (usually male) who insist that the purposes of alimony do not encompass the award of lifetime annuities to idle spouses.[83]

work and earn has not been substantially interrupted by the marriage. See, e.g., Huerta v. Huerta, 15 Ariz.App. 211, 487 P.2d 432 (1971); Behrle v. Behrle, 228 N.W.2d 25 (Iowa 1975); Fotinos v. Fotinos, 184 Neb. 486, 168 N.W.2d 698 (1969); Ford v. Ford, 112 N.H. 270, 293 A.2d 605 (1972).

For other cases on the plaintiff's financial resources, see Annot., 28 A.L.R.4th 786, 807 (1984).

In the unusual case in which the wife remarries before the alimony decision is made, she should not receive any alimony. Claughton v. Claughton, 393 So.2d 1061 (Fla. 1980), on remand 395 So.2d 308 (1981).

74. Abuzzahab v. Abuzzahab, 359 N.W.2d 12 (Minn. 1984); McClelland v. McClelland, 359 N.W.2d 7 (Minn. 1984); Otis v. Otis, 299 N.W.2d 114 (Minn.1980); Kover v. Kover, 29 N.Y.2d 408, 328 N.Y.S.2d 641, 278 N.E.2d 886 (1972).

75. Sisson v. Sisson, 336 So.2d 1129 (Fla.1976).

76. Lindsay v. Lindsay, 115 Ariz. 322, 565 P.2d 199 (App.1977) (refuses permanent alimony but holds that the trial court should reserve jurisdiction so that the wife could continue to receive alimony if unable to find work); In re Marriage of Brantner, 67 Cal.App.3d 416, 136 Cal. Rptr. 635 (1977) (reverses the trial court's limitation of alimony to a fixed period); Rosan v. Rosan, 24 Cal.App.3d 885, 101 Cal.Rptr. 295 (1972); Arundel v. Arundel, 281 N.W.2d 663 (Minn.1979); Swanstrom v. Swanstrom, 359 N.W.2d 634 (Minn.App.1984); Marriage of Cromwell, 180 Mont. 40, 588 P.2d 1010 (1979); Conrad v. Conrad, 471 P.2d 892 (Okl.1969); Matter of Marriage of McNamara, 65 Or.App. 785, 672 P.2d 722 (1983).

Even where the wife's employment prospects appear bleak, some courts put a fixed time limit on alimony. In re Beeh's Marriage 214 N.W.2d 170 (Iowa 1974).

77. Lanphear v. Lanphear, 303 N.W.2d 576 (S.D.1981); Annot., 28 A.L.R.4th 786, 809 (1984).

78. Danielson v. Danielson, 174 Conn. 427, 389 A.2d 750 (1978) (denial of alimony error where it prevented the wife from exercising her visitation rights); Benvenuto v. Benvenuto, 389 A.2d 795 (D.C.App.1978); Walton v. Walton, 354 So.2d 464 (Fla.App.1978).

79. See note 65, supra.

80. Matter of Marriage of Grove, 280 Or. 341, 571 P.2d 477 (1977), opinion modified, rehearing denied 280 Or. 769, 572 P.2d 1320 (1977).

81. Sisson v. Sisson, 336 So.2d 1129 (Fla.1976); Marriage of Cromwell, 180 Mont. 40, 588 P.2d 1010 (1979); Pyke v. Pyke, 212 Neb. 114, 321 N.W.2d 906 (1982).

82. In re Marriage of Bramson, 100 Ill.App.3d 657, 56 Ill.Dec. 205, 427 N.E.2d 285 (1981) (wife after a twenty-year marriage and two children, of whom she has custody, working as a sales clerk at $7,825.00 per year, is awarded $750 per month in alimony and child support for the children's minority, and then $500 per month when husband's income is $67,000 per year); Otis v. Otis, 299 N.W.2d 114 (Minn.1980) (wife of a twenty-six year marriage who has not worked receives $2000 per month for two years, then $1000 per month for two years when husband's income is $120,000 per year); Hickland v. Hickland, 39 N.Y.2d 1, 382 N.Y.S.2d 475, 346 N.E.2d 243 (1976), reargument denied 39 N.Y.2d 943, 386 N.Y.S.2d 1028, 352 N.E.2d 896 (1976) (wife receives $50 per week alimony when earning $8,000 per year, husband's income $35,000 per year).

83. Otis v. Otis, 299 N.W.2d 114 (Minn.1980).

4. Limits on Duration: Rehabilitative Alimony

Traditionally "permanent" alimony was not permanent but indefinite, ending with the death of either spouse or the remarriage of the recipient. It could also be reduced or terminated by the court which awarded it on proof of a change in relevant circumstances, for example, on proof that the wife had obtained work and was self-supporting. Nevertheless some courts continued to speak of alimony as if it really were permanent. Their stereotype is that of the ex-wife who is living in indolent luxury on the proceeds of her ex-husband's labor.[84] Needless to say, this stereotype can rarely be found in real life.

This contemporary hostility to alimony and the greatly increased entry of married women into the work force has led a few states to pass statutes imposing relatively short limits on the duration of alimony.[85] In many more states the courts, without the need to rely upon specific statutory authority, have imposed time limits on alimony awards. In some of these states the courts refer to such limited awards as rehabilitative alimony,[86] either pursuant to statutes authorizing this sort of alimony,[87] or without statutory authority on the ground that alimony in this form is within the broad discretion of the courts respecting alimony awards.[88]

Rehabilitative alimony is defined by some cases as alimony which is awarded only for a fixed period, usually short, on the basis of evidence indicating that the recipient will, at the end of that period, be able by the exercise of reasonable efforts to support herself.[89] Its purposes are to provide to the husband a measure of predictability concerning his financial obligations; to save further court time by permitting the divorcing court to take account of reasonably foreseeable changes in the recipient's circumstances; and above all to put some pressure on the recipient of alimony, usually assumed to be the wife, to find employment or to undertake education or training which will lead to employment.[90] The concept of rehabilitative alimony and its purposes are unexceptionable. The risk that the concept creates is that trial courts, in their zeal to restrict alimony and under the influence of the notion that most married women today work outside the home, will award rehabilitative alimony when the wife has no realistic expectation of earning enough to support herself in an acceptable degree.[91] That this is a substantial risk is demonstrated by the cases which have reversed rehabilitative alimony awards, either on the ground that the evidence did not support the claim that the wife was employable,[92] or that her earnings were likely to be far below her standard of living during marriage.[93]

---

84. E.g., Grinold v. Grinold, 32 Conn.Supp. 225, 348 A.2d 32 (1975).

85. Del.Code tit. 13, § 1512(a)(3) (1981) (alimony limited to two years where the divorce is granted for incompatibility and the marriage lasted less than twenty years). The period runs from the date of the divorce decree, according to Michael J. F. v. Carmela L. F., 437 A.2d 579 (Del.1981).

86. E.g., Hunt v. Hunt, 698 P.2d 1168 (Alaska 1985); Kuvin v. Kuvin, 442 So.2d 203 (Fla.1983); Smith v. Smith, 326 N.W.2d 697 (N.D.1982). Other cases are cited in Annot., 97 A.L.R.3d 740 (1980).

87. West's Ann.Cal.Civ.Code § 4801(a), (d) (Supp.1987); West's Fla.Stat.Ann. § 61.08 (1985); Official Code Georgia Ann. § 30–209(a)(5) (Supp.1986); Ill.—Smith Hurd Ann.Stat. ch. 40, § 504(b) (Supp.1986); West's Ann.Ind. Code § 31–1–11.5–11(e) (Supp.1986); Iowa Code Ann. § 598.21(3)(e) (Supp.1986); Md.Code Fam.Law, § 11–106(b) (1984); N.Y.—McKinney's Dom.Rel.L. § 236 Part B(6) (1986); Or.Rev.Stat. § 107.105(1)(d) (1983); Pa.Stat. tit. 23, § 501(b) (Supp.1986); Wis.Stat.Ann. § 767.26 (1981). See also Uniform Marriage and Divorce Act § 308(b), 9A Unif.L.Ann. 160 (1979).

88. Turner v. Turner, 158 N.J.Super. 313, 385 A.2d 1280 (1978), citing other cases. A dictum in Lepis v. Lepis, 83 N.J. 139, 416 A.2d 45 (1980) seems to approve rehabilitative alimony. See also Annot., 97 A.L.R.3d 740 (1980).

89. Kulakowski v. Kulakowski, 191 N.J.Super. 609, 468 A.2d 733 (1982); Turner v. Turner, 158 N.J.Super. 313, 385 A.2d 1280 (1978).

90. Turner v. Turner, 158 N.J.Super. 313, 385 A.2d 1280 (1978). The court in this case emphasized the need to force divorced women to find work and become self-supporting.

91. The risk is discussed at considerable length in the context of the new California statute in In re Marriage of Morrison, 20 Cal.3d 437, 143 Cal.Rptr. 139, 573 P.2d 41 (1978). That statute attempts to protect the ex-wife by providing that although support orders having specific time limits expire at the end of the time specified, the court which enters the order may expressly retain juris-

---

92.–93. See notes 92–93 on page 651.

In some of these cases the court dealt with the problem by requiring the trial court to retain jurisdiction, so that the wife's needs could be met by modifying the award.[94] Where the marriage is of short duration and the wife young enough to have reasonably good prospects for becoming self-supporting, or where she is older but the evidence shows that she clearly will be able to meet her financial needs either through employment or the possession of income producing property or a combination of the two, then rehabilitative alimony is appropriate and many cases have approved such awards.[95]

5. Reimbursement Alimony

The decisions of several cases holding that a spouse's education or professional training or license to practice a profession is not "property" which may be divided on divorce[96] strike many people as unfair when the education leading to the profession has been financed by the earnings of the other spouse. As a result the statutes of some states have been amended to authorize, as one of the factors on which an alimony award may be based, the contribution of a spouse to the education, training or professional license of the other spouse.[97] The alimony awarded in such cases is calculated on the basis of the amount of the other spouse's contribution rather than the value of the professional degree or license.[98] This can produce awards which leave the spouses in widely disparate circumstances.[99] A few cases award alimony of this kind even without statutory authority.[1]

diction to extend the award. West's Ann.Cal.Civ.Code § 4801(d) (Supp.1987).

92. Wikle v. Wikle, 390 So.2d 297 (Ala.Civ.App.1980) (held error to limit alimony to two years where the wife was fifty years old, had not worked during the fifteen-year marriage, had no marketable skills and was in doubtful health, and where the husband had a gross income of $80,000 per year and a net worth in excess of $1,250,000); In re Marriage of Carney, 122 Ill.App.3d 705, 78 Ill.Dec. 477, 462 N.E.2d 596 (1984) (limited alimony is proper only where the wife can find employment at compensation which will provide a standard of living comparable to that in the marriage, and in this case the wife's medical history and ability to support herself made that highly uncertain); Bowman v. Bowman, ___ Mont. ___, 633 P.2d 1198 (1981) (abuse of discretion to limit alimony to two years for a forty-one year old woman with a bachelor's degree in economics where the husband's income was in excess of $70,000 per year); Guindon v. Guindon, 256 N.W.2d 894 (S.D.1977) (reverses a two-year limit on alimony where the wife's chance of becoming self-supporting was speculative); Olson v. Olson, 704 P.2d 564 (Utah 1985) (two-year award made permanent); Molnar v. Molnar, ___ W.Va. ___, 314 S.E.2d 73 (1984) (rehabilitative alimony an abuse of discretion where the wife was earning $438 per month, was fifty-three, and would require another ten years to obtain qualifications as a computer programmer, while the husband earned $45,600 per year). Other cases are cited in Annot., 97 A.L.R.3d 740, 753 (1980).

93. In re Marriage of Carney, 122 Ill.App.3d 705, 78 Ill.Dec. 477, 462 N.E.2d 596 (1984).

94. In re Marriage of Morrison, 20 Cal.3d 437, 143 Cal.Rptr. 139, 573 P.2d 41 (1978); In re Marriage of Webb, 94 Cal.App.3d 335, 156 Cal.Rptr. 334 (1979).

95. Campbell v. Campbell, 432 So.2d 666 (Fla.App. 1983), petition for review dismissed 453 So.2d 1364 (1984); Cann v. Cann, 334 So.2d 325 (Fla.App. 1976); Beard v. Beard, 262 So.2d 269 (Fla.App. 1972); Kulakowski v. Kulakowski, 191 N.J.Super. 609, 468 A.2d 733 (1983);

Turner v. Turner, 158 N.J.Super. 313, 385 A.2d 1280 (1978); Matter of Marriage of Watrous, 23 Or.App. 241, 541 P.2d 1082 (1975). But rehabilitative alimony is not to be the presumptively proper form of award according to Walter v. Walter, 464 So.2d 538 (Fla. 1985). Other cases are cited in Annot., 97 A.L.R.3d 740, 746 (1980). See also Note, Rehabilitative Alimony—A Matter of Discretion or Direction, 12 Fla.State U.L.Rev. 285 (1984).

96. In re Marriage of Weinstein, 128 Ill.App.3d 234, 83 Ill.Dec. 425, 470 N.E.2d 551 (1984), citing cases. See section 15.5, supra.

97. West's Ann.Cal.Civ.Code § 4801 (Supp.1987); Official Code Ga.Ann. § 30–209 (Supp. 1986); Iowa Code Ann. § 598.21 (1981 and Supp.1986); N.Y.—McKinney's Dom. Rel.Law § 236 Part B(6) (1986); Or.Rev.Stat. § 107.105(1) (d) (1983); Pa.Stat. tit. 23, § 501 (Supp. 1986); Wis.Stat. Ann. § 767.26 (1981).

98. Hodge v. Hodge, 337 Pa.Super. 151, 486 A.2d 951 (1984), order affirmed 513 Pa. 264, 520 A.2d 15 (1986).

99. Hodge v. Hodge, 337 Pa.Super. 151, 160, 486 A.2d 951, 955 (1984), order affirmed 513 Pa. 264, 520 A.2d 15 (1986), concurring and dissenting opinion.

1. Mahoney v. Mahoney, 91 N.J. 488, 453 A.2d 527 (1982); Reiss v. Reiss, 195 N.J.Super. 150, 478 A.2d 441 (1984), judgment affirmed in part and remanded 205 N.J. Super. 41, 500 A.2d 24 (1985) (wife receives one-half of her earnings for the period in which she supported the husband in medical school plus an amount for supplementing his income during his residency); Hubbard v. Hubbard, 603 P.2d 747 (Okl.1979) (payments characterized as "property division alimony"). Morgan v. Morgan, 52 A.D.2d 804, 383 N.Y.S.2d 343 (1st Dept.1976), appeal dismissed 40 N.Y.2d 843, 387 N.Y.S.2d 839, 356 N.E.2d 292 (1976) refused to grant the wife alimony as reimbursement for her support of her husband in law school on the ground that it was not contemplated that she would later go to medical school while they were married. The case may be overruled by the New York statuted cited supra in note 97.

6. The Fault of the Parties

When the first edition of this work was published a large majority of states took the position that the wife's fault in the sense of marital misconduct either disqualified her for alimony entirely or was a factor to be considered in evaluating her claim for alimony. Conversely, the husband's marital misconduct was held by some courts to justify a larger award of alimony than would otherwise be granted, either on a theory of compensating the wife for the wrongs done to her or as punishment for the husband.

Although marital fault still appears quite often as a subject of comment in appellate cases dealing with alimony, its influence on alimony judgments seems to have diminished. In the first place the statutes of some states, under the influence of the Uniform Marriage and Divorce Act,[2] expressly provide that the award of alimony is to be made without regard to marital misconduct.[3] In a few other states it has been held that marital fault is no longer relevant to the alimony decision when

all reference to it was omitted from the alimony statute, even though consideration of it was not expressly forbidden.[4] In those states which have adopted one or more of the non-fault grounds for divorce, it may be argued that this indicates a legislative intent to eliminate acrimony and recriminations from divorce proceedings, and that it follows that fault should be irrelevant to the financial aspects of the litigation as well.[5]

Marital fault does continue to be a factor in the alimony decisions of a substantial number of state courts. Statutes in some jurisdictions either require or permit the courts to take account of marital conduct of either spouse in assessing alimony.[6] Even without express statutory authority some courts hold that fault is a relevant circumstance.[7] But the cases do not agree on the sort of marital misconduct which warrants consideration in the alimony decision. According to some, conduct which would constitute one of the fault grounds for divorce bars alimony.[8] Other cases consider it relevant to alimony that

2. Uniform Marriage and Divorce Act § 308(b), 9A Unif.L.Ann. 160 (1979).

3. Ariz.Rev.Stat. § 25.319 (1976); Alaska Stat. § 25.24.160 (1983); Colo.Rev.Stat. § 14–10–114(2) (1973); Ill.—Smith Hurd Ann. ch. 40, § 504 (Supp.1986); Minn. Stat.Ann. § 518.552(2) (Supp.1987); West's Rev.Code Wash.Ann. § 26.09.090(1) (1986).

4. In re Marriage of Tjaden, 199 N.W.2d 475 (Iowa 1972); Chapman v. Chapman, 498 S.W.2d 134 (Ky.1973); Wilson v. Wilson, 101 A.D.2d 536, 476 N.Y.S.2d 120 (1st Dept.1984) (dictum), appeal dismissed 63 N.Y.2d 768, 481 N.Y.S.2d 688, 471 N.E.2d 460 (1984); Dixon v. Dixon, 107 Wis.2d 492, 319 N.W.2d 846 (1982). See also cases cited in Annot., 86 A.L.R.3d 1116, 1129 (1978).

5. Murphy v. Murphy, 116 N.H. 672, 366 A.2d 479 (1976).

6. West's Fla.Stat.Ann. § 61.08 (1985) (court may consider the adultery of a spouse and the circumstances thereof); Official Code Ga.Ann. § 30–201 (Supp.1986) (no alimony where the separation was caused by a party's adultery or desertion); Md.Code, Fam.Law § 11–106 (1984) (court may consider the circumstances which contributed to the estrangement of the parties); Mass.Gen. Law Ann. c. 208, § 34 (Supp.1986) (court may consider the conduct of the parties during the marriage); Vernon's Ann.Mo.Stat. § 452.335 (court may consider the conduct of the parties during the marriage); Pa. Stat. tit. 23, § 501 (Supp.1986) (court may consider marital misconduct during the marriage but not after the separation); R.I.Gen.L.1986, § 15–5–16 (Supp.) (court may consider the conduct of the parties during the marriage); W.Va.Code, § 48–2–15(i) (1986).

The Florida statute was held constitutional in Pacheco v. Pacheco, 246 So.2d 778 (Fla.1971), appeal dismissed 404 U.S. 804, 92 S.Ct. 85, 30 L.Ed.2d 36 (1971). Anderson v. Anderson, 237 Ga. 886, 230 S.E.2d 272 (1976) held, notwithstanding the Georgia statute cited supra, that fault was not relevant to alimony when the divorce itself was granted on a non-fault ground.

7. Magruder v. Magruder, 190 Neb. 573, 209 N.W.2d 585 (1973), 54 Neb.L.Rev. 126 (1974) (semble); Mahne v. Mahne, 147 N.J.Super. 326, 371 A.2d 314 (1977), cert. denied 75 N.J. 22, 379 A.2d 253 (1977); Mees v. Mees, 325 N.W.2d 207 (N.D.1982).

8. E.g., Linda v. Linda, 352 So.2d 1208 (Fla.App.1977), cert. denied 360 So.2d 1249 (1978); Nethken v. Nethken, 307 So.2d 563 (La.1975); Higginbotham v. Higginbotham, 457 So.2d 165 (La.App.1984); Bender v. Bender, 282 Md. 525, 386 A.2d 772 (1978); Mahne v. Mahne, 147 N.J. Super. 326, 371 A.2d 314 (1977), cert. denied 75 N.J. 22, 379 A.2d 253 (1977); Annot., Adulterous Wife's Right to Permanent Alimony, 86 A.L.R.3d 97 (1978).

But some courts seem disposed to soften the requirement. See, e.g., Smith v. Smith, 378 So.2d 11 (Fla.App. 1979), cert. denied 388 So.2d 1118 (1980) (adultery occurring after separation is not relevant to alimony); Wallace v. Wallace, 290 Md. 265, 429 A.2d 232 (1981) (where adultery or abandonment are the sole cause of marriage breakup, there should be no alimony except in extremely extenuating circumstances); Moore v. Moore, 36 Md.App. 696, 375 A.2d 37 (1977) (condoned adultery does not bar alimony); Lynn v. Lynn, 165 N.J.Super. 328, 398 A.2d 141 (1979), certification denied 81 N.J. 52, 404 A.2d 1152 (1979) (post-separation adultery of the wife does not bar

the conduct of one of the spouses brought about their separation.[9] Still other courts ask whether there has been substantial inequitable conduct by a spouse.[10] This lack of agreement gives evidence of a recognition that the breakup of marriage is usually not attributable to the conduct of one spouse. It is more often the result of conflicts in the marriage relationship for which both spouses are responsible. At the same time these courts share a persistent conviction that there are circumstances, perhaps rarer than used to be thought, in which the conduct of a spouse seeking alimony has been so inimical to the marriage that fairness dictates she should not benefit financially from the relationship.[11] And in a few cases courts have a similar conviction that egregious conduct by a defendant should justify a larger than usual award of alimony.[12] This same ambivalence appears when the question is the division of property on divorce rather than alimony.[13] In both contexts the divorce process could be expedited and simplified if notions of fault could be forgotten.

7. The Form Which Alimony May Take

This section has already described the circumstances in which limited or rehabilitative alimony as distinguished from permanent or indefinite alimony may be awarded.[14] At this point other differences in the form of alimony awards will be briefly described.

Alimony is most commonly awarded in the form of periodic payments, indefinite in time and subject to future modification or termination by the court which granted it.[15] The statutes of many states authorize it to be ordered either in that form or as a lump sum.[16] Some cases have held that without statutory authority it may not be awarded in gross or as a lump sum.[17] Even where there is statutory authority to make awards in a single sum, there are courts which insist that periodic alimony is the preferred form of payment.[18] The reason is that awards in that form permit the court to amend the award in the future, thereby preventing hardship to either spouse in the event of a change in their circumstances. Lump sum alimony or alimony in gross is not subject to this control be-

alimony); Gugliotta v. Gugliotta, 160 N.J.Super. 160, 388 A.2d 1338 (1978), judgment affirmed 164 N.J.Super. 139, 395 A.2d 901 (1978) (adultery of the wife may be considered but did not bar alimony here); Kazin v. Kazin, 81 N.J. 85, 405 A.2d 360 (1979) (adultery not a per se bar to alimony, merely one circumstance to be weighed). In Kingsley v. Kingsley, 45 Md.App. 199, 412 A.2d 1263 (1980) the court stated that fault is to be considered only when it affects economic need.

9. Bryan v. Bryan, 242 Ga. 826, 251 S.E.2d 566 (1979); Nutter v. Nutter, ___ W.Va. ___, 327 S.E.2d 160 (1985).

10. Peremba v. Peremba, ___ W.Va. ___, 304 S.E.2d 880 (1983). Use of a standard as vague as this of course gives the trial court very broad discretion to consider or reject fault.

11. D'Arc v. D'Arc, 164 N.J.Super. 226, 395 A.2d 1270 (1978), modified on other grounds 175 N.J.Super. 598, 421 A.2d 602 (1980), cert. denied 451 U.S. 971, 101 S.Ct. 2049, 68 L.Ed.2d 350 (1981) in which both alimony and a division of property were denied to a husband when the trial court found that he had attempted to hire another person to murder the wife.

12. Claughton v. Claughton, 344 So.2d 944 (Fla.App. 1977); Pro v. Pro, 300 So.2d 288 (Fla.App.1974); Singer v. Singer, 8 Mass.App.Ct. 113, 391 N.E.2d 1239 (1979); Mees v. Mees, 325 N.W.2d 207 (N.D.1982); Dyer v. Tsapis, 162 W.Va. 289, 249 S.E.2d 509 (1978). Mahne v. Mahne, 147 N.J.Super. 326, 371 A.2d 314 (1977), cert. denied 75 N.J. 22, 379 A.2d 253 (1977) takes the untenable position that the wife's fault is relevant when she seeks alimony, but the husband's fault is not when he is the defendant.

13. See section 15.3, supra.

14. See the text at note 84, supra.

15. Green v. Green, 41 Ill.App.3d 154, 354 N.E.2d 661 (1976).

16. E.g., Alaska Stat. § 25.24.160 (Supp.1986); West's Fla.Stat.Ann. § 61.08 (1985); Ill.—Smith Hurd Ann. ch. 40, § 504 (Supp.1986); Mich.Code Law Ann. § 25.103 (Supp.1986); N.Y.—McKinney's Dom.Rel.Law § 236 Part B(6) (1986); Or.Rev.Stat. § 107.105(1)(d) (1983). The Uniform Marriage and Divorce Act contains no express authority for alimony in gross.

17. Welsh v. Welsh, 160 Fla. 380, 35 So.2d 6 (1948); Roberts v. Roberts, 160 Md. 513, 154 A. 95 (1931); Parmly v. Parmly, 125 N.J.Eq. 545, 5 A.2d 789 (Err. & App.1939). But see Roubicek v. Roubicek, 246 Ala. 442, 21 So.2d 244 (1945). There seems to be no substantial reason for requiring specific statutory authority and the modern cases seem to ignore any such requirement, in view of the broad discretion which trial courts are conceded in framing alimony awards. See, e.g. Moss v. Moss, 190 Colo. 491, 549 P.2d 404 (1976), decided under the Uniform Act.

18. Carlson v. Carlson, 178 Colo. 283, 497 P.2d 1006 (1972); Brandis v. Brandis, 51 Ill.App.3d 467, 9 Ill.Dec. 728, 367 N.E.2d 162 (1977); Green v. Green, 41 Ill.App.3d 154, 354 N.E.2d 661 (1976). But see Reed v. Reed, 457 S.W.2d 4 (Ky.1969), affirmed 484 S.W.2d 844 (Ky.1972), cert. denied 410 U.S. 931, 93 S.Ct. 1375, 35 L.Ed.2d 594 (1973), stating that lump sum alimony is favored.

cause it is usually held to be final and not modifiable.[19] An award of alimony in gross is therefore impossible to distinguish from a property division on divorce where the latter is to be accomplished by cash payments.[20]

Alimony in gross does have such substantial advantages for both parties that it is hard to understand why it is regarded as the less favored form of alimony. It offers the payer the assurance that he can plan his future life without the uncertainty caused by the possibility that his obligations under the divorce decree may be modified. The advantage to the payee is that she does not have to face the difficulty and expense of enforcing a periodic decree or the possibility that the payments will diminish with changes in the payer's circumstances. Obviously alimony in gross can only be awarded in those relatively unusual cases in which the payer's property is large enough to enable him to pay a substantial sum at once [21] or in installments.[22]

The choice between periodic alimony and alimony in gross is within the broad discretion of the trial court, reversible only where abuse of that discretion appears.[23] A major reason for choosing this form of alimony over a periodic award is that the uncertainty of the latter form is greater than usual due to the payer's resistance to complying with the decree, or to the hazards of his business, or to the possibility that he may leave the forum and thereby make enforcement of a periodic order difficult and expensive.[24] Many cases have found that awards of alimony in gross are appropriate for these and other reasons.[25]

The alimony decree may take still other forms. Although there is some authority that the husband may not be ordered to purchase an annuity to satisfy his alimony obligation,[26] this seems unnecessarily rigid,[27] at least in those states which permit alimony in gross. The decree may also order the husband to obtain or maintain life insurance for the benefit of the wife.[28] Alimony trusts may also be used to provide for the spouse, combining security with flexibility.[29] In order to protect the payee of alimony against inflation, some courts have held it within the trial court's discretion to insert in the alimony decree a provision that the alimony will increase in a specified degree when the payer's income increases.[30] This sort of provision has the additional virtue of lessening the need for modification proceedings, thereby saving court time and expense for the parties.

19. Scoville v. Scoville, 179 Conn. 277, 426 A.2d 271 (1979).

20. See section 16.1, supra. See Canakaris v. Canakaris, 382 So.2d 1197 (Fla.1980), in which the lump sum alimony award was used to accomplish an equitable division of property.

21. Miles v. Miles, 185 Or. 230, 202 P.2d 485 (1949).

22. Whitney v. Whitney, 164 Cal.App.2d 577, 330 P.2d 947 (1958).

23. Cummings v. Lockwood, 84 Ariz. 335, 327 P.2d 1012 (1958); La Bella v. La Bella, 134 Conn. 312, 57 A.2d 627 (1948); Canakaris v. Canakaris, 382 So.2d 1197 (Fla. 1980); Green v. Green, 41 Ill.App.3d 154, 354 N.E.2d 661 (1976); Reed v. Reed, 457 S.W.2d 4 (Ky.1969), affirmed 484 S.W.2d 844 (Ky.1972), cert. denied 410 U.S. 931, 93 S.Ct. 1375, 35 L.Ed.2d 594 (1973).

24. Green v. Green, 41 Ill.App.3d 154, 354 N.E.2d 661 (1976).

25. Moss v. Moss, 190 Colo. 491, 549 P.2d 404 (1976); Canakaris v. Canakaris, 382 So.2d 1197 (Fla.1980); Storer v. Storer, 353 So.2d 152 (Fla.App.1977), cert. denied 360 So.2d 1250 (1978); Hall v. Hall, 18 Ill.App.3d 583, 310 N.E.2d 186 (1974), appeal after remand 43 Ill.App.3d 97, 1 Ill.Dec. 874, 356 N.E.2d 1156 (1976); Reed v. Reed, 457

S.W.2d 4 (Ky.1969), affirmed 484 S.W.2d 844 (Ky.1972), cert. denied 410 U.S. 931, 93 S.Ct. 1375, 35 L.Ed.2d 594 (1973); Beals v. Beals, 682 P.2d 862 (Utah 1984).

Cases denying the equity of lump sum alimony include Carlson v. Carlson, 178 Colo. 283, 497 P.2d 1006 (1972); Brandis v. Brandis, 51 Ill.App.3d 467, 9 Ill.Dec. 728, 367 N.E.2d 162 (1977); Green v. Green, 41 Ill.App.3d 154, 354 N.E.2d 661 (1976); Miller v. Miller, 83 S.D. 227, 157 N.W.2d 537 (1968).

26. Elmer v. Elmer, 132 Colo. 57, 285 P.2d 601 (1955), appeal after remand 163 Colo. 430, 431 P.2d 470 (1967).

27. Note, 28 Rocky Mt.L.Rev. 423 (1956).

28. Annot., 59 A.L.R.3d 9 (1974), collecting cases.

29. Bowman v. Bowman, 29 Cal.2d 808, 178 P.2d 751 (1947); Annot., 170 A.L.R. 253 (1948).

30. Stanton-Abbott v. Stanton-Abbott, 372 Mass. 814, 363 N.E.2d 1311 (1977); Annot., Validity and Enforceability of Escalation Clause in Divorce Decree Relating to Alimony and Child Support, 19 A.L.R.4th 830 (1983). Contra, holding that an award may not be based upon uncertain future circumstances, In re Marriage of Davis, 44 Colo.App. 355, 618 P.2d 692 (1980); Jacobs v. Jacobs, 219 Va. 993, 254 S.E.2d 56 (1979).

8. Other Factors [31]

In addition to the factors already mentioned, courts also take into account in awarding alimony such considerations as the ages and health of the parties; [32] the duration of the marriage; [33] the standard of living maintained during the marriage; [34] what the wife gave up when she married the husband; [35] the property of the parties and whether the plaintiff contributed to its accumulation; [36] and the parties' other financial responsibilities. [37] Actually all of these factors are just specific indications of the needs of the plaintiff and the means of the defendant. They add little to analysis under the more general headings, provided that that analysis is conducted with care.

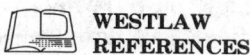

WESTLAW REFERENCES

The Functions of Alimony
di(function purpose /s alimony /s rehabilitat!)

alimony /s manner style standard /5 accustomed living /s maintain! /s marri! marital

ti(kover +s kover)

Factors to be Considered in Awarding Alimony
2. The Defendant's Ability to Pay
sy(husband /8 ability able capab! /3 pay /3 alimony)

3. The Plaintiff's Needs
alimony /s wife /s ability able capab! /5 work job employ****

to(134 /p sum amount) /p wife plaintiff /s (poor bad /3 health) sick! ill illness /s alimony

4. Limits on Duration: Rehabilitative Alimony
ti(grinold +s grinold)

6. The Fault of the Parties
sy(statute /s alimony /s misconduct conduct fault /s award)

§ 16.5 Modification of Alimony Decrees

Power to Modify Awards

The authority to modify periodic awards of alimony on account of subsequent changes in circumstance is granted to the courts in many states by statute.[1] The English courts had

---

31. See, e.g., West's Ann.Cal.Civ.Code § 4801 (Supp. 1987); Official Code Ga.Ann. § 30–209 (Supp.1986); Ill.—Smith Hurd Ann. ch. 40, § 504 (Supp.1986); Iowa Code Ann. § 598.21 (1981 and Supp.1986); N.Y.—McKinney's Dom.Rel.Law § 236 Part B(6) (1986); Or.Rev.Stat. § 107.105(1)(d) (1983); Pa.Stat. tit. 23, § 501 (Supp.1986) for comprehensive lists of relevant factors.

32. Hall v. Hall, 42 Cal.2d 435, 267 P.2d 249 (1954); Poppe v. Poppe, 114 Ind.App. 348, 52 N.E.2d 506 (1944); Waters v. Waters, 191 Md. 436, 62 A.2d 250 (1948); Wood v. Wood, 288 Mich. 14, 284 N.W. 627 (1939).

33. Fox v. Fox, 9 Ill.2d 509, 138 N.E.2d 547 (1956); Waters v. Waters, 191 Md. 436, 62 A.2d 250 (1948); Nickerson v. Nickerson, 152 Neb. 799, 42 N.W.2d 861 (1960); Pinion v. Pinion, 92 Utah 255, 67 P.2d 265 (1937).

34. Flanders v. Flanders, 241 Iowa 159, 40 N.W.2d 468 (1950); Prosser v. Prosser, 156 Neb. 629, 57 N.W.2d 173 (1953); Miles v. Miles, 185 Or. 230, 202 P.2d 485 (1949).

35. Prosser v. Prosser, 156 Neb. 629, 57 N.W.2d 173 (1953); Pinion v. Pinion, 92 Utah 255, 67 P.2d 265 (1937).

36. Roubicek v. Roubicek, 246 Ala. 442, 21 So.2d 244 (1945); Fox v. Fox, 9 Ill.2d 509, 138 N.E.2d 547 (1946); Poppe v. Poppe, 114 Ind.App. 348, 52 N.E.2d 506 (1944); Meads v. Meads, 182 Kan. 361, 320 P.2d 830 (1958); Baldridge v. Baldridge, 313 Ky. 604, 233 S.W.2d 95 (1950); Prosser v. Prosser, 156 Neb. 629, 57 N.W.2d 173 (1953).

37. Rovder v. Rovder, 78 N.E.2d 422 (Ohio App.1946).

§ 16.5

1. E.g., Ala.Code 1983, § 30–2–55; Alaska Stat. § 25.24.170 (1983); Ariz.Rev.Stat. § 25–327 (Supp. 1986) Ark.Stats. § 34–1213 (Sup. 1985); West's Ann.Cal.Civ. Code §§ 4801, 4801.5 (Supp. 1987); Colo.Rev.Stat. § 14–

10–122 (1973); Conn.Gen.Stat.Ann. § 46b–86 (1986); West's Fla.Stat.Ann. § 61.14 (Supp. 1987); Ill.—Smith Hurd Ann. ch. 40, § 510 (Supp. 1986); Iowa Code Ann. § 598.21 (Sup. 1986); Kan.Stat.Ann. § 60–1610 (Supp. 1986); Mass.Gen.Laws Ann. c. 208, § 37 (1981 and Supp. 1986); Mich.Comp.Law Ann. § 25.106 (1984); Minn.Stat. Ann. § 518.64 (Supp. 1987); Vernon's Ann.Mo.Stat. § 452.370 (Supp. 1987); N.J.Stat.Ann. § 2A:34–23 (Supp. 1986); N.Y.—McKinney's Dom.Rel.Law §§ 236 Part B 9b, 244 (1986); N.C.Gen.Stat. § 50–16.9 (1984); Ohio Rev. Code §§ 3105.18(C), (D) (Supp. 1986), (but there is no power to modify where the decree is for dissolution and is based on agreement); Knapp v. Knapp, 24 Ohio St.3d 141, 493 N.E.2d 1353 (1986); Okl.Stat. tit. 12, § 1277.6 (Supp. 1987); Or.Rev.Stat. § 107.135 (1983); Pa.Stat. tit. 23, § 501(e) (Supp. 1986); Tenn.Code Ann. § 36–5–101 (Supp. 1986); Utah Code Ann. 1986, § 30–3–5 (Supp.); Va.Code 1983, § 20–109; West's Rev.Code Wash.Ann. § 26.09.170 (1986); Wis.Stat.Ann. § 767.32 (Supp. 1986); Wyo.Stat.1977, § 20–2–116; Uniform Marriage and Divorce Act § 316, 9A Unif.L.Ann. 183 (1979).

The power to modify is usually not affected by the fact that the decree was based upon an agreement of the parties. Erickson v. Erickson, 181 Minn. 421, 232 N.W. 793 (1930), 15 Minn.L.Rev. 347 (1931); Annot., 61 A.L.R.3d 520 (1975). See also section 18.8, infra.

Where the state's statute authorizes alimony only for limited periods, modifications extending the period may be made before the period expires. See, e.g., Clevesy v. Clevesy, 118 N.H. 112, 383 A.2d 705 (1978); Healey v. Healey, 117 N.H. 618, 376 A.2d 140 (1977); Madsen v. Madsen, 111 N.H. 315, 282 A.2d 667 (1971); Ployer v. Ployer, 110 N.H. 338, 266 A.2d 848 (1970); Madsen v. Madsen, 109 N.H. 457, 255 A.2d 604 (1969); Homewood v.

this authority[2] and the practice of regarding alimony as modifiable came to this country along with other features of English divorce practice. Before the reform of the English divorce law in 1857 alimony was an incident to divorce *a mensa* only.[3] In this country it became an incident to divorce *a vinculo* also, but modifiability was generally retained, presumably on the familiar theory that alimony is a substitute for support and, support being subject to modification, alimony should be too.[4]

Where no authority to modify is given by statute, but the divorce decree expressly reserves jurisdiction to make further orders with respect to alimony, it is generally held that the decree may later be modified.[5] Alimony awards may be burdensome to the paying spouse and crucial to the welfare of the receiving spouse, so that changes in the situation of either can produce hardship if the decree is not modifiable. For this reason policy considerations should favor modifiability when jurisdiction is reserved in the decree. If the decree is unclear on whether jurisdiction has been reserved, doubts should therefore be resolved in favor of the power to modify.[6]

If no statute authorizes modification and the power to modify is not reserved in the original decree, most cases take the position that the alimony award may not be modified.[7] The reasoning underlying this position is conceptual rather than pragmatic. The status of husband and wife having terminated and the decree having become final in form, the argument goes, there is no authority upon which the court can base an order of modification. Although this argument is not convincing, the point is largely academic and unimportant, due to the prevalende of statutory authority to modify alimony.[8]

Where there is authority to modify alimony decrees, there is the further question whether the modification may be retroactive, that is, whether it is confined to future installments, or whether accrued, unpaid installments may be modified. Some of the statutes on modification answer this question, either by providing expressly that accrued installments may not be modified,[9] or by providing that they may be modified.[10] Where the statute does not contain any provision on the point, the majority of jurisdictions refuse to allow modification of accrued installments.[11] The reason usually given for this result is that as each installment accrues it is transformed into a final judgment for a fixed sum.[12] A better reason is the prevention of hardship to the recipient of alimony, most often the wife, by enabling her to rely upon the continuing alimony obligation of the husband. There are many unavoidable obstacles to her enforcement of the alimony decree without adding the risk that the husband may be able to have

---

Homewood, 11 Mass.App.Ct. 864, 420 N.E.2d 915 (1981) (New Hampshire law).

2. Cox v. Cox, 3 A. 276, 162 Eng.Rep. 480 (1826); De Blaquiere v. De Blaquiere, 3 Hagg.Ecc. 322, 162 Eng.Rep. 1173 (1830).

3. See section 12.1, supra.

4. Friedman v. Schneider, 52 So.2d 420 (Fla.1951); Emerson v. Emerson, 120 Md.584, 87 A. 1033 (1913).

5. In re Marriage of Vomacka, 36 Cal.3d 459, 204 Cal. Rptr. 568, 683 P.2d 248 (1984); Brinn v. Brinn, 147 Va. 277, 137 S.E. 503 (1927). The Virginia statute now authorizes modification. See note 1, supra.

6. In re Marriage of Vomacka, 36 Cal.3d 459, 204 Cal. Rptr. 568, 683 P.2d 248 (1984).

7. In re Marriage of Vomacka, 36 Cal.3d 459, 204 Cal. Rptr. 568, 683 P.2d 248 (1984); Brinn v. Brinn, 147 Va. 277, 137 S.E. 503 (1927) (citing other cases); Ruge v. Ruge, 97 Wash. 51, 165 P. 1063 (1917); Annots., 127 A.L.R. 741 (1940), 71 A.L.R 723 (1931); 18 A.L.R.2d 10 (1951). Contra: Garlington v. Garlington, 246 Ala. 665,

22 So.2d 89 (1945); Hunt v. Hunt, 169 Ohio St. 276, 159 N.E.2d 430 (1959). The similar rule that a divorce decree which is silent on the issue of alimony may not be modified later so as to include an award of alimony is discussed in section 16.3, supra. Compare McCarthy v. McCarthy, 293 Minn. 61, 196 N.W.2d 305 (1972), with Kaleal v. Kaleal, 73 Mich.App. 181, 250 N.W.2d 799 (1977).

8. See the statutes cited in note 1, supra.

9. E.g., the Arizona, California, Colorado, Illinois, Kansas, Missouri, Oklahoma, Oregon, Pennsylvania, Virginia, and Washington statutes, and the Uniform Marriage and Divorce Act cited in note 1, supra.

10. E.g., the New York statute cited in note 1, supra.

11. Sanchione v. Sanchione, 173 Conn. 397, 378 A.2d 522 (1977). Many other cases are collected in Annot., 52 A.L.R.3d 156 (1973). Contra: Rust v. Rust, 47 Wis.2d 565, 177 N.W.2d 888 (1970).

12. E.g., Bean v. Bean, 86 R.I. 334, 134 A.2d 146 (1957), 38 B.U.L.Rev. 152 (1958).

the accrued installments reduced.[13] But regard for the wife's position should not obscure the legitimate interests of the husband. Refusing to modify accrued installments may cause great hardship to him [14] and in some circumstances may result in a gratuitous and unfair windfall to the wife, as where she has remarried but he does not learn of her remarriage until after some installments have accrued.[15] Either because he does not know of changes in the wife's circumstances, or from ignorance of the necessity of a modification proceeding as a condition on reducing or terminating payments, the husband will usually fail to seek modification so long as the wife does not enforce the decree against him. When she does ask for enforcement of the accrued installments, the husband may have appealing reasons for being allowed a reduction, but most cases would hold that he must pay the full amount. Thus far the law seems to have been unable to devise a procedure flexible enough to protect the interests of both parties.[16]

An important distinction must be observed in deciding whether a particular decree is modifiable. As we have seen, if the decree orders the payment of periodic alimony, it may be modified on proof of changed circumstances.[17] But if the decree orders the payments as a means of carrying out a division of the parties' property, under many statutes [18] and the majority of cases [19] it may not be modified. The confusion in the cases which occurs when the courts attempt to articulate a distinction between an award of alimony and a division of property has been described in detail in an earlier section.[20] As matters now stand in the courts, there is no satisfactory way to be sure that a specific order will be characterized one way rather than the other, and therefore clearly modifiable or not modifiable. To some extent the label placed on the award by the parties or the court will carry weight in characterizing the award as alimony or property, but it will not usually be controlling.[21] And if the award is expressly made terminable on the remarriage of the

13. The relationship between modifiability and full faith and credit is important here. If the accrued installments are not modifiable, full faith and credit must be accorded to them. Enforcement in a foreign state is thus faster and simpler for the wife. If accrued installments are modifiable, full faith and credit need not be given. Compare on this point Griffin v. Griffin, 327 U.S. 220, 66 S.Ct. 556, 90 L.Ed. 635 (1946), rehearing denied 328 U.S. 876, 66 S.Ct. 975, 90 L.Ed. 1645 (1946), with Allingham v. Allingham, 141 Colo. 345, 348 P.2d 259 (1959). See the discussion of enforcement in foreign states in section 16.7, infra.

14. E.g., Stewart v. Stewart, 1 Ill.App.2d 283, 117 N.E.2d 579 (1954).

15. In Nelson v. Nelson, 282 Mo. 412, 221 S.W. 1066 (1920) the husband was required to pay alimony which had accrued over the preceding eleven yeas, even though the wife had been supported by her second husband during all that time. But cf. Swenson v. Swenson, 241 Mo.App. 21, 227 S.W.2d 103 (1950). In some states remarriage, by statute, automatically cuts off any right to alimony. See, e.g., the Arizona and California statutes and the Uniform Marriage and Divorce Act cited in note 1, supra, and Greene v. Greene, 102 Idaho 891, 643 P.2d 1061 (1982). Where the wife's remarriage automatically terminates her right to alimony but the husband continues to pay it in ignorance of the remarriage, it would seem that he should be entitled to restitution of the payments so made. Restatement, Restitution § 20 (1973); III G. Palmer, Law of Restitution ch. 14 (1978). In a state where the duty to pay continues until modification, no restitution could be granted. And in the intermediate situation, where the decree is modifiable as to arrears,

restitution should also be granted after modification has been obtained, but Schneider v. Schneider, 204 Misc. 918, 125 N.Y.S.2d 739 (1953) held otherwise. See also David v. David, 74 A.D.2d 542, 424 N.Y.S.2d 916 (1st Dept. 1980). Cf. Byrd v. Byrd, 78 Ohio App. 73, 69 N.E.2d 75 (1945) for a contrary holding on child support.

16. See Note, 22 Univ. of Chi.L.Rev. 246 (1954).

17. See the discussion at note 1, supra.

18. E.g., the Arizona, Colorado, Illinois, Minnesota, Oklahoma and Washington statutes and the Uniform Marriage and Divorce Act cited in note 1, supra.

19. Mackey v. Hall, 694 P.2d 1275 (Colo.1985); Bunche v. Bunche, 180 Conn. 285, 429 A.2d 874 (1980); Friedman v. Schneider, 52 So.2d 420 (Fla.1951); Duncan v. Duncan, 239 Ga. 789, 238 S.E.2d 902 (1977); Walters v. Walters, 409 Ill. 298, 99 N.E.2d 342 (1951); In re Marriage of Redmer, 111 Ill.App.3d 317, 66 Ill.Dec. 912, 443 N.E.2d 1075 (1982); Merrill v. Merrill, 449 A.2d 1120 (Me. 1982); Colizoli v. Colizoli, 15 Ohio St.3d 333, 474 N.E.2d 280 (1984) (dictum); Annot., 48 A.L.R.2d 270, 302 (1956).

A decree for the division of property may be vacated for reasons which justify the reopening of any judgment, however. See the statutes cited in note 18, supra, and the discussion in section 14.6, supra.

20. See section 15.1, supra. The confusion is especially acute when the courts speak of alimony in lieu of property. See, e.g., Isenhower v. Isenhower, 666 P.2d 238 (Okl.App.1983); Acker v. Acker, 594 P.2d 1216 (Okl.1979); Shea v. Shea, 537 P.2d 417 (Okl.1975).

21. Wagner v. Wagner, 25 Wash.App. 439, 607 P.2d 1251 (1980), judgment reversed on other grounds 95

recipient or on some other occurrence, this also may lead a court later to hold that it is alimony rather than property.[22] It is said by some courts that the distinction between alimony and property is to be made in reliance upon the intent of the parties and the circumstances of the case,[23] but of course the difficulties arise because the parties usually do not clearly express their intent and the circumstances of the cases are equivocal or ambiguous. Even if the payments may be characterized as alimony, many cases hold that they may not be modified where the award is a lump sum payable in installments.[24] These cases are not in accord with statutes authorizing the modification of alimony and they have no basis in policy.[25]

It may well be desirable to provide some procedure for achieving finality in awards of alimony. If it is true that a major purpose of alimony is to ease the adjustment to single status for the recipient,[26] that purpose may often be better served by a series of payments over a short period which both parties may count on as fixed and unalterable[27] than by the conventional periodic alimony lasting in-

definitely and always open to increase or decrease with the parties' changing circumstances. The alimony-property distinction is a judicially designed device for accomplishing this, but it is based on the fiction that there is some perceptible difference between awards of alimony and of property. There is no such difference. This purpose is much better achieved in several other ways already available in the various states. Rehabilitative alimony is one.[28] Another is the stricter standard for modifying alimony now prevailing in some states.[29] A third is the provision in the Uniform Marriage and Divorce Act[30] which permits the parties to agree that alimony will not be modifiable and which permits that agreement to be incorporated in the divorce decree itself, thereby achieving the finality which the alimony-property distinction aims for.

Procedure for Modification of Alimony

Proceedings for the modification of alimony decrees may be commenced by the filing of a motion or petition in the original divorce ac-

---

Wash.2d 94, 621 P.2d 1279 (1980). Similar difficulties of construction may arise when the parties deliberately omit to place a label on the award, which is sometimes done for tax purposes. See, e.g., Carter v. Carter, 215 Va. 475, 211 S.E.2d 253 (1975). In Greer v. Greer, 32 Colo. App. 196, 510 P.2d 905 (1973) an award labeled alimony by the parties was held to be a division of property when its purpose was shown to be the reimbursement of the wife for supporting the husband when he was in medical school. The parties' characterization of the award was persuasive to the court in Thompson v. Thompson, 82 Wash.2d 352, 510 P.2d 827 (1973), however.

22. Wagner v. Wagner, 25 Wash.App. 439, 607 P.2d 1251 (1980), judgment reversed on other grounds 95 Wash.2d 94, 621 P.2d 1279 (1980); Duncan v. Duncan, 239 Ga. 789, 238 S.E.2d 902 (1977) (absence of a provision for termination on remarriage indicated a division of property); Colizoli v. Colizoli, 15 Ohio St.3d 333, 474 N.E.2d 280 (1984) (award was made for a fixed amount over a definite number of years and was therefore a division of property).

23. Thus the purpose of the award is sometimes thought to be indicative. But compare In re Marriage of Redmer, 111 Ill.App.3d 317, 66 Ill.Dec. 912, 443 N.E.2d 1075 (1982) with Remmem v. Remmem, 73 Wash.2d 560, 439 P.2d 983 (1968). In Wagner v. Wagner, 25 Wash. App. 439, 607 P.2d 1251 (1980), judgment reversed on other grounds 95 Wash.2d 94, 621 P.2d 1279 (1980) the court characterized the award as alimony even though it conceded that the recipient had such a large estate that

an award of alimony would have seemed inappropriate since she had no need of support.

In Reiss v. Reiss, 200 N.J.Super. 122, 490 A.2d 378 (1984), affirmed 205 N.J.Super. 41, 500 A.2d 24 (1985) the court held that reimbursement alimony was not modifiable on the wife's remarriage, saying that it was neither alimony nor a marital asset. And in Bullock v. Bullock, 376 N.W.2d 30 (N.D.1985) the court held that rehabilitative alimony could continue after the wife's remarriage, as did In re Marriage of Orgren, 375 N.W.2d 710 (Iowa 1985).

24. Cummings v. Lockwood, 84 Ariz. 335, 327 P.2d 1012 (1958); Whitney v. Whitney, 15 Ill.App.2d 425, 146 N.E.2d 800 (1957); Ball v. Ball, 183 Neb. 216, 159 N.W.2d 297 (1968); Kishner v. Kishner, 93 Nev. 220, 562 P.2d 493 (1977).

25. Sinn v. Sinn, 696 P.2d 333 (Colo.1985).

26. See section 16.4, supra.

27. Ziegenbein v. Damme, 138 Neb. 320, 292 N.W. 921 (1940).

28. See section 16.4, supra.

29. See the Uniform Marriage and Divorce Act § 316, 9A Unif.L.Ann. 183 (1979), permitting modification only where the circumstances have changed so substantially and continuously as to make the original award unconscionable. See the discussion infra at note 47.

30. Uniform Marriage and Divorce Act § 306(f), 9A Unif.L.Ann. 136 (1979).

tion.[31] Since the modification is deemed to be a continuation of the original divorce action, a new assertion of personal jurisdiction over the defendant is not required,[32] provided of course that personal jurisdiction over the defendant was acquired when the alimony decree was granted.[33] But reasonable notice of the motion for modification must be given to the adverse party.[34] The notice may be served on the adverse party's attorney in the divorce action.[35]

The questions whether the alimony decree should be modified and if so, to what extent are held to be within the sound discretion of the trial court, to be reversed on appeal only where there has been an abuse of that discretion.[36] The party seeking the modification has the burden of proof.[37]

To avoid relitigation of matters already settled, courts in modification proceedings allow the parties only to present evidence going back to the latest petition for modification. Thus if the wife moves for an increase in alimony and loses, a subsequent motion by the husband for a reduction would have to be based upon changes in circumstances occurring after the wife's petition.[38] This means that when either party asks for a modification the other party must also seek modification on pain of losing any further opportunity based upon conditions existing up to that time. When modification is granted, the court has discretion to make it effective as of the date of the petition for modification as well as the date of the order.[39]

Interstate Modification of Alimony [40]

The mobility of the American population makes it inevitable that the courts of one state will be asked to modify the divorce decrees of another state. This raises two questions: a) May the divorce decree in state A be modified by the courts of state B? b) What law is to be applied in answering this question?

Although it seems clear that the courts of one state do not have the power directly to modify the decrees of another state, since the states are sovereign in our federal system, the same result may be reached indirectly. Pursuant to the much cited opinion in Worthley v. Worthley,[41] the second state may first makes the alimony decree of the first state its own decree and then proceeds to modify its own decree. In order to do this the second state must of course acquire personal jurisdiction over the defendant. The same result may be reached by the use of the procedure provided in the Uniform Reciprocal Enforcement of Support Act.[42]

The choice of law question is more difficult. The Worthley case and others have taken the

---

31. Van Divort v. Van Divort, 165 Ohio St. 141, 134 N.E.2d 715 (1956).

32. Heuchan v. Heuchan, 38 Wash.2d 207, 228 P.2d 470 (1951); State ex rel. Ravitz v. Fox, 166 W.Va. 194, 273 S.E.2d 370 (1980) (state's jurisdiction to modify continues even after the defendant moves out of the state); Annot., 62 A.L.R.2d 544 (1958).

33. Annot., 62 A.L.R.2d 544 (1958).

34. Kosch v. Kosch, 113 So.2d 547 (Fla.1959), conformed to 114 So.2d 18 (Fla.App.1959); Annot., 62 A.L.R.2d 544 (1958).

35. Reynolds v. Reynolds, 21 Cal.2d 580, 134 P.2d 251 (1943); Scarth v. Scarth, 211 Or. 121, 315 P.2d 141 (1957).

36. Nace v. Nace, 107 Ariz. 411, 489 P.2d 48 (1971); Grinold v. Grinold, 172 Conn. 192, 374 A.2d 172 (1976); Williams v. Williams, 444 A.2d 977 (Me. 1982); Esslinger v. Esslinger, 9 Mich.App. 11, 155 N.W.2d 702 (1967); Lovato v. Lovato, 98 N.M. 11, 644 P.2d 525 (1982); Vander Perren v. Vander Perren, 105 Wis.2d 219, 313 N.W.2d 813 (1982). An even more limited role for appellate courts is announced in Smith v. Smith, 419 A.2d 1035 (Me.1980).

37. Scott v. Scott, 121 Ariz. 492, 591 P.2d 980 (1979); Olsen v. Olsen, 98 Idaho 10, 557 P.2d 604 (1976); In re Marriage of Lasota, 125 Ill.App.3d 37, 80 Ill.Dec. 537, 465 N.E.2d 649 (1984).

38. Heuchan v. Heuchan, 38 Wash.2d 207, 228 P.2d 470 (1951).

39. Movius v. Movius, 163 Mont. 463, 517 P.2d 884 (1974).

40. This subject is closely related to the interstate enforcement of alimony decrees discussed infra in section 16.7.

41. 44 Cal.2d 465, 283 P.2d 19 (1955), per Traynor, J. See also Brisco v. Brisco, 355 So.2d 506 (Fla.App.1978); Malmgren v. Malmgren, 628 P.2d 164 (Colo.App.1981); Bohner v. Bohner, 18 Mass.App.Ct. 545, 468 N.E.2d 653 (1984), review denied 393 Mass. 1102, 470 N.E.2d 798 (1984), applying Mass.Gen.Laws Ann. ch. 208, § 37 (Supp. 1985); Gray v. Gray, 32 Mich.App. 466, 189 N.W.2d 145 (1971).

42. The conflict problems created by this Act are discussed in section 6.6, supra.

position that either party may raise any question of modification in the second state which they could have raised in the first state.[43] At the least this means that if the original decree was modifiable where entered, it may be modified in the second state. If not modifiable in the first state, the Full Faith and Credit Clause would foreclose modification in the second state.[44]

The further question, whether the second state's court may apply its own law in determining the grounds for modification, is not often discussed in the cases. It would seem that if both parties have become domiciliaries of the second state, that state's interests should prevail to the extent that modification should be granted or denied on the basis of that state's law.[45] Where only one party is domiciled in the state, there is no rational basis for choosing the law of either state except perhaps to vindicate the original expectations of the parties. This would indicate continuing to rely on the law of the divorcing state.[46]

Factors Influencing Modification

Alimony may only be modified upon proof that the relevant circumstances have changed substantially since the original decree was granted, that the changes will continue, that the changes were not contemplated or provided for changes will continue, and that the changes were not contemplated or provided for in the original decree.[47] There may not be a retrial of questions already decided.[48] In general the same sorts of circumstances are relevant in deciding whether the decree may be modified as are relevant in making the initial award of alimony.[49] These have to do with the needs and financial resources of the parties. Some changes in the parties circumstances raise specific issues peculiar to modification, however. These are discussed below.

1. Changes in the Recipient's Needs and Resources [50]

To the extent that the recipient's needs have increased since the divorce, alimony may be increased, provided that the other party is able to pay the larger amount.[51] The increase may be due to ill health,[52] a general

43. Worthley v. Worthley, 44 Cal.2d 465, 283 P.2d 19 (1955); Brisco v. Brisco, 355 So.2d 506 (Fla.App.1978); Lumpkins v. Lumpkins, 83 N.M. 591, 495 P.2d 371 (1972); Gorvin v. Stegmann, 74 Wash.2d 177, 443 P.2d 821 (1968). See also E. Scoles and P. Hay, Conflict of Laws §§ 15.37, 15.38 (1982). The conflicts which arise when modification is granted, producing a situation in which there are two different state court alimony decrees outstanding, are discussed in connection with the Uniform Reciprocal Enforcement of Support Act in section 6.6, supra.

44. Lumpkins v. Lumpkins, 83 N.M. 591, 495 P.2d 371 (1972).

45. E. Scoles and P. Hay, Conflict of Laws § 15.38 (1982) seem not to deal with this situation.

46. E. Scoles and P. Hay, Conflict of Laws § 15.38 (1982).

47. Cummock v. Cummock, 180 Conn. 218, 429 A.2d 474 (1980), appeal after remand 188 Conn. 30, 448 A.2d 204 (1982); Withers v. Withers, 390 So.2d 453 (Fla.App. 1980), review denied 399 So.2d 1147 (1981); Lepis v. Lepis, 83 N.J. 139, 416 A.2d 45 (1980); Naylor v. Naylor, 700 P.2d 707 (Utah 1985).

In an effort to discourage repeated or insubstantial motions for modification, the Uniform Marriage and Divorce Act § 316, 9A Unif.L.Ann. 183, 184 (1979) requires proof of changed circumstances so substantial and continuing as to make the terms of the original decree unconscionable before modification may be granted. The term "unconscionable" is not defined, although in relation to

another provision of the Act the term has been defined to mean that the alimony provision is not fair, just and reasonable. In re Marriage of Manzo, 659 P.2d 669 (Colo. 1983), citing other cases.

48. Colton v. Colton, 252 Ala. 442, 41 So.2d 398 (1949); Lyons v. Lyons, 240 Iowa 698, 37 N.W.2d 309 (1949); Yendes, Res Judicata in the Divorce Courts as Affects the Modification of Alimony Awards, 38 Neb.L.Rev. 989 (1959). But there may be relief from the original judgment on the same grounds and in compliance with the same conditions as in the case of relief from judgments in general. Larson v. Larson, 661 P.2d 626 (Alaska 1983); Roth v. Roth, 45 Ill.2d 19, 256 N.E.2d 838 (1970).

49. Cummock v. Cummock, 180 Conn. 218, 429 A.2d 474 (1980), appeal after remand 188 Conn. 30, 448 A.2d 204 (1982); Haskell v. Haskell, 119 Minn. 484, 138 N.W. 787 (1912); Bonanno v. Bonanno, 4 N.J. 268, 72 A.2d 318 (1950); Desvernine, Grounds for the Modification of Alimony Awards, 6 J. & Contemp.Prob. 236, 239 (1939).

50. For extensive citation of the earlier cases see Annot., Change in Financial Condition or Needs of Husband or Wife as Ground for Modification of Decree for Alimony or Maintenance, 18 A.L.R.2d 10 (1951).

51. McArthur v. McArthur, 95 So.2d 521 (Fla.1957); Lepis v. Lepis, 83 N.J. 139, 416 A.2d 45 (1980); Annot., 18 A.L.R.2d 10, 59 (1951).

52. McArthur v. McArthur, 95 So.2d 521 (Fla.1957); Louthan v. Louthan, 130 Ill.App.2d 281, 264 N.E.2d 797 (1970); Cecil v. Cecil, 179 Va. 274, 19 S.E.2d 64 (1942). In

increase in the cost of living,[53] additional expenses attributable to the children [54] (when they are not separately provided for in the divorce decree), and other similar factors.[55] In assessing the recipient's need for increased alimony the court should not be limited to the bare necessities of life but rather should consider the recipient's reasonable needs in relation to the payer's income, just as is the case when alimony is initially being granted.[56] Where the wife's increase in need is due to a voluntary change in her way of life, however, the courts have been reluctant to grant her an increase in alimony.[57]

Conversely, where the alimony recipient gets an appropriate job and thereby becomes self-supporting, the cases generally find that a reason to reduce or wholly terminate alimony.[58] Some cases go further, using a reduction or termination of alimony as a means of forcing the wife to find a job.[59] Other changes in circumstance which reduce the wife's need and therefore justify a reduction or termination of alimony include the inheri-

tance of property.[60] If the wife continues to be responsible for the care of children, it may be unwarranted to expect her to become self-supporting, however.[61] In all such cases the courts should exercise careful judgment in arriving at realistic assessments of the wife's ability to live reasonably and adequately on her own earnings.

2. Changes in the Payer's Needs and Resources

If after the divorce the husband's income declines to such an extent that he is materially less able to pay the alimony awarded, he may have the award reduced.[62] Whether merely temporary financial difficulties are sufficient to justify reduction of alimony depends upon how severe they are and upon the extent to which they interfere with the husband's ability to pay.[63] Though not strictly speaking a change in circumstances, a reduction in alimony may be granted when the initial decree was based upon expectations

---

what appears an extraordinary case the court cut off alimony where the wife's psychiatric condition caused her to lose many jobs and to undergo a reduction of earnings. Jeppson v. Jeppson, 684 P.2d 69 (Utah 1984). The wife's alcoholism was held not to be a reason for suspending or reducing alimony in Roberts v. Roberts, 35 Md.App. 497, 371 A.2d 689 (1977).

53. Siegel v. Siegel, 26 Cal.App.3d 88, 102 Cal.Rptr. 613 (1972); Arnold v. Arnold, 332 Ill.App. 586, 76 N.E.2d 335 (1947); Lane v. Lane, 439 S.W.2d 550 (Mo.App.1969); Lepis v. Lepis, 83 N.J. 139, 416 A.2d 45 (1980); Naylor v. Naylor, 700 P.2d 707 (Utah 1985). But see Grinold v. Grinold, 172 Conn. 192, 374 A.2d 172 (1976).

54. Siegel v. Seigel, 26 Cal.App.3d 88, 102 Cal.Rptr. 613 (1972); Cummock v. Cummock, 180 Conn. 218, 429 A.2d 474 (1980), appeal after remand 188 Conn. 30, 448 A.2d 204 (1982); Lane v. Lane, 439 S.W.2d 550 (Mo.App. 1969); Lepis v. Lepis, 83 N.J. 139, 416 A.2d 45 (1980).

55. E.g., Bonanno v. Bonanno, 4 N.J. 268, 72 A.2d 318 (1950).

56. Siegel v. Siegel, 26 Cal.App.3d 88, 102 Cal.Rptr. 613 (1972).

57. Nace v. Nace, 107 Ariz. 411, 489 P.2d 48 (1971); Sistrunk v. Sistrunk, 235 So.2d 53 (Fla.App. 1970).

58. Hornbaker v. Hornbaker, 25 Ariz.App. 577, 545 P.2d 425 (1976); Anderson v. Anderson, 333 So.2d 484 (Fla.App. 1976) (alimony terminated when the wife became self-supporting even though the husband had a much larger income); Moran v. Moran, 681 S.W.2d 510 (Mo.App. 1984); Cooper v. Cooper, 219 Neb. 64, 361 N.W.2d 202 (1985); Ward v. Ward, 41 Or.App. 447, 599 P.2d 1150 (1979); Dehm v. Dehm, 545 P.2d 525 (Utah

1976). But alimony was reduced rather than terminated in Carter v. Carter, 584 P.2d 904 (Utah 1978) when the wife obtained a job, the court saying that a wife who is enterprising and finds work should not be penalized for her efforts.

Lane v. Lane, 35 Ill.App.3d 276, 340 N.E.2d 705 (1975), cert. denied 429 U.S. 886, 97 S.Ct. 238, 50 L.Ed.2d 167 (1976) held that alimony would not be reduced when the wife entered a convent preparatory to becoming a nun.

59. Lasota v. Lasota, 125 Ill.App.3d 37, 80 Ill.Dec. 537, 465 N.E.2d 649 (1984); Lovato v. Lovato, 98 N.M. 11, 644 P.2d 525 (1982).

60. Brady v. Brady, 94 Cal.App.2d 1, 210 P.2d 69 (1949); In re Marriage of Horowitz, 159 Cal.App.3d 368, 205 Cal.Rptr. 874 (1984).

61. Jourdan v. Jourdan, 251 S.W.2d 380 (Mo.App. 1952). In Lovato v. Lovato, 98 N.M. 11, 644 P.2d 525 (1982) the court ordered the reduction of alimony notwithstanding that the wife did not have a job and still had custody of three of seven children.

62. In re Marriage of Dixon, 683 P.2d 803 (Colo.App. 1983); Vilas v. Vilas, 153 Fla. 102, 13 So.2d 807 (1943); Scalfaro v. Scalfaro, 123 Ill.App.2d 23, 259 N.E.2d 644 (1970); Smith v. Smith, 419 A.2d 1035 (Me.1980); Nelson v. Nelson, 225 Or. 257, 357 P.2d 536 (1960); Annot., 18 A.L.R.2d 10, 30 (1951). But a prediction of changed circumstances may not be relied upon to reduce alimony. Scott v. Scott, 121 Ariz. 492, 591 P.2d 980 (1979).

63. Cf. McDonald v. McDonald, 6 N.J.Super. 11, 69 A.2d 593 (1949) with Kelly v. Kelly, 194 Mich. 94, 160 N.W. 397 (1916) and Dillon v. Dillon, 21 Wash.2d 311, 150 P.2d 594 (1944).

concerning the husband's future earnings which were not fulfilled.[64]

The traditional view of the courts was that a voluntary reduction of income on the husband's part, as for example when he retired from active employment, did not warrant a reduction in alimony.[65] This is too broad a rule to fit contemporary circumstances, in which early retirements and abrupt career changes are not uncommon. A husband who is paying alimony ought to be entitled to make, in good faith, the same decisions about his career that he could have made if the divorce had not occurred.[66] The question always is the meaning and application of the term "good faith". If the husband's primary purpose in making the change is to frustrate his ex-wife's claim for alimony, then the change should not result in a reduction.[67] If that is not the primary purpose, the reduction may be appropriate, depending in part of course upon the wife's circumstances. Determining what the purposes of the change are and distinguishing between proper and improper purposes are the kinds of factual issues that trial courts are accustomed to resolving in all kinds of contexts. Very often there will be external circumstances which are helpful in resolving them, such as the age,

health and work situation of the husband and his conduct of his financial affairs.[68]

The payer's remarriage is also a voluntarily undertaken change of circumstances. Since it produces additional demands on the payer's resources, it is a factor to be considered in the reduction of alimony,[69] but it does not necessarily require a reduction.[70] If the second spouse has income, that income should be taken into account in determining the resources of the payer, since that spouse of course has a duty to provide for the payer's support.[71]

A complex issue is raised when, after divorce, the payer-husband's fortunes greatly improve. In a leading case the Illinois court held that when that happened the wife was entitled only to be supported on the scale which she enjoyed at the time of the divorce, and that she could not be granted an increase in alimony solely on the basis of the husband's greater wealth.[72] Although alimony necessarily must decline with the husband's declining prosperity, it does not follow that it should rise if he strikes it rich.[73] The purpose of alimony is to care for the wife's needs after divorce, not to provide her with a lifetime

---

64. Bratnober v. Bratnober, 48 Cal.2d 259, 309 P.2d 441 (1957); Douglas v. Douglas, 109 N.H. 41, 242 A.2d 78 (1968). But some cases take the position that inability to pay the sums decreed in the divorce is not a change in circumstances and therefore does not justify reduction. E.g., D'Arezzo v. D'Arezzo, 107 R.I. 422, 267 A.2d 683 (1970).

65. Tydings v. Tydings, 349 A.2d 462 (D.C.App.1975); Olsen v. Olsen, 98 Idaho 10, 557 P.2d 604 (1976); Ellis v. Ellis, 262 N.W.2d 265 (Iowa 1978); Smith v. Smith, 299 Ky. 715, 187 S.W.2d 271 (1945); Nelson v. Nelson, 225 Or. 257, 357 P.2d 536 (1960) (dictum); Annot., 18 A.L.R.2d 10, 51 (1951). Some courts put the same point in somewhat different terms by saying that they will be guided by the husband's potential for earning income rather than by his actual income. See, e.g., Schuler v. Schuler, 382 Mass. 366, 416 N.E.2d 197 (1981).

66. Giacalone, The Drop-Out Ex-Husband's Right to Reduce Alimony and Support Payments, 1 Fam.L.Rptr. 4065 (1975).

67. Smith v. Smith, 419 A.2d 1035 (Me.1980), containing a careful and discriminating discussion of this issue.

68. Such facts were present in In re Marriage of Kowski, 123 Ill.App.3d 811, 79 Ill.Dec. 286, 463 N.E.2d 840 (1984); Smith v. Smith, 419 A.2d 1035 (Me.1980);

Villano v. Villano, 98 Misc.2d 774, 414 N.Y.S.2d 625 (1979).

69. Philbin v. Philbin, 19 Cal.App.3d 115, 96 Cal.Rptr. 408 (1971); Tan v. Tan, 3 Ill.App.3d 671, 279 N.E.2d 486 (1972); Cooper v. Cooper, 219 Neb. 64, 361 N.W.2d 202 (1985); Berg v. Berg, 116 R.I. 607, 359 A.2d 354 (1976). The same question arises in connection with the modification of child support. See section 17.2, infra.

70. Williams v. Williams, 444 A.2d 977 (Me.1982).

71. Gammell v. Gammell, 90 Cal.App.3d 90, 153 Cal. Rptr. 169 (1979).

72. Arnold v. Arnold, 332 Ill.App. 586, 76 N.E.2d 335 (1947). In accord are Russell v. Russell, 79 U.S.App.D.C. 44, 142 F.2d 753 (1944); Burr v. Burr, 313 Mich. 330, 21 N.W.2d 150 (1946); Kaiser v. Kaiser, 290 Minn. 173, 186 N.W.2d 678 (1971); Annot., 18 A.L.R.2d 10, 25 (1951).

73. But some cases accept this argument. See Lott v. Lott, 17 Md.App. 440, 302 A.2d 666 (1973); Martindell v. Martindell, 21 N.J. 341, 122 A.2d 352 (1956); Balmer v. Balmer, 12 Misc.2d 226, 179 N.Y.S.2d 234 (1958), modified 7 A.D.2d 741, 180 N.Y.S.2d 1017 (2d Dept. 1958), affirmed 7 N.Y.2d 833, 196 N.Y.S.2d 707, 164 N.E.2d 725 (1959); Commonwealth ex rel. Levy v. Levy, 240 Pa.Super. 168, 361 A.2d 781 (1976) (semble).

profit-sharing plan.[74] But if the original award was less than she really needed because of the husband's inability to pay more, then his later prosperity should justify an increase up to the amount necessary to provide the wife with adequate support.[75] To that extent improvement in the husband's earning power is sufficient to support a modification of alimony.

3. Violation of the Original Divorce Decree

The husband sometimes seeks to reduce or terminate alimony payments on the ground that the wife has violated the divorce decree, usually by refusing to honor its provisions for the husband's visitations with the children. The courts are usually reluctant to modify the decree on such grounds,[76] but on occasion they will suspend alimony on this ground.[77] Presumably it may be reinstated when the violation of the decree ends. In the very similar case where the husband seeks to end his child support payments on the wife's frustration of his visitation rights, the courts almost always refuse modification, since modification would normally prejudice the child's welfare.[78]

In the converse situation, where the husband is in default on his alimony obligation, the courts will entertain a motion to modify, but of course that would not excuse the husband from any past defaults except in those states where retroactive modification is permitted.[79]

4. The Recipient's Remarriage

The change in circumstance which most obviously calls for a modification of alimony is the remarriage of the recipient, usually the wife.[80] The cases sometimes give as reasons for terminating alimony when the wife remarries that she has "elected" to be supported by her second husband,[81] or that she has "abandoned" her claim for support against her first husband.[82] A better reason is that the purpose of alimony has been achieved when she contracts a second marriage. That purpose is to mitigate the hardship caused by the termination of the marriage.[83] When the wife contracts a new marriage, those hardships are over and all incidents of the first marriage should likewise terminate. If this were not so, she would be in the very odd position of being entitled to support from her first husband in the form of alimony at the same time she is entitled to support from her second husband.

Termination of alimony upon the wife's remarriage is automatic under the statutes of some states.[84] This means that the husband may stop paying at once, without having the decree modified.[85] In the absence of a statute of this kind, it is usually held that the decree must be modified in order to end the hus-

---

74. Calderwood v. Calderwood, 114 N.H. 651, 327 A.2d 704 (1974), appeal after remand 115 N.H. 550, 345 A.2d 166 (1975) (dictum).

75. McCann v. McCann, 191 Conn. 447, 464 A.2d 825 (1983); Hardisty v. Hardisty, 183 Conn. 253, 439 A.2d 307 (1981); Howat v. Howat, 1 Conn.App. 400, 472 A.2d 799 (1984); Fender v. Fender, 256 S.C. 399, 182 S.E.2d 755 (1971); Naylor v. Naylor, 700 P.2d 707 (Utah 1985).

76. Blank v. District Court In & For Boulder County, 190 Colo. 114, 543 P.2d 1255 (1975).

77. Gordon v. Gordon, 368 So.2d 1356 (Fla.App.1979); Ruquist v. Ruquist, 367 Mass. 662, 327 N.E.2d 742 (1975); Noble v. Noble, 86 Nev. 459, 470 P.2d 430 (1970).

78. See section 17.2, infra.

79. Sanchione v. Sanchione, 173 Conn. 397, 378 A.2d 522 (1977).

80. See the cases cited in Annot., 48 A.L.R.2d 270 (1956). Remarriage of the parties to each other may also be a ground to terminate the alimony. Annot., 52 A.L.R.3d 1334 (1973).

81. Voyles v. Voyles, 644 P.2d 847 (Alaska 1982).

82. Cary v. Cary, 112 Conn. 256, 152 A. 302 (1930); Hunt v. Hunt, 169 Ohio St. 276, 159 N.E.2d 430 (1959).

83. See section 16.4, supra, and In re Marriage of Shima, 360 N.W.2d 827 (Iowa 1985); Bubar v. Plant, 141 Me. 407, 44 A.2d 732 (1945); Wolfe v. Wolfe, 124 N.E.2d 485 (Ohio Com.Pl.1954); Nelson v. Nelson, 181 Or. 494, 182 P.2d 416 (1947); Austad v. Austad, 2 Utah 2d 49, 269 P.2d 284 (1954).

84. See the Alabama, Arizona, California, Colorado, Illinois, Minnesota, Missouri, New York, Oklahoma, Utah, Virginia and Washington statutes cited in note 1, supra. See also the Uniform Marriage and Divorce Act § 316, 9A Unif.L.Ann. 183 (1979).

85. Tomkins v. Tomkins, 89 Cal.App.2d 243, 200 P.2d 821 (1948). The reason given is that the statutory limitation becomes a part of the alimony decree, making it read, in effect, that alimony is granted only so long as the wife remains unmarried.

band's obligation.[86] If the parties are in a state which only permits the modification of future, unaccrued installments, this requirement may lead the husband to be liable for alimony accruing after the wife's remarriage.

Some of the statutes which provide for the automatic termination of alimony upon the recipient's remarriage also provide a method by which the remarriage can be prevented from having that effect. Usually this may be done by an express agreement in writing or by an express provision in the divorce decree.[87]

If there is no statute which specifically provides for the termination of alimony upon the recipient's remarriage, the question arises whether termination is to be automatically granted by the courts or whether there may be some situations in which the remarriage does not end the right to alimony. Some cases do hold that the court has no choice but to terminate the alimony when the wife remarries.[88] These cases are clearly correct.

There is no good reason why alimony should continue in such circumstances.

Many courts are oddly reluctant to reach this result, however. They say that although the wife's remarriage is generally a good reason to terminate the alimony, there may be situations in which this should not be done.[89] Such statements usually prove to be dictum, but there are some cases in which the first husband is required to continue supporting his ex-wife even after her marriage to another man.[90] Some of these cases occur when the second marriage is annulled, the courts taking the position that the annulment amounts to a declaration that the second marriage never existed.[91] It has been shown in an earlier section [92] that contemporary cases generally reject that view and treat the effect of annulment as analogous to the effect of divorce. By that analysis the annulment of the wife's second marriage would not revive her rights under the alimony decree, and the better reasoned cases so hold.[93]

86. Hartigan v. Hartigan, 145 Minn. 27, 176 N.W. 180 (1920); Nelson v. Nelson, 282 Mo. 412, 221 S.W. 1066 (1920); Bean v. Bean, 86 R.I. 334, 134 A.2d 146 (1957); Annot., 48 A.L.R.2d 270, 292 (1956).

87. Uniform Marriage and Divorce Act § 316(b), 9A Unif.L.Ann. 183 (1979); Mason v. Mason, 40 Wash.App. 450, 698 P.2d 1104 (1985).

88. Voyles v. Voyles, 644 P.2d 847 (Alaska 1982); White v. Murden, 190 Ga. 536, 9 S.E.2d 745 (1940); Wolfe v. Wolfe, 124 N.E.2d 485 (Ohio Com.Pl.1954) (semble). If the wife enters into a relationship in another state than the one in which alimony was granted, and that relationship constitutes a marriage by the law of the divorcing state, alimony will thereby be terminated. Fahrer v. Fahrer, 36 Ohio App.2d 208, 304 N.E.2d 411 (1973).

89. In re Marriage of Shima, 360 N.W.2d 827 (Iowa 1985) (remarriage does not result in automatic termination, but shifts the burden to the wife to show that "extraordinary circumstances" require the continuation of alimony); Beck v. Beck, 208 Kan. 148, 490 P.2d 628 (1971); Bubar v. Plant, 141 Me. 407, 44 A.2d 732 (1945); Matter of Marriage of Grove, 280 Or. 341, 571 P.2d 477 (1977), opinion modified, rehearing denied 280 Or. 769, 572 P.2d 1320 (1977) (public policy does not require that a woman whose first marriage has been dissolved be free to remarry only if her new husband is able to support her); Annot., 48 A.L.R.2d 270, 282 (1956).

90. In Sutton v. Leib, 199 F.2d 163 (7th Cir.1952) the first husband was required to pay more than three years'

back alimony which accrued while his wife lived with her second husband in a "void" marriage. The peculiar Oregon rule seems to be that alimony will not be terminated on remarriage if the second husband is not able to support the wife, this being the construction given to the phrase "extraordinary circumstances" in that state. Most of the Oregon cases find that extraordinary circumstances in that sense do not exist, but one of them did find that alimony would be reduced but not terminated when the wife married a second husband whose earning capacity did not fully meet her needs. Matter of Marriage of Stephens-Tiley, 50 Or.App. 503, 623 P.2d 1105 (1981). Compare with that case Matter of Marriage of Bates, 73 Or.App. 530, 699 P.2d 678 (1985), and In re Marriage of Wilson, 62 Or.App. 201, 660 P.2d 188 (1983). See also In re Marriage of Shima, 360 N.W.2d 827 (Iowa 1985), holding that the wife's devotion and dedication as a homemaker and mother did not constitute "extraordinary circumstances" justifying the continuation of alimony after her remarriage.

91. In re Moncrief's Will, 235 N.Y. 390, 139 N.E. 550 (1923); Sleicher v. Sleicher, 251 N.Y. 366, 167 N.E. 501 (1929).

92. See section 3.5, supra.

93. Sefton v. Sefton, 45 Cal.2d 872, 291 P.2d 439 (1955). But see Heistand v. Heistand, 384 Mass. 20, 423 N.E.2d 313 (1981).

5. Cohabitation by the Recipient After Divorce [94]

As we have shown,[95] the remarriage of the alimony recipient almost always result in the termination of alimony. This was a simple and workable rule so long as the traditional moral principle prevailed that if a man and woman wished to live together they should get married. Unfortunately for simplicity and workability, however, that moral principle no longer does prevail. Today people of all ages and backgrounds in society find it desirable for one reason or another to form households or "living together arrangements" without troubling to go through a wedding ceremony. Notwithstanding the prevalence of the practice, neither the law nor popular usage has devised a term for describing these relationships or the people who engage in them.[96] For lack of a better term, cohabitation will be used here even though that word may be somewhat ambiguous.[97]

Once the social pressure toward marriage had diminished or disappeared, the temptation for alimony recipients to replace a possible second marriage with cohabitation became obvious. The question then is, what are to be the consequences for the continuation of alimony when the recipient does cohabit rather than marry?

Some states have attempted to deal with this question by enacting statutes authorizing or requiring the modification of alimony awards when the recipient cohabits with a person of the opposite sex.[98] The language of these statutes varies considerably, making it impossible to draw from them a single coherent notion of their purpose and application. For example, some of the statutes make modification mandatory, while others leave modification to the discretion of the trial court.[99] Some statutes seem to emphasize the meretricious nature of the relationship or its immorality, while others make modification depend

---

94. This subject has been thoroughly discussed in Oldham, The Effect of Unmarried Cohabitation By a Former Spouse Upon His or Her Right to Continue to Receive Alimony, 17 J.Fam.J. 249 (1978–1979), and Oldham, Cohabitation By an Alimony Recipient Revisited, 20 J.Fam. L. 615 (1981–1982). The older cases on the subject are collected in Annot., 98 A.L.R.3d 453 (1980).

95. See the text at note 80, supra.

96. At one time the Census Bureau adopted POSSLQ, Person of Opposite Sex Sharing Living Quarters, as a way of describing persons in these relationships. Oldham, Cohabitation By an Alimony Recipient Revisited, 20 J.Fam.L. 615, 646 (1981–1982).

97. The term is generally defined to refer to a man and woman living together as if they were husband and wife but without being legally married. II Oxford English Dictionary 598 (1961); Webster's Third New International Dictionary 440 (1976). Haddow v. Haddow, 707 P.2d 669 (Utah 1985) defines cohabitation as involving two elements—a common residency and sexual relations evidencing a conjugal association.

98. Ala.Code 1983, § 30–2–55 (decree shall be modified on proof that the receiving spouse is living openly or cohabiting with a member of the opposite sex); West's Ann.Cal.Civ.Code § 4801.5 (Supp.1987) (rebuttable presumption of decreased need for support if the supported party is cohabiting with a person of the opposite sex; holding oneself out to be the husband or wife of such a person is not necessary to constitute cohabitation); Conn. Gen.Stat.Ann. § 46b–86 (1986) (court may modify, suspend, reduce or terminate alimony on a showing that the recipient is living with another person where the living arrangements cause such a change in circumstances as to alter the recipient's financial needs); Ill.—Smith Hurd Ann. ch. 40, § 510 (Supp.1986) (alimony terminates of the

recipient cohabits with another person on a resident, continuing, conjugal basis); N.Y.—McKinney's Dom.Rel. Law § 248 (1986) (court may modify alimony on proof the recipient is habitually living with another man and holding herself out as his wife although not married); Okl. Stat.1987, tit. 12, § 1289 (Supp.) (voluntary cohabitation with a person of the opposite sex is a ground for modification on proof of a substantial change in circumstances related to need for support or ability to support; cohabitation means dwelling together continuously and habitually in a private conjugal relation not a marriage); Pa. Stat. tit. 23, § 507 (Supp.1986) (no petitioner is entitled to receive alimony when he has entered into cohabitation with a person of the opposite sex not a member of petitioner's immediate family); Tenn.Code Ann. § 36–5–101 (Supp.1986) (where recipient lives with a third person, rebuttable presumption is raised that the third person is contributing to support and that recipient does not need alimony); Utah Code Ann.1986, § 30–3–5 (Supp.) (alimony terminates when recipient resides with a person of the opposite sex unless it is established that there is no sexual contact).

99. For example, Alabama and Utah seem to make modification mandatory while Connecticut makes it discretionary on proof of the requisite form of cohabitation. California compromises the issue by setting up a rebuttable presumption of decreased need when cohabitation is proved. The presumption was held not to be rebutted in In re Marriage of Leib, 80 Cal.App.3d 629, 145 Cal.Rptr. 763 (1978) where the court saw the evidence as indicating an agreement that the recipient would contribute her services as a homemaker to her cohabitant, using her alimony to pay her share of the expenses of the new household. The court said that she could not give away her services and thereby create the appearance of continuing need.

upon changes in the recipient's need for support.[1] The New York statute makes it easy for the recipient to evade modification by imposing two requirements: a) It must be shown that the recipient was habitually living with another man; and b) was holding herself out as his wife.[2] If the recipient is careful to make it clear that she is not married, she can apparently continue to collect her alimony no matter how prosperous she and her cohabitant may be.[3] Application of the term "cohabitation" also may be different under the various statutes depending upon the context in which it is used and upon the courts' view of the recipients' needs.[4]

The cohabitation statutes have occasionally been subjected to attack on constitutional grounds but have been held valid.[5] There seems no substantial basis for contending that they violate the Equal Protection or Due Process Clauses or that they unconstitutionally intrude on the parties' privacy[6]

The decisions in states which have no statute on cohabitation exhibit many inconsistencies, but there are some commonly accepted views. Since the parties are no longer married to each other, nearly all courts take the position that the payer of alimony has no legitimate reason for terminating or reducing alimony solely because he objects to the morality of the recipient's cohabitation.[7] She owes her former husband no particular obligations the violation of which should excuse him from complying with the alimony decree. Her alleged immorality is not adultery[8] and is of no greater concern to him than to any other member of society.

If any general proposition can be deduced from the cases, it is that the recipient's cohabitation may justify reduction or termination of alimony if it reduces or ends her need for alimony.[9] But even on this point there is some disagreement since some courts argue that the cohabitant has no legal duty to provide support for the ex-wife and therefore the

1. E.g., the Utah Statute cited in note 98, supra. See Hathcock v. Hathcock, 249 Ga. 74, 287 S.E.2d 19 (1982); Gray v. Gray, 451 So.2d 579 (La.App.1984), writ denied 457 So.2d 13 (1984); Wacker v. Wacker, 668 P.2d 533 (Utah 1983).

2. Northrup v. Northrup, 43 N.Y.2d 566, 402 N.Y.S.2d 997, 373 N.E.2d 1221 (1978). Bliss v. Bliss, 66 N.Y.2d 382, 497 N.Y.S.2d 344, 488 N.E.2d 90 (1985).

3. Citron v. Citron, 91 Misc.2d 785, 398 N.Y.S.2d 624 (1977).

4. Cohabitation was held not proved when a man lived in the recipient's house for only three weeks, in Atkinson v. Atkinson, 372 So.2d 1106 (Ala.Civ.App.1979). But cohabitation need not be "habitual" according to Parish v. Parish, 374 So.2d 348 (Ala.Civ.App.1979), writ denied 374 So.2d 351 (1979). Cohabitation did not occur when the ex-wife lived with two male boarders without evidence of sexual involvement. In re Marriage of Thweatt, 96 Cal. App.3d 530, 157 Cal.Rptr. 826 (1979). But cohabitation was held to have occurred "on a conjugal basis" when the ex-wife lived with an impotent man, the court saying that the term "conjugal" does not necessarily require evidence of sexual conduct. In re Marriage of Sappington, 106 Ill. 2d 456, 88 Ill.Dec. 61, 478 N.E.2d 376 (1985). See also In re Marriage of Olson, 98 Ill.App.3d 316, 53 Ill.Dec. 751, 424 N.E.2d 386 (1981); Schoenhard v. Schoenhard, 74 Ill. App.3d 296, 30 Ill.Dec. 109, 392 N.E.2d 764 (1979); In re Support of Halford, 70 Ill.App.3d 609, 27 Ill.Dec. 168, 388 N.E.2d 1131 (1979). Maintaining separate households normally does not constitute cohabitation. Kaplan v. Kaplan, 186 Conn. 387, 441 A.2d 629 (1982). Findings on this point are within the sound discretion of the trial court. Lupien v. Lupien, 192 Conn. 443, 472 A.2d 18 (1984).

5. Roberts v. Roberts, 657 P.2d 153 (Okl.1983). A provision for modification inserted in a separation agreement was held not to violate the constitution in Matter of Marriage of Edwards, 73 Or.App. 272, 698 P.2d 542 (1985). An earlier version of the Georgia statute was held unconstitutional when it applied only to wives and not husbands, as a form of gender discrimination. Sims v. Sims, 243 Ga. 275, 253 S.E.2d 762 (1979).

6. Cf. Griswold v. Connecticut, 381 U.S. 479, 85 S.Ct. 1678, 14 L.Ed.2d 510 (1965).

7. Drummond v. Drummond, 267 Ark. 449, 590 S.W. 2d 658 (1979); Alibrando v. Alibrando, 375 A.2d 9 (D.C. App.1977); Mitchell v. Mitchell, 418 A.2d 1140 (Me.1980); Meyer v. Meyer, 41 Md.App. 13, 394 A.2d 1220 (1978); Abbott v. Abbott, 282 N.W.2d 561 (Minn. 1979).

8. Some courts are oddly confused on this point, seeming to think that the ex-wife commits adultery when she cohabits with another man. E.g., Drummond v. Drummond, 267 Ark. 449, 590 S.W.2d 658 (1979). But of course an unmarried woman cannot commit adultery. Of course the cohabitation of unmarried persons may constitute some other crime, such as fornication, in those few states in which such crimes still exist.

A case which may be contra the text statement is Taake v. Taake, 70 Wis.2d 115, 233 N.W.2d 449 (1975), but it may be questioned by Van Gorder v. Van Gorder, 110 Wis.2d 188, 327 N.W.2d 674 (1983).

9. Alibrando v. Alibrando, 375 A.2d 9 (D.C.App.1977); Meyer v. Meyer, 41 Md.App. 13, 394 A.2d 1220 (1978); Abbott v. Abbott, 282 N.W.2d 561 (Minn.1979); Bisig v. Bisig, 124 N.H. 372, 469 A.2d 1348 (1983); Gayet v. Gayet, 92 N.J. 149, 456 A.2d 102 (1983); Van Gorder v. Van Gorder, 110 Wis.2d 188, 327 N.W.2d 674 (1983).

cohabitation can have no effect on her need for alimony.[10] Even if this argument is rejected, the most common arrangement made by cohabitants is that they will share the expenses of their joint household, in which event they can plausibly assert that the ex-wife's need for alimony persists unchanged.[11] Notwithstanding these arguments there are cases in which courts have found that the recipient's need for financial support has decreased or ended when she cohabited with another man, usually on the ground that he did in fact contribute to her support.[12] In order to rely upon this line of cases the payer should be required to show that the recipient occupied living quarters with the cohabitant over a substantial period of time up to the date of the petition for modification.[13] It clearly is not sufficient that the recipient merely had sexual relations with the cohabitant and perhaps also attended social affairs with him.[14] On the other hand these cases do not seem to require that the cohabiting parties represent that they are married.[15]

It would seem logical to apply the same reasoning to homosexual cohabitation as to heterosexual relationships, but the authorities are not numerous enough to draw any conclusions on the point. Many of the statutes refer only to cohabitation with a person of the opposite sex and therefore do not apply to homosexual unions.[16]

In view of the uncertainty produced by statute and case law concerning the effect of cohabitation on the continuance of alimony, it seems obvious that the careful lawyer for the husband should attempt to include in any separation agreement some provision covering the question. In fact there are cases which suggest that a separation agreement which merely provides in the usual terms that alimony will continue until the death of either party or the remarriage of the recipient contains the negative inference that cohabitation will have no effect on alimony regardless of the circumstances in which it occurs.[17] If a separation agreement does contain a provision for modification in the event of cohabitation by the recipient of alimony, it will be honored by the courts, but of course care must be taken to draft the provision precisely enough to cover the kind of conduct which should fairly result in modification.[18]

10. Fleming v. Fleming, 221 Kan. 290, 559 P.2d 329 (1977); Mitchell v. Mitchell, 418 A.2d 1140 (Me.1980); Allgood v. Allgood, 626 P.2d 1323 (Okl.1981) (Oklahoma statute did not control this case); Porter v. Porter, 137 Vt. 375, 406 A.2d 398 (1979). Even Marvin v. Marvin, 18 Cal.3d 660, 134 Cal.Rptr. 815, 557 P.2d 106 (1976) did not suggest that there would be some duty of support between cohabitants in the absence of a contract. That case and others are discussed in sections 1.2 and 15.7, supra.

11. E.g. Lydic v. Lydic, 664 S.W.2d 941 (Ky.App.1983); Mitchell v. Mitchell, 418 A.2d 1140 (Me.1980); Porter v. Porter, 137 Vt. 375, 406 A.2d 398 (1979).

12. Bentzoni v. Bentzoni, 442 So.2d 235 (Fla.App. 1983); Bisig v. Bisig, 124 N.H. 372, 469 A.2d 1348 (1983); Garlinger v. Garlinger, 137 N.J.Super. 56, 347 A.2d 799 (1975), cited with approval in Gayet v. Gayet, 92 N.J. 149, 456 A.2d 102 (1983). Where the recipient uses the alimony to support the cohabitant, the alimony likewise should be modified, since that fact shows that she does not need the award or all of it. See the Garlinger case, supra. In Husband B. W. D. v. Wife B. A. D., 436 A.2d 1263 (Del. Super.1981) the court held that alimony should be reduced when the ex-wife shared living quarters and expenses with a cohabitant who paid part of the housing costs. The same court divided evenly on the question whether this living arrangement justified terminating alimony entirely, leaving in effect the trial court's decision that it did not.

13. Brister v. Brister, 92 N.M. 711, 594 P.2d 1167 (1979); Matter of Vann's Marriage, 24 Or.App. 31, 544 P.2d 175 (1976).

14. See the cases cited in note 7, supra.

15. See the cases cited in note 12, supra.

16. People ex rel. Kenney v. Kenney, 76 Misc.2d 927, 352 N.Y.S.2d 344 (1974).

17. E.g., In re Marriage of Sasson, 129 Cal.App.3d 140, 180 Cal.Rptr. 815 (1982); Bisig v. Bisig, 124 N.H. 372, 469 A.2d 1348 (1983); Matter of Paul S. v. Roberta S., 91 Misc.2d 211, 397 N.Y.S.2d 568 (Fam.Ct.1977).

18. O'Connor Bros. Abalone Co. v. Brando, 40 Cal. App.3d 90, 114 Cal.Rptr. 773 (1974) (court construes "appearing to maintain a marital relationship with anyone" to include cohabitation); Quisenberry v. Quisenberry, 449 A.2d 274 (Del.Fam.Ct.1982) (provision for termination of alimony when the wife cohabits with an unrelated adult male warrants termination without any proof of change in the wife's financial circumstances). Under the unique Oregon view that a court may not in advance provide for termination of alimony on remarriage it has been held that a decree so providing on the ground of cohabitation is invalid, but that a separation agreement so providing may be enforced. "Cohabitation" was also held to have a sufficiently precise meaning to be enforceable. Matter of Marriage of Edwards, 73 Or.App. 272, 698 P.2d 542 (1985).

It is curious that in all the judicial discussion of the effect of cohabitation on alimony there is little or no consideration of the purpose of alimony. If, as has been argued in an earlier section,[19] the purpose of alimony where no children are being provided for by it is to mitigate the social and financial hardship caused by divorce, then it would seem to follow that alimony should terminate when that hardship no longer exists. The reason for terminating alimony on the remarriage of the recipient is that remarriage clearly signifies that the alimony recipient has successfully worked through the hardships of divorce and has rearranged her life in a way satisfactory to herself. Alimony is therefore no longer needed. The same analysis should be applied to cohabitation. If the alimony recipient has entered into what appears to be a stable relationship with another man, regardless of what they may agree about sharing expenses, she has weathered the disruption and adversity caused by the divorce and should no longer need alimony. Although the relationship of cohabitation results in no legal obligation of support and although it may end at any time, that is the choice the recipient has made. If she wants greater legal status and stability in the relationship, she can hold out for marriage. A legal doctrine which holds adults responsible for the choices they make hardly seems objectionable. But admittedly the courts have not taken this view of the situation.

6. The Effect of Attempts at Reconciliation

Where the parties resume living together after the divorce in an attempt at reconciliation and then separate, it is held that alimony must be resumed in accordance with the terms of the divorce decree.[20] Whether the payer will be held liable for the installments which accrued during the period of reconciliation seems to depend upon whether the payer supported the recipient during that time.[21]

7. Post-Decree Agreement of the Parties

An agreement between the former husband and wife, made after the divorce decree has been entered and alimony awarded, does not prevent the divorce court from exercising its jurisdiction to modify.[22] The leading case on the point is Hoops v. Hoops,[23] in which the wife agreed to accept $7,500 in full settlement of her claims to alimony past and future. The New York court held that this did not prevent her from later obtaining additional alimony. Likewise the wife's agreement to accept periodic alimony in a sum less than was given her by the decree does not of itself alter the husband's alimony obligation.[24] If the parties wish to make such agreements binding, they should present them to the court and have the decree modified to correspond with the agreement.[25] Just as the courts are normally willing to accept the parties' initial agreement as to the amount of alimony,[26] so here they should accept the sum agreed on as a basis for modification in the absence of any showing of fraud, unfairness or overreaching.

8. The Payer's Death

It is a much litigated question whether alimony continues beyond the husband's death.[27] More precisely, there are two questions, although too many courts fail to distinguish between them. Does the divorce court have

---

19. See section 16.4, supra.

20. Rice v. Rice, 603 P.2d 1125 (Okl.1979).

21. Ross v. Ross, 592 P.2d 600 (Utah 1979).

22. O'Hara v. O'Hara, 137 N.J.Eq. 369, 44 A.2d 169 (1945); Nichols v. Nichols, 11 App.Div.2d 149, 202 N.Y.S.2d 124 (4th Dept. 1960), reargument denied 11 App. Div.2d 974, 209 N.Y.S.2d 540, 541 (4th Dep't 1960) (applying former McKinney's Civil Practice Act (N.Y.) 1170); Feves v. Feves, 198 Or. 151, 254 P.2d 694 (1953). Other cases are cited in Annot., 166 A.L.R. 370 (1947) and in Desvernine, Ground for the Modification of Alimony Awards, 6 Law & Contemp. Prob. 236, 247 (1939).

23. 292 N.Y. 428, 55 N.E.2d 488 (1944), modification granted in Hoops v. Hoops, 269 App.Div. 968, 58 N.Y.S.2d 151 (1st Dept. 1945), rehearing denied 269 App.Div. 980, 59 N.Y.S.2d 294 (1st Dep't 1945).

24. Sirianni v. Sirianni, 127 N.Y.S.2d 387 (1953).

25. Feves v. Feves, 198 Or. 151, 254 P.2d 694 (1953).

26. See section 18.1, infra.

27. Cases on the question are collected in Annots., 18 A.L.R. 1040 (1922) and 39 A.L.R.2d 1406 (1955).

authority to award alimony for a period extending beyond the payer's death? If it does, is the particular decree to be construed as having that effect?

The statutes of several states now state that unless it is otherwise expressly provided in a written agreement or in the divorce decree itself, alimony terminates upon the death of either party.[28] That seems to mean that the trial court does have authority to order alimony to continue beyond the payer's death if the decree expressly so provides.[29] This authority might also be deduced from statutes which in general terms give the courts broad discretion to fix the amount and terms of alimony decrees.[30] It does seem necessary to find some statutory basis for the authority in view of the general principle that the courts have no inherent authority to grant alimony in divorces *a vinculo* in the absence of statute.[31]

Where no specific statutory authority for extending alimony beyond the payer's death is in force, some early influential cases held that the courts have no power to award alimony in this form.[32] Other courts which did not take such a broad position were sufficiently doubtful of their authority as to "construe" decrees as ending on the payer's death even though such a "construction" was hardly warranted by the literal terms of the decree.[33]

The reason usually given for this result was that alimony could continue no longer than the husband's duty of support would have continued if the parties had remained married, and that duty clearly ends with his death.[34] Other more recent cases have been willing to find that the courts do have the authority to award alimony which survives the husband's death, either on the basis of general statutory provisions [35] or without specifying just where the authority originates.[36]

Thus there remains a substantial conflict among the states concerning the wisdom of giving the courts the authority to continue alimony beyond the payer's death, representing differing views of the underlying policy. The cases and statutes permitting alimony to continue recognize that a rigid rule may involve hardship at times since there may be cases in which the extension of alimony beyond the husband's death is desirable for the protection of the wife. The argument that the duty of support ends at death is not conclusive since if the parties remain married the wife receives other forms of protection at the husband's death, such as dower or a statutory forced share in his estate. These forms of financial support are not available to the divorced wife.

---

28. See the Arizona, California, Colorado, Illinois, Minnesota, Missouri, and Washington statutes cited in note 1, supra, as well as the Uniform Marriage and Divorce Act § 316(b), 9A Unif.L.Ann. 183 (1979).

29. But see In re Marriage of Clarke, 125 Ill.App.3d 432, 80 Ill.Dec. 629, 465 N.E.2d 975 (1984) which seems to say, notwithstanding the Illinois statute, that the court has no authority to order alimony extending beyond the husband's death.

30. E.g., Stoutland v. Stoutland, 103 N.W.2d 286 (N.D.1960); Matter of Gustafson's Estate, 287 N.W.2d 700 (N.D.1980); Murphy v. Shelton, 183 Wash. 180, 48 P.2d 247 (1935) (under an earlier Washington statute); Hale v. Hale, 108 W.Va. 337, 150 S.E. 748 (1929). Massachusetts also may reach this result. See Du Mont v. Godbey, 382 Mass. 234, 415 N.E.2d 188 (1981).

31. Wilson v. Hinman, 182 N.Y. 408, 75 N.E. 236 (1905). See also section 16.1, supra.

32. Emerson v. Emerson, 120 Md. 584, 87 A. 1033 (1913); Wilson v. Hinman, 182 N.Y. 408, 75 N.E. 236 (1905); Annot., 39 A.L.R.2d 1406 (1955). Later cases which seem to take the position that alimony may not continue beyond the payer's death, unless the parties have agreed that it will, include Kuhns' Estate v. Kuhns,

550 P.2d 816 (Alaska 1976); O'Malley v. Pan American Bank of Orlando, N.A., 384 So.2d 1258 (Fla.1980); Dolvin v. Dolvin, 248 Ga. 439, 284 S.E.2d 254 (1981); Ehrler v. Ehrler, 69 Misc.2d 234, 328 N.Y.S.2d 728 (1972); Funnell v. Funnell, 584 P.2d 1319 (Okl.1978).

The alimony decree may be attacked for fraud after the payer's death on the same grounds and with the same limitations applicable to attack on other decrees for non-jurisdictional reasons. State ex rel. Smith v. Delaware County Superior Court, 442 N.E.2d 978 (Ind. 1982).

33. Parsons v. Parsons' Estate, 70 Colo. 333, 201 P. 559 (1921); Watrous' Estate, 95 Pa.Super. 11 (1928), 77 U.Pa.L.Rev. 924 (1929) (Nebraska law).

34. Daggett v. Commissioner, 128 F.2d 568 (9th Cir. 1942), cert. denied 317 U.S. 673, 63 S.Ct. 78, 87 L.Ed. 540 (1942) (New York law).

35. See the statutes and cases cited in notes 28 and 30, supra.

36. Garber v. Robitshek, 226 Minn. 398, 33 N.W.2d 30 (1948), decided before the present Minnesota statute was enacted; Prather v. Prather, ___ W.Va. ___, 305 S.E.2d 304 (1983).

Although the authority to make the award is available in a substantial number of states today, it does not automatically follow that alimony will survive the husband's death. If the decree expressly provides that alimony is for joint lives, then it ends on the husband's death.[37] The more common form of alimony decree orders the alimony to be paid until the wife's death or remarriage. Literally construed, this would mean that the alimony remains in effect after the husband's death and some cases so hold.[38] Other cases have held that it is not to be so contrued. Perhaps influenced by the thought that such decrees may not be carefully drafted and that the trial court in entering the decree does not think of the possibility of the husband's prior death, these cases have held that a decree so worded does not authorize the continuance of alimony beyond his death.[39] They require specific language or at the very least a clear implication that the alimony is to survive. If such language is found in the decree, the alimony remains payable [40] and, on a showing of changed circumstances, modifiable.[41]

The reluctance to honor the wife's claim which is expressed in this approach to construction seems justified.[42] In most cases the continuation of alimony causes hardship, inconvenience and expense to those closer to the husband than his ex-wife, such as the wife and children of a second marriage. It requires either that the estate be held open for a substantial time or that a lump sum be paid in satisfaction of the ex-wife's claim. Either alternative may frustrate the scheme of distribution set up by the husband's will. Although there may be circumstances in which the alimony ought to continue, due to the necessities of the ex-wife and the absence of hardship on others having claims on the husband, such cases are probably rare. The rule should be that alimony ends on the husband's death unless the decree plainly provides otherwise.

This problem is one which could and should be eliminated by more careful drafting of separation agreements and alimony decrees. In the majority of cases the decree should expressly provide that alimony end on husband's death. In those unusual cases where some further provision for the wife is needed, an insurance policy on the husband's life is more satisfactory to all parties than continuing the alimony. But if it is advisable in any event to have the alimony continue, the decree should say so in so many words, thereby avoiding any issue of construction.

The foregoing discussion has been concerned with periodic alimony. Although lump sum awards payable in installments should be subject to the same rules as periodic alimony, some cases treat them differently, holding that the husband's death does not terminate the obligation.[43] Likewise, if the payments are characterized as a division of property, they do not terminate.[44]

37. Harrison v. Union & New Haven Trust Co., 147 Conn. 435, 162 A.2d 182 (1960).

38. Johnson v. Every, 93 So.2d 390 (Fla.1957); Matter of Gustafson's Estate, 287 N.W.2d 700 (N.D.1980).

39. Kuhns' Estate v. Kuhns, 550 P.2d 816 (Alaska N.A., 1976); O'Malley v. Pan American Bank of Orlando, N.A., 384 So.2d 1258 (Fla.1980); Dolvin v. Dolvin, 248 Ga. 439, 284 S.E.2d 254 (1981); Kendall v. Kendall, 218 Kan. 713, 545 P.2d 346 (1976); Annot., 39 A.L.R.2d 1406, 1410 (1955). Likewise a decree ordering alimony to be paid "until the further order of this court" has been construed as not surviving the husband's death. Masters v. Masters, 155 Neb. 569, 52 N.W.2d 802 (1952). Alimony "so long as the wife remains unmarried" does not survive the husband's death under Luce v. Providence Union National Bank, 122 F.Supp. 21 (D.R.I.1954), affirmed p.c. 217 F.2d 648 (1st Cir.1954); Carrell v. Carrell, 250 Iowa 983, 96 N.W.2d 315 (1959); Deriemer v. Old Nat. Bank of Spokane, 60 Wash.2d 686, 374 P.2d 973 (1962).

40. McDonnell v. McDonnell, 166 Conn. 146, 348 A.2d 575 (1974); Garber v. Robitshek, 226 Minn. 398, 33 N.W.2d 30 (1948).

41. Welsh v. Welsh, 346 Mich. 292, 78 N.W.2d 120 (1956).

42. Note, 43 Iowa L.Rev. 421 (1958). For an argument that construction of the decree has no relevance to the issue of modification, see section 18.8, supra. Unfortunately the alimony cases do not recognize that this is not a question of construing the decree but rather of modifying it.

43. Hagerty v. Hagerty, 222 Mich. 166, 192 N.W. 553 (1923). For a discussion of modifiability of lump sum alimony awards, see the text at note 25, supra.

44. Farrand v. Farrand, 246 Iowa 488, 67 N.W.2d 20 (1954). The supposed distinction between alimony and a division of property is criticized supra at note 20.

Where the alimony decree is based upon an agreement of the parties which expressly states that the payments are to survive the husband's death, the decree will be given that effect even in a state where his death would ordinarily terminate alimony payments.[45]

**WESTLAW
REFERENCES**

Procedure for Modification of Alimony

di(burden /3 prove* proving proof /s chang! modif! /s alimony)

Interstate Modification of Alimony

sy("full faith and credit" /p chang! modif! /s alimony)

Factors Influencing Modification

2. Changes in the Payer's Needs and Resources

sy(chang! /5 circumstance /s reduc! lower decreas! /s alimony /5 husband)

4. The Recipient's Remarriage

find 360 nw2d 827

---

45. International Trust Co. v. Liebhardt, 111 Colo. 208, 139 P.2d 264 (1943); Taylor v. Gowetz, 339 Mass. 294, 158 N.E.2d 677 (1959); Snouffer v. Snouffer, 132 Ohio St. 617, 9 N.E.2d 621 (1937). See also the cases cited in notes 39 and 40, supra.

§ 16.6

1. By "domestic" in this context, we intend to refer to enforcement of decrees by courts of the state which granted the decrees. Interstate enforcement problems are discussed in section 16.7, infra. The enforcement of child support decrees is governed by somewhat similar rules and to that extent the discussion in this section is relevant to that subject. But child support has also come to involve special enforcement techniques, including some federal procedures and it is therefore discussed separately in section 17.3, infra.

The federal remedies outlined in section 17.3, except for the federal refund intercept program, are available for the enforcement of alimony as well as child support, where there is a state alimony decree in force, where the minor child of the obligor is living with the alimony recipient, and where the support enforcement services are provided for child support by the state's title IV–D agency. 42 U.S.C.A. § 654(4)(B), and (6)(A).

2. E.g., West's Ann.Cal.Civ.Code § 4380 (1983); Colo.Rev.Stat. § 14–10–117 (1974 and Supp.1986); D.C.Code 1981, §§ 16–911, 16–912; Neb.Rev.St. § 42–370 (1984); N.Y.—McKinney's Dom.Rel.L. § 245 (1986); Wis.Stat.Ann. § 767.30 (Supp.1986). See the Uniform Marriage and Divorce Act § 311, 9A Unif.L. Ann. 173 (1979).

The procedure and limitations on contempt enforcement are discussed in detail infra, at note 23.

3. 4380 (1983); Conn.Gen.Stat.Ann. § 46b–69a (1986); Mass.Gen. Laws Ann. c. 208, § 33 (1981); Mich.Comp.Law Ann. § 25.105 (1984); Neb.Rev.St.

---

alimony /s remarri! remarry! /s "extraordinary circumstance"

5. Cohabitation by the Recipient After Divorce

sy(wife /s co-habit! /s alimony /5 terminat! modif! chang!)

8. The Payer's Death

to(134 205) /p alimony /10 continu! surviv! /s death dead die* dying /5 husband

---

§ 16.6   Enforcement of Domestic Alimony and Property Division Decrees [1]

Enforcement—In General

The divorce statutes of many states provide for the enforcement of claims for alimony or property by a wide variety of processes, including contempt,[2] execution,[3] garnishment,[4] orders for the assignment of wages or in-

§ 42–371 (1984); N.Y.—McKinney's Dom.Rel.L. § 244 (1986); Wis.Stat.Ann. § 767.30 (Supp.1986).

4. E.g., D.C.Code 1981, §§ 16–911, 16–912; N.C.Gen. Stat. § 50–16.7(e) (1984). A federal statute permits garnishment to be used for the enforcement of alimony and child support claims with respect to money due from the United States or the District of Columbia to the obligor. 42 U.S.C.A. § 659; United States v. Morton, 467 U.S. 822, 104 S.Ct. 2769, 81 L.Ed.2d 680 (1984), rehearing denied 468 U.S. 1226, 105 S.Ct. 27, 82 L.Ed.2d 920 (1984). The federal Consumer Credit Protection Act, 15 U.S.C.A. § 1673(b) provides a maximum amount of wages garnishable, the amount being 50% where the obligor of alimony is supporting other dependents and 60% where he is not supporting other dependents. These maxima may be increased by 5% if the payments are more than twelve weeks in arrears. The statute applies only to alimony and child support claims. It seems not to apply to claims based on a division of property, or, according to Dyche v. Dyche, 570 S.W.2d 293 (Mo.1978), to claims for attorney fees. If the claims are not for alimony, the statute permits only 25% of the wages to be garnished. The statute seems to have been enacted by people who were ignorant of the essential similarity between alimony on the one hand the property divisions and attorney fees on the other. Title IV–D of the Social Security Act requires the state to collect spousal support as well as child support where there is already a support order outstanding, where the support obligor's minor child is living with the spousal support claimant and where support collection services are being provided on the child's behalf by the state IV–D agency. 42 U.S.C.A. § 654(4)(B) and (6) (A). Title IV–D is discussed in detail in section 17.3, infra. Wages being paid in another state may be garnished if the court has personal jurisdiction of the garnishee. Champion International Corp. v. Ayars, 587 F.Supp. 1274 (D.Conn.1984).

come,[5] attachment,[6] imposition of liens,[7] or the requirement of security.[8] Many of the same enforcement remedies, and some others, are available under the general statutes of the states,[9] or by virtue of established common law principles.[10]

In most states accrued and unpaid installments of alimony are final judgments, not subject to modification, upon which execution may issue without further proceedings.[11] It has been held that this procedure does not violate due process by permitting execution to issue without further notice or opportunity to be heard,[12] in distinction to the cases in which the Supreme Court has held that pre-judgment attachment or garnishment may not be accomplished without notice and hearing.[13] In a few states accrued installments of alimony may be modified.[14] In those states the alimony claimant, before being able to get execution, must make a motion to have a judgment for the arrears of alimony docketed, giving notice to the obligor.[15] When the judgment is docketed, execution may issue. The enforcement of a judgment for alimony or a division of property is normally a continuation of the original suit and therefore need not rest up-

---

5. E.g., Colo. Rev.Stat. § 14–10–118 (Supp.1986); Conn.Gen.Stat.Ann. § 46b–69a (1986); Wis.Stat.Ann. § 767.265 (Supp.1986–1987). The Uniform Marriage and Divorce Act § 311, 9A Unif.L.Ann. 173 (1979) and the statutes of several states authorize the court to order alimony to be paid to the clerk of the court, with authority to the clerk or other public official to follow up on nonpayment and bring enforcement proceedings. The same Act, in § 312, 9A Unif.L.Ann. 175 (1979) authorizes the courts to order the spouse to make an assignment of wages or trust income to the alimony obligee. An assignment of part of a workers' compensation award was approved in Donovan v. Donovan, 15 Mass.App.Ct. 61, 443 N.E.2d 432 (1982). For a general discussion of wage assignments, see Note, Domestic Relations—Wage Assignment After Divorce, 1968 Wis.L.Rev. 261.

6. E.g., D.C.Code 1981, §§ 16–911, 16–912; Mass.Gen. Laws Ann. c. 208, § 33 (1981); N.C.Gen.Stat. § 50–16.7(e) (1984).

7. E.g., Mich.Comp.Law Ann. § 25.105 (1984); Neb. Rev.St. § 42–371 (1984). For a more thorough discussion of alimony liens see the text at second note 11, infra.

8. E.g., Colo.Rev.Stat. § 14–10–118 (Supp.1986); N.J. Stat.Ann. § 2A:34–23 (Supp.1986); N.Y.—McKinney's Dom.Rel.L. § 243 (1986).

9. E.g., In re Marriage of Valley, 633 P.2d 1104 (Colo. App.1981) (lien imposed where husband threatened to dispose of his assets and leave the state); Chirekos v. Chirekos, 33 Ill.App.3d 606, 338 N.E.2d 140 (1975) (Illinois court imposes a lien on land in Arizona); Grosvenor v. Grosvenor, 206 Neb. 395, 293 N.W.2d 96 (1980) (lien); Hidy v. Hidy, 184 Neb. 527, 169 N.W.2d 285 (1969) (statute of limitations on liens is constitutional). Contra the text statement, denying authority to impose a lien: Uhrich v. Uhrich, 173 Ind.App. 133, 362 N.E.2d 1163 (1977).

Sequestration was held authorized by a general statute in In re Marriage of Hilkovitch, 124 Ill.App.3d 401, 79 Ill. Dec. 891, 464 N.E.2d 795 (1984) and In re Marriage of Hellwig, 100 Ill.App.3d 452, 55 Ill.Dec. 762, 426 N.E.2d 1087 (1981), where the husband was dissipating his assets, and in Campbell v. Campbell, 353 A.2d 276 (D.C. App.1976).

Garnishment was held available under a general statute in Holt v. Holt, 84 S.D. 671, 176 N.W.2d 51 (1970).

Prather v. Prather, ___ W.Va. ___, 305 S.E.2d 304 (1983) held that a trust could be imposed under a general statute, citing other cases.

10. Gredone v. Gredone, 361 A.2d 176 (D.C.App.1976) (ne exeat); Chlupacek v. Reed, 225 Ga. 512, 169 S.E.2d 782 (1969) (ne exeat); Ralston Purina Co. v. Detwiler, 173 Ind.App. 513, 364 N.E.2d 180 (1977) (must be execution and levy on corporate stock in order to impose a lien); In re Prybil's Marriage, 230 N.W.2d 487 (Iowa 1975) (receivership); Brady v. Brady, 380 Mass. 480, 404 N.E.2d 75 (1980) (dictum that the court could impose a lien on real estate to secure alimony payments); Cohen v. Cohen, 319 Mass. 31, 64 N.E.2d 689 (1946) (ne exeat); Kerr v. Kerr, 309 Minn. 124, 243 N.W.2d 313 (1976) (husband's lien on land awarded to wife was modifiable); Walker v. Walker, 119 N.H. 551, 404 A.2d 1103 (1979) (appointed a commissioner to sell real estate under the divorce decree where the husband was recalcitrant); Schumacher v. Schumacher, 242 N.W.2d 136 (N.D.1976) (receivership where property was being badly managed); Kinne v. Kinne, 27 Wash.App. 158, 617 P.2d 442 (1980) (lien to secure alimony or property settlement only where the parties impress a particular fund or piece of property with a charge to secure payment).

11. See section 16.5, supra, at notes 9 and 11. See also DiCorpo v. DiCorpo, 33 Cal.2d 195, 200 P.2d 529 (1948) (dictum); Burke v. Burke, 127 Colo. 257, 255 P.2d 740 (1953).

12. Halpern v. Austin, 385 F.Supp. 1009 (N.D.Ga. 1974); In re Marriage of Wyshak, 70 Cal.App.3d 384, 138 Cal.Rptr. 811 (1977). For a more thorough discussion of this issue in general terms, see Duranceau v. Wallace, 743 F.2d 709 (9th Cir.1984) and Brown v. Liberty Loan Corp. of Duval, 539 F.2d 1355 (5th Cir.1976), cert. denied 430 U.S. 949, 97 S.Ct. 1588, 51 L.Ed.2d 797 (1977).

13. Fuentes v. Shevin, 407 U.S. 67, 92 S.Ct. 1983, 32 L.Ed.2d 556 (1972), rehearing denied 409 U.S. 902, 93 S.Ct. 177, 34 L.Ed.2d 165 (1972); Sniadach v. Family Finance Corp. of Bay View, 395 U.S. 337, 89 S.Ct. 1820, 23 L.Ed.2d 349 (1969).

14. See section 16.5, supra, at note 10.

15. Joseph Harris & Sons v. Van Loan, 23 N.J. 466, 129 A.2d 571 (1957); Winter v. Winter, 162 N.J.Super. 456, 393 A.2d 593 (1978); N.Y.—McKinney's Dom.Rel.L. § 244 (Supp.1984–1985).

on a new assertion of personal jurisdiction over the defendant.[16]

The federal government has provided additional methods of enforcing those support obligations owing to a parent who has custody of a child, where that parent has been receiving support from the state and has consequently assigned her support claim to the state. Federal statutes provide in such circumstances that any federal tax refunds owed by the United States to the obligor responsible for the payment of such support may be intercepted and paid by the United States to the state in question.[17] This and other programs will be discussed in greater detail in connection with the enforcement of child support claims.[18]

Transfers made for inadequate consideration and while the transferor was insolvent, or made with intent to hinder or delay creditors of the transferor are generally considered fraudulent conveyances, and may be reached by the creditors of the transferor.[19] This principle applies to transfers made by a spouse who has been ordered to pay alimony, so that the obligee spouse may recover back the transferred property to the extent necessary to satisfy her claim.[20] The transferee is a necessary party in such a case.[21]

Alimony decrees and decrees dividing property, where they are money decrees, carry interest at the rate prescribed for judgments from the date on which the decrees are entered.[22]

Enforcement by Contempt Proceedings

Contempt proceedings are a common method of enforcing alimony decrees. This is recognized in almost all states, whose courts hold that this use of contempt does not violate constitutional prohibitions upon imprisonment for debt.[23] This is so even though the alimony decree may be based upon an agreement of the spouses.[24] The courts which reach this result sometimes base their decisions upon an assertion that alimony is not a "debt" and thus not within the constitutional prohibition.[25] Of course alimony is a kind of debt, but the purpose of the constitutional prohibition is served if, as is usually the case, the contempt sanction is only applied against defendants who are able to comply with the alimony decree. The honest debtor who is unable to pay is given a defense, which is all

16. Bjordahl v. Bjordahl, 308 N.W.2d 817 (Minn.1981) (divorce decree enforced against a non-resident twenty-two years after its entry).

17. I.R.C. § 6402(c) (West 1985); 42 U.S.C.A. § 664 (West 1985). For discussion of the tax intercept program and of its constitutionality, see Nelson v. Regan, 560 F.Supp. 1101 (D.Conn.1983), affirmed 731 F.2d 105 (2d Cir.1984), cert. denied 469 U.S. 853, 105 S.Ct. 175, 83 L.Ed.2d 110 (1984); Marcello v. Regan, 574 F.Supp. 586 (D.R.I.1983). Many states require welfare recipients to assign to the state their support claims, on which the state may then recover from the obligor of support. See, e.g., Schiavo v. Schiavo, 71 Wis.2d 136, 237 N.W.2d 702 (1976). Mandatory wage withholding may also be available to the custodial parent for enforcement of alimony

18. See section 17.3, infra.

19. 4 Collier, Bankruptcy ch. 548 (15th ed.1985).

20. Elliott v. Elliott, 365 F.Supp. 450 (S.D.N.Y.1973); Scavello v. Scott, 194 Colo. 64, 570 P.2d 1 (1977); Jorden v. Ball, 357 Mass. 468, 258 N.E.2d 736 (1970).

21. Becker v. Becker, 138 Vt. 372, 416 A.2d 156 (1980).

22. Ballard v. Ballard, 224 Tenn. 390, 455 S.W.2d 592 (1970); Annot., 33 A.L.R.2d 1455 (1954).

23. Ryan v. Ryan, 267 Ala. 677, 104 So.2d 700 (1958); Application of Hendricks, 5 Cal.App.3d 793, 85 Cal.Rptr.

220 (1970); Heflinger v. Heflinger, 172 Ga. 889, 159 S.E. 242 (1931); Keltner v. Keltner, 589 S.W.2d 235 (Mo.1979); State ex rel. Stanhope v. Pratt, 533 S.W.2d 567 (Mo.1976), 42 Mo.L.Rev. 325 (1977); Adams v. Adams, 80 N.J.Eq. 175, 83 A. 190 (1912), 12 Colum.L.Rev. 638 (1912); Potter v. Wilson, 609 P.2d 1278 (Okl.1980); State ex rel. Hambrecht v. Hambrecht, 128 Or. 305, 274 P. 507 (1929), 9 Ore.L.Rev. 188 (1930); Schroeder v. Schroeder, 95 Wis.2d 415, 290 N.W.2d 548 (App.1980), decision reversed on other grounds 100 Wis.2d 625, 302 N.W.2d 475 (1981); Annot., 30 A.L.R. 130 (1924). Orders for the payment of attorney fees are also enforcible by contempt. Application of Hendricks, 5 Cal.App.3d 793, 85 Cal.Rptr. 220 (1970); Hartt v. Hartt, 121 R.I. 220, 397 A.2d 518 (1979).

Indiana seems to be the only state which persists in holding that the use of contempt to enforce alimony decrees violates the state's constitutional prohibition. State ex rel. Shaunki v. Endsley, 266 Ind. 267, 362 N.E.2d 153 (1977); Neal v. Neal, 412 N.E.2d 319 (Ind.App.1980).

For a general account of contempt, see R. Goldfarb, The Contempt Power (1963).

24. Holloway v. Holloway, 130 Ohio St. 214, 198 N.E. 579 (1935).

25. State ex rel. Stanhope v. Pratt, 533 S.W.2d 567 (Mo.1976).

that the constitutional provision is intended to ensure.

There is a conflict in the cases as to whether decrees dividing the property of the spouses on divorce may be enforced by contempt proceedings. Some cases which deny contempt enforcement to decrees for the division of property rely on the argument that the decree creates a "debt" which may not constitutionally be the basis for imprisonment.[26] Since this kind of decree, no less than an alimony award, does create a debt, this argument fails to address the real purpose of the constitutional provision. Other cases advance the more plausible reason that while alimony decrees are modifiable, property decrees are not, and that the severe sanction of contempt should not be applied to a decree which is not modifiable.[27] Although this reasoning has some appeal, it really does not furnish a persuasive basis for denying the use of contempt to enforce divisions of property. It has been shown in an earlier section [28] that in most states today the division of property has the same functions as the award of alimony, and that it is often virtually impossible to draw a rational distinction between an

award of alimony and an award of property.[29] The distinction can be drawn no more sensibly for granting or withholding the contempt sanction than in other contexts.[30] The better and more workable result therefore is to enforce divisions of property by contempt and a growing number of courts do so.[31] This is particularly desirable in view of the need for effective enforcement of all the financial aspects of divorce decrees which is so crucial today.[32] Of course if contempt is used to enforce divisions of property, the same defense of inability to pay should be available to the defendant as is available when he is charged with the failure to pay alimony.[33]

The procedure for conducting contempt proceedings varies with the different states,[34] but in all states it follows the same general pattern. The form of contempt asserted is usually civil contempt, which is defined as contempt whose purpose is to coerce the defendant into complying with the divorce decree.[35] Where there have been repeated or aggravated episodes of disobedience to decrees, the courts may also resort to criminal contempt, whose purpose is the punishment of past violations and which requires the court

26. Proffit v. Proffit, 105 Ariz. 222, 462 P.2d 391 (1969); Plumer v. Superior Court In and For Los Angeles County, 50 Cal.2d 631, 328 P.2d 193 (1958); Bradley v. Superior Court, 48 Cal.2d 509, 310 P.2d 634 (1957), 10 Stan.L.Rev. 321 (1958), 42 Minn.L.Rev. 929 (1958); In re Fontana, 24 Cal.App.3d 1008, 101 Cal.Rptr. 465 (1972); (But see In re Marriage of Verner, 77 Cal.App.3d 718, 143 Cal.Rptr. 826 (1978)); Linton v. Linton, 166 Ind.App. 409, 336 N.E.2d 687 (1975), rehearing denied 166 Ind.App. 409, 339 N.E.2d 96 (1975); McAlear v. McAlear, 298 Md. 320, 469 A.2d 1256 (1984); Thomas v. Thomas, 337 Mich. 510, 60 N.W.2d 331 (1953); Seablom v. Seablom, 348 N.W.2d 920 (N.D.1984) (relying on a state statute); State ex rel. Stirewalt v. Stirewalt, 7 Or.App. 544, 492 P.2d 802 (1972).

Even in these jurisdictions the courts would enforce an act decree, as distinguished from a money decree, by contempt, as, for example, where the decree called for a conveyance of real estate. See the Proffit and Linton cases, supra.

27. E.g., McAlear v. McAlear, 298 Md. 320, 469 A.2d 1256 (1984) (semble).

28. See section 15.1, supra.

29. See sections 15.1, supra, and 16.8, infra. The same confusion between alimony and divisions of property is exhibited in the bankruptcy cases, discussed infra at note 67.

30. See, e.g., Seablom v. Seablom, 348 N.W.2d 920 (N.D.1984) and State ex rel. Stirewalt v. Stirewalt, 7 Or.

App. 544, 492 P.2d 802 (1972), in both of which cases the parties called the payments alimony but the court characterized them as property.

31. In re Marriage of Ramos, 126 Ill.App.3d 391, 81 Ill.Dec. 214, 466 N.E.2d 1016 (1984), cert. denied 471 U.S. 1017, 105 S.Ct. 2023, 85 L.Ed.2d 305 (1985); Haley v. Haley, 648 S.W.2d 890 (Mo.App.1982); Harris v. Harris, 58 Ohio St.2d 303, 390 N.E.2d 789 (1979); Hanks v. Hanks, 334 N.W.2d 856 (S.D.1983); In re Gorena, 595 S.W.2d 841 (Tex.1979); Decker v. Decker, 52 Wash.2d 456, 326 P.2d 332 (1958).

32. See the discussion of the difficulties facing the alimony and property claimant in section 16.1, supra.

33. See the cases cited infra, at note 44.

34. E.g., Note, Enforcement of Alimony Judgments in New Jersey, 11 Rutgers L.Rev. 726 (1957); Note, Enforcement of Alimony Provisions of Matrimonial Decrees in New York, 3 Syra.L.Rev. 136 (1951); Note, 10 So.Cal.L. Rev. 496 (1937).

35. Johansen v. State, 491 P.2d 759 (Alaska 1971); Elzey v. Elzey, 291 Md. 369, 435 A.2d 445 (1981); McDaniel v. McDaniel, 256 Md. 684, 262 A.2d 52 (1970); Schroeder v. Schroeder, 100 Wis.2d 625, 302 N.W.2d 475 (1981) (in civil contempt the act required must be within the defendant's power to perform, and the contempt order must state what the defendant must do to purge himself of the contempt).

to observe all of the procedural and due process safeguards of the usual criminal proceeding.[36] The proceedings in civil complaint are begun by a verified motion, by an application, or by affidavits setting forth the decree and its breach and asking for a citation or an order to show cause.[37] The alleged violation of the divorce decree must be described in the citation,[38] which must be served on the defendant.[39] Since the contempt proceeding is a continuation of the divorce action, the personal jurisdiction acquired in that action to serve as the basis for the alimony or property award is sufficient to support the contempt proceeding without a new assertion of personal jurisdiction.[40] It is sufficient that the defendant receives notice from the citation and is given an opportunity to be heard.[41] It is generally held today that an indigent defendant in a civil contempt proceeding is entitled to have counsel appointed to represent him at state expense if, as is usually the case, imprisonment may follow his conviction.[42]

The offense to which civil contempt is addressed is often characterized as the wilful

failure or refusal to comply with the order for alimony or support.[43] What this means is that the defendant may not be found guilty of contempt if at the time of the hearing on the citation he is unable to make the payments.[44] Although local practice varies with respect to the duty of pleading ability or inability to pay, the burden of proving inability to pay is generally placed upon the defendant.[45] This is proper so long as it is recognized that the proceeding is civil and not criminal contempt. Some of the cases which place the burden of proving ability to pay upon the plaintiff are based on the view that the proceeding is criminal, thereby invoking the rule that all elements of the defendant's guilt must be proved beyond a reasonable doubt.[46]

It is impossible to give a comprehensive definition of "inability to pay", but some helpful generalizations may be drawn from the cases. The defendant must show in good faith that he was unable to make the payments, not merely that it was inconvenient or

36. Hopkins v. Jarvis, 648 F.2d 981 (5th Cir.1981); Hopkins v. Hopkins, 244 Ga. 66, 257 S.E.2d 900 (1979); Anderson v. Anderson, 667 P.2d 660 (Wyo.1983). See also Murray v. Murray, 60 Hawaii 160, 587 P.2d 1220 (1978).

37. Annot., 41 A.L.R.2d 1263 (1955).

38. Wright v. District Court of Second Jud.Dist., 192 Colo. 553, 561 P.2d 15 (1977).

39. Lubbehusen v. Lubbehusen, 16 Ariz.App. 45, 490 P.2d 1173 (1971), petition for review denied 108 Ariz. 430, 501 P.2d 14 (1972) (defendant must be given reasonable notice of the proceeding); Richardson v. Richardson, 276 A.2d 231 (D.C.App.1971) (reasonable notice required); Womack v. Celanese Corp. of America, 205 Ga. 514, 54 S.E.2d 235 (1949), cert. denied 338 U.S. 937, 70 S.Ct. 346, 94 L.Ed. 578 (1950) (notice not required if the defendant had knowledge of the restraining order).

40. Lubbehusen v. Lubbehusen, 16 Ariz.App. 45, 490 P.2d 1173 (1971), petition for review denied 108 Ariz. 430, 501 P.2d 14 (1972); Application of Jess, 11 Cal.App.3d 819, 91 Cal.Rptr. 72 (1970); Richardson v. Richardson, 276 A.2d 231 (D.C.App.1971); State ex rel. Brubaker v. Pritchard, 236 Ind. 222, 138 N.E.2d 233 (1956); People ex rel. Kazubowski v. Ray, 48 Ill.2d 413, 272 N.E.2d 225 (1971), cert. denied 404 U.S. 818, 92 S.Ct. 78, 30 L.Ed.2d 118 (1971). Contra, requiring personal jurisdiction to be obtained at the time of the contempt citation, Strauss v. Strauss, 231 Ga. 248, 200 S.E.2d 878 (1973).

41. Yoder v. Cumberland County, 278 A.2d 379 (Me. 1971); Sodones v. Sodones, 366 Mass. 121, 314 N.E.2d 906 (1974) (criminal contempt); Mills v. Howard, 109 R.I. 25, 280 A.2d 101 (1971).

42. Walker v. McLain, 768 F.2d 1181 (10th Cir. 1985), cert. denied ___ U.S. ___, 106 S.Ct. 805, 88 L.Ed.2d 781 (1986); Ridgway v. Baker, 720 F.2d 1409 (5th Cir.1983); Parker v. Turner, 626 F.2d 1 (6th Cir.1980); Vela v. District Court In and For Arapahoe County, 664 P.2d 243 (Colo.1983), citing other cases; Rutherford v. Rutherford, 296 Md. 347, 464 A.2d 228 (1983). Duval v. Duval, 114 N.H. 422, 322 A.2d 1 (1974) held that a trial court could appoint counsel for an indigent defendant in a contempt proceeding if the case was complicated.

43. Connolly v. Connolly, 191 Conn. 468, 464 A.2d 837 (1983).

44. E.g., Blalock v. Blalock, 214 Ga. 586, 105 S.E.2d 721 (1958); Elzey v. Elzey, 291 Md. 369, 435 A.2d 445 (1981); Clausen v. Clausen, 250 Minn. 293, 84 N.W.2d 675 (1957); State ex rel. Varner v. Janco, 156 W.Va. 139, 191 S.E.2d 64 (1972). Other cases are cited in Annot., 53 A.L.R.2d 591 (1957); Note, 37 Yale L.J. 509, 511 (1928); and Moscowitz Contempt of Injunctions, Civil and Criminal, 43 Colum.L.Rev. 780, 795 (1943).

45. Application of Martin, 76 Idaho 179, 279 P.2d 873 (1955); In re Marriage of Logston, 103 Ill.2d 266, 82 Ill. Dec. 633, 469 N.E.2d 167 (1984); In re Marriage of Hilkovitch, 124 Ill.App.3d 401, 79 Ill.Dec. 891, 464 N.E.2d 795 (1984); Rainwater v. Rainwater, 236 Miss. 412, 110 So.2d 608 (1959); Pugh v. Pugh, 15 Ohio St.3d 136, 472 N.E.2d 1085 (1984); Bailey v. Bailey, 77 S.D. 546, 95 N.W.2d 533 (1959). Other cases are cited in Annot., 53 A.L.R.2d 591, 605 (1957).

46. E.g. Frye v. Frye, 158 Neb. 694, 64 N.W.2d 468 (1954).

difficult to make them.[47] In proving this he is required to make a full disclosure of the details of his financial situation.[48] It is not enough for him to assert in general terms that he was unable to comply with the decree. The defense in contempt requires a proof of greater financial hardship than does a motion to reduce alimony. A defendant who is able to pay part but not all of the alimony is guilty of contempt if he fails to pay what he can.[49] If his inability to pay arises from his own extravagance, neglect, fraud, misconduct or refusal to work when able to, it is contumacious and not a defense.[50] He may not plead inability when he has sufficient funds, even if those funds are capital assets or constitute property which is exempt from the claims of creditors.[51]

There is some conflict in the cases concerning the availability of contempt to enforce alimony decrees where other methods of enforcement, such as execution, security or a lien, are available.[52] Some cases take the view that contempt is an extraordinary remedy to be used only when others fail or are not possible.[53] The better view is that contempt

is cumulative. The plaintiff should be able to rely on it whether or not she has other remedies.[54] It seems particularly short-sighted to force her to proceed against property securing her claim before seeking contempt, since this leaves her without protection for the future.[55]

The extent and form of the penalty in contempt proceedings are within the discretion of the trial court, which may condition the penalty upon the defendant's non-performance of his alimony obligation within a specific time.[56]

Property Available for the Enforcement of Alimony Claims

In general of course execution or garnishment are effective to reach any property owned by the alimony obligor. In a few instances, however, his property may be subject to statutory or contractual provisions excluding alienation or assignment. The question then is whether these provisions operate to prevent the alimony claimant from enforcing her claim against such property.

As has been indicated,[57] Congress has passed a statute permitting money due as

47. Faircloth v. Faircloth, 321 So.2d 87 (Fla.App.1975), decision quashed on other grounds 339 So.2d 650 (1976); In re Marriage of Logston, 103 Ill.2d 266, 82 Ill.Dec. 633, 469 N.E.2d 167 (1984); Katz v. Katz, 113 N.J.Eq. 75, 166 A. 176 (1933).

48. Shaffner v. Shaffner, 212 Ill. 492, 72 N.E. 447 (1904).

49. Gibson v. Clark, 216 Miss. 430, 62 So.2d 585 (1953); State ex rel. Wolf v. Wolf, 11 Or.App. 477, 503 P.2d 1255 (1972); Bailey v. Bailey, 77 S.D. 546, 95 N.W.2d 533 (1959).

50. Faircloth v. Faircloth, 321 So.2d 87 (Fla.App.1975), decision quashed on other grounds 339 So.2d 650 (1976); In re Marriage of Logston, 103 Ill.2d 266, 82 Ill.Dec. 633, 469 N.E.2d 167 (1984); Wohlfort v. Wohlfort, 116 Kan. 154, 225 P. 746 (1924); Terrell v. Terrell, 239 S.W.2d 975 (Ky.1951); Bailey v. Bailey, 77 S.D. 546, 95 N.W.2d 533 (1959). But see Clausen v. Clausen, 250 Minn. 293, 84 N.W.2d 675 (1957), and Snook v. Snook, 188 P. 502 (Wash. 1920).

51. Ex parte Smallbone, 16 Cal.2d 532, 106 P.2d 873 (1940); Krokyn v. Krokyn, 378 Mass. 206, 390 N.E.2d 733 (1979).

52. Annot., 136 A.L.R. 689 (1942).

53. Andrews v. Andrews, 198 Misc. 223, 98 N.Y.S.2d 254 (1950); Zuehls v. Zuehls, 227 Wis. 473, 278 N.W. 880 (1938).

54. Larson v. Larson, 248 Wis. 352, 21 N.W.2d 725 (1946). Although there should be no election of remedies

requirement, if the alimony claimant first seeks contempt and loses on the ground that the decree has been complied with, res judicata will bar a later attempt to obtain execution. Silva v. Silva, 122 R.I. 178, 404 A.2d 829 (1979).

55. Erickson v. Erickson, 8 Wash.2d 255, 111 P.2d 757 (1941).

56. Kephart v. Kephart, 89 U.S.App.D.C. 373, 193 F.2d 677 (1951), cert. denied 342 U.S. 944, 72 S.Ct. 557, 96 L.Ed. 702 (1952); Wohlfort v. Wohlfort, 116 Kan. 154, 225 P. 746 (1924); Grattan v. Grattan, 307 P.2d 541 (Okl. 1957); Shaw v. Shaw, 81 R.I. 487, 104 A.2d 754 (1954); Keller v. Keller, 52 Wash.2d 84, 323 P.2d 231 (1958).

57. See note 4, supra, and 42 U.S.C.A. § 659 (1982). This statute does not permit the garnishment of federal compensation to enforce property division claims, however, as indicated in note 4. This distinction has led to conflict in the cases dealing with Texas decrees dividing community property, since Texas does not award alimony, some cases holding that the Texas decree is "tantamount" to alimony, while others hold that it is not and is therefore not within the garnishment statute. Compare Williams v. Williams, 338 So.2d 869 (Fla.App.1976) with Marin v. Hatfield, 546 F.2d 1230 (5th Cir.1977) and United States v. Stelter, 567 S.W.2d 79 (Tex.Civ.App.1978). There may be various state restrictions against attachment or garnishment of pensions to enforce alimony or property claims of spouses, based upon state statutes or common law doctrines. E.g. Watson v. Watson, 424 F.Supp. 866 (E.D.N.C.1976) (state law does not permit compensation for employment to individuals from the United States or the District of Columbia to be reached for the enforcement of alimony claims. Some types of pension are covered by federal or other statutes forbidding alienation or assignment, however. Railroad Retirement Act pensions have for this reason been held not to be available to spouses seeking a division of property, for example.[58] For a time federal military retirement pensions were not subject to spousal property claims [59] but today they are so available to some extent, pursuant to a change in the federal statute.[60] The federal Employee Retirement Income Security Act of 1974 (ERISA) governs employee pensions where the employer is engaged in commerce and contains provisions apparently forbidding alienation or assignment.[61] Until 1984 there was some question in the case law as to whether an alimony claimant could reach pensions subject to that Act to enforce her claims.[62] In 1984 ERISA was amended by the Retirement Equity Act of that year (REA) to provide that ERISA pensions must provide for the payment of benefits in accordance with a "qualified domestic relations order", that is, the decree of a court ordering the payment of alimony, child support or a division of property to a spouse or child, if such an order meets the highly de-

tailed requirements set out in the statute as conditions upon qualification.[63]

There is considerable disagreement among the states concerning the enforcement of alimony claims against property held in spendthrift trusts, with a substantial number of cases holding that the spouse's claim for alimony stands in no better position than the claim of any other creditor.[64] Although it is generally true that one person may transfer property to another upon such terms as he may deem wise, there is something repugnant in the spectacle of an ex-spouse enjoying affluence on the proceeds of a trust while his exspouse or child are in need. Claims for alimony are of such social importance that the better result is to grant the ex-spouse execution or garnishment against the principal or income of the spendthrift trust.[65]

Most, if not all, jurisdictions have statutes exempting from the claims of creditors a state proportion of the debtor's real estate, of his wages, and in some instances other kinds of property. The purpose of these statutes is broadly the preservation from destitution not only of the individual owner of the property but also of his spouse and family. That being so, it follows, as many cases have held,[66] that the claims of the spouse and children for

---

garnishment of federal military retirement pay); Sochor v. International Business Machines Corp., 60 N.Y.2d 254, 469 N.Y.S.2d 591, 457 N.E.2d 696 (1983) (retirement benefits may not be garnished before the earning spouse retires); Udall v. Udall, 613 P.2d 742 (Okl.1980) (state public employees' pension may not be attached under the statute). For a case holding that social security disability payments may not be garnished for spousal support, see Sharlot v. Sharlot, 122 Misc.2d 350, 470 N.Y.S.2d 544 (Fam.Ct.1984), order reversed 110 A.D.2d 299, 494 N.Y.S.2d 238 (1985).

Weinberg v. Weinberg, 67 Cal.2d 557, 63 Cal.Rptr. 13, 432 P.2d 709 (1967) and In re Marriage of Barnes, 83 Cal. App.3d 143, 147 Cal.Rptr. 710 (1978) have stated that a first wife may enforce her alimony claim against the community property of her ex-husband and his second wife.

58. Hisquierdo v. Hisquierdo, 439 U.S. 572, 99 S.Ct. 802, 59 L.Ed.2d 1 (1979). Amendments to the Railroad Retirement Act subsequent to Hisquierdo have made divorced wives eligible for annuities under that Act under conditions established by the Social Security Act. 45 U.S.C.A. § 231a(c)(4) (West 1985).

59. McCarty v. McCarty, 453 U.S. 210, 101 S.Ct. 2728, 69 L.Ed.2d 589 (1981).

60. 10 U.S.C.A. § 1408. See section 16.6, supra, at note 7.

61. 29 U.S.C.A. § 1144, preempting state law; 29 U.S. C.A. § 1056(d)(1); I.R.C. § 401(a)(13).

62. American Tel. & Tel. Co. v. Merry, 592 F.2d 118 (2d Cir.1979), holding that a state divorce court could garnish ERISA pension benefits to satisfy spousal support claims, and citing other cases both ways. See also section 15.6, supra, at note 15.

63. 29 U.S.C.A. § 1056(d)(3) (West 1985); Pub.L. 98–397, 98 Stat. 1433 (1984). See also I.R.C. § 401(a)(13)(B) (West 1985).

64. Dinwiddie v. Baumberger, 18 Ill.App.3d 933, 310 N.E.2d 841 (1974); Bucknam v. Bucknam, 294 Mass. 214, 200 N.E. 918 (1936); In Matter of Campbell's Trusts, 258 N.W.2d 856 (Minn.1977); Eaton v. Lovering, 81 N.H. 275, 125 A. 433 (1924).

65. Bacardi v. White, 463 So.2d 218 (Fla.1985), citing other cases. See also E. Griswold, Spendthrift Trusts § 339 (2d ed.1947).

66. Schlaefer v. Schlaefer, 71 U.S.App.D.C. 350, 112 F.2d 177 (1940); Kendrick v. Kendrick, 271 Ala. 372, 124 So.2d 78 (1960); Henry v. Henry, 182 Cal.App.2d 707, 6 Cal.Rptr. 418 (1960); In re Bagnall's Guardianship, 238

alimony and support may be enforced against such exempt property. Alimony claims are held not to be "debts" for purposes of these statutes.

Bankruptcy and Other Defenses to the Enforcement of Alimony and Property Claims

Although the bankruptcy law may affect divorce proceedings in several ways,[67] at this point we are chiefly concerned with the question whether obligations imposed upon the spouses in a divorce decree are dischargeable in bankruptcy. The Bankruptcy Code, in peculiarly convoluted language, provides that a discharge in bankruptcy does not discharge liabilities "actually in the nature of alimony, maintenance, or support" to spouses or children in connection with a separation agreement, divorce decree, or other order of a court of record, or property settlement agreement.[68] This requires lawyers and courts to determine whether a particular liability is for alimony or child support, or rather for some other

kind of obligation arising out of marriage. Since the only other obligation likely to be asserted in divorce is one for the division of property, we are faced with the same kind of alimony-property distinction which has proved so unworkable in other contexts.[69]

The federal courts usually state, when deciding whether payments are for alimony or a division of property, that the question turns on federal law.[70] This is correct in the sense that it is a federal statute which is being construed. It is more precise to say, however, that state law governs the extent, purpose, qualifications and limitations of the obligation being characterized. It is the evaluation of those factors which persuades the bankruptcy courts to place the obligation in one category or the other.[71] For that reason the distinction between alimony and property involves both state and federal law. Some cases adopt a somewhat different analysis in reliance upon the Bankruptcy Code. In re Calhoun[72] held that the bankruptcy court must first decide, on the basis of the intention of

Iowa 905, 29 N.W.2d 597 (1947). Many other cases are collected in Annot., 54 A.L.R.2d 1422 (1957). See Albrecht v. Albrecht, 99 N.W.2d 229 (N.D.1959) holding separate maintenance claims enforceable against the homestead. But the alimony claim cannot be asserted against the homestead over the objection of a second wife and children. The later going marriage is properly preferred. Yager v. Yager, 7 Cal.2d 213, 60 P.2d 422 (1936).

67. E.g., the statute provides that a petition in bankruptcy operates as a stay of proceedings against the debtor. 11 U.S.C.A. § 362 (1982 and West 1985). The provision is very broad and could apply to divorce proceedings, although it probably should not apply to the status and custody aspects of such proceedings. Cases applying the section include In re Pagitt, 3 B.R. 588 (Bkrtcy.W.D.La.1980); Graves v. Graves, 239 Ga. 869, 239 S.E.2d 35 (1977).

Where a divorce decree has ordered property of the debtor to be turned over to the spouse before a bankruptcy petition is filed, this may prevent the property from becoming part of the bankruptcy estate, depending upon the effect of such an order under state law. Compare In re Paderewski, 564 F.2d 1353 (9th Cir.1977); In re Barasch, 439 F.2d 1393 (9th Cir.1971); Decker v. Occidental Life Ins. Co., 70 Cal.2d 842, 76 Cal.Rptr. 470, 452 P.2d 686 (1969) with In re Arnold C. Harms, 7 B.R. 398 (Bkrtcy.Colo.1980).

For the relationship of bankruptcy to marital property see Riesenfeld, Who Owns What Under Chapter 7?, 5 Fam. Advocate 28 (1983).

68. 11 U.S.C.A. § 523(a)(5) (1982 and West 1985). The phrase "or other order of a court of record" was added to

the Bankruptcy Code in 1984 to cover child support for illegitimate children ordered in paternity or other proceedings. The former Bankruptcy Act also provided for the non-dischargeability of alimony and child support payments, requiring the courts to observe the same alimony-property distinction. 11 U.S.C.A. § 35(a)(7).

The Code provision states that the debt for alimony is discharged if it is assigned voluntarily or by operation of law to another entity, except where the assignment is of a child support claim to a state in order to enable the assignor to become eligible for Aid to Families With Dependent Children (AFDC) payments under 42 U.S.C.A. § 402(a)(26). In re Spong, 661 F.2d 6 (2d Cir.1981) held that an order requiring a husband to pay the attorney fees of his wife directly to her attorney was not to be deemed an assignment under this provision so that the debt was not discharged. The same result has been reached respecting other kinds of direct payments pursuant to divorce decrees. In re Calhoun, 715 F.2d 1103 (6th Cir.1983); Annot., 69 A.L.R.Fed. 403, 489 (1984).

69. E.g., sections 15.1, 16.5 and this section at note 26, supra. See also section 16.8, infra.

70. E.g., In re Williams, 703 F.2d 1055 (8th Cir.1983).

71. Matter of Albin, 591 F.2d 94 (9th Cir.1979). See also Nichols v. Hensler, 528 F.2d 304 (7th Cir.1976). It follows that the bankruptcy court is not bound by the label the state court puts on the payments. Erspan v. Badgett, 647 F.2d 550 (5th Cir.1981), rehearing denied 659 F.2d 26 (5th Cir.1981).

72. 715 F.2d 1103 (6th Cir.1983). In re Harrell, 754 F.2d 902 (11th Cir.1985) rejected the Calhoun reasoning.

the parties or of the divorce court, whether the obligation constitutes alimony or a division of property. If it is found to be a property division, then it is discharged by the bankruptcy. If it is found to be alimony, the bankruptcy court must go on to decide whether the award made by the state court was "manifestly unreasonable." If so, or if it exceeded the bankrupt spouse's ability to pay, the bankruptcy court must then hold that the excess is dischargeable, and only that portion of the payments which is reasonably within the bankrupt's ability to pay is non-dischargeable. In effect this view of the Code gives the bankruptcy court the power to modify divorce decrees ex post facto, provides incentives for recalcitrant husbands to disobey alimony decrees and creates one more obstacle to divorced wives' attempts to collect their alimony.[73]

The purpose of the bankruptcy laws is obviously to give the bankrupt a "fresh start" free of his old debts.[74] The reason for excepting from that fresh start the obligations he owes to his ex-spouse and children is that those obligations are regarded as having greater social importance than his obligations to ordinary creditors.[75] This being so, the crucial issue then is whether the obligation imposed by the divorce court has the purpose and effect of providing support for the spouse. Theoretically it should be possible to decide this issue with reasonable certainty, but in practice it usually cannot be done, as the

hopeless conflict and confusion in the bankruptcy cases demonstrates.[76] The reason that it cannot be done is that nearly all financial provisions in divorce decrees have as their purpose and effect the support of the recipient. The statutes on division of property make this clear,[77] as do the opinions of the judges in divorce cases, which often state that the level of alimony and the amount of property awarded are to be arrived at interdependently.[78] If the spouse is given more property, she will usually receive less alimony, and vice versa. Some of the bankruptcy cases recognize this fact implicitly, though not expressly, when they characterize as alimony a property award made in a state in which alimony is not permitted.[79] Unfortunately the drafters of the Bankruptcy Code were not aware of it.

The bankruptcy cases attempt to make this distinction in the first instance by saying that the intent of the parties or the divorce court is controlling.[80] But they also say that the label placed on the payments by the parties or the court is not controlling.[81] They then look at the form of the award for clues to its character, on the theory that alimony awards generally assume a certain form. Thus if the decree provides that the payments terminate on the remarriage or death of the recipient, or is modifiable for changed circumstances, this is evidence that it is alimony.[82] If the agreement or decree contains other provisions labeled property, the payments may be held

---

73. See section 16.1, supra. Rather than try to interfere in the state courts' handling of their divorce proceedings, the bankruptcy courts should follow the salutary advice of In re MacDonald, 755 F.2d 715, 717 (9th Cir. 1985): "It is appropriate for bankruptcy courts to avoid incursions into family law matters 'out of consideration of court economy, judicial restraint, and deference to our state court brethren and their established expertise in such matters'".

74. In re Harrell, 754 F.2d 902 (11th Cir.1985).

75. Shaver v. Shaver, 736 F.2d 1314 (9th Cir.1984).

76. An extensive collection of cases illustrating the text statement may be found in Annot., Debts for Alimony, Maintenance and Support as Exceptions to Bankruptcy Discharge Under 523(a)(5) of the Bankruptcy Code of 1978, 11 U.S.C.A. § 523(a)(5), 69 A.L.R.Fed. 403 (1984).

77. See section 15.1, supra.

78. See section 15.3, supra.

79. E.g., Shaver v. Shaver, 736 F.2d 1314 (9th Cir. 1984); Erspan v. Badgett, 647 F.2d 550 (5th Cir.1981), cert. denied 455 U.S. 945, 102 S.Ct. 1443, 71 L.Ed.2d 658 (1982).

80. E.g., In re Calhoun, 715 F.2d 1103 (6th Cir.1983); Melichar v. Ost, 661 F.2d 300 (4th Cir.1981), cert. denied 456 U.S. 927, 102 S.Ct. 1974, 72 L.Ed.2d 442 (1982); In re Lelak, 38 B.R. 164 (Bkrtcy.S.D.Ohio 1984).

81. In re Williams, 703 F.2d 1055 (8th Cir.1983); Erspan v. Badgett, 647 F.2d 550 (5th Cir.1981), cert. denied 455 U.S. 945, 102 S.Ct. 1443, 71 L.Ed.2d 658 (1982).

82. Shaver v. Shaver, 736 F.2d 1314 (9th Cir.1984). But see Matter of Albin, 591 F.2d 94 (9th Cir.1979); Stein v. Fellerman, 144 N.J.Super. 444, 365 A.2d 1382 (1976), certification denied 73 N.J. 50, 372 A.2d 315 (1977).

alimony.[83] Periodic payments look more like alimony than lump sum payments, in the view of some courts.[84] Other courts take a practical approach, holding that if the recipient's means appear inadequate for her support without the payments, then it must be alimony.[85] Perhaps the most difficult case arises when the parties have agreed on a lump sum payable in installments over more than ten years with the objective of having the payments treated as alimony for tax purposes, but with the provision that the payments are not modifiable except on certain remote contingencies.[86] Although bankruptcy should be considered by the parties as a possibility when they are negotiating a separation agreement, the cases create so much uncertainty about its impact on the financial provisions in divorce decrees that they can do little more than attach the label they wish to have applied and hope that the bankruptcy court will be persuaded by it.[87]

Attorney fees are generally and properly held to be alimony.[88] They certainly have the purpose of providing a specific item of support for the recipient and therefore meet the Bankruptcy Code's requirement. Child support orders do not often pose any difficulties of characterization except perhaps in the rare case when they run beyond the age of majority. But even then they should properly be held to be child support.[89]

Another defense which may be advanced to bar the enforcement of alimony decrees is that of the statute of limitations.[90] The statute begins to run on each installment of alimony when it accrues, rather than when the decree is originally granted.[91] The running of the statute is tolled while the husband is out of the jurisdiction or where he in other ways makes it impossible for the wife to enforce the decree against him.[92]

Dicta in many cases has it that laches may bar enforcement of alimony decrees.[93] The fact that laches is an equitable doctrine caused some early cases difficulty either in deciding whether the alimony claim was equitable,[94] or in deciding whether laches might apply to enforcement by execution as well as contempt.[95] Now that we are accustomed to recognizing that the old distinctions between law and equity have long been abolished, these difficulties should no longer trouble the

83. In re Bonhomme, 8 B.R. 645 (Bkrtcy.W.D.Okl. 1981). Conversely, if the divorce decree contains a provision which is clearly for alimony, other provisions may be characterized as a division of property. Nitz v. Nitz, 568 F.2d 148 (10th Cir.1977). And if the dovrce decree fails to provide specifically for alimony, the bankruptcy court may find that awards of property are for the support of the spouse. Shaver v. Shaver, 736 F.2d 1314 (9th Cir. 1984). But see Abrams v. Burg, 367 Mass. 617, 327 N.E.2d 745 (1975).

84. Annot., 69 A.L.R.Fed. 403, 464 (1984).

85. Nitz v. Nitz, 568 F.2d 148 (10th Cir.1977); Nichols v. Hensler, 528 F.2d 304 (7th Cir.1976).

86. Shaver v. Shaver, 736 F.2d 1314 (9th Cir.1984) (held alimony although apparently not modifiable); Melichar v. Ost, 661 F.2d 300 (4th Cir.1981), cert. denied 456 U.S. 927, 102 S.Ct. 1974, 72 L.Ed.2d 442 (1982) (held alimony where modifiable); In re Cox, 543 F.2d 1277 (10th Cir.1976) (held not to be alimony where not modifiable, though described as alimony in the divorce decree).

87. Compare Erspan v. Badgett, 647 F.2d 550 (5th Cir. 1981), cert. denied 455 U.S. 945, 102 S.Ct. 1443, 71 L.Ed. 2d 658 (1982) with Matter of Albin, 591 F.2d 94 (9th Cir. 1979).

88. Matter of Steingesser, 602 F.2d 36 (2d Cir.1979); In re Spong, 661 F.2d 6 (2d Cir.1981); In re Kaytes, 28 B.R. 140 (Bkrtcy. S.D.Fla.1983); Goldman v. Rodriques,

370 Mass. 435, 349 N.E.2d 335 (1976); Annot., 69 A.L.R. Fed. 403, 416 (1984).

89. In re Harrell, 754 F.2d 902 (11th Cir.1985); Annot., 69 A.L.R.Fed. 403, 468 (1984).

90. Annots., 137 A.L.R. 884, 888 (1942), 70 A.L.R.2d 1250, 1255 (1960).

91. McKee v. McKee, 154 Kan. 340, 118 P.2d 544 (1941); Annots., 137 A.L.R. 884, 890 (1942), 70 A.L.R.2d 1250, 1258 (1960).

92. Stephenson v. Stephenson, 52 So.2d 684 (Fla.1951). Contra: Knipfer v. Buhler, 227 Minn. 334, 35 N.W.2d 425 (1948).

93. Cases are collected innot., Laches or Acquiescence as Defense, So As To Bar Recovery of Arrearages of Permanent Alimony or Child Support, 5 A.L.R.4th 1015 (1981).

94. Smith v. Smith, 168 Ohio St. 447, 156 N.E.2d 113 (1959); Durham v. Durham, 104 Ohio St. 7, 135 N.E. 280 (1922).

95. Compare Brandt v. Brandt, 276 F.2d 488 (D.C.Cir. 1960); Kephart v. Kephart, 89 U.S.App.D.C. 373, 193 F.2d 677 (1951), cert. denied 342 U.S. 944, 72 S.Ct. 557, 96 L.Ed. 702 (1952); Hopkins v. Hopkins, 116 Cal.App.2d 174, 253 P.2d 723 (1953); Jenner v. Jenner, 138 Colo. 149, 330 P.2d 544 (1958); Piacquadio v. Piacquadio, 22 Conn. Supp. 47, 159 A.2d 628 (1960).

courts.[96] Either the spouse is fairly entitled to the amount due or she is not. If she is not, then the equitable doctrine of laches should bar the legal as well as the equitable method of enforcement.

The elements of the defense of laches are (a) an excessive delay in enforcing the decree; and (b) a consequent prejudice to the interests of the judgment debtor.[97] Some cases involve reasoning based on waiver[98] or estoppel[99] or acquiescence.[1] It is doubtful whether there is a discernible difference between these doctrines and laches. The cases upholding the defense of laches generally turn on failure to enforce the decree for periods of more than ten years,[2] although there are other cases in which even longer periods have been held insufficient to establish laches.[3] When the courts speak of prejudice to the judgment debtor's interests, they seem to be insisting on proof that, due to the passage of time and change of conditions, the enforcement of the alimony decree causes substantially greater hardship to the judgment debtor than it would have earlier.[4]

A long delay in enforcing the decree which is explained by the judgment debtor's absence from the jurisdiction or by the claimant's poverty or illness or inability to enforce the decree does not amount to laches.[5] This, together with the requirement that the hardship to the judgment debtor be substantial, has meant that the defense of laches is very rarely successful.

Where there is an agreement between the parties for a reduction in alimony, there is no very convincing reason why this should not be a defense to an attempt to enforce the decree for the original amount, provided of course that the modifying agreement was arrived at without fraud, duress or any over-reaching, and that the modifying agreement has been complied with. Some courts take this position.[6] Others hold that unless the new agreement is approved by a court and the original decree modified, the obligor must continue to pay the amount originally ordered.[7] On this state of the law in order to be fully protected the alimony obligor should be advised not to rely on such agreements, but to seek a court imposed modification, even though such ad-

---

96. Rupp v. Rupp, 129 Cal.App.2d 23, 276 P.2d 144 (1954); Larsen v. Larsen, 5 Utah 2d 224, 300 P.2d 596 (1956), second appeal, Larsen v. Larsen, 9 Utah 2d 160, 340 P.2d 421 (1959).

97. Papcun v. Papcun, 181 Conn. 618, 436 A.2d 282 (1980) (delay must also be inexcusable); Rybinski v. Rybinski, 333 Mich. 592, 53 N.W.2d 386 (1952); Miller v. Miller, 153 Neb. 890, 46 N.W.2d 618 (1951); Connin v. Bailey, 15 Ohio St.2d 34, 472 N.E.2d 328 (1984); Openshaw v. Openshaw, 105 Utah 574, 144 P.2d 528 (1943); Annot., 5 A.L.R.4th 1015 (1981).

98. Bethell v. Bethell, 268 Ark. 409, 597 S.W.2d 576 (1980); Kaminski v. Kaminski, 8 Cal.App.3d 563, 87 Cal. Rptr. 453 (1970).

99. Ellingwood v. Ellingwood, 25 Ill.App.3d 587, 323 N.E.2d 571 (1975) (although wife accepted a lesser amount of alimony for sixteen years without objection, she was not estopped to enforce the full arrears). Estoppel is obviously closely related to the defense of agreement, discussed infra, at note 6. Papcun v. Papcun, 181 Conn. 618, 436 A.2d 282 (1980) treated estoppel as a separate defense rejecting it on the facts for lack of reliance by the judgment debtor.

1. Annot., 5 A.L.R.4th 1015, 1042 (1981). Alig v. Alig, 220 Va. 80, 255 S.E.2d 494 (1979) enforced an alimony decree after a wife had vehemently rejected the payments for three years, finding that neither estoppel nor acquiescence applied.

2. E.g., Rupp v. Rupp, 129 Cal.App.2d 23, 276 P.2d 144 (1954) (fourteen years); Hamilton v. Hamilton, 104 Colo. 615, 94 P.2d 127 (1939) (seventeen years).

3. E.g., Smith v. Smith, 168 Ohio St. 447, 156 N.E.2d 113 (1959) (fourteen years).

4. Prouty v. Drake, 18 Misc.2d 887, 182 N.Y.S.2d 271 (Sup.Ct.1959).

5. Kephart v. Kephart, 89 U.S.App.D.C. 373, 193 F.2d 677 (D.C.Cir.1951), cert. denied 342 U.S. 944, 72 S.Ct. 557, 96 L.Ed. 702 (1952); Gregg v. Gregg, 220 Md. 578, 155 A.2d 500 (1959); Annot., 5 A.L.R.4th 1015, 1025 (1981).

6. Hill v. Hill, 106 Colo. 492, 107 P.2d 597 (1940); Faucette v. Faucette, 226 Ga. 127, 172 S.E.2d 665 (1970); Beiter v. Beiter, 24 Ohio App.2d 149, 265 N.E.2d 324 (1970); Masse v. Masse, 112 R.I. 599, 313 A.2d 642 (1974); Annot., 5 A.L.R.4th 1015, 1042 (1981). Where the agreement relates to past due installments of alimony or to provisions of a property settlement agreement, it should likewise constitute a defense to enforcement, but it may be difficult to reach that result because of the doctrine that such obligations are not modifiable. Nevertheless, the current policy favoring the parties' settling their own financial affairs, and the general contract principle permitting the knowing release of claims should warrant the courts' approval of this kind of agreement. See Uniform Commercial Code § 1–107, 1 Unif.L.Ann. 38 (1976).

7. Sterling v. Sterling, 2 Ark.App. 168, 621 S.W.2d 1 (1981) (semble); Meredith v. Meredith, 238 Ga. 595, 234 S.E.2d 510 (1977); Annot., 5 A.L.R.4th 1015, 1045 (1981).

vice may legitimately strike him as requiring unnecessary expense.

Other defenses are occasionally asserted when enforcement of alimony decrees is sought, but they are rarely successful. For example, it has been held not a defense that the wife frustrated the husband's visitation rights; [8] or that the husband objected to the manner in which she spent the alimony.[9] The husband is usually not permitted to set off against his alimony obligation amounts paid to the wife in other forms.[10]

Alimony Decrees as Creating Judgment Liens [11]

It seems clear that if the procedure previously described [12] for obtaining a writ of execution to collect accrued installments of alimony is followed, the money judgment for unpaid installments thereby entered becomes a lien under the general judgment lien statute.[13] Likewise, if the alimony decree orders the payment of a lump sum, or the payment of a specified amount in installments, the general judgment lien statute imposes a lien on the husband's property.[14] The reason is that in all such cases the wife has a money judgment which is indistinguishable from any other money judgment.

Difficulties arise, however, when the divorce decree orders the payment of alimony installments for an indefinite period in the future, usually continuing until the wife's death or remarriage. The question then is, does such a decree, as to future installments

of alimony, constitute a lien on the husband's property, enforceable against purchasers from him? [15] Judgment liens being entirely creatures of statute, the answer to this question is ultimately referable to the applicable state statute. If the local statute expressly provides that alimony decrees of this kind constitute liens, the courts will give them that effect.[16] Conversely, if the statute expressly provides that such decrees do not constitute liens, no lien results.[17]

If no statute specifically authorizes or forbids the lien, the authorities are divided on whether the general judgment lien statute may be construed so that alimony decrees constitute liens. A careful distinction must be made here between a lien to secure accrued and unpaid installments, and a lien for future installments. This distinction is sometimes overlooked by the courts, as in the leading case of Boyle v. Baggs.[18] When a lien is asserted to secure unpaid installments, the outcome depends initially upon whether such installments automatically become money judgments, enforceable as such. If they do,[19] then it follows that just as execution may be obtained, so a lien is created for the amount unpaid. On the other hand, if the rule of the jurisdiction requires the docketing of a judgment for the unpaid installments, before such a docketing, a lien will exist only if the alimony decree itself creates a lien for all future installments.

Boyle v. Baggs [20] was this kind of a case. The majority opinion, arguing that alimony decrees are different from ordinary money

---

8. Stancill v. Stancill, 286 Md. 530, 408 A.2d 1030 (1979).

9. Mixson v. Mixson, 253 S.C. 436, 171 S.E.2d 581 (1969).

10. Glaeser v. Glaeser, 449 So.2d 428 (Fla.App.1984).

11. For an extensive collection of cases on this subject see Annot., 59 A.L.R.2d 656 (1958).

12. See note 15, supra. In the majority of states described in the first note 11, supra, where each installment of alimony becomes a final judgment on accrual, without opportunity for modification, a lien for each installment results when that installment comes due and is unpaid. See the first note 7, supra.

13. Leifert v. Wolfer, 74 N.D. 746, 24 N.W.2d 690 (1946) (dictum); Boyle v. Baggs, 10 Utah 2d 203, 350 P.2d 622 (1960) (dictum).

14. Esselstyn v. Casteel, 205 Or. 344, 286 P.2d 665 (1955); 2 A. Freeman, Judgments § 932 (5th ed.1925).

15. 2 A. Freeman, Judgments § 916 (5th ed.1925).

16. Spencer v. Spencer, 165 Neb. 675, 87 N.W.2d 212 (1957). If the judgment does constitute a lien, it runs against homestead property as well as other real estate. Annot., 54 A.L.R.2d 1422, 1430 (1957).

17. Annot., 59 A.L.R.2d 656, 669 (1958).

18. 10 Utah 2d 203, 350 P.2d 622 (1960). The case involved child support payments, but the same principles apply to alimony.

19. See the text at first note 11, supra.

20. 10 Utah 2d 203, 350 P.2d 622 (1960).

judgments in that they are indefinite in amount, continue for long periods and are modifiable, denied the lien on the ground that otherwise the purchaser of property could not protect himself and the alienability of property would be impaired. These arguments have force in support of the position that the alimony decree itself does not constitute a lien as to all installments coming due in the future. But in the Boyle case the wife was only asserting a lien as to a definite sum then due and unpaid. The real issue there was, as the dissent argued, whether the amount due and unpaid could be considered a judgment giving rise to a lien.

Other cases hold, though not unanimously, that under the general lien statute the alimony decree does not create a lien as to future installments.[21] Aside from the technical considerations of whether such decrees can be labeled "judgments" under the general lien statute, the choice between conflicting cases turns on an evaluation of conflicting policies. As the Boyle case shows, the policy favoring marketability of land and limiting liens to those which can be ascertained from an examination of the record opposes the lien. The policy emphasizing the social importance of alimony and the need for providing effective methods of enforcing alimony decrees favors creation of the lien. Specific statutes establishing and defining the prevailing policy would seem to be badly needed in this area.

Where only a general judgment lien statute exists, an alimony decree will establish a lien as to future installments if the decree itself

specifically so provides. There is general agreement among the cases on this rule.[22]

 WESTLAW REFERENCES

Enforcement by Contempt Proceedings
to(134 /p contempt) /p enforc! comp*l! /s alimony & sy(contempt)

Property Available for the Enforcement of Alimony Claims
find 567 sw2d 797
spend-thrift /3 trust /s enforc! comp*l! /s alimony
exempt! /3 property /s enforc! comp*l! /s alimony

Bankruptcy and Other Defenses to the Enforcement of Alimony and Property Claims
sy,di(alimony /s bankrupt! /s discharg!)
find 715 f2d 1103
di(statute period action /5 limitation /s alimony)

Alimony Decrees as Creating Judgment Liens
134k256 /p alimony /s lien!

§ 16.7 Enforcement of Foreign [1] Alimony and Property Division Decrees

Application of the Full Faith and Credit Clause

The Full Faith and Credit Clause of the United States Constitution [2] applies to alimony decrees as well as to other judgments. Where the decree is based on jurisdiction over the subject matter of the action and the person of the defendant, the Constitution requires that it be enforced by the courts of states other than the stated in which it was rendered to the extent that it is final and not modifiable. This was the decision in Sistare v. Sistare.[3] The Supreme Court in that case

---

21. Morris v. Henry, 193 Va. 631, 70 S.E.2d 417 (1952). For cases taking this position, see 2 Freeman, Judgments, § 932 (5th ed. 1925); Annot., 59 A.L.R.2d 656, 678 (1958). Contra: Chero-Cola Co. v. May, 169 Ga. 273, 149 S.E. 895 (1929); Cases cited in Annot., 59 A.L.R.2d 656, 675 (1958).

22. Slack v. Mullenix, 245 Iowa 1180, 66 N.W.2d 99 (1954); Owens v. Owens, 234 Miss. 261, 106 So.2d 59 (1958); Kerr v. Kerr, 74 S.D. 454, 54 N.W.2d 357 (1952); Bunde v. Bunde, 270 Wis. 226, 70 N.W.2d 624 (1955). Other cases are cited in Annot., 59 A.L.R.2d 656, 680 (1958).

§ 16.7

1. "Foreign" here means that the decree was entered by the court of another state, not of a foreign country. Enforcement of the alimony decrees of other nations is governed by the doctrines of comity discussed in the

second part of this section, Ehrenzweig, Conflict of Laws, § 83 (1962), and may be affected by the existence of reciprocity between the countries involved. See Gull v. Constam, 105 F.Supp. 107 (D.Colo.1952), 38 Corn.L.Q. 423 (1953).

2. U.S.Const. art. IV, § 1; 28 U.S.C.A. § 1738.

3. 218 U.S. 1, 30 S.Ct. 682, 54 L.Ed. 905 (1910). Earlier cases are Lynde v. Lynde, 181 U.S. 183, 21 S.Ct. 555, 45 L.Ed. 810 (1901) and Barber v. Barber, 62 U.S. (21 How.) 582, 16 L.Ed. 226 (1858). Cases following the Sistare rule include Gargis v. Gargis, 367 So.2d 476 (Ala.Civ.App. 1979), writ denied 367 So.2d 479 (1979) (judgment terminating alimony entitled to full faith and credit); McElroy v. McElroy, 256 A.2d 763 (Del.Ch.1969); Varone v. Varone, 296 A.2d 174 (D.C.App.1972); Wolk v. Leak, 70 So. 2d 498 (Fla.1954); Connell v. Connell, 119 Ga.App. 485,

found that the law of New York was that alimony decrees were not modifiable with respect to accrued and unpaid installments. Since they were final, the Court held that Connecticut was bound to enter a judgment enforcing the New York separation decree and ordering the payment of the accrued installments of alimony. On the other hand if the original divorce decree was not based upon jurisdiction over the person of the defendant,[4] or over the subject matter of the action,[5] or was entered without observing the requirements of due process,[6] full faith and credit need not be extended to it under the Sistare rule.

An earlier section[7] has shown that there are two rules among the various states concerning the modification of alimony decrees. In some states as each installment accrues and is unpaid, it automatically becomes a judgment debt which is not modifiable. The Sistare case requires that full faith and credit be given to such decrees to the extent of the unpaid installments. In other states, such as New York and New Jersey, the accrued installment remains modifiable and does not become final until a judgment for the particular installment is entered. The Sistare case

does not require that full faith and credit be given to such alimony decrees until the judgment for the unpaid installment has been entered. Thus under the Sistare rule an initial determination of finality must be made on the basis of the law of the state in which the divorce decree was originally entered. Once the decree is found to be final by that law, the Full Faith and Credit Clause requires that it be enforced in all other states.

It is a logical inference from the Sistare holding, supported by dictum in the case,[8] that if the alimony decree is modifiable in the state which originally entered it, it is not entitled to full faith and credit. Thus the usual alimony decree need not be given automatic enforcement by the courts of other states to the extent that it imposes a duty to pay future installments of alimony, since the rule in most jurisdictions is that such decrees are modifiable upon a showing of changed circumstances.[9] This is unfortunate since it limits the ability of the alimony recipient to enforce her decree and provides an incentive, if any were needed, to the obligor to evade his obligation.[10] There is nothing in the language either of the Full Faith and Credit

---

167 S.E.2d 686 (1969) (full faith and credit due to a South Carolina decree modifying an earlier Georgia child support order); Wicker v. Wicker, 85 Nev. 141, 451 P.2d 715 (1969); Corliss v. Corliss, 89 N.M. 235, 549 P.2d 1070 (1976); Ceyte v. Ceyte, 222 Va. 11, 278 S.E.2d 791 (1981) (full faith and credit due to a denial of alimony). If the prior decree fails to address the claim made in the second state, the requirement of full faith and credit to the first decree does not prevent the second state from enforcing the omitted claim. Pierrakos v. Pierrakos, 148 N.J. Super. 574, 372 A.2d 1331 (1977).

The Sistare rule applies to distribution of property as well as to alimony. Wicker v. Wicker, 85 Nev. 11, 451 P.2d 715 (1969).

For discussion of these principles see Foster and Freed, Modification, Recognition and Enforcement of Foreign Alimony Orders, 11 Cal.W.L.Rev. 280 (1975); Note, Interstate Enforcement of Modifiable Alimony and Child Support Decrees, 54 Iowa L.Rev. 597 (1969).

The doctrine of Sistare may be relevant in a three-judgment situation. For example, state A grants a divorce decree to the wife, ordering the husband to convey certain property to her. The husband then sues in state B and gets a decree that he is entitled to the property, the court in state B erroneously refusing to give full faith and credit to state A's judgment. The wife then brings another suit in state A seeking the property. Porter v.

Porter, 101 Ariz. 131, 416 P.2d 564 (1966), cert. denied 386 U.S. 957, 87 S.Ct. 1028, 18 L.Ed.2d 107 (1967) held that in such circumstances state A was not required to give full faith and credit to the judgment of state B, but the case is clearly wrong. For discussion of this "last case" problem, see section 12.2, supra, at note 90.

4. Benefield v. Harris, 143 Ga.App. 709, 240 S.E.2d 119 (1977). For a discussion of personal jurisdiction as a basis for alimony and property decrees, see section 12.4, supra.

5. Krueger v. Krueger, 179 Conn. 488, 427 A.2d 400 (1980). The rules governing subject matter jurisdiction in divorce are discussed in section 12.2, supra.

6. Brown v. Brown, 96 Nev. 713, 615 P.2d 962 (1980). This point is more fully discussed in connection with the Griffin case infra, at note 15.

7. See section 16.5, supra.

8. Sistare v. Sistare, 218 U.S. 1, 17, 30 S.Ct. 682, 690, 54 L.Ed. 905 (1910). See also Overman v. Overman, 514 S.W.2d 625 (Mo.App.1974), 40 Mo.L.Rev. 335 (1975).

9. See section 16.5, supra.

10. For criticism of the limited effect of Sistare see Foster and Freed, Modification, Recognition and Enforcement of Foreign Alimony Orders, 11 Cal.W.L.Rev. 280 (1975).

Clause [11] or the implementing statute [12] which excludes modifiable decrees from mandatory enforcement. For these reasons Justice Jackson, concurring, in Barber v. Barber [13] stated that an alimony decree is entitled to full faith and credit whether or not it is modifiable. The leading case of Light v. Light [14] takes the same position. Justice Schaefer, finding no square authority to the contrary and relying upon the strong policy considerations favoring the enforcement of modifiable alimony decrees, held that neither the Constitution nor the implementing statute imposes any requirement of finality for full faith and credit. The court's opinion went on to hold that a Missouri alimony decree was constitutionally entitled to enforcement in Illinois even though by Missouri law the decree remained modifiable. This case made the interstate enforcement of alimony decrees more effective by closing an avenue of possible evasion. In this way it helped to accomplish the purposes of the Full Faith and Credit Clause in an area of the law where respect for the decrees of other states was clearly needed.

It has been indicated [15] that full faith and credit need not be given to a judgment which has been entered without observing the requirements of due process. In Griffin v. Griffin [16] a New York alimony decree was docketed in the District of Columbia without notice to the defendant husband. Under New York law such a decree was modifiable with respect to accrued and unpaid installments until such time as a further judgment was entered for such installments. The Supreme Court held that the entry of the judgment in the District of Columbia, thereby cutting off the husband's right to seek modification, without notice to him was a violation of the Due Process Clause.[17] The judgment so entered was therefore not entitled to enforcement in the District. The effect of Griffin is that alimony decrees entered in violation of due process may not be enforced in other states even as a matter of comity. Whether this is the case will depend on the law of the state in which the decree was originally entered. If by that law the accrued installments of alimony automatically become final money judgments not subject to modification, enforcement in other states without further notice is not a violation of due process provided of course that personal jurisdiction is obtained in the second state.[18] The finality of the original decree distinguishes this case from Griffin.

If the decree for which enforcement is sought commands the doing of an act other than the payment of money, such as the conveyance of land, the traditional view has been that it may not be enforced in another state by a suit on the decree.[19] Or, to put it another way, the cause of action does not merge in the decree.[20] As a result there has been doubt whether such decrees are entitled to full faith and credit. The major source of this doubt has been Fall v. Eastin.[21] In that case a divorce decree of a Washington court ordered the husband to convey Nebraska land to his wife in order to carry out a property division between the spouses. The husband refused to obey the decree and a conveyance

11. U.S.Const. art. IV, § 1.

12. 28 U.S.C.A. § 1738.

13. 323 U.S. 77, 86, 65 S.Ct. 137, 141, 89 L.Ed. 82 (1944).

14. 12 Ill.2d 502, 147 N.E.2d 34 (1957), 27 Univ.Chi.L. Rev. 136 (1958), citing other cases.

15. See note 6, supra.

16. 327 U.S. 220, 66 S.Ct. 556, 90 L.Ed. 635 (1946), rehearing denied 328 U.S. 876, 66 S.Ct. 975, 90 L.Ed. 1645 (1946).

17. U.S.Const.Amend. XIV, § 1.

18. Allingham v. Allingham, 141 Colo. 345, 348 P.2d 259 (1959).

19. Restatement of Conflict of Laws § 449(1) (1934). Many early authorities are cited in Lorenzen, Application

of Full Faith and Credit Clause to Equitable Decrees for the Conveyance of Foreign Land, 34 Yale L.J. 591 (1934), which also explains the reason for this peculiar rule. It rested on the historical distinction between judgments at law, which were said to operate on the matter in issue, and equity decrees, which had the effect merely of ordering the defendant to perform a personal duty, in other words operated on the defendant's conscience. This distinction went back at least to the time of Lord Coke and the early development of equity as a system of jurisprudence separate from law.

20. Restatement of Judgments § 46 (1942).

21. 215 U.S. 1, 30 S.Ct. 3, 54 L.Ed. 65 (1909). See Currie, Full Faith and Credit to Foreign Land Decrees, 21 U.Chi.L.Rev. 620 (1954).

was then made by a commissioner of the Washington court. The wife later sued in Nebraska to enforce the Washington decree, and the Nebraska court refused relief. On appeal the United States Supreme Court held that Nebraska was not bound to enforce the decree. The rationale for the decision is unclear and therefore its reach is also. It seems to stand for the broad proposition that equity act decrees are not entitled to full faith and credit.[22] The analysis might be that Nebraska law did not sanction the award of alimony in the form of land, and that therefore Nebraska was not obliged to honor a decree which violated the state's policy.[23] Or the decision may only mean that Nebraska need not recognize a conveyance Nebraska law made by a Washington commissioner.[24]

Whatever the rationale of Fall v. Eastin may be, the case places an unfortunate and unnecessary limitation upon the enforcement of foreign divorce decrees. The case has been vigorously criticized on this ground and on the ground that it was based upon long outmoded distinctions between judgments at law

and decrees in equity.[25] Many courts today refuse to follow it and instead do enforce, on theories of res judicata or comity, the divorce decrees of other states ordering the conveyance of forum land.[26] The case is thus in the category of legal antiquities and, we may hope, will no longer influence the enforcement of divorce decrees.

Where land titles are not involved, the objection to enforcement of the act decrees of other states has even less justification, being based entirely on the historic maxim "equity acts in personam".[27] This maxim and the distinction which it emphasizes between the effect of judgments at law and decrees in equity have no place in the modern world.[28] If equity money decrees are entitled to full faith and credit, there is no excuse for a different rule with respect to act decrees. Although the courts of the United States generally grant recognition to act decrees under doctrines of comity,[29] those doctrines do not require recognition as would the Full Faith and Credit Clause. That Clause should be applied to such decrees in order to ensure

---

22. This seems to be the reading given the case by Gammon v. Gammon, ___ Mont. ___, 684 P.2d 1081 (1984), and Allis v. Allis, 378 F.2d 721 (5th Cir.1967), cert. denied 389 U.S. 953, 88 S.Ct. 337, 19 L.Ed.2d 363 (1967).

23. This view of the cases is taken by Weesner v. Weesner, 168 Neb. 346, 95 N.W.2d 682 (1959).

24. This seems to be the analysis of the case in Redwood Investment Co. of Stithton, Ky. v. Exley, 64 Cal. App. 455, 221 P. 973 (1923). Even today the cases continue to hold that one state's court may not directly accomplish the conveyance of land either by purporting to have its decree act as a conveyance or by appointing an official of the first state to execute a deed. E.g. Gammon v. Gammon, ___ Mont. ___, 684 P.2d 1081 (1984); Whitmer v. Whitmer, 243 Pa.Super. 462, 365 A.2d 1316 (1976), cert. denied 434 U.S. 822, 98 S.Ct. 67, 54 L.Ed.2d 79 (1977); Kane v. Kane, 577 P.2d 172 (Wyo.1978), affirmed 616 P.2d 780 (Wyo.1980). It has been clear of course since the days of Penn v. Lord Baltimore, 1 Ves.Sr. 444, 27 Eng. Rep. 1132 (1750), that a court of equity could order the conveyance of land in another jurisdiction and enforce its order by contempt proceedings against the defendant. See Annot., Power of Divorce Court to Deal With Real Property Located in Another State, 34 A.L.R.3d 962 (1970).

25. Currie, Full Faith and Credit to Foreign Land Decrees, 21 U.Chi.L.Rev. 620 (1954); Barbour, The Extra-Territorial Effect of the Equitable Decree, 17 Mich.L.Rev. 527 (1919).

26. Allis v. Allis, 378 F.2d 721 (5th Cir.1967), cert. denied 389 U.S. 953, 88 S.Ct. 337, 19 L.Ed.2d 363 (1967);

Gammon v. Gammon, ___ Mont. ___, 684 P.2d 1081 (1984); Weesner v. Weesner, 168 Neb. 346, 95 N.W.2d 682 (1959); McElreath v. McElreath, 162 Tex. 190, 345 S.W.2d 722 (1961), 50 Geo.L.J. 157 (1961), 47 Iowa L.Rev. 712 (1962); Kane v. Kane, 577 P.2d 172 (Wyo.1978), affirmed 616 P.2d 780 (Wyo.1980); Annot., 32 A.L.R.3d 1330 (1970). The Restatements have also abandoned their support of Fall v. Eastin. Restatement (Second) of Conflict of Laws § 102, comment d (1971); Restatement (Second) of Judgments § 18, comment b (1982) (semble).

Although the Weesner opinion and some others continue to repeat the tired cliché that the courts of one state cannot affect the title to land in another state, the result of the case is inconsistent with this principle. It is hard to see just what policy underlies the principle. What does the state of the situs care who owns land in the state so long as the title is clearly revealed by the land records? Specifically, what difference does it make to the policy of the situs as such whether land is in the hands of the husband or the wife? The state whose interests are really involved in that question is the state in which the parties live.

27. See note 19, supra, and Note, Equitable Decree as a Cause of Action in Another State, 21 Harv.L.Rev. 210 (1908), and Buswell v. Buswell, 377 Pa. 487, 105 A.2d 608 (1954).

28. Currie, Full Faith and Credit to Foreign Land Decrees, 21 U.Chi.L.Rev. 620, 625 (1954).

29. Rozan v. Rozan, 49 Cal.2d 322, 317 P.2d 11 (1957); Matson v. Matson, 186 Iowa 607, 173 N.W. 127 (1919), 18 Mich.L.Rev. 142 (1920).

that the claimant spouse receives what he or she was awarded by the divorcing state.

It may make a substantial difference in the relief available whether comity or the Full Faith and Credit Clause is the basis for the enforcement of a divorce decree. The Supreme Court has made it clear that the meaning of full faith and credit is that the decree must be given the same effect in the state where enforcement is sought as it would have had in the state where it was rendered. Aldrich v. Aldrich [30] makes the point. There the wife had obtained a Florida divorce and an order for alimony which by its terms was to continue beyond the husband's death. According to Florida law a decree in those terms was erroneous but could not be collaterally attacked. No appeal was taken in Florida and the alimony order thus became immune to attack. The husband moved to West Virginia and died there. The West Virginia court refused to enforce the alimony decree against his estate, but the Supreme Court held that such enforcement was mandatory under the Full Faith and Credit Clause because enforcement against the husband's estate would have been required in Florida. If West Virginia had been enforcing this decree solely as a matter of comity, it could have refused to grant enforcement where its own public policy opposed the granting of alimony beyond the death of the obligor, as was apparently the case in Aldrich.[31] The impact of the Full Faith and Credit Clause as applied in Aldrich is to force all states to effectuate the policy of the decree-granting state irrespective of later changes in domicile and of differences in policy.

Enforcement Through Comity

"Comity" is the principle that one court should ordinarily respect the judgment of another court even in the absence of a binding obligation to do so.[32] It is not so much a legal rule as a recognition of the need for cooperation among jurisdictions. It rests on the same policies as res judicata and the Full Faith and Credit Clause, i.e. the need for finality in legal proceedings and the avoidance of the waste in time and money caused by the duplication of trials. In divorce litigation it rests on still another and more important policy, that which demands that spouses and parents shall not evade judicially established obligations of support. There is no reason why a spouse who has obtained an alimony decree in one state should be forced to relitigate the merits of the claim in every other state into which the obligor may wander. Comity says she need not do so.

Comity has become more important as the basis for the interstate enforcement of alimony decrees than the Full Faith and Credit Clause because of the United States Supreme Court's restriction of that Clause to the enforcement of final decrees for the payment of money. As has already been indicated,[33] the state courts today generally enforce the act decrees of other states as a matter of comity even though not required to do so by the Full Faith and Credit Clause as the Supreme Court has construed it. Similarly, decrees ordering the payment of alimony in the future, which under the Sistare case [34] are generally thought not to be entitled to full faith and credit because not final, are enforced in many jurisdictions as a matter of comity.[35] Worthley v. Worthley [36] exemplifies this en-

30. 378 U.S. 540, 84 S.Ct. 1687, 12 L.Ed.2d 1020 (1964), reversing Aldrich v. Aldrich, 147 W.Va. 269, 127 S.E.2d 385 (1962). The Restatement (Second) of Conflict of Laws § 103 (1971), without citing Aldrich, seems to permit a state to refuse recognition of a sister state's judgment if recognition would "involve an improper interference with important interests" of the state in which enforcement is sought. This seems a very dubious doctrine, to say the least, particularly in the divorce context.

31. The Aldrich case did not discuss the point, but Robinson v. Robinson, 131 W.Va. 160, 50 S.E.2d 455 (1948) seems to indicate that in West Virginia alimony ends on the husband's death.

32. Walzer v. Walzer, 173 Conn. 62, 376 A.2d 414 (1977).

33. See notes 26 and 29, supra.

34. Sistare v. Sistare, 218 U.S. 1, 30 S.Ct. 682, 54 L.Ed. 905 (1910), discussed at note 3, supra.

35. Many cases are collected in Foster and Freed, Modification, Recognition and Enforcement of Foreign Alimony Decrees, 11 Cal.W.L.Rev. 280 (1975) and Note, Interstate Enforcement of Modifiable Alimony and Child Support Decrees, 54 Iowa L.Rev. 597 (1969).

36. 44 Cal.2d 465, 283 P.2d 19 (1955). Similar results were reached in Hopkins v. Hopkins, 46 Cal.2d 313, 294

lightened approach. In this case the plaintiff was a wife who was the obligee under a New Jersey separate maintenance decree which was modifiable both prospectively and retroactively. She sued in California to enforce the decree as to both the accrued and the future installments. The California Supreme Court granted enforcement. It went on to hold, however, that due process as applied by the Griffin case [37] required the enforcing court to give the husband an opportunity to present any defenses or grounds for reduction of alimony which would have been available to him in the state where the alimony decree was originally entered. It might be argued that if both husband and wife had become domiciled in California, the law of California rather than that of New Jersey should govern the extent to which the alimony obligation should be modifiable.[38] If both parties were in California only temporarily, New Jersey law would be more clearly applicable. And if only one party were domiciled in California, weighing the conflicting interests of the two states would be difficult, but for lack of a clearly prevailing interest in a single state, the obligation should be dealt with according to the law of the place where the original decree was granted. In any case Worthley avoids these problems by referring to the law of the state in which the decree was originally rendered.

Another application of comity has enlarged the range of remedies in the enforcing state.

By the more rigid traditional view the money decree of another state was enforced only by an action at law as upon a judgment.[39] This produced a money judgment of the enforcing court for the amount then due and unpaid. This remedy fell far short of protecting the obligee spouse's interests, however, since it required him to sue again and again to collect the installments of alimony as they came due. Under the leadership of the courts of California [40] and Florida [41] more effective remedies have been devised. In those states and some others [42] the foreign alimony decree is enforced by the full range of legal and equitable remedies. When suit is successfully brought on the foreign decree, a decree in equity is entered which is enforced like similar domestic equity decrees. The decree includes not only an order for the payment of accrued installments which may be collected by execution by also pursuant to an order that payments be made in the future on the same terms as in the decree sued on. This order may then be the basis of a contempt proceeding if obeyed.

The next step for the state which is enforcing a foreign alimony decree is to subject it to the same modification as is available for domestic decrees. Although it is technically impossible for the courts of one state directly to modify decrees entered by the courts of other states, if the foreign decree is first entered made a decree of the enforcing state, there is no reason why the court of that state

P.2d 1 (1956); Walzer v. Walzer, 173 Conn. 62, 376 A.2d 414 (1977); McElroy v. McElroy, 256 A.2d 763 (Del.Ch. 1969); Sackler v. Sackler, 47 So.2d 292 (Fla.1950); Hudson v. Hudson, 36 N.J. 549, 178 A.2d 202 (1962); Hecox, Interstate Modification of Support Decrees, 28 Rocky Mt. L.Rev. 355 (1956); Note 18 Vand.L.Rev. 830 (1965).

37. Griffin v. Griffin, 327 U.S. 220, 66 S.Ct. 556, 90 L.Ed. 635 (1946), rehearing denied 328 U.S. 876, 66 S.Ct. 975, 90 L.Ed. 1645 (1946), discussed at note 16, supra.

38. Cf. Stone, J., dissenting in Yarborough v. Yarborough, 290 U.S. 202, 54 S.Ct. 181, 78 L.Ed. 269 (1933); Kinross-Wright v. Kinross-Wright, 248 N.C. 1, 102 S.E.2d 469 (1958), 37 N.C.L.Rev. 329 (1959); Picker v. Vollenhover, 206 Or. 45, 290 P.2d 789 (1955). But see Aldrich v. Aldrich, 378 U.S. 540, 84 S.Ct. 1687, 12 L.Ed.2d 1020 (1964).

39. Page v. Page, 189 Mass. 85, 75 N.E. 92 (1905); Lynde v. Lynde, 162 N.Y. 405, 56 N.E. 979 (1900), affirmed 181 U.S. 183, 21 S.Ct. 555, 45 L.Ed. 810 (1901).

40. Worthley v. Worthley, 44 Cal.2d 465, 283 P.2d 19 (1955), citing other cases.

41. Sackler v. Sackler, 47 So.2d 292 (Fla.1950).

42. Cases are collected in Harrison v. Harrison, 214 F.2d 571 (4th Cir. 1954), cert. denied 348 U.S. 896, 75 S.Ct. 217, 99 L.Ed. 704 (1954) and Annot., 18 A.L.R.2d 862 (1951). See also Parker v. Parker, 233 Ga. 434, 211 S.E.2d 729 (1975). Equitable remedies are made available by statute in New York. N.Y.—McKinney's Dom.Rel. L. §§ 243, 245 (Supp.1984–1985); Mittenthal v. Mittenthal, 99 Misc.2d 778, 417 N.Y.S.2d 175 (1979). Contra: Scholla v. Scholla, 201 F.2d 211 (D.C.Cir.1953), cert. denied 345 U.S. 966, 73 S.Ct. 951, 97 L.Ed. 1384 (1953). Mock v. Mock, 155 N.J.Super. 282, 382 A.2d 702 (1977) refused to enforce by garnishment a New York alimony decree which would have been enforcible by that means in New York, on the ground that the public policy of New Jersey did not permit that method of enforcement.

may not modify its own decree on the same terms as it would modify any other alimony decree. Lopez v. Avery [43] and other similar cases [44] use this technique, modifying the decree only upon proof of the same change in circumstances which would warrant a modification by the court which originally awarded alimony or support.

The approach taken by Lopez v. Avery [45] leads to the possibility that at any one time there may be two conflicting alimony decrees outstanding. The conflict may be particularly acute when the wife is a resident of one state and the husband a resident of another. The husband might contend that he need pay only the alimony imposed by the court of his own state while the wife might insist upon collecting the larger amount awarded by the court of her state. The Full Faith and Credit Clause [46] partially resolves such conflicts by enabling the wife to collect as a matter of right the installments of alimony ordered by the court of her residence to the extent that they become final. [47] If the court of the husband's state later reduces the award, the court of the wife's state should, as a matter of comity, recognize the validity of the reduction and enforce only the smaller decree. The same conflict arises under the Reciprocal Enforcement of Support Act. [48]

The vague principle of comity is also relied upon for the enforcement by American state courts of foreign country alimony judgments. Those judgments will usually be enforced in the United States even though they are not covered by the Uniform Foreign Money-Judgments Act [49] except where the foreign country's judgment is not based upon personal jurisdiction or was awarded without observance of what our courts would consider due process. [50]

Statutory Remedies

Two modern statutes expedite the interstate enforcement of alimony decrees. The first of these, the Uniform Enforcement of Foreign Judgments Act, [51] in force in more than half of the states, provides a summary method of enforcement. The statute authorizes the judgment creditor to file a petition for registration of the foreign judgment (which includes alimony decrees), after which a summons is served personally upon the judgment debtor. If he then fails to plead, the foreign judgment becomes a final personal judgment of the court in which it is registered. Any defenses the judgment debtor has may be raised and determined under this statute, but it is assumed that there generally will be none. In that event the statutory procedure results more quickly in the entry of a local judgment than would follow from the usual course of pleading and practice.

---

43. 66 So.2d 689 (Fla.1953).

44. Kniffen v. Courtney, 148 Ind.App. 358, 266 N.E.2d 72 (1971); Blackburn v. Blackburn, 113 Misc.2d 619, 449 N.Y.S.2d 827 (1982). Rudolf v. Rudolf, 348 N.W.2d 740 (Minn.1984) held that Minnesota could modify a Nevada alimony decree notwithstanding that it was not modifiable by Nevada law. The case is clearly wrong in denying full fail and credit to the final Nevada decree, violating the principle of Sistare. See Aldrich v. Aldrich, 378 U.S. 540, 84 S.Ct. 1687, 12 L.Ed.2d 1020 (1964); Yarborough v. Yarborough, 290 U.S. 202, 54 S.Ct. 181, 78 L.Ed. 269 (1933).

45. 66 So.2d 689 (Fla.1953).

46. U.S.Const. art. IV, § 1.

47. Sistare v. Sistare, 218 U.S. 1, 30 S.Ct. 682, 54 L.Ed. 905 (1910), discussed supra at note 3.

48. That Act is discussed in section 6.6, supra.

49. Wolff v. Wolff, 40 Md.App. 168, 389 A.2d 413 (1978), judgment affirmed 285 Md. 185, 401 A.2d 479 (1979), citing many cases; Nicol v. Tanner, 310 Minn. 68, 256 N.W.2d 796 (1976) (enforcing a German judgment

even though that country would not extend reciprocity to Minnesota's judgments. The Uniform Foreign Money-Judgments Recognition Act § 1(2), 13 Unif.L.Ann. 419 (1980) excepts from its operation judgments for support in matrimonial or family matters. See Annot., Construction and Application of Uniform Foreign Money-Judgments Recognition Act, 100 A.L.R.3d 792 (1980).

50. Hager v. Hager, 1 Ill.App.3d 1047, 274 N.E.2d 157 (1971); Peterson, Foreign Country Judgments and the Second Restatement of Conflict of Laws, 72 Colum.L.Rev. 220 (1972).

51. 13 Unif.L.Ann. 173 (1980). Cases relying on the Act to enforce the alimony decrees of other states are Ehrenzweig v. Ehrenzweig, 86 Misc.2d 656, 383 N.Y.S.2d 487 (1976), order affirmed 61 A.D.2d 1003, 402 N.Y.S.2d 638 (1978); Andrysek v. Andrysek, 280 Or. 61, 569 P.2d 615 (1977); Salmeri v. Salmeri, 554 P.2d 1244 (Wyo.1976). Other cases are cited in Annot., 31 A.L.R.4th 706, 768 (1984). Matson v. Matson, 333 N.W.2d 862 (Minn.1983) has held that the foreign judgment being enforced under this Act may not be modified. Contra on this point: Gorvin v. Stegmann, 74 Wash.2d 177, 443 P.2d 821 (1968).

The other statute referred to is the Uniform Reciprocal Enforcement of Support Act [52] which is now in force in all states. This statute was expressly designed to deal with the national problem created by the evasion of support obligations. Its operation is described in detail in an earlier section.[53]

Enforcement of Alimony Decrees in the Federal Courts

Although the United States Supreme Court has said in several cases that the federal courts do not have a general jurisdiction to act in domestic relations cases, thereby creating the domestic relations exception to federal jurisdiction,[54] suits to enforce state court alimony and property decrees may be brought in the federal courts, where there is diversity of citizenship and the requisite amount in controversy.[55] There is disagreement in the cases as to whether the federal court may order alimony to be paid in the future in accordance with an existing state court decree, some cases taking the position that pursuant to Erie Railroad Co. v. Tompkins [56] the federal courts may give that form of relief which might be given by the courts of the state in which they sit,[57] while other cases limit relief to enforcement of past due final installments of alimony.[58] The objection to having the federal courts make orders for the future payment of alimony is that such orders are normally modifiable.[59] Since modification of alimony payments seems clearly to be within the domestic relations exception to federal jurisdiction,[60] it seems equally clear that fed-

eral courts should not give relief which might lead them into a consideration of that issue.

 WESTLAW REFERENCES

Application of the Full Faith and Credit Clause
sistare +s sistare /p foreign /3 decree judgment
ti(light +s light) & "full faith and credit"

Enforcement Through Eastin
di(comity /s alimony)
lopez /s avery

Statutory Remedies
"uniform enforcement of foreign judgment" /s alimony

Enforcement of Alimony Decrees in the Federal Courts
find 647 f2d 561

§ 16.8 Federal Tax Aspects of Separation and Divorce

Introduction and Background

The impact of federal taxes, particularly the federal income tax, is a major concern in the preparation of a separation agreement on divorce. It may lead the parties to choose one form of agreement rather than another. Even in those cases where the financial provisions incident to the divorce are arrived at by litigation rather than agreement, the effect of federal taxes should be taken into account by the court. For these reasons a brief description of the federal taxation treatment of separate maintenance and divorce is included in this section. Space limitations foreclose an exhaustive discussion of the subject. For that the reader is referred to the books and arti-

---

52. The Revised Uniform Reciprocal Enforcement of Support Act of 1968 is in 9A Unif.L.Ann. 647 (1979).

53. See section 6.6, supra. Some typical cases in which the Act has been used to enforce alimony decrees include Lumpkins v. Lumpkins, 83 N.M. 591, 495 P.2d 371 (1972); Everson v. Everson, 494 Pa. 348, 431 A.2d 889 (1981); Alig v. Alig, 220 Va. 80, 255 S.E.2d 494 (1979).

54. This exception to federal jurisdiction is discussed in detail in section 12.2, supra.

55. Erspan v. Badgett, 647 F.2d 550 (5th Cir.1981), cert. denied 455 U.S. 945, 102 S.Ct. 1443, 71 L.Ed.2d 658 (1982); Dorey v. Dorey, 609 F.2d 1128 (5th Cir.1980), rehearing denied 613 F.2d 314 (5th Cir.1980); Harrison v. Harrison, 214 F.2d 571 (4th Cir.1954), cert. denied 348 U.S. 896, 75 S.Ct. 217, 99 L.Ed. 704 (1954); Smith v. Smith, 217 F.2d 917 (6th Cir.1954); Wilson v. Wilson, 532

F.Supp. 152 (M.D.La.1980), affirmed p.c. 667 F.2d 497 (5th Cir. 1982), cert. denied 458 U.S. 1107, 102 S.Ct. 3485, 73 L.Ed.2d 1368 (1982); Zimmerman v. Zimmerman, 395 F.Supp. 719 (E.D.Pa.1975).

56. 304 U.S. 64, 58 S.Ct. 817, 82 L.Ed. 1188 (1938).

57. Keating v. Keating, 542 F.2d 910 (4th Cir.1976); Harrison v. Harrison, 214 F.2d 571 (4th Cir.1954), cert. denied 348 U.S. 896, 75 S.Ct. 217, 99 L.Ed. 704 (1954).

58. Jagiella v. Jagiella, 647 F.2d 561 (5th Cir. 1981), rehearing denied 654 F.2d 723 (5th Cir.1981); Maner v. Maner, 401 F.2d 616 (5th Cir.1968).

59. See section 16.5, supra.

60. Jagiella v. Jagiella, 647 F.2d 561 (5th Cir. 1981), rehearing denied 654 F.2d 723 (5th Cir.1981).

cles cited in connection with specific tax issues later in this section and to general treatments of the subject.[1]

The law prevailing before 1942 was that alimony paid by a husband was not deductible by him for federal income tax purposes and was not taxable to the wife who received it.[2] As income tax rates increased this produced hardships for divorced husbands. The 1942 Revenue Act changed the law so that in general and with many qualifications the husband was entitled to a deduction for alimony paid to the wife and she was required to pay an income tax on the sums paid to her as alimony.[3] This general scheme of taxation, with statutory and judicial developments over the years, has remained in effect. In 1984 Congress responded to many criticisms of this scheme of taxation by enacting comprehensive reforms of its details[4] without, however, changing the basic rule that the payer of alimony is entitled to deduct it and the recipient must pay a tax on what she receives.[5] This enactment was part of a broader tax act

entitled the Deficit Reduction Act of 1984, but the sections of that Act applicable to divorce and separation are usually referred to as the Domestic Relations Tax Reform Act of 1984[6] and will be so referred to in this section.

Alimony and Separate Maintenance Payments: Before 1984

Before the 1984 amendments the operative law was the Internal Revenue Code of 1954. This law provided that a wife[7] who was divorced or legally separated from her husband pursuant to a decree of divorce or separate maintenance must include in her gross income periodic payments received after such a decree in discharge of a legal obligation imposed upon the husband under the decree, or by a written instrument incident to the divorce or separation, by virtue of the marital or family relationship.[8] Payments made under a written separation agreement executed after August 16, 1954, the effective date of the Internal Revenue Code of 1954, were likewise includable in her gross income,[9] as were pay-

§ 16.8

1. See, e.g., M. O'Connell, Divorce Taxation (1985 with frequent supplements), a loose leaf service; F. Sander and H. Gutman, Tax Aspects of Divorce and Separation (1975), giving extensive treatment of the pre-1984 law; J. Chommie, The Law of Federal Income Taxation § 159 (2d ed.1973), outlining the pre-1984 law; L. Thomas, Tax Consequences of Marriage, Separation, and Divorce (1986) (dealing with the changes made by the Domestic Relations Tax Reform Act of 1984); Vogel and Roche, Domestic Relations Tax after TRA 1984 and TRA 1986, 21 Fam.L.Q. 1 (1987); Note, 1984 Deficit Reduction Act: Divorce Taxation, 1986 Wis.L.Rev. 177; Addendum: Tax Reform Act of 1986 Revisions to the Deficit Reduction Act of 1984 Marital Dissolution Tax Provisions, 1986 Wis. L.Rev. 1061.

2. Gould v. Gould, 245 U.S. 151, 38 S.Ct. 53, 62 L.Ed. 211 (1917); Douglas v. Willcuts, 296 U.S. 1, 56 S.Ct. 59, 80 L.Ed. 3 (1935).

3. Revenue Act of 1942 § 120, 56 Stat. 816, 817 (1942), amending I.R.C. §§ 22(k), 23(w).

4. For an account of the genesis and passage of this Act see O'Connell, The Domestic Relations Tax Reform Act: How We Got It and What We Can Do About It, 18 Fam.L.Q. 473 (1985).

In 1986 the Tax Reform Act of that year amended I.R.C. § 71(f) respecting excess front-loading of alimony payments. See the discussion at note 53, infra.

5. O'Connell, Divorce Taxation: The Domestic Relations Tax Reform Act of 1984), and Florescue, Divorce and the Internal Revenue Code: Divorce Your Spouse

and Marry the Commissioner, in 2 N.Y.U. Forty-Third Institute on Federal Taxation ch. 43, 47 (1985); Hjorth, Divorce, Taxes and the 1984 Tax Reform Act: An Inadequate Response to an Old Problem, 61 Wash.L.Rev. 151 (1986).

6. Pub.L. 98–369, 98 Stat. 494, 98th Cong., 2d Sess. (1984). The Domestic Relations Tax Reform Act is section 421 of the Deficit Reduction Act, at 98 Stat. 793. It will be referred to as DRTRA in this section, and amends the Internal Revenue Code.

7. The definition section of the Code provided that "wife" may be read as "husband" or vice versa, and that "husband" may be read as "ex-husband" and "wife" may be read as "ex-wife". I.R.C. § 7701(a)(17).

8. I.R.C. § 71(a)(1). The definition of "periodic" is discussed below at note 20. This provision covered temporary alimony as well as alimony and payments made pursuant to interlocutory divorce decrees.

9. I.R.C. § 71(a)(2). This subsection applied only to separation agreements executed after August 16, 1954, the effective date of the Revenue Code of 1954. It did not apply if the parties filed a joint return for the year.

A separation agreement was held adequate for this purpose when it contained a standard of payments even though no dollar amount was fixed in Jacklin v. Commissioner, 79 T.C. 340 (1982), 58 Wash.L.Rev. 871 (1983).

Payments pursuant to an oral modification of an earlier separation agreement were not deductible under § 71. Blanchard v. United States, 424 F.Supp. 916 (D.Md.1976); Bishop v. Commissioner, 46 T.C.Mem. 15 (1983).

ments made pursuant to a decree for support or maintenance entered after March 1, 1954, provided husband and wife were separated.[10]

Payments which met these requirements were deductible by the husband.[11]

The statutory phrase which required that the husband's payments must be in discharge of a legal obligation imposed by the marital or family relationship was construed to mean that they had to be for support and not in furtherance of a division of property.[12] This construction involved the Internal Revenue Service and the federal courts in the alimony-property distinction.[13] If the payments were what is normally characterized as alimony or maintenance, they qualified for the tax treatment just outlined.[14] If they were used to divide the property of the spouses, they did not.[15] The cases were numerous and resulted in almost total confusion, the reason being that by the 1970's the law of most states provided that awards of alimony and of prop-erty had almost identical purposes.[16] Some cases held that the intent of the parties or of the divorce court controlled the characterization;[17] others relied on the circumstances of the award;[18] still others were persuaded by the modifiability of the award.[19]

The former Revenue Code also required the payments to be "periodic" in order to be taxable to the wife and deductible by the husband, omitting to provide a definition of "periodic".[20] The payments were said not to be periodic if they constituted a principal sum payable in installments,[21] but if they were payable over a period ending more than ten years after the date of the decree or agreement, they were to be treated as periodic.[22] Where the alimony was payable over a period of ten years or less, it was held to be periodic if subject to termination or modification on the death of either spouse, the remarriage of the wife, or a change in economic circumstances of either spouse.[23]

10. I.R.C. § 71(a)(3). Cases dealing with the meaning of "separated" include Sydnes v. Commissioner, 577 F.2d 60 (8th Cir.1978); Hertsch v. Commissioner, 43 T.C.Mem. 703 (1982); Dunn v. Commissioner, 70 T.C. 361 (1978).

11. I.R.C. § 215. But the husband was not entitled to the deduction of any amounts which would not have been includable in his gross income.

12. Treas.Reg. § 1.71–1(c)(4); Wright v. Commissioner, 543 F.2d 593 (7th Cir.1976). See Hjorth, Tax Consequences of Post-Dissolution Support Payment Arrangements, 51 Wash.L.Rev. 233 (1976); Note, Taxation of Divorce Settlements and the Property/Support Distinction, 55 So.Cal.L.Rev. 939 (1982).

13. See section 15.1, supra.

14. E.g., Schatten v. United States, 746 F.2d 319 (6th Cir.1984); Benedict v. Commissioner, 82 T.C. 573 (1984); Schottenstein v. Commissioner, 75 T.C. 451 (1980).

15. Griffith v. Commissioner, 749 F.2d 11 (6th Cir. 1984); Boucher v. Commissioner, 710 F.2d 507 (9th Cir. 1983); Gammill v. Commissioner, 710 F.2d 607 (10th Cir. 1982); Riley v. Commissioner, 649 F.2d 768 (10th Cir. 1981).

16. See section 15.1, supra.

17. Griffith v. Commissioner, 749 F.2d 11 (6th Cir. 1984); Schatten v. United States, 746 F.2d 319 (6th Cir. 1984); Boucher v. Commissioner, 710 F.2d 507 (9th Cir. 1983); White v. United States, 550 F.Supp. 96 (M.D.Ala. 1982); Benedict v. Commissioner, 82 T.C. 573 (1984); Lewis v. Commissioner, 47 T.C.Mem. 744 (1983); Middleman v. Commissioner, 46 T.C.Mem. 1383 (1983).

18. Slawski v. United States, 6 Cl.Ct. 433 (1984), judgment affirmed 770 F.2d 180 (C.A.Fed.1985); Goninen v. Commissioner, 47 T.C.Mem. 737 (1983); Houston v. Com-missioner, 47 T.C.Mem. 662 (1983); Benson v. Commissioner, 47 T.C.Mem. 294 (1983); Griffith v. Commissioner, 46 T.C.Mem. 189 (1983); Ward v. Commissioner, 44 T.C. Mem. 1299 (1982); Graff v. Commissioner, 44 T.C.Mem. 701 (1982).

19. Gammill v. Commissioner, 710 F.2d 607 (10th Cir. 1982); Riley v. Commissioner, 649 F.2d 768 (10th Cir. 1981). To compound the confusion, it is possible for a court to find part of an award to be alimony and part property. Hall v. Commissioner, 44 T.C.Mem. 1418 (1982).

20. I.R.C. § 71(a)(1). For the treatment of lump sum payments in satisfaction of past or future alimony obligations, see Olster v. Commissioner, 751 F.2d 1168 (11th Cir. 1985).

21. I.R.C. § 71(c)(1).

22. I.R.C. § 71(c)(2). This subsection also provided that only ten percent of the principal sum could be deducted in any one taxable year.

23. Treas. Reg. § 1.71–1(d)(3). These contingencies could be expressed in the decree or separation agreement, or could be the product of the state divorce law. Where some of the payments were subject to these contingencies and some were not, the cases disagreed as to whether they would be taxable to the wife. Compare Bernstein v. Bernstein, 622 F.2d 442 (9th Cir. 1980); Oman v. Commissioner, 767 F.2d 290 (6th Cir. 1985), and Coker v. United States, 327 F.Supp. 169 (D. Neb. 1971), affirmed 456 F.2d 676 (8th Cir. 1972), with White v. Commissioner, 82 T.C. 222 (1984), reversed 770 F.2d 685 (7th Cir. 1985). See also Crouser v. Commissioner, 668 F.2d 239 (6th Cir. 1981), holding fixed weekly payments not to be periodic, and Yoakum v. Commissioner, 82 T.C. 128 (1984), holding

To the extent that the divorce decree or separation agreement fixed a part of the payments to the wife as being for the support of children of the marriage, the payments were not includible in the wife's gross income or deductible by the husband.[24] Commissioner v. Lester[25] held that "fixed" as used in the Code meant that the decree or agreement had to designate specifically and expressly part of the payments as being for the support of the children before the wife could be excused from paying the tax and the husband deprived of his deduction. It was not sufficient under Lester that the decree or agreement contained provisions creating an inference that some portion of the payments were to be allocated to the support of the children.

The statutory requirement that the alimony payments had to be made under a decree, or a written instrument which was "incident to" the divorce or separation was liberally construed to mean only that the agreement had to be related to the divorce decree or to

the status of divorce.[26] Thus an agreement could qualify as incident to a divorce where it was made in a state in which alimony was not usually granted,[27] or where the agreement was invalid as conducive to divorce,[28] or where it was made after the divorce and altered the payments called for in the divorce decree.[29]

Alimony and Separate Maintenance Payments: After 1984

As has been indicated,[30] the rules for the taxation of alimony and maintenance payments were extensively changed in 1984, and again in 1986, but the essential pattern remained. If the payments comply with the statute they are taxable to the recipient and deductible by the payer.[31] The new rules apply to payments made with respect to divorce or separation instruments executed after December 31, 1984.[32] They also apply to payments pursuant to a modification of any divorce or separation instrument executed be-

alimony payments not to be periodic because not modifiable.

24. I.R.C. § 71(b). See also Treas. Reg. § 1.71–1(e).

25. 366 U.S. 299, 81 S.Ct. 1343, 6 L.Ed.2d 306 (1961). In this case the agreement provided that one-sixth of the payments would cease on the marriage, death or emancipation of each of the parties' three children, but the Supreme Court held that this did not "fix" the payments as being for support of the children. See also Brock v. Commissioner, 566 F.2d 947 (5th Cir.1978); Commissioner v. Gotthelf, 407 F.2d 491 (2d Cir.1969), cert. denied 396 U.S. 828, 90 S.Ct. 78, 24 L.Ed.2d 79 (1969). Sperling v. Commissioner, 726 F.2d 948 (2d Cir.1984) held that payments of college expenses made directly to the college constituted child support, without reliance on the Lester rule. Strealdorf v. Commissioner, 726 F.2d 1521 (11th Cir.1984) held that the payments were child support and not alimony when they continued after the wife's remarriage, on the ground that by state law a husband was not required to pay alimony after his wife's remarriage unless the divorce decree specifically so provided and the decree failed to do so in this case.

26. I.R.C. § 71(a)(1). Note, 69 Yale L.J. 153 (1959). Borax' Estate v. Commissioner, 349 F.2d 666 (2d Cir. 1965), cert. denied 383 U.S. 935, 86 S.Ct. 1064, 15 L.Ed.2d 852 (1966), 18 Stan.L.Rev. 750, 44 Tex.L.Rev. 564 (1966) held that payments were incident to a Mexican divorce even after the ex-wife had obtained a New York decree that the Mexican divorce was invalid.

27. Tuckie G. Hesse, 7 T.C. 700 (1946).

28. Robert Wood Johnson, 10 T.C. 647 (1948).

29. Newton v. Pedrick, 212 F.2d 357 (2d Cir.1954); Hollander v. Commissioner, 248 F.2d 523 (9th Cir.1957).

30. See the text at note 4, supra. For discussions of the new statute see M. O'Connell, Divorce Taxation pars. 452–455 (1984); O'Connell, Divorce Taxation: The Domestic Relations Tax Reform Act of 1984, 43 Inst. on Fed. Taxation 43–1 (N.Y.Univ.1985); Florescue, Divorce and the Internal Revenue Code: Divorce Your Spouse and Marry the Commissioner, 43 Inst. on Fed. Taxation 47–1 (N.Y.Univ.1985); Note, The Effect of the Tax Reform Act of 1984 on Alimony and Transfers of Property Incident to Divorce, 19 U.Rich.L.Rev. 129 (1984); Hopkins, Tax Reform/1984 Alimony, 7 Fam. Advocate 8 (1984).

31. I.R.C. §§ 71 and 215.

32. Pub.L. 98–369, § 422(e)(1), 98 Stat. 798. I.R.C. § 71(b)(2) defines divorce or separation instrument as a divorce or separate maintenance decree, a written instrument incident to such a decree, a written separation agreement, or a decree requiring one spouse to make support or maintenance payments to the other spouse. Presumably a decree of annulment or an order for temporary alimony qualify as divorce or separation instruments under this provision.

If a decree of divorce or separate maintenance executed after December 31, 1984 incorporates or adopts without change the terms of alimony or separate maintenance payments under a divorce or separation instrument executed before January 1, 1985, such a decree will be treated as executed before January 1, 1985. But a change in the amount of alimony or separate maintenance payments, or in the time period in which they are to continue, or the addition or deletion of conditions on payment is a change in the terms of the payments and they will be subject to the rules of the new section 71 of the Domestic Relations Tax Reform Act. Treas.Reg. § 71.1–1T, A–26.

fore January 1, 1985 if the modification expressly provides that the new rules shall apply to that modification.[33]

Although the 1984 amendments clear up some of the confusion of the prior tax law, for example by eliminating any further relevance of the alimony-property division distinction which produced so much litigation,[34] by eliminating the requirement of periodicity in the payments,[35] and by clarifying the distinction between alimony and child support,[36] they are far from simple. They inject many new and technical complications into the federal taxation of alimony payments.

The new statute provides that gross income includes alimony or separate maintenance payments, meaning that such payments will be included in the gross income of the recipient.[37] If so included, they are deductible by the payer.[38] In order to receive this tax treatment, the payments must meet these requirements: a) They must be made in cash.[39]

b) They must be received by or on behalf of the spouse pursuant to a divorce or separation instrument.[40]

c) If a court or the parties designate the payments in a divorce or separation instrument as not includible in gross income and not deductible by the payer, they will not be so includible or deductible.[41] If there is no such designation, the payments, if they meet all other requirements, will be so includible and deductible.[42]

d) If the spouses are legally separated by virtue of a decree of divorce or separate maintenance, payments will not be includible in gross income as alimony if they are members of the same household at the time the payments are made.[43] But if the payments are made pursuant to a written separation agreement or a decree for support, they are includible in gross income and deductible by the payer even though the spouses continue to live together.[44]

e) The payments must terminate on the death of the recipient.[45] There may be no

---

33. Pub.L. 98–369, § 422(e)(2), 98 Stat. 798; Treas.Reg. § 71.1–1T, A–26.

34. See note 12, supra, and Treas.Reg. § 1.71–1T, A–3.

35. See note 20, supra, and Treas.Reg. § 1.71–1T, A–3.

36. See note 24, supra, and I.R.C. § 71(c).

37. I.R.C. § 71(a).

38. I.R.C. § 215. This section also requires the alimony recipient to furnish his taxpayer identification number to the payer, who must then include it in his return.

39. I.R.C. § 71(b)(1). "Cash" includes checks or money orders, but does not include services or property, or debt instruments of third parties, or annuity contracts. Treas.Reg. § 1.71–1T, A–5.

40. I.R.C. § 71(b)(1)(A). Under the prior law payments could qualify for the alimony deduction if they were made to third parties for the benefit of the other spouse, under certain circumstances. Thus where the husband was required to pay the premiums on a whole life policy of insurance on his own life, the premiums were held to be alimony and deductible by him, provided that the wife was the sole owner and irrevocable beneficiary of the policy, in Piel v. Commissioner, 340 F.2d 887 (2d Cir.1965). See also Sperling v. Commissioner, 726 F.2d 948 (2d Cir.1984). The same is true of mortgage payments on a home owned by the wife. If the wife does not have the sole ownership of the property, however, the payments are considered not to have been made for her benefit. See note, Alimony Taxation of Indirect Benefits: A Critique and a Proposal, 66 Colum.L.Rev. 1118 (1966). The rules are the same under the Tax Reform Act.

Treas.Reg. 1.71–1T, A–6. Of course the payments must comply with the other requirements of that Act.

41. For the definition of divorce or separation instrument, see note 32, supra. These instruments are the same as those which were required in the prior law. Treas.Reg. § 1.7–1T, A–4. The designation must be in such an instrument. I.R.C. § 71(b)(1)(B). If the spouses have a written separation agreement, a writing signed by both spouses which designates the payments thereunder as nondeductible and excludible will be treated as a divorce or separation instrument for this purpose. Treas. Reg. § 1.71–1T, A–8.

42. I.R.C. § 71(b)(1)(B).

43. I.R.C. § 71(b)(1)(C). A payment made at a time when the parties are members of the same household may not qualify as an alimony payment if the parties are legally separated under a divorce or separate maintenance decree. They will be considered to be living in the same household even though they physically separate themselves within the home in which they have been living before the decree. But they will not be treated as members of the same household if one is preparing to leave and does leave within a month after the payment is made. Treas.Reg. § 1.71–1T, A–9.

44. Treas.Reg. § 1.71–1T, A–9.

45. I.R.C. § 71(b)(1)(D) (Tax Reform Act of 1986). This subsection of the DRTRA required also that the decree or agreement must state that the payments end on the recipient's death, but this requirement was removed by the Tax Reform Act of 1986.

substitute payments in cash or property after the death of the recipient.[46]

Just as under the prior law, the spouses may not have the includibility-deductibility advantages for alimony if they file a joint return. This is obvious in view of the fact that only one return is being filed, but the statute makes it explicit.[47]

The 1984 Act continues to provide that to the extent that a divorce or separation instrument shall "fix" part or all of payments to a spouse as payable for the support of children, those payments are not alimony and so not includible in gross income or deductible by the payer.[48] This Act makes an attempt to expand and clarify the meaning of "fix", however.[49] In order to do this it provides that if any amount prescribed by the divorce or separation instrument will be reduced on the occurrence of such contingencies as a child's reaching a specific age or marrying or dying or leaving school, the amount of the reduction will be treated as intended for the support of the child and therefore will not be considered alimony.[50] In addition the Act provides that

if the payments are to be reduced at a time which can clearly be associated with such contingencies, the amount of the reduction will also be deemed to be child support.[51] The Treasury has attempted to give some more specific content to this vague standard by creating presumptions respecting the sort of reduction in payments which are "clearly associated" with the contingencies referred to.[52]

The rules outlined to this point define alimony and provide for its deductibility by the payer and includibility by the payee. Unfortunately for clarity and simplicity, however, the DRTRA in 1984 added two other rules for alimony deductibility. These rules were in turn repealed and new rules imposed by the Tax Reform Act of 1986. The purpose of both statutes was apparently to prevent what they called "excess front-loading of alimony payments", that is, to prevent the deduction of large alimony payments in the early years after divorce in contrast to small payments in the later years.[53] To the extent that they apply to a particular set of alimony payments these rules limit deductibility, the DRTRA

46. I.R.C. § 71(b)(1)(D).

47. I.R.C. § 71(e).

48. The prior law, as construed by Commissioner v. Lester, 366 U.S. 299, 81 S.Ct. 1343, 6 L.Ed.2d 306 (1961), is discussed at note 24, supra. Under the 1984 Act payments will continue to be held child support rather than alimony where the instrument specifically provides that they are child support. Treas.Reg. § 1.71–1T, A–16 (1985).

49. I.R.C. § 71(c)(2). The attempt at clarification is only partially successful, however.

50. I.R.C. § 71(c)(2)(A). It does not matter whether the specified event is either certain or likely to occur. Treas.Reg. § 71.1–1T, A–17.

51. I.R.C. § 71(c)(2)(B) (DRTRA, as amended by Tax Reform Act of 1986).

52. Treas.Reg. § 71.1–1T, A–18 (1985), creating two kinds of rebuttable presumption: a) If the payments are to be reduced not more than six months before or after the date on which the child will reach the age of eighteen, twenty-one, or the local age of majority, they are presumed, to the extent of the reduction, to be child support. This presumption is conclusively rebutted if the reduction is a complete cessation of alimony or separate maintenance payments during the sixth post-separation year or upon the expiration of a seventy-two-month period. It may also be rebutted by proof of other circumstances, such as by showing that alimony payments are to be made for a period customarily provided in the local jurisdiction.

b) If the payments are to be reduced on two or more occasions occurring not more than one year before or after a child of the payer spouse reaches a certain age between the ages of eighteen and twenty-four inclusive, they are presumed, to the extent of the reduction, to be child support. The regulations contain an illustration of how this complicated and peculiar provision would work in practice. These two presumptions together offer a sort of "safe harbor" to the court or lawyer attempting to set up payments which will qualify as alimony or be labeled child support. If the payments do not fall within either of the presumptions, reductions will not be treated as "clearly associated" with the occurrence of a contingency related to the child. Treas.Reg. § 71.1–1T, A–18.

53. The quoted phrase is in both the DRTRA and the Tax Reform Act of 1986. The Tax Reform Act of 1986 § 1843(c)(1), Pub.L. 99–514. In order to avoid confusion which might result from the enactment of two conflicting provisions within two years of each other, the DRTRA version of I.R.C. § 71(f) will be cited I.R.C. § 71(f) (DRTRA), and the Tax Reform Act version will be cited I.R.C. § 71(f) (Tax Reform Act).

Both versions of I.R.C. § 71(f)(5)(B) state that for purposes of the "excess front-loading" subsection of the Code the term "alimony or separate maintenance payment" does not include any payment received under a decree described in I.R.C. § 71(b)(2)(C), that is, a decree for the support or maintenance of the other spouse. One effect of this, among others, is to exempt from the front-end loading rules temporary alimony or alimony pendente lite.

rules drastically, the Tax Reform Act rules much less drastically.

The DRTRA imposed two rules to prevent "front-end loading".[54] The first, known as the six-year rule, provided that if alimony or separate maintenance payments in any calendar year exceeded $10,000, the excess over $10,000 could not be treated as an alimony or separate maintenance payment unless the payments were to be made in each of the six post-separation years, without taking into account any termination contingent upon the death of either spouse or the remarriage of the payee.[55] This meant, for example, that if the divorce decree ordered the payment of a single sum of $8,000 which complied with the rules for alimony outlined earlier, the entire sum was deductible by the payer and includible by the payee. But if the single payment was set at $15,000, only $10,000 of it was deductible and includible. If the alimony were $12,000 per year for six years, to end on the death of either spouse or the remarriage of the payee, it also qualified as deductible and includible.[56] For purposes of this rule the six post-separation years were the six consecutive calendar years during which the payer

paid alimony qualifying as such under the statute.[57]

In addition to the "six-year rule" the DRTRA included what has come to be called the "recapture rule".[58] This rule in effect provided that if any of the alimony payments made during any of the six post-separation years (or any subsequent year) was less than a payment made in any preceding year by an amount greater than $10,000, the amount of the difference less $10,000 would be "recaptured."[59] "Recapture" meant that the amount in excess of $10,000 by which the alimony decreased in the "computation year"[60] in relation to the amount in any preceding year was taxable to the payer and deductible by the payee for the taxable year in which the decreased payment was made. The excess amount determined with respect to a particular prior post-separation year was the excess of the amount of alimony or separate maintenance payments made during the prior year over the amount of the payments in the computation year plus $10,000. In making this calculation the amount of the payments made in a prior year was reduced by any excess amount previously determined with respect to such year.[61]

54. For a vigorous criticism of these rules and the difficulties they created for divorced spouses, see O'Connell, The Domestic Relations Tax Reform Act: How We Got It and What We Can Do About It, 18 Fam.L.Q. 473, 497 (1985).

55. I.R.C. § 71(f)(1) (DRTRA).

56. Treas.Reg. § 1.71–1T, A–23 seems to expand the statutory qualification on the six-year rule by providing: "For purposes of determining whether alimony or separate maintenance payments are to be made in any year, the possible termination of such payments upon the happening of a contingency (other than the passage of time) which has not yet occurred is ignored (unless such contingency may cause all or a portion of the payment to be treated as a child support payment)." Under this Regulation alimony payable over six years, but terminable in the event that the payee lives on a conjugal basis with someone not her husband, would seem to qualify as deductible by the payer and includible by the payee.

57. I.R.C. § 71(f)(4)(A) (DRTRA). Treas.Reg. § 71.1–1T, A–22. The Regulation, in A–23, contains illustrations of the operation of the six-year rule. Thus a decree ordering payments of $15,000 per year for each calendar year from 1985 through 1990 would result in 10,000 being deductible and includible, but the additional $5,000 would be neither deductible nor includible. If the decree in addition ordered a payment of $1 in 1991, the six-year rule would be complied with and all payments would be deductible and includible. But that form of decree would

invoke the application of the recapture rule as outlined in the discussion immediately following.

58. The term "recapture" does not appear in the statute but does appear in the regulations. It means that alimony payments deducted and included in one year may be given the opposite treatment in a later year to some extent, that is, the payer will have to include them in his income for the later year and the payee may deduct them in his return. Treas.Reg. § 71.1–1T, A–24.

59. I.R.C. § 71(2), (3), (4) (DRTRA). See O'Connell, Divorce Taxation: The Domestic Relations Tax Reform Act of 1984, 43 Inst. of Fed. Taxation 43–1, 43–6 (N.Y. Univ.1985).

60. "Computation year" is defined as "the post-separation year for which the excess under paragraph (3) is being determined." I.R.C. § 71(f)(4)(B) (DRTRA). "Post-separation year" is defined as "any calendar year in the 6 calendar year period beginning with the first calendar year in which the payor spouse paid to the payee spouse alimony or separate maintenance payments to which this section applies." I.R.C. § 71(f)(4)(A) (DRTRA).

61. I.R.C. § 71(f)(2), (3), (4) (DRTRA); Treas.Reg. § 71.1–1T, A–24 (1985). The process of recapture can only be properly understood by applying the rules to specific states of fact. The Regulations put a relatively simple illustration: Alimony payments by A to B are $25,000 in 1985; $12,000 in 1986; and $1,000 in 1987. In 1986 $3,000 is recaptured ($25,000 − ($12,000 +

There were three exceptions to the recapture (in addition to the fact that it had no application to payments of less than $10,000). If a case fell within one of them, the taxes were not recomputed and deductibility-includibility were not affected. These occurred when a) the payments ceased by reason of the death of either spouse or the remarriage of the payee; b) the payments were made, not pursuant to a decree of divorce or separate maintenance, but to a decree for the support of a spouse; or c) the payments fluctuated because the divorce or separate maintenance decree based them upon a fixed proportion of the payer's compensation for services or of his business or property.[62]

Both the six-year rule and the recapture rule could have devastating consequences for the parties, through no fault of their own, and for the administration of the states' divorce and alimony laws. The six-year rule could limit awards of rehabilitative alimony where the period of rehabilitation which seemed appropriate was less than six years. The recapture rule could impose heavy tax burdens on the payer of alimony without giving a corresponding benefit to the payee also in circumstances beyond the control of either.

Presumably for these reasons the Tax Reform Act of 1986 eliminated the six-year rule and drastically amended the recapture rule,[63] effective with respect to divorce or separation instruments executed after December 31, 1986.[64] The new recapture rule reduces the

recapture period from six to three years and increases the amount by which the earlier payments must exceed later ones from $10,000 to $15,000, in both respects giving the ex-spouses more leeway when alimony payments fluctuate. The computations required for determining excess payments are more complex, however.

Specifically the statute now provides that if there are excess alimony payments the payer must include the amount of the excess in his gross income for his taxable year beginning in the third post-separation year. The payee is correspondingly allowed a deduction for the excess in her taxable year beginning in the third post-separation year.[65]

The excess alimony payments are those for the first and second post-separation years. The excess for the first post-separation year is the excess of payments made during that year over the sum of the average of the payments made during the second post-separation year reduced by the excess payments for the second post-separation year plus the payments made during the third post-separation year plus $15,000.[66] The excess for the second post-separation year is the excess of the alimony paid during the second post-separation year over the sum of the payments made during the third post-separation year plus $15,000.[67] As was true of the DRTRA recapture rules, the 1986 rules may only be understood by attempting their application to specific examples.[68]

$10,000)). For later computations this reduces the amount deemed paid in 1985 to $22,000. Then in 1987 $12,000 will be recaptured. This is the sum of an $11,000 excess of 1985 over 1987 ($22,000 − ($1,000 + $10,000)), and a $1,000 excess of 1986 over 1987 ($12,000 − ($1,000 + $10,000)). Treas.Reg. § 71.1–1T, A–24. Other more complicated examples are worked out in O'Connell, The Domestic Relations Tax Reform Act: How We Got It and What We Can Do About It, 18 Fam.L.Q. 473, 502 (1985).

62. I.R.C. §§ 71(f)(5)(A), 71(f)(5)(B), 71(f)(5)(C) (DRTRA). Treas.Reg. § 71.1–1T, A–25 states that if the payments decline or cease for other reasons, such as a modification of the divorce decree, a reduction in the needs of the payee or in the ability of the payer to make payments, the recapture rules will apply.

63. I.R.C. § 71(f) (Tax Reform Act of 1986).

64. Tax Reform Act of 1986 § 1843(c)(2) and (3), Pub. L. 99–514, 100 Stat. 2853.

The effective date provision also states that divorce or separation instruments executed before January 1, 1987 but modified after that date may be governed by the new Act if the modification expressly so provides. For the definition of divorce or separation instrument, see note 32, supra.

65. I.R.C. § 71(f)(1)(A) and (B) (Tax Reform Act of 1986). The term "first post-separation year" is defined to mean the first calendar year in which the payer paid alimony or separate maintenance. The second and third post-separation years are the first and second succeeding calendar years respectively. I.R.C. § 71(f)(6) (Tax Reform Act of 1986).

66. I.R.C. § 71(f)(3) (Tax Reform Act of 1986).

67. I.R.C. § 71(f)(4) (Tax Reform Act of 1986).

68. The Conference Committee Report of Congress on the Tax Reform Act of 1986, Pub.L. 99–514, 2 Prentice-Hall, Federal Taxes par. 7702.19 gives the following ex-

The Tax Reform Act of 1986 also establishes three exceptions to its recapture rule: [69] a) If either spouse dies before the end of the third post-separation year or the payee remarries before the end of that year and the alimony payments end by reason of the death or remarriage, the recapture rules do not apply. b) The term "alimony or separate maintenance payment" does not include, for purposes of the recapture rule, payments received pursuant to a decree requiring payments for the support or maintenance of a spouse. c) The term "alimony or separate maintenance payment" also does not include, for purposes of the recapture rule, any payment to the extent made pursuant to a continuing liability over not less than three years to pay a fixed portion of the income from business, property, from compensation for employment or from self-employment.

Transfers of Property on Divorce: Before 1984

United States v. Davis held that when one spouse transfers to the other, as part of a property settlement on divorce, property whose value has increased, such a transfer is a taxable event.[70] The analysis, such as it was, seemed to draw an analogy between this kind of transfer and a sale, indicating that the transferor conveyed the property in exchange for the transferee's release of any claims to the property. The Supreme Court then went on to hold that in this situation the transferor was liable for a tax on the difference between his basis, usually the cost of the property, and the fair market value at the time of the transfer to his spouse.[71] The logical consequence of this holding was that the transferee's basis in the property would be its fair market value when transferred to her.[72] The tax consequences followed whether the transfer was made pursuant to a separation agreement as in Davis, or to a divorce decree without an agreement.[73] Although one might think that the transferee of appreciated property would also recognize gain when she gave up claims against the spouse, in the amount of the difference between her basis, presumably zero, and the value of the property transferred, the Internal Revenue Service and the courts held that she would not be taxable on the transfer.[74]

The Supreme Court in the Davis case implied that if the husband and wife held property in some form of joint ownership, the division of that property on divorce would not be a taxable event.[75] Whether the property

---

amples of the application of the new recapture rule: "Thus, for example, if the payor makes alimony payments of $50,000 in the first year and no payments in the second or third year, $35,000 will be recaptured (assuming none of the exceptions apply). If instead the payments are $50,000 in the first year, $20,000 in the second year and nothing in the third year, the recapture amount will consist of $5,000 from the second year (the excess over $15,000) plus $27,500 for the first year (the excess of $50,000 over the sum of $15,000 plus $7,500). (The $7,500 is the average payment for years two and three after reducing the payments by the $5,000 recaptured from year two)."

69. I.R.C. § 71(f)(A), (B), and (C) (Tax Reform Act of 1986).

70. 370 U.S. 65, 82 S.Ct. 1190, 8 L.Ed.2d 335 (1962), rehearing denied 371 U.S. 854, 83 S.Ct. 14, 9 L.Ed.2d 92 (1962), discussed in Solomon, Property Transfer Pursuant to Divorce—Taxable Event? 17 Stan.L.Rev. 478 (1965).

71. United States v. Davis, 370 U.S. 65, 72, 82 S.Ct. 1190, 1194, 8 L.Ed.2d 335 (1962), rehearing denied 371 U.S. 854, 83 S.Ct. 14, 9 L.Ed.2d 92 (1962). The tax would usually be assessed at the capital gains rates if the property transferred is a capital asset. I.R.C. § 1221. If the property transferred has depreciated in value the transferor may be entitled to deduct the loss. McKinney

v. Commissioner, 64 T.C. 263 (1975). But if the transfer were made while the parties were still married to each other, the deduction would have been disallowed as a sale between family members. I.R.C. § 267. If the transfer had been of depreciable property, the gain would be taxable as ordinary income rather than a capital gain. I.R.C. § 1239, Deyoe v. Commissioner, 66 T.C. 904 (1976).

The Supreme Court in Davis assumed that the claims which the transferee gave up in exchange for the property she received were equal in value to the fair market value of the property. United States v. Davis, 370 U.S. 65, 72, 82 S.Ct. 1190, 1194, 8 L.Ed.2d 335 (1962), rehearing denied 371 U.S. 854, 83 S.Ct. 14, 9 L.Ed.2d 92 (1962).

72. United States v. Davis, 370 U.S. 65, 73, 82 S.Ct. 1190, 1194, 8 L.Ed.2d 335 (1962), rehearing denied 371 U.S. 854, 83 S.Ct. 14, 9 L.Ed.2d 92 (1962).

73. Wallace v. United States, 439 F.2d 757 (8th Cir. 1971), cert. denied 404 U.S. 831, 92 S.Ct. 71, 30 L.Ed.2d 60 (1971).

74. Howard v. Commissioner, 447 F.2d 152 (5th Cir. 1971); Rev.Rul. 67-221, 1967-2 C.B. 63.

75. United States v. Davis, 370 U.S. 65, 69-71, 82 S.Ct. 1190, 1192-93, 8 L.Ed.2d 335 (1962), rehearing denied 371 U.S. 854, 83 S.Ct. 14, 9 L.Ed.2d 92 (1962).

was so held in a particular case would turn on state law.[76] This had the effect of creating a distinction between those states in which the divorce merely required a spouse to transfer property to the other spouse and those states in which the division of property constituted a recognition of some kind of ownership in the transferee spouse. The distinction can be stated in the abstract, but it had no validity in practice since the division of property on divorce had the same general purpose in all states, which was to give the spouse some financial security.[77] Following the distinction as stated, however, some courts held that a division of property in community property states would not usually be a taxable event because it was a division of property between co-owners rather than a transfer from one spouse to the other.[78] The same result was reached where property held by the spouses in joint tenancy or tenancy by the entireties was divided on divorce.[79]

Several states, disliking the apparent inequity of the Davis rule, succeeded in evading it by creating a new form of co-ownership. These cases held that even though the two spouses in a non-community property state were not considered to be co-owners of property when title was held by one or the other of them, once a divorce suit was commenced, they became co-owners.[80] The effect of this was that when the property was divided pur-

suant to the divorce decree or a separation agreement, a division of property between co-owners rather than a taxable transfer occurred, at least where the property was equally divided.[81] The federal courts accepted the states' characterization of these transactions and they were held not to be taxable.[82] These cases exposed the essential artificiality (if any exposure were necessary) of the distinction drawn by the Davis case.

Transfers of Property on Divorce: After 1984

The Domestic Relations Tax Reform Act of 1984 eliminated the problems and the metaphysical distinctions required by the Davis case. In general that Act provides that no gain or loss will be recognized a) by reason of transfers to a spouse or in trust for the benefit of a spouse, or b) by reason of transfers to a former spouse if the transfers are incident to a divorce.[83] The non-recognition rules do not apply if the transferee spouse is a nonresident alien.[84]

In general the non-recognition provisions of the DRTRA are effective with respect to transfers occurring after July 18, 1984, the date on which the Act was passed.[85] There are two exceptions to the general rule concerning effectiveness: a) The Act does not apply to transfers occurring after July 18,

76. Ibid.; Beth W. Corp. v. United States, 350 F.Supp. 1190 (S.D.Fla.1972), affirmed p.c. 481 F.2d 140 (5th Cir. 1973), cert. denied 415 U.S. 916, 94 S.Ct. 1412, 39 L.Ed.2d 470 (1974).

77. See the discussion of property divisions in the various states in sections 15.1 and 15.3, supra.

78. Wren v. Commissioner, 24 T.C.Mem. 290 (1965). See also Showalter v. Commissioner, 33 T.C.Mem. 192 (1974) (dictum). But if the division were not an equal one, or where the division involved the transfer of separate property, it was held that the transaction was a transfer rather than a division and was therefore a taxable event. Siewert v. Commissioner, 72 T.C. 326 (1979); Showalter v. Commissioner, 33 T.C.Mem. 192 (1974); Schact v. Commissioner, 47 T.C. 552 (1967).

79. Rev.Rul. 74–347, 1974–2 C.B. 26. Likewise the conversion of a joint tenancy into a tenancy in common and the severance of a tenancy in common are not taxable events. Rev.Rul. 56–437, 1956–2 C.B. 507.

80. In re Questions Submitted by United States District Court, 184 Colo. 1, 517 P.2d 1331 (1974); Cady v. Cady, 224 Kan. 339, 581 P.2d 358 (1978); Miller v. Miller,

352 N.W.2d 738 (Minn.1984); Collins v. Oklahoma Tax Commission, 446 P.2d 290 (Okl.1968); Matter of Marriage of Engle, 293 Or. 207, 646 P.2d 20 (1982); Krueger v. Wisconsin Department of Revenue, 124 Wis.2d 453, 369 N.W.2d 691 (1985).

81. Miller v. Miller, 352 N.W.2d 738 (Minn.1984). See Vernon's Ann.Mo.Stat. § 452.330(3) (Supp.1985).

82. Serianni v. Commissioner, 765 F.2d 1051 (11th Cir. 1985) (Florida law); Imel v. United States, 523 F.2d 853 (10th Cir.1975); Collins v. Commissioner, 412 F.2d 211 (10th Cir.1969); Cook v. Commissioner, 80 T.C. 512 (1983), affirmed without opinion Cook v. Tax, 742 F.2d 1431 (2d Cir.1984); McIntosh v. Commissioner, 85 T.C. 31 (1985) (Montana law).

83. I.R.C. § 1041, and I.R.C. § 267(g) (Tax Reform Act of 1986). See O'Connell, Divorce Taxation: The Domestic Relations Tax Reform Act of 1984, 43 Inst. on Fed. Taxation 43–1, 43–13 to 43–18 (N.Y.Univ.1985).

84. I.R.C. § 1041(d).

85. Pub.L. 98–369, § 421(d) (1984), 98 Stat. 795. Treas.Reg. § 1.1041–1T, A–15.

1984 if they are made pursuant to an instrument in effect on or before that date, unless both spouses or former spouses elect to have it apply.[86] b) If both spouses elect to have the Act apply to transfers made after December 31, 1983, it will so apply.[87]

Transfers during marriage, to be within the Act, must be transfers of property, real, personal, tangible or intangible, but may not be transfers of services.[88] The transfer may take the form of a gift or of a sale or exchange and in either event is non-taxable.[89] It is important to note that the Act would apply to a transfer pursuant to an antenuptial contract provided that it occurred after the parties were married. A transfer in exchange for the relinquishment of marital rights is within the Act.[90]

Transfer which are "incident to divorce" (divorce here including annulment) are defined as a) transfers occurring within one year of the divorce;[91] and b) transfers which are "related to the cessation of the marriage".[92] The Regulations provide that a transfer is related to the cessation of a marriage if it occurs pursuant to a divorce or separation instrument[93] and occurs not more than six years after the marriage ends.[94] If the transfer is not pursuant to such an instrument or occurs more than six years after the divorce, there is a rebuttable presumption that it is not related to the cessation of the marriage.[95]

Transfers to a third person on behalf of a spouse or former spouse may qualify under

DRTRA if a) the transfer is required by a divorce or separation instrument; or b) the transfer to the third party is made pursuant to a written request of the other spouse or former spouse; or c) the transferor receives from the other spouse or former spouse a written consent to or ratification of the transfer to the third party, under conditions outlined in the Regulations.[96] If the transfer meets these conditions, it will be treated as made directly to the other spouse or former spouse and then immediately transferred by him to the third party. The pretended transfer from the spouse to the third party does not qualify for nonrecognition of gain under the Act.[97]

Transfers which qualify under the DRTRA result in no taxable gain or loss to the transferor. They likewise result in no taxable gain or loss to the transferee. And in all cases the transferee takes the property with the adjusted basis which it had in the hands of the transferor, regardless of whether that basis is less than, equal to or more than the property's fair market value at the time of the transfer and regardless of whether the property is subject to liabilities which exceed the adjusted basis.[98] The transferor must provide the transferee with records sufficient to determine the adjusted basis of the property transferred and the holding period.[99]

Alimony Trusts: Before 1984

Although the discharge of an alimony obligation by the creation of a trust is generally not desirable from the payer's point of view, it

---

86. Pub.L. 98–369, § 421(d)(3), 98 Stat. 795. Treas. Reg. § 1.1041–1T, A–16. An election under either of these two exceptions must be made in accordance with Treasury Regulations. Pub.L. 98–369, § 421(d)(4), 98 Stat. 795. The method of making these elections and the forms to be used are found in Treas.Reg. § 1.1041–1T, A–18.

87. Pub.L. 98–369, § 421(d)(2), 98 Stat. 798; Treas. Reg. § 1.1041–1T, A–16, A–17. Partial elections are not permitted under these Regulations.

88. I.R.C. § 1041(a); Treas.Reg. § 1.1041–1T, A–4.

89. Treas.Reg. § 1.1041–1T, A–2.

90. Ibid.

91. I.R.C. § 1041(c)(1). For a statement that annulments are included as divorces see Treas.Reg. § 1.1041–1T, A–8.

92. I.R.C. § 1041(c)(2).

93. Divorce or separation instrument is defined by I.R.C. § 71(b)(2) to mean a divorce or separate maintenance decree, a written instrument incident to such a decree, a written separation agreement, or a decree ordering one spouse to make payments for the support or maintenance of the other spouse.

94. Treas.Reg. § 1.1041–1T, A–7.

95. Ibid.

96. Treas.Reg. § 1.1041–1T, A–9.

97. Ibid.

98. I.R.C. § 1041(a), (b); Treas.Reg. § 1.1041–1T, A–10, A–11, A–12. Adjusted basis is defined by I.R.C. §§ 1011, 1012, 1016.

99. Treas.Reg. § 1.1041–1T, A–14.

offers the advantage of security for the payee and may sometimes be used for that reason. If the trust is set up specifically for this purpose, it is referred to as a section 71 trust. The tax consequences formerly were that the entire payments from such a trust were taxable to the payee, including not only payments out of trust income but payments from principal and from tax exempt securities.[1] The spouse who set up the trust was not entitled to a deduction for the payments, however.[2] Where the trust was in existence before the divorce and was not set up for the purpose of providing alimony, it was usually referred to as a section 682 trust. When this type of trust was used to provide alimony in a divorce, the payee was held taxable only upon payments out of the income of the trust.[3] Payments from this type of trust were not deductible by the other spouse.[4] Transfers of property in trust for this purpose could involve a taxable gain to the transferor under the Davis case[5] if the trust property had appreciated in his hands and if the trust beneficiary were given the principal or a general power of appointment over it.[6]

Alimony Trusts: After 1984

Under the DRTRA no distinction is made between trusts set up specifically for alimony purposes and pre-existing trusts which are used for that purpose. Three conditions must be complied with in order to have the new provisions apply:[7] a) The spouses must be divorced or legally separated under a decree of divorce or separate maintenance or separated under a written separation agreement; b) the payer would be taxable on the income of the trust except for the provisions of section 682; and c) the provisions do not apply to any part of the trust income which is fixed as a sum payable for the support of the children. If these conditions are met, the trust income is taxed to the payee spouse and is not includible in the gross income of the payer.[8] The payer receives no deduction for the trust income paid to the payee.[9] The effective date of these rules is the same as for other provisions of the alimony section.[10]

Since the Davis case has been eliminated by the changes in the DRTRA, no taxable gain or loss is recognized when property is transferred into an alimony trust.[11]

Dependency Exemption: Before 1984

The general rule before the DRTRA amendments was that following a divorce, legal separation or separation under a written agreement the parent having custody for the greater part of the calendar was entitled to the exemption for a dependent child of the marriage.[12] There were two exceptions to this general rule: a) If the divorce or separate maintenance decree or the separation agreement provided that the non-custodial parent should have the exemption, and if that parent

1. I.R.C. § 71(a)(1); Treas.Reg. § 1.71–1(c); Gunn, Douglas v. Willcuts Today: The Income Tax Problems of Using Alimony Trusts, 63 Corn.L.Rev. 1022 (1978); Note, Tax Aspects of Alimony Trusts, 66 Yale L.J. 881 (1957). The Regulation provides that payments pursuant to such a trust are not included in the settlor's gross income.

2. Treas.Reg. § 1.215–1.

3. Treas.Reg. § 1.71–1(c)(4); I.R.C. § 682.

4. Treas.Reg. § 1.215–1.

5. See the discussion of the Davis case in the text at note 70, supra. A transfer to a trustee in trust for the education of children pursuant to a divorce settlement was held to result in capital gain to the transferor by St. Joseph Bank and Trust Co. v. United States, 716 F.2d 1180 (7th Cir.1983).

6. Commissioner v. Patino, 186 F.2d 962 (4th Cir. 1950); Note, Tax Aspects of Alimony Trusts, 66 Yale L.J. 881, 884 (1957).

7. I.R.C. § 682(a).

8. Ibid.

9. I.R.C. § 215(d).

10. Pub.L. 98–369, § 421(e), 98 Stat. 798.

11. I.R.C. § 1041. See the discussion supra, at note 70. But under the Tax Reform Act of 1986 the transferor must recognize gain on a transfer in trust incident to divorce to the extent that the liabilities assumed by the trust exceed the transferor's basis. I.R.C. § 1041(e) (Tax Reform Act of 1986).

12. I.R.C. § 152(e)(1); Treas.Reg. § 1.152–4(c). "Child" was defined as a son, stepson, daughter or stepdaughter of the taxpayer under age nineteen at the close of the year, or a student. I.R.C. § 151(e). Where no decree of divorce or separate maintenance and no separation agreement is in effect, the parent furnishing more than half of the support is entitled to the exemption under I.R.C. § 152(a). Muracca v. Commissioner, 47 T.C. Mem. 1762 (1984).

furnished at least $600 in child support during the calendar year, that parent could take the exemption.[13] b) If the non-custodial parent furnished at least $1,200 in child support for the calendar year and the custodial parent could not clearly establish that he furnished more for child support than the non-custodial parent during the year, the non-custodial parent was entitled to the exemption.[14]

The general rule and exceptions did not apply where the child was in the custody of a person or persons other than his parents for half or more of the calendar year[15] or where the child received half or more of his support during the year from persons other than his parents.[16] For purposes of the general rule and exceptions, amounts expended for the support of the child were treated as received from the non-custodial parent to the extent that parent furnished those amounts.[17] Where the second exception was invoked, each parent was entitled to have from the other an itemized statement of the other's claimed expenditures.[18] A stepparent's contributions to the child's support could be included in determining whether the custodial parent contributed half of the child's support, where the custodial parent had married the stepparent.[19] The provisions of the general rule and exceptions did not apply where there was a multiple support agreement in force.[20]

Dependency Exemptions: After 1984

The DRTRA has attempted to simplify the process of determining dependency exemp-tions for children of divorced parents by eliminating the necessity for controversies over which parent furnishes the greater part of the child's support. The general rule under that Act now is that the custodial parent is entitled to the dependency exemption if the parents are divorced, or legally separated under a decree of separate maintenance, or are separated under a written separation agreement, or live apart at all times during the last six months of the calendar year, and if the child is in the custody of one or both parents for more than half of the calendar year.[21] "Child" is defined as a son, stepson, daughter or stepdaughter of the taxpayer.[22]

There are three exceptions to the rule that the custodial parent is entitled to the exemption: a) Where a multiple support agreement is in force, the exemption will be allocated in accordance with the provisions governing such agreements.[23] b) Where a decree or agreement executed before January 1, 1985 provides that the custodial parent releases his claim to the dependency exemption to the non-custodial parent and the non-custodial parent furnishes at least $600 of support for the child during the calendar year, the dependency exemption may be taken by the non-custodial parent.[24] c) Where the custodial parent signs a written declaration in a form complying with the regulations that he will not claim the exemption for any taxable year beginning with the calendar year and the non-custodial parent attaches the declaration to his tax return for the calendar year, the

13. I.R.C. § 152(e)(2)(A); Treas.Reg. § 1.152–4(d)(2). See also Schneier v. Commissioner, 735 F.2d 375 (9th Cir. 1984), cert. denied 469 U.S. 1190, 105 S.Ct. 962, 83 L.Ed. 2d 967 (1985) and Zimmerman v. Commissioner, 48 T.C. Mem. 25 (1984).

14. I.R.C. § 152(e)(2)(B); Treas.Reg. § 1.152–4(d)(3).

15. I.R.C. § 152(e)(1)(B). If custody was divided or if the decree or agreement failed to allocate custody, it was deemed to be with the parent having physical custody of the child for the greater part of the year.

16. I.R.C. § 152(e)(1)(A).

17. I.R.C. § 152(e)(2).

18. I.R.C. § 152(e)(3); Treas.Reg. § 1.152–4(e). Under some circumstances the Regulation required the itemized statement to be attached to the parent's tax return.

19. Rev.Rul. 73–175, I.R.B.1973–16, p. 6; Colton v. Commissioner, 56 T.C. 471 (1971).

20. I.R.C. § 152(e)(4). Multiple support agreements are governed by I.R.C. § 152(c). Their requirements are described in detail in Treas.Reg. § 1.152–3.

21. I.R.C. § 152(e)(1); Treas.Reg. § 1.152–4T, A–1.

22. I.R.C. § 151(e)(3).

23. I.R.C. § 152(e)(3); Treas.Reg. § 1.152–4T, A–2.

24. I.R.C. § 152(e)(4); Treas.Reg. § 1.152–4T, A–2. For purposes of this exception amounts expended for support of a child are treated as received from the non-custodial parent to the extent that that parent furnished amounts for support.

non-custodial parent may take the dependency exemption.[25]

The amendments respecting the dependency exemption are effective for taxable years beginning after December 31, 1984.[26]

The DRTRA also permits either parent to deduct payments for the medical expenses of a child if the child is one to whom the exemption provision applies, without regard to whether the parent making the medical payment is entitled to the exemption for the child.[27] Likewise a child to whom the exemption provision applies is treated as a child of both parents for purposes of excluding from income amounts paid by health insurance as reimbursement for the costs of medical care, where such insurance is provided by the parent's employer.[28]

The DRTRA also liberalizes the requirements for head of household filing status. It reduces the time during which the child must reside in the household from one year to one-half of the taxable year.[29] It also provides that a parent may qualify as a head of household even though he has released the dependency exemption to the other spouse.[30]

Innocent Spouse Provisions: After 1984

The income tax statute provides, as it logically must, that spouses who sign joint returns are jointly and severally liable for the tax on the income of both of them.[31] This can produce hardship for a spouse who signs a

return in ignorance of the fact that the other spouse has greatly understated his tax liability. The hardship is particularly acute when the spouses are in the process of separation or divorce since in such circumstances the non-earning spouse may lack any means for ascertaining the source and amount of the other spouse's income. In order to mitigate these hardships Congress in 1971 passed what have come to be called the "innocent spouse" provisions of the statute, giving spouses who sign joint returns relief from liability for taxes where substantial income was omitted from the return without their knowledge.[32]

In 1984 the DRTRA enacted broader and more complex rules for the protection of the innocent spouse. These rules apply to all taxable years beginning after 1939.[33]

The DRTRA relieves the innocent spouse of liability for tax, interest, penalties and other amounts if, in the first place, he can meet these general requirements: [34] a) A joint return was filed for the particular taxable year.[35]

b) On this return there was a substantial understatement of the tax attributable to the grossly erroneous items of one spouse.[36] "Substantial understatement" is defined by the statute as any understatement in excess of $500.[37] "Grossly erroneous items" are defined as i. an item of gross income attributable to that spouse which is omitted from gross

---

25. I.R.C. § 152(e)(2); Treas.Reg. § 1.152–4T, A–3, A–4. The exemption may be released for one or more years, as specified in the declaration.

26. Pub.L. 98–369, § 423, 98 Stat. 801.

27. I.R.C. § 213(d)(4). In order to come within this provision the parents of the child must be divorced or legally separated under a decree of divorce or legal separation, or separated under a written separation agreement and must provide over half of the child's support during the calendar year. Treas.Reg. § 1.152–4T, A–5.

28. I.R.C. § 105(b). The parents must meet the same requirements here as for the application of I.R.C. § 213(d) (4). Treas.Reg. § 1.152–4T, A–5. Both of these provisions are effective for taxable years beginning after December 31, 1984.

29. I.R.C. § 2(b)(1); Treas.Reg. § 1.2–2(b).

30. I.R.C. § 2(b)(1)(A)(i).

31. I.R.C. § 6013(d)(3).

32. I.R.C. § 6013(e). The regulations explaining the statute are in Treas.Reg. § 1.6013–5. For a discussion of the background and operation of the statute, see Note, Section 6013(e): Congressional Response to Joint and Several Liability and the Innocent Spouse, 5 Val.U.L.Rev. 616 (1971); Note, The Innocent Spouse Act, 45 Temp.L.Q. 448 (1972). Cases applying the statute are collected in Annot., Validity, Construction, and Application of Innocent Spouse Statute (26 U.S.C.A. § 6013(e)), Under Which Innocent Spouse is Relieved of Federal Income Tax Liability in Certain Cases, 31 A.L.R.Fed. 14 (1977).

33. Pub.L. 98–369, § 424(c)(1), 98 Stat. 803.

34. The burden of proving that the requirements have been met is on the taxpayer. Ballard v. Commissioner, 740 F.2d 659 (8th Cir.1984).

35. I.R.C. § 6013(e)(1)(A).

36. I.R.C. § 6013(e)(1)(B).

37. I.R.C. § 6013(e)(3).

income;[38] or ii. a claim of a deduction, credit or basis by that spouse in an amount for which there is no basis in fact or law.[39]

c) The alleged innocent spouse establishes that in signing the return he did not know, and had no reason to know, that there was a substantial understatement.[40]

d) Taking into account all the facts and circumstances, it would be inequitable to hold the alleged innocent spouse liable for the deficiency in tax attributable to the substantial understatement, for the taxable year in question.[41] The proceeding version of this requirement expressly required the courts to take into account whether the alleged innocent spouse benefited from the items of income omitted from the other spouse's return,[42] but this has been left out of the DRTRA provision. It does not seem likely that this omission signals any change in the intent of Congress, however.[43]

Where the understatement of gross income is attributable to claims of deduction, credit or basis rather than to the omission of items from gross income, further limitations of amount are imposed by DRTRA. If the alleged innocent spouse had adjusted gross income for the preadjustment year of $20,000 or less, he will be given relief from liability only if the liability asserted is greater than ten percent of the adjusted gross income.[44] If his adjusted gross income from the preadjustment year is more than $20,000, the relevant percentage is twenty-five rather than ten.[45] If the innocent spouse is married to another

spouse at the end of the preadjustment year, the innocent spouse's adjusted gross income must include the income of the new spouse, whether or not they file a joint return.[46] The determination of the spouse to whom items of gross income are attributable is made without regard community property laws.[47]

Attorney Fees

The question here is whether the attorney fees of husband or wife incurred in divorce litigation are deductible for federal income tax purposes. The DRTRA has not addressed this question.

The question arises because the statute makes a distrinction between personal, living or family expenses, which are not deductible,[48] and expenses incurred for the production of income or for the management, conservation or maintenance of property held for the production of income, which are deductible.[49] Whether the attorney fees in a divorce case are deductible turns on which of these categories it is assigned to. Obviously a divorce case in which alimony or property claims are made may result in attorney fees which are attributable to both categories.

The Supreme Court has adopted an analysis which in general terms attempts to assign attorney fees to one or the other of these categories by reference to whether the fees "arise in connection with the taxpayer's profit-seeking activities", rather than to whether they have consequences which might affect

---

38. I.R.C. § 6013(e)(2)(A).

39. I.R.C. § 6013(e)(2)(B).

40. I.R.C. § 6013(e)(1)(C). Cases applying this criterion are collected in Annot., 31 A.L.R.Fed. 14, 31 (1977). See also Ratana v. Commissioner, 662 F.2d 220 (4th Cir. 1981); Shea v. Commissioner, 780 F.2d 561 (6th Cir.1986).

41. I.R.C. § 6013(e)(1)(D). "Inequitable" is further defined in Treas.Reg. § 1.6013–5(b). Cases dealing with this requirement are collected in Annot., 31 A.L.R.Fed. 14, 37 (1977). See also Ballard v. Commissioner, 740 F.2d 659 (8th Cir.1984); Ratana v. Commissioner, 662 F.2d 220 (4th Cir.1981); Busse v. United States, 542 F.2d 421 (7th Cir.1976).

42. I.R.C. § 6013(e)(1)(C).

43. Possible benefits will undoubtedly be taken into account as among the other "facts and circumstances".

Compare Ballard v. Commissioner, 740 F.2d 659 (8th Cir. 1984).

44. I.R.C. § 6013(e)(4)(A). "Preadjustment year" is defined as the most recent taxable year of the innocent spouse ending before the date the deficiency notice is mailed. I.R.C. § 6013(e)(4)(C).

45. I.R.C. § 6013(e)(4)(B).

46. I.R.C. § 6013(e)(4)(D).

47. I.R.C. § 6013(e)(5). Compare United States v. Mitchell, 403 U.S. 190, 91 S.Ct. 1763, 29 L.Ed.2d 406 (1971); Brent v. Commissioner, 630 F.2d 356 (5th Cir. 1980).

48. I.R.C. § 262.

49. I.R.C. § 212(1), (2).

the taxpayer's property.[50] In other words, it is the "origin and character of the claim with respect to which an expense was incurred, rather than its potential consequences upon the fortunes of the taxpayer"[51] which controls whether the fees will be deductible.

The effect of this analysis is that attorney fees of a husband which might appear to be deductible are held not to be.[52] For example, his successful resistance to his wife's claim to controlling stock interests in several corporations of which he was an officer as well as a stockholder was held not to be the sort of litigation in which his attorney fees would be deductible.[53] The same result was reached where the fees represented services in arranging stock transfers and a lease as part of a property settlement on divorce.[54] In these cases the character of the claim being made or resisted by the husband was held to arise out of the marital relationship, not out of any income-producing activity by him. There is some authority that the husband should be able to add the non-deductible attorney fees to the basis of property which he obtains in the litigation,[55] but this possibility may be very limited.[56]

The husband may deduct fees paid to his attorney in the divorce to the extent that they were paid for advice or representation on the determination of taxes.[57] In order to get the deduction, the tax work must be accurately segregated from other work done by the attor-ney.[58] But the husband may not deduct fees which he paid to his wife's attorney for tax advice given to her concerning a property settlement in divorce.[59]

Where the wife in a divorce seeks to deduct her attorney fees, the courts and the Internal Revenue Service seem to shift the rules. According to the regulations, she may deduct attorney fees to the extent they are attributable to the production of payments from the husband which will be includible in her gross income and therefore taxable to her.[60] This is apparently so even though her claim to alimony clearly arises out of the marital relationship, rather than from any income-producing activity. She may also deduct that part of her attorney fees representing tax advice to her.[61]

Gift and Estate Taxes: After 1984

Gift tax liability for transfers made in connection with property settlements or divorce actions may be avoided by ensuring that the transfers take either of two forms. In the first place, if the transfer is ordered by the divorce decree, it is not considered a gift even though the decree is based upon an agreement of the parties.[62] A second method of avoiding the gift tax is by making the transfer pursuant to a property settlement in settlement of marital property rights or to provide for the support of children.[63] Under the DR-TRA the property settlement agreement must

---

50. United States v. Gilmore, 372 U.S. 39, 83 S.Ct. 623, 9 L.Ed.2d 570 (1963).

51. 372 U.S. at 49, 83 S.Ct. at 629. See also United States v. Patrick, 372 U.S. 53, 83 S.Ct. 618, 9 L.Ed.2d 580 (1963).

52. Treas.Reg. § 1.262–1(b), 7. See also F. Sander, H. Gutman, Tax Aspects of Divorce and Separation A–41 (1975). It should go without saying that attorney fees for services in obtaining a divorce or the custody of children or in other non-financial aspects of divorce litigation are not deductible by the husband.

53. United States v. Gilmore, 372 U.S. 39, 83 S.Ct. 623, 9 L.Ed.2d 570 (1963). The husband's attorney fees incurred in resisting post-divorce claims for child support, or in seeking to vacate an alimony judgment are not deductible. Smith v. Commissioner, 40 T.C.Mem. 395 (1980); Favrot v. United States, 550 F.Supp. 809 (E.D.La. 1982).

54. United States v. Patrick, 372 U.S. 53, 83 S.Ct. 618, 9 L.Ed.2d 580 (1963).

Clark, Domestic Rel., 2nd Ed. HBSE—24

55. Gilmore v. United States, 245 F.Supp. 383 (N.D. Cal.1965).

56. F. Sander, H. Gutman, Tax Aspects of Divorce and Separation A–42 (1975).

57. I.R.C. § 212(3); Munn v. United States, 455 F.2d 1028 (Ct.Cl.1972).

58. Rev.Rul. 72–545, 1972–2 C.B. 179.

59. Davis v. United States, 370 U.S. 65, 82 S.Ct. 1190, 8 L.Ed.2d 335 (1962), rehearing denied 371 U.S. 854, 83 S.Ct. 14, 9 L.Ed.2d 92 (1962); Martin v. Commissioner, 73 T.C. 255 (1979).

60. Treas.Reg. § 1.262–1(b), 7; Hahn v. Commissioner, 35 T.C.Mem. 509 (1976).

61. F. Sander, H. Gutman, Tax Aspects of Divorce and Separation A–42 (1975).

62. Harris v. Commissioner, 340 U.S. 106, 71 S.Ct. 181, 95 L.Ed. 111 (1950).

63. I.R.C. § 2516; Treas.Reg. §§ 25.2516–1, 25.2516–2.

be made within one year after the divorce or two years before it.[64]

The estate tax consequences of transfers of property resulting from divorce now parallel the gift tax consequences of such transfers. If the transfers made by the divorced spouse's estate are made pursuant to the divorce decree, they are deductible from the deceased's gross estate.[65] This is the case even where the divorce decree is based on an agreement of the spouses, so long as the decree rather than the agreement is the authority for the transfer.[66] This was the law before 1984 and has not been changed by the DRTRA.

Before 1984 transfers pursuant to separation agreements rather than divorce decrees did not produce deductions from the deceased spouse's gross estate. There was no estate tax provision analogous to that in the gift tax which exempted certain transfers from that tax when made pursuant to separation agreements.[67] The relevant provisions of the estate tax statute made it clear that such transfers were not deemed to have been made in consideration of money or money's worth when the consideration consisted of a release of dower, curtesy or marital property rights.[68] A release of claims for support was held to be valid consideration, however, and the value of property transferred in exchange for a release of that kind was deductible from the gross estate.[69]

The DRTRA has amended the estate tax statute so that it now permits a deduction from the gross estate of the value of property transferred pursuant to a separation agreement if the agreement satisfies the new gift tax provisions of the statute.[70] This means that the deduction is allowed if the transfer is made pursuant to an agreement of husband and wife in settlement of marital property rights or of claims for child support and if the divorce occurs within a three-year period beginning one year before execution of the agreement.[71] The purpose of the amendment was of course to bring the estate tax into congruence with the gift tax. The amendment applies to the estates of decedents dying after the date of the enactment of the statute, which is July 18, 1984.[72]

The Validity of Marriages for Tax Purposes

Since the impact of federal taxes of all kinds often turns on whether a particular taxpayer is married, it is necessary for the federal courts on occasion to determine the validity of asserted marriages. It would seem obvious, at least at first glance, that the determination should be made by reference to the law of some state rather than by trying to establish some federal tax law of valid or invalid marriages. Some courts have been oddly reluctant to adopt such a rule,[73] although in the end they usually are guided by

---

64. I.R.C. § 2516. The effect of the DRTRA is to expand the time period within which the agreement might be made. The former rule was that the divorce had to be granted within two years after the execution of the property settlement agreement.

The amendment of the gift tax provision applies to transfers occurring after the enactment of the statute, July 18, 1984. Pub.L. 98–369, §§ 425(b), 425(c)(2), 98 Stat. 804.

The gift tax exclusion under section 2516 applies to former husbands and wives as well as to husbands and wives. I.R.C. § 7701(a)(17) (Tax Reform Act of 1986).

65. Robinson's Estate v. Commissioner, 63 T.C. 717 (1975).

66. F. Sander, H. Gutman, Tax Aspects of Divorce and Separation A–54 (1975).

67. The former gift tax provision was I.R.C. § 2516, discussed supra, at note 64.

68. I.R.C. §§ 2043(b), 2053(c)(1)(A); Treas.Reg. § 20.2043–1(b); F. Sander, H. Gutman, Tax Aspects of

Divorce and Separation A–54 (1975). See also In re Mathay's Estate, 463 Pa. 486, 345 A.2d 623 (1975).

69. Estate of Iversen, 552 F.2d 977 (3d Cir.1977). Cf. Gray v. United States, 541 F.2d 228 (9th Cir.1976), on remand 440 F.Supp. 684 (C.D.Cal.1977).

70. I.R.C. §§ 2043(b)(2), 2053(e), 2516.

71. I.R.C. § 2516; O'Connell, Divorce Taxation: The Domestic Relations Tax Reform Act of 1984, 43 Inst. on Fed. Taxation 43–1, 43–19 (N.Y.Univ.1985).

72. Pub.L. 98–369, § 425(c)(1), 98 Stat. 804.

73. E.g., Steffke v. Commissioner, 538 F.2d 730 (7th Cir.1976), cert. denied 429 U.S. 1022, 97 S.Ct. 639, 50 L.Ed.2d 624 (1976), stating that state law only controls where the tax statute expressly or by necessary implication so provides. A case in which the court found that the tax statute did so provide is Ensminger v. Commissioner, 610 F.2d 189 (4th Cir.1979), cert. denied 446 U.S. 941, 100 S.Ct. 2166, 64 L.Ed.2d 796 (1980).

local law.[74] This approach seems clearly correct but there may be difficulties in deciding which state's law should control.[75] And in some cases there may also be thought to be factors of tax policy which warrant ignoring the state law of marriage or divorce.[76]

The validity of marriages arises in many different tax contexts, and the courts' approach sometimes varies from one context to another. Where the question is whether the parties have contracted a valid common law marriage, for example, it seems clear that the federal court should decide whether the law of the state in which the parties live recognizes that form of marriage and whether the parties have complied with the requirements established by that state's courts.[77] Where a dependency exemption is claimed for a cohabitant, there may be no question of a valid marriage, but the local law may provide guidance on the extent to which Marvin relationships [78] are recognized in the jurisdiction.[79]

The most commonly encountered problem is raised by attacks upon the validity of divorces which, if successful will invalidate subsequent marriages. In the much cited Borax case [80] the Second Circuit recognized for various tax purposes the validity of a second marriage notwithstanding that a court of the parties' domicile, New York, had held that a Mexican divorce obtained by the taxpayer from his first wife was invalid, thereby by necessary implication establishing the invalidity of the second marriage.[81] The Second Circuit was moved in part by the desirability of validating existing de facto relationships, and in part by the consideration that federal tax questions should be decided uniformly throughout the United States, unaffected by differences among the states respecting the validity of migratory divorces.[82] Although both of these arguments make sense, Borax has received a mixed treatment by later cases, even those in the Second Circuit.[83] It therefore appears more likely than not that state law will be

---

74. The Steffke case, supra, note 73, chose to follow the law of the state in which an estate was being administered, where the question involved was the validity of an estate tax deduction. A case squarely holding that state law controls is Lee v. Commissioner, 550 F.2d 1201 (9th Cir.1977).

75. As in Steffke v. Commissioner, 538 F.2d 730 (7th Cir.1976), cert. denied 429 U.S. 1022, 97 S.Ct. 639, 50 L.Ed.2d 624 (1976).

76. E.g. Boyter v. Commissioner, 668 F.2d 1382 (4th Cir.1981) (semble); Borax' Estate v. Commissioner, 349 F.2d 666 (2d Cir.1965), cert. denied 383 U.S. 935, 86 S.Ct. 1064, 15 L.Ed.2d 852 (1966).

77. Purdy v. Commissioner, 39 T.C.Mem. 808 (1979).

78. The term is adapted from Marvin v. Marvin, 18 Cal.3d 660, 134 Cal.Rptr. 815, 557 P.2d 106 (1976) which held that property claims might be recognized where a man and woman lived together for a substantial period, either on a contract theory or on some vague theory of equity. The case is discussed in sections 1.2 and 15.7, supra.

79. Ensminger v. Commissioner, 610 F.2d 189 (4th Cir. 1979), cert. denied 446 U.S. 941, 100 S.Ct. 2166, 64 L.Ed. 2d 796 (1980). In this case the taxpayer claimed a dependency exemption for the adult woman with whom he lived. The court relied in part on I.R.C. § 152(b)(5) which provided that an individual is not to be considered a member of a taxpayer's household if their relationship violates local law, and found that the relationship in this case would be a misdemeanor under North Carolina law. The court referred to the principle that the regulation of marriage is a matter for the states rather than the federal government. See section 12.2 for a discussion of this principle in the divorce context.

State law has also been held to control the question whether two persons are "legally separated" and therefore not married under I.R.C. § 143. Capodanno v. Commissioner, 602 F.2d 64 (3d Cir.1979), relying on Weinkrantz v. Weinkrantz, 129 N.J.Super. 28, 322 A.2d 184 (1974).

80. Borax' Estate v. Commissioner, 349 F.2d 666 (2d Cir.1965), cert. denied 383 U.S. 935, 86 S.Ct. 1064, 15 L.Ed.2d 852 (1966), 34 U.Chi.L.Rev. 64 (1966), 66 Colum.L. Rev. 150 (1966). See also Spolter, Invalid Divorce Decrees, 24 Tax L.Rev. 163 (1969).

81. The tax questions in Borax which turned on the validity of the second marriage were whether the parties to that marriage were entitled to file joint returns, whether certain dependency exemptions based on that marriage could be claimed, and whether payments to the first wife were deductible as alimony or separate maintenance payments. 349 F.2d at 668, 669.

82. For a discussion of the validity of such divorces, see sections 12.2 and 12.3, supra.

83. The Internal Revenue Service has refused to acquiesce in Borax, Rev.Rul. 67–442, 1967–2 C.B. 65, but in the same ruling it has indicated that it will generally not question the validity of a divorce decree until a court of competent jurisdiction has declared it to be invalid. The cases of Lee v. Commissioner, 550 F.2d 1201 (9th Cir. 1977) and Steffke v. Commissioner, 538 F.2d 730 (7th Cir. 1976), cert. denied 429 U.S. 1022, 97 S.Ct. 639, 50 L.Ed.2d 624 (1976) refused to follow Borax, both cases affirming Tax Court decisions to that effect. The Second Circuit position is difficult to summarize. Estate of Spalding, 537 F.2d 666 (2d Cir.1976) held that the second marriage following a Nevada ex parte divorce would be recognized for estate tax purposes even though a New York court

looked to in order to determine the validity of divorces and subsequent marriages, except in those situations in which a strong and well defined tax policy calls for a different result.[84]

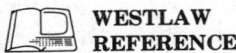 **WESTLAW REFERENCES**

Alimony and Separate Maintenance Payments: Before 1984

da(bef 1984) & wife /s inclu! /s income /s period! /3 payment

find 81 sct 1343

Alimony and Separate Maintenance Payments: After 1984

da(aft 1984) & wife /s inclu! /s alimony /s income

Transfers of Property on Divorce: Before 1984

find 82 sct 1190

Dependency Exemption: Before 1984

da(bef 1984) & 152(e)(2)(a)

Innocent Spouse Provisions: After 1984

da(after 1984) & "innocent spouse"

Attorney Fees

attorney counsel lawyer /2 fee /s divorc! dissol! /s deduct!

find 83 sct 623

---

had held the Nevada divorce invalid and that the first marriage continued to exist. Spalding relied in part on Borax and in part on the fact that at the time of the deceased's death the husband and his second "wife" were domiciled in California, having left New York. But Estate of Goldwater, 539 F.2d 878 (2d Cir.1976), cert. denied 429 U.S. 1023, 97 S.Ct. 641, 50 L.Ed.2d 624 (1976), decided in the same year, the same court held that a husband's estate was not entitled to the marital estate tax deduction for property devised to the second wife after a New York state court had held that his Mexican divorce from his first wife was invalid so that he was still married to her. In this case the court distinguished Borax on the ground that it involved the income tax rather than the estate tax, although why this distinction should matter remains a mystery. It distinguished Spalding on the ground that there the parties had moved to California, where the estate was being administered.

84. This may be the explanation for the inconclusive opinion in Boyter v. Commissioner, 668 F.2d 1382 (4th Cir.1981). In that case a husband and wife who were subject to the "marriage penalty", that is, the necessity of paying a higher income tax on their two incomes than if they were not married, obtained Haitian divorces near the end of each of two years, remarrying each other during the following years. The Fourth Circuit began by saying that state law generally controls the marital status, but found that in this case state law, the law of

Maryland, did not provide a clear rule as to the validity of these migratory divorces. But it went on to say that perhaps the "sham transaction doctrine" as developed in the tax law would apply to these divorces and remarriages, on the theory that the parties only intended to procure divorce papers rather than actually to end their marriage, solely for the purpose of appearing to be unmarried at the end of each tax year. The court then remanded the case to the Tax Court for a finding on this issue. See Note, The Haitian Vacation: The Applicability of Sham Doctrine to Year-End Divorces, 77 Mich.L. Rev. 1332 (1979).

The "marriage penalty" is described in Boyter v. Commissioner, 74 T.C. 989 (1980), and in Bittker, Federal Income Taxation and the Family, 27 Stan.L.Rev. 1389, 1416–1444 (1975). It was held not to violate any constitutional provision in Druker v. Commissioner, 697 F.2d 46 (2d Cir.1982), cert. denied 461 U.S. 957, 103 S.Ct. 2429, 77 L.Ed.2d 1316 (1983) and Mapes v. United States, 576 F.2d 896 (Ct.Cl.1978), cert. denied 439 U.S. 1046, 99 S.Ct. 722, 58 L.Ed.2d 705 (1978). This "penalty" has been mitigated by permitting a deduction for two-earner married couples. I.R.C. § 221. The provision mitigating the "penalty" and permitting a deduction has been repealed by the Tax Reform Act of 1986, § 131, repealing I.R.C. § 221. The repeal is effective for tax years beginning on or after 1987.

Chapter 17

CHILD SUPPORT ORDERS IN DIVORCE DECREES

Table of Sections

§ 17.1 Child Support Orders in Divorce Decrees—In General [1]

Introduction

The statutes of the various states authorize the courts in divorce actions to enter orders for the support of children of the marriage.[2] Such orders may be entered pendente lite, to ensure support of the children while the divorce action continues,[3] and they may also provide for support to continue after the divorce becomes final.[4]

§ 17.1

1. Influential treatments of this subject may be found in D. Chambers, Making Fathers Pay (1979) and H. Krause, Child Support in America (1981). For other general considerations of the subject see J. Cassetty, ed., The Parental Child-Support Obligation (1983); Bruch, Developing Standards for Child Support Payments: A Critique of Current Practice, 16 U.C.D.L.Rev. 49 (1982). A useful bibliography of the subject is R. Horowitz, D. Dodson, National Legal Resource Center for Child Advocacy and Protection, American Bar Association, U.S.Dep't of Health and Human Services, Office of Child Support Enforcement, Child Support: An Annotated Legal Bibliography (1984).

For general discussion of the obligations of parents to support their children, see Chapter 6, supra, especially sections 6.2, 6.3 and 6.6.

2. Ala.Code § 30-3-1 (1983); Alaska Stat. §§ 25.24.140, 25.24.160 (1983); Ariz.Rev.Stat. §§ 12-2451, 12-2453, 25-320 (1982 and Supp.1986); Ark.Stat. §§ 34-1211, 34-1222 (Supp.1985); West's Ann.Cal.Civ.Code §§ 196, 246, 4700, 4703 (1983 and Supp.1986); Colo.Rev. Stat. § 14-10-115 (1974 and Supp.1986); Conn.Gen.Stat. Ann. §§ 46b-84, 46b-215 (1986); Del.Code tit. 13, §§ 501, 514 (1981); D.C.Code § 16-916 (1981); West's Fla.Stat. Ann. §§ 61.09, 61.052, 61.13 (Supp.1987); Official Code Ga.Ann. §§ 30-206, 30-207, 74-105 (Supp.1986); Hawaii Rev.Stat. § 580-47 (Supp.1984); Idaho Code § 32-706 (Supp.1986); Ill.Ann.Stat. ch. 40, § 505 (Supp.1986); West's Ann.Ind.Code § 31-1-11.5-12 (Supp.1986); Iowa Code Ann. § 598.21 (1981 and Supp.1986); Kan.Stat.Ann. § 60-1610 (Supp.1986); Ky.Rev.Stat. § 403.210 (1984); La.S.A.—Civ.Code Ann. art. 227 (1952); Me.Rev.Stat.Ann. tit. 19, § 214 (Supp.1986-1987); Md.Code Fam.L., §§ 12-101, 12-102, 12-103 (1984); Mass.Gen.Law Ann. c. 208, § 28 (Supp.1986); Mich.C.L.A. §§ 25.95, 25.96 (1984); Minn.Stat.Ann. § 518.17 (Supp.1986); Miss.Code, § 93-5-23 (Supp.1986); Vernon's Ann.Mo.Stat. § 452.340 (1986); Mont.Code Ann. § 40-4-204 (1985); Neb.Rev.Stat. § 42-364 (1984); Nev.Rev.Stat. §§ 126.241, 126.251, 125.040, 125.450, 125.510 (1986); N.H.Rev.Stat.Ann. §§ 458:17, 458:35 (1983 and Supp.1986); N.J.Stat.Ann. §§ 2A:34-23, 2A:34-24 (Supp.1986); N.M.Stat.Ann., § 40-4-7 (1986); N.Y.—McKinney's Fam.Ct.Act §§ 413, 461 (1983 and Supp.1987); N.Y.—McKinney's Dom.Rel.L. § 240 (1986); N.C.Gen.Stat. § 50-13.4 (1984); N.D.Cent.Code §§ 14-09-08, 14-09-09.7, 14-05-23, 14-08-01 (1981 and Supp.1985); Ohio Rev.Code §§ 3103.03, 3109.05 (1980 and Supp.1986); Okl.Stat. tit. 10, § 4, tit. 12, § 1277 (Supp.1987); Or.Rev. Stat. § 107.105 (1984); Pa.Stat. tit. 23, § 401 (Supp.1986); R.I.Gen.L., § 15-5-16.2 (Supp.1986); S.C.Code, §§ 20-3-160, 20-7-40 (1985); S.D.Comp.L. §§ 25-4-38, 25-4-39, 25-4-40, 25-4-41, 25-7-7 (1984); Tenn.Code Ann. §§ 36-6-101, 36-5-101 (Supp.1986); Vernon's Tex.Code Ann., Family Code §§ 3.55, 11.03, 11.01(5), 4.02 (1975 and 1986); Utah Code Ann., § 30-3-5 (Supp.1986); Vt.Stat.Ann. tit.

3.–4. See notes 3–4 on page 710.

Traditionally in our law the father was primarily responsible for the support of the children of the family.[5] Although it is still possible to find courts which say that he has the primary responsibility for support,[6] it is clear today that both parents are equally obliged to support their children. Most of the state statutes impose the burden equally,[7] but if they do not, either the equal rights provisions of state constitutions [8] or the Equal Protection Clause [9] of the federal constitution clearly prohibit any gender distinction respecting the duty of support.[10] This means that to the extent of her financial resources the mother is as responsible for the support of her children as the father,[11] not only when she has custody following divorce but when he has custody as well.[12] It is also clear that there can be no gender distinction between

male and female children concerning their right to be supported by their parents.[13]

Stepparents are responsible for the support of stepchildren pursuant to some statutes, but in the absence of statute they are generally not held liable for support after their divorce from the children's natural parents, except in the case where an equitable estoppel may be based upon representations as to parentage by the stepparent and reliance upon such representations by the stepchild.[14]

Although of necessity the account of child support in this chapter is concerned primarily with the legal principles and technicalities governing the award, modification and enforcement of child support, it is most important for the reader to be aware of the fact that the amount of child support awarded in divorce actions is usually quite inadequate to

15, § 651 (Supp.1986); Va.Code, § 20–107.2 (Supp.1986); West's Rev.Code Wash.Ann. § 26.09.100 (1986); W.Va. Code, §§ 48–2–13, 48–2–15, 48–2–16 (1986); Wis.Stat.Ann. § 767.25 (Supp.1986); Wyo.Stat., § 20–2–113 (1977).

3. Ibid.

4. Ibid.

5. Slater v. Slater, 327 Mich. 569, 42 N.W.2d 742 (1950); Com. ex rel. Yeats v. Yeats, 168 Pa.Super. 550, 79 A.2d 793 (1951); Matthews v. Matthews, 71 S.D. 115, 22 N.W.2d 27 (1946); Baldwin v. Baldwin, 253 Wis. 200, 33 N.W.2d 198 (1948).

There seems at one point to have been some question whether the duty of the father to support his children was a duty imposed by the common law or merely a moral or natural obligation. Kelley v. Davis, 49 N.H. 187 (1870); Conwell v. Conwell, 3 N.J. 266, 69 A.2d 712 (1949); Haxton by Haxton v. Haxton, 299 Or. 616, 705 P.2d 721 (1985); Gordon v. Potter, 17 Vt. 348 (1845). Blackstone is not clear on this question, however. 1 W. Blackstone, Commentaries 446–448 (3d ed.Cooley 1884). In any event the duty is clearly imposed both by statute and common law today.

6. E.g., State ex rel. Division of Family Services v. Standridge, 676 S.W.2d 513 (Mo.1984); Pendexter v. Pendexter, 363 A.2d 743 (Me.1976)

7. See the statutes cited in note 2, supra.

8. Seventeen states have such amendments to their state constitutions. Kurtz, The State Equal Rights Amendments and Their Impact on Domestic Relations Law, 11 Fam.L.Q. 101 (1977).

9. U.S.Const. amend. XIV, sec. 1.

10. Barnhard v. Barnhard, 252 Ark. 167, 477 S.W.2d 845 (1972); Conway v. Dana, 456 Pa. 536, 318 A.2d 324 (1974). Cases which impose the support obligation on both parents by virtue of statute include Sims v. Sims, 457 So.2d 163 (La.App.1984); In re Marriage of Westby, 30 Or.App. 431, 567 P.2d 145 (1977). The Supreme Court

of the United States has made it clear in Orr v. Orr, 440 U.S. 268, 99 S.Ct. 1102, 59 L.Ed.2d 306 (1979), on remand 374 So.2d 895 (Ala.App.1979) that the United States Constitution forbids gender discrimination with respect to support obligations within the family. State cases which reach the same result as Orr in the child support context include In re Aguilar, 80 Cal.App.3d 58, 145 Cal. Rptr. 197 (1978); Carole v. Arnold K., 85 Misc.2d 643, 380 N.Y.S.2d 593 (Fam.Ct.1976), on remand 87 Misc.2d 547, 385 N.Y.S.2d 740 (1976). The Carole K. case was disapproved in Carter v. Carter, 58 A.D.2d 438, 397 N.Y.S.2d 88 (2d Dep't 1977) but the Appellate Division reached the same result by construction of the statute. See the present N.Y.—McKinney's Fam.Ct.Act § 413 (1983).

11. Conway v. Dana, 456 Pa. 536, 318 A.2d 324 (1974).

12. In re Marriage of Westby, 30 Or.App. 431, 567 P.2d 145 (1977); Annot., 98 A.L.R.3d 1146 (1980).

13. Stanton v. Stanton, 421 U.S. 7, 95 S.Ct. 1373, 43 L.Ed.2d 688 (1975). The Utah Supreme Court did not comply with the United States Supreme Court's mandate, Stanton v. Stanton, 552 P.2d 112 (1976), after which the Supreme Court again vacated the Utah Supreme Court's judgment and remanded the case for further proceedings. Stanton v. Stanton, 429 U.S. 501, 97 S.Ct. 717, 50 L.Ed. 7 (1977).

14. See section 6.2, supra, at notes 50, 57 and 58. In a few states a husband may be held responsible for the support of his wife's child even though it is not his if he married her knowing that she was pregnant by another man. The reason for this rule seems to be that by marriage in these circumstances the wife loses her right to bring a paternity suit against the child's father. State v. Shoemaker, 62 Iowa 343, 17 N.W. 589 (1883); Gustin v. Gustin, 108 Ohio App. 171, 161 N.E.2d 68 (1958). The rule was rejected in Kucera v. Kucera, 117 N.W.2d 810 (N.D.1962); Farris v. Farris, 58 Wash.2d 837, 365 P.2d 14 (1961).

provide for the children involved. Thorough, comprehensive studies of awards being given fully corroborate this fact.[15] They show that even where the family has enjoyed a substantial income the child support ordered does not begin to cover the expenses of feeding, clothing and educating the child. The result is that the child's custodian, most often the mother, is forced to work or driven into poverty or both as she attempts to provide the support which should come from the noncustodial parent. Inflation and the reduction in the age of majority (which may end child support long before the child is fully educated) add to the burdens of the custodial parent.[16] The reasons for the inadequacy of awards seem to lie in the reluctance of judges to recognize what the real needs of the children are and to make orders which reflect those needs. Whatever the reasons, lawyers, judges and legislators must face up to this problem as they are facing up to the problem of enforcing child support orders.

Some Questions of Procedure

Orders for child support, like orders for alimony and division of property, must be based upon personal jurisdiction over the obli-gor spouse.[17] The leading case is Kulko v. Superior Court,[18] which held that due process requires that the defendant in a suit for child support have sufficient contacts with the state in which the suit is brought that the maintenance of the suit does not offend traditional notions of fair play and substantial justice. The existence of such contacts enables the state to enter a decree for child support where the state's statute governing service is complied with and where the defendant is given proper notice of the suit.[19] But an order for child support may be entered notwithstanding the absence of jurisdiction to terminate the marriage, as where the parents are found not to be domiciled in the state.[20] If the parents have so transient a relationship to the jurisdiction that a child support order is not likely to be enforceable, the court may properly refuse to exercise jurisdiction, but aside from this the domicile of the parents is irrelevant to the granting of child support.[21]

Unlike alimony,[22] child support may be awarded even though the complaint in the divorce action contains no demand for child support and the defendant fails to appear, provided of course that personal jurisdiction exists.[23] The reasons for the difference lie

---

15. The leading study is L. Weitzman, The Divorce Revolution (1985), of which chapter 9 deals with child support, and illustrates in great detail the statements made in the text. See also D. Chambers, Making Fathers Pay 38–68 (1979); Bruch, Developing Normative Standards for Child-Support Payments: A Critique of Current Practice, in J. Cassetty, ed., The Parental Child-Support Obligation 119 (1983). The costs of raising children are carefully calculated in Espenshade, The Value and Cost of Children, 32 Population Bull. 3, 25 (1977), concluding that the direct costs of raising a child to age eighteen range from about $35,000 to about $54,000 in 1977 dollars, with additional costs of $7,000 or $8,000 for four years of college. Professor Weitzman makes a persuasive argument that child support should be computed in such a way that after the divorce all members of the family achieve an equal standard of living per capita.

16. L. Weitzman, The Divorce Revolution 283–285 (1985). It is important to note also that the inadequacy of child support has a serious impact on the children of the marriage, not only materially but psychologically as well. L. Weitzman, The Divorce Revolution 318–321 (1985); J. Wallerstein and J. Kelly, Surviving the Breakup: How Children and Parents Cope With Divorce 22 (1980).

17. Gleiser v. Gleiser, 402 Ill. 343, 83 N.E.2d 693 (1949). Other cases are collected in Annot., 62 A.L.R.2d 544 (1958).

18. Kulko v. Superior Court of California In and For City and County of San Francisco, 436 U.S. 84, 98 S.Ct. 1690, 56 L.Ed.2d 132 (1978), rehearing denied 438 U.S. 908, 98 S.Ct. 3127, 57 L.Ed.2d 1150 (1978).

19. See section 12.4, supra, for a more extensive discussion of the jurisdictional requirements. See also State ex rel. Hubbard v. Hubbard, 110 Wis.2d 683, 329 N.W.2d 202 (1983). Personal jurisdiction once acquired in a divorce action continues to exist and may be the basis for a later support order even though the defendant has left the state and obtained a domicile in some other state. Glading v. Furman, 282 Md. 200, 383 A.2d 398 (1978).

20. Hampshire v. Hampshire, 70 Idaho 522, 223 P.2d 950 (1950); Sauvageau v. Sauvageau, 59 Idaho 190, 81 P.2d 731 (1938). Contra: Cobb v. Cobb, 145 W.Va. 107, 113 S.E.2d 193 (1960). In this respect as in others divorce should be regarded as divisible, with entirely different jurisdictional rules for the termination of status from those applicable to financial relief and to custody.

21. Conwell v. Conwell, 3 N.J. 266, 69 A.2d 712 (1949); Landes v. Landes, 1 N.Y.2d 358, 153 N.Y.S.2d 14, 135 N.E.2d 562 (1956), appeal dismissed 352 U.S. 948, 77 S.Ct. 325, 1 L.Ed.2d 241 (1956).

22. See section 17.3, Practitioner's Edition.

23. Rinker v. Rinker, 3 N.J.Super. 251, 64 A.2d 910 (1949); Darty v. Darty, 33 Tenn.App. 321, 232 S.W.2d 59 (1949).

both in the greater social importance of child support orders and in the fact that parents ought to assume that they will be required to support their children whether or not they are given notice of the demand for support in the divorce complaint. For the same reasons child support may be claimed in a suit which begins as a custody matter, provided again that personal jurisdiction is obtained.[24]

It may often be just as necessary to make some provision for the support of children when a divorce decree is denied as when it is granted, for example when it is clear that the spouses intend to live apart whether or not they succeed in getting the divorce. The question then arises whether the court may make a child support order in the divorce action without at the same time granting the divorce. A well drafted divorce statute will give the court this power.[25] If no such authority is to be found in the statute, many cases have held that the courts have general equity power to order child support when the divorce is denied.[26] This is certainly the sensible course, although there are a few cases which do refuse to award child support when the divorce is denied, thereby forcing the child's custodian to undergo the delay and expense of bringing another suit.[27]

The usual plaintiff in a child support suit is the spouse who has custody of the child.[28] The child support order replaces and makes definite the obligation to support the child which the law imposes on all parents. Obviously it follows that the defendant is not excused from that obligation by the fact that he does not have custody of his child,[29] even though many non-custodial spouses feel that it is unfair for the law to impose upon them the burden of supporting children whom they see only during prescribed visitation periods, and over whose training and education they have little practical control. The non-custodial spouse's jealousy and bitterness is understandable, particularly when the custodial spouse remarries and the children then live with a stepparent, but it cannot be allowed to jeopardize the future of the children. Some separation of the children from one parent is inevitable in the divorce situation, although it can be reduced where the parents are willing to make genuine joint custody work.[30] The best that can be hoped for in this situation is that resentment and hostility between the parents can be kept to a minimum in order not to interfere with the care and support of the children. In any event the child support payments, although usually made to the child's custodian,[31] are to be used for the

---

24. Matter of Marriage of Quenzer, 42 Or.App. 3, 599 P.2d 1217 (1979). See also Annot., Court's Power in Habeas Corpus Proceedings Relating to Custody of Child to Adjudicate Questions as to Child's Support, 17 A.L.R.3d 764 (1968).

25. See the statutes cited in note 2, supra. The Uniform Marriage and Divorce Act § 309, 9A Unif.L.Ann. 167 (1979) authorizes child support in divorce without reference to whether the divorce is granted. Of course this will not normally present a problem in those states having marriage breakdown divorce statutes since the divorce will rarely or never be denied.

26. Chopp v. Chopp, 257 Minn. 526, 102 N.W.2d 318 (1960). See also Goecker v. Goecker, 227 Iowa 697, 288 N.W. 884 (1939); Urbach v. Urbach, 52 Wyo. 207, 73 P.2d 953 (1937); Annots., 113 A.L.R. 901 (1938) and 151 A.L.R. 1380 (1944).

27. Lewis v. Lewis, 103 Ohio App. 129, 144 N.E.2d 887 (1956); White v. White, 70 R.I. 48, 36 A.2d 661 (1944). See also cases cited in the Annotations cited supra in note 26.

28. It is odd, in view of the tendency of many states to make the child a party to a custody proceeding, that the child is not usually a party to a child support proceeding. The traditional view was that the parent represented the

child's interests in the support claim, and that a court's jurisdiction over the parent constituted jurisdiction over the child. See Yarborough v. Yarborough, 290 U.S. 202, 54 S.Ct. 181, 78 L.Ed. 269 (1933). But there may be circumstances today in which it is highly desirable to make the child a party to the suit for support purposes. See, e.g., Matter of Marriage of Thomas, 70 Or.App. 317, 689 P.2d 348 (1984); Franklin v. Franklin, 605 S.W.2d 170 (Mo.App.1980), and the cases dealing with res judicata of paternity discussed infra at note 52.

29. Bartlett v. Bartlett, 94 U.S.App.D.C. 190, 221 F.2d 508 (1954); Addy v. Addy, 240 Iowa 255, 36 N.W.2d 352 (1949), overruled on other grounds by Brown v. Brown, 269 N.W.2d 819 (Iowa 1978); Lide v. Lide, 201 Miss. 849, 30 So.2d 51 (1947); Landes v. Landes, 1 N.Y.2d 358, 153 N.Y.S.2d 14, 135 N.E.2d 562 (1956), appeal dismissed 352 U.S. 948, 77 S.Ct. 325, 1 L.Ed.2d 241 (1956). The parent's duty of support in such circumstances may also be enforced under state criminal non-support statutes. Annot. 73 A.L.R.2d 960 (1960).

30. Joint custody is discussed in section 19.5, infra.

31. In rare cases, as where the child is living apart from the parent, the payments may be made directly to the child. Cornett v. Cornett, 398 So.2d 303 (Ala.App. 1981).

benefit of the child rather than the custodian, and the custodian may be accountable if the payments are not so used.[32]

Where the original divorce decree omits any reference to child support, or expressly states that no child support is awarded, two questions may later arise. The first is whether at some later time the custodian may obtain an order for child support running in the future. The second is whether, if such an order may be obtained, it may also include sums reimbursing the custodian for expenditures already made for support of the child. The answer to the first question is clear. If the child needs support and the non-custodial parent is able to provide it under the usual principles, the order should be entered.[33] This is true even if the divorce decree expressly denied support.[34] This result recognizes the general principle that child support orders are always modifiable[35] and the strong public policy that the child's need for support should be met whenever possible. As some cases have said, support is a right which belongs to the child, independent of the rights of the custodian.[36]

Where the custodian of the child is seeking reimbursement for expenditures made in the past rather than an order for future support, the cases are in disagreement over the proper result. Some state statutes control the question by providing that modification of custody decrees may be had only with respect to the future and may not be retroactive, which presumably prevents a court from ordering reimbursement.[37] It should be emphasized that in this situation the welfare or interests of the child are not at stake. The child has already been supported by the custodian. The only issue therefore is, as between husband and wife, who should equitably bear the expense. In former days when the husband was held to be primarily responsible for the support of the child most courts held that the wife was entitled to reimbursement, although a minority of cases refused her relief on a variety of grounds.[38] Today, now that both husband and wife are responsible for the support of the child, the result should turn on what is equitable under the circumstances, provided that retroactive modification of the divorce decree is permitted. For example, if at the time of the divorce the custodian was unable to obtain personal jurisdiction over the other parent, he should be granted at least partial reimbursement at a later time when personal jurisdiction may be obtained.[39] Even if personal jurisdiction over the non-custodial parent is obtained in the divorce action, but no support order is entered, reimbursement may be appropriate later if the circumstances make reimbursement equitable in view of the relative means of the two parents.[40] On the

---

32. Rosenblatt v. Birnbaum, 16 N.Y.2d 212, 264 N.Y.S.2d 521, 212 N.E.2d 37 (1965). The Uniform Marriage and Divorce Act § 308(b)(1), 9A Unif.L.Ann. 160 (1979) seems to contemplate that child support orders may include sums for the support of the child's custodian, thereby obscuring the distinction between child support and alimony and making the custodian's responsibility for the use of payments less clear than it should be. Payments labeled alimony may in fact be child support. See Kohn v. Kohn, 242 Pa.Super. 435, 364 A.2d 350 (1976).

33. Dimon v. Dimon, 40 Cal.2d 516, 254 P.2d 528 (1953); Scheer v. District Court In and For City and County of Denver, 147 Colo. 265, 363 P.2d 1059 (1961); Addy v. Addy, 240 Iowa 255, 36 N.W.2d 352 (1949), overruled on other grounds by Brown v. Brown, 269 N.W.2d 819 (Iowa 1978); Glading v. Furman, 282 Md. 200, 383 A.2d 398 (1978); Ebel v. Brown, 70 Mich.App. 705, 246 N.W.2d 379 (1976). Other cases are collected in Annots., 69 A.L.R.2d 203 (1960); 91 A.L.R.3d 530 (1979).

34. Ebel v. Brown, 70 Mich.App. 705, 246 N.W.2d 379 (1976), holding that the court could order support even though the earlier divorce decree and the wife's agree-

ment released the husband from any obligation for child support.

35. See the statutes cited in note 2, supra, and the discussion in section 17.2, infra.

36. Scheer v. District Court In and For City and County of Denver, 147 Colo. 265, 363 P.2d 1059 (1961).

37. In re Marriage of Serfoss, 642 P.2d 44 (Colo.App. 1981); Meyer v. Meyer, 17 Ohio St.3d 222, 478 N.E.2d 806 (1985). The Uniform Marriage and Divorce Act § 316(a), 9A Unif.L.Ann. 183 (1979) limits modification of child support to installments accruing after the motion for modification. See also statutes cited in note 2, supra.

38. Cases are collected in Annot., 69 A.L.R.2d 203 (1960).

39. Gill v. Gill, 56 Ill.2d 139, 306 N.E.2d 281 (1973).

40. Cases are collected in Annot., 91 A.L.R.3d 530 (1979). See also Brown v. Brown, 269 N.W.2d 819 (Iowa 1978). The unfairness of denying reimbursement as a general principle is illustrated by Children's Hospital of Akron v. Johnson, 68 Ohio App.2d 17, 426 N.E.2d 515 (1980). In that case the child's mother had custody and

other hand if there is a child support order in the divorce decree and it is complied with, reimbursement of the custodian's expenditures for the child would not normally appear equitable.[41]

Child support litigation may have important consequences for the child's legitimacy as a result of doctrines of res judicata. The husband's support obligation usually extends only to children of the marriage[42] (and of course also to illegitimate children of whom he is the father).[43] It follows that in divorce actions in which a claim for child support is made the court has jurisdiction to determine paternity.[44] When the divorce court makes a finding on the question of paternity, the issue arises to what extent this finding is res judicata in later litigation involving the husband, the wife, or the child.

The need for finality of judgments dictates that a fact once litigated and determined cannot be relitigated between the same parties in the same or a different action.[45] This principle has been applied in a number of cases to foreclose relitigation of the paternity of children. Thus if the paternity of a child is in issue in a divorce action and the child is found to be legitimate, the husband may not later reopen the question by a motion to ter-

minate the child support payments on the ground that the child is not his.[46] A similar result will be reached on the basis of ordinary estoppel where the parties to the divorce action acted on the assumption of paternity for an appreciable period of time.[47] One case, in reliance on a requirement of the Uniform Parentage Act[48] that the child must be made a party to paternity suits, held that the husband was not bound by a finding of paternity in a divorce action when the child was not a party.[49] This would be correct if the child were raising the issue, but the Uniform Parentage Act requirement was enacted for the protection of the child not the alleged father, and therefore the doctrine of collateral estoppel should apply to this situation.

Conversely there is authority that if paternity is actually litigated and a finding of illegitimacy made, the wife cannot later relitigate the issue.[50] To this extent husband and wife are mutually bound by the decree. But a line of cases has held that if the child is not made a party to the divorce action, he is not bound by a finding in that action that he is illegitimate. In a later suit against the husband or against a third party, he is allowed to establish his legitimacy notwithstanding the earlier decree to the contrary.[51] If it were in

---

the court held that she was liable to the hospital for the child's medical expenses, notwithstanding that the divorce decree ordered the father to pay the medical bills. If the mother were not entitled to reimbursement in such a situation, she would be forced to bear an expense which the father clearly should bear.

41. Penn v. Morgan, 7 Wash.App. 794, 502 P.2d 1238 (1972).

42. Butler v. Butler, 254 Ala. 375, 48 So.2d 318 (1950); Pilgrim v. Pilgrim, 118 Ind.App. 6, 75 N.E.2d 159 (1947); Farris v. Farris, 58 Wash.2d 837, 365 P.2d 14 (1961); Taylor v. Taylor, 58 Wash.2d 510, 364 P.2d 444 (1961). The possible support obligations of stepparents are discussed in the text at notes 14–16, supra.

43. Curley v. Curley, 37 N.J.Super. 351, 117 A.2d 407 (1955); Carter v. Carter, 232 N.C. 614, 61 S.E.2d 711 (1950).

44. Cases are collected in Annot., 65 A.L.R.2d 1381, 1383 (1959).

45. Restatement (Second) of Judgments § 27 (1982). In the terminology of this Restatement the rule is called "issue preclusion", replacing the former "collateral estoppel".

46. Washington v. Washington, 170 Cal.App.2d 652, 339 P.2d 169 (1959); Peercy v. Peercy, 154 Colo. 575, 392

P.2d 609 (1964); McNeece v. McNeece, 39 Colo.App. 160, 562 P.2d 767 (1977); Farmer v. Farmer, 177 Kan. 657, 281 P.2d 1075 (1955); Martin v. Martin, 561 S.W.2d 396 (Mo.App.1977); Sandra I. v. Harold I., 54 A.D.2d 1040, 388 N.Y.S.2d 376 (3d Dep't 1976); Arnold v. Arnold, 207 Okl. 352, 249 P.2d 734 (1952); Limberg v. Limberg, 10 Wis.2d 63, 102 N.W.2d 103 (1960). Other cases are cited in Annot., 65 A.L.R.2d 1381, 1395 (1959) and 78 A.L.R.3d 846, 853 (1977). The presumption of legitimacy may also be invoked to hold the husband responsible for child support. Perkins v. Perkins, 198 Neb. 401, 253 N.W.2d 42 (1977) (wife pregnant at the time of divorce).

47. McDonald v. Hester, 115 Ga.App. 740, 155 S.E.2d 720 (1967); In re Adoption of Young, 469 Pa. 141, 364 A.2d 1307 (1976).

48. Uniform Parentage Act § 9, 9A Unif.L.Ann. 599 (1979).

49. In re Marriage of Burkey, 689 P.2d 726 (Colo.App. 1984).

50. Daniels v. Daniels, 143 Cal.App.2d 430, 300 P.2d 335 (1956); Savage v. Purcell, 9 S.W.2d 823 (Mo.App. 1928); Annot., 78 A.L.R.3d 846, 853 (1977).

51. Gonzales v. Pacific Greyhound Lines, 34 Cal.2d 749, 214 P.2d 809 (1950); Daniels v. Daniels, 143 Cal.App. 2d 430, 300 P.2d 335 (1956) (dictum); Doornbos v.

his interest, he would likewise be permitted to establish his illegitimacy after a divorce decree had found him legitimate so long as he had not been a party to the divorce action.[52] If the child is properly made a party to the divorce action, and the question of legitimacy is litigated in that action, then of course he is bound by the result.[53] The rules of res judicata in this situation are not applied with complete mutuality. The child may rely upon them to prevent the husband from attacking a prior finding of legitimacy, but he himself is free to attack a prior finding of legitimacy or illegitimacy, where he was not a party to the prior suit. It seems obvious that to avoid conflicting judgments and to protect all parties, the child should be made a party to the divorce action whenever any question of his legitimacy is anticipated.[54]

Where the paternity question is not contested in the divorce action, but a finding of paternity is made, the cases are not in agreement on the effect of the decision. The Restatement (Second) of Judgments limits collateral estoppel to those cases in which an issue is "actually litigated",[55] defining that phrase to mean that the issue was properly raised by pleadings or otherwise, was submitted for determination and was determined.[56] Some of the divorce cases would apparently go beyond the Restatement and hold that if a finding of paternity is made, even though not contested, it is binding on the husband in later proceedings.[57] Others have held that if paternity was not actually contested in the divorce action, a husband or wife may raise and litigate the issue in later proceedings.[58] In view of the serious consequences of a finding of paternity, it seems the better result to give the husband an opportunity to litigate the issue in these situations. Of course the child is not bound by the earlier proceeding if he was not made a party to it.[59]

Where the husband signs an agreement acknowledging the child to be his and later seeks to disprove paternity, and the agreement is incorporated in the divorce decree, the result turns on the arguments advanced in the preceding paragraphs.[60] In the converse case, where the wife purports to waive any claim of paternity and this is incorporated in the decree, the same results would be reached as to her,[61] but of course the child would not be bound by either waiver or de-

Doornbos, 12 Ill.App.2d 473, 139 N.E.2d 844 (1956); Ryke v. Ream, 212 Iowa 126, 234 N.W. 196 (1931); Sayles v. Sayles, 323 Mass. 66, 80 N.E.2d 21 (1948) (dictum); Schlenker v. Ferdon, 21 Ohio App. 222, 153 N.E. 113 (1926); In re Cogan's Estate, 267 Wis. 20, 64 N.W.2d 454 (1954). Other cases are cited in Annot., 65 A.L.R.2d 1381, 1396 (1959). The Uniform Parentage Act, cited in note 48, supra, requires the child to be made a party to a paternity suit, but it is not clear whether it requires him to be made a party to a divorce action.

52. In re Marriage of Burkey, 689 P.2d 726 (Colo.App. 1984) would have this effect, although the case confused issues of res judicata with those of jurisdiction.

53. Limberg v. Limberg, 10 Wis.2d 63, 102 N.W.2d 103 (1960).

54. This may be done in some jurisdictions. See Ohms v. Ohms, 287 App.Div. 839, 137 N.Y.S.2d 397 (2d Dep't 1955); Limberg v. Limberg, 10 Wis.2d 63, 102 N.W.2d 103 (1960). Other cases are cited in Annot., 65 A.L.R.2d 1381, 1392 (1959). See also the Uniform Parentage Act, cited in note 48, supra.

55. Restatement (Second) of Judgments § 27 and comment e (1982).

56. Restatement (Second) of Judgments § 27, comment d and e (1982).

57. Washington v. Washington, 170 Cal.App.2d 652, 339 P.2d 169 (1959) (semble); Garcia v. Garcia, 148 Cal. App.2d 147, 306 P.2d 80 (1957); Miller v. Miller, 96 Idaho 10, 523 P.2d 827 (1974); Farmer v. Farmer, 177 Kan. 657, 281 P.2d 1075 (1955) (dictum); Baum v. Baum, 20 Mich. App. 68, 173 N.W.2d 744 (1970); In re Adoption of Young, 469 Pa. 141, 364 A.2d 1307 (1976); Thompson v. Thompson, 572 S.W.2d 761 (Tex.Civ.App.1978). Mancini v. Mancini, 2 Ohio App.3d 124, 440 N.E.2d 1232 (1981) stated in dictum that a divorce court's finding of legitimacy would be binding on the husband, even though apparently the issue was not litigated, but held that neither the child nor a second husband would be bound by such a finding.

58. Everett v. Everett, 57 Cal.App.3d 65, 129 Cal.Rptr. 8 (1976), 1977 B.Y.U.L.Rev. 612; In re Marriage of Moser, 469 N.E.2d 762 (Ind.App.1984); Matter of Evans, 267 N.W.2d 48 (Iowa 1978); Gilbert v. Warren, 95 Nev. 296, 594 P.2d 696 (1979).

59. Mancini v. Mancini, 2 Ohio App.3d 124, 440 N.E.2d 1232 (1981). See also the discussion at note 51, supra.

60. Peercy v. Peercy, 154 Colo. 575, 392 P.2d 609 (1964) refused to allow the husband to reopen the question of paternity in this situation.

61. See the discussion at note 50, supra.

cree.[62] If such agreements are not incorporated in the divorce decree equitable considerations should govern the case. If the wife should change her position in reliance on the husband's stipulation as to paternity, he should not later be heard to claim he is not the father. The mere passage of time and attendant difficulty of proof might amount to such a change of position. On the other hand if the husband signed the stipulation under a mistake of fact and there has been no such reliance, equitable principles would permit him to prove non-paternity. In any such case, however, the child's interests should be the crucial factor.

Form and Duration of the Child Support Order

The usual form for child support orders directs payment of a stated sum periodically to the custodian of the child.[63] The custodian is then a fiduciary with respect to the amounts paid, with a duty to apply them for the child's support.[64] In times of inflation in general price levels this form or order can cause hardship to the child and the custodian as the rise in prices erodes the real value of the payments. Although child support may be modifiable in such circumstances[65] this puts a burden of expense and delay on the child and the custodian before the payments can be increased. These hardships may be avoided by framing the original decree so as to anticipate such changes through the inclusion of an escalation clause. The escalation clause provides in advance that the payments shall increase by a stated proportion related to the Consumer Price Index of the United States Department of Labor, preferably with the limitation that if the child support obligor's income increases by a lesser proportion, then the increase will be computed at that lesser proportion. Although some courts have expressed disapproval of decrees in this form,[66] the obvious advantages have led other courts to approve of them where the increase in living costs is not the only basis for the increase in payments and the decree recognizes the limits imposed by the obligor's earnings.[67] It has been held error to include in the child support order a provision for six percent interest on amounts in default, on the ground that this does not take into account the facts leading to the default.[68] It has also been held error to enter a lump sum child support order since this violates the principle that such orders should remain modifiable.[69]

The duration of child support orders in divorce decrees is normally limited to the period of the child's minority.[70] During the 1970's the age of majority was changed in most states from twenty-one to eighteen,[71] ap-

---

62. State ex rel. Fabian v. Fabian, 116 N.H. 516, 363 A.2d 1007 (1976).

63. E.g., Addy v. Addy, 240 Iowa 255, 36 N.W.2d 352 (1949), overruled on other grounds by Brown v. Brown, 269 N.W.2d 819 (Iowa 1978); Sonenfeld v. Sonenfeld, 331 Mich. 60, 49 N.W.2d 60 (1951); Knight v. Armstrong, 303 P.2d 421 (Okl.1956).

It is not uncommon for courts to enter an order for periodic payment of a single sum to cover both alimony and child support. Though this is productive of later difficulties of apportionment, courts are reluctant to hold such orders invalid. See cases cited in Annot., 124 A.L.R. 1324 (1940). For a discussion of apportionment see section 17.2, infra.

64. Corbridge v. Corbridge, 230 Ind. 201, 102 N.E.2d 764 (1953); Rosenblatt v. Birnbaum, 16 N.Y.2d 212, 264 N.Y.S.2d 521, 212 N.E.2d 37 (1965).

65. See section 17.2, infra.

66. Stanaway v. Stanaway, 70 Mich.App. 294, 245 N.W.2d 723 (1976); Falls v. Falls, 52 N.C.App. 203, 278 S.E.2d 546 (1981) pet. for review denied 304 N.C. 389, 285 S.E.2d 831 (1981).

67. In re Marriage of Nesset, 345 N.W.2d 107 (Iowa 1984); Roya v. Roya, 145 Vt. 488, 494 A.2d 132 (1985); Edwards v. Edwards, 99 Wash.2d 913, 665 P.2d 883 (1983). See Note, Inflation-Proof Child Support Decree: Trajecting to a Polestar, 66 Iowa L.Rev. 131 (1980).

68. Kline v. Kline, 92 Mich.App. 62, 284 N.W.2d 488 (1979).

69. Gibson v. Gibson, 147 Neb. 991, 26 N.W.2d 6 (1947).

70. Cases are collected in Annot., 1 A.L.R.2d 910, 914 (1948).

71. See section 8.1, supra, at notes 6 to 11. When the various states lowered the age of majority from twenty-one to eighteen, the question immediately arose whether this would affect child support decrees entered before the statutory change. In a few instances the legislature had the foresight to provide that such decrees would not be affected. E.g., Ganschow v. Ganschow, 14 Cal.3d 150, 120 Cal.Rptr. 865, 534 P.2d 705 (1975), appeal dismissed 423 U.S. 887, 96 S.Ct. 181, 46 L.Ed.2d 118 (1975); Monticello v. Monticello, 271 Md. 168, 315 A.2d 520 (1974), cert. denied 419 U.S. 880, 95 S.Ct. 145, 42 L.Ed.2d 121 (1974).

parently on the assumption that young people were maturing at the earlier age and should therefore have full legal capacity at that age. At the same time, however, it is clear that large numbers of young people, regardless of how mature they might be considered, are remaining financially dependent upon their parents beyond the age of eighteen and in fact beyond twenty-one as well.[72] This inconsistency between legislative action and social conditions raises the much litigated question whether or under what circumstances the courts may order child support to continue beyond the age of majority.

The statutes of some states seem to control this question by providing that the divorce court may enter a decree for support of the *minor* children of the marriage, thereby implying that support orders must terminate on the child's reaching majority.[73] In states hav-

ing this type of divorce statute there may be other statutes authorizing support for adult children, thereby leading to the use of two lawsuits and the concomitant waste of everyone's time and money.[74] In a few states there are statutes which expressly authorize support orders for adult children who are disabled or incompetent.[75] In many states, however, the statutes merely provide that support may be ordered for children of the marriage, without indicating whether or not the support may continue beyond the age of majority.[76]

Where statutes do not expressly either authorize or forbid the courts to order support for adult children, the cases are not in agreement. The majority of the cases are willing to order support for an adult child who is mentally or physically incapable of supporting himself.[77] A greater disagreement arises over the question whether the parents may be

Where the statute did not expressly deal with the question, the cases are about evenly divided on whether the statutes applied to existing decrees. Holding that the support must continue until the child reaches twenty-one: Finn v. Finn, 312 So.2d 726 (Fla. 1975); Waldron v. Waldron, 13 Ill.App.3d 964, 301 N.E.2d 167 (1973); In re Marriage of Harless, 251 N.W.2d 212 (Iowa 1977); Orlandella v. Orlandella, 370 Mass. 225, 347 N.E.2d 665 (1976) (citing many cases); Walker v. Walker, 116 N.H. 717, 367 A.2d 211 (1976); Gulf Oil Corp. v. Rota-Cone Field Operating Co., 85 N.M. 636, 515 P.2d 640 (1973); Nokes v. Nokes, 47 Ohio St.2d 1, 351 N.E.2d 174 (1976); Cunningham v. Cunningham, 12 Wash.App. 778, 532 P.2d 652 (1975). Holding that support terminates at eighteen: Stanley v. Stanley, 112 Ariz. 282, 541 P.2d 382 (1975); Sillman v. Sillman, 168 Conn. 144, 358 A.2d 150 (1975); Munck v. Munck, 62 Ill.App.3d 223, 19 Ill.Dec. 377, 378 N.E.2d 1252 (1978); Baker v. Baker, 217 Kan. 319, 537 P.2d 171 (1975); Jungjohann v. Jungjohann, 213 Kan. 329, 516 P.2d 904 (1973), 23 Kan.L.Rev. 181 (1974); Baril v. Baril, 354 A.2d 392 (Me. 1976); Chrestenson v. Chrestenson, 180 Mont. 96, 589 P.2d 148 (1979); Eaton v. Eaton, 215 Va. 824, 213 S.E.2d 789 (1975); Garey v. Garey, 482 S.W.2d 133 (Tenn. 1972); Schmitz v. Schmitz, 70 Wis.2d 882, 236 N.W.2d 657 (1975). Other cases are collected in Annot., 75 A.L.R.3d 228 (1977). The Colorado statute reduced the age of majority for all purposes except support. See Colo. Rev. Stat. Ann. § 13–22–101 (1974).

72. See, e.g., United States Department of Commerce, Bureau of Census, Statistical Abstract of the United States 134 (1985), indicating that the percentage of persons with four or more years of college has increased fourfold between 1940 and 1983.

73. The statutes of California, Connecticut, Delaware, Florida, Georgia, Indiana, Kansas, Maine, Michigan, Nebraska, New Mexico, New York, North Carolina, North Dakota, Oklahoma, Oregon, Pennsylvania, Texas, Utah,

Virginia and West Virginia cited supra in note 2 contain this kind of language.

74. Perla v. Perla, 58 So.2d 689 (Fla.1952); Baril v. Baril, 354 A.2d 392 (Me.1976).

75. See the Arizona and Hawaii statutes cited in note 2, supra, and Vernon's Tex.F.Code Ann., Fam.Code § 14.05(b) (1975). Ill.—S.H.A. ch. 40, § 513 (Supp.1985) authorizes the divorce court to order support for adult children where they are mentally or physically disabled, and to make provision for the education and maintenance of adult children as equity may require. This statute was held constitutional in Kujawinski v. Kujawinski, 71 Ill.2d 563, 17 Ill.Dec. 801, 376 N.E.2d 1382 (1978), the court saying that if the parents could have been expected to provide for their adult children in the absence of a divorce it is not unreasonable to require them to do so after the divorce.

76. See the divorce statutes of Alabama, Alaska, Arizona, Arkansas, Colorado, Idaho, Illinois, Iowa, Kentucky, Maryland, Minnesota, Mississippi, Missouri, Montana, Nevada, New Hampshire, New Jersey, Ohio, Rhode Island, South Carolina, South Dakota, Tennessee, Vermont, Washington, Wisconsin, Wyoming. The New York—McKinney's Domestic Relations Law § 240 (Supp.1984–1985) contains no limitation, but the New York—McKinney's Family Court Act § 413 (Supp.1985) authorizes support only for a child under 21. The Uniform Marriage and Divorce Act § 309, 9A Unif.L.Ann. 167 (1979), which served as a model for some of the statutes just referred to, authorizes the court to order parents owing a duty of support to a child to make reasonable payments for child support, thereby leaving open the question of support for an adult child.

77. Koltay v. Koltay, 667 P.2d 1374 (Colo.1983); Abbott v. Abbott, 673 S.W.2d 723 (Ky.1983); Stern v. Stern, 58 Md.App. 280, 473 A.2d 56 (1983); Feinberg v. Diamant, 378 Mass. 131, 389 N.E.2d 998 (1979); McCarthy v. Mc-

ordered to support an adult child in college or graduate school without express statutory authority. Some cases rely on the argument that if the marriage had continued, the parents would have been free to decide not to send their child to college, and that divorce should not deprive them of that discretion.[78] About an equal number of cases rely on the assumption that absent the divorce the parents would have been likely to finance the child's education and argue that the divorce should not deprive the child of a benefit he would otherwise have received.[79] The real question here is whether the courts should order a parent to provide a college education for his child.[80] If it is proper to do so, then in order to do it effectively, the order must run beyond the age of majority since many young people only begin their college careers at age eighteen.

Even in those states which do not permit the courts to order child support beyond the age of majority, the courts should be permit-

ted to enter such decrees if the parties agree to it in a valid separation or property settlement agreement.[81] Conversely, support orders may be terminated before majority if the child becomes emancipated by events other than attaining majority, such as contracting a marriage or leaving home becoming self-supporting.[82]

The duration of child support payments also raises problems when there is a decree ordering a parent to keep in force life insurance policies for the benefit of the child. Some cases have held such decrees invalid, either because they are not limited to the child's minority or because they provide benefits after the parent's death and child support must end with his death.[83] The first of these objections can be met by limiting the payment of premiums to the child's minority. The second objection is obviated by the Uniform Marriage and Divorce Act[84] and statutes like it which permit child support to run beyond the parent's death.[85] Even without such stat-

Carthy, 301 Minn. 270, 222 N.W.2d 331 (1974); Fower v. Fower Estate, 448 S.W.2d 585 (Mo.1970); Maberry v. Maberry, 183 Mont. 219, 598 P.2d 1115 (1979); Wiedrich v. Wiedrich, 179 N.W.2d 728 (N.D.1970); Castle v. Castle, 15 Ohio St.3d 279, 473 N.E.2d 803 (1984); Haxton by Haxton, v. Haxton, 299 Or. 616, 705 P.2d 1307 (1985). Sininger v. Sininger, 300 Md. 604, 479 A.2d 1354 (1984), applying the Maryland statute, held that a parent could be ordered to support an adult, disabled child even where the disability did not commence until after the child reached adulthood.

Cases contra the text: Murrah v. Bailes, 255 Ala. 178, 50 So.2d 735 (1951); Red v. Red, 552 S.W.2d 90 (Tex.1977) (semble); Ex Parte Williams, 420 S.W.2d 135 (Tex.1967).

78. H.P.A. v. S.C.A., 704 P.2d 205 (Alaska 1985); Dowling v. Dowling, 679 P.2d 480 (Alaska 1984); Riegler v. Riegler, 259 Ark. 203, 532 S.W.2d 734 (1976); Grapin v. Grapin, 450 So.2d 853 (Fla.1984); Phillips v. Phillips, 339 So.2d 1299 (La.App.1976); Carlson v. Carlson, 584 P.2d 864 (Utah 1978) (semble). See also Plummer v. Plummer, 735 P.2d 165 (Colo.1987).

79. Elkins v. Elkins, 262 Ark. 63, 553 S.W.2d 34 (1977); In re Marriage of Coram, 86 Ill.App.3d 485, 42 Ill. Dec. 40, 408 N.E.2d 418 (1980) (relying on the statute); French v. French, 117 N.H. 696, 378 A.2d 1127 (1977); Ross v. Ross, 167 N.J.Super. 441, 400 A.2d 1233 (1979) (child ordered supported in law school); Lord v. Lord, 96 Misc.2d 434, 409 N.Y.S.2d 46 (Sup.Ct.1978); Risinger v. Risinger, 273 S.C. 36, 253 S.E.2d 652 (1979); Childers v. Childers, 89 Wash.2d 592, 575 P.2d 201 (1978).

80. This question is discussed infra at note 19.

81. H.P.A. v. S.C.A., 704 P.2d 205 (Alaska 1985); Bethune v. Bethune, 96 Misc.2d 507, 413 N.Y.S.2d 800 (Sup.

Ct.1976), reversed 60 A.D.2d 588, 399 N.Y.S.2d 902 (2d Dep't 1977), reversed, judgment of trial court reinstated 46 N.Y.2d 897, 414 N.Y.S.2d 905, 387 N.E.2d 1220 (1979); Jameson v. Jameson, 306 N.W.2d 240 (S.D.1981). Contra: Kennedy v. Kennedy, 177 Conn. 47, 411 A.2d 25 (1979); Nokes v. Nokes, 47 Ohio St.2d 1, 351 N.E.2d 174 (1976).

82. In re Marriage of Fetters, 41 Colo.App. 281, 584 P.2d 104 (1978); In re Marriage of Weisbart, 39 Colo.App. 115, 564 P.2d 961 (1977); Hoffmann v. Hoffman, 32 Ohio App.2d 186, 289 N.E.2d 397 (1972). Where a daughter was married but unable to support herself and not supported by her husband, Suire v. Miller, 363 So.2d 945 (La. App.1978) held that her father had a continuing obligation of support. And In re Marriage of O'Connell, 80 Cal. App.3d 849, 146 Cal.Rptr. 26 (1978) held that a judicial declaration that a parent's children were free of his custody did not emancipate them for support purposes.

83. Hudson v. Aetna Life Ins. Co., 545 F.Supp. 209 (E.D.Mo.1982) (Missouri law); Budig v. Budig, 481 S.W.2d 95 (Ky.1972); Miller v. Miller, 154 Ohio St. 530, 97 N.E.2d 213 (1951).

Lockwood v. Lockwood, 205 Neb. 818, 290 N.W.2d 636 (1980) held it error for the trial court to order a parent to keep in force life insurance on the lives of the children and assign the policies to them when they should reach majority.

84. Uniform Marriage and Divorce Act § 316(c), 9A Unif.L.Ann. 183 (1979). See In re Marriage of Meek, 669 P.2d 628 (Colo.App.1983).

85. In re Icke's Marriage, 189 Colo. 319, 540 P.2d 1076 (1975); Merchant v. Merchant, 130 Mich.App. 566, 343 N.W.2d 620 (1983); Grotsky v. Grotsky, 58 N.J. 354, 277 A.2d 535 (1971); Puckett by and through Puckett v.

utes the use of life insurance as an aspect of child support is appropriate where the parent is able to pay the premiums and in fact does not cause the support to continue beyond the parent's death since obviously the premiums, which constitute the support, must end with the parent's death.[86] If the parties in their separation agreement provide that a parent is to maintain insurance on his life for the benefit of the children, and the agreement is incorporated in the divorce decree, it will be given effect even in those states which do not permit the court to order the maintenance of life insurance.[87]

Relevant Factors in Awarding Child Support

The amount to be awarded for the support of a child in a divorce action lies in the sound discretion of the trial court, to be reversed on appeal only where the court finds that discretion to have been abused.[88] In practice this means that the amount of child support may vary widely from case to case [89] and that a relatively small proportion of the cases are appealed, so that legal principles play a correspondingly small part in the decision of cases.

In some states the statutes describe in more or less general terms the factors which the courts are to take into account in awarding child support. After adjuring the courts to make awards in amounts reasonable and necessary for the case, nature and education of children,[90] the statutes list such factors as the financial resources and needs of the child, the standard of living enjoyed by the child during the marriage, the child's educational and medical needs, and finally the financial resources and needs of the parents.[91] Some statutes expressly authorize the court to order parents to provide health insurance for the children although in these days of enormous medical costs it would not seem necessary to make express provision for this crucial element of support.[92] The meaning of all these statutes is that within the limits of the parents' resources the support order should be sufficient to meet the child's needs, construing "needs" to mean the expenses of food, shelter, clothing, medical care and education at the level enjoyed before the divorce or as near to that level as possible.[93] Where the parents have agreed on the amount of child support, the court will usually enter an order corresponding to their agreement,[94] but it is not bound to do so and if it finds the agree-

---

Puckett, 41 Wash.App. 78, 702 P.2d 477 (1985), overruled on another ground, Porter v. Porter, 107 Wash.2d 43, 726 P.2d 459 (1986); Caldwell v. Caldwell, 5 Wis.2d 146, 92 N.W.2d 356 (1958). See also cases cited in Annot., 59 A.L.R.3d 9 (1974).

Cases which permit child support orders to run beyond the death of the obligor parent include Bailey v. Bailey, 86 Nev. 483, 471 P.2d 220 (1970), citing other cases; Guggenheimer v. Guggenheimer, 99 N.H. 399, 112 A.2d 61 (1955).

86. See Note, Child Support, Life Insurance and the Uniform Marriage and Divorce Act, 67 Ky.L.J. 239 (1978).

87. Robrock v. Robrock, 167 Ohio St. 479, 150 N.E.2d 421 (1958).

88. Martin v. Martin, 225 Ark. 677, 284 S.W.2d 647 (1955); Koester v. Koester, 99 Idaho 654, 586 P.2d 1370 (1978); Sims v. Sims, 457 So.2d 163 (La.App.1984); Whitney v. Whitney, 325 Mass. 28, 88 N.E.2d 647 (1949); In re Marriage of Carlson, ___ Mont. ___, 693 P.2d 496 (1984), appeal after remand ___ Mont. ___, 714 P.2d 116 (1986).

89. See Yee, What Really Happens in Child Support Cases: An Empirical Study of Establishment and Enforcement of Child Support Orders in the Denver District Court, 57 Den.L.J. 21 (1979). A great number of cases are collected in Annot., Excessiveness or Adequacy of

Money Awarded as Child Support, 27 A.L.R.4th 864 (1984).

90. E.g., the Alaska, Arizona, Arkansas, California (support suitable to the child's circumstances); Colorado; District of Columbia, Illinois, Iowa; Kentucky; Michigan; Minnesota; Missouri; Montana; New Hampshire; New Jersey; New Mexico (court should award just and proper support); New York; Oregon (just and proper support); Rhode Island; Vermont; Virginia (such orders as the court may deem expedient); Washington; Wisconsin statutes cited in note 2, supra.

91. E.g., the Arizona, Colorado, Connecticut, Delaware, Idaho, Illinois, Indiana, Iowa, Kansas, Kentucky, Minnesota, Missouri, Montana, New York, Ohio, Oregon, Rhode Island, Vermont, Virginia, West Virginia and Wisconsin statutes cited in note 2, supra. See also the Uniform Marriage and Divorce Act § 309, 9A Unif.L. Ann. 167 (1979).

92. E.g., the Arizona, Illinois, Maryland, Massachusetts, Ohio, and Tennessee statutes cited in note 2, supra.

93. Matter of Marriage of Gatti, 73 Or.App. 581, 699 P.2d 1151 (1985); Puckett v. Puckett, 76 Wash.2d 703, 458 P.2d 556 (1969).

94. Webb v. Daiger, 173 A.2d 920 (D.C.Mun.Ct.App. 1961); Commonwealth v. Cameron, 197 Pa.Super. 403, 179 A.2d 270 (1962).

ment does not serve the child's best interests, it may make a different award.[95]

Since it is now settled that both parents are responsible for the support of their children,[96] the court in entering child support orders must take into account the property and income of both parents.[97] This does not mean of course that both parents must contribute equally to the child's support but rather that they must contribute equitably in proportion to the property and income which they possess.[98] Some courts express the same principle by a formula.[99] The cases do not seem to take into account in computing child support the services provided to the child in kind by the custodial parent, although it would seem that these should not be totally ignored since they obviously can be translated into dollars. In determining the resources of the custodial parent the courts do take account of resources provided by the divorce decree itself in the division of property or award of alimony.[1] The fact that custody is awarded jointly to both spouses does not affect their relative responsibility for child support, but it does entail a further calculation based on the proportionate amounts of time the child spends with each parent.[2]

In rare cases the child himself may have some financial resources, but it has been held that this may only be taken into account to a limited extent. If the parent has sufficient means to provide adequate support, then he must be required to do so.[3] If he has not, the child's income may be resorted to.

The court in determining the ability of the non-custodial parent to pay support must evaluate the property of the parent,[4] must determine the disposable income available for support,[5] and must give due consideration to the health and physical condition of the parent.[6] Where it appears that the parent's income is less than his earning capacity indicates that it should be, the court must determine whether his actual earnings demonstrate a good faith choice of career or whether the parent's earnings are being held at a low level for the purpose of frustrating a child support order. If the court finds that the parent is acting in bad faith in this manner, the child support order may be based upon earning capacity rather than actual earnings.[7] In view of the fact that both spouses now have an obligation to support each other, one element of the parent's resources which is sometimes taken into ac-

---

95. Metcalf v. Commissioner, 271 F.2d 288 (1st Cir. 1959) (Massachusetts law); Blumenthal v. Blumenthal, 155 A.2d 525 (D.C.Mun.Ct.App.1959); Barbee v. Barbee, 201 Ga. 763, 41 S.E.2d 126 (1947). See also the Uniform Marriage and Divorce Act § 306(b), 9A Unif.L.Ann. 135 (1979).

96. See the discussion in section 6.2, supra.

97. Silvia v. Silvia, 9 Mass.App.Ct. 339, 400 N.E.2d 1330 (1980); Henderson v. Lekvold, 99 N.M. 269, 657 P.2d

125 (1983); Fernau v. Fernau, 39 Wash.App. 695, 694 P.2d 1092 (1984).

98. But where each spouse has equal resources, the support obligation may be equally divided. See Williams v. Williams, 510 S.W.2d 452 (Mo.1974).

99. Smith v. Smith, 290 Or. 675, 626 P.2d 342 (1981), using the following formula, where N is the noncustodial parent and C is the custodial parent:

$$\text{Obligation of N} = \frac{\text{Income of N}}{\text{Income of N} + \text{Income of C}} \times \text{Needs of the Child.}$$

1. Puckett v. Puckett, 76 Wash.2d 703, 458 P.2d 556 (1969).

2. Matter of Marriage of Belt, 65 Or.App. 606, 672 P.2d 1205 (1983), modified on other grounds, 68 Or.App. 42, 680 P.2d 390 (1984).

3. Armstrong v. Armstrong, 15 Cal.3d 942, 126 Cal. Rptr. 805, 544 P.2d 941 (1976).

4. Annot., 27 A.L.R.4th 864, 880 (1984). For a discussion of the process of valuation for purposes of dividing marital property, see section 15.4, supra.

5. William R. T. v. Bonnie R. T., 494 A.2d 150 (Del. 1985); Topper v. Topper, 478 A.2d 640 (Del.Super.1984); Emsley v. Emsley, 467 A.2d 700 (Del.Fam.Ct.1983); Butler

v. Butler, 339 Pa.Super. 312, 488 A.2d 1141 (1985); Annot., 27 A.L.R.4th 864, 877, 882 (1984).

6. Annot., 27 A.L.R.4th 864, 881 (1984).

7. Pierce v. Pierce, 241 Ga. 96, 243 S.E.2d 46 (1978) (relatively large child support award upheld on the ground of the parent's earning capacity); Glass v. Peitchel, 42 Ill. App.3d 240, 355 N.E.2d 750 (1976), appeal after remand 63 Ill.App.3d 57, 20 Ill.Dec. 442, 380 N.E.2d 420 (1978) (trial court must make a finding on the parent's good faith with respect to obtaining work); Dunn v. Dunn, 105 Mich.App. 793, 307 N.W.2d 424 (1981) (child support based on actual income rather than potential income where the parent had in good faith joined a religious order and taken a vow

count in determining his ability to pay child support is the income of a second spouse.[8] This does not mean that a second spouse has an obligation to support the child of a first marriage. It does mean that the income of the second spouse is a source of support for the child's parent, reducing pro tanto the demands on that parent's earnings, and therefore making a larger portion of that parent's income available for child support.

The marital misconduct of parents is today generally held to be irrelevant in awarding child support and some statutes so provide.[9] Where a custodial parent acts to frustrate or prevent the visitation rights of the other parent, however, or attempts to alienate the child from the other parent, the natural reaction of the non-custodial parent is to withhold support. The cases are not in agreement as to whether fault in this sense is a reason for denying child support. Although the question usually arises in connection with the modification or enforcement of support orders, conduct of this sort should be relevant in arriving at a support order in the first place, but only to the extent that it does not jeopardize the welfare of the child.[10] If the custodial parent is able to support the child without

contribution from the other parent, this sort of conduct should be a reason for not ordering that support or for ordering a lesser amount.[11]

Within the limits of the parents' ability to furnish support, the order should provide for the reasonable needs of the child in proportion to the family's standard of living. Statistically it is more likely than not that the amount arrived at by the trial courts will be inadequate to meet these needs, either because there is too little money available from the parents' resources, or because the judges seem to be unaware of what it costs to care for and educate a child,[12] or because the judges make the odd assumption that awards large enough to be adequate will not be complied with by the parent.[13] Now that the needs of children are being nationally recognized and that efficient enforcement techniques are being developed,[14] it is time that child support awards do correspond to realistic needs.

The child support award should cover the ordinary expenses of childhood and youth, including medical expenses,[15] taking into account the obvious fact that child raising ex-

---

of poverty); Lainson v. Lainson, 219 Neb. 170, 362 N.W.2d 53 (1985) (quadriplegic father had earning capacity in the form of investments which could be taken into account in awarding child support, although incapable of earning wages); Stanley v. Stanley, 51 N.C.App. 172, 275 S.E.2d 546 (1981), dismissed for want of jurisdiction 454 U.S. 959, 102 S.Ct. 496, 70 L.Ed.2d 374 (1981).

8. Silvia v. Silvia, 9 Mass.App. 339, 400 N.E.2d 1330 (1980).

9. E.g., the Arizona, Colorado, Idaho, Illinois, Indiana, Minnesota, Missouri, Montana and Washington statutes cited in note 2, supra. Some cases may take the broad position that the duty to permit visitation is independent of the duty of support. See, e.g., Comiskey v. Comiskey, 48 Ill.App.3d 17, 8 Ill.Dec. 925, 366 N.E.2d 87 (1977); Heller v. Heller, 367 N.W.2d 179 (N.D.1985); Hester v. Hester, 663 P.2d 727 (Okl.1983).

10. See sections 17.2 and 17.3 infra, dealing with the modification and enforcement of support orders.

11. State ex rel. Division of Family Services v. Standridge, 676 S.W.2d 513 (Mo.1984) (dictum that when the wife leaves the husband without his consent and takes the children, the father is not liable for necessaries furnished to the children); Young v. Young, 200 Neb. 787, 265 N.W.2d 666 (1978); Barbara M. v. Harry M., 117 Misc.2d 142, 458 N.Y.S.2d 136 (Fam.Ct.1982); C.J.S. v. E.K., 3 Fam.L.Rptr. 2413 (N.Y.Fam.Ct.1977).

12. Bruch, Developing Normative Standards for Child-Support Payments: A Critique of Current Practice, in J. Cassetty, The Parental Child-Support Obligation 119 (1983); Weitzmann, The Economics of Divorce: Social and Economic Consequences of Property, Alimony and Child Support Awards, 28 U.C.L.A.L.Rev. 1181, 1233 (1981); D. Chambers, Making Fathers Pay (1979).

13. Bruch, Developing Normative Standards for Child-Support Payments: A Critique of Current Practice, in J. Cassetty, The Parental Child-Support Obligation 119, 120 (1983).

14. See section 17.3, infra.

15. Bertram v. Bertram, 334 So.2d 70 (Fla.App.1976) (daughter's obesity treatments); Manacher v. Manacher, 35 A.D.2d 705, 314 N.Y.S.2d 955 (1st Dep't 1970) (psychiatrist); Hester v. Hester, 663 P.2d 727 (Okl.1983) (orthodontist). For other cases see Annot., 39 A.L.R.4th 502 (1985).

Matter of Marriage of Godwin, 30 Or.App. 425, 567 P.2d 144 (1977) held that a father who agreed to pay only the cost of an abortion could not limit his support obligation in such a way and would have to pay the cost of supporting the child.

An interesting case involving constitutional rights of privacy is Pamela P. v. Frank S., 110 Misc.2d 978, 443 N.Y.S.2d 343 (Fam.Ct.1981). In an opinion by Judge

penses increase as the child grows older.[16] The states are now under compulsion to develop "guidelines" as an aid to the computation of the appropriate levels of child support, pursuant to title IV–D of the Social Security Act, and many have done so.[17] Guidelines are useful in assisting trial judges to arrive at a reasonable child support amount, but they should not be permitted to become fixed rules which have the effect of putting ceilings on awards or of neglecting the special circumstances indicating the wisdom of a larger or smaller award.[18] The risks of using guidelines are particularly acute because in the hands of many hard pressed trial judges they are likely to become rigid and automatic rules.

As has already been indicated, some courts are willing to order the payment of child support past the age of majority to enable the child to attend college.[19] The broader question is whether the parent should be ordered to pay college expenses at all.

When the first edition of this work was published there were a substantial number of cases which held that trial courts could not make such orders, either on the ground that a college education is not a "necessary" or because the parent would be entitled to decide that the child should not attend college if the family remained intact and he should have no greater obligation when the family ends in divorce. Today only a very few jurisdictions take this position.[20] In some states the courts seem excessively cautious about imposing this duty, saying that it will only be imposed where there are "special circumstances" justifying an order that the parent provide a college education for his child.[21] But in most such cases the "special circumstances" turn out to be little more than the usual factors in any child support decision. It must be shown that the parent has sufficient means to afford the expense of college, and that the child gives evidence of being able to benefit from it by making satisfacto-

---

Dembitz the court held that a father who was deliberately deceived by a sexual partner concerning her use of contraception was liable for support of the child only to the extent the child could not be supported by the mother, in effect permitting the defense of fraud to a child support claim so far as the child's interests were not prejudiced. The case was modified in this respect, however. In re Pamela P., 88 A.D.2d 865, 451 N.Y.S.2d 766 (1st Dep't 1982), affirmed 59 N.Y.2d 1, 462 N.Y.S.2d 819, 449 N.E.2d 713 (1983).

16. Espenshade, The Value and Cost of Children, 32 Population Bull. 43 (Pop.Ref.Bureau 1977); C. Edwards, USDA Estimates of the Cost of Raising a Child: A Guide to Their Use and Interpretation (USDA Misc.Pub. No. 1411, (1981).

17. 42 U.S.C.A. § 667; 45 C.F.R. §§ 302.53, 302.56 (1985). See section 17.3, infra, for a discussion of this program. For discussion of guidelines see Sawhill, Developing Normative Standards for Child-Support Payments, in J. Cassetty, The Parental Child-Support Obligation 79 (1983); H. Krause, Child Support in America 11–5 (1981); D. Chambers, Making Fathers Pay 38–42 (1979).

It is most important for counsel to realize that the guidelines adopted by some states may have substantive, rather than merely procedural, effects. For example, the Colorado guidelines give the guideline amounts the effect of a rebuttable presumption for the establishment or modification of the amount of child support, to be deviated from only where its application would be inequitable. Colo.Sess.L. 1986, H.B. No. 1275, § 1, amending Colo.Rev. Stat. § 14–10–115(3)(a) (Supp. 1986).

Cases construing the guidelines include Perkins v. Perkins, 15 Ark.App. 82, 690 S.W.2d 356 (1985); Smith v. Smith, 290 Or. 675, 626 P.2d 342 (1981); Melzer v. Wits-

berger, 505 Pa. 462, 480 A.2d 991 (1984), 58 Temp.L.Q. 435 (1985) (with strong and persuasive dissent).

The Illinois guidelines were held constitutional in Boris v. Blaisdell, 142 Ill.App.3d 1034, 97 Ill.Dec. 186, 492 N.E.2d 622 (1986).

18. Powell v. Powell, 433 So.2d 1374 (Fla.App.1983) (parties must be given an opportunity to challenge the guidelines); In re Marriage of Drier, 119 Wis.2d 312, 351 N.W.2d 745 (1984) (Dep't of H & H S guidelines are advisory only).

19. See the discussion at notes 70 to 80, supra.

20. E.g., Spence v. Spence, 266 A.2d 29 (D.C.App.1970); Berger v. Hollander, 391 So.2d 716 (Fla.App.1980); Genoe v. Genoe, 373 So.2d 940 (Fla.App.1979); Kern v. Kern, 360 So.2d 482 (Fla.1978).

21. Van Orman v. Van Orman, 30 Colo.App. 177, 492 P.2d 81 (1971) (semble); Boleware v. Boleware, 450 So.2d 92 (Miss.1984); Kaplan v. Wallshein, 57 A.D.2d 828, 394 N.Y.S.2d 439 (2d Dep't 1977); Dugan v. Dugan, 126 Misc. 2d 600, 483 N.Y.S.2d 619 (Sup.Ct.1984). Hutchinson v. Hutchinson, 263 Pa.Super. 299, 397 A.2d 1218 (1979) takes the position that a parent may be required to provide a college education for his child only where he can do it without undue hardship, but does not explain why the standard is stricter for this element of child support than for others. Sunderwirth v. Williams, 553 S.W.2d 889 (Mo.App.1977) lists the relevant factors as the parent's financial ability, the child's capacity for college work, the nearness of the child to majority, whether the child is self-supporting and the parent's willingness to provide for college. It is not clear whether the parent's unwillingness would foreclose an order.

ry academic progress.[22] Many states recognize that providing a college education is just a specific application of general child support principles.[23] A few states might even include graduate school in the obligation.[24] Where the child has special needs, some form of private school training before college may be ordered.[25] In those states in which there is still reluctance to order the parent to pay for college, the courts may enter such orders if the spouses have included the obligation in their separation agreement and presented the agreement to the court for approval.[26] Whether the parent may be required to pay for a particular kind of college education, as for example by permitting the child or the child's custodian to choose an expensive private college over a cheaper state university, depends on the parent's resources and whether the child's needs demand the more expensive college.[27]

The great majority of cases which permit child support orders to include a college edu-

cation where the parent has sufficient resources are certainly correct. It would be extraordinary in these days to maintain that a college education is not a "necessary". It is necessary both from the child's and from society's point of view that every child receive all the education he is able to absorb. It is of course true that college expenses have risen sharply in the last two decades. It is also true that by virtue of scholarships, loans and part-time work the student can often succeed in getting a college degree without parental support. Nevertheless there is no reason why a parent who is able to make a contribution to his child's college education should be allowed to avoid doing so by shifting the burden either to society in general, or to the child himself, in the latter event reducing the time and energy which the child can devote to his education.

22. A parent was held not obliged to pay for college expenses where he had insufficient means in Commonwealth ex rel. Grossi v. Grossi, 218 Pa.Super. 728, 272 A.2d 239 (1970). Sakovits v. Sakovits, 178 N.J.Super. 623, 429 A.2d 1091 (1981) held that a parent need not provide a college education when the child had been out of high school four years before she decided she wanted to go to college. Greiman v. Friedman, 90 Ill.App.3d 941, 46 Ill.Dec. 355, 414 N.E.2d 77 (1980) held that the trial court could properly consider the child's academic record in deciding whether to order the parent to pay the college expenses, but found that the trial court had not abused its discretion in ordering the payments even though the academic record was not outstanding. Thiele v. Thiele, 479 N.E.2d 1324 (Ind.App.1985) held that the parent was not relieved of his obligation to pay a child's college expenses when she dropped out of college for a brief time and then returned.

23. Ogle v. Ogle, 275 Ala. 483, 156 So.2d 345 (1963); Jenkins v. Jenkins, 233 Ga. 902, 214 S.E.2d 368 (1975); Imes v. Imes, 52 Ill.App.3d 792, 10 Ill.Dec. 466, 367 N.E.2d 1075 (1977); Dorman v. Dorman, 251 Ind. 272, 241 N.E.2d 50 (1968); Charlton v. Charlton, 397 Mich. 84, 243 N.W.2d 261 (1976); Khalaf v. Khalaf, 58 N.J. 63, 275 A.2d 132 (1971); Irby v. Martin, 500 P.2d 278 (Okl.1972); Risinger v. Risinger, 273 S.C. 36, 253 S.E.2d 652 (1979). Many other cases are collected in Annot., 99 A.L.R.3d 322 (1980).

A state statute which expressly provided that a parent should pay his child's college expenses was held constitutional in In re Marriage of Vrban, 293 N.W.2d 198 (Iowa 1980).

24. Ross v. Ross, 167 N.J.Super. 441, 400 A.2d 1233 (1979). Contra, holding that the parent might be re-

quired to support a child in college, but not in law school, Brown v. Brown, 327 Pa.Super. 51, 474 A.2d 1168 (1984).

25. Wooddy v. Wooddy, 258 Md. 224, 265 A.2d 467 (1970) (special school for a Down's syndrome child); Spingola v. Spingola, 91 N.M. 737, 580 P.2d 958 (1978), appeal after remand 93 N.M. 598, 603 P.2d 708 (1979) (private school for the youngest child when the two older children went to private school and the parent was easily able to provide it); Com. ex rel. Stump v. Church, 333 Pa. Super. 166, 481 A.2d 1358 (1984) (private school to prepare child for college). Where there is not a special reason for private schooling and the parents have a bona fide difference of opinion as to its desirability, the court may properly refuse to order the parent to pay for it. Hardisty v. Hardisty, 183 Conn. 253, 439 A.2d 307 (1981). Horseback riding lessons were held not necessary or reasonable in Howard v. Reeck, 439 N.E.2d 727 (Ind.App. 1982).

26. Cooke v. Pieters, 123 Misc.2d 351, 473 N.Y.S.2d 726 (Fam.Ct.1984); Emrick v. Emrick, 445 Pa. 428, 284 A.2d 682 (1971); Hutchinson v. Hutchinson, 263 Pa. Super. 299, 397 A.2d 1218 (1979); Barnes v. Craig, 202 Va. 229, 117 S.E.2d 63 (1960). Contra: Nokes v. Nokes, 47 Ohio St.2d 1, 351 N.E.2d 174 (1976).

27. Greiman v. Friedman, 90 Ill.App.3d 941, 46 Ill. Dec. 355, 414 N.E.2d 77 (1980); Willcutts v. Willcutts, 88 Ill.App.3d 813, 43 Ill.Dec. 924, 410 N.E.2d 1057 (1980); Rohn v. Thuma, 408 N.E.2d 578 (Ind.App.1980); Commonwealth ex rel. Larsen v. Larsen, 211 Pa.Super. 30, 234 A.2d 18 (1967). The non-custodial parent may in some cases be entitled to be consulted about the choice of a college where he is to pay the bills. Cleveland v. Cleveland, 161 Conn. 452, 289 A.2d 909 (1971).

Some Questions of Procedure

di(child /3 support /s jurisdiction! /s determin! establish!
settl*** /7 paternity)

child /3 support /s paternity /s res +l adjudicata
judicata

Relevant Factors in Awarding Child Support

child /3 support /s best /3 interest /s agree! amenab!
/5 divorc! dissol! separat!

child /3 support /s "disposable income"

support! /s subsequent second +2 spous!

§ 17.2 Child Support Orders in Divorce Decrees—Modification

Jurisdiction and Procedure in Modification

It is obvious that modification of child support decrees is closely related to their enforcement. The material in this section should therefore be considered in conjunction with the material in the next two sections, which deal with the enforcement of domestic and foreign child support decrees.

As in the case of alimony awards,[1] child support orders in divorce decrees are modifiable. The power to modify rests upon statute in some states [2] and upon the common law in

others.[3] Modification proceedings may not be used to obtain a redetermination of the original award,[4] but require proof of a change in circumstances occurring after the original order was entered.[5] The change of circumstance must normally be permanent rather than temporary or variable,[6] and must relate to factors which are relevant to any determination of the level of child support.[7] The grant or denial of modification of child support is a matter for the discretion of the trial court, to be reversed only where that discretion is abused.[8]

The support order is modifiable notwithstanding that it was originally based upon a separation agreement or stipulation signed by the husband and wife.[9] An order for child support may be made or modified even when the parties have previously contracted for the payment of a different amount and the contract has not been incorporated in the divorce decree if the court finds that the child's needs and the parent's ability to pay justify the different amount.[10] The court's judgment on what is necessary and reasonable clearly takes precedence over the parties' agreement.

The power to modify a divorce decree with respect to child support exists whether or not the decree originally included a provision for

§ 17.2

1. See section 16.5, supra. Many of the principles governing the modification of alimony decrees are applicable to the modification of child support orders.

2. E.g., Alaska Stat. § 25.24.140 (1983); Ariz.Rev.Stat. § 25–327(a) and (c) (Supp.1986); West's Ann.Cal.Civ.Code § 4700.1 (Supp.1987); Colo.Rev.Stat. § 14–10–122 (Supp. 1986); Conn.Gen.Stat.Ann. § 46b–86 (1986); West's Fla. Stat.Ann. § 61.13 (Supp.1987); Official Code Ga.Ann. § 30–220 (Supp.1986); Ill–S.H.A. Ch. 40, §§ 510, 511 (1980 and Supp.1986); Mich.C.L.A. § 25.106 (1984); N.M. Stat.Ann., § 40–4–7 (1986); N.Y.—McKinney's Dom.Rel. L. § 240 (1986); Vernon's Tex.Code Ann., Fam.Code § 14.08 (1986); Va.Code, § 20–108 (Supp.1986); Wis.Stat. Ann. § 767.32 (Supp.1986). See also Uniform Marriage and Divorce Act § 316(a), 9A Unif.L.Ann. 183 (1979).

3. E.g., Reiter v. Reiter, 225 Ark. 157, 278 S.W.2d 644 (1955); Knabe v. Knabe, 176 Md. 606, 6 A.2d 366 (1939); 3 Md.L.Rev. 367 (1939); Miller v. Miller, 153 Neb. 890, 46 N.W.2d 618 (1951); Seitz v. Seitz, 156 Ohio St. 516, 103 N.E.2d 741 (1952). Other cases are collected in Annot., 71 A.L.R.2d 1370, 1376 (1960).

4. Warren v. Warren, 218 Md. 212, 146 A.2d 34 (1958); Tedford v. Dempsey, 437 So.2d 410 (Miss.1983); Roberts v. Roberts, 292 S.W.2d 596 (Mo.App.1956).

5. Reiter v. Reiter, 225 Ark. 157, 278 S.W.2d 644 (1955); Pearson v. Pearson, 247 Iowa 437, 74 N.W.2d 224 (1956); Grunder v. Grunder, 186 Kan. 766, 352 P.2d 1067 (1960); Warren v. Warren, 218 Md. 212, 146 A.2d 34 (1958); Udy v. Udy, 195 Or. 156, 244 P.2d 615 (1952).

6. Holesinger v. Holesinger, 252 Iowa 374, 107 N.W.2d 247 (1961); Van Tinker v. Van Tinker, 31 Wash.2d 12, 195 P.2d 96 (1948).

7. Pearson v. Pearson, 247 Iowa 437, 74 N.W.2d 224 (1956); Tedford v. Dempsey, 437 So.2d 410 (Miss.1983).

8. In re Marriage of Wiley, 444 N.E.2d 315 (Ind.Ann. 1983); Tedford v. Dempsey, 437 So.2d 410 (Miss.1983); Christensen v. Christensen, 628 P.2d 1297 (Utah 1981).

9. Reiter v. Reiter, 225 Ark. 157, 278 S.W.2d 644 (1955); Singer v. Singer, 7 Cal.App.3d 807, 87 Cal.Rptr. 42 (1970); Meehan v. Meehan, 425 N.E.2d 157 (Ind.1981); Kern v. Kern, 65 Misc.2d 765, 319 N.Y.S.2d 178 (Fam.Ct. 1970). Compare Boden v. Boden, 42 N.Y.2d 210, 397 N.Y.S.2d 701, 366 N.E.2d 791 (1977) with Brescia v. Fitts, 56 N.Y.2d 132, 451 N.Y.S.2d 68, 436 N.E.2d 518 (1982), on remand 89 A.D.2d 894, 453 N.Y.S.2d 458 (1982). Other cases are cited in Annot., 71 A.L.R.2d 1370, 1396 (1960).

10. Annot., 166 A.L.R. 675, 686 (1947).

child support or specifically reserved jurisdiction to include such a provision.[11] Although the rule as to alimony decrees is otherwise,[12] the necessity for providing for children of the marriage persuades most courts that they may enter a child support order subsequent to divorce whenever the child's welfare requires it and the parent's resources permit it. The most frequent illustration of this rule occurs when a child of the marriage is born after the divorce, the divorce decree not mentioning the wife's pregnancy,[13] but the rule applies to other cases as well.

Just as in most states accrued and unpaid installments of alimony may not be modified,[14] accrued and unpaid installments of child support may not usually be modified.[15] In both situations this may inflict serious hardship on the obligor, as where the child's custodian appears to acquiesce for long periods in the non-payment, or where the obligor is not aware that the child's circumstances have changed in a relevant way.[16] If the hardship is particularly severe, the courts sometimes devise a way to protect the obligor,[17] but in most instances the courts hold that retroactive modification of this kind is beyond their power [18] and indeed the governing statute may so provide.[19] The court's modification in these cases takes effect as of the date on which the petition for modification was filed.[20]

The procedure for obtaining a modification of child support orders varies somewhat from state to state, but it is generally agreed that the proceeding constitutes a continuation of the original divorce action [21] when it is brought in the same state as the divorce action.[22] It is commenced by a motion or peti-

11. Krog v. Krog, 32 Cal.2d 812, 198 P.2d 510 (1948); Effland v. Effland, 171 Kan. 657, 237 P.2d 380 (1951); Havens v. Havens-Anthony, 335 Mich. 445, 56 N.W.2d 346 (1953); Roberts v. Roberts, 292 S.W.2d 596 (Mo.App. 1956); Walker v. Walker, 198 Misc. 414, 97 N.Y.S.2d 208 (Dom.Rel.Ct.1950). Many other cases are cited in Annot., 71 A.L.R.2d 1370 (1960). For cases contra, see Hall v. Hall, 101 Ohio App. 237, 139 N.E.2d 60 (1956), and Annot., 71 A.L.R.2d 1370, 1378 (1960). The reasoning of the contrary cases is not persuasive, since they concede, as they must, that if child support is denied in the divorce action, the child may still obtain support in another action. Thus nothing is accomplished by the rule of these cases except to increase the expense, the hardship and the burdens upon crowded courts. Some cases, e.g., Mund v. Mund, 252 Minn. 442, 90 N.W.2d 309 (1958), and Riding v. Riding, 8 Utah 2d 136, 329 P.2d 878 (1958) hold that child support may be ordered even after a prior request for such support has been refused, either in the original divorce suit, or in a modification proceeding.

12. See section 16.3, supra.

13. E.g., Moore v. Moore, 231 Or. 302, 372 P.2d 981 (1962). But see Havens v. Havens-Anthony, 335 Mich. 445, 56 N.W.2d 346 (1953).

14. See section 16.5, supra.

15. Hoos v. Hoos, 86 Ill.App.3d 817, 42 Ill.Dec. 174, 408 N.E.2d 752 (1980); In re Marriage of Wiley, 444 N.E.2d 315 (Ind.App.1983); Strecker v. Wilkinson, 220 Kan. 292, 552 P.2d 979 (1976); Wood v. Wood, 407 A.2d 282 (Me.1979); Abright v. Abright, 454 S.W.2d 957 (Mo. App.1970); Schrader v. Schrader, 148 Neb. 162, 26 N.W.2d 617 (1947); Corbin v. Corbin, 288 N.W.2d 61 (N.D. 1980); McPherson v. McPherson, 153 Ohio St. 82, 90 N.E.2d 675 (1950); Matter of Marriage of Cope, 49 Or. App. 301, 619 P.2d 883 (1980), affirmed 291 Or. 12, 631 P.2d 781 (1981); Cofer v. Cofer, 205 Va. 834, 140 S.E.2d 663 (1965). Contra, allowing reduction of payments after they became due, Sawyer v. Kuhnle, 324 Mass. 53, 84

N.E.2d 546 (1949); Barker v. Barker, 366 Mich. 624, 115 N.W.2d 367 (1962); State ex rel. Larsgaard v. Larsgaard, 298 N.W.2d 381 (S.D.1980).

16. E.g., Finley v. Finley, 81 Ill.2d 317, 43 Ill.Dec. 12, 410 N.E.2d 12 (1980); State ex rel. Larsgaard v. Larsgaard, 298 N.W.2d 381 (S.D.1980).

17. E.g., Hill v. Hill, 106 Colo. 492, 107 P.2d 597 (1940) (retroactive modification where the wife agreed to accept the smaller amount); Corbridge v. Corbridge, 230 Ind. 201, 102 N.E.2d 764 (1952) (contempt may not be used to collect); Wood v. Wood, 407 A.2d 282 (Me.1979) (arrears accruing after a child's death or emancipation may be forgiven); Hartman v. Smith, 100 Wash.2d 766, 674 P.2d 176 (1984) (wife estopped to collect past due installments). Contra, arrears may not be released by contract, Weaver v. Garrett, 13 Md.App. 283, 282 A.2d 509 (1971).

For defenses to the enforcement of child support see section 17.3, supra.

18. E.g., Haynes v. Haynes, 168 Kan. 219, 212 P.2d 312 (1949); Wilburn v. Wilburn, 59 Wash.2d 799, 370 P.2d 968 (1962).

19. West's Ann.Cal.Civ.Code § 4700 (1983); Colo.Rev. Stat. § 14–10–122(1) (1973); Uniform Marriage and Divorce Act § 316(a), 9A Unif.L.Ann. 183 (1979). But N.Y.—McKinney's Dom.Rel.L. § 240(1) (Supp.1984–1985) expressly permits the modification of accrued installments under certain conditions.

20. Wood v. Wood, 407 A.2d 282 (Me.1979).

21. E.g., Houghton v. Houghton, 37 S.D. 184, 157 N.W. 316 (1916); Hacking v. Hacking, 78 R.I. 325, 82 A.2d 168 (1951), and cases cited in Annot., 71 A.L.R.2d 1370, 1406 (1960).

22. Of course if the suit is brought in another state to enforce, and then to modify, the child support order in the divorce, it is a wholly new action requiring the assertion of personal jurisdiction anew over the defen-

tion filed in the divorce suit.[23] Where both parties were personally subject to the court's jurisdiction in the divorce, personal jurisdiction need not be acquired again at the time of the petition for modification.[24] The original personal jurisdiction continues and supports the decree in the modification proceeding. But there must be adequate notice to the non-moving party,[25] and an opportunity for a hearing on the petition,[26] in order to meet the requirements of procedural due process. The burden of proof is on the party seeking the modification.[27]

When the original divorce decree orders payment of a single sum for the support of two or more children, and one of the children reaches the age of majority, the payer of support sometimes makes the mistake of thinking that he is entitled to reduce the payments pro rata without obtaining a modification of the order. The cases hold that he may not do this, and that he must continue to make the prescribed payments until the appropriate court modifies the decree.[28]

A more difficult question is created when the divorce decree orders the payment of a single sum for alimony and child support.[29] Although such decrees are objectionable on the ground that they do not accurately define the parties' rights and obligations, many

courts seem to think that they are not invalid.[30] In any event they raise the question whether a court may subsequently allocate part of the monthly sum to alimony and part to child support, for the purpose of increasing or reducing one or the other. The majority of courts hold that they do have the power to make such an allocation in a proceeding for the modification of the decree.[31] Once the court determines that it does have this power, the payments will not and should not be reduced or increased without further consideration of changes in needs and ability to pay, just as would be necessary to support any modification of child support or alimony.[32] When the parties have moved to another state, making it inconvenient or impossible to seek modification in the original divorce proceeding, the court of the second state may grant a decree in the same terms as the original divorce decree, and then allocate the combined payments between alimony and child support for the purpose of modifying what is determined to be child support on the same basis as any other modification of child support.[33]

It is not uncommon for the child support obligor to seek a reduction in child support at a time when he is in arrears on the original child support decree. The recipient of child

dant. In re Marriage of Bussey, 108 Ill.2d 286, 91 Ill.Dec. 594, 483 N.E.2d 1229 (1985).

23. Annot., 71 A.L.R.2d 1370, 1406 (1960).

24. Watson v. Watson, 88 So.2d 133 (Fla.1956); McClellan v. McClellan, 125 Ill.App.2d 477, 261 N.E.2d 216 (1970); Carpenter v. Carpenter, 240 So.2d 13 (La.App. 1970); Atwood v. Atwood, 253 Minn. 185, 91 N.W.2d 728 (1958); Van Divort v. Van Divort, 165 Ohio St. 141, 134 N.E.2d 715 (1956); Davi v. Davi, 456 S.W.2d 238 (Tex.Civ. App.1970); Lynde v. Lynde, 492 S.W.2d 641 (Tex.Civ.App. 1973).

25. Thurman v. Thurman, 73 Idaho 122, 245 P.2d 810 (1952); Miller v. Miller, 153 Neb. 890, 46 N.W.2d 618 (1951); Annot., 71 A.L.R.2d 1370, 1400 (1960).

26. Strecker v. Wilkinson, 220 Kan. 292, 552 P.2d 979 (1976).

27. In re Marriage of Mizer, 683 P.2d 382 (Colo.App. 1984); Freeman v. Freeman, 397 A.2d 554 (D.C.App. 1979); Jenkins v. Jenkins, 453 S.W.2d 619 (Mo.App.1970); Christensen v. Christensen, 628 P.2d 1297 (Utah 1981); Manners v. Manners, 706 P.2d 671 (Wyo.1985).

28. Delevett v. Develett, 156 Conn. 1, 238 A.2d 402 (1968); Finley v. Finley, 81 Ill.2d 317, 43 Ill.Dec. 12, 410

N.E.2d 12 (1980); Lewis v. Staub, 95 Ill.App.3d 243, 50 Ill. Dec. 774, 419 N.E.2d 1223 (1981); Hoos v. Hoos, 86 Ill. App.3d 817, 42 Ill.Dec. 174, 408 N.E.2d 752 (1980); Corbin v. Corbin, 288 N.W.2d 61 (N.D.1980). Contra: Brady v. Brady, 225 Kan. 485, 592 P.2d 865 (1979).

29. Cases are collected in Annot., 124 A.L.R. 1324 (1940).

30. E.g., Knabe v. Knabe, 176 Md. 606, 6 A.2d 366 (1939).

31. Ginsberg v. Ginsberg, 127 So.2d 137 (Fla.App. 1961); In re Marriage of Kessler, 110 Ill.App.3d 61, 65 Ill. Dec. 707, 441 N.E.2d 1221 (1982); Roth v. Roth, 10 N.J. Super. 406, 76 A.2d 818 (1950); Ditmar v. Ditmar, 48 Wash.2d 373, 293 P.2d 759 (1956); Vaccaro v. Vaccaro, 67 Wis.2d 477, 227 N.W.2d 62 (1975); Annot., 78 A.L.R.2d 1110 (1961).

32. Lockwood v. Lockwood, 160 F.2d 923 (D.C.Cir. 1947); Cooper v. Matheny, 220 Or. 390, 349 P.2d 812 (1960); Annot., 78 A.L.R.2d 1110, 1123–1132 (1961).

33. Hopkins v. Hopkins, 46 Cal.2d 313, 294 P.2d 1 (1956); Grossman v. Grossman, 242 S.C. 298, 130 S.E.2d 850 (1963); Evans v. Evans, 116 Wash. 460, 199 P. 764 (1921).

support in such cases invokes the "unclean hands" doctrine, arguing that before the obligor may seek the aid of equity to reduce his obligation, he should be required to do equity by complying with the original decree. In those states which do not permit the modification of accrued installments, this argument is properly rejected.[34] In the states which permit retroactive modification the argument is obviously unavailable.[35]

Grounds for Modification

The reader is here referred to the section dealing with the modification of alimony decrees.[36] Many of the same considerations apply to the modification of both alimony and child support decrees. In both proceedings the moving party has the burden of proof.[37] And in recent times both courts and legislatures have acted to raise the standards for modifying alimony and child support decrees, thereby giving evidence of a policy unfavorable to modification.[38] This seems to place greater emphasis on the need for finality in the tension which necessarily arises between modification and the policies underlying res

judicata. It also reflects the need to achieve some reduction in the level of divorce litigation which now raises serious problems of judicial administration in nearly all states.

The grounds for modification of child support orders are those factors which are relevant to the making of the orders in the first place, such as changes in the child's needs and resources, in the needs and resources of both parents, and in the child's physical, emotional and educational requirements.[39] As in the case of modifications of alimony decrees, it is difficult to assign specific weight to any of these factors since more than one of them are found in any particular case, so that the decisions represent interactions among a variety of factors.

The most obvious reason for modifying a child support order is an increase in the child's needs, which may be caused by inflation,[40] an increase in educational or medical expenses,[41] or just by virtue of the higher expenses which are inevitable as the child grows older.[42] Of course the payments may not be increased unless the parent has suffi-

34. Cooper v. Cooper, 59 Ill.App.3d 457, 16 Ill.Dec. 818, 375 N.E.2d 925 (1978); Edwards v. Edwards, 125 Ill. App.2d 91, 259 N.E.2d 820 (1970); In re Marriage of Carlson, ___ Mont. ___, 693 P.2d 496 (1984). Of course the obligor in such a case remains subject to all of the usual remedies for enforcement of the unpaid installments of support.

35. See the cases cited in note 15, supra.

36. See section 16.5, supra.

37. See note 27, supra.

38. E.g., the Uniform Marriage and Divorce Act § 316, 9A Unif.L.Ann. 183 (1983) authorizes modification of either alimony or child support only on proof of changed circumstances so substantial and continuing as to make the terms of the original decree unconscionable. See also Deatherage v. Deatherage, 395 So.2d 1169 (Fla. App.1981), appeal dismissed 402 So.2d 609 (Fla.1981) (changes must be substantial, significant, material, involuntary and permanent); Fuller v. Fuller, 101 Idaho 40, 607 P.2d 1314 (1980) (changes must be permanent, material and substantial); In re Marriage of Habben, 260 N.W.2d 401 (Iowa 1977) (changes must be material and substantial). Of course the changes must have occurred *after* the entry of the original decree. Sheridan v. Sheridan, 267 A.2d 343 (D.C.App.1970).

The substantive law of modification may be changed in some states by the adoption of guidelines pursuant to title IV–D of the Social Security Act. See, e.g., Colo.Rev. Stat. § 14–10–115(3)(a) (Supp.1986), which provides that

the guidelines must be relied upon as a rebuttable presumption for the modification of child support, unless their application would be inequitable. See also Colo. Rev.Stat. § 14–10–122 (Supp.1986).

39. In re Marriage of Bussey, 108 Ill.2d 286, 91 Ill.Dec. 594, 483 N.E.2d 1229 (1985).

40. Reynolds v. Reynolds, 203 Mont. 97, 660 P.2d 90 (1983); Craven v. Craven, 119 Utah 476, 229 P.2d 301 (1951); Foregger v. Foregger, 48 Wis.2d 512, 180 N.W.2d 578 (1970).

41. Kuespert v. Roland, 222 Ark. 153, 257 S.W.2d 562 (1952); Pencovic v. Pencovic, 45 Cal.2d 97, 287 P.2d 501 (1955); Maitzen v. Maitzen, 24 Ill.App.2d 32, 163 N.E.2d 840 (1959); Davis v. Davis, 8 Mich.App. 104, 153 N.W.2d 879 (1967). The expense of a college education as an element of the child support award is discussed in section 17.1, supra.

42. Tyler v. Tyler, 203 Kan. 565, 455 P.2d 538 (1969); Shapera v. Levitt, 260 Pa.Super. 447, 394 A.2d 1011 (1978). Graber v. Graber, 220 Neb. 816, 374 N.W.2d 8 (1985) takes the odd position that child support may not be increased because of the additional expenses incurred for older children, on the ground that it must have been contemplated at the time of divorce that the children would grow older and that factor must have entered into the original award of support.

Child support may also be increased when a child of the marriage is born after the divorce. Weaver v. Weaver, 15 Mich.App. 15, 166 N.W.2d 4 (1968).

cient income to cover them.[43] In the somewhat unusual case of a decline in the child's needs, as where he receives income from other sources, the support award may be reduced,[44] although the courts seem reluctant to make such reductions unless the existing payments are at a level which is burdensome to the parent.[45] In general the child's need is viewed as ending entirely when he is emancipated, justifying the termination of child support at that time,[46] although there are cases in which the courts are willing to continue child support beyond majority when the child is still in college or is unable to support himself.[47]

Now that the duty to support children rests equally upon both parents to the extent of their respective means, changes in the financial resources of the custodial parent are relevant to the modification of awards. Thus where the custodial parent increases his income or acquires additional property, this may justify reducing the support award on the ground that the custodial parent may then be able to undertake an increased share of the support obligation.[48] Conversely, where the custodial parent's income is re-

duced or lost, this is a relevant circumstance in determining whether child support should be increased at the expense of the non-custodial parent.[49] The remarriage of the custodial parent may often have some effect on the resources available for support of the child even though the stepparent does not normally have any legal duty to support the child.[50] For example, it may mean that the custodial parent no longer faces the expense of paying rent for himself and the child, and therefore the need for support is pro tanto reduced. Or it may mean that the custodial parent ceases to work outside the home and is therefore less able to contribute to child support. Notwithstanding these obviously relevant circumstances the courts are oddly reluctant to take account of the custodial parent's remarriage in proceedings to modify child support.[51] If the stepparent adopts the child, the duty of support then becomes his and the adoption is a ground for terminating the payments.[52] In rare instances the same result may be reached when the second husband agrees to support the child and stands in loco parentis to him though without going through an adoption proceeding.[53] In the equally rare

43. Moore v. Moore, 173 Conn. 120, 376 A.2d 1085 (1977); Jackman v. Jackman, 533 S.W.2d 361 (Tex.Civ. App.1975).

44. Cash v. Cash, 234 Ark. 603, 353 S.W.2d 348 (1962); Henzgen v. Henzgen, 62 Cal.App.2d 214, 144 P.2d 428 (1944); McMann v. McMann, 285 Mich. 562, 281 N.W. 327 (1938).

45. Matthews v. Matthews, 71 S.D. 115, 22 N.W.2d 27 (1946); Pearson v. Pearson, 247 Iowa 437, 74 N.W.2d 224 (1956).

46. Berglund v. Berglund, 28 Colo.App. 382, 474 P.2d 800 (1970); In re Marriage of Christianson, 89 Ill.App.3d 167, 44 Ill.Dec. 397, 411 N.E.2d 519 (1980); Ellis v. Ellis, 292 Or. 502, 640 P.2d 1024 (1982).

Cases terminating support at the age of majority include Worthington v. Worthington, 207 Ark. 185, 179 S.W.2d 648 (1944); Codorniz v. Codorniz, 34 Cal.2d 811, 215 P.2d 32 (1950); Green v. Green, 234 S.W.2d 350 (Mo. App.1950). Holding emancipation a ground for terminating child support is Codorniz v. Codorniz, 34 Cal.2d 811, 215 P.2d 32 (1950). Emancipation may occur by virtue of the child's marriage, Ditmar v. Ditmar, 48 Wash.2d 373, 293 P.2d 759 (1956), his entrance into the armed forces, Corbridge v. Corbridge, 230 Ind. 201, 102 N.E.2d 764 (1952), his obtaining a job and becoming self-supporting, Blue v. Blue, 152 Neb. 82, 40 N.W.2d 268 (1949), and in other ways, Annot., 165 A.L.R. 723 (1946).

47. See section 17.1, supra, at note 70.

48. Wood v. Wood, 407 A.2d 282 (Me.1979).

49. Taylor v. Luntz, 89 Ill.App.3d 278, 44 Ill.Dec. 584, 411 N.E.2d 950 (1980).

50. See section 6.2, supra.

51. Gebhardt v. Gebhardt, 198 Colo. 28, 595 P.2d 1048 (1979) (child support may be reduced on the wife's remarriage where it was in fact intended in part as alimony); Mears v. Mears, 213 N.W.2d 511 (Iowa 1973) (wife's remarriage was contemplated at the time of the original child support decree, even though this resulted in her loss of income); Thies v. MacDonald, 51 Wis.2d 296, 187 N.W.2d 186 (1971) (wife's remarriage did not justify reducing child support).

A carefully reasoned and realistic opinion which holds relevant evidence concerning the custodial parent's remarriage and its effect on his ability to support the children is Gardner v. Perry, 405 A.2d 721 (Me.1979).

52. Byrd v. Byrd, 78 Ohio App. 73, 69 N.E.2d 75 (1945); Anderson v. Anderson, 27 Wash.2d 122, 177 P.2d 83 (1947). But it has been held that the adoption is not ground for canceling the accrued and unpaid arrears of child support. Napier v. Kilgore, 284 S.C. 313, 326 S.E.2d 171 (1985).

53. Ladd v. Welfare Com'r, 3 Conn.Cir. 504, 217 A.2d 490 (1965); Commonwealth v. Cameron, 197 Pa.Super. 403, 179 A.2d 270 (1962). Contra: Zeller v. Zeller, 195 Kan. 452, 407 P.2d 478 (1965).

case where husband and wife remarry each other, child support payments may be terminated in a modification proceeding, but if they are not and the parents later are divorced again, the obligation under the first decree remains.[54]

Just as a change in the circumstances of the child or the custodial parent may justify modification, so a change in the circumstances of the noncustodial parent may have this effect. A decline in the income of the noncustodial parent may be a ground for reducing the child support payments if it is large enough to impose a permanent and substantial burden on his ability to support himself.[55] When the decline is caused by the obligor's taking a job carrying a smaller income, or by his choosing to acquire further education, the cases are not in agreement. Some courts reduce the payments even if the decline in income is voluntary, so long as it is not brought about in bad faith, that is, for the very purpose of depriving the other spouse of child support payments.[56] Other courts are more strict and refuse to reduce the award where they find that the obligor has the capacity to earn the higher amount.[57] Where the change in income is incurred in good faith, on the basis of substantial reasons, it should be taken into account in modifying child support unless the effect of modification would be to leave the child and custodial parent so little support as to create serious hardship. After all a similar career change might have been undertaken during the marriage notwithstanding that it caused a reduction in living standards for the family and the same result should be tolerable after divorce.

An increase in the supporting parent's income may also be taken into account as a reason for modifying the child support payments, but the cases which do so are usually also based upon an increase in the needs of the child.[58] But if the original award was limited to the extent that it did not fully cover the child's realistic needs, it would seem proper to increase the level of support on the basis of the obligor's increased income even without proof that the child's needs had increased.[59]

Another form of voluntary change by the non-custodial parent occurs when that parent remarries. The effect of this may be to reduce his capacity to pay child support because he incurs support responsibilities to a new spouse and perhaps to the children of the newly contracted marriage. Some courts take a doctrinaire approach to these circumstances, saying that the remarriage can never be a reason for reducing support payments to the children of the first marriage and that the claims of the first family are "paramount".[60] This may be true in the unlikely event that the noncustodial parent's income is sufficient

54. Benjamin v. Benjamin, 99 N.H. 117, 106 A.2d 187 (1954).

55. Nelson v. Nelson, 225 Or. 257, 357 P.2d 536 (1960); Annot., Change in Financial Condition or Needs of Parents or Children as Ground for Modification of Decree for Child Support Payments, 89 A.L.R.2d 7 (1963).

56. Coons v. Wilder, 93 Ill.App.3d 127, 48 Ill.Dec. 512, 416 N.E.2d 785 (1981) (father left his job to enter law school); Mosley v. Mosley, 348 So.2d 225 (La.App.1977), writ denied 350 So.2d 1213 (La.1977) (father left his job to enter law school); Moncada v. Moncada, 81 Mich.App. 26, 264 N.W.2d 104 (1978), 25 Wayne L.Rev. 951 (1979) (no evidence of bad faith in the loss of a job). Pencovic v. Pencovic, 45 Cal.2d 97, 287 P.2d 501 (1955) increased child support payments on the ground that the father had earning capacity sufficient to pay the larger amount, in circumstances suggesting bad faith.

57. In re Marriage of Mizer, 683 P.2d 382 (Colo.App. 1984) (court *increased* child support when the father left the army to enroll in college, on the basis of his earning capacity); Freeman v. Freeman, 397 A.2d 554 (D.C.App. 1979).

58. In re Sharp, 65 Ill.App.3d 945, 22 Ill.Dec. 581, 382 N.E.2d 1279 (1978) (contains a thorough discussion of the issue); Tedford v. Dempsey, 437 So.2d 410 (Miss.1983); In re Marriage of Burroughs, 691 S.W.2d 470 (Mo.App.1985); Lane v. Lane, 4 Wash.App. 632, 483 P.2d 644 (1971); Manners v. Manners, 706 P.2d 671 (Wyo.1985).

59. In re Marriage of Bussey, 108 Ill.2d 286, 91 Ill.Dec. 594, 483 N.E.2d 1229 (1985).

60. Kephart v. Kephart, 89 U.S.App.D.C. 373, 193 F.2d 677 (1951), cert. denied 342 U.S. 944, 72 S.Ct. 557, 96 L.Ed. 702 (1952); Green v. Green, 232 Ark. 868, 341 S.W.2d 41 (1960); Warren v. Warren, 218 Md. 212, 146 A.2d 34 (1958); Renn v. Renn, 318 Mich. 230, 27 N.W.2d 618 (1947); McKey v. McKey, 228 Minn. 28, 36 N.W.2d 17 (1949); Testut v. Testut, 34 N.J.Super. 95, 111 A.2d 513 (1955); Monfette v. Van Sickle, 76 Misc.2d 275, 351 N.Y.S.2d 46 (Fam.Ct.1973); Christensen v. Christensen, 628 P.2d 1297 (Utah 1981); Dillon v. Dillon, 34 Wash.2d 12, 207 P.2d 752 (1949). See also section 16.5, supra, where similar issues with respect to alimony are discussed. Other cases are cited in Annot., Remarriage of Parent as Basis for Modification of Amount of Child

to provide adequate support for both families. If it is not, then the needs of the "second" family must be considered and the available resources apportioned between the two families on an equitable basis, which may require a reduction in the child support award. Many of the more modern and well considered cases recognize this.[61] The remarriage of the noncustodial parent may increase his resources or mitigate his obligations rather than aggravate them. If his second spouse is working or has income from property, her income is now legally subject to the noncustodial parent's claims for his own support, although of course it is not subject to the child support claims arising out of the first marriage. Under these circumstances it seems clear that the income of the second spouse is relevant to a consideration of a petition for modification of child support, and at least some cases so hold.[62] This does not mean that the second spouse's income automatically justifies an increase in child support, but only that it may be taken into account as improving the financial circumstances of the noncustodial spouse.

Although a divorce decree may place the children of the marriage in the custody of one spouse, it is not uncommon for the other spouse to care for them for shorter or longer periods either with or without a modification of the custody provisions of the decree. If this is contemplated in the original decree, it should have no effect on the support provisions.[63] If not so contemplated, the change in the custody arrangements may be a reason for modifying the support provisions if it has an effect on the expense of caring for the child.[64] If the change is only for a short term, it may often not have that effect if the original custodian's expenses are of longer term duration. On the other hand if the change in custody is for substantial and regular periods, or is permanent, the support order will generally be modified proportionately.[65] Whether such a change in custody should excuse past noncompliance with the support order is the subject of conflicting decisions, discussed in another section.[66]

An agreement between the father and mother to change the support payments required by the divorce decree will usually be accepted as a ground for modification if the court finds that the child's welfare will not be prejudiced by the change.[67] Agreements of this kind should be dealt with on the same basis as separation agreements providing for child support. As indicated in another section[68] separation agreements cannot prevent the courts from inquiring into what the

Support Provisions of Divorce Decrees, 89 A.L.R.2d 106 (1963).

61. Evans v. Evans, 264 Ala. 2, 84 So.2d 337 (1955); McCutcheon v. McCutcheon, 226 Ark. 276, 289 S.W.2d 521 (1956); Lewis v. Lewis, 73 Idaho 165, 248 P.2d 1061 (1952); Greiman v. Friedman, 90 Ill.App.3d 941, 46 Ill. Dec. 355, 414 N.E.2d 77 (1980); S. v. C., 70 Misc.2d 19, 332 N.Y.S.2d 773 (Fam.Ct.1972); Udy v. Udy, 195 Or. 156, 244 P.2d 615 (1952); Cambra v. Cambra, 114 R.I. 553, 336 A.2d 842 (1975); Hanson v. Hanson, 47 Wash.2d 439, 287 P.2d 879 (1955).

62. Williams v. Williams, 155 Cal.App.3d 57, 202 Cal. Rptr. 10 (1984); Morace v. Morace, 220 So.2d 775 (La. App.1969); Gardner v. Perry, 405 A.2d 721 (Me.1979); Reynolds v. Reynolds, 203 Mont. 97, 660 P.2d 90 (1983); Felisa L. v. Allen M., 107 Misc.2d 217, 433 N.Y.S.2d 715 (Fam.Ct.1980); Renaud v. Renaud, 118 R.I. 365, 373 A.2d 1198 (1977). Contra: In re Whitney, 90 Ill.App.3d 734, 46 Ill.Dec. 118, 413 N.E.2d 872 (1980); Edwards v. Edwards, 125 Ill.App.2d 91, 259 N.E.2d 820 (1970).

63. Rabon v. Ledbetter, 9 N.C.App. 376, 176 S.E.2d 372 (1970).

64. Rock v. Rock, 107 R.I. 172, 265 A.2d 640 (1970). See also Daniel v. Daniel, 239 Ga. 466, 238 S.E.2d 108

(1977) where the court held that the father was not liable for arrears in child support which accrued while he had custody with the consent of the mother, although the decree had not been modified to reflect the change in custody.

65. Hixson v. Hixson, 38 Cal.2d 444, 240 P.2d 586 (1952); Perry v. Perry, 213 Ga. 847, 102 S.E.2d 534 (1958); Schlom v. Schlom, 149 Mass. 111, 115 So. 197 (1928); State v. Superior Court of Skagit County, 159 Wash. 277, 292 P. 1011 (1930).

66. See section 17.3, infra.

67. Hill v. Hill, 106 Colo. 492, 107 P.2d 597 (1940); Annot., 100 A.L.R.3d 1129, 1156 (1980), citing many cases. Herb v. Herb, 251 Iowa 957, 103 N.W.2d 361 (1960) refused modification where it found the agreement reducing payments would jeopardize the child's welfare. Hartman v. Smith, 100 Wash.2d 766, 674 P.2d 176 (1984) contains dictum that agreements for the modification of prospective child support are invalid, but that such agreements are valid with respect to past due installments of child support. Both statements are too sweeping. The question in either case should be whether the agreement is or is not conducive to the child's welfare.

68. See section 18.5, infra.

child's welfare demands, but they will generally be approved by the courts if they make adequate provision for the child in the light of all the circumstances. In any case there may be a difficult question of fact whether the parties' acquiescence in a level of payments different from that ordered by the divorce decree can be construed as an agreement to modify the decree.[69] Different issues are raised where no attempt to modify the agreement is made, the agreement to reduce the payments being relied upon as a defense to a proceeding for the enforcement of the child support order.[70]

Disputes over the custody and visitation provisions of divorce decrees often lead to motions for the modification of child support orders. In the typical case the mother is given custody of the child, with rights of visitation to the father. She then moves out of the state. The divorce decree may or may not forbid the move so that she may or may not be in violation of that decree. She may have substantial reasons for moving, as where she returns to her parents' home, or remarries and moves to another state to be with her second husband. In any event her move makes it either impossible or inconvenient and impracticable for the father to exercise his visitation rights. His natural response is to move for an order terminating child support. In dealing with the question so raised the courts have not taken wholly consistent positions. Most of them refuse to modify the child support order,[71] but merely counting the

authorities is to ignore the controlling factors. One such factor is the provision of the divorce decree. If it contains no prohibition upon removal of the child from the state, some cases hold that the mother does not violate it by moving, and that the husband is therefore not excused from continuing the payments, notwithstanding that the removal effectively ends his contact with his child.[72] Even if the decree does forbid her to take the child out of the state, however, she may be able to have it modified so as to permit the move.[73]

Another controlling factor is the child's welfare. If the mother is unable to provide adequately for the child out of her own property or earnings, the courts will not allow the father to stop making child support payments when the mother has been guilty of a violation of the custody decree.[74] This causes particular hardship to the father if the mother not only prevents him from visiting the child but also attempts to alienate the child's affection for his father. The father is compelled to continue complying with the divorce decree when he can see his former wife violating it. He feels with reason that if he were to cut off the support payments that might effectively end the mother's misconduct. Although the child should not be allowed to go without support because of his mother's misconduct,[75] the support payments may be reduced or terminated for her violation where she has sufficient funds to support the child so that the modification will not prejudice the child's welfare.[76]

69. Compare Meyer v. Meyer, 493 S.W.2d 42 (Mo.App. 1973) with Severson v. Severson, 71 Wis.2d 382, 238 N.W.2d 116 (1976), 15 J.Fam.L. 629 (1977).

70. The enforcement question is discussed in section 17.3, infra.

71. E.g., Reiter v. Reiter, 225 Ark. 157, 278 S.W.2d 644 (1955); Lucy K. H. v. Carl W. H., 415 A.2d 510 (Del.Fam. Ct.1979); Comiskey v. Comiskey, 48 Ill.App.3d 17, 8 Ill. Dec. 925, 366 N.E.2d 87 (1977); Matter of Marriage of Doley, 30 Or.App. 989, 569 P.2d 627 (1977); Commonwealth ex rel. Firestone v. Firestone, 158 Pa.Super. 579, 45 A.2d 923 (1946); Newton v. Newton, 202 Va. 515, 118 S.E.2d 656 (1961); Gaidos v. Gaidos, 48 Wash.2d 276, 293 P.2d 388 (1956). Other cases are collected in Annot., 8 A.L.R.4th 1231 (1981).

72. Corson v. Corson, 46 Wash.2d 611, 283 P.2d 673 (1955); Lear v. Lear, 29 Wash.2d 692, 189 P.2d 237 (1948). In Lucy K. H. v. Carl W. H., 415 A.2d 510 (Del.Fam.Ct.

1979), although the mother took the child to Norway in clear violation of the decree, the court seemed to excuse her conduct, and also relied upon the fact that the decree itself provided for the forfeiture of marital property as a penalty for the violation.

73. Iverson v. Iverson, 243 Minn. 54, 66 N.W.2d 549 (1954); Sanges v. Sanges, 44 Wash.2d 35, 265 P.2d 278 (1953). See also section 19.9, infra.

74. Levell v. Levell, 183 Or. 39, 190 P.2d 527 (1948); Gaidos v. Gaidos, 48 Wash.2d 276, 293 P.2d 388 (1956).

75. Reiter v. Reiter, 225 Ark. 157, 278 S.W.2d 644 (1955); Lucy K. H. v. Carl W. H., 415 A.2d 510 (Del.Fam. Ct.1979).

76. Cortina v. Cortina, 108 So.2d 63 (Fla.App.1958); Wick v. Wick, 19 Ill.2d 457, 167 N.E.2d 207 (1960); Cooper v. Cooper, 59 Ill.App.3d 457, 16 Ill.Dec. 818, 375 N.E.2d 925 (1978); Ryan v. Ryan, 300 Minn. 244, 219 N.W.2d 912

The only other solution to the problem is to modify the custody order by transferring custody from mother to father. A few courts have done this,[77] but it is usually not feasible, either because the father is unable to assume custody, or because the change would not promote the child's interest, or because the court is understandably reluctant to use a custody order as a form of punishment. In any event it will be done only in extreme cases. The sad fact is that if divorced persons are determined to hurt each other through their children, there is often little that the courts can do to prevent it.

It is a much litigated question whether child support terminates automatically on the death of the obligor. Analytically the cases break the question down into two more specific questions: (1) Does the divorce court have the power to make a child support order which will continue to be enforceable against the obligor's estate after his death? (2) If so, is the particular order to be construed as having that effect?

On the first question there are cases and arguments both ways, as is true of the corresponding alimony problem. The arguments opposed to automatic termination are stronger in the case of child support than in the

case of alimony, but there are certainly cases involving both alimony and child support in which the courts should have the authority to continue the payments beyond the obligor's death.[78] A substantial number of cases have held that the courts do have this authority with respect to child support under statutes which do not expressly either grant or withhold it.[79] And contemporary well considered statutes now expressly grant the authority[80] at the same time providing that on the death of the obligor the court may modify, revoke or commute the payments to a lump sum, thereby giving the courts discretion to reach equitable results in the light of the particular circumstances. Once it is decided that the statutory authority exists, the strongest argument against the termination of child support on the obligor's death rests upon the needs of the children. As a dissent in a leading case put it: "It is inconsistent with the whole theory of our law that infants become charges on society if the parent has an estate that may be made available to them."[81]

A substantial number of cases do hold, however, that the courts have no authority to make child support orders which will be enforceable after the obligor's death.[82] Their argument is that the child, if there were no

(1974); Barela v. Barela, 91 N.M. 686, 579 P.2d 1253 (1978); Levell v. Levell, 183 Or. 39, 190 P.2d 527 (1948); Sanges v. Sanges, 44 Wash.2d 35, 265 P.2d 278 (1953). Conversely, the father's visitation rights were conditioned on his making support payments in Reardon v. Reardon, 3 Ariz.App. 475, 415 P.2d 571 (1966).

77. See section 19.9, infra. The court refused this relief also in Comiskey v. Comiskey, 48 Ill.App.3d 17, 8 Ill.Dec. 925, 366 N.E.2d 87 (1977).

78. For a discussion of the survival of alimony see section 16.5, supra, at note 27.

79. Newman v. Burwell, 216 Cal. 608, 15 P.2d 511 (1932); Garber v. Robitshek, 226 Minn. 398, 33 N.W.2d 30 (1948) (under an earlier statute); Guggenheimer v. Guggenheimer, 99 N.H. 399, 112 A.2d 61 (1955); Morris v. Henry, 193 Va. 631, 70 S.E.2d 417 (1952); Caldwell v. Caldwell, 5 Wis.2d 146, 92 N.W.2d 356 (1958); Edelman v. Edelman, 65 Wyo. 271, 199 P.2d 840 (1948), rehearing denied 65 Wyo. 271, 295, 203 P.2d 952 (1949), 62 Harv.L. Rev. 1079 (1949); Annot., 18 A.L.R.2d 1126 (1951).

80. E.g., Ill.—S.H.A. ch. 40, § 510(c) (Supp.1985); Uniform Marriage and Divorce Act § 316(c), 9A Unif.L.Ann. 183 (1979), providing that the child support survives the obligor's death unless otherwise expressly provided in the separation agreement or divorce decree. The Illinois

statute was held constitutional in Kujawinski v. Kujawinski, 71 Ill.2d 563, 17 Ill.Dec. 801, 376 N.E.2d 1382 (1978). West's Rev.Code Wash.Ann. § 26.09.170 (Supp.1986) provides that the child support terminates unless otherwise expressly provided in the agreement or decree.

81. Justice Terrell, dissenting, in Guinta v. Lo Re, 159 Fla. 448, 452, 31 So.2d 704, 706 (1947).

82. Pittman v. Pittman, 419 So.2d 1376 (Ala.1982); Gordon v. Valley National Bank of Arizona, 16 Ariz.App. 195, 492 P.2d 444 (1972); Guinta v. Lo Re, 159 Fla. 448, 31 So.2d 704 (1947); Oetter v. Sandlin's Adm'x, 262 Ky. 355, 90 S.W.2d 350 (1936); Gardine v. Cottey, 360 Mo. 681, 230 S.W.2d 731 (1950) (semble); Lee v. Coffield, 245 N.C. 570, 96 S.E.2d 726 (1957); Robinson v. Robinson, 131 W.Va. 160, 50 S.E.2d 455 (1948), 62 Harv.L.Rev. 1079 (1949); Annot., 18 A.L.R.2d 1126 (1951).

Even in those jurisdictions which hold that the order may not be made enforceable against the obligor's estate the parties may be able to accomplish that result by a provision in their separation agreement which is incorporated in the divorce decree. See, e.g., Hill v. Matthews, 76 N.M. 474, 416 P.2d 144 (1966); Lee v. Coffield, 245 N.C. 570, 96 S.E.2d 726 (1957); Silberman v. Brown, 34 Ohio Op. 295, 72 N.E.2d 267 (1946).

divorce, could only assert a claim for support during the parent's life, and that he should have no better claim when the marriage has ended in divorce.[83] The contrary rule, it is said, leads to inequality in the distribution of estates and upsets dispositions made by the obligor's will.[84] This view is in accord with the generally accepted view in American law that a parent may disinherit his minor children if he wishes, even though this results in their becoming charges on the state.[85] But disinherited children are in fact protected where the marriage does not end in divorce, since in most states the surviving spouse is given a statutory forced share of the deceased's estate which can then be subjected to the child's claim for support.[86]

Where the obligor remarries and has a second family before he dies, the continuation of child support obligations to the children of the first family may result in hardship to those of the second family, where the estate is not large. But this is the same problem which is created when the existence of the second family is asserted as a ground for reducing the child support, and should be dealt with in the same manner.[87] The sensible solution is to give the courts the discretion to apportion the scarce resources in an equitable way in both situations.

As has been indicated, if the court is held to have the power to make a support order which will survive, some cases raise the further question whether the particular order is to be construed as surviving the obligor's death. This should not be the relevant question at all. The relevant question should be whether the death of the obligor is the sort of change in circumstances which justifies a modification of the child support order, the same question with which this entire section is concerned. At the time of the original divorce decree and child support order the court cannot know what the circumstances will be at the time of the obligor's death. It is therefore a mistake to decide whether the support will terminate by reference to what the original order provided. The determining factors should be what equity and fairness demand at the time of the obligor's death, in the light of the circumstances then prevailing.

It must be conceded that the cases do not adopt this analysis. Some of them give the order a literal construction resulting in its survival.[88] Others construe the order more restrictively.[89] It may be easier to read the order so that it does not survive if it contains other financial benefits for the child, such as by requiring the maintenance of a life insurance policy payable to the child.[90] Of course in those states where survival is not permitted as a matter of law, there is no room for construction, but the court in any case may avoid the question of statutory authority by relying upon a construction of the decree.[91]

Treating the question of survival as one of construction of the decree cannot help but produce unwise results in many cases because of the inability of the divorce court to foresee future circumstances. In those states which permit the child support to survive the obligor's death the divorce decree should so provide, with the understanding that, like any other child support decree, the death of the obligor may be a change in circumstances which should lead to a reduction, termination or change in form of the support order.

83. Robinson v. Robinson, 31 W.Va. 160, 50 S.E.2d 455 (1948).

84. Gardine v. Cottey, 360 Mo. 681, 230 S.W.2d 731 (1950).

85. See Uniform Probate Code § 2–302, 8 Unif.L.Ann. 90 (1983), permitting children to be disinherited provided the will states that it is done intentionally.

86. This argument was relied upon in Kujawinski v. Kujawinski, 71 Ill.2d 563, 376 N.E.2d 1382 (1978).

87. See the discussion supra, at notes 60 and 61.

88. Guggenheimer v. Guggenheimer, 99 N.H. 399, 112 A.2d 61 (1955). At some points in the opinion this case seems to support the analysis in the text.

89. Bailey v. Bailey, 86 Nev. 483, 471 P.2d 220 (1970); Prime v. Prime, 172 Or. 34, 139 P.2d 550 (1943); In re Moore's Estate, 34 Tenn.App. 131, 234 S.W.2d 847 (1949); Colombo v. Walker Bank and Trust Co., 26 Utah 2d 350, 489 P.2d 998 (1971); O'Neal v. Morris, 7 Wash.App. 157, 498 P.2d 326 (1972).

90. Riley v. Riley, 131 So.2d 491 (Fla.App.1961).

91. E.g., Prime v. Prime, 172 Or. 34, 139 P.2d 550 (1943).

WESTLAW
REFERENCES

Jurisdiction and Procedure in Modification

child /3 support /10 modifi! modify! amend***
    amendment /s pro +1 rate* rata rating

modifi! modify! amend*** amendment /s support /3 child
    /s "unclean hand" laches (estop! /3 equitab! pais)

Grounds for Modification

child /3 support /s modifi! modif! amend*** amendment
    /s custod! /s remarry! remarri!

sy,di(modifi! modify! /s child /3 support! /s custod! /s
    transfer*** transferab!)

child /3 support! /s terminat! end ending ended stop
    stopp! ceas! cessation discontinu! /s automatic! /s
    dead death die* dying deceas!

fi 419 so2d 1376

§ 17.3 Child Support Orders in Divorce Decrees—Enforcement of Domestic Decrees

Introduction—Scope of the Problem

An earlier section [1] has indicated that many child support awards are insufficient to maintain the child and his custodian, usually his mother, above the level of poverty, making it necessary for the custodian to work outside the home and often also making her dependent upon welfare assistance. Even where the child support award is generous enough to provide a standard of living above the poverty level, it usually is not large enough to permit the child and the custodian to live as well as they did before the divorce. In any event the adequacy or inadequacy of the award is only the beginning of the difficulties which the custodian and child must face. Whatever the award may be, it is obviously of no value to the custodian and child unless it is paid and paid in full. There is ample evidence showing that a very large proportion of child support awards are not paid or not paid in full and on time.[2] This is too often the case even where the non-custodial parent is able to make the payments.[3] The scale and magnitude of the child support orders outstanding which are not being paid have become so great as to constitute a serious national social problem.[4]

The reasons for this are not a mystery. In the first place it is difficult or impossible for the child support payee to obtain legal representation for the enforcement of the child support order. She is often unable to pay a lawyer's fee and there is not enough at stake to resort to the contingent fee device.[5] Although the Uniform Reciprocal Enforcement of Support Act is available in all states,[6] it has not proved to be as effective as its drafters hoped. In the second place, the mobility of child support obligors make it very difficult to locate them even if some lawyer can be persuaded to take the case.[7] In the third place too many judges have been reluctant to impose the stringent penalties, primarily contempt convictions, which might induce a

---

§ 17.3

1. See section 17.1, supra, at note 15.

2. Sorenson and MacDonald, An Analysis of Child-Support Transfers, in Cassetty, The Parental Child-Support Obligation 35, 41 (1983), showing less than 75% of all mothers receiving some payment on their child support awards, and less than 40% of women living below the poverty line receiving payment. L. Weitzman, The Divorce Revolution 283 (1985) cites statistics indicating that less than half of the women awarded child support had received payment in full.

The reasons why fathers fail to pay child support are discussed in D. Chambers, Making Fathers Pay 71–78 (1979) and in L. Weitzman, The Divorce Revolution 295–298 (1985).

3. H. Krause, Child Support in America ch. VII (1981); L. Weitzman, The Divorce Revolution 295 (1985).

4. L. Weitzman, The Divorce Revolution 283 (1985); U.S.Department of Health and Human Services, Office of Child Support Enforcement, Eighth Annual Report to Congress, Child Support Enforcement 1 (1983).

It is important to note that the enforcement problem also involves support for illegitimate children, and that the enforcement procedures discussed here are also available to the custodians of those children. Paternity suits and support for illegitimate children are discussed in section 4.4, supra.

5. Although contingent fees are not generally available in divorce actions, some authorities permit them when the claim is for past due child support. See section 14.7, at note 1, supra. In many states child support claimants may be represented by public officials, such as district or county attorneys, but these officials are often so busy that the representation they can provide is not very effective. See L. Weitzman, The Divorce Revolution 289–290 (1985).

6. This Act is of course available for the enforcement of past due child support payments, but its chief use is in interstate enforcement. It is discussed in detail in section 6.6 supra.

7. L. Weitzman, The Divorce Revolution 286–287 (1985).

higher proportion of obligors to comply with support decrees.[8] Finally, the court delays encountered in enforcement proceedings place such proceedings out of the reach of many, probably most, child support claimants.[9]

The Federal Child Support Enforcement Program

Public and Congressional recognition of the deficiencies in child support enforcement just described led Congress in 1974 to add title IV–D to the Social Security Act.[10] In 1984 title IV–D was amended by the Child Support Enforcement Amendments of 1984.[11] These statutes are parts of the program known as Aid to Families With Dependent Children (AFDC). AFDC uses the familiar device of providing for appropriations of cash to those states which adopt "plans" approved by the Secretary of Health and Human Services for aid to needy families with children.[12] Since the states can hardly afford not to receive the federal funds, the effect of the statutes is to impose upon the states federal requirements concerning, among many other subjects, the enforcement of child support decrees. The 1984 amendments to title IV–D made those requirements very specific and highly detailed[13] and, since the requirements apply to persons who are not receiving AFDC benefits,[14] extremely pervasive. In sum, it is now

federal law rather than state law which governs the methods of enforcing state child support orders.

Although the major function of title IV–D is to force the states to adopt more effective child support enforcement procedures, it also authorizes the creation of federal and state institutions for the provision of assistance to child support claimants. One of these is the Office of Child Support Enforcement (OCSE), created within the Department of Health and Human Services as the chief enforcement agency for the federal-state program.[15] The responsibilities of OCSE include the establishment of standards for the state programs, the evaluation of those programs, the maintenance of records of their operations, the approval of applications to use the United States courts for the enforcement of child support orders,[16] and the operation of the Parent Locator Service.[17] The Parent Locator Service, another such institution, provides for "authorized persons"[18] the address and place of employment of any absent parent and is permitted to use for obtaining this information the records of the Department of Health and Human Services and of all other departments and agencies of the United States government.[19] The effect of this is to make available to the claimant for child support the facilities of the Social Security Administration, the In-

---

8. Id. at 283–285, 292–295.

9. Id. at 291.

10. Pub.L. 93–647, 88 Stat. 2337 (1974), which appears as 42 U.S.C.A. §§ 651–665.

11. Pub.L. 98–378, 98 Stat. 1305 (1984). The 1974 version of title IV–D was amended in some respects between 1974 and 1984, but in the discussion which follows the 1984 version of the law, including all prior provisions will be the basis for analysis.

12. 42 U.S.C.A. §§ 601, 652.

13. The provisions of these Acts are described in detail in Dodson and Horowitz, Child Support Enforcement Amendments of 1984: New Tools for Enforcement, 10 Fam.L.Rptr. 3051 (1984); U.S.Department of Health and Human Services, Office of Child Support Enforcement, Horowitz, Dodson, Haynes, Remedies Under the Child Support Enforcement Amendments of 1984 (1985).

The effective date of the 1984 amendments imposing these sweeping requirements upon the state procedures for the enforcement of child support decrees was October 1, 1985. Pub.L. 98–378 § 3(g), 98 Stat. 1311 (1984), set out as a note to 42 U.S.C.A. § 654.

14. 42 U.S.C.A. § 666(a); 45 C.F.R. § 302.33(a) (1985).

15. 42 U.S.C.A. § 652. OCSE has regional offices as well as the central office in Washington. See 45 C.F.R. § 301.1 (1985), and U.S.Department of Health and Human Services, Office of Child Support Enforcement, Adams, Cooper and Kaye, A Guide for Judges in Child Support Enforcement ch. II (1982).

16. 42 U.S.C.A. § 652(a).

17. 42 U.S.C.A. § 652(a)(9).

18. 42 U.S.C.A. § 653(c), defining authorized person to include an agent or attorney of a state; a court having authority to issue a child support order, or a parent, guardian, attorney or agent for a child other than a child receiving aid under the statute. For a discussion of the sources of information available to support claimants see U.S. Department of Health and Human Services, Office of Child Support Enforcement, Horowitz, Dodson, Haynes, Remedies Under the Child Support Enforcement Amendments of 1984 ch. 7 (1984).

19. 42 U.S.C.A. § 653.

ternal Revenue Service, the armed forces or of any other federal government agency for the purpose of locating any non-paying support obligor. Title IV–D also requires the states to set up Parent Locator Services to call on state agencies to furnish addresses and places of employment of child support obligors.[20]

Other institutional arrangements imposed upon the states by title IV–D include the establishment of state IV–D agencies designed to assist child support claimants in enforcing their claims;[21] the requirement that the states set up "expedited processes" for the enforcement of support orders;[22] the establishment of some system for keeping track of support payments and the amounts withheld from the obligor's income and, with the assistance of the federal government the establishment of automatic data processing services for this purpose;[23] and the development by the states of child support guidelines to be used in arriving at child support awards by the state courts.[24]

In addition to these institutional or organizational devices in aid of child support collection, title IV–D requires the states to adopt certain procedural methods for enforcing support awards. The states must now authorize their courts to impose liens upon both real and personal property to cover amounts of overdue support,[25] and must also authorize their courts to require absent parents to provide security in the form of a bond or other guarantee as a means of securing the payment of overdue support.[26] These enforcement methods have been available in some states in the past, although not often used. Title IV–D also requires two new forms of enforcement, the interception of income tax refunds, both state and federal,[27] and, most important of all the methods, mandatory income withholding.[28]

The income withholding provisions of title IV–D are rigorous, specific and prescribe in detail the procedure to be followed. Although space does not permit an exhaustive discussion of the procedural steps, an account will be given here of their major aspects.[29] The attorney on either side of a child support enforcement case must of course be familiar not only with the federal statutory provisions but also with the provisions of his state statutes enacted in compliance with the federal program.

The system for mandatory withholding of child support from the income of the obligor begins with the requirement that all state child support decrees must contain a provision for withholding amounts from wages.[30] This may include withholding from other forms of income than wages.[31] Even those orders entered before the effective date of title IV–D must be enforceable by withholding regardless of the fact that no provision for withholding was included in the original or-

---

20. 45 C.F.R. § 320.35 (1985). Parents and guardians need not exhaust state remedies before applying to the federal Parent Locator Service. 42 U.S.C.A. § 653(f).

21. 42 U.S.C.A. § 654(3). The regulations impose various duties on "IV–D agencies". 45 C.F.R. §§ 302.31, 302.32, 302.33 (1985). 45 C.F.R. § 301.1 (1985) defines "IV–D agency" as the state organizational unit having the responsibility for administering the state plan under title IV–D of the Social Security Act.

22. 42 U.S.C.A. § 666(a)(2). Expedited processes are defined as administrative or judicial processes which increase effectiveness and speed collections sufficiently to meet the deadlines set by the regulations. 45 C.F.R. § 303.101, (a), (b)(2) (1985).

23. 42 U.S.C.A. §§ 654(16), 666(b)(5).

24. 42 U.S.C.A. § 667. The state guidelines must be set up by October 1, 1987. 45 C.F.R. § 302.56 (1985).

25. 42 U.S.C.A. § 666(a)(4). See also 45 C.F.R. § 303.103 (1985). This and the other procedures for bonds, tax refund intercepts, and income withholding

went into effect on October 1, 1985. Pub.L. 98–378, § 3(g) (1) and (2), 98 Stat. 1311 (1984).

26. 42 U.S.C.A. § 666(a)(6); 45 C.F.R. § 303.104 (1985).

27. 42 U.S.C.A. §§ 664(a), 666(a)(3).

28. 42 U.S.C.A. § 666(a)(1), (b).

29. The account in the text is indebted to the excellent article, Dodson and Horowitz, Child Support Enforcement Amendments of 1984: New Tools for Enforcement, 10 Fam.L.Rptr. 3051 (1984).

For a discussion of the constitutional validity of the withholding procedure, see Motz and Baida, The Due Process Rights of Post Judgment Debtors and Child Support Obligors, 45 Md.L.Rev. 61 (1986).

30. 42 U.S.C.A. § 664(a)(8).

31. 45 C.F.R. § 303.100(f) (1985) provides that the state may extend the system of withholding to include withholding from forms of income other than wages. See also 42 U.S.C.A. § 666(b)(8).

der.[32] The withholding system must apply to those obligees whose child support decrees are being enforced by the state IV–D agency, but the state may extend the benefits of the system to other obligees as well, such as those being represented by private attorneys.[33]

The withholding system normally will come into operation when arrears under the child support order equal one month's support.[34] This means, for example, that the procedure begins when one month's support is one day late, or when the arrears resulting from partial payments have accumulated to an amount totaling one month's support. This obviously makes it essential that each state set up a system from which the state IV–D agency can immediately determine whether arrears have accrued, since the state is not permitted to wait to act until the support claimant applies for withholding or until some other action is taken.[35]

As soon as the arrears accrue, the state must take steps to send an "advance notice" to the obligor, containing a statement of the amount due, the potential withholding, and other information, including the procedures available to the obligor to contest the with-

holding.[36] If the obligor notifies the state that he wishes to contest the withholding, within forty-five days he must be given a hearing and a determination must be made as to whether the withholding shall occur.[37] If there is no contest, or if the contest is unsuccessful, a notice must then be sent to the obligor's employer indicating the amount to be withheld and including certain other information.[38] The only grounds for contesting the withholding are that mistakes of fact have been made concerning the amount of current or overdue support, or concerning the identity of the obligor.[39] Where the obligor contends that his or the child's circumstances have so changed as to justify reducing or terminating the support, this is not a defense to withholding. He must make these claims in a proceeding to modify the order.[40]

The amount to be withheld must equal the current support installments, with a maximum (including the employer's fee)[41] set by the Consumer Credit Protection Act.[42] If the current support does not equal the maximum, an additional amount may be withheld in order to reduce the arrears.[43] The state law

---

32. 45 C.F.R. § 303.100(h) (1985).

33. 42 U.S.C.A. § 666(c), permitting the states to establish procedures for support payments to be made through the state agency where either the obligor or the child's custodian requests it. See also 45 C.F.R. § 303.100(h) (1985), and U.S. Department of Health and Human Services, Office of Child Support Enforcement, Horowitz, Dodson, Haynes, Remedies Under the Child Support Enforcement Act of 1984, 9 (1985).

34. 42 U.S.C.A. § 666(b)(3)(A). This provision of the Act also permits the inception of the procedure to be when the absent parent requests it, if earlier, or on such earlier date as the state may select.

35. 42 U.S.C.A. § 666(b)(2). 45 C.F.R. § 303.100(a)(4) (1985).

36. 42 U.S.C.A. § 666(b)(4)(A). This section also requires that all procedural due process requirements of the state must be complied with. 42 U.S.C.A. § 666(b)(4)(B) excuses the advance notice requirement if the state had a withholding system in effect on August 16, 1984 which provided procedural due process. The cases which arose under the earlier version of the tax refund intercept provision seem to indicate that procedural due process requires some form of notice in advance of the withholding, however. See, e.g., Nelson v. Regan, 731 F.2d 105 (2d Cir.1984), cert. den. 105 S.Ct. 175 (1984); Marcello v. Regan, 574 F.Supp. 586 (D.R.I.1983). But see Jahn v. Regan, 584 F.Supp. 399 (E.D.Mich.1984).

Clark, Domestic Rel., 2nd Ed. HBSE—25

37. 42 U.S.C.A. § 666(b)(4)(A); 45 C.F.R. § 303.100(c) (1985). See Varner v. Bard, 622 F.Supp. 1518 (M.D.Pa. 1985).

38. 42 U.S.C.A. § 666(b)(6)(A); 45 C.F.R. § 303.100(c) (1985).

39. 42 U.S.C.A. § 666(b)(4)(A); 45 C.F.R. § 303.100(a) (5) (1985).

40. Modification of child support orders is discussed in section 17.2, supra.

41. 42 U.S.C.A. § 666(b)(1). The employer's fee is to be set by the state.

42. 15 U.S.C.A. § 1673(b) provides that the maximum proportion of aggregate disposable earnings for any week which may be garnished for support may not exceed fifty percent if the person is supporting a spouse or dependent child; sixty percent if the person is not supporting a spouse or dependent child; with the additional provision that the proportions are fifty-five and sixty-five percent if the support is more than twelve weeks in arrears.

43. 42 U.S.C.A. § 666(b)(1); 45 C.F.R. § 303.100(a) (1985). If there is more than one withholding notice outstanding against the same obligor, the state must allocate the amounts available, giving priority to current support up to the maximum limits.

must contain provisions governing the termination of withholding.[44]

The employer who receives the notice of withholding must withhold the prescribed amount from the obligor's wages and pay the amount to the proper state agency, after retaining his fee.[45] He is liable to the state for any amount which he fails to withhold after receiving proper notice.[46] The state must provide for a fine against any employer who discharges or takes disciplinary action against an employee because of the burdens imposed by the withholding process.[47] If there is more than one notice for withholding against a parent, the state must allocate the amounts available for withholding among the claimants, giving priority to current support up to the statutory limits.[48]

As has been indicated,[49] another method of collecting unpaid child support is provided by the federal and state tax refund intercept programs.[50] Both programs permit the state IV–D agencies to initiate action which will result in the diversion of any tax refunds payable to support obligors either to the state itself if the child has been supported by AFDC, or to the child's custodian in the case of non-AFDC claimants. The benefits of either the federal or the state programs are open only to the states themselves or to clients of state IV–D agencies.[51] This means that if an attorney for a private client wishes to collect child support by reaching the obligor's tax refund, he must refer her to the state IV–D agency. Under either federal or

state program the tax refund may be reached only to pay overdue support.[52] It may not be relied on to pay current support, unlike the income withholding program. The federal and state tax refund intercept programs also differ from the income withholding program in that there is no limit imposed by the Consumer Credit Protection Act on the amount of the refund which may be applied to the child support obligation, so that if necessary the entire refund may be so applied.

A state as assignee of an AFDC recipient, or a client of a IV–D agency becomes eligible for the federal income tax refund intercept program only when a prescribed amount of child support has been due and unpaid for a prescribed period.[53] Interception of the federal refund is initiated by the state IV–D agency.[54] A written advance notice must be sent by the Office of Child Support Enforcement or by the state IV–D agency to the taxpayer, telling him that his overdue support debt will be referred to the Internal Revenue Service for collection by the tax refund interception.[55] In addition the notice must contain other prescribed information, including the taxpayer's right to contest the determination that he owes the support. A later notice is given the taxpayer by the Internal Revenue Service that the interception of the revenue has been made.[56] At the time of interception the Internal Revenue Service must inform the spouse of the obligor of the steps he may take to protect his share of the refund, where the refund arises on a joint return.[57] It is uncer-

---

44. 42 U.S.C.A. § 666(b)(10). But the payment of overdue support may not be made the sole basis for terminating withholding. 45 C.F.R. § 303.100(a)(9) (1985).

45. 42 U.S.C.A. § 666(b)(6)(A)(i). 45 C.F.R. § 303.100(d)(ii) (1985) requires that the amount withheld be sent to the state within ten days.

46. 42 U.S.C.A. § 666(b)(6)(C).

47. 42 U.S.C.A. § 666(b)(6)(D).

48. 45 C.F.R. § 303.100(a)(6) (1985).

49. See the text at note 27, supra.

50. These programs are described in detail in U.S. Department of Health and Human Services, Office of Child Support Enforcement, Horowitz, Dodson, Haynes, Remedies Under the Child Support Enforcement Amendments of 1984, ch. 3, 4 (1985). The intercept program has been held to reach excess earned-income credits, treating

them as overpayments of tax, when authorized by I.R.C. § 6401(b). Sorenson v. Secretary of the Treasury of U.S., 475 U.S. 851, 106 S.Ct. 1600, 89 L.Ed.2d 855 (1986).

51. 42 U.S.C.A. §§ 664, 666(a)(3), 657(B)(4).

52. 42 U.S.C.A. §§ 664(a), 666(a)(3)(A). "Overdue support" is defined in 45 C.F.R. § 301.1 (1985).

53. 45 C.F.R. § 303.72(a) (1985).

54. 45 C.F.R. § 302.72(b) (1985).

55. 42 U.S.C.A. § 664(a)(3)(A); 45 C.F.R. § 303.72(e)(1) (1985).

56. 45 C.F.R. § 303.72(e)(2) (1985).

57. 42 U.S.C.A. § 664(a)(3)(A), (B) and (C); 45 C.F.R. § 303.72(e)(4) (1985). The courts have not provided us with a clear analysis of the availability of the refund for child support when it results from a joint return by the obligor and his second spouse. See, e.g. Jahn v. Regan,

tain whether the refund intercept program may be applied to refunds resulting from the earned income credit.[58]

The federal taxpayer may, either before or after the interception of his refund, contest the interception and then must be given a hearing on his complaint.[59] The hearing must meet the requirements of procedural due process.[60] The cases are not very specific on just what this means, but it seems to mean that an administrative hearing on the basis of the relevant documents plus an opportunity for the taxpayer to discuss the case with the state official would be sufficient.[61] Presumably some judicial review would also be available.[62]

The states are also required to provide a state income tax refund intercept program.[63] Like the federal program, this is available only to the state if there has been an assignment of the support obligation by an AFDC

recipient, or to a parent applying for IV–D agency services.[64] The obligor must be given advance notice of the intercept [65] and an opportunity to contest the intercept.[66] Distribution of the refund and return of any excess to the taxpayer are also required.[67]

State Methods of Enforcement

Since most states have begun to enact legislation responding to the requirements of title IV–D of the Social Security Act, many of the remedies just described in the discussion of that Act now exist in the states. Thus many states have prescribed mandatory income withholding,[68] some have provisions for the interception or offset of state income tax refunds,[69] some now provide expedited judicial or administrative processes,[70] some provide the courts with authority to impose liens for the collection of child support [71] and with authority to require the posting of a bond or

584 F.Supp. 399 (E.D.Mich.1984); Sorenson v. Secretary of the Treasury of U.S., 557 F.Supp. 729 (W.D.Wash. 1982), affirmed on other grounds 752 F.2d 1433 (9th Cir. 1985).

58. Sorenson v. Secretary of the Treasury of U.S., 752 F.2d 1433 (9th Cir.1985), cert. granted 472 U.S. 1016, 105 S.Ct. 3475, 87 L.Ed.2d 611 (1985) and cases cited.

59. 45 C.F.R. § 303.72(f) (1985), providing for an administrative review.

60. The leading case on this is Mathews v. Eldridge, 424 U.S. 319, 96 S.Ct. 893, 47 L.Ed.2d 18 (1976), discussing in detail the varying requirements of due process in a variety of circumstances. The program has been held constitutional in McClelland v. Massinga, 786 F.2d 1205 (4th Cir.1986).

61. Presley v. Regan, 604 F.Supp. 609 (N.D.N.Y.1985); Nelson v. Regan, 560 F.Supp. 1101 (D.Conn.1983), affirmed 731 F.2d 105 (2d Cir.1984), cert. denied 469 U.S. 853, 105 S.Ct. 175, 83 L.Ed.2d 110 (1984); Marcello v. Regan, 574 F.Supp. 586 (D.R.I. 1983).

62. Marcello v. Regan, 574 F.Supp. 586 (D.R.I.1983).

63. 42 U.S.C.A. § 666(a)(3).

64. 45 C.F.R. § 303.102(a)(1) (1985). Most of the details of this program are left to the state statutes.

65. 45 C.F.R. § 303.102(d) (1985).

66. 45 C.F.R. § 303.102(e) (1985).

67. 45 C.F.R. § 303.102(g) (1985).

68. E.g., Alaska Stat. § 47.23.062 (Supp.1986) (includes all income); Ariz.Rev.Stat. § 12–2454 (Supp.1986) (includes all income); West's Ann.Cal.Civ.Code § 4701 (Supp.1987); Colo.Rev.Stat. § 14–14–107 (Supp.1986); Conn.Gen.Stat.Ann. § 52–362 (1986); West's Fla.Stat. Ann. § 61.181 (Supp.1987); Ill.—S.H.A. ch. 40, § 706.1 (Supp.1986); Kan.Sess.L. ch. 115, § 2 ff. (1985); Mass.G.L.

A. ch. 208, § 36 (Supp.1986), ch. 209, § 32E (Supp.1986); N.J.Stat.Ann. §§ 2A:17–56.7 to 2A:17–56.151 (Supp.1986); N.Y.—McKinney's Civ.P.L. & R. §§ 5241, 5242 (Supp. 1987) (includes all income); Or.Rev.Stat. § 25.050 (1985); Vernon's Tex.Code Ann., Fam.Code § 14.43 (Supp.1987); Va.Code, § 63.1–250.3 (Supp.1986); West's Rev.Code Wash.Ann. § 26.18.060 (1986).

Cases dealing with the procedure in wage withholding or garnishment, including the requirement of a pre-garnishment hearing, are Lang v. Superior Court, 153 Cal. App.3d 510, 200 Cal.Rptr. 526 (1984); In re Marriage of Barnes, 692 P.2d 329 (Colo.App.1984) (no hearing required); In re Marriage of McCue, 645 P.2d 854 (Colo. App.1982); Skinner v. Skinner, 252 Ga. 512, 314 S.W.2d 897 (1984); Sheahan v. Department of Liquor Control, 44 Ohio App.2d 393, 339 N.E.2d 840 (1974); Hehr v. Tucker, 256 Or. 254, 472 P.2d 797 (1970) (no hearing required); State ex rel. Cox v. Cox, 31 Or.App. 473, 570 P.2d 988 (1977); Cardenas v. Cardenas, —— R.I. ——, 478 A.2d 968 (1984).

69. E.g., West's Ann.Cal.Govt.Code § 12419.5 (1980); Colo.Rev.Stat. §§ 26–13–111 to 26–13–116 (Supp.1986); Ill.—S.H.A., ch. 15, § 210.05 (Supp.1986); Kan.Stat.Ann. §§ 75–6202 to 75–6214 (Supp.1986); Mass.G.L.A. ch. 62D, §§ 1 to 12 (Supp.1986); N.Y.—McKinney's Tax L. § 171–C (1986 and Supp.1987); and N.Y.—McKinney's Soc.Serv. L. § 111–b (Supp.1987); Or.Rev.Stat. § 293.250 (1986); Va.Code, § 63.1–256 (Supp.1986).

70. E.g., N.Y.—McKinney's Fam.Ct.Act §§ 433, 435 (Supp.1987).

71. E.g., West's Ann.Cal.Civ.Pro.Code § 697.510 (Supp. 1987); Colo.Rev.Stat. § 13–52–102 (1974); Conn.Sess.L., Pub.Act 85–548 (1985); Kan.Sess.L. ch. 115 § 29 (1985); Mass.G.L.A. ch. 209, § 33 (Supp.1986); N.Y.—McKinney's Fam.Ct.Act § 460 (Supp.1987); Ohio Rev.Code § 2329.02 (1981); Or. Rev.Stat. § 416.180 (1985).

other security in certain cases.[72] Liens and bonds for security are of course not novel remedies in child support cases. The statutes and the case law of many states have authorized them for years.[73] Other similar remedies have also been available for a long time, such as attachment,[74] sequestration,[75] or the appointment of a receiver.[76] If the obligor attempts to transfer his property to another with inadequate consideration, the child support claimant may reach the property on a theory of fraudulent conveyance.[77]

Enforcement of child support may also be accomplished by a writ of execution.[78] As is the case with alimony,[79] in some jurisdictions the accrual of each installment pursuant to the child support order results in a final judgment for the amount accrued and unpaid, without the necessity of further court action.[80] The effect of this is that a writ of execution may be issued as a matter of course and that

the child's custodian has vested right to the accrued payments.[81] Interest on each installment runs from the date on which it accrues.[82]

In other jurisdictions the accrued installment does not constitute a final judgment which can be the subject of a writ of execution, but the child's custodian must first file a motion for the entry of a judgment for the arrears.[83] Notice of this motion must be given to the obligor, although new personal service on him is not necessary.[84] The amounts due and unpaid may be modified in this proceeding,[85] but when the judgment is given, it may be enforced by execution like other judgments.

There is substantial authority that the child support obligation may be enforced against spendthrift trust property of which the obligor is the beneficiary.[86] "Spendthrift

72. E.g., Conn.Gen.Stat.Ann. § 46b–215 (1986); West's Fla.Stat.Ann. § 61.13(1)(b) (1985); Ill.—S.H.A. ch. 40, § 1361 (1980); Mass.G.L.A. ch. 208, § 36 (Supp.1986); N.J.Stat.Ann. § 9:17–53(c) (Supp.1986); N.Y.—McKinney's Fam.Ct.Act § 471 (1983); Or.Rev.Stat. § 25.230 (1985); Vernon's Tex.Code Ann., Fam.Code § 14.42 (1986); Va.Code, § 63.1–267.1 (Supp.1986); West's Rev. Code Wash.Ann. § 26.18.150 (1986).

73. This may be by virtue of statute, or by an express provision in the decree. Annot., 59 A.L.R.2d 656, 665 (1958). The lien may not attach to equitable interests in property. Action Realty Co., Inc. v. Miller, 191 Neb. 381, 215 N.W.2d 629 (1974). On the requirement of a bond, see State ex rel. Lay v. District Court, Fourth Judicial District in and for Ravalli County, 122 Mont. 61, 198 P.2d 761 (1948); Dubois v. Dubois, 121 N.H. 664, 433 A.2d 1277 (1981).

74. Langville v. Langville, 191 Md. 103, 60 A.2d 206 (1948).

75. Fox v. Fox, 276 App.Div. 859, 93 N.Y.S.2d 620 (2d Dep't 1949).

76. Bruton v. Tearle, 7 Cal.2d 48, 59 P.2d 953 (1936), 10 So.Cal.L.Rev. 496 (1937).

77. Robertson v. Robertson, 123 Ill.App.3d 323, 78 Ill. Dec. 593, 462 N.E.2d 712 (1984).

78. Wolfe v. Wolfe, 30 Cal.2d 1, 180 P.2d 345 (1947); Gray v. Gray, 238 Iowa 723, 27 N.W.2d 123 (1947). A decree providing for payment on a sliding scale dependent upon the husband's earnings was held sufficiently definite to be enforced in Vollenhover v. Vollenhover, 4 Ill.App.2d 44, 123 N.E.2d 114 (1954). Execution was stayed in Harmon v. Harmon, 26 Utah 2d 436, 491 P.2d 231 (1971) on the ground that this preserved in the obligor's hands assets which could be used to support the child in the future, certainly a very dubious ground for in effect excusing a past duty of support. The execution

may finally result in a judicial sale of the judgment debtor's property. Gonzalez v. Gonzalez, 103 N.M. 157, 703 P.2d 934 (1985).

79. See section 16.5, supra, at note 9.

80. Brandt v. Brandt, 276 F.2d 488 (D.C.Cir.1960); Ortiz v. Ortiz, 180 Kan. 334, 304 P.2d 490 (1956); Martin v. Martin, 59 Wash.2d 468, 368 P.2d 170 (1962); Korczyk v. Solonka, 130 W.Va. 211, 42 S.E.2d 814 (1947).

81. Martin v. Martin, 59 Wash.2d 468, 368 P.2d 170 (1962). There is apparently no constitutional requirement that the obligor be given a hearing before execution is issued. Brown v. Liberty Loan Corp. of Duval, 539 F.2d 1355 (5th Cir.1977), cert. denied 430 U.S. 949, 97 S.Ct. 1588, 51 L.Ed.2d 797 (1977), notwithstanding Sniadach v. Family Finance Corp. of Bay View, 395 U.S. 337, 89 S.Ct. 1820, 23 L.Ed.2d 349 (1969) and Fuentes v. Shevin, 407 U.S. 67, 92 S.Ct. 1983, 32 L.Ed.2d 556 (1972).

82. Larsen v. Larsen, 9 Utah 2d 160, 340 P.2d 421 (1959). But see Griffin v. Avery, 120 N.H. 783, 424 A.2d 175 (1980).

83. Smith v. Smith, 217 F.2d 917 (6th Cir.1954) (New York law); Brun v. Rembert, 227 Ark. 241, 297 S.W.2d 940 (1957); Langville v. Langville, 191 Md. 103, 60 A.2d 206 (1948); Federbush v. Federbush, 5 N.J.Super. 107, 68 A.2d 473 (1949).

84. Smith v. Smith, 217 F.2d 917 (6th Cir.1954); Sewell v. Trimble, 172 F.2d 27 (D.C.Cir.1948).

85. Federbush v. Federbush, 5 N.J.Super. 107, 68 A.2d 473; Annot., 6 A.L.R.2d 1277 (1949). The corresponding rule with respect to alimony is discussed in section 16.5, supra.

86. In re Matt, 105 Ill.2d 330, 85 Ill.Dec. 505, 473 N.E.2d 1310 (1985); Howard v. Spragins, 350 So.2d 318 (Ala.1977), citing other cases; Hurley v. Hurley, 107 Mich.App. 249, 309 N.W.2d 225 (1981); E. Griswold,

trust" here means a trust in which the interest of the beneficiary cannot be assigned by him or reached by his creditors.[87] On the other hand, if the trust is a discretionary one, that is, by its terms the beneficiary is entitled only to so much of the income or principal as the trustee in his uncontrolled discretion may decide to give him, some cases seem to take the position that the trust may not be reached to pay for the support of the beneficiary's child,[88] but the better view is certainly that the trust property is subject to the claim for child support, either because the settlor would have wished this result, or because the restriction in the trust should be overridden by the policy that child support claims are more important that other claims and must be enforced wherever possible.[89]

Although ordinarily the child's custodian is the proper party to initiate proceedings to enforce the child support decree,[90] on occasion a public officer may be the property party,[91] or the child himself may do so.[92]

Until title IV–D of the Social Security Act transformed the enforcement of child support claims, the usual sanction for non-payment was a proceeding for contempt. Contempt is

still widely used and has been found to be effective if it results in a high proportion of jail sentences and if the enforcement process begins without delay when payments are missed.[93] The use of contempt for this purpose, with the possibility that the obligor will be sentenced to jail, does not violate state constitutional provisions forbidding imprisonment for debt.[94] Contempt may be relied upon to enforce the child support decree even where that decree contains provisions which the court would not be permitted to include, so long as the decree is based upon an agreement of the parties.[95] And so long as the child support decree was based upon jurisdiction of the person and subject matter, it is enforceable by contempt even though it may have been erroneously entered.[96]

Contempt proceedings which arise out of the enforcement of child support decrees may be either criminal or civil in nature. The distinction is well recognized and turns on the purpose of the proceeding.[97] If the alleged contempt consists in the past wilful violation of the child support decree, so that the purpose of the proceeding is to punish an affront to the court's authority, the contempt is criminal.[98] If, on the other hand, the purpose of

Spendthrift Trusts §§ 333–336 (2d ed.1947); Annot., 91 A.L.R.2d 262, 271 (1963).

87. II A. Scott, The Law of Trusts § 151 (3d ed.1967).

88. Cases are cited in Howard v. Spragins, 350 So.2d 318, 321 (Ala.1977), and in Annot., 91 A.L.R.2d 262, 281 (1963). See also Restatement (Second) of Trusts § 155 (1959); II A. Scott, The Law of Trusts § 155 (3d ed.1967). Even under this view of the law the trustee may be liable to the child support claimant if he pays the beneficiary after he has been served with process in a proceeding by the claimant to reach the trust property. Restatement (Second) of Trusts § 155(2) (1959).

89. E. Griswold, Spendthrift Trusts § 337 (2d ed.1947). Where the child's father is both beneficiary and settlor of the trust, it has been held that the trust property may be reached to collect child support. McLean v. McLean, 273 S.C. 571, 257 S.E.2d 751 (1979).

90. Savell v. Savell, 213 Miss. 869, 58 So.2d 41 (1952); Knight v. Armstrong, 303 P.2d 421 (Okl.1956); Korczyk v. Solonka, 130 W.Va. 211, 42 S.E.2d 814 (1947); Annot., 61 A.L.R.2d 1083, 1096 (1958). It has been held that the custodian has standing to institute contempt proceedings even though she has assigned to the state under AFDC her right to support payments. Erb v. Erb, 573 P.2d 849 (Wyo.1978).

91. Jenkins v. Jenkins, 19 Conn.Supp. 213, 111 A.2d 21 (1954).

92. Gibbs v. Giles, 96 Nev. 243, 607 P.2d 118 (1980). Contra, where the claim is for arrears in support payments, In re Marriage of Utigard, 126 Cal.App.3d 133, 178 Cal.Rptr. 546 (1981).

93. D. Chambers, Making Fathers, Pay ch. 6 (1979). This study found that the population of the county involved also was related to the effectiveness of support enforcement.

94. Application of Martin, 76 Idaho, 179, 279 P.2d 873 (1955); Brown v. Brown, 287 Md. 273, 412 A.2d 396 (1980). For similar cases dealing with alimony, see section 16.6, supra. The Brown case held, however, that contempt does not lie to enforce a stepfather's contractual duty to support his stepdaughter.

95. Ovaitt v. Ovaitt, 43 Mich.App. 628, 204 N.W.2d 753 (1972).

96. Robinson v. Robinson, 169 W.Va. 425, 288 S.E.2d 161 (1982).

97. Furtado v. Furtado, 380 Mass. 137, 402 N.E.2d 1024 (1980).

98. Marshall v. Marshall, 191 Colo. 165, 551 P.2d 709 (1976); Furtado v. Furtado, 380 Mass. 137, 402 N.E.2d 1024 (1980).

the proceeding is to compel future compliance with the child support decree, the contempt is civil.[99] It is important to maintain this distinction because in most jurisdictions the criminal contempt proceeding must comply with all of the procedural requirements of a criminal prosecution.[1] These include the appointment of counsel for indigent defendants,[2] adequate notice of the charges and an opportunity to meet them,[3] proof beyond a reasonable doubt that the violation occurred and was wilful,[4] and in most jurisdictions a trial by jury.[5] The character of the proceeding must ordinarily be established before the trial.[6] The sentence in a criminal contempt case must be for a definite period.[7]

If the contempt proceeding is civil in the sense just defined, it must ordinarily be brought in the court which entered the decree for support.[8] The defendant must have notice or knowledge of the proceeding and an opportunity to be heard.[9] Some courts have held that if he is indigent he is entitled to have counsel furnished by the state,[10] while others take the position that his right to counsel must be determined on a case by case basis, the outcome depending upon the complexity of the case and similar factors.[11] Before finding the defendant in contempt the court must find that he has the present ability to comply with the child support decree.[12] Without such a finding the result of the proceeding would be to sentence the defendant to jail for an indefinite period, thereby violating the constitutional prohibition on imprisonment for debt.[13] The contempt decree of course should

---

99. Marshall v. Marshall, 191 Colo. 165, 551 P.2d 709 (1976); Eliker v. Eliker, 206 Neb. 764, 295 N.W.2d 268 (1980); Barrett v. Barrett, 470 Pa. 253, 368 A.2d 616 (1977).

1. Furtado v. Furtado, 380 Mass. 137, 402 N.E.2d 1024 (1980); Note, The Indigent Defendant's Right to Court-Appointed Counsel in Civil Contempt Proceedings for Nonpayment of Child Support, 50 U.Chi.L.Rev. 326 (1983).

2. Argersinger v. Hamlin, 407 U.S. 25, 92 S.Ct. 2006, 32 L.Ed.2d 530 (1972); In re Gault, 387 U.S. 1, 87 S.Ct. 1428, 18 L.Ed.2d 527 (1967); Bowen v. Bowen, 454 So.2d 565 (Fla.App.1984), affirmed on other grounds 471 So.2d 1274 (Fla.1985); Note, The Indigent Defendant's Right to Court-Appointed Counsel in Civil Contempt Proceedings for Nonpayment of Child Support, 50 U.Chi.L.Rev. 326, 330 (1983).

3. Furtado v. Furtado, 380 Mass. 137, 402 N.E.2d 1024 (1980).

4. Bowen v. Bowen, 471 So.2d 1274 (Fla.1985). "Wilful" in this context means that at the time of the failure to make the payments the defendant had the means of making them.

5. Bloom v. Illinois, 391 U.S. 194, 88 S.Ct. 1477, 20 L.Ed.2d 522 (1968). But see State ex rel. Dwyer v. Dwyer, 299 Or. 108, 698 P.2d 957 (1985).

6. Furtado v. Furtado, 380 Mass. 137, 402 N.E.2d 1024 (1980).

7. State ex rel. Dwyer v. Dwyer, 299 Or. 108, 698 P.2d 957 (1985).

8. Gonzales v. District Court In and For Otero County, 629 P.2d 1074 (Colo.1981).

9. Courtney v. Courtney, 16 Ohio App.3d 329, 475 N.E.2d 1284 (1984). The defendant must also have knowledge or notice of the child support order before he may be charged with violating it. People in Interest of F. S. B., 640 P.2d 268 (Colo.App.1981). But new acquisition of in personam jurisdiction in the contempt proceeding is not necessary if there was personal jurisdiction for pur-

poses of the child support order, the contempt proceeding being considered a continuation of the support proceeding. Brown v. Brown, 183 Colo. 356, 516 P.2d 1129 (1973). On arrest in a contempt proceeding see Lester v. Bennett, 1 Va.App. 47, 333 S.E.2d 366 (1985).

10. Ridgway v. Baker, 720 F.2d 1409 (5th Cir.1983); Lake v. Speziale, 580 F.Supp. 1318 (D.Conn.1984) (semble); Mastin v. Fellerhoff, 526 F.Supp. 969 (S.D.Ohio 1981); Young v. Whitworth, 522 F.Supp. 759 (S.D.Ohio 1981); Otton v. Zaborac, 525 P.2d 537 (Alaska 1974); Schock v. Sheppard, 7 Ohio App.3d 45, 453 N.E.2d 1292 (1982); Tetro v. Tetro, 86 Wash.2d 252, 544 P.2d 17 (1975); Note, The Indigent Defendant's Right to Court-Appointed Counsel in Civil Contempt Proceedings for Nonpayment of Child Support, 50 U.Chi.L.Rev. 326 (1983); Hermann and Donahue, Fathers Behind Bars: The Right to Counsel in Civil Contempt Proceedings, 14 N.M.L.Rev. 275 (1984). Although counsel may be waived in such cases, the waiver must be made knowingly and intelligently. Padilla v. Padilla, 645 P.2d 1327 (Colo.App. 1982).

11. Sword v. Sword, 399 Mich. 367, 249 N.W.2d 88 (1976); Duval v. Duval, 114 N.H. 422, 322 A.2d 1 (1974); Jolly v. Wright, 300 N.C. 83, 265 S.E.2d 135 (1980). Meyer v. Meyer, 414 A.2d 236 (Me.1980) seems to take the view that counsel should never be provided in these cases.

12. Marshall v. Marshall, 191 Colo. 165, 551 P.2d 709 (1976); Lamb v. Eads, 346 N.W.2d 830 (Iowa 1984); Eliker v. Eliker, 206 Neb. 764, 295 N.W.2d 268 (1980); Courtney v. Courtney, 16 Ohio App.3d 329, 475 N.E.2d 1284 (1984). The implications of the requirement of ability to pay are discussed infra, at note 29.

13. Although the cases which hold that the constitutional prohibition is not violated by the enforcement of child support or alimony by civil contempt often rely on some distinction between a "debt" and a child support or alimony obligation, the real reason for their result is that imprisonment for debt was prohibited because it could be indefinite, it being no defense that the debtor was unable

state that the defendant is only sentenced to remain in jail until he purges himself of the contempt, that is, until he begins making the support payments.[14] The contempt order may, in appropriate circumstances, include a provision that the party violating the child support order pay the other party's counsel fees.[15]

Defenses Against Enforcement

Events subsequent to the child support order may provide the obligor with a defense against its enforcement. To some extent these are the same kinds of events which might entitle him to a reduction or termination of the order in a proceeding for modification.[16] The issue here, however, is whether the events relied upon are sufficient to warrant the court in refusing contempt, execution or other methods of enforcement in the absence of any proceeding for modification of the order.

It must be emphasized at this point that the defenses to be discussed may apply to some forms of enforcement, such as contempt or execution, but that they are not permitted to apply to those forms of enforcement imposed upon the states by title IV–D of the Social Security Act. As has been indicated,[17] the possible defenses to mandatory income withholding are sharply limited.

The obligor's inability to make the payments is a defense to contempt.[18] The burden of proving inability to pay the child support is sometimes said to rest on the defendant,[19] but some courts seem to mean by this only that the defendant has the burden of producing evidence on the issue, after which the court should make its determination on the basis of all the evidence, with the ultimate burden of persuasion resting on the claimant.[20] The courts seldom define what they mean by inability to pay,[21] which must in any event be excusable and not brought about by the defendant's own fault.[22] The matter is largely left to the trial court's discretion,[23] but that discretion should be exercised on the basis of evidence relating to the defendant's employment history, his education and work skills, the opportunities for work which are available to him, his diligence in trying to find work, and his health and physical capacity for work.[24] If the evidence shows that he is unable to make the payments because he made no diligent effort to find work, he may be held in contempt.[25] The obligor, in order to support the defense, must make a full disclosure of his circumstances, since he is best able to

---

to pay his debts. But in the case of alimony or child support the debtor is said to carry the keys of the prison in his pocket, meaning that he will only be jailed if he is able to pay and he can always purge himself of contempt by making the payments. See, e.g., Ridgway v. Baker, 720 F.2d 1409 (5th Cir.1983); Brown v. Brown, 287 Md. 273, 412 A.2d 396 (1980).

14. Barrett v. Barrett, 470 Pa. 253, 368 A.2d 616 (1977), 81 Dick.L.Rev. 851 (1977). The contempt order must also prescribe conditions for the obligor's release from jail which he is reasonably able to meet. Mays v. Mays, 193 Conn. 261, 476 A.2d 562 (1984).

15. Blair v. Blair, 8 N.C.App. 61, 173 S.E.2d 513 (1970).

16. See section 17.2, supra.

17. See the discussion at notes 39, 55 and 59, supra, indicating that the only grounds for contesting either mandatory income withholding or the tax refund intercept are that the support is not owed, or not owed in the alleged amount, or that there is a mistake in the identity of the obligor.

18. Feazell v. Feazell, 225 Ark. 611, 284 S.W.2d 117 (1955); Gehrkin v. Gehrkin, 216 La. 950, 45 So.2d 89 (1950); Butler v. Butler, 80 Mich.App. 696, 265 N.W.2d 17

(1978); State ex rel. Blackwell v. Blackwell, 181 Or. 157, 179 P.2d 1023 (1947); Bailey v. Bailey, 77 S.D. 546, 95 N.W.2d 533 (1959).

19. Duncan v. Duncan, 417 So.2d 908 (Miss.1982); Ex Parte Lindsey, 561 S.W.2d 572 (Tex.Civ.App.1978).

20. Skinner v. Ruigh, 351 N.W.2d 182 (Iowa 1984); Barrett v. Barrett, 470 Pa. 253, 368 A.2d 616 (1977). Cases both ways are collected in Annot., 53 A.L.R.2d 591 (1957). The similar question arising out of enforcement of alimony decrees is discussed in section 16.6, supra, at note 45.

21. See also section 16.6, at notes 47 to 51, dealing with alimony enforcement.

22. Dyer v. Dyer, 92 Ariz. 49, 373 P.2d 360 (1962); Federbush v. Federbush, 5 N.J.Super. 107, 68 A.2d 473 (1949) (payments not suspended while husband was in jail for a prior contempt).

23. Bailey v. Bailey, 77 S.D. 546, 95 N.W.2d 533 (1959).

24. Sword v. Sword, 399 Mich. 367, 249 N.W.2d 88 (1976).

25. Butler v. Butler, 80 Mich.App. 696, 265 N.W.2d 17 (1978).

prove what his financial means are.[26] If he proves that he is unable to support himself and at the same time make the child support payments, he will not be held in contempt.[27] He may be held in contempt, however, for not paying as much as he was able to even if he was not able to pay the entire amount ordered by the decree.[28]

Although inability to pay bars a conviction for contempt, there is authority that it does not relieve the obligor of his obligation.[29] If he later acquires assets sufficient to satisfy the amount due, they can be subjected to execution. This is the logical outcome of characterizing each installment of child support as a judgment when it comes due and is unpaid, a characterization which inflicts hardship on the husband in other contexts,[30] but which does not operate unfairly here.

In most jurisdictions the statute of limitations applicable to judgments will bar enforcement of the child support decree, to the extent of installments which remain due and unpaid for the statutory period, at least where the jurisdiction adopts the rule that each installment becomes a final judgment when it falls due and is not paid.[31] If the

obligor is outside the state or the custodian is ignorant of his whereabouts, the statute does not run.[32]

If the statute of limitations does not apply for one or another reason, the defendant often raises the defense of laches, perhaps also combined with defenses labeled waiver, estoppel or acquiescence. These defenses are seldom successful.[33] In the first place, it is clear that they cannot be applied to foreclose future support for the child since that would usually prejudice the child's welfare and that may not be allowed solely on the basis of some default on the part of the custodian.[34] The defenses may be applied to claims by the custodian for arrears in support since if successful that will only preclude the custodian from being reimbursed for support already furnished.[35] In most cases this will not affect the child's welfare. The governing principle is that the custodian's failure to enforce the claim may not be allowed to harm the child or deprive him of support. Laches is effective to bar enforcement when there has been a substantial and inexcusable delay in enforcing the claim to arrears of support and the delay has prejudiced the defendant or led him to change his position to such an extent that enforce-

---

26. State ex rel. Blackwell v. Blackwell, 181 Or. 157, 179 P.2d 278 (1947), rehearing denied 181 Or. 157, 179 P.2d 1023 (1947).

27. In re Marriage of Crowley, 663 P.2d 267 (Colo.App. 1983); Haynes v. Haynes, 168 Kan. 219, 212 P.2d 312 (1949).

28. Bailey v. Bailey, 77 S.D. 546, 95 N.W.2d 533 (1959).

29. Gehrkin v. Gehrkin, 216 La. 950, 45 So.2d 89 (1950); Weinand v. Weinand, 286 Minn. 303, 175 N.W.2d 506 (1970).

30. As in the case of laches, for example. For a discussion of this problem in connection with alimony see section 16.6, supra.

31. Hauck v. Schuck, 143 Colo. 324, 353 P.2d 79 (1960); Riney v. Riney, 205 Kan. 671, 473 P.2d 77 (1970) (the statutory revival of dormant judgments may apply to child support); Rybinski v. Rybinski, 333 Mich. 592, 53 N.W.2d 386 (1952); In re Marriage of Holt, 635 S.W.2d 335 (Mo.1982); Britton v. Britton, 100 N.M. 424, 671 P.2d 1135 (1983). But Griffin v. Avery, 120 N.H. 783, 424 A.2d 175 (1980) held that the statute does not begin to run until a judgment is obtained for the arrears, even though each installment may be deemed final for full faith and credit purposes. This unfortunately imposes additional delay and expense on the custodian and of course on the child. Schmidt v. Forehan, 549 S.W.2d 320 (Ky.1977)

held that the statute does not begin to run until the child's emancipation. In a few states it is held that the statute of limitations does not apply to child support decrees. Gehrkin v. Gehrkin, 216 La. 950, 45 So.2d 89 (1950); Miller v. Miller, 153 Neb. 890, 46 N.W.2d 618 (1951). See also Annot., 70 A.L.R.2d 1250 (1960).

Payment by the obligor may amount to an acknowledgment of the debt which tolls the statute of limitations. Duncan v. Roane, 127 So.2d 191 (La.App.1961).

32. Stephenson v. Stephenson, 52 So.2d 684 (Fla.1951); Halmu v. Halmu, 247 Wis. 124, 19 N.W.2d 317 (1945) (semble).

33. Cases are collected in Annot., Laches or Acquiescence as Defense, So As To Bar Recovery of Arrearages of Permanent Alimony or Child Support, 5 A.L.R.4th 1015 (1981).

34. Larsen v. Larsen, 5 Utah 2d 224, 300 P.2d 596 (1956).

35. Padgett v. Padgett, 472 A.2d 849 (D.C.App.1984), appeal after remand 478 A.2d 1098 (D.C.App. 1984). Some jurisdictions do not make this distinction but hold that laches is never a defense to the collection of child support, apparently assuming that the child's welfare is at stake whether the claim is for future payments or for arrears. Lyon v. Lyon, 143 Vt. 458, 466 A.2d 1186 (1983); Paterson v. Paterson, 73 Wis.2d 150, 242 N.W.2d 907 (1976).

ment of the decree would be inequitable or unjust.[36] Estoppel and acquiescence are defined in somewhat different terms but generally come down to the same requirement that enforcement must be shown to be inequitable under all the circumstances.[37] Most cases which refuse to uphold the defense of laches do so on the ground that although there may have been delay in enforcement, the delay did not cause hardship or unfairness to the defendant.[38] There is is also a tendency in some cases to hold that even if laches does prevent enforcement of the order by contempt proceedings, it does not affect enforcement by execution, being only an equitable doctrine.[39] This distinction makes no sense and should be abandoned. All of these defenses are generally left to the discretion of the trial court, meaning that its decision will be reversed only where it appears that that discretion has been abused.[40]

Similar policies are at work when the custodian's release is asserted as a defense to her enforcement of child support. A good illustration is Pappas v. Pappas.[41] In that case the wife had custody and an order for child support. She then remarried and gave a release of further child support in consideration for the husband's promise to consent to the child's adoption by the stepfather. For some reason the adoption decree was never entered. Two years later the wife sought to set aside the release and collect the arrears of child support. The court rejected her claim on the ground that the release was valid, it was supported by consideration, and the wife and her second husband were well able to support the child. The court was careful to say, however, that such release is effective only as to the wife. If the child should later need support, the husband would have to provide it notwithstanding the release. This result effectuates the husband's interest in being able to rely upon the wife's agreement that she would not attempt to collect the arrears, at the same time ensuring that the child's welfare will not be prejudiced. As in the cases on laches or estoppel, the wife's acts were given legal effect so far as they could be without inflicting harm on the child.

Other cases accept the principles of Pappas.[42] But there are authorities which refuse

---

36. Bozzi v. Bozzi, 177 Conn. 232, 413 A.2d 834 (1979); In re Marriage of Cuberly, 135 Ill.App.3d 55, 90 Ill.Dec. 30, 481 N.E.2d 830 (1985) (laches as applied to the original claim for support); Kinney v. Mathias, 10 Ohio St.3d 72, 461 N.E.2d 901 (1984).

37. Estoppel: Carey v. Carey, 29 Colo.App. 328, 486 P.2d 38 (1971) (estoppel requires a representation to the defendant on which he relied); Merrifield v. Troutner, 269 N.W.2d 136 (Iowa 1978) (distinguishes promissory estoppel from equitable estoppel, holds that promissory estoppel requires a promise by the custodian, reliance by the defendant, with equities favoring the defendant); Davidson v. Van Lengen, 266 N.W.2d 436 (Iowa 1978) (wife held equitably estopped by her twenty-year acquiescence in non-payment); Conrad v. Conrad, 208 Neb. 588, 304 N.W.2d 674 (1981) (requires a representation on which the defendant relies in good faith).

Acquiescence: Davidson v. Van Lengen, 266 N.W.2d 436 (Iowa 1978) (acquiescence produces an estoppel); Rodgers v. Rodgers, 505 S.W.2d 138 (Mo.App.1974) (wife was barred by acquiescing the husband's non-payment of child support). Other cases are cited in Annot., 5 A.L.R.4th 1015, 1042 (1981).

38. E.g., Bozzi v. Bozzi, 177 Conn. 232, 413 A.2d 834 (1979); Jones v. Meade, 126 Ill.App.3d 897, 81 Ill.Dec. 786, 467 N.E.2d 657 (1984); Ruster v. Ruster, 91 Ill.App. 3d 355, 46 Ill.Dec. 874, 414 N.E.2d 927 (1980); Thurn v. Thurn, 310 N.W.2d 539 (Iowa 1981); Harrison v. Smith, 201 Neb. 21, 265 N.W.2d 855 (1978); Kinney v. Mathias, 10 Ohio St.3d 72, 461 N.E.2d 901 (1984).

39. Hauck v. Schuck, 143 Colo. 324, 353 P.2d 79 (1960); Carey v. Carey, 29 Colo.App. 328, 486 P.2d 38 (1971); Korczyk v. Solonka, 130 W.Va. 211, 42 S.E.2d 814 (1947).

40. Jones v. Meade, 126 Ill.App.3d 897, 81 Ill.Dec. 786, 467 N.E.2d 657 (1984); Ruster v. Ruster, 91 Ill.App.3d 355, 46 Ill.Dec. 874, 414 N.E.2d 927 (1980); Kinney v. Mathias, 10 Ohio St.3d 72, 461 N.E.2d 901 (1984) (semble).

41. 247 Iowa 638, 75 N.W.2d 264 (1956), overruled on other grounds by Brown v. Brown, 269 N.W.2d 819 (Iowa 1978).

42. Malekos v. Chloe Ann Yin, 655 P.2d 728 (Alaska 1982); Bartlett v. Bartlett, 70 Ill.App.3d 661, 27 Ill.Dec. 329, 389 N.E.2d 15 (1979); Nichols v. Nichols, 400 So.2d 1109 (La.App.1981); Weber v. Weber, 203 Neb. 528, 279 N.W.2d 379 (1978) (treats the case as one of accord and satisfaction); Hartman v. Smith, 100 Wash.2d 766, 674 P.2d 176 (1984) (void adoption). Other cases are cited in Annot., 57 A.L.R.2d 1139, 1143 (1958). Herb v. Herb, 251 Iowa 957, 103 N.W.2d 361 (1960) refused to enforce the agreement because the child's welfare required continuation of the payments. The Malekos case, supra, reached the same result by holding that the agreement could be withdrawn at any time, after which the payments would have to be renewed. A distinction may be made between future payments which may not be released and past payments, which may be. Larsen v. Larsen, 5 Utah 2d 224, 300 P.2d 596 (1956).

to honor agreements by which the custodian attempts to relinquish claims for child support.[43] These cases fail to realize that there is no substantial objection to such agreements so long as they do not affect the child's maintenance. Still other cases refuse to enforce the custodian's release if it is given without consideration,[44] although the insistence upon observance of contract principles in this setting seems unnecessary and undesirable.[45] The further requirement is made in a few states that such agreements must be in writing.[46]

It is a much disputed question whether the conduct of a child's custodian gives rise to a defense against enforcement of a child support decree. In the most common case the custodian moves out of the jurisdiction or away from the obligor's residence, thereby making it either impossible or very difficult for him to exercise his rights of visitation and causing him to lose contact with the child. When this occurs he is understandably angry. He may often have no effective way of enforcing his visitation rights other than to stop support payments. The great majority of the cases hold that he may not do this, and that

he must continue to make the payments even though he is cut off from contact with his child.[47] Their reasoning seems to be that the child's welfare is the paramount consideration. The child should not be allowed to suffer from lack of support because of the custodian's action. In some cases the custodian's removal from the state may not be in violation of the decree and may be taken for substantial and valid reasons.[48] In those cases it seems correct to hold that the support payments must continue, but it may be possible to require the parents to share the expense of visitation.[49] If the removal is in violation of the decree or if there is a deliberate compaign to frustrate visitation rights by hiding the child or by other means, and if the custodian is capable of supporting the child, it seems proper to deny enforcement of the child support decree.[50] As a practical matter the cases are probably rare in which the custodian is so clearly able to support the child as to justify excusing the payment of support by the non-custodial parent. It is therefore not surprising that the obligor is so seldom able to base a successful defense to contempt proceed-

Of course the court may find that the custodian made no release, and for this reason continue enforcement. Guri v. Guri, 122 N.H. 552, 448 A.2d 370 (1982); Maule v. Kaufman, 33 N.Y.2d 58, 349 N.Y.S.2d 368, 304 N.E.2d 234 (1973), reargument denied 33 N.Y.2d 940, 353 N.Y.S.2d 1027, 309 N.E.2d 143 (1974).

43. Johnson v. Johnson, 233 Ga. 664, 212 S.E.2d 835 (1975); Pickett v. Pickett, 470 N.E.2d 751 (Ind.App.1984); Hailey v. Holden, 457 So.2d 947 (Miss.1984); Peebles v. Disher, 279 S.C. 611, 310 S.E.2d 823 (App.1983); Ditmar v. Ditmar, 48 Wash.2d 373, 293 P.2d 759 (1956). Napier v. Kilgore, 284 S.C. 313, 326 S.E.2d 171 (App.1985) held that a father could be required to pay child support arrears after the child had been adopted by the mother's second husband, the arrears accruing before the adoption.

44. Johnson v. Johnson, 26 Ill.App.3d 64, 324 N.E.2d 450 (1975); Ruehle v. Ruehle, 161 Neb. 691, 74 N.W.2d 689 (1956).

45. Malekos v. Chloe Ann Yin, 655 P.2d 728 (Alaska 1982).

46. Rehill v. Rehill, 306 N.Y. 126, 116 N.E.2d 281 (1953).

47. Allison v. Binkley, 222 Ark. 383, 259 S.W.2d 511 (1953); Bozzi v. Bozzi, 177 Conn. 232, 413 A.2d 834 (1979); Raymond v. Raymond, 165 Conn. 735, 345 A.2d 48 (1974); Slavis v. Slavis, 12 Ill.App.3d 467, 299 N.E.2d 413 (1973); State ex rel. Southwell v. Chamberland, 361 N.W.2d 814 (Minn.1985) (no defense to a state's AFDC claim that the mother removed and concealed the child); Moir v.

Kowalkowski, 282 Minn. 243, 164 N.W.2d 69 (1969) (children's rejection of the father not a defense); Fitzgerald v. Fitzgerald, ___ Mont. ___, 618 P.2d 867 (1980); Lippman v. Kay, ___ R.I. ___, 415 A.2d 738 (1980); Stach v. Stach, 369 N.W.2d 132 (S.D.1985); Gaidos v. Gaidos, 48 Wash.2d 276, 293 P.2d 388 (1956); State ex rel. Hubbard v. Hubbard, 110 Wis.2d 683, 329 N.W.2d 202 (1983).

48. Clark v. Clark, 46 Ala.App. 432, 243 So.2d 517 (1970); Baures v. Baures, 13 Ariz.App. 515, 478 P.2d 130 (1970); Potts v. Potts, 266 S.W.2d 114 (Ky.1954); Von Trotha v. Hansen, 171 N.W.2d 744 (N.D.1969); Commonwealth ex rel. Firestone v. Firestone, 158 Pa.Super. 579, 45 A.2d 923 (1946); Corson v. Corson, 46 Wash.2d 611, 283 P.2d 673 (1955).

49. Schwartz v. Schwartz, 91 A.D.2d 628, 456 N.Y.S.2d 811 (2d Dep't 1982).

50. Sharum v. Dodson, 264 Ark. 57, 568 S.W.2d 503 (1978) (recognizes a defense to the collection of arrears by contempt); Sears v. Sears, 462 A.2d 1099 (Del.Fam.Ct. 1983) (removal and concealment a defense to enforcement of arrears); Atwell v. Hill, 226 Ga. 560, 176 S.E.2d 60 (1970); Wick v. Wick, 19 Ill.2d 457, 167 N.E.2d 207 (1960); Hasse v. Hasse, 232 Minn. 234, 45 N.W.2d 383 (1950); Hudson v. Hudson, 97 Misc.2d 558, 412 N.Y.S.2d 242 (1978) (construing a statute); Goodwin v. Fayerman, 88 Misc.2d 690, 389 N.Y.S.2d 527 (Fam.Ct.1977); Sperry v. Hlutke, 19 Ohio App.3d 156, 483 N.E.2d 870 (1984) (based on statute).

ings upon the custodian's violation of the divorce decree. In the converse situation, where the custodian of the child seeks to terminate visitation rights on the ground that the support payments are not being made in accordance with the decree, the courts have similarly held that this may not be done, on the ground that visitation is important for the child's welfare and should not be affected by the default of the support obligor.[51]

The parent's duty to make child support payments normally ends when the child reaches majority or is emancipated.[52] The cases generally permit the child's custodian to collect, after the child reaches majority or emancipated, arrears of support which accrued before majority or emancipation,[53] although in some states the enforcement may only be by execution and not by contempt proceedings.[54] Even in those states (the majority) in which the accrued and unpaid installments of child support are characterized as final, non-modifiable judgments, it has been held that installments accruing after the child reaches majority or is emancipated may not be collected from the supporting parent.[55]

A discharge in bankruptcy is not a defense to enforcement of a child support decree, just as it is not a defense to an alimony obliga-

tion.[56] This is true even though the claim has been assigned to the state by the child's custodian pursuant to the Social Security Act.[57] It likewise follows that arrears of child support may not be included in the obligor's Chapter 13 plan.[58]

The last defense to be discussed in this section is that of complete or partial compliance with the decree. To the extent that the obligor has made the child support payments commanded by the divorce decree he should not be made to pay again. The problems arise, however, when he provides some or all of the support in a form different from that prescribed by the decree.[59] The decree normally orders him to make periodic payments in a stated amount to the child's custodian. Should he receive credit for payments made directly to the children, either by himself or by someone else on his behalf? Should he have a defense when he takes custody of the child for a time and supports them in kind? Should he be credited with sums paid to third parties for the education or medical expenses of the child? These questions and others have often arisen. The answers which the courts have given are by no means wholly satisfying.

51. Johnson v. Johnson, 52 Ohio App.2d 180, 368 N.E.2d 1273 (1977); Ledsome v. Ledsome, ___ W.Va. ___, 301 S.E.2d 475 (1983).

52. Codorniz v. Codorniz, 34 Cal.2d 811, 215 P.2d 32 (1950); Rybinski v. Rybinski, 333 Mich. 592, 53 N.W.2d 386 (1952); Swenson v. Swenson, 241 Mo.App. 21, 227 S.W.2d 103 (1950). See also section 17.1, supra, which indicates that under some circumstances the parent's duty of support may continue beyond majority or emancipation.

53. Tande v. Bongiovanni, 142 Ariz. 120, 688 P.2d 1012 (1984); Finley v. Finley, 81 Ill.2d 317, 43 Ill.Dec. 12, 410 N.E.2d 12 (1980); Cullinan v. Cullinan, 226 N.W.2d 33 (Iowa 1975); Ex parte Hooks, 415 S.W.2d 166 (Tex. 1967); Annot., 32 A.L.R.3d 888 1970). On the meaning of emancipation for this purpose see McGregor v. McGregor, 237 Ga. 57, 226 S.E.2d 591 (1976). Emancipation in general is discussed in section 8.3, supra. See also Broyles v. Broyles, 711 P.2d 1119 (Wyo.1985).

54. Smith v. Morgan, 379 So.2d 1052 (Fla.App.1980); Annot., 32 A.L.R.3d 888, 889 (1970).

55. Crook v. Crook, 80 Ariz. 275, 296 P.2d 951 (1956); Corbridge v. Corbridge, 230 Ind. 201, 102 N.E.2d 764 (1952); Swenson v. Swenson, 241 Mo.App. 21, 227 S.W.2d 103 (1950); Ditmar v. Ditmar, 48 Wash.2d 373, 293 P.2d

759 (1956); Annot., 58 A.L.R.2d 355 (1958); Annot., 6 A.L.R.2d 1277 (1949). Byrd v. Byrd, 78 Ohio App. 73, 69 N.E.2d 75 (1945) carried the analysis one step further, saying that the obligor could recover back amounts paid in ignorance of the fact that his duty to support had terminated, in this instance by the child's adoption.

Contra: Ortiz v. Ortiz, 180 Kan. 334, 304 P.2d 490 (1956); State ex rel. Casey v. Casey, 175 Or. 328, 153 P.2d 700 (1944).

56. 11 U.S.C.A. § 523(a)(5)(A). The impact of this provision on alimony obligations is discussed in section 16.6, supra, at note 67.

57. 11 U.S.C.A. § 523(a)(5)(A); In re Wilson, 29 B.R. 254 (Bkrtcy.D.Kan.1983). The Social Security Act provision governing such assignments is 42 U.S.C.A. § 602(a) (26)(A). The custodian's claim to arrears of child support in equity belongs to the child not to her, and therefore is not part of the custodian's assets on her bankruptcy, and so is not "asigned" to her trustee in bankruptcy. Zimmerman v. Starnes, 35 B.R. 1018 (Bkrtcy.D.Colo.1984).

58. Caswell v. Lang, 757 F.2d 608 (4th Cir.1985).

59. Cases on this subject are collected in Annots., 47 A.L.R.3d 1031 (1973) and 2 A.L.R.2d 831 (1948).

All of these questions may be reduced to a single broad inquiry: Has there been, in whole or in part, substantial compliance with the child support decree? Presumably no court would insist on exact and meticulous compliance in every case, although a few cases have required a literal compliance which does violence to the purpose of the decree and serves no interest of the parties.[60]

In undertaking the difficult task of defining "substantial compliance", the courts should not restrict themselves to a literal interpretation of the decree. Nor should they be influenced by such irrelevancies as the retroactive modification bugaboo.[61] When the obligor raises the defense that he has made support payments directly to the children, for example, he is not asking for a modification of accrued installments, but on the contrary is arguing that he has made the payments and complied with the decree. A holding that he should receive credit for payments made to the children does not constitute a modification of the accrued installments any more than would a finding that he made the payments to the custodian.

"Substantial compliance", when divorced from excessive literalness and irrelevancies, has a sufficiently precise meaning to furnish a useful guide in the decision of cases. Properly understood, it means that the child support obligor's claimed performance accomplished the spirit and purpose of the support order (the maintenance of the child), without at the same time violating any other provision of the divorce decree. A look at the cases demonstrates that this is another example of the law's refusal to insist upon the observance of technicalities when such insistence would inflict hardship on the obligor and confer no corresponding benefit on the custodian and the child.[62]

The most common case arises when the obligor fails to make the payments called for by the order but does make presents directly to the child, either money or property. The majority of cases hold that he gets no credit for such gifts.[63] This result is based upon either or both of two sound reasons. First, the gifts may be so inconsequential that they have no significance for the support of the children and therefore do not tend to fulfill the purpose of the support order.[64] Second, even if they are large enough to be of some value in supporting the children, they have the effect of removing a part of the child's support from the custodian's control. The substitute for joint parental control which the divorce decree sets up gives the custody and supervision of the child to the custodian.[65] The other parent has the duty of providing support in the amount specified by the decree, but he does not have the right to say how the money shall be spent. If he is permitted to make presents or other direct payments to the child, this violates the custodian's authority and responsibility for the care to be given to the child.[66] On the other hand, where the payments are made directly to the custodian rather than through an agency of the state, this objection does not apply and the payments should be credited against the child support obligation.[67] Likewise, where the payments are made by a third party to the

---

60. E.g., Hains v. Hains, 187 Kan. 379, 357 P.2d 317 (1960); Nichols v. Nichols, 306 N.Y. 490, 119 N.E.2d 351 (1954).

61. Cases which seem to treat the issue of credit for payments as an attempt at retroactive modification include Skinner v. Skinner, 252 Ga. 512, 314 S.E.2d 897 (1984); Matter of Marriage of Cope, 291 Or. 412, 631 P.2d 781 (1981); Koon v. Koon, 50 Wash.2d 577, 313 P.2d 369 (1957).

62. See, e.g., the doctrine of estoppel against attack upon divorce decrees rendered without jurisdiction, which has a similar purpose, discussed in section 12.3, supra.

63. Young v. Williams, 583 P.2d 201 (Alaska 1978); Skinner v. Skinner, 252 Ga. 512, 314 S.E.2d 897 (1984); Duncan v. Roane, 127 So.2d 191 (La.App.1961); Gardner

v. Perry, 405 A.2d 721 (Me.1979); Bradford v. Futrell, 225 Md. 512, 171 A.2d 493 (1961), citing other cases; Williams v. Budke, 186 Mont. 71, 606 P.2d 515 (1980); Ruehle v. Ruehle, 169 Neb. 23, 97 N.W.2d 868 (1959); Martin v. Martin, 59 Wash.2d 468, 368 P.2d 170 (1962). Other cases are cited in Annot., 47 A.L.R.3d 1031 (1973).

64. Fussell v. State, 102 Neb. 117, 166 N.W. 197 (1918).

65. See section 19.2, infra.

66. Gardner v. Perry, 405 A.2d 721 (Me.1979); Bradford v. Futrell, 225 Md. 512, 171 A.2d 493 (1961).

67. Payson v. Payson, 442 N.E.2d 1123 (Ind.App.1982); Castro v. Castro, 436 N.E.2d 366 (Ind.App.1982).

custodian, as where they are made from social security disability benefits [68] or from a trust set up for the benefit of the child [69] they may be credited against the support obligation since they do not give rise to any interference with the custodian's authority. And if substantial payments are made directly to the child or for the child's benefit to third parties with the consent of the custodian, these payments also may be credited against the obligation under the decree.[70]

Some contemporary joint custody decrees may give both parents equal authority with respect to the child's upbringing while at the same time giving one of them physical custody of the child.[71] The parent not having physical custody may then make direct payments to the child and seek to have them credited against the child support decree, arguing that he has as much right to decide how the money should be spent as the other parent. This creates a conflict which can only be resolved in the same way as other conflicts over the details of the child's care, that is, generally by placing the authority in the hands of the person who is actually caring for the child on a daily basis.[72]

For similar reasons the courts have generally refused to permit the obligor's over-payments of child support to be applied to reduce amounts accruing subsequently.[73] Where the obligor attempts to set off against his child support obligation amounts which the custodian owes him, the courts refuse to permit it for another reason, which is that the child support payments are for the benefit of the child not the custodian, so that they are not, properly speaking, cross demands.[74]

The same sort of analysis explains the cases which refuse the obligor credit for support provided in kind while the child is in his custody. If he takes the child in violation of the custody decree, the court will not credit the support given against amounts due under the support decree.[75] The courts cannot condone violations of their orders in this fashion. But if the obligor has custody with the consent of the other parent, or because the other parent has abandoned the child or is unable to care for him, or because there is some other emergency, there is no violation of the custody decree and credit for the support so provided is allowed.[76] Where there is a custody decree denominated joint custody, but one parent has physical custody for the greater proportion of the time, it may be very unfair to allow the other parent credit for the time he cares for the child, since the expenses of undertaking the child's care are not usually

But in Matter of Marriage of Cope, 291 Or. 412, 631 P.2d 781 (1981) the court was foreclosed from giving credit by a statute which expressly provided that payments to the obligee rather than to the state agency could not be credited to the obligor.

68. In re Marriage of Robinson, 651 P.2d 454 (Colo. App.1982) (social security payments may be credited toward the support obligation, but may not be relied on to reduce arrears); Potts v. Potts, 240 N.W.2d 680 (Iowa 1976); Andler v. Andler, 217 Kan. 538, 538 P.2d 649 (1975); Cohen v. Murphy, 368 Mass. 144, 330 N.E.2d 473 (1975); Griffin v. Avery, 120 N.H. 783, 424 A.2d 175 (1980); Mask v. Mask, 95 N.M. 229, 620 P.2d 883 (1980) (credit against current payments permitted, but not against arrears); Annot., 77 A.L.R.3d 1315 (1977). Contra: Matter of Marriage of Cope, 291 Or. 412, 631 P.2d 781 (1981), relying in part upon the statute.

69. Nielsen v. Nielsen, 93 Idaho 419, 462 P.2d 512 (1969).

70. Ediger v. Ediger, 206 Kan. 447, 479 P.2d 823 (1971), citing other cases; Goodson v. Goodson, 32 N.C. App. 76, 231 S.E.2d 178 (1977).

In an unusual case in which support payments were deducted from the obligor's weekly wages but then em-

bezzled by the employer's office manager so that no money was paid to the custodian, the court held that the obligor had to bear that loss. Szigyarto v. Szigyarto, 64 N.Y.2d 275, 486 N.Y.S.2d 164, 475 N.E.2d 777 (1985).

71. E.g., Griffin v. Griffin, 699 P.2d 407 (Colo.1985). Joint custody is discussed in section 19.5, infra.

72. Griffin v. Griffin, 699 P.2d 407 (Colo.1985).

73. See cases cited in Annot., 47 A.L.R.3d 1031, 1055 (1973). Contra: In re Marriage of Peet, 84 Cal.App.3d 974, 149 Cal.Rptr. 108 (1978).

74. Williams v. Williams, 8 Cal.App.3d 636, 87 Cal. Rptr. 754 (1970); Broyles v. Broyles, 711 P.2d 1119 (Wy. 1985); Annot., 100 A.L.R.2d 925 (1965).

75. Finkbeiner v. Finkbeiner, 226 Ark. 165, 288 S.W.2d 586 (1956). Other cases are cited in Annot., 47 A.L.R.3d 1031, 1048 (1973).

76. Daniel v. Daniel, 239 Ga. 466, 238 S.E.2d 108 (1977); White v. White, 34 Md.App. 635, 368 A.2d 1061 (1977); McNeal v. Robinson, 628 P.2d 358 (Okl.1981); French v. French, 74 Wash.2d 708, 446 P.2d 332 (1968). Other cases are cited in Annot., 47 A.L.R.3d 1031, 1039 (1973).

reduced merely because the child is staying with the other parent for short periods.[77]

Occasionally the divorced parents may remarry each other. The effect of this, according to most cases, is that the support order is thereby made unenforceable.[78] If they later separate for a second time, the question of support must be litigated de novo.

 **WESTLAW REFERENCES**

The Federal Child Support Enforcement Program

ci(42 +5 651)

child /3 support /s property /s arrear! "past due" overdue /s lien!

sy,di(child /3 support /s wage salary earning income /5 withh*ld!)

State Methods of Enforcement

child /3 support /s enforc! /p writ /2 execution

sy(child /3 support /s contempt /s crime criminal!)

Defenses Against Enforcement

sy,di(child /3 support /s statute period action /5 limitation /s toll!)

child /3 support /p pappas

child /3 support /s credit! /s (third +1 person party) "social security disability"

child /3 support /s off-set off-setting set-off setting-off /s custod!

---

§ 17.4 Child Support Orders in Divorce Decrees—Enforcement of Foreign Decrees [1]

The Federal Child Support Enforcement Program

As has been indicated in an earlier section,[2] title IV–D of the Social Security Act has im-

posed upon the states detailed and complex requirements for the enforcement of child support claims. The most effective of these, the income withholding provisions, are required by the federal Act to be made available in each state for the enforcement of child support decrees of other states.[3] In addition the federal tax refund intercept provisions apply to the child support decrees of states other than the state of the obligor's residence at the time of the intercept.[4] And the state income tax intercept provisions may also be relied upon to enforce the decrees of states other than that of the obligor's residence, by using the Uniform Reciprocal Enforcement of Support Act to register the child support decree as a judgment in the state of his residence.[5]

The federal courts may be used to enforce child support decrees, either under title IV–D [6] or where diversity of citizenship and amount in controversy exist, pursuant to the usual rules of federal jurisdiction.[7]

State Enforcement

The rules applicable to the enforcement of child support orders entered in other jurisdictions are very similar to those applicable to the enforcement of alimony decrees. For this reason the reader is referred to the corresponding section on alimony decrees [8] to supplement the discussion which follows.

The Full Faith and Credit Clause [9] governs the enforcement of child support orders as well as alimony decrees. To the extent that the order is valid and final by the law of the

---

77. Hyde v. Hyde, 143 Kan. 660, 56 P.2d 437 (1936) (semble).

78. Davis v. Davis, 68 Cal.2d 290, 66 Cal.Rptr. 14, 437 P.2d 502 (1968), citing other cases; Annot., 26 A.L.R.4th 325, 332 (1983).

§ 17.4

1. "Foreign" in this section means that the decree is that of another state of the United States not of another nation. But aside from the application of the United States Constitution, the principles discussed in this section apply to the decrees of other nations.

2. See section 17.3, supra, at note 10.

3. 42 U.S.C.A. § 666(b)(9); 45 C.F.R. § 303.100(g) (1985).

4. 42 U.S.C.A. § 664; 45 C.F.R. § 303.72(d), (g) (1985).

5. 42 U.S.C.A. § 666(a)(3); 45 C.F.R. § 303.102 (1985). The procedure in Uniform Reciprocal Enforcement of Support Act cases is discussed in section 7.6, supra.

6. 42 U.S.C.A. § 660. Various conditions on the use of the federal courts under this statute are spelled out in 45 C.F.R. § 303.73 (1985).

7. Harrison v. Harrison, 214 F.2d 571 (4th Cir.1954), cert. denied 348 U.S. 896, 75 S.Ct. 217, 99 L.Ed. 704 (1954) (alimony); Jagiella v. Jagiella, 647 F.2d 561 (5th Cir. 1981), rehearing denied 654 F.2d 723 (5th Cir.1981). See also Note, Enforcing State Domestic Relations Decrees in Federal Courts, 50 U.Chi.L.Rev. 1357 (1983).

8. See section 16.6, supra.

9. U.S.Const. art. IV, sec. 1; 28 U.S.C.A. § 1738.

state where it was originally entered, it must be enforced by all other states.[10] Decrees which are not valid because not based upon personal jurisdiction in the state which entered them are not entitled to full faith and credit.[11] In the leading case for full faith and credit, Sistare v. Sistare,[12] a New York decree made a single award for both child support and alimony. The Supreme Court found that the New York decree was final and not modifiable and as a result held that Connecticut was required by the Constitution to enforce it. Support decrees entered in those states which hold that each installment of support constitutes a final judgment when it accrues [13] are thus constitutionally entitled to enforcement in all other states as to such accrued and unpaid installments. Decrees of those relatively few states which require the entry of a judgment for arrears before the amount becomes finally due are not entitled to enforcement as a matter of the Full Faith and Credit Clause until such a judgment is entered.[14]

The Full Faith and Credit Clause has been given particularly broad application to child support orders by the Supreme Court in Yarborough v. Yarborough.[15] In this case a Geor-

gia divorce and child support decree ordered the child's father to transfer certain property for the child's support. According to Georgia law this decree was final and nonmodifiable. The child moved to South Carolina where she sued her father for further support, asking for funds for her education. The Supreme Court held that the Full Faith and Credit Clause required South Carolina to respect the Georgia decree as ending all support obligations of the father notwithstanding that the child had a domicile in South Carolina and that South Carolina would order support in this situation. The Court also held that the Georgia decree was binding on the child although she was not made a party to the divorce suit. Justice Stone dissented from the opinion.[16] He expressed some doubt as to whether the Georgia decree could affect the rights of a child not a party to the suit,[17] but his chief reliance was upon the view that South Carolina had a legitimate interest in the child's welfare when she became a domiciliary of the state which the state was entitled to vindicate. In his opinion the Court's decision allowed Georgia to interfere in the internal affairs of South Carolina. He supported this

10. Sistare v. Sistare, 218 U.S. 1, 30 S.Ct. 682, 54 L.Ed. 905 (1910); Smith v. Smith, 217 F.2d 917 (6th Cir.1954); Huggins v. Deinhard, 134 Ariz. 98, 654 P.2d 32 (App. 1982); Sevison v. Sevison, 396 A.2d 178 (Del.Super.1978); Watson v. McDowell, 110 So.2d 680 (Fla.App.1959); Connell v. Connell, 119 Ga.App. 485, 167 S.E.2d 686 (1969), 21 Mercer L.Rev. 675 (1970); Conwell v. Conwell, 3 N.J. 266, 69 A.2d 712 (1949); Armstrong v. Armstrong, 117 Ohio St. 558, 160 N.E. 34 (1927); Annot., 90 A.L.R. 939 (1934). But see Picker v. Vollenhover, 206 Or. 45, 290 P.2d 789 (1955).

11. Benefield v. Harris, 143 Ga.App. 709, 240 S.E.2d 119 (1977) (alimony decree). See also Restatement (Second) of Conflict of Laws §§ 27, 104 (1971); Restatement (Second) of Judgments §§ 1, 81 (1982). Full faith and credit may also be refused if the court which entered the child support decree did not have subject matter jurisdiction. Bierl v. McMahon, 270 Cal.App.2d 97, 75 Cal.Rptr. 473 (1969). For the requirements of personal jurisdiction in child support cases, see Kulko v. Superior Court of California In and For City and County of San Francisco, 436 U.S. 84, 98 S.Ct. 1690, 56 L.Ed.2d 132 (1978), rehearing denied 438 U.S. 908, 98 S.Ct. 3127, 51 L.Ed.2d 1150 (1978).

12. 218 U.S. 1, 30 S.Ct. 682, 54 L.Ed. 905 (1910).

13. See section 17.2, supra, at note 14.

14. Smith v. Smith, 217 F.2d 917 (6th Cir.1954); Keller v. Guernsey, 227 Kan. 480, 608 P.2d 896 (1980). Scott v. Sylvester, 220 Va. 182, 257 S.E.2d 774 (1979) held that such a non-final decree would be enforced under principles of comity, including the installments which accrued while the obligor resided in the state in which the decree was entered. Wilson v. Wilson, 143 Me. 113, 56 A.2d 453 (1947) held that if such a non-final decree is to be enforced as a matter of comity, notice and an opportunity to be heard as to modification must be given to the obligor.

15. 290 U.S. 202, 54 S.Ct. 181, 78 L.Ed. 269 (1933).

16. Yarborough v. Yarborough, 290 U.S. 202, 213, 54 S.Ct. 181, 185, 78 L.Ed. 269 (1933).

17. Yarborough v. Yarborough, 290 U.S. 202, 214, 54 S.Ct. 181, 186, 78 L.Ed. 269, footnote 1 (1933). Justice Stone's doubts seem clearly justified. The Supreme Court now recognizes children's due process rights to a greater degree than at the time of Yarborough. Application of Gault, 387 U.S. 1, 87 S.Ct. 1428, 18 L.Ed.2d 527 (1967). The state courts have taken the view that the child is not bound if he is not a party to the suit. Gonzales v. Pacific Greyhound Lines, 34 Cal.2d 749, 214 P.2d 809 (1950); Nappe v. Nappe, 20 N.J. 337, 120 A.2d 31 (1956); Annot., 65 A.L.R.2d 1381, 1396 (1959). See also Restatement (Second) of Judgments § 34, Reporter's Note (1982).

position by references to other judicially created limitations on full faith and credit, by operation of which a judgment of one state is not enforced in another.[18]

The significance of Yarborough is reduced by the later decision in Elkind v. Byck.[19] The parties in that case were also divorced in Georgia, the husband being required to set up a trust for the support of their child. He complied with the decree. Under Georgia law this was a final and conclusive determination of his support obligation. The wife and child then moved to New York and the husband to California. She brought suit in New York under the Uniform Reciprocal Enforcement of Support Act or its New York equivalent and New York sent the petition to California for proceedings under the California URESA.[20] The California Supreme Court held that additional support could be ordered notwithstanding the final nature of the Georgia decree, in part because Georgia's adoption of URESA left it to the state of the husband's residence to impose a further duty of support, and in part on the ground that the rule in Yarborough does not apply when both parents have left the state of the original decree. A further and probably conclusive reason for the result was the policy view that "the divorce state should not be permitted to determine the welfare of the child for all time and in all states".[21] The Yarborough case may still apply to the accrued and unpaid installments of child support where by the law of the divorcing state such installments are final and not subject to modification[22] unless Justice Traynor was correct in Elkind in his opinion that Yarborough is limited to the case where the obligor remains in the divorcing state. Since many of the comments on the Yarborough case were critical of the majority opinion and favorable to Justice Stone's dissent,[23] perhaps the Elkind result should prevail. In any event Yarborough's impact is not great as a practical matter since all states permit modification of the future installments of child support.[24]

If the decree for which enforcement is sought is not final, the inference from the Sistare case[25] is that it is not entitled to full faith and credit.[26] Likewise it is frequently said that the Full Faith and Credit Clause does not require that any particular remedy be made available to enforce the decrees of other states.[27] The combination of these two principles produces the result that child support orders are not entitled to interstate enforcement as a matter of right, nor are they entitled to equitable enforcement, so far as they look to the future. The child or the

---

18. E.g., cases holding that a state need not give effect to judgments for conviction of a crime or for penalties entered in a sister state, as in Wisconsin v. Pelican Insurance Co. of New Orleans, 127 U.S. 265, 8 S.Ct. 1370, 32 L.Ed. 239 (1888). One case on which he relied has been overruled. Haddock v. Haddock, 201 U.S. 562, 26 S.Ct. 525, 50 L.Ed. 867 (1906), overruled by Williams v. North Carolina, 317 U.S. 287, 63 S.Ct. 207, 87 L.Ed. 279 (1942). To some extent his point is supported by Estin v. Estin, 334 U.S. 541, 68 S.Ct. 1213, 92 L.Ed. 1561 (1948) and Vanderbilt v. Vanderbilt, 354 U.S. 416, 77 S.Ct. 1360, 1 L.Ed.2d 1456 (1957) holding that an ex parte divorce in one state, although valid as a divorce, does not foreclose a sister state from awarding a spouse alimony or separate maintenance. More recently, however, the Court has given less limited application to the Full Faith and Credit Clause, suggesting that Justice Stone's view in Yarborough is not favored. See Aldrich v. Aldrich, 378 U.S. 540, 84 S.Ct. 1687, 12 L.Ed.2d 1022 (1964).

19. 68 Cal.2d 453, 67 Cal.Rptr. 404, 439 P.2d 316 (1968).

20. For a discussion of URESA and its procedure, see section 6.2, supra.

21. Elkind v. Byck, 68 Cal.2d 453, 459, 67 Cal.Rptr. 404, 408, 439 P.2d 316, 320 (1968).

22. A list of such states is found in section 17.2 at note 15, supra.

23. E.g., Notes, 47 Harv.L.Rev. 712 (1934); 34 Colum. L.Rev. 164 (1934); Reese and Johnson, The Scope of Full Faith and Credit to Judgments, 49 Colum.L.Rev. 153, 169 (1949).

24. See section 17.2, supra.

25. Sistare v. Sistare, 218 U.S. 1, 30 S.Ct. 682, 54 L.Ed. 905 (1910). See also Lynde v. Lynde, 181 U.S. 183, 21 S.Ct. 555, 45 L.Ed. 810 (1901).

26. Williamson v. Williamson, 247 Ga. 260, 275 S.E.2d 42 (1981), cert. denied 454 U.S. 1097, 102 S.Ct. 669, 70 L.Ed.2d 638 (1981); Windham v. Blakeney, 354 So.2d 786 (Miss.1978); Silverstein v. Silverstein, 246 Pa.Super. 503, 371 A.2d 948 (1977). But Hill v. Hill, 153 W.Va. 392, 168 S.E.2d 803 (1969) held that full faith and credit would be given to a non-final decree.

27. German v. German, 122 Conn. 155, 188 A. 429 (1936). See also 2 J. Beale, Conflict of laws 1377 (1935) and Jacobs, The Enforcement of Foreign Decrees for Alimony, 6 Law & Contemp.Prob. 250, 267 (1939).

custodian on his behalf has as his sole constitutional remedy the right to bring an action in the second state to recover those installments which have accrued and become final. Not one but many suits may be necessary. The inconvenience, hardship, and waste of time and money both of litigants and court which are produced by so limiting the custodian's remedies in the second state have led the courts to go beyond what the Full Faith and Credit Clause requires. As a matter of comity and respect for the decrees of other states they will now enter a child support order for future installments even though the Constitution does not demand it.[28] In addition they will enforce orders so made by the full range of equitable and legal sanctions applicable to any other domestic support decree.[29] The result is that the custodian and the child have as effective a remedy in the second state as in the first. This is the only efficient way of handling the problem of child support in these days of highly mobile child support obligors. It parallels a similar line of authority in the enforcement of foreign alimony decrees.[30] Of course the second state may only enforce the sister state's decree where it is able to acquire personal jurisdiction over the obligor.[31]

To a substantial degree the Uniform Reciprocal Enforcement of Support Act[32] and the revised version of that Act[33] have occupied the field of interstate child support enforcement.[34] The Act provides two methods of enforcement for the child's custodian, either registration of the decree in the state of the obligor's domicile[35] or the unique two-state proceeding commencing in the state of the custodian's residence and concluding in the state of the obligor's residence.[36] The resulting decree is then enforceable by whatever remedies the local law makes available. Under this Act the child support decree is enforceable whether it is final or not.[37]

The courts of the various states have taken one further step in the application of comity to child support decrees. Not only do they enforce such decrees even though they are not final, but once having entered a decree based upon the sister state decree, they now feel free to modify the decree so entered.[38] The usual rule is that modification may be had on the same basis as would have been available in the state which originally entered the decree.[39] A different rule is adopted by the Uniform Reciprocal Enforcement of Support Act. That Act provides that the duties of support applicable under its procedure are

---

28. Sackler v. Sackler, 47 So.2d 292 (Fla.1950); Keller v. Guernsey, 227 Kan. 480, 608 P.2d 896 (1980); Cousineau v. Cousineau, 155 Or. 184, 63 P.2d 897 (1936); Scott v. Sylvester, 225 Va. 304, 302 S.E.2d 30 (1983), cert. denied 464 U.S. 961, 104 S.Ct. 395, 78 L.Ed.2d 338 (1983).

29. Cases are collected in Annot., 18 A.L.R.2d 862, 867 (1951). See also Feder v. Skyway Container Corp., 218 N.Y.S.2d 362 (1961) and Jacobs, The Enforcement of Foreign Decrees for Alimony, 6 Law & Contemp.Prob. 250, 267 (1939).

30. See section 16.7, supra.

31. Garlitz v. Rozar, 18 Ariz.App. 94, 500 P.2d 354 (1972); Morrill v. Tong, 390 Mass. 120, 453 N.E.2d 1221 (1983).

32. 9A Unif.L.Ann. 747 (1979).

33. 9A Unif.L.Ann. 647 (1979).

34. The operation of the Act is described in detail in section 6.6, supra. All states now have one version or another of this Act, so that there is reciprocity among all the states.

35. Revised Uniform Reciprocal Enforcement of Support Act §§ 36 to 40, 9A Unif.L.Ann. 741–744 (1979).

36. Revised Uniform Reciprocal Enforcement of Support Act §§ 11 to 32, 9A Unif.L.Ann. 681–736 (1979).

37. Government of Virgin Islands v. Lorillard, 358 F.2d 172 (3d Cir.1966).

38. Elkind v. Byck, 68 Cal.2d 453, 67 Cal.Rptr. 404, 439 P.2d 316 (1968); Lopez v. Avery, 66 So.2d 689 (Fla. 1953); Thomas v. Thomas, 248 N.C. 269, 103 S.E.2d 371 (1958); Scott v. Sylvester, 225 Va. 304, 302 S.E.2d 30 (1983), cert. denied 464 U.S. 961, 104 S.Ct. 395, 78 L.Ed.2d 338 (1983). Cases reaching the same result in a proceeding under the Uniform Reciprocal Enforcement of Support Act include Glickman v. Mesigh, 200 Colo. 320, 615 P.2d 23 (1980); Ainbender v. Ainbender, 344 A.2d 263 (Del.Super.1975); Hall v. Hall, 585 S.W.2d 384 (Ky.1979). In Shulman v. Miller, 191 F.Supp. 418 (E.D.Wis.1961) a child support order was entered in Wisconsin, enforced with modifications in Florida, and then the Florida decree as modified was enforced in Wisconsin. Contra: Pace v. Pace, 222 Va. 524, 281 S.E.2d 891 (1981), applying the erroneous principle that the sister state's decree was not entitled to full faith and credit to the extent that it modified an earlier Virginia decree.

39. Stevens v. Stevens, 44 Colo.App. 252, 611 P.2d 590 (1980) (semble); Burton v. Burton, 189 Conn. 129, 454 A.2d 1282 (1983); Scott v. Sylvester, 225 Va. 304, 302 S.E.2d 30 (1983), cert. denied 464 U.S. 961, 104 S.Ct. 395, 78 L.Ed.2d 338 (1983). Contra: Thompson v. Thompson, 645 S.W.2d 79 (Mo.App.1982).

those imposed by the law of the state in which the obligor was present for the period during which support is sought.[40] Where enforcement is sought in accordance with that Act, modification may be granted pursuant to the law of the state in which enforcement is sought.[41] The confusion which may often result from the consequent entry of conflicting support decrees in various states and from the statutory rule that a decree under the Act does not supersede earlier decrees in other states[42] is dealt with in an earlier section of this work.[43]

The defenses to the enforcement of sister state decrees are in general those applicable to domestic decrees, such as, for example, that payment of the proper amounts has been made.[44] One defense which has caused litigation and which raises questions peculiar to interstate enforcement is the statute of limitations. There is a conflict in the cases as to whether the applicable statute of limitations is that of the state in which the decree was entered[45] or that of the state in which enforcement is sought.[46] If the parties have their principal contacts with the state of enforcement, it would seem that its statute of limitations is the appropriate one. In any event a statute which attempts to distinguish between domestic and sister state judgments respecting the period of limitations is likely to be held in violation of the Equal Protection Clause of the state or federal constitution.[47]

WESTLAW REFERENCES

State Enforcement

di(child /3 support /s "full faith and credit" /s final!)

"foreign decree" /s enforc! /s child /3 support

sy,di("uniform reciprocal enforcement" u.r.e.s.a. /s modif! amend! /s jurisdiction!)

---

40. Revised Uniform Reciprocal Enforcement of Support Act § 7, 9A Unif.L.Ann. 672 (1979).

41. Elkind v. Byck, 68 Cal.2d 453, 67 Cal.Rptr. 404, 439 P.2d 316 (1968). Contra: Matter of Marriage of Tavares, 293 Or. 484, 651 P.2d 133 (1982); Oman v. Oman, 333 Pa.Super. 356, 482 A.2d 606 (1984).

42. Revised Uniform Reciprocal Enforcement of Support Act § 31, 9A Unif.L.Ann. 734 (1979).

43. See section 6.6, supra, at note 84. For an example of the occurrence of conflicting decrees see Haughton v. Haughton, 76 Ill.2d 439, 31 Ill.Dec. 183, 394 N.E.2d 385 (1979), cert. denied 444 U.S. 1102, 100 S.Ct. 1069, 62 L.Ed. 2d 789 (1980).

44. Robbins v. Robbins, 647 P.2d 589 (Alaska 1982). See also Bahr v. Bahr, 85 S.D. 240, 180 N.W.2d 465 (1970), and the discussion in section 17.3, supra.

45. Cf. Yarborough v. Yarborough, 290 U.S. 202, 54 S.Ct. 181, 78 L.Ed. 269 (1933), applying the law of the state in which the decree was entered to determine whether the decree could be enforced in another state.

46. Morris v. Cohen, 149 Cal.App.3d 507, 196 Cal.Rptr. 834 (1983), cert. denied 469 U.S. 879, 105 S.Ct. 243, 83 L.Ed.2d 182 (1984); Treaster v. Laird, 33 Colo.App. 297, 519 P.2d 1231 (1974). See also D. R. T. v. O. M., 244 So.2d 752 (Fla.App.1971), 25 Ark.L.Rev. 322 (1971), holding that the Florida age of majority applies to suit in Florida to enforce a child support decree of California.

47. Watkins v. Conway, 385 U.S. 188, 87 S.Ct. 357, 17 L.Ed.2d 286 (1966) (semble); Haughton v. Haughton, 76 Ill.2d 439, 31 Ill.Dec. 183, 394 N.E.2d 385 (1979), cert. denied 444 U.S. 1102, 100 S.Ct. 1069, 62 L.Ed.2d 789 (1980).

Chapter 18

SEPARATION AGREEMENTS

Table of Sections

§ 18.1 Separation Agreements—Validity—In General—Consideration

The statement was made in an earlier section of this work that a great proportion of all divorce cases, probably about ninety percent, are not contested.[1] Some of the uncontested cases may involve no property or child custody issues. Many of them will doubtless be uncontested because the issues of alimony, child support, property and child custody have been settled by agreement of the parties and the settlement embodied in a separation agreement. Although there do not seem to be statistics revealing what proportion of uncontested cases are disposed of by separation agreements, it seems fair to assume that the proportion is large, certainly greater than fifty percent. The facts that separation agreements are so widely used in preference to litigation and that lawyers generally agree that it is cheaper, faster and less destructive

to the parties' relationship to compromise cases than to try them serve to demonstrate the importance of separation agreements in divorce practice.

Since most separation agreements are the result of negotiations between the lawyers for the spouses, it is important that lawyers in domestic relations practice develop skill at negotiating, particularly since the negotiating and compromise of divorce cases present difficulties greater than the settlement of other kinds of lawsuits. The parties are ordinarily emotional, often hostile and unused to litigation. The lawyer generally finds it far from easy to persuade his client to accept a reasonable settlement of the issues in the case. At the same time those issues usually have a greater impact on the future lives of both spouses and of their children than the issues in the ordinary kinds of litigation. The recent interest in the psychology and tactics of

§ 18.1

1. See section 14.8, supra, at note 76. See also P. Jacobson, American Marriage and Divorce 120–121 (1959), indicating that even when divorce was more of an adversary proceeding than it is now, only from thirteen to fifteen percent of the cases were contested. The same

conclusion was drawn in 1 L. Marshall and G. May, The Divorce Court 199 (1932).

Arbitration provisions in separation agreements provide a means for avoiding litigation in divorce actions. The validity and construction of arbitration agreements are discussed supra in section 14.8.

negotiation which has been taken by the bar and the law schools is beginning to be reflected in a body of writing on the subject.[2] Some familiarity with current writing is of course helpful in developing negotiating techniques, but constant practice informed by self-awareness and self-criticism is essential to the production of skill in such a complex activity. Above all one must have a thorough knowledge of the applicable legal principles and of the facts of the particular case if he is to obtain a satisfactory and fair agreement for his client.

Some cases and authorities produce unnecessary confusion by attempting to draw distinctions between separation agreements, property settlements, stipulations, consent judgments or other forms of agreement in divorce actions.[3] None of these is a technical term. They all refer to methods of compromising divorce litigation. In this chapter only one term will be used: separation agreement. We mean by this an agreement which settles whatever issues may arise in the course of a divorce case, including those relating to alimony, to a division of property, to child support and to child custody. There are obvious differences, both practical and legal,[4] between these issues, but at the same time they are very closely related to each other both practically and legally, and are usually resolved in a single agreement. Treating them as giving rise to different kinds of agreement obscures these relationships and produces no benefits of either clarity or efficiency.[5]

The obvious need for and advantages of separation agreements as devices for compromising marital disputes and for avoiding the expense, delay and stress of litigation convinced the courts long ago that such agreements are in general valid and to be encouraged.[6] More recently the same view has been expressed in a variety of ways in many state statutes.[7] An important consequence of

2. E.g., R. Fisher and W. Ury, Getting to Yes: Negotiating Agreement Without Giving In (1981); X. Frascogna and H. Hetherington, Negotiation Strategy for Lawyers (1984); R. Haydock, Negotiation Practice (1984); G. Nierenberg, Fundamentals of Negotiating (1973); H. Raiffa, The Art and Science of Negotiating (1982); G. Williams, Legal Negotiation and Settlement (1983). Although not really concerned with techniques of negotiation, Mnookin and Kornhauser, Bargaining in the Shadow of the Law: The Case of Divorce, 88 Yale L.J. 950 (1979) discusses some of the factors relevant to reaching a separation agreement.

3. Distinctions of this sort are described in Sharp, Divorce and the Third Party: Spousal Support, Private Agreements and the State, 59 N.C.L.Rev. 819 (1981).

4. The differences are described at great, one might say inordinate, length in chapters 15, 16, 17 and 19 of this work.

5. For example, it is obvious that only after custody is allocated between the parents can child support be determined. As a practical matter all of the financial aspects of divorce, alimony, division of property and child support, are viewed as elements of a single determination, who gets what, even though in form, modification, enforcement and taxation they all have differences. But both the differences and the singleness of purpose must be taken account of in a single agreement, the separation agreement.

6. Rash v. Bogart, 226 Ala. 284, 146 So. 814 (1933); Brimble v. Sickler, 83 Colo. 494, 266 P. 497 (1928); Lasprogato v. Lasprogato, 127 Conn. 510, 18 A.2d 353 (1941); Beverly v. Beverly, 290 Ga. 468, 74 S.E.2d 89 (1953); Shaffer v. Shaffer, 135 Kan. 35, 10 P.2d 17 (1932); Hayden v. Hayden, 215 Ky. 299, 284 S.W. 1073 (1926); Vanderburgh v. Vanderburgh, 152 Minn. 189, 188 N.W. 276

(1922); Ward v. Ward, 81 Mont. 587, 264 P. 667 (1928); Hemingway v. Ball, 119 N.J.Eq. 471, 183 A. 172 (Ct.Err. & App.1936), adopting the opinion of the court below, 118 N.J.Eq. 378, 179 A. 374 (Ch.1935); McDaniel v. McDaniel, 36 N.M. 335, 15 P.2d 229 (1932); Galusha v. Galusha, 116 N.Y. 635, 22 N.E. 1114 (1889); Brown v. Brown, 205 N.C. 64, 169 S.E. 818 (1933); Tefft v. Tefft, 73 Ohio App. 399, 54 N.E.2d 423 (1943); Murphy v. McElroy, 185 Okl. 388, 92 P.2d 369 (1939); Hill v. Hill, 124 Or. 364, 264 P. 447 (1928); Miller v. Miller, 284 Pa. 414, 131 A. 236 (1925); Rinehart v. Rinehart, 52 Wyo. 363, 75 P.2d 390 (1938). See also 15 S. Williston, Contracts § 1742 (3d ed.1972) and 1 A. Lindey, Separation Agreements and Ante-Nuptial Contracts 4–8 (1985).

7. E.g., Alaska Stat. §§ 25.24.210, 25.24.220 (1983) (authorizing and regulating the parties' agreement); Ariz. Rev.Stat. § 25–317 (1976); Ark.Stat. § 34–1212 (Supp. 1985); West's Ann.Cal.Civ.Code § 4728 (1985) (recognizing separation agreements); Official Ga.Code Ann. § 19–6–8 (Supp.1986) (authorizing separation agreements); Ill.—S.H.A. ch. 40, § 502 (Supp.1986) (encourages amicable settlements on dissolution of marriage); West's Ann. Ind.Code § 31–1–11.5–10 (1980); Iowa Code Ann. § 598.21 (1981 and Supp.1986); Kan.Stat.Ann. § 23–207 (1981) (marriage settlements approved); Md.Code, Fam.L. § 8–101 (1984) (authorizing separation agreements); Vernon's Ann.Mo.Stat. § 452.325 (1986) (authorizing separation agreements); Mont.Code Ann. § 40–4–201 (1985) (encourages amicable settlement); Neb.Rev.Stat. § 42–366 (1984); N.Y.—McKinney's Dom.Rel.L. § 236, Part B, 3 (1986) (separation agreements valid and enforceable); N.C.Gen. Stat. §§ 50–20, 52–10.1 (1984 and Supp.1985); Vernon's Ann.Tex.Stat., Fam.Code § 3.631 (Supp.1987); Va.Code 1983, § 20–109.1 (authorizing the court to approve separation agreements); West's Rev.Code Wash.Ann. § 26.09.070 (1986); The Ohio statute authorizes a dissolu-

the judicial and legislative approval of separation agreements has been that the courts usually accept the parties' resolution of their financial and custody conflicts in individual cases.[8] Although their negotiations are carried on against a background of legal principles, they are aware that within very broad limits any agreement reached is likely to be approved by the court to which it is presented.

In the days when the grounds for divorce were predominantly fault based it was customarily held that the separation agreement would only be valid if at the time it was made the parties had actually separated or were on the point of separating.[9] Agreements made before that point were said to be invalid because conducive to divorce.[10] It was never made quite clear why an agreement to divide property or pay for support made while the parties were still living together was always and necessarily conducive to divorce, but the courts assumed that it was. Now that fault is no longer the basis for the grounds for divorce and in many states divorce may be had for the asking by either spouse,[11] little is to be served by continuing to reject separation agreements on the ground that they are con-

ducive to divorce. The new statutes make it plain that there is no longer any general public policy opposed to divorce.[12] This reasoning has been accepted by the growing number of states which permit the financial aspects of divorce to be controlled not merely by agreements made before separation, but by agreements made before marriage.[13] It therefore seems no longer rational to require that the parties separate before they may make a valid separation agreement.[14] For the same reasons provisions in reconciliation agreements purporting to govern the spouses' financial relations during marriage should be valid and not open to the objection that they are conducive to divorce.[15] This having been said, it is perhaps the better part of discretion to advise the spouses to separate before they executed their agreement, since there are doubtless courts which may cling to outdated notions about separation agreements conducive to divorce.[16]

In general of course separation agreements are governed by the principles of the law of contracts.[17] This means among other things that the agreement must be supported by consideration to the extent that it is executo-

tion of marriage when the parties both petition for it and execute a separation agreement. Ohio Rev.Code § 3105.63 (Supp.1986).

The Uniform Marriage and Divorce Act § 306, 9A Unif.L.Ann. 135 (1979) authorizes the execution of separation agreements in order to promote the amicable settlement of disputes between spouses.

8. Under some statutes the court is required to approve the parties' agreement except for the provisions dealing with child support and custody, unless the court finds it to be inconscionable. Uniform Marriage and Divorce Act § 306(b), 9A Unif.L.Ann. 135 (1979). See also Hopson, Economics of Divorce: A Pilot Empirical Study at the Trial Court Level, 11 Kan.L.Rev. 107, 118 (1962); Newey v. Newey, 161 Colo. 395, 422 P.2d 641 (1967); Dominick v. Dominick, 18 Mass.App.Ct. 85, 463 N.E.2d 564 (1984).

9. See the cases cited in note 6, supra.

10. Maynard v. Maynard, 329 Mich. 247, 45 N.W.2d 56 (1950); Beck v. Beck, 98 N.J.Eq. 474, 131 A. 520 (Ch. 1925); Garlock v. Garlock, 279 N.Y. 337, 18 N.E.2d 521 (1939); Myles v. Arnold, 162 S.W.2d 442 (Tex.Civ.App. 1942).

11. See the statutes cited in section 13.1, supra, at notes 47 to 54.

12. Posner v. Posner, 233 So.2d 381 (1970).

13. See section 1.1, supra, at note 44.

14. Some courts are beginning to recognize this. E.g., Sanders v. Colwell, 248 Ga. 376, 283 S.E.2d 461 (1981), overruling earlier cases.

15. Schichtel v. Schichtel, 3 Ark.App. 36, 621 S.W.2d 504 (1981); Whalen v. Whalen, 581 S.W.2d 578 (Ky.App. 1979); Nicholson v. Nicholson, 199 N.J.Super. 525, 489 A.2d 1247 (1985). Of course the reconciliation agreement must be free from fraud and made in good faith. Blaising v. Mills, 176 Ind.App. 141, 374 N.E.2d 1166 (1978); Marshall v. Marshall, 166 W.Va. 304, 273 S.E.2d 360 (1980). One would think that the courts would wish to encourage reconciliation agreements, but some of them seem unaccountably hostile to them. E.g., Clark v. Clark, 425 S.W.2d 745 (Ky.1968); Snyder v. Snyder, 196 Neb. 383, 243 N.W.2d 159 (1976); Towles v. Towles, 256 S.C. 307, 182 S.E.2d 53 (1971).

16. E.g., Stenson v. Stenson, 45 Ill.App.3d 249, 3 Ill. Dec. 928, 359 N.E.2d 787 (1977).

17. In re Marriage of Deines, 44 Colo.App. 98, 608 P.2d 735 (1980); McNevin v. McNevin, 444 N.E.2d 320 (Ind.App.1983); Fraunhofer v. Price, 182 Mont. 7, 594 P.2d 324 (1979); Blount v. Blount, 72 N.C.App. 193, 323 S.E.2d 738 (1984), review denied 313 N.C. 506, 329 S.E.2d 389 (1985); Mikeska v. Mikeska, 584 S.W.2d 565 (Tex.Civ. App.1979).

ry.[18] For the most part however this requirement is only relied upon by the courts as a convenient excuse for upsetting separation agreements which appear unfair to wives. The courts seldom hold a separation agreement invalid for lack of consideration when that would benefit the husband.[19] The doctrine of consideration in this context is only an interesting relic of the age of chivalry.

The form which consideration may take varies with the particular agreement. Cases have found sufficient consideration in (1) mutual promises of various kinds;[20] (a) a release by a spouse of rights in the property of the other spouse, usually without much discussion of just what rights, if any, existed;[21] (3) a promise by the wife to care for the children of the marriage[22] even though the care of the children may be a duty imposed by law upon

both parents;[23] (4) a spouse's acceptance of the agreement in satisfaction of his claims for alimony or support;[24] (5) a spouse's legal obligation to support the other spouse,[25] although such a holding is contrary to the usual rules of contracts;[26] and (6) either the promise to live separately or the fact that the parties have separated and will continue to live apart.[27] In any event nearly any separation agreement containing provisions of any consequence will necessarily meet the requirements of consideration. If no other provision seems appropriate, the ordinary promise to live apart may always be inserted.

Although the traditional statute of frauds does not require separation agreements to be in writing,[28] some of the divorce statutes do so[29] and in addition may require other formalities such as notarization.[30] Where there

---

18. Lampkin v. Lampkin, 480 S.W.2d 35 (Tex.Civ.App. 1972). Landa v. Astin, 193 F.2d 369 (D.C.Cir.1951) enforced a sealed separation agreement without consideration. For an executed agreement see Price v. Price, 24 Cal.App.2d 462, 75 P.2d 655 (1938). For a separation agreement which was no more than an agreement to agree and unenforceable for that reason, see Simmons v. Simmons, 37 Md.App. 202, 376 A.2d 1147 (1977).

19. E.g., Morrow v. Morrow, 40 Cal.App.2d 474, 105 P.2d 129 (1940); Frank v. Frank, 203 Md. 361, 101 A.2d 224 (1953), second appeal 207 Md. 124, 113 A.2d 411 (1955); Cronin v. Hebditch, 195 Md. 607, 74 A.2d 50 (1950), 11 Md.L.Rev. 350 (1950); Johns v. McNabb, 247 S.W.2d 640 (Mo.1952); Cohen v. Cohen, 6 N.J.Super. 26, 69 A.2d 752 (App.Div.1949); Rehill v. Rehill, 306 N.Y. 126, 116 N.E.2d 281 (1953). In Kay v. Kay, 460 Pa. 680, 334 A.2d 585 (1975) the court enforced a separation agreement over the husband's objection when there was no consideration.

20. Chilwell v. Chilwell, 40 Cal.App.2d 550, 105 P.2d 122 (1940); Gummerson v. Gummerson, 14 Cal.App.2d 450, 58 P.2d 394 (1936); Cooper v. Cooper, 112 Colo. 140, 146 P.2d 986 (1944); Peters v. Peters, 20 Del.Ch. 28, 169 A. 298 (1933); Salinas v. Salinas, 187 Misc. 509, 62 N.Y.S.2d 385 (Sup.Ct.1946), affirmed 271 App.Div. 917, 67 N.Y.S.2d 692 (1st Dep't 1947); Cleary v. LaFrance, 109 Vt. 422, 199 A. 242 (1938).

21. Kirkland v. Kirkland, 236 Ala. 120, 181 So. 96 (1938); Laleman v. Crombez, 6 Ill.2d 194, 127 N.E.2d 489 (1955); Mayhew v. Chapman, 117 N.J.Eq. 27, 174 A. 733 (Ct.Err. & App.1934); Blankenship v. Blankenship, 234 N.C. 162, 66 S.E.2d 680 (1951); Tullis v. Tullis, 138 Ohio St. 187, 34 N.E.2d 212 (1941); Lampkin v. Lampkin, 480 S.W.2d 35 (Tex.Civ.App.1972); Eschner v. Eschner, 146 Va. 417, 131 S.E. 800 (1926).

22. Whitten v. Bird, 23 Del.Ch. 36, 2 A.2d 83 (1938); Shankland v. Shankland, 301 Ill. 524, 134 N.E. 67 (1922); Campbell v. Campbell, 234 N.C. 188, 66 S.E.2d 672 (1951). But see Coombs v. Coombs, 120 Me. 103, 113 A. 20 (1921).

23. See section 17.1, supra, on the duty of both spouses to support the children of the marriage.

24. Bennett v. Bennett, 219 Cal. 153, 25 P.2d 426 (1933); Peters v. Peters, 20 Del.Ch. 28, 169 A. 298 (1933); Folds v. Folds, 187 Ga. 463, 1 S.E.2d 4 (1939); Vanderburgh v. Vanderburgh, 152 Minn. 189, 188 N.W. 276 (1922).

25. Hayes v. Hayes, 65 Ga.App. 222, 15 S.E.2d 626 (1941), transferred from 191 Ga. 237, 11 S.E.2d 764 (1940); North v. North, 339 Mo. 1226, 100 S.W.2d 582 (1936); In re Lineaweaver's Estate, 284 Pa. 384, 131 A. 378 (1925).

26. 1A A. Corbin, Contracts § 189 (1963); J. Calamari, J. Perillo, The Law of Contracts 145 (2d ed.1977); Ferson, Consideration and Contracts, 28 Rocky Mt.L.Rev. 31, 47–51 (1955).

27. Hagen v. Viney, 124 Fla. 747, 169 So. 391 (1936) (semble); Murphy v. Murphy, 308 Ky. 194, 213 S.W.2d 601 (1948); Hoskins v. Hoskins, 201 Ky. 208, 256 S.W. 1 (1923); Fisher v. Fisher, 53 N.D. 631, 207 N.W. 434 (1926); Huffman v. Huffman, 311 Pa. 123, 166 A. 570 (1933) (semble); Granat v. Granat, 189 Wash. 308, 65 P.2d 220 (1937) (semble). Contra: Landes v. Landes, 94 Misc. 486, 159 N.Y.S. 586 (1916), affirmed 172 App.Div. 758, 159 N.Y.S. 230 (1st Dep't 1916).

28. Statute of Frauds, 29 Car. II, c. 3 (1677).

29. E.g. Uniform Marriage and Divorce Act § 306(a), 9A Unif.L.Ann. 135 (1979). But see In re Marriage of Chambers, 657 P.2d 458 (Colo.App.1982), holding that the Uniform Act does not require a written agreement. See also Carter v. Carter, 656 S.W.2d 257 (Ky.App.1983); Dominick v. Dominick, 18 Mass.App.Ct. 85, 463 N.E.2d 564 (1984), review denied 392 Mass. 1103, 456 N.E.2d 262 (1984); Turpin v. Turpin, 570 S.W.2d 831 (Mo.App.1978).

30. E.g., Mass.Gen.L.Ann. ch. 208, § 1A (1981).

is no such statutory requirement, an oral agreement may be enforceable.[31] As a practical matter, for the protection of all parties the separation agreement should be in writing whatever the local law may require or permit.

 WESTLAW REFERENCES

"separation agreement" /s law /2 contract

di(separation /2 agreement /p sufficien! insufficien! adequa! inadequa! /p consideration)

separation /2 agreement /p "statute of fraud" (oral! /s enforc!)

§ 18.2 Separation Agreements—Fraud, Duress and Unfairness [1]

The statement was made in the preceding section that in general the law of contracts applies to separation agreements.[2] The most significant qualification on that statement is the subject of this section. Although fraud and duress and to some extent unfairness may be grounds for the courts' refusal to enforce contracts today,[3] they are much more likely to have that effect on separation agreements than on ordinary commercial contracts. The reason for this is that in spite of the enactment of non-fault grounds for divorce in most states and the corresponding freedom which that gives to the spouses to end their marriage, the state still asserts an interest in the terms on which the marriage ends. This is most obviously true respecting custody and

the support of children, but it is true of alimony and the division of property as well. In part the state's interest is a survival from the days when it exerted complete control over the process of divorce and the incidents of marriage.[4] More importantly, it reflects a legitimate desire to ensure, as far as may be equitable, that the purposes of alimony, child support and property divisions are fulfilled so that the ex-spouse and the children of the marriage do not have to be supported by the state.[5] The avoidance of support obligations by means of separation agreements resulting from fraud, duress or less obvious forms of unfairness is no more to be countenanced than when it is accomplished by outright refusal to comply with divorce decrees.[6]

Some courts prefer to base their concern with the terms of separation agreements upon the view that the relationship of husband and wife is a confidential one requiring the spouses to make a full disclosure of the extent of their property and of other relevant facts in the negotiations leading to their separation agreement.[7] It has been argued in an earlier section that prospective spouses who make an antenuptial agreement have such a confidential relationship and that the reason for this is that each of them is likely to have placed a special reliance or trust in the other as they enter the marriage.[8] When the marriage is in the process of breaking up and the spouses

---

31. Rice v. Rice, 219 Kan. 569, 549 P.2d 555 (1976); Di Giacomo v. Di Giacomo, 80 N.J. 155, 402 A.2d 922 (1979); Smith v. Phelps, 218 Tenn. 369, 403 S.W.2d 747 (1966).

§ 18.2

1. For a thorough and thoughtful discussion of the subject of this section see Sharp, Fairness Standards and Separation Agreements: A Word of Caution on Contractual Freedom, 132 U.Pa.L.Rev. 1399 (1984).

2. See section 18.1, supra, at note 17.

3. For fraudulent contracts, see E. Farnsworth, Contracts §§ 4.9 to 4.15 (1982). Duress in contracts is discussed in the same work in §§ 4.16 to 4.20. And unfairness and unconscionability in contracts generally is discussed in §§ 4.27 and 4.28 of the same work. The influence of the Uniform Commercial Code § 2–302, 1 Unif.L.Ann. 252 (1976) on the law of contracts has been much commented on. See, e.g., Leff, Unconscionability and the Code—The Emperor's New Clause, 115 U.Pa.L. Rev. 485 (1967). That provision authorizes the court to refuse to enforce a contract which it finds to have been unconscionable at the time it was made.

4. See the historical discussions in sections 2.1, 2.2, and 12.1, supra, and Christian v. Christian, 42 N.Y.2d 63, 396 N.Y.S.2d 817, 365 N.E.2d 849 (1977) which asserts the traditional state's interest.

5. See sections 15.1, 16.1 and 17.1, supra.

6. The problems of enforcement of alimony, property divisions and child support decrees are discussed supra, in sections 16.6, 16.7, 17.3 and 17.4.

7. Francois v. Francois, 599 F.2d 1286 (3d Cir.1979), cert. denied 444 U.S. 1021, 100 S.Ct. 679, 62 L.Ed.2d 653 (1980); Bodine v. Bodine, 103 Idaho 185, 646 P.2d 427 (App.1982), judgment affirmed 150 Idaho 477, 670 P.2d 884 (1983); Daffin v. Daffin, 567 S.W.2d 672 (Mo.App. 1978); Hall v. Otterson, 52 N.J.Eq. 522, 28 A. 907 (1894), affirmed 53 N.J.Eq. 695, 35 A. 1130 (1895); Christian v. Christian, 42 N.Y.2d 63, 396 N.Y.S.2d 817, 365 N.E.2d 849 (1977).

8. See section 1.1, supra, at note 15.

are coming to an agreement about such matters as alimony and the division of their property, it is less clear that such a special trust exists between them. In some cases it may continue in spite of their estrangement.[9] In other cases each spouse may be represented by an attorney and any negotiations may be carried on as much at arm's length as if they were engaged in a business transaction.[10] This being the case, it is difficult realistically to hold that a confidential relationship exists whenever the spouses make a separation agreement.[11]

It therefore seems preferable not to rest a requirement of full disclosure and essential fairness in separation agreements upon a finding of confidential relationship but rather upon the public interest in having spouses and children adequately provided for after divorce. There is a further reason for imposing a requirement of essential fairness in the spouses' negotiations with each other which does not seem to have been noticed in the cases but which is equally important. It is generally conceded that the law should encourage the resolution of financial, property and custody issues in divorce through the processes of mediation, negotiation and agreement rather than by litigation.[12] Those processes will be more likely to succeed if the parties and their lawyers know in advance

that a full disclosure and fairness will be insisted upon by the courts when they are called upon to approve the agreement. That knowledge should give them the confidence to proceed without fear of being imposed upon. The statutes of many states do in fact impose this requirement when they forbid the approval of "unconscionable" agreements.[13]

The degree to which the courts will recognize fraud, duress and unfairness as grounds for invalidating separation agreements may often be affected by the manner in which the case arises. If the separation agreement is incorporated in the divorce decree and one of the spouses later contends that fraud or unfairness or duress led to the execution of the agreement, the correct analysis is that before relief may be granted the complaining spouse must prove the sort of fraud which justifies setting aside a judgment.[14] This analysis may sometimes not be followed and a certain amount of confusion thereby created.[15] Conversely, if the agreement is attacked when it is presented to the divorce court for that court's approval in the first instance, that court generally has great freedom pursuant to the applicable statute to reject the agreement, to accept it, or to accept it with modifications.[16] In these cases also the court may not make clear just what it thinks the procedural posture of the case is.[17]

---

9. A good example occurs in Daffin v. Daffin, 567 S.W.2d 672 (Mo.App.1978).

10. The court found this to be the case in Bell v. Bell, 38 Md.App. 10, 379 A.2d 419 (1977), although it seems doubtful on the facts.

11. Several states take the position that whether or not there is a confidential relationship between husband and wife is a question of fact to be determined in each case. See, e.g., In re Marriage of Connolly, 23 Cal.3d 590, 153 Cal.Rptr. 423, 591 P.2d 911 (1979); Blum v. Blum, 59 Md.App. 584, 477 A.2d 289 (1984); Craft v. Craft, 478 So. 2d 258 (Miss.1985); Butler v. Butler, 464 Pa. 522, 347 A.2d 477 (1975). At least one state holds that there is no confidential relationship between the parties to a divorce suit. Harder v. Harder, 49 Or.App. 582, 619 P.2d 1367 (1980). See also Sharp, Fairness Standards and Separation Agreements: A Word of Caution on Contractual Freedom, 132 U.Pa.L.Rev. 1399, 1414 (1984).

12. See section 14.8, supra.

13. Uniform Marriage and Divorce Act § 306(b), 9A Unif.L.Ann. 135 (1979).

14. Cases of this kind are discussed in section 19.14, infra. See also section 14.6, supra.

15. Cases which set aside agreements which have been incorporated in divorce decrees without mention of the rules relating to vacating judgments include Bellow v. Bellow, 40 Ill.App.3d 442, 352 N.E.2d 427 (1976); Adams v. Adams, 376 So.2d 1204 (Fla.App.1979), cert. denied 388 So.2d 1109 (Fla. 1980), Hager v. Hager, 6 Mass.App. 903, 378 N.E.2d 459 (1978); Alexander v. Sagehorn, 600 S.W.2d 198 (Mo.App.1980). It may well be that these cases give evidence that the strict rules governing attack on judgments are being changed where the judgment in question resulted from an agreement between the parties, at least when those parties were formerly husband and wife. But the cases cited omit to tell us whether such an important change in the law of judgments and of res judicata is contemplated.

16. Cases of this kind are discussed in section 18.5, infra.

17. E.g., In re Marriage of Kesler, 59 Ohio Misc. 33, 392 N.E.2d 905 (1978), in which the court sets aside the separation agreement on the ground of the wife's lack of counsel and the unfairness of the provision for her.

The cases under discussion in the present section arise in ways intermediate between attacks on divorce decrees and objections to the divorce courts' approval of agreements. They arise when a spouse seeks to cancel the separation agreement or to make a claim for support or property inconsistent with the agreement on the ground that the agreement was reached as a result of fraud, duress or other inequitable conduct.

It is clear that separation agreements are vitiated by fraud in the sense of a misrepresentation of fact, just as ordinary contracts would be. The misrepresentation usually concerns the amount or the value of the property being divided,[18] but it may relate to other matters material to the execution of the agreement.[19] An innocent misrepresentation may be grounds for upsetting the agreement in the view of some cases.[20] Concealment of

material facts may also be a ground for invalidating the agreement.[21]

Duress as a reason for attack upon separation agreements calls forth a great diversity of responses in judicial decisions. Some courts define duress in a way which would be appropriate for business contracts, as requiring proof of a wrongful act which deprives the complaining spouse of his ability to enter voluntarily into the contract.[22] Others place their reliance upon undue influence, which seems to mean that the circumstances surrounding the execution of the contract indicated that one spouse was dominant over the other.[23] In those cases there is often little attempt to find wrongful conduct in the usual sense of that phrase. The finding of duress or undue influence is made easier if the complaining spouse was not given the opportunity to be represented by counsel.[24] In at least a few cases the courts are beginning to recog-

---

18. In re McNutt's Estate, 36 Cal.App.2d 542, 98 P.2d 253 (1940); Baker v. Baker, 394 So.2d 465 (Fla.App.1981), review denied 402 So.2d 607 (Fla. 1981); Adams v. Adams, 376 So.2d 1204 (Fla.App.1979), cert. denied 388 So.2d 1109 (Fla. 1980); Bodine v. Bodine, 103 Idaho 185, 646 P.2d 427 (1982), judgment affirmed 150 Idaho 477, 670 P.2d 884 (1983); James v. James, 14 Ill.2d 295, 152 N.E.2d 582 (1958), on remand 24 Ill.App.2d 445, 164 N.E.2d 505 (1960); Bellow v. Bellow, 40 Ill.App.3d 442, 352 N.E.2d 427 (1976); Hager v. Hager, 6 Mass.App. 903, 378 N.E.2d 459 (1978); Alexander v. Sagehorn, 600 S.W.2d 198 (Mo. App.1980).

The claim of fraud may be barred by laches. Toomey v. Toomey, 13 Cal.2d 317, 89 P.2d 634 (1939).

19. If marital misconduct is not material to the division of property or to the award of alimony, it would seem that this need not be disclosed in the course of negotiations leading to the separation agreement. Bearden v. Bearden, 272 S.C. 378, 252 S.E.2d 128 (1979) held that a wife had no duty to disclose pre-separation marital misconduct in this situation. But In re Marriage of Brewer, 592 S.W.2d 529 (Mo.App.1979) upset an agreement where the husband had misrepresented his relationship with a woman other than his wife.

20. Matt v. Matt, 115 Colo. 589, 178 P.2d 419 (1947).

21. Kerslake v. Kerslake, 609 P.2d 559 (Alaska 1980); Best v. Best, 202 Mont. 109, 656 P.2d 201 (1982). But see In re Marriage of Bashwiner, 107 Ill.App.3d 772, 63 Ill. Dec. 559, 438 N.E.2d 490 (1982). Wales v. Wadham [1977] 1 W.L.R. 199, [1977] 2 All E.R. 125 held that the wife's concealment of her intention to remarry did not warrant cancelling the separation agreement.

22. E.g., In re Marriage of Gonzalez, 57 Cal.App.3d 736, 129 Cal.Rptr. 566 (1976); Blum v. Blum, 59 Md.App. 584, 477 A.2d 289 (1984); Eckstein v. Eckstein, 38 Md. App. 506, 379 A.2d 757 (1978).

If the complaining party signed the separation agreement voluntarily, the claim of duress must fail. Bell v. Bell, 38 Md.App. 10, 379 A.2d 419 (1977); Surlak v. Surlak, 95 A.D.2d 371, 466 N.Y.S.2d 461 (2d Dep't 1983); Johnson v. Johnson, 67 N.C.App. 250, 313 S.E.2d 162 (1984).

The cases are also in conflict concerning the burden of proof of undue influence or fraud. If, as some courts hold, there is a confidential relationship between the spouses in the execution of the separation agreement, the burden of proof may be imposed upon the spouse seeking to uphold the agreement. Robert O. v. Ecmel A., 460 A.2d 1321 (Del.Sup.1983). If the court finds no such confidential relationship, the party attacking the agreement has the burden of proof. In re Ratony's Estate, 443 Pa. 454, 277 A.2d 791 (1971); McGannon v. McGannon, 241 Pa.Super. 45, 359 A.2d 431 (1976); DiPietro v. DiPietro, 10 Ohio App.3d 44, 460 N.E.2d 657 (1983). The latter two cases require proof by clear and convincing evidence.

23. Francois v. Francois, 599 F.2d 1286 (3d Cir.1979), cert. denied 444 U.S. 1021, 100 S.Ct. 679, 67 L.Ed.2d 653 (1980); Robert O. v. Ecmel A., 460 A.2d 1321 (Del.Sup. 1983); McGowan v. McGowan, 663 S.W.2d 219 (Ky.App. 1983); Link v. Link, 278 N.C. 181, 179 S.E.2d 697 (1971).

A spouse who consents to a separation agreement as a result of a trial judge's indication in advance of trial of the way he would divide the parties' property may be voidable on the ground of duress. In re Marriage of Hitchcock, 265 N.W.2d 599 (Iowa 1978), appeal after remand 309 N.W.2d 432 (Iowa 1981).

24. Where the spouse thought that the other spouse's lawyer was representing both parties, though that was not the case, the court found the contract oppressive and unfair in Jensen v. Jensen, 97 Idaho 922, 557 P.2d 200 (1976). Where the complaining spouse was represented by counsel at all times, the court denied the claim of

nize that a separation agreement may be set aside when one of the spouses threatens to assert a claim to custody for the purpose of winning an advantage in negotiations over property.[25] The contemporary popularity of statutes encouraging awards of joint custody may often give one spouse or the other a potent weapon in bargaining about property,[26] since demands for joint custody may easily be made by a spouse who has no serious intention of taking on full time child care. This weapon may be used in many cases.[27] This places a heavy burden on trial courts to distinguish those cases from others in which bona fide claims to custody are being made.

Fraud and duress as grounds for the invalidation of separation agreements shade off into another ground which, for lack of a more precise term, may best be labeled "unfairness".[28] The term "unfairness", when relied upon to justify the avoidance or cancellation of separation agreements, covers a wide range of evidentiary circumstances, many of which arise in combination in the cases, making it difficult to establish just which circumstance

might be decisive.[29] The statutes in many states provide that when, in the divorce suit, the parties present a separation agreement to the court for its approval the court must determine whether the agreement is "unconscionable".[30] Although these statutes do not literally apply to the situation under discussion in this section, i.e. one in which a party sues to cancel the agreement or seeks to avoid its application to him, the courts today tend to apply the term "unconscionable" to this situation as well.[31] "Unconscionable" has been defined in several ways. One leading case defines it as referring to a bargain which no person in his senses and not under a delusion would make, on the one hand, and, on the other hand, such as no honest and fair person would accept.[32] Although this is not a helpful definition, it does suggest that a separation agreement would be set aside if it just provides an amount of alimony or property for a spouse which appears to be very much larger or very much smaller than a court would consider appropriate. Another important case has defined "unconscionable" as re-

duress in Wile v. Wile, 100 A.D.2d 932, 474 N.Y.S.2d 821 (2d Dep't 1984).

The physical and emotional condition of the complaining spouse is also relevant in determining whether undue influence or overreaching has occurred. Link v. Link, 278 N.C. 181, 179 S.E.2d 697 (1971). Cases in which the spouse's condition was not sufficient to support such a finding include Filko v. Filko, 127 Ill.App.2d 10, 262 N.E.2d 88 (1970); Reiner v. Miller, 478 S.W.2d 283 (Mo. 1972).

25. Robert O. v. Ecmel A., 460 A.2d 1321 (Del.Sup. 1983); McGowan v. McGowan, 663 S.W.2d 219 (Ky.App. 1983); Link v. Link, 278 N.C. 181, 179 S.E.2d 697 (1971).

26. Joint custody is discussed infra in section 19.5.

27. See the discussion of the leverage which this weapon gives to husbands in R. Neely, The Divorce Decision 60–67 (1984). The courts are sometimes, but not always, tolerant of the use of this weapon in negotiations. Compare In re Marriage of Lawrence, 197 Mont. 262, 642 P.2d 1043 (1982), seeming to accept this bargaining ploy, with In re Marriage of Carlson, 101 Ill.App.3d 924, 57 Ill. Dec. 325, 428 N.E.2d 1005 (1981) which sets aside an agreement where the wife got a very small share of the property when the husband threatened to take the children.

28. Harding v. Harding, 461 S.W.2d 235 (Tex.Civ.App. 1970), appeal after remand 485 S.W.2d 297 (Tex.Civ.App. 1972). The complaining spouse may be required to plead the facts on which he relies for the claim of unfairness, the pleading of conclusory statements not being sufficient. Robinson v. Robinson, 111 A.D.2d 316, 489

N.Y.S.2d 301 (2d Dep't 1985); appeal dismissed 66 N.Y.2d 613, 498 N.Y.S.2d 1030, 489 N.E.2d 258 (1985).

29. Dominick v. Dominick, 18 Mass.App.Ct. 85, 463 N.E.2d 564 (1984), review denied 392 Mass. 1103, 465 N.E.2d 262 (1984) lists as the circumstances to be taken into account in determining the fairness of an agreement the following: 1) the nature and substance of the complaining party's complaint; 2) the financial and property division provisions of the agreement; 3) the context in which the negotiations took place; 4) the complexity of the issues involved; 5) the background and knowledge of the parties; 6) the abilities and experience of counsel; 7) the need for and availability of experts; 8) certain other statutory factors.

30. E.g., Uniform Marriage and Divorce Act § 306(b), 9A Unif.L.Ann. 135 (1979). The Commissioners' Note to this section, after referring to the Uniform Commercial Code standard of unconscionability as including protection against overreaching, concealment of assets and sharp dealing, states that the courts may consider the economic circumstances of the parties resulting from the agreement, the conditions under which the agreement was made and the knowledge of the defendant spouse.

31. In re Marriage of Wigner, 40 Colo.App. 253, 572 P.2d 495 (1977).

32. Christian v. Christian, 42 N.Y.2d 63, 396 N.Y.S.2d 817, 365 N.E.2d 849 (1977). The court in this case characterized the husband-wife relationship as a confidential one and said that the separation agreement could be set aside if manifestly unfair due to overreaching.

quiring, first, evidence of fraud, overreaching, concealment of assets or other sharp dealing, and second, evidence that the resulting agreement is not fair, just and reasonable for both parties.[33] It seems likely that in practice if the result is unfair in its provision for one of the spouses, there will also have been fraud, duress or some lesser form of inequality in the bargaining process.

When these standards are applied in specific cases, the results will not usually be much in doubt. Thus if a full disclosure of assets is not made, this should be a sufficient ground for the cancellation of the agreement, where the separation agreement fails to make a reasonably adequate provision for the complaining spouse.[34] In some states it is sufficient to prove either that there was a full disclosure or that the complaining spouse had independent legal advice [35] but that approach holds out the temptation to engage in chicanery when there are lawyers on both sides and for that reason seems unsound. In the rare case in which there is a full disclosure but the financial provisions of the agreement are unreasonably disproportionate to the spouse's means, the court may set the agreement aside if there is evidence that the complaining spouse did not understand the agreement or was not properly represented.[36] Where the

unfairness relates to the provision for child support, the court will be even more likely to set the agreement aside.[37]

Conversely, if the separation agreement makes a reasonably adequate provision for the spouse, the fact that he was not represented by an attorney does not make the agreement unfair.[38] The courts in general will not approve attempts to revise separation agreements when one of the parties thinks he should have received a greater share of the property unless there is a substantial unfairness either in the procedure leading to the execution of the agreement or in the amount of the provision for the complaining spouse or (as is usually the case) in both respects.[39] Although the parties and their lawyers should be required to observe ordinary standards of fair treatment in the negotiation and preparation of separation agreements, this requirement should not be relied upon by trial courts to rewrite such agreements unless this sort of unfairness is demonstrated.

 **WESTLAW REFERENCES**

separation /2 agreement /s confiden! /3 relationship

separation /2 agreement /s full! scope complete! /3 disclos!

separation /2 agreement /s unconscionab! /s statut!

33. In re Marriage of Manzo, 659 P.2d 669 (Colo.1983), relying in part upon the Commissioners' Note to the Uniform Marriage and Divorce Act cited in note 30, supra. In re Marriage of Carlson, 101 Ill.App.3d 924, 57 Ill.Dec. 325, 428 N.E.2d 1005 (1981) specifically holds that a determination of unconscionability requires consideration of two factors: 1) the conditions under which the agreement was made, and 2) the economic circumstances of the parties resulting from the agreement. Accord: In re Marriage of Riedy, 130 Ill.App.3d 311, 85 Ill.Dec. 614, 474 N.E.2d 28 (1985).

34. In re Cover's Estate, 188 Cal. 133, 204 P. 583 (1922); In re Brimhall's Estate, 62 Cal.App.2d 30, 143 P.2d 981 (1943); Pilati v. Pilati, 181 Mont. 182, 592 P.2d 1374 (1979); Hall v. Otterson, 52 N.J.Eq. 522, 28 A. 907 (1894), affirmed 53 N.J.Eq. 695, 35 A. 1130 (1895); Christian v. Christian, 42 N.Y.2d 63, 396 N.Y.S.2d 817, 365 N.E.2d 849 (1977) (dictum); In re Marriage of Eltzroth, 67 Or.App. 520, 679 P.2d 1369 (1984) (dictum).

35. Collins v. Collins, 48 Cal.2d 325, 309 P.2d 420 (1957); O'Connor v. O'Connor, 435 So.2d 344 (Fla.App. 1983); Annot., 123 A.L.R. 1505, 1517 (1939).

36. Crawford v. Crawford, 39 Ill.App.3d 457, 350 N.E.2d 103 (1976); In re Kesler, 59 Ohio Misc. 33, 392 N.E.2d 905 (1978); Matter of Marriage of Olsen, 24 Wash.

App. 292, 600 P.2d 690 (1979). If an exculpatory provision is included in the separation agreement, such as an acknowledgment by both parties that the agreement is fair, this may cause the burden of proof of invalidity to shift to the spouse attacking the decree or may in other ways affect the court's decision on validity. Weinstein v. Weinstein, 109 A.D.2d 881, 487 N.Y.S.2d 75 (2d Dep't 1985). It would seem, however, that if the entire agreement is induced by fraud, duress or unfairness the exculpatory clause should fall along with the rest of the agreement.

37. Debry v. Debry, 27 Utah 2d 337, 496 P.2d 92 (1972).

38. Wilke v. Wilke, 51 Ill.App.3d 438, 9 Ill.Dec. 462, 366 N.E.2d 973 (1977); Levine v. Levine, 56 N.Y.2d 42, 451 N.Y.S.2d 26, 436 N.E.2d 476 (1982).

39. Cases which illustrate the application of this principle include In re Marriage of Weck, 706 P.2d 436 (Colo. App.1985); In re Marriage of Brandt, 140 Ill.App.3d 1019, 95 Ill.Dec. 340, 489 N.E.2d 902 (1986); In re Marriage of Kloster, 127 Ill.App.3d 583, 82 Ill.Dec. 847, 469 N.E.2d 381 (1984); Miller v. Miller, 98 Ill.App.3d 1084, 54 Ill.Dec. 439, 424 N.E.2d 1342 (1981); In re Marriage of Cohn, 18 Wash.App. 502, 569 P.2d 79 (1977).

```
separation /2 agreement /s incorporat! /s divorc! dissol!
    /2 order decree /s fraud!

separation /2 agreement /s unfair! /s set setting +1
    aside
```

§ 18.3 Separation Agreements—Validity of Particular Provisions

Particular provisions of separation agreements may be invalid even though the circumstances under which an agreement is executed are not objectionable. In the heyday of the fault grounds for divorce the most common of the invalid provisions were those which aimed in one way or another at the procurement of a divorce. The courts found many of them to "promote" or "facilitate" divorce and therefore to run afoul of the policy discussed in an earlier section.[1] Of course most separation agreements facilitate divorce in the sense that they settle incidental disputes which might otherwise make the time and expense of the proceedings onerous.[2]

§ 18.3

1. See section 18.1, supra, at note 10.

2. Hill v. Hill, 23 Cal.2d 82, 142 P.2d 417 (1943); Mnookin, Divorce Bargaining: The Limits on Private Ordering, 18 U.Mich.J.L.Ref. 1015 (1985).

3. Alexander, Let's Get the Embattled Spouses Out of the Trenches, 18 Law & Contemp.Probs. 98, 101 (1953).

4. E.g., Uniform Marriage and Divorce Act § 306(a), and Commissioners' Note, 9A Unif.L.Ann. 135, 136 (1979).

5. Plant v. Plant, 57 A.2d 204 (D.C.Mun.Ct. of App. 1948); Hood v. Roleson, 125 Ark. 30, 187 S.W. 1059 (1917); Beard v. Beard, 65 Cal. 354, 4 P. 229 (1884); Brainard v. Brainard, 82 Cal.App.2d 478, 186 P.2d 990 (1947); Green v. Green, 66 Cal.App.2d 50, 151 P.2d 679 (1944); Law v. Law, 186 Ga. 113, 197 S.E. 272 (1938); Morrissey v. Morrissey, 299 Ill.App. 173, 19 N.E.2d 835 (1939); Chrysler Corp. v. Disich, 295 Mich. 261, 294 N.W. 673 (1940); Gardine v. Cottey, 360 Mo. 681, 230 S.W.2d 731 (1950); Hemingway v. Ball, 118 N.J.Eq. 378, 179 A. 374 (Ch.1935); affirmed without opinion, 119 N.J.Eq. 471, 183 A. 172 (Ch.1936); Riggle v. Riggle, 148 N.E.2d 72, 76 O.L.A. 530 (Ohio App.1957); Campbell v. Campbell, 75 N.E.2d 698 (Ohio C.P.1947); Giddings v. Giddings, 167 Or. 504, 114 P.2d 1009 (1941); Perry v. Perry, 183 Tenn. 362, 192 S.W.2d 830 (1946).

6. Hill v. Hill, 23 Cal.2d 82, 142 P.2d 417 (1943) (dictum), 17 So.Cal.L.Rev. 184 (1944).

7. Williams v. Williams, 261 App.Div. 470, 25 N.Y.S.2d 940 (4th Dep't 1941), judgment affirmed 287 N.Y. 799, 40 N.E.2d 1017 (1942). But a grievance committee has found that it is not improper for the wife's lawyer to accept the husband's agreement to furnish, in consideration of a money settlement, witnesses to acts by

This hardly seems a reason to hold such provisions invalid. As Judge Alexander once said, no sensible purpose is served by saying to the spouses, "The minute you begin to behave like civilized humans, we will deny your divorce."[3] In fact today many legislatures have adopted the more enlightened view that the settlement of marital disputes by agreement is to be encouraged rather than discouraged.[4]

In one group of cases the courts generally held invalid provisions in the agreement which promised to relinquish or abandon a defense,[5] which called for the concealment or destruction of evidence supporting a defense,[6] or which contemplated the procurement of evidence demonstrating the grounds for divorce.[7] On the other hand the courts distinguished provisions which merely recited that the parties contemplated divorce or which conditioned the operation of the agreement on the granting of the divorce to one spouse or the other, holding such provisions to be valid,[8]

him which would constitute grounds for divorce. Opinion No. 86, N.Y. County Lawyers' Committee; Drinker, Legal Ethics 123 (1953).

A promise by the wife to accept $10,000 in settlement of all claims if the husband should be guilty of further misconduct giving grounds for divorce is also invalid. Pereira v. Pereira, 156 Cal. 1, 103 P. 488 (1909). See also Wolkovisky v. Rapaport, 216 Mass. 48, 102 N.E. 910 (1913) holding invalid a trust under which $2000 was to be paid to the wife when she should get a divorce.

The courts also held void contracts in which a spouse agreed to get the divorce. Miller v. Criswell, 54 Cal.App. 2d 524, 129 P.2d 450 (1942); People v. Walker, 409 Ill. 413, 100 N.E.2d 621 (1951); Wagner v. Shelly, 241 Mo. App. 259, 235 S.W.2d 414 (1950) (dictum); Harris v. Harris, 287 N.Y. 444, 40 N.E.2d 245 (1942); Shelton v. Stewart, 193 Va. 162, 67 S.E.2d 841 (1951). In the well known case of Viles v. Viles, 14 N.Y.2d 365, 251 N.Y.S.2d 672, 200 N.E.2d 567 (1964), 51 Corn.L.Q. 135, 63 Mich.L. Rev. 735, 50 Va.L.Rev. 1448 (1965) a collateral promise by the wife to get a Virgin Islands divorce was held invalid. Contra: Arnold v. Arnold's Ex'x., 314 Ky. 734, 237 S.W.2d 58 (1951); Moore v. Moore, 197 Tenn. 360, 273 S.W.2d 148 (1954); Annot., 130 A.L.R. 1008 (1941). This result was sometimes reached without regard to whether grounds for divorce did or did not exist. Bishop v. Bishop, 162 S.W.2d 332 (Mo.App.1942).

8. Divorce contemplated: Huntsberger v. Huntsberger, 2 Cal.2d 655, 43 P.2d 258 (1935); Briner v. Briner, 63 Cal.App.2d 429, 146 P.2d 709 (1944); Ward v. Goodrich, 34 Colo. 369, 82 P. 701 (1905); Gallemore v. Gallemore, 94 Fla. 516, 114 So. 371 (1927); Watson v. Burnley, 150 Ga. 460, 104 S.E. 220 (1920); Craig v. Craig,

although the practical difference between these and the first type of provision was non-existent in most cases. In still a third group of cases the separation agreements provided that one of the spouses would assist the other in obtaining the divorce, by filing an appearance in the divorce action or by paying litigation expenses or counsel fees for the other spouse. Some courts held these provisions valid [9] and some held them invalid.[10] These provisions also could not really be distinguished from others which were routinely held valid. These provisions were usually inserted in separation agreements in order to assure the plaintiff that he would get the benefit of the Sherrer rule [11] protecting migratory divorces.

With the enactment of no-fault divorce statutes in most of the states, much, if not all, of

the legal lore just described became either obsolete or irrelevant. For example, in a state which has abolished the defenses to divorce,[12] there is no reason to include in the separation agreement a promise not to defend any divorce suit which might be brought. Promises related to obtaining out of state divorces are no longer necessary when there is little reason for getting such a divorce, as is now the fact in most states.[13] More fundamentally, the enactment of no-fault grounds for divorce and the ready availability of divorce to either spouse without the need for any contest about the grounds has demonstrated that provisions in separation agreements which look to the obtaining of a divorce, whatever their precise purpose or effect may be, no longer violate the public policy of most states.[14] There are cases which take this position,[15] although they are not numer-

53 Ga.App. 632, 186 S.E. 755 (1936); Greene v. Greene, 150 Pa.Super. 182, 27 A.2d 525 (1942).

Agreement conditioned on divorce: Frothingham v. Anthony, 69 F.2d 506 (1st Cir. 1934); Prudential Ins. Co. of America v. Rader, 98 F.Supp. 44 (D.Minn.1951); Thornton v. Rodgers, 251 Ala. 553, 38 So.2d 479 (1949); Hill v. Hill, 23 Cal.2d 82, 142 P.2d 417 (1943); Cookinham v. Cookinham, 219 Cal. 723, 28 P.2d 1045 (1934); Reynolds v. Owen, 328 Mass. 451, 104 N.E.2d 146 (1952); Kull v. Losch, 328 Mich. 519, 44 N.W.2d 169 (1950); Bishop v. Bishop, 162 S.W.2d 332 (Mo.App.1942); Koeppel v. Koeppel, 138 N.Y.S.2d 366 (1954); Dora v. Dora, 392 Pa. 433, 141 A.2d 587 (1958); Zlotziver v. Zlotziver, 355 Pa. 299, 49 A.2d 779 (1946); Evens v. Evens, 55 S.D. 482, 226 N.W. 725 (1929). Schmoker v. Schmoker, 359 Pa. 272, 59 A.2d 55 (1948) held there was no objection to an agreement that the divorce could be obtained for any ground except adultery.

Contra: Ewell v. State, 207 Md. 288, 114 A.2d 66 (1955) (semble); Silverman v. Silverman, 95 S.W.2d 1237 (Mo. App.1936); Gould v. Gould, 261 App.Div. 733, 27 N.Y.S.2d 54 (1st Dep't 1941), appeal denied 262 App.Div. 833, 29 N.Y.S.2d 503 (1st Dep't 1941).

9. Holding such an agreement valid when it provided for the reopening of the foreign divorce and entry of appearance by the defendant: Hudson v. Hudson, 36 N.J. 549, 178 A.2d 202 (1962); In re Rhinelander's Estate, 290 N.Y. 31, 47 N.E.2d 681 (1943).

Sells v. Sells, 206 Ga. 650, 58 S.E.2d 186 (1950) enforced a contract for the payment of litigation expenses, while Wasserstrom v. Pearce, 47 N.E.2d 660 (Ohio App.1942), motion denied 51 N.E.2d 236 (Ohio App.1943) held such a provision invalid.

10. An agreement for an appearance in the foreign action was held invalid by Montgomery v. Wilmerding, 26 N.J.Super. 214, 97 A.2d 745 (1953); Roberts v. Roberts, 206 Misc. 779, 134 N.Y.S.2d 877 (1954), appeal dismissed 285 App.Div. 980, 139 N.Y.S.2d 284 (1955); Reed v. Rob-

ertson, 195 Misc. 885, 91 N.Y.S.2d 583 (1949), reversed 276 App.Div. 902, 94 N.Y.S.2d 905 (1st Dep't 1950), affirmed 302 N.Y. 596, 96 N.E.2d 894 (1951).

11. Sherrer v. Sherrer, 334 U.S. 343, 68 S.Ct. 1087, 92 L.Ed. 1429 (1948), discussed in section 13.2, supra. See, e.g., Rifkin v. Rifkin, 155 Conn. 7, 229 A.2d 358 (1967), in which the court seems to have held the separation agreement invalid because it facilitated divorce on the ground that the parties had decided that the wife would obtain an out of state divorce, although the agreement contained no provision to that effect.

12. The current status of the traditional divorce defenses is discussed in sections 13.8 to 13.11, supra.

13. For the states recognizing such non-fault grounds as irretrievable breakdown of the marriage, irreconcilable differences, or incompatibility, see sections 13.5 and 13.6, supra. Where these grounds exist, the spouses have no need to resort to migratory divorce in most instances.

14. Hayes v. Beresford, 184 Conn. 558, 440 A.2d 224 (1981), holding that the validity of the separation agreement was not affected by the fact that it was quickly followed by a Mexican divorce, the court saying that after the enactment of non-fault grounds out of state divorces became both less likely and less opprobrious.

15. Browning v. Browning, 250 Ga. 450, 298 S.E.2d 496 (1983) (distinction between contracts incident to divorce and contracts facilitating divorce abolished); Sanders v. Colwell, 248 Ga. 376, 283 S.E.2d 461 (1981) (wife's agreement not to contest the divorce does not invalidate the separation agreement); Cooley v. Cooley, 220 Va. 749, 263 S.E.2d 49 (1980) (wife's promise not to contest the divorce does not invalidate the separation agreement).

Other cases reach similar results less directly. See, e.g., Walden v. Lattarulo, 6 Conn.Cir. 118, 268 A.2d 250 (1969) (upholds a separation agreement which was part of a plan to obtain a Mexican divorce); Groves v. Alexander, 255 Md. 715, 259 A.2d 285 (1969), cert. denied 397 U.S.

ous presumably because provisions of this kind are no longer being included in the agreements. In spite of these changes, there still may be courts which choose to follow the older cases in some situations, a fact which suggests some caution in including provisions about divorce in contemporary separation agreements.[16]

Another specific provision common to many separation agreements is occasionally held invalid. This is one in which a spouse releases all claims for support or takes the payments under the agreement in lieu of support. In the majority of jurisdictions such provisions are valid.[17] To some extent they have been held invalid in New York [18] in reliance upon a statute which requires that result,[19] and in New Jersey [20] and Illinois [21] under early cases which should not be controlling today.[22] The

only tenable objection to such a release should be that it resulted from fraud, duress or unfairness.[23] If the provision for the spouse is not subject to these infirmities, it should be as binding as any other financial or property provision in the separation agreement.

In negotiating their separation agreement the parties sometimes find that they wish to include provisions which a court, absent the agreement, would not have authority to impose. The question then is, may the court approve the agreement and make it part of its decree? The majority of the cases hold that the court may approve the agreement and that it and the resulting decree may be enforced according to their terms. For example, the agreement may provide that periodic payments be made to a spouse until his death or

1023, 90 S.Ct. 1263, 25 L.Ed.2d 532 (1970) (parol evidence rule bars evidence showing a collateral agreement to facilitate divorce); Narins v. Narins, 116 N.H. 200, 356 A.2d 665 (1976); Lurie v. Lurie, 246 Pa.Super. 307, 370 A.2d 739 (1976) (agreement not invalid because collaterally conducive to divorce).

The New York cases in this field are sui generis, largely due to a statute, N.Y.—McKinney's Gen.Oblig.L. § 5–311 (Supp.1986), which provides that a husband and wife may not contract to dissolve their marriage, but that a contract is not considered to be for the altering or dissolving of a marriage unless it expressly requires a dissolution of the marriage or provides for the procurement of grounds for divorce. Viles v. Viles, 14 N.Y.2d 365, 251 N.Y.S.2d 672, 200 N.E.2d 567 (1964), 51 Corn. L.Q. 135, 63 Mich.L.Rev. 735 (1965). That case invalidated a separation agreement on the authority of the statute where there was a collateral agreement that the wife would obtain a Virgin Islands divorce. The statute was amended so that the agreement is valid unless the promise to dissolve the marriage or procure grounds for divorce is in the agreement itself. Culhane v. Culhane, 119 N.H. 389, 402 A.2d 490 (1979), citing New York cases and applying New York law. But New York law seems still to void separation agreements which look toward divorce. See, e.g., Matter of Wilson's Estate, 50 N.Y.2d 59, 427 N.Y.S.2d 977, 405 N.E.2d 220 (1980) (contract for future separation is unenforceable); Shapiro v. Shapiro, 110 Misc.2d 726, 442 N.Y.S.2d 928 (1981), modified on other grounds 88 A.D.2d 592, 449 N.Y.S.2d 806 (2d Dep't 1982) (dictum that the agreement may not offer an inducement to end the marriage by providing a larger sum under the agreement than if the suit were litigated).

It is odd that the New York courts, notwithstanding the statute and the cited cases, have held that an agreement between husband and wife to the effect that one of them will obtain a "Get", a Jewish religious divorce, is enforceable and does not have a tendency to promote a divorce. Avitzur v. Avitzur, 58 N.Y.2d 108, 459 N.Y.S.2d 572, 446 N.E.2d 136 (1983), cert. denied 464 U.S. 817, 104

S.Ct. 76, 78 L.Ed.2d 88 (1983) (antenuptial agreement); Waxstein v. Waxstein, 90 Misc.2d 784, 395 N.Y.S.2d 877 (Sup.Ct.1976), affirmed 57 A.D.2d 863, 394 N.Y.S.2d 253 (2d Dep't 1977), appeal denied 42 N.Y.2d 806, 398 N.Y.S. 2d 1027, 367 N.E.2d 660 (1977); Annot., 27 A.L.R.4th 746 (1984).

16. In addition to the New York cases cited supra in note 15, see Wife, B.T.L. v. Husband, H.A.L., 287 A.2d 413 (Del.Ch.1972), judgment affirmed 336 A.2d 216 (Del.Supr. 1975) (dictum that an agreement not to defend the divorce makes the separation agreement unenforceable); Baker v. Baker, 187 Conn. 315, 445 A.2d 912 (1982) (separation agreement concealed from the divorce court is unenforceable).

17. Cases are collected in Annots., 50 A.L.R. 351 (1927) and 120 A.L.R. 1334 (1939).

18. Kyff v. Kyff, 286 N.Y. 71, 35 N.E.2d 655 (1941).

19. N.Y.—McKinney's Gen.Oblig.L. § 5–311 (Supp. 1986). This statute provides that husband and wife may not contract with each other to relieve either of them of the duty of support if the effect of the contract is that a spouse will become incapable of self-support or will be likely to become a public charge.

20. Lester v. Lester, 122 N.J.Eq. 532, 195 A. 381 (Ch. 1937).

21. Lagow v. Snapp, 400 Ill. 414, 81 N.E.2d 144 (1948). South Carolina may take the same position. Towles v. Towles, 256 S.C. 307, 182 S.E.2d 53 (1971) held that a reconciliation agreement was void when it provided that the wife would not thereafter bring any suit against the husband.

22. Illinois has the Uniform Marriage and Divorce Act, which requires the court to accept the parties' separation agreement if it is not unconscionable. Ill.—S.H.A. ch. 40, § 502(b) (Supp.1985). For the contemporary New Jersey position see Wertlake v. Wertlake, 137 N.J.Super. 476, 349 A.2d 552 (1975).

23. See section 18.2, supra.

remarriage. A few cases have had trouble determining whether under such a provision the payments should survive the payer's death.[24] Most courts construe that and similar provisions as surviving his death and hold them valid.[25] The cases likewise enforce separation agreements which provide that child support should continue beyond the age of majority, although without such an agreement the court might not be authorized to make such an order.[26] Escalation clauses providing for the increase of alimony or support are also enforced, provided that they are fair and equitable, whether or not a court could impose them in the absence of an agreement.[27] And agreements extending or limiting alimony are enforced as well.[28] But of course if the agreement is unfair in its omission of child support, it will not be enforced.[29]

It is not uncommon for separation agreements to impose conditions upon the payment of alimony. Some agreements make the amount vary with the payer's income (the escalation clause),[30] others make it depend on the amount of the payee's income,[31] or on the ages and needs of the children.[32] Nearly all provide that the payments end on the payee's remarriage.[33] They are generally conceded to be valid.[34] Performance of the custody provisions in the agreement may be a valid condition on the other spouse's liability for support of the children.[35] On the other hand it is doubtful whether the breach of a non-molestation clause in the agreement will serve as an excuse for failure to pay alimony.[36] And a leading New York case has held that the wife's breach of a covenant not to compete with her husband in business did not provide the husband with a defense to her alimony

24. In re Shideler's Estate, 172 Kan. 695, 242 P.2d 1057 (1952) held that such a provision continues the payments beyond the payer's death. Contra: In re Kettering's Estate, 151 Colo. 202, 376 P.2d 983 (1962); Billow v. Billow, 97 Ohio App. 277, 125 N.E.2d 558 (1953).

25. Daggett v. Commissioner, 128 F.2d 568 (9th Cir. 1942), cert. denied 317 U.S. 673, 63 S.Ct. 78, 87 L.Ed. 540 (1942); Anthony v. Anthony, 94 Cal.App.2d 507, 211 P.2d 331 (1949); In re Wise's Estate, 99 Colo. 562, 64 P.2d 594 (1937); Allen v. Allen, 111 Fla. 733, 150 So. 237 (1933); In re Estate of Yoss, 237 Iowa 1092, 24 N.W.2d 399 (1946); McCune v. McCune, 284 S.C. 452, 327 S.E.2d 340 (1985) (dictum); Annot., 5 A.L.R.4th 1153 (1981). Reed v. Reed, 29 Colo.App. 199, 481 P.2d 125 (1971) held that the parties could not by agreement make the wife an irrevocable beneficiary of the husband's national service life insurance, in view of the provisions of the federal statute. See also Prince v. Prince, 572 S.W.2d 908 (Tenn.1978) enforcing an agreement that the husband would insure his life in favor of the wife without discussing whether a court could order him to do so. Contra the text statement: Dolvin v. Dolvin, 248 Ga. 439, 284 S.E.2d 254 (1981).

26. Rice v. Rice, 213 Kan. 800, 518 P.2d 477 (1974); Rand v. Rand, 18 Ohio St.3d 356, 481 N.E.2d 609 (1985) (agreement required parent to pay child's tuition for religious education); Bugay v. Bugay, 53 Ohio App.2d 285, 373 N.E.2d 1263 (1977) (relying on statute); Grant v. Grant, 60 Ohio App.2d 277, 396 N.E.2d 1037 (1977).

27. Aldredge v. Aldredge, 477 So.2d 73 (La.1985) (enforced agreement that child support could be modified without proof of change of circumstances); Petersen v. Petersen, 85 N.J. 638, 428 A.2d 1301 (1981).

28. Glickman v. Collins, 13 Cal.3d 852, 120 Cal.Rptr. 76, 533 P.2d 204 (1975) (enforces an agreement by which the second wife guaranteed the husband's obligation to the first wife for child support and alimony); Scharnweber v. Scharnweber, 65 N.Y.2d 1016, 494

N.Y.S.2d 100, 484 N.E.2d 129 (1985) (separation agreement may condition alimony upon the wife's refraining from living with another man); Beard v. Worrell, 158 W.Va. 248, 212 S.E.2d 598 (1974) (separation agreement may provide for alimony notwithstanding the wife's fault, where fault would be a bar under the statute).

29. Frink v. Frink, 128 Vt. 531, 266 A.2d 820 (1970); Grosz v. Grosz, 506 P.2d 46 (Wyo.1973).

30. E.g., Alexander v. Alexander, 158 F.2d 429 (10th Cir.1946), cert. denied 330 U.S. 845, 67 S.Ct. 1086, 91 L.Ed. 1290 (1947); Hardy v. Hardy, 23 Cal.2d 244, 143 P.2d 701 (1943); Yost v. Yost, 116 Cal.App.2d 572, 253 P.2d 696 (1953); Axell v. Axell, 114 Cal.App.2d 248, 250 P.2d 182 (1952); Kohn v. Kohn, 95 Cal.App.2d 708, 214 P.2d 71 (1950); Kirkland v. Kirkland, 209 Ga. 526, 74 S.E. 2d 453 (1953); Krell v. Krell, 192 Misc. 1, 80 N.Y.S.2d 168 (1948); Hoffstaedter v. Hoffstaedter, 188 N.Y.S. 251 (1st. Dep't 1921). If the level of support is keyed to the husband's taxable income, problems of construction may arise. See e.g. Berry v. Berry, 50 Wash.2d 158, 310 P.2d 223 (1957), and Annot., 79 A.L.R.2d 609 (1961).

31. E.g., Towne v. Towne, 117 Mont. 453, 159 P.2d 352 (1945); Zuckerman v. Zuckerman, 96 N.Y.S.2d 190 (1950).

32. E.g., Craver v. Craver, 186 App.Div. 847, 175 N.Y.S. 26 (3d Dep't 1919), appeal dismissed 226 N.Y. 631, 123 N.E. 860 (1919).

33. E.g., Jones v. Jones, 1 Colo.App. 28, 27 P. 85 (1891); Watson v. Burnley, 150 Ga. 460, 104 S.E. 220 (1920).

34. See notes 30 to 33, supra.

35. Annot., 105 A.L.R. 901 (1936).

36. Cygielman v. Cygielman, 111 A.D.2d 1057, 490 N.Y.S.2d 356 (3d Dep't 1985) holds that the non-molestation and the maintenance provisions are independent, unless expressly made interdependent. Contra: Forsland v. Forsland, 46 Cal.App. 405, 189 P. 327 (1920).

claims, on the ground that the covenant not to compete was not reasonably related to the marriage.[37] The case runs counter to the contemporary judicial tolerance of provisions in separation agreements and therefore should not be followed.

The moral of the cases discussed in this section is that within the limits of the fairness standard the spouses have broad latitude in the kinds of provision which they will be permitted to insert in their separation agreements. This is consistent with the long term trend in our law in the direction of giving spouses greater control over all of the incidents of their marriages and their divorces.[38]

**WESTLAW
REFERENCES**

di(separation /2 agreement /p re-marry! re-marri! /p
  period! /3 pay paid payment)

separation /2 agreement /p molest! non-molestation /2
  provision clause

sy(separation /2 agreement /s releas! waiv! /s support!)

---

§ 18.4   Separation Agreements—Effect of Reconciliation or Offer of Reconciliation

This section presents two problems: First, what do we mean by reconciliation? Second, assuming that the parties to a separation agreement are reconciled according to our definition, what effect does that have upon the obligations and transfers pursuant to that agreement?

37. Haas v. Haas, 298 N.Y. 69, 80 N.E.2d 337 (1948), 49 Colum.L.Rev. 130 (1949), 24 N.Y.U.L.Rev. 384 (1949).

38. See, e.g., sections 2.2 and 14.8, supra.

§ 18.4

1. Agreements to rescind contracts are discussed in E. Farnsworth, Contracts 288–289 (1982).

2. E.g., Larson v. Goodman, 28 Colo.App. 418, 475 P.2d 712 (1970), cert. dismissed 177 Colo. 219, 493 P.2d 365 (1972); In re Wilson's Estate, 50 N.Y.2d 59, 427 N.Y.S.2d 977, 405 N.E.2d 220 (1980); Markowitz v. Markowitz, 52 A.D.2d 521, 381 N.Y.S.2d 678 (1st Dep't 1976) (parties must have the intent to be reconciled, to "destroy the validity of the separation agreement").

3. E.g., White v. White, 350 So.2d 326 (Ala.1977); Will of Granchelli, 90 Misc.2d 103, 393 N.Y.S.2d 894 (Surr.Ct. 1977); Whitt v. Whitt, 32 N.C.App. 125, 230 S.E.2d 793 (1977); Potts v. Potts, 24 N.C.App. 673, 211 S.E.2d 815 (1975). In Travis v. Travis, 227 Ga. 406, 181 S.E.2d 61

One might suppose at the outset that the effect of reconciliation is to be determined by the same criteria as are applicable to agreements to rescind contracts.[1] Some judicial opinions, by emphasizing the importance of the parties' intent,[2] lend force to this supposition, but there is seldom any explicit discussion of rescission or its technical requirements in the reconciliation cases. Other cases talk in terms of the "abrogation" of the separation agreement, suggesting that this occurs by operation of law rather than as a result of the parties' agreement to rescind.[3] If the abrogation does occur by operation of law, there is remarkably little discussion in the opinions of the purposes or policies lying behind the legal rules which are being applied. It also seems strange that if there is some public policy involved in these problems no state has dealt with them by statute.[4]

It is not difficult to define reconciliation, although the application of the definition to specific cases may sometimes be difficult. For the present purpose reconciliation means a voluntary resumption of marital cohabitation in the fullest sense.[5] This ordinarily requires living together as husband and wife, engaging in sexual relations, and where possible, establishing a joint domicile. The parties must intend to resume married life entirely and not merely to enjoy each other's society temporarily, for limited purposes, or as an experiment to determine whether they wish to be reconciled.[6] Acts of intercourse alone are not suffi-

(1971) the court speaks of reconciliation annulling the separation agreement.

4. One state does have a statute providing that the subsequent voluntary cohabitation of the spouses, where there has been no divorce, sets aside all provisions for permanent alimony in a deed or decree, providing however that this does not affect the rights of children. Official Ga.Code Ann. § 30–217 (Supp.1985). See also Travis v. Travis, 227 Ga. 406, 181 S.E.2d 61 (1971).

5. Keller v. Keller, 122 Cal.App. 712, 10 P.2d 541 (1932); Miller v. Miller, 189 Mont. 356, 616 P.2d 313 (1980); Hughes v. Cuming, 36 App.Div. 302, 55 N.Y.S. 256 (2d Dep't 1899), reversed on other grounds 165 N.Y. 91, 58 N.E. 794 (1900); Annot., 35 A.L.R.2d 707, 746–753 (1954); Annot., 40 A.L.R. 1227, 1238–1239 (1926).

6. Frana v. Frana, 12 Md.App. 273, 278 A.2d 94 (1971); Zlotziver v. Zlotziver, 355 Pa. 299, 49 A.2d 779 (1946);

cient.[7] In one case the court found no reconciliation when the spouses did not occupy a common home but did have frequent marital relations, enjoyed social activities together and often ate together.[8] But a reconciliation may be found to exist without the resumption of a matrimonial domicile if the parties live together as constantly as the circumstances permit.[9]

The effect of reconciliation upon separation agreements is a more difficult question. The cases [10] do not agree in their analysis of precisely how reconciliation affects agreements but their results are in general not inconsistent. One line of cases holds that the intention of the parties determines what consequences their resumption of cohabitation will have.[11] If the parties express their intention in the separation agreement itself, this of course should govern the effect of their reconciliation.[12] Or if, at the time of the reconciliation, they indicate by their words or their conduct that they wish the reconciliation to bring about the rescission of part or all of the separation agreement, this constitutes an ordinary agreement to rescind and it should

have that effect.[13] These are easily decided cases. If, however, the parties indicate nothing whatever about their intentions, it does not help to pretend that their intentions control the impact of the reconciliation on the agreement. Talk of intention in these circumstances is just as fictional as when it is used to justify the construction of a statute.

Another line of cases has determined the effect of reconciliation on separation agreements by reference to the rule that reconciliation avoids a separation agreement but not a property settlement.[14] There are at least two fatal objections to this rule. One is that it tells us nothing about why the result is reached. The other is that it assumes that some realistic distinction exists between separation agreements and property settlements. There is no such distinction. A separation agreement is a contract made by the spouses when they separate, usually in contemplation of a divorce. The separation agreement normally contains provisions governing whatever issues may be in dispute between them, such as the award of alimony, a division of the marital property, and awards of child custody

Barnes v. American Fertilizer Co., 144 Va. 692, 130 S.E. 902 (1925).

7. Peterson v. Peterson, 583 S.W.2d 707 (Ky.App. 1979); Roberts v. Pace, 193 Va. 156, 67 S.E.2d 844 (1951). There may be some confusion on this point since some courts used "cohabitation" synonymously with sexual intercourse. See, e.g., Busot v. Busot, 338 So.2d 1332 (Fla. App.1976). North Carolina is apparently the exception to the text statement, its courts taking the position that sexual relations between the parties is of itself sufficient to abrogate the separation agreement, at least to the extent that the agreement is executory. Murphy v. Murphy, 295 N.C. 390, 245 S.E.2d 693 (1978). This position is sharply criticized in Pitts v. Pitts, 54 N.C.App. 163, 282 S.E.2d 488 (1981). The more general rule is stated in Matter of Adamee's Estate, 291 N.C. 386, 230 S.E.2d 541 (1976).

8. In re Boeson's Estate, 201 Cal. 36, 255 P. 800 (1927). Contra: Weeks v. Weeks, 143 Fla. 686, 197 So. 393 (1940).

9. Walsh v. Walsh, 108 Cal.App.2d 575, 239 P.2d 472 (1952) (dictum).

10. Cases are collected in 1 A. Lindey, Separation Agreements and Antenuptial Contracts 8–14 to 8–24 (Rev.ed.1985); 15 S. Williston, Contracts 76–77 (3d ed. 1972); Annot., 35 A.L.R.2d 707 (1954).

11. In addition to the cases cited in note 2, supra, see Peterson v. Peterson, 583 S.W.2d 707 (Ky.App.1979) and cases cited in Annot., 35 A.L.R.2d 707, 719–727 (1954). Some courts confuse the question somewhat by emphasizing the parties' intent to be reconciled, thereby implying that the intent to be reconciled in some way is evidence of intent to rescind the separation agreement. See, e.g., Miller v. Miller, 189 Mont. 356, 616 P.2d 313 (1980); Will of Granchelli, 90 Misc.2d 103, 393 N.Y.S.2d 894 (Surr.Ct. 1977).

12. Simpson v. Weatherman, 216 Ark. 684, 227 S.W.2d 148 (1950); Hartley v. Hartley, 305 Ky. 350, 203 S.W.2d 770 (1947); Garland v. Garland, 50 Mass. 694 (1874); Eaves v. Eaves [1939] P. 361 (C.A.).

13. In re Marriage of Carl, 67 Cal.App.3d 542, 136 Cal. Rptr. 703 (1977); In re Valentine's Estate, 123 Cal.App.2d 418, 266 P.2d 880 (1954); Blumenthal v. Blumenthal, 194 Misc. 322, 48 N.Y.S.2d 43 (1944), modified 268 App.Div. 973, 52 N.Y.S.2d 577 (1st Dep't 1944), appeal denied 268 App.Div. 1027, 53 N.Y.S.2d 307 (1st Dep't 1945). The restoration of the status quo or the continued disregard of obligations under the agreement might indicate that they intended to rescind the separation agreement by mutual consent. Lo Vasco v. Lo Vasco, 46 Cal.App.2d 242, 115 P.2d 562 (1941); In re Whiteford's Estate, 35 A.D.2d 751, 314 N.Y.S.2d 811 (3d Dep't 1970).

14. White v. White, 350 So.2d 326 (Ala.1977); Simpson v. Weatherman, 216 Ark. 684, 227 S.W.2d 148 (1950); Larson v. Goodman, 28 Colo.App. 418, 475 P.2d 712 (1970), cert. dismissed 177 Colo. 219, 493 P.2d 365 (1972); Matter of Estate of Morrell, 687 P.2d 1319 (Colo.App. 1984); In re Marriage of Reeser, 635 P.2d 930 (Colo.App. 1981); Annot., 35 A.L.R.2d 707, 714–719 (1954).

and support. A property settlement is just that portion of the separation agreement dealing with the property of the spouses. The division of property bears a close relation to the agreement concerning alimony, so that a spouse may receive more alimony when he receives less property and vice versa.[15] It is therefore both misleading and unhelpful to talk as if there were two different kinds of agreement and as if the impact of reconciliation upon one should be different from the impact on the other. Specious distinctions of this kind ought to be abandoned and the courts should talk about the merits of these cases in more realistic terms.

Still other cases adopt the view that reconciliation abrogates the executory portions of the separation agreement but does not affect those portions which have been executed.[16] In application this tends to reach about the same result as the separation agreement-property settlement rule. This rule not only does not account for the cases but may produce a very inequitable result in some circumstances, for example, where the division of property and the award of alimony are closely related, and the effect of the rule is to leave the property transfer in effect but to terminate the alimony award.

In the absence of statute,[17] the effect of reconciliation should be governed by the circumstances in which it is asserted. If, as an aspect of reconciliation, the parties by their words or their conduct express the intention of rescinding the separation agreement in whole or in part, effect should be given to their action.[18] This is just an ordinary application of contract principles.[19] A different question arises when the agreement provides for property transfers between the spouses and for payments of alimony. If the parties are reconciled after the property transfers have been made and there is no evidence as to their intentions with respect to the agreement, the cases generally have held that the property transfers will not be disturbed but that the claim for alimony is abrogated.[20] Although the opinions rely on the unenlightening distinction between executed and executory provisions, the real reason for this result is that after the reconciliation the agreement is subject to the traditional objection that it is a contract for a future separation. As has been indicated in an earlier section it was formerly held that a separation agreement could only be enforced if at the time it was made the spouses were already separated or were on the point of separation.[21] If the parties were living together without the prospect of an immediate divorce, the agreement was held to be "conducive to divorce" and for that reason contrary to public policy and unenforceable. A reconciliation has the same effect on a separation agreement previously made. Where the courts adhere to the notion that agreements made before separation are conducive to divorce and unenforceable for that reason, it still follows that reconciliation will prevent the enforcement of an agreement for future support.[22]

Today, however, a large number of states have rejected the notion that the parties must be on the point of divorce before they can make an agreement respecting either the property or the alimony incidents of divorce.[23] In fact in many states such an agreement is held valid even when it is made before the marriage.[24] In those states there is no valid

---

15. See the discussion of the property division in section 15.1, supra.

16. Travis v. Travis, 227 Ga. 406, 181 S.E.2d 61 (1971); Peterson v. Peterson, 583 S.W.2d 707 (Ky.App.1979); Miller v. Miller, 189 Mont. 356, 616 P.2d 313 (1980) (semble); Matter of Adamee's Estate, 291 N.C. 386, 230 S.E.2d 541 (1976); Walker v. Walker, 59 N.C.App. 485, 297 S.E.2d 125 (1982); 15 S. Williston, Contracts 76–77 (3d ed.1972).

17. The only statute which has been found is that cited in note 4, supra.

18. See notes 12 and 13, supra.

19. See note 1, supra.

20. Cases are collected in Annot., 35 A.L.R.2d 707, 714–715 (1954). See also the cases cited in notes 14 and 16, supra.

21. See section 18.1, supra, at note 9.

22. In re Wilson's Estates, 50 N.Y.2d 59, 427 N.Y.S.2d 977, 405 N.E.2d 220 (1980) seems to support the text statement in effect.

23. See section 18.1, supra, at note 12.

24. See section 1.1, supra.

reason why the separation agreement should not remain in force notwithstanding the parties' reconciliation. This result vindicates two important policies which are recognized almost universally. One is that the law should encourage the settlement of marital disputes by agreement.[25] The other is that reconciliation should also be encouraged.[26] If the parties know in advance that their agreement will survive a reconciliation, they will more readily make it and they will more readily attempt reconciliation. The only exception to this view should arise where, when the parties' reconciliation later fails, the adherence to the provisions of the separation agreement would be unconscionable, as that term has been defined in an earlier section.[27] In that situation the separation agreement should be held to be unenforceable just as any other unconscionable separation agreement would be. In the unusual case in which the reconciliation succeeds, the parties live together until one of them dies, and the survivor claims an intestate share in the estate of the deceased, the separation agreement should not be applicable because the basic assumption of fact on which the agreement was made, that is, that the parties would separate and then obtain a divorce, has not occurred.[28] In that situation the separation agreement has become irrelevant to their status.

In general the same result should be reached where the effect of the separation agreement on the children of the marriage is in question. If the parties are reconciled but the reconciliation later fails and they separate for a second time, the provisions for child custody and support should again become effective unless a court finds that the provisions

are unconscionable or do not adequately serve the child's interests. This result may or may not be in accord with contracts principles concerning the discharge of third party beneficiary contracts,[29] but in any event the child's position is unlike the usual beneficiary of such a contract. His claim exists whether or not there is a contract recognizing it and it is a claim with respect to which the state has important interests.

There is some authority that an offer of reconciliation has the same effect on a separation agreement as reconciliation itself.[30] On principle the opposite should be the case. It is axiomatic in contracts that one party may not unilaterally terminate the contract in contravention of its terms. There is no reason why, when the separation agreement contains no provision for termination other than that alimony payments shall continue until the death of the parties or the remarriage of the payee, any shorter period of duration should be forced on one party by the other's offer of reconciliation. Unless both wish to be reconciled such an offer would not lead to a restoration of the marital relationship. If an offer did terminate obligations pursuant to the agreement, there would be substantial risk that such offers would be made for the sole purpose of evading agreements, thereby causing the litigation and controversy which it is the chief function of separation agreements to avoid.

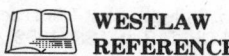 **WESTLAW REFERENCES**

separation /2 agreement /s reconcil! /s void!
separation /2 agreement /s reconcil! /s co-habit! (liv***
  /3 together)

---

25. Uniform Marriage and Divorce Act § 306(a), and Commissioners' Note, 9A Unif.L.Ann. 135 (1979).

26. See section 14.8, supra.

27. See section 18.2, supra.

28. In re Wilson's Estate, 50 N.Y.2d 59, 427 N.Y.S.2d 977, 405 N.E.2d 220 (1980); Matter of Adamee's Estate, 291 N.C. 386, 230 S.E.2d 541 (1976).

29. The older authorities took the position that a contract made for the benefit of a donee beneficiary could not be rescinded without the consent of the donee. 4 A.

Corbin, Contracts § 814 (1951); 2 S. Williston, Contracts § 396 (3d ed.1959). More recent authorities state the rule to be that such a contract may be rescinded up until the time when the donee learns of the contract and relies upon it. E. Farnsworth, Contracts 738–740 (1982); Restatement (Second) of Contracts § 311 (1981).

30. E.g., Finnegan v. Finnegan, 42 Cal.2d 762, 269 P.2d 873 (1954) (dictum); Vanderburgh v. Vanderburgh, 152 Minn. 189, 188 N.W. 276 (1922); Devine v. Devine, 89 N.J.Eq. 51, 104 A. 370 (Ch.1918) (dictum); Carl v. Carl, 166 N.Y.S. 961 (1917).

§ 18.5 Separation Agreements—Effect Upon the Custody, Property and Support Aspects of Divorce Decrees

The subject of discussion in this section is, to what extent should a court accept the parties' agreement concerning the division of property, alimony and the custody and support of children when presented to it in the divorce action? Traditionally the courts of some states, concerned that their authority over these incidents to the divorce might be impaired and hostile to agreements deemed to be "conducive to divorce", took the position that agreements could be freely disregarded when presented to them for approval.[1] Courts in other states were willing to concede presumptive validity to such agreements, but in practice the trial courts in both groups of states gave more or less routine approval to agreements unless one of the parties asserted strong objection.[2] Today nearly all states recognize that it is generally preferable to settle these matters by agreement rather than by litigation.[3] If this opinion is to be vindicated, the law should let the parties know in advance that their agreement will be approved by the divorce court unless it can be shown to be subject to some serious infirmity. To a great extent this has been the prevailing view since the promulgation of the Uniform Marriage and Divorce Act.[4] If the great majority of divorce cases were not disposed of by agreement of the parties, court congestion would be intolerable rather than merely inconvenient as it is now.[5]

The degree to which the courts are free to disregard the spouses' agreement depends in the first instance upon which aspects of that agreement are being challenged. It is axiomatic that the courts have an obligation in divorce litigation to place the highest importance upon the welfare of the children of the marriage.[6] To the extent that their welfare can be accomplished by the arrangements for custody and child support made by the spouses, the courts will approve such arrangements.[7] But if the court finds that the custody and support provided for in the separation agreement does not serve the child's welfare in view of the relevant circumstances, the court is free to disregard the agreement and make a different decree respecting custody or support or both.[8] An additional reason for disregarding the agreement is that the child is not usually a party to it.[9] Although this is the courts' official view of the question, as a practical matter it must be recognized that busy overworked trial courts will accept the parties' agreement concerning custody and child support in most cases unless there is

§ 18.5

1. For a discussion of these factors see Comment, Divorce Agreements: Independent Contract or Incorporation in Decree, 20 U.Chi.L.Rev. 138 (1952); Note, Control of Post-Divorce Level of Support by Prior Agreement, 63 Harv.L.Rev. 337 (1949); Pilpel and Zavin, Separation Agreements: Their Function and Future, 18 Law & Contemp.Prob. 33 (1953); Mason, The Paradoxical Separation Agreement, 21 Rocky Mt.L.Rev. 434 (1949).

2. Ibid.

3. Persuasive argument for this position is presented in Mnookin and Kornhauser, Bargaining in the Shadow of the Law: The Case of Divorce, 88 Yale L.J. 950 (1979). See also the discussion of mediation in section 14.8, supra.

4. Uniform Marriage and Divorce Act § 306, Commissioners' Note, 9A Unif.L.Ann. 136 (1979).

5. Mnookin and Kornhauser, Bargaining in the Shadow of the Law: The Case of Divorce, 88 Yale L.J. 950, 951 (1979), indicating that divorce cases compose a high proportion of all civil cases and that eighty or ninety percent of such cases are disposed of by agreement, with only administrative approval by the courts.

6. See section 17.1, supra, and section 19.1, infra.

7. Forte v. Forte, 320 So.2d 446 (Fla.App.1975), cert. denied 351 So.2d 406 (Fla.1977); Pegram v. Pegram, 310 Ky. 86, 219 S.W.2d 772 (1949); Kane v. Kane, 314 Mich. 529, 22 N.W.2d 773 (1946); Laurance v. Laurance, 198 Or. 630, 258 P.2d 784 (1953); Ruch v. Ruch, 183 Or. 240, 192 P.2d 272 (1948). In drafting custody provisions of separation agreements counsel should keep in mind their effect on subsequent attempts by stepparents to adopt the children. See section 20.4, infra.

8. Miller v. Miller, 208 Ark. 1058, 189 S.W.2d 371 (1945); Daily v. Daily, 175 Ark. 161, 298 S.W. 1012 (1927); Graves v. Elmer, 81 Colo. 158, 253 P. 1067 (1927); Barbee v. Barbee, 201 Ga. 763, 41 S.E.2d 126 (1947); Hendricks v. Hendricks, 69 Idaho 341, 206 P.2d 523 (1949); Johns v. McNabb, 247 S.W.2d 640 (Mo.1952); Marshall v. Marshall, 236 S.W. 378 (Mo.App.1922); Muller v. Ashurst, 208 Misc. 283, 143 N.Y.S.2d 713 (1955) (dictum); Madsen v. Madsen, 2 Utah 2d 423, 276 P.2d 917 (1954).

9. Story v. Story, 221 N.C. 114, 19 S.E.2d 136 (1942). See Pappas v. Pappas, 247 Iowa 638, 75 N.W.2d 264 (1956), 42 Iowa L.Rev. 442 (1956).

clear and persuasive reason for not doing so.[10] Trial judges hearing one divorce case after another generally cannot afford the luxury of a careful evaluation of custody and support provisions reached by agreement in even a substantial proportion of their case load. This limitation on the courts' time and energy places the responsibility upon the spouses and their lawyers to arrive at agreements concerning the children which serve the children's welfare as well as may be done with the resources available. In some cases agreements have been made and upheld which provide greater benefits to the children of the marriage than would be authorized in the absence of an agreement, the most common example being agreements for support of the children beyond their majority to enable them to obtain a college education.[11]

Where the spouses attempt in their separation agreement to prescribe their child's religious training after the divorce, most courts have refused to enforce the agreement, either on the ground that enforcement might violate the First Amendment or that it would create psychological conflicts and insecurity in the child.[12] In order to avoid conflicts and psychological stress of this kind, such contracts ought not to be enforced, and the child's religious training should be left to the person having custody.

The provisions of separation agreements dealing with the financial and property claims of the spouses inter se have been treated differently from the provisions dealing with child custody and support.[13] In the past some courts would merely state in a perfunctory way that the agreement should be approved if free from fraud or duress and if fair and equitable.[14] Others asserted the right to refuse approval of the agreement on the sole ground that they would have made a different award of property or alimony than the agreement did.[15] No distinction was generally made for this purpose between awards of

---

10. See the account of the negotiating process by an experienced judge in R. Neely, The Divorce Decision 67–79 (1984). Witmayer v. Witmayer, 320 Pa.Super. 372, 467 A.2d 371 (1983) takes the position that the courts should encourage the parents to settle custody by agreement, and that in order to do that their agreements should be given great weight in determining who should have custody.

11. E.g., Ovaitt v. Ovaitt, 43 Mich.App. 628, 204 N.W.2d 753 (1972); Bugay v. Bugay, 53 Ohio App.2d 285, 373 N.E.2d 1263 (1977); West v. West, 131 Vt. 621, 312 A.2d 920 (1973). Contra: Helber v. Frazelle, 118 Ariz. 217, 575 P.2d 1243 (1978).

12. Lynch v. Uhlenhopp, 248 Iowa 68, 78 N.W.2d 491 (1956); Miles v. Liebolt, 230 N.Y.S.2d 342 (1962). Contra: Shearer v. Shearer, 73 N.Y.S.2d 337 (1947). Other cases are collected in Annot., 66 A.L.R.2d 1410, 1426, 1432 (1959) and Note, 50 Yale L.J. 1286 (1941). The problem is discussed in Friedman, The Parental Right to Control the Religious Education of a Child, 29 Harv.L.Rev. 485 (1916); Note, Religion as a Factor in Adoption, Guardianship and Custody, 54 Colum.L.Rev. 377, 385, n. 59 (1954).

13. The Uniform Marriage and Divorce Act § 306(b), 9A Unif.L.Ann. 135 (1979) makes the separation agreement binding on the court unless unconscionable, except for the provisions relating to custody, visitation and child support.

14. E.g., Hobbs v. Hobbs, 72 Colo. 190, 210 P. 398 (1922); Warner v. Warner, 219 Minn. 59, 17 N.W.2d 58 (1944); Dunlap v. Dunlap, 145 Neb. 735, 18 N.W.2d 51 (1945); Elliott v. Dunham, 191 Okl. 395, 130 P.2d 534 (1942); Smith v. Smith, 125 W.Va. 489, 24 S.E.2d 902 (1943); Rinehart v. Rinehart, 52 Wyo. 363, 75 P.2d 390 (1938) (dictum).

15. Russell v. Russell, 247 Ala. 284, 24 So.2d 124 (1945) (dictum that judge's discretion to give alimony cannot be controlled by agreement); Adams v. Adams, 29 Cal.2d 621, 177 P.2d 265 (1947) (agreements should be carefully scrutinized); Moog v. Moog, 203 Cal. 406, 264 P. 490 (1928) (court could award more than agreement gave wife where she needed more); Cameron v. Cameron, 85 Cal.App.2d 22, 192 P.2d 89 (1948) (court could award additional amount); Hobbs v. Hobbs, 72 Colo. 190, 210 P. 398 (1922) (additional allowance made apparently because the amount given by the agreement was insufficient); Weeks v. Weeks, 143 Fla. 686, 197 So. 393 (1940) (dictum that inadequacy raises presumption of concealment); McHie v. McHie, 106 Ind.App. 152, 16 N.E.2d 987 (1938) (court entitled to disregard alimony and property provisions of the agreement); Messer v. Messer, 238 Iowa 783, 28 N.W.2d 329 (1947) (court not bound by the property settlement); Cessna v. Cessna, 155 Kan. 856, 130 P.2d 560 (1942) (agreement invalid if inadequate); Oakes v. Oakes, 266 Mass. 150, 165 N.E. 17 (1929) (dictum that court can consider agreement, but it does not control as matter of law); Hellman v. Hellman, 250 Minn. 422, 84 N.W.2d 367 (1957); Barber v. Barber, 92 N.H. 523, 30 A.2d 278 (1943) (agreement relevant but not controlling); Kirshbaum v. Kirshbaum, 125 N.J.Eq. 558, 5 A.2d 792 (Ct.Err. & App. 1939) (court's inquiry not limited to fraud); Lum v. Lum, 138 N.J.Eq. 198, 47 A.2d 555 (Ch.1946), reversed on other grounds 140 N.J.Eq. 137, 53 A.2d 309 (Ct.Err. & App. 1947) (agreement does not control the court, but is evidence of what is reasonable); Polyckronos v. Polyckronos, 17 N.J.Misc. 250, 8 A.2d 265 (Ch.1939) (agreement is a yardstick, but not control); Scanlon v. Scanlon, 60 N.M. 43, 287 P.2d 238 (1955) (court may disregard agreement and award what is fair); Seyler v. Seyler, 190 Okl. 250, 122 P.2d 804 (1942) (court may approve, reject, or

property and awards of alimony.[16] In a third, smaller, group of jurisdictions it was held that the courts must approve separation agreements in the absence of fraud, duress or a breach of some confidential relation existing between the spouses.[17]

The first edition of this work advocated a greater willingness on the part of divorce courts to accept and enforce the separation agreements of the spouses so far as they relate to the division of property and alimony. To a substantial extent the law today has taken that position. The Uniform Marriage and Divorce Act led the way by providing that the separation agreement is binding on the court unless found to be unconscionable.[18] Several states in addition to those which have enacted the Uniform Act have taken a similar position, either by statute[19] or judicial decision.[20] This development in the law is a striking example of the contemporary movement toward giving the spouses greater authority over their divorce and its incidents, and is consistent with the adoption of the various non-fault grounds for divorce in nearly all states. It is likewise consistent with the position taken in many states that the spouses may exercise a substantial degree of control over their financial and property relations during marriage by means of contracts executed even before their marriage occurs.[21] It is not clear that this signals a decline in the importance attributable to marriage and divorce.[22] It is more likely that it rests on two very practical factors. One is the recognition that within broad limits the spouses are as likely to arrive at equitable financial and property arrangements as a trial court. The other and more important is the necessity for avoiding litigation in divorce actions wherever that is reasonably possible, as a way of saving expense for the parties and scarce judicial resources for the state. The Commissioners' Note to the Uniform Act gives elliptical expression to these factors by stating the Act's purpose to be "to reduce the adversary trappings of marital dissolution".[23]

modify agreement); Barraclough v. Barraclough, 100 Utah 196, 111 P.2d 792 (1941) (agreement is only a recommendation to the court); Hughes v. Hughes, 173 Va. 293, 4 S.E.2d 402 (1939) (dictum that court is not bound if it finds the agreement makes insufficient provision for the wife.)

Many courts took the same view when an agreement was made *after* the alimony decree in an attempt to change the obligations of the parties under the decree. Cahill v. Cahill, 316 Ill.App. 324, 45 N.E.2d 69 (1942); Apfelbaum v. Apfelbaum, 111 N.J.Eq. 529, 162 A. 543 (Ct. Err. & App.1932); Feves v. Feves, 198 Or. 151, 254 P.2d 694 (1953); Wilson v. Woolf, 274 S.W.2d 154 (Tex.Civ.App. 1954); Casilear v. Casilear, 168 Va. 46, 190 S.E. 314 (1937).

16. E.g., McHie v. McHie, 106 Ind.App. 152, 16 N.E.2d 987 (1938); Messer v. Messer, 238 Iowa 783, 28 N.W.2d 329 (1947). But see Adams v. Adams, 29 Cal.2d 621, 177 P.2d 265 (1947).

17. Dunn v. Dunn, 174 Ark. 517, 295 S.W. 963 (1927); Apperson v. Apperson, 169 Ga. 593, 150 S.E. 827 (1929) (semble); Belcher v. Belcher, 242 Ky. 54, 45 S.W.2d 841 (1932); Alverson v. Alverson, 249 S.W.2d 472 (Mo.App. 1952) (semble); Lee v. Lee, 55 Mont. 426, 178 P. 173 (1919); Nellis v. Nellis, 98 Ohio App. 247, 129 N.E.2d 217 (1955); Lowman v. Lowman, 98 Ohio App. 254, 129 N.E.2d 213 (1955); Matthews v. Matthews, 24 Tenn. App. 580, 148 S.W.2d 3 (1940).

18. Uniform Marriage and Divorce Act § 306, 9A Unif.L.Ann. 135 (1979). The Act has been adopted in Arizona, Colorado, Illinois, Kentucky, Minnesota, Missouri, Montana and Washington. Uniform Marriage and Divorce Act, 9A Unif.L.Ann. 56 (Supp.1986). See also the Uniform Marital Property Act § 10, 9A Unif.L.Ann. 37 (Supp.1986).

19. E.g., Alaska Stat. § 25.24.220 (1983); Ark.Stat. § 34–1212 (Supp.1985) (semble); West's Ann.Cal.Civ.Code §§ 4728, 4811 (Supp.1987); Conn.Gen.Stat.Ann. § 46b–66 (1986); Official Ga.Code Ann. § 19–6–8 (Supp.1986); West's Ann.Ind.Code § 31–1–11.5–10 (1980); Kan.Stat. Ann. § 23–207 (1981); Md.Code Ann. (Family Law) § 8– 101 (1984); Miss.Code 1986, § 93–5–2 (Supp.); Neb.Rev. Stat. § 42–366 (1984); N.Y.—McKinney's Dom.Rel.L. § 236, Part B(3) (1986); N.C.Gen.Stat. §§ 50–20, 52–10.1 (1984); Ohio Rev.Code §§ 3105.63, 3105.65 (Supp.1986); Pa.Stat. tit. 23, § 401 (Supp.1986); Tenn.Code Ann. §§ 36–4–121, 36–5–101 (Supp.1986); Va.Code 1983, § 20– 109.1; W.Va.Code, §§ 48–2–16, 48–2–32 (1986).

20. Costello v. Costello, 186 Conn. 773, 443 A.2d 1282 (1982); Burtoff v. Burtoff, 418 A.2d 1085 (D.C.App.1980) (antenuptial agreement); Baker v. Baker, 394 So.2d 465 (Fla.App.1981), review denied 402 So.2d 607 (1981) (dictum); Frey v. Frey, 298 Md. 552, 471 A.2d 705 (1984) (antenuptial agreement); Di Giacomo v. Di Giacomo, 80 N.J. 155, 402 A.2d 922 (1979); Wertlake v. Wertlake, 137 N.J.Super. 476, 349 A.2d 552 (1975); Skillman v. Skillman, 136 N.J.Super. 348, 346 A.2d 408 (1975); Patino v. Patino, 687 S.W.2d 799 (Tex.Civ.App.1985).

21. See section 1.1, supra.

22. Cf. M. Glendon, The New Family and the New Property 5–68 (1981).

23. Uniform Marriage and Divorce Act § 306, Commissioners' Note, 9A Unif.L.Ann. 136 (1979).

Although it is clear that the financial aspects of divorce are usually left to the parties' agreement by the divorce court, as has been shown in an earlier section, there are limits to the courts' willingness to accept such agreements.[24] These limits are expressed by general statements to the effect that the agreement must be fair, equitable, not unconscionable and free from fraud, duress or overreaching.[25] In applying such general doctrine to the infinite variety of circumstances found in divorce the courts no longer seem to make any distinction between the case in which a suit is brought on the separation agreement and the case in which the agreement is presented to the divorce court for its approval.[26] It is difficult to translate the general doctrine into precise formulae, but it seems to have both a procedural and a substantive aspect. The trial court should consider whether there was an inequality of bargaining power, whether there was misrepresentation or concealment of property, whether one of the parties was acting under duress or coercion, and whether both parties had an opportunity to consider the terms of the agreement, to obtain legal or other advice, and whether they both understood its terms. If so, the court should further consider whether, under the economic circumstances in existence at the time the

agreement was made and also at the time of the decree, the agreement made fair, just and reasonable provision for the spouses.[27] It must be recognized that in the great majority of cases the agreement will be approved unless one of the spouses raises an objection to it. In practice few trial courts will have the time or inclination to make a detailed study of the separation agreement if it is presented as being consented to by both parties. To this extent there remains a gap between the law on the books and the law in action at the trial court level.

Under the statutes of some states some forms of marital fault are still relevant in awarding alimony and dividing property on divorce.[28] The question is thereby raised whether, if a spouse guilty of marital fault may not be awarded alimony or a share of property, a separation agreement making a provision for such a spouse may be approved in the divorce decree. The cases are in conflict on the issue.[29] Those which deny approval do so because the divorce court has no jurisdiction, they say, to make an award to a guilty spouse and because the parties may not by their agreement confer jurisdiction. This analysis is unsound. The matter is not one of jurisdiction. If the parties have agreed, no one is imposed upon. The case is like any

---

24. See sections 18.1 and 18.2, supra.

25. E.g., In re Marriage of Hadley, 88 Wash.2d 649, 565 P.2d 790 (1977), 53 Wash.L.Rev. 763 (1978).

26. See the cases cited in section 18.2, supra. There is likewise no distinction made between the maintenance and the property division aspects of the agreement when the courts come to evaluate its fairness and equity. See, e.g., Blum v. Blum, 59 Md.App. 584, 477 A.2d 289 (1984).

27. The leading case which spells out these factors is In re Marriage of Manzo, 659 P.2d 669 (Colo.1983), construing "unconscionability" as found in the Uniform Marriage and Divorce Act § 306, 9A Unif.L.Ann. 135 (1979). The court relies upon the Commissioners' Note to that section and cites many other cases, including some cases from states not having the Uniform Act. The court expressly adopts a stricter standard of review for separation agreements than for antenuptial agreements, on the ground that the interests of a spouse making a separation agreement need greater protection from the courts because of the more stressful circumstances in which the agreement is made. On this point the case seems very doubtful, since the antenuptial agreement is usually made in circumstances of trust and confidence such as to make it easy for one party to take advantage of the other, just as much as is true of the separation agreement.

Other cases adopting standards similar to those in Manzo include Sands v. Sands, 188 Conn. 98, 448 A.2d 822 (1982); In re Marriage of Wigner, 40 Colo.App. 253, 572 P.2d 495 (1977); In re Marriage of Foster, 115 Ill. App.3d 969, 71 Ill.Dec. 761, 451 N.E.2d 915 (1983); Blum v. Blum, 59 Md.App. 584, 477 A.2d 289 (1984); In re Clapper, 674 S.W.2d 656 (Mo.App.1984); Turpin v. Turpin, 570 S.W.2d 831 (Mo.App.1978); In re Marriage of Myers, ___ Mont. ___, 682 P.2d 718 (1984); Dobesh v. Dobesh, 216 Neb. 196, 342 N.W.2d 669 (1984); In re Marriage of Kesler, 59 Ohio Misc. 33, 392 N.E.2d 905 (1978); In re Marriage of Hadley, 88 Wash.2d 649, 565 P.2d 790 (1977), 53 Wash.L.Rev. 763 (1978).

28. See sections 15.3 and 16.4, supra.

29. Denying approval: Feldman v. Feldman, 236 N.C. 731, 73 S.E.2d 865 (1953) (semble); Gibson v. Gibson, 193 Or. 139, 237 P.2d 498 (1951); Garner v. Garner, 182 Or. 549, 189 P.2d 397 (1948); Bernard v. Bernard, 74 S.D. 449, 54 N.W.2d 351 (1952). Many of these states today would not find marital fault relevant to the financial incidents of divorce, but these cases remain relevant on the separation agreement issue.

Allowing approval: McKinney v. McKinney, 152 Kan. 372, 103 P.2d 793 (1940); Stratton v. Stratton, 77 Me. 373 (1885). See also Annot., 34 A.L.R.2d 313, 326 (1954).

other in which the parties' agreement does beyond what a court would be authorized to grant. If the agreement is fair and equitable to both spouses, it should be approved by the divorce court.

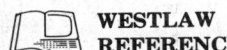

WESTLAW
REFERENCES

separation /2 agreement /s presum! /s valid!
separation /2 agreement /s approv! stipulat! /s divid!
  division /s land property

§ 18.6 Separation Agreements—Effect of Divorce Decrees Upon Separation Agreements—Introduction

The foregoing sections have indicated some ways in which the decisions of divorce courts are affected by the prior formation of separation agreements between the spouses. The sections which follow will attempt to show how divorce decrees may affect the rights of parties under separation agreements entered into in contemplation of divorce. The two subjects are obviously closely related. The distinction is emphasized here in the interests of clear analysis.

§ 18.7 Separation Agreements—Enforcement of Divorce Decrees Based Upon Separation Agreements

As has been shown in an earlier section of this work, a separation agreement may be sued on at law or in equity in the same manner as other contracts.[1] In the present section it is assumed that no such suit has

been brought, but that the parties have presented their agreement to the court in which one or both of them has brought suit for divorce, and that the court has entered a decree which dissolves the marriage and settles the alimony and property questions in accordance with the agreement. The questions then raised are how such a decree may be enforced and whether the agreement may still be sued on.

If the separation is "incorporated"[2] in the divorce decree, the courts find that the contractual obligations of the agreement are converted into obligations based upon the decree by a process called "merger".[3] Although this process resembles merger as that term is used in the law of judgments,[4] it is not really the same. The word is therefore not entirely appropriate in this context. It will nevertheless be used here, both for the sake of convenience and because it is generally current in judicial opinions.

If the separation agreement is found to have been merged in the divorce decree, its enforcement is governed by the same rules as is the enforcement of any divorce decree.[5] Conversely, if merger has not occurred, the agreement remains enforceable by the usual contract remedies,[6] but it may not be enforced by the remedies available for the enforcement of judgments, particularly that of contempt.[7]

In many states a distinction is made between decrees which order the payment of money, as for example to accomplish a division of property, and decrees which order the

---

§ 18.7

1. See section 18.8, Practioner's Edition.

2. The term "incorporated" upon which depends the manner of enforcement is defined below at notes 21 to 29.

3. Helber v. Frazelle, 118 Ariz. 217, 575 P.2d 1243 (1978); Flynn v. Flynn, 42 Cal.2d 55, 265 P.2d 865 (1954). But see Silvestri v. Slatowski, 423 Pa. 498, 224 A.2d 212 (1966).

4. Restatement (Second) of Judgments § 18 (1982).

5. Kemp v. Kemp, 287 Md. 165, 411 A.2d 1028 (1980) (semble); Walters v. Walters, 307 N.C. 381, 298 S.E.2d 338 (1983); Harris v. Harris, 58 Ohio St.2d 303, 390 N.E.2d 789 (1979). See also Uniform Marriage and Divorce Act § 306(e), 9A Unif.L.Ann. 136 (1979) and In re Marriage of Haggard, 585 S.W.2d 480 (Mo.1979). McGoodwin v. McGoodwin, 671 S.W.2d 880 (Tex.1984) appears to be contra the statement in the text. Thus

where the agreement is not merged in the decree its enforcement is subject to the contract statute of limitations rather than the statute applicable to judgments. Tauber v. Lebow, 65 N.Y.2d 596, 493 N.Y.S.2d 1008, 483 N.E.2d 1140 (1985).

6. Helber v. Frazelle, 118 Ariz. 217, 575 P.2d 1243 (1978); Shacknow v. Shacknow, 248 App.Div. 827, 289 N.Y.S. 95 (2d Dep't 1936); Greiner v. Greiner, 61 Ohio App.2d 88, 399 N.E.2d 571 (1979); Mobley v. Mobley, 221 S.W.2d 565 (Tex.Civ.App.1949); Matter of Marriage of Olsen, 24 Wash.App. 292, 600 P.2d 690 (1979). See section 19.8, Practioner's Edition, at note 24.

7. E.g., Frykberg v. Frykberg, 76 N.C.App. 401, 333 S.E.2d 766 (1985). See also Uniform Marriage and Divorce Act § 306(e), 9A Unif.L.Ann. 136 (1979), which provides that an agreement set forth in the divorce decree may be enforced both by the methods appropriate to judgments and those appropriate to contracts.

payment of alimony or child support. The former, sometimes characterized as property settlements, are held by some states not to be enforceable by contempt proceedings.[8] The reason for this seems to be that the use of the contempt remedy in such a case violates constitutional prohibitions against imprisonment for debt.[9] This reason does not apply where the decree orders the conveyance of property *in specie*, since that is not a money decree, but an act decree.[10] In such a case contempt should be allowed, or, where the defendant spouse is recalcitrant and the statute authorizes it, the court should be able to make the conveyance.[11]

When the decree based upon a separation agreement orders the payment of alimony or the support of children, nearly all states agree that it may be enforced by contempt proceedings.[12] The courts usually regard these sections of the divorce decree not as ordering the payment of money, but as enforcing the defendant's obligation to support his spouse and children. Although some of the cases seem concerned with whether alimony and child support are to be considered a "debt" for purposes of the constitutional prohibition against imprisonment for debt, this should

not be the focus of analysis. Permitting contempt to be used simply recognizes that alimony and child support are kinds of debts of especial importance to society, for the collection of which the law should provide severe sanctions, against which the obligor always has the defense that if he is unable to pay, he may not be imprisoned.[13]

The difficulty of making any realistic distinction between the alimony and the property provisions of divorce decrees in many cases has been extensively discussed in earlier sections of this work.[14] In view of that difficulty the sensible approach is to permit contempt enforcement of both property and alimony awards. Some courts have taken this approach.[15] If this is done, a defense to contempt of inability to pay should be extended to defendants who are subject to property decrees, just as is the case where alimony decrees are enforced by contempt. This defense avoids the objection that contempt enforcement violates the constitutional prohibition on imprisonment for debt. Further protection to the obligor subject to the property decree could be afforded by permitting modification of the property decree on the

---

8. Luna v. Luna, 125 Ariz. 120, 608 P.2d 57 (App. 1979); Bradley v. Superior Court In and For City and County of San Francisco, 48 Cal.2d 509, 310 P.2d 634 (1957); Foote v. Foote, 190 Md. 171, 57 A.2d 804 (1948); Bushman v. Bushman, 157 Md. 166, 145 A. 488 (1929); Shafer v. Shafer, 257 Mich. 372, 241 N.W. 144 (1932); Goldfish v. Goldfish, 193 App.Div. 686, 184 N.Y.S. 512 (1st Dep't 1920), affirmed 230 N.Y. 606, 130 N.E. 912 (1921); Glynn v. Glynn, 8 N.D. 233, 77 N.W. 594 (1898); Huchteman v. Huchteman, 557 P.2d 427 (Okl.1976); Brown v. Brown, 198 Tenn. 600, 281 S.W.2d 492 (1955). Contra: Harris v. Harris, 58 Ohio St.2d 303, 390 N.E.2d 789 (1979); Decker v. Decker, 52 Wash.2d 456, 326 P.2d 332 (1958) (semble). Other cases are cited in section 17.7, supra, at note 26.

9. Stone v. Stidham, 96 Ariz. 235, 393 P.2d 923 (1964); Bradley v. Superior Court In and for City and County of San Francisco, 48 Cal.2d 509, 310 P.2d 634 (1957); Harris v. Harris, 58 Ohio St.2d 303, 311, 390 N.E.2d 789, 794 (1979) (dissenting opinion).

10. Luna v. Luna, 125 Ariz. 120, 608 P.2d 57 (1980) (dictum); Buswell v. Buswell, 377 Pa. 487, 105 A.2d 608 (1954). Contra: Norris v. Norris, 695 P.2d 506 (Okl.1984); Pierce v. Pierce, 609 P.2d 732 (Okl.1979).

11. Robinson v. Robinson, 37 Wash.2d 511, 225 P.2d 411 (1950). But see Ex Parte Jones, 163 Tex. 513, 358 S.W.2d 370 (1962).

12. Thomas v. Thomas, 246 Ark. 1126, 443 S.W.2d 534 (1969); In re Marriage of Alper, 116 Cal.App.3d 925, 172 Cal.Rptr. 402 (1981) (Arizona law); Petry v. Superior Court of Los Angeles County, 46 Cal.App.2d 746, 116 P.2d 954 (1941); McClain v. McClain, 235 Ga. 659, 221 S.E.2d 561 (1975); Application of Martin, 76 Idaho 179, 279 P.2d 873 (1955); Scheldrup v. Gaffney, 243 Iowa 1297, 55 N.W.2d 272 (1952); Honaker v. Honaker, 267 Ky. 129, 101 S.W.2d 679 (1937); Wilson v. Wilson, 140 Me. 250, 36 A.2d 774 (1944); Soldana v. Soldana, 258 Md. 145, 265 A.2d 263 (1970); Britt v. Britt, 49 N.C.App. 463, 271 S.E.2d 921 (1980); Holloway v. Holloway, 130 Ohio St. 214, 198 N.E. 579 (1935); Skidmore v. Skidmore, 197 Or. 409, 253 P.2d 903 (1953); Ex Parte Gorena, 595 S.W.2d 841 (Tex.1979).

13. See the discussion of the enforcement of alimony decrees in section 16.6, supra.

14. See sections 15.1, 16.5 and 16.6, supra.

15. Campbell v. Goodbar, 110 Colo. 403, 134 P.2d 1060 (1943) (dictum); Harris v. Harris, 58 Ohio St.2d 303, 390 N.E.2d 789 (1979); Decker v. Decker, 52 Wash.2d 456, 326 P.2d 332 (1958) (semble).

The Uniform Marriage and Divorce Act § 306(e), 9A Unif.L.Ann. 136 (1979) seems to take this position, authorizing the enforcement of all terms in the decree by contempt.

same terms as are applied to alimony decrees, but the cases do not reach this result.[16]

There are a few cases which do not define the alimony-property distinction by reference to the purpose of the payments, but which exclude from the category of alimony any payments which the court could not have awarded in the absence of the agreement, whether or not the payments were intended for the support of the payee spouse.[17] For example, if the divorce is granted for the marital misconduct of the defendant spouse and the statute does not allow alimony in such a case, payments provided by the separation agreement for the defendant's support would be held property payments, not alimony, and not enforceable by contempt.[18] Or if the payments are to continue unconditionally until the payee's death or remarriage, while continuation of statutory alimony beyond the payer's death is forbidden, these courts would hold that the payments are not alimony and that contempt does not lie to enforce them.[19] This reasoning wrongly disregards the purpose of the payments. It also fails to take account of the fact that the statutory limits are imposed on alimony for the protection of the obligor. If he wishes to forego that protection by providing support beyond what the

statute requires, there is no reason why the agreed payments should not be treated as alimony when incorporated in the divorce decree.[20]

There is a substantial difference of opinion among courts on what will constitute "incorporation" of the separation agreement into the divorce decree so as to make contempt proceedings available for its enforcement. In part the difference is due to different emphases which the courts place upon such factors as the parties' intent as expressed in the agreement,[21] the extent to which and the method by which the agreement is included in the decree,[22] and whether the decree specifically orders performance of the agreement.[23] It seems clear that merger will occur if the parties intend the separation agreement to be incorporated in the decree, if the agreement is included verbatim in the decree and if the decree orders the parties to perform the agreement.[24] But there are cases which hold that it is sufficient if the court approves the agreement and incorporates it by reference.[25] On the other hand some courts would not hold that merger had occurred unless the divorce court expressly ordered the parties to perform the agreement.[26] And in at least one state it appears that approval of the agree-

---

16. See the discussion of modification of decrees based upon agreements in section 18.8, infra.

17. Foote v. Foote, 190 Md. 171, 57 A.2d 804 (1948); Goldfish v. Goldfish, 193 App.Div. 686, 184 N.Y.S. 512 (1st Dep't 1920), affirmed 230 N.Y. 606, 130 N.E. 912 (1921); Glynn v. Glynn, 8 N.D. 233, 77 N.W. 594 (1898); Lemons v. Lemons, 205 Okl. 485, 238 P.2d 790 (1951); Brown v. Brown, 198 Tenn. 600, 281 S.W.2d 492 (1955).

18. Glynn v. Glynn, 8 N.D. 233, 77 N.W. 594 (1898).

19. Dickey v. Dickey, 154 Md. 675, 141 A. 387 (1928).

20. Sloan v. Mitchell, 28 Cal.App.3d 47, 104 Cal.Rptr. 418 (1972) (payments held to be alimony for bankruptcy purposes); McClain v. McClain, 235 Ga. 659, 221 S.E.2d 561 (1975) (child support); Wilson v. Wilson, 140 Me. 250, 36 A.2d 774 (1944); Edmundson v. Edmundson, 222 N.C. 181, 22 S.E.2d 576 (1942). O'Connor v. O'Connor, 48 Wis. 2d 535, 180 N.W.2d 735 (1970) held that attorney fees arrived at by agreement and ordered paid in the divorce decree could be enforced by contempt without violation of the constitutional prohibition against imprisonment for debt.

The most persuasive support for the view expressed in the text is Justice Traynor's dissent in Bradley v. Superior Court In and For City and County of San Francisco, 48 Cal.2d 509, 523, 310 P.2d 634, 643 (1957).

21. E.g. Helber v. Frazelle, 118 Ariz. 217, 575 P.2d 1243 (1978).

22. E.g., Tilghman v. Superior Court for Los Angeles County, 40 Cal.App.3d 599, 115 Cal.Rptr. 195 (1974).

23. E.g., Thomas v. Thomas, 246 Ark. 1126, 443 S.W.2d 534 (1969); Oedekoven v. Oedekoven, 538 P.2d 1292 (Wyo.1975).

24. This appears to be substantially what is required by the Uniform Marriage and Divorce Act § 306(d)(1), 9A Unif.L.Ann. 136 (1979), the intent of the parties being presumed under that provision unless a contrary intent is indicated. See also Helber v. Frazelle, 118 Ariz. 217, 575 P.2d 1243 (1978). Contra: In re Seymour's Marriage, 36 Colo.App. 104, 536 P.2d 1172 (1975). The Arizona version of the Uniform Act seems designed to create confusion. Young v. Burkholder, 142 Ariz. 415, 690 P.2d 134 (App. 1984).

25. Ferree v. Ferree, 71 N.C.App. 737, 323 S.E.2d 52 (1984), review denied 313 N.C. 328, 327 S.E.2d 889 (1985); Greiner v. Greiner, 61 Ohio App.2d 88, 399 N.E.2d 571 (1979).

26. Thomas v. Thomas, 246 Ark. 1126, 443 S.W.2d 534 (1969); Shoosmith v. Scott, 217 Va. 789, 232 S.E.2d 787 (1977) (semble); Oedekoven v. Oedekoven, 538 P.2d 1292 (Wyo.1975). The New York practice seems to be that the

ment by the court is sufficient to convert the agreement into a decree, whatever that may involve.[27]

In spite of statements in the cases, the intention of the parties is not relevant to whether contempt should be available to enforce a decree based upon the agreement, but only to the question whether the court should make the agreement a part of the decree.[28] Once that question is decided in favor of approval, the further question arises concerning just what action by the court should be required for merger to occur and for contempt to become available. Since contempt is a relatively severe sanction, the person who is to be subject to it is entitled to have his obligations spelled out in detail in the decree and to have a specific order of the court that he perform those obligations. In other words, before merger can occur, the agreement should reproduce verbatim the parties' agreement and the obligor should be expressly ordered to perform its requirements. If the agreement is merely incorporated by reference, its provisions may not be available in the court file and in any event will not be ascertainable solely by an inspection of the decree. In such circumstances the obligor will not have sufficient notice of his duties under the decree. For this reason incorporation by reference or any lesser form of approval of the agreement should not be given the effect of merger, at least for purposes of enforcement. Where modification is sought the result may be different.[29] Certainly counsel

for either spouse in a divorce action should take care to have the agreement set forth in toto in the divorce decree and to have that decree specifically order the parties to comply with the agreement as so set forth.

A divorce decree which incorporates a separation agreement may be the subject of an independent suit under the same circumstances as may any other divorce decree.[30] Thus if the decree orders the payment of money, a suit upon it for accrued installments may be brought in another state, according to the usual principles governing the enforcement of money decrees.[31] But if the decree calls for the performance of acts, such as the conveyance of specific property, some of the older cases hold that an action may not be brought on the decree in another state.[32] This view is being replaced by the holding that the first decree at least may be treated as establishing a right to the property in the second state by virtue of the doctrines of res judicata and collateral estoppel.[33]

It has already been indicated that if the divorce decree does not incorporate the separation agreement so as to bring about merger, suit may be brought on the agreement.[34] The same principle is followed where the divorce is obtained in a state other than that in which the suit to enforce the agreement is brought.[35] But if the divorce action is joined with a claim for enforcement of rights under the separation agreement and the entire action is adju-

agreement is incorporated in the decree but not merged in it. See Tauber v. Lebow, 65 N.Y.2d 596, 493 N.Y.S.2d 1008, 483 N.E.2d 1140 (1985).

27. Walters v. Walters, 307 N.C. 381, 386, 298 S.E.2d 338, 342 (1983): "* * * we now establish a rule that whenever the parties bring their separation agreements before the court for the court's approval, it will no longer be treated as a contract between the parties. All separation agreements approved by the court as judgments of the court will be treated similarly, to-wit, as court ordered judgments." See also Frykberg v. Frykberg, 76 N.C.App. 401, 333 S.E.2d 766 (1985).

28. See section 18.5, supra, and Uniform Marriage and Divorce Act § 306(d)(1), 9A Unif.L.Ann. 136 (1979).

29. See section 18.8, infra.

30. In re Marriage of Alper, 116 Cal.App.3d 925, 172 Cal.Rptr. 402 (1981); German v. German, 122 Conn. 155, 188 A. 429 (1936); Van Wagner v. Van Wagner, 1 Conn.

App. 578, 474 A.2d 110 (1984); Knight v. Knight, 70 Ohio L.A. 271, 114 N.E.2d 616 (1953), rehearing denied 115 N.E.2d 34 (Ohio App.1953); Wallihan v. Hughes, 196 Va. 117, 82 S.E.2d 553 (1954). For a complete discussion of the interstate enforcement of alimony and property division decrees see section 16.7, supra.

31. Ibid.

32. Buswell v. Buswell, 377 Pa. 487, 105 A.2d 608 (1954). See the discussion of this point in section 16.7, at note 19.

33. See section 16.7, at notes 26 to 29.

34. See the discussion at notes 6 and 7, supra.

35. Whitney v. Whitney, 316 Mass. 367, 55 N.E.2d 601 (1944); Welch v. Chapman, 296 Mass. 487, 6 N.E.2d 438 (1937); Russo v. Russo, 62 N.Y.S.2d 514 (City Ct.1946), 47 Colum.L.Rev. 158 (1947); Allen v. Allen, 196 Okl. 36, 162 P.2d 193 (1945).

dicated on the merits, any later action to enforce the agreement is barred.[36]

A spouse's rights under a separation agreement are not impaired when the marriage ends in annulment rather than divorce. The obligor may not succeed with the argument that the annulment eliminated any consideration for the agreement by establishing that he, never having been married, never had an obligation to support the other spouse.[37] The agreement in those circumstances is valid as a compromise of a doubtful claim.

Occasionally the divorce court may give alimony without mentioning an existing separation agreement. This would not amount to incorporation or merger but might raise doubts about whether the rights based on the agreement were affected. To the extent that it is inconsistent with the agreement, the decree clearly should prevail.[38] If the parties so intend, the spouses might have rights under both agreement and decree.[39] In such a case payments made under one should be applied in satisfaction of the obligations on the other.[40]

WESTLAW REFERENCES

separation /2 agreement /s merg! /s incorporat! /s oblig!

di(separation /2 agreement /s contempt /s alimony)

---

36. Holcomb v. Holcomb, 93 U.S.App.D.C. 242, 209 F.2d 794 (D.C.Cir.1954).

37. Reighley v. Continental Illinois Nat. Bank & Trust Co. of Chicago, 390 Ill. 242, 61 N.E.2d 29 (1945).

38. Miller v. Miller, 134 F.2d 583 (9th Cir. 1943), cert. denied 320 U.S. 744, 64 S.Ct. 46, 88 L.Ed. 441 (1943).

39. Freeman v. Sieve, 323 Mass. 652, 84 N.E.2d 16 (1949).

40. Miller v. Miller, 134 F.2d 583 (9th Cir. 1943), cert. denied 320 U.S. 744, 64 S.Ct. 46, 88 L.Ed. 441 (1943).

§ 18.8

1. See the discussion in section 16.5, supra.

2. See the discussion in section 15.1, supra, at note 20.

3. The cases are extensively collected in Annot., Divorce: Power of Court to Modify Decree for Alimony or Support of Spouse Which Was Based on Agreement of Parties, 61 A.L.R.3d 520 (1975).

4. These cases are discussed in section 18.7, supra.

5. Gertrude L.Q. v. Stephen P.Q., 466 A.2d 1213 (Del. 1983); Turner v. Turner, 90 Idaho 308, 410 P.2d 648

§ 18.8 Separation Agreements—Modification of Divorce Decrees Based Upon Separation Agreements

As has been indicated in earlier sections of this work, the alimony, child support and custody provisions of divorce decrees are generally modifiable by the court which granted them,[1] whereas the property provisions of such decrees are not modifiable.[2] The questions with which this section is concerned are whether and to what extent the power to modify and the limitations on modifiability are affected by the fact that the divorce decree was based upon a separation agreement or incorporated a separation agreement in its terms. These questions have generated a large number of cases with varying results.[3] To some extent the analysis of these questions parallels that in the cases dealing with the enforcement of divorce decrees based upon separation agreements,[4] but there is a surprising disparity in the outcomes of the modification and enforcement cases.

The alimony and property provisions of separation agreements are not modifiable when the agreements are not merged in divorce decrees,[5] unless a provision authorizing modification is inserted in the agreement itself.[6] But provisions in separation agreements for the custody and support of children are modifiable whether or not incorporated in divorce

(1966); Moller v. Moller, 121 N.J.Eq. 175, 188 A. 505 (Ch. 1936); Cohen v. Cronin, 39 N.Y.2d 42, 382 N.Y.S.2d 724, 346 N.E.2d 524 (1976); Stark v. Stark, 185 Okl. 348, 91 P.2d 1064 (1939). If a decree is entered without referring to or incorporating the agreement, the decree may be modified on the usual terms, Lasprogato v. Lasprogato, 127 Conn. 510, 18 A.2d 353 (1941), the original agreement remaining as an unmodified contract obligation, Simpson v. Superior Court of Arizona In and For Pima County, 87 Ariz. 350, 351 P.2d 179 (1960). But Lindsley v. Lindsley, 374 A.2d 311 (Me.1977) held, in partial reliance on a Florida statute, that a decree ordering a larger amount of alimony than an agreement had the effect of modifying the agreement.

6. Crook v. Crook, 211 Ga. 406, 86 S.E.2d 223 (1955); Aseltine v. Second Judicial District Court In and For Washoe County, Dept. No. 1, 57 Nev. 269, 62 P.2d 701 (1936); Collyer v. Proper, 109 A.D.2d 1010, 486 N.Y.S.2d 808 (3d Dep't 1985).

decrees.[7] There are two reasons for this, one being the courts' overriding interest in the protection and welfare of children,[8] and the other the fact that the children are not parties to separation agreements and should not be bound by them.[9] The grounds for modification of the custody and support provisions are those described in an earlier section dealing with the modification of support orders,[10] and in a later section dealing with modification of custody orders.[11] In fact a few cases go so far as to say that child support provisions in separation agreements may be modified not only when conditions have changed but also when it appears that the execution of the separation agreement prevented material facts from being presented to the court in the divorce action.[12]

Assuming for the moment that the separation agreement has been so fully incorporated in the divorce decree as to make it a part of that decree,[13] an examination of the cases reveals that the alimony or maintenance provisions of the agreement and decree have been treated in at least five different ways when modification is sought by one of the parties: [14]

(a) The majority of courts hold that the alimony or maintenance provisions of a decree into which a separation agreement has been merged may be increased or reduced upon the same terms as any other alimony decree.[15] A few courts would even reach this result where the agreement contains a provision forbidding modification.[16] Where either a statute or a line of judicial decisions authorizing the modification of alimony awards

---

7. Curley v. Curley, 588 P.2d 289 (Alaska 1979); Guille v. Guille, 196 Conn. 260, 492 A.2d 175 (1985); G. W. F. v. G. P. F., 271 A.2d 38 (Del.1970); Knox v. Remick, 371 Mass. 433, 358 N.E.2d 432 (1976); Berkowitz v. Berkowitz, 55 N.J. 564, 264 A.2d 49 (1970); Brescia v. Fitts, 56 N.Y.2d 132, 451 N.Y.S.2d 68, 436 N.E.2d 518 (1982), on remand 89 A.D.2d 894, 453 N.Y.S.2d 458 (1982); Boden v. Boden, 42 N.Y.2d 210, 397 N.Y.S.2d 701, 366 N.E.2d 791 (1977), 27 Buff.L.Rev. 411 (1978); Kozak v. Kozak, 111 A.D.2d 842, 490 N.Y.S.2d 583 (2d Dep't 1985), appeal dismissed 66 N.Y.2d 913, 498 N.Y.S.2d 794, 489 N.E.2d 763 (1985); Rutter v. Rutter, 53 Ohio Op.2d 32, 261 N.E.2d 202 (1970); Parrillo v. Parrillo, 1 Va.App. 226, 336 S.E.2d 23 (1985); Morris v. Morris, 216 Va. 457, 219 S.E.2d 864 (1975). See also N.Y.—McKinney's Fam.Ct. Act § 461 (1983). The Uniform Marriage and Divorce Act §§ 306(f) and 316, 9A Unif.L.Ann. 136, 183 (1979) seem to support the text position. Many other cases are collected in Annot., 61 A.L.R.3d 657 (1975).

A small minority of cases are contra the statement in the text, but they are clearly wrong. See, e.g., McInturff v. McInturff, 7 Ark.App. 116, 644 S.W.2d 618 (1983); Lanahan v. Nevius, 317 A.2d 521 (D.C.App.1974). Murphy v. Murphy, 467 A.2d 129 (Del.Fam.Ct.1983), in a confused opinion, seems to hold that child support may be modified if merged, but not if incorporated in the divorce decree.

8. The importance of this factor has led some courts to hold that the presence of a separation agreement will prevent child support from being reduced, but that it does not prevent the court from increasing the support. E.g., Forrester v. Buerger, 241 Ga. 34, 244 S.E.2d 345 (1978); Grijalva v. Grijalva, ___ W.Va. ___, 310 S.E.2d 193 (1983).

9. Guille v. Guille, 196 Conn. 260, 492 A.2d 175 (1985).

10. Section 17.2, supra.

11. Section 19.9, infra.

12. Hendricks v. Hendricks, 69 Idaho 341, 206 P.2d 523 (1949); Annot., 9 A.L.R.2d 623 (1950).

13. The extent to which and circumstances in which incorporation must occur for this purpose are discussed infra at note 30. See also section 18.7, supra, at note 21.

14. For general discussions of the modification of incorporated agreements see Note, Control of Post-Divorce Level of Support by Prior Agreement, 63 Harv.L.Rev. 337 (1949); Note, Power of Court to Modify Decree for Alimony or Property Settlement as Affected by Agreement of the Parties, 39 Mich.L.Rev. 120 (1940).

The law of the place where the separation agreement was executed has been applied to determine the effect of such an agreement upon the modifiability of alimony in Knodel v. Knodel, 14 Cal.3d 752, 122 Cal.Rptr. 521, 537 P.2d 353 (1975).

15. Viles v. Viles, 316 F.2d 31 (3d Cir.1963); Thomas v. Thomas, 281 Ala. 397, 203 So.2d 118 (1967); Frizzell v. Bartley, 372 So.2d 1371 (Fla.1979) (pursuant to statute); Baird v. Baird, 209 Kan. 604, 498 P.2d 83 (1972); Taylor v. Taylor, 392 So.2d 1145 (Miss.1981); Smith v. Smith, 72 N.J. 350, 371 A.2d 1 (1977); Walters v. Walters, 307 N.C. 381, 298 S.E.2d 338 (1983); Wolfe v. Wolfe, 46 Ohio St.2d 399, 350 N.E.2d 413 (1976), limited on other grounds by Grant v. Grant, 60 Ohio App.2d 277, 396 N.E.2d 1037 (1977), 37 Ohio St.L.J. 382 (1976), 45 U.Cin.L.Rev. 717 (1977); Garnett v. Garnett, 270 Or. 102, 526 P.2d 549 (1974); Jeanes v. Jeanes, 255 S.C. 161, 177 S.E.2d 537 (1970); Corbin v. Corbin, 157 W.Va. 967, 206 S.E.2d 898 (1974); Johnson v. Johnson, 717 P.2d 335 (Wyo.1986). Many other cases are cited in Annot., 61 A.L.R.3d 520, 533 (1975). The parties, by an agreement incorporated in the divorce decree, may extend the court's power to modify alimony beyond what would normally be permissible under the applicable statute or case law. See, e.g. Raymond v. Raymond, 447 A.2d 70 (Me.1982); Matter of Marriage McDonnal, 293 Or. 772, 652 P.2d 1247 (1982).

16. Ward v. Ward, 48 R.I. 60, 135 A. 241 (1926).

based upon separation agreements has long been in existence, the agreement of the parties may be considered to have been made pursuant to this legal principle. For this reason the principle does not violate the Contracts Clause of the state or federal constitution.[17] There is an apt analogy to the principle of corporation law which permits the amendment of articles of incorporation pursuant to statute even when the amendment may affect "vested" rights of shareholders.[18] Where modification is permitted by this line of cases, the grounds on which it may be granted are those required to be proved for any such modification, that is, a change in the relevant circumstances of the parties.[19]

(b) A substantial number of states authorizes alimony awards based upon separation agreements to be modified upon the same terms as other alimony awards but with the qualification that this may not be done if the parties' agreement expressly limits or precludes modification.[20]

(c) New York has adopted the rule that an order incorporating a separation agreement dealing with maintenance may only be modi-

fied upon proof of "extreme hardship" to either party.[21]

(d) In a very few states the alimony decree may be modified but without prejudice to obligations under the separation agreement.[22]

(e) In an equally small number of states the courts attempt to make a distinction between a "stipulation" and an "independent agreement" for modification purposes. An alimony decree based upon a stipulation may be modified, but one based upon an independent decree may not be.[23] This distinction has been seen to be overly technical and irrelevant in at least one state.[24]

(f) There may be one or two jurisdictions in which modification of an alimony decree is denied on the sole ground that it was based upon a separation agreement which was merged in the decree, although the language of the opinions is so imprecise that one may be in error in characterizing the cases in that way.[25]

The reason for all this diversity in the treatment of the relationship between separation agreements and alimony decrees with respect to modification is, as in so many other

---

17. Frizzell v. Bartley, 372 So.2d 1371 (Fla.1979); Lindsley v. Lindsley, 374 A.2d 311 (Me.1977).

18. See N. Lattin, The Law of Corporations §§ 158, 159 (2d ed.1971).

19. For modification of alimony decrees in general, see section 16.5, supra.

20. West's Ann.Cal.Civ.Code § 4811(b) (Supp.1986); Uniform Marriage and Divorce Act §§ 306(f), 316(a), (b), 9A Unif.L.Ann. 136, 183 (1979). See also McLoughlin v. McLoughlin, 234 Ga. 259, 214 S.E.2d 925 (1975); Kitfield v. Kitfield, 237 Ga. 184, 227 S.E.2d 9 (1976). Some courts get the same result by holding that the agreement is only merged in the decree if the parties intend it to be merged. Johnston v. Johnston, 297 Md. 48, 465 A.2d 436 (1983). The Illinois version of the Uniform Act was held constitutional in Josic v. Josic, 78 Ill.App.3d 347, 33 Ill.Dec. 871, 397 N.E.2d 204 (1979). Cases construing this and similar statutes include In re Marriage of Farrell, 171 Cal.App.3d 695, 217 Cal.Rptr. 397 (1985); In re Marriage of Hufford, 152 Cal.App.3d 825, 199 Cal.Rptr. 726 (1984); In re Marriage of Kozloff, 101 Ill.2d 526, 79 Ill.Dec. 165, 463 N.E.2d 719 (1984); In re Marriage of Mass, 102 Ill.App.3d 984, 58 Ill.Dec. 941, 431 N.E.2d 1 (1981); In re Marriage of Chalkley, 99 Ill.App.3d 478, 55 Ill.Dec. 262, 426 N.E.2d 237 (1981); Berman v. Berman, 701 S.W.2d 781 (Mo.App. 1985); Wagner v. Wagner, 95 Wash.2d 94, 621 P.2d 1279 (1980).

21. N.Y.—McKinney's Dom.Rel.L. § 236, Part B, 9(b) (Supp.1986); Pintus v. Pintus, 104 A.D.2d 866, 480 N.Y.S.2d 501 (2d Dep't 1984).

22. Stansel v. Stansel, 385 Mass. 510, 432 N.E.2d 691 (1982) and Moore v. Moore, 389 Mass. 21, 448 N.E.2d 1255 (1983) seem to be cases of this kind, but these cases may simply be examples of the rule stated in paragraph (b) supra. This was formerly also the New York rule. See Kleila v. Kleila, 50 N.Y.2d 277, 428 N.Y.S.2d 896, 406 N.E.2d 753 (1980).

23. Law v. Law, 248 Ark. 894, 455 S.W.2d 854 (1970), 24 Ark.L.Rev. 557 (1971).

24. Walters v. Walters, 307 N.C. 381, 298 S.E.2d 338 (1983).

25. Compare Rice v. Rice, 219 Kan. 569, 549 P.2d 555 (1976) with Baird v. Baird, 209 Kan. 604, 498 P.2d 83 (1972), and Stuart v. Stuart, 555 P.2d 611 (Okl.1976) with Acker v. Acker, 594 P.2d 1216 (Okl.1979). In Ohio a distinction is made between divorce decrees, which may be modified though they incorporate separation agreements, and dissolution of marriage which may not be so modified. Compare Wolfe v. Wolfe, 46 Ohio St.2d 399, 350 N.E.2d 413 (1976), limited on other grounds by Grant v. Grant, 60 Ohio App.2d 277, 396 N.E.2d 1037 (1977), with McClain v. McClain, 15 Ohio St.3d 289, 473 N.E.2d 811 (1984). Dissolution of marriage is granted on the ground of separation pursuant to a separation agreement. This distinction would appear to be without substance.

domestic relations issues, that the courts are faced with conflicting policies, both of which are entitled to respect. The courts' analyses reflect this conflict. The cases allowing modification usually argue that decrees incorporating agreements are not different from other decrees, that the jurisdiction to modify alimony is expressly given by statute, and that the parties' own arrangements should not be permitted to oust that jurisdiction. The presence of the statutes certainly makes it difficult for the courts to deny some power of modification, regardless of how the decree is arrived at. Underlying both the statutes and the expressions in the opinions is the view that it is desirable for the courts to retain some control over the continuing obligation of alimony for the obvious reason that the parties' circumstances will sometimes so change that the original award will produce hardship to either of them. For example, in times of inflation the payer may find it extremely difficult, even impossible to make the payments, or the payee may be unable to exist on the amounts originally awarded. No one can completely foresee what may happen to him economically after divorce. Some authorities would add the dogma that the state has an interest in such matters. Unless the parties' hardship reaches such an acute degree that the state must provide public assistance [26] (and most modification cases fall short of this) the interest of the state is hard to define. Whatever the policies, the interests favoring modification are strong enough to make it the prevailing rule.

The countervailing policies are by no means to be ignored, however. All agree that it is desirable to adopt rules which encourage the parties to settle their financial differences by agreement rather than by litigation. It seems likely that a rule assuring them that they could make an agreement which would not later be changed by a court would offer that encouragement. Such a rule not only gives both parties the opportunity to plan for the future but it allows them to assume financial responsibilities after the divorce free from the threat of subsequent litigation and from the prospect that some court may make substantial changes in their ability to meet those responsibilities. Of course they may achieve the same result in many states by seeing to it that the agreement is not merged in the decree,[27] but this precludes later reliance upon the remedies for the enforcement of judicial decrees and leaves them to a suit on the contract for their protection.[28]

The Uniform Marriage and Divorce Act seems to offer the most workable compromise among these conflicting policies.[29] It enables the parties to have the remedies for enforcement of decrees and at the same time to control the extent to which that decree based upon their agreement may be modified. If they wish the alimony provisions of the decree to be fully modifiable, to be modifiable only on certain eventualities, or not modifiable at all, their separation agreement may accomplish any of these aims. The Act does have one important consequence, however. It requires counsel for the spouses to exercise more than ordinary care in the drafting of separation agreements in order to provide for the problems that control of modifiability presents.

In the foregoing discussion it has been assumed that the agreement was "merged" in the divorce decree, that is, was made a part of the divorce decree to the fullest possible extent. The question left to be answered is how the agreement must be handled in order to allow the courts to modify the alimony provisions to whatever extent the local law permits it. Here again there is disagreement. What constitutes merger of the agreement for purposes of enforcement has been outlined in an earlier section.[30] Merger should be defined in the same way when the question is the court's power to modify the alimony award, since the severity of contempt enforcement should only be available when the court has the power to

---

26. See the New York statute cited in note 21, supra.

27. See note 5, supra.

28. See section 18.7, supra.

29. See the text at note 20, supra.

30. See section 18.7, supra, at note 21.

amend upon a proper showing of changed circumstances. Just as in the case of enforcement, some courts take the view that the decree must set forth the agreement in full [31] or must expressly merger the agreement [32] before modification of the provisions on alimony may be accomplished. Other courts find that merger has occurred when the agreement is incorporated in the decree by reference [33] or when the decree "ratifies and confirms" the agreement.[34] Still others make the issue turn on the intent of the parties, either as expressed in the separation agreement or as inferred from their conduct.[35] As has been argued in connection with enforcement,[36] the more workable rule is to require that the agreement be set forth in full in the decree, together with an order for payment of the alimony before the agreement may be held to merge in the decree. This gives the parties notice of their obligations and rights and avoids later conflict concerning the enforcement and modification of the alimony provisions.

As where enforcement of the decree is at stake,[37] it is necessary to distinguish for modification purposes between agreements dividing the property of the parties and agreements providing for the support of spouse or children. This distinction has been discussed in several other sections where it has impor-

tant consequences.[38] Where the separation agreement provides for the division of property between spouses and the agreement is then merged in the divorce decree, it is generally held that this provision in the decree may not subsequently be modified.[39] This result is only a specific application of the general principle that property division provisions in divorce decrees in general are not modifiable.[40] In some states the rule has been carried a step further. If the spouses' separation agreement contains both property division provisions and alimony provisions, and both types of provision are "integrated", that is each is arrived at in consideration for the other, then neither the property division nor the alimony is modifiable when the agreement is merged in the divorce decree.[41]

While it is easy to state the rule that alimony is modifiable but a property division is not, defining the distinction between the two kinds of provision may often be difficult or even impossible on any basis which appears reasonable. The form of the provision may be decisive, as where the agreement and decree provide that one spouse will transfer specific personal or real property to the other.[42] But in most of those cases no problem of modification arises. The difficult cases are those in which installment payments continuing over a period of time are provided for. Some

---

31. Simpson v. Superior Court of Arizona In and For Pima County, 87 Ariz. 350, 351 P.2d 179 (1960) (under an earlier statute); McWilliams v. McWilliams, 110 Colo. 173, 132 P.2d 966 (1942) (under an earlier statute).

32. Corbin v. Corbin, 157 W.Va. 967, 206 S.E.2d 898 (1974).

33. Wise v. Watson, 286 Ala. 22, 236 So.2d 681 (1970); Flynn v. Flynn, 42 Cal.2d 55, 265 P.2d 865 (1954), 43 Cal. L.Rev. 524, 528 (1954); Lasprogato v. Lasprogato, 127 Conn. 510, 18 A.2d 353 (1941); Underwood v. Underwood, 64 So.2d 281 (Fla.1953); Fabrizio v. Fabrizio, 316 Mass. 343, 55 N.E.2d 604 (1944). Compare Madnick v. Madnick, 339 Pa.Super. 130, 488 A.2d 344 (1985) with Commonwealth ex rel. Tokach v. Tokach, 326 Pa.Super. 359, 474 A.2d 41 (1984).

34. Phillips v. Phillips, 93 Idaho 384, 462 P.2d 49 (1969).

35. Johnston v. Johnston, 297 Md. 48, 465 A.2d 436 (1983); Kirk v. Kirk, 598 S.W.2d 153 (Mo.App.1980).

36. See section 18.7, supra, at notes 28 and 29.

37. See section 18.7, supra.

38. See sections 15.1, 16.5 and 16.6, supra.

39. Salomon v. Salomon, 196 So.2d 111 (Fla.1967); Covalt v. Covalt, 171 Ind.App. 37, 354 N.E.2d 766 (1976); Wardwell v. Wardwell, 458 A.2d 750 (Me.1983); Garnett v. Garnett, 270 Or. 102, 526 P.2d 549 (1974); Kinne v. Kinne, 82 Wash.2d 360, 510 P.2d 814 (1973).

40. See section 16.5, supra.

41. Lincoln v. Lincoln, 24 Ariz.App. 447, 539 P.2d 921 (1975) (pursuant to and earlier statute); In re Marriage of Matthews, 74 Cal.App.3d 683, 141 Cal.Rptr. 634 (1977); White v. White, 296 N.C. 661, 252 S.E.2d 698 (1979). Where the separation agreement indicates that the alimony and property provisions are separable, the alimony provision may be modified. Levitt v. Levitt, 62 Cal.2d 477, 42 Cal.Rptr. 577, 399 P.2d 33 (1965). California law on integrated agreements was applied to an agreement executed in California and merged in a California divorce decree by Barbash v. Barbash, 91 Nev. 320, 535 P.2d 781 (1975). Other cases are cited in Annot., 61 A.L.R.3d 520, 589 (1975).

42. E.g. Wardwell v. Wardwell, 458 A.2d 750 (Me. 1983).

courts make the distinction depend upon the purpose of the payments, often without perceiving that the purpose nearly always is the support of the payee spouse.[43] Other courts are persuaded by the intent of the parties as indicated in the separation agreement.[44] Still others fall into a sort of circular reasoning which leads them to say that the payments are part of a property division if the agreement does not provide for termination on such eventualities as the death or remarriage of the payee, the result being that the payments are held not modifiable for the reason claimed because they are not modifiable for other reasons.[45] When the agreement and the divorce decree provide for the establishment of a trust with the income payable to the spouse the courts have reached varying conclusions on modification.[46]

In these cases involving installment payments the alimony-property distinction is neither sensible nor workable, and in fact is largely illusory.[47] Nevertheless it persists in the cases. This presents a serious difficulty for the draftsman of the separation agreement. Although he can include in the agreement a statement expressly labelling the payments property or alimony, and although such a statement will be persuasive to some courts, others will feel free to ignore it.[48] Under the statutes and judicial decisions of many states he may be able to provide expressly that modification is to occur, either without limitation or under specified circumstances, or that it is not to occur at all, and the courts will be required to follow the prescriptions in the separation agreement.[49] But in other states, due to the uncertainty inherent in the alimony-property distinction, it may be difficult or impossible for counsel to assure the spouses that their wishes concerning modification will be carried out.

WESTLAW REFERENCES

separation /2 agreement /s merg! /s divorc! /s modif! /s alimony maintenance

separation /2 agreement /s merg! /s divorc! dissol! /s modif! /s child /s support custod!

separation /2 agreement /s hardship

---

43. E.g., Salomon v. Salomon, 196 So.2d 111 (Fla.1967) (monthly payments to the wife held a property settlement because made for the purpose of enabling her to meet the expenses of her residence); Bockoven v. Bockoven, 444 So.2d 30 (Fla.App.1983) (payments for maintenance of the marital residence held a property settlement and not modifiable); Garnett v. Garnett, 270 Or. 102, 526 P.2d 549 (1974) (payments for the wife's household and automobile expenses held alimony and modifiable).

44. Flowers v. Flowers, 334 So.2d 856 (Ala.1976); Kinne v. Kinne, 82 Wash.2d 360, 510 P.2d 814 (1973).

45. E.g., Hamblett v. Lewis, 114 N.H. 258, 319 A.2d 629 (1974); Matter of Marriage of Pope, 73 Or.App. 242, 698 P.2d 518 (1985). A more workable definition of this distinction is made in Stebbins v. Stebbins, 121 N.H. 1060, 1063, 438 A.2d 295, 297 (1981): "A property settlement therefore exists when a spouse agrees to make monetary payments which are ascertainable in amount, payable within a definite period, and binding on the estate of the paying spouse. * * * In contrast to prop-

erty settlements, continuing obligations, such as alimony and child support, involve indefinite payments which remain modifiable by the court. * * * Furthermore, unless otherwise provided, support payments terminate upon the death of either spouse, and the estates of the spouses have no rights or responsibilities concerning those payments."

46. Holding the trust payments modifiable: Reynolds v. Reynolds, 53 R.I. 326, 166 A. 686 (1933). Holding them property and not modifiable: Douglas v. Willcuts, 296 U.S. 1, 56 S.Ct. 59, 80 L.Ed. 3 (1935) (Minnesota law); Stebbins v. Stebbins, 121 N.H. 1060, 438 A.2d 295 (1981).

47. See section 15.1, supra, following note 18.

48. Kinne v. Kinne, 82 Wash.2d 360, 510 P.2d 814 (1973) respected the parties' characterization expressed in the agreement. But Fagan v. Lewis, 374 So.2d 18 (Fla. App.1979) and Schaffer v. Schaffer, 57 Or.App. 43, 643 P.2d 1300 (1982) refused to do so.

49. See the text at note 20, supra.

Chapter 19

CUSTODY OF CHILDREN

Table of Sections

§ 19.1 Custody of Children—Introduction

Litigation concerning the custody of children arises in many contexts, but suits for divorce account for most of it. The jurisdictional aspects of the subject have already been dealt with at inordinate length in another chapter.[1] The procedural and substantive aspects of it will be discussed in this chapter in the hope of giving a complete view of what is really a single subject even though custody issues will often arise in connection with adoption, with neglect and dependency cases, between unmarried parents and occasionally on the death of natural parents.

The magnitude of potential custody litigation is demonstrated by the fact that annually the parents of more than one million children under eighteen are now obtaining divorces in the United States.[2] If anything this may understate the number of cases since as indicated custody may be an issue in suits other than divorces and since a sizeable number of divorced parents bring more than one custody proceeding.[3] In any case it is evident that half or nearly half of all divorces involve children.[4]

The power to protect children and act for their welfare goes back several centuries in Anglo-American law. It was acknowledged to be part of equity jurisdiction in England at least as early as the Seventeenth Century, although the origin of the jurisdiction re-

---

§ 19.1

1. See section 12.5, supra.

2. Statistical Abstract of the United States 1986, 79, indicating that in 1982 1,108,000 children under eighteen were involved in divorce in the thirty-one states reporting, or .94 children per marriage. See also Department of Health and Human Services, Vital Statistics of the United States 1981, Table 2–9 on page 2–10, giving a figure for 1981 of 1,180,000 children under eighteen in divorce.

3. Many cases of this kind are discussed in section 12.5, supra.

4. P. Jacobson, American Marriage and Divorce 130–131 (1959).

mains in dispute.[5] It is usually explained as being derived from the Crown's prerogative as *parens patriae* to protect those of the Crown's subjects who were unable to protect themselves.[6] Although this is an explanation which explains nothing, we leave it at that, except to add that it is more likely to have been due to the range and flexibility of remedy available in equity. The jurisdiction has likewise been recognized from earliest times in the United States,[7] and is now largely covered by state statutes.

Awarding custody under the early English law in the infrequent cases where the issue arose presented few difficulties to the courts. The rule was that the child's father was entitled to custody.[8] The rule was not absolute, however.[9] This rule was not adopted in the United States, the courts holding that custody could be awarded to the mother as well as the father where the good of the child required it, although there was apparently some sort of a *prima facie* right in the father.[10] In any event by late in the Nineteenth Century custody could be awarded to either parent in this country and in fact under what came to be called the tender years doctrine there was a rebuttable presumption that the custody of a young child should normally go to the mother.[11] The tender years doctrine is now on the wane, partly due to constitutional doctrines of

gender equality and partly due to changes in state statutes,[12] so that ostensibly at least both mother and father are considered to be equal candidates for custody. As a practical matter, however, the mother still receives custody of the children in the large majority of cases.[13]

Judges and lawyers have many times characterized custody cases as the most difficult cases they face.[14] The reasons for this are not hard to find. The future lives of children are at stake, imposing heavy responsibilities on all concerned. The cases arise in an atmosphere of strongly felt emotions. Since no two cases are exactly alike, the decisions must be made on a highly individualized basis by the trial court, which is often not assisted very much by appellate decisions or statutes. Finally, there is a greater than usual element of prediction required in custody cases, although it is easy to over-emphasize this source of difficulty.

One consequence of the difficulty in these cases has been a search by lawyers both in practice and in academic life for some workable rules which could reduce the *ad hoc* aspects of custody determination. For the most part the search has not been very successful.[15] The difficulties have also led lawyers to turn hopefully to other disciplines for help in par-

---

5. 3 J. Story, Equity §§ 1743–1749 (14th ed.1918); Hochheimer, Custody of Infants (2d ed.1891).

6. Ex Parte Skinner, 9 Moore C.P. 278 (1824); Eyre v. Shaftesbury, 2 P.Wms. 102, 24 Eng.Rep. 659 (1722); Falkland v. Bertie, 2 Vern. 333, 23 Eng.Rep. 814 (1696). Occasionally there was dispute as to whether the jurisdiction over custody was limited to cases where property of the child was also involved. See In re Spence, 2 Ph. 247, 41 Eng.Rep. 937 (1847), holding it was not so limited, and Wellesley v. Beaufort, 2 Russ. 1, 38 Eng.Rep. 236 (1827), saying that it was. See also Custer, The Origins of the Doctrine of *Parens* Patriae, 27 Emory L.J. 195 (1978).

7. People v. Mercein, 8 Paige 46 (N.Y.Ch.1839); Finlay v. Finlay, 240 N.Y. 429, 148 N.E. 624 (1925).

8. King v. De Manneville, 5 East 221, 102 Eng.Rep. 1054 (K.B.1804).

9. In Shelley v. Westbrooke, Jacob 265, 37 Eng.Rep. 850 (Ch.1817) the poet was denied custody of his children on the ground of his immorality, atheism and denial of the Christian revelation.

10. 2 J. Bishop, Commentaries on the Law of Marriage and Divorce §§ 526–530 (4th ed.1864), citing cases, and Zainaldin, The Emergence of a Modern American

Family Law: Child Custody, Adoption and the Courts, 1796–1851, 73 Nw.U.L.Rev. 1038 (1979).

11. J. Bishop, Commentaries on the Law of Marriage and Divorce § 544 (4th ed.1864), indicating also that marital fault as established in the divorce suit should be relevant on the custody issue.

12. See section 19.4, infra.

13. Weitzman and Dixon, Child Custody Awards: Legal Standards and Empirical Patterns for Child Custody, Support and Visitation After Divorce, 12 U.C.D.L.Rev. 471, 489 (1979), stating that in California between 1968 and 1972 only from 12% to 20% of fathers asked for custody, and that physical custody was awarded to mothers in from 84% to 89% of the cases. See also P. Jacobson, American Marriage and Divorce 131 (1959) stating that mothers received custody in about 80% of all cases.

14. E.g., R. Neely, The Divorce Decision 58 (1984).

15. The most exhaustive and analytical attempt to work out some rules is Chambers, Rethinking the Substantive Rules for Custody Disputes in Divorce, 83 Mich. L.Rev. 477 (1984), finding only that a preference for the

ticular cases and for empirical studies which might suggest general principles applicable to custody determinations. Although it is now commonplace (where the expense is not an obstacle) to have psychiatric or psychological testimony in custody litigation,[16] the chief result has been to convert the suit into a battle of the experts rather than to give the trial court any very conclusive assistance.[17] And although there are now many psychological studies of the effects of divorce upon children, they do not generally seem to provide reliable data on which to base legal principles.[18] This leaves the legal profession with two avenues of approach to custody cases. It can, and certainly should, seek to resolve as many cases as possible by negotiation and agreement, perhaps with the aid of mediation.[19] Where agreement cannot be reached, the only alternative is the application to the decision of cases of as much knowledge, intelligence and sensitivity as the bar and bench, primarily the trial bench, can muster. After all, these are qualities which the public expects from the legal profession and, one might add, which it pays for. It does not seem unreasonable to expect lawyers and judges to develop their capacities to such an extent that they are able to achieve as satisfactory results in custody cases as in other kinds of complex litigation.

Nearly all judicial discussion of custody cases begins with the statement that custody must be so awarded as to promote the child's best interests.[20] Viewed as a principle, the statement is often criticized as providing no real guidance to the courts and as being difficult to define.[21] Other formulations have been suggested.[22] A little reflection is enough to reveal, however, that this is not a legal principle in the usual sense but merely a statement that when the child's welfare seems to conflict with the claims of one or both parents, the child's welfare must prevail. It would be an odd legal system indeed which would announce that custody would *not* be awarded with regard to the child's best interests. But having made the statement, few if any experienced judges or lawyers think that it goes very far toward deciding cases. That can only be done by considering the facts of the individual case against the background of factors held to be relevant in earlier cases, and most importantly, with an awareness of the biases which the judge brings to his deliberations. Biases are the product of training and experience and can no more be eliminated in these cases than in any other litigation. Their destructive effect can be reduced, however, by a thorough and conscientious self-awareness on the part of the judge, and for that matter on the part of counsel.

The best interests ideal is not to be taken too literally for another reason. The child's interests are not the only consideration to be taken into account in every circumstance,

"primary caretaker" might be useful in awarding custody of young children.

16. See section 19.3, infra.

17. R. Neely, The Divorce Decision 74 (1984), suggesting that there is a Gresham's law of experts.

18. E.g., J. Wallerstein, J. Kelly, Surviving the Breakup: How Children and Parents Cope With Divorce (1980), reviewed in Bruch, Parenting At and After Divorce: A Search for New Models, 79 Mich.L.Rev. 708 (1981); D. Luepnitz, Child Custody (1982). Two other books written from psychiatric and psychological points of view have been influential with courts and lawyers although they are not studies based upon empirical data, J. Goldstein, A. Freud, A. Solnit, Beyond the Best Interests of the Child (2d ed.1979) emphasized the child's psychological needs as the focus of custody determinations. The book was reviewed and ciriticized in Dembitz, Beyond the Best Interests of the Child, 83 Yale L.J. 1304 (1974), and P. Strauss and J. Strauss, Beyond the Best Interests of the Child, 74 Colum.L.Rev. 996 (1974). J. Goldstein, A. Freud, A. Solnit, Before the Best Interests of the Child

(1979) attempted to answer the related question of what circumstances should justify the state in intervening in the parent-child relationship. For a comprehensive citation and critique of empirical studies of child custody see Chambers, Rethinking the Substantive Rules for Custody Disputes in Divorce, 83 Mich.L.Rev. 477 (1984).

19. See the discussion in sections 14.8 and 18.1, supra.

20. Mnookin, Child Custody Adjudication: Judicial Functions in the Face of Indeterminacy, 39 Law & Contemp.Probs. No. 3, 226, 236 (1975); Uniform Marriage and Divorce Act § 402, 9A Unif.L.Ann. 197 (1979). See section infra.

21. Chambers, Rethinking the Substantive Rules for Custody Disputes in Divorce, 83 Mich.L.Rev. 477, 480–486 (1984).

22. J. Goldstein, A. Freud, A. Solnit, Beyond the Best Interests of the Child 53 (2d ed.1979), suggesting "the least detrimental alternative" in place of best interests, not exactly a world-shaking change.

even though some non-legal writers think that they are.[23] For example, the parents' interests must be regarded procedurally, since due process requires that their claims be heard.[24] When they are heard, they must be given some weight, not merely because they are related to the child's welfare, but because we recognize that a parent's interest in the training, upbringing and companionship of his child has an independent importance in our society which must be respected. The interplay between the child's interests and those of the parents is a major source of the difficulty which courts have in deciding custody cases.

Another source of difficulty in recent years has been the growth of political factions and the intrusion of a narrow kind of partisanship into custody cases. Fathers' rights organizations have often had this effect.[25] Advocates of the claims of mothers are open to the same reproach.[26] Grandparents' political pressure has produced grandparent visitation statutes which in some circumstances can have destructive consequences in custody litigation.[27] Any forms of factionalism in these emotionally charged cases can only make the courts' task more difficult and reduce the opportunities for successful child placement.

Finally, we must recognize the obvious fact that child custody is inextricably connected with child support. Neither can be determined without close attention to the other. In fact in some cases claims to custody can be and are used to win a bargaining advantage in reducing the level of child support or even

alimony, when the claimant has no real expectation or desire that he will obtain custody.[28] Tactics of this kind raise serious ethical questions and impair public confidence in courts and lawyers.

 WESTLAW REFERENCES

"tender year" maternal /2 presumption preference principle doctrine rule /p unconstitutional! constitution!

sy("due process" "fourteenth amendment" /s hear*** /s custod! /5 child)

§ 19.2 Custody of Children—Definition

It is strange but the term "custody", which is used about as much as any word in the law of divorce, is seldom defined by cases or statutes. It has been characterized as a slippery word[1] as indeed it is, especially now that joint custody has become a popular option in divorce. The chief reason for the uncertainty or ambiguity in the term is that it expresses a complex of both rights and obligations the combination of which varies considerably from case to case.

In its broadest sense custody refers to the relationship which exists between parents and child in a normal intact family. It means that the parents and child live together[2] and that the parents together have the right and the obligation to supervise, care for, and educate the child.[3] Conversely, the child has a right to parental care and a duty to respect the parents' supervision.[4] In the intact family both parents have the duty to support the child and the right to his earnings.[5]

23. Batt, Child Custody Disputes: A Developmental-Psychological Approach to Proof and Decisionmaking, 12 Willamette L.J. 491 (1976), relying on theories of child development; J. Goldstein, A. Freud, A. Solnit, Beyond the Best Interests of the Child 38 (1973), taking the position that the custodial parent alone should decide whether the non-custodial parent visits the child.

24. Armstrong v. Manzo, 380 U.S. 545, 85 S.Ct. 1187, 14 L.Ed.2d 62 (1965); Smith v. Organization of Foster Families for Equality and Reform, 431 U.S. 816, 97 S.Ct. 2094, 53 L.Ed.2d 14 (1977).

25. R. Doyle, The Rape of the Male (1976); M. Franks, Winning Custody (1983).

26. Cf. Uviller, Fathers' Rights and Feminism: The Maternal Presumption Revisited, 1 Harv.Women's L.J. 107 (1978).

27. See section 19.7, infra.

28. R. Neely, The Divorce Decision 63–73 (1984).

§ 19.2

1. Justice v. Hobbs, 245 Iowa 707, 63 N.W.2d 882 (1954).

2. For the rules concerning choice of domicile see section 4.3, Practitioner's Edition.

3. The parent's rights and obligations of this kind are discussed in sections 9.1 through 10.6, Practitioner's Edition.

4. See section 9.5, supra.

5. See sections 6.2 and 8.2, supra.

When the family breaks up through death, divorce, separation, abandonment of the child by the parents or through the emancipation of the child, all of the rights and obligations formerly subsisting between parents and child must be separately allocated by the courts to one parent or the other, or on occasion to non-parents or even to the representatives of the state. For example, the most common disposition made by divorce courts is to give custody of a young child to the mother, with rights of visitation to the father at prescribed times. This form of decree is usually characterized as giving the mother custody without regard to the obvious fact that the mother no longer has the full or exclusive range of rights with respect to the child that the parent in the intact family would have. And even in this situation courts do define custody as embracing the sum or parental rights respecting the rearing of the child, including its care, the right to services and earnings, and the right to direct the child's activities, to and to make decisions concerning the care, control education, health and religion of the child.[6]

The confusion and ambiguity in the term custody increase when the divorce decree makes a different disposition of the child's parental contacts. This is particularly evident when "joint custody" is authorized by statute or awarded by a court. Does "joint custody" mean that the child will live with each parent on some sort of alternate schedule? Or does it mean only that the child will live with one parent, will visit with the other as under the traditional custody decree, but that the other parent will share in the decisions about care, education, health, religion concerning the child? Some statutes attempt to clarify these questions by distinguishing between "physical custody", which refers to the parent with whom the child lives, and "legal custody", which refers to the parent who is authorized to make decisions about the child's care.[7] Where there is not a statute of this kind, an award of "joint custody" without specific directions concerning which parent has authority to make decisions about the child's care, or concerning the way in which such decisions are to be made in the event of disagreement between the parents can result in an impasse which may have adverse effects on the child and on parental cooperation.[8]

Since it may be crucial in many circumstances to determine which parent has custody in the absence of precise provisions in the divorce decree, a general rule of thumb on the subject would be useful. Without such provisions, custody should be deemed to be in the parent who is authorized to have the child live with him during the larger part of the year in which the question arises. Such a rule is definite, workable and avoids the circularity which would result if the allocation of custody were to depend upon which parent has authority to make decisions concerning the child's care. It also accords with the result of those few cases which have attempted a definition of custody.[9]

A variety of consequences may follow from a determination that one or the other parent has custody of the child. It has already been indicated that the parent who does not have custody may be guilty of abduction when he removes the child from the state.[10] Another consequence is that if the decree is silent concerning which parent is authorized to make decisions about the child's care, education, religion or training, that authority will

---

6. Burge v. San Francisco, 41 Cal.2d 608, 262 P.2d 6 (1953) (per Traynor, J.); Adoption of Van Anda, 62 Cal. App.3d 189, 132 Cal.Rptr. 878 (1976). Cases which seem to say that a parent who has rights of visitation does not have custody include Spencer v. Spencer, 567 P.2d 112 (Okl.App.1977); Leithold v. Plass, 413 S.W.2d 698 (Tex. 1967).

7. E.g. West's Ann.Cal.Civ.Code § 4600.5 (Supp.1986); Conn.Gen.Stat.Ann. § 46b–56 (Supp.1986).

8. See Griffin v. Griffin, 699 P.2d 407 (Colo.1985), holding that an agreement between the parents that they would jointly select the child's school was unenforceable,

and that the authority to control the child's education in the event of disagreement remained with the child's custodian. "Joint custody" was defined in People v. Harrison, 82 Ill.App.3d 530, 37 Ill.Dec. 820, 402 N.E.2d 822 (1980) as including an award of custody to the mother and of visitation rights to the father, the result of which definition was to hold the father guilty of abduction when he removed his children from the state.

9. See note 6, supra.

10. People v. Harrison, 82 Ill.App.3d 530, 37 Ill.Dec. 820, 402 N.E.2d 822 (1980). Cf. State v. Al-Turck, 220 Kan. 557, 552 P.2d 1375 (1976).

be attributed to the child's custodian.[11] The allocation of custody may also determine which parent is entitled to the dependency exemption under the federal tax laws.[12] And the statutes of some states give the child's custodian the right to grant or withhold consent to the child's adoption.[13]

 WESTLAW REFERENCES

joint! /2 custod! /3 defin! mean***

§ 19.3 Custody of Children—Remedies and Procedure

The requirements for obtaining jurisdiction to determine custody are discussed in an earlier section.[1] In this section we outline the various remedies made available by state statutes for the decision of custody disputes. Although contemporary cases try to avoid overemphasis on technicalities of procedure in the interest of protecting children, established rules of procedure must be observed. A brief account of the various remedies follows. There is sufficient local variation in their nature and limits to require a careful study of the applicable statutes and rules of practice before undertaking to answer any specific question on remedies.

Divorce

The divorce statutes in all states authorize the divorce court to enter custody orders, both temporarily pending the litigation, and governing the child's custody after divorce.[2] Custody orders may also be made after the divorce decree has been granted, the fact that the decree is silent as to custody not barring the party from moving for an award of custody at some later time.[3] Likewise custody may be provided for in the decree even though the divorce plaintiff has not included a prayer for custody in the complaint.[4] In any case, however, the defendant must be given adequate notice and an opportunity to be heard on the custody question.[5]

In former days, under less carefully drawn divorce statutes a surprising number of cases held that when the divorce was refused, but the parties still sought a custody order, such

---

11. Burge v. San Francisco, 41 Cal.2d 608, 262 P.2d 6 (1953) (right to settle child's tort claim); Griffin v. Griffin, 699 P.2d 407 (Colo.1985) (right to control child's education); Bentley v. Bentley, 86 A.D.2d 926, 448 N.Y.S.2d 559 (3d Dep't 1982) (religious training); Angel v. Angel, 140 N.E.2d 86 (Ohio Com.Pl.1956) (religious instruction). The question of the child's religious training has given the courts difficulty, in part because they have anticipated First Amendment objections. Thus they have generally refused to enforce after divorce antenuptial agreements providing that the child must be brought up in a particular faith, preferring to leave that decision to the custodial parent. Lynch v. Uhlenhopp, 248 Iowa 68, 78 N.W.2d 491 (1956), 57 Colum.L.Rev. 595 (1957); Martin v. Martin, 308 N.Y. 136, 123 N.E.2d 812 (1954), affirming p.c. 283 App.Div. 721, 127 N.Y.S.2d 851 (2d Dep't 1954); Hackett v. Hackett, 146 N.E.2d 477 (Ohio Com.Pl.1957), judgment affirmed 150 N.E.2d 431 (Ohio App.1958). On the other hand a few courts have held that the non-custodial parent ought not to be prevented from talking with the child about religion or giving him religious instruction where no harm to the child results. In re Marriage of Murga, 103 Cal.App.3d 498, 163 Cal. Rptr. 79 (1980); Compton v. Gilmore, 98 Idaho 190, 560 P.2d 861 (1977). Cf. Munoz v. Munoz, 79 Wash.2d 810, 489 P.2d 1133 (1971).

12. See section 16.8, supra.

13. Adoption of Van Anda, 62 Cal.App.3d 189, 132 Cal.Rptr. 878 (1976).

§ 19.3

1. See section 12.5, supra.

2. E.g., Alaska Stat. § 25.24.150 (1983); West's Ann. Cal.Civ.Code § 4600 (Supp.1987); Conn.Gen.Stat.Ann. § 46b–56 (1986); Ill.—S.H.A. ch. 40, §§ 601, 603 (Supp. 1986); N.Y.—McKinney's Dom.Rel.L. § 240 (1986); Wis. Stat.Ann. §§ 767.02, 767.24 (Supp.1985–1986). See also the Uniform Marriage and Divorce Act § 401(d), 9A Unif. L.Ann. 194 (1979).

3. Enos v. Enos, 44 R.I. 450, 118 A. 676 (1922).

4. Remus v. Remus, 325 Mich. 641, 39 N.W.2d 211 (1949); Annot., 12 A.L.R.2d 340, 343 (1950).

5. Anonymous v. Anonymous, 353 So.2d 515 (Ala. 1977) appeal after remand 353 So.2d 519 (Ala.Civ.App. 1977); State ex rel. Shelhamer v. District Court of Fourteenth Judicial Dist. of Musselshell County, 159 Mont. 11, 494 P.2d 928 (1972); Coble v. Coble, 229 N.C. 81, 47 S.E.2d 798 (1948); Sheldon v. Sheldon, 47 Wash.2d 699, 289 P.2d 335 (1955); Annot., 76 A.L.R. 242 (1932). A parent is also entitled to notice and hearing on his application for custody pendente lite. Annot., 31 A.L.R.3d 1378 (1970). Where the parent is represented in the proceeding, some courts have held that it is not necessary that the parent himself be present at the custody hearing. Annot., 15 A.L.R.4th 864 (1982). It has also been held that a foster parent is entitled to notice and a hearing before the child is removed from her custody. Rivera v. Marcus, 696 F.2d 1016 (2d Cir. 1982), citing other cases.

an order could not be granted.[6] The reason was either that the statute only authorized custody orders "when a divorce is decreed"[7] or because the custody order was held to be merely incident to a decree of divorce.[8] More enlightened courts proceeded to determine the custody issue even though the divorce was denied, either in reliance on statute[9], or on the ground that since equity has inherent power to award custody and divorce is equitable in nature, the case may be retained for the giving of appropriate relief in order to avoid a multiplicity of suits.[10] By this analysis custody awards may be made regardless of statutory language, whether the divorce is denied for substantive reasons[11] or because of a lack of jurisdiction[12] provided of course that jurisdiction to award custody exists.[13]

One of the consequences of the rule that divorce actions abate on the death of a party is that, in the view of some courts at least, the custody provisions of the divorce decree no longer operate.[14] This means that the surviving parent has neither right nor disability under the decree but does have the claim to custody which any parent would have.[15] This is an unnecessary and undesirable application of the abatement rule. It is also held that the custody decree becomes inoperative when the parents are reconciled and resume living together.[16]

Habeas Corpus

A second remedy by which equity exercises it power to protect children is the writ of habeas corpus. The common law writ of habeas corpus was originally used only for the purpose of obtaining release from illegal arrest or imprisonment.[17] It was in the Eighteenth Century that the writ was first put to the analogous use of releasing infants from the custody of private persons,[18] although at that time there seems to have been some question whether the court on a petition for habeas corpus might go into all the facts to determine what the child's welfare required, or whether the court was limited to the question of the legality of the child's confinement.[19] The use of habeas corpus in custody matters became a part of American practice and by the late Nineteenth Century it had become well established. Today it is recognized as a remedy by which a person claiming custody of a child who is in the possession of another may have the court pass on his claim. Some limitations of the procedure make it less useful than a petition in equity. It is not available against a person who does not have

6. Johnson v. Levis, 240 Iowa 806, 38 N.W.2d 115 (1949), 35 Iowa L.Rev. 111 (1949), 35 Va.L.Rev. 921 (1949), decided under a statute which has since been repealed. See Iowa Code Ann. § 598.41 (Supp.1986–1987) for the present statute. A few states still retain statutes phrased in these unfortunate terms. Ala.Code 1983, § 39–3–1; Mass.Gen.Law Ann. Ch. 208, § 28 (Supp.1986).

7. Ollman v. Ollman, 396 Ill. 176, 71 N.E.2d 50 (1947), Johnson v. Levis, supra, note 6.

8. Payne v. Payne, 121 Colo. 212, 214 P.2d 495 (1950) (under an earlier statute); Harrison v. Harrison, 201 Ga. 21, 38 S.E.2d 817 (1946); Annots., 151 A.L.R. 1380, 1381 (1944) and 113 A.L.R. 901, 905 (1944).

9. E.g., Stetson v. Stetson, 103 N.H. 290, 171 A.2d 28 (1961); Settle v. Settle, 117 W.Va. 476, 185 S.E. 859 (1936); Annots., 151 A.L.R. 1380 (1944) and 113 A.L.R. 901 (1938).

10. Sovereign v. Sovereign, 354 Mich. 65, 92 N.W.2d 585 (1958); Atwood v. Atwood, 229 Minn. 333, 39 N.W.2d 103 (1949), 34 Minn.L.Rev. 347 (1949) (the leading case). See also Bartlett v. Bartlett, 94 U.S.App.D.C. 190, 221 F.2d 508 (D.C.Cir.1954), and cases cited in Annot., 113 A.L.R. 901 (1938), and 151 A.L.R. 1380 (1944). A case which refused to follow this reasoning is Urbach v. Urbach, 52 Wyo. 207, 73 P.2d 953 (1937), but the court reached the correct result by virtue of a statute.

11. E.g. Harmon v. Harmon, 111 Kan. 786, 208 P. 647 (1922); Subrt v. Subrt, 275 Wis. 628, 83 N.W.2d 122 (1956).

12. E.g. Sauvageau v. Sauvageau, 59 Idaho 190, 81 P.2d 731 (1938).

13. See section 12.5, supra.

14. Leclerc v. Leclerc, 85 N.H. 121, 155 A. 249 (1931). Contra: Snead v. Davis, 265 Ala. 229, 90 So.2d 825 (1956).

15. Stone v. Duffy, 219 Mass. 178, 106 N.E. 595 (1914); Petition of Hohmann's Petition, 255 Minn. 165, 95 N.W.2d 643 (1959).

16. Rasch v. Rasch, 250 Miss. 885, 168 So.2d 738 (1964); Annot., 26 A.L.R.4th 325, 328 (1983).

17. 1 Holdsworth, History of English Law 227 (7th ed. 1956); 9 Id. 108. See also In re Burrus, 136 U.S. 586, 602, 10 S.Ct. 850, 34 L.Ed. 500 (1890) for an excellent account of the development of habeas corpus as a remedy for custody disputes.

18. Rex v. Smith, 2 Strange 982, 93 Eng.Rep. 983 (1734); Rex v. Delaval, 3 Burrow 1434, 97 Eng.Rep. 913 (1763). For a discussion of the development of habeas corpus see Hochheimer, Custody of Infants 38–68 (2d ed. 1891).

19. Ibid.

custody of the child,[20] it may not be used to enforce a claimed right of visitation,[21] and it may not be used to relitigate a prior custody order, although it does open to scrutiny both jurisdiction and compliance with constitutional requirements in prior proceedings.[22]

The development of the writ of habeas corpus as applied to custody cases has been such as to distinguish it sharply from the older form of the writ used in criminal cases.[23] In the first place, the writ in custody cases is generally considered equitable rather than legal.[24] Second, although there are some states in which habeas corpus addresses only the limited question of who has a legal right to the child under a prior decree or on some other basis providing a clear legal right,[25] in most jurisdictions the petition for the writ opens up the broad question of what disposition will best serve the child's interest, just as in any other custody remedy.[26] In the latter jurisdictions the question is not one of personal freedom, but of whose custody will be best

for the child. The nature of the writ has thus been completely transformed.[27] Third, the usual rules of res judicata apply in habeas corpus involving custody, at least to the extent that the judgment is final, while in criminal habeas corpus the person under confinement may petition again and again.[28] Fourth, there has been a tendency to relax the requirements of pleading in habeas corpus for custody,[29] although correct form in most states requires first a petition for the writ stating the basis for the claim, followed by a return of the writ or the production of the child in court, and finally by an answer to the return.[30] The case is then tried on the issues made by the return and answer.[31]

For a time there was thought to be a possibility that federal habeas corpus might be available as a remedy for custody cases.[32] The Supreme Court has now laid this possibility to rest in Lehman v. Lycoming County Children's Services Agency,[33] however, by holding that the federal habeas corpus stat-

20. Gibson v. Wood, 209 Ga. 535, 74 S.E.2d 456 (1953).

21. Donnelly v. Donnelly, 4 Mass.App.Ct. 162, 344 N.E.2d 195 (1976).

22. J. V. by Levine v. Barron, 112 Wis.2d 256, 332 N.W.2d 796 (1983).

23. For historical accounts of the distinction see New York Foundling Hospital v. Gatti, 203 U.S. 429, 27 S.Ct. 53, 51 L.Ed. 254 (1906); In re Burrus, 136 U.S. 586, 10 S.Ct. 850, 34 L.Ed. 500 (1890); Pukas v. Pukas, 129 W.Va. 765, 42 S.E.2d 11 (1947).

24. E.g., Wood v. Wood, 241 Mo.App. 367, 231 S.W.2d 882 (1950) (semble); People v. Mercein, 8 Paige 47 (N.Y. Ch.1839); Turner v. Hendryx, 86 Or. 590, 167 P. 1019 (1917); State ex rel. Lipscomb v. Joplin, 131 W.Va. 302, 47 S.E.2d 221 (1948).

25. E.g., Chamblee v. Chamblee, 248 S.W.2d 422 (Ky. 1952); State ex rel. White v. Swink, 241 Mo.App. 1048, 256 S.W.2d 825 (1953) (semble); May v. Anderson, 345 U.S. 528, 73 S.Ct. 840; 97 L.Ed. 1221 (1953) (Ohio law); Vernon's Tex.Code Ann., Family Code § 14.10 (1986); Trevino v. Garcia, 627 S.W.2d 147 (Tex.1982); McElreath v. Stewart, 545 S.W.2d 955 (Tex.1977); Standley v. Stewart, 539 S.W.2d 882 (Tex.1976).

26. Application of Miracle, 208 Kan. 168, 490 P.2d 638 (1971); Stelly v. Montgomery, 347 So.2d 1145 (La.1977); Griffith v. Roy, 263 La. 712, 269 So.2d 217 (1972); New York Foundling Hospital v. Gatti, 203 U.S. 429, 27 S.Ct. 53, 51 L.Ed. 254 (1906); Commonwealth ex rel. Children's Aid Society v. Gard, 362 Pa. 85, 66 A.2d 300 (1949); Morris v. Jackson, 66 Wyo. 369, 212 P.2d 78 (1949); Annot., Child Custody Provisions of Divorce or Separation Decree as Subject to Modification on Habeas Corpus, 4 A.L.R.3d 1277 (1965). In special circumstances the

inquiry on habeas corpus may be limited to the legal right of the custodian, as for example where the writ is used to enforce compliance with an existing custody order. E.g., Ex parte Quinn, 192 Or. 254, 233 P.2d 767 (1951).

27. In re Flynn, 87 N.J.Eq. 413, 100 A. 861 (1917).

28. Sheehy v. Sheehy, 88 N.H. 223, 186 A. 1 (1936).

29. Wolfe v. Wolfe, 250 Ala. 223, 34 So.2d 8 (1948); Application of Enke, 129 Mont. 353, 287 P.2d 19 (1955), cert. denied 350 U.S. 923, 76 S.Ct. 212, 100 L.Ed. 808 (1955). Contra: State ex rel. Doran v. Doran, 215 La. 151, 39 So.2d 894 (1949), requiring compliance with the general habeas corpus statute.

30. Application of Enke, 129 Mont. 353, 287 P.2d 19 (1955), cert. denied 350 U.S. 923, 76 S.Ct. 212, 100 L.Ed. 808 (1955); Application of Bruno, 153 Neb. 445, 45 N.W.2d 178 (1950). In Application of Habeck, 75 S.D. 535, 69 N.W.2d 353 (1955) the failure to file a return was disregarded, illustrating the courts' willingness to excuse technical irregularities where necessary to protect children. In some states pleading after the return may not be required. Hochheimer, Custody of Infants 72–76 (2d ed. 1891). See also Barnes v. Raymer, 214 S.W.2d 341 (Tex.Civ.App.1948).

31. State ex rel. White v. Swink, 241 Mo.App. 1048, 256 S.W.2d 825 (1953); Application of Enke, 129 Mont. 353, 287 P.2d 19 (1955), cert. denied 350 U.S. 923, 76 S.Ct. 212, 100 L.Ed. 808 (1955); Ex parte Quinn, 192 Or. 254, 233 P.2d 767 (1951).

32. The cases are discussed in Note, Federal Habeas Corpus in Child Custody Cases, 67 Va.L.Rev. 1423 (1981).

33. 458 U.S. 502, 102 S.Ct. 3231, 73 L.Ed.2d 928 (1982).

ute [34] does not apply to controversies over child custody. The Court's reasons were that that statute had not historically been so applied, that such application would run counter to concerns with federalism since custody has traditionally been a matter for the states and the use of federal habeas would permit the federal courts to relitigate final state court custody decrees. The Court also referred to the states' interest in the finality of their custody decrees, but seeming to notice that state custody decrees are not final but are generally modifiable upon proof of changed circumstances. [35]

Other features of habeas corpus as used in custody litigation may be summarily described. As in divorce, orders governing the custody of the child pending suit may be made where necessary for the child's welfare. [36] Proper notice and an opportunity to be heard must be afforded both parties. [37] The judgment in habeas corpus is enforceable by contempt, [38] and on appeal the scope of review is like that in other equity cases. [39]

The habeas corpus has been largely assimilated to that in divorce or equity proceedings for the custody of children. The courts have first adopted and then refashioned an ancient remedy into a form more or less appropriate to the determination of the issues raised in such cases. The courts have stopped short of a completely pragmatic treatment of habeas corpus by refusing to make orders for the child's support in the habeas corpus proceeding. [40] Other limitations apparently inherent in habeas, such as its inapplicability to cases in which the petitioner has custody but wishes a custody determination, make it less than completely effective for the purpose.

Petition in Equity

Since habeas corpus does have limitations as a remedy for custody, the better procedure, one which exists in most states today, and one which has largely replaced habeas corpus, is what used to be called a petition in equity, and now that the law-equity distinction has been abolished, is just a petition in a civil action. [41] This remedy is based upon the inherent power of equity to act for the protection of children and needs no statutory authority. [42] In its practical consequences it is much like a declaratory judgment suit, and in fact the declaratory judgment may be used for this purpose. [43] Equity may also act indirectly by enjoining a threatened interference with the custody of a child, [44] although this is rarely done since other remedies usually provide adequate relief. [45]

---

34. 28 U.S.C.A. § 2254.

35. On modification of custody decrees see section 19.9, infra.

36. In re Allen, 238 N.C. 367, 77 S.E.2d 907 (1953).

37. Ex parte Moilanen, 104 Cal.App.2d 835, 233 P.2d 91 (1951); Griffin v. Griffin, 95 Or. 78, 187 P. 598 (1920).

38. People ex rel. McKee v. McKee, 338 Ill.App. 654, 89 N.E.2d 197 (1949); Application of Hebo, 95 N.Y.S.2d 545 (1950); Brown v. Cook, 123 Utah 505, 260 P.2d 544 (1953).

39. Ashbaugh v. McKinney, 182 Or. 652, 189 P.2d 583 (1948); Commonwealth ex rel. Bendrick v. White, 403 Pa. 55, 169 A.2d 69 (1961).

40. Ex parte Kelly, 261 P.2d 452 (Okl.1953); Pugh v. Pugh, 133 W.Va. 501, 56 S.E.2d 901 (1949). Contra: Waller v. Waller, 220 Ark. 19, 245 S.W.2d 814 (1952). Other cases are collected in Annot., 116 A.L.R. 699 (1938).

41. E.g., Alaska Stat. § 25.20.060 (1983); Ariz.Rev. Stat. § 25–331 (Supp.1986); West's Ann.Cal.Civ.Code § 4603 (1983); Colo.Rev.Stat. § 14–10–123 (1973); Conn. Gen.Stat.Ann. § 46b–56 (1986); Del.Code tit. 13, § 721

(1981); Hawaii Rev.Stat. § 571–46 (Supp.1984); Ill.— S.H.A. ch. 40, § 601 (Supp.1986); Mont.Code Ann. § 40–4–211 (1985); N.Y.—McKinney's Dom.Rel.L. § 240 (1986); N.C.Gen.Stat. § 50–13.1 (1984); Vernon's Tex.Code Ann., Family Code § 14.01 (1986); West's Rev.Code Wash.Ann. § 26.09.180 (1986); W.Va.Code, § 48–2–15 (1986); Wis. Stat.Ann. § 767.24 (Supp.1986); Uniform Marriage and Divorce Act § 401(d), 9A Unif.L.Ann. 194 (1979). Cases recognizing the equity courts' power to make such orders include Seidenberg v. Seidenberg, 219 F.2d 769 (App.D.C. 1955); Atwood v. Atwood, 229 Minn. 333, 39 N.W.2d 103 (1949), 34 Minn.L.Rev. 347 (1949); In re Badger, 286 Mo. 139, 226 S.W. 936 (1920); Finlay v. Finlay, 240 N.Y. 429, 148 N.E. 624 (1925).

42. Atwood v. Atwood, 229 Minn. 333, 39 N.W.2d 103 (1949), 34 Minn.L.Rev. 347 (1949).

43. Johnson v. Cook, 274 Ky. 841, 120 S.W.2d 675 (1938).

44. Shelley v. Westbrooke, 1 Jac. 266, 37 Eng.Rep. 850 (Ch.1821).

45. See Prescott v. Prescott, 174 La. 653, 141 So. 88 (1932).

Parties, Evidence and Procedure in Custody Litigation

Of course the usual parties to custody litigation, at least where the remedy is divorce, are the child's parents. That being so, the question arises whether if one of the parents is indigent the state must provide counsel for him. Although it has been held that there is a limited due process right to counsel in custody cases under state constitutions,[46] the Supreme Court's opinion in Lassiter v. Department of Social Services of Durham County, North Carolina[47] implies that there is no such right under the Fourteenth Amendment of the federal constitution. Nevertheless trial courts may have the authority in their discretion to appoint counsel in cases in which the parent shows particular need for representation.[48]

In addition to the parents, other persons having an interest in the custody of the child may be made parties. Thus a grandparent who has custody of the child should be made a party[49] or should be allowed to intervene in the case.[50] Some courts take a hypertechnical approach to notice where third parties are permitted to participate in the case, to the detriment to the child's interests.[51]

When we reflect on the child's position in custody litigation, it is hard to avoid the conclusion that he is the one with the greatest interests at stake, and consequently that he should be made a party to the proceeding. There is remarkably little case law taking this position, however.[52] Instead, the focus of attention in both cases and statutes has been the appointment of independent counsel for the child without consideration for whether he should technically be made a party to the suit. There is little reason to suppose that there is a constitutional duty to appoint counsel for the child in custody cases,[53] but statutes in many states give the trial courts discretion to provide independent counsel or a guardian ad litem where the child's welfare makes it desirable.[54] The fees of counsel so appointed must be paid by the child's parents.[55] If they are indigent, some of the stat-

---

46. Flores v. Flores, 598 P.2d 893 (Alaska 1979) held that the Alaskan constitution required court-appointed counsel for an indigent wife in a custody case, but limited its holding to the case in which the opposing party was represented by counsel provided by a public agency, the Alaska Legal Services Corporation.

47. 452 U.S. 18, 101 S.Ct. 2153, 68 L.Ed.2d 640 (1981), rehearing denied 453 U.S. 927, 102 S.Ct. 889, 69 L.Ed.2d 1023 (1981). The Court held that the failure to appoint counsel for an indigent parent in a proceeding to terminate parental rights did not deprive the parent of due process, but in the contemporary style hedged its holding with so many qualifications that it is virtually worthless as a precedent. Even so, if counsel need not be provided in the relatively final and crucial litigation leading to complete severance of parental bonds, it seems likely that due process does not require it in the less sweeping litigation of a custody case.

48. See the cases cited in Annot., Appointment of Counsel for Indigent Husband or Wife in Action for Divorce or Separation, 85 A.L.R.3d 983 (1978). In Guardianship of H. L., 143 Vt. 62, 460 A.2d 478 (1983) the court held that it was reversible error not to appoint a guardian ad litem for a mentally incompetent mother in a custody case.

49. Smith v. Watson, 425 So.2d 1030 (Miss.1983).

50. Uniform Marriage and Divorce Act § 401(e), 9A Unif.L.Ann. 194 (1979). But see Marshall v. Superior Court In & For Yavapai County, 145 Ariz. 309, 701 P.2d 567 (1985).

51. Tautfest v. Tautfest, 215 Neb. 233, 338 N.W.2d 49 (1983).

52. Roe v. Roe, 49 Misc.2d 1070, 269 N.Y.S.2d 40 (1966) held that the child had a constitutional right to be made a party in a divorce action in which his status was in issue, but no other case to this effect has been found. de Montigny v. de Montigny, 70 Wis.2d 131, 233 N.W.2d 463 (1975) refers to children in divorce proceedings as "indispensable parties" who must be represented in their own capacity as parties.

53. A cryptic comment in In re Gullette, 173 Mont. 132, 566 P.2d 396 (1977) states that it would be a violation of the state constitution to fail to appoint counsel for the child where a contested proceeding for a change in custody is involved, but Matter of M. D. Y. R., 177 Mont. 521, 582 P.2d 758 (1978) seems to be contra. See also Leigh v. Aiken, 54 Ala.App. 620, 311 So.2d 444 (1975) indicating that the child's due process rights are not involved in such a proceeding.

54. E.g., Alaska Stat. § 25.24.310 (1983); West's Ann. Cal.Civ.Code § 4606 (Supp.1986); Iowa Code Ann. § 598.12 (Supp.1986); Neb.Rev.Stat. § 42–358 (1984); Or. Rev.Stat. § 107.425 (1985); V.T.C.A., Fam.Code § 11.10 (1986); Utah Code Ann. 1984, § 30–3–11.2; Vt.Stat.Ann. tit. 15, § 594 (1974); Wis.Stat.Ann. § 767.045 (1981). See also the Uniform Marriage and Divorce Act § 310, 9A Unif.L.Ann. 172 (1979).

55. Ibid.; Gibson v. Barton, 118 Ill.App.3d 576, 74 Ill. Dec. 252, 455 N.E.2d 282 (1983).

utes would require the fees to be paid by the state or county.[56]

The reported cases naturally find it difficult to define in general terms what conditions call for the appointment of counsel for the child in a custody case. The question in any case is whether the circumstances are such that counsel for the child would be likely to provide substantial assistance in arriving at a disposition conducive to the child's welfare.[57] Some courts would apply this principle broadly.[58] Others are more cautious, recognizing that there are costs in such appointments, not merely in the fees to be paid to counsel but in delays and additional complications of trial, and that in many, perhaps a majority of cases, the benefits to be expected from the child's counsel may be minimal.[59] The more cautious cases have the better of the argument.[60] In spite of the law review commentary urging more frequent appointments of counsel for the child, in the great majority of cases it is difficult to see how the presence of another lawyer could improve the process enough to be worth the cost.[61]

The cases usually treat the terms "guardian ad litem" and "counsel for the child" as synonymous.[62] The responsibility of the person

so appointed is to represent the child just as he would represent the party to any litigation.[63] He must act as advocate for the child's preference if the child is old enough to have and express a preference,[64] but if not, he must advocate whatever custody disposition he finds to be in the child's best interests.[65] In doing this he of course must investigate, interview witnesses, take part in the hearing, and make arguments on the facts and law. Where appropriate, he may arrange for investigations and interviews of the child by psychologists or other experts.[66] In other words, a more than perfunctory performance of his professional duties is demanded of him.

Other issues which frequently arise in connection with evidence and the trial of custody cases, including the use of custody investigations and psychological testimony, are discussed in an earlier section of this work.[67]

Although custody orders are subject to modification upon a showing of change in circumstances,[68] they are final in the sense that appeals may be taken from them.[69] In most states the award of custody is held to be a matter for the discretion of the trial court, to be upset on appeal only where an abuse of that discretion is shown.[70] In a few states the

56. E.g., the Alaska, Iowa, Vermont and Wisconsin statutes, supra, note 80, as well as the Uniform Marriage and Divorce Act.

57. Matter of Appeal in Yavapai County Juvenile Action No. J–8545, 140 Ariz. 10, 680 P.2d 146 (1984).

58. de Montigny v. de Montigny, 70 Wis.2d 131, 233 N.W.2d 463 (1975).

59. Veazey v. Veazey, 560 P.2d 382 (Alaska 1977).

60. Dembitz, Beyond Any Discipline's Competence, 83 Yale L.J. 1304, 1312 (1974), in which a distinguished New York family court judge indicates that Goldstein, Freud and Solnit, in Beyond the Best Interests of the Child, have an exaggerated and unrealistic view of the utility of counsel for the child in cases involving child placement. Judge Dembitz expresses the opinion that usually there is little that such counsel can contribute to the fact finding process and that his presence may delay and complicate the trial of the case.

61. E.g., In re Richard E., 21 Cal.3d 349, 146 Cal.Rptr. 604, 579 P.2d 495 (1978), appeal dismissed 439 U.S. 1060, 99 S.Ct. 822, 59 L.Ed.2d 26 (1979).

62. Veazey v. Veazey, 560 P.2d 382 (Alaska 1977). But Provencal v. Provencal, 122 N.H. 793, 451 A.2d 374 (1982) seems to impose upon the guardian ad litem a dual function, of representing the interests of the child, but also of assisting the court and the parties in reaching a

prompt and fair determination, apparently by filing some sort of report with the court.

63. Veazey v. Veazey, 560 P.2d 382 (Alaska 1977); de Montigny v. de Montigny, 70 Wis.2d 131, 233 N.W.2d 463 (1975).

64. Matter of Appeal in Yavapai County Juvenile Action No. J–8545, 140 Ariz. 10, 680 P.2d 146 (1984). See also Mlyniec, The Child Advocate in Private Custody Disputes: A Role in Search of a Standard, 16 J.Fam.L. 1 (1977).

65. Veazey v. Veazey, 560 P.2d 382 (Alaska 1977).

66. Veazey v. Veazey, 560 P.2d 382 (Alaska 1977).

67. See section 14.4, supra.

68. See section 19.9, infra.

69. Lerner v. Superior Court In and For San Mateo County, 38 Cal.2d 676, 242 P.2d 321 (1952); Burkholder v. Burkholder, 231 Minn. 285, 43 N.W.2d 801 (1950). There is some authority that an appeal may be taken by persons interested in the child's custody though not parties to the suit, but this seems doubtful. Ramey v. Ramey, 170 Kan. 1, 223 P.2d 695 (1950).

70. E.g. Adams v. Adams, 206 Ga. 881, 59 S.E.2d 366 (1950); Finnegan v. Finnegan, 134 W.Va. 94, 58 S.E.2d 594 (1950).

case is considered to be equitable and the appellate court may hear it de novo on the record made below,[71] but as a practical matter even in these states great deference is properly given to the trial court's decision. Certainly any appellate court should be reluctant to substitute its judgment for that of a trial court in cases so entirely dependent upon particular facts and the subtle inferences to be drawn from those facts. If the custody decision is appealed, the trial court is often given the authority in its discretion to stay the enforcement of its order pending the appeal.[72]

WESTLAW REFERENCES

Divorce

custod! /5 decree! order! /s reconcil!

Habeas Corpus

"habeas corpus" /p enforc! claim*** compel! /s right entitl! /s visit!

71. E.g., Jensen v. Jensen, 237 Iowa 1323, 25 N.W.2d 316 (1946); Rutstein v. Rutstein, 324 S.W.2d 760 (Mo.App. 1959); Young v. Young, 166 Neb. 532, 89 N.W.2d 763 (1958).

72. E.g., West's Ann.Cal.Civ.Pro.Code § 917.7 (Supp. 1986); Goetz v. Goetz, 181 Kan. 128, 309 P.2d 655 (1957); Kaufman v. Kaufman, 239 La. 500, 118 So.2d 901 (1960); Application of Nelson, 132 Mont. 252, 316 P.2d 1058 (1957); Sewell v. Sewell, 28 Wash.2d 394, 184 P.2d 76 (1947), 23 Wash.L.Rev. 145 (1948).

§ 19.4

1. This section is limited to a discussion of the factors to be considered when the parents are in conflict concerning the custody of their child, and when the decision will award custody to one or the other of them. Today of course there is an increasing tendency to award "joint custody" to both parents. Although the distinction is for practical purposes somewhat artificial, the definition of joint custody and the circumstances in which it may be awarded are postponed to the succeeding section, 20.5.

2. Many of the relevant factors are discussed in the following articles and notes. Batt, Child Custody Disputes: A Developmental-Psychological Approach to Proof and Decisionmaking, 12 Willamette L.J. 491 (1976); Bersoff, Representation for Children in Custody Decisions: All That Glitters is Not Gault, 15 J.Fam.L. 27 (1976); Brodsky, Alford, Sharpening Solomon's Sword: Current Considerations in Child Custody, 81 Dick.L.Rev. 683 (1977); Brown, The Custody of Children, 2 Ind.L.J. 325 (1926); Chambers, Rethinking the Substantive Rules for Custody Disputes in Divorce, 83 Mich.L.Rev. 477 (1984); Kay, Phillips, Poverty and the Law of Child Custody, 54 Cal.L.Rev. 717 (1966); Mnookin, Child-Custody Adjudication: Judicial Functions in the Face of Indeterminacy, 39

to(197) /p custod! /5 child minor /p equit!

Petition in Equity

petition! complain*** /s custod! /s civil +1 action suit proceeding

Parties, Evidence and Procedure in Custody Litigation

custod! /s indigen! (unable cannot +2 afford!) /s "due process" "fourteenth amendment" /s counsel lawyer attorney

§ 19.4   Custody of Children—Factors in Awarding Custody—Dispute Between Natural Parents [1]

The outcome of a custody case is a product of the influence exerted on the court by many different factors, all of them related more or less closely to a judgement as to what the child's welfare requires.[2] Many statutes[3] and most of the case law[4] have adopted as the ultimate criterion for custody awards "the best interests of the child", even though, as an

L. & Contemp.Prob. #3 226 (1975); Weinman, The Trial Judge Awards Custody, 10 L. & Contemp.Prob. 721 (1944); Note, The California Custody Decree, 13 Stan.L.Rev. 108 (1960).

3. E.g., Ala.Code 1983, § 30–3–1 (safety and well-being of the child); Alaska Stat. § 25.20.060 (1983); West's Ann.Cal.Civ.Code § 4600 (Supp.1987); Conn.Gen.Stat. Ann. § 46b–56 (1986); Del.Code tit. 13, § 722 (1981); D.C. Code 1981, § 16–911; Official Ga.Code Ann. § 19–9–3 (Supp.1986); Hawaii Rev.Stat. § 571–46 (Supp.1984); Ill.—S.H.A. ch. 40, § 602 (Supp.1986); West's Ann.Ind. Code § 31–1–11.5–21 (Supp.1986); Iowa Code Ann. § 598.41 (Supp.1986–1987); Kan.Stat.Ann. § 60–1610 (1983); Ky.Rev.Stat. § 403.270 (1984); Me.Rev.Stat.Ann. tit. 19, § 752 (Supp.1986); Mass.G.L.A. ch. 208, § 31 (Supp.1986); Mich.C.L.A. § 25.312(3) (1984); Miss.Code Ann. § 93–5–24 (Supp.1986); Neb.Rev.Stat. § 42–364 (Supp.1986); Nev.Rev.Stat. § 125.480 (1986); N.H.Rev. Stat.Ann. § 458:17 (1983 and Supp.1986); N.J.Stat.Ann. § 9:2–4 (1976); N.M.Stat.Ann. § 40–4–9 (1986); N.Y.— McKinney's Dom.Rel.L. § 240 (1986); N.C.Gen.Stat. § 50–13.2 (1984); Or.Rev.Stat. § 107.137 (1983); Pa.Stat. tit. 23, §§ 5301, 5303 (Supp.1986); V.T.C.A., Fam.Code § 14.07 (1986); Utah Code Ann. § 30–3–10 (1984); Vt. Stat.Ann. tit. 15, § 665 (Supp.1986); Va.Code 1986, § 20–107.2 (Supp.); Wis.Stat.Ann. § 767.24 (1981 and Supp. 1986). See also the Uniform Marriage and Divorce Act § 402, 9A Unif.L.Ann. 197 (1979).

4. E.g., In re Marriage of Ellerbroek, 377 N.W.2d 257 (Iowa App.1985); Pikula v. Pikula, 374 N.W.2d 705 (Minn.1985); Bergstrom v. Bergstrom, 296 N.W.2d 490 (N.D.1980); Commonwealth ex rel. Pierce v. Pierce, 493 Pa. 292, 426 A.2d 555 (1981). Many other cases could be cited for this obvious proposition, which is the starting

earlier section has indicated,[5] the phrase has been much criticized and attempts have been made to replace it with something less vague. The courts' persistent reliance on this phrase suggests that no more appealing formulation is likely to be devised, in spite of its vagueness, and also that it is not much less workable than other standards the law has adopted such as, for example, negligence as conduct "which falls below the standard established by law for the protection of others against unreasonably great risk of harm."[6] That some such standard as the child's best interests is inescapable is demonstrated by those cases which ostensibly rely upon some other standard for the custody award, such as the presumption that custody should go to the child's "primary caretaker". Those cases adopt that presumption out of the conviction that the child will be better off if he remains in the custody of the parent who has been caring for him than if he is subjected to the psychological stress of adjustment to a new caretaker.[7] In other words even in that case the child's welfare is the ultimate test for custody.

The vagueness of the ultimate standard and the number and variety of the individual factors which may be relevant to its application to the particular case have led appellate courts to follow the principle that awards of custody are within the discretion of the trial court, to be reversed only where an abuse of this discretion appears.[8] With occasional dis-

agreement[9] appellate courts recognize that the subtle and sensitive evaluation of the evidence which custody cases demand is best left to trial courts except where the trial court's decision is based upon an erroneous view of the law, or is contrary to the great weight of the evidence.[10] As a consequence custody cases are largely won or lost in the trial courts and the opinions of appellate courts in custody cases, although useful as guides to the kinds of facts which should be taken into account, do not often have the conclusive influence which such opinions have in more formal areas of the law.

The pages which follow describe the factors which are generally held to be relevant to the decision of custody cases when the controversy lies between the child's parents. Many of them are also relevant when the contestants are persons other than parents but in such cases additional elements often come into play. It should be understood that these factors, while they do not mechanically decide cases, do tell counsel and trial courts what to look for when custody is litigated. In this day of increased statutory treatment of custody, many originate in the state statutes.[11] The discussion of individual factors found in judicial opinions is more helpful, however, since it can convey some notion of the weight to be given a particular factor in some circumstances and of the relationship among the various factors.

---

point for the discussion in nearly all the opinions cited in this section.

5. See section 19.1, supra.

6. Restatement (Second) of Torts § 282 (1965).

7. E.g., Pikula v. Pikula, 374 N.W.2d 705 (Minn.1985).

8. E.g., Horutz v. Horutz, 560 P.2d 397 (Alaska 1977); Ridgeway v. Ridgeway, 180 Conn. 533, 429 A.2d 801 (1980); Menne v. Menne, 194 Colo. 304, 572 P.2d 472 (1977); Ballou v. Ballou, 95 N.H. 105, 58 A.2d 311 (1948); Jorgensen v. Jorgensen, 599 P.2d 510 (Utah 1979); McAllister v. McAllister, 166 W.Va. 569, 276 S.E.2d 321 (1981).

9. Commonwealth ex rel. Pierce v. Pierce, 493 Pa. 292, 426 A.2d 555 (1981): "Our scope of review in a custody matter is of the broadest type, and we are not bounded by

deductions or inferences made by a trial court. ∗ ∗ ∗ We must exercise an independent judgment based on the evidence and and make such an order on the merits of the case as right and justice dictate."

10. Allen v. Allen, 78 Wis.2d 263, 254 N.W.2d 244 (1977).

11. E.g., Uniform Marriage and Divorce Act § 402, 9A Unif.L.Ann. 197 (1979), listing the wishes of the child's parents, the wishes of the child, the relationship of the child with his parents and with his siblings, the child's adjustment to home, school and community, and the mental and physical health of all individuals involved as relevant factors. The Commissioners' Note to this section states that this list is not intended to be exhaustive and that other factors may be considered.

(a) The Relative Weight of the Claims of Father and Mother

At common law the father had a right to the custody of his child which was nearly absolute.[12] He could be deprived of custody only where danger to the child or corruption of the father were proved.

At the time of the first edition of this work although the courts followed the general principle that both parents had an equal right to the custody of their children, they also widely accepted a rule of thumb or presumption that the welfare of a child of "tender years" was normally best served by placing him in the custody of his mother.[13] The presumption was sometimes stated that it applied where other factors appeared to be equal as between the parents.[14] Few courts attempted a definition of "tender years". The presumption would clearly apply to a child under five years, might apply to one under ten years and perhaps in a very few cases might even apply to a child of eleven or twelve.[15] Since the

presumption was ostensibly relied upon because it was thought to provide a clue to what the child's interests would require, it did not apply when the circumstances indicated that the child's interests would be better served by placing him in the custody of his father or of some other person.[16] The presumption offered considerable benefit to hard pressed trial judges when the evidence indicated that both parents would be good custodians and provided no clear reason for preferring one over the other.

The last twenty years have seen the law recognizing gender equality in a great variety of contexts.[17] At the same time fathers have begun to assert a stronger claim for custody of their children in divorce.[18] The result has been a significant diminution in the importance of the tender years doctrine. Although it continues to exist in some states, it is less often decisive even there.[19] In many states it has been abolished by statute.[20] In others the same result has been reached by judicial deci-

---

12. Rex v. Greenhill, 4 Ad. & El. 624, 111 Eng.Rep. 922 (1836); Shelley v. Westbrooke, Jacob Ch. 266, 37 Eng. Rep. 850 (1821); Brown, The Custody of Children, 2 Ind. L.J. 325 (1926).

13. Boone v. Boone, 80 U.S.App.D.C. 152, 150 F.2d 153 (1945); Brashear v. Brashear, 71 Idaho 158, 228 P.2d 243 (1951); Vanden Heuvel v. Vanden Heuvel, 254 Iowa 1391, 121 N.W.2d 216 (1963); Hild v. Hild, 221 Md. 349, 157 A.2d 442 (1960); Mullen v. Mullen, 188 Va. 259, 49 S.E.2d 349 (1948); Settle v. Settle, 117 W.Va. 476, 185 S.E. 859 (1936); Chapman v. Chapman, 3 Wis.2d 559, 89 N.W.2d 207 (1958). Many of these same cases recognized the general principle that both spouses have an equal right to the custody of their children.

14. Allen v. Allen, 78 Wis.2d 263, 254 N.W.2d 244 (1977).

15. Annot., Modern Status of Maternal Preference Rule or Presumption in Child Custody Cases, 70 A.L.R.3d 262, 287 (1976). Williams v. Williams, 223 Pa.Super. 29, 296 A.2d 870 (1972) held that the tender years doctrine might continue to apply until the child reached age fourteen.

16. Commonwealth ex rel. Parikh v. Parikh, 449 Pa. 105, 296 A.2d 625 (1972); McCreery v. McCreery, 218 Va. 352, 237 S.E.2d 167 (1977); Allen v. Allen, 78 Wis.2d 263, 254 N.W.2d 244 (1977).

17. E.g., Orr v. Orr, 440 U.S. 268, 99 S.Ct. 1102, 59 L.Ed.2d 306 (1979).

18. Roth, The Tender Years Presumption in Child Custody Disputes, 15 J.Fam.L. 423, 432 (1977), citing many of the tender years cases. See also M. Roman, W. Haddad, The Disposable Parent (1978). One study has concluded that it could find no evidence which would support the presumption favoring mothers. D. Luepnitz, Child Custody 149 (1982).

19. Albright v. Albright, 437 So.2d 1003 (Miss.1983); Smith v. Smith, 564 P.2d 307 (Utah 1977). Other cases are collected in Annot., Modern Status of Maternal Preference Rule or Presumption in Child Custody Cases, 70 A.L.R.3d 262 (1976).

20. See, e.g., Ariz.Rev.Stat. § 25–332 (Supp.1986); West's Ann.Cal.Civ. Code § 4600 (Supp.1986); Colo.Rev. Stat. § 14–10–124 (Supp.1986); Del.Code tit. 13, § 722 (1981); Kan.Stat.Ann. § 60–1610 (1983); Me.Rev.Stat. Ann. tit. 19, § 752 (Supp.1986); Mass.G.L.A. ch. 208, § 31 (Supp.1986); Neb.Rev.Stat. § 42–364 (Supp.1986); Nev. Rev.Stat. § 125.480 (1986); N.H.Rev.Stat.Ann. § 458:17 (1983 and Supp.1986); N.Y.—McKinney's Dom.Rel.L. § 240 (1986); N.C.Gen.Stat. § 50–13.2 (1984); Or.Rev. Stat. § 107.137 (1983); V.T.C.A., Fam.Code § 14.01 (1986); Va.Code § 20–107.2 (Supp.1986); Wis.Stat.Ann. § 767.24 (1981 and Supp.1986). The Uniform Marriage and Divorce Act § 402 does not mention the presumption in its list of relevant factors, but the Commissioners' Note states that there was no intention thereby to eliminate the presumption. 9A Unif.L.Ann. 198 (1979).

sion.[21] Many of the states which have adopted Equal Rights Amendments to their state constitutions have found the tender years doctrine to be a violation of those Amendments.[22] Notwithstanding these developments, the custody of young children continues to be awarded to their mothers in the majority of cases.[23] The reason seems to be that in the majority of families the mother still has the primary responsibility for child care and the award of custody reflects that fact, the tender years doctrine being thereby transformed into the doctrine known as the "primary caretaker" principle.[24] For this reason the demise of the tender years doctrine is not likely to have much impact upon the outcome of custody cases even though it will affect the reasoning by which results are reached.

In another less numerous class of cases the gender of the parties may be urged as the ground for the custody award. There is some evidence in the non-legal literature that the children of divorce will be more likely to come through the family's disruption successfully if the custody of boys is awarded to their fathers and that of girls to their mothers.[25] The objections to making awards on this principle are the same as those applicable to the tender years doctrine, however, either statutory or constitutional.[26] But, as with the tender years doctrine, the same result may be reached by focusing solely upon the child's best interests in the light of available psychological information.[27] There is an additional obstacle to the application of this principle in that the courts are generally reluctant to split the custody of siblings between the parents,[28] a result which this principle would make necessary if the children of the marriage were of both sexes.

(b) The Primary Caretaker Presumption

The recurrent longing of lawyers and judges to avoid the pains of exercising judgment in custody cases has replaced the tender years doctrine with another presumption which often reaches the same result but which does not incur the reproach of gender discrimination.[29]

21. Faro v. Faro, 579 P.2d 1377 (Alaska 1978); Blonsky v. Blonsky, 84 Ill.App.3d 810, 40 Ill.Dec. 20, 405 N.E.2d 1112 (1980); Bazemore v. Davis, 394 A.2d 1377 (D.C.App.1978); In re Bowen's Marriage, 219 N.W.2d 683 (Iowa 1974); Stafford v. Stafford, 618 S.W.2d 578 (Ky. App.1981) (relying on statute); Elza v. Elza, 300 Md. 51, 475 A.2d 1180 (1984) (relying on statute); Arnold v. Arnold, 95 Nev. 951, 604 P.2d 109 (1979); Commonwealth ex rel. Spriggs v. Carson, 470 Pa. 290, 368 A.2d 635 (1977), 25 Vill.L.Rev. 752 (1980).

22. Cases are collected in Annot., 90 A.L.R.3d 158, 186 (1979). There is also some authority that the tender years presumption violates the Equal Protection Clause of the Fourteenth Amendment to the United States Constitution. Ex parte Devine, 398 So.2d 686 (Ala.1981), on remand 398 So.2d 697 (Ala.Civ.App.1981); State ex rel. Watts v. Watts, 77 Misc.2d 178, 350 N.Y.S.2d 285 (Fam. Ct.1973) (semble). Cases contra on this point include Gordon v. Gordon, 577 P.2d 1271 (Okl.1978), cert. denied 439 U.S. 863, 99 S.Ct. 185, 58 L.Ed.2d 172 (1978); Cox v. Cox, 532 P.2d 994 (Utah 1975); J. B. v. A. B., 161 W.Va. 332, 242 S.E.2d 248 (1978). See also Jones, The Tender Years Doctrine: Survey and Analysis, 16 J.Fam.L. 695 (1978).

23. J. Wallerstein, J. Kelly, Surviving the Breakup 110 (1980) indicates that most of the custodial parents in their study were women and documents the stress that this imposed upon them. See also P. Jacobson, American Marriage and Divorce 131 (1959).

24. Klaff, The Tender Years Doctrine: A Defense, 70 Cal.L.Rev. 335 (1982). The primary caretaker principle is discussed infra at note 29.

25. The literature is discussed in Chambers, Rethinking the Substantive Rules for Custody Disputes in Divorce, 83 Mich.L.Rev. 477, 512–515 (1984).

26. See notes 20 and 21, supra.

27. A case which gives some attention to the sex of the child and to the importance of the mother as a role model for the five-year-old girl is Matter of Marriage of Clement, 52 Or.App. 101, 627 P.2d 1263 (1981), review denied 291 Or. 368, 644 P.2d 1126 (1981). Brooks v. Brooks, 319 Pa.Super. 268, 466 A.2d 152 (1983) rejects the suggestion that there should be a preference for placing male children with the father and female children with the mother.

28. Holliday v. Huffstickler, 245 So.2d 598 (Miss.1971); J. v. E., 417 S.W.2d 199 (Mo.App.1967); Boroff v. Boroff, 197 Neb. 641, 250 N.W.2d 613 (1977); In re Marriage of Little, 26 Wash.App. 814, 614 P.2d 240 (1980), reversed on other grounds 96 Wash.2d 183, 634 P.2d 498 (1981). Where exceptional circumstances relevant to the children's welfare indicate the desirability of divided custody, it will be approved. E.g., In re Marriage of Wahl, 246 N.W.2d 268 (Iowa 1976); In re McFarland's Marriage, 239 N.W.2d 175 (Iowa 1976). Other cases are cited in Annot., 98 A.L.R.2d 926 (1964).

29. See Cochran, The Search for Guidance in Determining the Best Interests of the Child at Divorce: Reconciling the Primary Caretaker and Joint Custody Preferences, 20 U.Rich.L.Rev. 1 (1985).

This is the presumption that the child's welfare will be best served by placing him in the custody of the parent who, before the divorce proceeding, has been his primary caretaker.[30] "Primary caretaker" is generally defined as the parent who has had the primary responsibility for the day to day and hour to hour care of the child, who has fed him, clothed him, arranged for his medical care, taken him to and from school, taught him in the home and been responsible for his discipline.[31] The presumption is justified by some courts on the ground that it provides a measure of certainty upon which the spouses may depend in making agreements about custody.[32] It is also advocated on the ground that it prevents a spouse from making custody claims in bad faith as a way of inducing the other spouse to reduce her child support and alimony or property demands, a practice which is unfortunately prevalent, in the opinion of some authorities.[33] A related advantage is that the primary caretaker will have been closest to the child before the divorce and therefore presumably will suffer the most by being deprived of custody by the divorce decree.[34] Finally, this presumption is said to enable the courts and lawyers to decide custody cases without having to make precise and supposed-ly unreal judgments about the relative fitness of the contending spouses in those cases in which both spouses appear to be reasonably and psychologically adequate parents.[35]

There are differing views about what it takes to rebut the primary caretaker presumption. One view is that the presumption prevails unless the primary caretaker fails to meet a minimum objective standard for being a fit parent.[36] Other cases have found the presumption rebutted where it ran counter to the child's preference,[37] or where it appeared that the welfare of the child would be better served by placement with the non-caretaker parent.[38] In any event of course the question of fitness of a parent is hardly one which can be clearly distinguished from the question of what the child's welfare dictates.

At first glance this presumption seems to offer a welcome refuge to hard pressed lawyers and judges. Further reflection generates some doubts about its clarity and therefore about its efficacy in accomplishing the purposes just outlined. Determination of which parent is the primary caretaker is relatively easy for the old fashioned conventional family in which the husband works outside the home and the wife is the homemaker.[39] It is not

---

30. E.g., Pikula v. Pikula, 374 N.W.2d 705 (Minn. 1985); Brauer v. Brauer, 384 N.W.2d 595 (Minn.App. 1986); Brooks v. Brooks, 319 Pa.Super. 268, 466 A.2d 152 (1983); Commonwealth ex rel. Jordan v. Jordan, 302 Pa. Super. 421, 448 A.2d 1113 (1982); Rose v. Rose, ___ W.Va. ___, 340 S.E.2d 176 (1986); Graham v. Graham, ___ W.Va. ___, 326 S.E.2d 189 (1984); Garska v. McCoy, 167 W.Va. 59, 278 S.E.2d 357 (1981). Many other cases are cited in Annot., 41 A.L.R.4th 1129 (1985).

31. Pikula v. Pikula, 374 N.W.2d 705 (Minn.1985); Garska v. McCoy, 167 W.Va. 59, 278 S.E.2d 357 (1981). Cochran, The Search for Guidance in Determining the Best Interests of the Child at Divorce: Reconciling the Primary Caretaker and Joint Custody Preferences, 20 U.Rich.L.Rev. 1, 33 (1985).

32. Garska v. McCoy, 167 W.Va. 59, 278 S.E.2d 357 (1981).

33. R.Neely, The Divorce Decision 63 (1984), also discussed supra in section 17.1 in connection with child support. Justice Neely makes the same argument in Garska v. McCoy, 167 W.Va. 59, 278 S.E.2d 357 (1981). The argument is that the primary caretaker presumption makes it so clear in most cases when the child is very young that the mother will get custody that the father will have no opportunity to exert unfair bargaining leverage by bad faith claims to custody.

34. Garska v. McCoy, 167 W.Va. 59, 278 S.E.2d 357 (1981); Chambers, Rethinking the Substantive Rules for Custody Disputes in Divorce, 83 Mich.L.Rev. 477, 543 (1984). There is also of course an often repeated assertion that the child, especially the very young child, needs stability in his relationships. The primary caretaker presumption provides this stability above all other considerations. See J. Goldstein, A. Freud, A. Solnit, Beyond the Best Interests of the Child 19, 31 (2d ed.1979).

35. Garska v. McCoy, 167 W.Va. 59, 278 S.E.2d 357 (1981). See also Pikula v. Pikula, 374 N.W.2d 705 (Minn. 1985).

36. Garska v. McCoy, 167 W.Va. 59, 278 S.E.2d 357 (1981); J. B. v. A. B., 161 W.Va. 332, 242 S.E.2d 248 (1978); R. Neely, The Divorce Decision 81 (1984).

37. Rose v. Rose, ___ W.Va. ___, 340 S.E.2d 176 (1985).

38. Brooks v. Brooks, 319 Pa.Super. 268, 466 A.2d 152 (1983).

39. R. Neely, The Divorce Decision 79 (1984); Chambers, Rethinking the Substantive Rules for Custody Disputes in Divorce, 83 Mich.L.Rev. 477, 534 (1984), both indicating that although the presumption is not discriminatory with respect to gender, in the majority of cases the mother will turn out to be the primary caretaker.

easy for the increasingly common contemporary family in which both spouses work outside the home and share the care of the children. Rebuttal of the presumption is not so difficult that it will inevitably discourage a spouse from making nuisance claims for custody as a way of gaining leverage in financial negotiations, particularly now that joint custody is preferred by statute in many states.[40] A claim for joint custody may plausibly be made where one spouse has been the primary caretaker solely as a means of acquiring this sort of leverage. There appears to be no substantial evidence that an award of custody to the primary caretaker will promote the child's best interests more effectively than an award to the other parent,[41] nor is it clear that such an award will inflict less suffering on the non-caretaker spouse than an award to him would inflict on the primary caretaker. Although the claims which have been made in favor of this presumption may not be entirely supported by a careful analysis of the probabilities, perhaps it provides sufficient benefits to be worth seriously considering in any custody case in which one of the spouses can be clearly identified as the primary caretaker for a young child.[42]

(c) The Character and Conduct of the Parents and Their Relationships With Their Children

The most important contribution to custody litigation made by the Goldstein, Freud, Solnit book[43] was its insistence that the primary emphasis of the courts' inquiry should be the relationship, in particular the psychological relationship, between parents and children. Many state statutes expressly require the courts to take account of that relationship in awarding custody,[44] recognizing that this is the crucial factor in determining what the child's best interests demand.[45]

If the parent-child relationship is to be the focus of inquiry, the courts must then confront the most difficult of the many issues which complicate custody litigation, the extent to which the character and conduct of the parents affects the parent-child relationship. It is easy to say, as the Uniform Act does,[46] that the parents' conduct is only relevant when it bears some relation or has some effect on the parent-child relationship. It is equally easy to condemn many of the older decisions which denied custody to a parent solely on the ground that she was the losing defendant in a fault-based divorce,[47] or on the ground that the child's mother had been guilty of adultery.[48] And we certainly ought

---

40. See the dissenting opinion in Rose v. Rose, ___ W.Va. ___, 340 S.E.2d 176 (1985), arguing that the primary caretaker presumption was rebutted by the father's "psychological ploys" aimed at destroying the child's affection for the mother. See also Graham v. Graham, ___ W.Va. ___, 326 S.E.2d 189 (1984) which seemed to find that there was no primary caretaker, a conclusion with which the dissent took exception. Joint custody is discussed infra in section 19.5, infra.

41. Chambers, Rethinking the Substantive Rules for Custody Disputes in Divorce, 83 Mich.L.Rev. 477, 533–538 (1984).

42. This seem to be the ultimate conclusion of Chambers, Rethinking the Substantive Rules for Custody Disputes in Divorce, 83 Mich.L.Rev. 477, 568 (1984).

43. J. Goldstein, A. Freud, A. Solnit, Beyond the Best Interests of the Child (2d ed.1979).

44. E.g., Alaska Stat. § 25.24.200 (1983); Del.Code tit. 13, § 721 (1981); West's Ann.Ind.Code § 31–1–11.5–21 (1980); Kan.Stat.Ann. § 60–1610 (1983); Me.Rev.Stat. Ann. tit. 19, § 752 (Supp.1986); Mich.C.L.A. § 25.312(3) (1984); Ohio Rev.Code § 3109.04 (Supp.1986); Or.Rev. Stat. § 107.137 (1985); Vt.Stat.Ann. tit. 15, § 652 (Supp. 1986); Va.Code 1986, § 20–107.2 (Supp.); Wis.Stat.Ann. § 767.24 (1981 and Supp.1986). See also Uniform Mar-

riage and Divorce Act § 402(3), 9A Unif.L.Ann. 198 (1979).

45. Seymour v. Seymour, 180 Conn. 705, 433 A.2d 1005 (1980), rejecting objective guidelines in custody in favor of flexible, individualized adjudication of the particular facts of each case.

46. Uniform Marriage and Divorce Act § 402, 9A Unif.L.Ann. 198 (1979): "The court shall not consider conduct of a proposed custodian that does not affect his relationship to the child." The Commissioners' Note to this section adds the curious qualification that the limitation in the provision could not be overcome if the parent's behavior has been circumspect or unknown to the child.

47. Settle v. Settle, 117 W.Va. 476, 185 S.E. 859 (1936); Annot., 41 L.R.A.(N.S.) 565, 590 (1913); Weinman, The Trial Judge Awards Custody, 10 L. & Contemp.Prob. 720, 731 (1944). See also the large number of cases cited in Annot., Award of Custody of Child to Parent Against Whom Divorce is Decreed, 23 A.L.R.3d 6 (1969).

48. E.g., Hild v. Hild, 221 Md. 349, 157 A.2d 442 (1960); Bunim v. Bunim, 298 N.Y. 391, 83 N.E.2d 848 (1949); Beck v. Beck, 175 Neb. 108, 120 N.W.2d 585 (1963). The extreme position of the Hild case has been modified in Davis v. Davis, 280 Md. 119, 372 A.2d 231

to agree with the contemporary decisions that custody should not be granted or withheld as a reward or a punishment for conduct which a court finds worthy of praise or blame,[49] notwithstanding the Uniform Child Custody Jurisdiction Act's unfortunate injection of the clean hands doctrine into custody decisions.[50] But it is an entirely different and much more troubling matter for the courts to determine whether and how much the parent-child relationship is and will be affected by particular kinds of conduct or by alleged immorality on the part of a parent. If any proof of this statement were needed, the large number and confused condition of the reported cases would supply it.

The range of character or conduct which a conscientious court might find potentially relevant to the custody question is very wide. Thus a court might conceivably consider physical handicaps in their effect on the ability to care for children, but one would hope with some awareness of the success many people have in overcoming handicaps.[51] Psychiatric or emotional illness suffered by a parent will often affect his relationship with and his ability to care for the children and thus will be relevant to the custody decision.[52] The dangers here are that the court may have inadequate resources to determine the nature and prognosis of the illness,[53] and that even if it does have comprehensive and helpful evidence on those points, it may either exaggerate or under-estimate the effect of the illness on the relations between parent and child.[54]

There are even greater dangers when the courts confront claims that the "life styles" of the contending parents are objectionable in some way. The term itself is so vague as to be nearly meaningless.[55] When such claims are made the courts must discriminate between serious and relevant conditions like alcoholism or drug addiction on the one hand,[56] and essentially unimportant and irrelevant forms of personal behaviour on the other.[57] A fortiori the courts should avoid appeals to local chauvinism [58] or cultural bias.[59]

Parental conduct raising questions of sexual morality has produced more custody litigation than any other types of conduct. This is

(1977), cert. denied 434 U.S. 939, 98 S.Ct. 430, 54 L.Ed.2d 299 (1977).

49. In re Gutermuth's Marriage, 246 N.W.2d 272 (Iowa 1976); Tolos v. Tolos, 11 Mass.App.Ct. 708, 419 N.E.2d 304 (1981); Dees v. Dees, 41 Wis.2d 435, 164 N.W.2d 282 (1969). An extreme example of the use of custody as compensation to a parent is Gydesen v. Gydesen, 188 Neb. 538, 198 N.W.2d 67 (1972), in which a trial court awarded custody to the husband on the ground he had had a vasectomy and was unable to have any more children. Fortunately the Nebraska Supreme Court reversed.

50. See section 12.5, supra. It is surprising how often courts continue to treat a denial of custody as a punishment, as for example where a parent violates a court order. See, e.g., In re Custody of Rose, 9 N.C.App. 413, 176 S.E.2d 249 (1970); Barstad v. Barstad, 74 Wash.2d 295, 444 P.2d 691 (1968).

51. Bednarski v. Bednarski, 141 Mich.App. 15, 366 N.W.2d 69 (1985) (mother's deafness held not a bar to an award of custody).

52. E.g., Smith v. Smith, 172 Colo. 516, 474 P.2d 619 (1970); Dees v. Dees, 41 Wis.2d 435, 164 N.W.2d 282 (1969). See Malmquist, The Role of Parental Mental Illness in Custody Proceedings, 2 Fam.L.Q. 360 (1968).

53. The courts in many states are authorized to order psychiatric examinations of parents in custody cases where the parents' mental or emotional condition is in question. Annot., Right to Require Psychiatric or Mental Examination for Party Seeking to Obtain or Retain Custody of Child, 99 A.L.R.3d 268 (1980). Family counseling may also be ordered in appropriate cases. Lewis v. Lewis, 271 Pa.Super. 519, 414 A.2d 375 (1979), cert. denied 449 U.S. 877, 101 S.Ct. 221, 66 L.Ed.2d 99 (1980). But psychiatric testimony may sometimes be lacking in specific details and therefore disregarded. Foy v. Foy, 22 Mich.App. 514, 177 N.W.2d 681 (1970).

54. Cf. Sheridan v. Sheridan, 466 P.2d 821 (Alaska 1970) with McManus v. McManus, 250 So.2d 498 (La.App. 1971).

55. Webster's Third New International Dictionary of the English Language Unabridged 2271, "style", 4(c)(2) (1976) defines it as "an individual's typical way of life: his attitudes and their expression in a self-consistent manner as developing from childhood."

56. Sheridan v. Sheridan, 466 P.2d 821 (Alaska 1970) (semble); In re Marriage of Welbes, 327 N.W.2d 756 (Iowa 1982); In re Marriage of Seidenfeld, 241 N.W.2d 881 (Iowa 1976).

57. E.g., Weber v. Weber, 256 Ark. 549, 508 S.W.2d 725 (1974); Horen v. Horen, 73 Wash.2d 455, 438 P.2d 857 (1968).

58. Painter v. Bannister, 258 Iowa 1390, 140 N.W.2d 152 (1966), cert. denied 385 U.S. 949, 87 S.Ct. 317, 17 L.Ed.2d 227 (1966) is the most famous example of a court's finding that life for the child would be preferable in its jurisdiction to life in another state.

59. Carle v. Carle, 503 P.2d 1050 (Alaska 1972).

particularly true in some states where the courts have had great trouble in arriving at ways of talking about the issue which take account of contemporary changes in moral standards without at the same time abandoning all moral standards entirely.[60] Notwithstanding contemporary changes in sexual mores sexual morality still generates strong emotions in the minds of judges which are reflected in their judgments either expressly or under the surface. At the same time the courts do have to recognize that at least in many regions of the country extramarital and nonmarital sexual relationships have come to be accepted as no longer immoral.[61] Nearly all the cases recognize this to the extent of holding that adultery or the participation in a nonmarital relationship are not of themselves ground for denying custody to a parent,[62] even though many of them continue to insist that such conduct is relevant to the custody issue.[63] There are even some cases which continue to

give such conduct sufficient weight to make it the decisive factor in awarding custody.[64] The more sensible and workable approach to this problem is taken by the authorities which hold that the parents' sexual relations are only relevant when they have a direct effect upon the care of the child or upon the parent-child relationship.[65] It cannot be emphasized too strongly, however, that this factor never exists in isolation from others, is always affected by the other factors in the case, and may be given more or less weight in relation to the context in which it occurs. Thus sexual immorality might be given greater weight in a case in which the original custody order is being entered than in one involving a claimed modification of an existing order, in view of the policy disfavoring modification.[66]

Examples of sexual immorality which has had a direct and adverse effect on the parent-child relationship or on the child's welfare do

60. The states of Louisiana, Maryland and Nebraska have produced large numbers of reported cases on the subject. See Schexnayder v. Schexnayder, 371 So.2d 769 (1979); Davis v. Davis, 280 Md. 119, 372 A.2d 231 (1977); Greenfield v. Greenfield, 199 Neb. 648, 260 N.W.2d 493 (1977), citing many other cases.

61. Marvin v. Marvin, 18 Cal.3d 660, 134 Cal.Rptr. 815, 557 P.2d 106 (1976).

62. Davis v. Davis, 280 Md. 119, 372 A.2d 231 (1977); Lockard v. Lockard, 193 Neb. 400, 227 N.W.2d 581 (1975); In re Dahlman's Marriage, 20 Or.App. 375, 531 P.2d 909 (1975); Commonwealth ex rel. Myers v. Myers, 468 Pa. 134, 360 A.2d 587 (1976); Gunter v. Gunter, 240 Pa. Super. 382, 361 A.2d 307 (1976). Many other cases are collected in Annot., Custodial Parent's Sexual Relations With Third Person as Justifying Modification of Child Custody Order, 100 A.L.R.3d 625 (1980).

Certainly the standard of relevance and consequences should be the same for both husband and wife. Krueger v. Stevens, 90 S.D. 641, 244 N.W.2d 763 (1976).

63. See the cases cited in note 62, supra.

64. The leading case is Jarrett v. Jarrett, 78 Ill.2d 337, 400 N.E.2d 421 (1979), cert. denied 449 U.S. 927, 101 S.Ct. 329, 66 L.Ed.2d 155 (1980), rehearing denied 449 U.S. 1067, 101 S.Ct. 329, 66 L.Ed.2d 612 (1980), in which the court granted a change of custody from mother to father on the ground that the mother was living with a man to whom she was not married. The court relied heavily on the Illinois criminal statute making "open and notorious" cohabitation a crime as establishing the state's moral standards in such a case. The court also found that the mother's demonstration of improper moral values would affect the child's mental and emotional health. See also Olson v. Olson, 180 N.W.2d 427 (Iowa 1970); Dalton v. Dalton, 214 Kan. 805, 522 P.2d 378 (1974); Schexnayder

v. Schexnayder, 371 So.2d 769 (La.1979); Carr v. Carr, 480 So.2d 1120 (Miss.1985); In re H Children, 65 Misc.2d 187, 317 N.Y.S.2d 535 (Fam.Ct.1970); Larson v. Larson, 294 N.W.2d 616 (N.D.1980); Beaber v. Beaber, 41 Ohio Misc. 95, 322 N.E.2d 910 (1974); Pfeifer v. Pfeifer, 62 Wis. 2d 417, 215 N.W.2d 419 (1974) (semble). The parent's conduct may in some cases cause the court to impose restrictions on his rights of visitation. Gallo v. Gallo, 184 Conn. 36, 440 A.2d 782 (1981); DeVita v. DeVita, 145 N.J. Super. 120, 366 A.2d 1350 (1976). Such restrictions were held to be improper in In re Marriage of Wellman, 104 Cal.App.3d 992, 164 Cal.Rptr. 148 (1980). And in a few cases the courts, while they have refused to modify custody, have subjected the custodian to restrictions or supervision on the ground of immorality. Ketron v. Aguirre, 15 Ark.App. 325, 692 S.W.2d 261 (1985); Greenfield v. Greenfield, 199 Neb. 648, 260 N.W.2d 493 (1977).

65. This seems to be the effect of the Uniform Marriage and Divorce Act § 402, 9A Unif.L.Ann. 198 (1979). See also Anonymous v. Anonymous, 106 Ariz. 284, 475 P.2d 268 (1970); In re Moore's Marriage, 35 Colo.App. 280, 531 P.2d 995 (1975); Elizabeth A. S. v. Anthony M. S., 435 A.2d 721 (Del.1981); Dinkel v. Dinkel, 322 So.2d 22 (Fla.1975); Moore v. Moore, 577 S.W.2d 613 (Ky.1979); Feldman v. Feldman, 45 A.D.2d 320, 358 N.Y.S.2d 507 (2d Dep't 1974); Whaley v. Whaley, 61 Ohio App.2d 111, 399 N.E.2d 1270 (1978); Brown v. Brown, 218 Va. 196, 237 S.E.2d 89 (1977) (semble). See also Lauerman, Nonmarital Sexual Conduct and Child Custody, 46 U.Cin. L.Rev. 647 (1977); Wadlington, Sexual Relations After Separation or Divorce: The New Morality and the Old and New Divorce Laws, 63 Va.L.Rev. 249, 263 (1977).

66. Compare Madson v. Madson, 313 N.W.2d 42 (S.D. 1981) with Youngberg v. Youngberg, 193 Neb. 394, 227 N.W.2d 396 (1975). See also Annot., 100 A.L.R.3d 625 (1980).

appear in the cases.[67] The child who is aware of the parent's conduct may well be affected by it psychologically.[68] The parent's activities may prevent him from giving the child the affection and attention the child needs.[69] In some instances the effect on the child may be caused by the presence of another person in the home in place of the absent parent, as would be true if the custodial parent had remarried.[70] In such cases any immorality should be ignored and the court should deal with the "stepparent" problem.

The courts' treatment of custody claims made by homosexual parents constitutes an unfortunate example of judicial involvement in matters of sexual morality. Despite somewhat increased social tolerance of homosexuality in recent years, it still meets with hostility on the part of the law in many different contexts.[71] This is reflected by the substantial number of cases which continue to deny custody or visitation to homosexual parents on the sole ground of their homosexuality.[72] The reasoning of these cases is that the homosexual parent is likely to attempt to convert his child to homosexuality,[73] or that the child

will be subjected to social disapproval and harassment if he lives with the homosexual parent,[74] or just that the homosexual parent is engaging in immoral conduct which presumably will contaminate the morals of the child.[75] The first of these reasons has generally been characterized as unfounded by authoritative psychological opinion.[76] Psychological testimony, which should be helpful in this type of case, has usually been that homosexual parents are as capable of competent loving care of their children as any other parents.[77] The argument based upon harassment of the children may be borne out by experience, but a similar argument has been rejected by the Supreme Court where it was advanced to justify racial discrimination,[78] and it should be rejected here as well. The third reason is merely a concession that the court is punishing what it considers to be the immorality of homosexuality by withholding custody. Nearly all courts agree that custody should not be granted or withheld as a reward or a punishment for good or bad behaviour. To treat it so is to revert to practices abandoned more than a half century ago.

67. See the Commissioners' Note to § 402 of the Uniform Marriage and Divorce Act, 9A Unif.L.Ann. 198 (1979), which suggests that the parent's conduct would only have an effect on his relationship with the child if the child knew of the conduct. Lauerman, Nonmarital Sexual Conduct and Child Custody, 46 U.Cin.L.Rev. 647, 660 (1977) gives as examples cases in which the child knew and disapproved of the parent's conduct, or in which the child exhibited symptoms of psychological disturbance attributable to the parent's conduct. The same article, at 661, indicates the ambiguity of language in some judicial opinions which speak of sexual conduct occurring in the child's "presence". See also Dinkel v. Dinkel, 322 So.2d 22 (Fla.1975).

68. S. v. J., 81 Misc.2d 828, 367 N.Y.S.2d 405 (1975); Madson v. Madson, 313 N.W.2d 42 (S.D.1981).

69. In re Bowen's Marriage, 219 N.W.2d 683 (1974).

70. See J. Wallerstein, J. Kelly, Surviving the Breakup 287–296 (1979), describing the conflicts which occur when the custodial parent, usually the mother, remarries. Of course in many cases the second husband will have "earlier lived in the household as lover and companion." Id. at 288.

71. E.g., Bowers v. Hardwick, ___ U.S. ___, 106 S.Ct. 2841, 92 L.Ed.2d 140 (1986), rehearing denied ___ U.S. ___, 107 S.Ct. 29, 92 L.Ed.2d 779 (1986), upholding the constitutionality of sodomy laws as applied to the sexual activities of adults in private, and citing the statutes of the twenty-four states which make such conduct criminal.

72. N. K. M. v. L. E. M., 606 S.W.2d 179 (Mo.App. 1980); Newsome v. Newsome, 42 N.C.App. 416, 256 S.E.2d 849 (1979); Jacobson v. Jacobson, 314 N.W.2d 78 (N.D.1981); M. J. P. v. J. G. P., 640 P.2d 966 (Okl.1982); Constant A. v. Paul C. A., 344 Pa.Super. 49, 496 A.2d 1 (1985); Roe v. Roe, 228 Va. 722, 324 S.E.2d 691 (1985). The homosexual parent's visitation was limited in J. L. P. (H.) v. D. J. P., 643 S.W.2d 865 (Mo.App.1982) and in Roberts v. Roberts, 22 Ohio App.3d 127, 489 N.E.2d 1067 (1985). Other cases are cited in Annots., 6 A.L.R.4th 1297 (1981) and 36 A.L.R.4th 997 (1985).

73. E.g., S. v. S., 608 S.W.2d 64 (Ky.App.1980), cert. denied 451 U.S. 911, 101 S.Ct. 1982, 68 L.Ed.2d 300 (1981).

74. Jacobson v. Jacobson, 314 N.W.2d 78 (N.D.1981); M. J. P. v. J. G. P., 640 P.2d 966 (Okl.1982).

75. Roe v. Roe, 228 Va. 722, 324 S.E.2d 691 (1985).

76. Note, Assessing Children's Best Interes When a Parent is Gay or Lesbian: Toward a Rational Custody Standard, 32 U.C.L.A.L.Rev. 852, 870–876 (1985) cites some of the relevant literature.

77. See the testimony recounted in Bezio v. Patenaude, 381 Mass. 563, 410 N.E.2d 1207 (1980).

78. Palmore v. Sidoti, 466 U.S. 429, 104 S.Ct. 1879, 80 L.Ed.2d 421 (1984), appeal after remand 472 So.2d 843 (Fla.App.1985). See M. P. v. S. P., 169 N.J.Super. 425, 404 A.2d 1256 (1979).

The better approach to this question is the one which most courts now take when heterosexual conduct is alleged as a ground for denying custody.[79] Homosexuality should only be relevant to the custody decision when it can be shown to have a direct effect on the child's welfare or on the parent-child relationship. This will not often be the case. In fact the more enlightened judicial opinions take this view of the question.[80] Here again of course many other factors may also influence the custody decision, which may also be affected by the fact that a change in custody is being sought rather than an original custody award.[81]

In addition to the factors just described, the courts may occasionally consider the physical conditions to be provided for the child by the prospective custodian,[82] or the remarriage of a parent and the willingness of the new spouse to accept the child,[83] but such factors as these are and should be of relatively little weight except in the unusual circumstance of clearly harmful conditions. Superior financial or material resources are sometimes urged as a reason for favoring one parent over the other and a few cases in fact do find this relevant.[84]

Inequality of resources should not be given any weight in the custody decision[85] but should be corrected by an appropriate award of child support.

In nearly all the cases which have been discussed under this heading it is either expressly stated or assumed that the crucial factor in awarding custody is the relationship between parent and child as revealed by the parents' past conduct and by the strength and sincerity of the parents' desire to have custody.[86] Evaluation of these intangible factors is difficult and challenging for the courts, but of course that process may be assisted by what the evidence of the parents' past conduct shows. A factor of almost equal importance, where it exists, is the child's need for stability and continuity in his relationships with his parents.[87] This means that the award of temporary custody pending the outcome of the litigation may assume much greater significance than it should have if in the particular jurisdiction long delays in coming to trial are common. In such circumstances the final decision on custody may be little more than a perfunctory reaffirmance of the temporary custody award.[88]

---

79. See the text at note 65, supra.

80. D. H. v. J. H., 418 N.E.2d 286 (Ind.App.1981); Bezio v. Patenaude, 381 Mass. 563, 410 N.E.2d 1207 (1980); Doe v. Doe, 16 Mass.App.Ct. 499, 452 N.E.2d 293 (1983); M. P. v. S. P., 169 N.J.Super. 425, 404 A.2d 1256 (1979); DiStefano v. DiStefano, 60 A.D.2d 976, 401 N.Y.S.2d 636 (4th Dep't 1978); A. v. A., 15 Or.App. 353, 514 P.2d 358 (1973), rehearing denied 15 Or.App. 353, 515 P.2d 730 (1973). Cases taking this position where visitation is in issue include In the Matter of J. S. & C., 129 N.J.Super. 486, 324 A.2d 90 (1974), affirmed 142 N.J. Super. 499, 362 A.2d 54 (1976); Matter of Marriage of Cabalquinto, 100 Wash.2d 325, 669 P.2d 886 (1983), appeal after remand 43 Wash.App. 518, 718 P.2d 7 (1986), 20 Willamette L.Rev. 598 (1984). See also Hunter, Polikoff, Custody Rights in Lesbian Mothers: Legal Theory and Litigation Strategy, 25 Buff.L.Rev. 691 (1976); Annot., 36 A.L.R.4th 997 (1985).

81. See, e.g., Schuster v. Schuster, 90 Wash.2d 626, 585 P.2d 130 (1978).

82. Stifflemire v. Williamson, 250 Ala. 409, 34 So.2d 685 (1948); Sanders v. Felzman, 308 Ky. 25, 213 S.W.2d 428 (1948); Thalassinos v. Thalassinos, 77 N.Y.S.2d 311 (1947), affirmed 279 App.Div. 807, 81 N.Y.S.2d 155 (2d Dep't 1948); Mullen v. Mullen, 188 Va. 259, 49 S.E.2d 349 (1948).

83. Jenks v. Brown, 250 Ala. 534, 35 So.2d 359 (1948).

84. Blain v. Blain, 205 Ark. 346, 168 S.W.2d 807 (1943); White v. White, 160 Kan. 32, 159 P.2d 461 (1945); Salk v. Salk, 89 Misc.2d 883, 393 N.Y.S.2d 841 (1975), affirmed 53 A.D.2d 558, 385 N.Y.S.2d 1015 (1st Dep't 1976); Kightlinger v. Kightlinger, 249 Or. 521, 439 P.2d 614 (1968).

85. Anderson v. Anderson, 309 So.2d 1 (Fla.1975). The statutes in some jurisdictions may require the courts to give some consideration to the relative material prosperity of the parents. See, e.g. Mich.C.L.A. § 25.312(3)(c) (1984) and Dempsey v. Dempsey, 96 Mich.App. 276, 292 N.W.2d 549 (1980), modified 409 Mich. 495, 296 N.W.2d 813 (1980).

86. E.g., Seymour v. Seymour, 180 Conn. 705, 433 A.2d 1005 (1980); Commonwealth ex rel. Parikh v. Parikh, 449 Pa. 105, 296 A.2d 625 (1972).

87. Miller v. Miller, 202 N.W.2d 105 (Iowa 1972). This factor is given extreme if not exclusive emphasis in J. Goldstein, A. Freud, A. Solnit, Beyond the Best Interests of the Child 31 (2d ed.1979).

88. See, e.g., Berman v. Berman, 84 Mich.App. 740, 270 N.W.2d 680 (1978), in which the standard for reviewing a temporary custody order was required to be the same as for modifying custody.

(d) The Effect of an Agreement of the Parents Concerning Custody

Agreements between parents as to custody of their children, usually made as part of their separation agreement are usually encouraged by the courts and therefore enforced,[89] so long as they appear to serve the child's interests. Although the courts are free to disregard such contracts when they find that the child's interests are not being served,[90] as a practical matter the courts are only too happy to enforce the contracts and avoid litigating custody.[91] Today many such contracts provide for some form of joint custody.[92]

(e) The Child's Preference as a Factor in Awarding Custody

The statutes of several states either require the court to honor the child's wishes as to his custodian or authorize the court to take his wishes into account in making the award, provided either that the child has reached a specified age,[93] or that he has sufficient intelligence and understanding to form a judgment on the question.[94] Where no age is specified by statute, the cases do not lay down absolute rules but give more or less weight to the child's preference depending upon his age and maturity of judgment. The desire of a six-year-old boy to live with his father would not ordinarily weigh heavily with a court.[95] A similar desire on the part of a twelve-year-old would be given much more weight.[96] Where the child's preference does not seem wholly voluntary,[97] or runs counter to other very persuasive factors,[98] even the older child's preference may not be honored. In any event it is ordinarily desirable for the court to attempt some inquiry into the reasons underlying the preference in order to avoid the argument often made that giving weight to the child's wishes is an invitation to the parents to engage in a campaign to win the child's favor and an invitation to the child to extort favors from the parents.[99] Although it is undoubtedly wise practice to take account of the child's desire, this is one of those situations in which the substantive merits are less important than the procedure by which the court learns what the child thinks about his future custody. The methods by which the court may do this are discussed in an earlier section.[1]

---

89. Witmayer v. Witmayer, 320 Pa.Super. 372, 467 A.2d 371 (1983).

90. See section 18.5, supra, at note 8.

91. R. Neely, The Divorce Decision 67–79 (1984).

92. See section 19.5, infra.

93. Official Ga.Stat.Ann. § 74–107 (Supp.1986) (child of fourteen has the right to select his custodian); Ohio Rev.Code § 3109.04 (Supp.1986) (child of twelve may choose his custodian unless the parent chosen is unfit or the choice would not be in the child's best interests). The child does not have an absolute right to choose under the Georgia statute. Prater v. Wheeler, 253 Ga. 649, 322 S.E.2d 892 (1984) (selection is subject to the judge's determination that the parent selected is not unfit).

94. Alaska Stat. § 25.24.150 (1983); West's Ann.Cal. Civ.Code § 4600 (Supp.1987); Conn.Gen.Stat.Ann. § 46b–56 (1986); West's Fla.Stat.Ann. § 61.13(3)(i) (1985); Hawaii Rev.Stat. § 571–46 (1976 and Supp.1984); Neb.Rev. Stat. § 42–364 (Supp.1986); N.J.Stat.Ann. § 9:2–4 (1976); Okl.Stat. 1987, tit. 12, § 1277.1 (Supp.); Utah Code Ann. § 30–3–10 (1984). The Uniform Marriage and Divorce Act § 402(2), 9A Unif.L.Ann. 197 (1979) requires the court to consider the child's wishes but does not indicate that the child must be of any particular age or level of understanding.

95. Poliakoff v. Poliakoff, 221 S.C. 391, 70 S.E.2d 625 (1952); Hild v. Hild, 221 Md. 349, 157 A.2d 442 (1960)

(seven-year-old not old enough). Many other cases are cited in Annot., Child's Wishes as Factor in Awarding Custody, 4 A.L.R.3d 1396 (1965) and Speca, The Role of the Child in Selecting His or Her Custodian in Divorce Cases, 27 Drake L.Rev. 437 (1978).

96. Sanders v. Felzman, 308 Ky. 25, 213 S.W.2d 428 (1948); Guinan v. Guinan, 254 S.C. 554, 176 S.E.2d 173 (1970) (sixteen-year-old boy's wishes should have great weight). The child's wishes should have even greater weight when they are enforced by other considerations. See Commonwealth ex rel. Pierce v. Pierce, 493 Pa. 292, 426 A.2d 555 (1981).

97. Jordana v. Corley, 220 N.W.2d 515 (N.D.1974).

98. In re Marriage of Ellerbroek, 377 N.W.2d 257 (Iowa App.1985), rejecting the preference of a sixteen-year-old boy to live with his father.

99. Lacy v. Lacy, 553 P.2d 928 (Alaska 1976). See the dissent in Jordana v. Corley, 220 N.W.2d 515, 523 (N.D.1974), the dissenting judge concluding: "It would be better, I believe, to leave the children out of the matter entirely." One such argument refers to the guilt the child must feel in being pressured to express a preference for one parent over the other. For arguments favoring heavy reliance on the child's wishes, see Speca, The Role of the Child in Selecting His or Her Custodian in Divorce Cases, 27 Drake L.Rev. 437 (1978).

1. See section 14.4, supra, at note 21.

The courts give similar consideration to the child's desire concerning the place in which he is to live,[2] even where this involves imposing serious restrictions on the child's custodian.[3]

(f) Race, Religion and Political or Social Views of the Parents

Some early cases have held that in a custody dispute between parents of different races the race of the parties would be relevant although it should not be the sole ground on which custody is awarded.[4] The reason for this was sometimes stated to be that where the child is born of an interracial marriage society will consider him black rather than white and that he would therefore be subjected to less stress and prejudice if he were placed in the custody of the black parent.[5] The Supreme Court of the United States in Palmore v. Sidoti[6] has now made that reasoning unacceptable by holding that a custody

decision based solely on race out of a recognition of such private biases or prejudices violates the Equal Protection Clause of the Fourteenth Amendment.[7] The Court, without citing lower court cases dealing with custody and race, said:[8]

"The effects of racial prejudice, however real, cannot justify a racial classification removing an infant child from the custody of its natural mother found to be an appropriate person to have such custody."

In nearly all cases the only possible basis for taking race into account is the argument from racial prejudice rejected in Palmore. Even before Palmore was decided several courts recognized that the argument was not permissible and in sweeping terms stated that race is not a relevant consideration in custody cases.[9] There may conceivably be cases in which race is directly and closely related to the welfare of the child in other ways, but certainly they will be rare.[10] The better re-

---

2. Cases are collected in Annot., Desire of Child as to Geographical Location of Residence or Domicile as Factor in Awarding Custody or Terminating Parental Rights, 10 A.L.R.4th 827 (1981).

3. Bergstrom v. Bergstrom, 296 N.W.2d 490 (N.D. 1980).

4. Murphy v. Murphy, 143 Conn. 600, 124 A.2d 891 (1956); Fountaine v. Fountaine, 9 Ill.App.2d 482, 133 N.E.2d 532 (1956). Other early cases are cited in Annot., 57 A.L.R.2d 678 (1956).

5. Even today the child of mixed white and black parents will often be considered black. Palmore v. Sidoti, 466 U.S. 429, 433 104 S.Ct. 1879, 1882, 80 L.Ed.2d 421 (1984); appeal after remand 472 So.2d 843 (Fla.App.1985). See also G. Myrdal, An American Dilemma 113 (1944). A case which relied on the prejudice to be suffered by a mixed race child in a white family is Ward v. Ward, 36 Wash.2d 143, 216 P.2d 755 (1950).

6. 466 U.S. 429, 104 S.Ct. 1879, 80 L.Ed.2d 421 (1984), appeal after remand 472 So.2d 843 (Fla.App.1985). In this case a white couple was divorced in Florida and custody of their three-year-old daughter was given to the mother. A year or so later the mother began living with a black man, whom she married two months later. The father then sought modification of the decree which would give him custody. The Florida court, after finding that both parents were devoted to the child and able to care for her, awarded custody to the father on the ground that the child would suffer from social stigmatization if allowed to remain with her mother and the mother's black husband. The Supreme Court reversed on the ground of the reason stated in the text.

7. U.S.Const.amend. XIV, § 1.

8. 466 U.S. at 434, 104 S.Ct. at 1882.

9. Cases rejecting the argument from racial prejudice when a white parent married or lived with a black include In re Marriage of Kramer, 297 N.W.2d 359 (Iowa 1980); Edel v. Edel, 97 Mich.App. 266, 293 N.W.2d 792 (1980), questioned on other grounds Blaskowski v. Blaskowski, 115 Mich.App. 1, 320 N.W.2d 268 (1982); Farmer v. Farmer, 109 Misc.2d 137, 439 N.Y.S.2d 584 (1981); Commonwealth ex rel. Myers v. Myers, 468 Pa. 134, 360 A.2d 587 (1976); Commonwealth ex rel. Lucas v. Kreischer, 450 Pa. 352, 299 A.2d 243 (1973). Other cases are cited in Annot., Race as a Factor in Custody Award or Proceedings, 10 A.L.R.4th 795 (1981). The Edel, Myers and Kreischer cases cited above contain broad language that race is not a relevant consideration in custody cases as does Milligan v. Davison, 244 Pa.Super. 255, 367 A.2d 299 (1976).

Of course race may have some effect on a custody decision even though the trial court does not admit it. Schexnayder v. Schexnayder, 371 So.2d 769 (La.1979) and Brokenleg v. Butts, 559 S.W.2d 853 (Tex.Civ.App.1977), cert. denied 442 U.S. 946, 99 S.Ct. 2894, 61 L.Ed.2d 318 (1979) may be cases of this kind.

10. In re Marriage of Mikelson, 299 N.W.2d 670 (Iowa 1980) may be such a case. In that case the divorcing spouses had adopted two mixed race children. In the custody dispute the father argued that he should be granted custody because he had made an active and successful effort to make friends in the black community and was therefore in a better position than the mother to help the children recognize, understand and appreciate their black identity. The court seems to have recognized the relevance of this argument but did not modify the earlier decree to give custody to the father. It seems doubtful that arguments of this kind can survive the Palmore ruling, however. Farmer v. Farmer, 109 Misc.

sult in all cases is to exclude race as a relevant factor in custody disputes, placing the child with the parent whose affection and care will best serve his interests irrespective of race.

Religion raises different questions.[11] The English courts historically had no compunction about denying a person the custody of his children when they found his religious or social views unacceptable even though his conduct might have been quite moral and upright.[12] In our system, however, the United States Constitution [13] and the various state constitutions all forbid the state from assisting or interfering with religious establishments. The extent to which the courts are thereby prevented from taking account of religious factors in awarding custody is far from clear.[14]

It is usually held that the Establishment Clause [15] as applied to the states prevents the courts from favoring one religion or one religious denomination over another in custody

cases, even where one of the religions is relatively obscure or unpopular.[16] At the same time the Supreme Court in Prince v. Commonwealth of Massachusetts has taught us that the state may regulate the activities of parents, even activities having a religious purpose, if that is reasonably necessary for the protection of children.[17] The question then is, may the court in a custody case take into consideration the religious practices of a parent where those practices are shown to have a direct effect upon the health or the development of the child? There is a line of contemporary cases which hold that the courts may do so. For example, the parent's religion may require the withholding of some forms of medical care and if this carries a serious potential for harm to the child it may be relevant to the custody decision.[18] In other cases the parent's religious practices may adversely affect the child's own religious beliefs and training if the child is old enough to have such beliefs.[19] In all such cases, however, the court should take great care to focus on the

---

2d 137, 439 N.Y.S.2d 584 (1981) seems to preserve some influence for race in custody cases by saying that it is of no significance in conflicts between the parents, but it may be important in conflicts between a parent and a stranger.

Statutes in a few states may continue to make race a relevant factor when child custody is in issue. E.g., Colo. Rev.Stat. § 19–4–103 (1986).

11. Cases are collected in Annot., Religion as a Factor in Child Custody and Visitation Cases, 22 A.L.R.4th 971 (1983). See also Religion in Adoption and Custody Cases, 1 Institute of Church and State Conference Proceedings 56 (1958); List, A Child and a Wall: A Study of "Religious Protection" Laws, 13 Buff.L.Rev. 9 (1963); Pfeffer, Religion in the Upbringing of Children, 35 B.U.L.Rev. 333 (1955); Mangrum, Exclusive Reliance on Best Interest May be Unconstitutional: Religion as a Factor in Child Custody Cases, 15 Creighton L.Rev. 25 (1981).

12. Shelley v. Westbrooke, Jacob Ch. 266, 37 Eng.Rep. 850 (1821); In re Besant, 11 Ch.D. 508 (1879). The background of the Shelley case is described in Burch, The Case of Shelley v. Westbrooke, 23 Case and Comment 181 (1916).

13. U.S.Const.amend. I, XIV.

14. Note, The Establishment Clause and Religion in Child Custody Disputes, 82 Mich.L.Rev. 1702 (1984).

15. U.S.Const.amend. I, amend. XIV, § 1.

16. Johnson v. Johnson, 564 P.2d 71 (Alaska 1977), cert. denied 434 U.S. 1048, 98 S.Ct. 896, 54 L.Ed.2d 800 (1978) (mother a Jehovah's witness); Smith v. Smith, 90 Ariz. 190, 367 P.2d 230 (1961); Quiner v. Quiner, 59 Cal. Rptr. 503 (Cal.App.1967); Waites v. Waites, 567 S.W.2d

326 (Mo.1978); In re Sisson, 152 Misc. 806, 274 N.Y.S. 857 (1934); Frantzen v. Frantzen, 349 S.W.2d 765 (Tex.Civ. App.1961); In re Marriage of Hadeen, 27 Wash.App. 566, 619 P.2d 374 (1980). Other cases are cited in Annot., 22 A.L.R.4th 971, 977 (1983).

In some states there may be statutes which in some situations may authorize or require the courts to take religion into account in awarding custody. E.g., Alaska Stat. § 25.24.150(c)(1) (1983) (court to consider the religious needs of the child); Colo.Rev.Stat. § 19–4–103(1) (1986) (placement after relinquishment); Ill.—S.H.A. ch. 40, § 1519 (Supp.1986) (adoption); N.Y.—McKinney's Dom.Rel.L. § 113 (1977). Of course such statutes may always raise constitutional questions in their application, but the Alaska statute was held not to be unconstitutional on its face in Bonjour v. Bonjour, 592 P.2d 1233 (Alaska 1979).

17. 321 U.S. 158, 167, 64 S.Ct. 438, 442, 88 L.Ed. 645 (1944), rehearing denied 321 U.S. 804, 64 S.Ct. 784, 88 L.Ed. 1090 (1944).

18. In re Marriage of Short, 698 P.2d 1310 (Colo.1985); Birch v. Birch, 11 Ohio St.3d 85, 463 N.E.2d 1254 (1984). Burnham v. Burnham, 208 Neb. 498, 304 N.W.2d 58 (1981) awarded custody to the father in reliance upon extreme religious views of the mother which the court regarded as harmful to the child. The case is strongly criticized in Mangrum, Exclusive Reliance on Best Interest May be Unconstitutional: Religion as a Factor in Child Custody Cases, 15 Creighton L.Rev. 25 (1981).

19. Bonjour v. Bonjour, 592 P.2d 1233 (Alaska 1979). T. v. H., 102 N.J.Super. 38, 245 A.2d 221 (1968), affirmed on other grounds 110 N.J.Super. 8, 264 A.2d 244 (1970) awarded custody of two children, ages eight and ten, to

harm to the child and put aside its views about the merits or demerits of the religion involved, even though this distinction may be a difficult one to observe.[20] And where the parent's faith forbids recourse to medical or surgical care, rather than deny custody to that parent, the court may grant custody and impose conditions which ensure that the child will receive such care when he needs it.[21]

Although some courts seem to have been much too willing to favor a parent who espouses some religious belief over one who is an atheist or agnostic,[22] these decisions are clearly wrong and should not be followed. Unless the parent's lack of religious conviction has a direct effect on the child's welfare or health, it should be disregarded in the custody decision.[23] Thus if the child were old enough to have some religious beliefs, and a parent refused to permit the child to continue to practice his religion, this might be a relevant circumstance in awarding custody. But the courts should not be in the business of preferring religion over non-religion in custody cases.

Controversies over children's religious training sometimes erupt after the divorce. Normally the custodian of the child has the right to control the child's religious training just as he does other aspects of the child's education.[24] This does not mean that the non-custodial parent is not permitted to have any influence on the child's religious upbringing. Several cases have refused to enjoin him from giving the child some religious training or from taking the child to religious observances even though the custodial parent seeks to prevent it and even though this subjects the child to religious beliefs and practices other than those of the custodial parent, so long as no real harm to the child occurs or is threatened.[25] The refusal of injunctions is usually based upon a reluctance to invade parental privacy and on the reasoning that the non-custodial parent should have continuing contacts with the child and with the child's religious training.[26] The custodian's right to control religious education, within these limits, has also generally persuaded the courts to refuse to enforce antenuptial agreements concerning the religious training to be given children of the marriage.[27]

Whether a parent's political or social opinions or the social or cultural environment in which he proposes to raise the child should be taken into account in awarding custody is a question to which a few cases give some attention. Certainly the parent's opinions should

their father on the ground that their upbringing in the Jewish religion could better be continued in New Jersey, where he lived, than in Idaho where the mother planned to live.

20. In re Marriage of Short, 698 P.2d 1310 (Colo.1985).

21. Osier v. Osier, 410 A.2d 1027 (Me.1980) (suggests devices other than withholding custody which would minimize the risk to the child); Levitsky v. Levitsky, 231 Md. 388, 190 A.2d 621 (1963); Gluckstern v. Gluckstern, 17 Misc.2d 83, 158 N.Y.S.2d 504 (1956), affirmed 3 A.D.2d 999, 165 N.Y.S.2d 432 (1957), appeal denied 4 A.D.2d 832, 166 N.Y.S.2d 299 (1957). Custody was awarded without restriction to a mother who was a Jehovah's Witness in Waites v. Waites, 567 S.W.2d 326 (Mo.1978). Other cases are cited in Annot., 22 A.L.R.4th 971, 998 (1983). See also Harris v. Harris, 343 So.2d 762 (Miss.1977).

22. Murphy v. Murphy, 143 Conn. 600, 124 A.2d 891 (1956); Schreifels v. Schreifels, 47 Wash.2d 409, 287 P.2d 1001 (1955).

23. Welker v. Welker, 24 Wis.2d 570, 129 N.W.2d 134 (1964); Wilson v. Wilson, 473 P.2d 595 (Wyo.1970); Pfeffer, Religion in the Upbringing of Children, 35 B.U.L.Rev. 333, 364 (1955).

24. Griffin v. Griffin, 699 P.2d 407 (Colo.1985); Wilhelm v. Wilhelm, 504 S.W.2d 699 (Ky.1973); Clements v.

Young, 481 So.2d 263 (Miss.1985) (custodian makes day to day decisions concerning the child's care, but decisions may be reviewed for reasonableness); Pogue v. Pogue, 147 N.J.Super. 61, 370 A.2d 539 (1977); Siegel v. Siegel, 122 Misc.2d 932, 472 N.Y.S.2d 272 (1984).

25. In re Marriage of Mentry, 142 Cal.App.3d 260, 190 Cal.Rptr. 843 (1983); In re Marriage of Murga, 103 Cal. App.3d 498, 163 Cal.Rptr. 79 (1980); Felton v. Felton, 383 Mass. 232, 418 N.E.2d 606 (1981); Robert O. v. Judy E., 90 Misc.2d 439, 395 N.Y.S.2d 351 (Fam.Ct.1977); Munoz v. Munoz, 79 Wash.2d 810, 489 P.2d 1133 (1971). Contra: Morris v. Morris, 271 Pa.Super. 19, 412 A.2d 139 (1979).

26. In re Marriage of Mentry, 142 Cal.App.3d 260, 190 Cal.Rptr. 843 (1983); Felton v. Felton, 383 Mass. 232, 418 N.E.2d 606 (1981).

27. Stanton v. Stanton, 213 Ga. 545, 100 S.E.2d 289 (1957); Jacobs v. Jacobs, 25 Ill.App.3d 175, 323 N.E.2d 21 (1974); Lynch v. Uhlenhopp, 248 Iowa 68, 78 N.W.2d 491 (1956); Miles v. Liebolt, 230 N.Y.S.2d 342 (1962). Other cases are cited in Annot., 22 A.L.R.4th 971, 1028 (1983). Contra: Spring v. Glawon, 89 A.D.2d 980, 454 N.Y.S.2d 140 (2d Dep't 1982).

not be relevant, even if they are unpopular or unconventional,[28] although there is a little evidence that in some courts they may be,[29] unless again they have a direct impact on the child's emotional or physical development. Cultural biases of the particular judge should certainly not enter into the custody decision.[30]

(g) Effect of a Finding That Neither Parent is a Suitable Custodian

Where the court finds that neither parent is a suitable custodian, it may place the child in the custody of relatives if they are willing and are appropriate custodians,[31] or as a last resort in the custody of a state or private child care agency.[32] Most courts will only place the child with persons other than the parents where both parents are unfit to have custody or where extraordinary reasons exist for removing the child from his parents.[33] And most judges are properly very reluctant to make a decree which will institutionalize a child.[34]

(h) Visitation and Removal From the Jurisdiction [35]

The award of custody after consideration of the factors already described in this section does not conclude the divorce court's task but still leaves open the important question of what the decree should say concerning the contact between the child and the non-custodial parent.[36] In conventional legal terms, what rights of visitation with the child are to be conferred in the decree? Although the Goldstein, Freud, Solnit book [37] has had great influence with the courts, its rigid view that there should be no rights of visitation has not only had no influence, but the courts have recently tended to expand the scope of visitation and give it strong support.[38] In spite of the conflicts and hostility between the parents which are often caused or exacerbated by the requirement and the enforcement of visitation rights, the courts and many non-legal students of divorce continue to advocate its use.[39] In addition to the benefits of regular visitation for the child, decrees which grant it

---

28. Weinman, The Trial Judge Awards Custody, 10 L. & Contemp.Prob. 721, 733 (1944).

29. Eaton v. Eaton, unreported, discussed in 49 Harv. L.Rev. 831 (1936); People ex rel. Portnoy v. Strasser, 303 N.Y. 539, 104 N.E.2d 895 (1952).

30. Carle v. Carle, 503 P.2d 1050 (Alaska 1972).

31. Ford v. Ford, 194 Colo. 134, 571 P.2d 717 (1977); Collins v. Collins, 76 Kan. 93, 90 P. 809 (1907); Ballard v. Ballard, 233 Or. 74, 377 P.2d 24 (1962). But see West v. Griffin, 207 Ark. 367, 180 S.W.2d 839 (1944) and Boone v. Boone, 8 N.C.App. 524, 174 S.E.2d 833 (1970), holding it was error to place a child in the possession of one not a party to the suit, since such a decree would be unenforceable.

Cases dealing with controversies between parents and non-parents for custody are discussed infra, in section 19.6, infra.

32. In re Douglas, 164 N.E.2d 475 (Ohio Juv.Ct.1959). Wilson v. Wilson, 269 N.C. 676, 153 S.E.2d 349 (1967) placed the child with an agency when both parents were found unfit.

33. In re Marriage of Carrico, 284 N.W.2d 251 (Iowa 1979); Wilson v. Wilson, 269 N.C. 676, 153 S.E.2d 349 (1967); James v. James, 230 Va. 51, 334 S.E.2d 551 (1985) (hostility of parents toward each other did not justify awarding custody to grandparents).

34. Withrow v. Withrow, 212 La. 427, 31 So.2d 849 (1947).

35. Visitation by grandparents, involving as it does controversy between parents and grandparents, will be discussed in section 19.7, infra. An extensive discussion

of visitation rights is found in Novinson, Post-Divorce Visitation: Untying the Triangular Knot, 1983 U.Ill.L. Rev. 119.

36. The closely related subject of joint custody, dealing with the same question, is discussed in section 19.5, infra. Visitation may have an important relationship to the level of child support, since the statutory child support guidelines in force in many states may reduce the level of child support sharply when overnight visitation reaches a certain proportion of the total custody time in one year. See, e.g., Colo. Rev. Stat. §§ 14–10–115(15) (Supp. 1986).

37. J. Goldstein, A. Freud, A. Solnit, Beyond the Best Interests of the Child 38 (2d ed. 1979): "Thus, the noncustodial parent should have no legally enforceable right to visit the child, and the custodial parent should have the right to decide whether it is desirable for the child to have such visits." This view is cogently criticized in Novinson, Post-Divorce Visitation: Untying the Triangular Knot, 1983 U.Ill.L.Rev. 119, 140.

38. J. Wallerstein, J. Kelly, Surviving the Breakup 121 (1980) found that over eighty percent of divorces involved custody to the mother with visitation rights to the father.

39. See, e.g., Weiss v. Weiss, 52 N.Y.2d 170, 436 N.Y.S.2d 862, 418 N.E.2d 377 (1981), emphasizing the importance of visitation to both parent and child. A discussion of both the difficulties of and the need for visitation may be found in J. Wallerstein, J. Kelly, Surviving the Breakup chs. 7, 8 (1980). See also D. Luepnitz, Child Custody 33–35 (1982).

represent a recognition that the child's interests are not the only factors to be considered in divorce, and that the parents also have important interests which should be vindicated where that can be done without harm to the child.

The statutes of many of the states authorize the award of visitation rights in varying terms.[40] They also, in some states, require the court to take into account in awarding custody the willingness and ability of the parents to facilitate and encourage a close relationship between the child and the other parent, thereby presumably indicating a policy favoring amicable and effective visitation.[41]

As the language of many of the statutes suggests, visitation should be awarded to the non-custodial parent unless the award would seriously harm the child.[42] This means in practice that the parent resisting visitation has the burden of showing that it should not be granted.[43] Although the grant of visitation should take into account many of the factors relevant to the award of custody,[44] many courts will grant it even where it involves

some inconvenience to the custodial parent and some objections from the child's point of view.[45] In this sort of case as in custody cases generally it is impossible to lay down precise rules. It is perhaps enough to say that visitation will be granted when the advantages to the non-custodial parent and to the child can be found to outweigh the disadvantages to the child, given what seems to be a relatively strong bias in favor of visitation.

Specific examples of the difficulties surrounding visitation are produced by the mobility of contemporary American society. There are essentially two questions to be faced by lawyers and courts. May custody be awarded to a parent who intends to leave the jurisdiction and reside at a distance great enough to make visitation by the other parent difficult or impossible? And if a parent having custody proposes to make such a move, under what circumstances may a court enjoin it or impose conditions upon it? Most of the cases speak in terms of moves outside the state, but of course in practice a move within a large state may have a greater impact on

---

40. E.g., Alaska Stat. § 25.24.150 (1982); Ariz.Rev. Stat. § 25–337 (1973); Conn.Gen.Stat.Ann. § 46b–56 (1986); Official Ga.Code Ann. § 19–9–1 (Supp.1986); Hawaii Rev.Stat. § 571–46 (1976); Ill.—S.H.A. ch. 40, § 607 (1982); Iowa Code Ann. § 598.41 (1984); N.Y.—McKinney's Dom.Rel.L. § 241 (1986) (enforcement of visitation by suspending alimony or maintenance payments); N.D. Cent.Code § 14–05–22 (1981); Or.Rev.Stat. § 107.105 (1984); V.T.C.A., Fam.Code § 14.03 (1986); Utah Code Ann.1984, § 30–3–5; W.Va.Code, § 48–2–15 (Supp.1985); Wis.Stat.Ann. § 767.245 (Supp.1986). The Uniform Marriage and Divorce Act § 407, 9A Unif.L.Ann. 207 (1979) provides that the non-custodial parent is entitled to reasonable visitation unless visitation would seriously endanger the child's physical, mental, moral or emotional health.

41. E.g., West's Ann.Cal.Civ.Code § 4600 (Supp.1987); Me.Rev.Stat.Ann. tit. 19, § 752 (Supp.1986); Mich.C.L.A. § 25.312(3) (1984); Pa.Stat. tit. 23, § 1004 (Supp.1986).

42. French v. French, 452 So.2d 647 (Fla.App.1984); Cox v. Moulds, 490 So.2d 866 (Miss.1986); Pettry v. Pettry, 20 Ohio App.3d 350, 486 N.E.2d 213 (1984).

43. Pettry v. Pettry, 20 Ohio App.3d 350, 486 N.E.2d 213 (1984). Visitation, like other custody decisions, is a matter for the trial court's discretion. Frail v. Frail, 54 Ill.App.3d 1013, 370 N.E.2d 303 (1977). Deacon v. Deacon, 207 Neb. 193, 297 N.W.2d 757 (1980) held it was error for the trial court to delegate to a psychologist the authority to determine visitation.

44. Larisa F. v. Michael S., 120 Misc.2d 907, 466 N.Y.S.2d 899 (Fam.Ct.1983). Thus the children's prefer-

ence is an important factor in awarding visitation. Frail v. Frail, 54 Ill.App.3d 1013, 370 N.E.2d 303 (1977).

45. French v. French, 452 So.2d 647 (Fla.App.1984) (child had observed the father engaged in sexual activities with his girl friend); Frail v. Frail, 54 Ill.App.3d 1013, 370 N.E.2d 303 (1977) (children to visit their mother in prison for homicide); Hock v. Hock, 50 Ill.App.3d 583, 8 Ill.Dec. 639, 365 N.E.2d 1025 (1977) (child to visit blind and disabled father); Smith v. Smith, 258 Iowa 1315, 142 N.W.2d 421 (1966) (visitation granted several years after divorce to father who had been in mental hospitals); Cox v. Moulds, 490 So.2d 866 (Miss.1986); M___ L___ B___ v. W___ R___ B___, 457 S.W.2d 465 (Mo.App.1970) (visitation to father in prison); Wilke v. Culp, 196 N.J.Super. 487, 483 A.2d 420 (1984), certification denied 99 N.J. 243, 491 A.2d 728 (1985); Fusco v. Fucso, 186 N.J.Super. 321, 452 A.2d 681 (1982) (visitation to father in prison for murder); Matter of Marriage of A., 41 Or.App. 679, 598 P.2d 1258 (1979) (visitation to father even though this contributed to the child's psychological problems).

Courts are reluctant to impose controls on the place and manner of visitation, preferring to leave the details to the non-custodial parent, subject to reasonable limits in the decree. In re Marriage of Mentry, 142 Cal.App.3d 260, 190 Cal.Rptr. 843 (1983); Cox v. Moulds, 490 So.2d 866 (Miss.1986). But Bergstrom v. Bergstrom, 320 N.W. 2d 119 (N.D.1982) approved the trial court's restriction of a mother's visitation to the United States where she intended to move to Dubai, on the ground of the child's strong desire not to leave the United States.

the exercise of visitation rights than many interstate moves.

When the question relates to the initial award of custody, there may be considerations other than visitation which the courts will take into account, such as the possible loss of the child's American citizenship,[46] the child's preference,[47] and the court's loss of control over the child.[48]

On the award of custody to a parent who intends to leave the state the courts are about evenly divided.[49] It is very difficult to explain the differences in the cases except on the basis of differences in all the relevant factors including this one. Certainly where the evidence shows that the child's interests would best be served by being in the custody of the parent who intends to move, that intention should not prevent the court from giving custody to that parent, even if visitation is thereby made more difficult.[50] The denial of custody solely on the ground of residence is also improper where the move is being made in good faith and out of a desire to improve the material or psychological life of the custodian, so long as the child's interests are not prejudiced thereby.[51] On the other hand it

might well justify a court in denying custody if the parent were intending to move for the purpose of frustrating visitation rights and without countervailing benefits to himself or the child.[52]

Very similar analysis should be applied to the question whether a court ought to enjoin or restrict the movements of a parent who has already been given custody. In fact the two kinds of cases are analogous, since the original award of custody could be made on condition that the custodian not leave the state or the region. Here again the cases take different positions, some sharply restricting the custodian's choice of residence,[53] others, perhaps the majority, permitting the custodian to move where the move is not undertaken for the purpose of breaking contact between the child and the other parent or for insubstantial reasons.[54]

A leading New Jersey case, which may be to some but not a great extent affected by statute,[55] adopts the following standard to resolve the conflict of interests of the custodian and non-custodian:

"* * * we hold that to establish sufficient cause for the removal, the custodial parent

---

46. Cases are collected in Annot., 20 A.L.R.4th 677, 685 (1983).

47. Bergstrom v. Bergstrom, 320 N.W.2d 119 (N.D. 1982).

48. Presutti v. Presutti, 181 Conn. 622, 436 A.2d 299 (1980) (court permits the mother to take the child to Italy, on the ground that there was no indication that Italian courts would not enforce the court's orders).

49. Cases are collected in Annot., 20 A.L.R.4th 677 (1983), so far as they deal with removal to a foreign country. Other cases are cited in Presutti v. Presutti, 181 Conn. 622, 436 A.2d 299 (1980), dealing with the impact of the move on visitation.

50. Presutti v. Presutti, 181 Conn. 622, 436 A.2d 299 (1980); Helentjaris v. Sudano, 194 N.J.Super. 220, 476 A.2d 828 (1984), certification denied 99 N.J. 200, 491 A.2d 699 (1984). Removal of the child from the United States was held not to violate any constitutional rights of the child in Schleiffer v. Meyers, 644 F.2d 656 (7th Cir.1981), cert. denied 454 U.S. 823, 102 S.Ct. 110, 70 L.Ed.2d 96 (1981).

51. Ibid.

52. People ex rel. Ragona v. De Saint-Cyr, 207 Misc. 194, 137 N.Y.S.2d 275 (1955).

53. E.g., Ziegler v. Ziegler, 107 Idaho 527, 691 P.2d 773 (1985) (both parents ordered not to move more than one hundred miles from Coeur d'Alene with the child);

Carlson v. Carlson, 8 Kan.App.2d 564, 661 P.2d 833 (1983) (mother given custody only as long as she resided in McPherson County, Kansas, that being found in the children's best interests); Weiss v. Weiss, 52 N.Y.2d 170, 436 N.Y.S.2d 862, 418 N.E.2d 377 (1981) (mother enjoined from moving to Las Vegas where she sought an opportunity for employment, reversing the trial court's denial of the injunction); Courten v. Courten, 92 A.D.2d 579, 459 N.Y.S.2d 464 (2d Dep't 1983) (relocation will only be permitted on a compelling showing of exceptional circumstances); Bergstrom v. Bergstrom, 320 N.W.2d 119 (N.D.1982); Matter of Marriage of Smith, 290 Or. 567, 624 P.2d 114 (1981) (move turns on the child's best interests). See also D.H. v. State, 723 P.2d 1274 (Alaska 1986).

54. E.g., Presutti v. Presutti, 181 Conn. 622, 436 A.2d 299 (1980); In re Marriage of Brady, 115 Ill.App.3d 521, 71 Ill.Dec. 297, 450 N.E.2d 985 (1983); Johnson v. Johnson, 105 Ill.App.2d 399, 245 N.E.2d 580 (1969); Helentjaris v. Sudano, 194 N.J.Super. 220, 476 A.2d 828 (1984), certification denied 99 N.J. 200, 491 A.2d 699 (1984); Powell v. Powell, 336 N.W.2d 166 (S.D.1983); Whitman v. Whitman, 28 Wis.2d 50, 135 N.W.2d 835 (1965). See also Bodenheimer, Equal Rights, Visitation and the Right to Move, Fam.Advocate, Summer 1978 at 18.

55. N.J.Stat.Ann. § 9:2–2 (1976).

initially must show that there is a real advantage to that parent in the move and that the move is not inimical to the best interests of the children. Removal should not be allowed for a frivolous reason. The advantage, however, need not be a substantial advantage but one based on a sincere and genuine desire of the custodial parent to move and a sensible good faith reason for the move." [56]

This makes it clear that the judgments in removal cases should give substantial consideration to the interests of the custodial parent as well as to those of the child and the non-custodial parent. It is not without importance that if the non-custodial parent should choose to leave the jurisdiction, thereby making contact with the child less frequent or impossible, no court would attempt to enjoin him from doing so.[57] It is also not without significance that most custodial parents are women and that many courts find it much too easy to ignore their employment and other interests when they forbid them to move.[58] Emphasis on fathers' rights over the interests of mothers should long since have been ended.[59] In fact it has been suggested with some force that a custody decree might well include a provision *requiring* fathers to have frequent contact with their children.[60] In any event the quoted sentences are about as sensible, workable and comprehensive a general statement of the principle which ought to guide the courts in these cases as can readily be devised.

When the courts do attempt to restrict the custodian in his choice of a residence, the argument is sometimes made that the restriction constitutes an unconstitutional infringement on the custodian's right to travel. Although the Supreme Court has on occasion announced that some kinds of state or federal regulation are unconstitutional when they have the effect of limiting travel among the states,[61] an injunction against removal of a child from the state, entered for the protection of a parent's right of visitation with his child, can hardly be held within whatever principle these cases may stand for. The state's interest in such a case is certainly "compelling" and the restriction is clearly in furtherance of that interest.[62] The constitutional argument should therefore be rejected, as it has been by the state courts.[63]

 WESTLAW REFERENCES

"best interest" /3 child /s primary +1 care-taker care-giver

a. *The Relative Weight of the Claims of Father and Mother*

"tender year" maternal /2 presumption preference principle doctrine rule /s equal +1 right protection

sy,di(custod! /s sibling sister brother /s split! divid! division separat!)

b. *The Primary Caretaker Presumption*

primary +1 care-taker care-giver /s presum! prefer! /s custod!

c. *The Character and Conduct of the Parents and Their Relationships with Their Children*

di(parent! /s conduct! /s relationship /s child minor /s custod!)

56. Cooper v. Cooper, 99 N.J. 42, 56, 491 A.2d 606, 613 (1984). Similar standards were adopted in In re Marriage of Burgham, 86 Ill.App.3d 341, 408 N.E.2d 37 (1980); Yannas v. Frondistou-Yannas, 395 Mass. 704, 481 N.E.2d 1153 (1985); Henry v. Henry, 119 Mich.App. 319, 326 N.W.2d 497 (1982).

57. Cooper v. Cooper, 99 N.J. 42, 55, 491 A.2d 606, 613 (1984).

58. Weiss v. Weiss, 52 N.Y.2d 170, 436 N.Y.S.2d 862, 418 N.E.2d 377 (1981).

59. Bruch, Parenting At and After Divorce: A Search for New Models, 79 Mich.L.Rev. 708, 724 (1981).

60. Bruch, Making Visitation Work: Dual Parenting Orders, Fam.Advocate, Summer 1978 at 22. Similar results might be achieved by requiring the non-custodial parent who fails to visit on schedule to pay the child care expenses occasioned by his failure.

61. Shapiro v. Thompson, 394 U.S. 618, 89 S.Ct. 1322, 22 L.Ed.2d 600 (1969); Dunn v. Blumstein, 405 U.S. 330, 92 S.Ct. 995, 31 L.Ed.2d 274 (1972); Memorial Hospital v. Maricopa County, 415 U.S. 250, 94 S.Ct. 1076, 39 L.Ed.2d 306 (1974). But see Sosna v. Iowa, 419 U.S. 393, 95 S.Ct. 553, 42 L.Ed.2d 532 (1975) holding constitutional Iowa's durational residence requirement for divorce. For a discussion of these cases see L. Tribe, American Constitutional Law §§ 15–15, 16–8 (1978).

62. See Sosna v. Iowa, 419 U.S. 393, 95 S.Ct. 553, 42 L.Ed.2d 532 (1975).

63. Ziegler v. Ziegler, 107 Idaho 527, 691 P.2d 773 (1985); Carlson v. Carlson, 8 Kan.App.2d 564, 661 P.2d 833 (1983).

di(custod! /s child minor /s homo-sexual! gay lesbian! bisexual!)

f. *Race, Religion and Political or Social Views of the Parents*

find 104 sct 1879

custod! /s child infant minor /s religio! /s unconstitutional! constitution!

h. *Visitation and Removal From the Jurisdiction*

visit! /s non-custod! /s remov! tak** taking leave leaving left /7 jurisdiction! state area /s child infant minor

visit! /s non-custod! /s child infant minor /s danger! endanger!

custod! /p right /5 travel! /s constitution! unconstitutional!

§ 19.5 Custody of Children—Factors in Awarding Custody—Joint Custody

Joint custody has become a significant option for trial courts in custody cases during the years since 1975. This has been due in large part to the influence of fathers' rights advocates,[1] to the large amount of legal and non-legal writing favorable to awards of joint custody,[2] and to the enactment of statutes in more than half of the states encouraging the

courts to award custody jointly to both parents.[3] The statutes vary considerably in form from state to state. A few create a rebuttable presumption in favor of joint custody.[4] Some list in considerable detail the factors which the courts are to take into account in deciding whether joint custody is to be awarded.[5] Some merely state that joint custody is an option for the courts to consider.[6] Some require the parties to submit a detailed plan indicating how joint custody is to operate.[7] Some include a provision requiring mediation when joint custody is contemplated.[8] And some authorize joint custody only when the parties agree to it.[9] It seems clear that under the usual broad custody provision in divorce statutes the courts have the power to award custody jointly even without express authorization.[10] Nevertheless the existence of express statutory authorization has the practical effect of directing the courts' attention to joint custody as a desirable alternative to sole custody. As experience with joint custody statutes accumulates the statutes will undoubtedly be amended in many respects.[11]

---

§ 19.5

1. M. Roman, W. Haddad, The Disposable Parent—The Case for Joint Custody (1978); M. Morgenbesser, N. Nehls, Joint Custody (1981).

2. Folberg, Graham, Joint Custody of Children Following Divorce, 12 U.C.D.L.Rev. 523 (1979) and Bratt, Joint Custody, 67 Ky.L.J. 271 (1978–1979) were relatively early and influential articles. Many other articles are cited in Scott, Derdeyn, Rethinking Joint Custody, 45 Ohio St.L.J. 455, note 2 (1984), most of them advocating a greater use of joint custody. Joint custody was studied along with sole custody by fathers and mothers in D. Luepnitz, Child Custody (1982), concluding that joint custody at its best is superior to single-parent custody at its best.

It should come as no surprise, in view of the tendency of some law review writers to expand constitutional doctrines to and beyond their uttermost limits, to find that there are advocates of a fundamental constitutional right to joint custody except where harmful to the child. Note, Joint Custody as a Fundamental Right, 23 Ariz.L.Rev. 785 (1981); Robinson, Joint Custody: Constitutional Imperatives, 54 U.Cin.L.Rev. 27 (1985). The courts have not gone this far.

J. Goldstein, A. Freud, A. Solnit, Beyond the Best Interests of the Child (2d ed.1979) is a leading work which takes a position incompatible with joint custody.

3. The statutes are cited and abstracted in Folberg, Joint Custody Law—The Second Wave, 23 J.Fam.L. 1, 14 (1984–1985). See also Scott, Derdeyn, Rethinking Joint Custody, 45 Ohio St.L.J. 455, 4472–474 (1984).

4. E.g., West's Ann.Cal.Civ.Code § 4600.5(a) (Supp. 1987) (rebuttable presumption favoring joint custody when the parties have agreed); Idaho Code § 32–717B(4) (1983); L.S.A.—Civ.Code art. 146 A 1 (Supp.1986).

5. E.g., Alaska Stat. § 25.20.090 (1983), listing such factors as the child's preference and needs, the stability of the home environment, the child's education, the advantages of keeping the child in the community, the optimal time for the child to be with each parent, findings of a mediator, and whether there is a history of violence between the parents. See also Ill.—S.H.A. ch. 40, § 602.1 (Supp.1986) directing consideration of the ability of the parents to cooperate for the child's best interests and of the residential circumstances of the parents.

6. E.g., Ill.—S.H.A. ch. 40, § 602.1(b) (Supp.1986).

7. E.g., Colo.Rev.Stat. § 14–10–123.5(3) (Supp.1986); Vt.Stat.Ann. tit. 15, § 666(b) (Supp.1986).

8. E.g., Colo.Rev.Stat. § 14–10–123.5(4) (Supp.1986); Conn.Gen.Stat.Ann. § 46b–56a(c) (1986).

9. E.g., Wis.Stat.Ann. § 767.24(1)(b) (1981).

10. Beck v. Beck, 86 N.J. 480, 432 A.2d 63 (1981). Contra, holding that joint custody may only be ordered where authorized by statute or agreed on by the parties, Lord v. Lord, 443 N.E.2d 847 (Ind.App.1982).

11. See the California experience. Cal.Stats. 1979, c. 204, p. 448; Cal.Stats. 1981, c. 714, § 56.

The statutes, and the cases as well, differ over the definition of joint custody. It is most often defined as meaning only that both parents will share in the decisions concerning the child's care, education, religion, medical treatment and general welfare.[12] This definition says nothing about sharing the physical possession of the child. Other definitions distinguish between joint legal custody and joint physical custody, the former meaning that decisions will be jointly made, the latter that each parent will have the actual care of the child for substantial periods.[13] In some jurisdictions joint custody means both sharing in the decisions and sharing in the care of the child.[14] A well drawn statute should be specific in its definition of terms. It is even more important that the courts preserve clear distinctions in their opinions on joint custody. A court which is only providing for joint decision-making respecting the child should take into account circumstances quite different from those which are relevant to an order by which the parents are to share in the daily physical care of the child. Unfortunately many courts do not seem to recognize the distinction.

Many benefits to both parents and children are alleged to accrue from joint custody, although they are more likely to result from an award of joint physical custody than from an award limited to joint legal custody. Joint custody is said to enable both parents to share in the pleasures and responsibilities of child-rearing and, by preserving the contacts between both parents and their child, to give the child assurance that he is still cherished by both parents, avoiding the traumatic sense of loss experienced by the child who is in the custody of one parent and who seldom sees the other parent.[15] The psychological tie between both parents and child remains a reality and a source of emotional stability to both. There may also be practical benefits in that one parent does not have the sole responsibility for daily care, freeing her for work outside the home or for other activities foreclosed to the sole custodian of a small child.[16] Joint custody may also reduce the hostility which arises between the parents when one of them has sole custody and the other only the right to visit the child, by recognizing that both have rights which are entitled to respect, and by putting pressure on the parents to cooperate for the good of their child.[17]

Critics of joint custody emphasize the child's need for stability and argue that joint custody deprives him of it.[18] They point out

12. E.g., Colo.Rev.Stat. § 14–10–123.5(1) (Supp.1986); Wis.Stat.Ann. § 767.24 (1981); Bazant v. Bazant, 80 A.D.2d 310, 439 N.Y.S.2d 521 (4th Dep't 1981). The Florida statute speaks of "shared parental responsibility". West's Fla.Stat.Ann. § 61.13(2)(a) (1985). Illinois defines joint custody as custody determined pursuant to a joint parenting agreement or joint parenting order, which seems to mean that joint custody is whatever the parties or the court says it is. Ill.—S.H.A. ch. 40, § 602.1(b) (Supp.1986).

13. West's Ann.Cal.Civ.Code § 4600.5 (Supp.1986) (joint custody includes both joint legal custody and joint physical custody); Idaho Code § 32–717B (1983); Beck v. Beck, 86 N.J. 480, 432 A.2d 63 (1981).

14. Conn.Gen.Stat.Ann. § 46b–56a (1986); Idaho Code § 32–717B (1983); In re Marriage of Lampton, 704 P.2d 847 (Colo.1985); In re Marriage of Burham, 283 N.W.2d 269 (Iowa 1979); Strosnider v. Strosnider, 101 N.M. 639, 686 P.2d 981 (App.1984).

15. Beck v. Beck, 86 N.J. 480, 432 A.2d 63 (1981); Steinman, Joint Custody: What We Know, What We Have Yet to Learn, and the Judicial and Legislative Implications, 16 U.C.D.L.Rev. 739, 746 (1983); Scott, Derdeyn, Rethinking Joint Custody, 45 Ohio St.L.J. 455, 484 (1984), citing other articles.

16. D. Luepnitz, Child Custody 42–45 (1982).

17. Nestor, Developing Cooperation Between Hostile Parents at Divorce, 16 U.C.D.L.Rev. 771 (1983). There seems to be disagreement among the experts on whether joint custody awards, by continuing both parents' relationship with the child, result in more frequent compliance with child support obligations. Suggesting that they have this effect: Kelly, Further Observations on Joint Custody, 16 U.C.D.L.Rev. 762, 764 (1983). Stating that joint custody does not affect compliance with child support orders: L. Weitzman, The Divorce Revolution 255 (1985).

18. Steinman, Joint Custody: What We Know, What We Have Yet To Learn, and the Judicial and Legislative Implications, 16 U.C.D.L.Rev. 739, 747–748 (1983). J. Goldstein, A. Freud, A. Solnit, Beyond the Best Interest of the Child 38 (2d ed.1979) is perhaps the strongest expression of the need for stability in the child's life and takes the position not only that the child should be in the custody of one parent, but that that parent should have the sole right to decide whether and to what extent the child visits the non-custodial parent.

For a vigorous criticism of the social science studies on joint custody, see Clingempeel, Repucci, Joint Custody After Divorce: Major Issues and Goals for Research, 91 Psychology Bull. 102, 124 (1982).

the practical difficulties in arranging joint custody when the parents live at a distance from each other. They assert that when the mother has been the child's primary caretaker the demand by the father for joint custody, encouraged by statutory provisions in many states, may be used as a form of extortion, forcing her to reduce her claims for maintenance or child support out of fear that the child will be partially lost to her.[19] Where the parents do not have a strong commitment to make joint custody work, the arrangement may continue the conflicts which led to the divorce, causing the child intense distress, anxiety, a conflict in his loyalties and impairing his ability to adjust to the divorce.[20]

Several studies of the nature and effect of joint custody have been made by social scientists.[21] They have generally reached the conclusion that joint custody is superior to sole custody in its consequences for children,[22] but they have been based on small samples, have not precisely defined what types of joint custody are involved, have not compared joint custody orders arrived at by agreement with those imposed by the courts, and have usually not compared the effects of joint custody with matched samples of parents having sole custody orders.[23] Further research may remedy some of these deficiencies, but research of this kind is extraordinarily difficult.[24] Joint cus-

tody does offer advantages over sole custody when the parents not only agree to joint physical custody but share a sincere commitment to cooperate in arranging the child's residential changes, to communicate with each other concerning the child's care, and to meet future developments with consideration for each other and for the child. Cases which meet these requirements are undoubtedly not numerous. Cases which do not meet them are not likely to justify the enthusiasm which joint custody has evoked in the law reviews.[25] Decrees awarding only joint legal custody achieve few of the values usually attributed to joint custody. Their effect is generally to leave the mother in her traditional role as primary caretaker but to remove from her the authority to make decisions concerning the child which the custodian normally has authority to make. The benefits to the child from this form of decree seem minimal.

The courts, when they come to apply the statutes to specific claims of joint custody, are usually cautious. A rough consensus has developed that where the parents are so antagonistic or hostile toward each other that cooperation in carrying out a joint custody decree is unlikely, such a decree should not be granted.[26] In fact some courts would deny joint custody whenever the parties do not agree to

---

19. L. Weitzman, The Divorce Revolution 246–247 (1985); Scott, Derdeny, Rethinking Joint Custody, 45 Ohio St.L.J. 455, 479 (1984). This tendency of joint custody statutes may be aggravated where there is a preference favoring joint custody or when the statute contains a "friendly parent" provision, by which the court is required to take account of a parent's willingness to preserve contact between the child and the other parent in awarding custody. See section 19.4, supra, at note 41.

20. L. Weitzman, The Divorce Revolution 251–253 (1985); Scott, Derdeyn, Rethinking Joint Custody, 45 Ohio St.L.J. 455, 486 (1984).

21. Chambers, Rethinking the Substantive Rules for Custody Disputes in Divorce, 83 Mich.L.Rev. 477, 551–552, note 84 (1984) contains an exhaustive list of these studies.

22. E.g., D. Luepnitz, Child Custody 46–48 (1982). Some of the cases described in this study involved what could be called custody plus visitation rather than joint physical custody. Of course as visitation is extended it comes to resemble joint physical custody more closely.

23. The existing studies are reviewed critically in Chambers, Rethinking the Substantive Rules for Custody Disputes in Divorce, 83 Mich.L.Rev. 477, 550–558 (1984).

24. Scott, Derdeyn, Rethinking Joint Custody, 45 Ohio St.L.J. 455, 484–498 (1984) describes some of the difficulties.

25. D. Luepnitz, Child Custody 48–52 (1982) describes the adverse effect upon children occurring when joint custody is imposed by a court without the agreement or against the consent of the parents.

26. Davis v. Davis, 63 Ill.App.3d 465, 20 Ill.Dec. 437, 380 N.E.2d 415 (1978); In re Marriage of Weidner, 338 N.W.2d 351 (Iowa 1983); Kline v. Kline, 686 S.W.2d 13 (Mo.App.1984); In re Custody and Support of B.T.S., ___ Mont. ___, 712 P.2d 1298 (1986); Mastropole v. Mastropole, 181 N.J.Super. 130, 436 A.2d 955 (1981); Braiman v. Braiman, 44 N.Y.2d 584, 407 N.Y.S.2d 449, 378 N.E.2d 1019 (1978); Robinson v. Robinson, 111 A.D.2d 316, 489 N.Y.S.2d 301 (2d Dep't 1985), appeal dismissed 66 N.Y.2d 613, 498 N.Y.S.2d 1030, 489 N.E.2d 258 (1985); Sooy v. Sooy, 101 A.D.2d 287, 475 N.Y.S.2d 920 (3d Dep't 1984), affirmed 64 N.Y.2d 946, 488 N.Y.S.2d 637, 477 N.E.2d

it.[27] Several cases have adopted general standards to guide them in determining what circumstances should be considered in determining whether to grant or deny joint custody. These include such factors as the fitness of both parents, parental agreement or disagreement on joint custody, their ability to communicate with each other and to cooperate respecting the child's welfare, their geographical proximity, the similarity or dissimilarity in the two homes and surroundings, the possible harm to the child's psychological or emotional development from a joint custody award, the child's wishes, and the parents' ability to meet the physical demands of joint custody.[28] The court may also consider whether one of the parents has been the child's primary caretaker in the past.[29]

Most courts approve claims for joint custody when both parents agree that they should be granted,[30] although even then joint custody

may be denied if the parents' circumstances do not offer stability and good care for the children.[31] A well known New Jersey case has found an award of joint physical and legal custody to be within a trial court's discretion notwithstanding that neither parent requested it and both children opposed it.[32] The court held that the award was supported by the testimony of two psychologists and a psychiatric social worker which, for the most part, merely repeated the current arguments in favor of joint custody. Other cases have also awarded joint custody over the objections of one or both of the parents.[33] There is evidence in the studies of joint custody that compulsory awards of this kind are often harmful to the children involved.[34] They may be intended to force the parents to compromise their custody conflicts but if so, the compromise is no more likely to be successful than strict divorce laws were successful in

1091 (1985); Dodd v. Dodd, 93 Misc.2d 641, 403 N.Y.S.2d 401 (1978); Matter of Marriage of Handy, 44 Or.App. 225, 605 P.2d 738 (1980). A trial court's decree that the family home be maintained after the divorce as the home of the children, with the parents to alternate living in the home with the children each month, was held unworkable in Fuhrman v. Fuhrman, 254 N.W.2d 97 (N.D.1977).

27. In re Marriage of Neal, 92 Cal.App.3d 834, 155 Cal.Rptr. 157 (1979); In re Marriage of Lampton, 704 P.2d 847 (Colo.1985). But see Colo.Rev.Stat. § 14–10–124 (Supp.1987).

Cases which take the position that joint custody is disfavored rather than favored include In re Marriage of Manuele, 107 Ill.App.3d 1090, 438 N.E.2d 691 (1982); Trimble v. Trimble, 218 Neb. 118, 352 N.W.2d 599 (1984); Starkeson v. Starkeson, 119 N.H. 78, 397 A.2d 1043 (1979); Ponder v. Rice, 479 S.W.2d 90 (Tex.Civ.App.1972); Lumbra v. Lumbra, 136 Vt. 529, 394 A.2d 1139 (1978).

28. In re Marriage of Burham, 283 N.W.2d 269 (Iowa 1979); Beck v. Beck, 86 N.J. 480, 432 A.2d 63 (1981); In re Wesley J. K., 299 Pa.Super. 504, 445 A.2d 1243 (1982).

29. In re Marriage of Hickey, 386 N.W.2d 141 (Iowa App.1986).

Many cases on joint custody are collected in Annot., 17 A.L.R.4th 1013 (1982).

30. McClain v. McClain, 716 P.2d 381 (Alaska 1986) (joint custody awarded though the father renounced his agreement); Smith v. Smith, 307 Pa.Super. 544, 453 A.2d 1020 (1982) (joint custody awarded after agreement even when the parents lived one hundred and twenty miles apart).

31. Elebash v. Elebash, 450 So.2d 1268 (Fla.App.1984); In re Marriage of Nalivka, ___ Mont. ___, 720 P.2d 683 (1986). Timm v. Timm, 195 Conn. 202, 487 A.2d 191 (1985) held that a purported agreement for joint custody

should be disregarded when it did not represent a meeting of the parties' minds.

32. Beck v. Beck, 86 N.J. 480, 432 A.2d 63 (1981).

33. In re Marriage of Wood, 141 Cal.App.3d 671, 190 Cal.Rptr. 469 (1983) (under a statute providing for a preference for joint custody); In re Marriage of Behn, 385 N.W.2d 540 (Iowa 1986) (joint physical custody, the mother having custody during the school year, the father in the summer vacations, though the mother lived in the state of Washington and the father in Iowa); In re Marriage of Ertmann, 376 N.W.2d 918 (Iowa App.1985) (joint legal custody though the parents had difficulty in communicating and the mother opposed joint custody); In re Marriage of Short, 373 N.W.2d 158 (Iowa App.1985) (joint legal custody, physical custody to the father); In re Marriage of Fish, 350 N.W.2d 226 (Iowa App.1984) (joint legal custody, physical to the mother); In re Marriage of Estlund, 344 N.W.2d 276 (Iowa App.1983) (joint legal custody, physical custody to the mother); Martinez v. Martinez, 470 So.2d 374 (La.App.1985), writ denied 472 So.2d 923 (La.1985) (joint custody ordered although the trial court had ordered sole custody, under a statute giving preference to joint custody); Bazant v. Bazant, 80 A.D.2d 310, 439 N.Y.S.2d 521 (4th Dep't 1981) (joint legal custody, physical custody to the mother during the school year, with physical custody to the father during the summer and school holidays, although the mother lived in Saskatchewan and the father in Buffalo, New York); Odette v. Odette, 91 Misc.2d 792, 399 N.Y.S.2d 93 (Fam. Ct.1977) (joint legal custody, physical custody divided, to the father during the school year, to the mother during vacations).

34. See note 25, supra, and Chambers, Rethinking the Substantive Rules for Custody Disputes in Divorce, 83 Mich.L.Rev. 477, 556 (1984).

forcing spouses to get along with each other in the first half of this century.

Under the preference type of statute found in a few states, the parent opposing joint custody has the burden of proof.[35]

A major defect of joint custody arises out of the propensity of Americans to change residences. Joint physical custody may become unworkable if one of the parents chooses to live at a distance from the other, and even joint legal custody may become so difficult that it is no longer feasible. When this occurs the courts must necessarily award sole physical custody to one parent or the other, and may also have to terminate the provision for joint decision-making concerning the child. This may be difficult or impossible in those states which have the rigid restrictions on modification of custody decrees modeled on the Uniform Marriage and Divorce Act.[36] This may require proof that the existing custody award has seriously endangered the health of the child.[37] If joint custody is to be at all workable, statutes and case law must permit modification of joint legal or physical custody decrees where the circumstances have changed so that the child's interests dictate modification.[38] If modification is available under the applicable statute, it should not be used to punish either parent for moving, so long as the move is reasonable in view of that parent's circumstances.[39] Unfortunately some of the cases do not accept this view, seeming to think that there is something reprehensible in moving, at least where it is the child's mother who moves.[40]

One of the risks of joint legal custody is that the parties will be unable to agree on important decisions concerning the child's education or care. If the joint custody is based upon the parties' separation agreement, that agreement might contain a provision for the resolution of disagreements, such as mediation or submission of the question to arbitration, although the latter solution may not be satisfactory.[41] Whatever solution is agreed upon, the parties' disagreement may be so fundamental that it cannot be resolved, and the question then is, what should the courts do to protect the child's interests and end the conflict? There are at least three possible answers to this question, with some authority supporting each answer. The first possibility is that the court might delay action, in the hope that the parents would eventually come to some agreement, ultimately perhaps intending to modify the decree from awarding

---

35. Owen v. Gallien, 477 So.2d 1240 (La.App.1985).

36. Uniform Marriage and Divorce Act, § 409, 9A Unif.L.Ann. 211 (1979) provides that within two years a custody decree may only be modified on the ground that the child's environment seriously endangers his health. After two years the decree may be modified if the parties agree, or if the child has been integrated into the family of the non-custodial parent, or if the child's environment seriously endangers his health and the harm caused by the change is outweighed by its advantages. For a discussion of modification of custody decrees, see section 19.9, infra.

37. In re Marriage of Gahm, ___ Mont. ___, 722 P.2d 1138 (1986).

38. See Colo.Rev.Stat. § 14–10–131.5 (Supp.1986), which takes essentially this position, imposing the burden of proof on the party seeking modification. Cases taking this position include Sanborn v. Sanborn, 123 N.H. 740, 465 A.2d 888 (1983); Andrews v. Andrews, 74 A.D.2d 546, 425 N.Y.S.2d 120 (1st Dep't 1980), motion to dismiss appeal denied 50 N.Y.2d 841, 430 N.Y.S.2d 52, 407 N.E.2d 1348 (1980), affirmed 52 N.Y.2d 787, 439 N.Y.S.2d 918, 422 N.E.2d 578 (1981); Matter of Marriage of Bohn, 43 Or.App. 561, 603 P.2d 781 (1979), modified on other grounds 288 Or. 697, 607 P.2d 1375 (1980).

39. See Yannas v. Frondistou-Yannas, 395 Mass. 704, 481 N.E.2d 1153 (1985), awarding joint legal custody, physical custody to the mother, and permitting her to remove the children to Greece.

40. E.g. Yeo v. Cornaire, 91 A.D.2d 1153, 458 N.Y.S.2d 743 (3d Dep't 1983), affirmed 59 N.Y.2d 875, 466 N.Y.S.2d 315, 453 N.E.2d 544 (1983), in which the mother remarried and moved with her new husband from New York to California, whereupon the New York court modified the custody order, changing physical custody from mother to father but retaining the provision for joint legal custody. In In re Marriage of Stafford, 386 N.W.2d 118 (Iowa App. 1986) the father remarried and secretly moved from Iowa to the state of Washington, causing the mother to take them back to Iowa. Physical custody was retained in the father, joint legal custody was retained, but the mother's visitation rights were limited.

For a further discussion of the issues raised by removal of a parent from the jurisdiction, see section 19.4, supra.

41. For a discussion of the problems involved in arbitration of custody disputes, see section 14.8, supra.

joint custody to awarding sole custody.[42] The sole custodian would then have the right to decide the disputed question, as in other sole custody cases.[43] The second possibility is that the court might itself decide the question in disagreement, ordering the child to be sent to the parochial school or the public school for example, in accordance with what the court thought the child's best interests indicated.[44] The difficulty with this course of action is that it is expensive of court time, does not solve the underlying problem of parental non-cooperation, and involves the court in overseeing the details of family life, an activity for which courts generally do not have the qualifications. The third possibility is for the court to let the question be decided by the parent having physical custody, provided of course that joint physical custody has not been awarded.[45] If the parents have joint physical custody as well as joint legal custody, the only solution to the conflict is to terminate joint custody and order some form of sole custody, since the parents have shown by their disagreement that they are unable to make the joint custody decree work successfully.

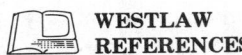

**WESTLAW
REFERENCES**

di(presum! prefer! /s joint! /2 custod! /s rebut!)

joint! /2 custod! /s award! grant*** /s factor element criterion

§ 19.6 Custody of Children—Factors in Awarding Custody—Dispute Between a Parent and a Non-parent [1]

In the two immediately preceding sections we were concerned with the factors to be considered by the courts when a child's natural parents are contending for his custody. In this section those same factors may still be relevant, but a new element is injected into the dispute by virtue of the fact that one of the parties is a person other than the child's natural parent.[2] The question which this presents is whether or to what extent the natural parent's claim to custody is to be preferred over that of the non-parent. This question should be dealt with in some fashion before the further issue of the child's best interests may be considered, although some courts are understandably reluctant or unable to treat it separately from the child's interests.[3] It arises not only as a consequence of divorce, but in guardianship proceedings,[4] in dependency and neglect proceedings,[5] in proceedings leading to adoption,[6] and the child involved may be born in or out of wedlock.[7]

---

42. Strosnider v. Strosnider, 101 N.M. 639, 686 P.2d 981 (App.1984). Where the parties disagreed over visitation, the court apparently found that the disagreement was the fault of the mother who had physical custody and punished her by ordering physical custody transferred to the father, retaining joint legal custody. Hindsley v. Hindsley, 145 Ariz. 428, 701 P.2d 1236 (App.1985).

43. The powers of the sole custodian are discussed in section 19.4, supra.

44. Burchell v. Burchell, 684 S.W.2d 296 (Ky.App. 1984) (semble); Asch v. Asch, 164 N.J.Super. 499, 397 A.2d 352 (1978).

45. Griffin v. Griffin, 699 P.2d 407 (Colo.1985).

§ 19.6

1. "Non-parent" as used in this section may include friends, relatives, grandparents, stepparents or child-care agencies, or in other words any person or agency other than the child's natural parent. As in other contexts "custody" may be an ill defined term when used by some courts. Trompeter v. Trompeter, 218 Kan. 535, 545 P.2d 297 (1976). For an attempt at defining custody see section 19.2, supra.

2. Brief mention was given to the rare circumstances in which a court, in a custody dispute between natural

parents, finds both unsuitable as custodians and awards custody to a third person, in section 19.4, supra, at note 31. Those cases are analytically analogous to the cases discussed in this section.

3. E.g., Bresnock v. Bresnock, 346 Pa.Super. 563, 500 A.2d 91 (1985).

4. In re Guardianship of Pankey, 38 Cal.App.3d 919, 113 Cal.Rptr. 858 (1974); Evans v. Santoro, 6 Conn.App. 707, 507 A.2d 1007 (1986); Styck v. Karnes, 462 N.E.2d 1327 (Ind.App.1984); Matter of Guardianship of Sams, 256 N.W.2d 570 (Iowa 1977); Custody of a Minor, 389 (Mass. 755, 452 N.E.2d 483 (1983); Hosey v. Myers, 240 So.2d 252 (Miss.1970); Matter of Guardianship of J.R.G., —— Mont. ——, 708 P.2d 263 (1985); In re Guardianship of Wonderly, 67 Ohio St.2d 178, 423 N.E.2d 420 (1981).

5. In Interest of A. B., 444 So.2d 981 (Fla.App.1983); Matter of Joseph, 416 N.E.2d 857 (Ind.App.1981).

6. In re Jennings, 68 Ill.2d 125, 11 Ill.Dec. 256, 368 N.E.2d 864 (1977).

7. State ex rel. Acton v. Flowers, 154 W.Va. 209, 174 S.E.2d 742 (1970).

Since all these kinds of proceedings raise this one question, they are all included in this section even though most of the cases do arise out of the destruction of the family caused by divorce. Analogous questions arise when there is a proceeding for the involuntary termination of parental rights, but the discussion of these cases is postponed to a later section by reason of their relation to the law of adoption.[8]

As a preliminary matter, before the court can decide on the merits of custody, there must be a determination that the non-parent has standing to bring the custody proceeding or to intervene in it. This turns initially on whatever local statute there may be governing the proceeding.[9] The provisions of the statutes governing divorce may well differ from those governing guardianship or dependency, so that the form of the proceeding may control whether the non-parent may have his claim heard.[10] Although it may not be wise to permit persons having no prior relationships to the child to raise issues concerning his custody,[11] there is also a danger that the

statutes may exclude from standing persons who have a prior relationship or a legitimate interest in the child's welfare.[12] Those cases which do not turn on statutory provisions attempt to effectuate this distinction with more or less success.[13]

As has been shown in the immediately preceding sections,[14] when custody is disputed between the natural parents of a child, the child's welfare is the sole factor on which the court makes its decision. Odd as it may seem, when the custody dispute arises between a parent and a non-parent, the outcome no longer turns exclusively on the child's interests but instead the courts give substantial, sometimes decisive, weight to the interests of the natural parent. A partial explanation for this sharp change in emphasis is the development in recent years of the doctrine that a natural parent has a constitutional right to the custody of his child, although the "parental right" doctrine antedated those cases which based it on the Constitution.[15] There were earlier statements of the constitutional doctrine [16] but the most explicit reliance upon

8. Termination of parental rights is discussed in section 20.6, infra. In a particular case the questions of custody and of termination of parental rights may be inextricably mingled. E.g., In re J. and J. W., 134 Vt. 480, 365 A.2d 521 (1976). See also Bandel v. Bandel, 211 Kan. 672, 508 P.2d 487 (1973), holding that an award of permanent custody to a non-custodian does not sever parental rights, so that the custodian may not adopt the child without another finding of unfitness of the parent.

9. In re Custody of Peterson, 112 Ill.2d 48, 96 Ill.Dec. 690, 491 N.E.2d 1150 (1986); In re Jennings, 68 Ill.2d 125, 11 Ill.Dec. 256, 368 N.E.2d 864 (1977); In re Custody of Menconi, 117 Ill.App.3d 394, 73 Ill.Dec. 10, 453 N.E.2d 835 (1983); Henderson v. Henderson, 174 Mont. 1, 568 P.2d 177 (1977).

10. Compare In re Custody of Peterson, 112 Ill.2d 48, 96 Ill.Dec. 690, 491 N.E.2d 1150 (1986) with In re Jennings, 68 Ill.2d 125, 11 Ill.Dec. 256, 368 N.E.2d 864 (1977) and with Matter of Welfare of E. G. and K. B., 268 N.W.2d 420 (Minn.1978).

11. Ruppel v. Lesner, 421 Mich. 559, 364 N.W.2d 665 (1984) (grandparents have no standing to sue for custody when the parents are living together and caring for the child).

12. See the Uniform Marriage and Divorce Act § 401(d), 9A Unif.L.Ann. 194 (1979), permitting a child custody proceeding to be commenced by a non-parent only if the child is not in the custody of his parent. Welfare of E. G. and K. B., 268 N.W.2d 420 (Minn.1978) refused to permit foster parents to intervene in a neglect

proceeding although they had had the child in their care for ten years.

13. R. A. D. v. M. E. Z., 414 A.2d 211 (Del.Super.1980) (maternal grandmother has standing); Harper v. Ballensinger, 226 Ga. 828, 177 S.E.2d 693 (1970) (child's sister has standing); Freeman v. Chaplic, 388 Mass. 398, 446 N.E.2d 1369 (1983) (material stepgrandmother has standing); Ruppel v. Lesner, 421 Mich. 559, 364 N.W.2d 665 (1984) (maternal grandparents do not have standing where the child is living with his parents, no divorce is pending, and there has been no finding of parental unfitness in an appropriate proceeding); J. L. E. v. D. J. E., 675 S.W.2d 456 (Mo.App.1984) (grandparents who already had visitation rights may intervene when father seeks to modify an award of custody to the mother); Pierce v. Pierce, 198 Mont. 255, 645 P.2d 1353 (1982) (man claiming equitable adoption has no standing); In re Schmidt, 25 Ohio St.3d 331, 496 N.E.2d 952 (1986) (grandparents having visitation rights had no standing to intervene in neglect proceeding); In re Marriage of Allen, 28 Wash. App. 637, 626 P.2d 16 (1981) (stepmother has standing).

14. See Sections 19.4 and 19.5, supra.

15. A leading case is Roche v. Roche, 25 Cal.2d 141, 152 P.2d 999 (1944), 33 Cal.L.Rev. 306 (1945), 19 So.Cal.L. Rev. 72 (1945), citing other cases, and applying the "parental right" doctrine.

16. Prince v. Commonwealth of Massachusetts, 321 U.S. 158, 166, 64 S.Ct. 438, 442, 88 L.Ed. 645 (1944), rehearing denied 321 U.S. 804, 64 S.Ct. 784, 88 L.Ed. 1090 (1944): "It is cardinal with us that the custody, care and

it occurs in Stanley v. Illinois [17] and the cases which followed it.[18] This right of a parent may even be characterized as a "fundamental right", which normally means that it may only be overcome where necessary to effectuate a "compelling state interest." [19] In this context as in many others the force or extent of this "right" cannot be precisely defined, nor can one be sure how it will be applied in specific cases.[20] Nor has the Supreme Court given us an adequate explanation of just why this "right" is superior to the child's interest in having the courts focus their attention exclusively upon his welfare. We do know, however, that this "right" is not absolute, that under some circumstances the custody of a child will be awarded to a person not a parent over the objections of the parent.[21] In fact so many cases continue to be decided

without reliance upon the constitutional doctrine that it is an open question whether that doctrine adds anything of substance to the long-standing principle of parental right.[22] Unfortunately one can say that the injection of a vague constitutional "right" into these difficult cases may often interfere with the achievement of a sensible, workable custody disposition. The fact is that these are not "rights" in any proper sense of the word. They are claims or interests. Calling them rights gives them unwarranted status and creates unnecessary confusion.

This is not to say that the natural parent's interests should be ignored. In our legal system there is a firmly held belief that with all their faults and mistakes parents will generally be more successful in caring for their

---

nurture of the child reside first in the parents, whose primary function and freedom include preparation for obligations the state can neither supply nor hinder." This case of course had nothing to do with custody disputes, and in fact the child was in the custody of her aunt, not a parent. The case held that Massachusetts could convict the aunt of violating a state statute prohibiting child labor without infringing the aunt's federal constitutional rights.

17. 405 U.S. 645, 92 S.Ct. 1208, 31 L.Ed.2d 551 (1972). The case held that an Illinois statute violated the Due Process Clause when it authorized the termination of the parental rights of the father of an illegitimate child without a determination of his unfitness. Among other things, the Court said: "The private interest here, that of a man in the children he has sired and raised, undeniably warrants deference and, absent a powerful countervailing interest, protection." 405 U.S. at 651, 92 S.Ct. at 1212. And at 405 U.S. 652, 92 S.Ct. at 1213: "These authorities make it clear that, at the least, Stanley's interest in retaining custody of his children is cognizable and substantial."

18. Quilloin v. Walcott, 434 U.S. 246, 98 S.Ct. 549, 54 L.Ed.2d 511 (1978), rehearing denied 435 U.S. 918, 98 S.Ct. 1477, 55 L.Ed.2d 511 (1978); Caban v. Mohammed, 441 U.S. 380, 99 S.Ct. 1760, 60 L.Ed.2d 297 (1979). These cases are discussed in more detail in section 20.2, infra.

Cases which apply this constitutional doctrine to custody conflicts between parents and non-parents include Lossman v. Pekarske, 707 F.2d 288 (7th Cir.1983) (suggesting there may be a conflict between the parent's constitutional liberty and that of the child); Ruffalo by Ruffalo v. Civiletti, 702 F.2d 710 (8th Cir.1983), on remand 565 F.Supp. 34 (W.D.Mo. 1983) (mother's constitutional right to contact with her son vindicated as against the federal government's witness protection program); Duchesne v. Sugarman, 566 F.2d 817 (2d Cir.1977) (mother deprived of due process when her children were taken by the welfare department without a hearing followed by their refusal to return them); Custody of a Minor, 389

Mass. 755, 452 N.E.2d 483 (1983) (parents have a "natural right" to custody of their children); In re Guardianship of Doney, 174 Mont. 282, 570 P.2d 575 (1977) (children may not be taken from the custody of a natural parent without proof of dependency, abuse or neglect, and this is constitutionally required); McBride v. Magnuson, 282 Or. 433, 578 P.2d 1259 (1978).

19. Franz v. United States, 707 F.2d 582 (D.C.Cir. 1983); Sheppard v. Sheppard, 230 Kan. 146, 630 P.2d 1121 (1981), cert. denied 455 U.S. 919, 102 S.Ct. 1274, 71 L.Ed.2d 459 (1982); Chapman v. Perera, 41 Wash.App. 444, 704 P.2d 1224 (1985). Doe v. Staples, 717 F.2d 953 (6th Cir.1983), cert. denied 465 U.S. 1033, 104 S.Ct. 1301, 79 L.Ed.2d 701 (1984) held that the relationship of mother and child is not of a kind to invoke the rule of strict scrutiny or compelling state interest, appearing to modify in that respect Doe v. Staples, 706 F.2d 985 (6th Cir.1983), cert. 465 U.S. 1033, 104 S.Ct. 1301, 79 L.Ed.2d 701 (1984).

20. E.g., Hao Thi Popp v. Lucas, 182 Conn. 545, 438 A.2d 755 (1980) (parent's constitutional right must yield when the child's welfare requires custody to be given to the non-parent); Custody of a Minor, 377 Mass. 876, 389 N.E.2d 68 (1979) (state may remove child from parental custody only on a showing of unfitness of the parents, citing Stanley v. Illinois, supra, note 17); Ellerbe v. Hooks, 490 Pa. 363, 416 A.2d 512 (1980) (parents have a prima facie right to custody which may be forfeited if the child's interests lie in being in the custody of the non-parent).

21. Sorentino v. Family & Children's Society of Elizabeth, 74 N.J. 313, 378 A.2d 18 (1977), affirmed 77 N.J. 483, 391 A.2d 497 (1978).

22. The analysis in the following cases places about equal emphasis on both the constitutional and the non-constitutional arguments. Hao Thi Popp v. Lucas, 182 Conn. 545, 438 A.2d 755 (1980); Custody of a Minor, 377 Mass. 876, 389 N.E.2d 68 (1979); Sorentino v. Family & Children's Society of Elizabeth, 74 N.J. 313, 378 A.2d 18 (1977), affirmed 77 N.J. 483, 391 A.2d 497 (1978).

children than strangers or agencies of the state.[23] There is also a conviction that the profound and elemental emotional ties between parent and child should be respected by the state even though the child might have greater material advantages and perhaps might receive better care in the custody of someone else.[24]

When the courts attempt to translate these assumptions into legal standards, agreement breaks down and diversity prevails. The diversity is increased by the familiar principle that the award of custody is largely within the trial court's discretion, to be reversed only when abuse of that discretion appears,[25] a principle which sharply affects both the general language and the application of that language to appellate opinions. There is also the further principle, not open to dispute, that whatever is done by the trial court must only be done after the parent has been afforded full due process in the form of notice and an opportunity to be heard.[26]

These assumptions about the importance of the parent-child relationship have led many courts to adopt what is essentially a rule, that as between a parent and a non-parent, the parent may only be deprived of the custody of his child if he is shown to be unfit to perform the duties that custody imposes.[27] This is often referred to as the parental right theory.[28] Although there is some flexibility in applying the rule of unfitness to individual states of fact, it generally requires proof of such serious parental inadequacy as child neglect,[29] child abuse,[30] parental inability to care for the child,[31] or conditions such that the child will suffer severe physical or emotional harm if left in the care of the parent.[32] Abandonment of the child is the equivalent of unfitness.[33] A voluntary relinquishment of the child may also be the basis for an award of custody to the non-parent.[34] Unfitness is a rigorous standard, one which goes beyond a mere determination of the child's best inter-

23. In re Guardianship of Smith, 42 Cal.2d 91, 94, 265 P.2d 888, 891 (1954) (concurring opinion).

24. State ex rel. Nelson v. Whaley, 246 Minn. 535, 75 N.W.2d 786 (1956).

25. Hao Thi Popp v. Lucas, 182 Conn. 545, 438 A.2d 755 (1980); Montgomery County Department of Social Services v. Sanders, 38 Md.App. 406, 381 A.2d 1154 (1977); Phillips v. Choplin, 65 N.C.App. 506, 309 S.E.2d 716 (1983); Chapman v. Perera, 41 Wash.App. 444, 704 P.2d 1224 (1985).

26. Franz v. United States, 707 F.2d 582 (D.C.Cir. 1983).

27. Turner v. Pannick, 540 P.2d 1051 (Alaska 1975); Nolan v. Nolan, 240 Ark. 579, 401 S.W.2d 13 (1966); Roche v. Roche, 25 Cal.2d 141, 152 P.2d 999 (1944), 33 Cal.L.Rev. 306 (1945), 19 So.Cal.L.Rev. 72 (1945); Kersey v. State, 124 So.2d 726 (Fla.App.1960); Blackburn v. Blackburn, 249 Ga. 689, 292 S.E.2d 821 (1982); Bramblet v. Cox, 461 S.W.2d 349 (Ky.1970); State in Interest of Toler, 261 So.2d 659 (La.App.1972); Freeman v. Chaplic, 388 Mass. 398, 446 N.E.2d 1369 (1983); Matter of Guardianship of Doney, 174 Mont. 282, 570 P.2d 575 (1977); Nielsen v. Nielsen, 207 Neb. 141, 296 N.W.2d 483 (1980); Matter of D. T., 200 N.J.Super. 171, 491 A.2d 7 (1985); Masitto v. Masitto, 22 Ohio St.3d 63, 488 N.E.2d 857 (1986); Engelhardt v. Bergeron, 113 R.I. 50, 317 A.2d 877 (1974); Bailes v. Sours, 231 Va. 96, 340 S.E.2d 824 (1986) (semble); Rozas v. Rozas, ___ W.Va. ___, 342 S.E.2d 201 (1986); Barstad v. Frazier, 118 Wis.2d 549, 348 N.W.2d 479 (1984). A statute which authorized the court to award custody to a non-parent solely on the ground that this would serve the child's best interests was held to violate the Due Process Clause of the United States

Constitution because it infringed the fundamental right of the parent without requiring proof of unfitness in Sheppard v. Sheppard, 230 Kan. 146, 630 P.2d 1121 (1981), cert. denied 455 U.S. 919, 102 S.Ct. 1274, 71 L.Ed. 2d 459 (1982).

28. E.g., Barstad v. Frazier, 118 Wis.2d 549, 348 N.W.2d 479 (1984); Annot., Award of Custody of Child Where Contest is Between Child's Father and Grandfather, 25 A.L.R.3d 7, 33 (1969).

29. State in Interest of Toler, 261 So.2d 659 (La.App. 1972); Matter of D. T., 200 N.J.Super. 171, 491 A.2d 7 (1985).

30. Hosey v. Myers, 240 So.2d 252 (Miss.1970); Matter of Guardianship of Doney, 174 Mont. 282, 570 P.2d 575 (1977).

31. Custody of a Minor, 377 Mass. 876, 389 N.E.2d 68 (1979); Masitto v. Masitto, 22 Ohio St.3d 63, 488 N.E.2d 857 (1986); Engelhardt v. Bergeron, 113 R.I. 50, 317 A.2d 877 (1974).

32. Bramblet v. Cox, 461 S.W.2d 349 (Ky.1970) (father indicted for murder of the child's mother, and the child was a witness); Bezio v. Patenaude, 381 Mass. 563, 410 N.E.2d 1207 (1980) (lesbian relationship of mother was not a ground to remove child from her custody).

33. Turner v. Pannick, 540 P.2d 1051 (Alaska 1975); Nielsen v. Nielsen, 207 Neb. 141, 296 N.W.2d 483 (1980); Sorentino v. Family & Children's Society of Elizabeth, 74 N.J. 313, 378 A.2d 18 (1977), affirmed 77 N.J. 483, 391 A.2d 497 (1978); Barstad v. Frazier, 118 Wis.2d 549, 348 N.W.2d 479 (1984).

34. Masitto v. Masitto, 22 Ohio St.3d 63, 488 N.E.2d 857 (1986).

ests.[35] The parent's claim is strengthened even further by the rule adopted in some states that the unfitness must be proved by clear and convincing evidence.[36] In applying this and less rigid preferences, it is clear that an adoptive parent is to be given the same status as a natural parent of the child.[37] The decision on these matters should reflect the facts as they exist at the time of the hearing, not as they exist at the time a petition is filed.[38]

The rule that a parent may only be deprived of custody on proof of his unfitness is not universally adhered to. A significant number of cases take the position that not even a parent has a "right" to custody and that custody disputes between a parent and a non-parent should be decided in the way which best serves the child's interests.[39] This point of view has received strong support from the Goldstein, Freud, Solnit book.[40] It is based primarily on the broad proposition, often referred to, that the state has a responsibility to promote the welfare of children when the family breaks up.[41] Even the cases which take this position, however, do not ignore the natural parent's interest.[42] They express their respect for that interest in a variety of ways which probably represent different degrees of respect for it.[43] For example, some courts state that the child's welfare is the ultimate test for custody, but that there is a rebuttable presumption or a preference that that welfare will be best served by the natural parent.[44] Others reverse the factors and say that the parent should prevail unless that

---

35. Blackburn v. Blackburn, 249 Ga. 689, 292 S.E.2d 821 (1982); Sheppard v. Sheppard, 230 Kan. 146, 630 P.2d 1121 (1981), cert. denied 455 U.S. 919, 102 S.Ct. 1274, 71 L.Ed.2d 459 (1982); Freeman v. Chaplic, 388 Mass. 398, 446 N.E.2d 1369 (1983); In Interest of LaRue, 244 Pa. Super. 218, 366 A.2d 1271 (1976).

36. Custody of a Minor, 389 Mass. 755, 452 N.E.2d 483 (1983); Doe v. Mitchell, 397 Mich. 225, 244 N.W.2d 827 (1976).

37. Ruppel v. Lesner, 421 Mich. 559, 364 N.W.2d 665 (1985) (semble).

38. Custody of a Minor, 5 Mass.App.Ct. 741, 370 N.E.2d 712 (1977).

39. Matson v. Matson, 639 P.2d 298 (Alaska 1982); R. A. D. v. M. E. Z., 414 A.2d 211 (Del.Super.1980); In re Custody of Townsend, 86 Ill.2d 502, 56 Ill.Dec. 685, 427 N.E.2d 1231 (1981); Painter v. Bannister, 258 Iowa 1390, 140 N.W.2d 152 (1966), cert. denied 385 U.S. 949, 87 S.Ct. 317, 17 L.Ed.2d 227 (1966), 79 Harv.L.Rev. 1710 (1966); Chapsky v. Wood, 26 Kan. 650 (1881); Matter of Guardianship of J. R. G., ___ Mont. ___, 708 P.2d 263 (1985); Hoy v. Willis, 165 N.J.Super. 265, 398 A.2d 109 (1978); Ellerbe v. Hooks, 490 Pa. 363, 416 A.2d 512 (1980); Elm v. Key, 480 P.2d 104 (Wyo.1971). For further discussion of the issue and a vehement criticism of Chapsky v. Wood, supra, see Sayre, Awarding Custody of Children, 160 Annals 66 (1932), Association of American Law Schools, Selected Essays on Family Law 588 (1950). Roche v. Roche, 25 Cal.2d 141, 152 P.2d 999 (1944), Stewart v. Stewart, 41 Cal.2d 447, 260 P.2d 44 (1953), and In re Guardianship of Smith, 42 Cal.2d 91, 265 P.2d 888, 891 (1954) put both sides of the issue in extensive and well reasoned majority and dissenting opinions.

40. J. Goldstein, A. Freud, A. Solnit, Beyond the Best Interests of the Child 7, 27, 31–35, 51, 71–96 (2d ed.1979).

41. Halstead v. Halstead, 259 Iowa 526, 144 N.W.2d 861 (1966); Chapsky v. Wood, 26 Kan. 650 (1881).

42. E.g., In re Custody of Townsend, 86 Ill.2d 502, 56 Ill.Dec. 685, 427 N.E.2d 1231 (1981).

43. These cases probably also reflect differing reactions to different states of fact. See, e.g., Ellerbe v. Hooks, 490 Pa. 363, 416 A.2d 512 (1980). And we should not expect to find agreement among the cases in a single jurisdiction on the verbal formulae to be applied to the parent-non-parent cases. Compare Chapsky v. Wood, 26 Kan. 650 (1881) with Sheppard v. Sheppard, 230 Kan. 146, 630 P.2d 1121 (1981), cert. denied 455 U.S. 919, 102 S.Ct. 1274, 71 L.Ed.2d 459 (1982), and Halstead v. Halstead, 259 Iowa 526, 144 N.W.2d 861 (1966) with Matter of Guardianship of Sams, 256 N.W.2d 570 (Iowa 1977).

44. Hao Thi Popp, 186 Conn. 545, 438 A.2d 755 (1980); In re Guardianship of Sams, 256 N.W.2d 570 (Iowa 1977) (rebuttable presumption favoring natural parents places the burden on the non-parent of establishing that the child's best interests require his custody); Doe v. Mitchell, 397 Mich. 225, 244 N.W.2d 827 (1976) (child's best interests presumed served by placement with the parent unless otherwise shown by clear and convincing evidence, pursuant to statute); Phillips v. Choplin, 65 N.C.App. 506, 309 S.E.2d 716 (1983) (children's preference rebutted the presumption); Albright v. Commonwealth ex rel. Fetters, 491 Pa. 320, 421 A.2d 157 (1980) (parent has a prima facie right to custody, non-parent has a heavy burden of producing evidence and of persuasion); Commonwealth ex rel. Holschuh v. Holland-Moritz, 448 Pa. 437, 292 A.2d 380 (1972) (parent has a prima facie right to custody which can be overcome only in the most extreme circumstances); Hutchison v. Hutchison, 649 P.2d 38 (Utah 1982) (presumption favors the natural parent, to be rebutted only by evidence that the parent-child bond does not exist, that the parent is not willing to sacrifice his interest for the child, and that parent lacks sympathy for an understanding of the child); Paquette v. Paquette, 146 Vt. 83, 499 A.2d 23 (1985) (presumption favoring the natural parent rebuttable only by clear and convincing evidence of unfitness or extraordinary circumstances).

would be detrimental to the child,[45] or unless there are "extraordinary circumstances" calling for an award to the non-parent.[46] It is interesting that we seldom find any discussion of the possibility of an award of joint custody to parent and non-parent.[47]

The differences between the various versions of the best interests standard represent more a difference in emphasis and in standards for tolerable parental performance than a clash of opposing rules of law. But the conflict between the several versions of the best interests standard on the one hand and the parental right doctrine on the other is more than that. The parental right doctrine has acquired rigidity from the dubious and amorphous principle that the natural parent has some sort of a constitutional "right" to the custody of his child.[48] This principle comes dangerously close to treating the child in some sense as the property of his parent, an unhappy analogy which the Supreme Court has been guilty of in another context.[49] Although adherence to the best interests of the child does not guarantee wise custody dispositions between parent and non-parent,[50]

it at least places the emphasis where it should be, on the child's welfare rather than on the parent's interests. And, as Chapsky v. Wood made clear more than one hundred years ago,[51] the best interests standard is based upon the recognition that there is no analogy between a custody award and a decision concerning the title to property.

There would not be insuperable obstacles to the development of workable principles in these cases if the courts could manage to avoid doctrinaire statements about parental rights. In general this would require recognition that the child's welfare is the principle guiding the process of decision, but in addition that the emotional and psychological advantages to the child of a parent's care should be placed high in the scale of factors which contribute to that welfare.[52] The application of these principles should vary with the specific type of case before the court. When the case is brought by the state for the purpose of removing a child from the custody of his parent or parents, the courts must normally follow the state's dependency and neglect statute, which usually requires a finding of

45. West's Ann.Cal.Civ.Code § 4600(c) (Supp.1986) (before the court may award custody to a non-parent, it must find that the award to the parent would be detrimental and that the award to the non-parent is required to serve the child's best interests). See also Ross v. Hoffman, 280 Md. 172, 372 A.2d 582 (1977), and Matson v. Matson, 639 P.2d 298, 300 (Alaska 1982) (dissenting opinion), in which an award to a parent was in effect an award to non-parents who were actually caring for the child.

46. This line of cases originated with Bennett v. Jeffreys, 40 N.Y.2d 543, 387 N.Y.S.2d 821, 356 N.E.2d 277 (1976), appeal after remand 59 A.D.2d 492, 399 N.Y.S.2d 697 (1977), which held that one such "extraordinary circumstance" was the eight-year separation of parent and child, during which the child was cared for by an unrelated older woman. The court's expression of the guiding principle was: "The State may not deprive a parent of the custody of a child absent surrender, abandonment, persisting neglect, unfitness or other like extraordinary circumstances." On its face this seems like little more than the conventional unfitness doctrine, but some lower court cases in New York read it as giving greater emphasis to the child's interest than would be done under the fitness doctrine. E.g., Bennett v. Marrow, 59 A.D.2d 492, 399 N.Y.S.2d 697 (2d Dep't 1977); In re Paschen, 116 Misc.2d 421, 455 N.Y.S.2d 168 (Surr.Ct. 1982). But later cases in the New York Court of Appeals seem to have rejected that view. Matter of Adoption of L., 61 N.Y.2d 420, 474 N.Y.S.2d 447, 462 N.E.2d 1165 (1984); Dickson v. Lascaris, 53 N.Y.2d 204, 440 N.Y.S.2d

884, 423 N.E.2d 361 (981); Matter of Sanjivini K., 47 N.Y. 2d 374, 418 N.Y.S.2d 339, 391 N.E.2d 1316 (1979). It is notable that a distinguished family court judge in Christina L. v. James H., supra, 115 Misc.2d 248, 454 N.Y.S.2d 379 (Fam.Ct.1982), found that the child's welfare would be so seriously endangered by a return to his natural mother that his constitutional interest in liberty would be infringed.

Bailes v. Sours, 231 Va. 96, 340 S.E.2d 824 (1986) appears to hold that custody should go to the non-parent where extraordinary circumstances exist, proved by clear and convincing evidence, that the child's best interests would thereby be promoted.

47. Stanley D. v. Deborah D., 124 N.H. 138, 467 A.2d 249 (1983) awarded joint legal custody to a child's mother and stepfather, with physical custody to the stepfather. Simmons v. Balcarran, 105 A.D.2d 639, 481 N.Y.S.2d 701 (1st Dep't 1984) reversed a trial court decree awarding joint legal custody to a father and maternal grandparents, although the grandparents had cared for the child for the first three years of her life.

48. See the cases cited at notes 15 to 22, supra.

49. May v. Anderson, 345 U.S. 528, 73 S.Ct. 840, 97 L.Ed. 1221 (1953).

50. E.g., Painter v. Bannister, 258 Iowa 1390, 140 N.W.2d 152 (1966).

51. Chapsky v. Wood, 26 Kan. 650, 652–653 (1881).

52. See the cases cited in note 44, supra.

abandonment, abuse or serious neglect of parental obligations, or, in other words, unfitness.[53] Even in these cases the child may not be permanently removed from the custody of his parents if an alternative plan or disposition can be worked out which will provide the child with adequate care.[54] In such dependency and neglect proceedings it is not improper to give the highest significance to the parent's claim and to characterize that claim as one of parental right.

On the other hand, when a child has been living with a natural parent and a stepparent for a substantial number of years and the parent dies, so that a custody question arises between the other parent and the stepparent, the child may have strong psychological ties to the stepparent, perhaps stronger than his ties to the other natural parent. In such circumstances we should not talk of parental rights but rather should ask, what disposition best serves the child's interests, taking into account and giving weight to the child's relations with the other natural parent, but not ignoring the strength of the attachment to the stepparent. In fact some cases do reach this result.[55] Although the stepparent relationship often involves the closest contact between the child and a non-parent to be found in the cases, similar close contact and psychological bond may occur with other persons, such as relatives or friends of the natural parents. The same approach should be taken to these cases.[56] In such cases it may well be

53. Dependency and neglect petitions may be aimed at the involuntary termination of parental rights, with a view to the later adoption of the child. Cases of this kind are discussed in section 20.6, infra. Typical dependency and neglect statutes are West's Ann.Cal.Welfare & Inst. Code § 300 (Supp.1987); Colo.Rev.Stat. § 19–1–103 (1986); N.Y.—McKinney's Soc.Serv.L. § 384–b (1983 and Supp. 1986). Cases supporting the text statement include petition of New Bedford Child & Family Service to Dispense with Consent to Adoption, 385 Mass. 482, 432 N.E.2d 97 (1982); Custody of a Minor, 377 Mass. 876, 389 N.E.2d 68 (1979); Matter of Guardianship of Doney, 174 Mont. 282, 570 P.2d 575 (1977); Dickson v. Lascaris, 53 N.Y.2d 204, 440 N.Y.S.2d 884, 423 N.E.2d 361 (1981). Similar principles apply to visitation by natural parents when custody has been awarded to a state agency, Matter of Joseph, 416 N.E.2d 857 (Ind.App.1981), and when, in a divorce action, the court proposes to award custody to neither parent but to a third party, Fox v. Fox, 466 N.E.2d 789 (Ind.App.1984).

A case which makes the distinction suggested in the text, between custody disputes between parent and state on the one hand, and between parent and other third parties on the other, is Ellerbe v. Hooks, 490 Pa. 363, 416 A.2d 512 (1980), concluding that the standards to be applied in the second kind of a case do not place as much emphasis on the parent's rights as in the first kind of a case.

54. See, e.g., In Interest of A. B., 444 So.2d 981 (Fla. App.1983).

55. Root v. Allen, 151 Colo. 311, 377 P.2d 117 (1962), 73 Yale L.J. 151 (1963); Doe v. Doe, 92 Misc.2d 184, 399 N.Y.S.2d 977 (1977); Bailes v. Sours, 231 Va. 96, 340 S.E.2d 824 (1986); Patrick v. Byerley, 228 Va. 691, 325 S.E.2d 99 (1985). Other cases are collected in Annot., Award of Custody of Child Where Contest is Between Natural Parent and Stepparent, 10 A.L.R.4th 767 (1981).

Several cases have awarded visitation rights to stepparents: Bryan v. Bryan, 132 Ariz. 353, 645 P.2d 1267 (App. 1982); Collins v. Gilbreath, 403 N.E.2d 921 (Ind.App. 1980); Spells v. Spells, 250 Pa.Super. 168, 378 A.2d 879 (1977); Gribble v. Gribble, 583 P.2d 64 (Utah 1978).

But other cases rely heavily on the parents' right doctrine to deny custody to a stepparent, sometimes in circumstances which appear shockingly prejudicial to the child's welfare. E.g., Pape v. Pape, 444 So.2d 1058 (Fla. App.1984); In re Custody of Krause, 111 Ill.App.3d 604, 67 Ill.Dec. 408, 444 N.E.2d 644 (1982); Simpson v. Simpson, 586 S.W.2d 33 (Ky.1979); Simpson v. Rast, 258 So.2d 233 (Miss.1972); Tyrrell v. Tyrrell, 67 A.D.2d 247, 415 N.Y.S.2d 723 (4th Dep't 1979), affirmed 47 N.Y.2d 937, 419 N.Y.S.2d 969, 393 N.E.2d 1041 (1979). Commonwealth ex rel. Patricia L. F. v. Malbert J. F., Jr., 278 Pa. Super. 343, 420 A.2d 572 (1980) held that a stepparent would not be considered a natural parent solely on the basis of being in loco parentis with the child.

56. R. A. D. v. M. E. Z., 414 A.2d 211 (Del.Super.1980); In re Custody of Menconi, 117 Ill.App.3d 394, 73 Ill.Dec. 10, 453 N.E.2d 835 (1983) (grandparent); Painter v. Bannister, 258 Iowa 1390, 140 N.W.2d 152 (1966), cert. denied 385 U.S. 949, 87 S.Ct. 317, 17 L.Ed.2d 227 (1966), 79 Harv. L.Rev. 1710 (1966); Ross v. Hoffman, 280 Md. 172, 372 A.2d 582 (1977); Degrange v. Kline, 254 Md. 240, 254 A.2d 353 (1969) (aunt and uncle); Hosey v. Myers, 240 So. 2d 252 (Miss.1970) (child's adult sister); Masitto v. Masitto, 22 Ohio St.3d 63, 488 N.E.2d 857 (1986) (grandparents); Ellerbe v. Hooks, 490 Pa. 363, 416 A.2d 512 (1980) (grandmother); Dyer v. Howell, 212 Va. 453, 184 S.E.2d 789 (1971) (aunt and uncle); Elm v. Key, 480 P.2d 104 (Wyo.1971). Other cases involving disputes between parents and grandparents are collected in Annot., 25 A.L.R.3d 7 (1969).

Contra: Turner v. Pannick, 540 P.2d 1051 (Alaska 1975); In re Custody of Townsend, 86 Ill.2d 502, 56 Ill. Dec. 685, 427 N.E.2d 1231 (1981); Montgomery County Department of Social Services v. Sanders, 38 Md.App. 406, 381 A.2d 1154 (1977) (rejects the Goldstein, Freud, Solnit thesis); Powers v. Hadden, 30 Md.App. 577, 353 A.2d 641 (1976); Nielsen v. Nielsen, 207 Neb. 141, 296 N.W.2d 483 (1980); Chapman v. Perera, 41 Wash.App. 444, 704 P.2d 1224 (1985).

In some cases the court must use some discrimination in determining who will be the true custodian of the child. Compare Matson v. Matson, 639 P.2d 298 (Alaska

that custody should be given to the natural parent, but this should only be done after a thorough consideration of the child's relationship to both the parent and the non-parent and of the child's welfare.[57]

The most difficult cases are those in which a parent places his child temporarily in the custody of another person, perhaps with the understanding that the parent will resume custody when he is able to, or in which a parent places the child with prospective adoptive parents. The problems arise when the parent seeks to reclaim the child or to revoke his consent to adoption and the non-parent refuses to restore the child to the custody of the parent. In the temporary placement cases, if the child is not returned to the parent, the parent's expectations will be frustrated thereby deepening the parent's heartache and bitterness. And in the adoption cases the parent may have consented to the adoption under the stress of circumstances and may have tried to change her mind relatively soon after giving the consent. Due to these factors, the parent's interest should perhaps be given greater weight than in the stepparent

cases, and the child retained in the custody of the non-parent only where his welfare clearly dictates that result.[58] Even in these circumstances, however, it should not be necessary to prove the parent unfit as a condition of awarding custody to the non-parent. If the child has been in the non-parent's care for a substantial period of time, taking into account that time may have a different significance for a child,[59] and if the child is strongly attached to the non-parent emotionally and psychologically, so that the child will suffer serious harm by being shifted to another's custody, then the non-parent should be awarded custody.[60] It should not matter for this purpose that delays in the process of litigation account for much of the time during which the child remains with the non-parent, since the effect on the child is the same regardless of the source of the delay.[61] It must be conceded that some of the cases would strongly disagree with an award of custody to the non-parent in these circumstances, absent proof of unfitness, thereby exhibiting a startling lack of concern for the interests of children.[62]

1982) with Freeman v. Chaplic, 388 Mass. 398, 446 N.E.2d 1369 (1983).

57. Bezio v. Patenaude, 381 Mass. 563, 410 N.E.2d 1207 (1980); Nielsen v. Nielsen, 207 Neb. 141, 296 N.W.2d 483 (1980); Barstad v. Frazier, 118 Wis.2d 549, 348 N.W.2d 479 (1984).

58. E.g., Hoy v. Willis, 165 N.J.Super. 265, 398 A.2d 109 (1978), refusing to remove a child from the care of his aunt, with whom he had lived for four and one-half of his six years after a placement by his mother. Another temporary placement case suggested the possibility of this treatment of such cases, but remanded the case for further evidence. Bennett v. Jeffreys, 40 N.Y.2d 543, 387 N.Y.S.2d 821, 356 N.E.2d 277 (1976), appeal after remand 59 A.D.2d 492, 399 N.Y.S.2d 697 (1977). The case has been sharply limited by later New York cases. See note 46, supra. The concurring opinion in that case supports the position taken in the text. 40 N.Y.2d at 553, 387 N.Y.S.2d at 829, 356 N.E.2d at 285.

Sorentino v. Family & Children's Society of Elizabeth, 74 N.J. 313, 378 A.2d 18 (1977), affirmed 77 N.J. 483, 391 A.2d 497 (1978) seems to support the text statement in the context of a consent to adoption by the natural parent followed by a revocation of that consent. The revocation of consent to adoption is discussed at greater length in section 20.4, infra.

59. J. Goldstein, A. Freud, A. Solnit, Beyond the Best Interests of the Child 40–52 (2d ed.1979) describes the child's sense of time and of continuity, and the changes which occur in that sense as the child grows older.

60. A graphic statement of this position is made by Judge Dembitz in Christina L. v. James and Susan H., 115 Misc.2d 248, 454 N.Y.S.2d 379 (Fam.Ct.1982), but she felt obliged to return the child to the natural mother by the New York Court of Appeals' decisions notwithstanding her conviction that removal of the child from his custodians would disrupt his attachment to them, would cause him short-term distress, and might result in serious and permanent psychological and emotional damage. Her infliction of this result on the child was affirmed in Matter of Adoption of Landaverde, 95 A.D.2d 29, 465 N.Y.S.2d 6 (1st Dep't 1983), and in affirmed 61 N.Y.2d 420, 474 N.Y.S.2d 447, 462 N.E.2d 1165 (1984).

61. Contra the text statement: Matter of Adoption of L., 61 N.Y.2d 420, 474 N.Y.S.2d 447, 462 N.E.2d 1165 (1984), which seems to say that litigation delays do not count, and also that the custodians were to blame for not handing over the child when the natural parent demanded him. This case thus uses removal from custody as a sort of punishment. In re Custody of Townsend, 86 Ill.2d 502, 56 Ill.Dec. 685, 427 N.E.2d 1231 (1981) also seems to consider the passage of time irrelevant when it was due to the delays of litigation.

62. E.g., Custody of a Minor, 389 Mass. 755, 452 N.E.2d 483 (1983); Matter of Adoption of L., 61 N.Y.2d 420, 474 N.Y.S.2d 447, 462 N.E.2d 1165 (1984); Dickson v. Lascaris, 53 N.Y.2d 204, 440 N.Y.S.2d 884, 423 N.E.2d 361 (1981); Interest of LaRue, 244 Pa.Super. 218, 366 A.2d 1271 (1976). Matter of Guardianship of J. R. G., —— Mont. ——, 708 P.2d 263 (1985) seems to adopt the best

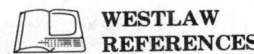

§ 19.7 Custody of Children—Visitation by Grandparents or Other Non-parents

There is conflict in the case law on the question whether a court may, without express statutory authority, grant rights of visitation to a grandparent or other non-parent.[1] In a few cases visitation was granted when the parents consented,[2] but such awards were not usually made over the opposition of the custodial parent.[3] An award of visitation to a grandparent was made where the grandparent had cared for the child after the separation of his parents, however.[4]

During the past ten years nearly all states have enacted statutes which in varying terms

provide for the award of rights of visitation to grandparents or to other non-parents.[5] Since these statutes are the product of a combination of the lobbying efforts of grandparent groups[6] and the sentimentality of the state legislatures, they take so many different forms and limit visitation to so many different kinds of circumstances that it is extremely difficult to classify them. For example, most of the statutes only speak of visitation orders to grandparents,[7] but a few of the others include great-grandparents,[8] siblings,[9] or, in a very few states authorize visitation to any interested person.[10] The statutes are generally limited in their application to situations in which the child's parents are being or have been divorced or separated,[11] or in which one or both parents have died.[12] Some statutes provide that only the parents of a non-custodial parent or of a deceased parent may be granted visitation rights.[13] Some statutes apply to the grandparents of children born out of wedlock,[14] while others expressly or by implication do not.[15] The condition imposed by nearly all the statutes is that visitation must be found to be in the child's best inter-

interests test, but affirms a return of the child to the natural parent after being in the care of the non-parent for the first five years of his life. A case which seems to reach the correct result in ordering the return of the child to the natural parent is Matter of Sanjivini K., 47 N.Y.2d 374, 418 N.Y.S.2d 339, 391 N.E.2d 1316 (1979), where the child was older and the natural parents had maintained consistent contact with him.

§ 19.7

1. Holding that the courts did have jurisdiction: L. v. G., 203 N.J.Super. 385, 497 A.2d 215 (1985) (sibling visitation held not in the child's best interests). Holding that the courts did not have this jurisdiction: Matter of Guardianship of Brown, 402 So.2d 354 (Miss.1981).

2. Cases are collected in Annot., 98 A.L.R.2d 325, 328 (1964).

3. Succession of Reiss, 46 La.Ann. 347, 15 So. 151 (1894); Foster, Freed, Grandparent Visitation: Vagaries and Vicissitudes, 23 St.L.U.L.J. 643, 645 (1979).

4. Benner v. Benner, 113 Cal.App.2d 531, 248 P.2d 425 (1952).

5. Extensive citations to the statutes may be found in Note, The Constitutional Constraints on Grandparents' Visitation Statutes, 86 Colum.L.Rev. 118, 119–121 (1986); Ingulli, Grandparent Visitation Rights: Social Policies and Legal Rights, 87 W.Va.L.Rev. 295, 302–304 (1985). Apparently only Nebraska is without a statute authorizing grandparents or other non-parents to be awarded visitation.

6. See A. Kornhaber, K. Woodward, Grandparents/Grandchildren (1985).

7. E.g., Ala.Code 1983, § 30–3–4; Colo.Rev.Stat. § 19–1–116 (1986); Del.Code tit. 10, § 950(7) (Supp.1984); West's Fla.Stat.Ann. § 61.13(2)(b) 2c (1985); Pa.Stat. tit. 23, §§ 5311, 5312, 5313 (Supp.1986).

8. E.g., Ariz.Rev.Stat. § 25–337.01 (Supp.1985).

9. E.g., Ark.Stat. § 57–137 (Supp.1985).

10. E.g., Alaska Stat. § 25.24.150(a) (1983) (grandparent "or other person"); West's Ann.Cal.Civ.Code § 4601 (1983) (any other person having an interest in the welfare of the child); Conn.Gen.Stat.Ann. § 46b–59 (Supp.1986) (may grant visitation to any person subject to equitable limitations); Me.Rev.Stat.Ann. tit. 19, § 752 (Supp.1985) (any third person).

11. E.g., Ala.Code, § 30–3–4 (1983); Alaska Stat. § 25.24–150(a) (1983); Ariz.Rev.Stat. § 25–337.01 (Supp. 1985); Colo.Rev.Stat. § 19–1–116 (1986); Iowa Code Ann. § 598.35 (1981); N.Y.—McKinney's Dom.Rel.L. §§ 72, 240 (1977 and Supp.1986); Or.Rev.Stat. § 109.121 (1984).

12. See the statutes cited in note 11, supra.

13. E.g., Ariz.Rev.Stat. § 25–337.01 (Supp.1985).

14. E.g., Ark.Stat. § 34–1211.2 (Supp.1985); Del.Code tit. 10, § 950(7) (Supp.1984); La.S.A.—Rev.Stat. § 9:572(C) (Supp.1986).

15. Okl.Stat.1985, tit. 10, § 60.16(3) (Supp.) provides that grandparent visitation does not apply to the illegitimate child. Presumably those statutes which authorize

ests.[16] A few statutes add the requirement that visitation must not interfere with the parent-child relationship [17] or that the court may consider the amount of prior personal contact between the grandparent and the child.[18] Many statutes provide that grandparent visitation is not to be permitted when the child has been adopted, at least where the adoption is by someone other than a stepparent or a grandparent.[19]

The procedure by which non-parent visitation may be sought is not usually provided for in the statutes.[20] It may be done by seeking to intervene in a divorce action,[21] or by filing an original petition in the appropriate court.[22] The grandparent or other person seeking visitation has the burden of proof [23] and apparently the weight of that burden may sometimes vary depending upon the extensiveness of the visitation being asked.[24] The award or denial of visitation is generally held to be a matter for the discretion of the trial court, to be reversed only where that discretion is abused.[25]

Although it has been argued that there are constitutional limitations on the doctrine that grandparents may be entitled to visitation rights respecting their grandchildren,[26] no cases have been found which directly impose such limitations. One case involving the construction of a statute authorizing grandparent visitation does state that the "parenting right", whatever that may be, is a fundamental liberty interest protected against unwarranted state intrusion, presumably by the United States Constitution.[27] The case seems to take the position that to avoid infringing this liberty interest the statute is to be construed to apply only where there is a disruption of the family unit which deprives the grandparents of their normal access to the child, that access being through the grandpar-

grandparent visitation only upon the death or divorce of the parents would not apply to illegitimate children, since their parents obviously could not be divorced, never having been married. See Olds v. Olds, 356 N.W.2d 571 (Iowa 1984). Whether the statute would apply to an illegitimate child one of whose parents had died is unclear. This kind of careless drafting is not uncommon in these statutes.

16. See most of the statutes cited supra, in notes 7 to 16. Some statutes speak only of granting "reasonable" visitation to grandparents, as does Del.Code tit. 10, § 950(7) (Supp.1984), but this has been construed to mean that the child's best interests must be proved by the applicant in Rosemary E. R. v. Michael G. Q., 471 A.2d 995 (Del.1984). West's Ann.Cal.Civ.Code § 4601 (1983) also refers to reasonable visitation.

17. E.g., Pa.Stat. tit. 23, §§ 5311, 5312, 5313 (Supp. 1986).

18. E.g., Idaho Code § 32–1008 (1983); Minn.Stat.Ann. § 257.022 (1982); Pa.Stat. tit. 23, §§ 5311, 5312 (Supp. 1986).

19. E.g., Ariz.Rev.Stat. § 25–337.01 (Supp.1985); Colo. Rev.Stat. § 19–1–116 (1986); Ill.—S.H.A. ch. 110½, § 11–7.1 (Supp.1986); Mass.G.L.A. ch. 119, § 39D (Supp.1986); Minn.Stat.Ann. § 257.022 (1982); Pa.Stat. tit. 23, § 5314 (Supp.1986). A more complete discussion of the effect of adoption placement and adoption may be found in section 20.10, infra.

20. But see Colo.Rev.Stat. § 19–1–116 (1986) authorizing the grandparent to seek an order for visitation, with the ruling to be based either on affidavits or on a hearing.

21. Krieg v. Glassburn, 419 N.E.2d 1015 (Ind.App. 1981). But see Perry v. Superior Court of Kern County, 108 Cal.App.3d 480, 166 Cal.Rptr. 583 (1980).

22. Roberts v. Ward, 126 N.H. 388, 493 A.2d 478 (1985); Nation v. Nation, 715 P.2d 198 (Wyo.1986).

23. Krieg v. Glassburn, 419 N.E.2d 1015 (Ind.App. 1981). It is especially important that the grandparents have the burden of proof in these cases, since they may be seeking seriously to interfere with the parents' care of the child and since the standard for permitting that interference is under the circumstances a vague one. But Globman v. Globman, 158 N.J.Super. 338, 386 A.2d 390 (1978), cert. denied 77 N.J. 493, 391 A.2d 507 (1978) states that the statute creates a presumption that the child's best interests are ordinarily served by maintaining contact with the grandparent. The Illinois statute may create the same sort of presumption by providing that where both parents are deceased, visitation shall be granted unless it would be detrimental to the child's best interests and welfare. Ill.—S.H.A. ch. 110½, § 11–7.1 (Supp.1986).

24. Commonwealth ex rel. Williams v. Miller, 254 Pa. Super. 227, 385 A.2d 992 (1978), approved in Commonwealth ex rel. Zaffarano v. Genaro, 500 Pa. 256, 455 A.2d 1180 (1983).

25. Lo Presti v. Lo Presti, 40 N.Y.2d 522, 387 N.Y.S.2d 412, 355 N.E.2d 372 (1976), on remand 54 A.D.2d 582, 387 N.Y.S.2d 153 (1976); Looper v. McManus, 581 P.2d 487 (Okl.App.1978).

26. Note, The Constitutional Constraints on Grandparents' Visitation Statutes, 86 Colum.L.Rev. 118 (1986).

27. Olds v. Olds, 356 N.W.2d 571 (Iowa 1984).

ents' offspring. By this analysis, on divorce, the grandparents only may sue for visitation when the grandchild is in the custody of the parent who is not the grandparents' offspring. This case provides graphic illustration, if any is needed, of the distortions and unreality resulting when notions of constitutional "rights" are injected into custody disputes. The parents, the child, and perhaps the grandparents all have interests in these cases, but it is quite unrealistic to translate these interests into constitutional "rights" having uncertain origins and vague outlines.[28]

The extraordinarily diverse qualifications and limitations imposed by the statutes providing for grandparent (and non-parent) visitation raise the initial question whether these statutes are to be construed as exclusive sources of judicial authority or whether there remains some reservoir of common law authority under which the courts may order visitation in cases which do not fit into the statutory scheme. Many such cases can easily be imagined. In a state whose statute provides only for grandparent visitation may the court award visitation rights to some other relative or to a foster parent? In a state whose statute does not provide for visitation with grandchildren born out of wedlock, may the grandparent enforce visitation claims respecting such a child? And perhaps the most difficult question of all, where the statute provides for grandparent visitation if the parents' marriage has ended by death or divorce, may the grandparents be awarded visitation

rights when neither of these circumstances has occurred? The statutes themselves do not attempt to deal with such questions, except for those statutes like California's which give the courts unlimited discretion to grant visitation to any person having an interest in the welfare of the child, in effect passing the buck to the courts to deal with the problem.[29]

The normal inference, when the legislature enacts a statutory program dealing with a perceived problem, is that the statutory provisions must be complied with as a condition on the grant of remedies for that problem.[30] It might be argued that the statutes merely made explicit what was assumed to be the common law respecting grandparent visitation.[31] The objection to this argument is that in the view of many courts the common law did not authorize the courts to grant visitation to persons other than parents.[32] The person seeking grandparent or non-parent visitation should for these reasons be required to meet the statutory conditions. The case law on the issue is not only inconclusive but notably unhelpful. Some of the cases are so convinced that grandparent visitation is a good thing that they grant it even where the statute does not authorize it, usually without dicussion of whether the statute provides the exclusive remedy.[33] Others take the position that if the person seeking visitation is unable to comply with the statutory conditions, visitation should be denied, without consideration of the child's best interests.[34] One virtue of the latter position is that it may induce the

28. The same point is made in section 19.6, supra, in connection with controversies over custody between parents and non-parents. See also Commonwealth ex rel. Zaffarano v. Genaro, 500 Pa. 256, 266, 455 A.2d 1180, 1185 (1983) (concurring opinion of Nix, J.).

29. West's Ann.Cal.Civ.Code § 4601 (1983): "* * * In the discretion of the court, reasonable visitation rights may be granted to any other person having an interest in the welfare of the child." But West's Ann.Cal.Civ.Code § 4351.5(b) (Supp.1987) authorizes the grandparent to petition for visitation in divorce or when the child is dependent.

30. 2A Sutherland, Statutory Construction § 50.05 (4th ed.Sands, N. Singer 1984).

31. Hughes v. Hughes, 316 Pa.Super. 505, 463 A.2d 478 (1983) (dictum).

32. See notes 1 to 4, supra.

33. Roberts v. Ward, 126 N.H. 388, 493 A.2d 478 (1985) (court has jurisdiction to award grandparent visitation in an independent proceeding notwithstanding that the statute only authorized it as part of a divorce action); L. v. G., 203 N.J.Super. 385, 497 A.2d 215 (1985) (court could grant visitation to siblings although the statute authorized only visitation to grandparents under some circumstances); In re Bomgardner, 711 P.2d 92 (Okl.1985) (dictum that there is equity jurisdiction apart from statute to award grandparent visitation.

34. Towne v. Cole, 133 Ill.App.3d 380, 88 Ill.Dec. 404, 478 N.E.2d 895 (1985) (court had no jurisdiction to grant visitation to a grandmother where the statute was not applicable because the child's parents were neither divorced nor deceased); In re Visitation of J. O., 441 N.E.2d 991 (Ind.App.1982) (no jurisdiction to grant visitation where the child is illegitimate); Olds v. Olds, 356 N.W.2d

legislatures to enact statutes which more satisfactorily define the circumstances in which non-parent visitation is desirable.

As has been indicated,[35] the statutes on grandparent visitation as well as the judicial decisions agree that visitation should only be granted where it is in the child's best interests.[36] The question then is, how do the courts translate this broad standard into specific decisions?

In making these decisions the courts must necessarily arrive at some distinction between visitation and custody, since if the grandparents are seeking custody, the statutes do not apply and the strong preferences favoring parents described in the preceding section[37] would often bar the grandparent's claim. Here again the statutes are deficient, since they do not attempt to define visitation.[38] As one case has put it, visitation is at one end of a continuum of orders respecting children and custody is at the other end.[39] Somewhere in between lies something called partial custody. Any distinction between partial custody and visitation is arbitrary, but perhaps some help could be had from customary usage. By that test visits of the child with the grandparents lasting no longer than a weekend or a brief school vacation might be considered visita-

tion. Any period longer than that would have to be considered a substantial inroad on the parents' custody and therefore more than just visitation.

The application of the best interests standard to grandparent visitation cases has led the courts to look for the existence of specific factors which in their opinions seem to have a crucial bearing on the child's welfare.[40] One of these is the existence or non-existence on the grandparent's part of prior interest in the child. If the grandparent has shown little interest in the child in the past, visitation may be denied,[41] but if he has cared for the child or visited the child regularly in the past, the courts will be more sympathetic to his claim.[42] In the latter circumstance there may be a psychological bond between grandparent and grandchild which in the courts' view is important to the child's welfare. The child's preference may also be a relevant factor in these cases.[43] If the non-custodial parent has rights of visitation after divorce, at least some courts would refuse to permit his parents to be awarded visitation rights, since this would result in a multitude of relatives competing for his company.[44] And if the parent's parental rights have been judicially terminated, it would seem clear that his parents should not

571 (Iowa 1984) (visitation with illegitimate child not covered by statute).

35. See note 16, supra.

36. Representative decisions announcing the best interests rule, whether or not a statute is involved, include Bookstein v. Bookstein, 7 Cal.App.3d 219, 86 Cal.Rptr. 495 (1970); Kudler v. Smith, 643 P.2d 783 (Colo.App. 1981), cert. denied 459 U.S. 837, 103 S.Ct. 83, 74 L.Ed.2d 78 (1982); Hawkins v. Hawkins, 102 Ill.App.3d 1037, 58 Ill.Dec. 670, 430 N.E.2d 652 (1981); Roberts v. Ward, 126 N.H. 388, 493 A.2d 478 (1985); Commonwealth ex rel. Zaffarano v. Genaro, 500 Pa. 256, 455 A.2d 1180 (1983); Weichman v. Weichman, 50 Wis.2d 731, 184 N.W.2d 882 (1971). Other cases are cited in Ingulli, Grandparent Visitation Rights: Social Policies and Legal Rights, 87 W.Va.L.Rev. 295 (1985), and in Annot., Grandparents' Visitation Rights, 90 A.L.R.3d 222 (1979).

37. See section 19.6, supra.

38. Pennsylvania's statute is the exception, defining partial custody (not wholly satisfactorily) as the right to take possession of the child away from the custody of a parent for a certain period of time. Pa.Stat. tit. 23, § 5302 (Supp.1986).

39. Commonwealth ex rel. Zaffarano v. Genaro, 500 Pa. 256, 455 A.2d 1180 (1983).

40. The grandparent visitation statutes do not usually contain a list of relevant factors such as are found in the custody statutes. Some of them do direct the courts to be guided by the child's wishes if he is old enough to form an intelligent opinion. E.g., Conn.Gen.Stat.Ann. § 46b–59 (Supp.1986).

41. Hughes v. Hughes, 316 Pa.Super. 505, 463 A.2d 478 (1983) (lack of prior interest combined with great bitterness between grandparent and custodian); Dolman v. Dolman, 586 S.W.2d 606 (Tex.Civ.App.1979) (grandmother hardly knew the child).

42. Bookstein v. Bookstein, 7 Cal.App.3d 219, 86 Cal. Rptr. 495 (1970); Hawkins v. Hawkins, 102 Ill.App.3d 1037, 58 Ill.Dec. 620, 430 N.E.2d 652 (1981); Roberts v. Ward, 126 N.H. 388, 493 A.2d 478 (1985); Looper v. McManus, 581 P.2d 487 (Okl.App.1978).

43. L. v. G., 203 N.J.Super. 385, 497 A.2d 215 (1985) (sibling visitation denied where the sixteen-year-old child's views were given weight by the court).

44. In the Matter of Adoption of a Child by M, 140 N.J.Super. 91, 355 A.2d 211 (1976). But Looper v. McManus, 581 P.2d 487 (Okl.App.1978) granted visitation to a non-custodial parent, to his parents, and to a former stepmother of the child. One wonders when the custodial parent was supposed to see her child. See also Bennett v.

be able to enforce rights of visitation,[45] although even here it appears that some courts would continue to grant such rights to those grandparents, just as they would if the child had been adopted.[46]

The major issue created by the grandparent visitation statutes is to what extent the hostility of the custodial parent toward visitation should be sufficient to prevent an award. It would seem obvious at the outset that grandparent visitation is usually to be viewed as appropriate only when the family has broken down by death or divorce, and not when a grandparent wishes to intrude his visits against the opposition of the parents in a going family.[47] Many of the visitation statutes do not so limit grandparents, however, and it is possible to find cases in which the courts have ordered the parents in an intact family to honor grandparent visitation.[48] When the marriage has broken up as a result of divorce or death, the custodial parent may still have serious objections to enforced visitation by a grandparent, so serious as to create real hostility and antagonism between parent and grandparent. Although this is bound to

have adverse effects on the child, many courts tend to reject it as a reason to deny visitation and grant the visitation to the grandparent.[49] The cases the other way emphasize the harm to the child's welfare in granting visitation in such circumstances.[50]

The contrast between the treatment by both courts and legislatures of custody disputes between a parent and a non-parent on the one hand and disputes over visitation between a parent and a non-parent on the other is indeed striking. In the one case the parent's claim is given a very strong preference, in some jurisdictions to be denied only where the parent is unfit to undertake the responsibilities of custody. In the other case many courts, acting pursuant to the statutes, come very close to reversing the preference, ordering visitation unless it is convincingly proved that this will adversely affect the child's welfare. The advocates of grandparent visitation rest their case in part upon studies which allegedly show that the child benefits from continued contact with his grandparents.[51] The method of such studies and therefore their conclusion have been criti-

Bennett, 150 N.J.Super. 509, 376 A.2d 191 (1977), certification denied 75 N.J. 526, 384 A.2d 506 (1977).

45. J. v. M., 157 N.J.Super. 478, 385 A.2d 240 (1978), certification denied 77 N.J. 490, 391 A.2d 504 (1978).

46. Matter of Guardianship and Conservatorship of Ankeney, 360 N.W.2d 733 (Iowa 1985); Mimkon v. Ford, 66 N.J. 426, 332 A.2d 199 (1975). But see Ryback v. Cobb County Dep't of Family & Children's Services, 163 Ga. App. 165, 293 S.E.2d 563 (1982), holding that grandparent visitation should not be granted when the child had been placed for adoption.

47. Towne v. Cole, 133 Ill.App.3d 380, 88 Ill.Dec. 404, 478 N.E.2d 895 (1985).

48. E.g. Matter of Guardianship and Conservatorship of Ankeney, 360 N.W.2d 733 (Iowa 1985) (grants visitation rights over the objection of the natural father and the adoptive mother); Roberts v. Ward, 126 N.H. 388, 493 A.2d 478 (1985) (holding that the maternal grandparents may be granted visitation over the objection of the natural mother and stepfather of the child); Bucci v. Bucci, 351 Pa.Super. 457, 506 A.2d 438 (1986) (grants visitation to the paternal grandparents over the objection of the child's mother and stepfather).

49. In re Robert D., 151 Cal.App.3d 391, 198 Cal.Rptr. 801 (1984); Bookstein v. Bookstein, 7 Cal.App.3d 219, 86 Cal.Rptr. 495 (1970); Hawkins v. Hawkins, 102 Ill.App.3d 1037, 58 Ill.Dec. 620, 430 N.E.2d 652 (1981); Barry v. Barrale, 598 S.W.2d 574 (Mo.App.1980); Globman v. Globman, 158 N.J.Super. 338, 386 A.2d 390 (1978), certifi-

cation denied 77 N.J. 493, 391 A.2d 507 (1978); Lo Presti v. Lo Presti, 40 N.Y.2d 522, 387 N.Y.S.2d 412, 355 N.E.2d 372 (1976), on remand 54 A.D.2d 582, 387 N.Y.S.2d 153 (1976) (visitation turns on whether it has an adverse effect on the child's welfare, as determined by the trial court in its discretion); Commonwealth ex rel. Williams v. Miller, 254 Pa.Super. 227, 385 A.2d 992 (1978). Other cases are cited in Ingulli, Grandparent Visitation Rights: Social Policies and Legal Rights, 87 W.Va.L.Rev. 295 (1985); Annot., Grandparents' Visitation Rights, 90 A.L.R.3d 222 (1979); Bean, Grandparent Visitation: Can the Parent Refuse? 24 J.Fam.L. 393 (1985–1986). The problems of enforcement of decrees which such decisions create are discussed in Note, Rights of a Grandparent Over the Objections of a Parent: The Best Interests of the Child, 15 J.Fam.L. 51 (1976).

50. Kudler v. Smith, 643 P.2d 783 (Colo.App.1981), cert. denied 459 U.S. 837, 103 S.Ct. 83, 74 L.Ed.2d 78 (1982); In re Griffiths, 47 Ohio App.2d 238, 353 N.E.2d 884 (1975); Commonwealth ex rel. Zaffarano v. Genaro, 500 Pa. 256, 455 A.2d 1180 (1983) (grandparent seeking partial custody, friction between parent and grandparent outweighed benefits to the child); Hughes v. Hughes, 316 Pa.Super. 505, 463 A.2d 478 (1983); In re Custody of Thompson, 34 Wash.App. 643, 663 P.2d 164 (1983). In most of these cases the courts seemed to place greater weight on the child's welfare than on the grandparent's wishes, unlike the cases cited supra in note 49.

51. A. Kornhaber, K. Woodward, Grandparents/ Grandchildren (1985). J. Wallerstein, J. Kelly, Surviving

cized.[52] One may go so far as to accept the studies without also accepting the view that judicial enforcement of a grandparent's claim to visitation rights, made over the objection of the parent who is attempting to meet the responsibilities of custody, is for the child's or the custodian's best interests. The studies do not reveal what the consequences of that kind of interference with parental privacy and discretion may be. In fact the movement for wider grandparent visitation is in large part based upon a desire to vindicate the claims of the grandparents rather than to benefit the children. The institution of this sort of a lawsuit alone imposes heavy financial burdens on the custodian, who in most cases will have inadequate financial resources even to meet the daily demands for support. In addition the lawsuit imposes serious psychological stresses on the children at a time when they are least able to sustain them. If the grandparent's claim is upheld, the custodian, who is often a hard-pressed single parent, will then be subjected to deadlines and requirements which will interfere with her own relationship with the child. For all these reasons the statutes and the decisions dependent upon them are singularly ill advised. The law should return to the position taken before grandparent visitation statutes were enacted.[53] If the custodial parent has a firm objection to the visitation claim, that claim should be denied except perhaps in the rare case in which the child is old enough to have a strong preference and wishes to visit the grandparent. In conflicts of this kind between custodial parent and grandparent mediation may be helpful, just as it is in resolv-

ing father-mother custody disputes. But if mediation is unsuccessful, the wishes of the custodial parent, who, after all, bears all the responsibility of caring for the child, should be respected.

 **WESTLAW REFERENCES**

sy(right entitl! /5 visit! /s statut! law legislat! /s child infant minor /s grand-parent grand-mother grand-father)

grand-parent grand-mother grand-father non-parent! (not / 3 parent) /s interven! /s visit*** visitation

grand-parent grand-mother grand-father /s visit! /s hostil! antagoni!

---

§ 19.8 Custody of Children—Factors in Awarding Custody—Dispute Between Persons Other Than Parents

This section deals with the custody problems which arise when both parents are out of the picture and the litigation is between parties who are not the parents of the child. In most cases this is a question of determining what the child's welfare requires,[1] many of the same factors being relevant here as when the parents are contending for custody.[2] But in some cases the fact that it is non-parents who are seeking custody may give rise to different factors having relevance to the placement of the child. Where a relative of the child is contending with a non-relative for custody, it may be argued that some weight should be given to the fact of blood relationship, but the cases usually find that there is not a relative preference.[3] In fact the burden of proof in all these cases has been held to be

---

the Breakup 43 (1980) found that that some grandparents who lived close to the custodian and children after divorce were helpful and that the contacts with such grandparents benefited the children.

52. Ingulli, Grandparent Visitation Rights: Social Policies and Legal Rights, 87 W.Va.L.Rev. 295, 298 (1985) provides a citation and critique of the social studies.

53. See, e.g., Chodzko v. Chodzko, 66 Ill.2d 28, 4 Ill. Dec. 313, 360 N.E.2d 60 (1976). West v. King, 220 Va. 754, 263 S.E.2d 386 (1980); Brotherton v. Boothe, 161 W.Va. 691, 250 S.E.2d 36 (1978).

§ 19.8

1. Petition of Schomer, 89 Ill.App.3d 92, 44 Ill.Dec. 432, 411 N.E.2d 554 (1980); In re Moore, 8 N.C.App. 251,

174 S.E.2d 135 (1970); Commonwealth ex rel. Kuntz v. Stackhouse, 176 Pa.Super. 361, 108 A.2d 73 (1954), cert. denied 348 U.S. 981, 75 S.Ct. 571, 99 L.Ed. 763 (1955); State ex rel. Van Loh v. Prosser, 78 S.D. 35, 98 N.W.2d 329 (1959). Many other cases are collected in Annot., Award of Custody Where Contest is Between Child's Grandparent and One Other Than the Child's Parent, 30 A.L.R.3d 290 (1970).

2. See section 19.4, supra.

3. People in Interest of A. D., 706 P.2d 7 (Colo.App. 1985) (semble); Matter of Peter L., 59 N.Y.2d 513, 466 N.Y.S.2d 251, 453 N.E.2d 480 (1983); In Interest of Tremayne Quame Idress R., 286 Pa.Super. 480, 429 A.2d 40 (1981).

evenly divided, which is really to say that each party enters the case with no preferences in his favor.[4] Other factors found to be relevant include the ages of the parties,[5] the race of the child and the persons claiming custody,[6] the psychological attachments between the child and the prospective custodians,[7] the need for stability in the life of the child,[8] and to some degree at least, the desires of the natural parents, although this factor generally is not conclusive.[9]

The most complex of the custody conflicts falling within this section have arisen out of modern child care and adoption techniques. The question is, what is to be done when foster parents, who have temporary custody of a child under a "boarding home" agreement with a child placement agency which requires them to return the child on demand, become attached to the child and refuse to return him?

At the outset in this sort of dispute the foster parents may attack the procedure pursuant to which the child was removed from their custody, arguing that it violated the Due Process Clause. The United States Supreme Court had this contention before it in Smith v. Organization of Foster Families for Equality and Reform.[10] The plaintiff foster parents and their organization brought a civil rights suit against state and city officials alleging that removal procedures used by the defendants violated the Due Process Clause. The Court discussed whether the foster parent has a "liberty interest" in the custody of the child, without ever deciding the question. The Court conceded that a foster parent and child

may develop a "deeply loving and interdependent relationship" even though not related by blood. But it then attempted to draw a distinction between the position of the unrelated foster parent and a person related to the child by blood. It found the foster parent relationship different because it was based on state law and contract rather than on intrinsic human rights. The Court also emphasized the "virtually unavoidable" conflict between the interest of the foster parent and that of a natural parent which would result if the interest of the foster parent were afforded constitutional sanction. Where the natural parent gave up custody only on the understanding that the child would be returned, there would be great difficult in recognizing a liberty interest in the foster parent. After all this, however, the Court disclaimed deciding whether the foster parent had such a liberty interest, holding instead that even assuming that he did, the New York procedure met the demands of procedural due process. New York City law gave the foster parent a trial-type administrative review before removal, while the New York state law provided for a pre-removal judicial hearing. Subsequent cases in the lower federal courts read the Smith case as meaning that foster parents have no liberty interest in children placed in their custody by the state.[11]

Notwithstanding the Smith case and those which followed it, if the state should propose to remove a child from the custody of a foster parent without notice or any form of hearing, if the child is related in some way to the foster parent and has been in the custody of

---

4. In Interest of Tremayne Quame Idress R., 286 Pa. Super. 480, 429 A.2d 40 (1981).

5. In re Davis, 502 Pa. 110, 465 A.2d 614 (1983).

6. Ibid.

7. Smith v. Holt, 225 N.W.2d 906 (Iowa 1975), affirmed 240 N.W.2d 644 (Iowa 1976); In re Augustus, 158 N.W.2d 625 (Iowa 1968).

8. In re Hatzopoulos, 4 Fam.L.Rptr. 2075 (Colo.Juv.Ct. 1977). In re Guardianship of Stanger, 299 Minn. 213, 217 N.W.2d 754 (1974) appointed a custodian in part on the ground that he would be most likely to preserve the child's contacts with the grandparents.

9. People in Interest of A. D., 706 P.2d 7 (Colo.App. 1985); In re Erich, 310 A.2d 910 (Del.Ch.1973); Matter of

Peter L., 59 N.Y.2d 513, 466 N.Y.S.2d 251, 453 N.E.2d 480 (1983), 13 Hofstra L.Rev. 375 (1985); In re Guardianship of Schmidt, 71 Wis.2d 317, 237 N.W.2d 919 (1976).

10. 431 U.S. 816, 97 S.Ct. 2094, 53 L.Ed.2d 14 (1977).

11. Backlund v. Barnhart, 778 F.2d 1386 (9th Cir. 1985) (foster parents could be ordered by state court to refrain from corporal punishment of foster child without constitutional violation); Drummond v. Fulton County Dep't of Family & Children's Services, 563 F.2d 1200 (5th Cir.1977), cert. den. 437 U.S. 910 (1978) (child removed without a trial-type hearing, but after investigation and consultation with the foster parents).

the foster parent for a substantial period, such action by the state should be held to be a deprivation of procedural due process.[12] The form of notice and hearing might well vary with variation in the circumstances, so long as some opportunity to object to the removal is afforded the foster parent. Even in the absence of a relationship between foster parent and child, such an opportunity should be given, for the protection of the child as well as of the foster parent.[13]

Whether or not the foster parent is entitled to due process by virtue of having a liberty interest in his relationship with the child, the removal of the child from his custody may, in cases where the child has been with the foster parent for a substantial period, cause psychological harm to the child and great unhappiness to the foster parent. If the agency which placed the child in the foster home is acting only to provide temporary care for the child and if the natural parent of the child retains parental rights, then the agency must return the child to the parent. Presumably the foster parent will be informed that this is the situation, and will have accepted the child on these terms. Under these circumstances there is no alternative to the return of the child notwithstanding the emotional hardship to both foster parent and child.[14]

Where the natural parent's rights as a parent have been terminated, either voluntarily or involuntarily,[15] the solution to this conflict is not so clear. In the typical case the agency has a child which it intends eventually to place for adoption. It turns the child over to foster parents under a boarding home contract by which they are paid for their expenses and they agree to return the child on demand. The child is then left with them long enough so that a strong psychological attachment grows up between the child and the foster parents.[16] The agency later asks for the return of the child and the foster parents refuse. If the child's welfare is the only factor to be considered, the court is usually justified in giving custody to the foster parents, and some courts have done this.[17] But there is an important countervailing factor in the need to preserve the foster home system. If foster parents can violate their agreements and thereby acquire children for adoption, the agencies will not be able to make these temporary placements. Some

---

12. Rivera v. Marcus, 696 F.2d 1016 (2d Cir.1982), 50 Bklyn.L.Rev. 483 (1984) (foster parent related to the child who had had custody of the child for six years held to have a liberty interest in the child); Ellis v. Hamilton, 669 F.2d 510 (7th Cir.1982), cert. denied 459 U.S. 1069, 103 S.Ct. 488, 74 L.Ed.2d 631 (1982) (court assumes that some form of notice and hearing is due in these cases, but finds the state has provided adequate remedies). Eason v. Welfare Commissioner, 171 Conn. 630, 370 A.2d 1082 (1976), cert. denied 432 U.S. 907, 97 S.Ct. 2953, 53 L.Ed.2d 1079 (1977) also held that the state remedies were adequate, so that there was no violation of due process. Wilson v. Family Services Division, Region Two, 554 P.2d 227 (Utah 1976), appeal after remand 572 P.2d 682 (Utah 1977) held that a grandmother was entitled to be heard before a child whose parents' rights had been terminated was placed for adoption.

13. In Interest of R.K.W., 689 S.W.2d 647 (Mo.App. 1985). Contra: Nye v. Marcus, 198 Conn. 138, 502 A.2d 869 (1985); State by St. Louis County Welfare Dep't v. Niemi, 284 Minn. 225, 169 N.W.2d 758 (1969) (foster parents have no standing to litigate the custody of a child placed with them).

14. In re Jewish Child Care Ass'n of New York, 5 N.Y.2d 222, 183 N.Y.S.2d 65, 156 N.E.2d 700 (1959). But see the discussion of this problem in In re P., 71 Misc.2d 965, 337 N.Y.S.2d 203 (Fam.Ct.1972) by Judge Polier. See also J. Goldstein, A. Freud, A. Solnit, Beyond the Best Interests of the Child 39–45 (2d ed.1979) arguing

that during temporary placements the state should develop procedures for maintaining the relationship between child and absent parent, and that when the tie with his parents has been broken (using the child's scale of values respecting time) the temporary placement can no longer be considered temporary. Brief discussion of this problem is also found in State by St. Louis County Welfare Dep't v. Niemi, 284 Minn. 225, 169 N.W.2d 758 (1969).

15. Relinquishment and involuntary termination of parental rights are discussed in chapter 20, infra.

16. The agency could presumably prevent this by shifting the child from foster parent to foster parent, but this would certainly be harmful to the child, and is condemned by J. Goldstein, A. Freud, A. Solnit, Beyond the Best Interests of the Child 39 (2d ed.1979). This and other practices of placement agencies are criticized in Smith v. Organization of Foster Families for Equality and Reform, 431 U.S. 816, 831–838, 97 S.Ct. 2094, 2102–06, 53 L.Ed.2d 14 (1977).

17. People ex rel. I v. Convent of Sisters of Mercy in Brooklyn, 200 Misc. 115, 104 N.Y.S.2d 939 (1951); Commonwealth ex rel. Children's Aid Society v. Gard, 362 Pa. 85, 66 A.2d 300 (1949); Hammond v. Dep't of Public Assistance of Doddridge County, 142 W.Va. 208, 95 S.E.2d 345 (1956). See also Katz, Foster Parents Versus Agencies, 65 Mich.L.Rev. 145 (1966); Taylor, Guardianship or "Permanent Placement" of Children, 54 Cal.L.Rev. 741 (1966).

people may even seek to become foster parents for the sole purpose of short-cutting the adoption process, which involves long, even prohibitive, delay in obtaining a child. Foster homes play a useful part in child care, since they furnish neglected child with a home-like atmosphere and care superior to that in institutions. In order to protect this system and to make sure that foster home contracts are carried out in good faith, some courts have enforced agency demands for the child's return even when this did not seem immediately to serve the best interests of the particular child.[18] In this clear conflict of policies between the demands of the child's interests and the need to maintain the foster home system, it is not surprising that case authority may be found on each side.

A possible resolution of this conflict might lie in a consideration of the future prospects of the child. If it could be shown that adoption is probable, then removal of the child from the foster parents might be in the child's long run interests even though harmful to him in the short run.[19] But if the child's prospects appear to be only a succession of foster homes without a probability of the sta-

bility of an adoption, the child's welfare dictates permitting him to remain with the foster parents, looking forward perhaps to adoption by them.[20]

 WESTLAW REFERENCES

sy(custod! /5 child infant minor /s non-relative unrelated stranger)

foster +1 parent care home child /s remov! /p "due process" "fourteenth amendment"

find 97 sct 2094

foster +1 parent care home child /s notic! notif! /s hear*** /s remov! custod!

§ 19.9   Custody of Children—Modification of Custody Decrees

Custody orders, whether included in divorce decrees or in other kinds of judgment, are modifiable pursuant to statute in most states,[1] or, in the absence of statute, pursuant to the common law.[2]

The authority of a court to modify a custody order may be affected by events which have occurred since the original order was entered, as the Uniform Child Custody Jurisdiction

---

18. Convent of Sisters of Mercy v. Barbieri, 200 Misc. 112, 105 N.Y.S.2d 2 (1950); In re Adoption of Johnson, 144 W.Va. 625, 110 S.E.2d 377 (1959); In re Adoption and Custody of Underwood, 144 W.Va. 312, 107 S.E.2d 608 (1959); State Dep't of Public Assistance v. Pettrey, 141 W.Va. 719, 92 S.E.2d 917 (1956). In re St. John, 51 Misc. 2d 96, 272 N.Y.S.2d 817 (Fam.Ct.1966), reversed on other grounds 26 A.D.2d 980, 274 N.Y.S.2d 798 (3d Dep't 1966) held that the return of the child to the agency was in the child's long term best interests even though it would have adverse effects on the child in the short term.

19. Compare In re Henwood's Guardianship, 49 Cal.2d 629, 320 P.2d 1 (1958). Adoption was assumed to be probable and the text analysis was applied in In re St. John, 51 Misc.2d 96, 272 N.Y.S.2d 817 (Fam.Ct.1966), reversed on other grounds, 26 A.D.2d 980, 274 N.Y.S.2d 798 (3d Dep't 1966)

20. Hammond v. Department of Public Assistance of Doddridge County, 142 W.Va. 208, 95 S.E.2d 345 (1956) rested on facts of this nature.

§ 19.9

1. Alaska Stat. §§ 25.20.110, 25.24.170 (1983); Ariz. Rev.Stat. § 25–332 (Supp.1986); West's Ann.Cal.Civ.Code §§ 4600.5, 4603 (Supp.1987); Colo.Rev.Stat. §§ 14–10–131, 14–10–131.5 (Supp.1986); Conn.Gen.Stat.Ann. § 46b–56(a) (1986); Del.Code tit. 13, §§ 727, 729 (1981); D.C.Code 1973, § 16–914; Official Ga.Code Ann. § 19–9–3 (Supp. 1986); Hawaii Rev.Stat. §§ 571–46(6), 571–46.1(c) (1976);

Ill.—S.H.A. ch. 40, § 610 (Supp.1986); West's Ann.Ind. Code § 31–1–11.5–21.1, 31–1–11.5–24 (1980); Iowa Code Ann. § 598.21 (1980 and Supp.1986); Kan.Stat.Ann. § 60–1610 (1983); Ky.Rev.Stat. § 403.340 (1980); L.S.A.— La.Civ.Code art. 146 (1952 and Supp.1985); Me.Rev.Stat. Ann. tit. 19, § 752 (Supp.1986); Md.Code, § 9–103 (Supp. 1985); Mich.C.L.A. § 25.97, 25.312(7) (1984); Minn.Stat. Ann. § 518.18 (Supp.1985); Miss.Code 1983, §§ 93–5–23, 93–5–24; Vernon's Ann.Mo.Stat. § 452.410 (Supp.1986); Mont.Code Ann. § 40–4–219 (1983); Nev.Rev.Stat. § 125.510 (1981); N.M.Stat.Ann.1983, § 40–4–7; N.Y.— McKinney's Dom.Rel.L. § 240 (1986); N.C.Gen.Stat. § 50–13.7 (1984); Ohio Rev.Code § 3109.04(B)(1) (Supp. 1986); Okl.Stat.1986, tit. 12, § 1277 (Supp.); Pa.Stat. tit. 23, § 1011 (Supp.1986); S.D.Codif.L. § 24–4–45 (1984); Tenn.Code Ann. § 36–6–101 (1984); V.T.C.A., Fam.Code § 14.08 (1986); Utah Code Ann.1984, § 30–3–5; Vt.Stat. Ann. tit. 15, § 1014 (Supp.1985); West's Rev.Code Wash. Ann. § 26.09.26 (Supp.1986); W.Va.Code, § 48–2–15 (Supp.1985); Wis.Stat.Ann. § 767.245 (Supp.1986); Wyo. Stat.1977, § 20–2–113.

2. Boone v. Boone, 80 U.S.App.D.C. 152, 150 F.2d 153 (D.C.Cir.1945); In re Burket's Guardianship 58 Cal.App. 2d 726, 137 P.2d 475 (1943), 17 So.Cal.L.Rev. 73 (1943); Butterick v. Butterick, 127 N.H. 731, 506 A.2d 335 (1986). For a discussion of modification of custody decrees see Wexler, Rethinking the Modification of Child Custody Decrees, 94 Yale L.J. 757 (1985).

Act may apply to it.[3] And although, strictly speaking, the courts of one state cannot modify the decrees of courts of another state, the awards of custody made by courts of another state may be changed, but only if this is permitted by the Uniform Child Custody Jurisdiction Act and by the Parental Kidnapping Prevention Act.[4] As has been shown in an earlier section,[5] the purpose of those Acts is to reduce the opportunities of parents to relitigate custody issues after the breakup of families. The breadth and complexity of the rules contained in those Acts causes jurisdictional issues to overshadow or to be indistinguishable from the merits of the modification of custody decrees in many cases.[6] Where modification of another state's custody decree is sought, a new action must be brought, in the form of a habeas corpus petition or a petition in equity.[7] The court of the forum may modify the decree on the same grounds as would be available in the courts of the state in which the custody decree was originally granted.[8]

Modification of the custody aspects of a domestic divorce decree may be made on the motion of a party[9] or, according to some authorities, on the court's own motion.[10] It is accomplished by filing a verified petition in the original action.[11] Fresh service on the party having custody is not necessary,[12] but adequate notice and an opportunity to be heard are constitutional requirements.[13] Whether notice to the attorney who represented the party in the original divorce or custody action is sufficient is a point of disagreement among the cases.[14] Some hold that since the jurisdiction to modify is continuous, the attorney's authority continues until he expressly withdraws from the case.[15] Others take what seems a more realistic position that there is no presumption that his authority continues and that notice to him is not sufficient unless he is still representing a party in the litigation.[16]

The courts are in general agreement that the party seeking to modify a custody decree has the burden of proof.[17] As in the case of the original custody determination,[18] the deci-

---

3. 9 Unif.L.Ann. 116 (1979). This Act is now in force in all states.

4. Ibid.; 28 U.S.C.A. § 1738A.

5. See the discussion in section 12.5, supra.

6. E.g., Martin v. Martin, 45 N.Y.2d 739, 408 N.Y.S.2d 479, 380 N.E.2d 305 (1978), reargument denied 45 N.Y.2d 839, 409 N.Y.S.2d 1031, 381 N.E.2d 630 (1978); Nehra v. Uhlar, 43 N.Y.2d 242, 401 N.Y.S.2d 168, 372 N.E.2d 4 (1977).

7. Eddards v. Suhr, 193 N.W.2d 113 (Iowa 1971); Annot., 4 A.L.R.3d 1277 (1965).

8. People of State of N.Y. ex rel. Halvey v. Halvey, 330 U.S. 610, 67 S.Ct. 903, 91 L.Ed. 1133 (1947).

9. Papaik v. Papaik, 235 Minn. 393, 51 N.W.2d 68 (1952); State ex rel. Edwards v. Superior Court of King County, 37 Wash.2d 8, 221 P.2d 518 (1950). Geark v. Geark, 318 Mich. 614, 29 N.W.2d 89 (1947) held that the grandmother with whom the children lived could not move for modification because not a party, but it would see she should have been allowed to intervene. See, e.g., Harris v. Harris, 151 Neb. 191, 36 N.W.2d 849 (1949).

10. Cases are cited in Annot., 16 A.L.R.2d 664 (1951).

11. State ex rel. Edwards v. Superior Court of King County, 37 Wash.2d 8, 221 P.2d 518 (1950). But see Damm v. Damm, 77 R.I. 24, 72 A.2d 839 (1950), holding that this is a new and independent proceeding.

12. Atwood v. Atwood, 253 Minn. 185, 91 N.W.2d 728 (1958). But see Damm v. Damm, 77 R.I. 24, 72 A.2d 839 (1950).

13. Lamoreaux v. Schadt, 442 So.2d 117 (Ala.Civ.App. 1983); Ashlock v. District Court, Fifth Judicial District, 717 P.2d 483 (Colo.1986); Kalousek v. Kalousek, 77 Idaho 433, 293 P.2d 953 (1956); Heilman v. Heilman, 181 Kan. 467, 312 P.2d 622 (1957) (paternal grandmother who had custody under prior order entitled to notice, but note father who had no rights under prior order); Geark v. Geark, 318 Mich. 614, 29 N.W.2d 89 (1947); Thompson v. Thompson, 238 Minn. 41, 55 N.W.2d 329 (1952); Miller v. Miller, 153 Neb. 890, 46 N.W.2d 618 (1951).

14. Cases both ways are collected in Annot., 42 A.L.R.2d 1115 (1955).

15. E.g., State ex rel. Jones v. Superior Court, 78 Wash. 372, 139 P. 42 (1914); Sweeny v. Sweeny, 43 Wash. 2d 542, 262 P.2d 207 (1953).

16. E.g., Moore v. Lee, 72 So.2d 280 (Fla.1954).

17. Ex Parte McLendon, 455 So.2d 863 (Ala.1984), on remand 455 So.2d 867 (Ala.Civ.App. 1984); Speelman v. Superior Court of Santa Clara County, 152 Cal.App.3d 124, 199 Cal.Rptr. 784 (1983); Norris v. Norris, 12 Ill.App. 2d 226, 257 N.E.2d 545 (1970); In re Marriage of Bolin, 336 N.W.2d 441 (Iowa 1983); Kenney v. Hickey, ___ R.I. ___, 486 A.2d 1079 (1985).

18. Davis v. Davis, 280 Md. 119, 372 A.2d 231 (1977), cert. denied 434 U.S. 939, 98 S.Ct. 430, 54 L.Ed.2d 299 (1977), rehearing denied 434 U.S. 1025, 98 S.Ct. 754, 54 L.Ed.2d 774 (1978).

sion on modification of custody is a matter for the trial court's discretion, to be reversed only where that discretion has been abused or where it is based upon an erroneous legal rule.[19] Other courts come to about the same conclusion when they hold that the trial court's determination may be reversed only where clearly erroneous[20] or where there was not substantial probative evidence supporting that determination.[21] Notwithstanding these statements emphasizing the discretion of the trial court, a reading of a large number of appellate cases leaves the impression that there is a greater tendency to reverse trial court decisions where they concern modification than where they make an initial award of custody. This may be attributable to the adoption by appellate courts of stricter standards for the allowance of modification than have prevailed in the past.

The death of a party to a divorce action, as has been shown,[22] may affect the substantive right of the other parent to custody of the child. It also may have the effect in some states of depriving the divorce court of jurisdiction to modify the custody order.[23] According to these authorities any further change in custody after the death of a parent must be accomplished by a new suit, usually a petition for habeas corpus or a petition in equity. In view of the general flexibility of remedies for custody conflicts and of the desirability of rapid and inexpensive relief, the position taken by other courts that the power to modify is not affected by the death of a party, seems preferable.[24]

If the courts do have a general power to modify custody decrees where there is jurisdiction over the subject matter,[25] the question then is whether in exercising that power they may consider only facts which have occurred since the entry of the initial custody decree, that is, only changed circumstances in the usual meaning of that phrase, or whether they may take account of circumstances in existence before the initial decree was entered. Obviously this question evokes a conflict between the policy favoring the finality of judgments and decrees, and the social concern for the welfare of children. Although equity decrees are sometimes modifiable when circumstances change after the entry of the decree,[26] the general rules of res judicata do not ordinarily permit parties to reopen such decrees on the basis of circumstances in existence before the case was decided, even if those circumstances were not known to the parties or were not the subject of evidence in the case.[27]

The policy which favors the finality of judgments has caused a few courts to hold that custody orders may only be modified upon proof of a change in circumstances which has occurred after the original decree, of such a character that the child's welfare requires a change in his custody.[28] The statutes of a small number of states also seem to require

19. Ebert v. Ebert, 38 N.Y.2d 700, 382 N.Y.S.2d 472, 346 N.E.2d 240 (1976) (trial court findings to be accorded the greatest respect); Rice v. Rice, 603 P.2d 1125 (Okl. 1979); Tanner v. Tanner, 482 P.2d 443 (Wyo.1971); Gould v. Gould, 116 Wis.2d 493, 342 N.W.2d 426 (1984).

Some courts do not give so much weight to the trial court's determination. E.g., Hobson v. Hobson, 248 N.W.2d 137 (Iowa 1976) (appellate review is de novo, giving weight to the fact findings); Hille v. Hille, 116 N.H. 109, 352 A.2d 703 (1976) (trial court's discretion may be limited according to the circumstances of the case).

20. Gratrix v. Gratrix, 652 P.2d 76 (Alaska 1982); Tucker v. Tucker, 453 So.2d 1294 (Miss.1984) (findings will be set aside only where manifestly wrong).

21. Gunter v. Gunter, 93 Ill.App.3d 1043, 49 Ill.Dec. 505, 418 N.E.2d 149 (1981) (trial court's decision stands unless against the manifest weight of evidence or manifest injustice will result); Poret v. Martin, 434 N.E.2d 885 (Ind.1982) (appellate court to determine whether there

was substantial probative evidence supporting the trial court's conclusion).

22. See section 19.6, supra, at note 55.

23. Woodford v. Superior Court In and For Graham County, 82 Ariz. 181, 309 P.2d 973 (1957); Edgil v. Ragsdill, 256 Ark. 958, 511 S.W.2d 625 (1974), 29 Ark.L.Rev. 104 (1975); Baram v. Schwartz, 151 Conn. 315, 197 A.2d 334 (1964). See also Annot., 74 A.L.R. 1352 (1931).

24. Evans v. Cone, 62 So.2d 907 (Fla.1953); Jarrett v. Jarrett, 415 Ill. 126, 112 N.E.2d 694 (1953).

25. See section 12.5 supra.

26. E.g., United States v. Swift & Co., 286 U.S. 106, 52 S.Ct. 460, 76 L.Ed. 999 (1932).

27. See section 14.6, supra, dealing with attack on divorce decrees on non-jurisdictional grounds.

28. In re Marriage of Simmons, 487 N.E.2d 450 (Ind. App.1985); McKee v. McKee, 239 Iowa 1093, 32 N.W.2d

such proof.[29] Even in these states, however, it may be doubted whether the courts would hold that events occurring before the initial decree could not be looked at if these events tended to show a probability of serious physical or emotional harm to the child.[30] And under this more restricted rule some evidence related to conditions before the decree may be admissible, as where one of the parties has undergone a change in his character or living conditions. The former conditions may be proved in order to show that a change has occurred.[31] If a party was induced by fraud not to submit evidence in the earlier proceeding, he may be entitled to prove in the modification proceeding facts in existence at the time of the earlier decree.[32]

A larger number of cases have taken the broader view that the needs of the child outweigh the principles of res judicata in this context, and have held that existing custody arrangements may be modified if the child's welfare requires it, not only for changes in circumstances occurring after the initial decree, but also on the ground of facts existing at the time of that decree if those facts were not presented to or known by the court which issued that decree.[33] Some statutes expressly contemplate the admission of evidence relating to conditions in existence before the entry of the initial decree.[34] According to this line of cases a custody decree is only res judicata as to facts actually brought to the court's attention. If, for example, the decree were issued as a matter of law to enforce a still earlier decree, a complete reexamination of the facts could later be made.[35]

The question whether a custody decree may be modified only on the ground of changed circumstances occurring after its entry, or on the ground of facts existing before the decree but not known to the court at that time may sometimes be related to the settlement of custody disputes in separation agreements. If

---

379 (1948) (dictum); Kavanaugh v. Carraway, 435 So.2d 697 (Miss.1983); Agati v. Agati, 342 Pa.Super. 132, 492 A.2d 427 (1985); Wellnitz v. Wellnitz, 71 S.D. 430, 25 N.W.2d 458 (1946) (dictum); Hogge v. Hogge, 649 P.2d 51 (Utah 1982) (trial court must first decide whether there are changed circumstances warranting reconsideration of the custody award, after which it must decide how custody should be modified). The earlier cases of Sullivan v. Sullivan, 141 Conn. 235, 104 A.2d 898 (1954) and Krasnow v. Krasnow, 140 Conn. 254, 99 A.2d 104 (1953), requiring proof of a change in circumstances, seem to have been overruled by Simons v. Simons, 172 Conn. 341, 374 A.2d 1040 (1977). In some cases it may be difficult to determine just what rule the court was following. Pridgeon v. Superior Court, 134 Ariz. 177, 655 P.2d 1 (1982) (seems to take the same position as Hogge v. Hogge, supra); Friederwitzer v. Friederwitzer, 55 N.Y.2d 89, 447 N.Y.S.2d 897, 432 N.E.2d 765 (1982) (suggests that the effect of the initial decree may be less entitled to respect if it was based on an agreement of the spouses).

29. See the statutes of Alaska, Iowa and Texas, cited in note 1, supra.

30. See Valencia v. Valencia, 71 Ill.2d 220, 16 Ill.Dec. 467, 375 N.E.2d 98 (1978), in which the man with whom the child's mother was living had abused and may have killed the child's sibling but this was not proved at the original custody hearing.

31. Sullivan v. Sullivan, 141 Conn. 235, 104 A.2d 898 (1954).

32. Hendricks v. Hendricks, 69 Idaho 341, 206 P.2d 523 (1949) (dictum).

33. People of State of N.Y. ex rel. Halvey v. Halvey, 330 U.S. 610, 67 S.Ct. 903, 91 L.Ed. 1133 (1947) (Florida law); Porter v. Porter, 46 Ala.App. 22, 237 So.2d 507 (1970) (semble); Henkell v. Henkell, 224 Ark. 366, 273 S.W.2d 402 (1954); Gantner v. Gantner, 39 Cal.2d 272, 246 P.2d 923 (1952); Simons v. Simons, 172 Conn. 341, 374 A.2d 1040 (1977); Hendricks v. Hendricks, 69 Idaho 341, 206 P.2d 523 (1949); Valencia v. Valencia, 71 Ill.2d 220, 16 Ill.Dec. 467, 375 N.E.2d 98 (1978); Harwell v. Harwell, 253 Iowa 413, 112 N.W.2d 868 (1962); Young v. Young, 166 Neb. 532, 89 N.W.2d 763 (1958); Jackson v. Jackson, 200 Okl. 333, 193 P.2d 561 (1948); McDaniel v. McDaniel, 14 Wash.App. 194, 539 P.2d 699 (1975); Laughton v. Laughton, 71 Wyo. 506, 259 P.2d 1093 (1953). Other cases are cited in Annot., 9 A.L.R.2d 623 (1950).

34. See the Illinois, Missouri and Ohio statutes cited in note 1, supra. The Uniform Marriage and Divorce Act § 409, 9A Unif.L.Ann. 211 (1979) provides that: "* * * the court shall not modify a prior custody decree unless it finds, upon the basis of facts that have arisen since the prior decree or that were unknown to the court at the time of entry of the prior decree, that a change has occurred in the circumstances of the child or his custodian, and that the modification is necessary to serve the best interest of the child." Although the section is far from clear, it seems to mean that there must be proof of a change, and that the evidence of circumstances in existence before entry of the initial decree is admissible to show that the change occurred. It does not seem to permit modification where the basis for the child's unsatisfactory condition is wholly proved by evidence of circumstances existing before the initial decree. It would thus not permit modification on a state of facts such as existed in Valencia v. Valencia, 71 Ill.2d 220, 16 Ill.Dec. 467, 375 N.E.2d 98 (1978), even though the child appears to be in very serious danger.

35. Boone v. Boone, 80 U.S.App.D.C. 152, 150 F.2d 153 (D.C.Cir.1945).

the separation agreement executed by the parties provides for custody, the divorce court will normally accept that agreement and award custody accordingly,[36] although it is clear that it is not required to do so. The divorce court may, if it finds the child's best interests call for some other disposition, enter a decree different from the parties' agreement.[37] In practice many custody cases, probably a large majority, are disposed of by agreement with the encouragement of the law, especially now that the mediation movement has gained much popular and legal support.[38] Since this usually means that the divorce court has not heard much, if any, evidence on the child's best interests, some courts hold that custody awards based upon agreement may more readily be modified than awards occurring after a trial based on evidence and a finding concerning the child's interests.[39] This is unsound, both because it may discourage the settlement of custody conflicts by agreement and because it may produce instability in agreed custody dispositions.[40] Certainly the fact that the original custody decree was based upon the agreement of the parties does not immunize that decree from later modification.[41] Modification of those decrees should be made on the same grounds as are applied to other decrees, however.

Although at some point circumstances occurring before entry of the initial custody decree may justify a finding of serious risk of harm to the child and therefore be admissible and sufficient to support the modification of the decree, a broad rule permitting reliance upon such evidence may paradoxically result in harm to the child if it encourages courts to be too ready to upset existing custody arrangements. A court may, for example, tolerate an initially undesirable or doubtful custody disposition on the ground that it can always be changed later if necessary. An even more serious danger is that courts will be so ready to modify custody orders that the child will be disturbed and upset by the changes brought about by modification.[42] Many courts are aware of these dangers and especially in recent years have become more reluctant to modify existing custody arrangements.

In view of the conflict between the genuine need to protect children from harmful circumstances and the equally important policy favoring stability and discouraging attempts to relitigate custody decisions, the legislatures and courts have attempted to devise verbal formulas expressing in general terms the sort of evidence which will be sufficient to justify a modification of custody. The traditional position taken by many courts was and still is that a custody decree may be modified where modification is proven to promote the child's best interests, either on the basis of changed circumstances or of evidence not considered by the court in entering the original decree.[43] In the view of other courts and legislatures in

---

36. See section 19.4, supra, at note 89.

37. Ibid.

38. On the use of mediation in custody cases see section 14.8, supra.

39. Cases are collected and discussed in Sharp, Modification of Agreement-Based Custody Decrees: Unitary or Dual Standard, 68 Va.L.Rev. 1263 (1982).

40. Id. at 1288. In re Marriage of Carney, 24 Cal.3d 725, 157 Cal.Rptr. 383, 598 P.2d 36 (1979) and Millikin v. Millikin, 115 Wis.2d 16, 339 N.W.2d 573 (1983) held that no distinction is to be made for modification purposes between custody decrees which have been actually contested and those based upon the agreement of the parents.

41. Anderson v. Anderson, 14 Ariz.App. 195, 481 P.2d 881 (1971); Eschbach v. Eschbach, 56 N.Y.2d 167, 451 N.Y.S.2d 658, 436 N.E.2d 1260 (1982); Friederwitzer v. Friederwitzer, 55 N.Y.2d 89, 447 N.Y.S.2d 893, 432

N.E.2d 765 (1982). Earlier cases are cited in Annot., 73 A.L.R.2d 1444 (1960).

42. See J. Goldstein, A. Freud, A. Solnit, Beyond the Best Interests of the Child ch. 3 (2d ed.1979); Watson, The Children of Armageddon: Problems of Custody Following Divorce, 21 Syra.L.Rev. 55 (1969). See also Poesy v. Bunney, 98 Idaho 258, 561 P.2d 400 (1977).

43. E.g., Ex Parte McLendon, 455 So.2d 863 (Ala. 1984), on remand 455 So.2d 867 (Ala.Civ.App. 1984); Simons v. Simons, 172 Conn. 341, 374 A.2d 1040 (1977); Smith v. Todd, 464 So.2d 1155 (Miss.1985); Gibbons v. Gibbons, 442 P.2d 482 (Okl.1968); Kenney v. Hickey, __ R.I. __, 486 A.2d 1079 (1985); Keel v. Keel, 225 Va. 606, 303 S.E.2d 917 (1983); Holstein v. Holstein, 152 W.Va. 119, 160 S.E.2d 177 (1968). If one of the parents has de facto custody of the child, so that there has been no prior decree, one court has treated the case as an original decision on custody rather than as a modification. If that is done, there may be a broader power to remove the

other states, this formula gives the courts too great an opportunity to relitigate custody and is for that reason too broad. Many courts have responded to this objection by limiting modification to cases in which substantial or continuing changes of circumstance are proved,[44] or in which persuasive and substantial changes are proved,[45] or in which it is proved that there is a strong possibility that the child will be harmed if the existing custody arrangements are not changed.[46] Some state statutes have also been amended so as to restrict the circumstances in which custody decrees may be modified.[47]

Perhaps the strictest limitation on modification is found in the Uniform Marriage and Divorce Act.[48] That Act, in terms that are not very clear, seems to contain two limitations on the conventional standard of the child's best interests. In its first subsection it provides that no modification may be made in the first two years after the initial decree unless the child's environment may seriously endanger his physical, mental, moral or emotional health.[49] In its second subsection the Act states the traditional standard that modi-

fication must be necessary to serve the child's best interests, but then limits it by providing that the same custodian must be retained unless he agrees to the modification, or the child has been integrated into the petitioner's family with the consent of the custodian, or the child's environment seriously endangers his physical, mental, moral or emotional health and the harm caused by the change is outweighed by the advantages to the child.[50] The test of serious endangerment imposed by both subsections of the statute is intended to establish a presumption that the existing custodian should continue to care for the child.[51]

Joint custody decrees and provisions for visitation create special problems for the court which is asked to modify them. Where joint legal custody is awarded originally it would seem clear that it should be modifiable when the parents are no longer able to reach amicable agreement on decisions relating to the child, regardless of what the general custody modification statute provides.[52] In such a case modification may be accomplished without the adverse effect on the child which modification usually produces. Where joint

child from the existing custody even though as a practical matter that may produce as much disruption and psychological trauma for the child as does the usual modification of custody. State ex rel. Laughlin v. Hugelman, 219 Neb. 254, 361 N.W.2d 581 (1985).

44. E.g., Rice v. Rice, 460 N.E.2d 1228 (Ind.App.1984); In re Marriage of Davis, 441 N.E.2d 719 (Ind.App.1982). In re Marriage of Gonzales, 373 N.W.2d 152 (Iowa App. 1985) adopts a similar rule and in addition requires that the petitioner show a superior parenting ability.

45. E.g., In re Marriage of Carney, 24 Cal.3d 725, 157 Cal.Rptr. 383, 598 P.2d 36 (1979).

46. Forde v. Sommers, 117 N.H. 356, 373 A.2d 358 (1977), qualified by Richards v. Richards, 125 N.H. 331, 480 A.2d 155 (1984).

47. E.g. Wis.Stat.Ann. § 767.32(2) (Supp.1986–1987), as construed in Gould v. Gould, 116 Wis.2d 493, 342 N.W.2d 426 (1984) and Millikin v. Millikin, 115 Wis.2d 16, 339 N.W.2d 573 (1983) to require a showing that the existing custody arrangement is in some way harmful to the child. Matter of a Proceeding for Custody and/or Visitation of Minors Under Article 6 of Family Court Act, 87 Misc.2d 822, 386 N.Y.S.2d 928 (Fam.Ct.1976) takes a similar position.

48. Uniform Marriage and Divorce Act § 409, 9A Unif.L.Ann. 211 (1979).

49. Uniform Marriage and Divorce Act § 409(a), 9A Unif.L.Ann. 211 (1979), requiring that the petitioner present affidavits showing the required harm to the child. In

re Custody of Sexton, 84 Ill.2d 312, 49 Ill.Dec. 709, 418 N.E.2d 729 (1981). That this subsection is to be strictly enforced is the position of the Montana court. Strouf v. Strouf, 176 Mont. 406, 578 P.2d 746 (1978); Olson v. Olson, 175 Mont. 444, 574 P.2d 1004 (1978); Holm v. Holm, 172 Mont. 81, 560 P.2d 905 (1977).

50. A case which applies this subsection literally is In re Custody of Harne, 77 Ill.2d 414, 33 Ill.Dec. 110, 396 N.E.2d 499 (1979). But In re Custody of Sussenbach, 108 Ill.2d 489, 92 Ill.Dec. 556, 485 N.E.2d 367 (1985) seems to go back to the best interests test. Montana cases applying the section rigorously include In re Marriage of Sarsfield, ___ Mont. ___, 671 P.2d 595 (1983), appeal after remand ___ Mont. ___, 695 P.2d 473 (1985); Weber v. Weber, 176 Mont. 144, 576 P.2d 1102 (1978); Gianotti v. McCracken, 174 Mont. 209, 569 P.2d 929 (1977); In re Custody of Dallenger, 173 Mont. 530, 568 P.2d 169 (1977).

51. Uniform Marriage and Divorce Act § 409, Commissioners' Note, 9A Unif.L.Ann. 212 (1979).

52. Some states have enacted statutes addressed specifically to the modification of joint custody decrees. One such statute is Colo.Rev.Stat. § 14–10–131.5 (Supp.1986), which seems to take the position advocated in the text. Without such a statute it might be necessary to meet the restrictive standards imposed by the Uniform Marriage and Divorce Act, which would preserve the unworkable joint custody arrangement. See Darner v. District Court In & For Montrose County, Seventh Judicial Dist. 680 P.2d 235 (Colo.1984).

physical custody is originally awarded, the same should be true although here some adverse effect on the child is to be expected. But if the parties fall into such discord that they are unable to cooperate amicably in sharing the physical care of the child, this of itself should be considered a change of circumstance of such seriousness as to affect the child's welfare and therefore to be ground for modifying the custody decree.[53] A modification of sole custody to some form of joint custody should require the same sort of evidence which modifications of custody require under the state's statute or case law.[54]

If the parties are operating under a joint legal or physical custody decree and one of them proposes to move to a distant place, the cases disagree on whether or to what extent this should justify a modification of the joint custody order. Some of them refuse to modify the order on the theory that the move does not constitute a sufficient change in circumstances to meet the statutory test.[55] The effect of this may be to cut off one parent or the other from the close contact with the child which he had previously enjoyed.[56] Other cases take the more sensible course of attempting to rearrange the custody decree in such a way as to make the removal feasible but at the same time to maintain the child's contacts with both parents.[57] Analytically the effect of removal in these cases is very similar to its effect on the usual sole custody order when the custodian wishes to move and the non-custodial parent seeks to prevent the move in order to preserve his visitation rights.

Visitation provisions in divorce decrees raise two issues when a party seeks modification. The first is whether modification of visitation requires evidence of the same quality and force as modification of custody provisions. Of course there may be cases in which the exercise of visitation causes the child serious harm, and if so, the visitation could be restricted or terminated on the same grounds as would justify a change in custody.[58] Many changes in visitation assume such variety, however, that it is impossible to force them into a single standard such as the statutory standards for modification of custody. Thus visitation may be expanded or limited where the child has strong preferences even though there has not been the sort of extreme change in circumstances which would be required for a custody modification.[59] In other cases the removal of a parent from the jurisdiction may justify changes in visitation in order to meet the needs of that parent even though it cannot be said that the child's interests dictate the change.[60] In still other cases visitation may be expanded or limited where some effect on the child's welfare is shown to result thereby, without meeting the requirements for a custody modification.[61] In all such situations the questions may be made more complex by

---

53. In re Marriage of Dickman, 670 P.2d 20 (Colo.App. 1983); Rice v. Rice, 603 P.2d 1125 (Okl.1979); Matter of Marriage of Heinel, 55 Or.App. 275, 637 P.2d 1313 (1981); Moody v. Moody, 715 P.2d 507 (Utah 1986).

54. Hornbeck v. Hornbeck, 702 P.2d 42 (Okl.1985).

55. Sydnes v. Sydnes, 388 N.W.2d 3 (Minn.App.1986); Hegerle v. Hegerle, 355 N.W.2d 726 (Minn.App.1984).

56. See, e.g., Sydnes v. Sydnes, 388 N.W.2d 3 (Minn. App.1986).

57. In re Marriage of Frederici, 338 N.W.2d 156 (Iowa 1983); In re Marriage of Bolin, 336 N.W.2d 441 (Iowa 1983); Gordon v. Gordon, 339 N.W.2d 269 (Minn.1983); In re Marriage of Paradis, ___ Mont. ___, 689 P.2d 1263 (1984).

58. E.g., Tischendorf v. Tischendorf, 321 N.W.2d 405 (Minn.1982), cert. denied 460 U.S. 1037, 103 S.Ct. 1426, 75 L.Ed.2d 787 (1983); Hotze v. Hotze, 57 A.D.2d 85, 394 N.Y.S.2d 753 (4th Dep't 1977), appeal denied 42 N.Y.2d 805, 398 N.Y.S.2d 1027, 367 N.E.2d 660 (1977); Morris v. Morris, 271 Pa.Super. 19, 412 A.2d 139 (1979) (visitation

limited where conflicting religious beliefs caused harm to the child). The Tischendorf case refused to honor a claim that the child had a constitutional right not to be removed from the United States, the child there being an intelligent eleven-year-old.

59. In re Two Minor Children, 249 A.2d 743 (Del. 1969). But see Fanning v. Warfield, 252 Md. 18, 248 A.2d 890 (1969).

60. In the Interest of C. E. B., 604 S.W.2d 436 (Tex. Civ.App.1980). But Partridge v. Partridge, 257 Ind. 81, 272 N.E.2d 448 (1971) refused to expand visitation to include an eight-week stay with the father when the father moved out of the state.

61. Taraboletti v. Taraboletti, 56 Ill.App.3d 854, 14 Ill. Dec. 350, 372 N.E.2d 155 (1978); Flanagan v. Flanagan, 123 Ill.App.2d 17, 259 N.E.2d 610 (1970).

Dicta in Manson v. Manson, 35 Colo.App. 144, 529 P.2d 1345 (1974) and Olson v. Olson, 175 Mont. 444, 574 P.2d 1004 (1978) state that the two-year limitation imposed by

the difficulty of distinguishing clearly between visitation and custody.[62] When, for example, a parent's visitation is expanded from weekends and Christmas holidays to include a month in the summer as well, does this constitute a modification of visitation or of custody?[63] No rules can be devised which will satisfactorily solve all these questions. The courts must remain flexible and try to respect the parents' interests in maintaining contact with their children while at the same time preserving the children's welfare. Since the major factor in determining whether modification should be granted is its effect on the child's stability, the courts should be more liberal in expanding or limiting visitation when the effect on stability is slight and less liberal when the effect is great.

The second issue raised by proposed modification of visitation rights is whether the court should grant modification permitting the custodial parent to move out of the state where that would make the exercise of visitation inconvenient, difficult or impossible for the non-custodial spouse. The closely related question whether the proposed move out of state should be relevant to the initial grant of custody is discussed in an earlier section.[64] Although one might think that removal from the state would not be held to violate a decree which did not expressly forbid such a move,

there is a little authority that if the decree provides for visitation and if the move would prejudice visitation, the move should be considered to violate the decree.[65] If that is the law, then parties contemplating a move would be well advised to seek modification of the decree.

As might be expected where there is such a clear conflict between the interests of the custodial parent and those of the non-custodial parent, the courts are far from agreement on what standards to apply in deciding whether removal of the custodian and child from the state should be permitted, some courts within a single state exhibiting disagreement on the question.[66] In some states removal is permitted only when it is shown to be in the child's best interests.[67] If this standard is applied literally, it will usually serve to prevent removal, since any removal inflicts a certain amount of disruption on the child and requires him to adjust to a new environment, especially if he is of school age.[68] The effect of this standard may also be to place conclusive weight on the deprivation of visitation which the removal causes.[69] On the other hand, some courts apply the standard rather loosely, permitting the removal when it does not appear to benefit the child to any great extent.[70] In New York the standard seems to be that the custodian who wishes to move

the Uniform Marriage and Divorce Act, supra, note 48 does not apply to modifications of visitation.

But see Colo.Rev.Stat. § 14–10–129 (1974), providing that rights of visitation may be modified when it would serve the child's best interests, but that visitation rights may not be restricted except where visitation would endanger the child's physical health or significantly impair his emotional development.

62. See Partridge v. Partridge, 257 Ind. 81, 272 N.E.2d 448 (1971); Olson v. Olson, 175 Mont. 444, 574 P.2d 1004 (1978); In Interest of C. E. B., 604 S.W.2d 436 (Tex.Civ. App.1980).

63. Partridge v. Partridge, 257 Ind. 81, 272 N.E.2d 448 (1971) held this to be a change in custody.

64. See section 19.4, supra at notes 49 to 60.

65. Scheiner v. Scheiner, 336 So.2d 406 (Fla.App. 1976), cert. denied 342 So.2d 1103 (Fla. 1977), enjoining the move even though the initial decree did not expressly forbid it. See also Giachetti v. Giachetti, 416 So.2d 27 (Fla.App.1982).

66. Compare In re Marriage of Harris, 670 P.2d 446 (Colo.App.1983) with Casida v. Casida, 659 P.2d 56 (Colo.

App.1982), and Matter of Marriage of Meier, 286 Or. 437, 595 P.2d 474 (1979) with Marriage of Ditto, 52 Or.App. 609, 628 P.2d 777 (1981), review denied 291 Or. 504, 634 P.2d 1347 (1981). See also Spitzer, Moving and Storage of Postdivorce Children: Relocation, the Constitution and the Courts, 1985 Ariz.L.J. 1; Note, The Judicial Role in Post-Divorce Child Relocation Controversies, 35 Stan.L. Rev. 949 (1983).

67. Casida v. Casida, 659 P.2d 56 (Colo.App.1982); Reddig v. Reddig, 12 Ill.App.3d 1009, 299 N.E.2d 353 (1973); Matter of Marriage of Meier, 286 Or. 437, 595 P.2d 474 (1979); Fritschler v. Fritschler, 60 Wis.2d 283, 208 N.W.2d 336 (1973); Carpenter v. Carpenter, 220 Va. 299, 257 S.E.2d 845 (1979).

68. Matter of Marriage of Meier, 286 Or. 437, 595 P.2d 474 (1979).

69. In re Marriage of Burgham, 86 Ill.App.3d 341, 41 Ill.Dec. 691, 408 N.E.2d 37 (1980).

70. See Marriage of Ditto, 52 Or.App. 609, 628 P.2d 777 (1981), review denied 291 Or. 504, 634 P.2d 1347 (1981), in which the mother was permitted to take the children to New Zealand.

must establish "exceptional circumstances" which would warrant the removal, even where the move seems to be made in good faith and for reasons relating to her own welfare.[71] Some states take a more liberal approach to the custodian's move by holding that it should be permitted unless it significantly harms the child's physical, mental, moral or emotional health.[72] The most comprehensive and sensitive set of standards seems to be that of New Jersey, which approves removal from the state if it leads to a better and more comfortable life style for the custodian and child, even if it prevents daily or weekly visitation by the other parent, at least where alternative visitation can be arranged, although it would not approve removal if undertaken primarily to frustrate the other parent's visitation rights.[73] The court in this case emphasized that since the non-custodial parent is free to move away to seek better opportunities for himself, the custodial parent should be entitled to equivalent freedom, at least where some visitation arrangements can be made.

Even though the competing standards can be described in this way, it must be recognized that any standard is capable of manipulation, and that the outcome of any particular case will be as much affected by the circumstances of that case as by the general view which the court takes of removal and visitation. This is illustrated by the differing results exhibited by the reported cases.[74]

The specific kinds of changed circumstances which will persuade courts to modify custody orders vary with the degree of finality which courts feel constrained to give to initial decrees,[75] and with the courts' freedom to take account of some circumstances existing before the initial decree but not known to the court in that proceeding.[76] In general these are the kinds of circumstances which affect the child's welfare as described in detail in an earlier section.[77] The development of a strong preference by the child for life with the other parent may lead to modification,[78] although some courts seem reluctant to recognize this as a ground for modification.[79] Changes in the custodian's ability or willing-

71. Weiss v. Weiss, 52 N.Y.2d 170, 436 N.Y.S.2d 862, 418 N.E.2d 377 (1981), denying the mother the chance to move to Las Vegas in order to make a a career change, reversing a contrary decision by the trial court.

72. In re Marriage of Harris, 670 P.2d 446 (Colo.App. 1983); Auge v. Auge, 334 N.W.2d 393 (Minn.1983); Schmidt v. Schmidt, 7 Ohio App.3d 175, 454 N.E.2d 970 (1982); Long v. Long, 127 Wis.2d 521, 381 N.W.2d 350 (1986) (the fact that this case adopts a different standard from that in the Wisconsin case cited in note 67, supra, may be due to an amendment of the modification statute in that state).

73. D'Onofrio v. D'Onofrio, 144 N.J.Super. 200, 365 A.2d 27 (1976), affirmed on the opinion of the court below, 144 N.J.Super. 352, 365 A.2d 716 (1976). See also Hale v. Hale, 12 Mass.App.Ct. 812, 429 N.E.2d 340 (1981).

74. Cases either refusing to permit removal or shifting custody when the custodian proposes to move: In re Marriage of Nodot, 81 Ill.App.3d 883, 37 Ill.Dec. 96, 401 N.E.2d 1189 (1980); Temple v. Temple, 52 Ill.App.3d 851, 10 Ill.Dec. 706, 368 N.E.2d 192 (1977); In re Marriage of Malone, 340 N.W.2d 798 (Iowa App.1983); Vanderzee v. Vanderzee, 221 Neb. 738, 380 N.W.2d 310 (1986); Daghir v. Daghir, 56 N.Y.2d 938, 453 N.Y.S.2d 609, 439 N.E.2d 324 (1982); Weiss v. Weiss, 52 N.Y.2d 170, 436 N.Y.S.2d 862, 418 N.E.2d 377 (1981); O'Shea v. Brennan, 88 Misc. 2d 233, 387 N.Y.S.2d 212 (Sup.Ct.1976); Matter of Marriage of Meier, 286 Or. 437, 595 P.2d 474 (1979); Carpenter v. Carpenter, 220 Va. 299, 257 S.E.2d 845 (1979).

Cases permitting removal: Casida v. Casida, 659 P.2d 56 (Colo.App.1982); Arquilla v. Arquilla, 85 Ill.App.3d

1090, 41 Ill.Dec. 450, 407 N.E.2d 948 (1980); Lubeznik v. Liddy, 477 N.E.2d 947 (Ind.App.1985); In re Marriage of Lower, 269 N.W.2d 822 (Iowa 1978); Hale v. Hale, 12 Mass.App.Ct. 812, 429 N.E.2d 340 (1981); Meyer v. Meyer, 346 N.W.2d 369 (Minn.App.1984); Pender v. Pender, 598 S.W.2d 554 (Mo.App.1980); Hicks v. Hicks, 223 Neb. 189, 388 N.W.2d 510 (1986); Boll v. Boll, 219 Neb. 468, 363 N.W.2d 542 (1985); Middlekauff v. Middlekauff, 161 N.J.Super. 84, 390 A.2d 1202 (1978); D'Onofrio v. D'Onofrio, 144 N.J.Super. 200, 365 A.2d 27 (1976), affirmed on the opinion of the court below 144 N.J.Super. 352, 365 A.2d 716 (1976); Schmidt v. Schmidt, 7 Ohio App.3d 175, 454 N.E.2d 970 (1982); Marriage of Ditto, 52 Or.App. 609, 628 P.2d 777 (1981), review denied 291 Or. 504, 634 P.2d 1347 (1981); Long v. Long, 127 Wis.2d 521, 381 N.W.2d 350 (1986).

75. See the discussion at note 43, supra.

76. See the discussion at note 36, supra.

77. See sections 19.4, 19.6 and 19.8, supra.

78. Goto v. Goto, 52 Cal.2d 118, 338 P.2d 450 (1959); Butterick v. Butterick, 127 N.H. 731, 506 A.2d 335 (1986); Richards v. Richards, 125 N.H. 331, 480 A.2d 155 (1984); Allen v. Allen, 200 Or. 278, 268 P.2d 358 (1954); S. H. v. R. L. H., 169 W.Va. 550, 289 S.E.2d 186 (1982).

79. Filipello v. Filipello, 130 Ill.App.2d 1089, 268 N.E.2d 478 (1971); Ebert v. Ebert, 38 N.Y.2d 700, 382 N.Y.S.2d 472, 346 N.E.2d 240 (1976).

ness to care for the child is also a reason to modify,[80] especially where it is of a magnitude to justify a finding that the custodian is unfit to care for the child.[81] Conversely, some courts have modified custody where the noncustodial parent's ability or capacity to care for the child has substantially improved since the initial decree.[82] Evidence that the child's condition has changed for the worse under the custodian's care may be a ground for modifying custody.[83] The fact that a parent is inducted into the armed forces does not of itself justify modifying a decree giving him custody of his children.[84] Some earlier cases based modification on religious factors,[85] but it seems clear that the courts should not prefer one religion over another or prefer a custodian who professes a religious belief over an agnostic or atheist as a ground for the modification of custody.[86]

As is the case where the question is the original grant of custody,[87] contemporary courts are not of one mind on whether a custodian's sexual relations outside marriage are grounds for removing the child from his custody. Most of the cases seem to involve mothers, and many courts even today find that a mother's sexual conduct is immoral and justifies removal of the child from her custody.[88] Other courts are more willing to recognize that moral standards have changed and to hold that a mother's sexual activities are not grounds for modification when they do not affect the child.[89]

The remarriage of one of the parents is often asserted as a ground for modifying the custody decree.[90] A few cases contain overly broad language to the effect that remarriage alone is not enough to warrant modification.[91] It may not justify modification in all cases, but it may be an important factor leading to modification if it enables a parent to provide a satisfactory home for the child if the stepparent is willing to accept and help to care for

80. Simons v. Simons, 172 Conn. 341, 374 A.2d 1040 (1977); In re Custody of Harne, 77 Ill.2d 414, 33 Ill.Dec. 110, 396 N.E.2d 499 (1979); People ex rel. Rathbun v. Rathbun, 48 Ill.App.3d 328, 6 Ill.Dec. 314, 362 N.E.2d 1136 (1977); In re Marriage of Davis, 441 N.E.2d 719 (Ind. App.1982); Hobson v. Hobson, 248 N.W.2d 137 (Iowa 1976); Warren v. Warren, 191 N.W.2d 659 (Iowa 1971); Friederwitzer v. Friederwitzer, 55 N.Y.2d 89, 447 N.Y.S. 2d 893, 432 N.E.2d 765 (1982).

In re Marriage of Carney, 24 Cal.3d 725, 157 Cal.Rptr. 383, 598 P.2d 36 (1979) held that a father's physical handicap preventing him from engaging in physical activities with the children was not sufficient reason to modify custody.

81. Berigan v. Berigan, 185 Neb. 411, 176 N.W.2d 1 (1970). Cases on the mental health of the parent are cited in Annot., 74 A.L.R.2d 1073, 1078 (1960).

82. Perdue v. Perdue, 254 Ind. 77, 257 N.E.2d 827 (1970); Hille v. Hille, 116 N.H. 109, 352 A.2d 703 (1976); Kenney v. Hickey, ___ R.I. ___, 486 A.2d 1079 (1985); Hogge v. Hogge, 649 P.2d 51 (Utah 1982).

83. In re Marriage of Padiak, 101 Ill.App.3d 306, 56 Ill.Dec. 826, 427 N.E.2d 1372 (1981); Lee v. Lee, 92 Misc. 2d 551, 400 N.Y.S.2d 680 (1977); Valeo v. Valeo, 132 Vt. 526, 322 A.2d 306 (1974).

84. Goto v. Goto, 52 Cal.2d 118, 338 P.2d 450 (1959).

85. Sullivan v. Sullivan, 141 Conn. 235, 104 A.2d 898 (1954); Frank v. Frank, 26 Ill.App.2d 16, 167 N.E.2d 577 (1960).

86. Gould v. Gould, 116 Wis.2d 493, 342 N.W.2d 426 (1984).

87. See section 19.4, supra.

88. Scherm v. Scherm, 12 Ark.App. 207, 671 S.W.2d 224 (1984); Jarrett v. Jarrett, 78 Ill.2d 337, 400 N.E.2d 421 (1979), cert. denied 449 U.S. 927, 101 S.Ct. 329, 66 L.Ed.2d 155 (1980) rehearing denied 449 U.S. 1067, 101 S.Ct. 797, 66 L.Ed.2d 612 (1980); Poret v. Martin, 434 N.E.2d 885 (Ind.1982); M. L. G. v. J. E. G., 671 S.W.2d 312 (Mo.App.1984); Anderson v. Anderson, 85 S.D. 152, 179 N.W.2d 1 (1970), appeal after remand 86 S.D. 757, 201 N.W.2d 394 (1972); Shioji v. Shioji, 712 P.2d 197 (Utah 1985). Other cases are collected in Annot., 100 A.L.R.3d 625 (1980). See also Watts v. Watts, 17 Ark.App. 253, 707 S.W.2d 777 (1986), distinguishing the Scherm case.

89. Dunlap v. Dunlap, 475 N.E.2d 723 (Ind.App.1985); Molloy v. Molloy, 460 S.W.2d 15 (Ky.1970); Stewart v. Stewart, 430 So.2d 189 (La.App.1983); Greenfield v. Greenfield, 200 Neb. 608, 264 N.W.2d 675 (1978); Matter of Marriage of Niedert, 28 Or.App. 309, 559 P.2d 515 (1977) (father's immorality not sufficient grounds for modification). Christian v. Randall, 33 Colo.App. 129, 516 P.2d 132 (1973) held that it was error for the trial court to modify the custody of the children's mother on the ground that she had gone through a transsexual change from female to male and had married a woman, where the change had not adversely affected the children.

90. Cases are collected in Annot., 43 A.L.R.2d 363 (1955).

91. North v. North, 209 Ga. 883, 76 S.E.2d 617 (1953); Peterson v. Peterson, 77 Idaho 89, 288 P.2d 645 (1955); Maikos v. Maikos, 260 Iowa 382, 147 N.W.2d 879 (1967); Gianotti v. McCracken, 174 Mont. 209, 569 P.2d 929 (1977) (Uniform Marriage and Divorce Act).

the child.[92] Conversely, the marriage of the custodial parent to an abusive or neglectful spouse may often be a reason to shift custody to the other parent.[93]

It is not uncommon for hostility between the spouses arising out of their divorce to continue after the divorce has been granted and to affect their performance of obligations imposed by the custody decree. This hostility may be manifested by attempts to alienate the child from the other parent or by attempts to prevent the other parent from exercising visitation rights or from seeing the child. Although this sort of conduct usually constitutes a violation of the custody decree and therefore could be the basis for punishment by contempt, it may be difficult to prove and courts seem reluctant to impose fines or jail terms as punishment.[94] In such circumstances the aggrieved parent, finding himself without an effective remedy, seeks to modify the custody decree in his favor. The courts often disavow any intention to use modification of the decree as punishment.[95] Where the violation of the decree is deliberate and repeated, however, they will sometimes rely upon the custodian's conduct to modify it in the noncustodial parent's favor.[96] And if a parent's attempts to alienate the child from the other parent affect the psychological or emotional health of the child, the courts will also modify the decree.[97] It is paradoxical that these cases usually reject the custodian's violation of the custody decree as a ground for modification when the statutes in all states now provide that "unclean hands" may be a ground for refusing to permit a parent to seek modification of the decree, unclean hands being defined to include a violation of an ex-

92. Stewart v. Stewart, 41 Cal.2d 447, 260 P.2d 44 (1953); McGuire v. McGuire, 190 Kan. 524, 376 P.2d 908 (1962). But in states having a strict rule for modification, the sole fact that the non-custodial parent is in a better position to care for the child than before would not be sufficient grounds for shifting custody.

93. In re Marriage of Utzinger, 721 P.2d 703 (Colo. App.1986) (sexual abuse by stepfather); In re Custody of Sussenbach, 108 Ill.2d 489, 912 Ill.Dec. 556, 485 N.E.2d 367 (1985); Valencia v. Valencia, 71 Ill.2d 220, 16 Ill.Dec. 467, 375 N.E.2d 98 (1978); Norenberg v. Norenberg, 168 N.W.2d 794 (Iowa 1969) (hostility of stepmother toward mother); Steagall v. Steagall, 442 So.2d 732 (La.App.1983) (sexual abuse by stepfather); In re Custody of Dumont, __ Mont. __, 700 P.2d 167 (1985) (harsh physical discipline by stepfather); In re Marriage of Sarsfield, __ Mont. __, 671 P.2d 595 (1983) (mother living with child molester), appeal after remand __ Mont. __, 695 P.2d 473 (1985); In re Furrow, 187 Neb. 64, 187 N.W.2d 586 (1971) (violence by stepfather). Millikin v. Millikin, 115 Wis.2d 16, 339 N.W.2d 573 (1983) upheld a trial court's refusal to modify custody when the children had "problems" with their stepfather, finding that the modification was not necessary to the child's best interests.

94. See, e.g., Egle v. Egle, 715 F.2d 999, 1008 (5th Cir. 1983), writ denied 469 U.S. 1032, 105 S.Ct. 549, 83 L.Ed. 2d 371 (1984), in which the trial court held the mother in contempt for egregious violations of the decree but imposed no punishment.

95. Ashlock v. District Court, Fifth Judicial District, 717 P.2d 483 (Colo.1986) (mother's removal from the state in violation of the decree may not be punished by modification); In re West, 245 A.2d 636 (D.C.App.1968) (court refuses to consider reprehensible conduct having no effect on the child's welfare); Kalousek v. Kalousek, 77 Idaho 433, 293 P.2d 953 (1956); Norris v. Norris, 12 Ill.App.2d 226, 257 N.E.2d 545 (1970) (refuses modification on the ground the mother had removed the child from the

jurisdiction); Marshall v. Reeves, 262 Ind. 107, 311 N.E.2d 807 (1974) (violation of a decree is not of itself a ground for modification); Everett v. Everett, 433 So.2d 705 (La.1983) (trial court erred in changing custody from mother to father on the ground mother had frustrated father's visitation rights); Bylinski v. Bylinski, 25 Mich. App. 227, 181 N.W.2d 283 (1970) (trial court erred in changing custody as a punishment for contempt in frustrating visitation rights); Smith v. Smith, 282 Minn. 190, 163 N.W.2d 852 (1968) (no error to deny modification where the mother took the children to Egypt in frustration of visitation rights); Knoblauch v. Jones, 613 S.W.2d 161 (Mo.App.1981) (removal from the state without permission is not of itself a ground for modification); In re Custody of Poole, 8 N.C.App. 25, 173 S.E.2d 545 (1970) (modification improper when based upon mother's violation of an order not to associate with a certain person); Pamela J. K. v. Roger D. J., 277 Pa.Super. 579, 419 A.2d 1301 (1980) (father's frustration of mother's visitation rights was not of itself a ground to modify custody); Sweeny v. Sweeny, 43 Wash.2d 542, 262 P.2d 207 (1953).

Other cases are collected in Annot., Interference by Custodian of Child With Non-Custodial Parent's Visitation Rights as Ground For Change of Custody, 28 A.L.R. 4th 9 (1984).

96. Egle v. Egle, 715 F.2d 999 (5th Cir.1983), petition for mandamus denied 469 U.S. 1206, 105 S.Ct. 1234, 84 L.Ed.2d 371 (1985); Garrett v. Garrett, 464 S.W.2d 740 (Mo.App.1971).

97. In re Marriage of Ciganovich, 61 Cal.App.3d 289, 132 Cal.Rptr. 261 (1976); Tyree v. Jackson, 226 Ga. 690, 177 S.E.2d 160 (1970); Hotze v. Hotze, 57 A.D.2d 85, 394 N.Y.S.2d 753 (4th Dep't 1977), appeal denied 42 N.Y.2d 805, 398 N.Y.S.2d 1027, 367 N.E.2d 660 (1977); Hoog v. Hoog, 460 P.2d 946 (Okl.1969); Matter of Marriage of Birge, 34 Or.App. 581, 579 P.2d 297 (1978). But see Labow v. Labow, 59 N.Y.2d 956, 466 N.Y.S.2d 304, 453 N.E.2d 533 (1983).

isting custody decree.[98] As has been argued, the doctrine of unclean hands is not a sound basis for deciding custody disputes.[99] It should not be relied upon in the decision of modification claims, either as a ground for modification or as a reason for denying a parent standing to seek modification. But where either the violation of a decree or attempts to alienate the child from a parent, or both together, have a direct effect on the child's welfare, these factors clearly should qualify as a ground for modification. If both parents are determined to hurt each other or get revenge on each other through the child, no really satisfactory resolution of the conflict may be possible, leaving the trial court only a choice of evils.[1]

 WESTLAW REFERENCES

134k303 /p "uniform child custody jurisdiction" u.c.c.j.a. /p modif!

134k303 /p modif! /p noti! /p hear***

di(modif! /s sole! one /3 custod! /s joint!)

134k300 134k303 285k2(17) /p modif! /p custod! /p "best interest" /p move* moving remov!

modif! /s custod! /s sex sexual! /s abus!

modif! /s custod! /s clean unclean +1 hand

§ 19.10   Custody of Children—Enforcement of Custody Decrees

If one defines enforcement broadly, it is accurate to say that there are several methods for the enforcement of custody decrees, some of which have been discussed in earlier sections of this work. Thus the removal of a child from the custody of a parent in violation of a custody decree, either by the other parent or a third person, may now be a crime if the removal is wilful or with knowledge of the decree.[1] The parent who has custody pursuant to a decree may recover damages from the other parent or a third person who takes or withholds the child in violation of the decree.[2] The writ of habeas corpus provides a specific remedy enabling such a parent to recover possession of the child.[3] The enforcement of the custody orders of other states either by habeas corpus or a petition in equity in the forum state is governed by the Uniform Child Custody Jurisdiction Act and the Parental Kidnapping Prevention Act, both of which are discussed in the section on custody jurisdiction.[4] In many states the courts are authorized to require a bond of a parent to secure the production of the child at trial or the return of the child to a custodial parent after a period of visitation, the bond to be forfeited if the court's order is not complied with.[5]

It is a question of some difficulty whether a court may enforce custody rights, usually rights of visitation, by authorizing child support to be withheld by the other spouse until his visitation rights are honored. As might be expected, there are cases on both sides of

98. Uniform Child Custody Jurisdiction Act § 8, 9 Unif.L.Ann. 142 (1979), discussed in section 13.5, supra. Cases applying the unclean hands doctrine include Application of Stone, 14 Ariz.App. 109, 481 P.2d 280 (1971); Martin v. Martin, 45 N.Y.2d 739, 408 N.Y.S.2d 479, 380 N.E.2d 305 (1978), reargument denied 45 N.Y.2d 839, 409 N.Y.S.2d 1031, 381 N.E.2d 630 (1978); Nehra v. Uhlar, 43 N.Y.2d 242, 401 N.Y.S.2d 168, 372 N.E.2d 4 (1977). Cases refusing to apply it include King v. King, 477 P.2d 356 (Alaska 1970); Lunnie v. Lunnie, 127 Vt. 207, 243 A.2d 795 (1968).

99. See section 12.5, supra.

1. E.g., Egle v. Egle, 715 F.2d 999 (5th Cir.1983), petition for mandamus denied 469 U.S. 1206, 105 S.Ct. 1234, 84 L.Ed.2d 371 (1985).

§ 19.10

1. State v. McLaughlin, 125 Ariz. 505, 611 P.2d 92 (1980); People v. Coyle, 654 P.2d 815 (Colo.1982); People v. Williams, 105 Ill.App.3d 372, 61 Ill.Dec. 259, 434 N.E.2d 412 (1982); Marchand v. State, 435 N.E.2d 284

(Ind.App.1982). Other cases are cited in section 11.2 supra, at notes 2 and 3, and in Annot., 20 A.L.R.4th 823 (1983). People v. Howard, 36 Cal.3d 852, 206 Cal.Rptr. 124, 686 P.2d 644 (1984) held that when husband and wife were reconciled after an interlocutory divorce decree, the custody order in that decree was no longer in effect, and the father could therefore not be criminally convicted for violating the order when he removed the children from the custody of the mother.

2. E.g., Fenslage v. Dawkins, 629 F.2d 1107 (5th Cir. 1980). Other cases are cited in section 11.2, supra, at note 19.

3. See section 19.3, supra, at note 18 and State ex rel. Butler v. Morgan, 34 Or.App. 393, 578 P.2d 814 (1978); Marshall v. Wilson, 616 S.W.2d 932 (Tex.1981).

4. See section 12.5, supra.

5. Langley v. Denton, 263 Ark. 904, 568 S.W.2d 19 (1978); Herring v. Morton, 248 Ark. 718, 453 S.W.2d 400 (1970); Brooks v. Brooks, 131 Vt. 86, 300 A.2d 531 (1973).

the question.[6] If the children are so dependent upon the child support payments that they will be in need without them, it seems clear that the payments should not be used as a method of enforcement. On the other hand, if the custodial parent is able to support the children adequately, so that the question is merely who should bear the burden of the support, ordering the non-custodial parent to withhold payments pending recognition of his visitation rights may be an effective method of support and would not impose hardship on the child.[7]

The usual method of enforcing custody decrees is by contempt proceedings. In order to use contempt, the custody decree must be reasonably clear and definite in informing the parent what he is required to do.[8] Contempt as a device for enforcing compliance with the custody order is civil,[9] but the court may also punish past violations of the decree by a criminal contempt conviction.[10] The criminal contempt must be proved beyond a reasonable doubt[11] and is punishable by a fine or specifically limited jail term.[12] The sanctions in civil contempt must be conditioned on the defendant's compliance with the custody decree.[13] If the custody order is violated by a person other than a party to the divorce action, that person may be held in contempt if he had knowledge of the order and acted in concert with a party to the divorce action.[14]

Personal jurisdiction over the defendant is required in order to find him in contempt.[15] Some cases hold that if he was personally subject to the court's jurisdiction in the divorce action, that jurisdiction continues so that personal jurisdiction over him need not be acquired again for purposes of the contempt proceeding,[16] although of course he must be given notice and an opportunity to be heard.[17] Other cases take the position that he must be properly subjected to personal jurisdiction again when the contempt proceeding is initiated.[18] Under the Uniform Child Custody Jurisdiction Act[19] the custody decree of another state may be filed in the clerk's office of a court in the state of the forum and when this is done, it may be enforced by contempt in the same manner as a decree of the forum, provided of course the defendant is made personally subject to the court's jurisdiction.[20]

A conviction for contempt must be based upon evidence that the failure to comply with the custody order was wilful,[21] and that the

6. Appert v. Appert, 80 N.C.App. 27, 341 S.E.2d 342 (1986), citing cases both ways on the subject.

7. Cf. Note, Making Parents Behave: The Conditioning of Child Support and Visitation Rights, 84 Colum.L. Rev. 1059 (1984).

8. Kranis v. Kranis, 313 So.2d 135 (Fla.App.1975); Dey v. Cunningham, 93 Idaho 684, 471 P.2d 71 (1970); Clark v. Clark, 404 N.E.2d 23 (Ind.App.1980).

9. Blankenship v. Blankenship, 63 Ill.App.3d 803, 20 Ill.Dec. 956, 380 N.E.2d 1165 (1978); Mather v. Mather, 70 N.C.App. 106, 318 S.E.2d 548 (1984).

10. In re Marriage of Joseph, 44 Colo.App. 128, 613 P.2d 344 (1980); Mather v. Mather, 70 N.C.App. 106, 318 S.E.2d 548 (1984).

11. Dennison v. Mobley, 257 Ark. 216, 515 S.W.2d 215 (1974); Abbott v. Abbott, 129 Ill.App.2d 96, 262 N.E.2d 502 (1970).

12. In re Marriage of King, 44 Wash.App. 189, 721 P.2d 557 (1986).

13. Blankenship v. Blankenship, 63 Ill.App.3d 803, 20 Ill.Dec. 956, 380 N.E.2d 1165 (1978); Curlee v. Howle, 277 S.C. 377, 287 S.E.2d 915 (1982).

14. Dennison v. Mobley, 257 Ark. 216, 515 S.W.2d 215 (1974) (criminal contempt); Wilkerson v. Tolbert, 239 Ga. 702, 238 S.E.2d 338 (1977). Other cases are cited in

Annot., 7 A.L.R.4th 893 (1981). But see Demarest v. Superior Court for Los Angeles County, 103 Cal.App.3d 791, 165 Cal.Rptr. 641 (1980).

15. Brown v. Brown, 183 Colo. 356, 516 P.2d 1129 (1973); Smith v. Smith, 244 Ga. 230, 259 S.E.2d 480 (1979).

16. Blank v. District Court In and For Boulder County, 190 Colo. 114, 543 P.2d 1255 (1976); Brown v. Brown, 183 Colo. 356, 516 P.2d 1129 (1973).

17. Ex Parte Cox, 479 S.W.2d 110 (Tex.Civ.App.1972).

18. Smith v. Smith, 244 Ga. 230, 259 S.E.2d 480 (1979); Tuten v. Tuten, 227 Ga. 228, 180 S.E.2d 233 (1971).

19. Uniform Child Custody Jurisdiction Act § 15, 9 Unif.L.Ann. 158 (1979).

20. State ex rel. Butler v. Morgan, 34 Or.App. 393, 578 P.2d 814 (1978). See also Gedeon v. Gedeon, 630 P.2d 579 (Colo.1981), appeal dismissed for want of a substantial federal question 454 U.S. 1050, 102 S.Ct. 592, 70 L.Ed.2d 585 (1981), which enforced fines imposed by a New Mexico contempt proceeding.

21. Entwistle v. Entwistle, 61 A.D.2d 380, 402 N.Y.S.2d 213 (2d Dep't 1978) (dictum that removal was wilful if the mother never intended to remain in the state).

defendant was able to comply with it.[22] Where the order directs the defendant to turn over the children to the other parent, it must be proved that he was in control of the children and that he violated an express order to deliver them.[23] A violation may also occur when a period of visitation ends and the noncustodial parent then refuses to return the child to the custodian.[24] It is not a defense to a failure to return the child that the child did not wish to return to the other parent.[25] Of course if the child is delivered into court by the time of the hearing, the defendant may not be held in contempt.[26]

The reader should be referred at this point to other recent developments which have had a salutary effect in causing parties to custody disputes to comply with court orders. An earlier section has discussed at length the Uniform Child Custody Jurisdiction Act and the Parental Kidnapping Prevention Act, both of which are designed to prevent violations of custody orders.[27] And the enactment in many jurisdictions of criminal statutes imposing heavy sanctions upon parents who carry off their children in violation of custody decrees has certainly reduced the incidence of "seize and run" attempts by parents.[28]

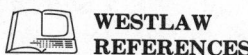

WESTLAW REFERENCES

di(custod! /s child minor infant /s contempt /s civil!)
custod! /s child minor infant /s contempt /3 crime criminal!

---

22. Glesner v. Dembrosky, 73 N.C.App. 594, 327 S.E.2d 60 (1985).

23. Pereira v. Pereira, 35 N.Y.2d 301, 361 N.Y.S.2d 148, 319 N.E.2d 413 (1974); Ex Parte Karr, 663 S.W.2d 534 (Tex.App.1983).

24. Copic v. Iowa District Court for Polk County, 356 N.W.2d 223 (Iowa 1984).

25. Clark v. Atkins, 489 N.E.2d 90 (Ind.App.1986).

26. Blankenship v. Blankenship, 63 Ill.App.3d 803, 20 Ill.Dec. 956, 380 N.E.2d 1165 (1978).

27. See section 12.5, supra.

28. See section 11.2, supra.

Chapter 20

TERMINATION OF PARENTAL
RIGHTS AND ADOPTION

Table of Sections

§ 20.1 Termination of Parental Rights and Adoption—Background and Contemporary Problems

Adoption is the legal process by which a child acquires parents other than his natural parents and parents acquire a child other than a natural child. As a result of the adoption decree the legal rights and obligations which formerly existed between the child and his natural parents come to an end, and are replaced by similar rights and obligations with respect to his new adoptive parents. It is common, in considering adoption, to focus attention on the second of these steps, that is, the formation of the legal bond with the adoptive parents, but since in our legal system it is generally the case that the parent-child relationship may exist with only one set of parents at a time, adoption also neces-

sarily involves the termination of the bond with the natural parents. In some jurisdictions the two steps are accomplished by two separate lawsuits, the first being referred to as a proceeding for termination of parental rights, the second as adoption. Both steps will be considered in this chapter under the general heading of adoption.

It is also possible in many jurisdictions to bring a legal proceeding for the adoption of an adult.[1] This is done for inheritance purposes and is a simple procedure, raising none of the difficult problems inherent in child adoptions.

There are some pre-Roman traces of adoption, but the most thorough early development of adoption is found in the Roman law, where it was recognized in two forms.[2] The form called *adoptio* applied to unemancipated children, and brought about their transfer

§ 20.1
1. See section 21.10, Practitioner's Edition.

2. There are several historical accounts of adoption. See, e.g., Presser, The Historical Background of the

850

from the family and authority of their natural father to that of their adoptive father. The formalities for *adoptio*, fictional and elaborate in classical times, were simplified by Justinian, but still required court action. It is this form of adoption which is the precursor of our modern adoption proceeding. The other form of Roman adoption, called *adrogatio*, applied to adults and is of less importance to us.

The Roman adoption proceeding was carried over into the law of those countries, like France, Germany and Spain, in which the Roman legal system survived, and of those American states having a civil law background.[3] Adoption did not, however, become a part of the English common law.[4] It was not until 1926 that an adoption statute was passed in England itself.[5] Likewise in the United States, in those states not influenced by the Roman law, adoption was not recognized by the common law, and adoption statutes were a relatively late development, although not as late as in Britain. The lack of any common law background may explain the hostility toward adoption legislation which is evident in many judicial opinions up until very recent times.

Early adoption legislation in the United States authorized the transfer of children by deed from one set of parents to another, without legal proceedings, very much as one might transfer a chattel.[6] Even before enabling legislation was enacted, such transfers occurred and were recognized by the courts.[7] More modern statutes, generally taken to date from the passage of the Massachusetts statute in 1851,[8] provide for the institution of a legal proceeding leading to a decree of adoption, thereby giving the courts some powers in the supervision of the adoption process. The purpose of such statutes is to protect the interests of all parties to the adoption, the natural parents, the adoptive parents, and particularly the child who is the subject of the proceedings.[9]

Since the early legislation there have been many changes in the statutory pattern. The most striking of these has been in the direction of giving social agencies an active and responsible role in the adoption proceedings. Adoptions have come to require the cooperation of many persons and organizations in the community.[10] They are no longer the exclusive province of lawyers and judges.[11] This development has improved the adoption pro-

American Law of Adoption, 11 J.Fam.L. 443 (1971), citing many sources; Huard, The Law of Adoption: Ancient and Modern, 9 Vand.L.Rev. 743 (1956); Brosnan, The Law of Adoption, 22 Colum.L.Rev. 332 (1922); II C. Sherman, The Roman Law in the Modern World 83–91 (1922); W. Buckland, A Text-Book of Roman Law from Augustus to Justinian 121–128 (3d ed.1963); R. Leage, Roman Private Law 114–120 (3d ed. Prichard 1961); H. Jolowicz and B. Nicholas, Historical Introduction to the Study of Roman Law 119–120 (3d ed.1972); J. Thomas, Textbook of Roman Law 439–440 (1976).

3. Huard, The Law of Adoption: Ancient and Modern, 9 Vand.L.Rev. 743, 747 (1956); Witmer, Herzog, Weinstein, Sullivan, Independent Adoptions, 20 (1963).

4. But there is some reason to think that fictions were used to reach the same result as adoption in extreme cases. Huard, op. cit. note 2 at page 746.

5. The Adoption of Children Act, 16 & 17 Geo. 5, c. 29 (1926).

6. E.g. Texas Laws, 1850, ch. 39; II Abbott, The Child and The State, 172 (1938).

7. Witmer, Herzog, Weinstein, Sullivan, Independent Adoptions, 24–29 (1963).

8. Huard, The Law of Adoption: Ancient and Modern, 9 Vand.L.Rev. 743, 748 (1956). There is a suggestion by Huard that Mississippi had a slightly earlier statute.

New York's first adoption statute was passed in 1873. W. Gellhorn, Children and Families in the Courts of New York City 239 (1954). Today all states have adoption statutes of this general pattern. E.g., West's Ann.Cal. Civ.Code § 227 (1982); Colo.Rev.Stat. §§ 19–4–112, 19–4–113 (1986); Ill.—S.H.A. c. 40, §§ 1516, 1517 (Supp.1986); Mass.Gen.Laws Ann. c. 210, §§ 5A, 6 (1981 and Supp. 1986); N.Y.—McKinney's Dom.Rel.L. §§ 112, 115 (1977 and Supp.1986); N.C.Gen.Stat. §§ 48–17, 48–18, 48–21 (1984); V.T.C.A., Fam.Code § 16.08 (1986).

9. Witmer, Herzog, Weinstein, Sullivan, Independent Adoptions, 32–33 (1963). See also Wilson v. Pierce, 14 Utah 2d 317, 383 P.2d 925 (1963).

10. Katz, Community Decision-Makers and the Promotion of Values in the Adoption of Children, 4 J.Fam.L. 7 (1964).

11. Elson and Elson, Lawyers and Adoption: The Lawyer's Responsibility, 41 A.B.A.J. 1125 (1955). Since adoption is so extensively a non-legal matter, the lawyer who conducts an adoption practice should be familiar with some of the non-legal literature. A representative list might include the following: Schapiro, A Study of Adoption Practice (1956); Smith, Readings in Adoption (1963); Brooks and Brooks, Adventuring in Adoption (1939); Buck, Children for Adoption (1965); Gallagher, The Adopted Child (1936); Maas, Children in Need of Parents (1959); Riese, Heal and Hurt Child (1962).

cess but at the same time has created conflicts between legal and non-legal agencies which had to be resolved in such a way as to accomplish the purposes of the adoption statutes.

A major decline in the availability of children for adoption has occurred in the United States since the publication of the first edition of this work. Adoption statistics are incomplete, but they exist in sufficient volume to indicate that there are now far fewer children being adopted by non-relatives than was the case twenty years ago. In 1951 the total number of adoptions in the United States was estimated to be about 80,000.[12] By 1962 the number had risen to about 121,000,[13] and by 1970 to about 175,000.[14] The number declined to 169,000 for 1971[15] and to an estimated 142,000 in 1982.[16] Approximately half of these totals would normally be stepparent adoptions, so that the actual numbers of children available for adoption by non-relatives would be fewer than these figures might suggest. The decline is the more striking in view of the increases in children born out of wedlock in recent years.[17] Those children have in the past been the largest source of adoptable newborns. In California, one of the states which continues to maintain adoption statistics, adoptions by other than stepparents declined from about 12,000 per year to about 5,400 per year between 1968 and 1973,[18] de-

clined further to 4,700 in 1981[19] and to 4,200 in 1982.[20]

The reasons for the decrease in the number of babies available for adoption are said to be that many women who become pregnant out of wedlock whose babies would formerly have been available for adoption are now choosing either to have abortions or to keep their babies, the stigma attached to illegitimate births having been greatly reduced in recent years.[21] Whatever the reasons may be, it is clear that childless couples wishing to adopt a newborn child face long waiting lists or outright rejection in places where the adoption agencies have so many applications that they no longer accept new ones.[22]

Although in the world inhabited by the University of Chicago school of economists the sale of babies for adoption is viewed as a solution rather than a problem,[23] the shortage of adoptable newborns has given rise to what others more realistically consider the serious problem of a "black market" in babies. It is difficult to determine how serious this is, but legislative investigations have indicated that children were being sold in various parts of the country and that this traffic often has tragic consequences for the parents and children involved in it.[24] Although relatively few children may be affected, this does constitute a social evil which ought to be eliminated. A

Books advising adoptive parents include Doss, If You Adopt a Child (1957) and Raymond, Adoption and After (1955).

12. Children's Bureau Statistical Series No. 14 (1953), giving figures for 1951.

13. Children's Bureau Statistical Series No. 75, 17 (1964). Kirk, Shared Fate 2 (1964) estimated that about 2.5% of the child population of the United States was adopted.

14. Statistical Abstract of the United States 305 (1972).

15. Statistical Abstract of the United States 363 (1978).

16. New York Times, Dec. 4, 1985, sec. 3, p. 14, col. 1.

17. Statistical Abstract of the United States 65 (1978), stating that for 1976 illegitimate live births amounted to 14.8% of all births.

18. Bodenheimer, New Trends and Requirements in Adoption and Proposals for Legislative Change, 49 S.Cal. L.Rev. 10, 13 (1975).

19. California Statistical Abstract Table E–16 (1984).

20. Ibid. See also Cole, Advocating for Adoption Services, in M. Hardin, D. Dodson eds., Foster Children in the Courts 454–455 (1983). The author concludes among other things that the adoption system is failing to find homes for children who need them.

21. Select Committee on Children, Youth, and Families, U.S.House of Representatives, Ninety-Ninth Cong., 1st Sess., Teen Pregnancy: What Is Being Done? A State-By-State Look 18–19 (1986); Johnson, The Business in Babies, New York Times Magazine, August 17, 1975, 11.

22. New York Times, October 13, 1985, sec. XXI, p. 24, col. 3 describes long waiting lists in some regions.

23. Landes, Posner, The Economics of the Baby Shortage, 7 J. of Legal Studies 323 (1978).

24. Hearings on Juvenile Delinquency (Interstate Adoption Practices) Before the Subcommittee to Investigate Juvenile Delinquency of the Committee on the Judiciary, Eighty-Fourth Cong., 2d Sess., July 15 and 16, 1955; November 14 and 15, 1955, and Eighty-Fourth Cong., 2d Sess., May 16, 1956, on S.B. 3021, 1123, 2281. See also State of New York, Legislative Document No. 44, Report

legislative change which would achieve this result is the abolition of independent or private placements and the restriction of all adoption placements (other than with relatives or stepparents) to licensed public or private agencies.[25] Few states have been willing to go this far.[26] Another more commonly enacted statute requires investigation of all adoption placements by social agencies before a decree may be entered.[27] In the absence of these kinds of statutes, the suppression of the black market must depend on the enforcement of state and federal statutes imposing criminal penalties for the sale of children,[28] a solution which can never be wholly effective due to the difficulties and expenses inherent in any criminal enforcement program.

The shortage of adoptable babies has led some childless couples to arrange for the adoption of children from foreign countries. In the aftermath of the Vietnam war many Vietnamese children were brought to this country and adopted by American citizens.[29] These adoptions sometimes posed difficulties for both children and adoptive parents going beyond the usual difficulties of adjustment inherent in the adoption process.[30] The fact that the adoption of small children from other countries can cause legal and social difficulties for both the children and the adoptive parents may not be a reason for condemning all such adoptions. Instead it suggests the need for a thorough preparation on the part of the adoptive parents and a scrupulous observance of the legal requirements both in the United States and the other country.[31]

Reforms of the adoption laws have been proposed for the purpose of increasing the number of adoptions and of providing permanent homes for hard-to-place children, that is, older children, minority children and children having mental or physical disabilities. One such reform which has been carried out with some success is based upon a federal statute authorizing reimbursement to states which set up programs giving financial assistance to persons who adopt children with special needs.[32] The states have responded to federal pressure by providing this sort of assistance.[33] Interracial adoptions have been advocated as

of the Joint Legislative Committee on Matrimonial and Family Laws 33–65 (1959); New York Times, April 25, 1976, p. 50, col. 3; August 30, 1985, sec. I, p. 14, col. 5; December 17, 1985, sec. I, p. 2, col. 3.

25. This proposal was embodied in the Children's Bureau's proposed adoption statute. Goldberg, U.S. Department of Health, Education and Welfare, Social Security Administration, Children's Bureau, Legislative Guides for the Termination of Parental Rights and Responsibilities and the Adoption of Children, Children's Bureau Publication No. 394–1961 53 (1961), hereinafter cited as Children's Bureau Publication No. 394–1961. See also Child Welfare League of America, Standards for Adoption Service 5, 71 (1968).

26. Conn.Gen.Stat.Ann. § 45–61i (1981) and Del.Code tit. 13, § 904 (Supp.1984) seem to limit placements for non-relative adoptions to public or licensed private agencies. See also Katz, Judicial and Statutory Trends in the Law of Adoption, 51 Geo.L.J. 64, 67 (1962). The draft of the American Bar Association Model State Adoption Act, § 31, 19 Fam.L.Q. 128 (1985) makes it a misdemeanor for anyone other than a parent, a grandparent or an agency to place a child for adoption, but it permits any person to assist a parent in locating or evaluating potential adoptive parents and in transferring legal custody of the child to them. This distinction is not very clear, to say the least.

27. This is the technique of the Uniform Adoption Act, as revised in 1969 and amended in 1971, § 11, 9 Unif.L.Ann. 36 (1979). This sort of requirement is made in many states. Katz, Judicial and Statutory Trends in

the Law of Adoption, 51 Geo.L.J. 64, 67 (1962). The Uniform Act § 10, 9 Unif.L.Ann. 35 (1979) also requires the petitioner for adoption to file with the court a report of all expenditures he has made in connection with the adoption, the purpose being to discourage payments for babies.

28. For a discussion of such statutes see section 20.7, infra.

29. Johnson, The Business in Babies, New York Times Magazine, August 17, 1975, 11, 70.

30. The immigration of such children into the United States is one such difficulty. Congress has passed legislation encouraging the immigration of alien orphans for the purpose of adoption in this country, in 8 U.S.C.A. § 1101(b)(1)(E) and (F) (1982). Other complexities are discussed in Note, International Adoption—United States Adoption of Vietnamese Children: Vital Considerations for the Courts, 52 Denver L.J. 771 (1975).

31. See, e.g., Kim, Carroll, Intercountry Adoption of South Korean Orphans: A Lawyer's Guide, 14 J.Fam.L. 223 (1975).

32. 42 U.S.C.A. §§ 670, 671, 673.

33. E.g., West's Ann.Cal.Welf. & Inst.Code § 16120 (Supp.1986); Colo.Rev.Stat. §§ 26–7–101 to 26–7–108 (1982); N.Y.—McKinney's Soc.Serv.L. §§ 450 to 458 (1983 & Supp.1986); Pa.Stat. tit. 62, §§ 771 to 774 (Supp.1986); V.T.C.A., Human Res.Code § 47.004 (1980 & Supp.1986); Wis.Stat.Ann. § 48.975 (Supp.1986). The subsidy program is described in U.S.Dep't of Health, Education & Welfare, Subsidized Adoption in America (1976), Office of

a means of providing permanent homes for minority children, and adoption agencies at one time began to abandon their standards of racial matching in order to accomplish this, but opposition to the placing of minority children in white families has developed.[34] If adoption placements are not made available for hard-to-place children, they are relegated to long term foster care, often in a series of foster homes, a prospect especially undesirable in view of the serious criticisms being leveled at foster care programs.[35] If it is true that the primary purpose of adoption is to provide stable family relationships for the children who need them, the persistence of rigid racial and religious matching requirements and reluctance to place children across racial and religious lines seem hard to justify.

Other proposals for change in adoption practices are aimed at inducing larger numbers of parents, usually mothers, of illegitimate children to relinquish their children for adoption. These proposals have come to be referred to as advocating open adoption, meaning adoptions which permit the continuation of some contacts between the natural parent and the child.[36] Traditional adoption agency standards required that the natural

parents of a child who was placed for adoption with non-relatives should not know the identity of the adoptive parents and the adoptive parents and adopted child should not know the identity of the natural parents.[37] Advocates of open adoption would eliminate such standards, arguing that such knowledge benefits the adopted child as well as leading the natural parent to be more willing to permit the child's adoption.[38] Social and psychological studies are often cited in support of open adoptions[39] and the American Bar Association's proposed model act may permit them.[40] It remains to be seen whether many adoptive parents would be willing to adopt a child with the knowledge that the child's natural parents would continue to be in contact with the child and perhaps to interfere in the child's upbringing.[41]

The current controversy over the confidentiality of the birth records of adopted children is obviously closely related to the open adoption movement. The argument is that birth records should be freely available to adopted children once they reach adulthood rather than to be open only at the discretion of the courts for good cause shown as is now the case in many states.[42] Adopted children are said

Human Development, Office of Child Development, Children's Bureau No. (OHD) 76–30087; Note, Foster Care and Adoption Reform, 16 J.Fam.L. 751 (1978).

34. Note, Racial Matching and the Adoption Dilemma: Alternatives for the Hard To Place, 17 J.Fam.L. 333, 338 (1979); Note, Matching for Adoption: A Study of Current Trends, 22 Cath.Law. 70 (1976); Howard, Transracial Adoption: Analysis of the Best Interests Standard, 59 Notre Dame L.Rev. 503 (1984).

35. Smith v. Organization of Foster Families for Equality and Reform, 431 U.S. 816, 833, 97 S.Ct. 2094, 2103, 53 L.Ed.2d 14 (1977).

36. Stoxen, The Best of Both "Open" and "Closed" Adoption Worlds: A Call for the Reform of State Statutes, 13 J. of Legislation 292 (1986). See also Bodenheimer, New Trends and Requirements in Adoption Law and Proposals for Legislative Change, 49 So.Cal. L.Rev. 10, 49 (1975).

37. Child Welfare League of America, Standards for Adoption Service 2.3 (1958).

38. Smith, Adoption—The Case for More Options, 1986 Utah L.Rev. 495; Stoxen, The Best of Both "Open" and "Closed" Adoption Worlds: A Call for the Reform of State Statutes, 13 J. of Legislation 292 (1986).

39. Smith, Adoption—The Case for More Options, 1986 Utah L.Rev. 495, 531. Other studies of adoption

practice and its consequences for the parties include T. Bradley, An Exploration of Caseworkers' Perceptions of Adoptive Applicants (1966); B. Jaffee, How They Fared in Adoption: A Follow-Up Study (1970); A. Kadushin, Adopting Older Children (1970); E. Lawder, A Followup Study of Adoptions (1969); B. Tizard, Adoption: A Second Chance (1977).

40. Draft American Bar Association Model State Adoption Act § 9, 19 Fam.L.Q. 110 (1985) seems to permit a natural parent to consent to adoption by a specified person, so that contact between the natural parent and the adopted child might be possible after the adoption. The statute is not wholly clear on this, however, just as it is far from clear on other aspects of adoption law and practice.

41. Schur, The ABA Model State Adoption Act: Observations from an Agency Perspective, 19 Fam.L.Q. 131, 132 (1985) argues that open adoption is not suitable for many natural and adoptive parents.

42. A. Sorosky, A. Baran, R. Pannor, The Adoption Triangle: The Effects of the Sealed Record on Adoptees, Birth Parents, and Adoptive Parents (1978); Research Center, Child Welfare League of America, Inc., The Sealed Adoption Record Controversy: Report of a Survey of Agency Policy, Practice and Opinion (1976); Note Adoption Records Reform: Impact on Adoptees, 67 Mar. L.Rev. 110 (1983). The statutes on adoption records are

to have legitimate and important interests in knowing not merely such general information as their medical or genetic backgrounds but in knowing specifically who their natural parents are so that they may establish contact with those parents.[43] Several adopted children have written about their emotions and difficulties as they attempted to trace their parents in spite of the obstacles placed in their way by courts and state agencies.[44] Proposals of this kind have begun to make some headway in the statutes,[45] but opposition to them persists.[46]

§ 20.2   Termination of Parental Rights and Adoption—Constitutional Limitations

The Constitutional Position of the Father of an Illegitimate Child

As has already been indicated,[1] adoption involves two steps, the termination of parental rights on the part of the child's natural parents, and the establishment of parental rights on the part of the adoptive parents. Both steps may take place in one proceeding,[2] but it is more common to have them occur in two separate proceedings.[3] The process by which the parental rights of a natural parent are terminated may either be voluntary or involuntary. They may be voluntarily terminated when the natural parent files a consent to adoption in the adoption proceeding itself,[4] or when he brings a separate proceeding usually referred to as relinquishment, the decree which approves his petition to give up his

parental rights to the child.[5] They may be involuntarily terminated by a proceeding brought usually on behalf of the state to establish that the child has been abandoned, or that he is dependent or neglected, or that the natural parent has failed to meet his obligations in other ways as outlined in the state's statutes.[6] In any event the voluntary and involuntary proceedings for the termination of parental rights are *in pari materia* in the sense that they both result in freeing the child for adoption, and that the involuntary method need not be resorted to if the voluntary method is available. All of this is elementary learning but is rehearsed here in order to provide a background for the understanding of the United States Supreme Court's treatment of the rights of the father of the illegitimate child.

Until 1972 the statutes in the various states generally provided that the consent of the mother of an illegitimate child would alone be sufficient to make the child available for adoption[7] and, as a logical consequence, that the involuntary termination of her parental rights would have the same effect. In other words the father of the illegitimate child had, under these statutes, no legally enforceable right to assert his parental rights in the child if the mother wished to place the child for adoption or if she failed in her parental duties sufficiently to warrant terminating her parental rights. Nevertheless some courts did award custody of the illegitimate child to the father on occasion,[8] or did award him rights of

---

cited in Stoxen, The Best of Both "Open" and "Closed" Adoption Worlds: A Call for the Reform of State Statutes, 13 J. of Legislation 292, 298 (1986).

43. A. Sorosky, A. Baran, R. Pannor, The Adoption Triangle: The Effects of the Sealed Record on Adoptees, Birth Parents, and Adoptive Parents (1978).

44. E.g., F. Fisher, The Search for Anna Fisher.

45. Stoxen, The Best of Both "Open" and "Closed" Adoption Worlds: A Call for the Reform of State Statutes, 13 J. of Legislation 292, 301 (1986).

46. Howe, Adoption Practice, Issues, and Laws 1958–1983, 17 Fam.L.Q. 173, 190–191 (1983).

§ 20.2

1. See section 19.1, supra.

2. See section 21.4, Practitioner's Edition.

3. Ibid.

4. For a discussion of consent and its revocation, see section 20.5, infra.

5. See section 21.4, Practitioner's Edition.

6. The grounds for involuntary termination of parental rights are discussed in section 20.6, infra.

7. The statutes are cited and discussed in Note, The Emerging Constitutional Protection of the Putative Father's Parental Rights, 70 Mich.L.Rev. 1581 (1972).

8. Cases are collected in Annot., 37 A.L.R.2d 882 (1954). See also In re Zink, 269 Minn. 535, 132 N.W.2d 795 (1964) and Embick, The Illegitimate Father: Conditions Under Which the Courts Will Recognize Paternal Rights to the Illegitimate Child in Washington, Oregon and California, 3 J.Fam.L. 321 (1963).

visitation.[9] The purposes of the adoption statutes were to facilitate the adoption of illegitimate children, to protect the privacy of mothers of such children, and to enable the courts to provide the adoptive parents with unassailable rights to their adopted children.[10]

The law governing the rights of fathers with respect to their illegitimate children was sharply altered by Stanley v. Illinois [11] in 1972. In that case an unmarried man and woman had had three children while "intermittently" [12] living together over eighteen years. The children's mother died and the state of Illinois, pursuant to its statute recognizing no parental rights in fathers of illegitimate children, declared the children to be wards of the state and assumed their custody. Mr. Stanley then sued to obtain custody of the children and the Illinois Supreme Court denied his claim. The Supreme Court of the United States reversed, holding that a parent has a due process right under the Fourteenth Amendment to a hearing on his fitness as a parent before the state may remove children from his custody and that the state, in denying such a hearing to Mr. Stanley, while granting it to the fathers of legitimate children, violated the Equal Protection Clause of

the Fourteenth Amendment.[13] The Court's logic is hard to understand. If the premise is correct, that due process requires a hearing on fitness for all fathers, then the Illinois procedure was clearly unconstitutional, whether or not the Equal Protection Clause was invoked. In any event, although the decision ostensibly dealt with the right of the father of an illegitimate child to the custody of that child, its major impact was and still is on the termination of parental rights and the availability of children for adoption. Most of the newborn children who will be adopted by non-relatives are illegitimate. By invalidating the procedures then existing for making such children available for adoption, the Stanley case imposed upon the states the necessity for comprehensively revising their rules concerning the persons whose consent had to be obtained or whose rights had to be terminated before such children could be placed for adoption.

Many criticisms and questions can be directed to the Stanley opinion.[14] For example, it cited with approval May v. Anderson [15] which had held that custody decrees must be based upon personal jurisdiction over the defendant. Then in a footnote [16] Stanley stated that custody of an illegitimate child may be

9. Commonwealth v. Rozanski, 206 Pa.Super. 397, 213 A.2d 155 (1965), 39 Temp.L.J. 222 (1966).

10. These purposes are eloquently stated in In re Adoption of Malpica-Orsini, 36 N.Y.2d 568, 370 N.Y.S.2d 511, 331 N.E.2d 486 (1975), appeal dismissed for want of a substantial federal question 423 U.S. 1042, 96 S.Ct. 765, 46 L.Ed.2d 631 (1976).

11. 405 U.S. 645, 92 S.Ct. 1208, 31 L.Ed.2d 551 (1972), 34 U.Pitt.L.Rev. 303 (1973), 59 Va.L.Rev. 517 (1973), 1973 Wis.L.Rev. 908. Justice White wrote the Court's opinion which was concurred in by Justices Brennan, Stewart, Marshall and in part by Justice Douglas. Justices Powell and Rehnquist did not participate in the decision. Chief Justice Burger and Justice Blackmun dissented. The Court had before it at the same time as Stanley, State ex rel. Lewis v. Lutheran Social Services of Wisconsin and Upper Michigan, 47 Wis.2d 420, 178 N.W.2d 56 (1970), vacated 405 U.S. 1051, 92 S.Ct. 1488, 31 L.Ed.2d 786 (1972), in which an illegitimate child had been placed for adoption without notice to the father, pursuant to a Wisconsin statute like the Illinois statute in Stanley. The Supreme Court remanded the case for further consideration in the light of Stanley. On remand the Wisconsin courts terminated the father's parental rights on the ground of abandonment. State ex rel. Lewis v. Lutheran Social Services of Wisconsin and Upper Michigan, 68 Wis.

2d 36, 227 N.W.2d 643 (1975). The remand of this case suggests that the Supreme Court thought Stanley did apply to fathers who had disclaimed paternity and evinced no interest in the child, since the father in this case was in that position. The Supreme Court also remanded Vanderlaan v. Vanderlaan, 126 Ill.App.2d 410, 262 N.E.2d 717 (1970), vacated 405 U.S. 1051, 92 S.Ct. 1488, 31 L.Ed.2d 787 (1972). After the remand the court gave custody of the child to his father. Vanderlaan v. Vanderlaan, 9 Ill.App.3d 260, 292 N.E.2d 145 (1972).

12. 405 U.S. at 646, 92 S.Ct. at 1210.

13. 405 U.S. at 658, 92 S.Ct. at 1216.

14. Some of them may be found in Schwartz, Rights of Father With Regard to His Illegitimate Child, 36 Ohio State L.J. 1 (1975).

15. 345 U.S. 528, 73 S.Ct. 840, 97 L.Ed 1221 (1953). This case is discussed and criticized at length in section 12.5, supra. If it were applied to termination of parental rights and adoption, it would cripple those procedures, since in a large proportion of illegitimate births the identity or the whereabouts of the fathers involved are unknown and therefore personal jurisdiction would be unobtainable.

16. 405 U.S. at 657, footnote 9, 92 S.Ct. at 1215, footnote 9.

based upon service by publication, apparently failing to notice that this statement was quite inconsistent with May v. Anderson. The statement in the Stanley opinion that due process requires a hearing on fitness before the father of an illegitimate child may be deprived of custody is too broad.[17] Grounds other than unfitness as a basis for depriving a parent of custody hardly violate due process.[18] Finally, the Stanley decision failed to indicate whether it was to be retroactive. If it had been, the effect on prior adoptions would have been severe, since many of them would have been based upon statutes like the one held unconstitutional in Stanley.

But the most important question raised by the Stanley decision was whether it applied to *all* fathers of illegitimate children or only to those who had had some substantial contact with their children. This was an important question because if the decision were given the first construction, entirely different notice requirements would be necessary than if the second construction were the correct one. The opinion itself contained inconsistent clues. When it referred to a father's interest "in the children he has sired and raised"[19], this implied that it applied only to fathers who had helped to care for their children, as

was true of Mr. Stanley. But in footnote 9 the Court recommended service by publication on unknown fathers, implying that they too must be given notice before their parental or custodial rights may be terminated.[20]

The various states, not surprisingly, responded in different ways to the uncertain notice requirements in Stanley. Some assumed that the Stanley case meant that all biological fathers had to be given notice before their parental rights could be terminated and therefore enacted statutes requiring notice to fathers whose identity or whereabouts was known by personal service or registered mail and to fathers whose identity or whereabouts was not known by publication, the publication sometimes including the child's name and the mother's name.[21] Other states construed the Stanley opinion in a more limited way and required notice to be given only to fathers who had in some fashion indicated some interest in the child or provided some care or support for the child or the mother during her pregnancy.[22] Of course the requirement of service by publication in this context is not only foolish in the extreme since such notice will never be seen by the father, but constitutes an egregious infringement of the privacy of mother and child.[23] It

---

17. 405 U.S. at 658, 92 S.Ct. at 1216: "We have concluded that all Illinois parents are entitled to a hearing on their fitness before their children are removed from their custody."

18. For a discussion of many cases which deprive parents of the custody of their children without a finding of unfitness, see section 19.6, supra.

19. 405 U.S. at 651, 92 S.Ct. at 1212.

20. 405 U.S. at 657, 92 S.Ct. at 1215.

21. Freeman, Remodeling Adoption Statutes After Stanley v. Illinois, 15 J.Fam.L. 385 (1976–1977) discusses the New York, Illinois, Wisconsin and Michigan attempts to comply with Stanley. Barron, Notice to the Unwed Father and Termination of Parental Rights: Implementing Stanley v. Illinois, 9 Fam.L.Q. 527 (1975) describes the delays caused in many states' adoptions by Stanley and the attempts of Illinois, Wisconsin and Michigan to meet Stanley's requirements. This article discusses in detail the conflict between a service by publication requirement and the privacy interests of the mother and child, in view of the absurdity of a published notice which fails to identify mother and child, without concluding whether or not the mother has such right or whether it might be overridden by the need to notify the father. The Wisconsin statute passed in response to Stanley authorizes service by publication in some cases and further authorizes

the court to order the publication to name the mother where that is necessary to give effective notice, which would seem to include all cases. Wis.Stat.Ann. §§ 48.41, 48.42 (Supp.1986–1987). The Uniform Parentage Act § 24(f), 9A Unif.L.Ann. 616 (1979) attempts to comply with Stanley by requiring service by publication or by posting only where the court finds that such service would be likely to lead to the identification of the father. Illinois seems to have gone farther than other states in requiring service by publication where the father is unknown. Ill.—S.H.A. c. 40, § 1509 (Supp.1986). See also In Interest of Woodard, 231 Kan. 544, 646 P.2d 1105 (1982).

22. E.g., Alaska Stat. §§ 25.23.040, 25.23.050 (1983); Mich.C.L.A. §§ 27.3178 (555.36), 27.3178 (555.37) (1980 and Supp.1986–1987). A statute of this type was held constitutional in Department of Health & Rehabilitative Services v. Herzog, 317 So.2d 865 (Fla.App.1975).

23. See, e.g., In re Adoption of Cecilie Ann T., 101 Misc.2d 472, 421 N.Y.S.2d 167 (Surr.Ct.1979); Slawek v. Stroh, 62 Wis.2d 295, 215 N.W.2d 9 (1974). Cf. Doe v. Norton, 365 F.Supp. 65 (D.Conn.1973), vacated and remanded for further consideration in the light of Pub.L. 93–647, 22 U.S. 391, 95 S.Ct. 2221, 45 L.Ed.2d 268 (1975), vacated and remanded 432 U.S. 526, 97 S.Ct. 2474, 53 L.Ed.2d 534 (1977).

seems strange that most of the comments on the Stanley case have been favorable when it makes such uncertain, unrealistic and unnecessary requirements that adoptions are delayed and made more expensive at a time when adoption law changes are being proposed for the purpose of encouraging and expediting adoptions as the most satisfactory solution for many illegitimate children.[24]

The Supreme Court has attempted on four subsequent occasions to clarify some of the issues raised by the Stanley case but has succeeded only in compounding the confusion. In the first of these cases the New York Court of Appeals had upheld the constitutionality of the New York statute which provided that illegitimate children might be adopted on the basis of the consent of their mothers alone.[25] In this case the child's father was given notice and participated in the adoption hearing, and the adoption was approved on the ground that it was in the child's best interests. The New York court held that Stanley's due process requirement was complied with when the father was given a hearing. The Supreme Court dismissed the appeal from his case on the ground that there was no substantial federal question.[26]

Quilloin v. Walcott,[27] the next case, unanimously upheld a Georgia statute which provided that only the mother of an illegitimate child need consent to the adoption of that child. The adoption was sought by the husband of the child's mother after the child had been living with his mother and her husband for about nine years. The child's father had notice of the adoption petition and participated in a hearing in which he asked that he be declared the child's legitimate father, that he be granted visitation and that the adoption be denied. The child's father had made some support payments and had visited with the child on "many occasions".[28] The child himself, who was about eleven years old, expressed a desire to be adopted. The trial court granted the adoption on the ground that it served the child's best interests, the Georgia Supreme Court affirmed, and the United States Supreme Court affirmed. The Court found that the father's due process rights were not violated because the adoption gave recognition to a family unit already in existence. It made no real attempt to distinguish Stanley. It rejected the father's equal protection argument on the ground that this father's interests were "readily distinguishable"[29] from those of a father who had been married to the mother and divorced. The decision is inexplicable in its ignoring of Stanley and of Stanley's reasoning, leaving the impression that the Court thought Stanley just required notice and a hearing to the father of the illegitimate child rather than substantive rights equivalent to those of the father of a legitimate child. At least the opinion did seem to reject the position taken in Stanley that a father of an illegitimate child is entitled to a hearing on his fitness as a parent. The effect of Quilloin seemed to be that such a father could be deprived of his parental rights whenever that would serve the child's best interests.

Only a little more than a year after Quilloin the Supreme Court, in Caban v. Mohammed,[30] invalidated the same New York statute

See also Lutheran Social Services of New Jersey v. Doe, 172 N.J.Super. 343, 411 A.2d 1183 (1979), approving service by publication where the child's mother refused to reveal the name of the father.

24. See the discussion in section 20.1, supra.

25. In re Adoption of Malpica-Orsini, 36 N.Y.2d 568, 370 N.Y.S.2d 511, 331 N.E.2d 486 (1975), appeal dismissed for want of a substantial federal question 423 U.S. 1042, 96 S.Ct. 765, 46 L.Ed.2d 631 (1976), 25 Buff.L.Rev. 787 (1976).

26. Ibid. The Court later conceded that this was a ruling on the merits and entitled to weight as a precedent, but then said that it is not entitled to the same deference as a ruling embodied in a written opinion.

Caban v. Mohammed, 441 U.S. 380, 390, footnote 9, 99 S.Ct. 1760, 1767, footnote 9, 60 L.Ed.2d 279 (1979). The Court then overruled Malpica-Orsini to the extent that it was inconsistent with the result of Caban.

27. 434 U.S. 246, 98 S.Ct. 549, 54 L.Ed.2d 511 (1978), rehearing denied 435 U.S. 918, 98 S.Ct. 1477, 55 L.Ed.2d 511 (1978), 58 Neb.L.Rev. 610 (1979).

28. 434 U.S. at 251, 98 S.Ct. at 552.

29. 434 U.S. at 256, 98 S.Ct. at 555.

30. 441 U.S. 380, 99 S.Ct. 1760, 60 L.Ed.2d 297 (1979). Justice Powell wrote the Court's opinion. Justices Stewart, Stevens, Rehnquist and Chief Justice Burger dissented.

it had upheld in Malpica-Orsini,[31] a statute quite similar to the one it had also upheld in Quilloin v. Walcott.[32] The New York statute [33] provided that an illegitimate child could be adopted by virtue of the consent of his mother alone, without the consent of his father. The two children in the case were born when their parents were living together, the father supporting them for a time and having them for visits after he stopped living with their mother. At one point the father had custody of the children in violation of an agreement with their mother, following which a court in New York gave custody to the mother and her husband, with visitation rights to the father and his wife. The mother and her husband then filed an adoption petition respecting the two children pursuant to the New York statute.[34] The father filed a cross-petition for adoption and after a hearing the trial court approved the adoption by the mother and her husband. At the time of the adoption proceedings the children were four and six years old respectively. The Supreme Court held that the distinction made by the statute between the mothers and fathers of illegitimate children violated the Equal Protection Clause of the Fourteenth Amendment. It rejected the argument that the statute could be justified as promoting the state's interest in providing for the adoptions of illegitimate children on the ground that the statute bore no reasonable relation to that interest. Conceding for purposes of argument that the fathers of such children might be hard to locate or identify, the Court said that that factor had no application to the fathers of

older children who have not participated in the care of such children.[35] The Court further said that in cases where the fathers had not so participated, his consent could be dispensed with by the statute. In other words the Court found that this was gender discrimination which relied upon an "over-broad generalization".[36]

Justice Stewart's dissent took the position that the distinction between married and unmarried fathers and between fathers and mothers of illegitimate children is constitutional.[37] Justice Stevens' dissent also argued that the many differences between mothers and fathers before and just after the birth of children and the necessities of the adoption process justified the gender discrimination made by the New York statute.[38] Justice Stevens' analysis was quite similar to that of the New York Court of Appeals in Malpica-Orsini.[39] Finally, Justice Stevens construed the majority opinion to apply only so far as statutes like that of New York deprived the fathers of older children of the right to veto their adoption, leaving unaffected the much larger proportion of adoptions in which the children are in the custody of their mothers.[40] He also strongly asserted that the majority opinion should have no retroactive effect [41] and a subsequent New York case has so held.[42]

Lehr v. Robertson,[43] the latest attempt by the Supreme Court to provide some guidance for state adoption procedures, concerned the amended New York statute on notice of adoption to fathers of illegitimate children. That statute provides, so far as relevant to this

---

31. In re Adoption of Malpica-Orsini, 36 N.Y.2d 568, 370 N.Y.S.2d 511, 331 N.E.2d 486 (1975), appeal dismissed for want of a substantial federal question 423 U.S. 1042, 96 S.Ct. 765, 46 L.Ed.2d 631 (1976).

32. 434 U.S. 246, 98 S.Ct. 549, 54 L.Ed.2d 511 (1978), rehearing denied 435 U.S. 918, 98 S.Ct. 1477, 55 L.Ed.2d 511 (1978).

33. N.Y.—McKinney's Dom.Rel.L. § 111(1)(c) (1977).

34. The New York statute authorized a mother to adopt her illegitimate child. 441 U.S. at 383, footnote 1, 99 S.Ct. at 1763 footnote 1.

35. 441 U.S. at 392, 99 S.Ct. at 1768.

36. 441 U.S. at 394, 99 S.Ct. at 1769.

37. 441 U.S. at 394, 397, 398, 99 S.Ct. at 1769, 1770.

38. 441 U.S. at 406, 99 S.Ct. at 1775.

39. See note 25, supra, and 441 U.S. at 410, footnote 20, 99 S.Ct. at 1777 footnote 20.

40. 441 U.S. at 415, 99 S.Ct. at 1780.

41. 441 U.S. at 416, 99 S.Ct. at 1780.

42. Matter of Adoption of Jessica XX, 54 N.Y.2d 417, 446 N.Y.S.2d 20, 430 N.E.2d 896 (1981), affirmed without discussion of this issue sub.nom. Lehr v. Robertson, 463 U.S. 248, 103 S.Ct. 2985, 77 L.Ed.2d 614 (1983).

43. 463 U.S. 248, 103 S.Ct. 2985, 77 L.Ed.2d 614 (1983). Justice Stevens wrote the majority opinion in the case. Justices White, Marshall and Blackmun dissented.

case, that notice of adoption be given to a father who had filed in the state's putative father registry a notice of intent to claim paternity of the child.[44] The child in this case was born out of wedlock. Her mother married a man not the father and when the child was two years old, the mother's husband filed a petition to adopt her. Up to that point the child's father had not supported the child, or lived with her or, so far as the Supreme Court's opinion reveals, cared for the child. He had also failed to file any notice of intent to claim paternity pursuant to the statute. Shortly after the adoption petition was filed the father did file a petition in a different New York court claiming paternity and seeking rights of visitation. The adoption was granted without notice to the father, and the father appealed to the United States Supreme Court alleging that he had been deprived of both due process and equal protection by the state court's decision. The Supreme Court held that due process had not been violated by the failure to give notice because the mere biological relationship between father and child did not warrant the same constitutional protection as a father-child relationship in which the father had cared for, supported, and associated with the child. The Court seemed to hold that the New York statute, by specifying various categories of fathers including those who file a notice of intent to claim paternity, provided an adequate method for determining those fathers who have developed an emotional as distinguished from a merely biological relationship with their children.[45] The statute's notice provision was for this reason approved.

The Court held that the Equal Protection Clause was not violated in this case because the mother and father here were not similarly situated and the statute could therefore validly make a distinction between them. Here the mother had had custody of the child and cared for her while the father had never had a custodial, personal or financial relationship with her.[46] In short, the Lehr case seems to stand for the proposition that an illegitimate child may be placed for adoption on the basis of the mother's consent alone and without notice to the father if a) the father has failed to comply with a state statute which authorizes such placement upon the father's failure to demonstrate his interest in or support for the child in relevant ways specified in the statute;[47] and b) the father has not in fact maintained "any custodial, personal or financial relationship"[48] with the child.

It is difficult if not impossible to arrive at an accurate or useful assessment of the Supreme Court's decisions from Stanley to Lehr. A few points of support for hard pressed legislatures and adoption agencies may exist. It is clear that the rights of a father of an illegitimate child may not be ignored in all cases, as was the effect of the Illinois statute in Stanley.[49] It is also clear that where the father has persistently and consistently supported and cared for the child, he must be given notice if his parental rights or rights to custody may be cut off.[50] Whether he must be given such notice when his identity or whereabouts are unknown remains as uncertain as

---

44. N.Y.—McKinney's Dom.Rel.L. § 111–a 2(c) (1977). The registry of such notices was provided for by N.Y.—McKinney's Soc.Serv.L. § 372–c (1983).

45. 463 U.S. at 262, 103 S.Ct. at 2993.

46. 463 U.S. at 267, 103 S.Ct. at 2996.

47. 463 U.S. at 263–265, 103 S.Ct. at 2994–2995.

48. 463 U.S. at 267, 103 S.Ct. at 2996.

49. Cases applying Stanley to various states of fact include Miller v. Miller, 504 F.2d 1067 (9th Cir.1974); In re Richard M., 14 Cal.3d 783, 122 Cal.Rptr. 531, 537 P.2d 363 (1975) (father had legitimated the child); Matter of Barlow, 404 Mich. 216, 273 N.W.2d 35 (1978); State ex rel. J. D. S. v. Edwards, 574 S.W.2d 405 (Mo.1978); Adoption of Walker, 468 Pa. 165, 360 A.2d 603 (1976) (relies in

part on the Equal Rights Amendment to the state constitution); Rogers v. Lowry, 546 S.W.2d 881 (Tex.Civ.App. 1977); Matter of Daft's Adoption, 159 W.Va. 895, 230 S.E.2d 475 (1976) (approves service by publication). Commonwealth v. Hayes, 215 Va. 49, 205 S.E.2d 644 (1974) limited Stanley to its facts and approved an adoption over the father's objection. And see Matter of Karen A. B., 513 A.2d 770 (Del.1986).

50. This is the narrowest construction of Stanley v. Illinois, 405 U.S. 645, 92 S.Ct. 1208, 31 L.Ed.2d 551 (1972). Whether the converse is true, that is, whether notice need not be given if the father has not cared for the child, is answered more or less unclearly by Lehr v. Robertson, 463 U.S. 248, 103 S.Ct. 2985, 77 L.Ed.2d 614 (1983).

it was left by Stanley.[51] It is equally uncertain whether, if he is given notice and an opportunity to be heard, his rights may be terminated on the ground that the child's best interests demand it, or whether he must be proved to be unfit or to have a detrimental effect on the child, as would be the case if the child were legitimate.[52]

It was held in Lehr that if the father has had no "custodial, personal, or financial relationship"[53] with the child, the state may authorize the mother alone to consent to adoption and may dispense with notice to the father. But Lehr gives us no clues as to how much of a relationship is enough to entitle the father to veto an adoption or have notice of the adoption petition.[54] The Lehr case also leaves unanswered the question of the father's rights respecting adoption placements

of newborn children. In such cases he usually will have had no opportunity to develop a relationship with the child if the mother relinquishes the child straight from the hospital to an adoption agency, the procedure favored for non-relative adoptions by many agencies.[55] One well-reasoned case has held that if the applicable state statute authorizes such a placement by the mother alone when the father has failed to register his claim of paternity, that procedure meets the constitutional requirements of Lehr v. Robertson.[56]

One negative but helpful proposition emerging from all this litigation is that there seems little prospect that May v. Anderson[57] will be relied upon to require personal jurisdiction over fathers in proceedings for adoption or for termination of parental rights.[58] Even

---

51. The Uniform Parentage Act § 24, 9A Unif.L.Ann. 615 (1979) is a careful and thoughtful attempt to deal with that problem. See Michael U. v. Jamie B., 39 Cal.3d 787, 218 Cal.Rptr. 39, 705 P.2d 362 (1985) for a construction of this statute.

52. In Quilloin v. Walcott, 434 U.S. 246, 98 S.Ct. 1477, 54 L.Ed.2d 511 (1978), rehearing denied 435 U.S. 918, 98 S.Ct. 1477, 55 L.Ed.2d 511 (1978) the father's objection to the adoption was overridden largely on the ground that this was dictated by the child's best interests. But In re Baby Girl M., 37 Cal.3d 65, 207 Cal.Rptr. 309, 688 P.2d 918 (1984) it was held that the court must find that the father's custody would be detrimental to the child before his rights could be terminated, just as would be the case for the father of a legitimate child. Matter of Lathrop's Adoption, 2 Kan.App.2d 90, 575 P.2d 894 (1978) held that the father's rights could only be terminated if he were shown to be an unfit parent, relying upon the Stanley case. Aside from constitutional doctrines, the cases in the various states differ on what sort of evidence will justify an award of custody to a non-parent. See section 19.6, supra.

But the Stanley rule was held not to give an alleged natural father the right to assert paternity when the child was born while the mother was married to someone else and the husband acknowledged paternity in Petitioner F. v. Respondent R., 430 A.2d 1075 (Del.1981); P. B. C. v. D. H., 396 Mass. 68, 483 N.E.2d 1094 (1985), cert. denied ___ U.S. ___, 106 S.Ct. 1286, 89 L.Ed.2d 593 (1986). See also In Interest of K, 535 S.W.2d 168 (Tex.1976), cert. denied 429 U.S. 907, 97 S.Ct. 273, 50 L.Ed.2d 189 (1976), rehearing denied 429 U.S. 1010, 97 S.Ct. 542, 50 L.Ed.2d 620 (1976).

Michelle W. v. Ronald W., 39 Cal.3d 354, 216 Cal.Rptr. 748, 703 P.2d 88 (1985), appeal dismissed for want of a substantial federal question ___ U.S. ___, 106 S.Ct. 774, 88 L.Ed.2d 754 (1986), held that the Stanley case did not render unconstitutional the presumption of legitimacy

applicable to a child born while its mother was married to someone other than the alleged natural father.

53. Lehr v. Robertson, 463 U.S. 248, 267, 103 S.Ct. 2985, 2996, 77 L.Ed.2d 614 (1983).

54. In Quilloin v. Walcott, 238 Ga. 230, 232 S.E.2d 246 (1977), for example, the child visited with his father on occasion, his father provided him with some support and gave him presents from time to time. But the Supreme Court held that the father's rights could nevertheless be cut off. On the other hand that Court placed great emphasis on the father-child relationship in Caban v. Mohammed, 441 U.S. 380, 99 S.Ct. 1760, 60 L.Ed.2d 297 (1979), on remand 47 N.Y.2d 880, 419 N.Y.S.2d 74, 392 N.E.2d 1257 (1979) as a reason for not permitting an adoption over the father's objection although the children had not lived with their father in an "unbroken family" continuously up to the time of the adoption petition.

55. See section 20.4, infra.

56. Wells v. Children's Aid Society of Utah, 681 P.2d 199 (Utah 1984). See also Catholic Charities of Archdiocese of Dubuque v. Zalesky, 232 N.W.2d 539 (Iowa 1975), 25 Drake L.Rev. 497 (1976); Collins v. Division of Foster Care, Jefferson Parish, Family Division, 377 So.2d 1266 (La.App.1979); Shoecraft v. Catholic Social Services Bureau, Inc., 222 Neb. 574, 385 N.W.2d 448 (1986), appeal dismissed as moot ___ U.S. ___, 107 S.Ct. 49, 93 L.Ed.2d 10 (1986), rehearing denied ___ U.S. ___, 107 S.Ct. 612, 93 L.Ed.2d 610. But see In re Adoption of Baby Boy Doe, 717 P.2d 686 (Utah 1986).

57. 345 U.S. 528, 73 S.Ct. 840, 97 L.Ed. 1221 (1953). This case is discussed at length in connection with custody jurisdiction in section 12.5, supra.

58. Cases which reject any application of May v. Anderson to adoption or termination of parental rights proceedings include In Interest of J. B., 140 Ga.App. 668, 231 S.E.2d 821 (1976); Wenz v. Schwartze, 183 Mont. 166, 598 P.2d 1086 (1979), cert. denied 444 U.S. 1071, 100 S.Ct.

though Stanley v. Illinois [59] cited the case with approval, reliance upon it in this context would be so destructive of adoption practice that the courts seem just to be ignoring it.

The two issues of consent to adoption and notice to the child's father are closely related. If his consent is not required, notice to him should not be necessary. Unfortunately the Supreme Court's decisions do not reveal any perception of this relationship. As a result the states have had to enact elaborate notice requirements regardless of the existing rules concerning consent.[60] The effect is to delay, handicap and discourage the adoption of children by non-relatives, all of which could have been avoided if the Supreme Court had been able to comprehend that adoption involves the interests of children and that those interests are more deserving of protection than those of the father when the two are in conflict.

Notice and Hearing as Constitutional Requirements

Although, as has been indicated,[61] there seems to be either a tacit or an express con-

sensus that May v. Anderson [62] is to be ignored in the adoption context and that personal jurisdiction over the defendant is not required, it is clear that reasonable notice and an opportunity to be heard are required by the Due Process Clause of the Fourteenth Amendment.[63] Under the law of some states the notice must specifically state that termination of parental rights may occur as a result of the proceeding.[64] If proper notice is not given, the adoption decree may be open to collateral attack by the natural parent with consequent hardship and suffering for both the child and the adoptive parents.[65] Some statutes authorize seizure of the child in advance of notice where his welfare requires it, and these statutes have on occasion been held to be unconstitutional either under the Due Process Clause on procedural grounds or for other reasons.[66]

Assuming that there is a general requirement of notice for termination of parental rights, or for adoption when parental rights have not been terminated, the next question is, what form should the notice take? [67] Personal service either within or without the

1015, 62 L.Ed.2d 753 (1980). Cases which seem to assume that personal jurisdiction over the defendant parent is required in such proceedings are Donlon v. Miller, 42 Ill. App.3d 64, 355 N.E.2d 195 (1976); In re Guardianship of Ellick, 69 Misc.2d 175, 328 N.Y.S.2d 587 (Fam.Ct.1972) (Polier, J.).

59. 405 U.S. 645, 92 S.Ct. 1208, 31 L.Ed.2d 551 (1972).

60. E.g., Ill.—S.H.A. c. 40, § 1509 (Supp.1986); Mich. C.L.A. §§ 27.3178 (555.36) (Supp.1986–1987), 27.3178 (555.37) (1980); West's Rev.Code Wash.Ann. §§ 26.33.020, 26.33.110, 26.33.310 (1986); Wis.Stat.Ann. §§ 48.41, 48.42 (Supp.1986–1987).

61. See the text at notes 57 to 59, supra.

62. 345 U.S. 528, 73 S.Ct. 840, 97 L.Ed. 1221 (1953).

63. Armstrong v. Manzo, 380 U.S. 545, 85 S.Ct. 1187, 14 L.Ed.2d 62 (1965); Huynh Thi Anh v. Levi, 586 F.2d 625 (6th Cir.1978); Schrum v. Bolding, 260 Ark. 114, 539 S.W.2d 415 (1976); Leithold v. Plass, 488 S.W.2d 159 (Tex. Civ.App.1972), decided on other grounds 505 S.W.2d 376 (Tex.Civ.App.1974). If notice is voluntarily and understandingly waived, it is not required. Matter of a Male Child's Adoption, 102 Idaho 225, 628 P.2d 1059 (1981). Where the adoption statute is silent on notice but notice is in fact given, there is no unconstitutionality. People in Interest of M. M., 726 P.2d 1108 (Colo.1986).

64. Robinson v. People in Interest of Zollinger, 173 Colo. 113, 476 P.2d 262 (1970); In re Martin, 3 Wash.App. 405, 476 P.2d 134 (1970). In Interest of Hewitt, 272 N.W.2d 852 (Iowa 1978) held that the notice must include

a general statement of the facts relied on in support of the petition and must notify the parent of her rights regarding counsel. See also Matter of Trapp, 593 S.W.2d 193 (Mo.1980), appeal dismissed for want of a substantial federal question 456 U.S. 967, 102 S.Ct. 2226, 72 L.Ed.2d 840 (1982), rehearing denied 458 U.S. 1116, 102 S.Ct. 3499, 73 L.Ed.2d 1377 (1982) on the notice requirements for a proceeding to terminate parental rights, and Doe v. Staples, 706 F.2d 985 (6th Cir.1983), cert. denied 465 U.S. 1033 (1984), imposing detailed notice requirements for a removal of children from the custody of their parents by a state agency.

65. In re Hampton's Estate, 55 Cal.App.2d 543, 131 P.2d 565 (1943); Leonard v. Leonard, 88 Idaho 485, 401 P.2d 541 (1965); Edwards v. Cockburn, 264 Mass. 112, 162 N.E. 225 (1928); In re Ives, 314 Mich. 690, 23 N.W.2d 131 (1946); In re Adams, 237 S.W.2d 232 (Mo.App.1951); In re Adoption of Bascom, 126 Mont. 129, 246 P.2d 223 (1952); Application of Osborne, 284 App.Div. 143, 130 N.Y.S.2d 450 (3d Dep't 1954) appeal denied 283 App.Div. 1121, 131 N.Y.S.2d 909 (1954); In re Meyers' Estate, 197 Or. 520, 254 P.2d 227 (1953); Beatty v. Davenport, 45 Wash. 555, 88 P. 1109 (1907); Schiltz v. Roenitz, 86 Wis. 31, 56 N.W. 194 (1893). Persons other than the one entitled to notice may be estopped to attack the decree. See section 20.11, infra.

66. Roe v. Conn, 417 F.Supp. 769 (M.D.Ala.1976); White v. Minter, 330 F.Supp. 1194 (D.Mass.1971).

67. The Children's Bureau's proposed statutes spell out the notice requirements in helpful detail. Children's

state is the most reliable and is clearly adequate.[68] In default of personal service, service by registered mail is effective, and as a last resort where the persons entitled to notice cannot be located, notice by publication may be relied upon.[69] It should be recognized that for all practical purposes service by publication is little better than no notice at all and is merely a fictional method of meeting the constitutional requirements, made necessary by the fact that a party's whereabouts is unknown. In any event the requirements of the local statute must be complied with exactly.[70] Due to the importance of adoption in the lives of all parties, and to the need for finality of adoption decrees, courts should be vigilant in insisting that every effort be made to fulfill notice requirements. The notice should of course be given in sufficient time to afford the recipient the opportunity to be heard.

Holding that notice is required in adoptions leads to the further question of some difficulty, namely, what persons are entitled to receive notice. The question is affected by both statutory provisions and constitutional principles. The cases occasionally confuse requirements of notice with consent requirements, two entirely separate and distinct issues.[71]

The extent to which the father of the illegitimate child is entitled to notice of adoption or of termination proceedings has already been discussed.[72] The mother of the illegitimate child and the natural parents of the legitimate child are ordinarily entitled to receive such notice.[73] If their parental rights have been terminated by a judicial proceeding, as for dependency or neglect, then no notice need be given them.[74] Notice also need not be given them if they have voluntarily terminated their parental rights in a judicial proceeding for relinquishment.[75] Closer cases arise when there is an allegation of abandonment or neglect in the adoption proceeding itself. Here it is the adoption proceeding which terminates parental rights, not a prior proceeding, and therefore notice is constitutionally required,[76] notwithstanding some judicial expressions to the contrary.[77] The point is that

Bureau, Legislative Guides for the Termination of Parental Rights and Responsibilities and the Adoption of Children 42, 55 (Children's Bureau Publication No. 394–1961). The Uniform Adoption Act, 9 Unif.L.Ann. 17 (1979) contains no notice provisions on the theory that parental rights are to be terminated by a prior separate proceeding or by consent, and that there is thus no need for notice.

68. In re Interest of Baby Boy Bryant, 9 Kan.App.2d 768, 689 P.2d 1203 (1984) (service in accordance with the rules of civil procedure). Notice to a defendant parent's counsel may be sufficient. Mahoney v. Linder, 14 Or. App. 656, 514 P.2d 901 (1973).

69. D. A. v. D. R. L., 727 P.2d 768 (Alaska 1986); Young v. Foster, 148 Ga. 737, 252 S.E.2d 680 (1979); Greene v. Graham, 140 Ga.App. 375, 231 S.E.2d 74 (1976); Matter of Lathrop's Adoption, 2 Kan.App. 90, 575 P.2d 894 (1978); Smith v. Benson, 542 S.W.2d 571 (Mo.App.1976).

70. In re Soderberg, 26 Ariz. 404, 226 P. 210 (1924); Augusta County Dep't of Social Services v. Unnamed Mother, 3 Va.App. 40, 348 S.E.2d 26 (1986); Matter of Adoption of Hickey, 18 Wash.App. 259, 567 P.2d 260 (1977). See also the discussion of notice to the father of the illegitimate child at note 20, supra.

71. E.g., Finn v. Rees, 65 Idaho 181, 141 P.2d 976 (1943).

72. See the discussion at notes 1 to 60, supra.

73. In re Adoption of a Minor, 82 U.S.App.D.C. 110, 160 F.2d 928 (D.C.Cir.1947); Edwards v. Cockburn, 264 Mass. 112, 162 N.E. 225 (1928); In re Adoption of Bascom,

126 Mont. 129, 246 P.2d 223 (1952); In re Meyers' Estate, 197 Or. 520, 254 P.2d 227 (1953); Schiltz v. Roenitz, 86 Wis. 31, 56 N.W. 194 (1893). If the parent of the child is incompetent, notice may have to be made on a guardian. In Interest of Baby Boy Bryant, 9 Kan.App.2d 768, 689 P.2d 1203 (1984). Notice may be waived by a general appearance and participation in the adoption or dependency proceeding. Stubbs v. Hammond, 257 Iowa 1071, 135 N.W.2d 540 (1965); In re Adoption of Cannon, 243 Iowa 828, 53 N.W.2d 877 (1952); In re Rose, 161 Pa. Super. 204, 54 A.2d 297 (1947).

74. In Interest of Workman, 56 Ill.App.3d 1007, 14 Ill. Dec. 908, 373 N.E.2d 39 (1978), affirmed on other grounds 76 Ill.2d 256, 28 Ill.Dec. 541, 390 N.E.2d 900 (1979), cert. denied 444 U.S. 992, 100 S.Ct. 525, 62 L.Ed.2d 422 (1979) (semble); In re Matthews, 203 Tenn. 161, 310 S.W.2d 185 (1957).

75. Smith v. Welfare Department of Denver, 144 Colo. 103, 355 P.2d 317 (1960).

76. In re Hampton's Estate, 55 Cal.App.2d 543, 131 P.2d 565 (1942); Davis v. Neely, 387 P.2d 494 (Okl.1963), appeal dismissed, cert. denied 379 U.S. 2, 85 S.Ct. 31, 13 L.Ed.2d 21 (1964).

77. E.g., Modacsi v. Taylor, 104 So.2d 664 (Fla.App. 1958); Smith v. Smith, 67 Idaho 349, 180 P.2d 853 (1947); Finn v. Rees, 65 Idaho 181, 141 P.2d 976 (1943); Lucius v. Wistner, 97 N.H. 128, 82 A.2d 602 (1951) (dictum); Nugent v. Powell, 4 Wyo. 173, 33 P. 23 (1893) (dictum). It may be clear from the applicable statute that consent to the adoption is not required in these cases, but this does not mean that notice is unnecessary.

the parent is entitled to notice and a day in court on the question whether he has abandoned or neglected his child and on whether his rights in relation to that child should be cut off.[78] The same reasoning should apply to those situations in which, after a divorce, a child of the marriage is adopted without the consent of the non-custodial parent. Under some statutes the non-custodial parent's consent is not required to be obtained and the adoption may be decreed even though he objects.[79] Nevertheless, until the adoption decree is entered, his parental rights continue to exist since, for example, the custody order might be modified or he might resume custody on the death of the other parent. It therefore certainly seems the better practice to insist upon notice to him even though his consent to the adoption is not required,[80] and in fact it seems clear that notice to him is constitutionally required as is true in any other case substantially affecting one's legal rights.[81]

A parent who has consented to the adoption is generally held not entitled to notice of the proceedings.[82] This rule has some utility since it helps to preserve the anonymity of the adoption process, keeping the adoptive parents from knowing who the natural parents are and vice versa. In practice the consenting parent would seldom wish to receive notice. As a matter of properly protecting legal rights, however, this seems erroneous. The consent of itself does not terminate parental rights unless it is given in a prior relinquishment proceeding or is given that effect specifically by statute. This being so, it would seem that notice ought to be given the parent even if he did consent on the principle that judgments affecting a person's legal rights are only entered after due notice and an opportunity to be heard. Anonymity may be preserved by terminating parental rights in a prior, separate proceeding as recommended by the Children's Bureau [83] or by obtaining a waiver of notice from the parent when he gives his consent to the adoption.[84]

The final problem with notice concerns the identity of those, other than the natural parents, who are entitled to receive notice of adoption proceedings. The Supreme Court has looked at the constitutional aspects of this question in Smith v. Organization of Foster Families for Equality and Reform.[85] The issue in that case was whether a foster parent having custody of a child pursuant to the authority given by a state agency had a "liberty interest" in the child such that he was entitled under the Due Process Clause of the Fourteenth Amendment to notice and a hearing before the child could be removed from his custody. The Court did not reach that question, deciding the case on the narrower ground that however the foster parent's inter-

78. Carpenter v. Forshee, 103 Ga.App. 758, 120 S.E.2d 786 (1961), overruled on other grounds by Davey v. Evans, 156 Ga.App. 698, 275 S.E.2d 769 (1980).

79. E.g., In the Matter of the Adoption of Smith, 229 Or. 277, 366 P.2d 875 (1961).

80. Hammer v. Hammer, 16 Alaska 203 (1956); In re Adoption of Thevenin, 189 Cal.App.2d 245, 11 Cal.Rptr. 219 (1961); In re Adoption of Burton, 147 Cal.App.2d 125, 305 P.2d 185 (1956); In re Adams, 237 S.W.2d 232 (Mo. App.1951). Other cases are cited in Annot., 76 A.L.R. 1077, 1081 (1932). Contra the text: Mowery v. Ealey, 91 Ohio App. 266, 108 N.E.2d 143 (1948); Byrd v. Byrd, 78 Ohio App. 73, 69 N.E.2d 75 (1945).

81. Cf. the discussion in Smith v. Organization of Foster Families for Equality and Reform, 431 U.S. 816, 97 S.Ct. 2094, 53 L.Ed.2d 14 (1977).

82. In re Adoption of a Minor, 345 Mass. 706, 189 N.E.2d 505 (1963); Matter of Anonymous, 55 A.D.2d 383, 390 N.Y.S.2d 433 (2d Dep't 1977) (with a strong dissent); Whetmore v. Fratello, 204 Or. 316, 282 P.2d 667 (1955); Austin v. Collins, 200 S.W.2d 666 (Tex.Civ.App.1947).

83. Winter v. Director, Department of Welfare of Baltimore City, 217 Md. 391, 143 A.2d 81 (1958), cert. denied 358 U.S. 912, 79 S.Ct. 242, 3 L.Ed.2d 233 (1958); Children's Bureau, Legislative Guides for the Termination of Parental Rights and Responsibilities and the Adoption of Children 9, 49 (Children's Bureau Publication No. 394–1961).

84. See note 61, supra, and In re Adoption of Smith, 314 S.W.2d 464 (Mo.App.1958). Alaska Stat. §§ 25.23.050(b) and 25.23.100(a) (1983) provide that notice is not required for a person whose consent is filed with the adoption petition. This seems to have the effect that a consent is an automatic waiver, but it seems a dubious procedure. Petition of Foley, 123 Colo. 533, 232 P.2d 186 (1951) invalidated a waiver by a minor when the statute authorized minors to make binding consents to adoption but said nothing about waivers.

85. 431 U.S. 816, 97 S.Ct. 2094, 53 L.Ed.2d 14 (1977), 79, Colum.L.Rev. 1191 (1979).

est might be defined, the procedure employed by New York in removing children from foster parents was not constitutionally defective. Although the Supreme Court was wise to avoid imposing a constitutional rule of notice and hearing when the facts of the cases and the interests involved may vary widely, it may be going too far to hold, as some lower courts have,[86] that notice and a hearing are never to be granted when the child is taken from the custody of a foster parent. It may be appropriate to deny a hearing to a foster parent having only temporary custody under the general supervision of a state agency, especially when the state seeks to return the child to its natural parent.[87] On the other hand if the child has been for some years in the custody of a foster parent, perhaps a grandparent, so that both child and foster parent view the relationship as permanent, the child certainly should not be removed

without notice and a hearing.[88] Relationships of this latter type may have the strength and permanence of the natural parent-child relationship and should be entitled to the same respect by the courts.

Right of Indigent Parent or Child to Have Counsel Provided

Until 1981 it was generally held in the state courts and the lower federal courts that a parent facing the possible termination of his parental rights had a right under the Due Process Clause of the Fourteenth Amendment to have counsel provided for him by the state, where he was indigent and unable to obtain counsel for himself.[89] Although some of these cases did take some account of the possibility that criminal liability might be imposed in the termination proceedings,[90] the major emphasis in all of them was on the crucial, even fundamental, interest which would be affect-

---

86. Drummond v. Fulton County Dep't of Family and Children's Services, 563 F.2d 1200 (5th Cir.1977), cert. denied 437 U.S. 910, 98 S.Ct. 3103, 57 L.Ed.2d 1141 (1978); Sherrard v. Owens, 644 F.2d 542 (6th Cir.1981), cert. denied 454 U.S. 828, 102 S.Ct. 120, 70 L.Ed.2d 103 (1981); Eason v. Welfare Commissioner, 171 Conn. 630, 370 A.2d 1082 (1976), cert. denied 432 U.S. 907, 97 S.Ct. 2953, 53 L.Ed.2d 1079 (1977); Nye v. Marcus, 198 Conn. 138, 502 A.2d 869 (1985); W. C. v. P. M., 155 N.J.Super. 555, 383 A.2d 125 (1978).

87. Smith v. Organization of Foster Families for Equality and Reform, 431 U.S. 816, 97 S.Ct. 2094, 53 L.Ed.2d 14 (1977) emphasized the temporary nature of the foster parent's care for the child and the fact that the relationship was expressly terminable and under state supervision. The Drummond case, cited in note 86, supra, was a similar kind of case, in which the child was being removed from the foster parents for the purpose of making an adoption placement. See also Barriner v. Stedman, 580 P.2d 514 (Okl.1978), in which the court held that a grandparent having visitation rights was not entitled to notice of adoption proceedings respecting the grandchild.

88. Rivera v. Marcus, 696 F.2d 1016 (2d Cir.1982) held that the Constitution requires a full hearing before an impartial decisionmaker, with the foster parent represented by counsel and having the right to confront witnesses where the child was related to the foster parent and had been in her custody for six years. The action of the agency in this case seems to have been egregiously high-handed. See also Ellis v. Hamilton, 669 F.2d 510 (7th Cir.1982), cert. denied 459 U.S. 1069, 103 S.Ct. 488, 74 L.Ed.2d 631 (1982) Brown v. County of San Joaquin, 601 F.Supp. 653 (E.D.Cal.1985); In Interest of Orcutt, 173 N.W.2d 66 (Iowa 1969); Cennami v. Department of Public Welfare, 5 Mass.App. 403, 363 N.E.2d 539 (1977); Muggenborg v. Kessler, 630 P.2d 1276 (Okl.1981).

89. Davis v. Page, 640 F.2d 599 (5th Cir.1981), cert. granted and judgment vacated 458 U.S. 1118, 102 S.Ct. 3504, 73 L.Ed.2d 1380 (1982), on remand 714 F.2d 512 (5th Cir.1983), cert. denied 464 U.S. 1052, 104 S.Ct. 735, 79 L.Ed.2d 194 (1984) (counsel must be provided where prolonged or indefinite deprivation of custody is threatened); Cleaver v. Wilcox, 499 F.2d 940 (9th Cir.1974) (due process requires appointed counsel whenever an indigent parent faces a substantial possibility of loss of custody and is unable to present his case properly); Smith v. Edmiston, 431 F.Supp. 941 (W.D.Tenn.1977); State v. Anonymous, 179 Conn. 155, 425 A.2d 939 (1979); In Interest of D. B., 385 So.2d 83 (Fla.1980) (due process requires counsel in proceedings for the termination of parental rights); In Interest of Howard, 382 So.2d 194 (La.App.1980) (due process requires counsel for indigent parents where they may lose custody for an indefinite or prolonged period); Department of Public Welfare v. J. K. B., 379 Mass. 1, 393 N.E.2d 406 (1979) (indigent parent entitled to counsel at state expense when contesting a petition to dispense with consent to adoption); In re B., 30 N.Y.2d 352, 334 N.Y.S.2d 133, 285 N.E.2d 288 (1972); Matter of Chad S., 580 P.2d 983 (Okl.1978); State v. Jamison, 251 Or. 114, 444 P.2d 15 (1968); In re Adoption of R. I., 455 Pa. 29, 312 A.2d 601 (1973), appeal after remand 468 Pa. 287, 361 A.2d 294 (1976), dismissed, cert. denied 429 U.S. 1032, 97 S.Ct. 722, 50 L.Ed.2d 743 (1977); In re Welfare of Luscier, 84 Wash.2d 135, 524 P.2d 906 (1974).

California has held that there is no due process right to counsel in such cases. In re T., 25 Cal.App.3d 120, 101 Cal.Rptr. 606 (1972). But see note 93, infra.

90. In re B., 30 N.Y.2d 352, 334 N.Y.S.2d 133, 285 N.E.2d 288 (1972).

ed by a judgment adverse to the parent.[91] Cases holding that the state must furnish counsel also held that effective counsel is required.[92] In some states the issue is moot since the statute on termination provides for the assistance of counsel to indigent defendants.[93]

In 1981 in a curiously unconvincing opinion the Supreme Court held that the federal constitution does not require that counsel be furnished in all proceedings for the termination of parental rights.[94] Instead the Court left "the decision whether due process calls for the appointment of counsel for indigent parents in determination proceedings to be answered in the first instance by the trial court, subject, of course, to appellate review."[95] Since the Court relied for this result on the factors set forth in Mathews v. Eldridge,[96] presumably it is those factors which should guide trial courts in deciding whether in a given case counsel should be furnished. Those factors are a) the importance of the private interests at stake; b) the importance of the government's interest; and c) the risk that the procedures used will lead to erroneous decisions.[97] In view of the very great importance to the parents and also to the child of the interests involved in these cases, and of the difficulty with which any parent

would face in presenting his case without counsel, one would suppose that the Mathews v. Eldridge factors would always lead to the furnishing of counsel. This is particularly obvious when the necessarily vague nature of dependency and neglect statutes is considered,[98] making a defense in these cases assume a complex mixture of legal and factual arguments. The impact of the Lassiter case is somewhat lessened by the Court's closing concession that a "wise public policy" may require higher standards than the Court itself demands and that the Court's opinion does not invalidate higher standards now being followed by the states.[99]

If the parent in a termination of rights proceeding were always entitled to have counsel furnished, there might be less reason to require the appointment of counsel for the child. But if neither parent nor child is entitled to have counsel appointed, it is difficult to see how the proceeding can be fairly conducted. Nevertheless some cases have held that counsel for the child need not be appointed.[1] Other courts take the position that due process does require counsel for the child, on the grounds that most serious interests are involved, and that the child's interests will often not be represented adequately by the parents.[2] It seems clear that there may often

---

91. E.g., Danforth v. State Dep't of Health and Welfare, 303 A.2d 794 (Me.1973), 5 Tex.Tech.L.Rev. 857 (1974).

92. State v. Anonymous, 179 Conn. 155, 425 A.2d 939 (1979). An indigent parent may be entitled to a transcript at state expense. Smith v. Superior Court of Los Angeles County, 41 Cal.App.3d 109, 115 Cal.Rptr. 677 (1974).

93. E.g., West's Ann.Cal.Civ.Code § 237.5 (1982); Colo. Rev.Stat. § 19–1–106(d) (1986).

94. Lassiter v. Department of Social Services of Durham County, N.C., 452 U.S. 18, 101 S.Ct. 2153, 68 L.Ed.2d 640 (1981), rehearing denied 453 U.S. 927, 102 S.Ct. 889, 69 L.Ed.2d 1023 (1981), 23 B.C.L.Rev. 1177 (1982), 14 Conn.L.Rev. 733 (1982), 15 U.C.D.L.Rev. 1123 (1982). Cases following Lassiter include In re Blake C., 178 Cal. App.3d 608, 224 Cal.Rptr. 167 (1986); In Interest of Cooper, 230 Kan. 57, 631 P.2d 632 (1981); Brown v. McLennan County Children's Protective Services, 627 S.W.2d 390 (Tex.1982) (counsel need not be furnished when the parent relinquishes the child). In some states counsel must still be furnished. V. F. v. State, 666 P.2d 42 (Alaska 1983); In re Interest of Burbanks, 209 Neb. 676, 310 N.W.2d 138 (1981) (delay in appointment of guardian ad litem for parents and children was a depriva-

tion of due process). Counsel must be effective and may not be permitted to withdraw. Appeal in Gila Cty. Juvenile Action No. J 3824, 130 Ariz. 530, 637 P.2d 740 (1981); In re Welfare of Hall, 99 Wash.2d 842, 664 P.2d 1245 (1983). The People of The State of Illinois v. Alvis Ray Lackey, 79 Ill.2d 466, 39 Ill.Dec. 769, 405 N.E.2d 748 (1980) held it was reversible error for the public defender to represent both the parents and the child in a termination proceeding.

95. 452 U.S. at 32, 101 S.Ct. of 2162.

96. 424 U.S. 319, 96 S.Ct. 893, 47 L.Ed.2d 18 (1976).

97. 424 U.S. at 335, 96 S.Ct. at 903.

98. See the discussion in section 20.5, infra.

99. 452 U.S. at 33, 34, 101 S.Ct. at 2162, 2163.

1. In re Richard E., 21 Cal.3d 349, 146 Cal.Rptr. 604, 579 P.2d 495 (1978), appeal dismissed 439 U.S. 1060, 99 S.Ct. 822, 59 L.Ed.2d 26 (1979), rehearing denied 440 U.S. 940, 99 S.Ct. 1290, 56 L.Ed.2d 500 (1979), relying in part on the statute, which required counsel for the parent but not for the child.

2. Ricketts v. Ricketts, 265 Ark. 28, 576 S.W.2d 932 (1979); Matter of Guardianship of Gullette, 173 Mont. 132, 566 P.2d 396 (1977) (semble, though the opinion is

be a conflict between the interests of the child and those of the parent. A third line of cases adopts the approach of the Lassiter case,[3] holding that the issue is to be decided on a case by case basis, depending upon whether independent counsel for the child will be able to bring out evidence or make arguments which would otherwise not be made or brought out in the proceeding.[4] Since a termination proceeding differs from a custody case in that it may result in a final, nonmodifiable decree which ends all of the child's contact with his parent, it would seem the better part of wisdom to provide independent counsel for the child, either as a matter of due process or pursuant to statute.[5]

Standard of Proof and Other Evidentiary Principles

According to the Supreme Court in Santosky v. Kramer[6] the Due Process Clause requires that before a parent's rights may be terminated the state's allegations must be proved by clear and convincing evidence. The Court in this case may have been trying to atone for its insensitivity to the interests of both parents and children in Lassiter, but the fact is that the requirement of a higher standard of proof than a preponderance of the

evidence is of relatively little protection for the rights involved if the parent is not represented by counsel. The Court reasoned that the parent's interest in the custody of his child is an interest more precious than property rights and that when the factors outlined in Mathews v. Eldridge[7] are "balanced",[8] the advantage is heavily on the side of the state, thereby justifying the higher standard of proof. As in other cases,[9] the Court largely ignored the fact that the child's interests as well as those of the parent are at stake in these cases. When one reads the opinion, one has a strong impression that its arguments more than justify providing counsel for indigent parents and for children as well, but the Court was oddly reluctant to impose such an obligation on the states.[10] Even before Santosky was decided some states had required proof by clear and convincing evidence in termination proceedings,[11] while others went even further to require proof beyond a reasonable doubt in reliance upon the state due process clause.[12]

The Supreme Court in Santosky gratuitously suggests in a footnote that it is not "clear that the State constitutionally could terminate a parent's rights *without* showing paren-

---

unclear); New Jersey Division of Youth and Family Services v. Wandell, 155 N.J.Super. 302, 382 A.2d 711 (1978).

3. Lassiter v. Department of Social Services of Durham County, N.C., 452 U.S. 18, 101 S.Ct. 2153, 68 L.Ed.2d 640 (1981), rehearing denied 453 U.S. 927, 102 S.Ct. 889, 69 L.Ed.2d 1023 (1981).

4. Matter of D., 24 Or.App. 601, 547 P.2d 175 (1976), cert. denied 429 U.S. 907, 97 S.Ct. 273, 50 L.Ed.2d 189 (1976), overruling on this point State ex rel. Juvenile Dep't of Multnomah County v. Wade, 19 Or.App. 314, 527 P.2d 753 (1974), dismissed for want of a substantial federal question 423 U.S. 806, 96 S.Ct. 16, 46 L.Ed.2d 27 (1975). See also In re Adoption of Female Infant, 237 A.2d 468 (D.C.App.1968).

5. See Colo.Rev.Stat. § 19–1–106(b) (1986).

6. 455 U.S. 745, 102 S.Ct. 1388, 71 L.Ed.2d 599 (1982), on remand 89 A.D.2d 738, 453 N.Y.S.2d 942 (1982), appeal denied 58 N.Y.2d 605, 459 N.Y.S.2d 1029, 445 N.E.2d 656 (1983).

7. The factors are listed at note 97, supra. Mathews v. Eldridge, 424 U.S. 319, 96 S.Ct. 893, 47 L.Ed.2d 18 (1976).

8. 455 U.S. at 754, 102 S.Ct. at ___. The Court's "balancing" metaphor is particularly inappropriate in these circumstances as well as in many others, since the

process consists not in balancing but in deciding that the private interests involved should be given preference over those of the state.

9. E.g., May v. Anderson, 345 U.S. 528, 73 S.Ct. 840, 97 L.Ed. 1221 (1953), criticized at length in section 12.5, supra.

10. The Court points out that the stricter standard of proof can be imposed without placing fiscal burdens on the state. 455 U.S. at 767.

11. The Court in Santosky v. Kramer, 455 U.S. 745, 749, footnote 3, 102 S.Ct. 1388, ___, footnote 3, 71 L.Ed.2d 599 (1982), on remand 89 A.D.2d 738, 453 N.Y.S.2d 942 (1982), appeal denied 58 N.Y.2d 605, 459 N.Y.S.2d 1029, 444 N.E.2d 656 (1983) lists thirty-five states which have required this standard of proof or its equivalent by statute or judicial decision. After Santosky People in Interest of A. M. D., 648 P.2d 625 (Colo.1982) has held that a finding of dependency or neglect as a predicate for termination of parental rights may be based upon a preponderance of the evidence so long as the termination decision rests on clear and convincing evidence, but it seems very doubtful that this procedure meets the standard set by Santosky.

12. E.g., State v. Robert H., 118 N.H. 713, 393 A.2d 1387 (1978).

tal unfitness." [13]   Although this remark is certainly no more than dictum, it may be a forecast of what at least some Supreme Court justices think the law ought to be. It is inconsistent with the views of some distinguished state courts [14] and ignores the child's interests. For these reasons it should not be taken as authoritative.

Other state court decisions have held that a termination proceeding may be held in the absence of the parent under some circumstances; [15] that various kinds of evidence may be relied upon without violation of the Constitution; [16] and that the parent is entitled to an expeditious hearing on the question of termination of parental rights. [17]

 WESTLAW REFERENCES

The Constitutional Position of the Father of an Illegitimate Child

da(bef 1972) & di(adopt! /s consent! /s mother /s illegitimate /3 child infant baby)

find 92 sct 1208

"equal protection" "due process" "fourteenth amendment" /p father /s adopt! /s illegitimate /3 child infant minor

ti(quilloin /s walcott)

find 103 sct 2985

Notice and Hearing as Constitutional Requirements

notic! notif! /s father /s illegitimate /2 child infant minor /p adopt!

di(notic! notif! /s parent father mother /s adopt! /s abandon! neglect!)

Right of Indigent Parent or Child to Have Counsel Provided

di("due process" /s counsel lawyer attorney /s terminat! (cut cutting +3 off) /s parent! /3 entitl! right)

Standard of Proof and Other Evidentiary Principles

find 102 sct 1388

sy(standard /2 proof prove* proving /s terminat! (cut cutting +3 off) /s parent! mother father /3 right entitl!)

§ 20.3   Termination of Parental Rights and Adoption—Jurisdiction

Jurisdiction in this section broadly refers to the court's authority to pass upon the adoption.[1] This depends upon a variety of factors, which may be summarized under the headings of jurisdiction over the subject matter of the action, and jurisdiction over the persons of the parties. The question whether jurisdiction is present arises in two contexts. It may be raised at the outset of the adoption proceeding, forcing the court to determine whether it is authorized to hear the case, or it may

13. Santosky v. Kramer, 455 U.S. 745, 760, footnote 10, 102 S.Ct. 1388, ___, footnote 10, 71 L.Ed.2d 599 (1982), on remand 89 A.D.2d 738, 453 N.Y.S.2d 942 (1982), appeal denied 58 N.Y.2d 605, 459 N.Y.S.2d 1029, 445 N.E.2d 656 (1983). The Court relied for this statement on Quilloin v. Walcott, 434 U.S. 246, 98 S.Ct. 549, 54 L.Ed.2d 511 (1978), rehearing denied 435 U.S. 918, 98 S.Ct. 1477, 55 L.Ed.2d 511 (1978), which is discussed in section 20.2, at note 27, and which not only does not support the statement in the Santosky footnote, but took a position exactly opposite to that statement.

14. E.g., Matter of Adoption of McMullen, 236 Kan. 348, 691 P.2d 17 (1984) (statute not unconstitutional in providing that a court need not find total and absolute abandonment as a condition to permitting adoption of a child without parental consent); Sorentino v. Family and Children's Society of Elizabeth, 74 N.J. 313, 378 A.2d 18 (1977), affirmed 77 N.J. 483, 391 A.2d 497 (1978) (not unconstitutional to place upon the parents the burden of proving that the child would not be harmed by removal from the adoptive home).

15. State in Interest of A. E., 448 So.2d 183 (La.App. 1984) (mother comatose); Matter of Welfare of HGB, 306 N.W.2d 821 (Minn.1981) (mother in an out-of-state jail); Matter of Rich, 604 P.2d 1248 (Okl.1979); In Interest of

Darrow, 32 Wash.App. 803, 649 P.2d 858 (1982) (father in an out-of-state jail).

16. In re Neglected Child, 129 Vt. 234, 276 A.2d 14 (1971) (use of social worker's report not a violation of due process). But Matter of Ana Maria R., 98 Misc.2d 910, 414 N.Y.S.2d 982 (Fam.Ct.1979) held that it was a denial of equal protection to base the termination of parental rights of a Spanish-speaking mother in part upon a standardized intelligence test as a way of proving mental retardation.

17. In re Willis, 157 W.Va. 225, 207 S.E.2d 129 (1973).

§ 20.3

1. For general treatment of jurisdiction in adoption, see Ehrenzweig, Conflict of Laws, 85–88 (1962); Stumberg, Principles of Conflict of Laws, 338–341 (3d ed. 1963); Goodrich, Conflict of Laws, 288–290 (4th ed. Scoles, 1964); Taintor, Adoption in the Conflict of Laws, 15 U.Pitts.L.Rev. 222 (1954) (the most sensible and coherent discussion); Kennedy, Adoption in the Conflict of Laws, 34 Can.B.Rev. 507 (1956); Note, Foreign Adoptions, 28 Bklyn.L.Rev. 324 (1962); and Baade, Interstate and Foreign Adoptions in North Carolina, 40 N.C.L.Rev. 691 (1962).

come up after an adoption has been decreed when a court is asked to recognize the decree. In the latter situation familiar doctrine has it that if jurisdiction over the adoption was originally lacking, the decree need not be recognized, but that if jurisdiction was present the decree will be recognized.[2] In a few cases the Full Faith and Credit Clause has been held to require interstate recognition of adoption decrees.[3]

Jurisdiction over the subject matter of the adoption turns in the first instance on the provisions of the local statute. All states have statutes authorizing particular courts to grant adoptions. The proper court may be one of general jurisdiction,[4] or, a specialized court such as the probate court [5] or the juvenile or domestic relations court.[6] In addition the statutes require the filing of the adoption petition in a specific locality. This is most commonly the county of the petitioner's residence,[7] but authority may also be given for filing in the county of the child's residence,[8] or the county in which is located the office of the child placement agency having custody or guardianship of the child.[9] A few statutes impose the further requirement that the petitioner must have been a resident of the state for one year.[10] The term "residence" usually found in such statutes apparently means domicile.[11]

---

2. Refusing to recognize a decree of its own courts: Hughes v. Industrial Commission, 69 Ariz. 193, 211 P.2d 463 (1949). Refusing to recognize the decree of another state for lack of jurisdiction: Goclanney v. Desrochers, 135 Ariz. 240, 660 P.2d 491 (Ariz.App.1983); Brown v. Hall, 385 Ill. 260, 52 N.E.2d 781 (1944); Foster v. Waterman, 124 Mass. 592 (1878). Refusing to grant comity to the decree of a foreign country: Barry E. (Anonymous) v. Ingraham, 43 N.Y.2d 87, 400 N.Y.S.2d 772, 371 N.E.2d 492 (1977). Holding that the jurisdiction of another state may be inquired into: Ross v. Pick, 199 Md. 341, 86 A.2d 463 (1952). Recognizing the decree of another state upon finding that jurisdiction existed: Woodward's Appeal, 81 Conn. 152, 70 A. 453 (1908); Succession of Caldwell, 114 La. 195, 38 So. 140 (1903); Anderson v. French, 77 N.H. 509, 93 A. 1042 (1915); Zanzonico v. Neeld, 17 N.J. 490, 111 A.2d 772 (1955); Matter of Neuwirth's Estate, 155 N.J.Super. 410, 382 A.2d 972 (1978); In re Chinsky's Estate, 159 Misc. 591, 288 N.Y.S. 666 (Surr.Ct.1936); Cribbs v. Floyd, 188 S.C. 443, 199 S.E. 677 (1938); Finley v. Brown, 122 Tenn. 316, 123 S.W. 359 (1909).

For a useful statute authorizing the approval of an adoption decree of a foreign country, see Colo.Rev.Stat. § 19–4–107.5 (1986). The question of what effect the valid adoption decree of another state or country will be given is discussed in a later section. See section 20.10, infra.

Even a decree given without jurisdiction will be immune to attack by parties or those in privity with them where the usual doctrines of estoppel apply. See section 20.11, infra.

3. E.g., Glas v. Sankey, 148 Ill. 536, 36 N.E. 628 (1893); Orme v. Northern Trust Co., 25 Ill.2d 151, 183 N.E.2d 505 (1962), cert. denied 371 U.S. 935, 83 S.Ct. 308, 9 L.Ed.2d 271 (1962); Ross v. Pick, 199 Md. 341, 86 A.2d 463 (1952). See Leflar, The Law of Conflict of Laws, 342 (1959).

4. E.g., West's Ann.Cal.Civ.Code § 226 (Supp.1987); West's Fla.Stat.Ann. § 63.102 (1985); Ill.—S.H.A. ch. 40, § 1505 (1980).

5. E.g., Conn.Gen.Stat.Ann. § 45–63 (Supp.1986); Mass.Gen.Laws Ann. ch. 210, § 1 (1981); Mich.C.L.A.

§ 27.3178 (555.24) (1980); Ohio Rev.Code §§ 3107.01, 3107.04 (1980).

6. E.g., Colo.Rev.Stat. § 19–1–104(h) (1986); D.C.Code 1981, § 11–1101(9); N.Y.—McKinney's Fam.Ct.Act § 641 (Supp.1987) (family court and surrogate's court have concurrent jurisdiction).

There may be conflicts over jurisdiction among the courts of a single state. These must be settled by reference to the applicable local statutes. See, e.g. In re Adoption of Biddle, 168 Ohio St. 209, 152 N.E.2d 105 (1958), on remand 163 N.E.2d 188 (Ohio App.1959); Petition of Parks, 262 Minn. 319, 114 N.W.2d 667 (1962); Williamson v. Laughlin, 192 Tenn. 580, 241 S.W.2d 576 (1951); Morrisette v. Superior Court In and For Kern County, 236 Cal.App.2d 597, 46 Cal.Rptr. 153 (1965).

7. See, e.g., the statutes cited in notes 4 and 5, supra.

8. E.g., West's Fla.Stat.Ann. § 63.102 (1985); Ill.—S.H.A. ch. 40, § 1505 (1980); N.Y.—McKinney's Dom.Rel. L. § 115 (1977); West's Rev.Code Wash.Ann. § 26.33.030 (1986); Wis.Stat.Ann. § 48.83 (Supp.1986–1987).

9. E.g., Conn.Gen.Stat.Ann. § 45–63 (Supp.1986); Ill.—S.H.A. ch. 40, § 1505 (1980); N.J.Stat.Ann. § 9:3–42 (Supp.1986); N.Y.—McKinney's Dom.Rel.L. § 113 (1977); Pa.Stat. tit. 23, § 2302 (Supp.1986).

10. E.g., D.C.Code 1981, § 16–301; Minn.Stat.Ann. § 259.22 (1982); N.C.Gen.Stat. § 48–4 (1984) (six months' residence required).

11. Hughes v. Industrial Commission, 69 Ariz. 193, 211 P.2d 463 (1949); Johnson v. Smith, 94 Ind.App. 619, 180 N.E. 188 (1932); Krakow v. Department of Public Welfare, 326 Mass. 452, 95 N.E.2d 184 (1950); In re Adoption of _____, 22 N.J.Misc. 181, 37 A.2d 645 (1944); Cribbs v. Floyd, 188 S.C. 443, 199 S.E. 677 (1938); In re Adoption of Mullins, 219 Tenn. 666, 412 S.W.2d 896 (1967).

Pennsylvania apparently takes the position that "residence" means either temporary or permanent residence. Wolf's Appeal, 13 A. 760 (Pa.1888); In re Wagner's Petition, 381 Pa. 107, 112 A.2d 352 (1955). Stearns v. Allen, 183 Mass. 404, 67 N.E. 349 (1903) construes "residence" in the statute in its popular sense, not as meaning domi-

The headings of these statutes often read "Jurisdiction and Venue",[12] suggesting that the requirement of filing in a certain county is merely one of venue which might be waived by the parties. The cases in the various states are in complete conflict as to whether the requirement is one of jurisdiction or merely one of venue which may be waived.[13] One of the undesirable consequences of holding it jurisdictional is that this may later vitiate the adoption decree, with great hardship to all concerned.

The next question is whether there are jurisdictional requirements for adoption beyond those found in particular statutes. It has been assumed in many text discussions that there are,[14] an assumption which is somewhat odd in view of the fact that, as the cases are fond of repeating, there was no common law of adoption, and the practice and procedure in adoption cases are entirely statutory. Conceivably in those states whose adoption statutes include provisions construed as gov-

erning venue only, it might be easier to argue that there is a body of common law on jurisdiction. Where the adoption statute imposes residence requirements which have been construed as jurisdictional, however, one would normally argue that these are the only jurisdictional requirements, excluding by implication any additional limits on jurisdiction. The cases on this issue are not very helpful. One Maryland case does state that the statute is the sole source of adoption jurisdiction.[15] Several other cases assume this to be so without any discussion.[16] And there is a line of cases which assumes without discussion that there are additional common law requirements for adoption jurisdiction,[17] some of them following the Restatement.[18]

The theoretical basis for the assumption that there are common law rules governing adoption jurisdiction is the idea that since adoption affects status, and since a person's status is generally governed by the law of his domicile, the status of adopted child may only

---

cile. See also Herrin v. Graham, 87 Ga.App. 291, 73 S.E.2d 572 (1952).

Goclanney v. Desrochers, 135 Ariz. 240, 660 P.2d 491 (App.1982) held that residence in the Texas adoption statute is to be construed to mean domicile.

12. See generally the statutes cited in notes 4 to 10, supra.

13. Holding the requirement is jurisdictional: Hughes v. Industrial Commission, 69 Ariz. 193, 211 P.2d 463 (1949); In re Webb's Adoption, 65 Ariz. 176, 177 P.2d 222 (1947); Ozment v. Mann, 235 Ark. 901, 363 S.W.2d 129 (1962); Pardo v. Creamer, 228 Ark. 746, 310 S.W.2d 218 (1958); In re McGrew, 183 Cal. 177, 190 P. 804 (1920); Portman v. Mobley, 158 Ga. 269, 123 S.E. 695 (1924); Hook v. Wright, 329 Ill. 299, 160 N.E. 579 (1928) (semble); Foster v. Waterman, 124 Mass. 592 (1878) (applying the New Hampshire statute); Adoption of Klinger, 5 D. & C.2d 767 (Pa. Orphans' Ct.1956). And In re Adoption of Johnson, 399 Pa. 624, 161 A.2d 358 (1960) seems to assume that the requirement is one of jurisdiction, as does Thompson's Adoption, 290 Pa. 586, 139 A. 737 (1927).

Holding the requirement merely one of venue: In re Robertson, 127 F.Supp. 39 (W.D.Mo.1954) (applying Missouri law); In re Adoption of Curtis, 143 Mont. 330, 390 P.2d 209 (1964); Adoption of Eckstein, 2 D. & C.2d 651 (Pa. Orphans' Ct.1955). In re McQuiston's Adoption, 238 Pa. 304, 86 A. 205 (1913) holds the requirement not mandatory but only directory, apparently meaning that it is not jurisdictional.

14. An earlier authoritative discussion is in 2 J. Beale, Conflict of Laws 713–714 (1935). See also E. Scoles, P.

Hay, Conflict of Laws 541 (1982); Restatement (Second) of Conflict of Laws § 78 (1971).

15. Waller v. Ellis, 169 Md. 15, 179 A. 289 (1935). See also In re Estate of Youmans, 218 Minn. 172, 15 N.W.2d 537 (1944), applying Illinois law. State ex rel. True v. Lakosky, 301 Minn. 450, 224 N.W.2d 128 (1974) may also be a holding that the statute is the sole source of jurisdiction.

16. Carter Oil Co. v. Norman, 131 F.2d 451 (7th Cir. 1942) (applying Illinois law); Matter of Appeal in Maricopa County Juvenile Action No. A–27789, 140 Ariz. 7, 680 P.2d 143 (1984); Matter of Appeal in Pima County, Adoption of B–6355 and H–533, 118 Ariz. 111, 575 P.2d 310 (1978) cert. denied 439; U.S. 848, 99 S.Ct. 149, 58 L.Ed.2d 150 (1978); Hopkins v. Gifford, 309 Ill. 363, 141 N.E. 178 (1923); Haney v. Knight, 197 Md. 212, 78 A.2d 643 (1951); Farnsworth v. Goebel, 240 Mass. 18, 132 N.E. 414 (1921); Stearns v. Allen, 183 Mass. 404, 67 N.E. 349 (1903); In Desoe's Estate, 134 Neb. 371, 278 N.W. 852 (1938). It is sometimes impossible to tell whether the court is relying solely on the statute or is following some common law rule of jurisdiction, as in Matter of Adoption of E. W. C., 89 Misc.2d 64, 389 N.Y.S.2d 743 (Surr.Ct.1976).

17. Brown v. Hall, 385 Ill. 260, 52 N.E.2d 781 (1944); A. v. M., 74 N.J.Super. 104, 180 A.2d 541 (1962); Adoption of Klinger, 5 D. & C.2d 767 (Pa.Orphans' Ct.1955); Adoption of Eckstein, 2 D. & C.2d 651 (Pa.Orphans' Ct. 1955).

18. Matter of Neuwirth's Estate, 155 N.J.Super. 410, 382 A.2d 972 (1978); In re Adoption of Baby Boy C., 31 Wash.App. 639, 644 P.2d 150 (1982).

be created at the domicile.[19] There is an obvious analogy to divorce, also largely a statutory action but one in which jurisdiction is often said to be based upon domicile.[20] The difficulties with this view of adoption are both theoretical and practical. First, when one says that the domicile has jurisdiction, which domicile is meant, that of the child, that of the adoptive parents, or that of the natural parents? Although it seems to be generally conceded that a state in which none of these parties is domiciled would not have jurisdiction over adoption,[21] that does not help to answer the question which domicile is determinative. The confusion caused by attempting to make domicile the test of adoption jurisdiction is especially great because of the number of parties involved in adoption cases and therefore more domiciles which are potentially relevant. As a practical matter it is more true today than ever that domicile may in many instances be a highly technical concept of little relevance to the lives of litigants. This is particularly true where children are concerned. A nice example of this is Stearns

v. Allen,[22] in which the child was domiciled in Scotland although it had lived all its life in Massachusetts. The court held that the Massachusetts residence was a sufficient basis for adoption jurisdiction when the Massachusetts statute was complied with.

It is also occasionally said that adoption is an action in rem [23] (or perhaps quasi in rem),[24] with the child's status the res. On this theory the state of the child's domicile would alone have jurisdiction to grant the adoption.[25] Needless to say, such pseudo-analysis is not only irrelevant but harmful. It obscures the factors which ought to be weighed in the rules about jurisdiction over the subject matter. In many cases the state of the child's domicile is the last place which ought to have adoption jurisdiction.

Against the foregoing theoretical background subject matter jurisdiction over adoption has been held to be based on the child's domicile by some authorities,[26] and on the adoptive parents's domicile by others.[27] Jurisdiction has also been based upon the child's

---

19. This reasoning is spelled out by 2 J. Beale, Conflict of Laws 713, 714 (1935) and the much cited early case of Ross v. Ross, 129 Mass. 243 (1880). See also A. v. M., 74 N.J.Super. 104, 180 A.2d 541 (1962); Taintor, Adoption in the Conflict of Laws, 15 U.Pitt.L.Rev. 222, 246 (1954); E. Scoles, P. Hay, Conflict of Laws 541–543 (1982).

20. See section 12.2, supra.

21. Barry E. (Anonymous) v. Ingraham, 43 N.Y.2d 87, 400 N.Y.S.2d 772, 371 N.E.2d 492 (1977); Matter of Adoption of E. W. C., 89 Misc.2d 64, 389 N.Y.S.2d 743 (Surr.Ct. 1976) (dictum). In re Blalock, 233 N.C. 493, 64 S.E.2d 848 (1951) and Culver v. Culver and Gammie [1933] 2 D.L.R. 535 seem to hold that the adoption is void unless both child and adoptive parents are domiciled in the state. Conversely, it is apparently conceded that if all parties, natural parents, adoptive parents, and child, are domiciled in the same state, that state has jurisdiction to decree the adoption. See E. Scoles, P. Hay, Conflict of Laws 541 (1982).

22. 183 Mass. 404, 67 N.E. 349 (1903). To the same effect is Davey v. Evans, 156 Ga.App. 698, 275 S.E.2d 769 (1980). For cases on the residence or domicile of the child and the adoptive parents see Annot., 170 A.L.R. 403 (1947).

23. In re Adoption of Barnett, 54 Cal.2d 370, 6 Cal. Rptr. 562, 354 P.2d 18 (1960); In re Adoption of _____, 22 N.J.Misc. 181, 37 A.2d 645 (1944).

24. In re Smith's Estate, 86 Cal.App.2d 456, 195 P.2d 842 (1948).

25. This seems to be the purport of Adoption of Eckstein, 2 D. & C.2d 651 (Pa.Orphans' Ct.1955).

26. Goclanney v. Desrochers, 135 Ariz. 240, 660 P.2d 491 (App.1982) (semble); In re Adoption of Burton, 147 Cal.App.2d 125, 305 P.2d 185 (1956) (semble); Jensen v. Sorenson, 211 Iowa 354, 233 N.W. 717 (1930); Krakow v. Department of Public Welfare, 326 Mass. 452, 95 N.E.2d 184 (1950) (semble); In re Adoption of _____, 22 N.J. Misc. 181, 37 A.2d 645 (1944).

A nice example of the unreality with which the whole question of adoption jurisdiction is dealt with is In re Pratt, 219 Minn. 414, 18 N.W.2d 147 (1945), which upholds Minnesota's jurisdiction on the ground that the child was physically present in the state and in need of court protection. At the same time a Tennessee adoption decree was denied recognition on the ground that the child was not domiciled in Tennessee, though at times the court also seemed to rely on the fact the child was not physically present in Tennessee. The prevailing impression left by much of the jurisdictional discussion is that of shadow-boxing.

27. Woodward's Appeal, 81 Conn. 152, 70 A. 453 (1908) (semble); Welch v. Welch, 208 Miss. 726, 45 So.2d 353 (1950); Brown v. Hall, 385 Ill. 260, 52 N.E.2d 781 (1944); A. v. M., 74 N.J.Super. 104, 180 A.2d 541 (1962).

A few cases base jurisdiction on the domicile of both adoptive parents and adopted child, without indicating whether either one alone would be sufficient. E.g., McNamara v. McNamara, 303 Ill. 191, 135 N.E. 410

presence in the state by some courts.[28] The case law supporting any of these views is by no means extensive, however. In fact the majority of cases which have discussed adoption jurisdiction with any thoroughness have done so solely in terms of making certain that the local statute was complied with. For that reason the Restatement's position that jurisdiction exists in the state of the domicile of either the adopted child or the adoptive parent if the adoptive parent and either the child or the person having legal custody of the child are subject to the court's personal jurisdiction is not very solidly based on the case law.[29] Some cases have followed the Restatement, however.[30] The Restatement's requirement of personal jurisdiction is not supported by the case law in any substantial respect, as will be shown later in this section.[31]

Subject matter jurisdiction over adoption can fairly be characterized as both confused and uncertain, largely because the statutes are unclear and because there is little reasoned discussion in the cases. Under these circumstances the question arises whether any sensible and workable principles can be devised, bearing in mind the obvious fact that time spent in litigating over jurisdiction is time wasted.

The purpose of jurisdictional rules, in this field at least, is to authorize adoption decrees by the court best able to evaluate the conflicting claims. In practice this means the court which can investigate and judge the qualifications of the prospective adoptive parents. The rights of the natural parents are terminated in adoption cases either by their consent, or involuntarily upon proof of abandonment, neglect, non-support or the like. The only issues raised with respect to the natural parents are therefore whether the consent is genuine, or whether the alleged abandonment or neglect did occur. These resemble the issues in the ordinary transitory lawsuit and there is thus no need for any requirement of domicile or residence on the part of the natural parents.[32] In order to judge the qualifications of the prospective parents, their home and their capacities to act as parents, however, they must be in the court's jurisdiction on a more than temporary basis. In many states the adoptive parents have the child during an interlocutory period ranging from six months to a year, while the court, usually acting through an agency, observes their care of the child. Even where a step-parent adoption or a non-agency placement is involved, the court needs to be able to judge the environment into which the child is to move. This again

(1922); Gray v. Holmes, 57 Kan. 217, 45 P. 596 (1896); In re Adoption of P. J. K., 359 S.W.2d 360 (Mo.App.1962).

Other cases are collected in Annot., Requirements as to Residence or Domicil of Adoptee or Adoptive Parent for Purposes of Adoption, 33 A.L.R.3d 176 (1970).

28. Matter of Appeal in Maricopa County Juvenile Action No. A–27789, 140 Ariz. 7, 680 P.2d 143 (1984); Matter of Appeal in Pima County Adoption of B–6355 any H–533, 118 Ariz. 111, 575 P.2d 310 (1978); State ex rel. True v. Lakosky, 301 Minn. 450, 224 N.W.2d 128 (1974) (residence of parents plus presence of child).

29. Restatement (Second) of Conflict of Laws § 78 (1971).

30. In re Smith's Estate, 86 Cal.App.2d 456, 195 P.2d 842 (1948); Ross v. Pick, 199 Md. 341, 86 A.2d 463 (1952); Matter of Neuwirth's Estate, 155 N.J.Super. 410, 382 A.2d 972 (1978); Matter of Adoption of E. W. C., 89 Misc. 2d 64, 389 N.Y.S.2d 743 (Surr.Ct.1976) (semble); In re Adoption of Baby Boy C., 31 Wash.App. 639, 644 P.2d 150 (1982) (dictum).

31. See the discussion at note 45, infra.

32. The text statement is supported by the fact that no cases require domicile or residence of the natural

parents as a condition for adoption jurisdiction, nor do the statutes make this requirement. In re Soderberg, 26 Ariz. 404, 226 P. 210 (1924) terminates the parental rights of a non-resident parent. And the statutes governing relinquishment and dependency actions, where the only issue is termination of natural parents' rights, do not require proof that the natural parent is domiciled or resident in the state. The common jurisdictional basis is merely that the child be physically present in the state. Peterson v. Schwartzmann, 116 Colo. 235, 179 P.2d 662 (1947); In re Mathers, 371 Mich. 516, 124 N.W.2d 878 (1963), rehearing denied 371 Mich. 516, 126 N.W.2d 722 (1964); Blanchard v. State ex rel. Wallace, 30 N.M. 459, 238 P. 1004 (1925); In re Wolfe, 26 Ohio Op.2d 274, 187 N.E.2d 658 (Juv.Ct.1962). See also West's Ann.Cal.Civ. Code § 224m (1982); Colo.Rev.Stat. § 19–4–102 (1986); Ohio Rev.Code § 5103.15 (Supp.1985). The Children's Bureau statute on voluntary and involuntary termination of parental rights requires only that the child be present in the state. Children's Bureau, Legislative Guides for the Termination of Parental Rights and Responsibilities and the Adoption of Children 40 (Children's Bureau Publication No. 394–1961).

implies that the adoptive parents have their home in the state.

Since adoption consists of matching a child with a new parent or set of parents, the court or adoption agency also needs a thorough opportunity to study the child and his background. To give the court this opportunity, the child must be present and available in the jurisdiction. This is especially important when the child is old enough to express his own desires concerning the adoption, as where adoption by a step-parent is in issue.

If the rationale of jurisdictional rules has been correctly outlined, it points to subject matter jurisdiction in adoption where a) the prospective adoptive parents, the petitioners, reside in the jurisdiction, and b) the child is physically present in the jurisdiction. "Reside" should be construed here to mean not technical domicile, but residence in the popular sense, of a person's home for the time being, the purpose of this construction being merely to require a sufficient connection with the jurisdiction to enable the court to make the necessary judgments about the child's prospective environment. It would seem entirely proper, for example, to allow an Army couple to adopt a child at the place of their duty station for the time being, even though that might often not be their domicile.

To a degree at least the analysis just suggested seems to be in the process of being adopted. The vehicles for this are the Uniform Child Custody Jurisdiction Act[33] and the Parental Kidnapping Prevention Act of 1980.[34] Although these statutes were enacted to solve the problems and abuses which had arisen out of interstate custody conflicts, and although the termination of parental rights, both voluntary and involuntary, and the adoption process itself do not lead to these abuses nearly so often, it appears clear that

both statutes provide the governing rules for jurisdiction in such cases and for the effect to be given to decrees of adoption or for the termination of parental rights. Since some version of the UCCJA is now in force in all states and since the PKPA, being a federal statute, also applies to all states, together they provide a nationwide basis for jurisdiction in such cases.

The basic jurisdictional provision of the UCCJA states that a court having local competence in custody matters has jurisdiction to make a "child custody determination by initial or modification decree"[35] under certain circumstances. The definition section of the Act defines "child custody determination" as follows:

"(2) 'custody determination' means a court decision and court orders and instructions providing for the custody of a child, including visitation rights; it does not include a decision relating to child support or any other monetary obligation of any person;"[36]

The same section contains this definition as well:

"(3) 'custody proceeding' includes proceedings in which a custody determination is one of several issues, such as an action for divorce or separation, and includes child neglect and dependency proceedings;"[37]

There is no question that these definitions could be more specific. They do, however, seem literally to apply to proceedings for the involuntary termination of parental rights on the grounds of dependency or neglect, the most common grounds for that kind of remedy. And certainly most of the cases in which parental rights are voluntarily relinquished, or in which an adoption is in issue also result in orders "for the custody of a child" along with orders respecting the parental rights over that child. For these reasons it seems

---

33. Uniform Child Custody Jurisdiction Act, 9 Unif.L. Ann. 116 (1979), referred to hereinafter as the UCCJA.

34. 28 U.S.C.A. § 1738A.

35. UCCJA § 3(a), 9 Unif.L.Ann. 122 (1979).

36. UCCJA § 2(2), 9 Unif.L.Ann. 119 (1979).

37. UCCJA § 2(3), 9 Unif.L.Ann. 119 (1979). The Commissioners' Note to this section states: "Subsection

(3) indicates that 'custody proceeding' is to be understood in a broad sense. The term covers habeas corpus actions, guardianship petitions, and other proceedings available under general state law to determine custody. See Clark, Domestic Relations 576–582 (1968)." 9 Unif.L.Ann. 120 (1979).

justified to believe that the UCCJA now governs adoption and similar proceedings.

The PKPA contains a definition of "custody determination" similar to, but not identical with, the definition in the UCCJA.[38] The differences do not seem substantial enough to exclude adoption decrees and decrees terminating parental rights from it jurisdictional requirements.

There is little case law supporting the position that these statutes govern jurisdiction for adoption and for the termination of parental rights, but there are beginning to be some decisions which do so, albeit without comprehensive discussion of the problem. For example the statutes have been relied upon in controversies between prospective adoptive parents and the natural parent of a child, after the child has been placed for adoption.[39] They have been relied upon in adoption cases themselves.[40] And the PKPA has been relied upon in a dependency proceeding which resulted in a change in the custody of the child.[41] Taking these admittedly fragmentary indications together with the obvious need for authoritative jurisdictional rules, one may reasonably conclude that the statutes should apply both to adoptions and to decrees terminating parental rights voluntarily and involuntarily.

If the foregoing argument is sound and the UCCJA and PKPA do apply to adoption and termination of parental rights, then the usual basis for jurisdiction over such proceedings will be proof that the child's "home state" is the state of the form.[42] Under the UCCJA jurisdiction may also be based on proof that the state of the forum has a "significant connection" with the child and at least one of the contesting parties.[43] The use of either of these bases for jurisdiction should go far to achieve the purposes outined above [44] as being the purposes which jurisdictional rules governing adoption should serve.

In addition to the problem of subject matter jurisdiction there is the troublesome question of jurisdiction over the person in adoption and termination of parental rights proceedings. The "persons" referred to are the child's natural parents, since the adoptive parents or the state, being the moving parties, will always be subject to the personal jurisdiction of the court. Specifically then the question is, must the natural parents always be subject to the personal jurisdiction of the court, by personal service within the state, by a general appearance, or pursuant to some applicable long-arm statute in order to meet the requirements of due process? This question arises out of May v. Anderson [45] which was discussed at length

---

38. 28 U.S.C.A. § 1738A(b)(3): "(3) 'custody determination' means a judgment, decree or other order of a court providing for the custody or visitation of a child, and includes permanent and temporary orders, and initial orders and modifications."

39. Martinez v. Reed, 623 F.Supp. 1050 (E.D.La.1985), affirmed without opinion 783 F.2d 1061 (5th Cir.1986); Martinez v. Reed, 490 So.2d 303 (La.App.1986); E. E. B. v. D. A., 89 N.J. 595, 446 A.2d 871 (1982), cert. denied 459 U.S. 1210, 103 S.Ct. 1203, 75 L.Ed.2d 445 (1983), rehearing denied 460 U.S. 1104, 103 S.Ct. 1806, 76 L.Ed.2d 369 (1983); Decatur v. Ahearn, 89 A.D.2d 742, 453 N.Y.S.2d 946 (3d Dep't 1982). Lemley v. Barr, ___ W.Va. ___, 343 S.E.2d 101 (1986) recognizes an Ohio decree invalidating parental consent, on the basis of jurisdiction under UCCJA.

40. In re C. C. B., 164 Ga.App. 3, 296 S.E.2d 198 (1982).

41. Matter of Pima County Juvenile Action No. J–78632, 147 Ariz. 527, 711 P.2d 1200 (Ariz.App.1985), modified on other grounds 147 Ariz. 584, 712 P.2d 431 (1986); State ex rel. Dep't of Human Serv. v. Avinger, 104 N.M. 355, 721 P.2d 781 (1985), affirmed 104 N.M. 255, 720 P.2d 290 (1986). But see Petition of Catholic Charitable Bu-

reau of Archdiocese of Boston, Inc., to Dispense with Consent to Adoption 392 Mass. 738, 467 N.E.2d 866 (1984), holding in another context that a petition to dispense with a parent's consent to adoption is not a "child custody case".

42. UCCJA § 3(a)(1), 9 Unif.L.Ann. 122 (1979). This and other provisions of the UCCJA and the PKPA are discussed at length in section 12.5, supra. The PKPA also adopts as its preferred basis for jurisdiction the home state of the child. 28 U.S.C.A. § 1738A(c)(2)(A).

43. UCCJA § 3(a)(2), 9 Unif.L.Ann. 122 (1979). The PKPA differs somewhat from the UCCJA in this respect in that "significant connection" is only recognized if there is no other state which would have jurisdiction as the home state. 28 U.S.C.A. § 1738A(c)(2)(B).

44. See the text discussion at note 32, supra.

45. 345 U.S. 528, 73 S.Ct. 840, 97 L.Ed. 1221 (1953). Restatement (Second) of Conflict of Laws § 78 (1971) requires personal jurisdiction over the adoptive parent and either the child or the person having legal custody of the child. As has been indicated, there is little case support for this rule. See note 31, supra.

in the earlier section dealing with custody jurisdiction.[46] That case held that a custody decision need not be given full faith and credit if the court in which it was entered did not have personal jurisdiction over the defendant. This is generally taken to mean that personal jurisdiction over the defendant in custody proceedings and (by logical extension) in proceedings for the termination of parental rights and adoption, is required by the Due Process Clause of the Fourteenth Amendment.[47]

It has already been argued that such an application of May v. Anderson to adoption termination proceedings would be a catastrophe.[48] An unknown but certainly large proportion of adoptions and terminations involve children whose natural parents are either out of the state or cannot be located. A requirement of personal jurisdiction over such parents would make adoption of their children or at least deprive the adoption decree of the protection of the Full Faith and Credit Clause. These results are so undesirable that many state courts have refused to extend the rule of May v. Anderson to adoption.[49] Only in a small number of cases has personal jurisdiction been insisted upon.[50] And, as has already been pointed out,[51] neither the UCCJA nor the PKPA makes any requirement of personal jurisdiction for custody determinations. If, as has been argued, these statutes apply to jurisdiction over termination

of parental rights and adoption, then personal jurisdiction should not be required in those proceedings. It is difficult to imagine the courts holding these statutes unconstitutional on this ground.

Notice as a constitutional requirement in termination and adoption proceedings, as distinguished from personal jurisdiction, is discussed in the preceding section of this work.[52]

Jurisdiction Concerning Indian Children

The Indian Child Welfare Act of 1978[53] provides that exclusive jurisdiction respecting child custody proceedings involving an Indian child who resides or is domiciled on a tribal reservation is vested in the Indian tribe unless jurisdiction is otherwise vested by federal law.[54] "Child custody proceeding" is defined to include foster care placements, proceedings for the termination of parental rights, preadoptive placements and adoptive placements.[55] Where the Indian child is not domiciled or residing on the reservation, a state court in a proceeding for foster care placement or termination of parental rights must, in the absence of good cause to the contrary, on the petition of either parent, an Indian custodian, or the child's tribe, transfer the proceeding to the jurisdiction of the tribe.[56] The purpose of this legislation is to promote the stability of the Indian tribes, protect the

---

46. Section 12.5, supra.

47. B. Currie, Selected Essays on the Conflict of Laws 678 (1963).

48. See section 12.5, supra, and Hazard, May v. Anderson: Prelude to Family Law Chaos, 45 Va.L.Rev. 379 (1959).

49. Cases ignoring or rejecting May v. Anderson where custody is involved are cited in section 12.5, supra. Cases which base adoption decrees on some form of substituted service in which personal jurisdiction is not acquired include In re Soderberg, 26 Ariz. 404, 226 P. 210 (1924); Barrett v. Asbell, 121 Ga.App. 269, 173 S.E.2d 735 (1970); In re Benfield, 468 S.W.2d 156 (Tex.Civ.App.1971).

Stanley v. Illinois, 405 U.S. 645, 657, footnote 9, 92 S.Ct. 1208, 1215, footnote 9, 31 L.Ed.2d 551 (1972), discussed in section 20.2 supra, at note 16 stated that a proceeding to terminate parental rights may be based upon service by publication, which means without personal jurisdiction over the natural parent, seeming to relegate May v. Anderson to the rubbish heap, although the case cited May v. Anderson with approval.

50. Donlon v. Miller, 42 Ill.App.3d 64, 355 N.E.2d 195 (1976) (semble); Matter of Adoption of a Child by McKinley, 157 N.J.Super. 293, 384 A.2d 920 (1978).

51. See section 12.5, supra, and Bodenheimer and Neeley-Kvarme, Jurisdiction Over Child Custody and Adoption After Shaffer and Kulko, 12 U.C.D.L.Rev. 229 (1979).

52. See section 20.2, supra, at note 61.

53. 25 U.S.C.A. §§ 1901 ff.

54. 25 U.S.C.A. § 1911(a). See also Matter of Adoption of Baby Child, 102 N.M. 735, 700 P.2d 198 (1985). But see D. E. D. v. State, 704 P.2d 774 (Alaska 1985); Matter of Adoption of Baby Boy L., 231 Kan. 199, 643 P.2d 168 (1982). A case decided before the Act was passed is Fisher v. District Court of the Sixteenth Judicial District of Montana, In and For Rosebud County, 424 U.S. 382, 96 S.Ct. 943, 47 L.Ed.2d 106 (1976), rehearing den. 425 U.S. 926, 96 S.Ct. 1524, 47 L.Ed.2d 772 (1976).

55. 25 U.S.C.A. § 1903(1).

56. 25 U.S.C.A. § 1911(b).

children's best interest and to place the children in foster homes or adoptive families reflecting the unique values of Indian culture.[57] Congress found, as a basis for the legislation, that many Indian children had been removed from their families, and the families broken up, by the placement of such children in nontribal foster homes and adoptive families by state public and private agencies.[58]

  WESTLAW REFERENCES

"full faith and credit" /s adopt! /2 decree! order!
adopt! /s statut*** law legislat! /s domicil! /s resid****
di(person! /3 jurisdiction! /s adopt!)
to(17) /p subject-matter /5 jurisdiction! /s adopt!

Jurisdiction Concerning Indian Children
"indian child welfare" /s jurisdiction!

§ 20.4 Adoption—Consent and Its Revocation

An earlier section [1] has indicated that adoption comprises two legal steps: a) making the child available for adoption by ending the parental rights of his natural parents; and b) establishing his relationship with the adoptive parents. The statutes in the United States in general, albeit with considerable differences in detail, provide that the first of these steps may be taken either by obtaining the consent of the natural parents or by terminating the parental rights of those parents involuntarily upon proof of specified kinds of conduct harmful to the child. The present

section is concerned with the legal issues arising out of the requirement of parental consent, including the form which the consent must take, the identity of those who must consent, and the circumstances under which consent may be revoked before the entry of an adoption decree. One might say that this section deals with the voluntary termination of parental rights. The conditions in which adoption may occur without the consent of a parent or guardian are discussed in a later section.[2] Obviously in any given case one may find it necessary to think about both voluntary and involuntary termination of parental rights. Their separation in these sections is merely for convenience in analysis and presentation.

The subject of attack on adoption decrees on the ground of lack of consent or for other reasons is also discussed in another section.[3] It is sufficient at this point to mention the statement often made in judicial opinions that consent is "jurisdictional" in adoption,[4] postponing until later a consideration of what this may mean when it is advanced as the reason for attacking an adoption decree.

Formalities of Consent

Most adoption statutes require the consent of the natural parents, guardians or others as a prerequisite to adoption, with certain statutory exceptions.[5] The statutes sometimes prescribe formalities for consents, such as that

---

57. 25 U.S.C.A. § 1902.

58. 25 U.S.C.A. § 1901.

§ 20.4

1. See section 20.1, supra.

2. See section 20.5, infra.

3. See section 20.11, infra.

4. E.g., Westerlund v. Croaff, 68 Ariz. 36, 198 P.2d 842 (1948); In re Adoption of Barnett, 54 Cal.2d 370, 6 Cal. Rptr. 562, 354 P.2d 18 1960); Storey v. Shumaker, 131 Colo. 131, 279 P.2d 1057 (1955); Oeth v. Erwin, 6 Ill.App. 2d 18, 126 N.E.2d 526 (1955); Matter of Adoption of Trent, 229 Kan. 224, 624 P.2d 433 (1981). See also In re Adoption of E. M. A., 487 Pa. 152, 409 A.2d 10 (1979), appeal dismissed for want of a substantial federal question 449 U.S. 802, 101 S.Ct. 46, 66 L.Ed.2d 6 (1980), holding that the court has no authority to decree an adoption in the absence of statutory consents.

The death of a parent who has consented to the adoption of her child does not affect her consent. Degolyer v. Chesney, 527 P.2d 844 (Okl.1974).

5. E.g., Ala.Code 1986, § 26–10–3; Alaska Stat. § 25.23.040 (1983); Ariz.Rev.Stat. § 8–106 (Supp.1986); West's Ann.Cal.Civ.Code § 224 (1982); Colo.Rev.Stat. § 19–4–107 (1986); Ill.—S.H.A. ch. 40, § 1510 (Supp. 1986); N.J.Stat.Ann. § 9:2–41 (Supp.1987); N.Y.—McKinney's Dom.Rel.L. § 111 (1977 and Supp.1987); Ohio Rev. Code § 3107.06 (Supp.1985); Pa.Stat. tit. 23, § 2501 (Supp.1986).

The exceptions are generally based on the involuntary termination of parental rights, or the mental incompetence of the parent. A statute authorizing the guardian ad litem of an incompetent to consent was held unconstitutional in Helvey v. Rednour, 86 Ill.App.3d 154, 41 Ill. Dec. 671, 408 N.E.2d 17 (1980). The Arizona statute authorizes the court to waive the requirement of consent

they must be in writing,[6] before witnesses,[7] or that they must be acknowledged before a person authorized to take acknowledgments.[8] In a few states the voluntary relinquishment of parental rights is accomplished by a legal proceeding having that purpose rather than by the execution of consent to adoption[9] thereby providing the additional safeguard of some court supervision of the process and greater assurance that the parents will not be able to change their minds or revoke their consents. It has been held that a statute on consent to adoption is not unconstitutional in failing to require that the consenting parent be given advice and consultation by an attorney before consenting.[10]

The minority of the person consenting to the adoption does not invalidate the consent according to the law of most states,[11] although when coupled with other factors it may lead a court to allow the consent to be revoked.[12]

The cases have naturally and properly insisted that there be compliance with the statutory formalities and requirements as a condition upon recognizing the validity of the consents,[13] the purposes of these requirements being to emphasize the seriousness and finality of the consent to adoption and to avoid, so far as possible, later disputes over the validity and effect of the consent.[14] For these reasons various attempts to rely upon informal consents, such as consents inserted in separation agreements, have often been held ineffective.[15] The validity of any consent is to be judged as of the time it is executed, which is

---

after notice and a hearing where it finds that the interests of the child will be promoted by the adoption. Ariz. Rev.Stat.Ann. § 8–106 (Supp.1986). A similar statute was held constitutional in Petition of J. O. L., 409 A.2d 1073 (D.C.App.1979), vacated and remanded, 449 U.S. 989, 101 S.Ct. 523, 66 L.Ed.2d 286 (1980), cert. denied 454 U.S. 832, 102 S.Ct. 131, 70 L.Ed.2d 110 (1981). But see In re Hyatt's Adoption, 24 Ariz. 170, 536 P.2d 1062 (App. 1975). In some states the consent of the parents is said to be "jurisdictional", Shelley v. Nowlin, 494 So.2d 453 (Ala. Civ.App.1986), but this is a misuse of the concept of jurisdiction.

6. E.g., Ill.—S.H.A. ch. 40, § 1512 (Supp.1986) (prescribes forms); Me.Rev.Stat.Ann. tit. 19, § 532 (1981).

7. E.g., West's Ann.Cal.Civ.Code § 224m (1982).

8. E.g. Alaska Stat. § 25.23.060 (1983); West's Ann. Cal.Civ.Code § 224m (1982); Minn.Stat.Ann. § 259.24 (1982).

9. E.g., Colo.Rev.Stat. § 19–4–102 (1986); Conn.Gen. Stat.Ann. § 45–61c (Supp.1986); Pa.Stat. tit. 23, § 2501 (Supp.1986); West's Rev.Code Wash.Ann. § 26.33.080 (1986). See also Sees v. Baber, 74 N.J. 201, 377 A.2d 628 (1977).

10. Matter of Adoption of Hewitt, 396 N.E.2d 938 (Ind. App.1979).

11. E.g., Ill.—McKinney's Ann.Stat. ch. 40, § 1513 (Supp.1986); In re Adoption of Holman, 80 Ariz. 201, 295 P.2d 372 (1956); Martin v. Ford, 224 Ark. 993, 277 S.W.2d 842 (1955); In re Duarte's Adoption, 229 Cal.App.2d 775, 40 Cal.Rptr. 671 (1964); Petition of Foley, 123 Colo. 533, 232 P.2d 186 (1951); In re Adoption of Anderson, 235 Minn. 192, 50 N.W.2d 278 (1951); In re Adoption of Morrison, 260 Wis. 50, 49 N.W.2d 759 (1951), rehearing denied 260 Wis. 50, 51 N.W.2d 713 (1952). But such statutory safeguards as requiring the consent of the minor parent's guardian must be observed. Adoption of Harvey, 375 Pa. 1, 99 A.2d 276 (1953).

12. See the text at note 62, infra.

13. In re Pior's Adoption, 43 Cal.2d 472, 274 P.2d 637 (1954) (failure to file copy of relinquishment with state welfare department); Petition of Foley, 123 Colo. 533, 232 P.2d 186 (1951) (absence of proper jurat); McKinney v. Weeks, 130 So.2d 310 (Fla.1961), 10 Kan.L.Rev. 607 (1962) (only one witness where two were required); Doan Thi Hoang Anh v. Nelson, 245 N.W.2d 511 (Iowa 1976); Wright v. Howard, 711 S.W.2d 492 (Ky.App.1986) (no sworn consent); Petition of Thompson, 337 Ill.App. 354, 86 N.E.2d 155 (1949); State ex rel. Simpson v. Salter, 211 La. 918, 31 So.2d 163 (1947); Petition of Alsdurf, 270 Minn. 236, 133 N.W.2d 479 (1965) (requirement of two witnesses not satisfied by execution of two different consents, each with one witness); In re Adoption of Mc-Cauley, 177 Neb. 759, 131 N.W.2d 174 (1964) (consent not signed in the presence of the officer taking the acknowledgment); Taylor v. Waddoups, 121 Utah 279, 241 P.2d 157 (1952) (consent not given before a court). In In re Long's Adoption, 56 So.2d 450 (Fla.1952) the consent was held valid though signed in an assumed name, where the signer was identified as the child's mother. And in Riley v. Byrne, 145 Mont. 138, 399 P.2d 980 (1965) a consent was held valid though not acknowledged. See also Baker v. Compton, 247 Ind. 39, 211 N.E.2d 162 (1965) holding consent valid though not strictly in accordance with the statute. Other cases are cited in Annot., 24 A.L.R.2d 1127 (1952).

Where there is doubt about the validity of consent, Massachusetts authorizes a judicial determination of validity in advance of the adoption proceeding. In re Adoption of a Minor, 345 Mass. 706, 189 N.E.2d 505 (1963).

14. Petition of Foley, 123 Colo. 533, 232 P.2d 186 (1951). Even if the formalities are observed, the consent may be invalid if given from ulterior motives or without the intention of effectuating a true adoption. Gutierrez v. New Mexico Dept. of Public Welfare, 74 N.M. 273, 393 P.2d 12 (1964).

15. In Anonymous, 9 Misc.2d 420, 170 N.Y.S.2d 270 (Surr.Ct.1958); People ex rel. Hydock v. Greenberg, 273

usually before the adoption petition is filed,[16] and it is not affected by events occurring after the proceedings have begun.[17] Notwithstanding the importance of the statutory requirements for consent, some cases have given effect to consents which do not fully meet those requirements where compliance with the statute was substantial and where the consent was shown to have been executed freely, voluntarily and advisedly.[18] The states differ on whether and to what extent counseling must be provided for a parent who is relinquishing his child or consenting to an adoption.[19]

Parents occasionally attempt to condition their consent to adoption on adoption by a specified person, or on the retention of visitation rights. The few cases disagree on the effect of such conditions, some holding that they vitiate the consent,[20] others that the condition should be enforced.[21] Consent which is conditioned in this way is undesirable because it may result in later conflicts between natural and adoptive parents detrimental to the child's welfare. Whether a conditioned consent is valid depends in the first instance on the applicable state statute. If the statute does not invalidate the consent, its enforcement should depend upon what the child's welfare requires under the circumstances.

The mobility of the American population has led to a few cases having to apply choice of law principles to adoption. Where the consent to adoption may be questionable under the law of the state in which it was executed, but valid by the law of the forum, the cases properly hold that the forum law applies and the consent is recognized.[22] Where the forum law has jurisdiction under the principles discussed in an earlier section [23] that is the state with the controlling interest in the child's welfare and therefore the state whose law should control the validity of consent.

Restrictions on the Time of Giving Consent

There is some inclination on the part of the people involved in adoption placements to seek consent from natural parents before the

App.Div. 710, 79 N.Y.S.2d 389 (1st Dep't 1948). See also Haney v. Knight, 197 Md. 212, 78 A.2d 643 (1951). But consent which does not comply with the statute may nevertheless be some evidence of abandonment. See section 20.5, infra. A consent to adopt procured by the payment of money has been held invalid in Downs v. Wortman, 228 Ga. 315, 185 S.E.2d 387 (1971); Gray v. Maxwell, 206 Neb. 385, 293 N.W.2d 90 (1980).

16. In re Burdette, 83 Ohio App. 368, 83 N.E.2d 813 (1948).

17. Storey v. Shumaker, 131 Colo. 131, 279 P.2d 1057 (1955) (later dependency decree cannot validate earlier adoption not based on consent); In re Roger's Adoption, 47 Wash.2d 207, 286 P.2d 1028 (1955) (consent may not be filed nunc pro tunc). In In re Adoption of Graham, 58 Cal.2d 899, 27 Cal.Rptr. 163, 377 P.2d 275 (1962) (it was held that the entry of a nunc pro tunc divorce decree did not invalidate an earlier relinquishment for adoption). The death of the natural parent did not invalidate her consent in Wallace v. Lougee, 107 N.H. 251, 221 A.2d 780 (1966).

18. San Diego County Dep't of Public Welfare v. Superior Court of San Diego County, 7 Cal.3d 1, 101 Cal.Rptr. 541, 496 P.2d 453 (1972); Matter of Adoption of Trent, 229 Kan. 224, 624 P.2d 433 (1981); In re Cox, 327 So.2d 776 (Fla.1976); Hale v. Hale, 57 Ill.App.3d 730, 15 Ill.Dec. 85, 373 N.E.2d 431 (1978); Matter of Adoption of Christopher P., 480 Pa. 79, 389 A.2d 94 (1978); Matter of Application of Santore, 28 Wash.App. 319, 623 P.2d 702 (1981).

19. E.g. Doe v. Catholic Family Services, Inc., 36 Conn.Supp. 93, 412 A.2d 714 (1979) (counseling was required and was adequate); Kathy O. v. Counseling and Family Services, 107 Ill.App.3d 920, 63 Ill.Dec. 764, 438 N.E.2d 695 (1982) (no counseling required); Matter of Guardianship of C. M., 158 N.J.Super. 585, 386 A.2d 913 (1978) (legal counsel constitutionally required to represent a parent contemplating a surrender of her child); In re Adoption of Hernandez, 25 Wash.App. 447, 607 P.2d 879 (1980) (no constitutional requirement of legal counsel for the parent at a relinquishment hearing).

20. K. W. E. v. People, 31 Colo.App. 219, 500 P.2d 167 (1972) (conditional relinquishment not permitted by statute); McLaughlin v. Strickland, 279 S.C. 513, 309 S.E.2d 787 (App.1983).

21. In re Adoption of Driscoll, 269 Cal.App.2d 735, 75 Cal.Rptr. 382 (1969); In re Adoption of a Minor, 362 Mass. 842, 291 N.E.2d 729 (1973).

22. Matter of Adoption of Gates, 6 Kan.App.2d 945, 636 P.2d 818 (1981); In re Adoption of Hunter, 421 Pa. 287, 218 A.2d 764 (1966); In re Adoption of MM, 652 P.2d 974 (Wyo.1982). Wojciechowski v. Allen, 238 Ga. 556, 234 S.E.2d 325 (1977) applied California law where the child was born there and the parents lived there. See also In re Adoption of a Minor Child, 127 F.Supp. 256 (D.D.C.1954) and Haney v. Knight, 197 Md. 212, 78 A.2d 643 (1951). Restatement (Second) of Conflict of Laws § 289 (1971): "A court applies its own local law in determining whether to grant an adoption."

23. See section 20.3, supra.

birth of the child, so that the child can be taken by the adoptive parents directly from the hospital to their home. Although this may seem desirable as a means of achieving immediate integration of the child into the adoptive home and of vindicating the adoptive parents' interest in forming a bond with the child, it creates serious risk that the natural parent, once the child is born, will have second thoughts about giving him up and will attempt to revoke the consent. For this reason many adoption statutes provide that the consent may not be given earlier than a specified period after the child is born.[24] Even without such a statutory restriction some courts have held that a prenatal consent is invalid.[25]

"Blanket" Consent

A recurring issue affecting consent to adoption is whether a consent is valid where, at the time it is executed by the natural parent, it does not name the prospective adoptive parents. A few statutes expressly authorize consent in this form.[26] The same result may be reached under statutes providing for a separation relinquishment proceeding in which the natural parents' rights are terminated and the child's custody awarded to a placement agency with a view to later adoption placement.[27] The policy behind such statutes is to prevent the natural parent

knowing who the adoptive parents are and vice versa, so that there will not be later conflicts which might prejudice the child's complete integration into his new family. This policy of course has no application in stepparent or relative adoptions, but is an important one and one to be effectuated if at all possible in those placements where the adoptive parents are not related to the child.[28] In fact modern agency adoption practice maintains anonymity on both sides, so that the natural parent does not know the identity of the adoptive parents and the adoptive parents do not know the identity of the natural parents (although they may be given considerable background information about the natural parents.)[29]

Where the adoption statute does not expressly authorize blanket consents, the courts have not reached uniform results. Some cases have held blanket consents are invalid on the ground that adoption statutes must be strictly construed.[30] The better reasoned view of most of the cases is that such consents have a useful purpose and should be upheld.[31]

Who Must Consent to Adoption

As with other aspects of adoption practice, there is general agreement among the states on the persons whose consent must be obtained for a valid adoption to occur, but there is considerable variation in details of lan-

---

24. E.g., Alaska Stat. § 25.23.060 (1983) (consent must be given after the birth of the child); Ariz.Rev.Stat. § 8–107 (Supp.1986) (not before seventy-two hours after birth); Ill.—S.H.A. ch. 40, § 1511 (Supp.1986) (not less than seventy-two hours after birth); Ohio Rev.Code § 3107.08 (1980) (not less than seventy-two hours after birth). See also Uniform Adoption Act § 7, 9 Unif.L.Ann. 31 (1979), requiring consent after the birth of the child. See also Ex Parte Sullivan, 407 So.2d 559 (Ala.1981), on remand 407 So.2d 565 (Ala.Civ.App. 1981) (applying Indiana law).

25. Anonymous v. Anonymous, 108 Misc.2d 1098, 439 N.Y.S.2d 255 (1981); Matter of Adoption of BGD, 713 P.2d 1191 (Wyo.1986). But an invalid consent executed before the birth of the child may be ratified and become effective after the birth. In re Adoption of Krueger, 104 Ariz. 26, 448 P.2d 82 (1968).

26. E.g., Alaska Stat. § 25.23.060 (1983); N.Y.—McKinney's Dom.Rel.L. § 111(3) (Supp.1987); Uniform Adoption Act § 7(b), 9 Unif.L.Ann. 31 (1979).

27. E.g., West's Ann.Cal.Civ.Code § 224m (1982); Colo.Rev.Stat. § 19–4–102 (1986); Conn.Gen.Stat.Ann. § 45–61c (Supp.1986); Iowa Code Ann. § 600.3 (1981);

N.J.Stat.Ann. § 9:3–41 (Supp.1986); Pa.Stat. tit. 23, § 2501 (Supp.1986); V.T.C.A., Fam.Code § 15.01 (1986); Wis.Stat.Ann. §§ 48.41, 48.42 (Supp.1986).

28. See In re K. W. S., 370 S.W.2d 698 (Mo.App.1963).

29. I Schapiro, A Study of Adoption Practice 86, 87 (1956).

30. Sampson v. Holton, 185 N.W.2d 216 (Iowa 1971), 57 Iowa L.R. v. 171 (1971); Annot., 24 A.L.R.2d 1127, 1138 (1952).

31. In re Adoption of a Minor Child, 127 F.Supp. 256 (D.D.C.1954); McKinney v. Weeks, 130 So.2d 310 (Fla. 1961), 10 Kan.L.Rev. 607 (1962); S. O. v. W. S., 643 P.2d 997 (Alaska 1982); McKinney v. Weeks, 130 So.2d 310 (Fla.1961), 10 Kan.L.Rev. 607 (1962); Cohen v. Janic, 57 Ill.App.2d 309, 207 N.E.2d 89 (1965); Johnson v. Cupp, 149 Ind.App. 611, 274 N.E.2d 411 (1971); Matter of Adoption of Baby Girl Chance, 4 Kan.App. 576, 609 P.2d 232 (1980); Barwin v. Reidy, 62 N.M. 183, 307 P.2d 175 (1957); Matter of Jackson's Adoption, 89 Wash.2d 945, 578 P.2d 33 (1978). See also Embick, The "In Blank" Consent and the Independent Adoption, 5 Willamette L.J. 50 (1968).

guage and application. A legitimate child may only be adopted with the consent of both parents [32] unless one of them has lost his parental rights through abandonment or other conduct dispensing with his consent.[33] If one parent is dead, the other must consent.[34] A child conceived through artificial insemination by the semen of a third party with the husband's consent may only be adopted with the consent of the mother's husband.[35] The parent's refusal to consent blocks the adoption, even though the child might be better off in the care of adoptive parents, so long as no grounds for involuntary termination of parental rights exist.[36] The courts rightly refuse to remove a child from his parents' care solely for the reason that someone else might have superior means or ability to care for him.

Adoption statutes also generally require that the consent of the child himself be obtained if he has reached a specified age at the time of the adoption, usually twelve or fourteen years old.[37] Conversely if the person being adopted is an adult, many statutes waive the requirement of parental consent,

adoptions of adults being for entirely different purposes from adoptions of children.[38]

The law of some states permits parents to relinquish their children even though they are married and able to care for the children themselves.[39] The questions of policy which are raised by such relinquishments seem not to have been faced by the courts. Certainly the children's welfare should be carefully considered before parents are permitted to avoid their parental responsibilities by this means.[40] If the children do not appear to be adoptable, such a relinquishment might condemn them to years of foster homes, possibly shifting from one foster home to another, a face which hardly seems preferable to a more stable life with their natural parents.

If parental rights are terminated, either voluntarily or involuntarily, in a proceeding brought for that purpose, the court is generally authorized and required by statute to place the child in the custody of a public or licensed private adoption agency and to give the agency the authority to consent to the child's adoption.[41] Likewise when a guardian of the person of the child other than a person has

---

32. See, e.g., the statutes cited in note 5, supra. Grandparents standing in loco parentis are not persons required to consent to adoption, but they may have standing to intervene and be heard in the adoption proceeding. Quarles v. French, 272 Ark. 51, 611 S.W.2d 757 (1981).

33. The termination of parental rights may be accomplished in a separate proceeding, as is illustrated by the statutes cited in note 27, supra, or in the adoption proceeding itself, depending upon the local practice. For a discussion of involuntary termination of parental rights as well as other cases in which parental consent is dispensed with, see section 20.5, infra.

34. See the statutes cited in note 5, supra.

35. In re Adoption of Anonymous, 74 Misc.2d 99, 345 N.Y.S.2d 430 (Surr.Ct.1973). The Uniform Parentage Act § 5, 9A Unif.L.Ann. 592 (1979), while it does not deal directly with the adoption question, seems to reach the same result by providing that the husband of a woman artificially inseminated with the husband's consent is treated in law as the father of the child so conceived.

36. Ex Parte Sullivan, 407 So.2d 559 (Ala.1981), on remand 407 So.2d 565 (Ala.Civ.App.1981); In re McDonald's Adoption, 43 Cal.2d 447, 274 P.2d 860 (1954) (dictum); Oeth v. Erwin, 6 Ill.App.2d 18, 126 N.E.2d 526 (1955); Matter of Adoption of BGD, 713 P.2d 1191 (Wyo. 1986).

37. See the statutes cited in note 5, supra. The statutes also usually require that the spouse of an adopting person consent to the adoption. See Annot., Necessity

and Sufficiency of Consent to Adoption By Spouse of Adopting Parent, 38 A.L.R.4th 768 (1985). In some jurisdictions a child who has reached the "age of discretion" must be asked whether he objects to having his parent's rights terminated. Deahl v. Winchester Dep't of Social Services, 224 Va. 664, 299 S.E.2d 863 (1983).

38. E.g., Ill.—McKinney's ch. 40, § 1510 (Supp.1986). On the adoption of adults see section 21.10, Practitioner's Edition.

39. E.g., Smith v. Welfare Department of Denver, 144 Colo. 103, 355 P.2d 317 (1960).

40. See McKay, Today's Controversial Clients: Married Parents Who Place Legitimate Children for Adoption, in Smith, Readings in Adoption 87 (1963).

41. E.g., Ala.Code 1986, § 26–10–3; Alaska Stat. § 25.23.040 (1983); Ariz.Rev.Stat. § 8–106 (Supp.1986); West's Ann.Cal.Civ.Code § 224n (Supp.1986); Colo.Rev. Stat. § 19–4–107(d) (1986); Conn.Gen.Stat.Ann. § 45–63(a)(3) (Supp.1986); West's Fla.Stat.Ann. § 63.062(3) (1985); Ill.—S.H.A. ch. 40, § 1510 (Supp.1986); Md.Code, Fam.L., § 5–31 (Supp.1986); Mass.Gen.Laws Ann. c. 210, § 2A (1981); Mich.C.L.A. § 27.3178 (555.43) (Supp.1986); Minn.Stat.Ann. § 259.24 (1982); N.J.Stat.Ann. § 9:3–47 (Supp.1986); N.Y.—McKinney's Dom.Rel.L. § 111 (Supp. 1987); Ohio Rev.Code § 3107.06 (Supp.1985); West's Rev. Code Wash.Ann. § 26.33.160 (1986). See also Uniform Adoption Act § 5(a)(3), 9 Unif.L.Ann. 23 (1979) and Annot., 83 A.L.R.3d 373 (1978).

been appointed, the consent of the guardian may be required for adoption.[42] Under most cases the fact that the child is living with a relative, as for example a grandparent, does not of itself mean that the consent of that relative is essential for the child's adoption.[43] Once the child has been legally committed to an agency or a guardian has been properly appointed, the parents' consent to adoption is no longer required.[44]

A question then arises concerning the consequences for the adoption if the agency or the guardian refuses to give consent. Is their consent to be dealt with on the same footing as that of a natural parent? Or may the adoption be decreed in spite of the refusal if the court thinks it beneficial for the child? Initially the answer to these questions depends on a close examination of the particular statute. In a few states the statutes spell out the procedure to be followed when the agent's or guardian's consent is refused, generally providing that the court may nevertheless grant the adoption if that is found to be in the child's best interests.[45] Where the statute is silent on the question, some courts have de-

nied the petition where consent is refused, treating the agency's or guardian's consent as analogous to that of a parent and therefore an essential condition to the adoption.[46] The larger number of cases, and the more modern ones, hold that the agency's refusal of consent is not conclusive and that the adoption should be granted if the agency's refusal can be characterized as arbitrary or capricious, or, according to some courts, if the child's welfare would be promoted by the adoption.[47] In practical terms the question usually arises where an agency has placed the child for adoption and later decides that the persons with whom the child was placed are not satisfactory adoptive parents for that child. Or it may arise out of a dispute between an agency and a prospective adoptive parent as to the latter's qualifications. The underlying issue is thus whether in the last analysis the agency or a court should determine the merits of a particular adoption. The writer's view, with full awareness of the value of agency expertise, is that the court should make the ultimate decision, since in some cases it is not uncommon for agency rules to be applied too

42. Ibid.

43. Quarles v. French, 272 Ark. 51, 611 S.W.2d 757 (1981); Adoption of Anonymous, 208 Misc. 357, 143 N.Y.S.2d 857 (Surr.Ct.1955); Webb v. Barnett, 207 S.W.2d 706 (Tex.Civ.App.1947); Annot., 104 A.L.R. 1464 (1936).

44. Hogg v. Peterson, 245 Ind. 515, 198 N.E.2d 767 (1964); In re Whitcomb, 271 App.Div. 11, 61 N.Y.S.2d 1 (4th Dep't 1946); In re Ramsey, 164 Ohio St. 567, 132 N.E.2d 469 (1956); In re Magee, 74 S.D. 286, 52 N.W.2d 99 (1952).

45. E.g., West's Ann.Cal.Civ.Code § 226.4 (Supp.1986) (court may grant the petition if in the child's best interests); Mass.Gen.Laws Ann. c. 210, § 2A (1981) (person aggrieved by refusal of consent may appeal to the court); Mich.C.L.A. § 27.3178 (555.45) (Supp.1986) (court may order the adoption if consent is arbitrarily withheld); Minn.Stat.Ann. § 259.24 (1982) (consent is not to be unreasonably withheld); N.J.Stat.Ann. § 9:3–47 (Supp.1986) (refusal to consent does not preclude action for adoption); Wis.Stat.Ann. § 48.85 (1979) (court may take testimony as to the child's best interests).

46. In re Adoption of Greybull, 29 Or.App. 889, 565 P.2d 773 (1977); In re Dougherty Adoption Case, 358 Pa. 620, 58 A.2d 77 (1948); In re Adoption of Tschudy, 267 Wis. 272, 65 N.W.2d 17 (1954) (under the former Wisconsin statute). Many other cases are cited in Annot., 83 A.L.R.3d 373 (1978). Agency consent may not be needed if the agency has only temporary custody. Morgan v. South Carolina Dep't of Social Services, 280 S.C. 577, 313 S.E.2d 350 (App.1984).

47. Ex parte Dep't of Pensions and Security of Ala., 437 So.2d 544 (Ala.Civ.App.1983) (denial of consent arbitrary and capricious); Matter of Roberts, 349 So.2d 1170 (Ala.Civ.App.1977) (agency may not arbitrarily withhold consent); Ratcliffe v. Williams, 220 Ark. 807, 250 S.W.2d 330 (1952); Bland v. Department of Children & Family Services, 141 Ill.App.3d 818, 96 Ill.Dec. 122, 490 N.E.2d 1327 (1986) (denial of consent is not binding of not reasonable); Matter of Adoption of Smith, 38 Ill.App.3d 217, 347 N.E.2d 292 (1976), cert. denied 431 U.S. 939, 97 S.Ct. 2651, 53 L.Ed.2d 256 (1977); Bernhardt v. Lutheran Social Services of the National Capital Area, Inc., 39 Md. App. 334, 385 A.2d 1197 (1978); Ritchie v. Children's Home Society of St. Paul, 299 Minn. 149, 216 N.W.2d 900 (1974); M. v. Family and Children's Service, Inc., 130 N.J. Super. 214, 326 A.2d 74 (1974) (decision to withhold consent may be set aside if arbitrarily exercised); Mundie v. Nassau County Dep't of Social Services, 88 Misc.2d 273, 387 N.Y.S.2d 767 (1976); In re Adoption of Daughtridge, 25 N.C.App. 141, 212 S.E.2d 519 (1975); State ex rel. Portage County Welfare Dept. v. Summers, 38 Ohio St.2d 144, 311 N.E.2d 6 (1974), 36 Ohio St.L.J. 451 (1975); State ex rel. Dep't of Inst., Soc. & R. Serv. v. Griffis, 545 P.2d 763 (Okl.1975). Other cases are collected in Annot., 83 A.L.R.3d 373 (1978). A case finding the agency denial of consent not to be arbitrary or capricious is O'Rourke v. Kirby, 54 N.Y.2d 8, 444 N.Y.S.2d 566, 429 N.E.2d 85 (1981).

rigidly or to operate unwisely.[48] The courts provide a single tribunal in which all points of view can be heard and weighed, and in which the agency objection may be overridden where that appears beneficial to the child. The agency determination should be presumptively effective, however, with the person seeking to upset it having the burden of proof.

The question whether the consent of the father of an illegitimate child must be obtained before the child may be adopted is a special case. Before 1972 the statutes of the various states provided that it need not be, and that the child could be adopted upon the consent of his mother alone. In that year Stanley v. Illinois [49] was decided, seeming to say that the consent of the father must also be obtained. That and the later decisions of the United States Supreme Court dealing with this problem are discussed in an earlier section of this work.[50] As is indicated in that section, it is difficult to arrive at general principles from a reading of those decisions since the Supreme Court has vacillated in its views as different factual situations came before it. It is also fair to say that the Court has overemphasized the interests of the father at the expense of those of the child, seeming oblivious to the damage it was doing to the process of adoption.[51]

Since the Stanley decision and the cases following it the states have attempted to enact statutes which will preserve a workable adoption process while at the same time will give to the father of the illegitimate child the protection the Supreme Court has appeared to demand. In very broad outline this means that these statutes require the consent of the father when he has exhibited an interest in and a willingness to care for the child but not otherwise. Perhaps the most thoroughly considered statute is the Uniform Parentage Act.[52] That Act requires that consent to adoption be obtained from a person who is the presumed father of the child,[53] from a person whose paternity has been established by a court,[54] or a person as to whom the child is legitimate under the law of the forum or of other states. The Act also provides for notice of the adoption to other persons identified as the child's father and requires the court to terminate the parental rights of any unknown natural fathers, with complete finality as to the termination after the expiration of six months.[55] Other statutes attempt to accomplish the same purposes by a great variety of means.[56] It is impossible to predict which of these statutes will be held constitutional by the Supreme Court since one cannot predict the factual circumstances in which the ques-

48. E.g., In re Adoption of Barnett, 54 Cal.2d 370, 6 Cal.Rptr. 562, 354 P.2d 18 (1960); In re Adoption of Tschudy, 267 Wis. 272, 65 N.W.2d 17 (1954), in both of which the agency action appeared to be of doubtful soundness.

49. 405 U.S. 645, 92 S.Ct. 1208, 31 L.Ed.2d 551 (1972), 34 U.Pitt.L.Rev. 303 (1973), 59 Va.L.Rev. 517 (1973), 1973 Wis.L.Rev. 908.

50. See section 20.2 at note 11.

51. A case which describes in detail the harm being done is In re Adoption of Malpica-Orsini, 36 N.Y.2d 568, 331 N.E.2d 486 (1975), appeal dismissed for want of a substantial federal question 423 U.S. 1042, 96 S.Ct. 765, 46 L.Ed.2d 631 (1976).

52. Uniform Parentage Act § 24(a), 9A Unif.L.Ann. 615 (1979).

53. Uniform Parentage Act § 4, 9A Unif.L.Ann. 590 (1979) defines the presumed father in a variety of ways, including the father who receives the child into his home and holds the child out as his, and who acknowledges paternity in specified fashion.

54. This provision is found in other statutes as well but makes little sense. A putative father who is the losing defendant in a paternity suit hardly seems one

who should be entitled to object to the adoption and future welfare of the child.

55. Uniform Parentage Act § 24(b), (c), (d), (e), (f), 9A Unif.L.Ann. 615, 616 (1979).

56. E.g., Ala.Code 1986, § 26–10–3 (mother's consent for adoption of the illegitimate is alone sufficient, but the father must be given notice); Alaska Stat. § 25.23.040 (1983) (no consent required of a parent who fails to communicate with or support the child); Ariz.Rev.Stat. § 8–106 (Supp.1986) (consent required from both natural parents); West's Fla.Stat.Ann. § 63.062 (1985) (paternity has been established by a court; father has acknowledged or supported the child); Iowa Code Ann. § 600.7 (1981) (if person whose consent is required refuses, or cannot be located, the court may determine whether in the child's and petitioner's best interests consent is unnecessary); Mass.Gen.Laws Ann. c. 210, § 4A (1981) (provides for the filing of a paternal responsibility claim); Mich.C.L.A. §§ 27.3178 (555.36), 27.3178 (555.37), 27.3178 (555.39) (1980 and Supp.1986) (complex provisions on notice to the father and termination of his parental rights under some conditions); Mont.Code Ann. §§ 40–6–125 to 40–6–130 (Supp.1985) (highly complex provisions amplifying the Uniform Parentage Act); N.Y.—McKinney's Dom.Rel.L. § 111(1)(d) (Supp.1987) (putative father may veto the

tions may arise. One hopes that they would be so held wherever they are reasonably calculated to go no further than to protect the caring father as outlined above. As it is, they undoubtedly impose delay and expense on the adoption process which may in some cases be discouraging to adoptive parents.[57] Any attempt to give further rights of consent to fathers of illegitimate children would place unacceptable impediments to the children's opportunities for a suitable placement and a stable family life, even though the rights of the father of the illegitimate child can usually be terminated involuntarily if he neglects or abandons the child.[58]

One further difficulty is caused by the adoption of an illegitimate child when the child's mother is married but asserts that her husband is not the father of the child. In such circumstances must the husband be given notice and his consent to the adoption obtained? The argument of course is that there is a strong presumption that the child of a married woman is legitimate [59] and therefore that the husband should have an opportunity to present evidence in support of legitimacy if he

wishes to. This argument has been persuasive notwithstanding that the evidence of non-access by the husband was strong.[60] Where the evidence is not so clear, there is even more reason to insist that the husband have notice and an opportunity to be heard on paternity.[61]

Revocation of Consent [62]

Attempts to revoke consent to adoption have produced more litigation than any other aspect of consent. Two factors may be responsible for this. One is the contemporary unwillingness to recognize that we all are and should be responsible for our decisions, that our actions have consequences which cannot be evaded. The other is the profound emotional bonds which prospective adoptive parents feel for the children placed with them for adoption, bonds which spring up with extraordinary quickness after the placement. It is not surprising that these psychological factors produce vigorously litigated conflicts even after some states have made serious and thoughtful efforts to avoid them.[63]

adoption where he has supported, visited, or communicated with the child); Ohio Rev.Code § 3107.06 (Supp.1985) (consent required if the putative father acknowledged the child, signed a birth certificate etc.).

Cases in the state courts dealing with these statutes are not numerous. See, e.g., Unwed Father v. Unwed Mother, 177 Ind.App. 237, 379 N.E.2d 467 (1978); Catholic Charities of Archdiocese of Dubuque v. Zalesky, 232 N.W.2d 539 (Iowa 1975); Aslin v. Seamon, 225 Kan. 77, 587 P.2d 875 (1978) (before enactment of the Uniform Parentage Act); Matter of Adoption of B., 152 N.J.Super. 546, 378 A.2d 90 (1977); Matter of Andrew Peter H. T., 64 N.Y.2d 1090, 489 N.Y.S.2d 882, 479 N.E.2d 227 (1985); Lemley v. Kaiser, 6 Ohio St.3d 258, 452 N.E.2d 1304 (1983); In Interest of T. E. T., 603 S.W.2d 793 (Tex.1980), cert. denied 450 U.S. 1025, 101 S.Ct. 1732, 68 L.Ed.2d 220 (1981).

California cases construing the Uniform Parentage Act provision on consent include Michael U. v. Jamie B., 39 Cal.3d 787, 218 Cal.Rptr. 39, 705 P.2d 362 (1985); W. E. J. v. Superior Court of Los Angeles County, 100 Cal.App.3d 303, 160 Cal.Rptr. 862 (1979); Matter of Adoption of Marie R., 79 Cal.App.3d 624, 145 Cal.Rptr. 122 (1978); Matter of Tricia M., 74 Cal.App.3d 125, 141 Cal.Rptr. 554 (1977), cert. denied 435 U.S. 996, 98 S.Ct. 1649, 56 L.Ed.2d 86 (1978).

57. See, e.g. the Michigan and Montana statutes cited in note 56, for example.

58. A proceeding for involuntary termination can be a slow, complex and expensive proceeding, in which the

defendant may raise many factual and legal questions. Any significant delay in the adoption proceeding is very likely to have an adverse effect on the child. Prospective adoptive parents, especially those who might be willing to adopt a "hard to place" child may well be discouraged from the attempt when faced with such complex litigation.

59. The presumption is discussed in section 4.4, supra, at note 32.

60. In re Adoption of Minor, 29 Wash.2d 759, 189 P.2d 458 (1948); Annot., 51 A.L.R.2d 497, 509 (1957).

61. Adoption of Reagan, 88 D. & C. 315 (Pa.Orphans' Ct.1953); Peters v. Campbell, 80 Wyo. 492, 345 P.2d 234 (1959).

62. "Revocation" here refers to revocation of consent before the decree of adoption has been entered. Attempts are revocation after the adoption decree are discussed in section 20.11, infra, in connection with attacks on adoption decrees.

Many cases on this issue are collected in Comment Note- Right of Natural Parent to Withdraw Valid Consent to Adoption of Child, 74 A.L.R.3d 421 (1976).

63. See, e.g., the New York statute passed to avoid unfortunate results like that in People ex rel. Scarpetta v. Spence-Chapin Adoption Service, 28 N.Y.2d 185, 321 N.Y.S.2d 65, 269 N.E.2d 787 (1971), cert. denied 404 U.S. 805, 92 S.Ct. 54, 30 L.Ed.2d 38 (1971); Foster, Adoption and Child Custody: Best Interests of the Child? 22 Buff. L.Rev. 1 (1972).

Whether consent to adoption may be revoked is to be determined initially by reference to the applicable state statute. Relatively few statutes deal with the question explicitly, although this is certainly a matter as to which the courts should be given statutory guidance. Those statutes which do mention revocation take a variety of approaches. Some provide that the consent may only be withdrawn with court approval, that approval to be given only if the court finds that that is in the child's best interests.[64] Others impose a relatively short period within which revocation may occur, on the expiration of which it is not permitted.[65] Still others permit it only on the ground of fraud or duress.[66] The New York statute provides for execution of consent before a judge, with various safeguards, after which revocation is not permitted, with a somewhat less strict rule if the consent is not executed before a judge.[67] Constitutional attacks on these statutes based on due process have generally been unsuccessful.[68]

In the absence of statute the earlier cases often took the position that the parent's consent could be revoked at any time up to the entry of the adoption decree and for any reason which seemed sufficient to the parent.[69] This amounted to saying that revocation is a matter of right. A few courts seem to adhere to this view.[70] Their reasoning seems to be that consent in the adoption proceedings is a continuing condition which must exist not only at the outset but also at the entry of the decree. The opinions in these cases also place some emphasis on the doctrine of parental right which has been influential in custody litigation.[71]

Today the principle is strongly held in the great majority of jurisdictions not controlled by statute that the natural parent may not withdraw his consent to adoption arbitrarily[72] and without careful scrutiny by the courts.[73] The grounds upon which revocation will be upheld are variously stated, but the emphasis has shifted from some vague "right"

64. E.g., West's Ann.Cal.Civ.Code § 226a (1982); Ohio Rev.Code § 3107.09 (1980); Uniform Adoption Act § 8, 9 Unif.L.Ann. 32 (1979). The California statute has been construed to permit revocation of consent on the ground of fraud by the agency which took the consent, with relatively slight consideration for the child's best interests in Matter of Cheryl E., 161 Cal.App.3d 587, 207 Cal. Rptr. 728 (1984). See also Adoption of Jennie L., 111 Cal. App.3d 422, 168 Cal.Rptr. 695 (1980); Guardianship of Baby Boy M., 66 Cal.App.3d 254, 135 Cal.Rptr. 866 (1977).

65. E.g., Official Code Ga.Ann. § 19–8–4(b) (Supp. 1986) (ten days); Minn.Stat.Ann. § 259.24 (1982) (ten days, after which consent is irrevocable except for fraud); Or.Rev.Stat. § 418.270 (1985) (no revocation after placement for adoption except for fraud or duress); West's Rev.Code Wash.Ann. § 26.33.160 (1986) (revocation before court approval or within forty-eight hours after the birth, and within one year after approval of consent for fraud or duress). On the Oregon provision, see State ex rel. Tanzer v. Williams, 263 Or. 394, 502 P.2d 596 (1972). The Minnesota provison is construed in Matter of J. M. S. Welfare, 268 N.W.2d 424 (Minn.1978).

66. E.g., Ariz.Rev.Stat. § 8–107 E (Supp.1986); Ill.— S.H.A. ch. 40, § 1513 (Supp.1986). What constitutes fraud or duress is discussed below at notes 83, 85.

67. N.Y.—McKinney's Dom.Rel.L. § 115–b (Supp. 1987). Application of this statute to prevent the withdrawal of consent was approved in Matter of Sarah K., 66 N.Y.2d 223, 496 N.Y.S.2d 384, 487 N.E.2d 241 (1985); cert. denied ___ U.S. ___, 106 S.Ct. 1515, 89 L.Ed.2d 914 (1986); Matter of Adoption of Daniel C., 63 N.Y.2d 927, 483 N.Y.S.2d 679, 473 N.E.2d 31 (1984). But see Janet G. v. New York Foundling Hospital, 94 Misc.2d 133, 403 N.Y.S. 2d 646 (Fam.Ct.1978), 28 Drake L.J. 211 (1978).

68. B. J. B. A. v. M. J. B., 620 P.2d 652 (Alaska 1980); Golz v. Children's Bureau of New Orleans, Inc., 326 So.2d 865 (La.1976), appeal dismissed for want of a substantial federal question 426 U.S. 901, 96 S.Ct. 2220, 48 L.Ed.2d 827 (1976); Matter of Myers, 131 Mich.App. 160, 345 N.W.2d 663 (1983).

69. Cases are collected in Annot., 138 A.L.R. 1038 (1942).

70. Adoption of Vaida, 34 Or.App. 631, 579 P.2d 313 (1978); In re R. W. B., 485 Pa. 168, 401 A.2d 347 (1979); K. N. v. Cades, 288 Pa.Super. 555, 432 A.2d 1010 (1981); Griggs v. Griggs, 374 S.W.2d 937 (Tex.Civ.App.1964). Other cases are cited in Comment Note- Right of Natural Parent to Withdraw Valid Consent to Adoption of Child, 74 A.L.R.3d 421, 435 (1976).

71. See section 19.6, supra. People ex rel. Scarpetta v. Spence-Chapin Adoption Service, 28 N.Y.2d 185, 321 N.Y.S.2d 65, 269 N.E.2d 787 (1971) emphasized parental right in permitting a natural mother to revoke her consent.

72. Rhodes v. Shirley, 234 Ind. 587, 129 N.E.2d 60 (1955); In re Adoption of Cannon, 243 Iowa 828, 53 N.W.2d 877 (1952); In re Adoption of D____, 122 Utah 525, 252 P.2d 223 (1953).

73. Matter of Gibson's Adoption, 239 N.W.2d 540 (Iowa 1976); In re Adoption of Baby C., 125 N.H. 216, 480 A.2d 101 (1984). Cases holding that the decision whether to permit revocation rests in the discretion of the court are cited in Comment Note- Right of Natural Parent to Withdraw Valid Consent to Adoption of Child, 74 A.L.R.3d 421, 434 (1976).

on the part of the natural parent to the interests of the child, particularly his interest in a stable, continuing relationship with his psychological parents. The Goldstein, Freud, Solnit writing has had a wide and useful influence in persuading courts that stability of environment is a most important aspect of the child's welfare, and that shifting the child from one set of parents to another is harmful even for the very young child.[74] The courts quite properly think that he should not be subjected to this sort of uncertainty merely because his natural parent has undergone a change of heart. The avoidance of hardship to the adoptive parents is also now being recognized as a significant factor in evaluating the validity of a revocation of consent.[75] In any event it seems clear that in judging the validity of an attempted withdrawal of consent the courts should not draw an analogy to the custody disputes between parents and non-parents, but rather should treat the natural parent and the prospective adoptive parent as asserting comparable claims, with no sort of presumptive advantage to the natural parent.[76] This is borne out by the generally accepted view that the burden of proof in these cases lies on the natural parent claiming that the consent was revoked.[77]

When one looks at the facts of cases on revocation of consent, one finds the same lack of agreement and consistency which characterize the custody cases.[78] Nevertheless a few generalizations may be drawn from the great variety of decisions. Thus the minority of the natural parent is not of itself a ground for permitting revocation,[79] but youth, immaturity, lack of understanding of the effect of consent and the pressure of external circumstances may lead the courts to permit revocation.[80] Fraud or duress in the usual meanings of those terms will often justify a revocation of consent,[81] and in the opinions of some courts only fraud or duress will have that effect.[82] Fraud is usually defined as speech or conduct which is false with respect to a material fact, is known by the party making it to be false, and is intended to induce the other party to rely on it.[83] Fraud does not include, for this purpose, so-called

---

74. In re Adoption of Child, 114 N.J.Super. 584, 277 A.2d 566 (1971); J. Goldstein, A. Freud, A. Solnit, Beyond the Best Interests of the Child (2d ed.1979).

75. In re Adoption of Lauless, 216 Or. 188, 338 P.2d 660 (1959) (parent may be estopped to revoke); In re Adoption of F_____, 26 Utah 2d 255, 488 P.2d 130 (1971) (adoptive parents led to change position in reliance on the consent).

76. Adoption of Jennie L., 111 Cal.App.3d 422, 168 Cal.Rptr. 695 (1980). Contra the text statement: D_____ P_____ v. Social Service & Child Welfare Dep't of Relief Soc. General Bd. Ass'n of Church of Jesus Christ of Latter-Day Saints, 19 Utah 2d 311, 431 P.2d 547 (1967).

77. Regenold v. Baby Fold, Inc., 68 Ill.2d 419, 369 N.E.2d 858 (1977), appeal dismissed for want of a substantial federal question 435 U.S. 963, 98 S.Ct. 1598, 56 L.Ed. 2d 54 (1978) (natural parent has burden of proof by clear and convincing evidence); In re Hoffman's Adoption, 61 Ill.2d 569, 338 N.E.2d 862 (1975), cert. denied 425 U.S. 958, 96 S.Ct. 1738, 48 L.Ed.2d 202 (1976); Matter of Adoption of Baby Boy Irons, 235 Kan. 540, 684 P.2d 332 (1984); Matter of Adoption of D. P., 583 P.2d 706 (Wyo. 1978).

78. See section 19.4, supra.

79. Adoption of Holman, 80 Ariz. 201, 295 P.2d 372 (1956); Ridgley v. Helms, 168 Ga.App. 435, 309 S.E.2d 375 (1983); Batt v. Nebraska Children's Home Society, 185 Neb. 124, 174 N.W.2d 88 (1970); Matter of Adoption of T. W. C., 38 N.Y.2d 128, 379 N.Y.S.2d 1, 341 N.E.2d 526 (1975).

80. Janet G. v. New York Foundling Hospital, 94 Misc.2d 133, 403 N.Y.S.2d 646 (Fam.Ct.1978).

81. Matter of Cheryl E., 161 Cal.App.3d 587, 207 Cal. Rptr. 728 (1984); In Interest of Sims, 30 Ill.App.3d 406, 332 N.E.2d 36 (1975); Wuertz v. Craig, 458 So.2d 1311 (La.1984); Sorentino v. Family and Children's Society of Elizabeth, 72 N.J. 127, 367 A.2d 1168 (1976), appeal after remand 74 N.J. 313, 378 A.2d 18 (1977), affirmed 77 N.J. 483, 391 A.2d 497 (1978).

82. In re Adoption of Holman, 80 Ariz. 201, 295 P.2d 372 (1956); In re Adoption of Shea, 86 So.2d 164 (Fla. 1956) (semble); Regenold v. Baby Fold, Inc., 68 Ill.2d 419, 12 Ill.Dec. 151, 369 N.E.2d 858 (1977), appeal dismissed 435 U.S. 963, 98 S.Ct. 1598, 56 L.Ed.2d 54 (1978); People ex rel. Drury v. Catholic Home Bureau, 34 Ill.2d 84, 213 N.E.2d 507 (1966); Mabbitt v. Miller, 246 Iowa 712, 68 N.W.2d 740 (1955); In re Surrender of Minor Children, 344 Mass. 230, 181 N.E.2d 836 (1962); C. C. I. v. Natural Parents, 398 So.2d 220 (Miss.1981); Catholic Charities of Diocese of Galveston v. Harper, 161 Tex. 21, 337 S.W.2d 111 (1960), 30 U.Cin.L.Rev. 257 (1961). For cases on duress and undue influence see Annots., 74 A.L.R.3d 527 (1976), 50 A.L.R.3d 918 (1973).

83. Regenold v. Baby Fold, Inc., 68 Ill.2d 419, 12 Ill. Dec. 151, 369 N.E.2d 858 (1977), dismissed for want of a substantial federal question 435 U.S. 963, 98 S.Ct. 1598, 56 L.Ed.2d 54 (1978); In re Hoffman's Adoption, 61 Ill.2d 569, 338 N.E.2d 862 (1975), cert. denied 425 U.S. 958, 96 S.Ct. 1738, 48 L.Ed.2d 202 (1976); In Interest of Nolan, 94 Ill.App.3d 1081, 50 Ill.Dec. 442, 419 N.E.2d 550 (1981).

constructive fraud, that is, a failure to reveal such information as the identity of the adoptive parents, at least where there is no fiduciary relation between the parties.[84]

Duress is more difficult to define than fraud. The cases are numerous, turn on a great variety of facts and are often decided by courts who naturally but unfortunately are moved by sympathy for the plight of the natural mother without giving enough consideration to the welfare of the child. Most of the cases nevertheless define duress as wrongful conduct or threats of wrongful conduct which overcome the voluntary judgment or decision of the natural parent.[85] But others recognize a situation which might be called "duress of circumstances" as justifying the revocation of consent.[86] These cases arise when the natural parent, finding herself without resources or assistance, sometimes under pressure from friends or relatives to give up the child, consents to adoption as a way out of her troubles and then later changes her mind when her situation improves. Adoption agencies obviously should exercise the greatest possible

care to counsel natural parents in these troubled circumstances in order to avoid attempts at revocation, but when the attempts are made despite all the agencies can do, revocation should not be permitted, especially after an adoption placement has occurred.[87] The effect on the child when such revocations occur is likely to be severe and this factor justifies denying the attempt at revocation. The court's sympathy for the natural parent may be reinforced by some notion that granting the adoption is an expression of class bias prejudicial to the natural mother, but this is merely another way of evading responsibility to the child.[88] It must be conceded, however, that the distinction between duress as properly defined and "duress of circumstances" is, in its application to the multitude of factual circumstances which may arise, a difficult one to draw and one which must generally be left to the discretion of trial courts.

In a very small number of cases a natural parent's mistake concerning the effect of a consent to adoption not induced by misrepresentations or duress has been held to justify

Matter of Adoption of D. P., 583 P.2d 706 (Wyo.1978) takes the position that the fraud must relate to past or existing facts rather than to misrepresentations about the future but it is unclear why this should be so.

84. In Interest of C. K., 315 N.W.2d 37 (Iowa 1982). The dangers for an attorney in representing both the natural and the adoptive parents are illustrated by Matter of Adoption of Baby Boy Irons, 235 Kan. 540, 684 P.2d 332 (1984). A case contra the text statement is Matter of Cheryl E., 161 Cal.App.3d 587, 207 Cal.Rptr. 728 (1984), in which the court held that negligent misrepresentations could be a ground for revoking consent.

85. Regenold v. Baby Fold, Inc., 68 Ill.2d 419, 369 N.E.2d 858 (1977), dismissed for want of a substantial federal question 435 U.S. 963, 98 S.Ct. 1598, 56 L.Ed.2d 54 (1978); People ex rel. Drury v. Catholic Home Bureau, 34 Ill.2d 84, 213 N.E.2d 507 (1966); Wuertz v. Craig, 458 So.2d 1311 (La.1984) (threat of unjustified criminal charges amounts to duress); C. C. I. v. Natural Parents, 398 So.2d 220 (Miss.1981).

In Interest of Sims, 30 Ill.App.3d 406, 332 N.E.2d 36 (1975) the court found that a sixteen-year-old mother was subjected to duress by her parents when they conditioned their love and financial support upon her consenting to the adoption of her baby. Sorentino v. Family & Children's Society of Elizabeth, 72 N.J. 127, 367 A.2d 1168 (1976), appeal after remand 74 N.J. 313, 378 A.2d 18 (1977), judgment affirmed 77 N.J. 483, 391 A.2d 497 (1978) found duress by an adoption agency in threats of harassment and litigation and in failure to inform the sixteen-year-old mother of options other than adoption.

For other cases see Annots., 74 A.L.R.3d 527 (1976) and 50 A.L.R.3d 918 (1973).

86. Matter of Cheryl E., 161 Cal.App.3d 587, 207 Cal. Rptr. 728 (1984); Duncan v. Harden, 234 Ga. 204, 214 S.E.2d 890 (1975); Huebert v. Marshall, 132 Ill.App.2d 793, 270 N.E.2d 464 (1971); People ex rel. Scarpetta v. Spence-Chapin Adoption Service, 28 N.Y.2d 185, 321 N.Y.S.2d 65, 269 N.E.2d 787 (1971), dismissed for want of jurisdiction and cert. denied 404 U.S. 805, 92 S.Ct. 54, 30 L.Ed.2d 38 (1971); Matter of Adoption of R. P. R., 98 Wis. 2d 613, 297 N.W.2d 833 (1980) ("rejection trauma"). Failure to comply with requirements of the statute concerning a relinquishment proceeding was held to justify revocation in In re D. L. F——, 85 S.D. 44, 176 N.W.2d 486 (1970).

87. Matter of Appeal in Yuma County, Juvenile Action Nos. J–81–339 and J–81–340, 140 Ariz. 378, 682 P.2d 6 (Ariz.App.1984); Petition of Steve B. D., 111 Idaho 285, 723 P.2d 829 (1986); Boatwright v. Walker, 715 S.W.2d 237 (Ky.App.1986); Kane v. United Catholic Social Services of Omaha, Inc., 187 Neb. 467, 191 N.W.2d 824 (1971); Matter of Adoption of Child, 114 N.J.Super. 584, 277 A.2d 566 (1971); In re Doe's Adoption, 87 N.M. 253, 531 P.2d 1226 (1975), cert. denied 87 N.M. 239, 531 P.2d 1212 (1975); In re Adoption of K——, 24 Utah 2d 59, 465 P.2d 541 (1970); In re Adoption of Baby Girl K., 26 Wash.App. 897, 615 P.2d 1310 (1980); Wooten v. Wallace, —— W.Va. ——, 351 S.E.2d 72 (1986).

88. Matter of Cheryl E., 161 Cal.App.3d 587, 207 Cal. Rptr. 728 (1984).

revocation of the consent.[89] Other cases refuse to accept this ground for revocation.[90] And when the consent is shown to be voluntary in the sense that the consequences were explained to the consenting parent or were understood by her, the courts uphold the consent.[91]

Whether required to do so by statute or in order to effectuate what the courts regard as good policy, many cases refuse to permit the revocation of consent unless the natural parent sustains the burden of proving that such revocation and the return of the child to the natural parent will be in the child's best interests.[92] A major factor in determining what the child's best interests demand in such circumstances is the length of time the child has been in the care of adoptive or foster parents.[93] These cases demonstrate that the courts have understood and are giving effect to considerations of psychological parenthood as being as significant or even more significant in many cases than biological parenthood.[94]

89. In re Adoption by Emanuel T., 81 Misc.2d 535, 365 N.Y.S.2d 709 (Fam.Ct.1975) granted revocation on this ground, but the decision was reversed in 48 A.D.2d 425, 370 N.Y.S.2d 93 (1st Dep't 1975). Other cases are cited in Annot., Mistake or Want of Understanding as Ground for Revocation of Consent to Adoption or of Agreement Releasing Infant to Adoption Placement Agency, 74 A.L.R.3d 489 (1976).

90. Davis v. Turner, 337 So.2d 355 (Ala.1976) cert. denied 337 So.2d 362 (Ala.1976) Anonymous v. Anonymous, 23 Ariz.App. 50, 530 P.2d 896 (1975); Stotler v. Lutheran Social Service of Iowa, 209 N.W.2d 121 (Iowa 1973).

91. Matter of Adoption of Hewitt, 396 N.E.2d 938 (Ind. App.1979); In re Revocation of Appointment of a Guardian, 360 Mass. 81, 271 N.E.2d 621 (1971); In re Adoption of Hecker, 448 S.W.2d 280 (Mo.App.1969); People ex rel. Stone v. Maglio, 62 Misc.2d 292, 308 N.Y.S.2d 604 (Fam. Ct.1970); In re K., 31 Ohio Misc. 218, 282 N.E.2d 370 (1969).

92. Matter of Gibson's Adoption, 239 N.W.2d 540 (Iowa 1976); Van Wey v. Van Wey, 656 S.W.2d 731 (Ky. 1983), cert. denied 465 U.S. 1066, 104 S.Ct. 1416, 79 L.Ed. 2d 742; In re Child, 1 Mass.App. 256, 295 N.E.2d 693 (1973); Application of Hendrickson, 159 Mont. 217, 496 P.2d 1115 (1972); In re Adoption of Baby C., 125 N.H. 216, 480 A.2d 101 (1984); In re Adoption of Child, 114 N.J.Super. 584, 277 A.2d 566 (1971), 26 Rutgers L.Rev. 693 (1973); Roe v. New York Foundling Hospital, 36 A.D. 2d 100, 318 N.Y.S.2d 508 (1st Dep't 1971); Webb v. Wiley, 600 P.2d 317 (Okl.1979). In Lemley v. Barr, ___ W.Va. ___, 343 S.E.2d 101 (1986) the court felt obliged to enforce an Ohio decree revoking consent to adoption, but held

Indian Child Welfare Act

This Act,[95] passed by Congress to protect Indian families from breakup, establishes formalities for voluntary placement or relinquishment of Indian children, including that consent to adoption may not be given earlier than ten days after the child's birth.[96] The Act also provides that the parent's consent to the adoption of an Indian child may be withdrawn at any time, upon which the child must be returned to the natural parent or custodian.[97]

 **WESTLAW REFERENCES**

Formalities of Consent

di(statut*** law legislat*** /s consent! /s
   acknowledg! notar!)
find 396 ne2d 938

Who Must Consent to Adoption

di(legitima! /3 child minor infant /s adopt! /s consent! /s
   parent mother father)
find 345 nys2d 430

that this did not mean that the child should be returned to the custody of his natural parent, and remanded the case for determination of what the child's best interests would dictate in these circumstances.

93. Van Wey v. Van Wey, 656 S.W.2d 731 (Ky. 1983); In re Adoption of Child, 114 N.J.Super. 584, 277 A.2d 566 (1971); Lemley v. Barr, ___ W.Va. ___, 343 S.E.2d 101 (1986). Contra, insisting on the prior right of the biological parent: Spence-Chapin Adoption Service v. Polk, 29 N.Y.2d 196, 324 N.Y.S.2d 937, 274 N.E.2d 431 (1971); D_____ P_____ v. Social Service & Child Welfare Dep't of Relief Soc. General Bd. Ass'n of Church of Jesus Christ of Latter-Day Saints, 19 Utah 2d 311, 431 P.2d 547 (1967). In Szemler v. Clements, 214 Va. 639, 202 S.E.2d 880 (1974) the court held that revocation was ineffective, but permitted the natural parent to oppose the adoption, finally holding that the child's interests would be best served by permitting the adoption.

94. In re Adoption of Child, 114 N.J.Super. 584, 277 A.2d 566 (1971). Contra, vehemently rejecting the idea of psychological parenthood and disparaging reliance upon psychological analysis generally, Commonwealth ex rel. Grimes v. Yack, 289 Pa.Super. 495, 433 A.2d 1363 (1981).

95. 25 U.S.C.A. § 1901 ff.

96. 25 U.S.C.A. § 1913(a).

97. 25 U.S.C.A. § 1913(b). See also A. B. M. v. M. H., 651 P.2d 1170 (Alaska 1982), cert. denied 461 U.S. 914, 103 S.Ct. 1893, 77 L.Ed.2d 283, (1983); Matter of Appeal in Pima County Juvenile Action No. S-903, 130 Ariz. 202, 635 P.2d 187 (App.1981), cert. denied 455 U.S. 1007, 102 S.Ct. 1644, 71 L.Ed.2d 875 (1982).

sy(parent father mother /s refus! withh*ld! /3 consent! /s
adopt!)

find 92 sct 1208

di(father /s illegitima! wedlock bastard! /s notic! notif! /s
adopt!)

Revocation of Consent

di(fraud! duress /s revok! revoca! withdr*w! /s consent!
/s adopt!)

di(right /5 revok! revoca! withdr*w! /5 consent! /s adopt!
/s parent! mother father)

---

§ 20.5 Involuntary Termination of Parental Rights—Constitutionality of Statutes

Children may become available for adoption without the consent of their natural parents if, pursuant to statutes found in all states, parent-child relationships are terminated involuntarily. Since court decrees accomplishing this are final and obviously affect a most important legal relationship, the statutes only authorize such decrees upon proof of parental failures so drastic as to cause serious harm to the children. The states have naturally found it difficult to devise statutory formulations which will strike a balance between protecting the rights of parents against state intrusion and protecting children against parental misconduct. The efforts of national consultative bodies to produce workable model statutes have not been conspicuously more successful than those of the state legislatures.[1] Under these conditions it is not surprising that a very wide diversity of statutory language should be adopted, and that, especially in the decades of the 1960's and 1970's, that language should come under frequent constitutional attack.

The greatest number of constitutional attacks upon involuntary termination statutes have been based upon what has come to be known as the "void-for-vagueness" doctrine. This doctrine originally appeared in the criminal law as a development from the Due Process Clause of the Fourteenth Amendment. Briefly stated, it is that a criminal statute must be drafted with sufficient precision to inform people fairly and reasonably concerning the kind of conduct which is prohibited.[2] If the statute is not so drafted, the argument goes, the person convicted pursuant to it is being deprived of his liberty without due process of law.[3] To a limited extent this doctrine has been applied in civil litigation to mean that statutes depriving people of certain kinds of civil rights must be drafted with similar precision.[4] Since it is now well established that the interest which a parent has in his relationship with his child is of such fundamental importance in our society as to be entitled to constitutional protection in other respects,[5] the state courts and some federal courts have had no hesitation in applying the void-for-vagueness doctrine to termination of

---

§ 20.5

1. Katz, Freeing Children for Permanent Placement Through a Model Act, 12 Fam.L.Q. 203, 216 (1978); Wald, State Intervention on Behalf of "Neglected" Children: A Search for Realistic Standards, 27 Stan.L.Rev. 985, 1039 (1975). See also Wald, State Intervention on Behalf of Neglected Children: Standards for Removal of Children From Their Homes, Monitoring the Status of Children in Foster Homes and Termination of Parental Rights, 28 Stan.L.Rev. 623 (1976); Ketcham, Babcock, Statutory Standards for the Involuntary Termination of Parental Rights, 29 Rut.L.Rev. 530 (1976); Boskey, McCue, Alternative Standards for the Termination of Parental Rights, 9 Seton Hall L.Rev. 1 (1978); Derdeyn, Rogoff, Williams, Alternatives to Absolute Termination of Parental Rights After Long-Term Foster Care, 31 Vand.L.Rev. 1165 (1978).

2. W. LaFave, A. Scott, Criminal Law § 11 (1972), describing the purposes of the doctrine as giving fair warning to those potentially subject to a statute, and as preventing the enactment of statutes so broad that they are susceptible to arbitrary or discriminatory enforcement. See also L. Tribe, American Constitutional Law 513 (1978) and Lanzetta v. New Jersey, 306 U.S. 451, 458, 59 S.Ct. 618, 621, 83 L.Ed. 888 (1939), holding that a criminal statute referring to a person "known to be a member of any gang" was unconstitutionally vague.

3. The doctrine is thus closely related to the procedural due process requirements of notice and an opportunity to be heard. L. Tribe, American Constitutional Law 512 (1978).

4. Giaccio v. Pennsylvania, 382 U.S. 399, 86 S.Ct. 518, 15 L.Ed.2d 447 (1966) (statute was too vague to meet due process standard when it authorized the imposition of costs on one guilty of "some misconduct"); A. B. Small Co. v. American Sugar Refining Co., 267 U.S. 233, 45 S.Ct. 295, 69 L.Ed. 589 (1925) (statutory language unconstitutionally vague as a standard for the enforcibility of contracts).

5. Stanley v. Illinois, 405 U.S. 645, 92 S.Ct. 1208, 31 L.Ed.2d 551 (1972) and other cases discussed in section 20.2, supra.

parental rights statutes on the same theory, that parents have a due process right to be informed about the standards of child care being imposed by the state.[6] There is a certain unreality in this reasoning when applied to these statutes. It seems unlikely that parents will ever be guided in caring for their children by what these statutes tell them about their obligations. On the contrary, the real thrust of the void-for-vagueness doctrine in this context is to limit the state's power to establish standards for child care and to enforce those standards by removal of children from their parents.

Notwithstanding this obvious application of the void-for-vagueness rule to termination statutes, some courts define the precision required of the statutes in terms of their meaning for parents.[7] More discerning courts are concerned with the breadth of discretion which the statutes given to judges as they decide whether to terminate the rights of parents.[8] The definitions used are largely tautological and probably cannot be otherwise. Borrowing from the criminal cases, some courts hold that the statute must give a person of ordinary intelligence fair notice that his contemplated conduct is forbidden, so that he may act accordingly.[9] Others hold that the statute must establish sufficient standards so that judges are not completely free to determine what is prohibited on a case by case basis.[10] Even a broad statute may pass

muster if it can be narrowly construed to establish reasonable standards.[11] And statutes should not be subjected to impossibly precise standards of construction.[12] It is important to emphasize that the void-for-vagueness rule performs its functions in termination cases quite differently from its performance in criminal cases. In termination cases if the rule is rigidly applied the result may be that children will be subjected to serious harm which might have been prevented. In criminal cases a rigid void-for-vagueness rule does not present that danger. Much greater caution should therefore be used in invalidating termination of parental rights statutes than in invalidating ordinary criminal statutes.

The type of statute most often attacked for vagueness authorizes termination of parental rights on the ground that a child has been neglected, defining neglect in a multitude of different ways, some more specific than others. The case of Alsager v. District Court of Polk County,[13] much cited but seldom followed, held the Iowa neglect statute unconstitutionally vague. The objectionable parts of the statute were those authorizing termination of parental rights of parents who "have continuously or repeatedly refused to give the child necessary parental care and protection", and who "are unfit by reason of * * * conduct found by the court likely to be detrimental to the physical or mental health or morals

6. Some termination statutes carry criminal as well as civil sanctions, so that the void-for-vagueness doctrine is applicable on both grounds. See In re B., 30 N.Y.2d 352, 334 N.Y.S.2d 133, 285 N.E.2d 288 (1972).

7. Linn v. Linn, 205 Neb. 218, 286 N.W.2d 765 (1980); In re Interest of Metteer, 203 Neb. 515, 279 N.W.2d 374 (1979) (statute is valid if it uses ordinary terms which find adequate interpretation in common usage and understanding).

8. Thompson v. Arkansas Social Services, 282 Ark. 369, 669 S.W.2d 878 (1984), appeal dismissed 469 U.S. 926, 105 S.Ct. 316, 83 L.Ed.2d 254 (1984); In re Doe, 123 N.H. 634, 465 A.2d 924 (1983).

9. Davis v. Smith, 266 Ark. 112, 583 S.W.2d 37 (1979); Matter of Gentry, 142 Mich.App. 701, 369 N.W.2d 889 (1985).

10. Alsager v. District Court of Polk County, Iowa (Juvenile Division), 406 F.Supp. 10 (S.D.Iowa 1975), affirmed on other grounds 545 F.2d 1137 (8th Cir.1976).

11. Matter of Gentry, 142 Mich.App. 701, 369 N.W.2d 889 (1985).

12. Thompson v. Arkansas Social Services, 282 Ark. 369, 669 S.W.2d 878 (1984), appeal dismissed 469 U.S. 926, 105 S.Ct. 316, 83 L.Ed.2d 254 (1984).

13. 406 F.Supp. 10 (S.D.Iowa 1975), affirmed on other grounds 545 F.2d 1137 (8th Cir.1976). The case arose as a suit by the parents whose rights had been terminated against various state officials under the federal Civil Rights Act, 42 U.S.C.A. § 1983, claiming that the state's action in terminating the parents' rights violated various constitutional principles.

A similar case which relied upon Alsager and found the Alabama child neglect law unconstitutionally vague is Roe v. Conn, 417 F.Supp. 769 (M.D.Ala.1976), although this case involved the additional factor that a child was removed from the custody of his parents in part on the ground that he was white and was living in an interracial family.

of the child." [14] The court found that these phrases would not inform the ordinary parent concerning, for example, the kind of discipline he might adopt for correcting his child's behavior. It also held that the statutory language would permit state officials to determine subjectively what sort of conduct by a parent is necessary and what detrimental. And finally, the court thought that the statute was so vague that it would deter parents from engaging in conduct essential to the exercise of their fundamental right to family integrity. This list of statutory deficiencies is indeed impressive but it seems to ignore the obvious difficulty of designing a statute which protects children against the wide variety of parental acts of omission and commission to which child welfare workers in Iowa and elsewhere could undoubtedly testify. The court in Alsager also found that the evidence in the case failed to show harm

to the children serious enough to support a compelling state interest in terminating the parent-child relationship, a section of its opinion announced under the heading of "Substantive Due Process".[15]

The Alsager case has had beneficial effects by showing that some juvenile and trial courts are much too ready to terminate parental rights on the basis of inadequate harm to the children,[16] and that the facilities and supervision available for the care of children after termination are often far less conducive to their welfare than continued care by their natural parents would have been. The case has not been widely followed by other courts on the issue of the void-for-vagueness rule, however. Even in Iowa its effect has been mixed.[17] The neglect statutes of other states having terminology not greatly different from the Iowa statute have generally been held not to be unconstitutionally vague.[18]

14. 406 F.Supp. at 14, 18.

15. 406 F.Supp. at 21. On this point the Eighth Circuit affirmed the district court, relying on the district court's opinion to hold that the state had failed to prove the sort of harm necessary to give the state a compelling interest sufficient to terminate the parent-child relationship. It also characterized the vagueness attack on the statute as "serious" but expressed no opinion on the point. Alsager v. District Court of Polk County, Iowa, 545 F.2d 1137 (8th Cir.1976). This holding has the dubious consequence of transforming questions of fact in termination proceedings into broad constitutional issues, a process indulged in by the Supreme Court on occasion. See Stanley v. Illinois, 405 U.S. 645, 92 S.Ct. 1208, 31 L.Ed.2d 551 (1972) and its progeny, discussed in section 20.2, supra.

16. The Alsager case is discussed and grounds for state intervention proposed which would limit such intervention in J. Goldstein, A. Freud, A. Solnit, Before the Best Interests of the Child 83, 187 (1979).

17. In Interest of Hochmuth, 251 N.W.2d 484 (Iowa 1977) found the Iowa statute not too vague as applied, while In Interest of Crooks, 262 N.W.2d 786 (Iowa 1978) held it unconstitutionally vague. In Interest of Ponx, 276 N.W.2d 425 (Iowa 1979) upheld a later version of the statute containing a bit more detail but not substantially different from the former one. State v. Winters, 346 So. 2d 991 (Fla.1977) held unconstitutional a statute which imposed criminal penalties on parents who deprived their children of "necessary food, clothing, shelter or medical treatment", but State v. Joyce held a substantially similar statute not too vague.

Statutes which authorize termination of parental rights where the parents fail or refuse to provide a "proper home" for the child have also been held unconstitutional for vagueness. Davis v. Smith, 266 Ark. 112, 583

S.W.2d 37 (1979). But such phrases as "proper care" and "unfit home" were held sufficiently specific in Matter of Gentry, 142 Mich.App. 701, 369 N.W.2d 889 (1985).

18. Thompson v. Arkansas Social Services, 282 Ark. 369, 669 S.W.2d 878 (1984), dismissed for want of a substantial federal question 469 U.S. 926, 105 S.Ct. 316, 83 L.Ed.2d 254 (1984) ("basic essential needs" of a child not too vague); In re Camm, 294 So.2d 318 (Fla.1974), cert. denied 419 U.S. 866, 95 S.Ct. 121, 42 L.Ed.2d 103 (1974); Woodruff v. Keale, 64 Hawaii 85, 637 P.2d 760 (1981) ("failure to provide for care and support" not too vague); Matter of Trapp, 593 S.W.2d 193 (Mo.1980), appeal dismissed for want of a substantial federal question 456 U.S. 967, 102 S.Ct. 2226, 72 L.Ed.2d 840 (1982), rehearing denied 458 U.S. 1116, 102 S.Ct. 3499, 73 L.Ed. 2d 1377 (1982) ("proper care, custody or support" and similar language not too vague); In Interest of Souza, 204 Neb. 503, 283 N.W.2d 48 (1979) (abandonment and neglect language constitutional); Matter of Doe, 100 N.M. 92, 666 P.2d 771 (1983) ("parent/child relationship has disintegrated" not too vague); In re Wright, 64 N.C.App. 135, 306 S.E.2d 825 (1983) (termination of parental rights for "neglect" not too vague); Matter of Daniel, Deborah and Leslie H., 591 P.2d 1175 (Okl.1979) (definition of dependent or neglected child not too vague); In re William L., 477 Pa. 322, 383 A.2d 1228 (1978), cert. denied 439 U.S. 880, 99 S.Ct. 216, 58 L.Ed.2d 192 (1978) (definition of incapacity or neglect not too vague); In re David, ___ R.I. ___, 427 A.2d 795 (1981) ("neglect to provide proper care and maintenance for one year" not too vague); Knox v. Lynchburg Division of Social Services, 223 Va. 213, 288 S.E.2d 399 (1982) (neglect statute not too vague); Matter of A. M. K., 105 Wis.2d 91, 312 N.W.2d 840 (1981) (inability to give parental care and protection not too vague). Other cases are collected in Annot., Validity of State Statute Providing for Termination of Parental Rights, 22 A.L.R.4th 774 (1983).

The so-called substantive due process claim vindicated by the Alsager court [19] has been made in a few other cases. In the present context the doctrine amounts to the assertion that a) the parent has a fundamental right to the custody and society of his child; b) this right may not be cut off without a determination that there is a compelling state interest for doing so; and c) the particular termination statute, at least as applied in the case, requires no proof of a compelling state interest.[20] This line of argument is based by some courts upon the Equal Protection Clause of the Fourteenth Amendment.[21] Like so many other questions raised by the application of constitutional doctrine to children's cases, this one receives no unified or coherent treatment from the courts. The major issue in most of the cases is whether the termination statute effectuates a compelling state interest. Most courts concede that the welfare of children is a compelling state interest, but the question is whether in the circumstances of a particular case that welfare is promoted by the statute. The situation is made more complicated by the tendency of some courts to

base the decision invalidating a statute both upon the void-for-vagueness rule and on substantive due process, so that the reader cannot be certain whether the result would have been the same under either doctrine by itself.[22] Nor can one be sure whether the statute would be held unconstitutional under either doctrine if it were to be applied to a different set of facts.

There are many illustrations of this confusion. The statutes of a few states authorize termination of parental rights, or sometimes temporary custody orders in favor of state agencies, when the best interests of the child demand those forms of relief. The uncertainty of the phrase "best interests" has been demonstrated in the discussions of custody.[23] In the present context some courts have held that this is insufficient to meet the constitutional standard of precision or to comply with substantive due process requirements.[24] Other courts have held such statutes valid.[25] A closely related line of cases is concerned with whether "unfitness" must be proved before parental rights may be terminated. Here also the cases are in disagreement.[26] In some

19. See note 15, supra. The substantive due process claim was sustained in Roe v. Conn, 417 F.Supp. 769 (M.D.Ala.1976). It was not sustained and the state statute was held constitutional in In re William L., 477 Pa. 322, 383 A.2d 1228 (1978), cert. denied 439 U.S. 880, 99 S.Ct. 216, 58 L.Ed.2d 192 (1978) and in Knox v. Lynchburg Division of Social Services, 223 Va. 213, 288 S.E.2d 399 (1982).

20. In re William L., 477 Pa. 322, 383 A.2d 1228 (1978), cert. denied 439 U.S. 880, 99 S.Ct. 216, 58 L.Ed.2d 192 (1978) contains a clear statement of the doctrine free of constitutional jargon. In re Lester, 417 A.2d 877 (R.I.1980) rejected the view of some courts that state statutes on dependency and neglect should be subjected to "strict scrutiny" in determining whether they comply with due process.

21. In Interest of J. C., 242 Ga. 737, 251 S.E.2d 299 (1978), appeal dismissed 441 U.S. 929, 99 S.Ct. 2046, 60 L.Ed.2d 657 (1979); Matter of Joyce T., 65 N.Y.2d 39, 489 N.Y.S.2d 705, 478 N.E.2d 1306 (1985); Matter of Carl and Annette N., 91 Misc.2d 738, 398 N.Y.S.2d 613 (Fam.Ct. 1977).

22. Roe v. Conn, 417 F.Supp. 769 (M.D.Ala.1976); Alsager v. District Court of Polk County, Iowa (Juvenile Division), 406 F.Supp. 10 (S.D.Iowa 1975); affirmed 545 F.2d 1137 (8th Cir.1976).

23. See sections 19.1 and 19.4, supra.

24. In re Juvenile Appeal, 181 Conn. 638, 646, 436 A.2d 290, 294 (1980) (dissenting opinion) (parental rights

may be terminated when "there is no ongoing parent-child relationship"); Linn v. Linn, 205 Neb. 218, 286 N.W.2d 765 (1980) (termination on the ground of the child's best interests is unconstitutionally vague); In re J. P., 648 P.2d 1364 (Utah 1982) (parent has a fundamental right not to be deprived of the society of his child without proof of unfitness, abandonment or substantial neglect; the child's best interests are not sufficient). In Interest of R. W., 495 So.2d 133 (Fla.1986) (unconstitutional to terminate parental rights where the parent violated a performance agreement with a state agency for the care of the child).

25. Matter of Adoption of J. S. R., 374 A.2d 860 (D.C. App.1977) ("best interests" is not unconstitutionally vague); Petition of Department of Public Welfare, 376 Mass. 252, 381 N.E.2d 565 (1978) (may dispense with consent to adoption where that is in the child's best interests); Petition of New England Home for Little Wanderers, 367 Mass. 631, 328 N.E.2d 854 (1975) ("best interests" test is constitutional). See also Wells v. Children's Aid Society of Utah, 681 P.2d 199 (Utah 1984). Taking temporary custody of a child where his best interests require it was held constitutional in In re Juvenile Appeal, 189 Conn. 276, 455 A.2d 1313 (1983).

26. Holding a finding of unfitness constitutionally required: Custody of a Minor, 378 Mass. 712, 393 N.E.2d 379 (1979); In Interest of J. L. W., 102 Wis.2d 118, 306 N.W.2d 46 (1981). Holding such a finding not required: In Matter of K. A., 484 A.2d 992 (D.C.App.1984). "Unfitness" was held not to be unconstitutionally vague in

states a parent's rights may be involuntarily terminated when he has been imprisoned and when the child's best interests would thereby be promoted. These statutes have generally been held not to violate either substantive due process or equal protection.[27] Likewise statutes which expressly authorize the termination of parental rights when the parent is unable to care for the child by reason of mental illness, mental retardation or the habitual use of drugs or alcohol are generally held not to be void for vagueness and not to violate substantive due process or equal protection.[28]

Statutes in a few states provide that when a child has been in temporary foster care or in the custody of an agency for a specified period varying from six months to two years, this gives rise to a rebuttable presumption that the child's best interests will be served by terminating the parent's rights or by adoption

without the parent's consent.[29] Some courts have held these statutes to be unconstitutional, either as violative of substantive due process or as too vague or as inconsistent with the rule of Santosky v. Kramer.[30] Other cases have held them to be valid as against all constitutional attacks.[31] Although one may appreciate the desire to provide children in those circumstances with permanent homes, the presumption may in many cases prevent a parent from keeping his children after undergoing temporary difficulties and therefore seems unwise. The principles of constitutional law as applied to termination of parental rights are so uncertain that it is impossible to determine whether lack of wisdom or sound policy equals unconstitutionality.

Although it is extraordinary that constitutional principles should be so uncertain when applied to the most fundamental of human relationships, perhaps we can take some com-

---

People in Interest of M. S. H., 656 P.2d 1294 (Colo.1983); In re Dingee, 328 A.2d 139 (Del.1974); Matter of Ladewig, 34 Ill.App.3d 393, 340 N.E.2d 150 (1975); In the Interest of Brooks, 228 Kan. 541, 618 P.2d 814 (1980); In re Interest of J. L. L., 209 Neb. 76, 306 N.W.2d 175 (1981).

27. Chandler v. Cochran, 247 Ga. 184, 275 S.E.2d 23 (1981), cert. denied 454 U.S. 872, 102 S.Ct. 342, 70 L.Ed. 2d 177 (1981), rehearing denied 454 U.S. 1094, 102 S.Ct. 665, 70 L.Ed.2d 635 (1981); People v. Ray, 88 Ill.App.3d 1010, 44 Ill.Dec. 182, 411 N.E.2d 88 (1980), appeal dismissed for want of a substantial federal question 452 U.S. 956, 101 S.Ct. 3102, 69 L.Ed.2d 967 (1981); Matter of Adoption of Joseph LL, 97 A.D.2d 263, 470 N.Y.S.2d 784 (3d Dep't 1983), affirmed 63 N.Y.2d 1014, 484 N.Y.S.2d 508, 473 N.E.2d 736 (1984); Matter of D., 24 Or.App. 601, 547 P.2d 175 (1976), cert. denied 429 U.S. 907, 97 S.Ct. 273, 50 L.Ed.2d 189 (1976); Matter of A. M. K., 105 Wis.2d 91, 312 N.W.2d 840 (1981).

28. Holding the statute not unconstitutional for vagueness: Matter of Appeal in Maricopa County Juvenile Action No. JS–5209 and No. JS–4963, 143 Ariz. 178, 692 P.2d 1027 (App.1984); Thompson v. Arkansas Social Services, 282 Ark. 369, 669 S.W.2d 878 (1984), appeal dismissed for want of a substantial federal question 469 U.S. 926, 105 S.Ct. 316, 83 L.Ed.2d 254 (1984); In re Mark K., 159 Cal.App.3d 94, 205 Cal.Rptr. 393 (1984); Custody of a Minor, 378 Mass. 712, 393 N.E.2d 379 (1979); In Interest of Metteer, 203 Neb. 515, 279 N.W.2d 374 (1979).

Holding the statute did not deprive the parent of substantive due process or of equal protection: Matter of Appeal in Maricopa County Juvenile Action Nos. JS 1308 and JS 1412, 27 Ariz.App. 420, 555 P.2d 679 (1976); In re Mark K., 159 Cal.App.3d 94, 205 Cal.Rptr. 393 (1984); In Interest of J. C., 242 Ga. 737, 251 S.E.2d 299 (1978), appeal dismissed for want of a substantial federal ques-

tion 441 U.S. 929, 99 S.Ct. 2046, 60 L.Ed.2d 657 (1979); Matter of Montgomery, 311 N.C. 101, 316 S.E.2d 246 (1984).

Holding the statute not unconstitutional as applied: Matter of J. L. B., 182 Mont. 100, 594 P.2d 1127 (1979); Matter of Joyce T., 65 N.Y.2d 39, 489 N.Y.S.2d 705, 478 N.E.2d 1306 (1985). Contra, holding the statute, as applied, unconstitutionally vague: In re Doe, 123 N.H. 634, 465 A.2d 924 (1983).

Holding the statute constitutional when it provided that parental rights may be terminated when the parent is disabled from caring for the child through habitual intemperance or drug use: In re S. M., 39 Cal.App.3d 40, 113 Cal.Rptr. 847 (1974); In Interest of D. L. H., 198 Neb. 444, 253 N.W.2d 283 (1977).

Other cases are cited in Annot., 22 A.L.R.4th 774, 819 (1983).

29. E.g., Mass.Gen.L.Ann. c. 210, § 3(c) (1981), basing the presumption upon one year in the care of a public or private child care agency.

30. Washington County Dep't of Social Services v. Clark, 296 Md. 190, 461 A.2d 1077 (1983), 43 Md.L.Rev. 632 (1984); Petitions of Dep't of Social Services to Dispense with Consent to Adoption, 389 Mass. 793, 452 N.E.2d 497 (1983) (dictum); In re Laflure, 48 Mich.App. 377, 210 N.W.2d 482 (1973); Santosky v. Kramer, 455 U.S. 745, 102 S.Ct. 1388, 71 L.Ed.2d 599 (1982), on remand 89 A.D.2d 738, 453 N.Y.S.2d 942 (1982), appeal denied 58 N.Y.2d 605, 459 N.Y.S.2d 1029, 445 N.E.2d 656 (1983) held that clear and convincing evidence is constitutionally required in order to terminate parental rights. The case is discussed in section 20.2, supra.

31. In re Clark, 303 N.C. 592, 281 S.E.2d 47 (1981); Matter of J. F. C., 577 P.2d 1300 (Okl.1978).

fort from the large measure of agreement among courts that reasonable legislative attempts to define the circumstances in which parental rights may be terminated will not be held void for vagueness, pursuant to that vaguest of all constitutional principles. The interests of both parents and children are best served by an informed and sensitive judiciary operating under statutes giving them workable standards. No more than such standards can be expected from the legislatures. The search for ideal statutes which will produce perfect results in the hands of all courts in all circumstances is a waste of energy which might be better used in the training of judges.

WESTLAW REFERENCES

statute statutor! law legislat! /s vague! /s terminat! (cut cutting +3 off) /5 parent! /3 right

sy("due process" /s terminat! (cut cutting +3 off) /5 parent! /3 right) & 211k178 211k155 92k274(5) 92k82(10)

find 406 fsupp 10

sy(terminat! (cut cutting +3 off) /5 parent! /3 right /s clear /3 convincing) & santosky /s kramer

§ 20.6 Involuntary Termination of Parental Rights—Grounds

The statutes authorizing the involuntary termination of parental rights offer an alternative method of making children available for adoption when their parents refuse to consent, but they have other aspects and raise other issues as well. They enable the courts permanently to remove children from harmful parents or damaging environments, whether or not adoption is possible. If adoption is not immediately possible for such children, foster care is the usual resort of social workers. Although the majority of placement agencies are conscientious and diligent in their efforts to arrange care for the children committed to them, it is fashionable today to criticize foster care programs on a variety of grounds, primarily on the ground that they tend to shift children about from one foster home to another, thereby preventing the children from forming stable parental attachments and causing serious adverse effects on their psychological development.[1] This brings up the question whether or to what extent the courts are free to consider the child's best interests and the placement possibilities when terminating parental rights. Many courts continue to require exact proof of the statutory grounds for termination, refusing to terminate parental rights on the ground of the child's best interest, even though the refusal may often subject the child to instability, very poor home conditions, or life in a succession of foster homes.[2] Once parental rights have been terminated, the placement possibilities may be considered during the dispositional phase of the case.[3] On the other hand in some states parental rights may be terminated solely on the ground that this will serve the child's best

§ 20.6

1. Wald, State Intervention on Behalf of "Neglected" Children: A Search for Realistic Standards, 27 Stan.L. Rev. 985 (1975); Wald, State Intervention on Behalf of Neglected Children: Standards for Removal of Children from Their Homes, Monitoring the Status of Children in Foster Homes and Termination of Parental Rights, 28 Stan.L.Rev. 623 (1976); Mnookin, Child-Custody Adjudication: Judicial Functions in the Fact of Indeterminacy, 39 L. & Contemp.Prob. 226 (1975); Ketcham and Babcock, Statutory Standards for the Involuntary Termination of Parental Rights, 29 Rut.L.Rev. 530 (1976); Derdeyn, Rogoff, Williams, Alternatives to Absolute Termination of Parental Rights after Long-Term Foster Care, 31 Van.L. Rev. 1165 (1978); Garrison, Why Terminate Parental Rights? 35 Stan.L.Rev. 423 (1983). See also Smith v. Organization of Foster Families for Equality and Reform, 431 U.S. 816, 97 S.Ct. 2094, 53 L.Ed.2d 14 (1977). A graphic account of some instances of long term foster care and agency failure to place children for adoption occurs in the Wall Street Journal, September 9, 1978, page 1, column 1.

2. E.g., In re Hyatt's Adoption, 24 Ariz.App. 170, 536 P.2d 1062 (1975); Chancey v. Department of Human Resources, 156 Ga. 338, 274 S.E.2d 728 (1980) (parental rights not terminated although the two-year-old child had never been in the custody of its mother and there was no prospect that the mother could care for it); Matter of Yarber, 341 So.2d 108 (Miss.1977); Matter of Adoption of L., 61 N.Y.2d 420, 474 N.Y.S.2d 447, 462 N.E.2d 1165 (1984) (child returned to natural mother although proposed adoptive parents had had custody for all of its two years and the trial court found that return to the mother was contrary to the child's best interests); Interest of R. D. S., 259 N.W.2d 636 (N.D.1977); In Interest of C. E. W., 124 Wis.2d 47, 368 N.W.2d 47 (1985).

3. In Interest of C. E. W., 124 Wis.2d 47, 368 N.W.2d 47 (1985).

interests[4] or because the child has been in foster care for a long time[5] but even in these cases evidence of serious parental neglect or harm is usually found.[6] The close relationship between cases of this kind and the cases dealing with custody disputes between parents and non-parents is obvious.[7] In some cases courts may refuse to terminate parental rights for lack of evidence supporting the statutory grounds, but then award custody to a person who has cared for the child for a substantial period, the result being that the child lives with an adult who is psychologically and practically his parent but who cannot have the legal status of parent.[8] This state of the law is hardly in anyone's interest but it is the inevitable result of rigid insistence upon strict compliance with termination statutes.

The statutes which authorize the involuntary termination of parental rights are so varied that they are difficult to summarize. The difficulty is compounded by the endless variety of circumstances in which the parent-child relationship is played out. Although most of the statutes include in the grounds for termination only serious forms of parental misconduct, the courts exhibit wide divergences of approach to essentially similar statutes. Consequently the usual principles of stare decisis have less impact here than in cases where the conflicts are less emotional and the interests involved less complex. Still another source of difficulty in dealing with termination is the vast number of reported cases. Exhaustive citations are impossible in such circumstances. Citations will therefore be limited to those cases which reveal policy, illuminate analysis and illustrate factual diversity.

One further aspect of the termination cases must be emphasized. Particular conduct or omissions by a parent may often fall well within a reasonable construction of the termination statute, but a court may nevertheless refuse to terminate parental rights, choosing instead to order less drastic remedies, such as temporary custody, protective custody, counseling and help for the parent from whatever state agencies may be available.[9] In many of the reported cases these less drastic remedies will have been attempted and failed to succeed. For this reason the reported cases give a somewhat more rigid impression of the state's readiness to terminate rights than the actual practice in the state's agencies and trial courts would justify.

4. E.g., In re David C., 152 Cal.App.3d 1189, 200 Cal. Rptr. 115 (1984); Petition of R. H. N., 710 P.2d 482 (Colo. 1985) (stepparent adoption); Washington County Dep't of Social Services v. Clark, 296 Md. 190, 461 A.2d 1077 (1983); Adoption of a Minor, 378 Mass. 793, 389 N.E.2d 90 (1979). Other cases are cited in section 20.5, supra, at note 23. Such statutes are generally held constitutional.

5. E.g., Petition of Dep't of Public Welfare, 371 Mass. 651, 358 N.E.2d 794 (1976); Matter of J. R. Guardianship, 174 N.J.Super. 211, 416 A.2d 62 (1980); Matter of Roy, 90 Misc.2d 35, 393 N.Y.S.2d 515 (Fam.Ct.1977). See also West's Ann.Cal.Civ.Code § 232(7) (Supp.1987); N.Y.—McKinney's Soc.Serv.L. § 384–b 7(a) (1983).

6. E.g., Care and Protection of Three Minors, 392 Mass. 704, 467 N.E.2d 851 (1984); Jolliff v. Crabtree, 224 Va. 654, 299 S.E.2d 358 (1983) (withholding consent to adoption contrary to the child's best interests construed as requiring proof that it would be detrimental to the child).

7. See section 19.6, supra.

8. In the much cited case of Bennett v. Jeffreys, 40 N.Y.2d 543, 387 N.Y.S.2d 821, 356 N.E.2d 277 (1976), appeal after remand 59 A.D.2d 492, 399 N.Y.S.2d 697 (1977) the natural parent, fifteen years old, placed her newborn child with an older woman who cared for the child for eight years, after which the mother sued to reclaim custody. The New York Court of Appeals announced that a non-parent might be granted custody not only on the ground of abandonment, surrender, unfitness, neglect, but also for "other like extraordinary circumstances." This was thought to enlarge the circumstances in which a parent's "right" to custody might be lost, but later New York cases do not support that view. Christina L. v. James and Susan H., 115 Misc.2d 248, 454 N.Y.S.2d 379 (Fam.Ct.1982) refused to award custody to non-parents after the natural mother had consented to adoption but then changed her mind even though it found that such an award would be in the child's best interests, on the ground that the New York cases required that result. The case was affirmed in 95 A.D.2d 29, 465 N.Y.S.2d 6 (1st Dep't 1983), and in 61 N.Y.2d 420, 474 N.Y.S.2d 447, 462 N.E.2d 1165 (1984). Custody was ultimately awarded to the foster parent in the Bennett case. Bennett v. Marrow, 59 A.D.2d 492, 399 N.Y.2d 697 (2d Dep't 1977). See J. Goldstein, A. Freud, A. Solnit, Before the Best Interests of the Child 44, 45, 51, 224, 233 (1979).

9. E.g., Colo.Rev.Stat. §§ 19–3–111, 19–11–105(b) (1986); N.Y.—McKinney's Soc.Serv.L. § 384–b 7 (1983 and Supp.1987); Wis.Stat.Ann. § 48.425 (Supp.1986). See also In re M., 65 Ohio Misc. 7, 416 N.E.2d 669 (1979).

Child Abuse

Child abuse, at least where it is likely to be repeated or where the parents have not responded to counseling and assistance, clearly is and should be a ground for termination of parental rights.[10] Child abuse in this context means the infliction of serious physical harm on the child[11] and includes sexual molestation or abuse.[12] The abuse of one child in the family may justify the termination of parental rights of other children where it appears likely that they will also be abused.[13] In many instances child abuse may exist along with other grounds for terminating parental rights, such as neglect or unfitness.[14] The failure of one parent to protect the children from abuse by the other parent when such protection was realistically possible may lead the courts to terminate the parental rights of the non-abusing parent.[15] The fact that the child abuse was inflicted by a psychotic parent should not prevent parental rights from being terminated.[16]

Abandonment

Abandonment as such is a ground for the involuntary termination of parental rights in many states[17] and grounds resembling it are found in other states in somewhat different forms, such as failure to communicate with the child for a specified period[18] or as demonstrating a settled purpose of relinquishing his parental claim.[19] The lines of distinction between abandonment and the many forms of child neglect are often not very clear so that failure to support or to care for a child may sometimes be characterized as abandonment and sometimes as neglect.[20]

General definitions of abandonment have been advanced in many cases. In the abstract it signifies having the established intention to give up all parental rights and to avoid all parental obligations.[21] Although on rare occasions the parent makes this state of mind

---

10. In Interest of N. H., 383 N.W.2d 570 (Iowa 1986); Long v. Long, 255 N.W.2d 140 (Iowa 1977); Custody of Two Minors, 396 Mass. 610, 487 N.E.2d 1358 (1986); Interest of R. W. B., 241 N.W.2d 546 (N.D.1976) (child deprived).

11. New Jersey Division of Youth and Family Services v. Torres, 185 N.J.Co. 234, 447 A.2d 1372 (Juv. & Dom. Rel.Ct.1980), affirmed 185 N.J.Super. 182, 447 A.2d 1343 (1982).

12. In re Interest of Goodon, 208 Neb. 256, 303 N.W.2d 278 (1981) (sexual molestation by the father coupled with severe alcohol addiction, mother failed to protect the children); Annot., Sexual Abuse of Child By Parent as Ground for Termination of Parent's Right to Child, 58 A.L.R.3d 1074 (1974). Parental rights were terminated when the parents sold their twelve-year-old daughter into marriage with an older man in In Interest of Flynn, 22 Ill.App.3d 994, 318 N.E.2d 105 (1974). Some courts seem oddly reluctant to terminate parental rights on this ground. E.g., In re Involuntary Termination of Parental Rights, 449 Pa. 543, 297 A.2d 117 (1972) (mother pleaded guilty to the charge of accessory to the rape of one of her daughters, statute required repeated abuse); Robinette v. Keene, 2 Va.App. 578, 347 S.E.2d 156 (1986). Sexual molestation of an eight-year-old by her stepfather was held to be a ground for placing the child in the custody of the state where the child's mother planned to resume living with the stepfather, but the court remanded the case for findings on whether custody should remain with the state or be returned to the mother, in In Interest of K. B., 276 Pa.Super. 380, 419 A.2d 508 (1980).

13. People in Interest of C. R., 38 Colo.App. 252, 557 P.2d 1225 (1976); Custody of Two Minors, 396 Mass. 610, 487 N.E.2d 1358 (1986).

14. Champagne v. Welfare Division of Nevada State Dep't, 100 Nev. 640, 691 P.2d 849 (1984).

15. In re Brown, 86 Ill.2d 147, 56 Ill.Dec. 4, 427 N.E.2d 84 (1981); In Interest of Armentrout, 207 Kan. 366, 485 P.2d 183 (1971); Matter of MLM, 682 P.2d 982 (Wyo. 1984).

16. In re Theresa S., 196 Conn. 18, 491 A.2d 355 (1985).

17. E.g., Uniform Adoption Act §§ 6, 19, 9 Unif.L. Ann. 26, 51 (1979).

18. In re Male Child's Adoption, 56 Hawaii 412, 539 P.2d 467 (1975). See also West's Ann.Cal.Civ.Code § 232 (Supp.1987) creating a presumption of abandonment where there is a failure to communicate for six months. See Matter of Rose Lynn G., 57 Cal.App.3d 406, 129 Cal. Rptr. 338 (1976); In re Adoption of Oukes, 14 Cal.App.3d 459, 92 Cal.Rptr. 390 (1971).

19. Pa.Stat.Ann. tit. 23, § 2511(a)(1) (Supp.1986) (parent has for six months evidenced a settled purpose of relinquishing his parental claim); Matter of Adoption of David C., 479 Pa. 1, 387 A.2d 804 (1978).

20. E.g., Nada A. v. State, 660 P.2d 436 (Alaska 1983) (disregard of parental obligations is abandonment); Matter of S., 476 Pa. 138, 381 A.2d 1263 (1977). Matter of Anonymous, 40 N.Y.2d 96, 386 N.Y.S.2d 59, 351 N.E.2d 707 (1976) distinguishes the two grounds, finding that neglect is less strict in its evidentiary requirements.

21. Adoption of V. M. C., 528 P.2d 788 (Alaska 1974) (conscious disregard of parental obligations); Matter of Appeal in Pima County Severance Action No. S–1607, 147 Ariz. 237, 709 P.2d 871 (1985) (intentional conduct which evinces settled purpose to forego all parental duties and

explicit,[22] the courts must usually infer the intention from the parent's conduct.[23] As might be expected, the courts reach a variety of different results when they apply the standard definitions to specific states of fact. Where the parent consistently fails, over a substantial period of time, to communicate with the child, to support him, or to take any real interest in him, most courts will hold that this is sufficient basis for a finding of abandonment.[24] This result will normally be reached even though the parent's lack of attention to the child is attributable to the parent's mental illness, at least where there is no evidence that the illness is likely to re-spond to treatment in the foreseeable future.[25] On the other hand there are many cases in which the courts, out of what sometimes seems an excessive concern with biological relationships, find that no abandonment has occurred when the parent's contacts with his child have been intermittent, sporadic and seem to evince relatively little concern for the child's welfare.[26] The difficulty of deciding whether the contacts between natural parent and child have been sufficient to forestall a finding of abandonment are illustrated by the cases in which "a flicker of interest" by the natural parent is held sufficient for that pur-pose[27] and the contrast with very similar

relinquish all parental claims); In re Adoption of Childers, 441 N.E.2d 976 (Ind.App.1982) (same as in Arizona); In re Shannon R., 461 A.2d 707 (Me.1983) (abandonment must be "wilful"); In re Jessica B., 121 N.H. 291, 429 A.2d 320 (1981) (parents must have left child without provision for its identification or for support or for communication with the parent); Matter of Anonymous, 40 N.Y.2d 96, 386 N.Y.S.2d 59, 351 N.E.2d 707 (1976) (settled purpose to be rid of all parental obligations and to forego all parental rights); Pritchett v. Executive Director of Soc.Serv.Bd. of State of N.D., 325 N.W.2d 217 (N.D.1982) (must have an intent to abandon); In re Adoption of Holcomb, 18 Ohio St.3d 361, 481 N.E.2d 613 (1985) (failure to communicate with the child for one year without justifiable cause); In re A. M. B., 479 Pa. 193, 387 A.2d 1289 (1978) (settled purpose for six months of relinquishing parental claim to the child); Bevis v. Bevis, 254 S.C. 345, 175 S.E.2d 398 (1970) (voluntary act or conscious disregard of parental obligations); Matter of Voss' Adoption, 550 P.2d 481 (Wyo.1976) (wilful abandonment and nonsupport).

22. E.g., In re Adoption of "Anonymous", 71 Misc.2d 448, 336 N.Y.S.2d 364 (Sur.Ct.1972).

23. E.g., Nada A. v. State, 660 P.2d 436 (Alaska 1983); Matter of Appeal in Pima County Severance, 147 Ariz. 237, 709 P.2d 871 (1985).

24. Nada A. v. State, 660 P.2d 436 (Alaska 1983) (parent fled, leaving the child with a babysitter for eight and one-half months); Matter of Appeal in Pima County Severance Action No. S–1607, 147 Ariz. 237, 709 P.2d 871 (1985) (father visited son only five or six times in two years, contributed little to support); People in Interest of F. M., 44 Colo.App. 142, 609 P.2d 1123 (1980) (child "abandoned" to care of relatives); In re Adoption of Dove, 174 Ind.App. 464, 368 N.E.2d 6 (1977), rehearing denied 174 Ind.App. 464, 371 N.E.2d 387 (1978) (unjustifiable failure to communicate for more than a year); Ainsworth v. Natural Father, 414 So.2d 417 (Miss.1982) (disregard of child's welfare for more than three and one-half years, including failure to support); In re Adoption of W. B. L., 647 S.W.2d 531 (Mo.1983), affirmed 681 S.W.2d 452 (1984) (sporadic contacts with the child for a year and a half); Blunk v. Stuchlick, 185 Neb. 139, 174 N.W.2d 194 (1970)

(mother failed to provide food, shelter, or care for seven children); In re Jessica B., 121 N.H. 291, 429 A.2d 320 (1981) (mother made no attempt to communicate with the child for more than two years when living within thirty miles); In re K. W. V., 92 Misc.2d 292, 399 N.Y.S.2d 593 (Sur.Ct.1977) (long separation from the child and the child's attachment to the foster family); Pritchett v. Executive Director of Soc.Serv.Bd., 325 N.W.2d 217 (N.D.1982) (only slight communication for more than three years); Matter of Adoption of David C., 479 Pa. 1, 387 A.2d 804 (1978) (father had no contract with the child for several years); Matter of Kapcsos, 468 Pa. 50, 360 A.2d 174 (1976) (no contact with or interest in the child for eighteen months); In re Adoption of Battle, 456 Pa. 553, 321 A.2d 622 (1974) (mother had only sporadic contacts with the child for six years, then seized the child and kept her for two years); In re Adoption of Jagodzinski, 444 Pa. 511, 281 A.2d 868 (1971) (two and one-half years of no communication).

25. In re Wardship of B. C., 441 N.E.2d 208 (Ind.1982).

26. In re Adoption of Minor Child, 50 Hawaii 255, 438 P.2d 398 (1968) (father did not support the child, but sent cards and gifts); Matter of Burney, 259 N.W.2d 322 (Iowa 1977) (child left with mother's friends for two and one-half years, mother visited the child once or twice each month, sent him toys, clothing and some support); Matter of T. C. M., 651 S.W.2d 525 (Mo.App.1983) (stepparent adoption, mother did not abandon where she did not visit the children under some pressure from the father and his second wife); Adoption of R. A. B. v. R. A. B., 562 S.W.2d 356 (Mo.1978) (finding of abandonment reversed, numerous contacts between parent and children); Matter of Custody of Tricia Lashawnda M., 113 Misc.2d 287, 451 N.Y.S.2d 553 (Fam.Ct.1982), appeal dismissed 96 A.D.2d 1100, 467 N.Y.S.2d 71 (2d Dep't 1983) (extreme case, disapproved by the Appellate Division); Bevis v. Bevis, 254 S.C. 345, 175 S.E.2d 398 (1970) (stepmother sought to adopt, mother had continued to visit and call the children in spite of attempts of stepmother to frustrate these contacts).

27. Matter of Adoption of Goldman, 41 N.Y.2d 894, 393 N.Y.S.2d 989, 362 N.E.2d 619 (1977) (semble); W. v. G., 34 N.Y.2d 76, 356 N.Y.S.2d 34, 312 N.E.2d 171 (1974).

cases reaching the opposite result.[28] One situation in which most courts find that no abandonment has occurred is where the natural parent temporarily leaves the child with friends or relatives while he or she attempts to acquire the ability to care for the child, even where the child remains with the foster parents for a considerable time.[29] The courts also seem reluctant to make a finding of abandonment when a parent relinquishes the child and then within a relatively short time changes her mind and seeks to obtain custody of the child.[30]

The courts are divided on whether a parent's imprisonment, causing him to be unable to communicate with, or support, or care for the child justifies a holding that he has abandoned the child. The difference may lie in whether the parent uses whatever limited resources are available to him to keep in touch with his child. If he seems to do so, he may not be held to have abandoned the child.[31] If he does not, or if the prison term is a long

one, courts often find him guilty of abandonment.[32]

Abandonment, once it exists, is not cured by a single act of repentance, such as the payment of a sum for child support.[33] But there may be a defense to the charge of abandonment if the parent's attempts at maintaining contact with the child have been prevented by actions of the other parent.[34]

Neglect, Dependency, Deprivation, Nonsupport and Similar Grounds

Parental rights may also be terminated upon proof of various kinds of parental failure to care for children, described in a great variety of terms. The most common of such statutes refer to neglect, usually accompanied by some attempt at statutory definition,[35] but the term deprivation may be used[36] as well as nonsupport,[37] and dependent.[38] Although the statutory terms do vary, which sometimes leads to different results when they are applied to specific cases, there is a considerable

28. Corey L. v. Martin L., 45 N.Y.2d 383, 408 N.Y.S.2d 439, 380 N.E.2d 266 (1978) (controlled by a new statute). In re Shannon R., 461 A.2d 707 (Me.1983) rejected the flicker of interest test but held that abandonment had not been proved. See also In re A. M. B., 479 Pa. 193, 387 A.2d 1289 (1978), in which an evenly divided court had to affirm a finding of abandonment.

29. Adoption of V. M. C., 528 P.2d 788 (Alaska 1974); Solomon v. McLucas, 382 So.2d 339 (Fla.App.1980); Matter of Burney, 259 N.W.2d 322 (Iowa 1977); Matter of Interest of Worrell, 198 Neb. 507, 253 N.W.2d 843 (1977); In re Adoption of Wolfe, 454 Pa. 550, 312 A.2d 793 (1973); In re Adoption of Female Child X, 537 P.2d 719 (Wyo. 1975).

30. Meyers v. State, 124 Ga.App. 146, 183 S.E.2d 42 (1971) (revocation of consent within a few days); Hendricks v. Curry, 401 S.W.2d 796 (Tex.1966); In re Adoption of Baby Girl Fleming, 471 Pa. 73, 369 A.2d 1200 (1977) (revocation of consent after eighteen months); In re Adoption of R. W. B., 485 Pa. 168, 401 A.2d 347 (1979) (revocation after six months). In re R. R. R.'s Adoption, 18 Cal.App.3d 973, 96 Cal.Rptr. 308 (1971) held that where the parent consented to adoption by a relative this did not constitute an unconditional relinquishment sufficient to amount to abandonment and adoption by someone else.

31. Nada A. v. State, 660 P.2d 436 (Alaska 1983) (battered wife shot and killed her husband, dictum that abandonment is not wilful if due to incarceration); In re M. T. T.'s Adoption, 467 Pa. 88, 354 A.2d 564 (1976) (father did what he could to retain his rights); In re Adoption of Jameson, 20 Utah 2d 53, 432 P.2d 881 (1967) (abandonment not voluntary if caused by imprisonment). Moody v. Voorhies, 257 Or. 105, 475 P.2d 579 (1970) held

that abandonment was not voluntary when caused by confinement in a mental hospital.

32. In re Adoption of Baby Boy, 106 Ariz. 195, 472 P.2d 64 (1970) (child held dependent when mother was in prison); In re Staat, 287 Minn. 501, 178 N.W.2d 709 (1970) (imprisonment of itself is not abandonment, but may be combined with other evidence of neglect and withholding of affection); In Interest of F. H., 283 N.W.2d 202 (N.D.1979) (father abandoned the child before its birth by virtue of being incarcerated; abandonment may turn on incarceration plus other factors); In re Adoption of Infant Male M., 485 Pa. 77, 401 A.2d 301 (1979) (father made no attempt to fulfill parental duties); Hutson v. Haggard, 475 S.W.2d 330 (Tex.Civ.App.1971); Matter of Interest of Pawling, 101 Wash.2d 392, 679 P.2d 916 (1984) (imprisonment alone does not require a finding of abandonment, but may be combined with other factors).

33. In re Adoption of Searle, 83 N.C.App. 273, 346 S.E.2d 511 (1986); Abercrombie v. LaBoon, 290 S.C. 35, 348 S.E.2d 170 (1986).

34. Cocozza v. Antidormi, 35 A.D.2d 810, 316 N.Y.S.2d 471 (2d Dep't 1970); In re Adoption of Holcomb, 18 Ohio St.3d 361, 481 N.E.2d 613 (1985).

35. E.g., Alaska Stat. § 47.10.010 (1984); West's Ann. Cal.Civ.Code § 232(a)(2) (Supp.1987); N.Y.—McKinney's Soc.Serv.L. § 384–b 7 (1983, Supp.1987); Pa.Stat. tit. 23, § 2511(a) (Supp.1986).

36. McGurren v. S. T., 241 N.W.2d 690 (N.D.1976).

37. See Note, Termination of Parental Rights: Should Nonpayment of Child Support Be Enough? 67 Iowa L.Rev. 827 (1982).

38. Ill.—Smith Hurd Ann. ch. 37, § 702–5 (Supp.1987).

amount of agreement among the state courts in the approaches taken to neglect and its equivalents. As has been indicated,[39] there are also cases in which the kinds of facts which will support a finding of neglect are not very different from those which will support a finding of abandonment.

Since the concepts of neglect, deprivation or dependency are necessarily somewhat indeterminate, this creates the risk that children may be taken from their parents too readily and in violation of the parents' fundamental rights to family integrity so well established by the United States Supreme Court.[40] In order to minimize this risk, most state courts, in addition to adopting various procedural safeguards,[41] have insisted that the statutory grounds be clearly proved before parental rights may be terminated.[42] Thus a finding that the child's best interests will be promoted by the termination is not sufficient,[43] nor may the parent's rights be terminated on the grounds that the parent is poor or uneducated or that someone else could provide a better life for the child.[44] Even in those states whose statutes authorize termination on the ground of the child's best interests the courts require additional evidence that the continued custody of the parent will be detrimental

to the child.[45] The same reluctance to terminate parental rights is demonstrated by courts which find the child neglected or dependent but refuse to terminate parental rights,[46] or which refuse to terminate parental rights on the ground that the state agencies did not do enough to provide child care training for the parent.[47]

It is easy to state these principles, particularly in the broad ranging style favored by some courts, but it is quite another matter to apply them in a discriminating and sensitive spirit to specific states of fact.[48] The obvious danger is that unless they are applied in that spirit, serious and preventable harm may be inflicted upon the children. These cases do not present a simple conflict between the interests of parents and those of children. Since it is generally the case that the natural parents who have had the care of the child will best serve his interests unless there are strong indications to the contrary, to a substantial degree the parents' interests are often congruent with those of the child. The difficulty lies precisely in determining at what point this is no longer the case.

Not many courts venture to formulate a general definition of neglect or deprivation, since any definition is helpful only in the

---

39. See the discussion at note 20, supra.

40. See the cases cited in section 2.2, supra, and Stanley v. Illinois, 405 U.S. 645, 92 S.Ct. 1208, 31 L.Ed.2d 551 (1972).

41. See section 20.2, supra.

42. In re Juvenile Appeal, 177 Conn. 648, 420 A.2d 875 (1979); Matter of Welfare of Solomon, 291 N.W.2d 364 (Minn.1980); Petition of Linehan, 280 N.W.2d 29 (Minn.1979); Matter of Sanjivini K., 47 N.Y.2d 374, 418 N.Y.S.2d 339, 391 N.E.2d 1316 (1979); In re Cunningham, 59 Ohio St.2d 100, 391 N.E.2d 1034 (1979); In Interest of La Rue, 244 Pa.Super. 218, 366 A.2d 1271 (1976). It was thought at one time that Bennett v. Jeffreys, 40 N.Y.2d 543, 387 N.Y.S.2d 821, 356 N.E.2d 277 (1976), appeal after remand 59 A.D.2d 492, 399 N.Y.S.2d 697 (1977) signalled a willingness by the New York Court of Appeals to recognize that the child's best interests are superior to the parent's right to custody, but subsequent cases such as Sanjivini, supra, seem to have rejected that position at least where the issue is termination of parental rights, as distinguished from custody.

43. In Interest of La Rue, 244 Pa.Super. 218, 366 A.2d 1271 (1976) develops this idea at length, with emphasis on the parents' fundamental right to the custody of their children.

44. In re Hyatt's Adoption, 24 Ariz.App. 170, 536 P.2d 1062 (1975); In Interest of J. K. S., 274 N.W.2d 244 (N.D.1979); State in Interest of Baby Girl Marie, 561 P.2d 1046 (Utah 1977).

45. E.g., In re Baby Girl M., 37 Cal.3d 65, 207 Cal. Rptr. 309, 688 P.2d 918 (1984); In re Burrell, 58 Ohio St. 2d 37, 388 N.E.2d 738 (1979).

46. In re People in Interest of M. M., 184 Colo. 298, 520 P.2d 128 (1974), appeal after remand 188 Colo. 199, 533 P.2d 913 (1975); In Interest of M. N., 294 N.W.2d 635 (N.D.1980).

47. State in Interest of Walter B., 577 P.2d 119 (Utah 1978).

48. The point is illustrated by In re Adoption of Michael J. C., 326 Pa.Super. 143, 473 A.2d 1021 (1984), reversed 506 Pa. 517, 486 A.2d 371 (1984). Vigorous dissenting opinions were filed at both levels of this proceeding, showing that neither termination nor leaving the child with his mother was able to command complete agreement. The final result was the termination of the mother's parental rights, however. A case which seems to illustrate too great a readiness to terminate rights is In re Appeal in Maricopa County, Juv. Action No. J–75482, 111 Ariz. 588, 536 P.2d 197 (1975).

context of the specific case. It has been defined to mean the failure to exercise the care of the child which the circumstances fairly demand, including both wilful and unintentional failure.[49] It has also been characterized as the failure to meet the minimal standards of care in the community.[50] It is usually held that neglect implies that the conditions in which the child lives are not likely to improve in the future.[51] To a substantial degree the definition of neglect turns on the impact which the parent's conduct has had upon the child.[52] Although all of these elements must be taken into account, the nature and characteristics of neglect can only be understood by examining the cases in which parental rights have been terminated on this ground.

The most obvious forms of child neglect occur when the parent fails to provide for the child's elementary needs, either remaining away from the child altogether[53] or maintaining entirely inadequate or harmful living conditions.[54] In most such cases there is also a

finding that the parent's acts or omissions have seriously harmed the child, physically or psychologically.[55] The situation may be even more serious if the child is handicapped and therefore requires more care or more expert care than the normal child.[56] This does not mean that the courts should be in the business of holding parents to a high standard of housekeeping or child training and care.[57] It does mean that where the conditions of care are so inadequate or harmful that the child is presently suffering and that his future development is jeopardized, the court will find that the child is neglected. Evidence on these matters frequently includes the testimony of psychiatrists or psychologists which may be helpful but which should not be accepted as the final word in such cases[58] The charge is sometimes made that the courts in neglect cases are imposing middle class standards of child care upon parents in other classes of society having different standards of child care.[59] In some cases this may undoubtedly occur,[60] but the courts are generally able to

49. In re Stilley, 66 Ill.2d 515, 6 Ill.Dec. 873, 363 N.E.2d 820 (1977). In re Adoption of Brown, 22 Or.App. 219, 538 P.2d 1268 (1975) seems to say that the neglect must be intentional, deliberate or wilful, but this cannot be correct. Failure to give the child the minimum of care, resulting in serious harm to him cannot be excused on the ground that it was only negligent or unknowing.

50. In Interest of J. K. S., 274 N.W.2d 244 (N.D.1979). In some states neglect appears to be considered as synonymous with an even vaguer term, unfitness. In Interest of Bachelor, 211 Kan. 879, 508 P.2d 862 (1973).

51. Matter of L. F. G., 183 Mont. 239, 598 P.2d 1125 (1979); McGurren v. S. T., 241 N.W.2d 690 (N.D.1976); In re H., 206 N.W.2d 871 (N.D.1973).

52. New Jersey Division of Youth and Family Services v. A. W., 103 N.J. 591, 512 A.2d 438 (1986); McGurren v. S. T., 241 N.W.2d 690 (N.D.1976). ·

53. In Interest of Clouse, 244 Pa.Super. 396, 368 A.2d 780 (1976); Gonzalez v. Texas Department of Human Resources, 581 S.W.2d 522 (Tex.Civ.App.1979), cert. denied 445 U.S. 904, 100 S.Ct. 1079, 63 L.Ed.2d 319 (1980).

54. In re Stilley, 66 Ill.2d 515, 6 Ill.Dec. 873, 363 N.E.2d 820 (1977) (mother taking drugs); In Interest of J. K. S., 274 N.W.2d 244 (N.D.1979) (parental rights not terminated though child found deprived, mother unable to give the newborn adequate care); In Interest of C. and K., 322 N.W.2d 76 (Iowa 1982), appeal dismissed for want of a substantial federal question 459 U.S. 1094, 103 S.Ct. 711, 74 L.Ed.2d 942 (1983) (children living in unsanitary conditions, malnourished); In Interest of Bachelor, 211 Kan. 879, 508 P.2d 862 (1973) (child living in unhealthy conditions, subjected to some violence); In re Tricia and

Trixie H., 126 N.H. 418, 493 A.2d 1146 (1985) (parents refused to improve after counselling and assistance by state agencies; In Interest of Black, 273 Pa.Super. 536, 417 A.2d 1178 (1980) (newborn found deprived immediately after birth on the ground that parents' two previous children had died of neglect).

55. People in Interest of C. O., 36 Colo.App. 298, 541 P.2d 330 (1975) (failure to thrive); Adoption of Gregory, 23 Mass.App.Ct. 948, 501 N.E.2d 1179 (1986) (serious psychological effects on the children); Matter of D. H., 354 N.W.2d 185 (S.D.1984) (child exhibited serious emotional symptoms).

56. In Interest of M. N., 294 N.W.2d 635 (N.D.1980) (child required special education, found deprived but parental rights not terminated; father alcoholic, mother schizophrenic); In Interest of J. K. S., 274 N.W.2d 244 (N.D.1979) (child born prematurely and needed special care); In Interest of Pernishek, 268 Pa.Super. 447, 408 A.2d 872 (1979) (child a psychosocial dwarf, but parental rights not terminated); In re Aschauer's Welfare, 93 Wash.2d 689, 611 P.2d 1245 (1980) (children retarded and afflicted with psychosocial dwarfism).

57. Matter of Sherol A. S., 581 P.2d 884 (Okl.1978); DS and RS v. Department of Public Assistance and Social Services, 607 P.2d 911 (Wyo.1980).

58. In Interest of Winger, 558 P.2d 1311 (Utah 1976), refusing to rely on psychological findings, although the child's prospects did not look very promising.

59. See the materials cited in note 1, supra.

60. In re Appeal in Maricopa County, Juv. Action No. J–75482, 111 Ariz. 588, 536 P.2d 197 (1975) (semble). Of

distinguish between family conditions caused by poverty or by differences in customs based on racial or national origin and those harmful enough to constitute neglect.[61]

Even though a parent has shown a serious inability to meet the responsibilities of caring for his child, parental rights will often not be terminated if he shows affection for the child, and a willingness to become an acceptable parent.[62] In order to assist in this process many states require designated state agencies to develop a plan according to which such a parent might be helped to care for his child adequately before the courts are permitted to terminate parental rights. If the parent is unable to care for the child despite this assistance, then his parental rights may be terminated.[63] If the court finds that the agency did not provide sufficient assistance or an adequate plan, it may deny the termination petition on that ground,[64] on the assumption that greater diligence by the agency might succeed in giving the child a home with his natural parents. Likewise, termination should be denied where there is insufficient evidence that

the conditions which seem to harm the child are likely to continue indefinitely or for a long period.[65]

Neglect of a child is sometimes alleged on the ground that the child has been separated from his natural parent for a period. Where the period of separation has been extended and without justification on the part of the parent, parental rights will often be terminated.[66] Some courts seem extremely reluctant to terminate the parent's rights in such cases if token attempts at maintaining contact with the child have been made by the parent, at least where the child is in the custody of an agency.[67] A distinction should be made in these cases between the child who has been taken from his natural parents by a state or licensed private adoption agency and who has been in the care of foster parents on the one hand, and a child who has been cared for by relatives or who has been living with one natural parent and a stepparent on the other. In the second of these kinds of case the child has very likely been integrated into a new family on a permanent basis and the risk so

course one can find cases refusing to terminate parental rights which appear to give too little consideration to the child's interests. E.g., Matter of Yarber, 341 So.2d 108 (Miss.1977).

61. New Jersey Division of Youth and Family Services v. A. W., 103 N.J. 591, 512 A.2d 438 (1986) contains a thorough and thoughtful discussion of this question. See also In re Jertrude O., 56 Md.App. 83, 466 A.2d 885 (1983), cert. denied 298 Md. 309, 469 A.2d 863 (1984); Mcguire v. Brown, 580 S.W.2d 425 (Tex.Civ.App.1979) (semble).

62. Matter of Gerald G. G., 61 A.D.2d 521, 403 N.Y.S.2d 57 (2d Dep't.1978), appeal dismissed 46 N.Y.2d 1036, 416 N.Y.S.2d 586, 389 N.E.2d 1106 (1979); In re Adoption of Pyott, 475 Pa. 197, 380 A.2d 311 (1977).

63. In re Laura F., 33 Cal.3d 826, 191 Cal.Rptr. 464, 662 P.2d 922 (1983) (mother failed to cooperate with social work agencies); People in Interest of C. A. K., 652 P.2d 603 (Colo.1982) (mother unable to become a competent parent in spite of the plan; plan need not provide an express standard by success is to be measured); Petitions of Department of Soc. Serv. to Dispense with Consent to Adoption, 389 Mass. 793, 452 N.E.2d 497 (1983) (mother unable to cooperate with agency); Matter of J. L. B., 182 Mont. 100, 594 P.2d 1127 (1979) (mother unable to meet parental responsibilities even with agency assistance); Matter of Guardianship of Star Leslie W., 63 N.Y.2d 136, 481 N.Y.S.2d 26, 470 N.E.2d 824 (1984) (parent failed to cooperate with the agency); Matter of Ray A. M., 37 N.Y.2d 619, 376 N.Y.S.2d 431, 339 N.E.2d 135 (1975) (parent failed to comply with the plan); In re Adoption of

J. J., 511 Pa. 590, 515 A.2d 883 (1986) (parent failed to cooperate with the agency).

64. Matter of Jamie M., 63 N.Y.2d 388, 482 N.Y.S.2d 461, 472 N.E.2d 311 (1984); Matter of Sheila G., 61 N.Y.2d 368, 474 N.Y.S.2d 421, 462 N.E.2d 1139 (1984); Matter of Star A., 55 N.Y.2d 560, 450 N.Y.S.2d 465, 435 N.E.2d 1080 (1982); Matter of L. Children, 131 Misc.2d 81, 499 N.Y.S.2d 587 (Fam.Ct.1986).

65. People in Interest of E. A., 638 P.2d 278 (Colo. 1981); In Interest of R. D. S., 259 N.W.2d 636 (N.D.1977); In re H., 206 N.W.2d 871 (N.D.1973). Where the condition seems likely to continue, termination should be granted. Matter of Welfare of J. J. L. B., 394 N.W.2d 858 (Minn.App.1986).

66. E.g., People in Interest of C. S., 200 Colo. 213, 613 P.2d 1304 (1980); Petition of Dep't of Public Welfare To Dispense With Consent to Adoption, 383 Mass. 376, 419 N.E.2d 285 (1981) (six years in foster care); In re Interest of D., 218 Neb. 23, 352 N.W.2d 566 (1984) (three years in foster care); Petition of Lutheran Children and Family Service of Eastern Pennsylvania, 456 Pa. 429, 321 A.2d 618 (1974) (long foster care); State in Interest of P. L. L., 597 P.2d 886 (Utah 1979) (long foster care, child adoptable); Matter of Kegel, 85 Wis.2d 574, 271 N.W.2d 114 (1978).

67. Matter of Adoption of L., 61 N.Y.2d 420, 474 N.Y.S.2d 447, 462 N.E.2d 1165 (1984); Matter of Leon R R, 48 N.Y.2d 117, 421 N.Y.S.2d 863, 397 N.E.2d 374 (1979); In re Adoption of Pyott, 475 Pa. 197, 380 A.2d 311 (1977).

often alluded to by commentators of shifting about between foster homes does not exist.[68] In those circumstances the courts should be much more ready to terminate parental rights than in the foster care cases notwithstanding some contact between the natural parent and the child. These are common cases in times of high divorce rates and correspondingly high remarriage rates for younger spouses. Stepparents who form strong psychological attachments with the child in contrast with natural parents who provide only token amounts of support and contact should in such circumstances be permitted to legitimate their relationships with stepchildren by adoption.[69] A few states have statutes which are designed to achieve this result by providing that the consent of a parent to adoption is not necessary where he has been deprived of custody by divorce proceedings.[70] The courts have been generally unwilling to apply such statutes literally and usually require evidence that the non-custodial parent has failed to comply with support provisions of the decree or in other ways has failed in his parental obligations before they will terminate his parental rights.[71] This properly recognizes that the non-custodial parent continues to have interests in the child which are important both to himself and the child and which should not be cut off without continued and substantial failure to maintain the relationship with the child. In those cases in which the natural parent who becomes unable to care for his child places the child temporarily with a relative or friend, the courts usually hold that this does not constitute neglect, treating the situation as one in which the parent is caring for the child through the efforts of the friend or relative.[72] Arrangements of this kind may run on for quite long periods and leading to the formation of strong ties between the caretaker and the child, so that the court may ultimately be justified in terminating parental rights.[73]

Non-support

The failure to provide support for a child without justifiable cause for a specified period, usually a year, is made a ground for termination of parental rights by the statutes of many states.[74] This has been construed to mean that the court should look at the twelve-month period immediately preceding the adoption petition to determine whether support was withheld during that time as a whole.[75] Since this provision is often invoked to make possible an adoption by a stepparent, the courts in such cases are influenced by what appears to be the child's best interests in regularizing his relationship to the stepparent with whom he is living.[76] Where the

---

68. Matter of J. J. J., 718 P.2d 948 (Alaska 1986), requiring the natural parent to have maintained "meaningful" contact with the child and to have made regular support payments in order to block an adoption by a stepparent. The court discusses the stepparent adoption claim thoroughly and intelligently.

69. Matter of J. J. J., 718 P.2d 948 (Alaska 1986). See also Bodenheimer, New Trends and Requirements in Adoption Law and Proposals for Legislative Change, 49 S.Cal.L.Rev. 10, 44–46 (1975).

70. E.g., Or.Rev.Stat. § 109.314 (1984). Other statutes seeming to make possible the termination of parental rights on the ground of the child's best interests or without the consent of the non-custodial parent are cited in Note, A Survey of State Law Authorizing Stepparent Adoptions Without the Non-Custodial Parent's Consent, 15 Akron L.Rev. 567 (1982).

71. E.g., Moody v. Voorhies, 257 Or. 105, 475 P.2d 579 (1970).

72. Welfare Commissioner v. Anonymous, 33 Conn. Supp. 100, 364 A.2d 250 (1976); In re Howard, 468 Pa. 71, 360 A.2d 184 (1976); In re Adoption of Farabelli, 460 Pa. 423, 333 A.2d 846 (1975).

73. See In re Adoption of R. I., 468 Pa. 287, 361 A.2d 294 (1976), cert. denied 429 U.S. 1032, 97 S.Ct. 722, 50 L.Ed.2d 743 (1977).

74. E.g., Colo.Rev.Stat. § 19–4–107(e)(II) (1986); West's Ann.Ind.Stat. § 31–3–1–6(g)(1) (1980); Mont.Code Ann. § 40–8–111(1)(a)(v) (1985); Ohio Rev.Code § 3107.07(A) (Supp.1986); Okl.St.Ann. tit. 10, § 60.6 (Supp.1987). The Oklahoma statute was held constitutional in Matter of Adoption of Blevins, 695 P.2d 556 (Okl.App.1984). See also Note, Termination of Parental Rights: Should Nonpayment of Child Support Be Enough? 67 Iowa L.Rev. 827 (1982).

75. Petition of R. H. N., 710 P.2d 482 (Colo.1985). Contra, holding that any payments made during the immediately preceding year blocks the adoption: In re Adoption of Anthony, 5 Ohio App.3d 60, 449 N.E.2d 511 (1982); Wiley v. Spratlan, 543 S.W.2d 349 (Tex.1976).

76. Petition of R. H. N., 710 P.2d 482 (Colo.1985). But see Young v. Young, 174 Ind.App. 112, 366 N.E.2d 216 (1977).

termination of parental rights will result in an award of custody to an agency or to some other relative, the courts seem to apply the statutes in ways more favorable to the natural parent.[77]

All such statutes require proof that the failure to support occurred when the obligor was able to pay. Even if he was unable to pay an amount equal to an outstanding child support order, his rights may be terminated if he failed to pay what his means made possible.[78] Some courts also take into account what he was able to earn in distinction to his actual earnings.[79] It is not generally viewed as an excuse for non-payment that the other spouse refused to honor visitation rights,[80] or discouraged the payments from being made.[81]

Incarceration of the Natural Parent

The incarceration of a parent as an aspect of abandonment has been discussed earlier in this section.[82] The effect of imprisonment when other similar grounds for termination

are relied upon is similar. It is usually not of itself a reason to terminate parental rights, but it does not justify the parent in failing to do what he can to maintain contact with the child,[83] nor does it prevent the adoption when the parent is unable to provide any necessary care for the child.[84]

A few states have statutes which specifically make the parent's imprisonment a ground for termination of his parental rights, usually with qualifications concerning the term of imprisonment or the nature of the offense.[85] The former New York statute of this type has been held constitutional.[86]

Mental or Physical Illness of the Parent

Some states also have enacted statutes which authorize the courts to terminate parental rights when the parent's mental illness or mental retardation disables him from caring for his child.[87] Such statutes have been held constitutional.[88]

77. Eacret v. Dews, 10 Or.App. 511, 500 P.2d 481 (1972); Heard v. Bauman, 443 S.W.2d 715 (Tex.1969).

78. Petition of R. H. N., 710 P.2d 482 (Colo.1985); In re Adoption of Lay, 25 Ohio St.3d 41, 495 N.E.2d 9 (1986); In re Adoption of McDermitt, 63 Ohio St.3d 301, 408 N.E.2d 680 (1980).

79. Karkanen v. Valdesuso, 33 Colo.App. 47, 515 P.2d 128 (1973); Matter of Adoption of B. L. P., ___ Mont. ___, 728 P.2d 803 (1986).

80. Petition of R. H. N., 710 P.2d 482 (Colo.1985); Matter of Adoption of K. L. J. K., ___ Mont. ___, 730 P.2d 1135 (1986).

81. Kirkland v. Lee, 160 Ga.App. 446, 287 S.E.2d 365 (1981); In re Adoption of Infants Reynard, 252 Ind. 632, 251 N.E.2d 413 (1969). Contra: T. C. H. v. J. M. S., 190 Colo. 246, 545 P.2d 1357 (1976).

82. See the text at notes 31 and 32, supra. See also Note, On Prisons and Parenting: Preserving the Tie That Binds, 87 Yale L.J. 1408 (1978).

83. Matter of J. J. J., 718 P.2d 948 (Alaska 1986); In re Adoption of Baby Boy, 106 Ariz. 195, 472 P.2d 64 (1970); In Interest of Kester, 228 N.W.2d 107 (Iowa 1975); In re Randy Scott B., 511 A.2d 450 (Me.1986); Matter of Taurus F., 415 Mich. 512, 330 N.W.2d 33 (1982), dismissed for want of a substantial federal question 464 U.S. 1064, 104 S.Ct. 747, 79 L.Ed.2d 204 (1984). Other cases are cited in Annots., 79 A.L.R.3d 417 (1977) and 78 A.L.R.3d 712 (1977).

84. A. B. v. Arkansas Social Services, 273 Ark. 261, 620 S.W.2d 271 (1981); Petition of R. H. N., 710 P.2d 482 (Colo.1985); People in Interest of M. C. C., 641 P.2d 306 (Colo.App.1982); Matter of Herman's Adoption, 406

N.E.2d 277 (Ind.App.1980); In re Adoption of McCray, 460 Pa. 210, 331 A.2d 652 (1975).

85. E.g, West's Ann.Cal.Civ.Code § 232(a)(4) (Supp. 1987) (conviction of a felony where the crime shows unfitness); Colo.Rev.Stat. § 19–11–105(2)(g) (1986) (long term confinement of the parent); Or.Rev.Stat. § 109.322 (1985) (in prison not less than three years, where the child's welfare will be promoted by termination).

86. In re Anonymous, 79 Misc.2d 280, 359 N.Y.S.2d 738 (Sur.Ct.1974).

87. West's Ann.Cal.Civ.Code § 232(a)(5) (Supp.1987); Colo.Rev.Stat. § 19–11–105(2)(a) (1986); N.Y.—McKinney's Dom.Rel.L. § 111(2)(d) (Supp.1987); N.Y.—McKinney's Soc.Serv.L. § 384–b(4)(c) (1983); Or.Rev.Stat. § 109.322 (1985). These statutes were construed in In re Heidi T., 87 Cal.App.3d 864, 151 Cal.Rptr. 263 (1978); People in Interest of L. D., 671 P.2d 940 (Colo.1983); Matter of Hime Y., 52 N.Y.2d 242, 437 N.Y.S.2d 286, 418 N.E.2d 1305 (1981), on remand 81 A.D.2d 313, 440 N.Y.S. 2d 635 (1981), order affirmed 54 N.Y.2d 282, 445 N.Y.S.2d 114, 429 N.E.2d 792 (1981); Matter of Daniel A.D., 106 Misc.2d 370, 431 N.Y.S.2d 936 (Fam.Ct.1980). Termination of parental rights for this reason was denied in In re Carmaleta B., 21 Cal.3d 482, 146 Cal.Rptr. 623, 579 P.2d 514 (1978); Matter of Star A., 55 N.Y.2d 560, 450 N.Y.S.2d 465, 435 N.E.2d 1080 (1982) (state failed to provide care for the mother); Matter of Hime Y., 52 N.Y.2d 242, 437 N.Y.S.2d 286, 418 N.E.2d 1305 (1981), on remand 81 A.D.2d 313, 440 N.Y.S.2d 635 (1981), order affirmed 54 N.Y.2d 282, 445 N.Y.S.2d 114, 429 N.E.2d 792

88. See note 88 on page 903.

When a parent is unable to care for his child by reason of mental illness or mental retardation, most courts have held that this may constitute neglect or dependency, provided that the evidence demonstrates that the parent is not likely to become able to care for the child in the reasonable future. In such circumstances the parent's rights respecting the child may be terminated on one of those grounds.[89] The courts are much more reluctant to terminate parental rights when the parent's impaired capacity to care for the child results from physical rather than mental illness,[90] out of natural sympathy for the parent or from the lack of sufficient evidence that arrangements can be made to care for the child in the parent's home.

Unfitness, Depravity and Similar Grounds

Unfitness as a ground for the termination of parental rights is perhaps the least precise of all grounds and the most capable of confu-

sion with other grounds.[91] It has been said to connote a condition of the parent while neglect connotes a condition of the child, to require evidence indicating that the parent is unsuitable to continue the parental relationship,[92] surely a tautological definition if there ever was one. It has also been defined to mean that the return or continuance of the child in the care of his natural parents would be seriously detrimental to his welfare,[93] a definition which seems to equate unfitness with the test of the child's best interests.[94] Perhaps no better definition can be devised than that unfitness signifies active conduct by the parent which seriously and repeatedly harms the child either physically or psychologically. A definition in these terms enables unfitness to be applied to situations which justify termination without clearly fitting into the other statutory standards such as abandonment, neglect or non-support.

The applications of the unfitness standard in specific cases tend to bear out this defini-

(1981) (mother's inability to care for the child in the future not proved); Matter of Anderson, 35 Or.App. 561, 582 P.2d 29 (1978) (father's inability to care for his child in the future not proved, trial court's termination reversed).

The significance of these statutes is underlined by the rule that without statutory authority an incompetent person is incapable of giving consent to adoption just as he is incapable of other juridical acts. Annot., 45 A.L.R.2d 1379, 1381 (1956).

88. In re W., 29 Cal.App.3d 623, 105 Cal.Rptr. 736 (1972); People ex rel. Nabstedt v. Barger, 3 Ill.2d 511, 121 N.E.2d 781 (1954); In re Sylvia M., 82 A.D.2d 217, 443 N.Y.S.2d 214 (1st Dep't 1981), affirmed 57 N.Y.2d 636, 454 N.Y.S.2d 61, 439 N.E.2d 870 (1982).

89. In Interest of Love, 50 Ill.App.3d 1018, 9 Ill.Dec. 25, 366 N.E.2d 139 (1977); In Interest of Kerns, 225 Kan. 746, 594 P.2d 187 (1979); Matter of Welfare of J. J. B., 390 N.W.2d 274 (Minn.1986); Matter of L. F. G., 183 Mont. 239, 598 P.2d 1125 (1979); In re Kristopher B., 125 N.H. 678, 486 A.2d 277 (1984) (court emphasizes the psychological effect on the child); In Interest of R. L. D., 253 N.W.2d 870 (N.D.1977); In re Campbell, 13 Ohio App. 3d 34, 468 N.E.2d 93 (1983) (mother unable to care for a newborn child); In re Castillo, 632 P.2d 855 (Utah 1981); In re Rathburn, 128 Vt. 429, 266 A.2d 423 (1970); In re Welfare of Frederiksen, 25 Wash.App. 726, 610 P.2d 371 (1979).

Contra: Matter of J. N. M., 655 P.2d 1032 (Okl.1982); Matter of Baby Girl Williams, 602 P.2d 1036 (Okl.1979); Drake v. Drake, 8 Or.App. 57, 491 P.2d 1203 (1971). The court in Matter of Swartzfager, 290 Or. 799, 626 P.2d 882 (1981) refused to terminate parental rights in the face of persuasive evidence that the mother, suffering from lu-

pus erythematosus affecting her central nervous system, had not properly cared for her daughter and that the daughter had undergone psychological harm therefrom.

90. In re Michael G., 147 Cal.App.3d 56, 194 Cal.Rptr. 745 (1983); Leyva v. Brooks, 145 Ga.App. 619, 244 S.E.2d 119 (1978) (mother deaf and mute); Matter of McDuel, 142 Mich.App. 479, 369 N.W.2d 912 (1985) (multiple sclerosis).

91. See, e.g., Ill.—Smith Hurd Ann. ch. 40, §§ 1501, 1510 (Supp.1986), providing that consent to adoption is not needed if the parent is unfit and defining unfit to include abandonment, neglect, child abuse and nearly all other possible bases for terminating parental rights. One case has held that if unfitness is not listed as a ground in the statute, it may not be relied upon. Ricky Ralph M. v. Onondaga County Department of Social Services, 56 N.Y. 2d 77, 451 N.Y.S.2d 41, 436 N.E.2d 491 (1982).

92. Champagne v. Welfare Division of Nevada State Dep't. of Human Resources, 100 Neb. 640, 691 P.2d 849 (1984).

93. Petition of Department of Public Welfare to Dispense With Consent to Adoption, 383 Mass. 573, 421 N.E.2d 28 (1981); Custody of a Minor, 383 Mass. 595, 421 N.E.2d 63 (1981).

94. Mass.Gen. Laws Ann. ch. 210, § 3(a)(ii), (c) (1981 and Supp.1986) provides that consent to adoption is not required if allowance of the adoption is in the child's best interests, and that the fitness of the parents should be considered in determining the child's best interests. But see Care and Protection of Three Minors, 392 Mass. 704, 467 N.E.2d 851 (1984) in which the court seems at pains to distinguish between unfitness and the child's welfare.

tion. They include those cases in which the parent lives a disorganized, violent, life, harmful to the child, sometimes involving periods of neglect or abuse.[95] The habitual use of alcohol and drugs, often combined with violence toward the child may constitute unfitness.[96] But minor faults of parenting or the choice of unusual ways of living not harmful to the child do not amount to unfitness.[97]

Criminal violence not directed against the child may be held to justify the termination of parental rights, either on the ground of unfitness or of some other statutory standard. The clearest cases are those surprisingly common ones in which the child's father kills the child's mother,[98] sometimes in circumstances of shocking brutality.[99] A few courts have held that this conduct does not support a finding of unfitness, however.[1] When the criminal conduct is not directed against either the child or another parent, the cases generally hold that it is not sufficient to warrant termination of parental rights.[2]

The claim is occasionally made that various kinds of sexual immorality are indications of unfitness which should lead the courts to terminate parental rights. Such claims are usually rejected for a variety of reasons, either because they do not fit within the existing statutory grounds for termination,[3] or that the alleged immorality does not affect the parent's competence in child care.[4]

95. E.g., In Interest of Dixon, 81 Ill.App.3d 493, 36 Ill. Dec. 750, 401 N.E.2d 591 (1980); Petition of the Catholic Charitable Bureau of the Archdiocese of Boston, 395 Mass. 180, 479 N.E.2d 148 (1985); Care and Protection of Three Minors, 392 Mass. 704, 467 N.E.2d 851 (1984); Custody of a Minor, 383 Mass. 595, 421 N.E.2d 63 (1981); Champagne v. Welfare Division of the Nevada State Department of Human Resources, 100 Nev. 640, 691 P.2d 849 (1984); Matter of Adoption of RHA, 702 P.2d 1259 (Wyo.1985) (father convicted of incest, taking indecent liberties and sexual relations, all with his twelve-year-old daughter). Compare In re Harpman, 146 Ill.App.3d 504, 100 Ill.Dec. 177, 496 N.E.2d 1242 (1986).

96. In re Interest of Brungardt, 211 Neb. 519, 319 N.W.2d 109 (1982); In re Adoption of Michael J. C., 506 Pa. 517, 486 A.2d 371 (1984); Matter of Welfare of Tarango, 23 Wash.App. 126, 595 P.2d 552 (1979).

97. Paul v. Steele, 101 Ill.2d 345, 78 Ill.Dec. 149, 461 N.E.2d 983 (1984); Department of Public Welfare to Dispense With Consent to Adoption, 383 Mass. 573, 421 N.E.2d 28 (1981).

98. In re Geoffrey G., 93 Cal.App.3d 412, 159 Cal.Rptr. 460 (1979); Turner v. Adoption of Turner, 352 So.2d 957 (Fla.App.1977); Brown v. Department of Human Resources, 157 Ga.App. 106, 276 S.E.2d 155 (1981); Matter of Mudge, 116 Mich.App. 159, 321 N.W.2d 878 (1982); In re Interest of Ditter, 212 Neb. 279, 322 N.W.2d 642 (1982); Matter of B. A. M., 290 N.W.2d 498 (S.D.1980); Adoption of Bowling v. Bowling, 631 S.W.2d 386 (Tenn.1982); In Interest of B. J. B., 546 S.W.2d 674 (Tex.Civ.App.1977); In re Sego, 82 Wash.2d 736, 513 P.2d 831 (1973).

99. In re Juvenile Appeal (84–6), 2 Conn.App. 705, 483 A.2d 1101 (1984), certification denied 195 Conn. 801, 487 A.2d 564 (1985) (father stabbed mother in the presence of the child); In re Abdullah, 85 Ill.2d 300, 53 Ill.Dec. 246, 423 N.E.2d 915 (1981).

1. Bryant v. Lenza, 90 Ill.App.3d 275, 45 Ill.Dec. 572, 412 N.E.2d 1154 (1980); Interest of Jones, 34 Ill.App.3d 603, 340 N.E.2d 269 (1975); Matter of Adoption of J. by J., 73 N.J. 68, 372 A.2d 607 (1977), reversing In re Adoption of J, 139 N.J.Super. 533, 354 A.2d 662 (1976).

2. Petition of Boston Children's Service Association, 20 Mass.App.Ct. 566, 481 N.E.2d 516 (1985), review denied 397 Mass. 1102, 484 N.E.2d 102 (1985) (mother convicted of first degree murder but made arrangements for the care of her children); Boyd v. Texas Department of Human Services, 715 S.W.2d 711 (Tex.App.1986) (burglary convictions did not "endanger" the child under the statute). But In Interest of M. B. C., 125 Ill.App.3d 512, 80 Ill.Dec. 821, 466 N.E.2d 273 (1984), appeal dismissed 471 U.S. 1062, 105 S.Ct. 2129, 85 L.Ed.2d 493 (1985) held that convictions for armed robbery, rape, deviate sexual assault and intimidation were sufficient to constitute "depravity" under the statute and that this ground for termination was not unconstitutionally vague. A case which found depravity on very dubious evidence is Tiernan v. Stewart, 33 Ill.App.3d 545, 338 N.E.2d 153 (1975).

3. S. J. v. L. T., 727 P.2d 789 (Alaska 1986) (refuses to terminate parental rights of a stepfather whose child was conceived by intercourse with his fifteen-year-old stepdaughter either because it was not proved that this was criminal, or because this ground was not provided for in the statute); Johnson v. Eidson, 235 Ga. 820, 221 S.E.2d 813 (1976), on remand 137 Ga.App. 595, 224 S.E.2d 518 (1976) (moral unfitness is not "abandonment" under the statute); Matter of Adoption of W., 573 P.2d 1290 (Utah 1978) (refuses to terminate parental rights on the ground that the child was conceived in a criminal relationship, but does so on the ground that the father failed to show any interest in the child).

But Daly v. Daly, ___ Nev. ___, 715 P.2d 56 (1986), cert. denied ___ U.S. ___, 107 S.Ct. 250, 93 L.Ed.2d 176 (1986) terminated a father's parental rights on the ground he had undergone a sex change.

4. In re Burrell, 58 Ohio St.2d 37, 388 N.E.2d 738 (1979), 40 Ohio St.L.J. 1017 (1979) (child's mother living with her boy friend, no evidence of detriment to the child); Doe v. Doe, 222 Va. 736, 284 S.E.2d 799 (1981) (refuses to terminate parental rights of lesbian mother on the ground she was in all respects a good mother).

Best Interests of the Child

As has been indicated,[5] the statutes in some states provide that a parent's rights respecting his child may be terminated when that is required in order to serve the child's best interests. This might seem to create the risk that the courts are being authorized to take children away from their parents on relatively insubstantial grounds, or where their removal would give them material or educational advantages. The Massachusetts cases have shown that this need not occur. They have held that there is a strong component of unfitness in determining what the child's best interests demand.[6] Most commonly they have terminated parental rights on this ground where the child has been in foster care for a substantial period and the parent has developed no realistic plan for caring for him.[7]

Defenses

Although, as has been shown,[8] failure to make support payments is not excused by interference with visitation rights, at least some cases have held that a deliberate and effective attempt by a child's custodian or relatives to prevent the other parent from communicating with the child will operate as a defense to the termination of that parent's rights.[9] Removal of the child from the state and successfully frustrating the parent's desire to locate the child may have the same effect.[10] On the other hand a parent's belated attempts to see or communicate with the child after a statutory period of neglect has run will not normally be a defense to the termination of parental rights.[11]

5. See the text at notes 4, 5 and 6, supra.

6. Petition of New England Home for Little Wanderers, 367 Mass. 631, 328 N.E.2d 854 (1975).

7. Compare Custody of a Minor (No. 2), 392 Mass. 719, 467 N.E.2d 1286 (1984) with Petition of the Department of Public Welfare to Dispense with Consent to Adoption, 371 Mass. 651, 358 N.E.2d 794 (1976).

8. See the text at notes 80, 81, supra.

9. In re Adoption of B. D. S., 494 Pa. 171, 431 A.2d 203 (1981); In re D. J. Y., 487 Pa. 125, 408 N.E.2d 1387 (1979).

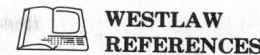

WESTLAW REFERENCES

Child Abuse

di(child infant minor /5 abus! /s ground! base* basis basing /s terminat! (cut cutting +3 off) /s parent! /s right)

Abandonment

211k157 211k180 /p willful! inten!

Neglect, Dependency, Deprivation, Non-Support and Similar Grounds

211k156 211k179 /p depriv! /s terminat! (cut cutting +3 off) /s parent! /s right entitl!

Non-Support

non-support (fail*** lack*** /3 support!) /s ground** base* basis basing /s terminat! (cut cutting +3 off) /s parent** /s right entitl!

Incarceration of the Natural Parent

211k157 211k178 211k180 /p incarcerat! imprison! prison jail! /s terminat! (cut cutting +3 off) /s parent! /s right

Unfitness, Depravity and Similar Grounds

parent! /s unfit! /s habitual! /s dr*nk! drug alcohol narcotic "controlled substance"

ti(doe +s doe) & lesbian!

Defenses

defense /s terminat! (cut cutting +3 off) /s parent! /s entitl! right

§ 20.7 Adoption—The Placement Process

In General

When once it has been determined that a child is eligible for adoption, either because the appropriate person or agency has consented, or because parental rights have been involuntarily terminated, the next step in the process of adoption is the establishment of the child's relationship with the adoptive parents. This step may occur in the same hearing which made him eligible for adoption so that

10. D. A. v. D. R. L., 727 P.2d 768 (Alaska 1986); In re Adoption of Brown, 22 Or.App. 219, 538 P.2d 1268 (1975). Contra: Brown v. Johnson, 10 Ark.App. 110, 661 S.W.2d 443 (1983); Dodson v. Donaldson, 10 Ark.App. 64, 661 S.W.2d 425 (1983); In re Adoption of Faith M., 509 Pa. 238, 501 A.2d 1105 (1985).

11. In re Adoption of J. J., 511 Pa. 590, 515 A.2d 883 (1986).

the two steps may be taken together. Or it may occur at a later time as a result of subsequent legal proceedings. The timing and method of placement depend upon the relationships of the parties, upon the method of placement and of course upon the governing law in the particular state.

An important distinction must be made concerning the method of placement. The child may be placed for adoption by a licensed private or public child placing agency, in which case the process is referred to as an agency placement. When the child is placed for adoption by his parents or by some other private individual, this is called a private placement or an independent placement.[1] A large proportion of private placements occur when the child is adopted by relatives or by a stepparent.[2] These cases raise few problems, not merely because of the relationship between the child and the adoptive parents, but also because the adoption usually has the effect of giving legal status to an already existing de facto relationship.[3] The child in such cases has usually been living with the adoptive parent for some time and there is thus every reason to grant the adoption decree.

Other private placements may not be of this type, however.[4] They occur when the parent picks out a person with whom he wishes to place the child or more commonly when a lawyer or physician brings parent and adoptive parents together or in some cases actually makes the placement. Usually in such cases no very extensive or thorough investigation of the adoptive parents is made by the individual arranging the placement.[5] As has been indicated [6] the laws of some states require agency investigations and reports in all adoption cases including private placements. Although pursuant to such laws the private placement may be scrutinized by an agency, the placement having been made, the investigation may be more limited than if the agency had made the placement.[7] For that reason and because of the risk that private placements may award the child to unsuitable adoptive parents, some states have enacted "Baby Broker Acts" forbidding private placements by persons other than licensed agencies, with exceptions for the natural parents, certain relatives and stepparents.[8] Such statutes carry criminal penalties and have been held to be constitutional.[9] But a violation of this statute may not be the basis for denying a decree of adoption if the prospective adoptive parents are found to be in all respects suitable and able to care for the child.[10] Private placements may also be objectionable on

§ 20.7

1. Witmer, Herzog, Weinstein, Sullivan, Independent Adoptions 15 (1963).

2. For adoption statistics see section 20.1, supra.

3. Children's Bureau Publication No. 394–1961, 23 which would allow non-agency placements with relatives or stepparents.

4. I Schapiro, A Study of Adoption Practice 109 (1956).

5. Witmer, Herzog, Weinstein, Sullivan, Independent Adoptions 91–100 (1963).

6. See section 21.4, Practitioner's Edition; Commonwealth Dep't of Child Welfare v. Lorenz, 407 S.W.2d 699 (Ky.1966); I Schapiro, A Study of Adoption Practice 110–112 (1956); Colby, Problems and Procedures in Adoption, Children's Bureau Publication No. 262 (1940).

7. I Schapiro, A Study of Adoption Practice 112–116 (1956).

8. E.g., Ill.—Smith Hurd Ann. ch. 40, §§ 1701, 1702, 1703, 1704 (1980), forbidding the "placing out" of children for compensation by persons other than adoption agencies. "Placing out" is defined as arranging for free care of a child for the purpose of adoption. The statute excepts placements with parents, stepparents, brothers,

sisters, aunts, uncles, grandparents and legal guardians of the child. Similar statutes are N.J.Stat.Ann. § 9:3–39 (Supp.1986); N.Y.—McKinney's Soc.Serv.L. §§ 371(12), 374(2) (1983). See also Montana Department of Social and Rehabilitation Services v. Angel, 176 Mont. 293, 577 P.2d 1223 (1978).

9. State v. Schwartz, 64 Ill.2d 275, 1 Ill.Dec. 8, 356 N.E.2d 8 (1976), cert. denied 429 U.S. 1098, 97 S.Ct. 1116, 51 L.Ed.2d 545 (1977); Annot., Criminal Liability of One Arranging for Adoption of Child Through Other Than Licensed Child Placement Agency ("Baby Broker Acts"), 3 A.L.R.4th 468 (1981). Under the law of some states the statutes may forbid advertising of private placements. Cal.Civ.Code § 224p (1982). And lawyers procuring children for private placement adoptions may be subject to discipline. Matter of Mountain, 239 Kan. 412, 721 P.2d 264 (1986). The proper role of the lawyer in a private placement is described in Carsola, Lewis, Independent Adoptions: An Alternative for Adoptive Parents, 9 Fam. L. Reporter 4019 (1983).

10. Matter of Adoption of a Child By I. T., 164 N.J. Super. 476, 397 A.2d 341 (1978), relying in part on the argument that unclean hands should have no part in such a decision. See also Matter of Adoption of a Child by N. P., 165 N.J.Super. 591, 398 A.2d 937 (1979).

the ground that they do not preserve the anonymity of both natural parents and adoptive parents which the policy of many states finds desirable as a means of ensuring the completeness and finality of the child's integration into his new family.[11] They may also fail to provide the sort of counseling for the natural parent which an agency might provide, thereby perhaps increasing the possibility that the natural parent might change her mind and seek to revoke her consent.[12]

For all these reasons many social workers experienced in adoption work advocate laws requiring all adoption placements other than those with close relatives to be made through adoption agencies.[13] On the other hand, in periods when adoptable children are in such short supply that childless couples seeking to adopt face long waiting lists in adoption agencies, often without any realistic likelihood of receiving a child, the private placement alternative also has its advocates.[14] This view is reinforced by the opinion held by some authorities that adoption agencies tend to follow too rigid and narrow rules in approving adoptions and that exclusive reliance upon agency placements prevents the adoption of many

children for whom suitable homes might be found.[15] These arguments have led some agencies to revise their rules and procedures and to make a greater effort to place children who were formerly thought not to be adoptable.[16]

When the adoption placement is made by an agency, of necessity courts and agencies must cooperate.[17] Neither can function effectively without the help and understanding of the other. The agency and indeed other community organizations are as significant participants in the adoption process as the courts or lawyers.[18] Agency services cannot be described in detail here, but in general they consist of investigations and evaluations by trained persons of the child, his natural parents, and the adoptive parents, with the goal of making the best possible placement for the child.[19] In addition the agencies offer counseling services to the natural parents (particularly to the unmarried mother) to help in the decision on relinquishment of the child for adoption, and to the adoptive parents before and after the adoption to prepare them for their newly assumed rule as parents.[20]

---

11. See Petition of the Department of Social Services to Dispense With Consent to Adoption, 384 Mass. 707, 429 N.E.2d 685 (1981).

12. See the private placement procedure outlined in Matter of Anonymous (G.), 89 Misc.2d 514, 393 N.Y.S.2d 900 (1977). These and other risks of private placements are discussed in Rocky Mountain Adoption Ethics Committee, Family Law Newsletter, 11 Colo. Lawyer 641 (1974).

13. Children's Bureau Publication No. 394–1961, 23. For a description of the methods of inspection and licensing for adoption agencies see I Schapiro, A Study of Adoption Practice 19–40 (1956). See also section 20.1, supra, at notes 25, 26.

14. Charney, The Rebirth of Private Adoptions, 71 A.B.A.J. 52 (1985); Carsola and Lewis, Independent Adoptions: An Alternative for Adoptive Parents, 9 Fam.L. Reporter 4019 (1983).

15. Cole, Advocating for Adoption Services, in M. Hardin, D. Dodson, Foster Children in the Courts 455–469 (1983); Isaac, Children Who Need Adoption, The Atlantic Monthly November 1963, 45; P. Buck, Children for Adoption Ch. IX (1965); Witmer, Herzog, Weinstein, Sullivan, Independent Adoptions Ch. XIV (1963). See also Child Welfare League of America, Standards for Adoption Services (1978).

16. Cole, Advocating for Adoption Services, in M. Hardin, D. Dodson, Foster Children in the Courts Ch. 18

(1983); The Wall Street Journal, January 9, 1970, page 1, col. 1.

17. Elson and Elson, Lawyers and Adoption: The Lawyer's Responsibility in Perspective, 41 A.B.A.J. 1125 (1955); National Conference of Lawyers and Social Workers, Responsibilities and Reciprocal Relationships in Adoption-Lawyer and Social Worker (1965); Duquette, Collaboration Between Lawyers and Mental Health Professionals: Making It Work, in M. Hardin, D. Dodson, Foster Children in the Courts Ch. 19 (1983).

18. Katz, Community Decision-Makers and the Promotion of Values in the Adoption of Children, 4 J.Fam.L. 7 (1964); Schapiro, A Study of Adoption Practice, passim.

19. Cole, Advocating for Adoption Services, in M. Hardin, D. Dodson, Foster Children in the Courts 456–488 (1983); I. Smith, Readings in Adoption Ch. 1, 2, 9–21 (1963); I Schapiro, A Study of Adoption Practice Ch. V, VI, VII (1956). The federal government has provided for assistance to the states in these respects by the Adoption Assistance and Child Welfare Act of 1980, 42 U.S.C.A. §§ 670 ff. This Act is summarized and discussed in National Legal Resource Center for Child Advocacy and Protection, Protecting Children Through the Legal System 769–823 (1981).

20. I. Smith, Readings in Adoption Ch. 4, 7, 23, 28, 32 (1963); I Schapiro, A Study of Adoption Practice 46–48, 86–89 (1956).

Legal Regulation of Placement—In General

Adoption statutes contain surprisingly few restrictions on the persons eligible to receive children for adoption. These usually include only the requirement that they be adults, that, if married, both husband and wife join in the petition to adopt, and in a few states residence and age restrictions.[21] But these statutes allow an unmarried person to adopt a child.[22] Presumably the reason for the absence of qualifications in the statutes is the intention to rely upon adoption agencies, either as part of the placement process itself or in investigating and making recommendations to the courts, to screen out the unsuitable adoptive parents. Since particular adoption agencies may have many standards or rules of thumb respecting the qualifications of prospective adoptive parents,[23] this gives the agencies considerable legal power over the grant or denial of adoptions. The agency's

refusal to place a child with prospective adoptive parents, although it may theoretically be reviewable by the courts,[24] as a practical matter will seldom be challenged. People in this situation must undertake the risks and uncertainty of a private placement if it is permitted in the jurisdiction, and even then may have to face an adverse agency recommendation to which the court in the adoption proceeding will give some weight. The difficult position in which this places the would-be adoptive parent is not much ameliorated by the legal rule that ultimately the adoption decision rests in the sound discretion of the trial court as guided and informed by the agency's report.[25]

What then are the agencies' rules? In the first place they vary from state to state, but judging from the non-legal literature certain rules prevail in most places. Perhaps "rules" is too strong a word, and it might be better to

---

21. E.g., Ala.Code 1986, § 26–10–1; Alaska Stat. § 25.23.020 (1983); West's Ann.Cal.Civ.Code § 222 (1982) (adoptive parent must be ten years older than the child); Conn.Gen.Stat.Ann. § 45–62 (1981); Del.Code tit. 13, § 903 (1981) (must be a resident of the state); Ill.—Smith Hurd Ann. ch. 40, § 1502 (Supp.1986) (must be a resident, reputable person of legal age, or minor by leave of court); N.J.Stat.Ann. § 9:3–43 (Supp.1986) (must be ten years older than the child); N.Y.—McKinney's Dom.Rel.L. § 110 (Supp.1987); Ohio Rev.Code § 3107.03 (1980); Wis. Stat.Ann. § 48.82 (Supp.1986) (must be a resident). But the Massachusetts statute requires the judge to consider the needs of the child for loving and responsible parental care and all factors relevant to physical, mental and moral health of the child. Mass.Gen.Laws Ann. ch. 210, § 5B (1981).

22. The fact that the statute permits an unmarried person to adopt does not mean that an agency or a court would approve such a placement in a specific case, however. See Annot., Marital Status of Prospective Adoptive Parents as Factor in Adoption Proceedings, 2 A.L.R.4th 555 (1980).

23. Cole, Advocating for Adoption Services, in M. Hardin, D. Dodson, Foster Children in the Courts 463–469 (1983), suggesting among other points that the criteria are subjective. See also Child Welfare League of America, Standards for Adoption Service 43–48 (1968), listing a large number of criteria, many of them quite vague.

24. Of course in a jurisdiction which takes the position that the agency's denial of consent to adoption is conclusive, no review would be available. But in states where the courts may override the agency's denial of consent (vide section 20.4, supra) the prospective adoptive parent should be able to bring a declaratory judgment

suit if the agency refuses to consider him eligible for placement. This is clearly a "case of actual controversy" under 28 U.S.C.A. § 2201 or other similarly worded declaratory judgment statutes. The suit constitutes a petition for judicial review of the action of an administrative agency. 4 K. Davis, Administrative Law Treatise §§ 23:6, 24:2, 24:3 (2d ed.1983); E. Borchard, Declaratory Judgments 896–899 (2d ed.1941). It would at least require the agency to give the prospective adoptive parent a hearing and set forth its reasons for rejecting him, and if the reasons were arbitrary or amounted to an abuse of discretion the court could so declare. See, for example, In re Adoption of Barnett, 54 Cal.2d 370, 6 Cal.Rptr. 562, 354 P.2d 18 (1960), in which the court held that the agency rule against adoption by single persons was not to be followed in the particular circumstances; Fleming v. Hursh, 271 Minn. 337, 136 N.W.2d 109 (1965) which held foster parents entitled to a hearing on an agency's refusal of consent; and Rockefeller v. Nickerson, 36 Misc.2d 869, 233 N.Y.S.2d 314 (1962), which denied mandamus where the plaintiffs asked that the Commissioner of Welfare be directed to accept their petition to adopt a negro child. But denial was on the ground that the Commissioner's refusal was not arbitrary, thus implicitly recognizing that there was a remedy. In re Cooper, 17 Utah 2d 296, 410 P.2d 475 (1966) implicitly recognized the foster parents' standing to sue. Conceivably a court might hold that the existence of private placement prevents the agency's refusal from causing irreparable injury, but this does not seem justified by the practicalities of the situation. See also Note, Judicial Review of Adoption Agency Decisions, 25 Case W.Res.L.Rev. 650 (1975).

25. Appeal in Pima County Juvenile Action B–10489, 151 Ariz. 335, 727 P.2d 830 (App.1986).

refer to "standards",[26] although in social work as in other activities standards and principles tend to harden into rules. Most agencies impose, as requirements for eligibility to adopt, physical and emotional health, that the petitioners be married, some evidence of financial stability and that the petitioners be below a certain maximum age.[27] Other facts considered by some agencies include length of marriage, infertility, legal residence, citizenship, minimum age, race and religion.[28] In addition to these rather specific matters the agencies also look at such intangibles as the motives of the petitioners, and their capacity for parenthood.[29] It is generally considered important to match the child with the adoptive parents, which of course brings into play a large number of other intangible factors such as level of intelligence, temperament, cultural background, and physical resemblance.[30] Finally, although it is difficult to document the assertion, there is what may be called a common law of custom and usage within particular agencies which undoubtedly plays an important part in making decisions on placement.[31] It seems clear that agency standards are under constant scrutiny by the agencies and by experts in social work, and therefore may be changed either by virtue of

refinements in theory and technique, or in response to changing conditions.[32] In short, the adoption agencies resemble other administrative agencies, with the obvious differences that they function in a non-adversary context, that their decisions are based upon highly intangible and non-measurable factors, and that they often fail to realize that they are part of a legal process.

In adoption as in custody the ultimate standard for both agencies and courts is the best interests and welfare of the child.[33] Although both are working for the same purpose, there obviously may be conflicts between them in some cases. In those states where the refusal of agency consent conclusively bars the adoption of children in agency custody[34] the agency's principles must necessarily prevail and in effect are translated into law. On the other hand where the courts have the authority to scrutinize agency refusal to place or to consent, or where the issue revolves around an agency recommendation regarding a private placement,[35] the cases provide some insight into the courts' reaction to agency standards. Under some circumstances the courts are reluctant to permit an agency standard to override all other factors. For example, where

---

26. I Schapiro, A Study of Adoption Practice, 74 (1956) refers to "factors considered important and given emphasis" rather than requirements.

27. I Schapiro, A Study of Adoption Practice, 72–86 (1956); Child Welfare League of America, Standards for Adoption Service (1959); Michaels, Casework Considerations in Rejecting the Adoption Application, in Smith, Readings in Adoption, 300 (1963). For arguments favoring age differentials see Wadlington, Minimum Age Difference as a Requisite for Adoption, 1966 Duke L.J. 392.

28. I Schapiro, A Study of Adoption Practice, 75 (1956).

29. Simon, Evaluation of Adoptive Parents, and Beck, Evaluating an Individual's Capacity for Parenthood, reprinted in II Schapiro, A Study of Adoption Practice, 160 and 72 (1955).

30. I Schapiro, A Study of Adoption Practice, 83, 84 (1956); Costin, Implications of Psychological Testing for Adoptive Placements, and Reid, Principles, Values, and Assumptions Underlying Adoption Practice, reprinted in Smith, Readings in Adoption, 452, 26 (1963). For a practical application of the matching process see Crump v. Montgomery, 220 Md. 515, 154 A.2d 802 (1959).

But apparently the matching ideal is changing. In the Revised Section 4.3 of the Child Welfare League of America, Standards For Adoption Service (1963) it is

stated: "Similarities of background or characteristics of children should not be a major consideration in the selection of a family." See also Note, Adoptions for the Hard-To-Place: The Role of the Court and the Trend Against Matching, 25 U. Miami L.Rev. 749 (1971).

31. Evidence of this can be found in the excellent study, Broeder, Barrett, Impact of Religious Factors in Nebraska Adoptions, 38 Neb.L.Rev. 641 (1959).

32. For example, the emphasis in some agencies on early placement has of necessity changed ideas about matching. Reid, Principles, Values, and Assumptions Underlying Adoption Practice, cited supra note 26.

33. Appeal in Pima County Juvenile Action B–10489, 151 Ariz. 335, 727 P.2d 830 (App.1986); In Interest of J. R., 315 N.W.2d 750 (Iowa 1982); In re Adoption of a Minor (No. 2), 367 Mass. 684, 327 N.E.2d 875 (1975); In re Adoption of Kreyche, 15 Ohio St.3d 159, 472 N.E.2d 1106 (1984). See Edwards, Adaption—The Welfare and Best Interest of the Child, 5 Willamette L.J. 93 (1968).

34. See section 20.4, supra, and Petition of Sherman, 241 Minn. 447, 63 N.W.2d 573 (1954); In re Dougherty Adoption Case, 358 Pa. 620, 58 A.2d 77 (1948).

35. The court ordered a remand to consider an agency report in In re Adoption of a Minor (No. 2), 367 Mass. 684, 327 N.E.2d 875 (1975).

the agency refuses to approve an adoption which in most respects impresses the court as conducive to the child's welfare solely on the ground that the petitioner is unmarried, the court may nevertheless approve the adoption.[36] An agency refusal to permit adoption was also overridden when it was based solely on the petition's place on the agency waiting list.[37] The marital status of the petitioner is relevant, however, and in some circumstances may lead to a denial of the adoption.[38] The age of the prospective adoptive parent is also relevant, on the theory that there should be a natural age span between parent and child both to provide against a too early loss of the parents and also to simulate the natural family relationship.[39] The courts concede this factor, denying adoptions at least in part on this ground in some cases,[40] but where other factors strongly preponderate in favor of the

adoption, they may be unwilling to let petitioner's age stand in the way.[41]

Other factors which courts and agencies find relevant in evaluating candidates for adoption include sexual orientation,[42] emotional stability,[43] moral character,[44] methods of discipline in the home,[45] and the relative merits of separating siblings or keeping them together.[46] The courts have taken differing approaches to the unusual situation in which a natural parent seeks to adopt his own child, being swayed in the result by the parent's motive for the adoption.[47] The cases are about evenly divided on whether a grandparent has some sort of a preference to the adoption of a grandchild which should be taken into account by agencies or courts, and which might counteract the factor of age.[48] The difference in result reflects differences in the total mixture of factors.

36. In re Adoption of Barnett, 54 Cal.2d 370, 6 Cal. Rptr. 562, 354 P.2d 18 (1960); In re McDonald's Adoption, 43 Cal.2d 447, 274 P.2d 860 (1954). In re Adoption of Tschudy, 267 Wis. 272, 65 N.W.2d 17 (1954) was a similar case on the facts but the court had to deny the adoption since the agency's consent was, under the statute, a prerequisite to any adoption.

37. In re Harshey, 45 Ohio App.2d 97, 341 N.E.2d 616 (1975).

38. E.g., Middlecoff v. Leofanti, 133 Ill.App.2d 822, 272 N.E.2d 289 (1971); Matter of Interest of L. B. T., 318 N.W.2d 200 (Iowa 1982); In re Adoption of H., 69 Misc.2d 304, 330 N.Y.S.2d 235 (Fam.Ct.1972). See Annot., Marital Status of Prospective Adopting Parents as Factor in Adoption Proceedings, 2 A.L.R.4th 555 (1980) for other cases.

39. I Schapiro, A Study of Adoption Practice 77 (1956).

40. Clark v. Buttry, 121 Ga.App. 492, 174 S.E.2d 356 (1970), judgment affirmed 226 Ga. 687, 177 S.E.2d 89 (1970); Frantum v. Department of Public Welfare of Baltimore City, 214 Md. 100, 133 A.2d 408 (1957), cert. denied 355 U.S. 882, 78 S.Ct. 149, 2 L.Ed.2d 112 (1957); In re Adoption of Ann, 461 S.W.2d 338 (Mo.App.1970); In re Adoption of K. B. I. D. v. M. G., 417 S.W.2d 702 (Mo.App. 1967) (effect of age is a matter for the trial court's discretion); In re Adoption of H., 69 Misc.2d 304, 330 N.Y.S.2d 235 (Fam.Ct.1972); In re Adoption of Shields, 4 Wis.2d 219, 89 N.W.2d 827 (1958). See also Annot., Age of Prospective Adoptive Parent as Factor in Adoption Proceedings, 84 A.L.R.3d 665 (1978).

41. In re Adoption of Michelle Lee T., 44 Cal.App.3d 699, 117 Cal.Rptr. 856 (1975); In re Brown's Adoption, 85 So.2d 617 (Fla.1956); Madsen v. Chasten, 7 Ill.App.3d 21, 286 N.E.2d 505 (1972); Williams v. Neumann, 405 S.W.2d 556 (Ky.1966); In re Haun, 31 Ohio App.2d 63, 286 N.E.2d 478 (1972); Wilson v. Pierce, 14 Utah 2d 317, 383 P.2d 925 (1963).

42. Matter of Appeal in Pima County Juvenile Action B–10489, 151 Ariz. 335, 727 P.2d 830 (App.1986) (refusing to place child with a bisexual man). See also Note, Second Parent Adoption for Lesbian-Parented Families: Legal Recognition of the Other Mother, 19 U.C.D.L.Rev. 729 (1986).

43. Commonwealth, Dep't of Child Welfare v. Jarboe, 464 S.W.2d 287 (Ky.1971); Van Kleek v. State Public Welfare Commission, 252 Or. 497, 450 P.2d 549 (1969).

44. In re Adoption of Childers, 441 N.E.2d 976 (Ind. App.1982); Dickey v. Boxley, 481 S.W.2d 283 (Ky.1972).

45. Alan D. M. v. Nassau County Department of Social Services, 58 A.D.2d 111, 395 N.Y.S.2d 666 (2d Dep't 1977) (mother's spanking child not a basis for denial of adoption, but requires delay and counseling).

46. Petition of Department of Public Welfare to Dispense With Consent to Adoption, 376 Mass. 252, 381 N.E.2d 565 (1978).

47. In re Adoption of J. H., 313 A.2d 874 (D.C.App. 1974); In re Jessica W., 122 N.H. 1052, 453 A.2d 1297 (1982) and Matter of A. J. J., 108 Misc.2d 657, 438 N.Y.S.2d 444 (Sur.Ct.1981) permitted the father of an illegitimate child to adopt the child where this would not affect the child's relationship with the mother. In re Adoption of Graham, 63 Ohio Misc. 22, 409 N.E.2d 1067 (1980) refused to permit a mother to adopt her own child for the purpose of cutting off the father's parental rights.

48. Granting a preference: In Interest of J. R., 315 N.W.2d 750 (Iowa 1982); Wilson v. Family Services Division, Region Two, 554 P.2d 227 (Utah 1976), appeal after remand 572 P.2d 682 (1977); In re Adoption of Tachick, 60 Wis.2d 540, 210 N.W.2d 865 (1973). Denying any preference: Matter of W. E. G., 710 P.2d 410 (Alaska 1985); Matter of M. N., 199 Mont. 407, 649 P.2d 749 (1982); Matter of Peter L., 59 N.Y.2d 513, 466 N.Y.S.2d

The question whether the courts should follow agency recommendations in placement arises in its most acute form when a petition for adoption is filed by foster parents who have had custody of a child pursuant to a contract or other arrangements with the agency. The constitutional position of such foster parents when the agency removes the child from their custody without a hearing has been discussed in an earlier section.[49] At this point the questions are a) do the foster parents have standing to seek an adoption; and b) if so, should the court grant the adoption over the objection of the agency which placed the child and which is ultimately responsible for the care of the child. The standing of the foster parent may be excluded by statute.[50] If it is not, the question is whether the foster parent is prevented from seeking adoption by the contract which many agencies require foster parents to sign and which provides that the child's placement with them is only temporary, may be terminated by the agency at any time, and that the foster parent agrees not to seek to adopt the child.[51] There are cases which hold that the foster parent, either because of the contract or out of a desire to preserve the agency's discretion in the control of adoption placements, has no standing to seek to adopt the child placed with him.[52] Other cases, probably more numerous, hold that the foster parent may file a petition to adopt.[53] These cases rest on the analysis that the ultimate purpose of the adoption process is to find the best possible home for the children it serves. If the foster parents are able to furnish that home, bearing in mind the importance of continuity in child care and the fact that the foster parents' ability to care for the child can be evaluated rather than merely predicted, they should be permitted to adopt the child.[54] The agency's position should be given considerable weight by the courts in view of the agency's experience and expertise.[55] If the agency's plan for the child is found to be more conducive to the child's welfare, the foster parents' petition should be denied.[56] If the agency is seeking to remove the child from the custody of the foster parents in order to return it to the natural parents, many courts would consider that an additional important reason for supporting the agency's position, although that might seriously interfere with the stability and continuity of care for the child.[57]

Unusual difficulties arise when a child is acquired by petitioners in one state and they file an adoption petition in another state. If the placement was made in accordance with the statutes in the first state and if the adop-

251, 453 N.E.2d 480 (1983); In re Adoption of Randolph, 68 Wis.2d 64, 227 N.W.2d 634 (1975).

49. See section 20.2, supra, at note 85.

50. E.g., West's Ann.Cal.Civ.Code § 224n (Supp.1987); Oxendine v. Catawba County Department of Social Services, 303 N.C. 699, 281 S.E.2d 370 (1981).

51. Such a contract is described but not specifically enforced in Knight v. Deavers, 259 Ark. 45, 531 S.W.2d 252 (1976).

52. Drummond v. Fulton County Department of Family and Children Services, 237 Ga. 449, 228 S.E.2d 839 (1976), cert. denied 432 U.S. 905, 97 S.Ct. 2949, 53 L.Ed.2d 1077 (1977), rehearing denied 434 U.S. 881, 98 S.Ct. 243, 54 L.Ed.2d 164 (1977); People ex rel. Ninesling v. Nassau County Department of Social Services, 46 N.Y.2d 382, 413 N.Y.S.2d 626, 386 N.E.2d 235 (1978), reargument denied 46 N.Y.2d 836, 414 N.Y.S.2d 1055, 386 N.E.2d 1105 (1978). Other cases are cited in Annot., 21 A.L.R.4th 535, 546 (1983).

53. Knight v. Deavers, 259 Ark. 45, 531 S.W.2d 252 (1976); People in Interest of M., 34 Colo.App. 91, 522 P.2d 1234 (1974); Fleming v. Hursh, 271 Minn. 337, 136 N.W.2d 109 (1965); Stapleton v. Dauphin County Child Care Service, 228 Pa.Super. 371, 324 A.2d 562 (1974); In

re Joseph, ___ R.I. ___, 420 A.2d 85 (1980); Harris County Child Welfare Unit v. Caloudas, 590 S.W.2d 596 (Tex.Civ. App.1979). Other cases are cited in Annot., 21 A.L.R.4th 535, 543 (1983).

54. Katz, Foster Parents Versus Agencies: A Case Study in the Judicial Application of "The Best Interests of the Child" Doctrine, 65 Mich.L.Rev. 145 (1966).

55. See In re Adoption of Reinius, 55 Wash.2d 117, 346 P.2d 672 (1959), holding the agency's consent may be dispensed with only on proof that its refusal to consent is unreasonable.

56. Marten v. Thies, 99 Cal.App.3d 161, 160 Cal.Rptr. 57 (1979), cert. denied 449 U.S. 831, 101 S.Ct. 99, 66 L.Ed. 2d 36 (1980); In re MCK, 444 So.2d 1362 (La.App.1984); Matter of Aaron and Alfred Z., 81 Wis.2d 194, 260 N.W.2d 246 (1977). Cases in which the agency agreed that the foster parents should adopt include Lloyd v. Schutes, 24 Md.App. 515, 332 A.2d 338 (1975); In re Niskanen, 301 Minn. 53, 223 N.W.2d 754 (1974).

57. See Schneider v. S. L. M., 347 N.W.2d 126 (N.D.1984), in which the court ordered the return of the child so that it might be placed with persons chosen by the natural mother.

tion is appropriate according to the law of the second state, the adoption may be granted without difficulty.[58] In order to determine whether the laws of both states are complied with, however, the Interstate Compact on Placement of Children, now in force in nearly all states [59] must be complied with.[60] The Compact provides that before a child may be brought into the state for the purpose of adoption the sending agency must furnish specified information to the public authorities in the receiving state.[61] The child may not be brought into the receiving state until the public authorities in that state notify the sending agency that the proposed placement is not contrary to the child's interests.[62] The Compact does not apply to a child brought into a state for adoption placement by his parent or by certain relatives if left with such relative or a non-agency guardian in the receiving state.[63] If the Compact is not complied with, the child must be returned to the natural parent or to the placement agency in the first state.[64] International adoption placements are not covered by the Compact, but the laws of both the country in which the child is

obtained and of the state in which the adoption proceeding is brought must be complied with.[65] Failure to observe this rule led to suffering and hardship when Viet Namese children were brought to the United States without being properly made available for adoption in Viet Nam.[66]

Race and Religion in Adoption Placements [67]

The factors of race and religion in adoption placements raise hard questions. Race is injected into the adoption process in two ways. A few states have enacted statutes either directly or indirectly providing, or at least suggesting, that race is among the factors to be considered in evaluating placements, either by the court or by an agency investigating the placements.[68] Even if no such statute is involved, adoption agencies may take race into account. Although at one point racial matching of adoptive parents with children to be adopted was not favored in the official pronouncements of adoption organizations,[69] the not uncommon appearance of cases dealing with race gives evidence that the agencies

58. In re Adoption of Lunger, 28 N.J.Super. 614, 101 A.2d 370 (1953).

59. Council of State Governments, Interstate Compacts and Agencies 3 (1983).

60. Pima County Juvenile Action No. 18635 v. Fisher, 125 Ariz. 430, 610 P.2d 64 (1980); Matter of Adoption of T. M. M., 186 Mont. 460, 608 P.2d 130 (1980). But a court may approve an adoption which does not comply with the Compact if the child has been with the petitioners for an appreciable time and they appear to be suitable parents. Matter of Adoption of Baby "E", 104 Misc.2d 185, 427 N.Y.S.2d 705 (Fam.Ct.1980). See also Weiland and White, The Law of Interstate Placements of Children, 39 Ohio St.L.J. 327 (1978).

61. Interstate Compact on the Placement of Children Art. III.

62. Interstate Compact on the Placement of Children Art. III.

63. Interstate Compact on the Placement of Children Art. VIII.

64. See note 60, supra.

65. Note, International Adoptions-United States Adoption of Vietnamese Children: Vital Considerations for the Courts, 52 Denver L.J. 771 (1975); Kim and Carroll, Intercountry Adoption of South Korean Orphans: A Lawyer's Guide, 14 J. of Fam.L. 223 (1975).

66. See, e.g., Doan Thi Hoang Anh v. Nelson, 245 N.W.2d 511 (Iowa 1976).

67. For a discussion of race in adoption see R. Simon, H. Altstein, Transracial Adoption (1977); D. Fanshel, A Study in Negro Adoptions (1957); Howard, Transracial Adoption: Analysis of the Best Interests Standard, 59 N. Dame L.Rev. 503 (1984); Note, Racial Matching and the Adoption Dilemma: Alternatives for the Hard to Place, 17 J.Fam.L. 333 (1979). For a discussion of religious factors see Note, Religious Matching Statutes and Adoption, 51 N.Y.U.L.Rev. 262 (1976); Note, A Reconsideration of the Religious Element in Adoption, 56 Corn.L.Q. 780 (1971).

68. Ariz.Rev.Stat. § 8–105(D)(4) (Supp.1986) (agency investigation to report on the heritage of the child); Colo. Rev.Stat. § 19–4–103(1) (1986) (court to take race into account); D.C.Code 1981, § 16–305 (petition to state child's race); West's.Ann.Ind.Code § 31–3–1–4 (1980) (agency report to state whether child is hard to place because of race); Md.Rule D72 (petition to state child's race); Vernon's Ann.Mo.Stat. § 453.070 (1986) (agency report to include race); Okl.St.Ann. tit. 10, § 60.12 (1966) (petition to show child's race); Pa.Stat. tit. 23, § 2531 (Supp.1986) (report to show child's race); V.Tex.C.A., Fam.Code § 16.032 (1986) (agency report to show genetic history, i.e. ethnic background).

69. Child Welfare League of America, Standards for Adoption Service 33 (1968), stating that in most instances similarity in background and characteristics should not be a consideration in the selection of a family. But see Child Welfare League of America, Standards for Adoption Service § 4.5 (1972) stating that it is preferable to

still do pay attention to racial characteristics in placing children.[70] It is also clear that minority organizations oppose the placement of minority children with white parents, either out of fear of losing ethnic identity or on the ground that in such circumstances the minority children will not be as well prepared to encounter racial prejudice in later life as they would be if brought up in minority households.[71] And the Indian Child Welfare Act mandates racial preferences in the adoption placements of Indian children.[72] The federal adoption subsidy program as implemented by state subsidy statutes has provided a means by which greater numbers of minority parents may be enabled to adopt minority children who might otherwise be hard to place,[73] thereby to some extent ameliorating the hardship to minority children imposed by racial matching practices. Yet the fact remains that under contemporary conditions there are many children of minority races who could benefit from adoption but who are not likely to be placed, either because of opposition by minority organizations, or as a result of the application of racial matching criteria by adoption agencies.[74] This is especially unnecessary in times when the number of parents seeking to adopt a child far exceeds the number of adoptable children of the same race, so that without the racial restrictions

some of the children of minority races might well find adoptive homes which would better serve their psychological welfare than the alternatives of institutions or foster care.[75]

Against this background of heavy emphasis on race in adoption agencies, racial minority organizations and the United States Congress, legal doctrines as announced by statutes[76] and cases[77] seem almost irrelevant. Yet there is the United States Constitution[78] which has been construed to invalidate most forms of racial discrimination and to subject all racial criteria to strict scrutiny.[79] The relatively few lower court cases which have had to face the question of what the Constitution requires when race is advocated as a reason for granting or denying adoption have held that the courts may consider it as one of the relevant factors in the decision. The Drummond case[80] so held when white foster parents sued under the Civil Rights Act[81] to regain custody of a mixed race child on the ground that his removal from their custody had violated the Constitution because based upon his race. The Fifth Circuit en banc found that race was not relied upon "in an automatic fashion", it was not considered in a discriminatory way, there was no racial slur or stigma involved, and that "It is a natural thing for children to be raised by parents of

place a child with parents of the same race. See also Note, Matching for Adoption: A Study of Current Trends, 22 Cath.Law. 70 (1976).

70. Cases are collected in Annot., Race as Factor in Adoption Proceedings, 34 A.L.R.4th 167 (1984). See also Child v. Beame, 425 F.Supp. 194 (S.D.N.Y.1977).

71. R. Simon, H. Altstein, Transracial Adoption 186 (1977): "As a highly visible social movement transracial adoption appears to be dead." Howard, Transracial Adoption: Analysis of the Best Interests Standard, 59 N. Dame Law Rev. 503, 517 (1984), quoting from the National Association of Black Social Workers condemning transracial adoption and indicating that as a result very few transracial placements are being made.

72. 25 U.S.C.A. § 1915(a) provides that in any adoptive placement of an Indian child preference shall be given, in the absence of good cause to the contrary, to a placement with a member of the child's extended family, to other members of the tribe, or to other Indian families. See Howard, Transracial Adoption: Analysis of the Best Interests Standard, 59 N. Dame L.Rev. 503, 518–527 (1984).

73. See section 20.1, supra, at notes 32, 33.

74. Howard, Transracial Adoption: Analysis of the Best Interests Standard, 59 N. Dame L.Rev. 503, 513, 535 (1984).

75. Id. at 545–555, examining the best interests of the child in the context of transracial adoption.

76. Two states have statutes to some extent excluding race from consideration in adoption placement. Conn. Gen.Stat.Ann. § 45–63(3) (Supp.1986) (court shall not deny adoption solely because of a difference in race); Ky. Rev.Stat. §§ 199.471, 199.473 (Supp.1986) (adoption not to be denied for racial background unless contrary to the expressed wishes of the natural parent).

77. Annot., 34 A.L.R.4th 167 (1984).

78. U.S.Const.amend. XIV, § 1 (Equal Protection Clause).

79. Many of the relevant cases are cited in Petition of R. M. G., 454 A.2d 776, 784–786 (D.C.App.1982).

80. Drummond v. Fulton County Department of Family & Children's Services, 563 F.2d 1200 (5th Cir.1977), cert. denied 437 U.S. 910, 98 S.Ct. 3103, 57 L.Ed.2d 1141 (1978).

81. 43 U.S.C.A. § 1983.

their same ethnic background." [82] The court stated, on the basis of professional literature not cited, that race is directly relevant to the question whether prospective adoptive parents will be able to care for the child.[83] The District of Columbia Court of Appeals, in Petition of R. M. G.,[84] reached a conclusion similar to that of the Drummond case. The child in that case was born to black parents and placed by a state agency with white foster parents who, after three months sought to adopt her. At first the agency approved, but later when the child's paternal grandparents sought to adopt her, the agency social worker changed her mind and recommended approval of adoption by the black grandparents. The trial court granted a decree to the grandparents. The court of appeals held a) that the Delaware statute authorizing consideration of race is not facially invalid when subjected to a strict standard of review; b) that race may be relevant in an adoption proceeding; and c) that when race is relevant, the court must ask how each family's race is likely to affect the child's development of identity, how the families compare in this respect, and how significant the racial factors are when all other relevant factors are considered.[85] The court then reversed the trial court's decision on the ground that it did not make findings on how the racial difference would affect this child, nor did it specifically follow the suggested analysis. The court then remanded the case for consideration of these points.

The Supreme Court's decision in Palmore v. Sidoti [86] casts considerable doubt on the positions taken by the Drummond and R. M. G. cases. In Palmore white parents were divorced, with custody of their three-year-old daughter awarded to the child's mother. The

father sought custody a little more than a year later when mother and child began living with a black man whom the mother married two months later. The trial court awarded custody to the father on the ground that the child would suffer social stigma by having to live with a mixed race couple. The Supreme Court reversed. It stated that the trial court found no unfitness on the mother's part nor any deficiency in the care given the child by the mother. It then said, in very sweeping terms, that while it is obvious that racial and ethnic prejudices exist, and that there is a risk that a child living with a stepparent of a different race might face pressures and stresses not present if she were living with parents of the same race, under the Constitution the courts may not consider removing a child from the custody of her parent because of the effect of these biases. It stated that whatever problems a child might face in a racially mixed household, those problems may not justify a denial of constitutional rights nor the removal of the child from the custody of her mother. Of course we all know that the Supreme Court is capable of beating a retreat from advanced positions taken without thorough consideration, and certainly Palmore contains little consideration or citation of authority, nor was it addressed to a situation like that in R. M. G., where the contending parties were not biological parents of the child. Nevertheless, fairly read, the opinion may be construed to say that the impact on a child caused by living in a mixed race household, which is described in Drummond, R. M. G., and in commentators on transracial adoption, is not a factor which the Constitution permits the courts to take into account.

---

82. 563 F.2d at 1204, 1205. The court also referred with approval to the agency practice of matching parent and child in adoptions apparently without being aware of the fact that this practice has been severely criticized by adoption authorities.

The former Louisiana statute forbidding all transracial adoptions was held unconstitutional in Compos v. McKeithen, 341 F.Supp. 264 (E.D.La.1972).

83. 563 F.2d at 1205.

84. 454 A.2d 776 (D.C.App.1982), 32 Cath.U.L.Rev. 1022 (1983). Other cases are collected in Annot., 34

A.L.R.4th 167 (1984). There is a strong dissent to Petition of R. M. G., taking the position that the trial court's award of adoption should have been affirmed since there was evidence that racial differences would be detrimental to the black child in a white family.

85. 454 A.2d at 791–793.

86. 466 U.S. 429, 104 S.Ct. 1879, 80 L.Ed.2d 421 (1984), appeal after remand 472 So.2d 843 (Fla.App.1985), also discussed in section 19.4, supra, at note 6.

The Palmore case, read as suggested, would exclude racial considerations from adoption entirely. As in other cases,[87] it hardly seems good policy to excuse racial discrimination on the ground that there is racial prejudice in the community and that therefore the child of a racially mixed household may suffer. This is especially true where, as in R. M. G.[88] the testimony concerning the effect on the child was general, not specific, bore no relation to the family and child in the case and amounted to a reliance on stereotypes of human behavior which might or might not have relevance in particular situations. It is hard to avoid the conclusion that Palmore as applied to adoptions would achieve a useful result in eliminating racial considerations entirely. A court faced with a transracial adoption case could then focus its attention as in other adoption cases upon whether the adoption is the best available placement for the particular child, in view of the needs of that child and the capacities of the prospective adoptive parents. Perhaps then the courts and agencies could devote their energies to finding good homes for children of all races, thereby leading the law of adoption to fulfill its major purpose of improving the lives of all children regardless of race.

Religion produces even more complexities in adoption than race, not so much because of the legal questions it raises but because of the essentially irrelevant claims which seem to follow in its train. A reading of the cases and some of the large number of articles on the subject creates the impression that the child being placed for adoption is too often treated as merely a potential recruit by contending religious sects intent on augmenting their membership.[89] It is not surprising that in such a contest the interests of the child get lost, and rationalization replaces reasoning.

The difficulties begin with the statutes. Two states have statutes which provide that adoption is not to be denied solely on religious grounds.[90] A substantial number of other states have statutes which contemplate in some form or other that religion will be brought to the attention of the court in adoption proceedings or that the adoption shall be awarded "when practicable" to a person of the same religious faith as the child.[91] Delaware seems to be the only state which presently requires the child to be placed with a person of the same religion as the parents, unless the parents indicate indifference to the matter.[92] Many of these statutes are either unclear concerning what part religion should play in the placement of a child or they leave to the agencies the discretion to apply religious matching rules to whatever extent they wish, or they are open to both reproaches. Since many of the agencies are sponsored by religious denominations, it seems obvious that they will at least be favoring their own denomination when they come to place children for adoption.[93] Whether they do or not, the application of religious matching principles

---

87. E.g., Buchanan v. Warley, 245 U.S. 60, 38 S.Ct. 16, 62 L.Ed. 149 (1917).

88. 454 A.2d at 781, where the court recounts the testimony of a psychiatrist who had never seen either the child or the contending parties and who said that transracial adoption would always be harmful to the child.

89. E.g., in Cooper v. Hinrichs, 10 Ill.2d 269, 140 N.E.2d 293 (1957) a sectarian adoption agency intervened in the suit, although it had had nothing to do with the placement of the child involved. See Pfeffer, Religion in the Upbringing of Children, 35 B.U.L.Rev. 333, 336 (1955).

The closely related question of religion as a factor in awarding custody is discussed in section 19.4, supra, at note 11.

90. Conn.Gen.Stat.Ann. § 45–63(3) (Supp.1986); Ky. Rev.Stat. §§ 199.471, 199.473 (Supp.1986).

91. Ariz.Rev.Stat. § 8–105 (Supp.1986); Colo.Rev.Stat. § 19–4–103(1) (1986); D.C.Code 1981, § 16–305; Ill.—

Smith Hurd Ann. ch. 40, § 1519 (Supp.1986); Md. Rule D72; Mass.Gen.L.Ann. c. 210, § 5B (1981); Mich.Comp. Laws Ann. § 27.3178 (555.46) (1980); Minn.Stat.Ann. § 260.181 (1982 and Supp.1987); Vernon's Ann.Mo.Stat. § 211.221 (1983); N.Y.—McKinney's Const. Art. 6, § 32; N.Y.—McKinney's Fam.Ct.Act § 116 (1983); N.Y.—McKinney's Dom.Rel.L. § 113 (1977); Pa.Stat. tit. 23, § 2531 (Supp.1986); R.I.Gen.L. 1981, § 14–1–41; V.Tex.C.A., Fam.Code § 16.032 (1986); Va.Code 1982, § 16.1–288; Wis.Stat.Ann. § 43.82 (Supp.1986).

92. Del.C.Ann. tit. 13, § 911 (1981).

93. See Scott v. Family Ministries, 65 Cal.App.3d 492, 135 Cal.Rptr. 430 (1976), involving a denominational adoption agency which refused to accept applications for adoption from people who were not members of an evangelical Protestant church. The court held this practice to be in violation of the California administrative regulation which permitted only religious matching.

cannot but reduce the range of alternative placements for children, and equally reduce the chances that a prospective adoptive parent will receive a child.

If adoption usually concerned children old enough to have received religious training and to have formed some religious beliefs, the effect of religious protection statutes would be to further the sort of matching of child to adoptive parent formerly favored by the agencies and now less favored.[94] It would have some relation to the child's interests, though it would be hard to say how close or strong the relation might be.[95] Or if the courts were merely enjoined to take the adoptive parent's religious beliefs into consideration as part of the process of evaluating his qualifications to receive a child, much as the courts do in custody cases, this might be relevant though not of overwhelming importance.[96] But neither of these purposes underlies the statutes. Many adoptions affect children too young to have formed religious beliefs.[97] Many agencies consider it desirable for the newborn child to go direct from the hospital to his adoptive home. It makes little sense to talk of the religion of a child so young. In

fact many of the statutes do not purport to be concerned with the child's religion but require only that the religion of natural parents and adoptive parents be the same. And it is identity of religion that is insisted upon, not merely that the adoptive parent have some religious belief. Requiring identity of belief is sometimes justified by the argument that the parent should be entitled to control the religious training of his child.[98] But the natural parent is not allowed to control any other aspect of his child's training after the child has been adopted. The common form of statute declaring the consequences of adoption makes this plain.[99] The natural parent would not be entitled to insist, for example, that the child be sent to a particular school or college or be trained for a particular career. Why should he be entitled to insist that the child be raised in a particular religious faith? That the parent's right of control is not the real basis for the statutes is further shown by the fact that the statutes sometimes forbid adoption by persons of a different religion from the natural parents even when the natural parents are willing to consent.[1]

94. See Child Welfare League of America, Standards for Adoption Service 35 (1968): "The family selected for a child should be one in which the child will have an opportunity for religious or spiritual and ethical development; but religious background alone should not be the basis for the selection of a family for a child."

95. See Broeder and Barrett, Religious Factors in Nebraska Adoptions, 38 Neb.L.Rev. 641, 654 (1959).

96. See Section 16.3, supra, dealing with custody, and II Schapiro, A Study of Adoption Practice, 119, 130, 134 (1955). Broeder and Barrett, Religious Factors in Nebraska Adoptions, 38 Neb.L.Rev. 641, 667 (1959) cites many cases in which church attendance and membership have been deemed crucial in deciding what is for the child's best interests, and goes on to suggest that there is no solid evidence supporting a correlation between religious training and morality, although there is some indication that persons with little religious interest have the highest divorce and separation rates. The same article, 38 Neb.L.Rev. at page 658 raises the question whether the existence of a mixed marriage between adoptive parents is significant and finds that the law seems to give this factor little consideration. See also Landis, Religiousness, Family Relationships and Family Values in Protestant, Catholic, and Jewish Families, 22 Marr. & Family Living 341 (1960).

In re Adoption of "E", 59 N.J. 36, 279 A.2d 785 (1971) held that the trial court could not constitutionally deny an adoption petition on the sole ground that the prospec-

tive adoptive parents did not believe in a Supreme Being when they were otherwise suitable parents for the child.

97. Young children may, in the view of a particular church, become members of that church before being able to have religious convictions, as by being baptized. It may be questionable whether the law should recognize their membership, but in any event the religious protection statutes do not turn on baptism. See the discussion by Father Joseph M. Snee, S. J., to the effect that children are not born Catholic, but are regarded as pagans until baptized, in 1 Institute of Church and State Proceedings of Villanova University School of Law, Religion in Adoption Cases, 61, 110 (1957). The courts are not well equipped to decide such theological questions. An example is Matter of Glavas, 203 Misc. 590, 121 N.Y.S.2d 12 (N.Y.Dom.Rel.Ct.1953).

98. E.g., In re Doe, 167 N.E.2d 396 (Ohio Juv.1956).

99. Statutes in most states provide that adoption terminates all rights and obligations between natural parents and child and substitutes therefor rights and obligations between adoptive parents and child. See section 21.10, Practitioner's Edition.

1. In Petitions of Goldman, 331 Mass. 647, 121 N.E.2d 843 (1954), cert. denied 348 U.S. 942, 75 S.Ct. 363, 99 L.Ed. 737 (1955) the court refused to approve the adoption of a "Catholic" child by a Jewish couple even though the Catholic mother had consented.

Why then is there such extensive adherence to the maintenance of religious identity between natural parents and adoptive parents? It clearly has nothing to do with the child's welfare except in those cases where an older child is adopted, and those cases most often involve stepparent adoptions in which the religious protection statute usually does not apply. The only explanation which seems to fit the facts is that the statutes impose a truce upon proselytizing by maintaining the status quo during adoption.[2] The ultimate purpose is to avoid conflict between religious groups through the historically respectable device of the legal fiction, the fiction that in this context the child's religion is that of his parent.

Since the adoption agencies play a leading role, often the conclusive role, in adoptions, it is important to know how they apply the religious protection statutes in practice. Private sectarian agencies usually place children with persons of the same denomination as their supporting church.[3] Many agencies, both sectarian and non-sectarian, prefer to see some evidence of church membership or attendance.[4] But some agencies will place children across religious lines where placement with persons of the same faith as the child's parents cannot be made.[5] The Nebraska study indicated that agencies handling about one-third of all adoptions would refuse

adoption in any case where the child's parent and the adoptive parents did not have the same basic religious faith.[6] Both the public adoption agencies and the state's judges attached relatively little importance to the fact of religious difference between natural and adoptive parents, however.[7] But the Nebraska study found that where the adoptive parents were not church members at all, the agencies would nearly always refuse placement and the judges would be likely to deny the adoption, although they would place less emphasis on church membership than the agencies.[8] If, as seems to be the case, about half of the population belongs to no church,[9] agency policy excludes more potential adoptive parents than is wise, from the point of view of the otherwise qualified persons seeking to adopt a child as well as of the children thereby condemned to grow up in institutions or a succession of foster homes.

There are remarkably few cases dealing with the constitutionality of religious protection statutes in adoption, presumably because the application of these statutes by adoption agencies are not often sufficiently exposed to the light of day to be effectively attacked in litigation. It has been held, however, that an agency's refusal to accept applications from adoptive parents who were not members of an evangelical Protestant sect was contrary to

---

2. I Schapiro, A Study of Adoption Practice, 58 (1956) nicely supports the text analysis by reporting that in New York it is the custom, when placing foundlings whose parents' religion is not known, to allocate them among Catholic, Protestant and Jewish applicants in the proportion which the three groups appear in the general population, that is, 1:1:1.

3. Note, A Reconsideration of the Religious Element in Adoption, 56 Cornell L.Rev. 780, 801 (1971); I Schapiro, A Study of Adoption Practice 59 (1956). The child's plight in this situation is illustrated by In re P, 52 Misc.2d 528, 276 N.Y.S.2d 257 (Fam.Ct.1966).

4. Note, A Reconsideration of the Religious Element in Adoption, 56 Cornell L.Rev. 780, 798 (1971); Michael, The Religious Factor in Adoptions, 3 Osgoode Hall LJ. 14 (1964).

5. I Schapiro, A Study of Adoption Practice 59 (1956); Duker, Jewish Attitudes to Child Adoption in II Schapiro, A Study of Adoption Practice 134 (1956).

6. Broeder and Barrett, Religious Factors in Nebraska Adoptions, 38 Neb.L.Rev. 641, 652 (1959).

7. Ibid. Apparently religious differences play some part in independent placements, certainly where reli-

gious protection statutes exist, but it is hard to say how great a part. See Witmer, Herzog, Weinstein, Sullivan, Independent Adoptions 90–91, 307–308, 351–352 (1963).

8. Broeder and Barrett, Religious Factors in Nebraska Adoptions, 38 Neb.L.Rev. 641, 677–683 (1959). See also Chaikoff, Adoption in Ontario: An Agnostic's Position, 3 Osgoode Hall L.J. 23 (1964). Both the Nebraska study and Dr. Chaikoff's article indicate that an atheist or agnostic has no chance whatever to obtain a child by agency placement. This is further borne out by a recent New Jersey case in which petitioners having no religious affiliation were refused a child by a state agency. The attorney general ordered a change in agency practice after suit was filed, however. Burke v. N.J., Docket No. A491–65, Superior Court, Appellate Division, Welfare Law Bulletin, Dec. 1966, later decided by the New Jersey Supreme Court, holding that the refusal to place a child with agnostic parents was unconstitutional. In re Adoption of "E", 59 N.J. 36, 279 A.2d 785 (1971).

9. Broeder and Barrett, Religious Factors in Nebraska Adoptions, 38 Neb.L.Rev. 641, 672–674 (1959).

the state's administrative regulation on adoptions, with a dictum that any such practice which went beyond matching religions of child and adoptive parents would violate the Constitution.[10] And a leading New Jersey case held that a violation of the First Amendment [11] occurred when a trial court denied the adoption petition of suitable adoptive parents solely on the ground that they did not believe in a "Supreme Being".[12] The opinion in the case makes clear, however, that the court was not holding that religion could not be inquired into in adoption. In fact it stated that the religion of applicants for adoption is relevant, and "questions concerning religion as it bears on ethics are not constitutionally forbidden because they serve a valid secular purpose." [13] The New York Court of Appeals has upheld the New York religious preference statute [14] on the ground that it serves a valid secular purpose and preserves a benevolent neutrality toward religion.[15] The opinion in this case is not very enlightening on just what the valid secular purpose of the statute is, however. A third case also holds a religious protection statute constitutional on unimpressive reasoning that all religions are treated alike, that there is no burden on religion, no exercise of religion is required and that the statute does not interfere with the natural parent's right to determine the religion of her offspring.[16]

None of the arguments in these cases reach the main point, which is that the religious protection statutes put the state in the position of determining the future disposition of the homeless child by reference to the factor of a religious faith attributed to the child by a fiction.[17] Further, the statutes may relegate some children to life in institutions or foster homes where the religion attributed to them does not coincide with the religion of those in the community who are potential adoptive parents. In some localities, for example, there may be a surplus of children of Catholic parents who cannot be placed because of the agencies' unwillingness to cross religious lines. As has been argued,[18] the only purpose discernible behind the statutes is the avoidance of proselytizing among children who are available for adoption. To accomplish this purpose it is necessary in some cases to choose one adoptive parent in preference to another on the ground of religion, a wholly irrelevant ground. The avoidance of religious proselytizing is outside the states' powers under the First and Fourteenth Amendments. As the concurring opinion in the New Jersey case argues,[19] "it is not the State's business to prowl among anyone's thoughts and to label him fit or unfit, in whole or in part, because his views are distasteful to someone in a placement agency or in the judiciary." For these reasons the religious preference statutes violate the First Amendment's "free exercise" and "establishment" clauses and ought to be repealed, even where they include some such qualification as "where practicable" or "whenever possible". In fact they also violate the Equal Protection Clause of the Fourteenth Amendment since they discriminate between prospective adoptive parents on grounds which have no relation to any legitimate state purpose.[20]

---

10. Scott v. Family Ministries, 65 Cal.App.3d 492, 135 Cal.Rptr. 430 (1976).

11. U.S.Const.amend. I.

12. In re Adoption of "E", 59 N.J. 36, 279 A.2d 785 (1971), 17 Vill.L.Rev. 591 (1972), 76 Dick.L.Rev. 529 (1972).

13. 59 N.J. at 57, 279 A.2d at 796.

14. Dickens v. Ernesto, 30 N.Y.2d 61, 330 N.Y.S.2d 346, 281 N.E.2d 153 (1972), appeal dismissed 407 U.S. 917, 92 S.Ct. 2463, 32 L.Ed.2d 803 (1972). N.Y.—McKinney's Fam.Ct.Act § 116 (1983).

15. Dickens v. Ernesto, 30 N.Y.2d 61, 330 N.Y.S.2d 346, 281 N.E.2d 153 (1972), appeal dismissed for want of a substantial federal question 407 U.S. 917, 92 S.Ct. 2463, 32 L.Ed.2d 803 (1972). The New York statute was also

held constitutional on its face in Wilder v. Sugarman, 385 F.Supp. 1013 (S.D.N.Y.1974).

16. Petitions of Goldman, 331 Mass. 647, 121 N.E.2d 843 (1954), cert. denied 348 U.S. 942, 75 S.Ct. 363, 99 L.Ed. 737 (1955).

17. See the discussion at note 2, supra.

18. See the discussion at note 2, supra.

19. In re Adoption of "E", 59 N.J. 36, 58, 279 A.2d 785, 797 (1971).

20. Note, A Reconsideration of the Religious Element in Adoption, 56 Cornell L.Q. 780 (1971); Note, Religious Matching Statutes and Adoption, 51 N.Y.U.L.Rev. 262 (1976); Note, Religion and Adoption—Constitutionality of Religious Matching Practices, 17 Wayne L.Rev. 1509 (1971).

Since the existing cases hold religious preference statutes to be for the most part constitutional, it becomes important to see how they are construed. There are lines of authority on the point. The Massachusetts rule is that if there is evidence in the case that in general there are potential adoptive parents of the same religious faith as the child, adoption by a person of a different faith must be denied.[21]

The New York statute spells out in some detail how the statute is to be applied. If a child is committed to an agency or placed by the agency, the commitment or placement must be made, when practicable, with an agency or person of the same religious faith as the child.[22] The statute provides that the term "when practicable" is to have no effect if there is an agency or a proper or suitable person of the same religious faith to whom the child may be committed or with whom it may be placed.[23] In other words if there is such an agency or person available, the statute is mandatory. If the court should place the child with a person of a different faith, it must recite the facts which led it to make the decision.[24] The provisions of the statute must be applied, so far as is consistent with the child's best interests and where practicable, to give effect to the wishes of the parent.[25] In other words the religion of the child is assumed to be that of the parent. A case which was decided before the present version of this statute was adopted held that "where practicable" was intended to give the courts discretion to approve interreligious adoptions in exceptional situations.[26] It is not clear

whether this construction can survive the present statutory language, but in some cases it probably cannot. A later case has held that statute constitutional on its face.[27]

The Illinois statute requires placement with persons of the same religious belief "whenever possible".[28] This has been held to mean that the religious faith of the adopting parents is one factor among many others to be considered, but that it alone does not bar an interreligious adoption if such an adoption will best promote the child's welfare.[29]

The Massachusetts rule is much too strict and would rule out adoption by entirely suitable parents of a different religion on wholly hypothetical grounds, making it possible that the child might not find equally good placement later. The New York rule is somewhat better but it remains uncertain in application. It seems to mean that if there is a suitable person of the same religious faith available for the adoption, he must be given the child notwithstanding the application of a superior adoptive parent. The Illinois rule is preferable because it gives the agencies and the courts the widest latitude in the placement of children and limits the effect or religion more strictly than the other two states.

Placing Children for Money

Many states have statutes which either forbid or impose criminal penalties for paying or receiving money in connection with the placement of children for adoption.[30] The purposes of such statutes are to cause children to be placed in homes which will promote their

---

21. Petitions of Goldman, 331 Mass. 647, 121 N.E.2d 843 (1954), cert. denied 348 U.S. 942, 75 S.Ct. 363, 99 L.Ed. 737 (1955).

22. N.Y.—McKinney's Fam.Ct.Act § 116(a), (b) (1983).

23. N.Y.—McKinney's Fam.Ct.Act § 116(e) (1983).

24. N.Y.—McKinney's Fam.Ct.Act § 116(f) (1983).

25. N.Y.—McKinney's Fam.Ct.Act § 116(g) (1983).

26. In re Adoption of Maxwell, 4 N.Y.2d 429, 176 N.Y.S.2d 281, 151 N.E.2d 848 (1958), 25 Bklyn.L.Rev. 334 (1959), 6 U.C.L.A.L.Rev. 459 (1959). The earlier New York cases are discussed in Ramsey, The Legal Imputation of Religion to an Infant in Adoption Proceedings, 34 N.Y.U.L.Rev. 649 (1959). Other cases are cited in Annot., Religion As Factor in Adoption Proceedings, 48 A.L.R.3d 383 (1973).

27. Dickens v. Ernesto, 30 N.Y.2d 61, 330 N.Y.S.2d 346, 281 N.E.2d 153 (1972), appeal dismissed for want of a substantial federal question 407 U.S. 917, 92 S.Ct. 2463, 32 L.Ed.2d 803 (1972).

28. Ill.—Smith Hurd Ann. ch. 40, § 1519 (Supp.1986).

29. Cooper v. Hinrichs, 10 Ill.2d 269, 140 N.E.2d 293 (1957), citing cases from other states. Cf. In re Adoption of Stone, 398 Pa. 190, 156 A.2d 808 (1959).

30. E.g., West's Ann.Cal.Penal Code § 273 (1970); Colo.Rev.Stat. § 19–4–115 (1986); Ill.—Smith Hurd Ann. ch. 40, §§ 1701, 1702, 1703, 1704 (1980); Mass.Gen.L.Ann. c. 210, § 11A (Supp.1986); Mich.Comp.Laws Ann. §§ 27.3178(555.54), 27.3178(555.69) (1980); N.J.Stat.Ann. § 9:3–54 (Supp.1986); N.Y.—McKinney's Soc.Serv.L. § 374(6) (1983); Pa.Stat. tit. 18, § 4305 (1983); Wis.Stat.

welfare and to prevent them from being placed with parents whose major qualification is the possession of a substantial sum of money.[31] In addition of course our society has traditionally found the purchase and sale of human beings repugnant to our ideals, at least since the abolition of slavery.[32] These statutes have been held constitutional.[33] They have not been wholly effective in preventing the interstate sale of children, however, in part because of the difficulty in some cases in establishing just where the violation occurred.[34] They have generally been construed to permit the payment of medical or hospital expenses of the mother of the child being adopted to the extent the expenses were incurred in the birth of the child[35] and they

also permit a lawyer to charge a fee for his legal services in connection with the adoption proceeding.[36] They do not permit the placement of children for money by intermediaries such as lawyers or doctors, where the fee is paid for the placement and not for legal or medical services.[37]

Adoption agencies often charge fees in connection with placements as a method of financing their operations.[38] Usually the fees are graduated in proportion to the parents' ability to pay.[39] This seems not to violate the statutes forbidding the sale of children and in general seems to meet with approval[40], but the practice has been criticized and is capable of abuse when the fees charged have no rela-

Ann. § 946.716 (1982). See also notes 8 and 9, supra, and Annot., 3 A.L.R.4th 468 (1981).

31. In re Baby Girl D., ___ Pa. ___, 517 A.2d 925 (1986).

32. Ibid. But see Landes and Posner, The Economics of the Baby Shortage, 7 J. of Legal Studies 323 (1978).

33. People v. Schwartz, 64 Ill.2d 275, 1 Ill.Dec. 8, 356 N.E.2d 8 (1976), cert. denied 429 U.S. 1098, 97 S.Ct. 1116, 51 L.Ed.2d 545 (1977); State v. Wasserman, 75 N.J.Super. 480, 183 A.2d 467 (1962), affirmed 39 N.J. 516, 189 A.2d 218 (1963).

34. People v. Keane, 144 Mich.App. 12, 373 N.W.2d 228 (1985). See also Hearings on Juvenile Delinquency (Interstate Adoption Practices) before the Subcommittee to Investigate Juvenile Delinquency of the Committee on the Judiciary, Eighty-Fourth Congress, First Session, July 15 and 16, 1955; November 14 and 15, 1955, and Eighty-Fourth Congress, Second Session, May 16, 1956, on S.B. 3021, 1123, 2281; State of New York Legislative Document No. 44, Report of the Joint Legislative Committee on Matrimonial and Family Laws, 33–65 (1959); New York Times, April 25, 1976, page 50, col. 3, reporting a flourishing black market in babies, with payments ranging from $5000 to $50,000 for eligible babies; Note, Black-Market Adoptions, 22 Catholic Lawyer 48 (1976).

Galison v. District of Columbia, 402 A.2d 1263 (D.C. App.1979) held that a New York lawyer had violated the District of Columbia baby broker statute by arranging an adoption of the baby of a Florida mother, the child to be born in the District.

Advertising for adoption services may be prohibited in some states. Adoption Hot Line, Inc. v. State Department of Health and Rehabilitative Services, 402 So.2d 1307 (Fla.App.1981).

An Illinois lawyer was held extraditable to New Jersey for a violation of the baby broker statute in Newman v. Elrod, 72 Ill.App.3d 616, 28 Ill.Dec. 838, 391 N.E.2d 37 (1979), cert. denied 445 U.S. 942, 100 S.Ct. 1338, 63 L.Ed. 2d 776 (1980).

35. Cohen v. Janic, 57 Ill.App.2d 309, 207 N.E.2d 89 (1965); State v. Segal, 78 N.J.Super. 273, 188 A.2d 416

(1963), certification denied 40 N.J. 224, 191 A.2d 63 (1963); Gorden v. Cutler, 324 Pa.Super. 35, 471 A.2d 449 (1983) (holding that the adoptive parents were entitled to a return of the expense money when the natural parents broke their agreement).

36. In re Adoption of B. A. B., 352 Pa.Super. 444, 508 A.2d 556 (1986).

37. State v. Segal, 78 N.J.Super. 273, 188 A.2d 416 (1963), certification denied 40 N.J. 224, 191 A.2d 63 (1963), sustaining a conviction where all but $100 of the consideration was paid in Pennsylvania, but the child was actually placed in New Jersey. But People v. Scopas, 11 N.Y.2d 120, 227 N.Y.S.2d 5, 181 N.E.2d 754 (1962) held a defendant had not been guilty of "placing out" children when he arranged Greek adoptions of Greek children for New York residents, taking compensation for his services. See also State of New York, Legislative Document (1962) No. 34, Report of Joint Legislative Committee on Matrimonial and Family Laws, 51–58. Some rather fine distinctions have to be made under these statutes. Thus it is proper for a lawyer to give to a parent the names of persons wanting to adopt a child, and to perform legal services in connection with the adoption for which he receives a fee. But if the fee is in fact compensation for the placement rather than for legal services, presumably the statute would be violated. Although payments made to the child's mother for her medical expenses are not illegal, other payments, as for her time lost from work, may be. See Report of California State Bar Committee on Adoption, 36 J. State Bar of Calif. 970 (1961).

38. Crosier, Fee Charging for Adoption Service, reprinted in Smith, Readings in Adoption, 371 (1963); Child Welfare League of America, A Study of Adoption Fees (1961).

39. State of New York, Legislative Document (1963) No. 34, Report of the Joint Legislative Committee on Matrimonial and Family Laws 63–78.

40. Matter of Adoption of Infant V., 91 Misc.2d 209, 397 N.Y.S.2d 575 (Fam.Ct.1977).

tion to the expenses of the particular adoption.[41]

Little authority exists on the effect of the sale of a child on the subsequent adoption proceedings. The sale may vitiate the consent to adoption, but it may constitute abandonment so that parental rights could be terminated in any event.[42] Since the ultimate disposition of the child, if parental rights are terminated, must be governed by the child's best interests, this might lead to approval of the adoption by the persons who made the illegal payments, especially if the child has been in their custody an appreciable time and they appear to be otherwise suitable parents.[43]

Tort Liability Arising Out of Adoption Placement

Although there seems to be no legal right to be adopted,[44] there may be a few circumstances in which liability may arise out of adoption placements. Thus an agency may be liable for a negligent placement which causes harm to the child.[45] And there may be liability for discriminatory failure to place in violation of statute or constitution.[46]

41. In re Baby Girl D., ___ Pa. ___, 517 A.2d 925 (1986) held that the fees paid must promote the child's welfare, and on that ground invalidated fees charged by an agency calculated as 7–½% of the adoptive parents' income, with a ceiling of $7,500.

42. Barwin v. Reidy, 62 N.M. 183, 307 P.2d 175 (1957).

43. Cohen v. Janic, 57 Ill.App.2d 309, 207 N.E.2d 89 (1965); People ex rel. Hydock v. Greenberg, 273 App.Div. 710, 79 N.Y.S.2d 389 (1st Dep't 1948). Cases denying adoption where the statutes were violated include Bryant v. Cameron, 473 So.2d 174 (Miss.1985); Matter of Jose L., 126 Misc.2d 612, 483 N.Y.S.2d 929 (Fam.Ct.1984); In re Adoption of Anonymous, 46 Misc.2d 928, 261 N.Y.S.2d 439 (Fam.Ct.1965).

44. Child v. Beame, 412 F.Supp. 593 (S.D.N.Y.1976).

45. Koepf v. York County, 198 Neb. 67, 251 N.W.2d 866 (1977) (dictum); Annot., Governmental Tort Liability for Social Service Agency's Negligence in Placement, or Supervision After Placement, of Children, 90 A.L.R.3d 1214 (1979).

46. Child v. Beame, 412 F.Supp. 593 (S.D.N.Y.1976). See also Joseph A. v. New Mexico Department of Human Services, 575 F.Supp. 346 (D.N.M.1982).

WESTLAW REFERENCES

Legal Regulation of Placement—In General
find 315 nw2d 750
foster /2 mother father parent /s standing /s adopt!
"inter-state compact" +2 placement +2 children

Race and Religion in Adoption Placements
find 425 fsupp 194
drummond /s fulton
find 279 a2d 785

Placing Children for Money
agency /s fee /s placement /s adoption
barwin /s reidy

§ 20.8 Adoption—The Surrogate Mother Contract

If the soundness of the solutions to legal problems varied directly with the number of words devoted to the problems and with the number of persons engaged in producing the words, we would need to have no fears about being able to cope with the difficulties created by surrogate mother contracts.[1] The legal and nonlegal output on the subject has been enormous[2] and will doubtless continue at the same rate until some other fascinating and unanswerable question appears. Unfortunately, however the ability to solve legal problems probably varies inversely with the num-

§ 20.8

1. One student author has had the courage to offer a solution. Note, Developing a Concept of the Modern "Family": A Proposed Uniform Surrogate Parenthood Act, 73 Geo.L.J. 1283 (1985).

2. Citations to the legal works appear in Note, Rumpelstiltskin Revisited: The Inalienable Rights of Surrogate Mothers, 99 Harv.L.Rev. 1936 (1986); Note, Redefining Mother: A Legal Matrix for New Reproductive Technologies, 96 Yale L.J. 187 (1986). See also Note Surrogate Motherhood and the Baby-Selling Laws, 20 Colum.J.L. & Soc.Probs. 1 (1986); Note, Developing a Concept of the Modern "Family": A Proposed Uniform Surrogate Parenthood Act, 73 Geo.L.J. 1283 (1985); Note, Parenthood by Proxy: Legal Implications of Surrogate Birth, 67 Iowa L.Rev. 385 (1981); Note, In Defense of Surrogate Parenting: A Critical Analysis of the Recent Kentucky Experience, 69 Ky.L.J. 877 (1981); Black, Legal Problems of Surrogate Motherhood, 16 N.Eng.L.J. 373 (1980); Keane, Legal Problems of Surrogate Motherhood, 1980 S.Ill.U.L.J. 147; Coleman, Surrogate Motherhood: Analysis of the Problems and Suggestions for Solutions, 50 Tenn.L.Rev. 71 (1982); Martin, Surrogate Motherhood: Contractual Issues and Remedies Under Legislative Proposals, 23 Washburn L.J. 601 (1984).

ber of words expended. Generally acceptable methods of dealing with these contracts therefore do not seem likely to be devised.

Surrogate mother contracts are made between a woman (and her husband if she is married) and a man not her husband (and his wife if he is married), by which the woman agrees to be artificially inseminated, to bear the child so conceived and to deliver the child at its birth to the other contracting parties in consideration of substantial payments of money.[3] For want of a better term the other contracting parties are referred to as the initiating couple or the initiating person. The term surrogate mother is not an apt one, since the surrogate mother is the biological mother, but it has been popularized by the news media to the point where it must be retained to avoid confusion. The usual assumption is that the artificial insemination will be accomplished with the sperm contributed by the male member of the initiating couple. In conventional legal terms therefore the child will be the illegitimate child of that man and the surrogate mother. But if the surrogacy process is approved there seems to be no reason why it should not be accomplished by the use of sperm from an anonymous donor, or from a sperm bank. It is also usually assumed that the surrogate mother contract is resorted to because the wife in the initiating couple is infertile, but if the process has social utility, it may be used because the initiating couple has other reasons for not wanting to have a child in the usual manner.[4]

In fact we may see cases in which the contract is not initiated by married persons but by a single person, male or female, who wishes to have a child. The social forces leading to the use of such contracts include both the apparent increase in infertility of women, perhaps due to the postponement of child-bearing to later years, and the shortage of adoptable newborn babies.

Attorneys active in the surrogate mother process have worked out the surrogate mother contract in considerable detail. Among other provisions the contract provides that the surrogate will take steps to terminate her parental rights in the child, and her husband will do likewise.[5] She agrees that she will not attempt to form a parent-child relationship with the child.[6] Various provisions attempt to deal with such eventualities as the death during pregnancy of the natural father,[7] the illness of the surrogate mother during the pregnancy and the occurrence of an abnormal fetus,[8] the surrogate mother's expenses during the pregnancy and her possible miscarriage.[9] The payments called for by the contract are customarily placed in escrow on its execution, with payment to the surrogate mother on termination of her parental rights or the delivery of the child.[10] There may be an attempt to preserve anonymity between the surrogate mother and the initiating couple so that neither will know the identity of the other,[11] but this is apparently not always done, and of course it cannot be done if the

---

3. Graham, Surrogate Gestation and the Protection of Choice, 22 Santa Clara L.Rev. 291 (1982); Brophy, A Surrogate Mother Contract to Bear a Child, 20 J. of Fam. L. 263 (1981–1982), hereinafter cited as Brophy, p. ——, Fleming, Our Fascination With Baby M, New York Times Magazine, March 29, 1987, 32 describes the activities of one well known provider of surrogate mother services and indicates that the fees are ten thousand dollars each to the provider and to the surrogate mother, with an additional five thousand dollars to the surrogate for her expenses.

4. In the celebrated Baby M case, Stern v. Whitehead, the wife of the sperm donor had had multiple sclerosis and feared the consequences of a pregnancy.

5. Brophy, pages 267, 268.

6. Brophy, page 267. Some organizations which provide surrogate mother services engage in psychological and physical testing to match the surrogate mother with

the initiating couple, but other arrangers do not do this. Cf. Graham, Surrogate Gestation and the Protection of Choice, 22 Santa Clara L.Rev. 291, 293 (1982) with Fleming, Our Fascination With Baby M, N.Y. Times Magazine, March 29, 1987, 32.

7. Brophy, page 275. The contract may also require the surrogate mother to observe certain rules of good health during the pregnancy, such as not drinking, smoking or taking medication except on physician's orders. Graham, supra, note 6, at 295.

8. Brophy, page 280, providing that if the fetus is determined to be abnormal, the surrogate mother agrees to have an abortion.

9. Brophy, pages 270, 271, 272, 276, 277.

10. Brophy, page 271.

11. Brophy, pages 278, 285.

contract is not performed and becomes the focus of a lawsuit.[12]

Under present circumstances, in which there are no state statutes addressed to the surrogate mother process, these contracts face some difficulties of accomplishment where all parties wish to comply with them in accordance with their terms, and even greater difficulties if there is non-performance on one side or the other and an attempt is made to enforce them. Some of the risks are as follows: [13]

1. There may be problems of terminating the parental rights of the surrogate mother. The contract may be considered a consent to adoption, but some states do not permit consents to be made before the birth of the child.[14] In that event a subsequent consent would have to be provided after the birth or the parental rights would have to be terminated involuntarily, which would require proof of abandonment, neglect or unfitness.[15] Proof of such conduct with respect to a newborn might be difficult.

2. If parental rights are properly terminated, the court in which the petition to adopt is filed may be unable to grant it if the state law does not permit private placements.[16] Even if private placements are permitted, the court may exercise its discretion not to award the adoption to the initiating couple. Although this may be unlikely, this result may not be so unlikely if the surrogacy process is initiated by a single person or if an agency is

asked to investigate the placement and returns an adverse report.

3. The major problem of course is that surrogate mother contracts contemplate payments of relatively substantial amounts of money and may be considered to constitute the sale of the baby. The sparse judicial authority on this point does not provide solutions. One case has held that the Michigan statute forbidding the payment or receipt of money in connection with adoption is not, as applied to a surrogate mother contract, an infringement on the right of privacy of the initiating couple.[17] Another case has held that the payments made pursuant to a surrogate mother contract do not constitute a sale of the baby on the ground that the agreement is entered into before conception and is indistinguishable from artificial insemination by a donor other than the woman's husband, which is not characterized as the sale of a baby.[18] Since the payment is apparently not made until the baby is handed over to the initiating couple, it seems difficult to avoid characterizing the transaction as a sale of the child, which is generally held to be a crime.[19] The policy basis underlying the prohibition on baby selling, namely that it prevents babies from being placed in homes whose only virtue is the wealth of their owners rather than in homes which will best provide for the child's interests, seems to apply to the surrogate mother contract as well as to ordinary payments of money in relation to adoption.[20] Certainly the delivery of a baby already born

12. N. Keane, D. Breo, The Surrogate Mother (1981), describing in detail the negotiation and performance of many surrogate mother contracts; Fleming, Our Fascination With Baby M, New York Times Magazine, March 29, 1987, 32.

13. See N. Keane, D. Breo, The Surrogate Mother 235–237 (1981).

14. See section 20.4, supra. The husband of the surrogate mother might have to consent as well if the state has a statute, as some do, providing that the husband of a woman who is artificially inseminated with the husband's consent is deemed the father of the child. See Syrkowski v. Appleyard, 420 Mich. 367, 362 N.W.2d 211 (1985), in which this issue was dealt with by having the husband file an affidavit of non-consent to the artificial insemination, which seems an awkward way of proceeding.

15. See section 20.6, supra.

16. See section 20.7, supra.

17. Doe v. Kelley, 106 Mich.App. 169, 307 N.W.2d 438 (1981), cert. denied 459 U.S. 1183, 103 S.Ct. 834, 74 L.Ed. 2d 1027 (1983), 1981 Det.Coll. of Law L.Rev. 1131.

18. Surrogate Parenting Associates, Inc. v. Commonwealth ex rel. Armstrong, 704 S.W.2d 209 (Ky.1986). This was a suit by the state attorney general to revoke the charter of the surrogate parenting organization on the ground that it was violating the Kentucky baby broker statute. The court held that there was no violation. Two justices dissented.

19. See section 20.7, supra, and Galison v. District of Columbia, 402 A.2d 1263 (D.C.App.1979).

20. In re Baby Girl D., ___ Pa. ___, 517 A.2d 925 (1986). The surrogate mother is seen by some members of the women's movement as an exploited victim of people with money enough to pay the substantial sums for surrogate motherhood, lending some political force to the argument that it is the passage of money which is the

for cash is not analogous to the sale of sperm for the purpose of artificial insemination, in the latter of which cases no one can know whether a child will be produced.

4. A question which seems not to have been raised relates to legal ethics. Some of the persons arranging surrogate mother contracts are lawyers. It is not at all clear in the negotiations and legal work leading to the contract whom the lawyer is representing. If, as has been suggested earlier in this work, there are serious potential conflicts of interest when a single lawyer represents both parties to an antenuptial contract,[21] or to a separation agreement,[22] representing both parties to a surrogate mother contract would seem to involve even more serious questions of conflict of interests.

5. Finally, if the surrogate mother should refuse to deliver the baby to the initiating couple, extremely complex legal issues would arise.[23] This might be characterized as a revocation of the consent to the adoption by the surrogate mother, in which event the state's rules regarding revocation would come into play.[24] If the revocation were effective, there would have to be a trial on the issues of a) whether the contract could and should be enforced specifically, or if not, b) whether the surrogate mother's parental rights could be terminated involuntarily. Specific performance of the contract would be inconsistent

with an extensive body of law dealing with separation agreements as to custody which are not enforced without judicial scrutiny concerning the child's best interests.[25] The involuntary termination of parental rights would require proof of the usual grounds under the applicable state statute.[26] If the surrogate mother's parental rights could not be terminated involuntarily, there might still be a question whether she or the initiating couple or perhaps an adoption agency should be given custody of the child, this question to turn on the child's best interests. One celebrated case in a New Jersey trial court has held that the contract should be enforced, that it does not involve the sale of a child, that the state's adoption laws do not apply to such contracts, and that under the circumstances revealed by the evidence the child's interests would be best served in the custody of the initiating couple.[27]

At the present writing there are no statutes in the United States dealing expressly with the surrogate mother contract. Many authorities assert that statutes should be passed, that the uncertainties in trying to apply the existing law of adoption to this situation are too great to be tolerable.[28] Several state legislatures have bills before them, either forbidding surrogate mother contracts as the English have done [29] or providing for regulation in

objectionable feature of surrogate mother contracts. See New York Times, March 20, 1987, p. 16, col. 1.

21. See section 1.1, supra.

22. See section 14.7, supra.

23. N. Keane, D. Breo, The Surrogate Mother 236 (1981).

24. See section 20.4, supra. The Kentucky Supreme Court in Surrogate Parenting Associates, Inc. v. Commonwealth ex rel. Armstrong, 704 S.W.2d 209 (Ky.1986) seems not to understand the situation which arises when the surrogate mother refuses to deliver the baby. The court says that no question of adoption is involved, the only issue then being whether the surrogate mother or the father should have custody of the child. But of course the father's wife also wishes to be a parent of the child, which requires both the termination of the surrogate's parental rights and a decree of adoption.

25. See section 18.5, supra.

26. See section 20.6, supra.

27. This is the case known as the case of Baby M, or Stern v. Whitehead. The judge's memorandum of decision is excerpted in the New York Times, April 1, 1987, p. 13, col. 1, and discussed in the New York Times, April, 1987, p. 1, col. 6. The background of the case is discussed in The National Law Journal, September 29, 1986, p. 1, col. 1.

28. N. Keane, D. Breo, The Surrogate Mother ch. 12 (1981); Coleman, Surrogate Motherhood: Analysis of the Problems and Suggestions for Solutions, 50 Tenn.L.Rev. 71 (1982); Graham, Surrogate Gestation and the Protection of Choice, 22 Santa Clara L.Rev. 291, 322, 323 (1982).

29. Surrogacy Arrangements Act of 1985, making it a crime to negotiate for surrogacy arrangements but exempting from the statute surrogate mothers and initiating couples. In other words the intermediaries are forbidden to engage in the negotiations leading to surrogate mother contracts, but the mothers and those who wish children are not.

a variety of respects.[30] In view of the profound emotional drives which are satisfied by the surrogate mother's services, together with the large amounts of money to be made from such arrangements, it seems more likely that regulation rather than prohibition will result, although there are important segments of society strongly opposed to surrogacy arrangements.[31]

 WESTLAW REFERENCES

stern /s whitehead
"surrogate mother!"
find 307 nw2d 438

§ 20.9 Equitable Adoption

The parents of a child turn him over to foster parents who agree to care for him as if he were their own child. Perhaps they also agree to adopt him. They do care for him, support him, educate him, and treat him in all respects as if he were their child, but they never adopt him. Upon their death he seeks to inherit their property on the theory that he should be treated as if he had been adopted. Many courts would honor his claim, at least under some circumstances, characterizing the

case as one of equitable adoption, or adoption by estoppel, or virtual adoption, or specific enforcement of a contract to adopt.[1] The circumstances could more accurately be described as de facto adoption, since it is the facts of the child's position in the foster family which control his status rather than the requirements of adoption statutes.

At the outset equitable adoption must be distinguished from the contract to make a will. In some cases a contract to make a will in the child's favor may be part of the transfer from natural to foster parents. Such contracts are usually enforceable if they meet the requirements for contracts in general.[2] If so, the child's claim to a share of the foster parent's property can be vindicated in reliance upon the contract to make a will, and the effect of the promise to adopt need not be considered. The latter issue only becomes crucial when there is no contract to make a will and the child claims under the intestacy statute.[3]

The arguments pro and con equitable adoption are easily stated. The courts refusing to grant inheritance claims to children asserting equitable adoption rely upon the old notion that adoption was unknown to the common law, that there can be no adoption without

---

30. Pierce, Survey of State Activity Regarding Surrogate Motherhood, 11 Fam.L. Reporter 3001 (1985) indicates that there is activity in twenty-one states. The proposed regulations pertain to the identity of the parties, medical and psychological screening, limitation on fees, requirement of a home for the initiating couple, requirements that the child be legitimated, testing of the baby and confidentiality. There is considerable diversity in the proposals. Prohibition has been proposed in a few states.

31. Opposition has come from the Catholic Church, some influential members of the women's movement, and the Child Welfare League of America. See the New York Times, March 11, 1987, p. 1, col. 6; the New York Times March 20, 1987, p. 16, col. 1; Pierce, Survey of State Activity Regarding Surrogate Motherhood, 11 Fam.L. Reporter 3001, 3002 (1985).

§ 20.9

1. The term equitable adoption is used in this section to accord with the usage in most of the cases. For citation of cases on equitable adoption see Annots., 27 A.L.R. 1325, 2365 (1923); 142 A.L.R. 84 (1943); 171 A.L.R. 1315 (1947); 97 A.L.R.3d 347 (1980); Bailey, Adoption "By Estoppel", 36 Tex.L.Rev. 30 (1957); Note, 47 Mich.L. Rev. 962 (1949); Note, 45 Iowa L.Rev. 159 (1959); Note, Equitable Adoption: They Took Him Into Their Home and Called Him Fred, 58 Va.L.Rev. 727 (1972) (listing

twenty-six states which have recognized equitable adoption in one form or another). In states which recognize equitable adoption it may apply to adoption of adults. Nichols v. Pangarova, 443 P.2d 756 (Wyo.1968). But see Goldberg v. Robertson, 615 S.W.2d 59 (Mo.1981).

2. 2 A. Corbin, Contracts § 439 (1950); 1 W. Page, Wills ch. 10 (Bowe-Parker rev. 1960 and Supp.1986). See also Reimche v. First National Bank of Nevada, 512 F.2d 187 (9th Cir.1975), 1976 B.Y.U.L.Rev. 583, upholding a contract by which the father of an illegitimate child agreed to provide for the child and her mother by will in return for the mother's consent to adoption by the father. The father adopted the child and left a will in her favor but did leave anything to the child's mother. The court rejected the argument that the contract amounted to a sale of the child.

3. See Bank of Maryville v. Topping, 216 Tenn. 597, 393 S.W.2d 280 (1965) where the court held there could be no inheritance without proof of both a contract to adopt and a contract "of inheritance." It is wholly fictional of course to talk of a contract of inheritance unless one means a contract to make a will. What the courts seem to mean by this sort of talk is that the contract to adopt must specifically refer to the child's right to inherit. See, for example, Chehak v. Battles, 133 Iowa 107, 110 N.W. 330 (1907), and Note, 47 Mich.L.Rev. 962 (1949). Cf. Chambers v. Byers, 214 N.C. 373, 199 S.E. 398 (1938).

statutory authority and that therefore a negative inference arises from adoption statutes that if they are not complied with, the status of parent and child is not created for any purpose whatever.[4] This is certainly logical. The trouble with the argument is that it leads to serious hardship in many cases. In the strongest case, for example, a child may be left destitute upon the death of persons occupying, for all practical purposes, the position of parents, the property of these persons going to remote collateral relatives.[5] Many courts try to avoid such results. We have seen other well established doctrines in the law of domestic relations which have as their purpose the vindication of the expectations of individuals when their relationships fail to comply with legal rules. Common law marriage [6] and estoppel to attack invalid divorce decrees [7] illustrate this tendency of the law. The impulse to reach this result is especially strong when the person whose interests are at stake was a child when the operative facts occurred.

Although a majority of the states in which the issue of equitable adoption has been raised have accepted the concept in general,[8]

a close reading of the cases leaves the impression that there is little appreciation of the basis for the doctrine and correspondingly little enthusiasm about applying it beyond a very limited range of cases. The clearest cases for equitable adoption occur when there is an express written or oral promise by the foster parents to adopt the child.[9] In fact a substantial number of cases make this a rigid requirement for finding an equitable adoption.[10] It does some violence to concepts of contract to say that on the death of the foster parent a contract to adopt may be specifically enforced, since in fact such a contract could probably not be specifically enforced in all respects, as for example in a suit by the natural parent against the foster parents.[11] Furthermore it is clear that such a contract would not prevent the natural parent from reclaiming the child if he should change his mind.[12] Thus for some purposes no such contract would be recognized. For this reason some courts rely on a broader and vaguer equitable principle of estoppel. This is none other than the de facto principle already referred to [13] dressed up in traditional equity

4. E.g., Crozier v. Cohen, 299 F.Supp. 563 (W.D.Okl. 1969) (Oklahoma law); Fuller v. Fuller, 247 A.2d 767 (D.C.App.1968) (no equitable adoption when the husband accepted the wife's illegitimate child into the family); Glass v. Glass, 125 N.E.2d 375 (Ohio App.1952); Geiger v. Estate of Connelly, 271 N.W.2d 570 (N.D.1978); In re Estate of Schultz, 220 Or. 350, 348 P.2d 22 (1959); Bank of Maryville v. Topping, 216 Tenn. 597, 393 S.W.2d 280 (1965); In re Estate of Libert, 269 Wis. 448, 69 N.W.2d 467 (1955). Maddox v. Maddox, 224 Ga. 313, 161 S.E.2d 870 (1968) refused to enforce an oral contract to adopt where it was made as an incident to the marriage of husband and wife, holding it within the statute of frauds as a contract in consideration of marriage.

Apparently equitable adoption is not recognized in Louisiana, and the resultant discrimination for social security purposes which this causes between Louisiana children and those living in other states has been held constitutional. See King v. Schweiker, 647 F.2d 541 (5th Cir. 1981).

5. In In re Estate of Libert, 269 Wis. 448, 69 N.W.2d 467 (1955) the property was held to have escheated to the state rather than be given to the foster daughter.

6. See section 2.4, supra.

7. See section 12.3, supra. One might also add the presumption of validity of later marriages. See section 2.6, supra.

8. E.g., Calista Corp. v. Mann, 564 P.2d 53 (Alaska 1977); Barlow v. Barlow, 170 Colo. 465, 463 P.2d 305 (1969); Prince v. Black, 256 Ga. 79, 344 S.E.2d 411 (1986),

on remand 180 Ga.App. 265, 349 S.E.2d 550 (1986); Wheeling Dollar Savings & Trust Co. v. Singer, 162 W.Va. 502, 250 S.E.2d 369 (1978). Other cases are cited in Annot., 97 A.L.R.3d 347 (1980).

9. E.g., Habecker v. Young, 474 F.2d 1229 (5th Cir. 1973) (Florida law); Davis v. Celebrezze, 239 F.Supp. 608 (S.D.W.Va.1965) (West Virginia law); In re Prewitt's Estate, 17 Ariz.App. 396, 498 P.2d 470 (1972); Long v. Willey, 391 S.W.2d 301 (Mo.1965); Mitchell v. Burleson, 466 S.W.2d 646 (Tex.Civ.App.1971). Long v. Willey, supra, held that the contract to adopt was not within the statute of frauds. But see Maddox v. Maddox, 224 Ga. 313, 161 S.E.2d 870 (1968). If the contract is within the statute of frauds, the doctrine of part performance will apply to render it enforcible. Monahan v. Monahan, 14 Ill.2d 449, 153 N.E.2d 1 (1958).

10. E.g., Glaze v. Richardson, 438 F.2d 120 (5th Cir. 1971); Wilks v. Langley, 248 Ark. 227, 451 S.W.2d 209 (1970); First National Bank of Denver v. People, 183 Colo. 320, 516 P.2d 639 (1973) (must prove oral contract which is fully performed except for compliance with the adoption statute); In re Estate of Staehli, 86 Ill.App.3d 1, 41 Ill.Dec. 243, 407 N.E.2d 741 (1980); Defoeldvar v. Defoeldvar, 666 S.W.2d 668 (Tex.App.1984) (no written agreement to adopt and no corroboration of an oral agreement).

11. Bailey, Adoption "By Estoppel", 36 Tex.L.Rev. 30, 31 (1957).

12. Id. at 34.

13. See the text at notes 1, 6 and 7, supra.

language. The consent of the natural parents must normally be given in such cases.[14]

It would be more productive of fairness and would create fewer conceptual problems if the courts would candidly base relief in these cases upon the de facto principle.[15] The reason for the elaborate procedure established by the adoption statutes is the protection primarily of the child and secondarily of the interests of both the natural and the adoptive parents. The equitable adoption cases arise in such a way that the interests of natural and foster parents are not in jeopardy, and the interests of the child are harmed if the exclusive nature of statutory adoption is insisted upon. Since the policy of the statutes is not prejudiced, but rather promoted, by determining inheritance rights as if the adoption had occurred, this should be done without worrying about whether a more or less fictional contract can be spelled out. Some courts do come very close to doing this, finding that equitable adoption has occurred when the parties have acted as if the child had been adopted, whether or not an express contract is proved.[16]

Most courts hold that the elements of equitable adoption must be proved by "clear cogent and convincing" evidence,[17] although Texas finds the usual civil rule of preponderance appropriate.[18] According to those courts insisting upon proof of a contract, consideration for the promise to adopt must also be proved.[19] This generally consists of the relinquishment of the child to the foster parents

and the child's performance of his filial obligations.[20] The more realistic courts recognize that in contemporary society the child performs no services and in fact is an expense to the family, so that it is fictional to speak of his performance of filial obligations as consideration.[21]

WESTLAW REFERENCES

di equitable adoption
di de facto adoption

§ 20.10 Consequences of Adoption

In General

At the outset of this chapter adoptions was described as the process by which a child's rights and obligations with respect to his natural parents are terminated and similar rights and obligations with respect to his adoptive parents are created. In this section we will show what this means in detail and indicate to what extent there may still be a few circumstances in which it is not wholly true.

The consequences of the adoption decree rest in the first instance upon the applicable state statute. All adoption statutes contain more or less specific provisions governing the effect of the decree. A common form of statute in earlier days, a few of which remain in force, contained only a brief statement that the final decree of adoption divests the natural parents of their rights and duties respect-

---

14. Blair v. Califano, 650 F.2d 840 (6th Cir.1981) (Michigan law); Hayes v. Secretary of Health, Education and Welfare, 413 F.2d 997 (5th Cir.1969).

15. Note, 45 Iowa L.Rev. 159, 162 (1959); Bailey, Adoption "By Estoppel", 36 Tex.L.Rev. 30, 36 (1957); Uhlenhopp, Adoption in Iowa, 40 Iowa L.Rev. 228, 291 (1955).

16. Calista Corp. v. Mann, 564 P.2d 53 (Alaska 1977) (contract may be implied from the facts); Roberts v. Sutton, 317 Mich. 458, 27 N.W.2d 54 (1947); In re Firle's Estate, 197 Minn. 1, 265 N.W. 818 (1936); Mize v. Sims, 516 S.W.2d 561 (Mo.App.1974) (contract may be proved by the acts, conduct or admissions of the foster parent); Flynn v. State, 667 S.W.2d 235 (Tex.App.1984), judgment affirmed 707 S.W.2d 87 (1986) (treated like a son, use of the father's name, holding out as an adopted child); Wheeling Dollar Savings & Trust Co. v. Singer, 162 W.Va. 502, 250 S.E.2d 369 (1978) (evidence that the child was treated in all respects as adopted).

17. In re Estate of Fox, 164 Ind.App. 221, 328 N.E.2d 224 (1975); Matter of Van Cleave's Estates, 610 S.W.2d 620 (Mo.1980); Wheeling Dollar Savings & Trust Co. v. Singer, 162 W.Va. 502, 250 S.E.2d 369 (1978); Annot. 97 A.L.R.3d 347, 357 (1980).

18. Moran v. Adler, 570 S.W.2d 883 (Tex.1978).

19. In re Lamfrom's Estate, 90 Ariz. 363, 368 P.2d 318 (1962); Chehak v. Battles, 133 Iowa 107, 110 N.W. 330 (1907).

20. See the cases cited in notes 9 and 10, supra. Where the persons caring for the child do not do so in the capacity of foster parents, no equitable adoption occurs. Hegger v. Kausler, 303 S.W.2d 81 (Mo.1957).

21. Blair on Behalf of Brown v. Califano, 650 F.2d 840 (6th Cir.1981).

ing the child and vests equivalent rights and duties in the adoptive parents.[1] In some states some aspects of the parent-child relationship between the adopted child and his natural parents were preserved.[2] It is still possible to find an occasional case holding that the adopted child retains some ties with his natural parents.[3] In general, however, the state legislatures have spelled out in detailed and sometimes complex language the mandate that the adopted child will for all purposes have all the rights and obligations with respect to his adoptive parents that a natural child of those parents would have, and that he will correspondingly have no further rights and obligations with respect to his natural parents,[4] with the single exception

that if a stepparent adoption occurs, it does not affect the parent-child relationships between the child and his natural parent.[5] The legislatures have, in other words, made plain their intention that the courts are to recognize and accept the adoption process as one by which the ties of blood are cut off and adoptive ties substituted. For the most part the courts have applied the statutes in ways which effectuate this intention.[6]

Custody, Support and Visitation

The adoptive parents of adopted children become entitled to their custody[7] and are responsible for their support.[8] Normally the

§ 20.10

1. E.g., West's Ann.Cal.Civ.Code §§ 228, 229 (1982); Colo.Rev.Stat. § 19–4–113 (1986); N.M.Stat.Ann. § 40–7–52 (1986); Pa.Stat. tit. 23, § 2902 (Supp.1986); S.D.Codif. L. §§ 25–6–16, 25–6–17 (1984).

2. Note, The Adopted Child's Inheritance from Intestate Natural Parents, 55 Iowa L.Rev. 739 (1970).

3. E.g., Warren v. Foster, 450 So.2d 786 (Miss.1984) (adopted child inherits from his natural parent); Meadow Gold Dairies v. Oliver, 535 P.2d 290 (Okl.1975) (adopted child may have a workers' compensation award on the death of his natural parent); Matter of Estate of Marriott, 515 P.2d 571 (Okl.1973) (adopted child inherits from his natural parent); Harrell v. McDonald, 90 S.D. 482, 242 N.W.2d 148 (1976) (adopted child inherits from her natural mother).

4. E.g., Alaska Stat. § 25.23.130 (1983); Ariz.Rev.Stat. § 8–117 (1974); West's Fla.Stat.Ann. § 63.172 (1985); Md. Code, Family Law, § 5–308 (1984), Md.Code, Estates and Trusts, § 1–207 (1974); Vernon's Ann.Mo.Ann.Stat. § 453.090 (1986); Neb.Rev.St. §§ 43–110, 43–111 (1984); N.J.Stat.Ann. § 9:3–50(a) (Supp.1986); N.Y.—McKinney's Dom.Rel.Law § 117 (Supp.1987); N.C.Gen.Stat. § 48–23 (1984); Ohio Rev.Code § 3107.15 (1980); Okl.St.Ann. tit. 10, § 60.16 (Supp.1987); V.Tex.C.A., Fam.Code § 16.09 (1986); West's Rev.Code Wash.Ann. §§ 11.04.085 (1967), 26.33.260 (1986); Wis.Stat.Ann. § 48.92 (1979 and Supp. 1986), § 851.51 (1971 and Supp.1986). See also Uniform Adoption Act § 14, 9 Unif.L.Ann. 44 (1979) and Uniform Probate Code § 2–109, 8 Unif.L.Ann. 66 (1983). But see Ala.Code 1982, § 43–4–3 permitting the adopted child to inherit from his natural parents or other kindred, and Ohio Rev.Code § 3107.15(B) (1980) preserving the child's rights from or through a deceased natural parent after a stepparent adoption.

5. This is found as an express exception to most of the statutes cited in note 4, supra.

6. E.g., Holder v. Industrial Commission of Arizona, 125 Ariz. 366, 609 P.2d 1066 (App.1980) (adopted children not entitled to workers' compensation for death of natural father); Gessner v. Powell, 238 So.2d 101 (Fla.1970) (adopted child may not sue for wrongful death of his natural parent); Willson v. Carmichael, 665 S.W.2d 52

(Mo.App.1984) (no inheritance through an adopted child by blood kindred); Matter of Estate of Best, 66 N.Y.2d 151, 495 N.Y.S.2d 345, 485 N.E.2d 1010 (1985), cert. denied ___ U.S. ___, 106 S.Ct. 1463, 89 L.Ed.2d 720 (1986) (child adopted out of the family does not take under a class gift to issue); Crumpton v. Mitchell, 303 N.C. 657, 281 S.E.2d 1 (1981) ("issue" in deed does not include children adopted out of the family); Cox v. Cox, 262 S.C. 8, 202 S.E.2d 6 (1974) (adopted children did not inherit from natural parents); Department of Revenue v. Martin, 3 Or.App. 594, 474 P.2d 355 (1970) (adopted child not a child of natural mother for inheritance tax purposes); Patton v. Shamburger, 431 S.W.2d 506 (Tex.1968) (adopted child not entitled to workers' compensation claim for death of natural father); In re Estates of Donnelly, 81 Wash.2d 430, 502 P.2d 1163 (1972) (adopted child does not inherit from natural kindred). A few cases for special reasons may still recognize the blood relationship of the adopted child. E.g., Monroney v. Mercantile-Safe Deposit and Trust Co., 291 Md. 546, 435 A.2d 788 (1981) (gift to children in a will included adopted child of natural parent where testatrix knew the child had been adopted and did not exclude him); Matter of Avery's Estate, 176 N.J. Super. 469, 423 A.2d 994 (1980), certification denied 85 N.J. 499, 427 A.2d 587 (1981) (adoption child could inherit from natural father under former adoption statute in force at the time of adoption); Alberino v. Long Island Jewish-Hillside Medical Center, 87 A.D.2d 217, 450 N.Y.S.2d 857 (2d Dep't 1982) (child adopted after natural parent's death may sue for wrongful death of parent, since he has a vested right in the claim). See also Annot., Right of Adopted Child to Inherit from Intestate Natural Grandparent, 60 A.L.R.3d 631 (1974).

7. Douglas v. Harrelson, 454 So.2d 984 (Ala.Civ.App. 1984), writ quashed 454 So.2d 988 (1984); People ex rel. Bachelda v. Dean, 48 Ill.2d 16, 268 N.E.2d 11 (1971); Spencer v. Franks, 173 Md. 73, 195 A. 306 (1937), 36 Mich.L.Rev. 1308 (1938); Munson v. Johnston, 16 N.J. 31, 106 A.2d 1 (1954). The adoptive parents are also entitled to the child's services and may recover for loss of these services by seduction or enticement. Cook v. Bartlett, 179 Mass. 576, 61 N.E. 266 (1901).

8. Betz v. Horr, 276 N.Y. 83, 11 N.E.2d 548 (1937). But the natural parent may continue to be liable for

natural parents have no right to the children's custody after adoption [9] although there are cases which gave granted visitation to natural parents either on the basis of contract,[10] or because the circumstances indicated that this would be especially beneficial for the welfare of the child.[11] For the most part it would seem highly doubtful to do this because of the disruptive effect it would be likely to have on the adoptive family, and of the inconsistency between such orders and the sweeping terms of the state adoption statutes.[12] The natural parent is also not responsible for the child's support after adoption [13] except of course where the adoption is by a stepparent in which case the rights and duties of the natural parent who is married to the stepparent are not affected by the adoption.[14] One might think that if courts are going to grant visitation to natural parents after adoption, they might order the natural parent to continue contributing to the child's support, but no case has been found on this point.

The adoption decree also normally provides that the child's name will be changed to that of the adoptive parents [15] and it may also provide for the issuance of a new birth certificate showing the child to be the child of the adoptive parents.[16]

The adoption may have other peripheral effects. The marriage of an adopted child within the nuclear family should be held to be within the incest prohibitions found in the statutes.[17] The immigration laws make certain concessions to adopted children, both with respect to entry outside the quotas and to naturalization.[18] Persons adopted as adults should have the same rights and obligations as those who are adopted as children unless the statutes provide otherwise,[19] although there are a few cases to the contrary.[20]

A major change in adoption practice has been produced by the statutes which grant visitation rights to grandparents.[21] These statutes raise the questions whether existing rights of visitation held by natural grandparents are affected by the adoption of the child and whether grandparents may seek visitation after an adoption has occurred. A few statutes deal with these questions explicitly, either by providing that grandparents do not have visitation after adoption,[22] or that they

arrearages in support which accrued before the adoption. C. v. R., 169 N.J.Super. 168, 404 A.2d 366 (1979).

9. Marckwardt v. Superior Court for County of Los Angeles, 150 Cal.App.3d 471, 198 Cal.Rptr. 41 (1984); Jones v. Allen, 277 So.2d 599 (Fla.App.1973); Spencer v. Franks, 173 Md. 73, 195 A. 306 (1937).

10. Weinschel v. Strople, 56 Md.App. 252, 466 A.2d 1301 (1983); Petition of the Department of Social Services to Dispense With Consent to Adoption, 392 Mass. 696, 467 N.E.2d 861 (1984); In re Jessica W., 122 N.H. 1052, 453 A.2d 1297 (1982).

11. Matter of Adoption of Children by F., 170 N.J. Super. 419, 406 A.2d 986 (1979); Kattermann v. DiPiazza, 151 N.J.Super. 209, 376 A.2d 955 (1977); Matter of Custody of Dana Marie, 128 Misc.2d 1018, 492 N.Y.S.2d 340 (Fam.Ct.1985). Similar considerations have led one court to grant visitation rights to the adopted child's siblings. Matter of Adoption of Anthony, 113 Misc.2d 26, 448 N.Y.S.2d 377 (Fam.Ct.1982).

12. See the statutes cited in note 4, supra.

13. C. v. R., 169 N.J.Super. 168, 404 A.2d 366 (1979); Betz v. Horr, 276 N.Y. 83, 11 N.E.2d 548 (1937).

14. See the statutes cited in note 4, supra. But see Uniform Probate Code § 2–109, 8 Unif.L.Ann. 66 (1983), and Jones, Stepparent Adoption and Inheritance: A Suggested Revision of Uniform Probate Code § 2–109, 8 W. New Eng.L.Rev. 53 (1986).

15. Cases are collected in Annot., 53 A.L.R.2d 927 (1957).

16. Matter of Adoption of a Child by L. C. and E. R. C., 85 N.J. 152, 425 A.2d 686 (1981).

17. See section 2.9, supra, and Wadlington, The Adopted Child and Intra-Family Marriage Prohibitions, 49 Va.L.Rev. 478 (1963).

18. 8 U.S.C.A. § 1101(b)(1)(E) and (F); 8 U.S.C.A. § 1433.

19. McLaughlin v. People, 403 Ill. 493, 87 N.E.2d 637 (1949). See section 21.10, supra.

20. Martin v. Cuellar, 131 Colo. 117, 279 P.2d 843 (1955); Wilson v. Johnson, 389 S.W.2d 634 (Ky.1965).

21. Grandparent visitation is discussed in section 19.7, supra. The statutes on grandparent visitation are cited in Note, Grandparents' Statutory Visitation Rights and the Rights of Adoptive Parents, 49 Bklyn.L.Rev. 149 (1982); Note, Grandparent Visitation Statutes: Remaining Problems and the Need for Uniformity, 67 Marq.L. Rev. 730, 740 (1984); Note, Visitation After Adoption: In the Best Interests of the Child, 59 N.Y.U.L.Rev. 633 (1984).

22. Only two states seem to do this. Ariz.Rev.Stat. § 337.01 (Supp.1986); N.M.Stat.Ann. § 40–9–4 (1986), and the New Mexico statute seems to be ignored in Pillars v. Thompson, 103 N.M. 704, 712 P.2d 1366 (1986).

may have such rights.[23] Most of the grandparent visitation statutes are silent on the question. If the statutes dealing with the consequences of adoption are given their literal effect, that is, that the rights of natural parents and natural kindred are cut off by adoption, the result would be that grandparents could have no rights of visitation after adoption. Some cases have so held.[24]

The courts in other states take the position that the grandparent visitation statutes authorize visitation to be continued after adoption over the objection of the adoptive parents, where the child's interests are served thereby.[25] Although the child's best interests are ostensibly relied upon as the reason for ordering grandparent visitation, at least some of the cases justify the inference that it is the grandparent's interest which is the deciding factor in the decision.[26] Grandparent visitation is most often granted where the adoption has been by a stepparent,[27] but it may also be granted where neither adoptive parent is related to the child by blood.[28] The finding that visitation will promote the child's best interests is usually based upon evidence of long continued and relatively close contact between the grandparent and the child.[29]

One can appreciate the benefits of affection between grandparent and child without approving of these visitation orders. They represent a significant infringement of the principle that adoptive parents replace the blood parents for all purposes. Although grandparent visitation is probably sought more often where there has been a stepparent adoption than where strangers to the child's blood have adopted, it is equally disruptive of the family relationship in both cases when it is forced on the child's parents by judicial decision. The mere bringing of the suit imposes strains on family solidarity and on family resources. Grandparent visitation after adoption is a unique instance of court interference in a properly functioning nuclear family and should be rarely, if ever, permitted.

Adoption and Intestate Succession

If the adoption of a child is to have any consequences at all for inheritance purposes, it must mean that the adopted child inherits from his adoptive parents. In fact this is the universal rule today.[30] Where a child is

23. Note, Grandparent Visitation Statutes: Remaining Problems and the Need for Uniformity, 67 Marq.L. Rev. 730, 750 (1984).

24. Ex parte Bronstein, 434 So.2d 780 (Ala.1983), on remand 434 So.2d 784 (1983); Irvan v. Kizer, 286 Ark. 105, 689 S.W.2d 548 (1985); Wilson v. Wallace, 274 Ark. 48, 622 S.W.2d 164 (1981); Mitchell v. Erdmier, 253 Ga. 335, 320 S.E.2d 163 (1984); Matter of Adoption of Gardiner, 287 N.W.2d 555 (Iowa 1980); Browning v. Tarwater, 215 Kan. 501, 524 P.2d 1135 (1974); Smith v. Trosclair, 321 So.2d 514 (La.1975); Bikos v. Nobliski, 88 Mich.App. 157, 276 N.W.2d 541 (1979); Olson v. Flinn, 484 So.2d 1015 (Miss.1986); Acker v. Barnes, 33 N.C.App. 750, 236 S.E.2d 715 (1977), review denied 293 N.C. 360, 238 S.E.2d 149 (1977); Leake v. Grissom, 614 P.2d 1107 (Okl.1980); Deweese v. Crawford, 520 S.W.2d 522 (Tex.Civ.App.1975); Mitchell v. Doe, 41 Wash.App. 846, 706 P.2d 1100 (1985). The refusal to recognize grandparent visitation with respect to adopted child was held constitutional in Cox v. Stayton, 273 Ark. 298, 619 S.W.2d 617 (1981).

25. Johnson v. Fallon, 129 Cal.App.3d 71, 181 Cal. Rptr. 414 (1982); Lingwall v. Hoener, 108 Ill.2d 206, 91 Ill.Dec. 166, 483 N.E.2d 512 (1985); Morse v. Daly, 101 Nev. 320, 704 P.2d 1087 (1985); Mimkon v. Ford, 66 N.J. 426, 332 A.2d 199 (1975); People ex rel. Sibley v. Sheppard, 54 N.Y.2d 320, 445 N.Y.S.2d 420, 429 N.E.2d 1049 (1981); In re Thornton, 24 Ohio App.3d 152, 493 N.E.2d 977 (1985); Chavis v. Witt, 285 S.C. 77, 328 S.E.2d 74 (1985).

26. E.g., Mimkon v. Ford, 66 N.J. 426, 332 A.2d 199 (1975).

27. E.g., Lingwall v. Hoener, 108 Ill.2d 206, 91 Ill.Dec. 166, 483 N.E.2d 512 (1985); Mimkon v. Ford, 66 N.J. 426, 332 A.2d 199 (1975); Layton v. Foster, 61 N.Y.2d 747, 472 N.Y.S.2d 916, 460 N.E.2d 1351 (1984).

28. E.g., Morse v. Daly, 101 Nev. 320, 704 P.2d 1087 (1985). But Lingwall v. Hoener, 108 Ill.2d 206, 91 Ill.Dec. 166, 483 N.E.2d 512 (1985) seems to indicate that visitation should not be granted where the adoption is by strangers to the child's blood, but that a different approach should be taken for stepparent adoptions. Mimkon v. Ford, 66 N.J. 426, 332 A.2d 199 (1975) seems to take a similar position.

29. E.g., Morse v. Daly, 101 Nev. 320, 704 P.2d 1087 (1985); People ex rel. Sibley v. Sheppard, 54 N.Y.2d 320, 445 N.Y.S.2d 420, 429 N.E.2d 1049 (1981); In re Thornton, 24 Ohio App.3d 152, 493 N.E.2d 977 (1985).

30. See the statutes cited in note 4, supra, and Williams v. Nash, 247 Ark. 135, 445 S.W.2d 69 (1969); In re Kruse's Estate, 120 Cal.App.2d 254, 260 P.2d 969 (1953) (dictum); Welch v. Funchess, 220 Miss. 691, 71 So.2d 783 (1954); Maurer v. Becker, 26 Ohio St.2d 254, 271 N.E.2d 255 (1971); In re Estate of Hamilton, 73 Wash.2d 865, 441 P.2d 768 (1968) (adopted child is within the pretermitted child statute). But see Morris v. Ulbright, 558 S.W.2d 660 (Mo.1977).

adopted more than once, the proper result is that he inherit from his second adoptive parents and not from those who adopted him earlier.[31] Most cases would also hold that the children of a deceased adopted child inherit from the adoptive parent as the adopted child would have if he had survived.[32]

In the past when an adopted child claimed an intestate share in the estate of a person related to his adoptive parents, or, in other words, when he sought to inherit through the adoptive parents, he was somewhat less successful.[33] Today, however, many of the earlier cases have been overruled by express statutory amendment, so that the adopted child may inherit through as well as from his adoptive family. The correct analysis in all cases would effectuate the spirit and purpose of the adoption statutes by allowing the inheritance as if the adopted child had been born a natural child of his adoptive parent, and a majority of states take this position.[34]

The social security acts also permit the adopted child to receive benefits derived from his adoptive parent, but with certain detailed and complex limitations,[35] which have been held not to violate the Equal Protection Clause.[36]

Adoption Records: Confidentiality

In order to protect the interests of both natural and prospective adoptive parents by preventing each from knowing the identity of the other, the records of adoption proceedings have traditionally been confidential, except of course for stepparent and other relative adoptions and sometimes private placements as well. This has been accomplished by the enactment of statutes providing that such records must be sealed and may only be opened for inspection upon court order "for good cause shown" or some similar qualification.[37] During the expansive era of constitutional doctrine in the 1970's these statutes came under attack in many states on a variety of constitutional grounds. The state and federal courts have held that they do not violate the First Amendment,[38] the Equal Protection and Due Process Clauses of the Fourteenth Amendment[39] and that they do not

---

31. Quintrall v. Goldsmith, 134 Colo. 410, 306 P.2d 246 (1957); In re Estate of Orzoff, 116 Ill.App.3d 265, 72 Ill.Dec. 150, 452 N.E.2d 82 (1983); Matter of Adolphson's Estate, 403 Mich. 590, 271 N.W.2d 511 (1978); In re Talley's Estate, 188 Okl. 338, 109 P.2d 495 (1941), 26 Minn.L.Rev. 114 (1941).

32. In re Estate of Miner, 359 Mich. 579, 103 N.W.2d 498 (1960); Annot., 94 A.L.R.2d 1200 (1964).

33. See Smith and Fawsett, Florida Adoption and Intestate Succession Laws: A Legal Paralogism, 24 U.Fla. L.Rev. 603 (1972); Note, Inheritance Rights of an Adopted Child in Texas, 6 Hous.L.Rev. 350 (1968); Note, Domestic Relations—The Legal Consequences of Adoption in Georgia—Inheritance Rights and Wrongful Death Actions, 23 Mercer L.Rev. 1003 (1972); Note Intestate Succession and Adoption in Utah: A Need for Legislation, 1969 Utah L.Rev. 56; Note, Intestate Succession, Sociology and the Adopted Child, 11 Vill.L.Rev. 392 (1966). See also Binavince, Adoption and the Law of Descent and Distribution: A Comparative Study and a Proposal for Model Legislation, 51 Cornell L.Q. 152 (1966). The earlier form of statute was held constitutional in Nunnally v. Trust Company Bank, 244 Ga. 697, 261 S.E.2d 621 (1979), cert. denied 445 U.S. 964, 100 S.Ct. 1654, 64 L.Ed.2d 240 (1980).

34. See the statutes cited in note 4, supra.

35. The statutes and cases are collected in Annot., Denial of Social Security Benefits to Adopted Children Who Are Neither Natural Children Nor Stepchildren of Eligible Individual and Who Do Not Meet Dependency Requirements, Under § 202(d)(8) of the Social Security

Act, As Amended (42 U.S.C.A. § 402(d)(8)), 57 A.L.R.Fed. 942 (1982).

36. Johnson v. Califano, 656 F.2d 569 (10th Cir.1981); Tsosie v. Califano, 630 F.2d 1328 (9th Cir.1980), cert. denied 451 U.S. 940, 101 S.Ct. 2022, 68 L.Ed.2d 328 (1981); Clayborne v. Califano, 603 F.2d 372 (2d Cir.1979).

37. E.g., Colo.Rev.Stat. § 19–4–104 (1986); N.J.Stat. Ann. § 9:3–52 (Supp.1986); S.C.Code 1986, § 20–7–1780; N.Y.—McKinney's Dom.Rel.Laws § 114 (1977 and Supp. 1987); Va.Code 1980, § 63.1–236; West's Rev.Code Wash. Ann. § 26–33–330 (1986); Uniform Adoption Act § 16, 9 Unif.L.Ann. 48 (1979).

38. Schechter v. Boren, 535 F.Supp. 1 (W.D.Okl.1980); Application of Maples, 563 S.W.2d 760 (Mo.1978). The First Amendment claim was that these statutes prevent the adopted child from receiving information and therefore abridged freedom of speech.

39. Alma Society, Inc. v. Mellon, 601 F.2d 1225 (2d Cir.1979), cert. denied 444 U.S. 995, 100 S.Ct. 531, 62 L.Ed.2d 426 (1979); In re Roger B., 84 Ill.2d 323, 49 Ill. Dec. 731, 418 N.E.2d 751 (1981), appeal dismissed for want of a substantial federal question 454 U.S. 806, 102 S.Ct. 80, 70 L.Ed.2d 76 (1981); Linda F. M. v. Department of Health of the City of New York, 52 N.Y.2d 236, 437 N.Y.S.2d 283, 418 N.E.2d 1302 (1981), appeal dismissed for want of a substantial federal question 454 U.S. 806, 102 S.Ct. 79, 70 L.Ed.2d 76 (1981); In re Assalone, ___ R.I. ___, 512 A.2d 1383 (1986); Bradey v. Children's Bureau of South Carolina, 275 S.C. 622, 274 S.E.2d 418 (1981); Application of Sage, 21 Wash.App. 803, 586 P.2d 1201 (1978). The Alma case also rejected a claim that the New

unconstitutionally infringe the adopted child's right of privacy.[40] The courts in these cases recognized that a natural parent who is considering the placement of his child for adoption may have many legitimate reasons for not having his identity known to those with whom the child will be placed.[41] Maintaining confidentiality in this way thus avoids what might otherwise be a factor working against the placement and against the child's welfare. Correspondingly the integration of the child into his adoptive family and the resulting solidarity of that family are aided by the adoptive parents' awareness that the natural parent will not know who received the child and therefore will not be able to disrupt the adoptive family. For these reasons the sealing of adoption records used to be thought no more than good administration of the adoption process.

The courts are naturally reluctant to put forward a general definition of "good cause" for giving access to the records in view of the conflicting interests of natural parents, adoptive parents and adopted child.[42] The burden of proving cause is held to be on the person, usually the adopted child, who sought to have the records opened to his inspection.[43] At least one court indicated that if, after a confidential inquiry of the natural parent, a waiver of the confidentiality of the record is not obtained, inspection by the adopted child will

normally not be granted.[44] If the petition for inspection of the records is the product of no more urgent motive than a desire to know who one's natural parents are, the courts usually deny the request.[45] On the other hand if the evidence sought is needed for substantial medical or psychological reasons, the courts have been willing to permit inspection.[46] One case suggests that if there is property in the state which the adopted child might inherit from his natural parents, that might constitute a sufficient reason to look at the records.[47] A lower court in New Jersey has adopted the procedure of referring requests to see adoption records to the agency which arranged the adoption, with authority to solicit permission from the natural parent to reveal his identity to the adopted child.[48] If the permission is granted, disclosure would be automatic, but if not, the agency is to be given the authority to "broker a contract" with the natural parent. If the natural parent or the agency refuses permission, the adopted child may appeal to the court. Although this procedure has some superficial appeal, it seems to place undue pressure and undue risk of revealing identity on the parent and therefore should be disapproved.

The adoption records laws began to come under criticism during the 1970's at the instigation of organizations formed to end confidentiality and to achieve accessibility for

---

York statute imposed upon adopted children badges or incidents of slavery, thereby violating the Thirteenth Amendment.

40. Application of Maples, 563 S.W.2d 760 (Mo.1978); Mills v. Atlantic City Department of Vital Statistics, 148 N.J.Super. 302, 372 A.2d 646 (1977).

41. Linda F. M. v. Department of Health of the City of New York, 52 N.Y.2d 236, 437 N.Y.S.2d 283, 418 N.E.2d 1302 (1981), appeal dismissed for want of a substantial federal question 454 U.S. 806, 102 S.Ct. 79, 70 L.Ed.2d 76 (1981).

42. Linda F. M. v. Department of Health of the City of New York, 52 N.Y.2d 236, 437 N.Y.S.2d 283, 418 N.E.2d 1302 (1981), appeal dismissed for want of a substantial federal question 454 U.S. 806, 102 S.Ct. 79, 70 L.Ed.2d 76 (1981).

43. Application of Maples, 563 S.W.2d 760 (Mo.1978). But Mills v. Atlantic City Department of Vital Statistics, 148 N.J.Super. 302, 372 A.2d 646 (1977) held that the burden of proof is on the adopted child before he reaches majority, but if he seeks to see the record after becoming

an adult, the burden is on the state to show that there is not good cause.

44. Application of Maples, 563 S.W.2d 760 (Mo.1978). See also Application of Sage, 21 Wash.App. 803, 586 P.2d 1201 (1978).

45. Linda F. M. v. Department of Health of the City of New York, 52 N.Y.2d 236, 437 N.Y.S.2d 283, 418 N.E.2d 1302 (1981), appeal dismissed for want of a substantial federal question 454 U.S. 806, 102 S.Ct. 79, 70 L.Ed.2d 76 (1981); Application of Romano, 109 Misc.2d 99, 438 N.Y.S.2d 967 (Sur.Ct.1981); In re Assalone, ___ R.I. ___, 512 A.2d 1383 (1986); Bradey v. Children's Bureau of South Carolina, 275 S.C. 622, 274 S.E.2d 418 (1981) (petitioner must show a compelling need to see the records).

46. Application of Anonymous, 92 Misc.2d 224, 399 N.Y.S.2d 857 (Sur.Ct.1977). But see Matter of Dixon, 116 Mich.App. 763, 323 N.W.2d 549 (1982).

47. Massey v. Parker, 369 So.2d 1310 (La.1979).

48. Mills v. Atlantic City Department of Vital Statistics, 148 N.J.Super. 302, 372 A.2d 646 (1977).

those adopted persons wishing to discover the identity of their natural parents.[49] Publicity and political influence followed, in part by virtue of the leadership of individuals in the movement who published books about their experiences in trying to locate their natural parents.[50] Other books [51] and a large amount of law review commentary followed, nearly all of it favoring some relaxation of the existing restrictions on access to adoption records.[52] It is odd that the discussion was addressed exclusively to court records in view of the fact that most of the information of interest to adopted children was in the possession of adoption agencies which largely continued to follow a policy of confidentiality although somewhat less strictly than would be permitted by the statutes on court records prevailing in some states.[53] But the agencies did not release information about the circumstances of birth or the identity of the natural parents.[54]

As a result of these activities a substantial number of states changed their statutes on adoption records in an attempt to meet the objections so far as that could be done without invading the privacy of the natural parents. The interest of adoptive parents in continuing to be viewed as the parents of adopted children was apparently considered of too little importance to be taken into account. The statutes largely took two approaches to confidentiality.[55] Some of them provided for the release of medical and other information about the adopted person but excluded from the material released any information which would lead to the identification of the natural parents.[56] The second approach was to create a system by which adopted persons and natural parents could each indicate their consent to be identified by the other and by which these indications of consent could be inspected by the persons involved. The usual device for accomplishing this is the maintenance of a state registry of natural parents and adopted persons, with provision for notification of the individuals involved when a match of parent and child is determined.[57] The information is

49. Klibanoff, Genealogical Information in Adoption: The Adoptee's Quest and the Law, 11 Fam.L.Q. 185 (1977).

50. The most influential of these was probably F. Fisher, The Search for Anna Fisher (1973), describing the author's attempt, finally successful, to find her natural parents.

51. B. Lifton, Twice Born (1975); Triseliotis, In Search of Origins: The Experience of Adopted People (1973).

52. Note, The Adoptee's Right to Know: In re Adoption of a Female Infant, 1 Antioch L.J. 107 (1981); Note, Arizona Adoption Records Statute: A Call for Reform, 1979 Ariz.St.L.Rev. 459; Levin, The Adoption Trilemma: The Adult Adoptee's Emerging Search for His Ancestral Identity, 8 U. Baltimore L.Rev. 496 (1979); Note, The State's Interest in Adoption and Washington's Sealed Records Statute, 4 U.Puget Sound L.Rev. 351 (1981); Note, Sealed Adoption Records and the Constitutional Right of Privacy of the Natural Parent, 34 Rut.L.Rev. 451 (1982); Smith, In re the Application of Annetta Louise Maples: The Adoptee's Right to Know, 23 St.L.U.L.J. 731 (1979); Note, Discovery Rights of the Adoptee—Privacy Rights of the Natural Parent: A Constitutional Dilemma, 4 U. of San Fernando Valley L.Rev. 65 (1975) (suggests mediation); Note, The Adult Adoptee's Constitutional Right to Know His Origins, 48 So.Cal.L.Rev. 1196 (1975); Note, Confidentiality of Adoption Records: An Examination, 52 Tul.L.Rev. 817 (1978); Note, The Adoptee's Right to Sealed Adoption Records in North Carolina, 16 Wake Forest L.Rev. 563 (1980). See also Sorosky, Baran, Pannor, Identity Conflicts in Adoptees, 45 Amer.J. of Orthopsychiatry 18 (1975).

53. M. Jones, The Sealed Adoption Record Controversy: Report of a Survey of Agency Policy, Practice and Opinion (Research Center, Child Welfare League of America, July, 1976).

54. Klibanoff, Genealogical Information in Adoption: The Adoptee's Quest and the Law, 11 Fam.L.Q. 185 (1977).

55. Pierce, Survey of State Laws and Legislation on Access to Adoption Records, 10 Fam.L.Reporter 3035 (1984) gives a useful review of the activities in the various states on this subject. It is notable that two states authorize the adult adopted person to see his original birth certificate. Ala.Code 1986, § 26–10–4; Kan.Stat. Ann. § 65–2423 (1985), and one state opens court records to the adoptee at his majority. Va.Code 1980, § 63.1–236.

56. E.g., West's Ann.Cal.Civ.Code § 224t (Supp.1987); Conn.Gen.Stat.Ann. § 45–68e (Supp.1987); Mich.Comp. Laws Ann. §§ 27.3178 (555.27), 27.3178 (555.67), 27.3178 (555.68) (Supp.1986); Vernon's Ann.Mo.Stat. § 453.090 (1986); Ohio Rev.Code § 3107.17 (Supp.1986); Pa.Stat. tit. 23, § 2905 (Supp.1986); Wis.Stat.Ann. § 48.93 (Supp. 1986).

57. West's Ann.Cal.Civ.Code § 227 (Supp.1987); Colo. Rev.Stat. § 25–2–113.5 (Supp.1986); Conn.Gen.Stat.Ann. §§ 65i, 65j, 65k, 65l (1981); West's Fla.Stat.Ann. § 63.162 (1985); Me.Rev.Stat.Ann. tit. 22, § 2706–A (1980 and Supp.1986). The construction and administration of the Connecticut statute are dealt with in Sherry H. v. Probate Court, 177 Conn. 93, 411 A.2d 931 (1979).

A physician who revealed the identity of a natural parent to her daughter after the daughter had been

of course not available to anyone other than those determined to be parent and child.

Whether the systems which have so far been developed will satisfy adopted persons searching for their "roots" remains to be seen. One suspects that it is only a relatively small proportion of adopted persons who are concerned with these matters and that the notoriety given to the problem is somewhat in excess of its social significance.

WESTLAW REFERENCES

Adoption and Intestate Succession

di(adopt! /s child minor infant /s statut! law legislat! /s "intestate succession")

§ 20.11 Attack on Adoption Decrees

Statutes of Limitations

The obvious necessity for finality of adoption decrees has led the legislatures of many states to enact statutes which provide that adoptions may not be set aside after the running of a relatively short period of limitations, usually not in excess of five years.[1] The statutes which forbid all attack, jurisdictional as well as merely procedural, raise a difficult constitutional issue. To put the hardest case, a husband and wife are divorced and the wife given custody of their child. The wife runs off with the child, hides from the husband, remarries and the second husband adopts the

child without notice to the child's father and by means of fraudulent statements to the adoption court. The father does not located the child despite diligent attempts to do so until the period of limitations has run. As soon as he does so he sues in equity to set the decree aside for lack of notice and is met with the defense of the statute of limitations.[2] The statutes of states like California or Oregon would bar his suit unless the application of the statute to this situation violates the state or federal constitution. A substantial number of cases has held that the application of the statute of limitations to cases of this kind does not violate the Due Process Clause of the Fourteenth Amendment on the ground that the statute has a reasonable relation to a legitimate state purpose, establishing a stable environment for the adopted child.[3] There are cases either holding or assuming that such an application of the statute is unconstitutional, however.[4]

Notwithstanding the broad language in some cases to the effect that a judgment void for want of jurisdiction is a nullity at all times and for all purposes, these statutes barring attack on adoption decrees should be held valid and the cases so holding should be followed. The adoption decree is sui generis because it closely concerns the life of someone other than the contending parties. A rule that an individual's right to set aside a judgment entered without jurisdiction over him

adopted was held liable for breach of a confidential relationship in Humphers v. First Interstate Bank, 298 Or. 706, 696 P.2d 527 (1985).

§ 20.11

1. E.g., Alaska Stat. § 25.23.140 (1983); West's Ann. Cal.Civ.Code § 227d (1982); Colo.Rev.Stat. § 19–4–116 (1986); D.C.Code 1981, § 16–310; West's Fla.Stat.Ann. § 63.182 (1985); Md.Code, Family Law, § 5–325 (1984); Neb.Rev.Stat. § 43–116 (1984); N.C.Gen.Stat. § 48–28 (1984); Or.Rev.Stat. § 109.381 (1984); V.Tex.C.A., Fam. Code § 16.12 (1986). See also Uniform Adoption Act § 15(b), 9 Unif.L.Ann. 47 (1979).

2. This is essentially the case of McClary v. Follett, 226 Md. 436, 174 A.2d 66 (1961) which set aside the adoption without passing on the constitutional question. Failure to give notice would be considered a violation of due process under Armstrong v. Manzo, 380 U.S. 545, 85 S.Ct. 1187, 14 L.Ed.2d 62 (1965).

3. Syrovatka v. Erlich, 608 F.2d 307 (8th Cir.1979), cert. denied 446 U.S. 935, 100 S.Ct. 2152, 64 L.Ed.2d 788

(1980), rehearing denied 448 U.S. 910, 100 S.Ct. 3056, 65 L.Ed.2d 1140 (1980); Walter v. August, 186 Cal.App.2d 395, 8 Cal.Rptr. 778 (1960) (semble); In Interest of Voyles, 417 So.2d 497 (La.App.1982), writ denied 420 So.2d 981 (1982); Hogue v. Olympic Bank, 76 Or.App. 17, 708 P.2d 605 (1985), review denied 300 Or. 545, 715 P.2d 92 (1986) (citing other cases); Stewart v. Rouse, 469 S.W.2d 615 (Tex.Civ.App.1971), modified on other grounds 475 S.W.2d 574 (Tex.1972).

4. Sumter v. Allton, 278 Ark. 621, 648 S.W.2d 55 (1983); Matter of Adoption of Lori Gay W., 589 P.2d 217 (Okl.1978), cert. denied 441 U.S. 945, 99 S.Ct. 2165, 60 L.Ed.2d 1047 (1979); Hughes v. Aetna Casualty & Surety Co., 234 Or. 426, 383 P.2d 55 (1963); Campbell v. Kindred, 26 Or.App. 771, 554 P.2d 599 (1976). See also Annot., 83 A.L.R.2d 945 (1962) and White v. Davis, 163 Colo. 122, 428 P.2d 909 (1967).

cannot be cut off by lapse of time does not and should not apply to the case where interests exist superior to those of the party whose rights are terminated. A court faced with this problem could solve it partially even if the statute is held invalid by treating it as a question of custody. If the child's welfare requires it, his custody could be left with the foster parents even though the adoption is set aside. Subsequently a new adoption proceeding could be brought if that also were consistent with the child's best interests and the natural parent's rights could then be terminated if the applicable termination statute so provided.[5]

Where the adoption is attacked on grounds other than lack of notice or of jurisdiction, the statute of limitations of course protects the decree.[6] In the absence of a statute of limitations the attack may be barred by laches[7] or waiver.[8]

Parties and Grounds

Most attempts to set aside adoption decrees are made by the natural parents. The correct procedure is an independent suit in equity to set aside the decree, a form of direct attack.[9] A motion in the original adoption suit is normally not the correct method of attack.[10] Collateral attack is also occasionally attempted but does not succeed unless the decree was entered without jurisdiction.[11] Some courts seem to have an extraordinarily broad definition of jurisdictional attack, however.[12]

The natural parent clearly has standing to attack the decree.[13] In the rare case where he joined in the petition to adopt, he may be estopped, however.[14] The older cases held that the father of the illegitimate child had no standing to attack the adoption,[15] but of course this is no longer true and he has the same standing that the father of a legitimate child would have.[16]

The clearest justification for setting an adoption aside at the instance of the natural parent is that the parent was not given notice of the adoption proceeding.[17] The decree may also be set aside where no consent to the

5. See section 20.6, supra, on termination of parental rights.

6. Cottrell v. Cottrell, 258 Ark. 116, 522 S.W.2d 433 (1975); Beatty v. Brooking, 9 Mich.App. 579, 157 N.W.2d 793 (1968); In re Kerr, 547 S.W.2d 837 (Mo.App.1977); In re Adoption of Hiatt, 157 Neb. 914, 62 N.W.2d 123 (1954). Cf. McClary v. Follett, 226 Md. 436, 174 A.2d 66 (1961).

7. Garcia v. De Enriquez, 313 S.W.2d 918 (Tex.Civ. App.1958); Bull v. Fenich, 34 Wash.App. 435, 661 P.2d 1012 (1983).

8. Shuttleworth v. Catholic Family Services, 439 So.2d 1292 (Ala.Civ.App.1983), cert. denied 466 U.S. 950, 104 S.Ct. 2151, 80 L.Ed.2d 537 (1984).

9. Laffoon v. Hayden, 337 P.2d 736 (Okl.1959).

10. Shaw v. Pilcher, 9 Utah 2d 222, 341 P.2d 949 (1959). But a motion may be used to set aside the interlocutory decree of adoption. Powell v. Powell, 99 Ga.App. 730, 109 S.E.2d 827 (1959).

11. Liberty Mutual Ins. Co. v. Klem, 288 F.Supp. 533 (N.D.Tex.1968); In re Smith's Estate, 86 Cal.App.2d 456, 195 P.2d 842 (1948); In re Harris' Estate, 339 Ill.App. 162, 89 N.E.2d 197 (1949); Hogg v. Peterson, 245 Ind. 515, 198 N.E.2d 767 (1964); Hamilton v. Craig, 257 S.W.2d 500 (Tex.Civ.App.1953). Petition of Stern, 2 Ill.App.2d 311, 120 N.E.2d 62 (1954) seems to hold that collateral attack will lie only where the error is apparent on the face of the record. For a cogent argument that the direct collateral distinction should be abandoned here, see Uhlenhopp, Adoption in Iowa, 40 Iowa L.Rev. 228, 279 (1955).

12. Batton v. Massar, 149 Colo. 404, 369 P.2d 434 (1962), 35 Rocky Mt.L.Rev. 314 (1963) (dictum that consent is jurisdictional); Blue v. Boisvert, 143 Me. 173, 57 A.2d 498 (1948) (decree is void if adoption proceedings are not in compliance with the statute); In re Ramsey, 164 Ohio St. 567, 132 N.E.2d 469 (1956) (may attack the decree collaterally for lack of consent); Hughes v. Aetna Casualty & Surety Co., 234 Or. 426, 383 P.2d 55 (1963) (lack of parents' consent or appointment of agency as guardian). Lack of consent was held not jurisdictional in Hogg v. Peterson, 245 Ind. 515, 198 N.E.2d 767 (1964).

13. Durham v. Barrow, 600 S.W.2d 756 (Tex.1980) (parent may attack the decree terminating his parental rights and then if successful attack the adoption).

14. In re Adoption of Curtis, 143 Mont. 330, 390 P.2d 209 (1964).

15. In re Cotes' Estate, 144 Me. 297, 68 A.2d 18 (1949).

16. Stanley v. Illinois, 405 U.S. 645, 92 S.Ct. 1208, 31 L.Ed.2d 551 (1972); Kozak v. Catholic Social Services of St. Clair County, 92 Mich.App. 579, 285 N.W.2d 378 (1979).

17. Armstrong v. Manzo, 380 U.S. 545, 85 S.Ct. 1187, 14 L.Ed.2d 62 (1965); Lee v. Superior Court in and for Pima County, 25 Ariz.App. 55, 540 P.2d 1274 (1975); Smith v. Tisdal, 484 N.E.2d 42 (Ind.App.1985); Kozak v. Catholic Social Services of St. Clair County, 92 Mich.App. 579, 285 N.W.2d 378 (1979). Persons other than the natural parent who are entitled to notice may attack the decree if notice is not given them. Annot., 92 A.L.R.2d 813, 817 (1963).

adoption was obtained.[18] More commonly there is consent, but it is alleged to have been obtained by fraud or duress. Where the evidence sustains the claim on the facts, the court will set aside the adoption, reasoning that this is extrinsic fraud since it prevented the natural parent from having a fair hearing.[19] But in the absence of fraud, duress or undue influence the adoption or the decree terminating parental rights will not be set aside.[20] Thus, for example, the decree will not be set aside on the ground that the natural parent changed his mind about consenting to the adoption or did not understand the full impact of his consent.[21] Oddly enough, one finds little consideration for the child's needs or interests in these cases, the courts focusing exclusively on the question whether fraud in fact occurred.[22] But a consent originally genuine and not affected by fraud or duress may not be revoked after entry of the adoption decree or relied upon as a reason for setting aside the adoption.[23] Care must be taken to distinguish dealing with revocation of consent before the decree is entered from those in which revocation is attempted after adoption. Revocation after adoption is refused even where the natural parent has undergone a

change in his circumstances affecting his ability and desire to care for the child.[24] It is also generally held that irregularities in the form or execution of the consent do not justify setting aside the adoption,[25] nor do other formal defects in the proceedings.[26]

In the rare cases which have arisen the courts have been willing to allow natural parents to set aside adoption decrees upon proof that the adoptive parents were not qualified,[27] or had neglected or mistreated the child subsequent to the adoption.[28] The reasoning seems to be that the natural parents are, even after their parental rights have been terminated by adoption, more interested in the welfare of the child than anyone else and therefore have standing to attack the decree. In such cases of course setting the adoption aside is also in the child's interests.

Suits by adoptive parents to set aside adoptions present different questions. California authorizes such suits where the child shows evidence of "developmental disability" or mental illness resulting from conditions existing before the adoption, if the suit is filed within five years of the adoption.[29] This section has been held to permit the court to set

---

18. Lee v. Superior Court in and for Pima County, 25 Ariz.App. 55, 540 P.2d 1274 (1975); Leonard v. Leonard, 88 Idaho 485, 401 P.2d 541 (1965); In re Adoption of Thornton, 184 Kan. 551, 337 P.2d 1027 (1959); Blue v. Boisvert, 143 Me. 173, 57 A.2d 498 (1948); In re Ramsey, 164 Ohio St. 567, 132 N.E.2d 469 (1956).

19. Arnold v. Howell, 98 Cal.App.2d 202, 219 P.2d 854 (1950); People ex rel. Karr v. Weihe, 30 Ill.App.2d 361, 174 N.E.2d 897 (1961); Matter of Kozak, 92 Mich.App. 579, 285 N.W.2d 378 (1979); In re Novak, 536 S.W.2d 33 (Mo.1976); Adoption of Robin, 571 P.2d 850 (Okl.1977). But perjury in the adoption hearing is not the sort of fraud which warrants setting the decree aside. Davis v. Winningham, 483 S.W.2d 535 (Tex.Civ.App.1972).

20. Matter of Welfare of K. T., 327 N.W.2d 13 (Minn. 1982); In re Adoption of C. L. R., 218 Neb. 319, 352 N.W.2d 916 (1984); In re Adoption of Minor Child, 109 R.I. 443, 287 A.2d 115 (1972).

21. BB v. SS and JS, 171 Colo. 534, 468 P.2d 859 (1970); Matter of Male Child Born July 15, 1985, ___ Mont. ___, 718 P.2d 660 (1986); Matter of Nicky, 81 Misc. 2d 132, 364 N.Y.S.2d 970 (Sur.Ct.1975).

22. See People ex rel. Karr v. Weihe, 30 Ill.App.2d 361, 174 N.E.2d 897 (1961). See Uhlenhopp, Adoption in Iowa, 40 Iowa L.Rev. 279–281 (1955).

23. Batton v. Massar, 149 Colo. 404, 369 P.2d 434 (1962), 35 Rocky Mt.L.Rev. 314 (1963); Riley v. Byrne, 145

Mont. 138, 399 P.2d 980 (1965); Bidwell v. McSorley, 194 Va. 135, 72 S.E.2d 245 (1952). But see Smith v. Consul General of Spain, 110 N.H. 62, 260 A.2d 95 (1969), which held that if the parent revoked her consent before the adoption decree was entered, the decree should be set aside.

24. Annot., 2 A.L.R.2d 887, 892, 894 (1948).

25. Riley v. Byrne, 145 Mont. 138, 399 P.2d 980 (1965).

26. In re Adoption of Hiatt, 157 Neb. 914, 62 N.W.2d 123 (1954).

27. Adoption of Montgomery, 167 Pa.Super. 635, 76 A.2d 240 (1950) (adoptive parents not married, a fact concealed from the court). Other cases are cited in Annot., 2 A.L.R.2d 887, 896 (1948).

28. Gillen v. Edge, 214 Ark. 776, 217 S.W.2d 926 (1949), and Annot., 2 A.L.R.2d 887, 896 (1948).

29. West's Ann.Cal.Civ.Code § 227b (1982). See also West's Ann.Cal.Civ.Code 227c (1982). Several other states have statutes authorizing the abrogation of adoption decrees on these or different grounds. Levy, Duncan, Constitutional Implications of Adoption Revocation Statutes, 8 Pac.L.J. 611, 625 (1977); Note, Annulment of Adoption Decrees on Petition of Adoptive Parents, 22 J.Fam.L. 549, 565 (1984).

aside an adoption at the suit of one of the two adoptive parents after their marriage had ended in divorce, with the other parent as an indispensable party.[30] The statute has been criticized on the ground that it does not require the child to be made a party,[31] a criticism which seems sound both as a matter of constitutional law and of decent regard for the rights of the adopted child. Presumably the child's welfare would be a key factor in the court's decision to set aside the adoption. In any event the policy underlying this kind of statute is doubtful and certainly inconsistent with the philosophy of the adoption process which is to create a family in all possible respects like the natural family.

There is in some states the remedy of relinquishment which provides a method for voluntarily terminating parental rights.[32] This should be as readily available to adoptive parents as to natural parents.[33] Since in relinquishment the child's welfare is clearly the focus of inquiry, this should be the exclusive

method for terminating the parental rights of adoptive parents, at least where no infirmity in the adoption decree is alleged. No case has been found which takes this position, however.

In the absence of statutory authority the courts have understandably taken a dim view of attempts by adoptive parents to set aside adoption decrees.[34] A few cases have permitted attack on adoption decrees by the adoptive parents where fraud or undue influence were alleged.[35] But adoptions have been held immune to attack where the child proved to be mentally retarded,[36] where the child later rejected the adoptive parents,[37] or where the adoptive parents merely wanted to be freed from a burdensome responsibility.[38]

Attack on the adoption decree by the person adopted rarely occurs. When it does, the success of the attack should depend on the grounds on which it is made. If, for example, the contention is that there was some defect in notice to or consent of the natural parents,

---

30. Department of Social Welfare v. Superior Court of Contra Costa County, 1 Cal.3d 1, 81 Cal.Rptr. 345, 459 P.2d 897 (1969).

31. Levy, Duncan, Constitutional Implications of Adoption Revocation Statutes, 8 Pac.L.J. 611 (1977).

32. See section 20.4, supra.

33. Hammerlund v. Washington Children's Home Society, 56 Wash.2d 609, 354 P.2d 945 (1960) involved an adopted child relinquished in this way. In re Welfare of Alle, 304 Minn. 254, 230 N.W.2d 574 (1975) takes a position contra the text statement, refusing to permit a relinquishment but suggesting an attack on the adoption decree on the ground of the fraud of a natural parent leading to a stepparent adoption.

34. Allen v. Allen, 214 Or. 664, 330 P.2d 151 (1958) held that there is jurisdiction to set the decree aside only in order to protect the child and that the adoptive parents, having invoked the court's jurisdiction, may not attack the decree. A similar decision is Matter of Marriage of Haley, 66 Or.App. 37, 672 P.2d 1222 (1983), review denied 296 Or. 486, 677 P.2d 702 (1984), which also denied the adoptive father standing to attack on the ground that he was attempting to assert the rights of the natural father. See also Cribbs v. Floyd, 188 S.C. 443, 199 S.E. 677 (1938). Cowhey v. Tator, 36 Ill.App.3d 962, 344 N.E.2d 501 (1976) held that the annulment of the marriage of the adoptive parents was not a reason to set aside the adoption, since it did not affect the adoptive relationship to the child. Estoppel to attack the jurisdiction in the adoption proceeding was also relied upon to prevent attack by the adoptive stepfather in Matter of Adoption of Hobson, 8 Kan.App.2d 772, 667 P.2d 911 (1983). Other cases are cited in Note, Annulment of

Adoption Decrees on Petition of Adoptive Parents, 22 J.Fam.L. 549 (1984).

35. Adoption of Jason R., 88 Cal.App.3d 11, 151 Cal. Rptr. 501 (1979); County Department of Public Welfare v. Morningstar, 128 Ind.App. 688, 151 N.E.2d 150 (1958); Pierce v. Pierce, 522 S.W.2d 435 (Ky.1975); In re Welfare of Alle, 304 Minn. 254, 230 N.W.2d 574 (1975). The adopted children were held entitled to appeal from a decree setting aside their adoption at the suit of the adoptive father in Matter of Appeal in Pima County, 138 Ariz. 291, 674 P.2d 845 (1983). But it was held that an adoption would not be set aside for fraud where the alleged fraud was not "extrinsic" in In re Adoption of Hammer, 15 Ariz.App. 196, 487 P.2d 417 (1971).

36. In re McDuffee, 352 S.W.2d 23 (Mo.1961) (child's welfare is the crucial factor, should not annul the adoption where he would become a public charge); In re Adoption of G, 89 N.J.Super. 276, 214 A.2d 549 (1965); Allen v. Allen, 214 Or. 664, 330 P.2d 151 (1958). Burr v. Stark County Board of Commissioners, 23 Ohio St.3d 69, 491 N.E.2d 1101 (1986) held that adoptive parents could recover for the fraud of a placement agency including them to adopt a mentally retarded and physically handicapped child.

37. In re Adoption of L, 56 N.J.Super. 46, 151 A.2d 435 (1959) (abrogation refused where the child wanted to return to her natural mother to avoid the more severe discipline of her adoptive parents); In re Eaton, 305 N.Y. 162, 111 N.E.2d 431 (1953) (court refused to annul adoption after the child had reached majority).

38. Cases are cited in Annot., 2 A.L.R.2d 887, 903 (1948).

this might entitle the child to have the adoption set aside, since the requirements of notice and consent are imposed for his protection as well as for the protection of his natural parents' interest. One case has allowed the child to have the decree set aside for defects in consent, saying that consent is jurisdictional.[39] It would appear the better rule to let the child also attack the decree for other grounds relevant to his welfare, as for example on the ground that the adoptive parents had been guilty of fraud with respect to their qualifications as parents. Agencies have been able to have adoptions vacated on this ground[40] and there seems no reason why the child should not also be a proper party plaintiff.

Attack on adoption decrees by persons other than natural parents, adoptive parents or the adopted child has been permitted occasionally where such persons have a natural interest in the child, as in the case of a grandparent who has received no notice of the adoption.[41] Most such attacks come from relatives of the adoptive parents who wish to upset the adoption in order to inherit from or through the adoptive parents at the expense of the child. In a considerable number of cases persons in this category have been permitted to attack decrees, at least where the defect was such that the court could find a lack of jurisdiction and thereby label the adoption void.[42] A smaller number of cases have held that since the adoptive parent would be estopped to attack the decree which he obtained, persons claiming under him would likewise be estopped.[43] In the rare cases which have arisen the courts are in disagreement as to whether a foster parent has standing to seek to vacate an adoption decree or a decree for commitment of a child in the care of such foster parent.[44]

Strangers to the adoption probably should not be permitted to attack the decree on the ground of non-compliance with such requirements as notice or consent since those requirements are not imposed for their protection, but for the protection of the natural parents or the child. There is not much authority for this position, however.[45] Statutory treatment of the subject would be useful.

---

39. Hughes v. Aetna Casualty & Surety Co., 234 Or. 426, 383 P.2d 55 (1963). See also Annot., 92 A.L.R.2d 813, 824 (1963).

40. In re Doe's Adoption, Storey 132, 197 A.2d 469 (Del.Orph.Ct.1964), judgment affirmed 8 Storey 487, 210 A.2d 863 (1964). In re Adoption of O., 88 N.J.Super. 30, 210 A.2d 440 (1965) refused to return an adopted child to the agency which had placed it when the agency attacked the decree on the ground of fraud. The court said that it reached this result on the ground of the child's welfare. See also Note, Family Law—Vacation of a Judgment of Adoption for Fraud—Welfare of the Child, 51 Iowa L.Rev. 735 (1966).

41. Cotton v. Hamblin, 234 Ark. 109, 350 S.W.2d 612 (1961). Attack by a grandmother was refused in Petition for Revocation of a Judgment for Adoption of a Minor, 393 Mass. 556, 471 N.E.2d 1348 (1984), partly on the ground of her delay in suing and partly on the ground that she was not a person entitled to notice of the adoption proceeding. See also Annot., 92 A.L.R.2d 813, 820–823 (1963).

42. In re Adoption of Sewall, 242 Cal.App.2d 208, 51 Cal.Rptr. 367 (1966) (attack niece of adoptive father); Succession of Bush, 222 So.2d 642 (La.App.1969) (attack by wife of adoptive father); Annots., 92 A.L.R.2d 813, 820–823 (1963), 16 A.L.R. 1020, 1024 (1922).

43. In re Smith's Estate, 86 Cal.App.2d 456, 195 P.2d 842 (1948); Dahl v. Grenier, 126 Ill.App.3d 891, 81 Ill.Dec. 870, 467 N.E.2d 992 (1984); Annots., 92 A.L.R.2d 813, 830 (1963), 16 A.L.R. 1020, 1030 (1922).

44. Holding that there is standing: Siebert v. Benson, 243 Ark. 843, 422 S.W.2d 683 (1968). Denying standing: Eason v. Welfare Commissioner, 171 Conn. 630, 370 A.2d 1082 (1976), cert. denied 432 U.S. 907, 97 S.Ct. 2953, 53 L.Ed.2d 1079 (1977).

45. In re Smith's Estate, 86 Cal.App.2d 456, 195 P.2d 842 (1948); Locke v. Merrick, 223 N.C. 799, 28 S.E.2d 523 (1944).

Appendix

WESTLAW REFERENCES

Information Contained on WESTLAW

WESTLAW is a computer assisted legal research service of West Publishing Company. Federal and state cases, statutes, and information of interest to those in specialized law practices are available on WESTLAW. For example, WESTLAW contains separate federal topical databases for areas of the law such as tax, patents and copyrights, bankruptcy, communications, labor, energy and utilities, securities, antitrust and business regulation, environment law, national defense, financial services, admiralty, and government contracts. WESTLAW also contains the text of the U.S. Code and the Code of Federal Regulations, West's Insta-Cite, Shepard's Citations, Black's Law Dictionary, and many other legal sources.

The case law databases consist of cases from the National Reporter System and some unpublished decisions from both state and federal courts. Most include a synopsis and headnotes written by West editors. The headnotes are classified according to West's Key Number system.

You may research cases from all states by accessing the ALLSTATES database. The database identifier for an individual state database consists of the state's postal abbreviation followed by a hyphen and the letters CS (e.g. IL–CS for Illinois cases).

You may research decisions from all federal courts in the ALLFEDS database. Individual federal case law databases include: Supreme Court Reporter (SCT), U.S.

Courts of Appeals (CTA), and U.S. District Courts (DCT). There are also individual databases for each U.S. Court of Appeals. The database identifier for an individual Court of Appeals consists of the letters CTA followed by the number of the federal circuit (e.g., CTA4 for the Fourth Circuit Court of Appeals).

The most helpful databases for the queries presented in this publication are the multistate database on family law and the individual state family law databases. The multistate database contains family law cases from all of the states. The database identifier for this database is MFL–CS. To access family law cases from an individual state, use an identifier consisting of the state's postal abbreviation followed by FL followed by a hyphen and the letters CS (e.g. MDFL–CS for Maryland family law cases).

The WESTLAW System

To research case law, select the appropriate database by typing its identifier and pressing ENTER. Then, type a query, and press ENTER to send it to the WESTLAW computer. The computer processes the query and identifies documents that satisfy the search request. The retrieved documents are then stored on magnetic discs and transmitted to your terminal. When the documents appear on the terminal you can decide whether or not to continue your research. If another search is necessary, the query may be recalled for editing, or an entirely new query may be formed.

You may immediately print documents displayed on the terminal, store them offline and print them later, or request West Publishing Company to print them and mail them to you. If you are using a personal computer to communicate with WESTLAW, you may store the documents on the magnetic discs of the personal computer.

Improving Legal Research With WESTLAW

WESTLAW adds a dynamic aspect to the text of this hornbook. Since new legislation and newly decided cases are continuously being added to WESTLAW databases, the queries at the end of many chapter sections provide a self-contained updating service. Queries are the messages you send to the computer to research an issue. Since a query may be addressed to the entire range of cases contained in the database designated for a search—from the earliest decisions to the most recent—search results will include the most current law available on any given issue. By directing the user to a wide range of supporting authorities, WESTLAW queries add to the customary role of hornbook footnotes.

In addition to its function as an efficient updating service, WESTLAW permits you to tailor your research to a specific legal issue or fact situation. WESTLAW permits access to the many cases that are not indexed or digested in texts, treatises, case digests, encyclopedias, citators, annotated law reports, looseleaf services, and periodicals. It gives you the flexibility to search for significant terms or combinations of terms in a variety of ways, instead of limiting you to the static index of a bound volume.

You may use the queries supplied in this edition "as is," but they are not meant to be anything more than illustrative. They are, however, examples upon which you can model your own queries, depending upon the legal issues and the facts you are researching. WESTLAW queries may be made as broad or as specific as desired.

Query Formulation: (a) In General

A query instructs the WESTLAW computer to retrieve documents containing terms ordered in the manner you have specified. The terms in a query are words and/or numbers that pinpoint the legal issue to be researched. These words or numbers are tied together by connectors that tell WESTLAW the order in which the terms must appear.

Below is a preformulated query that appears in this publication.

```
sy(ante-nuptial pre-nuptial  /s  alimony support
maintenance  /s  divorce dissolution separated
separation)
```

This query is taken from Chapter 1, § 1.9. Related WESTLAW queries appear at the end of many sections of the text. The above query asks WESTLAW to find documents where, within the synopsis field, the term ANTE–NUPTIAL or PRE–NUPTIAL occurs within the same sentence as the term ALIMONY or MAINTENANCE or SUPPORT, and also within the same sentence as DIVORCE or DISSOLUTION or SEPARATED or SEPARATION.

Query Formulation: (b) A Recommended Strategy

When you do research on WESTLAW, as with any research method, it is important to reduce your problem to its underlying legal issues. You may want to begin by consulting a hornbook. After refining the issues, the next step is determining the correct database. Among other considerations, this choice depends on the type of documents you want to retrieve, and the court or courts from which you want to retrieve them. You will then be ready to formulate a query.

Terms. When formulating a query the first step is to choose search terms that identify a particular issue. WESTLAW searches only the terms you enter. Specific words, terms of art, and relevant numbers should be included.

Root Expansion. Once the initial terms have been chosen, the root expander,(!), or universal character,(*), should be used to retrieve alternate forms of words. For example, if you are searching for various forms of the word "STERILIZE," use the root expander with the root STERILIZ!. This form retrieves STERILIZE, STERILIZATION, STERILIZING, and STERILIZED.

Universal Character. The universal character can be used at the end of a word or within a word to retrieve alternate forms. For example, searching ABUS* * * * retrieves ABUSING, ABUSIVE, ABUSE and ABUSED. This form is helpful where alternate forms are desired and using the root expander retrieves too many terms. It is unnecessary to use the root expander or the universal character to retrieve plurals, because they are retrieved automatically.

Alternative Terms. Alternative terms should be added if it is possible that the concept being searched is likely to be expressed in more than one way or using different language. For example, if you are looking for cases discussing tort actions between parent and child, the query

```
parent  /2  child  /5  immun!  /p  harmon
```

retrieves relevant documents. However, the query

```
(parent  /2  child) inter-famil! intra-famil!
 /5  immun!  /p  harmon
```

retrieves a greater number of relevant documents than the previous query.

You can easily search for compound words that may appear in various forms. Whenever your search terms include a compound word, use a hyphen between the words. This way, the search generates the other forms of the compound word. For example, inserting a hyphen between the words HEART and BALM generates HEARTBALM, HEART BALM, and HEART–BALM.

Connectors. You must use connectors to specify the relationship between the terms in the query. When choosing connectors, consider the grammatical context in which the search terms are likely to appear.

Query Formulation: (c) Proximity Connectors

Proximity connectors allow search terms to be ordered so that relevant documents will be retrieved from WESTLAW. The connectors and their meanings appear below.

Space (or).

> Example: alimony support

A space between search terms means **"or."** Leaving a space between the query terms ALIMONY and SUPPORT instructs the computer to retrieve documents that contain either the word ALIMONY or the word SUPPORT (or both).

& (and).

> Example: alimony & divorce

> Example: alimony support & divorce dissolution

Placing **&** between two terms instructs the computer to retrieve documents that contain both of the terms from anywhere in the document. The terms on either side may be in reverse order. As shown above, the **&** may be placed between groups of alternative terms as well as between individual terms.

/p (same paragraph).

> Example: alimony /p divorce

> Example: alimony support /p divorce dissolution

One or more search terms placed on each side of **/p** retrieves terms within the same paragraph. The terms on each side of **/p** may appear in the document in any order within the paragraph. As with **&**, the **/p** connector may be placed between groups of alternative terms.

/s (same sentence).

> Example: marry /s affinity

> Example: marry marri! marital /s affinity consanguinity

The **/s** symbol requires that one or more search terms on each side of **/s** appear in the same sentence. The **/s** may be placed between groups of alternative terms.

+s (precedes within sentence).

> Example: marvin +s marvin

The +**s** symbol requires that one or more terms to the left of this symbol precede one or more terms to the right of +**s** within the same sentence. The +**s** connector, like the other connectors, may be used between groups of alternative terms.

/n (numerical proximity within n words).

Example: informed /2 consent

The /**n** symbol means "within n words." **N** represents a whole number. The /**n** symbol requires that terms to the left of /**n** appear within the designated number of words as terms to the right of the connector. For example, placing /2 between the terms INFORMED and CONSENT instructs the computer to retrieve all documents in which the term INFORMED occurs within two words of the term CONSENT. Numerical proximities may also be used between groups of alternative search terms.

+n (precedes within n words).

Example: blood +2 test

The +**n** symbol may be used to require that terms to the left of the numerical proximity symbol precede the terms to the right of the symbol. Thus, the above query instructs the computer to retrieve cases in which the word BLOOD precedes and occurs within two words of the term TEST.

" " (restricted phrase).

Example: "wrongful life"

Using quotation marks is the most restrictive way to search terms. Placing terms within quotation marks instructs the computer to retrieve all documents in which the terms appear in the precise order in which they are typed. It should therefore be limited to those instances in which it is certain that the terms always appear adjacent to each other and in the same order. Please note that WESTLAW automatically generates standard plural forms for search terms, even when those terms are contained in quotation marks.

Spaces within quotation marks are not interpreted by the computer to mean "or." For example, the above query instructs the computer to retrieve all documents in which the term WRONGFUL appears adjacent to, and precedes, the term LIFE. However, phrases that are constructed with quotation marks may be used as alternatives by leaving a space between them.

Example: "wrongful life" illegitima!

Thus, the above query instructs the computer to retrieve all documents in which the phrase WRONGFUL LIFE or the term ILLEGITIMA! (or BOTH) occur. Since the space is not within quotation marks, it still means "or."

% (exclusion).

Example: "loco parentis" % guardian

The % symbol means "but not." It instructs the computer to exclude documents that contain terms appearing after the % symbol. In the above query, documents containing phrase LOCO PARENTIS would be retrieved, but not documents containing the term GUARDIAN.

Field Searching: (a) In General

WESTLAW can be instructed to search for terms within designated fields, or sections of a document. Moreover, in reviewing the documents that have been retrieved in a search, you may instruct the computer to display specified fields. The fields available for WESTLAW case law databases are described below.

Title Field. The title field contains the title of the case (e.g., *Griswold v. Connecticut*).

Citation Field. The citation field contains the citation of the case (e.g., 85 S.Ct. 1678).

Court Field. The court field contains abbreviations that allow searches for case law to be restricted to particular states, districts, or courts.

Judge Field. The judge field contains the names of judges or justices who wrote the majority opinion.

Synopsis Field. The synopsis field contains the synopsis of the case, prepared by West editors.

Topic Field. The topic field contains the West Digest Topic name and number, the Key Number, and the text of the key line for each digest paragraph.

Digest Field. The digest field contains digest paragraphs prepared by West editors. It includes the headnotes, the corresponding Digest Topics and Key Numbers, the title and citation of the case, the court, and the year of decision.

Headnote Field. The headnote field contains the headnotes prepared by West editors. It does not include Digest Topic lines, Key Number lines, or case identification information.

Opinion Field. The opinion field contains the text of the case, court and docket numbers, names of attorneys appearing in the case, and judges participating in the decision.

The format for a query that instructs the computer to search for terms within a specified field consists of the field name, or the first two letters of the field name, followed by a set of parentheses containing the search terms and grammatical connectors, if any. For example, to retrieve the case appearing at 85 S.Ct. 1678, type **citation** or **cite** or **ci,** followed by a set of parentheses containing the volume and page numbers of the citation, separated by the +5 connector.

```
citation(85  +5  1678)
cite(85  +5  1678)
ci(85  +5  1678)
```

Correspondingly, to retrieve the case entitled *Griswold v. Connecticut*, type **title** or **ti** followed by a set of parentheses containing the names in the title, separated by the & connector.

```
title(griswold  &  connecticut)
ti(griswold  &  connecticut)
```

Specific U.S. Code sections may also be retrieved. For example, the query

```
ci(42  +s  654)
```

retrieves section 654 of Title 42 of the U.S. Code.

Field Searching: (b) Combination Field Searching

Fields may be combined in a query. For example, terms may be searched in the headnote field and, at the same time, the query may be limited to search only for cases in which the opinions were written by a particular judge. Terms may also be searched in clusters of fields by joining any number of field names by commas. One application of this latter technique is to search for terms in the synopsis and digest fields. This technique is illustrated below:

```
sy,di(heart-balm)
```

This query instructs the computer to retrieve documents containing the term HEART–BALM in either the digest or synopsis fields. Any number of different fields may be combined with this method. Many of the queries presented include field restrictions for the synopsis and digest fields. Because cases are regularly added to WESTLAW before these editorial enhancements are added by West editors, these queries will not retrieve recently added cases or unreported decisions. In addition to other uses, researchers should consider using these searches without these restrictions either with a date restriction to retrieve only recent cases or in a database containing unreported decisions. This will insure more accurate results.

Consult the WESTLAW Reference Manual for further instruction on performing searches using field restrictions.

Date Restriction

Queries may be restricted to retrieve documents appearing before, after, or on a specified date, or within a range of dates. The date restriction format consists of the word DATE followed by the appropriate restriction(s) within parentheses. The words BEFORE and AFTER may be used to designate the desired date relationships. Alternatively, the symbols < and > may be used. Moreover, the month and day and year may be spelled out (e.g., January 1, 1984) or they may be abbreviated as follows: 1–1–84, or 1/1/84. The date restriction is joined to the rest of the query by the & symbol. For example, to retrieve documents decided or issued after December 31, 1981, that discuss a parent's liability for the torts of his child, any of the following formats may be used.

```
parent!  /7  responsib! liab!  /7  tort tortious!  /5  child  &  date(after 12/31/81)
parent!  /7  responsib! liab!  /7  tort tortious!  /5  child  &  date(>december 31, 1981)
parent!  /7  responsib! liab!  /7  tort tortious!  /5  child  &  date(>12–31–81)
```

To retrieve documents decided after December 31, 1981, and before April 1, 1983, the following format may be used:

```
parent!  /7  responsib! liab!  /7  tort tortious!  /5  child  &  date(after 12/31/79  &  before 4/1/83)
```

Digest Topic and Key Number Searching

Searches may be performed using West Digest Topic and Key Numbers as search terms. Because digest paragraphs are classified by West editors, digest topic and key number searches can quickly find cases classified under a particular point of law. Digest Topic numbers are available in numerous places including the WESTLAW Directory, any volume of the West Digest System and the WESTLAW Reference Manual. Key numbers can be found through the West Digest System and are also listed in other sources including reference materials (e.g., *Corpus Juris Secundum*) and annotated statutes.

To search a Digest Topic and Key Number on WESTLAW, type the topic number followed by the letter 'k' followed by the key number. For example,

    345k160

retrieves every case in the selected database that contains a digest paragraph classified under this Digest Topic and Key Number. As a follow-up to this type of search, the appropriate West Digest volume or pocket part should be checked for reclassifications or changes to a particular topic.

Retrieving Citing Documents

Case Law. To find cases that refer to other decisions, search the names of the parties and the citation numbers. For example, the query

    meyer /s nebraska

retrieves cases that cite *Meyer v. Nebraska*, 43 S.Ct. 625, 262 U.S. 390.

U.S. Code. To retrieve decisions that cite a section of the U.S. Code, search the title and section number. For example, the query

    42 +5 654

retrieves documents that refer to this section of Title 42. Searching title and number is a useful way of eliminating irrelevant documents containing references to '654' alone.

Shepard's Citations on WESTLAW

From any point in WESTLAW, case citations may be entered to retrieve Shepard's listings for those citations. To enter a citation to be Shepardized, the following formats may be used:

    sh 92 s ct 1526
    sh 92 s.ct. 1526
    sh92sct1526

When the citation is entered, Shepard's listings for the citation will be displayed. To Shepardize a citation it is not necessary to be in the same database as that of the citation. For example, a Supreme Court citation may be entered from any state database.

West's Insta-Cite

Insta-Cite, West Publishing Company's case history system, allows users to trace the prior and subsequent history of an individual case. It also contains parallel citations.

For example, Insta-Cite reveals if a case has been affirmed or reversed, if judgment has been vacated, or if certiorari has been denied. A list of Insta-Cite case history and precedential treatment notations appears in the WESTLAW Reference Manual.

The format to access the Insta-Cite display for a case citation consists of the letters **ic** followed by the citation, with or without spaces and periods:

    ic 92 s ct 1526
    ic 92 s.ct. 1526
    ic92sct1526

West's FIND—Retrieving Specific Court Decisions

The fastest way to retrieve a court decision from any of the case law databases is to use the FIND command. For example, the following queries

find 93 s.ct. 705

fi93sct705

retrieve the cited decisions directly. Using this method, you can quickly move between your search results and cases that may be cited in the documents produced in your search without having to enter new database information. To retrieve specific statutes or to retrieve a specific case by entering a standard query without using FIND, consult the "Field Searching (a) In General" section of this appendix.

Black's Law Dictionary

WESTLAW contains an online version of Black's Law Dictionary. The dictionary incorporates definitions of terms and phrases of English and American law.

Included within the preformulated queries in this publication are references to Black's Law Dictionary. To use Black's Law Dictionary online, type the letters **di** followed by the term to be defined, then press ENTER.

di antenuptial

To see the definition of a phrase, type the letters **di** followed by the phrase (without quotation marks):

di parens patriae

If the precise spelling of a term to be defined is not known, or a list of dictionary terms is desired, a truncated form of the word may be entered followed by the root expansion symbol(!):

di marr!

This produces a list of all dictionary terms beginning with the term MARRIAGE. From the list of terms, a number corresponding to the desired term can be entered to obtain the appropriate definitions.

WESTLAW Hornbook Queries: (b) Textual Illustration

This section explains how the queries provided in this hornbook may be used in researching issues in family law that a practitioner might encounter. Examples from the text of this edition have been selected to illustrate how the queries can be expanded, restricted, or altered to meet the specific needs of the reader's research.

A segment of the text from Chapter 5, section 5.5, of *Domestic Relations* by Clark appears below:

Whatever the constitutional position may be, changing social conditions have caused many courts, either explicitly or implicitly, to abandon maternal preference as a guide to the award of custody of illegitmate children. Illegitimacy has become much more prevalent than ever before in the United States. And more fathers of illegitimate children are taking an interest in their children and seeking custody or rights of visitation, although one suspects that these fathers are still a small proportion of all fathers of illegitimate children. The result has been that in a growing body of cases the courts are awarding custody of illegitimate children on the basis of the same sort of reasoning they would use in awarding custody of legitimate children. In many instances, perhaps the majority, the mother's claim is found to be most conducive to the child's welfare and custody is awarded to the mother. In other instances the father is given custody when that is found to be in the child's best interests.

The text of this section discusses a trend towards awarding custody to fathers of illegitimate children. In order to retrieve cases where fathers in this situation have been awarded custody, the following query

```
sy,di(father dad  /s  right  /3  custody  /s  illegitima!)
```

is given as a suggested search strategy on WESTLAW.

A sample screen showing a headnote from a document retrieved from the MFL–CS database using this query appears below:

```
              R 4  of 59     p 4 of 5     MFL–CS     T     427 So.2d 227

(3)
205Ak20
ILLEGITIMATE CHILDREN
k. Right to custody.
Fla.App. 3 Dist. 1983
Best interest of the child doctrine would not operate to terminate paramount custody rights of natural father of
illegitimate child, where the natural father had not abandoned the child but has contributed to the child's support
in a repetitive, customary manner.  West's F.S.A. s. 63.062.
Stevens v. Johnson
427 So.2d 227
```

The relevant portion of the opinion that corresponds to this headnote appears below:

There is competent and substantial evidence in the record to support the trial court's determination that appellee, the natural father of the minor child born out of wedlock, had not abandoned the child after the mother's death, but in fact had contributed to the child's support in a repetitive, customary manner. Section 64.062, Fla.Stat. (1979). Therefore, appellee had standing to contest the petition for adoption of the child filed by appellants, relatives of the deceased mother. On these facts the "best interest of the child" doctrine will not operate to terminate the paramount custody rights of the natural parent.

The query can be altered to meet the needs of the individual researchers. For example, a practitioner may wish to find cases that discuss joint custody of an illegitimate child. In this instance, the preformulated query can be modified as follows:

```
parent father dad  /s  illegitima!  /s  joint!
mutual!  /s  custody
```

The search terms PARENT, JOINT, and MUTUAL are added to retrieve documents related to this particular parental right. Below is a portion of a document retrieved by this query from the MFL–CS database:

```
              R 1 of 7    P 5 of 10    MFL–CS     T     471 So.2d 270

LSA–C.C. Art. 245 provides that where custody of an illegitmate child formally acknowledged by other
parents is sought, it shall be awarded in accordance with LSA–C.C. Art. 146, which sets forth a
preference for joint custody in both parents, according to the best interest of the children.  LSA–C.C. Art.
146(A)(2), however, permits an award of custody to either parent upon the court's consideration of the
factors involved in the case.  LSA–C.C. Art. 146(C)(2) further provides that the presumption in favor of
joint custody may be rebutted by showing that it is not in the best interest of the child after consideration
of the factors enumerated therein.  Furthermore, as this court pointed out in Plemer v. Plemer, 436 So.2d
```

1348 (La.App. 4th Cir.1983), even the phrase "joint custody" does not necessarily mean a "fifty-fifty sharing of time" between the parents, but rather each case depends on the child's age, the parents' availability and desires and other factors.

Conclusion

This appendix reviews methods you can use to obtain the most effective legal research concerning family law. Clark's *Domestic Relations* combines the familiar hornbook publication with an effective and easily accessed law library. The WESTLAW references at the end of many sections of this hornbook provide a basic framework upon which you can structure additional WESTLAW research. The queries may be used as provided or they may be tailored to meet your specific research needs. The power and flexibility of WESTLAW affords you a unique opportunity to greatly enhance your access to and understanding of the family law.

*

Table of Cases

A

B

*

Index

References are to Pages

EQUAL PROTECTION CLAUSE—Cont'd

Discrimination in filing fees in divorce cases, 532

Distinctions between mothers and fathers of illegitimate children in adoption, 858

Duty of support of illegitimate child on both parents, 176

Effect of on choice of law in Uniform Reciprocal Enforcement of Support Act cases, 284

Effect on criminal nonsupport statutes, 270

Effect on custody of illegitimate children, 197

Effect on disabilities of married women, 292

Effect on illegitimate child's right under wrongful death statute, 155

Effect on married women's contracts, 299

Effect on modification of decrees in paternity suits, 169

Effect on rights of illegitimate child, 155

Effect on statutes of limitations in paternity suits, 168

Effect on support obligations, 252, 259, 710

Invalidating gender distinctions on marriageable age, 90

Involuntary sterilization statutes, 222

Management of community property, 298

Notice to father of illegitimate child concerning adoption, 860

Parents' duty to support illegitimate child, 176

Right of both spouses to alimony, 622

Right of father of illegitimate child to custody, 856

Right to treatment, 367

Validity of marriage breakdown as ground for divorce, 514

Validity of prohibition on marriage of adopted siblings, 84

EQUAL RIGHTS AMENDMENT

Application to homosexual marriage, 79

Effect on custody of illegitimate child, 197

Effect on property of spouses, 292

Effect on suits for loss of consortium, 392

Effect on support obligations, 252, 259

Gender discrimination, 291

Invalidity of the tender years doctrine, 800

Proposed federal amendment, 291

State constitutional provisions, 291

EQUITABLE ADOPTION

Child of artificial insemination, 153

Definition of, 925

Purposes of, 926

EQUITABLE DISTRIBUTION LAWS

See Division of Property

EQUITABLE ESTOPPEL

Support of stepchildren by stepparent, 264

EQUITY DECREES

Interstate enforcement of Equity Act decrees, 685

EQUITY JURISDICTION

Over marriage, 24

Protection of children, 786

Remedy in custody cases, 794

ESCALATION CLAUSE

Inclusion in separation agreement, 767

Use of in child support decrees, 716

ESSENTIALS

Fraud respecting as grounds for annulment, 107

ESTABLISHMENT CLAUSE

Application to homosexual marriage, 77

Validity of religion as a factor in custody determinations, 809

ESTOPPEL

Against minor's disaffirmance, 319

Application to divorce decrees, 434

Basis for duty to support illegitimate child on marriage to mother, 200

Basis for, as bar to attack on divorce decrees, 435

Defense to annulment for non-age, 96

Defense to enforcement of child support, 744

Rationale of, as barring attack on divorce decrees, 441

To deny paternity on marriage to a pregnant woman, 192

EUGENICS

Basis for statutes on involuntary sterilization, 221

EVASION

Of incest regulations by foreign marriage, 86

Of licensing regulations, 42

EVASION OF MARRIAGE REGULATIONS

Availability of, 34

EVIDENCE

Anthropological evidence in paternity suits, 185

Blood-grouping tests in paternity suits, 186

Common law marriage, 48, 49

EXCEPTIO PLURIUM CONCUBENTIUM

Defense to paternity proceedings, 183

EXCUSABLE NEGLECT

Ground for attack on judgments, 551

EXECUTION

Enforcement of alimony claims, 672

Enforcement of child support, 740

Enforcement of temporary alimony, 626

EXEMPT PROPERTY

Enforcement of alimony against, 676

Enforcement of child support against, 740

EXPERT TESTIMONY

Use in custody disputes, 787

RIGHT OF PRIVACY—Cont'd
Mothers of illegitimate children, 170
Sterilization of minors, 217
Validity of court-ordered contraception, 213
Validity of laws regulating distribution of contraceptives, 211
Validity of restrictions on abortion funding, 235

RIGHT TO COUNSEL
For child in proceeding under statutes defining child in need of supervision, 364
For children in divorce action of parents, 564
Of child in paternity suit, 180
Right of indigent parent in proceeding for termination of parental rights, 865
Under Uniform Reciprocal Enforcement of Support Act, 277

RIGHT TO TRAVEL
Validity of restrictions on child's custodian in choice of a residence, 814

RIGHT TO TREATMENT
As applied to child in need of supervision, 366
Definition of, 368

ROMAN LAW
Emancipation of minors, 322

RUNAWAY CHILDREN
Statutes regarding, 361

SALPINGECTOMY
Definition of, 214

SCHOOL ATTENDANCE LAWS
See Compulsory Education Laws

SEARCH AND SEIZURE
Home inspection by caseworker, 262

SEDUCTION
Parent's right to sue for seduction of child, 387

SELF–INCRIMINATION
In paternity suits, 185

SEPARATE MAINTENANCE
Effect of divorce decree on, 639
Period of, calculation of desertion time, 501

SEPARATE PROPERTY
Existence of, as defense to claims for temporary alimony, 625
Property acquired while living together before marriage where marriage follows, 618
Significance of time of acquisition, 597

SEPARATION
Definition for purposes of desertion, 503
Ground for divorce, definition of, 518
Required for validity of separation agreements, 757

SEPARATION AGREEMENTS
Arbitration provision in, 576
Collusive provisions in, 764
Defense to temporary alimony, 625
Definition of, 756
Effect of, on modification of custody decrees, 840
Effect in support obligations, 256
Grounds on which courts may disregard, 772, 774
Inclusion of provisions not within court authority, 766
Merger defined, 783
Modification of child support based on, 724
Presumptive validity of, 772, 774
Validity of provisions contemplating obtaining a divorce, 765

SERVICE
Under Uniform Reciprocal Enforcement of Support Act, 278

SERVICE BY PUBLICATION
On unknown fathers of illegitimate children, 857

SERVICE OF PROCESS
Annulment actions, 131
Claims for temporary alimony or attorney's fees, 623

SETTLEMENT
Of paternity claims, 193

SEXUAL ABUSE OF CHILDREN
Background of, 346

SEXUAL CHILD ABUSE
As constituting child abuse, 353

SEXUAL MORALITY
As unfitness in proceeding for termination of parental rights, 904
Effect of on modification of custody decrees, 845
Factor in custody determinations, 803

SEXUAL RELATIONS
Capacity for and definition of impotence, 100
Factor in legal definition of marriage, 26

SHAM MARRIAGE
Validity of, 120

SHELTERS
Victims of domestic violence, 308

SHOTGUN MARRIAGE
As duress, 103

SIGNIFICANT CONNECTION
Basis for custody jurisdiction under Uniform Child Custody Jurisdiction Act, 466

†